BREWER'S CONCISE
PHRASE
& FABLE

BREWER'S CONCISE
PHRASE
& FABLE

EDITED BY
BETTY KIRKPATRICK

CASSELL&CO

Cassell & Co.
Wellington House
125 Strand
London
WC2R 0BB

First published as *Brewer's Concise Dictionary of Phrase and Fable*, 1992
© Cassell 2000

Brewer's Dictionary of Phrase and Fable first published 1870
16th edition 1999, reprinted 2000

Brewer's is a registered trademark of Cassell & Co.

British Library Cataloguing-in-Publication Data
A catalogue entry for this book is available from the British Library

ISBN 0-304-35725-1

Printed and bound in Great Britain by Mackays of Chatham PLC, Kent

Contents

Preface

Preface

These days much emphasis is placed on the importance of communicative skills. Such skills do not come naturally to most people and in order to acquire and maintain them it is necessary to have a well-stocked reference library to hand — preferably in the home.

In response to this need bookshops are abundantly stocked with many types of reference books — from dictionaries to thesauruses to guides to the use of the English language. A wide selection of each of these categories is available but there is only one Brewer.

Brewer's Dictionary of Phrase and Fable has enjoyed great popularity ever since its first publication, and Cassell is now seeking to extend its already wide market. For those who prefer their reference books more compact or cheaper this Concise edition of Brewer is ideal.

To have simply reduced the type size of the existing text would not have resulted in a small enough book — and would have caused much eyestrain. Instead it has been necessary to remove some of the text to achieve the optimum size.

Removing material from a reference book is always an agonizing task for an editor. Not only does the mere fact of being in print convey an aura of authority and so of indispensability to everything, but creative people hate to undo the work of other creative people.

In any case it is extremely difficult to decide what to leave and what to take out. Editors of reference books, almost by definition, are hoarders of information and it is heart-breaking for them to delete anything. Besides, it is all too easy with a book like Brewer to get absorbed in the content and forget the task at hand.

When it came to shortening the text of Brewer to produce a Concise edition my greatest concern was to retain the very individual flavour and personality of the book. In a world where so much is a conveyor-belt copy of other things it is important to preserve uniqueness where it exists.

Retaining the personality of Brewer whilst shortening it was in some ways a relatively easy task. No one-volume reference book is totally comprehensive or even consistent in its coverage and there are always some entries that can be lost without upsetting the balance of the book.

Brewer has the added dimension of being rather idiosyncratic, a fact which increases its charm greatly and makes it easier to shorten. It is in fact a treasure house of interesting pieces of information — some snippets, some larger articles — put together by people by people for whom all information is of interest.

Lovers of the parent volume of Brewer may not forgive me for some of the deletions but them no change is acceptable to those who love and admire something/someone. I can only hope that they will appreciate the plight of someone faced with the necessity of effecting such change.

For the most part I have deleted the quotations. They seemed inappropriate in a smaller volume and in any case they did not always add significantly to the explanation of an entry, particularly to modern users less steeped in literature.

I have also tended to remove entries which simply give the meanings of words readily obtainable in ordinary English-language dictionaries. In the same spirit I have removed other material which is available elsewhere or has no particular literary or historical allusions associated with it.

Apart from these deletions I have removed some of the more idiosyncratic material, which was personally interesting, but not absolutely essential. In addition I have excluded some of the more archaic and recherché information and some of the more modern information which did not quite fit the scheme of the smaller volume.

Inevitably the deletions have been as individual and idiosyncratic as the existing entries themselves. My hope is that I have left the book as I found it — a unique and fascinating collection of information invaluable to anyone who reads or writes.

Betty Kirkpatrick
EDINBURGH 1992

Key to Pronunciation

VOWELS

a	as in	far (far).	ē	as in	beef (bēf).	u	as in	bull (bul).
ă	"	fat (făt).	i	"	bit (bit).	ŭ	"	sun (sŭn).
ā	"	fate (fāt).	ī	"	bite (bīt).	ū	"	muse (mūz).
aw	"	fall (fawl).	o	"	not (not).	ou	"	bout (bout).
â	"	fair (fâr).	ō	"	no (nō).	oi	"	join (join).
e	"	bell (bel).	ô	"	north (nôrth).			
ĕ	"	her (hĕr).	oo	"	food (food).			

A dot placed over a, e, o, or u (ȧ, ė, ȯ, u̇) signifies that the vowel has an obscure, indeterminate, or slurred sound, as in:—

advice (ȧd vīs'), current (kŭr' ėnt), notion (nō' shȯn).

y when used as a vowel is rendered by i as in Polycrates (pol i' krȧ tēz), or by ī as in Gyges (gī' jēz).

CONSONANTS

b, d, f, h (see the combinations below), k, l, m, n, p, r, t, v, w, x, z, and y when used as a consonant, have their usual values.

c (except in the combinations ch and *ch*) is not used, the hard c being rendered by k as in cachet (kăsh' ā), and the soft c by s as in Circe (sĕr' si).

q is not used and is rendered by k as in quey (kwā).

s is used only for the sibilant s, as in toast (tōst); the sonant is rendered by z, as in toes (tōz).

x is not used and is rendered by z or ks as in Xerxes (zĕrks' ēz).

ch is rendered by k when thus pronounced, as in Acheron (ăk' er on), and by sh in words of French origin as in panache (păn ăsh).

ph is rendered by f as in Pharaoh (fâr' ō).

ch	as in	church (chĕrch).	sh	as in	shawl (shawl).
ch	"	loch (lo*ch*).	zh	"	measure (mezh' u̇r).
g	"	get (get).	th	"	thin (thin).
j	"	join (join).	*th*	"	thine (*th* īn).
hw	"	white (hwīt).			

The soft g is rendered by j as in gin (jin) and in words of French origin by zh as in gendarme (zhon' darm); j is also rendered by zh in words of French origin as in jeunesse (zhĕr nes').

The accent (') follows the syllable to be stressed.

Abbreviations

Arab.	Arabic	L. Lat.	Late Latin
Austr.	Australian	M.E.	Middle English
c.	*circa* (about)	Med. Lat.	Mediæval Latin
cp.	compare	Mod. Fr.	Modern French
Dan.	Danish	O.E.	Old English
Dut.	Dutch	O.Fr.	Old French
e.g.	*exempli gratia* (for example)	O.H.Ger.	Old High German
		O. Slav.	Old Slavonic
Fr.	French	O.W.	Old Welsh
Gael.	Gaelic	Pers.	Persian
Ger.	German	Port.	Portuguese
Gr.	Greek	*q.v.*	*quod vide* (which see)
Heb.	Hebrew	Russ.	Russian
Hind.	Hindustani	Sans.	Sanskrit
Icel.	Icelandic	Scot.	Scottish
i.e.	*id est* (that is)	Sp.	Spanish
Ital.	Italian	Swed.	Swedish
Jap.	Japanese	Turk.	Turkish
Lat.	Latin	*viz.*	*videlicet* (namely)

Cross-References

These are indicated in the text by the use of SMALL CAPITALS unless *Cp.* is used.

NOTE. All biblical references are to the *Authorized Version* unless otherwise stated. Entries concerning liturgical customs of the Church of England refer to those associated with the *Book of Common Prayer*. Ecclesiastical usages are those of the Church of England except where otherwise indicated.

A

Abbreviation

A. This letter is modified from the Egyptian hieroglyph representing the EAGLE. The Phœnician (Hebrew) symbol was א (*aleph* = an ox), doubtfully assumed to represent an ox-head. The Greek A (*alpha*) was the symbol of a bad AUGURY in the sacrifices. *See also* SCARLET LETTER.

A in logic denotes a universal affirmative.

A1 means first-rate—the very best. In LLOYD'S *Register of British and Foreign Shipping* the state of a ship's hull is designated by *letters* and that of the anchors, cables, etc. by *figures*. Thus A1 is a mark of the first class.

A.M.D.G. An abbreviation for *ad majorem Dei gloriam* (Lat.) meaning "to the greater glory of God".

A.U.C. Abbreviations of the Lat. *ab urbe condita*, or *Anno urbis conditae*, "from the foundation of the city" (ROME) "in the year of the city's foundation". It is the starting point of the Roman system of dating, and corresponds with 753 B.C.

A from a windmill, Not to know. To be very obtuse or ignorant. Possibly suggested by the similarity between the shape of a capital A and that of a distant tower windmill.

Aalu, or **Aaru.** In ancient Egyptian religion the fields of Aalu, where food was grown for the dead to supplement the votive offerings of their descendants, correspond roughly with the ELYSIAN FIELDS of Greek mythology.

Aaron (âr' on). The patriarch of the Jewish priesthood (*Exod*. xxviii), possibly connected with *haaron*, "the ark".

Aaron's Beard. The popular name of many wild plants, including Great St. John's Wort (Rose of Sharon), the Ivy-leaved Toadflax, Meadowsweet, *Saxifrage sarmentosa*, etc. The reference is to *Ps*. cxxxiii, 2.

Aaron's Rod. The name given (with reference to *Num*. xvii, 8) to various flowering plants including Golden Rod and Great Mullein. Also a name for the DIVINING ROD.

Aaron's serpent. Something so powerful as to swallow up minor powers (*Exod*. vii, 10–12). [Thus Prussia was the Aaron's serpent that swallowed up the lesser German States between 1866 and 1870.]

Aaru. *See* AALU.

Aarvak. *See* HORSE.

Aback, To be taken, to be astounded, taken by surprise. From the sailing-ship term *aback*, when the sails press against the mast (or the clew of a fore and aft sail is to windward) and progress is suddenly stayed.

Abaddon (á băd' ŏn). The angel of the bottomless pit (*Rev*. ix, 11), from Heb. *abad*, he perished. Milton used the name for the pit itself.

Abaris (ăb' á ris). **The dart of Abaris.** A mythical priest of APOLLO mentioned by Herodotus, PINDAR, etc. and surnamed "the Hyperborean". Apollo gave him a magic arrow which rendered him invisible and on which he rode through the air. He cured diseases and spoke oracles. Abaris gave the dart to PYTHAGORAS.

Abatement (O.Fr. *abatre*, to beat down). In HERALDRY, a *difference* in coat armour for illegitimate birth, granted to a petitioner after establishing paternity but indicating that the possessor is outside the legitimate line of succession.

Abaton (ăb' á ton) (Gr. *a*, not; *baino*, I go). **As inaccessible as Abaton.** Said of various places of antiquity difficult of access.

Abbassides (ăb' á sīdz). A dynasty of caliphs who ruled the Arabian Empire from 750 to 1258, descended from Abbas, uncle of MOHAMMED. Haroun al-Raschid (b. 765, reigned 786–808), of the ARABIAN NIGHTS, was one of their number.

Abbot of Misrule. See KING OF MISRULE.

Abbot's Bromley Horn, or **Antler Dance.** One of the rare European animal dances surviving from remote times. Originally danced on Twelfth Day at Abbot's Bromley, Staffordshire, it now takes place on the first Monday after 4 September. The six dancers, all male as in MORRIS DANCES, hold antlers (three of which are painted blue or red and three white) to their heads as they dance. It may originally have been a form of fertility rite since the dancers go the round of neighbouring farms before the dance.

Abdallah (ăb dăl′ à). The father of MOHAMMED. He was so beautiful that when he married Amina 200 virgins broke their hearts from disappointed love. He died before his son was born.

Abdals (ăb′ dălz). The name given by MOSLEMS to certain mysterious persons whose identity is known only to God and through whom the world is able to continue in existence. When one dies another is secretly appointed by God to fill the vacant place.

Abdera (ăb dēr′ à). A maritime town of Thrace, mythically founded by HERCULES in memory of ABDERUS. The *Abderites* or *Abderitans* were proverbial for stupidity, said to be caused by the air, but among them were DEMOCRITUS, the laughing philosopher (hence *Abderitan laughter* = scoffing laughter, and *Abderite* = scoffer) and Hecatæus, the historian.

Abderus. A friend of HERCULES, who was devoured by the horses of DIOMEDES when keeping guard over them.

Abdiel (ăb′ dēl). See ABD. In Milton's *Paradise Lost* (V, 805, 896, etc.) the faithful seraph who withstood SATAN when he urged the angels to revolt.

Abe, Old or **Honest Abe.** Abraham Lincoln, President of the US from 1861 to 1865.

Abecedarian (ă bē si dâr′ i àn). A teacher or learner of the A B C or rudiments. Also an ANABAPTIST sect, the ZWICKAU

PROPHETS, founded in 1520. Led by Nicholas Stork, a weaver, they relied on direct inspiration from God, rejecting all learning as a hindrance.

Abecedarian Hymns. Hymns the lines or divisions of which begin with the letters of the alphabet in regular succession. In Hebrew the 119th Psalm is abecedarian. See ACROSTIC POETRY.

Abelard and Héloïse (ăb′ e lard, ă lō ēz). Peter Abelard (1079–1142), eminent scholar, theologian and philosopher, studied under William of Champeaux and Anselm, and founded an internationally famous school of theology in Paris. At the age of thirty-six he became tutor to Héloïse, the beautiful and accomplished seventeen-year-old niece of Canon Fulbert of Notre Dame. They fell in love, a son was born and they were secretly married, but Héloïse soon disavowed the marriage that she might not hinder Abelard's advancement. Fulbert, enraged at her husband's seeming connivance, caused him to be emasculated. Abelard entered the monastery of St. Denis. Héloïse became a nun. Abelard continued his highly controversial teaching and later founded another school near Nogent-sur-Seine called PARACLETE, which, after his departure to take charge of the Abbey of St. Gildas in Brittany, was given to a sisterhood under Héloïse. His stormy career ended in 1142 and Héloïse was laid by his side in 1164. Their remains were transferred from Paraclete and re-buried in the PÈRE LACHAISE cemetery (Paris) in 1817.

Abelites (ăb′ e lītz), **Abelians,** or **Abelonians.** A Christian sect of the 4th century living in North Africa. They married but remained virgin, as they affirmed Abel did. Children were adopted.

Abenezra. See ADMIRABLE.

Abhidhamma (ăb id a′ ma). The third pitaka of the three texts (TRIPITAKA) which together form the sacred canon of the Buddhists. In seven treatises it is essentially concerned with metaphysics.

Abhorrers. See PETITIONERS.

Abif. See HIRAM ABIF.

Abigail (ăb′ i găl). A lady's maid. Abigail (I *Sam*. xxv, 24–28) repeatedly called herself David's handmaid, hence the usage. It was used by Swift, Fielding and others. Probably the usage was popularized by the political notoriety of Abigail Hill (Mrs. Masham), waiting-woman to QUEEN ANNE and royal favourite.

Abingdon Law. *See* CUPAR JUSTICE.

Abiogenesis (Gr. *a*, without, *bios*, life + *genesis*), a term applied by T. H. Huxley in 1870 to the ancient theory that non-living matter could produce living. An example of such spontaneous generation is found in VIRGIL'S *Georgics* (Bk. IV), when the shepherd Aristæus, son of APOLLO and CYRENE, having lost his bees through disease and famine, slew four bulls at his mother's orders. On the ninth morning bees poured forth from the decomposing cattle.

Abolitionists. In Great Britain historically applied to supporters of the anti-slavery movement; in the US specifically applied to those who agitated for the abolition of Negro slavery in the period 1830–1861; in Australia, to those, in the 19th century, who sought to end the transportation of British convicts.

Abominable Snowman. Name, popularized by Shipton's Everest Expedition of 1951, for the yeti, a rare, elusive, and supposedly bear-like animal of the Himalayas.

Abou-Bekr (ă boo bekr), (*c.* 573–634), called Father of The Virgin (AYESHA). He was the immediate successor of MO-HAMMED or first CALIPH (632–634) and was supported by the SUNNITES.

Abou Hassan (ă boo hăs' ăn). A rich merchant (in the ARABIAN NIGHTS, *The Sleeper Awakened*), transferred while asleep to the bed of the Caliph HAROUN AL-RASCHID. Next morning he was treated as the CALIPH and every effort was made to make him forget his identity.

Abou ibn Sina. *See* AVICENNA.

About the size of it. How matters stand, approximately the facts of the case.

Above-board. Honest and open. According to Johnson "borrowed from gamesters, who, when they put their hands under the table, are changing their cards."

Above oneself, To be. Temporarily more than ordinarily high-spirited, self-confident, or conceited.

Above your hook. *See* HOOK.

Ab ovo (Lat. from the egg). Laboriously from the very beginning. Stasinus in his *Cypria*, an introduction to the ILIAD, begins with the eggs of LEDA, from one of which HELEN was born. If Leda had not laid this egg Helen would never have been born, therefore PARIS could not have eloped with her, therefore there would have been no TROJAN WAR, etc.

Abracadabra. A cabbalistic charm, said to be made up from the initials of the Hebrew words Ab (Father), Ben (Son), and Ruach ACadsch (Holy Spirit), and formerly used against ague, flux, tooth-ache etc. The word was written on parchment as shown and hung from the neck by a linen thread. *See* CABBALA.

```
A B R A C A D A B R A
  A B R A C A D A B R
    A B R A C A D A B
      A B R A C A D A
        A B R A C A D
          A B R A C A
            A B R A C
              A B R A
                A B R
                  A B
                    A
```

Abracax. *See* ABRAXAS.

Abraham. In addition to the BIBLE stories about the Hebrew patriarch, Mohammedan legend adds the following: His parents were Prince Azar and his wife Adna. As King Nimrod had been told that one shortly to be born would dethrone him, he proclaimed a "massacre of the innocents". Adna retired to a cave where Abraham was born and was nourished by sucking two of her fingers, one giving milk and the other honey. At fifteen months the boy was the size of a lad of fifteen, and so wise that Azar introduced him to Nimrod's court. Further, that Abraham and his son "Ismail" rebuilt for the fourth time the KAABA; that Abraham destroyed the idols made and worshipped by his father Terah; and that the mountain on which he offered up his son ("Mount Moriah" in the Bible) was "Arfaday".

The GHEBERS say that the infant Abraham was thrown into the fire by Nimrod's order but it turned into a bed of roses on which he went to sleep.

To sham Abraham. *See* ABRAM-MAN.

Abrahamic Covenant. The promise given by God to ABRAHAM because he left his father's house to live in a strange land as God told him, and interpreted to mean that the MESSIAH should spring from Abraham's seed (*Gen.* xii, 1–3 and xvii).

Abraham's bosom. The repose of the happy in death.

The allusion is to the ancient custom of allowing a dear friend to recline on one's bosom (*Luke* xvi, 22), as did John on the bosom of Jesus.

There is no leaping from Delilah's lap into Abraham's bosom—*i.e.* those who live and die in notorious sin must not expect to go to HEAVEN at death.

Abram-colour. "Abram" here is a corruption of *auburn*.

Abram-man, or **Abraham cove.** In Tudor and early Stuart times a pretended maniac who wandered about begging; a TOM O'BEDLAM; hence **to sham Abraham** meaning to sham illness in order to dodge work.

Inmates of BEDLAM who were not dangerous were kept in the "Abraham Ward" and occasionally allowed out in distinctive dress and permitted to beg.

Abraham, Plains of, or **Heights of,** south-west of the city of Quebec, the scene of the decisive battle (13 September 1759) between the British under Wolfe and the French under Montcalm, as a result of which the conquest of Canada was effected. They were named after a pilot known as Maître Abraham (A. Martin).

Abraxas (á brăks' ás). A cabbalistic word used by the GNOSTICS to denote the Supreme Being, the source of 365 emanations, the sum of the numbers represented by the Greek letters of the word.

Absalom. The third son of DAVID, remarkable for his good looks, who rose in rebellion against his father, aided by AHITHOPHEL. In his flight after defeat, Absalom was trapped in the branches of a tree and slain by Joab, the King's general. David's great sorrow was thus expressed (II *Sam*. xviii, 33):

O my son Absalom, my son, my son Absalom! would God I had died for thee, O Absalom my son, my son!

In Dryden and Tate's *Absalom and Achitophel*, Absalom stands for the Duke of Monmouth.

Absent. The absent are always wrong. From the French proverb, *les absents ont toujours tort*. It implies that it is always easy to blame those not present, who cannot defend themselves.

Absence makes the heart grow fonder. A tag from the song, *the Isle of Beauty*, by T. Haynes Bayly (1797–1839).

Absinthe (ăb' sinth). A green liqueur flavoured with wormwood (*Artemisia absinthium*) together with angelica root, etc. It appears frequently in accounts of the life of French literary and artistic circles at the end of the 19th century and the early 20th century, and was first popularized by being prescribed as a febrifuge to French troops during the Algerian War (1830–1847). *L'Absinthe* is the title by which the painting "Au Café" by Degas (exhibited in London in 1893) is better known. Émile Zola vividly described the horrors of absinthe poisoning in *L'Assommoir*. Its sale and manufacture are now illegal in France.

Abstinence. Ecclesiastically *Days of Abstinence* are those when the eating of meat is not permitted; on *Fasting Days* only one full meal is allowed in the twenty-four hours.

Abstract. Things are said to be **taken in the abstract** when considered absolutely without relation to other things.

An abstract of title is a legal phrase meaning a précis of the evidences of ownership of real property.

Abstraction. An empty abstraction, a mere ideality of no practical use and thus often eventually rejected as unsatisfying.

Abyla. *See* CALPE.

Abyssinian Christians. A branch of the Coptic Church. *See* COPTS.

Academy. Originally a garden near Athens where PLATO taught (named after *Academos*). Hence the philosophical school or system of Plato, and later a place, society or institution where the arts and sciences are taught or fostered.

The teaching of Plato and his early followers came to be known as the Old Academy; the modified Platonic system founded by Arcesilaus (*c.* 224 B.C.), as the Middle; the half-sceptical school founded by Carneades (*c.* 160 B.C.), as the New. Plato's followers were known as *Academics*. In addition to its usage in reference to an academy or university the adjective academic has come to mean "theoretical, scholarly, abstract, unpractical". *See* PLATONISM.

Acadia (à kā' dià), **Acadie.** A former French settlement which now forms part of the provinces of Nova Scotia and New Brunswick. Ceded to Great Britain in 1713, the French inhabitants continued to intrigue against the British, and in 1755 were dispossessed and dispersed among the British colonies to the southward. This deportation provides the subject for Longfellow's *Evangeline*.

Acadine (ăk' à dīn). A Sicilian fountain mentioned by Diodorus Siculus as having magic properties. Writings were thrown into it to be tested; if genuine they floated, if spurious they sank to the bottom.

Acanthus (à kăn' thùs). The representation of the leaf of *Acanthus mollis* used to decorate the capitals of CORINTHIAN and composite columns. The story is that an acanthus sprang up around a basket of flowers that Callimachus had placed on his daughter's grave. This so struck the fancy of the architect that he introduced the design into his buildings.

Accessory after the fact is one who screens a felon or helps him in any way to profit from his crime. A receiver of stolen goods, knowing or even suspecting them to be stolen, is an accessory *ex post facto*.

Accessory before the fact is one who is aware that another intends to commit an offence, but is absent when the offence is committed.

Accident. A logical accident is some quality or property which a thing possesses but which is not essential to it, the removal or change of which would not necessarily affect it, as the height of our bodies, the whiteness of paper or the redness of a brick. *See* TRANSUBSTANTIATION.

Accidental colours. *See* COLOURS.

Accius Nævius (ăk' kiùs nē' vi ùs). A legendary Roman augur who forbade TARQUIN the Elder (616–579 B.C.) to increase the number of centuries (*i.e.* divisions of the army) instituted by ROMULUS, without consulting the augurs. Tarquin asked him if, according to the augurs, the thought then in his (Tarquin's) mind was feasible of accomplishment. "Undoubtedly", said Accius after consultation. "Then cut through this whet-stone with the razor in your hand". The priest gave a bold cut and the block fell in two (Livy, I, 36). *See* AUGURY.

To be called to one's last account. To die.

To be sent to one's account. To have final judgment passed on one. The ghost in *Hamlet* (I, v) uses the phrase as a synonym for death:

To square accounts with someone means to get even with or retaliate upon. Derived from "square accounts" in which debit balances credit.

Ace. The unit of cards or dice from *as*, the Latin unit of weight. In World War I the French word *as*, applied to an airman who had brought down ten enemy aeroplanes, was imported in its English equivalent *ace*, then extended to any especially expert flier, golfer, etc.

Within an ace. Within a hair's breadth of; he who wins with an ace wins within a single mark.

To bate an ace. To make an abatement or to give a competitor some start or advantage making the combatants more equal. *See* BOLTON.

Aceldama (à sel' dà mà). The Aramaic for the "field of Blood" figuratively used for any place of great slaughter. It was the POTTER'S FIELD near Jerusalem bought to bury strangers in (*see Matt. xxvii*, 7, 8 and *Acts* i, 18, 19), and was used by Christians during the CRUSADES and as late as the 17th century.

Acephalites (à sef' à lītz) (Gr. *akephale*, without a head). A name given to various schismatical Christian bodies, principally to (i) those MONOPHYSITES who rejected the authority of Peter Mongus, Bishop of Alexandria, in 482, and were later absorbed by the JACOBITES; (2) those NESTORIANS rejecting patriarchal condemnation of Nestorius in 431; (3) priests rejecting episcopal authority or bishops that of their metropolitans; (4)

a group of English LEVELLERS in the reign of Henry I, who acknowledged no leader.

The name is also given to various legendary headless monsters.

Acestes (à ses' tēz). **The arrow of Acestes.** In a trial of skill Acestes, the Sicilian, shot his arrow with such force that it took fire (*Æneid*, V, 525).

Achates (à kā' tēz). **A fidus Achates** is a faithful companion, a bosom friend. Achates (in VIRGIL's *Æneid*) was the chosen comrade of ÆNEAS.

Achemon (à ke' mon). According to Greek legend, Achemon and his brother Basalas were two Cercopes (a people of Ephesus) for ever quarrelling. One day they saw HERCULES asleep under a tree and insulted him, so he tied them by their feet to his club and walked off with them, heads downwards. Everyone laughed at the sight, and it became a proverbial cry among the Greeks, when two men were seen quarrelling—"Look out for Melampygos!" (*i.e.* Hercules):

Ne incidas in Melampygum.

Acheri. The ghost of a little girl, who, according to folk tradition of India, comes down at night from her mountain haunts to bring sickness to children in human habitations. A bright-red thread worn round the neck is believed to be a protection against such molestation.

Acheron (ăk' er on). The "woeful river" of the underworld into which flow the PHLEGETHON and COCYTUS. Also HADES itself. *See* CHARON; STYX.

They pass the bitter waves of Acheron
Where many souls sit wailing woefully.
SPENSER: *Faerie Queene* I, v, 33.

See also VIRGIL's *Æneid*, Bk. VI.

Acherontian Books. *See* TAGES.

Acherusia (ăk er ooz' i à). A cavern on the borders of Pontus, through which HERCULES dragged CERBERUS from the infernal regions to earth.

Acheulean (à shĕr' li àn). The name given to stages of PALAEOLITHIC hand-axe culture typified by the tools found at St. Acheul, near Amiens.

Achillea (ăk il ē' à). A genus of plants of the aster family, including common yarrow (*Achillea millifolium*), so called from ACHILLES. The tale is that the Greeks, on the way to TROY, landed in Mysia and were opposed by Telephus, son of HERCULES. DIONYSUS caused Telephus to stumble and he was wounded by Achilles with his spear. Told by the ORACLE that Achilles (the wounder) would be the healer (meaning milfoil or yarrow), Telephus sought out the Greek leader, promising to lead him to Troy in return for his help. Achilles agreed, scraped some rust from his spear from which sprang the plant milfoil, and this healed the wound. It is called carpenters' wort by the French (*herbe aux charpentiers*) because it is supposed to heal wounds made by carpenters' tools.

Achilles (à kil'ēz). Hero of the ILIAD, the son of Peleus, King of the MYRMIDONS in Thessaly, and grandson of Æacus. Brave and relentless, his quarrel with AGAMEMNON, the Greek commander-in-chief, caused him to withdraw from the struggle. The TROJANS prevailed and Achilles allowed PATROCLUS to lead the Myrmidons back. Patroclus was killed by HECTOR. Achilles then returned, routed the Trojans, and slew Hector. According to later poems Achilles was killed by PARIS at the Scæan gate. *See* ACHILLES TENDON.

Achilles and the tortoise. Alludes to a paradox by ZENO. In a race Achilles, who can run ten times as fast as a tortoise, gives the latter 100 yards start; but cannot win the race because while he is running the first 100 yards, the tortoise runs ten, while Achilles runs that ten the tortoise runs one, while Achilles is running one, the tortoise runs one-tenth of a yard, and so on *ad infinitum*.

Achilles tendon (*tendo Achillis*). A strong sinew connecting the heel and calf frequently strained by athletes. The tale is that THETIS took her son Achilles by the heel, and dipped him in the river STYX to make him invulnerable, but the heel in her hand remained dry. The hero was slain by an arrow wound in the heel—the one weak spot (a post-Homeric story).

Achilles's horses. Balios and XANTHIUS. *See* HORSE.

Achilles's spear. *See* ACHILLEA.

Achilles's tomb. In Sigeum, over which no bird ever flies. *Pliny*, X, 29.

The heel of Achilles. The vulnerable spot in the character of a man or a nation. *See* ACHILLES TENDON.

Achitophel. *See* AHITHOPHEL.

Achor (ā kôr). Said by Pliny to be the deity prayed to by the Cyreneans for the averting of insect pests. *See* FLIES, GOD OF.

Acid. Acid test. Gold is not attacked by most acids but reacts to AQUA FORTIS (and AQUA REGIA)—the acid test. Hence applied to a decisive or searching test.

To come the acid. To adopt an acid manner, to exaggerate one's authority, to be overbearing or offensive.

To put the acid on. Used originally in Australia and New Zealand meaning to ask for a loan. It has since come to mean to make excessive demands on. Possibly derived from ACID TEST.

Acis (ā′ sis). The son of FAUNUS, in love with GALATEA, crushed to death with a rock by his rival, POLYPHEMUS the CYCLOPS, and changed into the river Acis (Ovid, *Metam.* xiii, 750–968).

Ack Ack. Slang from World Wars I and II meaning Anti-Aircraft Guns. Field telephonese, *cp.* ACK EMMA.

Ack Emma. *See* PIP EMMA.

Acknowledge the corn. To admit the truth of the point at issue, an American expression. In a Congressional debate in 1828 one of the states which claimed to export corn admitted that the corn was actually used to feed hogs, and exported in that form.

> "I hope he will give up the argument, or to use a familiar phrase *acknowledge the corn*" (Mr Speight of Mississippi speaking in the U.S. Senate in 1846).

Acme (ăk′ mi) (Gr. a point). The highest pitch of perfection. Old medical writers divided the progress of a disease into the *arche*, or beginning; the *anabasis* or increase; the *acme*, or crisis; and the *paracme*, or decline.

Aconite (ăk ónīt). The herb Monkshood or Wolfsbane. According to classic fable when HERCULES, at the command of Eurystheus, dragged CERBERUS from the infernal regions, the poisonous aconite grew from the foam which dropped from his mouths.

Acrasia (à krā′ zi à). The personification of intemperance, the name signifying "lack of self control".

Acre. O.E. *æcer*, akin to Lat. *ager*, a field.

God's acre, a cemetery or churchyard. A modern borrowing from Germany, wrongly called by Longfellow an "ancient Saxon phrase".

Acre-Fight. *See under* FIGHT.

Acres, Bob. A coward is sometimes called "a regular Bob Acres" after a character in Sheridan's *The Rivals*, whose courage always "oozed out at his fingers' ends".

Across someone, To get. To quarrel with or annoy a person; *cp.* "cross" in the sense of obstruct or thwart.

Across, To put, or **get something.** Generally used of a speaker making his point and carrying his audience with him. Probably derived from the theatre where actors must reach their audience across the footlights, or possibly from the game of baseball.

Acrostic (Gr. *akros*, outermost; *stichos*, line of verse). Verse in which the initial letters of each line read downwards to form a word; if the final letters also form a word it is a double acrostic; if the middle letters also, it is a triple acrostic. The term was first applied to the obscure prophecies of the Erythræan SIBYL written on loose leaves, which made a word when sorted into order (*Dionys.* IV, 62).

Acrostic Poetry among the Hebrews consisted of twenty-two lines or stanzas beginning with the letters of the alphabet in succession (*cp.* ABECEDARIAN HYMNS).

Act of God. A term applied by lawyers to happenings indisputably outside human control, for which there is no legal redress (*e.g.*, losses caused by flood, hurricane, earthquake, etc.).

Act of Parliament. A law or statute made by PARLIAMENT. Introduced as a BILL, it becomes an Act when passed, after it has received the royal assent. *See* REGNAL YEAR *under* YEAR.

Act of Truth. An event which, following a solemn oath, was held to prove or disprove its truth as in trial by ORDEAL.

Actæon (ăk tē′ on). In Greek mythology a huntsman who, having surprised DIANA bathing (or according to Euripides boasted his superiority in the chase) was changed into a stag and torn to pieces by his own hounds. Thus (as a stag) he became representative of men whose wives are unfaithful. *See* TO WEAR THE HORNS *under* HORN.

Actian Games (ăk′ ti ăn). The games celebrated at Actium in honour of APOLLO, renewed by AUGUSTUS after his naval victory over Antony off Actium (31 B.C.).

Action Sermon. In the Scottish PRESBYTERIAN Church the sermon sometimes preached before administering the Communion.

Actresses. Thomas Coryate says "When I went to a theatre [in Venice] I observed certain things that I never saw before; for I saw women act... I have heard that it hath sometimes been used in London" (Coryate's *Crudities*, 1611). Female parts on the English stage were always taken by boys until the RESTORATION. The first actress to perform in public was Margaret Hughes (Prince Rupert's mistress) playing Desdemona in *Othello* at a theatre in Clare Market, London (8 December 1660). Edward Kynaston (d. 1706) seems to have been the last actor to take female parts in serious drama.

> Whereas, women's parts in plays have hitherto been acted by men in the habits of women... we do permit and give leave for the time to come that all women's parts be acted by women.
>
> *Charles II's licence of 1662.*

Ad inquirendum (ăd′in kwī ren′ dum) (Lat.). A judicial writ commanding an inquiry to be made into some complaint.

Ad Kalendas Græcas (ăd ka len′dăs grē′ kăs) (Lat.). (Deferred) to the Greek Calends—*i.e.* for ever. (It shall be done) on the Greek Calends—*i.e.* never—for the Greeks had no CALENDS. Suetonius says AUGUSTUS used this reply if asked when he was going to pay his creditors.

Ad libitum (ăd lib′ i tum) (Lat.). To choice, at pleasure, without restraint.

Ad libbing. From *ad libitum*. In theatrical, broadcasting and musical parlance, to depart from the script or music and improvise.

Ad valorem (ăd văl ôr′ em) (Lat.). According to the value. A term used in imposing customs and stamp duty, the duty increasing according to the value of the transaction or goods involved.

Adam. The Talmudists say that Adam lived in PARADISE only twelve hours before he was thrust out. Islamic legend says that:

> God sent GABRIEL, MICHAEL, and ISRAFEL in turn to fetch seven handfuls of earth from different depths and of different colours for the creation of Adam (hence the varying colours of mankind), but they returned empty-handed because Earth foresaw that the creature to be made from her would rebel against God and draw down his curse on her. AZRAEL was then sent and he fulfilled the task, and so was appointed to separate the souls from the bodies, hence becoming the ANGEL of Death. The earth he fetched was taken to ARABIA to a place between MECCA and Tayef, kneaded by angels, fashioned into human form by God and left to dry for either 40 days or 40 years. The tradition holds that Adam was buried on Aboucais, a mountain in Arabia.

For the Bible story of Adam, see *Gen*. i-v.

Adam. The elegant neo-classical style of architecture and interior decoration created by the brothers Adam, especially Robert Adam (1728–1792). *See* ADELPHI.

As old as Adam. Means that something was well known long ago.

The curse of Adam. The necessity of working for a living. "In the sweat of thy face shalt thou eat bread, till thou return unto the ground" (*Gen*. ii, 19).

Not to know someone from Adam. To regard someone as a complete stranger, to be completely unacquainted.

The old Adam. The offending Adam, etc.

> Consideration, like an angel, came
> And whipped the offending Adam out of him.
>
> SHAKESPEARE: *Henry V*, I, i.

Adam, as the head of unredeemed man, stands for "original sin", or "man without regenerating grace".

The Second Adam, the New Adam, etc. Jesus Christ is so called.

> The Tempter set
> Our second Adam in the wilderness,
> To show him all earth's Kingdoms and their glory.
>
> *Paradise Lost*, XI, 383.

In the same way Milton calls MARY our "second Eve" (*Paradise Lost*, V, 387 and X, 183).

When Adam delved:

When Adam delved and Eve span,
Who was then the gentleman?

This, according to the *Historia Anglicana* of Thos. Walsingham (d. 1422), was the text of John Ball's speech at Blackheath to the rebels in the PEASANTS' REVOLT (1381).

Cp. JACK'S AS GOOD AS HIS MASTER—*under* JACK(1).

Adam Bell. *See* CLYM OF THE CLOUGH.

Adam Cupid, *i.e.* Archer CUPID, probably alluding to ADAM BELL. In all early editions the line in *Romeo and Juliet* (II, i, 13) "Young Adam Cupid, he that shot so trim", reads "Young Abraham Cupid". The emendation was suggested by George Stevens (1736–1800).

Adam's ale. Water; first man's only drink, sometimes called *Adam's wine* in Scotland.

Adam's apple. The protuberance in the forepart of the throat; so called from the supposition that a piece of the forbidden fruit stuck in Adam's throat.

Adam's bridge. *See* RAMA.

Adam's needle. A name given chiefly to the Yucca and to certain other plants with needle-like spines. *Gen*. iii, 7 tells us that Adam and EVE "sewed fig leaves together".

Adam's Peak. A mountain in Sri Lanka where, according to Mohammedan legend, ADAM, after his expulsion from PARADISE, expiated his crime by standing on one foot for 200 years until GABRIEL took him to Mount Ararat, where he found EVE. In the granite there is a large impression resembling a human foot. Hindus assert that it was made by BUDDHA when he ascended into heaven.

Adam's profession. Gardening or agriculture. *See Gen*. ii, 15 and *Gen*. iii, 23.

Adamites (ăd′ à mīts). The name given to various heretical sects, possibly of misguided ascetics, who practised nudity and rejected marriage. Such were the 2nd-century Adamites in North Africa, but similar ideas, leading to licentiousness, were revived in Europe by the *Bre-*

thren and Sisters of the Free Spirit in the 13th century; the BEGHARDS in France, Germany and the Netherlands; and the PICARDS of Bohemia in the 14th and 15th centuries, etc.

Adamastor (ăd à măs′ tôr). The spirit of the Cape of Storms (Good Hope), described by Camoëns (1524–1580) in the LUSIADS, who appeared to Vasco da Gama and foretold disaster to all attempting the voyage to India.

Add insult to injury. To wound by word or deed someone who has already suffered an act of violence or injustice. PHÆDRUS quotes the fable of ÆSOP about a bald man who, in attempting to kill a fly which had bitten his head, missed and dealt himself a sharp smack. Whereupon the fly said: "You wished to kill me for a mere touch. What will you do to yourself since you have added insult to injury?"

Add up, It does not. No sensible answer can be arrived at from the known facts, it does not make sense.

Addisonian termination. The name given by Bishop Hurd (1720–1808) to the construction, frequently employed by Joseph Addison (1672–1719), which closes a sentence with a preposition, *e.g.*, "which the prophet took a distinct view of".

Addled Parliament (5 April–7 June 1614). So called for its sterility, being dissolved by James I without passing a single Act. It refused to grant supplies unless the king abandoned IMPOSITIONS.

Adept. One who has attained (Lat. *adeptus*). The alchemists applied the term *vere adeptus* to those who professed to have found out the ELIXIR OF LIFE or the PHILOSOPHER'S STONE.

Adiaphorists (ăd ĭ ăf′ or ists) (Gr. indifferent). Moderate Lutherans, followers of Melanchthon, who accepted the Interim of Leipzig (1548) on ceremonies indifferent (*i.e.* neither sanctioned nor forbidden by the Scriptures), causing controversy among the Lutherans, which substantially ended in 1555. *See* AUGSBURG.

Aditi. The great earth mother of Hindu mythology, sometimes an abstract concept of limitless space and time. Variously described as the mother, wife, and daughter of VISHNU.

Adityas. In the VEDAS they are the divine sons of ADITI, the chief being VARUNA, sustainer of the moral law, who is often called *Aditya*.

Admass. Coined by J. B. Priestley in *Journey Down a Rainbow* (1955) to describe the vast mid-20th-century proliferation of commercial advertising and high-pressure salesmanship, especially in the U.S.A. The word has now come to mean the vast mass of the general public to which advertisers address their publicity.

Admirable, The. Abraham ben Meir ibn Ezra (1092–1167), a celebrated Spanish Jew was so called. He was a noted mathematician, philologist, poet, astronomer, and commentator on the BIBLE, and the Rabbi Ben Ezra of Robert Browning's poem of that name.

The Admirable Crichton. James Crichton (1560–1585), Scottish traveller, scholar and swordsman. So called and wonderfully portrayed by Sir Thomas Urquhart (1611–1660) in *The Exquisite Jewel*. Hence one distinguished by all-round talents. Harrison Ainsworth was much indebted to Urquhart for his novel, *The Admirable Crichton* (1837). Sir J. M. Barrie's play of this name appeared in 1902.

> And was in short (in their eyes at least) a very Admirable Crichton of the nineteenth century.
>
> CUTHBERT BEDE: *Adventures of Mr. Verdant Green*, ch. v.

Admirable Doctor (*Doctor Admirabilis*). Roger Bacon (*c.* 1214–1294), the great English philosopher.

Admiral. Admiral of the Blue facetiously used for a butcher or a tapster from their blue aprons.

> As soon as customers begin to stir
> The Admiral of the Blue cries "Coming Sir!"
>
> *Poor Robin* (1731).

Yellow Admiral, nickname for those promoted from Captain to Admiral but not employed actively (in allusion to the yellow QUARANTINE Flag). The Retired List proper dates from 1870.

Admonitionists, or **Admonitioners.** Those who in 1572 sent *admonitions* to PARLIAMENT condemning EPISCOPACY and advocating the doctrines and practices of Geneva.

Adonai (á dō nī) (Heb. pl. of *adon*, lord). A name for the Deity used by the Hebrews, instead of *Yahweh* (JEHOVAH), "the ineffable name", wherever it occurs. *See* TETRAGRAMMATON.

Adonists. Those Hebraists who maintain that the vowels of the word ADONAI are not those necessary to make the TETRAGRAMMATON J H V H into the name of the Deity. *See* JEHOVAH.

Adonais (àd ō nā' is). The name given by Shelley to Keats in his elegy (*Adonais*, 1821) lamenting the latter's death, probably in allusion to the mourning for ADONIS.

Adonia (àd ō' ni à). An eight-day feast of ADONIS, celebrated in Assyria, Alexandria, Egypt, Judæa, Persia, Cyprus, Greece and Rome. The women first lamented the death of ADONIS then wildly rejoiced at his resurrection—a custom referred to in the BIBLE (*Ezek.* viii, 14), where Adonis appears under his Phœnician name, Tammuz. *See* THAMMUZ.

Adonis (à dō' nis). In classical mythology, a beautiful youth, son of MYRRHA (or Smyrna), he was beloved by APHRODITE (Venus) and killed by a boar while hunting. Hence, usually ironical, any beautiful young man. Leigh Hunt was sent to prison for libelling the Prince Regent by calling him "a corpulent Adonis of fifty" (*Examiner*, 1813).

Adonis Flower, the rose, once white, but coloured red by the blood of APHRODITE when pricked by a thorn rushing to help the fallen ADONIS; the anemone which sprang from his blood or the tears of Aphrodite; and more commonly Pheasant's Eye (*Adonis autumnalis*), which arose from the hunter's blood.

Adonis garden. A worthless toy; very perishable goods.

Adonis River, the stream near Byblos which ran red with the soil brought down from Lebanon.

Adoption. Adoption by arms. An ancient custom of giving arms to a person of merit, which put him under the obligation of being your champion and defender.

Adoption by baptism. Being godfather or godmother to a child.

Adoption by hair. Boso, King of Provence (879–889), is said to have cut off his hair and given it to Pope John VIII (872–882) as a sign that the latter had adopted him.

Adoption controversy. Elipand, Archbishop of Toledo, and Felix Bishop of Urgel (in the 8th century), maintained that Christ in his human nature was the son of God by adoption only (*Rom*. viii, 29), though in his pre-existing state he was the "begotten Son of God" in the ordinary Catholic acceptation. The **adoptionists** were condemned by the Council of Frankfurt in 794.

Adoptive Emperors. The five Emperors—Nerva, Trajan, Hadrian, Antoninus Pius, Marcus Aurelius—each of whom (except Nerva, who was elected by the Senate) was the adopted son of his predecessor. Their period (96–180) is said to have been the happiest in Roman history.

Adrammelech (à drăm' e lek). A Babylonian deity to whom infants were burnt in sacrifice (II *Kings* xvii, 31). Possibly the sun god worshipped at Sippar (Sepharvaim).

Adrastus (à drăs' tus). (i) A mythical Greek king of Argos, leader of the expedition of the SEVEN AGAINST THIEBES. (ii) An Indian prince, slain by RINALDO (in Tasso's JERUSALEM DELIVERED, Bk, XX), who aided the king of Egypt against the crusaders.

Adriatic. *See* BRIDE OF THE SEA.

Adullamites (à dŭl' à mĭts). A group of some thirty LIBERALS led by R. Lowe and E. Horsman, who led the opposition to Lord Russell's Reform Bill in 1866; likened by John Bright to the malcontents who joined David when he escaped to the cave of Adullam.

> And every one that was in distress, and every one that was in debt, and every one that was discontented, gathered themselves unto him.
>
> I *Sam*. xxii, 1, 2

Adulterous Bible. *See* BIBLE, SOME SPECIALLY NAMED EDITIONS.

Advent (Lat. *adventus*, arrival). The four weeks before CHRISTMAS, beginning on St. ANDREW'S Day (30 November), or the Sunday nearest to it, commemorating the first and second coming of Christ; the first to redeem, and the sec-

ond to judge the world.

Advent Sunday. The first Sunday in Advent, the beginning of the Church Year, except in the Greek Church where it begins on St. MARTIN'S Day (11 November).

Adventists. Those who expect a second coming of Christ on earth as imminent. They originated in the U.S.A. as MILLERITES. *See* MILLENARIANS; SEVENTH-DAY ADVENTISTS.

Adversary, The. SATAN or the DEVIL (from I *Pet*. v, 8).

Advocate. The Devil's Advocate. A carping or adverse critic, from *Advocatus Diaboli* (Devil's Advocate). In the ROMAN CATHOLIC CHURCH, the popular name given to the Promoter of the Faith whose duty it is to promote vigorously the arguments against a proposed BEATIFICATION or CANONIZATION. The supporter was (until 1983) called *Advocatus Dei* (God's Advocate).

Advocates' Library, was founded in Edinburgh (1682) by Sir George Mackenzie, Dean of the Faculty of Advocates (*i.e.* members of the Scottish bar). In 1925 it became the National Library of Scotland and has received a copy of all books published since the Copyright Act of 1709. *See* FAMOUS LIBRARIES *under* LIBRARY.

Advowson (Lat. *advocatio*, a summoning). The right of presentation to a church BENEFICE. Thus named because the patron was the advocate or defender of the living and of the claims of his candidate.

Adytum (Gr. *aduton*, not to be entered). The HOLY OF HOLIES in Greek and Roman temples, into which the public was not admitted; hence a sanctum.

Ægeus (ē' jūs). A mythical king of Attica, who sent his son THESEUS to Crete to deliver ATHENS from the yearly tribute of seven youths and seven maidens exacted by MINOS. If successful, Theseus was to hoist white sails (in place of black) on his return, as a signal of his safety. He omitted to do so. Ægeus, thinking his son was lost, threw himself into the sea. The story is repeated in the tale of TRISTRAM and Isolde.

Æginetan Sculptures consist of two groups of figures from the east and west pediments of the temple of ATHENE, on the island of Ægina, representing exploits of the Greek heroes at TROY. They date from c. 500 B.C., being found in 1811, and are preserved in the Glyptothek, in Munich.

Ægir (ē′ jir, ē′ gir). In Norse mythology the god of the ocean, husband of Ran. They had nine daughters (the billows), who wore white robes and veils.

Ægis (ē′ jis) (Gr. goat skin). The shield of ZEUS, made by HEPHÆSTOS and covered with the skin of the goat AMALTHEA, who had suckled the infant Zeus. With the GORGON'S head in the centre, it was also carried by his daughter ATHENE. By shaking his ægis Zeus produced storms and thunder. In relation to Athene it is usually represented as a cloak fringed with serpents and the Gorgon's head. It is symbolic of divine protection, hence *under my ægis*, under my protection.

Ægyptus (ē jip′ tus). In Greek legend a son of Belus and twin brother of Danaus who was king of that part of Africa named after him (Egypt).

Æneas (ē nē′ as). In Greek mythology the son of Anchises, King of Dardanus, and APHRODITE. According to HOMER he fought in the TROJAN WAR, and after the sack of TROY withdrew to Mount IDA and reigned in the Troad. The post-Homeric legends are largely embodied in the ÆNEID.

Æneid (ē′ ne id or ē nē′ id). VIRGIL'S epic poem in twelve books, accounting for the settlement of ÆNEAS in Italy, thus claiming Trojan origins for the Roman state. The story tells how Æneas escaped from the flames of TROY carrying his father Anchises to Mount IDA. With his Trojan followers he sailed to Crete but learnt in a vision that he was destined for Italy, and eventually reached Sicily where his father died. Heading for the mainland, he was wrecked on the coast of Carthage. He left secretly, at JUPITER'S behest, whereupon the lovelorn queen DIDO of Carthage killed herself. Reaching Latium he was betrothed to LAVINIA, daughter of king LATINUS; but war arose with Turnus, king of the Rutuli, who also wished to marry Lavinia. Turnus was finally killed by Æneas.

Æolian Harp. A musical instrument rather like a zither consisting of a wooden resonating box with strings of different thickness tuned to the same note. Taking its name from ÆOLUS, when exposed to the wind the strings vibrate producing a series of chords depending on the speed of the wind. It developed to its present form at the end of the 16th century.

Æolian Mode, in music, the ninth of the "church modes" according to the classification established by Henricus Glareanus in 1547, the range being from A to A with dominant E.

Æolian Rocks. Those which have been deposited or eroded largely by the wind.

Æolus (ē′ ō lùs), in Homeric legend, was appointed ruler of the winds by ZEUS, and lived on his Æolian island.

Æon (ē′ on) (Gr. *aion*). An age of the universe, an infinite length of time. Also the personification of an age, a god, any being that is eternal. Basilides, in the early 2nd century, held that there had been 365 such Æons but Valentinus, the 2nd-century GNOSTIC, restricted the number to 30.

Æschylus (ēs′ ki lùs) (525–456 B.C.), the main father of Greek tragic drama. Only seven plays, of over seventy known titles, are extant. Fable says he was killed by a tortoise dropped by an eagle (to break the shell) on his bald head (mistaken for a stone).

Æsculapius (ēs kū lā′ pi us). The Latin form of the Greek *Asklepios*, god of medicine and of healing, son of APOLLO and father of HYGEIA. The usual offering to him was a cock, hence "to sacrifice a cock to Æsculapius"—to give thanks (or pay the doctor's bill) after recovery from an illness.

> When men a dangerous disease did scape,
> Of old, they gave a cock to Æsculape.
>   BEN JONSON: *Epigram*.

Introduced to ROME (293 B.C.), in the form of a snake, during a pestilence, the SERPENT entwined round a staff became his attribute.

Æsir (ē′zēr). The collective name of the mythical gods of Scandinavia, who lived in ASGARD. (1) ODIN the chief; (2) THOR; (3) TIU; (4) BALDER; (5) BRAG, god of poetry; (6) VIDAR, god of silence; (7) Hoder the blind (slayer of Balder); (8) Hermoder, Odin's son and messenger; (9) Hœnir, a minor god; (10) Odnir, husband of FREYJA; (11) LOKI; (12) Vali (Odin's youngest son).

Æsop's Fables (ē′ sop). These popular animal fables are traditionally the work of Æsop, a deformed Phrygian slave (c. 620–560 B.C.), but many are far older, being found on Egyptian papyri of 800–1,000 years earlier. SOCRATES, in prison, began committing them to verse. A collection made in CHOLIAMBIC by BABRIUS (early 3rd century A.D.), was found in a monastery on Mount Athos in 1844. See PHÆDRUS.

Aetites (ā ē tī′ tēz) (Gr. aetos, an eagle). Eagle stones, also called gagites: according to fable found in eagle's nests, possessing magical and medical properties.

Affluent Society. A phrase, popular from the later 1950s, denoting the overall growth in material prosperity of British society as evidenced by the growingly widespread ownership of motor cars, television sets, washing machines, refrigerators, etc.; a society further cushioned by its "free" social services. J. K. Galbraith's The Affluent Society was published in 1958.

Afreet, Afrit (ăf′ rēt). In Mohammedan mythology the second most powerful of the five classes of JINN or devils. They were of gigantic stature, malicious and inspiring great dread.

Africa. Teneo te, Africa. When CÆSAR landed at Adrumetum, in Africa, he tripped and fell—a bad omen; but with great presence of mind pretended that it was intentional. He kissed the soil, exclaiming, "Thus do I take possession of thee, O Africa." The story is told also of Scipio and again of Cæsar on his landing in Britain.

Africa semper aliquid novi affert. "Africa is always producing some novelty." A Greek proverb quoted by Pliny, in allusion to the belief that Africa abounded in strange monsters.

African Sisters, The. The HESPERIDES, who dwelt in Africa.

Afrikander Bond. A party founded in Cape Colony in 1874 to promote "a united South Africa under its own Flag", essentially under Boer domination.

After. After-clap. A catastrophe or misfortune after an affair is supposedly over. In thunderstorms a "clap" is often heard after the rain stops, and the clouds break.

After-guard. The men who tended the gear in the after part of a ship, also the officers, who had their quarters aft.

After meat, mustard. See under MUSTARD.

After me the deluge. See APRÈS MOI LE DÉLUGE.

Aft-meal. An extra meal; a meal taken after and in addition to the ordinary meals.

> At aft-meals who shall pay for the wine?
> THYNNE: Debate (c. 1608).

Agamemnon (ăg à mem′ non). In Greek legend, the King of Mycenæ, son of Atreus, grandson of PELOPS, brother of MENELAUS, and leader of the Greeks at the siege of TROY. He married CLYTEMNESTRA. ORESTES was their son. Their daughters were IPHIGENIA and/or Iphianassa, Laodice (in later legend ELECTRA), and Chrysothemis. He returned from Troy with CASSANDRA (daughter of King PRIAM) and both were murdered by his wife Clytemnestra and her paramour Ægisthus. The guilty pair were killed by Orestes, called Agamemnonides.

Vixere fortes ante Agamemnona, a quotation from HORACE (Od. IV, ix), paraphrased by Byron in Don Juan (i, 5);

> Brave men were living before Agamemnon
> And since, exceeding valorous and sage,
> A good deal like him too, though quite the same none;
> But then they shone not on the poet's page,
> And so have been forgotten.

In general, we are not to suppose our own age or locality monopolizes all that is good.

Aganippe (ăg à nip′ i). In Greek legend a fountain of BŒOTIA at the foot of Mount HELICON, dedicated to the MUSES because it imparted poetic inspiration. Hence the Muses are sometimes called Aganippides. Also the NYMPH of this fountain.

Agape (ăg' à pi). A love-feast (Gr. *agape*, love). The early Christians held a love-feast in conjunction with the Lord's Supper when the rich provided food for the poor. Eventually they became a scandal and were condemned by the Council of Carthage, 397. *Agape* was the mother of Priamond, Diamond, Triamond and Cambina in Spenser's *Faerie Queene* (IV, ii, 4188).

Agapetæ (ăg à pē' tē). (Gr. beloved). A group of 3rd-century ascetic women who, under vows of virginity, contracted spiritual marriage with monks and attended to their wants. The practice became widespread and the scandals arising led to their condemnation in the 4th century and suppression by the LATERAN COUNCIL of 1139.

Agate (ăg' àt). So called, says Pliny (XXXVII, 10), from Achates or Gagates, a river in Sicily, near which it is found in abundance. It was supposed to render a person invisible, and to turn the sword of foes against themselves.

A diminutive person has been called an *agate* from the custom of carving small figures on seals made from agate.

Agatha, St. (ăg 'à thà), was tortured and murdered at Catania in Sicily, possibly during the Decian persecution of 250–253. She is sometimes represented holding a salver containing her severed breasts, and the shears or pincers with which she was mutilated. Her feast day is 5 February.

Agdistes (ăg dis' tēz). The god who kept the "Bower of Bliss" in Spenser's *Faerie Queene*.

Agdistis (ăg dis' tis). A Phrygian mother goddess sometimes identified with CYBELE the goddess of fertility. Originally hermaphrodite, she was made female by castration.

Age, a word used in mythology, geology, archaeology, history, etc. to denote a period of time marked by particular characteristics, *e.g.*, GOLDEN AGE, ICE AGE, STONE AGE, DARK AGES, MIDDLE AGES, Elizabethan Age, AUGUSTAN AGE, Machine Age, Atomic Age, etc.

Hesiod (? 8th century B.C.) names five ages: the Golden or patriarchal; the SILVER or voluptuous; the Brazen, warlike and violent; the Heroic or renaissant;

the IRON or present, an age of misery and crime when justice and piety have vanished.

Lucretius (*c.* 94–55 B.C.) distinguishes three ages, stone, bronze, and iron, according to the material from which implements were made (V, 2128).

Varro (116–27 B.C.) recognizes three—from the beginning of mankind to the DELUGE; from the Deluge to the first OLYMPIAD, called the mythical period; from the first Olympiad to his own time, called the historic period (*Fragments*, p. 219 Scaliger's edition, 1623).

Ovid (B.C. 43–A.D. 18) describes four ages—Golden, Silver, Bronze and Iron (*Metamorphoses* I, 89–150).

Thomas Heywood (*c.* 1572–1650) has a series of plays based on classical mythology called *The Golden Age, The Silver Age, The Brazen Age,* and *The Iron Age*.

Shakespeare's seven ages of man are described in *As You Like It*, II, vii.

Age of Animals. According to an old CELTIC rhyme:

Thrice the age of a dog is that of a horse;
Thrice the age of a horse is that of a man;
Thrice the age of a man is that of a deer;
Thrice the age of a deer is that of an eagle.

Age of Consent. The age at which a girl's consent to seduction is legal. In English and Scottish law the age is 16.

Age of Discretion. In English law, a child of 14 years is deemed to have sufficient discretion to be prosecuted for offences of commission.

Age of Reason, for Roman Catholics the end of the seventh year when they begin to assume moral responsibility, the obligation of confession, etc.

The 18th century is also called the *Age of Reason* as a period of ENLIGHTENMENT when philosophy was in vogue throughout Europe.

Canonical Age. Ages fixed by Canon Law when individuals may undertake various functions, duties, etc. In the CHURCH OF ENGLAND a man may become a deacon at 23, a priest at 24, and a BISHOP at 30. In the ROMAN CATHOLIC CHURCH a novice must be 16, a deacon 22, and a bishop 30. FASTING begins at the age of 21.

Age hoc (a' jē hok). "Attend to this." In sacrifice the Roman crier perpetually repeated these words to arouse attention.

Agelasta (ăj e lăs' tà), (Gr. joyless). The stone on which CERES (Demeter) rested when wearied in the search for her daughter, PERSEPHONE.

Agenor (ă jen' or). King of Tyre, son of POSEIDON (Neptune).

Agent provocateur (Fr. provocative agent). A person used to incite or stir up others by posing as a partisan in order to induce them to commit treasonable or indictable actions.

Aglaia (à glī' à). One of the three GRACES.

Aglaonice (ăg lā ō nī' si), the Thessalian, being able to calculate eclipses, claimed power over the MOON and to be able to draw it from HEAVEN. Her vaunting became a laughing-stock and gave rise to the Greek proverb cast at braggarts, "Yes, as the Moon obeys Aglaonice."

Agnes, St., patron saint of young virgins, possibly martyred in the Diocletian persecution (*c.* 304) at the age of 13. There are various unreliable and conflicting accounts on the manner of her death; some say she was burnt at the stake and others that she was beheaded or stabbed. She vowed that her body was consecrated to Christ and rejected all her suitors. Her festival is on 21 January. Upon St. Agnes's night, says Aubrey in his *Miscellanies* (1696), you take a row of pins, and pull out every one, one after another. Saying a PATERNOSTER, stick a pin in your sleeve, and you will dream of him or her you shall marry. In Keats' *The Eve of St. Agnes*, we are told:

> how upon St. Agnes' Eve,
> Young virgins might have visions of delight,
> And soft adorings from their loves receive
> Upon the honey'd middle of the night,
> If ceremonies due they did aright;
> As, supperless to bed they must retire.

Tennyson has a poem called *St. Agnes' Eve*.

Agnoitæ (ăg' nō tē) (Gr. *a*, not; *gignoskein*, to know).—(1) Certain 4th-century Eunomian heretics, who maintained that God was not completely omniscient.

(2) A group of 6th-century MONOPHYSITES, who maintained that Christ, by the limitations of his human nature, had incomplete knowledge of both present and future.

Agnostic (Gr. *a*, not; *gignoskein*, to know). A term coined by T. H. Huxley in 1869 (with allusion to St. PAUL'S mention of an altar "To the Unknown God" in *Acts* xvii, 23) to indicate the mental attitude of those who withhold their assent from whatever is incapable of proof, *e.g.* the existence of God, a First Cause, etc. An agnostic simply says 'I do not know". *See* THEIST.

Agnus Bell. *See* AGNUS DEI.

Agnus-castus. *See* VITEX.

Agnus Dei (ăg' nùs de' ī) (Lamb of God). (1) A title of Jesus; (2) the figure of a lamb bearing a cross or flag, the symbol of Christ; (3) the cake of wax or dough bearing this imprint, distributed by the POPE on the Sunday after EASTER—a relic of the ancient custom of distributing the wax of the Paschal candle, which was stamped with the lamb; (4) that part of the MASS introduced by the ringing of the *Agnus bell*, beginning with the words, *Agnus Dei, qui tollis peccata mundi* (O Lamb of God, that takest away the sins of the world); also part of the *Gloria* in the English Communion service.

Agonistes (ă gon is' tēz), (Gr. champion). The title of Milton's last poem, *Samson Agonistes* (1671), simply means "Samson the Champion". Similarly *Sweeney Agonistes*, a poem by T. S. Eliot (1888–1965).

Agony aunt. A woman who conducts an advice column, page or pages in newspapers or magazines (especially women's) answering correspondents who seek help with their problems. Most of the letters are from girls and women and are mainly concerned with family relationships, marital problems, sex and boy friends. Nowadays agony aunts tend to adapt their advice to the circumstances of the PERMISSIVE SOCIETY.

Aguecheek. Sir Andrew Aguecheek, a straight-haired country squire, stupid even to silliness, self-conceited, living to eat, and wholly unacquainted with the world of fashion. The character is in

Shakespeare's *Twelfth Night*.

Agur's Wish (ā' gĕrz) (*Prov*. xxx, 8). "Give me neither poverty nor riches."

Ahasuerus (à hăs ū ēr' ùs). Under this name the Emperor XERXES (485–465 B.C.), husband of Esther, appears in the Biblical books of *Ezra* and *Esther*. The Ahasuerus of *Daniel* has not been identified. It is also traditionally the name of the WANDERING JEW.

Ahithophel. A treacherous friend and adviser. Ahithophel was the traitorous counsellor of King DAVID, who deserted to ABSALOM but hanged himself when Absalom disregarded his advice (II *Sam*. xvii, 23). In Dryden and Tate's *Absalom and Achitophel*, Achitophel (Ahithophel) stands for Lord Shaftesbury.

Ahmed, Prince (a' med), in the ARABIAN NIGHTS, is noted for the tent given him by the fairy Paribanou, which would cover a whole army, but might be carried in one's pocket; and for the apple of Samarkand (*see* APPLE, PRINCE AHMED'S), which would cure all diseases. Similar qualities to those of the tent are common to many legends. *See* BAYARD; CARPET; SKIDBLADNIR.

Aholah and Aholibah (à hō' la, a hō - lī' bà) (*Ezek*. xxiii). Personifications of prostitution. Used by the prophet to signify religious adultery or running after false faiths.

Ahriman (a' ri màn). In the dualism of later ZOROASTRIANISM, the spirit of evil, also called Angra Mainyu. He is in eternal conflict with Ahura Mazda or ORMUZD. The spirit of deceit and wickedness was earlier personified as Druj.

Ahura Mazda. *See* ORMUZD.

Aidan, St. A monk of Iona who was chosen in 635 in answer to King Oswald's request to spread and rekindle Christianity in Northumbria. He established a monastery on the island of Lindisfarne (HOLY ISLAND) and founded many churches and schools on the mainland. He died at Bamburgh in 651.

Aide-mémoire (Fr. *aider*, to help; *mémoire*, memory). A memorandum or reminder. In diplomatic parlance, a memorandum sent by one government through its ambassador to the Foreign Minister of another government summarizing the points he has been instructed to make by word of mouth.

Aide-toi, le Ciel t'aidera (ād twa lè sē el tā dè ra'). A line from LA FONTAINE (*Fables*, vi, 18). Literally "Help yourself, heaven will help you"; motto of a French liberal political society founded in 1824 to secure the advancement of the working classes.

Aim. To give aim. To stand aloof. In archery, meaning to stand within a suitable distance from the butts, to inform the archers how near their arrows fall to the target.

To cry aim. To applaud, encourage. In archery those chosen to cry "aim" to encourage the archer.

All my neighbours shall cry aim.
SHAKESPEARE: *Merry Wives of Windsor*,
III, ii.

Air. Held by Anaxagoras (*c*. 500–*c*. 428 B.C.) to be the primary form of matter and one of the four elements according to Empedocles and ARISTOTLE. *See* ELEMENT.

Air-brained. A mis-spelling of HAREBRAINED.

Hot Air. *See* HOT.

The air of the court, the air of gentility; hence **to give oneself airs**—to assume a manner, appearance, tone, superiority to which one has no real claim.

Aitch-bone. Corruption of "naitch-bone", *i.e.* the haunch-bone (Lat. *nates*). For other instances of the coalescence of the "n" of "an" with an initial vowel (or the coalescence of the "n" with the article), *see* APRON, NICKNAME.

Ajax (ā jăks). (1) *The Greater*. A famous hero of the TROJAN WAR. Son of Telamon and King of Salamis, a man of giant stature, daring and slow-witted. In the ODYSSEY, when the armour of ACHILLES was awarded to Odysseus (ULYSSES), as the champion, Ajax killed himself.

(2) *The Lesser*. In HOMER, son of Oileus, King of Locris, in Greece, and of small stature. In consequence of his attack on PRIAM'S daughter CASSANDRA he was drowned by POSEIDON after being shipwrecked.

Akbar (ăk' bar). An Arabic title, meaning "Very Great", especially applied to

Jelaled-din-Mohammed, Akbar Khan, MOGUL emperor of India (1556–1605).

Aladdin (à lăd' in), in the ARABIAN NIGHTS, obtains a magic lamp and has a splendid palace built by the genie of the lamp. He marries the daughter of the SULTAN of China, who disposes of the lamp, and his palace is transported to Africa. He subsequently recovers the lamp and returns with both wife and palace to China to live happily for many years.

Aladdin's lamp. The source of wealth and good fortune. After his good luck and marriage Aladdin neglected his lamp and allowed it to rust.

Alamo (al' ămo). American cottonwood tree, hence the name *Alamo Mission* for the Franciscan mission at San Antonio, Texas, which stood in a grove of cottonwood trees. Founded in 1718, it was later used as a fort. During the Texas rebellion against Mexico in 1836 a garrison of 187 Texans, including David CROCKETT, was wiped out by 3,000 Mexicans under Santa Anna, after a thirteen-day siege. "Remember the Alamo" became the war cry with which Sam Houston led the Texans to victory. Alamo is sometimes called the "THERMOPYLÆ of America" and the buildings are now a national monument.

Alans. Large hunting dogs introduced to Britain from Spain, whither they are said to have been brought by the Alani, a barbarian tribe which entered Spain *c.* 410. Chaucer in *The Knight's Tale* describes Lycurgus on his throne guarded by "alaunts, twenty and mo, as grete as any steer". Scott mentions them in *The Talisman* (ch. vi). *Cp.* RACHE.

Al Araf (al' ă' răf) (Arab. the partition). In the KORAN, a region between PARADISE and Jahannam (HELL), for those who are neither morally good nor bad, such as infants, lunatics and idiots. Also where those whose good and evil deeds are equally balanced can await their ultimate admission to HEAVEN—a kind of LIMBO.

Alasnam (à lăs' năm). In the ARABIAN NIGHTS Alasnam had eight diamond statues, but was required to find a ninth more precious still, to fill the vacant pedestal. The prize was found in the woman who became his wife, at once the most beautiful and perfect of her race.

Alasnam's mirror. The "touchstone of virtue", given to him by one of the genii. If he looked into this mirror and it remained unsullied so would the maiden he had in mind; if it clouded she would prove faithless.

Alastor (à lăs' tor). The evil genius of a house; a NEMESIS, the Greek term for an avenging power who visits the sins of the fathers on their children. Shelley has a poem entitled *Alastor; or the Spirit of Solitude*.

Alauda. A Roman legion raised by Julius CÆSAR in GAUL, so called from the lark's tuft worn on top of their helmets.

Alban, St. (ôl' bàn). Britain's first martyr, beheaded *c.* 305 at Verulamium during the Diocletian persecution, for harbouring a Christian priest. The monastery of St. Albans was built by Offa in 795 on the spot where he died. His feast is on 22 June, although the CHURCH OF ENGLAND keeps 17 June.

Albany, Albainn, or **Albin** (Celtic *alp* or *ailp*, rock or cliff). An ancient name applied to the northern part of Scotland, inhabited by PICTS, and called CALEDONIA by the Romans. The name Albany survives in Breadalbane, the hilly country of Albainn, *i.e.* western Perthshire.

In Spenser's *Fairie Queene* (II, x, 14, etc.) northern Britain is called Albania.

Albatross. The largest of web-footed birds, called the Cape Sheep by sailors from its frequenting the CAPE of Good Hope. It was said to sleep in the air without any apparent motion of its wings, and sailors say that to shoot one is fatal. *See* ANCIENT MARINER.

Alberich. In Scandinavian mythology, the all-powerful King of the DWARFS. In Wagner's version of the NIBELUNGENLIED he appears as a hideous GNOME and steals the magic GOLD guarded by the Rhine Maidens but is later captured by the gods, and forced to give up all he has in return for freedom.

Albert, An. A watch-chain across the waistcoat from one pocket to another or to a buttonhole; so called from Albert, Prince Consort, who set the fashion. He was presented with such a chain by the jewellers of Birmingham, when visiting the town in 1849.

Albert the Good. The Prince Consort (1819–1861).

> Beyond all titles, and a household name,
> Hereafter, thro' all times, Albert the Good.
> TENNYSON: Dedication to *Idylls of the King*.

Albert the Great. (1) Albertus Magnus (c. 1206–1280), Albert of Cologne, famous DOMINICAN scholastic philosopher, also called *doctor universalis*.

(2) A nickname, by analogy with Albert the Good, given to Albert Chevalier (1861–1923), the coster's LAUREATE and great favourite of the late Victorian and Edwardian MUSIC HALLS. Among the most famous of his songs are *Knock'd 'em in the Old Kent Road* and *My Old Dutch*.

Albigenses (ăl bi jen' sēs). A common name for various 12th- and 13th-century MANICHEAN sects in southern France and northern Italy; so called from the city of Albi in LANGUEDOC, where their persecution began. Violent opponents of the CATHOLIC Church, they were subjected to a crusade by Innocent III in 1208 and they were finally exterminated by the end of the 14th century. They were also called Cathari and Bulgarians.

Albin. *See* ALBANY.

Albion. An ancient and poetical name for Great Britain, probably from the white (Lat. *albus*) cliffs that face GAUL, but possibly from the CELTIC *alp*. Albion or ALBANY originally may have been the Celtic name of all Great Britain.

One legend is that a giant son of NEPTUNE, named Albion, discovered the country and ruled over it for forty-four years. Another such derivation is that the fifty daughters of the King of Syria (the eldest of whom was named Albia), were all married on the same day, and murdered their husbands on their wedding night. They were set adrift in a ship as punishment and eventually reached this western isle where they duly married natives.

Perfide Albion. Although the sentiment is often traced back to a mid-17th-century sermon by Bossuet, where the phrase "la perfide Angleterre" is used, he is referring to England's adoption of

Protestantism, and there is no real connection with the subsequent expression which is first noticed in a poem of 1793 by the Marquis de Ximenez— "Attaquons dans ses eaux la perfide Albion". It attracted no particular attention and next appears in 1809 in both a poem by Henri Simon and a song. Its popular currency stems from its wide use in the Napoleonic recruiting drive of 1813 and it was well established by the end of the war in 1815.

Al Borak. *See* BORAK.

Alcaic Verse (ăl kā' ik) or **Alcaics.** A Greek and Latin lyrical metre so called from Alcæus (7th century B.C.) who supposedly invented it.

Alcestis. In Greek legend the daughter of Pelias and wife of Admetus, King of Pheræ in Sicily to whom the FATES agreed to grant deliverance from death if his mother, father, or wife would die for him instead. Alcestis thus sacrificed her life but was restored to her husband from the lower world by PERSEPHONE (another version says by HERCULES).

Alchemilla (ăl kẻ mil'ả). A genus of plants of the rose family; so called because alchemists collected the dew of its leaves for their operations. Also called "Lady's Mantle", from the Virgin MARY, to whom the plant was dedicated.

Alchemy (ăl'kẻ mi). The derivation of this word is obscure; *al* is the Arabic article the, and *kimia* the Arabic form of the Greek *chemeia*, which seems to have meant "Egyptian art"; hence "the art of the Egyptians". Its main objects were the transmutation of base metals into gold, and the search for the PHILOSOPHER'S STONE, the universal solvent or ALKAHEST, the PANACEA, and the ELIXIR OF LIFE. It was the forerunner of the science of chemistry. Ben Jonson wrote a play called *The Alchemist* (1610).

Alcimedon (ăl sim' ẻ don). A generic name for a first-rate carver in wood.

Alcinoo poma dare (ăl'sin' ō ō pō' mả da' re) (to give apples to Alcinous). "To carry COALS to Newcastle." The gardens of Alcinous, legendary king of the Phæacians, by whom ULYSSES was entertained, were famous for their fruits.

Alcmena (ălk mē' nả). In Greek mythology, daughter of Electryon (King of

Mycenæ), wife of AMPHITRYON, and mother (by ZEUS) of HERCULES. The legend is that at the conception of Hercules, Zeus (in the guise of Amphitryon), for additional pleasure with Alcmena, made the night the length of three ordinary nights.

Alcofribas Nasier (ălko'frebăs nã'syer). The anagrammatic pseudonym used by Rabelais under which the first two books of GARGANTUA and PANTAGRUEL appeared.

Aldebaran (al'deb' á răn) (Arab. *al*, the; *davaran*, the follower, because its rising follows that of the PLEIADES). A red star of the first magnitude, α Tauri, it forms the bull's eye in the constellation of TAURUS.

Aldine Editions. Internationally famous and reliable octavo editions of the Greek and Latin classics printed and published at Venice by the firm founded by Aldus Manutius in 1490. The type called *italics*, once called *Aldine*, was devised by his type-designer, Francesco Griffo. The founder's grandson (Aldus, the Younger) closed the business on taking charge of the VATICAN press in 1590.

Ale is the Old English *alu*, connected with the Scandinavian *ol*. Beer is the Old English *beor* connected with the German *bier*. A beverage made from barley is mentioned by Tacitus (*c.* 55–120?) and even Herodotus (5th century B.C.). Ale in Britain is of pre-Roman origin and was a malt brew without hops. Hopped or bitter beer was introduced by the Flemings in the 15th century. Fuggles hops are now used for most beers and goldings for pale ales—ale and beer now being largely synonymous terms, although the word ale is not used for the thick black beers (STOUT and porter) which became so popular in the 18th century. In some areas ale is used for the stronger malt liquors and beer for the weaker, in others the terms are reversed. *See also* AUDIT-ALE, CHURCH-ALE, ENTIRE.

Aleberry. A corruption of *ale-bree*. A drink made of hot ale, spice, sugar and toast. Burns speaks of the barley-bree (A.S. *briw*, broth).

Ale-silver. Formerly, the annual fee paid to the Lord MAYOR of London for the privilege of selling ale within the city.

Ale-stake, or **ale-pole.** The pole set up before an ale-house by way of a sign, often surmounted by a bush or garland. Thus, Chaucer says of the Sompnour:

> A garland hadde he sette upon his hede
> As gret as it were for an ale-stake.
> *Canterbury Tales, Prologue,* 666.

Ale-wife. The landlady of an ale-house. In America a fish of the herring family, possibly from supposed resemblance to a stout landlady; or from a corruption of aloofe, a North American Indian name; or from the French *alose*, a shad.

Alecto (á lek' tō). In Greek mythology "she who rests not", one of the three ERINYES, goddesses of vengeance, the Latin FURIES.

Alectorian Stone (á lek tôr' i án) (Gr. *alector*, a COCK). A stone, fabled to be of talismanic power, found in the stomach of cocks. Those who possess one are strong, brave, and wealthy. MILO of Crotona owed his strength to one.

Alectryomancy (á lek' tri ō măn si). DIVINATION by a COCK. Draw a circle, and write in succession round it the letters of the alphabet, on each of which lay a grain of corn. Then put a cock in the centre of the circle, and watch what grains he eats. The letters will prognosticate the answer. Libanus and Jamblicus thus discovered who was to succeed the emperor Valens. The cock ate the grains over the letters t, h, e, o, d = Theod (orus).

Alexander. So PARIS, son of PRIAM, was called by the shepherds who brought him up.

Alexander the Great. Alexander III of Macedon (356–323 B.C.).

The continence of Alexander. Having won the battle of Issus (333 B.C.), the family of Darius III fell into his hand; but he treated the women with the greatest decorum. His CONTINENCE drew respect from Darius.

You are thinking of Parmenio and I of Alexander.—*i.e.* you are thinking of what you ought to receive, and I of what I ought to give; you are thinking of those castigated or rewarded, but I of my position, and what reward is consistent with my rank. The allusion is to the tale that Alexander said to Parmenio, "I consider not what Parmenio should receive, but what Alexander should give."

Alexander of the North. The warloving Charles XII of Sweden (1682–1718), whose army was annihilated by Peter the Great at Pultawa (1709).

Alexander's beard. A beardless, smooth chin—an AMAZONIAN CHIN.

> I like this trustie glass of Steele …
> Wherein I see a Sampson's grim regarde
> Disgraced yet with Alexander's bearde.
> GASCOIGNE: *The Steele Glas* (1576).

Alexandra Day. A day in June when rose emblems are sold for the hospital fund inaugurated in 1912 by Queen Alexandra (1844–1925), Danish consort of Edward VII, to celebrate the fiftieth year of her residence in England.

Alexandra limp. In the 1860s Queen Alexandra (then Princess of Wales), after a minor accident, developed a very slight limp, which was imitated in sycophantic fashion by many women about the court. Hence the description "Alexandra limp".

Alexandrian. Anything from the East was so called by the old writers because Alexandria was the depot from which Eastern goods reached Europe. Thus ARIOSTO says:

> Reclined on Alexandrian carpets (*i.e.* Persian).
> *Orlando Furioso*, X, 37.

Alexandrian Codex. A Greek MS. of the Scriptures, probably of the 5th century, written in UNCIALS on parchment, and supposed to have originated at Alexandria. It was presented to Charles I in 1628 by the PATRIARCH of Constantinople, and was placed in the BRITISH MUSEUM on its foundation.

Alexandrian School. An academy of learning founded about 310 B.C. at Alexandria by Ptolemy I (Soter) and Demetrius of Phaleron, especially noted for its literary scholars and mathematicians. Of the former the most noted were Aristarchus (*c.* 217–145 B.C.), Eratosthenes (*c.* 275–194 B.C.), and Harpocration (2nd century A.D.); and of its mathematicians EUCLID (fl. *c.* 300 B.C.), the author of the *Elements*, the celebrated treatise on geometry, and Claudius Pto-

lemæus (2nd century A.D.), the astronomer. Alexandria remained a centre of learning until 640 A.D. when the library was, supposedly, finally destroyed.

Alexandrine. In prosody, an IAMBIC or trochaic line of twelve syllables or six feet with, usually, a caesura (break) at the sixth syllable. So called either from the 12th-century French metrical romance, *Li Romans d'Alixandre* (commenced by Lambert-li-Cort and continued by Alexandre de Bernay), or from the old Castilian verse chronicle, *Poema de Alexandro Magno*, both of which are written in this metre. Pope sometimes used it but wrote:

> A needless Alexandrine ends the song
> That, like a wounded snake, drags its slow length along.
> *Essay on Criticism* (1709), ii, 356.

Alexandrine Age. When the Alexandrine school was the centre of literature, science and philosophy.

Alexandrine Philosophy. A school of philosophy which developed at Alexandria in the early centuries of the Christian era. It gave rise to Gnosticism and Neoplatonism and attempted to reconcile Christianity and Greek philosophy.

Alexis, St. Patron saint of hermits and beggars. According to the story in the GESTA ROMANORUM (*Tale* XV) he lived on his father's estate as a hermit until he died, but was never recognized.

Alfadir (al fa' der) (father of all). In Scandinavian mythology, one of the epithets of ODIN.

Alfana. *See* HORSE.

Alfar. The elves of the northern mythology. In German legend the *döckalfar* frequent dark underground caverns and mines. The O.E. *Ælfric* means "ruler of the elves".

Alfonsin, Alfonsine Tables. *See* ALPHONSIN, etc.

Alfred the Great (849–899), King of WESSEX, especially noted for his resistance to the Danish invaders who in the winter of 877–8 occupied much of Wessex. Alfred withdrew to his base at Athelney and it is to this period that the story of Alfred and the cakes belongs— the first known version probably dating from the 11th/12th century. The story is that the king, unrecognized, took refuge in a cowherd's hut. He was sitting by the fire seeing to his equipment and allowed the housewife's loaves to burn. For this he was vigorously scolded. The story is not found in Asser's *Life of Alfred* (written in 893). After the defeat of the Danes Alfred commanded the building of a monastery at Athelney.

The beautiful gold enamelled relic, known as *Alfred's Jewel*, and bearing his name, was dug up at Athelney in 1693. It is now in the ASHMOLEAN MUSEUM, Oxford.

Alhambra (ăl hăm′ brà) (Arab. *Kal′-at al hamra*, the red castle). The citadel and palace built at Granada by the Moorish kings in the 13th century. Also the name of a famous theatre and music hall in Leicester Square, built in Moorish style. *See* PANOPTICON.

Ali (a′ lē). MOHAMMED'S cousin and son-in-law, famed among Persians for the beauty of his eyes, hence *Ayn Hali* (eyes of Ali) as the highest expression for beauty.

Ali Baba (ă′ lē ba′ ba). The hero of a story in the ARABIAN NIGHTS ENTERTAINMENTS, who sees a band of robbers enter a cave by means of the magic password "Open SESAME". When they have gone away he enters the cave, loads his ass with treasure and returns home. The Forty Thieves discover that Ali Baba has learned their secret and resolve to kill him, but they are finally outwitted by the slave-girl MORGIANA.

Alias (ā′ li ăs), "You have as many aliases as Robin of Bagshot," said to one who passes under many names. The phrase is from Gay's *Beggar's Opera*: Robin of Bagshot, one of Macheath's gang, was *alias* Gordon, *alias* Bluff Bob, *alias* Carbuncle, *alias* Bob Booty and intended for Sir Robert Walpole.

Alibi (ă′ li bī) (Lat. elsewhere). A plea of having been elsewhere at a time that an offence is alleged to have been committed. A clock which strikes an hour, while the hands point to a different time, has been humorously called *an alibi clock*. A modern usage of the word is for an excuse or pretext.

Aliboron. The name of a jackass in LA FONTAINE'S *Fables*; hence Maître Aliboron = Mr. Jackass.

Alice. Alice in Wonderland. *Alice's Adventures in Wonderland* (1865) and *Through the Looking Glass* (1871), widely read children's classics, originally illustrated by Sir John Tenniel, were written by C. L. Dodgson, an Oxford mathematician, under the pseudonym of Lewis Carroll. The original of Alice was Alice Liddell, daughter of Dean Liddell, famous as joint author of Liddell and Scott's Greek Lexicon. The Alice stories are noted for their whimsical humour and the "nonsense" verse included in them.

"Alice in Wonderland" schemes, projects, ideas etc., are those which are unreal, totally impractical, things which can only exist in the realm of fantasy. *Cp.* CLOUD-CUCKOO-LAND; LOOKING-GLASS.

Alien priory. A priory which was dependent upon a monastery in a foreign country.

Alifanfaron (ăl i fan′ fà ron). Don QUIXOTE attacked a flock of sheep, and declared them to be the army of the giant Alifanfaron. Similarly AJAX, in a fit of madness, fell upon a flock of sheep, mistaking them for the sons of Atreus.

Al Kadr (ăl kădr) (the divine decree). A particular night in the month RAMADAN when Mohammedans say that angels descend to earth and GABRIEL reveals to man the decrees of God. — *Al Koran*, ch. xcvii.

Alkahest (ăl′ kà hest). A sham-Arabic word attributed to PARACELSUS. *See* ALCHEMY.

All. All abroad. To be confused in mind, or wide of the mark.

All and Some. An old expression meaning "one and all", confused sometimes with "all and sum", meaning the whole total.

> They that wolde nought Crystene become,
> Richard lect sleen hem alle and some.
> *Cœur de Lion.* 14th cent.

All Fools' Day (1 April). *See* APRIL FOOL.

To go on all fours is to crawl about on all four limbs like a quadruped or an infant. The phrase used to be *all four*, as in *Lev.* xi, 42, "whatsoever goeth upon all four".

It does not go on all fours means it does not suit in every particular; it limps like a lame quadruped. Thus the Latin saying, *Omnis comparatio claudicat* (all similes limp) was translated by Macaulay as "No simile can go on all fours".

All-Hallows' Day. All Saints' Day (1 November), "hallows" being the Old English *halig*, a holy (man), a saint. Pope Boniface IV converted the PANTHEON at Rome into a Christian church, dedicated to all the martyrs, in 610. The festival of All Saints, originally held on 1 May, was changed to 1 November in 834.

All-Hallows' Eve or **Hallowe'en** (31 October), also called "NUTCRACK NIGHT" and "Holy Eve", is associated with many ancient customs including bobbing for apples (*see* BOB), cracking nuts (mentioned in *The Vicar of Wakefield*), finding one's lover by various rites, etc. Burns portrays the Scottish customs in his poem *Hallowe'en*, and Scottish tradition says that those born on HALLOWE'EN have the gift of second sight. Thus Mary Avenel, in Scott's *The Monastery* (1820), is made to see the WHITE LADY.

All-Hallows Summer. Another name for St. Martin's SUMMER or an INDIAN SUMMER, so called because it set in about All-Hallows; similarly there is a St. Luke's Summer (from 18 October).

> Farewell, thou latter spring! farewell,
> All-hallow Summer!
> SHAKESPEARE: *Henry IV, Part I*, I, ii.

All Heal. The common Valerian, formerly supposed to have many medicinal virtues, also called *Hercules Woundwort*, because HERCULES is supposed to have learned its virtues from CHIRON. Spikenard, mentioned in the BIBLE (*Mark* xiv, 3), and extracted from a Himalayan member of the family, was used in perfumes by the ancient Egyptians, Greeks and Romans.

All in. Completely exhausted.

All my eye and Betty Martin. All nonsense, BOSH, rubbish. A curious phrase of uncertain origin. A common explanation was that it was a British soldiers' or sailors' rendering of "O mihi, beate Martine" an invocation to ST. MARTIN heard abroad. "All my eye" is the older

saying:

> That's all my eye, the King only can pardon, as the law says.
> GOLDSMITH: *The Good Natur'd Man* (1767).

All-overish. Not to be at one's best, beset with lassitude and indifference as before the onset of an illness.

All Saints. *See* ALL HALLOWS.

All serene (Sp. *sereno*). In Spain the word was used by night watchmen to indicate that the weather was fine and is equivalent to our "All's well". It was a popular CATCHPHRASE from the late 19th century.

All ship-shape and Bristol fashion. Everything stowed and the ship in every way ready for sea, thus "to be completely organized and ready". It derives from the port of Bristol's reputation for efficiency in the days of sail.

All Sir Garnet, meaning "everything is as it should be" began as an army phrase of the 1880s arising from Sir Garnet Wolseley's skilfully organized operations in Egypt.

All Souls' Day (2 November). The day which Roman Catholics devote to prayer and almsgiving on behalf of the faithful departed. According to tradition, a pilgrim returning from the HOLY LAND took refuge on a rocky island during a storm. There he met a hermit, who told him that among the cliffs was an opening to the infernal regions, through which flames ascended, and where the groans of the tormented were distinctly audible. The pilgrim told Odilo, abbot of Cluny, who appointed the day following (2 November 998) to be set apart for the benefit of those souls in PURGATORY.

All Souls' Parish Magazine. *The Times* was so nicknamed during the editorship (1923–1941) of G.G. Dawson, Fellow of All Souls. He and some of his associates, who were also fellows of the college, frequently met there for discussions.

All standing. A nautical expression meaning "fully equipped", "all sails set".

To be brought up all standing is to be suddenly checked when unprepared, or to be taken by surprise.

To turn in all standing is to go to one's

hammock, bunk or bed fully dressed.

All Stuarts are not sib (O.E. *gesibb*, related), *i.e.* related to the Royal Family. An old Scottish proverb rebuking those who, sharing a surname with a famous person, advance false claims of kinship to inflate their self-esteem.

All the Talents. The unsuitable name given to Lord Grenville's ministry (1806–1807) formed on the death of the younger Pitt. It was an attempt at a broadly-based administration but largely consisted of the followers of Charles James Fox, who was Foreign Secretary. Its one great measure was the abolition of the slave trade in 1807.

All this for a song! *See* WHAT! ALL THIS FOR A SONG? *under* SONG.

Allah (ăl′ à). The Arabic name of the Supreme Being (*al*, the, *ilah*, god). The Mohammedan war-cry *Allah il Allah* is a form of *la illah illa allah* "there is no God but the God"—the first clause of their confession of faith. *Allah akbar* means "God is most mighty".

Allan-a-Dale. A minstrel in the ROBIN HOOD ballads who also appears in Scott's *Ivanhoe*. Robin Hood helped him to carry off his bride when she was on the point of being married against her will to a rich old knight.

Alleluiah. *See* HALLELUJAH.

Alley, or **Ally.** A choice, large playing-marble made of stone or alabaster (from which it takes its name). The alley for (taw) beloved of Master Bardell (*Pickwick Papers*, xxxiv) was a special alley that had won many taws or games. Also in Australia, a group of gamblers, or their den.

Alley, Right up one's. A variation of *right up one's street*, meaning some kind of activity in which one is specially skilled or particularly well informed. Current since the early 19th century.

Alley, The. An old name for Change Alley in the City of London, where dealings in the public funds, etc. used to take place.

Alley up. In Australia, to pay up one's debts.

Alliensis, Dies (ăl i en′ sis, dī′ ēz). The day when the Romans were cut to pieces by the Gauls (390 B.C.) near the banks of the river Allia. It was ever after held to be a DIES NEFASTUS, or unlucky day.

Alliteration. The rhetorical device of commencing adjacent accented syllables with the same letter or sound, as ridiculed by Quince in *A Midsummer Night's Dream* (V, i):

> Whereat with blade, with bloody blameful blade,
> He bravely broach'd his boiling bloody breast.

Alliteration was a SINE QUA NON in Old and Middle English poetry, and is frequently used in modern poetry with great effect, as in Coleridge's *Ancient Mariner*:

> The fair breeze blew, the white foam flew,
> The furrow followed free.

Many fantastic examples of excessive alliteration are extant (*see* AMPHIGOURI). Henry Harder composed a poem of 100 lines in Latin hexameters on cats, each word beginning with c, called *Canum cum Catis certamen carmine compositum currente calamo C Catulli Caninii*.

Thomas Tusser (1524–1580) has a rhyming poem of twelve lines, every word of which begins with a *t*; and in the 1890s a Serenade of twenty-eight lines was published "sung in M flat by Major Marmaduke Muttinhead to Mademoiselle Madeline Mendoza Marriott", which contained only one word not beginning with *M*—in the line "Meet me by moonlight, marry me". The alliterative alphabetic poem beginning:

> An Austrian army awfully arrayed
> Boldly by battery besieged Belgrade;
> Cossack commanders, cannonading come,
> Dealing destruction's devastating doom;

was published in *The Trifler* (7 May 1817), ascribed to the Rev. B. Poulter, later revised by Alaric A. Watts.

Ally Pally. A familiar and affectionate name for the Alexandra Palace in North London, first opened in 1863 but burnt down and rebuilt in 1873. A popular amusement centre like the CRYSTAL PALACE and partly used as a broadcasting and television centre, it was devastated by another disastrous fire in July 1980.

Ally Sloper's Cavalry. In the GREAT WAR, a nickname of the Army Service

Corps which provided transport for men, rations and supplies generally. Ally Sloper was the jester in a pre-war comic paper of this name.

Alma Mater (Lat. bounteous mother). A collegian so calls his university. Also applied to one's school and other "fostering mothers".

> You might divert yourself, too, with Alma Mater, the Church.
> HORACE WALPOLE: *Letters* (1778).

Almagest (ăl′ mȧ jest). The English form of the Arabic name (*al Majisti*) given to Ptolemy's *Mathematike syntaxis*, his classic astronomical treatise in thirteen books, of the mid-2nd century. An Arabic translation was made about 820. In the third book the length of the year was first fixed at 365¼ days. His geocentric astronomy lasted until the introduction of the COPERNICAN SYSTEM.

Almanac. A mediæval Latin word of obscure origin for a calendar of days and months with astronomical data, etc.

> A calendar, a calendar! look in the almanac; find out moonshine, find out moonshine.
> SHAKESPEARE: *A Midsummer Night's Dream*, III, i.

Some early almanacs before the invention of printing are:

By Solomon Jarchi	in and after 1150
Peter de Dacia	about 1307
Walter de Elvendene	1327
John Somers, Oxford	1380
Nicholas de Lynna	1386
Purbach	1457–1461

Examples after the invention of printing are:

By Regiomantanus at Nuremberg	1474
Zainer at Ulm	1478
Richard Pynson (Sheapeherd's Kalendar)	1497
Stoffler at Venice	1499
Poor Robin's Almanac (*q.v.*)	1652
Francis Moore's Almanack	1698–1713
Poor Richard's Almanack (U.S.A.)	1732–1757
Almanach de Gotha (Successively suppressed by Hitler, Stalin and Adenauer)	1764–1944
Whitaker's Almanack	from 1869

Almanzor (ăl măn′ zor). The word, derived from the Arabic, means "the invincible" and was adopted as a title by several MOSLEM rulers, notably the second Abasside Caliph Abu Jafar Abdullah (712–775), who founded Baghdad.

Almesbury. It was in a SANCTUARY at Almesbury that Queen GUINEVERE, according to Malory, took refuge after her adulterous passion for LANCELOT was revealed to King ARTHUR. Here she died; but her body was buried at GLASTONBURY.

Almighty Dollar. *See under* DOLLAR.

Almonry. The place where the almoner resides. In monasteries, one-tenth of the income was distributed to the poor by the almoner. *Almonry* is from the Latin *eleemosynarium*, a place for alms but the word became confused with AMBRY, thus "Ambry Close" in WESTMINSTER used to be called "Almonry Close".

Alms. To live on the alms basket. To live on charity.

  Alms-drink. Leavings; the liquor which a drinker finds too much, and therefore hands to another.

  Alms-man. One who lives on alms.

Alnaschar's Dream. Counting your chickens before they are hatched. In the ARABIAN NIGHTS, Alnaschar, the Talkative Barber's fifth (and deaf) brother, spent all his money on a basket of glassware, on which he was to make a profit which was to be invested to make more, and so on until he grew rich enough to marry the VIZIER's daughter. Being angry with his imaginary wife he gave a kick, overturned his basket and broke all his wares.

Aloe (Gr. *aloe*). A genus of very bitter plants of the family Liliaceæ; hence the line in Juvenal's sixth satire (181), *Plus aloes quam mellis habet*, "He has in him more bitters than sweets", said of a writer with a sarcastic pen. The French say, "*La côte d'Adam contient plus d'aloès que de miel*", where *côte d'Adam* means woman or one's wife.

Alombrados. *See* ALUMBRADO; ILLUMINATI.

À l'outrance (a loo′ trons). To the uttermost, to the death. An incorrect English form of the French *à outrance*.

Alpha (ăl′ fȧ). "I am Alpha and Omega, the first and the last" (*Rev.* i, II). *Alpha* (A) is the first and *Omega* (Ω) the last letter of the Greek alphabet. *See* TAU.

Alphabet. Compounded from *alpha* and

beta, the first two letters of the Greek alphabet. *Ezra* vii, 21 contains all the letters of the English alphabet except j.

The number of letters in an alphabet varies in different languages. Although the English alphabet is capable of innumerable combinations and permutations, we have no means of differentiating our vowel sounds; take *a*, we have *fate, fat, Thames, war, orange, ware, abide, calm, swan*, etc. So with *e*, we have *era, the, there, prey, met, England, sew, herb, clerk*, etc. The other vowels are equally indefinite. *See* LETTER.

Alpheus and Arethusa (ăl fē' us, ăree-thū' za). Greek legend says that the river-god Alpheus fell in love with the nymph Arethusa, who fled from him in affright to Ortygia, an island near Syracuse, where ARTEMIS changed her into a fountain. Alpheus flowed under the sea from Peloponnesus to rise in Ortygia and so unite with his beloved. The myth seems to derive from the fact that the Alpheus, in places, does flow underground.

Alphonsin (ăl fon' sin). An old surgical instrument for extracting shot from wounds, named after Alphonso Ferri, a surgeon of Naples, who invented it in 1552.

Alphonsine Tables. Astronomical tables completed in 1252 by a group of Jewish, Arabian and Christian astronomers under the patronage of Alphonso X of Castile.

Alpine Race. Another name for the broadheaded CELTIC Race, because of its distribution in the mountainous regions from Armenia to the Pyrenees. They were a midway race between the Scandinavian Nordics and the dark Mediterranean folk. The LA TÈNE period (500 B.C.-? A.D.) witnessed the zenith of their culture.

Alruna-wife, An (ăl roo' nà). The Alrunes were the LARES or PENATES of the ancient Germans; and an Alruna-wife, the household goddess.

> She looked as fair as the sun, and talked like an Alruna-wife.
> KINGSLEY: *Hypatia* (1853), ch. xii.

Alsatia (ăl sā' shà). The Whitefriars district of London, which retained privileges derived from being a converted

SANCTUARY until 1697, and was the haunt of debtors and law-breakers. Bounded on the north and south by FLEET STREET and the THAMES, on the east and west by the Fleet river (now New Bridge Street) and the TEMPLE, it was probably named after Alsace (Lat. *Alsatia*), which was for centuries a disputed frontier and refuge of the disaffected.

Al-Sirat (Arab. the path). In Mohammedan mythology, the bridge leading to PARADISE; a bridge over a mid-HELL, no wider than the edge of a sword, across which all who enter HEAVEN must pass.

Also ran, An. In horse-racing this refers to a runner who fails to come in among the first three, hence, metaphorically, it denotes one who has failed to make his mark or to distinguish himself.

Altar. Led to the altar, *i.e.* married, said of a woman, who as a bride is led up to the altarrail, where marriages are solemnized.

Alter ego (ăl'ter eg' ō) (Lat. other I, other self). One's double, one's intimate and thoroughly trusted friend; one who has full power to act for another. *Cp.* ONE'S SECOND SELF (*see* SECOND).

Alternative Services Book. *See* BOOK OF COMMON PRAYER.

Althæa's Brand (ăl' thē à), a fatal contingency. Althæa's son MELEAGER was to live just so long as a log of wood, then on the fire, remained unconsumed, so she snatched it from the fire. Years later, to avenge her brothers (slain by Meleager) she threw the brand into the fire, and her son died as it was consumed (Ovid: *Metamorphoses*, viii).

> As did the fatal brand Althæa burned.
> SHAKESPEARE: *Henry VI, Part II*, 1, i.

Althea. The divine Althea of Richard Lovelace (1618–1658) was Lucy Sacheverell, also called by the poet "Lucasta".

> When love with unconfinèd wings
> Hovers within my gates,
> And my divine Althea brings
> To whisper at my grates

Lovelace was imprisoned in the Gatehouse, Westminster, by the LONG PARLIAMENT for his royalist activities; hence the grates or railings referred to.

Altis. The sacred precinct of ZEUS at OLYMPIA combining the altar of Zeus, the temples of Zeus and HERA, the Pelopion (grave of PELOPS), etc. It was connected by an arched passage with the STADIUM, where the games were held.

Altmark, The. In the Royal Navy an opprobrious synonym for a ship or an establishment with a reputation for very strict discipline. It derives from a famous naval exploit of February 1940 when Captain Vian, commanding the destroyer *H.M.S. Cossack*, entered Norwegian territorial waters to effect the release of 299 British prisoners of war from the German auxiliary-cum-prison ship *Altmark*, which had taken refuge in Josing Fiord.

Alto relievo. Italian for "high relief". A term used for sculptures so cut as to project more than one-half their thickness from the background. The ELGIN MARBLES are notable examples. *See* BAS-RELIEF.

Alumbrado (Sp. illuminated, enlightened). A perfectionist; so called from a Spanish sect claiming special "illumination", which arose in 1575.

Alvina weeps, or "Hark! Alvina weeps", *i.e.* the wind howls loudly, a Flemish saying. Alvina was the daughter of a king, who was cursed by her parents because she married unsuitably. From that day she roamed about the air invisible to the eye of man, but her moans are audible.

Alzire (ăl′ zēr). A daughter of Montezuma, invented by VOLTAIRE and the central character of his play *Alzire* (1736), which is set in Peru instead of Mexico.

Amadis of Gaul (à ma′ dis). The hero of the famous prose romance of the same title. The oldest extant edition (1508) is in Spanish by Montalvo but is probably an adaptation of a 14th-century Portuguese or Spanish original with his own additions. Many details are derived from ARTHURIAN legend, and subsequent writers increased the romance to fourteen books by adding other exploits. It long enjoyed popularity and exerted a wide influence on literature.

Amadis, called the "Lion-Knight", from the device on his shield, and "Beltenebros" (darkly beautiful), was a love-child of Perion, King of Gaula (Wales), and Elizena, Princess of Britta-

ny. He was cast away at birth and became known as the Child of the Sun. After many adventures he secured the hand of ORIANA. He is represented as a poet and musician, a linguist and a gallant, a knight-errant and a king, the very model of CHIVALRY.

Other names by which Amadis was called were the *Lovely Obscure*, the *Knight of the Green Sword*, the *Knight of the Dwarf*, etc.

Amadis of Greece. A supplemental part of the romance *Amadis of Gaul* supposedly added by the Spaniard Feliciano de Silva in 1530.

Amaimon (à mī′ i mon). A DEVIL, king of the eastern portion of HELL in mediæval demonology. He might be bound or restrained from doing hurt from the third hour till noon, and from the ninth hour till evening. ASMODEUS is his chief officer. *See* BARBASON; LUCIFER.

> Amaimon sounds well; Lucifer well; Barbason well; yet they are devils' additions, the names of fiends.
> SHAKESPEARE: *Merry Wives of Windsor*, II, ii.

Amalfitan Code (à măl′ fi tàn). The oldest existing collection of maritime law, compiled in the 11th century at Amalfi, then an important trading centre.

Amalthea (ăm ăl thē′ à). In Greek mythology a NYMPH, the nurse of ZEUS; (alternatively the she-goat which suckled him). In Roman legend a SIBYL of Cumæ who offered the SIBYLLINE Books to Tarquin II.

Amalthea's horn. The cornucopia or HORN OF PLENTY. The infant ZEUS was fed with goat's milk by Amalthea, daughter of Melisseus, King of Crete. Zeus, in gratitude, broke off one of the goat's horns, and gave it to Amalthea, promising that the possessor should always have in abundance everything desired. *See* ÆGIS.

> When Amalthea's horn
> O'er hill and dale the rose-crowned flora pours,
> And scatters corn and wine, and fruits and flowers.
> CAMOËNS: *Lusiad*, Bk. II.

Amaranth (ăm′ à rănth) (Gr. *amarantos*, everlasting). In Pliny the name of some real or imaginary fadeless flower. Clement of Alexandria says:

Amarantus flos, symbolum est immortalitatis.

It is so called because its flowers retain to the last much of their deep blood-red colour.

Amaryllis (ăm à ril′ is). A rustic sweetheart, from a shepherdess in the pastorals of Theocritus and VIRGIL.

To sport with Amaryllis in the shade.
MILTON: *Lycidas*, 68.

Amasis, Ring of (à mā′ sis). Herodotus tells us (III, iv) that Polycrates, tyrant of Samos, was so fortunate in everything that Amasis, King of Egypt, fearing such unprecedented luck boded ill, advised him to part with something which he highly prized. Polycrates accordingly threw into the sea an extremely valuable RING, but a few days afterwards a fish was presented to him, in which the ring was found. Amasis now renounced friendship with Polycrates, as a man doomed by the gods; and not long afterwards the latter was crucified by his host, the satrap Oroetes.

Amati (à ma′ ti). A first-rate violin; properly one made by the brothers Andrea and Nicolo Amati or their successors at CREMONA. *Cp.* STRAD.

Amaurote (ăm ô rō′ te) (Gr. the shadowy or unknown place). The chief city of Sir Thomas More's *Utopia*. Rabelais introduces Utopia and "the great city of the Amaurots" into his *Pantagruel* (Bk. II, ch. xxiii).

Amazement. Not afraid with any amazement (I *Pet.* iii, 6), introduced at the end of the marriage service in the BOOK OF COMMON PRAYER. The meaning is, you will be God's children so long as you do his bidding, and are not drawn aside by any distraction.

Amazon (ăm′ à zon). A Greek word meaning *without breast*. In Greek mythology a race of female warriors living in Scythia, although some writers mention an older nation of Amazons in Africa. There were no men in the nation, but any sons born of their union with their neighbours were killed or sent to their fathers. The girls had their right breasts burnt off, that they might better draw the bow. The term is now applied to any strong brawny woman of masculine habits.

She towered, fit person for a Queen
To lead those ancient Amazonian files;
Or ruling Bandit's wife among the
Grecian isles.
WORDSWORTH: *Beggars*.

Amazonia (ăm à zō′ ni à). An old name for the regions about the river Amazon in South America, which was so called by the early Spanish explorers under Orellana who claimed to have seen female warriors on its banks.

Amazonian chin. A beardless chin like that of a woman warrior.

When with his Amazonian chin he drove
The bristled lips before him.
SHAKESPEARE: *Coriolanus*, II, ii.

Amber. A yellow, translucent, fossilized vegetable resin, the name of which originally belonged to ambergris. Legend says that amber is a concretion of the tears of birds who were the sisters of MELEAGER and who never ceased weeping for the death of their brother (Ovid: *Metamorphoses*, viii, 170).

Amber meaning a repository is an obsolete spelling of AMBRY.

Ambree, Mary. An English heroine whose valour in the siege of Ghent of 1584 is recorded in the ballad *Mary Ambree* in PERCY'S RELIQUES.

Her name was proverbial for a woman of heroic spirit or a virago.

My daughter will be valiant
And prove a very Mary Ambry in the
business.
BEN JONSON: *Tale of a Tub*, I, ii.

Ambrose, St. (*c.* 340–397) became BISHOP of Milan in 374. He was noted for the penance he imposed on the Eastern Emperor Theodosius, for the massacre of the Thessalonians; also for his victory over the ARIANS at the synod of Aquileia (381), and for his organization of church music. The **Ambrosian Chant** was used until the GREGORIAN CHANT became the basis of church music two centuries later. His feast day is 7 December. His emblems are (1) a beehive, in allusion to the legend that a swarm of bees settled on his mouth when he was lying in his cradle—a favourable OMEN; (2) a scourge, by which he expelled the ARIANS from Italy.

Ambrosia (ăm brō′ zi à) (Gr. *a*, not, *brotos*, mortal). The food of the gods, so called because it made them immortal.

Hence anything delicious to the taste. *See* NECTAR.

Ambrosius Aurelianus. A shadowy 5th-century figure, according to GILDAS the last of the Roman nation in Britain, under whose leadership the Britons rallied to resist the SAXON invaders.

Ambry (am' bri) (Lat. *armarium*, cupboard, chest). A cupboard, wall-press, or locker. In church a closed recess for keeping books, vestments, sacramental plates, consecrated oil, etc. There are several variant forms such as *aumbry, awmry, almery*, etc., the latter leading to confusion with ALMONRY.

Ambs-as, or **ace**, or **Ames-ace** (ămz ās) (Lat. *ambo-asses*, both or two aces). Two aces, the lowest throw in dice; figuratively, bad luck.

> I had rather be in this choice than throw amesace for my life.
> SHAKESPEARE: *All's Well that Ends Well*, II, iii.

Also the name of a card game sometimes spelt **aumo-ace**.

Amelia. A model of conjugal affection in Fielding's last novel, *Amelia* (1751). It is said that the character was intended for his own wife. Amelia Sedley, "one of the best and dearest creatures", appears in Thackeray's *Vanity Fair* (1847–8).

Amen Corner, at the west end of PATERNOSTER ROW, London, was where the monks finished the PATER NOSTER, on CORPUS CHRISTI Day, as they went in procession to St. Paul's Cathedral. They began in *Paternoster* Row with the *Lord's Prayer* in Latin, which was continued to the end of the street; then said *Amen* at the corner of the Row; on turning down *Ave Maria* Lane, commenced chanting the *Hail Mary*! then, crossing LUDGATE entered *Creed* Lane chanting the CREDO. Paternoster Row, Amen Corner and much of Ave Maria Lane were destroyed in an air raid on 28 December 1940.

Amen-Ra, or **Amon-Ra.** The King of the gods during the ancient Egyptian Empire, a development from *Amon* ("the hidden one"), patron of Thebes. Usually figured as human-headed, with two long ostrich plumes rising above his head, sometimes with a ram's head. The ram was sacred to him and his ORACLE

was at the oasis of Jupiter AMMON. The Greeks identified him with ZEUS.

Amende honorable. An anglicized French phrase for a full and public apology. In mediæval France the term was applied to the degrading punishment inflicted on traitors, parricides and the sacrilegious, who were brought into court with a rope round their necks, stripped to the shirt and made to beg pardon of God, the King and the court.

A mensa et thoro. *See* A VINCULO.

Amenthes (a men' thēz). The HADES of the ancient Egyptians, the abode of the spirits of the dead where judgment was passed by OSIRIS.

America. *See* UNITED STATES OF AMERICA.

Americans, Good—when they die go to Paris. Not an original witticism of Oscar Wilde, who used it in *A Woman of No Importance*, but attributed by Oliver Wendell Holmes to Thomas Appleton (1812–1884).

American Dream, The. A phrase epitomizing the democratic ideals and aspirations on which America had been founded, the American way of life at its best.

> It [the American dream] has been a dream of being able to grow to fullest development as man and woman, unhampered by the barriers which had slowly been erected in older civilizations, unrepressed by social orders which had developed for the benefit of classes rather than for the simple human being of any and every class.
> J.T. ADAMS: *The Epic of America, Epilogue* (1938).

Amerindian (ăm ér in' di án). A PORTMANTEAU WORD combining *American* and *Indian* applied to native peoples of the NEW WORLD as distinct from those of India and the East Indies.

Amethea. *See* FAMOUS HORSES *under* HORSE.

Amethyst (ăm' e thist) (Gr. *a*, not; *methusko*, intoxicate). A violet-blue variety of quartz supposed by the ancients to prevent intoxication. Drinking-cups of amethyst were a charm against inebriety and it was especially cherished by Roman matrons from the belief that it would preserve inviolate the affection of their husbands.

Aminadab (a min' á dăb). A QUAKER.

The Scripture name has a double *m*, but in old comedies, where the character represents a Quaker, the name has generally only one. Obadiah was also used to signify a Quaker and Rachel a Quakeress.

Amis and Amile. *See* AMYS.

Amish, The. Followers of Jakob Ammann; a strictly conservative sect which separated from the MENNONITES in the late 17th century. They first appeared in Pennsylvania in *c*. 1714 and settlements in other parts of America followed. They are conspicuous for their colourful customs, industry, and frugality. They still use the German language, wear old-fashioned dress and beards without moustaches, use hooks and eyes instead of buttons, and employ horse-drawn vehicles.

Ammon, or **Hammon.** The Greek form of the name of the Libyan and Egyptian god Amun or Amon.

Son of Ammon. ALEXANDER the Great was thus greeted by the priests of the Libyan temple of JUPITER Ammon.

Ammonites (ăm′ ăn ītz). Fossil molluscs allied to the nautilus and cuttlefish. So called because they resemble the horn upon the ancient statues of Jupiter Ammon.

Also the children of Ammon; the descendants of Ben-ammi, the son of Lot by his younger daughter (*Gen*. xix, 38).

Amour-propre (a′ moor propr) (Fr.). One's self-love, vanity, or opinion of what is due to oneself.

Ampersand. The character "&" for *and*. In the old HORNBOOKS, after giving the twenty-six letters, the character & was added (... x, y, z, &), and was called "Ampersand", a corruption of "and per se &" (and by itself, and). The symbol is an adaptation of *et* (Lat. *and*), as can be seen if we look at the italic ampersand—*&*—where the "e" and the cross of the "t" are clearly recognizable. *See* TIRONIAN.

Amphictyonic Council (ăm fik ti on′ ik) (Gr. *amphiktyones*, dwellers round about). In Greek history, the council of the Amphictyonic League, consisting of the deputies of the twelve member tribes, who met twice a year, at DELPHI or THERMOPYLAE. With Delphi it administered the sanctuary of the Pythian APOLLO and it also conducted the PYTHIAN GAMES. It was named after its supposed founder Amphictyon, son of DEUCALION.

Amphigouri (ăm fi goor′ i). Verses which, while sounding well, contain no meaning. A good example is Swinburne's *Nephelidia*, a well-known parody of his own style, which begins:

> From the depth of the dreamy decline of the dawn through a notable nimbus of nebulous noonshine,
> Pallid and pink as the palm of the flag-flower that flickers with fear of the flies as they float,
> Are they looks of our lovers that lustrously lean from a marvel of mystic miraculous moonshine? *etc*.

Amphion (ăm fī′ on). The son of ZEUS and Antiope who, according to Greek legend, built Thebes by the music of his lute, which was so melodious that the stones danced into walls and houses of their own accord.

Amphisbæna (ăm fis bē′ nà), (Gr. *amphis*, both ways; *baino*, go). A fabulous venomous serpent with a head at each end and able to move in either direction. The name is applied to a genus of South American lizards.

Amphitrite (ăm fi trī′ ti). In classical mythology, the goddess of the sea, wife of POSEIDON, daughter of NEREUS and Doris (Gr. *amphi-trio* for *tribo*, rubbing or wearing away [the shore] on all sides).

Amphitryon (ăm fit′ ri on). Son of Alcæus and husband of ALCMENA.

> Le véritable Amphitryon
> Est l'Amphitryon où l'on dine.
> MOLIÈRE: *Amphitryon*.

That is, the person who provides the feast (whether master of the house or not) is the real host. The tale is that ZEUS assumed the likeness of Amphitryon, in order to visit Alcmena, and gave a banquet; but Amphitryon came home and claimed the honour of being master of the house. As far as the servants and guests were concerned "he who gave the feast was to them the host".

Amphrysian Prophetess (ăm fri′ zi àn). The Cumæan SIBYL; so called from Amphrysus, a river of Thessaly, on the banks of which APOLLO fed the herds of Admetus.

Ampoule, La Sainte (la sant am pool'). The vessel containing oil used in anointing the kings of France, and said to have been brought from heaven by a dove for the coronation service of St. LOUIS. It was preserved at Rheims till the French Revolution, when it was destroyed.

Amram's Son. Moses (*Exod*. vi, 20). Milton's reference in *Paradise Lost*, I, 338–40:

> As when the potent rod
> Of Amram's son, in Egypt's evil day,
> Waved round the coast,

is to *Exod*. x, 13.

Amrita (ăm rē' tà). In Hindu mythology the ELIXIR of immortality, corresponding to the AMBROSIA of classical mythology.

Amulet (Lat. *amuletum*, a charm). Something worn, usually round the neck, as a preventive charm. The word was formerly connected with the Arabic *himalah*, the name given to the cord that secured the KORAN to the person.

The early Christians used to wear amulets called ICHTHUS. *See also* TALISMAN.

Amun, or **Amon**. *See* AMEN-RA.

Amyclæan Silence (ăm i klē' àn). Amyclæ in the south of Sparta was so often alarmed by false rumour of the approach of the SPARTANS, that a decree was issued forbidding mention of the subject. When the Spartans actually came no one dared give warning and the town was taken. Hence the proverb, *more silent than Amyclæ*.

Ruled by the mythical Tyndareus, CASTOR AND POLLUX were born there and are hence sometimes called the **Amyclæan Brothers.**

Amys and Amylion, or **Amis et Amiles.** A late 12th-century French romance telling the story of the friendship of two knights in the reign of CHARLEMAGNE. At the end of the story Amylion slays his children to cure his friend of leprosy.

Anabaptists. At the time of the REFORMATION the name given to various sects which did not believe in infant baptism, and noted for their extremist views, especially at Zwickau and Munster in Germany. On coming to years of discretion they were re-baptized (Gr. *ana*, over again). In 17th-century England Baptists were often abusively called Anabaptists.

Anacharsis (ăn à kar' sis). A Scythian PHILOSOPHER (*c*. 600 B.C.) and admirer of Greek civilization. He studied at Athens and became acquainted with SOLON.

Anacharsis Cloots. Anarcharsis Jean Baptiste Du Val De Grâce, baron de Cloots (1755–1794), also known as "the Orator of the human race". A Prussian noble and apostle of revolution, who travelled Europe as a young man and became a member of the CONVENTION. He was guillotined by Robespierre in 1794.

Anachronism (Gr. *ana chronos*, out of time). Something wrongly dated, thus in the wrong chronological relationship with other things and events, and most commonly found in imaginative works which are in an historical setting. Thus in Shakespeare's *Henry IV, Pt. I*, II, i, the carrier complains "The turkeys in my pannier are quite starved", but turkeys were introduced from America, which was not discovered until nearly a century after Henry IV's time. In *Julius Cæsar*, II, i, the clock strikes and Cassius says "The clock has stricken three", yet striking clocks were not invented until 1400 years after the days of Cæsar. Mediæval romances abound with anachronisms.

Anaclethra. Another name for the AGELASTA.

Anacreon (ă năk' ri on). A Greek lyric poet (born *c*. 570 B.C.) who wrote chiefly in praise of love and wine. Hence *Anacreontics* as a name for this kind of verse or the metrical form in which they were written.

Anadyomene (Gr. rising). In ancient Greece a name given to APHRODITE in allusion to her having risen from the sea as portrayed in the famous painting by APELLES.

Anagram (Gr. *ana graphein*, to write over again). A word or phrase formed by transposing letters of another word or phrase. Some famous examples are:

> Dame Eleanor Davies (prophetess in the reign of Charles I)=*Never so mad a ladie*.

Gustavus=*Augustus*.
Horatio Nelson=*Honor est a Nilo*.
Florence Nightingale=*Flit on cheering angel*.
Queen Victoria's Jubilee=*I require love in a subject*.
Quid est Veritas (*John* xviii, 38)=*Vir est qui adest*.
Marie Touchet (mistress of Charles IX of France)=*Je charme tout* (made by Henry IV).
Voltaire is accepted as an anagram of *Arouet l(e) j(eune)*.

These are *interchangeable words*: Alcuinus and Calvinus; Amor and Roma; Eros and Rose; Evil and Live.

Anastasia, St. (ăn a stā′ zi a), a Roman matron said to have been beheaded with St. Basilissa for having buried the bodies of St. PETER and St. PAUL.

Anathema (à năth′ i mà). A denunciation or curse. A Greek word meaning "a thing set up or hung up", an offering to the gods. Thus Gordius (*see* GORDIAN KNOT) hung up his yoke and beam; the shipwrecked hung up their wet clothes; retired workmen hung up their tools, cripples their crutches, etc. Later it came to mean a thing devoted to evil since animals offered up were destined for death.

In the Catholic and Calvinistic churches it became a more extreme form of denunciation than EXCOMMUNICATION.

Ancæus (ăn sē′ às). Helmsman of the ship ARGO, after the death of Tiphys. He was told by a hard-pressed slave that he would never live to taste the wine of his vineyards, and when wine, made from his own grapes, was set before him he sent for the slave to laugh at the latter's prognostications; but the slave made the answer "there's many a slip 'twixt the CUP and the lip". At this very instant a messenger informed Ancæus that the Calydonian BOAR was devastating his vineyard, whereupon he set down his cup, went out against the boar, and was slain in the encounter.

Anchises. In Greek mythology, ruler of DARDANUS. APHRODITE became enamoured of his beauty and bore him ÆNEAS, the Trojan hero. According to one legend Anchises was blinded or killed by lightning for naming his son's mother. Virgil gives a different legend.

Anchor. In Christian symbolism the anchor is the sign of hope, in allusion to *Heb*. vi, 19, "Hope we have as an anchor of the soul". It also symbolizes security. In art it is an attribute of Pope CLEMENT I who was said to have been tied to an anchor and cast into the sea (1st century); and St. Nicholas of Bari, the patron SAINT of sailors.

Anchor light. A white light visible all round the horizon, shown from the forepart of an anchored vessel. Vessels over 150 feet in length must carry two, one being aft.

Anchor watch. A watch kept when a vessel is anchored as a precaution against dragging, etc.

Swallowing the anchor. A sailor is said to do so when he retires from the sea.

The anchor comes home. When an anchor does not hold and drags out of the ground. Figuratively, the enterprise has failed, notwithstanding the precautions employed.

To weigh anchor. To haul in the anchor. When broken out of the ground it is *aweigh*. Figuratively to begin an enterprise which has hung on hand.

Ancien Régime (Fr.). The old order of things; a phrase used during the French Revolution for the system of government, with all its evils and shortcomings, which existed under the BOURBON monarchy.

Ancient. In the now obsolete sense of a flag or standard or bearer of same, is a corruption of *ensign*. Pistol was Falstaff's ancient and Iago Othello's.

> 'Tis one Iago, ancient to the general.
> SHAKESPEARE: *Othello*, II, i.
> My whole charge consists of Ancients, corporals, lieutenants, gentlemen of companies...
> SHAKESPEARE: *Henry IV, Pt. I*, IV, ii.

Ancient Lights on a notice board in England means that for at least 20 years uninterruptedly a certain building has enjoyed light, and no structure may be erected which substantially deprives it of such light.

Ancient Mariner. Having shot an albatross, he and his companions were subjected to fearful penalties. On repentance he was forgiven, and on reaching land told his story to a hermit. At times, however, distress of mind drove him from land to land, and wherever he abode told his tale of woe, to warn from cruelty and persuade men to love God's creatures. This story in Coleridge's *Rime of the Ancient Mariner*, which was first published in *Lyrical Ballads* (1798), is partly based on a dream told by his friend Cruickshank, and partly gathered from his reading. Wordsworth told him the story of the privateer George Shelvocke, who shot an albatross while rounding Cape Horn in 1720, and was dogged by bad weather. Other suggested sources are Thomas James's *Strange and Dangerous Voyage* (1683) and the *Letter of St. Paulinus to Macarius, in which he relates astounding wonders concerning the shipwreck of an old man* (1618). A full and definitive examination of the sources is to be found in *The Road to Xanadu* (1927) by J. L. Lowes.

Ancient of Days. A scriptural name given to God (*Dan*. vii, 9).

Ancile (ăn′ sīl). The PALLADIUM of ROME; the sacred buckler said to have fallen from heaven in the reign of Numa. To prevent its being stolen, as the safety of the state depended on it, he caused eleven others, exactly similar, to be made, and entrusted them to twelve priests called SALII.

Ancren Riwle, or **Ancrene Wisse.** The rule of the Anchoresses; a mediæval treatise (? early 13th century) in rhythmical prose of great charm, written for the guidance of women who were trying to live the strict religious lives of anchoresses.

Andrew, a name used in old plays for a valet or man-servant. *Cp.* ABIGAIL. *See also* MERRY ANDREW.

St. Andrew was a fisherman and brother of St. PETER, depicted in Christian art as an old man with long white hair and beard, holding the Gospel in his right hand, and leaning on a St. Andrew's cross. His day is 30 November. It is said that he was crucified in Patræ (*c*. A.D. 70) on a *crux decussata* (*see* CROSS). He is also the patron saint of Russia and Scotland. *See* RULE, ST.; CONSTANTINE'S CROSS *under* CROSS.

The Andrew meaning "the Royal Navy" derives from the time of the French Revolutionary and Napoleonic Wars when one Andrew Miller acquired such a reputation in the Portsmouth area as a PRESSGANG operator that it came to be said that his victims had been snatched into "the Andrew".

Androcles and the Lion (ăn drō′ klěz). Androcles was a runaway slave who took refuge in a cavern. A lion entered and, instead of tearing him to pieces, lifted up his forepaw that Androcles might extract from it a thorn. The slave, being subsequently captured, was doomed to fight with a lion in the Roman arena. It so happened that the same lion was led out against him, and recognizing his benefactor, showed towards him every demonstration of love and gratitude.

Android. An old name for an AUTOMATON figure resembling a human being (Gr. *andros-eidos*, a man's likeness).

Andromache (ăn drom′ à ki). In Greek legend she was the wife of HECTOR, on whose death she was given to Pyrrhus (Neoptolemus). The latter was killed by ORESTES and she became the wife of Helenus, Hector's brother. It is the title of a play by Euripides.

Andromeda (ăn drom′ e dà). Daughter of CEPHEUS and CASSIOPEIA. Her mother boasted that her beauty surpassed that of the NEREIDS; so the Nereids induced NEPTUNE to send a sea-monster to the country, to which the oracle of Jupiter AMMON declared ANDROMEDA must be surrendered. She was accordingly chained to a rock but was delivered by PERSEUS, who married her and slew Phineus, her uncle, to whom she had been promised. After death she was placed among the stars.

Angel. In post-canonical and apocalyptic literature angels are grouped in varying orders. The commonly used hierarchy of nine orders is that popularized by the Pseudo-Areopagite or Pseudo-Dionysius (early 5th century) in his *De Hierarchia Celesti*, which arranges them in three triads:

(1) Seraphim, Cherubim, and Thrones in the first circle.

(2) Dominions, Virtues, and Powers in the second circle.

(3) Principalities, Archangels, and

Angels in the third circle. The names are taken from the *Old Testament* and *Eph*. i, 21 and *Col*. i, 16.

The seven holy angels are MICHAEL, GABRIEL, RAPHAEL, URIEL, Chamuel, Jophiel and ZADKIEL. Michael and Gabriel are mentioned in the BIBLE, Raphael in the APOCRYPHA and all appear in *Enoch* (viii, 2).

Milton in *Paradise Lost*, Bk. I, 392, gives a list of the fallen angels.

Moslems say that angels were created from pure bright gems; the genii from fire, and man from clay.

Angel. An English gold coin copied from the French *ange* and minted from 1465 to the reign of Charles I. It was to replace the NOBLE and was first called *angel noble*. Valued at 6s. 8d. and later at 10s., it bore the figure of the archangel MICHAEL slaying the dragon, and was the coin presented to persons touched for the KING'S EVIL.

Angel. In modern theatrical parlance denotes the financial backer to a play.

Angel. *See* PUBLIC-HOUSE SIGNS.

Angel of the Schools. St. Thomas Aquinas.

A flying angel. A ride given to a youngster seated astride someone's shoulders, holding hands with arms held high at full stretch.

On the side of the angels. *See* SIDE.

To entertain an angel unawares. To meet and talk with someone famed for saintliness of life while unaware of their identity; nowadays more usually applied to the entertainment of persons of note rather than sanctity.

Angels of Mons. The 3rd and 4th Divisions of the OLD CONTEMPTIBLES, under the command of General Dorrien-Smith, were sorely pressed in the retreat from Mons (26–27 August 1914). Their losses were heavy and that they survived at all was by some attributed to divine intervention. Arthur Machen, writing from FLEET STREET, described with great verisimilitude St. GEORGE and the angels, who, clad in white, with flaming swords held back the might of the German First Army. For some, the imaginary became a reality, and the *Angels of Mons* became a phrase and fable.

Angel visits. Delightful intercourse of short duration and rare occurrence.

> Like angel visits, few and far between.
> T. CAMPBELL: *Pleasures of Hope*
> (1799), II, 378.

Angelic. Angelic Doctor. Thomas Aquinas (*c*. 1225–1274) was so called, probably because of the purity and excellence of his teaching. His exposition of the most recondite problems of theology and philosophy was judged to be the fruit of almost more than human intelligence and in 1879 Pope Leo XIII directed that the teachings of Aquinas should be the basis of theology. His *Summa Theologica* is the culmination of SCHOLASTICISM.

Angelic Hymn, The. The hymn beginning with *Glory to God in the highest* (*Luke* ii, 14), so called because the former part of it was sung by the angel host that appeared to the shepherds of Bethlehem.

Angelic Salutation, The. The AVE MARIA.

Angelica (ăn jel' i kà). The name of a plant (*Archangelica officinalis*) cultivated for its aromatic stalks which when candied are used in decorating cakes and confectionery. Called the **angelic herb** from a belief in its medicinal virtues, especially against plague and pestilence, it was also used as an ingredient of ABSINTHE, of gin and of "bitters".

Angelical Stone. The speculum of Dr. DEE. He asserted that it was given him by the angels RAPHAEL and GABRIEL. It passed into the possession of the Earl of Peterborough, thence to Lady Betty Germaine, by whom it was given to the Duke of Argyll, whose son presented it to Horace Walpole. It is now in the BRITISH MUSEUM.

Angelico, Fra. The name by which Giovanni da Fiesole (*c*. 1400–1455), who was famed for the spiritual quality of his paintings, is better known.

Angelus, The (ăn' je lùs). A Roman Catholic devotion in honour of the Annunciation. It begins with the words *Angelus Domini nuntiavit Mariae*. It is recited thrice daily, usually at 6 a.m., noon, and 6 p.m. at the sound of the *Angelus* bell.

Angevin Kings of England (ăn' je vin). The early PLANTAGENET kings from

Henry II to John. Henry II (1154–1189) was the son of Matilda (daughter of Henry I) and Geoffrey "Plantagenet", Count of Anjou. John lost Anjou in 1204.

Angle. Angle with a silver hook. To buy fish at the market; said of an unsuccessful angler who buys fish to conceal his failure.

The Father of Angling. Izaak Walton (1593–1683). *See* THE GENTLE CRAFT.

Angles. Non Angli, sed angeli (Not Angles, but angels). The legend is that when Pope GREGORY THE GREAT (590–604) saw some fair-complexioned youths in the slave-market he asked whence they had come. He was told that they were Angles and also heathen. "Not Angles, but angels" was his comment and on becoming Pope he sent St. AUGUSTINE to effect their conversion.

Anglo-Saxon Chronicle. The first history in the English language to use the dating system ANNO DOMINI. It was probably begun in the reign of ALFRED THE GREAT (871–899). There are seven manuscript versions extant, which substantially deal with events from the time of Julius Cæsar to 1154, and four of these are usually distinct chronicles. It is the basic source for the history of Anglo-Saxon England.

Angra Mainyu. *See* AHRIMAN.

Angry Young Men. A name applied to certain living British dramatists, particularly John Osborne, from whose play *Look Back in Anger* (1956) the term was derived. They are characterized by dissatisfaction with established social, moral, political and intellectual values. By association it is also applied to some American writers of protest.

Angurvadel. FRITHIOF'S sword, inscribed with runic letters, which blazed in time of war, but gleamed with a dim light in time of peace. *See* SWORD.

Anima Mundi (ăn' i mä mŭn' dī) (Lat. the soul of the world), with the oldest of the ancient philosophers meant "the source of life"; with PLATO it meant "the animating principle of matter", inferior to pure spirit, with the STOICS it meant "the whole vital force of the universe".

G. E. Stahl (1660–1734) taught that the phenomena of animal life are due to

an immortal *anima* or vital principle distinct from matter.

Animal Farm. A satirical "fairy story" by George Orwell (1903–1950) of totalitarianism of the Russian kind under Stalin. A modern fable in which the pigs, by cunning, treachery and ruthlessness, lord it over the more honest, gullible and hardworking farm animals. It was first published in 1945.

Animals in Christian Art. Some animals are appropriated to certain saints: as the calf or ox to St. LUKE; the cock to St. PETER; the eagle to St. JOHN the Divine; the lion to St. MARK and St. JEROME; the raven to St. Benedict, etc. *See* SYMBOLS OF SAINTS *under* SAINT.

Animals in Heaven. According to Mohammedan legend the following ten animals have been allowed to enter paradise: Jonah's whale; Solomon's ant; the ram caught by ABRAHAM and sacrificed instead of Isaac; the lapwing of BALKIS; the camel of the prophet Saleh; Balaam's ass; the ox of MOSES; the dog KRATIM of the SEVEN SLEEPERS; Al BORAK, MOHAMMED'S steed; and Noah's dove.

Animals in symbolism.

The lamb, the pelican, and the unicorn, are symbols of Christ.

The dragon, serpent, and swine, symbolize Satan and his crew. The ant symbolizes frugality and prevision; ape, uncleanness, malice, lust, and cunning; ass, stupidity; bantam cock, pluckiness, priggishness; bat, blindness; bear, ill-temper, uncouthness; bee, industry; beetle, blindness; bull, strength, straight-forwardness; bulldog, pertinacity; butterfly, sportiveness, living in pleasure; calf, lumpishness, cowardice; camel, submission; cat, deceit; cicada, poetry; cock, vigilance, overbearing insolence; crocodile, hypocrisy; crow, longevity; cuckoo, cuckoldom; dog, fidelity, dirty habits; dove, innocence, harmlessness; duck, deceit (French, *canard*, a hoax); eagle, majesty, inspiration; elephant, sagacity, ponderosity; fly, feebleness, insignificance; fox, cunning, artifice; frog and toad, inspiration; goat, lasciviousness; goose, conceit, folly; grasshopper, old age; gull, gullibility; hare, timidity; hawk, rapacity, penetration; hen, maternal care; hog, impurity; horse, speed, grace; jackdaw, vain assumption, empty conceit; jay, senseless chatter; kitten, playfulness; lamb, innocence, sacrifice; lark, cheerfulness; leopard, sin; lion, noble courage; lynx, suspicious vigilance; magpie, garrulity; mole, blindness, obtuseness; monkey, tricks; mule, obstinacy; nightingale, forlornness; ostrich, stupidity; owl, wisdom; ox, patience, strength, pride; parrot, mocking verbosity; peacock, pride; pig, obstinacy, dirtiness, gluttony; pigeon, cowardice (pigeon-livered); puppy, conceit; rabbit, fecundity; raven, ill-luck; robin redbreast, confiding trust; serpent, wisdom; sheep, silliness, timidity; sparrow, lasciviousness; spider, wiliness; stag, cuckoldom; swan, grace; tiger, ferocity; tortoise, chastity; turkey cock, official insolence; turtledove, conjugal fidelity; vulture, rapine; wolf, cruelty, ferocity; worm, cringing; etc.

Animals sacred to special deities:

To Æsculapius, the serpent; to Apollo, the wolf, the griffon, and the crow; to Bacchus, the dragon and the panther; to Diana, the stag; to Hercules, the deer; to Isis, the heifer; to Juno, the peacock and the lamb; to Jupiter, the eagle; to the Lares, the dog; to Mars, the horse and the vulture; to Mercury, the cock; to Minerva, the owl; to Neptune, the bull; to Tethys, the halcyon; to Venus, the dove, the swan, and the sparrow; to Vulcan, the lion, etc.

Animal, Cries of.

To the cry, call or voice of many animals a special name is given; to apply these names indiscriminately is always wrong and frequently ludicrous. Thus, we do not speak of the "croak" of a dog or the "bark" of a bee. Apes gibber; asses bray; bears growl; bees hum; beetles drone; bitterns boom; blackbirds and thrushes whistle; bulls bellow; calves bleat; cats mew, purr, swear and caterwaul; chaffinches chirp and pink; chickens peep; cocks crow; cows moo or low; crows caw; cuckoos cry cuckoo; deer bell; dogs bark, bay, howl and yelp; doves coo; ducks quack; eagles, vultures and peacocks scream; falcons chant; flies buzz; foxes bark and yelp; frogs croak; geese cackle and hiss; grasshoppers chirp and pitter; guineafowls cry "Come back"; guineapigs and hares squeak; hawks scream; hens cackle and cluck; horses neigh and whinny; hyenas laugh; jays and magpies chatter; kittens mew; linnets chuckle in their call; lions and tigers roar and growl; mice squeak and squeal; monkeys chatter and gibber; nightingales pipe and warble—we also speak of their "jug-jug"; owls hoot and screech; oxen low and bellow; parrots talk; peewits cry peewit; pigs grunt, squeak and squeal; pigeons coo; ravens croak; rooks caw; screech owls screech or shriek; sheep and lambs baa or bleat; snakes hiss; sparrows chirp; stags bellow and call; swallows twitter; swans cry and are said to sing just before death (*see*

SWAN); turkey-cocks gobble; wolves howl. Most birds, besides many of those here mentioned, sing, but we speak of the chick-chick of the blackcap, the drumming of the grouse, and the chirr of the whitethroat.

Animosity meant originally animation, spirit, as the fire of a horse, called in Latin *equi animositas*. Its present exclusive use in a bad sense is an instance of the tendency by which words originally neutral have come to assume a bad meaning.

Animula, vagula, etc. (an im' ū lă , văg' ū lă). The opening of a poem to his soul, ascribed to the dying Emperor Hadrian (A.D. 76–138):

> Animula, vagula, blandula,
> Hospes, comesque, corporis;
> Quae nunc abibis in loca,
> Pallidula, rigida, nudula?

> Sorry-lived, blithe little, flittering sprite,
> Comrade and guest in this body of clay,
> Whither, ah! whither, departing in flight,
> Rigid, half-naked, pale minion, away?
>
> E.C.B.

Annates (ăn' ātz) (Lat. *annus*, a year), also called FIRST FRUITS. Payments to the POPE, on the appointment of a BISHOP or other ecclesiastic, of a year's income of the SEE or BENEFICE. In England these payments were finally stopped in 1534 and transferred to the Crown.

Annie Laurie was the eldest of three daughters of Sir Robert Laurie of Maxwelton, born 16 December 1682. William Douglas of Fingland (Kirkcudbright) wrote the popular verses which were altered by Lady Scott (1810–1900), who composed the air. In 1709 Annie married Alexander Fergusson of Craigdarroch. She was the grandmother of Alexander Fergusson, the hero of Burns's song called *The Whistle*.

Annie Oakley. *See* OAKLEY.

Anno Domini (ăn' ō dom' i nī) (Lat.). In the Year of our Lord; *i.e.* in the year after the Nativity; or A.D. This system of dating was introduced by the monk Dionysius Exiguus who lived in the first half of the 6th century. *Anno Domini* is also used colloquially as a synonym for old age, *e.g.*, "Anno Domini is his complaint." *See* ANGLO-SAXON CHRONICLE.

Annunciation, The Feast of the. 25 March, also called LADY DAY, on which the angel GABRIEL announced to the Virgin MARY that she would be the mother of the MESSIAH (*Luke* i, 26–38).

Sisters of the Annunciation. *See* FRANCISCANS.

Annus Luctus (ăn' ŭs lŭk' tŭs) (Lat. the year of mourning). The period during which a widow is supposed to remain unmarried. If she marries within about nine months from the death of her husband and a child is born, a doubt might arise as to its paternity. Such a marriage is not illegal.

Annus Mirabilis (ăn' ŭs mir ăb'i lis). The year of wonders. Such was 1666, memorable for the Great FIRE OF LONDON and the successes of English arms over the Dutch, commemorated in Dryden's poem entitled *Annus Mirabilis*.

Annwn (ăn' oon), or **Annwyfn** (ăn oi' vŭn). In Welsh legend, the land of the departed, the Celtic HADES.

Anodyne Necklace, An. An anodyne relieves pain: an anodyne necklace was an AMULET supposedly efficacious against suffering.

Anschluss, The. This German word meaning "junction" or "union" in a modern historical context refers to the seizure of Austria by Germany in March 1938.

Answer like a Norman, To, that is, evasively.

Answer more Scotico, To. Avoiding the direct question by starting another question or subject.

> "Hark you sirrah", said the doctor, "I trust you remember you are owing to the laird four stones of barleymeal and a bow of oats...". "I was thinking" replied the man *more Scotico* (in the Scottish fashion), that is returning no direct answer on the subject on which he was addressed "my best way would be to come to your honour, and take your advice yet, in case my trouble should come back".
> SIR WALTER SCOTT: *The Abbot*, ch. xxvi.

Answer to a Maiden's Prayer, The. A young good-looking and wealthy bachelor or generally anything which exactly meets requirements.

Ant. For many centuries the ant has been a symbol of thrift and industry. The *Bible* says "Go to the ant, thou sluggard; consider her ways and be wise" (*Proverbs* vi, 6). Æsop has a fable on the "Ant and the Grasshopper" in which the indolent grasshopper, in the winter, went to the busy little ants to beg food.

Antæus (ăn tē' us), in Greek mythology, a gigantic wrestler, son of Earth and Sea (GÆA and POSEIDON), who became stronger whenever he touched the earth. HERCULES lifted him from the ground and slew him.

Antediluvian. Before the DELUGE. Colloquially used for anything hopelessly outdated.

Anthony Eden. Popular name for the style of black felt homburg worn by Sir Anthony Eden (Lord Avon) when Foreign Secretary in the 1930s.

Anthony the Great, St. (*c.* 250–356), the patron saint of herdsmen and hermit of Upper Egypt; also the father of Christian monasticism. The story of his temptations by the devil was a popular subject in literature and art. His day is 17 January.

St. Anthony's Cross. The TAU cross, T, called a lace.

St Anthony's fire. In mediæval times a pestilential disease, so called from the belief that those who sought the intercession of St. Anthony recovered from this epidemic or sacred fire. It was commonly supposed to be erysipelas (Gr. red skin) or the ROSE (from its colour) but in fact the disease was ergotism, a poisoning due to eating rye bread with fungal infection. *Cp.* ST. VITUS'S DANCE *under* VITUS.

St. Anthony's pig. A pet pig, the smallest of the litter, also called the TANTONY PIG.

Anthroposophy (ăn'thrō pos' ŏ fi). (Gr. *anthropos*, man; *sophia*, knowledge). The name given to the "spiritual science" developed by the Austrian philosopher Rudolf Steiner (1861–1925), a former theosophist. *See* THEOSOPHY.

Antic Hay. *See* HAY.

Antichrist, or the Man of Sin, due to appear at the end of time, is mentioned in the *Epistles of St. John* (I, ii, 18, 22) and is derived from Hebrew teachings. The belief that the arrival of Antichrist was to precede the second advent is chiefly founded on II *Thess*. ii, 1–12, and *Rev*. xiii. In the early Christian Church the ROMAN EMPIRE and its rulers were frequently referred to as Antichrist and later the title was bestowed upon the Emperor Frederick II and various Popes. With the REFORMATION the PROTESTANT conception of the papacy as Antichrist became widespread and its later use is largely as an abusive term and it has been applied even to NAPOLEON and William II of Germany. The Mohammedans have a legend that Christ will slay the Antichrist at the gate of the Church at Lydda, in Palestine. *See also* NUMBER OF THE BEAST.

Antigone (ăn tig′ ò ni). The subject of a tragedy by Sophocles: she was the daughter of ŒDIPUS by his mother, Jocasta. She slew herself to avoid being buried alive for disobeying an edict of Creon. She was famed for her devotion to her brother Polynices, hence the Duchess of Angoulême (1778–1851) was called *the Modern Antigone* for her attachment to her brother Louis XVII.

Antimony (an′ ti mon i). A word probably from the Arabic as it was introduced through ALCHEMY, but Johnson's *Dictionary* derives it erroneously from the Greek *antimonachos* (bad for monks). The explanation copied from earlier writers was that a prior gave some of this mineral to his convent pigs, who thrived upon it and became very fat. He next tried it on the monks, who died from its effects.

Antinomian (an ti no′ mi an) (Gr. *antinomos*, exempt from the law). One who believes that Christians are not bound to observe the "law of God", but "may continue in sin that grace may abound". The term was first applied to John Agricola by Martin Luther, and was given to a sect that appeared in Germany about 1535. It was put forward as an excuse for immorality by extremist sects from early Christian times and appeared in England during the COMMONWEALTH period.

Antinous (ăn tin′ ō ùs). A model of manly beauty. He was favourite and companion of Hadrian, the Roman Emperor.

Anti-pope. A usurping or rival pontiff set up in opposition to one canonically elected. Of the thirty-nine anti-popes, those residing at Avignon during the Great SCHISM (1378–1417) are perhaps best known. When John XXIII (a schismatic) summoned the Council of Constance (1414) to end the schism, there were three rival popes. John and Benedict XIII were deposed as schismatics, Gregory XIII resigned and a new POPE, Martin V, was elected in 1417.

Antisthenes (ăn tis′ the nēz). Athenian philosopher (*c.* 455–*c.* 360 B.C.), founder of the CYNIC School. He wore a ragged cloak, and carried a wallet and staff like a beggar. SOCRATES, whose pupil he was, wittily said he could "see rank pride peering through the holes of Antisthenes' rags".

Antonine's Wall. A turf wall fronted by a deep ditch with forts at intervals stretching from Carriden on the Forth, to Old Kilpatrick on the Clyde (*c.* 36 miles). Built between 140 and 142 by Lollius Urbicus, governor of Britain under the Emperor Antoninus Pius, it was abandoned before the end of the 2nd century. *See* HADRIAN'S WALL.

Anu. Chief God of the Sumerians and Babylonians, king of heaven and ruler of destiny. The centre of his cult was at Erech, mentioned in *Genesis* (x, 10) as part of Nimrod's kingdom.

Anubis (à nū′ bis). An Egyptian god similar to HERMES of Greece with whom he was sometimes identified. His office was to take the souls of the dead before the judge of the infernal regions. The son of OSIRIS, the judge, he was represented with a human body and a jackal's head.

Anvil. It is on the anvil, under deliberation, the project is in hand.

Anzac. A word coined in 1915 from the initials of the Australian and New Zealand Army Corps. It was also applied to the cove and beach in Gallipoli where they landed.

Anzac Day. 25 April, commemorating the landing of the Anzacs in Gallipoli in 1915.

Aonian (ā ō′ ni an). Poetical, pertaining to the MUSES. The Muses, according to Greek mythology, dwelt in Aonia, that part of Bœotia which contains Mount HELICON and the MUSES' fountain.

Apache (à păch′ i). The name of a group of tribes of North American Indians, given to (or adopted by) the HOOLIGANS of Paris about the end of the 19th century (here pronounced à păsh'). This usage has a close parallel in the MO-HOCKS of the 18th century.

Apartheid (Afrikaans, apart-hood). A policy adopted by the Afrikaner National Party in 1948 to ensure the dominance of the white minority. It divided South Africa into separate areas for whites and blacks causing its departure from the British Commonwealth in 1961 and leading to rioting, repression and isolation from other nations. Limited constitutional rights were granted to non-whites in 1985.

To lead apes in hell. It is an old saying (frequent in the Elizabethan dramatists) that it is the fate of old maids. Hence *ape-leader*, an old maid.

To play the ape, to play practical jokes or silly tricks, to pull faces like an ape.

To put an ape into your hood or **cap**, *i.e.* to make a fool of you. Apes were formerly carried on the shoulders of fools and simpletons.

Apelles. *See* CHAN PAINTER.

A-per-se (ā pĕr sē). An AI; a person or thing of unusual merit. "A" all alone with no one who can follow, *nemo proximus aut secundus*. Chaucer calls Cresseide "the floure A-per-se of Troi and Greek".

> London, thou art of towns A-per-se.
> DUNBAR: *In honour of the city of London* (1501).

Aphrodite (ăf' rō dī ti) (Gr. *aphros*, foam). The Greek VENUS; so called because she sprang from the foam of the sea. In HOMER she is the daughter of ZEUS and DIONE.

Aphrodite's girdle. The CESTUS.

Apicius (a pis' i ùs). A gourmand. The name of three famous Roman gourmands.

A-pigga-back. *See* PICK-A-BACK.

Apis (ā'pis). In Egyptian mythology, Hap, the bull of Memphis, sacred to Ptah (later associated and identified with OSIRIS) of whose soul it was supposed to be the image. SERAPIS was the dead Apis. The sacred bull had to be black with special markings. Sometimes it was not suffered to live more than twenty-five years, when it was sacrificed and embalmed with great ceremony. Cambyses, King of Persia (529–521

B.C.), and conqueror of Egypt, slew the bull of Memphis, and is said to have been punished with madness.

Apocalypse, Four Horsemen of. *See under* FOUR.

Apocalyptic Number. The mysterious number 666 (*Rev.* xiii, 15). *See* NUMBER OF THE BEAST.

Apocrypha (à pok' ri fà) (Gr. *apokrupto*, hide away); hence the meaning "withheld from general circulation" (for various reasons), and therefore coming to be regarded as of doubtful origin, false or spurious. In the early 5th century JEROME was responsible for its inappropriate application to the non-canonical books of the Old Testament found in the SEPTUAGINT and VULGATE and not usually included in PROTESTANT Bibles. In the preface to the Apocrypha in the 1539 Bible the explanation that the books are so called "because they were wont to be read not openly" is untenable. The Apocrypha was included in the AUTHORIZED VERSION of 1611. The Apocrypha proper consists of:

> I and II Esdras, Tobit, Judith, additions to Esther, WISDOM OF SOLOMON, Ecclesiasticus, Baruch, part of the Epistle of Jeremiah, the SONG OF THE THREE HOLY CHILDREN, the History of Susanna, Bel and the Dragon, the Prayer of Manasses, I and II Maccabees.

Apart from other Old Testament Apocryphal books there are numerous New Testament Apocryphal Gospels, Acts and Teachings of the APOSTLES, Epistles and Apocalypses.

Apocryphal. Applied to a story or anecdote, especially one concerning a celebrity or well-known individual to indicate that it is in character but fictitious. *See* APOCRYPHA.

Apollinarians (à pol in âr' i ànz). An heretical 4th-century sect, followers of Apollinaris, Bishop of Laodicea, a vigorous opponent of Arianism. They denied that Christ had a human soul and asserted that the *Logos* supplied its place. This heresy was condemned at the Council of Constantinople (381) and subsequently.

Apollo (à pol' ō). In Greek mythology, son of ZEUS and Leto (LATONA), and sometimes identified with HELIOS the sun god. He was the brother of Artemis (see DIANA), half-brother of HERMES, and father of ÆSCULAPIUS. He was the god of music, poetry, archery, prophecy and the healing art. His plant was the LAUREL and he is represented as the perfection of youthful manhood.

> the fire rob'd god,
> Golden Apollo.
> SHAKESPEARE: *A Winter's Tale*, IV, iii.

A perfect Apollo is a model of manly beauty, referring to the APOLLO BELVEDERE.

Apollonius of Tyana. A Pythagorean philosopher (born shortly before the Christian era), accredited with exceptional powers of magic. It was he who discovered that the Phœnician woman whom Menippus Lycius intended to wed was in fact a serpent or LAMIA.

Apollyon (à pol' yon). The Greek name of ABADDON, King of HELL. It is used by Bunyan in *The Pilgrim's Progress*.

Aposiopesis. *See* QUOS EGO.

A posteriori (ā pos tē' ri ôr' i) (Lat. from the latter). An *a posteriori* argument is proving the cause from the effect. Thus if we see a watch, we conclude there was a watchmaker.

Apostles. The word *apostle* (Gr. *apostolos*, envoy, messenger, one sent) was especially applied to the Twelve Disciples of Christ as those sent forth to preach the gospel. They are named in *Matthew* x, 1–4; *Mark* iii, 14–19; *Luke* vi, 13–16; and *Acts* i, 13. The original list comprises PETER, ANDREW, JAMES and JOHN (the sons of Zebedee), PHILIP, BARTHOLOMEW, THOMAS, MATTHEW, James (the son of Alphæus), Judas or JUDE, SIMON and JUDAS Iscariot. The Gospels of *St. Matthew* and *St. Mark* give Thaddæus in place of Jude, and the Gospel of *St. John* (xxi, 1–2) has Nathanael, who by some has been identified with Bartholomew. James the Less has also been identified, somewhat dubiously, with James, the son of Alphæus. MATTHIAS and PAUL were subsequent additions. The badges or symbols of the fourteen apostles (*i.e.* the original twelve with Matthias and Paul) are as follows:

> Andrew, *an* × *-shaped cross* because he was crucified on one.
> Bartholomew, *a knife*, because he was flayed with a knife.

James the Great, *a scallop shell, a pilgrim's staff*, or *a gourd bottle*, because he is the patron saint of pilgrims.

James the Less, *a fuller's pole*, because he was killed by a blow on the head with a pole, dealt him by Simeon the fuller.

John, *a cup with a winged serpent flying out of it*, in allusion to the tradition about Aristodemos, priest of Diana, who challenged John to drink a cup of poison. John made the sign of a cross on the cup, Satan like a dragon flew from it, and John then drank the cup which was quite innocuous.

Judas Iscariot, *a bag*, because he "had the bag and bare what was put therein" (*John* xii, 6).

Jude, *a club*, because he was martyred with a club.

Matthew, *a hatchet* or *halberd* because he was slain at Nadabar with a halberd.

Matthias, *a battleaxe*, because he was first stoned, and then beheaded with a battle axe.

Paul, *a sword*, because his head was cut off with a sword. The convent of La Lisla in Spain boasts of possessing the very instrument.

Peter, *a bunch of keys*, because Christ gave him "the keys of the kingdom of heaven". *A cock*, because he went out and wept bitterly when he heard the cock crow (*Matt.* xxvi, 75).

Philip, *a long staff surmounted with a cross*, because he suffered death by being suspended by the neck from a tall pillar.

Simon, *a saw*, because he was sawn to death, according to tradition.

Thomas, *a lance*, because he was pierced through the body, at Mylapore, with a lance.

According to tradition:

> ANDREW lies buried at Amalfi (Naples).
> BARTHOLOMEW, at Rome, in the church of Bartholomew, on the Tiber Island.
> JAMES THE GREAT was buried at St. Jago de Compostella, in Spain.
> JAMES THE LESS, at Rome, in the church of SS. Philip and James.
> JOHN, at Ephesus.
> JUDE, at Rome.
> MATTHEW, at Salerno (Naples).
> MATTHIAS, at Rome, in the church of St. Peter.
> PAUL, at Rome, in the church of S. Paolo fuori le Mura.
> PETER, at Rome, in the church of St. Peter.
> PHILIP, at Rome.
> SIMON or SIMEON, at Rome.
> THOMAS, at Ortona (Naples). (?Madras).
> The supposed remains of MARK THE EVANGELIST were buried at Venice, about 800.
> LUKE THE EVANGELIST is said to

have been buried at Padua.

See EVANGELISTS; SYMBOLS OF SAINTS *under* SAINT.

Apostles of

Abyssinians, St. Frumentius (*c.* 300–*c.* 360).
Alps, Felix Neff (1798–1829).
Andalusia, Juan de Avila (1500–1569).
Ardennes, St. Hubert (d. 727).
Armenians, Gregory the Illuminator (*c* 257–*c.* 337).
Brazil, José de Anchieta, Jesuit missionary (1533–1597).
English, St. Augustine (d. 604); St. George (d. *c.* 300).
Free Trade, Richard Cobden (1804–1865).
French, St. Denis (? 3rd century).
Frisians, St. Willibrod (*c.* 657–738).
Gauls, St. Irenæus (*c.* 130–*c.* 200); St. Martin of Tours (*c.* 316–400).
Gentiles, St. Paul (d. 67).
Germany, St. Boniface (680–754).
Highlanders, St. Columba (521–597).
Hungary, St. Stephen (975–1038), the Apostle King.
Indians (American), Bartolomé de Las Casas (1474–1566); John Eliot (1604–1690).
Indies (East), St. Francis Xavier (1506–1552).
Infidelity, Voltaire (1694–1778).
Ireland, St. Patrick (*c.* 389–461).
North, St. Ansgar or Anscarius (801–865), missionary to Scandinavia; Bernard Gilpin (1517–1583), Archdeacon of Durham, evangelist of the Scottish border.
Peru, Alonso de Barcena, Jesuit, missionary (1528–1598).
Picts, St. Ninian (? 5th century).
Rome, St. Philip Neri (1515–1595) for his good works there. (*See* ORATORIANS).
Scottish Reformers, John Knox (1505–1572).
Slavs, St. Cyril (827–869).
Spain, St. James the Great (d. 44).
The Sword, Mohammed (*c.* 570–632).
Temperance, Father Mathew (1790–1856).
Yorkshire, Paulinus, Archbishop of York (d. 644).
Wales, St. David (*c.* 500–*c.* 600).

Prince of the Apostles. St. PETER (*Matt.* xvi, 18, 19).

The Apostles or **The Society.** *See* CAMBRIDGE APOSTLES.

Apostle spoons. Silver spoons having the figure of one of the APOSTLES at the top of the handle, formerly given at christenings. Sometimes twelve spoons, representing the twelve apostles; sometimes four, representing the four EVAN-GELISTS; and sometimes only one was presented. Occasionally a set occurs, containing in addition the "Master Spoon" and the "Lady Spoon". Silver spoons were given to children of the wealthier classes, hence the saying BORN WITH A SILVER SPOON IN ONE'S MOUTH. *See under* BORN.

Apostles' Creed. A Christian creed supposed to be an epitome of doctrine taught by the apostles. It was received into the Latin Church, in its present form, in the 11th century, but a formula somewhat like it existed in the 2nd century. Items were added in the 4th and 5th centuries, and verbal alterations much later. *See* ATHANASIAN CREED; NICENE CREED.

Apostolic Fathers. Christian writers born in the 1st century supposedly in contact with the original APOSTLES. Polycarp, the last of the Apostolic Fathers, born about 69, was believed to be the disciple of St. John the Apostle. Clement of Rome died *c.* 101, Ignatius *c.* 120, and Polycarp *c.* 155. Others are Barnabas, Hermas (author of *The Shepherd*) and Papias (a bishop of Hierapolis, mentioned by Eusebius).

Apostolic Succession. The doctrine that the mission given to the APOSTLES by Christ (*Matt.* xxviii, 19) must extend to their legitimate successors in an unbroken line. Thus the only valid ministry is that of clergy ordained by properly consecrated BISHOPS.

Appeal to the Country, An. To ask the nation to express its opinion on some particular issue or issues by dissolving PARLIAMENT and holding a general election.

Appiades (ăp′ i à dēz). Five divinities whose temple stood near the Appian aqueduct in ROME. Their names are VENUS, PALLAS, Concord, Peace, and VESTA. They were represented on horseback, like AMAZONS. Also a name for the courtesans of this locality.

Appian Way (ăp′ i àn). The "queen of long-distance roads" leading from Rome to Brundusium (Brindisi). This most famous Roman road was begun by the censor Appius Claudius about 312 B.C.

Apple. There is no mention of an apple in the Bible story of Eve's temptation. She took "the fruit of the tree which is in the midst of the garden" (*Gen.* iii, 3).

Apple, Newton and the. The well-known story of Newton and the apple originated with VOLTAIRE, who says that Mrs. Conduit, Newton's niece, told him that Newton was at Woolsthorpe (visiting his mother) in 1666 when, seeing an apple fall, he was led into the train of thought which resulted in his contribution to the laws of gravitation.

Apple, Prince Ahmed's, a cure for every disorder. In THE ARABIAN NIGHTS story of Prince Ahmed, the Prince purchased his apple at Samarkand.

Apple of Discord. A cause of dispute; something to contend about. At the marriage of THETIS and Peleus, where all the gods and goddesses assembled, Discord (Eris), who had not been invited, threw on the table a golden apple "for the most beautiful". Hera (JUNO), Pallas Athene (MINERVA), and Aphrodite (VENUS) put in their claims and PARIS, as referee, gave judgment in favour of Aphrodite. This brought upon him the vengeance of Hera and PALLAS, to whose spite the fall of TROY was attributed.

Apple of the eye. The pupil, because it was anciently supposed to be a round solid ball like an apple. Figuratively anything held extremely dear or much cherished.

Apple Tree Gang. The name given to John Reid and his Scottish friends who introduced golf into the U.S.A. in 1888, at Yonkers, N.Y. The name was coined in 1892 when they moved to their third "course" at Yonkers—a 34-acre orchard which yielded six holes.

Apple-cart, To upset the. To ruin carefully laid plans. To have one's expectations blighted, as a farmer's might be when his load of apples was overturned.

Apple-islanders. NICKNAME for the inhabitants of Tasmania, who are also known as Tassies and Mountain-devils.

Apple-john. An apple so called from its being mature about St. JOHN THE BAPTIST'S Day, 24 June. The French call it *Pomme de Saint Jean.* We are told that apple-johns will keep for two years, and are best when shrivelled.

I am withered like an old apple-john.
SHAKESPEARE: *Henry IV, Part I,* III, iii.

Apple-pie bed, or **pie bed.** A bed in which the sheets are so folded that a person cannot get his legs down. Perhaps a corruption of *nappe pliée* (French), a folded sheet or cloth.

Apple-pie order. Everything just so, in perfect order. The origin of the phrase is uncertain. Perhaps the suggestion *nappes pliées* (Fr. folded linen), neat as folded linen, is near the mark. *See* APPLE-PIE BED.

Apple-polishing. An attempt to win favour by gifts or flattery. From the practice of American schoolchildren bringing shiny apples to their teachers.

Apples, Isle of. *See* AVALON.

Apples of Iduna. *See* IDUNA.

Apples of Istakhar are "all sweetness on one side, and all bitterness on the other".

Apples of Paradise, according to tradition, had a bite on one side, to commemorate the bite given by Eve.

Apples of perpetual youth. *See* IDUNA.

Apples of Pyban, says Sir John MANDEVILLE, fed the pigmies with their odour only.

Apples of Sodom. Possibly the *madar* or *oschur* (*Caloptris procera*). The fruit of trees reputed to grow on the shores of the Dead Sea "which bear lovely fruit, but within are full of ashes". Josephus, Strabo and Tacitus refer to them.

Après moi le déluge. After me the deluge—I care not what happens after I am dead. Madam de Pompadour (1721–1764), mistress of Louis XV, used the phrase, *Après nous le déluge*, when remonstrated with on account of the extravagances of the Court, possibly having heard her royal lover use it. Metternich (1773–1859), the Austrian statesman, used the expression, meaning that the existing order would collapse when his guiding hand was removed.

April. The opening month (probably derived from Lat. *aperire*, to open) when trees unfold and the earth opens with new life. The old Dutch name was *Gras-maand* (Grass month). In the French Republican CALENDAR it was called *Germinal*, the time of budding

A priori

(21 March to 19 April).

April fool, called in France *un poisson d'avril*, and in Scotland a *gowk* (cuckoo), a person befooled or tricked on *All Fools' Day* (1 April). In India similar tricks are played at the Holi Festival (31 March), so that it cannot refer to the uncertainty of the weather, nor yet to a mockery of the trial of Christ, the two most popular explanations. A better solution is this: as 25 March used to be New Year's Day, 1 April was its octave, when its festivities culminated and ended.

It may be a relic of the Roman CEREALIA, held at the beginning of April. The tale is that PROSERPINA was sporting in the Elysian meadows, and had just filled her lap with daffodils, when PLUTO carried her off to the lower world. Her mother, CERES, heard the echo of her screams, and went in search of the voice; but her search was a fool's errand, it was "hunting the gowk", or looking for the "echo of a scream".

A priori (ā prī ôr′ i) (Lat. from an antecedent). An *a priori* argument is one in which a fact is deduced from something antecedent, as when we infer certain effects from given causes. Mathematical proofs are of this kind whereas judgments in the law courts are usually A POSTERIORI; we infer the animus from the act.

Apron. Tied to one's mother's apron strings. Completely under one's mother's thumb, particularly of a young man dominated by his mother.

Aqua Fortis (ăk′ wà for′ tis) (Lat. strong water). Nitric acid.

Aqua Regia (ăk′ wà rē′ jà) (Lat. royal water). A mixture usually of one part concentrated nitric acid with three parts concentrated hydrochloric acid; so called because it dissolves GOLD.

Aqua Tofana (ăk′ wà tof′ ā nà). A poisonous liquid containing arsenic, much used in Italy in the 18th century by young wives who wanted to get rid of their husbands. It was invented about 1690 by a Greek woman named Tofana, who called it the *Manna* of St. Nicholas of Bari, from a widespread notion that an oil of miraculous efficacy flowed from the tomb of that saint.

Aqua vitæ (ăk′ wà vī′ tē) (Lat. water of life). Brandy or distilled spirits. EAU DE VIE, *whisky*, and the Irish USQUEBAUGH have the same meaning. Also certain ardent spirits used by the alchemists.

Aquarius (à kwâr′ i ùs) (Lat. the water-bearer). The eleventh sign of the ZODIAC (21 January to 18 February). Its symbol is a man pouring water from a vessel, its sign ⚒ representing a stream of water.

Aquila non captat muscas (ăk′ wi là non kăp′ tăt mŭs′ kăs). A Latin phrase—"an eagle does not hawk at flies", a proverbial saying implying that little things are beneath a great man's contempt.

Aquiline. *See* FAMOUS HORSES *under* HORSE.

Aquinas, St. Thomas. *See under* THOMAS.

Aquinian Sage, The. Juvenal is so called because he was born at Aquinum, a town of the Volscians, in Latium.

Arabesque. A term now applied to forms of design derived from classical grotesque.

Arabia. It was Ptolemy who was the author of the threefold division into **Arabia Petræa,** or Stony (Hejaz); **Arabia Felix,** or Fruitful (Hasa, Hadramaut, Oman and Yemen); **Arabia Deserta** or Desert (Nejd).

Arabian Bird, The. The PHŒNIX; hence, figuratively, a marvellous or unique person.

> All of her that is out of door most rich!
> If she be furnish'd with a mind so rare,
> She is alone the Arabian bird.
> SHAKESPEARE: *Cymbeline*, I, vi.

Arabian Nights Entertainments, The, or **The Thousand and One Nights.** These ancient Oriental tales were first introduced into western Europe in a French translation by Antoine Galland (12 vols., 1704–1717), derived from an Egyptian text probably of 14th- or 15th-century origin. English translations based on Galland were made by R. Heron (1792) and W. Beloe (1795). The later English translations by Henry Torrens (1838), E.W. Lane (1839–1841), John Payne (1882–1884), and Sir Richard Burton's unexpurgated edition published at Benares (16 vols., 1885–1888) are based on a late 18th-century Egyptian text. The standard French translation by J. C. Mardrus (1899–1904) has been severely criticized.

The framework of the tales is that they were told by SCHEHERAZADE, bride of Sultan Schahriah, to stave off her execution.

Arabians. An obscure Arabian Christian sect of the 3rd century who maintained that the soul dies with the body but rejoins the body on the last day. This heresy was overcome by Origen (*c*. 185–*c*. 254).

Arabic figures. The figures 0, 1, 2, 3, 4, etc., so called because they were introduced to Europe by the Arabs who brought them from India. They were familiar in Europe by the 12th century but did not generally supersede the Roman numerals (I, II, III, IV, V, VI, etc.) until the 16th century. The cipher or nought was an immensely valuable gain and the introduction of place value made possible a decimal system, the positional value of the numbers (*e.g.* 444) increasing tenfold to the left and decreasing correspondingly to the right. *See* NUMBERS.

Street Arabs. Children of the houseless poor; street urchins. So called from the nomadic habits of the Arabs.

Arachne's Labours (à răk′ ni). Spinning and weaving. The story is that Arachne challenged ATHENE to a weaving contest and hanged herself when the goddess destroyed her web. Athene then changed her into a spider, hence Arachnida, the scientific name for spiders, scorpions and mites.

Arawn (ă′ roun). King of ANNWN.

Arbor Day. A day set apart in Canada, the United States and New Zealand, for planting trees, first observed in Nebraska in 1872 where it became a legal holiday in 1885. The date varies according to locality.

Arbor Judæ. *See* JUDAS TREE.

Arcadia (ar′ kā′ di ā). A district of the Peloponnesus named after Arcas, son of JUPITER, chiefly inhabited by shepherds and the abode of PAN. According to VIRGIL it was the home of pastoral simpli-

city and happiness. The name was used by Sidney for the title of his romance (1590) and soon became a byword for rustic bliss.

Arcades ambo (ar′ kà dēz ăm′ bō) (Lat.). From VIRGIL'S seventh ECLOGUE: "*Ambo florentes ætatibus, Arcades ambo*" (Both in the flower of youth, Arcadians both), meaning "both poets or musicians", now extended to two persons having tastes or habits in common. BYRON gave the phrase a whimsical turn:

> Each pulled different ways with many an oath,
> "Arcades ambo"—*id est*, blackguards both.
>
> *Don Juan*, iv, 93.

Arcadian beasts. An old expression to be found in Plautus, Pliny, etc. *See* Persius, iii, 9:

> Arcadiae pecuaria rudere credas,

and Rabelais, V, vii. So called because the ancient Arcadians were renowned as simpletons.

Arcas. *See* CALISTO.

Archangel. In Christian story the title is usually given to MICHAEL, the chief opponent of SATAN and his angels, and to GABRIEL, RAPHAEL, URIEL, Chamuel, Jophiel and ZADKIEL. *See* ANGEL.

According to the KORAN, there are four archangels; Gabriel, the angel of revelations, who writes down the divine decrees; Michael, the champion, who fights the battle of faith; AZRAEL, the angel of death; and ISRAFEL, who is commissioned to sound the trumpet of the resurrection.

Archbishop Parker's Table. *See under* TABLE.

Archers. The best archers in British legend are ROBIN HOOD, and his two companions LITTLE JOHN and Will Scarlet.

The story of TELL reproduces the Scandinavian tale of EGIL, who at the command of King Nidung performed a precisely similar feat.

Arches, Court of. The ecclesiastical court of appeal for the province of Canterbury, which was anciently held in the church of St. Mary-le-Bow (*Beata Maria de Arcubus*, St. Mary of the Arches), Cheapside, London.

Archeus (ar kē′ us). According to PARA-

CELSUS (*c.* 1490–1541), the immaterial principle which energizes all living substances. There were supposed to be numerous *archei*; the chief one was said to reside in the stomach.

Archies. In World War I anti-aircraft guns and batteries were thus nicknamed—probably from Archibald, the hero of one of George Robey's songs.

Archilochian Bitterness (ar ki lō′ ki ǎn). Ill-natured SATIRE or bitter mockery, so named from Archilochus, a Greek satirical poet (fl. *c.* 650 B.C. and after).

Archimago (ar ki mā′ gō). The enchanter in Spenser's *Faerie Queene* (Bks. I and II), typifying hypocrisy.

Archimedes' Principle (ar ki mē′ dēz). The apparent loss in weight of a body immersed in liquid will equal the weight of the displaced liquid. This discovery was made by Archimedes of Syracuse (*c.* 287–212 B.C.). *See* EUREKA.

Architecture, Orders of. In classical architecture, DORIC, IONIC, CORINTHIAN, TUSCAN and Composite (a compound of Ionic and Corinthian).

Archontics. A 2nd-century GNOSTIC sect attributing the Creation to God's agents or *archons* (Greek *archon*, a chief magistrate or ruler).

Arcite (ar sī′ ti, ar′ sīt). A Theban knight made captive by Duke THESEUS, and imprisoned with Palamon at ATHENS. Both captives fell in love with Emily, the duke's sister (or daughter in some versions), and after gaining their liberty Emily was promised by the duke to the victor in a tournament. Arcite won but was thrown from his horse and killed when riding to receive his prize. Emily became the bride of Palamon. Chaucer, in his *Knight's Tale*, borrowed the story from Boccaccio's *Teseide* (1341), and it is told by Fletcher in his *Two Noble Kinsmen* (1634), and Dryden in his *Fables* (1699).

Arcos Barbs. War steeds of Arcos, in Andalusia, famous in Spanish ballads. *See* BARB.

Arctic Region means the region of the Bear stars, from *arktos*, bear (meaning both the animal and the constellation), hence northern. Arcturus (the bearward) or Alpha Boötes is the brightest star in the Northern Hemisphere and can be found by following the curve of the Great Bear's tail. In *Job* xxxviii, 32, Arcturus is used for the Great Bear itself. *See under* BEAR.

Arden, The Forest of. In north Warwickshire, once part of a large Midland forest, famous as the probable setting of Shakespeare's *As You Like It*.

Arden, Enoch. The story in Tennyson's poem of this name (1864), of a husband who mysteriously and unwillingly disappears, and returns years later to find that his wife (who still treasures his memory) is married to another, is not an uncommon theme. It is reminiscent of Crabbe's *The Parting Hour*, and a similar story appeared in Adelaide Anne Procter's *Homeward Bound* (in her *Legends and Lyrics*, 1858), and Mrs. Gaskell's *Manchester Marriage*.

Areopagus (ǎr e op′ ǎ gus) (Gr. the hill of Mars or Ares). The seat of a famous tribunal in ATHENS; so called from the tradition that MARS was tried there for causing the death of NEPTUNE'S son Halirrothius.

Ares (âr′ ēz). The Greek god of war, son of ZEUS and HERA and identified with the Roman MARS.

Arethusa. *See* ALPHEUS AND ARETHUSA.

Aretinian Syllables. *Ut, re, mi, fa, sol, la*, used by Guido d'Arezzo or Aretino in the 11th century for his hexachord, or scale of six notes. These names were taken from the Latin hymn by Paulus Diaconus, addressed to St. JOHN, which Guido used in teaching singing:

Ut queant laxis, Re-sonare fibris,
Mi-ra gestorum Fa-muli tuorum,
Sol-ve pollutis La-biis reatum
Ut-tered be thy wondrous story,
Re-prehensive though I be,
Me make mindful of thy glory,
Fa-mous son of Zacharee;
Sol-ace to my spirit bring,
La-bouring thy praise to sing.

E.C.B.

Si was added in the 16th century and *do* (doh), probably from *dominus*, took the place of *ut* in the 17th century. In England *te* replaced *si* in the 19th century (*ti* or *si* are used in the U.S.A.).

Argenis (ar′ jen is). A political allegory by John Barclay (1582–1621) written in Latin and published in 1621. It deals with the state of Europe, and France in particular, in the time of the CATHOLIC LEAGUE.

Argentine, Argentina (ar'jen tīn, ar jen tē' nà). This South American republic, The Silver Republic, takes its name from the Rio de la Plata, or River of Silver, so called from the Indian silver work sent to Spain by Sebastian Cabot in 1526, assumed to indicate vast future wealth.

Argo (Gr. *argos*, swift). The galley of JASON in which he sailed in search of the GOLDEN FLEECE and finally succeeded with the help of MEDEA. Hence a sailing ship on any particularly adventurous voyage; also the name of a Southern constellation (the Ship).

Argonauts. The sailors of the ship Argo, who sailed from Iolcos to Colchis in quest of the GOLDEN FLEECE. Apollonius of Rhodes wrote an epic poem on the subject. The name is also given to a family of cephalopod molluscs (cuttle-fish).

Argosy. A merchant ship. A corruption of *ragusea*. Large merchant ships were built and sailed from Ragusa (Dubrovnik) in Dalmatia.

Argus-eyed. Jealously watchful. According to Grecian fable, Argus had 100 eyes, and JUNO set him to watch IO, of whom she was jealous. MERCURY, however, charmed him to sleep with his lyre, and slew him. Juno then set the eyes of Argus on the peacock's tail.

Argyle. God bless the Duke of Argyle, a phrase supposed to have been used by Scottish Highlanders when they scratched themselves. The story is that a Duke of Argyle (now Argyll) had posts erected on a treeless part of his estates so that his cattle might rub against them to ease themselves of the "torment of flies". The herdsmen saw the value of the practice, and as they rubbed their itching backs against the posts they thankfully uttered the above words.

Ariadne (ă ri ăd' ni). In Greek mythology, daughter of the Cretan King, MINOS. She helped THESEUS to escape from the LABYRINTH, and later went with him to Naxos where he deserted her. Here DIONYSUS found her and married her.

Arians (âr' i ànz). The followers of Arius, a presbyter of the Church of Alexandria in the 4th century. He maintained (1) that the Father and Son are distinct beings; (2) that the Son, though divine, is not equal to the Father; (3) that the Son had a state of existence prior to His appearance on earth, but not from eternity; (4) that the MESSIAH was not real man, but a divine being in a veil of flesh. The heresy was condemned by the Council of Nicæa (325), which upheld the orthodox view of Athanasius that the Son was "of the same substance" with the Father.

Ariel (âr' iel). A Hebrew name signifying "lion of God". In *Isaiah* xxix, 1–7, it is applied to Jerusalem; in astronomy a satellite of URANUS; in demonology and literature, the name of a spirit. Thus Ariel is one of the seven angelic "princes" in Heywood's *Hierarchie of the Blessed Angels* (1635); one of the rebel angels in Milton's *Paradise Lost*, VI, 371 (1667); a SYLPH, the guardian of Belinda, in Pope's *Rape of the Lock* (1712); but best known as "an ayrie spirit" in Shakespeare's *Tempest*. According to the play Ariel was enslaved to the witch Sycorax (I, ii) who overtasked him, and in punishment for not doing what was beyond his power, shut him up in a pine-rift for twelve years.

Aries (âr' ēz). The RAM. The first sign of the ZODIAC in which the sun is from 21 March to 20 April. The legend is that the ram with the GOLDEN FLEECE, which bore Phrixus and Helle on its back, was finally sacrificed to ZEUS, who set it in the heavens as a constellation.

Arimanes (a ri ma' nēz). Another form of AHRIMAN.

Arimaspians (ăr im ăs' pi ànz). A one-eyed people of Scythia constantly at war with the GRIFFINS who guarded a hoard of gold. Rabelais (IV, lvi, and V, xxix) so names the peoples of northern Europe who had accepted the REFORMATION, the suggestion being that they had lost one eye—that of faith.

> As when a gryphon, through the wilderness
> With winged course, o'er hill or moory dale
> Pursues the Arimaspian, who by stealth
> Had from his wakeful custody purloin'd
> The guarded gold.
> MILTON: *Paradise Lost*, II, 943–7.

Arioch (ăr′ i ok). The name means "a fierce lion" and was used for one of the fallen angels in *Paradise Lost* (VI, 371); Milton took it from *Dan*. ii, 14, where it is the name of the captain of the guard.

Arion (à rī′ on). A Greek poet and musician (7th century B.C.) reputed to have been cast into the sea by mariners but carried to Taenaros on a dolphin's back. *See* FAMOUS HORSES *under* HORSE.

Ariosto, Ludovico (ăr i os′ tō) (1474–1533). Italian poet, author of ORLANDO FURIOSO.

Aristides (à ris′ ti dēz). Athenian statesman and general, surnamed "the Just" (*c*. 520–*c*. 468 B.C.).

Aristophanes (ăr is tof′ à nēz) (*c*. 450–*c*. 385 B.C.). The great Athenian comic dramatist.

The French Aristophanes. MOLIÈRE (Jean Baptiste Poquelin) (1622–1673).

Aristotle (ăr′ is totl) (384–322 B.C.). The great Greek philosopher, pupil of Plato, and founder of the PERIPATETIC SCHOOL.

Aristotelian philosophy (ăr is tot ē′ li àn). Aristotle maintained that four separate causes are necessary before anything exists: the material cause, the formal, the final, and the moving cause. The first is the antecedents from which the thing comes into existence; the second, that which gives it its individuality; the moving or efficient cause is that which causes matter to assume its individual forms; and the final cause is that for which the thing exists. According to Aristotle, matter is eternal.

Aristotelian Unities. *See* DRAMATIC UNITIES.

Arm, Arms. This word, with meaning of the limb, has given rise to numerous common phrases, such as:

Arm of the sea. A narrow inlet.

To chance your arm. *See* CHANCE.

To make a long arm. *See under* LONG.

At arm's length. At a good distance; hence with avoidance of familiarity.

With open arms. Cordially, as a dear friend is received, with arms open for an embrace.

Arm-shrines. In the MIDDLE AGES bodily relics of saints were often put in metal containers modelled on the shape of the contents. Arm-shrines were normally cylinders of silver ending in the shape of a hand. Head-shrines were called *Chefs*.

A passage of arms. A literary controversy; a battle of words.

An assault at arms (or **of arms**). A hand-to-hand military exercise.

Coat of Arms. *See* ARMOUR.

Small arms. Those which do not, like artillery, require carriages.

To appeal to arms. To decide an issue by resorting to the test of war.

To arms. Make ready for battle.

To lay down arms. To cease from armed hostilities; to surrender.

Under arms. Prepared for battle; in battle array.

Up in arms. In open rebellion; figuratively, roused to anger.

King of Arms. *See* HERALDRY.

The right to bear arms. This is based on proven descent, through the male line, from an ancestor entitled to bear certain arms; or by a grant from the College of Arms (Heralds' College) in England and Wales; the NORROY and ULSTER King of Arms in Ulster; and the LYON King of Arms in Scotland. A person having such right is said to be *armigerous*. *See* HERALDRY.

In the U.S.A. the right to bear arms means the right of a citizen to have a gun and is still zealously championed by many.

The Royal Arms of England. The systematic use of Royal Arms begins with Richard I, who introduced the three lions passant gardant. In 1340 Edward III styled himself "of Great Britain, France and Ireland, King", and quartered the arms of France with those of England. This title and practice was abandoned in 1801 when the Arms were re-marshalled consequent upon the Union with Ireland. During Mary Tudor's reign the arms of Philip II of Spain were impaled on the existing Arms. James I of England and VI of Scotland introduced the LION rampant of Scotland and the harp of Ireland (derived from the badge assigned to Ireland in the reign of Henry VIII). During the reign of William III and Mary II the arms of Nassau were added, and on the accession of George I the White Horse of Hanover was superimposed until the Hanoverian connection ended with the accession of Victoria in 1837. The lion supporter for England and the UNICORN for Scotland were introduced by James I. The lion statant gardant on the crest was first used by Edward III.

The corrct emblazoning of the arms of the United Kingdom of Great Britain and Northern Ireland is:

Quarterly, first and fourth gules, three lions passant gardant in pale, or, for England; second or, a lion rampant with a double tressure flory-counter-flory gules, for Scotland; third azure, a harp or, stringed argent, for Ireland; all surrounded by the Garter. *Crest.*—Upon the royal helm, the imperial crown proper, thereon a lion statant gardant or, imperial crown proper. *Supporters.*—A lion rampant gardant, or, crowned as the crest. Sinister, a unicorn argent, armed, crined, and unguled proper, gorged with a coronet composed of crosses patée and fleur de lis, a chain affixed thereto passing between the forelegs, and reflexed over the back, also or. *Motto.*—"Dieu et mon Droit" in the compartment below the shield, with the Union rose, shamrock, and thistle engrafted on the same stem.

Armageddon (ar má ged′ ón). The name given in the Apocalypse (*Rev.* xvi, 16) to the site of the last great "battle of that great day of God almighty" between the forces of good and evil. Hence any great battle or scene of slaughter.

Armchair general. A person who thinks he knows how to direct affairs in which he is not taking part.

Armida (ar mē′ da). In Tasso's JERUSALEM DELIVERED a beautiful sorceress, with whom RINALDO fell in love and wasted his time in voluptuous pleasure. After his escape from her, Armida followed him, but being unable to lure him back, set fire to her palace, rushed into a combat, and was slain.

Arminians. Followers of Jacobus Hermansen or Arminius (1560–1609), anti-Calvinist theologian and professor at Leiden. They asserted that God bestows forgiveness and eternal life on all who repent and believe; that He wills all men to be saved and that His predestination is founded on His foreknowledge. His Dutch followers came to be called "Remonstrants" after their "remonstrance" of 1610 embodying their

five points of difference from orthodox Calvinism. In England the name was applied to the supporters of William Laud, Archbishop of Canterbury (1633–1645).

Armistice Day. 11 November, the day set aside to commemorate the fallen in World War I, marked by a two-minute silence at 11 a.m. and religious ceremonies. The armistice ending the war was signed at 11 o'clock on 11 November 1918. In 1946 the name was changed to REMEMBRANCE DAY. In the U.S.A. and Canada 11 November is a legal holiday, its name being changed to *Veterans' Day* in 1954.

Armory. The old name for HERALDRY, the word originally used to describe arms, military equipment and their employment.

Armour, Coat, or a **Coat of Arms,** was originally a coat of silk or linen used to cover the Knight's armour from the heat of the sun, or from rust and dirt, and it was colourfully embroidered with the distinguishing device of the wearer.

Arnauts (ar′ nawts) (Turk. brave men). Albanian mountaineers.

Arnold of Rugby. Dr. Thomas Arnold (1795–1842), father of the poet Matthew Arnold, and famous headmaster and reformer of Rugby School portrayed as "The Doctor" in *Tom Brown's Schooldays* by Thomas Hughes. His avowed aim in education was "if possible to form Christian men, for Christian boys I can scarcely hope to make."

Aroint thee. Get ye gone, be off. The phrase occurs in Shakespeare's *Macbeth* (I, iii, 6) and *King Lear* (III, iv, 129), on both occasions in connexion with witches. Its origin is unknown.

Arondight (ar′ on dīt). The sword of Sir LANCELOT OF THE LAKE.

Arras (ar′ ás). Tapestry, so called from Arras in Artois, once famed for its manufacture. When rooms were hung with tapestry it was easy for persons to hide behind it; Polonius was slain by Hamlet while concealed behind the arras (*Hamlet*, III, iv).

Arrière-ban. *See* BAN.

Arrière-pensée. (Fr. behind-thought). A hidden or reserved motive, not apparent on the surface.

Arrow. *See* BROAD ARROW; JONATHAN'S ARROWS.

Art. Art Deco. The decorative style of the 1920s and 1930s in painting, glass, pottery, silverware, furniture, etc. It is distinguished by bold colours, ornateness, geometrical lines and lack of symmetry.

Art Nouveau (ăr noo vō′) (Fr.). New art. A decorative art style of the 1890s and early 1900s freely ornamented with leaf-like and organic or natural forms. It is characterized by the use of curves and the absence of geometrical lines.

Art trouvé (ar troo vā′) (Fr.). Found art. Not the direct creation of the artist but adapted from "found" or natural objects which have been primarily shaped by circumstances, nature, and the elements. Items found on the seashore are obvious examples of the raw material of *art trouvé*.

Art Union. Originally, in Europe and Great Britain, associations formed to promote art by purchasing paintings, etc., and dispersing them among the membership by lottery. In Australia, after a while, all kinds of prizes were offered and consequently *Art Union* came to be applied to a lottery with money prizes.

Artaxerxes (àr tàks ĕrks′ ēz), younger son of XERXES and king of the Persians (465–425 B.C.) called the long-handed (*Longimanus*) because his right hand was longer than his left.

Artemis. *See* DIANA.

Artemus Ward. The name of an imaginary YANKEE showman and writer, the guise adopted by the American humorist, Charles Farrer Browne (1834–1867).

Artesian State, The. South Dakota, better known as the *Coyote State*.

Artful Dodger. A young thief up to every sort of wicked dodge. Such was the character of Jack Dawkins, pupil of Fagin, in Dickens's *Oliver Twist*.

Arthegal. *See* ARTEGAL.

Arthur. As a shadowy "historical" figure is first mentioned under the Latin name Artorius in the late 7th-century *Historia Britonum* (usually known by the name of Nennius, its 9th-century editor). Arthur, as *Dux Bellorum*, not king, is said to have led the Britons against the Saxons in twelve great battles culminating in the great victory of *Mons Badonicus* (fought between 493 and 516). He is mentioned again by William of Malmesbury (early 12th century), but ARTHURIAN ROMANCES owe most to Geoffrey of Monmouth. *See* CAMELOT.

Arthur's Seat. A hill overlooking Edinburgh from the East. The name is a corruption of the GAELIC *Ard-na-said*, the height of the arrows, a convenient shooting ground.

Arthurian Romances. The stories which have King Arthur as their central figure appear as early as 1136 in Geoffrey of Monmouth's mainly fabulous *Historia Regum Britanniæ*, which purported to be a translation (in Latin) of an ancient CELTIC history of Britain, lent to him by Walter Map, Archdeacon of Oxford. This was versified in French in Wace's *Roman de Brut* or *Brut d'Angleterre* (1155), which is the first to mention the ROUND TABLE. These were used by Layamon, the Worcestershire priest, whose BRUT (in English) was completed in about 1205, with additions such as the story of the fairies at Arthur's birth, who transported him to AVALON at his death. In France, in the late 12th century, Robert de Borron introduced the legend of the GRAIL and gave prominence to MERLIN; Chrestien de Troyes brought in the tale of ENID and GERAINT, the tragic loves of LANCELOT and GUINEVERE, the story of PERCEVAL and other material which was probably drawn from Welsh sources including the MABINOGION. Thus Walter Map and the Arthurian writers introduced the romantic spirit of CHIVALRY and courtly manners into European literature and King Arthur became the embodiment of the ideal Christian KNIGHT. Many other Welsh and Breton ballads, lays and romances popularized the legend and the whole corpus was collected and edited by Sir Thomas Malory (d. 1471), whose great prose romance *Le Morte d'Arthur* was produced by Caxton in 1485. Tennyson's *Morte d'Arthur* and *Idylls of the King* (1857–1885) were based upon it.

Articles of Roup. The conditions of sale at a ROUP, as announced by a crier.

The Six Articles. *See under* SIX.

The Thirty-nine Articles. *See under* THIRTY.

Artists, the Prince of. Albrecht Dürer (1471–1528) of Nuremberg was so called by his countrymen.

Arts, Degrees in. In the mediæval universities the seven liberal arts consisted of the TRIVIUM (grammar, logic and rhetoric), and the QUADRIVIUM (arithmetic, geometry, music and astronomy).

Arundel. *See* HORSE.

Arundelian Marbles. A collection of ancient sculptures made at great expense by Thomas Howard, 14th Earl of Arundel (1585–1646), and presented to Oxford University in 1667 by his grandson Henry, 6th Duke of Norfolk. They include the famous *Marmor Chronicon* or *Parian Chronicle* (said to have been executed in the island of Paros about 263 B.C.) which recorded events in Greek history from 1582 to 264 B.C., although now incomplete and ending at 354 B.C.

Arval Brothers (*Fratres Arvales*). An ancient Roman college of Priests, revived by AUGUSTUS.

Aryans. A name used for the parent stock of the Indo-European family of nations and popular with 19th-century philologists for the Indo-European languages (also sometimes called Indo-Germanic and JAPHETIC but more accurately Indo-Hittite). They include Sanskrit, Zend, Latin, Greek, Celtic, Persian, Hindu and all the European languages except Basque, Turkish, Hungarian, Finnish and Estonian. The name Aryan means "noble" and was used by early Hindus and Persians, to whose descendants it can be more properly applied. Anti-Semites prostituted the word and it was used by the German NAZIS to denote any people or thing that was not Semite, even the Japanese being classified as Aryans.

Asaph. In the Bible, a famous musician in David's time (I *Chron*, xvi, 5 and xxv, 1, 2). He is supposed to be the founder of the hereditary choir of *b'ne Asaph* in the Second Temple (*Ezra* iii, 10, 11 and *Neh*. vii, 44). *Psalms* 50 and 73–83 are ascribed to Asaph.

Tate lauds Dryden under this name in *Absalom and Achitophel*, Pt. II, 1063.

St. Asaph. A 6th-century Welsh saint, Abbot and first Welsh bishop of the see of Llanelwy which came to be called St. Asaph in the 12th century.

Ascalaphus. In Greek mythology, a son of ACHERON who said that PROSERPINE had partaken of a pomegranate when PLUTO had given her permission to return to the upper world if she had eaten nothing. In revenge Proserpine turned him into an owl by sprinkling him with the water of PHLEGETHON.

Ascendant. In casting a HOROSCOPE the point of the ECLIPTIC or degree of the ZODIAC which is nearest the eastern horizon at the time of birth is called the ascendant, and the easternmost star represents the house of life (*see* HOUSES, ASTROLOGICAL; STAR), because it is in the act of ascending. This is a person's strongest star, and when the outlook is bright, we say *one's star is in the ascendant*.

The house of the Ascendant, includes five degrees of the ZODIAC above the point just rising, and twenty-five below it. Usually, the point of birth is referred to.

Ascension Day, or Holy Thursday (*q.v.*). The day set apart by the Christian Churches to commemorate the ascent of Christ from earth to HEAVEN. It is the fortieth day after EASTER.

Asclepiads, or Asclepiadic Metre (ăs kle pī′ ădz). A Greek and Latin verseform, possibly invented by Asclepiades (3rd century B.C.) consisting of a spondee, two (or three) choriambi, and an iambus, usually with a central cæsura, thus:

$$- -|- \cup \cup -||- \cup \cup -|\cup -$$

The first ode of HORACE is Asclepiadic. Its first and last two lines have been translated in the same metre:

> Dear friend, patron of song, sprung from the race of kings;
> Thy name ever a grace and a protection brings...
> My name, if to the lyre haply you chance to wed,
> Pride would high as the stars lift my exalted head.
>
> E.C.B.

Ascot, Royal. A very fashionable race meeting held in June at Ascot Heath,

Berkshire, instituted by Queen Anne in 1711.

Asgard (ăs' gard) (*As*, a god; *gard*, or *gardh*, an enclosure, garth or yard). The realm of the ÆSIR or the Northern gods, the OLYMPUS of Scandinavian mythology. It is said to be situated in the centre of the universe, and accessible only by the rainbow bridge, BIFROST. It contains many regions, and mansions such as Gladsheim and VALHALLA.

Ash Tree, or **Tree of the Universe.** *See* YGGDRASIL.

Ash Wednesday. The first day of LENT, so called from the Roman Catholic custom of sprinkling on the heads of penitents the consecrated ashes of palms remaining from the previous PALM SUNDAY. The custom is of uncertain date but is commonly held to have been introduced by GREGORY THE GREAT (Pope 590–604).

Ashes. Ashes to ashes, dust to dust. A phrase from the English burial service, used sometimes to denote total finality. It is founded on scriptural texts such as "dust thou art, and unto dust thou shalt return" (*Gen.* iii, 19).

Dust and Ashes. *See under* DUST.

The Ashes. The mythical prize contended for in the test CRICKET matches between England and Australia. When England was beaten at the Oval in 1882 a humorous epitaph on English cricket appeared in the *Sporting Times*, winding up with the remark that "The body will be cremated and the ashes taken to Australia".

To wear sackcloth and ashes. *See under* SACK.

Ashtaroth, or **Ashtoreth.** The goddess of fertility and reproduction among the Canaanites and Phœnicians, called by the Babylonians ISHTAR (VENUS) and by the Greeks ASTARTE. She is referred to in I *Sam.* xxi, 10; I *Kings* xi, 5 and II *Kings* xxiii, 13; and she may be the "queen of heaven" mentioned by *Jeremiah* (vii, 18; xliv, 17, 25). Formerly she was supposed to be a moon-goddess, hence Milton's reference in his *Hymn on the Nativity*.

And moonèd Ashtaroth,
Heav'ns Queen and Mother both.

Ashur. *See* ASSHUR.

Asir. *See* ÆSIR.

Askance at, To look. To regard obliquely, with suspicion or disapproval. Of uncertain origin but the expression of ill-will sometimes used by gypsies "May the Lord look upon you sideways" probably stems from the same root idea.

Asleep at the switch. A failure in alertness of mind or lack of awareness of threatened danger. An American expression derived from the railroads. "To switch a train" is to transfer it to another set of rails by operating a switch. Failure to do this according to schedule might well lead to a catastrophe.

Also a derisive nickname for the American Defense Medal, given to those in the armed forces on Pearl Harbour Day (7 December 1941).

Asmodeus (ăs mō dē' us, ăs mō'di ùs). The evil demon who appears in the Apocryphal book of TOBIT and is derived from the Persian *Aeshma*. In *Tobit* Asmodeus falls in love with Sara, daughter of Raguel, and causes the death of seven husbands in succession, each on his bridal night. He was finally driven into Egypt through a charm made by Tobias of the heart and liver of a fish burnt on perfumed ashes, as described by Milton in *Paradise Lost* (IV, 167–71). Hence Asmodeus often figures as the spirit of matrimonial jealousy or unhappiness.

Asoka (ås' ō kà). Emperor of India *c.* 274–232 B.C., who was converted to BUDDHISM by a miracle and became its "nursing father", as Constantine was of Christianity.

Aspasia (ă spä' zi à). A courtesan. The most celebrated of the Greek Hetæræ. She lived at Athens as mistress of Pericles and after his death (429 B.C.) with Lysicles, the democratic leader.

Aspatia (ă spä' shà), in the *Maid's Tragedy*, of Beaumont and Fletcher, is noted for her deep sorrows, her great resignation, and the pathos of her speeches. Amyntor deserts her, women point at her with scorn, she is the jest and byword of everyone, but she bears it all with patience.

Aspen, or **trembling poplar.** The aspen leaf is said to tremble, from shame and horror, because our Lord's cross was made of this wood. In fact, owing to the shape of the leaf and its long, flexible leafstalk, it is peculiarly liable to move with the least breath of air.

Asphaltic Lake. The DEAD SEA, where asphalt abounds both on the surface of the water and on the banks.

Asphodel (ăs' fō del). A plant genus of the lily family, particularly associated with death and the underworld in Greek legend. It was planted on graves, and the departed lived their phantom life in the *Plain of Asphodel*. The name DAFFO-DIL is a corruption of asphodel.

Aspidistra. It was a very popular house plant from late Victorian times until the 1920s owing to its ability to survive in heated gas-lit rooms. It has become a symbol of Victorian lower-middle-class philistinism, respectability and stuffiness. George ORWELL wrote a novel called *Keep the Aspidistra Flying*.

Ass. According to tradition the dark stripe running down the back of an ass, crossed by another at the shoulders, was the cross communicated to the creature when Christ rode on the back of an ass in His triumphant entry into Jerusalem.

Ass, deaf to music. This tradition arose from the hideous noise made by "Sir Balaam" in braying. *See* ASS-EARED.

An ass in a lion's skin. A coward who hectors, a fool that apes the wise man. The allusion is to the fable of an ass that put on a lion's skin, but was betrayed by his braying.

An ass with two panniers. A man out walking with a lady on each arm, called in Italy *a pitcher with two handles*, and formerly in London *walking bodkin* (*see* BODKIN). Our expression is from the French *faire le panier à deux anses*.

Ass-eared. MIDAS had the ears of an ass. The tale says APOLLO and PAN had a contest, and chose Midas to decide which was the better musician. Midas gave sentence in favour of Pan; and Apollo, in disgust, changed his ears into those of an ass.

Golden Ass. *See* GOLDEN.

Sell your ass. Get rid of your foolish ways.

That which thou knowest not perchance thine ass can tell thee. An allusion to BALAAM's ass (*Num.* xxii, 21–33).

The ass waggeth his ears. A proverb applied to those who lack learning, and yet talk as if they were very wise; men wise in their own conceits. The ass, proverbial for having no "taste for music", will nevertheless wag its ears at a "concord of sweet sounds", just as if it could well appreciate it.

Till the ass ascends the ladder—*i.e.* NEVER. A rabbinical expression. The Romans had a similar one, *cum asinus in tegulis ascenderit* (when the ass climbs to the tiles).

Ass's bridge. *See* PONS ASINORUM.

Well, well! honey is not for the ass's mouth. Persuasion will not persuade fools.

Wrangle for an ass's shadow. To contend about trifles. The tale told by Demosthenes is that a man hired an ass to take him to Megara; and at noon, the sun being very hot, the traveller dismounted, and set himself down in the shadow of the ass. Just then the owner came up and claimed the right of sitting in this shady spot, saying that he let out the ass for hire, but there was no bargain made about the ass's shade. The two men then fell to blows to settle the point in dispute. While they were wrangling the ass took to its heels and ran away, leaving them both in the glare of the sun.

Asses as well as pitchers have ears. Children and even the densest minds hear and understand many a word and hint which the speaker supposed would pass unheeded. *Cp.* WALLS HAVE EARS.

Feast of Asses. *See under* FOOL.

Asses that carry the mysteries (*asini portant mysteria*). A classical knock at the Roman clergy. The allusion is to the custom of employing asses to carry the *cista* which contained the sacred symbols, when processions were made through the streets (WARBURTON: *Divine Legation*, ii, 4).

Assassins (à săs' inz). Killers by treachery and violence. Originally a sect of MOSLEM fanatics founded in Persia, about 1090, by Hassan ben Sabbah (better known as *the Old Man of the* MOUN-TAIN), their terrorism was mainly directed against the SELJUK authority. From Persia and Iraq they extended their activities to Syria in the early 12th century. Their power was broken by 1273 through the attacks of the Mongols and the MAMELUKE Sultan Bibars. Their name *hashishin* is derived from their reputed habit of dosing themselves with *hashish* or *bhang* prior to their murderous assaults.

Assay (à sā), or **Essay** (through O.Fr. from Lat. *exagium*, weighing). To try or test metals, coin, etc.; and formerly to taste food or drink before it was offered to a monarch; hence, *to take the assay* is to taste wine to prove it is not poisoned.

The aphetic form of the word, "say", was common until the 17th century. Thus Edmund in *King Lear* (V, iii), says to Edgar, "thy tongue some say of breeding breathes"; *i.e.* thy speech gives indication of good breeding—it savours of it.

Assay as a noun means a test or trial.

> (He) makes vow before his uncle never more
> To give the assay of arms against your majesty.
> SHAKESPEARE: *Hamlet*, II, ii.

For the last 300 years the spelling *essay* (from French) has been used for the noun, except in connexion with the assaying of metals.

Assemblage, Nouns of. Long custom and technical usage have ascribed certain words to assemblages of animals, things, or persons. Some of the principal are:

Animals, birds, etc.
antelopes: a herd.
asses: a pace or herd.
badgers: a cete.
bears: a sloth.
bees: a swarm, a grist.
birds: a flock, flight, congregation, volery.
bitterns: a sedge or siege.
boars: a singular.
bucks: a brace or leash.
cattle: a drove or herd.
chickens: a brood.
choughs: a chattering.
coots: a covert.
cranes: a herd, sedge, or siege.
crows: a murder.
cubs: a litter.
curlews: a herd.
deer: a herd.
doves: a flight.

ducks: (in flight) a team, (on water) a paddling.
elk: a gang.
ferrets: a fesnyng.
fishes: a shoal, draught, haul, run, or catch.
flies: a swarm.
foxes: a skulk.
geese: (in flight) a skein; (on the ground) a gaggle.
gnats: a swarm or cloud.
goats: a herd or tribe.
goldfinches: a charm.
grouse: (a single brood) a covey; (several broods) a pack.
hares: a down or husk.
hawks: a cast.
hens: a brood.
herons: a sedge or siege.
hounds: a pack or mute.
kangaroos: a troop.
kine: a drove.
kittens: a kindle.
larks: an exaltation.
leopards: a leap.
lions: a pride.
mares: a stud.
moles: a labour.
monkeys: a troop.
nightingales: a watch.
oxen: a yoke, drove, team or herd.
partridges: a covey.
peacocks: a muster.
pheasants: a nye or nide.
plovers: a wing or congregation.
porpoises: a school.
pups: a litter.
quails: a bevy.
rabbits: a nest.
rooks: a building or clamour.
seals: a herd or pod.
sheep: a flock.
starlings: a murmuration.
swans: a herd or bevy.
swifts: a flock.
swine: a sounder or drift.
teals: a spring.
whales: a school, gam or pod.
wolves: a pack, rout or herd.
woodcock: a fall.

Things.
aeroplanes: a flight, squadron.
arrows: a sheaf.
bells: a peal.
bowls: a set.
bread: a batch.
cars: a fleet.
cards: a pack, a deck (Am.).
eggs: a clutch.
flowers: a bunch, bouquet or nosegay.
golf-clubs: a set.
grapes: a cluster or bunch.
onions: a rope.
pearls: a rope or string.
rags: a bundle.
sails: a suit.
ships: a fleet, squadron or flotilla.
stars: a cluster or constellation.
steps: a flight.
trees: a clump.

Persons.

actors: a company, cast or troupe.
angels: a host.
baseball: team, a nine.
beaters: a squad.
bishops: a bench.
cricket team: an eleven.
dancers: a troupe.
football: (Association) an eleven or squad; (Rugby) a fifteen or squad.
girls: a bevy.
labourers: a gang.
magistrates: a bench.
minstrels: a troupe.
musicians: a band, an orchestra.
police: a posse.
rowing: an eight, a four, a pair.
runners: a field.
sailors: a crew.
savages: a horde.
servants: a staff.
worshippers: a congregation.

Asshur. Originally the local god of Asshur, the capital of Assyria, he became the chief god of the kingdom. His symbol was the winged sun disc enclosing a male figure wearing a horned cap, often with a bow in his hand. His name was frequently linked with the goddess ISHTAR of Nineveh. *See* ASHTAROTH.

Assumption, Feast of the. 15 August, celebrated in the ROMAN CATHOLIC CHURCH to commemorate the death of the Virgin MARY and the assumption of her body into HEAVEN when it was reunited to her soul.

Assurance. To make assurance doubly sure. To make security doubly sure or secure.

But yet I'll make assurance double sure
And take a bond of fate.
SHAKESPEARE: *Macbeth*, IV, i.

Astarte (à star' ti). The Greek and Roman name for the supreme goddess of the Phoenicians, ASHTAROTH.

BYRON gave the name to the lady beloved by Manfred in his drama, *Manfred*. It has been suggested that Astarte was drawn from the poet's half-sister, Augusta (Mrs. Leigh).

Astley's. The popular name for an enterprising and much patronized place of entertainment from 1770 to 1862, opened and developed by Philip Astley (1742–1814). Astley, with his charger Gibraltar, opened a theatre with an unroofed circus at Lambeth in 1770 for equestrian displays. Eventually called the Royal Grove Theatre, it was burnt down in 1794 and rebuilt as the Royal Amphitheatre. It grew in repute as a centre for equestrian and circus entertainment under Astley's pioneering management—he was the best horse-tamer of his day. Astley's was destroyed again by fire in 1803 but was re-opened in 1804. *Cp.* SADLER'S WELLS.

But many other "cunning tricks" ... have been performed by dogs some few years ago, at Sadler's Wells, and afterwards at Astley's, to the great amusement of the polite spectators.
STRUTT: *Sports and Pastimes* (1801), Bk. III, Ch. vi, vii.

Astolat (ăs' tō lăt). This town, mentioned in the ARTHURIAN ROMANCES, is generally identified with Guildford, in Surrey.

The Lily Maid of Astolat. ELAINE.

Astoreth. *See* ASHTAROTH.

Astræa (ă s trē' à). Justice, innocence. During the GOLDEN AGE this goddess dwelt on earth, but when sin began to prevail, she reluctantly left it, and was metamorphosed into the constellation VIRGO.

Astral Body. In theosophical parlance, the phantasmal or spiritual appearance of the physical human form, that is existent both before and after the death of the material body, though during life it is not usually separated from it; also the "Kamarupa" or body of desires, which retains a finite life in the astral world after bodily death.

Astral spirits. The spirits animating the stars. According to occultists, each star had its special spirit; and PARACELSUS maintained that every man had his attendant star, which received him at death, and took charge of him until the great resurrection.

Astrea, Incomparable. Mrs. Aphra Behn (1640–1689), playwright and novelist, author of *Oroonoko*, the first English novel written by a woman.

Hymnes of Astrea in Acrosticke Verse, twenty-six poems written by Sir John Davies (1569–1626), in honour of Elizabeth I, the ACROSTICS being based on the name Elizabeth Regina.

Astrology. The pseudo-science of the ancient and mediæval world, concerned with DIVINATION, etc., based on the stars and heavenly bodies. *Natural*

Astrology dealt with the movements and phenomena of the heavenly bodies, time, tides, eclipses, the fixing of EASTER, etc., and was the forerunner of the science of astronomy (*cp.* ALCHEMY); *Judicial Astrology* dealt with what is now known as astrology, the influence of the stars upon human affairs. *See* ASCENDANT; HOUSES, ASTROLOGICAL; HOROSCOPE.

Astrophel (ăs' trō fel). Sir Philip Sidney (1554–1586). "Phil. Sid." being a contraction of *Philos Sidus*, and the Latin *sidus* being changed to the Greek *astron*, we get *astron-philos* (star-lover), the "star" being Penelope Devereux, whom he called Stella in his collection of sonnets known as *Astrophel and Stella*. Spenser wrote a pastoral called *Astrophel* to the memory of his friend and patron, who fell at Zutphen.

Asur (ăs' ŭr). *See* ASSHUR.

Asurbanipal. *See* SARDANAPALUS.

Asynja (ăs in' yà). The goddesses of ASGARD; the feminine counterparts of the ÆSIR.

At Home. *See* HOME.

Atalanta's Race (ăt à lăn' tà). In Greek myth the daughter of Iasus or of Schoenus. She took part in the hunt of the Calydonian BOAR and, being very swift of foot, refused to marry unless the suitor should first defeat her in a race. Milanion (or HIPPOMENES) overcame her by dropping at intervals during the race three golden apples, the gift of VENUS. Atalanta stopped to pick them up, lost the race and became his wife.

Atargatis (ăt ar găt' is). The "Syrian Goddess", the "fish goddess". A fertility goddess represented at Ascalon as half woman, half fish.

Atatürk. Father of the Turks. A surname adopted in 1934 by Mustapha Kemal (1881–1938), the maker of modern Turkey, when all Turks were made to assume surnames.

Ate (ā' tē). In Greek mythology, the goddess of vengeance and mischief; she was cast down to earth by ZEUS.

Atellane, or **Atellan Farces** (ă tē la' nē). Coarse improvised interludes in the Roman theatres introduced from Atella, in Campania. The characters of Macchus and Bucco are the forerunners of our PUNCH and CLOWN.

Athanasian Creed (ăth à nā' shàn). One of the three creeds accepted by the Roman and Anglican churches; so called because it embodies the opinions of Athanasius (*c.* 298–373) respecting the TRINITY. It is of unknown authorship. *See* APOSTLES' CREED; NICENE CREED.

Atheling (O.E. *æthel*, noble). In Anglo-Saxon England a title of distinction to those of noble family but subsequently restricted to royal princes or the heirs apparent. The island of Athelney, a marsh near Taunton, means *royal* or *princes'* island and it is where King Alfred took refuge from the Danes (878–879) and is supposed to have burnt the cakes.

Athena. *See* ATHENE.

Athenæum (ăth ė nē' ŭm). (1) A temple in Athens which became a meeting place of learned men. (2) A famous academy in Rome founded by Hadrian *c.* 135 A.D. The name is still used for literary and scientific institutions.

The Athenæum Club in PALL MALL was founded in 1824; the literary review called *The Athenæum* was founded by James Silk Buckingham in 1828 and was incorporated with *The Nation* in 1921, which merged with the *New Statesman* in 1931.

Athene, or **Pallas Athene** (à thē' nē). The patron goddess of ATHENS and patroness of arts and crafts; the goddess of wisdom and subsequently identified with MINERVA by the Romans.

Athens. When ATHENE and POSEIDON disputed for the honour of being the city's patron, the goddess of wisdom produced an olive branch, the symbol of peace and prosperity, and the sea-god created a horse, symbolic of war. The gods deemed the olive the better boon, and the city was called Athens.

The Modern Athens, the Athens of the North. Edinburgh.

Athenian Bee. PLATO (*c.* 429–347 B.C.), a native of ATHENS, was so called from the tradition that a swarm of bees alighted on his mouth when he was in his cradle, consequently his words flowed with the sweetness of honey. The same tale is told of St. AMBROSE, and others. *See* BEE. Xenophon (*c.* 430–*c.*

354 B.C.) was also called "the Athenian Bee" or "Bee of Athens". *See* ATTIC BEE.

Atkins. *See* TOMMY ATKINS.

Atlantean Shoulders. Shoulders able to bear a great weight, like those of ATLAS.

Atlantes (ăt lăn' tēz). Figures of men, used in architecture as pillars. So called from ATLAS. Female figures are called CARYATIDES.

Atlantic Ocean, is named after the Atlas mountains or the mythical ATLANTIS.

Atlantis. According to ancient myth, an extensive island in the Atlantic Ocean, mentioned by PLATO in the *Timaeus* and *Critias*. It was said to have been a powerful kingdom before it was overwhelmed by the sea. The story was brought from Egypt by Solon. In the 16th century it was suggested that America was Atlantis and there have been a number of other implausible identifications. More recently, and more likely, the work of archaeologists and scientists has placed it in the Eastern Mediterranean. The centre of the former island of Stronghyle (Santorin) collapsed after catastrophic volcanic action and was submerged (c. 1500 B.C.). The civilization of the island was Minoan and the Minoan Empire suffered overwhelming disaster at this time. The general conclusion equates Atlantis with Stronghyle-Santorin and Minoan Crete.

The New Atlantis. An allegorical romance by Francis Bacon (written in 1624) in which he describes an imaginary island where was established a philosophical commonwealth bent on the cultivation of the natural sciences. *See* UTOPIA; CITY OF THE SUN.

Mrs. Manley, in 1709, published under the same title a scandalous chronicle, in which the names of contemporaries are so thinly disguised as to be readily recognized.

Atlas. In Greek mythology, one of the TITANS, condemned by ZEUS for his part in the war of the Titans to uphold the heavens on his shoulders. His abode became the Atlas mountains in Africa, which accorded with the legend that they supported the heavens.

A book of maps is so called because the figure of Atlas with the world on his back was put on the title page by Rumold Mercator when he published his father's maps in 1595.

Atli. *See* ETZEL.

Atman. In Buddhist philosophy the noumenon of one's own self. Not the EGO, but the Ego divested of all that is objective; the "spark of heavenly flame". In the UPANISHADS the Atman is regarded as the sole reality.

Atomy. *See* ANATOMY.

Atonement (at-one-ment). Reconciliation, expiation, making amends. In Christian usage the *Atonement* denotes the reconciliation of God and man through the life, sufferings and crucifixion of Jesus Christ. It presupposes man's alienation from God through sin.

Day of Atonement or **Yom kippur** (Heb. *yom*, day; *kippur*, atonement). The great Jewish fast day held on the tenth day of *Tishri*, the seventh month (Sept.–Oct.). The day is one of prayer, confession and repentance and the closing service of this most sacred day ends with the sounding of the SHOFAR. The ceremonies are described in *Leviticus*, xvi.

> And this shall be a statute for ever unto you: that in the seventh month, on the tenth day of the month ye shall afflict your souls, and do no work at all, whether it be one of your own country, or a stranger than sojourneth among you.
>
> *Leviticus*, xvi, 29.

Atossa. Sarah, Duchess of Marlborough (1660–1744), is said to be intended by Pope (*Moral Essays*, ii). Her friend, Lady Mary Wortley Montagu, is called SAPPHO. Somewhat convincingly the Duchess of Buckingham has also been suggested for Atossa.

Atropos (ăt' rō pos). In Greek mythology the eldest of the Three FATES, and the one who severs the thread of life.

Attic. Of ATHENS or Attica.

The Attic Bee. Sophocles (c. 496–406 B.C.), the Athenian tragic poet, so called from the sweetness of his compositions. *See also* ATHENIAN BEE.

The Attic Bird. The NIGHTINGALE; so called because Philomel was the daughter of the King of Athens, or because of the abundance of nightingales in Attica.

The Attic Boy. Cephalos, beloved by

AURORA or Morn; passionately fond of hunting.

Attic faith. Inviolable faith, the very opposite of PUNIC FAITH.

The Attic Muse. Xenophon (c. 430–c. 354 B.C.), the historian, a native of Athens; so called because the style of his composition is a model of elegance. *See* ATHENIAN BEE.

Attic salt. Elegant and delicate wit. Salt, both in Latin and Greek, was a common term for wit, or sparkling thought well expressed, thus CICERO says, *Scipio omnes sale superabat* (Scipio surpassed all in wit). The Athenians were noted for their wit and elegant turns of thought.

Atticus (ăt′ i kus). An elegant Roman scholar and master of Greek, publisher, and patron of the arts (109–32 B.C.).

The English Atticus. Joseph Addison (1672–1719), so called by Pope (*Prologue to Satires*), on account of his refined taste and philosophical mind.

Attila. *See* ETZEL.

Attis. *See* ATYS.

Attorney (a tĕr′ ni). **Power of Attorney.** Legal authority given to another to collect rents, pay wages, etc. or to act in matters stated in the legal instrument of **Warrant of Attorney,** according to his own judgment.

Atys (ă′ tis). A youth beloved by AGDISTIS (Cybele). Driven mad by her jealousy he castrated himself with a sharp stone. According to Ovid's *Metamorphoses* Cybele changed him into a pine tree as he was about to commit suicide.

Au courant (ō koo′ ron) (Fr.), "acquainted with" (literally, in the current of events). To keep one *au courant* of everything is to keep one informed of passing events.

Au fait (Fr.). Skilful, a thorough expert in, conversant with.

Au pair (Fr.). An arrangement by which foreigners who wish to learn the language or study the way of life of another country offer their services as domestic help in return for board and lodging, and usually a small payment as well.

Au pied de la lettre (Fr.). *Litteratim et verbatim*; according to the strict letter of the text.

Au revoir (Fr.). "Good-bye for the present". Literally, *till seeing you again*.

Aubaine. *See* DROIT D'AUBAINE.

Aubry's Dog. *See* DOG.

Auburn. The hamlet described by Goldsmith in *The Deserted Village*, said to be Lissoy, County Westmeath, Ireland.

Audit Ale. A strong ALE which was brewed at some of the Oxford and Cambridge colleges and originally broached on audit day when college accounts had to be paid up by the students.

Audley. We will John Audley it. A theatrical phrase meaning to abridge, or bring to a conclusion, a play in progress. It is said that an 18th-century travelling showman named Shuter used to lengthen out his performance until sufficient newcomers were waiting for the next house. An assistant would then call out, "Is John Audley here?" and the play was ended as soon as possible.

Audrey. In Shakespeare's *As You Like It*, an awkward country wench who jilted William for Touchstone. *See also* TAWDRY.

Auf Wiedersehen (ouf vē′ der zän). The precise German equivalent of the French AU REVOIR.

Augean Stables (aw jē′ ån). The stables of Augeas, the mythological King of Elis, in Greece, which housed his great herd of oxen. They were never cleaned and it was one of the labours of HERCULES to cleanse them, which he did by diverting the course of a river through them. Hence *to cleanse the Augean stables* means to clear away an accumulated mass of rubbish or corruption, physical, moral, religious or legal.

Augsburg Confession. The historical confession of faith compiled by MELANCHTHON in consultation with Luther and presented to Charles V at the Diet of Augsburg in 1530.

Augury (aw′ gū ri) (etymology uncertain), means properly the function of an augur, a Roman religious official. The duty of members of the college of Augurs was to pronounce, by the observation of signs called AUSPICES, whether the gods favoured or disfavoured a proposed course of action. *See* DIVINATION; INAUGURATE; OMENS; SINISTER.

August. Formerly called *sextilis* in the Roman calendar, the sixth month from MARCH (when the year began). It was changed to *Augustus* in 8 B.C. in honour of AUGUSTUS (63 B.C.–A.D. 14), the first Roman Emperor, whose "lucky month" it was. *Cp*. JULY. It was the month in which he began his first consulship, celebrated three TRIUMPHS, received the allegiance of the legions on the Janiculum, reduced Egypt, and ended the civil wars.

The old Dutch name for August was *Oostmaand* (harvest month); the old Saxon *Weodmonath* (weed-month, weed meaning vegetation in general); the French Republicans called it THERMIDOR (hot month, 19 July to 17 August).

Augusta. A name given to many Roman provincial towns. London was called *Augusta Trinobantia*.

Augustan Age. The GOLDEN AGE of Latin literature, so called from the Emperor AUGUSTUS, in whose reign (27 B.C.–A.D. 14) HORACE, Ovid, VIRGIL, Livy, Propertius, Tibullus, etc., flourished.

Augustan Age of English Literature. The period of the classical writers of the time of Queen Anne and George I, or to interpret it more widely, from Dryden to Johnson.

Augustan Age of French Literature. The period of Corneille (1606–1684), MOLIÈRE (1622–1673), and Racine (1639–1699).

Augustine, St. (354–430). Bishop of Hippo, DOCTOR OF THE CHURCH, and the greatest of the Latin fathers. He was baptized in 387 after an earlier life of self-indulgence and in due course (396) became Bishop of Hippo in N. Africa; distinguished by his zealous opposition to the heresies of his time and by his prolific writings.

Augustine of Canterbury, St. (d. 604). APOSTLE of the English and first Archbishop of Canterbury. He was sent from ROME by POPE Gregory the Great with a band of 40 monks to convert the English. They first landed on the Isle of Thanet, gained the support of King Aethelbert of Kent and established themselves at Canterbury in 597 when Aethelbert was baptized. Differences with the older British Church became apparent before Augustine's death.

Augustine, The Second. THOMAS AQUINAS, the ANGELIC DOCTOR.

Augustus. A title, meaning venerable, bestowed upon Gaius Julius Cæsar Octavianus, the first Roman Emperor, in 27 B.C., and borne by his successors. In the reign of Diocletian (284–305) the two emperors, of the East and the West, were called *Augustus*, each with his *Cæsar* or colleague.

Augustus was the name given to Philip II of France (1165–1223) and to Sigismund II of Poland (1520–1527), both of whom were born in August.

Auld Hornie. After the establishment of Christianity, the heathen deities were degraded by the Church into fallen angels; and PAN, with his horns, crooked nose, goat's beard, pointed ears, and goat's feet, was transformed to his Satanic majesty, and called Old Horny.

The Auld Kirk. The CHURCH OF SCOTLAND.

Auld Lang Syne. Old long since — the days of long ago. Words immortalized in the famous 18th-century Scottish ballad by Robert Burns, still frequently sung at the end of social gatherings and dances.

Auld Reekie. Edinburgh old town; so called because it generally appeared to be capped by cloud of "reek" or smoke.

Aulis (aw' lis). The port in BŒOTIA where the Greek fleet assembled before sailing against TROY. Becalmed by the intervention of ARTEMIS, because AGAMEMNON had killed a stag sacred to her, she was propitiated by the sacrifice of his daughter IPHIGENIA.

Aums-ace. *See* AMBS-AS.

Aunt Sally. A game in which sticks or cudgels are thrown at a wooden (woman's) head mounted on a pole, the object being to hit the nose of the figure, or break the pipe stuck in its mouth. The word *aunt* was anciently applied to any old woman. An Aunt Sally as a popular expression is applied to one who is an object of ridicule or a target of abuse.

Aureole (Fr. through Latin *aura*, air). A luminous radiance surrounding the whole figure in paintings of the Saviour and sometimes of the SAINTS. Du Cange (1610–1688) informs us that the aureole of nuns is white, of martyrs red, and of doctors green. *See* HALO; NIMBUS; VESICA PISCIS.

Auri sacra fames (aw' ri săk' ră fā' mēz). A Latin tag from the ÆNEID (III, 57), meaning "the cursed hunger for wealth", which almost amounts to monomania.

Aurignacian (aw rig nā' shăn). An upper PALÆOLITHIC culture characterized by the very extensive use of flint scrapers, blade flakes, and bone tools, probably originating in Palestine. It is the period of CRO-MAGNON man, notable for his cave paintings like those of Altamira in Spain.

Aurora (aw rôr' ă). Early morning. According to Greek mythology, the dawn-goddess Eos (Lat. *Aurora*) called by HOMER "rosy-fingered", sets out before the sun to proclaim the coming of day.

Aurora's tears. The morning dew.

Aurora borealis. Bands of light usually seen in high latitudes, hence the name *Northern Lights*. (*See* MERRY DANCERS; DERWENTWATER.) The similar phenomenon in the southern hemisphere is called *Aurora Australis*. Both are forms of *Aurora Polaris* and the lights are probably due to electrically charged solar particles.

Ausonia (aw sō' ni ă). An ancient name of Italy; so called from Auson, son of ULYSSES, and father of the Ausones.

Auspices (aw' spi sēz) (Lat. *avis*, a bird; *specere*, to observe). In ancient ROME the name for the interpreters of signs from birds, animals, and other phenomena, who were later called augurs.

Aussie (aw' si, os' i). A familiar name given to Australian soldiers during and after World War I. Their own colloquial term was "DIGGER".

Auster (Gr. *austeros*, hot, dry). A wind pernicious to flowers and health. In Italy one of the south winds was so called; its modern name is the *Sirocco*. In England it is a damp wind, generally bringing wet weather.

Australia. The States of Australia have their own familiar names:

South Australia, the Wheat State.
Queensland, Bananaland.
Victoria, the Cabbage Patch.
New South Wales, Ma State.
Northern Territory, The Top End, Land of the White Ant.
Western Australia, Westralia, Groperland.

Among the cities, Perth is called The Swan City; Adelaide, the City of the Churches; Melbourne, City of the Cabbage Garden.

Australia Day. 26 January, commemorating the first landing at Sydney Cove in 1788.

Australian Capital Territory. The name given to an area in New South Wales, of just over 900 square miles, which is Federal territory, containing Canberra, the Federal capital and seat of government.

Austrian Lip. A characteristic of the royal family of HABSBURGS, one of the most famous cases of hereditary physical deformity, said to have been derived through marriage with a daughter of the Polish princely house of Jagellon. Motley (*The Rise of the Dutch Republic*) describing the Emperor Charles V, at the age of fifty-five, says, "the lower jaw protruding so far beyond the upper, that it was impossible for him to bring together the few fragments of teeth which still remained, or to speak a whole sentence in an intelligible voice."

Aut Cæsar aut nullus (awt sē' săr awt nŭl' us) (Lat. either Cæsar or a nobody). Everything or nothing; all or not at all. CÆSAR used to say, "he would sooner be first in a village than second at Rome". The phrase was used as a motto by Pope Alexander VI's natural son, Cesare Borgia (1476–1507).

Authentic Doctor. A title bestowed on the scholastic philosopher, Gregory of Rimini (d. 1358).

Authorized Version, The. *See* BIBLE, THE ENGLISH.

Auto da fe (aw' tō da fā) (Port. an act of faith). The ceremonial procedure of the Spanish INQUISITION when sentences against heretics were read. Persistent HERETICS were subsequently delivered to the secular ARM for punishment. The reason why their victims were *burnt* was because inquisitors were forbidden to "shed blood"; a tergiversation based on the axiom of the ROMAN CATHOLIC CHURCH, *Ecclesia non novit sanguinem* (The Church is untainted with blood).

Autolycus (aw tol' i kŭs). In Greek mythology, son of MERCURY, and the craftiest of thieves. He stole his neighbours' flocks and altered their marks;

but SISYPHUS outwitted him by marking his sheep under their feet. Delighted with this device, Autolycus became friends with Sisyphus. Shakespeare uses his name for a rascally pedlar in *The Winter's Tale* (IV, ii).

Auto State, The. An alternative nickname to "the Wolverine State" for Michigan, in which Detroit is situated, and where Ford automobiles were originally made.

Autumn. The third season of the year, in the Northern Hemisphere AUGUST or SEPTEMBER, OCTOBER and NOVEMBER; astronomically 22/23 September to 21/22 DECEMBER.

Avalon (ăv' à lon). Called *Avilion* in Tennyson's *Morte d'Arthur*, a CELTIC word meaning the "island of apples", and in Celtic mythology the *Island of Blessed Souls*. In the ARTHURIAN ROMANCES it is the abode and burial place of ARTHUR, who was carried thither by MORGAN LE FAY. Its identification with GLASTONBURY is due to etymological error. OGIER THE DANE and OBERON also held their courts at Avalon.

Avant-garde (ă' von gard) (Fr.). The advanced guard of an army, usually nowadays shortened to *vanguard*. The term is also applied to ultra-modern and experimental young artists and writers.

Avars. *See* BANAT.

Avatar (Sans. *avatara*, descent; hence incarnation of a god). In Hindu mythology the advent to earth of a deity in a visible form. The ten avatars of VISHNU are the most celebrated. He appeared as (1) the fish (Matsya); (2) the tortoise (Kurma); (3) the boar (Varaha); (4) half-man, half-lion (Nrisinha); (5) the dwarf (Vamana); (6) RAMA with the Axe (Parasurama); (7) again as Rama (Ramachandra); (8) KRISHNA; (9) BUDDHA; the tenth advent is to occur at the end of the four ages and will be in the form of a white horse with wings (Kalki), to destroy the earth.

The word is used metaphorically to denote a manifestation or embodiment of some idea or phrase:

> I would take the last years of Queen Anne's reign as the zenith, or palmy state of Whiggism, in its divinist avatar of common sense.
>
> COLERIDGE: *Table-talk*.

Ave (ā' vi, a'vā). Latin for "Hail!"

Ave atque vale. *See* VALE.

Ave Maria (Lat. Hail, Mary!). The first two words of the Latin prayer to the Virgin MARY used in the ROMAN CATHOLIC CHURCH. (*See Luke* i, 28.) The phrase is applied to the smaller beads of a ROSARY, the larger ones being termed PATERNOSTERS.

Avenger of Blood, The. The man who, in the Jewish polity, had the right of taking vengeance on him who had slain one of his kinsmen (*Josh.* xx, 5, etc.). The Avenger in Hebrew is called GOEL.

Avernus (à vĕr' nŭs) (Gr. *a-ornis*, without a bird). A lake in CAMPANIA, so called from the belief that its sulphurous and mephitic vapours caused any bird that attempted to fly over it to fall into its waters. Latin mythology made it the entrance to Hell.

Avesta (à ves' tà). The sacred writings of ZOROASTER, sometimes called ZENDAVESTA. The present fragment is from the Avesta compiled under the SASSANIDES, using earlier sources from the time of Zoroaster onwards and adding to them. It essentially comprises (1) the Yasna, the chief liturgical portion including the *Gathas*, or hymns; (2) the Vispered, another liturgical work; (3) the Vendidad, which like the Christian PENTATEUCH, contains the laws; (4) the Yashts, dealing with stories of the different gods, etc.; (5) the Khordah Avesta (Little Avesta), containing short prayers.

Avicenna (**Abu Ibn Sina**) (980–1037). A great Moslem PHILOSOPHER, mathematician, astronomer and physician. About 100 treatises are attributed to him and his *Canon of Medicine* remained a standard text-book into the 17th century.

Avignon Popes (ă vē' nyon). In 1309 Pope Clement V (1305–1314), a Gascon, under pressure from Philip the Fair of France, transferred the papal court to Avignon, where it remained until 1377. This BABYLONIAN CAPTIVITY weakened the papacy and led to the GREAT SCHISM.

Other Avignon popes were:

John XXII	1316–34
Benedict XII	1334–42
Clement VI	1342–52
Innocent VI	1352–62

Urban V	1362–70
Gregory XI	1370–78

A vinculo matrimonii (ā vin′ kū lō măt rimō′ niī) (Lat.). A total divorce from the marriage bond. A divorce *a mensa et thoro* (*i.e.* from table and bed), equivalent to a modern decree of judicial separation, was formerly granted by the Church courts until the Matrimonial Causes Act of 1857 transferred this jurisdiction to the King's Court.

Awar. One of the sons of EBLIS.

Axe. To have an axe to grind. To have some selfish motive in the background; some personal interest to answer. Benjamin Franklin tells of a man who wanted to grind his axe, but had no time to turn the grindstone. Going to the yard where he saw young Franklin, he asked the boy to show him how the machine worked, kept praising him till his axe was ground, and then laughed at him for his pains.

To hang up one's axe. To retire from business. The allusion is to the battle-axe, hung up when fighting was over.

To put the axe on the helve. To solve a problem, "hit the nail on the HEAD".

To send the axe after the helve. To spend more money in the hope of recovering bad debts.

Axinomancy (ăks′ in ō măn si). DIVINATION by the axe, practised by the ancient Greeks with a view to discovering crime. An agate or piece of jet was placed on a red-hot axe which indicated the guilty person by its motion.

Axis. The alliance of the FASCIST states of Germany and Italy (October 1936), described by Mussolini an "an axis round which all European states animated by the will to collaboration and peace can also assemble". It became the Rome–Berlin–Tokyo axis in 1937.

Axle grease. Money; an Australian colloquial expression. Money makes life run more smoothly, as axle grease helps the running of a wagon.

Ayesha, or **A'isha** (ī yesh′ a). Favourite wife of MOHAMMED, daughter of ABOU BEKR.

Aymon, The Four Sons of (ā′ mon). The *geste* of *Doon de Mayence* (13th century) describes the struggle of certain feudal VASSALS against CHARLEMAGNE, including Doon of Mayence and Aymon of Dordone. The exploits of the four sons of Aymon—Renauld or RINALDO, Alard, Guichard, and Richard with their famous horse BAYARD is a central feature.

Ayrshire poet. Robert Burns (1759–1796), who was born at Alloway in Ayrshire.

Azazel (à zăz′ el). In *Lev.* xvi, 7–8, we read that AARON, as an atonement, "shall cast lots" on two goats "one lot for the Lord, and the other lot for the scapegoat" (Azazel). Milton uses the name for the standard-bearer of the rebel angels (*Paradise Lost*, I, 534). In Mohammedan demonology Azazel is the counterpart of the DEVIL, cast out of HEAVEN for refusing to worship ADAM. His name was changed to EBLIS (Iblis), which means "despair".

Azaziel (à zăz′ i el). In BYRON's *Heaven and Earth*, a seraph who fell in love with Anah, a granddaughter of Cain. When the flood came he carried her under his wing to another planet.

Azilian (à zil′ i àn). A MESOLITHIC culture of the transitional period between PALÆOLITHIC and NEOLITHIC. Named from the bone and flint implements found in the cave at Mas d'Azil in the south of France.

Azoth (ăz′oth) (Arab.). The alchemists' name for mercury; also the PANACEA or universal remedy of PARACELSUS.

Azrael (ăz′ rāl). The Mohammedan ANGEL of death.

The Wings of Azrael. The approach or signs of death.

Azrafil. *See* ISRAFEL; ADAM.

Aztec State, The. One of the names by which Arizona, the *Apache State*, has been known. Also called the *Grand Canyon State* and the *Valentine State*, the latter because it was admitted as a state of the U.S.A. on St. VALENTINE'S DAY (14 February) 1912.

Azure (ăzh′ ūr, ā′ zūr). From the Arabic *lazura* (lapis-lazuli). Heraldic term for the colour blue. Also used as a synonym for the clear blue sky.

B

B. The form of the Roman capital "B" can be traced through early Greek to Phœnician and Egyptian hieratic; the small "b" is derived from the cursive form of the capital. In Hebrew the letter is called *beth* (a house); in Egyptian hieroglyphics it was represented by the crane. **B** in Roman notation stands for 300; with a *line above*, it denotes 3,000.

Marked with a B. In the MIDDLE AGES, and as late as the 17th century (especially in America), this letter was branded on the forehead of convicted blasphemers.

Not to know B from a battledore, or **from a bull's foot.** To be quite illiterate.

B. and S. Brandy and soda.

B.C. In dating an abbreviation for "Before Christ", before the Christian era.

Marked with B.C. When a soldier disgraced himself by insubordination he was formerly marked with "B.C." (bad character) before he was finally drummed out of the regiment.

B Flats. Bugs; which obnoxious insects are characterized by their flatness.

Ba. The SOUL, which according to more primitive Egyptian belief roamed the burial places at night. Later belief held that it travelled to the realm of OSIRIS, after a harrowing journey, where its happiness was assured.

Baal. A Semitic word meaning proprietor or possessor, primarily the title of a god as lord of the place (*e.g. Baal-peor*, lord of Peor), or as possessor of some distinctive attribute (*e.g. Baal-zebub* or BEELZEBUB). The worship of local Baals was firmly established in Canaan when the Israelites arrived. The latter adopted many rites of the Canaanites and grafted them to their own worship of Jahweh (JEHOVAH), who thus tended to become merely the national Baal. It was this form of worship that Hosea and other prophets denounced as heathenism. BEL is the Assyrian form of the name. *See also* BELPHEGOR.

Baal, or **Bale Fires.** Fires lighted on the highest moorland hill-tops on Midsummer Eve, etc. The custom still survives in Cornwall. *See* BELTANE.

Baalbec. *See* CHILMINAR.

Baba Yaga. A cannibalistic ogress of Russian folk-lore who stole young children and cooked them.

Babbitt (băb' it). The leading character in Sinclair Lewis's novel of this name (1922). He is a prosperous "realtor" or estate agent in the Western city of Zenith, a simple likeable fellow, with faint aspirations to culture that are forever smothered in the froth and futile hustle of American business life. Drive (which takes him nowhere), hustle (by which he saves no time) and efficiency (which does not enable him to do anything) are the keynotes of his life.

Babe the Blue Ox. A legendary and indeed remarkable beast that belonged to Paul BUNYAN.

Babel. A perfect Babel. A thorough confusion. "A Babel of sounds", a confused uproar and hubbub. The allusion is to the confusion of tongues at Babel (*Gen.* xi).

Babes in the Wood. *See* CHILDREN. The phrase has been humorously applied to simple trustful folks, never suspicious and easily gulled.

Babes, Protecting deities of. According to Varro (116–27 B.C.), Roman infants were looked after by Vagitanus, the god who caused them to utter their first *cry*; FABULINUS, who presided over their *speech*; CUBA, the goddess who protected them in their cots; and Domiduca, who brought young children safe *home*, and guarded them when out of their parents' sight. In the Christian Church St. NICHOLAS is the patron SAINT of children.

Babies in the Eyes. Love in the expression of the eyes.

Babrius. Ancient fabulist, probably a Hellenized Roman of the early 3rd century, possibly dwelling in Syria. *See* ÆSOP'S FABLES.

Baby. To be left holding the baby. *See under* HOLD.

To throw out the baby with the bath-water. Over-zealous reform, reorganization or action, which in getting rid of unwanted elements casts away the essentials as well.

Babylon (băb' i lŏn). **The Modern Babylon.** London is sometimes so called on account of its wealth, luxury and dissipation.

The hanging gardens of Babylon. *See* HANGING.

The whore of Babylon. A PURITAN epithet for the ROMAN CATHOLIC CHURCH. The allusion is to *Rev*. xvii–xix (*cp*. SCARLET WOMAN), where Babylon stands for Rome, the embodiment of luxury, vice, splendour, tyranny and all that the early Church held was against the spirit of Christ.

Babylonian Captivity. The period beginning from 597 B.C., when the Jews became captives in Babylon after the attacks by NEBUCHADNEZZAR, until their return (from 538 B.C.) after their release by Cyrus, consequent upon his conquest of Babylon.

Babylonian numbers. *Nec Babylonios temptaris numeros* (HORACE: *Odes*, Bk. I, xi, 2). Do not make trial of Babylonian calculations, *i.e.* do not consult astrologers or fortune-tellers. The Babylonians or Chaldeans were the most noted of astrologers.

Baca, The Valley of (ba' ka). An unidentified place mentioned in *Ps*. lxxxiv, 6, meaning the "Valley of Weeping".

Bacbuc (băk' bŭc). A Chaldean or Assyrian word for an earthenware pitcher, cruse, or bottle, taken by Rabelais as the ORACLE of the Holy Bottle (and of its

priestess). PANURGE consulted the Holy Bottle on the question whether or not he ought to marry and it answered with a click, like the noise made by glass snapping. Bacbuc told Panurge the noise meant *trinc* (drink), and that was the response, the most direct and positive ever given by the oracle. Panurge might interpret it as he liked, the obscurity would always save the oracle.

Bacchus (băk' ŭs). In Roman mythology, the god of wine, the Dionysus of the Greeks, son of ZEUS and SEMELE. The name "Bacchus" is a corruption of the Gr. *Iacchus* (from *Iache*, a shout) and was originally merely an epithet of Dionysus as the noisy and rowdy god. As MARS is the guardian power of Christianity, Bacchus is the guardian power of Mohammedanism.

Bacchus sprang from the thigh of Zeus. The tale is that SEMELE, at the suggestion of JUNO, asked JUPITER to appear before her in all his glory, but the foolish request proved her death. Jupiter saved the child, which was prematurely born, by sewing it up in his thigh till it came to maturity.

What has that to do with Bacchus? *i.e.* What has that to do with the matter in hand? When Thespis introduced recitations in the vintage songs, the innovation was suffered to pass, so long as the subject of recitation bore on the exploits of BACCHUS; but when, for variety's sake, he wandered to other subjects, the Greeks pulled him up with the exclamation, "What has that to do with Bacchus?"

Bacchanalia. Roman festivals in honour of BACCHUS, the equivalent of the Greek Dionysia, characterized by drunkenness and licentiousness (although it must be noted that Greek drama had its origins in the Dionysia). Hence *Bacchanalian orgy* now denotes any wild and drunken revelry.

Bacchanals (băk' à nàlz), **Bacchants, Bacchantes.** Priests and priestesses, or male and female votaries of BACCHUS; hence drunken roysterers. *See also* BAG O'NAILS *under* PUBLIC HOUSE SIGNS.

Bachelor. The word was applied to aspirants to knighthood, and KNIGHTS of the lowest rank were known as *knights* *bachelor*, those too young to display their own banners.

Bachelor of Arts, Science, Medicine, etc. In most British and American universities one who has taken a first degree in the appropriate faculty. Originally the degrees of "master" and "doctor" were for those further qualified to teach at the university.

Bachelor's buttons. Buttons, similar in principle to press-studs used in dressmaking, and affixed without the need of sewing, hence the name.

Also several button-shaped flowers are so called—red bachelor's buttons (double red campion), yellow (the upright crowfoot and buttercup), white (white ranunculus and white campion). Rustics were wont to put them in their pockets and their growth was an indication that they would find favour with their sweethearts. Maidens wore them under their aprons.

Bachelor's fare. Bread and cheese and kisses.

Bachelor's porch. An old name for the north door of a church. Menservants and old men used to sit on benches down the north aisle, and maidservants and poor women on the south side. After service the men formed one line and the women another, through which the clergy and gentry passed.

Bachelor's wife. A hypothetical ideal or perfect wife.

Back. Back-of-beyond. A phrase originating in Australia to describe the vast inland spaces, the *great Outback*. The term *back-block* is found in 1850, referring to those territories divided up by the government into blocks for settlement.

Back to Square One. Back to where one started from. Popularised from the early days of broadcast commentaries on football matches when, in order to make the course of the game easier to follow, a diagram of the pitch, divided into numbered squares, was printed in radio programmes. Possibly derived from earlier board games.

Laid on one's back. Laid up with ill health; helpless.

Thrown on one's back. Completely beaten. A figure taken from wrestling.

To back and fill. A nautical phrase, denoting a mode of tacking when the tide is with the vessel and the wind against it. Metaphorically, to be irresolute.

To back down. To yield a point contrary to the stand one had previously made.

To back out. To withdraw from an engagement, commitment, etc.; to retreat from a difficult position.

To back the field. *See under* FIELD.

To back the oars, or **to back water,** is to row backwards to check way, or go astern.

To back the sails. In a fore and aft rigged vessel, to sheet the sails to windward to check its way; in a square-rigged ship, to brace the yards so that the wind will press on the front of the sail thereby retarding the ship's course.

To back up. To uphold, to support. As one who stands at your back to support you. In CRICKET an advance by the batsman not taking strike, in order to take a quick run if the striker makes an opportunity.

To be a back number. To be superseded, relegated, out of the SWIM, to be a person with outdated ideas. From old back numbers of newspapers which carry news that is no longer current.

To break the back of. To finish the hardest part of (one's work).

To get one's back up. To become annoyed or angry. The allusion is to a cat, which sets its back up when attacked by a dog or other animal.

To go back on one's word. To withdraw from what one has promised or said. **To go back on a person** is to betray him.

To have one's back to the wall. To act on the defensive against odds. One beset with foes tries to get his back against a wall to prevent attack from behind.

To take a back seat. To withdraw from a position one has occupied into relative obscurity; to submit to humiliation.

To turn one's back on. To have nothing more to do with.

Back-bencher. *See under* BENCH.

Back end, The. Autumn. Widely used

in the North of England.

Back-friend. A secret enemy. SHAKE-SPEARE uses it in this sense.

Back-hander. A blow with the back of the hand.

A back-handed compliment. One so phrased as to imply depreciation. Also shortened, *a backhander*.

Backroom boys. A name given to the unpublicized scientists and technicians in World War II who contributed so much to the development of scientific warfare and war production, and since applied generally to such anonymous laboratory workers. The phrase comes from a speech by Lord Beaverbrook on war production (24 March 1941): "To whom must praise be given ... to the boys in the backroom."

Back-seat driver. One who gives a car driver advice and instructions from the back seat.

Back-slang. A form of slang which consists in pronouncing the word as spelt backwards. Thus *police* becomes *ecilop* (hence the term *slop* for a policeman), *parsnips*, *spinsrap*, etc. It was formerly much used by "flash" cockneys (*see* COCKNEY), thieves, etc. The widely-used epithet *yob* may be aptly defined as a "backward boy".

Backstairs influence. Private or unrecognized influence, especially at Court. Royal palaces have more than one staircase, and backstairs would be used by those who sought the sovereign upon private matters.

Backward. Not to be backward in coming forward. Not reluctant to make oneself prominent, or to draw attention to oneself.

Backward blessing. A curse. To say the Lord's Prayer backwards was to invoke the DEVIL.

Backwater. Properly a pool or stretch of water fed by the backflow of a stream or river. Figuratively **to be in a backwater** is to be isolated from the active flow of life. *See above* TO BACK THE OARS.

Bacon. To baste your bacon. To strike or scourge one. Bacon is the outside portion of the sides of pork, and may be considered generally as the part which would receive a blow. Here *baste* means "to thrash".

Falstaff's remark to the travellers at Gadshill, "On, bacons, on!" (*Henry IV, Pt. I*, II, ii) is an allusion to the fact that formerly bacon was the normal meat of English rustics, hence such terms as *bacon-brains* and CHAW-BACON for a country yokel.

To bring home the bacon. To bring back the prize; to succeed. Possibly a reference to the DUNMOW flitch, or to the sport of catching a greased pig at country fairs.

To save one's bacon. To save oneself from injury; to escape loss. The allusion may be to the care taken by our forefathers to save from the dogs of the household the bacon which was stored for winter use.

He may fetch a flitch of bacon from Dunmow. He is so amiable and good-tempered he will never quarrel with his wife. *See* DUNMOW.

Baconian Philosophy. Inductive philosophy as formulated by Francis Bacon (1561–1626) in the second book of the *Novum Organum*. He did not invent it but gave it a new importance.

Baconian Theory. *See* SHAKESPEARE.

Bacon's Brazen Head. *See* BRAZEN HEAD.

Bactrian Sage. ZOROASTER or Zarathustra, founder of the ancient Persian religion, who was probably either a Bactrian or a Mede.

Bad. Among rulers called "the Bad" are William I, King of Sicily from 1154 to 1166; Albert, Landgrave of Thuringia and Margrave of Meissen (d. 1314); Charles II, King of Navarre from 1349 to 1387.

Bad blood. Vindictiveness, ill-feeling.

In one's bad books. Under disgrace, in disfavour. Similarly "in one's BLACK BOOKS".

Bad debts. Debts unlikely to be paid.

Bad egg. A disreputable character.

A bad excuse is better than none. An adage first appearing in Nicholas Udall's *Ralph Roister Doister*, the first English comedy, performed *c.* 1553.

Bad form. Not in good taste.

Bad hat. A rascal or good-for-nothing.

Bad Lands, The. In particular the *Mauvaises Terres*, of the early French trappers in the west of South Dakota;

extensive tracts of sterile, rocky and desolate hill-country.

A bad lot. One morally or commercially unsound. Also a commercial project or stock that is worthless. Perhaps from auctioneering meaning a lot for which no one will bid.

A bad shot. A wrong guess. A sporting phrase for a shot that misses the mark.

To go to the bad. To mix with bad companions and acquire bad habits.

To the bad. On the wrong side of the account; in arrears.

Badge-men. Licensed beggars, or almshouse men; so called from their special dress or badge, worn to indicate that they belonged to a particular foundation.

Recipients of parish relief formerly wore a badge on the shoulder of the right sleeve, consisting of the letter P, with the initial of their parish, in red or blue cloth. *See* DYVOUR. In the Royal Navy a rating who holds Good Conduct Badges is called a "one", "two", or "three badgeman" according to the number of chevrons he wears on his left arm.

Badger, A. A hawker, huckster, or itinerant dealer, especially in corn, but also in butter, eggs, fish, etc. Its derivation is uncertain.

To badger. To tease, annoy, or persistently importune, in allusion to badger-baiting. The badger was kennelled in a tub and dogs were set upon him to "draw him out". When dragged from his tub the badger was allowed to retire to recover and then the process was repeated several times.

Badinguet (ba' din gä). A nickname given to NAPOLEON III, reputedly the name of the workman whose clothes he wore when he escaped from the fortress of Ham in 1846.

Badminton. The Gloucestershire seat of the Dukes of Beaufort which has given its name to a claret-cup and the game played with rackets and shuttlecocks. In pugilistic parlance blood, which is sometimes called CLARET, from the colour, is also called "badminton".

Badoura (ba doo' rà). "The most beautiful woman ever seen upon earth", heroine of the story of Camaralzaman and Badoura in the ARABIAN NIGHTS.

Baedeker (bā' dè kèr). Karl Baedeker (1801–1859) published the first of the famous series of guidebooks, modelled on John Murray's *Handbooks*, at Coblenz in 1839. Noted for reliability and thoroughness, they became widely used by tourists the world over.

Baffle. Originally a punishment or degradation of a recreant KNIGHT including hanging him or his effigy by the heels from a tree.

Bag and Baggage. In entirety (*cp.* LOCK, STOCK AND BARREL). Originally a military phrase signifying the soldier with all his belongings or the whole of the equipment and stores of an army. (*See* BAGGAGE.)

A bag of bones. Very emaciated.

Bag o'Nails. *See* PUBLIC HOUSE SIGNS.

A bag of tricks, or **the whole bag of tricks.** The whole lot, the entire collection. An allusion to the conjuror's bag, in which he carried his equipment for performing tricks.

An old bag. A slang term for an elderly and unattractive or slovenly woman; also a lady of easy virtue.

In the bag. As good as certain. In horse-racing parlance in Australia it means that the horse referred to will not be running.

The bottom of the bag. The last expedient, after having emptied one's bag of all others. A trump card held in reserve.

To be left holding the bag. To be deserted by one's comrades and left with the entire onus of what was originally a group responsibility.

To empty the bag. To tell everything and conceal nothing.

To give the bag now means to give the sack, but it seems formerly to have meant the reverse. An employee who left without giving notice was said to have given his master "the bag".

To let the cat out of the bag. *See* CAT.

To bag. To secure for oneself, to purloin; probably from sporting or poaching use, to put into one's bag what one has shot or trapped. Hence, **a good bag,** a large catch of game, fish, etc.

To set one's bag. In America is used of someone setting out to secure political office or preferment.

Bag-man, A. A commercial traveller, from the bag of samples that he carries. Formerly the horses of commercial travellers often bore outsize saddle-bags.

Bags. Slang for "trousers" which may be taken as the bags of the body. When the pattern was strong and "loud" they were once called *howling-bags*.

Bags I. Schoolboy slang assertion of a claim. *See* FAINS.

Oxford bags were wide-bottomed flannel trousers, popularized by Oxford undergraduates in the 1920s.

Bags of mystery. Slang for sausages and savelos; the allusion is obvious.

Baga de Secretis. Records in the Public Record Office of treason and other State trials from 1477 to 1813.

Baggage, as applied to a worthless or flirtatious woman, dates from the days when soldiers' wives, taken on foreign service with the regiment, travelled with the regimental stores and baggage.

Bail up! The Australian BUSHRANGER'S equivalent for the highwayman's "Stand and deliver!"

Bailey (probably ultimately from O.Fr. *bailler*, to enclose). The external wall of a mediæval castle, also the outer court, the space immediately within the outer wall. Subsequently the word was attached to the buildings as the OLD BAILEY (London), the Bailey (Oxford).

Bailey bridge. In World War II a metal bridge of amazing strength made of easily portable sections and capable of speedy erection, invented by the British engineer D. C. Bailey.

Bailiff. *See* BUM-BAILIFF.

Baily's Beads. *See* BEAD.

Bairam (bī răm). The name given to two Mohammedan feasts. The word in Turkish means "festival". The Lesser begins on the new moon of the month Shawwal, immediately after the feast of RAMADAN and lasts three days. The Greater (seventy days after the Lesser) lasts three days, beginning on the tenth day of the twelfth month, and forms the concluding ceremony of the pilgrimage to MECCA.

Bajadere. *See* BAYADERE.

Bajan, or **Bajanella.** *See* BEJAN.

Bajazet (băj' á zet), or **Bayezid I.** Ottoman SULTAN from 1389 to 1403, and a great warrior, noted for his victories especially against the Hungarians and their allies at Nicopolis in 1396. He was overwhelmed by TIMUR at Ankara in 1402 and held prisoner until his death. There is no evidence for the story, popularized by Christopher Marlowe (1564–1593) and Nicholas Rowe (1674–1718), that Timur carried him about in an iron cage.

Baked Meats, or **Bake meats.** Meat pies.

Baker, The. Louis XVI was so called and his Queen "the baker's wife", and the DAUPHIN the "shop boy"; because they gave bread to the starving men and women who came to VERSAILLES on 6 October 1789.

Baker's dozen. Thirteen for twelve. In earlier times when a heavy penalty was inflicted for short weight, bakers used to give a surplus number of loaves, called the *inbread*, to avoid all risk of incurring a fine. The 13th was the *vantage loaf*.

To give one a baker's dozen. To give one a sound drubbing, *i.e.* all he deserves and one stroke more.

Baker's knee. Knock-knee. Bakers were said to be particularly liable to this deformity owing to the constrained position in which they had to stand when kneading bread.

Bakha. The sacred bull of Hermonthis in Egypt, an incarnation of Menthu, a personification of the heat of the sun. He changed colour every hour of the day.

Baksheesh (băk' shēsh). A Persian word for a gratuity.

Balaam (bā lăm). A misleading prophet or ally as Balaam was in *Numb.* xxii–xxiv. In Dryden's *Absalom and Achitophel* (l. 574), Balaam stands for the Earl of Huntingdon. The "citizen of sober fame" called Balaam in Pope's *Moral Essays*, Ep. iii, is partly drawn on DIAMOND PITT.

Balaamite. One who makes a profession of religion for profit or gain, as did Balaam.

Balaclava. *See* CARDIGAN.

Balan (bā' lăn). A strong and courageous giant in many old romances. In the Arthurian cycle, brother of BALIN.

Balance, The. LIBRA, an ancient zodiacal constellation between VIRGO and SCOR-

PIO representing a pair of scales, the 7th sign of the ZODIAC, which the sun enters a few days before the autumnal equinox.

According to Persian mythology, at the LAST DAY there will be a huge balance as big as the vault of HEAVEN. The two scale pans will be called that of light and that of darkness. In the former all good will be placed, in the latter all evil; and everyone will be rewarded according to the verdict of the balance.

In commercial parlance one's *balance* is the money remaining after all assets are realized and liabilities discharged. Hence the phrases:

Balance of payments. The difference over a given period between a nation's gross receipts from other countries and its gross payments to them.

Balance of power. Such an adjustment of power among sovereign states that no state has such a preponderance as to endanger the independence of the rest.

Balance of trade. The money-value difference between the exports and imports of a nation.

Balclutha (băl cloo' thà). A fortified town on the banks of the Clutha (*i.e.* the Clyde) mentioned in *Carthon*, one of the OSSIAN poems. It was captured and burnt by Comhal, father of FINGAL, in one of his forays against the Britons.

Bald. Charles le Chauve. Charles II of France (823, 840–877), son of Louis the Pious or le Débonnaire, was named "the Bald".

Bald as a coot. Completely bald. The common coot, a water bird, has a white bill and frontal shield which give the impression of baldness.

Baldfaced Stag. Common among old PUBLIC-HOUSE SIGNS. *Baldfaced* was applied to horses and other animals with a white strip down the forehead. *Cp.* BLAZE.

Baldheaded. To go for someone baldheaded, that is, without constraint or compunction, probably dating from the days when men wore wigs, and any energetic action or fray required that the wig should be thrown aside.

Balder (bol' der). A Scandinavian god of light, son of ODIN and FRIGG who dwelt at Breidhablik, one of the mansions of ASGARD. One legend says that Frigg

bound all things by oath not to harm him, but accidentally omitted MISTLETOE, with a twig of which he was slain. Another tells that he was slain by his rival Hodhr while fighting for the beautiful Nanna. His death was the final prelude to the overthrow of the gods.

Baldwin. (1) In the CHARLEMAGNE romances, nephew of ROLAND and the youngest and comeliest of Charlemagne's PALADINS.

(2) First King of Jerusalem (1100–1118), brother of Godfrey of Bouillon, the previous ruler, who declined the title of king.

Bale. When bale is highest, boot is nighest. An old Icelandic proverb appearing in Heywood and other English writers. It means, when things have come to the worst they must needs mend. *Bale* means "evil", *boot* is the M.E. *bote*, relief, remedy, good.

Bale out. Literally to empty water out of a boat with pails, etc.; also an airman's phrase meaning to parachute from an aircraft in an emergency. In army usage it means hastily escaping from a tank when it is hit.

Balfour of Burley, John. Leader of the COVENANTERS in Sir Walter Scott's *Old Mortality* (1816).

Balfour's Poodle. The HOUSE OF LORDS. From 1906 the CONSERVATIVE leader A. J. Balfour exploited their majority in the House of Lords to block the legislation of the LIBERAL government which had an overwhelming majority in the Commons. When the Lords rejected the Licensing Bill of 1908, Mr. Henry Chaplin, M.P., claimed that the House of Lords was the "watchdog of the constitution", to which Mr. Lloyd George replied, "You mean it is Mr. Balfour's poodle! It fetches and carries for him. It barks for him. It bites anybody that he sets it on to!"

Balin (bal' in). In the ARTHURIAN ROMANCES devoted brother of BALAN. They accidentally slew one another in ignorance of each other's identity and were buried in one grave by MERLIN.

Balios. *See* HORSE.

Balisarda. *See* SWORD.

Balk (bawlk, bawk). Originally a ridge, the word came to be applied to any obstacle, stumbling-block or check on one's actions. Thus in billiards, the balk is the part of the table behind the balk-line from which one has to play when in certain circumstances one's freedom is checked. So *to balk* is to place obstacles in one's way.

A balk of timber is a large roughly squared piece of timber.

To make a balk. To miss a part of the field in ploughing. Hence, to disappoint, to withhold deceitfully.

Balker. One who from an eminence on shore directs fishermen where shoals of herrings have gathered together.

Balkis (bol′ kis). The Mohammedan name of the Queen of SHEBA, who visited SOLOMON.

Ball. A ball of fortune. One tossed like a ball, from PILLAR to post; one who has experienced many vicissitudes of fortune.

The ball is with you, or **in your court.** It is your turn now.

To have the ball at your feet. To have an opportunity, a METAPHOR from football.

To keep the ball rolling. To continue without intermission. To keep the fun, conversation, or the matter going. A metaphor from ball games.

To open the ball. To lead off the first dance at a ball, hence to begin the matter by taking the lead.

To play ball. A colloquial phrase, meaning to agree to a suggestion or to co-operate in some plan or action.

To strike the ball under the line. To fail in one's object. The allusion is to the earlier game of tennis in which a line was stretched across the middle of the court, and the players on each side had to strike and return the ball over the line.

To take the ball before the bound. To anticipate an opportunity; to be over-hasty. A metaphor from CRICKET.

Ball's Bull. A person with no ear for music. According to an old tale this bull kicked a fiddler, whose music angered him, over a bridge.

The Three Golden Balls. The once familiar pawnbroker's sign was taken from the coat of arms of the MEDICI family and first introduced to London by the

LOMBARD bankers and money-lenders. The positioning of the balls was popularly explained in that there were two chances to one that what was brought to UNCLE would be redeemed.

Balloon, A pilot. Metaphorically, a feeler to ascertain opinion. *Cp.* TO FLY A KITE *under* KITE.

Ballot. This method of voting was common in ancient Greece and Rome. (*See* BEANS.) The name comes from the use of small balls put secretly in a box (Fr. *ballotte*, a little ball). In more modern times secret voting at governmental elections was first used in South Australia in 1856, hence the term *Australian Ballot*. Although one of the six points of CHARTISM, voting by ballot was not adopted in Great Britain until the Ballot Act of 1872, and not until after 1884 in the U.S.A.

Ballyhoo (băli hoo′). The word is said to come from Ballyhooly, a village in Co. Cork, but in its present sense of a noisy demonstration to attract attention, extravagant advertisement or publicity, originates from the U.S.A.

Balm. Is there no balm in Gilead? (*Jer.* viii, 22). Is there no remedy, no consolation? "Balm" here is the Geneva Bible's translation of the Heb. *sori*, which probably means "mastic", the resin yielded by the mastic tree, *Pistacia lentiscus*. In Wyclif's Bible the word is translated "gumme" and in Coverdale's "triacle". (*See* BIBLE, THE ENGLISH; TREACLE.)

The gold-coloured resin now known as "Balm of Gilead" is that from *Balamodendron gileadense*.

Balmerino (băl mer′ i nō). The story was long current that when Lord Balmerino was executed for his part in the JACOBITE rebellion of 1745, the executioner bungled and only half cut off his head, whereupon his lordship turned round and grinned at him.

Balmy. I am going to the balmy—*i.e.* to "balmy sleep"; one of Dick Swiveller's pet phrases (Dickens: *Old Curiosity Shop*). *See also* BARMY.

Balnibarbi (băl ni bar′ bi). A land occupied by projectors (Swift: *Gulliver's Travels*).

Balthazar (băl thăz′ ăr). One of the three

kings of COLOGNE. *See* MAGI.

Bamberg Bible, The. *See* BIBLE, SOME SPECIALLY NAMED EDITIONS.

Bambocciades (băm boch' i ădz). Pictures of scenes in low life, such as country WAKES, PENNY WEDDINGS, and so on; so called from the Ital. *bamboccio*, a cripple, nickname given to Pieter van Laar (1592–*c.* 1675), a noted Dutch painter of such scenes.

Bamboo Curtain, The. Formed by analogy with IRON CURTAIN to denote the veil of secrecy and mistrust drawn between the Chinese Communist block and the non-Communist nations. *Cp.* GARLIC WALL, IRON CURTAIN.

Ban, King. In the ARTHURIAN ROMANCES, father of Sir LANCELOT DU LAC. He died of grief when his castle was taken and burnt through the treachery of his seneschal.

Banagher, That beats (băn' à her). Wonderfully inconsistent and absurd—exceedingly ridiculous. Banagher is a town in Ireland, on the Shannon, in Offaly. It formerly sent two members to PARLIAMENT and was a notorious POCKET BOROUGH. When a member spoke of a family borough where every voter was a man employed by the owner, it was not unusual to reply, "Well, that beats Banagher."

According to Francis Grose, however, Banagher (or Banaghan) was an Irish minstrel famous for telling wonderful stories of the MÜNCHAUSEN kind.

> "Well," says he, "to gratify them I will. So just a morsel. But Jack, this beats Banagher."
>
> W. B. YEATS: *Fairy Tales of the Irish Peasantry*.

Bananalanders. Nickname for the inhabitants of Queensland, Australia, who are also known as *Canecutters*.

Banana oil. Used colloquially in Australia and America for "nonsense" or "insincere talk".

Banat (băn' àt). A territory governed by a *ban* (Persian for lord, master) particularly certain districts of Hungary and Croatia. The word was imported by the Avars who settled in Dacia in the latter half of the 6th century.

Banbury. A town in Oxfordshire, proverbially known for its PURITANS, its "cheese-paring", its cakes and its cross. Hence a *Banbury man* is a Puritan or bigot.

Banbury cake is a kind of spiced pastry turnover, once made exclusively at Banbury.

Banbury Cross of nursery rhyme fame was removed by the PURITANS as a heathenish memorial in 1646. Another CROSS was erected on the site in 1858.

Banbury Tinkers. People who try to put things right but only make them worse. The Banbury tinkers were said to make three holes in a pot while mending one.

Banco. A commercial term denoting bank money of account as distinguished from currency.

In Banco, or **in Banc.** A Late Latin legal phrase, meaning "on the bench"; it is applied to sittings of a superior court of COMMON LAW in its own bench or court, and not on circuit or at NISI PRIUS. The work of the courts *in Banco* was transferred to Divisional Courts of the High Court of Justice by the Judicature Act of 1873.

Bancus Communium Placitorum. The BENCH OF COMMON PLEAS.

Bancus Regius, or **Bancus Reginae.** The King's or Queen's Bench.

Bandbox. To look as if one were just out of a. To look neat and carefully dressed like something carefully kept in a bandbox, a cardboard box for millinery formerly used by parsons for keeping their BANDS in.

Bandicoot. Bald as a bandicoot (Austr.). Quite bald. An alliterative variant of BALD AS A COOT. Meaning is sacrificed to euphony since the bandicoot is not bald. The expression *busy as a bandicoot* similarly means "extremely busy".

To bandicoot is an Australian phrase meaning to steal vegetables—often by removing the roots and leaving the tops standing so that the theft is not noticed. The bandicoot ravages garden and farm produce.

Band of Hope. The name given (*c.* 1847) to children's temperance societies in the UNITED KINGDOM. The movement grew steadily and the Band of Hope Union was founded in 1855.

Bands. Clerical bands are a relic of the ancient *amice*, a square linen tippet tied about the neck of priests during the saying of MASS. Disused by ANGLICAN clergy in the late 19th century, they have partially come back into fashion of late and are also worn by PRESBYTERIAN ministers and continental clergy.

Legal bands are a relic of the wide falling collars which formed a part of the ordinary dress in the reign of Henry VIII, and which were especially conspicuous in Stuart times. In the showy days of Charles II the plain bands were changed for lace ends.

Bandwagon. To climb on the bandwagon is to show support for a popular movement or trend with intent to profit or reap easy material benefit. It was customary in the U.S.A., particularly in southern States, for a band to play on a wagon through the streets to advertise a forthcoming meeting, political or otherwise. At election time local leaders would show their support of a candidate by climbing on the wagon and riding with the band.

Bandy. I am not going to bandy words with you, *i.e.,* to wrangle. The META-PHOR is from the Irish game bandy (the precursor of hockey), in which each player has a stick with a crook at the end. The ball is *bandied* from side to side, each party trying to beat it home to the opposite goal. It was earlier a term in tennis as is shown by the line in John Webster's *Victoria Corombona* (IV, iv):

> That while he had been bandying at tennis. (1612).

Banian, or **Banyan** (băn' yàn) (Sanskrit *vanij*, a merchant). A name applied to a caste of Hindu traders and moneylenders, who wore a particular dress, were strict in their observance of fasts, and abstained from eating any kind of flesh. It is from this circumstance that sailors speak of BANYAN DAY.

The word is also applied to a form of loose house-coat worn by Anglo-Indians.

Bank. Originally meaning "bench" or "shelf", in Italy the word BANCO was applied specially to a tradesman's counter, and hence to a money-changer's bench or table, from which the modern meaning of an establishment dealing with money, etc., is derived.

Banker. In Australia, a river in flood running as high as its banks. In North America, a cod fisherman of the Newfoundland Banks, or his ship.

Bank Holidays. Properly, when banks are legally closed. In 1830 Bank of England closures were limited from more than 40 to 18 and in 1834 to 4. By the Bank Holiday Act of 1871 days were again fixed for England, Wales and Ireland and with a slight variation for Scotland. These Bank Holidays soon became general public holidays. Alterations have taken place from 1967.

Bankrupt. In Italy, when a moneylender was unable to continue business, his bench or counter was broken up, and he was spoken of as a *bancorotto—i.e.* a bankrupt.

Bank of river. Stand with your back to the source, and face to the sea or outlet: the *left* bank is on your left, and *right* bank on your right hand.

Bankside. An historic part of the borough of SOUTHWARK on the right bank of the Thames between Blackfriars and London bridges. At one end stood the CLINK prison and the church of St. Mary OVERIE (now Southwark Cathedral). Also famous in Shakespeare's England for BULL-BAITING and the Globe theatre, and notorious for its brothels and evil-doers. Hence **Sisters of the Bank,** an old term for prostitutes.

Banks's Horse. A horse called Marocco, belonging to one Banks about the end of Queen Elizabeth I's reign, and trained to do all manner of tricks. One of his exploits is said to have been the ascent of St. Paul's steeple. A favourite story of the time is of an apprentice who called his master to see the spectacle. "Away, you fool," said the shopkeeper, "what need I go to see a horse on the top when I can see so many horses at the bottom!"

Bannatyne Club. The literary club founded by Sir Walter Scott, Archibald Constable and others in 1823 and named after George Bannatyne (1545?–1608), to whose manuscript we owe the preservation of much 15th- and early 16th-century Scottish poetry. The club had convivial meetings and printed 116 rare works of Scottish history and literature.

Banner of the Prophet, The. What purports to be the actual standard of MOHAMMED is present in the Eyab mosque of Istanbul. It is twelve feet in length and made of four layers of silk, the topmost being green, embroidered with GOLD. In times of peace it is kept in the hall of the "noble vestment" as the Prophet's garb is styled, along with his stirrup, sabre, bow and other relics.

Banner of France, The Sacred. The ORIFLAMME.

Banners in churches. These are suspended as thank offerings to God.

Banner State. In the U.S.A. the State which, in a presidential election, gives the victor the biggest majority or vote.

Banneret. One who leads his vassals to battle under his own banner. Also an order of Knighthood conferred on the field of battle for deeds of valour by tearing off the points of the recipient's pennon. This mediæval order lapsed after the reign of Elizabeth I, and was last properly conferred by Charles I in 1642 on Colonel John Smith for his recovery of the Royal Standard at Edgehill.

Banns of Marriage. The publication in the parish church for three successive Sundays of an intended marriage. It is made after the second lesson of the Morning Service, or of Evening Service (if there be no Morning Service). The word is from the same root as BAN.

To forbid the banns. To object formally to the proposed marriage.

Banquet in addition to its present meaning once also meant dessert. Thus in the *Pennyles Pilgrimage* (1618) John Taylor, the WATER POET, says: "Our first and second course being three-score dishes at one boord, and after that, always a banquet." The word is from the Italian *banco*, a bench or table (*see* BANK).

Banshee. In Irish folklore and that of the Western Highlands of Scotland, a female fairy who announces her presence by shrieking and wailing under the windows of a house when one of its occupants is awaiting death. The word is a phonetic spelling of the Irish *bean-sidhe*, a woman of the fairies.

Bantam. A little bantam cock. A plucky little fellow that will not be bullied by a person bigger than himself. The bantam cock will encounter a dunghill cock five times his own weight, and is therefore said to "have a great soul in a little body". The bantam originally came from Bantam in Java.

Banting. Reducing superfluous fat by living on an essentially protein diet, and abstaining from beer, port, etc., and farinaceous food, according to the method adopted by William Banting (1797–1878).

A greater benefactor to mankind was Sir Frederick Grant Banting (1891–1941), the Canadian scientist who discovered insulin in 1922.

Banyan Day. An English nautical phrase to describe a day on which no meat was issued in the rations. In Australia it is found in official documents of the late 18th century. On Australian outstations Banyan Day for the hands was when meat supplies were exhausted, before the end of the ration period. *See* BANIAN.

Baphomet (Fr. *Baphomet*; O.Sp. *Matomat*). A corruption of Mahomet, the imaginary idol which the TEMPLARS were said to worship with licentious rites.

Baptes. Priests of the goddess COTYTTO, the Thracian goddess of lewdness, whose midnight orgies were so obscene that they disgusted even the goddess herself. The name is derived from the Greek verb *bapto*, to wash, because of the so-called ceremonies of purification connected with her rites (*Juvenal*, ii, 91).

Baptism. This SACRAMENT of the Christian Church dates back in one form or another to pre-apostolic times.

Baptism for the dead was a kind of vicarious baptism of a living person for the sake of one dead. An heretical and superstitious custom referred to in I *Cor. xv,* 29.

Baptism of blood. Martyrdom for the sake of Christ which supplied the place of the sacrament if the martyr was unbaptized.

Baptism of desire is the grace or virtue of baptism acquired by one who earnestly desires baptism by water but dies before receiving it.

Baptism of fire is really martyrdom, but usually means experiencing the fire of battle for the first time. It was so used by NAPOLEON III. It has now been extended to include other first experiences.

Baptists. English Baptists are of 16th-century origin. Their first independent church, however, was founded from a group of separatists under John Smythe at Amsterdam in 1609, from whence an offshoot returned to London in 1612 to form the General Baptists. Their Arminianism (*see* ARMINIANS) led to the growth of the Strict, Particular, or Calvinistic Baptists in the 1630s. In the 18th century many General Baptists became UNITARIANS and the more orthodox formed the New Connection in 1770. The Baptist Union (1832) eventually led to closer co-operation and the Particular Baptists joined forces with the New Connection in 1891. Church government is congregational and baptism (by total immersion) is only for believers. *Cp.* BARROWISTS; BROWNISTS; CONGREGATIONALISTS; PRESBYTERIANS.

Bar. The prisoner at the bar. The prisoner in the dock before the judge.

To be called within the bar. To be appointed QUEEN'S COUNSEL, *i.e.* to be admitted within the bar which separated the members of the court from the prisoners, junior counsel and public. Q.C.s are thus of the inner bar.

Trial at Bar. By full court of judges in the QUEEN'S BENCH division. These trials are for very difficult causes, before special juries, and occupy the attention of the four judges in the superior court, instead of at NISI PRIUS.

Bar. Excepting. In the language of the TURF, "two to one, bar one" means betting two to one against any horse in the field with one exception.

Bar. In HERALDRY, a horizontal band across the shield taking up not more than one-fifth of the Field. A diminutive of the fesse.

Bar sinister. An heraldic term popularly mistaken as an indication of bastardy, correctly denoted by a baton sinister. *See* BEND SINISTER.

Barring out. In bygone days, the practice of barricading the masters out of the classroom or the school.

Bar Mitzvah (Heb. Son of duty). The ceremony celebrating the arrival of a Jewish boy at the age of responsibility, 13 years.

Barataria. SANCHO PANZA'S island-city, in Don QUIXOTE, over which he was appointed governor. The table was presided over by Doctor Pedro Rezio de Aguero, who caused every dish set upon the board to be removed without being tasted—some because they heated the blood, and others because they chilled it, some for one ill effect, and some for another; so that Sancho was allowed to eat nothing. The word is from Sp. *barato*, cheap.

Barataria is also the setting of Act II of *The Gondoliers*. *Cp.* BARMECIDE'S FEAST.

Barathron, or **Barathrum.** A deep ditch behind the Acropolis of ATHENS into which malefactors were thrown; somewhat in the same way as criminals at ROME were cast from the TARPEIAN ROCK.

Barb (Lat. *barba*, a beard). Used in early times in England for the beard of a man and thus for the feathers under the beak of a HAWK (beard feathers). Its first English use was for a curved-back instrument such as a fish-hook. The barb of an arrow had two iron "feathers" or hooks near the point to hinder extraction.

Barb. A Barbary steed, noted for docility, speed, endurance and spirit; also called a *Barbary*. *See* BARBARY ROAN.

Barbara Allen. The heroine of an old ballad given in PERCY'S RELIQUES called *Barbara Allen's Cruelty*. She died of remorse after showing no pity for the young man who was dying of love for her.

Barbara, St. Virgin and martyr (*c.* 4th century). Her father, a fanatical heathen, delivered her up to Martian, governor of Nicomedia, for being a Christian. After she had been subjected to the most cruel tortures, her unnatural father was about to strike off her head, when a lightning flash laid him dead at her feet. Hence she is invoked against lightning and is the patron saint of arsenals and artillery.

Barbari. Quod non fecerunt barbari, fecerunt Barberini. *i.e.* What the barbarians left standing, the Barberini contrived to destroy. A PASQUINADE current in ROME at the time when Pope Urban VIII (1623–1644) (Barberini) converted the bronze girders from the portico of the PANTHEON, which had remained in splendid condition since 27 B.C., into cannon and into pillars for the Baldacchino, or canopy of St. Peter's.

Barbarian. The Greeks and Romans called all foreigners *barbarians* (babblers; men who spoke a language not understood by them). The word was probably merely imitative of unintelligible speech. The extension of meaning to imply uncivilized, uncultured, is a natural consequence.

Barbarossa (Red-beard). The surname of Frederick I (*c.* 1123–1190), Holy Roman EMPEROR. He was drowned whilst on the Third CRUSADE. Also the name applied by the Christians to a family of Turkish sea rovers, especially well known being the famous corsair Khair ud-Din Barbarossa, who became Bey of Algiers in 1518 and High ADMIRAL of the Turkish fleet in 1537.

Barbary Coast. The western Mediterranean coast of Africa which was infested by MOSLEM sea rovers from the 16th century until the early 19th century. The native Berbers derive their name from the Roman habit of referring to indigenous peoples as *barbari*.

Barbason (bar' bà son). A fiend mentioned by Shakespeare in *The Merry Wives of Windsor*, II, ii, and in *Henry V*, II, i.

Barbecue (bar' be kū) (Sp. *barbacoa*, a wooden framework set up on posts). A West Indian term formerly used in America for a wooden bedstead, and also for a large gridiron upon which an animal could be roasted whole or meat etc. cooked. Hence an animal, such as a hog, so cooked; also the feast at which it is roasted and eaten. Popularly applied to an outdoor party when the food is cooked on a fire in the open.

Barber. (Ultimately from Lat. *barba*, beard). One who cuts and trims beards, a hairdresser. Originally barbers also practised dentistry and surgery. The Company of Barber-Surgeons in London was first incorporated in 1461 and in 1540 it became the Company of Barbers and Surgeons limited (other than in its proper functions) to drawing teeth. In 1745 it was renamed the Barbers Company which is still one of the London LIVERY COMPANIES.

Every barber knows that. From ancient Roman times the barber's shop has been a centre for the dissemination of scandal, and the talk of the town.

Barber's pole. This pole, painted spirally with two stripes of red and white, and displayed outside barber's shops as a sign, derives from the days when they also practised phlebotomy. The pole represents the staff gripped by persons in venesection, which was painted red since it was usually stained with blood. The white spiral represents the bandage twisted round the arm previous to blood-letting. The gilt knob at the end of the pole represents the brass basin which sometimes actually suspended from it. The basin had a notch in it to fit the throat, and was used for lathering customers before shaving.

Barber of Seville. The comedy of this name (*Le Barbier de Séville*) was written by Beaumarchais and produced in Paris in 1775. In it appeared as the barber the famous character of FIGARO. Paisello's opera appeared in 1780 but was eclipsed by Rossini's *Barbiere di Siviglia*, with words by Sterbini. The latter was hissed on its first appearance in 1816 under the title of *Almaviva*.

Barber-shop. A term used to denote a style of close-harmony part singing by male quartets. Informal music-making existed in barber shops in the 16th and 17th centuries in Britain as well as Europe. It lapsed in the 18th century but continued in the U.S.A. where the barber-shop quartet came into being.

Barcelona. A fichu, piece of velvet for the neck, or small necktie, made at Barcelona, and common in England in the early 19th century. Also a neckcloth of some bright colour, as red with yellow spots.

Barchester. An imaginary cathedral town

(modelled on Winchester), in the county of Barsetshire; the setting of Anthony Trollope's "Barchester Novels".

Barcochebah, or **Barcochebas** (barkoch' e ba). In Hebrew means "Son of a star". One Simeon, a heroic Jewish leader against the Romans, who is reputed to have claimed to be the "Star out of Jacob" mentioned in *Num*. xxiv, 17, was so called. He took Jerusalem in 132 and was acclaimed by some as the MESSIAH. He was overwhelmed and slain by the forces of Julius Severus in 135.

Bard. The minstrel of the ancient Celtic peoples, the Gauls, British, Welsh, Irish and Scots. They celebrated the deeds of the gods and heroes, incited to battle, acted as heralds, and sang at festivities. The oldest extant bardic compositions are of the 5th century. *See* EISTEDDFOD.

Bard of Avon. William Shakespeare (1564–1616), who was born and buried at Stratford-upon-Avon.

Bard of Erin. Thomas Moore (1779–1852). Born in Dublin, writer of *Irish Melodies*, *Lalla Rookh*, etc. He spent most of his life in England.

Bard of Hope. Thomas Campbell (1777–1844), author of *The Pleasures of Hope* (1799).

Bard of Prose. Boccaccio (1313–1375), author of the DECAMERON.

Bard of Rydal Mount. William Wordsworth (1770–1850); so called because Rydal Mount was his home.

Bard of Twickenham. Alexander Pope (1688–1744), who had a house at Twickenham. Also called the **Wasp of Twickenham** by some of his contempraries.

Bardolph. One of FALSTAFF'S inferior officers. He is a low-bred, drunken swaggerer, without principle, and "POOR AS A CHURCH MOUSE".

Barebones Parliament (4 July–11 December 1653). The Nominated or Little PARLIAMENT of 140 members approved by Cromwell and the officers and derisively named after one of its members, Praise-God Barebon.

Barefooted. Certain FRIARS and nuns (some of whom wear sandals instead of shoes), especially the reformed section of the CARMELITES (White Friars) founded by St. TERESA in the 16th century, known as the *Discalced Carmelites* (Lat. *calceus*, a shoe). The practice is defended by the command of our Lord to His disciples "Carry neither purse, nor scrip, nor shoes" (*Luke* x, 4). The Jews and Romans used to put off their shoes in mourning and public calamities, by way of humiliation.

Bare poles, Under. When a ship has no sails set due to bad weather and gale conditions. Figuratively applied to a person reduced to the last extremity.

Bargain. Into the bargain. In addition thereto; besides what was bargained for.

King's, or **Queen's bad bargain.** *See under* KING.

To make the best of a bad bargain. To make the best of a matter in which one has been worsted.

To stand to a bargain. To abide by it; the Lat. *stare conventis, conditionibus stare, pactis stare*, etc.

Barisal Guns. The name given to certain mysterious booming sounds which occur at Barisal (Eastern Bengal) and seem to come from the sea. Similar phenomena at Seneca Lake, New York, are called *Lake guns*; on the coast of Holland and Belgium *mistpoeffers*; and in Italy *bombiti, baturlio marina*, etc.

Bark. Dogs in their wild state never bark, but howl, whine, and growl. Barking is an acquired habit.

Bark and the tree, Put not thy hand between the. Do not interfere in disputes between the closely related.

Barker. A pistol, which barks or makes a loud report. Also the man who stands at the entrance to a sideshow of a circus, etc., or touts outside a shop, shouting to attract custom. In the U.S.A. it is also applied to a baseball coach.

Barking dogs seldom bite. Huffing, bouncing, hectoring fellows rarely possess cool courage.

His bark is worse than his bite. He scolds and abuses roundly, but does not bear malice or act harshly.

To bark at the moon. To rail uselessly, especially at those in high places, as a dog thinks to frighten the moon by baying at it. There is a superstition that when a dog does this it portends death or ill-luck.

To bark up the wrong tree. To waste

energy, to be on the wrong scent. The phrase comes from raccoon hunting, which takes place in the dark. The dogs are used to mark the tree where the raccoon has taken refuge, but they can mistake the tree in the dark and bark up the wrong one.

Barkis is willin'. The message sent by Barkis to Peggotty through David Copperfield, expressing his desire to marry. It has become a proverbial expression indicating willingness.

Barlaam and Josaphat (bar' lăm, jós à făt). An Indian romance telling how Barlaam, an ascetic of the desert of Sinai, converted Josaphat, a Hindu prince, to Christianity. Probably translated into Greek by the 6th century, and put into its final form by St. John of Damascus, a Syrian monk of the 8th century, in part it corresponds closely with the legendary story of BUDDHA'S youth. It became a widely popular mediæval romance. The Story of the Three Caskets was used by SHAKESPEARE in *The Merchant of Venice*.

Barley. To cry barley. An old country game akin to "Prisoners' Base", having a "home" which was called "hell". Herrick has a poem, *Barley-break, or Last in Hell*. Barley, a corruption of parley, was, in rough games, a cry for a truce.

Barley-bree. ALE: malt liquor brewed from barley, also called *barley-broth*.

John, or **Sir John Barleycorn.** A personification of malt liquor. The term was popularized by Burns.

Barmecide's Feast. An illusion, particularly one containing a great disappointment. In the ARABIAN NIGHTS, *The Barber's story of his sixth Brother*, a prince of the great Barmecide family in Baghdad, desirous of sport, asked Schacabac, a poor starving wretch, to dinner. Having set before him a series of empty plates, the merchant asked, "How do you like your soup?" "Excellently well," replied Schacabac. "Did you ever see whiter bread?" "Never, honourable sir," was the civil answer. Illusory wine was later offered, but Schacabac excused himself by pretending to be drunk already, and knocked the Barmecide down. The latter saw the humour of the situation, forgave Schacabac, and pro-

vided him with food to his heart's content.

Barmy. Mad, crazy, *i.e.* full of froth. Sometimes incorrectly spelled "balmy". Hence, in prison slang, **to put on the barmy stick** is to feign insanity. There is a popular misconception that the word comes from *Barming* (near Maidstone) because the county lunatic asylum was built at Barming Heath.

Barnabas. St. Barnabas's Day, 11 June. St. Barnabas was a fellow-labourer of St. PAUL. His symbol is a rake, because 11 June is the time of hay-harvest.

Barnabites. An order of regular clerks of St. PAUL, recognized by Clement VII in 1533. Probably so called from the Church of St. Barnabas in Milan which became their centre.

Barnaby Rudge. This novel by Charles Dickens, which first appeared in 1840, centres round the Gordon riots of 1780, and he drew upon the memories of survivors of these times. Barnaby was a half-witted lad whose companion was a raven.

Barnacle. A species of wild GOOSE allied to the Brent Goose, called in Germany the "duck-mussel". Also the popular name of the *Cirripedes*, especially those attached by a stalk to floating balks of timber and the bottoms of ships. In mediæval times it was held that the goose developed from it as a frog does from a tadpole.

The name is given figuratively to close and constant companions, hangers-on; and also to PLACEMEN who cling to office, like barnacles sticking to the bottoms of ships.

Barnacles. Spectacles, especially those of heavy make and clumsy appearance. A slang term from their supposed resemblance to the twitches or barnacles formerly used by farriers to restrain unruly horses while being shod, etc. This instrument, consisting of two branches joined at one end by a hinge, was used to grip the horse's nose. Probably a diminutive of the O.Fr. *bernac*, a kind of muzzle for horses.

Barnard's Inn. One of the old Inns of CHANCERY, formerly situated on the south side of HOLBORN.

Barn-burners. Destroyers, who, like the

Dutchmen of story, would burn down their barns to rid themselves of the rats. In the U.S.A. the term was applied to the radical section of the Democratic party in New York State in the Presidential election of 1844 by their conservative opponents, who were called HUNKERS. The Barn-burners finally joined the Republican party in the 1850s to further the cause of anti-slavery.

Barney. A dispute, argument or rumpus. A contraction of BARNABAS, current in England and Australia. Barney was a fairly common name among Irish settlers in the 19th century, and the usage is probably an allusion to their reputed temperament and behaviour.

Barnstormer. A strolling player, and hence any second-rate actor, especially one whose style is an exaggerated declamatory kind. From the itinerant actors who performed in village barns.

In the U.S.A. the term has also been applied to a stunt pilot touring country districts or one giving trips for a fee; also to someone carrying out a speaking tour in rural areas, etc.

Baron is from Late Lat. *baro*, a man (especially opposed to something else, as a freeman to slave, etc.). After the Norman CONQUEST it denoted the man or VASSAL of a great noble, especially the king, and by the 13th century the distinction between greater and lesser barons was well established. The greater barons came to be summoned to the GREAT COUNCIL by individual writs and the term *baronage* became equated to peerage. It is now the lowest order of nobility.

In colloquial speech in the U.S.A. it is equivalent to "magnate" as in "beef baron" and "soap baron".

Baron and feme. An heraldic term for husband and wife, an example of the older use of the word BARON.

Baron Münchausen. *See* MÜNCHAUSEN.

Baron of beef. A double SIRLOIN, left uncut at the backbone, and of great size, roasted at special festivities. Jocosely, but wrongly, said to be a pun upon *baron* and *sir* loin.

Barons of the Cinque Ports. The name given to the representatives of the CINQUE PORTS in the HOUSE OF COMMONS until the Reform Act of 1832.

Barons' War. The name applied to the civil war (1264–1267) between the baronial supporters of Simon de Montfort and the supporters of Henry III. Drayton's poem *The Barrons Wars* appeared in 1603.

Court Baron. A court dealing with matters concerning the duties and services relating to a MANOR, and with personal actions under 40 shillings. Freeholders were not subject to it but were under the COMMON LAW.

Baronet. An hereditary title instituted by James I in 1611, the sale of which was to provide funds for the defence of the plantation of ULSTER. The Red Hand of Ulster became the badge of Baronets of England; of Great Britain; of the United Kingdom; and of Ireland (instituted in 1619). Baronets of Scotland and Nova Scotia were created from 1625. Nova Scotian patents ceased in 1638 after the colony had fallen to the French. Scottish creations ceased in 1707 and Irish from 1801, consequent upon the respective Acts of UNION.

Barrack. To barrack, is to jeer at, to receive with derisive applause, to interrupt with rude comments, particularly the players of games. In Australia, where the word came into use during the 1880s, it is nearly always used in the opposite sense meaning to cheer or support a team. It stems from the days when army supporters of the Victoria Barracks team entered the S. Melbourne cricket ground and were greeted with shouts of "here come the barrackers".

Barrack Hack. A lady who attends all barrack social events and hangs on the sleeves of the officers.

Barrack-room lawyer. A soldier with a real or professed knowledge of regulations who makes complaints against authority. A grouser. In American army parlance, a *latrine lawyer*.

Barrel House. A name applied in the U.S.A. in the late 19th century to a small squalid drinking saloon, where customers drew their own liquor from the cask. Also given to a rough uninhibited type of JAZZ.

Barricade. To block up a street, building,

etc., against attack. The term arose in France in 1588, when Henri de Guise returned to Paris in defiance of Henry III. The King called out the SWISS GUARDS, and the Parisians tore up the pavements, threw chains across the streets, and piled up barrels (Fr. *barriques*) filled with earth and stones, from behind which they shot down the Swiss.

Barrister. One who has been "called to the BAR", and is thereafter entitled to plead in any court, having received his brief from a solicitor. Formerly called "outer" or "UTTER" barristers, after ten years as junior counsel they may apply to "take SILK" to become QUEEN'S (King's) COUNSEL. Until 1877 there was a superior third group called SERGEANTS-AT-LAW. The Q.C. is a senior barrister and is entitled to wear a silk gown and full-bottomed wig. Other barristers wear a stiff gown and short wig.

A Revising Barrister. One appointed to revise the list of electors for members of PARLIAMENT.

Barrowists. In the reign of Elizabeth I, PURITAN followers of Henry Barrow, holding CONGREGATIONALIST views similar to the BROWNISTS.

Bartholomew, St. The symbol of this SAINT is a knife, in allusion to the knife with which he was flayed alive, reputedly in A.D. 44. His day is 24 August.

Bartholomew doll. A TAWDRY overdressed woman; like one of the flashy bespangled dolls offered for sale at Bartholomew Fair.

Bartholomew Fair. A FAIR opened annually at SMITHFIELD on St. Bartholomew's Day, from 1133 to 1752; after the reform of the CALENDAR it began on 3 September. It was removed to Islington in 1840 and was last held in 1855 (*see* CALEDONIAN MARKET). One of the great national fairs dealing in cloth, livestock, etc., accompanied by a variety of amusements and entertainments, it long held its place as a centre of London life. The PURITANS failed to suppress it. Ben Jonson's *Bartholomew Fair*, a comedy of manners, was first acted in 1614.

Bartholomew, Massacre of St. The slaughter of the French HUGUENOTS begun on St. Bartholomew's Day, 24 August 1572, in Paris and the provinces, at the instigation of Catherine de' MEDICI, mother of Charles IX. Probably some 50,000 people perished.

Bartholomew pig. A very fat person. At BARTHOLOMEW FAIR one of the chief attractions used to be a pig, roasted whole and sold piping hot.

Bartolist. One skilled in law, or specifically a student of Bartolus. Bartolus (1314–1357) was an eminent Italian lawyer who greatly enhanced the status of the law school of Perugia, particularly by his *Commentary on the Code of Justinian*.

Bas Bleu. *See* BLUE-STOCKING.

Base Tenure. Originally tenure not by military, but by base service, such as a serf or VILLEIN might give; later, villein tenure became COPYHOLD tenure.

Bashaw. An arrogant, domineering man; a corruption of the Turkish PASHA, a viceroy or provincial governor.

The Three Bashaws of Somerset House. A popular nickname for the three Poor Law Commissioners (T. Frankland Lewis, J. G. Shaw Lefevre, George Nicholls) appointed under the Poor Law Amendment Act of 1834. SOMERSET HOUSE was their headquarters.

Bashi-bazouk (băsh' i bă zook'). A savage and brutal ruffian (Turkish *bashi*, headdress; *bozuq*, unkempt). It was applied in Turkey to non-uniformed irregular soldiers who made up in plunder what they did not get in pay. The term came into prominence at the time of the Crimean War and again through the Bulgarian atrocities of 1876.

Basic English. A fundamental selection of 850 English words designed by C. K. Ogden as a common first step in the teaching of English and as an auxiliary language. The name comes from the initials of the words British, American, Scientific, International, Commercial. *Cp.* ESPERANTO; INTERLINGUA; VOLAPÜK.

Basilian Monks. A monastic order founded by St. Basil in *c.* 360 whose rule became the basis of monasticism in the Greek and Russian churches.

Basilica (bà zil' i kà) (Gr. *basilikos*, royal). Originally a royal palace, but afterwards (in ROME) a large building with nave, aisles, and an apse at one end used as a court of justice and for public meetings. Some were adapted by the early Christians and many churches were modelled on them. Constantine built the great basilicas of St. PETER (rebuilt in the 16th century), St. PAUL, and St. John Lateran.

Basilisco. A braggart. Basilisco was a cowardly, bragging KNIGHT in Kyd's (?) tragedy *Solyman and Perseda* (?1588).

Basilisk (baz' i lisk). The fabulous king of serpents (Gr. *basileus*, a king), also called a COCKATRICE and alleged to be hatched by a SERPENT from a cock's egg. It was reputed to be capable of "looking anyone dead on whom it fixed its eyes".

Also the name given to a genus of Central American lizard and to a large brass cannon of Tudor times.

Basin Street. A street in the RED-LIGHT DISTRICT of the French quarter of New Orleans which is possibly the original home of American JAZZ music. The well-known *Basin Street Blues* was composed by Spencer Williams in 1928.

Basket. To be left in the basket. To be neglected or uncared for. Formerly foundling hospitals used to place baskets at their doors for the reception of abandoned infants.

To give a basket. To refuse to marry. In Germany it was an old custom to fix a basket on the roof of one who had been jilted.

To go to the basket. Old slang for consignment to prison: referring to the dependence of the lowest grade of poor prisoners upon what passers-by put in the basket for their sustenance.

To put all your eggs in one basket. *See* EGG.

Bast. *See* BUBASTIS.

Bastard. An illegitimate child, from the Old French *bast*, a pack-saddle, used by muleteers as a bed; hence, one begotten on a pack-saddle bed. Also an old name for a sweetened Spanish wine made from the bastard muscadine grape.

Baste. I'll give you a thorough basting, *i.e.* beating. The word is of uncertain origin but may derive from the fact that lazy scullions and TURNSPITS were sometimes beaten by the enraged cook with the basting-stick.

Bastille (băs tēl') (O.Fr. *Bastir*, now *bâtir*, to build). A fortress, but specifically the famous state prison in Paris built as a royal castle by Charles V between 1370 and 1383, seized and sacked by the mob in the French Revolution, 14 July 1789. Regarded as a symbol of tyranny, *bastille*, when used of a building or establishment, implies prison-like qualities. *Cp.* ALTMARK.

Bat. HARLEQUIN'S lath wand (Fr. *batte*, a wooden sword).

Off his own bat. By his own exertions; on his own account. A cricketer's phrase, meaning runs made by a single player.

Parliament of Bats. *See* CLUB PARLIAMENT.

To bat along, to get along at a great bat. Here the word means beat, pace, rate of speed.

To bat on a sticky wicket. To have to take action or carry on in difficult circumstances where things make success unlikely. In CRICKET the batsman playing on recently rained-on turf finds the movement of the ball very tricky.

To carry one's bat (in cricket). A batsman who goes in first and is "not out" at the end of the innings.

To have bats in the belfry, or **attic.** To be crazy in the head, bats here being the nocturnal variety.

Without batting an eyelid. Without betraying surprise. Here *batting* is derived from the now obsolete *bate* (from O.Fr. *batre*) meaning to beat the wings, to flutter.

Batman (Fr. *bat*, pack-saddle). Originally a soldier in charge of a **bat-horse** (pack-horse) and its load of officer's baggage. The name came to denote an army officer's servant in World War I through its inaccurate use by non-regular wartime officers. *Cp.* BASTARD.

Bate me an Ace. *See* BOLTON.

Bath. Knights of the Bath. This order derives its name from the ceremony of bathing which was formerly practised at the inauguration of a KNIGHT as a symbol of purity. Established in the reign of Henry IV, the last knights were created in the ancient manner at the coronation of Charles II in 1661. G.C.B. stands for Grand Cross of the Bath (the first class); K.C.B., Knight Commander of the Bath (the second class); C.B., Companion of the Bath (the third class).

Bath brick. A scouring brick made at Bridgwater, Somerset, used for cleaning steel knives, metals, etc. made from sand and clay taken from the River Parret, which runs through the town.

Also a naval nickname for Malta, derived from the particular hue of its stone buildings.

Bath chair. An invalid chair mounted on wheels, first used at Bath, frequented by invalids on account of its hot springs.

Bath King-of-Arms. *See* HERALDRY.

Bath metal. An alloy like PINCHBECK consisting of copper, zinc, lead and tin. Also called mosaic gold, DUTCH GOLD, etc.

Bath Oliver. A special kind of biscuit invented by Dr. William Oliver (1695–1764), founder of the Royal Mineral Water Hospital, Bath; an authority on GOUT, he left his biscuit recipe to his coachman, Atkins.

Bath post. A letter paper with a highly glazed surface, used by the ultra-fashionable visitors of Bath when that spa was in its prime.

Bath shillings. Silver tradesmen's tokens coined at Bath in 1811–1812 with face values of 4s., 2s., 1s.

Bath stone. An attractive, but not very durable building stone, quarried in the Lower Oolite, near Bath.

There, go to Bath with you! Don't talk nonsense. Insane persons used to be sent to Bath for the benefit of its mineral waters.

Bathia (băth' i à). The name given in the TALMUD to the daughter of PHARAOH who found MOSES in the ark of bulrushes.

Bathos (bā' thos) (Gr. *bathos*, depth). First used by Pope (1727) in the sense of a ludicrous descent from grandiloquence to the commonplace.

> And, thou Dalhousie, the great god of war,
> Lieutenant-general to the Earl of Mar.
> *Bathos*, ix.

Bathyllus (băth' i lùs). A beautiful boy of Samos, greatly beloved by Polycrates the tyrant, and by the poet ANACREON (Horace: *Epistle* xiv, 9).

Bat-Kol (băt kol') (daughter of the voice). A heavenly or divine voice announcing the will of God. It existed in the time of the Jewish prophets but was also heard in post-prophetic times. The expression "daughter of a voice", meaning a small voice, differentiated it from the customary voice. Bat-Kol also denoted a kind of OMEN or AUGURY. After an appeal to Bat-Kol the first words heard were considered oracular.

Batrachomyomachia (bă' trak ō mi' ō mă kyà). A "STORM IN A TEACUP"; much ado about nothing. The word means *The Battle of the Frogs and Mice* and is the name of a mock heroic Greek epic once attributed to HOMER but probably by Pigres of Caria.

Batta (băt' à). An Anglo-Indian term for perquisites. Properly an extra allowance once paid to officers of the British army in India which varied according to where they were stationed, etc. Also spelt *batty*.

Battersea. You must go to Battersea to get your simples cut. A reproof to a simpleton, or one who makes a very foolish observation. The market gardeners of Battersea used to grow simples (medicinal herbs), and the London apothecaries went there to cut or select such as they wanted.

Battle. A pitched battle. A battle which has been planned, and the ground pitched on or chosen beforehand.

A close battle. Originally a naval engagement **at close quarters** in which opposing ships engage each other alongside.

Half the battle. *See* THE FIRST BLOW IS HALF THE BATTLE *under* BLOW.

Line of battle. The formation of ships in line ahead or line abreast in a naval engagement. A *line of battle ship* was a CAPITAL SHIP built and equipped to take part in a main attack. Also a line or lines of troops drawn up for battle.

Trial by battle or **by Combat; Wager of battle.** An ancient usage abolished by 59 Geo. III, c. 46 (1819), after a man accused of murder escaped conviction in 1818, by appealing to *wager of battel* by throwing down the glove, which his accuser did not take up. Originally one of the forms of ORDEAL, when the accuser and accused could settle a case by personal combat in the presence of the court under the assumption that God would give the victory to the innocent.

Battle above the clouds. *See* CLOUDS.

Battle bowler. A nickname given in World War I to the soldier's steel helmet or tin hat. In World War II it was also called a "tin topee".

Battle of Britain. The attempt of the German Luftwaffe by their prolonged attack on S.E. England (August–October 1940) to defeat the R.A.F., as a prelude to invasion. R.A.F. Fighter Command gained the victory and universal admiration. The name arose from Sir Winston Churchill's speech (18 June 1940)—"What General Weygand called the 'Battle of France' is over. I expect that the Battle of Britain is about to begin."

Battle of the Books. A satire by Swift (written 1697, published 1704) on the current literary dispute as to the relative merits of ancient and modern authors. In the battle, ancient and modern books assail each other in St. James's Library. *See* BOYLE CONTROVERSY.

Battle of the Frogs and Mice. *See* BATRACHOMYOMACHIA.

Battle of the Giants. *See* GIANTS.

Battle of the Herrings. *See* HERRINGS.

Battle of the Nations. *See* NATIONS.

Battle of the Poets, The. A satirical poem (1725) by John Sheffield, Duke of Buckingham, in which the versifiers of the time are brought into the field.

Battle of the Spurs. *See* SPURS.

Battle of the Standard. *See* STANDARD.

Battle of the Standards. The nickname given to the presidential election contest of 1896. The Republican candidate, William McKinley, upheld the single GOLD STANDARD, and the Democratic candidate, William Jennings Bryan, fought for the free and unrestricted coinage of silver. The latter was defeated by a comparatively small margin. It was regarded as a victory for "big property".

Battle of the Three Emperors. *See* THREE EMPERORS.

Battle-painter, The. *See* MICHAEL ANGELO.

Battle Royal. In COCKFIGHTING, a certain number of birds are pitted together and left to fight until there is one survivor, the victor of the battle royal (*cp.* WELSH MAIN). Metaphorically the term is applied to any contest of wits, a general mêlée, etc.

Battledore-book. A name sometimes used for a HORN-BOOK, because of its shape like a shuttlecock bat or battledore. Hence, perhaps, the phrase "not to know B from a battledore". *See* CRISSCROSS.

Batty. *See* BATTA. Also slang for crazy, to have "bats in the belfry" (*see* BAT).

Baturlio marina. *See* BARISAL GUNS.

Baubee. *See* BAWBEE.

Bauble. A fool should never hold a bauble in his hand. "'Tis a foolish bird that fouls its own nest", a fool should not advertise his folly. The bauble was a short stick, ornamented with ass's ears, carried by licensed fools (O.Fr. *bable*, or *baubel*, a child's toy; perhaps confused with M.E. *babyll* or *babulle*, a stick with a thong).

If every fool held a bauble, fuel would be dear. The proverb indicates that the world contains a vast number of fools.

To deserve the bauble. To be so foolish as to qualify for the fool's emblem.

Baucis. *See* PHILEMON.

Bauld Willie. *See* BELTED WILL.

Baulk. *See* BALK.

Bavieca. *See* FAMOUS HORSES (under HORSE).

Bawbee. A Scottish small coin or halfpenny first issued in 1541. The word is probably derived from a mint-master of that time, the laird of Sillebawby.

Jenny's bawbee. Her marriage portion.

Bawtry. Like the saddler of Bawtry, who was hanged for leaving his liquor (Yorkshire proverb). It was customary for criminals on their way to execution to stop at a certain tavern in York for a "parting draught". The saddler of Bawtry refused to accept the liquor and was hanged. If he had stopped a few minutes at the tavern, his reprieve, which was on the road, would have arrived in time to save his life.

Baxterians. Followers of Richard Baxter

(1615–1691), eminent divine of PRESBY-TERIAN sympathies, who took a prominent part in the SAVOY CONFERENCE, but was ejected by the Act of Uniformity (1662). His chief doctrines were—(1) That Christ died in a spiritual sense for the elect, and in a general sense for all; (2) that there is no such thing as reprobation; (3) that even saints may fall from grace.

Bay. A shrub of the LAUREL family, *Laurus nobilis*, used for flavouring, was the bay of the ancients. As the tree of APOLLO (*see* DAPHNE) it was held to be a safeguard against thunder and lightning. Hence, according to Pliny, Tiberius and other Roman emperors wore a wreath of bay as an AMULET. The withering of a bay tree was supposed to be an OMEN of evil or death. Holinshed's reference to this superstition is used by SHAKESPEARE in *King Richard II* (II, iv).

In another sense *bay* is a reddish-brown colour, generally used of horses. The word is the Fr. *bai*, from Lat. *badius*, a term used by Varro in his list of colours appropriate to horses. Thus BAYARD means "bay-coloured".

Crowned with bays. A reward of victory: from the ancient Roman custom of so crowning a victorious general.

To bay at the moon. *See under* BARK.

To flourish like a green bay tree. To prosper exceedingly. The bay throws out many fresh green branches every year from both base and trunk.

Bay Psalm Book, or **The Whole Booke of Psalmes.** A translation for colonial churches by Thomas Welde, Richard Mather and John Eliot and the first book published in NEW ENGLAND, printed by Stephen Daye and his family at Cambridge, Mass., in 1640, and of which only eleven copies are known to have survived. Now highly prized, a copy changed hands in 1947 for $151,000.

The Bay State. Massachusetts.

Bay-window. An old nickname for a fat belly, which sticks out, as a bay-window does, from the house-front; the same as BOW-WINDOW.

Bayadere (bā ya′ dâr). A Hindu professional dancing girl or nautch-girl employed for religious dances and private

amusements. The word is a French corruption of the Portuguese *bailadeira*, a female dancer.

Bayard (bā′ yard). A horse of incredible swiftness, given by CHARLEMAGNE to the four sons of AYMON. If only one of the sons mounted, the horse was of ordinary size; but if all four mounted, his body became elongated to the requisite length. The name is used for any valuable or wonderful horse. *See* BAY.

Bold as a Blind Bayard. Foolhardy. If a blind horse leaps, the chance is that he will fall into a ditch.

Keep Bayard in the stable. Keep what is valuable under lock and key.

Bayardo. The famous steed of RINALDO, which once belonged to AMADIS OF GAUL. *See* BAYARD.

Bayonets. A synonym of "rank and FILE," that is, privates and corporals of infantry. As, "the number of bayonets was 25,000". In former times the strength of a cavalry force was indicated similarly by "Sabres".

Bayou State (bī′ yoo). The State of Mississippi; so called from its numerous bayous. A bayou is a creek or sluggish and marshy offshoot of a river or lake. The word is probably a corruption of the Fr. *boyau*, gut.

Bazooka. (1) A comedian's trombone-type wind instrument. The name is perhaps modelled on *Kazoo*, a once popular submarine-shaped toy producing sounds of the "comb and paper" variety. (2) American infantry light rocket-firing tube used as an anti-tank weapon in World War II. It was then applied to the British P.I.A.T. (projectile, infantry anti-tank) and the German *Panzerfaust*.

To be bazookaed. To be in a tank struck by such a weapon and thus metaphorically to be "scuppered", put out of action, done for.

Beachcomber. One who subsists on what FLOTSAM AND JETSAM he can find on the seashore. The word originated in New Zealand, where it is found in print in 1844; an earlier form (1827) was beach ranger, analogous to BUSHRANGER.

Bead. From O.E. -*bed* (in *gebed*), a prayer. "Bead" thus originally meant "a prayer"; but as prayers were "told" (*i.e.* account was kept of them) on a PATER-

NOSTER, the word came to be transferred to the small globular object which, threaded on a string, made up the paternoster or ROSARY.

To count one's beads. To say one's prayers. *See* ROSARY.

To draw a bead on. *See* DRAW.

To pray without one's beads. To be out of one's reckoning.

Baily's beads. When the disc of the moon has (in an eclipse) reduced that of the sun to a thin crescent, the crescent assumes a resemblance to a string of beads. This phenomenon, caused by the sun shining through the depressions between the lunar mountains, was first accurately described by Francis Baily in 1836, hence the name.

St. Cuthbert's beads. *See under* CUTH-BERT.

St. Martin's beads. *See under* MARTIN.

Bead-house. An almshouse for BEADS-MEN.

Bead-roll. A list of persons to be prayed for; hence also any list.

Beadsman, or **Bedesman.** Properly, one who prays; hence an inmate of an ALMSHOUSE, since most of these charities, under the terms of their foundation, required the inmates to pray for the soul of the founder. *See* BEAD.

Beak. Slang for a police magistrate, but formerly (16th and 17th cent.) for a constable. Of uncertain origin.

Beam. In nautical usage, that part of the ship's side between the bows and quarter; also the extreme breadth of a ship. Thus **on the port beam** means away on the left-hand side of the ship when facing the bows; **on the starboard beam** is similarly away on the right-hand side. **On the weather beam** is the side of the ship from which the wind is blowing.

To be on one's beam ends. To be virtually destitute. The *beams* of a wooden ship are the transverse timbers which support the decks and retain the sides, and a vessel is said to be on her beam ends when heeling excessively, or laid on her side—an extremely dangerous situation.

To be on the beam is to be on the right course or track. A modern phrase coming from the directing of aircraft by means of a radio beam.

To kick the beam. *See* KICK.

Bean. Every bean has its black. *Nemo sine vitis nascitur* (everyone has his faults). The bean has a black eye (*Ogni grano ha la sua semola*).

He has found the bean in the cake. He has got a prize in the lottery, has come to some unexpected good fortune. The allusion is to the custom of hiding a bean in TWELFTH-NIGHT cakes.

Jack and the bean-stalk. *See* JACK.

Old bean. A colloquial expression of good-natured familiarity. Very common early in the 20th century.

Bean-feast. Much the same as WAYZ-GOOSE. Properly an annual dinner given by an employer to his employees, possibly because beans or a BEAN-GOOSE were prominent in the meal. Now applied to various annual outings and jollifications or *beanos*.

Bean-goose. A grey goose (*Anser faba-lis*) which arrives in England in the autumn; so named from a mark on its bill like a horse-bean. It is also reputed to be fond of newly sown beans.

Beans. Slang for property, money; also for a sovereign and a GUINEA, probably the O.Fr. cant, *biens*, meaning property. In such phrases as *not worth a bean*, the allusion is to the bean's small value. Similarly *without a bean* means penniless or "broke".

PYTHAGORAS forbade the use of beans to his disciples—not as a food, but the use of beans for political elections. Magistrates and other public officers were elected by beans cast by the voters into a helmet, and what Pythagoras advised was that his disciples should not interfere with politics or "love beans" (*i.e.* office). According to ARISTOTLE, the word *bean* implied venery and that the prohibition "to abstain from beans" was equivalent to "keeping the body chaste".

Blue Beans. Lead shot. *Cp.* BLUEY.

Beans are in flower. A catch-phrase intended to account for a person's silliness. Our forefathers imagined that the perfume of bean flowers made people silly or light-headed.

He knows how many beans make five. He is no fool; he is "up to SNUFF"; he is not to be imposed upon. The reference is to an old catch. Everyone knows five beans make five, and on getting the correct answer the questioner says "But you don't know how many blue beans make five white ones." The correct answer to this is "Five—if peeled."

Full of beans. Said of a fresh and spirited horse; hence in good form; full of health and spirits.

I'll give him beans. I'll give him a thrashing. There is a similar French proverb, *S'il me donne des pois, je lui donnerai des fèves* (if he gives me peas I will give him beans), I will give him TIT FOR TAT, A ROLAND FOR AN OLIVER.

To spill the beans. To give away a secret, to let the cat out of the bag.

Bear. In STOCK EXCHANGE parlance, a speculator for a fall (*cp.* BULL). Thus **to operate for a bear,** or **to bear the market,** is to use every effort to depress prices so as to buy cheap and profit on the rise. Such a transaction is known as a **Bear account.** The term was current at least as early as the SOUTH SEA BUBBLE and probably derives from the proverb "Selling the SKIN before you have caught the bear". One who sold stocks in this way was formerly called a *bearskin jobber*.

The Great Bear and Little Bear. These constellations were so named by the Greeks and their word, *arktos,* a bear, is still kept in the names, *Arcturus,* the bearward or guard, and *Arctic. See* ARCTIC REGION, CHARLES'S WAIN, NORTHERN WAGONER.

> The wind-shak'd surge, with high and monstrous mane,
> Seems to cast water on the burning bear
> And quench the guards of th'ever-fixed pole.
>
> SHAKESPEARE: *Othello,* II, i.

The "guards" referred to in this quotation are β and γ of URSA MINOR. One classical fable is that the nymph CALISTO had a son by ZEUS called Arcas. She was changed into a bear by the angry HERA. Calisto and her son were then set in the sky as constellations by Zeus.

> 'Twas here we saw Calisto's star retire
> Beneath the waves, unawed by Juno's ire.
>
> CAMOËNS: *Lusiad,* Bk. V.

The Northern Bear. An old nickname for Russia. In political cartoons the U.S.S.R. is still usually depicted as a bear.

A bridled bear. A young nobleman under the control of a travelling tutor. *See* BEAR-LEADER.

The bear and the tea-kettle. Said of a person who injures himself by foolish rage. The story is that one day the bear entered a hut in Kamchatka, when a kettle was on the fire. Master Bruin smelt at it and burnt his nose; greatly irritated he seized it and squeezed it against his breast, scalding himself terribly. He growled in agony till some neighbours killed him with their guns.

A bear sucking his paws. It was once held that when a bear was deprived of food it sustained life by sucking its paws. The same was said of the badger. The phrase is applied to industrious idleness.

As savage as a bear with a sore head. Unreasonably ill-tempered.

As a bear has no tail, for a lion he'll fail. The same as *Ne sutor supra crepidam* (let not the cobbler aspire above his last). Robert Dudley, Earl of Leicester, a descendant of the Warwick family, is said to have changed his own crest (a green lion with two tails) for the Warwick bear and ragged staff. Given command of the expedition to the Netherlands (1585), he was suspected of wider ambitions when the Netherlanders granted him "absolute authority" (1586). As the lion is monarch among beasts, some wit wrote under his crest set up in public, *Ursa caret cauda non queat esse leo, i.e.:*

> Your bear for lion needs must fail,
> Because your true bears have no tail.

If it were a bear it would bite you. An old expression applied to a person looking for something right in front of him, just under his nose.

To take the bear by the tooth. Needlessly to run into danger.

Bear garden, This place is a perfect. That is, full of confusion, noise, tumult and quarrels. In Tudor and Stuart times the gardens where bears were kept and baited for public amusement were notorious for noise and riotous disorder.

Bear-leader. In the 18th century denoted the tutor who conducted a young nobleman or youth of wealth and fashion on the GRAND TOUR. It is taken from the old custom of leading muzzled bears about the streets and making them show off to attract notice and money. (This practice was only made illegal in 1925.)

Bear. To bear arms. To do military service; to be entitled to heraldic coat of arms and crest.

To bear away (nautical). The same as TO BEAR UP but applied to the ship instead of the helm.

To bear one company. To be one's companion.

To bear down. To overpower.

To bear down upon (nautical). To approach from the weather side.

To bear in mind. Not to forget; to remember for consideration.

To bear out. To corroborate, to confirm.

To bear up. To support; to keep the spirits up. In nautical language, to keep further away from the wind by putting the helm up. *Cp.* TO BEAR AWAY.

To bear with. To show forbearance.

To bear the bell. *See* BELL.

Beard. Among the Jews, Turks, Persians and many other peoples the beard has long been a sign of manly dignity and to cut it off wilfully is a deadly insult. MOSLEMS swore by the beard of the Prophet and to swear by one's beard was an assurance of good faith. To pluck or touch a man's beard was an extreme affront, hence the phrase *to beard one*, to defy or insult or contradict flatly.

To beard the lion in his den. To defy personally or have it out FACE TO FACE.

To make one's beard. To have one wholly at your mercy, as a barber when holding a man's beard to dress it, or shaving the chin of a customer. So, to be able to do what you like with one, to outwit or delude him.

I told him to his beard. I told him to his face, regardless of the consequences; openly and fearlessly.

Maugre his beard. In spite of him.

Old Man's Beard. *Clematis vitalba*, so called from its head of long-bearded fruits. Also known as Traveller's Joy.

To laugh in one's beard. To laugh up one's SLEEVE, that is, surreptitiously.

To lie in one's beard. To accuse some-

one of doing so is to stress the severity of the accusation.

To run in one's beard. To offer opposition to a person; to do something obnoxious to a person before his face.

With the beard on the shoulder (Sp.). In the attitude of listening to overhear something; with circumspection, looking in all directions for surprises and ambuscades.

Tax upon beards. Peter the Great (1672–1725) encouraged shaving in Russia by imposing a tax upon beards. Clerks were stationed at the gate of every town to collect the tax. He personally cut off the beards of his chief boyars.

Bearded Master. So Persius styled SOCRATES, under the notion that the beard is a symbol of wisdom.

Bearings. I'll bring him to his bearings. I'll bring him to his senses, put him on the right track. In navigation bearings are taken of the direction in which an object is seen. Thus to keep one's bearings is to keep on the right course, in the right direction.

To lose one's bearings. To be off course, to become lost, bewildered, to get perplexed.

To take the bearings. To ascertain the relative position of an object.

Beast. The number of the Beast. *See under* NUMBERS.

Beast of Belsen. In World War II the name given to Joseph Kramer, commandant of the infamous Belsen concentration camp.

Beasts of heraldry. In English HERALDRY all manner of creatures (many derived from BESTIARIES) have been borne as charges or as crests, notably the lion, leopard, bear, bull, boar, cat, eagle, swallow (called a martlet), pelican, unicorn, stag, griffin, wyvern. The attitude or position of the animal is thus described: *couchant*, lying down with head erect; *dormant*, sleeping, with head lowered; *passant*, walking; *passant gardant*, walking but looking at the beholder; RAMPANT, on its hind legs; *rampant combattant*, two beasts rampant facing one another; *rampant endorsed*, two beasts rampant back to back. A beast can be *proper*, that is, emblazoned in its natural colour; *naissant*, emerging out of a fesse or ordinary; *erased*, a head or limb torn from the body; etc.

Beauty and the Beast. *See under* BEAUTY.

Beat (O.E. *beatan*). The first sense of the word was that of striking; that of overcoming or defeating was a natural extension. Also a track, range or walk, trodden or beaten by the feet, as a **policeman's beat.**

Beat group. A type of "pop music" group of the 1950s and 1960s, characterized by a marked emphasis on rhythm or beat.

Dead beat. *See under* DEAD.

Dead beat escapement. *See under* DEAD.

Not in my beat. Not in my line; not in the range of my talents or inclination.

Off his beat. Not on duty; not in his appointed walk; not his speciality or line.

Out of his beat. In his wrong walk; out of his proper sphere.

That beats Banagher. *See* BANAGHER; TERMAGANT.

To beat about. A nautical phrase meaning to TACK against the wind.

To beat about the bush. To approach a matter cautiously in a roundabout way, to SHILLY-SHALLY; perhaps because one goes carefully when beating a bush to find if any game is lurking within.

To beat an alarm. To give notice of danger by beat of a drum.

To beat a retreat is to withdraw from or abandon a position, undertaking, etc.

To beat retreat, in the military sense, was originally to summon men by drum beat to withdraw to camp or behind the lines when hostilities temporarily ceased at the approach of darkness; also to give warning to the guards to collect and be posted for the night.

The drums were later augmented by fifes and more recently, with the advent of military bands, *beat retreat* became an impressive ceremonial display.

To beat down. To make a seller abate his price.

To beat, or **drum a thing into someone.** To repeat as a drummer repeats his beats on the drum.

To beat hollow, or **to a mummy, a frazzle, to ribbons, a jelly,** etc. To beat wholly, utterly, completely.

To beat the air. To strike out at nothing as pugilists do before a fight; to toil without profit; to work to no purpose.

To beat the band. To excel, to exceed or surpass; from the idea of making more noise than the band.

To beat the booby. *See* BOOBY.

To beat the bounds. *See* BOUNDS.

To beat the bush. To allow another to profit by one's exertions; "one beat the bush and another caught the hare". The allusion is to beaters who start the game from the bushes for a shooting party.

To beat the devil's tattoo. *See* DEVIL.

To beat the Dutch. To "draw a very long BOW"; to say something very incredible.

To beat time. To indicate time in music by beating or moving the hands, feet or a baton.

To beat up someone. To make one the victim of vicious and brutal assault.

To beat up recruits, or **supporters.** To hunt them up or call them together, as soldiers are summoned by beat of drum.

To beat one with his own staff. To confute him with his own words. An *argumentum ad hominem*.

Beati Possidentes (bē a′ tī pos i den′ tēz). Blessed are those who have (for they shall receive). "Possession is nine points of the law." (*See under* NINE.)

Beatific Vision. The sight of God, or of the blessed in the realms of HEAVEN, especially that granted to the SOUL at the instant of death. See *Is.* vi, 1–3 and *Acts* vii, 55, 56.

Beatification (bē ăt i fi kā′ shùn). In the ROMAN CATHOLIC CHURCH this is a solemn act by which a deceased person is formally declared by the POPE to be one of the blessed departed and therefore a proper subject for a MASS and OFFICE in his honour, generally with some local restriction. Beatification is usually, though not necessarily, a step to CANONIZATION.

Beatitude (bē ăt′ i tūd). Blessedness, perfect felicity.

The Beatitudes are the eight blessings

pronounced by Our Lord at the opening of the Sermon on the Mount (*Matt.* v, 3–11).

Beatnik. A "beat" person, one who lives a beat life, akin to the American *hipster*. Socially, politically, intellectually and artistically the beatnik stands apart, and is an ANGRY YOUNG MAN or woman, ultra-BOHEMIAN, flouting all or most of the established conventions and values. The beatnik is distinguished by unconventional dress and slovenliness. The term may derive from the "beat generation" (meaning dissatisfied young people) and a Russian suffix (*nik*, as in SPUTNIK).

Beatrice. *See* DANTE.

Beau (bō) (Fr. fine or beautiful). In England and America used for a lover or admirer; formerly prefixed to the name of a fop or man of fashion, such as the following:

Beau Brummel. George Brummel (1778–1840), an intimate of the Prince Regent.

Beau Nash. Richard Nash (1674–1762). Born at Swansea and educated at Jesus College, Oxford. As a noted gambler, he nevertheless achieved distinction as Master of Ceremonies at Bath, which he made the leading English spa.

Beau Tibbs, in Goldsmith's *Citizen of the World*, noted for his finery, vanity and poverty.

Beau ideal. "The ideal Beautiful" is the proper meaning of the original French, but often used in English to mean the beautiful ideal.

Beau monde. The fashionable world; people who make up the coterie of fashion.

Beau trap. An old name for a loose paving-stone under which water lodged and which squirted up filth when trodden on, to the discomfort of the smartly dressed.

Beauclerc (bō' klĕrk) (good scholar). Applied to Henry I, King of England (1100–1135) for his scholarly accomplishments.

Beaumontague, Beaumontage, or **Beaumontique**. A filling compound used in joinery and metalwork said to be named after the French geologist Elie de

Beaumont (1798–1874), who also gave his name to *beaumonlite*, a silicate of copper. As it can be used for disguising bad workmanship, it has the added meanings of bad joinery, literary padding and bad work generally.

Beautiful Parricide. Beatrice Cenci, daughter of Francesco Cenci, a dissolute Roman nobleman. Because of her father's cruelties to the family, she and two of her brothers contrived his murder. She was beheaded in 1599. Their story has been a favourite theme in literature and art; Shelley's tragedy, *The Cenci* (1819), is particularly noteworthy.

Beauty. Beauty is but skin deep.

> O formose puer, nimium ne crede colori.
> VIRGIL: *Bucolics, Eclogue* ii.

(O my pretty boy, trust not too much to your pretty looks.)

Beauty and the Beast. A handsome woman with an uncouth or uncomely male companion.

The heroine and hero of the well-known fairy tale in which Beauty saved the life of her father by consenting to live with the Beast; and the Beast, being disenchanted by Beauty's love, became a handsome prince, and married her. The story is found in Straparola's *Piacevoli Notti* (1550), and this is probably the source of Mme. deprince de Beaumont's popular French version (1757). It is the basis of Grétry's opera *Zémire et Azor* (1771). The story is of great antiquity and takes various forms. *Cp.* LOATHLY LADY.

Beauty sleep. Sleep taken before midnight. Those who habitually go to bed after midnight, especially during youth, are supposed to become pale and haggard.

Beaux Esprits (bō zā sprē') (Fr.). Persons of wit or genius (singular, *Un bel esprit*, a wit, a genius).

Beaux yeux (bō zyĕr') (Fr.). Beautiful eyes or attractive looks. "I will do it for your *beaux yeux*" (because you are so pretty, or because your eyes are so attractive).

Beaver. The lower and movable part of a helmet; so called from Fr. *bavière*, which meant a child's bib, to which it had some resemblance.

Beaver is also an old name for a man's hat because some hats used to be made of beaver fur.

The Beaver. Name given in journalistic circles to Lord Beaverbrook (William Maxwell Aitken, 1879–1964), Canadian-born politician and newspaper magnate.

Bed. The great bed of Ware. A fourposter bed eleven feet square and capable of holding twelve people. It dates from the late 16th century and was formerly at Rye House, Hertfordshire, but in 1931 it came into the possession of the Victoria and Albert Museum.

As you make your bed, so you must lie on it. Everyone must bear the consequences of his own acts.

To bed out. To transfer plants raised in pots or a greenhouse out into the open ground.

You got out of bed the wrong way, on the wrong side, or **with the left leg foremost.** Said of a person who is moody or grumpy. It was held to be unlucky to set the left foot on the ground first when getting out of bed. The same superstition applies to putting on the left shoe first. AUGUSTUS Caesar was very superstitious in this respect.

Bed of Justice. See LIT.

A bed of roses. A situation of ease and pleasure.

A bed of thorns. A situation of great anxiety and apprehension.

Bedchamber Crisis, or **Question.** In May 1839, Lord Melbourne's insecure WHIG ministry resigned and when Sir Robert Peel accepted office he requested that some of the Whig ladies of the bedchamber be replaced by TORIES. Queen Victoria refused and Peel resigned, whereupon Melbourne was recalled to office. The question was resolved, with the intervention of the Prince Consort, before Melbourne's resignation in 1841.

Beddgelert (beth gel' ert). The name of a village in Caernarvonshire (the grave of Gelert). According to Welsh folklore, Prince Llewelyn returned to his castle to find his dog Gelert's jaws dripping with blood. His son had been left in Gelert's care but the baby was not to be found. In his distress, Llewelyn slew the faithful hound and found his son, close to the body of a wolf, which the hound had

killed. This story has many variants in other ancient literatures.

Bede, The Venerable (c. 673–735). Also called the *English* DOCTOR. This most renowned of early English scholars became a monk at Jarrow and devoted his life to religion and learning. His industry, output and range were remarkable, but he is probably best known for his *Ecclesiastical History of the English People*, a work of unusual merit and value, which has led him to be called the *Father of English History*. His book is a major source of information to the year 731. The title "venerable" is by one tradition assigned to an angelic hand; it is certainly not due to great age as is often thought.

Bedivere, or **Bedver.** In the ARTHURIAN ROMANCES, a knight of the ROUND TABLE, butler and staunch adherent of King ARTHUR. It was he who, at the request of the dying king, threw EXCALIBUR into the lake, and afterwards bore his body to the ladies in the barge which was to take him to AVALON.

Bedlam (A contraction of *Bethlehem*). A lunatic asylum, a madhouse; hence a place of hubbub and confusion. The priory of St. Mary of Bethlehem outside Bishopsgate was founded in 1247 and began to receive lunatics in 1377. It was given to the City of London as a hospital for lunatics by Henry VIII in 1547. In 1676 it was transferred to Moorfields and became one of the sights of London, where for twopence, anyone might gaze at the poor wretches and bait them. It was a place for assignations and one of the disgraces of 17th-century London.

> All that I can say of Bedlam is this; 'tis an almshouse for madmen, a showing room for harlots, a sure market for lechers, a dry walk for loiterers.
> NED WARD: *The London Spy* (1698).

In 1815 Bedlam was moved to St. George's Fields, Lambeth, the present site of the Imperial War Museum, when in 1931 the occupants were moved to West Wickham. Hannah SNELL died in Bedlam in 1792.

Bedlamite. A madman, a fool, an inmate of Bedlam. See ABRAM-MAN.

Bedlam, Tom o'. See TOM.

Bedouin (bed' oo in). French (and thence English) form of an Arabic word meaning "a dweller in the desert", applied to the nomadic tribes of Arabia and Syria. Formerly also the homeless street poor. *Cp.* STREET ARABS.

Bedrock. American slang for one's last dollar. "I'm come down to bedrock", the end of one's resources. Bedrock is the miner's term for the hard basis rock which is reached when the mine is exhausted.

Bee. Legend has it that JUPITER was nourished by bees, similarly PINDAR was nourished by bees with honey (instead of milk). The Greeks consecrated bees to the MOON. With the Romans a flight of bees was considered a bad OMEN. Appian (*Civil War*, Bk. II) says a swarm of bees lighted on the altar and prognosticated the fatal issue of the battle of Pharsalia. *See* AMBROSE; ATHENIAN BEE; ATTIC BEE.

The name *bee* is given, particularly in America, to a social gathering for some useful work (*see* ANIMALS IN SYMBOLISM), *e.g.* a *sewing bee*. A *spelling-bee* is a competition or gathering to compete in spelling.

Bee-line. The shortest distance between two given points such as a bee is supposed to take in making for its hive. *See* AIRLINE.

To have your head full of bees, or **to have a bee in your bonnet.** To be cranky; to have an idiosyncrasy; to be full of devices, crotchets, fancies, inventions and dreamy theories. The connection between bees and the soul was once generally maintained; hence MOHAMMED admits bees to PARADISE. Porphyry says of fountains, "they are adapted to the NYMPHS or those souls which the ancients called bees." *Cp.* MAGGOT.

Beef. From the O.Fr. *boef*, an ox. Like mutton (O.Fr, *moton*) it is a reminder of the period after the Norman Conquest when the Saxon was the servant of the conquerors. The Saxon was the herdsman and used the word for the beast under his charge, the Normans had the cooked meat and used the appropriate French name for it.

Beefeaters. The popular name of the Yeomen of the Guard, first formed as a royal bodyguard at Henry VII's coronation in 1485; also of the Yeomen Extraordinary of the Guard, who were appointed as Warders of the TOWER of London by Edward VI, and wear the same Tudor-period costume. The name was probably first specifically applied to the Yeomen of the Guard about the middle of the 17th century.

That "eater" was formerly a synonym for "servant" is shown by the O.E. word *hláf-oeta* (loaf-eater), which meant "a menial servant" and by the passage in Ben Jonson's *Silent Woman*, III, ii (1609), where Morose, calling for his servants, shouts:

> Bar my doors! bar my doors! Where are all my eaters? My mouths, now? Bar up my doors you varlets!

The literal meaning "eaters of beef" is the probable origin of the word, rather than the Fr. word *buffetier*.

Beelzebub. Other forms are *Beelzebul, Baalzebub*. Baalzebub was the god of Ekron (II *Kings* i, 3), and the meaning is obscure although it has been popularly held to mean "lord of FLIES". In any event it was probably a derisory title. The most likely explanation so far is that Baalzebul means "lord of the lofty dwelling" and refers to the Syrian BAAL. This was altered to Baalzebub by the Jews, as the former title seemed only proper to JAHWEH. To the Jews he came to be the chief representative of the false gods. In *Matt.* xii, 24, he is referred to as "the prince of the devils" and similarly in *Mark* iii, 22, and *Luke* xi, 15. Hence Milton places him next in rank to SATAN.

> One next himself in power, and next in crime,
> Long after known in Palestine, and named Beelzebub.
> *Paradise Lost*, I, 79.

Beer. *See* ALE.

Beer-money. An allowance of one penny per day paid to British soldiers and N.C.O.s between 1800 and 1823 instead of an issue of beer. Now sometimes used to denote "spending money" for refreshment or pleasure.

Life is not all beer and skittles, *i.e.* not all eating, drinking, and play; not all pleasure.

Small beer. *See* SMALL.

Beeswing. Thus named from its appearance. A crust or film of tartar which forms in port and other wines after long keeping. It is not detrimental if it passes into the decanter.

Beetle, To. To overhang, to threaten, to jut over. The word seems to have been first used by SHAKESPEARE:

> Or to the dreadful summit of the cliff
> That beetles o'er his base into the sea.
> *Hamlet*, I, iv.

It is formed from the adjective *beetle-browed*, having prominent or shaggy eyebrows. The derivation of *beetle* in this use is uncertain, but it probably refers to the tufted antennæ which, in some beetles, stand straight out from the head.

Beeton, Mrs. *The Book of Household Management*, a classic mid-Victorian work on "domestic economy", was written by Mrs. Isabella Beeton (1836–1865) and first published in 1861. The bulk of its contents consisted of some 4,000 recipes and it readily established itself as the most famous of all English cookery books. The name of Mrs. Beeton became synonymous with this book, although she compiled other lesser ones during her short life. In its revised editions it is still widely used. Mrs Beeton was doubtless familiar with the books written by the famous French cook, Alexis Soyer (1809– 1858), who came to England after the French Revolution of July 1830.

Befana (be fa′ na). The good fairy of Italian children, who is supposed to fill their stockings with toys when they go to bed on TWELFTH NIGHT. Someone enters the children's bedroom for the purpose and the wakeful youngsters cry out, "*Ecco la Befana.*" According to legend, Befana was too busy with house affairs to look after the MAGI when they went out to offer their gifts, and said she would wait to see them on their return; but they went another way, and Befana, every Twelfth Night, watches for them. The name is a corruption of *Epiphania*.

Before the Lights. *See* LIGHTS.

Before the Mast. *See* MAST.

Beg the Question, To. To assume a proposition which, in reality, involves the conclusion. Thus, to say that parallel lines will never meet because they are parallel, is simply to assume as a fact the very thing you profess to prove. The phrase is the common English equivalent of the Latin term, PETITIO PRINCIPII.

Beggar. A beggar may sing before a pick-pocket. *Cantabit vacuus coram latrone viator* (*Juvenal*, x, 22). A beggar may sing in the presence of thieves because he has nothing in his pocket to lose.

Beggars cannot be choosers. Beggars must take what is given to them and be thankful. They are not in a position to pick and choose or dictate terms to the giver.

Beggars' barm. The yeast-like scum which collects on the surface of ponds, brooks, etc. where the current is arrested. Unfit for use, it is only beggarly barm (froth) at best.

Beggars' bullets. Stones.

Beggars of the Sea. *See* GUEUX.

Beggar's Opera, The. Produced in 1728, its enormous success gave a new impetus to English comic opera. The hero is a highwayman, MacHeath, and it centres around NEWGATE. This topical satire by John Gay was produced by Rich (*see* BEEFSTEAK CLUB). It is said to have made Gay rich and Rich gay. The music was made up of traditional ballads and popular tunes of the day arranged by Pepusch.

Begging Friars. *See* MENDICANT ORDERS.

King of the Beggars. Bampfylde Moore Carew (1693–1770), a famous English vagrant who became King of the GIPSIES. Transported to Maryland, he escaped and is said to have joined the Young PRETENDER and followed him to Derby.

Set a beggar on horseback, and he'll ride to the de'il. There is no one so proud and arrogant as a beggar who has suddenly grown rich.

To go by beggar's bush, or **Go home by beggar's bush**—*i.e.* to go to ruin.

Beghards (be gardz). Monastic fraternities which first arose in the Low Countries in the late 12th century, named after Lambert le Bègue, a priest of Liège, who also founded the BÉGUINES. They took no vows and were free to leave the society at will. In the 17th century, those who survived Papal persecution joined the TERTIARIES of the FRANCISCANS. The word *beggar* possibly derives from beghards. Le Bègue means "the stammerer". *Cp.* LOLLARDS; ORATORIANS.

Beglerbeg. *See* BASHAW.

Beguine (bĕ gēn'). A popular Martinique and South American dance, or music for this dance in bolero rhythm. It inspired Cole Porter's success of the 1930s, *Begin the Beguine*.

Béguines (bā gēn'). A sisterhood founded in the late 12th century by Lambert le Bègue (*see* BEGHARDS). They were free to quit the cloister and to marry, and formerly flourished in the Low Countries, Germany, France, Switzerland and Italy. There are still communities in Belgium. The cap called a *béguin* was named from this sisterhood.

Behemoth (be hē' moth). The animal described under this name in *Job* xl, 15–24, is probably the hippopotamus. The poet James Thomson apparently took it to be a rhinoceros.

> Behold! in plaited mail,
> Behemoth rears his head.
> *The Seasons: Summer*, 709, 710.

The word is more often pronounced Be' hemoth; but Milton, like Thomson, places the accent on the second syllable.

> Scarce from his mould
> Behemoth, biggest born of earth, upheaved
> His vastness.
> *Paradise Lost*, VII, 471.

Behmenists (bā' men ists). A sect of theosophical mystics, called after their founder Jacob Behman or Boehme (1575–1624). Jane Leade founded a Behmenist sect in England in 1697 called the Philadelphists.

Behram (bā' răm). The most holy kind of fire according to the PARSEES. *See also* GUEBRES.

Bel. The name of the Assyrio-Babylonian gods En-lil and MARDUK. It has the same meaning as BAAL. The story of Bel and the Dragon, in which we are told how Daniel convinced the King that Bel was not an actual living deity but only an image, was formerly part of the book of *Daniel*, but is now relegated to the APOCRYPHA.

Bel Esprit (bel es prē') (Fr.). *See* BEAUX ESPRITS.

Belch, Sir Toby. A reckless, roistering jolly fellow; from the knight of that name in Shakespeare's *Twelfth Night*.

Bel-fires. *See* BELTANE.

Belfry. Originally a movable tower used in sieges from which the attackers threw missiles. (O.Fr. *berfrei*. Mid. High Ger. *Bercfrit*, a place of safety. Thence a watch-tower, beacon or alarm bell-tower.) Thus a church bell tower is called a belfry not because bells are hung in it.

Belial (bē li ăl) (Heb.). In Old Testament usage it has the meaning of worthlessness, wickedness, but later it is used as a proper noun in the sense of the wicked one.

> What concord hath Christ with Belial?
> II *Cor.* vi, 15.

Milton thus uses it as a proper name:

> Belial came last—than whom a spirit more lewd
> Fell not from heaven, or more gross to love
> Vice for itself.
> *Paradise Lost*, I, 490.

Sons of Belial. Lawless, worthless, rebellious people.

> Now the sons of Eli were sons of Belial; they knew not the Lord.
> I *Sam.* ii, 12.

Belisha Beacon. An amber-coloured globe mounted on a black and white banded pole, the sign of a pedestrian crossing. Named after Leslie Hore-Belisha, Minister of Transport (1934–1937), who introduced them.

Bell, Acton, Currer, and **Ellis.** These were the names under which Anne, Charlotte, and Emily Brontë wrote their novels.

Bell. As the bell clinks, so the fool thinks, or **As the fool thinks, so the bell clinks.** The tale says when Dick WHITTINGTON ran away from his master, and had got as far as Highgate Hill, he was hungry, tired, and wished to return. BOW BELLS began to ring, and Whittington fancied they said, "Turn again, Whittington, Lord Mayor of London." The bells clinked in response to the boy's thoughts.

At three bells, at five bells, etc. At sea a bell is rung at half-hourly intervals to mark the passing of time in the WATCH. Five of the seven watches last four hours. Thus "three bells" (three strokes on the bell) denotes the third half-hour of the watch, "five bells" the fifth, etc. "Eight bells" marks the ending of a watch. The two Dog watches are each of two hours duration (4 p.m. to 6 p.m. and 6 p.m. to 8 p.m.). The passing of the 1st DOG WATCH is marked by four bells and the 2nd or Last Dog by eight.

Bell, book, and candle. The popular phrase for ceremonial EXCOMMUNICATION in the ROMAN CATHOLIC CHURCH. After pronouncing sentence the officiating cleric closes his book, quenches the candle by throwing it to the ground and tolls the bell as for one who has died. The book symbolizes the book of life, the candle that the soul is removed from the sight of God as the candle from the sight of man.

Hence, **in spite of bell, book and candle** signifies in spite of all opposition the Christian hierarchy can offer.

Give her the bells and let her fly. Don't throw good money after bad; make the best of the matter but don't try to bolster it up. In falconry, when a HAWK was worthless it was allowed to escape, even at the expense of bells attached to it.

Like sweet bells jangled, out of tune and harsh (*Hamlet*, III, i). A metaphor for a deranged mind.

One bell in the Last Dog Watch. It is a common story in the Royal Navy that one bell has been struck at 6.30 p.m. instead of five since the mutinies of 1797, because in one port five bells in the dog watches was to be the signal for mutiny. This was prevented by the foreknowledge of officers, who caused one bell to be struck instead.

Passing bell. The hallowed bell which used to be rung when persons were *in extremis*, to scare away evil spirits which might be lurking ready to snatch the SOUL while *passing* from the body. A secondary object was to announce to the neighbourhood that all good Christians might pray for the safe passage of the soul into PARADISE. The bell rung at a funeral is sometimes improperly called the "passing bell".

Athenians used to beat on brazen kettles at the moment of decease to scare away the FURIES.

Ringing the bell backwards is ringing a muffled peal. *Backwards* is often used to denote "in a reverse manner", as, "I hear you are grown rich"—"Yes, backwards", meaning "quite the reverse". A muffled peal is one of sorrow, not of joy, and was formerly sometimes employed as a tocsin or notice of danger.

Ringing the hallowed bell. Consecrated bells were believed to be able to disperse storms and pestilence, drive away devils (*see* PASSING BELL) and extinguish fire. It is said that as late as 1852 the Bishop of Malta ordered the church bells to be rung for an hour to "lay a gale of wind".

Sound as a bell. Quite sound. A cracked bell is useless.

That rings a bell, that strikes a chord, that sounds familiar, that reminds me of something. It may have derived from the fairground, where a bell on top of a tall column could be struck by a contestant hammering a pivot at the base and sending a projectile upwards.

To bear, or **carry away the bell.** To be first fiddle; to carry off the palm; to be the best. The BELLWETHER bore the bell, hence the phrase; but it has been confused with an old custom of presenting to winners of horse-races, etc., a little GOLD or SILVER bell as a prize.

Tolling the bell for church. The "church-going bell" as Cowper called it (*Verses by Alexander Selkirk*) was in pre-Reformation days rung as an Ave Bell to invite worshippers to a preparatory prayer to the Virgin.

Warming the bell. A nautical phrase, doing something before the proper time, *e.g.* preparing to leave early, etc. Possibly from the idea that a bell, like a clock, if warmed moves faster.

Who is to bell the cat? Who will risk his own life to save his neighbour's? Anyone who encounters great personal hazard for the sake of others undertakes to "bell the cat". The allusion is to the fable of the cunning old mouse (given in *Piers Plowman* and elsewhere), who suggested that they should hang a bell on the cat's neck to give notice to all mice of her approach. "Excellent," said a wise young mouse, "but who is to undertake the job?"

Bell-the-Cat. Archibald Douglas, fifth Earl of Angus (d. 1514), was so called. James III made favourites of architects and masons, Cochrane, a mason, being created Earl of Mar. The Scottish nobles held a council in the church of Lauder for the purpose of putting down these upstarts, when Lord Gray asked "Who will bell the cat?" "That will I," said Douglas, and he fearlessly put to death, in the king's presence, the obnoxious minions.

Bell-man. *See* TOWN CRIER.

Bell Savage. *See* LA BELLE SAUVAGE.

Bell-wavering. Vacillating, swaying from side to side like a bell.

Bellwether of the flock. A jocose and rather deprecatory term applied to the leader of a party. The allusion is to the wether, or sheep, which leads the flock with a bell fastened to its neck.

Belladonna. The Deadly Nightshade. The name is Italian and means "beautiful lady". Its power of enlarging the pupils was put to use by would-be glamorous females. This is the usual explanation of the name but another is that it was used by an Italian poisoner named Leucota to poison beautiful women.

Bellarmine (bel' ar mĭn). A large Flemish GOTCH, or stone beer-jug, originally made in Flanders in ridicule of CARDINAL Bellarmine (1542–1621), a great defender of the ROMAN CATHOLIC CHURCH. It carried a rude likeness of the Cardinal. *Cp.* DEMIJOHN; GREYBEARD.

Belle (bel) (Fr.). A beauty.

The Belle of the ball. The most beautiful woman in the room.

Belles-lettres (bel letr). Polite literature; poetry and standard literary works: the study or pursuit of such.

Bellerophon (be ler' ō fon). The JOSEPH of Greek mythology; Antæa, spouse of Prœtus, being the "POTIPHAR'S WIFE" who tempted him and afterwards falsely accused him. Prœtus sent Bellerophon with a letter to Iobates, King of Lycia, his wife's father, narrating the charge, and praying that the bearer might be put to death. Iobates, reluctant to slay Bellerophon himself, gave him many hazardous tasks, including the killing of the CHIMÆRA, but as he succeeded in all of them Iobates made him his heir. Later Bellerophon attempted to fly to heaven on PEGASUS, but ZEUS sent a gadfly to sting the horse, and the rider was thrown.

Bellerophon. The name of the former seventy-four-gun ship of the Royal Navy which took part in the Battle of the Nile and Trafalgar and to whose captain NAPOLEON finally surrendered himself after Waterloo. The name was corrupted by sailors to "Billy Ruffian", "Bully-ruffran", "Belly-ruffron", etc.

Letters of Bellerophon. Letters or documents either dangerous or prejudicial to the bearer. *See* BELLEROPHON.

Bellona. The Roman goddess of war, wife (or sometimes sister) of MARS.

Belly. The belly and its members. The fable of Menenius Agrippa to the Roman people when they seceded to the Sacred Mount. "Once upon a time the members refused to work for the lazy belly; but, as the supply of food was thus stopped, they found there was a necessary and mutual dependence between them." The fable is given by ÆSOP and by Plutarch, whence Shakespeare introduced it in his *Coriolanus*, I, i.

The belly has no ears. A hungry man will not listen to advice or arguments.

Belomancy (bel' ō măn si) (Gr.). DIVINATION by arrows. Labels being attached to a given number of arrows, the archers let them fly, and the advice on the label of the arrow which flies farthest is accepted.

Beloved Disciple. St. JOHN (*John* xiii, 23).

Beloved Physician. St. LUKE (*Col.* iv, 14).

Belphegor (bel' fe gôr). The Assyrian form of *Baal-Peor* (*see* BAAL), the Moabitish god to whom the Israelites became attached in Shittim (*Numb.* xxv, 3), which was associated with licentious orgies (*Hos.* ix, 10).

The name was given in mediæval Latin legend to a demon sent into the world by his fellows to test rumours concerning the happiness of married life on earth. After a thorough trial, he fled to the happy regions where female companionship was non-existent. Hence the name is applied to a misanthrope and to a nasty, obscene, licentious fellow. The story is found in MACHIAVELLI, and occurs in English in Barnabe Rich's *Farewell to the Militarie Profession* (1581) and is used in *Grim, The Collier of Croyden* (1600), Jonson's *The Divell is an Asse* (1616), and John Wilson's *Belphegor, or the Marriage of the Devil* (1691).

Belt. To hit below the belt. To strike unfairly. It is prohibited in the QUEENSBERRY RULES of prize-fighting to hit below the waist-belt.

To hold the belt. To be the champion. In pugilism, a belt usually forms part of the prize in big fights.

Belted earl, or **knight.** This refers to the belt and spurs with which KNIGHTS, etc., were invested when raised to the dignity. In American usage, *belted earl* is a person who claims noble birth.

Beltane (bel' tān) (Gaelic, *bealtainn*). The derivation is uncertain but it is not connected with *baal*. In Scotland, May Day (O.S.); also an ancient Celtic festival when *bel-fires* were kindled on the hill-tops and cattle were driven between the flames, either to protect them from disease, or as a preparatory to sacrifice.

Ben trovato. Well invented. A phrase from the Italian rendered in French as *bien trouvé*. The full Italian saying *Se non è vero, è molto ben trovato* means "If it is not true, it is very well invented".

Benares (ben âr' ēz). The holy city of the Hindus, being to them what MECCA is to the MOSLEMS. It contains many temples including the Golden Temple of SIVA and is much frequented by pilgrims. It is of great antiquity and was for centuries a Buddhist centre.

Bench. Originally the same word as BANK; properly, a long wooden seat, hence the official seat of judges or magistrates in court, BISHOPS in the HOUSE OF LORDS, aldermen in the council chamber, etc.; hence by extension judges, bishops, etc., or the dignity of holding such official status.

The front bench. In the HOUSE OF COMMONS the leading members of the government occupy the front bench to the right of the SPEAKER. This is called the Treasury Bench. The OPPOSITION leaders occupy the opposite front bench; hence, by extension, the leaders of the government, or of the opposition.

To be raised to the bench. To be made a judge.

To be raised to the Episcopal bench. To be made a BISHOP.

Bench and Bar. Judges and barristers. *See* BAR; BARRISTER.

Benchers. Senior members who administer the INNS OF COURT and call students to the BAR. They also exercise powers of expulsion.

Back-benchers. Ordinary members of the House of Commons who do not hold office and occupy the back benches. *Cp.* THE FRONT BENCH.

Bench-mark. A surveyor's mark cut in some lasting material such as rock, the wall of a building etc. as a located point of reference and to act as a starting point in a line of levels for determining the altitudes of an area. In Britain it consists of cuts in the shape of a broad arrow with a horizontal incision across its apex. When making the reading an angle-iron is inserted in the horizontal cut to form the *bench* on which the levelling-staff is rested. Hence the name.

Bend. In HERALDRY, an ORDINARY formed between the two parallel lines drawn across the shield from the DEXTER chief (*i.e.* the top left-hand corner when looking at the shield) to the SINISTER base (the opposite corner). It is said to represent the sword-belt.

Bend sinister. A bend running across the shield from the SINISTER chief, *i.e.* from right to left. It is occasionally an indication of bastardy (*cp.* BAR SINISTER) though more often a *baton sinister* is used. *He has a bend sinister* means he was not born in lawful wedlock.

To bend over backwards. To make exceptional or unnecessary efforts to please or appease.

To go round the bend, or **to be driven round the bend.** To go mad or to be driven crazy. Here *bend* is used in the sense of "taking a turn".

Bendy, Old. The DEVIL; who is willing to bend to anyone's inclination.

Benedicite (ben e dīs' i ti) (Lat.). "Bless

you", or "may you be blessed". In the first sense it is the opening word of many old graces; hence a grace or a blessing. The second sense accounts for its use as an expression of astonishment.

> The god of love, A benedicite,
> How myghty and how great a lord is he!
> CHAUCER: *Knight's Tale*, 927.

Benedick, or **Benedict**. A sworn bachelor caught in the snares of matrimony; from Benedick in SHAKESPEARE'S *Much Ado about Nothing*.

Benedictines. Monks who follow the rule of St. Benedict of Nursia (*c.* 480–*c.* 553), also known as the "Black Monks". Monte Cassino became their chief centre and they were renowned for their learning.

Benefice. Under the Romans certain grants of land made to veteran soldiers were called *beneficia*, and in early feudal times an estate held for life, in return for military service, was called a *benefice*. The term came to be applied to the possessions of the Church held by individuals as a recompense for their services. Hence a church "living".

Benefit of Clergy. Formerly, the privilege enjoyed by the English clergy of trial in an ecclesiastical court, where punishments were less harsh than in the secular courts, and where bishops could not impose the death penalty. A clerk came to be identified with one who could read the NECK VERSE. By an Act of Henry IV's reign, no woman was to suffer death for circumstances in which a man could "plead his clergy", and a blind man could avoid the rope if able to speak Latin "congruously". Benefit of clergy was steadily curtailed from the time of Henry VII and by the end of the 17th century most of the serious crimes were excluded, but it was not totally abolished until 1827.

Benefit Societies. *See* FRIENDLY SOCIETIES.

Benevolence. A royal expedient for raising money without consent of PARLIAMENT. First so called in 1473, when Edward IV raised such a forced loan as a mark of goodwill towards his reign. Last levied by James I in 1622, it was declared illegal by the BILL OF RIGHTS, 1689.

Bengodi (ben gō' di). A "land of COCKAIGNE" mentioned in Boccaccio's *Decameron* (viii, 3), where "they tie the vines with sausages, where you may buy a fat goose for a penny and have a gosling into the bargain; where there is also a mountain of grated Parmesan cheese, and people do nothing but make cheese-cakes and macaroons. There is also a river which runs MALMSEY wine of the very best quality," etc., etc.

Benjamin. The pet, the youngest; in allusion to Benjamin, the youngest son of Jacob (*Gen.* xxxv, 18). Also (in early and mid-19th century), an overcoat, so called from a tailor of this name, and rendered popular by its association with JOSEPH'S "coat of many colours".

Benjamin's mess. The largest share. The allusion is to the banquet given by Joseph, viceroy of Egypt, to his brethren. "Benjamin's mess was five times so much as any of theirs" (*Gen.* xliii, 34).

Benjamin tree. A tree of the Styrax family that yields benzoin, of which the name is a corruption. Friar's Balsam or Jesuit's Drops is compounded from its juice.

Beowulf (bā' ō wulf). The hero of the Old English epic poem of the same name of unknown date and authorship, but certainly originally written before the Saxons came to England and modified subsequent to the introduction of Christianity. In its present form, it probably dates from the 8th century. It is the oldest epic in English and also in the whole Teutonic group of languages.

The scene is laid in Denmark or Sweden; the hall of King Hrothgar is raided nightly by GRENDEL, whom Beowulf mortally wounds after a fierce fight. Next night Grendel's mother comes to avenge his death. Beowulf pursues her to her lair under the water and slays her with a magic sword. He eventually becomes king and fifty years later is killed in combat with a DRAGON, which had ravished the land.

Berchta. A goddess of South German mythology akin to the HULDA of North Germany, but after the introduction of Christianity she was degraded into a BOGY to frighten children. She was sometimes represented with a long iron nose and one large foot. *See* BERTHA; WHITE LADY.

Berchtesgaden. A charmingly situated resort in Bavaria known for its salt mines, royal castle and abbey but subsequently for Adolf Hitler's strongly guarded and fortified retreat. His mountain villa could only be entered by an elevator and then a tunnel hewn through the rock.

Berecynthian Hero. MIDAS, the mythological king of Phrygia; so called from Mount Berecynthus in Phrygia.

Berenice. The wife of Ptolemy III Euergetes (246–221 B.C.). She vowed to sacrifice her hair to the gods, if her husband returned home the vanquisher of Asia. She suspended her hair in the temple, but it was stolen the first night and Conon of Samos told the king that the winds had wafted it to heaven, where it still forms the seven stars near the tail of LEO, called *Coma Berenices*.

Bergomask (ber' gō mask). A rustic dance (*see Midsummer Night's Dream*, V, i); so called from Bergamo, a Venetian province, whose inhabitants were noted for their clownishness. Also a CLOWN.

Berlin. A four-wheeled carriage with a hooded seat behind. It was introduced into England by a German officer about 1670.

Bermoothes (bĕr mō ooth' ēz). The name of the island in *The Tempest*, feigned by SHAKESPEARE to be enchanted and inhabited by WITCHES and DEVILS. He almost certainly had the newly discovered Bermudas in mind.

Bermuda Triangle. The triangular sea area between Bermuda, Florida and Puerto Rico where the currents are very strong. It gained notoriety in the 1960s on account of the disappearance of numerous ships and aircraft without any trace of wreckage.

Bernard, St. (1090–1153). Abbot of Clairvaux. Renowned for his wisdom and abilities, he did much to promote the growth of the Cistercian Order, and exercised great influence in Church matters. He was nicknamed the "MELLI-FLUOUS DOCTOR".

Bernardine. A monk of the Order of

ST. BERNARD of Clairvaux; a CISTERCIAN.

Bonus Bernardus non videt omnia. The good Bernard does not see everything. We are all apt to forget sometimes; events do not always turn out according to plan. *Cp.* HOMER SOMETIMES NODS.

Bernardo del Carpio. A semi-mythical Spanish hero of the 9th century and a favourite subject of minstrels. Lope de Vega wrote several plays around his exploits. He is credited with having defeated ROLAND at Roncesvalles.

Bernesque Poetry. Serio-comic poetry; so called from Francesco Berni (*c.* 1497–1536), the Italian cleric and poet who greatly excelled in it. BYRON'S *Beppo* is a good example of English bernesque, with reference to which he wrote to John Murray, his publisher:

> Whistlecraft is my immediate model, but Berni is the father of that kind of writing.

Berserk, Berserker. In Scandinavian mythology, the sons of Berserk, grandson of the eight-handed Starkadder and Alfhilde. The name probably means bear-sark, or bear-coat. Berserk always fought ferociously and recklessly, without armour. Hence *berserk* for a savage and reckless fighter, one with the fighting fever on him.

Berth. He has fallen into a good berth. A good situation or fortune. Nautically, a good berth is one that is safe and favourable.

To give a wide berth. Not to come near a person; to keep at a safe distance from; literally to give a ship plenty of room to swing at anchor.

Bertha. A German impersonation of the EPIPHANY with some of the attributes of BERCHTA, and corresponding to the Italian BEFANA. She is a WHITE LADY, who steals softly into nurseries and rocks infants to sleep, but is the terror of all naughty children.

Berthe au Grand Pied (bert ō gronpē ā'). Mother of CHARLEMAGNE, and great-granddaughter of Charles Martel; she had a club-foot and died in 783.

Besaile. A word once used in England for a great-grandfather; it is the French *bisaïeul*.

Besant. *See* BEZANT.

Beside the Cushion. An odd phrase first used by Judge Jeffreys in the sense of "beside the question", "not to the point".

Besom. Jumping the besom. Omitting the marriage service after the publication of BANNS, and living together as man and wife. In Lowland Scots, *besom* is a name applied to a prostitute or woman of low character.

To hang out the besom. To have a fling when your wife is gone on a visit.

Bess, Good Queen. Queen Elizabeth I (1533–1603).

Bess o'Bedlam. A female lunatic vagrant. *See* BEDLAM.

Bess of Hardwick. Elizabeth Talbot, Countess of Shrewsbury (1518–1608), to whose husband's charge Mary Queen of Scots was committed in 1569. The countess treated the captive queen harshly, through real or feigned jealousy of her husband. Known as "building Bess of Hardwick", she built Hardwick Hall, Oldcotes, Worksop, Bolsover, and completed Chatsworth.

Black Bess. Dick Turpin's mythical but celebrated mare, created by Harrison Ainsworth in his romance *Rookwood* (1834), particularly known for Dick's famous ride to York. *See* TURPIN.

Bessie with the braid apron. *See* BELTED WILL.

Best. At best, or **At the very best.** Looking at the matter in the most favourable light. Making every allowance.

> Man is a short-sighted creature at best.
> DEFOE: *Colonel Jack*.

At one's best. On top form in all respects.

For the best. With the best of motives; with the view of obtaining the best results.

To best somebody. To get the better of him; to outwit him and so have the advantage.

To have the best of it, or **to have the best bargain.** To have the advantage or best of a transaction.

To make the best of the matter. To submit to ill-luck with the best grace in your power.

Best Man (at a wedding). The bridegroom's chosen friend who waits on him as the bridesmaids wait on the bride.

Bestiaries, or **Bestials.** Books which had a great vogue between the 11th and 14th centuries, describing the supposed habits and peculiarities of animals both real and fabled, with much legendary lore and moral symbolism. They were founded on the *Physiologi* of earlier centuries and those in English were mostly translations of continental originals. Among the most popular were those of Philippe de Thaun, Guillaume le Clerc, and Richard de Fournival's satirical *Bestiaire d'Amour* (*c*. 1250).

Bête Noire (bāt nwar) (Fr. black beast). The thorn in the side, the bitter in the cup, the SPOKE IN THE WHEEL, the BLACK SHEEP, one's pet aversion.

Beth Gelert. *See* BEDDGELERT.

Bethel (Heb. house of God). A hallowed place where God is worshipped (see *Gen*. xxviii, 18, 19). The name has frequently been given to Nonconformist chapels, especially in Wales, and also to religious meeting houses for seamen.

Better. Better off. In easier circumstances.

For better for worse. Forever. From the English marriage service, expressive of indissoluble union.

My better half. My wife. As the twain are one, each is half. Horace calls his friend *animæ dimidium meæ* (*Odes* I, iii, 8).

No better than he or **she should be.** A phrase of disparagement implying immorality or an amoral character.

To be better than his word. To do more than he promised.

To think better of the matter. To give it further consideration; to form a more correct opinion respecting it, and usually to revise one's intentions as a result.

Betubium (be tū' bi um). The old poetic name for the Cape of St. Andrew, Scotland.

> The north-inflated tempest foams
> O'er Orka's and Betubium's highest peak.
> THOMSON: *Autumn*, 891, 2.

Between. Between hay and grass Between. Neither one thing nor yet another; a hobbledehoy, neither a man nor yet a boy.

Between cup and lip. *See* SLIP.

Between Scylla and Charybdis. Between equal dangers. *See* CHARYBDIS; SCYLLA. *Cp.* HOBSON'S CHOICE.

Between the devil and the deep (blue) sea. Similar in use to BETWEEN SCYLLA AND CHARYBDIS. *See under* DEVIL.

Between two fires. Between two dangers as soldiers caught between fire from opposite sides.

Between two stools, you fall to the ground. As when accidentally, or as the victim of a practical joke, you miss both stools and fall to the ground. To miss both chances through hesitance or indecision.

Between you and me. In confidence. Alternatively, **Between you and me and the gatepost**, or **bed-post**; between ourselves. Often an indication that some gossip or slander about a third person is to follow.

Betwixt and between. Neither one nor the other, but somewhere between the two. Thus, grey is neither white nor black, but *betwixt and between* the two.

Betwixt wind and water. In a most dangerous spot. The phrase refers to that part of a sailing ship's hull around the waterline, which is alternately wet and dry according to the motion of both ship and waves. A dangerous place for a ship to be holed.

Beulah. *See* LAND OF BEULAH.

Bevin Boys. Nickname for the young men directed to work in coal mines under the Emergency Powers (Defence) Act (1940). Ernest Bevin (1881–1951) was Minister of Labour and National Service at the time.

Bevis (bē′ vis). In Scott's *Marmion*, Lord Marmion's red-roan charger.

Bevoriskius (be vôr is′ ki ùs), whose *Commentary on the Generations of Adam* is referred to by Sterne in the *Sentimental Journey*, was Johan van Beverwyck (1594–1647), a Dutch physician and author.

Bevy. A throng or company of ladies, roebucks, quails, or larks. The word is the Italian *beva*, a drink; possibly it acquired this meaning because timid, gregarious animals go down to the river to drink in company. Ladies in former times were regarded as timid creatures.

Bezant (be zănt′) (from Byzantium, the old name of Constantinople, now Istanbul). A gold coin of varying value struck by the Byzantine Emperors and current in England until the time of Edward III. In HERALDRY the name is given to a plain gold ROUNDEL on the shield.

Bezoar (bē′ zōr). A stone from the stomach or gall-bladder of an animal (usually goats and antelopes), set as a jewel and believed to be an antidote against poison. The word is of Persian origin (*pad-zahr*) and means "counter-poison".

Bezonian (be zō′ ni àn). A raw recruit; applied originally in derision to young, ill-equipped soldiers sent from Spain to the Italian Wars, who arrived in want of everything (Ital. *bisogni*, from *bisogno*, need; Fr. *besoin*). Hence a beggar, a knave, etc.

> Great men oft die by vile bezonians.
> SHAKESPEARE: *Henry VI, Pt. II*, IV, i.

Bhagavad Gita (The Song of the Blessed). One of the great religious and philosophical poems of India which occurs in the sixth book of the MAHABHARATA. In it, KRISHNA, in the form of a charioteer, instructs Arjuna, chief of the Pandus, in his duties and elaborates his ethical and pantheistic philosophy, finally revealing himself as the Supreme Being.

Bianchi (bē äng′ ki) (It. the Whites). In 1300 the GUELPH family in Florence split into two factions, "Whites" and "Blacks" (Neri). The Bianchi, among whom Dante was prominent, allied with their GHIBELLINE opponents. After the triumph of the Neri in 1301, Dante was exiled from Florence.

Bib. Best bib and tucker. *See* TUCKER.

Biberius Caldius Mero. The punning nickname of Tiberius Claudius Nero (Roman Emperor, A.D. 14–37). Biberius (Tiberius) drink-loving, Caldius Mero (Claudius Nero), by METATHESIS for *calidus mero*, hot with wine.

Bible. The word is derived from the Greek *Ta Biblia* through mediæval Latin and means *The Books*. *See* APOCRYPHA; DEAD SEA SCROLLS; NEW TESTAMENT; OLD TESTAMENT; PENTATEUCH; PSALMS; PSEUDEPIGRAPHA; "Q"; SEPTUAGINT; VULGATE.

Bible, The English. The principal versions in chronological order are:

Wyclif's Bible. The name given to two translations of the VULGATE. The earlier one completed c. 1384 is the first complete English Bible, although there were renderings of parts of the Scriptures from Anglo-Saxon times. Wyclif may have translated parts of it and one of his circle, Nicholas of Hereford, is known to have participated. The second and improved version, probably written between 1395 and 1397, is considered to owe much to John Purvey, a LOLLARD scholar. As a whole it remained unprinted until a monumental edition of both versions, prepared by Forshall and Madden, appeared in 1850.

Tyndale's Bible. This consists of the New Testament printed at Cologne in 1525 (Revisions 1534 and 1535); the PENTATEUCH, printed at Marburg, 1530; the Book of Jonah, 1531; Epistles of the Old Testament (after the Use of Salisbury), 1534; and a MS. translation of the Old Testament to the end of Chronicles, which was afterwards used in MATTHEW'S BIBLE. His work was chiefly based on Greek originals, while making use of the Greek and Latin versions of the New Testament by Erasmus, Luther's Bible, and the VULGATE. His work fixed the language of subsequent English versions.

Coverdale's Bible. This first printed edition of a complete English Bible appeared in 1535, translated "out of Douche (German) and Latyn", by Miles Coverdale. It was based on Luther, the ZÜRICH BIBLE, the VULGATE, the Latin version of Pagninus, and Tyndale. The first edition was probably printed at Zürich, the second was printed by Nicolson at Southwark in 1537 (the first Bible printed in England).

Matthew's Bible. Printed in Antwerp in 1537 as the translation of Thomas Matthew, most probably an alias, for self-preservation, of John Rogers, an assistant of Tyndale. It is essentially made up from the work of Tyndale and Coverdale. Like Coverdale's third edition it appeared under the King's licence, but was soon superseded by the GREAT BIBLE. It is important as a basis of the approved editions which culminated in the AUTHORIZED VERSION. See BUG BIBLE.

Taverner's Bible. A revision of MATTHEW'S BIBLE by Richard Taverner printed in 1539, notable for its idiomatic English.

The Great Bible. Published by Grafton and Whitchurch in 1539 as an authorized Bible sponsored by Cranmer and Cromwell, being a revision by Coverdale substantially based on MATTHEW'S BIBLE.

Cromwell's Bible. The GREAT BIBLE of 1539. The title-page includes a portrait of Thomas Cromwell, under whose direction the Bible was commissioned.

Cranmer's Bible. The name given to the 1540 edition of the GREAT BIBLE. It and later issues contained a prologue by Cranmer, and, on the woodcut title-page by Holbein, Henry VIII is shown seated handing copies to Cranmer and Cromwell. Its Psalter is still incorporated in the BOOK OF COMMON PRAYER.

The Geneva Bible. An important revision in the development of the English Bible, undertaken by English exiles in Geneva during the Marian persecutions, first published in 1560; largely the work of William Whittingham, assisted by Anthony Gilby and Thomas Sampson. Whittingham had previously (1557) published a translation of the New Testament. Based on the GREAT BIBLE, MATTHEW'S BIBLE, etc., it was the first English Bible to be printed in roman type instead of black letter, in QUARTO size, and the first in which the chapters were divided into verses.

The Bishops' Bible. A revision of the GREAT BIBLE to counter the growing popularity of the GENEVA BIBLE. Organized by Archbishop Matthew Parker, it appeared in 1568 and was the basis of the AUTHORIZED VERSION. See TREACLE BIBLE.

Matthew Parker's Bible. THE BISHOPS' BIBLE.

The Douai Bible (dou' ā). A translation of the VULGATE by English Roman Catholics. The New Testament was published at the English College at Rheims in 1582, the Old Testament at

Douai in 1609; hence called the **Rheims and Douai version.** *See* ROSIN BIBLE.

The Authorized Version. This version, still in general use in England, was produced by some 47 scholars, working at the command of King James I, and was a by-product of the HAMPTON COURT CONFERENCE. Begun in 1607 and published in 1611, since 1984 it has been published as the *Authorized King James Version*.

King James's Bible. The AUTHORIZED VERSION.

The Revised Version. This revision of the AUTHORIZED VERSION resulted from a resolution passed by Houses of Convocation in 1870. It was the work of two companies of English scholars, with American co-operators. The New Testament appeared in 1881 the Old Testament in 1885, and the APOCRYPHA in 1895.

The American Standard Version (1901). Essentially a modification of the Revised Version of 1881.

The New Testament in Modern Speech (1903). A new translation from the Greek by R. F. Weymouth.

Knox Version. A new Roman Catholic translation of the VULGATE by Monsignor R.A. Knox.

The Revised Standard Version. The work of American scholars issued between 1946 and 1952. It was to embody the results of modern scholarship "and to be in the diction of the simple classic English style of the King James version".

The New Testament in Modern English. A translation by J.B. Phillips aiming at clarity of expression, first published in 1958 with a revised version in 1973.

The New English Bible. A translation into contemporary English first proposed by the CHURCH OF SCOTLAND and directed by a joint committee of the PROTESTANT Churches of Great Britain and Ireland. The N.T. appeared in 1961 and the translations of the O.T. and the APOCRYPHA were finished in 1966. The complete bible was published in 1970. The 1989 edition was revised to eliminate "sexist language" such as *man*, *sons*, *brothers*, etc.

The Jerusalem Bible. A new translation of the Bible, prepared from the ancient originals by Roman Catholic scholars, largely in contemporary English. First published in 1966, it derives its notes and introduction from the French *La Bible de Jérusalem*.

The Revised Standard Version Common Bible. Published in 1973, based on both the Protestant and Roman Catholic (1966) editions of the REVISED STANDARD VERSION, and intended for interdenominational use.

The Good News Bible: Today's English Version. An illustrated version, produced by the American Bible Society, designed to be easily understood, including by those whose first language is not English. The N.T. was published in 1966 and the complete Bible in 1976.

The New International Version. A new translation, the work of an Anglo-American team seeking to present a modernized version in good English. First published by the New York Bible Society in 1978 followed by a British edition in 1979.

The Adulterous Bible. The WICKED BIBLE.

The Affinity Bible, of 1923, which contains a table of affinity with the error, "A man may not marry his grandmother's wife."

The Bad Bible. A printing of 1653 with a deliberate perversion of *Acts* vi, 6, whereby the ordination of deacons was ascribed to the disciples and not to the apostles.

The Bear Bible. The Spanish Protestant version printed at Basle in 1569; so called because the woodcut device on the title-page is of a bear.

Bedell's Bible. An Irish translation of the Old Testament carried out under the direction of Bishop William Bedell (1571–1642).

The Breeches Bible. The popular name for the GENEVA BIBLE because in it *Gen*. iii, 7, was rendered, "and they sowed figge-tree leaves together, and made themselves breeches."

The Brothers' Bible. The KRALITZ BIBLE.

The Bug Bible. COVERDALE'S BIBLE of 1535 is so called because *Ps*. xci, 5, is

Bible

translated: "Thou shalt not nede to be afrayed for eny bugges by night."

Camel's Bible, of 1823. *Gen.* xxiv, 61, reads: "And Rebekah arose, and her camels (for *damsels*)."

Complutensian Polyglot. Published between 1514 and 1517 at Alcalá (the ancient Complutum), near Madrid, at the expense of Cardinal Ximenes. In six FOLIO volumes, it contains the Hebrew and Greek texts, the Septuagint, the VULGATE, and the Chaldee paraphrase of the PENTATEUCH with a Latin translation, together with Greek and Hebrew grammars and a Hebrew dictionary.

The Denial Bible. Printed at Oxford in 1792, in *Luke* xxii, 34, the name *Philip* is substituted for *Peter*, as the apostle who should deny Jesus.

The Discharge Bible. An edition of 1806 containing *discharge* for *charge* in I *Tim.* v, 21: "I dis-charge thee before God, ... that thou observe these things."

The Ears to Ear Bible. An edition of 1810, in which *Matt.* xiii, 43, reads: "Who hath ears to *ear*, let him hear."

The Ferrara Bible. The first Spanish edition of the Old Testament (1553) for the use of Spanish Jews.

The Fool Bible. An edition of Charles I's reign in which *Psalm* xiv, 1, reads: "The fool hath said in his heart there is a God." (instead of *no god*).

The Forgotten Sins Bible, of 1638. *Luke* vii, 47, reads: "Her sins which are many, are forgotten (instead of *forgiven*)."

The Forty-two-line Bible. The MAZARIN BIBLE.

The Goose Bible. The editions of the GENEVA BIBLE printed at Dort: the Dort press had a goose for its device.

The Gutenberg Bible. The MAZARIN BIBLE.

The He Bible. In the first of the two editions of the AUTHORIZED VERSION in 1611, known as "the He Bible", *Ruth* iii, 15, reads: "and he went into the city." The other, and nearly all modern editions (except the REVISED VERSION) have "she". "He" is the correct translation of the Hebrew.

The Idle Bible. An edition of 1809, in which "the idol shepherd" (*Zech.* xi, 17) is printed "the idle shepherd".

The Incunabula Bible. The date on the title page reads 1495 instead of 1594. The word INCUNABULA came to be applied to all books printed before 1500, the period when typography was in its "swaddling-clothes", or its beginnings.

The Indian Bible. The first complete Bible printed in America, translated into the dialect of the Indians of Massachusetts by the Rev. John Eliot and published by Samuel Green and Marmaduke Johnson in 1663.

Judas Bible, of 1611. *Matt.* xxvi, 36, reads "Judas" instead of "Jesus".

The Kralitz Bible, also called the *Brothers' Bible*, was published by the United Brethren of Moravia at Kralitz, 1579–1593.

The "Large Family" Bible. An Oxford edition of 1820 prints *Isaiah* lxvi, 9: "Shall I bring to the birth and not cease (for *cause*) to bring forth?"

The Leda Bible. The third edition (second folio) of the BISHOPS' BIBLE, published in 1572, and so called from the decoration of the initial at the Epistle to the Hebrews which is a startling and incongruous woodcut of JUPITER visiting LEDA in the guise of a swan.

The Leopolita Bible. A Polish translation of the VULGATE by John of Lemberg (Jan Nicz of Lwów) published at Cracow in 1561. So called from the Latin name, *Leopolis*, of his birthplace.

The Lions Bible. A Bible issued in 1804 containing many printers' errors such as: I *Kings* viii, 19, "but thy son that shall come forth out of thy lions (for *loins*)".

The Mazarin Bible. The first known book to be printed from movable type, probably by Fust and Schöffer at Mainz, who took over most of Gutenberg's presses in 1455. This edition of the VULGATE was on sale in 1456 and owes its name to the copy discovered in the Mazarin Library in Paris in 1760. It was for long credited to Gutenberg and is frequently called the **Gutenberg Bible**. It is usually known to bibliographers as the **Forty-two-line Bible** (it having 42 lines to the column) to differentiate it from the THIRTY-SIX-LINE BIBLE.

The Murderers' Bible. An edition of

1801 in which *Jude* 16 reads: "These are murderers (for *murmurers*), complainers", *etc*.

The Placemaker's Bible. The second edition of the GENEVA BIBLE, 1562. *Matt*. v, 9, reads: "Blessed are the placemakers (peacemakers). It has also been called the WHIG BIBLE.

The Printers' Bible. An edition of about 1702 which makes David complain that "printers (princes) have persecuted me without a cause". (*Ps*. cxix, 161.)

The Proof Bible (Probe-Bibel). The revised version of the first impression of Luther's German Bible.

The Rosin Bible. The DOUAI BIBLE, 1609, is so called because it has in *Jer*. viii, 22: "Is there noe rosin in Galaad?" The AUTHORIZED VERSION translates the word by "balm".

Sacy's Bible. A French translation by the JANSENIST, Louis Isaac le Maistre de Sacy, director of PORT ROYAL (1650–1679). He began his work when imprisoned in the BASTILLE.

Schelhorn's Bible. The THIRTY-SIX-LINE BIBLE.

The September Bible. Luther's German translation of the New Testament, published anonymously at Wittenberg in September 1522.

The She Bible. *See* HE BIBLE.

"Sin on" Bible. The first printed in Ireland was dated 1716. *John* v,14, reads: "sin on more", instead of "sin no more". The mistake was undiscovered until 8,000 copies had been printed and bound.

The Standing Fishes Bible. An edition of 1806 in which *Ezek*. xlvii, 10, reads: "And it shall come to pass that the fishes (fishers) shall stand upon it," *etc*.

The Sting Bible of 1746. *Mark* vii, 35, "the sting of his tongue", instead of "string".

The Thirty-six-line Bible. A Latin Bible of 36 lines to the column, probably printed by A. Pfister at Bamberg in 1460. It is also known as the Bamberg, and Pfister's, Bible and sometimes as Schelhorn's, as it was first described by the German bibliographer J. G. Schelhorn, in 1760.

The Treacle Bible. A popular name for the BISHOPS' BIBLE, 1568, because *Jer*. viii, 22, reads: "is there no tryacle in Gilead, is there no phisition there?"

The Unrighteous Bible. A Cambridge printing of 1653 contains: "know ye not that the unrighteous shall inherit the Kingdom of God?", instead of "shall not inherit" (I *Cor*. vi, 9). This edition is also sometimes known as the WICKED BIBLE.

The Vinegar Bible. An Oxford printing of 1717 in which part of the chapter heading to *Luke* xx reads: "The parable of the Vinegar" (for *Vineyard*).

The Whig Bible. Another name for the PLACEMAKERS' BIBLE. The jibe is obvious. *See* PLACEMEN.

The Wicked Bible. So called because the word "not" was omitted in the seventh commandment (*Exod*. xx, 14) making it, "Thou shalt commit adultery." It was printed by Barker and Lucas, the King's printers at Blackfriars in 1631. It is also called the *Adulterous Bible*. *See* UNRIGHTEOUS BIBLE.

Wujek's Bible. An authorized Polish translation by the Jesuit, Jacub Wujek, printed at Cracow in 1599.

The Zürich Bible. A German version of 1530 composed of Luther's translation of the New Testament and portions of the Old, with the remainder and the APOCRYPHA by other translators.

Bible, Statistics of. The following statistics are those given in the *Introduction to the Critical Study and Knowledge of the Bible*, by Thos. Hartwell Horne, D.D., first published in 1818. They apply to the English AUTHORIZED VERSION.

	O.T.	N.T.	Total
Books	39	27	66
Chapters	929	260	1,189
Verses	23,214	7,959	31,173
Words	593,493	181,253	774,746
Letters	2,728,100	838,380	3,566,480

APOCRYPHA. Books, 14; chapters, 183; verses, 6,031; words, 125,185; letters, 1,063,876.

	O.T.	N.T.
Middle book	*Proverbs*	*II Thess.*
Middle Chapter	*Job* xxix	*Rom*. xiii and xiv
Middle verse	II *Chron*. xx, 17 & 18	*Acts* xvii, 17
Shortest verse	I *Chron*. i, 25	*John* xi, 35

Shortest chapter   *Psalm* cxvii
Longest chapter   *Psalm* cxix

Ezra vii, 21, contains all the letters of the alphabet except j.

II *Kings* xix and *Isaiah* xxxvii are exactly alike.

The last two verses of II *Chron.* and the opening verses of *Ezra* are alike.

Ezra ii and *Nehemiah* vii are alike.

The word *and* occurs in the O.T. 35,543 times, and in the N.T. 10,684 times.

The word *Jehovah* occurs 6,855 times, and *Lord* 1,855 times.

About thirty books are mentioned in the Bible, but not included in the canon.

In addition it is noteworthy that by the end of 1965 the United Bible Societies had circulated the Scriptures in 1,251 languages.

Bible-backed. Round-shouldered, like one who is always poring over a book.

Bible belt. In the U.S.A. the south central Mid-west, south of the MASON AND DIXON line reputedly associated with puritanism and religious fundamentalism.

Bible-carrier. A scornful term for an obtrusively pious person.

Bible Christians. An evangelical sect founded in 1815 by William O'Bryan, a Cornish METHODIST; also called Bryanites. The movement grew steadily, beginning in the fishing and farming districts of Devon and Cornwall. They joined the United Methodist Church in 1907.

Bible-Clerk. A student at Oxford or Cambridge who formerly got pecuniary advantages for reading the Bible at chapel, etc.

Bible-puncher. A modern equivalent of BIBLE-CARRIER.

Biblia Pauperum (Lat., poor man's Bible). A MISNOMER coined long after the first appearance in the 1460s of these late mediæval BLOCK BOOKS. They contain a series of NEW TESTAMENT scenes from the life of Christ, each surrounded by their OLD TESTAMENT antetypes, and with a brief text engraved in the same block below the illustration. Despite their name, the *Biblia Pauperum* can hardly have been intended for the illiterate, their iconography and text being replete with allegory and symbol, and must rather have served itinerant preachers and the lower orders of clergy. *See* SPECULUM HUMANÆ SALVATIO-NIS.

Bibliomancy. DIVINATION by means of the Bible. *See* SORTES.

Bibulus. Colleague of Julius Caesar, a mere cipher in office; hence proverbial for one in office who is a mere *fainéant*.

Bickerstaff, Isaac. A name assumed by Dean Swift in a satirical pamphlet against Partridge, the ALMANAC-maker.

Bicorn (bī kôrn). A mythical beast, fabled by the early French romancers to grow very fat through living on good and enduring husbands. It was the antitype of CHICHEVACHE.

Bi-corn (two-horns) contains an allusion to the horned CUCKOLD.

Bid. To bid fair. To seem likely; as "He bids fair to do well"; "It bids fair to be a fine day".

To bid for (votes). To promise to support certain measures in PARLIAMENT in order to obtain votes.

To bid against one. To offer a higher price for an article at auction.

I bid you good night. I wish you good night, or I pray that you may have a good night.

Neither bid him God speed.
II *John* 10.

To bid one's beads. To tell off one's prayers by beads. *See* BEAD; ROSARY.

To bid the (marriage) banns. To ask if anyone objects to the marriage of the persons named. *Cp.* SI QUIS.

To bid to the wedding. To ask to the wedding feast.

Bid-ale (or **Help-ale**). A gathering to drink ALE and to collect for the relief of some poor man or other charity. They frequently became an excuse for excessive conviviality.

There was an ancient custom called a Bidale or Bidder-ale... when any honest man decayed in his estate was set up again by the liberal benevolence and contributions of friends at a feast to which those friends were bid or invited. It was most used in the West of England, and in some counties called a Help-ale.
BRAND: *Popular Antiquities* (1777).

Bidding-prayer (O.E. *biddan; see* BID). In the CHURCH OF ENGLAND this term is now commonly applied to a prayer for the souls of benefactors said before the sermon, in cathedrals, university churches, and on special occasions. It stems from the pre-REFORMATION vernacular prayer of the "bidding of the beads". "Bidding" was here used in the sense of "praying" and the priest told the people what to remember in their prayers. By the time of Elizabeth I the "bidding of prayers" came to mean the "directing" or "enjoining" of prayers, hence the modern meaning.

Biddy (*i.e.* Bridget). A generic name for an Irish servant-maid. Such names were once very common: for example: JACK TAR, a sailor; TOMMY Atkins, a soldier; *See* NICKNAME.

Biddy also denotes a hen; sometimes *chick-a-biddy*, and also, in English dialect, a louse. In Australia it denotes a female teacher.

> The English hens had a contented cluck as if they never got nervous like Yankee biddies.
>
> L. M. ALCOTT: *Little Wives*.

Old Biddy. A term applied to an elderly woman who is somewhat of a busybody.

Bidpay. *See* PILPAY.

Bifrost (Icel. *bifa*, tremble; *rost*, path). In Scandinavian mythology, the bridge between HEAVEN and earth, ASGARD and MIDGARD. The rainbow may be considered to be this bridge, and its various colours are the reflections of its precious stones. HEIMDALL is its keeper.

Big. To look big. To assume a consequential air.

To talk big. To boast or brag.

Big Bang (in the City of LONDON). The deregulation of the STOCK EXCHANGE, the removal of fixed commissions charged by stockbrokers and the merging of the functions of STOCKJOBBER and STOCKBROKER operating with negotiated rates of commission. Foreign investment companies may now join the Stock Exchange and also own British brokers and jobbers. The intention was to maintain London's position as a leading international financial centre. It took place on 26 Oct. 1986 and its long term effects remain to be seen.

Big Bang (in cosmology). The theoretical origin of the universe. It presupposes that a very small fireball of an extraordinary high temperature was formed and when this exploded (the Big Bang) the result was the formation of the universe.

Big Ben. Properly, the famous hour bell in the Clock Tower (St. Stephen's Tower) of the Houses of PARLIAMENT, which came to be so called after Sir Benjamin Hall who was Chief Commissioner of Works at the time. The original casting of 1856, weighing some 15 tons, when being tested in Palace Yard developed serious cracks and was scrapped. The new bell weighing *c*. 13 tons was installed in October 1858. This also developed a crack, but of a less serious nature. There are also four Quarter bells whose weight varies between *c*. 4 tons and 1 ton. The clock as a whole is popularly and generally now called "Big Ben".

Big Bertha. The name given by the French to the large howitzers used by the Germans against Liége and Namur in 1914. In reality made at the Skoda works, they were mistakenly thought to be a product of the famous German armament firm, hence the allusion to Frau Bertha Krupp. In American slang "Big Bertha" means a fat woman.

Big bird, To get the (*i.e.* the goose). To be hissed; to receive one's *congé*; originally a theatrical expression. Today the usual phrase is "to get the bird".

Big Brother is watching you. Authority, totalitarian and bureaucratic, has you under its observation from which there is no escape. One of the telling phrases from George Orwell's *Nineteen Eighty-Four* (1949). The allusion is to the U.S.S.R. but its application is not without significance in other modern states.

Big-endians. In Swift's *Gulliver's Travels*, a party in the empire of Lilliput who made it a matter of conscience to break their eggs at the *big end*; they were looked on as heretics by the orthodox party, who broke theirs at the *little end*. The *Big-endians* typify the CATHOLICS and the *Little-endians* the PROTESTANTS.

Big Gooseberry Season, The. The "SILLY SEASON", the dead season, when newspapers are glad of any subject to fill their columns; monster gooseberries will do for such a purpose.

Big head. A conceited person.

Big House. American slang for a prison. Also the name given to the large structure formerly erected by the Delaware Indians for their twelve-night ceremony to propitiate the Great Spirit (*see* MANITOU).

Big nob. Big noise. *See* BIG-WIG.

Big shot. *See* BIG-WIG.

Big Smoke, The. One of the nicknames of London, more commonly "the SMOKE"; also of Sydney, N.S.W. *Cp.* AULD REEKIE.

Big stick diplomacy. Backing negotiations or policy with the threat of military force. The term was popularized by Theodore Roosevelt's declaration in 1900 that he had always been fond of the West African proverb "speak softly and carry a big stick".

Big Triangle. A sailorman's term denoting the round trip frequently made by sailing ships from a British port to Australia, thence with New South Wales coal to South America, and back home with a cargo of nitrates.

Big-wig. A person in authority, an important person. The term arises from the custom of judges and BISHOPS, and so on, wearing large WIGS.

Bight (bīt). **To hook the bight**—*i.e.* to get entangled. A nautical term; the bight is the loop or doubled part of a rope, and when the fluke of one anchor gets into the bight of another's cable it is "hooked".

Bikini. This atoll in the Marshall Islands, the scene of American nuclear weapon testing in 1946 (and 1954), has given its name to a scanty two-piece bathing outfit worn by women, apparently from the devastating effects of the atomic explosion and the overpowering effect of the costume.

Bilbo. A rapier or sword. So called from Bilbao, in Spain, once famous for its finely tempered blades.

Bilboes. A bar of iron with sliding fetters attached to it, by which mutinous sailors or prisoners were linked together. Possibly derived from Bilbao where they may have been first made. Some of the bilboes from the Spanish Armada are kept in the TOWER of London.

Bile. It rouses my bile. It makes me angry or indignant. According to ancient theory, bile is a HUMOUR of the body and black bile is indicative of melancholy. When excited abnormally, bile was supposed to produce choler or rage.

Bilge-water. Stale dregs; bad beer; any distasteful or nauseating drink. The bilge is the inside or curve of the ship immediately above the keel, where the rain or seawater collects and becomes foul. In slang *bilge* means worthless stuff or rubbish.

Bilk. Originally a term in cribbage meaning to spoil your adversary's score, to BALK him; perhaps the two words are mere variants.

It now usually means to cheat, to obtain goods and depart without paying.

Bill. The nose, also called the *beak*. Hence *billy* is slang for a pocket-handkerchief.

Bill, A. The draft of an ACT OF PARLIAMENT. When a Bill is passed and receives the royal assent it becomes an Act.

A Private Member's Bill is a public bill introduced by a private member as distinct from a member of the Government. Few reach the STATUTE Book.

A True Bill. Under the old judicial system before a case went to the Criminal Assizes it was examined by the Grand Jury. If they decided that there was enough evidence to justify a trial they were said "to find a true bill"; if they decided to the contrary they were said to ignore the bill and it was endorsed *ignoramus*. Hence *to find a true bill* is a colloquial way of saying that something after examination can go forward as true.

Bill of Attainder. In mediæval England felons under sentence of death, outlaws, etc., were *attainted* and subject to forfeiture of goods, etc. Bills of Attainder were used for arbitrarily destroying political enemies of the government, for criminal offences against the State and public peace, PARLIAMENT acting as both judge and jury. First introduced in 1549, the last Bill of Attainder was passed against Lord Edward Fitzgerald, Irish rebel leader, in 1798.

Bill of Exchange. An order transferring a named sum of money at a given date from the debtor (drawee) to the creditor (drawer). The drawee having signed the bill becomes the "acceptor", and the document is then negotiable in commercial circles just as money itself.

Bill of Fare. A list of dishes provided in a restaurant, etc.; a menu.

Bill of Health. A document signed by the proper authorities to the master of a ship certifying that when the ship sailed no infectious disorder existed in the place. This is a *clean bill of health*, and the term is often used figuratively. *See* YELLOW JACK. **A foul bill of health,** or the absence of a clean bill, means that the place from which the vessel sailed was infected.

Bill of Lading. A document signed by the master of a ship in acknowledgment of goods laden in his vessel. In this document he binds himself to deliver the articles in good condition to the persons named, subject to certain circumstances. These bills are generally in triplicate—one for the sender, one for the receiver, and one for the master of the vessel.

Bill of Pains and Penalties. A Parliamentary proceeding like a BILL OF ATTAINDER imposing punishment less than capital. The last such bill against Queen Caroline, wife of George IV, was dropped in 1820.

Bill of Rights (Oct. 1689). A constitutional enactment of fundamental importance consolidating the GLORIOUS REVOLUTION of 1688. It asserted the liberties and rights of the nation, declared William and Mary King and Queen, and settled the succession.

A Bill of Rights, designed to guarantee civil liberties, was embodied in the American Constitution in 1791. It consists of the first ten amendments, proposed in 1789.

Bill of Sale. When a person borrows money and delivers goods as security, he gives the lender a "bill of sale", *i.e.* permission to sell the goods if the money is not returned on the stated day.

Bills of Mortality. In 1592, on the occasion of a great pestilence, the Company of Parish Clerks, representing 109 parishes in and around London, began to publish weekly returns of all deaths occurring; later they included births or baptisms. They were very inaccurate

and were superseded by the Registrar-General's returns after 1836. **Within the Bills of Mortality** means within the districts covered by the Bills of Mortality, which grew with the growth of London.

Bills receivable. Promissory notes, bills of exchange, or other acceptances held by a person to whom the money stated is payable.

Billet-doux (Fr. a sweet note). A love letter, now usually given a humorous use.

Billingsgate. The site of an old passage through that part of the city wall that protected London on the river side, named from an early property-owner in the area; also the site of a fish-market for many centuries, where porters were famous for their foul and abusive language at least four centuries ago.

Billingsgate pheasant. A red herring; a bloater.

Billy. Billies and Charlies. *See under* FORGERY.

Billy Barlow. A street droll, A MERRY ANDREW; so called from a half-idiot of that name well known in the East End of London for witty and droll behaviour, in the early half of the 19th century.

Billy Blue. Admiral Sir William Cornwallis (1744–1819).

Billy boy. A bluff-bowed North Country coaster of river-barge build.

Billy goat. A male goat. From this came the term once common for a tufted beard—a "billy" or goatee.

Billycock Hat. A round, low-crowned, hard felt hat with a wide brim. One account says the name is the same as "bully-cocked", that is, as worn by a bully or swell, a term used in Amhurst's *Terrae Filius* (1721). Another says that it was first used by Billy Coke (Mr. William Coke) at the great shooting parties at Holkham about 1850. Old established West End hatters used to call them "Coke hats". *See* BOWLER HAT; COKE'S CLIPPINGS.

Billy the Kid. William H. Bonney (1859–1881), baby-faced killer, who committed his first murder at the age of twelve. Prominent in the Lincoln County cattle war in New Mexico, he boasted that he had killed a man for every year of his life. He was finally shot (aged 21) by

Sheriff Pat Garrett.

Billy Williams's Cabbage Patch. The English Rugby Football Union's ground at Twickenham, the headquarters of the game, also known as *Twickers*. Popularly so-called after W. (Billy) Williams (1860–1951), who discovered the site and through whose persistence the ground was acquired in 1907; also from the ground's former partial use as a market garden.

Bi-metallism. The employment for coinage of two metals, SILVER and GOLD which would be of fixed relative value; both being standard money or legal tender.

Bimini. A legendary island of the Bahamas where the fountain of youth gave everlasting life to all who drank from it.

Bing Boys. The nickname of the Canadian troops in World War I from the name of their commanding officer, Lord Byng of Vimy. Also from the revue, *The Bing Boys Are Here*, which opened at the ALHAMBRA in 1915.

Birchin Lane. I must send you to Birchin Lane. *i.e.* whip you. The play is on *birch* (a rod), but the derivation of the name really means "the lane of barbers".

A suit in Birchin Lane. Birchin Lane was once famous for all sorts of apparel and was known for second-hand clothing in Shakespearean times.

Bird. The now obsolete use as an endearing name for a girl is connected with BURD. In modern slang "bird" is often a somewhat disparaging term for a young female.

Bird is also a name for the shuttlecock used in Badminton.

A bird in the hand is worth two in the bush; a pound in the purse is worth two in the book. Possession is better than expectation.

A bird of ill omen. One who is regarded as unlucky or who is in the habit of bringing bad news. The phrase comes from the custom of AUGURY and even today OWLS, crows and RAVENS are often regarded as unlucky birds, SWALLOWS and STORKS as lucky ones. Ravens by their acute sense of smell can often locate dead and decaying bodies at a great distance, hence, perhaps, they indicate

death. Owls screech when bad weather is at hand and, as foul weather often precedes sickness, so the owl is looked on as a funeral bird.

A bird of passage. A person who shifts from place to place, a temporary visitant, like a cuckoo, swallow, swift, etc.

A little bird told me so. From *Eccles*. x, 20:

> Curse not the King, no not in thy thought;...for a bird of the air shall carry the voice, and that which hath wings shall tell the matter.

Birdie. A hole at golf which the player has completed in one stroke less than par (the official figure). Two strokes less is an *eagle*.

Bird's-eye view. A mode of perspective drawing in which the artist is supposed to be over the objects drawn, in which case he beholds them as a bird in the air would see them; a general or overall view.

Birds of a feather flock together. Those of similar character, taste or station associate together. Hence, *of that feather*, of that sort.

Bird walking weather. A flying expression of American origin, indicating CEILING ZERO, coined from the phrase, "the weather is so bad, even the birds are walking."

Fine feathers make fine birds. *See* FEATHER.

Old birds are not to be caught with chaff. Experience teaches wisdom.

One beats the bush, another takes the bird. The workman does the work, the master makes the money. *See* BEAT.

The Arabian bird. The PHŒNIX.

The bird of Juno. The peacock. MINERVA'S bird is either the COCK or the owl; that of VENUS is the DOVE.

The bird of Washington. The American or bald-headed EAGLE.

Thou hast kept well the bird in thy bosom. Thou has remained faithful to thy allegiance or faith.

'Tis the early bird that catches the worm. It is the early riser or one who acts promptly who attains his objective.

To get the bird. To be hissed; to be given a hostile reception. *See* BIG BIRD.

To kill two birds with one stone. To achieve two ends with one effort or outlay.

Birds Protected by Superstitions:

The **Chough** was protected in CORN-WALL because the soul of King ARTHUR was fabled to have migrated into one.

The **Falcon** was held sacred by the Egyptians because it was the form assumed by RA and HORUS; and the **Ibis** because the god THOTH escaped from the pursuit of TYPHON disguised as an Ibis.

Mother Carey's Chickens, or Stormy Petrels, are protected by sailors from a superstition that they are the living embodiment of the souls of dead mariners. *See also* MOTHER.

The **Robin** is protected on account of Christian tradition and nursery legend. *See* ROBIN REDBREAST.

The **Stork** is held sacred in Sweden, from the legend that it flew round the cross crying, "Styrka, Styrka!" when Jesus was crucified. *See* STORK.

Swans are protected in Ireland from the legend of the FIONNUALA (daughter of LIR) who was metamorphosed into a swan and condemned to wander the waters until the advent of Christianity. Moore wrote a poem on the subject.

Birmingham by way of Beachy Head. Metaphorically, a roundabout approach. It is a quotation from G. K. Chesterton's poem *The Rolling English Road*.

> He (Mr. George Brown) grows impatient with a Civil Service that makes him travel to Birmingham by way of Beachy Head.
>
> *The Times*, London, 22 February 1965.

Birrellism. A good-humoured but penetrating comment tinged with kindly irony. Named after Augustine Birrell (1850– 1933), Professor of Law at University College, London, politician, and man of letters.

Birthday suit. In one's birthday suit. Quite nude, as when born.

Originally, the magnificent suit of clothes specially ordered by courtiers to be worn on the sovereign's birthday.

> The Sun himself, on this auspicious Day,
> Shines, like a Beau in a new Birth-day Suit.
>
> FIELDING: *Tom Thumb the Great*, I, i.

Bis (Lat. twice). French and Italians use this as English audiences use *encore*.

Bis dat, qui cito dat. He gives twice who gives promptly—*i.e.* quick relief will do as much good as twice the sum later.

Bishop. The name is given to one of the men in CHESS (formerly called the *archer*); to the LADYBIRD (*see* BISHOP BARNABEE); to a lady's bustle (sometimes called a "stern reality"); and to a drink made by pouring red wine, such as CLARET or burgundy, either hot or cold, on ripe bitter oranges, the liquor being sugared and spiced to taste. Similarly a *Cardinal* is made by using *white* wine instead of *red* and a *Pope* by using *tokay*. *See also* BOY BISHOP.

Bishop Barker. An Australian term used around Sydney for the largest glass of beer available, named from Frederick Barker (1808–1882), Bishop of Sydney, who was a very tall man.

Bishop Barnabee. The May-bug, lady-bird, etc.

Bishop in Partibus. *See* IN PARTIBUS.

The bishop has put his foot in it. Said of milk or porridge that is burnt, or of meat over-roasted. Tyndale says, "If the porage be burned to, or the meate over rosted we saye the byshope hath put his fote in the potte"; and explains it thus, "because the bishopes burnt who they lust". Such food is also said to be *bishopped*.

The Bishops' Bible. *See* BIBLE, THE ENGLISH.

The Bishops' Wars. The name given to Charles I's two short wars (1639–1640) against the Scots when they renounced EPISCOPACY. The wars ended with his defeat and caused the summoning of the LONG PARLIAMENT.

To Bishop was formerly used in the sense of to confirm, to admit into the Church. There are two verbs *to bishop*, both from proper names. One is obsolete and meant to murder by drowning; from the name of a man who drowned a little boy in Bethnal Green and sold the body to the surgeons for dissection. The other means to conceal a horse's age by "faking" his teeth.

Bissextile (bi seks' tīl). LEAP YEAR. We add a day to February in leap year, but the Romans counted 24 FEBRUARY twice, and called it *dies bissextus* (*sexto calendas Martias*), the sextile or sixth day before 1 MARCH. This day was reckoned twice (*bis*) in leap year, which was called *annus bissextus*.

Bistonians (bis tō' ni ånz). The Thracians; after Biston, son of MARS, who allegedly built Bistonia on Lake Bistonis.

Bit. *Bit* is old thieves' slang for money and a coiner is called a "bit-maker".

In the 1920s *bit* was slang for a girl, short for a "bit of fluff", now a "bit of stuff". "Piece (or bit) of skirt" is similarly used but now considered sexist.

Bit (of a horse). **To take the bit between**, or **in one's teeth.** To be obstinately self-willed; to make up one's mind not to yield. When a horse has a mind to run away, he catches the bit between his teeth and the driver no longer has control over him.

Bite. A cheat; one who bites us. "The biter bit" explains the origin. We say a man was "bitten" when "he burns his fingers", meddling with something that promised well but turned out a failure. "The biter bit" is the moral of ÆSOP'S fable *The* VIPER AND THE FILE.

Once bitten, twice shy. Having been caught, led up the garden path, or seen off once, to be wary or cautious in order not to be tricked a second time.

To bite off more than one can chew. To undertake more than one is capable of doing, or seeing through.

To bite on the bullet. To endure pain courageously, to face trouble or adversity with fortitude, to behave stoically.

To bite one's thumb at another. To insult or defy by putting the thumbnail into the mouth and clicking it against the teeth. Why this should be so provocative is not clear.

To bite the dust or **the ground.** To fall, to be struck off one's horse, to be vanquished.

To bite the lip, indicative of suppressed chagrin, passion, or annoyance.

To bite upon the bridle. To champ the bit, like an impatient or restless horse.

Bitter end, The. *À outrance*, with relentless hostility; also applied to affliction, as "she bore it to the bitter end", meaning to the last stroke of adverse fortune.

In nautical parlance the "bitter end" is that part of the cable abaft the bitts (*i.e.* the inboard end) when the vessel is riding at anchor.

In the Bible, *Proverbs* v, 4, reads: "But her end is bitter as wormwood." This may have some share in the present use of the phrase.

Black. *See* COLOURS for its symbolism. Its use for mourning was a Roman custom (*Juvenal*, x, 245), borrowed from the Egyptians. At funerals mutes who wore black cloaks were sometimes known as the *blacks*, and sometimes as *Black Guards. See* BLACKGUARDS.

> I do pray ye
> To give me leave to live a little longer.
> You stand about me like my Blacks.
> BEAUMONT and FLETCHER: *Monsieur Thomas*, III, i.

In several of the Oriental nations it is a badge of servitude, slavery and low birth. Our word *blackguard* seems to point to this meaning, and the Lat. *niger*, black, also meant bad, impropitious.

Beaten black and blue. A very severe beating when the skin is bruised black and blue.

Black as a crow, etc. Among the common similes used to denote "blackness" are black as a crow, a RAVEN, a raven's wing, ink, HELL, HADES, death, the grave, your hat, thunder or a thundercloud, Egypt's night, a NEWGATE KNOCKER, ebony, coal, pitch, soot, tar, etc. Most of these are self-explanatory.

Black in the face. Extremely angry.

A black dog for a white monkey. A fair swop or exchange is no robbery.

I must have it in black and white, *i.e.* in writing; the paper being white and the ink black.

Not as black as he or **she is painted.** Not as bad or disreputable as he or she is said to be.

The pot calling the kettle black. *See under* POT.

To say black's his eye, *i.e.* to vituperate, to blame. **Black's the white of someone's eye** is a modern variant. To say the eye is black or evil is to accuse a person of an evil heart or great ignorance.

To swear black is white. To swear to

any falsehood no matter how glaring.

All Blacks, The. New Zealand's Rugby XV which first played in England in 1905.

Black and Tans. The name of a pack of hounds in County Limerick, applied to the irregulars enlisted by the British government in 1920 to supplement the Royal Irish Constabulary. This force (sometimes called the "Auxis") was so called from their dark blue uniforms with the black belts and dark-green caps of the R.I.C. Later the Irish used the name indiscriminately for all the armed constabulary.

Black Act. An Act of 1722 (9 Geo. I, c. 22) imposing the death penalty for certain offences against the Game Laws, and specially directed against the Waltham deer-stealers who blackened their faces and, under the name of *Blacks*, carried out their depredations in Epping Forest. Dick TURPIN was a member of such a gang at the outset of his career. This Act was repealed in 1827.

Blackamoor. Washing the blackamoor white—*i.e.* engaged upon a hopeless and useless task. The allusion is to one of ÆSOP'S FABLES of that name.

Black art, The. Magic, NECROMANCY. The name seems to have derived from Med. Lat. *nigromantia* used erroneously for Gr. *nekromanteia*. The devil was also portrayed as black.

Black Assize. 6 July 1577, when a putrid pestilence broke out at Oxford and the SHERIFF and a large number of gentry died during the Assize.

Black-balled. Not admitted to, or rejected by a CLUB or suchlike. In the BALLOT those who accepted a candidate dropped a red or white ball into the box, those rejecting dropped a black one.

Blackbirds. Slang for negro slaves or indentured labourers. Hence **Blackbirding**, capturing or trafficking in slaves. *Cp.* BLACK CATTLE.

Blackboard Jungle, The. Schools in which delinquency is rife and discipline is difficult to impose. The name is taken from the title of a novel by Evan Hunter published in 1954 and filmed in 1955, based on a New York school.

Black books. To be in one's black books. Out of favour, in disgrace. A black book is one recording the names of those who are in disgrace or have merited punishment.

Black Canons. The AUGUSTINIANS, from their black cloaks.

Black cap. A small square of black cloth. In Britain it was worn by a judge when passing the death sentence; it is part of a judge's full dress and is also worn on 9 November, when the new Lord Mayor of London takes the oath at the Law Courts. Covering the head was a sign of mourning among the Israelites, Greeks, Romans, and Anglo-Saxons. *Cp.* II *Sam*. xv, 30.

Black coat. An old name for a parson.

Black-coated worker. A clerical worker as opposed to a manual worker, from their former convention of wearing a black jacket with pin-striped trousers. *Cp.* WHITE-COLLAR WORKER.

Black Country, The. The crowded manufacturing district in the Midlands comprising parts of South Staffordshire, Warwickshire and Worcestershire of which Dudley is the geographical centre. The collieries, blast furnaces, foundries and metal industries grimed and blackened the area with smoke, hence the name.

Black Death. The plague, both pneumonic and bubonic, which came from Asia and ravaged Europe between 1348 and 1351. It reached England in 1348 where it probably carried off one-eighth of the population, the clergy being particularly badly hit. The name does not appear before the 16th century and may be due to the devastating nature of the visitation but it is usually said that it comes from the dark skin haemorrhage (ecchymosis). Coughing and sneezing were doubtless accompanying symptoms, hence the somewhat improbable suggestion that the nursery rhyme:

> Ring a ring o'roses,
> A pocket full of posies,
> A-tishoo! A-tishoo!
> We all fall down.

was some form of folk memory of the Black Death. It reappeared in 1361–1362 and 1379, and there were periodic epidemics until the GREAT PLAGUE.

Black Diamonds. Coal. Coal and diamonds are both forms of carbon.

Truffles are also called black DIAMONDS.

Black Dick. Richard, Earl Howe (1726–1799), British admiral and victor of the Battle of the First of June, 1794. So called from his swarthy complexion.

Black Dog. An early 18th-century name for a counterfeit SHILLING or other "silver" coin made of pewter. Also another name for the BLUES. See also A BLACK DOG HAS WALKED OVER HIM *under* DOG.

Black Doll. The sign of a MARINE STORE. The doll was a dummy dressed to indicate that cast-off garments were bought. *See* DOLLY SHOP.

Black Douglas. *See* DOUGLAS.

Black Dwarf. *See under* DWARF.

Black Flag. The pirate's flag; the JOLLY ROGER. A black flag was formerly hoisted over a prison immediately after an execution.

Chinese mercenaries who opposed the French in Tongkin in the 1880s were known as the *Black Flags*, as also were the troops of the CALIPH of Baghdad, because his banner, that of the ABASSIDES, was black.

Blackfoot. A Scottish term for a matchmaker, or an intermediary in love affairs; if he chanced to play traitor he was called a *whitefoot*. Also the name of one of the Irish agrarian secret societies of the early 19th century.

Blackfeet. The popular name of two North American Indian tribes, one the Algonkin (Algonquin) calling themselves the *Silksika*, and the other, the *Sihasapa*.

Black Friars. The DOMINICAN Friars, from their black mantle. The London district of this name is on the site of the former Dominican monastery.

Black Friday. Notably (1) 6 December 1745, the day on which the news arrived in London that the Young PRETENDER had reached Derby; (2) 11 May 1866, when widespread financial panic was caused by Overend, Gurney and Co., the bankers, suspending payments; (3) 15 April 1921 was Black Friday for the British Labour Movement when the threatened General Strike was cancelled; (4) in the U.S.A., 24 September 1869, when many speculators were ruined by the Government's release of gold into the open market in order to bring down the price, which had been forced up by stock manipulators. *See also* RED FRIDAY.

Black Game. Heath-Fowl; in contradistinction to *red* game, as grouse. The male bird is called a *black cock*.

Black Genevan. A black preaching gown formerly used in many Anglican churches and still used by NONCONFORMISTS. So called from Geneva, where Calvin preached in such a robe.

Blackguards. The origin of this term, long applied to rogues and scoundrels, is uncertain. In the 16th and 17th centuries it was applied to lowest menials in great houses, army hangers-on, scullions, camp-followers, etc. It was also given to the link-boys and torch-bearers at funerals.

Black Hand. The popular name of the Slav secret society largely responsible for contriving the assassination of the Archduke Franz Ferdinand in Sarajevo, 28 June 1914. This was the event which precipitated World War I.

Blackheath. A district of S.E. London once the haunt of footpads and highwaymen. The followers of Wat Tyler in 1381 and Jack CADE in 1450 assembled there. Here also the Londoners welcomed Henry V after Agincourt and Charles II met the army on his way to London in 1660.

Black Hole of Calcutta (20–21 June 1756). Surajah Dowlah, Nawab of Bengal, thoughtlessly confined 146 British prisoners, including one woman, in the small prison (eighteen feet by fourteen feet ten inches) of the East India Company's Fort William, after its capture. Only 22 men and the woman escaped suffocation in the Black Hole.

Black Ivory. Negro slaves from Africa.

Black jack. A large leather can for beer, so called from the outside being tarred. Cornish miners called blende or sulphide of zinc "Black Jack", the occurrence of which was considered a favourable indication. Hence the saying *Black Jack rides a good horse*, the blende rides upon a lode of good ore.

A blackjack is a small club or cosh, usually leather covered; and the American scrub oak is called Black Jack.

The nickname Black Jack was given to the American General J. A. Logan (1826–1886) on account of his dark complexion and hair, and to General Pershing (1860–1948) who commanded the Americans in World War I.

Blacklead. *See* MISNOMERS.

Black-leg. An old name for a swindler, especially at cards or races; now almost solely used for a non-union member who works for less than trade-union rates, or especially one who works during a strike.

Black letter. Gothic or German type which in the early days of printing was the most commonly used. The term dates from *c*. 1600 because of its heavy black appearance in comparison with roman type.

Black letter day. An inauspicious or unlucky day. The allusion is to the old liturgical CALENDARS in which major saints' days and festivals were distinguished by being printed in red. Black was used for holy days of lesser importance. (*See* RED-LETTER DAY.) The Romans marked the unlucky days with a piece of charcoal and their lucky ones with white chalk.

Black list. A list of those in disgrace, or who have incurred censure or punishment; a list of bankrupts for the private guidance of the mercantile community. *Cp*. BLACK BOOKS.

Black looks. Looks of displeasure.

Blackmail. "Mail" here is the Old English and Scottish word meaning rent, tax, or tribute. In Scotland *mails* and *duties* are rents of an estate in money or otherwise. Blackmail was originally a tribute paid by the BORDER farmers to FREEBOOTERS in return for protection or immunity from molestation. Hence payment extorted by intimidation or threat, or extractions and exorbitant charges.

Black Maria. The police van used for the conveyance of prisoners. It is suggested that the name is derived from that of Maria Lee, a Boston negress who kept a lodging-house. She was of such great size that when the police required help they sent for Black Maria, who soon collared the refractory men and led them to the lock-up. The term was certainly in use at Boston in the 1840s.

Black market. A World War II phrase to describe illicit dealing in rationed goods. *See* UNDER THE COUNTER.

Black Mass. A sacrilegious MASS in which the DEVIL is invoked in place of God and various obscene rites performed in ridicule of the proper ceremony. *See* MEDMENHAM MONKS.

It is also a REQUIEM Mass from the custom of wearing black vestments.

Black Monday. Supposedly Easter Monday, 14 April 1360, when Edward III was besieging Paris. The day was so dark, windy and bitterly cold that many men and horses died. In fact 14 April 1360 fell on the Tuesday of the week after Easter. The Monday after Easter Monday is called "Black Monday" in allusion to this fatal day.

Black money. *See* BLACK DOG.

Black Monks. The BENEDICTINES.

Black Nell. Wild Bill Hickok's famous mare. *See* DEAD MAN'S HAND.

Black-out. The term was first used in the theatre, certainly from the early 1920s, when the lighting was extinguished to darken the whole stage, but it is now largely associated with its wartime use. From the outbreak of war against Germany (3 September 1939) until 23 April 1945 (coastal areas, 11 May), it was obligatory throughout Great Britain to cover all windows, skylights, etc., before dark so that no gleam of light could be seen from outside.

Black-out also denotes a complete loss of consciousness.

Black ox. The black ox has trod on his foot, *i.e.* misfortune has come to him. Black oxen were sacrificed to PLUTO and other infernal deities.

Black Parliament. A name given to the REFORMATION Parliament (1529–1536) which effected the breach with ROME.

Black Pope. The General of the JESUITS.

Black Prince. Edward, Prince of Wales (1330–1376), eldest son of Edward III. He is popularly supposed to be named from wearing black armour, but there is no evidence for this. Froissart says he was "styled black by terror of his arms" (*c*. 169).

Black Rod. The short title of the "Gentleman Usher of the Black Rod", named from his staff of office—a black wand surmounted by a gold lion. He is responsible for maintaining order in the HOUSE OF LORDS and summoning the Commons to the Peers when the royal assent is given to bills, etc. He is also chief gentleman usher to the sovereign and usher to the order of the GARTER.

Black Rood of Scotland. The "piece of the true cross" or ROOD, set in an ebony crucifix, which St. MARGARET, wife of King Malcolm Canmore, left to the Scottish nation in 1093. It fell into English hands at the battle of Neville's Cross (1346) and was kept in Durham Cathedral until the REFORMATION when it was lost.

Black Saturday. In Scotland 4 August 1621, because a violent storm occurred at the very moment the PARLIAMENT was sitting to force EPISCOPACY upon the people.

Black Sea, The. Formerly called the EUXINE and probably given its present name by the Turks, possibly from its dangers and lack of shelter.

Black sheep. A disgrace to the family or community; a *mauvais sujet*. Black sheep are not as valuable as white and in times of superstition were looked on as bearing the devil's mark. A black sheep in a white flock is the ODD MAN OUT. *Cp.* BÊTE NOIRE.

Black Shirts. The distinguishing garment worn by Mussolini's Italian FASCISTS and adopted in England by their imitators. Also a name for the German S.S. or *Schutzstaffeln*, led by Himmler. *See* BROWN SHIRTS.

Blacksmith. A smith who works in black metal (such as iron). A mixture of Guinness and barley wine is called a *Blacksmith*.

Black Stone. The famous stone kissed by every pilgrim to the KAABA at MECCA. Moslems say that it was white when it fell from heaven but it turned black because of the sins of mankind. The stone was worshipped centuries before MOHAMMED. In Persian legend it was an emblem of SATURN.

Black strap. A sailor's term for any strong dark liquor, especially dark red wines. In North America, a mixture of

rum or whisky with molasses, sometimes with vinegar added.

Black Swan. *See* RARA AVIS.

Black Tom Tyrant. Thomas Wentworth (1593–1641), Earl of Strafford, Lord Lieutenant of Ireland, from his policies in support of Charles I.

Black velvet. A drink of champagne and Guinness in equal parts. It was the favourite drink of Bismarck, the IRON CHANCELLOR.

Black Watch. Originally companies, recruited from the WHIG clans, employed from 1729 by the English Government to watch the HIGHLANDS and to enforce the Disarming Act. Named Black Watch from their dark tartan, they were enrolled under the Earl of Crawford as the 42nd Regiment in 1739, later the Royal Highland Regiment. They are distinguished by the red hackle (small group of red feathers) on their bonnets.

Blade. A knowing blade, a sharp fellow; **a regular blade,** a BUCK or fop. Originally the word conveyed a sense of somewhat bullying bravado, and probably the name arose from the sword a swaggering buck would carry.

Bladud (blā'dŭd). A mythical English king, father of King LEAR.

Blanch, To. A method of testing the quality of money paid in taxes to the King, used by Roger of Salisbury in the reign of Henry I. 44 shillings' worth of SILVER coin was taken from the amount being paid in, a pound's weight of it was melted down and the impurities were skimmed off. If then found to be light, the taxpayer had to throw in enough pennies to balance the scale.

Blanchefleur (blonsh' flĕr). The heroine of the Old French metrical romance, *Flore et Blanchefleur*, used by Boccaccio for his prose romance, *Il Filocolo*. It is substantially the same as that of Dianora and Ansaldo in the DECAMERON and that of DORIGEN and Aurelius by Chaucer. The tale is of a young Christian prince who is in love with the SARACEN slave-girl with whom he has been brought up. They are parted, but after many adventures he rescues her unharmed from the harem of the Emir of Babylon.

Blank. To draw blank. *See* DRAW.

Blank cartridge. Cartridge with powder only, without shot, bullet, or ball; used in drill and saluting. Thus figuratively, empty threats.

Blank cheque. A signed cheque, leaving the amount to be filled in by the payee. Thus **to give a blank cheque** is, figuratively, to give CARTE BLANCHE.

Blank verse. Rhymeless verse in continuous decasyllables with IAMBIC or trochaic rhythm, first used in English by the Earl of Surrey about 1540 in his version of Books II and IV of the ÆNEID.

Blanket. To be born on the wrong side of the blanket. To be illegitimate.

A wet blanket. A discouragement; a MARPLOT or spoilsport. A person who discourages a proposed scheme is a *wet blanket*. A wet blanket smothers fire and has a dampening effect.

Blanketeers. The starving handloom weavers and spinners who assembled in St. Peter's Field, Manchester, 10 March 1817, each equipped with a blanket for their march to London to present a petition to the Prince Regent.

Blarney. Soft wheedling speeches to gain some end; flattery or lying with unblushing effrontery. Legend has it that Cormac Macarthy in 1602 undertook to surrender Blarney Castle (near Cork) to the English, as part of an armistice. Daily the Lord President Carew looked for the fulfilment of the terms, but received nothing but soft speeches, till he became the laughing-stock of Elizabeth's ministers, and the dupe of the Lord of Blarney.

Among American criminals "to blarney" means to pick locks.

To kiss the Blarney Stone. In the wall of Blarney Castle about twenty feet from the top and difficult of access is a triangular stone inscribed, "Cormac Macarthy *fortis me fieri fecit*, A.D. 1446". Tradition says that whoever kisses it is endowed with wonderful powers of cajolery. As it is almost impossible to reach, a substitute has been provided, which is said to be as effective as the original. *Cp.* SHANNON.

Blasphemous Balfour. Sir James Balfour (d. 1583), Scottish judge, was so called for his apostasy. He "served with all parties, deserted all, and yet profited by all".

Blast. To strike by lightning; to cause to wither, *e.g.* the "blasted oak". This is the sense in which the word is used as an expletive.

In full blast. In full swing, all out. "The speakers at MARBLE ARCH on Sunday were in full blast." A METAPHOR from the blast furnace in full operation.

Blatant Beast. In Spenser's *Faerie Queene* (Bks. V, VI) "a dreadful fiend of gods and men, ydrad"; the type of calumny or slander. He was born of CERBERUS and CHIMÆRA, and had a hundred tongues and a sting. The word *blatant* seems to have been coined by Spenser and is probably from the provincial word *blate*, to bellow.

Blaze (Icel. *blesi*). A white spot on the forehead of a horse, also called a *star* (*cp.* CLOUD). Similarly, a white mark made on a tree by chipping off a piece of bark is called a *blaze*.

To blaze a trail. To notch trees as a guide. In America trees so marked are called *blazed trees*.

To blaze abroad (Icel. *blasa*, to blow), to broadcast or spread.

Blazes. Go to blazes. Go to HELL. Here the word is from O.E. *blaese*, a torch.

Bleed. To bleed someone white is to extort the last penny from someone.

It makes my heart bleed. It makes me very sorrowful.

Bleeding of a dead body. It was once believed that at the approach of a murderer, the blood of the murdered body gushed out. If there was the slightest change observable in the eyes, mouth, feet, or hands of a corpse the murderer was supposed to be present.

Bleeding the monkey. The same as *Sucking the Monkey. See* MONKEY.

Blefuscu (ble fūs' kū). An island in Swift's *Gulliver's Travels*. In describing it he satirized France.

Blemmyes (blem' iz). An ancient Ethiopian tribe mentioned by Roman writers as inhabiting Nubia and Upper Egypt. They were fabled to have no head, their eyes and mouth being placed in the breast. *Cp.* ACEPHALITES; CAORA.

Blenheim Palace (blen' im). This mansion, given to the Duke of Marlborough for his great victory over the French at

Blenheim (1704), has given its name to the *Blenheim spaniel*, and to a golden-coloured apple, the *Blenheim Orange*.

Blenheim Steps. Going to Blenheim Steps meant going to be dissected, or unearthed from one's grave. Sir Astley Cooper (1768–1841), the great surgeon, presided over an anatomical school at Blenheim Steps, Bond Street. Here "RESURRECTIONISTS" were sure to find a ready mart for their gruesome wares.

Bless. He has not a penny or **a sixpence to bless himself with,** *i.e.* in his possession; wherewith to make himself happy; he has no financial resources. Perhaps this expression goes back to the times when such coins were of silver and carried a cross on the reverse.

Blessing with three fingers in Christian churches is symbolical of the TRINITY.

Blest. I'll be blest if I do it. I will not do it. A EUPHEMISM for *damned*.

Blighty. Soldier's name for England or the homeland widely current in World War I, but was well known to soldiers who had served in India long before. It is the Hind. *bilayati*, foreign, from Arab. *wilayet* meaning "provincial", "removed at some distance"; hence adopted by the military for England.

Blimp. A word originally applied to an observation balloon in World War I. "Colonel Blimp" was created by David Low, the cartoonist, between the wars, to embody the elderly dyed-in-the-wool TORY, opposing all and any change. A *blimp* has come to mean an elderly, unprogressive, reactionary "gentleman" of somewhat limited intelligence.

Blind. Blind Alley, A. A *cul-de-sac*. It is blind because it has no "eye" or passage through it. "A blind alley occupation" is one that leads nowhere; there are no prospects of promotion.

Blind as a bat, or **beetle,** or **mole,** or **owl.** Blind, with very poor sight. None of these creatures is actually blind. The phrase is often used sarcastically of one who is unable to see what is under his nose.

Blind Department, The. In Post Office parlance, the Returned Letter Office (formerly Dead Letter Office), the department where efforts are made to trace the proper destination of inaccurately or illegibly addressed mail.

Blind ditch. One which cannot be seen. Here *blind* means concealed, obscure.

Blind drunk. Very drunk, so drunk as to be unable to distinguish things clearly.

Blind Harper, The. John Parry, who died in 1782. He lived at Ruabon, and published collections of Welsh music.

Blind Harry. A Scottish minstrel who died *c.* 1492 and left in MS. an epic of 11,858 lines on Sir William Wallace.

Blind Hedge. A ha-ha. Milton used the word blind for *concealed*.

Blind leaders of the blind. Those who give advice to others or who take the lead but who are unfitted to do so, or incapable themselves. The allusion is to *Matt.* xv, 14.

Blind Magistrate, The. Sir John Fielding (1722–1780), Bow Street Magistrate, blinded in his youth, was reputed to know countless thieves by their voices.

Blindman's buff. A very old-established children's game. "Buff" here is short for "buffet", and is an allusion to the three buffs or pats which the "blind man" gets when he has caught a player.

Blindman's holiday. The hour of dusk when it is too dark to work, and too soon to light candles.

Blindmen's Dinner, The. A dinner unpaid for, the landlord being the victim. EULENSPIEGEL, being asked for alms by twelve blind men, said "Go to the inn; eat, drink and be merry, my men; and here are twenty florins to pay the bill." They thanked him, each supposing one of the others had received the money. After having provided them with food and drink at the inn, the landlord asked for payment, whereupon they all said, "let him who received the money pay for the dinner." But none had received a penny.

Blind spot. This is a small area not sensitive to light, situated on the retina where the optic nerve enters the eye. The term is used figuratively to denote some area in one's understanding where judgment and perception are always lacking.

To go it blind. To enter upon some

project without sufficient forethought, inquiry, or preparation.

To turn a blind eye. To pretend tactfully not to see; to ignore, in order to avoid embarrassment to all concerned.

When the devil is blind. A circumlocution for NEVER.

You came on my blind side. My tenderhearted side. Said of persons who wheedle some favour out of another.

Blitzkrieg (Ger. *blitz*, lightning; *krieg*, war). A concentrated military offensive designed to produce a knock-out blow. The term was particularly applied to the attacks by Hitler's Germany on various European countries between 1939 and 1941.

The Blitz. The name (an abbreviation of BLITZKRIEG) given to the intensive German air raids on London between July and December 1940 which resulted in the destruction of many buildings and the death of some 23,000 civilians.

To have a blitz or **thorough blitz**. To make a real attack on something, to go the whole HOG. An expression often used when a thorough clean-up or clear-out is needed.

Block. To block a bill. In parliamentary language means to postpone or prevent the passage of a bill by giving notice of opposition, thus preventing its being taken after ten o'clock at night.

A chip of the old block. *See* CHIP.

A stumbling block. An obstacle in the path of progress, a snag or cause of difficulty.

To cut blocks with a razor. *See* CUT.

Block books. Late mediæval books printed from wood-blocks in which both text and illustrations (if any) were carved in relief. The impression was taken by laying the paper on the block moistened with a brown or grey waterbased ink and rubbing the verso by hand with a cloth, though some later block books were produced with black oilbased printer's ink in a press. As the water-based ink tended to soak through the paper, impressions were generally taken on one side of the leaf only. The most important block books were pictorial works of devotion, such as the BIBLIA PAUPERUM, *Ars Moriendi*, *Apocalypse*, *et al.*, but the same method was also used for printing various scientific works, Latin grammars, etc., with or without illustrations.

Blockhousers. The oldest Negro Regiment in the U.S. Army, nicknamed from its gallant assault on a blockhouse in the Spanish-American War.

Blondin (blon' din). One of the most famous acrobats of all time. Born at St. Omer in 1824, his real name was Jean François Gravelet; he died at Ealing in 1897. His greatest feat was in 1859, when he crossed the Niagara Falls on a tightrope, embellishing the performance by repeating it blindfolded, wheeling a barrow, twirling an umbrella, and carrying a man on his back.

Blood. In figurative use came to denote members of the same family or race, family descent generally, and thence one of noble or gentle birth, finally a BUCK or aristocratic rowdy.

It also denotes royalty, and the once popular "PENNY DREADFULS".

A blood horse. A thoroughbred; a horse of good parentage or stock.

A prince of the blood. One of a royal family.

Bad blood. Anger, etc., as, *It stirs up bad blood*. It provokes ill-feeling and resentment.

Blood and iron policy. A policy requiring war as its instrument. The phrase was coined by Bismarck in 1886.

Blood and thunder. Melodrama, sensational and blood-curdling stuff.

Bloodhound. Figuratively, one who follows up someone or something with real pertinacity.

Blood is thicker than water. The interest we take in a stranger is "thinner" and more evanescent than that which we take in a blood relation.

Bloodless Revolution. The revolution of 1688 when William of Orange, invited over by leading WHIGS and TORIES, landed at Torbay (5 November) and the army of James II deserted without firing a shot. James was captured but eventually escaped and fled to France.

Blood money. Money paid to a person for giving such evidence as shall lead to the conviction of another; or for the betrayal of another, as JUDAS was paid for his betrayal of Jesus. Also at one time money paid to the next of kin as compensation for the murder of a relative.

Blood-red wedding. *See under* WEDDING.

Blood relation. One in direct descent from the same father or mother.

Blood Royal. The royal family or royalty; also called "the blood".

Bloodstone. *See* HELIOTROPE.

Bloodsucker. A leech-like animal which, if allowed, will rob a person of all vitality. Hence a sponger, a parasite, an extortioner.

Blood, toil, tears and sweat. The words used by Sir Winston Churchill in his speech to the HOUSE OF COMMONS, on becoming Prime Minister, 13 May 1940.

Blue blood. *See* BLUE.

In cold blood. Deliberately; not in the excitement of passion or battle.

It makes one's blood boil. It provokes indignation and anger.

It runs in the blood. It is inherited or is characteristic of the family or race.

Laws written in blood. Demades said that the laws of Draco were written in blood, because every offence was punishable by death. *See* DRACONIAN CODE.

Man of Blood. Any man of violent temper. David was so called in II *Sam*. xvi, 7 (REVISED VERSION), and the PURITANS applied the term to Charles I.

My own flesh and blood. My near kindred.

Nelson's blood. The Royal Navy's nickname for rum.

The Field of Blood. ACELDAMA, the piece of ground purchased with the blood-money of our Saviour.

The battlefield of CANNAE, where Hannibal defeated the Romans, 216 B.C., is also so called.

Young blood. Young members.

Bloody. Several fanciful derivations are suggested for this expletive, that it is a corruption of "By our Lady", or associated with "bloods" or aristocratic rowdies; but the obvious meaning of the word with its unpleasant and lurid associations is a sufficient explanation of its origin and its use as an intensive.

It was bloody hot walking today.
SWIFT: *Journal to Stella*, letter xxii.

As a title the adjective has been bestowed on Otto II, Holy Roman Emperor (973–983) and Queen Mary Tudor (1553–1558) was called "Bloody MARY".

Bloody Assizes. The Assizes conducted in the western circuit under Judge Jeffreys after MONMOUTH'S REBELLION, 1685. Named from the brutality, severity, and unfairness of the proceedings.

Bloody Balfour. In 1887, when A. J. Balfour became Chief Secretary for Ireland, the police fired on a riotous mass meeting at Mitchelstown, County Cork, occasioned by the prosecution of a nationalist leader, William O'Brien. Three people were killed. As a consequence of Balfour's resolute support of authority the nickname *Bloody Balfour* soon became current in Ireland.

Bloody Bill, The. Better known as the Act of the SIX ARTICLES (31 Henry VIII, c. 14), it made the denial of TRANSUBSTANTIATION a heresy punishable by death.

Bloody Hand. A term in Old Forest Law denoting a man whose hand was bloody, and who was therefore presumed to be the one guilty of killing the deer. In HERALDRY it is the badge of a BARONET and the armorial device of ULSTER. *See* HAND.

Bloody Mary. *See under* MARY.

Bloody Pots, The. *See* KIRK OF SKULLS.

Bloody Sunday. (1) 13 November 1887. The dispersal of a socialist demonstration in Trafalgar Square which had been prohibited by the Commissioner of Police led to baton charges being made, Footguards and Life Guards being brought in, and the arrest of two M.P.s, R. Cunninghame-Graham and John Burns. Two of the crowd died of injuries. (2) 22 January 1905. A deputation of workers led by Father Gapon marched to St. Petersburg to present a petition to the Czar. They were attacked by troops and hundreds of unarmed peasants were killed. (3) 30 January 1972. The dispersal of anti-internment marchers in the Bogside, Londonderry by British troops when 13 civilians were killed.

Bloody Thursday. The Thursday in

the first week of LENT, that is, the day after ASH WEDNESDAY, used to be so called.

Bloody Tower. *See under* TOWER.

Bloomers. Originally a female costume consisting of jacket, skirt and Turkish trousers gathered closely round the ankles, introduced by Mrs. Amelia Bloomer of New York in 1849. Associated with the Woman's Rights Movement, the outfit met with little success. Nowadays "bloomers" is applied to the trouser portion of the outfit, or drawers.

Bloomsbury Group. The name given to a group of various callings — writer, artist, philosopher, economist, who, from about 1904 met at the Bloomsbury home of Clive and Vanessa Bell (née Stephen) in Gordon Square, that of Virginia and Adrian Stephen in Fitzroy Square and elsewhere. Virginia Stephen married Leonard Woolf; others prominent in the circle were Roger Fry, Duncan Grant, J.M. Keynes, David Garnett, Lytton Strachey and to a lesser extent E.M. Forster. They saw themselves as advocates of a new rational, civilized society and many of them had Cambridge links. The group had lost its cohesion by the end of the 1920s. They were considerably influenced by G.E. Moore's *Principia Ethica* (1903).

Blot. To blot one's copybook. *See* COPYBOOK.

Blow. A blow-out. A "tuck in" or feast which swells out the paunch. Also the sudden collapse of a pneumatic tyre when the inner tube is punctured.

Blowing Stone. A roughly square block of red sarsen about 3½ ft. high, perforated with two or three holes. If blown properly it produces a lingering moaning sound. It is situated at Kingston Lisle in the Vale of the WHITE HORSE.

Blow me down. An expletive of nautical origin, as in the sea shanty "Blow the man down" of sailing ship days.

Blown herrings. Herrings bloated, swollen or cured by smoking; another name for bloaters.

Blown upon. Blown upon by the breath of slander. *Cp.* FLY-BLOWN.

Blow-point. A game similar to peashooting, only instead of peas small skewers of pointed wood were puffed

through the tube.

Fly-blown. *See under* FLY.

It will soon blow over. It will soon cease to be talked about, as a gale blows over or ceases.

I will blow him/her (up) sky high. Give him/her a good scolding. The metaphor is from blasting by gunpowder.

To blow a cloud. To smoke a cigar, pipe, etc.

To blow a trumpet. To sound a trumpet, but **to blow one's own trumpet** is to go in for self-advertisement, to boast.

To blow great guns. Said of a wind that blows so violently that its noise resembles the roar of artillery.

To blow hot and cold. To be inconsistent, to be irresolute, unable to make up one's mind. The allusion is to the fable of a traveller who was entertained by a SATYR. Being cold the traveller blew his fingers to warm them, and afterwards blew his hot broth to cool it. The satyr, in great indignation turned him out of doors, because he blew both hot and cold with the same breath.

To blow off steam. To get rid of superfluous temper. The allusion is to the forcible escape of superfluous steam no longer required. *See also under* LET.

To blow one's top. To lose one's temper.

To blow the gaff. To let out a secret; to inform against a companion. Here *gaff* is a variant of GAB.

To blow up. To inflate, to explode, to burst into fragments; to censure severely. *See* I WILL BLOW HIM UP (*above*).

You be blowed. A mild imprecation or expletive.

Blow it!Blow is similarly used.

Full-blown. In full flower, hence fully developed or qualified. "He is a fullblown doctor now" means he is no longer a student but fully qualified to practise.

A body-blow. *See under* BODY.

At one blow. By one stroke.

The first blow is half the battle. Well begun is half done, a good lather is half the shave.

Without striking a blow. Without coming to a contest.

Bluchers (bloo' kerz). Half-boots; named after the Prussian Field-Marshal von

Blücher (1742–1819), of Waterloo fame. *See* WELLINGTON.

Bludger (Austr.). Originally (19th century) a pimp, but later any scrounger or one profiting without risk.

Blue, or AZURE. *See* COLOURS for its symbolisms.

The COVENANTERS wore blue as their badge in opposition to the scarlet of royalty. They based their choice on *Numb.* ix, 38. "Speak unto the children of Israel, and bid them that they make them fringes on the borders of their garments...and that they put upon the fringe...a ribband of blue." It was one of the traditional Whig colours, also blue and buff. The LIBERAL colours are now blue and yellow, and the CONSERVATIVES blue. It was also the colour of the Unionists in the American CIVIL WAR; the CONFEDERATE colour was grey.

A blue, or **a true blue,** politically speaking usually means a TORY. Also at Oxford and Cambridge *a blue* is a man who has been chosen to represent his 'VARSITY in rowing, CRICKET, etc. In the general sense "a true blue" is a person of unimpeachable integrity and staunch fidelity, probably from the idea of such qualities being characteristic of BLUE BLOOD.

Bluebeard. A BOGEY, a murderous tyrant in Charles Perrault's *Contes du Temps* (1697). In this version Bluebeard goes on a journey leaving his new wife the keys of his castle, but forbidding her to enter one room. Curiosity overcomes her and she opens the door to find the bodies of all Bluebeard's former wives. On his return he finds a blood spot on the key which tells him of his wife's disobedience. He is about to cut off her head when her two brothers rush in and kill him. The tale is of an internationally widespread and ancient type and it is unprofitable to regard Gilles de Rais or Henry VIII as the historical Bluebeard.

Bluebeard's Key. When the bloodstain of this key was rubbed out on one side, it appeared on the other; so prodigality being overcome will appear in the form of meanness; and friends, over-fond, will often become enemies.

Blue beans. *See under* BEAN.

Blue Billy. *See under* BILLY.

Blue Bird of Happiness. This is an idea elaborated from Maeterlinck's play of that name, first produced in London in 1910. It tells the story of a boy and girl seeking "the blue bird" which typifies happiness.

Blue blood. High or noble birth or descent; it is of Spanish origin, from the fact that the veins of the pure-blooded Spanish aristocrat, whose race had suffered no Moorish admixture, were more blue than those of mixed ancestry.

Blue Boar. A cognizance of Richard, Duke of York, father of Edward IV. The cognizance of Richard III was a white boar—a popular inn sign. After his defeat at Bosworth, White Boars were changed into Blue Boars.

Blue Bonnets, or **Blue Caps.** The Highlanders of Scotland, or the Scots generally; from the blue woollen cap formerly in very general use in Scotland.

Blue Books. In Great Britain parliamentary reports and other official parliamentary publications. Each volume is in FOLIO with a blue cover.

Bluebottle. A constable, a policeman; also formerly an almsman, or anyone else whose distinctive dress was blue.

Blue Caps. *See* BLUE BONNETS.

Blue-Coat School. Christ's Hospital is so called because the boys there wear a long blue coat girded at the loins with a leather belt. Formerly in the City of London, it moved to Horsham in 1902.

Blue Devils. *See* BLUES.

Blue-eyed Boy, The. The favourite, one highly thought of and shown preference or marks of favour.

Blue-eyed Maid. MINERVA, the goddess of wisdom, is so called by HOMER.

Blue gown. A harlot. Formerly a blue gown was a dress of ignominy for a prostitute who had been put in the HOUSE OF CORRECTION.

The bedesmen to whom the Scottish kings distributed certain alms were known as *blue gowns* from their dress of coarse blue cloth. *See* GABERLUNZIE.

Blue Hen's Chickens. The inhabitants of the State of Delaware. It is said that in the Revolutionary War, one Captain Caldwell, commander of a very efficient Delaware regiment, used to say that no cock could be truly game whose mother was not a blue hen.

Blue jackets. Sailors in the naval service; from the colour of their jackets (worn 1857–1890 and subsequently replaced by jumpers).

Blue John. A blue fluorspar, found in the Blue John Mine near Castleton, Derbyshire; so called to distinguish it from BLACK JACK. Called John from John Kirk, a miner who first noticed it.

Bluemantle. One of the four English PURSUIVANTS attached to the College of Arms or Heralds' College, so called from his official robe.

Blue Monday. The Monday before LENT, spent in dissipation, which is said to give everything a blue tinge. Hence "Blue" means tipsy.

Blue Monkey, The. The nickname given to the Marquis Luis Augusto Pinto de Soveral (d. 1922), from his swarthy complexion and blue-black hair. Portuguese ambassador at London almost continuously from 1884 to 1909, and intimate of King Edward VII, he was noted for his wit, discretion and ability as a raconteur.

Blue moon. Once in a blue moon. Very rarely indeed.

Blue murder. To scream or **shout blue murder.** Indicative of terror and alarm rather than real danger. It appears to be a play on the French exclamation *morbleu*.

Blue-noses. The Nova Scotians.

Blue Peter. A blue flag with a white square in the centre, hoisted as a signal that a ship is about to sail. Here "Peter" is a corruption of "repeater", the flag having been originally used to mean that a signal had not been read and should be repeated. Also the letter "P" in the International Code of Signals.

Blue-pencil. The mark of editing or censorship.

Blue-pictures. Indecent cinema shows. The name derives from the custom of Chinese brothels being painted blue externally.

Blue-print. Properly the reproduction of a detailed architectural or engineering drawing, etc., in white lines on a blue ground. Now increasingly used for any project, scheme, or design.

Blue Riband of the Atlantic. The liner gaining the record for the fastest Atlantic crossing is said to hold the "Blue Riband of the Atlantic".

Blue Ribbon. The blue ribbon is the GARTER, the most coveted Order of Knighthood in the gift of the British Crown; hence the term is used to denote the highest honour attainable in any profession or walk of life, etc. The Blue Ribbon of the Church is the Archbishopric of Canterbury, that of the Law, the office of Lord Chancellor. *See* CORDON BLEU.

A weal from a blow has had the term "blue ribbon" applied to it, because a bruise turns the skin blue.

Blue Ribbon Army. A TEETOTAL society founded in the U.S.A. and extending to Great Britain by 1878, whose members wore a piece of narrow blue ribbon as a badge. It became the Gospel Temperance Union in 1883.

Blue Shirts. An Irish FASCIST organization under General Eoin O'Duffy, former Commissioner of the Garda, which developed from the Army Comrades Association in the early 1930s. A Blue Shirt battalion led by O'Duffy fought for General Franco in the Spanish Civil War, 1936–1939.

Blue Sky Laws. In the U.S.A., laws passed to protect the inexperienced buyer of stocks and bonds against fraud. The name is said to have its origin in a phrase used by one of the supporters of the earliest of these laws, who said that certain business operators were trying to capitalize "the blue skies".

Blue-stocking. A female pedant or learned woman. In 1400 a society of men and women was formed in Venice, distinguished by the colour of their stockings and called *della calza*. A similar society appeared in Paris in 1590 and was the rage among lady *savants*. The name is derived directly from such a society, founded by Mrs. Montagu about 1750, from the fact that a prominent member, Mr. Benjamin Stillingfleet, wore blue stockings. The last of the clique was Miss Monckton, afterwards Countess of Cork, who died in 1840. Mrs. Montagu is also said to have deliberately adopted the badge of the

French *Bas-bleu* club.

Blues. A traditional form of American folk-song expressive of the unhappiness of the black man in the Deep South. Blues usually consist of 12 bars made up of three 4-bar phrases in 4/4 time.

Also low spirits, **to have a fit of the blues** is to be downcast or depressed. Here a contraction of **blue-devils**. *See also* REGIMENTAL AND DIVISIONAL NICKNAMES.

Bluey. A slang word for lead. Also an Australian name for blue-coloured blankets widely used in the 19th century, hence the SWAG which tramps carried in their blankets. In Tasmania a *bluey* was a blue shirt-like garment issued to convicts.

The Boys in blue. The police, from the colour of their uniforms.

To be blue in the face. To have made a great effort; to be breathless and exhausted.

To look or **feel blue.** To be depressed.

True blue will never stain. A really noble heart will never disgrace itself. The reference is to blue aprons and blouses worn by butchers. They do not show bloodstains.

True as Coventry blue. The reference is to a blue cloth and blue thread made at Coventry, noted for its permanent dye.

'Twas Presbyterian true blue (*Hudibras*, I, i). The allusion is to the blue apron which some PRESBYTERIAN preachers used to throw over their preaching-tub before they began to address the people.

Bluff, To. In poker and other card-games, to stake on a bad hand. This is a ruse to lead an adversary to throw up his cards and forfeit his stake rather than risk them against the "bluffer".

So, by extension, to bluff is to deceive by pretence. **To call someone's bluff** is to unmask his deception.

Bluff Harry, or **Bluff King Hal.** Henry VIII (1509–1547), from his bluff hearty manner.

Blunderbore. A nursery-tale giant, brother of CORMORAN, who put JACK THE GIANT KILLER to bed and intended to kill him; but Jack thrust a billet of wood into the bed, and crept under the bedstead. Blunderbore came with his club and broke the billet to pieces and was amazed to see Jack next morning at breakfast. He asked Jack how he had slept. "Pretty well," said the Cornish hero, "but once or twice I fancied a mouse tickled me with its tail." This increased the giant's surprise. Hasty pudding being provided for breakfast, Jack stowed away such a bulk in a bag concealed within his dress that the giant could not keep pace. Jack cut the bag open to relieve the "gorge" and the giant, to effect the same relief, cut his throat and thus killed himself.

Blurb. A publisher's note on the dustjacket or cover of a book purporting to tell what the book is about and usually of a laudatory nature. The word was coined by Gelett Burgess, the American novelist (1866–1951).

Blush. At first blush. At first sight, on the first glance. The word is from the M.E. *blusche*, a gleam, a glimpse.

To blush like a blue dog. Not to blush at all.

Bo. You cannot say Bo!, or **Boo! to a Goose.** A proverbial saying implying timidity.

Boadicea (bō à disē' à), or **Boudicca**. The famous British warrior queen, wife of Prasutagus, king of the Iceni. On her husband's death (A.D. 61) the Romans had seized the territory, scourged the widow for her opposition and violated her two daughters. Boudicca raised a revolt of the Iceni and Trinovantes, burned Camulodunum (Colchester), Londinium (London), and Verulamium (St. Albans), but when finally routed by Suetonius Paulinus, she took poison.

Boanerges (bō à nĕr' jēz). A name given to James and John, the sons of Zebedee, because they wanted to call down "fire from HEAVEN" to consume the Samaritans for not "receiving" the Lord Jesus. It is said in the Bible to signify "sons of thunder", but "sons of tumult" would be a better rendering. (*Luke* ix, 54; *Mark* iii, 17.)

Boar, The. Richard III. *See* BLUE BOAR.

Buddha and the boar. A Hindu legend relates that BUDDHA died from eating dried boar's flesh. The third AVATAR of VISHNU was in the form of a boar, and in the legend "dried boar's flesh" probably typifies ESOTERIC knowledge prepared for popular use. None but Buddha himself must take the responsibility of giving out occult secrets, and he died while preparing for the general esoteric knowledge.

The Calydonian boar. In Greek legend, Œneus, King of Calydon in Ætolia, having neglected the sacrifices to ARTEMIS, was punished by the goddess sending a ferocious boar to ravage his lands. A band of princes collected to hunt the boar, which was wounded by Atalanta (*see* ATALANTA'S RACE), and killed by MELEAGER.

Boar's Head. The old English custom of serving this as a Christmas dish is said to derive from Norse mythology. FREYR, the god of peace and plenty, used to ride on the boar Gullinbursti: his festival was held at YULETIDE, when a boar was sacrificed to his honour. The English custom is described in Washington Irving's *Sketch Book* (*The Christmas Dinner*). The Boar's Head was brought in ceremoniously to a flourish of trumpets and a carol was sung.

The Boar's Head Tavern. Made immortal by SHAKESPEARE and Prince Hal, this used to stand in Eastcheap. Destroyed in the Great Fire (*see* FIRE), it was rebuilt and annual Shakespeare Dinners were held there until 1784. It was demolished in 1831.

Board of Green Cloth. So called from the green covered table at which the board originally sat under the Lord Steward. It examined all the accounts of the English Royal Household and formerly dealt with all offenders within the verge of the palace, which extended 200 yards from the palace gate. Its powers were curtailed in 1782 and it is now concerned with the royal domestic arrangements under the Master of the Household.

In modern slang *the board of green cloth* is the card-table or the billiard-table.

He is on the boards. He is an actor by profession.

To sweep the board. To win and carry off all the stakes in a game of cards, or all the prizes at some meeting.

To board. To feed and lodge. From the custom of dining at table or board.

Boarding School. One where the pupils are fed and lodged as well as being taught. The term is sometimes applied euphemistically to prison.

Board Wages. Wages paid to servants which include the cost of food. Servants "on board wages" provided their own victuals.

Board in many nautical phrases is that part of the sea which a ship passes over in tacking.

To go by the board. To go for good, to be completely destroyed or finished with, thrown overboard. When a ship's mast is carried away it is said "to go by the board", *board* here meaning the ship's side.

To make a long, good, or **short board.** To make a long or short tack.

To make a stern board, *i.e.* to go backwards. To sail stern foremost.

To run aboard of. To run foul of another ship.

Boast of England, The. A name given to TOM THUMB or Tom-a-lin by Richard Johnson, who in 1599 published a "history of this ever-renowned soldier, the Red Rose Knight, surnamed The Boast of England".

Boaz. *See* JACHIN.

Bob. Slang for a SHILLING. This use, of unknown origin, dates from about 1800. Also a term used in campanology denoting certain CHANGES in the long peals. A *bob minor* is rung on six bells, a *bob triple* on seven, a *bob major* on eight, a *bob royal* on ten, and a *bob maximus* on twelve.

Bob-a-Job-Week. An imaginative way of raising funds by self-help, instituted by the BOY SCOUTS in 1949. All kinds of jobs were undertaken, some for their publicity value, for the payment of one shilling. It became an annual effort but with the declining value of the "bob" and the advent of DECIMAL CURRENCY, *Scout Job Week* took its place in 1972 thus encouraging patrons to give a fairer return for work done.

To bob for apples or cherries is to try and catch them in the mouth while they swing backwards and forwards. *Bob* here means to move up and down buoy-antly; hence the word also means to "curtsy".

To bob for eels is to fish for them with a *bob*, which is a bunch of lobworms like a small mop.

A bob wig. One in which the bottom locks are turned up into bobs or short curls.

Bear a bob. Be brisk. The allusion is to bobbing for apples which requires great agility and quickness.

Bobbed hair is hair that has been cut short; docked like a bobtailed horse.

Bobbing John. John Erskine, Earl of Mar (1675–1732), was so called from his frequent change of allegiance. He began as a WHIG but eventually led the JACO-BITES in the rebellion of 1715.

Pretty bobbish. Pretty well (in spirits and health), from *bob* as in BEAR A BOB.

Bob's your uncle. That will be all right; you needn't bother any more, just leave it to me! The phrase was occasioned by A. J. Balfour's promotion by his uncle Robert (Lord Salisbury), the TORY Prime Minister, to the post of Chief Secretary for IRELAND. Balfour had previously been made President of the Local Government Board in 1886, then Secretary for SCOTLAND with a seat in the CABINET.

Bobbery. Kicking up a bobbery. Making a squabble, kicking up a SHINDY. It was much used in India and probably comes from Hind. *bapre*, "Oh, father!" a common exclamation of surprise.

Bobby. A policeman, from Sir Robert Peel, Home Secretary, who established the Metropolitan Police in 1829. *Cp.* PEELER.

Bobby-sox. Long white cotton socks or ankle socks affected by teenage girls in the U.S.A. in the early 1940s. Hence the name *Bobby-soxers* for the young females who distinguished themselves for their intemperate and moronic behaviour at the public appearances of crooners and suchlike.

Bobadil. A military braggart of the first water, Captain Bobadil is a character in Ben Johnson's *Every Man in his Humour*. This name was probably derived from Bobadilla, the first governor of Cuba, who sent Columbus home in chains.

Bocland, or **Bookland.** Denotes land of inheritance granted from FOLKLAND in Anglo-Saxon England by the King and the Witan by written charter or book. It was at first given to the CHURCH, but also to lay subjects. The place-name *Buckland* is derived from this.

To ride bodkin. To ride in a carriage between two others. Probably the allusion is to the bodkin, something so slender that it can be squeezed in anywhere.

Bodle, or **Boddle.** A former Scottish COPPER coin of low value; said to be so-called from Bothwell, a mint-master.

Body. Body-blow. In boxing a punch between the breast-bone and the navel; figuratively, a shattering blow, a severe setback or shock.

Body colour. Paint containing body or density.

Body corporate. A group of individuals legally united into a corporation.

Body line. In CRICKET, fast bowling at the batsman rather than the wicket with the intention of forcing him to give a catch while defending his person. The accurate but dangerous bowling of Larwood and Voce won the ASHES for England 1932–1933, but roused a storm of indignation in Australia which caused a modification in the laws of cricket.

Body politic. A whole nation considered as a political corporation; the State.

Body-snatcher. One who stole newly buried corpses to sell them for dissection. *See* RESURRECTIONISTS; *Cp.* BURKE.

By a play on the words, a BUM-BAILIFF was so called, because his duty was to snatch or capture a delinquent.

A regular body, in geometry means one of the five regular solids called PLATONIC BODIES.

The heavenly bodies. The SUN, MOON, stars, etc.

The seven bodies (of alchemists). The seven metals supposed to correspond with the "seven planets".

	Planets	Metals
1.	Apollo, or the Sun	Gold
2.	Diana, or the Moon	Silver
3.	Mercury	Quicksilver
4.	Venus	Copper
5.	Mars	Iron
6.	Jupiter	Tin
7.	Saturn	Lead

To body forth. To give mental shape to an ideal form.

To keep body and soul together. To sustain life; from the notion that the SOUL gives life. The Lat. *anima*, and the Gr. *psyche*, mean both soul and life. According to Homeric mythology and the common theory of "ghosts", the departed soul retains the shape and semblance of the body. See ASTRAL BODY.

Bœotia (bē ō' shà). The ancient name for a district in central Greece, probably so called from its abundance of cattle. The fable is that CADMUS was conducted thence by an ox (Gr. *bous*) to the spot where he built THEBES.

Bœotian (bē ō' shàn). Rude and unlettered, a dullard. The ancient Bœotians were an agricultural and pastoral people, so the Athenians used to say that they were as dull and thick as their own atmosphere.

Boethius (bō ē' thi ùs). Roman philosopher and writer (c. 475–c. 525 A.D.). His manuals and translations from the Greek were widely used in the MIDDLE AGES. Both King Alfred and Chaucer translated his *De Consolatione Philosophiae*.

Boffin. A nickname used by the R.A.F. in World War II for research scientists or BACKROOM BOYS. It passed into general use in the 1940s and is said to be from the practice of a certain scientist giving his colleagues Dickensian nicknames, Mr Boffin being a character in *Our Mutual Friend*. There is a family of HOBBITS called Boffins.

Boggard or **Boggart**. A North of England name for a GOBLIN or spectre, especially one haunting a particular place. It is the same as a BROWNIE or KOBOLD and the Scottish *bogle*.

Bogey. See BOGY.

Bogomils. A long-lasting heretical sect which sprang up in Thrace and Bulgaria in the 10th century, named after the priest Bogomil. As a result *Bulgar* became an abusive term in the West, being identified with Bogomilism and evil practices generally. Hence the word *bugger* as a low term of abuse, etc. See *also* MANICHÆANS.

Bog-trotters. Irish tramps; from their skill in Irish bogs, trotting from tussock to tussock, either as guides or to escape pursuit.

Bogy. A HOBGOBLIN; a person or object of terror; a bugbear. The word first appeared in the 19th century and is perhaps connected with the Scottish *bogle* and so with the obsolete BUG. A more recent suggestion is that *bogy* derives from the *Boogie* tribesmen's privateering and piratical activities in S.E. Asian waters.

Colonel Bogey. A name given in golf to an imaginary player whose score for each hole is settled by the committee of the particular club and is supposed to be the lowest that a good average player could do it in. It is usually one stroke above par at a hole.

Colonel Bogey is also the name of a well-known military march tune by K. J. Alford.

Bohemian. A term applied to artists, writers and others of unconventional, loose or irregular habits. Originally the name was applied to a GIPSY from the belief that Bohemia was the home of the gipsies, or because the first to arrive in France (1427) came by way of Bohemia.

Bohemian Brethren. A religious sect formed from the HUSSITES which arose in Prague in the 15th century. They were the forerunners of the MORAVIANS.

Boiling point. He was at boiling point. Very angry indeed. Properly the point at which water under ordinary conditions boils (212° Fahrenheit, 100° Centigrade, 80° Réaumur).

Bold. Bold as Beauchamp. It is said that Thomas Beauchamp, Earl of Warwick, with one squire and six archers, overthrew 100 armed men at Hogges, in Normandy, in 1346.

Bold as brass. Downright impudent; without modesty. Similarly we say *brazen-faced*.

Boldon Book. A record of the possessions of the see of Durham in 1183. The DOMESDAY BOOK did not include the counties of Durham, Northumberland, Cumberland and Westmorland, probably because of their devastation by WILLIAM THE CONQUEROR.

Bollandists. JESUIT WRITERS of the *Acta Sanctorum* or *Lives of the Saints*, the original editor being John Bolland, a Dutchman. The first two volumes giving the SAINTS commemorated in January were published in 1643. The disturbances of the French Revolution of 1789 led to cessation of the work in 1794 but the society was reconstituted in 1837. Sixty-seven volumes (from 1 Jan. to 10 Nov.) had been completed by 1967.

Bollen. Swollen. The past participle of the obsolete English verb, *bell*, to swell. The seed capsule of flax or cotton is called a *boll*.

> The barley was in the ear, and the flax was bolled.
>
> *Exod.* ix, 31.

Bolognese School. There were three periods to the Bolognese School in painting—the Early, the Roman, and the ECLECTIC. The first was founded by Marco Zoppo in the 15th century, and its best exponent was Francia. The second was founded in the 16th century by Bagnacavallo, and its chief exponents were Primaticcio, Tibaldi, and Niccolò dell'Abbate. The third was founded by Carracci at the close of the 16th century, and its best masters were Domenichino, Lanfranco, Guido, Schidone, Guercino, and Albani.

Boloney. It is all boloney. It is all nonsense, rubbish or pretence. Originally the name for a Bologna sausage. "Bunk" and "hooey" are similarly used.

Bolshevik (bol' she vik), or less correctly **Bolshevist.** Properly a member of the Russian revolutionary party under Lenin that seized power in 1917, aiming at the establishment of the supreme power of the proletariat and declaring war on capitalism. The Bolsheviks were so called from the fact that at the party conferences of 1902–1903 the Leninists were the majority group (*Bolsheviki* = majority). The defeated minority were called MENSHEVIKS.

Bolshie, or **Bolshy.** A derogatory contraction of "Bolshevik". Also used to denote a person with "red" or revolutionary tendencies, or sometimes a troublemaker.

Bolt. Bolted arrow. A blunt arrow for shooting young rooks with a cross-bow; called "bolting rooks".

Bolt in tun. In HERALDRY, a bird-bolt, in pale, piercing through a tun, often used as a PUBLIC-HOUSE SIGN.

Bolt upright. Straight as an arrow.

A bolt from the blue. A sudden and wholly unexpected event or catastrophe, like a thunderbolt from the blue sky, or a flash of lightning without warning. Here "bolt" is used for lightning, although strictly a meteorite is a thunderbolt.

A fool's bolt is soon shot or **spent.** *See under* FOOL.

The horse bolted. The horse shot off like a bolt or arrow.

To bolt food. To swallow it quickly without waiting to chew it; hence **to bolt a Bill,** a political phrase used of Bills passed without adequate time or opportunity for consideration.

To bolt out the truth. To blurt it out; also to bolt out, to exclude or shut out by bolting the door.

To have shot one's bolt. To have tried; to have done all that one can but with no avail. The bolt here is that of the archer.

Bolton. Bate me an ace, quoth Bolton. Give me some advantage. What you say must be qualified, as it is too strong. Ray says that a collection of proverbs was once presented to the VIRGIN QUEEN, with the assurance that it contained all the proverbs in the language; but the Queen rebuked the boaster with the proverb, "Bate me an ace, quoth Bolton", a proverb omitted in the compilation. John Bolton was one of the courtiers who used to play cards and dice with Henry VIII, and flattered the King by asking him to allow him an ACE or some advantage in the game.

Bomb. Bombshell, To drop a. Suddenly to deliver or release some shattering or surprising news. *Cp.* A BOLT FROM THE BLUE.

King Bomba. A nickname given to Ferdinand II, King of Naples, for his cruel and wanton bombardment of Messina in 1848. His son Francis II was called Bomba II, or *Bombalino* (Little Bomba), for his bombardment of Palermo in 1860.

Bombay Duck. A fish, the bummalo, which is dried and eaten with curries.

Bombiti. *See* BARISAL GUNS.

Bon mot (bon mō) (Fr.). A good or

witty saying; a pun; a clever repartee.

Bon ton (Fr.). Good manners or manners accredited by good society; also, the fashionable world.

Bon vivant (Fr.). A boon companion; one who indulges in the good things of the table.

Bon viveur (Fr.). One who enjoys high living, a fast man about town.

Bon voyage (Fr.). Have a good journey! Often used as a send-off to a departing traveller.

Bona Dea (Lat. the good goddess). A Roman goddess supposed to preside over the earth and all its blessings. She was worshipped by the VESTALS as the goddess of chastity and fertility. Her festival was 1 May and no men were allowed to be present at the celebration.

Bona Fide (bō' nà fī' di) (Lat.). Without subterfuge or deception; really and truly. Literally, *in good faith*. **To produce bona fides** is to produce credentials, to give proof of identity or ability to perform what one professes.

Bona-roba (bō' nà rō' ba) (Ital. *buona roba*, good stuff, fine gown, fine woman). A courtesan; so called from the smartness of her dress.

Bonanza (Sp. a fair weather at sea, prosperity). The term was applied in the mining areas of the U.S.A. to the discovery of a rich vein or pocket when the mine was said to be *in bonanza*. Subsequently a *bonanza farm* was so called when it was very profitable and had all the latest machinery. Now in colloquial usage it implies an unexpected source of wealth or success, a run of good luck.

Bonduca (bon dū' ka). Another form of BOADICEA, or Boudicca. Fletcher wrote a tragedy of this name in 1616.

Bone. Old thieves' slang for "good", "excellent". From the Fr. *bon*. The lozenge-shaped mark chalked by tramps on the walls of houses where they have been well received is known among the fraternity as a "bone".

Also slang for dice and counters used at cards.

Bone, To. To filch, as, *I boned it*. SHAKESPEARE (*Henry VI, Pt. II*, I, iii) says, "By these ten bones, my lords," meaning the fingers and calls the ten fingers "pickers and stealers" (*Hamlet*,

III, ii). So "to bone" may mean to finger, that is, "to pick and steal". Another explanation is that it is an allusion to the way a dog makes off with a bone.

A bone in her mouth, or **teeth.** Said of a ship speeding along throwing up spray or foam under the bows. *Cp.* TO CUT A FEATHER *under* FEATHER.

A bone of contention. A disputed point; a point not yet settled. The METAPHOR is taken from two dogs fighting for a bone.

Bone-shaker. An "antediluvian", dilapidated four-wheel cab; an old bicycle of the days before pneumatic tyres, spring saddles, etc.; any "old crock" of a vehicle.

Bred in the bone. A part of one's nature. "What's bred in the bone will come out in the flesh." A natural propensity cannot be repressed.

I have a bone in my leg. An excuse given to children for not moving from one's seat. Similarly "I have a bone in my arm", and must be excused using it for the present.

I have a bone in my throat. I cannot talk; I cannot answer your question.

Napier's bones. *See* NAPIER.

One end is sure to be bone. It won't come up to expectation. "All is not gold that glitters."

To give one a bone to pick. To throw a sop to CERBERUS; to give a lucrative appointment to a troublesome opponent to silence him, or to a colleague who is for any reason an embarrassment. It is used in political life, by removing members of the Commons to the Lords by gift of a peerage or by giving appointments in nationalized industries, etc.

To have a bone to pick with someone. To have an unpleasant matter to discuss and settle. This is another allusion from the kennel. Two dogs and one bone invariably form an excellent basis for a fight.

To make no bones about the matter. To do it, say it, etc., without hesitation or scruple; to offer no opposition, present no difficulty. Dice are called bones and the Fr. *flatter le dé* (to slide the dice, to soften a thing down) is the opposite of our expression. *To make no bones* of a thing is not to "make much of" or coax the dice in order to show favour. Hence *without more bones*, without further scruple or objection.

To make old bones. To live to a ripe old age.

To point a bone at (Austr.). To place a death curse on someone. In an Australian aboriginal ceremony a small sharp bone was pointed at the person to whom ill was wished while the curse was uttered.

Boney (bō′ni). "If you aren't a good boy Boney will catch you," was an old threat from a children's nurse or harassed parent; Boney being NAPOLEON Bonaparte, whose threatened invasion of England was a real scare in the early years of the 19th century.

Bonfire. Originally a *bone-fire*, that is, a fire made of bones. The *Festyvall* of 1493, printed by Wynkyn de Worde in 1515, says, "in the worship of St. John the people ... made three manner of fires: one was of clean bones and no wood, and that is called a bone fire; another of clean wood and no bones, and that is called a wood-fire ... and the third is made of wood and bones, and is called St. John's fire." Also:

> In some parts of Lincolnshire ... they make fires in the public streets ... with bones of oxen, sheep, etc, ... heaped together ... hence came the origin of bonfires.
>
> LELAND (1546).

Bonhomme. *See* JACQUES.

Boniface. St. Boniface. The APOSTLE of Germany, a West Saxon whose English name was Wynfrith (680–754).

St. Boniface's cup. An extra cup of wine; an excuse for an extra glass. Pope Boniface, we are told in the *Ebrietatis Encomium*, instituted an indulgence to those who drank his good health after grace, or the health of the POPE of the day. This probably refers to Boniface VI, an abandoned profligate, who was elected Pope by the mob in 896 and died fifteen days later. The two Saints Boniface to be Pope were Boniface I (418–422) and Boniface IV (608–615).

Bonne Bouche (Fr.). A delicious morsel; a titbit.

Bonnet. In slang, a player at a gaming table or an accomplice at auctions, to lure others to play or bid, so called because

he blinds the eyes of his dupes, just as if he had "bonneted them" or crashed their hats down over their eyes.

Balmoral bonnet. A flat Scottish cap.

Bonnet lairds. Local magnates or petty squires of SCOTLAND who wore the BRAID BONNET, like the common people.

Bonnet-piece. A gold coin of James V of SCOTLAND, on which the king's head wears a bonnet.

Bonnet Rouge. The red CAP OF LIBERTY worn by the leaders of the French Revolution in 1789.

Glengarry bonnet. The highland bonnet, which rises to a point; named after the valley in Inverness.

He has a bee in his bonnet. *See* BEE.

He has a green bonnet. He has failed in trade. In France it used to be customary, even in the 17th century, for bankrupts to wear a green bonnet (cloth cap).

To cast one's bonnet over a windmill. To throw caution to the winds. To decide on a hazardous course of action.

Bonnie Dundee. John Graham of Claverhouse, Viscount Dundee (1649–1689). A noted supporter of the Stuart cause and a relative of Montrose. He was killed at the battle of Killiecrankie.

Booby. A spiritless fool, who suffers himself to be imposed upon. The player who comes in last in whist-drives, etc.; the lowest boy in the class.

A species of gannet (*Sula piscator*) is called a booby, from its apparent stupidity.

Booby-prize. A prize, often of a humorous or worthless kind, given to the "booby" at whist-drives, parties, etc., *i.e.* to the player who has the lowest score, etc.

Booby trap. A trap set to discomfit an unsuspecting victim, such as placing an object on top of a door to fall on whoever opens it. More deadly "booby traps" are used in warfare.

To beat the booby. A sailor's term for warming the hands by striking them under the armpits.

Boogie-woogie. A style of piano playing. The left hand maintains a heavy repetitive pattern of eight beats to the bar over which the right hand improvises at will.

Probably developed in the Middle West by JAZZ musicians early in the 20th century. It owes its name to Clarence "Pinetop" Smith's *Pinetop's Boogie-Woogie* (1928). *Boogie* in U.S. slang is a negro performer and *woogie* a rhyming additive. *Cp.* BLUES; RAGTIME; SWING.

Boojum. *See* SNARK.

Book. Bell, book and candle. *See under* BELL.

Beware of a man of one book. Never attempt to controvert the statement of anyone in his own special subject. A shepherd who cannot read will know more about sheep than the wisest bookworm. This caution is given by St. THOMAS AQUINAS.

Bookworm. One who is always poring over books, so called in allusion to the maggot that eats holes in books, and lives in and on their leaves.

To be in my books, or **in my good books.** The former is the older phrase; both mean to be in favour. The word book was at one time used more widely, a single sheet or even a list being called a book. *To be on my books* is to be on my list of friends.

To be in my black, or **bad books.** In disfavour. *See* BLACK BOOKS.

On the books. On the list of a club, on the list of candidates, or any official or members' list.

Out of my books. Not in favour; no longer on my list of friends.

That does not suit my book. Does not accord with my arrangements. The reference is to the betting-book of the BOOKMAKER in which bets are formally entered.

The Battle of the Books. *See under* BATTLE; BOYLE CONTROVERSY.

The Book of Books. The BIBLE; also called simply "the Book", or "the good Book".

The Book of Common Prayer. The official liturgy of the CHURCH OF ENGLAND first issued in 1549 under Cranmer. Modified in 1552, 1559, and 1604 it was revised after the RESTORATION and reissued in 1662. The amended Prayer Books of 1927 and 1928 were approved by Convocation but rejected by PARLIAMENT.

Since the 1960s *The Book of Common Prayer* has been increasingly displaced by alternative forms of service commonly known as Series 1, Series 2 and Series 3. The *Alternative Services Book* of 1980 contains three alternative forms of Communion Service, namely, revised versions of Series 1 and 2 (largely based on the *Book of Common Prayer*), and the more controversial Series 3 (Revised) in modern English. The other services are all in the Series 3 idiom, those for the Visitation and Communion of the Sick being dropped. None of the readings (formerly called *lessons*) is from the AUTHORIZED VERSION (*see* BIBLE) and perhaps more properly it should have been called "The Replacement Service Book", although this was not supposed to be the intention.

The Book of Kells. An exceptionally fine illustrated copy of the Gospels in Latin. It is kept in the Library of Trinity College, Dublin, and probably dates from the 8th century.

The Book of Life, or **of Fate.** In BIBLE language, a register of the names of those who are to inherit eternal life (*Phil.* iv, 3; *Rev.* xx, 12).

The Book of the Dead. A collection of ancient Egyptian texts, both religious and magical, concerned with guidance for the safe conduct of the soul through Amenti (the Egyptian HADES). The Egyptians called it *The Book of Going Forth by Day* and copies, or parts of it, were buried with the mummy. There is a variety of texts.

To be booked. Not to be available; to have a previous commitment in one's engagement book or diary. Also to have something booked or entered up against one, hence caught. Currently applied to being entered in a policeman's notebook for an offence and subsequently charged.

To book a ticket, or **seat.** Now means to purchase a ticket for a theatre, railway journey, etc. In coaching days and in the early days of railways, tickets sold at Booking Offices were written out and entered up in the books by clerks.

To bring someone to book. To call someone to account; to make someone prove his words. Make him show that what he says accords with the records, the written agreement, or the book which treats of the subject.

To kiss the book. *See* KISS.

To know one's book. To know one's own interest; to know on which side one's bread is buttered (*see under* BREAD). Also, to have made up one's mind.

To speak by the book. To speak with meticulous exactness. To speak *literatim*, according to what is in the book.

To speak like a book. To speak with great precision and accuracy; to be full of information. Often used of a pedant.

To take one's name off the books. To withdraw from a club, from an organization or register, etc. In the passive voice it means to be excluded. *See* ON THE BOOKS, *above*.

To take a leaf out of someone else's book. To follow someone else's example; to copy.

Boom. Boom passenger. A convict on board a transport ship, who was chained to a boom when made to take his daily exercise.

Boomer. Since the early 19th century an Australian name for the kangaroo, the national animal; possibly of Tasmanian aboriginal origin.

Boomerang. Metaphorically a *boomerang* is a scheme or proposal that recoils upon its originator. A scheme can also be said *to boomerang* upon its author, *i.e.* to have repercussions to his disadvantage.

Boon Companion. A convivial or congenial companion. (Fr. *bon*, good.)

Boon work, or **Bene work,** or **Precariæ.** Special work at request (*ad precem* or *at bene*), *i.e.*, extra work done by the mediæval VILLEIN from Saxon times for the lord at haytime and harvest, etc. *Boon days* were in addition to the normal WEEK WORK.

Boondoggling. An expression used in the early 1930s to denote useless spending, usually with reference to the U.S. government's expenditure in the effort to combat the depression. It apparently derives from the Scottish word *boondoggle*, meaning a marble youreceive as a gift without having worked for it.

Boone, Daniel (1733–1820). American pioneer and frontiersman renowned for his prowess and exploits, who became a hunter when only twelve years old and at one time was captured and adopted by the Shawnees.

Boosening (M.E. *bousen*, to drink or tipple). An old method of treating insanity by immersing the patient in cold water. *See* BOOZE.

Boot. An instrument of torture made of four pieces of narrow board nailed together, of a length to fit the leg. Wedges were inserted till the victim confessed or fainted.

Boot and saddle. The order to cavalry to get packed and ready to go. It is a corruption of the Fr. *boute selle* (put on the saddle), and has nothing to do with boots.

Boot-hill (western U.S.A.). A frontier cemetery, thus called because so many of its occupants "died with their boots on".

Boot-jack. *See* JACK.

Bootless errand. An unprofitable or futile errand. *Cp.* I WILL GIVE YOU THAT TO BOOT, *below*.

Bootlegger. One who traffics illegally in alcoholic liquor, derived from the smuggling of flasks of liquor in boot legs.

Bootlegging became a major racket in the U.S.A. during the years of prohibition (1920–1934), MOONSHINERS and RUM-RUNNERS playing their part. Criminal elements took over and the profits of bootlegging fostered the growth of underworld bosses like CAPONE.

Bootlicker. A TOADY or creep. *See* TO LICK A MAN'S BOOTS *under* LICK.

Boots. An inn or hotel servant whose duty it is to clean the boots.

The BISHOP with the shortest period of service in the HOUSE OF LORDS, whose duty it is to read prayers, is colloquially known as the "Boots"; the name is also applied to the youngest officer in a regimental mess.

I will give you that to boot, *i.e.* in addition. The O.E. *bot* means advantage, good, profit.

It also meant compensation paid for injury; reparation. *Cp.* HOUSE-BOTE.

Like old boots. Slang for vigorously.

Puss in Boots. *See under* PUSS.

Seven-leagued boots. The boots worn by the giant in the fairy tale called *The*

Seven-leagued Boots. A pace taken in them measured seven leagues.

The boot is on the other foot. The CASE is altered; you and I have changed places.

The order of the boot. "The sack"; notice of dismissal from one's employment or office.

To die with one's boots on. To die fighting.

To go to bed in one's boots. To be very tipsy.

To have one's heart in one's boots. To be utterly despondent.

When bale is highest boot is nighest. *See* BALE.

Boötes (bō oo' tēz). Greek for "the ploughman"; the name of the constellation which contains the bright star, Arcturus (*see* ARCTIC REGION). According to ancient mythology Boötes invented the plough, to which he yoked two oxen, and at death was taken to HEAVEN with his plough and oxen and made a constellation. HOMER calls it "the wagoner", *i.e.* the wagoner of CHARLES'S WAIN, the Great Bear. *See* BEAR.

Bor. An East Anglian form of address to a lad or young man as, "Well, bor, I saw the mauther you spoke of"—*i.e.* "Well, boy, I saw the lass...". It is apparently O.E. *gebur*, neighbour, similar in use to Dut. *buur*, neighbour.

Borachio (bô ra' chō). Originally a wine bottle made of goat-skin; hence a drunkard, one who fills himself with wine. Sp. *borracha*; Ital. *borraccia*.

Borak, or **Al Borak** (bôr' ak) (the lightning). The animal brought by GABRIEL to carry MOHAMMED to the seventh HEAVEN, and itself received into PARADISE. It had the face of a man but the cheeks of a HORSE; its eyes were like jacinths, but brilliant as the stars; it had the wings of an EAGLE, spoke with the voice of a man, and glittered all over with radiant light.

To poke Borak at. To make fun of or jeer at. From an Australian aboriginal word for "banter". It has been suggested as a possible source of BARRACK.

Bordar. In Anglo-Saxon England, a VILLEIN of the lowest rank who did menial service to his lord in return for his cottage; the *bordars* or *bordarii* were the la-

bourers, and the word is from the Med. Lat. *bordarius*, a cottager. *See* COTTAR.

Border, The. The frontier of England and Scotland which from the 11th to the 15th century was a field of constant forays.

Border Minstrel. Sir Walter Scott (1771–1832), because he sang of the Border.

Boreas (bôr' ē ăs). In Greek mythology, the god of the north wind, and the north wind itself. He was the son of Astræus, a TITAN, and Eos, the morning, and lived in a cave of Mount Hæmus, in Thrace.

Hence *boreal*, of or pertaining to the north.

Borgias (bôr' jăz). **A glass of wine with the Borgias** was a great and sometimes fatal honour, for Caesar and Lucretia Borgia, children of Pope Alexander VI, were reputed to be adept in ridding themselves of foes or unwanted friends by inducing them to pledges in poisoned wine.

Born in the purple. *See under* PURPLE; PORPHYROGENITUS.

Born with a silver spoon in one's mouth. Born to good luck; born with hereditary wealth. The reference is to the usual gift of a silver spoon by the godparents (*see* APOSTLE SPOONS). The lucky child does not need to wait for the gift for it inherits it at birth. A phrase with a similar meaning is **born under a lucky star;** here the allusion is to ASTROLOGY.

In all my born days. Ever since I was born; in all my experience.

Not born yesterday. Not inexperienced and gullible; not to be taken in.

Poets are born, not made. One can never be a poet by mere training if one has been born without the "divine afflatus". A translation of the Lat. phrase *Poeta nascitur non fit*, of which an extension is *Nascimur poetae fimus oratores*, we are born poets, we are made orators. The idea has, of course, been extended to other callings.

Borough or **Burgh.** Originally, a corporate town with privileges granted by royal charter. By the Local Government Act of 1888 many large towns became county boroughs with the same governing powers as a county, but they were abolished by an act of 1972. By the same act non-county boroughs lost their status except in the Greater London Council area set up by the London Government Act of 1963. Subsequently various District Councils have been granted the title of borough by royal charter, thus enabling their chairmen to become mayors. The word *borough* has lost its historical meaning since it has been bestowed upon rural districts.

A Parliamentary Borough was one that sent at least one "burgess" or member to PARLIAMENT.

A Rotten, or **Pocket Borough** was a borough of much diminished population with the parliamentary seat at the disposal of a patron (frequently the Crown).

Borough English. A custom abolished in 1925 by which real estate passed to the youngest instead of the eldest son. It was of English origin and was so called to distinguish it from Norman custom. If there was no son, then the youngest daughter was sole heiress; failing a daughter, the youngest brother, then the youngest sister, etc. Land held by Borough English was sometimes termed *Cradle-Holding* or *Cradle-land*.

Borrow. Originally a noun (O.E. *borg*) meaning a pledge or security; the modern sense of the verb depended originally on the actual pledging of something as security for the loan. Even today the idea that a loan is the property of the lender and must be returned some day is always present. The noun sense is seen in the old oath *St. George to borowe*, which is short for "I take St. George as pledge," or "as surety"; also in:

> Ye may retain as borrows my two priests.
> SCOTT: *Ivanhoe*, ch. xxxiii.

Borrowed, or **borrowing days.** The last three days of MARCH are said to be "borrowed from APRIL", as is shown by the proverb in Ray's Collection:
"March borrows three days of April, and they are ill." One old rhyme says:

> March borrowed frae Aprile
> Three days an' they were ill;
> The first o' them was wind and weet,
> The second o' them was snaw an' sleet,
> The third o' them was sic a freeze,
> That the birds' legs stack to the trees.

In Scotland, FEBRUARY also has its "borrowed days", the 12th, 13th, and 14th, which are said to be borrowed from JANUARY. If these prove stormy the year will be one of good weather; if fine, the year will be foul. They are called *Faoilteach*.

Borrowed time, To live on. To continue to live after every reasonable presumption is that one should be dead, *i.e.* living on time borrowed from Death.

Bosey (Austr.). In CRICKET, another name for a GOOGLY, so named from its inventor, the English bowler B. J. T. Bosanquet, who toured Australia in 1903–1904. The term was also applied in World War II to a single bomb dropped from a plane.

Bosh. A Turkish word meaning empty, worthless. It was popularized by James Morier in his novel *Ayesha* (1834), and other Eastern romances.

To talk bosh. To talk rubbish, to be quite on the wrong track.

Bosky. On the verge of drunkenness. A slang term possibly connected with the legitimate *bosky* meaning bushy, hence overshadowed, obscured.

Bosom friend. A very dear friend. Nathan says it "lay in his bosom, and was unto him as a daughter" (II *Sam*. xii, 3). St. JOHN is represented in the New Testament as the "bosom friend" of Jesus.

Bosom sermons. Sermons committed to memory and learnt by heart; not extempore or delivered from notes.

Bosporus (bos' pôr ús), or less correctly **Bosphorus**, is a Greek compound meaning "ox-ford". The Thracian Bosporus unites the Sea of Marmora with the EUXINE or BLACK SEA. Greek legend says that ZEUS, enamoured of Io, changed her into a white heifer from fear of HERA, to flee from whom Io swam across the strait, which was thence called *bos porus*, the passage of the cow. Hera discovered the trick, and sent a gadfly to torment Io, who was made to wander, in a state of frenzy, from land to land, ultimately finding rest on the banks of the Nile. The wanderings of the Argive princess were a favourite theme among ancient writers.

Boss. Boss-eyed. Slang for having a bad squint or one eye injured, or only one eye. Hence, **boss one's shot,** to miss one's aim, as a person with a defective eye might be expected to do; and **a boss,** a bad shot. In archery the *boss* is the straw-packed base to which the target proper is affixed. Thus to shoot clumsily, missing the target altogether and lodging one's arrow in the boss, would be a "boss shot", and the archer derisively dubbed "boss-eyed" by the more expert.

Boston Tea-Party (1773). An incident serving to worsen the relations between Great Britain and her American colonies. By the Tea Act of 1773 the East India Company was enabled to ship its surplus stocks of tea direct to America to the disadvantage of American merchants. At Boston, patriots, disguised as Indians, boarded the tea ships and dumped all the tea into the harbour. As a consequence the British PARLIAMENT passed the INTOLERABLE ACTS.

Botanomancy (bot' ǎn ō mǎn si). DIVINATION by leaves. One method was by writing sentences on leaves which were exposed to the wind, the answer being gathered from those which were left; another was through the crackling made by leaves of various plants when thrown on the fire or crushed in the hands.

Botany Bay. An inlet in the coast of New South Wales five miles south of Sydney discovered by Captain Cook in 1770, and so named by him on account of the great variety of new plants observed there. Although the first convicts landed there in 1788 the settlement was established at Sydney, Port Jackson. In contemporary parlance Botany Bay was an alternative name for New South Wales and **to be sent to Botany Bay** meant sentence of transportation to Australia.

Both ends against the middle, To play (western U.S.A.). A method of rigging a pack of cards in faro, from which the expression became common for any sharp practice with a risk of being found out.

Bothie (perhaps from Gaelic *Bothag*). A humble cottage or hut. Particularly applied to the one-room farm servants' dwelling in the north-east of Scotland which was often part of the stabling. The *bothie system* was formerly wide-

spread, and the unmarried men were crowded into these sparsely furnished habitations, often preparing their own food.

Bo-tree. The pipal tree or *Ficus religiosa* of India, allied to the banyan and so called from Pali *Bodhi*, perfect knowledge, because it is under one of these trees that GAUTAMA attained enlightenment and so became the BUDDHA. At the ruined city of Anuradhapura in Sri Lanka is a bo-tree reputed to have grown from a cutting sent by King ASOKA in 288 B.C.

Bottle. The accepted commercial size of a wine bottle is one holding 26⅔ fluid ounces per reputed quart. Large bottles are named as follows:

Magnum	holding	2 ordinary bottles.	
Double-magnum			
or *Jeroboam*	,,	4	,, ,,
Rehoboam	,,	6	,, ,,
Methuselah	,,	8	,, ,,
Salmanazar	,,	12	,, ,,
Balthazar	,,	16	,, ,,
Nebuchadnezzar	,,	20	,, ,,

A *Nip* is ¼ of a bottle, a *Baby* is ⅛.

Bottle-chart. A chart of ocean surface currents made from the track of sealed bottles thrown from ships into the sea.

Bottle-holder. One who gives moral but not material support. The allusion is to boxing or prize-fighting, where the attendant on each combatant, whose duty it is to wipe off blood, to refresh him with water, and to do other services to encourage his man to persevere and win, is called "the bottle-holder".

Bottle-neck. Metaphorically, a narrowing of the main highway impeding the smooth flow of traffic; an impediment holding up production or trade.

Bottle-washer. Chief agent; the principal person employed by another; a factotum. The full phrase—which is usually applied more or less sarcastically—is "chief cook and bottle-washer".

Bottled moonshine. Unpractical social and benevolent schemes.

Looking for a needle in a bottle of hay, or **in a haystack.** Looking for a very small article amidst a mass of other things. Bottle here is a diminutive of the Fr. *botte*, a bundle.

To be bottled. A colloquialism for being drunk.

To bottle up one's feelings, emotions, etc. To suppress them; to hold them well under control.

To put new wine into old bottles. A saying found in *Matt*. ix, 17; typical of incongruity. New wine expands as it matures. If put in a new skin (bottle), the skin expands with it; if in an old skin, when the wine expands, the skin bursts.

Bottom. Of a ship, the lower part of the hull, usually below the waterline; hence the hull itself or the whole ship as in such phrases as *goods imported in British bottoms* or *in foreign bottoms*.

At bottom. Radically, fundamentally.

From the bottom of my heart. Without reservation.

To be at the bottom of it. To instigate it or prompt it.

Never venture all in one bottom. Do not put all your eggs in one basket. This has allusion to the marine use of the word.

> My ventures are not in one bottom trusted.
>
> SHAKESPEARE: *Merchant of Venice*, I, i.

To have no bottom. To be unfathomable; to be unstable.

To get to the bottom of the matter. To ascertain the entire truth; to "BOLT (sieve) a matter to its bran".

To knock the bottom out of anything. *See under* KNOCK.

To touch bottom. To reach the lowest depth.

Bottom drawer. *See under* DRAWER.

Bottom the Weaver. A man who fancies he can do everything, and do it better than anyone else. Shakespeare has drawn him as profoundly ignorant, brawny, mock heroic, and with an overflow of self-conceit. He is in one part of *Midsummer Night's Dream* represented with an ass's head, and Titania, queen of the fairies, under a spell caresses him as an ADONIS.

The name is very appropriate, as one meaning of *bottom* is a ball of thread used in weaving, etc. Thus in Clark's *Heraldry* we read, "The coat of Badland is argent, three bottoms in fess gules, the thread or."

Bottomless Pit, The. Hell is so called in *Revelation*, xx, 1. *See* ABADDON. William Pitt, the younger (1759–1806), was humorously called **the bottomless Pitt**, in allusion to his thinness.

Boudicca. Nowadays the preferred form of BOADICEA.

Bought and Sold, or **Bought, Sold, and Done For.** Ruined, done for, outwitted.

Bouillabaisse (boo′ ya bās). A soup, for which Marseilles is celebrated, made of fish boiled with herbs in water or white wine.

Boulangism (boo lonj′ izm). The name given to a wave of political hysteria that swept over France, especially in Paris, in 1886–1887, and to the movement in support of General Boulanger (1837–1891). As Minister of War (1886–1887), he achieved some popularity for army reforms, but more particularly for his handsome military figure and identification with the policy of revenge against Germany. Deprivation of command (1888) increased his popularity, but his plans for a COUP D'ÉTAT were never realized. His flight abroad, when sentenced to exile (1889) for crimes against the Republic, lost him his supporters, and he shot himself in Brussels in 1891.

Boule, or **Boulle** (bool). A kind of marquetry in which brass, GOLD, or enamelled metal is inlaid into wood or tortoiseshell, named after André Charles Boulle (1642–1732), the celebrated cabinet-maker who worked for Louis XIV on the decorations and furniture at VERSAILLES. With English furniture dealers **buhl** (a Germanized form of the name) or **buhlwork** came to denote inlay work of this sort, however inferior or cheap.

Bounce. Brag, swagger; boastful and mendacious exaggeration.

That's a bouncer. A gross exaggeration, a braggart's lie. A *bouncing* lie is a *thumping* lie and a *bouncer* is a *thumper*. A *bouncer* is also a "chucker-out" at a dance-hall, etc.

Boundary Rider. An employee on an Australian pastoral station who looks for and repairs damaged fences, attends to water supplies and treats sick stock.

Bounds, Beating the. An old custom still kept up in a few English parishes, of going round the parish boundaries on

Holy Thursday or ASCENSION DAY. The schoolchildren, accompanied by the clergymen and parish officers, walked round the boundaries, which the boys struck with peeled willow-wands. The boys were sometimes "whipped" at intervals and water was sometimes poured on them from house windows "to make them remember" the boundaries.

In Scotland beating the bounds was called *Riding the marches* (bounds), and in England the day is sometimes called *gang-day*.

Bounty, The Mutiny of the. This celebrated mutiny broke out on 28 April 1789, and was as much due to the mutineers' attachment to the damsels of Otaheite as to the exacting discipline of Captain William Bligh. The *Bounty* had been engaged in a bread-fruit collecting voyage in the South Seas and Bligh was unaware of the impending mutiny. The mutineers reached Tahiti and some of them, accompanied by native men and women, sailed to Pitcairn Island, where they were not discovered until 1808, John Adams being the only surviving mutineer. Bligh, with 18 loyal companions, was set adrift in an open boat and made the remarkable passage of 3,618 nautical miles to Timor near Java.

Bourbon (boor' bon). The family name of the kings of France from 1589 to 1793 (Henry IV, Louis XIII, XIV, XV, XVI), and from 1814 to 1830 (Louis XVIII, Charles X), derived from the seigniory of Bourbon, in the Bourbonnais in central France; the family is a branch of the house of CAPET. Bourbons also ruled in Spain, Naples and Sicily, and later in Lucca, Parma and Piacenza, as a result of the accession of Philip of Anjou (grandson of Louis XIV) to the Spanish throne in 1700.

In the U.S.A. the term *Bourbon* is also used for a whisky made from Indian corn, sometimes with rye or malt added. The first Kentucky whisky was made by a BAPTIST clergyman named Elijah Craig at Royal Spring, near Georgetown, in 1789. Georgetown (now County seat of Scott County) was then in Bourbon (*pron.* bĕr' bŭn) County.

Bourgeois (Fr.). Our *burgess*; a member of the class between the "upper" and "working" classes. It includes merchants, shopkeepers and professional people, the so-called "middle class".

Bourgeoisie (Fr.). The merchants, manufacturers, master-tradesmen, etc., considered as a class; much maligned since the days of Karl Marx who portrayed it as the exploiting class.

More recently the word has also been used to denote the conventional, narrow-minded and philistine elements of the middle classes. *See* PHILISTINES.

Bouse. *See* BOOZE.

Boustrapa. A nickname of NAPOLEON III; in allusion to his unsuccessful attempts at a COUP D'ÉTAT at *Bou*logne (1840) and *Stra*sbourg (1836) and the successful one at *Pa*ris (1851).

Boustrophedon (boo strof' e dŏn). A method of writing found in early Greek inscriptions in which the lines run alternately from right to left and left to right, like the path of oxen in ploughing. (Gr. *boustrophos*, ox-turning.)

Bouts-rimés (boo rē' mā) (Fr. rhymed endings). A parlour game which had a considerable vogue in 18th-century literary circles as a test of skill. A list of words that rhyme with one another is drawn up; this is handed to the competitors, and they have to make a poem to the rhymes, each rhyme-word being kept in its place on the list.

Bow. Draw not your bow till your arrow is fixed. Have everything ready before you begin.

He has a famous bow up at the castle. Said of a braggart or pretender.

He has two strings to his bow. Two means of accomplishing his object; if one fails, he can try the other. The allusion is to the custom of bowmen carrying a reserve string for emergency.

To be too much of the bow-hand. To fail in a design; not to be sufficiently dexterous. The bow-hand is the left hand, the hand which holds the bow.

To draw a bow at a venture. To attack without proper aim; to make a random remark which may hit the truth.

To draw the longbow. To exaggerate. The tales told about longbow exploits, especially in the ROBIN HOOD stories, fully justify the application of the phrase. *See* TELL.

To unstring the bow will not heal the wound (Ital.). René of Anjou (1409–1480), king of Sicily, on the death of his wife, Isabella of Lorraine, adopted the emblem of a bow with the string broken with the words given above for the motto, by which he meant, "Lamentation for the loss of one's wife is but poor satisfaction."

Bow Bells (bō). **Born within sound of Bow Bells.** Said of a true COCKNEY. St. Mary-le-Bow, Cheapside, long had one of the most celebrated bell-peals in London, until an air raid destroyed the bells and the interior of the church in 1941. John Dun, mercer, in 1472 gave two tenements to maintain the ringing of Bow Bell every night at nine o'clock, to direct travellers on the road to town. In 1520 William Copland gave a bigger bell for the purpose of "sounding a retreat from work". It is said that the sound of these bells, which seemed to say "Turn again, Whittington, Lord Mayor of London", encouraged the young Dick WHITTINGTON to return to THE CITY and try his luck again.

Bow Street Runners (bō). The first regular police and detective force in London, organized in the mid-18th century under the chief magistrate at Bow Street, near COVENT GARDEN. They were eventually superseded (1829–1839) by the Metropolitan Police.

Bow-wow (bou-wou). A word in imitation of the sound made, as hiss, cackle, murmur, cuckoo, etc. Hence *the bow-wow school* is derisively applied to those philologists who sought to derive speech and language from the sounds made by animals. The terms were first used by Max Müller. *See* ONOMATOPEIA.

Bowdlerize (bou' dler īz). To expurgate a book. Thomas Bowdler, in 1818, published a ten-volume edition of Shakespeare's works "in which nothing is added to the original text; but those words are omitted which cannot with propriety be read aloud in a family". He also expurgated Gibbon's *Decline and Fall*, hence the words bowdlerist, bowdlerizer, bowdlerism, etc.

Bowels of Mercy. Compassion, sympathy. The affections were once supposed to be the outcome of certain secretions or organs, as the bile, the kidneys, the heart, the liver, the bowels, the SPLEEN etc. Hence the word *melancholy* or "black bile"; the Psalmist says that his *reins*, or kidneys, instructed him (*Ps*. xvi, 7), meaning his inward conviction; the *head* is the seat of understanding, the *heart* of affection and memory (hence "learning by heart"); the *bowels* of mercy, the *spleen* of passion or anger, etc. *See* HUMOUR.

Bower of Bliss. In Spenser's *Faerie Queene* (Bk. II), the enchanted home of Acrasia.

Bowery, The (Dut. *bouwerij*, a farm). A densely populated cosmopolitan street in New York city which runs through the former farm or *bouwerij* of Governor Peter Stuyvesant (1592–1672). Noted for its many cheap lodging houses, saloons and shops, it was once the haunt of the notorious ruffians called the *Bowery Boys*.

Bowie Knife. James Bowie (*pron*. Booee) was a Southerner who for some years from 1818 smuggled negro slaves with the great pirate Jean Laffitte. In 1827 he was present at a duel on a sandbar in Mississippi near Natchez which ended in a general mêlée. Six of the seconds and spectators were killed and fifteen wounded. Bowie killed one Major Norris Wright with a knife fashioned from a blacksmith's rasp some 10 to 15 inches long, with one sharp edge curving to the point. This knife attracted such attention that Bowie sent it to a cutler in Philadelphia who marketed copies as the *Bowie knife*. Bowie was with Davy CROCKETT at the fall of the ALAMO on 6 March 1836.

Bowing (bou' ing). We uncover the head when we wish to salute anyone with respect; but the Jews, Turks, Siamese, etc., uncover their feet. The reason is that with us the chief act of investiture is crowning or placing a cap on the head, but in the East it is the putting on of slippers.

Bowled. To be bowled out, or **to be clean bowled** are METAPHORS from CRICKET, meaning to be defeated in argument or detected in a falsehood.

Bowled over. To be knocked down; or figuratively to be overcome by a sudden assault on the emotions.

Bowler Hat. A hard felt hat, known in the U.S.A. as the DERBY hat. Like the BILLY-COCK HAT it is said to have been introduced by the Norfolk landowner, William Coke. Because he found his tall riding hat frequently swept off by overhanging branches, he asked (1850) Locks, the famous hatters of St. James's to design him a lower-crowned hat. The first "Coke" or bowler was made from felt supplied by Thomas and William Bowler.

To be bowler-hatted. To be discharged from the forces with a gratuity before the normal termination of one's commission, a bowler hat being the emblem of CIVVIE STREET. *Cp.* GOLDEN HANDSHAKE.

Bowling, Tom (bō ling). The type of a model sailor; from the character of that name in Smollett's *Roderick Random*.

The Tom Bowling referred to in the long-famous sea-song was Captain Thomas Dibdin, brother of Charles Dibdin (1768–1833), who wrote the song, and father of Thomas Frognall Dibdin, the BIBLIOMANIAC.

Bowyer God. The "archer god", usually applied to CUPID.

Bowyang (Austr.). A string or strap used by labourers to hitch the trouser leg below the knee, hence a symbol of manual labour.

From bowyangs to bowyangs. The Australian equivalent of CLOGS TO CLOGS IS ONLY THREE GENERATIONS.

Box, The. An everyday name for a television set.

"Box about, 'twill come to my father anon." During an argument with his son, Sir Walter Ralegh gave him a blow on the head. Not wishing to strike his father back, young Walter hit the man on his other side at table making the above remark, intending that the blow should go right round the table and get back to his father. According to Aubrey this became a common proverb in the 17th century.

Box and Cox has become a phrase which can only be explained by the story. Mrs Bouncer, a deceitful lodging-house land-lady, let the same room to two men, Box and Cox, who unknown to each other occupied it alternately, one being out at work all day, the other all night. It is from the farce by J. M. Morton (1811–1891) called *Box and Cox* (adapted from the French).

Box Days. A custom established in the Scottish Court of Session in 1690, providing two days in spring and autumn, and one at CHRISTMAS (during vacation) on which pleadings could be filed. Informations were to be placed in a box for each judge and examined in private.

I've got into the wrong box. I am out of my element, or in the wrong place or in a false position.

To be in the same box. To be in the same predicament as somebody else; to be equally embarrassed. *To be in the same boat* is a similar phrase.

To box the compass. A nautical phrase meaning to name the thirty-two points of the compass in their correct order. Hence a wind is said to "box the compass" when it blows from every quarter in rapid succession; hence, figuratively, to go right round in political views, etc., and end at one's starting-place.

Boxing Day. *See* CHRISTMAS BOX.

Boxer Hat (Austr.). A BOWLER HAT.

Boxers. A branch of the White Lotus sect in China which took a prominent part in the rising against foreigners in 1900 and was suppressed by joint European action. The Chinese name was *I Ho Chuan* or "Righteous Harmony Fists", implying training for the purpose of developing righteousness and harmony.

Boy. The Boy, meaning champagne, takes its origin from a shooting-party at which a boy with an iced bucket of wine was in attendance. When the Prince of Wales (Edward VII) needed a drink, he shouted "Where's the boy?", and thence the phrase found its way into would-be smart parlance.

Boy Bishop. St. NICHOLAS of Bari was called "the Boy Bishop" because from his cradle he manifested marvellous indications of piety.

Boy Scouts. An outstandingly imaginative and successful youth movement started by General Sir Robert Baden-Powell (Lord Baden-Powell of Gilwell) in 1908. The aim was to train boys to be good citizens with high ideals of honour, service to others, cleanliness and self-reliance, based essentially on training in an outdoor setting. The movement became world-wide with a membership now of over eight million young people. A complete Scout Group now consists of Cub Scouts (formerly Wolf Cubs), age 8 to 11; Scouts 11 to 16; Venture Scouts (formerly Rover Scouts), 16 to 20. These new designations, as well as that of Scout Association, were introduced in 1967.

Naked boy. *See* NAKED.

The Boys in blue. *See under* BLUE.

The Gazelle Boy. *See* GAZELLE.

Boycott. To boycott is to coerce by preventing any social or commercial dealings with a person, group, or nation. The term dates from 1880, when such methods were used by the Irish Land League under Parnell, who advocated that anyone taking over a farm from an evicted tenant should be "isolated from his kind as if he were a leper of old". This treatment was first used against Captain Boycott, a land agent in County Mayo. *Cp.* TO SEND TO COVENTRY *under* COVENTRY.

Boyle Controversy. A book-battle between Charles Boyle, fourth Earl of Orrery (1676–1731), and Richard Bentley (1662–1742), respecting the *Epistles of Phalaris* which were edited by Boyle in 1695. In 1697 Bentley wrote an essay declaring the Epistles to be spurious, and finally routed his opponents in his famous *Dissertation* of 1699. Swift's BATTLE OF THE BOOKS was one result of the controversy.

Boyle Lectures. A course of eight sermons to be delivered annually, in defence of the Christian religion; endowed by the Hon. Robert Boyle, the natural philosopher, and first given in 1692.

Boz. Charles Dickens (1812–1870). "Boz, my signature in the *Morning Chronicle*," he tells us, "was the nickname of a pet child, a younger brother, whom I had dubbed Moses, in honour of the Vicar of Wakefield, which being pronounced Boses, got shortened into Boz."

Bozzy. James Boswell (1740–1795), the biographer of Dr. Johnson.

Brabançonne, La (bra ban son). The national anthem of Belgium, composed by Van Campenhout in the revolution of 1830, and so named from Brabant, of which Brussels is the chief city.

Braccata. *See* GENS BRACCATA; GALLIA.

Bradamante (brăd′ à mănt). The sister of RINALDO in ORLANDO FURIOSO and ORLANDO INNAMORATO. She is represented as a wonderful Christian AMAZON, possessed of an irresistible spear which unhorsed every KNIGHT it struck.

Bradbury. A £1 note, as issued by the Treasury 1914–1928, bearing the signature of J. S. Bradbury (first Baron Bradbury), who as Joint Permanent Secretary to the Treasury began the issue.

Bradshaw's Guide. This famous railway guide was started in 1839 by George Bradshaw (1801–1853), printer, in Manchester. The *Monthly Guide* was first issued in December 1841, and consisted of thirty-two pages, giving tables of forty-three lines of English railway. Publication ceased in 1961.

Brag. A game at CARDS; so called because the players *brag* of their cards to induce the company to make bets. The principal sport of the game is occasioned by any player *bragging* that he holds a better hand than the rest of the party, which is declared by saying "I brag", and staking a sum of money on the issue.

Braggadocio (brăg à dō′ si ō). A braggart; one who is valiant with his tongue but a great coward at heart. *Cp.* ERYTHYNUS. The character is from Spenser's *Faerie Queene* and a type of the "Intemperance of the Tongue". It is thought that the poet had the Duke of Alençon, a suitor of Queen Elizabeth I, in mind when he drew this character (*Faerie Queene*, II, iii; III, v, viii, x; IV, ii, iv; V, iii, etc.).

Bragi. In Norse mythology, the god of poetry and eloquence, son of ODIN and husband of IDUNA. He welcomes the slain heroes who arrive in VALHALLA.

Brahma (bra′ mà). In Hinduism Brahma, properly speaking, is the Absolute, or God conceived as entirely impersonal. This theological abstraction was later endowed with personality and became the Creator of the universe, the first in the divine Triad, of which the other partners were VISHNU the maintainer, and SIVA, the destroyer. As such the Brahmins claim Brahma as the founder of their religious system.

Brahma Somaj (Sans., the Society of Believers in the One God). A Hindu theistic religious movement founded in 1828 by Ram Mohan Roy (1772–1833), a wealthy and well-educated BRAHMIN who wished to purify his religion and found a national church which should be free from idolatry and superstition. It was further developed after 1841 by Debendra Nath Tagore, but schisms occurred before the end of the century.

Brahmin. A worshipper of BRAHMA, the highest CASTE in the system of Hinduism and of the priestly order.

Braille. A system of writing made up of varying combinations of raised dots enabling the blind to read by touch, invented by Louis Braille in 1829. It has been likened to a domino block as it consists of different groups of one to six raised points. Braille devised his system after becoming acquainted with a twelve dot system invented by Captain Charles Barbier for passing messages at night.

Brain-child. A project, scheme, invention, etc., the product of an individual's brain.

Brain Drain. A phrase used to denote the drift abroad (from the early 1960s), of British-trained scientists, technologists, doctors and university teachers (especially to the U.S.A.), attracted by higher salaries and often better facilities for their work.

Brain-washing. The subjection of a person to an intensive course of indoctrination in order to transform his opinions and transfer his political loyalties to those approved by the "washers".

Brain-wave. A sudden inspiration; "a happy thought".

Brains Trust. Originally the name "Brains Trust" was applied by James M. Kieran of the *New York Times* to the advisers of F. D. Roosevelt in his election campaign; later to the group of college professors who advised him in administering the NEW DEAL. In Britain it became the name of a popular B.B.C. programme in which well-known public figures aired their views on questions submitted by listeners. Now in general use for any such panel of experts or team which answers questions impromptu.

Bran-new, or **Brand-new** (O.E. *brand*, a torch). Fire new, new from the forge. Originally applied to metals and things manufactured in metal which shine. Subsequently applied generally to things quite new.

Brand. He has the brand of villain in his looks. It was once customary to brand vagabonds and convicted offenders with a red-hot iron. In Tudor times vagabonds were branded with a V on the breast, and brawlers or "fray-makers in church" with an F, and so on. In the reign of William III it was enacted that branding for theft and larceny should be on the left cheek (1698). This was replaced in 1707 and in the 18th century "cold branding" was often passed as a normal sentence until branding was finally abolished in 1829. In the Army deserters were "branded" by tattooing below the left nipple until 1879. Deserters were branded with a D and incorrigibly bad characters with B.C. *Cp.* MAVERICK.

Brandan, St., or **Brendan.** A semi-legendary Irish saint, said to have been born at Tralee in 484. He founded the abbey of Clonfert and died in 577. The *Rule of St. Brendan* was dictated to him by an angel and he is said to have presided over 3,000 monks in the various houses of his foundation.

He is best known for the mediæval legend, widespread throughout Europe, of his seven-year voyage in search of the "Land of the Saints", the Isle of St. Brendan, reputed to be in mid-Atlantic. The very birds and beasts he encountered observed the Christian fasts and festivals. The earliest surviving version of the story is the *Navigatio Brendani* (11th century). *See* MAELDUNE.

Brandenburg Confession. A formulary of faith drawn up in the city of Brandenburg in 1610, by order of the elector, with the view of reconciling the tenets of Luther with those of Calvin, and to put an end to the disputes occasioned by the AUGSBURG CONFESSION.

Branding. *See* BRAND.

Brandy Nan. Queen Anne, who was very fond of brandy. On her statue in St. Paul's Churchyard a wit once wrote:

> Brandy Nan, Brandy Nan, left in the lurch,
> Her face to the gin-shop, her back to the church.

A "gin palace" used to stand at the south-west corner of St. Paul's Churchyard. *See* EST-IL POSSIBLE; QUEEN ANNE.

Brank (Scot.). A gag for scolds consisting of an iron framework fitting round the head with a piece projecting inward which went into the mouth and prevented the tongue wagging. There is one dated 1633 in the church vestry at Walton-on-Thames, inscribed:

> Chester presents Walton with a bridle
> To curb women's tongues that talk too idle.

Brasenose College (brāz' nōz) (Oxford). Over the gate is a brass nose, the arms of the college; but the word is a corruption of *brasenhuis*, a brasserie or brewhouse, the college having been built on the site of a brewery. For over 550 years the original nose was at Stamford, for in the reign of Edward III the students migrated thither in search of religious liberty, taking the nose with them. It was re-acquired by the college in 1890.

Brass. A slang term for money.

A church brass. A memorial brass plate engraved with details of the person commemorated. The earliest complete specimen is late 13th century in Stoke d'Abernon Church, Surrey.

Brassbounder. Formerly, a premium apprentice on a merchant ship, called by courtesy midshipman.

Brass Hat. A service term for an officer of high rank. It dates from the first Boer War (1880–1881), and refers to the gold oak leaves on the brim of senior officers' caps, sometimes nicknamed "scrambled egg". Officers of the highest rank are called **top brass.**

The Man of Brass. Talus, the work of Hephæstus (VULCAN). He was the guardian of Crete and threw rocks at the ARGONAUTS to prevent their landing; he used to make himself red-hot, and then hug intruders to death.

As bold as brass. With barefaced effrontery or impudence. Said to derive from Brass Crosby, Lord Mayor of LONDON in 1770, at which time publishing of reports of Parliamentary proceedings was still forbidden but Crosby, as chief magistrate, released the printer of the *London Evening Post* for so doing. Crosby was committed to the TOWER but public outcry soon secured his freedom.

To get down to brass tacks. To get down to the essentials. Probably from cockney RHYMING SLANG where *brass tacks* are *facts*.

Brazen Age. The age of war and violence. It followed the SILVER AGE. *See* AGE.

Brazen-faced. Bold (in a bad sense), without shame. *Cp.* BRASS.

> What a brazen-faced varlet art thou!
> SHAKESPEARE: *King Lear*, II, ii.

Brazen head. The legend of the wonderful head of brass that could speak and was omniscient, found in early romances, is of Eastern origin. Ferragus in VALENTINE AND ORSON is an example but the most famous in English legend is that fabled to have been made by the great Roger Bacon. It was said if Bacon heard it speak he would succeed in his projects; if not, he would fail. His familiar, Miles, was set to watch, and while Bacon slept the Head spoke thrice: "Time is"; half an hour later it said, "Time was". In another half-hour it said, "Time's past", fell down and was broken to atoms. Byron refers to this legend.

> Like Friar Bacon's head, I've spoken,
> "Time is", "Time was", "Time's past."
> *Don Juan*, i, 217.

See also SPEAKING HEADS.

Breach of Promise. A contract to marry was as binding in English law as any other contract, and the man or woman who broke an engagement was liable in law. The plaintiff was entitled to recover any pecuniary loss due to outlay in anticipation of marriage and a woman might be awarded substantial damages in certain circumstances. "Breach of Promise" was abolished for England and Wales as from 1 January 1971.

Breaches, meaning *creeks* or *small bays*, is to be found in *Judges* v, 17. Deborah, complaining of the tribes who refused to assist her in her war with Sisera, says that Asher "abode in his breaches", that is, creeks on the seashore.

Spenser has the same usage:

> The headful boateman strongly forth did
> stretch
> His brawnie armes, and all his body
> straine,
> That the utmost sandy breach they
> shortly fetch.
> *Faerie Queene*, II, xii, 21.

Bread. Bread is the staff of life (17th-century proverb).

Bread and cheese. The barest necessities of life.

Bread and circuses. Free food and entertainment. *Panem et circenses* were, according to Juvenal's *Satires*, the two things the Roman populace desired.

Bread and point. *See* TO DINE ON POTATOES AND POINT *under* POINT.

Bread-basket. The stomach.

Bread never falls but on its buttered side. An old north country proverb.

Breaking of bread. The EUCHARIST. In scriptural language *to break bread* is to partake of food.

Cast thy bread upon the waters; for thou shalt find it after many days (*Eccles*. xi, 1). The interpretation of this well-known passage is obscure. Perhaps the most likely meaning is "do not be afraid to give generously without hope of immediate gain, sooner or later you will reap as you have sown." Another common explanation is that seed cast on flooded land will take root and profit the sower when the waters recede, bread in this context meaning "corn" or "seed".

Don't quarrel with your bread and butter. Don't foolishly give up your job or take action that will deprive you of your living.

He took bread and salt, *i.e.* he took his oath. In Eastern lands bread and salt were once eaten when an oath was taken.

To know which side one's bread is buttered. To be mindful of one's own interest.

To take the bread out of someone's mouth. To forestall another; to take away another's livelihood.

Break. To break a butterfly on a wheel. To employ superabundant effort in the accomplishment of a small matter.

To break a journey. To stop before the journey is accomplished, with the intention of completing it later.

To break a matter to a person. To be the first to impart it, and to do so cautiously and piecemeal.

To break away. To escape, to go away abruptly; to start too soon in a race.

To break bread. *See* BREAD.

To break cover. To start forth from a hiding-place.

To break down. To lose all control of one's feelings; to collapse, to become hysterical; also to demolish or to analyse. A *breakdown* is a temporary collapse in health; it is also the name given to a wild kind of Negro dance.

To break faith. To violate one's word or pledge; to act traitorously.

To break ground. To commence a new project, as a settler does.

To break in. To interpose a remark. To train a horse or animal to the saddle, harness, etc., or to train a person to a way of life. To enter as a burglar does.

To break off. To stop a conversation, etc. To end an engagement or friendship.

To break one's fast. To take food after long abstinence; to eat one's *breakfast* after the night's fast.

To break one's neck. To dislocate the bones of one's neck. To be in a violent hurry.

To break on the wheel. To torture on a "wheel" by breaking the long bones with an iron bar. *See* COUP DE GRÂCE.

To break out. To escape from prison. To throw off restraint.

To break the ice. To prepare the way; to get through the stiffness and reserve of a first meeting with a stranger; to impart distressing news to another delicately and tactfully.

To break through. To force a passage. To overcome major obstacles especially in the field of scientific or technical progress.

To break one's back. To make one bankrupt; to reduce one to a state of impotence. The METAPHOR is from carrying burdens on the back.

To break up. To break into pieces, to smash; to discontinue classes at the end of term and go home; to separate. A meeting is said to break up when it dissolves or disperses. Also to become rapidly decrepit and infirm.

To break with someone. To quarrel or discontinue relations.

To get a break. To have an unexpected chance; to have an opportunity of advancing oneself.

To make a break. To make a complete change; to commit a social error or make an unfortunate mistake.

To run up a score in billiards or snooker.

Breaking a Stick. Part of the marriage ceremony of certain North American Indians, as breaking a wineglass is part of the marriage ceremony of the Jews.

One of Raphael's pictures shows an unsuccessful suitor of the Virgin Mary breaking his stick. This alludes to the legend that suitors were each to bring an almond stick to be laid up in the sanctuary overnight. The owner of the stick which budded was to be accounted the suitor approved by God. It was thus Joseph became the husband of Mary.

Breast. To make a clean breast of it. To make a full confession, concealing nothing.

Breath. All in a breath. Without taking breath (Lat. *continenti spiritu*).

It takes one's breath away. The news is so astounding it causes one to hold one's breath with surprise.

Out of breath. Panting from exertion; temporarily short of breath.

Save your breath to cool your porridge. Don't talk to me, it is only wasting your breath.

To catch one's breath. To check suddenly the free act of breathing.

To hold one's breath. Voluntarily to cease breathing for a time, as in fear, etc.

To take breath. To cease for a little time from some exertion in order to recover from exhaustion of breath.

Under one's breath. In a whisper or undertone.

To breathe fire and brimstone. To be manifestly wrathful.

To breathe one's last. To die.

Breeches. She wears the breeches or **trousers.** Said of a woman who usurps the prerogative of her husband. *Cp.* THE

GREY MARE IS THE BETTER HORSE, *under* MARE.

Breeches Bible. *See* BIBLE.

Brehon Laws (brē' hon). The English name for the ancient laws of Ireland, which prevailed until the mid-17th century. They cover every phase of Irish life and provide an invaluable source of historical information.

Brendan, St. *See* BRANDAN, ST.

Bren-gun. A World War II light machine-gun, fired from the shoulder. Originally made in Brno, Czechoslovakia, then in Enfield, England. *Bren* is a blend of Brno and Enfield.

Br'er Fox, he lay low. A hint that silence in speech or action is the wise course. The expression was in fairly common use in the early 1900s and was derived from the popular stories, largely concerning Br'er Fox and Br'er Rabbit, by the American writer Joel Chandler Harris (1848–1908). These animal stories in the Negro dialect, which began to appear in 1879, were supposedly told to a plantation owner's little boy by Uncle Remus, a kindly old Negro.

Bretwalda (bret wol' dà). The title given in the *Anglo-Saxon Chronicle* to Egbert of Wessex (802–839) and seven earlier English kings, who exercised a supremacy, often rather shadowy, over other English kings south of the Humber. The title probably means "overlord of the Brets (Britons)" and was sometimes assumed by later kings. *See* HEPTARCHY.

Breviary (brē' vi àr i). A book containing the ordinary and daily services of the ROMAN CATHOLIC CHURCH, which those in orders are bound to recite. It omits the EUCHARIST, which is contained in the MISSAL, and the special services (marriage, ordination, etc.), which are found in the *Ritual* or *Pontifical*. It is called a breviary because it is an abbreviation in the sense that it contains prayers, hymns, and lessons, etc., thus obviating the need to use a separate hymn book, and BIBLE.

Brew. As you brew, so you will bake. As you will go on; you must take the consequences of your actions; "as you make your BED so you will lie on it."

Brian Boru, or **Boroma** (brī' àn bo roo',

bo ro' ma) (926–1014). This great Irish chieftain became king of Munster in 978 and chief king of all Ireland in 1002. On Good Friday 1014, his forces defeated the Danes of Dublin at the battle of Clontarf, but Brian, too old to fight, was killed in his tent.

Briareus (brī âr' ē ús), or **Ægeon**. A giant with fifty heads and a hundred hands. Homer says the gods called him Briareus, but men called him Aegeon (*Iliad*, I, 403). He was the offspring of HEAVEN and Earth and was one of the race of TITANS, against whom he fought in their war with ZEUS.

Bold Briareus. Handel (1685–1759), so called by Pope:

> Strong in new arms, lo! giant Handel stands,
> Like bold Briareus, with a hundred hands;
> To stir, to rouse, to shake the soul he comes.
> And Jove's own thunders follow Mars's drums.
> *Dunciad*, IV, 65.

Bric-à-brac. Odds and ends of curiosities. In French, a *marchand de bric-à-brac* is a seller of junk, old stores, etc., usually of small value; we employ the phrase for odds and ends of virtu. *Bricoler* in French means *faire toute espèce de métier*, to be Jack of all trades. *Brac* is the RICOCHET of *bric*, as FIDDLE-FADDLE and scores of other double words in English. Littré says that it is formed on the model of *de bric et de broc*, by hook or by crook.

Brick. A regular brick. A jolly good fellow; perhaps because a brick is solid, four-square, plain and reliable.

Brickfielder (Austr.). A southerly gale experienced at Sydney which used to blow dust into the city from the nearby brickfields.

Brick tea. The inferior leaves of the plant mixed with a glutinous substance (sometimes bullock's or sheep's blood), pressed into cubes and dried. In this form it was sent overland from China to Russia and these blocks were frequently used as a medium of exchange in central Asia.

To drop a brick. To make a highly tactless remark.

To make bricks without straw. To attempt to do something without having the necessary material supplied. The allusion is to the Israelites in Egypt, who were commanded by their taskmasters so to do (*Exod.* v, 7).

Bride. Bride, or **wedding favours** represent the TRUE-LOVER'S KNOT and symbolic union.

Bride-ale. *See* CHURCH-ALE. It is from this word that we get the adjective *bridal*.

Bride cake. A relic of the Roman *confarreatio*, a mode of marriage practised by the highest class in Rome. It was performed by the *Pontifex Maximus* before ten witnesses and the contracting parties mutually partook of a cake of salt, water, and flour (*far*). Only those born in such wedlock were eligible for the high sacred offices.

Bride of the Sea. Venice; so called from the ancient ceremony of the wedding of the sea by the Doge, who threw a ring into the Adriatic saying, "We wed thee, O sea, in token of perpetual domination." This took place annually on ASCENSION DAY, and was enjoined upon the Venetians in 1177 by Pope Alexander III, who gave the Doge a gold ring from his own finger in token of the Venetian fleet's victory over Frederick Barbarossa, in defence of the Pope's quarrel. At the same time his Holiness desired the event to be commemorated each year. *See* BUCENTAUR.

Bridegroom's men. In the Roman marriage by *confarreatio*, the bride was led to the *Pontifex Maximus* by bachelors, but was conducted home by married men. Polydore Virgil says that a married man preceded the bride on her return, bearing a vessel of GOLD and SILVER. *See* BRIDE CAKE.

Bridewell. A generic term for a HOUSE OF CORRECTION, or a prison, so called from the City Bridewell, BLACKFRIARS, formerly a royal palace built over the holy well of St. Bride (Bridget). After the REFORMATION, Edward VI made it a penitentiary for unruly apprentices and vagrants. It was demolished in 1863 although much of the palace was destroyed in the GREAT FIRE OF LONDON. *See under* FIRE.

Bridge of Gold. According to a German

tradition, CHARLEMAGNE's spirit crosses the Rhine on a golden bridge at Bingen, in seasons of plenty, to bless the vineyards and cornfields.

To make a bridge of gold for him is to enable a man to retreat from a false position without loss of dignity.

Bridge of Jehennam. Another name for AL SIRAT.

Bridge of Sighs. Over this bridge, which connects the Doge's palace with the state prisons of Venice, prisoners were conveyed from the judgment hall to the place of execution. The passageway which used to connect the Tombs prison in New York with the criminal court was so dubbed for similar reasons.

A bridge over the Cam at St. John's College, Cambridge, which resembles the Venetian original, is called by the same name.

Waterloo Bridge, London, was also called *The Bridge of Sighs* when suicides were frequent there. Hood gave the name to one of his poems.

Bridget, St. (Bridig, Bride, Brigid) (453–523). The second patron saint of Ireland whose day is 1 February. She became a nun renowned for her piety and founded an abbey at Kildare — the first for women in Ireland. She is the protectress of dairy workers and became popular in England as St. Bride.

Bridle road, or **path.** A way for a ridinghorse, but not for a HORSE and cart.

To bite on the bridle is to suffer great hardships. Horses bit on the bridle when trying, against odds, to get their own way.

To bridle up. In Fr. *se rengorger*, to draw in the chin and toss the head back in scorn or pride. The METAPHOR is from a HORSE pulled up suddenly and sharply.

A scold's bridle. A most uncomfortable metal bridle with an even more unpleasant tongue plate put upon shrewish women as a punishment. They were used from mediæval times until the 18th century. There was a ring over the nose aperture for a rope or chain by which the wearer was led through the streets. *See* SKIMMINGTON; STANG.

Bridport. Stabbed with a Bridport dagger, *i.e.* hanged. Bridport in Dorsetshire was famous for its hempen goods, supplying ropes and cables for the Royal Navy, and it is still a centre for netmaking. The hangman's rope, being made at Bridport, gave rise to the phrase.

Brigade of Guards. *See* HOUSEHOLD TROOPS.

Brigand. A French word from the Ital. *brigante*, pres. part. of *brigare*, to quarrel. The 14th-century FREE COMPANIES of France, such as *The White Company* in Conan Doyle's story, were brigands, *i.e.* irregular troops addicted to marauding. In the course of time the Ital. *brigante* came to mean a robber or pirate; hence *brig, brigandine, brigantine* for a pirate ship, then a type of sailing vessel. *Brigade* and *Brigadier* are also derivatives.

Brighton. Doctor Brighton The town of Brighton in Sussex, from its popularity as a health resort. Originally the fishing village of Brighthelmstone, it changed its name at the beginning of the 19th century. Dr. Richard Russell drew attention to its possibilities as a wateringplace in the 1750s and it rapidly gained in favour after the PRINCE OF WALES first spent a holiday there in 1782. Subsequently he built the Royal Pavilion, in which he resided on his annual visits, thereby making the town fashionable.

Bring. To bring about. To cause a thing to be done.

To bring down the house. To cause rapturous applause in a theatre.

To bring forth. To produce or give birth.

To bring in. To introduce, to pronounce a verdict.

To bring into play. To cause to act, to set in motion.

To bring off. To achieve successfully.

To bring on. To cause an event or speed it up.

To bring round. To restore to consciousness or health; to cause one to recover from a faint or fit, etc.

To bring to. To restore to consciousness, to resuscitate.

Nautically, to luff, to heave to, to bend a sail to its yard; or used of a ship about to anchor, etc.

To bring to bear. To apply oneself to,

to focus one's efforts or attention upon, as guns or searchlights are trained on a target.

To bring to book. To detect one in a mistake, to bring one to account.

To bring to pass. To cause to happen.

To bring to the hammer. To offer or sell by public auction.

To bring under. To bring into subjection.

To bring up. To rear from birth or an early age. To moor or anchor a ship. Also numerous other meanings.

Brinkmanship. A term coined by Adlai Stevenson in 1956 (though he disclaimed originality), with especial reference to the policy of J. Foster Dulles as leading to the brink of war. It is now generally used for policies leading to the verge, and possible outbreak, of war.

Briny. I'm on the briny. The sea, which is salt like brine.

Brioche (brē′ osh). A kind of pâtisserie made with flour, butter and eggs. The French phrase *Qu'ils mangent de la brioche*, popularly translated as "Let them eat cake", has been commonly, but apocryphally, attributed to Queen Marie Antoinette. The remark was said to have been occasioned at the time of the bread riots at Paris (October 1789) when she was told that the starving populace could not afford bread. The saying in various forms has also been attributed to Yolande, duchesse de Polignac; the Princess Victoire; Queen Maria Theresa and others, but seems to have a considerably earlier ancestry. It is also said that Princess Charlotte (1796–1817), daughter of the then Prince Regent (later George IV), avowed that she would for her part "rather eat beef than starve" and wondered why the people should insist on bread when it was so scarce.

Briseis. The patronymic name of Hippodamia, daughter of Briseus. She was the cause of the quarrel between AGAMEMNON and ACHILLES, and when the former robbed Achilles of her, Achilles withdrew from battle and the Greeks lost ground daily. Ultimately, Achilles sent his friend PATROCLUS to supply his place; he was slain, and Achilles, towering with rage, rushed to battle, slew HECTOR, and TROY fell.

Brissotins. A name given to the republican group in the French Revolution led by Jaques Pierre Brissot (1754–1793), more commonly known as the GIRONDISTS.

Bristol cream is a particularly fine rich brand of SHERRY. *See* BRISTOL MILK.

Bristol diamonds. Brilliant crystals of colourless quartz found in St. Vincent's Rock, Clifton, Bristol. Spenser refers to them as "adamants".

Bristol fashion. *See* ALL SHIP-SHAPE AND BRISTOL FASHION *under* ALL.

Bristol Milk. Sherry; the nickname arose in the 17th century when sherry SACK was a major import at Bristol.

> This metaphorical milk, whereby Xeres or Sherry-sack is intended.
> FULLER: *Worthies*.

Bristol waters. Mineral waters of Clifton, Bristol, formerly celebrated in cases of pulmonary consumption.

Britain (M.E. *Bretayne* through O.Fr. *Bretaigne* from Lat. *Britannia*). An anglicized form of the Latin name for what is now England, WALES and SCOTLAND, called *Britannia* by CAESAR and other Roman writers. In the 4th century B.C. the inhabitants were known as *Pritani* or *Priteni*, and under the Roman occupation they were known as *Britones*.

Great Britain consists of "Britannia prima" (England), "Britannia secunda" (Wales), and "North Britain" (Scotland), united under one sway. The term was first officially used in 1604 when James I was proclaimed "King of Great Britain" and was previously used by some writers to distinguish Britain from "Brittannia Minor", or Brittany, in France.

Britannia. The earliest figure of Britannia as a female figure reclining on a shield is on a Roman coin of Antoninus Pius, who died in A.D. 161. The figure reappeared on our copper coin in the reign of Charles II, 1665, and the model was Frances Stewart, afterwards Duchess of Richmond. The engraver was Philip Roetier.

British. British disease. An uncomplimentary term used abroad with reference to the prevalence of strikes and INDUSTRIAL ACTION in Great Britain during the 1970s. *Cp.* TO WORK LIKE A BRI-

TON *under* BRITON.

British Legion. *See under* LEGION.

British Lion, The. The pugnacity of the British nation, as opposed to the JOHN BULL, which symbolizes their substantiality, solidity and obstinacy.

To twist the tail of the British lion, or **to twist the lion's tail** used to be a favourite phrase particularly in America for attempting to annoy the British people or provoke them by abuse or to inflict a rebuff. This was a device used to gain the support of Irish Americans.

British Museum. This famous institution began in Montague House, Great Russell Street. It resulted from an Act of 1753 and its first collections were purchased from the proceeds of a public lottery.

Britomart (brit′ ō mart). In Spenser's *Faerie Queene*, a female knight, daughter of King Ryence of Wales. She is the personification of chastity and purity.

Spenser got the name, which means "sweet maiden", from Britomartis, a Cretan NYMPH of Greek mythology, who was very fond of the chase. King MINOS fell in love with her, and persisted in his advances for nine months, after which she threw herself into the sea.

Brittany, The Damsel of. Eleanor, daughter of Geoffrey, second son of Henry II of England and Constance, daughter of Conan IV of Brittany. At the death of Prince Arthur (1203) she became heiress to the English throne, but King John confined her within Bristol castle, where she died in 1241.

Broach. To broach a subject. To open up a subject or start a topic in conversation. The allusion is to beer barrels which are tapped by means of a peg called a *broach*.

Broad Arrow. The symbol with which Government stores are marked as a precaution against theft, also once forming a pattern on convicts' uniforms. There are various explanations of its origin but in 1698 an Act was passed imposing heavy penalties on anyone found in possession of naval stores or other goods marked with the broad arrow. *See* ROGUE'S YARN.

Broad Bottom Ministry. A name particularly applied to Henry Pelham's administration (1743–1754) from 1744, which was reinforced by the admission of members of various opposition groups.

Broad Church. A group within the CHURCH OF ENGLAND favouring theological liberalism and tolerance, typified by the writers of *Essays and Reviews* (1860). The name dates from the mid-19th century and the party have certain affinities with the LATITUDINARIANS of former times. They were the forerunners of the MODERNISTS. *Cp.* HIGH CHURCH; LOW CHURCH.

Broadside. In naval language, the whole side of a ship, thus *to fire a broadside* is to discharge all the guns on one side simultaneously; figuratively, a telling verbal onslaught. It is also another name for a *broadsheet*, a large sheet of paper printed on one side, once a popular form of selling printed ballads, etc.

Brobdingnag. In Swift's *Gulliver's Travels*, the country of the giants, to whom Gulliver was a pigmy "not half so big as a round little worm plucked from the lazy finger of a maid". Hence the adjective, *Brobdingnagian*, colossal.

Brocken. *See* SPECTRE.

Broken Music. In Tudor England this term meant: (1) Part, or concerted music, *i.e.* music performed on instruments of different classes such as the consorts given in Morley's *Consort Lessons* (1599), which are written for the treble lute, cithern, pandora, flute, treble viol, and bass viol; (2) Music played by a string orchestra, the term in this sense probably originating from harps, lutes, etc., played without a bow and unable to sustain a long note. Bacon uses it in this sense.

> Dancing to song is a thing of great state and pleasure. I understand it that the song be in quire, placed aloft and accompanied with some broken music.
> *Essays: Of Masques and Triumphs.*

SHAKESPEARE makes verbal play with the term:

> *Pand:* Fair prince, here is good broken music.
> *Paris:* You have broke it cousin: and by my life, you shall make it whole again.
> *Troilus and Cressida*, III, i.

Broker. This word originally meant a man who broached wine and then sold it;

hence one who buys to sell again, a retailer, a second-hand dealer, a middleman. The word is formed in the same way as *tapster*, one who *taps* a cask. Thus bill-broker, cotton-broker, pawn-broker, ship-broker, STOCK-BROKER, etc.

Bromide. One given to trite remarks, then the remark itself. It was first used in this latter sense by Gelett Burgess (1866–1951) in his novel *Are You a Bromide?* (1906).

Brontes (bron' tēz). A blacksmith personified; in Greek mythology, one of the CYCLOPS. The name signifies *Thunder*.

Brontës, The. The three novelist sisters and their brother Branwell. *See* BELL.

Bronx cheer. The American term for a vulgar derisive sound made with the tongue between the lips, known in England as a "RASPBERRY".

Broom. The small wild shrub with yellow flowers (Lat. *planta genista*) from which the English royal dynasty unhistorically called PLANTAGENETS were named. The founder of the dynasty, Geoffrey of Anjou (father of Henry II), was nicknamed Plantagenet because he wore a sprig of broom in his hat, but it was not until about 1448 that the name was assumed by Richard, Duke of York (father of Edward IV) as a surname. It is more correct to refer to ANGEVIN, LANCASTRIAN, and YORKIST kings.

Broom. A broom hung at the masthead of a ship indicates that it is for sale or to be "swept away". The idea is popularly taken to be an allusion to Admiral Van Tromp (*see* PENDANT). It is more probably due to the custom of hanging up something special to attract notice, as a bush meant wine for sale; an old piece of carpet outside a window meant furniture for sale; a wisp of straw meant oysters for sale, etc.

New brooms sweep clean. Those new in office are generally very zealous at first, and sometimes ruthless in making changes.

Brother. Brother Jonathan. It is said that when Washington was in want of ammunition, he called a council of officers, but no practical suggestion was forthcoming. "We must consult brother Jonathan," said the general, meaning

His Excellency Jonathan Trumbull, governor of the State of Connecticut. This was done and the difficulty was remedied. Hence the set phrase "To consult Brother Jonathan", and *Brother Jonathan* became the JOHN BULL of the United States until replaced by UNCLE SAM. (*See under* SAM.)

Brougham (brō' ăm, brum). A closed four-wheel carriage drawn by one horse, very similar to the old GROWLERS. It was named after Lord Brougham (1778–1868), a prominent WHIG politician and one-time Lord CHANCELLOR.

Brow-beat. To beat or put down with sternness, arrogance, in a bullying manner, etc.; from knitting the brows and frowning on one's opponent.

Brown. A copper coin; a penny; so called from its colour.

Browned off. A slang phrase (derivation uncertain) widely current in World War II, signifying "fed up" or "bored stiff". *Cheesed off* is a similar expression. *See* COOKING.

To be done brown. To be deceived, taken in; seen off, to be "roasted". One of the many expressions connected with cooking. *See* ROAST; COOK.

Brown Bagger. A "swot" type of undergraduate, especially at the modern universities. The term is derived from the brown attaché case in which students (especially non-resident students) used to carry their books.

> A "Brown Bagger" I must explain, is a peculiar person; he is one who arrives at 10 a.m. (or earlier) and leaves at 5 p.m., takes no active part in the social life of the college, works at home or elsewhere on Boat Race and Athletic Days when the college is shut and perhaps knows only by hearsay where the Union is.
>
> *Westminster City School Magazine*,
> Dec. 1930.

In the U.S.A. a *brown bagger* is a workman who takes his lunch from a brown paper bag rather than use the cafeteria, etc.; or one who similarly takes his own liquor to a club or restaurant, usually where alcoholic drinks are not available.

Brown Bill. A kind of halberd used by foot-soldiers before muskets took their place. The *brown* probably refers to their rusty condition though it may equally stand for *burnished* (Dut. *brun*, shining) as in the old phrases "my bonnie brown sword", "brown as glass", etc. Keeping the weapons *bright*, however, is a modern habit; our forefathers preferred the honour of bloodstains.

Brown Bomber. Joe Louis (1914–1981), undefeated heavyweight champion of the world from 1937 until his retirement in 1949. On his return in 1950 he was defeated by Ezzard Charles. He began his career in 1934, winning 27 fights, all but four by knockouts. The phrase comes from his being a NEGRO and from the great power of his punches.

Brown George. A large earthenware vessel such as that mentioned by Thomas Hughes in *Tom Brown at Oxford* (1861).

Brown, Jones, and Robinson. The typification of middle-class Englishmen; from the adventures of three Continental tourists of these names which were told and illustrated by Richard Doyle in *Punch* in the 1870s. These sketches hold up to ridicule the gaucherie, insularity, vulgarity, extravagance, conceit, and snobbery of the middle class, and are in themselves an outstanding example of Victorian snobbery in their ill-mannered sneers at the uneducated.

Brown Shirts. Hitler's NAZI Party in Germany, so called from the colour of their shirts.

Brown study. Absence of mind; apparent thought but real vacuity. The corresponding French phrase explains it—*sombre rêverie. Sombre* and *brun* both mean sad, melancholy, gloomy, dull.

Brownie. The home spirit in Scottish superstition; is called in England ROBIN GOODFELLOW. At night he is supposed to busy himself on little jobs for the family over which he presides. Brownies are brown or tawny spirits and farms are their favourite abode. *See also* GIRL GUIDES.

Brownists. Followers of Robert Browne, who established a congregational society at Norwich in 1580. Both episcopal and presbyterian organization was rejected. Browne eventually left his own society and returned to the Church. *See* INDEPENDENTS.

> I had as lief be a Brownist as a politician.
> SHAKESPEARE: *Twelfth Night*, III, ii.

Bruderhof (Ger. Society of Brothers). A Christian sect founded in Germany in 1920 with beliefs similar to the MENNONITES. They came to Gloucestershire in 1937 when driven out by the NAZIS, but to avoid internment in World War II left for Paraguay in 1941. They re-established themselves in Sussex in 1971. The men wear beards and dark trousers with braces, the women are simply clad with long skirts and head-scarves or caps. They support themselves by making quality wooden toys in community workshops and the children first go outside the community at the secondary school stage. There are four other groups in the Eastern U.S.A. and they are linked with the Hutterian Anabaptists in the Western U.S.A. and Canada. *Cp.* KIBBUTZ.

Bruin. Sir Bruin. The bear in the famous mediæval beast-epic, REYNARD THE FOX.

Brumaire (brü' mâr). In the French Revolutionary CALENDAR, the month from 23 October to 21 November; named from *brume*, fog (Lat. *bruma*, winter). The celebrated COUP D'ÉTAT of 18 Brumaire (9 November 1799) was when NAPOLEON overthrew the DIRECTORY and established the Consulate, thus ending the sway of the revolutionary oligarchy.

Brumby. An Australian wild horse. The origin of the word is obscure.

Brummagem (brŭm' à jem). Worthless or inferior metal articles made in imitation of better ones. The word is a local form of the name *Birmingham*, formerly noted for its output of cheap trinkets, toys, imitation jewellery, etc.

Brummel, George Bryan. *See* BEAU.

Brunhild (broon' hild). Daughter of the King of Islant, and of superhuman physique, beloved by GUNTHER, one of the two great chieftains in the NIBELUNGENLIED. She was to be won by strength, and SIEGFRIED contrived the matter but Brunhild never forgave him for his treachery.

Brunt. To bear the brunt. To bear the worst stress, the worst of the shock. The *brunt of the battle* is the hottest part of the fight.

Brush. He brushed by me. He just touched me as he hurried by. Hence also *brush*, a slight skirmish.

To brush aside. To sweep out of the way; to take no account of.

To brush up. To renovate or revive; to bring back into use that which has been neglected, as, "I must brush up my French."

To get the brush-off (of American origin). To be given a curt rebuff; to be put aside, rejected or dismissed.

Brut. A rhyming chronicle of British history beginning with the mythical Brut, or BRUTE, and so named from him. Wace's *Le Roman de Brut*, or *Brut d'Angleterre* is a rhythmical translation of Geoffrey of Monmouth's *History*, with additional legends. Wace's work formed the basis of Layamon's *Brut* (early 13th century), a versified history of England from the fall of TROY to A.D. 698. (*See* ARTHURIAN ROMANCES.)

Brute (broot), or **Brutus**. In the mythological history of Britain the first king was Brute, the son of Sylvius (grandson of Ascanius and great-grandson of ÆNEAS). Having inadvertently killed his father, he first took refuge in Greece, and then in Britain. In remembrance of TROY he called the capital of his kingdom TROY NOVANT, now London.

Brutum fulmen (broo' tum fŭl' men) (Lat.). A noisy but harmless threatening; an innocuous thunderbolt. The phrase is from Pliny II, xliii, 113: "*Bruta fulmina et vana, ut quae nulla veniant ratione naturae*"—Thunderbolts that strike blindly and harmlessly, being traceable to no natural cause.

Brutus, Junius (broo' tus, joo' ni ŭs). In legend, the first consul of ROME, fabled to have held office about 509 B.C.

Brutus, Marcus (85–42 B.C.). Caesar's friend, who joined the conspiracy to murder him.

Et tu Brute. Thou, too, Brutus! Caesar's exclamation when he saw that his old friend was one of his assassins. "Does my old friend raise his hand against me?"

Bryanites. *See* BIBLE CHRISTIANS.

Bub. Drink; particularly strong beer.

Bubastis. The ancient capital of Lower Egypt named after Bast, the local cat-headed goddess. The Greeks identified her with ARTEMIS and the CAT was sacred to her.

Bubble, or **Bubble Scheme.** A worthless, unstable, unsound project—an ephemeral scheme, frail as a bubble. *See* MISSISSIPPI; SOUTH-SEA.

The Bubble Act. An Act of 1719 which was designed to check the formation of "bubble" companies or schemes. It proved to be ineffectual and was repealed in 1825.

Bubble and Squeak. Cold boiled potatoes and greens fried up together (sometimes with meat). They first *bubbled* in water when boiled and afterwards hissed or *squeaked* in the frying pan.

Bubbles. The name given to the portrait of a curly-headed boy, clad in velvet, with pipe and bowl, blowing bubbles. It was painted by Sir John Millais in 1886 and it became widely familiar when used as an advertisement for Pears' Soap. The boy concerned came to be Admiral Sir William James (1881–1973), affectionately known in the Royal Navy as "Bubbles James".

Bubbly. Sparkling champagne. Until well into the 18th century champagne was fashionable as a still drink.

Bucca (bŭk' à). A GOBLIN of the wind, once supposed by Cornish people to foretell shipwrecks; also a sprite fabled to live in the tin mines.

Bucentaur (bū sen' tôr) (Gr. *bous*, ox; *centauros*, centaur). The name of the Venetian state galley used by the Doge on ASCENSION DAY when Venice was made BRIDE OF THE SEA. The original galley was probably ornamented with a manheaded ox. The third and last Bucentaur was destroyed by the French in 1798.

Bucephalus (bull-headed). A HORSE. The famous charger of ALEXANDER THE GREAT.

Buchmanism. *See* OXFORD GROUP.

Buck. A DANDY; a GAY and spirited fellow; a fast young man.

The word is also American slang for a DOLLAR, derived from the time when skins were classified as "bucks" and "does", the former being the more valuable.

Buck-basket. A linen-basket. To *buck* is to wash clothes in lye. The word is probably connected with the Ger. *beuchen*, Fr. *buer*, to steep in lye, and perhaps with O.E. *bue*, a pitcher.

Buck board. An open four-wheeled horse-drawn vehicle formerly used in the U.S.A.; named from the "bucking" motion endured by the occupants due to the springy structure of the floorboards.

Buckeye State. Ohio, from the abundance of *buckeyes* or horse-chestnut trees that grow there. A *buckeye* is a native of Ohio.

Buck horn. *See* STOCKFISH.

Buckhorse, A. A severe blow or slap on the face, from an 18th-century pugilist, John Smith, whose nickname was "Buckhorse". For a small sum he would allow anyone to strike him heavily on the side of the face.

Buck-tooth. A large projecting front-tooth, once called a butter-tooth.

To pass the buck. To evade a task or responsibility and shift it on to someone else. The term is from poker and was the equivalent of passing (*i.e.* not bidding) in a game of bridge.

Bucket, To. An obsolete slang term for *to cheat*, of American origin.

Bucket-shop. Probably derived from TO BUCKET, it denoted the office of an "outside" STOCKBROKER, *i.e.* a non-member of the STOCK EXCHANGE. As these offices are used for gambling in stocks rather than investing, the name usually implies a shady establishment.

To give the bucket, to get the bucket. To give (or receive) notice of dismissal from employment. Here *bucket* is synonymous with SACK.

To kick the bucket. To die. *Bucket* here is a beam or yoke (O.Fr. *buquet*, Fr. *tré-buchet*, a balance), and in East Anglia the beam on which a pig is suspended by the heels for slaughter is called a bucket. Another theory is that the bucket was kicked away by a suicide, who stood on it the better to hang himself. A third explanation is that when a bucket was put out to collect for the widow of a workmate some who passed by kicked the bucket instead of throwing in a coin.

Buckle. I can't buckle to. I can't give my mind to work. The allusion is to buckling on one's armour or belt.

To cut the buckle. To caper about, to

heel and toe it in dancing. In jigs the two feet buckle or twist into each other with great rapidity.

To talk buckle. To talk about marriage.

Bucklersbury (London) was at one time the noted street for druggists and herbalists; hence Falstaff says:

> I cannot cog, and say thou art this and that, like a many of these lisping haw-thorn buds, that come like women in men's apparel, and smell like Bucklers-bury in simple time.
> SHAKESPEARE: *Merry Wives of Windsor*, III, iii.

Buckley's Chance (Austr.). An extremely remote chance. One explanation of the phrase is that it comes from a convict named Buckley who escaped in 1803 and lived over thirty years with aborigines. The second explanation derives it from the Melbourne business house of Buckley and Nunn—hence the pun, "There are just two chances, Buck-ley's or None."

"To have two chances—mine and Buckley's" is a way of emphasizing that there is only one feasible course of action to take.

Buckram. A strong coarse kind of cloth.

Men in buckram. Imaginary men, as in Falstaff's vaunting tale to Prince Henry. Hence a "buckram army", one which exists only in the imagination.

> Four rogues in buckram let drive at me.
> SHAKESPEARE: *Henry IV, Pt. I*, II, iv.

Buckshee. Free, gratis. Military slang derived from BAKSHEESH.

Buckskin. A Virginian.

Buddha (bud' à) (Sans. the enlightened). The title given to Prince Siddhartha or GAUTAMA (*c.* 563–483 B.C.), the founder of BUDDHISM; also called Sakyamuni from the name of his tribe, the Sakyas.

Buddhism. A religion inaugurated by Buddha in India in the 6th century B.C. It holds that the way to *enlightenment* consists in knowledge of the *Four Truths*:

(1) That life is characterized by un-satisfactoriness.

(2) That this is due to desire or craving.

(3) That the state of unsatisfactoriness can be removed by eliminating desire.

(4) That NIRVANA, the state of non-, desire is attainable by means of the *Noble Eightfold Path*: right understanding, right thought, right speech, right action, right livelihood, right effort, right mindfulness and right concentration.

Esoteric Buddhism. *See* THEOSOPHY.

Budge. Lambskin with the wool dressed outwards, worn on the edges of capes, graduates' hoods, etc. Hence the word is used attributively to denote pedantry, stiff formality, etc.

Budge Bachelors. A company of men clothed in long gowns lined with *budge* or lamb's wool, who used to accompany the Lord MAYOR at his inauguration.

Budget (O.Fr. *bougette*, a wallet). The present meaning of the (normally) annual estimate of revenue and expenditure and statement on financial policy, which the CHANCELLOR OF THE EXCHEQUER lays before the HOUSE OF COMMONS, arose from the custom of bringing the relevant papers to the House in a leather bag and laying them on the table. Hence to *budget*, to estimate, or to make proper provision for meeting one's expenses.

A budget of news. A bagful of news, a large stock of news.

Cry budget. A watchword or shibboleth; short for MUMBUDGET. Slender says to Shallow:

> We have a nay-word how to know one another. I come to her in white and cry *mum*: she cries *budget*; and by that time we know one another.
> SHAKESPEARE: *Merry Wives of Windsor*, V, ii.

Buff. Properly, soft stout leather prepared from the skin of a buffalo; hence any light-coloured leather; then figuratively, the bare skin. **To stand in buff** is to stand without clothing; **to strip to the buff** is to strip to the skin.

To stand buff. To stand firm; unflinching. Here buff means a blow or buffet. *Cp.* BLINDMAN'S BUFF.

The phrase also occurs as **to stand bluff.** Here the allusion is probably nautical; a "bluff shore" is one with a bold and upright front.

Buffalo Bill. William Frederick Cody (1847–1917) earned this name for his hunting the buffalo to provide meat for the labourers constructing the Kansas Pacific Railway in 1876–1878. He is held to have killed 4,280 buffaloes in 18 months. He was born in Iowa and, when little more than a boy, was a rider of the PONY EXPRESS. In 1861 he became a scout for the U.S. army and fought in the CIVIL WAR. Later on he was fighting once more in the Indian wars and single-handed killed Yellowhand, the Cheyenne chief. In 1883 he organized his Wild West Show, which he brought to Europe for the first time in 1887. He paid various subsequent visits and toured the Continent in 1910. His show, with its Indians, cowboys, sharpshooters and roughriders was outstanding.

Buffer. A chap, a silly old fellow. In M.E. it is used for a stammerer or stutterer.

Buffer State. A small state between two larger neighbours acting as a shock-absorber between the two.

Bug. An old word for GOBLIN, SPRITE, BOGY; probably from the Welsh *bwg*, a ghost. The word is used in the BUG BIBLE (*see* BIBLE, SPECIALLY NAMED), and survives in *bogle*, *bogy*, and in *bugaboo*, a monster or goblin, and *bugbear*, a scarecrow, or sort of HOBGOBLIN in the form of a bear.

> Warwick was a bug that feare'd us all.
> SHAKESPEARE: *Henry VI, Pt. III*, V, ii.

In common usage the word *bug* is applied to almost any kind of insect or germ, especially an insect of the creeping crawling sort, and notably the *bed bug*. Also it is colloquially used to refer to anyone "bitten" with a particular craze or obsession, from the *love-bug* to the *money-bug*. *See* BUGHOUSE.

A big bug. A person of importance, especially in his own eyes, a SWELL, a conceited man. There is an old adjective *bug*, meaning pompous, proud.

Bug-eyed Monster. Generic for the creatures of the science-fiction writers' imaginations, inhabitants of, or visitors from, outer space; from the American slang "bug" (*i.e.* bulging) eyes. It is known as BEM to science-fiction addicts.

Bughouse (U.S.A.). Crazy or demented. Also used in England for the old-time cheap cinema in the same way as *fleapit*.

Fire-bug. A person with a mania for incendiarism. A term of American origin.

Buggane. *See* BOGGARD.

Buhl. An incorrect form of BOULE.

Bull. (1) A blunder, or inadvertent contradiction of terms, for which the Irish are proverbial. *The British Apollo* (No. 22, 1708) says the term is derived from one Obadiah Bull, an Irish lawyer of London in the reign of Henry VII, whose blundering in this way was notorious, but there is no corroboration of this story which must be put down as BEN TROVATO. Another explanation is that it is suggested by the contradiction in a PAPAL BULL in which the POPE humbly styles himself "servant of servants" while asserting complete authority. There was a M.E. verb *to bull*, to befool, to cheat, and there is the O.Fr. *boule* or *bole*, fraud, trickery; the word may be connected with one of these.

(2) Slang for a five-shilling piece. Possibly from *bulla* (*see* PAPAL BULL); but as BULL'S EYE was an older slang term for the same thing, this is doubtful. Hood, in one of his comic sketches, speaks of a crier who, being apprehended, "swallowed three hogs (shillings) and a bull".

(3) It is also short for BULL'S EYE.

(4) *Bull* (short for bull-shit), originally army slang for excessive spit and polish and unnecessary cleaning of equipment, etc. Now used also for anything useless, unnecessary, or just rubbish and pretence.

(5) In STOCK EXCHANGE language, a *bull* is a speculative purchase for a rise; also a buyer who does this, the reverse of a BEAR. A *bull-account* is a speculation made in the hope that the stock purchased will rise before the day of settlement. Since the early 18th century the terms *bull* and *bear* have been broadly used on the Stock Exchange to describe an optimist or pessimist in share-dealing.

(6) In astronomy, the English name of the northern constellation (Lat. Taurus) which contains ALDEBARAN and the PLEIADES; also the sign of the ZODIAC that the sun enters about 22 April.

(7) *Bull* is also the name given to a

drink from the swillings of empty spirit casks.

Bulling the barrel. Pouring water into a nearly empty rum cask to prevent it leaking. The water which gets impregnated with the spirit is called *bull*. Hence the seaman's phrase of *bulling the teapot* (making a second brew).

A bull in a china shop. One who behaves clumsily or acts in a gauche manner, without finesse, or even with violence.

To roar like a bull of Bashan. To roar loudly and excessively. In OLD TESTAMENT times Bashan was a territory in northern Palestine noted for its breed of cattle.

In the SCRIPTURES a bull of Bashan also denoted a loud-mouthed, tyrannical oppressor.

To score a bull. *See* BULL'S EYE.

To take the bull by the horns. To attack or encounter a threatened danger fearlessly; to go forth boldly to meet a difficulty, just as a MATADOR will grasp the horns of a bull about to toss him.

A brazen bull. An instrument of torture.

Bull sessions. In the U.S.A. this phrase is applied to long talks, among men only, about life in general or some particular problem.

Geneva Bull. *See under* GENEVA.

John Bull. *See* JOHN BULL.

Papal Bull. An edict issued by the POPE, named from the seal (Lat. *bulla*) appended to the document. *See* GOLDEN BULL.

Bull-ring. In Spain the arena where bull-fights take place; in England, the place where bulls used to be baited. The name survives in many English towns, as in Birmingham. *See* MAYOR OF THE BULL-RING.

Bull-Roarer. A flat piece of wood, about eight inches long, attached to a cord and whirled above the head, producing a moaning or humming sound. It was used by the primitive peoples of Australia (called *tundun*) and North America in rain-making, initiation and fertility ceremonies.

Bull's eye. The inmost disc or centre of a target. Also a black and white streaked peppermint-flavoured sweet; a small

Bun

cloud appearing seemingly in violent motion, and expanding till it covers the entire vault of heaven, producing a tumult of wind and rain (I *Kings* xviii, 44); and a thick disc or boss of glass. Hence a *bull's-eye lantern*, also called a *bull's-eye*.

To make a bull's-eye, or **to score a bull.** To gain some signal advantage; a successful coup. To hit the centre of the target.

Bulldog. A man of relentless, tenacious disposition is sometimes so called. A bulldog courage is one that flinches from no danger. The bulldog was formerly used for BULL-BAITING.

Boys of the bulldog breed. Britons, especially with reference to their pugnacity. This phrase comes from Arthur Reece's music-hall song *Sons of the Sea, All British born* which had a tremendous vogue in late Victorian and Edwardian England.

Bullet. Every bullet has its billet. Nothing happens by chance and no act is altogether without effect.

To get the bullet. To be dismissed, TO GET THE SACK. (*See under* SACK.)

Bully. To overbear with words. A *bully* is a blustering menacer. The original meaning of the noun was "sweetheart" as in

> I kiss his dirty shoe, and from my heart-strings
> I love the lovely bully.
> SHAKESPEARE: *Henry V*, IV, i.

It is probably from the Dut. *boel*, a lover; and the later meaning may have been influenced by Dut. *bul*, a bull, also a clown, and *bulderen*, to bluster.

Bully-beef. Tinned corned beef. Probably from Fr. *boulli*, boiled meat.

Bully-rag. To intimidate; *bully-ragging* is abusive intimidation. A *rag* is a scold.

Bully-rook. SHAKESPEARE uses the term (*Merry Wives*, I, iii, 2) for a jolly companion, but later it came to mean a hired ruffian.

Bum. Bum-bailiff. The Fr. *pousse-cul* seems to favour the view that *bum-bailiff* is no corruption. These officers, who made an arrest for debt by touching the debtor on the back, are frequently referred to as *bums*.

Scout me for him at the corner of the orchard, like a bum-bailiff.
SHAKESPEARE: *Twelfth Night*, III, iv.

Bum-boat. A small wide boat used to carry provisions to vessels lying off shore. Also called "dirt boats", being used for removing filth from ships lying in the Thames.

Bum-freezer. A short jacket, an Eton jacket, especially as formerly worn by schoolboys at Eton and elsewhere.

Bumble. A BEADLE. So called from the officious, overbearing beadle in Dickens's *Oliver Twist*; hence **bumbledom**, fussy officialism, especially on the part of parish officers; also parochial officials collectively.

Bummaree. Middlemen or fishjobbers in BILLINGSGATE Market. It has been suggested that the word is a corruption of *bonne marée*, good fresh fish, *marée* being a French term for all kinds of fresh seafish.

Bump off. To murder, a EUPHEMISM deriving from "to take for a ride" (*see* RIDE).

Bump Suppers. Festivities which follow the BUMP RACES, often accompanied by hilarious behaviour from the undergraduates.

Bun. Hot cross buns on GOOD FRIDAY were supposed to be made of the dough kneaded for the HOST, and were marked with a cross accordingly. As they are said to keep for twelve months without turning mouldy, some persons still hang up one or more in their house as a "charm against evil".

The Greeks offered cakes with "horns" on them to APOLLO, DIANA, HECATE and the MOON. Such a cake was called a *bous*, and (it is said) never grew mouldy. The round bun represented the full moon, and the cross symbolized the four quarters.

> Good Friday comes this month: the old woman runs.
> With one a penny, two a penny "hot cross buns",
> Whose virtue is, if you believe what's said,
> They'll not grow mouldy like the common bread.
> *Poor Robin's Almanack*, 1733.

Bun fight. A tea party on a fairly large scale such as that of a SUNDAY SCHOOL, social club, parish organization, etc.

To put a bun in the oven. To make a woman pregnant.

Bunce. A slang term for money; particularly for something extra or unexpected in the way of profit. Also sometimes used in the sense of perquisites, which can be sold for money. Thought to be a corruption of *bonus* (in the sense of extra dividend).

Bunch. Bunch of Fives. Slang for the hand or fist.

Bundle. Bundle of Sticks. ÆSOP, in one of his fables, shows that sticks one by one may be readily broken; not so when several are bound together in a bundle. The lesson taught is that "Union gives strength".

The bundle of rods with an axe or *Fasces*, the Roman symbol of absolute authority, was adopted by Mussolini's party. Hence the name FASCIST.

Bundling. The curious and now obsolete New England custom of engaged couples going to bed together fully dressed and thus spending the night. It was a recognized proceeding to which no suggestion of impropriety was attached.

> Stopping occasionally in the villages to eat pumpkin pie, dance at country frolics, and bundle with the Yankee lasses.
> WASHINGTON IRVING: *Knickerbocker*.

The same custom existed in Wales and the remoter parts of Scotland.

Bung. A CANT term for a publican; also for a toper. "Away, … you filthy bung," says Doll to Pistol (SHAKESPEARE: *Henry IV, Pt. II*, II, iv).

Bung up. Close up, as a bung closes a cask.

Bungalow (Hind. *bangla*, of, or belonging to, Bengal). Originally, the house of a European in India, generally of one storey only with a verandah all round it, and the roof thatched to keep off the hot rays of the sun. A *dak-bungalow* is a caravansary or house built by the government for the use of travellers.

Bungay. *See* FRIAR BUNGAY.

Bungay play. Leading with the highest scoring cards in WHIST, instead of attempting any finesse. It may be a corruption of "bungling" or a reference to the supposed rustic slow-wittedness of the people of Bungay in Suffolk.

Castle of Bungay. *See* CASTLE.

Friar Bungay. *See under* FRIAR.

Go to Bungay with you!—*i.e.* get away and don't bother me; don't talk such stuff. Bungay in Suffolk was famous for the manufacture of leather breeches, once very fashionable. Persons who required new ones or old ones re-seated went or sent to Bungay for them. Hence rose the cant saying, "Go to Bungay, and get your breeches mended", shortened into "Go to Bungay with you!"

Bunkum. Claptrap. Now more commonly shortened to *bunk*. A representative at Washington being asked why he made such a flowery and angry speech, so wholly uncalled for, made answer, "I was not speaking to the House, but to Buncombe," which he represented (North Carolina).

Bunny. A rabbit. So called from the provincial word *bun*, a tail, especially of a hare, which is said to "cock her bun". *Bunny*, a diminutive applied to a rabbit, means the animal with the "little tail".

Bunny girl. A somewhat scantily dressed waitress or attendant in certain night clubs and Playboy clubs, equipped with a fluffy tail and a headdress with long ears to suggest a rabbit.

Bunting. In Somersetshire *bunting* means sifting flour. Sieves were once made of a strong gauzy woollen cloth, which was tough and capable of resisting wear. It has been suggested that this cloth was found suitable for making flags, hence its present meaning of a material for this purpose.

Bunyan, Paul. A legendary hero of the lumber camps of the north-western U.S.A.

Bunyip. According to Australian aboriginal folk-lore, a man-eating bellowing monster who drags his victims down to the bottom of the lake or swamp that he inhabits. It is also used to mean an "impostor".

Burble (bĕr'bĕl). To mutter nonsense. In its modern use this is a word invented by Lewis Carroll (*Through the Looking Glass*) with the meaning to make a sound somewhere between a bubble and a gurgle.

The Jabberwock, with eyes of flame,

Came whiffling through the tulgy wood
And burbled as it came.

Burd. A poetic word for a young lady (*cp.*
BIRD). Obsolete except in ballads.

Burden of a song. A line repeated at intervals constituting a refrain or chorus.
It is the Fr. *bourdon*, the big drone of a
bagpipe, or double diapason of an organ, used in *forte* parts and choruses.

Burden of Isaiah. "The Burden of Babylon, which Isaiah the son of Amoz did
see" (*Isaiah* iii, 1, etc.). Burden here is a
literal translation of the Heb. *massa*
(rendered in the Vulgate by *onus*),
which means "lifting up", either a burden or the voice; hence utterance, hence
a prophecy announcing a calamity, or a
denunciation of hardships on those to
whom the burden is uttered.

The burden of proof. The obligation
to prove something.

Burgoyne, Gentleman Johnny. General
John Burgoyne (1722–1792), who surrendered to General Gates at Saratoga
(1777). He later devoted his time to writing light literature and plays. He
earned his nickname for his elegant
manner and fondness of fashionable life.

Burgundian. A Burgundian blow, *i.e.*
decapitation. The Duc de Biron, who
was put to death for treason by Henry
IV, was told in his youth by a fortune-
teller, "to beware of a Burgundian
blow". When going to execution, he
asked who was to be his executioner,
and was told he was a man from Burgundy.

Burial of an Ass. No burial at all, just
thrown on a refuse heap.

Buridan's Ass. A man of indecision; like
one on "double business bound, who
stands in pause where he should first begin, and both neglects". Buridan was a
French scholastic philosopher who died
c. 1360, incorrectly reputed to be the
father of the well-known SOPHISM:

> If a hungry ass were placed exactly be-
> tween two haystacks in every respect
> equal, it would starve to death, because
> there would be no motive why it should
> go to one rather than to the other.

Burke. To murder by smothering. So
called from William Burke, an Irish
NAVVY, who with his accomplice William Hare, used to suffocate his victims

and sell the bodies to Dr. Robert Knox,
an Edinburgh surgeon. Aided by their
wives they lured fifteen people to their
deaths before discovery. Hare turned
King's EVIDENCE and Burke was hanged
in 1829. *Cp.* RESURRECTIONISTS.

To burke a question. To smother it at
birth. *The publication was burked*, suppressed before it was circulated.

To be in Burke. To be of an aristocratic family. Burke's *Peerage, Baronetage and Knightage* has, since 1826, been
a recognized authority on Britain's titled
classes with their family pedigrees. *Cp.*
DEBRETT.

Burlaw. *See* BYRLAW.

Burlesque. Father of burlesque poetry.
Hipponax of Ephesus (6th cent. B.C.).

Burlington Bertie. A would-be MASHER.
Portrayed in Vesta Tilly's song of that
name.

Burma Road. This great highway was
made in 1937–1939 to open up the western interior of China by communication
with the sea, and ran from Lashio to
Kunming in Yunnan, a distance of 770
miles. It was the chief highway for supplies to China during World War II until the Japanese cut it in 1941. It was recaptured in 1945.

Burn. His ears must be burning. *See*
under EAR.

**His money burns a hole in his pock-
et.** He cannot keep it in his pocket, he
cannot refrain from spending it.

The burnt child dreads fire. Once
caught twice shy. "What! wouldst thou
have a serpent sting thee twice?"

To burn used adjectivally as in such
phrases as *money to burn* or *time to burn*
means to have much more than is
needed and therefore it can be expended
without causing any hardship or sense of
deprivation.

To burn one's boats. To take an irrevocable step; to cut oneself off from all
chance of retreat. When invading forces
burned their boats they were impelled to
conquer or die—there could be no going
back. *Cp.* RUBICON.

To burn one's fingers. To suffer loss
or mischance. The allusion is to taking
chestnuts from the fire.

To burn the midnight oil. To work or
study late into the night.

To burn the Thames. To set the Thames on fire.

The burning question. A question under hot discussion, the vital question.

You cannot burn the candle at both ends. You cannot do two opposite things at one and the same time, or more commonly, you cannot exhaust your energies in one direction and yet reserve them unimpaired for something else. If you overdo it your health will suffer. *To burn the candle at both ends* often implies a hectic and somewhat dissipated existence.

Burnt Candlemas. The name given by the Scots to the period around CANDLEMAS DAY, 1355–1356, when Edward III marched through the Lothians with fire and sword.

Burns' Night. The evening of 25th January, the birthday of the Scottish poet Robert Burns (1759–1796). In Scotland it is a celebration for many accompanied by feasting and drinking, the HAGGIS being a prominent dish on the bill of fare. *See* AULD LANG SYNE.

Bursa (Gr. a *hide*). So the citadel of Carthage was called. The tale is that when DIDO came to Africa she bought from the natives "as much land as could be encompassed by a bull's hide". The agreement was made, and Dido cut the hide into thongs so as to enclose a space sufficient for a citadel. *Cp.* DONCASTER.

Burton. Gone for a Burton. Absent, missing or lost (referring to persons or things), dead or presumed dead. Widely used by the services in World War II it is of uncertain origin and date. Often claimed as an R.A.F. coinage derived from the training of Radio Telegraph operators in Burton's clothing premises at Blackpool. Those who failed their tests were said to have *gone for a Burton* and it was subsequently applied to those who were killed. It may also possibly be connected with Burton beer meaning he has gone for a drink as an explanation of absence. Another interesting suggestion is that when George Cadbury was standing for Birmingham Council in 1878 and supporting the temperance interest his opponent, Dr. Burton, was openly backed by the licensed victuallers. The Birmingham Post (22 July) says "Dur-

ing the whole of the polling day men were seen coming from Dr. Burton's committee room, and, parading Steward St. with jugs of beer in their hands, on which were painted papers 'Vote for Burton'". This could have given rise to the expression "he's gone for a Burton" when inquiring of someone's whereabouts.

Bury the Hatchet. Let bygones be bygones. The "GREAT SPIRIT" commanded the North American Indians, when they smoked their calumet or peace-pipe, to bury their hatchets, scalping-knives, and war clubs, that all thought of hostility might be put out of sight.

Burying at the cross roads. *See* CROSS ROADS.

Bus. A contraction of *omnibus*. An affectionate term for a car, aeroplane, etc.

Busman's holiday. There is a story that in the old horse-bus days a driver spent his holiday travelling to and fro on a bus driven by one of his pals. From this has arisen the phrase, which means to occupy one's spare or free time on the same or similar work to one's everyday occupation, *i.e.* a holiday in name only.

To miss the bus. To miss a chance or opportunity.

Bush. One beats the bush but another has the hare. *See* BEAT THE BUSH.

Good wine needs no bush. That which has real worth, quality or merit does not need to be advertised. An ivy-bush (in the ancient world sacred to BACCHUS) was once the common sign of taverns and ale and wine vendors.

> Some ale-houses upon the road I saw,
> And some with bushes showing they
>   wine did draw.
> *Poor Robin's Perambulations* (1678).

The proverb is a Latin one, and shows that the Romans introduced the custom into Europe. *Vino vendibili hedera non opus est* (Columella).

Bush. An Australian term for wild wooded and sparsely populated country, derived from the Dut. *bosch* and imported from South Africa before 1820. It has given rise to a whole vocabulary.

Bush Baptist. A person of dubious religious convictions.

Bush Brotherhood. An association formed to take the Christian religion to the OUTBACK and remote cattle stations. Its members sacrifice their own personal and domestic comforts in so doing.

Bush carpenter. A clumsy, inept joiner.

Bush lawyer. One who argues glibly on a slight or inaccurate basis.

Bushed. An Australian word meaning "lost" or "confused". It has become so general that we find, "a small ship became bushed in the great Van Diemen's Gulf" (Barratt: *Coast of Adventure*, 1944).

Bushmen (Dut. *boschjesman*). The Cape of Good Hope Aborigines; dwellers in the Australian bush; bush farmers.

Bushrangers. Originally escaped convicts in Australia who lived as robbers in the wilds to avoid recapture, in which sense it is found in the *Sydney Gazette* in 1805. The word has a modern sense of those who take advantage of their fellows by sharp practice or crime. *See* KELLY.

Bush telegraph. In early Australian slang, one who informed the BUSHRANGERS of police movements. Now widespread to indicate any unofficial and undisclosed source of information.

Bush-whacker (Dut. *bosch wachter*, forest-keeper). In Australia, one who lives in the bush, especially an axeman engaged in clearing scrub. In the U.S.A. a deserter in the CIVIL WAR, who looted behind the lines.

To take to the bush. To become a BUSH-RANGER and live by plunder like a runaway convict.

Bushel. To hide one's light under a bushel. To conceal one's talents; to be self-effacing and modest about one's abilities. The bushel was measured in a wooden or earthenware container, hence *under a bushel* is to hide something.

> Neither do men light a candle and put it under a bushel, but on a candlestick.
> *Matt.* v, 15.

To measure other people's corn by one's own bushel. To make oneself the standard of right and wrong; to appraise everything as it accords or disagrees with one's own habits of thought and opinions.

Bushido. The code of conduct of the SA-MURAI of Japan. Courage, self-discipline, courtesy, gentleness, and keeping one's word were among the virtues enjoined. *Cp.* CHIVALRY.

Bushnell's Turtle. A Dutchman, Cornelius van Drebel, successfully demonstrated a submarine in the THAMES in the reign of James I; but the first to be used in naval warfare was David Bushnell's *Turtle* built at Saybrook, Conn., in 1775 and used to attack (unsuccessfully) the British 64-gun *Eagle* in New York harbour (1776). It was employed subsequently for laying mines in the Delaware River. It was made of oak, coated with tar and looked like two turtle shells joined together.

Business. O.E. *bisignes* and *bisigian*, to occupy, to worry, to fatigue. In theatrical parlance "business" or "biz" means by-play, *e.g.* Hamlet trifling with Ophelia's fan. The "business" is usually the creation of the actor who plays the part and it is handed down by tradition.

Business tomorrow. When the SPARTANS seized upon Thebes they placed Archias over the garrison. Pelopidas with eleven others banded together to put Archias to the sword. A letter giving full details of the plot was given to Archias at the banquet table but he thrust the letter under his cushion, saying "Business tomorrow." But long ere the sun rose he was dead.

The business end. The end of the tool, etc., with which the work is done. The *business end* of a chisel is the cutting edge, of a rifle the barrel.

Busiris (bū si' ris). A mythical king of Egypt who, in order to avert a famine, used to sacrifice to the gods all strangers who set foot on his shores. HERCULES was seized by him; and would have fallen a victim, but he broke his chain and slew the inhospitable king.

Buskin. Tragedy. The Greek tragic actors used to wear a similar thick-soled boot or *cothurnus* to elevate their stature. *Cp.* SOCK.

> Or what (though rare) of later age
> Enobled hath the buskind stage.
> MILTON: *Il Penseroso*

Buss. To kiss. An obsolete word, probably of onomatopœic origin, but *cp.* Lat. *basium*, Ital. *bacio*, Sp. *beso*, and

Fr. *baiser*.

Bust. A frolic; a drunken debauch. The word is a vulgarization of BURST.

Busted. Done for, exploded.

To be bust. To be spent up with no money left, to be "broke".

Buster. Anything of large or unusual size or capacity; a "whacking great lie".

To come a buster. To come a CROPPER; to meet with a serious set-back or fall.

Butcher. A title given to many soldiers and others noted for their bloodthirstiness. Achmed Pasha was called *djezzar* (the butcher), and is said to have whipped off the heads of seven wives. He was killed at the siege of Acre in 1804.

The Bloody Butcher. The Duke of Cumberland (1721–1765), second son of George II. So called for his ruthless suppression of the Highlanders after the rising under the Young PRETENDER. *See* JACOBITES.

Butter. Often used figuratively for flattery or "soft-soap", in order to appease or win somebody over. *To butter up* a person is to flatter them and smooth them down.

Butter-fingers. Said of a person who lets things fall out of his hands or slip through his fingers. Often used in the CRICKET field.

> I never was a butter-fingers, though a bad batter.
>
> H. KINGSLEY.

He knows which side his bread is buttered. He knows his own interest.

He looks as if butter would not melt in his mouth. He seems suspiciously amiable. He looks quite harmless, but his innocence is probably misleading. He seems too good to be true.

Soft, or fair words butter no parsnips. Saying "Be thou fed" will not feed a hungry man. Mere words will not find salt for our porridge, or butter our parsnips.

To butter one's bread on both sides. To be wastefully extravagant and luxurious; also to run with the HARE and hunt with the hounds, to gain advantages from two sides at once.

Buttercups. So called because they were once supposed to increase the butter content of milk. Miller, in his *Gardener's Dictionary*, says that they were named "under the notion that the yellow colour of butter is owing to these plants".

Butterfly. A light, flippant, objectless young person who flutters from pleasure to pleasure. One who is bright when conditions are favourable but is "done for" when the clouds gather.

The name was once used in the cab trade for those drivers who took up the occupation at the best of the season, in summertime only.

> The feeling of the regular drivers against these "butterflies" is very strong.
>
> *Nineteenth Century* (March 1893, p.177).

Butterfly kiss. A kiss with the eyelashes, that is, stroking the cheek with one's eyelashes.

Button. A decoy in an auction room was known as a *button*, because he "buttoned" or tied the unwary to "bargains" offered for sale. The button fastens or fixes what otherwise would slip away.

Buttons. A page whose jacket in front is remarkable for a display of small round buttons, as close as they can be fixed, from chin to waist. In the pantomime of CINDERELLA, Buttons, the page, is a stock character.

Bachelor's buttons. *See* BACHELOR.

He has not all his buttons. He is half-silly; "not all there"; he is a "button short", a "screw loose".

The buttons come off the foils. Figuratively, the courtesies of controversy are neglected. The *button* of a foil is a ball of waxed thread about one third of an inch in diameter drawn round and over the tip of the blade to prevent injury in fencing.

The button of the cap. The tip-top. Thus in *Hamlet* (II, ii), Guildenstern says, "On fortune's cap we are not the very button" *i.e.* the most highly favoured. The button on the cap was a mark of honour. In Imperial China the first grade of literary honour was the privilege of adding a gold button to the cap, and the several grades of MANDARINS are distinguished by a different coloured button on top of their caps. The idea has been used on schoolboys' caps.

See PANJANDRUM.

'Tis in his buttons. He is destined to obtain the prize; he is the accepted lover. Boys used to count their buttons, as plum-stones, etc., are counted on one's dish, to see what trade they were to follow, whether to do a thing or not, and whether some favourite favoured them.

> 'Tis in his buttons; he will carry't.
> SHAKESPEARE: *Merry Wives of Windsor*,
> III, ii.

To have a soul above buttons. To be worthy, or rather, to consider oneself worthy, of better things; to believe that one has abilities too good for one's present employment. This is explained by George Colman in *Sylvester Daggerwood* (1795): "My father was an eminent button-maker ... but I had a soul above buttons ... and panted for a liberal profession."

To have something buttoned up. To have something organized; to have it under control, everything tied up.

To press the button. To set in motion, literally or figuratively; generally by simple means, as the pressing of a button will start electrically driven machinery.

To take by the button. TO BUTTON-HOLE A PERSON.

Buttonhole. A flower or nosegay worn in the coat buttonhole.

To buttonhole a person. To detain him in conversation; to deliberately waylay someone to speak to them. The allusion is to a former habit of holding a person by the button or buttonhole while in conversation.

Buy. To buy in. To collect stock by purchase; to withhold the sale of something offered at auction because the bidding has not reached the reserve price. On the STOCK EXCHANGE *buying in* is the term used when, a seller having sold stock that he is unable to deliver, the buyer purchases the stock himself in the market and charges the extra cost, if any, to the original seller.

Buying a pig in a poke. *See* PIG.

To buy off. To give a person money or some form of reward to drop a claim, put an end to contention, or throw up a partnership.

To buy over. To induce one by a bribe to renounce a claim; to gain over by bribery.

To buy up. To purchase stock to such an amount as to obtain a virtual monopoly, and thus command the market; to make a CORNER, as to "buy up corn", etc.

Buzfuz (bŭz'fŭz). Sergeant Buzfuz was the windy, grandiloquent counsel for Mrs Bardell in the famous breach of promise trial described in *Pickwick Papers*. He represented a type of barrister of the early 19th century, seeking to gain his case by abuse of the other side and a distortion of the true facts.

Buzz. A rumour, a whispered report. An old usage.

Buzzard. Between hawk and buzzard. Not quite the equal of master or mistress nor quite a servant.

Buzzard called hawk by courtesy. It is a EUPHEMISM, a brevet rank, a complimentary title.

> The noble Buzzard ever pleased me best;
> Of small renown, 'tis true; for, not to lie
> We call him but a hawk by courtesy.
> DRYDEN: *The Hind and the Panther*, III,
> 1221.

By-and-by now means a little time hence, but at the time of the preparation of the AUTHORIZED VERSION of the Bible it meant *instantly*. "When tribulation or persecution ariseth ... by-and-by he is offended" (*Matt*. xiii, 21); rendered in *Mark* iv, 17, by the word "immediately". Our *presently* means in a little time, soon, but formerly it meant at present, at once; in this sense it is not an uncommon usage in the U.S.A.

By the street of by and by one arrives at the house of never. A Spanish proverb which is roughly the equivalent of "Procrastination is the thief of time." Things postponed never get done.

By and large. Taking one thing with another, generally speaking. This is really a nautical phrase. When a vessel is close-hauled, to sail by and large is to sail slightly off the wind, making it easier for the helmsman to steer and less likely for the vessel to be taken ABACK.

To sail "by" is to sail close to the wind, to sail large (*see under* LARGE) is to sail with the wind free or on the quarter. A ship's capability was evaluated from her performance sailing "by and large" *i.e.* from an overall or general view, hence the usage as an everyday expression.

> Taking it 'by and large', as the sailors say, we had a pleasant ten days run from New York to the Azores islands....
>
> MARK TWAIN: *The Innocents Abroad*, ch. V.

By-blow. A bastard.

By-laws. Local laws. From *by*, a town (*e.g.* Selby). Laws of local or restricted application introduced by local government authorities, joint-stock companies, etc. They must not conflict with the laws of the land. *See* BYRLAW.

By-line. A journalist's signature. When a newspaper reporter progresses from anonymous to signed contributions, he is said to have got a *by-line*.

By-the-by. *En passant*, laterally connected with the main subject. *By-play* is side or secondary play; *by-roads* and streets are those which branch out of the main thoroughfare. The first *by* means *passing from one to another*, as in the phrase "Day by day". Thus *By-the-by* is passing from the main subject to a *by* or secondary one.

By-the-way. An introduction to an incidental remark thrown in, and tending the same way as the discourse itself.

Bycorne. *See* BICORN.

Bye Plot, or **Watson's Plot.** So called from its presumed connection with Cobham's plot or the MAIN PLOT. In 1603, William Watson, a Roman Catholic priest, and others, plotted to capture James I and to secure toleration from him. Some PURITANS collaborated but the plans were revealed by a JESUIT and Watson was beheaded.

Byerly Turk. *See* DARLEY ARABIAN.

Byrlaw. A local law in the rural districts of Scotland. The inhabitants of a district used to make certain laws for their own observance, and appoint one of their neighbours, called the *Byrlawman*, to carry out the pains and penalties. *Byr = by*, common in such names as *Derby*, the town on the Derwent, Grimsby, Aswardby, Spilsby, etc., and is present in BY-LAWS.

Byron. Lord George Gordon Byron (1788–1824). The great English poet, much admired by his European contemporaries, who died at Missolonghi, serving the cause of Greek Independence.

Byrsa. *See* BURSA.

Byzantine (bi zǎn′ tin). Another name for the BEZANT.

Byzantine Art (from Byzantium, the former name of Constantinople, now Istanbul). A blend of Roman and Eastern influence and Christian symbolism by the early Greek or Byzantine artists. Its chief features are the circle, dome and round arch; and its chief symbols the LILY, CROSS, VESICA and NIMBUS. St. Sophia at Istanbul and St. Mark at Venice are excellent examples of Byzantine architecture and decoration. Westminster Cathedral, the great Roman Catholic cathedral in Ashley Gardens, Westminster, first used in 1904, is a fine modern example of Early Byzantine style. It was designed by J. F. Bentley, who died in 1903. Cardinal Wiseman and Cardinal Manning are buried there.

Byzantine Empire. The Eastern or Greek Empire, which lasted from the separation of the eastern and western Roman Empires on the death of Theodosius in 395 until the capture of Constantinople by the Turks in 1453.

C

C. The form of the letter is a rounding of the Gr. *gamma* (Γ), which was a modification of the Phœnician sign for *gimel*, a camel. It originally corresponded with the Gr. *gamma*, as its place in the alphabet indicates.

C in Roman notation stands for *centum*, 100. Hence the Fr. *cent*, etc. When the French *c* has a mark called a cedilla under it, thus, ç, it is to be pronounced as an *s*. There are poems written in which every word begins with C. There is one by Hamconius called "*Certamen catholicum cum Calvinistis*" and another by Henry Harder in Latin on Cats. *See* ALLITERATION.

C₃. Signifies a physical weakling or something of third-rate quality. The lowest category in the medical examination for service in the armed forces. *Cp.* A1.

Ca'canny. A Scots expression meaning "go easy", "don't exert yourself", much the same as "go slow". *Ca'* is *caw*, to drive, and *canny* here means "gently".

Ça ira (it will go). The name and refrain of a popular French patriotic song which became the *Carillon National* of the French Revolution. It went to the tune of the *Carillon National*, which Marie Antoinette was for ever strumming on her harpsichord.

Caaba. *See* KAABA.

Cab. A contraction of *cabriolet*, a small one-horse carriage, from the Ital. *capriola*, a caper, the leap of a kid, from the lightness of the carriage compared with its lumbering early predecessors. Cabs were introduced into London in the 19th century.

Cabal. A JUNTO, a council of intriguers. The famous Cabal (1667–1673) of Charles II's reign, the group of five ministers, the initial letters of whose names (Clifford, Ashley, Buckingham, Arlington, Lauderdale) by coincidence spelt this word, did not give rise to the usage. It was often applied in the 17th century to the king's inner group of advisers. *See* CABALA.

Cabala, Cabalist. *See* CABBALA.

Cabbage. An old term for odd bits of cloth, etc., left over after making up suits and other garments, appropriated by working tailors as perquisites. Hence a tailor was sometimes nicknamed "cabbage", and *to cabbage* means to pilfer. It was formerly so used in schoolboy slang as well as for something "cribbed". *See* TO CRIB *under* CRIB.

Cabbage-patch, Billy Williams's. *See under* BILLY.

Cabbage-patchers. Nicknames for the inhabitants of Victoria, Australia, who are also known as YARRA-YABBIES.

Cabbala. The word is the Heb. *qabbalah* or *kabbalah*, which means "accepted by tradition." It is particularly applied to a Jewish mystical system of theology and metaphysics, dating from the 11th and 12th centuries, but with much older antecedents in the teachings of the Neoplatonists and Neopythagoreans, etc. Its aim was to relate the finite and the infinite, which was brought about by emanations from the Absolute Being. Scriptural passages were treated as symbolic and interpretation was based on the significance of numbers. The most important Cabbalistic work is the *Zohar*, written in the 13th century, but based on earlier material. Our CABAL is from *Cabbala*.

Cabbalist. From the later MIDDLE AGES the cabbalists were chiefly occupied in concocting and deciphering charms, mystical anagrams, etc., by unintelligible combinations of letters, words and numbers; in searching for the PHILOSO-PHER'S STONE; in prognostications, attempted or pretended relations with the dead, and suchlike fantasies.

Cabinet, The. In Britain, the inner committee of ministers, headed by the Prime Minister, who hold the highest executive offices and largely determine national policy. The Prime Minister chooses the many ministers and decides the composition of the Cabinet, which has varied in size, but latterly contained about twenty. Those included in 1979 were the Chancellor of the Exchequer; the Secretaries of State for Foreign and Commonwealth Affairs, Home Department, Scotland, Wales, Northern Ireland, Defence, Employment, Environment, Industry, Social Services, Trade, Energy, Education; the Minister of Agriculture, Fisheries and Food; the Chancellor of the Duchy of Lancaster; the Chief Secretary to the Treasury; the Paymaster General; the Lord High Chancellor; the Lord President of the Council; and the Lord Privy Seal. The Cabinet is collectively responsible to Parliament and its decisions are binding on all members of the government.

The word *cabinet* originally meant a small room and eventually came to apply to the group of politicians who met in the room. The Cabinet has its real origins in the reign of Charles II (1660–1685) and it developed steadily from Hanoverian times with the growth of the Prime Minister's influence, and by the latter part of the 18th century ministerial responsibility was fairly well established.

In the U.S.A. the Cabinet consists of the heads of the great departments of state (twelve in number), who are appointed by the President and serve as his advisers. Unlike their British counterparts they are not members of the legislature and cannot take part in debates. A new Cabinet post must be authorized by an Act of Congress. They hold office during the President's pleasure. If the President is elected for a second term they continue in office, except the Postmaster General, who has to be reappointed. The President is more inde-pendent of his cabinet's advice than is the British Prime Minister.

Shadow Cabinet. A potential cabinet formed from leaders of the OPPOSITION party in PARLIAMENT, who also take the lead as critics of particular features of government policy.

Cabiri (ka bī' ri). Certain deities, probably of Phrygian origin, worshipped in Asia Minor, Greece and the islands. Samothrace was the centre of their worship, which involved scandalous obscenities. The traditional four deities are Axierus, Axiocersa, Axiocersus and Cadmilus who promoted fertility and safeguarded mariners.

Cable. In nautical usage commonly denotes the rope or chain to which the anchor is secured. Ship's cable is measured in *shackles*, a shackle being 12½ fathoms.

A cable's length. Eight shackles or 100 fathoms, one-tenth of a nautical mile.

To slip the cable. To release the cable from the inboard end letting it run out through the hawse, thus releasing the anchor.

Figuratively, to slip one's cable is to die.

Caboched (O.Fr. *caboche*, head). A term in HERALDRY when a beast's head is borne full face, without any part of the neck.

Caboodle (ka boodl'). **The whole caboodle.** The whole lot, the whole collection. Possibly from the Dut. *boedel*, possession, household goods, property.

Caboshed, or **Cabossed.** *See* CABOCHED.

Cachecope Bell (kăsh'kōp). In some parts of England it was customary to ring a bell at a funeral when the PALL was thrown over the coffin. This was called the cachecope bell, from Fr. *cache corps*, conceal the body.

Cachet (kăsh'ā) (Fr.). A seal; hence a distinguishing mark, a stamp of individuality.

Lettres de cachet (letters sealed). Under the old régime in France, letters or orders issued by the king under the royal seal (*cachet*). The name is best known for those used to imprison or punish a subject without trial, there being no HABEAS CORPUS in France. In the 18th century they were often issued as blank warrants, leaving the name to be filled in subsequently by the authorities or parties concerned. They were used against lunatics and prostitutes, and obtained by heads of families against their relatives; thus Mirabeau was consigned to prison by his father. During the administration of Cardinal Fleury (1726– 1734) 80,000 of these cachets are said to have been issued, mostly against the JANSENISTS. They were abolished by the CONSTITUENT ASSEMBLY (January 1790).

Cacodæmon (kăkō dē'mon) (Gr. *kakos daimon*). An evil spirit. Astrologers gave this name to the Twelfth House of HEAVEN, from which only evil prognostics proceed.

> Hie thee to hell for shame, and leave this world, Thou cacodemon.
> SHAKESPEARE: *Richard III*, I, iii.

Cacoethes (kăk ō ēth' ēz) (Gr.) A bad habit.

> As soon as he came to town, the political Cacoethes began to break out upon him with greater violence because it had been suppressed.
> SWIFT: *Life of Steele*.

Cacoethes loquendi. A passion for making speeches or talking.

Cacoethes scribendi. The love of rushing into print; a mania for authorship.

Cacus (kā'kus). In classical mythology, a famous robber, son of VULCAN, represented as three-headed and vomiting flames. He lived in Italy and was strangled by HERCULES for stealing some of his cattle. The curate of La Mancha says of Lord Rinaldo and his friends, "They are greater thieves than Cacus" (*Don Quixote*).

Cad. A low, vulgar, nasty fellow; also, before the term fell into disrepute, an omnibus conductor. The word is like the Scots CADDIE, probably from CADET.

Caddice-garter, or **caddis.** A servant, a man of mean rank (*caddice*, worsted yarn or binding, crewel). When garters were worn in sight, the cheaper variety was worn by small tradesmen, servants, etc. Prince Henry calls Poins a "caddis-garter" (SHAKESPEARE: *Henry IV*, Pt. I, II, iv).

> Dost hear,
> My honest caddis-garter?
> CLAPTHORNE: *Wit in a Constable* (1639).

Caddie. This is now almost solely associated with the boy or man who carried a golfer's clubs on the links, and now and then gave the tyro advice, and the two-wheeled container which has largely replaced them. It is another form of CADET and was formerly commonly used in Scotland for errand boys, odd-job men, chairmen, etc.

Caddy. In some English dialects, a ghost, a bugbear; from *cad*, a word of uncertain origin which in the 17th century meant a FAMILIAR spirit. It is not connected with *caddis*, a grub, which is from *caddice*, the allusion being to the similarity of the caddis-worm to the larva of the silkworm.

Cadency, Marks of. *See* DIFFERENCE.

Cader Idris (Kă'der id' ris). *Cader* in Welsh means chair, and *Idris* is the name of one of the old Welsh giants. The legend is that anyone who passes the night in this "chair" will either be a poet or a madman.

Cadet (kȧ det). Younger branches of noble families are called cadets from Fr. *cadet*, a diminutive, ultimately from Lat. *caput*, head, hence little head, little chieftain. Their armorial shields bore the marks of cadency (Lat. *cadere*, to fall). *See* DIFFERENCE.

The word is now commonly used to denote certain categories of military trainees, etc.

Cadmus. In Greek mythology, the son of AGENOR, King of Phœnicia and Telephassa, founder of THEBES (Bœotia) and the introducer of the alphabet into Greece. Legend says that, having slain the dragon which guarded the fountain of Dirce, in BŒOTIA, he sowed its teeth, and a number of armed men sprang up with intent to kill him. By the counsel of ATHENE, he threw a PRECIOUS STONE among them and they killed each other in the struggle to gain it, except five who helped to build the city. *See also* JASON.

Cadmean victory. A victory purchased with great loss. The allusion is to the armed men who sprang from the dragon's teeth sown by CADMUS.

Caduceus. A white wand carried by Roman heralds when they went to treat for peace; the wand placed in the hands of MERCURY, the herald of the gods, with which, poets feign, he could give sleep to whomsoever he chose; wherefore Milton styles it his "opiate rod" (*Paradise Lost*, XI, 133). It is generally pictured with two SERPENTS twined about it (a symbol thought to have originated in Egypt), and—with reference to the serpents of ÆSCULAPIUS—it was adopted as the badge of the Royal Army Medical Corps.

Caedmon (kăd'mon) (d. 680). Anglo-Saxon poet famed for his *Hymn* preserved in Bede's Latin. All his other work is lost. BEDE says he was an ignorant man knowing nothing of poetry, but was commanded in a dream, by an ANGEL, to sing the Creation, which he straightway did. On waking he remembered his verses and composed more. He was received into the monastery at Whitby, where he spent his life praising God in poetry. He has been called the "father of English song".

Cærleon (kâr' lē on). The Isca Silurum of the Romans, about three miles N.E. of Newport in South Wales. It is the traditional residence of King ARTHUR, where he lived in splendid state, surrounded by hundreds of knights, twelve of whom he selected to be KNIGHTS OF THE ROUND TABLE. *See* CAMELOT.

Cæsar (sē' zàr). The cognomen of Caius Julius Cæsar, assumed by his male successors, and by the heir-apparent to the imperial throne. The titles KAISER and *Czar* or *Tsar* are variants of the name.

Cæsar's wife must be above suspicion. The name of Pompeia having become involved with an accusation against P. Clodius, Cæsar divorced her, not because he believed her guilty, but because the wife of Cæsar must not be even suspected of crime (Suetonius, *Julius Cæsar*, 74).

Cæsarian operation. The extraction of a child from the womb by cutting the abdomen; supposedly so called because Julius Cæsar was thus brought into the world, but the obstetric use of the word *cæsarian* is most probably derived from Lat. *cæsus* (past participle of *cædere*, to cut).

Cage. To whistle, or **sing in the cage.** The *cage* is a jail, and to *whistle in a cage* is to turn King's EVIDENCE, or

peach against a comrade. The lift in which miners descend the pit shaft is termed a *cage*.

Cagmag (kăg' măg). Offal, bad meat; also a tough old goose; food which none can relish.

Cagots (ka' gō). In the MIDDLE AGES, a sort of GYPSY race, living in Gascony and Béarn, supposed to be descendants of the Visigoths and shunned as something loathsome, possibly because they may have been leprous. *Cp.* CAQUEUX; COLLIBERTS. In modern French, a hypocrite or ultra-devout person is called a *cagot*. From this came the word *cagoule*, meaning a penitent's hood or cowl, and from this the terrorist political organization of the latter 1930s, the *Cagoulards*, took their name.

Cahoot (Fr. *cahute*, cabin or small hut). In the U.S.A. **to go cahoots** is to share equally, to become partners.

In cahoots is to be in partnership or in league with someone.

Cain-coloured Beard. Yellowish, or sandy red, symbolic of treason. In the ancient tapestries Cain and JUDAS are represented with yellow beards. *See* YELLOW.

Cainites (kā' nītz). An heretical sect of the 2nd century so named because they held that Cain was made by an almighty power and Abel by a weak one. They renounced the NEW TESTAMENT in favour of *The Gospel of Judas* which justified the false disciple and the crucifixion of Jesus, and held that the way to salvation was to give way to every lust and make a trial of everything.

To raise Cain. To "raise the devil", to "play hell", to make an angry fuss or noisy disturbance. Cain here is either used as an alternative to "the DEVIL", or is a direct allusion to Cain's violent anger which drove him to kill his brother. (*See Gen.* iv, 5.)

Cake. Obsolete slang for a fool, a poor thing.

Cakes and ale. A good time. *Life is not all cakes and ale.* Life is not all BEER AND SKITTLES—all pleasure.

It's a piece of cake. It's easy, it can be done with little trouble or effort—as easy as eating cake.

My cake is dough. All my swans are

turned to geese. *Occisa est res mea*; my project has failed; *mon affaire est manquée*.

The land of cakes. Scotland, famous for its oatmeal cakes.

Land o'cakes and brither Scots.

BURNS.

To go like hot cakes. To be a great success, to sell well.

To take the cake, bun, or **biscuit.** To carry off the prize (ironically). That beats everything. The reference is to the negro *cake walk*, the prize for which was a cake. The competitors walk round the cake in pairs while the judges decide which couple walk the most gracefully. From this a dance developed which was popular in the early 20th century before the coming of JAZZ.

In ancient Greece, a cake was the award to the toper who held out longest, and in Ireland the best dancer in a dancing competition was rewarded, at one time, by a cake.

You cannot eat your cake and have it too. You cannot spend your money and yet keep it. You cannot serve God and MAMMON. You cannot have it both ways.

Calainos (kà li' nos). The most ancient of Spanish ballads. Calainos the Moor asked a damsel to wife; she consented on condition that he should bring her the heads of the three PALADINS of CHARLEMAGNE—RINALDO, ROLAND, and OLIVER. Calainos went to Paris and challenged them. First Sir Baldwin, the youngest Knight, accepted the challenge and was overthrown; then his uncle Roland went against the Moor and smote him.

Calas. The case of Jean Calas (căl' aš'). A celebrated case in French history. Jean Calas (1698–1762), a HUGUENOT cloth-merchant of Toulouse, was tortured, broken on the wheel and burnt in 1762, having been found guilty of the murder of his twenty-nine-year-old son Marc-Antoine. The motive was supposed to be that Jean was determined to prevent his son becoming a Roman Catholic. The evidence was circumstantial although suicide was perhaps the most obvious conclusion to draw. The widow's case was taken up by Voltaire in his book *Sur la Tolérance*, with the re-

sult that the family, who had also suffered the penalties of intolerance, were declared innocent and given 30,000 livres by Louis XV.

Calatrava, Order of (kăl á tra' va). A Spanish military order of knighthood, founded by Sancho III of Castile in 1158 from the many warriors who had concentrated there for the town's defence against the MOORS. They at first entered the order of Cîteaux and wore a white scapulary and hood; in 1397 they were permitted to wear secular dress, their badge being a red cross fleury. The knights took vows of poverty, obedience and conjugal chastity. It became an order of merit in 1808.

Calchas. The famous Greek soothsayer in the TROJAN WAR who told the Greeks that the aid of ACHILLES was essential for the taking of the city, that IPHIGENIA must be sacrificed before the fleet could sail from AULIS, and that the siege would take ten years. He died of disappointment when beaten in a trial of skill by the prophet Mopsus.

Calculate is from the Lat. *calculi* (pebbles), used by the Romans for counters. In the ABACUS the round balls were called *calculi*. The Greeks voted by pebbles dropped into an urn—a method adopted both in ancient Egypt and Syria; counting these pebbles was *calculating* the number of voters.

Caledonia. SCOTLAND; the ancient Roman name, now only used in poetry and in a few special connections, such as the Caledonian Canal, etc.

Caledonian Market. Until its closure at the outbreak of World War II, this Islington cattle and general market was especially noted for miscellaneous secondhand goods and was much frequented by bargain hunters. Dubbed the "thieves' market", it was partially a relic of the pedlar's part of London's BARTHOLOMEW FAIR, which ceased in 1855, the year in which the Caledonian Market opened.

Calembour (ka lom boor') (Fr.). A pun, a jest. From Wigan von Theben, a priest of Kahlenberg in Lower Austria, who was introduced in *Till* EULENSPIEGEL and other German tales. He was noted for his jests, puns, and witticisms.

In the French translation he appeared as the Abbé de Calembourg or Calembour.

Calendar.

The Julian Calendar. *See* JULIAN.

The Gregorian Calendar. *See* GREGORIAN.

The Jewish Calendar. This dates from the Creation, fixed at 3761 B.C. and consists of 12 months of 29 and 30 days alternately, with an additional month of 30 days interposed in EMBOLISMIC years to prevent any great divergence from the months of the Solar year. The 3rd, 6th, 11th, 14th, 17th, and 19th years of the METONIC CYCLE are Embolismic Years.

The Mohammedan Calendar, used in Moslem countries, dates from 16 July 622, the day of the HEGIRA. It consists of 12 lunar months of 29 days 12 hours 44 minutes each; consequently the Mohammedan year consists of only 354 or 355 days. A cycle is 30 years.

The French Revolutionary Calendar. Adopted by the National CONVENTION on 5 October 1793, retrospectively as from 22 September 1792, and in force in France till 1 January 1806, when NAPOLEON restored the GREGORIAN CALENDAR. It consisted of 12 months of 30 days each, with 5 intercalary days, called SANSCULOTTIDES. Every fourth or Olympic Year was to have six such days. It was devised by Gilbert Romme (1750–1795), the months being named by the poet Fabre d'Eglantine (1755–1794).

The Newgate Calendar. *See* NEWGATE.

Calender. The Persian *galandar*, a member of a begging order of dervishes founded in the 13th century by Qalander Yusufal-Andalusi, a native of Spain. The took a vow of perpetual wandering and feature in the story of the *Three Calenders* in the ARABIAN NIGHTS.

Calends (from Lat. *calare*, to call). The first day of the Roman month. Varro says the term originated in the practice of calling the people together on the first day of the month, when the *pontifex* informed them of the time of the new moon, the day of the NONES, with the festivals and sacred days to be observed. The custom continued till A.U.C. 450, when the FASTI or *calendar* was posted in public places. *See* GREEK CALENDS.

Calepin, A (kăl' e pin). A dictionary. Ambrosio Calepino of Calepio in Italy was the author of a famous Latin dictionary (1502), so that *my Calepin* was used in earlier days as my EUCLID, my Liddell and Scott, my Lewis and Short, my Kennedy, etc., became common later.

Calf. Slang for a dolt, a "mutton-head", a raw, inexperienced, childish fellow. *See also* CALVES.

The golden calf. *See* GOLDEN.

There are many ways of dressing a calf's head. Many ways of saying or doing a foolish thing; a simpleton has many ways of showing his folly; or, generally, if one way won't do we must try another. The allusion is to the banquets of the CALVES' HEAD CLUB.

To eat the calf in the cow's belly. To be over-ready to anticipate; to count one's chickens before they are hatched. *See under* CHICKEN.

To kill the fatted calf. To celebrate, to welcome with the best of everything. The phrase is from the parable of the prodigal son (*Luke* xv, 30).

Calf-love. Youthful fancy, immature love as opposed to lasting attachment.

Calf-skin. Fools and jesters used to wear a calf-skin coat buttoned down the back. In SHAKESPEARE's *King John*, III, i. Constance says scathingly to the Archduke of Austria:

> Thou wear a lion's hide! Doff it for shame,
> And hang a calf's skin on those recreant limbs!

Caliban (kăl' i băn). Rude, uncouth, unknown. The allusion is to SHAKESPEARE's Caliban in *The Tempest*, the deformed half-human son of a DEVIL and a WITCH, slave to Prospero.

Caliburn (kăl' i bĕrn). Same as EXCALIBUR, King ARTHUR's well-known sword.

Caligula (kȧ lig' ū lȧ). Roman Emperor (A.D. 37–41); so called because, when with the army as a boy, he wore a military sandal called a *caliga* which had no upper leather and was only used by the common soldiers.

Caligula was a voluptuary whose cruelties and excesses almost amounted to madness. Hence Horace Walpole coined the word *Caligulism*. Speaking of Frederick, Prince of Wales, he says:

> Alas! it would be endless to tell you all his Caligulisms.
> *Letter to France*. 29 Nov. 1745.

Calipash and Calipee (kăl i păsh, kăl i pē). These are apparently fancy terms (though the former may come from *carapace*, the upper shell of a tortoise and crustaceans), to describe choice portions of the turtle. Calipash is the fatty, dull-greenish substance of the upper shield; calipee is the light-yellow fatty stuff belonging to the lower. Only epicures and aldermen can tell the difference!

> Cut off the bottom shell, then cut off the meat that grows to it (which is the callepy or fowl).
> MRS. RAFFALD: *English Housekeeping* (1769).

Caliph (kā lif). A title given to the successors of MOHAMMED (Arab. *Khalifah*, a successor). The caliphate of Baghdad reached its highest splendour under Haroun al-Raschid (786–809). From the 13th century the titles of *Caliph*, *Sultan*, *Imam* came to be used indiscriminately, but in the 19th century Ottoman Sultans sought to revive their claim to the title, especially Abdul Hamid II (1876–1908). In 1924 the Turks declared the abolition of the Caliphate.

Calisto and Arcas. Calisto was an Arcadian NYMPH metamorphosed into a she-bear by JUPITER. Her son Arcas having met her in the chase, would have killed her, but Jupiter converted him into a he-bear, and placed them both in the heavens, where they are recognized as the Great and Little Bear. *See* ARCTIC REGION.

Call. A summons, or invitation felt to be divine, as a "call to the ministry".

A call bird. A bird trained as a decoy.

A call-boy. A boy employed in theatres to call or summon actors in time for them to appear on the stage.

A call-box. A public telephone booth.

A call-girl. A prostitute who uses her telephone for arranging to receive her customers.

A call of the House. An imperative summons sent to every Member of PARLIAMENT to attend. This is done when the opinion of the whole house is required.

A call on shareholders. A demand to pay the balance of money due for shares allotted in a company, or a part thereof.

A call to the pastorate. An invitation to a clergyman by the members of a PRESBYTERIAN or NONCONFORMIST congregation to serve as their minister.

A curtain call. *See under* CURTAIN.

Called to the Bar. *See under* BAR.

Payable at call. To be paid on demand.

The call of God. An invitation, exhortation, or warning by the dispensations of Providence (*Isa*. xxii, 12); divine influence on the mind to do or avoid something (*Heb*. iii, 1).

To call a man out. To challenge him; to appeal to a man's honour to come forth and fight a duel.

To call God to witness. To declare solemnly that what one states is true.

To call in question. To doubt the truth of a statement; to challenge the truth of a statement. *"In dubium vocare"*.

To call in. To summon a doctor or invite for consultation, etc. In banking, to take coins or notes out of circulation.

To call it a go, or **a day.** To give in, to give up, to stop work.

To call off. To cancel a forthcoming event, to withdraw from a deal.

To call over the coals. *See* COALS.

To call to account. To demand an explanation; to reprove.

To be called, or **sent to one's account.** To be removed by death, to be called to the judgement seat of God to give an account of one's deeds.

To call to arms. To summon, to prepare for battle. *"Ad arma vocare."*

To call to mind. To recollect, to remember.

To call up. To summon for military service.

Caller herrings. Fresh herrings. The adjective is also applied in SCOTLAND to fresh air, water, etc.

Calliope (kả lĩō pi) (Gr. beautiful voice). Chief of the nine MUSES; the muse of epic or heroic poetry, and of poetic inspiration and eloquence. Her emblems are a stylus and wax tablets.

The name is also applied to a steam organ, making raucous music on steam whistles.

Callippic Period (kȧ lip′ ik). A correction of the METONIC CYCLE by Callippus, the Greek astronomer of the 4th century B.C. To remedy the defect in the Metonic Cycle, Callippus quadrupled the period of Meton, making his cycle one of seventy-six years, and deducted a day at the end of it, by which means he calculated that the new and full moons would be brought round to the same day and hour. His calculation, however, is not absolutely accurate, as there is one whole day lost every 553 years.

Calotte (kȧ lot′). **Régime de la calotte.** Administration of government by ecclesiastics. The *calotte* is the small skullcap worn over the TONSURE.

Caloyers (kȧ lō′ yĕrz). Monks in the Greek church, who follow the rule of St. Basil. They are divided into *cenobites*, who recite the offices from midnight to sunrise; *anchorites*, who live in hermitages; and *recluses*, who shut themselves up in caverns and live on alms (Gr. *calos* and *geron*, beautiful old man).

Calpe (kăl′ pi). Gibraltar, one of the PILLARS OF HERCULES; the other, the opposite promontory in Africa (Jebel Musa, or Apes' Hill), was anciently called Abyla. According to one account these two were originally one mountain which HERCULES tore asunder; but some say he piled up each mountain separately.

Caltrop, Caltrap, or **Chevaltrap**. A mediæval four-pronged iron device placed on the ground so that the horses of the attacking cavalry might be lamed. There is a similar modern one for puncturing pneumatic tyres.

Calumet (kăl′ u met). The "pipe of peace" of the North American Indians. The word is of French Canadian origin, being the Norman form of the Fr. *chalumeau* (Lat. *calamus*, a reed); it was the name they gave to certain plants used by the natives as pipe stems, and hence, the pipe itself. The calumet is about two-and-a-half feet long, the stem is reed and the bowl is of highly polished red marble. To present the calumet to a stranger is a mark of hospitality and goodwill; to refuse the offer is an act of hostile defiance. *Cp.* MATÉ.

Calvary. The Latin translation of the Gr. GOLGOTHA, which is a transliteration of the Hebrew word for a skull. It is the name given to the place of our Lord's crucifixion. Legend has it that the skull of ADAM was preserved here, but the name is probably due to a fancied resemblance of the configuration of the ground to the shape of a skull.

The actual site may be that occupied by the Church of the Holy Sepulchre, or possibly an eminence above the grotto of Jeremiah not far from the Damascus Gate.

A Calvary. A representation of the successive scenes of the PASSION of Christ in a series of pictures, etc., in a church; the shrine containing such representations. Wayside calvaries or crosses, representing the Crucifixion, are common in parts of Europe and some notable examples are to be found in Brittany.

A calvary cross. A Latin CROSS mounted on three steps (or grises).

Calvary clover. A common trefoil, *Medicago echinus*, said to have sprung up in the track made by PILATE when he went to the cross to see his "title affixed" (Jesus of Nazareth, King of the Jews). Each of the three leaves has a little carmine spot in the centre; in the daytime they form a sort of cross; and in the flowering season the plant bears a little yellow flower, like a "crown of thorns". Julian tells us that each of the three leaves had in his time a white cross in the centre, and that the centre cross remains visible longer than the others.

Calves. The inhabitants of the Isle of Wight were sometimes so called from a tradition that a CALF once got its head firmly wedged in a wooden pale, and instead of breaking up the pale, the farmhand cut off the calf's head.

His calves are gone to grass. Said of a spindle-legged man. And another mocking taunt is, "Veal will be dear, because there are no calves."

Calvinism. The doctrines of the Reformer Jean Calvin (1509–1564), particularly as expressed in his *Institutio Religionis Christianæ* (1536). Some chief points of his teaching are:

(1) the transcendence of God;
(2) the total depravity of natural man. He can achieve nothing without God;
(3) predestination of particular election.

Before the world began God chose some men for salvation through Christ;
(4) the scriptures and the Holy Spirit are the sole authority;
(5) the community must enforce the Church's public discipline.

Calydon (kal' i don). In classical geography, a city in Ætolia, near the forest which was the scene of the legendary hunt of the CALYDONIAN BOAR (*see* BOAR). Also in Arthurian legend, the name given to a forest in northern England.

Calypso (kȧ lip' sō). In classical mythology, the queen of the island Ogygia on which ULYSSES was wrecked. She kept him there for seven years and promised him perpetual youth and immortality if he would remain with her for ever. She bore him two sons and was inconsolable when he left. Ogygia is generally identified with Gozo, near Malta.

A **calypso** is a type of popular song developed by the coloured folk of Trinidad, improvised on topical subjects.

Cam and Isis. The universities of Cambridge and Oxford; so called from the rivers on which they stand.

Cama. The god of young love in Hindu mythology. His wife is Rati (voluptuousness), and he is represented as riding on a sparrow, holding in his hand a bow of flowers and five arrows. (*i.e.* the five senses).

Camacho (kȧm a' chō). A rich but unfortunate man in one of the stories in *Don Quixote*, who is cheated of his bride just when he has prepared a great feast for the wedding; hence the phrase **Camacho's wedding** to describe useless show and expenditure.

Camarina. *Ne moveas Camarinam* (Don't meddle with Camarina). Camarina, a lake in Sicily, was a source of malaria to the inhabitants, who, when they consulted APOLLO about draining it, received the reply, "Do not disturb it." Nevertheless, they drained it, and ere long the enemy marched over the bed of the lake and plundered the city. The proverb is applied to those who remove one evil, but thus give place to a greater—"LEAVE WELL ALONE".

Cambalo's Ring. Cambalo was the second son of CAMBUSCAN in Chaucer's unfinished *Squire's Tale*. He is introduced

as Cambel in the *Faerie Queene*. The ring, which was given him by his sister Canace, had the virtue of healing wounds.

Camber. In British legend, the second son of BRUTE. WALES fell to his portion; which is one way of accounting for its name of Cambria.

Cambria. The ancient name of WALES, the land of the Cymry.

Camden Society. An historical society founded in 1838 for the publication of early historical texts and documents, named after William Camden (1551–1623), schoolmaster, antiquary and author of *Britannia*, a survey of the British Isles. In 1897 it amalgamated with the Royal Historical Society, and its long series of publications were transferred to that body.

Camel. MOHAMMED's favourite camel was Al Kaswa. The mosque at Koba covers the spot where it knelt when he fled from MECCA. He considered the kneeling of the camel as a sign sent by God, and remained at Koba in safety for four days. The swiftest of his camels was Al Adha, who is fabled to have performed the whole journey from JERUSALEM to Mecca in four bounds, thereby gaining a place in heaven along with BORAK, Balaam's ass, Tobit's dog, and the DOG OF THE SEVEN SLEEPERS.

It is easier for a camel to go through the eye of a needle, than for a rich man to enter into the Kingdom of God (*Matt.* xix, 24 and *Mark* x, 25). In the KORAN we find a similar expression: "The impious shall find the gates of heaven shut; nor shall he enter till a camel shall pass through the eye of a needle." The meaning of the passage is reinforced by *Mark* x, 24, "How hard is it for them that trust in riches to enter into the Kingdom of God!" In the Rabbinical writings there is a variant of the expression, "Perhaps thou are one of the Pampedithians, who can make an elephant pass through the eye of a needle."

Camelot (kăm' e lot). In British fable, the legendary spot where King ARTHUR held his court. It has been tentatively located at CAERLEON, the hill-fort known as Cadbury castle in Somerset, and Camelford in Cornwall, where the Duke of

Cornwall resided in his castle of TINTA-GEL, etc. The Cadbury site is the most probable. It is mentioned in Shakespear's *King Lear*, II, ii, and Tennyson's *Idylls of the King*, etc. *See also* CAMLET.

Cameron Highlanders. The 79th Foot, raised by Allan Cameron of Errock in 1793. It became the Queen's Own Highlanders (Seaforth and Cameron).

Cameronians, or Reformed PRESBYTERIANS, were organized by the strict COVENANTER and field preacher, Richard Cameron, who was slain in battle at Aird's Moss in 1680. He objected to the alliance of Church and State under Charles II and seceded from the Kirk. His followers refused to take the Oath of Allegiance and thus deprived themselves of some of the privileges of citizenship. In 1876 the majority of Cameronians united with the Free Church.

Cameronian Regiment. The 26th Infantry, which had its origin in a body of CAMERONIANS in the Revolution of 1688, called the Cameronians (Scottish Rifles) from 1881.

Camford. A name, made up from Cambridge and Oxford, which has never acquired the same currency as OXBRIDGE. *Cp.* REDBRICK.

Camilla (kȧ mil' ȧ). In Roman legend a virgin queen of the Volscians. She helped Turnus against ÆNEAS. VIRGIL (*Aeneid* VII, 809) says she was so swift that she could run over a field of corn without bending a single blade, or make her way over the sea without even wetting her feet.

Camisard, or **Camisardo** (kăm' i sard, kăm i sa' dō). A night attack; so called because the attacking party wore a *camise* or *camisard* over their armour, both to conceal it, and that they might better recognize each other in the dark.

Camisards. In French history the PROTESTANT insurgents of the Cévennes, who resisted the violence of the DRAGONNADES occasioned by the Revocation of the Edict of NANTES in 1685 and carried on a fierce war of reprisals with Louis XIV's forces until finally suppressed in 1705. Their leader was Jean Cavalier (1681–1740), afterwards governor of Jersey and later of the Isle of

Wight. So called from the *camise* or blouse worn by the peasantry.

Camlan, Battle of. In Arthurian legend the battle which put an end to the KNIGHTS OF THE ROUND TABLE, and at which ARTHUR received his death wound from the hand of his nephew MODRED, who was also slain.

Camlet, camelot. A fabric. As far back as the 13th century camlet was a rich stuff made of silk and camel's hair. Later it was a durable cotton and woollen cloth mixture, etc.; also the name of a waterproof material before the introduction of indiarubber.

> After dinner I put on my new camelott suit, the best that I ever wore in my life, the suit costing me above £24.
>
> PEPYS: *Diary* (1 June 1664).

Cammock. As crooked as a cammock. A cammock is a staff or stick with a crook-end like a hockey stick or shinty club.

> Though the cammock, the more it is bowed the better it serveth; yet the bow, the more it is bent and occupied the weaker it waxeth.
>
> LYLY: *Euphues*.

Camorra (kȧ mor' ȧ). A lawless secret society of the 19th century, run on gangster lines, which terrorized Naples. It began amongst prisoners in the gaols about 1820, and exacted tribute from traders and brothel-keepers alike. From 1848 it began to intervene in politics and continued to be a very real menace until 1911, when severe judicial action led to its extinction. The name is probably from the Sp. *Camorra*, a quarrel, and now has the same significance as THUG, APACHE, gangster, etc. *Cp.* MAFIA.

Camp. The origin of the use of this word in the following expressions is a matter of surmise.

High camp. Ostentatiously exaggerated movements and gestures akin to those of the ballet.

To camp it up is to use *camp* gestures in an affected and effeminate way.

Camp-followers. The old-time armies which lived on the country, moved in a leisurely fashion and laid up in winter quarters, were accompanied by numerous civilian followers, such as washerwomen and sutlers who sold liquor and provisions, etc. These were called camp-followers.

Campaign Wig. This style of WIG came from France in the early 18th century. It was very full, curled, and 18 inches in length at the front with deep locks. Sometimes the back part was put in a black silk bag. The name refers to Marlborough's campaign in the Netherlands.

Campania (kăm pā′ ni à) (Lat. level country). The ancient geographical name for the fertile district south-east of the Tiber, containing the towns of Cumæ, Capua, Baiæ, Puteoli, Herculaneum, Pompeii, etc.

Campaspe (kăm păs′ pe). A beautiful concubine, favourite of ALEXANDER THE GREAT, whom he handed over to APELLES, who it is said modelled his VENUS Anadyomene from her.

Campbellites. Followers of John McLeod Campbell (1800–1872), who taught the universality of the atonement, for which he was ejected from the CHURCH OF SCOTLAND in 1831.

Campbells are coming, The. This stirring song is supposed to have been composed in 1715 when John Campbell, Duke of Argyll, defeated the Earl of Mar and the JACOBITES. It became the regimental march of the Sutherland Highlanders (93rd Regiment) and after 1881 of the Argyll and Sutherland Highlanders when the two regiments merged.

At the second relief of Lucknow in November 1857 the beseiged in the Residency became aware of the approach of Sir Colin Campbell and the Sutherland Highlanders when they heard the distant sound of bagpipes playing "The Campbells are coming".

Campeador. The CID.

Canard (kăn′ ar) (Fr. a duck). A hoax, a ridiculously extravagant report. The French lexicographer Emile Littré (1801–1881) says that the term comes from an old expression, *vendre un canard à moitié*, to half-sell a duck. As this was no sale at all, it came to mean "to take in", "to make a fool of". Another explanation is that a certain Cornelissen, to try the gullibility of the public, reported in the papers that he had twenty ducks, one of which he cut up and threw to the nineteen, who devoured it gree-

dily. He then cut up another, then a third, and so on till the nineteenth was gobbled up by the survivor—a wonderful proof of duck voracity.

Canary. Wine from these islands was very popular in the 16th and 17th centuries.

> Farewell, my hearts, I will to my honest knight Falstaff, and drink canary with him.
> SHAKESPEARE: *Merry Wives of Windsor*, III, ii.

It was also at one time slang for a GUINEA or SOVEREIGN, from its yellow colour.

Cancan. A fast and extremely dexterous dance, sometimes accompanied by extravagant and often indecent postures, originally performed in the casinos of Paris. The most famous example is in Offenbach's opera *Orpheus in the Underworld* (1858).

Cancer (Lat. crab). One of the twelve signs of the ZODIAC, the Crab. It appears when the sun has reached its highest northern limit, and begins to go backward to the south; but like a crab the return is sideways (21 June to 23 July).

According to fable, JUNO sent Cancer against HERCULES when he combated the HYDRA of Lerna. It bit the hero's foot, but Hercules killed the creature, and Juno took it up to heaven.

Candid Camera. An unseen camera which is used to photograph an unsuspecting subject. Candid camera shots, which are often ridiculous, are much used in pictorial journalism.

Candidate (Lat. *candidatus*, clothed in white). One who seeks or is proposed for some office, appointment, etc. Those who solicited the office of consul, quæstor, prætor, etc., among the Romans, arrayed themselves in a loose white robe. It was loose that they might show the people their scars, and white in sign of fidelity and humility.

Candide (kan′ dēd). The hero of VOLTAIRE's philosophical novel, *Candide, ou l'Optimisme* (1759). All sorts of misfortunes are heaped upon him which he bears philosophically. It was written at the time of the Lisbon earthquake to satirise philosophical optimism.

Candle. Bell, book, and candle. *See* BELL.

He is not fit to hold a candle to him.
He is very inferior. The allusion is to
link boys who held candles in theatres
and other places of night amusement.

The game is not worth the candle. *Le
jeu n'en vaut pas la chandelle*. The effort is not worth making; not worth
even the cost of the candle that lights the
players.

To burn the candle at both ends. *See*
BURN.

To hold a candle to the Devil. To aid
or countenance that which is wrong.

To sell by the candle. A form of sale
by auction. A pin is thrust through a
candle about an inch from the top, and
bidding goes on till the candle is burnt
down to the pin; when the pin drops
into the candlestick the last bidder is declared the purchaser. Such an auction
was held at Aldermaston and reported in
the *Reading Mercury* (16 Dec.) in 1893.

To vow a candle to the Devil. To seek
to bribe or propitiate the DEVIL.

What is the Latin for candle? *See*
TACE.

Candle-holder. An abettor. The reference is to the practice of holding a candle to assist a reader or worker where
light is needed. In ordinary parlance it
applies to one who assists in some slight
degree but is not a real sharer in an action or undertaking.

Candlemas Day. 2 February, formerly
the Feast of the Purification of the Virgin Mary, now called the Presentation of
Our Lord; one of the QUARTER DAYS in
SCOTLAND. In ROMAN CATHOLIC
churches all the candles which will be
needed in the church throughout the
year are consecrated on this day; they
symbolize Jesus Christ, called "the light
of the world", and "a light to lighten the
Gentiles". The ancient Romans had a
custom of burning candles to scare away
evil spirits.

> If Candlemas Day be dry and fair,
> The half o'winter's come and mair;
> If Candlemas Day be wet and foul,
> The half o'winter was gone at Youl.
> *Scotch Proverb*.

> The badger peeps out of his hole on
> Candlemas Day, and, if he finds snow,
> walks abroad; but if he sees the sun shin-
> ing he draws back into his hole.
> *German Proverb*.

Candour, Mrs. In *The School for Scandal*
Sheridan drew the perfect type of female back-biter, concealing her venom
under an affectation of frank amiability.

Canecutters. Nickname for the inhabitants of Queensland, Australia, who are
also known as *Bananalanders*.

Canephorus (kå nef' ôr ůs). A sculptured
figure of a youth or maiden bearing a
basket on the head. In ancient ATHENS
the *canephori* bore the sacred things necessary at the feasts of the gods.

Canicular Days (Lat. *canicula*, dim. of
canis, a dog). The DOG-DAYS.

Canicular Period. The ancient Egyptian cycle of 1,461 years or 1,460 Julian
years, also called a SOTHIC PERIOD, during which it was supposed that any given day had passed through all the seasons of the years.

Canicular Year. The ancient Egyptian
year computed from one heliacal rising
of the DOG STAR to the next.

Canmore. *See* GREAT HEAD.

Cannæ. The place where Hannibal defeated the Romans under Varro and
Æmilius with great slaughter in 216 B.C.
Any fatal battle that is the turning point
of a great general's success may be called
his *Cannæ*. Thus Moscow was the Cannæ of NAPOLEON.

Canned music. Music recorded and reproduced, as opposed to "live music",
i.e. played by musicians present in person. Canned music, like canned foods,
can be stored and used when required.
See DISC JOCKEY.

To cannon into, or **against someone.**
An unexpected collision of persons or a
chance encounter.

Canny. *See* CA'CANNY.

Canoe. Paddle your own canoe. Rely
upon yourself. The caution was given
by President Lincoln, but it is an older
saying and was used by Captain Marryat
(*Settlers in Canada*, ch. viii) in 1844.
Sarah Bolton's poem in *Harper's Magazine* for May 1854 popularized it:

Canon. The canon. The body of books in
the BIBLE which are accepted by the
Christian Church generally as genuine
and inspired; the whole Bible from *Genesis* to *Revelation*, excluding the APO-
CRYPHA. Called also the *sacred canon*
and the *Canonical Books*.

The Church dignitary known as a *Ca-*

non is a capitular member of a cathedral or COLLEGIATE CHURCH, usually living in the precincts, and observing the rule or *canon* of the body to which he is attached. The canons, with the DEAN or provost at their head, constitute the governing body, or CHAPTER, of the cathedral. These are the *canons-residentiary*; there are also *honorary canons* who have no share in the cathedral government, or emoluments. *Minor canons* are mainly concerned with the singing of the services and have no part in the decisions of the chapter.

The title once had a much wider application and was used to designate most of the diocesan clergy. When its use came to be limited to the secular clergy of a cathedral, they were called *secular canons* as distinct from the *canons regular* such as the Austin or AUGUSTINIAN CANONS.

Also in music, from the same derivation, a composition written strictly according to rule, for two or three voices which sang exactly the same melody, one a few beats after the other, either at the same or different pitch. Simple forms are the catch and the round such as *Three Blind Mice* and *London's Burning*. A London choral club was founded in 1843 called the "Round, Catch and Canon Club".

Canoness. The title was given to certain women living under rule, less strict than that of nuns, in the Frankish empire from the late 8th century. Like their male counterparts they came to be divided into canonesses *regular* and *secular*.

Canon law, or canons. A collection of ecclesiastical laws which serve as the rule of church government. The professors or students of canon law are called *canonists*.

Book of Canons. A collection of 178 canons enacted by the councils of Nicæa, Ancyra, Neocesarea, Laodicea, Gangra, Antioch, Constantinople, Ephesus, and Chalcedon. It was first published in 1610 and is probably of late 4th or early 5th-century origin.

The CHURCH OF ENGLAND "Book of Canons" was adopted in 1604 as the basis of ecclesiastical law. A *Book of Ca-*nons for the Scottish Church was drawn up under Charles I's command and issued in 1636. It mainly helped to precipitate religious strife in Scotland.

Canons of the Mass. The fixed form of consecratory prayer used in the GREEK and ROMAN CATHOLIC CHURCHES—from the *Sanctus* to the PATERNOSTER.

Canonical Age. *See under* AGE.

Canonical dress. The distinctive or appropriate costume worn by the clergy according to the direction of the canon; BISHOPS, DEANS and archdeacons, for instance, wear canonical hats. This distinctive dress is sometimes called simply "canonicals"; Macaulay speaks of "an ecclesiastic in full canonicals".

The same name is given also to the special parts of such robes, such as the pouch on the gown of an M.D., originally designed for carrying drugs; the lamb-skin on some B.A. hoods, in imitation of the *toga candida* of the Romans; the tippet on a BARRISTER'S gown, meant for a wallet to carry briefs in.

Canonical Epistles. The seven CATHOLIC EPISTLES as distinct from those of Paul which were addressed to particular churches or individuals.

Canonical hours. The different parts of the Divine Office which follow, and are named after the hours of the day. They are seven—MATINS, PRIME, tierce, sext, NONES, VESPERS and COMPLINE. Prime, tierce, sext and nones are the first, third, sixth and ninth hours of the day, counting from six in the morning. (*See* BREVIARY.) The reason why there are seven canonical hours is that David says, "Seven times a day do I praise thee" (*Ps.* cxix, 164).

In England the phrase means more especially the time of the day within which persons can be legally married, *i.e.* from 8 in the morning to 6 p.m.

Canonization. The solemn act by which the Pope proclaims the sanctity of a person, subsequent to the lesser act of BEATIFICATION; whereupon he or she is worthy to be honoured as a SAINT and is put upon the *Canon* or Catalogue of Saints of the Church.

Canopus (kà nō′ pus). Alpha Argus or Canopus, in the constellation Argo Navis, is the brightest star in the heavens after SIRIUS.

Canopy properly means a gnat curtain. Herodotus tells us (II, 95) that the fishermen of the Nile used to lift their nets on a pole, and form thereby a rude sort of tent under which they slept securely, as gnats will not pass through the meshes of a net. Subsequently the hangings of a bed were so called, and lastly the canopy borne over kings (Gr. *konops*, a gnat).

Canossa (kà nos' à). Canossa, in the duchy of Modena, is where the Holy Roman Emperor Henry IV humbled himself to Pope Gregory VII (Hildebrand) by standing for three days barefooted in the courtyard of the palace in the garb of a penitent (January 1077). This was during the INVESTITURE CONTROVERSY.

Hence, **to go to Canossa** is to undergo humiliation, to EAT HUMBLE PIE, to submit after having refused to do so. During Bismarck's quarrel with Pope Pius IX at the time of the KULTURKAMPF he said in the Reichstag (14 May 1872): "*Nach Canossa gehen wir nicht.*" (We shall not go to Canossa!)

Cant. Language peculiar to a social class; profession, sect, etc., jargon; technical language; insincere talk, hypocrisy. As its derivation (Lat. *cantus*, song) shows, the earlier application of the word was to music and thereby intonation. Soon the term came to be applied to the whining speech of beggars, who were known as the CANTING CREW.

The term was in use to denote professional slang by the 17th century.

Cantabrian Surge. The Bay of Biscay. So called from the Cantabri who dwelt about the Biscayan shore.

Cantate Sunday (kăn'ta' te). ROGATION Sunday, the fifth Sunday after EASTER. So called from the first word of the introit of the MASS: "Sing to the Lord". Similarly "LÆTARE SUNDAY", the fourth in LENT, is so called from the first word of the introit of the mass. *Cp*. QUASIMODO SUNDAY.

Canterbury Tales. Chaucer represented that he was in company with a party of pilgrims going to Canterbury to pay their devotions to the shrine of St. Thomas à Becket. The party assembled at the TABARD INN, SOUTHWARK, and there agreed to tell one tale each, both in going and returning. He who told the best story was to be treated with a supper on the homeward journey. The work is incomplete and we have none of the tales told on the way home.

Canucks (ka nŭks'). The name given to Canadians generally, sometimes derogatively, but in Canada to Canadians of French descent. Possibly a corruption of *Connaught*, a name originally applied by the French Canadians to Irish immigrants.

Canvas. To be under canvas. To be in camp, in a tent.

To canvas a subject is to strain it through a hemp strainer, to sift it.

To canvass a constituency is to solicit votes. In the U.S.A. it is also used to mean scrutinizing voting papers after the ballot.

Caora (ka ŏr' à). A river described in Hakluyt's *Voyages*, on the banks of which dwelt a people whose heads grew beneath their shoulders. Their eyes were in their shoulders, and their mouths in the middle of their breasts. Ralegh, in his *Description of Guiana*, gives a similar account of a race of men. *Cp*. BLEMMYES.

Cap. The word is used figuratively by SHAKESPEARE for the top, the summit (of excellence, etc.).

Black cap. *See* BLACK.

Cap acquaintance. A bowing acquaintance. One just sufficiently known to touch one's cap to.

Cap and bells. The insignia of a professional fool or jester.

Cap and feather days. The time of childhood.

Cap and gown. The full academical costume of a university student, tutor or graduate, worn on formal occasions, etc.

Cap in hand. Submissively. Like a servant.

Cap money. Money collected in a cap or hat; hence an improvised collection.

Cap of liberty. When a slave was manumitted by the Romans, a small Phrygian cap, usually of red felt, called a *pileus*, was placed on his head and he was termed *libertinus* (a freed-man). When Saturninus, in 100 B.C., possessed himself of the Capitol, he hoisted a similar cap to the top of his spear, to indicate that all slaves who joined his standard should be free. Marius employed the same symbol against Sulla, and when CÆSAR was murdered, the conspirators marched forth with a cap elevated on a spear in token of liberty.

In the French Revolution the cap of liberty (*bonnet rouge*) was adopted as an emblem of freedom from royal authority.

Cap of maintenance. A cap of dignity anciently belonging to the rank of duke; the fur cap of the Lord MAYOR of London, worn on days of state; a cap carried before the British sovereigns at their coronation. The significance of *maintenance* here is not known, but the cap was an emblem of very high honour, for it was conferred by the POPE three times on Henry VII and once on Henry VIII. By certain old families it is borne in the COAT OF ARMS, either as a charge or in place of the wreath.

Canterbury cap. A soft flat cloth cap sometimes worn by dignitaries of the CHURCH OF ENGLAND.

Cater cap. A square cap or MORTAR-BOARD (Fr. *quartier*).

College cap. A TRENCHER, like the caps worn at the English universities.

Dunce's cap. A conical cap worn by the class "dunce" as a symbol of disgrace and stupidity. *See* DUNCE.

Fool's cap. A conical cap with feather and bells, such as licensed fools used to wear.

Forked cap. A bishop's MITRE.

John Knox cap. An early form of the TRENCHER, MORTAR-BOARD, or COLLEGE CAP worn at the Scottish universities.

Monmouth cap. *see* MONMOUTH.

Phrygian cap. CAP OF LIBERTY.

Scotch cap. A cloth cap worn in Scotland as part of the national dress.

Square Cap. A TRENCHER or MORTAR-BOARD.

Statute cap. A "cap of wool knit", the wearing of which on holidays was enforced on all over six years of age (with certain exceptions for rank and sex) by a statute of Elizabeth I of 1571, for the benefit of the woollen trade.

Trencher cap, or MORTAR-BOARD. A cap with a square board on top, generally covered with black cloth, and with a tassel, worn with academical dress; a COLLEGE CAP.

A feather in one's cap. An achievement to be proud of; something creditable.

I must put on my thinking cap. I must consider before I give a final answer. The allusion is to the official cap of the judge, formerly donned when passing sentence, later reserved for passing the death sentence.

If the cap fits, wear it. If the remark applies to you, apply it to yourself. Hats and caps vary only slightly in size but everyone knows his own when he puts it on.

Setting her cap at him. Trying to catch for a sweetheart or husband. In the days when ladies habitually wore caps they would naturally put on the most becoming to attract the attention of the favoured gentleman.

To cap. To take off, or touch one's cap to, in token of respect; also to excel.

I cap to that. I assent to it. The allusion is to the custom among French judges. Those who assent to the opinion stated by any of the bench signify by lifting their toques from their heads.

To cap a story. To go one better; to follow a good story with a better one of the same kind.

To cap it all. To surpass what has gone before; to make things even worse.

To cap verses. Having the metre fixed and the last letter of the previous line given, to add a line beginning with that letter, thus:

> The way was long, the wind was cold (D).
> Dogs with their tongues their wounds do heal (L).
> Like words congealed in northern air (R).
> Regions Cæsar never knew (W).
> With all a poet's ecstasy (Y).
> You may decide my awkward pace, *etc., etc.*

There are parlour games of capping names, proverbs, etc., in the same way, as: Plato, Otway, Young, Goldsmith, etc., "Rome was not built in a day", "Ye are the salt of the earth", "Hunger is the best sauce", "Example is better than precept", "Time and tide wait for no man", etc.

To send the cap round. To make a collection. From the custom of street musicians, singers, etc., sending a cap round to collect pennies among the onlookers.

Wearing the cap and bells. Said of a person who is the butt of the company, or one who excites laughter at his own expense. The reference is to licensed jesters, formerly attached to noblemen's establishments, who wore the CAP AND BELLS.

> One is bound to speak the truth—whether he mounts the cap and bells or a shovel hat [like a bishop].
>
> THACKERAY.

Your cap is all on one side. Many workmen, when they are perplexed or bothered, scratch their heads and in so doing push their cap on one side of the head, generally over the right ear, because the right hand is occupied.

Capful of wind. Olaus Magnus tells us that Eric, King of Sweden, was so familiar with evil spirits that whatsoever way he turned his cap the wind would blow, and for this he was called *Windy Cap*. The Laplanders drove a profitable trade in selling winds, and even so late as 1814, Bessie Millie of Pomona (Orkney), used to sell favourable winds to mariners for the small sum of sixpence.

To be capped. A player who has represented ENGLAND, SCOTLAND, IRELAND, or WALES in an international match at any of the major field sports may wear a cap bearing the national emblem. Hence the phrase, *he was capped for England*, etc.

Capability Brown. Lancelot Brown (1715– 1783), landscape gardener and architect, patronized by most of the rich men of taste. He set their great country houses in a surround of parkland and informal pastoral charm. He was given this nickname because he habitually assured prospective employers that their land held "great capabilities".

Cap-à-pie (kăp á pē). From head to foot; usually with reference to arming or accoutring. From O.Fr. *cap-à-pie* (Mod. Fr. *de pied en cap*).

> Armed at all points exactly cap-a-pie.
>
> SHAKESPEARE: *Hamlet*, II, i.

Cape. The Cape. Cape of Good Hope (originally known as the Cape of STORMS), Cape Province.

Cape cart. A two-wheeled, hooded cart with a single shaft or pole, much used in Cape Colony and South Africa in colonial days.

Cape Gooseberry. *Physalis peruviana*, a plant much prized for its decorative bladder-like calyx, it takes its name from the Cape, but is of South American origin.

Cape Doctor. A bracing S.E. wind blowing at the Cape of Good Hope; so named from the time when the British in India used the Cape as a health resort, to recuperate from the more exacting climate of India, until hill stations came to be used for the same purpose.

Spirit of the Cape. *See* ADAMASTOR.

Capel Court. A lane adjacent to the London STOCK EXCHANGE where dealers congregate to do business; so called from Sir William Capel, Lord Mayor in 1504. Hence used sometimes for the Stock Exchange itself.

Caper. The weather is so foul not even a Caper would venture out Caper. A Manx proverb. A *Caper* is a fisherman of Cape Clear in Ireland, who will venture out in almost any weather.

Caper Merchant. A dancing master who "cuts capers".

Cut your capers! Be off with you!

I'll make him cut his capers, *i.e.* rue his conduct.

To cut capers. To spring upwards in dancing, and rapidly interlace one foot with the other; figuratively to act in a manner with the object of attracting notice. *Caper* here is from the Ital. *capra*, a she-goat, which will jump about in an erratic way.

Capet. Hugh Capet (938–996), the founder of the Capetian dynasty of France, is said to have been named from the *cappa*, or monk's hood, which he wore as a lay abbot of St. Martin de Tours. The Capetians of the direct line ruled from 987 till 1328 when they were succeeded by the collateral house of VALOIS and by that of BOURBON in 1589 (Henry of Navarre). Louis XVI was arraigned before the National CONVENTION under the name of Louis Capet.

Capital. Active capital. Ready money or property readily convertible into it.

Capital cross. *See under* CROSS.

Capital levy. A State exaction on capital. First proposed in the British HOUSE OF COMMONS in 1914. A Capital Gains tax was introduced in 1965.

Capital punishment. The imposition of the death penalty for crime (Lat. *caput*, head).

Circulating capital. Wages or raw material. This sort of capital is not available a second time for the same propose.

Fixed, capital. Land, buildings, and machinery, which are only gradually consumed.

To make capital out of. To turn to account; thus, in politics, one party is always ready to make *political capital* out of the errors or misfortunes of the other.

Capitán, El Gran (el grăn kăp i ta' n) (the Great Captain). The name given to the famous Spanish general Gonsalvo de Cordova (1453–1515), through whose efforts Granada and Castile were united.

Capitulary (kăp it' ū lår i). A collection of ordinances or laws, especially those of the Frankish kings. The laws were known as *capitulars*, from their being arranged in chapters (Med. Lat. *capitularius*). *See* CHAPTER.

Capon. (kā' pon). Properly a castrated cock; but the name has been given to various fish, perhaps originally by humorous friars who wished to avoid the Friday fast and so eased their consciences by changing the name of the fish and calling a chicken a *fish out of the coop*. Thus we have:

A Crail's capon. A haddock dried and split, Crail being the borough in Fife, Scotland, which flourished from its fishing.

A Glasgow capon. A salt herring.

A Norfolk or **Yarmouth capon.** A red herring.

A Severn capon. A sole.

Capone, Alphonse (1899–1947). Al (Scarface) Capone, notorious Chicago gangster and racketeer of Sicilian origin. He rose to power in the heyday of BOOTLEGGING in the 1920s and made himself master of the rackets in the city by organizing the killing of most of the rival gunmen. After the St. Valentine's Day Massacre of 1929, when seven rival gangster leaders were machine-gunned, he was left in supreme control of the protection racket, speakeasies, brothels, etc. The suburb of Cicero was completely dominated by him. *See also* MAFIA.

Capricorn (kăp' ri kôrn). Called by Thomson in his *Winter*, "the centaur archer". Anciently the winter SOLSTICE occurred on the entry of the sun into Capricorn, *i.e.* the Goat; but the stars having advanced a whole sign to the east, the winter now falls at the sun's entrance into SAGITTARIUS (the Centaur Archer), so that the poet is strictly right, though we commonly retain the classical manner of speaking. Capricorn is the tenth, or strictly, eleventh sign of the ZODIAC (21 December–20 January).

In classical mythology Capricorn was PAN, who, from fear of the great TYPHON, changed himself into a goat, and was made by JUPITER one of the signs of the Zodiac.

Captain. Captain Cauf's Tail. In Yorkshire, the chief MUMMER who led his following from house to house on PLOUGH MONDAY He was most fantastically dressed, with a cockade and many coloured ribbons; and he always had a genuine calf's (*cauf's*) tail affixed behind.

Captain Moonlight. In Ireland a mythical person to whom was attributed the performance of atrocities by night especially in the latter part of the 19th century. Arson, murder, and the maiming of cattle were his specialities.

Captain of the Heads. In naval ships, the rating in charge of the *Heads* or lavatories. The name Heads arises from the original position of the ship's latrines, right forward in the beakhead or heads of the vessel.

Capua (kăp' ū à). **Capua corrupted Hannibal.** Luxury and self-indulgence will ruin anyone. Hannibal was everywhere victorious until he wintered at Capua, the most luxurious city of Italy, after which his star began to wane. Another form of the saying is **Capua was the Cannæ of Hannibal.** (*See* CANNÆ.)

Capuchin (kăp' ū chin). A friar of the

strict group of FRANCISCANS that arose about 1520; so called from the *capuce* or pointed cowl. They became a separate order in 1619.

Capulet (kăp′ ū let). A noble house in Verona, the rival of that of Montague; in Shakespeare's *Romeo and Juliet*, Juliet is of the former, and ROMEO of the latter.

Caput Mortuum (kăp′ ut môr tū um) (Lat. dead head). An alchemist's term for the residuum left after exhaustive distillation or sublimation; hence, anything from which all that made it valuable has been removed.

Caqueux (ka kè). A sort of gipsy race in Brittany, similar to the CAGOTS of Gascony and COLLIBERTS of Poitou.

Carabinier. *See* CARABINEER.

Caracalla (kăr′ a kăl′ à). Aurelius Antonius, Roman Emperor (211–217), was so called because instead of the Roman TOGA he adopted the Gaulish *caracalla*. It was a large, close-fitting, hooded mantle, reaching to the heels, and slit up before and behind to the waist.

Caradoc (kà răd′ ok). A Knight of the ROUND TABLE, noted for being the husband of the only lady in the queen's train who could wear "the mantle of matrimonial fidelity".

Also in history, the British king whom the Romans called Caractacus, who was taken captive to Rome in A.D. 51.

Carat. For precious stones, a measure of weight, about 1/142 of an ounce; for GOLD it is a ratio or proportional measure of 1/24th. Thus 22 carats of gold means 22 parts gold, 2 parts alloy. The name is perhaps from the Arab. *qirat*, meaning the seed of the locust tree, which was used for weighing gold and PRECIOUS STONES.

Carbineer, Carabineer, or **Carabinier.** In the 16th century light cavalry armed with *carabins*, later becoming troops armed with a short rifle called a *carbine*. The 9th Horse (subsequently the 6th Dragoon Guards) were named the *Carabiniers* by William III in 1692. Louis XIV's Royal Carabiniers were so named in 1693. In 1939 the 3rd and 6th Dragoon Guards amalgamated to form the 3rd Carabineers.

Carbonari (kar bo na′ rē). The name means *charcoal burners* and was assumed by a political secret society in Naples formed about 1808 with the aim of overthrowing despotic and foreign government. Their meeting-place was called a "hut", the inside "the place of selling charcoal", the outside "the forest", their opponents "wolves", etc. Much of their ritual was drawn from FREEMASONRY and kindred societies grew up throughout Italy and also France. The Italian Carbonari were largely merged into YOUNG ITALY in the 1830s. BYRON and Mazzini were members, and NAPOLEON III was associated with the movement in his earlier days.

Card. Slang for a queer fellow, an eccentric, a "character".

A cooling card. An obsolete expression for something that cools one's ardour, probably derived from some old game of cards. It is quite common in Shakespeare's day.

A knowing card. A sharp fellow, next door to a sharper. The allusion is to card-sharpers and their tricks.

A leading card. The strongest point in one's argument, etc.; a star actor. In card games a person leads from his strongest suit.

A queer card. An eccentric person, "indifferent honest"; one who may be "all right", but whose proceedings arouse mild suspicion and so not inspire confidence.

A sure card. A person one can fully depend on; one sure to command success. A project certainly to be depended on, as a winning card in one's hand.

Court cards. *See* COURT.

He played his cards well. He acted judiciously and skilfully, like a WHIST-player who plays his hand with judgment.

On the cards. Likely to happen, projected, and talked about as likely to occur. Probably derived from fortune-telling by cards, but possibly an allusion to a racing programme or *card*.

That's the card. The right thing. It probably refers to card games—"that's the right card to play"—but it means the same as "that's the ticket" and may refer to a ticket, or a race-card, etc.

That was my trump card. My best chance, my last resort.

The cards are in my hands. I hold the disposal of events which will secure success; I have the upper hand, the whip-end of the stick.

The Devil's Four-poster. *See under* DEVIL.

To ask for one's cards. To resign one's job. The reference is to the National Insurance cards kept by a person's employer. Similarly **to be given one's cards** means to be dismissed or sacked.

To count on one's cards. To anticipate success under the circumstances; to rely on one's advantages.

To go in with good cards. To have good patronage; to have excellent grounds for expecting success.

To have a card up one's sleeve. To have resources unsuspected by one's opponents, to have a last stroke in reserve. From cheating at cards, but with no implication of dishonesty in the figurative use.

To play one's best card. To do that which one hopes is most likely to secure victory.

When Osric tells Hamlet (V, ii) that Laertes is "the card and calendar of gentry" the compass card is implied with all its points.

Cardi. A native of Cardiganshire (now part of Dyfed), Wales. *Cardis* are popularly reputed to be clannish, parsimonious and excessively thrifty. Thus, among Welsh people "an old Cardi" denotes one reluctant to pay his turn of drinks, a stingy person.

Cardigan. A knitted woollen overwaistcoat with sleeves, named after the 7th Earl of Cardigan, who led the Light Brigade in the famous charge of Balaclava (1854). It appears to have been first worn by the British to protect themselves from the bitter cold of the Crimean winter. The Balaclava helmet or cap, a knitted woollen covering for the head and neck, has a similar origin.

Cardinal (Lat. *cardo*, a hinge). The adjective *cardinalis* meant originally "pertaining to a hinge" hence "that on which something turns or depends", thus "the principal or chief". In Rome, a cardinal church was a parish church as distinct from an oratory attached to it and the word was next applied to the senior priest of such a church. From the mid-8th century it denoted urban as distinct from rural clergy, and subsequently the clergy of a diocesan town and its cathedral but it was later restricted to the cardinals of the Roman see. In 1567 Pius V formally reserved the title for members of the Pope's Council, the COLLEGE OF CARDINALS.

The Cardinal's red hat was made part of the official vestments by Innocent IV in 1245. This 30-tasselled hat (not worn) was abolished in 1969. *See also* BISHOP.

College of Cardinals, or **Sacred College.** Originally formed from the clergy of the see of ROME, it now contains members from many nations who take their titles, as has always been customary, from a Roman parish. It consists of Cardinal-Bishops, Cardinal-Priests, and Cardinal-Deacons (the latter possibly deriving from the seven deacons appointed by St. PETER), but these terms are essentially of historical significance only, as all cardinals are now consecrated bishops. The number of cardinals was fixed at 70 by Sixtus V in 1586. John XXIII (1958–1963) raised it to 87, and in 1969 it reached 136. The POPE is elected by and from the College of Cardinals.

Cardinal humours. An obsolete medical term for the four principal humours of the body. *See* HUMOUR.

Cardinal points of the compass. Due north, south, east, and west, so called because they are the points on which the intermediate ones (NE., NW., NNE., etc.) hinge. The poles, being the points on which the earth turns, were called in Latin *cardines* (*See* CARDINAL.) The cardinal points are those which lie in the direction of the poles and of sunrise and sunset. Thus the winds which blow due north, east, west, and south, are called *cardinal winds*. It is probably from the fact that there are four cardinal points that there are four cardinal humours, virtues, etc.

Cardinal signs (of the ZODIAC). The two equinoctial and the two solstitial signs ARIES and LIBRA, CANCER and CA-

PRICORN.

Cardinal virtues. Justice, prudence, temperance, and fortitude, on which all other virtues hang or depend. A term of the SCHOOLMEN, to distinguish the "natural" virtues from the "theological" virtues (faith, hope and charity).

Care. Care killed the cat. It is said that "a cat has nine lives", yet care would wear them all out.

Care Sunday. The fifth Sunday in LENT. "Care" here means trouble, suffering; and Care Sunday means PASSION SUNDAY (as in O.H. Ger. *kar-fritag* is GOOD FRIDAY).

Care Sunday is also known as *Carle* or *Carling Sunday*. It was an old custom, especially in the north, to eat parched peas fried in butter on this day, and they were called *Carlings*.

Care-cloth. In the ROMAN CATHOLIC CHURCH, the fine silk or linen cloth formerly laid over the newly-married, or held over them as a canopy.

Carey Street, To be in. To be bankrupt. Carey Street is in the City of London, off Chancery Lane, and the bankruptcy court is situated there.

Carle Sunday; Carlings. *See* CARE SUNDAY.

Carlists. Don Carlos (1788–1855), second son of Charles IV of Spain, would have become king on the death of his brother Ferdinand VII, had not the SALIC LAW been set aside in favour of Ferdinand's daughter, Isabella. Don Carlos was supported by the Church, and the Carlist Wars ensued (1833–1840), but Isabella's supporters triumphed. Carlist intrigues continued until the death of Don Carlos II in 1909 and in 1937 the Carlists supported General Franco's FALANGE, maintaining Carlos Hugo de Borbón-Parma as claimant to the throne. On General Franco's death in 1975, Alphonso XIII's grandson became King of Spain as Juan Carlos I, his succession having been accepted by Franco in 1969.

Carlovingians (kar lo vin′ jiänz). **Carolingians,** or **Karlings.** The dynasty named from *Carolus Magnus* or CHARLEMAGNE. They were descended from Arnulf, a 7th-century bishop of Metz, and ruled in France (751–987), Germa-

ny (752–911), and Italy (744–887).

Carmagnole (kar ma nyōl). Originally the name of a workman's jacket introduced into France from Carmagnola in Piedmont and adopted by French revolutionaries. Thus the name came to be applied to them, to the soldiers of the Republic, and to a widely popular song and dance which was almost invariably used at the executions of 1792 and 1793. The first verse of the song is:

Madame Veto avait promis
De faire égorger tout Paris,
Madame Veto avait promis
De faire égorger tout Paris,
Mais son coup a manqué.
Dansons la carmagnole, Vive le son, vive le son,
Dansons la carmagnole, Vive le son du canon.

Madame VETO was their name for Marie Antoinette, as she was supposed to have instigated the king's unfortunate use of the veto. Carmagnole was subsequently applied to other revolutionary songs such as ÇA IRA, the MARSEILLAISE, the CHANT DU DÉPART, also to the speeches in favour of the execution of Louis XVI, called by Barère *des Carmagnoles*.

Carmelites (kar′ me lītz). A mendicant order of friars of 12th-century origin, taking its name from Mount Carmel in Syria and with a mythical history associating them with the prophet Elijah. Also called WHITEFRIARS from their white mantle. *See* BAREFOOTED.

Carmen Sylva (kar′ men sil′ và). The penname of Queen Elizabeth of Roumania (1843–1916). She was a musician, painter, and writer of poems and stories.

Carnaby Street. In the 1960s the much publicized clothing centre for fashion-conscious young men, situated east of Regent Street. It became associated with trendy unisex costumes and was somewhat showily refurbished by Westminster City Council in 1973, but its popularity had declined by 1975 when boutiques in King's Road, Chelsea, began to attract this type of trade.

Carnival. The season immediately preceding LENT, ending on SHROVE TUESDAY and a period in many Roman Catholic countries devoted to amusement; hence revelry, riotous amusement. From the Lat. *caro, carnis*, flesh; *levare*, to remove; signifying the abstinence from meat during Lent. The earlier word *carnilevamen* was altered in Italian to *carnevale* as though connected with *vale*, farewell—farewell to flesh.

Carol (O.Fr. *carole*, probably from Lat. *choraula*, a flute-player). The earliest use of the word in English was for a round dance, then later a light and joyous hymn particularly associated with the Nativity. The following verse is a translation from Old English of our earliest extant Christmas carol:

> Lordlings listen to our lay—
> We have come from far away
> To seek Christmas;
> In this mansion we are told
> He his yearly feast doth hold;
> 'Tis today!
> May joy come from God above,
> To all those who Christmas love.

The first printed collection came from the press of Wynkyn de Worde in 1521; it included the *Boar's Head Carol*, which is still sung at Queen's College, Oxford. *See* BOAR'S HEAD.

Carolingians. *See* CARLOVINGIANS.

Carolus (kå rō′ lus). A GOLD coin of the reign of Charles I. It was at first worth 20s., later 23s.

Carpathian Wizard. PROTEUS, who lived in the island of Carpathus (now Scarpanto), between Rhodes and Crete, and could transform himself into any shape he pleased. He is represented as carrying a sort of crook in his hand, because he was an ocean shepherd and had to manage a flock of sea-calves.

Carpe diem (kar′ pā dī′ em) (Lat.). Seize the present day. Enjoy yourself while you have the chance. "*Dum vivimus, vivamus*".

> Carpe diem, quam minimum credula postero.
> HORACE: *Odes* I, xi, 8.
> Seize the present, trust tomorrow e'en as little as you may.
> CONNINGTON.

Carpet. The magic carpet. The apparently worthless carpet, which transported whoever sat upon it wheresoever they wished, is one of the stock properties of Eastern story-telling. It is sometimes *Prince Housain's carpet*, because

of the popularity of the *Story of* PRINCE AHMED in the ARABIAN NIGHTS, when it supplies one of the main incidents; but the chief magic carpet is that of King SOLOMON which, according to legend, was of green silk. His throne was placed on it when he travelled, and it was large enough for all his forces to stand upon, the men and women on his right hand, and the spirits on his left. When ready, Solomon told the wind where he wished to go, and the carpet rose in the air, and landed at the place required. The birds of the air, with outspread wings, protected the party from the sun.

To be on the carpet, or **to be carpeted.** To be reprimanded, to be "called over the COALS".

To sweep under the carpet. To conceal or put something out of sight so that it will not be noticed; to try and forget unpleasant difficulties or realities.

Carpet-bagger. The name given in the U.S.A. to the northern political adventurers who sought a career in the southern states after the CIVIL WAR ended (1865). Their only "property qualification" was their "carpet bag" of personal belongings, and they were regarded by the southerners as parasites and exploiters. The southern state governments of this time are called *carpet-bagger* governments from the presence of these Republican office-holders from the north.

Hence a general term for one who comes to a place for political or particular ends, as a political candidate who has no real roots in the constituency he seeks to represent.

Carpet bombing. Delivery by the postman of unsolicited (and mainly unwanted) advertising matter. Increasingly prevalent from the 1980s.

Carpet-knight. One dubbed at Court by favour, not having won his spurs by military service in the field. Perhaps because non-military knighthoods were conferred "on the carpet", rather than "in the field", but more probably in allusion to the attachment shown to the carpeted drawing-room by non-martial knights.

Carriage. This used to mean things carried, luggage.

Carriage company. People who kept their own carriage for visiting, etc.

Carronade (kăr o năd). A short gun of large calibre like a mortar, having no trunnions and thus differing from howitzers. First made in 1779 at the Carron iron foundry in Scotland, carronades were fastened to their carriages by a loop underneath, and were chiefly used on ships to enable heavy shot to be thrown at close quarters.

Carry. Carry arms! Carry swords! Military commands directing that the rifle or drawn sword is to be held in a vertical position in the right hand and against the right shoulder.

To carry both ends of the log (Austr). To do all the work supposed to be shared by two.

To carry coals. *See* COAL.

To carry everything before one. To carry off all the prizes, to be highly successful in any form of sport, contest, or examination.

To carry fire in one hand and water in the other. To say one thing and mean another; to flatter, to deceive; to lull suspicion in order the better to work mischief.

To carry on. (1) To continue an activity from the point already reached. (2) To make a scene, lose one's temper— "he carried on something dreadful".

To carry on with someone. To indulge in an amorous affair.

To carry one's bat. Said of a cricketer who goes in first and is "not out" at the innings close. Hence, figuratively, to outlast one's opponents, to succeed in one's undertaking.

To carry one's point. To succeed against opposition, to overrule, to win. Candidates in ROME were balloted for and the votes marked on a tablet by points. Hence, *omne punctum ferre* meant "to be carried *nem. con.*", or to gain every vote; and "to carry one's point" is to carry off the points at which one aimed.

To carry out, or **through.** To continue a project to its completion.

To carry the can. To receive the blame for the misdeeds or mistakes in which others have participated. Probably from the performance of menial tasks in the services, which benefit others.

To carry the day. To win the contest; to carry off the honours of the day.

To carry weight. To have influence. In horse-racing, to equalize the weight of two or more riders by adding to the lighter ones.

Cart. To put the cart before the horse is to reverse the right or natural order of things.

> This methinks is playnely to sett the carte before the horse.
> *The Babees Book* (Early English Tract Society, p.23).

In other languages we have:

French:	Mettre la charrette avant les bœufs.
Latin:	Currus bovem trahit praepostere.
Greek:	HYSTERON PROTERON.
German:	Die Pferde hinter den Wagen spannen.
Italian:	Metter il carro innanzi ai buoi.

Carte. Carte blanche (Fr.). Literally a blank paper. A paper with only the signature written on it, so that the recipient may write his own terms upon it, knowing they will be accepted. Of military origin, referring to unconditional surrender, but now entirely used in a figurative sense meaning to confer absolute freedom of action on someone. *Cp.* BLANK CHEQUE.

Cartesian Philosophy (kar tē′ zhăn). The philosophical system of René Descartes (1596–1650), often called the father of modern philosophy. The basis of his system is COGITO ERGO SUM. Thought must proceed from SOUL and therefore man is not wholly material; that soul must be from some Being not material, and that Being is God. As for physical phenomena, they must be the result of motion excited by God, and these motions he termed *vortices*, to explain the movement of heavenly bodies. This latter theory was replaced by Newton's theory of gravitation. *See* NEWTONIAN PHILOSOPHY.

Carthaginem esse delandam. *See* DELENDA EST CARTHAGO.

Carthaginian faith. Treachery. *See* PUNIC FAITH.

Carthusians. An order of monks founded about 1084 by St. Bruno of Cologne, who with six companions retired to the solitude of La Grande Chartreuse, thirteen miles north-east of Grenoble, and there built his famous monastery. It was here they made the famous liqueur called CHARTREUSE. In 1902 monks were evicted by order of the French government and they moved to the Certosa (Charterhouse) near Lucca.

The first English Charterhouse was founded by Sir Walter de Menny at London in 1371 and the Carthusians were among the staunchest opponents of Henry VIII at the time of the Dissolution of the Monasteries. In 1833 the Carthusians were re-established in the Charterhouse at Parkminster, Sussex.

Carucate (Med. Lat. *caruca*, a plough). The same as a HIDE.

Carvilia. *See* MORGAN LE FAY.

Caryatides, or **Caryatids** (kăr i ăt' idz). Figures of women in Greek costume, used in architecture to support entablatures. Caryæ, in Laconia, sided with the Persians at THERMOPYLÆ, in consequence of which the Greeks destroyed the city, slew the men, and made the women slaves. Praxiteles, to perpetuate the disgrace, employed figures of these women instead of columns. *Cp.* ATLANTES, CANEPHORUS, TELAMONES.

Casanova. To be regarded as a "regular Casanova" is to have a reputation for amorous escapades, in allusion to the notorious Giovanni Jacopo Casanova de Seingalt (1725–1798), who secured his own reputation as an insatiable amorist by the writing of his lengthy *Mémoires*. Expelled from a Venetian seminary for his immoral conduct, after a period in the household of Cardinal Acquaviva, he wandered the capitals of Europe mixing with aristocratic and wealthy society, posing as alchemist, preacher, gambler, diplomatist, etc., and generally leading a vicious life. He was also a knight of the papal order of the Golden Spur, and was acquainted with Stanislaus Poniatowski and Frederick the Great, but he soon exhausted the goodwill of those around him and found it necessary to move on.

Case. The case is altered. *See* PLOWDEN.

To case. To skin an animal; to deprive it of its "case". *See* FIRST CATCH YOUR HARE *under* CATCH.

To case a joint A criminal's expression for investigating, reconnoitring or inspecting a "joint" (the building or property concerned) preparatory to the intended robbery, etc.

Case-hardened. Impenetrable to all sense of honour or shame. The allusion is to steel hardened by carbonizing the surface.

Casket. A small chest or box.

Casket Homer. *See* HOMER.

Casket, Children of the. Between 1728 and 1751 the Mississippi Company sent regular shipments of respectable middle-class girls to New Orleans to provide wives for the French settlers in Louisiana; each was presented on her departure with a *casket* of suitable clothing. They were known as *filles à la cassette*, to distinguish them from the women of bad character shipped out from the Salpêtrière prison during the same period. Louisiana families like to claim descent from a casket girl as New Englanders do from a MAYFLOWER pilgrim.

Casket Letters, The. Letters supposed to have been written between Mary Queen of Scots and Bothwell, at least one of which was held to prove the complicity of the Queen in the murder of Darnley, her husband. They were kept in a *casket* which fell into the hands of the Earl of Morton in 1567; they were examined in England and used as evidence (though denounced as forgeries by the Queen, who was never allowed to see them), and they disappeared after the execution of the Earl of Gowrie (1584), into whose possession they had passed on Morton's execution in 1581. Their authenticity is still in dispute.

Cassandra (kà săn' drà). A prophetess. In Greek legend the daughter of PRIAM and HECUBA, gifted with the power of prophecy. She refused APOLLO's advances and he brought it to pass that no one believed in her predictions, although they were invariably correct. She appears in SHAKESPEARE's *Troilus and Cressida*. In the figurative sense the name is usually applied to a prophet of doom.

Cassation. The Court of Cassation, in France, is the highest Court of Appeal, the court which can *casser* (quash) the judgment of other courts.

Cassiopeia (kaš i ō pē′ à). In Greek mythology, the wife of CEPHEUS, King of Ethiopia, and mother of ANDROMEDA. In consequence of her boasting of her beauty, she was sent to the heavens as the constellation Cassiopeia, the chief stars of which form the outline of a woman sitting in a chair and holding up both arms in supplication.

Cassiterides (kăs i ter′ i dēz). The tin islands, generally supposed to be the Scilly Islands and CORNWALL; but possibly the isles in Vigo Bay are meant. It is said that the Veneti procured tin from Cornwall and carried it to these islands, keeping its source a profound secret. The Phœnicians were the chief customers of the Veneti.

Cast. A cast of the eye. A squint. One meaning of the word cast is to twist or warp.

Cast down. Dejected (Lat. *dejectus*).

Cast not a clout till May is out. *See under* MAY.

Casting vote. The vote of the presiding officer or chairman when the votes of the assembly are equal. The final vote casts, turns, or determines the issue.

To cast about. To deliberate, to consider, as, "I am casting about me how I am to meet the expenses." A sporting phrase. Dogs, when they have lost scent, "cast for it", *i.e.* spread out and search in different directions to recover it.

To cast anchor. To throw out the anchor in order to bring the vessel to a standstill (Lat. *anchoram jacere*).

To cast a sheep's eye at one. *See* SHEEP.

To cast beyond the moon. To form wild conjectures. One of Heywood's proverbs. At one time the MOON was supposed to influence the weather, to affect the ingathering of fruits, to rule the time of sowing, reaping and slaying cattle, etc.

To cast in one's lot. To share the good or bad fortune of another.

To cast in one's teeth. To throw reproof at one. The allusion is to knocking one's teeth out by stones.

To cast pearls before swine. To offer what is precious to those who are unable to understand its value or appreciate it;

a Biblical phrase (*Matt*. vii, 6). If pearls were cast to swine, the swine would trample them underfoot.

Castaly (kăs′ tà li). A fountain of PARNASSUS sacred to the MUSES. Its waters had the power of inspiring with the gift of poetry those who drank of them.

Caste (Port. *casta*, race). One of the hereditary classes of society among Hindus; hence any hereditary or exclusive class. The four Hindu castes are BRAHMINS (the priestly order), *Shatriya* (soldiers and rulers), *Vaisya* (husbandmen and merchants), *Sudra* (agricultural labourers and artisans). The first issued from the mouth of BRAHMA, the second from his arms, the third from his thighs, and the fourth from his feet. Below this come thirty-six inferior classes, to whom the VEDAS are sealed, and who are held cursed in this world and without hope in the next.

To lose caste. To lose position in society. To be degraded from one caste to an inferior one.

Castle. Castle in the air. A visionary project, day-dream, splendid imagining which has no real existence. In fairy tales we often have these castles built at a word and vanishing as soon, like that built for ALADDIN by the Genie of the Lamp. Also called *Castles in Spain*; the French call them *Châteaux en Espagne* or *Châteaux en Asie*.

Castle of Indolence. In Thomson's poem of this name (1748) it is situated in the land of Drowsiness, where every sense is steeped in enervating delights. The owner was an enchanter, who deprived all who entered his domains of their energy and free will.

Castle Terabil, or **Terrible,** in ARTHURIAN legend stood in Launceston, Cornwall. It had a steep keep environed with a triple wall. Sometimes called Dunheved Castle.

Castor and Pollux (kăs′ tòr, pol′ uks). In classical mythology, twin sons of JUPITER and LEDA, also known as the DIOSCURI. They had many adventures including sailing with JASON in quest of the GOLDEN FLEECE, were worshipped as gods, and finally placed among the constellations as the GEMINI.

Their names used to be given by sailors to the ST. ELMO'S FIRE, or CORPO-SANT. If only one flame showed itself, the Romans called it HELEN, and said that the worst of the storm was yet to come; two or more luminous flames they called *Castor and Pollux*, and said that they boded the termination of the storm.

Casus belli (kā′ sŭs bel′ i) (Lat.). A ground for war; an occurrence warranting international hostilities.

Cat. Called a "FAMILIAR", from the mediæval superstition that SATAN's favourite form was a black cat. Hence witches were said to have a cat as their familiar. The superstition may have arisen from the classical legend of Galenthias who was turned into a cat and became a priestess of HECATE.

In ancient Rome the cat was a symbol cᶠ liberty and the goddess of Liberty was represented with a cat at her feet. No animal is so opposed to restraint as a cat.

In Ancient Egypt the cat was held sacred. The goddess Bast (*see* BU-BASTIS), representative of the life-giving solar heat, was portrayed as having the head of a cat, probably because that animal likes to bask in the sun. Diodorus tells us that in Egypt whoever killed a cat, even by accident, was punished by death. According to tradition DIANA assumed the form of a cat, and thus excited the fury of the GIANTS.

The male, or Tom, cat in SCOTLAND is called a Gib cat; the female is a Doe cat. *Cat* is also a term for a spiteful woman, a spiteful remark is said to be "catty" and "cat" was once a slang term for a harlot.

A cat has nine lives. A cat is more tenacious of life than many animals, it is careful and hardy and after a fall generally lands upon its feet without injury, the foot and toes being well padded.

A cat may look at a king. An impertinent remark by an inferior, meaning, "I am as good as you." There was a political pamphlet published with this title in 1652.

All cats love fish but fear to wet their paws. An old adage said of one who is anxious to obtain something of value but does not care to incur the necessary

trouble or risk. It is to this saying that SHAKESPEARE referred in *Macbeth*, I, vii:

> Letting "I dare not" wait upon "I would",
> Like the poor cat i' the adage.

Before the cat can lick her ear. Never; before the GREEK CALENDS. No cat can lick her ear. *See* NEVER.

Care killed the cat. *See* CARE.

Cat i' the adage. *See* ALL CATS LOVE FISH, ETC.

Dick Whittington and his cat. *See* WHITTINGTON.

Enough to make a cat laugh. Incongruously ridiculous.

Enough to make a cat speak. Said of something (usually good liquor) that will loosen one's tongue.

Hang me in a bottle like a cat. (*Much Ado about Nothing*, I, i). In olden times a cat was for sport enclosed in a bag or leather bottle, and hung to the branch of a tree, as a mark for bowmen to shoot at.

It is raining cats and dogs. Very heavily. *See under* RAIN.

Like a cat on hot bricks. Very uneasy; not at all "at home" in the situation; very restless.

Like something the cat brought in. Said of a slovenly person or one of uncouth or unkempt appearance. Also used in fun.

Muffled cats catch no mice (Ital. *Gatta guantata non piglia sorce*). Said of those who work in gloves for fear of soiling their fingers.

Not room to swing a cat. Used to indicate that a space, room, house, etc., is very restricted and small. There are various suggested origins of the phrase. Swinging cats by their tails as a mark for sportsmen was once a popular amusement. Cat was an abbreviation for CAT-O'-NINE-TAILS and in view of the restricted space in the old sailing ships where the cat was often administered, it is most likely derived from swinging this particular kind of cat. *Cat* is also an old Scottish word for rogue, and if the derivation is from this, the "swing" is that of the condemned rogue hanging from the gallows.

See how the cat jumps. See "which way the wind blows"; await the course of events, but see what is going to happen before you pass an opinion, support a course of action or commit yourself. The allusion is either to the game of "tip-cat", in which before you strike you must watch which way the "cat" has jumped up, or to the cruel pastimes mentioned under NOT ROOM TO SWING A CAT.

Sick as a cat. Cats are very prone to vomiting. Hence one is said *to cat* or *to shoot the cat* when vomiting.

The cat's pyjamas. Something superlatively good; first rate; attractive. An American colloquialism in use by 1900 and current in England in the 1920s and 1930s. **The cat's whiskers** is used in the same way and with the same meaning.

To bell the cat. *See* BELL.

To be made a cat's paw of. *See under* CAT'S PAW.

To fight like Kilkenny cats. To fight till both sides have lost their all; to fight with the utmost determination and pertinacity. The story is that during the Irish rebellion of 1798 Kilkenny was gar- risoned by a troop of Hessian soldiers, who amused themselves by tying two cats together by their tails and throwing them across a clothes-line to fight. When an officer approached to stop the "sport", a trooper cut the two tails with a sword and the two cats bolted. When an explanation of the two bleeding tails was asked for, he was told that two cats had been fighting and devoured each other all but the tails.

To grin like a Cheshire cat. An old simile popularized by Lewis Carroll:

> "please would you tell me," said Alice a little timidly,... "why your cat grins like that?" "It's a Cheshire cat," said the Duchess, "and that's why."
> *Alice in Wonderland* (1865), ch. vi.

The phrase has never been satisfactorily explained, but it has been said that Cheshire cheese was once sold moulded like a cat that appeared to be grinning. The waggish explanation is that the cats know that Cheshire is a COUNTY PALATINE and find the idea a source of perpetual amusement.

To lead a cat and dog life. To be always snapping and quarrelling, as a cat and a dog.

To let the cat out of the bag. To disclose a secret. *See* A PIG IN A POKE *under* PIG.

To live under the cat's foot. To be under PETTICOAT GOVERNMENT; to be HENPECKED. A mouse under the cat's paw lives but by sufferance and at the cat's pleasure.

To put the cat among the pigeons. To stir up trouble, to cause dissension. The allusion is obvious.

To turn cat-in-pan. To turn traitor, to be a TURNCOAT. The phrase seems to be the Fr. *tourner côté en peine* (to turn sides in trouble).

Touch not a cat but a glove. The punning motto of the Mackintosh clan, whose crest is a "cat-a-mountain salient guardant proper", with "two cats proper" for supporters. Their clan was the clan *Cattan* or *Chattan*, thus "touch not the clan Cattan". The meaning of "but" here is "without" or "except with".

What can you have of a cat but her skin? Said of something that is useless for any purpose but one. The cat's fur was used for trimming cloaks, etc., but the flesh was no good for anything.

When the cat's away the mice will play. Advantage will be taken of the absence of the person in authority.

Cat and Fiddle. There are several fanciful derivations for this inn sign but it most probably comes from the nursery rhyme:

> Heigh diddle diddle
> The cat and the fiddle, *etc.*

There is a possible reference to the once popular game of tip-cat or trap-ball and the fiddle for a dance that were provided as attractions for customers.

Cat and Kittens. A PUBLIC-HOUSE SIGN alluding to the large and small pewter pots in which beer was served. Stealing these pots was called "cat and kitten sneaking".

Cat and Mouse Act. Popular name for the Prisoners (Temporary Discharge for Ill-Health) Act of 1913, passed during the SUFFRAGETTE disturbances to avoid the imprisoned law-breakers from achieving martyrdom through hunger strikes. They were released on licence when necessary, subject to re-arrest if need arose. **To play cat and mouse** is to do what you like with someone in your power.

Cat-call. A kind of whistling noise sometimes used by theatre audiences, etc., to express displeasure or impatience.

Cat-eyed. Able to see in the dark.

Cat-ice. Very thin, almost transparent ice, from under which the water has receded; unable to bear the weight of a cat.

Cat-lap. A contemptuous name for tea, or other "soft" drink such as a cat would drink; non-alcoholic liquor.

Cat o'mountain. The wild-cat; also the leopard, or panther; hence a wild, savage sort of man.

Cat-o'-nine-tails. A whip with nine lashes used for punishing offenders, briefly known as the "cat". Once used for flogging in the Army and Navy and not formally abolished as a civil punishment for crimes of violence until 1948. Popular superstition says that the nine tails were because flogging by "a trinity of trinities" would be both more efficient and more efficacious. *See* NOT ROOM TO SWING A CAT *above*.

Cat Stane. Certain monoliths in Scotland (there is one near Kirkliston, Linlithgow), so called from the Celtic *cath*, a battle, because they mark the site of a battle. They are not Druidical stones.

Cat's-brains. This curious name is given to a geological formation of sandstone veined with chalk. It is frequently met with in old agricultural deeds and surveys.

Cats' concert. A noisy jangle, a discordant din; like the caterwauling of cats at night.

Cat's cradle. A game played with a piece of twine by two children. It has been suggested that the name is a corruption of *cratch-cradle*, or the manger cradle in which the infant Saviour was laid (*cratch* is the Fr. *crèche*, a rack or manger), but this is no more than surmise.

Cat's eye. A gem which possesses chatoyancy, or a changeable lustre. The true or precious cat's eye is a variety of chrysoberyl. The semi-precious kind is a form of quartz.

It is also the trade name of a reflector embedded in the road as a guide for motorists after lighting-up time or in fog.

Cat's paw. A light air, seen afar off, indicated by a ripple on a calm sea, and often heralding the end of the prevailing calm, is so called by sailors. It is also a nautical term for a loop formed in a rope for attaching a hook, etc.

To be made a cat's paw of, *i.e.* the tool of another, to do another's dirty work. The allusion is to the fable of the monkey who wanted to get some roasted chestnuts from the fire, and used the paw of his friend the cat for the purpose.

Cat's whisker. In the old fashioned "crystal" wireless sets, this was the name given to the very fine wire that made contact with the crystal. *See also* CAT'S PYJAMAS *above*.

Catacomb (kăt′ à cōm). A subterranean gallery for the burial of the dead, especially those at ROME. The origin of the name is unknown but the cemetery of St. SEBASTIAN on the APPIAN WAY was called the *Catacumbas*, probably a place-name and in the course of time the name was applied to similar cemeteries. Their extensive development in Rome took place in the 3rd and 4th centuries and was due to the spread of Christianity. At times they were used by the Christians for their meetings. They suffered much destruction from the GOTHS and Lombards and eventually came to be forgotten until rediscovered in 1578 as the result of a landslip.

Cataian (kàt ā′ yan) A native of CATHAY or China; hence a thief, liar or scoundrel, because the Chinese were supposed to have these characteristics.

> I will not believe such a Cataian, though the priest of the town commended him for a true man.
> SHAKESPEARE: *Merry Wives of Windsor*, II, i.

Catalogue raisonné (rā′ zò nā) (Fr.). A catalogue of books, paintings, etc., classed according to their subjects and often with explanatory notes or comments.

Catastrophe (kà tăs trò fi) (Gr. *kata* downwards; *strephein*, to turn). A turning upside down. Originally used of the change which produces the *dénouement* of a drama, which is usually a "turning upside down" of the beginning of the plot.

Catch. Catch as catch can. Get by HOOK OR CROOK all you can; a phrase from the child's game of this name, or from the method of wrestling so called, in which the wrestlers are allowed to get a grip anyhow or anywhere.

Catch me at it. Most certainly I shall never do what you say, I will never do that.

Catch weights. A term in racing, wrestling or boxing, meaning without restrictions as to weight.

First catch your hare. This direction is generally attributed to Hannah Glasse, habit-maker to the Prince of Wales, and author of *The Art of Cookery made Plain and Easy* (1747). Her actual directions are, "Take your hare when it is cased, and make a pudding,... etc." To "case" means to take off the skin, as in Shakespeare's *All's Well that Ends Well*, iii, vi, "We'll make you some sport with the fox ere we case him." "First catch your hare," is a very old phrase and in the 13th century Bracton (Bk. IV, tit. i, ch. xxi, sec. 4) has these words:

> Vulgariter, quod primo oportet cervum capere, et postea, cum captus fuerit, illum excoriare. (It is commonly said that you must first catch your deer, when it is caught, skin it.)

To be caught bending. To be caught at a disadvantage. If you catch a small boy bending over it is easy to smack him on that portion of his anatomy provided by nature for the purpose. Some time about 1903 one of George Robey's songs declared:

> My word! If I catch you bending!

The expression also occurs, of course, in *Knees up, Mother Brown*.

To be caught napping. To suffer some disadvantage while off one's guard. Pheasants, hares, and other animals are sometimes surprised "napping".

To be caught out. To be unmasked in a lie or subterfuge, from CRICKET, etc., in which the striker is out when a catch is caught by a fieldsman.

To catch a crab. In rowing when the oarsman fails to strike the blade deeply enough into the water and falls backwards as a result, or too deeply and risks being thrown overboard.

To catch a tartar. To catch a troublesome prisoner; to have dealings with a person who is more than a match for one; to think one is going to manage a person, only to find it is no easy job.

To catch a Yankee. The equivalent of TO CATCH A TARTAR, before Yankee lost its derogatory implication.

To catch on. To make its way; something which becomes popular, such as a song, a phrase, a fashion, etc.

To catch someone with their pants down. A metaphor meaning to take someone at a great disadvantage.

To catch the Speaker's eye. *See* SPEAKER.

To lie upon the catch. To lie in wait; to try to catch one tripping.

You'll catch it. You'll get severely punished. Here "it" stands for the undefined punishment, such as a whipping, a scolding, etc.

Catch penny. A worthless article puffed up to catch the pennies of those who are foolish enough to buy it.

Catch -22. Whichever alternative you choose you can't win or you are in a different situation or tight spot — you lose either way. It is the title of Joseph Heller's book published in 1955. The story centres around Captain Yossarian of the 256th United States (Army) bombing squadron in World War II and his main aim is to avoid being killed. "There was only one catch and that was Catch -22 which specified that concern for one's own safety in the face of dangers that were real and immediate was the process of a rational mind. Orr was crazy and could be grounded. All he had to do was to ask and as soon as he did he would no longer be crazy and would have to fly more missions".

Catchphrase. A phrase which has caught on and is repeated by all and sundry. Virtually the same as CATCHWORD.

Catchpole. A constable; a law officer whose business it was to apprehend criminals. This is nothing to do with a pole or staff, nor with *poll*, the head, but is the mediæval Latin *chassipullus*, one who hunts or chases fowls.

Catchword. A popular cry, a word or CATCHPHRASE, particularly adopted as a political slogan. "Three acres and a cow", "your food will cost you more", "CHINESE SLAVERY", "Scholarships not battleships", 'the NEW MORALITY", "the AFFLUENT SOCIETY", are examples.

In printing, the first word on a page which is printed at the foot of the preceding page is known as the catchword; the first printer to employ catchwords may be either Balthazar Azoguidus of Bologna (in his Italian and Latin editions of Antoninus' *Confessionale*, 1472) or Vindelinus de Spira of Venice (in his undated editions of Philelphus' *Epistolae*, and Tacitus' *Opera* printed before 1474).

Some printers also use the name for the main words in a dictionary; *i.e.* those at the head of each article, printed in bold type so as to catch the eye.

In the theatre, the cue (the last word or so of an actor's lines) is called the *catchword*.

Catechumen (kăt e kū' men). One taught by word of mouth (Gr. *katecheein*, to din into the ears). Those about to be baptized in the Early Church were first taught by word of mouth, and then *catechized* on their religious faith and duties.

Caterans, or **Catherans** (kăt' e ránz). Highland Scottish FREEBOOTERS; the word occurs in Scottish romances and ballads.

Cater-cousin. An intimate friend, a remote kinsman. The word probably refers to persons being *catered* for together, "friends so familiar that they eat together".

Alternatively it may derive from *cater* or *quater* (Fr. *quatre*, four) meaning a fourth cousin or remote relation; or from the dialect word *cater* meaning "diagonally", hence an indirect relation.

Catgut. Cords of various thicknesses, made from the intestines of animals (usually sheep, but never cats) and used for the strings of musical instruments and racquets for ball-games. Why it is called catgut has never been satisfactorily explained, but it may be a corruption of *kitgut, kit* being an old word for a small fiddle.

SHAKESPEARE, however, gives catgut its true origin:

> Now divine air! Now is his soul ravished! Is it not strange that Sheep's guts should hale souls out of men's bodies? Well, a horn for my money when all's done.—*Much Ado*, II, iii.

Catgut scraper. A fiddler.

Catharine. *See* CATHERINE.

Cathay (kà thā'). The name used by Marco Polo for what roughly corresponds to northern China, and the name for that part of China which the 16th-century navigators sought to discover via a NORTH-EAST or NORTH-WEST PASSAGE. The word comes from *Khitai*, a Manchurian Tartar kingdom of the 10th century. It was also used less specifically for China in general. *See* MANGI.

An English Cathay Company was founded by Michael Lok in 1577 to develop Frobisher's discoveries. In more modern times the name remained as a poetic usage.

> Better fifty years of Europe than a cycle of Cathay.
>
> TENNYSON: *Locksley Hall*.

Cathedrals of the Old Foundation. The ancient cathedrals that existed in England before Henry VIII founded and endowed new cathedrals out of some of the revenues from the Dissolution of the Monasteries. These latter are known as **Cathedrals of the New Foundation;** they are Chester, Gloucester, Peterborough, Bristol and Oxford.

Catherine, St. Virgin and martyr of noble birth in Alexandria. She adroitly defended the Christian faith at a public disputation (*c*. 310) with certain heathen philosophers at the command of the Emperor Maximinus, for which she was put on a wheel like that of a chaff-cutter. Legend says that as soon as the wheel turned, her bonds were miraculously broken; so she was beheaded. Hence the name CATHERINE WHEEL. She is the patron saint of wheel-wrights.

Catherine of Siena, St. (1347–1380). A patron saint of Italy, she was canonised in 1461 and in 1970 the second woman to be made a DOCTOR OF THE CHURCH. As well as serving the poor she was instrumental in bringing about the return of the POPE from AVIGNON to

ROME.

Catherine wheel. A kind of firework, in the form of a wheel, which is driven round by the recoil from the explosion of the various squibs of which it is composed.

Catherine-wheel window. A wheel window, sometimes called a *rose-window*, with radiating divisions.

To braid St. Catherine's tresses. To live a virgin.

Catherine Théot (tā' ō). A French prophetess like the English Joanna Southcott, calling herself "The Mother of God" and changing her name to Theos (God). In the height of the Revolution she preached the worship of the Supreme Being and announced that Robespierre was the forerunner of The Word. She called him her well-beloved son and chief prophet. She died in prison in 1794.

Catholic. The word (Gr. *katholikos*) means general, universal, comprehensive. It is used in this sense in the following extract:

> Creed and test
> Vanish before the unreserved embrace
> Of Catholic humanity.
> WORDSWORTH: *Ecclesiastical Sonnets*, III, xxxvi.

Hence from the Church viewpoint it distinguishes (1) the whole body of Christians as apart from "Jews, heretics and infidels", (2) a member of a church which claims the APOSTOLIC SUCCESSION and direct descent from the earliest body of Christians; (3) the ROMAN CATHOLIC CHURCH, *i.e.* the Western or Latin branch of the ancient Catholic or universal Church.

A person of catholic tastes is one who is interested in a wide variety of subjects.

Catholic Church. The whole body of Christians as distinct from the Churches and sects into which they are divided. The Latin Church called itself Catholic after the separation from the Eastern or ORTHODOX CHURCH. At the REFORMATION the Reformers called the Western Church under papal jurisdiction the ROMAN CATHOLIC CHURCH as opposed to their own Reformed or PROTESTANT Churches. Members of the CHURCH OF ENGLAND hold themselves to be Catholics but in popular usage Catholic usually means Roman Catholic.

> I believe in the Holy Ghost; The holy Catholic Church; *etc.*
> *Book of Common Prayer: Apostles' Creed.*

Catholic Association (1823–1829). Founded in Ireland by Daniel O'Connell and supported by the Roman Catholic clergy to promote the political emancipation of Roman Catholics. It became a powerful organization, aided by the monthly subscriptions of the peasantry called "Catholic Rent", and achieved its objective with the passing of the Catholic Emancipation Act in 1829.

Catholic Epistles. Those Epistles in the NEW TESTAMENT not addressed to any particular church or individual; the epistles of James, Peter, and Jude and the first of John; II John is addressed to a "lady", and III John to Gaius, but they are often included. *See* CANONICAL.

Catholic King, or **His Most Catholic Majesty.** A title given by Pope Innocent VIII to Ferdinand of Aragon and Isabella of Castile, and confirmed by Pope Alexander VI on account of their conquest and subsequent expulsion of the MOORS in 1492. Those who remained and became nominal Christians were called Moriscos. The title was thereafter used as an appellation of the kings of Spain. *Cp.* RELIGIOUS.

Catholic League. (1) The party headed by the Guise faction in France (1584) in alliance with Philip II of Spain. Their object was to prevent the succession of Henry of Navarre to the French crown and place the Cardinal of BOURBON on the throne on the death of Henry III. (2) A Catholic confederacy formed in Germany in 1609 to counterbalance the Protestant Union of 1608. These rival groupings resulted in the THIRTY YEARS WAR (1618–1648).

Catholic Roll. A document which Roman Catholics were obliged to sign on taking their seats as Members of PARLIAMENT. It was abolished when a single oath was prescribed to all members by an Act of 1866.

Old Catholics. In the Netherlands, the Church of Utrecht which separated from ROME in 1724 after allegations of Jansenism. (*See* JANSENISTS). The term is more particularly associated with members of the German, Austrian and Swiss Churches who rejected the dogmas of papal INFALLIBILITY after the VATICAN COUNCIL of 1870 and were joined by others as a result of the KULTURKAMPF. Their episcopal succession is derived from the Church of Utrecht and they are in communion with the CHURCH OF ENGLAND. There are also others in the U.S.A. and small groups of Poles and Croats.

Catholicon (kà thol' i kòn). A PANACEA, a universal remedy, from the Greek word meaning universal, all-embracing.

Also the name of a comprehensive work of the encyclopaedic dictionary type.

Catiline's Conspiracy (kăt' i līn). Lucius Sergius Catilina conspired with a number of dissolute young nobles (64 B.C.) to plunder the Roman treasury, destroy the senate, and fire the city as part of a political revolution. CICERO, who was consul, got full information of the plot and delivered his first Oration against Catiline (8 November 63 B.C.), whereupon Catiline left ROME. Next day Cicero delivered his second Oration, and several of the conspirators were arrested. His third Oration respecting the punishment to be accorded was made on 4 December and, after his fourth Oration the following day, sentence of death was passed. Catiline was slain with his supporters at Pistoria in Etruria (62 B.C.).

Cato Street Conspiracy. A plot by Arthur Thistlewood (1770–1820) and his associates to murder the CABINET while the members were dining with the Earl of Harrowby in Grosvenor Square (23 February 1820). Hand grenades were to be used. The conspirators met in a loft in Cato Street, a small MEWS near the Edgware Road, where some were arrested. Thistlewood and others escaped, but he was caught the following morning. Five, including Thistlewood, were hanged and decapitated and five others were transported for life.

Caucasian (kaw kā' shàn). The white or European race is so called. The term

originated with J. F. Blumenbach (1752–1840) who, in 1775, selected a Georgian skull as the perfect type of Indo-European. His views are no longer held, but the word has been used with certain qualifications by later anthropologists.

Caucus (kaw' kùs). An American word, first recorded as having been used in Boston about 1750 and popularized in England by Joseph Chamberlain about 1878 in Birmingham. In America it means a meeting of some division, large or small, of a political or legislative body for the purpose of agreeing upon a united course of action in the main assembly. In England it is applied opprobriously to an inner group which seeks to manipulate affairs behind the backs of its party. The origin of the word is unknown, but it may be connected with the Algonquin word *cau-cau-as-u*, one who advises.

Caudillo (kaw dil' yō). The title adopted by General Franco, head of the FALANGIST government in Spain, in imitation of Mussolini's DUCE and Hitler's FÜHRER. Like them it means "Leader".

Caudine Forks. A narrow pass in the mountains near Capua, now called the Valley of Arpaia. It was here that the Roman army, under the consuls T. Veturius Calvinus and Sp. Postumius, fell into the hands of the Samnites (321 B.C.), and were made to pass "under the YOKE".

Caudle. Any sloppy mess, especially that sweet mixture of gruel and wine or spirits once given by nurses to recently confined women and their "gossips" who called to see the baby during the first month. The word means "something warm" (Lat. *calidus*).

Caudle lecture. A curtain lecture. The term is derived from a series of papers by Douglas Jerrold, *Mrs. Caudle's Curtain Lectures*, which were published in *Punch* (1846). These papers represent Job Caudle as a patient sufferer of the lectures of his nagging wife after they had gone to bed and the curtains were drawn.

Caught bending, napping, etc. *See under* CATCH.

Caul. The word was formerly used for a

net in which women enclosed their hair, now called a SNOOD.

It was also used to describe any membrane enclosing the viscera, *e.g.* "The caul that is above the liver", *Exod.* xxix, 13.

The membrane on the head of some new-born infants is the *caul* and is held to be a charm, especially against death by drowning. They were once advertised for sale and frequently sought after by mariners. To be born with a caul was with the Romans tantamount to being BORN WITH A SILVER SPOON IN ONE'S MOUTH.

Cauld-lad, The, of Hilton Hall. A house-spirit who moved about the furniture during the night. Being resolved to banish him, the inmates left for him a green cloak and hood, before the kitchen fire, which so delighted him that he never troubled the house any more; but sometimes he might be heard singing:

Here's a cloak, and here's a hood,
The cauld-lad of Hilton will do no more good.

Cauliflower ear. An ear permanently thickened and deformed by boxing injuries.

Caurus (kaw′ rŭs). The Latin name for the west-north-west wind, anglicized as Chorus.

Causa causans (kaw′ ză kaw′ zănz). The initiating cause, the primary cause.

Causa causata. The cause which owes its existence to the CAUSA CAUSANS; the secondary cause.

Causa vera. (*a*) The immediate predecessor of an effect; (*b*) a cause verifiable by independent evidence (Mill).

In theology, God is the *causa causans*, and creation the *causa causata*. The presence of the sun above the horizon is the *causa vera* of daylight, and its withdrawal below the horizon is the *causa vera* of night.

Cause. Aristotelian causes.

(1) **The Efficient Cause.** That which immediately produces the effect.

(2) **The Material Cause.** The matter on which (1) works.

(3) **The Formal Cause.** The Essence or "Form" (or group of attributes) introduced into the matter by the *efficient cause*.

(4) **The Final,** or **Ultimate Cause.** The purpose or end for which the thing exists or the causal change takes place. But God is called the Ultimate Final Cause, since, according to ARISTOTLE, all things tend, so far as they can, to realize some Divine attribute.

God is also called the **First Cause,** or the **Cause Causeless,** beyond which even imagination cannot go.

Cause, The. A mission; the object or project.

The Cause, or **The Good Old Cause** in the 17th century is the PURITAN cause, and was commonly used by the supporters of the Puritan Revolution in Cromwellian times and afterwards.

To make common cause. To work for the same object. Here "cause" is the legal term meaning the cause or side of the question advocated.

Cause célèbre (Fr.). Any famous law case or trial, such as the TICHBORNE CASE or the case of Jean CALAS.

Caution. So-and-so's a caution, meaning that he is odd in his ways, likely to do something unexpected, often with a quaint twist to it. The phrase is originally American and had a somewhat wider application:

The way the icy blast would come down the bleak shore was a caution.
C. F. HOFFMAN: *Winter West* (1835).
His wife was what the Yankees call a Caution.
MORTIMER COLLINS: *Vivien* (1870).

Caution money. A sum deposited with college authorities, at an INN OF COURT, etc., as a safeguard against misbehaviour.

Cavalier. A horseman; whence a knight, a gentleman (Span. *caballero, b* and *v* being pronounced alike in that language).

Cavalier, or **Chevalier of St. George.** James Francis Edward Stuart, called the PRETENDER, or the Old Pretender (1688–1766). See WARMING-PAN.

The Laughing Cavalier. The name given to the famous portrait of an unknown gallant, by the Dutch painter Frans Hals, now in the Wallace Collection, London.

The Young Cavalier, or **the Bonnie Chevalier.** Charles Edward Stuart, the Young Pretender (1720–1788). *See*

PRETENDER.

Cavalier Parliament (1661–1679). The first PARLIAMENT of Charles II after the RESTORATION and thus named from its Royalist majority. It was also called the PENSIONARY PARLIAMENT or LONG PARLIAMENT of Charles II.

Cavaliers. The Royalists or adherents of Charles I at the time of the CIVIL WARS. Their opponents were called ROUNDHEADS.

Cave of Adullam. *See* ADULLAMITES.

Caveat (kā′ vē ăt) (Lat. let him beware). A notice directing the recipient to refrain from some act pending the decision of the court. Hence, **to enter a caveat,** to give legal notice that the opponent is not to proceed with the suit in hand until the party giving notice has been heard; to give warning or admonition.

Caveat emptor (Lat. let the purchaser beware). The buyer must keep his eyes open, for the bargain he agrees to is binding. The full legal maxim is: *Caveat emptor, quia ignorare non debuit quod ius alienum emit*. (Let a purchaser beware, for he ought not to be ignorant of the nature of the property which he is buying from another party.)

Caviare (kăv′ i ar). Sturgeon's roe, pickled, salted and used as a savoury or HORS D'ŒUVRE, etc. Caviare is usually only appreciated by those who have acquired a taste for it, hence Shakespeare's *caviare to the general* (*Hamlet*, II, ii), above the taste or comprehension of ordinary people.

In the days of Tsarist Russia certain matter in imported periodicals was blacked out by over-stamping. Such matter came to be known as *caviare* because its appearance was reminiscent of black, salted caviare on a slice of bread.

Cavo-rilievo (ka′ vō ril yā′ vō). "Relief", cut below the original surface, the highest parts of the figure being on a level with the surface.

Caxton, William. Father of English printing, hence his name is widely applied to branded articles in the printing and paper trades. Born in the Weald of Kent, he learnt his printing in Cologne and Bruges. He set up shop at the sign of the Red Pole in the shadow of West-

minster Abbey about 1476 and died in 1491, by which time he had printed about a hundred books. He was printer, publisher, retailer and translator.

Cayuse. An Indian pony. The Cayuses were a North American Indian tribe. Since about 1880 the word has meant "a horse of little value".

Cean (sē′ an). **The Cean poet.** Simonides of Ceos, *c*. 556–468 B.C.

The Cean and the Teian muse.
BYRON: *Don Juan* (Song: *The Isles of Greece*).

Cecilia, St. (se sil′ i à). Patron SAINT of the blind and patroness of music and especially of Church music. Born in Rome, she is usually supposed to have been martyred in A.D. 230, but the date is uncertain. She was blind, and according to tradition, was inventor of the organ. An ANGEL fell in love with her for her musical skill; her husband saw the heavenly visitant, who gave to both a crown of martyrdom which he brought from PARADISE. Her day is 22 November, on which the Worshipful Company of Musicians, a LIVERY COMPANY of the CITY of LONDON, meet and go in procession for divine service in St. Paul's Cathedral. Both Dryden and Pope wrote odes in her honour.

Cecil's Fast. A dinner of fish. William Cecil, Lord Burghley, for nearly forty years chief minister to Queen Elizabeth I, introduced a law to enjoin the eating of fish on certain days in order to promote the fishing industry.

Ceelict, St. An English name of St. Calixtus, who is commemorated on 14 October, the day of the Battle of Hastings.

Ceiling. Ceiling zero means that the clouds or mist are down to ground level.

Celestial City. HEAVEN is so called by John Bunyan in his *Pilgrim's Progress*.

Celestial Empire. China; a translation of the Chinese *Tien Chao*, literally "heavenly dynasty", alluding to the belief that the old Emperors were in direct descent from the gods. Hence the Chinese are sometimes called *Celestials*.

Celestines. An order of reformed BENEDICTINES founded about 1260 by Pietro di Murrone, who became Pope Celestine V in 1294.

Celt (selt, kelt). A piece of stone, ground

artificially into a wedge-like shape with a cutting edge, used for axes, chisels, etc. The term is also loosely applied to metal axe-heads, especially of bronze.

Celtic (sel′tik, kel′ tik). Applied to the peoples and languages of that branch of the Aryan family which includes the Irish, Manx, Welsh, Cornish, Breton, and Scottish Gaels. Anciently the term was applied by the Greeks and Romans to the peoples of western Europe generally, but when CÆSAR wrote of the Celtæ he referred to the people of middle GAUL only. The word *Celt* probably means a warrior; fable accounts for it by the story of Celtina, daughter of Britannus, who had a son by HERCULES, named Celtus, who became the progenitor of the Celts.

Celtic Fringe. Those parts of Great Britain and Ireland whose population is predominantly of Celtic stock, namely WALES, CORNWALL, SCOTLAND and IRELAND.

Celtic Sea. Formally defined as "that part of the continental shelf lying between the 200 fathom contour, S. Ireland, the S.W. tip of Wales, Land's End and Ushant". The term derives from the neighbouring Celtic areas—Brittany, CORNWALL, WALES and IRELAND, and was first used by E. W. L. Holt in 1921.

Cemetery properly means a sleeping-place (Gr. *koimeterion*, a dormitory). The Persians call their cemeteries "the Cities of the Silent".

Cenci. *See* BEAUTIFUL PARRICIDE.

Cenomanni (sen ō ma′ ni). The name given to the inhabitants of Norfolk, Suffolk, and Cambridge by CÆSAR in his *Commentaries*.

Cenotaph (sen′ o tăf) (Gr. *kenos*, empty; *taphos*, tomb). A sepulchral monument raised to the memory of a person or persons buried elsewhere. By far the most noteworthy to all of British race is that in Whitehall, designed by Sir E. Lutyens, which was dedicated on 11 November 1920, to those who fell in World War I. It has since been adapted to commemorate the fallen of World War II.

Centaur. Mythological beast, half horse and half man. Centaurs are said to have dwelt in ancient Thessaly; a myth the origin of which is probably to be found in the expert horsemanship of the inhabitants. (*See* IXION). The Thessalian centaurs were invited to a marriage feast and one of their number attempted to abduct the bride, whereupon conflict ensued and the centaurs were duly driven out of the country by the LAPITHAE.

Cent Nouvelles Nouvelles (son noo-vel′). This collection of "a hundred new tales" first appeared in the MS. dated 1456. It is on much the same lines as the DECAMERON and tells in French some of the stories already made familiar by the Italian novelists. Saintsbury calls it the best of all the late mediæval prose works. Nicolas of Troyes produced his *Grand Parangon de Nouvelles Nouvelles* in 1535, containing tales of his own and drawing from the GESTA ROMANORUM and *Decameron*.

Cento (Lat. a patchwork). Poetry made up of lines borrowed from established authors, an art freely practised in the decadent days of Greece and Rome. Ausonius, who has a nuptial idyll composed from verses selected from VIRGIL, made rules for their composition. Well-known examples are the *Homerocentones*, the *Cento Virgilianus* by Proba Falconia (4th century), and the hymns made by Metellus out of the *Odes* of HORACE.

Centre Party. In politics, the party occupying a place between two extremes: the *left centre* is the most radical wing, and the *right centre* the more conservative. In the French Revolution *the Centre* of the Legislative Assembly included the friends of order.

Centurion (sen tū′ ri on) (Lat. *centum*, a hundred). A Roman officer who had the command of 100 men. There were sixty centurions, of varying ranks, to a legion, the chief being the first centurion of the first maniple of the first cohort; his title was *Primus pilus prior* or *Primipilus*. The centurion's emblem of office was a vinestaff.

Cephalus and Procris (sel′ a lùs, prok′ ris). Cephalus was husband of PROCRIS, who deserted him through jealousy. He went in search of her and rested awhile under a tree. Procris crept through some bushes to ascertain if a rival was with him and Cephalus, hearing the noise and thinking it was made by some wild beast, hurled his javelin into the bushes and slew Procris. When he discovered what he had done he slew himself with the same javelin.

Cepheus (sē′ fūs). A northern constellation; named from Cepheus, king of Ethiopia, husband of CASSIOPEIA and father of ANDROMEDA.

Cepola (sep′ ō là). **Devices of Cepola.** Quips of law are so called from Bartholomew Cepola whose law-quirks, teaching how to elude the most express law, and to perpetuate lawsuits *ad infinitum*, have been frequently reprinted—once in 8vo, in BLACK LETTER, for John Petit of Paris, in 1503.

Cerberus (sĕr′ bĕr ùs). A grim, watchful keeper, house-porter, guardian, etc. Cerberus according to classical mythology is the three-headed dog that keeps the entrance of the infernal regions. HERCULES dragged the monster to earth and let him go again. (*See* ACONITE.) ORPHEUS lulled Cerberus to sleep with his lyre and the SIBYL who conducted ÆNEAS through the INFERNO also threw the dog into a profound sleep with a cake seasoned with poppies and honey. (*See* SOP.)

The origin of the fable of Cerberus may be found in the custom of the ancient Egyptians of guarding graves with dogs.

Ceremony (Lat. *cærimonia*). By way of accounting for this word, which is probably connected with the Sans. *karman*, a religious action, a rite, Livy tells us that when the Romans fled before Brennus, one Albinus, who was carrying his wife and children in a cart to a place of safety, overtook at Janiculum the VESTALS bending under their load. He took them up and conveyed them to *Cære* in Etruria, where they remained and continued to perform their sacred rites, which were consequently called *Cæremonia*.

Master of the Ceremonies. A court official, first appointed by James I to superintend the reception of ambassadors and strangers of rank, and to prescribe the formalities to be observed in LEVEES and other public functions. The title is now given to one whose duty it is to superintend at a ball and similar social gatherings; usually now abbreviated to "M.C.".

Dont' stand on ceremony. Make yourself at home, be natural, don't be formal.

Ceres (sē′ rēz). The Roman name of MOTHER EARTH, the protectress of agriculture, and of all the fruits of the earth. She is the Corn Goddess and she had a daughter by JUPITER, called PROSERPINE. She is identified with the Greek DEMETER.

Cess. A tax, contracted from assessment; as, a "church-cess". In Ireland the word is sometimes used as a contraction of success, meaning luck, as, "Bad cess to you!" It is also a common contraction of *cesspit* or *cesspool*.

C'est magnifique. C'est magnifique, mais ce n'est pas la guerre. "It is magnificent, but it is not war." The criticism on the charge of the Light Brigade at Balaclava (25 October 1854), made on the field at the time, by the French General Bosquet to A. H. Layard.

Cestui que vie. This and the two following are old Anglo-French legal terms (*cestui* = he, or him). The person for whose life any lands or hereditaments may be held.

Cestui que use, the person to whose use anyone is infeoffed of lands or tenements.

Cestui que trust, the person for whose benefit a trust has been created.

Cestus (ses′ tus). The girdle of VENUS, made by her husband VULCAN; but when she wantoned with MARS it fell off, and was left on the "Acidalian Mount". It was of magical power to move to ardent love. By poetical fiction, all women of irresistible attraction are supposed to be wearers of Aphrodite's girdle, or the cestus. *Cp.* CHASTITY GIRDLE.

The word is also used for the Roman boxing-glove composed of leather thongs wound round the hand and wrist, and sometimes loaded with iron.

Ceteris paribus (set′ĕris pă′ ribus) (Lat.). Other things being equal.

Chacun a son goût (shăk′ ùn a son goo). "Everyone has his taste" is the correct French phrase. "Everyone to his taste" (*à*, to, instead of *a*, has) is English-

French. The phrase is more common with us than it is in France, where we meet with the phrases, *Chacun a sa chacunerie* (everyone has his own idiosyncrasy), and *chacun a sa marotte* (everyone has his hobby). In Latin *sua cuique voluptas*, every man has his own pleasures.

Chad, St. (*Ceadda*). A Northumbrian by birth and a pupil of St. Aidan, he subsequently became BISHOP of MERCIA with Lichfield as his SEE. He died in 672 and was the patron SAINT of springs.

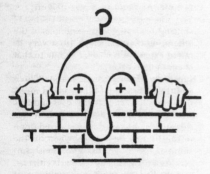

WOT NO CHAR?

Chad. A character whose bald head and large nose were depicted appearing over a wall and inquiring, "Wot, no [word filled in to suit the circumstances]?", as a comment or protest against a shortage or shortcoming. Widely current during World War II, especially among the forces, Chad provided scope for humorous relief in many a difficult situation. It was the happy creation (1938) of "Chat" the cartoonist (George Edward Chatterton). *Cp.* KILROY; *see also* GRAFFITI.

Chadband. This synonym for a religious hypocrite is taken from a character in Dickens's *Bleak House*—a gluttonous, unctuous, illiterate rogue, minister of some indeterminate sect.

Chaff. An old bird is not to be caught with chaff. An experienced man, or one with his wits about him, is not to be deluded by humbug. The reference is to throwing chaff instead of birdseed to al-

lure birds. Hence perhaps:

You are chaffing me. Making fun of me. A singular custom used to exist in Nottinghamshire and Leicestershire. When a husband ill-treated his wife, the villagers emptied a sack of chaff at his door, to intimate that "thrashing was done within".

Chain letter. A letter, frequently anonymous, which the recipient is asked to copy and send to one or more friends, requesting that they should do the same, good luck being supposed by the superstitious to follow the faithful fulfilment of the conditions. It is sometimes used by the unscrupulous as a device for obtaining money from the credulous.

Chair, The. The seat of authority, or the office of same. The person in authority or the president of an assembly or meeting whose decisions, like those of the SPEAKER of the HOUSE OF COMMONS, are final in all points of doubt.

A university professorship is also called a chair.

To take the chair. To be the chairman of a meeting or assembly, committee, etc. Colloquially **to be in the chair** means to act as host or to be the one paying for the round of drinks.

Chair of St. Peter. The office of the POPE of Rome, founded by St. PETER, the apostle; but *St. Peter's Chair* means the Catholic festival held in commemoration of the two episcopates founded by the apostle, one at Rome, and the other at Antioch (18 January; 22 February). The reputed chair itself in St. Peter's at ROME is kept locked away and only exhibited once every century. It is of wood with ivory carvings, the wood being much decayed. It is probably 6th-century BYZANTINE work.

Chalk. Chalk it up. Put it on the SLATE, put it to his credit.

Chalk and talk. A common phrase in the scholastic profession to denote teaching essentially relying upon oral instruction and the use of the blackboard, a method not always popular with the professors of pedagogy, but likely to remain the basis of most good teaching.

I beat him by a long chalk. Thoroughly. A reference to the custom of making merit marks with chalk, before lead pencils were so common.

I'll chalk out your path for you, *i.e.* lay it down or plan it out, as a carpenter or shipwright plans out his work with a piece of chalk.

I can walk a chalk as well as you. I am no more drunk than you are. The allusion is to a test given to those suspected of drunkenness which consists of walking steadily along a line chalked on the floor.

I cannot make chalk of one and cheese of the other. I must treat both alike; I must show no favouritism.

I know the difference between chalk and cheese. Between what is worthless and what is valuable, between a counterfeit and a real article.

A popular phrase, no doubt helped by its alliteration.

They are no more alike than chalk and cheese is another common variant.

Walk your chalk. Get you gone. Lodgings wanted for the royal retinue were once taken arbitrarily by the marshal and sergeant-chamberlain and the occupants of houses marked with the chalk were sent to the right-about. The phrase is "Walk, you're chalked", corrupted to *Walk your chalk*.

At one time it was customary for a landlord to give the tenant notice to quit by chalking the door.

Challenge. This meant originally an accusation or charge, and secondly a claim, a defiance, etc. It comes through French from the Lat. *calumnia*, a false accusation, and is etymologically the same word as "calumny".

Cham (kăm). The sovereign prince of Tartary, now written Khan.

The great Cham of Literature. An epithet applied to Dr. Johnson (1709–1784) by Tobias Smollett.

Chamber of Horrors. *See* MADAME TUSSAUD'S.

Chambre Ardente (shombr ar dont') (Fr.). In French history, the name given to certain courts of justice held under the ANCIEN RÉGIME, for trying exceptional cases such as charges of heresy, poisoning, etc. They were usually held at night, and both then and when held in daytime were lighted by torches. These courts were devised by the Cardi-

nal of Lorraine and first used by Francis I in 1535. Louis XIV used a Chambre Ardente in 1679 to investigate suspected poisoners as a result of the scare caused by the trial of the Marquise de BRINVILLIERS. These courts were abolished in 1682.

Chambre Introuvable (shombr an' troo vab là) (Fr. the chamber not to be found again). The French Chamber of Deputies, which met in 1815 after the second return of Louis XVIII, was so named by the king for its fervent royalist sympathies. It was afterwards used to denote any ultra-royalist assembly.

Chameleon. You are a chameleon, *i.e.* very changeable, like a VICAR OF BRAY, shifting according to the opinions of the others, as the chameleon (to a very limited extent) can change its hue to that of contiguous objects.

Champ de Mars (shon dĕ mars). Clovis and the early Frankish kings held meetings in MARCH when feudal gifts and fees were paid and homage received. It was this ancient custom that was seized upon in the French Revolution when, in the summer of 1790, an enormous amphitheatre was dug by the Paris citizens, and the Federation of Freedom sworn at the altar of the Fatherland.

NAPOLEON gave the name of **Champ de Mai** to the assembly he called together on 1 May 1815, when he proclaimed the result of the plebiscite ratifying the liberal *Acte additionnel* on his return from Elba.

Champagne Charlie. The 4th Marquess of Hastings was the first so named (*see* PLUNGER) and another was Charles Philip Yorke, 5th Earl of Hardwicke (1836, 1873–1897), who was one time Comptroller of the Royal Household and prominent in the social circle around the Prince of Wales. He wasted his inheritance mostly by gambling and riotous living and finally went bankrupt in 1893.

Champak (chăm' păk). An Indian magnolia (*Michelia champaca*). The wood is sacred to BUDDHA, and the strongly scented golden flowers are worn in the black hair of Indian women.

The Champak odours fail.
SHELLEY: *Lines to an Indian Air*.

Champion of England, or **King's Champion.** A person whose office it was to ride up Westminster Hall on a Coronation Day, and challenge anyone who disputed the right of succession. The office was established by William the Conqueror but last observed at the coronation of George IV. Instead the Champion bears the sovereign's standard at the coronation.

Chamuel. *See* ARCHANGEL.

Chance. *See* MAIN CHANCE.

To chance your arm, or **your luck.** To run a risk in the hope of "bringing it off' and obtaining a profit or advantage of some sort.

Chancel means a lattice screen. In the Roman law courts the lawyers were cut off from the public by such a screen (Lat. *cancellus*).

Chancel of a church. That part of the church (usually at the eastern end) containing the altar and choir, which is often separated from the nave by a screen of wood or iron lattice-work and often with a raised floor level.

Chancellor. Originally an official (*cancellarius*) in the Roman law courts stationed at the CHANCEL as usher of the court and in the Eastern Empire a secretary or notary, subsequently invested with judicial functions. The name has been used in most European countries for an officer of state with varying powers and functions. In England, the office of Chancellor was introduced by Edward the Confessor and under the Normans the Chancellor became the chief secretary in charge of all important legal documents, head of CHANCERY, and keeper of the GREAT SEAL. In France, the Chancellor was the royal notary, president of the councils, and keeper of the Great Seal. Bismarck was made Chancellor of the newly created German Empire in 1871.

There are also diocesan chancellors who preside over the bishop's court, chancellors of cathedrals, academic chancellors who are usually the titular heads of universities, etc.

Chancellor, Dancing. *See* DANCING.

The Lord Chancellor, or **the Lord High Chancellor.** The highest judicial functionary of Great Britain, who ranks above all peers, except princes of the BLOOD and the Archbishop of Canterbury. He is keeper of the GREAT SEAL, is called "Keeper of His (or Her) Majesty's Conscience", and presides on the WOOLSACK in the House of Lords and in the CHANCERY Division of the Supreme Court of Judicature or High Court of Justice.

Chancellor of the Exchequer. The minister of finance in the British CABINET; the highest financial official of state in the kingdom.

Chancery. One of the three divisions of the High Court of Justice. It is mainly concerned with Equity and is presided over by the LORD CHANCELLOR. Not all its work is done in London; there is also a Chancery Court in Manchester, such jurisdiction having existed in the COUNTY PALATINE of Lancashire since the end of the 15th century. The word is shortened from Chancellery.

A Ward of Chancery is the term applied to a minor whose guardianship is vested in the Court of CHANCERY for various legal reasons. It is contempt of court to marry a ward of Chancery without the court's consent.

Change. Ringing the changes. Repeating the same thing in differing ways. The allusion is to bell-ringing. For the sharper's meaning of the term, *see* RINGING.

To know how many changes can be rung on a peal, multiply the number of bells in the peal by the number of changes that can be rung on a peal consisting of one bell less, thus: 1 bell, no change; 2 bells, 1 by 2 = 2 changes; 3 bells, 2 by 3 = 6 changes; 4 bells, 6 by 4 = 24 changes; 5 bells, 24 by 5 = 120 changes; 6 bells, 120 by 6 = 720 changes, etc.

Changeling. A peevish, sickly child. The notion used to be that the fairies took a healthy child, and left in its place one of their starvelling elves which never thrived.

Chansons de Geste (shon son dĕ zhest) (Fr.). Narrative poems dealing with the heroic families of French history and legend, and composed at various times between the 11th and 15th centuries. The famous *Chanson de Roland* is generally

regarded as the finest. *See under* RO-
LAND.) *Gestes* (Lat. *gesta*) is used to
mean the deeds of a hero and the account of his deeds.

Chant du départ (shon dū dā par). After
the MARSEILLAISE, this was the most celebrated song of the French Revolution.
It was written by M. J. Chénier for a
public festival in 1794 to commemorate
the taking of the BASTILLE. The music is
by Méhul. A mother, an old man, a
child, a wife, a girl, and three warriors
sing a verse in turn, and the sentiment
of each is, "We give up our claims on the
men of France for the good of the Republic." *Cp.* CARMAGNOLE.

> La république nous appelle,
> Sachons vaincre ou sachons périr;
> Un Français doit vivre pour elle,
> Pour elle un Français doit mourir.

Chantage. BLACKMAIL; money accepted
by low-class journals to prevent the publication of scandals, etc. *Chantage* is the
common name in France for this form of
subsidy; and the word has been used in
the same way in England.

Chanticleer. The cock, in the tale of REY-
NARD THE FOX, and in Chaucer's *Nonnes
Prestes Tale*; also in Rostand's play
Chantecleer, produced in Paris in 1910
(Fr. *Chanter clair*, to sing clearly).

Chantry. A religious and often charitable
endowment usually connected with a
chapel (often part of the parish church)
and mainly to provide for the chanting
of masses for the founder. Their spolia-
tion was begun by Henry VIII in 1545
and completed under Edward VI in
1547. Little of the proceeds was used for
charitable or educational purposes.

Chaonian Bird (kā ō′ ni án). This is the
poetic name for a DOVE, and takes its origin from the legend that the dove bore
the oracles of Chaonia.

Chaonian food. Acorns. So called
from the acorns of Chaonia or DODONA.
Some think beech-mast is meant, and
tell us that the bells of the ORACLE were
hung on beech-trees, not on oaks.

Chap. A man, properly a merchant. A
chap-man (O.E. *ceap-mann*) is a
merchant or tradesman. "If you want to
buy, I'm your chap." A good chap-man
or chap became in time a good fellow.
Hence, *a good sort of chap, a clever*

chap, etc.
    An awkward customer is an analogous
phrase.

Chap-book. A cheap little book containing tales, ballads, lives, etc., sold by
chapmen.

Chapeau bras (shăp ō bra) (Fr.). A soft
three-cornered flat silk hat which could
be folded and carried under the arm
(Fr. *chapeau*, hat; *bras*, arm). It was
worn in France with the court dress of
the 18th century.

Chapel. Originally a chest containing relics or the shrine thereof, so called from
the *capella* (little cloak or cope) of St.
MARTIN, which was preserved by the
Frankish kings as a sacred relic. The
place in which it was kept when not in
the field was called the *chapelle*, and the
keeper thereof the *chapelain*. Hence the
name came to be attached to a sanctuary, or a private place of worship other
than a parish or cathedral church; and is
also used for a place of worship belonging to the Free Churches, as a METHOD-
IST Chapel, Baptist Chapel, etc., or a separately dedicated oratory within a
church.
    Among printers and journalists a
chapel is an association of journeymen
(compositors, machine-men, etc.), who
meet periodically to discuss matters of
common interest and take decisions affecting their conditions of employment,
etc. The chairman is called the "father
of the chapel". This use of the word possibly derives from the earliest days of
English printing when presses were set
up in chapels attached to abbeys. *See*
CAXTON; FRIAR; MONK.

Chapel of ease. A place of worship for
the use of parishioners residing at a distance from the parish church.

Lady chapel. A chapel dedicated to the
Virgin within a larger church.

Chapelle Ardente (shă pel′ ar dont′)
(Fr.). The chapel or resting-place of
kings or exalted personages when lying
in state, so called from the many candles
which were lit round the catafalque, a
custom at least dating from the funeral
rites of DAGOBERT, king of the FRANKS
in 638. The term is now also applied to
other mortuary chapels.

Chaperon (shăp′ e rōn). A married or

mature woman who escorted a young unmarried girl in public places and acted as adviser and protector. So called from the Spanish hood worn by the duennas in former days. Also the hood or cap worn by Knights of the GARTER.

Chapter. From Lat. *caput*, a head. The chapter of a cathedral, composed of the canons (*see* CANON) and presided over by the DEAN or provost is so called from the ancient practice of the canons and monks reading at their meetings a *capitulum* (*cp.* CAPITULARY) or chapter of their Rule or of Scripture. *Ire ad capitulum* meant to go to the meeting for the reading of the chapter, hence to the meeting, hence to the body which made up the meeting.

Chapter of accidents. A series of unforeseen events. *To trust to a chapter of accidents* is to rely on something unforeseen turning up in your favour.

To give chapter and verse. To give the exact authority for a statement, as the name of the author, the title of the book, the date, the chapter, etc., which may make verification readily possible.

Char. This is a common abbreviation for "charwoman", or woman who chars or chares, *i.e.* works by the hour or day at house-cleaning. The word comes from O.E. *cerr, cerran*, meaning to turn. It has come back to England from the U.S.A. in the form of "chores", monotonous but necessary tasks.

The slang word "char" meaning tea appears to derive from the army in India from the Hind. *cha*, meaning tea.

Character. An oddity. One who has a distinctive peculiarity of manner. Sam Weller is a character, so is Pickwick.

In character. In harmony with personality and habitual behaviour.

Out of character. Not in harmony with a person's usual actions, writing, profession, age, status, etc.

Chare Thursday. Another form of *Shear* or *Shere* Thursday; the same as MAUNDY THURSDAY.

Charge, To. To make an attack or onset.

To be on charge. To be up before a magistrate.

To be put on a charge. In the Armed Forces to be entered up as a defaulter and brought before the appropriate offi-

cer for a hearing. If the charge is held proven, punishment is then awarded in accordance with Sevice regulations.

To charge a person. To accuse him formally of a crime or misdemeanour. It must be answered before the appropriate court or authority.

To charge like a bull at a gate. To go at something BALDHEADED, head first; to tackle something in a precipitate manner without due forethought.

To charge oneself with. To take upon oneself the onus of a given task.

To return to the charge. To renew the attack.

To take in charge. To "take up" a person given in charge; to make an arrest; to take upon oneself the responsibility for something.

Charge-sheet. The form setting out in correct language and according to law the specific charges which an accused person has to answer.

Charing Cross. The original Charing Cross was erected in the centre of the ancient village of Charing, which stood midway between the cities of LONDON and WESTMINSTER, by Edward I to commemorate his Queen, Eleanor. It was the spot where her coffin was halted for the last time on it way from Harby, Notts., to Westminster.

The cross was sited where the statue of King Charles I now stands on the south side of Trafalgar Square, but it was destroyed by the PURITANS in 1647. The present Gothic cross in the courtyard of Charing Cross Station was designed by E. M. Barry and erected in 1865.

Chariot. According to Greek mythology, the chariot was invented by ERICHTHONIUS to conceal his feet, which were those of a dragon.

Chariot of the gods. So the Greeks appear to have called Sierra Leone, in Africa, a ridge of mountains of great height; but some suggest the title applies to Mount Cameroon.

Chariots, or cars. That of:

Admetus was drawn by lions and wild boars,
BACCHUS by panthers,
CERES by winged dragons,
CYBELE by lions,
DIANA by stags,

JUNO by peacocks,
NEPTUNE by sea-horses,
PLUTO by black horses.
The SUN by seven horses (the seven days of the week),
VENUS by doves.

Charity. Charity begins at home. "Let them learn first to show piety at home" (I *Tim*. v, 4).

Charivari (shǎ ri va' ri). A French term for an uproar caused by banging pans and kettles and accompanied by hissing, shouting, etc., to express disapproval. As a verb (*charivariser*) it means to subject someone to disapproval. Originally a common practice at weddings in mediæval France, it was later only used as a derisive or satirical demonstration at unpopular weddings. The fracas resembled what we would call a CAT'S CONCERT. The name *Charivari* was adopted for a satirical paper in Paris in 1832 and used in the subtitle for *Punch* which derided the shortcomings of society, the politicians, etc. *See* SHIVAREE; ROUGH MUSIC.

Charlatan (shar' lá tán). From the Ital. *ciarlare*, to prate, to chatter, to babble. One who pretends to knowledge or skill he does not possess; a MOUNTEBANK. It is usually applied to vendors of QUACK remedies who cover their ignorance in a spate of high-sounding and often meaningless words.

Charlemagne (sharl' mǎn) (742–814). Charles the Great became sole king of the Franks in 771 and first Holy Roman EMPEROR in 800. He ruled over most of western Europe and was noted as a lawgiver, administrator, protector of the Church and promoter of education. He was married nine times.

Charlemagne and his Paladins are the centre of a great series of chivalric romances. (*See* PALADIN). We are told that he was eight feet tall and of enormous strength and could bend three horseshoes at once in his hands. He was buried at Aix-la-Chapelle (Aachen), but according to legend he waits, crowned and armed, in Oldenburg, Hesse, for the day when ANTICHRIST shall appear; he will then go forth to battle and rescue Christendom. Another legend says that in years of plenty he crosses the Rhine on a BRIDGE OF GOLD, to bless the cornfields and vineyards.

Charles. Many rulers bearing this name have been afflicted with misfortune:
England:
CHARLES I was beheaded by the Cromwellians (1649).
Charles II lived long in exile. *See also* CHARLES AND THE OAK.
Charles Edward, the Young PRETENDER, died in poverty in Rome in 1788.
France:
Charles II, the Fat, reigned wretchedly, was deposed in 877, and died in poverty in 888.
Charles III, the Simple, died a prisoner in the castle of Péronne in 929.
Charles IV, the Fair, reigned six years (1322–1328), married thrice, buried all his children except one daughter, who was forbidden by THE SALIC LAW to succeed to the crown.
Charles VI (reigned 1380–1422) went mad in 1392.
Charles VII starved himself to death in 1461, partly through fear of being poisoned and partly because of a painful and incurable abscess in the mouth.
Charles VIII accidentally smashed his head against the lintel of a doorway in the Château d'Amboise, and died in agony (1498), leaving no issue.
Charles IX died at the age of twenty-four (1574), harrowed in conscience for the part he had taken in the Massacre of St. BARTHOLOMEW.
Charles X spent a quarter of a century in exile, and after less than six years on the throne, fled for his life and died in exile (1836).
Charles the Bold, of Burgundy, lost his life at Nancy in 1477, when he was utterly defeated by the Swiss.
Naples:
Charles I (1266–1285) lost Sicily as a result of the SICILIAN VESPERS and experienced only disasters.
Charles II, the Lame, was in captivity at the time of his father's death (died 1309).
Charles III, his great-grandson, was killed (1386).
Charles I of England. When Bernini's bust of Charles I was brought home, the king was sitting in the garden of WHITEHALL Palace. He ordered the bust to be uncovered, and at that moment a hawk

with a bird in its beak flew by, and a drop of blood fell on the throat of the bust. The bust was ultimately destroyed when the palace was burnt down.

Charles and the Oak. When Charles II fled from the Parliamentary army after the battle of Worcester (3 September 1651), he took refuge in Boscobel House; but it was unsafe to remain there, and he hid himself in an oak-tree.

Charles's Wain. An old popular name for the seven bright stars of the Great Bear (*see under* BEAR). The constellation forms the rough outline of a wheelbarrow or rustic wagon and the name is held to be a corruption of "Churl's wain" (peasant's cart). Another version derives it from "CHARLEMAGNE'S wain". It is also called the *Wagon*, the *Plough*, and the *Dipper*, and by the Romans the *Septentriones* (the seven plough-oxen). *See* SEPTENTRIONAL SIGNS.

Charleys, or **Charlies.** The old night watch, before the police force was organized in 1829. Possibly from Charles I, under whom London's WATCH system was reorganized in 1640.

Charlie, Bonnie Prince. *See* THE YOUNG PRETENDER *under* PRETENDER.

Charleston. A FOX-TROT popular *c.* 1925–1927, originated as a dance among the American Negroes. Charleston is the name of a cotton-trading seaport in South Carolina, one-third of the population of which is Negro.

Charon. In Greek mythology, the son of Erebus and Nox, the hideous old man who ferried the spirits of the dead over the rivers STYX and ACHERON for the fare of an *obolus*.

Charon's Toll. A coin placed in the mouth or hand of the dead by the ancient Greeks to pay Charon for ferrying the spirit across the rivers of the underworld to ELYSIUM.

Chartism. A working-class movement beginning in 1837 which embodied its agreed demands in the *People's Charter* of 1838. Its six points included: manhood suffrage, vote by ballot, annual parliaments, payment of M.P.s., equal constituencies and the abolition of the property qualification for M.P.s. It collapsed after the failure of their petition to Parliament in 1848.

Charybdis (kȧ rib' dis). A whirlpool on the coast of Sicily. SCYLLA and Charybdis are employed to signify two equal dangers. Thus HORACE says an author trying to avoid Scylla, drifts into Charybdis, *i.e.* seeking to avoid one fault, he falls into another.

The Homeric account says that Charybdis dwelt under an immense fig-tree on the rock, and that thrice every day he swallowed the waters of the sea and thrice threw them up again; but later writers have it that he stole the oxen of HERCULES, was killed by lightning, and changed into the gulf.

Chase (O.Fr. *chasier* from Lat. *captiare*, to chase). A small unenclosed deer forest held mainly by private individuals, and protected only by COMMON LAW. Forests were royal prerogatives and protected by the Forest Laws.

An iron frame used by printers for holding sufficient type for one side of a sheet, which is held tight by quoins, or small wedges of wood or metal, is also called a chase. Here the word is the Fr. *chasse* (Lat. *capsa*), a case.

Chasidim (chȧs i dim). *See* HASIDEANS.

Chastity Girdle. A padded metal appliance in the shape of a belt that a man could fasten around his wife in such a way as to preclude possibility of unfaithfulness during his prolonged absence. It is said to have come into vogue at the time of the CRUSADES when such protracted absence was common. One or two examples exist in museums. *Cp.* CESTUS.

Chasuble (chȧz' ū bl) (Fr. from Med. Lat. *casabula*, a little cottage). The principal vestment worn by the priests in celebrating MASS. It is a roughly rectangular sleeveless garment, with a hole for the head in the middle, thus hanging down both back and front. It is usually richly decorated with embroidery, and mediæval chasubles were finely ornamented with gold wire and gilded silver, this form of work being known throughout Europe as OPUS ANGLICANUM. The City of London was the home of some of the best work of the 12th and 13th centuries. The chasuble is said to represent the seamless coat of Christ.

Château (shȧ tō). French for castle, mansion, or country seat.

The wines of various districts of France, especially Bordeaux, are named after the château or homestead of the estate from which they are produced. *Mise en bouteille au Château* or *Mise du Château* means that they were also bottled there.

Château en Espagne. A castle in the air. *See* CASTLE.

Chatelaine (shăt' e lān). Originally the mistress of a château, a chatelaine now usually signifies a brooch or clasp from which a variety of trinkets hang on short chains. They are the things which the mistress of a castle was likely to use, keys, scissors, knives, etc.

Chatterbox. A talkative person. SHAKESPEARE speaks of the CLACK-DISH. "His use was to put a ducat in her clack-dish" (*Measure for Measure*, III, ii), *i.e.* the beggars' alms-dish which was clattered or rattled to attract attention. We also find *chatter-basket* in old writers, referring to the child's rattle.

Chautauqua (shȧ tawk' wȧ). In the U.S.A. the name given to an assembly for educational purposes with lectures, entertainments, etc., held largely out of doors, modelled on the Chautauqua Assembly. This was started in 1874 at the village and summer resort on Lake Chautauqua, New York State, which developed into the Chautauqua Literary and Scientific Circle in 1878 to promote home reading and study.

Chauvinism (shō' vin izm). Blind and exaggerated patriotism similar to jingoism (*see* JINGO). Nicholas Chauvin was a soldier of the French Republic and Empire well known by contemporaries for his devoted enthusiasm for NAPOLEON.

Chawbacon. A contemptuous name for an uncouth rustic, whose only meat was bacon. (*Chaw*, chew.)

Che sarà, sarà (kā sa ra', sa ra'). What will be, will be. The motto of the Dukes of Bedford and the Russell family.

Cheap as a Sardinian. A Roman phrase referring to the great crowds of Sardinian prisoners brought to ROME by Tiberius Gracchus, and offered for sale at almost any price.

Cheap-jack. A travelling vendor of small wares who is usually ready to "cheapen" his goods, *i.e.* take less for them than the price he first named.

Cheapside bargain. A weak pun meaning that the article was bought cheap or under its market value. Cheapside; on the south side of the *Cheap* (or *Chepe*), was the principal market-place of old LONDON, so called from O.E. *ceaptan*, to buy; *cypan*, to sell; *ceap*, a price or sale.

Cheater. Originally an Escheator, or officer of the King's EXCHEQUER appointed to receive dues and taxes. The present meaning shows how these officers were wont to fleece the people. *Cp.* PUBLICANS.

A windcheater. A warm semi-weather-proof garment of the blouse or jacket type. The derivation is obvious.

Check. A sudden stop, hindrance or control. From the game of CHESS in which a threat to the king is called a *check*. *Cp.* CHECKMATE.

Checkmate. A term in CHESS meaning to put your adversary's king into inescapable check. This wins the game. Figuratively "to checkmate" means to foil or outwit another. The term is from the Arabic *shāh māt*, the king is dead, and was introduced into Old Spanish and Portuguese as *xaque mate*.

In check. Under restraint.

To check in. To register on arrival at a hotel, conference, etc.

To check out. To settle one's account at a hotel on leaving, to register one's departure.

To check up on. To examine someone's personal record, etc.

Checks. To hand in one's checks. *See* HAND.

Cheek. Cheek by jowl. Side by side, close together.

None of your cheek. None of your insolence. A *cheeky* person is one who is saucy and presumptuous.

To cheek, or **to give cheek.** To be insolent, to be saucy.

To have the cheek. To have the face or assurance or presumption. "He hadn't the cheek to ask for more."

Cheese. A green cheese. An unripe cheese; also a cheese that is eaten fresh (like a cream cheese) and is not kept to

Chefs

mature.

Big Cheese (slang). The boss, or someone in an important position.

Bread and cheese. Food generally, but of a frugal nature.

Cheese it! Stop it! Stow it! Also (in thieves' slang) clear off, make yourself scarce.

Cheesed off. Services' slang for disgusted, disgruntled.

Hard cheese. Hard lines; rotten luck.

He is quite the cheese, or **just the cheese**—*i.e.* quite the thing. Here "cheese" is the Persian and Urdu *chiz* (*cheez*), meaning "thing". The phrase is of Anglo-Indian origin; but it has been popularly treated as being connected with Eng. *cheese*, and thus we get the slang varieties, *That's prime Stilton, or double Gloster*—*i.e.* SLAP UP. Hence:

It is not the cheese. Not the right thing; said of something of rather dubious propriety or morals.

The moon made of green cheese. *See* MOON.

'Tis an old rat that won't eat cheese. It must be a very old man that is inaccessible to flattery or who can abandon his favourite indulgence; only a very cunning rat knows that cheese is a mere bait.

Cheeseparer. A skinflint, one who would pare off the rind of his cheese so as to waste the minimum.

Cheese-toaster. A sword; also called a "toasting-fork", etc.

Cheesewring, The Devil's. A mass of eight stones towering to the height of thirty-two feet in the Valley of Rocks, Lynmouth, Devon, so called because it looks like a gigantic cheesepress.

Chefs. *See* ARM-SHRINES.

Chef d'œuvre (shā der vr) (Fr. a chief work). A masterpiece.

Chellean. (shell' ē ȧn). An early PALÆO-LITHIC core-tool culture named by G. de Mortillet, French anthropologist, from the site at Chelles-sur-Marne where the remains were found.

Chelsea Pensioner. *See under* PENSIONER.

Chemosh (kē mosh). The national god of the Moabites; very little is known of his cult, but human beings were sacrificed to him in times of crisis.

Next Chemos, the obscene dread of Moab's sons,
From Aroer to Nebo and the wild
Of southmost Abarim.
MILTON: *Paradise Lost*, I, 406–8.

Cheque. To give a blank cheque. *See under* BLANK.

Cheque-book journalism. A phrase introduced in the mid-1960s to describe the misuse of the wealth of the press to obtain copy by purchase, especially of exclusive rights, to the detriment of less wealthy competitors and possible corruption of the public. A particular abuse is the buying of stories from criminals, harlots, and notorious persons generally, thus financially rewarding the evil-doer and tending to encourage others in vicious activities with the prospect of gain. Such conduct has been condemned by the Press Council.

Chequers (chek' ėrz). A PUBLIC-HOUSE SIGN. The arms of Fitzwarren, the head of which house had the privilege of licensing ale-houses in the reign of Edward IV, probably helped to popularize this sign, but it is of much older origin. It has been found on houses in Pompeii and probably referred to some game like draughts being played on the premises. One explanation is that in mediæval times some innkeepers were also money-changers and used an "exchequer board" as a sign of their calling. Also certain public houses were used by the parish authorities for the payment of doles, etc., and a chequer-board was provided for that purpose and also adopted as a sign.

Chequers, the country seat of the Prime Minister of Great Britain, in the Chiltern country near Princes Risborough, was presented to the nation for this purpose by Sir Arthur and Lady Lee (Lord and Lady Lee of Fareham) in 1917, and first officially used by Lloyd George in 1921.

Cheronean (kē rō nē' ȧn). **The Cheronean Sage.** Plutarch (A.D. 46–120), who was born at Cheronea in BŒOTIA.

Cherry-trees and the cuckoo. The cherry-tree is strangely mixed up with the CUCKOO in many cuckoo stories, because of the tradition that the cuckoo must eat three good meals of cherries before he is allowed to cease singing.

The whole tree or not a cherry on it. "AUT CÆSAR AUT NULLUS." All in all or none at all.

To make two bites of a cherry. To divide something too small to be worth dividing.

To take two bites at a cherry. To take two spells over a piece of work that should be done in one.

Cheshire Cat. To grin like a Cheshire cat. *See under* CAT.

Chess. "The game of kings"; the word being the English equivalent of the Persian *shah* (*see* CHECKMATE), a king. In Arabic the word was pronounced *shag*, which gave rise to the late Lat. *scaccus*, whence the O.Fr. *eschec*, Mod. Fr. *échecs*, and E. *chess*. Derivatives in other languages are *scacco* (Ital.), *jaque* (Span.), *xaque* (Port.), *Schach* (Ger.).

Chestnut. A stale joke. The term is said to have been popularized in America by a Boston actor named Warren, who, on a certain apposite occasion, quoted from *The Broken Sword*, a forgotten melodrama by William Dimond, first produced at COVENT GARDEN in 1816, in which one of the characters, Captain Xavier, is forever telling the same jokes with variations, one of which concerned his exploits with a cork-tree. He is corrected by Pablo who says "A chestnut. I have heard you tell the joke twenty-seven times, and I am sure it was a chestnut."

Cheval (shĕ văl') (Fr. a horse).

Cheval de bataille (Fr. literally "horse of battle"). One's strong argument, one's favourite subject.

Cheval de frise. An apparatus consisting of a bar carrying rows of pointed stakes, set up so that the bar can revolve, and used in warfare as a defence against enemy cavalry. So called from its first use by the Frisians (who had few if any horses) in the siege of Groningen, Friesland, in 1594. A somewhat similar engine had been used before. In German it is "a Spanish horseman" (*ein spanischer Reiter*).

Cheval glass. A large, swinging mirror, long enough to reflect the whole of the figure; so called from the "horse" or framework which supports it.

Chevalier de St. George. *See* CAVALIER.

Chevy Chase. There had long been a ri-

valry between the families of Percy and Douglas, which showed itself by incessant raids into each other's territory. Percy of Northumberland once vowed he would hunt for three days in the Scottish border, without condescending to ask leave of Earl Douglas. The Scots warden said in his anger, "Tell this vaunter he shall find one day more than sufficient." The ballad called *Chevy Chase* mixes up this hunt with the battle of Otterburn, which, Bishop Percy justly observes, was "a very different event". The ballad of *The Battle of Otterburn* is also given in PERCY'S RELIQUES.

Chew. To chew the fat or **rag.** An old colloquialism meaning to grumble or to "belly-ache", to harp on an old sore; to argue the point. Also, to hold familiar conversation. *Cp.* JAW.

Chian Painter, The. Appelles, famous Grecian painter and contemporary of ALEXANDER THE GREAT, born at Colophon on the coast of Asia Minor.

Chicane (chi kān'). A term used in bridge for a hand containing no trumps. Its general meaning is the use of mean, petty subterfuge, especially legal dodges and quibbles. It is a French word which, before being used for sharp practice in lawsuits, meant a dispute in games, particularly mall, and originally the game of mall itself. (*See* PALL MALL). It seems to be ultimately from the Persian *chaugan*, the crooked stick used in polo, and it is also applied to an obstacle on a racecourse, particularly to the artificial bends introduced on motor-racing tracks.

Chichevache (chich' e vash). A fabulous monster that lives only on good women, and was hence all skin and bone, because its food was so extremely scarce; the antitype to BICORN. Chaucer introduced and changed the word from the French *chichifache* (thin or ugly face) into *chichevache* (lean or meagre-looking cow).

Chicken. Chicken-feed, chick-feed, or **chicken-corn.** Trivial amounts of money, SMALL BEER, or comparatively trifling costs; from the fact that chicken corn usually consists of the smaller and cheaper grains.

Chicken-hearted, or **chicken-livered.** Cowardly. Young fowls are remarkably timid and run to the hen on the slightest alarm.

Children and chicken must always be pickin'. They are always hungry and ready to eat.

Curses, like chickens, come home to roost. *See* CURSE.

Don't count your chickens before they are hatched. Make sure that a thing is actually yours before you speak or act as if it were already yours. The saying in a slightly different form is first found in the writings of Erasmus. "Don't crow till you are out of the wood" has a similar meaning.

His chickens have come home to roost. His sins have found him out; he has got what he asked for; his actions have caught up on him.

Mother Carey's chickens. *See* MOTHER CAREY.

She's no chicken, or **she's no spring chicken.** She's no youngster, she is not young.

Where the chicken got the axe. *See* NECK. TO GET IT IN THE NECK.

Which came first, the chicken or the egg? A suitable reply to an unanswerable question.

Chicken of St. Nicholas. So the Piedmontese call our "LADYBIRD", the little red beetle with spots of black. The Russians call it "God's little cow".

Child. At one time this was a provincial term for a female infant, and was the correlative of *boy*.

> Mercy on's, a bairn; a very pretty bairn!
> A boy or a child, I wonder?
> SHAKESPEARE: *Winter's Tale*, III, iii.

Child of God. In the CHURCH OF ENGLAND and the ROMAN CATHOLIC CHURCH, one who has been baptized; others consider the phrase to mean one converted by special grace and adopted into the holy family of God's Church.

That's child's play. Said of something which can be done very easily or simply.

Childe. In *Childe Harold, Childe Roland, Childe Tristram*, etc., "childe" is a title of honour like the Sp. "infante". In the days of CHIVALRY, a noble youth who was a candidate for knighthood, during his time of probation, was called

infans, valet, damoysel, bachelier, and *childe*.

Childe Harold. Byron's poem depicts a man sated of the world, who roams from place to place to escape from himself. The "Childe" was in fact BYRON himself, who was only twenty-one when he began the poem, and twenty-eight when he finished it.

Childermas. The Old English name for the festival, of MASS of the HOLY INNOCENTS (28 December).

Children. Three hundred and sixty-five at a birth. It is said that a countess of Henneberg accused a beggar of adultery because she carried twins, whereupon the beggar prayed that the countess might carry as many children as there are days in the year. According to the legend, this happened on Good Friday, 1276. All the males were named John, and all the females Elizabeth. The countess was forty-two at the time.

The Children, or **Babes in the Wood.** The story is that the master of Wayland Hall, Norfolk, left a little son and daughter to the care of his wife's brother; both were to have money, but if the children died first the uncle was to inherit. After twelve months the uncle hired two ruffians to murder the babes; one of them relented and killed his partner, leaving the children in a wood. They died during the night, and "ROBIN REDBREAST" covered them over with leaves. All things now went ill with the wicked uncle; his sons died, his barns were fired, his cattle died, and he finally perished in gaol.

Chiliasts (ki' li ásts) (Gr. *chilias*, a thousand). Also called MILLENARIANS. Those who believe that Christ will return to this earth and reign a thousand years in the midst of his SAINTS. Originally a Judaistic theory, it became a heresy in the early Christian Church, and though it was condemned by St. Damasus, who was POPE from 366 to 384, it was not extirpated. Article xli of the English Church further condemned Chiliasm in 1553; this Article was omitted in 1562.

Chillingham Cattle. A breed of cattle still preserved in the Northumberland park of the Earl of Tankerville, reputed to be the last remnant of the wild oxen of Britain.

Chillon (shē' yong). **Prisoner of Chillon.** François de Bonnivard (1493–1570), a Genevan prelate and politician. BYRON, in his poem, makes him one of six brothers, all of whom suffered for their opinions.

Chilminar and Baalbek (kil min ar', bāl' bek). According to legend, two cities built by the Genii, acting under the orders of Jinn bin Jann, who governed the world long before ADAM. Chilminar, or the "Forty Towers", is Persepolis. They were intended as lurking places for the Genii to hide in.

Chilo. One of the "Seven Sages of Greece". *See* WISE MEN.

Chiltern Hundreds. The HUNDREDS of Stoke, Desborough and Burnham, Buckinghamshire, over which a Steward was originally appointed to suppress the robbers who frequented the thickly wooded Chiltern Hills. The necessity has long since ceased, but the office remains. As a consequence of the Succession Act of 1701 and later Place Acts, the holding of most non-political offices of profit under the Crown meant resignation from the HOUSE OF COMMONS, and after 1750 application for the stewardship of the Chiltern Hundreds was used as a means of relinquishing membership of Parliament (since members cannot resign directly). The Stewardships of Old Shoreham, East Hendred, Hempholme, Poynings, and Northstead were also used for this purpose, as were (till 1838) the Escheatorships of Munster and Ulster. By the House of Commons Disqualification Act (1957), the Stewardship of the Chiltern Hundreds and the Manor of Northstead (Yorks), were retained for this use and their gift remains with the CHANCELLOR OF THE EXCHEQUER.

Chimæra (ki mē' rà) (Gr. *chimaira*, a she-goat). A fabulous monster in Greek mythology. According to HOMER it has a lion's head, a goat's body, and a dragon's tail. It was born in Lycia and slain by BELLEROPHON. Hence the use of the name in English for an illusory fancy, a wild incongruous scheme.

Chime in. To join in a conversation already in progress, or to be in accord with or agree to suggestions made by others. The allusion is to the chiming of bells.

Chimney Money, or Hearth Money. A yearly tax of two shillings on every fireplace in all houses liable to church and poor rates, or above a minimum value of 20s. per year. First levied in 1663, it was abolished in 1689 and replaced by the WINDOW TAX in 1696.

Chimneypot hat. The same as a STOVEPIPE HAT; the ordinary cylindrical black silk hat or top-hat.

Chinaman. A cricketing term (not to be confused with GOOGLY) denoting an offbreak bowled from the back or side of the hand by a left-handed bowler. It is said that the name derives from the Chinese bowler Ellis Achong, who played for the West Indies, and who practised this kind of bowling, although he was not the first to do so.

Chinatown. That part of any city which forms the Chinese quarter.

Chindit. A corruption of *chinthe*, the lion-headed DRAGON gracing the outside of Burmese pagodas. It was adopted as the device of the troops under Major-General Orde Wingate operating in Burma behind the Japanese lines (1943–1945).

Chinese Gordon. General Charles Gordon (1833–1885), who in 1863 was placed in command of the EVER-VICTORIOUS ARMY and after thirty-three engagements succeeded in suppressing the formidable TAI-PING rebellion by 1864.

After the MAHDI's revolt in the Sudan, he was sent out by Gladstone's government to effect the evacuation of the Egyptian garrisons, but allowed himself to be cut off in Khartoum and was killed (26 January) after a heroic defence lasting nearly a year. The relief force under Wolseley arrived two days too late, due to CABINET procrastination.

Chinese Slavery. Virtual slavery; excessively hard graft for negligible rewards. The phrase became widely used as a political slogan by the LIBERALS from 1903, when Balfour's CONSERVATIVE government (1902–1905) introduced indentured men from China to combat the shortage of Kaffir labour in the Rand gold mines after the dislocation caused by the South African War. They were kept in compounds and only allowed out under permit.

Chinook. A warm, dry wind which blows down the east side of the Rockies in winter causing rapid rises in temperature and sudden thawing of snow. It is a cooling wind in the summer and takes its name from the Chinook Indians of the Columbia River area.

Chintz. A plural word that has erroneously become singular. The Hindi *chint* (from Sans. *chitra*, variegated) was the name given in the 17th century to the painted and stained calico imported from the East; but as the plural *chints* was more common in commercial use it came to be taken for the singular, and was written *chince* or *chinse* and finally *chintz*.

Chip. A chip of the old block. A son or child of the same stuff as his father. The chip is the same wood as the block. Burke applied the words to William Pitt the younger.

He's had his chips. He is finished or come to an end as far as this is concerned, he is out of it. Probably from the game of poker. *See* TO CHIP IN.

The chips are down. The situation is urgent or desperate. Probably the same derivation as TO CHIP IN.

To chip in. It has two meanings; to make a contribution, and to interrupt. The former derives from the game of poker, in which the chips, representing money, are placed by the players in the "pot". The latter is obscure, but possibly from the same source.

To have a chip on one's shoulder. To be quarrelsome; to parade or have a grievance. Of 19th-century American origin, possibly as a man might carry a chip on his shoulder daring others to dislodge it.

Chiromancy. *See* PALMISTRY.

Chiron (kī'ron). The CENTAUR who taught ACHILLES, and many other heroes, music, medicine, and hunting. JUPITER placed him in heaven among the stars as SAGITTARIUS.

Dante, in his INFERNO, gives the name to the keeper of the lake of boiling blood, in the seventh circle of HELL.

Chivalry (shiv' ȧl ri). A general term for all things pertaining to the romance of the old days of knighthood. The word is of similar origin to *cavalry*, coming from the Fr. *cheval*, a horse, and *chevalier*, a horseman. Chivalry embodied the mediæval conception of the ideal life, where valour, courtesy, generosity and dexterity in arms were the summit of any man's attainment.

A great literature arose out of chivalry—the ROLAND epics, those of CHARLEMAGNE, and ARTHUR. It was, perhaps, prophetic of the fate of chivalry itself that in every case these great epics end in tragedy.

The PALADINS of CHARLEMAGNE were all scattered by the battle of RONCESVALLES.

The champions of Dietrich were all assassinated by the instigation of Chriemhild (KRIEMHILD), the bride of ETZEL, king of the Huns.

The KNIGHTS of the ROUND TABLE were all destroyed in the fatal battle of CAMLAN.

The flower of chivalry. *See* FLOWER.

Chivy. To chase or urge someone on; also a chase in the game of "Prisoner's Base". One boy "sets a chivy" by leaving his base, when one of the opposite side chases him, and if he succeeds in touching him before he reaches "home", the boy touched becomes a prisoner. The word is a variant of *chevy*, from CHEVY CHASE.

Chivy, or **chivvy.** The face. An example of RHYMING SLANG.

Chloe (klō' ē). The shepherdess beloved by DAPHNIS in the Greek pastoral romance of Longus called *Daphnis and Chloe*, and hence a generic name in literature for a rustic maiden—not always of the artless variety.

Chock-full. Chock-a-block. Full right up; no room for any more. When two blocks of a tackle meet preventing any more purchase being gained it is said to be *two blocks* or *chock-a-block*.

Chocolate. The produce of the cocoaberry was introduced into England from Central America in the early 16th century as a drink. It was sold in London coffee-houses from the middle of the 17th century.

Hobson's choice. *See* HOBSON'S CHOICE.

Choke. May this piece of bread choke me, if what I say is not true. In ancient times, a person accused of robbery had a piece of barley bread given him over which MASS had been said. He put it in his mouth uttering the above words, and if he could swallow it without being choked he was pronounced innocent.

Choke-pear. A kind of pear with a rough, astringent taste. From this the term was applied to anything that stopped speaking, such as an unanswerable argument or a biting sarcasm.

Choker. Formerly a broad neck-cloth, worn in full dress by waiters, clergymen and others; then a high stiff collar or necklace or scarf worn tight round the neck.

Chop. (1) **to chop,** meaning to cut a piece off with a sudden blow, is a variant spelling of *chap*, a cleft in the skin, and *to chap*, to open in long slits or cracks. From this we get:

Chops of the Channel. The short, broken motion of the waves experienced in crossing the English Channel; also the place where such motion occurs. In this use, however, the word may be *chops*, the jaw (*see below*), because the *Chops of the Channel* is an old and well-understood term for the entrance to the Channel from the Atlantic.

Chop house. An eating-house, originally one where chops and steaks were served.

(2) In the following phrases **chop** comes from the same root as *chap* in CHAPMAN and signifies to barter, exchange, or sell.

To chop and change. To barter by RULE OF THUMB; to fluctuate, to keep changing one's mind or vary continuously.

To chop logic. To bandy words; to altercate. Bacon says, "Let not the counsel chop with the judge."

(3) **Chop,** the face, and **chops,** the jaws or mouth, is a variant spelling of *chap* (as in *Bath chap*, the lower part of a pig's face, cured). From this come:

Chop-fallen, or **Chap-fallen.** CRESTFALLEN, down in the mouth.

To lick one's chops. To relish in anticipation.

(4) In the slang phrase **first chop**, meaning excellent, the word is the Hindi *chhāp*, a print or stamp, formerly used in India and China by English residents for an official seal, also for a passport or permit; and a Chinese customhouse is known as a *chop-house*.

Chop-chop. Hurry, hurry; get moving quickly. *See* PIDGIN ENGLISH.

Chopsticks. The name of a quick traditional waltz tune played as a duet by schoolchildren. The French call it *Côtelettes* (Cutlets), and the Germans *Koteletten Walzer*.

Choragus (kor ā' gŭs). The leader of the chorus in the ancient Athenian drama.

Choriambic Metre. HORACE gives us a great variety, but the main feature in all is the prevalence of the choriambus (—◡◡—). Specimen translations in two of these metres are subjoined:

(1) Horace, *Odes*, I, viii.

—◡◡—|◡——
—◡|——|—◡◡—|—◡◡—|◡——

> Lydia, why on Stanley,
> By the great gods, tell me, I pray, ruinous love you centre?
> Once he was strong and manly,
> Never seen now, patient of toil Mars' sunny camp to enter.
>
> E.C.B.

——|—◡◡—|◡—
——|—◡◡—|—◡◡—|◡—

> When you with an approving smile,
> Praise those delicate arms, Lydy, of Telephus,
> Ah me! how you stir up my bile!
> Heart-sick that for a boy you should forsake me thus.
>
> E.C.B.

Chouans (shoo' ong). French peasant bands in Brittany, under the leadership of Jean Cottereau (1767–1794), who rose in revolt in 1793 and joined the royalists of La VENDÉE. *Chouan* (a corruption of *chat-huant*, a screech-owl) was the nickname given to Cottereau, who imitated the screech of the owl to warn his companions of danger, and the name was extended to his followers.

Choughs. *See under* BIRD.

Chouse (chouz). To cheat or swindle. It derives from the Turkish *cha' ush*, an interpreter, messenger, etc. The interpreter of the Turkish embassy in Eng-

Chriem-hild

land in 1609 defrauded his government of £4,000, and the notoriety of the swindle gave rise to the term.

Chriem-hild. *See* KRIEMHILD.

Chrism, Chrisom (Gr. *chrisma*, anointing, unction). The mixture of oil and balm consecrated for use in baptism, confirmation, etc. Originally *chrisom* was merely a variant of *chrism* resulting from a frequent form of pronunciation but later differentiated from the latter when it came to designate the white cloth or robe worn at baptism. This was used as a shroud if the child died within the ensuing month. In the BILLS OF MORTALITY, as late as 1726, such infants were called *chrisoms*.

Chriss-cross, or **Christ-cross row.** The alphabet in a HORNBOOK, which had a cross like the MALTESE CROSS (✝) at the beginning and end.

The word appears as *Christ-cross, criss-cross*, etc., and Shakespeare shortened it to *cross-row*.

As the Maltese cross was also sometimes used in place of XII to mark that hour on clocks, chriss-cross has occasionally been used for noon.

Christadelphians, or **Brethren of Christ,** sometimes called *Thomasites* after their founder Dr. John Thomas (1805–1871), who migrated from London to Brooklyn and established the sect in 1848. They believe in "conditional immortality" for the faithful and the full inspiration of the BIBLE, and look for the return of Christ to reign on this earth.

Christendom. All Christian countries generally; formerly it also meant the state or condition of being a Christian.

Christian. A follower of Christ. So called first at Antioch (*Acts* xi, 26). Also the hero of Bunyan's *Pilgrim's Progress* who fled from the CITY OF DESTRUCTION and journeyed to the CELESTIAL CITY. He started with a heavy burden on his back, which fell off when he stood at the foot of the cross.

Christian Brothers. A secret society formed in London in the early 16th century to distribute the NEW TESTAMENT in English. The name is now better known as that of the Roman Catholic teaching congregation of laymen, founded by the Abbé de la Salle in 1684.

It still flourishes in France, Great Britain and elsewhere.

Christian Science. The religion founded at Boston by Mrs. Mary Baker Eddy in 1879, "the scientific system of divine healing". Her views were put forward in her book *Science and Health, with key to the Scriptures*, first published in 1875. Christian Science is founded on the BIBLE, but distinguishes between what is taught in the NEW TESTAMENT and what is taught in the creeds and later dogma. It now has a considerable following and is not limited, as is popularly assumed, to the healing of those who are ill.

Most Christian King. The style of the king of France since 1429, when it was conferred on Louis XI by POPE Paul II. Previously the title had been given in the 8th century to Pepin le Bref by Pope Stephen III (714–768), and again in the 9th century to Charles le Chauve. *See* RELIGIOUS.

Christiana (kris ti an' a). The wife of CHRISTIAN in Pt. II of Bunyan's *Pilgrim's Progress*, who journeyed with her children and Mercy from the CITY OF DESTRUCTION some time after her husband.

Christmas. 25 December is Christmas Day although almost certainly not the day on which Christ was born, as is popularly supposed. The date was eventually fixed by the Church in A.D. 440, the day of the winter SOLSTICE, which had anciently been a time of festival among heathen peoples. In Anglo-Saxon England, the year began on 25 December, but from the late 12th century until the adoption of the Gregorian Calendar in 1752 the year began on LADY DAY, 25 March. *See* GREGORIAN YEAR; OLD STYLE.

Christmas box. A gratuity given on Boxing Day (the day after Christmas Day), St. Stephen's Day. Boxes placed in churches for casual offerings used to be opened on Christmas Day, and the contents, called the "dole of the Christmas box", or the "box money", were distributed next day by priests. Apprentices also used to carry a box around to their masters' customers for small gratuities (*See* PIGGY-BANKS). Postmen received such gifts until after World War II, and some dustmen and errand-boys still call to collect them. *Cp.* HANDSEL.

Christmas cards. These boosters of post office and stationers' revenues are of comparatively recent origin. W. C. T. Dobson, R.A., is usually regarded as having sent the first such card in 1844. Sir Henry Cole and J. C. Horsley produced the first commercial Christmas card in 1846, although it was condemned by temperance enthusiasts because members of the family group in the centre piece were cheerfully drinking wine. After Tucks, the art printers, took to printing them in the 1870s, they really came into VOGUE.

Christmas Day in the Workhouse. The popular title of the much parodied long narrative poem (twenty-one verses) properly entitled *In the Workhouse: Christmas Day*, by George R. Sims (1847–1922). It was frequently burlesqued in the days of the MUSIC HALL and subsequently.

> It is Christmas Day in the Workhouse,
> And the cold bare walls are bright
> With garlands of green and holly,
> And the place is a pleasant sight:
> For with clean-washed hands and faces,
> In a long and hungry line
> The paupers sit at the tables
> For this is the hour they dine.

Christmas decorations. The Roman festival of SATURN was held in December and the temples were decorated with greenery; the DRUIDS are associated with MISTLETOE, and the Saxons used HOLLY and IVY. These customs have been transferred to the Christian festival. The holly or holy-tree is called Christ's thorn in Germany and Scandinavia, from its use in church decorations and its putting forth its berries about Christmas time. The early Christians gave an emblematic turn to the custom, referring to the "righteous branch", and justifying it from *Isaiah* lx, 13: "The glory of Lebanon shall come unto thee, the fir-tree, the pine-tree, and the box together, to beautify the place of my sanctuary."

The decorated Christmas tree was in use among the Romans and was introduced into England from Germany soon after Queen Victoria's marriage with Prince Albert of Saxe-Coburg-Gotha in 1840. SANTA CLAUS and his reindeer came to England at the same time.

Christopher, St. Legend relates that St. Christopher was a giant who one day carried a child over a brook, and said, "Chylde, thou hast put me in gret peryll. I might bere no greater burden." To which the child answered "Marvel thou nothing, for thou hast borne all the world upon thee, and its sins likewise." This is an allegory: Christopher means Christbearer; the child was Christ, and the river was the river of death.

Christy Minstrels. For many years the mid-Victorian publics of London and New York were entertained by the troupe of black-faced minstrels organized by the American Christy brothers (1815–1862). To an accompaniment of various stage-Negro antics they sang plantation songs and cracked innocent jokes with Bones, Sambo, and the rest. Stephen Collins Foster provided their best songs, of which *Beautiful Dreamer* is the most famous. They were succeeded by Moore and Burgess, and other troupes of the same genre.

Chronicle, Chronicon ex Chronicis. An early 12th-century chronicle from the creation to 1117 written by Florence, a monk of Worcester (d. 1118). It is largely based on Marianus Scotus, a lost version of the ANGLO-SAXON CHRONICLE, and Asser. His own contributions begin with 1106 and it was carried on to 1141 by John of Worcester.

Chronogram. A sentence or inscription in which certain letters stand for a date or epoch. In this double chronogram upon the year 1642 (one part in Latin and the other in the English of that Latin) the capitals in each produced the total of 1642.

TV DeVs IaM propItIVs sIs regI regnoq Ve hVIC VnIVerso.

O goD noVV sheVV faVoVr to the kIng anD thIs VVhoLe LanD.

VDVIMIIVIIVVICVIV   1642
DVVVVVVIDIVVLLD   1642

Chrysippus. *Nisi Chrisippus fuisset, Porticus non est.* If Chrysippus had not been, there would be no Porticus (STOIC philosophy—the portico was the place where ZENO taught.). Chrysippus of

Soli was a disciple of Zeno the Stoic and Cleanthes, his successor. He did for the Stoics what St. PAUL did for Christianity—that is, he explained the system, showed by plausible reasoning its truth, and how it was based on a solid foundation. Stoicism was founded by Zeno; but if Chrysippus had not been its advocate, it would never have taken root.

Chum. A crony, a familiar companion.

To chum up with. To become friendly with, to make a companion of.

Church. This is the O.E. *circe*, or *cirice*, which comes through W.Ger. *kirika*, from Gr. *kuriakon*, a church, the neuter of the adjective *kuriakos*, meaning of or belonging to the Lord. It denotes the whole body of Christians; the place of worship; a particular sect or group of Christians; the CLERGY.

Anglican Church The CHURCH OF ENGLAND.

Broad Church. *See* BROAD.

Catholic Church. *See* CATHOLIC.

Collegiate Churches. So called from having a college or chapter of CANONS or prebends under a DEAN. There were many such in mediæval England but they were mainly suppressed during the reign of Edward VI (1547–1553). St George's Chapel, Windsor and Westminster Abbey are surviving examples. Some of them eventually became cathedrals of new dioceses (*e.g.* at Manchester and Ripon).

Established Church. The church officially recognized and established by law and enjoying a privileged position. In England the established Church is Episcopalian, in Scotland it is PRESBYTERIAN. *See* EPISCOPACY.

Church of England. First severed its connection with ROME under Henry VIII and subsequently under Elizabeth I (1559). Doctrinal changes were largely effected in the reign of Edward VI (1547–1553) and embodied in the BOOK OF COMMON PRAYER of 1549 and the more definitely PROTESTANT version of 1552.

Church of Ireland. This became PROTESTANT in the same way as the Church of England and, although most of the Irish remained Roman CATHOLIC, it was not disestablished and largely disendowed until 1869.

Church of North America (Episcopalian), was established in November 1784, when Bishop Seabury, chosen by the churches of Connecticut, was consecrated in Scotland. The first convention was held at Philadelphia in 1787.

Church of Scotland. It first became PRESBYTERIAN in 1560, but EPISCOPACY was cautiously restored by James VI and I from 1599, to be rejected finally in 1638. It is an ESTABLISHED CHURCH.

Church in Wales was separated from the province of Canterbury in 1920, after the long-standing agitation for disestablishment, which resulted in the Act of 1914 for this purpose.

Church Commissioners. *See* ECCLESIASTICAL COMMISSIONERS; QUEEN ANNE'S BOUNTY.

Church-ale. Also called *Easter-ale* and *Whitsun-ale* from their being sometimes held at EASTER and WHITSUNTIDE; a church festivity akin to the WAKES, when specially brewed ale was sold to the populace and money was collected in addition for church purposes. The word "ale" is used in such composite words as *bride-ale, church-ale, clerk-ale, lamb-ale, Midsummer-ale, Scot-ale* etc., for revel or feast, ale being the chief liquor provided. Church-ales were unsuccessfully forbidden in 1603 but mostly came to an end during the INTERREGNUM.

Church scot. A tribute, earlier known as *food-rent*, paid on ST. MARTIN's Day (11 November) in corn and poultry, etc., to support the parish priests in Saxon times. It is named from the Early Saxon silver coin called a *sceat*.

High Church. *See* HIGH.

Low Church. *See* LOW.

Orthodox Church. *See* ORTHODOX.

The Church Army. A CHURCH OF ENGLAND evangelical body founded by the Rev. Wilson Carlile in 1882. It began its work among the poor of LONDON on somewhat similar lines to those of the SALVATION ARMY.

The Church Invisible. Those who are known to God alone as His sons and daughters by adoption and grace. *See* CHURCH VISIBLE.

There is...a Church visible and a

Church invisible; the latter consists of those spiritual persons who fulfil the notion of the Ideal Church—the former is the Church as it exists in any particular age, embracing within it all who profess Christianity.

F. W. ROBERTSON: *Sermons* (series IV, ii).

The Church Militant. The Church or whole body of believers who are said to be "waging the war of faith" against "the world, the flesh and the DEVIL". It is therefore militant, or in warfare.

The Church Triumphant. Those who are dead and gone to their rest. Having fought the fight and triumphed, they belong to the Church Triumphant in HEAVEN.

The Church Visible. All ostensible Christians; all who profess to be Christians; all who have been baptized and admitted into the communion of the Church. *Cp.* CHURCH INVISIBLE.

The Seven Churches of Asia. *See* SEVEN.

To church a woman. To read the appointed service when a woman comes to church to give thanks after childbirth.

To go into the Church. To take HOLY ORDERS; to enter the ministry.

Uniat Churches. *See* UNIAT.

Churchwarden. A long clay pipe, such as churchwardens used to smoke a century or so ago when they met together in the parish tavern, after they had made up their accounts in the VESTRY, or been elected to office at the EASTER meeting.

Churchyard cough. A deep, chesty cough of an ominous kind. The allusion is obvious.

Churn Supper. *See* MELL SUPPER.

Churrigueresque (chu rig er esk'). Over-ornate as applied to architecture. The word, frequently used by Richard Ford (1796–1858) in his writings on Spain, derives from José Churriguera (1665–1725), a Spanish architect of the Baroque school.

Ci-devant (sē de vong) (Fr.). Former, of times gone by. As *Ci-devant governor*, once a governor but no longer so; *cidevant philosophers*, philosophers of former days. In the time of the first French Republic the word was used as a noun meaning a nobleman of the ANCIEN RÉGIME.

Cicero (sis' er ō). Marcus Tullius, the great Roman orator, philosopher, and statesman (106–43 B.C.); said by Plutarch to have been called Cicero from Lat. *cicer* (a wart or vetch), because he had "a flat excrescence on the tip of his nose".

Cicerone. A guide who points out objects of interest to strangers. So called from the great orator Cicero, in the same way as PAUL was called by the men of Lystra, "Mercurius, because he was the chief speaker."

Cicisbeo (chich is bā' ō). A dangler about women; the professed gallant of a married woman. At one time in Italy it was unfashionable for a husband to associate with his wife in society or in public and she was accompanied by her cicisbeo. Also the knot of silk or ribbon which is attached to fans, walking sticks, umbrellas, etc.

Cid (sid). A corruption of *seyyid*, Arabic for lord. The title given to Roderigo or Ruy Diaz de Bivar (*c.* 1040–1099), also called El Campeador, the national hero of Spain and champion of Christianity against the MOORS. His exploits, real and legendary, form the basis of many Spanish romances and chronicles, as well as Corneille's tragedy *Le Cid* (1636).

Cid Hamet Benengeli. The supposititious author upon whom Cervantes fathered the *Adventures of Don Quixote*.

If the two bad cassocks I am worth ... I would have given the latter of them freely as even as Cid Hamet offered his ... to have stood by.

STERNE.

Cimmerian Darkness (sī mēr' i àn). HOMER (possibly from some story as to the Arctic night) supposes the Cimmerians to dwell in a land "beyond the ocean stream", where the sun never shone (*Odys.* XI, 14). Spenser refers to "Cymerian shades" in *Virgil's Gnat* and Milton to "Cimmerian desert" in *L'Allegro*.

The Cimmerians were known in post-Homeric times as an historical people on the shores of the BLACK SEA, whence the name *Crimea*.

Cinch. It's a cinch. Dead easy, an absolute certainty. A phrase of American origin derived from the Mexican saddle girth which was strong, tight and safe (Sp. *cincha*, girth).

Cinchona (sin chō' na), or **Quinine.** So named from the wife of the Conte del Chinchon, viceroy of Peru, who was cured of a tertian fever by its use, and who brought it to Europe in 1640. Linnæus erroneously named it *Cin*chona for *Chin*chona. *See* PERUVIAN BARK.

Cincinnatus (sin si nā' tus). A legendary Roman hero of about 500 to 430 B.C., who, after having been consul years before, was taken from his plough to be Dictator. After he had conquered the Æquians and delivered his country from danger, he laid down his office and returned to his plough.

Cinderella (sin der rel'à). Heroine of a fairy tale of very ancient, probably Eastern, origin, found in German literature in the 16th century and popularized by Perrault's *Contes de ma mère l'oye* (1697). Cinderella is drudge of the house, while her elder sisters go to fine balls. At length, a fairy enables her to go to the prince's ball; the prince falls in love with her, and she is found again by means of a glass slipper which she drops, and which will fit no foot but her own.

The glass slipper has been conjectured as a fur or sable slipper, supposedly from *pantoufle de vair* not *de verre*. Perrault's text of 1697 has "*de verre*", which is more in keeping with the story.

Cinquecento (ching' kwè chen' tō). The Italian name for the 16th century, applied as an epithet to art and literature with much the same significance as RENAISSANCE or Elizabethan. It was the revival of the classical or antique, but is also understood as a derogatory term, implying debased or inferior art.

Cinque Ports (sink). Originally the five Kent and Sussex seaports of Hastings, Sandwich, Dover, Romney, and Hythe, which were known by this name collectively from the 12th century and were granted special privileges in consideration of their providing ships and men for the defence of the Channel. Winchelsea and Rye were subsequently added and there were ultimately thirty-two lesser members. Their privileges were largely surrendered in 1685.

Barons of the Cinque Ports. *See un-*
der BARON.

Circe (sĕr' si). A sorceress in Greek mythology, who lived in the island of Æœa. When ULYSSES landed there, Circe turned his companions into swine, but Ulysses resisted this metamorphosis by virtue of a herb called MOLY, given him by MERCURY.

Circle. Circle of Ulloa. A white rainbow or luminous ring sometimes seen in Alpine regions opposite the sun in foggy weather. Named from Antonio de Ulloa (1716–1795), a Spanish naval officer who founded the observatory at Cadiz and initiated many scientific enterprises.

Circuit, Judicial. The journey through the counties formerly made by the judges twice a year to administer justice at the Assizes, a system changed by the Courts Act of 1971. Circuit Judges are now appointed having criminal jurisdiction in the Crown Courts and civil jurisdiction in the County Courts.

Circuit Rider. A METHODIST minister in America who rode on horseback round the outlying stations of his circuit to preach and perform other pastoral duties. Francis Asbury, a follower of John Wesley, began the practice in 1771.

Circumlocution Office. A term applied in ridicule by Charles Dickens in *Little Dorrit* to our public offices, because each person tries to shuffle off every act to someone else; and before anything is done it has to pass through so many departments with such consequent delays that it is hardly worth having bothered about it.

Cist (kist) (Gr. *kiste*, Lat. *cista*). A chest or box, generally used as a coffer for the remains of the dead by prehistoric man, made from flat stones placed on edge with another stone as a lid, and usually covered by a round barrow. The Greek and Roman cist was a deep cylindrical basket made of wickerwork. The basket into which voters cast their tablets was called a *cist*; but the mystic cist used in the rites of CERES was latterly made of bronze. *Cp.* KIST OF WHISTLES.

Cistercians. A monastic order, founded at Cistercium or Cîteaux (near Dijon) in 1098, by Robert, abbot of Molesme, as strict BENEDICTINES. They are also known as Grey or White Monks from their habit and as *Bernadines* from St. Bernard of Clairvaux, who with thirty companions joined the abbey of Cîteaux in 1113. They were noted agriculturalists, and in the 13th-century England became a great producer of wool.

Citizen King, The. Louis Philippe of France. So called because he was elected King of the French (1830–1848), not King of France, after the downfall of Charles X.

City. A town thus incorporated by charter; any large town is so called in ordinary speech. In England, the term is of historical and ceremonial rather than administrative significance. In the BIBLE, it means a town having walls and gates.

The City. The City of LONDON within its historic boundaries as distinct from other London boroughs; also a general term for the business and financial interests of the City of London.

The Big City. London.

The City of a Hundred Towers. Pavia, in Italy; famous for its towers and steeples.

The City of Bells. Strasbourg.

The City of Brotherly Love. Philadelphia. A somewhat ironical but quite etymological nickname for this city (Gr. *philadelphia*, brotherly love).

The City of David. Jerusalem. So called in compliment to King David (II *Sam.* v, 7, 9).

The City of Destruction. In Bunyan's *Pilgrim's Progress*, the world of the unconverted.

The City of Dreaming Spires. Oxford. A name derived from Matthew Arnold's *Thyrsis*: "that sweet City with her dreaming spires".

The City of Dreadful Knights. Cardiff. After World War I, Lloyd George, Prime Minister in the Coalition government, made lavish grants of honours in a cynical and blatant fashion. In 1922 Lord Salisbury opened an attack and it was alleged that the government had fixed prices for the sale of titles, the money being put into party political funds. The CONSERVATIVE PARTY profited as did Lloyd George's private party chest. As a consequence, a Royal Commission was set up in 1922 to re-

commend future procedure. Three people connected with prominent South Wales newspapers were among the recipients of these honours, hence Cardiff was dubbed the "City of Dreadful Knights", a punning allusion to *The City of Dreadful Night*, a poem by James Thomson (1834–1882).

The City of God. The Church, or whole body of believers; the Kingdom of Christ, in contradistinction to the CITY OF DESTRUCTION. The phrase is from St. Augustine's famous work, *De Civitate Dei*.

The City of Lanterns. A suppositious city in Lucian's *Verae Historiae*, situated somewhere beyond the ZODIAC. *Cp.* LANTERN-LAND.

The City of Legions. Caerleon-on-Usk, where King ARTHUR held his court.

The City of Lilies. Florence.

The City of Palaces. Agrippa, in the reign of AUGUSTUS, converted ROME from "a city of brick huts to one of marble palaces".
Calcutta is also called the "City of Palaces".

The City of Saints. Montreal is so named because of its streets named after SAINTS. Salt Lake City, Utah, U.S.A., is also so called, from its MORMON inhabitants.

The City of the Golden Gate. San Francisco. *See* GOLDEN GATE.

The City of the Prophet. MEDINA. *See* CITIES OF REFUGE.

The City of the Seven Hills. ROME, built on seven hills (*Urbs Septacollis*). The hills are the Aventine, Cælian, Capitoline, Esquiline, Palatine, Quirinal, and Viminal.

The City of the Sun. Baalbec, Rhodes, and Heliopolis, which had the sun for tutelary deity, were so called. It is also the name of a treatise on the Ideal Republic by the Dominican Friar Campanella (1568–1639), similar to the REPUBLIC of Plato, UTOPIA of Sir Thomas More, and the NEW ATLANTIS of Bacon.

The City of the Three Kings. Cologne; the reputed burial place of the MAGI.

The City of the Tribes. Galway; because it was anciently the home of the thirteen "tribes" or chief families, who settled there in 1232 with Richard de Burgh.

The City of the Violet Crown. Athens is so called by Aristophanes (*Equites*, 1323 and 1329; and *Acharnians*, 637). Macaulay refers to Athens as the "violet-crowned city". Ion (a violet) was a legendary king of ATHENS, whose four sons gave names to the four Athenian tribes; and Greece in Asia Minor was called Ionia. Athens was the city of "Ion crowned its king" or "of the Violet crowned".

Cities of Refuge. Six walled cities (*Joshua*, xxxv, 6), three on each side of the Jordan, set aside under MOSAIC LAW as a refuge for those who committed accidental homicide. Such refuges were necessitated by the primitive law which exacted blood vengeance by next of kin. All seeking asylum were tried, and if found guilty of murder right of asylum was withdrawn. The cities were Ramoth, Kedesh, Bezer, Shechem, Hebron, and Golam (*Joshua* xx, 7, 8). In *Numbers* xxxv, and other references, the choice of cities is attributed to Moses, but in *Joshua* xx, to Joshua.

Among Mohammedans, MEDINA, in Arabia, where MOHAMMED took refuge when driven by conspirators from MECCA, is known as "the City of Refuge". He entered it, not as a fugitive, but in triumph (622 A.D.). Also called the *City of the Prophet*.

The Cities of the Plain. Sodom and Gomorrah.

> Abram dwelled in the land of Canaan, and Lot dwelled in the cities of the plain, and pitched his tent towards Sodom.
> *Gen*. xiii, 12.

Civil List. The annual grant to the Crown and Royal Family, voted by PARLIAMENT for royal expenditure from the CONSOLIDATED FUND. It was so named in the early 18th century because the salaries of Civil Servants, Judges, etc., were paid from it (until 1831) and it has its origins in the reign of William III.

George III gave up most of the hereditary revenues in 1760 in return for an annual grant. In 1978 it was over £2,000,000. *See* ROYAL BOUNTY.

Civil Service. This name for all those employed in administering the civil business of the State was originally used by the English East India Company to distinguish its civilian employees from its soldiers.

Civil Service Estimates. The annual Parliamentary grant to cover the expenses of the diplomatic service, the Home Office, the prison service, education, the collection of the revenue, and various other expenses pertaining to neither the sovereign nor the armed services of the Crown.

Civil War. War between citizens (*civiles*) of the same state. In English history, the term is particularly applied to the war between Charles I and PARLIAMENT; but the BARONS' WAR and the Wars of the Roses (*see under* ROSE) were also civil wars. The U.S.A. was confronted with a costly civil war between 1861 and 1865, when the eleven CONFEDERATE STATES sought to secede from the Union.

Civis Romanus sum (siv' is rō-mā'nus sŭm). "I am a Roman citizen", a plea which sufficed to stop arbitrary condemnation, bonds, and scourging. No Roman citizen could be condemned unheard; by the Valerian Law he could not be bound; by the Sempronian Law it was forbidden to scourge him or beat him with rods. When the chief captain commanded PAUL "should be examined by scourging", he asked, "Is it lawful for you to scourge a man that is a Roman, and uncondemned?" (*Acts*, xxii, 24–25). *See also Acts* xvi, 37, etc.

The phrase gained an English fame from the peroration of Palmerston's great speech in the House of Commons (24 June, 1850) over the Don PACIFICO affair: "As the Roman, in days of old, held himself free from indignity, when he could say *Civis Romanus sum*, so also a British subject, in whatever land he may be, shall feel confident that the watchful eye and the strong arm of England will protect him against injustice and wrong."

Civvies. Civilians or civilian clothes as opposed to military uniform. *See* MUFTI.

Civvie Street (siv' i). The usual term by which members of the armed services refer to civilian life.

Clack Dish. A dish or basin with a movable lid. Some two or three centuries ago, beggars used to proclaim their want by clacking the lid of a wooden dish.

Clam. A bivalve mollusc like an oyster, which burrows in sand or mud. In America especially, clams are esteemed a delicacy and are gathered only when the tide is out. Hence the saying, "Happy as a clam at high tide." The word is also used as slang for the mouth, and for a close-mouthed person.

Close as a clam. Mean, close-fisted; from the difficulty with which a clam is made to open its shell.

Clameur de Haro *See* HARO.

Clan. This is from the mediæval Latin *planta*, a branch. The prevalent idea that the Scottish Highland clan consisted of the chief of a family and his followers, related by ties of kinship and bearing his name, is unsound. It comprised the chief and his followers irrespective of descent, and only in its narrowest sense applies to the chief, his family, and kindred. The legal power and hereditary jurisdiction of the head of a clan was abolished in 1747 after the '45 Rebellion. The phrase **a gathering of the clans** implies any assembly of like-minded persons, usually for convivial purposes.

Clan-na-Gael (Klăn′nà gāl′). An Irish FENIAN organization founded in Philadelphia in 1881, and known in secret as the "United Brotherhood". Its object was to secure "the complete and absolute independence of Ireland from Great Britain, and the complete severance of all political connexion between the two countries, to be effected by unceasing preparation for armed insurrection in Ireland".

Clapham Sect. The name bestowed by Sydney Smith upon the group of EVANGELICALS with common social and political interests most of whom lived in Clapham at the end of the 18th and in the early 19th centuries. William Wilberforce (1759–1833) the ABOLITIONIST was their leader. Their opponents derisively called them "the Saints".

Clapperclaw. To jangle, to claw or scratch; to abuse, revile; originally meaning to claw with a clapper of some sort.

Clapper-dudgeon. An ABRAM-MAN, a beggar from birth. The clapper is the tongue of the bell, and in CANT language the tongue. Dudgeon is the hilt of a dagger; and perhaps the original meaning is one who knocks his *clap dish* or CLACK DISH with a dudgeon.

Clap-trap. Something introduced to win applause: something really worthless but sure to take with the groundlings. A *trap* to catch applause.

Claque (klăk). A body of hired applauders at a theatre, etc.; said to have been originated or first systematized by a M. Sauton, who, in 1820, established in Paris an office to secure the success of dramatic performances. The manager ordered the required number of *claqueurs*, who were divided into *commissaires*, those who commit the piece to memory, and noisily point out its merits; *rieurs*, who laugh at the puns and jokes; *pleureurs*, chiefly women who hold their handkerchiefs to their eyes at the emotional parts; *chatouilleurs*, who are to keep the audience in good humour; and *bisseurs*, who are to cry BIS (encore). *Claque* is also the French for an opera-hat. Thackeray thus uses it.

> A gentleman in black with ringlets and a tuft stood gazing fiercely about him, with one hand in the armhole of his waistcoat and the other holding his claque.
>
> *Pendennis*, ch. xxv.

Clare. County Clare Election. The famous election of 1828 which resulted in the return of the CATHOLIC candidate, Daniel O'Connell, and which brought about the Catholic Emancipation Act of 1829.

Clare, Order of St. A religious order of women founded in 1212, the second that St. Francis instituted. The name derives from their first abbess, Clare of Assisi. The nuns are also called Clarisses, Poor Clares, Minoresses, or Nuns of the Order of St. Francis. *See* FRANCISCANS.

Clarenceux King of Arms (klăr′ en sū). The second of the three English Kings of Arms, under the head of the College of Arms, having jurisdiction over the counties east, west and south of the Trent. The office was instituted by the Duke of Clarence, third son of Edward

III. *See* HERALDRY.

Clarendon Code. The famous four acts passed by the CAVALIER PARLIAMENT, named after the King's minister, the Earl of Clarendon, although he was not their originator. They comprise the Corporation Act (1661), the Act of Uniformity (1662), the Conventicle Act (1664), and the Five-Mile Act (1665). They were directed against the NON-CONFORMISTS.

Clarendon type. A bold-faced condensed type, such as that used for a CATCHWORD or words.

The Constitutions of Clarendon. Laws made by Henry II at a council held at Clarendon in Wiltshire in 1164, to check the power of the Church and to restrain the prerogatives of ecclesiastics. These sixteen ordinances defined the limits of the patronage and jurisdiction of the POPE in England.

Claret. The English name for the red wines of Bordeaux, originally the yellowish or light red wines as distinguished from the white wines. The name (which is not used in France) is the O.Fr. *clairet*, diminutive of *clair*, from Lat. *clarus*, clear. The *colour* receives its name from the wine.

Claret cup. A drink made of claret, brandy, lemon, borage, sugar, ice, and carbonated water.

Clark(e). Nobby Clark(e) is the popular name used by British army and navy personnel for every man of the name of Clark(e). It originated in the dressy or "NOBBY" turn-out affected by clerks and other blackcoated workers of the early 19th century.

Classics. The best authors. The Romans were divided by Servius into five classes. Any citizen who belonged to the highest class was called *classicus*, all the rest were said to be *infra classem* (unclassed). From this the best authors were termed *classici auctores* (classic authors), *i.e.* authors of the best or first class. The high esteem in which Greek and Latin authors were held at the RENAISSANCE obtained for these authors the name of *classic*. When other first-rate works are intended some distinctive name is added, as the English, French, Spanish, etc., classics.

Claude Lorraine (*i.e.* of Lorraine). This incorrect form is generally used in English for the name of Claude Gellée (1600–1682), the French landscape painter, born at Chamagne in Lorraine.

Clause Rolls. *See* CLOSE ROLLS.

Clavie. Burning of the Clavie on New Year's Eve (old style) in the village of Burghead, on the southern shore of the Moray Firth. The clavie is a sort of bonfire made of casks split up. One of the casks is split into two parts of different sizes, and an important item of the ceremony is to join these parts together with a huge nail made for the purpose. Whence the name, from *clavus* (Lat.), a nail. Chambers in his *Book of Days* (vol. II, p. 789) minutely describes the ceremony and suggests that it is a relic of DRUID worship. The two unequal divisions of the cask possibly symbolize the unequal parts of the old and new year.

Claw. Claw me I will claw thee. "Praise me, and I will praise you", or "scratch my back, and I'll scratch yours". To claw meaning to tear or scratch, formerly also meant to stroke or tickle; hence to please, flatter or praise.

Clay, To have feet of. *See under* FOOT.

Clean. A clean tongue. Not abusive, not profane, not addicted to swearing.

To clean down. To sweep down, to swill down.

To clean out. To purify, to make tidy. Also, to win another's money till his pocket is quite empty; to completely impoverish someone.

To clean up. To wash up, to put in order; to wash oneself.

To have clean hands. To be quite clear of some stated evil.

To live a clean life. To live blameless and undefiled.

To make a clean breast of it. To make a full and unreserved confession.

To make a clean sweep. To dispose completely of anything; to get rid of materials, methods or staff regarded as obsolete or redundant. *See under* BROOM.

To show a clean bill of health. *See* BILL.

To show a clean pair of heels. To run away, to make one's escape by superior speed. Here *clean* means free from obstruction.

Clean and unclean animals. Among the Jews of the OLD TESTAMENT (*see Lev.* xi) those animals which chew the cud and part the hoof were clean and might be eaten. Hares and rabbits could not be eaten because (although they chew the cud) they do not part the hoof. Pigs and camels were unclean, because (although they part the hoof) they do not chew the cud. Birds of prey were accounted unclean. Fish with fins and scales were accounted fit food for man.

According to PYTHAGORAS, who taught the doctrine of the TRANSMIGRATION OF THE SOUL, it was lawful for man to eat only those animals into which the human soul never entered, the others being held unclean. This notion existed long before the time of Pythagoras, who learnt it in Egypt.

Cleanliness is next to godliness. An old saying, quoted by John Wesley (*Sermon* xcii, *On Dress*), Matthew Henry, and others. The origin is said to be found in the writings of Phinehas ben Yair, an ancient rabbi.

Clear (verb). **To be quite cleared out.** To have spent all one's money; to have nothing left. *Cleared out* means, my purse or pocket is cleared out of money.
To clear away. To remove, to melt away, to disappear.
To clear for action. To prepare for action, TO CLEAR THE DECKS.
To clear off. To make oneself scarce, to remove oneself or something.
To clear out. To eject; to empty out, to make tidy, to make off.
To clear out for Guam. An obsolete shipping phrase; used when a ship was bound for no specific port. In the height of the gold rushes ships carried passengers to Australia without making arrangements for return cargoes. They were, therefore, obliged to leave Melbourne in ballast, and to sail in search of homeward freights. The Customs regulations required that some port should be specified on clearing outwards, so it became the habit of captains to name Guam (a small island of the Ladrone group) as their hypothetical destination.
To clear the air. To get rid of sultriness, oppressiveness, etc.; figuratively, to remove misunderstandings or ambiguities of a situation, argument, etc.
To clear the court. To remove all strangers, or persons not officially concerned in the suit.
To clear the customs. To have been inspected and dealt with by the customs officers.
To clear the decks. To remove everything not required, especially when preparing for action; playfully used of eating everything available on the table at mealtimes.
To clear the room. To remove from it every thing or person not required.
To clear the table. To remove what has been placed upon it.
To clear up. To become fine after rain or cloudiness; to make manifest; to elucidate what was obscure; to tidy up.

Clear. A clear day. An entire, complete day. "The bonds must be left three clear days for examination", means that they must be left for three days not counting the first or last. It also means a cloudless day, or one free from engagements.
A clear head. A mind that is capable of understanding things clearly.
A clear statement. A straightforward and intelligible statement.
A clear style (of writing). A lucid method of expressing one's thoughts.
A clear voice. A voice of pure intonation, neither husky, mouthy, nor throaty.

Cleft stick, To be caught in a. Figuratively to be caught in two awkward situations which combine to embarrass one. The form of torture inflicted on ARIEL by the witch Sycorax in SHAKESPEARE'S *The Tempest* (I, ii) was to confine him in the trunk of a cleft pine tree.

Clement, St. Patron SAINT of tanners, being himself a tanner. His day is 23 November, and his symbol is an anchor, because he is said to have been martyred by being thrown into the sea tied to an anchor.

Cleopatra (klē ō păt′ rà). (69–30 B.C.). She was Queen of Egypt, being joint ruler with and wife of her brother Ptolemy Dionysius. In 48 B.C. she was driven from the throne, but was reinstated in 47 by Julius Cæsar, by whom she had a son. In 41 Mark Antony fell under her spell and repudiated his wife Octavia.

When he was defeated at Actium by Octavian, he committed suicide, and Cleopatra is supposed to have killed herself by means of the bite of an asp.

Cleopatra and her pearl. It is said that Cleopatra gave a banquet for Antony at Alexandria, the costliness of which excited his astonishment. When Antony expressed his surprise she took a pearl eardrop and dissolved it in her drink, the further to impress him.

A similar story is told of Sir Thomas Gresham when Queen Elizabeth I visited the ROYAL EXCHANGE. He is said to have pledged her health in a cup of wine in which a precious stone worth £15,000 had been crushed to atoms.

Cleopatra's Needle. The OBELISK so called, now on the Thames Embankment, was brought from Alexandria in 1877, whither it and its fellow (now in Central Park, New York) had been moved from Heliopolis by Augustus about 14 B.C. It has no connexion with Cleopatra other than having been in her capital, Alexandria, and was originally set up by Thotmes III about 1500 B.C.

Cleopatra's nose. Blaise Pascal (1623–1662) wrote, "If the nose of Cleopatra had been shorter, the whole face of the earth would have been changed" (*Pensées* viii, 29). The allusion is to the momentous effects brought about by her conquest, through her charm and beauty, first of Julius Cæsar, then of Mark Antony.

Clergy. Ultimately from Gr. *kleros*, a lot or inheritance, with reference to *Deut.* xviii, 21 and *Acts* i, 17; thus, the men of God's lot or inheritance. In St. Peter's First Epistle (ch. v, 3) the Church is called "God's heritage" or lot. In the OLD TESTAMENT the tribe of Levi is called the "lot or heritage of the Lord".

Clergy, Benefit of. *See* BENEFIT.

Clerical Titles. *Clerk.* In remote times the clergyman was usually one of the few who could read and write, so the word *clerical*, as used in "clerical error", came to mean an orthographical error. As the respondent in church was able to read, he received the name of clerk, and the assistants in writing, etc., were so termed in business (Late Lat. *clericus*, a clergyman).

Curate. One who has the cure of souls in a parish. Properly a rector, vicar, or perpetual curate, but the word curate is now generally used to denote an "assistant" curate or unbeneficed clergyman.

Parson. The same word as *person*. As Blackstone says, a parson is "*persona ecclesiae*, one that hath full rights of the parochial church".

> Though we write "parson" differently, yet 'tis but "person"; that is the individual person set apart for the service of such a church, and 'tis in Latin *persona*, and *personatus* is a parsonage. Indeed with the canon lawyers, *personatus* is any dignity or preferment in the church.
> SELDEN: *Table-talk*.

Rector. One who received the great TITHES. From Lat. *rector*, a ruler—the man who rules and guides the parish.

Vicar. Originally one who does the "duty" of a parish for the owner or owners of the tithes (Lat. *vicarius*, a deputy). *Perpetual Curates* are now termed Vicars.

The French *curé* equals our vicar, and their *vicaire* our curate.

In the U.S.A. a vicar is the priest of a chapel, dependent on a church.

Clerical vestments. *White*. Emblem of purity, worn on all feasts, saints' days, and sacramental occasions.

Red. The colour of blood and of fire, worn on the days of martyrs, and on WHIT SUNDAY, when the HOLY GHOST came down like tongues of fire. Now also used on GOOD FRIDAY.

Green. Worn on days which are neither feasts nor fasts.

Purple. The colour of mourning, worn on ADVENT Sundays, in LENT, and on EMBER DAYS. Now used on Good Friday in some churches.

Black. Formerly worn on Good Friday; worn when masses are said for the dead.

Clerihew (kler' i hū). The name given to a particular kind of humorous verse invented by E. Clerihew Bentley (1875–1956). It is usually satirical and often biographical, consisting of four rhymed lines of uneven length. For inclusion in this Dictionary Mr. Bentley suggested the following:

> It was a weakness of Voltaire's
> To forget to say his prayers,

And one which, to his shame,
He never overcame.

Clerk-ale *See* CHURCH-ALE.

Clerk of the Weather. A humorous personification of whatever forces govern the weather.

Clerkenwell (klark' en wel). At the holy well in this district the parish clerks of LONDON used to assemble yearly to play some sacred piece.

Clew up. To draw up the lower ends of square sails to the upper yard ready for furling. Figuratively, to finish something completely, to tie it up leaving no loose ends.

Cliff-hanger. Figuratively, a state of affairs producing anxiety. From the early serial adventure films where the hero was often left in such a hazardous plight in order to whet the cinema-goer's appetite for the next instalment.

Climacteric (klī măk' tèr ik). It was once believed by astrologers that the 7th and 9th years, with their multiples, especially the odd multiples (21, 27, 35, 45, 49, 63, and 81), were critical points in life; these were called the *Climacteric Years* and were presided over by SATURN, the malevolent planet. 63, which is produced by multiplying 7 and 9 together, was termed the *Grand Climacteric*, which few persons succeeded in outliving.

Climate of Opinion. The way people in general think and feel about matters, the state of opinion. A hackneyed vogue phrase much used in political speeches and writings of the mid-20th century.

Climb down, To. To abandon as untenable an attitude or opinion that one has hitherto vigorously supported.

Climbing the ladder. To progress in one's career or to move upwards, socially and financially.

Clink. Slang term for prison, derived from the famous gaol, the Clink in SOUTHWARK, destroyed in the Gordon Riots of 1780.

Clio (klī' ō). One of the nine MUSES, the inventress of historical and heroic poetry, the Muse of history. Hence the pun, "Can Clio do more than amuse?"

Addison adopted the name as a pseudonym, and many of his papers in the *Spectator* are signed by one of the four letters in this word, probably the initial letters of where they were written—of Chelsea, LONDON, Islington, Office. *Cp*. NOTARIKON.

Clip-joint. A night club or place of entertainment where patrons are grossly overcharged or cheated, *i.e.* clipped.

Clipper. A fast sailing-ship, first built at Baltimore about 1830; in Smyth's *Sailors Word Book* (1867) described as "formerly applied to the sharp-built raking schooners of America, and latterly to Australian passenger-ships" (*see* CUTTY SARK). The name was applied in the mid-20th century to a transatlantic flying-boat.

Clippie (klip' i). A popular nickname for bus conductresses during and since World War II, since they clipped or punched the tickets.

Cliveden Set. The name given to the right-wing politicians and journalists who gathered for week-end parties in the late 1930s at Cliveden, the country home of Lord and Lady Astor in Buckinghamshire. They were alleged to favour the appeasement of NAZI Germany.

Cloacina (klō a sī' nà). (Lat. *cloaca*, a sewer). Goddess of sewers.

Cloak and Sword Plays. Swashbuckling plays, full of fighting and adventure. The name comes from the comedies of the 17th-century Spanish dramatists, Lope de Vega and Calderón—*Comedias de capa y espada*. With them it signified merely a drama of domestic intrigue and was named from the rank of the chief characters, but in France (and, through French influence, in England) it was applied as above. They are also called **Cloak and dagger plays.** The intrigues, undercover and often melodramatic activities of those involved in espionage, etc., are similarly called **cloak and dagger operations.**

Clock. So church bells were once called (Ger. *Glocke*: Fr. *cloche*: Med. Lat. *cloca*).

The tale about St. Paul's clock striking thirteen is given in Walcott's *Memorials of Westminster*, and refers to John Hatfield, a soldier of William III's reign who died in 1770, aged 102. Accused before a court martial of falling asleep on duty upon Windsor Terrace, he asserted in proof of his innocence that he heard St. Paul's strike thirteen. His statement was confirmed by several witnesses.

To put the clock back. To revert to an earlier practice or way of life; also to put back the hands of a clock especially at the end of DAYLIGHT SAVING.

To put the clock on. To put forward the hands of a clock, particularly at the commencement of a period of DAYLIGHT SAVING.

Clockwork. Like clockwork. Used of any enterprise that runs as planned, without any hitch.

Clog Almanac. A primitive almanac or calendar, originally made of a four-square "clog" or log of wood. The sharp edges were divided by notches into three months each, every week being marked by a bigger notch. The faces contained the saints' days, the festivals, the phases of the moon, and so on, sometimes in Runic characters (*see* RUNE), whence the clog was also called a "Runic Staff".

Clogs to clogs is only three generations is an old Lancashire saying, implying that however a man may prosper and raise himself from poverty, his grandson will be wearing clogs, and back to the condition the family started from.

Clootie. Auld Clootie. OLD NICK (*see* NICK). The Scots call a cloven hoof a *cloot*, so that Auld Clootie is Old Clovenfoot.

Close Rolls. CHANCERY enrolments of royal letters closed with the GREAT SEAL. Close writs date from 1204 but in the 16th century the Close Rolls came to consist only of private deeds, enclosure awards, etc. They ceased in 1903. *Cp.* PATENT ROLLS.

Close Shave. A narrow escape; a figure based on the extremely small margin between a smooth, closely shaven skin and a painful gash.

Closed Shop. *See* SHOP.

Closure. The ending of a HOUSE OF COMMONS debate by a member moving "that the question be now put". The chair is not bound to accept the motion. The procedure was derived from the French *clôture* and first asked by Speaker Brand in 1881 against Parnell and his Irish obstructionists, consequent upon the fa-

mous sitting of February 1881 which lasted from 4 p.m. Monday until 9.30 a.m. on the following Wednesday. *See* FILIBUSTER; GUILLOTINE; KANGAROO.

Cloth, The. Once applied to the customary garb of any calling and similar in usage to the word LIVERY. In the 17th century it became restricted to the CLERGY and clerical office. Thus we say "having respect for the cloth".

Cloth of Gold, Field of. *See* FIELD.

Clotho (Gr. *klotho*, to draw thread from a distaff). One of the three FATES in classic mythology. She presided over birth and drew from her distaff the thread of life. *See* ATROPOS; LACHESIS.

Cloud. A dark spot on the forehead of a horse between the eyes. *Cp.* BLAZE.

A clouded cane. A malacca cane clouded or mottled from age and use. These canes were very popular in the first quarter of the 18th century and earlier.

Cloud-Cuckoo-Land. The *Nephelococcygia* of *The Birds*, by Aristophanes; an imaginary city built in the air by the birds. Hence any impractical Utopian scheme.

Every cloud has a silver lining. There is some redeeming brightness in the darkest prospect; while there is life there is hope.

He is in the clouds. In dreamland; entertaining visionary notions and so having no distinct idea about the matter in question.

He is under a cloud. Under suspicion, in disrepute.

The Battle above the Clouds. A name given to the battle of Lookout Mountain, part of the battle of Chattanooga, fought during the American CIVIL WAR, on 24 November 1863. The Union forces defeated the Confederates and part of the fighting took place in a heavy mist on the mountains, hence the name.

To blow a cloud. *See* BLOW.

Cloven Foot. To show the cloven foot, or **hoof.** *i.e.* to show a knavish intention; a base motive. The allusion is to SATAN, represented with the legs and feet of a goat. However disguised he could never conceal his cloven feet. *See* CLOOTIE.

Clover. He's in clover. In luck, in prosperous circumstances, in a good situation. The allusion is to cattle feeding in fields of clover.

Clown. The clown of circus and PANTOMIME, in his baggy costume, whitened face, grotesque red lips, and odd little tuft of black hair is probably a relic of the DEVIL as he appeared in mediæval miracle plays. He is the descendant of many court fools and jesters. Of all the clowns, Joseph GRIMALDI (1779–1837), and the Swiss "Grock", Adrien Wettach (1880–1959), were outstanding. *See* HARLEQUIN.

Club. In England the club has played an important part in social life. Clubs came into vogue in the reign of Queen Anne as is evidenced by the *Tatler* and *Spectator*. Dr. Johnson's Ivy Lane Club (1749) and the Literary Club (1764), which he founded with Sir Joshua Reynolds, set a new standard in social clubs where likeminded men of culture could meet and converse. For many years clubs met in taverns and COFFEE houses and did not begin to occupy their own premises until the REGENCY. Many more sprang up in the early 19th century, some being solely gaming clubs. The first exclusive modern ladies' club was the Alexandra (1883), to which no man was allowed admittance. Among the principal London clubs (with the dates of their foundation) are the following:

Army and Navy, 1838	Guards, 1813
ATHENÆUM, 1824	Junior Carlton, 1864
Bath, 1894	Lansdowne, 1935
BEEFSTEAK, 1876	National Liberal, 1822
Boodle's, 1762	Reform, 1832
BROOKS'S, 1764	Savage, 1857
Carlton, 1832	Savile, 1868
Cavalry, 1890	Thatched House, 1865
Conservative, 1840	Travellers, 1819
Constitutional, 1883	United Services, 1815
Devonshire, 1875	WHITE'S, 1693
Garrick, 1831	

Among the famous clubs associated with sport are:

M.C.C., 1787	Royal Automobile, 1897
Royal Aero, 1901	Turf, 1868

Clubs of many kinds have long been a common feature of national and provincial life among all classes and range from the serenity of the Athenæum to the less austere atmosphere of the STRIP-TEASE Club. *See also* CORDELIER; JACOBINS;

OTHER CLUB; THE RAG *under* RAG.

Club-bearer, The. In Greek mythology, Periphetes, the robber of Argolis, is so called because he murdered his victims with an iron club.

Club-land. That part of the West End of London centred around PALL MALL where the principal clubs are situated; also the members of such clubs.

Club-law. The law of might or compulsion through fear of chastisement; "might is right"; "do it or get a hiding".

Club men. The bands of rustics, formed in the southern and western counties in 1645 to resist the exactions of both CAVALIERS and ROUNDHEADS, were so called from their cudgels.

Club Parliament, or **the Parliament of Bats,** was held at Northampton in 1426, during the quarrel between the Duke of Gloucester and Cardinal Beaufort. Forbidden to bear arms by the Regent Bedford, the members came armed with clubs or "bats".

Club sandwich. A term for a "three decker" sandwich, usually with different fillings between the layers.

Clue. I have not yet got the clue; to give a clue, *i.e.* a hint. A clue is a ball of thread (O.E. *cleowen*). The only way of finding the way out of the Cretan LABYRINTH was by a skein of thread, which, being followed, led the right way.

I haven't a clue. A colloquial usage meaning "I haven't an inkling", "I haven't the vaguest idea" (of what you are asking or talking about, etc.).

Cluniacs. In 10th century France discipline in the Benedictine abbeys had declined almost completely and wealth and luxury predominated. At Cluny, N.W. of Mâcon a reformed abbey was established in 910 and in due course many old abbeys adopted the rigid rule of the Cluniacs. As with the BENEDICTINES wealth and laxity took over and the next major revival was that of the CISTERCIANS.

Cluricaune. An ELF in Irish folklore. He is of evil disposition and usually appears as a wrinkled old man. He has a knowledge of hidden treasure and is the fairies' shoemaker. Another name for him is LEPRECHAUN.

Clydesdale Horses. *See* SHIRE HORSES.

Clydesiders, The. A loosely attached

group of left-wing M.P.s representing Glasgow and Clydeside constituencies, who enlivened British politics and Parliament from 1922 until the were much diminished in numbers by the 1931 election. Notable among them were John Wheatley, of Housing Act fame, Campbell Stephen, Emanuel Shinwell, and best known of all James Maxton who became chairman of the Independent LABOUR Party. They acted as a GINGER GROUP on the Labour Party and were notable champions of the poor and unemployed.

Clym of the Clough. A noted archer and outlaw, who, with Adam Bell and WILLIAM OF CLOUDESLEY, forms the subject of a ballad in PERCY'S RELIQUES. The three became as famous in the north of England as ROBIN HOOD and LITTLE JOHN in the midland counties. They were presumed to have lived before Robin Hood and abode in Englewood Forest, near Carlisle. Clym of the Clough means Clement of the Cliff. He is mentioned in Ben Jonson's *Alchemist* (I, ii, 46).

Clytemnestra. In Greek legend, the faithless wife of AGAMEMNON. She was a daughter of Tyndarus and LEDA. *See also* ELECTRA.

Clytie. In classical mythology an ocean NYMPH, in love with APOLLO. She was deserted by him and changed into the heliotrope or sunflower, which, traditionally, still turns to the sun, following him through his daily course.

Cnidian Venus, The. The exquisite statue of VENUS by Praxiteles, formerly in her temple at Cnidus. It is known through the antique reproduction now in the VATICAN.

Coach. A slow coach. A dullard, an unprogressive person.

To drive a coach and four through an Act of Parliament. To find a way of flagrantly ignoring or evading its provisions wholesale, thereby reducing it to an absurdity. In effect, to make it useless. The term has been extended into more general usage.

Coade Stone. An artificial stone of great durability and firmness of outline, much used from the 1770s until the 1830s for statues and ornamentations for build-

ings (CARYATIDS, keystone masks, friezes, vases, etc.). Made from a kind of frost-resistant terra-cotta, and presumably invented by the sculptor John Bacon (1740–1799), it was produced in Mrs. Eleanor Coade's factory at Lambeth (later the firm of Coade and Sealy).

Coal. To blow the coals. To fan dissensions, to excite smouldering animosity into open hostility, as dull coals are blown into a blaze with a pair of bellows.

To call, or **haul over the coals.** To bring to task for shortcomings; to scold. At one time the Jews were "bled" whenever the kings or barons wanted money. One very common torture, if they resisted, was to haul them over the coals of a slow fire, to give them a "roasting".

To carry coals. To be put upon. "Gregory, o'my word, we'll not carry coals"—*i.e.* submit to be "put upon" (*Romeo and Juliet*, I, i). So in *Every Man out of his Humour*, "Here comes one that will carry coals, ergo, will hold my dog." The allusion is to the dirty, laborious occupation of charcoal carriers.

To carry coals to Newcastle. To do what is superfluous; to take something where it is already plentiful. The French say, "*Porter de l'eau à la rivière*" (to carry water to the river). ALCINOO POMA DARE is a Latin equivalent.

To heap coals of fire on one's head. To melt down one's animosity by deeds of kindness: to repay bad treatment with good.

Coal brandy. Burnt brandy. The old way to set brandy on fire was to drop in it a live or red-hot piece of charcoal.

Coaling, in theatrical slang, means telling phrases and speeches, as, "My part is full of *coaling lines*." Possibly from COLE (money), such a part being profitable.

Coalition Government. One formed of rival parties, usually in times of crisis, when party differences are set aside. Examples are those of Fox and North in 1783; of WHIGS and PEELITES under Aberdeen, 1852–1855; of CONSERVATIVES and LIBERAL-UNIONISTS under Salisbury 1895–1902; of LIBERALS, UNIONISTS, and LABOUR under Asquith 1915–1916 (reformed under Lloyd

George 1916–1922); Macdonald's NA-
TIONAL GOVERNMENT, 1931–1935; and
Winston Churchill's Coalition Govern-
ment, 1940–1945.

Coast. The coast is clear. There is no
likelihood of interference. It was originally a smuggling term, implying that no
coastguards were about.

Coastal Eastern. The form of American English which has much the same
relation to other variants of that language as Standard Received English has
to variants in England. Both developed
in those districts where academic and
cultural influences were strongest.

Coasting lead. A sounding lead used in
shallow water.

Coasting waiter. An officer of Customs in the Port of London, whose duty
it was to visit and make a return of coasting vessels which (from the nature of
their cargo) were not required to report
or make entry at the Custom House, but
which were liable to payment of certain
small dues. The coasting waiter collected these, and searched the cargo for
contraband. Like TIDE WAITERS, they
were abolished in the latter part of the
19th century and their duties taken over
by the examining officer.

Coat. Coat Card. *See* COURT CARDS.

**Cut your coat according to your
cloth.** Curtail your expenses to the
amount of your income; live within your
means. *Si non possis quod velis, velis id
quod ossis.*

To baste someone's coat. To beat
someone.

To trail one's coat. To try deliberately
to pick a quarrel. From an old Irish custom of trailing one's coat along the
ground as a sign that the owner was prepared to fight anyone daring to tread on
his coat-tails.

To wear the King's coat. To be a soldier.

Turning one's coat for luck. It was an
ancient superstition that this was a
charm against evil spirits. *See* TURN-
COAT.

Coat of Arms. Originally a linen or
silken surcoat worn by KNIGHTS to protect their armour from the sun's heat,
dirt, etc., with their arms embroidered
upon it. The use of coats of arms prob-

ably began in the 12th century. In HER-
ALDRY the coat of arms comprises
shield, helmet, crest, mantling and supporters. The shield is the central part.

Cob. A short-legged, stout variety of
horse, rather larger than a pony, from
thirteen to nearly fifteen hands high.
(*See* HAND.) The word means big,
stout. It also meant a tuft or head (from
cop), hence eminent, large, powerful.
The *cob of the county* is the great boss
thereof. A *rich cob* is a plutocrat. Hence
also a male is a *cobswan*.

Cobalt. From the Ger. *kobold*, a GNOME,
the demon of the mines. This metal,
from which a deep blue pigment is
made, was so called by miners partly because it was thought to be useless and
partly because the arsenic and sulphur,
with which it was found in combination,
had bad effects on their health and on
the silver ores. Its presence was therefore attributed to the mine demon.

Cobb and Co. The mail and passenger
coach company whose fame is legendary
in Australia. Founded by Freeman
Cobb and three other Americans in
1854, during the Ballarat gold rush,
they provided reliable and comfortable
transport between Melbourne and
Bendigo in American-built coaches.
Tales of the exploits of Cobb and Co.'s
crack drivers are as exciting as any told
of WELLS FARGO.

Cobber (Austr.). A friend or companion;
possibly from the old Suffolk *to cob*, to
form a friendship.

Cobbler. A drink made of sherry, sugar,
lemon and ice. *See* COBBLER'S PUNCH.

Also the name of a deep fruit pie with
no bottom crust and a top crust resembling scone or plain cake dough. The
name is possibly suggested by the resemblance of the uneven surface of the
top crust to cobble stones.

A cobbler should stick to his last. Let
no one presume to interfere in matters
of which he is ignorant.

Ne supra crepidam sutor judicaret
PLINY, XXV, X, 85.

There is the story of a cobbler who
detected a fault in a shoe-latchet in a
painting by APELLES. The artist rectified
the fault. The cobbler then ventured to
criticize the legs but Apelles answered,

"Keep to your trade—you understand about shoes, but not about anatomy."

Cobbler's punch. Gin and water, with a little treacle and vinegar.

Cobbler's toast. Schoolboy's bread and butter, toasted on the dry side and eaten hot.

Cobham's Plot. *See* MAIN PLOT.

Coburg. A corded or ribbed cotton cloth made in Coburg (Saxony), or an imitation thereof. Chiefly used for ladies' dresses.

Also a type of round loaf, said to have been named in honour of the Prince Consort, who was of the House of Saxe-Coburg-Gotha.

Cobweb. To blow away the cobwebs. To clear one's mind by taking fresh air; to freshen oneself up.

Cock (noun). In classical mythology the cock was dedicated to APOLLO because it gives notice of the rising sun. It was also dedicated to MERCURY, because it summons men to business by its crowing; and to ÆSCULAPIUS, because "early to bed and early to rise makes a man healthy".

Mohammedan legend says that the Prophet found in the first HEAVEN a cock of such enormous size that its crest touched the second heaven. The crowing of this celestial bird arouses every living creature except man. When this cock ceases to crow, the Day of JUDGMENT will be at hand.

Peter Le Neve (1661–1729), English antiquary, affirms that a cock was the warlike ensign of the GOTHS and therefore used in GOTHIC churches for ornament.

The weathercock is a very old symbol of vigilance. As the cock heralds the coming of day, so does the weathercock tell the wise man what the weather will likely be.

A cock and bull story. A long highly coloured or incredible story, a CANARD. It possibly derives from old fables in which cocks and bulls and other animals conversed.

The *Cock and Bull* inn sign is found in the 17th century and both *Cock* and *Bull* as separate signs were always popular. There is a story at Stony Stratford, Buckinghamshire that in the coaching days the London coach changed horses at the Bull Inn and the Birmingham coach at the Cock. From the exchange of jests and stories between the waiting passengers of both coaches the "Cock and Bull" story is said to have originated.

The French equivalents are *faire un coq à l'âne* and *un conte de ma mère l'oie* (a mother goose tale). In Scotland a satire or rambling story was a *cockalayne* from the Fr. *coq à l'âne*.

A cock of hay, or **haycock.** A small heap of hay thrown up temporarily (Ger. dialect *kocke*, a heap of hay; Norw. *kok*, a heap).

By cock and pie. We meet with *cock's bones, cock's wounds, cock's mother, cock's body, cock's passion,* etc., where there is no doubt that the word is a minced oath, and stands for God. The *pie* is the table or rule in the old Catholic office, showing how to find out the service for each day (from Med. Lat. *pica*).

> By cock and pie, sir, you shall not away to-night.
> SHAKESPEARE: *Henry IV, Pt. II*, V, i.

Cock and Bottle, Cock and Pie. Both are PUBLIC HOUSE SIGNS. The latter is probably "The Cock and Magpie" and the former probably means that draught and bottled beer are sold on the premises (here *cock* would mean the tap).

Cock of the North. George, fifth Duke of Gordon (1770–1836), who raised the Gordon Highlanders in 1795, is so called on a monument erected to his honour at Fochabers in Morayshire.

The brambling, or mountain finch, is also known by this name.

Cock of the walk. The dominant bully or master spirit. The place where barndoor fowls are fed is the *walk*, and if there is more than one cock, they will fight for the supremacy of this domain.

Every cock crows on its own dunghill, or **Ilka cock crows on its ain midden.** It is easy to brag of your deeds in your own castle when safe from danger and not likely to be put to proof.

Nourish a cock, but offer it not in a sacrifice. This is the eighteenth Symbolic Saying in the *Protreptics* of Iamblichus. The cock was sacred to MINERVA, and also to the SUN and MOON, and it would be impious to offer a sacrilegious offering to the gods. What is already consecrated to God cannot be employed in sacrifice.

The red cock will crow in his house.
His house will be set on fire.

> "We'll see if the red cock craw not in his bonnie barnyard ae morning." ... "What does she mean?" said Mannering ... "Fire-raising", answered the ... dominie
> SCOTT: *Guy Mannering*, ch. iii.

To cry cock. To claim the victory; to assert oneself to be the superior. To assert oneself as COCK OF THE WALK.

Cock-crow. The Hebrews divided the night into four watches: (1) The "beginning of the watches" or "even" (*Lam*. ii, 10); (2) the "middle WATCH" or "midnight" (*Judges* vii, 19); (3) the "cock-crowing"; (4) The "morning watch" or "dawning" (*Exod*. xiv, 24).

The Romans divided the day into sixteen parts, each one hour and a half, beginning at midnight. The third of these divisions (3 a.m.) they called *gallicinium*, the time when cocks begin to crow; the next was *conticinium*, when they ceased to crow; and the fifth was *diluculum*, dawn.

If the Romans sounded the hour on a trumpet three times it would explain the diversity of the Gospels: "Before the cock crow" (*John* xiii, 38; *Luke* xxii, 34; *Matt*. xxvi, 34) and "Before the cock crow twice" (*Mark* xiv, 30)—that is, before the trumpet has finished sounding.

Apparitions vanish at cock-crow. This is a Christian superstition, the cock being the watch-bird placed on church spires, and therefore sacred.

> The morning cock crew loud,
> And at the sound it [the Ghost] shrunk in haste away,
> And vanish'd from our sight.
> SHAKESPEARE: *Hamlet*, I, ii.

Cock-eye. A squint. **Cock-eyed,** having a squint; cross-eyed. It may mean that such an eye has to be *cocked*, as the trigger of a gun is cocked, before it can do its work effectively; or it may be from the verb *to cock* in the sense of "turning up" as in *to cock the nose*. *Cock-eyed* also means not straight, out of true, out of line, as well as nonsensical.

Cockfighting was a favourite sport with both Greeks and Romans and was introduced into Britain by the Romans.

It was made illegal in Britain in 1849.
See also BATTLE ROYAL; WELSH MAIN.

That beats cockfighting. That is most improbable and extraordinary. The allusion is to the extravagant tales told of fighting cocks.

To live like fighting cocks. To live in luxury. Fighting cocks were highly fed to increase their mettle and powers of endurance.

Cock-horse. To ride a cock-horse. A cock-horse is really a HOBBY-HORSE, but the phrase means to sit astride a person's foot or knee while he jigs it up and down.

A horse kept ready at the bottom of a steep hill to help a coach and its team to the top, was called a *cock-horse*. It was hitched to the front of the team.

Cock Lane Ghost. A tale of terror without truth; an imaginary tale of horrors. In Cock Lane, Smithfield (1762), certain knockings were heard, which Mr. Parsons, the owner, declared proceeded from the ghost of Fanny Kent, who died suddenly. Parsons, with the hope of blackmail, wished people to suppose that she had been murdered by her husband. All London was agog with the story. Royalty and the nobility made up parties to go to Cock Lane to hear the ghost. Dr. Johnson and others of learning and repute investigated the alleged phenomena. Eventually it was found that the knockings were made by Parson's eleven-year-old daughter rapping on a board which she took into her bed. Parsons was condemned to the pillory. *Cp*. STOCKWELL GHOST.

Cockpit of Europe. Belgium is so called because it has so frequently been the battleground of Europe.

Cockshut, or **Cockshut time.** Twilight; the time when the *cockshut* (a large net to catch woodcocks) was spread. The net was so named from being used in a glade through which the woodcocks might *shoot* or dart.

Cockshy. A free fling or "shy" at something. The allusion is to the once popular SHROVE TUESDAY sport of shying or casting stones or sticks at cocks.

The phrase was popular in military circles in World War II, implying an ill-considered, ill-prepared attempt at something.

Cock sure. As sure as a cock, brazenly self-confident; meaning either "with all the assurance of a game-cock", or "as sure as the cock is to crow in the morning". Shakespeare uses it in the sense of "sure as the cock of a fire-lock".

> We steal as in a castle, cock-sure,
> *Henry IV, Pt. I*, II, i.

The phrase "sure as a gun" seems to favour the latter explanation.

Cock (verb). In the following phrases, all of which connote assertiveness, obtrusiveness, or aggressiveness in some degree, the allusion is to game-cocks, whose strutting about, swaggering, and ostentatious pugnacity is proverbial.

To cock the ears. To prick up the ears, or turn them as a horse does when he listens to a strange sound.

To cock the nose, or **cock up the nose.** To turn up the nose in contempt. *See* TO COCK YOUR EYE.

To cock up your head, foot, etc. To lift up or turn up your head or foot.

To cock your eye. To shut one eye and look with the other in a somewhat cheeky fashion; to glance at questioningly. *Cp.* COCK-EYE.

To cock your hat. To set your hat on one side of the head; to look knowing and pert.

To cock a snook. To make a long nose; to put the thumb to the nose and spread wide the fingers. A gesture of contempt; also known as Anne's fan or Queen Anne's fan.

Cock-a-hoop. Jubilant; exultant; as a cock crowing boastfully; but the saying may come from the fact that when the spigot or *cock* is removed from the beer barrel and laid on a hoop of the barrel, the beer flows for jollity and high spirits.

Cocked hat. A hat with an upturned brim like that of a BISHOP, DEAN, etc.: also applied to the CHAPEAU BRAS. It now denotes the brimless triangular hat, pointed at the back and front, worn as part of full-dress by diplomats and naval and army officers, the *chapeau à cornes. Cocked* here means turned up.

Knocked into a cocked hat. To beat someone in a contest of skill, etc., by a wide margin. In the game of ninepins,

three pins were set up in the form of a triangle and when all the pins except these three were knocked down, the set was said to be "knocked into a cocked hat". From the idea of a hat being knocked out of shape.

Cockade (Fr. *cocarde*, a plume, rosette, or bunch of ribbons). A badge worn on the head-dress of menservants of Royalty, naval and military officers, diplomatists, lord-lieutenants, high sheriffs, etc. The English cockade is black and circular in shape with a projecting fan at the top, except for naval officers, for whom the shape is oval without the fan. This form was introduced from Hanover by George I; under Charles I the cockade was scarlet but Charles II changed it to white. Thus the white cockade became the badge of the House of Stuart; William III (as Prince of Orange) adopted an orange cockade. *See* DOG-VANE.

To mount the cockade. To become a soldier.

Cockaigne, Land of (kok ān). An imaginary land of idleness and luxury, famous in mediæval story. Ellis in his *Specimens of Early English Poets* gives an early translation of a 13th-century French poem called *The Land of Cockaign* in which "the houses were made of barley sugar cakes, the streets were paved with pastry, and the shops supplied goods for nothing".

LONDON has been so called, with punning reference to COCKNEY. Boileau applies the name to Paris.

The name may well mean the "land of cakes", ultimately from Lat. *coquere*, to cook. Scotland is called the "land of cakes" (*see under* CAKE).

Cockatoo. Old Australian slang for a convict serving his sentence on Cockatoo Island, Sydney, which was first used for convicts in 1839. Also used for small farmers in Australia who were "just picking up the grains of a livelihood like cockatoos do maize".

Cockatrice. A fabulous and heraldic monster with the wings of a fowl, tail of a DRAGON, and head of a cock; the same as BASILISK. Isaiah says, "The weaned child shall put his hand on the cockatrice' den" (xi, 8), to signify that the most obnoxious animal shall not hurt the most feeble of God's creatures.

Figuratively, it means an insidious, treacherous person bent on mischief.

Cocker. According to Cocker. All right according to Cocker. According to established rules, according to what is correct. Edward Cocker (1631–1675) published his *Arithmetick* which ran through over a hundred editions.

Cockle. Cockle hat. A pilgrim's hat. Pilgrims used to wear cockle (scallop) shells on their hats, the symbol of St. JAMES of COMPOSTELA in Spain. This supposed shrine of James, the son of Zebedee, was especially favoured by English pilgrims. The polished side of the shell was scratched with some crude drawing of the Virgin, the Crucifixion, or some other object related to the pilgrimage. Being blessed by the priest, the shells were considered as amulets against spiritual foes, and might be used as drinking vessels.

Cockle shell. A small boat or frail craft. *See also* COCKLE HAT.

To try cockles. To be hanged; from the gurgling noises made in strangulation.

To warm the cockles of one's heart. Said of good wine and anything which particularly warms and gratifies one's feelings (Lat. *cochleæ cordis*, the ventricles of the heart).

Cockney. This is the M.E. *cokeney*, meaning "a cock's egg" (-ey = O.E. *æg*, an egg), applied to the small malformed egg occasionally laid by young hens; hence applied to a foolish or spoilt child, or a simpleton.

The word then came to be applied by country folk, the majority of the population, to townsfolk generally for their reputed ignorance of country life, customs and habits. Its restriction to Londoners, particularly those born within the sound of the bells of St. Mary-le-Bow, dates from the 17th century. It is also used to denote London peculiarities of speech. *See* BOW BELLS: RHYMING SLANG.

As Frenchmen love to be bold, Flemings to be drunk, Welchmen be called Britons, and Irish to be costermongers; so cockneys, especially she cockneys, love not aqua-vitae when 'tis good for them.
DEKKER and WEBSTER: *Westward Hoe*,

II, ii (1607).

SHAKESPEARE uses the word for a squeamish woman.

Cry to it, nuncle, as the cockney did to the eels, when she put them i' the paste alive.
King Lear, II, iv.

The Cockney School. A nickname given by Lockhart to a group of writers including Leigh Hunt, Hazlitt, Shelley, and Keats. It was used derogatorily on account of the kind of rhymes they used in their verse, which smacked too much of everyday life instead of the classic purity preferred by the critics.

Cocktail. An aperitif, or short drink taken before a meal, usually concocted of spirits, bitters, fruit-juice or other flavourings, etc. There are many varieties of the American appetizer. The origin of the name is uncertain but suggestions vary from "a tail that cocks up" and "the tail of a cock" to the name of an Aztec princess Xochitl, who is supposed to have given a drink to the king with romantic results. *Coquetel*, a mixed drink from the wine-growing district of the Gironde, has also been suggested.

The name also applies to a horse with a docked tail which "cocks up"; and to a half-bred horse, from the custom of docking stage-coach horses and hunters.

Coconut. Milk in the coconut. *See* MILK.

Cocqcigrues. At the coming of the Cocqcigrues. (kok' sē groo). (More correctly *coquecigrues*.) Imaginary animals that have become labels for an idle story. The phrase *à la venue des cocquecigrues* used by Rabelais (*Gargantua*, Ch. V) means "NEVER".

Cocytus (ko si' tŭs). One of the five rivers of HELL, which flows into the ACHERON. The word means the "river of lamentation". The unburied were doomed to wander about its banks for 100 years. *See* CHARON; STYX.

Cod. You can't cod me. You can't take me in, or deceive me.

Codille (kŏdil'). Triumph. In the game of OMBRE, when one of the two opponents of ombre has more tricks than ombre, he is said to have won *codille* and takes all the stakes for which ombre played.

Codswallop. A lot, or **a load of cods-**

wallop. Simply nonsense or rubbish; said of something silly, far-fetched or fanciful when advanced as serious information or explanation. In 1875 Hiram Codd patented a mineral water bottle with a marble stopper. *Wallop* here is a slang term for beer. Thus *Codd's wallop* is said to have become a disparaging term among beer drinkers for mineral waters and weak drinks and in due course the term acquired a more general application.

Coehorn, or **Coehoorn.** A small mortar named after Baron von Coehoorn of Holland (1641–1704), who was called the Dutch Vauban, after Louis XIV's famous siege engineer and fortifications expert, Sebastien Le Prestre de Vauban (1633–1707).

Coelacanth (see'. lĕkanth). *See* FOUR-LEGS, OLD.

Cœnobites, or **Cenobites** (sen' ō bīts) (Gr. *koinos bios*). Monks who live in common, in contradistinction to hermits or anchorites.

Cœur de Lion (kĕr de lē' on). Richard I of England (1157, 1189–1199); called the lionhearted for his valour in the Third CRUSADE.

Coffee. From the Turkish form *kahveh* of the Arabic *qahwah*, the drink. The first coffee-house in England opened at Oxford in 1650 and the first in London about 1652. They soon became centres for social and political gossip and meeting places for the wits and literary men of the day.

Coffee housing. Talking and gossiping, especially when waiting for something to happen or when there is work to be done. The expression was used in the hunting field certainly from the 1860s when riders were waiting for the hounds to draw a fox from a covert and gossiping at the same time.

Pousse café. Liqueur served after coffee. Also a drink of various liqueurs in layers in a glass.

Coffin. A raised pie crust, like the lid of a basket (Gr. *kophinos*, a basket). Hence Shakespeare speaks of a "custard-coffin" (*Taming of the Shrew*, IV, iii) meaning a custard under a crust.

Coffin nail. A cigarette. An expression in use long before the association be-

tween cigarette smoking and lung cancer but probably connected with the risk to health.

To drive a nail into one's coffin. To do anything that would tend to hasten one's death, or finish one off, usually by annoyance and frustration.

Coggeshall (kog' shăl). **A Coggeshall job.** Something foolish. It is said that the Coggeshall (Essex) folk wanted to divert the current of a stream, and so fixed hurdles in its bed. Another tale is that a mad dog bit a wheelbarrow, and the people, fearing the wheelbarrow's madness, chained it up in a shed. *Cp.* GOTHAM.

Cogito, ergo sum. The axiom formulated by Descartes (1596–1650) as the starting point of his philosophic system: it means, "I think, therefore I am." He provisionally doubted everything until he concluded that "I think" presupposed the existence of "I". *See* PETITIO PRINCIPII.

Cognoscente (Latinized form of It. *conoscente* from *cognoscere*, to know). One with a critical, expert and thorough knowledge of a subject, especially in literature, music, works of art, etc. The plural form *cognoscenti* is the more widely used.

Coif. Serjeants of the Coif. SERJEANTS-AT-LAW were so called from the close-fitting white lawn or silk cap once worn as a symbol of their rank (O.Fr. *coife*, a cap).

Coinage (Fr. *coin*, corner). Derived from the practice in the STANNARY towns of Devon and Cornwall of collecting a "coinage" duty. In the towns appointed for the purpose the blocks of tin were weighed by the assay-master, then a piece called a *coign* was struck from the corner of each block. This was assayed for quality to fix the dues before stamping the block.

Paid in his own coin. TIT FOR TAT.

To coin a phrase. To invent a phrase. If it is a telling phrase it may *gain currency, i.e.* become popular and widespread.

To coin money. To make money with rapidity and ease.

Coke. Slang for cocaine.

Colbronde, or **Colbrand.** The Danish

giant slain by Guy of Warwick. By his death the land was delivered from Danish tribute.

Colcannon (kŏl kăn' ŏn). Potatoes and cabbage pounded together and then fried in butter (Irish). "Col" is cole or cale, *i.e.* cabbage. *Cp.* BUBBLE AND SQUEAK.

Colcannon Night. HALLOWEEN in parts of N.E. Canada, when it is traditional to eat this dish.

Cold. Cold as Charity. *See* CHARITY.

Cold blood. Done in cold blood (Fr. *sang froid*). Not in the heat of temper; deliberately, and with forethought. The allusion is to the old notion that the temperature of the blood ruled the temper.

Cold-blooded animals. As a rule, all invertebrates, and all fishes and reptiles, the temperature of their blood being about equal to the medium in which they live.

Cold-blooded people. Those not easily excited. Those with little feeling.

Cold chisel. A steel chisel made in one piece and so tempered that it will cut cold metal when struck with a hammer.

Cold comfort. Comfort that is found chilling by the receiver, discouraging, little or no consolation.

Cold feet, To have or **to get.** To be really discouraged, to be afraid, or in a state of fear.

Cold fish, He is a. He has no warm feelings, he is unemotional and impassive.

Cold shoulder. To show, or **to give one the cold shoulder.** To assume a distant manner, to indicate that you wish to CUT someone.

Cold steel. The persuasion of cold steel. Persuasion enforced at the point of the sword or bayonet.

Cold war. The term applied to the state of tension between states which behave with marked distrust and hostility towards each other without recourse to actual fighting.

Cold-water ordeal. An ancient method of testing guilt or innocence. The accused, being tied under the arms, was thrown into a river. If he sank, he was held guiltless and drawn up by the cord; if he floated, the water rejected him because of his guilt.

Cold water. To pour cold water on. To discourage. To damp the fires of enthusiasm.

Cold Comfort Farm. As a phrase, it is used to imply that a particular domicile is untidy and comfortless. It is from a humorous book of this title by Stella Gibbons (1932).

Coldbrand. *See* COLBRONDE.

Coldstream Guards. One of the five regiments of Foot Guards. General Monk's Regiment which crossed the border at Coldstream in Berwickshire to effect the RESTORATION of Charles II in 1660. It became the 2nd Regiment of Footguards in 1661 and in 1670 was officially called the Coldstream Guards.

Cole. An old canting term for money. *Cp.* COALING.

Cole, King. A legendary British king, described in the nursery rhyme as "a merry old soul" fond of his pipe, fond of his glass, and fond of his fiddlers three. Robert of Gloucester says he was father of St. HELENA (and consequently grandfather of the Emperor Constantine). Colchester was said to have been named after him.

Colettines. *See* FRANCISCANS.

Coliseum. *See* COLOSSEUM.

Collar. Against the collar. Somewhat fatiguing. When a horse travels uphill the collar distresses his neck, so foot travellers often find the last mile or so "against the collar", or distressing.

Out of collar. Out of work, out of a place.

Collar-day. A day on which KNIGHTS of the different orders when present at LEVEES or other Court functions wear all their insignia and decorations, including the collar.

In the late 18th century it was a slang term for execution day.

Collar of S's. A decoration restricted to the Lord Chief Justice, the Lord Mayor of London, the Kings of Arms, the HERALDS, the SERJEANTS-AT-ARMS, and the Serjeant Trumpeter. It is composed of a series of golden S's joined together, and was originally the badge of the adherents of the House of Lancaster.

To collar. To seize (a person) by the collar; to steal; to appropriate without leave; to acquire (of possessions).

To collar the bowling. In CRICKET, to hit the bowling all over the field so that it becomes easier to score, through the bowlers losing their length.

To collar the cole. To steal the money. *See* COLE.

To get hot under the collar. To become indignant, angry or irritated.

To slip the collar. To escape from restraint; to draw back from a task begun.

To work up to the collar. To work TOOTH AND NAIL; not to shirk the work in hand. A horse that lets his collar lie loose on his neck without bearing on it does not draw the vehicle at all, but leaves another to do the real work.

Dog-collar. *See under* DOG.

Spit and rub collar. A jocular term for the "celluloid" collar worn by clerics, which does not need laundering but can be cleaned by rubbing with a damp cloth.

White collar workers. *See* WHITE.

College. From Lat. *collegium*, a colleague; hence a body of colleagues with common duties and privileges, etc. In English the word has a wide range, as College of Surgeons, Heralds' College, College of Justice, College of Preceptors. It is most commonly used for a separate foundation of teachers and scholars within a university and for a wide range of educational institutions, including many schools.

In old slang a prison was known as a college, and the prisoners as *collegiates*. NEWGATE was "New College" and *to take one's final degree at New College* was to be hanged. The King's Bench Prison was "King's College" and so on.

College pudding. A small, sweet, individual-sized pudding. The name may be an abbreviation of New College Pudding.

Colliberts. A sort of GYPSY race similar to the CAQOTS and CAQUEUX, living in boats, chiefly on the rivers of Poitou. In feudal times a collibert was a partly free serf but still bound to certain services (Lat. *collibertus*, a fellow freedman).

Collins. A word sometimes applied to the "thank you letter" one writes after staying at another person's house. In *Pride and Prejudice* Mr. Collins appears as a bore and a snob of the first water; after a protracted and unwanted visit at the Bennets' his parting words are: "Depend upon it, you will speedily receive from me a letter of thanks for this, as for every mark of your regard during my stay in Hertfordshire" (ch. xxi).

Tom Collins. *See* TOM.

Colly. An old popular name for a blackbird. *Colly* is the black grime of coal (A.S. *Col*, coal). The traditional song, "The Twelve Days of Christmas", has:

> The Fourth day of Christmas my true love sent to me,
> Four colly birds, Three French hens, Two turtle doves,
> And a partridge in a pear tree.

Cologne (ko lōn'). **The Three Kings of Cologne.** The three Wise Men of the East, the MAGI, whose bones, according to mediæval legend, were deposited in Cologne Cathedral.

Eau de Cologne. *See* EAU DE COLOGNE.

Colonial Goose. A roast leg of mutton which has been boned and the cavity filled with a stuffing of onions, breadcrumbs and savoury herbs. A recipe intended to vary the monotony of too frequently recurring mutton on Australian sheep stations.

Colophon. Originally, as the name implies, the *tail-piece* at the end of a book giving the printer's name, the date and place of printing, etc., sometimes with laudatory remarks designed to promote sales. It survives in the brief information usually given on the front or back of the title-page. The term is now loosely applied to a printer's or publisher's house device.

Colophon, an Ionian city, was famed for its horsemen who were always reputed to turn the tide of battle by their last charge, hence this name for the final part of the book. **To add a colophon** means "to supply the finishing stroke".

Coloquintida, St. (col ō kwin' ti dà). Charles I was so called by the LEVELLERS, to whom he was as bitter as gall or coloquintida (colocynth), the bitter-apple.

Colorado (U.S.A.). The river (and hence the State) was so named by the Spanish explorers from its *coloured* (*i.e.* reddish) appearance.

Colosseum (kol o sē' ùm). The great Flavian amphitheatre of ancient ROME, said

to be named from the colossal statue of
NERO that stood close by in the Via Sacra. It was begun by Vespasian in A.D.
72, and for 400 years was the scene of
gladiatorial contests. The name has
since been applied to other amphitheatres and places of amusement. *Cp.*
PALLADIUM.

Colossus, or **Colossos** (ko los' ùs) (Lat.
and Gr. for a giant statue). The bronze
colossus of Rhodes, completed by
Chares about 280 B.C., was a representation of the sun-god HELIOS, and commemorated the successful defence of
Rhodes (305–304 B.C.) against Demetrius Poliorcetes. It was one of the Seven WONDERS of the World and probably
stood some 100 ft. high. It was destroyed by an earthquake in 224 B.C.
The story that it was built striding
across the harbour and that ships could
pass between its legs is of 16th-century
origin and is not found in Strabo or Pliny's descriptions,

> He doth bestride the narrow world
> Like a Colossus.
> SHAKESPEARE: *Julius Cæsar*, I, ii.

**Colour. His coward lips did from their
colour fly.** (Shakespeare: *Julius Cæsar*, I, ii). He was unable to speak. As
cowards run away from their regimental
colour, so Cæsar's lips, when he was ill,
ran away from their colour and turned
pale.

**I should like to see the colour of
your money.** I should like proof that
you have any; I should like to be paid.

Off colour. Not up to the mark; run
down; seedy. In the U.S.A. a risqué
joke is called *off colour*.

To change colour. To blush; especially to look awkward and perplexed
when found out in some deceit or meanness.

To colour up. To turn red in the face;
to blush.

To give colour, or **some plausible
colour to the matter.** To render it
more plausible; to give it a more specious appearance.

To put a false colour on a matter. To
misinterpret it, or put a false construction on it.

Under colour of. Under pretence of;
under the alleged authority of.

Colours. Accidental colours. Those
colours seen on a white ground after
looking for some time at a bright object
such as the sun. The accidental colour
of red is bluish green, of orange dark
blue, of violet yellow, and the converse.

Complementary colours. Colours
which in combination, produce white
light.

Fundamental colours. The seven
colours of the spectrum: violet, indigo,
blue, green, yellow, orange, and red.

Primary, or **simple colours.** Colours
which cannot be made by mixing other
colours. Usually red, yellow, and blue
(violet is sometimes substituted for
blue).

Secondary colours. Those which result from the mixture of two or more
PRIMARY COLOURS, such as orange,
green, and purple.

Regimental colours. The flags peculiar to regiments, carried into battle until 1881, on which they are entitled to
embroider their battle honours, by permission of the sovereign. The Royal
Regiment of Artillery has no colours,
regarding the capture of its guns as the
same disgrace as having one's colours
captured. The regimental colours of NA-
POLEON's Army were the famous eagle
standards, copied from the eagles of the
Roman legions. The capture of a Napoleonic eagle was such an unusual feat
that regiments which did so (such as the
Scots Greys) usually incorporated the
eagle into their regimental device. *See*
QUEEN'S COLOUR.

Colours.

To come off with flying colours. To
be completely triumphant, to win
"hands down". The allusion is to a victorious fleet sailing into port with their
flags still flying at the mastheads.

To come out in one's true colours.
To reveal one's proper character, divested of all that is meretricious.

**To describe (a matter) in very black
colours.** To see it with a jaundiced eye,
and describe it accordingly; to describe
it under the bias of strong prejudice.

To desert one's colours. To become a
TURNCOAT; to turn tail. The allusion is
to the military flag.

To get one's colours. To be rewarded

for prowess in sport by the privilege of wearing school, college, or university colours on the appropriate garment, blazer, etc. *See* TO BE CAPPED, *under* CAP; FLANNELS.

To paint in bright, or **lovely colours.** To see or describe things in COULEUR DE ROSE.

To sail under false colours. To try to attain your object by appearing to be other than you are, to act hypocritically. The allusion is to the practice of pirate ships approaching their unsuspecting victim with false colours at the mast.

To see things in their true colours. To see them as they really are.

With colours nailed to the mast. Holding out to the bitter end. Colours so fixed cannot be lowered in sign of defeat or submission.

Colours IN SYMBOLISM, ECCLESIASTICAL USE, etc.

Black:
In blazonry, sable, signifying prudence, wisdom and constancy; it is engraved by perpendicular and horizontal lines crossing each other at right angles.
In art, signifying evil, falsehood, and error.
In Church decoration it was used for GOOD FRIDAY.
As a mortuary colour, signifying grief, despair, death. (In the Catholic Church violet may be substituted for black.)
In metals it is represented by lead.
In precious stones it is represented by the DIAMOND.
In planets it stands for SATURN.

Blue:
Hope, love of divine works; (in dresses) divine contemplation, piety, sincerity.
In blazonry, azure, signifying chastity, loyalty, fidelity, it is engraved by horizontal lines.
In art (as an angel's robe) it signifies fidelity and faith; (as the robe of the Virgin Mary) modesty and (in the Catholic Church) humility and expiation.
In Church decoration, blue and green were used in differently for ordinary Sundays in the pre Reformation Church.
As a mortuary colour it signifies eternity (applied to Deity), immortality (applied to man).
In metals it is represented by tin.
In precious stones it is represented by sapphire.
In planets it stands for JUPITER.

Pale Blue:

Peace, Christian prudence, love of good works, a serene conscience.

Green:
Faith, gladness, immortality, the resurrection of the just; (in dresses) the gladness of the faithful.
In blazonry, vert, signifying love, joy, abundance; it is engraved by diagonal lines from left to right.
In art, signifying hope, joy, youth, spirit (among the Greeks and Moors it signifies victory).
In Church decoration it signifies God's bounty, mirth, gladness, the resurrection; used for week days and Sundays after TRINITY.
In metals it is represented by COPPER.
In precious stones it is represented by the emerald.
In planets it stands for VENUS.

Pale Green:
Baptism.

Purple:
Justice, royalty.
In blazonry, purpure, signifying temperance; it is engraved by diagonal lines from right to left.
In art signifying royalty.
In Church decoration it is used for ASH WEDNESDAY and HOLY SATURDAY.
In metals it is represented by quicksilver.
In precious stones it is represented by amethyst.
In planets it stands for MERCURY.

Red:
Martyrdom for faith, charity; (in dresses) divine love.
In blazonry, gules; blood-red is called sanguine. The former signifies magnanimity, and the latter fortitude; it is engraved by perpendicular lines.
In Church decoration it is used for martyrs and for WHIT SUNDAY.
In metals it is represented by iron (the metal of war).
In precious stones it is represented by the ruby.
In planets it stands for MARS.

White:
In blazonry, argent; signifying purity, truth, innocence; in engravings argent is left blank.
In art, priests, MAGI, and DRUIDS are arrayed in white. Jesus after the resurrection should be draped in white.
In Church decoration it is used for festivals of Our Lord, for MAUNDY THURSDAY, and for all Saints except Martyrs.
As a mortuary colour it indicates hope.
In metals it is represented by SILVER.
In precious stones it is represented by the pearl.
In planets it stands for DIANA or the MOON.

Yellow:
> *In blazonry*, or; signifying faith, constancy, wisdom, glory; in engravings it is shown by dots.
>
> *In modern art*, signifying jealousy, inconstancy, in continence. In France the doors of traitors used to be daubed with yellow, and in some countries Jews were obliged to dress in yellow. In Spain the executioner is dressed in red and yellow.
>
> *In Christian art* JUDAS is arrayed in yellow; but St. PETER is also arrayed in golden yellow.
>
> *In metals* it is represented by GOLD.
>
> *In precious stones* it is represented by the topaz.
>
> *In planets* it stands for APOLLO or the SUN.

Violet, Brown or Grey:
> are used in Church decoration for ADVENT and LENT; and in other symbolism violet usually stands for penitence, and grey for tribulation.

Colour-blindness. A term introduced by Sir David Brewster (1781–1868), the inventor of the kaleidoscope, to denote the various forms of defective colour vision or perception. Also known as *Daltonism* after John Dalton (1766–1844) the scientist, who first described it in 1794, and who also suffered from it.

Colour sergeant. From 1813 to 1915 the senior non-commissioned officer of an infantry company who had charge of the regimental colours. It is now a staff-sergeant's appointment whose badge is a sergeant's chevrons surmounted by a crown. The original badge was of crossed colours above the chevrons.

Colporteur. A hawker or PEDLAR; so called because he carried his basket or pack round his neck (Fr. *col*: neck; *porter*, to carry). The name is especially given to hawkers of religious books.

Colt. A person new to office; an awkward young fellow who needs "breaking in"; specifically in legal use, a BARRISTER who attended a SERJEANT-AT-LAW at his induction.

> I accompanied the newly made Chief Baron as his colt.
>
> POLLOCK.

In CRICKET and football a Colt team consists of a club's most promising young players.

Colt is also an abbreviation for "Colt's revolver", patented by the American Col. Sam Colt in 1835, as well as an old nautical term for an 18-inch length of knotted rope for use on the ship's boys; a CAT-O'-NINE-TAILS.

Colt-pixy. A PIXY, PUCK, or mischievous fairy. To *colt-pixy* is to take what belongs to the pixies, and is specially applied to the gleaning of apples after the crop has been gathered in.

Columbine. A stock character in old Italian comedy from about 1560 and transferred to English PANTOMIME. She was the daughter of PANTALOON and the sweetheart of HARLEQUIN, and, like him, was supposed to be invisible to mortal eyes. Columbina in Italian is a pet name for a lady-love, and means dove-like.

Columbus's Egg. An easy task once one knows the trick. The story is that Columbus, in reply to a suggestion that other pioneers might have discovered America had he not done so, is said to have challenged the guests at a banquet in his honour to make an egg stand on end. All having failed, he flattened one end of the egg by tapping it against the table and so standing it up, thus indicating that others might follow but he had discovered the way.

Column. The Column of Marcus Aurelius, or **Antonine Column.** Erected at Rome in honour of the Emperor Marcus Aurelius Antoninus (A.D. 121–180), covered like that of TRAJAN with spiral bas-reliefs representing the emperor's wars. It is a Roman DORIC column of marble 95 ft. in height on a square pedestal.

Sixtus V caused the original statue on this column to be replaced by a figure of St. PAUL in 1589.

The Column at Boulogne, or **The Column of the Grand Army,** a marble DORIC column 176 ft. high carrying a bronze statue of NAPOLEON I, to commemorate the camp at Boulogne 1804–1805, formed there for the invasion of England.

Columns, or **Pillars, of Hercules.** *See* PILLAR.

The Column of July. Erected in Paris in 1840 on the site of the BASTILLE to commemorate the July revolution of 1830 when Charles X abdicated. It is a bronze column 154 ft. high surmounted by a gilded statue of LIBERTY.

London's Column. *See* MONUMENT.

Nelson's Column. A CORINTHIAN column of Devonshire granite on a square base in Trafalgar Square, London, completed in 1843. The four lions, by Landseer, were added in 1867. It stands 185 ft. high overall; the column is a copy of one in the temple of MARS Ultor (the Avenger) at ROME. The statue, by E. H. Bailey, R.A., is 17 ft. high.

Column of the Place Vendôme. Erected in Paris (1806–1810) in honour of Napoleon I. Made of marble encased with bronze, the spiral outside in bas-relief represents his battles ending with Austerlitz (1805). This imitation of TRAJAN'S COLUMN is 142 ft. high and the statue of NAPOLEON at the top was hurled down by the COMMUNARDS in 1871 and replaced in 1874.

Trajan's Column. At ROME. Built of marble (A.D. 114) by Apollodorus of Damascus, it is a Roman DORIC column 127½ ft. high, on a square pedestal with a spiral staircase inside lighted by 40 windows. It was surmounted by a statue of the Emperor Trajan but Sixtus V substituted one of St. PETER. The outside spiral represents in bas-relief the emperor's battles.

Flying Column. A column of soldiers trained and equipped for rapid movement.

To dodge the column. To avoid one's duties or allotted tasks.

Coma Berenices. *See* BERENICE.

Comazant (kom′ à zănt). *See* CORPOSANT.

Reynard's wonderful comb. This comb existed only in the brain of Master Fox. He said it was made of the Panthera's bone (*see* PANTHER), the perfume of which was so fragrant that no one could resist following it; and the wearer of the comb was always cheerful and merry.—*Reynard the Fox* (*q.v.*).

Come. A come down. Loss of prestige or position.

Come February, Michaelmas, etc. A colloquialism for "next February", etc.

> Come Lammas-eve at night shall she be fourteen.
> SHAKESPEARE: *Romeo and Juliet*, I, iii.

Come hell or high water. No matter what happens.

Come home. Return to your house; to touch one's feelings or interest.

Come out. Formerly said of a young woman after she had been presented at Court, and more generally, when she comes out into society as a "grown up" person.

Come-ye-all. A type of ballad consisting of a strong simple narrative with little dialogue and usually ending with a moral reflection. Double ballad metre is the traditional form, and a typical first line is "Come all ye young maidens". Hence the name.

Don't try to come it over me. Don't try to boss me or order me about; don't set yourself in a position above me.

If the worst comes to the worst. *See* WORST.

Marry come up. *See* MARRY.

To come a cropper. *See* CROPPER.

To come by. To acquire, with a hint of premeditation in the transaction.

To come clean. To tell the whole truth, to make a full and frank admission, to reveal completely.

To come down. To leave the university finally or to commence vacation.

To come down upon one. To reproach, to punish severely, to make a peremptory demand.

To come it strong. To LAY IT ON THICK; to exaggerate or overdo. *See* DRAW IT MILD.

To come of good stock. To be descended from a good family.

To come off. To occur, as "my holiday didn't come off after all". Also to be accomplished successfully.

To come round. To recover consciousness; to recover from a fit of the sulks; return to friendship; "he is coming round to my way of thinking", he is beginning to think as I do.

To come short. Not to be sufficient. "To come short of" means to miss or fail to attain.

To come through the side door. To be born as an illegitimate child.

To come to. To amount to, as in "It will not come to much"; to obtain possession; to regain consciousness after fainting; etc.

To come to blows. To start fighting.

To come to grief. To meet with disaster; to be ruined.

To come to hand. *See under* HAND.

To come to pass. To happen, to befall, to come about.

> It came to pass in those days, that there went out a decree.
>
> *Luke* ii, I.

To come to stay. To come as a guest, also used of something which will be permanent or long-lasting.

To come to the point. *See* POINT.

To come under. To be classified under.

To come under the hammer. *See* HAMMER.

To come up against. To encounter opposition; to come across; to encounter by chance.

To come up smiling. To laugh at discomfiture or punishment; to emerge from disaster unruffled.

To come up to. To equal, to amount to the same quantity.

To come up to scratch. *See* SCRATCH.

To come Yorkshire over one. To bamboozle one, to overreach one. Yorkshire has been proverbial for shrewdness and sharp practice. "I's Yorkshire too" means I am as sharp as you and am not to be taken in.

To stage a come-back. To return successfully to former standing in political or professional life, etc., after withdrawing from it.

What's to come of it? What's to come of him? A contracted form of *become*.

Comedy (Gr. *komē-ōdē*). Originally a village song, referring to the village merry-makings, in which songs still take a conspicuous place. Greek comedy appears to have originated from such village revels and certain elements of the festivities connected with the worship of DIONYSUS. The chorus probably derives from the practice of Attic revellers masquerading as birds, frogs, fishes, etc. *Cp.* TRAGEDY.

The Father of Comedy. Aristophanes (*c.* 450–385 B.C.), the Athenian dramatist.

Comet Wine. A term denoting wine of a superior quality from the notion that grapes of "comet years" (*i.e.* years in which remarkable comets appear) are are better in flavour than those of other years.

Commandment, The Ten Commandments. *See* DECALOGUE; *also under* TEN.

The eleventh commandment. An ironical expression, signifying "Thou shalt not be found out".

Commando (Port. *commandar*, command). Originally armed units of Boer horsemen on military service. They achieved notable successes for their daring and nobility during the South African War (1899–1902).

> Lord Kitchener's relentless policy of attrition was slowly breaking the hearts of the commandos.
>
> DENEYS REITZ: *Commando*, ch. xxvi.

In World War II it was adopted as the name of the especially trained British assault troops formed from volunteers to undertake particularly hazardous tasks, and also used for a member of these units.

Comme il faut (kom ēl fō) (Fr.). As it should be; quite proper; quite according to etiquette or rule.

Commendam. A living in commendam is one temporarily held by someone (often a BISHOP) until an incumbent is appointed, and the practice arose of commending several livings to the bishops of poorer sees. The custom was abolished in 1836.

Commendation Ninepence. This was a bent ninepenny silver piece, commonly used in the 17th century as a love-token, giver and receiver saying. "To my love, from my love." Sometimes the coin was broken, each keeping a part.

Committee. A Committee of the whole House, in parliamentary language is when the SPEAKER leaves the chair, the mace is placed under the table, and the chair is taken by the Chairman of WAYS AND MEANS. Any member may speak more than once.

A Joint Committee is a committee nominated by the HOUSE OR LORDS and the HOUSE OF COMMONS, in practice a Select Committee of the Commons which meets a Select Committee of the Lords.

A Select Committee is fact-finding body of members selected from the whole House.

A Standing Committee in the Commons is formed so as to represent the different parties according to their relative strength in the House. They are appointed for the Session to deal with bills in the Committee stage.

Common. Short for common land which cannot be enclosed without an ACT OF PARLIAMENT. The enclosure of common land was a source of friction and discontent over the centuries and was not halted until the Com mons Preservation Act of 1876. *See* MANOR; OPEN FIELD SYSTEM.

Rights of Common are (1) Pasture, the right of feeding stock; (2) Piscary, the right of fishing; (3) Estovers, the right of cutting wood, furze, etc.; (4) Turbary, the right of cutting turves.

Common Law. Originally the unwritten law of custom of the King's courts (except of Equity). From the late 15th century precedent began to be accepted and gradually superseded local customs until the 19th century when precedent and case-made law predominated. *Cp.* STATUTE.

Common Law Wife. A common term applied to a woman cohabiting with a man as in a marriage relationship but based on mutual agreement and not on any civil or religious rite. Her partner has to maintain their children but she has no legal status under COMMON LAW.

Common Market. The popular name for the European Economic Community set up in 1957, consisting of Belgium, France, West Germany, Italy, Luxembourg and the Netherlands, to promote economic co-operation and common development with the ultimate aim of economic and a degree of political unity. It was joined by Great Britain, Denmark and the Irish Republic in 1974, by Greece in 1981 and by Spain and Portugal in 1985. Free Trade between members was established in 1984. A commission implements policies decided by a Council of Ministers which is subject to a European Parliament.

Common Pleas. Actions between subject and subject at Common Law. The Court of Common Pleas was for the trial of civil actions and was transferred to the High Court of Justice by the Judicature Act of 1873 and then merged in the Queen's Bench Division (1881).

Common Prayer. The Book of Common Prayer. *See under* BOOK.

Common sense. Good, sound, practical sense; general sagacity. Formerly it denoted a supposed internal sense held to be common to all the senses, or one that acted as a link between them. *See* SEVEN SENSES *under* SENSE.

Commoner. A member of the British HOUSE OF COMMONS; also one with RIGHTS OF COMMON and, at Oxford colleges, a student not on the foundation.

The Great Commoner. William Pitt the elder (1708–1778), Earl of Chatham, famous statesman, and, like Sir Winston Churchill, a great House of Commons man.

Commons. Doctors' Commons. *See under* DOCTOR.

To put someone on short commons. To stint him, to give him scanty meals. At the universities of Oxford and Cambridge the food provided for each student (at a common table) at breakfast was called his *commons*; hence food in general or meals.

Commonwealth, The. A term specifically applied to England in 1649 by the RUMP, after it had abolished the HOUSE OF LORDS and the monarchy and established the Council of State. Oliver Cromwell was styled Lord PROTECTOR of the Commonwealth in 1653, and the period of his rule is usually called the Protectorate.

In current usage the term is applied to the British Commonwealth, the free association of most nations of the former British Empire.

Ideal Commonwealths. The best known ideal or imaginary Commonwealths are those sketched by Plato in the *Republic* (from which later examples derive), by CICERO in his *De Republica*, by St. Augustine in his *De Civitate Dei*, by Dante in his *De Monarchia*, by Sir Thomas More in UTOPIA, by Bacon in the *New Atlantis* (*see under* ATLANTIS), by Campanella in his *Civitas Solis*, and by Samuel Butler in EREWHON.

Others are Johnson's *Rasselas*, Lytton's *Coming Race*, Bellamy's *Looking*

Backward, Wm. Morris's *News from Nowhere*, H. G. Wells's *In the Days of the Comet*, and *The World Set Free*.

Communards (From *commune*, in France, a unit of local government). After the Franco-Prussian War and the fall of Napoleon III, bitter political divisions arose between the people of Paris and the government at Versailles under Adolphe Thiers. Radicals, revolutionaries, socialists and workmen of the Paris Commune, adopting the name *Communards*, took control of the city in March 1871. They were ruthlessly suppressed by 29 May, with heavy loss of life, especially at the PÈRE LACHAISE cemetery.

Communism, in the general sense of a society or community based on common ownership of property and common labour with all sharing the common product, has been practised in many primitive societies and particular groups (*See* DIGGERS). Since the time of Plato's *Republic* various forms of communism have been elaborated, but in current usage it derives from the theories of Karl Marx (1818–1883) and Friedrich Engels (1820–1895) as set out in their *Communist Manifesto* (1848) and in the former's *Capital* (1867–1894). *See* MARXISM; MATERIALISM.

> The distinguishing feature of Communism is not the abolition of property generally, but the abolition of bourgeois property.
>
> *Communist Manifesto, II.*

Comparisons are odorous. So says Dogberry (SHAKESPEARE: *Much Ado About Nothing*, III, v) (a blunder for *odious*).

Complementary Colours. *See* COLOURS.

Complex. A combination of memories and wishes which exercise an influence on the personality. *See also under* (EDIPUS.

Inferiority complex. A feeling of inferiority in persons who appear overconscious of their own shortcomings.

To have a complex about something. To have a strong feeling either for or against something; to be over concerned about it.

Compline (kom' plin). The last of the CANONICAL HOURS, said about 8 or 9 p.m., and so called because it completes the series of the daily prayers or hours. From M.E. and O.Fr. *complie*, Lat.

completa (*hora*).

In ecclesiastical Lat. *vesperinus*, from *vesper*, means evening service, and *completinus* appears to be formed on this model.

Complutensian Polyglot. *See* BIBLE, SOME SPECIALLY NAMED EDITIONS.

Compos Mentis. *See* NON COMPOS MENTIS.

Comstockery. The vigorous suppression of books, plays, and other literature deemed to be salacious or corrupting, as advocated by the New York Society for the Suppression of Vice, whose moving spirit was Anthony Comstock (1844–1915). The word was coined by G. B. Shaw. *Cp.* BOWDLERIZE.

Comus (kō' mus) (Gr. *komos*, carousal). In Milton's masque of this name, the god of sensual pleasure, the son of BACCHUS and CIRCE.

Con amore (kon a môr' i) (Ital.). With heart and soul; as, "he did it *con amore*"—*i.e.* lovingly, with delight, and therefore in good earnest.

Con brio (Ital.). In music, forcefully and with spirit.

Con spirito (Ital.). With quickness and vivacity. A musical term.

Conceptionists. *See* FRANCISCANS.

Concert of Europe. In the 19th century, the name given to the general policy of the major European powers to maintain peace after the Vienna Settlement, and to regulate international relations by consultation and agreement, and to act in concert when the need arose. *See* CONGRESS SYSTEM.

Concert Pitch is the pitch, internationally agreed in 1939, to which musical instruments are usually tuned.

Hence figuratively **to screw oneself up to concert pitch** is to make oneself absolutely ready, prepared for any emergency or anything one may have to do.

Conchobar (kon ko' bar). In ancient Irish romance, son of Nessa, and king of ULSTER at the opening of the Christian era. He was uncle and guardian of CUCHULAIN and also responsible for the upbringing of DEIRDRE. He is said to have died of anger on the day of Christ's crucifixion.

Conchy. *See* CONSCIENTIOUS OBJECTOR.

Conclamatio

Conclamatio. Amongst the ancient Romans, the loud cry raised by those standing round a death-bed at the moment of death. It probably had its origin in the idea of recalling the departed spirit and was similar to the Irish howl over the dead. "One not howled over" (*corpus nondum clamatum*) meant one at the point of death; and "one howled for" was one given up for dead or actually deceased. Hence the phrase *conclamatum est*, he is dead past all hope, he has been called and gives no sign. VIRGIL makes the palace ring with howls when DIDO burnt herself to death.

> Lamentis, gemituque, et fœmineo ululato,
> Texta fremunt.
>
> *Æneid*, iv, 667.

Conclave. Literally, a room or set of rooms, all of which can be opened by one key (Lat. *cum clavis*). The word is applied to small cells erected for the CARDINALS who meet, after the death of a POPE, to elect a successor; hence the assembly of cardinals for this purpose; hence any private assembly for discussion. The conclave of cardinals dates from 1274 and was limited to 120 cardinals in 1973. Those assembled in the VATICAN are secluded in the conclave apartments and votes are taken morning and evening until one candidate has secured a two-thirds majority of votes. He is then acclaimed Pope.

To meet in solemn conclave is to meet together to decide matters of importance.

Concordat (kon kôr' dăt). An agreement, especially between a secular ruler and the POPE; as the Germanic Concordat of 1448 between the Emperor Frederick III and Nicholas V; the Concordat of 1516 between Francis I of France and Leo X to abolish the PRAGMATIC SANCTION; and the Concordat of 1801 between NAPOLEON and Pius VII. In 1929 a concordat between the Papacy and the Italian Government established the VATICAN City State.

Condottieri (It. *condotto*, hired). A name applied to the leaders of bands of FREEBOOTERS, mercenaries, or military adventurers of the 14th and 15th centuries. Notable among them were Sir John Hawkwood at Florence, Francesco of Carmagnola, and Francesco Sforza. Italy was particularly plagued by them. The singular is *condottiere*.

Confederate States. The eleven states which seceded from the Union in the American Civil War (1861–1865)—*viz.* Alabama, Arkansas, North and South Carolina, Georgia, Florida, Louisiana, Mississippi, Tennessee, Texas, Virginia.

Confederation of the Rhine. The sixteen German states which allied themselves with France in 1806. The confederation was dissolved in 1813.

The North German Confederation was formed in 1867 under the presidency of the King of Prussia, consequent upon the defeat of Austria in 1866. It consisted of all 22 states north of the river Main.

Confession, Seal of. The obligation which binds a priest not to divulge outside the confessional anything he may hear therein. He cannot be forced to reveal in the witness-box of a court of law any information he may have thus obtained.

Confetti. The practice of throwing confetti over the bridal pair after their wedding is a substitute for the old custom of throwing corn and later, rice. It derives from an ancient fertility rite the intent of which was to ensure prosperity and fruitfulness.

Confidence trick. Usually the work of a professional swindler, who creates a false impression to secure a person's trust with the direct purpose of cheating him. Often the victim is induced to hand over money, valuables, etc., as a mark of confidence but such trickery takes many forms. From this the current slang expression **all a con** is derived to imply *a take in*, *a see off*, or *a swindle*.

Confusion worse confounded. Disorder made worse than before.

Congé (kon zhā') (Fr. leave). "To give a person his congé" is to dismiss him from your service. "To take one's congé" is to give notice to friends of your departure by leaving a card at the friend's house inscribed P.P.C. (*pour prendre congé* to take leave) on the left-hand corner.

Congé d'élire (Fr. leave to elect). A

royal writ given to a CHAPTER to elect a named priest to a vacant SEE. Its use dates from 1533.

Congregationalists. Those PROTESTANT Dissenters maintaining that each congregation was independent with a right to govern its own affairs and choose its own minister. They derived from the BROWNISTS and BARROWISTS of Elizabeth I's reign. The Congregational Union was formed in 1832. *See* UNITED REFORMED CHURCH.

Congress System. Refers to the attempts made after the Vienna Settlement of 1815 to settle problems affecting the peace of Europe by congresses or conferences between the major powers. The experiment ended with the Congress of St. Petersburg (1825). *See* CONCERT OF EUROPE.

Congreve Rocket. A rocket invented in 1808 for use in war by Sir William Congreve (1772–1828). It was not very successfully used at Leipzig in 1813. He was Comptroller of the Royal Laboratory at Woolwich.

> But vaccination certainly has been
> A kind antithesis to Congreve's rockets.
> BYRON: *Don Juan*, I, cxxix.

Congreves. Predecessors of the LUCIFER-MATCH, invented by Sir William Congreve. The splints were dipped in sulphur then tipped with chlorate of potash paste, in which gum was substituted for sugar, then a small quantity of sulphide of antimony was added. The match was ignited by being drawn through a fold of sand-paper. *Cp.* PROMETHEAN.

Conker (kon' kĕr). A children's name for a horse-chestnut; possibly derived from the Fr. *conque*, a shell. Schoolboys thread a chestnut on a string knotted at one end, and then play conkers by each taking a turn at striking his opponent's conker until one or other is broken from the string. Perhaps **conk**, slang for nose, is similarly derived; hence, *conky*, a big- or beak-nosed person.

Old Conky. The Duke of Wellington (1769–1852) was so nicknamed from the shape of his nose or CONK.

To conk out, used of an engine or motor, means to break down or stop running. This usage is probably onomato-

poeic. It also means to die.

Connecticut (kȯ net' i kŭt) is the Mohegan dialect word *Quonaughicut*, meaning "long tidal river". *See* NUTMEG STATE.

Conquest, The. William of Normandy's conquest of England (1066).

Conscience. Conscience clause. A clause in an ACT OF PARLIAMENT to relieve persons with conscientious scruples from certain requirements in it (usually of a religious character). It acquired a wider significance in connexion with the Compulsory Vaccination Act of 1898.

Conscience money. Usually refers to money paid anonymously to the government by persons who have defrauded the revenue, most frequently by understating their income-tax liabilities. The sum is advertised in the *London Gazette*. It also has a more general connotation.

Court of Conscience. Courts of the recovery of small debts, established at LONDON and various other commercial centres, eventually superseded by County Courts.

Have you the conscience to [demand such a price]? Can your conscience allow you to [demand such a price]?

In all conscience. As, "And enough too, in all conscience", *i.e.* the demand made is as much as conscience would tolerate; verging on the border of sharp practice or of that fine line which divides honesty from dishonesty.

My conscience! An oath. I swear by my conscience.

To make a matter of conscience of it. To deal with it according to the dictates of conscience, to treat it conscientiously.

Conscientious objector. One who takes advantage of a conscience clause, and so evades some particular requirement of the law in question. Once specially applied to those who had a conscientious objection to vaccination, but since World War I it has come to mean one who obtains exemption from military service on grounds of conscience. Such people are also called. *C.O.*s or *Conchies*.

Conscript Fathers. Lat *Patres Conscrip-*

ti, the Roman Senate. One explanation is that ROMULUS is supposed to have instituted a senate of a hundred elders called *Patres* (Fathers). After the SABINES joined the State, another hundred were added. Tarquinius Priscus, the fifth king, added a third hundred, called *Patres Minorum Gentium*. When Tarquinius Superbus, the seventh and last king of Rome, was banished, several of the senate followed him, and the vacancies were filled up by Junius Brutus, the first consul. The new members were enrolled in the senatorial register and so called *conscripti*; the entire body was then addressed as *Patres [et] Conscripti* or *Patres, Conscripti. See* TARQUIN.

Consentes Dii. The twelve chief Roman deities, six male and six female, the same as the Athenian Twelve Gods:

> JUPITER, APOLLO, NEPTUNE, MARS,
> MERCURY, VULCAN, JUNO, DIANA,
> MINERVA, VENUS, CERES, VESTA.

Consenting Stars. Stars forming configurations for good or evil. In *Judges* v, 20, we read that "the stars in their courses fought against Sisera", *i.e.* formed unlucky or malignant configurations.

Conservative. One who essentially believes in amending existing institutions cautiously and who opposes doctrinaire changes. The name came to be applied to the TORY party from the 1830s after its use by J. W. Croker in the *Quarterly Review* of January 1830. "We have always been conscientiously attached to what is called Tory, and which might with more propriety be called the Conservative Party" (P. 276). Canning somewhat similarly used the word in a speech at Liverpool in March 1820.

Conservator of the Peace. The predecessor of the JUSTICE OF THE PEACE and usually a function of the KNIGHT OF THE SHIRE.

Consistory (Lat. *consistorium*, a place of assembly). As an ecclesiastical court in the Church of ROME it is the assembly in council of the POPE and CARDINALS; in England it is a diocesan court presided over by the CHANCELLOR of the diocese.

Consolidated Fund. The national revenue from all sources is paid into this fund and held in the EXCHEQUER account at the Bank of England. The fund, which dates from 1787, is pledged for meeting the interest and management costs of the National Debt, CIVIL LIST, etc.

Consols. A contraction of *Consolidated Annuities*, part of the public debt.

Constable (Lat. *comes stabuli*) means Court of the Stable or Master of the Horse. In the BYZANTINE EMPIRE the Constable was master of the imperial stables and a great officer of state, hence the use of the name for an official of a royal household or a military commander. It was adopted by the Frankish kings and the office grew steadily more important under their successors. (*See* CONSTABLE OF FRANCE.) Constable is also the term for a governor of a fortress, as the Constable of the TOWER of London. From Tudor times it became the designation of a parish officer, and later a policeman, as officers appointed to keep the peace. In England a *Special Constable* is one enrolled to help the regular constabulary in time of pressure or emergency.

The Constable of England, or **Lord High Constable** is first identifiable in Henry I's reign (1100–1135), but since 1521 has been appointed for coronation days only.

The Constable of France was once a great household official, judge of all matters pertaining to CHIVALRY, etc., and from the 14th century commander-in-chief of the army. The office was suppressed by Louis XIII in 1627, but temporarily revived by NAPOLEON.

The Lord High Constable of Scotland. An office similar to those of England and France instituted by David I about 1147. It was conferred by Robert Bruce in 1315 on Sir Gilbert Hay, created Earl of Erroll, in which family it was made hereditary and is still held.

Constantine, Donation of. *See* DECRETALS.

Constantine's Cross. *See* CROSS.

Constituent Assembly. The first of the National Assemblies of the French Revolution which sat from July 1789 until 1791; so called from its main objective of drawing up a new constitution.

Constitution. The fundamental law or

body of custom by which a state is organized and governed, *i.e.* constituted.

Apostolic Constitutions. A comprehensive rule in eight books concerning church doctrines and customs. Of unknown authorship, they are probably of Syrian origin and probably date from the 4th century. They are certainly post-Apostolic.

Constitutions of Clarendon. *See* CLARENDON.

Consummatum est. (kon sŭ-m ā' tum est) (Lat.). It is finished; the last words of our Lord on the CROSS (*John* xix, 30).

Contango. In STOCK EXCHANGE parlance, the sum paid by the purchaser of stock to the seller, for the privilege of deferring the completion of the bargain till the next, or some future settling day.

Contemplate. To meditate or reflect upon: to consider attentively. The word takes us back to the ancient Roman augurs (*see* AUGURY), for the *templum* (whence our *temple*) was that part of the heavens which he wished to consult. Having mentally divided it into two parts from top to bottom, he watched to see what would occur; and this watching of the *templum* was called *contemplating*.

Contempt of Court. A term of wide coverage which briefly defined consists of refusal to obey the rules, orders, and processes of the courts of law, or interference with the course of justice. Offenders can be jurors, parties, witnesses, solicitors, etc.

Contempt of Parliament. Any disobedience or disrespect or obstruction to the due course of proceedings or gross reflection on the character of a member is a breach of PRIVILEGE.

Contemptibles, The Old. Members of the British Expeditionary Force of 160,000 men that left Britain in 1914 to join the French and Belgians against Germany. The soldiers gave themselves this name from an army order (almost certainly apocryphal) said to have been given at Aix on 19 August by the Kaiser.

> It is my royal and imperial command that you exterminate the treacherous English, and walk over General French's contemptible little army.

It is said by some that actually he called the B.E.F. "a contemptibly little army", which is not nearly so disparaging.

Contest of Wartburg. Sometimes called the *Battle of the Minstrels*, the famous poetical contest of MINNESINGER held in 1207 at the Wartburg, a castle in Saxe-Weimar. The best of the contestants was Walther von der Vogelweide and the contest is commemorated in Wagner's TANNHÄUSER.

Continence of a Scipio. It is said that a beautiful princess fell into the hands of Scipio Africanus, and he refused to see her, "lest he should be tempted to forget his principles". Similar stories are told of many historical characters including Cyrus and ALEXANDER.

Continental System. The name given to NAPOLEON'S plan to cripple Britain by economic warfare when the invasion plan had failed. The Berlin Decrees of 21 NOVEMBER 1806 excluded all British goods from the ports of France and her allies, and declared the British Isles in a state of blockade.

Continuity Man, or **Girl.** The technique of cinematography allows of a play, etc., being photographed in scenes and incidents not necessarily in sequence and each scene, etc., may be "shot" many times. It is essential that every detail of costume, scenery, etc., is correctly repeated each time a scene is "shot". It is the task of the continuity man or girl to ensure this.

Contra (Lat.). Against: generally in the phrase *pro and contra* or *pro and con*. In bookkeeping a *contra* is an entry on the right-hand or credit side of the ledger. *See* PER CONTRA.

A contra-account is one kept by a firm which both buys from and sells to the same client, so that the transactions cancel out as paper entries.

Contra bonos mores (Lat.). Not in accordance with good manners; not COMME IL FAUT.

Contra jus gentium (Lat.). Against the law of nations; specially applied to usages in war which are contrary to the laws or customs of civilized peoples.

Contra mundum (Lat.). Against the world at large. Used of an innovator or reformer who sets his opinion against that of everyone else, and specially connected with Athanasius in his vehement opposition to the ARIANS.

Conventicle. The word was applied by the early Christians to their meeting places and inevitably acquired the derogatory sense of a clandestine meeting. With the advent of Protestantism in England it came to be applied to the meetings and meeting-places of DISSENTERS.

Conventicle Act. In 1593 such an Act was passed containing severe penalties against those attending religious conventicles. The better-known Act of 1664 forbade religious conventicles of more than five persons except in accordance with the BOOK OF COMMON PRAYER. It was repealed in 1812.

Convention Parliaments. Two parliaments were so called: one in 1660, because it was not summoned by the king, but was convened by General Monk to effect the RESTORATION of Charles II; and that authorized by William of Orange in January 1689 which offered the throne to William and Mary as joint sovereigns.

Cook, Cooking. Terms belonging to cuisine applied to man under different circumstances: Sometimes he is well *basted*; he *boils* with rage, is *baked* with heat, and *burns* with love or jealousy. Sometimes he is *buttered* and *well buttered;* he is often *cut up, devoured* with a flame and *done brown*. We *dress his jacket* for him; sometimes he is *eaten up* with care, sometimes he is *fried*. We *cook his goose* for him, and sometimes he makes a goose of himself. We make a *hash* of him, and at times he makes a hash of something else. He gets into *hot water*, and sometimes into a *mess*. Is made into *mincemeat*, makes mincemeat of his money, and is often in a *pickle*. We are often asked to *toast* him, sometimes he gets well *roasted*, is sometimes *set on fire*, put into a *stew*, or is in a *stew*.

A "softie" is *half-baked*, one severely handled is well *peppered*. To falsify accounts is to *cook* or *salt* them, wit is *Attic salt*, and an exaggerated statement must be taken *cum grano salis*.

A pert young person is a *sauce* box, a shy lover is a *spoon*, a rich father has to *fork out*, and is sometimes *dished* of his money.

A conceited man does not think small *beer* (or small *potatoes*) of himself, and one's mouth is called a *potato-trap*. A simpleton is a *cake*, a *gudgeon*, and a *pigeon*. Some are *cool as a cucumber*, others *hot as a quail*. A chubby child is a little *dumpling*. A woman may be a *duck*; a courtesan was called *mutton* or *laced mutton*, and a large coarse hand is a *mutton fist*. Side whiskers are called *mutton chops*. A greedy person is a *pig*, a fat one is a *sausage*, and a shy one, if not a sheep, is certainly *sheepish*; while a Lubin casts *sheep's eyes* at his lady-love. A coward is *chicken-hearted*, a fat person is *crummy*, and a cross one is *crusty*, while an aristocrat belongs to the *upper crust* of society. Yeomen of the Guard are BEEFEATERS, a soldier is a *red herring*, or a *lobster*, and a stingy, ill-tempered old man is a *crab*. A walking advertiser between two boards is a *sandwichman*. An alderman in his chain is a *turkey hung with sausages*. Two persons resembling each other are like as *two peas*. A chit is a mere *sprat*, a delicate maiden is a *titbit*, and a colourless countenenace is called a *wheyface*. Anything unexpectedly easy is a *piece of cake*.

Cooked. The books have been cooked. The accounts have been falsified.

Cook your goose. *See* GOOSE.

What's cooking? What's in hand? What's doing?

Cool. Cool card; cooling card. *See* CARD.

Cool as a cucumber. Perfectly composed; not in the least angry or agitated.

Cool hundred, thousand (or any other sum). The whole of the sum named, cool being emphatic; it may have originally had reference to the calm deliberation with which the sum was counted out.

> He had lost a cool hundred, and would play no longer.
> FIELDING: *Tom Jones*, VIII, xii.

Cool tankard, or **cool cup.** A drink made of wine and water, with lemon, sugar, and borage; sometimes also slices of cucumber.

Cooler. A slang term, of American origin, for a prison or prison cell.

Coon. Short for raccoon, a small North American arboreal animal, about the size of a fox, valued for its fur. The animal was adopted as a badge by the old WHIG party in the United States about 1840. In the 19th century the word became offensive slang for a Negro.

A gone coon. A person in a terrible fix; one on the verge of ruin. The coon being hunted for its fur is a "gone coon" when it is treed and so has no escape from its pursuers.

Coop. U.S. slang for prison.

To fly the coop is to escape from prison.

Coot. A silly coot, Stupid as a coot. The coot is a small waterfowl.

Bald as a Coot. *See under* BALD.

Cop. To catch, lay hold of, capture. To "get copped" is to get caught, especially by the police, whence *cop* and COPPER for a policeman. Perhaps connected with Lat. *capere*, to take, etc. The word is used for catching almost anything, as punishment at school, or even an illness. **A fair cop** is applied to one caught *in flagrante delicto*.

Cope, Johnnie. *See* JOHNNIE COPE.

Copenhagen (kō pèn hā´gèn). The famous chestnut horse ridden by the Duke of Wellington at Waterloo.

Copernican System, Copernicanism. The heliocentric or sun-centred theory of the universe postulated by Nicolaus Copernicus (1473–1543) in his book *De Revolutionibus Orbium*. This superseded the PTOLEMAIC SYSTEM in which the sun is supposed to move round the earth. The idea was not entirely new and was vaguely held by the School of PYTHAGORAS. Pope Gregory XIII used *De Revolutionibus* when constructing his CALENDAR but the book was placed on the INDEX in 1616. *See* ALMAGEST.

Cophetua (ko fet´ ū à). An imaginary king of Africa who fell in love with Penelophon (SHAKESPEARE'S Zenelophon in *Love's Labour's Lost*, IV, i) and married her. They lived happily and were widely lamented at death. The story is given in the ballad *King Cophetua and the Beggar-Maid* in PERCY'S RELIQUES and is referred to in Shakespeare's *Romeo and Juliet* (II, i) and *Richard II* (V, iii).

Copper. Among the old alchemists copper was the symbol of VENUS.

The name is also given to the large boiler used for laundry purposes, cooking, etc., which was originally made of copper but later of iron; also to pence, half-pence, farthings, etc., once minted of copper but from 1860 of bronze.

In slang a **copper** is a policeman, *i.e.* one who "cops" or catches offenders.

Copper Nose. Oliver Cromwell; also called "Ruby Nose", "Nosey", and "Nose Almighty", no doubt from *acne rosacea* which showed itself in a big red nose.

Copper-nose Harry. Henry VIII was notorious for his debasement of the coinage (from 1526). The copper content in the "silver" coins soon showed itself on the more prominent parts, especially the nose. Hence the king came to be called "Old Copper Nose" or "Copper-nose Harry".

Copperheads. Secret foes. Copperheads are North American poisonous snakes which attack without warning.

Copts. Christian descendants of the Ancient Egyptians who became MONOPHYSITES and JACOBITES and who have retained the patriarchal chair of Alexandria since the Council of Chalcedon in 451, which still has nominal jurisdiction over the Ethiopian Church. Coptic ceased to be a living language in the 16th or early 17th century but is still used in their liturgy. The word is derived from the Gr. *Agyiptos* which became *Qibt* after the 7th-century Arab invasion.

Copy-book. A book in which specimen entries of handwriting, letters, and figures are printed with blank spaces for the learner to imitate or copy them. Such exercise books were used in schools until the present century.

Copy-book maxims. Commonplace moral precepts, etc., of the sort found in copy-books. Actual examples are:

All good subjects love their country.
Your aim in life should be a noble one.
Britannia must ever rule the waves.

To blot one's copy-book. To make a

serious blunder, to mar one's reputation, to do something disgraceful. The derivation is obvious.

Copyhold estate. Land held by possession of a copy made by the steward of a manor from the court-roll of the manor. Copyhold was enfranchised in 1925.

Coq à l'âne. *See* A COCK AND BULL STORY *under* COCK.

Coral. The Romans used to hang beads of red coral on the cradles and round the necks of infants as a charm against sickness, etc., and soothsayers held that it was a charm against lightning, whirlwind, shipwreck and fire. PARACELSUS similarly advocated its use "against fits, sorcery, charms and poison". The bells on an infant's coral were a Roman Catholic addition to frighten away evil spirits.

Coram judice (kôr' am joo' di si) (Lat.). Under consideration; still before the judge.

Cordelia (kôr dē' li à). The youngest of King LEAR's three daughters, and the only one that loved him. *Cp.* GONERIL.

Cordon (Fr.). A ribbon or cord; especially the ribbon of an order of chivalry; also a line of sentries or military posts encircling some position, hence an encircling line.

Cordon bleu. Originally in France a knight of the Order of the *St. Esprit* (HOLY GHOST) from the fact that their insignia was suspended on a blue ribbon. Hence **un repas de cordon bleu** is a well-cooked and well-appointed dinner. The Commandeur de Souvé, Comte d'Olonne, and other *cordons bleus* (*i.e.* knights of St. Esprit), met together as a sort of club, and were noted for their excellent dinners. Hence when anyone has dined well he says, *"Bien, c'est un vrai repas de cordon bleu."* Thus the title was playfully bestowed on good cooks.

Cordon sanitaire. A sanitary cordon, a barrier line enclosing an infected area patrolled by watchers.

Un grand cordon. The highest grade in the French *Légion d'Honneur.* The cross is attached to a *grand* (broad) ribbon.

Corduroy. A corded fabric, originally made of silk, and worn by the kings of

France in the chase (Fr. *corde du roy*). It is also a coarse, thick, ribbed cotton stuff, capable of standing hard wear. Hence corduroys as a name for trousers made of such material.

Corduroy road. Roads formed of tree trunks sawn in two longitudinally and laid transversely, thus presenting a ribbed appearance like corduroy.

Corineus. A mythical hero in the suite of BRUTE, who conquered the giant GOEMAGOT, for which achievement the whole western horn of England was allotted to him. He called it Corinea, and the people Corineans from his own name. This is the legendary explanation of the name of the county of CORNWALL. *See also* BELLARUS.

Corinthian. A licentious libertine. The loose living of Corinth was proverbial both in Greece and ROME.

Corinthian brass. An alloy made of a variety of metals (said to be gold, silver and copper) melted at the conflagration of Corinth in 146 B.C., when the city was burnt to the ground by the consul Mummius. Vases and other ornaments, made of this metal by the Romans, were more highly prized than if they had been of SILVER and GOLD.

Corinthian Order. The most richly decorated of the five orders of Greek architecture. The shaft is fluted, and the capital is bell-shaped and adorned with ACANTHUS leaves. *See* DORIC; IONIC; TUSCAN.

Corked. This wine is corked, *i.e.* it tastes of the cork.

Corker. That's a corker. That's a tremendous example of whatever is in question—something very difficult to answer or deal with—said of a story, a problem, a ball in CRICKET, etc.

Corking-pins. Pins of the largest size, at one time used by ladies to keep curls on the forehead fixed and in trim.

Cormoran. The Cornish giant, who in the nursery tale fell into a pit dug by JACK THE GIANT-KILLER. For this doughty achievement Jack received a belt from King ARTHUR, with this inscription—

This is the valiant Cornish man
That slew the giant Cormoran.
Jack the Giant-killer

Corn. Acknowledge the corn. *See* ACK-NOWLEDGE.

There's corn in Egypt. There is abundance; there is a plentiful supply. The reference is to the BIBLE story of Joseph in Egypt (*Gen*. xliii, 2).

To tread on his corns. To irritate his prejudices; to annoy another by disregarding his pet opinions or habits or to offend his susceptibilities.

Corn Dolly. Customarily, when the last load of the corn harvest was carried home, a Corn Dolly (called in some areas a Kern Baby or Mel Doll) was made from the last sheaf and carried by one of those riding on top of the load. This female symbol of the Corn Spirit was hung in the farm kitchen until the next harvest. *See* CRYING THE NECK; HARVEST HOME; HARVEST THANKSGIVING; HOCKEY; MELL SUPPER.

Corn Laws. Enactments beginning in 1360 which were designed to regulate the export, and subsequently the import of grain. Particularly noteworthy and unpopular was the Corn Law of 1815 which forbade the import of foreign wheat until the home price reached 80s. per quarter. This kept the price of bread unduly high in times of bad harvests, thus increasing the hardships of the poor. A sliding scale was introduced in 1828 which was further modified in 1842. In 1839 the Anti-Corn Law League was founded in Manchester, and in 1846 Sir Robert Peel secured the virtual repeal of the duties. A nominal duty of 1s per quarter remained until 1869.

Cornage. A feudal rent for pasture paid by free men and fixed with relation to the number of horned cattle in their possession. It was most common in the north of England.

Cornelia, Mother of the Gracchi. The model of Roman matronly virtue. She was the second daughter of Scipio Africanus. On the death of her husband, T. Sempronius Gracchus, in 154 B.C. she refused to remarry and devoted herself to the education of her three surviving children, Tiberius, Gaius, and Sempronia. When asked to show her jewels, Cornelia produced her two sons, saying, "These are the only jewels of which I can boast."

Corner, To. To buy up the whole of any stock in the market, to buy up the available stocks of a commodity to secure a virtual monopoly in order to raise the price. The idea is that the goods are piled and hidden in a corner out of sight.

> The price of bread rose like a rocket, and speculators wished to corner what little wheat there was.
> *New York Weekly Times* (13 June 1894).

To be driven into a corner. Placed where there is no escape; driven from all subterfuges and excuses.

To turn the corner. To have got over the worst; after an illness, to be on the mend. In nautical parlance "turning the corner" implied sailing on, either to port or starboard, after reaching either the CAPE of Good Hope or CAPE HORN (*See under* HORN).

Corner-stone. A large stone laid at the base of a building to strengthen the two walls forming a right-angle. In figurative use, Christ is called (*Eph*. ii, 20) the chief corner-stone because He united the Jews and Gentiles into one family; and daughters are called corner-stones (*Ps*. cxliv, 12) because, as wives and mothers, they unite together two families.

Cornet. The Terrible Cornet of Horse. A nickname of William Pitt the Elder (1708–1778). He obtained a cornetcy in Cobham's Horse in 1731.

Cornish. The Cornish hug. A hug to overthrow you. Cornish men were noted wrestlers and tried to throttle their antagonist with a particular grip or embrace called the Cornish hug.

Cornish language. A Brythonic branch of the CELTIC language now only used as an acquired speech by a few. It is supposed that Dolly Pentreath (Dorothy Jeffery, 1685–1778) was the last to speak Cornish as a native language.

Cornish names.

> By Tre, Pol, and Pen
> You shall know the Cornishmen.

Thus *Tre* (a hamlet) gives Trebilcock, Tredinnick, Tregaskis, Tregenza, Trelawny, Treloar, Tremayne, Trenowth, Treseder, etc.

Pol (a pool) gives Polglase, Polkinghorne, Polmear, Polwhele, etc.

Pen (a top) gives Penberthy, Pengelly, Penhale, Penprase, Penrose, Penruddock, etc.

There are countless similarly formed place-names.

Cornstalks. In Australia, especially in New South Wales, from colonial times a name for youths, perhaps from their being taller and more slender than their parents.

Cornubian Shore. Cornwall, formerly famous for its tin mines.

> ... from the bleak Cornubian shore
> Dispense the mineral treasure, which of old
> Sidonian pilots sought.
> AKENSIDE: *Hymn to the Naiads.*

Cornucopia. *See* AMALTHEA'S HORN.

Cornwall (Cornish, *Kernow*). Probably from the tribal name *Cornovii*. The O.E. *Cornwealas* means "the Welsh in Cornwall". *See also* CORINEUS.

Barry Cornwall. The pseudonym of Bryan Waller Proctor (1787–1874), based on an inaccurate anagram of his name. Trained as a lawyer, he published poems, songs, memoirs of Edmund Kean and Charles Lamb, etc. He was very popular with the eminent poets and other writers of his time including Scott, Tennyson, Macaulay, Dickens and Thackeray.

Coronation Chair. *See* SCONE.

Coronet. A crown inferior to the royal crown. The coronet of the Prince of Wales has one arch less than the royal crown; those of other princes are without arches; a duke's coronet is adorned with strawberry leaves above the band; that of a marquis with strawberry leaves alternating with pearls; that of an earl has pearls elevated on stalks, alternating with strawberry leaves above the band; that of a viscount has a string of pearls above the band, but no leaves; that of a baron has only six pearls.

Coronis. (kôr ō′ nis). Mother of ÆSCULAPIUS by APOLLO, who slew her for her infidelity; also the daughter of Coronæus, King of Phocis, changed by ATHENE into a crow to enable her to escape from NEPTUNE.

Corporal Violet. *See* VIOLET.

Corporation. A body or succession of persons having legal existence, rights and duties, as distinct from the individuals from whom it is formed. In Britain its usual application is to the body of individuals elected for the local government of a city or town. In America it commonly applies to a company. The word *corporation* is also facetiously given to a fat paunch, from the tendency of civic bodies to indulge in well-provided feasts, thus acquiring generous figures.

Corposant. The ball of fire which is sometimes seen playing around the masts of ships in a storm. So called from the Ital. *corpo santo*, holy body. To the Romans the phenomenon was known as CASTOR AND POLLUX, and it is also known as ST. ELMO'S FIRE, HELEN'S FIRE, and Comazant.

Corps Diplomatique (Fr.). The diplomatic body in a capital made up of the diplomatic representatives of the various foreign states.

Corps législatif (Fr.). At various times in modern French history this name has been used for the lower house of the legislature. In 1799 NAPOLEON substituted a *Corps législatif* and a tribunal for the two councils of the DIRECTORY. In 1807 there was a *c.l.* and a *conseil d'état* (council of state); in 1849 a *c.l.* was formed with 750 deputies; and under NAPOLEON III the legislative power was vested in the Emperor, the Senate, and the *c.l.*

Corpse Candle. The IGNIS FATUUS is so called by the Welsh because it was supposed to forbode death, and to show the road the corpse would take. The large candle used at LICH WAKES was similarly named.

Corpse coins. An old name for the pennies placed on the eyelids of dead persons to prevent them from opening.

Corpus (Lat. a body). The whole body or substance; especially the complete collection of writings on one subject or by one person, as the *Corpus poetarum Latinorum*, the *Corpus historicum medii ævi*, etc.

Corpus Christi. A church festival kept on the Thursday after TRINITY SUNDAY, in honour of the Blessed Sacrament. It was instituted by Pope Urban IV in 1264. It was the regular time for the performance of religious dramas by the trade guilds and in England, many of the Corpus Christi plays of York, Coventry, and Chester are extant.

Corpus delicti (Lat. the body of the crime or offence). The material thing in respect to which a crime has been committed; thus a murdered body or some of the stolen property would be a "*corpus delicti*".

Corpuscular Philosophy. The theory promulgated by Robert Boyle which sought to account for all natural phenomena by the position and motion of corpuscles.

Corridors of Power. Collectively the ministries in WHITEHALL with their top-ranking civil servants. The phrase was first used by C. P. (Lord) Snow in his novel *Homecomings* (1956) and gained speedy acceptance. It was used in the title of a later novel *Corridors of Power* (1964).

> Boffins at Daggers Drawn in Corridors of Power.
> *The Times* (Headline 8 April 1965).

Corroboree. A dance practised by Australian aborigines on festal or warlike occasions; hence any hilarious or slightly riotous assembly.

Corruption of Blood. Loss of title and entailed estates in consequence of treason, by which a man's *blood was attainted* and his issue suffered.

Corsican. An epithet applied to NAPOLEON who was born in Corsica, which became a French possession in 1768. He was often referred to as "the Corsican upstart".

Corsned (kôrs' ned) (O.E. *cor*, choice, trial; *snaed*, piece). The piece of bread "consecrated for exorcism", formerly given to a person to swallow as a test of his guilt, a form of trial by ORDEAL. The words of "consecration" were: "May this morsel cause convulsions and find no passage if the accused is guilty, but turn to wholesome nourishment if he is innocent." *See* CHOKE.

Cortina (kôr' tī nà) (Lat. cauldron). The tripod of APOLLO, which was in the form of a cauldron; hence any tripod used for religious purposes by the ancient Romans.

Corvinus (kôr vī' nus). Matthias I, King of Hungary (1458–90), younger son of

John (Janos) Hunyadi, was so called from the raven (Lat. *corvus*) on his shield. He was one of the greatest of all book collectors and some of the earliest European gilt-tooled bindings were executed for his library. They may be recognized by the raven stamped in the centre of the covers.

Corvus, Marcus Valerius (c. 370–270 B.C.) was so called because while in combat with a gigantic Gaul during the Gallic War he was helped by a raven (*corvus*) which flew at the Gaul's face.

Corybantes (kor i băn' tēz). The Phrygian priests of CYBELE, whose worship was celebrated with orgiastic dances and loud, wild music. Hence a wild, unrestrained dancer is sometimes called a *corybant*. In 1890 Prof. T. H. Huxley referred to the members of the SALVATION ARMY as being "militant missionaries of a somewhat corybantic Christianity".

Corycian Cave (kor is' i àn). A cave on Mount PARNASSUS named after the NYMPH Corycia. The MUSES are sometimes in poetry called Corycides or the Corycian Nymphs.

> The immortal Muse
> To your calm habitations, to the cave
> Corycian...will guide his footsteps.
> AKENSIDE: *Hymn to the Naiads*.

Corydon (kor' i don). A conventional name for a rustic, a shepherd; a brainless lovesick fellow; from the shepherd in Virgil's *Eclogue* vii, and in Theocritus.

Coryphæus (kôr i fē' us). The leader and speaker of the chorus in Greek dramas; hence figuratively, the leader generally, the most active member of a board, company, expedition, etc.

Coryphée. A ballet dancer; strictly speaking, the leader of the ballet.

Coss, Rule of. An old name for algebra (also called the *Cossic Art*), from the Ital. *regola de cosa, cosa* being an unknown quantity, or a "thing".

Costard. A large ribbed apple, and metaphorically, a man's head. *Cp.* COSTERMONGER.

Costermonger. A street vendor of fruit, vegetables, fish, etc., properly an apple-seller; from COSTARD and *monger*, a dealer or trader (O.E. *mangian*, to trade), as in ironmonger, fishmonger, etc. Often abbreviated to *coster*, the word is generally applied in London to "barrow boys" and COCKNEY dealers. *See* PEARLIES.

Cotillion, Cotillon (ko til' yon) (Fr. petticoat). Originally a brisk dance by four or eight persons, in which the ladies held up their gowns and showed their under petticoats. It later became a form of quick waltz. The French phrase for PETTICOAT GOVERNMENT is *régime du cotillon*.

Cotset. A word found in DOMESDAY BOOK denoting one of the lowliest types of feudal bondsmen from O.E. *cot-saeta*, a cottage-dweller.

Cotswold. You are as long a-coming as Cotswold barley. The Cotswold Hills in Gloucestershire are bleak and cold, and wind-exposed. Backward in vegetation, they yield a good supply of late barley.

Cotswold lion. An ironical name for a sheep, for which the Cotswold hills are famous.

Cottage. Cottage loaf. A loaf of bread in two round lumps, the smaller being on top, and baked with a good crust.

Cottage Orné (Fr. *orné*, adorned). A picturesque country cottage or small house designed for the well-to-do.

Cottage piano. A small upright pianoforte.

Cottar. In England a class of VILLEIN, a cottager, virtually the same as a BORDAR; one who usually held a few acres in the village fields and who had to give one or two days each week to working for his lord.

In the Highlands of Scotland and in the Orkney and Shetland Isles the name applied to certain tenants with small patches of land owing no services.

Cotton. A cotton king. A rich Lancashire or Manchester cotton manufacturer, a king in wealth, style of living, equipage, etc. Sir Robert Peel, the statesman, could be so designated.

Cotton kingdom. In the U.S.A., the agricultural states of the South, where cotton production expanded rapidly from the close of the 18th century, and stimulated the support for slavery.

Cottonopolis. Manchester, the headquarters of cotton manufacture; Great Britain's largest single export during the 19th century.

To cotton on. To catch on, to grasp a line of thought.

To cotton on to a person. To cling to or take a fancy to someone. To stick to a person as cotton sticks to our clothes.

Cottonian Library. The remarkable library founded by Sir Robert Cotton (1571–1631), the antiquary. Rich in early MSS., and augmented by his son and grandson, it was secured for the nation in 1700 and transferred first to Essex House and then to Ashburnham House, Westminster, in 1730. A disastrous fire in 1731 destroyed over 100 volumes of irreplaceable MSS., and the remainder (some 800 volumes) were moved to Westminster School and finally lodged in the BRITISH MUSEUM in 1753.

Cottus (kot' ús). One of the hundred-handed giants, son of URANUS (HEAVEN) and GÆA (Earth). His two brothers were BRIAREUS and Gyes.

Cotytto (ko tī tō). The Thracian goddess of immodesty and debauchery, worshipped at Athens with licentious rites. *See* BAPTES.

Couéism. A form of psychotherapy dependent, upon auto-suggestion, propagated by Emile Coué (1857–1926), a French pharmacist. The key phrase of his system was, "Every day, and in every way, I am becoming better and better."

Couleur de rose (koo lĕr de rōz). (Fr. rose-coloured). Highly coloured; too favourably viewed; overdrawn with romantic embellishments, like objects viewed through rose-tinted spectacles.

Count (Lat. *comitem*, accusative of *comes*, a companion). The continental equivalent of the English EARL (O.E. *eorl*, a warrior), of which COUNTESS is still the feminine.

Count. Don't count your chickens before they are hatched. *See under* CHICKEN.

To count kin with someone. A Scots expression meaning to compare one's pedigree with that of another.

To count out the house. When the SPEAKER adjourns a sitting of the HOUSE OF COMMONS because there are not forty members present, after his attention has been called to the fact.

To be counted out is said of a boxer who, after being knocked down, fails to rise during the ten seconds counted out loud by the referee. **Count me out.** Do not reckon me in this.

To count upon. To rely with confidence on someone or something; to reckon on.

To count without one's host. *See* TO RECKON WITHOUT YOUR HOST, *under* HOST.

Countenance, To. To sanction, to support. Approval or disapproval is shown by the countenance. The Scriptures speak of "the light of God's countenance", *i.e.* the smile of approbation; and to "hide His face" (or countenance) is to manifest displeasure.

Out of countenance. Ashamed, confounded. With countenance fallen or cast down.

To keep one's countenance. To refrain from smiling or appearing downcast, to avoid revealing one's thoughts by the face.

To put one out of countenance is to make one ashamed or disconcerted. To *discountenance* is to set your face against something done or propounded.

Counter. Under the counter. A phrase that became current in World War II, to denote a common practice of dishonest tradesmen. Articles in short supply were kept out of sight, or under the counter, for sale to favoured customers, often at enhanced prices. *Cp.* BLACK MARKET.

Counter-caster. One who keeps accounts or casts up accounts by counters.

Counter-Reformation. *See under* REFORMATION.

Country. Black Country. *See* BLACK.

Country dance. A corruption of the Fr. *contre danse; i.e.* a dance where the partners face each other, as in the Sir Roger de Coverley. *See* COVERLEY.

To appeal, or **go to the country.** To dissolve PARLIAMENT in order to ascertain the wishes of the country by a general election.

County (Fr. *comté*). A SHIRE. After the Local Government Act of 1888 until 1972, certain of the larger towns had county status as county BOROUGHS. *See* *also* HUNDRED.

County family. A family belonging to the nobility or gentry with an ancestral seat in the county.

County Palatine, or **Palatinate** (Lat. *palatinus*, of the palace). Properly the dominion of an earl palatine over which he had quasi-royal jurisdiction. Cheshire, Shropshire, Durham and Kent became Counties Palatine after the Norman Conquest as frontier districts, and Lancaster in 1351. At one time Pembroke, Hexhamshire and the Isle of Ely were so designated but only Cheshire, Durham and Lancaster still retain the title, and the Chancellor of the Duchy of Lancaster is a member of the Government. Their jurisdictions are now vested in the Crown. *See* PALATINATE.

Coup (koo) (Fr.). A blow or stroke. Now used in English for a successful move or stroke in certain games (chess, billiards), a stroke of policy or a sudden and successful act, an illegal attempt to overthrow an established government. *See* COUP D'ÉTAT.

A good coup. A good hit or haul.

Coup d'essai. A trial-piece; a piece of work serving for practice.

Coup d'état. A state stroke, one of those bold measures taken by a government to forestall a supposed or actual danger to the régime; more commonly a violent or illegal seizure of power from above.

The famous *coup d'état* by which Louis Napoleon seized power occurred on 2 December 1851. *See* MAN OF DECEMBER *under* DECEMBER.

Coup de grâce. The finishing stroke; the stroke of mercy. When a prisoner was being tortured, the executioner finished him off with a *coup de grâce* to put him out of his misery.

Coup de main. A sudden stroke, a stratagem whereby something is effected suddenly; a *coup*.

> It appears more like a line of march than a body intended for a *coup de main*, as there are with it bullocks and baggage of different kinds.
>
> WELLINGTON: *Dispatches*, vol. I, p. 25.

Coup d'œil. A view, glance, prospect; the effect of things at the first glance; literally "a stroke of the eye".

Coup de pied de l'âne. A kick from

the ass's hoof; figuratively, a blow given to a vanquished or fallen man; a cowardly blow; an insult offered to one who has not the power of returning or avenging it. The allusion is to the fable of the sick lion kicked by the ass.

Coup de soleil. A sunstroke or any malady produced by exposure to the sun.

Coup de théâtre. An unforeseen or unexpected turn in a drama producing a sensational effect; something planned for effect, such as Burke's throwing down of the dagger in the HOUSE OF COMMONS.

Coup manqué. A false stroke, a miss, a failure.

Coupon Election. The General Election of 1918, when PRIME MINISTER Lloyd George and Mr. Bonar Law sent a certificate of coupon to all candidates supporting the Coalition. The coupon was not accepted by the Asquith LIBERALS nor by the LABOUR Party. A *couponeer* was a politician who accepted the coupon.

Course. In the course of nature. In the due of proper time or order, etc.; in the ordinary procedure of nature.

A matter of course is something that belongs to ordinary procedure, or that is customary.

To hold, or **keep on the course.** To go straight; to do one's duty in that course [path] of life in which we are placed. The allusion is to navigation.

Court. From Lat. *cohors, cohortis*, originally an enclosure for sheep or cattle; subsequently as many soldiers as could be cooped together in such an enclosure was called a *cohort*. The cattle-yard, being the nucleus of the farm, became the centre of a group of farm buildings and cottages, then of a hamlet, town, fortified place, and lastly of a royal residence.

Court Baron. *See* BARON.

Court cards. A corruption of *coat card*, because they bore the representation of a clothed or *coated* figure, and not because the king, queen, and knave belonged to a court.

The King of Clubs may originally have represented the arms of the Pope; of Spades, the king of France; of Dia-

monds, the king of Spain; and of Hearts, the king of England. The French kings of cards are called David (Spades), Alexander (Clubs), Cæsar (Diamonds), and Charles (Hearts)—representing the Jewish, Greek, Roman and Frankish empires. The queens or dames are Argine, *i.e.* Juno (Hearts), Judith (Clubs), Rachel (Diamonds), and Pallas (Spades)—representing royalty, fortitude, piety and wisdom. They were likenesses of Maria d'Anjou, the queen of Charles VII; Isabeau, the queen-mother; Agnès Sorel, the royal mistress; and Jeanne d'Arc, the dame of Spades or war.

Court Circular. Daily information concerning the official engagements of royalty for publication in the newspapers. George III introduced the custom in 1803 to prevent misstatements.

Court cupboard. A movable buffet to hold flagons, cans, cups, and beakers.

Court fools. *See* FOOLS.

Court-hand. A cursive form of handwriting which developed in England by the late 12th century as the legal script employed in the writing of the king's business, the law courts, etc. It was abolished in the reign of George II.

Court holy water. An obsolete term of Elizabeth I's reign for fair speeches, which look like promises of favour, but end in nothing.

Court-leet. *See* LEET.

Court martial. A court convened to try a person subject to military law. In Great Britain, such courts resulted from the Mutiny Act of 1689.

Court plaster. Sticking-plaster, so called from the fashion of court ladies patching their faces with fanciful shapes cut out from such plaster. This fashion was in vogue in the reign of Charles I and in Queen Anne's time was employed as a political badge.

Court of Arches. *See* ARCHES.

Court of Love. A judicial court for deciding affairs of the heart, established in Provence during the days of the TROUBADOURS. The following is a case submitted to their judgment: A lady listened to one admirer, squeezed the hand of another, and touched with her toe the foot of a third. Query: Which of these three was the favoured suitor?

Court of Piepowder. *See* PIEPOWDER.

Court of Session. The supreme court of civil jurisdiction in SCOTLAND, first established in 1532, and originally modelled on the PARLEMENT of Paris.

Out of court. Not admissible evidence within the terms of reference of the trial being conducted; ruled as being out of consideration.

They are but in the Court of the Gentiles. They are not wholly God's people; they are not the elect, but have only a smattering of the truth. The "Court of the Israelites" in the Jewish Temple was for Jewish men; the "Court of Women" for Jewish women; the "Court of the Gentiles" was for those who were not Jews.

To pay court to someone is to pay attention to or cultivate someone whose favour or interest is wanted.

To settle out of court. A case, almost always involving damages, which is settled by the respective litigants' solicitors, before it is called to court, agreeing on a sum to be paid by the litigant who admits himself to be in the wrong.

Courtesy titles. Titles assumed or granted by social custom, without legal status. The courtesy title of the eldest son of a peer is normally one of his father's inferior titles, usually his second, but sometimes lower ones are used. Younger sons of DUKES and MARQUISES have the courtesy title LORD. The daughters of Dukes, Marquises, and EARLS are styled LADY. Sons of Earls, VISCOUNTS and BARONS are entitled *Honourable* as are daughters of barons. Courtesy titles are allowed to the eldest son of courtesy marquises and earls. None of these titles carry the right to sit in the HOUSE OF LORDS.

Cousin. Sir William Blackstone (1723–1780) says that Henry IV, being related or allied to every EARL in the kingdom, artfully and constantly acknowledged the connection in all public acts. The usage has descended to his successors, and in royal writs and commissions an *earl* is addressed "Our right trusty and well-beloved cousin", a MARQUIS "Our right trusty and entirely-beloved cousin", and a DUKE "Our right trusty and

right-entirely-beloved cousin".

The word is also used by sovereigns in addressing one another formally.

Cousin-german. The children of brothers and sisters, first cousins or full cousins; kinsfolk (Lat. *germanus*, a brother, one of the same stock).

Cousin Jack. So Cornishmen are called in the western counties, and in places where they are working as miners.

Cousin Michael. The Germans were so called. *Michel*, in Old German, means "gross"; *Cousin Michael* is meant to indicate a slow, heavy, unrefined, coarse-feeding people.

I wouldn't call the king my cousin. I am perfectly satisfied with things as they are; they couldn't be bettered even if I were cousin to the king.

To call cousins. This formerly meant to claim relationship.

Cove. An individual; as a *flash cover* (a swell), a *rum cove* (a man whose position and character are not quite obvious, a queer fish), a *gentry cove* (a gentleman), a *downy cove* (a very knowing individual), etc. The word is old thieves' CANT.

> A ben cove, a brave cove, a gentry coffin.
> MIDDLETON and DEKKER: *The Roaring Girle*, V, i (1611).

Covenanters. A term applied to those Scottish PRESBYTERIANS subscribing to various bonds or covenants for the security and advancement of their cause. The first was entered into by the Lords of the Congregation in 1557 and another by ordinance of King James VI in 1581. In 1638 the National Covenant was directed against the Laudian prayer-book imposed by Charles I. In 1643 a Solemn League and Covenant pledged the Scots and their English Parlimentarian allies to preserve Presbyterianism in SCOTLAND and to establish it in ENGLAND and IRELAND.

The name Covenanter is particularly applied to those who adhered to the Covenants after they were declared unlawful in 1662. Between the RESTORATION and the Revolution of 1688 they were harried and proscribed but exhibited a brave and often fanatical resistance. *See* CAMERONIANS.

Covent Garden. A corruption of *Convent Garden*; the garden and burial ground attached to the convent or Abbey of WESTMINSTER, granted at the dissolution of the monasteries to the Duke of Somerset and on his attainder in 1552 it passed to the Earl of Bedford, in whose family it remained until 1910. The original church of St. Paul's Convent Garden was built by Inigo Jones between 1631 and 1638, separated from St. Martin's parish in 1645, and rebuilt after a disastrous fire in 1795. Its peculiar feature is that the portico that appears to be the front is really the back.

The fruit, flower, and vegetable market developed from the 17th century, when the square became popular with stallholders. The nucleus of the existing market buildings dates from 1850 but the market itself moved to Nine Elms, Battersea in 1974. In the 17th and 18th centuries the area was the stamping ground of the MOHOCKS and other semi-fashionable ruffians, and its COFFEE-houses, bagnios and taverns the favourite resorts of poets, actors and artists.

Coventry. Coventry Mysteries. Miracle plays supposed to have been acted at CORPUS CHRISTI at Coventry until 1591. Called *Ludus Coventriæ* by Sir Robert Bruce, Cotton's librarian in the time of James I, their special connexion with Coventry or Corpus Christi is doubtful, although there are two such plays extant, the play of the Shearman and Tailors, and the play of the Weavers. *See also* MYSTERY.

Peeping Tom of Coventry. *See* GODIVA.

To send one to Coventry. To take no notice of him; to make him feel that he is in disgrace by ignoring him. *Cp.* BOYCOTT. It is said that the citizens of Coventry once had so great a dislike of soldiers that a woman seen speaking to one was instantly tabooed; hence when a soldier was sent to Coventry he was cut off from all social intercourse. Clarendon, in his *History of the Great Rebellion*, says that Royalist prisoners captured in Birmingham were sent to Coventry, which was a Parliamentary stronghold.

Cover. To break cover. To start from the covert or temporary lair. The usual earthholes of a fox being blocked the night before a hunt, the fox seeks some other cover, and as soon as it quits it the hunt begins.

Coverley. Sir Roger de Coverley. A member of an imaginary club in the *Spectator*, "who lived in SOHO Square when he was in town". Sir Roger is the type of an English squire in the reign of Queen Anne.

The country dance of this name (or rather the *Roger of Coverly*) was well known before Addison's time.

Cow. The cow that nourished YMIR with four streams of milk was called Audhumla.

Always behind, like a cow's tail. A proverbial saying of ancient date. *Cp. Tanquam coda vituli* (Petronius).

Cow Cockie. A New Zealand or Australian dairy farmer. *See* COCKATOO.

Curst cows have curt horns. Angry men cannot do all the mischief they wish. Curst means "angry" or "fierce", and curt is "short", as curt-mantle, CURT-HOSE. The Latin proverb is, *Dat Deus immiti cornua curta bovi*.

Not until the cows come home. Not for a very long time, if at all.

The cow knows not the worth of her tail till she loses it, and is troubled with flies, which her tail brushed off.

The tune the old cow died of. *See* TUNE.

The whiter the cow, the surer it is to go to the altar. The richer the prey, the more likely it is to be seized. Pagan sacrifices demanded white cattle.

Cowboy. The term used for the cattlemen of the American West, much romanticized in popular ballad and story. Their "ten-gallon" hats, leather CHAPS, and high-heeled boots, were characteristic dress in the great days of the Cattle Kingdom. The name was also applied during the Revolutionary Wars to TORY partisans of New York State, notorious for their harsh treatment of their opponents. In current colloquial usage the term *cowboy* is applied to clumsy and unskilled lorry drivers and workers in many occupations.

Cow-lick. A tuft of hair on the forehead

that cannot be made to lie in the same direction as the rest of the hair.

Cowpuncher. A COWBOY, derived from the metal-tipped pole with which cattle are driven when being loaded on rail.

Cow with the iron tail, The. A pump, from its use in dishonestly watering-down milk.

Dun Cow, The Book of the Dun Cow, The Old Dun Cow. *See under* DUN.

Sacred Cow. *See under* SACRED.

Coward. Ultimately from Lat. *cauda*, a tail, either from an animal "turning tail" when frightened, or from cowering with its tail between its legs.

A beast *cowarded*, in HERALDRY, is one drawn with its tail between its legs.

Cowper Justice. *See* CUPAR JUSTICE.

Coxcomb. An empty-headed vain person. The ancient licensed JESTERS were so called because they wore a cock's comb in their caps.

> Let me hire him too; here's my cox-comb.
> SHAKESPEARE: *King Lear*, I, iv.

Coyne and livery. An old Irish term for food and entertainment for soldiers and forage for their horses, formerly exacted by Irish chiefs when on the march. *Coyne* is Irish *coinnemh*, billeting, or one billeted.

Coystril. A term of reproach, meaning a low fellow, a knave, a varlet.

> He's a coward and a coystril that will not drink to my niece.
> SHAKESPEARE: *Twelfth Night*, I, iii.

It is a variant of the obsolete *custrel*, an attendant on a KNIGHT, seemingly from O.Fr. *coustillier*, a soldier armed with a *coustille* (a two-edged dagger). Every soldier in the life-guards of Henry VIII was attended by a man called a *coystrel* or *coystril*.

Cozen. To cheat. This is the same word as *cousin*; the Fr. *cousiner* means "to sponge on" as well as "to call cousin" (*see under* COUSIN). In England one who *cozened* another was one who lived on another just as though they were "cousins". *See* SHAKESPEARE'S *Merry Wives*, IV, ii, and V, v.

Crab. A walking-stick made of crab-apple wood; a *crabstick*.

To catch a crab. *See* CATCH.

Crack. First-rate, excellent, quite at the top of its class; as a crack regiment, a crack shot, a crack hand of cards, etc. (*See* TO CRACK UP.) Formerly the word was used substantively for a lively young fellow, a WAG.

> Indeed, La! 'tis a noble child; a crack, madam.
> SHAKESPEARE: *Coriolanus*, I, iii.

Nowadays **a crack** or **a wisecrack** is a sharp, witty, or humorous saying, or just "a dig" at someone. Both derive from O.E. *cracian*, to make a sudden sharp noise.

A gude crack. In Scottish dialect, a good chat or conversation, also a good talker.

Crack-brained. Eccentric; slightly mad.

Cracked pots last longest. An old proverb. Long-sufferers from ill health or some disability often outlive the seemingly fit and healthy.

In a crack. Instantly. In a snap of the fingers, in the time taken by a crack or shot.

> Do pray undo the bolt a little faster—
> They're on the stair just now, and in a crack
> Will all be here.
> BYRON: *Don Juan*, I, cxxxvii.

To be given a fair crack of the whip. To be fairly treated; to receive just treatment; to be given a fair share of something.

To crack a bottle. In this phrase the word implies to open and drink.

To crack a crib. To break into a house and steal. (*See* CRIB.) Hence, *cracksman*, a burglar.

To crack up. To praise highly, to eulogize.

It also means to break down in health or mind.

Cracker-barrel philosophy (U.S.A.) is roughly the same as homespun philosophy. The barrels in which crackers, or biscuits, used to be kept, were often used as seats in the country stores by local folk who met there and exchanged views on topics of the day, etc. *See* CROSS-ROADS.

Crackers. In colloquial usage means CRACK-BRAINED.

Cradle Crown. In mediæval England a

fine paid by a priest (in lieu of penance) for fathering a child in his house and keeping a concubine. *Cp*. SIN RENT.

Cradle-holding. Land held by BOROUGH ENGLISH.

Cradle-snatching. Said of a grown man who consorts with a young girl well below his own age.

Craft. The Craft. A name given to FREEMASONRY by its members.

The Gentle Craft. *See under* GENTLE.

Crambo. A game which consists in someone setting a line which another is to rhyme to, but no word of the first line must occur in the second. The word is of uncertain origin.

Dumb crambo is a somewhat similar game where rhymes of the given word are pantomimed or acted in dumb show until guessed.

Cramp-rings. Rings blessed by English sovereigns and distributed on GOOD FRIDAY, supposed to cure cramp and "falling sickness" (epilepsy). The custom grew up after the time of Edward the Confessor, who was said to have been given such a ring by a pilgrim, and was continued until the reign of Queen Mary Tudor. *Cp*. KING'S EVIL.

Shackles or fetters, in colloquial usage, came to be called *cramp-rings*.

Cranmer's Bible. *See* BIBLE, THE ENGLISH.

Crannock. An Irish measure which, in the time of Edward II, contained either eight or sixteen pecks. *Curnock* is another form of the word: this was a dry measure of varying capacity, but usually 3 bushels for wheat, 4 bushels for corn, and from 10 to 15 bushels for coal, lime, etc.

Crapaud, or **Johnny Crapaud.** A Frenchman. *See* FLEUR-DE-LIS.

Les anciens crapauds prendront Sara. One of the cryptic prophecies of NOSTRADAMUS (1503–1566). Sara is *Aras* reversed, and when the French under Louis XIV took Arras from the Spaniards, this verse was remembered.

Crape. A saint in crape is twice a saint in lawn. (Pope: *Ep. to Cobham*, 136.) Crape (a sort of bombazine or alpaca) is the stuff of which cheap clerical gowns used to be made, lawn refers to the sleeves of a BISHOP. A saintly parson is all very well but the same goodness in a bishop is exalted into something much more noteworthy.

Craps. The American term for dice, a most popular form of gambling in the U.S.A. About 1800, when New Orleans was a French city, Bernard Marigny introduced dice-playing from France. He was a CREOLE and known as Johnny CRAPAUD, thus dice-playing, or Johnny Crapaud's game, became shortened into "craps". Burgundy Street in the Vieux Carré of New Orleans was, until 1860, known as Craps Street, after Marigny.

Cravat. This neckcloth was introduced into France in the 17th century. Croatian soldiers or Cravates (O.Slav. *khruvat*) guarded the Turkish frontier of HABSBURG territories and when France organized a regiment on the model of the Croats, their linen neckcloth was imitated, and the regiment was called "The Royal Cravat".

To wear a hempen cravat. To be hanged.

Craven. The word is derived from O.Fr. *cravant*, pres. part. of *craver* or *crever*, to burst or break, hence to be overcome.

When controversies were decided by an appeal to battle, the combatants fought with batons, and if the accused could either kill his adversary or maintain the fight till sundown he was acquitted. If he wished to call off, he cried out "Craven!" and was held infamous.

Crawler (Austr.). A convict who escaped with the connivance of the overseer, allowing himself to be recaptured in order that the overseer might collect the reward.

Creaking doors hang the longest. Delicate persons often outlive the more robust. *Cp*. CRACKED POTS.

Creatura Christi, or **Creature.** At one time newly-born children, in danger of dying before the arrival of a priest, were often baptized by a midwife. In the flurry of the moment mistakes could occur over the sex of the child, and to avoid the possibility of boys being baptized with girls' names, or the reverse, midwives often named them *Creature* or *Creatura Christi*—Christ's Creature being suitable in either case.

Creature. That which is created, animate or inanimate. Thus we speak of a man or animals as "God's creatures" and in the Communion Service (BOOK OF COMMON PRAYER), "these thy creatures of bread and wine".

Creature in the sense of whisky or other liquors is a facetious adaptation of the passage "Every creature of God is good" (I *Tim*. iv, 4), used in the defence of the drinking of alcoholic beverages.

> I find my master took too much of the creature last night, and is now angling for a quarrel.
>
> DRYDEN: *Amphitryon*, III, i.

Creature also has the meaning of a dependent or hanger-on.

Creature-comforts. Food and other things necessary for the comfort of the body. Man being supposed to consist of body and soul, the body is the creature, but the soul is the "vital spark of the heavenly flame".

Credat Judæus, or **Credat Judæus Apella** (Lat.). Let the Jew Apella believe it (HORACE, I *Satires*, v, 100); tell that to the Marines. (*See* HORSE MARINES.) Who this Apella was is not known.

Credence Table (kré' déns). The table near the altar on which the bread and wine are placed before they are consecrated. In former times food was placed on a credence table to be tasted prior to being set before the guests, to assure them that the meat was not poisoned (Ital. *credenza*, a shelf or buffet).

Credit Squeeze. A comprehensive term to cover governmental attempts to check internal consumption and spending in order to curb inflationary tendencies, and often with the further aim of improving the BALANCE OF PAYMENTS. Tight control over borrowing and lending is exercised by raising the bank rate, resulting in dearer money, the restriction of bank lending, hire purchase, etc.

Credo (Lat.). A statement of belief. Literally "I believe".

Credo quia impossibile (Lat.). I believe it because it is impossible. A paradox ascribed to St. Augustine, but founded on a passage in Tertullian's *De Carne Christi*, IV:

> Credibile est, quia ineptum est... certum est quia impossibile.

Crème de la Crème (krãm de la krãm) (Fr.). Literally "cream of the cream"; used figuratively for the very choicest part of something which itself is very choice; the very best.

Cremona (kre mõ' nà). A town in Lombardy famous for its violin makers (1550–1750). The most famous makers were Nicolo AMATI (1596–1684), teacher of Andreas GUARNIERI (*c.* 1626–1698) and Antonio Stradivari (1644–1737). The term is loosely applied to any good instrument. *See also* STRAD.

The organ-stop known as the cremona is a corruption of the German *krummhorn*, crooked horn. It is a reed stop of 8-foot tone.

Cremorne Gardens. Famous Victorian pleasure gardens opened in 1845 as a rival to VAUXHALL GARDENS on the land of Chelsea Farm, the former property of Thomas Dawson, Viscount Cremorne. A popular venue for fêtes and entertainments, their clientèle degenerated and they were closed in 1877 after many local complaints. Lots Road Power Station, on the left bank of the Thames near Battersea Bridge, largely occupies their site. Their memory is preserved in Whistler's *Nocturnes*.

Creole (krē ōl) (Fr. from Sp. *criollo*; W. Indian corruption of *criadillo* from *criado*, bred, brought up). Originally a person of Spanish parentage born in the West Indies as against those of mixed blood, Negroes, new immigrants, and aboriginals. It is often wrongly used to denote those of mixed blood but its usage varies in different places. In the West Indies it implies European descent; in Louisiana the French-speaking whites; in Mexico, whites of Spanish blood. Non-whites are called Negro creoles, but in Mauritius, Réunion, etc., creole is usually applied to Negroes. The Empress Josephine was a creole from Martinique and the liberated slaves of Liberia called themselves creoles.

Crescent. Tradition says that, "Philip, the father of Alexander, meeting with great difficulties in the siege of Byzantium, set the workmen to undermine the walls, but a crescent moon discovered the design, which miscarried; consequently the Byzantines erected a statue to DIANA, and the crescent became the symbol of the state."

Another legend is that Othman, the SULTAN, saw in a vision a crescent moon, which kept increasing till its horns extended from east to west, and he adopted the crescent of his dream for his standard, adding the motto, *"Donec repleat orbem"*.

The crescent as a symbol was used by the Seljuk Sultan Ala-ud-din in the mid-13th century, and it was reputedly adopted from this source by Osman, who founded the Ottoman dynasty in *c.* 1281. It is also said that the crescent was placed on the Turkish flag by Mohammed II, after the capture of Constantinople in 1453.

Crescent City. The descriptive name in the U.S.A. for New Orleans.

Cresset. A beacon light. The original cresset was an open metal cup at the top of a pole, the cup being filled with burning grease or oil. Hence the name; from O.Fr. *craisse* (Mod. Fr. *graisse*), grease.

Cressida, or **Cressid.** Daughter of Calchas, a priest, beloved by TROILUS. They vowed eternal fidelity and as pledges Troilus gave the maiden a sleeve, and Cressid gave the Trojan prince a glove. Scarce had the vow been made when an exchange of prisoners was agreed to. Diomed gave up three Trojan princes, and was to receive Cressid in lieu thereof. Cressid vowed to remain constant, and Troilus swore to rescue her. She was led off to the Grecian's tent and soon gave all her affections to Diomed—even bade him wear the sleeve that Troilus had given her in token of his love.

Cresswell, Madam. A notorious bawd and procuress who flourished in London between *c.* 1670 and 1684 and was much patronized by RESTORATION courtiers and politicians.

Crestfallen. Dispirited. The allusion is to fighting cocks, whose crest falls in defeat, and rises rigid and of a deep-red colour in victory.

Cretan Labyrinth. *See* LABYRINTH.

Crete. Hound of Crete. A bloodhound.

Coupe la gorge, that's the word. I thee

defy again, O hound of Crete.
SHAKESPEARE: *Henry V*, II, i.

The infamy of Crete. The MINOTAUR.

Cretinism (kret' in izm). Mental imbecility accompanied by goitre, so called from the Crétins of the Alps. The word is a corruption of Christian (*Chrétien*), because being baptized, and only idiots, they were "washed from original sin", and incapable of actual sin. Similarly, idiots are called *innocents*.

Crew Cut. A form of hair-cut popularized by U.S. athletes, particularly college rowing teams, in the decade following World War II. The hair is cut very short all over and brushed upright on top, reminiscent of a hedgehog.

Crewel Garters. Garters made of worsted or yarn. The resemblance in sound between *crewel* (the derivation of which is unknown) and *cruel* gave rise to many puns.

Ha, ha! he wears cruel garters.
SHAKESPEARE: *King Lear*, II, iv.

Crib. Thieves' slang for a house or dwelling as "Stocking Crib" (a hosier's shop), "Thimble Crib" (a silversmith's); also slang for a petty theft; and for a literal translation of a Greek or Latin text used as an aid in translating, either openly or surreptitiously.

The word originally denoted a fodder rack with bars in a stable or shippen; hence its application to a child's cot.

In the West Country a working man still has his mid-morning *crib* or refreshment during his *crib-break*. *See* BEVER.

To crack a crib. *See* CRACK.

To crib is to pilfer, purloin, or to copy someone else's work (especially applied to cheating or "copying" among school children), also to plagiarize.

Crichton. *See under* ADMIRABLE.

Cricket. Probably from O.E. *cric, cryec,* a staff or stick, and thus connected with *crutch*. Strutt in his *Sports and Pastimes of the People of England* (1801) suggests that cricket originated from the mediæval game of club-ball. John Derrick of Guildford in 1598 (being then aged *c.* 59) states that as a boy at school "hee and several of his fellowes did runne and play there at Crickett and other plaies". An earlier reference to *criquet* has been traced to 15th-century

Flanders. The game was certainly played at Winchester school before the Civil Wars. It began to come into its own in the 18th century and owed much to the Hambledon Club matches on Broad Halfpenny Down, which came to an end in 1793. The Marylebone Cricket Club (M.C.C.), which is regarded as the governing body of the game, was founded in 1787, and the present LORD'S CRICKET GROUND was opened in 1814.

Single and double wicket was played from early on, and sizes of wicket, etc., varied considerably. At the beginning of the 18th century two stumps, 12 inches high and 24 inches apart, were used. In the rules made in 1774 the stumps were to be 22 inches high with a bail of 6 inches. The third stump was added by the Hambledon Club in 1775 and the height of the stump raised from 27 to 28 inches in 1929. *See also* CHINAMAN; GOOGLY.

> Who would think that a little bit of leather and two pieces of wood, has such a delightful and delighting power!
>
> MISS MITFORD: *Our Village* (*A Country Cricket-Match*).

It's not cricket. It's not done in a fair and sportsmanlike way.

Merry as a cricket. *See* GRIG.

Crimen Læsæ Majestatis (krī' men lē' ze mǎj es tā' tis) (Lat.). *See* LÈSE-MAJESTÉ

Cripplegate. The origin of the name for this district in the City of London is uncertain. St. GILES is the patron SAINT of cripples, but the name is not derived from the former parish church of St. Giles, Cripplegate, which was spelt *Crupelgate* in the early 13th century. It is possibly from O.E. *crepel* (a burrow) or *crypele* (a den). The gate was demolished in 1760.

Crisis (Gr. *krinein*, to decide or to determine), properly means the "ability to judge". HIPPOCRATES said that all diseases had their periods, when the humours of the body (*see* HUMOUR) ebbed and flowed like the tide of the sea. These tidal days he called *critical days*, and the tide itself a *crisis*, because it was on these days the physician could determine whether the disorder was taking a good or bad turn. The seventh and all its multiples were critical days of a fa-

vourable character.

Crispin and Crispianus. Shoemakers who became patron saints of their craft. It is said that the two brothers born at Rome, went to Soissons in France to propagate the Christian religion, and they maintained themselves wholly by making and mending shoes. They were martyred in *c*.286.

St. Crispin's Day. 25 October, the day of the battle of Agincourt. SHAKESPEARE makes Crispin Crispian one person, and not two brothers. Hence Henry V says to his soldiers:

St. Crispin's holiday. Every Monday, with those who begin the working week on Tuesday, still a common practice with some butchers, fishmongers, etc.; a no-work day with shoemakers.

St. Crispin's lance. A shoemaker's awl.

Criss-cross Row. *See* CHRISS-CROSS.

Critic. A judge, an arbiter. (*See* CRISIS.) A captious, malignant critic is called a ZOILUS.

Prince of Critics. Aristarchus of Byzantium (2nd century B.C.), who compiled a critical edition of the Homeric poems, commentaries, etc.

Croak, To. In slang this means to die, the term probably coming from the hoarse death rattle or croak of the expiring breath. A HEDGE doctor or wandering QUACK is known as a *Crocus*, or one who makes his patients croak.

Croaker. A raven, so called from its croak; one who takes a despondent view of things.

Croakumshire. A name given to the county of Northumberland because the natives were alleged to speak with a peculiar croak.

Crockett, Davy (1786–1836). American folk hero famed as a marksman, bear hunter, and fighter. He served under Andrew Jackson in the Creek War (1813–1814). His popularity led him to Congress where his natural wit and homespun stories made him a noted character. He was killed at the ALAMO in 1836.

Crockford. The popular name for *Crockford's Clerical Directory*, published since 1838 and first compiled by John Crockford. It is a reference book of all the clergy of the CHURCH OF ENGLAND and of the other churches in communion with the SEE of Canterbury.

Crockford's was established as an exclusive gambling club at 50 St. James's Street in 1827 by William Crockford (1775–1844), the son of a fishmonger. It became the favourite haunt of the world of fashion, and fortunes were staked there. Crockford made more than £1,000,000 before he retired in 1840.

Crocodile. A symbol of deity among the Egyptians, because, says Plutarch, it is the only aquatic animal which has its eyes covered with a thin transparent membrane, by reason of which it sees and is not seen, as God sees all, Himself not being seen. To this he adds: "The Egyptians worship God symbolically in the crocodile, that being the only animal without a tongue, like the Divine Logos, which standeth not in need of speech." (*De Iside et Osiride*, vol. II, p. 381).

Achilles Tatius says, "The number of its teeth equals the number of days in a year." Another tradition is that, during the seven days held sacred to APIS, the crocodile will harm no one. At Crocodilopolis in the Faiyum, he was worshipped under the name of Sobek.

Crocodile tears. Hypocritical tears. The tale is that crocodiles moan and sigh like a person in deep distress, to allure travellers to the spot, and even shed tears over their prey while devouring it.

Crœsus (krē′ sŭs). **Rich as Crœsus.** Crœsus, the last king of Lydia (560–546 B.C.), was so rich and powerful that his name became proverbial for wealth. Many of the wise men of Greece were drawn to his court, including Æsop (*see under ÆSOP'S FABLES*) and SOLON. He was overthrown by Cyrus of Persia. *See* ORACLE.

Crofters. Smallholders in the Highlands of Scotland and the Western Isles, holding their land by a variety of ancient tenures; a COTTAR is somewhat similar to a crofter.

Cro-Magnon Man. A prehistoric race-type named after the Cro-Magnon cave near Les Eyzies in the Dordogne, France, where four of their skeletons were discovered in 1868. Cro-Magnon man is associated with the AURIGNACIAN culture. His skull was long and narrow and larger than that of the average European of today.

Cromlech (krom′ lek). A name formerly used by British archæologists for a NEOLITHIC AGE monument consisting of a large flat stone resting on top of two or more others, like a table (Welsh *crom*, bent; *llech*, a flat stone). They appear to be the uncovered remains of burial chambers or cairns, and the French name DOLMEN is now more commonly used.

WAYLAND SMITH's Cave (Berkshire), Trethevy Quoit (Cornwall), Kit's Coty House (Kent), and the "killing-stone" at Louth (Ireland), are examples among many.

Cromwell's Bible. *See* BIBLE, THE ENGLISH.

Cronian Sea. The north polar sea; so called from Cronos (*see* KRONOS). Pliny says, "*A Thule unius diei navigatione mare concretum, a nonnullis cronium appellatur.*" (*Nat. Hist.*, iv, 16.)

Cronos, or **Cronus.** *See* KRONOS.

Crook. By hook or crook. *See* HOOK.

There is a crook in the lot of every one. There is trial or vexation in every person's life. When LOTS were drawn by bits of stick it was desirable to get sticks which were smooth and straight; but one without a crook or some other defect is rare.

To crook the elbow, or **finger.** This occurs in England before the mid-1780s. It is the American equivalent to ELBOW-LIFTING. More recently in England *to crook the finger* means to drink from a tea or coffee cup with the little finger noticeably crooked. This is often regarded as a somewhat ostentatious mark of gentility.

Crop Up, or **Out.** To rise out of, to appear at the surface; hence to occur or arise. A mining term. Strata which appear near the surface are said to crop out. We say a subject *crops up* from time to time and such and such a thing *crops out* of what you were saying.

Cropper. To come a cropper. To get a bad fall, literally or metaphorically. "Neck and crop" means altogether, and "to come a cropper" is to come to the ground neck and crop.

Croquemitaine. A HOBGOBLIN, an evil sprite or ugly monster, used by French nurses and parents to frighten children into good behaviour. In 1863 M. L'Epine published a romance with this title, telling the story of a god-daughter of CHARLEMAGNE whom he called "Mitaine". It was translated by Tom Hood (the younger).

Croquet (krō′ki). The garden game takes its name from the Fr. *croc*, a hook, as the early croquet mallets were shaped like hockey-sticks. It is probably descended from the earlier game of pell mell or PALL MALL. It became popular in England from the 1850s.

Crosier, or **Crozier** (from L. Lat. *crocia*; connected with our *crook*; confused with Fr. *croisier* from *crois*, a cross). The pastoral staff of an abbot or BISHOP, and sometimes applied to an archbishop's staff, which terminates in a cross and not in a crook as does the bishop's crosier.

A bishop turns his staff outwards to denote his wider authority; an abbot turns it inwards to show that his authority is limited to his own convent. The abbot covers his staff with a veil when walking in the presence of a bishop, his superior.

Cross. The cross is not solely a Christian symbol originating with the crucifixion of the Redeemer. In Carthage it was used for ornamental purposes; runic crosses were set up by the Scandinavians as boundary marks, and were erected over the graves of kings and heroes. CICERO tells us (*De Divinatione*, ii, 27, and 80, 81) that the augur's staff with which they marked out the heaven was a cross; the Egyptians employed it as a sacred symbol, and two buns marked with a cross were discovered at Herculaneum. It was also a sacred symbol among the Aztecs; in Cozumel it was an object of worship; at Tabasco it symbolized the god of rain. It was one of the emblems of QUETZALCOATL, as lord of the four cardinal points, and the four winds that blow therefrom.

The cross of the crucifixion is said to have been made of palm, cedar, olive, and cypress, to signify the four quarters of the globe.

In his *Monasteries of the Levant* (1848) Curzon gives the legend that SOLOMON cut down a cedar and buried it on the spot where the pool of Bethesda stood later. A few days before the crucifixion the cedar floated to the surface of the pool, and was used as the upright of the Saviour's cross.

Constantine's Cross. It is said that Constantine on his march to ROME saw a luminous cross in the sky with the motto *In hoc vinces*, by this [sign] conquer. In the night before the battle of Saxa Rubra (312) he was commanded in a vision to inscribe the cross and motto on the shields of his soldiers. He obeyed the voice and prevailed. The LABARUM of Constantine was not really in the form of a cross but a monogram (XPI) formed of the first three letters of the word *Christ* in Greek. The legend of the DANNEBROG is similar and there are others. The Scots are said to have adopted St. ANDREW'S cross because it appeared in the heavens the night before Achaius, King of the Scots, and Hungus, King of the Picts, defeated Athelstan.

The Cross in heraldry. As many as 285 varieties of cross have been recognized, but the twelve in ordinary use, from which the others are derived, are: (1) the ordinary cross; (2) the cross humetté, or couped; (3) the cross urdé, or pointed; (4) the cross potent; (5) the cross crosslet; (6) the cross botoneé, or treflé; (7) the cross moline; (8) the cross potence; (9) the cross fleury; (10) the cross patté; (11) the Maltese cross (or eight-pointed cross); (12) the cross cleché and fitché.

The cross as a mystic emblem may be reduced to the four following:

1. **The Greek cross,** found on Assyrian tablets, Egyptian and Persian monuments, and on Etruscan pottery.

2. **The crux decussata,** generally called St. ANDREW'S cross, an x-shaped cross. Quite common in ancient sculpture.

3. **The Latin cross,** or **crux immissa.** This symbol is found on coins, monuments, and medals long before the Christian era.

4. **The tau cross** or **crux commissa.**

Very ancient indeed. It is also the cross of St. ANTHONY.

The tau cross with a handle, or **crux ansata**, is common to several Egyptian deities as ISIS, OSIRIS, etc.; and is the emblem of immortality and life generally. The circle on the top signifies the eternal preserver of the world, and the T is the monogram of THOTH, the Egyptian MERCURY, meaning wisdom.

Capital Cross. In HERALDRY, a Greek cross with terminations similar to the architectural capital of the TUSCAN ORDER. Also called *brick-axed* because the ends resembled a mason's brick-axe.

The Cross of Lorraine, with two bars, was adopted as the emblem of the Free French during World War II. It is the patriarchal cross.

Long Cross. *See* DAGGER.

The Red Cross on a white ground, sometimes called the *Cross of Geneva*, is the Swiss flag reversed, and indicates the neutrality of hospitals and ambulances. *See* GENEVA CONVENTION *under* GENEVA; *Cp.* THE RED CRESCENT *under* RED. The Red Cross is also the cross of St. GEORGE.

True Cross. *See* THE INVENTION OF THE CROSS.

Creeping to the Cross. The GOOD FRIDAY ceremony of the *Veneration of the Cross* was commonly so called in England, when priest and people kneel and kiss the cross on the sanctuary steps. The custom derives from the veneration of the True Cross at Jerusalem. *See* THE INVENTION OF THE CROSS.

> On Good Friday above all in holy Church men creep to the church and worship the cross.
> *Dives and Pauper* (printed by Wynkyn de Worde in 1496).

Everyone must bear his own cross. Everyone must carry his own burden or troubles. The allusion is to the practice of the person condemned to crucifixion being made to carry his cross to the place of execution.

Exaltation of the Cross. *See under* EXALTATION.

Hot cross buns. *See* BUN.

The Invention of the Cross. Until its abolition by Pope John XXIII in 1960, a church festival held on 3 May, in commemoration of the finding (Lat. *inve-nire*, to find) of the "true cross of Christ" by St. HELENA. At her direction, after a long and difficult search in the neighbourhood of the HOLY SEPULCHRE (which had been over-built with heathen temples), the remains of the three buried crosses were found. These were applied to a sick woman, and that which affected her cure was declared the True Cross. The Empress had this enclosed in a silver shring (after having taken a large piece to ROME) and placed in a church built on the spot for the purpose. *See* IRON CROWN OF LOMBARDY *under* CROWN.

The Judgment of the Cross. An ordeal instituted in the reign of CHARLEMAGNE. The plaintiff and defendant were required to cross their arms upon their breast; and he who could hold out the longest gained the suit.

The Stations of the Cross. *See under* STATION.

To take the Cross. In mediaeval times to take the pledge to become a crusader. *See* CRUSADES.

Veneration of the Cross. *See* CREEPING TO THE CROSS.

Cut on the cross. *See under* CUT.

On the cross. Not "on the square", not straightforward. To get anything "on the cross" is to get it unfairly or dishonestly.

To cross it off, or **out.** To cancel it by running your pen across it.

To cross swords. To fight a duel; metaphorically to encounter someone in argument or debate.

To cross the hand, or **palm.** Gipsy fortune-tellers always bid their dupe to "cross their hand with a bit of silver". This, they say, is for luck. The coin remains with the owner of the crossed hand. The sign of the cross warded off witches and all other evil spirits, and as fortune-telling belongs to the black arts, the palm is signed with a cross to keep off the wiles of the DEVIL.

Crossing the palm is also used colloquially to mean giving a tip or small "bribe".

To cross the line is to cross or pass the Equator. *See* CROSSING THE LINE *under* LINE.

Cross and Ball. The orb of royalty is a

sphere or ball surmounted by a cross, an emblem of empire introduced in representations of our Saviour. The cross stands above the ball, to signify that the spiritual power is above the temporal.

Cross and Pile. The obverse and reverse sides of a coin or head and tail; hence money generally and the game of PITCH AND TOSS in particular, to which Edward II was said to be partial. Coins were in former times stamped with a cross on one side. *Pile* (Lat. *pila*) is French for the reverse of a coin.

Cross-bench. Seats set at right angles to the rest of the seats in the HOUSE OF COMMONS and the HOUSE OF LORDS, and on which members independent of party usually sit. Hence *cross-bencher*, an independent, and the *cross-bench mind*, open or unbiased.

Crossbill. The red plumage and curious crossing of the upper and lower bill-halves are accounted for by a mediæval fable which says that these distinctive marks were bestowed on the bird by the Saviour at the Crucifixion, as a reward for its having attempted to pull the nails from the cross with its beak. The fable is best known to English readers through Longfellow's *Legend of the Crossbill*, a translation from the German of Julius Mosen.

Cross-biting. Cheating; properly cheating one who has been trying to cheat you—biting in return. Hence *cross-biter*, a swindler.

Cross-bones. See SKULL AND CROSS-BONES.

Cross-grained. Bad-tempered, self-willed. Wood only works smoothly with the grain; when the grain crosses we get a knot or curling which is hard to work.

Cross-legged Knights. Crusaders were generally represented on their tombs with crossed legs.

To dine with cross-legged knights. *See* DINE.

Cross questions and crooked answers. A parlour game which consists in giving ludicrous or irrelevant answers to simple questions. Hence the phrase is used of one who is "hedging" or trying by his answers to conceal the truth when questioned.

Cross-roads, Burial at. All excluded from holy rites (criminals and suicides) were at one time buried at cross-roads. The ancient Teutonic peoples used such places for holding sacrifice and they thus by association came to be places of execution.

Cross-roads of the Pacific. A nickname of Honolulu, from its position on shipping and air routes.

Dirty work at the cross-roads. Foul play; nefarious activity. Probably the phrase arose from the association with burial at cross-roads (*see above*), or from the fact that cross-roads were often the scene of foul play.

Cross-row. Short for CHRISS-CROSS ROW.

To cross a person's bows. To cause annoyance to another and incur his displeasure. A naval phrase. It is a breach of good manners for a junior ship to cross the bows of a senior.

To cross someone's path. To meet or to thwart a person.

Cross, meaning irritable, bad-tempered.

As cross as a bear with a sore head, as the tongs, as two sticks. Common phrases used of one who is very vexed, peevish, or cross. The allusions are obvious.

Cross-patch. A disagreeable, ill-tempered person. PATCH is an old name for a fool, and with the meaning "fellow" is common enough in SHAKESPEARE, as a "scurvy patch", "What patch is our porter?" etc.

Crotona's Sage (Kro tō′ nà). PYTHAGORAS. So called because he established his chief school of philosophy at Crotona in Italy (*c*. 530 B.C.). Such success followed his teaching that the whole aspect of the town became more moral and decorous in a very short time.

Crouchmas. An old name for the festival of the INVENTION OF THE CROSS, also for ROGATION Sunday and Rogation week. "Crouch", here from Lat. *crux*, means cross.

Crow. A crow symbolizes contention, discord, strife.

As the crow flies. The shortest distance between two places. The crow flies straight to its destination. *Cp.* AIR-LINE; BEE-LINE.

I must pluck a crow with you; I have

a crow to pick with you. I am displeased with you, and must call you to account. I have a small complaint to make against you. In Howell's proverbs (1659) we find the following used in the same sense, "I have a goose to pluck with you." *Cp.* TO HAVE A BONE TO PICK WITH SOMEONE *under* BONE.

> If a crow help us, sirrah, we'll pluck a crow together.
>
> SHAKESPEARE: *Comedy of Errors*, III, i.

Jim Crow. *See* JIM.

To crow over one. To exult over a vanquished or abased person. The allusion is to cocks who habitually crow when victorious.

To eat crow. To be forced to do something extremely distasteful. The expression derives from an incident during an armistice of the Anglo-American War of 1812–1814. A New Englander unwittingly crossed the British lines while hunting and brought down a crow. An unarmed British officer heard the shot and determined to punish the offender. He gained hold of the American's gun by praising his marksmanship and asking to see his weapon. The Britisher then told the American he was guilty of trespass and forced him at the point of the gun to take a bite out of the crow. When the officer returned the gun the American in his turn covered the soldier and compelled him to eat the remainder of the crow.

Crow-eaters. Nickname for the inhabitants of South Australia.

Crow's nest. A barrel or cylindrical box fitted to the crosstrees of the maintop mast of a sailing ship for the lookout man.

Crowd, Croud, or **Cruth** (*Crwth*). A mediæval rectangular shaped instrument, with from three to six strings, played with a bow. Hence *crowder*, a player of the *crowd*. It lingered on in WALES much longer than elsewhere. John Morgan who died in 1720 was a noted player, and the Welsh *crwth* survived until the end of the 18th century.

Crown. In HERALDRY, nine crowns are recognized: the oriental, the triumphal or imperial, the DIADEM, the obsidional crown, the civic, the crown vallary, the mural crown, the naval, and the crown

celestial.

Among the Romans of the Republic and Empire, crowns of various patterns formed marks of distinction for different services; the principal ones were:

1. *The blockade crown* (*corona obsidionalis*), given to the general who liberated a beleaguered army. This was made of grass and wild flowers gathered from the spot.

2. *A camp crown* (*corona castrensis*) was given to the first to force his way into the enemy's camp. It was made of GOLD, and decorated with palisades.

3. *A civic Crown* to one who saved a *civis* (Roman citizen) in battle. It was of oak leaves, and bore the inscription H.O.C.S.—*i.e., hostem occidit, civem servavit,* a foe he slew, a citizen saved).

4. *A mural crown* was given to the first to scale the wall of a besieged town. It was made of gold and decorated with battlements.

5. *A naval crown,* of gold, decorated with the beaks of ships, was given to him who won a naval victory.

6. *An olive crown* was given to those who distinguished themselves in battle in some way not specially provided for.

7. *An ovation crown* (*corona ovatio*), made of myrtle, was given to the general who won a lesser victory.

8. *A triumphal crown* was given to the general granted a triumph. It was made of LAUREL or bay leaves. Sometimes a massive gold crown was given to the victorious general.

The Iron Crown of Lombardy is the crown of the ancient Longobardic kings, said to have been bestowed by Pope GREGORY THE GREAT. CHARLEMAGNE was crowned (774) with it as King of Italy, as was Charles V in 1530. In 1805 NAPOLEON put it on his head with his own hands. It was restored to the King of Italy by the Emperor of Austria in 1866 and replaced in the cathedral at Monza. It is so called from the inner fillet of iron which is said to have been beaten out of a nail from the True Cross which was given to Constantine by his mother, St. HELENA (*See* INVENTION OF THE CROSS.) The outer circlet is of beaten GOLD, and set with PRECIOUS STONES.

The crown in English coinage when

first minted (1526) was valued at 4s. 6d. and called the *crown of the rose*, but in the same year it was replaced by one worth 5 s. It was a GOLD coin and did not disappear as such until the reign of Charles II. Silver crowns were struck from 1551. The name derives from the French gold coin (*couronne*) first issued by Philip of Valois in 1339, which bore a crown on the obverse.

In the paper trade **crown** was a standard size of printing paper measuring 15 by 20 inches (before metrification); so called from an ancient watermark.

Crown of the East. Antioch, ancient capital of Syria, which consisted of four walled cities, encompassed by a common rampart that "enrounded them like a coronet".

The Crown of St. Stephen. *See under* STEPHEN, ST.

Crown of Thorns. The crown of Christ upon the Cross.

Crown of Wild Olive. The satisfaction of having performed a worthwhile task for its own sake rather than for gain. This crown was the only prize awarded to victors in the ancient OLYMPIC GAMES, the wild olive being held sacred from its having been first planted by HERCULES. John Ruskin has a book of this title, first published in 1866, which is a series of four essays or lectures on work, traffic, war, and the future of ENGLAND.

Crozier. *See* CROSIER.

Crucial (kroo′ shàl). **A crucial test.** A very severe and undeniable test. The allusion is to a fancy of Francis Bacon, who said that two different diseases or sciences might run parallel for a time but would ultimately cross each other; thus, the plague might for a time resemble other diseases, but when the *bubo* or boil appeared, the plague would assume its special character. Hence the phrases *instantiacrucis* (a crucial or unmistakable symptom), a crucial experiment, example, question, etc. *Cp.* CRUX.

Cruel Garters. *See* CREWEL.

Cruft's. The usual name for the internationally famous Cruft's Dog Show, now held at Olympia and founded by Charles Cruft in 1891. Some years after his death in 1938, the show was taken over by the Kennel Club. Cruft's interest in

dogs largely arose from his apprenticeship to James Spratt in 1876. Spratt had recently started a "dog cake" business in HOLBORN, having got the idea from America.

Crummy. In obsolete slang, expressive of something desirable, as *that's crummy*, that's good; also meaning plump, well developed, as *she's a crummy woman*, a fine, handsome woman. No doubt from *crumb*, being the soft or fleshy part of the bread. Among soldiers the word has usually meant lousy, infested with lice, hence its present meaning of worthless or contemptible. It is probably from the likeness in appearance between breadcrumbs and the eggs of a louse.

Crusades. Wars undertaken by Christians in the late MIDDLE AGES to secure the right of Christian pilgrims to visit the Holy Sepulchre and to recover the HOLY LAND from its Mohammedan conquerors. The name is derived from the CROSS which the Crusaders wore on their dress. Ideas of CHIVALRY as well as hopes of material gain were prominent. According to Matthew Paris, each nation had its special colour, which was *red* for France; *white* for ENGLAND; *green* for Flanders; *blue* or *azure* for Italy; *gules* for Spain; for SCOTLAND, a *St. Andrew's cross*; for the Knights TEMPLAR, *red on white*. *See* TO TAKE THE CROSS *under* CROSS; PALMER.

There were eight principal crusades:

1. Proclaimed by Urban II in 1095. The futile expeditions under PETER THE HERMIT and Walter the Penniless were destroyed by the Turks, but the main expedition (1096–1099) under Raymond of Toulouse, Robert of Normandy, and Godfrey of Bouillon, ended with the capture of Jerusalem. The Latin Kingdom of Jerusalem was set up in 1100 under Baldwin I.

2. After the loss of Edessa an unsuccessful expedition (1147–1149) was promoted by St. BERNARD under the leadership of the Emperor Conrad III and Louis VII of France.

3. Inspired by the fall of Jerusalem in 1187, and led by Frederick Barbarossa, Philip Augustus of France and Richard I of England. Begun in 1188, it reached a stalemate in 1192.

4. Promoted by Innocent III in 1202 and led by Thibaut of Champagne and Baldwin of Flanders it was diverted, in spite of the Pope's prohibitions, into an attack on Constantinople. Baldwin became the first Latin Emperor of Constantinople in 1204.

5. Proclaimed by Innocent III for 1217 to recover Jerusalem. The main force was directed against Egypt. Damietta was taken but given up in 1221.

6. The Emperor Frederick II obtained Nazareth, Bethlehem and Jerusalem by negotiation (1222–1229), although he was under excommunication at the time, but was absolved on his return.

7. Followed the loss of Jerusalem in 1244. It was organized and led by St. LOUIS (Louis IX) of France in 1248. The main expedition against Egypt led to his capture in 1250. After release he made fruitless efforts to recover the Holy Land and returned home in 1254.

8. The Last Crusade. Undertaken by St. Louis, Charles of Anjou, and Prince Edward of England. St. Louis died in 1270 at Tunis and the project finally petered out in 1272.

The Children's Crusade of 1212 was due to misguided zeal. There were two main expeditions. Some 40,000 German children under one Nicholas, set off over the Alps for Italy. Only a few reached Genoa and ROME, where Innocent III ordered them home. Some hundreds possibly sailed from Brindisi to disappear from history. Another 30,000 French children, under Stephen of Cloyes, set out for Marseilles and about 5,000 were eventually offered passage by scoundrelly ship masters only to be wrecked or sold as slaves to the MOSLEMS. *See* PIED PIPER OF HAMELIN.

Crush. To crush a fly on a wheel. Another form of "to break a butterfly on a wheel". *See under* BREAK.

To have a crush on someone is to have an infatuation for someone–a schoolgirl's phrase.

Crush-room. An old term for a room in a theatre or opera-house, etc., where the audience can collect and talk during intervals, wait for their carriages, and so on.

Crust. The upper crust (of society). The aristorcracy; the UPPER TEN thousand. The phrase was first used in Haliburton's *Sayings and Doings of Sam Slick*. The upper crust was at one time the part of the loaf placed before the most honoured guests.

Crusted port. When port is first bottled its fermentation is not complete; in time it precipitates argol on the sides of the bottle, where it forms a crust. Crusted port, therefore, is port which has completed its fermentation.

Crusty. Ill-tempered, apt to take offence, cross, irritable, peevish. (*Cp.* CRUMMY) ACHILLES addresses the bitter THERSITES with:

> Thou crusty batch of nature, what's the news?
> SHAKESPEARE: *Troilus and Cressida*, V, i.

Crutched Friars. Crutched is the Lat. *cruciati*, crossed, from the cross at the top of their staves, later embroidered on their dress. They were a mendicant order established in Italy by 1169 and followed an Augustinian rule. They arrived in England in 1244 and the order was suppressed by the POPE in 1656.

Crux. A knotty point, an essential point, that on which a decision depends. It does not refer to the CROSS as an instrument of punishment, but to the crossing of two lines, called a *node* or knot; hence trouble or difficulty. *Quæ te mala crux agitat?* (Plautus); What evil cross distresses you?—*i.e.* what difficulty, what trouble are you under? *See* CRUCIAL.

Crux Ansata. *See* TAU CROSS *under* CROSS.

Crux Decussata. *See* CROSS.

Crux petoralis (Lat. *pectus*, breast). A cross suspended over the breast usually worn by BISHOPS, abbots and CARDINALS.

Cry. For the distinctive cries of animals, *see* ANIMALS.

A far cry. A long way; a very considerable distance; used both of space and time, as, "it is a far cry from David to Disraeli, but they were both Jews"; "it's a far cry from Clapham to Kamchatka".

Crying the Mare. *See* CRYING THE NECK.

Crying the Neck. Formerly, at the end of the harvest, especially in the north and west of England, the last sheaf of corn, the *Neck* (or the *Mare*) was held aloft by the leader or Harvest Lord, who shouted "I have it! I have it! I have it!" The harvesters around him cried "What have 'ee? What have 'ee? What have 'ee?". The leader shouted back, "A Neck! A Neck! A Neck!" The noise made it plain that the harvest on that particular farm was complete. There were numerous regional variants of these proceedings.

For crying out loud. A colloquial exclamation of astonishment or annoyance current since the 1920s, probably a subconscious EUPHEMISM for a blasphemous utterance.

Great cry and little wool. A proverbial equivalent expressive of contempt for one who promises great things but never fulfils the promises—*i.e.* "all talk and no do". Originally the proverb ran, "Great cry and little wool, as the Devil said when he sheared the hogs."

Hue and cry. *See* HUE.

In full cry. In full pursuit. A hunting phrase, with allusion to a yelping pack of hounds in full chase.

It's no good crying over spilt milk. It's useless lamenting what has happened, it is done and cannot be undone.

To cry aim. *See* AIM.

To cry cave (kā' vi). To give warning (Lat. *cave*, beware); a traditional schoolboy's warning given to his fellows on the approach of a master.

To cry down. To condemn, to belittle.

To cry havoc. *See* HAVOCK.

To cry off. To go back on a bargain or arrangement. In the U.S.A. it means to sell at auction.

To cry quits. *See under* QUIT.

To cry stinking fish. To belittle one's own endeavours, offerings, etc. "To cry" here is to offer for sale by shouting one's wares in the street.

To cry up. To praise loudly and publicly.

To cry wolf. *See under* WOLF.

Crystal Gazing, or, as it is sometimes called, **Scrying,** is a very ancient form of DIVINATION. By gazing fixedly and deeply into a polished crystal ball, was held that those possessing the gift could see what is about to happen or what was actually happening at some distant place, etc. *To gaze into the crystal ball* it is to see into the future, to seek inspiration to answer questions. *See* CRYSTALLOMANCY.

Crystal Palace. One of the glories of the Victorian era. It was designed entirely of glass and iron by Joseph Paxton, a former head gardener at Chatsworth, to house the Great Exhibition of 1851, or to give it its full name, the *Great Exhibition of the Works of Industry of All Nations.* It was originally erected in Hyde Park but moved to Sydenham in 1854 with some alterations, including the addition of two towers, and used as an exhibition, entertainment, and recreational centre. It became national property in 1911 and was destroyed by fire in 1936.

The Crystalline Sphere. According to Ptolemy, the ninth orb, identified by some with "the waters which were above the firmament" (*Gen.* i, 7); it was placed between the "PRIMUM MOBILE" and the firmament, or sphere, of the fixed stars, and was held to have a shivering movement that interfered with the regular motion of the stars.

Crystallomancy. DIVINATION by means of transparent bodies such as a crystal globe, polished quartz, and precious stones, especially a beryl. *See* CRYSTAL GAZING.

Cub. Properly the young of fox, wolf, bear, etc., figuratively a raw or unpolished young fellow. *See* TO LICK INTO SHAPE *under* LICK.

Cubbing, or **Cub-hunting.** Preliminary training for young foxhounds. Fox cubs have not the cunning nor the staying power of the grown fox, and thus offer better sport for young hounds and young riders.

Wolf Cub. *See* BOY SCOUT.

Cuba. The Roman deity who guarded infants in their cribs and sent them to sleep (Lat. *cubo*, I lie down in bed). *See* BABES, PROTECTING DEITIES OF.

Cubism. The style of an early 20th-century school of painters who depict surfaces, figures, tints, light and shade, etc., by means of a multiplicity of shapes of a cubical and geometrical character. The name was given somewhat disparagingly by Henri Matisse in 1908. It was essentially abstract and divorced from realism. It rejected any attempt to depict actual appearances and turned its back on all accepted canons of art. Its chief exponents were Braque, Derain, Léger, and notably Picasso.

Cubit (Lat. *cubitum*, elbow). An ancient measurement of length from the elbow to the tip of the longest finger. The Roman cubit was *c*. 17½ in., the Egyptian *c*. 21 in. (which was divided into seven palms), and that of the Hebrews *c*. 22 in. The English cubit was 18 in.

Cuchulain, or **Cú Chulainn** (koo kŭ lin, koo koo lin). A legendary Irish hero, called the "Hound of Culann" because, having accidentally slain the watchdog of the smith, Culann, in penance he had to take the animal's place. He was brought up in the court of King CON-CHOBAR of Ulster, whose kingdom he defended single-handed against the Queen of Connaught. He is called Cuthullin by OSSIAN.

Cucking-stool. A kind of stool once used for ducking scolds, disorderly women, dishonest apprentices, etc., in a pond. "Cucking" is from the old verb *cuck*, to void excrement, and the stool used was often a close-stool.

Cuckold. The husband of an adulterous wife; so called from the CUCKOO, whose chief characteristic is to deposit its eggs in other birds' nests. Johnson says, "it was usual to alarm a husband at the approach of an adulterer by calling out 'Cuckoo', which by mistake was applied in time to the person warned."

Cuckoo. Cuckoo folklore and superstitions abound and are often tokens of the bird's popularity as a herald of spring. There are many old rhymes and proverbs about this bird; one says:

> In April the cuckoo shows his bill;
> In May he sings all day;
> In June he alters his tune;
> In July away he'll fly;
> In August go he must.

Also:

> Turn your money when you hear the cuckoo, and you'll have money in your purse till he come again.

And:

> The cuckoo sings from St. Tiburtius' Day (14 April) to St. John's Day (24 June).

Cuckoo oats and woodcock hay make a farmer run away. If the spring is so backward that oats cannot be sown till the cuckoo is heard (*i.e.* April), or if the autumn is so wet that the aftermath of hay cannot be got in till woodcock shooting (middle of November), then the farmer is in a bad way.

Cuckoo-spit, or **Frog-spit.** A frothy exudation deposited on plants by certain insects, especially the froghopper (*Aphrophora spumaria*), for the purpose of protecting the larvæ. So called from an erroneous popular notion that the froth was spat out by cuckoos.

Cloud-cuckoo-land. *See under* CLOUD.

Don't be a cuckoo. Don't' be a silly ass; don't go and make a fool of yourself.

To wall in the cuckoo. *See* COURSE.

Cucullus non facit monachum (ku kul' lus non făk' it mo na' kum) (Lat. The cowl does not make the monk). Do not judge a person by external appearances. An old proverb quoted by SHAKESPEARE in *Twelfth Night*, I, v.

Cuddy, an abbreviation of Cuthbert, and the North Country and Scottish familiar name for a donkey, elsewhere called NEDDY or Jack. As an ass it also means a fool or dolt.

Cudgel. To cudgel one's brains. To make a painful effort to remember or understand something. The idea is from taking a stick to beat a dull boy under the notion that dullness is the result of temper or inattention.

To take up the cudgels. To maintain an argument or position. To fight, as with a cudgel, for one's own way or point of view.

Cue. Besides the usual dictionary meaning of a catchword for an actor or a hint, as SHAKESPEARE's "When my cue comes, call me, and I will answer" (*Midsummer Night's Dream*, IV, i), it also meant a humour or frame of mind.

Cuff. Speaking off the Cuff. Without previous preparation. Probably from the habit of some after-dinner speakers of making jottings on their stiff shirt cuffs as ideas occurred to them during the meal.

Cufuffle, Curfuffle, or **Carfuffle.** A fuss

or excitement. An old and expressive word of uncertain origin, but possibly from a verb used in Northern Ireland meaning to shake up and toss hay or straw. *Cufuffled* is also to be ruffled or rumpled.

Cui bono? (kwī bō' nō). Who is benefited thereby? To whom is it a gain? A common but wrong meaning attached to the phrase is, "What good will it do?" "For what good purpose?" It was the question of the Roman judge L. Cassius Pedanius (*see* Cicero, *Rosc. Am.*, xxv, 84).

> Cato, that great and grave philosopher, did commonly demand, when any new project was propounded unto him, *cui bono*, what good will ensue in case the same is effected?
>
> FULLER: *Worthies* (*The Design*, i).

Culdees (kŭl dēz'). A religious order in IRELAND and SCOTLAND from about the 8th century to the 13th, although they continued in Ireland until the REFORMATION. So called from the Old Irish *céle dé* servants of God.

Cullinan Diamond. The largest known DIAMOND, named after the chairman of the Premier Mine, Johannesburg, where it was found in 1905. Its uncut weight was 3,025¾ carats (about 1 lb. 6 oz.). It was presented to King Edward VII by the South African Government and was cut into a number of stones (the largest weighing some 516 carats), which now form part of the Crown Jewels.

Cullion. *See* CULLY.

Cully. A fop, a fool, a dupe, a strumpet. Possibly a contraction of *cullion*, a despicable creature, a sponger (Ital. *coglione*, Lat. *coleus*, a leather bag or sheath). SHAKESPEARE says "Away, base cullions!" (*Henry VI, Pt. II*, I, iii), and in *The Taming of the Shrew*, IV, ii—"And makes a god of such a cullion". *Cp.* GULL.

> You base cullion, you.
>
> JONSON: *Every Man in his Humour*, III, ii.

Cultures, The Two. The existence in England, and to a great extent in Western Europe, of two separate cultures with few points of contact between them; one based on the humanities and the other on the sciences. The phrase gained immediate popularity after C. P. (Lord) Snow's Rede Lecture, subsequently published as *The Two Cultures and the Scientific Revolution* (1959).

Cum grano salis (kŭm grā' nō sā' lis) (Lat. with a grain of salt). There is some truth in the statement but we must use great caution in accepting it. Similarly we "take something with a pinch of salt", *i.e.* it is not wholly palatable as it is, therefore it is accepted or believed with some reserve or allowance.

Cummer. A gude wife, old woman, midwife, gossip, neighbour (Fr. *commère*). Frequently used in Scott's novels. *Cp.* GAFFER; GAMMER.

Cunctator (kŭngk tā tôr) (Lat. the delayer). Used of one given to delay and especially of Quintus Fabius Maximus. He gained the epithet as an abusive title for his delaying tactics against Hannibal and avoidance of pitched battles, but subsequent events, such as Hannibal's great victory at CANNÆ (216 B.C.), seemed to justify his policy, and what started as a slur became an honour. Du Guesclin used similar tactics successfully against the English during the HUNDRED YEARS WAR. *See* FABIUS.

Cuneiform Letters. Wedge-shaped letters, also called arrow-headed (Lat. *cuneus*, a wedge). A name for the writing of ancient Babylonia, Assyria, Persia, and the Hittites, which was made up of wedge-shaped impressions made on soft clay. The name cuneiform is said to have been first used by the Orientalist Thomas Hyde, Regius Professor of Hebrew at Oxford (1636–1703). Cuneiform script was used from *c*. 3800 B.C. until the early years of the Christian era. The first to decipher the letters was Grotefend of Hanover in 1802.

Cunobelin (kŭ' nō bel' in). Cunobelinus, King of the Catuvellauni (A.D. 5–40), and the father of Caractacus (*see* CARADOC).

Cup. A mixture of strong ale with sugar, spice, and a lemon, properly served up hot in a silver cup. Sometimes a roasted orange takes the place of a lemon. *Cp.* BISHOP.

Cup Final. The final round of a football contest, etc., on the result of which a championship cup is awarded. In England the most popular is for the Football Association Cup. An engraved cup, usually of silver, is a common form of trophy for many sporting events.

Divination by cup. An ancient method of DIVINATION by floating certain articles on a cup of water and reading the signs. The practice survives in fortune-telling with a cup of tea. After the last of the liquid is disposed of, the arrangement of the sediment is examined for signs.

Grace Cup. *See* LOVING or GRACE CUP *under* LOVE.

He was in his cups. Drunk. *Inter pocula, inter vina* (Horace: *Odes* III, vi, 20).

Let this cup pass from me. Let this trouble or affliction be taken away, that I may not be compelled to undergo it. The reference is to Christ's agony in the Garden of GETHSEMANE (*Matt.* xxvi, 39).

Loving, or **Grace Cup.** *See under* LOVE.

My cup runs over. My blessings overflow. Here cup signifies portion or blessing.

> My cup runneth over. Surely goodness and mercy shall follow me all the days of my life.
>
> *Ps*. xxiii, 5, 6.

Not my cup of tea. This does not suit me, this is not my line, this is not the sort of thing I want.

Stirrup cup. *See under* STIRRUP.

The cup of vows. In Scandinavia it was anciently customary at feasts to drink from cups of mead, and vow to perform some great deed worthy of the song of the skald.

The Cups that cheer but not inebriate. Tea. A quotation from Cowper's *Task*, iv, 36, 40.

There's many a slip 'twixt the cup and the lip. Success is not always certain, things can go wrong at the last moment. *See* ANCÆUS.

We must drink the cup. We must bear our allotted burden, the sorrow which falls to our lot.

Cupar (koo' par). **He that will to Cupar maun to Cupar.** A wilful man must have his way, even to his own injury. A Scottish proverbial saying. Caleb Balderston uses it in Scott's *Bride of Lammermoor*, ch. xviii. The reference is to

the fact that the Fife Courts of Justice were formerly at Cupar.

Cupar justice, The same as "Jedburgh justice", hang first and try afterwards. It is sometimes called "Cowper law" and it owed its rise to a baron-baile in Coupar-Angus before heritable jurisdictions were abolished. *Abingdon Law* is a similar phrase. It is said that during the COMMONWEALTH Major-General Browne of Abingdon first hanged his prisoners, then tried them. *Cp*. JEDDART JUSTICE; LYDFORD LAW.

Cupboard Love. Love from self-interest or hope of gain. The allusion is to the love of children for some indulgent person who gives them something nice from the cupboard.

Cupid (Lat. *cupido*, desire, love). The Roman god of love, identified with the Greek EROS. He is usually represented as a beautiful winged boy, blindfolded, and carrying a bow and arrows. There are varying legends of his parentage.

Cupid and Psyche (sī' ki). The story is told in the GOLDEN ASS of Apuleius. *See* PSYCHE.

Cupid's golden arrow. Virtuous love.

Cupid's leaden arrow. Sensual passion.

Curate. *See* CLERICAL TITLES.

Curate's Egg. Among the catch-phrases that Punch (*see* MR. PUNCH *under* PUNCH) has introduced into the language, "Good in parts, like the curate's egg" is proverbial. The illustration shows a nervous young curate at his bishop's breakfast table. Asked by his lordship whether the egg is to his liking, he is terrified to say that it is bad and stammers out that, "Parts of it are excellent!"

Curfew (kĕr' fū). The custom of ringing a bell every evening as a signal to put out fires and go to bed; also the hour for this and the bell itself. The word is from O.Fr. *couvrefeu*, cover-fire, which reveals its Norman origin. WILLIAM THE CONQUEROR instituted the curfew in England in 1068, at the hour of 8 p.m. The word is now extended to mean the period commonly ordered by occupying armies or government authorities in time of war or civil commotion when civilians must stay within doors.

The curfew tolls the knell of parting day.
GRAY : *Elegy written in a Country Churchyard*.

Curmudgeon (kĕr mŭj' ŏn). A grasping, miserly fellow. A word of unknown origin, but of it Johnson's *Dictionary* says: "It is a vitious manner of pronouncing *cœur méchant*, Fr., an unknown correspondent", meaning that this suggestion was supplied by some corespondent unknown. By a ridiculous blunder, Ash (1775) copied it into his dictionary as "from Fr. *cœur*, unknown, *méchant*, correspondent"!

Curnock. *See* CRANNOCK.

Currency. A word applied in early colonial Australia to the wide variety of coins then in circulation, as distinct from English gold coins, which were called STERLING. Female convicts sent to Australia became known as the "currency" and the majority of first generation Australian-born whites were descended from them.

Currency lad, or **lass.** In the early 19th century this meant one of European descent born in Australia, as opposed to *sterling, i.e.* English-born settlers.

Curry Favour. A corruption of the M.E. *to curry favel*, to rub down Favel: *Favel* (or *Fauvel*) being the name of the CENTAUR in the early 14th-century French satirical romance *Fauvel*. This fallow-coloured creature symbolizes cunning and bestial degradation; hence to curry, or smooth down, Favel, was to enlist the services of duplicity, and so to seek to obtain by insincere flattery, to ingratiate oneself by sycophantic officiousness, etc.

Curse. Curses, like chickens, come home to roost. Curses rebound on the head of the curser, as chickens which stray during the day return to their roost at night.

Cursing by bell, book, and candle. *See under* BELL.

Curst cows have curt horns. *See under* COW.

Not worth a curse. I don't care (or **give**) **a** (**tinker's**) **curse** (or **cuss**), *i.e.* not worth anything, I care not at all. Similar expressions are "not a STRAW", "not a PIN", "not a bit", "not a RAP", "not a jot", "not a pin's point", "not a button".

The curse of Cain. One who is always on the move and has no abiding place is said to be "cursed with the curse of Cain". The allusion is to God's judgment on Cain after he had slain his brother Abel.

And now art thou cursed from the earth...a fugitive and a vagabond shalt thou be in the earth.
Gen, iv, 11–12.

The curse of Scotland. The nine of diamonds. The phrase seems to be first recorded in the early 18th century, for in Houston's *Memoirs* (1715–1747) we are told that Lord Justice Clerk Ormistone became universally hated in SCOTLAND and was called the Curse of Scotland; and when the ladies encountered the Nine of Diamonds at cards they called it Justice Clerk. Among the suggested origins of the phrase are:

(1) It may refer to the arms of Dalrymple, Earl of Stair—*viz*. or, on a saltire azure, nine lozenges of the first. The earl was justly held in abhorrence for his share in the massacre of GLENCOE.

(2) The nine of diamonds in the game of POPE JOAN is called the Pope, the ANTICHRIST of the Scottish reformers.

(3) In the game of *comette*, introduced by Queen Mary, it was the great winning card, and the game was the curse of Scotland because it was the ruin of many.

(4) The word "curse" is a corruption of cross, and the nine of diamonds is so arranged as to form a St. Andrew's Cross; but so are the other nines.

(5) Some say it was the card on which BUTCHER Cumberland wrote his cruel order after the battle of Culloden (1746); but the term was apparently already in vogue.

(6) Grose says somewhat inaccurately in his *Tour Thro' Scotland* (1789): "Diamonds...imply royalty...and every ninth king of Scotland has been observed for many ages to be a tyrant and a curse to the country."

The curse of Tutankhamun. A legend arising from the death of the 5th Earl of Carnarvon during the excavations at Tutankhamun's tomb. He died from pneumonia after an infection from a mosquito bite but Sir Arthur Conan Doyle, a convinced spiritualist, suggested that it might be attributed to elementals created by the priests of Tutankhamun. Coincidentally there was a power failure at Cairo when Carnarvon died and his dog in England expired at the same time. Howard Carter survived until 1939. *See also* THE VALLEY OF THE KINGS *under* VALLEY.

Cursor Mundi (Lat. *cursor*, runner, *mundus*, world). An early 14th-century English poem of some 24,000 lines in northern dialect. It describes the "Course of the World" from the Creation until Doomsday. It is essentially scriptural and designed to edify and supplant chivalric romance. The author wrote in English so those who had not the more fashionable French might understand. It is a valuable source of legend.

Curtain. Curtain Call. An invitation to an actor or actress to appear in front of the curtain and receive the applause of the audience.

Curtain Lecture. The nagging by a wife after she and her husband are in bed. *See* CAUDLE LECTURE.

To ring down the curtain. To bring a matter to an end. A theatrical term. *See* RABELAIS *under* DYING SAYINGS.

Curtal Friar (kĕr tál). A curtal was a horse with its tail docked, whence its application to other things that were cut down or shortened. A curtal friar was one who wore a short cloak. In later use, especially by Scott, it acquired a vaguely derisory or belittling significance.

Curtana (kĕr tā′ nà). The sword of mercy borne before kings of ENGLAND at their coronation; it has no point and is therefore shortened (O.Fr. *curt*; Lat. *curtus*). It is also called the sword of Edward the Confessor, which, having no point, was the emblem of mercy.

Curtmantle (kĕrt′ măn tál). Henry II (1133, 1154–1189), who introduced the Anjou mantle, which was shorter than the robe worn by his predecessors. *Cp.* CARACALLA.

Curule Chair. (kū′ rùl). A folding stool inlaid with ivory, and with curved legs, from Lat. *currus*, a chariot, because it was originally a chariot chair. It was the ancient Roman chair of office of the higher magistrates (*e.g.* dictators, consuls, prætors, censors, and the chief ædiles), termed *curules* or *curule* magistrates, and emperors.

Cushcow Lady. A Yorkshire name for a LADYBIRD.

Cushion Dance. A lively dance, popular in early Stuart times, in which kissing while kneeling on a cushion was a major feature.

Custard Coffin. *See* COFFIN.

Custer's Last Stand. In America in the late 19th century as favourite a subject for paintings and engravings as the "Relief of Ladysmith" became in England. Lt.-Col. George A. Custer was a dashing cavalry man with a popular reputation. The annihilation of his force of over 200 men by some 2,000 Indian warriors under Sitting Bull at the Battle of Little Big Horn, Montana (25 June 1876) made a tremendous impact, and the episode became part of the national epic. Custer's body was spared mutilation unlike most or all of the others.

Custom clothes, or **custom tailoring.** The American equivalent of "made to measure", or "bespoke tailoring". These terms were appearing in English fashion magazines by the 1960s.

Customer. A rum customer. A queer or strange fellow, one not to meddle with. Here *rum* is the old CANT term meaning "fine", "gallant", or "spirited".

A slim customer. A sly or crafty character, a "wily bird".

An ugly customer. One better left alone as he is likely to prove vicious if interfered with.

Custos Rotulorum (Lat. keeper of the rolls). Those officers charged with keeping the records of the courts in a county. The Lord-Lieutenant is now the Custos Rotulorum and the work is done by the Clerk of the Peace in his capacity of deputy.

Cut. Cut and come again. Take a cut from the joint, and come for another if you like it, *i.e.* "there's plenty of it, have as much as you like." It is used by Swift in his *Polite Conversation*, ii.

Cut and dried. All ready, fixed or arranged beforehand. "He had a speech all cut and dried." The allusion is to timber, cut, dried and ready for use.

The cuttings of the nails and hair were votive offerings to PROSERPINE, and it would excite the jealousy of NEPTUNE to make offerings to another in his own special kingdom.

Cut of his jib. The contour or expression of his face. "I don't like the cut of his jib" means, "I don't like the look of him." The phrase is of nautical origin. The cut of the jib or headsail betokened the quality or character of the vessel.

Cut-off. The American equivalent of the English "short cut".

Cut off with a shilling. Disinherited. To be left a shilling showed that the testator had not forgotten, but had intentionally disinherited a person by bequeathing a trifling sum.

Cut on the cross. A dressmaking and tailoring term. The material is folded so that the weft is parallel to the warp and the cut is then made along the fold.

Cut out. Left in the lurch; superseded. When there are too many for a game of cards (say whist or bridge), it is customary for the players to cut out after a rubber, in order that another may have a turn. The players cut the cards on the table the lowest turn-up gives place to a newcomer.

Cut your coat according to your cloth. *See* COAT.

Diamond cut diamond. *See under* DIAMOND.

He has cut his eye teeth. *See under* TOOTH.

He is cut, he is half cut. Drunk or nearly so.

His life was cut short. He died prematurely. The allusion is to ATROPOS, one of the three FATES, cutting the thread of life spun by her sister CLOTHO.

I must cut my stick, *i.e.* depart. The Irish usually cut a SHILLELAGH before starting on an expedition. *Punch* gives the following derivation: "Pilgrims on leaving the Holy Land used to cut a palmstick, to prove that they had really been to the Holy Sepulchre.

To be cut out for. To be naturally suited for, as, "He is cut out for a sailor." The allusion is to cutting out cloth for specific purposes.

To cut. To renounce or ignore acquaintance.

To cut blocks with a razor. To do something remarkable by insignificant means; to do something more eccentric than expedient.

To cut capers. *See under* CAPER.

To cut a dash. To make a show; to get oneself looked at and talked about for a showy or striking appearance. "Dashing" means showy or striking, as a "dashing fellow", a "dashing equipage".

To cut the ground from under one, or **from under his feet.** To leave an adversary no ground to stand upon, by disproving or forestalling all his arguments or undermining his case.

To cut no ice. Be of no account, make no impression, possibly borrowed from figure skating.

To cut the knot. To break through an obstacle. The reference is to the GORDIAN KNOT.

To cut the painter. *See under* PAINTER.

To cut up rough. To be disagreeable or quarrelsome about anything.

To cut and run. To escape in a hurry, to quit. In the days when a ship's anchor cable was made of hemp, the cable was cut, if the occasion demanded it, and the vessel allowed to run before the wind.

To cut it short means to bring to an end. *Cp.* AUDLEY.

To cut short is to shorten, to silence by interruption.

To cut a swath. To make an impression. An American expression usually used in the negative. A swath is the amount cut by one sweep of a scythe.

To cut your wisdom teeth. *See under* WISDOM.

Cuthbert. A name coined by "Poy", the cartoonist of the *Evening News*, during World War I for the fit men of military age, especially in Government offices, who were not called for military service, or who positively avoided it. These civilians were depicted as frightened-looking rabbits. *See* TO COMB OUT *under* COMB.

St. Cuthbert's Beads. Single joints of the articulated stems of encrinites (fossil crinoids), also called *stone lilies*. They are perforated in the centre and bear a fanciful resemblance to a CROSS; hence they were once used for ROSARIES. Legend relates that the 7th-century St. Cuthbert sits at night on a rock in HOLY ISLAND and uses the opposite rock as an anvil while he forges the beads.

St. Cuthbert's Duck. The eider duck, so called because it breeds in the Farne Islands, the headquarters of St. Cuthbert.

Cutpurse. A pickpocket nowadays. When purses were worn suspended from a girdle, thieves cut the strings by which the purse was attached. When purses, etc., came to be kept in pockets the cut-purse became a pickpocket.

Moll Cutpurse. The familiar name of Mary Frith (c. 1585–1660), a woman of masculine vigour, and who often dressed as one. In 1611 she was sentenced to do public penance by the Court of ARCHES for parading about FLEET STREET and the STRAND in male costume. She was a notorious thief and once attacked General Fairfax on Hounslow Heath, for which she was sent to NEWGATE. She escaped by bribery and finally died of dropsy.

Cuttle. Captain Cuttle. An eccentric, kind-hearted sailor in Dickens's *Dombey and Son*, simple as a child, credulous of every tale, and generous as the sun. He is immortalized by his saying "When found, make a note of" (*see* ch. xv.) This phrase was adopted by *Notes and Queries*.

Cutty. Scots for short, as *cutty pipe*, a short clay pipe; *cutty spoons*; *a cutty gun*, a popgun; a *cutty*, a dumpy girl or a woman of dubious character. *See* CUTTY SARK.

Cutty Sark (Scot.). A short petticoat or short-tailed shirt. The name of the famous clipper built at Dumbarton in 1869 for Captain John Willis, shipowner and master mariner. After a long career, mainly in the China tea trade and in shipping wool from Australia, she became a Portuguese trader in 1895 and was renamed the *Ferreira*. Purchased by Captain Dowman in 1922, and restored at Falmouth as a boys' training ship, she was towed round to the Thames in 1938 and taken over by the Cutty Sark Preservation Society in 1952—the last survivor of the clippers.

The name is taken from Burns' poem "Tam O'Shanter" which was illustrated on the carvings round the ship's bows, but the figurehead was of a woman in flowing garments with outstretched arm. The accompanying "witches" round the bows were naked. At one stage in the ship's career a short shirt emblem was flown at the main truck.

Cutty stool. A short-legged wooden stool; in Scotland the familiar name for the STOOL OF REPENTANCE.

Cyanean Rocks, The (sī ăn′ i ăn). Two rocky islands at the entrance of the EUXINE SEA, where the breakers make the passage very hazardous. It was anciently supposed that they floated and closed together to crush a vessel when it attempted to sail between them.

Cybele. Mother goddess of Phrygia, also goddess of fertility and of the mountains. Commonly identified with AGDISTIS her favourite was ATYS and her priests were called CORYBANTES. She is also associated with DEMETER.

Cycle. A period or series of events or numbers which recur everlastingly in the same order.

Cycle of the moon. The METONIC CYCLE, from its discoverer Meton of ATHENS (5th century B.C.). It is a period of nineteen years, at the expiration of which the phases of the MOON repeat themselves on the same days as they did nineteen years previously. *See* CALLIPPIC PERIOD.

Cycle of the sun. A period of twenty-eight years, at the expiration of which the days of the month fall on the same days of the week as they did twenty-eight years previously.

The Platonic Cycle, or **Great Year.** That space of time which, according to ancient astronomers, elapses before all the stars and constellations return to their former positions in respect to the equinoxes. Tycho Brahe calculated this period at 25,816 years, and Riccioli at 25,920 years.

Cyclic Poets (sī′ klik). Post-Homeric epic poets who wrote continuations, illustrations or additions to Homer's poems. These poets wrote between 800 and 550 B.C., and were called *cyclic* because they confined themselves to the cycle of the TROJAN WAR. The chief were Agias, Arctinus, Eugammon, Lesches, and Stasinus.

Cyclops (sī klops) (Gr. circular-eye). One of a group or race of GIANTS. They had only one eye each and that in the centre of the forehead, and their work was to forge iron for VULCAN. Hesiod limits their number to three: Arges, Steropes, and Brontes. *Cp.* ARIMASPIANS.

Cyclopean Masonry (sī klō′ piàn). The old Pelasgic ruins of Greece, Asia Minor, and Italy, such as the Gallery of Tiryns, the Gate of Lions at Mycenæ, the Treasury of ATHENS, and the tombs of Phoroneus and Danaos. They are made of huge blocks fitted together without mortar and are fabled to be the work of the CYCLOPS. The term is applied to similar huge structures elsewhere.

Cygnus. *See* PHAETON'S BIRD.

Cylleneius (sī lē′ ni ùs). MERCURY. So called from Mount Cyllene, in Peloponnesus, where he was born.

Cymbeline. *See* CUNOBELIN; CASSIBELAN.

Cymodoce (sī mod′ ō si). One of the NEREIDS, a companion of VENUS in Virgil's *Georgics* (IV, 338) and ÆNEID (V, 826). In Spenser's *Faerie Queene* (III, iv, and IV, xii), she is a daughter of Nereus and mother of Marinell by Dumarin. She frees Florimel from the power of PROTEUS. The word means "wave-receiving".

Cynic. The ancient school of Greek philosophers known as the *Cynics* was founded by ANTISTHENES and made famous by his pupil DIOGENES. They were ostentatiously contemptuous of ease, luxury or wealth, and convention. The name is either derived from their dog-like, slovenly, and uncouth habits or from the fact that Antisthenes held his school in the Gymnasium called *Cynosarges* (white dog), from the incident when a white dog carried away part of a victim which was then being offered to HERCULES. The effigy over the pillar of Diogenes was a dog with the inscription, (as rendered by Dr. Brewer):

"Say, dog, I pray, what guard you in that tomb?"
"A dog."—"His name?"—"Dio-genes."—"From far?"
"Sinope."—"What! who made a tub his home?"
"The same; now dead, amongst the stars a star."

Cynic Tub. The tub from which Diogenes lectured. Similarly we speak of the PORCH, meaning STOIC philosophy; the GARDEN, Epicurean philosophy; the ACADEMY, Platonic philosophy; and the *Colonnade*, meaning Aristotelian philosophy. *See* PERIPATETIC SCHOOL.

Cynosure (sin′ ō shur). The Pole star; hence the observed of all observers. Greek for *dog's tail*, and applied to the constellation called URSA MINOR. As mariners guide their ships by the north star, and observe it as well, the word "cynosure" is used for whatever attracts attention, as "The cynosure of neighbouring eyes" (Milton, *L'Allegro*), especially for guidance in some doubtful matter.

Cynthia. The MOON; a surname of Artemis or DIANA, who represented the moon, and was called Cynthia from Mount Cynthius in Delos, where she was born.

The name was one of many applied to Elizabeth I by contemporary poets.

Cypress. A funeral tree; dedicated by the Romans to PLUTO, because when once cut it never grows again. It is said that its wood was once used for making coffins; hence SHAKESPEARE's "In sad cypress let me be laid" (*Twelfth Night*, II, iv). The Greeks and Romans put cypress twigs in the coffins of the dead and it is much associated with cemeteries. It was also traditionally the wood from which CUPID's arrows were made.

Cyrene. A Thessalian nymph, daughter or granddaughter of the river god Peneus. She was carried off by APOLLO to the country which came to be called Cyrenaica, where she bore him a son named Aristæus. *See* ABIOGENESIS.

Cyrillic Alphabet. The form of letters traditionally used by the Slavonic peoples, a form of the Greek alphabet invented by two brothers, the apostles of the Slavs, Constantine (827–869) and Methodius (*c.* 825–885) of Thessalonica. Constantine was more popularly known by his religious name of Cyril.

D

D. This letter is the outline of a rude archway or door. It is called in Phœnician and Hebrew *daleth* (a door) and Gr. *delta*. In Egyptian hieroglyphics it is a man's hand.

D., or **d.** indicating a penny or pence is the initial of the Lat. *denarius*. As a Roman numeral **D** stands for 500, and represents the second half of **CIↃ**, the ancient Tuscan sign for one thousand. **Đ** stands for 5,000.

D.C. *See* DA CAPO.

D Day. In World War II, the day appointed for the Allied invasion of Europe and the opening of the long-awaited second front. It was eventually fixed for 5 June 1944, but owing to impossible weather conditions, it was postponed at the last moment until 6 June. *See* OVERLORD.

D.O.M. An abbreviation of the Lat., *Deo Optimo Maximo* (to God the best the greatest) or *Datur omnibus mori* (it is allotted to all to die). In the former sense it is inscribed on bottles of BENEDICTINE.

D.T.s. A contraction of *delirium tremens*.

D.V. *See* DEO VOLENTE.

Da Capo (D.C.) (Ital.). A musical term meaning from the beginning—that is, finish with a repetition from the beginning to the point indicated.

Dab. Clever, skilled; as "dab-hand at it". Possibly a contraction of the Lat. *adeptus*, an adept. *Dabster* is another form.

Dabbat (Arab. *Dabbatu'l-ard*). In Mohammedan mythology the monster, reptile of the earth, that shall arise at the last day and cry that mankind has not believed in the Divine revelations.

By some it is identified with the Beast of the Apocalypse (*Rev*. xix, 19; xx, 10).

Dactyls. Mythical beings connected with the worship of CYBELE in Crete, supposed to be the discoverers of iron and copper; also called *Idæan Dactyls* (the fingers of IDA), after their mountain home. Their number is given as ten or more but was originally three—the Smelter, the Hammer, and the Anvil.

In prosody a dactyl is a foot of three syllables, the first long and the others short (— ∪∪), again from the similarity to the joints of a finger.

Dad, or **Daddy.** A child's word for "father" common to many languages, Gaelic, *daidein*; Welsh, *tad*; Cornish, *tat*; Latin, *tata, tatula* (papa); Greek, *tata, tetta*, used by youths to an elder; Sanskrit, *tata*; Lap, *dadda*; are examples.

Daddy Long-legs. A crane-fly, applied also to the long-legged spiders called "harvestmen".

Dadaism (da' da izm). An anarchic and iconoclastic art movement which began at Zürich in 1916, arising from indignation and despair at the catastrophe of World War I. Its supporters, writers and painters, sought to free themselves from all artistic conventions, and what they considered cultural shams. Dadaism was influenced by CUBISM and FUTURISM and after about 1922 it was succeeded by SURREALISM. The name Dadaism was derived from *dada*, the French word for a hobby-horse, and was named by Tristan Tzara after opening a dictionary at random. Arp, Ernst and Janco were among their number. There was a similar outbreak at New York at the same time associated with Duchamp, Picabia and Man Ray. A plaque, showing a human navel, was unveiled at Zürich in February 1966, to

Daisy

commemorate the fiftieth anniversary of the movement. *Cp.* FAUVISM; IMPRESSIONISM; ORPHISM; SYNCHRONISM; VORTICISM.

Dædalus (dē' dà lùs). A legendary Athenian, father of ICARUS, who formed the Cretan LABYRINTH and made wings, by means of which he flew from Crete across the archipelago. He is said to have invented the saw, the axe, the gimlet, etc., and his name is perpetuated in our *dœdal*, skilful, fertile of invention; *dœdalian*, labyrinthine or ingenious.

Daffodil. Legend says that the daffodil, or LENT LILY was once white; but Persephone (PROSERPINA), who had wreathed her head with them and fallen asleep in the meadow, was captured by PLUTO and carried off in his chariot. She let fall some of the lilies and they turned to a golden yellow. Theophilus and Pliny tell us that they grow on the banks of ACHERON and that the spirits of the dead delight in the flower, called by them the ASPHODEL. In England it used to be called the Affodil (Fr. *asphodile*: Lat. *asphodelus*; Gr. *asphodelos*).

In the present century it has become an alternative to the LEEK as a Welsh emblem, because the leek was considered vulgar by some.

Dagger, or **Long Cross** (†), used for reference to a note after the asterisk (*), was originally used in church books, prayers of EXORCISM, at benedictions, and so on, to remind the priest where to make the sign of the cross. It is sometimes called an obelisk (Gr. *obelos*, a spit).

In the arms of the City of LONDON, the dagger supposedly commemorates Sir William Walworth's dagger, with which he slew Wat Tyler in 1381. Before this time the cognizance of the City was the sword of St. PAUL.

Dagger Money. The sum once paid to judges on the Northern Circuit for the purchase of weapons as a protection against thieves and robbers.

To be at daggers drawn. To be fiercely opposed, at great enmity.

To speak, or **look daggers.** To speak or look so as to wound, to convey open hostility.

I will speak daggers to her, but use none.
SHAKESPEARE: *Hamlet*, III, ii.

Daggle-tail, or **Draggle-tail.** A slovenly woman, the bottom of whose dress trails in the dirt. *Dag* (of uncertain origin) means loose ends, mire, dirt; whence *dag-locks*, the soiled locks of a sheep's fleece, and *dag-wool*, refuse wool.

Dagon. A semitic god worshipped by the PHILISTINES after their arrival in Canaan, supposed to have been symbolized as half man and half fish. Samson's vengeance on the Philistines occurred after their riotous celebrations to Dagon (*Judges* xvi, 23–30).

Dagonet, Sir. In ARTHURIAN ROMANCES, the fool of King Arthur, knighted by the king himself.

Daikoku (da ē' kō ku). One of the seven Japanese gods of luck. He is god of wealth and good fortune and is represented sitting on bags of rice.

Daisy. An emblem of deceit. Greene (*Quip for an Upstart Courtier*) speaks of the "dissembling daisie". "Light of love wenches" are warned by it "not to trust every fair promise that such amorous bachelors make them". Ophelia in SHAKESPEARE'S *Hamlet* gives the queen a daisy to signify, "that her light and fickle love ought not to expect constancy in her husband".

The word is *Day's eye* (O.E. *dœges eage*), and the flower is so called because it closes its pinky lashes and goes to sleep when the sun sets, but in the morning expands its petals to the light. *See* VIOLET.

That well by reason men call it maie,
The daisie, or else the eie of daie.
CHAUCER: *Legend of Good Women (Prol.)*.

Darling Daisy. Frances, Countess of Warwick, adulterous wife of the 5th Earl of Warwick and for nine years mistress of King Edward VII, whom he often addresed as "My Darling Daisy wife" when writing to her. In 1914 she sought to bring in money by threatening to publish her memoirs, which would include the late King's letters. This was prevented by three prominent courtiers acting on behalf of King George V.

Daisy-cutter. In CRICKET a ball that fails to rise when delivered, and in tennis a service which behaves similarly. In the 19th century a horse that lifted its feet very little above the ground was so described, and more recently it was applied colloquially by the R.A.F. to a perfect landing.

Daisy-roots. Legend says that these, like the berries of dwarf elder, stunt the growth, a superstition which probably arose from the notion that everything had the property of bestowing its own speciality on others. *Cp.* FERN SEED.

Pushing up the daisies. To be dead and buried.

Dak-bungalow. *See* BUNGALOW.

Dalai-Lama. *See* LAMAISM.

Daltonism. *See* COLOUR-BLINDNESS.

Damiens' Bed of Steel (Dăm′ i enz). Robert François Damiens, in 1757, attempted to stab Louis XV. As a punishment he was chained to an iron bed that was heated, his right hand was burned in a slow fire, his flesh was torn with pincers and the wounds dressed with molten lead, boiling wax, oil and resin. He was finally torn to pieces by wild horses.

> The uplifted axe, the agonising wheel,
> Luke's iron crown, and Damien's bed of steel.
> GOLDSMITH: *The Traveller* (1768).

Damn. Not worth a damn. Worthless; not even worth a curse. Goldsmith in his *Citizen of the World*, uses the expression "Not that I care three damns" and a common expression of the Duke of Wellington was "Not a twopenny damn". The derivation of these phrases from the coin, a dam, is without foundation.

To damn with faint praise. To praise in such restrained terms as to deprive the praise of any value.

> Damn with faint praise, assent with civil leer,
> And, without sneering teach the rest to sneer.
> POPE: *Epistle to Dr. Arbuthnot.*

Damocles. The Sword of Damocles. Impending evil or danger. Damocles, a sycophant of Dionysius the Elder, of Syracuse, was invited by the TYRANT to try the felicity he so much envied. Accepting, he was set down to a sumptuous banquet, but overhead was a sword suspended by a hair. Damocles was afraid to stir, and the banquet was a tantalizing torment to him.

Damon (dā′ mon). The name of a goatherd in VIRGIL's *Eclogues*, and hence used by pastoral poets for rustic swains. *Cp.* CORYDON.

Damon and Pythias. Models of devoted friendship. In the 4th century B.C. Pythias (correctly Phintias) was condemned to death by Dionysius, the TYRANT of Syracuse, but obtained leave to go home too arrange his affairs after his friend Damon had agreed to take his place and be executed should Pythias not return. Pythias returned in time to save Damon, and Dionysius was so struck with this honourable friendship that he released both of them.

A damp squib. *See under* SQUIB.

Damsel. A maiden or young woman, a waiting-maid or attendant. The word is the O.Fr. *damoisele*, the feminine of *damoisel*, a squire; this is from Med. Lat. *domicellus*, a contracted form of *dominicellus*, the dimunutive of *dominus*, lord (*cp.* DONZEL). In mediæval France the *domicellus* or *damoiseau* was the son of a king, prince, KNIGHT, or lord before he entered the order of knighthood; the king's bodyguards were called his *damoiseaux* or *damsels*. Froissart styles Richard II *le jeune damoisel Richart*, and Louis VII (Le Jeune) was called the *royal damsel*.

Dan. A title meaning *Sir* or *Master* (Lat. *dominus*; *cp.* Span. *Don*) common with the old poets, as Dan Phœbus, Dan Cupid, Dan Chaucer, etc. *Cp.* DOM.

> Dan Chaucer, well of English undefiled,
> On Fame's eternal beadroll worthy to be filed.
> SPENSER: *Faerie Queene*, IV, ii, 32.

From Dan to Beersheba. From one end of the kingdom to the other; everywhere. The phrase is scriptural, Dan being the most northern and Beersheba the most southern cities of the HOLY LAND. We have the similar expression, "From Land's End to John o'Groats".

Danace (Dăn′ ās). An ancient Persian coin, worth rather more than the Greek OBOLUS, and sometimes placed by the Greeks in the mouth of the dead to pay CHARON'S TOLL.

Danaë (Dăn′ á ē). Daughter of Acrisius,

King of Argos. He was told that his daughter's son would put him to death, and so resolved that Danaë should never marry. She was accordingly locked up in an inaccessible tower. ZEUS foiled the King by changing himself into a shower of gold, under which guise he readily found access to the fair prisoner, and she thus became the mother of PERSEUS.

Danaides (dăn ā' i dēz). The fifty daughters of Danaus, King of Argos. They married fifty sons of ÆGYPTUS, and all but HYPERMNESTRA, wife of LYNCEUS, at the command of their father murdered their husbands on their wedding night. They were punished in HADES by having to draw water everlastingly in sieves from a deep well.

Dance. I'll lead you a pretty dance. I'll bother or put you to trouble. The French say *Donner le bal à quelqu'un*. The reference is to the complicated dances of former times, when all followed the leader.

St. Vitus's Dance. *See* VITUS.

To dance and pay the piper. To work hard to amuse and have to take all the trouble and bear the expense as well. The allusion is to *Matt.* xi, 17: "We have piped unto you, and ye have not danced."

To dance attendance. To wait obsequiously, to be at the beck and call of another. It was an ancient custom at weddings for the bride, not matter how tired she was, to dance with every guest.

To dance the Tyburn jig. To be hanged. *See* TYBURN.

To dance upon nothing. To be hanged.

Dance of Death, or **Danse Macabre.** An allegorical representation of Death (usually a dancing skeleton or corpse) leading all sorts and conditions of men to the grave. It is first found in the 14th century, and there is a famous series of woodcuts on the subject by Hans Holbein the Younger (1497–1543). In the cloister of Old St. Paul's a "Dance of Death" called the "Dance of St. Paul's" was painted at the cost of John Carpenter, town clerk of London (15th century), with translations of French verses by John Lydgate. There is a copy in the LAMBETH PALACE library. W. H. Au-

den's poem *The Dance of Death* was published in 1933.

Floral Dance, or **Furry Dance.** *See* FURRY DANCE.

Horn Dance. *See* ABBOT'S BROMLEY.

Morris Dance. *See* MORRIS.

Dances of the Ancient World.

Astronomical dances, invented by the Egyptians, designed to represent the movements of the heavenly bodies.

Bacchic dances were of three sorts: grave (like the minuet), gay (like the gavotte), and a mixture of grave and gay.

The Danse champêtre, invented by PAN, quick and lively. The dancers (in the open air) wore wreaths of oak and garlands of flowers.

Children's dances, in Lacedæmonia, in honour of DIANA. The children were nude; and their movements were grave, modest, and graceful.

Corybantic dances, in honour of BACCHUS, accompanied with timbrels, fifes, flutes, and a tumultuous noise produced by the clashing of swords and spears against brazen bucklers.

Funeral dances, in Athens, slow, solemn dances in which the priests took part. The performers wore long white robes, and carried cypress slips in their hands.

Hymeneal dances were lively and joyous. The dancers were crowned with flowers.

Jewish dances. David danced in certain religious processions (II *Sam.* vi, 14). The people sang and danced before the GOLDEN CALF (*Exod.* xxxii, 19). And in the book of *Psalms* (cl, 4) we read, "Praise him with the timbrel and dance". Miriam, the sister of Moses, after the passage of the Red Sea, was followed by all the women with timbrels and dances (*Exod.* xv, 20).

Of the Lapithæ, invented by Pirithous. These were performed after some famous victory, designed to imitate the combats of the CENTAURS and LA-PITHÆ, and were both difficult and dangerous.

May-day dances at Rome. At daybreak lads and lasses went out to gather "May" and other flowers for themselves and their elders; and the day was spent in dances and festivities.

Military dances. The oldest of all dances, executed with swords, javelins and bucklers. Said to be invented by Minerva to celebrate the victory of the gods over the TITANS.

Nuptial dances. A Roman pantomimic performance representing the dances of our HARLEQUIN and COLUMBINE.

Pyrrhic dance. *See* PYRRHIC.

Salic dances, instituted by Numa Pompilius in honour of MARS. They were executed by twelve priests selected from the highest of the nobility, and were performed in the temple while sacrifices were being made and hymns sung to the god.

Dances, National. When Handel was asked to point out the peculiar taste of the different nations of Europe in dancing, he ascribed the *minuet* to the French, the *saraband* to the Spaniard, the *arietta* to the Italian, and the HORNPIPE and the MORRIS DANCE to the English. To these might be added the *reel* to the Scots, and the JIG to the Irish.

Dancing Dervishes. The Mawlawis, one of the many MOSLEM religious fraternities of dervishes for whom their dirge or *zikr* is a devotional rite. The chant is accompanied by a slow whirling movement with their eyes shut and arms stretched out. It lasts until a state of catalepsy is attained.

Dancing round the Maypole *See* MAYPOLE.

Dancing-water. A magic elixir, common to many fairy tales, which beautifies ladies, makes them young again and enriches them.

Dander. Is your dander up, or riz? Is your anger excited? Are you in a range? This is generally considered to be an Americanism but as a synonym for *anger* has been a common dialect word in several English counties. It is more likely that it was imported into America by the early Dutch colonists and is from their *donder*, thunder; the Dutch *op donderen* is to burst into a sudden rage.

Dandiprat. A small coin issued in the reign of Henry VII, value three halfpence. The term is also applied to a DWARF and a page and to a conceited little fellow, much as we speak of a "little twopenny-ha'penny fellow". Stanyhurst calls CUPID a "dandiprat" in his translation of VIRGIL's *Æneid*, Bk I (1582).

Dando. One who frequents hotels, restaurants, and such places, satisfies his appetite, and decamps without payment. From Dando, hero of many popular songs in the early 19th century, who was famous for this.

Dandy. A COXCOMB, a fop. Of late 18th-century Scottish origin; possibly one who has been spoilt by overmuch dandying, or from the name *Andrew*, or corruption of DANDIPRAT or the earlier JACK-A-DANDY.

Dandy traps. The same as BEAU TRAPS.

Danegeld. The geld or tax on land originally raised to buy peace from the Danes in the time of Ethelred II (978-1016) and continued as a tax long after it was needed for its original purpose.

> And that is called paying the Dane-geld;
> But we've proved it again and again,
> That if once you paid him the Dane-geld
> You never get rid of the Dane.
> KIPLING: *Dane-Geld.*

Danelaw, or **Danelagh** (O.E. *Dena lagu*, law of the Danes). That part of north and east England, roughly bounded by a line from LONDON to Chester, to which ALFRED THE GREAT (871–899) succeeded in containing the Danes and where Danish law was thus in force. The term was not used until the reign of King Cnut (1017–1035).

Danesblood, or **Danewort.** Dwarf elder (*Sambucus ebulus*), called Danesblood from a belief that it was supposed to flourish in places where there had been battles against the Danes; called Danewort because it is believed to have been introduced by the Danes.

Dane's skin. A freckled skin. Red hair and a freckled skin were regarded as the traditional characteristics of Danish blood.

Dannebrog, or **Danebrog.** (dăn' e brog). The national flag of Denmark (*brog* is Old Danish for cloth). The tradition is that Waldemar II of Denmark saw a fiery cross in the heavens which betokened his victory over the Estonians (1219). For similar legends of St. ANDREW and Constantine *see* CONSTANTINE'S CROSS *under* CROSS.

Daniel. A Daniel come to judgment. One who displays wisdom beyond his years.

In SHAKESPEARE's *Merchant of Venice*, IV, i, Shylock says:

> A Daniel come to judgement! yea, a Daniel!
> O wise young judge, how I do honour thee!

The History of Susanna in the APOCRYPHA tells how Susanna rejected the advances of two elders, was falsely accused by them and condemned to death. They claimed to have seen her lying under a tree with a young man. Her innocence was established by the youthful Daniel, who asked both accusers separately under what kind of tree the adultery took place. They each named a different tree.

Dante and Beatrice. Beatrice Portinari was only eight years old when Dante first saw her. The poet's love for her was pure as it was tender. Beatrice married a nobleman, Simone de Bardi, in 1287 and she died in 1290 (under the age of twenty-four). Dante, a few years later, married Gemma Donati. Beatrice is celebrated and idealized in Dante's *Vita Nuova* and *Divina Commedia*. In the latter work the poet is conducted first by VIRGIL (who represents human reason) through HELL and PURGATORY; then by the spirit of Beatrice (who represents the wisdom of faith); and finally by St. BERNARD (who represents the wisdom from on high).

Dantesque (Dăn tesk). Dante-like— that is, a minute lifelike representation of horrors, whether by words, as in the poet, or in visual form, as in Doré's illustrations of the *Inferno*.

Daphne (dăf' ni). Daughter of the river-god Peneus in Thessaly, beloved by APOLLO. She had resolved to spend her life in perpetual virginity and fled from him, seeking the protection of the gods, who changed her into a LAUREL or BAY-tree. Apollo declared that henceforth he would wear bay-leaves instead of the oak, and that all who sought his favour should follow his example.

Daphnis (dăf' nis). In Greek mythology, a Sicilian shepherd who invented pastoral poetry. He was a son of MERCURY and a Sicilian nymph and was protected by DIANA. He was taught by PAN and the MUSES.

Also the lover of CHLOE. Daphnis was the model of Allan Ramsay's *Gentle Shepherd* (1725), and the tale is the basis of Bernardin de St-Pierre's *Paul et Virginie* (1787).

Dapple. The name given in Smollett's translation of *Don Quixote* to SANCHO PANZA's donkey (in the original it has no name). The word is probably connected with Icel. *depill*, a spot, and means blotched, speckled in patches. A *dapple-grey* horse is one of a light grey

shaded with a deeper hue; a *dapple-bay* is of a light bay spotted with a bay of deeper colour.

Darbies. Handcuffs. Probably derived from a personal name.

Johnny Darbies, policeman, is a perversion of the Fr. *gendarmes*, in conjunction with the above.

Darby and Joan. The type of loving, old-fashioned, virtuous couples. The names belong to a ballad written by Henry Woodfall, first published in the *Gentleman's Magazine* in 1735. The characters are said to be John Darby, of Bartholomew Close, who died in 1730, and his wife "As chaste as a picture cut in alabaster. You might sooner move a Scythian rock than shoot fire into her bosom." Woodfall served his apprenticeship to John Darby; but another account localizes the couple in the West Riding of Yorkshire.

The French equivalent *C'est St. Roch et son chien* (*see* ROCH).

Darbyites (dar' bi iītz). A name sometimes given to the PLYMOUTH BRETHREN, from John Nelson Darby (1800–1882), their founder.

Dardanus. A son of ZEUS and ELECTRA and legendary founder of the royal house of TROY. He eventually married Batea, daughter of King Teucer, who gave him land near Abydos where he established the town of Dardania or Dardanus. Hence the name *Dardanelles* for what was once called the HELLESPONT.

Daric. An ancient Persian gold coin, probably so called from *dara*, a king (*see* DARIUS), much in the same way as our SOVEREIGN. There was also a silver daric, worth one-twentieth of the gold.

Darius (dà rī' ùs). A Greek form of Persian *dara*, a king, or of Sanskrit *darj*, the mountaineer. Darius the Great, son of Hystaspes (Vishtaspa), governor of Persia, assumed the name when he became king in 521 B.C.

Legend relates that he conspired with six other Persian nobles to overthrow Smerdis, the usurper, and that they agreed that he should be king whose horse neighed first; and the horse of Darius was the first to neigh. His exploits are recorded on the rock of BEHISTUN.

It is said that Darius III (Codomannus), the last king of the Persian empire, who was conquered by ALEXANDER the Great (331 B.C.), sent for the tribute of golden eggs on Alexander's accession. The Macedonian replied: "The bird which laid them is flown to the other world, where Darius must seek them." The Persian king then sent him a bat and ball, in ridicule of his youth; but Alexander told the messengers, with the bat he would beat the ball of power from their master's hand. Lastly, Darius sent him a bitter melon as emblem of the grief in store for him; but the Macedonian declared that he would make the Persian eat his own fruit.

Dark. A dark Horse. A racing term for a horse of possible promise, but of which nothing is positively known by the general public. The epithet is applied to a person whose abilities or probable course of action are unknown.

A leap in the dark. A step the consequences of which cannot be foreseen. *See* HOBBES *under* DYING SAYINGS. Lord Derby applied the words to the 1867 Reform Act.

Dark Ages, The. A term applied to the MIDDLE AGES, but more particularly to the early centuries; so called because of the intellectual darkness, held to be characteristic of the period, consequent upon the collapse of classical civilization. Hallam considered this term to apply to the period from the 5th to the 12th century, but it is now applied to a much more limited period "darkened" by the lack of contemporary written sources.

Dark Continent, The. Africa; concerning which the world was so long "in the dark", and much of which was an unknown land of mystery. It is also the land of dark races.

Dark Lady of the Sonnets. *See* LADY.

The darkest hour is that before the dawn. When things come to their worst, they must mend. In Lat., *Post nubila Phœbus.*

To keep dark. To lie perdu; to lurk in concealment.

To keep it dark. To keep it a dead secret; not to *enlighten* anyone about the matter.

To darken one's door. To cross one's threshold. Usually used in a threatening way as "Don't you dare to darken my door again!" The door is darkened by one's shadow.

Darling, Daisy. *See under* DAISY.

Grace Darling (1815–1842). An English heroine of almost legendary fame, the daughter of William Darling, keeper of the Longstone Lighthouse, Farne Islands, Northumberland. She and her father attempted the rescue of survivors of the wrecked *Forfarshire* in 1838. They launched their small boat in perilous seas and brought back five survivors to the lighthouse. Darling made a second trip with two of the *Forfarshire's* crew and saved four more, 43 being drowned. Grace died of consumption in 1842.

England's Darling. *See under* ENGLAND.

Darnex. *See* DORNICK.

Dart. *See* ABARIS.

Dartmoor. The extensive moorland in Devon, some 400 square miles in area, noted for its tors, hut circles, stone rows, barrows, pounds and stannaries and synonymous with the prison at Princetown. This was founded in 1809 to house prisoners during the Napoleonic Wars.

Darwinian Theory. The theory of evolution as put forward by Charles Darwin (1809–1882), notably in his famous book of 1859 *The Origin of Species by Natural Selection*, summed up by Herbert Spencer as "the survival of the fittest". Evolution was not a new idea to science but the shock to established science and orthodox Christian belief was profound.

Dash. Cut a dash. *See* CUT.

Dash it all, dash my wig, buttons, etc. In these expressions dash is a EUPHEMISM for "damn". *Wig, buttons,* etc., are relics of a fashion adopted by "MASHERS" of "swearing" without using profane or obscene language.

Date. Not up to date. Behind the times, not in the latest fashion, behindhand.

To date. As yet, up to the present time.

To have a date. To have an appointment, especially with one of the opposite sex.

Datum Line (Dā' tùm). A term used in surveying and engineering to describe a line from which all heights and depths are measured. The datum line upon which the Ordnance Survey maps of Great Britain were based until 1921 was the mean sea-level at Liverpool. Since 1921 it has been the mean sea-level at Newlyn, Cornwall.

Daughter. The daughter of Peneus. The bay-tree was so called because it grew in greatest perfection on the banks of the river Peneus. *See* BAY; DAPHNE.

The daughter of the horseleech. One very exigent; one for ever sponging on another, *Prov.* xxx, 15.

The scavenger's daughter. *See* SCA-VENGER.

Dauphin (daw' fin). The heir of the French crown under the VALOIS and BOURBON Dynasties. Guy IX, Count of Vienne, was the first so styled, and he wore a *dolphin* as his cognizance. The title descended in the family till 1349, when Humbert III sold his seigneurie, the Dauphiné, to Philippe VI (de Valois), one condition being that the heir of France assumed the title of *le Dauphin*. The first French prince so called was Jean, who succeeded Philippe; and the last was the Duc d'Angoulême, son of Charles X, and he renounced the title in 1830.

David. The youngest son of Jesse and slayer of GOLIATH. He temporarily rose in favour through comforting Saul by his skill as a harpist. Saul's eventual jealousy led to David's flight, effected with the aid of his wife Michal and her brother Jonathan, both children of Saul. After many vicissitudes David eventually became King of Israel (I *Sam.* xvi–xxxi, II *Sam.*; I *Kings* i–ii). The Davidic authorship of the *Psalms* has largely been discounted.

St. David, or **Dewi Sant.** Patron SAINT of WALES, whose day is 1 March. Historical information is scanty. He lived in the 6th century and died *c.* 600, and as the chief bishop of South Wales moved the ecclesiastical centre from CAERLEON to MENEVIA (St. David's). Legend is far more prolific and says that he was the son of Xantus, prince of Cereticu (Cardiganshire), and became an ascetic in

the Isle of Wight; that he visited Jerusalem, confuted Pelagius, and was preferred to the see of Caerleon. Geoffrey of Monmouth makes him the uncle of King ARTHUR.

David and Jonathan. A type of inseparable friends. *Cp.* DAMON AND PYTHIAS; PYLADES AND ORESTES.

> I am distressed for thee, my brother Jonathan; very pleasant hast thou been unto me. Thy love to me was wonderful, passing the love of women.
>
> II *Sam.* i, 26.

The Shield of David. *See under* SHIELD.

Davy Crockett *See* CROCKETT.

Davy Jones. An 18th-century sailor's term for the evil spirit of the sea. Of the many conjectures as to its derivation the most plausible are that Davy is a corruption of the West Indian *duppy* (devil) and that Jones is a corruption of Jonah, or that Davy Jones was a pirate.

Davy Jones's Locker. The sea, especially as the grave of drowned sailors.

Dawson, Bully. A noted London sharper, who swaggered and led a most abandoned life about Blackfriars in the reign of Charles II.

Day. When it begins. (1) At *sunset*: for the Jews in their "sacred year", and the Christian Church, hence the eve of feastdays; Tacitus tells us that the ancient Britons "*non dierum numerum, ut nos, sed noctium computant,*" hence "se'n-night" and "fort'night"; the ancient Greeks, Chinese, Mohammedans, etc.; (2) At *sunrise*: for the Babylonians, Syrians, Persians, and modern Greeks; (3) At *noon*: for the ancient Egyptians and modern astronomers; (4) At *midnight*: for the Romans, English, French, Dutch, Germans, Spaniards, Portuguese, Americans, etc.

A day after the fair. Too late; the fair you came to see is over.

Day in, day out. All day long and every day.

Day of Atonement, or **Day of Coverings.** *See under* ATONEMENT.

Day of the Barricades. *See under* BARRICADE.

Day of Dupes. *See* DUPES.

Days of Grace. *See* GRACE DAYS.

Every dog has its day. *See* DOG.

I have had my day. My prime of life is over. I am no longer in the SWIM and am of little account now.

I have lost a day. The exclamation (*Perdidi diem*) of the Roman emperor Titus, when on occasion he could recall nothing done during the past day for the benefit of his subjects. *See* DELIGHT.

Today a man, tomorrow a mouse. Fortune is so fickle that one day we may be at the top of the WHEEL, and the next day at the bottom. The French equivalent is, "*Aujourd'hui roi, demain rien.*"

To lose the day. To lose the battle, to be defeated.

To win, or **gain the day** is to be victorious or successful.

Daylight. In drinking bumpers, means the light seen between the wine and the rim of the glass when the wine-glass is not full. Toastmasters used to cry out "Gentlemen, no daylights nor heeltaps."

Daylight robbery. Flagrant overcharging or swindling.

Daylight Saving. The idea of making fuller use of the hours of daylight by advancing the clock originated with Benjamin Franklin, but its introduction was due to its advocacy from 1907 by William Willett (1856–1915), a Chelsea builder. It was adopted in 1916 in Germany, then England, as a wartime measure, when clocks were advanced one hour. In Britain it became permanent by an Act of 1925. *Summer Time*, as it was called, until 1939, and again in 1946 and from 1948 till 1959, began on the day following the third Saturday in April (unless that was Easter Day, in which case it was the day following the second Saturday in April). It ended on the day following the first Saturday in October. In 1961 Summer Time was extended by six weeks, beginning in March and ending in October, and similar extensions were made in 1962 and subsequent years. During World War II it extended from 25 February in 1940 and 1 January 1941–1944, until 31 December. In 1945 it ended in October. *Double Summer Time* (*i.e.* two hours in advance of G.M.T. instead of one hour) was in force during 1941–1945 and 1947 to save fuel. *See also* GREENWICH TIME.

In the U.S.A. Summer Time (March to October) was in force in 1917 and 1918 and again from 1942 to 1945 (all the year round and known as War Time). In 1966 the Uniform Time Act re-introduced Summer Time (from the last Sunday in April until the last Sunday in October) whilst allowing individual states the right of option. In the years following World War II a number of other countries have adopted some form of Summer Time.

Daylights. Pugilists' slang for eyes.

To beat the living daylights out of him, to chastise heavily.

To let daylight into him. To pierce a man with sword or bullet.

Daysman. An umpire, judge, or intercessor. The obsolete verb *to day* meant to appoint a day for the hearing of a suit, hence to judge between; the man who *dayed* was the *daysman*.

Dayspring. The dawn.

> The dayspring from on high hath visited us.
>
> *Luke* i, 78.

Daystar. The morning star; hence the emblem of hope and better prospects.

> Again o'er the vine-covered regions of France,
> See the day-star of Liberty rise.
> WILSON: *Noctes Ambrosianæ* (Jan. 1831).

De die in diem (dē dī′ ē in dī′ em) (Lat.). From day to day continuously, till the business is completed.

De facto (Lat.). Actually, in reality; as opposed to **de jure,** lawfully or rightfully. Thus John was *de facto* king, but Arthur was so *de jure*. A legal axiom says: "*De jure Judices, de facto Juratores, respondent*"; Judges look to the law, juries to the facts.

De gustibus non est disputandum (Lat.). There is no accounting for tastes; a somewhat similar English proverb is, "One man's meat is another man's poison". *Cp.* CHACUN A SON GOÛT.

De Jure. *See* DE FACTO.

De mortuis nil nisi bonum (dē môr′ tū is nil nī′sī bō′ num) (Lat.). Of the dead speak kindly or not at all. "Speak not evil of the dead" was one of the maxims of Chilo (*see* WISE MEN).

De novo (dē ñō′vō) (Lat.). Afresh; over again from the beginning.

Dead

De profundis (dē prō fŭn′ dis) (Lat.). Out of the deep; hence a bitter cry of wretchedness. *Ps* cxxx is so called from the first two words in the Latin version. It forms part of the Roman Catholic burial service.

These words were chosen as the title of Oscar Wilde's apologia, published posthumously in 1905.

De rigueur (dĕ rigēr′) (Fr.). According to strict etiquette; quite COMME IL FAUT, in the height of fashion.

De trop (dĕ trō) (Fr.). One too many; when a person's presence is not wished for, that person is *de trop*.

Dead. Dead as a door-nail. The door-nail is either one of the heavy-headed nails with which large outer doors used to be studded, or the knob on which the knocker strikes. As this is frequently knocked on the head, it cannot be supposed to have much life left in it. The expression is found in PIERS PLOWMAN.

> Old Marley was as dead as a door-nail.
> DICKENS: *Christmas Carol*, Stave i.

Other well-known similes are "Dead as a shotten herring", "as the nail in a coffin", "as mutton", and Chaucer's "as stoon [stone]", and "as the Dodo" (*see below*).

Dead as the Dodo. See DODO.

Let the dead bury their dead (*Matt*, viii, 22). Let bygones be bygones. Don't rake up old scores and dead grievances.

Dead beat. Completely exhausted, absolutely "whacked", like a dead man with no fight left in him. A *dead beat* is a down and out. In the U.S.A. it denotes a sponger, one who deliberately avoids settling his debts.

Dead beat escapement (of a clock or a watch). One in which there is no reverse motion of the escape-wheel.

Dead. Book of the Dead. *See under* BOOK.

Dead certainty. An absolute certainty.

Dead drunk. So drunk as to be totally incapable or senseless.

Dead duck. *See under* DUCK.

Dead end kids. Children from poverty-stricken back streets for whom the future seems to hold little promise.

Dead-eye. A wooden block with three holes but without sheaves used for the setting up of shrouds in sailing ships. The holes are the eyes.

Dead fire. CORPOSANT, believed at one time by the credulous to presage death.

Dead hand. A "dead hand" at anything can do it every time without fail.

> First-rate work it was too; he was always a dead hand at splitting.
> BOLDREWOOD: *Robbery Under Arms*, xv.

Dead-heads. Those admitted to theatres, etc., without payment; they are "dead" so far as box office receipts are concerned.

As a nautical usage, logs or obstructions floating low in the water, only a small part being visible.

Dead heat. A race in which two or more competitors tie for first place.

Dead horse. To flog a dead horse is to attempt to revive a question already settled or worn thin, thereby wasting time and energy.

To work a dead horse is to perform work already paid for, or to pay off a debt.

Dead knock. A knocking at the door caused by no visible agent, supposed to presage the death of an occupant of the house or someone closely connected with it.

Dead languages. Languages no longer spoken, such as Latin and Sanskrit.

Dead letter. A law or regulation no longer acted upon. A letter which the post office has been unable to deliver either because of an incorrect address or because the person addressed in untraceable.

Dead-letter office. *See* BLIND DEPARTMENT; DEAD LETTER.

Deadline. The final date or time when a task or assignment must be completed, etc. This sense of strict demarcation derives from the "deadline" round a military prison camp. The phrase was coined in the notorious Confederate prisoner of war camp, Andersonville, during the American CIVIL WAR. Some distance from the peripheral wire fence a line was marked out and any prisoner crossing this line was shot at sight.

Deadlock. A lock which has no spring catch. Metaphorically a state of things so entangled that there seems to be no solution; to reach a complete standstill.

Dead Man's Hand. In the western

283

states of U.S.A., a combination of aces and eights in poker, so called because when Sheriff Wild Bill Hickok was shot in the back at Deadwood, S. Dakota, he held such cards in his hand.

Dead man's handle. A handle on the controller of an electric train, etc., so designed that it cut off the current and applied the brakes if the driver released his pressure from illness or some other cause.

Dead Marines. Empty bottles. Of this it is said: "an empty bottle is no good to anyone", and "an empty bottle has done good service and is ready to do it again".

Dead men. Empty bottles. When the "spirit" is out of the bottle it is dead. In the U.S.A. *dead soldiers* has the same meaning.

Dead men's fingers. (1) The common British *Alcyonium digitatum*, a form of marine animal found attached to rocks and seaweed, so called from its appearance when out of the water. (2) The early purple orchis (*Orchis mascula*) which has tuberous roots somewhat resembling distorted hands.

Dead men's shoes. *See under* SHOE.

Dead pays. In the 15th and 16th centuries the pay of English officers on land and sea was augmented by permitting a fictitious increase in the numbers borne on the muster-roll. These "dead pays" were divided among the officers.

Dead Sea. The Palestinian Salt Sea or Sea of the Plain of the OLD TESTAMENT, in the ancient Vale of Siddim; called by the Romans *Mare Mortuum* and *Lacus Asphaltites*. It is about 46 miles long and 5 to 9 miles wide and is fed by the Jordan from the north, but has seemingly no outlet. The water is of bluish-green colour and its surface is about 1,300 ft. below the level of the Mediterranean. The northern end is some 1,300 ft. deep and its salt content is 25 per cent while that of sea-water is usually between 3 and 4 per cent. It supports no life other than microbes and a few very low organisms.

Dead Sea Fruit. *See* APPLES OF SODOM.

Dead Sea Scrolls. In 1947 a Bedouin goatherd, Muhammed the Wolf, made the first scroll discoveries in a cave at the N.W. end of the DEAD SEA, since when some hundreds more have been found and more discoveries are probable. Most scholars accept them as originating from the monastery of the Jewish sect of the ESSENES at Qumran. There is still much controversy over their interpretation but it is expected that these manuscripts (from the period 150 B.C. to A.D. 70) will add very considerably to the understanding of Old Testament textual criticism and the background of the NEW TESTAMENT.

To make a dead set upon someone. To concentrate steadfastly upon gaining someone's attention or notice; to concentrate on gaining someone's affection, particularly of the opposite sex; to make a prolonged and resolute onslaught. The allusion is to dogs, etc., set on each other to fight.

Dead soldiers. *See* DEAD MEN.

Dead to the world. In a deep sleep, or state of exhaustion or intoxication, so that a person is totally unconscious of his surroundings.

Dead water. The eddy-water which closes in round a ship's stern as it passes through the water.

Dead weight. The weight of something without life; a burden that does nothing towards easing its own weight; a person who encumbers us and renders no assistance. *Cp.* DEAD LIFT.

Deaf. Deaf as an adder. "Even like the adder that stoppeth her ears; which refuseth to hear the voice of the charmer: charm he never so wisely" (*Ps.* lviii, 4, 5). In the East, if a viper entered the house, the charmer was sent for, who enticed the serpent and put it into a bag. According to tradition, the viper tried to stop its ears when the charmer uttered his incantation, by applying one ear to the ground and twisting its tail into the other.

In the United States deaf adders are sometimes called COPPERHEADS.

Deaf as a post. Quite deaf; or so inattentive as not to hear what is said. One might as well speak to a gatepost or log of wood.

None so deaf as those who won't hear. The French have the same saying: *Il n'y a de pire sourd que celui qui ne veut pas entendre*.

Dean (Lat. *decanus*, one set over ten). The ecclesiastical dignitary who presides over the CHAPTER of a cathedral or COLLEGIATE CHURCH, this having formerly consisted of ten canons. In the more recent foundations decanal functions are carried out by a PROVOST.

In the colleges of Oxford and Cambridge, the resident don responsible for undergraduate discipline, or in charge of the chapel, is called a dean.

In Scottish and most modern English universities the title is given to the head of a faculty, as in America, where it is applied to certain other college and administrative officers. *Cp.* DOYEN.

Dean of the Arches. The judge presiding over the Court of ARCHES, formerly at Bow Church, once a PECULIAR.

Dean of Faculty. In Scotland the barrister who presides over the Faculty of Advocates.

Dean of Guild. One who formerly decided mercantile and maritime causes in a Scottish burgh, but more recently largely concerned with regulations affecting buildings.

Deans of Peculiars. Once numerous, and including those of Collegiate Churches such as Westminster and Windsor, surviving examples are those of Battle, Bocking, Jersey and Guernsey.

Dean of the Sacred College, is the senior cardinal-bishop who is given the title of Bishop of Ostia and Velletri. He ranks next to the POPE in the hierarchy. *See* CARDINAL.

Rural Dean. An incumbent who assists in adminstering part of an archdeaconry. An ancient office effectively revived from the mid-19th century.

Dear. Oh, dear me! A very common exclamation, most likely a EUPHEMISM for "Oh, damn me!"

Death. Angel of Death. *See* AZRAEL.

Black Death. *See* BLACK.

At death's door. On the point of death; very dangerously ill.

In at the death. Present when the fox was caught and killed; hence, present at the climax or final act of an exciting event.

Till death us do part. *See* DEPART.

To feel like death warmed up. To be utterly exhausted, to be quite done up, to feel ghastly.

Death from Strange Causes.

Æschylus was killed by a tortoise, dropped on his bald head by an eagle (Valerius Maximus, IX, xii, and Pliny, *History*, VII, vii).

Anacreon was choked by a grapestone (Pliny, *History*, VII, vii).

Bacon died of a cold contracted when stuffing a fowl with snow as an experiment in refrigeration.

Burton, author of the *Anatomy of Melancholy*, died on the very day that he had himself astrologically predicted.

Chalchas, the soothsayer, died of laughter at the thought of having outlived the predicted hour of his death.

Charles VIII, of France, conducting his queen into a tennis-court, struck his head against the lintel, which caused his death.

Fabius, the Roman prætor, was choked by the presence of a single goathair in the milk which he was drinking (Pliny, *History*, VII, vii).

Frederick Lewis, Prince of Wales, son of George II, died from the blow of a cricket-ball.

George, Duke of Clarence, brother of Edward IV, was drowned in a butt of MALMSEY.

King John, traditionally said to have died from a surfeit of lampreys but more probably from dysentery resulting from excessive fatigue and indulgence in food and drink.

Lepidus (*Quintus Æmilius*), going out of his house, struck his big toe against the threshold and died.

Lully (*Jean Baptiste*), the composer, when beating time by tapping the floor with his staff while directing a performance of the *Te Deum*, struck his foot and subsequently died from the abscess which set in.

Otway, the poet, in a starving condition, had a guinea given him, with which he bought a loaf of bread and died while swallowing the first mouthful.

Philomenes died of laughter at seeing an ass eating the figs provided for his own dessert (Valerius Maximus).

Prince Philip, eldest son of Louis VI of France, met his death when a pig ran between his horse's legs causing him to be thrown.

William III died from a fall from his horse which stumbled over a mole-hill.

Death in the pot. During a dearth in Gilgal, there was made for the sons of the prophets a potage of wild herbs, some of which were poisonous. When they tasted the potage, they cried out "there is death in the pot". Then Elisha put into it some meal and the poisonous qualities were counteracted (II *Kings* iv, 40).

Death under shield. Death in battle.

Death-bell. A tinkling in the ears, supposed by the Scottish peasantry to announce the death of a friend.

Death coach. A ghostly carriage, whose coachman is sometimes headless, which, in Irish and Breton superstition, is reputed to stop in front of a house where a death is about to occur.

Death-watch. Any species of *Anobium*, a genus of wood-boring beetles, that make a clicking sound, once supposed to presage death.

Death's head. A skull. Bawds and procuresses used to wear a ring bearing the impression of a death's head in the time of Queen Elizabeth I.

Death's-head Moth. *Acheronitia atropos* is so called from the markings on the back of the thorax which closely resemble a skull. It is the largest British Hawkmoth.

Death's-man. An executioner; a person who kills another brutally but lawfully.

Debatable Land. A tract of land between the Esk and Sark claimed by both ENGLAND and SCOTLAND and for long in dispute. It was the haunt of thieves and vagabonds.

Debon. *See* DEVONSHIRE.

Debrett. To be in Debrett is to be included in *Debrett's Peerage, Baronetage, Knightage, and Companionage, i.e.* to be of an aristrocatic or titled family. *Debrett's Peerage* was originally composed by John Debrett and first published in 1802, and followed by *Debrett's Baronetage* in 1808. *Cp.* TO BE IN BURKE *under* BURKE.

Debt of Nature. To pay the debt of Nature. To die. Life is a loan and the debt

is paid off by the death.

Decabrists, or **Dekabrists.** *See* DECEMBRISTS.

Decalogue (Gr. *deka logos*, ten words or sentences). The name given by the Greek Fathers to the TEN COMMANDMENTS referred to in *Exodus* xxxiv, 28 and elsewhere. They have sometimes been divided into those which define our duty to God and those which state our duty to others. The 'classic' version occurs in *Exodus* xx, 2–17; another is found in *Deuteronomy* v, 6–21. The form adopted by the CHURCH OF ENGLAND and most Protestant churches is that which Josephus says was used by his Jewish contemporaries.

Decameron (de kăm' ĕron). The collection of 100 tales by Boccaccio, completed *c.* 1353, represented as having been told in ten days (Gr. *deka*, ten, *hemera*, day) during the plague at Florence in 1348, seven ladies and three gentlemen each telling a tale daily. *Cp.* HEPTAMERON; CANTERBURY TALES.

Decathlon. An athletic contest in the modern OLYMPIC GAMES consisting of ten events: 100 metres race, long jump, putting the shot, high jump, 400 metres race, 110 metres hurdles, discus, pole vault, throwing the javelin, and 1,500 metres race.

December (Lat. the tenth month). So it was when the year began in MARCH with the vernal equinox; but, since JANUARY and FEBRUARY have been inserted before it, the name is somewhat misplaced. The old Dutch name was *Wintermaand* and the old Saxon *Wintermonath* (winter month), also called YULE month. After the Saxons became Christians it was known as *Helighmonath* (holy month). In Germany it is known as *Christmonat*. In the French Republican Calendar it was *Frimaire* (hoar-frost month, from 22 November to 20 December).

The Man of December. NAPOLEON III (1808–1873). He was elected President of the Second French Republic 10 December 1848; made his COUP D'ÉTAT 2 December 1851; and became Emperor 2 December 1852.

Decembrists. Conspirators in the Russian army who tried to overthrow the

Czar Nicholas I in December 1825.

Decimal Currency was introduced in Great Britain on 15 February 1971, the new POUND consisting of 100 pence. The new coins were the seven-sided 50p piece, the 10p piece (the same size as the former FLORIN), the 5p piece (the same size as the former SHILLING), the 2p piece, the 1p piece and the ½p piece. The first three coins are silver in colour and the remainder copper-coloured. The introduction of a decimal currency was first mooted by the Tory M.P., John Croker, 1816. The idea was again put forward in Parliament in 1824, 1847, 1853 and 1855.

Deck. A pack of cards, or that part of the pack left after the hands have been dealt.

Clear the decks. Get everything out of the way that is not essential, also to clear the decks of personnel. A nautical expression.

Decoration Day. *See* MEMORIAL DAY.

Decree nisi. *See* NISI.

Decretals. The name given to papal decrees or letters which embody decisions in ecclesiastical law.

Decuman Gate. The principal entrance to a Roman military camp, situated on the farthest side from the enemy, and so called because it was guarded by the 10th cohort of each legion (*decimus*, tenth).

Dedalian. *See* DÆDALUS.

Dee, Dr. John Dee (1527–1608), famous mathematician, alchemist and astrologer, was patronized by Queen Elizabeth I, but eventually died a pauper at Mortlake, where he was buried. He wrote 79 treatises on a variety of subjects. Dee's *Speculum* or Mirror, of solid pink-tinted glass, about the size of an orange, once in Horace Walpole's collection at Strawberry Hill, is now in the BRITISH MUSEUM.

Deed Poll. A deed made by one party, and so called because it was written on parchment with a *polled* or straight edge as opposed to an INDENTURE, one with an indented or wavy edge.

Deemster, Dempster, or **Doomster.** The two judges of the Isle of Man are called Deemsters and they take an oath to execute the laws "as indifferently as the herring backbone doth lie in the midst of the fish." (*See* DOOM.) Hall Caine's once popular romance *The Deemster* appeared in 1887.

In SCOTLAND, a Dempster or Doomster was formerly appointed to recite the sentence after it had been pronounced by the court. He combined this office with that of executioner.

Deer. Supposed by poets to shed tears. The drops, however, which fall from their eyes are not tears but an oily secretion from the so-called tear-pits.

> A poor sequester'd stag...
> Did come to languish... and the big round tears
> Cours'd one another down his innocent nose
> In piteous chase.
> SHAKESPEARE: *As You Like It*, II, ii.

Default. Judgment by default is when the defendant does not appear in court on the day appointed. The judge gives sentence in favour of the plaintiff, not because the plaintiff is right, but from the default of the defendent. Hence used of a judgement made in a person's absence.

Defender of the Faith (Lat. *fidei defensor*). A title given to Henry VIII by Pope Leo X (11 October 1521) for his treatise *Assertio Septem Sacramentorum* attacking Luther's teachings. The initials 'F.D.' continuously appeared on the British coinage from the reign of George I.

Defenders. An association of Irish Catholics (1784–1798), formed in Northern IRELAND in opposition to the PEEP-OF-DAY BOYS. In 1795 a pitched battle was fought between the two and the Defenders suffered severe losses.

Defenestration of Prague. An incident in Bohemia prior to the outbreak of the THIRTY YEARS WAR when the two leading Roman Catholic members of the Bohemian National Council were thrown out of a window of the castle of Prague by the PROTESTANT members. They landed in the moat and sustained only minor injuries.

Déficit, Madame. Marie Antoinette, because she was always in need of money. She was noted for her extravagance and popularly regarded as being responsible for the nation's bankruptcy.

Degrees, Songs of. Another name for the GRADUAL PSALMS.

Dei Gratia (dē ī grā' shà) (Lat.). By the grace of God. As early as *c.* 690 we find "I, Ine, by God's grace King of the West Saxons", and in an ordinance of William I, "*Willelmus gratia Dei Rex Anglorum*".It was first used on the GREAT SEAL by William II and all Great Seals from the reign of Edward I. It still appears on British coins, where it was originally introduced on the gold coins of Edward III in 1344. *See* GRACELESS FLORIN.

The style was also sometimes used by the Archbishops of Canterbury and York, until as late as the 17th century, and is still so used by BISHOPS of the RO-MAN CATHOLIC CHURCH.

Dei Judicium (dē ī yoo dis' i um) (Lat.). The judgment of God; so the judgment by ORDEAL was called, because it was taken as certain that God would deal rightly with appellants.

Deianira (dē ī ăn ira). Wife of HERCULES and the unwitting cause of his death. NESSUS, the CENTAUR, having carried her across a river, attempted to assault her and was shot by Hercules with a poisoned arrow. The expiring centaur gave Deianira his tunic, steeped in blood, telling her that it would reclaim her husband from illicit loves. When she had occasion to give it to Hercules, the poisoned blood brought about his death.

Deidamia (dē ī dā' mia). Daughter of Lycomedes, King of Scyros. ACHILLES, when sojourning there disguised as a woman, became the father of her son Pyrrhus, or Neoptolemus.

Deiphobus (dē ī fō' bus). Third husband of HELEN of Troy whom she married after the death of his brother PARIS. Helen betrayed Deiphobus to her first husband, MENELAUS who killed his rival.

Deirdre (dir' drē). In Irish romance the daughter of the king of ULSTER's storyteller. At her birth it was prophesied that she would bring ruin to IRELAND. King CONCHOBAR brought her up and planned to marry her, but she fell in love with Naoise, the eldest of the three sons of USNECH. She escaped to Scotland, with the three brothers but they were lured back by Conchobar with false promises. The jealous king killed the three young men. One version of the story says that Deirdre killed herself, another that she died the following year after living unhappily with Conchobar. Deirdre is the subject and title of a play by W.B. Yeats, and J.M. Synge also dramatized the legend in his *Deirdre of the Sorrows*.

Deist. *See* THEIST.

Deities. The more important classical, Teutonic, and Scandinavian deities appear under their own names; the present list is only intended to include certain collective names and some better-known gods, sprites, etc., of special localities, functions, etc.

Air: ARIEL; *Elves. See* ELF.
Caves or *Caverns*: HILL-FOLK or Hill-people, Pixies (*see* PIXIE).
Corn: CERES (Gr. DEMETER).
Domestic Life: VESTA.
Eloquence: MERCURY (Gr. HERMES).
Evening: Vesper.
Fairies. See FAIRY.
Fates: (*q.v.*); NORNS.
Fire: VULCAN (Gr. Hephaistos), VESTA, MULCIBER.
Furies: (*q.v.*), (Gr. EUMENIDES, ERINYES).
Gardens: PRIAPUS; VERTUMNUS; POMONA.
Graces: See under GRACE (Gr. Charites).
Hades (*q.v.*): PLUTO with his wife PROSERPINA (Gr. Aidēs and Persephóne).
Hills: Pixies (*see* PIXIE), TROLLS; also Wood Trolls and Water Trolls.
Home Spirits: LARES AND PENATES.
Hunting: DIANA (Gr. Artemis).
Justice: THEMIS, ASTRÆA, NEMESIS.
Love: VENUS (Gr. APHRODITE), CUPID (Gr. EROS).
Marriage: HYMEN.
Medicine: ÆSCULAPIUS.
Morning: AURORA (Gr. EOS).
Mountains: OREADS, TROLLS.
Ocean: OCEANIDES. *See* SEA *below*.
Poetry and Music: APOLLO, the nine MUSES.
Rainbow: IRIS.
Riches: PLUTUS.
Rivers and Streams: Fluviales (Gr. Potamēides, NAIADS, Nymphs).
Sea: NEPTUNE (Gr. POSEIDON), TRITON, *Nixies*, MERMAIDS, NEREIDS.
Shepherds and their flocks: PAN, the SATYRS.
Springs, Lakes, Brooks, etc.: NEREIDS, NAIADS. *See* RIVERS, *above*.
Time: SATURN (Gr. CHRONOS).
Trees: See WOODS, *below*.
War: MARS (Gr. ARES), BELLONA, THOR.

Water-nymphs: NAIADS, UNDINE.
Winds: ÆOLUS.
Wine: BACCHUS (Gr. DIONYSUS).
Wisdom: MINERVA (Gr. PALLAS, ATHENE, or PALLAS-ATHENE).
Woods: DRYADS (a Hamadryad presides over some particular tree), Wood Trolls.
Youth: HEBE.

Dekko, To take a. To glance at, to have a look at. This is one of the many phrases brought back from India by the British Army. In Hindustani *dekho* means "look".

Delectable Mountains. In Bunyan's *Pilgrim's Progress*, a range of mountains from which the "CELESTIAL CITY" may be seen.

Delenda est Carthago (dè len'dà est kar tha' gō) (Lat.). Carthage must be destroyed; the words with which Cato the Elder concluded every speech in the Senate after his visit to Carthage in 157 B.C. where he saw in her revived prosperity a standing threat to ROME. The phrase is now proverbial and means "that which stands in the way of our greatness must be removed at all costs".

Delilah, A. A beautiful but treacherous woman, from the story of Samson and Delilah (*Judges* xvi).

Delinquents. During the English civil wars (1642–1645) a term applied to the royalists by their opponents. Charles I was called the "chief delinquent".

Delirium. From the Lat. *lira* (the ridge left by the plough), hence the verb *delilare*, to make an irregular ridge in ploughing. Thus *delirus* for one who could not plough straight, and hence a crazy, dotty person, one whose mind wandered from the subject in hand. *Delirium* is that state of such a person. *Cp.* PREVARICATION.

Della Cruscans (del' a krŭs' kánz), or **Della Cruscan School.** A school of poetry started by some young Englishmen in Florence in the latter part of the 18th century. Their silly, sentimental affectations, which appeared in *The World* and *The Oracle*, created a temporary stir but were mercilessly pilloried in *The* BAVIAD and *The Mœviad*. The clique took its name from the famous Accademia della Crusca (Academy of Chaff) which was founded in Florence in 1582 with the object of purifying the

Italian language by sifting away its "chaff", and which in 1611 published an important dictionary.

Delos. The smallest island of the Cyclades, sacred to APOLLO. It comes from the Greek word for a ring, as the rest of the islands encircle Delos. It was fabled to have been called out of the deep by POSEIDON, and remained a floating island until ZEUS chained it to the bottom of the sea. It was the legendary birthplace of Apollo and Artemis (DIANA).

Delphi, or **Delphos** (now Kastri). A town of Phocis at the foot of Mount PARNASSUS famous for a temple of APOLLO and for its celebrated oracle which was silenced only in the 4th century by the Emperor Theodosius. Delphi was regarded by the ancients as the "navel of the earth", and in the temple there was a white stone bound with a red ribbon to represent the navel and umbilical cord.

A Delphic utterance is one which has the ambiguity associated with the words of the ORACLE.

Deluge. The Biblical story of the flood (*Gen.* vi, vii, viii) has its counterpart in a variety of mythologies. In Babylonia it appears in the 11th tablet of the GILGAMESH EPIC, but on a higher level of civilization, for UTNAPISHTIM takes both craftsmen and treasure into his ark.

Apollodorus tells the story of DEUCALION AND PYRRHA in some versions of which Deucalion is replaced by Ogyges. (*See* OGYGIAN DELUGE.) The story is also found in Ovid's *Metamorphoses*, Bk. I, 253–415.

In India one legend tells how MANU was warned by a fish of the approaching flood and the fish subsequently towed his vessel to safety.

Kindred stories are found in China, Burma, New Guinea, etc., and in both the American continents.

Delusion. A snare and a delusion. Something that raises hopes only to dash them.

Demesne. *See* MANOR.

Demeter (de mē' ter). The corn goddess of Greek legend, identified with the Roman CERES. She was the mother of Persephone (PROSERPINE) and the goddess of fruit, crops, and vegetation.

Demijohn (dem' i jon). A glass or stoneware vessel with a large body and a small neck enclosed in wickerwork and containing more than a bottle. A common capacity is five gallons. The word is probably from the Fr. *dame-jeanne*, Dame Jane. *Cp.* BELLARMINE.

Demi-monde (dem' i mond) (Fr. d*emi*, half; *monde*, world, society). As *le beau monde* is society, *le demi-monde* denotes that class of women whose social standing is only half acknowledged or who are of uncertain reputation. The term was first used by Dumas *fils* for the title of a play (*Le Demi-Monde*, 1855), and sometimes incorrectly applied to fashionable courtesans.

Demi-rep (dem' i rep). A woman whose character has been blown upon, one "whom everybody knows to be what nobody calls her" (Fielding). A contraction of *demi-reputable*.

Demiurge (demi' i ĕrj) (Gr. *demiourgos*, artisan, handicraftsman, etc.). In the language of the Platonists, that mysterious agent which made the world and all that it contains. The Logos, or Word, spoken of by St. JOHN in the first chapter of his gospel, is the *Demiurgus* of Platonizing Christians. Among the GNOSTICS JEHOVAH (as an eon or emanation of the Supreme Being) is the Demiurge. *See* MARCIONITES.

Certain officials in some of the ancient Greek states were called *Demiurgoi*.

Democritus (de mok' ri tus) (*c.* 460–370 B.C.). Called "Wisdom" during his life and later the "laughing philosopher". He was a follower of Leucippus and head of the school of ABDERA in Thrace. He should rather be termed the *deriding* philosopher, because he derided or laughed at people's folly or vanity. It is said that he put out his eyes that he might think the more deeply. He was no mere scoffer, and in many ways is to be ranked with PLATO and ARISTOTLE.

Democritus Junior. The name under which Robert Burton's (1577–1640) *The Anatomy of Melancholy* first appeared in 1621.

Demogorgon (dem ō gor' gon). A terrible deity, whose very name was capable of producing the most horrible effects. He is first mentioned by the 4th-century Christian writer, Lactantius, who in doing so broke with the superstition that the very reference to Demogorgon by name brought death and disaster.

Demons, Prince of. ASMODEUS, also called "the Demon of Matrimonial Unhappiness".

Demos, King (dē' mos). The electorate, the proletariat; those who choose the rulers of the nation and are therefore ultimately sovereign. A facetious or derisive term (Gr. *demos*, people).

Denarius (den âr' i ús). A Roman silver coin originally equal to ten ases (*deniases*). The word was used in France and England for the inferior coins whether of silver or copper, and for ready money generally. The initial "d" for PENNY (£ *s. d.*) is from *denarius*.

Denarius Dei (Lat. God's penny). An earnest of a bargain, which was given to the Church or poor.

Denarii St. Petri. Peter's pence. *See under* PETER.

Denis, St. *See* DENYS.

Denmark. According to the *Roman de la Rose*, Denmark means the country of Danaos, who settled there after the siege of TROY, as BRUTUS is said by the same sort of legend to have settled in BRITAIN. SAXO-GRAMMATICUS (*c.* 1150–*c.* 1206) in his *Gesta Danorum*, with equal fancifulness, explains the name by making Dan, the son of Humble, the first king. His work is largely a collection of myths and oral tradition dealing with kings, heroes and national gods.

Something is rotten in the state of Denmark. A hidden cause of uneasiness which is felt but cannot be precisely defined; there is a scent of corruption or something dubious going on. Often used facetiously. From SHAKESPEARE'S *Hamlet*, IV, i.

Denys, St. (dė nē') or **St. Dionysius.** The apostle to the Gauls and a traditional patron saint of France, said to have been beheaded at Paris in 272. Legendarily, after martyrdom he carried his head in his hands for two miles and laid it on the spot where stands the cathedral bearing his name. The tale may have arisen from an ancient painting of his martyrdom in which the artist placed the head between the hands so that the martyr might be identified. *See* CE N'EST QUE LE PREMIER PAS QUI COÛTE *under* PREMIER.

Montjoie Saint Denys! *See* MONTJOIE.

Deo gratias (dē' ō grä shăs) (Lat.). Thanks to God. *Cp.* DEI GRATIA.

Deo juvante, or **adjuvante** (dē' ō yoo-văn' te) (Lat.). With God's help.

Deo volente (dē' ō vō len' te) (Lat.). God be willing; by God's will; usually contracted into D.V.

Deoch-an-dorius. *See* DOCH-AN-DORIS.

Deodand (dē' ō dănd). Literally, something which should be given to God (Lat. *deo-dandum*). In English law a personal chattel responsible for the death of an individual was forfeited to the crown for some pious use. For example, if a man met his death from the fall of a ladder, the kick of a horse, etc., the cause of death was sold and the proceeds given to the Church. It originated from the idea that as the sufferer was sent to his account without the sacrament of extreme unction, the money could serve to pay for masses for his repose. Deodands were abolished in 1846.

Depart. Literally, to part thoroughly; to separate effectually. The marriage service in the old prayer-books had "till death us depart", which has been corrupted into "till death us do part".

Derby (dĕr' bi). The American name for the hat known as the BOWLER in England.

The Derby is the DERBY STAKES.

Derby Day (dar' bi) is the day when the DERBY STAKES are run for, during the great Epsom Summer Meeting.

Derby Dog. The stray dog that so often wanders on to the race-course on Epsom Downs as soon as it has been cleared for the main race. Something that inevitably "turns up".

Derby Stakes (dar' bi). One of the CLASSIC RACES, also called the BLUE RIBAND OF THE TURF, was instituted by the Twelfth Earl of Derby in 1780, one year after he established the OAKS. The Derby is for three-year-old colts and fillies only, therefore no horse can win it twice. *See* EPSOM RACES; HERMIT'S DERBY.

Kiplingcotes Derby. *See* KIPLINGCOTES.

Derbyite. In World War I, a soldier enlisted under the Derby Scheme of 1915. The Earl of Derby was Director of Recruiting and sought to promote a scheme of voluntary enlistment by age groups. The response was quite inadequate and conscription was instituted in May 1916.

Derbyshire neck. Goitre, from its occurrence in that county more commonly than in other parts of Britain.

Derrick. A contrivance or form of crane used for hoisting heavy objects; so called from Derrick, the TYBURN hangman of the early 17th century. The name was first applied to the gibbet and, from its similarity, to the crane.

Deseret. Deseret was the MORMON name for a honey bee and their original name for the State of Utah.

Desert Fathers. *See under* FATHER.

Desert Rats. *See* REGIMENTAL AND DIVISIONAL NICKNAMES.

Desmas. *See* DYSMAS.

Despair. Giant Despair, in Bunyan's *Pilgrim's Progress,* dwelt in DOUBTING CASTLE.

Destruction. Prince of Destruction. TAMERLANE, or Timur, the Tartar (1336–1405), the famous oriental conqueror of Persia and a great part of India. He was threatening China when he died.

Desultory. Roman circus-riders who used to leap from one horse to another were called *desultores*; hence used figuratively in Latin to mean an inconstant person, or one who went from one thing to another; and desultory thus means after the manner of a *desultor* (Lat. *desilio,* leap down, alight).

Deucalion and Pyrrha. Deucalion (the Greek counterpart of Noah) was a son of PROMETHEUS and married Pyrrha, daughter of Epimetheus. He was king of part of Thessaly. When ZEUS, angered at the evils of the Bronze Age (*See* AGE), caused the DELUGE, Deucalion built an ark to save himself and his wife, which came to rest on Mount PARNASSUS. Told by the ORACLE of THEMIS that to restore the human race they must cast the bones of their mother behind them (which they interpreted as the stones of Mother Earth), he and his wife obeyed the direction. The stones thrown by Deucalion became men and those thrown by Pyrrha became women.

Deuce. The two, in games with cards, dice, etc. (fr. *deux*). The three is called "tray" (Fr. *trois*).

Among the origins ascribed to the word *deuce* used as a EUPHEMISM for DEVIL is that it may come from the two at dice being an unlucky throw. Other suggestions are that it is from the Latin expletive *Deus*! My God!; from the Celtic *dus*, *teuz*, phantom, spectre; or from the Old German *Durce, Turse*, giant.

Deuce take you. Get away! you annoy me.

Go to the deuce. Go to the devil!

It played the deuce with me. It made me very ill; it disagreed with me. It gave me the devil of a time.

What the deuce is the matter? What the devil is up? What in the world is amiss?

Deus. Deux ex machina (Lat.). The intervention of some unlikely or providential event just in time to extricate one from difficulties or to save a situation; especially as contrived in a novel or a play. Literally it means "a god let down upon the stage from the machine", the "machine" being part of the stage equipment in an ancient Greek theatre.

Deus vult (Lat. God wills it). The warcry of the First CRUSADE, enjoined by Pope Urban II because these words were spontaneously used by the crowd in response to his address at Clermont in 1095.

Deva. The Roman legionary fortress on the site of the present Chester; the river Dee.

Devil, The. Represented with a cloven foot, because by the Rabbinical writers he is called *seirizzim* (a goat). As the goat is a type of uncleanness, the prince of unclean spirits is aptly represented under this emblem. As the Prince of Evil he is also called SATAN.

In legal parlance a counsel who prepares a brief for another is called a *devil* and the process is called *devilling*. It is also applied where one counsel transfers his brief to another to represent him in court.

A printer's devil. A printer's errand boy; formerly the boy who took the printed sheets from the tympan of the press.

DEVIL PHRASES.

As the Devil loves holy water. That is, not at all. HOLY WATER drives away the devil. The Latin proverb is, "*Sicut sus amaricinum amat*" (as swine love marjoram), which similarly means not at all, since Lucretius, VI, 974, says, "*amaricinum fugitat sus*."

Beating the Devil's tattoo. Drumming on the table with one's fingers a wearisome number of times, or on the floor with one's foot; repeating any rhythmical mechanical sound with annoying persistence.

Between the Devil and the deep (blue) sea. Between SCYLLA and CHARYBDIS; between two evils or alternatives, to be in a hazardous or precarious position. It is seemingly of nautical origin and means between the devil and the waterline of a ship. *See* THE DEVIL TO PAY AND NO PITCH HOT, *below.*

Cheating the Devil. Mincing an oath; doing evil for gain, and giving part of the profits to the Church, etc.

Rabelais (*Pantagruel*, Bk. IV, ch. xlvi), says that a farmer once bargained with the Devil for each to have on alternate years what grew under and over the soil. The canny farmer sowed carrots and turnips when it was his turn to have the under-soil share, and wheat and barley the year following.

Devil-may-care. Wildly reckless; also a reckless individual.

Give the Devil his due. Give even a bad person, or one hated like the devil, such credit as he deserves.

Go to the Devil. Go to ruin.

He needs a long spoon who sups with the Devil. *See* SPOON.

Here's the very Devil to pay. Here's a pretty KETTLE OF FISH. I'm in a pretty mess. *Cp.* **The devil to pay and no pitch hot,** *below.*

Needs must when the Devil drives. If I must, I must; there is no option.

Pull Devil, pull baker. Lie, cheat and wrangle away, "have a go at each other". Sometimes "parson" is substituted for "baker".

Talk of the Devil and he's sure to appear. Said of a person who has been the subject of conversation and who unexpectedly makes his appearance. An older proverb still is: "Talk of the Dule and he'll put out his horns"; and a more modern version is "Talk of an angel and you'll hear the fluttering of its wings."

Tell the truth and shame the Devil. A very old saying, of obvious meaning.

The Devil among the tailors. Said when a slanging match is in progress.

The phrase is said to have originated from a fracas made at a benefit performance about 1830 for the actor William Dowton (1764–1851). The piece was a burlesque called *The Tailors: a Tragedy for Warm Weather*, and the row was made outside the Haymarket Theatre by a large crowd of tailors, who considered the play a slur on their trade.

The Devil and all. Everything, especially everything bad.

The Devil and his dam. The Devil and something worse. Dam here may mean *mother* or *wife* and numerous quotations may be adduced in support of either interpretation. Rabbinical tradition relates that LILITH was the wife of ADAM, but was such a vixen that Adam could not live with her, and she became the Devil's dam. We also read that BELPHEGOR "came to earth to seek him out a dam". In many mythologies the Devil is typified by an animal, and in such cases *dam* for mother is not inappropriate.

The Devil catch the hindmost. A phrase from late mediæval magic. The Devil was supposed to have had a school at Toledo, or at Salamanca, where the students, after making certain progress in their mystic studies, were obliged to run through a subterranean hall, and the last man was seized by the Devil and became his imp. *See also under* SHADOW.

The Devil dances in an empty pocket. An old proverb. Poverty or an empty pocket leads to temptation or crime. Many coins bore a cross on the obverse and so the Devil could not gain entrance to the pocket if they were present.

The Devil is not so black as he is painted. Said in extenuation or mitigation, especially when it seems that exaggerated censure has been given.

The Devil's advocate. *See* ADVOCATE.

The Devil's dancing-hour. Midnight.

The Devil's door. A small door in the north wall of some old churches, which used to be opened at baptisms and communions to "let the Devil out". The north used to be known as "the Devil's side", where SATAN and his legion lurked to catch the unwary.

The Devil sick would be a monk.

> When the Devil was sick, the Devil a monk would be;
> When the Devil got well, the devil a monk was he.

Said of those persons who in times of sickness or danger make pious resolutions, but forget them when danger is past and health recovered.

The Devil to pay and no pitch hot. There will be serious trouble arising from this. The "devil" was the seam between the outboard plank and the waterways of a ship and very awkward of access. It also needed more pitch when caulking and paying, hence "the devil". *See* PAY.

To hold a candle to the Devil. *See* CANDLE.

To kindle a fire for the Devil. To offer sacrifice, to do what is really sinful, under the delusion that you are doing God's service.

To lead one the Devil's own dance. To give one endless trouble.

To play the very Devil with something. To thoroughly mar or spoil.

To pull the Devil by the tail. To struggle constantly against adversity.

To say the Devil's paternoster. To grumble; to rail at providence.

To vow a candle to the Devil. *See* CANDLE.

When the Devil is blind. Never.

Why should the Devil have all the good tunes? A saying originating with Charles Wesley about 1740, when he adapted the music of current popular songs to promote the use of his hymns.

DEVIL. SOME TOPOGRAPHICAL USAGES.

Devil's Arrows. Three remarkable "Druid" stones near Boroughbridge, Yorkshire.

Devil's Bridge. A popular name in mountainous areas for bridges built over ravines and chasms.

Devil's Cheesewring. *See* CHEESEWR-ING.

Devil's Coits. *See* HACKELL'S COIT.

Devil's Current. Part of the current of the BOSPORUS is so called, from its great rapidity.

Devil's Dyke. (1) An ancient earth-work in Cambridgeshire stretching from Reach to Wood Ditton. On the eastern side it is 18 ft. high. (2) A ravine in the South Downs to the N.W. of Brighton. The legend is that St. Cuthman, priding himself on having christianized the area and having built a nunnery where the dyke-house was later built, was con-fronted by the Devil and told that all his labour was vain for he would swamp the whole country before morning. St. Cuthman went to the nunnery and told the abbess to keep the sisters in prayer till after midnight and then illuminate the windows. The Devil came at sunset with mattock and spade, and began cut-ting a dyke into the sea, but was seized with rheumatic pains all over his body. He flung down his tools, and the cocks, mistaking the illuminated windows for sunrise, began to crow; whereupon the Devil fled in alarm, leaving his work not half done. (3) *See* GRIM'S DYKE *under* GRIM.

Devil's Island. A small island off the coast of French Guiana, formerly used as a convict settlement. Captain Alfred Dreyfus was confined there (*see* DREY-FUSARD).

Devil's Nostrils. Two vast caverns separated by a huge pillar of natural rock on the Mainland of Zetland.

Devil's Punch Bowl. A deep combe on the S.W. side of Hindhead Hills, in Sur-rey, scene of the murder of an unknown sailor in 1786. His assassins, Lonagan, Casey and Marshall, were hanged in chains on nearby Hindhead Common. A similar dell in Mangerton Mountain, near Killarney, has the same name.

DEVIL. IN PERSONAL NOMENCLATURE.

The Devil's Missionary. A nickname given to VOLTAIRE (1694–1778).

Robert the Devil. *See under* ROBERT.

White Devil. Vittoria Corombona, an Italian murderess whose story was dra-matized (1608) by John Webster under this name. "White devils" was 16th- and 17th-century slang for prostitutes.

DEVIL. IN MISCELLANEOUS TERMS AND NAMES.

Devil and bag o'nails. *See* BAG O'NAILS *under* PUBLIC-HOUSE SIGNS.

Devil on two sticks. *See* DIABOLO.

Devil's apple. The MANDRAKE; also the thorn apple.

Devil's bedpost. In card games, the four of clubs. *Cp.* DEVIL'S FOUR-POSTER *below*.

Devil's Bible. *See* DEVIL'S BOOKS *below*.

Devil's bird. A Scots name for the yel-low bunting; from its note, *deil*.

Devil's-bit. A species of scabious, *Sca-biosa succisa*, the root of which ends abruptly and is supposed to have been bitten off by the devil to destroy its use-fulness to mankind.

Devil's bones. Dice, which were made of bones and led to ruin.

Devil's books, or **Devil's picture-book.** Playing cards. A PRESBYTERIAN phrase, used in reproof of the name *King's Books*, applied to a pack of cards, from the Fr. *livre des quatre rois* (the book of the four kings). Also called the **Devil's Bible.**

Devil's candle. So the Arabs call the MANDRAKE from its shining appearance at night.

Devil's candlestick. The common stinkhorn fungus. *Phallus impudicus*; also called the **devil's horn** and the **devil's stinkpot.**

Devil's coach-horse. The cock-tail beetle, *Ocypus olens*. Also called **devil's cow.**

Devil's coach-wheel. The corn crow-foot.

Devil's daughter. A shrew.

Devil's dozen. Thirteen; twelve and one for the Devil. *Cp.* BAKER'S DOZEN.

Devil's dung. An old pharmaceutical nickname for the *asafœtida*, an evil-smelling resinous gum.

Devil's fingers. The starfish; also be-lemnites.

Devil's four-poster. A hand of cards containing four clubs. It is said that there never was a good hand at WHIST containing four clubs. *Cp.* DEVIL'S BED-POST, *above*.

Devil's guts. The long, thin, red stems

of the leafless, parasitic dodder plant; also the creeping buttercup.

Devil's horn. *See* DEVIL'S CANDLE-STICK, *above*.

Devil's livery. Black and yellow. Black for death, yellow for quarantine.

Devil's luck. Astounding good luck. Such lucky people were thought at one time to have compounded with the Devil.

Devil's Mass. Swearing at everybody and everything.

Devil's milk. The sun-spurge, from its poisonous milky juice.

Devil's Parliament. The parliament which met at Coventry in 1459 and passed Acts of Attainder against the YORKIST leaders.

Devil's shoestrings. Goats-rue *Tephrosia virginiana*, from its tough thin roots.

Devil's snuff-box. A puff-ball of the genus *Lycoperdon*; a fungus full of dust.

Devil's stinkpot. *See* DEVIL'S CANDLE-STICK *above*.

Devil's stones. The field gromwell, probably from its hard twin fruits. This plant is reputed to have contraceptive qualities.

Devonshire. The name is derived from the early CELTIC inhabitants, the Defnas. According to legend it is from Debon, one of the heroes who came with BRUTUS from TROY, and who was allotted this part of ALBION which was thus Debon's share.

Dew-beater. One who is out early and treads through the dew.

Dew-beaters. The feet; shoes to resist the wet.

Dew-cup, or **dew-drink.** An early morning allowance of beer formerly given to harvest-workers.

Dew Ponds. Artificial ponds or pools on the heights of the chalk downs of southern ENGLAND and elsewhere, which very rarely dry out even in the most severe drought. Formerly providing water for sheep, and known locally as "sheep ponds", their water supply depends upon rain and mist. Some date from the NEOLITHIC AGE. The pits were first lined with flints and stones, followed by a layer of straw, and finally a thick coating of puddled clay.

Dexter. A Latin word meaning "to the right-hand side", hence *dextrous* originally meant "right-handed". In HERALDRY the term *dexter* is applied to that side of the shield to the right of the person holding it, hence it is the left side of the shield as seen by the viewer.

Diabolo. A modern name for an old toy formerly called the "devil on two sticks". The "devil" is a hollow turned piece of wood, roughly the shape of two cones joined at the points. The player places the "devil" on a cord, held loosely between two sticks, and it is then made to spin by manipulating the sticks.

Diadem (Gr. *dia*, round; *deo*, bind). In ancient times the headband or fillet worn by kings as a badge of royalty was so called; it was made of silk, linen, or wool, and was tied at the back with the ends falling on the neck. The diadem of BACCHUS was a broad band which might be unfolded to make a veil. The diadem eventually became a flexible band of gold and its development and decoration became largely inseparable from that of the CROWN.

Dial of Ahaz. The only time-measuring device mentioned in the BIBLE. It was probably a form of sun-clock and its introduction by Ahaz may have been due to his contacts with the Assyrians. It is referred to in II *Kings* xx, 9–11 and *Is.* xxxviii, 8.

> And he brought the shadow ten degrees backward, by which it had gone down in the dial of Ahaz.
>
> II *Kings* xx, ii.

Dialectic, or **Dialectics** (Gr. *dialektikos*, belonging to discussion or disputation). Commonly used to mean abstract discussion, logic in general, or the investigation of truth by analysis, but the word has various technical implications in the language of philosophy. Under SOCRATES dialectic became a search for definition by the systematic use of question and answer, and for PLATO the method of the highest kind of speculation. For ARISTOTLE a dialectical proof was a probable deduction as opposed to a scientific or demonstrative proof. From the time of the STOICS until the end of the mediæval period dialectic was synonymous with logic.

Hegel (1770–1831) gave dialectic a new meaning—the action and reaction between opposites (thesis and antithesis), out of which the new or higher synthesis emerges. *See also* MATERIALISM.

Dialectical Materialism. *See under* MATERIALISM.

Diamond. A diamond of the first water. A specially fine diamond, one of the greatest value for its size (the colour or lustre of a diamond is called its "water"). Thus we speak of a "genius of the first water" meaning a very great genius; "a rogue of the first water" meaning one who excels in roguery; "a blunder of the first water" meaning an outstanding blunder, etc.

(Gr *adamas*, unconquerable.) A corruption of adamant. So called because the diamond, which cuts other substances, can only be cut or polished by one of its kind. *See* CULLINAN; FLORENTINE; FRENCH PASTE; GLAUCUS; HOPE DIAMOND; KOH-I-NOOR; PITT DIAMOND; SANCY; STAR OF SOUTH AFRICA.

A rough diamond. An uncultivated person but intrinsically of great merit; a person of excellent parts, but lacking social polish.

Black diamonds. *See under* BLACK.

Diamond cut diamond. Cunning outwitting cunning; a hard bargain overreached; an encounter of two acute minds. A diamond is so hard that it can only be ground by diamond dust or by rubbing one against another.

Diamond Jousts, The. Jousts instituted by King ARTHUR "who by that name had named them, since a diamond was the prize". The story as embroidered by Tennyson in his *Lancelot and Elaine* (from Malory, Bk. XVIII) is that Arthur once picked nine diamonds from the crown of a slain KNIGHT and when he became king he offered them as a prize for nine successive annual jousts, all of which were won by Sir LANCELOT. The knight attempted to present them to Queen GUINEVERE but she flung them out of the casement into the river below, through jealousy of ELAINE.

Diamond Jubilee. *See under* WEDDING ANNIVERSARIES.

Diamond Necklace, The Affair of the. A notorious scandal in French history (1784–1786) centering round Queen Marie Antoinette, Cardinal de Rohan, an ambitious profligate, and an adventuress, Jeanne, Countess de la Motte, who cleverly tricked Rohan by pretending to conduct for him a correspondence with the queen. Thus Rohan was induced to purchase for the queen (for 1,600,000 livres) the diamond necklace, originally intended for Madame du Barry, giving it to Jeanne de la Motte to pass to her. It was never delivered. When the jewellers, Boehmer and Bassenge of Paris, claimed payment, the queen denied all knowledge of the matter. The arrest of Rohan and Jeanne de la Motte followed. After a sensational trial, the Cardinal was acquitted and exiled to the abbey of *La Chaise-Dieu*, and the Countess was branded as a thief and consigned to the Salpêtrière, but subsequently escaped.

Diamond Sculls, The. An annual race for amateur single scullers at the Henley Royal Regatta, first rowed in 1844. The prize is a pair of crossed silver sculls nearly a foot in length, surmounted by an imitation wreath of LAUREL, and having a pendant of diamonds. The trophy passes from winner to winner but each winner retains a silver cup.

Diana. An ancient Italian goddess identified with Artemis. Commonly regarded as a moon-goddess, on somewhat slender evidence, she was also the goddess of hunting and the woodlands. Associated with fertility, she was largely worshipped by women, and was invoked by the Romans under her three aspects. *Cp.* SELENE.

Diana of Ephesus. This statue, we are told, fell from heaven. She is represented with many breasts and with trunk and legs enclosed in an ornamental sheath. The temple of Diana of Ephesus was one of the Seven Wonders of the World (*see under* WONDER), with a roof supported by 127 columns. It was set on fire by Eratostratus for the sake of perpetuating his name.

Diana's Worshippers. Midnight revellers. So called because they return home by moonlight, and so, figuratively, put themselves under the protection of

DIANA.

Great is Diana of the Ephesians. A phrase sometimes used to signify that self-interest blinds the eyes, from the story of Demetrius, the Ephesian silversmith in *Acts* xix, 24–28, who made shrines for the temple of DIANA. Demetrius stirred the people to riot, claiming that, "this Paul hath persuaded and turned away much people, saying that they be no gods, which are made with hands: so that not only this our craft is in danger to be set at naught; but also that the great goddess Diana should be despised ..." Hence their cry "Great is Diana of the Ephesians".

Diapason (dī à pā' zon). A Greek word (short for *dia pason chordon*, through all the strings) which means an harmonious combination of notes, hence harmony itself. According to the Pythagorean system (*see* PYTHAGORAS) the world is a piece of harmony and man the full chord.

Diavolo. Another form of DIABOLO.

Dibs. Money. *Cp*. TIP. The knuckle-bones of sheep used for gambling games were called *dibbs* and stones used for the same purpose were called *dibstones*.

Dicers' oaths. False as dicers' oaths. Worthless or untrustworthy, as when a gambler swears never to touch dice again (*see Hamlet*, III, iv).

Dick. Slang for detective.

A clever dick. A know-all, a SMART ALEC.

Dick Turpin. *See* TURPIN.

Dick Whittington. *See* WHITTINGTON.

King Dick. A scornful term for Richard Cromwell (1626–1712), who succeeded his father Oliver as Lord protector in September 1658 and showed no capacity to govern. *See also* TUMBLEDOWN DICK.

Queen Dick, That happened in the reign of Queen Dick, *i.e.* NEVER; there never was a Queen Richard.

Tumbledown Dick. Anything that will not stand firmly. "Dick" is KING DICK (*see above*), who was but a tottering wall at best.

Dickens. To play the dickens. To play the devil. *Dickens* here is probably a EUPHEMISM for the DEVIL or OLD NICK, and is nothing to do with Charles Dickens.

What the dickens. What the devil. *See* TO PLAY THE DICKENS *above*.

Dickey, or **Dicky.** In George III's time, a flannel petticoat.

> A hundred instances I soon could pick
> ye—
> Without a cap we view the fair,
> The bosom heaving also bare,
> The hips ashamed, forsooth to wear a
> dicky.
> PETER PINDAR: *Lord Auckland's Triumph.*

It was afterwards applied to what were called false shirts—*i.e.* a starched shirt front worn over another; also to leather aprons and children's bibs. It was also applied to the driver's seat in a carriage and the servant's seat behind. In the earlier "two-seater" motor-cars the dickey was the additional seating at the rear, where the occupants were exposed to the weather in the space corresponding to the *boot* of later models.

Dicky Sam. A native born inhabitant of Liverpool.

Dictys Cretensis (Dictys of Crete). A companion of Idomeneus at TROY and reputed author of an eyewitness account of the siege of Troy. The manuscript was probably written in the 2nd or 3rd century A.D. and translated into Latin in the 4th century. It is important as the chief source used by mediæval writers on the Trojan legend.

Didache (Gr. teaching). An early Christian treatise, also known as *The Teaching of the Twelve Apostles*, probably belonging to the late 1st or early 2nd century. It was discovered in the Patriarchal Library at Constantinople in 1875 and falls into two parts. The first is concerned with moral teachings and is based on an earlier document, seemingly of Jewish origin, called *The Two Ways*, with additions from the Sermon on the Mount, etc. The second part is concerned with church ordinances.

Dido, also called Elissa, was the legendary daughter of Belus of Tyre and founder Queen of Carthage, after the murder of her husband Sichæus by PYGMALION. According to VIRGIL's *Æneid* she fell in love with Æneas, who was driven by a storm to her shores, and committed herself to the flames through grief at his departure. Older legend says that she did it to avoid marriage with the king of Libya.

Porson (*see* DEVIL DICK) said he could rhyme on any subject; and being asked to rhyme upon the three Latin gerunds, which appeared in the old Eton Latin grammar as *-di, -do, -dum*, gave this couplet:

> When Dido found Æneas would not come,
> She mourned in silence and was Di-do-dum(b).

Cutting a dido, or **dancing dido.** The American equivalent of cutting a CAPER. The phrase appears as early as 1807 in the autobiographical work *A Narrative of the Life and Travels of John Robert Shaw, the Well-Digger*. Its origin is unknown but it has been fancifully suggested that Dido, Queen of Carthage, by a smart piece of work, managed to secure more land than she had agreed to buy, on which she built the city of Carthage.

Didymus (did' i mús). This Greek word for a twin was applied to St. THOMAS, as the name Thomas in Aramaic means a twin.

Die. The die is cast. The step is taken and there is no drawing back. So said Julius CÆSAR when he crossed the RUBICON—*jacta alea est! Die* here is ultimately from Lat. *datum*, given.

Die. Never say die. Never despair; never give up. *Die* here is "to cease to live".

To die in harness. To die working, while still in active employment or before retirement; like the draught horse which drops dead between the shafts of a cart, or the soldier who dies fighting in harness [armour].

To die in the last ditch. To fight to the death or last gasp.

What did your last servant die of? Said to someone who is expecting you to help and work like a galley slave doing one thing after another — asking a bit too much. An expression from the days when household servants were often grossly overworked from morning till night.

Whom the gods love die young. This is from Menander—*Hon hoi theoi philousin apothneskei neos*. Demosthenes has a similar apophthegm. Plautus has

the line, *Quem di diligunt adolescens moritur* (*Bacch*. IV, vii, 18).

Die-hards. In political phraseology those members of a party who refuse to abandon long-held theories and attitudes regardless of the changes that time and situation may bring. They would rather "DIE IN THE LAST DITCH" than give way.

Die-hards, The. *See* REGIMENTAL AND DIVISIONAL NICKNAMES.

Dies (dī' ēz). **Dies Alliensis.** *See* ALLIENSIS.

Dies Iræ (Lat. Day of Wrath). A famous mediæval hymn on the Last JUDGMENT, probably the composition of Thomas of Celano (in the Abruzzi), who died *c*. 1255. It is derived from the VULGATE version of *Zeph* i, 15, and is used by Roman Catholics in the MASS for the Dead and on ALL SOULS' DAY. Scott has introduced the opening into his *Lay of the Last Minstrel* (Canto vi, xxx).

> Dies iræ, dies illa
> Solvet sæclum in favilla.

Dies nefastus (Lat. *dies*, day, *nefas*, that which is contrary to divine law, sinful), An unlucky or inauspicious day. For the Romans *Dies nefasti* were days on which no judgment could be pronounced nor any public business transacted. *See* ALLIENSIS.

Dies non (Lat. a "not" day). A non-business day, a contracted form of *Dies non juridicus*, a non-judicial day, when the courts do not sit and legal business is not transacted, as SUNDAYS; the PURIFICATION in HILARY TERM; the ASCENSION, in EASTER term; and ALL SAINTS' Day, with ALL SOULS' in MICHAELMAS term.

Dieu. et mon droit (dyě ā mō drwa') (Fr. God and my right). The parole of Richard I at the battle of Gisors (1198), meaning that he was no vassal of France, but owed his royalty to God alone. The French were signally beaten, but the battle-word does not seem to have been adopted as the royal motto of ENGLAND till the time of Henry VI.

Difference. When Ophelia is distributing flowers (*Hamlet*, IV, v) and says: "You must wear your rue with a difference", she is using the word in the heraldic sense, probably implying that she and the queen were *to rue*; herself as the affianced of Hamlet, eldest son of the late king; the queen with a *difference* as the wife of Claudius, the late king's brother, and therefore the cadet branch.

In HERALDRY *differences* or *marks of cadency* indicate the various branches of a family. The eldest son, during the lifetime of his father, bears a *label, i.e.* a bar or fillet having three pendants often now shaped like a dovetail. The second son bears a *crescent*. The third, a *mullet* (*i.e.* a star with five points). The fourth, a *martlet*. The fifth, an *annulet*. The sixth, a *fleur-de-lis*. The seventh, a *rose*. The eighth, a *cross-moline*. The ninth, a *double quatrefoil*.

To difference is to make different by the superimposition of a further symbol.

Digest. A compendium, synopsis, or summary, especially the *Digest* of Roman Law, or PANDECTS, compiled by Tribonian and his sixteen assistants (530–533) by order of Justinian.

Digger. An Australian. The name was in use before 1850, consequent upon the discovery of GOLD, and was applied to ANZAC troops fighting in Flanders in World War I and again in World War II.

Diggings, or **digs.** Lodgings, rooms. A word imported from California and its gold diggings.

Digits (Lat *digitus*, a finger). The first nine numerals are so called from the habit of counting as far as ten on the fingers.

Dii Penates (dī′ i pe nā′ tēz) (Lat.). Household gods; now colloquially used for specially prized household possessions. *See* LARES AND PENATES.

Dilemma. The horns of a dilemma. A difficult choice in which the alternatives appear equally distasteful or undesirable. "Lemma" means an assumption, a thing taken for granted (Gr. *lambanein*, to take). "Dilemma" is a double lemma, a two-edged sword, called by the SCHOOLMEN *argumentum cornutum*, or a bull which will toss you whichever horn you lay hold upon. Thus:

> A young rhetorician said to an old sophist, "Teach me to plead, and I will pay you when I gain a cause." When his old tutor sued for payment, he argued, "If I gain the cause I shall not pay you, because the judge will say I am not to pay; and if I lose my case I shall not be required to pay, according to the terms of our agreement." To this the master replied: "Not so; if you gain your cause you must pay me according to the terms of our agreement; and if you lose your cause the judge will condemn you to pay me."

Diligence. A four wheeled stage-coach common in France before the days of the railway. The word meant speed, dispatch, promptitude, as in Shakespeare's "If your diligence be not speedy I shall be there before you" (*King Lear*, I, v).

Dilly. A stage-coach, as in the Derby Dilly. The word is an abbreviation of *diligence*.

Dime novel (U.S.A.). A cheap and lurid publication, formerly obtainable for a dime, a ten-cent piece. *Cp.* PENNY-DREADFUL.

Dimensions. *See* FOURTH DIMENSION.

Dimissory. A letter dimissory is a letter from the bishop of one diocese to some other bishop, giving leave for the bearer to be ordained by him (Lat. *dimittere*, to send away).

Dimity. Stout cotton cloth woven with raised patterns. It has been said to be so called from Damietta, in Egypt, but is really from Gr. *dimitos*, double-thread. *Cp.* SAMITE.

Dine. To dine with Democritus. To be cheated out of one's dinner. DEMOCRITUS was the derider, or philosopher who laughed at men's folly.

To dine with Duke Humphrey; to dine with Sir Thomas Gresham. To go dinnerless. *See* HUMPHREY.

To dine with Mohammed. To die, and dine in paradise.

To dine with the cross-legged knights. To have no dinner at all. The knights referred to are the stone effigies of the TEMPLE Church where lawyers once met their clients and where vagabonds loitered in the hope of being hired as witnesses. *See* CROSSLEGGED KNIGHTS. *Cp.* TO DINE WITH DUKE HUMPHREY.

Dingbats. An Australian colloquial term for *delirium tremens*.

Ding-dong. A ding-dong battle. A fight in good earnest. Ding-dong is an onomatopœic word reproducing the sound of a bell; the idea is that the blows fall regularly and steadily, like the hammer-strokes of a bell.

Dinkum (Austr.). Genuine, sincere, honest. The word probably derives from English country dialect. Also applied especially to the second shipment of AN-ZACS sent abroad in World War I. The third shipment were called "Superdink-ums". A "dinkum-Aussie" denotes a native-born Australian.

Dinos. *See* FAMOUS HORSES *under* HORSES.

Dint. By dint of war; by dint of argument; by dint of hard work. Dint means a blow or striking (O.E. *dynt*); whence perseverance, power exerted, force; it also means the indentation made by a blow, now *dent*.

Diogenes (dī oj′ ė nēz). Founder of the CYNIC sect at Athens (*c.* 400–*c.* 325 B.C.), who, according to Seneca, lived in a tub. ALEXANDER THE GREAT so admired him that he said, "If I were not Alexander I would wish to be Diogenes."

Diogenes Crab. A West Indian hermit crab which lives in another creature's shell as Diogenes in his tub.

Diogenes Cup. The cup-like hollow formed by the palm of the hand with closed fingers bent upward. An allusion to the philosopher's simple mode of life.

Diomedes (dī ō mē′ dēz), or **Diomed.** In Greek legend, a hero of the siege of TROY, second only to ACHILLES in bravery. With ULYSSES he removed the PAL-LADIUM from TROY. He appears as the lover of CRESSIDA in Boccaccio's *Filostrato* and in later works.

Also the name of a king in Thrace, son of ARES, who fed his horses on human flesh. One of the labours of HER-CULES was to destroy Diomedes and his body was thrown to his own horses to be devoured.

Diomedean exchange. One in which all the benefit is on one side. The expression is founded on an incident related in the ILIAD. GLAUCUS recognizes Diomed on the battlefield, and the friends change armour:

> For Diomed's brass arms, of mean device,

> For which nine oxen paid (a vulgar price),
> He gave his own, of gold divinely wrought,
> An hundred beeves the shining purchase bought.
>
> POPE: Iliad, VI.

Dione (dī ō′ ni). Daughter of OCEANUS and TETHYS and mother by JUPITER of VENUS. Also applied to Venus herself; Julius CÆSAR, who claimed descent from her, was sometimes called *Dionœus Cœsar*.

Dionysia. *See* BACCHANALIA.

Dionysius, St. *See* DENYS.

Dionysius's Ear. *See under* EAR.

Dionysus (Dī ō nī′ sùs). *See* BACCHUS.

Dioscuri. CASTOR AND POLLUX (Gr. *Dios Kouroi*, sons of ZEUS).

The horses of the Dioscuri. Cyllaros and Harpagus.

Dip, or **angle of dip.** The angle between a freely suspended needle and the horizontal. It is zero at the magnetic equator, where the needle rests horizontal, and 90 degrees at the magnetic poles. In geology it is the angle between the horizontal and the line of greatest slope of a stratum.

Dip. A candle made by dipping the cotton wick into melted tallow.

A farthing dip. A synonym for something almost valueless.

A lucky dip. A bran tub or other receptacle into which the hand is dipped to withdraw a prize or present at random.

The dip of the horizon is the apparent slope of the horizon as seen by an observer standing above sea-level. This slope is due to the convexity of the earth.

To dip a flag. *See under* FLAG.

To dip the headlights of a car is to lower them, usually when meeting oncoming traffic.

To go for a dip. To go bathing.

Diphthera (dif′ thē rà) (Gr.). A piece of prepared hide or leather; specifically the skin of the goat AMALTHEA on which JOVE wrote the destiny of man.

Diplomat. A diplomatic cold, illness, etc. When indisposition is pleaded as a tactful excuse for avoiding a meeting or engagement which might prove awkward or embarrassing.

Diplomatic. The scientific study of the official sources of history, namely characters, treaties, statutes, registers, etc., as opposed to literary and other sources. The name comes from an extended use of the Latin word *diploma* for an historical document. As a modern study it was largely stablished by one of the BOL-LANDISTS, Jean Mabillon, with his famous text-book *De re diplomatica* which appeared in 1681. His work was further advanced by Dom Toustain and Dom Tassin in their six-volume *Nouveau Traité de Diplomatique* (1750-1765).

Diplomatic Revolution. A phrase specifically applied to the reversal of alliances in 1756 under which Austria, France, Prussia and Great Britain had fought the War of the Austrian succession, with the result that, in the ensuing SEVEN YEARS WAR, France and her former enemy Austria fought against Great Britain and her former enemy Prussia.

Dipper. An old name for the seven principal stars of the constellation URSA MAJOR (Great Bear); also known as the Plough or CHARLES'S WAIN. The name is derived from the supposed resemblance to the kitchen utensil of this name—a pan with a long handle.

Dircæan Swan. Pindar (518-438 B.C.), so called from the fountain of Dirce near Thebes, the poet's birthplace. Dirce was changed into a fountain by the gods, out of pity for the sufferings inflicted upon her by the sons of Antiope, who were avenging torments she had imposed upon their mother.

Directory, The. The French constitution of 1795 which vested the executive authority in five Directors. The "Five Majesties" were Barras, Ruebell, Sieyès, Letourneur, and La Revellière. Sieyès retired at the outset and was replaced by Carnot. Its rule was ended by NAPOLEON's *coup d'état* of 18 BRUMAIRE (9 November) 1799 and the Consulate was established in its place.

Dirt (M.E. *drit* probably from Icel. *drit*, excrement). It has been extended to include filth generally, soil, dust, etc., and obscenity of any kind, especially language.

Pay dirt. Soil containing gold or diamonds, whichever is being sought.

Dirt cheap. Very low-priced, as cheap as dirt.

Throw plenty of dirt and some will be sure to stick. Scandal always leaves a trail behind; some of it will be believed. In Lat., *Fortiter calumniari, aliquid adhærebit.*

To eat dirt. To put up with insults and mortification.

Dirt-track racing. Motor-cycle racing on a track of cinders or similar material; introduced into England from Australia in 1928.

Dirty money. Money acquired by dishonest or disreputable means.

Dirty word. An obscene word; also currently used of something which has become socially or politically unpopular or suspect, often through unmerited criticism and denigration or from being out of line with current trends.

Disastrous Peace, The (*La Paix Malheureuse*). The Treaty of Cateau-Cambrésis (1559), essentially between France and Spain. It recognized Spanish supremacy in Italy and involved renunciation of the VALOIS claims there.

Disc. Disc Jockey. The established name for those who present broadcast programmes of gramophone records or discs, interspersed with commentary. Christopher Stone (1882—1965) was the pioneer of such performances in England.

Discalced. *See* BAREFOOTED.

Discharge Bible, The. *See* BIBLE, SOME SPECIALLY NAMED EDITIONS.

Disciples of Christ. *See* CAMPBELLITES.

Discipline, A. A scourge used for penitential purposes.

> Before the cross and altar, ... a lamp was still burning, ... and on the floor lay a discipline, or penitential scourge of small cord and wire, the lashes of which were stained with recent blood.
> SCOTT: *The Talisman*, ch. iv.

This is a transferred sense of one of the ecclesiastical uses of the word—the mortification of the flesh by penance.

Discipline, Books of. The books which formed the basis of the constitution and procedure of the CHURCH OF SCOTLAND after the REFORMATION. The first was drawn up under John Knox in 1566, and the second, which amplified the first, between 1575 and 1578.

Discord. Apple of Discord. *See* APPLE.

Discount. At a discount. Not in demand; little valued; less esteemed than formerly; below PAR (Med. Lat. *discomputare*, to deduct, to discount).

Dished. I was dished out of it. Cheated out of it; or rather, someone else contrived to obtain it. When one is *dished* or *dished up* he is completely done for, and the allusion is to food which, when it is quite *done*, is *dished*.

Disjecta membra (dis yek′ tà mem′ brà) (Lat.). Scattered limbs, remains, fragments. The phrase occurs in Ovid (*Met.*, III, 724) and HORACE has "*Etiam disjecti membra poetæ*" (*Sat.*, I, iv. 62).

Dismal Science. *See* SCIENCE.

Dismas, St. *See* DYSMAS.

Dispensation (Lat. *dispensatio*, from *dis-* and *pendere*, to dispense, distribute, arrange). The system which God chooses to dispense or establish between himself and man. The dispensation of ADAM was between Adam and God; the dispensation of ABRAHAM, and that of MOSES, were those imparted to these holy men; the GOSPEL dispensation is that explained in the Gospels.

A Papal dispensation. Permission from the POPE to dispense with something enjoined; a licence to do what is forbidden, or to omit what is commanded by the law of the ROMAN CATHOLIC CHURCH.

Displaced Persons. A phrase applied to the millions of homeless and uprooted people in Europe, India and Asia whose misfortunes were due to the havoc produced by World War II and subsequent events.

Dissenters. In England another name for the NONCONFORMISTS and commonly used from the RESTORATION until the 19th century, when it gradually fell into disuse.

Distaff. The staff from which the flax was drawn in spinning; hence, figuratively, woman's work, and a woman herself, in allusion to what was women's common daily task. *Cp.* SPINSTER.

St. Distaff's Day. 7 JANUARY. So called because the CHRISTMAS festival terminated on Twelfth Day, and on the day following the women returned to their distaffs or daily occupations.

It is also called ROCK DAY, "rock"

being an old name for the distaff.

The distaff side. The female side of a family; a branch descended from the female side. *See also* SPINDLE-SIDE.

To have tow on the distaff. To have work, or serious business on hand.

Distrain. To seize goods for nonpayment, to coerce by exacting fines, etc. (Lat. *distringere*, to pull asunder, to draw tight.)

Distraint of Knighthood. The compelling of persons with lands of certain value and tenants of KNIGHTS fees to become knights and assume the obligations and liabilities of such rank (relief, wardship, SCUTAGE, etc.). It was introduced in the reign of Henry III (1216–1272). The fines levied by Charles I on those who neglected this obligation angered many of the gentry. It was abolished by the LONG PARLIAMENT in 1641.

Dithyramb (dith i răm′) (Gr. *dithyrambos*, a choric hymn). *Dithyrambic poetry* was originally a wild impetuous kind of Dorian lyric in honours of BACCHUS, traditionally ascribed to the invention of ARION of Lesbos who gave it a more definite form (*c.* 600 B.C.) and who has hence been called the father of dithyrambic poetry.

Dittany (dit′ à ni). This plant (*Origanum dictamnus*), so named from Dicte in Crete, where it grew in profusion, was anciently credited with many medicinal virtues, especially in enabling arrows to be drawn from wounds and curing such wounds. In Tasso's JERUSALEM DELIVERED (Bk. IX) Godfrey is healed in this way.

Ditto (dit′ ō) (Ital. *detto*, said; from Lat. *dictum*). That which has been said before; the same or a similar thing. In writing the word is often contracted to *do*.

Dittoes, or **a suit of dittoes.** Coat, waistcoat, and trousers to match, all alike.

To say ditto. To endorse or agree with somebody else's expressed opinion.

Divan (Turk. and Pers.). A counting-house, a tribunal; hence the account book or register; the office or room where they are kept; a collection of poems; a long seat or bench covered with cushions; a court of justice and custom-house (whence, Fr. *douane*). The order of derivation is not certain but the word in its ramifications and extensions is rather like our BOARD. In England its chief meanings are a sofa without back or sides, a low bed, and formerly a coffee-house used for smoking.

Divan of the Sublime Porte. The former council of the Turkish Empire presided over by the Grand VIZIER.

Dives (Dī' vēz). The name popularly given to the rich man (Lat. *dives*) in the parable of the Rich Man and LAZARUS (*Luke* xvi, 19).

> Lazar and Dives liveden diversely
> And diverse guerdon haddon they therby.
>
> CHAUCER: *Somnour's Tale*, 169.

Divide. When the members in the British HOUSE OF COMMONS interrupt a speaker by crying out *Divide*, they mean, bring the debate to an end and put the motion to the vote—*i.e.* let the ayes divide from the noes, one group going into one LOBBY, and the others into another.

Divide and rule, or **govern** (Lat. *divide et impera*). Divide a nation into parties or set people at loggerheads and you can have your own way or exercise control.

> Every city or house divided against itself shall not stand.
>
> *Matt.* xii, 25.

Divination. There are numerous forms of divination. The following appear in the BIBLE:

ASTROLOGY (Judicial) (*Dan.* ii, 2).
CASTING LOTS (See LOTS) (*Josh*, xviii, 6).
HEPATOSCOPY (*Ezek.* xxi, 21–26).
ONEIROMANCY (*Gen.* xxxvii, 10).
NECROMANCY (I *Sam.* xxviii, 12–20).
RHABDOMANCY (*Hos.* iv, 12).
TERAPHIM (*Gen.* xxxi, *Zech.* x, 2).
WITCHCRAFT (I *Sam.* xxviii).

There are numerous other references including divination by fire, air, and water; thunder, lightning, meteors, etc. Consult: *Gen.* xxxvii, 5–11; xl, xli; I *Sam.* xxviii; II *Kings* xvii, 17; II *Chron.* xxxiii, 6; *Prov.* xvi, 33; *Ezek.* xxi; *Hos.* iii, 4, etc. *See also* ALECTRYOMANCY; AUGURY; AXINOMANCY; BELOMANCY; BIBLIOMANCY; BOTANOMANCY; CHIROMANCY; CRYSTALLOMANCY; DIVINATION BY CUP *under* CUP; EMPYROMANCY; EXTISPICY; GEOMANCY; GYROMANCY; HARUSPEX; OMENS; PALMISTRY; PYROMANCY; RUNE; SIEVE AND SHEARS; SINISTER; SORTES; URIM AND THUMMIN; XYLOMANCY; WITCH OF ENDOR. *See also* ORACLE.

The Divine Plant. Vervain.

The Divine Right of Kings. A theory, of mediæval origin, that kings reign by divine ordination, was first formulated in a rudimentary way during the struggle between the Papacy and the Empire. It was developed more fully to strengthen the European monarchies when they were later threatened by the activities of PROTESTANT and CATHOLIC extremists and others. Monarchy based on primogeniture was held to be divinely anointed and therefore unquestioning obedience could be demanded from subjects. Monarchs were responsible to God alone and their model was the patriarchal rule portrayed in the OLD TESTAMENT. The theory was expounded fully by James I in his *True Law of Free Monarchies* (1598) and in Sir Robert Filmer's *Patriarcha* (1642—published 1680). Divine Right was destroyed in Great Britain by the GLORIOUS REVOLUTION of 1688.

> The Right Divine of Kings to govern wrong.
>
> POPE: *Dunciad*, IV, 188.

Divining Rod, or **virgula divina,** also called AARON'S ROD or the *Wand of Mercury*. It is usually a forked branch of hazel or willow which when manipulated by the diviner or *dowser* inclines towards the place where a concealed spring or a metallic lode is to be found. The Romans used the *virgular divina* in AUGURY and the forked twig, or *virgula furcata*, was introduced into the Cornish mines from Germany in the reign of Elizabeth I.

Division. The sign ÷ for division was introduced by John Pell (1611–1685), the noted Cambridge mathematician who became professor of Mathematics at Amsterdam in 1643.

Division of labour. The division of an employment or manufacture into particular parts so that each individual is concerned with one part or process of the whole. Adam Smith in his *Wealth of Nations* (1776) argued strongly in its favour.

Divisions. In the Royal Navy the formal morning parade of officers and ship's company is so called, the custom being introduced by Kempenfelt in 1780. The name derives from the fact that the ship's complement is customarily divided or organized into parts of ship or divisions, usually Quarterdeck, Maintop, Foretop, and Forecastle. Divisions are subdivided into watches. *See* WATCH.

Divisionist technique. *See* POINTILLISME.

Divorcement. A Bill of Divorcement is a phrase from former days of divorce procedure. Before the Matrimonial Causes Act, 1857, "divorce", or in effect judicial separation, could be granted only by the ecclesiastical courts, but remarriage was prohibited except when a special bill was promoted and passed in PARLIAMENT for either of the parties. Few could afford such an expensive process. *See* A VINCULO MATRIMONII.

Divus (dī′ vŭs) (Lat. a god; godlike). After the Augustan period this was conferred as an epithet on deceased Roman Emperors proclaiming them "of blessed memory" rather than enrolling them among the gods.

Dix. One-time American slang for a ten-dollar bill, apparently derived from the fact that a bank in New Orleans used to issue ten-dollar bills with the French word *dix* (ten) printed on the back.

Dixie or **Dixieland** is a popular name for the southern states of the U.S.A., south of the MASON-DIXON LINE. One suggestion is that the name originated from *Dix*. Another is that it derives from *Dixieland*, the estate of a kind slave-owner, Dixie, on Manhattan Island, whose slaves lamented Dixie when transferred South. *Dixieland* also denotes the type of JAZZ played in New Orleans about 1910.

Dixie, the oval-shaped army cooking kettle is from the Hindi *degshi*, a pot or vessel. Its naval counterpart is called a FANNY.

Dizzy. A nickname of Benjamin Disraeli, Earl of Beaconsfield (1804–1881), Queen Victoria's favourite Prime Minster. *See* PRIMROSE DAY.

Djinn. *See* JINN.

Djinnestan. The realms of the jinns or genii of Oriental mythology.

Do. *See* DITTO, DOH.

A do. A regular swindle, a fraud; a party.

Do as you would be done by. Behave to others as you would have them behave to you.

Do-it-yourself. A post-World War II phrase applied primarily to the efforts of the amateur house-repairer, improver, and decorator, etc., but also more widely applied to many forms of self-help. A "do-it-yourself" shop is one which caters for the growing needs of the amateur decorator, furniture repairer, etc.

To do away with. To abolish, put an end to, destroy entirely.

To do for. To act for or manage for. *A man ought to do well for his children*; a landlady *does for* her lodgers. Also to ruin, destroy, wear out. *I'll do for him*, I'll ruin him utterly, or even, I'll kill him; *taken in and done for*, cheated and fleeced; *this watch is about done for*, it's nearly worn out.

To do it on one's head. Said of doing something with consummate ease; "I bet you couldn't walk a mile in seven minutes"; "Nonsense! I could do it on my head."

To do on. *See* DON.

To do one, to do one down, or **brown, to do one out of something.** To cheat or trick one out of something; to get the better of one.

To do one proud. To make much of one; to treat one in an exceptionally lavish and hospitable way.

To do oneself proud, or **well.** To give oneself a treat.

To do someone in. A common expression for killing a person.

To do the grand, amiable, etc. To act (usually with some ostentation) in the matter indicated by the adjective.

To do to death. To murder savagely, or to overcook excessively; to wear out or render stale by frequent repetition.

To do up. To repair, put in order, renovate. *This room wants doing up, i.e.* needs redecorating. Also to fasten a shoe-lace, a parcel, a button, etc., and to wear out or tire. *He has quite done himself up*, he is thoroughly worn out or exhausted.

To do up brown (U.S.A.). To do thoroughly in a good or bad sense—as beating someone up badly.

To do without so-and-so. To deny oneself something, to manage without it.

To have to do with. To have dealings with, to have relation to. "That has nothing to do with the case."

Well-to-do. In good circumstances, well off.

Dobbin. A steady old horse, a child's horse.

Dobby, a silly old man, also a GOBLIN or house-elf. Like DOBBIN, it is an adaptation of Robin, diminutive of Robert.

Docetes. An early GNOSTIC sect, which maintained that Jesus Christ was divine only, and that his visible form, the crucifixion, resurrection, etc., were merely illusions. Christ had no real body on earth, but only a phantom body. The word is Greek and means phantomists.

Doch-an-doris (Gael. *deoch*, drink, *an*, the, *doruis*, of the door). A Scottish term for a STIRRUP CUP or a final drink before departing, made familiar in England by one of Sir Harry Lauder's songs. Variants are *doch-an-doroch*, *deuch-an-doris*, etc.

Dock Brief. When a prisoner in the dock pleads inability to employ counsel, the presiding judge can instruct a BARRISTER present in court to undertake the defence, a fee for this being paid by the court.

Dock defence. The instruction of counsel by a prisoner in the dock without the aid of a solicitor.

Dockers' K.C. A nickname gained by Ernest Bevin (1881–1951) for his successful championing of the dockers' case before the Commission of Inquiry of 1920. Many of his union's demands were met.

Doctor. (Lat. *doctor*, a teacher, instructor). One who has obtained the highest university degree (a doctorate) in any Faculty (i.e. arts, science, law, medicine, etc.), but the word has acquired a special meaning by constant use in a particular context. In common parlance a doctor is a medical practitioner whether or not in possession of a doctorate. Because the doctor of medicine was most widely known the title came to be applied generally to members of the medical profession.

The name *Doctor* is also given to various adulterated or falsified articles because they are "doctored" *i.e.* treated in some way that strengthens them or otherwise makes them appear better than they actually are. Thus a mixture of milk, water, nutmeg, and rum is called *Doctor*; the two former ingredients being "doctored" by the two latter. Brown sherry is also called *Doctor* because it is concocted from thin wine with the addition of unfermented juice and some spirituous liquor.

In nautical parlance, the ship's cook is known as "the doctor" because he is supposed to doctor the food; and a seventh son used to be so dubbed from the popular belief that he was endowed with power to cure agues, the KING'S EVIL and other diseases.

Doctored dice, or **Doctors.** Loaded dice; dice which are so "doctored" as to make them turn up winning numbers.

To doctor the accounts. To falsify them, to COOK them; the allusion is to drugging wine, beer, etc., and adulteration generally.

To doctor the wine. To drug it, or strengthen it with brandy; to make wine stronger, and "sick" wine more palatable. The fermentation of cheap wines is increased by fermentable sugar. As such wines fail in aroma, connoisseurs smell at their wine.

To have a cat doctored. To have a TOM-cat "cut", or castrated.

To put the doctor on a man. To cheat him. The allusion is to DOCTORED DICE.

Who shall decide when doctors disagree? When authorities differ, the question SUB JUDICE must be left undecided. (POPE: *Moral Essays*, Ep. ii. line 1.)

Doctors of the Church. Certain early Christian Fathers, and other saints whose doctrinal writings gained special acceptance and authority.

Dr. Brighton. *See* BRIGHTON.

Dr. Dee. *See* DEE.

Dr. Faustus. *See* FAUST.

Dr. Fell. *See* FELL.

Dr. Syntax. *See* SYNTAX.

Doctors' Commons. The association and buildings established on St. Bennet's Hill, St. Paul's Churchyard, for practitioners of canon and civil law, under the presidency of the DEAN OF ARCHES. This self-governing body was established in the 16th century and dissolved after the passing of the Court of Probate Act and the Matrimonial Causes Act of 1857. The buildings were demolished in 1867. The name arises from the fact that the doctors had to dine there four days in each term.

Doddypoll. A blockhead, a silly ass. *Poll* is head and *doddy* is the modern dotty, silly, from the verb to dote, to be foolish or silly.

As wise as Dr. Doddypoll. Not wise at all; a DUNCE.

Dodger. The Artful Dodger. The sobriquet of John Dawkins, a young thief in Dicken's *Oliver Twist*.

Dodman. A snail; a word still used in Norfolk.

Hodmandod, a variant of DODMAN.

Dodo (Port. *doudo*, silly). *Didus ineptus*, a large bird about the size of a turkey last known to exist in Mauritius in the 1680s.

As dead as the dodo. Long since dead and forgotten and finished with; very much a thing of the past, completely extinct.

Dodona (do dō' nà). The site of a most ancient ORACLE of Epirus dedicated to ZEUS. The oracles were delivered from the tops of oak-trees, the rustling of the leaves being interpreted by the priests. The cooing of the sacred pigeons, and the clanging of brass plates suspended in the trees when the wind blew, gave further signs to the priests and priestesses. The Greek phrase *khalkos Dodones* (brass of Dodona), meaning a babbler, probably stems from this.

The black pigeons of Dodona. Two black pigeons, we are told, took their flight from Thebes, in Egypt; one flew to Libya, and the other to Dodona. On the spot where the former alighted, the temple of Jupiter AMMON was erected; in the place where the other settled the ORACLE of JUPITER was established, and there responses were made by the black pigeons that inhabited the surrounding groves. The fable is possibly based on a pun upon the word *peleiai* which usually meant "old women", but in the dialect of the Epirots signified pigeons or doves.

Doe. John Doe and Richard Roe. Any plaintiff and defendant in an action of ejectment. They were sham names formerly used to save certain "niceties of law". This legal fiction was abolished by the Common Law Procedure Act, 1852. The names "John o'Noakes" and "Tom Styles" were similarly used.

Doff is do-off, as "Doff your hat". So DON is do-on, as "Don your clothes". *Cp.* DUP, DOUT.

Dog. "Dog" entries are arranged as follows:
1. Dogs in Phrases and Colloquialisms.
2. Dogs of note in the Classics and in Legend.
3. Dogs of noted people and in Literature, etc.
4. Dogs in Symbolism and Metaphor.
5. Combinations of Dog or Dog's.

(i) IN PHRASES AND COLLOQUIALISMS.

A black dog has walked over him. Said of a sullen person. HORACE tells us that the sight of a black dog with its pups was an unlucky omen, and the DEVIL has been frequently symbolized by a black dog.

A dead dog. Something utterly worthless.

A dirty dog. One morally filthy, a CAD, a rotter, etc. In the East the dog is still the scavenger of the streets. "Him that dieth of Jeroboam in the city shall the dogs eat" (I *Kings* xiv, 11).

A dog in a doublet. A bold resolute fellow. In Germany and Flanders, the strong dogs used in hunting the wild boar wore a kind of buff doublet round their bodies. **A dog in one's doublet.** A false friend.

A dog in the manger. A mean-spirited individual who will not use what is wanted by another, nor yet let the other have it to use; one who prevents another enjoying something without any benefit to himself. The allusion is to the fable of the dog that fixed his place in a manger and would not allow the ox to come near the hay but would not eat it himself.

A dog's age. A long time.

A dog's chance. Virtually no chance at all.

A gay dog. Said of one who gets around and enjoys himself, especially with the ladies.

A living dog is better than a dead lion (*Eccles*. ix, 4). The meanest thing with life in it is better than the noblest without. The Italians say, "A live ass is worth more than a dead doctor."

A surly dog. A surly tempered fellow. Dog is often used for "chap" or "fellow" as in a *a dull dog*, A GAY DOG, etc.

A well-bred dog hunts by nature. Breeding "tells". The French proverb is "*Bon chien chasse de race.*"

Barking dogs seldom bite. *See under* BARK.

Dog eat dog. The equivalent of, "No quarter given."

Dog don't eat dog. The equivalent of, "There's honour among thieves."

Dogs howl at death. A widespread superstition.

> In the rabbinical book, it saith
> The dogs howl, when, with icy breath
> Great Sammael, the Angel of Death,
> Takes through the town his flight!
> LONGFELLOW: *Golden Legend*, III, vii.

Every dog has his day. You may crow over me today, but my turn will come by and by. In Latin, *Hodie mihi, cras tibi*, "Today to me, tomorrow to thee." *Nunc mihi, nunc tibi, benigna fortuna*, FORTUNE visits every man once; she favours me now, but she will favour you in your turn.

Give a dog a bad name and hang him. If you besmirch a person's reputation he will be as good as condemned. Give a person a bad reputation and he might as well be hanged as try to recover his good name.

He who has a mind to beat his dog will easily find a stick. If you want to abuse a person, you will easily find something to blame. Dean Swift, says, "If you want to throw a stone, every lane will furnish one."

Hungry dogs will eat dirty pudding. Those really hungry are not particular about what they eat, and are by no means dainty. "To the hungry soul every bitter thing is sweet" (Heywod,

Prov. xxvii, 7).

I am his Highness' dog at Kew; Pray tell me sir, whose dog are you? Frederick, Prince of Wales, had a dog given him by Alexander Pope, and these words are said to have been engraved on his collar. They are sometimes quoted with reference to an overbearing, bumptious person.

I don't keep dogs and bark myself. I don't keep servants to do their work for them, or to do the work myself.

In the doghouse. To be *in the doghouse* is to be in disgrace, as a dog confined to his kennel. Usually applied to a husband who has been misbehaving or has thoroughly displeased his wife, and is consequently treated with marked disfavour. In J.M. Barrie's PETER PAN, Mr. Darling lived in the dog kennel until his children returned, as a penance for his treatment of NANA.

Is thy servant a dog, that he should do this thing? Said in contempt when asked to do something derogatory or beneath one. The phrase (slightly modified) is from II *Kings* viii, 13.

When Landseer, the celebrated painter of dogs and animals, asked Lockhart if he would like to sit for his portrait, Lockhart's answer was: "Is thy servant a dog that he should do this thing?" The phrase was adopted and much used by Sydney Smith.

It was the story of the dog and the shadow. A case of one who gives up the substance for its shadow. The allusion is to the fable of the dog who dropped his bone into the stream because he opened his mouth to seize the reflection of it.

Let sleeping dogs lie; don't wake a sleeping dog. Let well alone. Don't stir up trouble by seeking to make changes. If your course of action is likely to cause trouble, let things be. *Cp.* QUIETA NON MOVERE.

Love me love my dog. *See under* LOVE.

Not to have a word to throw at a dog. Said of one who is sullen or sulky.

St. Roch and his dog. Emblematic of inseparable companions. *See* ROCH, ST.

Sick as a dog. Very sick. We also say, "Sick as a cat." (*See* CAT.) The Bible speaks of dogs returning to their vomit

(*Prov.* xxvi, 11; II *Pet.* ii, 22).

The dogs of war. The horrors of war, especially fire, sword and famine.

> Cry *Havoc* and let slip the dogs of war.
> SHAKESPEARE: *Julius Cæsar*, III, i.

The hair of the dog that bit you. *See under* HAIR.

The more I see of men the more I love dogs. A misanthropic saying of obvious meaning, attributed to Mme. de Sévigné (1626–1696). *Plus je vois les hommes, plus j'admire les chiens*; also to Mme Roland (1754–1793) and Frederick the Great of Prussia (1712–1786).

There are more ways of killing a dog than by hanging. There is more than one way of achieving your object. The proverb is found in Ray's *Collection* (1742).

Throw it to the dogs. Throw it away, it is useless and worthless.

> Throw physic to the dogs, I'll none of it.
> SHAKESPEARE: *Macbeth*, V, iii.

To blush like a dog, or **like a blue,** or **black dog.** Not to blush at all.

To call off the dogs. To desist from some pursuit or inquiry; to break up a disagreeable conversation. In the chase the huntsman calls off the dogs if they are on the wrong track.

To die like a dog. To have a shameful or miserable end.

To go to the dogs. To go to ruin, morally or materially.

To help a lame dog over a stile. To give assistance to one in distress; to hold out a helping hand; to encourage.

To lead a cat and dog life. *See under* CAT.

To lead a dog's life. To be harried from PILLAR to post, to be nagged constantly, never to be left in peace.

To put on the dog. To behave in a conceited or bumptious manner.

To rain cats and dogs. To rain very heavily. *See under* RAIN.

To wake a sleeping dog. To take action which stirs up or leads to trouble. *See* LET SLEEPING DOGS LIE, *above*.

Try it on the dog! A jocular phrase used of medicine that is expected to be unpalatable or of food that is suspect or dubious.

You can never scare a dog away from a greasy hide. It is difficult to free oneself from bad habits. The line is from HORACE'S *Satires* (II, v, 83): *Canis a corio nunquam absterrebitur uncto.*

You cannot teach old dogs new tricks. Elderly people are not adaptable. They do not readily take to new ways.

(2) DOGS OF NOTE IN THE CLASSICS AND IN LEGEND.

Aubry's Dog, or **the Dog of Montargis.** Aubry of Montdidier was murdered in 1371 in the forest of Bondy. His dog Dragon excited suspicion of Richard of Macaire by always snarling and flying at his throat whenever he appeared. Richard, condemned to a judicial combat with the dog, was killed, and, in his dying moments, confessed the crime.

Cuchulain's Hound. Luath.

Geryon's Dogs. Gargittios and the two-headed Orthos. Both were slain by HERCULES.

Icarius's Dog. Mœra (the glistener). *See* ICARIUS.

King Arthur's Favourite Hound. Cavall.

Llewelyn's Greyhound. Gelert. *See* BEDDGELERT.

Mauthe Dog. *See* MAUTHE.

Montargis, Dog of. AUBRY'S DOG.

Orion's Dogs. Arctophonos (bear-killer), and Ptoophagos (the glutton of Ptoon, in Bœtia).

Procris's Dog. Lælaps. *See* PROCRIS.

Roderick the Goth's Dog. Theron.

Seven Sleepers, Dog of the. Katmir who, according to Mohammedan tradition, was admitted to HEAVEN. He accompanied the seven noble youths (*see* SEVEN SLEEPERS) to the cavern in which they were walled up. He remained standing for the whole time, neither moving, eating, drinking nor sleeping.

Tristran's Dog. Hodain, or Leon.

Ulysses's Dog. Argos; he recognized his master after his return from TROY, and died of joy.

(3) DOGS OF NOTED PEOPLE AND IN LITERATURE, etc.

Boatswain. Byron's favourite dog; buried at Newstead Abbey. His master wrote the epitaph.

Bounce. Alexander Pope's dog.

Boy. Prince Rupert's dog, killed at the

battle of Marston Moor.

Brutus. Landseer's greyhound; jocularly called "The Invader of the Larder".

Dash. Charles Lamb's dog, also the much-loved spaniel of the young Queen Victoria.

Diamond. Sir Isaac Newton's little dog which one winter's morning upset a candle on his master's desk causing the destruction of the records of many years' experiments. On perceiving this disaster Newton exclaimed: "Oh, Diamond, Diamond, thou little knowest the mischief thou hast done!" And at once set to work to repair the loss.

Flush. Elizabeth Barrett Browning's dog.

Geist. One of Matthew Arnold's dachshunds. He wrote the poem *Geist's Grave* in memory of him.

Giallo. Walter Savage Landor's dog.

Greyfriars Bobby. A terrier who watched over the grave of his master (John Gray) in Greyfriars Kirkyard, Edinburgh, from 1852 to 1872. A drinking fountain surmounted by a statue of Bobby stands in nearby Candlemaker Row.

Hamlet. Sir Walter Scott's black greyhound.

Kaiser. Another of Matthew Arnold's dachshunds commemorated in his *Kaiser Dead. See* GEIST *above.*

Luath. The favourite of Robert Burns.

Lufra. The hound of Douglas, in Scott's *Lady of the Lake*.

Maida. Sir Walter Scott's favourite deerhound.

Mathe. Richard II's greyhound which left him in favour of Bolingbroke.

Nana. Mr. and Mrs. Darling's dog in J.M. Barrie's PETER PAN.

Rufus. Sir Winston Churchill's poodle.

St. Bernard Dogs. *See* PASSES, ST. BERNARD.

Toby. PUNCH's famous dog; named after the dog that followed TOBIT in his journeys, a favourite in mediæval Biblical stories and plays.

(4) DOGS IN SYMBOLISM AND METAPHOR.

Dogs in mediæval art, symbolize fidelity. A dog is represented as lying at the feet of St. BERNARD, St. Benignus, and St. Wendelon; as licking the wounds of St. ROCH; as carrying a lighted torch in representations of St. DOMINIC.

Dogs in effigy. In funeral monuments a dog in effigy is usually a memento of the dead person's pet with no symbolical significance.

Lovell the Dog. *See* RAT, CAT AND DOG *under* RAT.

The Derby Dog. *See under* DERBY

The Dog. DIOGENES (412–323 B.C.). When ALEXANDER of Macedon went to see him he introduced himself with these words: "I am Alexander, surnamed the Great." To which the philosopher replied: "And I am Diogenes, surnamed the Dog." The Athenians raised to his memory a pillar of Parian marble, surmounted by a dog. *See* CYNIC.

The Dog of God. So the Laplanders call the bear, which "has the strength of ten men and the wit of twelve".

The Thracian Dog. ZOILUS, the carping critic of ancient Greece.

> Like curs, our critics haunt the poet's feast,
> And feed on scraps refused by every guest;
> From the old Thracian dog they learned the way
> To snarl in want, and grumble o'er their prey.
> PITT: *To Mr. Spence.*

(5) COMBINATIONS OF DOG OR DOG'S.

Dog—or dog's—in combination, is used, besides in its literal sense (as in dog-biscuit) for

(a) denoting the male of certain animals, as dog-ape, dog-fox, dog-otter.

(b) denoting inferior plants, or those which are worthless as food for man, as dog-briar, dog-cabbage, dog-leek, dog-lichen, dog's mercury, dog-parsley, dog-violets (scentless), dog-wheat. *See below* DOG-GRASS, DOG-ROSE.

(c) expressing spuriousness or some mongrel quality, as dog's-logic, DOG-LATIN.

Dog-cart. A light one-horse trap popular for informal country use in Victorian and Edwardian times, originally designed for carrying sportsmen's dogs. Also the name of a small cart drawn by dogs.

Dog-cheap. Extremely cheap; "dirt-cheap".

Dog-collar. As well as its literal meaning, it is the popular name for a clergyman's "back to front" collar. Also the ornamental band or collar worn close to the throat by women.

Dog-days. Days of great heat. The Romans called the hottest weeks of the summer *caniculares dies*. Their theory was that the DOG-STAR, rising with the SUN, added to its heat, and the dog-days (about 3 July to 11 August) bore the combined heat of both.

Dog-ears. The corners of pages crumpled and folded down; *dog-eared* pages are so crumpled, like the turned-down ears of many dogs.

Dog-fall. A fall in wrestling when the two combatants touch the ground together.

Dog-grass. Couch-grass (*Triticum repens*), which is eaten by dogs when they have lost their appetite; it acts as an emetic and purgative.

Dog-head. In a flintlock, the part of the gun which bites or holds the flint.

Dog-Latin. Pretended or mongrel Latin. An excellent example is Stevens's definition of a kitchen:

> As the law classically expresses it, a kitchen is "camera necessaria pro usus cookare; cum saucepannis, stewpannis, scullero, dressero, coalholo, stovis, smoak-jacko; pro roastandum boilandum fryandum et plum-pudding-mixandum ...".
> *A Law Report* (Daniel *v.* Dishclout).

Dog-leech. A dog-doctor; formerly applied contemptuously to a medical practitioner.

Dog-rose. The common wild rose (*Rosa canina*, Pliny's *cynorrodon*), so called because it was supposed by the ancient Greeks to cure the bite of mad dogs.

Dogs, Isle of. *See* ISLE.

Dog's-nose. Gin and beer, etc.

> "Dog's-nose, which your committee find upon inquiry, to be compounded of warm porter, moist sugar, gin and nutmeg."
> DICKENS: *Pickwick Papers*, ch. xxxiii.

Dogsbody. A drudge, one who is generally exploited and used as a menial.

Dog-sleep. A pretended sleep; also a light, easily broken sleep. Dogs seem to sleep with "one eye open".

Dog-star. Sirius, the brightest star in the firmament in the constellation of the Big Dog, *Alpha Canis Majoris. See* DOG-DAYS *above.*

Dog-tags Identity discs of members of the U.S. armed forces (World War II).

Dog-tired. Exhausted, usually after exercise or hard manual labour; and wanting only to curl up like a dog and go to sleep.

Dog-vane. A nautical term for a small vane placed on the weather gunwale to show the direction of the wind. Sailors also apply it to a COCKADE.

Dog-watch. Two-hour watches (4–6 p.m. and 6–8 p.m.) instead of the usual four-hour watches introduced to enable seamen to vary their daily watch-keeping rota. Among various suggested origins are that it is a "docked" or shortened watch or a corruption of "dodge" watch. *See* WATCH.

Dog-whipper. A minor church officer of the days when sheepdogs, TURNSPITS and others accompanied their owners to church. His job was to keep order among the canine congregation, to eject the badly behaved and to exclude troublsome dogs generally. Whips and dog-tongs were used. The office became redundant in the 19th century. Even as late as 1856 Mr John Pickard was appointed dog-whipper in Exeter Cathedral.

Dog-whipping Day. 18 October (St. LUKE's Day). It is said that a dog once swallowed a consecrated wafer on this day.

Doggo. To lie doggo. To get into hiding and remain there; to keep quiet and out of sight.

Dog-goned. An American EUPHEMISM for "God-damned."

Dogaressa. The wife of a DOGE.

Dogberry. An officious and ignorant JACK IN OFFICE. The allusion is to the ignorant, self-satisfied, overbearing, but good-natured night-constable of this name in SHAKESPEARE's *Much Ado About Nothing.*

Doge (dōj) (Lat. *dux*, a leader or duke). The chief magistrate of the Venetian Republic. The first doge was Paolo Anafesto (Paoluccio), 697, and the last Luigi Manin, 1789. *See* BRIDE OF THE SEA.

The chief magistrate of Genoa was also called a doge from 1339 until 1796 when the French established the Ligurian Republic.

Dogie, or dogy (dō′ gi). In the western U.S.A. the term for an undersized calf. At round-up time all motherless calves were called "dough-guts", which became contracted into *dogie*. Being prematurely weaned, their stomachs could not digest and swelled accordingly.

Doh, or Do (dō). The first or tonic note of the solfeggio system of music. *See* ARETINIAN SYLLABLES.

Doily, or Doyley. A small ornamental mat or napkin used on cake dishes, etc., or on which to stand glasses, bottles, etc. In the 17th century it denoted a kind of woollen material; thus Dryden speaks of "doyley petticoats", and Steele in No. 102 of the *Tatler* speaks of his "doiley suit". The Doyleys, from which the stuff was named, were linen drapers in the STRAND from the time of Queen Anne until 1850.

Doit. An old Dutch coin of low value; hence any coin of little worth, a trifle.

Dolce far niente (dol′ chi far ni en′ ti) (Ital. sweet doing nothing). Delightful idleness. Pliny has "*Jucundum tamen nihil agere*" (*Ep.* viii, 9).

Doldrums, The. A condition of depression, slackness, or inactivity; hence applied by sailors to regions where ships were likely to be becalmed, especially those parts of the ocean near the Equator noted for calms, light winds, etc.

Dole (Lat. *dolor* grief, sorrow). Lamentation.

To make dole. To lament, mourn.

Dole (O.E. *dale*, a portion; *dael*, deal). A portion allotted, a charitable gift, alms. From Saxon times the strips of land, especially of common meadow, distributed annually were called *doles*. Since the National Insurance Act of 1911, it is the everyday name for "unemployment benefit".

Dollar. The sign $ is possibly a modification of the figure 8 as it appeared on the old Spanish "pieces of eight" which were of the same value as the dollar.

There are various other derivations put forward, most notably that it is the U of the United States superimposed on the S.

The word is a variant of *thaler* (Low. Ger. *Dahler*; Dan. *daler*), and means valley (our *dale*). The Counts of Schlick, at the close of the 15th century, coined ounce-pieces from the silver extracted from the mines at *Joachim's Tal* (Joachim's valley). These pieces called *Joachim's Talers* or *Schlickenthalers* gained such repute that they became standard coin. Other coins made like them came to be called *thalers*.

Bank of England dollars were struck as bank tokens in 1797 and subsequently. Dollars were first coined in the U.S.A. in 1794.

The Almighty Dollar. An expressive term emphasizing the power of money. Washington Irving seems to have first used this expression:

Ben Jonson (1573–1637) in his *Epistle to Elizabeth, Countess of Rutland*, speaks of "almighty gold".

Dollar Diplomacy. A term applied to governmental support and furtherance of commercial interest abroad for both political and economic ends. The phrase, popular with critics of American policy, stems from the Taft administration (1909–1913), which fostered such policies in the Far East and Latin America.

Dolly. Dolly shop. A MARINE STORE where rags and old clothes are bought; so called from the BLACK DOLL hung up as a sign. It is suggested that the name was originally a corruption of *tally shop*.

Dolly-tub. A wash-tub, the predecessor of the electric washing machine, with a *dolly* or revolving wooden disc with projecting dowels which stirred up its contents and was manually operated. The name was earlier applied to the keeve or tub which was part of the dollying-machine used in the Cornish tin-mining industry.

Dolmen (dol′ men). A word of CELTIC origin, the equivalent of the Welsh CROMLECH. The name is particularly used in Brittany. They are often called devils' tables, fairies' tables, etc.

Dolphin. *See* DAUPHIN. The dolphin in

mediæval art symbolizes social love.

Dom (Lat. *dominus*). A title applied in the MIDDLE AGES to the POPE, and later to other Church dignitaries. It is now largely restricted to monks of the BENEDICTINE and CARTHUSIAN Orders. The Sp. *don*, Port. *dom*, and M.E. *dan* are the same word. *See* DAN; DON.

Domboc. *See* DOOM.

Domdaniel. A fabled abode of evil spirits, GNOMES, and enchanters "under the roots of the ocean" off Tunis, or elsewhere. It first appears in Chaves and Gazotte's *Continuation of the Arabian Nights* (1788–1793), was introduced by Southey into his *Thalaba*, and used by Carlyle as synonymous with a den of iniquity. The word is made up from Lat. *domus*, a house, and *Danielis*, of Daniel, the latter being taken as a magician.

Domesday Book consists of one folio volume of 382 pp. and one quarto of 450 pp., written in Latin, now housed in the Public Record Office, but formerly kept in the EXCHEQUER. They contain the records of a survey of England begun in 1085 by order of WILLIAM THE CONQUEROR. Certain remote areas (Northumberland, Cumberland, Westmorland, and Durham) were omitted (*See* BOLDON BOOK).

Details of the ownership, extent, value, population, stock, etc., of all holdings are given for the time of Edward the Confessor and also at the time of the survey. The value is also given for the time of the Conquest. It was long used for taxation purposes and as a general governmental reference book. It is also called *The King's Book* and *The Winchester Roll* because it was once kept there. It was reproduced in typographical facsimile in 1783. The name is from O.E. *dom*, judgment. *Cp.* EXON DOMESDAY.

Dominations. *See* DOMINIONS.

Domine, quo vadis? (Lat. Master, whither goest thou?). According to tradition, when St. PETER was fleeing from NERO's persecution in ROME, he met Christ on the APPIAN WAY and greeted Our Lord with these words. The reply *"Veno Roman, iterum crucifigi"* (I am coming to Rome to be crucified again) so shamed the apostle that he returned to martyrdom in Rome. The meeting is commemorated by a church on the Appian Way. He is said to have requested to be crucified head downwards and to have given this account when nailed upon the cross. The story is found in the Gnostic *Acts* and other texts and is featured in an historical novel by H. Sienkiewicz, *Quo Vadis?* (1896).

Dominic, St., de Guzman (1170—1221), the founder of the Dominican Order, or Preaching Friars, noted for his vehemence against the ALBIGENSES and called by the POPE "Inquisitor-General". He was canonized by Gregory IX. He is represented with a sparrow at his side and a dog carrying in its mouth a burning torch. It is said that the DEVIL appeared to him in the form of a sparrow, and the dog refers to his mother's dream, during her pregnancy, that she had given birth to a dog which lighted the world with a burning torch.

Dominical Letters, or Sunday Letters. The first seven letters of the alphabet used in calendars, almanacs, etc., to mark the Sundays throughout the year (Lat. *Dominica Dies*, the Lord's Day, Sunday). If 1 January is a Sunday the Dominical Letter for the year will be A and if 2 January is a Sunday the Letter will be B, and so on. Dominical Letters are used for finding on what day of the week any day of the month falls in any particular year, also in determining EASTER. Tables and instructions are to be found in Prayer Books, Breviaries, etc.

Dominicans. The order of preaching friars founded by St. DOMINIC de Guzman in 1215, their rule being based on that of St. AUGUSTINE. Their first home in England was at Oxford (1221). They gained the name of BLACK FRIARS and in France they were called JACOBINS. They were also called *Domini canes* or Hounds of the Lord. Albertus Magnus, St. Thomas Aquinas and Savonarola were representatives of an order notable for its intellectual distinction.

Dominions. The sixth of the nine orders in the mediæval hierarchy of angels, also known as *Dominations* and symbolized in art by an ensign. *See* ANGEL.

From the formation of the Dominion

of Canada (1867) the word also came to be applied to the self-governing units of the British Empire as they were formed, and their relations with the mother country were handled by the Dominions Office. As the word *Empire* came to be replaced by that of COMMONWEALTH, the Dominions Office became the Commonwealth Relations Office in 1947 and Commonwealth Office in 1966, which was combined with the Foreign Office in 1968.

The Old Dominion. The State of Virginia, formerly an English colony.

Domino (Ital.). Originally a hooded clerical cloak; hence such a hooded garment worn at masquerades, then a hood only, and finally the half mask covering an inch or two above and below the eyes, worn as a disguise. The black ebony pieces used in the game of dominoes may have derived their name from some allusion to the black domino cloak or the black mask with the eyes showing through as the white pips.

Don is do-on, as "Don your bonnet". *See* DOFF; DOUT; DUP.

Don (Lat. *dominus* lord). A Spanish gentleman, any Spaniard, an aristocrat, a man of mark, a university tutor, fellow, etc.

Don Juan. *See under* JUAN.

Don Quixote. *See under* QUIXOTE.

Donatists. Schismatic followers of Donatus, a Numidian bishop of the 4th century who, on puritanical grounds, opposed the election of Cæcilianus to the bishopric of Carthage (311).

Their chief dogma was that the Church was a society of holy people and that mortal sinners were to be excluded. St. AUGUSTINE of Hippo vigorously combated their heresies.

Doncaster. The "City on the river Don" (Celt. *don*, that which spreads). Sigebert, monk of Gemblours, in 1100, derived the name from *Thong-ceaster*, "the castle of the thong", and says that HENGIST AND HORSA purchased from the British king as much as they could encompass with a leather thong, which they cut into strips and so encompassed the land occupied by the city.

Done. The done thing. That which is recognized as socially acceptable and proper. *Cp.* U AND NON-U.

Donkey. An ass. The word is first found in the later 18th century and is a diminutive probably derived from *dun* with reference to its colour. For the story concerning the cross on the donkey's back, *see* ASS.

A donkey's breakfast. A merchant navy term for a straw-filled mattress.

Not for donkey's ears. Not for a very long time. Probably from the mispronunciation of *years* with *ears* and an allusion to the length of a donkey's ears.

The donkey means one thing and the driver another. Different people see things from different standpoints, according to their interests. The allusion is to a fable in PHÆDRUS, where a donkey-driver exhorts his donkey to flee, as the enemy is at hand. The donkey asks if the enemy will load him with double pack-saddles. "No," says the man. "Then," replies the donkey, "what care I whether you are my master or some other?"

To ride the black donkey. To be pigheaded, obstinate like a donkey. Black is added in the sense of bad, as in BLACK BOOKS, BLACK LOOKS, etc.

To talk the hind leg off a donkey. To talk non-stop, to talk incessantly, and, less commonly, to wheedle. *Jackass, horse, cow*, etc. sometimes take the place of the donkey in this phrase.

Two more, and up goes the donkey. An old cry at fairs, the showman having promised his credulous hearers that as soon as enough pennies are collected his donkey will balance himself on the top of a pole or ladder. Always a matter of "two more pennies", the trick is never performed.

Who stole the donkey? An old gibe against policemen. The story is that in the early days of the force a donkey was stolen, but the police failed to discover the thief, and this gave rise to the laugh against them. The correct answer is "The man with the white hat", because white hats were made from the skins of donkeys, many of which were stolen and sold to hatters.

Donkey engine, pump, etc. Small auxiliary engines or pumps used for subsidiary work, just as the horse does more important work than the donkey.

Donkey-work. Uninteresting work; less responsible work, drudgery.

Donnybrook Fair. This FAIR, held in August from the time of King John till 1855, was noted for its bacchanalian routs and light-hearted rioting. Hence it is proverbial for a disorderly gathering or regular rumpus. The village is now one of the south-eastern suburbs of Dublin.

Donzel. A SQUIRE or young man of good birth not yet knighted (Ital. *doncello*, from Late Lat. *domicellus*). *See* DAMSEL.

Doolalli (Doolally) or Doolalli tap. An army expression for an unbalanced state of mind or mental derangement. Formerly, time-expired soldiers in India were sent to *Deolali*, a town near Bombay to await passage home. There were often long, frustrating delays, when boredom and the climate may have led to some odd behaviour, which caused some of them to become "doolalli". *Tap* when used in conjunction is the E. Indian word for fever.

Doom (O.E. *dom*). The original meaning was law, or judgment, and a *doomsman* was a judge. (*See* DEEMSTER.) The book of laws compiled by King Alfred was called the *Domboc*.

Crack of doom. The last trump, the signal for the final judgment.

To false a doom. A Scottish term meaning to protest against a sentence.

Doomsday Book. *See* DOMESDAY.

Doomsday Sedgwick (*c.* 1610–1669), a Puritan zealot during the COMMONWEALTH. He claimed to have had it revealed to him in a vision that doomsday was at hand; and going to the house of Sir Francis Russell, in Cambridgeshire, he called upon a party of gentlemen playing at bowls to leave off and prepare for the approaching dissolution.

Doones, The. Outlaws and desperadoes who supposedly settled in the Badgworthy area of Exmoor, Devon about 1620. They lived by highway robbery and plundering of farmsteads. They also abducted women. Numerous murders were attributed to them. When in *c.* 1699 they killed a child and seized the mother, the people of the district stormed their stronghold and those who were not destroyed fled. Some stories claim them to be of Scottish origin but the legends vary and they were adapted and romanticised by R.D. Blackmore in *Lorna Doone* (1869).

Door. Dead as a door-nail. *See* DEAD.

Door-money. Payment taken at the doors for admission to an entertainment, dance, etc.

Doors of Perception. The senses; the greatly increased sensitivity achieved by the taking of certain drugs, as described by Aldous Huxley in his book of that title.

He laid the charge at my door. He accused me of doing it.

Indoors. Inside the house; also attributively, as, *an indoor servant, indoor clothes*.

Next door to it. Within an ace of it (*see* ACE); very like it; next-door neighbour to it.

Outdoor, or **Out of doors.** Outside the house; in the open air.

Sin lieth at the door. (*Gen.* iv. 7). The blame of sin attaches to the wrongdoer, and he must take the consequences.

To darken one's door. *See under* DARK.

To make the door. To make it fast by shutting and bolting it.

To meet behind closed doors. In secret; without the press or public present.

To show someone the door. Peremptorily to ask a person to leave one's house; to get rid of someone whose presence is unwelcome.

To shut the door in someone's face. To shut the door deliberately and to refuse to have any dealings with the caller.

Dora. The popular name of the Defence of the Realm Acts (D.O.R.A.) which imposed many temporary restrictions. Their application to munitions factories and the drink trade caused particular irritation. It passed into common speech after being used in the Law courts by Mr Justice Scrutton. In numerous newspaper cartoons *Dora* was portrayed as a long-nosed elderly female, the personification of restriction (*Cp.* GRUNDY). There have been countless similar coinages since World War II and their derivation is usually, but not always, obvious. "Ernie" (Electronic Random Number Indicating Equipment), the selector of prizewinning numbers for holders of Government Premium Bonds; "Unesco" (United Nations Educational, Scientific and Cultural Organization); and "Sweb" (South Western Electricity Board) are typical examples. *Cp.* ENSA.

Dorado, El. *See* EL DORADO.

Dorcas Society. A woman's circle making clothing for charitable purposes. So called from Dorcas in *Acts* ix, 39, who made "coats and garments" for widows.

Dorian, Doric. Pertaining to Doris, a district of ancient Greece; or to the Doric or Dorian race, one of the four main divisions of the ancient Greeks, the others being the Aeolians, the Ionians, and the Achaeans. The Dorians maintained some of the characteristics of a simple-living, pastoral people and were dominant in the southern and western Peloponnesus, including Sparta, Megara, Corinth, Argos, Halicarnassus, Rhodes, Syracuse, Crete etc.

Dorian Mode. The scale represented by the white keys on a pianoforte, beginning with D. A simple, solemn form of music, the first of the authentic Church modes.

Doric Dialect The broad, hard dialect spoken by the natives of Doris, in Greece. Hence any broad rustic dialect, and especially that of Scotland, of which Robert Burns's verses are a notable example.

Doric Order. The oldest, strongest, and simplest of the Grecian orders of architecture. The Greek Doric is simpler than the Roman imitation. A characteristic of the Grecian is that the column stands directly on the pavement, whereas the Roman is placed on a plinth. *See* CORINTHIAN; IONIC; TUSCAN.

The Doric Land. Greece, of which Doris forms a part.

The Doric Reed. Pastoral poetry. Everything Doric was very plain, but cheerful, chaste and solid.

Doris. *See* NEREIDS.

Dorothea, St. (dor ō thē′ à). A martyr under Diocletian about 300. She is represented with a rose-branch in her hand, a wreath of roses on her head, and roses with fruit by her side. The legend is that Theophilus, the judge's secretary, scoffingly said to her as she was going to execution, "Send me some fruit and roses, Dorothea, when you get to Paradise." Immediately after her execution, a young angel brought him a basket of apples and roses, saying "From Dorothea in Paradise", and vanished. Theophilus was a convert from that moment.

Dorset. Once the seat of a British tribe, calling themselves *Dwr-trigs* (dwellers by the water). The Romans latinized *Dwrtrigs* into *Duro-triges*. Lastly came the Saxons, who translated the original words into their own tongue, *dorsaetta*, *saetta* being a seat or settlement.

The Dorsetshire Novelist. Thomas Hardy (1840–1928), of Dorset stock on both sides, who made the Dorset rustic and countryside a central feature of his novels.

Dot. Dot and carry one. An infant just beginning to toddle; one who limps in walking; a person who has one leg longer than the other.

On the dot. Precisely on time. A probable reference to the minute-hand of the clock being exactly over the dot marking the given minute on the dial.

To dot the i's and cross the t's. To be meticulous; to give most careful attention to detail; to finalize the details of an agreement. From the liability to confuse these letters if carelessly written without cross or dot.

Dotheboys Hall (doo′ the boiz). A private boarding school in Dickens's *Nicholas Nickleby* where boys were taken in and done for by Mr. Wackford Squeers, a brutish, ignorant, overbearing knave, who starved them and taught them nothing. The ruthless exposure of this kind of school led to the closing or reformation of many.

Dotterel. A doting old fool; an old man easily cajoled. So called from the bird, a species of plover, which is easily approached and caught.

Douai Bible. *See* BIBLE, THE ENGLISH.

Double (Lat. *duplus*, twofold). One's double is one's *alter ego*. The word is applied to such pairs as the Corsican brothers in the play *Les frères corses*, the DROMIO brothers, and the brothers Antipholus.

Double-barrelled. A double-barrelled gun is one with two barrels; to have a *double-barrelled name* is to have a hyphenated surname; a *double-barrelled compliment* is an ambiguous or two-edged compliment. *Cp.* BACK-HANDED COMPLIMENT.

Double dealing. Deceit or duplicity; professing one thing and practising another.

Double Dutch. Gibberish or jargon, as of infants or of a foreign tongue not understood by the hearer. Dutch is a synonym for foreign in this context; and double implies to an excessive degree.

Double-edged. Able to cut either way; used metaphorically of an argument which makes for and against the person employing it or of a compliment or statement with a double meaning.

Double entendre (doo' blòn tòn dra). An incorrect English version of the French *double entente*. Used of a word or phrase with a double meaning, one of which is usually coarse or indelicate.

A double first. Formerly in the first class both of the classical and mathematical triposes at Cambridge. Now, a first class in any two final examinations.

Double-headed Eagle. *See* THE TWO-HEADED EAGLE *under* EAGLE.

Double or quits. The winner stakes his stake, and the loser promises to pay twice the stake if he loses again; but if he wins the second throw, etc., his loss is cancelled and no money passes.

Double-quick. In military usage, means to proceed at double-quickstep or double-time, the quickest step next to a run. *See* TO DOUBLE-UP.

Double Summer Time. *See* DAYLIGHT SAVING.

Double take. An actor's trick. It is to look away from the person who has addressed a remark to you, and then to look back at him quickly when the purport of the remark sinks in. A second look occasioned by surprise or admiration.

Double-talk. An expression of American origin. Talk that sounds promising but in reality means nothing, or can be made to mean what the speaker wishes.

Double-think. A term used by George Orwell in his *Nineteen Eighty-four* (1949) to describe what unscrupulous propagandists achieved by "NEWSPEAK", a kind of DOUBLE-TALK. It denoted the mental ability to hold and accept simultaneously two entirely conflicting views or beliefs.

Double-time. As a military expression, the same as DOUBLE-QUICK.

Double-tongued. Making contrary declarations on the same subject at different times; deceitful; insincere.

> Be grave, not double-tongued.
> I *Tim*. iii, 8.

Double X. *See* X.

To double a part. Said of an actor playing two parts in the same piece.

To double and twist. To prevaricate, act evasively or to try to extract oneself from a difficulty by tortuous means. The phrase is taken from coursing—a hare "doubles and twists" in seeking to escape the hounds. In weaving, "to double and twist" is to add one thread to another and twist them together.

To double back. To turn back on one's course.

To double-cross. Properly to cheat or cross each of two parties, to betray both sides; but now commonly used to mean the betrayal or deception of an associate.

To double up. To fold together. "To double up the fist" is to clench the fist. "To double a person up" is to strike him in the wind and make him fold double with pain. In military language, "Double up" is an order to hurry or run.

To work double tides. To work extra hard, with all one's might. It implies doing three days work in two, or a minimum of two tides work in 24 hours. When a ship is left aground between tides for repairs below the waterline, a tide's work is that period of labour possible during the ebb and slack water.

Doubting Castle. In Bunyans's *Pilgrim's Progress*, the castle of the giant Despair and his wife Diffidence, in which CHRISTIAN and Hopeful were incarcerated, but from which they escaped by means of the key called Promise.

Doubting Thomas. *See* THOMAS.

Doughboy. Originally a dough cake baked for sailors, but from the late

1840s the name came to be given to American soldiers until World War II when "G.I." generally took its place. The common explanation is that the large brass buttons of the soldier's uniform resembled the dough cake.

Doughface (U.S.A.). An inhabitant of the northern states who was in favour of maintaining slavery in the South.

Douglas. The Scottish family name is from the river Douglas in Lanarkshire, which is the Celt. *dhu glaise*, black stream, a name in use also in IRELAND, the Isle of Man, etc., and in Lancashire corrupted to *Diggles*. Legend explains it by the story that in 770 an unknown chief came to the assistance of a Scottish king. After the battle the king asked who was the "Duglass" chieftain, his deliverer, and received for answer *Sholto Duglas* which means "Behold the dark grey man".

Black Douglas. Sir James Douglas (1286–1330), or "Good Sir James", champion of Robert Bruce, was called "Black Douglas" by the English of the Border to whom he became a figure of dread. He twice took Douglas Castle from its English occupants by stratagem. The story is told in Scott's *Castle Dangerous*.

Douse, or **dowse.** To strike, to *douse a sail* is to lower it hastily; to extinguish; to drench. The origin of the word is uncertain but possibly from Old Dut. *doesen*, to beat, to strike. *See also* DOWSE.

Douse the Glim. Put out the candle, put out the light, also to knock out a man's eye.

> "What though he has his humours, and made my eye dowse the glim in his fancies and frolics."
>
> SCOTT: *The Pirate*, ch. xxiv.

Dout. A contraction of *do out*. In some southern counties we find *dout the candle* and *dout the fire*, and extinguishers are called *douters*. *Cp.* DOFF; DON; DUP.

Dove. The name means "the diver-bird"; perhaps from its habit of ducking its head. So also Lat. *columba* is the Gr. *kolumbis*, a diver.

In Christian art the dove symbolizes the HOLY GHOST, and the seven rays proceeding from it the seven gifts of the Holy Ghost. It also symbolizes the SOUL and as such is sometimes represented coming out of the mouth of saints at death. A dove bearing a ring is an attribute of St. AGNES; St. DAVID is shown with a dove on his shoulder; St. DUNSTAN and St. Gregory the Great with one at the ear; St. Enurchus with one on his head; and St. REMIGIUS with the dove bringing him holy chrism.

The clergy of the CHURCH OF ENGLAND are allegorized as doves in Dryden's *The Hind and the Panther*, Pt. III, 947.

The dove is also the symbol of peace, tenderness, innocence, and gentleness.

To cause a flutter in the dovecot. To alarm, disturb, or cause confusion among those conventionally minded or settled in their ways, as would a bird of prey in a dovecot.

Down. Down and out. At the end of one's resources with no apparent chance of recovery. Homeless vagrants are termed down-and-outs. The allusion is to boxing.

Down at heel. In decayed circumstances, of which worn-down heels are a sign.

> A good man's fortune may grow out at heels
>
> SHAKESPEARE: *King Lear*, II, ii.

Down in the dumps. *See* DUMPS.

Down in the jib. The nautical equivalent of DOWN IN THE MOUTH.

Down in the mouth. Out of spirits; disheartened. When persons are very sad and low-spirited, the corners of the mouth are drawn down.

Down on his luck. In ill luck; short of cash and credit.

Down with! Away with! A cry of rage and exasperation, like the Fr. *à bas*.

He is run down. Out of condition. In need of a thorough rest. Like a clock that has *run down* and needs rewinding.

I was down on him in a minute. I pounced on him directly. I detected his trick immediately. The allusion is to birds of prey.

That suits me down to the ground. Wholly and entirely, like a well-tailored garment.

The down train. The train away from London or the local centre, in contradistinction to the *up train*, which goes to it. We also have the *down platform*, etc.

To be sent down. To be sent from a university as a punishment.

To down tools. To lay one's tools aside and stop work; to come out on strike.

To go down. In university parlance, to commence vacation or to leave the university finally.

To have a down on. To have a grudge or spite against.

To run a man down. To denigrate or discredit someone to a third party.

Ups and downs. The twists and turns of fortune; one's successes and reverses.

Down-easter. An American from New England.

Down-town. The business district of an American city, so called from New York, where financial houses are concentrated on the southern tip of Manhattan Island; the lower part of a town.

Down under. At the Antipodes; in Australia.

Downing Street. A street leading off WHITEHALL and a synonym for the British Government.

No. 10 was given in 1725 by George II to Sir Robert Walpole as the official residence of the PRIME MINISTER, and it is there that CABINET meetings are usually held. No. 11 is the official residence of the CHANCELLOR OF THE EXCHEQUER; No. 12 is the Government WHIP's Office. The street was named after Sir George Downing (*c.* 1623–1684), a noted parliamentarian and ambassador, who served under both Cromwell and Charles II, and owned property there.

Downright. Downright Dunstable. See DUNSTABLE.

Downy. A downy cove. A knowing or cunning fellow *up to* or, as formerly, *down to* every dodge. In Vaux's *Flash Dictionary* (1812) *down* is given as a synonym for "awake".

Dowsabell. A common name in 16th-century poetry for a sweetheart, especially an unsophisticated country girl. It is the Fr. *douce et belle*, sweet and beautiful.

Dowse (*see also* DOUSE). To search for water etc., with a DIVINING-ROD or *dowsing-rod*.

Doxology (Gr. *Doxologia*). The word means a hymn of praise to God. The Greater Doxology is the hymn *Gloria in Excelsis Deo* at the EUCHARIST. The Lesser Doxology is the *Gloria Patri* (Glory be to the Father, etc.) sung or said at the end of each psalm in the liturgy. The hymn "Praise God from whom all blessings flow" is also known as the Doxology.

Doyen. Fr. for DEAN (Lat. *decanus*). Denotes the senior accredited ambassador in a capital, but if there is a Papal Nuncio he is *ipso facto* the doyen. It is also applied to the senior member of a profession, etc.

Dozen. Twelve. The word is derived from the Lat. *duodecim*.

A long dozen is thirteen. *See* BAKER'S DOZEN.

To talk nineteen to the dozen. To talk at a tremendous speed or with excessive vehemence.

Drachenfels (Ger. Dragon's Rock). The German mountain on the right bank of the Rhine, south-east of Bonn. The legendary haunt of the DRAGON which SIEGFRIED slew. He bathed in its blood and so became invulnerable except in one spot on which a linden leaf had fallen. *See* NIBELUNGENLIED.

Draconian Code (drǎ kō′ ni ǎn). A very severe code. Draco was an Athenian of the 7th century B.C. who drew up a code of laws noted for their severity. As nearly every violation of his laws was a capital offence, Demades, the orator, said that Draco's code was written in blood.

Dracula. *See* VAMPIRE.

Drag. In slang, feminine dress worn by men; transvestite clothing.

Draggle-tail. *See* DAGGLE-TAIL.

Dragon. The Greek word *drakon* comes from a verb meaning "to see", to "look at", and more remotely "to watch" and "to flash".

In classical legend the idea of *watching* is retained in the story of the dragon who guards the golden apples in the Garden of the HESPERIDES, and in the story of CADMUS. In mediæval romance captive ladies were often guarded by dragons.

A dragon is a fabulous winged crocodile, usually represented as of large size, with a serpent's tail; whence the words dragon and SERPENT are sometimes interchangeable. In the Middle Ages the word was the symbol of sin in general and paganism in particular, the METAPHOR being derived from *Rev.* xii, 9, where SATAN is termed "the great dragon" and *Ps.* xci, 13, where it is said "the dragon shalt thou trample under feet". Hence, in Christian art it has the same significance.

Among the many SAINTS usually pictured as dragon-slayers are St. MICHAEL, St. GEORGE, St. MARGARET, St. Samson (Archbishop of Dol), St. Clement of Metz; St. Romain of Rouen, who destroyed the huge dragon La GARGOUILLE, which ravaged the Seine; St. PHILIP the Apostle; St. MARTHA, slayer of the terrible dragon Tarasque, at Aix-la-Chapelle; St. Florent, who killed a dragon which haunted the Loire; St. Cado, St. Maudet, and St. Pol, who performed similar feats in Brittany; and St. KEYNE of CORNWALL.

Among the ancient Britons and the Welsh the dragon was the national symbol on the war standard; hence the term PENDRAGON for the *dux bellorum*, or leader in war. *See* RED DRAGON.

Dragon's Blood. An old name in pharmacy for the resin from certain plants, formerly used in certain preparations, etc. The East Indian palm (*Calamus draco*) is used as a colouring matter for artists' varnishes, etc.

In German legend, when SIEGFRIED was told to bathe in the blood of a dragon in order to make him immune from injury, a linden leaf fell on him and the place it covered remained vulnerable. There is a possible connexion between this story and the term "dragon's blood" applied to a powder used in printing which, applied to a block for processing, prevents the etching of that portion covered.

A flying dragon. A meteor.

The Chinese dragon. In China, a five-clawed dragon is introduced into pictures and embroidered on dresses as an AMULET.

The Dragon of Wantley. *See* WANTLEY.

To sow dragon's teeth. To foment contentions; to stir up strife or war;

especially to do something which is intended to put an end to strife but which brings it about. The Philistines "sowed dragons' teeth" when they took SAMSON, bound him, and put out his eyes; Ethelred II did the same when he ordered the massacre of the Danes on St. Brice's Day (1002), as did the Germans when they took Alsace-Lorraine from France in 1871.

The reference is to the classical story of CADMUS.

Dragon's Hill. A site in Berkshire where one legend has it that St. GEORGE killed the dragon. A bare place is shown on the hill, where nothing will grow, for there the dragon's blood was spilled.

In Saxon annals we are told that Cerdic, founder of the West Saxon kingdom, there slew Naud or Natanleod, the PENDRAGON, and five thousand men.

Dragon Mountains. The Drakensberg Mountains in South Africa.

Dragonnades. The name given to Louis XIV's persecutions of the HUGUENOTS from 1681, until after the Revocation of the Edict of NANTES in 1685. The name arises from the billeting of DRAGOONS on those PROTESTANTS who refused to renounce their "heresy". The soldiery were given a free hand with the obvious results.

Dragoon. The name of certain cavalry regiments; originally a mounted infantryman. The name is taken from the carbine called a *dragon* which spouted fire like the fabulous beast of this name.

To dragoon is to persecute; to coerce. The derivation is obvious from the above. "He was dragooned into" means that he was coerced into it.

Drake. Drake Brass Plate. *See under* FORGERY.

Drake's Drum. *See under* DRUM.

Drama. Dramatic Unities. The three dramatic unities, the rules governing the so-called "classical' dramas, are founded on RENAISSANCE misconceptions of passages in ARISTOTLE's *Poetics*, and are hence often, though very incorrectly, styled the *Aristotelian Unities*. They are, that in dramas there should be (1) Unity of Action, (2) Unity of Time, (3) Unity of Place. Aristotle lays stress on the first, the second was deduced by

Castelvetro (1505–1571), the Italian scholar and critic, from an incidental reference to it by Aristotle, and the third followed almost perforce.

The convention of the three unities was adopted in France, especially after the triumph of Corneille's *Le Cid* (1636), but met with little success in ENGLAND. SHAKESPEARE, like Aristotle, was only concerned with the Unity of Action but the three unities were purposely adhered to in Ben Jonson's *Alchemist* (1610).

Dramatis personæ (drăm′ ȧ tis pĕr-sō′ nē). The characters of a drama, novel or, by extension, of an actual transaction.

Drapier's Letters (drā′ pēr). A series of letters written by Dean Swift to the people of Ireland, appearing in 1724 under the signature of M.B. Drapier, rousing them against the copper coinage called WOOD'S HALFPENCE.

Drat. A variant of *Od rot!* "Od" being a minced form of "God", and the vowel showing the same modifications as in "Gad!" or "Gadzooks!" *See* OD'S.

Draupnir (drawp′ nēr). ODIN'S magic ring, from which every ninth night dropped eight rings equal in size and beauty to itself. It was made by the DWARFS.

Draw. A drawn game, battle, etc. One in which neither side can claim a victory; perhaps so called from a battle in which the troops are drawn off on both sides when no decision seems possible.

A good draw. A first-rate attraction. "Performing elephants are always a good draw at circuses."

Draw it mild! Don't exaggerate! Don't make your remarks (or actions) stronger than necessary. The allusion is to the drawing of ALE.

Hanged, drawn, and quartered. Strictly, the phrase should read *Drawn, hanged, and quartered*; for the allusion is to the sentence usually passed on those guilty of high treason, which was that they should be drawn to the place of execution on a hurdle or at a horse's tail. Later, drawing (or disembowelling) was added to the punishment after the hanging and before the quartering. Thus the sentence (August 1305) on Sir William

WALLACE was that he should be drawn (*detrahatur*) from the Palace of WEST-MINSTER to the TOWER, then hanged (*suspendatur*), then disembowelled or drawn (*devaletur*), then beheaded and quartered (*decapitetur et decolletur*). His quarters were gibbeted at Newcastle, Berwick, Stirling and Perth.

Lord Chief Justice Ellenborough (1750–1818) used to say to those condemned:

> "You are drawn on hurdles to the place of execution, where you are to be hanged, but not till you are dead; for, while still living, your body is to be taken down, your bowels torn out and burnt before your face; your head is then cut off, and your body is divided into four quarters."
>
> *Gentleman's Magazine*, 1803.

To draw a badger. *See* BADGER.

To draw a bead on somebody. To take aim at him with a rifle or revolver. The *bead* referred to is the foresight.

To draw a bow at a venture; to draw the long bow. *See* BOW.

To draw a furrow. To plough or to make a furrow.

To draw a person out. To entice a person to speak on any subject, to encourage one too shy to talk, to obtain information.

To draw amiss. To take the wrong direction. A hunting term, *to draw* meaning to follow a scent.

To draw a veil over. To say no more about a matter; to conceal something from the knowledge of others as a veil conceals a woman's face.

To draw blank. To meet with failure in one's pursuit. The allusion is to sportsmen "drawing" a covert and finding no game. **To draw a blank** means having no luck in a lottery, etc., to fail in a search.

To draw in one's horns. *See under* HORN.

To draw the cork. To give one a bloody nose.

To draw the King's, or **Queen's picture.** To coin false money.

To draw the line. To set a definite limit beyond which one refuses to go; to impose a restriction on one's behaviour for fear of going too far.

To draw the nail. To release oneself

from a vow. It was a Cheshire custom to register a vow by driving a nail into a tree, swearing to keep your vow as long as it remained there. If you withdrew the nail, the vow was cancelled.

To draw rations, stores, etc. A military phrase; to go to the place of issue and collect same.

To draw rein. To pull up short, to check one's course.

To draw stumps. At the end of a game of CRICKET the wickets are dismantled, the stumps being drawn out of the ground.

Drawcansir. A bustling braggart, from the burlesque tyrant in Buckingham's *Rehearsal* (1671).

Drawer. Bottom Drawer. The most capacious drawer in a chest is usually at the bottom, and when a young woman who is engaged starts collecting articles for setting up her future home, she is said to be putting them in her bottom drawer.

> As soon as a girl passed her fifteenth birthday she began to sew for the "bottom drawer".
> ARNOLD BENNETT: *Anna of the Five Towns*, Ch.13.

Out of the top drawer. Upper class, to be of good family, to be of top grade socially. The expression probably derives from the fact that the top drawers of a chest often contain the more valued of one's personal effects.

Drawing-room. Originally the *withdrawing room* to which the ladies retired after dinner leaving the men to continue their drinking, etc.

Drawing-room of Europe. So NAPOLEON called St. Mark's Square in Venice.

Drawlatch. An old name for a robber, a house-breaker; *i.e.* one who entered by drawing up the latch with the string provided for the purpose.

Dreadnought. The name given to the 17,900-ton turbine-engined big-gun battleship completed in 1906, the first of a famous class, which greatly influenced subsequent naval construction. The first ship of this name was in use in the reign of Queen Elizabeth I.

Dreams, The Gates of. There are two, that of ivory and that of horn. Dreams which delude pass through the Ivory

gate, those which come true pass through the Gate of Horn. This fancy depends upon two puns: ivory in Greek is *elephas*, and the verb *elephairo* means "to cheat with empty hopes"; the Greek for horn is *keras*, and the verb *karanoo* means to accomplish.

The Immortal Dreamer. John Bunyan (1628–1688), whose allegory, *The Pilgrim's Progress*, is in the form of a dream.

Pipe dream. *See under* PIPE.

Drengage. An ancient form of tenure, connected with hunting services. Such service existed on the manors of the Bishop of Durham before the CONQUEST. The word is from Dan. *dreng*, a boy, a servant.

Dresden China. This fine hard porcelain, which attained such high repute in the 18th century and afterwards, was made at Meissen (some 12 miles from Dresden) from about 1709.

Dressed. Dressed to kill. Dress in the height of fashion. Very smartly dressed. The idea is from that of so dressing to make a conquest or "kill" of one of the opposite sex. **To dress to death** has a similar meaning. We also say **dressed up to the nines** which is perhaps a corruption of **to then eyne** (to the eyes).

Dreyfusard. An advocate of the innocence of Capt. Alfred Dreyfus (1859–1935), a French artillery officer of Jewish descent who was convicted in 1894 on a charge of betraying military secrets to Germany and sent to DEVIL'S ISLAND. In 1898 Clemenceau and Zola took up his case and Zola wrote his famous open letter *J'accuse*. In 1899 Dreyfus was retried, again condemned, but shortly afterwards pardoned. In 1906 the proceedings were finally quashed. The whole affair reflected the greatest discredit on the French military hierarchy of the time.

Drink. Drink-money. A "tip"; a small gratuity to be spent on drinking the health of the giver; a *pourboire* (Fr. for drink); also money allocated for drink.

Drinking of healths. *See* GABBARA; HEALTH.

In the drink. In the sea, in the water; long-established nautical slang.

It is meat and drink to me. Something that is almost essential to my well-being; something very much to my liking; just what I appreciate.

One must drink as one brews. One must take the consequences of one's actions; "as one makes one's bed so must one lie on it".

The big drink. An American expression for any large stretch of water, such as the Atlantic (*cp.* HERRING-POND) or Lake Superior.

To drink at Freeman's Quay. To get one's drink at someone else's expense. It is said, somewhat improbably, that at one time all porters and carmen calling at Freeman's Quay, near London Bridge, had a pot of beer given them gratis.

To drink deep. To take a deep draught; to drink heavily.

To drink like a fish. To drink abundantly or excessively. Many fish swim open-mouthed, thus appearing to be continually drinking.

To drink the cup of sorrow. To undergo affliction, to suffer one's share of sorrow. "To drink the cup" is used in the sense of "being allotted one's portion".

To drink the waters. To take medicinal waters, especially at a spa.

Drive. He is driving pigs, or **driving pigs to market.** Said of one who is snoring, because the grunt of a pig resembles the snore of a sleeper.

To drive a coach and four through an Act of Parliament. *See under* COACH.

To drive a good, or **hard bargain.** To exact more than is quite equitable.

To drive a nail into one's coffin. *See under* COFFIN.

To drive a point home. To stress a point with the utmost persistence; to ensure the acceptance of one's point and to make sure that it is understood; like driving a nail to its full extent.

To drive a roaring trade. To do a brisk business.

To drive a ship is to press on with full sail.

To drive someone up the wall. To drive a person to desperation; metaphorically, to drive one crazy.

To drive the swine through the hanks of yarn. To spoil what has been painfully done; to squander thrift. In Scotland, the yarn wrought in the winter (called *the gude-wife's thrift*) was laide down by the burn-side to bleach, and was thus exposed to damage from passing animals, such as a herd of pigs.

To drive to the wall. To push to extremity; to break or crush.

To let drive. To attack.

What are you driving at? What do you want to prove? What do you want to infer?

Droit. Droit d'Aubaine (drwa′ dō bān) (Fr.). *Aubain* means an "alien", a non-naturalized foreigner", and *droit d'aubaine* the "right over an alien's property". In France the king was entitled, at the death of foreign residents (except Swiss and Scots), to all their movable estates, a right that was not finally abolished until 1819.

Droit de fauteuil (drwa′ dĕ fotēē′). *See* TABOURET.

Droit du seigneur (drwa′ doo sen yĕr′) (Fr.). *See* JUS PRIMÆ NOCTIS.

Dromio (drō′ mi ō). **The brothers Dromio.** Two brothers who were exactly alike, who served two brothers who were exactly alike. The mistakes of masters and men form the fun of SHAKESPEARE's *Comedy of Errors*, based on the *Menæchmi* of Plautus.

A drop in one's eye. Not exactly intoxicated, but having had quite enough.

A drop in the ocean, or **bucket.** A negligible or tiny quantity; something that makes little difference.

A drop of the cratur. *See* CREATURE.

Drop-outs. A name for those who fail to complete their college courses or those who drift into hoodlum gangs on leaving school.

Prince Rupert's Drops. *See* RUPERT.

To drop across. To encounter accidentally or casually.

To drop an acquaintance. To allow acquaintanceship to lapse.

To drop in. To make a casual call or informal visit.

To drop off. To fall asleep (especially from weariness). When "friends drop off" they fall away gradually.

To drop someone a line. To write to them.

To drop the pilot. To dismiss a well-tried and trusted leader. The phrase was popularized by Tenniel's famous *Punch* cartoon (29 March 1890) showing Count von Bismarck, wearing pilot's uniform, being dismissed by Kaiser Wilhelm II.

To get the drop on someone. To have him in your power; a phrase taken from pistol shooting, where it means being ready to shoot before your opponent.

To take a drop. A EUPHEMISM for taking anything from a sip to a DUTCH-MAN'S DRAUGHT.

To take one's drops. To drink spirits in private.

Drown. Drowning men catch, or **clutch at straws.** People in acute danger or desperate circumstances cling in hope to trifles wholly inadequate to be of use.

To drown the miller. See MILLER.

Drows. See TROWS.

Drug. A drug in the market. Something which no one wants, something for which there is little or no demand, especially from there being a surfeit of the particular product in question.

Druids. The ancient order of priestly officials in pre-Roman Gaul, pre-Roman Britain, and IRELAND. They seem to have combined priestly, judicial, and political functions. The Druidic cult presents many obscurities and our main literacy sources are Pliny and the *Commentaries* of CÆSAR. We are told that their rites were conducted in oak-groves, that human sacrifices were offered up, and that they regarded the OAK and MISTLETOE with particular veneration. It is now suggested that the name Druid is derived from some "oak" word. They practised DIVINATION and ASTROLOGY and taught that the soul at death was transferred to another body. Their distinguishing badge was a serpent's egg. (*See* DRUID'S EGG).

In the 18th and 19th centuries there was a revival of interest in Druidism and a new romantic and unhistorical cult grew up associated with the Welsh Eisteddfodau. This is usually termed Neo-Druidism. *See* EISTEDDFOD.

Druid's Circles. A popular name for circles of standing stones, of which STONEHENGE is the most famous example.

The Druid's Egg. According to Pliny, who claimed to possess one, this wonderful egg was hatched by the joint labour of several serpents and was buoyed in the air by their hissing. The person who caught it had to escape at full speed to avoid being stung to death; but the possessor was sure to prevail in every contest, and to be courted by those in power.

United Ancient Order of Druids. A secret benefit society, akin to FREEMASONRY, founded in London in 1781 and introduced into the U.S.A. in 1833. It now has lodges, or "groves", in many parts of the world.

Druj. See AHRIMAN.

Drum. A popular name in the 18th century and later for a crowded evening party, so called from its resemblance in noise to the drumming up of recruits. The more riotous of these parties were called *drum-majors*.

A kettle drum. An afternoon tea. An obvious derivative of *drum* and a pun upon the tea kettle. A tea party was also called a *drum*.

Drake's Drum. Sir Francis Drake's (*c*. 1541–1596) drum of legendary fame.

> Take my drum to England, hang et by the shore.
> Strike et when your powder's runnin' low;
> If the Dons sight Devon, I'll quit the port o'heaven.
> An'drum them up the Channel as we drummed them long ago.
> SIR HENRY NEWBOLT: *Drake's Drum.*

Drum ecclesiastic. The pulpit cushion or pulpit, often vigorously thumped by "rousing preachers".

Drum-head court martial. One held in haste in the field to punish on the spot; from the one-time custom of holding it round the big drum.

To be drummed out. To be expelled ignominiously, as a soldier in disgrace was dismissed the regiment to the accompaniment of drum beats.

To drum up. To get together unexpectedly or in an emergency, as "to drum up a meal".

Drumsticks. Legs, especially thin ones. Also the legs of dress or cooked poultry.

Drummer. An old name for a BAGMAN. In former days pedlars often drew attention to their arrival by beating a drum. The word was also current in the U.S.A. until the early 20th century.

Drummond Light. *See* LIME-LIGHT.

Drunk. Drunk as a fiddler, or **fiddler's bitch.** The fiddler at WAKES, FAIRS, and aboard ship, used to be paid in liquor for playing to the dancers.

Drunk as a lord. Obviously the nobility of bygone days could afford to indulge in excessive drinking if they were so inclined. In the 18th and 19th centuries gross intoxication was common and many men of fashion prided themselves on the number of bottles of wine they could consume at a sitting.

Drunk as blazes. Very drunk. Blazes here means the DEVIL, or HELL, etc., or, as has been suggested, it is a corruption of "blaiziers", *i.e.* those gildsmen who took part in the feastings and revelry in honour of St. Blaize, the patron of wool-combers.

Drunk as David's sow. *See* DAVY'S SOW. There are many other common similes, such as *drunk as a coot, drunk as a newt, drunk as an owl*; Chaucer has *drunk as a mouse*, Massinger *drunk as a beggar*.

Drunkard's cloak. A tub with holes for the arms to pass through, used in the 17th century for drunkards and scolds by way of punishment.

Drunken Parliament, The. The Parliament assembled at Edinburgh, January 1661, of which Burnet says the members "were almost perpetually drunk".

Drury Lane. This famous London thoroughfare and its theatre takes its name from Drury House, built by Sir William Drury in the time of Henry VIII.

The parent of the present Drury Lane Theatre was opened in 1663 but was burned down nine years later. Its successor was designed by Wren but replaced by a new structure in 1794. This was destroyed by fire in 1809. The present theatre, designed by Wyatt, was opened in 1812. Many famous actors have appeared at Drury Lane, including Garrick, Kemble, and Kean.

Sweet Nell of Old Drury. Nell GWYN.

Druses. A people and sect of Syria of 11th-century origin, living about the mountains of Lebanon and Anti-Libanus. Their faith is a mixture of the PENTATEUCH, the GOSPEL, the KORAN and Sufism. They worship in both mosques and churches, but have their own SCRIPTURES. Their name is derived from their first apostle Ismail Ad-darazi.

Dry. I am dry with talking, *i.e.* I am thirsty after talking so long. Thus *to dry up* is to cease speaking. *Cp.* WET. **To go dry** is to adopt prohibition.

Not dry behind the ears. As innocent as a new-born child. When young animals are born, the last place to become dry after birth is the small depression behind each ear.

Dry lodgings. An old expression for sleeping accommodation without board. Gentlemen who took their meals at clubs lived in "dry lodgings".

Dry wine. Opposed to sweet. In sweet wine some of the sugar is not yet decomposed; in dry wine all the sugar has been converted into alcohol.

Dryad. In classical mythology, a tree nymph (Gr. *drus*, an oak-tree), who was supposed to die when the tree died. Also called Hamadryads (Gr. *hama*, with). EURYDICE, the wife of ORPHEUS, was a dryad.

Dryasdust. The name given by Scott to the fictitious "reverend doctor", a learned pundit to whom he addressed some of his prefaces, hence a heavy, plodding author, very prosy, very dull, and very learned; and antiquary without imagination.

Dual (Lat. *dualis*, twofold, divided in two).

Dual personality. Used of someone who, on different occasions, reveals two quite different characters.

Dual Monarchy. When two states share the same monarchy but remain politically separate, as in the case of England and Scotland from 1603. The Stuart kings reigned in both countries which, however, remained politically independent of each other until the Act of Union of 1707.

Historically the phrase is specifically applied to Austria-Hungary from the time of the *Ausgleich*, or Compromise, of 1867, until the collapse of 1918. During this period Francis Joseph was Emperor of Austria and King of Hungary.

Dualism. A system of philosophy which refers all things that exist to two ultimate principles, such as Descartes's Thought (*res cogitans*) and Extension (*res extensa*), or—in the theological sense—good and evil. In modern philosophy it is opposed to MONISM and insists that creator and creation, mind and body, are distinct entities. *See* MANICHÆANS.

Dub. The original meaning (from O.E. *dubban*, to equip with arms) was to confer knighthood by a stroke of a sword; whence it acquired figurative meanings, such as to nickname some thing or person, *e.g.* "he was dubbed a ladies' man".

Dub up. Pay down the money; "fork out". *Dub* another form of DUP.

Dubglas. *See* DUGLAS.

Ducat (dŭk' åt). A coin first minted in 1140 by Roger II of Sicily as Duke of the Duchy (*ducato*) of Apulia. In 1284 the Venetians struck a GOLD coin bearing the legend *Sit tibi, Christe, datus, quem tu regis, iste ducatus* (may this duchy which you rule be devoted to you, O Christ), and through this the name ducat gained wider use.

Duce (doo' chä) (Ital. leader). The title adopted by Benito Mussolini (1883–1945), the FASCIST dictator of Italy from 1922 to 1943.

Duck. *See* DUCK'S EGG.

A dead duck. Figuratively, something of no further interest. *To feel like a dead duck* is to be exhausted.

A lame duck. A STOCK-JOBBER or dealer who will not, or cannot, pay his losses, he has to "waddle out the alley like a lame duck". Also a defaulter or one who is disabled.

Duck's egg. Now always used in the shortened form of "a duck", meaning in CRICKET no score at all. It arose from the resemblance of 0 to a duck's egg. In American usage *goose-egg* is used for no score at all in a game. *See* SPECTACLES.

Ducks and Drakes. The ricocheting or rebounding of a stone thrown to skim along the surface of a pond, etc. **To play ducks and drakes with one's**

money is to throw it away carelessly, just for the sake of amusement and watching it make a splash.

Like a dying duck in a thunderstorm. Quite CHOP-FALLEN (*see under* CHOP (3)), very woebegone. Young ducks die speedily of chill if caught by a sudden downpour away from warmth and shelter.

Ducking stool, or **Scold's chair.** A specially made chair in which the culprit was bound and publicly "ducked" or immersed in the water. It was commonly used until the early 18th century, but its last recorded use in England was at Leominster, Herefordshire, in 1809, when Jenny Pipes was ducked.

Dudman and Ramhead. When Dudman and Ramhead meet, *i.e.* NEVER. The DODMAN and Ramehead (as they are now spelt) are two forelands on the south coast of CORNWALL about 23 sea miles apart.

Duds. A very old word of unknown origin once applied to coarse cloaks but now used for clothes of any kind, as "He was dressed in his best duds", or "He was wearing his oldest duds". A *dudder* or *dudsman* or *dudman* is a scarecrow, or a pedlar who sells dress materials, etc.

Duglas. According to the *Historia Brittonum* by Nennius, King ARTHUR fought twelve great battles against the Saxons. "The second, third, fourth, and fifth, were on another river, by the Britons called Duglas in the region Linius." The topography is vague and the whereabouts of the river Duglas (or Dubglas) is open to conjecture.

Duke (Lat. *dux*, leader). The title of the highest rank of nobility in Great Britain. The first English dukedom to be created was that bestowed by Edward III on his eldest son the BLACK PRINCE in 1338, when he was raised from Earl of CORNWALL to Duke of Cornwall. The title is very rarely conferred except for royal dukes; and since 1874 (when Hugh Lupus Grosvenor, 3rd Marquis of Westminster, was made Duke of Westminster), it has been conferred only on the Earl of Fife, who was created Duke of Fife on his marriage with Princess Louise in 1889. On his death in 1912, his daughter, Princess Arthur of Connaught, became Duchess of Fife in her own right, by special remainder. Prince Philip was created Duke of Edinburgh in 1947. Other than royal dukes there are twenty-six noble dukedoms.

Duke Humphrey. *See* HUMPHREY.

Duke or Darling. Heads or tails. When the scandals about the Duke of York (1763–1827) and his mistress, Mrs. Mary Anne Clarke, were the talk of the town, boys in the street used to cry *Duke or Darling*, instead of *Heads or Tails*.

Iron Duke. *See* THE GREAT DUKE.

The Duke of Exeter's daughter. The rack. It was introduced into England in 1447, when the Duke of Exeter was Constable of the TOWER, hence the name.

The Great Duke. The Duke of Wellington (1769–1852), the victor at the battle of Waterloo, who was also called the IRON DUKE.

To meet one in the Duke's Walk. To fight a duel. Duke's Walk, near Holyrood Palace, was the favourite promenade of the Duke of York (afterwards James II), during his residence in SCOTLAND and it became the common rendezvous for settling "affairs of honour", as did the fields behind the site of the BRITISH MUSEUM in ENGLAND.

Dukeries. That part of Nottinghamshire so called from the number of ducal residences established in the area from the 1680s, including Welbeck Abbey (Duke of Portland), Clumber (Duke of Newcastle), Thoresby (Duke of Kingston till 1773), Worksop Manor (formerly Duke of Norfolk). The land was formerly part of the Royal Forest of Sherwood.

Dulcarnon (dŭl kar′ non). The horns of a DILEMMA (or *syllogismum cornutum*); at my wit's end; a puzzling question. From an Arabic word meaning "the possessor of two horns". The 47th proposition of the First Book of EUCLID is called the Dulcarnon (the theorem of PYTHAGORAS), because the two squares which contain the right angle roughly represent horns.

To be at Dulcarnon. To be in a quandary, or on the horns of a dilemma.

"I am, til god me bettere mynde sende,

At dulcarnon, right at my wittes end."
CHAUCER: *Troilus and Criseyde*, Bk. III, 931.

Dulce est desipere in loco (dŭll′ si est dŏ sip′ ĕ ri in lō′ kō). It is delightful to play the fool occasionally; it is nice to throw aside one's dignity and relax at the proper time (HORACE: *Odes* IV, xii, 28).

Dulce et decorum est pro patria mori (dŭl si et de kôr′ um est prō păt′ ri ȧ môr′ ī). It is sweet and becoming to die on one's country's behalf, or to die for one's country (HORACE: III *Odes*, ii, 13).

Dulcinea (dŭl sin′ ē ȧ). A lady-love. Taken from the name of the lady to whom Don QUIXOTE paid his knightly homage. Her real name was Aldonza Lorenzo, but the knight dubbed her Dulcinea del Toboso.

Dulcinists (dŭl′ si nists). Heretical followers of Dulcinus (in northern Italy) who rejected papal authority and church rites and ceremonies. Dulcinus was burnt (1307) by order of Clement IV.

Dulia. *See* LATRIA.

Dullness. King of Dullness. So Pope called Colley Cibber (1671–1757), appointed Poet Laureate in 1730.

As dull as ditchwater. Applied to those who are boring and uninteresting, likewise to such tasks and employments. An allusion to the dull and muddy water in ditches.

Dum sola (Lat.). While single or unmarried.

Dum vivimus vivamus (dûm vi vī′ mùs vi vā′ mùs) (Lat.) While we live, let us enjoy life. This was the motto of the Epicureans.

Dumb. Dumb crambo. *See* CRAMBO.

Dumb Ox, The. St. Thomas Aquinas (1224–1274), known afterwards as "the ANGELIC DOCTOR", or "Angel of the Schools". Albertus Magnus, his tutor, said of him: "The dumb ox will one day fill the world with his lowing." So called from his great bulk and taciturnity.

Dumb-waiter. An 18th-century English contribution to the amenities of the DRAWING-ROOM. The mahogany dumb-waiter introduced in the 1730s consisted of two or three circular trays of graduated sizes pivoted on a central stem, the legs of which were on castors. The trays usually contained wine and glasses, etc., thus obviating the need for keeping servants hovering around the guests on social occasions. In the days when servants were noted for making improper use of overheard confidences, the dumb-waiter was a notable asset.

Dumdum. A half-covered steel-cased bullet which expands on impact and causes a very terrible wound. So called from the arsenal at Dumdum, near Calcutta, where they were first made in the 1890s. Their use was proscribed by the Second Hague Conference in 1899. At the time of the INDIAN MUTINY (1857), Dumdum was the scene of the first protests against the "greased cartridges".

Dumps. To be in, or down in the dumps. Out of spirits; Gay's Third Pastoral is *Wednesday, or the Dumps.*

Dun. One who importunes for payment of a bill. The tradition is that it refers to Joe Dun, a bailiff of Lincoln in the reign of Henry VII.

Squire Dun. The hangman between Richard Brandon (executioner of Strafford, Laud, and Charles) and JACK KETCH (executioner of Russell and Monmouth).

Dun Cow. The savage beast slain by GUY OF WARWICK. A huge tusk, probably that of an elephant, is still shown at Warwick Castle as one of the horns of the dun cow. The fable is that it belonged to a giant, and was kept on Mitchell Fold, Shropshire. Its milk was inexhaustible; but one day an old woman who had filled her pail wanted to fill her sieve also. This so enraged the cow that she broke loose from the fold and wandered to Dunsmore Heath, where she was slain.

The Book of the Dun Cow. An early 12th-century manuscript account of earlier Irish romance. It derives its name from the story that it is a copy of those written down on the hide of a cow by St. Kieran of Clonmacnoise in the 6th century.

To draw Dun out of the mire. To lend a helping hand to one in distress; to assist when things are at a standstill. The allusion is to an old English game, in which a log of wood, called Dun (a name formerly given to a cart-horse), is supposed to have fallen into the mire, and the players are to pull it out. Each does all he can to obstruct the other, and as often as possible the log is made to fall on someone's toes.

Dunce. A dolt; a stupid person. The word is taken from Duns Scotus (*c.* 1265–1308), the famous SCHOOLMAN so called from his birthplace, Dunse, in Scotland. His followers were called Dunsers or SCOTISTS. Tyndal says, when they saw that their hair-splitting divinity was giving way to modern theology, "the old barking curs raged in every pulpit" against the CLASSICS and new notions, so that the name indicated an opponent to progress, to learning, and hence a dunce.

Duns Scotus was buried at Cologne; his epitaph reads:

> Scotia me genuit, Anglia me suscepit,
> Gallia ma docuit, Colonia me tenet.

The Parliament of Dunces. Convened by Henry IV at Coventry in 1404, and so called because all lawyers were excluded from it. Also known as the Lawless, and Unlearned Parliament.

Dunciad. The dunce-epic, a satire by Alexander Pope, first published in 1728 with Theobald featuring as the Poet Laureate of the realm of Dullness, but republished with an added fourth part in 1741 with Colley Cibber in that role. Many contemporary writers who were pilloried in this poem would have otherwise been unnoticed by posterity.

Dunedin. *See* EDINBURGH.

Dunghill! Coward! Villain! This is a cockpit expression; all cocks, except gamecocks, being called dunghills.

Every cock crows on its own dunghill. *See under* COCK.

Dunheved Castle. *See* CASTLE TERABIL.

Dunkers. *See* TUNKERS.

Dunkirk. This once notorious haunt of pirates and privateers has acquired fresh associations since World War II. The name is now used figuratively to denote a forced military evacuation by sea to avoid disaster, a speedy and complete withdrawal, an entire abandonment of a position. The allusion is to the heroic evacuation of the main British expeditionary force (26 May–4 June 1940), in the face of imminent disaster, by Vice-Admiral Ramsay's motley force of destroyers, yachts, etc., with essential air cover from R.A.F. Fighter Command.

Dunmow (dŭn' mō). **To eat Dunmow bacon.** To live in conjugal amity, without even wishing the marriage knot to be less firmly tied. The allusion is to a custom said to have been instituted by Juga, a noble lady, in 1111, and restored by Robert de Fitzwalter in 1244. It was that any person going to Dunmow, in Essex, and humbly kneeling on two sharp stones at the church door, might claim a gammon of bacon if he could swear that for twelve months and a day he had never had a household brawl or wished himself unmarried.

Dunscore. The saut lairds o'Dunscore. Gentlefolk who have a name but no money. The tale is that the "puir wee lairds of Dunscore" (a parish near Dumfries) clubbed together to buy a stone of salt, which was doled out to the subscribers in spoonfuls, that no one should get more than his due quota.

Duns Scotus. *See* DOCTORS OF LEARNING; DUNCE.

Dunstan, St. (*d.* 925–988). Archbishop of Canterbury (961), and patron saint of goldsmiths, being himself a noted worker in GOLD. He is represented in pontifical robes, and carrying a pair of pincers in his right hand, the latter referring to the legend that on one occasion he seized the DEVIL by the nose with a pair of red-hot tongs and refused to release him till he promised never to tempt Dunstan again. *See also* HORSESHOE.

Dunsterforce. The name given to the men sent to Baku in 1918 under the command of Maj.-Gen. L.C. Dunsterville (1865–1946), who had been a schoolfellow of Rudyard Kipling and was the hero of *Stalky and Co.* The purpose of this expedition was to prevent the Turks and Germans seizing the oil-wells and Dunsterforce adequately accomplished its object.

Duodecimo (dū ō des' i mō). A book whose sheets are folded into twelve leaves each (Lat. *duodecim*, twelve), often called "twelvemo", from the contraction 12mo. The book is naturally a small one, hence the expression is some-

times applied to other things or persons of small size.

Dup is do up. Thus Ophelia says, "he ... dupp'd the chamber door", *i.e.* he did up or pushed up the latch, in order to open the door, that he might "let in the maid" (*Hamlet*, IV, v). *Cp.* DOFF, DON.

> Iche weene the porters are drunk. Will they not dup the gate today.
> RICHARD EDWARDS: *Damon and Pithias* (*c.* 1564).

Dupes, Day of the. In French history, 11 November 1630 when Marie de' MEDICI, the queen mother, and others sought the overthrow of Louis XIII's minister, Cardinal Richelieu. The cardinal's friends interviewed Louis at Versailles later in the day and by the evening Richelieu was reassured of the royal favour. This was the "day of dupes" for those who counted upon the minister's fall.

Durandal, or **Duranda,** or **Durenda,** etc. *See* ROLAND'S SWORDS *under* ROLAND.

Durden, Dame. A generic name for a good old-fashioned housewife.

Dust. Slang for money; probably in allusion to the moralist's contention that money is worthless.

Ashes to ashes, dust to dust. *See* ASHES.

Down with the dust! Out with the money; DUB UP! The expression is at least three hundred years old.

Dust and ashes. In Old Testament times, a person sprinkled earth, dust and ashes over the head as a sign of mourning. *Dust and ashes* was expressive of one's deep humiliation, insignificance and worthlessness. *Cp.* TO WEAR SACKCLOTH AND ASHES *under* SACK.

I'll dust your jacket for you. Give you a good beating; also used with *doublet, trousers, pants,* etc., in place of *jacket.*

To bite the dust. *See under* BITE.

To kiss, or **lick the dust.** *See under* KISS.

To raise a dust, to kick up a dust. To make a commotion or disturbance.

To shake the dust from one's feet. To show extreme dislike of a place, and to leave it with the intention of never returning. The allusion is to the Eastern custom.

> And whosoever shall not receive you,
> nor hear your words, when ye depart out
> of that house or city, shake off the dust
> of your feet.
>
> *Matt.* x, 14.

To throw dust in his eyes. To mislead, to dupe or trick. The allusion is to "the swiftest runner in a sandy race, who to make his fellows aloofe, casteth dust with his heeles into their envious eyes" (*Cotgrave*, 1611).

The Mohammedans had a practice of casting dust into the air for the sake of confounding the enemies of the Faith. This was done by the Prophet on two or three occasions, as in the battle of Honein; and the KORAN refers to it when it says: "Neither didst thou, O Mahomet, cast dust into their eyes; but it was God who confounded them."

The dustman has arrived, or more usually nowadays "The sandman is about", the "dustman" having lost popularity in nursery talk since the association with refuse collecting. The phrase means that it is bedtime, for the children rub their eyes, as if sand or dust are in them.

A dusty answer. To get a dusty answer is to receive an unsatisfactory reply akin to a BRUSH off; substantially the same as to be sent off with a flea in the ear.

Well, it is not so dusty, or **Not so dusty.** I don't call it bad; rather smart in fact, just as "not bad" is often used too mean "very good". Here *dusty* means soiled, bad, worthless.

A dust-up. A row, a bit of a SHEMOZZLE or a SHINDY.

Dustyfoot. *See* PIEPOWDER COURT.

Dusty Miller. A common nickname, particularly in the Royal Navy, for all those with the surname Miller, just as all Clarks are called "NOBBY", and Bells "Daisy" or "Dinger". Its origin is obvious and appropriate. The auricula is also known as *Dusty Miller* from the white mealiness of its leaves.

Dutch. This word, properly meaning "Hollandish", is the M.Dut. *Dutsch* or Ger. *Deutsch*, and formerly denoted the people of Germany or of Teutonic stock, not merely the Low Dutch or Netherlanders. (*See* PENNSYLVANIA DUTCH.) The derogatory implications of

some of the undermentioned phrases derive from the Anglo-Dutch wars of the 17th century.

Dutch auction. An auction in which the auctioneer offers the goods at gradually decreasing prices, the first bidder to accept becoming the purchaser; to reverse the process of a normal auction.

Dutch bargain, or **wet bargain.** A bargain settled over drinks, the Dutch being formerly reputed to be steady drinkers.

Dutch collar. A horse collar.

Dutch comfort. Cold comfort, *i.e.* things might have been worse.

Dutch concert. A great noise and uproar, like that made by a party of drunken Dutchmen, some singing, others quarrelling, speechifying, etc.

Dutch courage. The courage exerted by drink; POT VALOUR. The Dutch were considered heavy drinkers. *Cp.* DUTCH BARGAIN.

Dutch cousins. Close friends, a play upon COUSINS GERMAN.

Dutch defence. A sham defence.

Dutch gleek. Tippling. GLEEK is a game and the name implies that the game loved by Dutchmen is drinking.

Dutch gold. "German" gold, an alloy of copper and zinc, yellow in colour, which easily tarnishes unless lacquered. Imitation gold leaf is made from it, hence the name *Dutch leaf*. It is also called *Dutch metal*.

Dutch nightingales. Frogs. Similarly we have *Cambridgeshire nightingales; Liège nightingales*, etc.

Dutch talent. That which is not done in true nautical and shipshape fashion, more the result of brawn than brain.

Dutch treat. A meal, amusement, etc., at which each person pays for himself. *To go Dutch* has the same meaning.

Dutch wife. An open frame constructed of cane, originally used in the Dutch East Indies and other hot countries to rest the limbs in bed; also a bolster used for the same purpose.

Double Dutch. *See under* DOUBLE.

His Dutch is up. His DANDER is riz.

In Dutch. In trouble, out of favour, under suspicion.

My old Dutch. Here the word is a contraction of *duchess* and has nothing to do with Holland or Germany. It is a colloquial term for one's wife, especially the wife of a coster, as in the song *My Old Dutch*.

The Dutch have taken Holland. A quiz when anyone tells what is well known as a piece of wonderful news. Similar to *Queen Bess* (or *Queen Anne*) *is dead*.

To talk like a Dutch uncle. To reprove firmly but kindly. The Dutch were noted for their discipline.

Dutchman. I'm a Dutchman if I do. A strong refusal. During the Anglo-Dutch rivalry of the 17th century the name was synnonymous with all that was despicable and when a man said, "I would rather be a Dutchman than do what you ask me," he used the strongest possible terms of refusal.

If not, I'm a Dutchman. Used to strengthen an affirmation or assertion—if I am found to be wrong, then I am a Dutchman which I manifestly am not.

The Flying Dutchman. *See under* FLY.

Well, I'm a Dutchman! An exclamation of strong incredulity.

Dutchman's breeches, or **sailor's trousers.** Two patches of blue appearing in a stormy sky giving the promise of better weather, *i.e.* enough blue sky to make a Dutchman (or sailor) a pair of breeches.

The plant *dicentra cucullaria* is also called Dutchman's Breeches from its two-spurred flowers.

Dutchman's draught. A "big swig", a copious draught; an allusion to the Dutchman's reputed fondness for heavy drinking. *Cp.* DUTCH COURAGE; DUTCH GLEEK.

Dutchman's log. A rough method for finding a ship's speed by throwing a piece of wood, etc., into the sea well forward and timing its passage between two marks on the vessel of known distance apart.

Dwarf. Dwarfs have figured in the legends and mythology of nearly every people, and the success of Walt Disney's children's classic *Snow White and the Seven Dwarfs* (1938) is evidence of their enduring appeal. Pliny gives particulars of whole races of them, possibly following travellers' tales of African pygmies. They are prominent in Teutonic and Scandinavian legend and generally dwelt in rocks and caves, and recesses of the earth. They were guardians of mineral wealth and precious stones and very skilful at their work. They were not unfriendly to man, but could on occasions be intensely vindictive and mischievous.

In England, dwarfs or midgets were popular down to the 18th century as court favourites or household pets. In later times they were often exhibited as curiosities at circuses, etc.

Among those recorded in legend or history (with their reputed heights) the following are, perhaps, the most famous:

ALBERICH, the dwarf of the NIBELUNGENLIED.

ANDROMEDA and CONOPAS, each 2 ft. 4 in. Dwarfs of Julia, niece of Augustus.

BEBE, or NICHOLAS FERRY, 2 ft. 9 in. A native of France (1714–1737). He had a brother and sister, both dwarfs.

BORUWLASKI (*Count Joseph*), 3 ft. 3 in. (d. 1837).

CHE-MAH (a Chinaman), 2 ft. 1 in., weight 52 lb. Exhibited in London in 1880.

COLOBRI (*Prince*) of Sleswig. 2 ft. 1 in., weight 25 lb. at the age of twenty-five (1851).

CONOPAS. *See* ANDROMEDA, *above*.

COPPERNIN, the dwarf of the Princess of Wales, mother of George III. The last court dwarf in England.

CRACHAMI (*Caroline*). Born at Palermo; 1 ft. 8 in. (1814–1824). Exhibited in Bond Street, London, 1824.

DECKER or DUCKER (*John*), 2 ft. 6 in. An Englishman (1610).

FAIRY QUEEN (*The*), 1 ft. 4 in., weight 4 lb. Exhibited in Regent Street, London, 1850. Her feet were less than two inches.

GIBSON (*Richard*), a good portrait painter (1615–1690). His wife's maiden name was Anne Shepherd. Each measured 3 ft. 10 in. Waller sang their praises:

> Design or chance makes others wive,
> But Nature did this match contrive.

HOPKINS (*Harry*). Born at Llantrisant, Glamorgan: 2 ft. 7 in. (1737–1754).

HUDSON (*Sir Jeffrey*). Born at Oakham, Rutland; 3 ft. 9 in. at the age of thirty (1619–1682); he figures in

Scott's *Peveril of the Peak*.

JACKSON (*William E.*). Born at Dunedin, New Zealand; 2 ft. 3 in. and commonly known as *Major Mite* (1864–1900).

JARVIS (*John*), 2 ft. Page of honour to Queen Mary (1508–1556).

KELLY (*Mrs. Catherine, The Irish Fairy*), 2 ft. 10 in. (1756–1785).

LOLKES (*Wybrand*), 2 ft. 3 in., weight 57 lb. Exhibited at ASTLEY's in 1790.

LUCIUS, 2 ft., weight 17 lb. The dwarf of the Emperor Augustus.

MAGRI (*Count Primo*), *see* WARREN, *below*.

MARINE (*Lizzie*), 2 ft. 9 in., weight 45 lb.

MIDGETS (*The*). Lucia Zarate, the elder sister, 1 ft. 8 in., weight 4¾ lb., at the age of eighteen. Her sister was a little taller. Exhibited in London, 1881.

NUTT, COMMODORE. *See* TOM THUMB, *below*.

PAAP (*Simon*). A Dutch dwarf, 2 ft. 4 in., weight 27 lb.

SAWYER (*A.L.*), 2 ft. 6½ in., weight 39 lb. Editor in 1833 of the *Democrat* a paper of considerable repute in Florida.

STOBERIN (*C.H.*), of Nuremberg, 2 ft. 11 in. at the age of twenty.

STOCKER (*Nannette*), 2 ft. 9 in. Exhibited in ondon in 1815.

STRASSE DAVIT Family. Man 1 ft. 8 in.; woman, 1 ft. 6 in.; child at seventeen only 6 in.

TERESIA (*Madame*). A Corsican, 2 ft. 10 in., weight 27 lb. Exhibited in London, 1773.

TOM THUMB (*General*), whose name was Charles S. Stratton, born at Bridgeport in Connecticut, U.S.A. (1838–1883). Exhibited first in London in 1844. In 1863 he married Lavinia WARREN, and was then 31 in. in height, she being 32 in. and 21 years old. They visited England in the following year with their dwarf son, Commodore NUTT.

WANMER (*Lucy*), 2 ft. 6 in., weight 45 lb. Exhibited in London 1801, at the age of forty-five.

WARREN (*Lavinia*). *See* TOM THUMB *above*. In 1884 she married another dwarf, Count Primo Magri, who was 2 ft. 8 in.

WORMBERG (*John*), 2 ft. 7 in. at the age of thirty eight (Hanoverian period).

XIT was the dwarf of Edward VI.

ZARATE. *See* MIDGETS, *above*.

Cp. GIANTS; HEAVIEST MEN.

The Black Dwarf. A GNOME of the most malignant character, once held by the dalesmen of the BORDER as the author of all the mischief that befell their flocks and herds. In Scott's novel of this title (1816), the name is given to

Sir Edward Mauley, *alias* Elshander, the recluse, Cannie Elshie, and the Wise Wight of Mucklestane Moor.

Dye. A villain of the deepest dye. One steeped in villainy, a villain of the worst kind.

Dyed in the wool. Thorough-going 100 per cent (16th-century origin).

Dying Sayings. Many are either APOCRYPHAL or have survived in inaccurate versions.

ADAMS (*President*): "Independence for ever."

ADAMS (*John Q.*): "It is the last of earth. I am content."

ADDISON: "See in what peace a Christian can die."

ALBERT (*Prince Consort*): "I have such sweet thoughts." *Or*, "I have had wealth, rank, and power; but, if these were all I had, how wretched I should be!"

ALEXANDER I (of Russia; to his wife Elizabeth): "Que voux devez être fatiguée."

ALEXANDER II (of Russia): "I am sweeping through the gates, washed in the blood of the Lamb."

ALFIERI: "Clasp my hand, dear friend, I am dying."

ANAXAGORAS (the philosopher, who kept a school; being asked if he wished for anything, replied): "Give the boys a holiday."

ANTONY (of Padua): "I see my God. He calls me to Him."

ARCHIMEDES (being ordered by a Roman soldier to follow him, replied): "Wait till I have finished my problem."

AUGUSTUS (to his friends): "Do you think I have played my part pretty well through the farce of life?"

BACON (*Francis*): "My name and memory I leave to men's charitable speeches, to foreign nations and to the next age."

BECKETT (*Archbishop*; before he was struck dead by Sir William de Tracy): "I am prepared to die for Christ and His Church."

BEDE (*The Venerable*; having dictated the last sentence of his translation of St. John's Gospel, and being told by the Scribe that the sentence was now written): "It is well; you have said the truth: it is in deed."

BEECHER (*Henry Ward*): "Now comes the mystery."

BEETHOVEN (who was deaf): "I shall hear in heaven."

BLOOD (*Colonel*): "I do not fear death."

BOILEAU: "It is a great consolation to a poet on the point of death that he has never written a line injurious to good morals."

BOLEYN (*Anne*): "The executioner is, I believe, very expert; and my neck is very slender."

BURKE: "God bless you."

BURNS: "Don't let the awkward squad fire over my grave."

BYRON: "I must sleep now."

CÆSAR (to Brutus, his most intimate friend when he stabbed him): "Et tu, Brute?"

CASTLEREAGH (said to his doctor): "Bankhead, let me fall into your arms. It is all over."

CATESBY (a conspirator in the Gunpowder Plot): "Stand by me, Tom, and we will die together."

CATO THE YOUNGER (on seeing that the sword's point was sharp and before thrusting it into his body): "Now I am master of myself."

CAVELL (*Nurse*; before facing the German firing party in 1915): "Patriotism is not enough. I must have no hatred or bitterness towards anyone."

CHARLEMAGNE: "Lord, into Thy hands I commend my spirit." *Cp.* COLUMBUS, LADY JANE GREY, and TASSO.

CHARLES I: "From a corruptible to an incorruptible crown where no disturbance can be, no disturbance in the world". *See* REMEMBER.

CHARLES II: "I have been a most unconscionable time a-dying; but I hope you will excuse it." (To his brother, James II): "Do not, do not let poor Nelly starve."

CHARLES VIII (of France): "I hope never again to commit a mortal sin, nor even a venial one, if I can help it."

CHARLES IX (of France, in whose reign occurred the Massacre of St. BARTHOLOMEW): "Nurse, nurse, what murder! what blood! O! I have done wrong: God pardon me."

CHESTERFIELD (*Lord*): "Give Dayrolles a chair."

CHRYSOSTOM: "Glory to God for all things. Amen."

CICERO (to his assassins): "Strike."

COKE (*Sir Edward*): "Thy kingdom come; Thy will be done."

COLIGNY (to the German who assassinated him): "Honour these grey hairs, young man."

COLUMBUS: "Lord, into Thy hands I commend my spirit." *Cp.* CHARLEMAGNE and TASSO.

COPERNICUS: "Now, O Lord, set Thy servant free." (*See Luke* ii, 29.)

CRANMER (as he held in the flames his right hand which had signed his apostasy): "That unworthy hand! That unworthy hand!"

CROMWELL: "My design is to make what haste I can to be gone."

CUVIER (to the nurse who was applying leeches): "Nurse, it was I who discovered that leeches have red blood."

DANTON (to the executioner): "Be sure you show the mob my head. It will be a long time ere they see its like."

DARWIN: "I am not in the least afraid to die."

DEMONAX (the philosopher): "You may go home, the show is over" (*Lucian*). *Cp.* RABELAIS.

DIDEROT: "The first step towards philosophy is incredulity."

DOUGLAS: "Fight on, my merry men."

EDWARD I: "Carry my bones before you on your march, for the rebels will not be able to endure the sight of me, alive or dead."

EDWARDS (*Jonathan*): "Trust in God, and you need not fear."

ELDON (*Lord*): "It matters not where I am going whether the weather be cold or hot."

ELIZABETH I: "All my possessions for a moment of time."

ELLIOTT (*Ebenezer*); "A strange sight, sir, an old man unwilling to die."

ENGHIEN (*Duc d'*; shot by order of Napoleon I in (1804): "I die for my king and for France."

EPAMINONDAS (wounded; on being told that the Thebans were victorious): "Then I die happy." *Cp.* WOLFE.

ETTY: "Wonderful! Wonderful this death!"

FONTENELLE: "I suffer nothing, but I feel a sort of difficulty in living longer."

FOX (*C.J.*; to his wife): "It don't signify, my dearest, dearest Liz."

FOX (*George*, the Quaker): "Never heed! the Lord's power is over all weakness and death."

FREDERICK V (of Denmark): "There is not a drop of blood on my hands." *Cp.* PERICLES.

GAINSBOROUGH: "We are all going to heaven and Van Dyck is of the company."

GARTH (*Sir Samuel*; to his physicians—Garth was a doctor himself!): "Dear gentlemen, let me die a natural death."

GASTON DE FOIX: "I am a dead man! Lord, have mercy upon me!"

GEORGE IV (said to his page, Sir Walthen Waller): "Wally, what is this? It is death, my boy. They have deceived me."

GOETHE: "Light, more light!"

GRANT (*General*): "I want nobody distressed on my account."

GRATTAN: "I am perfectly resigned. I am surrounded by my family. I have served my country. I have reliance upon God and I am not afraid of the Devil."

GREELEY (*Horace*): "It is done."

GREGORY VII (he had retired to Salerno after his disputes with the Emperor, Henry IV): "I have loved justice and hated iniquity, therefore I die in exile."

GREY (*Lady Jane*): "Lord, into Thy hands I commend my spirit." *Cp.* CHARLEMAGNE.

GUSTAVUS ADOLPHUS: "I am sped, brother. Save thyself."

HALE (*Capt. Nathan*; hanged by the British Army in America for espionage): "I regret that I have but one life to give for my country."

HANNIBAL: "Let us now relieve the Romans of their fears by the death of a feeble old man."

HAVELOCK (*Sir Henry*): "Come, my son, and see how a Christian can die."

HAYDN died singing "God preserve the Emperor!"

HAZLITT: "Well, I've had a good life."

HENRY II (when told that his favourite son John was one of those who were conspiring against him): "Now let the world go as it will; I care for nothing more."

HENRY VIII: "All is lost! Monks, Monks, Monks!"

HERBERT (*George*): "Now, Lord, receive my soul."

HOBBES: "I am taking a fearful leap in the dark."

HOLLAND (*Lord*): "If Mr. Selwyn calls, let him in; if I am alive I shall be very glad to see him, and if I am dead he will be very glad to see me." [Selwyn was noted for his interest in viewing corpses and in attending executions.]

HUMBOLDT: "How grand these rays! They seem to beckon earth to heaven."

HUNTER (*Dr. William*): "If I had strength to hold a pen, I would write down how easy and pleasant a thing it is to die."

HUS (*John*; to an old woman thrusting another faggot on the pile to burn him): "Sancta simplicitas!"

JACKSON ("*Stonewall*"): "Let us pass over the river, and rest under the shade of the trees."

JAMES V (of Scotland; this he said when told that the Queen had given birth to a daughter—the future Mary Queen of Scots): "It [the crown of Scotland] came [to the Stewarts] with a lass and it will go with a lass."

JEFFERSON (of America): "I resign my spirit to God, my daughter to my country."

JEROME (of Prague): "Thou knowest, Lord, that I have loved the truth!"

JOAN OF ARC "Jesus! Jesus! Jesus! Blessed be God."

JOHNSON (*Dr.*; to Miss Morris): "God bless you, my dear."

JULIAN (called the "Apostate"): "Vicisti, O Galilæe." (Thou hast conquered, O Galilean.)

KEATS: "Severn—I—lift me up—I am dying—I shall die easy; don't be frightened—be firm, and thank God it has come."

KEN (*Bishop Thomas*): "God's will be done."

KNOX (*John*): "Now it is come."

LAMB (*Charles*): "My bed-fellows are cramp and cough—we three all in one bed."

LAMBERT (the Martyr; as he was pitched into the flames): "None but Christ! None but Christ!"

LATIMER (to Ridley at the stake): "Be of good comfort, Mr. Ridley, and play the man, we shall this day light a candle by God's grace in England, as I trust never shall be put out."

LAUD (*Archbishop*): "No one can be more willing to send me out of life than I am desirous to go."

LAWRENCE (*Sir Henry*): "Let there be no fuss about me, let me be buried with the men."

LEICESTER (*Earl of*): "By the arm of St. James, it is time to die."

LEOPOLD I (*Kaiser*): "Let me die to the sound of sweet music." *Cp.* MIRABEAU.

LOCKE (*John*; to Lady Masham, who was reading to him some of the Psalms): "Oh! the depth of the riches of the goodness and knowledge of God. Cease now."

LOUIS IX (he died in 1270 while on a crusade): "Jerusalem, Jerusalem."

LOUIS XIV: "Why weep you! Did you think I should live for ever? I thought dying had been harder."

LOUIS XVI (on the scaffold): "Frenchmen, I die guiltless of the crimes imputed to me. Pray God my blood fall not on France!"

MACAULAY: "I shall retire early; I am very tired."

MACHIAVELLI: "I love my country more than my soul."

MALESHERBES (to the priest): "Hold your tongue! your wretched chatter disgusts me."

MARIE ANTOINETTE: "Farewell, my children, for ever. I am going to your father."

MARTINEAU (*Harriet*): "I see no reason why the existence of Harriet Martineau should be perpetuated."

MARY I (*Queen of England*): "You will find the word Calais written on my heart."

MARY II (to Archbishop Tillotson, who had paused in reading a prayer): "My Lord, why do you not go on? I am not afraid to die."

MELANCHTHON (in reply to the question, "Do you want anything?"): "Nothing but heaven."

MICHELANGELO: "My soul I resign to God, my body to the earth, my worldly goods to my next of kin."

MIRABEAU: "Let me fall asleep to the sound of delicious music." *Cp.* LEOPOLD.

MOHAMMED: "O Allah! Pardon my sins. Yes, I come."

MONICA (*St.*): "In peace I will sleep with Him and take my rest". (St. Augustine: *Confessions*.)

MONMOUTH (*Duke of*; to his executioner): "There are six guineas for you and do not hack me as you did my Lord Russell."

MONTAGU (*Lady Mary Wortley*): "It has all been very interesting."

MOODY (the evangelist): "I see earth receding: Heaven is opening; God is calling me."

MOORE (*Sir John*): "I hope my country will do me justice."

MORE (*Sir Thomas*): "See me safe up [*i.e.* on ascending the scaffold]; for my coming down, let me shift for myself."

MOZART: "You spoke of a refreshment, Emile; take my last notes, and let me hear once more my solace and delight."

MURAT (*King of Naples*; said to the men detailed to shoot him): "Soldiers, save my face; aim at my heart. Farewell."

NAPOLEON I: "Mon Dieu! La Nation Française. Tête d'armée."

NAPOLEON III (to Dr. Conneau): "Were you at Sedan?"

NELSON: "I thank God I have done my duty. Kiss me, Hardy."

NERO: "Qualis artifex pereo." ("What an artist the world is losing in me!")

NEWTON: "I don't know what I may seem to the world. But as to myself I seem to have been only like a boy playing on the seashore and diverting myself in now and then finding a smoother pebble or prettier shell than ordinary, whilst the great ocean of truth lay all undiscovered before me."

PALMER (*John*, the actor): "There is another and a better world." (Said on the stage. It is a line in the part he was playing—*The Stranger*)

PALMERSTON: "Die, my dear doctor! that's the last thing I shall do."

PASCAL: "My God, forsake me not."

PERICLES: "I have never caused any citizen to put on mourning on my account." *Cp.* FREDERICK V.

PETERS (*Hugh*, the regicide; to his executioner): "Friend, you do not well to trample on a dying man."

PITT (*William, the Younger*): "My country! How I leave my country!"

PLATO: "I thank the guiding providence and fortune of my life, first, that I was born a man and a Greek, not a barbarian nor a brute; and next, that I happened to live in the age of Socrates."

POE (*Edgar Allan*): "Lord, help my soul!"

POMPADOUR (*Madame de*): "Stay a little longer, M. le Curé, and we will go together."

POPE: "Friendship itself is but a part of virtue."

QUIN (the actor): "I could wish this tragic scene were over, but I hope to go through it with becoming dignity."

RABELAIS: "Let down the curtain, the farce is over." *Cp.* DEMONAX. Also,

"I am going to seek the great perhaps."

RALEGH (said on the scaffold where he was beheaded): "It matters little how the head lies, so the heart be right."

RENAN: "We perish, we disappear, but the march of time goes on for ever."

REYNOLDS (*Sir Joshua*): "I know that all things on earth must have an end, and now I am come to mine."

RHODES (*C.J.*): "So little done, so much to do."

RICHARD I: "Youth, I forgive thee!" (Said to Bertrand de Gourdon, who shot him with an arrow at Chalus. Then, to his attendants, he added): "Take off his chains, give him 100 shillings, and let him go."

RICHARD III (at Bosworth, where his best men deserted him): "Treason! treason!"

ROLAND (*Madame*; on her way to the guillotine): "O Liberty! What crimes are committed in thy name!"

ROSCOMMON (*Earl of*):

"My God, my Father, and my Friend, Do not forsake me at my end."

(Quoting from his own translation of *Dies Iræ*.)

RUSSELL (*Lord*; executed 1683): "The bitterness of death is now past."

SALADIN: "When I am buried, carry my winding-sheet on the point of a spear, and say these words: Behold the spoils which Saladin carries with him! Of all his victories, realms and riches, nothing remains to him but this." *Cp.* SEVERUS.

SCARRON: "Ah, my children, you cannot cry for me so much as I have made you laugh."

SCHILLER: "Many things are growing plain and clear to my understanding."

SCOTT (*Sir Walter*; to his family): "God bless you all, I feel myself again."

SERVETUS (at the stake): "Christ, Son of the eternal God, Have mercy upon me." (Calvin insisted on his saying, "the eternal Son of God" but he would not, and was burnt to death.)

SEVERUS: "I have been everything, and everything is nothing. A little urn will contain all that remains of one for whom the whole world was too little." *Cp.* SALADIN.

SHERIDAN: "I am absolutely undone."

SIDNEY (*Sir Philip*; to his brother Robert): "Govern your will and affections by the will and word of your creator: in me beholding the end of this world with all her vanities."

SIWARD (the Dane): "Lift me up that I may die standing, not lying down like a cow." *Cp.* VESPASIAN.

SOCRATES: "Crito, I owe a cock to ÆSCULAPIUS."

STAËL (*Madame de*): "I have loved God, my father, and liberty."

STEPHEN (the first Christian martyr): "Lord, lay not this sin to their charge."

STRAFFORD (before his execution in 1641): "Put not your trust in princes."

TASSO: "Lord, into Thy hands I commend my spirit." Also recorded of Charlemagne, Lady Jane Grey, Columbus, and others.

TAYLOR (*General Zachary*): "I have tried to do my duty, and am not afraid to die. I am ready."

TAYLOR (the "Water-Poet"): "How sweet it is to rest!"

TENTERDEN (*Lord Chief Justice*): "Gentlemen of the jury, you may retire."

THERAMENES (the Athenian condemned by Critias to drink hemlock, said as he drank the poison): "'To the health of the fair Critias."

THISTLEWOOD (executed for high treason, 1820): "I shall soon know the grand secret."

THOREAU: "I leave this world without a regret."

THURLOW (*Lord*): "I'll be shot if I don't believe I'm dying."

TYNDALE: "Lord, open the eyes of the King of England [*i.e.* Henry VIII]."

VANE (*Sir Harry*): "It is a bad cause which cannot bear the words of a dying man."

VESPASIAN: "A king should die standing" (*see* SIWARD); but his last words were "Ut puto, deus fio," *i.e.* "I suppose I am now becoming a god," referring to the apotheosization of Cæsars after death.

VICTORIA (*Queen*; referring to the war in South Africa then in progress): "Oh, that peace may come."

VOLTAIRE: "Do let me die in peace."

WASHINGTON: "It is well, I die hard, but am not afraid to go."

WEBSTER (*Daniel*): "Life, life! Death, death! How curious it is!"

WESLEY (*Charles*): "I shall be satisfied with Thy likeness—satisfied."

WESLEY (*John*): "The best of all is, God is with us."

WILLIAM (*the Silent*): "O my God have mercy upon my soul! O my God, have mercy upon this poor people!"

WILSON (the ornithologist): "Bury me where the birds will sing over my grave."

WISHART (at the stake): "I fear not this fire."

WOLCOTT ("*Peter Pindar*"): "Give me back my youth!"

WOLFE (*General*): "What! do they run already? Then I die happy." *Cp.* EPAMINONDAS.

WOLSEY (*Cardinal*): "Had I but served God as diligently as I have served the King, He would not have given me over in my grey hairs."

WORDSWORTH: "God bless you! Is that you, Dora?"

ZISKA (*John*): "Make my skin into drum-heads for the Bohemian cause."

Dymoke. The name of the family which has held the office of CHAMPION OF ENGLAND since the coronation of Richard II (1377).

Dymphna (dimf' nà). The patron SAINT of the insane. She is said to have been the daughter of a 6th-century Irish chieftain, who fled to Gheel in Belgium to escape her father's incestuous attentions, and devoted herself to charitable works. She was eventually murdered by her father. In art she is shown dragging away a DEVIL. Gheel has long been a centre for the treatment of the mentally afflicted.

Dysmas (diz' măs). The traditional name of the Penitent Thief, who suffered with Christ at the Crucifixion. His relics are claimed by Bologna, and in some calendars he is commemorated on 25 March. In the apocryphal GOSPEL OF NICODEMUS he is called *Dimas* (and elsewhere *Titus*), and the Impenitent Thief *Gestas*.

Dyvour (dī' vôr). The old name in Scotland for a bankrupt (Fr. *devoir*, to owe). From the 17th century *dyvours* were by law compelled to wear an upper garment half yellow and half brown, with part-coloured cap and hose. This requirement was not formally abolished until 1836.

Dyzemas Day (diz' măs). Tithe day (Port. *dizimas*, tithes; Lat. *decima*, a tenth, a tithe).

E

E. This letter is derived from the Egyptian hieroglyph ☐, and the Phœnician and Hebrew sign called *he*.

The following legend is sometimes found in churches under the two tables of the Ten Commandments:

PRSVR Y PRFCT MN
VR KP THS PRCPTS TN
The vowel E
Supplies the key.

E pluribus unum (ē ploo′ ri bus ū′ nŭm) (Lat.) One out of many. It is taken from *Moretum* (l. 103), a Latin poem attributed to VIRGIL, and is the motto on the Great Seal of the United States of America.

Eager beaver. An American expression in World War II for an over-zealous recruit whose keenness was marked by volunteering on every possible occasion, and subsequently applied in civilian life to similar enthusiasts.

Eagle. In mythology, the eagle commonly represents the SUN, but in Scandinavian myth is usually associated with storm and gloom. It is also emblematic of courage, immortality, etc. In Christian art, it is the symbol of St. JOHN THE EVANGELIST (hence its use on church lecterns), St. Augustine, St. GREGORY THE GREAT, and St. PRISCA. Emblematically, or in HERALDRY, the eagle is a charge of great honour. It was called the Bird of JOVE by the Romans and was borne on their military standards; they used to let an eagle fly from the funeral pile of a deceased emperor, symbolizing the reception of his soul among the Gods. Dryden alludes to this custom in the opening stanza of his poem on the death of Oliver Cromwell:

> Like eager Romans ere all rites were past,

> Did let too soon the sacred eagle fly.

An *eagle* is also an American gold ten-dollar piece, first coined in 1795.

The Golden Eagle and **the Spread Eagle** are commemorative of the CRUSADES and were the devices of the Eastern Roman Empire. France (under the Empires), Germany, Austria, Prussia and Russia also adopted the eagle as a royal or imperial emblem. *See* THE TWO-HEADED EAGLE.

The white-headed American eagle, *Haliætus leucocephalus* (sometimes wrongly termed the Bald Eagle), with outspread wings or spread-eagle (the "eagle displayed" of HERALDRY) is specifically the emblem of the U.S.A.

The term **Spread-eaglism** denotes bombastic display and ostentation of speech or action, especially of vulgar patriotism, and in the United States was the counterpart of JINGOISM in Britain. In the navy a man was said to be **spread-eagled** when he was lashed to the rigging for flogging, with outstretched arms and legs.

The Two-headed Eagle. The German eagle has its head turned to our left hand and the Roman eagle to our right hand. CHARLEMAGNE, as successor to the Roman EMPERORS, is said to have adopted the eagle as a badge, but the two-headed eagle, reputedly symbolizing the eastern and western divisions of the empire, did not appear on the arms of the HOLY ROMAN EMPIRE until the early 15th century. It was retained by the Austrian Emperors as successors to the Holy Roman Emperors. In 1472 Ivan III of Russia assumed the two-headed eagle after his marriage to Sophia, daughter of Thomas Palæologus, and niece of Constantine XIV.

An eagle eye. One with keen and piercing sight; figuratively used of acute intellectual vision.

Eagle stones. See ÆTITES.

The Eagle and Child. The crest of the Stanley family and Earls of Derby, and a well-known PUBLIC-HOUSE SIGN. The legend is that Sir Thomas Latham, an ancestor of the house, caused his illegitimate son to be placed under the foot of a tree in which an eagle had built its nest. When out walking with his wife, they "accidentally" found the child, which he persuaded her to adopt as their heir. Later he changed his mind and left most of his wealth to his daughter, and the family altered the eagle crest of Sir Thomas to that of an eagle preying upon a child.

The eagle does not hawk at flies. See AQUILA NON CAPTAT MUSCAS.

Land of the White Eagle. See under LAND.

Thy youth is renewed like the eagle's (*Ps*. ciii, 5). This refers to the ancient superstition that every ten years the eagle soars into the "fiery region", and plunges into the sea, where, moulting its feathers, it acquires new life. *Cp*. PHOENIX.

Ear (O.E. *eare*). If your ears burn, someone is talking about you. This is a very old superstition; Pliny says, "When our ears do glow and tingle, some do talk of us in our absence."

About one's ears. Causing trouble. The allusion is to a hornet's nest buzzing about one's head; thus "to bring the house about one's ears" is to set the whole family against one.

Ass-eared. *See under* ASS.

Asses as well as pitchers have ears. *See under* ASS.

Bow down thine ear. Condescend to hear or listen (*Ps*. xxxi, 2).

By ear. To sing or play by ear is to sing or play without reading the music, depending on the ear alone.

Dionysius's Ear. A large ear-shaped underground cave cut in a rock and so connected that Dionysius, TYRANT of Syracuse, could overhear the conversation of his prisoners from another chamber. A similar whispering gallery exists beneath Hastings Castle. It is cut from the solid rock and the listening post is shaped like an ear.

Give ear to. Listen to; give attention to.

His ears must be burning. Said of someone being talked about in his absence.

I am all ear. All attention.

In one ear and out of the other. Forgotten as soon as heard.

Jew's ear. *See* ELDER TREE.

Lend me your ears. Pay attention to what I am about to say.

> Friends, Romans, countrymen, lend me your ears;
> I come to bury Cæsar, not to praise him.
> SHAKESPEARE: *Julius Cæsar*, III, ii.

Little pitchers have long ears. *See* PITCHER.

Mine ears hast thou bored. Thou hast accepted me as thy bond-slave for life. If a Hebrew servant declined to go free after six years' service, the master was to bore his ear with an awl, in token of his voluntary servitude for life (*Exod*. xxi, 6).

No ear. A bad ear for music, the opposite of a good ear.

Over head and ears, or **up to the ears.** Wholly, desperately; said of being in love, debt, trouble, etc.

To be sent off with a flea in your ear. *See under* FLEA.

To be willing to give one's ears. To be prepared to make a considerable sacrifice. The allusion is to the old practice of cutting off the ears for various offences.

To come to the ears of. To come to someone's knowledge, especially by hearsay.

To get the wrong sow by the ear. *See under* SOW.

To have itching ears. To enjoy scandalmongering, hearing news or current gossip (II *Tim*. iv, 3).

To have one's ear to the ground. To be alert and well informed of what is taking place, to be alive to the probable trend of events. A figure derived from woodcraft.

To prick up one's ears. To listen attentively to something not expected, as horses prick up their ears at a sudden sound.

To set people together by the ears. To create ill will among them; to set them quarrelling and, metaphorically, pulling each other's ears as dogs do when fighting.

To tickle the ears. To gratify the ear either by pleasing sounds or gratifying words.

To turn a deaf ear. To refuse to listen; to refuse to accede to a request.

Walls have ears. See under WALL.

Within earshot. Within hearing.

You cannot make a silk purse out of a sow's ear. See under SILK.

Ear-finger. The little finger, which, because of its convenient size, is thrust into the ear when it tickles.

Ear-marked. Marked so as to be recognized; figuratively, something allocated or set aside for a special purpose. The allusion is to owner's marks on the ears of cattle and sheep.

Ears to Ear Bible, The. See BIBLE, SOME SPECIALLY NAMED EDITIONS.

Earl (O.E. *eorl*, a man of position in opposition to a *ceorl* or churl; cp. Dan. *jarl*). The third in dignity in the British peerage, ranking next below MARQUESS. In later Anglo-Saxon England, earls became important administrative officers commanding the MILITIA of their areas, and their growing political power is exemplified by that of Earl Godwin. William the Conqueror tried to introduce the name COUNT unsuccessfully, but the wife of an earl is still called a *countess*. An earl's coronet has eight silver balls mounted on gold rays which reach to the top of the cap, with small strawberry leaves alternating between them. *Cp.* VISCOUNT.

Earl Marshal. The officer of State who presides over the College of Arms, grants armorial bearings and is responsible for the arrangements of State ceremonials, processions, etc. Since 1483 the office has been hereditary in the line of the Dukes of Norfolk. *See* MARSHAL.

Earth. Down to earth. Forthright and plain spoken.

Gone to earth. Gone into hiding. A figure derived from fox-hunting.

The ends of the earth. See under END.

To come back to earth. To abandon fantasy for reality.

To run something to earth. To trace something to its source, as a fox is chased or traced to its earth.

Earthquakes. According to Indian mythology the world rests on the head of a great elephant, "Muhu-pudma", and when, for the sake of rest, the huge monster refreshes itself by moving its head, an earthquake is produced.

The lamas say that the earth is placed on the back of a gigantic frog and when it moves its limbs or head it shakes the earth. Other Eastern myths place the earth on the back of a tortoise.

Greek and Roman mythologists ascribe earthquakes to the restlessness of the giants whom JUPITER buried under high mountains. Thus VIRGIL (*Aeneid*, III, 578) ascribes the eruption of Etna to the giant ENCELADUS.

Earwig. (O.E. *ear-wicga*, ear-beetle). So called from the erroneous notion that these insects are apt to enter the ears and penetrate the brain.

Metaphorically, one who whispers scandal, etc., in order to CURRY FAVOUR.

Ease. From O.Fr. *eise*, Mod. Fr. *aise*.

At ease. Resting; without pain or anxiety.

Chapel of Ease. See CHAPEL.

Ill at ease. Uneasy, anxious, uncomfortable.

Stand at ease! A military command for a position less rigid than attention, with the feet apart and the hands joined behind the back (unless arms are being carried).

Stand easy. In a military drill a position in which relaxation is permitted, short of moving away. In the Royal Navy a short break during working hours is called a *stand easy*.

To ease one of his money, or **purse**. To steal it.

East. In the Christian Church the custom of turning to the east when the creed is repeated is to express the belief that Christ is the Dayspring and Sun of Righteousness. The altar is placed at the east end of the church to remind us of Christ, the DAYSPRING and Resurrection; and persons are buried with their feet to the East to signify they died in the hope of the Resurrection.

The ancient Greeks always buried

their dead with the face upwards, looking towards HEAVEN; and the feet turned to the east, or the rising SUN, indicating that the deceased was on his way to ELYSIUM, and not to the region of night (Diogenes Laertius: *Life of Solon*).

East End. Specifically the inner London boroughs east of the CITY itself, essentially working-class areas, the inhabitants of which are known as *East Enders*. *Cp.* COCKNEY: WEST END.

East is East and West is West. A phrase from Rudyard Kipling, emphasizing the divergence of views on ethics and life in general between the Oriental and Western peoples.

Far East. South-East Asia, China, Japan, etc.

Middle East and **Near East.** The precise meaning of these terms has become blurred by recent usage, which has either treated them as interchangeable or used Middle East for what was formerly called the Near East. Iran, Iraq, Afghanistan, India, and Burma used to be called Middle East, and the Near East comprised Libya, Egypt, Arabia, Palestine, Syria and Turkey.

The Eastern Question, as an historical term, essentially refers to the problem created by the decay and disintegration of the Turkish Empire in south-eastern Europe and the NEAR EAST from the time of the Greek revolt in 1821, until the establishment of the Turkish Republic in 1922, which began a new chapter.

Eastern Association, The. Formed in December 1642 from the counties of Norfolk, Suffolk, Essex, Cambridge and Hertford to defend their territory against the ROYALISTS in the CIVIL WAR. Oliver Cromwell as the Puritan leader in East Anglia organized a disciplined army. His cavalry consisted of the pick of the yeomen of the area, voluntarily enlisted. *See* IRONSIDES; NEW MODEL.

Eastern Church. The Orthodox Church. *Cp.* GREEK CHURCH.

Eastern Empire. The East Roman or BYZANTINE EMPIRE.

Easter. The name was adopted for the Christian Paschal festival from O.E. *eastre*, a heathen festival held at the vernal equinox in honour of the Teutonic goddess of dawn, called *Eostre* by Bede, which fell about the same time.

Easter Day is the first Sunday after the Paschal full MOON, *i.e.* the full moon that occurs on the day of the vernal equinox (21 March) or on any of the next 28 days. Thus Easter Sunday cannot be earlier than 22 March, or later than 25 April, as laid down by the COUNCIL OF NICÆA in 325. The Eastern Church still celebrates Easter independently and in 1963 the VATICAN Council declared itself in favour of fixing the date of Easter when agreement with other churches could be reached.

Easter-ale. *See* CHURCH-ALE.

Easter Eggs, or **Pasch Eggs.** The egg as a symbol of fertility and renewal of life derives from the ancient world, as did the practice of colouring and eating eggs at the spring festival. The custom of eating eggs on Easter Sunday and of making gifts of Easter Eggs to children probably derives from the Easter payment of eggs by the VILLEIN to his overlord. The idea of the egg as a symbol of new life was adopted to symbolize the Resurrection. *Pasch Eggs* or *pace eggs*, hard-boiled and coloured, were rolled down slopes as one of the Easter games, a practice surviving in the yearly egg rolling held on the lawn of the WHITE HOUSE in Washington.

Eat. To eat together was, in the East, a sure pledge of protection. There is a story of a Persian grandee who gave the remainder of a peach which he was eating to a man who implored his protection, only to find that his own son had been slain by this man. The nobleman would not allow the murderer to be punished, but said, "We have eaten together; go in peace." *Cp.* CALUMET; TO EAT A MAN'S SALT *under* SALT.

Let us eat and drink, for tomorrow we shall die. *Is.* xxii, 13. A traditional saying of the Egyptians who, at their banquets, exhibited a skeleton to the guests to remind them of the brevity of life.

To eat a man's salt. *See under* SALT.

To eat dirt. *See under* DIRT.

To eat dog. An American Indian custom at councils of importance. Later, when white men took exception, they were allowed to avoid offence by placing a silver dollar on the dish; the next man ate dog and took the dollar. Hence the expression in American politics *to eat dog for another*.

To eat humble pie. To come down from a position you have assumed and to be obliged to defer to others, to submit to humiliation. Here "humble" is a pun on *umble*, the umbles being the heart, liver, and entrails of the deer, the huntsmen's perquisites. When the lord and his household dined off the venison on the dais, the huntsman and his fellows took lower seats and partook of the umbles made into a pie.

To eat its head off. Said of an animal (usually a horse) that eats more than it is worth, or whose work does not cover the cost of its keep.

To eat one out of house and home. Literally, to eat so much that the householder or host is ruined. A favourite complaint of the mother of a growing family.

To eat one's heart out. To fret or worry excessively; to allow grief or vexation to predominate and tincture all one's ideas, and absorb all other emotions.

To eat one's terms. To be studying for the BAR. Students are required to dine in the hall of an INN OF COURT at least thrice in each of the twelve terms before they are "called" to the bar.

To eat one's words. To retract in a humiliating manner; to unsay what you have said.

To eat out of someone's hand. To be submissive and compliant to someone, as a tame animal will eat from its master's hand.

To eat the leek. *See under* LEEK.

Eau de Cologne (Fr. water of Cologne). A perfumed spirit invented by an Italian chemist, Johann Maria Farina, who settled in Cologne in 1709.

Eau de vie (Fr. water of life). Brandy. A translation of the Lat. *aqua vitæ*. This is a curious perversion of the Ital. *acqua di vite* (water, or juice of the vine), rendered by the monks into *aqua vitæ* instead of *aqua vitis*, and confounding the juice of the grape with the alchemists' ELIXIR OF LIFE. *Cp.* USQUE-BAUGH.

Eavesdropper. One who listens stealthily to other people's conversation. The *eavesdrop* or *eavesdrip* was the space of ground around the house which received the water dripping from the eaves. An eavesdropper was one who stationed himself in the eaves-drip to overhear what was said in the house.

Ebenezer. A name often adopted by NONCONFORMIST chapels from the Heb. word meaning "stone of help" (I *Sam*. vii, 12) and thus sometimes used as a symbol of Nonconformity.

Ebionites (Heb. *ebion*, poor). In the early Church the name was given to the ultra-Jewish Christians, many of whom rejected the Virgin Birth and who kept the Jewish Sabbath as well as the Lord's Day. As a separate heretical sect from the 2nd century, they called themselves the Poor Men, and remained isolated from the Church, developing a mixture of creeds.

Eblis. A jinn of Arabian mythology, the ruler of the evil genii, or fallen angels. Before his fall he was called AZAZEL. When ADAM was created, God commanded all the angels to worship him; but Eblis replied, "Me thou hast created of smokeless fire, and shall I reverence a creature made of dust?" God turned the disobedient ANGEL into a Sheytan (DEVIL), and he became the father of devils.

> When he said unto the angels, "Worship Adam", all worshipped him except Eblis.
>
> *Al Koran*, ii.

E-boat. In World War II an abbreviation for "Enemy War Motorboat", the British name for the German motor torpedo boat.

Ebrew Jew, *i.e.* Hebrew Jew meaning a Jew of the purest stock, completely a Jew.

Ecce homo (ek' ki hō' mō) (Lat. Behold the man). The name given to many paintings of Our Lord crowned with thorns and bound with ropes, as He was shown to the people by PILATE, who said to them, "Ecce homo!" (*John* xix, 5). Especially notable are those by Correggio, Titian, Guido Reni, Van Dyck, Rembrandt, Poussin, and Albrecht Dürer. In 1865 Sir John Seeley published a study of Christ under this title.

Ecce signum (ek' ki sig' nùm). See it, in proof. Behold the proof.

Ecclesiastes. This book of the OLD TESTAMENT was formerly ascribed to SOLOMON, because it says (i, I), "The words of the Preacher, the son of David, King in Jerusalem." It is now generally assigned to an unknown author of about the 3rd century B.C.

Ecclesiastical. Ecclesiastical Commissioners, The, of the CHURCH OF ENGLAND were established in 1836 consisting of the archbishops, bishops and deans of Canterbury, St. Paul's and Westminster with certain judges and ministers of State together with eleven eminent laymen. Essentially they administered surplus episcopal and cathedral endowments for relief of the poorer clergy and parochial ministries. In 1948 they merged with QUEEN ANNE'S BOUNTY as the Church Commissioners, basically to manage the ancient endowments of the Church for the support of the ministry.

The Father of Ecclesiastical History. Eusebius of Cæsarea (*c*. 264–340).

Ecclesiasticus. The Latin name, probably meaning "church book" (from its frequent use in the church), for the Book of Sirach, traditionally ascribed to Jesus the son of Sira. It is perhaps the most important book of the OLD TESTAMENT APOCRYPHA and both the German hymn *Nun danket alle Gott* (Now thank we all our God) and the *Jubilee Rhythm* of St. BERNARD of Clairvaux are taken from it. It has been much used by the Lutheran Church.

Echidna (e kid' nà). In classical mythology, a celebrated monster, half woman, half SERPENT and mother of the CHIMÆRA, the many-headed dog ORTHOS, the hundred-headed DRAGON of the HESPERIDES, the Colchian dragon, the SPHINX, CERBERUS, SCYLLA, the GORGONS, the Lernæan HYDRA, the vulture that gnawed away the liver of PROMETHEUS, and the NEMEAN LION.

In zoology an echidna is a porcupine ant-eater found in Australia, Tasmania, and New Guinea, allied to the platypus.

Echo (ek' ō). The Romans say that Echo was a NYMPH in love with NARCISSUS,

but her love not being returned, she pined away until only her voice remained.

Eckhardt (ek' hart). **A faithful Eckhardt, who warneth everyone.** Eckhardt, in German legends, appears on the evening of MAUNDY THURSDAY to warn all persons to go home, that they may not be injured by the headless bodies and two-legged horses which traverse the streets on that night. He also warned those who followed Frau Holle or Holda (VENUS) of evils to come; sometimes he appears as the companion of TANNHÄUSER.

Eclectics (ek lek' tiks). The name given to those who do not attach themselves to any special school (especially philosophers and painters), but pick and choose from many (Gr. *eklegein*, to choose, select). The name was first given to such a group of Greek philosophers of the 2nd and 1st centuries B.C. The 17th-century Italian painters who followed the great masters are known as the *Eclectic School*.

Eclipse. Eclipses were considered by the Greeks and Romans as bad OMENS and the latter would never hold a public assembly during an eclipse. Some of their poets feign that an eclipse of the MOON is because she is on a visit to ENDYMION.

A general notion among some races was that the SUN or moon was devoured by some monster, hence the beating of drums and kettles to scare it away. The Chinese, Lapps and Persians call the evil beast a DRAGON. The East Indians say it is a black GRIFFIN.

The ancient Mexicans thought that eclipses were caused by quarrels between sun and moon.

Ecliptic. The track in the heavens along which the sun appears to perform its annual march. It lies in the middle of the ZODIAC and is an imaginary line produced by the earth's motion about the sun.

Eclogue (Gr. a selection). The word was originally used for VIRGIL's *Bucolics*, because they were selected poems; as they were all pastoral dialogues it came to denote such poems, and hence an *Eclogue* is now a pastoral or rustic dialogue in verse.

Economy. The Christian Economy.
The religious system based on the teachings of Jesus Christ as recorded in the NEW TESTAMENT.

The Economy of Nature. The laws and provisions of nature whereby the greatest amount of good is obtained, and by which the animal and vegetable kingdoms are regulated.

The Mosaic Economy. The religious system revealed by God to Moses and set forth in the OLD TESTAMENT.

Political Economy. The science of the production and distribution of wealth, etc., which in the 20th century came to be called *economics*.

Ecstasy (Gr. *ek*, out; *stasis*, a standing). Literally, a condition in which one stands out of one's mind, or is "beside oneself". St. PAUL refers to this when he says he was caught up to the third HEAVEN and heard unutterable words, "whether in the body, or out of the body, I cannot tell" (II *Cor.* xii, 2–4). St. JOHN also says he was "in the spirit"—*i.e.* in anecstasy—when he saw the apocalyptic vision (*Rev.* i, 10). The belief that the soul left the body at times was common in former ages, and there was a class of diviners among the ancient Greeks called **Ecstatici**, who used to lie in trances, and when they came to themselves gave strange accounts of what they had seen while they were "out of the body".

Ector, Sir. In ARTHURIAN ROMANCES the foster-father of King ARTHUR.

Edda. This name, which may be from Icel. *edda*, great-grandmother, or from Old Norse *odhr*, poetry, is given to two works or collections, *The Elder*, or *Poetic Edda*, and *The Younger Edda*, or *Prose Edda of Snorri*. The first-named was found in 1643 by an Icelandic bishop and consists of mythological and heroic poetry dating from about the 9th century. Erroneously attributed to Sæmund Sigfusson (d. 1133), it is sometimes called *Sæmund's Edda*. The *Younger Edda* by Snorri Sturluson (d. 1242) is in prose and verse and forms a guide to poets and poetry. Found in 1628, it consists of the *Gylfaginning* (an epitome of Scandinavian mythology), the *Skaldskaparmal* (a glossary of poetical expressions, etc.), the *Hattatal* (a list of metres with examples, lists of poets, etc.).

Eden. PARADISE, the country and garden in which ADAM was placed by God (*Gen.* ii, 15). The word means delight, pleasure.

Edge (O.E. *ecg*). **Back and edge.** *See* BACK.

It is dangerous to play with edged tools. It is dangerous to tamper with mischief or that which may bring you into trouble.

Not to put too fine an edge on it. Not to mince the matter; to speak plainly.

To be on edge. To be very eager or nervously impatient.

To edge away. To move away very gradually, as a ship moves away from the edge of the shore.

To edge on. *See* EGG ON.

To fall by the edge of the sword. By a cut from the sword; to be slain in battle.

To have the edge on someone. To have an advantage.

To set one's teeth on edge. To induce a tingling or grating sensation in one's teeth as from acids or harsh noises; to jar one's nerves or to feel aversion.

> I had rather hear a brazen canstick turn'd,
> Or a dry wheel grate on the axle-tree;
> And that would set my teeth nothing on edge,
> Nothing so much as mincing poetry.
> SHAKESPEARE: *Henry IV, Pt. I*, III, i.

Edge-bone. *See* AITCH-BONE.

Edinburgh. Edwin's burgh; the fort built by Edwin, king of Northumbria (616–632). Dunedin (Gael. *dun*, a fortress) and Edina are poetical forms. Also called the Modern ATHENS, or Athens of the North. *See* AULD REEKIE.

Edinburgh Review. An outstanding quarterly magazine founded at Edinburgh in 1802 by Francis Jeffrey, Sydney Smith, and Henry Brougham, and originally published in the buff and blue colours of the WHIG party by Constable. The first three numbers were edited by Smith, who then handed over to Jeffrey. Its brilliance and wit gave it great literary and political influence, especially in the earlier decades, but the unfairness and savageness of some of its reviews were particularly marked in the case of

Wordsworth and Southey, and it drew forth Byron's satire *English Bards and Scotch Reviewers* (1809). Its contributors included Hazlitt, Macaulay and Carlyle. It ceased publication in 1929.

Edward the Confessor. The last Anglo-Saxon king (1042–1066) of the old royal house, so called for his piety and monk-like virtues although conspicuously deficient as a ruler. He was canonized in 1161 by Pope Alexander III.

Edwardian. Belonging to the reign of King Edward VII (1901–1910). Edwardian style of dress was affected by many young men and youths in the 1950s, who soon came to be called *Teddy Boys*. They were as much distinguished for anti-social behaviour as for their peculiarities of costume. *Cp.* BEATNIK; MODS AND ROCKERS; MOHOCKS.

Eel. Holding the eel of science by the tail. To have a smattering of the subject, the kind which slips from the memory as an eel would wriggle out of one's fingers if held by the tail.

Effigy. To burn, or **hang one in effigy.** To burn or hang the dummy or representation of someone in order to show dislike or contempt. From earliest times it has been believed that magic was worked by treating an effigy as one would fain treat the original. In France the public executioner used to hang the criminal in effigy when the criminal himself could not be found.

Egeria (e jēr′ i à). The NYMPH who instructed Numa Pompilius, second king of ROME (753–673 B.C.), in his wise legislation; hence a counsellor, adviser.

Egg. A bad egg. *See under* BAD.
  A duck's egg. *See under* DUCK.
  Curate's egg. *See under* CURATE.
  Druid's egg. *See under* DRUIDS.
  Easter eggs. *See under* EASTER; EGG FEAST.
  Golden eggs. Great profits. *See under* GOOSE.
  Scrambled egg. *See* BRASS HAT.
  The mundane egg. The Phœnicians, Egyptians, Hindus, Japanese and others maintained that the world was egg-shaped and was hatched from an egg made by the Creator. In some mythologies a bird is represented as laying the mundane egg on the primordial waters.

Anciently this idea was attributed to ORPHEUS, hence the "mundane egg" is also called the *Orphic egg*.
  As sure as eggs is eggs. Very sure, certain in fact. It has been suggested that this is a corruption of the logician's formula "*x* is *x*".
  Don't put all your eggs in one basket. Don't venture all you have in one speculation or enterprise. The allusion is obvious.
  I have eggs on the spit. I am very busy, and cannot attend to anything else. The reference is to roasting eggs on a spit. They were first boiled, then the yolk was taken out, braided up with spices, and put back again; the eggs were then drawn on a spit and roasted. The process needed constant attention.
  Like as two eggs. Exactly alike.
  Show him an egg and instantly the whole air is full of feathers. Said of a very sanguine man, because he is "counting his chickens before they are hatched".
  Teach, or **tell your grandmother to suck eggs.** Said derisively to someone who tries to teach his elders or those more experienced than himself.
  There is reason in roasting egg. Even the most trivial thing has a reason for being done in one way rather than some other. When wood fires were usual, it was more common to roast eggs than to boil them, and some care was required to prevent their being "ill-roasted", "all on one side", as Touchstone says in SHAKESPEARE'S *As You Like It*, III, ii.
  To crush in the egg. TO NIP IN THE BUD; to ruin some scheme before it has been fairly started.
  To egg on. To incite, to urge on. Here *egg* is another form of edge, thus it means to encourage one to move little by little in the direction of the edge.
  To take eggs for money. To allow yourself to be imposed upon. The saying derives from the days when eggs were plentiful and exceedingly cheap.
  To tread upon eggs. To walk gingerly, as if walking over eggs, which are easily broken.
  Egg Feast, or **Egg Saturday.** The Saturday before SHROVE TUESDAY used to be so called, particularly in Oxfordshire,

as the eating of eggs was forbidden during LENT.

Egg-head. A bald person or an intellectual person. The latter derives from the former on the supposition that intellectuals are often bald. *See also* HIGH-BROW; SQUARE.

Egg-trot, or **Egg-wife's trot.** A cautious jog-trot pace, like that of a housewife riding to market with eggs in her panniers.

Egil. Brother of Weland (*see* WAYLAND), the VULCAN of Northern mythology. He was a great archer and in the Saga of Thidrik there is a tale told of him exactly similar to that about William TELL and the apple.

Ego (Lat. "I"). In various philosophical systems, *ego* is used of the conscious thinking subject and *non-ego* of the object. The term *ego* was introduced into philosophy by Descartes, who employed it to denote the whole man, body and mind. Fichte later used the term the *absolute ego*, meaning thereby

> the non-individual being, neither subject not object, which posits the world of individual egos and non-egos.

In psychoanalysis the ego is that part of the mind that perceives and takes cognizance of external reality and adjusts responses to it. *See* ID; QUIS.

Eight. One over the eight. Slightly drunk.

Eikon Basilike (ī' kon băz il' i ki) (Gr. royal likeness). *Eikon Basilike*: *The Pourtraicture of His Sacred Majestie in His Solitudes and Sufferings* appeared in 1649 very soon after the execution of Charles I. It purported to be his own account of his reflections and feelings during, and before, his imprisonment. It greatly strengthened royalist sentiment and led to Milton's less influential *Eikonoklastes*. Dr. John Gauden (1605–1662) afterwards claimed authorship at the time of his election to the bishopric of Worcester. It appears that he had edited the king's papers and his version received the royal approval.

Eisel (ī' sel). An old name for vinegar; through Old Fr. from Late Lat. *acetillum*, diminutive of *acetum* (vinegar).

Eisteddfod (ī steth' vod) (Welsh, a session; from *eistedd*, to sit). Eisteddfodau were held in mediæval Wales and later, largely to regulate the admission of aspirants seeking to qualify as bards or minstrels. Thus in 1568, the Council for the Marches of Wales commissioned the holding of an Eisteddfod at Caerwys because "vagraunt and idle persons, naming theim selfes mynstrelles Rithmrs, and Barthes, are lately growen into such an intollerable multitude ... that not only gentlemen and other by theire shameles disorders are oftentymes disquieted in their habitacione. But also thexpert mynstrelles and musicions in tonge and Conyng therby much discouraged ..." All such minstrels and bards were to appear before the experts and those found not worthy of their professions were "to returne to some honest Labor and due Exercise, such as they be most apt unto maytenaunce of their lyvinges, upon paine to be taken as sturdy and idle vacaboundes ..." Revival of the Eisteddfodau was largely due to the romantic movement and their modern development grew from the Corwen Eisteddfod of 1789, the druidic rites being introduced by Iolo Morgannwg in the early 19th century. They have been held annually since 1880, primarily for the encouragement of Welsh literature and music. *See* DRUIDS.

Elagabalus, or **Heliogabalus.** A Syro-Phœnician sun-god. Two temples were built at Rome for this god, who was represented by a huge conical stone.

Elaine. The Lily Maid of ASTOLAT, whose unrequited love for Sir LANCELOT caused her death.

Elbow. *See* ELL.

At one's elbow. Close at hand.

Elbow grease, use plenty of elbow grease, etc. The pressure and physical effort applied when rubbing, polishing, scrubbing, etc. A jocular expression in use for more than three centuries. A time-hallowed joke was to send the GREENHORN to the shop to buy "elbow-grease".

Elbow-lifting. Drinking. *To lift the elbow* is to drink and both expressions are used to indicate fondness of alcohol.

Elbow-room. Sufficient space for the work in hand; room to extend the elbows.

Elbow-shaker. A dicer, a sharper or gambler.

More power to your elbow. A jocular toast of encouragement and support implying that a stronger elbow will lift more glasses to the mouth.

Out at elbow. Shabbily dressed, like one who wears a coat worn out at the elbows. "Down at heel" has a similar meaning. *See under* HEEL.

To elbow one's way in. To push one's way through a crowd; to get a place by HOOK OR CROOK. *See under* HOOK.

To elbow out; to be elbowed out. To supersede; to be ousted by a rival. A thruster or pusher who selfishly pursues his own interest is said to *use his elbows*.

Up to one's elbows. Very busy, with work piled up to one's elbows. *Cp.* UP TO THE EYES *under* EYE.

Elder. The importance of elders as people of authority in ancient communities was a natural development. In the OLD TESTAMENT they appear as official authorities of a locality; and as the elders of the SYNAGOGUE they exercised religious discipline. The members of the SANHEDRIN were called elders. The name was also applied to officers of the early Christian Church and is still used in this sense by the PRESBYTERIAN CHURCH.

Elder Brethren. *See* TRINITY HOUSE.

Elder tree. There are many popular traditions and superstitions associated with this tree. The CROSS is supposed to have been made from its wood and, according to legend, JUDAS hanged himself on an elder, cup-shaped fungal excrescences on the bark still being known as Judas's (or Jew's) ears.

Warts are cured by being rubbed with elder and it is a protection against witchcraft. *See also* FIG-TREE; JUDAS TREE.

El Dorado (el dôr a' dō) (Sp. the gilded). Originally the name given to the supposed king of the fabulous city of MANOA believed to be on the Amazon. The king was said to be covered with oil and then periodically powdered with gold-dust so that he was permanently, and literally, gilded. Expeditions from Spain and England (two of which were led by Sir Walter Ralegh) tried to discover this territory. El Dorado and Manoa were used by the explorers as interchangeable names for the "golden city". Metaphorically it is applied to any place which offers opportunities of getting rich quickly or acquiring wealth easily.

Eleanor Crosses. The crosses erected by Edward I to commemorate his first wife Eleanor of Castile, who died at Hadby in Nottinghamshire in 1290. She was buried in Westminster Abbey and crosses were set up at each of the twelve places where her body rested on its journey—Lincoln, Grantham, Stamford, Geddington, Northampton, Stony Stratford, Woburn, Dunstable, St. Albans, Waltham, West Cheap (Cheapside) and CHARING CROSS. Only those at Geddington, Northampton and Waltham survive.

Eleatic Philosophy. A school of philosophy founded at Elea in Italy in the latter part of the 6th century B.C.

Elecampane (*Inula helenium*), one of the Compositae, allied to the aster. Its candied roots are used as a sweetmeat and were formerly held to confer immortality and to cure wounds. Pliny tells us that the plant sprang from HELEN'S tears. It was much used in old medicines and herb remedies.

Elector. In the HOLY ROMAN EMPIRE those rulers who formed an Electoral College to appoint the Emperor were called Electors. Their number was eventually regularized by the GOLDEN BULL of 1356 and the seven Electors were to be the archbishops of Mainz, Trier, and Cologne, with the rulers of the Rhine Palatinate, Saxony, Brandenburg and Bohemia. The ruler of Bavaria gained admission during the THIRTY YEARS WAR and Hanover became an Electorate in 1708. The office disappeared with the abolition of the Holy Roman Empire in 1806.

Electra (1) One of the PLEIADES, mother of Dardanus, the mythical ancestor of the Trojans. She is known as "the Lost Pleiad", for she is said to have disappeared a little before the TROJAN WAR to avoid seeing the ruin of her beloved city. She showed herself occasionally to mortal eye, but always in the guise of a comet. *See Odyssey*, V, and *Iliad*, XVIII.

(2) A sister of ORESTES who features in

the *Oresteia* of Aeschylus and the two other dramas entitled *Electra* by Sophocles and Euripides. The daughter of AGAMEMNON and CLYTEMNESTRA, she incited Orestes to kill their mother in revenge for the latter's murder of Agamemnon. In modern psychology, an *Electra Complex* is a girl's attraction towards her father accompanied by hostility towards her mother.

Electricity (Gr. *elektron*, amber). Thales of Miletus (600 B.C.) observed that amber when rubbed attracted small particles. From such observations of electrical phenomena the modern science of electricity has developed.

Electuary. Coming from a Greek word meaning to lick up, this term is applied in pharmacy to medicines sweetened with honey or syrup, and originally meant to be licked off the spoon by the patient.

Elegiacs. Verse consisting of alternate hexameters and pentameters, so called because it was the usual metre in which Greek and Roman elegies were written. In Latin it was commonly used by Ovid, Catullus, Propertius, Tibullus, and others.

Element (Lat. *elementum*, first principle). In ancient and mediæval philosophy, earth, air, fire and water were the four elements from which all other substances were composed. This conception was introduced by EMPEDOCLES in the 5th century B.C. Later a fifth immaterial element was added, called the QUINTESSENCE, or *quinta essentia*, supposed by ARISTOTLE to permeate everything.

The use of the word in chemistry to denote substances which resist analysis into simpler substances begins with Robert Boyle.

In one's element. One's natural surroundings, within one's ordinary range of activity, enjoying oneself thoroughly. The allusion is to the natural abode of any animals, as the air to birds, water to fish.

To brave the elements. To venture out into the weather, to defy adverse weather conditions. The elements here are the atmospheric powers; the winds, storms, etc.

Elephant. The Order of the Elephant. A Danish order of knighthood said to have been instituted by Christian I in 1462, but reputedly of earlier origin.

A white elephant. Some possession the expense or responsibility of which is not worth while; a burdensome possession. The allusion is to the story of a king of Siam who used to make a present of a white elephant to courtiers he wished to ruin.

Only an elephant can bear an elephant's load. An Indian proverb: Only a great man can do the work of a great man; also, the burden is more than I can bear; it is a load fit for an elephant.

To see the elephant (U.S.A.). To see all there is to see.

Elephant and Castle. The sign of a public house at Newington Butts that has given its name to a railway station and to a district in South London. The Elephant and Castle is the crest of the Cutlers' Company, into whose trade the use of ivory entered largely.

In ancient times, war-elephants bore "castles" on their backs containing bowmen and armed knights.

A legendary explanation is that it is a corruption of *Infanta de Castile*, Eleanor of Castile, who was the wife of Edward I.

Eleusinian Mysteries. The religious rites in honour of DEMETER or CERES, originally an agrarian cult, performed at Eleusis in Attica and later taken over by the Athenian state and partly celebrated at ATHENS. The rites included sea bathing, processions, religious dramas, etc., and the initiated obtained thereby a happy life beyond the grave. Little is known about the chief rites, hence the figurative use of the phrase to mean something deeply mysterious. The Eleusinian Mysteries were abolished by the Emperor Theodosius about the end of the 4th century A.D.

Elevation of the Host. In the MASS, after the consecration, the raising of the Host and the Chalice by the celebrant for the adoration of the faithful.

Eleven. At the eleventh hour. Just in time; from the parable in *Matt*. xx, 1–16.

Eleven Days. Give us back our ele-

ven days. When ENGLAND adopted the Gregorian CALENDAR (by Chesterfield's Act of 1751) in place of the JULIAN CALENDAR, eleven days were dropped, 2 September 1752 being followed by 14 September. Many people thought that they were being cheated out of eleven days and also eleven days' pay. Hence the popular cry from the populace, "Give us back our eleven days!"

The Eleven Plus. The name given to the selection tests set to school-children at the age of eleven, or just over that age, and used as a means of judging their suitability for the various types of secondary education provided by the Education Act of 1944 (secondary modern, secondary technical, secondary grammar, etc.).

The Eleven Thousand Virgins. *See* URSULA.

The Eleven Years' Tyranny. Denotes the period from 1629 to 1640 when Charles I, with the support of Strafford and Laud, governed without summoning a PARLIAMENT.

Elevenses. A popular name for a mid-morning refreshment snack with tea or coffee. *See also* CRIB.

Elf. Originally a dwarfish being of Teutonic mythology, possessed of magical powers which it used for the good or ill of mankind. Later the name was used for a malignant imp, and then for FAIRY creatures that dance on the grass in the full MOON, etc.

The derivation of elf and GOBLIN from GUELF AND GHIBELLINE is mentioned in Johnson (with disapproval); the word is O.E. *ælf*, from Icel. *alfr*, and Teut. *alp*, a nightmare.

Elf-fire. The IGNIS FATUUS.

Elf-locks. Tangled hair. It used to be said that one of the favourite amusements of Queen MAB was to tie people's hair in knots.

Elf-marked. Those born with a natural defect, according to ancient Scottish superstition, are marked by the elves for mischief.

Elgin Marbles. The 7th Earl of Elgin (1766–1841) was envoy to the Sublime PORTE from 1799 to 1803 and noticed that many of the classical sculptures at ATHENS were suffering from neglect and depredations. At his own expense, he made a collection of statuary and sculpture, including the frieze from the PARTHENON and works of Phidias, and brought them to England. He sold the "Elgin Marbles" to the BRITISH MUSEUM in 1816 for £36,000, a good deal less than they had cost him.

Elia. A *nom de plume* used by Charles Lamb (1775–1834), under which a series of essays appeared. The first of these (in the *London Magazine*, 1820) was a description of the Old South-Sea House, with which he associated the name of Elia, an Italian clerk, a "gay light-hearted foreigner", who was a fellow employee.

Eligius, St. *See* ELOI, ST.

Elijah's Mantle. Metaphorically the assumption of powers previously enjoyed by another, as Elisha took up the mantle of Elijah (II *Kings* ii, 13).

Elijah's Melons. Certain stones on Mount Carmel are so called from the legend that the owner of the land refused to supply food for the prophet, and for punishment his melons were turned into stones.

Eliot, George. The pseudonym of Mary Ann, or Marian, Evans (1819–1880). Her first novel appearing under this name was *Scenes of Clerical Life*, 1858.

Elissa. DIDO, Queen of Carthage, was sometimes called Elissa.

Elixir of Life. The supposed potion of the alchemists that would prolong life indefinitely. It was sometimes imagined as a powder, sometimes as a fluid (Arab. a powder for sprinkling on wounds). It also meant the PHILOSOPHER'S STONE, use for transmuting base metals into GOLD. The name is now given to any sovereign remedy—especially of the "QUACK" variety.

Elizabeth. St. Elizabeth of Hungary (1207–1231). Patron SAINT of the Third Order of St. FRANCIS of which she was a member. Her day is 19 November and she was noted for her good works and love of the poor. She is commemorated in Kingsley's poem *The Saint's Tragedy*. The story is told that her husband Louis at first forbade her abounding gifts to the poor. One day he saw her carrying away a bundle of bread and told her to open it asking what it contained. "Only flowers, my lord," said Elizabeth and, to save the lie, God converted the loaves into flowers and the king was confronted with a mass of red roses. This miracle converted him.

Ell. An old measure of length, which, like FOOT, was taken from a part of the body, *viz*. the forearm and was originally 18 inches. The word (O.E. *eln*) from a Teutonic word *alina*, the forearm to the tip of the middle finger, is cognate with Lat. *ulna*. The measure varied at different times and the English ell of 45 inches seems to have been introduced from France in the 16th century and was chiefly used as a measurement for cloth. The Scotch ell was 37 inches, the Flemish ell *c*. 27 inches and the French ell *c*. 47 inches.

Give him an inch and he'll taken an ell. Give him a little licence, and he will take great liberties or make great encroachments.

The King's Ell-wand. The group of stars called "ORION's Belt".

Elmo's Fire, St. *Elmo* through *Ermo*, is an Italian corruption of St. *Erasmus*, a 4th century Syrian bishop who came to be regarded as the patron SAINT of seamen, and St. Elmo's Fire was attributed to him. Through some confusion the name St. Elmo was also applied by Spanish sailors to the 13th century DOMINICAN, Blessed Peter Gonzalez, who revered him as their particular guardian for his labours among them. *See* CORPOSANT.

Elohim. The plural form of the Heb. *eloah*, God. It expresses the general notion of Deity in the same way as the more widely used *El*, which is found in Babylonian, Aramæan, Phœnician, Hebrew, and Arabic. JEHOVAH (*Jahweh* or *Yahve*), however, is used with the special meaning of the God of Israel.

Elohistic and Yahwistic Sources. The Mosaic authorship of the PENTATEUCH is no longer held by Biblical scholars and the first six books of the BIBLE (the Hexateuch) are usually regarded as a literary entity compounded of a variety of sources. Among the evidence used to support this view, is the use of the names ELOHIM and YAHWEH.

In some sections of the Hexateuch Elohim is used, in others Yahweh, and in some the names are used indifferently, the general conclusion being that the various sources, written at different periods, were subsequently blended. *See also* JEHOVAH, ADONAI.

Eloi, St., or **St. Eligius** (el' oi, el ij' i us) (588–659). Patron SAINT of goldsmiths and metal-workers, and apostle of Flanders.

Elysium (e liz' i ùm). In Greek mythology, the abode of the blessed; hence the **Elysian Fields**, the PARADISE or Happy Land in Greek poetry. *Elysian* means happy, delightful.

> Would take the prison'd soul,
> And lap it in Elysium.
> MILTON: *Comus*, 256, 7.

Embargo. To lay an embargo on. To prohibit, to forbid. The word comes from the Sp. *embargar*, to detain, and is especially applied to the prohibition of foreign ships to enter or leave a port, or to undertake any commercial transaction; also to the seizure of a ship, goods, etc., for the use of the State.

Embarras de richesse (om ba ra' de rē - shes') (Fr.). A perplexing amount of wealth, or too great an abundance of anything; more matter than can be conveniently employed. The phrase was used as the title of a play by the Abbé d'Allainval (1753).

Ember Days. The Wednesday, Friday, and Saturday of the four EMBER WEEKS once observed as days of fasting and abstinence, the following Sundays being the days of Ordination. The name is the M.E. *ymber*, from O.E. *ymbren*, a period, course or circuit (as the rotation of the seasons).

Ember Weeks. The weeks next after the first Sunday in LENT, WHIT SUNDAY, HOLY CROSS DAY (14 September), and St. Lucia's Day (13 December). Uniformity of observance was fixed by the Council of Placentia in 1095, but they were introduced into Britain by AUGUSTINE.

Ember goose. The northern diver or loon; called in Norway *imbre*, because it appears on the coast about the time of Ember days in ADVENT. In Germany it is called *Adventsvogel*.

Emblem. A symbolic figure or representation; a pictorial design with an allusive meaning which is inserted or "cast into" the visible device (Gr. *em*, in; *balein*, to cast). Thus a *balance* is an emblem of justice, *white* of purity, a *sceptre* of sovereignty.

Some of the most common and simple emblems of the Christian Church are:

A chalice. The eucharist.

The circle inscribed in an equilateral triangle, or *the triangle in a circle*. To denote the co-equality and co-eternity of the TRINITY.

A cross. The Christian's life and conflict; the death of Christ for man's redemption.

A crown. The reward of the perseverance of the SAINTS.

A dove. The HOLY GHOST.

A hand from the clouds. To denote God the Father.

A lamb, fish, pelican etc. The Lord Jesus Christ.

A phœnix. The resurrection.

Emblematical poems. Poems consisting of lines of different lengths so that the outline of the poem on the written page can be made to represent the object of the verse. Thus, George Herbert in the *Temple* wrote a poem on the *Altar* that is shaped like an altar, and one on *Easter Wings* like wings.

Embolismic (Late Lat. *embolismus*, intercalation). Pertaining to intercalation, that which is inserted; thus in the Jewish CALENDAR an embolismic year consists of thirteen lunar months, an ordinary year of twelve.

Emerald. According to legend, an emerald protected the chastity of the wearer. It also warded off evil spirits, and epilepsy, cured dysentery, and was anciently supposed to aid weak eyesight.

The Emerald Isle. Ireland, from its bright-green vegetation. The term was first used by Dr. Drennan (1754–1820) in his poem called *Erin*.

> Nor one feeling of vengeance presume to defile
> The cause or the men of the Emerald Isle.
> WILLIAM DRENNAN: *Erin*.

Émigré (ā' mē grā) (Fr.). An emigrant or refugee. The word is particularly applied to those royalists and members of the privileged classes who left France during the Revolution. Their co-operation with foreign powers led to severe laws against them. NAPOLEON, as First Consul, proclaimed a general amnesty, when many returned to France. After the fall of the Empire they were rewarded with political favours by Louis XVIII, but did not recover their estates and former privileges.

Eminence Grise (ā mē nos' grēz) (Fr.). *See* GREY EMINENCE.

Emmanuel, or **Immanuel** (Heb. God with us). The name of the child whose birth was foretold by Isaiah, and who was to be a sign from God to Ahaz (*Is*. vii, 14). The name was later applied in the NEW TESTAMENT to the Messiah.

> Behold, a virgin shall be with child, and shall bring forth a son, and they shall call his name Emmanuel, which being interpreted is, God with us.
> *Matt*. i, 23.

Emmets and Grockles. A current Westcountry expression applied to tourists and holiday-makers.

Emmet is an archaic word for an ant and such insects swarm everywhere. The word *Grockle* apparently derives from *Grock*, the famous CLOWN, implying someone to be laughed at.

Empedocles (em ped' ō klēz). Greek philosopher, statesman, and poet (*c*. 493–*c*. 433 B.C.). According to Lucian, he cast himself into the crater of ETNA, that people might believe he was returned to the gods; but Etna threw out his sandal and destroyed the illusion (HORACE, *Ars Poetica*, 404).

Emperor (Lat. *Imperator*). This title, borne by certain monarchs as a mark of the highest regal dignity, derives from its use by the rulers of the Roman Empire. In the days of the Roman Republic, the title *imperator* was given to magistrates vested with *imperium*, the supreme administrative power, which included military command. It came to be applied as a title of honour to military commanders after a victory until the celebration of their triumph. Julius Cæsar was the first to use the title permanently and it was adopted by Octavian as a *prænomen* (*i.e. imperator Cæsar*, not *Cæsar imperator*). In due course it became the monarchical title of the head of the Empire. Constantine Palæologus, the last of the emperors, fell in the siege of Constantinople in 1453.

CHARLEMAGNE was crowned Roman emperor in 800 but the first known use of the title HOLY ROMAN EMPIRE occurs in 1254. The so-called Holy Roman Emperors, whose office was abandoned by Francis II in 1806, were at best rulers of Germany, Burgundy and northern Italy, and from 1556 the HABSBURG emperors were but virtual presidents of a loose Germanic federation.

In 1804 the Holy Roman Emperor Francis II assumed the hereditary title of Emperor of Austria (as Francis I), a title last borne by Charles I (1916–1918).

In 1804 NAPOLEON crowned himself Emperor of the French. The First Empire lasted until 1815. NAPOLEON III ruled the Second Empire from 1852 until 1870.

Peter the Great was proclaimed "Emperor of All Russia" in 1721. The Russian Empire lasted until 1917.

In 1871 King William I of Prussia was proclaimed Emperor of Germany at Versailles. William II, the last German Emperor, abdicated in 1918.

King Victor Emmanuel III of Italy was declared Emperor of Abyssinia in 1936, when Italian forces invaded the country and the rightful Emperor, Haile Selassie I, went into exile until his return to his capital in 1941. Italy became a Republic in 1946.

Queen Victoria assumed the title of Empress of India in 1876. The title was relinquished by British sovereigns in 1947.

Emperors ruled Brazil from 1822 to 1889; Mexico from 1822 to 1823 and from 1864 to 1867 (the ill-fated Maximilian of Austria); Haiti from 1804 to 1806. The title has also been given to the Mogul of India, and to the sovereigns of China, Japan, Ethiopia, etc.

Emperor, not for myself, but for my people. The maxim of the Roman Emperor Hadrian (117–138).

Empire City, The. New York, the great commercial city of the United States, from its situation in the **Empire State,** the name given to New York State on account of its wealth and importance. Hence the name of the famous and tallest New York skyscraper.

Empire Day. Instituted by the Earl of Meath in 1902, after the end of the South African War, as a way to encourage schoolchildren to be aware of their duties and responsibilities as citizens of the British Empire. The day set aside was 24 May, Queen Victoria's birthday. In 1916 it was given official recognition in the United Kingdom, and was renamed Commonwealth Day in December 1958.

Empire Loyalist. See UNITED EMPIRE LOYALISTS.

Empire Style. The style of furniture, decoration, costume, etc., that came into vogue in Napoleonic France lasting from about 1800 until 1820. The Empire style followed the pseudo-classical fervour of the Revolution, but was much influenced by NAPOLEON's wish to emulate the splendour of Imperial Rome, hence the imitation of Roman architecture. The Egyptian campaign led to the introduction of Egyptian embellishments, notably the SPHINX. There was much use of bronze appliqué ornament, mirrors, and brocade, and court costume was rich and ornate. Women's fashions changed frequently, but the high-waisted Grecian style remained a constant motif.

Empirics. A school of medicine founded by Serapion of Alexandria (c. 200–150 B.C.) who made observation and experiment the first guide to treatment (Gr. *empeiros*, experienced). The statements of established authorities were placed second. Hence any medical QUACK or pretender is called an empiric.

Empyrean (em pi rē' àn). According to Ptolemy, there are five heavens, the last of which is pure elemental fire and the seat of deity; this fifth heaven is called the empyrean (Gr. *empuros*, fiery); hence in Christian angelology, the abode of God and the angels. See HEAVEN.

Empyromancy. An ancient method of DIVINATION by observing the behaviour of certain objects when placed on a sacrificial fire. Eggs, flour and incense were used for this purpose as well as a shoulderblade.

En avant (on ă von) (Fr.). Forward.

En bloc (on blok) (Fr.). The whole lot together. *Cp.* EN MASSE.

En famille (on fa mē) (Fr.). In the privacy of one's own home.

En grande toilette; en grande tenue (on grond twa let; on grond tĕ nŭ) (Fr.). In full dress; dressed for a great occasion.

En masse (on măs) (Fr.). The whole lot, just as it stands; the whole.

En papillotes (on papē yot) (Fr.). in a state of undress; literally, in curl-papers. Cutlets with frills on them are *en papillote*.

En passant (on păs' on) (Fr.). By the way. A remark made *en passant* is one dropped in, almost an aside.

En pension (on pon' si on) (Fr.). Pension is payment for board and lodging; hence, a boarding-house. "To live *en pension*" is to live at a boarding-house or hotel, etc., for a charge that includes board and lodging.

En rapport (on ra pôr) (Fr.). In harmony with; in agreement.

En route (on root) (Fr.). On the way; on the road or journey.

Enceladus (en sel' à dùs). The most powerful of the hundred-armed giants, sons of URANUS and GE, who conspired against ZEUS. The king of gods and men cast him down at Phlegra, in Macedonia, and threw Mount ETNA over him. The poets say that the flames of the volcano arise from the breath of this giant.

Encomium (en kō' mi ùm) (Gr. *komos*, revel). In ancient Greece, a eulogy or panegyric in honour of a victor in the games; hence, praise, eulogy, especially of a formal nature. The encomium was sung in the procession which escorted the victor home.

Encore (on kôr). A good example of "ENGLISH FRENCH". Our use of this word is not as in France, where they say *bis* (twice) if they wish a thing to be repeated. *Encore une tasse* is "another cup", *encore une fois*, "once again".

Encratites (en krăt' i tēz). In the early Church, and especially among the GNOSTICS, those ascetics who condemned marriage, forbade eating flesh

or drinking wine, and rejected all the luxuries and comforts of life. The name is Greek, and signifies "the self-disciplined" or "continent".

Encyclopedia (en sî klō pē' di à) or **Encyclopædia**. A book or books giving information on all branches of knowledge or on a particular subject, usually arranged alphabetically. The Greek word was used to denote a complete system of learning. The earliest encyclopedia extant is Pliny's *Naturalis historia* in 37 books (1st century A.D.). In *c.* 1360 Bartholomew de Glanville, an English Franciscan friar, wrote *De proprietatibus rerum*, in 19 books, starting with an article on God and ending with a list of birds' eggs, and the first encyclopedia in English was that of John Harris (*c.* 1667–1719) who in 1704 produced a *Lexicon technicum or an Universal English Dictionary of Arts and Sciences*. This was soon overshadowed by the work of Ephraim Chambers (d. 1740), who, in 1728, brought out his *Cyclopædia, or an Universal Dictionary of Art and Sciences, etc.*, in two volumes, the forerunner of *Chambers's Encyclopædia*. The *Encyclopædia Britannica*, edited by C. Macfarquhar, was first published at Edinburgh in three volumes (1768–1771). It was later taken over by Constable, then by A. and C. Black, and in 1920 it passed into American hands. The 11th edition (1908) in 29 volumes was issued by the Cambridge University Press, by arrangement. It is now published "with the editorial advice of the faculties of the University of Chicago and a committee of members of Oxford, Cambridge, and London Universities".

The French *Encyclopédie* developed from a translation of Chambers's *Cyclopædia*. The new work appeared at Paris between 1751 and 1772 in 28 volumes (including 11 volumes of plates) under the editorship of Diderot, assisted by d'Alembert, and many of the leading men of letters contributed to it. The **Encyclopedists** were exponents of sceptical, deistic and heretical opinions and their attacks on the Church and despotic government served the cause of revolution. Thus the name Encyclopedist designated a certain form of philosophy and gave their work conspicuous political importance resulting in censorship and attempts at suppression.

The above are but examples of the growth of a multitude of such reference books now too numerous to mention.

End. A rope's end. A short length of rope used for beating someone, a once convenient and common disciplinary weapon in a ship.

At a loose end. *See* LOOSE.

At my wits' end. In a quandary how to proceed further; not knowing what further to do; nonplussed.

East End. *See under* EAST.

End for end. In reverse position, as to turn a rope or plank so that each end occupies the opposite to its former position.

End it or mend it. Said when an *impasse* or a crisis is reached, when things are intolerable and something simply must be done.

He is no end of a fellow. A capital chap; a most agreeable companion.

Odds and ends. Fragments, remnants; bits and pieces of trifling value.

On end. Erect; also, in succession, without a break, as, "He'll go on talking for days on end."

One's latter end. The close of one's life.

> So the Lord blessed the latter end of Job more than his beginning.
>
> *Job* xlii, 12.

The end justifies the means. A false doctrine, frequently condemned by various Popes, which teaches that evil means may be employed to produce a good result.

The End of the World. According to rabbinical legend, the world was to last six thousand years. The reasons assigned are (1) because the name *Yahweh* contains six letters; (2) because the Hebrew letter *m* occurs six times in the book of *Genesis*; (3) because the patriarch Enoch, who was taken to heaven without dying, was the sixth generation from ADAM (Seth, Enos, Cainan, Mahalaleel, Jared, Enoch); (4) because God created the world in six days; (5) because six contains three binaries—the first 2,000 years were for the law of na-

ture, the next 2,000 the written law, and the last 2,000 the law of grace. *See* LAST TRUMP *under* TRUMP.

The ends of the earth. The remotest parts of the earth, the regions farthest from civilization.

> All the ends of the earth have seen the salvation of our God.
>
> *Ps.* xcviii, 3.

To begin at the wrong end. To take things in the wrong order; to attempt to do something without any method.

To burn the candle at both ends. *See under* BURN.

To come to the end of one's tether. *See* TETHER.

To go off the deep end. To get unnecessarily excited or angry.

To have something at one's fingers' ends. *See under* FINGER.

To make ends, or **both ends meet.** To make one's income cover expenses; to manage to live without getting into debt.

To put an end to. To terminate, or cause to terminate.

To the bitter end. *See* BITTER.

End-irons. Two movable iron cheeks or plates, formerly used in cooking-stoves to enlarge or contract the grate at pleasure. The term explains itself but must not be mistaken for "dogs".

End papers. The two leaves at the front and back of a book, one of which is pasted down on to the inside of the cover and the other is a fly-leaf. They were formerly usually coloured or marbled. Sometimes maps, plans, etc., are printed on them.

End-stopped. A term in prosody denoting that the sense of the line to which it is applied is completed with that line and does not run over to the next; the opposite of *enjambement*. In the following lines the first is an example of enjambement, and the second is end-stopped.

> Awake, my St. John, leave all meaner things
> To low ambition, and the pride of Kings.
>
> POPE: *Essay on Man*, I, i.

Endor, Witch of. *See under* WITCH.

Endymion (en dim' i on). In Greek mythology, the shepherd son of Aethlius, loved by SELENE, the Moon goddess who bore him fifty daughters. Another story is that ZEUS gave him eternal life and youth by allowing him to sleep perpetually on Mount Latmus and Selene came down nightly to embrace him.

Enemy. How goes the enemy? or **What says the enemy?** What o'clock is it? Time is the enemy of man, especially of those who are behindhand.

Enfant terrible (on fon te rēbl) (Fr.). Literally, a terrible child. An embarrassing person, one who says or does awkward things at embarrassing times; one who stirs up trouble for his cause or party by his impetuousness.

England. In O.E. it is *Engla land*, meaning the land of the Angles, a Germanic people who began to invade Britain in the late 5th century from the Baltic coastlands, Angeln at the south of the Danish peninsula being their chief centre. Their kingdoms were those of the East and Middle Angles, Mercia, and Northumbria.

England's Darling. A name given to Hereward the Wake (*fl.* 1070), the patriot who held the Isle of Ely against WILLIAM THE CONQUEROR and eventually escaped with a few followers when the isle was beset by William's forces.

England expects that every man will do his duty. Nelson's famous signal to his fleet before the battle of Trafalgar. The intended signal was "England confides, etc.", but the signal officer obtained permission to substitute "expects" in order to save seven hoists, as the word "confides" was not in the signal book.

Little Englander. A name applied to those RADICAL and LIBERAL politicians and propagandists of Victorian England who, influenced by the doctrines of LAISSER-FAIRE and the MANCHESTER SCHOOL, or from more positive and idealistic reasons, opposed IMPERIALISM and advocated retrenchment in the colonial field. Gladstone, Granville, Cobden, and Bright are examples.

English. The language of the people of ENGLAND. It is derived from the West Germanic branch of the Germanic or Teutonic division of the Indo-European or Aryan family of languages. Historically it is divided into three main stages

of development—*Old English*, or *Anglo-Saxon*, from the invasion to *c.* 1100; *Middle English* from *c.* 1100 to *c.* 1500; *Modern*, or *New English*, from *c.* 1500. It is the most widely used language in the world.

Basic English. *See* BASIC.

Borough English. *See under* BOROUGH.

King's or **Queen's English.** English as it should be spoken. The term occurs in SHAKESPEARE's *Merry Wives of Windsor* (I, iv), but it is older and was evidently common.

Plain English. Plain, unmistakable speech or writing. To tell a person *in plain English* what you think of him is to give your very candid opinion without any beating about the bush.

English French. A kind of perversity seems to pervade many of the words which we have borrowed from the French. Thus our *curate* is the Fr. *vicaire*, and our *vicar* the Fr. *curé*. Also note *epergne* (Fr. *surtout*); *surtout* (Fr. *pardessus*). *Screw* (Fr. *vis*), whereas the Fr. *écrou* we call a *nut*; and our vice is the Fr. *étau*. Some still say *à l'outrance* (Fr. *à outrance*). We say *double entendre*, the French *à double entente*. *See* ENCORE.

Englishman. The national nickname of an Englishman is JOHN BULL. The old nickname for him in France was GODDAM.

An Englishman's home, or **house is his castle.** Because so long as a man shuts himself up in his own house, no bailiff can break through the door to arrest him or seize his goods. It is generally used to mean that an Englishman is inviolable in his own home.

Nowadays, it is less of a "castle" than it was, various public authorities having right of entry under certain conditions; the premises may even be taken over and destroyed, consequent upon a compulsory purchase order.

Englishry. The differentiation between English and Normans or Anglo-Normans and Welsh. WILLIAM THE CONQUEROR introduced the *murdrum*, or fine for murder, to protect his fellow Normans. The fine was payable by the HUNDRED if the murderer could not be found. If it could be proved Englishry, *ie*, that the corpse was English, the Hundred was exempt.

Enid. The daughter and only child of Yniol, and wife of Prince GERAINT, one of the Knights of the ROUND TABLE. Ladies called her "Enid the Fair", but the people named her "Enid the Good". Her story is told in Tennyson's *Geraint and Enid (Idylls of the King).*

Enjambement. *See* END-STOPPED.

Enlightenment, The. The name given to the general intellectual and literary trend in Europe between *c*. 1690 and *c*. 1790. In England it is more commonly known as the AGE OF REASON. It was characterized by steadily increasing philosophical and radical criticisms of the existing order. In the political sphere the writings of Locke, Montesquieu, Voltaire, Diderot and Rousseau are typical. It led to the growth of Deism (*see* THEIST), MATERIALISM and humanitarianism, as well as ideas of popular sovereignty and somewhat facile ideas of progress. The better ENLIGHTENED DESPOT was influenced by these tendencies.

Enniskillens. *See* INNISKILLINGS.

Ennius. "The father of Roman poetry" (239–169 B.C.). Noted for his dramas and epic poetry.

Ensa Concerts. In World War II, concerts provided for the British fighting forces on active service by the Entertainments National Service Association (E.N.S.A.). Many famous figures in the entertainment and musical world took part, greatly helping to boost morale.

Entail. An estate in which the rights of the owner are *cut down* (Fr. *tailler*, to cut) by his being deprived of the right of the power of alienating them at pleasure and so depriving the rights of his issue; also the settlement of an estate in such a manner. *Tail males* or *tail females* were entails where the property passed exclusively to the males or females respectively.

Entente Cordiale (on tont' kôr di al') (Fr.) A cordial understanding between nations; not amounting to an alliance but something more than a *rapprochement*. The term is particularly applied to the Anglo-French Entente of 1904,

for which King Edward VII's visit to Paris in 1903 was a valuable preliminary.

Enter. To enter the lists. Figuratively, to enter any field of rivalry or controversy; an allusion to the arrival of a challenger in the tilting-ground in mediæval TOURNAMENTS.

Entertain. To entertain an angel unawares. *See under* ANGEL.

Enthusiast (Gr. *en theos*). Literally, one who is possessed or inspired by a god. "Inspired" is very similar, being the Lat. *in spirare*, to breathe in (the godlike essence). In the 17th and 18th centuries the word *enthusiasm* was applied disparagingly to emotional religion.

Entire. As the name of a beer, the term is now rarely used, but is still occasionally seen on public-house signs and advertisements. In the early 18th century the chief malt liquors were ALE, beer, and twopenny (a superior kind of ale sold at 2d. a pint). The constant demand for mixtures induced the brewers to combine the qualities of the three in a liquor called *entire* (from its being drawn from one cask). Being much drunk by porters it also came to be called *porter*.

Entrée (on' trä) (Fr.). **To have entrée.** To have the right or privilege of entry or admission.

Entre nous (on trė noo') (Fr.). Between you and me; in confidence.

Eolithic Age, The. The name given to the earliest part of the STONE AGE (Gr. *eos*, dawn; *lithos*, a stone). It is characterized by the rudest stone implements.

Eolus. *See* ÆOLUS.

Eon. *See* ÆON.

Epact (Gr. *epagein*, to intercalate). The excess of the solar over the lunar year, the former consisting of 365 days, and the latter of 354, or eleven days less. The epact of any year is the number of days from the last new moon of the old year to the first of the following January, and used in determining the date of EASTER. (See *Table of Movable Feasts* at the beginning of the BOOK OF COMMON PRAYER).

Epaulette (ep' aw let). A shoulder ornament worn by officers of the Royal Navy above the rank of sub-lieutenant, when in full dress. Epaulettes ceased to be worn in the army in 1855. Officers of the U.S. Navy above the rank of ensign wear epaulettes, but since 1872, in the army, they are worn by generals only.

Ephebi (e fē' bi) (Gr.). Youths who had reached the age of puberty. At Athens it denoted a youth who had reached the age of eighteen, and who had to spend a year in military training and a second year on garrison duty. When fully trained, he was given his shield and spear. He also attended public functions and was immune from taxation.

The system was adopted throughout the Greek world and, during the Roman period, athletic, cultural and religious studies took the place of military training, and admission for ephebi was by selection.

Ephesian. A jolly companion; a roysterer. The origin of the term is unknown.

Diana of the Ephesians. *See under* DIANA.

Ephialtes. A giant, son of POSEIDON and brother of Otus. When nine years old, they were nine fathoms tall and nine cubits broad. They were slain by APOLLO.

Ephors. In Sparta, the five magistrates annually elected from the ruling caste. They exercised control over the king, the *Gerousia* (Council of Elders) and the *Apella* (Assembly).

Epic Poetry. Narrative poetry of an elevated and dignified style dealing with heroic and historical events, real or fictitious and mythical. The ILIAD and ODYSSEY, Virgil's ÆNEID and Milton's *Paradise Lost* are outstanding examples.

Father of Epic Poetry. HOMER.

Epicurus (ep i kū' rus). The Greek philosopher (*c.* 341–*c.* 270 B.C.) who founded the *Epicurean School* and taught that "pleasure" was the natural aim and highest good, but a pleasure which consisted of right living which led to tranquillity of mind and body. The idea that "good living" and luxury were the pleasures to be sought was a corruption of his teaching.

Hence, *epicure*, one devoted to the pleasures of the table, but fastidious in his choice; *epicurean*, pertaining to good eating and drinking.

See DUM VIVIMUS VIVAMUS.

Epigoni. *See* THE SEVEN AGAINST THEBES *under* THEBES.

Epigram. A short piece of verse ending in a witty or ingenious thought, or WITH A STING IN ITS TAIL (*under* TAIL); or any short, pointed or witty saying. The original Greek verse epigrams were graceful lines for inscription on tombstones, etc.

> You beat your pate, and fancy wit will come:
> Knock as you please, there's nobody at home.
> ALEXANDER POPE.

> The Devil having nothing else to do
> Went off to tempt My Lady Poltargrue.
> My Lady, tempted by a private whim,
> To his extreme annoyance, tempted him.
> HILAIRE BELLOC.

Epimenides (e pi men' i dēz). A religious teacher and wonder worker of Crete (6th or 7th century B.C.). According to Pliny (*Natural History*), he fell asleep in a cave when a boy, and did not wake for 57 years. He is supposed to have lived for 299 years. *Cp.* RIP VAN WINKLE *under* WINKLE.

Epiphany (e pif' à ni) (Gr. *epiphaneia*, an appearance, manifestation). The manifestation of Christ to the Gentiles, *i.e.* to the Wise Men from East. 6 January is the feast of the Epiphany in commemoration of this. The vigil of the Epiphany (5 January) was the time for choosing the BEAN-KING. *See* TWELFTH NIGHT *under* TWELVE.

Episcopacy (Gr. *episkopos*, overseer, Late Lat. *episcopus*, bishop). Church government by BISHOPS. Hence an *episcopalian church* is a church governed by bishops and its supporters are designated *episcopalians*. Episcopacy in the CHURCH OF ENGLAND was contested early on by Calvinists, who advocated a PRESBYTERIAN system, and was abolished by PARLIAMENT in 1643, but restored with the return of the Stuarts. *See* ROOT AND BRANCH.

Episcopal Signatures. It is the custom of BISHOPS of the CHURCH OF ENGLAND to sign themselves with their Christian name and name of their SEE. In some of the older dioceses the Latin form is used, sometimes abbreviated:

Cantuar:	Canterbury.	*Gloucestr:*	Gloucester
Ebor:	York.	*Norvic:*	Norwich
Carliol:	Carlisle.	*Oxon:*	Oxford
Cestr:	Chester.	*Petriburg:*	Peterborough
Cicestr:	Chichester.	*Roffen:*	Rochester
Dunelm:	Durham.	*Sarum:*	Salisbury

Exon: Exeter. *Winton:* Winchester

Epistle (e pis' ĕl). This word, related in origin to APOSTLE, comes from a Greek verb meaning "to send to". The word is particularly applied to the NEW TESTAMENT letters, from which extracts are read at the Communion service. There are thirteen from St. PAUL, one from St. JAMES, two from St. PETER, three from St. JOHN, and one from St. JUDE, and the *Epistle to the Hebrews*, of unknown authorship, written to the various churches with which they were concerned.

Epitaph (ep' i taf). Strictly, an inscription on a tomb, but usually it refers to any brief verses or apt commemoration of the departed.

> Here a pretty baby lies
> Sung asleep with lullabies;
> Pray be silent, and not stir
> Th' easy earth that covers her.
>
> ROBERT HERRICK, *Upon a child*.

Epithalamium (e pi thà lā' mi um). In ancient Greece, a song sung by youths and maidens outside the bridal chamber. The poets developed it as a special literary form, notably SAPPHO, ANACREON, Stesichorus and Pindar. Spenser's *Epithalamion* (1595) is the most celebrated English poem of this kind. *Cp.* PROTHALAMION.

Epoch (ē' pok) (Gr. a stop or pause). A definite point in time. The succession of events in the period following, and reckoned from an epoch, is called an ERA. In general usage *epoch* and *era* are treated as interchangeable terms.

Epode (Gr. *epodos*; an aftersong). A Greek ode, the part after the strophe and antistrophe; in the epode the chorus returned to their places and remained stationary. Also a form of lyric poetry invented by Archilochus in which a longer verse is followed by a shorter one. The *Epodes* of HORACE are the best known examples.

Eppur si muove (e poor sē mwô' vē) (Ital. and yet it [the earth] does move). The phrase said to have been uttered by Galileo immediately after his recantation of belief in the COPERNICAN SYSTEM. He appeared before the INQUISITION at ROME in 1633, and record of the saying (certainly APOCRYPHAL), first occurs in 1761.

Epsom Races. Horse races instituted in the reign of James I and held on Epsom Downs (continuously from 1730, except during World Wars I and II). The main meeting is held in May or June. The second day (Wednesday) is DERBY DAY, and on the fourth the OAKS is run.

Epsom Salts. Magnesium sulphate; used as a purgative, etc., and so called because it was originally obtained by the evaporation of the water of a mineral spring at Epsom in Surrey. According to Fuller's *Worthies*, the spring was discovered by a farmer in 1618, who noticed that, in spite of the drought, his cows refused to drink water from the spring. On analysis, it was found to contain the bitter purgative, sulphate of magnesia.

Equality. The sign of equality in mathematics, two parallel lines (=), was invented by Robert Recorde, who died in 1558. As he said, nothing is more equal than parallel lines.

Equation of Time. The difference between mean time (as on a perfect clock) and apparent time (as indicated by a sundial). The greatest difference is at the beginning of November, when the sun is somewhat more than sixteen minutes slow. There are days in December, April, June, and September when the sun and the clocks agree.

Era. A series of years beginning from some EPOCH or starting-point as:

		B.C.
The Era of	the Chinese	2697
,,	Abraham (1 Oct.)	2016
,,	the Greek Olympiads	776
,,	the Foundation of Rome	753
,,	Nabonassar (Babylon)	747
,,	Alexander the Great	324
,,	the Selucidæ	312
,,	the Maccabees	166
,,	Tyre (19 Oct.)	125
,,	Julian	45
,,	Actium (1 Jan.)	30
,,	Augustus (27 June)	27
		A.D.
,,	Diocletian (29 Aug.)	284
,,	Armenia (9 July)	552
,,	the Hegira (16 July)	622
,,	Yezdegird (Persian) (16 June)	632
,,	American Independence (4 July)	1776
,,	the French Republic (22 Sept.)	1792

The Christian Era begins theoretically from the birth of Christ, though the actual date of the Nativity is uncertain and was probably B.C. 6 or 7. The EPOCH of the Christian Era was fixed by the calculations of Dionysius Exiguus in 527 A.D. and was inexact.

Erastianism. A term derived from Thomas Erastus (1524–1583), denoting the supremacy of the State in ecclesiastical affairs. *Erastus* (Gr. lovely, or beloved) was the name adopted by Thomas Lieber (Liebler, or Luber), professor of medicine at Heidelberg and at Basel, where he later held the chair of ethics. He was a follower of Zwingli, noted for his opposition to Calvinistic claims, and held that punishment for sin was the prerogative of the civil authority.

Erato. One of the nine MUSES; the Muse of erotic poetry, usually represented with a lyre.

Erebus. In Greek mythology, the son of Chaos and brother of Night; hence darkness personified. His name was given to the gloomy underground cavern through which the Shades had to walk in their passage to HADES.

Eretrian. The Eretrian Bull. Menedemus of Eretria (*c.* 319–*c.* 265 B.C.) was so called from his gravity. He was a follower of the MEGARIAN SCHOOL of philosophy and founder of the Eretrian School.

Erewhon (ēr' won, âr' e won). An ANAGRAM of "Nowhere", the name of the ideal commonwealth in Samuel Butler's philosophical novel of the same name (1872). *Cp.* IDEAL COMMONWEALTHS *under* COMMONWEALTH.

Erichthonius. Fathered by VULCAN and very deformed. ATHENE put him in a box and gave its charge to the daughters of Cecrops with strict orders not to open it but they did so and out of fright at what they saw jumped off the Acropolis to their death. He became King of ATHENS and established the worship of ATHENE. He was set up as the constellation *Auriga* (Lat. charioteer). *See* CHARIOT.

Erigena. Johannes Scotus, or John the Scot (*c.* 815–*c.* 877), philosopher and theologian. The name *Erigena* is taken to mean "born in Erin" (Ireland) but

nothing is known of his early life.

Erigone. *See* ICARIUS.

Erin. An ancient name for Ireland.

Erin go bragh. Ireland for ever. *See* MAVOURNIN.

Erinyes (e rin' yēz). In Greek mythology, avengers of wrong, the Latin FURIES. *See* EUMENIDES.

Erk. Originally "airk", an R.A.F. nickname of World War I given to aircraftmen and mechanics. It later became "erk" and is applied to beginners, juniors, and underlings generally.

Erlking. In German legend, a malevolent GOBLIN who haunts forests and lures people, especially children, to destruction. Goethe has a poem on him, set to music by Schubert.

Ermine (ēr' min). Another name for the stoat (*Putorius erminea*), but more usually used for its fur which is brown in summer and white in winter. It is one of the furs used in HERALDRY and is represented by a white field flecked with black ermine tails. Black tails on a white field is now called *ermines*. Other variants are *erminois*, a gold field with black tails; *erminites*, the same as *ermine* but with a red hair on either side of each black tail.

Ermine Street. The name of this essentially Roman road from LONDON to Lincoln, through Braughing and Huntingdon, is of later origin. It derives from *Earningastræt* (the road to Earn's people), a group of Anglo-Saxons who settled near part of its route through Cambridgeshire.

Eros. The Greek god of love, usually personified as a young boy with bow and arrows; the equivalent of the Roman CUPID. It is also the popular name for the winged archer surmounting the memorial fountain to the 7th Earl of Shaftesbury, in the centre of Piccadilly Circus, London, which is actually a symbol of Christian charity. It is the work of Sir Alfred Gilbert (1854–1934) and was unveiled in 1893.

Erra-Pater. The supposititious author of an ALMANAC published about 1535 as *The Pronostycacion for ever of Erra Pater: a Jewe born in Jewery, a Doctour in Astronomye and Physycke*. It is a collection of astrological tables, rules of health, etc., and is arranged for use in any year.

Erse. The native language of the HIGHLANDS and Western Isles of SCOTLAND. The word is a variant of Irish, the Scots coming originally from IRELAND. It was formerly applied by the Lowlanders to the CELTIC tongue of the Highlanders. It is now usually called GAELIC and the term Erse is more usually applied to the native language of Ireland.

Erudite. Most erudite of the Romans. Marcus Terentius Varro (116–27 B.C.), a man of vast and varied erudition in almost every department of literature, the greatest of Roman scholars.

Erythynus (e rith′ i nùs). **Have no doings with the Erythynus,** *i.e.* "don't trust a braggart". The Erythynus is mentioned by Pliny (ix, 77) as a red fish with a white belly, and PYTHAGORAS used it as a symbol of a BRAGGADOCIO, who fable says is white-livered.

Escorial, or **Escurial.** The royal palace, MAUSOLEUM, and monastery built by Philip II of Spain some 27 miles northwest of Madrid.

Escuage. *See* SCUTAGE.

Esculapius. *See* ÆSCULAPIUS.

Escutcheon. In HERALDRY, the shield on which armorial bearings are depicted. The word is from O.Fr. *escuchon* from Lat. *scutum* (Late Lat. *scutionem*), a shield.

Escutcheon of Pretence. In heraldry, the small shield of a wife, either heiress or co-heiress, placed in the centre of her husband's shield.

To blot one's escutcheon. To incur disgrace or mar one's reputation. *Cp.* TO BLOT ONE'S COPYBOOK *under* COPYBOOK.

Esoteric (Gr.) Secret, only for the initiated. Those within, as opposed to *exoteric*, those without. The term originated with PYTHAGORAS, who stood behind a curtain when he gave his lectures. Those who were allowed to attend lectures, but not to see his face, he called his *exoteric disciples*; but those who were allowed to enter the veil, his *esoteric*.

ARISTOTLE adopted the same terms; those who attended his evening lectures, which were of a popular character, he called his *exoterics*; and those who attended his more abstruse morning lectures, his *esoterics*.

Esoteric Buddhism. *See* THEOSOPHY.

Esperanto. A constructed international language first published in 1887 by L. L. Zamenhof which soon superseded VOLAPÜK. It means "the hopeful one", the pseudonym of its inventor.

Esprit (es′ prē) (Fr. spirit, mind, wit).

Esprit de corps (es′ prē de kôr) (Fr.). The spirit of pride in the organization with which you are associated, and regard for its traditions and associations, as a naval man speaks of "pride of ship".

Esprit d'escalier (es′ prē des kăl yā) (Fr., staircase wit). The effective rejoinder which comes too late, the witty retort which comes to one after the moment has passed. The correct French is *l'esprit de l'escalier*, the afterthought which occurs when going downstairs from the salon to the street door.

Beaux Esprits. *See* BEAUX.

Bel Esprit. *See* BEL.

Esquire. (O.Fr. *esquier* from Lat. *scutarius*, shield-bearer). One who carried the shield of a KNIGHT and who ranked immediately below him.

The term is now mainly used in correspondence (abbreviated to "Esq."), as an alternative to "Mr."

Essays. Bacon's essays were the first in English to bear this name.

Essenes. A Jewish fraternity originating about the 2nd century B.C. who lived a monastic kind of life and who rejected animal sacrifices. They were distinguished for their piety and virtue and were strict observers of the SABBATH. They were given to acts of charity and maintained themselves by manual labour (chiefly agriculture), lived in fellowship, and held their goods in common. Their way of life was akin to that of Jesus and His disciples. *See* DEAD SEA SCROLLS; HASIDEANS.

Essex Lions. Calves, for which the county is famous.

Valiant as an Essex lion. Said ironically of a timid person.

Establishment, The (O.Fr. *establissement*). A term long used to denote in particular the established CHURCH OF ENGLAND, but now a popular designation for the influential hierarchy or inner circle in any particular sphere of the community, or of the community in general. It has a somewhat derogatory significance associated with reaction, privilege, and lack of imagination.

Estate (O.Fr. *estat*; Lat. *status* from *stare*, to stand).

Estates General (*États généraux*. Fr.). The French assembly first summoned in 1302 as a consultative body consisting of clergy, nobility and THE THIRD ESTATE. It did not meet again after 1614 until 1789 when the Revolution began.

Estates of the Realm. Those classes, or orders, which have a recognized share or part in the body politic. In Britain the three estates are the Lords Spiritual, the Lords Temporal, and the Commons, although the term is now anachronistic.

> The King and the three estates of the realm assembled in parliament.
> *Collect for 5 Nov.*

The Third Estate. The Commons. Historically the term usually refers to the third chamber (*Tiers État*) of the French ESTATES GENERAL at the time of the Revolution.

The Fourth Estate. The Press. Burke, referring to the Reporters' Gallery in the HOUSE OF COMMONS, is reputed to have said, "Yonder sits the Fourth Estate, more important than them all", but it does not appear in his published works. In former days the phrase has also been applied to the working classes.

The Fifth Estate. The British Broadcasting Corporation has jocularly been so called.

Estotiland. An imaginary tract of land near the Arctic Circle in North America, said to have been discovered by John Scalve, a Pole.

Estrich. The old name for ostrich.

Eternal, The. God.

The Eternal City. ROME. The epithet occurs in Ovid, Tibullus, etc., and in many official documents of the Empire. It has also been applied to the "City of God".

The eternal fitness of things. The congruity between an action and the agent.

The Eternal Tables. In Mohammedan legend, a white PEARL extending from east to west, and from HEAVEN to earth,

on which God has recorded every event, past, present, and to come.

The Eternal Triangle. The oft-recurring comic or tragic situation of the amorous involvement of one of a married couple with another member of the opposite sex.

Etesian Wind (e tē' zhản). A Mediterranean wind which rises annually (Gr. *etos*, a year) about the DOG-DAYS, and blows mainly from the north for about 40 days. It is gentle and mild.

Ethon. The EAGLE or vulture that gnawed the liver of PROMETHEUS.

Etna, or **Ætna** (et' nả). The highest active volcano in Europe. It stands over the Straits of Messina, *c*. 10,700 ft. high, covering an area of 460 sq. miles. In Sicily, Etna is known as Monte Gibello and many towns and villages live under its continual threat. The last serious eruption was in 1928. VIRGIL (*Æneid* III, 578, etc.) ascribes its eruption to the restlessness of ENCELADUS, the most powerful of all the giants who plotted against JUPITER and who lies buried under the mountain. According to the Greek and Latin poets it is the site of the smithy of CYCLOPS and the forges of VULCAN.

Eton Crop. A short boyish hairstyle, fairly popular among women in the 1920s, called after the famous school for boys at Eton.

Etrenne. *See* STRENIA.

Ettrick Shepherd. The name given to James Hogg (1770–1835), the Scottish poet who was born at Ettrick, Selkirkshire, the son of a shepherd, and, for a time, a shepherd himself.

Etzel. In German heroic legend, Attila, King of the Huns (*d*. 453).

Eucharist (ū' kả rist) (Gr. *eucharistos*, grateful). An ancient name for the *Lord's Supper*, *Holy Communion*, or MASS; also the consecrated *Elements* in the Communion. Literally, a thank-offering. Our Lord gave thanks before giving the bread and wine to His disciples at the LAST SUPPER. The Church offers the Eucharist as a service of praise and thanksgiving. *See* IMPANATION.

Euchre (ū' kėr). A word of doubtful etymology and the name of the most popular card game in the United States before it was replaced by auction bridge.

To be euchred is when the side that makes the trumps fails to win three tricks. Hence, figuratively, to be beaten, to be at a disadvantage. *Cp.* TO TURN THE TABLES *under* TABLE.

> "See here, men" said Bradfield, a tall powerful native chiel wi' a black beard, a grand bushman, too: "this here battle's over, your euchred ..."
>
> BOLDREWOOD: *The Ghost Camp*, ch. iii.

Euclid (ū' klid). Many generations of schoolboys knew geometry only as "Euclid", because the teaching of that branch of mathematics was based on the *Elements* of Eucleides, a Greek mathematician, who taught at Alexandria about 300 B.C.

Eucrates (ū krā' tēz). **More shifts than Eucrates.** Eucrates, the miller, was one of the archons of Athens, noted for his shifts and excuses for neglecting the duties of his office.

Euhemerus (ū hē' mĕ rŭs). A Greek philosopher of the 4th century B.C., who lived at the court of Cassander, King of Macedonia. In his *Sacred History*, he maintained the theory that the gods were formerly kings and heroes of exceptional ability, reverenced after death and finally deified. Hence the term *euhemerism* for such explanations of primitive myth and the derivation of mythology from an historical basis.

Eulalia, St. (ū' lȧ lia). Eulalon (*i.e.* the sweetly spoken) is one of the names of APOLLO, and there are two 4th-century virgin martyrs called Eulalia both presumed to have been put to death under Diocletian in 304—St. Eulalia of Barcelona and St. Eulalia of Merida, whose ashes were scattered over a field upon which a pall of snow is said to have descended.

Eulenspiegel, Till (oi len shpē' gėl). The name (owl-glass) of a 14th-century villager of Brunswick round whom gathered a large number of popular tales of mischievous pranks and often crude jests, first printed in 1515.

Eumæus (ū mē' ŭs). The slave and swineherd of ULYSSES; hence a swineherd.

Eumenides (ū men' i dēz) (Gr. the good-tempered ones). The name given by the Greeks to the FURIES, as it would have been bad policy to call them ERINYES, their right name.

Euphemism (ū' fėmizm) (Gr. *euphemimos*, speaking fair). A word or phrase substituted to soften an offensive expression. Thus—His Satanic Majesty (the DEVIL); light-fingered gentry (pickpockets or thieves); an obliquity of vision (a squint); a lady of the town (a prostitute), are common examples. *Cp.* EUMENIDES; EUXINE SEA; FOUR-LETTER MAN.

Euphuism (u' fū izm). An affected and artificial literary style, characterized by alliteration, ornate language, lengthy similes taken from myth and fable, etc., after the manner of John Lyly (1554–1606), author of *Euphues: the Anatomy of Wit* (1578) and *Euphues and his England* (1580). Euphues, the hero of Lyly's romance, is taken from the Greek, implying a man "well-endowed by nature". Euphuism was much imitated by Lyly's contemporaries, including Queen Elizabeth I, Robert Greene and Thomas Lodge.

Eureka (ū rē'kȧ) (Gr. *Heureka*, I have found it). An exclamation of delight at having made a discovery; originally that of Archimedes, the Syracusan philosopher, when he discovered how to test the purity of Hiero's crown. The tale is, that Hiero gave some GOLD to a smith to be made into a votive crown, but suspecting that the gold had been alloyed with an inferior metal, asked Archimedes to test it. The philosopher did not know how to proceed, but in getting into his bath, which was full, observed that some of the water ran over and immediately concluded that a body must displace its own bulk of water when immersed; silver is lighter than gold, therefore a pound weight of silver is bulkier than a pound weight of gold and would consequently displace more water. Thus he found that the crown was deficient in gold. Vitruvius says:

> When the idea flashed across his mind, the philosopher jumped out of the bath exclaiming, "Heureka! heureka!" and, without waiting to dress himself, ran home to try the experiment.

Eurus (ū' rŭs). The east wind; connected with Gr. *eos* and Lat. *aurora*, the dawn.

Euryalus. *See* NISUS.

Eurydice (ū rid' i si). In Greek mythology the wife of ORPHEUS, killed by a serpent when fleeing from the attentions of Aristæus. Orpheus sought her in HADES, charmed PLUTO by his music, and was promised her return on condition that he did not look back until Eurydice had reached the upper world. Nearing the end of his journey he turned his head to see if Eurydice was following and she was instantly caught back into Hades.

Euterpe (ū tĕr' pi). One of the nine MUSES, daughter of JUPITER and MNEMOSYNE, inventress of the double flute, muse of Dionysiac music, patroness of joy and pleasure, and of flute-players.

Eutychians (ū tik' i ȧnz). Followers of Eutyches (c. 380–c. 456), archimandrite of Constantinople, and author of the Eutychian controversy. He fiercely opposed the NESTORIANS and held that Christ, after the incarnation, had only one nature, the divine. He was excommunicated, reinstated, and later exiled. They were the forerunners of the MONOPHYSITES.

Euxine Sea (ūks' in). The ancient Greek name for the BLACK SEA, meaning the "hospitable". It was originally called *Axeinos*, inhospitable, on account of its stormy character and rocky shores but the name was probably changed euphemistically to propitiate the powers supposedly controlling the elements. *Cp.* ERINYES; EUMENIDES.

Evangelical. From the time of the REFORMATION, Protestant Churches were often called Evangelical Churches from their insistence that their teachings were based on the *evangel*, or Gospel (*i.e.* the BIBLE). Those known as *Evangelicals* in the CHURCH OF ENGLAND emerged at the same time as the METHODISTS and they notably emphasized the importance of scriptural authority and salvation by faith in Christ, etc. *Cp.* CLAPHAM SECT; LOW CHURCH.

Evangelists. The four Evangelists, MATTHEW, MARK, LUKE and JOHN, are usually represented in art as follows:

Matthew. With pen in hand and scroll before him, looking over his left shoulder at an ANGEL.

Mark. Seated writing, and by his side a couchant winged LION.

Luke. With a pen, in deep thought, looking over a scroll, with a cow or ox nearby chewing the cud. Also shown painting a picture, from the tradition that he painted a portrait of the Virgin.

John. As a young man of great delicacy, with an EAGLE in the background to denote sublimity.

The more ancient symbols were: for Matthew, a man's face; for Mark, a lion; for Luke, an ox; and for John, a flying eagle, in allusion to the four living creatures before the throne of God, described by St. John the Divine.

> And the first beast was like a lion, and the second beast was like a calf, and the third beast had a face as a man, and the fourth beast was like a flying eagle.
> *Rev.* iv, 7.

Another explanation is that Matthew is symbolized by a man because he begins his gospel with the humanity of Jesus, as a descendant of David; Mark by a lion, because he begins with the scenes of JOHN THE BAPTIST and Jesus in the Wilderness; Luke by a calf, because he begins with the priest sacrificing in the temple; and John by an eagle, because he soars high, and begins with the divinity of the Logos. The four symbols are those of Ezekiel's cherubim (*Ezek.* i, 10).

Irenæus says: "The lion signifies the royalty of Christ; the calf His sacerdotal office; the man's face His incarnation; and the eagle the grace of the Holy Ghost."

The name evangelist was applied in the early Church to preachers of the Gospel and is often used today to denote a revivalist preacher.

Eve (Heb. *havvah*, life, lifegiving, or possibly, snake). The first woman, formed from one of the ribs of ADAM.

> And Adam called his wife's name Eve; because she was the mother of all living.
> *Gen.* iii, 20.

Daughter of Eve. Woman. Often used with reference to feminine curiosity.

Events. At all events. In any case; be the issue what it may; *utcumque ceciderit*.

In the event. "In the event of his being elected", means in case, or provided he is elected; if the result is that he is elected.

To be wise after the event. To give advice on what should have been done to prevent some happening after it has occurred.

Ever and anon. From time to time, every now and then. *See* ANON.

Everlasting staircase. The treadmill.

Everyman. The central character in the most famous English MORALITY PLAY (*c.* 1529) drawn from a late 15th-century Dutch original. Everyman is summoned by Death and invites all his acquaintances (such as Kindred, Good Deeds, Goods, Knowledge, Beauty, Strength, etc.) to accompany him on his journey, but only Good Deeds will go with him.

Every man Jack. Everyone, without exception.

> Sir Pitt had numbered every "Man Jack" of them.
>
> THACKERAY: *Vanity Fair*, ch. viii.

Evidence (Lat. *evidentia*, clearness). Evidence, meaning testimony in proof of something, has a wide variety of classifications, such as:

Circumstantial evidence. That based on relevant fact and circumstances to the fact in issue.

Conclusive evidence. That which establishes proof beyond doubt.

Demonstrative evidence. That which can be proved without leaving a doubt.

Direct evidence. Evidence of a fact in issue; that of an eyewitness.

Documentary evidence. Evidence supplied in written documents.

External evidence. That derived from history or tradition.

Hearsay evidence. That which is heard from another but not known to be true.

Internal evidence. That derived from conformity with what is known.

King's or *Queen's evidence.* That of an accessory against his accomplices.

Material evidence. That which is essential in order to carry proof.

Moral evidence. That which accords with general experience.

Presumptive evidence. That which is highly probable.

Prima facie evidence. That which seems likely unless it can be explained away.

Self evidence. That derived from the senses: manifest and indubitable.

In evidence. Before the eyes of the people; to the front; actually present.

Evil. Evil communications corrupt good manners. The words used by St. PAUL (I *Cor*. xv, 33); but he was evidently quoting Menander (*Thais*). Similar proverbs are, "he that toucheth pitch shall be defiled therewith" (*Ecclesiasticus*, xiii, 1); "one scabbed sheep infests a whole flock"; "the rotten apple injures its neighbours".

Evil Eye. An ancient and widespread belief that certain individuals had the power to harm or even kill with a glance.

The Evil One. The DEVIL.

Evil Principle. AHRIMAN.

King's Evil. *See under* KING.

Of two evils, choose the less. *See* CHOICE.

Ewe-lamb. A single possession greatly prized; in allusion to the story told in II *Sam*. xii, 1–14.

Ex (Lat. from, out of, after, or by reason of). It forms part of many adverbial phrases, of which those in common use in English are given below. As a prefix to the name of an office or dignity it denotes a former holder of that office (e.g. *an ex-president*), or the present holder's immediate predecessor (e.g. *the ex-president*).

Ex cathedra. With authority. The POPE speaking *ex cathedra* (from the chair, or Papal throne) is said to speak with an infallible voice—as the successor and representative of St. PETER. The phrase is applied to dicta uttered by authority and ironically to self-sufficient, dogmatic assertions.

Ex hypothesi. According to what is supposed or assumed; in consequence of assumption made.

Ex libris. Literally, "from the (collection of) books". It is written in books or on bookplates followed by the name of the owner (properly in the genitive). Hence, a bookplate is often called an *ex-libris*.

Ex officio. By virtue of office. As, "the Vicar shall be *ex officio* one of the trustees."

Ex parte. Proceeding only from one of the parties; hence likely to be prejudiced. An *ex-parte* statement is a one-sided or partial statement, made by one side without modification from the other.

Ex post facto. From what is done afterwards; retrospective. An *ex post facto* law is one made to operate retrospectively.

Ex professo. Avowedly, expressly.

Ex proprio motu. Of his (or its) own accord; voluntarily.

Ex uno (disce) omnes. From one instance you may infer the rest. A general inference from a particular example; if one OAK bears acorns, all oaks will.

Exaltation. In ASTROLOGY, a planet was said to be in its "exaltation" when it was in that sign of the ZODIAC in which it was supposed to exercise its strongest influence. Thus the exaltation of VENUS is in Pisces, and her "dejection" in Virgo.

Exaltation of the Cross. A feast held in the ROMAN CATHOLIC CHURCH on 14 September (HOLY CROSS DAY), in commemoration of the restoration of the true cross to CAVALRY in 629, after the victory of Heraclius over the Persians. The CROSS had been taken by Chosroes in 614.

Excalibur (ekskăl′ i bĕr). The name of King Arthur's sword (O.Fr. *Escalibor*), called by Geoffrey Monmouth *Caliburn*, and in the MABINOGION, *Caledvwlch*. There was also a legendary Irish sword called *Caladbolg* (hard-belly), *i.e.* capable of consuming anything.

According to Sir Thomas Malory's *Le Morte d'Arthur* (1470), Arthur, being the only one who could pull the sword from a great stone in which it had been magically fixed, was acclaimed king. The name *Excalibur* does not appear until later in the book. Later still, Chapter XXV is headed "How Arthur by the mean of MERLIN got Excalibur his sword of the LADY OF THE LAKE." After his last battle, when he lay sore wounded, it was returned at his command, by Sir Bedivere to the water. (See Malory, *Le Morte d'Arthur*, Bk. XXI, ch. v, and Tennyson's *Passing of Arthur*, *Idylls of the King*. There are some obvious inconsistencies in the story.

Excelsior (Lat. higher). Aim at higher things still. It is the motto of New York State and has been popularized by Longfellow's poem of this name:

> And from the sky, serene and far,
> A voice fell, like a falling star,
> Excelsior!

Exception. The exception proves the rule. The very fact of an exception proves or tests the rule.

To take exception. To feel offended; to find fault with or to object.

Exchequer. The name derives from the chequered cloth used for calculations. It dealt with the Crown's income and expenditure and was in being by Henry I's reign (1100–1135). It was presided over by the Treasurer until 1714 (when the Treasury board took over) and was abolished in 1833.

Chancellor of the Exchequer. *See under* CHANCELLOR.

Excommunication. An ecclesiastical censure which excludes a person from the communion of the Church and sometimes accompanied by other deprivations. If clerics, they are forbidden to administer the sacraments. As a form of discipline, it no doubt derives from the Jewish practice at the time of Christ, which entailed exclusion from religious and social intercourse. It was a common punishment in mediæval times and was on occasions applied to whole nations. Pope Adrian IV used it against ROME in 1155, and Pope Innocent III employed it against ENGLAND in 1208. (*See* I *Cor.* v, 5.) The practice was also adopted by PROTESTANT Churches at the REFORMATION. The thirty-third of the *Articles of Religion* in the *Book of Common Prayer* is headed "Of Excommunicate Persons, how they are to be avoided". *Cp.* INTERDICT; BELL, BOOK AND CANDLE.

Exempli gratia (Lat.). For the sake of example: abbreviated to "e.g." when used as the introduction to an example.

Exequatur (Lat. he may perform or exercise). The letter PATENT issued to a diplomat by the government to which he is accredited authorizing him to exercise his power; a temporal sovereign's recognition of a BISHOP under papal authority, or of a PAPAL BULL, thus implying the right of rejection.

The Exeter Book. A MS. collection of Old English poetry presented (*c.* 1060) by Bishop Leofric to Exeter Cathedral, and still preserved in the cathedral library. It includes riddles, proverbs, poems, and legal documents. Among them are Cynewulf's *Christ*, *Juliana*, *Guthlac*; Widsith, *Deor's Lament*, and *The Wanderer*. Widsith is the earliest

English poet known by name. The Exeter or EXON DOMESDAY is also sometimes called the "Exeter Book".

Exhibition. The Great Exhibition. The Exhibition of 1851, largely inspired by the Prince Consort and housed in the CYSTAL PALACE, Hyde Park, LONDON.

Existentialism. A philosophical attitude owing much to the writings of Søren Kierkegaard (1813–1855) which developed in Germany after World War I and somewhat later in France and Italy. Atheistic existentialism was popularized in France by Jean-Paul Sartre (1905–1980) during World War II. Existentialists emphasize the freedom and importance of individual "existence" and personality, and show a distrust of philosophical idealism. Much of their writing is characterized by disillusionment. The term is the translation of the German *Existenz-philosophie*.

Exon. One of the four officers in command of the YEOMEN OF THE GUARD, who are exempt from regimental duties. The word is an Anglicized pronunciation of the Fr. *exempt*, for former title of a junior officer who commanded in the absence of his superiors and was exempt from ordinary duty.

Exon Domesday. A magnificent MS. transcript of the Great, or Exchequer Domesday for the counties of Wiltshire, Dorset, Somerset, Devon, and Cornwall, preserved in the muniments of Exeter Cathedral. It was published in 1816. *See* DOMESDAY BOOK.

Exorcism. The expelling of evil spirits by prayers and incantations. An ancient practice taken over by the Christian Church, after the example of Jesus Christ and the APOSTLES who healed those possessed of evil spirits. The use of this rite in the ROMAN CATHOLIC CHURCH is now carefully regulated.

Exoteric. *See* ESOTERIC.

Expectation Week. Between ASCENSION and WHIT SUNDAY, when the APOSTLES continued praying "in earnest expectation of the Comforter".

Experimental Philosophy. Science founded on experiments or data, in contradistinction to moral and mathematical sciences; also called *natural philosophy*.

Experto crede (Lat.). Believe one who has had experience in the matter. The phrase is used to add significance or weight to a warning.

Extispicy. The ancient practice of Roman soothsayers of divination by the inspection of the entrails of sacrificed animals—the same as HARUSPEX.

Extreme Unction. The last sacramental unction, the anointing with oil when a person is *in extremis*, now usually called "The Anointing of the Sick". One of the seven SACRAMENTS of the ROMAN CATHOLIC CHURCH founded on *James* v, 14, "Is there any sick among you? let him call for the elders of the church; and let them pray over him, anointing him with oil in the name of the Lord."

Eye. Apple of the Eye. *See under* APPLE.

Bull's eye. *See under* BULL.

Cat's eye. *See under* CAT.

Eagle eye. *See under* EAGLE.

Evil eye. *see under* EVIL.

Eye of a needle, It is easier for a camel to go through the. *See under* CAMEL.

Eye of the storm. An opening between the storm clouds. *Cp.* BULL'S EYE.

Eyes and no eyes. Unobservant. "Eyes have they, but they see not". *Ps.* cxv, 5.

A green eye. A jealous or envious eye; jealousy is figuratively described as "a green-eyed monster".

An eye for an eye and a tooth for a tooth. Let the punishment be equal to the crime or offence. A phrase derived from the OLD TESTAMENT.

Eye for eye, tooth for tooth, hand for hand, foot for foot.

Exod. xxi, 24.

Do you see any green in my eye? Do I look credulous and easily bamboozled? Do I look a GREENHORN?

My eye! or **Oh, my eye!** An exclamation of astonishment.

All my eye and Betty Martin. *See* ALL.

One-eyed. An expression of contempt, as, "I've never seen such a one-eyed town," *i.e.* such a hopeless and lifeless place.

One-eyed peoples. *See* ARIMASPIANS; CYCLOPS.

In my mind's eye. In my perceptive thought.

In the twinkling of an eye. Immediately, in a very short time.

In the wind's eye. Directly opposed to the wind.

A sheet in the winds eye. An early stage of intoxication. An expression of nautical origin. *See* THREE SHEETS IN THE WIND, *under* SHEET.

A sight for sore eyes. A proverbial expression used of something that is very welcome, pleasant, and unexpected.

Mind your eye. Look out, be careful; keep your eyes open to guard against mischief.

There's more in that than meets the eye. There is more to it than appears at first sight or on the surface.

To cry one's eyes out. To cry immoderately or excessively.

To give the glad eye to. To cast inviting or amorous glances at.

To have, or **keep an eye on.** To keep watch over someone or something.

To have an eye for. To have due sense of appreciation and judgment for.

To have an eye to. To keep constantly in view; to act from motives of policy.

To have an eye to the future. To bear future circumstances in mind when acting or making a decision.

To have an eye to the main chance. To keep self-advantage or profit constantly in view.

To have bags under one's eyes. Bulges under the eyes, often a sign of dissipation.

To keep one's eyes skinned. To be particularly watchful.

To look babies in one's eyes. *See* BABIES.

To make eyes at. To look amorously or lovingly at. *Cp.* TO MAKE SHEEP'S EYES.

To make sheep's eyes. *See under* SHEEP.

To make someone open his eyes. To surprise him very much, and make him stare with wonder or admiration; to bring someone to realize what is happening, to enlighten him.

To meet the eye. To arrest the sight, to come into notice.

To pipe your eye. *See under* PIPE.

To see eye to eye. To be precisely of the opinion; to agree completely or think alike.

To see with half an eye. Easily, at a mere glance.

To set, or **lay eyes on.** To have sight of.

To throw dust in his eyes. *See under* DUST.

Up to the eyes. Wholly, completely; as, *up to the eyes in work*, very fully occupied; *up to the eyes in debt*, very heavily in debt.

Eyebrow. To raise an eyebrow. A natural sign of surprise.

Eyelid. Without batting an eyelid. Without the involuntary lowering or flicker of the eyelids that betrays surprise. "Batting" is from the O.Fr. *batre*, to beat or flap.

Eye-opener. Something that provides enlightenment; also, a strong mixed drink, especially a morning pick-me-up.

Eye-picking. An Australian expression in the days of the settlers for the practice of buying up the choice lots of land, leaving the waste parts in between to settlers of smaller means; it was called "picking the eyes out of the country". Those who adopted this practice were called *peacockers*. *Cp.* GRIDIRONER.

Eye-service. Unwilling service, of the sort only done when one's master is looking.

Eye-teeth. The canine teeth; so called because they are located (in the upper and lower jaw) just under the eyes.

He has cut his eye-teeth. *See under* TOOTH.

To draw one's eye-teeth. *See under* TOOTH.

Eye-wash. In colloquial usage means "BUNKUM", "humbug"; something to blind one to the real state of affairs.

Eyre (âr) (Lat. *iter*; O.Fr. *eire*, a journey).

Justices in Eyre. From the time of Henry II (1154–1189), itinerant judges travelled the country on circuit to hear pleas, etc., usually sitting in the SHIRE court. They lapsed in the mid-14th century, being made redundant by the Justices of Assize.

F

F. The first letter in the Runic FUTHORC, but the sixth in the Phœnician and Latin alphabets and their derivatives. The Egyptian hieroglyph represented a horned asp and the Phœnician character a peg. *Ph* represents the same sound.

Double F(Ff, or **ff)** as an initial in a few personal names, as *Ffoukes, ffrench,* etc., is a mistaken use in print of the mediæval or Old English capital F (F) as it appears written in engrossed leases, etc. In script the old capital F looked very much like two small F's entwined. Its modern use is an affectation.

F is written on his face. The letter F (for fraymaker) used to be branded on the cheek of brawlers in church or churchyard. The practice was begun in the reign of Edward VI (1547–1553) to check the violent outbursts occasioned by changes in ritual. It was abolished in 1822.

Fabius (fā′ bi ús). Quintus Fabius Maximus (*d.* 203 B.C.), surnamed CUNCTATOR. According to Ennius (*Annals,* XII):

> Unus homo nobis cunctando restituit rem.

i.e. one man by delaying saved the State for us.

The American Fabius. George Washington (1732–1799), whose tactics as commander-in-chief in the American War of Independence were somewhat similar to those of FABIUS.

Fabian Society. A society founded in January 1884 by a small group of middle-class intellectuals to propagate evolutionary socialism by transforming the State to an organization to promote social welfare through increasing state intervention in the economy. They took their name from Quintus FABIUS Maximus, believing that "long taking of counsel" was necessary before they could achieve their objective. George Bernard Shaw (1856–1950), Sidney Webb (1859–1947), Beatrice Webb (1858–1943), Graham Wallas (1858–1932), and Annie Besant (1847–1933) were prominent among them.

> It envisaged socialism as a heap of reforms to be built by the droppings of a host of successive swallows who would in the end make a Socialist summer.
> COLE and POSTGATE: *The Common People,* ch. xxiv.

Fabian tactics. Delaying tactics, masterly inactivity, winning by delay; after the manner of FABIUS called CUNCTATOR.

Fables (Lat. *fabula,* a narrative story or fable). Although this name is applied in a general sense to fictitious tales, legends and myths, it is more particularly applied to didactic stories of which a moral forms an integral part. In this more restricted class, human thoughts and attributes are usually portrayed by members of the animal and insect world. *See* ÆSOP; BABRIUS; LA FONTAINE; PILÆDRUS; PILPAY.

Fabliaux (fab′ lē ō). Mediæval French metrical tales, mostly comical and satirical, and intended primarily for recitation by the TROUVÈRES, or early poets north of the Loire, and essentially of the latter part of the 12th century to the latter half of the 14th. They have little connection with the fable proper, beyond the name, and were usually in octosyllabic couplets. They were essentially to entertain the common people and were characterized by coarseness and satirical treatment of the weaknesses of the clergy and feminine frailty, and the familiar incidents of ordinary life.

Fabricius (fà brish' ùs), Gaius Lusinus. A Roman consul (d. *c*. 270 B.C.) and hero of the war against Pyrrhus, representative of incorruptibility and honesty.

Fabulinus (*fabulari*, to speak). The god, mentioned by Varro, who taught Roman children to utter their first word. *See* BABES, PROTECTING DEITIES OF.

Face. A colloquialism for cheek, impudence, self-confidence, etc., as "He has face enough for anything", *i.e.* cheek or assurance enough. The use is quite an old one. *Cp.* NECK.

A brazen face. *See* BRAZEN-FACED. *Cp.* BRASS.

A pasty face. Pale faced, like paste; unhealthy looking.

A wry face. The features drawn awry, expressive of distaste.

Face to face. In the immediate presence of each other; two or more persons facing each other.

On the face of it. To all appearances; in the literal sense of the words.

That puts a new face on the matter. Said when fresh evidence has been produced, or something has happened which puts things in a new or different light.

The face that launched a thousand ships. That of HELEN, the ships being the Greek fleet which sailed for Troy to avenge Menelaus. The phrase is from Marlowe's *Faustus* (*l*. 1354).

To be doubled-faced, or **two-faced.** To be hypocritical. To say one thing and act differently.

To draw, or **wear a long face.** To look dissatisfied or sorrowful, as when the mouth is drawn down at the corners, and the eyes are dejected, giving the face an elongated appearance.

To face about. To turn round on one's ground.

To face down. To withstand with boldness and effrontery. To abash by fixity of look.

To face it out. To persist in an assertion which is not true. To maintain a bold front.

To face the music. To brave the consequences of one's actions or to put on a bold front in an unpleasant situation. Possibly derived from the stage.

To face up to something. To meet one's difficulties without weakening.

To fly in the face of. To set at defiance rashly; to oppose violently and unreasonably.

To have two faces, or **to keep two faces under one hood.** To pretend to be very religious, and yet live an evil life; TO BE DOUBLE-FACED.

To laugh on the wrong side of one's face. *See under* LAUGH.

To look a person in the face, or **full in the face.** To meet with a steady gaze, implying lack of fear, or, sometimes, a spirit of defiance.

To lose face. To be lowered in the esteem of others through an affront to one's dignity—a matter of especial concern in the Far East.

To make faces. To grimace or "pull faces".

To put a bold, or **a good face on the matter.** To make the best of a bad matter; to bear up under something disagreeable.

To save one's face. To avoid disgrace or discomfiture.

To set one's face against something. To oppose it firmly; to resist its being done.

To shut the door in someone's face. To put an end to negotiations; to refuse to have dealings with.

To take things at their face value. To judge matters on their apparent worth.

Face-lifting. A method of enhancing looks or concealing the marks of age by treatment which tightens the skin of the face and removes the wrinkles.

To give something a face-lift. To renovate and give it a new look.

Faced. With a facing; covering the surface of one material with another; dressing the surface of a material. *See* FACINGS.

Bare-faced. The present meaning, audacious, shameless, impudent, is a depreciation of its earlier sense of open or unconcealed. A "bare-face" is a beardless face, where the features are in no way hidden. The French equivalent is *à visage découvert*, with uncovered face.

Shame-faced. Having shame expressed in the face.

Face-card, or **Faced-card.** A COURT CARD, a card with a face on it; also a card which has been dealt face up.

Facile princeps (făk′ i lă prin keps) (Lat.). Easily first.

Facilis descensus Averno. *See* AVERNUS.

Façon de parler (fă son dė par lă) (Fr.). Idiomatic or unusual form of speech.

Fact. The Facts of life. The realities of a situation, knowledge of the details of reproduction, particularly of human reproductive functions.

Faction. In Roman and Byzantine history the *factiones* were originally the companies into which the charioteers were divided, each group having its special colour. The original two factions at ROME were the white (*albata*) and red (*russata*), to which the green (*prasina*) and blue (*veneta*) were added when the number of competing chariots was increased from two to four. From this the "factions" of the circus and hippodrome arose as political partisans.

Faerie (fă′ ėr i). The land of the fays or fairies, the dominions of OBERON. *See* AVALON.

> The land of faery,
> Where nobody gets old and godly and grave,
> Where nobody gets old and crafty and wise,
> Where nobody gets old and bitter of tongue.
> W. B. YEATS: *The Land of Heart's Desire*.

Faerie Queene, The. An allegorical romance of CHIVALRY by Edmund Spenser (*c.* 1552–1599), originally intended to have been in twelve books, each of which was to have portrayed one of the twelve moral virtues, but only six books were completed. It details the adventures of various knights, who personify different virtues (*e.g.* ARTEGAL, justice; Sir CALIDORE, courtesy), and who belong to the court of GLORIANA, who sometimes typifies Queen Elizabeth I.

Fag. A schoolboy drudge who performs menial tasks for his seniors in certain boarding schools. Perhaps from *flag* in the sense of "drooping", *to fag* is to work until weary.

Fag is also slang for a cigarette, possibly connected with "vag", a Devonshire term for a turf for burning. *Cp.* COFFINNAIL.

It's too much fag. Too much trouble, too much needless exertion.

Quite fagged out. Tired out, wearied with hard work.

Fag-end. Originally the coarse end of a piece of cloth; hence the remaining part of anything; as "the fag-end of a leg of mutton", "the fag-end of a conversation". It is also slang for a cigarette stub (*see* FAG *above*).

Faggot. A bundle of sticks. In the days when heretics were burnt at the stake, an embroidered representation of a faggot was worn on the arm by those who recanted, thus showing what they merited but had narrowly escaped. *Faggot* was also applied to a hireling who took the place of another at the muster of a regiment. An *old faggot* is a dreary old woman.

Faggot votes. Votes obtained by the nominal transfer of property to individuals in the days when this was a necessary qualification for voting rights, the minimum necessary being the forty-shilling freehold. The "faggot" was in this context a bundle of property divided into small lots.

Fainéant. Les Rois Fainéants. "Do-nothing" or puppet kings (Fr. *faire*, do; *néant*, nothing). An epithet particularly applied to the later MEROVINGIAN kings of France, whose powers were increasingly wielded by the MAYOR OF THE PALACE.

Fains. A schoolchildren's term of unknown origin exempting the first to call: "fains I goal-keeping". The opposite of "Bags I", by means of which a positive claim is asserted.

Faint. Faint heart never won fair lady. An old proverb with obvious meaning.

Fair. The Fair. The FAIR SEX.

Fair Isle. One of the Shetland islands, where a special pattern of knitting is done, which is believed to be of Moorish origin and to have been derived from contacts with shipwrecked sailors from the Spanish Armada of 1588. The Duke of Medina Sidonia, admiral of the Armada, was wrecked on Fair Isle.

Fair Maid of Kent. Joan (1328–1385), Countess of Kent, wife of the BLACK PRINCE, and only daughter of Edmund Plantagenet, Earl of Kent. The Prince was her second husband.

Fair Maid of Norway. Margaret (1283–1290), daughter of Eric II of Norway, and granddaughter of Alexander III of SCOTLAND. Acknowledged as heir to the throne of Scotland and affianced to Prince Edward, son of Edward I of England, she died in the Orkney islands on her way to Britain.

Fair Maid of Perth. Katie Glover, heroine of Scott's novel of this name, is supposed to have lived in the early 15th century, but is not a definite historical character, though her house is still shown at Perth. Bizet's opera, *La Jolie Fille de Perth* (1867), is based on the novel.

A fair field and no favour. Every opportunity being given.

By fair means. Straightforwardly; without deception or compulsion.

Fair and soft goes far in a day. Courtesy and moderation will help one to effect a good deal of one's purpose.

Fair and square. Honestly, justly, with straightforwardness.

Fair fall you. Good befall you; good luck to you.

Fair game. A worthy subject of banter; legitimately to be pursued or attacked.

Fair play. Honest or straight dealing. Fair or impartial treatment.

Fair to middling. Moderately good; reasonably well.

Fair trade. An old EUPHEMISM for smuggling. It also signifies reciprocal trading privileges with another country as a condition of free trade or tariff concessions.

Fair weather friends. *See under* WEATHER.

Fair words butter no parsnips. *See under* BUTTER.

The fair sex. Women; a phrase modelled on the French *le beau sexe*.

Pretty fair. Fairly well; reasonably satisfactory; "not bad".

To bid fair. To give good promise; to indicate future success as, 'He bids fair to be a good preacher."

To speak fair. To speak civilly or courteously.

Fairs (O.Fr. *feire*; Lat. *feria*, a holiday). These great periodical markets of former days were often held at the time of Church festivals and came to be associated with side-shows, amusements and merry-making. Although trade fairs or exhibitions are a link with the commercial aspect of the fairs of the past, the name is now largely associated with the travelling amusement fair. *See* BARTHOLOMEW FAIR; DONNYBROOK FAIR; GOOSE FAIR; PIE-POWDER COURT. *Cp.* PADDINGTON FAIR.

A day after the fair. *See under* DAY.

Hiring Fair. A STATUTE FAIR, virtually the same as a MOP FAIR; once an annual event in most market towns in England and Wales on MARTINMAS Day (11 Nov.), when men and maids stood in rows to be inspected by those seeking servants, farm workers, etc.

Mop Fair. A HIRING FAIR, probably taking its name from the tufts or badges worn by those seeking employment. Carters fastened a piece of whipcord to their hats; shepherds, a lock of wool; grooms, a piece of sponge. Others carried a pail, a broom, a mop, etc.

Statute Fair. A fair legalized by statute as opposed to custom or usage; a HIRING FAIR.

Fairy, or **Fay.** In folk-lore and legend, a diminutive supernatural being of human shape, with magical powers. The names of the principal fairies and sprites, etc., known in fable and legend appear in this dictionary as individual entries. *See also* BROWNIE, DEITIES, DWARF, ELF, FAUNI, GNOME, GOBLIN, LEPRECHAUN, PIXIE.

Fairy loaves, or **stones.** Fossil sea-urchins, said to be made by the fairies.

Fairy money. Found money, said to be placed by some good fairy at the spot where it is picked up. Also in legend, money given by the fairies which soon turned into "leaves" or other worthless forms.

Fairy rings. Circles of dark green grass often found in lawns and meadows and popularly supposed to be produced by fairies dancing on the spot. They are due to the growth of certain fungi below the surface. The spawn radiates from the centre at a similar rate annually and darker colour is due to the increased nitrogen produced by the action of the fungus.

Fairy sparks. The phosphoric light

from decaying wood, fish, and other substances. Thought at one time to be lights prepared for the fairies at their revels.

Fait accompli (fā tả kom' plē) (Fr.). An accomplished fact, something already done; often used in the sense of some act carried out in order to steal a march on some other party.

Faith. Act of faith. *See* AUTO DA FE.

Defender of the Faith. *See* DEFENDER.

In good faith. "*Bona fide*", "*de bonne foi*"; with no ulterior motive, with complete sincerity.

Punic Faith. *See* PUNIC.

To pin one's faith on. *See under* PIN.

Faithful. The active supporters of any cult are called *the faithful* and in former times a PURITAN was sometimes *Brother Faithful*.

Commander of the Faithful. The CA-LIPH was so called by Mohammedans.

Father of the Faithful. ABRAHAM (*Rom*. iv, 16; *Gal*. iii, 6–9).

Falange (Sp. *Phalanx*). At first a right-wing party in Spain formed in 1932 by José Antonio Primo de Rivera to uphold his father's memory against republican criticism, and later adopted by General Franco as the one official party in the State. Essentially representing a combination of European fascism and Spanish nationalism, it was used to counterbalance royalist, army, and Church influence and in 1937 forced the CARLISTS to join with it. Since 1957 the latter group has re-emerged. The Falange (latterly known as the National Movement) lost its unique position after the CAUDILLO's death in 1975, and was formally disbanded in 1977.

Falernian. A choice Italian wine esteemed by the ancient Romans and celebrated by VIRGIL and HORACE; so called because it was made of grapes from Falernus.

Fall. In the fall. In the autumn, at the fall of the leaf. Though now commonly classed as an Americanism, the term is found in the works of Drayton, Middleton, Ralegh, and others.

> What crowds of patients the town doctor kills,
> Or how, last fall, he raised the weekly bills.
>
> DRYDEN: *Juvenal*.

It fell off the back of a lorry. Said of

something picked up or acquired fortuitously or by somewhat questionable means. The origin is obvious.

The Fall of Man. The degeneracy of the human race in consequence of the disobedience of ADAM.

The fall of the drop. In theatrical parlance, means the fall of the drop-curtain at the end of the act or play.

To fall away. To lose flesh; to degenerate; to quit a party, as, "His adherents fell away one by one."

To fall back upon. To have recourse to.

To fall between two stools. To fail, through hesitating between two choices. The French say, *Être assis entre deux chaises*.

To fall flat. To fall prostrate; to fail to interest as "The last act fell flat."

To fall for. To be captivated by; to be taken in by; to become enamoured of.

To fall foul of one. To quarrel with; to make an assault on someone. A nautical term. A rope is said to be *foul* when it is entangled; one ship *falls foul* of another when they run against each other.

To fall from. To tumble or slip off; to violate, as "to fall from one's word"; to abandon or depart from, as "to fall from grace", to lapse into error or sin, to lose favour.

To fall in. To take one's place in the ranks; to take one's place with others. *Cp*. TO FALL OUT.

To fall in love with. To become enamoured of.

To fall in with. To meet accidentally; to come across; to agree with, as, "He fell in with my views."

To fall into a snare. To stumble accidentally into a snare. This is a Latin phrase, *insidias incidere*. Similarly, to fall into disgrace is the Latin *in offensionem cadere*.

To fall on deaf ears. To go unheeded or to be deliberately ignored.

To fall on evil days. To sink into poverty or suffer similar misfortune.

To fall on stony ground. Said of ideas, etc., which meet with no response and fail to take root. The allusion is to the parable of the sower (*Matt*. xiii, 5, 6).

To fall out. To quarrel; to happen.

Also, in military language, to be dismissed or to disperse from the ranks. *Cp*. TO FALL IN.

To fall short of. To be deficient of a supply; not to come up to standard. To *fall short of the mark* is a figure taken from archery, quoits, etc., where the missile falls to the ground before reaching the mark.

To fall sick. To be unwell. A Latin phrase, *in morbum incidere. Cp*. FALLING SICKNESS.

To fall through. To come to nothing; not to be carried out.

To fall to. To begin (eating, fighting, etc.).

To fall to the ground. To fail; to come to nothing, as, "His hopes fell to the ground."

To fall under. To incur, as, "to fall under the reproach of carelessness"; to become subject to, as, "He fell under the influence of bad companions."

To fall upon. To attack, as, "to fall upon the enemy"; to throw oneself on, as, "he fell on his sword"; to happen on, as, "On what day does Easter fall?"

To fall upon one's feet. To be unexpectedly lucky; to find oneself unexpectedly in a very favourable situation. Evidently from the old theory that the CAT always falls upon its feet unharmed.

To ride for a fall. *See under* RIDE.

To try a fall. To wrestle, when each tries to "fall", or throw the other.

Fall Guy (U.S.A.). A loser, dupe or victim. Towards the end of the nineteenth century professional wrestling became widely popular in America and many of the bouts were "rigged". One wrestler would promise to "take a fall" if the other agreed to deal with him gently, but the winner often broke his word and handled his opponent roughly. In such circumstances the loser came to be known as a "fall guy".

Fall-out. A name given to radioactive dust resulting from atomic and nuclear explosions. Figuratively, the effect of an action which extends beyond the intended range.

Fallen angels. Those cast out of HEAVEN; colloquially, women who have slipped from the paths of virtue.

Falling-bands. Neck bands or broad collars of cambric, lace or linen, made to lie upon the shoulders. Also called *falls* as distinct from the stiff ruff. They were common in the 17th century.

Falling sickness. Epilepsy, in which the patient falls suddenly to the ground. SHAKESPEARE plays upon the term.

Falling stars. Meteors. A wish made as a star falls is supposed to come true. Mohammedans believe them to be firebrands flung by good ANGELS against evil spirits when they approach too near the gates of HEAVEN.

False. False quantity. A term used in prosody to denote the incorrect use of a long for a short vowel or syllable, or vice versa.

To play false. To act treacherously, to be faithless.

To sail under false colours. *See under* COLOUR.

Falstaff. A fat, sensual, boastful, and mendacious KNIGHT; full of wit and humour; the boon companion of Henry, Prince of Wales (the future King Henry V); as portrayed by SHAKESPEARE in *Henry IV, Pts. I and II*, and *Merry Wives of Windsor*. Hence, **Falstaffian,** possessing the qualities and characteristics of Falstaff.

Falutin. *See* HIGH FALUTIN'.

Fame. Temple of Fame. A PANTHEON where monuments to the famous dead of a nation are erected and their memories honoured. Hence, *he will have a niche in the Temple of Fame* means his achievements will cause his people to honour him and keep his memory green.

Familiar, or familiar spirit (Lat. *famulus*, a servant). A spirit slave, sometimes in human shape, sometimes appearing as a cat, dog, raven, etc., attendant upon a WITCH, WIZARD, or magician, and supposed to be a demon in disguise.

> Away with him! he has a familiar under his tongue.
> SHAKESPEARE: *Henry VI, Pt. II*, IV, vii.

Familiarity. Familiarity breeds contempt. The proverb appears in English at least as early as the mid-16th century and was well known in Latin. The same idea is conveyed in the saying that a prophet is not appreciated in his own country.

Family Compact. (1) The name given to

the three agreements (1733, 1743, and 1761) between the BOURBON Kings of France and Spain to assert their interests. They were essentially directed against Austrian ascendancy in Italy and British mercantile and maritime supremacy.

Family of Love. *See* FAMILISTS.

Fancy. The Fancy. In early 19th-century slang parlance a collective name for prize-fighters and devotees of the prize-ring. It is now sometimes applied to supporters of other pastimes.

Fancy-free. Not in love.

Fancy-man. Originally a CAVALIERE SERVENTE or CICISBEO; one selected by a married woman to escort her to theatres, etc., to ride about with her, and to amuse her. It is now more usually applied to a lover, and a harlot's *souteneur*.

Fancy-sick. Love-sick.

To fancy oneself. To be conceited.

To tickle one's fancy. To tickle one's imagination, thus exciting amusement.

Fanfaron (Fr. *fanfare*, a flourish of trumpets). A swaggering bully, a cowardly boaster who blows his own trumpet. Scott uses the word for finery, especially for the gold lace worn by military men.

Hence **fanfaronade**, swaggering; vain boasting; ostentatious display.

Fanny. A naval mess kettle, somewhat similar in size and use to an army DIXIE. The name is said to have been applied to the tins in which preserved mutton or FANNY ADAMS was first issued. The sailors found them useful as mess traps and the name was transferred to the official kettle subsequently provided from naval stores.

Fanny Adams, or **Sweet Fanny Adams,** or **Sweet F.A.** means "nothing at all" or "sweet nothing" though (especially by its initials) it has a somewhat ambiguous connotation. It is a phrase of tragic origin. In 1867 Fanny Adams, a child of eight, was murdered in a hop-garden at Alton, Hants, and her body horribly dismembered. The Royal Navy, with gruesome humour, adopted her name as a synonym for tinned mutton, which was first issued at this time. Sweet Fanny Adams became, as a consequence, a phrase for anything worthless, and then for "nothing at all".

Fantom. An old spelling of PHANTOM.

Far. A far cry. *See* CRY.

Far and away. Beyond comparison; as "far and away the best", incomparably the best.

Far and wide. To a good distance in every direction. "To spread the news far and wide", to blazon it everywhere.

Far-fetched. Brought from afar; remotely connected, strained, as "a far-fetched simile", "a far-fetched conceit".

Far from it. Not in the least; by no means; quite the contrary. If the answer to, "Was he sober at the time?" is, "Far from it", the implication is that he was more than a little drunk.

Far gone. Deeply affected, as, "far gone in love".

Fare (O.E. *faran*, to go, to travel, etc., ultimately connected with Lat. *portare*, to carry). The noun formerly denoted a journey for which a sum was paid; then the sum itself, and by extension, the person who pays it. In certain English dialects, *e.g.* Suffolk, the verb *fare* is used in its original sense, "to go". The noun also means food and drink, the provisions of the table.

Farmer George. George III (1738, 1760–1820). A keen and progressive farmer who transformed his agricultural holdings. Under the name of *Ralph Robinson* he contributed the Robinson Letters to Arthur Young's *Annals of Agriculture*. His nickname of farmer was used by his political critics to arouse ridicule but:

> A better farmer ne'er brushed dew from lawn.
>
> BYRON: *Vision of Judgement.*

The Farnese Bull. A marble group executed by Apollonius of Tralles and his brother Tauriscus in the 2nd century B.C. The group represents Dirce bound to the horns of a bull by Zethus and AMPHION for ill-using their mother. It was discovered in the Baths of Caracalla in 1546, and placed in the Farnese Palace at ROME. It is now in the Museo Nazionale at Naples.

Farrago (fă ra' gō). **A farrago of nonsense.** A confused heap of nonsense. *Farrago* (Lat.) is properly a mixture of *far* (meal) with other ingredients for the use of cattle, *i.e.* mixed fodder.

Farthing (O.E. *feorthing*, a fourthling or fourth part). The early silver penny was divided into two or four parts on the reverse thus ⊕ on the lines of the cross. Each of these quarters was a farthing. Farthings were demonetized on 31 December 1960.

Not worth a brass farthing. Virtually worthless. Erasmus, when Professor of Greek at Cambridge, described his profits as "not worth a brass farthing" and the phrase is possibly an allusion to the Nuremberg Monastic token; the expression probably gained further use from the 17th-century farthing tokens or HARRINGTONS, and Gun-money. (*See under* GUN.)

Farthingale. The hooped understructure of the large protruding skirt fashionable in the reigns of Elizabeth I and James I. The word is the O.Fr. *verdugale*, a corruption of Span. *verdugado*, green rods, which were used for the framework before WHALEBONE took their place.

Fasces (Lat.). A bundle of rods tied round with a red thong from which an axe projected. In ancient ROME *fasces* were assigned to the higher magistrates as symbols of authority, representing power over life and limb. In modern times the fasces became the emblem of the Italian FASCISTS.

Fascines (făs′ ēnz). Bundles of faggots used to build up military defences or to fill ditches for impeding attack. They were much used in World War I for road foundations and for horse standings and also used to impede attack in World War II. The name derives from the Roman FASCES.

Fascist. Originally an Italian political movement taking its name from the old Roman FASCES. It was founded in 1919 by Benito Mussolini (1883–1945) who took advantage of the discontent in Italy after World War I to form a totalitarian nationalist party against left-wing radicalism and socialism. In 1922 the Fascists marched on ROME and demanded power, and King Victor Emmanuel III made Mussolini Prime Minister. He styled himself DUCE (leader) and made himself Dictator in 1925, suppressing all other political parties the following year. The Fascists controlled Italy until 1943.

The term Fascism soon came to be applied to similar totalitarian movements in other countries. Ruthlessness, inhumanity, and dishonest and disreputable practices were notable characteristics of its adherents. *See* HITLERISM; NAZI.

> Benito Mussolini provided Italy with a new theme of government which, while it claimed to save the Italian people from Communism, raised himself to dictatorial power. As Fascism sprang from Communism, so Nazism developed from Fascism.
> WINSTON CHURCHILL: *The Gathering Storm*, ch. i.

Fash. Dinna fash yoursel'! Don't get excited; don't get into a flurry about it. The word is not of Scottish origin, it is the O.Fr. *fascher* (Mod. Fr. *fâcher*), to anger.

Fashion. In a fashion, or **after a fashion.** "In a sort of way", as "He spoke French after a fashion."

In the fashion. Dressed in the latest style, modish; in accordance with current trends.

Fast. The adjective is used figuratively of someone of either sex who is addicted to pleasure and dissipation; of a young man or woman who "goes the pace", which amounts to the same thing.

To play fast and loose. To run with the HARE and hunt with the hounds; to blow both hot and cold; to say one thing and do another. The allusion is probably to an old cheating game once practised at FAIRS. A belt or strap was doubled and rolled up with the loop in the centre and placed on edge on a table. The player then had to catch the loop with a skewer while the belt was unrolled, but this was done in such a way by the trickster as to make the feat impossible.

To pull a fast one. *See under* PULL.

Fasti. In ancient ROME, working days when the law courts were open. Holy days (DIES NON) when the law courts, etc., were not open were called *nefasti*.

The *Fasti* were listed in calendars, and the list of events occurring during the year of office of a pair of consuls was called *fasti consulares*; hence, any chronological list of events of office-holders became known as *fasti*. The surviving

Fasting

six books of Ovid's *Fasti* are a poetical account of the Roman festivals of the first six months of the year. *Cp.* CALENDS.

Fasting. Strictly a complete abstention from food and drink, but the word is more usually applied to an extreme or fairly strict limitation of diet, and is of proved value in treating certain complaints. It is ancient and widespread as a form of penance, or purification, and was so used by the Jews. It was practised by Christ and adopted by the early Church. As currently practised in the Church, it is marked by abstinence from flesh meat and observance of a light diet. Throughout the ROMAN CATHOLIC CHURCH fasting is obligatory on ASH WEDNESDAY and GOOD FRIDAY. The main fast of the Mohammedans is during the month of RAMADAN.

Mahatma Gandhi (1869–1948) practised fasting, an ancient Hindu observance, as a form of asceticism and as a political protest. *See* HUNGER-STRIKE; CAT AND MOUSE ACT *under* CAT.

Fat. A bit of fat. An unexpected stroke of luck; also, the best part of anything, especially among actors, a good part in a play.

The fat is in the fire. Something has been let out inadvertently which will cause a "regular flare up"; it's all over, all's up with it, the damage is done. If, in cooking, the grease spills into the fire, it blazes up and smokes, there is a risk of trouble and the food is spoilt.

Fat-head. A silly fool, a dolt.

Fata (fa′ ta) (Ital. a fairy). Female supernatural beings introduced in Italian mediæval romance, usually under the sway of DEMOGORGON.

Fata Morgana. The fay, or fairy Morgana, sister of King ARTHUR; also a mirage often visible in the Straits of Messina, so named from MORGAN LE FAY who was fabled by the Norman settlers in England to dwell in Calabria.

Fates. The Cruel Fates. The Greeks and Romans supposed there were three Parcæ or Fates, who arbitrarily controlled the birth, life and death of everyone. They were CLOTHO, LACHESIS and ATROPOS; called cruel because they paid no regard to the wishes of anyone.

Father. In the HOLY TRINITY, God. The name is given as a title to Roman Catholic priests, and sometimes to CHURCH OF ENGLAND clergy of the HIGH CHURCH persuasion; also to the senior member of a body or profession, as the *Father of the House of Commons*; and to the originator or first leader of some movement or school, etc., as the *Father of Comedy*, the *Father of History*. In ancient Rome the title was given to the senators (*cp.* PATRICIAN; CONSCRIPT FATHERS), and in ecclesiastical history to the early Church writers and doctors.

Father of Angling. Izaak Walton (1593–1683).

Father of the Chapel. *See* CHAPEL.

Father of Comedy. Aristophanes (*c.* 450–*c.* 385 B.C.).

Father of English History. The Venerable Bede (673–735), author of the famous *Ecclesiastical History of the English People* (written in Latin).

Father of the English Novel. Both Samuel Richardson (1689–1761) and Henry Fielding (1707–1754) have been given the title.

Father of English Poetry. Chaucer (*c.* 1340–1400).

Father of Epic Poetry. HOMER.

Father of the Faithful. ABRAHAM.

Father of Greek Tragedy. Æschylus (*c.* 525–456 B.C.).

Father of History. Herodotus (*c.* 485–*c.* 424 B.C.).

Father of Lies. SATAN.

Father of Medicine. Hippocrates (469–399 B.C.).

Father of Moral Philosophy. St. THOMAS AQUINAS (*c.* 1225–1274).

Fathers of the Church. All those church writers of the first twelve centuries whose works on Christian doctrine are considered of weight and worthy of respect. But the term is more strictly applied to those teachers of the first twelve, and especially of the first six, centuries who added notable holiness and complete orthodoxy to their learning. Representative among them are:

1st cent., Clement of Rome; 2nd cent., Ignatius of Antioch, Justin, Irenæus, Polycarp; 3rd cent., Cyprian, Dionysius, Origen, Tertullian, Clement of Alexandria, Gregory Thaumaturgus; 4th cent., Hilary, Cyril of Jerusalem,

Gregory Nyssen, John Chrysostom, Eusebius, Jerome, Epiphanius, Athanasius, Basil, Ambrose; 5th cent., Rufinus, Augustine, Pope Leo the Great, Cyril of Alexandria, Vincent of Lerins; 6th cent., Cæsarius of Arles; 7th cent., Isidore, Pope Gregory the Great; 8th cent., John of Damascus, Venerable Bede; 11th cent., Peter Damian; 12th cent., Anselm, Bernard.

Cp. APOSTOLIC FATHERS.

Fathers of the Constitution. The framers of the constitution of the United States who took part in the Constitutional Convention at Philadelphia in 1787. In particular, James Madison (1751–1836) is known as *the Father of the Constitution* for the part he played in its formation.

Fathers of the Desert, or **Desert Fathers.** The monks and hermits of the Egyptian deserts in the 4th century from whom Christian monasticism derives.

Pilgrim Fathers. *See* PILGRIM.

Fatima. The last wife of BLUEBEARD. MOHAMMED's daughter was also called Fatima.

Fatimids, or **Fatimites.** An Arab dynasty ruling in Egypt and North Africa (909–1171), descended from Fatima and her husband ALI.

Fatted Calf. *See* TO KILL THE FATTED CALF *under* CALF.

Fault. At fault. Not on the right track. Hounds are *at fault* when the fox has jumped upon a wall, crossed a river, cut through a flock of sheep, or doubled like a hare, because the scent, *i.e.*, the track, is broken.

For fault of a better. For want of a better; no one (or nothing) better being available. SHAKESPEARE uses the expression in the *Merry Wives of Windsor* (I, iv).

In fault, at fault. To blame.

> Is Antony or we in fault for this?
> SHAKESPEARE: *Antony and Cleopatra*, III, xiii.

No one is without his faults. No one is perfect.

To a fault. In excess; as, "kind to a fault". Excess of every kind is almost a defect; there is a similar idea expressed in the phrase *to kill by kindness* (*see* KILL).

To find fault. To blame; to express disapprobation.

Fauna (faw' ná). The animals of a country at any given period. The term was first used by Linnæus in the title of his *Fauna Suecica* (1746), a companion volume to his *Flora Suecica* (1745), and is the name of a rural goddess, of like attributes to FAUNUS (*see* PAN).

> Nor less the place of curious plant he knows;
> He both his Flora and his Fauna shows.
> CRABBE: *The Borough*, Letter viii.

Fauni or **Fauns.** Minor Roman deities of the countryside, merry and mischievous, small counterparts of FAUNUS. *Cp.* SATYR.

Faunus. A good spirit of forest and field, and a god of prophecy. He had the form of a SATYR and is identified with the Greek PAN. FAUNA is sometimes given as his wife, sometimes as his daughter. At his festivals, called FAUNALIA, peasants brought rustic offerings and made merry. He was also fabled to have been a king of Latium subsequently deified for his devotion to agriculture.

Fauntleroy. Little Lord. *See under* LITTLE.

Faust (foust). The hero of Marlowe's *Tragical History of Dr. Faustus* (*c.* 1592) and Goethe's *Faust* (1772–1831) is founded on Dr. Johann Faust, or Faustus, a magician and astrologer, who was born in Württemberg and died about 1538, and about whom many stories soon began to circulate crediting him with supernatural gifts and evil living. The suggestion that Johann Fust, or Faust, the printer and one-time partner of Gutenberg, was the original upon whom the Faust stories were built, is now completely rejected. In 1587 *The History of Dr. Faustus, the Notorious Magician and Master of the Black Art* was published by Johann Spies at Frankfurt. It immediately became popular and was soon translated into English, French, and other languages. Many other accounts followed and the Faust, theme was developed by writers, artists and musicians over the years. It was Goethe who was responsible, however, for transforming the necromancer into a personification of the struggle between the higher and lower natures in man. Notable among musical compositions on the story are Spohr's opera *Faust*, 1813, Wagner's overture *Faust*, 1840; Berlioz's *Damnation de Faust*, 1846; Gounod's opera *Faust*, 1859; Boito's *Mefistofele*, 1868; and Busoni's *Doktor Faust*, 1925.

The idea of making a pact with a DEVIL for worldly reasons is of Jewish origin. The basis of the Faust story is that he sold his soul to the Devil in return for twenty-four years of further life during which he is to have every pleasure and all knowledge at his command. The climax comes when the Devil claims him for his own.

> O lente, lente currite noctis equi!
> The stars move still, time runs, the clock will strike,
> The Devil will come, and Faustus must be damned.
> O' I'll leap up to my God! Who pulls me down?
> See, see where Christ's blood streams in the firmament!
>
> MARLOWE: *Doctor Faustus*, V, iii.

Faute de mieux (fōt'dė mē ĕr) (Fr.). For want of something better. *Cp.* FOR FAULT OF A BETTER *under* FAULT.

Fauvism (fō' vizm). The name given to the work of a group of young French artists of the first decade of the 20th century, whose leader was Henri Matisse, and which included Derain, Braque, Vlaminck, Dufy, Marquet, Friez, and Rouault. There was a corresponding German movement known as *Die Brücke* (The Bridge). The French school derives from the influence of Van Gogh and their work was characterized by the imaginative use of brilliant colour, decorative simplicity, vitality and gaiety. The name *Fauves* (wild beasts) arose from a remark of the critic Vauxcelles at an exhibition of their work in 1905, *Donatello au milieu des fauves*, occasioned by the sight of their spectacularly coloured pictures. *Cp.* CUBISM; DADAISM; FUTURISM; IMPRESSIONISM; ORPHISM; SURREALISM; SYNCHRONISM; VORTICISM.

Faux pas (fō pa) (Fr. a false step). A breach of manners or good conduct.

> The fact is his Lordship, who hadn't, it seems,
> Form'd the slightest idea, not ev'n in his dreams,
> That the pair had been wedded according to law,

Conceived that his daughter had made a faux pas.
> BARHAM: *Ingoldsby Legends* (*Some account of a New Play*).

Favonius. The Latin name for the ZEPHYR or west wind. It means the wind favourable to vegetation.

Favour. Ribbons made into a bow are called favours from being bestowed by ladies on the successful champions of tournaments. *Cp.* TRUE-LOVERS' KNOT.
To curry favour. *See* CURRY.

Favourites. False curls on the temples; a curl of hair on the temples plastered with some cosmetic; whiskers made to meet the mouth.

Fay. *See* FAIRY.

Morgan le Fay. *See* FATA MORGANA *and* MORGAN.

Feal and Divot. In SCOTLAND, the right to cut turf or peat, from which, by jocular derivation, comes the *divot* of golf, a piece of turf removed by a player's club. Both words mean "turf".

Feast, or **Festival.** A day or days specially set apart for religious observances which is an ancient practice common to all religions. The number of Feasts in the ROMAN CATHOLIC and GREEK CHURCHES is extensive; the CHURCH OF ENGLAND after the REFORMATION only retained a certain number. The Feasts in the Christian CALENDAR have been divided in various ways, one of which is to group them as **movable** or **immovable.** All SUNDAYS are Feast Days.

The chief immovable feasts are the four quarter-days—*viz*. the ANNUNCIATION, or LADY DAY (25 March); The Nativity of ST. JOHN THE BAPTIST (24 June); MICHAELMAS DAY (29 September); CHRISTMAS DAY (25 December). Others are the Circumcision (1 January), EPIPHANY (6 January), ALL SAINTS (1 November), the several Apostles' days and the anniversaries of martyrs and saints.

The movable feasts depend upon EASTER Day and also among them are the Sundays after the EPIPHANY, SEPTUAGESIMA SUNDAY, the Sundays of LENT, Rogation Sunday, ASCENSION DAY, PENTECOST or WHIT SUNDAY, TRINITY SUNDAY, and the Sundays after Trinity.

Feather. A broken feather in one's wing. A scandal connected with someone.

A feather in your cap. An honour to you. The allusion is to the very general custom in Asia and among the American Indians of adding a feather to the headgear for every enemy slain. The ancient Lycians and many others had a similar custom, just as the sportsman who kills the first woodcock puts a feather in his cap. In Hungary, at one time, none might wear a feather but he who had slain a Turk. When CHINESE GORDON quelled the TAI-PING rebellion he was honoured by the Chinese Government with the "yellow jacket and peacock's feather".

Birds of a feather flock together. *See under* BIRD.

Fine feathers make fine birds. Said of an overdressed person who does not really match up to his or her clothes.

In full feather. Well supplied with money. In allusion to birds not on the moult.

In grand feather. Dressed "up to the nines" (*see under* NINE). Also, in perfect health, thoroughly fit.

In high feather. In exuberant spirits, joyous.

Of that feather. *See* BIRDS OF A FEATHER.

Prince of Wales's feathers. *See* WALES, PRINCE OF.

Tarred and feathered. *See* TAR.

Tickled with a feather. Easily moved to laughter. Pope in his *Essay on Man* (II, 276) has, "Pleased with a rattle, tickled with a straw."

To cut a feather. A ship moving at speed is said *to cut a feather* in allusion to the foam set up by her bows. Metaphorically "to cut a dash" (*see under* DASH). *Cp*. A BONE IN HER MOUTH *under* BONE.

To feather an oar. To turn the blade parallel with and move it along the surface of the water as the hands are moved forward for a fresh stroke. The oar throws off the water in a feathery spray.

To feather one's nest well. To provide for one's own interests, especially financial. The phrase is commonly used with implications of disapproval.

To feather one's propeller. In flying to rotate the aeroplane's propeller blades, when the engine is stopped, to an angle at which they produce minimum drag. In boats to perform a similar operation to lessen water resistance on the screw.

To make the feathers fly. To make a noisy scene when angered, to make the "fur fly": an allusion to the fighting of cock birds.

To show the white feather. *See* WHITE.

To smooth one's ruffled feathers. To recover one's equanimity after an insult, etc.

To featherbed. To pamper, to cushion; the allusion is obvious.

Featherweight. Something of extreme lightness in comparison with others of its kind. The term is applied to a jockey weighing not more than 4 st. 7 lb. or to a boxer weighing not more than 9 st. In the paper trade, the name is given to very light antique, laid, or wove book papers, which are loosely woven and made mainly from esparto.

February. The month of purification amongst the ancient Romans (Lat. *februo*, I purify by sacrifice).

2 February, CANDLEMAS DAY, is the feast of the Purification of the Blessed Virgin Mary. It is said that if the weather is fine and frosty at the close of JANUARY and the beginning of February, there is more winter ahead than behind.

Si sol splendescat Maria Purificante,
Major erit glacies post festum quam fuit ante.

SIR T. BROWNE: *Vulgar Errors*.

The Dutch used to call the month *Spokkel-maand* (vegetation-month); the Anglo-Saxons *Sprote-cal* (Sprout-Kale) from the sprouting of cabbage or kale and subsequently *sol-monath* (from the returning of the sun). In the French Republican Calendar it was called *Pluviôse* (rain-month, 20 January to 20 February). *See also* FILL-DYKE.

Fecit (fā′ kit) (Lat. he made it). A word often inscribed after the name of an artist, sculptor, etc., as David *fecit*, Goujon *fecit*; *i.e.*, David painted it, Goujon sculptured it, etc.

Federalists. Those Americans who supported the proposed new constitution of 1787, led by Alexander Hamilton, James Madison, John Adams, John Jay, and others.

Fee. An Anglo-French word, from Old High Ger. *Fehu*, wages, money, property, and it is connected with the O.E. *feoh*, cattle, goods, money. So in Lat. *pecunia*, money, from *pecus*, cattle. Capital is *capita*, heads (of cattle), and chattels is a mere variant.

At a pin's fee. *See* PIN.

Fee-farm. A tenure by which land is held in FEE SIMPLE without any services from the tenant other than a perpetual fixed rent.

Fee-penny. A fine for money overdue; an earnest or pledge for a bargain.

Fee simple. A property held by a person in his own right, free from condition or limitation. A conditional fee simple is one granted subject to conditions which if unfulfilled give the grantor the right to re-enter and is not a legal estate.

Fee-tail. An estate limited to a person and his lawful heirs; an entailed estate (*see* ENTAIL). Fee-tail as such was abolished by the Law of Property Act, 1925.

To hold in fee. To hold as one's lawful, absolute possession.

Feeble. Most forcible Feeble. Said of one whose language is pretentious but whose ideas are very jejune. Feeble is a woman's tailor brought to Sir John Falstaff as a recruit (SHAKESPEARE, *Henry IV, Pt. II*, III, ii). He tells Sir John he will do his good will, and the knight replies. "Well said, courageous Feeble! Thou wilt be as valiant as the wrathful or magnanimous mouse ... most forcible Feeble."

Fehmgerichte. *See* VEHMGERICHTE.

Felix, the Cat. Hero of early animated film cartoons which appeared in 1921 in a production by Pat Sullivan. Throughout his many adventures **Felix kept on walking** and thus originated the once-familiar catch-phrase.

Fell. Doctor Fell.

> I do not like thee, Dr. Fell,
> The reason why I cannot tell;
> But this I know, I know full well,
> I do not like thee, Dr. Fell.

These well-known lines are by the

"facetious" Tom Brown (1663–1704) and the person referred to was Dr. John Fell, Dean of Christ Church and Bishop of Oxford (1625–1686), who expelled him, but said he would remit the sentence if Brown translated the thirty-third Epigram of Martial:

> Non amo te, Sabidi, nec possum dicere-
> quare;
> Hoc tantum possum dicere, non amo te.

The foregoing translation is said to have been given impromptu.

Fellow-traveller. A person in sympathy with a political party but not a member of that party; usually restricted to Communist sympathizers. The term (Rus. *poputchik*) was coined by Leon Trotsky.

Felo de se (fē' lō dē sē). Self-destruction, the act of suicide; also the self-murderer himself. Murder is felony, and a man who murders himself commits this felony on himself. An Anglo-Latin expression.

Feme-covert (fem kŭv' ert). A married woman, one under the cover, authority, or protection of her husband. The expression is derived from Old French.

Feme sole (fem sōl). A single woman.

Feme sole merchant. A woman, married or single, who carries on a trade on her own account.

Feminine ending. An extra unaccented syllable at the end of a line of verse, *e.g.* in lines 1 and 3 of the following:

> With rue my heart is laden
> For golden friends I had,
> For many a rose-lipt maiden
> And many a light-foot lad.
> A. E. HOUSMAN.

Fen Nightingale. A frog, which sings at night in the fens, as nightingales sing in the groves.

Fence month, or **season.** The fawning time of deer, therefore the close time, *i.e.* from about fifteen days before midsummer until fifteen days after it. Also a close time for fishing, etc.

To sit on the fence. To take care not to commit oneself; to hedge. The characteristic attitude of "Mr. Facing-Both-Ways".

Fencibles. Companies of regular troops of horse and foot, raised for home service in 1759, again in 1778–1779, and 1794 for special emergencies. The word is short for *defensibles*.

Fenians. An anti-British secret society of Irishmen founded in New York in 1858 by John O'Mahony and in IRELAND by James Stephens, with the object of making Ireland a republic and bringing English domination to an end. The word is from the Old Irish *Fene*, a name of the ancient Irish, confused with *Fianna*, the legendary warriors who defended Ireland in the time of Finn.

The Fenian Brotherhood, or Irish Republican Brotherhood, attempted invasions of Canada in 1866 and 1870–1871. In 1867 there were insurrectionary attempts in Ireland, attacks on Chester Castle, Clerkenwell Gaol, and an attack on a policeman in Manchester, etc. The movement petered out in the late 1870s. *Cp.* CLAN-NA-GAEL; PHŒNIX PARK MURDERS; SINN FEIN.

Fennel. This herb was anciently supposed to be an aphrodisiac, thus "to eat conger and fennel" was provocative of sexual licence.

It was also emblematical of flattery, and may have been included among the herbs distributed by Ophelia (*Hamlet*, IV, v) for this reason.

Fenrir or **Fenris** (fen' rĕr). In Scandinavian mythology, the wolf of LOKI. He was the brother of HEL and when he gaped one jaw touched earth and the other HEAVEN. At the RAGNAROK he broke his fetters and swallowed ODIN, who was avenged by VIDAR thrusting his sword into the yawning gullet and piercing the beast's heart.

Feræ Naturæ (fer' ī nå tū' rī) (Lat. of savage nature). The legal term for animals living in a wild state, as distinguished from those which are domesticated.

Ferdiad. A hero of Irish legend who was persuaded to fight for Queen MAEVE against CUCHULAIN, his dearest friend. After a struggle lasting three days he was killed, to Cuchulain's bitter grief.

Fergus mac Roich. The heroic tutor of CUCHULAIN, who left CONCHOBAR'S court after the treacherous murder of the sons of USNECH.

Fern Seed. We have the receipt of fern seed, we walk invisible (SHAKESPEARE *Henry IV, Pt. I*, II, i). Fern seed was popularly supposed only to be visible on St. JOHN's Eve, and as it was thus so seldom seen it was believed to confer invisibility on those who carried it. Plants were often supposed to convey their own particular quality on their wearer. Thus the yellow celandine was said to cure jaundice; wood-sorrel, which has a heart-shaped leaf, to cheer the heart; liverwort to be good for the liver, etc.

Ferney. The Patriarch, or **Philosopher of Ferney.** VOLTAIRE (1694–1778); so called because for the last twenty years of his life he lived at Ferney, a village near Geneva.

Ferragus. The giant of Portugal in VALENTINE AND ORSON. The great BRAZEN HEAD, that told those who consulted it whatever they required to know, was kept in this giant's castle.

Ferrara Bible, The. *See* BIBLE, SOME SPECIALLY NAMED EDITIONS.

Ferrex and Porrex. Two sons of Gorboduc, a mythical British king, who divided his kingdom between them. Porrex drove his brother from Britain, and when Ferrex returned with an army he was slain, but Porrex was shortly after torn to pieces by his mother with the assistance of her women. The story is told in Geoffrey of Monmouth's *Historia Britonum* (ch. xvi), and it forms the basis of the first regular English tragedy, *Gorboduc, or Ferrex and Porrex*, written by Thomas Norton and Thomas Sackville, Lord Buckhurst, and acted in 1562.

Fescennine Verses. LAMPOONS; so called from Fescennium in Tuscany, where performers at merry-makings used to extemporize scurrilous jests of a personal nature to amuse the audience.

Fesse. *See* HERALDRY.

Festina Lente. (fes tēn' a len tā) (Lat.). Make haste slowly. It is the punning motto of the Onslow family.

Festschrift (fest'shrift) (Ger. *fest*, festival; *schrift*, writings). This term is commonly used for the volume of essays, papers, etc., prepared by colleagues and friends as a tribute to a scholar on some special occasion (usually on retirement or a particular anniversary).

Fetch. A WRAITH—the disembodied ghost

of a living person; hence *fetch-light*, or *fetch candle*, a light appearing at night supposed to foretell someone's death. *Fetches* most commonly appear to distant friends and relations at the very moment before the death of those they represent. The word is of uncertain origin.

It is also used in the sense of a stratagem, artifice, or trick.

Fetish (fet′ish) (Port. *fetico*, sorcery, charm; Lat. *facticius*, artificial). The name given by early Portuguese voyagers to AMULETS and other objects supposed by the natives of the Guinea Coast to possess magic powers: hence an idol, an object of devotion. Fetishism is found in all primitive nations in which the services of a spirit may be appropriated by the possession of its material emblem. In psycho-pathology the word is used to denote a condition or perversion in which sexual gratification is obtained from some object, etc., that has become emotionally charged.

Feu de joie (fĕr dĕ zhwa) (Fr. fire of joy). A ceremonial discharge of musketry into the air by a line of soldiers on an occasion of rejoicing.

Feudalism, or **Feudal system** (Med. Lat. *feodum*, fee). The name given to an institutional growth in Europe from the time of the decay of the Roman Empire. It arose from the need of the individual and society to gain protection from attack, occasioned by internal disorder and external threat. In return for protection from some powerful individual, the dependant offered services or surrendered to an overlord his land which was then held subject to conditions. English feudalism is commonly held to begin with WILLIAM THE CONQUEROR who acted on the principle that all land belonged to him. It was granted to the tenant-in-chief in return for homage and military service, etc., who passed on land to sub-tenants in return for other services. Thus a pyramidal social structure developed in which every man was bound to an overlord and ultimately to the King.

Feuillant (fĕr′ yon). A reformed CISTERCIAN order instituted in 1577 by Jean de la Barrière, Abbot of the Cistercian monastery of Feuillants in Languedoc.

The Club of the Feuillants in the French Revolution was formed by moderate JACOBINS in 1791. Among its members were Sieyès, Barère, Lafayette, Lameth and Barnave. The club's proper title, indicative of its attitude, was the *Société des Amis de la Constitution* and the popular name was derived from its premises in the Rue St. Honoré, formerly a convent of the Feuillants. In June 1792 all its members were disfranchised.

Few. The Few. The R.A.F. pilots of the BATTLE OF BRITAIN, so called from Prime Minister Winston Churchill's memorable tribute in the HOUSE OF COMMONS (20 August 1940), "Never in the field of human conflict was so much owed by so many to so few."

Fiacre (fē akr′). A French cab or HACKNEY coach, so called from the hotel of St. Fiacre, Paris, where the first station of these coaches was established by M. Sauvage, about 1650.

Legend has it that **St. Fiacre** was a 7th-century hermit of Irish origin. He settled in France and built a monastery at Breuil. His day is 30 August and he is the patron saint of gardeners.

Fiasco (Ital. a flask). A complete failure. In Italy an unpopular singer is sometimes greeted with the cry *Olà olà fiasco!* The word was used by the glassblowers of Venice to describe bad workmanship and it may have some allusion to the bursting of a bottle. Various incidents in the Italian theatre have been put forward as the origin of this usage.

Fiat (fī′ at) (Lat. let it be done). **I give my fiat to that proposal.** I consent to it. A fiat in law is a certificate of the ATTORNEY-GENERAL giving leave to take certain proceedings for which Crown permission is required.

Fiat justitia ruat coelum (Lat.). Let justice be done though the heavens should fall. *See* PISO'S JUSTICE.

Fico (Ital. a fig, from Lat. *ficus*). A popular term in Shakespeare's England for a gesture of contempt such as made by thrusting the thumb between the first and second fingers; much as we say, "I don't care that for you", snapping the fingers at the same time. *Figo* is another

form.
See also I DON'T CARE A FIG FOR YOU *under* FIG.

To fiddle. To manipulate accounts, etc., in a dishonest way in order to gain some advantage or to cover up a deficiency. **To work a fiddle** is substantially the same and usually implies some dishonest or "smart work".

To fiddle about. To trifle, fritter away one's time, mess about. **To fiddle with one's fingers** is to move them about as a fiddler does on the strings of a violin.

To fiddle while Rome burns. *See under* ROME.

Fit as a fiddle. In fine condition.

He was first fiddle. The leading or most distinguished of the company. The allusion is to the first violin, who leads the orchestra.

To play second fiddle. To take a subordinate part, but next after the leader.

Fiddle-de-dee! An exclamation signifying what you say is nonsense.

Fiddle-faddle. To busy oneself with nothing; to dawdle; to talk nonsense.

Fiddler. Slang for sixpence; also for a FARTHING.

Drunk as a fiddler. *See under* DRUNK.

Fiddler's fare, or **pay.** Meat, drink, and money.

Fiddler's Green. The happy land imagined by sailors where there is perpetual mirth, a fiddle that never stops playing for dancers who never tire, plenty of GROG, and unlimited tobacco.

Fiddler's news. Stale or late news, because fiddlers were long reputed to be purveyors of out-of-date news.

Fiddlesticks! Much the same as FIDDLE-DE-DEE, *i.e.* you are talking nonsense.

The devil rides on a fiddlestick. *See* DEVIL PHRASES *under* DEVIL.

Fidei Defensor. *See* DEFENDER OF THE FAITH.

Fiduciary. Fiduciary Issue. That part of a note issue which is not backed by coin or bullion although it may be backed by government securities, etc. If there is no such backing for the paper currency as a whole, then the whole issue is fiduciary. Fiduciary means that which is held or given in trust (Lat. *fiduciarius*).

Field. In huntsman's language *the field* means all the riders; in horse-racing it means all the horses in any one race. In military parlance it is the place of battle, the battle itself or the place of campaign. In HERALDRY it means the entire surface of the shield.

Field of Blood. *See* ACELDAMA.

Field of Cloth of Gold. The plain in Picardy between Guines and Ardres where Henry VIII met Francis I of France in June 1520. Francis hoped for English support against the Emperor, Charles V. A temporary palace was erected, lavish and spectacular arrangements were made for jousting, dancing, and banqueting, and Henry was accompanied by a magnificent retinue. Henry, however, later met the Emperor with whom he effected a treaty.

Field of fire. That part of the terrain before infantry or machine-guns which their weapons can cover, uninterrupted by contours, woods or other obstructions.

Field of force. A term used in physics to denote the range within which a force, such as magnetism, is effective.

Field of the Forty Footsteps, or **The Brothers' Steps.** The land at the back of the BRITISH MUSEUM, once called Southampton Fields, near the extreme north-east of the present Montague Street. The tradition is that at the time of the Duke of MONMOUTH'S REBELLION (1685) two brothers fought each other here until both were killed, and for many years forty impressions of their feet remained on the field. No grass would grow there, nor upon the bank where the young woman sat who was the object of their contest. The site was built upon about 1800.

Field of vision, or **view.** The space over which things can be seen; the space or range within which objects are visible when looking through an instrument such as a telescope or microscope, etc.

Master of the field. The winner; the conqueror in battle.

To back the field means to bet on all the horses except one, the favourite.

To keep back the field is to keep back the riders.

To take to the field. To make the

opening moves in a military campaign.

To win the field. To win the battle.

Field allowance. An extra allowance paid to officers in the field or on campaign.

Field-day. A military term for a day when troops have manœuvres or exercises. Generally, a day of unusual activity and success; to have a thorough turn-out and clean-up. In the U.S. Navy a day devoted to cleaning-ship and preparing for inspection.

Field works. Defensive or protective works, or temporary fortifications, made by an army to strengthen its positions.

Open-field System. *See under* OPEN.

Three-field System. *See under* THREE.

Fierabras, Sir (fī ĕr à brăs). The son of BALAN, King of Spain. For height of stature, breadth of shoulder, and hardness of muscle, he knew no equal, but his pride was laid low by OLIVER. He became a Christian, was accepted by CHARLEMAGNE as a PALADIN and ended his days in an odour of sanctity.

Fieri facias (fī′ er i făk′i ăs) (Lat. cause it to be done). A writ of execution to a sheriff to levy from the goods of a debtor the sum according to the judgment given. The phrase is often abbreviated to *fi fa*. The term was also punningly used in the 16th century in connection with red noses and "fiery faces" through drink.

Fiery Cross, The. An ancient signal in the Scottish Highlands when a chieftain wished to summon his clan in an emergency. It was symbolical of fire and sword and consisted of a light wooden cross the ends of which were dipped in the blood of a goat slain for the purpose. It was carried from settlement to settlement by swift runners. Disobedience to the summons implied infamy, hence the alternative name of *Cross of Shame*.

Scott's *Lady of the Lake* (canto iii) contains a graphic account of the custom.

When the KU KLUX KLAN arose after the American CIVIL WAR, it adopted this symbol.

Fifteen, The. The Jacobite rebellion of 1715 when James Edward Stewart, the Old PRETENDER, made an unsuccessful attempt to gain the throne. The Earl of Mar's Scottish forces were defeated at Sheriffmuir and the English JACOBITES under Squire Foster were beaten at Preston. *Cp.* BOBBING JOHN.

Fifth. Fifth-Amendment Communist. In the United States, one who refused to answer the charge of Communist activities by invoking the Fifth Amendment to the Constitution (1791), which states that no person "shall be compelled in any criminal case to be a witness against himself".

Fifth Column. Traitors; those within a country who are working for the enemy, often by infiltrating into key positions, and seeking to undermine the body politic from within. The origin of the phrase is attributed to General Mola, who, in the Spanish Civil War (1936–1939), said that he had four columns encircling Madrid, and a fifth column working for him in the city.

Fifth-Monarchy Men. Religious extremists of Cromwellian times who maintained that the time had come for the rule of Christ and His Saints—the Fifth Monarchy, succeeding those of Assyria, Persia, Macedonia, and Rome; as the four monarchies described in the *Book of Daniel* (ch. ii) give way to that set up by the "God of Heaven". VENNER'S RISING of 1661 marked the end of their attempts to establish the Fifth Monarchy.

Fig. Most phrases that include the word fig have reference to the fruit as being an object of trifling value; but in the phrases **in full fig,** meaning "in full dress", **figged out,** etc., "dressed up", the word is a variant of *feague*.

I don't care a fig for you; not worth a fig. Nothing at all. Here fig is either an example of something of little value, or alternatively the *fig of Spain* or FICO.

A fig for Peter.
SHAKESPEARE: *Henry VI, Pt. II*, II, iii.

To fig up a horse. To make it lively and spirited by artificial means.

Fig leaf. The leaf of the fig-tree was used by ADAM and EVE to cover their nakedness after the Fall (*Gen.* iii, 7). Hence its use in statuary and paintings in times when "modesty" was in fashion, notably in the Victorian period.

Fig Sunday. An old provincial name

for PALM SUNDAY. Figs were eaten on that day in commemoration of the blasting of the barren fig-tree by Our Lord (*Mark* xi). Many festivals still have their special dishes, as, the goose for MICHAELMAS, pancakes for SHROVE TUESDAY, hot cross BUNS for GOOD FRIDAY, etc.

Fig-tree. It is said that Judas hanged himself on a fig-tree. *See* ELDER-TREE; JUDAS TREE.

Mercury fig. *See under* MERCURY.

Figaro. A type of daring, cunning and witty roguery and intrigue. The character is in *Le Barbier de Séville* (1775), and *Le Mariage de Figaro* (1784) by Beaumarchais. There are several operas based on these dramas, as Mozart's *Nozze di Figaro*, and Paisiello's and Rossini's *Il Barbiere di Siviglia*.

Hence the name of the famous Parisian periodical which appeared from 1826 to 1833 and its successor which began life in 1854. *Le Figaro* is one of the foremost French dailies to survive World War II.

Fight. Acre-fight. A good example of a GHOST-WORD. It was wrongly explained by Cowell as a duel in the open field, fought with sword and lance by single combatants, on the Anglo-Scottish border. It is actually a transliteration of Med. Lat. *acram committere* where *acram* (for *pugnam*) is a poor translation of "camp combat" which was confused with Lat. *campus* (field), Fr. *champ* and so with the English *acre*. It is found only in Cowell and some modern dictionaries which have perpetuated the error.

He that fights and runs away may live to fight another day. An old saw found in many languages. Demosthenes, being reproached for fleeing from Philip of Macedon at Chæronea, replied, "A man that runs away may fight again."

Fighting French, or **La France Combattante.** All those Frenchmen at home and abroad who combined with the Allied nations in their war against the AXIS powers after the fall of France (in June 1940). General de Gaulle and others escaped to England and he formed them into "The Free French" with the CROSS OF LORRAINE for their emblem. The name was later changed to "The Fighting French" (14 July 1942).

To fight for one's own hand. To uphold one's own cause, to struggle for one's own interest.

To fight like Kilkenny cats. *See under* CAT.

To fight shy of. To avoid; to resist being brought into contest or conflict.

To fight with the gloves off. To dispute mercilessly "WITH NO HOLDS BARRED" (*see under* HOLD); without any regard to the courtesies of debate, not "PULLING ANY PUNCHES" (*see under* PULL).

To fight with the gloves on. Figuratively, to spar or dispute without open animosity, to observe the courtesies and to show some consideration for one's opponent.

To live like fighting cocks. *See under* COCK.

Figo. *See* FICO.

Figure. From Lat. *fingere*, to shape or fashion; not etymologically connected with Eng. *finger*, though fingers were used as a primitive method of calculating.

A figure of fun. Of droll appearance, whether from untidiness, quaintness or other peculiarity; one to be scoffed at.

A figure of speech. An established form of abnormal expression designed to produce a special effect, such as hyperbole, METAPHOR, METATHESIS, etc.

A figure of speech only, or **only a figure of speech** is another name for a piece of exaggeration.

To cut a figure. To make an imposing appearance through dress, bearing, etc. *Cp.* CUT A DASH *under* CUT.

To cut a pretty, or **a sorry figure.** To give a poor impression, little to one's credit.

To make a figure. To make a name or reputation, to be a notability.

What's the figure? How much am I to pay? What do I owe?

Figure-head. A carved figure on the head or bows of a sailing ship, which has ornamental value but is of no practical use (*see* CUTTY SARK). Hence, a nominal leader who plays no real part, but often one whose social or other position inspires confidence.

Figures, Roman. *See* NUMERALS.

Filch. To steal or purloin. A piece of 16th-century thieves' slang of uncertain origin (*cp*. FILE).

> With cunning hast thou filched my daughter's heart.
>
> SHAKESPEARE: *Midsummer Night's Dream*, I, ii.

A **filch**, or **filchman** was a staff with a hook at the end, for plucking clothes from hedges, articles from shop windows, etc.

File. Old slang for a rapscallion or worthless person; also a pickpocket. It comes from the same original as the word *vile*.

In single file. Single line; one behind another (Fr. *file*, a row). *Cp*. INDIAN FILE.

Rank and file. Soldiers and non-commissioned officers as apart from commissioned officers; hence the followers in a movement as distinct from its leaders. *Rank* refers to men in line abreast or side by side, *file* to men standing one behind another.

Filibuster (Dut. *vrijbuiter*, a freebooter). The earlier form of the word *flibuster* (Fr. *flibustier*) was applied to the pirates plundering in West Indian waters in the 17th century. *Filibuster* was later used of certain 19th-century bands organized from the United States, in defiance of international law, to invade and revolutionize certain Spanish-American territories. The most notable of these filibusters were those led by Narcisco Lopez against Cuba (1850–1851) and William Walker against Sonora (1853–1854). *See also* FREEBOOTER.

> After an abortive filibuster in Lower California he appeared in 1855 in Nicaragua with a few hundred hard-boiled Californians.
>
> L. D. BALDWIN: *Stream of American History*, I, xxiii, 2.

To filibuster. As a term meaning the use of obstructive tactics in a legislature, by excessive use of technicalities, lengthy speeches, etc., first came into use in the U.S.A. in 1841. Such tactics were notably employed by the Irish Nationalists under Parnell. In July 1877 the HOUSE OF COMMONS sat for 26 hours. *See* CLOSURE.

Filioque Controversy (fil i ō' kwė). An argument concerning the "Procession of the Holy Spirit" that long disturbed the Eastern and Western Churches, and the difference of opinion concerning which still forms one of the principal barriers between them. The point was: Did the HOLY GHOST proceed from the Father *and the Son* (*Filio-que*), or from the Father only? The argument basically is this: If the Son is one with the Father, whatever proceeds from the Father must proceed from the Son also. The *filioque* was first introduced by the Western Church at the Council of Toledo in 589 and was added to the NICENE CREED in the 11th century.

Fill-dyke. The month of FEBRUARY, when the rain and melted snow fills the ditches to overflowing.

> February fill dyke, be it black or be it white;
> But if it be white it's the better to like.
> *Old Proverb*.

Fille de joie (fē dė zhwa) (Fr. daughter of joy). A prostitute.

Fimbul-Winter. In Norse legend, such a severe winter of horrors as never before known which lasted three years without any summer to lessen its onslaught; trees, plants and men died of hunger. It was the forerunner of RAGNAROK.

Fin de siècle (făn dė sē ekl) (Fr. end of century). It has come to imply decadent, with particular reference to the end of the 19th century.

Finality Jack. Lord John Russell (1792–1878), 1st Earl Russell, who originally maintained that the Reform Act of 1832 was a finality, yet made further attempts to extend Parliamentary reform in 1854, 1860, and 1866.

Financial Year. *See* YEAR.

Find. Findings, keepings! An exclamation made when one has accidentally found something, implying that it is now the finder's property. This old saying is very faulty law.

Findabair. In Irish legend, the wondrously beautiful daughter of Queen MAEVE of Connacht. She was promised in marriage to the man who would challenge CUCHULAIN in the WAR OF THE BROWN BULL and died after her lover, Fraech, was slain in battle by Cuchulain.

Fine. Fine as fivepence. An old alliterative saying meaning splendidly dressed or turned out.

Fine feathers make fine birds. *See under* FEATHER.

In fine. In short; to sum up; to come to a conclusion.

One of these fine days. Some time or other; when the opportunity occurs; at some indefinite time in the future.

The Fine Arts. Those arts which depend upon creative imagination and the quest for the expression of beauty, as music, painting, poetry, sculpture and architecture, as opposed to the useful arts, *i.e.*, those which are practised primarily for their utility, as the arts of weaving, metal-working, etc.

He's got it down to a fine art. He has got it to a fine degree of proficiency. He's got the complete knack, he has got it completely "wrapped up".

Fingal. The great Gaelic legendary hero, father of OSSIAN, who was purported by Macpherson to have been the original author of the long epic poem *Fingal* (1762), which narrates the hero's adventures.

Fingal's Cave. The basaltic cavern on Staffa, said to have been a home of FINGAL. It is the name given to Mendelssohn's *Hebridean Overture* (1830).

Finger (O.E. *finger*). The old names for the fingers are:

Thuma (O.E.), the thumb.

Towcher (M.E. the finger that touches), *foreman*, or pointer. This was called the *scite-finger* (shooting finger) by the Anglo-Saxons, now usually known as the first or fore-finger and *index finger* because it is used for pointing.

Long-man, or *long-finger*.

Lech-man, or *ring-finger*. The former means the "medical finger" and the latter is the roman *digitus annularis*, called by the Anglo-Saxons the *gold-finger*. This finger was used as the ring finger (also *annular finger*) in the belief that a nerve ran through it to the heart. Hence the Greeks and Romans called it the *medical finger*, and used it for stirring mixtures under the notion that it would give instant warning to the heart if in contact with anything noxious. It is still

a popular superstition that it is bad to rub salve or scratch the skin with any other finger.

Little man, or *little finger*. Called by the Anglo-Saxons the EAR-FINGER. It is also known as the *auricular finger*.

The fingers each had their special significance in ALCHEMY, and Ben Jonson says:

> The thumb, in chiromancy, we give to Venus,
> The fore-finger to Jove; the midst to Saturn;
> The ring to Sol; the least to Mercury.
> *Alchemist*, I, ii.

Blessing with the fingers. *See* BLESSING.

Cry, baby, cry; put your fingers in your eye, etc. This nursery rhyme seems to be referred to in SHAKESPEARE's *Comedy of Errors*, II, ii:

> Come, Come, no longer will I be a fool,
> To put the finger in the eye and weep.

Fingers were made before forks. A saying used especially at mealtimes to imply that ceremony is unnecessary. Forks were not introduced into England until about 1620, before which period fingers were used.

Finished to the finger-nail. Complete and perfect in every detail, to all the extremities. The allusion is obvious.

His fingers are all thumbs. Said of a person who is clumsy with his hands.

Lifting the little finger. Tippling. Many people in holding a tankard or glass stick out or lift up the little finger. *Cp.* TO CROOK THE ELBOW, or FINGER *under* CROOK; ELBOW-LIFTING.

Lightfingered gentry. Pickpockets, thieves.

My little finger told me that. The same as "A little bird told me that" (*see under* BIRD), meaning, I know it, although you did not expect it. The popular belief was that an itching or tingling foretold that something was about to happen.

Not to lift a finger. Not to make the slightest effort; not to give any assistance.

To be finger and glove with another. To be in close collusion with, to be in the closest co-operation. The more common expression is TO BE HAND IN GLOVE WITH. (*See under* HAND).

To burn one's fingers. *See under* BURN.

To have a finger in. To be concerned in.

To have a finger in the pie. To have a share in doing something, usually with the implication of officious interference or meddling.

To have it at one's fingers' ends. To be completely familiar with it and able to do it adequately and readily. The Latin proverb is, *Scire tanquam ungues digitosque suos*, to know it as well as one's fingers and nails. The allusion is self-evident.

To keep one's fingers crossed. To hope for success, to try to ensure against disaster. From the superstition that making the sign of the CROSS will avert bad luck.

To lay, or put one's finger upon. To point out precisely the meaning, cause, etc.; to detect with complete accuracy.

To slip through one's fingers. To miss an opportunity, to let something elude one, just as a fielder in CRICKET fumbles a catch.

To twist someone round one's little finger. To do just what one likes with him.

With a wet finger. Easily, directly. The allusion is to spinning, in which the spinner constantly wetted the forefinger with the mouth.

Sailors find the wind by holding up a wet finger for the breeze to cool it, thus finding that side whence it comes.

Finger-print. An impression taken in ink of the whorls of lines on the finger. In no two persons are they alike, and they never change throughout life, hence their great value as a means of identifying criminals. From ancient times they were used for certifying documents by the Chinese and Japanese. Sir Francis Galton's *Finger Prints* (1892) and *Finger Print Directories* (1895) drew attention to their usefulness. Sir Edward Henry, Commissioner of the Metropolitan Police (1903–1918), devised a system for classifying impressions which was widely adopted. The American Federal Bureau of Investigation uses his method.

Fingle-fangle. A RICOCHET word from *fangle* meaning a fanciful trifle. It was fairly common in the 17th century and was evolved from *new fangle* (new-fangled).

Fionnuala. In Irish legend, the daughter of LIR, who was transformed into a swan and condemned to wander over the lakes and rivers until Christianity came to IRELAND. Moore has a poem on the subject in his *Irish Melodies*.

Firbolgs. *See* MILESIANS.

Fire (O.E. *fyr*; Gr. *pur*).

St. Anthony's Fire. *See under* ANTHONY.

St. Elmo's Fire; St. Helen's Fire. *See* CORPOSANT.

The Great Fire of London (Sept. 1666) broke out at Master Farryner's bakehouse in Pudding Lane, Thames Street, in the early hours of Sunday (2 Sept.) and aided by high winds spread from the TOWER to the TEMPLE and from the THAMES to SMITHFIELD. St. Pauls' Cathedral and eighty-nine other churches were destroyed and 13,200 houses. In five days it covered 387 acres within the walls and 73 without. It was not the reason for the disappearance of the Plague, as is commonly held, since most of the slum quarters escaped. The fire was halted by blowing up houses at Pie Corner, Smithfield.

Greek Fire. *See under* GREEK.

Between two fires. Subjected to attack, criticism, etc., from both sides at once.

The burnt child dreads the fire. *See under* BURN.

The fat is in the fire. *See under* FAT.

Fire away! Say on; say what you have to say. The allusion to the firing of a gun is obvious. You are loaded up to the muzzle with something to say; fire away and discharge your thoughts.

I have myself passed through the fire; I have smelt the smell of fire. I have had experience in trouble, and am all the better for it. The allusion is to the refining of GOLD, which is passed through fire and so purged of all its dross.

I will go through fire and water to serve you, *i.e.* through any hardships or any test. It may derive from the ORDEAL OF FIRE (*see under* ORDEAL).

If you would enjoy the fire you must put up with the smoke. You must take the rough with the smooth. Every convenience has its inconvenience.

Letter of fire and sword. In SCOTLAND, before the Union with ENGLAND (1707), an order issued by the Scottish Privy Council authorizing a sheriff to dispossess a tenant, or to proceed against a delinquent by all the means of force at his disposal.

Men stand with their backs to the fire. An old explanation is that when the dog's nose proved too small to stop a leak in the Ark, Noah sat on the hole to keep the water out. Ever since men have felt the need to warm their backs, and the dogs have had cold noses.

More fire in the bedstraw. More mischief brewing. A relic of the time when straw was used for beds.

No smoke without fire. To every scandal there is some foundation. Every effect is the result of some cause.

Out of the frying-pan into the fire. *See* FRYING-PAN.

To fire, or **to fire out.** To discharge from employment suddenly and unexpectedly. An expression originating in the U.S.A.

To fire up. To become indignantly angry; to flare up; to get unduly and suddenly excited.

To hang fire. To delay; to be irresolute; to be slow in taking action. An expression derived from gunnery, when the gun is slow in firing the charge.

To heap coals of fire on one's head. *See under* COAL.

To play with fire. To meddle with that which is perpetually dangerous or harmful.

To set the Thames on fire. *See* HE'LL NEVER SET THE THAMES ON FIRE *under* THAMES.

Fire-brand. An incendiary; one who incites to rebellion; like a blazing brand which sets on fire all it touches.

> Our fire-brand brother, Paris, burns us all
> SHAKESPEARE: *Troilus and Cressida*, II, ii.

Fire-bug. An habitual perpetrator of arson; a FIRE-RAISER. The term is also applied to a glow-worm.

Fire-cross. *See* FIERY CROSS.

Fire-drake, or **fire-dragon.** A fiery serpent, an IGNIS FATUUS of large proportions, superstitiously believed to be a flying DRAGON keeping guard over hidden treasures.

Fire-eaters. Those ready to quarrel with anyone; those looking for trouble; eager fighters. The allusion is to the jugglers who swallow flaming tow, etc.

Fire-new. SPICK AND SPAN NEW.

Fire-raiser. One guilty of arson, often to collect the insurance money.

Fire-ship. A ship filled with combustibles sent against enemy vessels to set them on fire. English fire-ships scattered the Spanish Armada in confusion when anchored off Calais in 1588. Also a venereally infected strumpet.

Fire-spaniel. Applied to one who hugs the fire and is loathe to stir from it.

Fire-watcher. The name given to those volunteers in Britain who kept watch for fires started by enemy air raids during World War II.

Fire-worship is said to have been introduced into Persia by Phœdima, widow of Smerdis, and wife of Hystaspes. It is not the SUN that is worshipped, but the god who is supposed to reside in it; at the same time the fire worshippers reverence the sun as the throne of the deity. *Cp.* PARSEES.

Fireside Chats. The name adopted by President F. D. Roosevelt for his broadcasts to the American people on topics of national interest and importance. They began in 1933 and became customary during his administration.

First. A diamond of the first water. *See under* DIAMOND.

At first hand. From one's own knowledge or personal observation.

First catch your hare. *See under* CATCH.

First cause. A cause that does not depend on any other. The Creator.

First come first served. Promptness reaps its own reward. Chaucer in *The Wife of Bath's Tale* (*Prologue*) says:

> Whoso first cometh to the mill, first grint.

The first stroke is half the battle. *See* THE FIRST BLOW IS HALF THE BATTLE *under* BLOW.

First Fleet. The first expedition of eleven ships under Captain Arthur Phillip, R.N. bringing convicts to Australia in 1788. The second fleet arrived in 1790. To have been a *first fleeter* became a matter of pride.

First floor. In Britain the first floor is that immediately above the ground floor; in America it is the ground floor.

First foot, or **first footer.** The first visitor at a house after midnight on New Year's Eve. In SCOTLAND and the North of ENGLAND the custom of *first footing* is still popular.

First-fruits. The first profitable results of labour. In husbandry, the first corn that is cut at harvest, which by the ancient Hebrews was offered to JEHOVAH. Such offerings became customary in the early Christian Church. ANNATES were also called First-fruits. The word is used figuratively as well in such expressions as "the first fruits of sin", "the first fruits of repentance".

First light. In the armed forces "first light" denotes the earliest time (roughly dawn) at which light is sufficient for movement of ships, or for military operations to begin. Similarly *last light* is the latest time when such movements can take place. The expression was current in World War II.

First nighter. One who makes a practice of attending opening performances of plays.

The First Gentleman of Europe. A nickname given to George IV, but Thackeray says in *The Four Georges*, "We can tell of better gentlemen."

The First Grenadier of the Republic. A title given by NAPOLEON to La Tour d'Auvergne (1743–1800) a man of extraordinary courage and self-effacement. He refused all promotion beyond that of captain, as well as this title.

Fish. The fish was used as a symbol of Christ by the early Christians because the letters of its Greek name *ichthus* (*see* ICHTHYS) formed an acronym of the initial letters of the words Jesus Christ, Son of God, Saviour.

Ivory and mother-of-pearl counters used in card games, some of which are more or less fish-shaped, are so called, not from this shape, but from Fr. *fiche*, a peg, a card counter. *La fiche de consolation* (a little piece of comfort or consolation) is the name given in some games to the points allowed for the rubber.

A fish out of water. Said of a person out of his usual environment and who thus feels awkward; also of one who is without his usual occupation and is restless in consequence.

A loose fish. A man of loose or dissolute habits. Fish as applied to a human being is mildly derogatory.

A pretty kettle of fish. *See under* KETTLE.

A queer fish. An eccentric person.

All is fish that comes to my net. I turn everything to some use; I am willing to deal in anything out of which I can make a profit.

He eats no fish. In the time of Elizabeth I, a way of saying he is an honest man and one to be trusted, because he is not a Papist. Roman Catholics were naturally suspect at this time, and PROTESTANTS refused to adopt their custom of eating fish on Fridays (*see* FISH DAY).

The government, however, sought to enforce the observance of fish days in order to help the fishing ports and the seafaring population; and to check the consumption of meat which encouraged the conversion of arable into pasture.

I have other fish to fry. I have other things to do. I am busy and cannot attend to anything else now.

Neither fish, flesh, nor fowl, or **neither fish, flesh nor good red herring.** Suitable to no class of people; neither one thing nor another. Not fish (food for the monk), nor flesh (food for the people generally), nor yet red herring (food for the poor).

The best fish swim near the bottom. What is most valuable is not to be found near the surface, nor is anything really worth having to be obtained without effort and trouble.

There's as good fish in the sea as ever came out of it. Don't be disheartened if you've lost the chance of something good, you'll get another. Those who get preferment are not the only capable people.

To cry stinking fish. *See under* CRY.

To drink like a fish. *See under* DRINK.

Five

To feed the fishes. To be sea-sick; to be drowned.

To fish for compliments. To try to obtain praise, usually by putting leading questions.

To fish in troubled waters. To scramble for personal advantage in times of stress, political unrest, etc.; to try to make a calamity a means to personal gain.

You must not make fish of one and flesh of the other. You must treat both alike. You must not discriminate.

Fish day. In France known as *jour maigre* (a lean day), a day when Roman Catholics and others used to abstain from meat and customarily eat fish. In the ROMAN CATHOLIC CHURCH there was a general law of abstinence on all Fridays (unless FEASTS), but BISHOPS now urge the faithful voluntarily to practise this or some other form of self-denial.

Fish Royal. Sturgeon and whale (although the latter is not a fish). If caught near the coast they are the property of the Crown.

Fish-wife. A woman who sells fish in a fish market or who hawks fish. Fish-wives are renowned for their flow of invective, hence the term is sometimes applied to a vulgar, scolding female.

Fisher King. In the legends of the Holy GRAIL, the uncle of PERCEVAL.

Fisherman's Ring. A seal-ring with which the POPE is invested at his election, bearing the device of St. PETER fishing from a boat. It is used for sealing papal briefs, and is officially broken up at the Pope's death by the Chamberlain of the Roman Church.

Fitz. The Norman form of the modern French *fils*, son of; as Fitz-Herbert, FitzWilliam, Fitz-Peter, etc. It is sometimes assumed by the illegitimate or morganatic children of royalty, as Fitz-Clarence, Fitz-roy, etc.

Fitzroy Cocktail (Austr.). One of the many concoctions drunk by strong men "OUT BACK". The recipe is methylated spirits, ginger beer, and one teaspoonful of boot polish.

Five. The pentad, one of the mystic numbers, being the sum of 2 and 3, the first *even* and first *odd* compound. Unity is God alone, *i.e.*, without creation. Two is diversity, and three (being 1 and 2) is the compound of unity and diversity, or the two principles in operation since creation, and representing all the powers of nature.

Bunch of fives. Pugilistic slang for the fist.

The Five Alls. *See* PUBLIC-HOUSE SIGNS.

The Five Boroughs. In English history, the Danish confederation of Derby, Leicester, Lincoln, Nottingham, and Stamford in the 9th and 10th centuries.

Five fingers. A fisherman's name for the starfish.

The Five Members. Pym, Hampden, Haselrig, Holles, and Strode; the five members of the LONG PARLIAMENT whom Charles I attempted to arrest in 1642.

The Five-Mile Act. An Act passed in 1665 (repealed in 1812), the last act of the CLARENDON CODE prohibiting NON-CONFORMIST clergy from coming within five miles of any corporate town or within that distance of the place where they had formerly ministered.

The Five Nations. A description applied by Kipling to the British Empire—the Old Country, with Canada, Australia, South Africa, and India.

In American history the term refers to the five confederated Indian tribes inhabiting the present State of New York, *viz*. the Mohawks, Oneidas, Onondagas, Cayugas, and Senecas; also known as the IROQUOIS Confederacy. HIAWATHA is traditionally regarded as the founder of this league, to which the Tuscarora were admitted as a Sixth Nation about 1715.

The Five Points of Calvinism. *See* CALVINISM.

The Five Senses. These are hearing, sight, smell, taste and touch.

The Five Towns. Towns in the Potteries which Arnold Bennett (1867–1931) used as the scene of the best known of his novels and stories. They are Tunstall, Burslem, Hanley, Stoke-upon-Trent, Longton, and Fenton—actually six—but for artistic purpose Bennett called them five. All are now part of Stoke-on-Trent. *Cp.* ETRURIA.

The Five Wits. Common sense, imagination, fantasy, estimation and memory; in general, the faculties of the mind; also an alternative expression for the five senses.

Five-Year Plans. In the U.S.S.R., plans for developing the whole of the nation's economy in a co-ordinated effort by a five-year programme. The first Five-Year Plan was launched by Stalin in 1928 with the aims of making the Soviet Union self-supporting, mechanizing agriculture, promoting literacy, etc. Further Five-Year Plans followed and the example was copied by other countries.

Fiver. A five-pound note.

Fix, A. In modern slang and of American origin, a shot of heroin or other narcotic drug.

In a fix. In an awkward predicament.

To fix on, or **upon.** To determine upon; to settle upon; to choose.

To fix up. To mend or repair; to arrange.

To obtain a fix. In navigation to fix one's exact position by the intersection at a suitable angle of two or more position lines obtained at the same time.

Fixed Air. An old name of carbonic acid gas (carbon dioxide), given to it by Dr. Joseph Black (1728–1799), because it is "fixed" in solid carbonates until driven out by heat.

Fixed Stars. Stars whose relative position to other stars is always the same, as distinguished from planets, which shift their relative positions.

Flaccus (flăk′ŭs). HORACE (65–8 B.C.), the Roman poet, whose full name was Quintus Horatius Flaccus.

Flag. A word of uncertain origin. National flags are flown as the symbols of a state and are particularly important as a means of recognition of ships at sea. Merchant ships usually wear their flag or ensign at the stern, warships wear their flag or jack at the bows and their ensign at the stern. Flags are also used as personal banners or standards, especially by royalty and high-ranking naval and military officers, by regiments, as house flags by companies, for signalling purposes, etc. That part of a flag which is nearest the mast is called the *hoist* and

the disc at the top of the flagstaff is the *truck*. The *fly* is the end of the flag furthest from the staff. *See* TRICOLOUR.

Flags on Church flagstaffs. In the CHURCH OF ENGLAND the proper flag to be flown is that of St. GEORGE, with the arms of the SEE in the first quarter.

A black flag is the emblem of piracy or of no QUARTER (*see under* BLACK); also the anarchists' flag. In World War II, submarines, on returning to base, sometimes hoisted a black flag to indicate a "kill".

A green flag is used on railways, roads, etc. for signalling "Go ahead".

A red flag is generally used to indicate danger or as a stop signal. It is also the symbol of international socialism and *The Red Flag* is a socialist anthem still used, somewhat incongruously, by the British LABOUR PARTY.

> Then raise the scarlet standard high,
> Beneath its shade we'll live and die
> Though cowards flinch and traitors sneer
> We'll keep the Red Flag flying here.
> JAMES CONNELL: *The Red Flag.*

A white flag is the flag of truce or surrender, hence **to hang out the white flag** is to sue for QUARTER, to give in.

A yellow flag is one of the three "quarantine flags".

A flag of convenience is a foreign flag under which a vessel is registered, usually to lessen taxation and manning costs. Liberia, Honduras and Panama are the most widely used flags of convenience and Liberia has the largest merchant fleet in the world.

The flag of distress. When a ship's ensign is flown upside down it is a signal of distress.

The flag's down. Indicative of distress; also the start of a race. When the face is pale the "flag is down"; alluding to the old custom of taking down the flag of theatres when they were closed during LENT.

To break a flag is to hoist it rolled up and to "break" it by pulling the halyard to release the hitch which holds it together.

To dip a flag is to haul it down to a half-mast position and then rehoist it. This is the usual salute between ships at sea. It is also flown **at the dip** as a sign of mourning.

To flag down. To stop someone, nowadays usually a motor-driver; from the practice of stopping a train or other vehicle by waving or displaying a flag. Formerly, trains which did not usually stop at little-used wayside stations did so if the appropriate flag was displayed. Such stations were known as *flag-stations* or *flag-stops*.

To fly the flag at half-mast is a sign of mourning.

To get one's flag. To become an admiral.

To lower one's flag. TO EAT HUMBLE PIE; *see under* HUMBLE), to yield or confess oneself in the wrong; to eat one's own words.

To strike the flag. To lower it completely. It is also a token of surrender; and when an admiral relinquishes his command he *strikes his flag*.

Trade follows the flag. *See under* TRADE.

Flag Day. In the U.S.A., 14 June, the anniversary of the adoption of the STARS AND STRIPES in 1777. In Britain **a flag day** is any day on which small paper flags or emblems for wearing on the apparel are sold for the support of charities, etc.

Flag Officer. An admiral, vice-admiral or rear-admiral who flies the flag appropriate to his rank. An Admiral of the Fleet flies a UNION JACK; an admiral a ST. GEORGE's Cross on a white ground, a vice-admiral the same, with on red ball in the upper canton next the staff, and a rear admiral a second red ball in the canton immediately below.

Flag-ship. A ship carrying the FLAG OFFICER.

Flagellants (flă jel' ănts). The Latin *flagellum* means a scourge, and this name is given to those extremists who scourged themselves in public processions in mediæval times, and subsequently, as penance for the sins of the world. There was a particular outbreak in Italy in 1260 and again in 1348–1349, at the time of the BLACK DEATH, when the movement spread over Europe. The Church has never encouraged such practices.

Flagellum Dei (Lat. the scourge of God). *See* SCOURGE OF GOD.

Flamboyant Architecture. The last phase of French GOTHIC architecture, named from O.Fr. *flambe* (flame). Characterized by the flame-like tracery and elaboration of detail, it flourished from about 1460 until the 16th century.

Flame. A sweetheart. **An old flame**, a quondam sweetheart.

Flaming swords. Swords with a wavy or flamboyant edge, used now only for state ceremonies. The Dukes of Burgundy carried such swords, and they were worn in Britain until the time of William III (1689–1702).

Flaminian Way. The great northern road, the *Via Flaminia*, of ancient Italy, constructed by G. Flaminius in 220 B.C. It led from the Flaminian gate of Rome to Ariminum (Rimini).

Flanders Mare. So Henry VIII called Anne of Cleves, his fourth wife whom he married in January 1540, and divorced the following July. She died at Chelsea in 1557.

Flanders Poppies. The name given to the red artificial poppies sold for REMEMBRANCE DAY to benefit ex-service men. The connexion with poppies comes from a poem by John McCrae, which appeared in *Punch*, 8 December 1915:

> If ye break faith with us who die
> We shall not sleep, though poppies grow
> In Flanders fields.

Flannel. That's all flannel. That's all soft soap. What you say does not really impress me. *Flannel* may have acquired this kind of connotation in the same way as BOMBAST and FUSTIAN.

Flannelled fools. Cricketers. This term, used either derisively or humorously, is taken from Kipling's poem *The Islanders*.

> Then ye returned to your trinkets; then ye contented your souls.
> With the flannelled fools at the wicket or the muddied oafs at the goals.

Flap. To be in a flap. A colloquial expression meaning to be in a state of anxious excitement, as birds flap and flutter when disturbed.

Flap-dragons. An old name for SNAP-DRAGON, *i.e.* raisins soaked in spirit, lighted and floating in a bowl of spirituous liquor. GALLANTS used to drink flap-dragons to the health of their mistresses, and would frequently have lighted candle-ends floating in the liquor to heighten the effect.

Flapjack. A flat cake of batter baked on a griddle or in a shallow pan, and so called from turning it by tossing it into the air.

In the 20th century the word has been applied to a woman's flat powder compact.

Flapper. In the early years of the 20th century a term applied to a girl in her teens, now called a teenager, from her plaited pigtail tied at the end with a large bow. When stepping along the pigtail flapped her back. Subsequently her hair was "put up" in a "bun" or other hairstyle. By the 1920s the name was commonly applied to a young woman, or "bright young thing". *See also* LAPUTA.

The Flapper Vote. An irreverent name for the vote granted to women of 21 by the Equal Franchise Act of 1928, sponsored by Baldwin's Conservative government. *See* FLAPPER.

Flash. Showy, smart, "swagger"; as a *flash wedding*, a *flash hotel*. In Australia the term *flash* or *flashy* is applied to

> anyone who is proud and has nothing to be proud of.
> J. KIRBY: *Old Times in the Bush of Australia*, 1895.

Also counterfeit, sham, fraudulent.

Flash notes are forged notes, a **flash man** is a thief or an associate of one; and a **flash-house** is one frequented by thieves and prostitutes.

> The excesses of that age [the Restoration] remind us of the humours of a gang of footpads, revelling with their favourite beauties at a flash-house.
> MACAULAY: *Essays (Hallam's Constitutional History)*.

A mere flash in the pan. A failure after a showy beginning; like the attempt to discharge an old flint-lock gun that ends with a flash in the lock-pan, the gun itself "hanging-fire" (*see* TO HANG FIRE *under* FIRE).

Flat. Flat as a flounder. I knocked him down "flat as a flounder". A flounder is one of the flatfish.

Flat as a pancake. Quite flat.

Flat out. At full speed, all out, fully extended.

He is a regular flatfish. A dull, stupid fellow. The play is upon *flat* (not sharp, *i.e.* dull), and such fish as plaice, dabs, etc.

To lie like a flatfish. To lie blatantly. The punning derivation is obvious.

To be caught flat-footed. To be caught unprepared, as a football player who is tackled by an opponent before he has been able to advance.

To be in a flat spin. To be very flurried, to be in a panic. In flying, a flat spin is when the longitudinal axis of an aircraft inclines downwards at an angle of less than $45°$. In the early days this inevitably involved loss of control. It is now an aerial manœuvre performed at low level in air combat as an evasive action.

Flat-foot. A policeman. Sometimes called a **flattie**.

Flat race. A race on the "flat" or level ground without obstacles, as opposed to hurdling, STEEPLECHASING, etc.

Flatterer. When flatterers meet, the devil goes to dinner. Flattery is so pernicious, so fills the heart with pride and conceit, so perverts the judgment and disturbs the balance of mind, that SATAN himself could do no greater mischief, so he may go to dinner and leave the leaven of wickedness to work its own mischief.

Flea. A flea's jump. It has been estimated that if a man, in proportion to his weight, could jump as high as a flea, he could clear St. Paul's Cathedral with ease (365 ft. high).

Aristophanes, in the *Clouds*, says that SOCRATES and Chærephon tried to measure how many times its own length a flea jumped. They took in wax the size of a flea's foot; then on the principle of EX PEDE HERCULEM, calculated the length of its body. They then measured the distance of a flea's jump from the hand of Socrates to Chærephon and the problem was resolved by simple multiplication.

A mere flea-bite. A thing of no moment, a very small portion or contribution.

Great fleas have lesser fleas. No matter what our station in life, we all have some hangers-on.

To be sent off with a flea in the ear.
Sent away discomfited by a reproof or
repulse. A dog which has a flea in the ear
is very restless, and runs off in terror
and distress.

An old phrase dating at least from the
15th century in English, and earlier in
French.

Flecknoe, Richard. A Roman Catholic
priest, and author of poems, plays and
other works. He died about 1678. He is
now only remembered through Dryden's satire *Mac Flecknoe*, where it is
said he reigned

> without dispute
> Through all the realms of Nonsense, ab-
> solute.

Fleet, The. A famous London prison of
mediæval origin which stood on the east
side of Farringdon Street, until its demolition (1845–1846), on the site now
partly occupied by the Memorial Hall.
It took its name from the river Fleet
which (now piped) enters the THAMES at
Blackfriars Bridge. As a royal prison it
housed some distinguished prisoners in
Tudor and Stuart times, including those
committed by STAR CHAMBER, but mainly owes its notoriety to its subsequent
use as a debtor's prison. It was destroyed in the GREAT FIRE OF LONDON
(*see under* FIRE), rebuilt, and again
burned during the Gordon Riots. The
Warden farmed out the prison to the
highest bidder which encouraged the
shameful treatment of its occupants. *Cp.*
FLEET MARRIAGES.

Fleet Book Evidence. No evidence at
all. The books of the Old Fleet prison
are not admissible as evidence of a marriage. *See* FLEET MARRIAGES *below.*

Fleet Marriages. Clandestine marriages, especially of minors, at one time
performed without BANNS or licence in
the chapel of the FLEET, but from the
latter part of Queen Anne's reign performed by the Fleet clergy in rooms of
nearby taverns and houses.

Fleet Street. The famous thoroughfare
which runs from Ludgate Circus to the
Strand taking its name from the Fleet river, once navigable for coal barges as far
as HOLBORN. Formerly noted for its
bookshops, it is now synonymous with
journalism and the newspaper world.

Flemish School. A school of painting
founded by the brothers van Eyck, in
the 15th century. The chief early masters were Memling, Weyden, Matsys,
and Mabuse; of the second period, Rubens and Van Dyck, Snyders, and the
younger Teniers. As well as the invention of oil painting by Jan van Eyck the
school was notable for the perfection
and unsurpassed representation of reality.

Flesh. A thorn in the flesh. *See* THORN.

To be one flesh. To be closely united,
as in marriage.

He fleshed his sword, *i.e.* used it for
the first time.

Men fleshed in cruelty. Those initiated or used to it when being trained.
Young sporting dogs and hawks are rewarded with the first game they catch.
This first introduction to flesh encour-
ages the taste for blood.

The Fleshly School. In the *Contemporary Review* for October 1871, Robert
Buchanan published a violent attack on
the poetry and literary methods of Swinburne, Rossetti, Morris, O'Shaugh-
nessy, John Payne, and one or two
others under the heading *The Fleshly
School of Poetry*, over the signature
"Thomas Maitland". The incident
created a literary sensation; Buchanan
first denied the authorship but was soon
obliged to admit it, and was reconciled
to Rossetti, his chief victim, some years
later. Swinburne's very trenchant reply
is to be found in his *Under the Microscope* (1872).

Fleur-de-lis, -lys, or **-luce** (flĕr de lē, lēs,
loos) (Fr. lily-flower). The name of several varieties of iris or flags, and also of
the heraldic LILY which was borne as a
charge on the old French royal COAT OF
ARMS. In the reign of Louis VII
(1137–1180) the national STANDARD was
thickly charged with lilies but in 1376
the number was reduced to three by
Charles V in honour of the TRINITY.
Guillim's *Display of Heraldrie* (1610)
says the device is "Three TOADS erect,
saltant"; in allusion to which NOSTRA-
DAMUS in the 16th century called
Frenchmen CRAPAUDS. The *fleur-de-lis*
was used to decorate the north point on
the mariner's card before the end of the

15th century and in the 20th century it was adopted as the badge of the BOY SCOUTS. *See also* FLORIN.

Flibbertigibbet. One of the five fiends that possessed "poor Tom" in *King Lear* (IV, i). SHAKESPEARE got the name from Harsnet's *Declaration of Egregious Popish Impostures* (1603), where we are told of forty fiends which the JESUITS cast out, and among the number was "Fliberdigibet", a name which had been previously used by Latimer and others for a mischievous GOSSIP. Elsewhere the name is apparently a synonym for PUCK.

Flicks. To go to the flicks. To go to a film show, an expression derived from the early days of such shows when the pictures "flickered" on the screen.

Fling. I must have a fling at. Metaphorically, throw a stone at, *i.e.* attack with words, especially sarcasm; to make a haphazard venture.

To have his fling. To have full freedom of action; to indulge in pleasure to the fullest extent; to sow his wild OATS. The Scots have a proverb:

Let him tak' his fling and find oot his ain wecht [weight]

meaning, give him a free hand and he'll soon find his level.

Flint. To skin a flint. *See under* SKIN.

Floating Academy. A convict ship, one of the HULKS.

Flogging a dead horse. *See under* HORSE.

Flogging round, or **through the fleet.** In the Royal Navy, according to the ancient practice of the sea, this barbarous punishment consisted of a number of lashes from the CAT-O'-NINE-TAILS administered alongside each ship present, usually to the accompaniment of the ROGUE'S MARCH. Death was a common result. It ceased before the end of the 18th century but flogging at the gangway was not finally "suspended" until 1879. After the mutiny at the Nore in 1797 one seaman of the *Monmouth* was sentenced to 380 lashes.

Flood, The. *See* DELUGE.

Floor. I floored him. Knocked him down on the floor; hence figuratively, to overcome or beat.

To cross the floor. In Parliamentary usage, means to change parties; from

the fact that government and OPPOSITION benches are on opposite sides of the floor of the HOUSE OF COMMONS.

To get in on the ground floor. *See under* GROUND.

To take the floor. To speak in a debate; to begin to dance.

Flora. The Roman goddess of flowers especially associated with Spring. Her festivals, the *Floralia*, were from 28 April to 3 May. The term *Flora* also denotes the native or indigenous plants of a country or region. *Cp.* FAUNA.

Flora Macdonald (1722–1790). The Scottish heroine who aided the escape of Prince Charles Edward after the failure of the FORTY-FIVE Rebellion. She conducted the YOUNG PRETENDER (*see* PRETENDER), disguised as Betty Bourke, an Irish woman, from Benbecula to Monkstadt in Skye and thence via Kingsburgh to Portree, often in imminent danger from the military search parties. She was subsequently imprisoned in the TOWER OF LONDON but released in 1747 under the Act of Indemnity. She married Allan Macdonald in 1750, emigrated to North Carolina, 1774, but returned to Scotland in 1779.

Florentine Diamond. A large and famous DIAMOND weighing 133 carats. It formed part of the Austrian crown jewels and previously belonged to Charles, Duke of Burgundy.

Florida. In 1512 Ponce de León sailed to the west in search of "the Fountain of Youth". He first saw land on Easter Day which was then popularly called in Spain *Pascua florida*, flowery EASTER, and on that account called the land "Florida". It is also called the "Peninsula State". Its city of St. AUGUSTINE is the oldest European settlement in the original UNITED STATES.

Florin (Ital. *fiorino*, a little flower). As a gold coin it was first minted in 13th-century Florence and named after the lily on the reverse. The FLEUR-DE-LIS was the badge of Florence. Edward III coined an English gold florin in 1344 valued at 6s. The English silver florin representing 2s. was first issued in 1849 as a tentative introduction of a DECIMAL CURRENCY.

Graceless, or **Godless florin.** The

first English silver florin struck in 1849, called "graceless" because the usual "*Dei Gratia*" (by God's grace) was omitted; and "Godless" because of the omission of F.D. (DEFENDER OF THE FAITH).

Some attributed the cholera outbreak of that year to the new florin. The coins were called in and the Master of the Mint, Richard Lalor Sheil (1791–1851), a Roman Catholic, left the MINT the following year.

Florizel. George IV, when Prince of Wales, corresponded under this name with Mrs. Robinson, the actress, generally known as PERDITA, in which character she first attracted his attention. The name comes from SHAKESPEARE's *Winter's Tale*.

Flotsam and Jetsam. Properly wreckage and other goods found in the sea. "Flotsam", goods found floating on the sea (O.Fr. *floter*, to float); "jetsam", things thrown overboard (Fr. *jeter*, to throw out). The term is now also applied to wreckage found on the shore. *Lagan*, a word of uncertain origin, applies to goods thrown overboard but tied to a float for later recovery.

Flowers and Trees, etc.

(1) Dedicated to heathen gods:

The Cornel cherry-tree	to	APOLLO
,, CYPRESS	,,	PLUTO
,, DITTANY	,,	DIANA
,, LAUREL	,,	APOLLO
,, LILY	,,	JUNO
,, Maidenhair	,,	PLUTO
,, MYRTLE	,,	VENUS
,, Narcissus	,,	CERES
,, OAK	,,	JUPITER
,, OLIVE	,,	MINERVA
,, POPPY	,,	CERES
,, VINE	,,	BACCHUS

(2) Dedicated to saints:

Canterbury Bells	to	St. AUGUSTINE of CANTERBURY
Crocus	,,	St. VALENTINE
Crown Imperial	,,	Edward the Confessor
DAISY	,,	St. MARGARET
Herb Christopher	,,	St. CHRISTOPHER
LADY'S-SMOCK	,,	the Virgin MARY
ROSE	,,	MARY MAGDALENE
St. John's-wort	,,	St. JOHN
St. Barnaby's Thistle	,,	St. BARNABAS

(3) National emblems:

LEEK, Daffodil	emblem of	Wales
LILY (FLEUR-DE-LYS)	,,	BOURBON France
,, (Giglio bianco)	,,	Florence
Lily, White	,,	GHIBELLINES
,, red	,,	the GUELPHS
LINDEN	,,	Prussia
Mignonette	,,	Saxony
Pomegranate	,,	Spain
Rose	,,	ENGLAND
,, red, LANCASTRIANS:		white, YORKISTS
SHAMROCK	emblem of	IRELAND
THISTLE	,,	SCOTLAND
VIOLET	,,	ATHENS
Sugar Maple	,,	Canada

(4) In Christian Symbolism:

Box	a symbol of	the Resurrection
Cedars	,,	the faithful
Corn-ears	,,	the Holy Communion
Dates	,,	the faithful
Grapes	,,	this is my blood
HOLLY	,,	the Resurrection
IVY	,,	the Resurrection
Lily	,,	purity
OLIVE	,,	peace
ORANGE-BLOSSOM	,,	virginity
PALM	,,	victory
Rose	,,	incorruption
Vine	,,	Christ our Life
YEW	,,	death

N.B.—The laurel, oak, olive, myrtle, rosemary, cypress, and amaranth are all funereal plants.

Flowers in Christian Tradition. Many plants and flowers play a part in Christian tradition. The ASPEN is said to tremble because the cross was made of its wood and there are other traditions connected with the ELDER-TREE, FIG-TREE, PASSION FLOWER, THISTLE, etc. *See also* FIG LEAF; GLASTONBURY.

The following are said to owe their stained blossoms to the blood which trickled from the CROSS: the red anemone; the arum; the purple orchis; the crimson-spotted leaves of the roodselken (vervain, or the "herb of the cross"); the spotted persicaria or snakeweed.

The Language of Flowers. The traditional symbolic meanings attached to numerous flowers and plants. Some examples are:

Asphodel	my regret follows you to the grave
Bay leaf	I change but in death
Bluebell	constancy
Foxglove	insincerity
Honeysuckle	generous and devoted affection
Jasmine	amiability
Nasturtium	patriotism
Oak leaves	bravery

Peony	shame, bashfulness
Quince	temptation
Snowdrop	hope
Veronica	fidelity

There's rosemary, that's for remembrance; pray love, remember; and there is pansies, that's for thoughts.

SHAKESPEARE: *Hamlet*, IV, v.

Flower people. Supporters of a brightly clad cult of the mid-1960s who advocated "universal love" as a substitute for materialism.

The Flowery Kingdom. China; a translation of the Chinese *Hwa-Kwo*.

Fluff. A little bit of fluff. A girl or woman. A colloquial expression of Edwardian origin, fluff being the light, downy, soft stuff; now considered derogatory.

Flush of, or **with money.** Very well supplied with money. Similarly *a flush of water* means a sudden and full flow of water (Lat. *fluxus*, flowing).

To flush game. A gun-dog is said to *flush game* when he disturbs them and they take to the air.

Flute. The Magic Flute. In Mozart's opera of this name (*Die Zauberflöte*, 1791) the magic flute was bestowed by the powers of darkness, and had the power of inspiring love. By it Tamino and Pamina are guided through all worldly dangers to knowledge of Divine Truth.

Flutter. A colloquial term for a small gamble.

To flutter, or **cause a flutter in the dovecotes.** To disturb the equanimity of a group of people.

Fly (*plural* flys). A one-horse hackney-carriage. A contraction of *Fly-by-night*, as sedan chairs on wheels used to be called in the REGENCY. These "Fly-by-nights", much patronized by the Regent and his boon companions at Brighton, were invented in 1809 by John Butcher, a carpenter.

Fly. An insect (*plural* flies). For the theatrical use, *see* FLYMAN.

It is said that no fly was ever seen in Solomon's temple, and according to Mohammedan legend, all flies shall perish except one, the bee-fly.

The God, or **Lord of Flies.** Every year, in the temple of Actium, the Greeks used to sacrifice an ox to ZEUS, who in this capacity was surnamed Apo-

myios, the averter of flies. Pliny tells us that at ROME sacrifice was offered to flies in the temple of HERCULES Victor, and the Syrians also offered sacrifice to these insects. *See* ACHOR; BEELZEBUB.

The fly in the ointment. The trifling cause that spoils everything; a Biblical phrase.

Dead flies cause the ointment of the apothecary to send forth a stinking savour; so doth a little folly him that is in reputation for wisdom and honour.

Eccles. x, 1.

The fly on the coach-wheel. One who fancies himself of great importance, one who is in reality of none at all. The allusion is to ÆSOP's fable of a fly sitting on a chariot-wheel and saying, "See what dust I make."

There are no flies on him. He's very shrewd and wide awake; he won't be CAUGHT NAPPING (*see under* CATCH).

To crush a fly on a wheel. An allusion to the absurdity of taking a wheel used for torturing criminals and heretics for killing a fly. *Cp.* TO USE A SLEDGEHAMMER TO CRUSH A NUT *under* NUT; TO BREAK A BUTTERFLY ON A WHEEL *under* BREAK.

To rise to the fly. To rise to the bait, to fall for a hoax or trap, as a fish rises to the angler's fly and is caught.

Fly-blown. Fouled by flyblows; hence tainted, spoiled. At one time naturalists thought that maggots were actually blown on to the meat by blow-flies.

Fly. A flying angel. *See under* ANGEL.

As the crow flies. *See under* CROW.

Fly bird. A knowing one, a WIDE BOY.

To fly a kite. *See under* KITE.

To fly blind. To pilot an aircraft solely by means of instruments; the opposite of visual navigation.

To fly in one's face. To get into a passion with someone; to insult; as a HAWK, when irritated, flies in the face of its master.

To fly in the face of danger. To defy danger in a foolhardy manner, as a hen flies in the face of a dog.

To fly in the face of providence. To act rashly, and throw away good opportunities; to court danger.

To fly off the handle. To burst out into angry and violent speech without

Folio

control, as a hammer loses its head when loose after a blow has been struck.

To fly out at. To burst or break into a passion.

To let fly. To make a violent attack upon, either literally or by a torrent of abuse, etc.

To make the feathers, or **fur fly.** To create a violent disturbance or to attack vigorously, either physically or by speech or writing, as when birds or animals are attacked.

No flying without wings. Nothing can be done without the proper means.

To come off with flying colours. *See under* COLOUR.

Fly-by-night. One who defrauds his creditors by decamping in the night; a dubious character. *See also* FLY (a cab).

Fly-flat. A racing man's term for a punter who thinks he knows all the ins and outs of the turf, but doesn't. *Cp.* FLAT.

Flying bedstead. Nickname of the experimental wingless and rotorless vertical take-off jet aircraft demonstrated in Britain in 1954. Built by Rolls-Royce, the name was inspired by its appearance.

Flying Column. *See under* COLUMN.

Flying-the-garter. *See under* GARTER.

The Flying Duchess. Mary du Caurroy Russell, Duchess of Bedford (1865–1937). After making record-breaking return flights to India (1929) and South Africa (1930) with Captain Barnard, she obtained an "A" pilot's licence in 1933 and disappeared on a solo flight over the North Sea in March 1937.

The Flying Dutchman. In maritime legend, a spectral ship that is supposed to haunt the seas around the Cape of Good Hope and to lure other vessels to their destruction or to cause other misfortune. According to Jal's *Scènes de la Vie Maritime*, he is said to be a Dutch captain, who persisted in trying to round the Cape, in spite of the violence of the storm, and the protests of passengers and crew. Eventually a form, said to be the Almighty, appeared on the deck, but the Captain did not even touch his cap but fired upon the form and cursed and blasphemed. For punishment, the Dutchman was con-

demned to sail and to be a torment to sailors until the Day of JUDGMENT. A skeleton ship appears in Coleridge's *Ancient Mariner*, and Washington Irving tells of "the Flying Dutchman of the Tappan Sea" in his *Chronicles of Woolfert's Roost*. Wagner has an opera *Der Fliegende Holländer* (1843) and Captain Marryat's novel *The Phantom Ship* (1839) tells of Philip Vanderdecken's successful but disastrous search for his father, the captain of the Flying Dutchman. Similar legends are found in many other countries.

> The Demon Frigate braves the gale;
> And well the doom'd spectators know
> The harbinger of wreck and woe.
> SCOTT: *Rokeby*, canto II, xi.

Flyman. In the theatre, the sceneshifter, or man in the "flies", *i.e.* the gallery over the proscenium where the curtains, scenery, etc., are controlled.

Fob. You are trying to fob, or **fub me off.** You are trying to put me off (with something inferior or by deception). *Fob* is connected with Ger. *foppen*, to hoax.

Fo'c's'le. *See* FORECASTLE.

Foil. That which sets off something to advantage. The allusion is to the metallic leaf used by jewellers to set off PRECIOUS STONES (Fr. *feuille*; Lat. *folium*; Gr. *phullon*, a leaf).

Folio. The word is the ablative of the Lat. *folium*, a leaf.

In bibliography and printing it has distinct applications. (1) A sheet of paper (for printing) in its standard size. (2) A book *in folio*, in [one] sheet, is a book, the sheets of which have been folded once only, so that each sheet makes two leaves; hence a book of large size. (3) It is also applied to the leaf of a book of any size. Until the mid-16th century, when printed pagination became common, books were *foliated, i.e.* numbered on the recto or front of the leaf only and not on the verso. (4) Printers call a page of MS. or printed matter a *folio* regardless of size.

In BOOK-KEEPING *Folio so-and-so* means page so-and-so, and also two pages which lie exposed at the same time, one containing the credit and the other the debit of one and the same account. So called because ledgers, etc., are made *in folio*.

In conveyances, MSS., type-written documents etc., 72 words, and in Parliamentary proceedings 90 words, make a *folio*, where it is used for assessing the length of a document. In the U.S.A. it is 100 words.

Folkland. An uncommon Anglo-Saxon term formerly explained as land which was the common property of the "folk" from which the king could grant land to his followers. The more accepted theory, initiated by Vinogradoff in 1893, is that folkland is land held by *folkright*. Folkland was subject to FOOD-RENT and other duties to the king, from which BOCLAND was exempt.

Folk-lore. The traditional beliefs, customs, popular superstitions and legends of a people. The word was coined in 1846 by W. J. Thomas (1803–1885), editor of the *Athenæum* (*see under* ATHENÆUM CLUB), and founder of *Notes and Queries*.

Folk-mote. The meeting of the free men in the shire MOOT.

Follow. Follow-my-leader. A parlour game in which each player must exactly imitate the actions of the leader, or pay a forfeit.

Follow your nose. Go straight on.

He who follows truth too closely will have dirt kicked in his face. Be not too strict to pry into abuse.

To follow suit. To do as the person before you has done. A phrase from cardplaying.

Follower. In addition to its usual meaning of one who follows a leader, the word was used in Victorian days to designate a maid-servant's young man.

Folly. A fantastic or foolishly extravagant country seat or costly structure, built for amusement or vainglory. Fisher's Folly, a large and beautiful house in Bishopsgate, with pleasure-gardens, bowling green and hothouses, built by Jasper Fisher, one of the six clerks of CHANCERY, is an historical example. Queen Elizabeth I lodged there; in 1625 it was acquired by the Earl of Devonshire and its site is now occupied by Devonshire Square.

Kirkby's castle, and Fisher's folly,
Spinola's pleasure, and Megse's glory.
STOWE: *Survey* (1603).

A classic example was that of Fonthill, Wiltshire, built by William Beckford (1760–1844), author of *Vathek*, at a cost of some £273,000. It took 18 years to complete and was sold in 1822 for £330,000. Three years later the tower, 260 ft. high, collapsed, destroying part of the house. With the growth of landscaping in the 18th century follies multiplied rapidly taking many forms. Towers, obelisks, mock ruins of castles and abbeys, chapels, temples, hermitages and grottoes became the pride of their owners. The style varied from "gothick" to classical and Chinese pagodas were not uncommon.

Palmerston's Follies. The nickname given to the line of forts surrounding Portsmouth and Plymouth, the building of which was supported by the Prime Minister, Lord Palmerston, in 1859 when he thought attack from NAPOLEON III's France was a possibility. They were called follies because they were never used for their original purposes. Fort Southwick, near Portsmouth, was used as the headquarters of the Commander-in-Chief, Portsmouth, during World War II.

Fond. A foolish, fond parent. Here fond does not mean affectionate, but silly, from the obsolete *fon*, to act the fool, to become foolish (connected with our fun). Chaucer uses the word *fonne* for a simpleton (Reeve's Tale, 169); SHAKESPEARE has "fond desire", "fond wretch", "fond madwoman", etc.

Fontange (fôn tonzh). A head-dress introduced in France about 1680, and named after Louis XIV's mistress, the Duchesse de Fontanges (1661–1681). It became progressively more extravagant in height and similar to the English *Tower* or *Commode* of the same period.

Fontarabia (font á rā' bi á). Now called Fuenterrabia (Lat. *Fons rapidus*), near the Gulf of Gascony. Here, according to legend, CHARLEMAGNE and all his chivalry fell by the swords of the SARACENS. The French romancers say that, the rear of the king's army being cut to pieces, Charlemagne returned to life and avenged them by a complete victory.

Food. Food for powder. Soldiers; especially raw recruits levied in time of war; cannon fodder.

Food for thought. Something to cogitate upon.

The food of the gods. *See* AMBROSIA; NECTAR.

To become food for worms, or **for the fishes.** To be dead and buried, or to be drowned.

Food-rent. In Anglo-Saxon England the victuals payable by a group of vills (townships) on the royal estates sufficient to provide for the king and his household for 24 hours. A food-rent used for the endowment of parish churches came to be called CHURCH SCOT.

Fool. A fool and his money are soon parted; Fortune favours fools; There's no fool like an old fool, etc., are among the "fool phrases" which need no explanation. Others are:

A fool's bolt is soon shot (SHAKE-SPEARE, *Henry V*, III, vii). Simpletons cannot wait for the fit and proper time, but waste their resources in random endeavours. The allusion is to bowmen, *bolt* being the arrow of a crossbow; the good soldier shot with a purpose, the foolish soldier at random. *Cp. Prov.* xxix, 11.

A fool's errand. A fruitless errand which is a waste of time.

A fool's paradise. A state of contentment or happiness founded on unreal, fanciful, or insecure foundations.

As the fool thinks, so the bell clinks. A foolish person believes what he desires. *See under* BELL.

At forty every man is a fool or his own physician. Said by Plutarch (*Treatise on the Preservation of Health*) to have been a saying of Tiberius. A man at the age of forty ought to have learnt enough about his own constitution to be able to keep himself healthy.

Every man hath a fool in his sleeve. No one is always wise; there is something of the fool in everyone.

Fools rush in where angels fear to tread. The unintelligent and thoughtless get involved where those with superior wisdom and understanding think twice.

To be a fool for one's pains. To have worked ineffectively; to have had no reward for one's labours.

To be a fool to. Not to come up to; to be very inferior to; as, "Bagatelle is a fool to billiards."

To make a fool of someone. To mislead him; to trick him; to make him appear foolish.

Young men think old men fools, old men know young men are. An old saying quoted by Camden in his *Remains* (1605), as by a certain Dr. Metcalfe.

To fool about, or **around.** To play the fool; to play around in an aimless fashion.

To fool away one's time, money, etc. To squander it; to fritter it away.

All Fools' Day. The first day of April. *See* APRIL FOOL.

April Fool. *See* APRIL.

Court Fools. From mediæval times until the 17th century licensed fools or jesters were commonly kept at court; and frequently in the retinue of wealthy nobles. Holbein painted Sir Thomas More's jester, Patison, in his picture of the chancellor; the Earl of Morton, Scottish Regent (executed 1581), had a fool called Patrick Bonny; and as late as 1728 Swift wrote an epitaph on Dickie Pierce, the Earl of Suffolk's fool, who is buried in Berkeley Churchyard, Gloucestershire. *See also* DAGONET.

Among the most celebrated court fools are:

Rahère (founder of St. Bartholomew's Hospital), of Henry I (according to a tradition); John Scogan (*see* SCOGAN'S JESTS), of Edward IV; PATCH, of Elizabeth, wife of Henry VII; Will Somers, of Henry VIII; Jenny Colquhoun and James Geddes, of Mary Queen of Scots; Robert Grene, of Queen Elizabeth I; Archie Armstrong and Thomas Derrie, of James I; Muckle John, of CHARLES I, who was probably also the last court fool in England.

In France, Miton and Thévenin de St. Léger were fools of Charles V; Haincelin Coq belonged to Charles VI, and Guillaume Louel to Charles VII, Triboulet was the jester of Louis XII and Francis I; Brusquet, of Henri II; Sibilot and Chicot, of Henri III and IV; and l'Angély, of Louis XIII and Louis XIV.

In chess the French name for the "bishop" is *fou* (a fool) and they used to represent it in a fool's dress. *See* GON-NELLA'S HORSE.

Gooseberry Fool. *See* GOOSEBERRY.

Tom Fool. *See under* TOM.

The Feast of Fools. A kind of clerical SATURNALIA, popular in the MIDDLE AGES and not successfully suppressed until the REFORMATION, and even later in France. The feast was usually centred on a cathedral and most commonly held on the Feasts of St. STEPHEN (26 December), St. JOHN (27 December), HOLY INNOCENTS (28 December). The mass was burlesqued and braying often took the place of the customary responses. Obscene jests and dances were common as well as the singing of indecent songs. The ass was a central feature and the **Feast of Asses** was sometimes a separate festival.

The wisest fool in Christendom. James I was so called by Henri IV of France, who learnt the phrase from Sully.

Foolscap. Properly the jester's cap and bells or the conical paper hat of a DUNCE. The standard size of printing paper measuring $13\frac{1}{2} \times 17$ in. and of writing paper measuring $13\frac{1}{4} \times 16\frac{1}{2}$ in. took their name from an ancient watermark showing a fool's head and cap.

Fool's gold. *See under* GOLD.

Foot. First foot. *See under* FIRST.

I have not yet got my foot in. I am not yet familiar and at home with the work. The allusion is to the preliminary exercises in Roman foot-races. While the starting signal was awaited the contestants made essays at jumping, running, etc., to limber up. This was "getting one's foot in" for the race. *Cp.* TO GET ONE'S HAND IN *under* HAND.

To be carried out feet foremost. To be dead.

To cast oneself at someone's feet. To be entirely submissive to him, to throw oneself on his mercy.

To fall, or **land on one's feet.** To secure a good position; to be fortunately placed. As a cat luckily lands on its feet.

To find one's feet. To get on one's

feet; to settle down and develop a grip on one's work.

To have feet of clay. Said of someone hitherto held in high regard or in an important position who shows disappointing weaknesses of character. The allusion is to *Dan.* ii, 31–45. The image in Nebuchadnezzar's dream had a head of gold, breast and arms of silver, belly and thighs of brass, legs of iron and feet of iron and clay.

To have one's foot on another's neck. To have him at one's mercy; to tyrannize over, or domineer over him completely. *See Josh.* x, 24.

To measure another's foot by one's own last. To apply one's personal standards to the conduct or actions of another; to judge people by oneself.

To put one's best foot foremost. To walk as fast as possible, with all dispatch; to try to make a good impression.

To put one's foot down. To take a firm stand, to refuse or insist upon something firmly and finally. In driving, to depress the accelerator and drive fast.

To put one's foot in it. To perpetrate a blunder, to make a FAUX PAS, to get into trouble. The allusion is obvious. There is a famous Irish BULL. "Every time I open my mouth I put my foot in it".

To set a man on his feet. To start him off in business, etc., especially after he has "come a CROPPER".

To set on foot. To set going.

To show the cloven foot, or **hoof.** To betray an evil intention. An allusion to the DEVIL who is represented with a cloven hoof.

To trample under foot. To oppress, or outrage; to treat with the greatest contempt and discourtesy.

With one foot in the grave. In a dying state.

To foot it. To walk the distance instead of riding; also to dance.

To foot the bill. To pay it; to promise to pay the account by signing one's name at the foot of the bill.

Washing the feet. *See* MAUNDY THURSDAY; MAUNDS.

To be on a good footing (with someone). To be on friendly terms with a person; to be in good standing.

Footloose and fancy free. Unfettered,

unattached to a member of the opposite sex.

Footmen. *See* RUNNING FOOTMEN.

Footlights. To appear before the footlights. To appear on the stage. The footlights are placed near the front edge of the stage.

Fop's Alley. An old name for a promenade in a theatre, especially the central passage between the stalls (right and left in the opera-house).

Forbidden. Forbidden City. Lhasa (the seat of the gods), the ancient religious and political capital of Tibet, some 12,000 ft. above sea level. The palace of the Dalai-Lama or Grand Lama stands on the neighbouring Potala hill. This sacred city of Lamaist BUDDHISM containing fifteen monasteries fell under Chinese control (*c.* 1720) and when, in 1959, the Tibetans unsuccessfully tried to cast off the Chinese yoke, the Dalai-Lama fled to India. Its first European mention was by Friar Odoric, the famous traveller (*c.* 1330). Long closed to Europeans, hence the epithet, it is still largely a forbidden city.

Forbidden Fruit. Forbidden or unlawful pleasure of any kind, especially illicit love. The reference is to *Gen.* ii, 17, "But of the tree of knowledge of good and evil, thou shalt not eat of it." According to Mohammedan tradition the forbidden fruit partaken of by ADAM and EVE was the banyan or Indian fig.

Forcible Feeble. *See* FEEBLE.

Fore! A cry of warning used by golfers before driving.

To come to the fore. To stand forth; to stand out prominently; to distinguish oneself.

To the fore. In the front rank; eminent.

Forecastle, or **fo'c's'le** (fōk' sŭl). So called because anciently the fore part of a ship was raised and protected like a castle, so that it could command the enemy's deck.

Forestick. The front log laid across the ANDIRONS on a wood fire, which holds the others in. Its opposite number at the back is the *backlog*.

Forest Courts. The ancient courts established for the conduct of forest business and the administration of the forest laws, the main aim of which was to preserve the wild animals for the royal chase. Such laws existed in Saxon England and were reinforced by the Norman kings. William I created the New Forest in the sense that he placed the area under Forest Law, and the forests reached their greatest extent under Henry II (1154–1189).

Forgery (O.F. *forgier*, Lat. *fabricare*, to fabricate or make). Generally speaking a forgery is an attempt to pass off as genuine some piece of spurious work or writing with the intent to deceive or defraud. It is not always easy to distinguish a forgery and an *imposture*. Among the notable examples given here, the ROWLEY POEMS (*see below*) are perhaps impostures rather than forgeries. *See also* OSSIAN.

Billies and Charlies. Bogus mediæval metal objects, chiefly plaques, cast in lead or an alloy of lead and copper known as cock metal, and artificially pitted with acid. Between 1847 and 1848 William Smith and Charles Eaton (Billy and Charley) produced these objects by the thousand and planted them on sites being excavated in and around London.

The Drake Brass Plate. Sir Francis Drake during his voyage of circumnavigation (1577–1580), anchored off the Californian coast in 1579 and set up a brass plate naming the territory New Albion and claiming it in the name of Queen Elizabeth. In 1936 the plate was said to have been found near San Francisco and the inscription seemed to be reasonably authentic although some authorities expressed doubt. A replica was, in due course, presented to Queen Elizabeth II which is kept in Buckland Abbey, Drake's Devonshire property, now a museum. In 1977 a reported analysis of the composition of the brass by the Lawrence Berkeley Institute of the University of California and the Research Laboratory for Archaeology at Oxford found that it was of late 19th- or early 20th-century manufacture.

Hitler Diaries. In April 1983 *The Sunday Times* reported the discovery of 60 volumes of Hitler's diaries which had been acquired by the Hamburg colour magazine *Stern* for £2,460,000 and delivered to them by their reporter Gert Heidemann. They were said to have been salvaged from an aircraft wrecked in 1945 and found in a hayloft. Professor Hugh Trevor-Roper (Lord Dacre) had vouched for their authenticity and *The Sunday Times* (after paying *Stern* for publication rights) obtained two volumes (1932 and 1935) for testing. Dr. Julius Grant, a chemical expert, proved that the paper in the diaries was not in use until after World War II. Two weeks after their alleged discovery the Bonn government also declared them to be forgeries. Heidemann revealed that he had obtained them from a Stuttgart dealer in military relics, Konrad Fischer, whose real name was Kujau and the latter confessed to forgery. Both were imprisoned in May 1983, brought to trial in August 1984 and sentenced in July 1985. Kujau was jailed for 4 years 6 months for forgery and Heidemann 4 years 8 months for fraud.

The Ireland Forgeries. One of the most famous literary forgers was William Henry Ireland (1777–1835), the son of a bookseller and amateur antiquarian. When only 19, young Ireland produced a number of seemingly ancient leases and other documents purporting to be in SHAKESPEARE's handwriting, including a love poem to "Anna Hatherrawaye". Emboldened by their acceptance he next came out with two "lost" Shakespeare plays—*Vortigern* and *Henry II*. Ignoring the suspicions of Kemble, Sheridan produced *Vortigern* at DRURY LANE in 1796. During the rehearsals Mrs. Siddons and Mrs. Palmer resigned their roles and Kemble helped to ensure the play was laughed off the stage. When he spoke the line "When this solemn mockery is o'er", the house yelled and hissed until the curtain fell. Meanwhile Malone and Steevens had studied the *Miscellaneous Papers*, said to be Shakespeare's, and had declared them forgeries. Ireland confessed later in the same year. His motive appears to have been a craving to secure the regard and admiration of his father, whose antiquarian interests amounted to an obsession.

The Pictures of Tom Keating. Kea-

ting (1918–1984), beginning as a picture restorer, produced about 2,000 drawings and paintings and sold them as originals by Constable, Gainsborough, Turner, Rembrandt and others. He admitted they were fakes in 1976.

The Pigott Forgeries. In April 1887, *The Times* published in facsimile a letter attributed to Charles Stewart Parnell, the Irish leader, condoning the PHOENIX PARK MURDERS. Parnell denounced this as a forgery, but *The Times* continued to publish its damaging articles on "Parnellism and Crime" which deeply influenced English opinion. In 1888 O'Donnell, one of those besmirched, sued *The Times* for libel. From the judicial inquiry which resulted, the letters were found to be forged by Richard Pigott, who sold them to *The Times* for a large sum, money being his only motive. *The Times* had to pay £250,000 in costs. Pigott fled to Madrid and shot himself when arrest was impending.

The Piltdown Skull, or Piltdown Man. In 1908 and 1911 Charles Dawson of Lewes "found" two pieces of a highly mineralized human skull in a gravel bed near Piltdown Common, Sussex. By 1912 he and Sir Arthur Smith Woodward had discovered the whole skull. This was thought to be that of a new genus of man and was called *Eoanthropus Dawsoni*. It came to be accepted as such by most prehistorians, archaeologists, etc., although a few were sceptical. In 1953 J. S. Weiner, K. P. Oakley and W. E. Le Gros Clark issued a report (*Bulletin of the British Museum* (Natural History), Vol. II, No. 3) announcing that the Piltdown mandible was a fake, in reality the jaw of a modern ape, the rest of the skull being that of *Homo sapiens*. The hoax, which took in most of the experts, was apparently planned by William Sollas, Professor of Geology at Oxford (1897–1937), through his dislike of Sir Arthur Smith Woodward.

The Poems of Ossian. *See* OSSIAN.

The Protocols of the Elders of Zion. *See under* PROTOCOL.

Psalmanazar, George. *See* PSALMANAZAR.

The Rowley Poems. Certain poems written by Thomas Chatterton (1752–

1770), and said by him to have been the work of a 15th-century priest of Bristol called Thomas Rowley (a fictitious character). Chatterton began to write them be _ fore he was 15 and, after having been refused by Dodsley, they were published in 1769. Many prominent connoisseurs and litterateurs, including Horace Walpole (until he consulted friends), were hoaxed.

The Turin Shroud. The shroud of twill linen kept in Turin Cathedral and claimed to be that which wrapped the body of Christ after His crucifixion. The POPE agreed to RADIOCARBON DATING in 1987 and in 1988 the Archbishop of Turin appointed the Oxford Research Laboratory for Archaeology, the Department of Physics of Arizona University and the Swiss Federal Institute of Technology at Zurich, to date the shroud, pieces of which were given to these institutes in April 1988. The results were announced on 13 October and the cloth was dated between 1260 and 1390. There is no historical evidence that it was known before the 14th century. Although not accepted by all the general conclusion is that the shroud is a mediæval forgery.

The Vermeer Forgeries. Hans (Henri) van Meegeren (1889–1947) began his series of brilliant fakes of Dutch masters in 1937 with *The Supper at Emmaus* which was sold as a "Vermeer" for 550,000 gulden. It was, of course, vetted by the experts! His intention seems to have been to indulge his contempt and hatred of the art critics by a superlative hoax, but the financial success of his first fake led to others, mostly "Vermeers". Discovery only came in 1945 when Allied commissioners were seeking to restore to their former owners the art treasures which had found their way to Germany during the war. Among Goering's collection was an unknown Vermeer—*The Woman taken in Adultery*—and its original vendor was found to be van Meegeren. Sale of such a work of national importance involved a charge of collaboration with the enemy. To escape the heavy penalty, van Meegeren confessed to the faking of 14 Dutch masterpieces, 9 of which had

been sold for a total of 7,167,000 gulden, and to prove his story agreed to paint another "old masterpiece" in prison in the presence of the experts. He was sentenced to one year's imprisonment in October 1947 but died on 30 December.

The Vinland Map. Norse exploration from the end of the 10th century led to the discovery of part of North America. According to the Norse Saga, *Flateyjarbók*, "When spring came they made ready and left, and Leif named the land after its fruits, and called it *Vinland*". In 1957 the discovery of a map of the N.E. American coast was announced and said to be the most exciting cartographic find of the century. Supposedly drawn about 1440, it substantially preceded the voyages of Columbus (1492) and of John Cabot (1497), thus conclusively establishing the extent of the Viking explorations. It was presented to Yale University by an anonymous giver in 1965. In 1974 Yale announced that it was a fake. The pigment of the ink with which it was drawn was found to contain titanium dioxide, first used in the 1920s.

The Zinoviev Letter, or **Red Letter Scare.** A letter, which purported to be signed by Zinoviev, president of the Presidium of the Third Communist International, summoning the British Communist Party to intensify its revolutionary activities and to subvert the armed forces of the crown, was published (25 October 1924), four days before a General Election. It helped to promote a "red scare" and possibly increased an almost certain CONSERVATIVE majority. Many Labour leaders held it to be a forgery and its authenticity was denied by the Russians. In December 1966 *The Sunday Times* published an article establishing that the letter was a forgery perpetrated by a group of WHITE RUSSIAN *émigrés*, at the same time suggesting that certain leaders at the Conservative Central Office knew that it was a fake, although the Conservative party as a whole assumed it to be genuine. The "informant" was paid for his services.

Forget-me-not. According to German legend this flower takes its name from the last words of a knight, who was drowned while trying to pick some from the riverside for his lady. The botanical name *myosotis* (mouse-ear) refers to the shape of the leaves.

Forgotten Man, The. A phrase derived from W. G. Summer (1840–1910), the American sociologist, to describe the decent, hardworking, ordinary citizen. It was later popularized by F. D. Roosevelt in 1932 during the Presidential election campaign, although he actually used the expression before his nomination. He advocated a NEW DEAL and appealed to the "forgotten man at the bottom of the economic pyramid".

Fork. To fork out. Fork is old thieves' slang for a finger, hence "to fork out" is to produce and hand over, to pay up.

Fingers were made before forks. *See* FINGERS.

Forked cap. A bishop's MITRE; so called by John Skelton (*c.* 1460–1529). It is cleft or forked.

The forks. The gallows (Lat. *furca*). Among the Romans the word also meant a kind of yoke, with two arms stretching over the shoulders, to which the criminal's hands were tied.

The Caudine Forks. *See* CAUDINE.

Forlorn Hope. This is the Dutch *verloren hoop*, the lost squad or troop. The French equivalent is *enfants perdus*, lost children. The *forlorn hope* was a picked body of men sent in front to begin an attack, particularly the body of volunteers who first entered the breach in the storming of defensive fortifications. The phrase is now usually applied to a body of men selected for some desperate enterprise.

Hoop means a troop or company, and word play or mistaken etymology have resulted in the phrase being used to mean a "faint hope" or an enterprise offering little chance of success.

Form (O.Fr. *forme*, Lat. *forma*). Shape, figure, manner, etc. *Good* or *bad form* is behaving in accordance—or otherwise —with the established conventions of good manners and behaviour.

Fortiter in re (fôr′ ti tĕr in rē) (Lat.). Firmness in doing what is to be done; an unflinching resolution to persevere to the end. *See* SUAVITER.

Fortunatus. A hero of mediæval legend (derived from Eastern sources) who possessed an inexhaustible purse, a wishing cap, etc.

Fortune. Fortune favours the brave. The expression is found in Terence— "Fortis fortuna adjuvat" (*Phormio*, I, iv); also in VIRGIL—"Audentis fortuna adjuvat" (*Æn*. X. 284), and many other classic writers.

Fortunate Islands. An ancient name for the Canary Islands; also, for any imaginary lands set in distant seas, like the "Islands of the Blest".

Forty. A number of frequent occurrence in the SCRIPTURES and hence formerly treated as, in a manner, sacrosanct. Moses was "in the mount forty days and forty nights"; Elijah was fed by ravens for forty days; the rain of the FLOOD fell forty days; and another forty days expired before NOAH opened the window of the ark; forty days was the period of embalming; Nineveh had forty days to repent; Our Lord fasted forty days; He was seen forty days after His Resurrection, etc.

St. SWITHIN betokens forty days' rain or dry weather; a QUARANTINE extended to forty days; in Old English law forty days was the limit for the payment of the fine for manslaughter; a stranger, at the end of forty days, was compelled to be enrolled in the TITHING; the privilege of SANCTUARY was for forty days; the widow was allowed to remain in her husband's house for forty days after his decease; a KNIGHT enjoined forty days' service of his tenant; a new-made burgess had to forfeit forty pence unless he built a house within forty days, etc., etc.

Forty stripes save one. The Jews were forbidden by MOSAIC LAW to inflict more than forty stripes on an offender, and for fear of breaking the law, they stopped short of the number. If the scourge contained three lashes, thirteen strokes would equal "forty save one".

The THIRTY-NINE ARTICLES of the CHURCH OF ENGLAND used sometimes to be called "the forty stripes save one" by theological students.

Forty winks. A short nap.

The Forty Immortals, or simply **The Forty.** The members of the French

Academy, who number forty.

The Hungry Forties. *See* HUNGRY.

The Roaring Forties. A sailor's term for the stormy regions between 40° and 50° south latitude, where heavy westerly winds (known as Brave West Winds) prevail. In the days of sail, owing to these winds, mariners used often to return to Europe via Cape Horn instead of the Cape of Good Hope. The term has also been applied to the North Atlantic crossing between Europe and America between 40° and 50° north latitude.

The Forty-Five. The name given to the rebellion of 1745 led by Charles Edward Stuart, the Young PRETENDER. He landed on Eriskay Island (23 July) and raised his standard at Glenfinnan (19 August). Joined by many Scottish clansmen, he proclaimed the Old Pretender King, as James III, and defeated Sir John Cope at Prestonpans (21 September), and marched south reaching Derby (4 December). His plan to proceed to London was frustrated by the advice of his supporters and lack of support from English JACOBITES. He retreated to SCOTLAND and was decisively defeated by the Duke of Cumberland at Culloden Moor (16 April 1746). The Young Pretender escaped to France (20 September) with the help of FLORA MACDONALD and others. Cumberland earned the nickname "Butcher" for the subsequent reprisals taken against the Highlanders.

Forty-niners. Those who took part in the Californian gold rush, after the discovery of gold there in 1848. Most of the adventurers arrived in 1849, coming from many parts of the world, including Australia and China.

Forty-two Line Bible, The. *See* BIBLE, SOME SPECIALLY NAMED EDITIONS.

Forty Years On. This oft quoted phrase forms the opening of the famous Harrow Football Song. It is also the school song. The words by Edward Bowen were set to music by his colleague John Farmer.

Forwards, Marshal. Blücher (1742–1819) was called *Marschall Vorwärts*, from his constant exhortation to his soldiers in the campaigns preceding Waterloo. *Vorwärts!* always *Vorwärts!*

Fosse, or **Foss Way.** One of the principal Roman roads in Britain. It runs on the line Axmouth — Ilchester — Bath — Cirencester — Leicester — Lincoln. Its name derives from the ditch (Lat. *fossa*) on each side of the road. *Cp.* ERMINE STREET.

Fountain of Arethusa. *See* ALPHEUS AND ARETHUSA.

Fountain of Youth. In popular legend, a fountain with the power of restoring youth. Much sought after, at one time it was supposed to be in one of the Bahama Islands. Ponce de León, discoverer of FLORIDA, set out in search of BIMINI.

Four. Four-eyes. An old and somewhat derisive nickname often used by children when teasing a bespectacled acquaintance.

The Four Corners of the Earth. Generally speaking, the uttermost ends of the earth, the remotest parts of the world.

In 1965 members of the Johns Hopkins Applied Physics Laboratory named the four corners of the earth as being in Ireland, south-east of the Cape of Good Hope, west of the Peruvian coast, and between New Guinea and Japan. Each of these "corners" (of several thousand square miles in area) is some 120 ft. above the geodetic mean and the gravitational pull is measurably greater at these locations.

The Four Freedoms. These were defined by President Franklin D. Roosevelt in his message to Congress, 6 January 1941, as the freedom of speech, and expression, the freedom of worship, and the freedom from fear and want. They were to be the aims of the U.S.A. and ultimately of the world. The occasion was his proposal to make the U.S.A. "the arsenal of democracy" and to extend Lease-Lend to Britain.

Four Horsemen of the Apocalypse. In *The Revelation of St. John the Divine* (ch. vi), four agents of destruction, two being agents of war and two of famine and pestilence. The first appeared on a white horse, the second on a red horse, the third on a black horse, and the fourth on a pale horse.

The Four Hundred. A late 19th-century term for New York's most exclusive social set, which came into general use as a designation of social exclusiveness. In 1892, Mrs. William Astor finding the need to limit her guests to the capacity of her ballroom, which was asserted to be suitable for 400 guests, asked Ward McAllister, the self-appointed organizer of New York society, to prune her invitations. McAllister is also reported to have claimed that there were only 400 people in New York city who could claim to be "society". *Cp.* UPPER TEN *under* TEN.

Four Letters, The. *See* TETRAGRAMMATON.

Four-letter words. The long established term for the blunt O.E. words for certain parts and functions of the body. Such words, not used in polite society, gained a much wider currency during the two World Wars and attained a degree of literary usage, especially after the *Lady Chatterley's Lover* case in 1960, when Penguin Books were acquitted of issuing an obscene publication. They are now in common use in informal contexts but are still considered taboo and labelled so in dictionaries.

Four-minute men. In the U.S.A. during World War I, the name given to the members of a volunteer organization some 75,000 strong who, in 1917–1918, set out to promote the sale of Liberty Loan Bonds and stir up support for the war in Europe. They gave talks of four minutes duration to church congregations, cinema audiences, lodges, etc.

Four-minute mile. The running of a mile in four minutes was for many years the hoped-for achievement of first-class athletes. The rigorous training and timed pacing of P. J. Nurmi (Finland) achieved a time of 4 mins. 10·4 secs. in 1924 but R. G. Bannister (b. 1929) was the first man to reach the goal in 1954. He achieved a *sub-four-minute mile* at Oxford in 1954 (3 mins. 59·4 secs.) after constant and carefully planned efforts. In July 1979 Sebastian Coe achieved a new world record of 3 mins. 49 secs. only to be beaten almost immediately by Steve Ovett, who reduced this time by one-fifth of a second. In 1981 Coe ran the mile in 3 mins. 47·33 secs.

The four-minute mile had become rather like an Everest—a challenge to the human spirit.
R. BANNISTER: *First Four Minutes*, ch. xiii.

Four Sons of Aymon. *See* AYMON.

Fourlegs, Old. Nickname for the coelacanth, a species of fish held to be extinct for millions of years until a specimen was caught in 1938 off East London, South Africa. Another was caught off the Comoro Islands, north of Madagascar, in 1952 and subsequently numerous others. The lobate fins, which could be used more or less as limbs, give rise to the name.

Fourth dimension. As a mathematical concept, a hypothetical dimension, whose relation to the recognized three of length, breadth and thickness, is analogous to their relation with each other. Albert Einstein in 1921 introduced time as the fourth dimension in his THEORY OF RELATIVITY. The expression is also sometimes used to describe something beyond the limits of normal experience.

Fourth Estate. *See under* ESTATE.

Fourth of July. *See* INDEPENDENCE DAY.

Fourth Party. The nickname of a group of four members of the CONSERVATIVE opposition, who harassed Gladstone's second administration (1880–1885). It consisted of Sir Henry Drummond Wolff, Sir John Gorst, A. J. Balfour and their leader, Lord Randolph Churchill. They seized their first opening during the disputes over Bradlaugh's admission to Parliament, when as an atheist he refused to take the Parliamentary oath of allegiance. They made every use of their political opportunities against the government, and strongly criticized their own front bench under the somewhat ineffective leadership of Sir Stafford Northcote. The name "Fourth Party" arose when a member of the Commons referred to two parties (LIBERAL and Conservative) and Parnell, the Irish leader, called out "three"; Randolph Churchill then interjected to make it "four".

Fourth Republic. The French Republic established in 1946 which replaced the provisional governments that followed the collapse of the VICHY régime after D-DAY. Essentially a continuation of the THIRD REPUBLIC, it gave way to the *Fifth Republic* in 1958.

Fourierism. A utopian socialist system advocated by François Marie Charles Fourier (1772–1837) of Besançon. Society was to be organized into "phalanges" each consisting of about 1,600 people sharing common buildings (the *phalanstère*) and working about 5,000 acres of land, with suitable facilities for the development of handicrafts and sources of amusement and a harmonious social life. The most menial tasks were to be the best rewarded out of the common gain and pleasant labour the least. The "phalanges" were to be linked together in suitable groups and finally into one great federation with the capital Constantinople. A number of short-lived Fourierist phalanges were established in the U.S.A. in the middle years of the 19th century but all had disappeared by 1860.

Fourteen Hundred. The cry raised on the Stock Exchange to give notice that a stranger has entered the "HOUSE". The term is said to have been in use in Defoe's time, and to have originated when, for a considerable period, the number of members had remained stationary at 1,399.

Fourteen Points. The 14 conditions laid down by President Woodrow Wilson (1856–1924) as those on which the Allies were prepared to make peace with Germany on the conclusion of World War I. He outlined them in a speech to Congress on 8 January 1918 and they were eventually accepted as the basis for the peace. They included the evacuation by Germany of all allied territory, the restoration of an independent Poland, freedom of the seas, reduction of armaments, and OPEN DIPLOMACY.

Fox. Reynard the Fox. *See* REYNARD.

A case of the fox and the grapes. Said of one who wants something badly, but cannot obtain it, and so tries to pretend that he does not really want it at all. *See* GRAPES.

A fox's sleep. A sleep with one eye open. Assumed indifference to what is going on. *Cp.* TO FOX.

A wise fox will never rob his neighbour's henroost. It would soon be

found out, so he goes farther afield where he is less likely to be discovered.

Every fox must pay his skin to the furrier. The crafty will be taken in by their own wiliness.

To set a fox to keep the geese (Lat. *ovem lupo committere*). Said of one who entrusts his money to sharpers.

To fox. To steal or cheat; to keep an eye on somebody without seeming to do so; to baffle. A dog, a fox, and a weasel sleep, as they say, "with one eye open".

Foxed. A print or page of a book stained with reddish-brown marks is said to be "foxed" because of its colour. *Foxed* is also used to imply "baffled" or "bewildered", and fuddled or the worse for liquor.

Fox-fire. The phosphoric light, without heat, which occurs on decaying matter. It is the Fr. *faux* or false.

Foxglove (*Digitalis purpurea*). The flower is named from the animal and the glove. It is not known how the fox came to be associated with it, but one suggestion is that it is a corruption of "folk's glove", folks being the fairies or little people. In Welsh it is called *menygellyllon* (elves' gloves) or *menyg y llwynog* (fox's gloves) and in Ireland it is called a *fairy thimble*.

Fox-hole. A small slit trench for one or more men.

Fox-trot. The short quick walking pace, as of a fox. "Only a fox's step away" means a very small distance away. It is also the name of a ballroom dance originating in America, popular from the 1920s until the 1950s.

Fra Diavolo. *See* DIAVOLO.

Frame-up. A cooked-up criminal charge against an innocent victim, a trumped-up affair. A term of American origin (from the early 1900s), derived from the framed photographs of criminals kept by law-enforcement agencies.

France. *See* FRANKS.

Francesca da Rimini (frăn ches' kà da rim' i ni). Daughter of Guido da Polenta, Lord of Ravenna. Her story is told in DANTE's *Inferno* (canto v). She was married to Giovanni Malatesta, Lord of Rimini, but her guilty love for his younger brother, Paolo, was discovered and both were put to death about 1289.

Francis of Assisi, St

Francis of Assisi, St. The founder of the FRANCISCANS. Born in 1182, son of a wealthy merchant, he was rejected by his father for his generous gifts to the poor folk of Assisi and his little chapel, called the *Portiuncula*, was soon thronged with disciples. His love of nature was a characteristic as was his purity and gentleness of spirit and his preaching to the birds became a favourite subject for artists. His begging friars lived in extreme poverty and he was canonized two years after his death (1226).

Franciscans (frăn sis' kănz). The Friars Minor, founded by St. FRANCIS OF ASSISI in 1209 and now divided into three distinct and independent branches, the Friars Minor, the Friars Minor Conventual and the Friars Minor CAPUCHIN. These constitute the First Order. The Franciscans first appeared in England in 1224 and were called *Grey Friars* from the indeterminate colour of their habit, which is now brown. They had 65 religious houses in England at the time of the REFORMATION. Especially notable for its preaching among the poor, the distinguishing feature of the order at the outset was insistence on poverty, which later produced dissension. Many of the stricter members called *Spirituals* or *Zealots*, the less strict FRATICELLI, and in 1517 the *Observants*, separated from the *Conventuals*, and in the 1520s the Capuchins became another Order. Later groups were the *Reformati*, the *Recollects*, and the *Discalced* (*see* BAREFOOTED). The whole Order was reorganized into its present branches by Pope Leo XIII in 1897. For the Second Order (or Nuns) *see* CLARE, ORDER OF ST.

Those nuns following a milder rule instituted by Urban IV in 1263 were called *Urbanists*, and a reformed order of *Colettines* founded by St. Colette arose in the 15th century, other offshoots being the *Grey Sisters, Capuchin Nuns, Sisters of the Annunciation*, and *Conceptionists*.

Francs-tireurs (frong tē rĕr) (Fr. free-shooters). Sharp-shooters, skirmishers, or irregular troops. Originally unofficial military units or rifle clubs formed in France during the Luxembourg crisis of 1867, they gave notable service in the Franco-German War of 1870–1871. At first wearing no uniform, until brought under proper French military control, they were shot if captured by the Germans.

Frankalmoin, or **frankalmoigne tenure** (frăngk' ăl moin) (free alms). A form of feudal tenure whereby the Church held land granted by pious benefactors in return for some form of praying service, usually praying for the soul of the donor. The Church also held some of its lands by KNIGHT SERVICE. *See* CHANTRY; MORTMAIN.

Frankenstein. The young student in Mary Wollstonecraft Shelley's romance of that name (1818), a classic horror story. Frankenstein made a soulless monster out of corpses from churchyards and dissecting-rooms and endued it with life by galvanism. The tale shows the creature longed for sympathy, but was shunned by everyone and became the instrument of dreadful retribution on the student who usurped the prerogative of the Creator. *Cp.* VAMPIRE.

Frankincense. The literal meaning of this is pure or true incense. It is a fragrant gum exuded from several trees of the genus *Boswellia*, abundant on the Somali coast and in South Arabia. It was ceremonially used by the Egyptians, Persians, Babylonians, Hebrews, Greeks, and Romans and is an ingredient of the modern incense used in certain churches.

> They presented unto him gifts; gold, and frankincense, and myrrh.
> *Matt.* ii, 11.

Frankpledge. A system originating in Anglo-Saxon times by which all men were to be grouped in a TITHING or frankpledge with the responsibility for each other's actions. If one of their number committed an offence the others would compel him to answer for it or see that reparation was made. Men of position were excused as were freeholders and the system came only to apply to the unfree, when over 12 years of age.

Franks. Free letters for government officials and Members of PARLIAMENT. The privilege of franking a letter was held by

408

numerous court officials in Tudor times. By writing their name and title on the corner of the letter they secured free delivery. This concession was abused from the outset and after the RESTORATION was increasingly exploited by members of both Houses of Parliament signing the letters of friends and others. By an act of 1764 each member of either house of Parliament was permitted to send 10 free letters daily and to receive 15. The abuse still continued and the right was abolished in 1840 on the introduction of the penny post although it still exists in the U.S.A. for Members of Congress and others.

Franks. The Germanic tribe which conquered GAUL after the fall of the Roman Empire, whence the name France.

Frater (frā'tèr). The refectory or dining-room of a monastery, where the brothers (Lat. *fratres*) met together for meals. Also called the *fratry*.

In old vagabond's slang a *frater* was much the same as an ABRAM-MAN, a usage derived from the friar's begging habits.

Fraternity, The. A term highwaymen used to apply to themselves as a body but the "Gentlemen of the road" were by no means always on friendly terms with one another.

Fraticelli (frăt i chel' ē) (Ital. Little Brethren). A name given to several groups of monks and friars in Italy in the 13th, 14th, and 15th centuries, many of whom were originally FRANCISCANS. They were mostly fanatical ascetics and came to be branded as HERETICS.

Frazzle. Beaten, or **licked to a frazzle.** Completely beaten and reduced to a state of exhaustion; an expression of American origin, *frazzle* being a "frayed edge".

Worn to a frazzle. Reduced to a state of nervous exhaustion.

Free. A free and easy. An informal social gathering where people chat and smoke together. A public-house social and sing-song. Thus **in a free and easy way** is with entire absence of ceremony.

A free fight. A fight in which all engage, rules being disregarded. **A free-for-all** is much the same whether applied to a scuffle or an argument.

Free on board, or **F.O.B.** Used of goods delivered on board ship or into a conveyance at the seller's expense.

To have a free hand. *See under* HAND.

To make free with. To take liberties with; to treat whatever it is as one's own.

Free Bench (*francus bancus*) (Lat.). A legal term denoting a widow's free right to the interest in a COPYHOLD estate. Called *bench* because, on acceding, she became a tenant of the MANOR, and entitled to sit on the bench at manorial courts. It was abolished by Acts of 1922 and 1925.

Free Churches. The NONCONFORMIST churches, so called because they are free from any kind of official connexion with the State.

Free Church of Scotland or **Free Church.** Formed by those who left the established CHURCH OF SCOTLAND after the disruption of 1843.

Free companies. A name given to groups of disbanded soldiery who in the mid-14th century roamed France, plundering and pillaging. Sir Arthur Conan Doyle's story, *The White Company*, is based upon the exploits of one of them, which had the white cross for its emblem. *Cp.* CONDOTTIERI.

Free French. *See* FIGHTING FRENCH.

Free House. A public house or inn which is not tied to a brewery; its landlord is thus free to sell any kind of beer he chooses.

Free lance. *See under* LANCE.

Free Soilers. In the U.S.A. members of the Free Soil Party which arose in 1847–1848 to oppose the extension of slavery into further territories.

Free Trade. The opposite of PROTECTION; when a government does not impose duties on imports to favour the home producer. Such a policy in Britain aroused increasing advocacy from the time of Adam Smith's *Wealth of Nations* (1776) when he attacked the existing protectionist policies which he called the *Mercantile System*.

The Apostle of Free Trade. Richard Cobden (1804–1865), the principal founder of the Anti-Corn Law League in 1838.

Free Verse. A breakaway from the regular classical metres, which dominated European and English poetry from the later mediæval period, and the substitution of ordinary speech rhythms and little or loose rhyme-patterns, in place of regular stanza forms. Milton experimented with irregular forms and much of Browning's poetry breaks away from the older tradition. From the early 20th century, free verse came into its own through the influence of Ezra Pound, T. S. Eliot, and others. There was a similar trend in France towards *vers libre*.

Wee Frees. A minority of the FREE CHURCH which refused to join the United Free Church in 1900. It had some 16,000 members in 1988.

Freebooter. A pirate, an adventurer who makes his living by plundering; literally one who obtains his booty free (Dut. *vrij*, free; *buit*, booty). *See also* FILIBUSTER.

Freehold. An estate held in FEE SIMPLE. *Cp.* COPYHOLD.

Freeman, Mrs. The name assumed by Sarah, Duchess of Marlborough (1660–1744), in her correspondence with Queen Anne. The Queen called herself Mrs. Morley.

Freemasonry. As a secret society it has existed for many centuries and professes to trace its origins to the building of SOLOMON'S TEMPLE. In mediæval times stonemasons banded together with their secret signs, passwords and tests. Freemasonry in its modern form, as a body with no trade connections, began to flourish in the 17th century.

Freischütz (frī' shutz) (the freeshooter). A legendary German marksman in league with the DEVIL, who gave him seven balls, six of which were to hit infallibly whatever the marksman aimed at, and the seventh was to be directed as the devil wished.

French. French of Stratford atte Bow. This has often been taken to mean French as spoken by an Englishman, and a COCKNEY at that, but it had no such connotation in Chaucer's day. Stratford and Bromley were then fashionable suburbs, and at Bromley was the convent of ST. LEONARDS' where the daughters of well-to-do citizens and others were taught French by the nuns. French was a common acquirement of the time and freely used at Court and in society; but it was somewhat archaic French, descending from Norman times, and not such as was current in Paris.

> And Frensh she [the nun] spake ful faire and fetisly,
> After the scole of Stratford atte Bowe,
> For Frensh of Paris was to hir unknowe.
> CHAUCER: *Canterbury Tales, Prologue*, 124–6.

To take French leave. To take without asking; also to leave without asking or announcing one's departure. This kind of backhander to the French was once common (*cp.* "French gout" for venereal disease).

The French returned the compliment similarly. The French equivalent of "to take French leave" is *s'en aller* (or *filer*) *à l'anglaise*. In the 16th century a creditor used to be called *un Anglais*.

French paste. A kind of glass into which a certain quantity of oxide of lead is introduced. It gives a very good imitation of a DIAMOND. *See* GLAUCUS.

Frenchman. *See* NATIONAL NICKNAMES *under* NICKNAME.

Done like a Frenchman, turn and turn again (*Henry VI, Pt. I*, III, iii). The French were frequently ridiculed as a fickle, wavering nation. Dr. Johnson says he once read a treatise, the object of which was to show that a weathercock is a satire on the word *Gallus* (a Gaul or cock).

Freyja (frā' yà). In Scandinavian mythology the sister of FREYR, goddess of love, marriage and of the dead. She was the wife of ODIN and always wore the shining necklace called *Brisingamen* and was consequently called "ornament loving". Her husband is also given in some legends as *Odhr*, and she shed golden tears when he left her. The counterpart of VENUS, she is also commonly identified with Frigg, wife of Odin, who in Scandinavian myth ranked highest among the goddesses. *See* FRIDAY.

Freyr. In Norse mythology, god of fruitfulness and crops, and of the sun and rain. His horse was called Bloodyhoof and his ship SKIDBLADNIR.

Friar (Lat. *frater*, a brother). A member

of one of the mendicant orders, notably the AUGUSTINIANS, CARMELITES, DOMINICANS, and FRANCISCANS. *See also* CRUTCHED FRIARS.

Crutched Friars. *See* CRUTCHED.

Curtal Friar. *See* BRAZEN HEAD.

Friar Bungay. Thomas de Bungay of Suffolk, a FRANCISCAN who lectured at Oxford and Cambridge in the 13th century, whose story is much overlaid with legend. He came to be portrayed as a magician and necromancer.

Friar Rush. A legendary house-spirit who originated as a kind of ultramischievous ROBIN GOODFELLOW in German folk-lore. He later acquired more devilish attributes and appeared in the habit of a Friar to lead astray those under religious vows.

Friar Tuck. Chaplain and steward of ROBIN HOOD.

Friar's Lanthorn. One of the many names given to the Will o' the Wisp. *See* IGNIS FATUUS.

Friars Major (*Fratres majores*). Sometimes applied to the DOMINICANS in contrast to the FRIARS MINOR.

Friars Minor (*Fratres minores*). The FRANCISCANS.

Friars of the Sack. *See under* SACK.

Friday. The sixth day of the week (until 1971 when it became the fifth (*see* SUNDAY); in ancient ROME called *dies Veneris*, the day dedicated to VENUS, hence the French *vendredi*. The northern nations adopted the same nomenclature and the nearest equivalent to Venus was Frigg or FREYJA, hence Friday (O.E. *frige dæg*).

Friday was regarded by the Norsemen as the luckiest day of the week, the day of weddings, etc., but among Christians it has been regarded as the unluckiest, because it was the day of the Crucifixion. While no longer a day of compulsory abstinence for Roman Catholics, they are urged to set Friday apart for some voluntary act of self-denial.

Friday is the SABBATH for Mohammedans and they say that ADAM was created on a Friday and it was on Friday that Adam and EVE ate the forbidden fruit, and on a Friday they died. It is also held unlucky among Buddhists and BRAH-MINS.

In England the proverb is that "a Friday moon brings foul weather"; but it is not unlucky to be born on this day, since "Friday's child is loving and giving". It is held to be a bad day for ships to put to sea, but in 1492 Columbus set sail on a Friday and sighted land on a Friday. It was also sometimes called *Hanging day* as it was a common day for executing condemned criminals.

Black Friday. *See under* BLACK.

Good Friday. *See under* GOOD.

Friday the Thirteenth. A particularly unlucky Friday. *See* THIRTEEN.

Long Friday. GOOD FRIDAY was so called by the SAXONS, probably because of the long fasts and offices associated with that day.

Man Friday. The young savage found by ROBINSON CRUSOE on a Friday and kept as his servant and companion on the desert island. Hence a faithful and willing attendant, ready to turn his hand to anything.

He who laughs on Friday will weep on Sunday. Sorrow follows in the wake of joy. The line is taken from Racine's comedy, *Les Plaideurs*.

Friend. A QUAKER, *i.e.* a member of the Society of Friends; also one's second in a duel. In the law courts counsel refer to each other as "my learned friend", though they may be entire strangers, just as in the HOUSE OF COMMONS one member speaks of another as "my honourable friend".

A friend at court. A friend who is in a position to help by influencing those in power or authority.

A friend of the court (*amicus curiæ*). A legal term to denote anyone not concerned in a case who brings to the attention of the court some point or decision of law which seems to have been overlooked.

A friend in need is a friend indeed. The Latin saying (from Ennius) is, *Amicus certus in re incerta cernitur*, a sure friend is made known when (one is) in difficulty.

Friends of the Earth. An organization founded in Great Britain in 1971, with some 250 local groups, to campaign for the protection of the environment. It now has branches in a number of other countries. Protests and propaganda are furthered by public meetings, demonstrations, etc. They are active against all forms of pollution (especially nuclear power), developments which ruin the countryside and the destruction of wildlife. *Cp.* GREENPEACE *under* GREEN.

The Society of Friends. The QUAKERS.

The Society of Friends of the People. A society founded at London (1792) largely of young aristocrats, and which included Lauderdale, Charles Grey, and Sheridan. They advocated reform of PARLIAMENT and estimated that 51 English and Welsh boroughs, with a total voting strength of under 1,500, returned 100 members to Parliament. It dissolved itself in 1795 after one of its members, Thomas Muir, was sentenced to 14 years transportation, it being held by Lord Braxfield that "to agitate for equal representation of the people in the House of the People was in the circumstances of itself sedition".

Friendly Societies. Voluntary self-help organizations providing insurance against sickness, infirmity, death, etc., payable from central funds. Preceded by the old village Benefit Clubs, they developed from the late 17th century and became widespread in the 19th and early 20th centuries.

Friendship. The classical examples of lasting friendship between man and man are ACHILLES and PATROCLUS, PYLADES and ORESTES, NISUS and EURYALUS, DAMON and PYTHIAS. To these should be added DAVID and JONATHAN.

Frigg. *See* FREYJA.

Fringe. The fringe, or more correctly twisted cords or tassels worn on the four corners of the Jewish outer garment (*tzitzith*) in OLD TESTAMENT times and later, were anciently supposed to have a special virtue. Hence the desire of the woman who had the issue of blood to touch the fringe of Our Lord's garment (*Matt*. ix, 20–22). From the 13th century an undergarment with tassels attached, the *arba kanfoth* (four corners) worn at all times by orthodox Jews, replaced the *tzitzith*.

Fringe benefits. Concessions and benefits given to employees, or extra "perks" that go with a job or appointment such as free coal, use of a motor car, pensions, insurances, medical benefits etc.

The lunatic fringe. The small section of the community who follow and originate extremist ideas, and whose behaviour is often markedly eccentric by conventional standards, but whose influence on the majority is of little account.

Frippery. Rubbish of a tawdry character, worthless finery; foolish levity. A *friperer* or *fripperer* was one who dealt in old clothes (*cp.* Fr. *friperie*, old clothes, cast-off furniture, etc.).

Also a shop where odds and ends, old clothes, and so on are dealt in.

Frithiof (frit' yof). A hero of Icelandic myth who married Ingeborg, daughter of a minor king of Norway, and widow of Sigurd Ring, to whose dominions he succeeded. His name signifies "the peacemaker" and his adventures are recorded in the saga which bears his name. It was paraphrased by Esaias Tegner in his famous poem (1825) of the same name.

Froebel System. The name given to a system of KINDERGARTEN teaching where children's abilities are developed by means of clay-modelling, mat-plaiting, and other forms of self-activity, developed by Friedrich Froebel (1782–1852), a German schoolmaster.

Frog. A frog and a mouse agreed to settle by a single combat their claims to a marsh; but, while they fought, a kite carried them both off (ÆSOP: *Fables*, clxviii).

Frenchmen, properly *Parisians*, have been nicknamed Frogs or Froggies, from their ancient heraldic device which was three frogs or toads. (*See* FLEUR-DE-LIS.) *Qu'en disent les grenouilles?* What do the frogs (people of Paris) say?—was in 1791 a common court phrase at VERSAILLES. There was point in the pleasantry, Paris having once been a quagmire, called *Lutetia* (mudland). Further point is given to the nickname by the fact that the back legs of the edible frog (*Rana esculenta*) form a delicacy in French cuisine that aroused much disparaging humour from the English. *See* NATIONAL NICKNAMES *under* NICKNAME.

Frog, or **frog's march.** Carrying an obstreperous prisoner face downwards by his four limbs.

A frog in the throat. A temporary loss of voice, hoarseness.

It may be fun to you, but it is death to the frogs. A caution, meaning that one's sport should not be at the expense of other people's happiness. The allusion is to ÆSOP's fable of a boy stoning frogs for amusement.

Frogmen. In World War II, strong swimmers dressed in rubber suits with paddles on their feet resembling the feet of frogs, who operated in enemy harbours by night attaching explosives to shipping, etc. They are now used in salvage operations, etc.

Fronde (frond). The name given to a civil contest in France (1648–1653) during the minority of Louis XIV. It began as a struggle against the Court party for the redress of grievances, but soon became a faction fight among the nobles to undo the work of Cardinal Richelieu and to overthrow Cardinal MAZARIN. *Fronde* means sling and the name arose from the occasion when the Paris mob pelted Cardinal Mazarin's windows with stones.

Frost Saints. *See* ICE SAINTS.

Frozen Words. A conceit used by the ancient Greeks. Antiphanes applies it to the discourses of PLATO: "As the cold of certain cities is so intense that it freezes the very words we utter, which remain congealed till the heat of summer thaws them, so the mind of youth is so thoughtless that the wisdom of Plato lies there frozen, as it were, till it is thawed by the ripened judgment of mature age." MÜNCHAUSEN relates an incident of the "frozen horn" and Rabelais (Bk. IV, ch. lvi) tells how PANTAGRUEL and his friends, on the confines of the Frozen Sea, heard the uproar of a battle, which had been frozen the preceding winter, released by a thaw.

> Where truth in person doth appear.
> Like words congeal'd in northern air.
> BUTLER: *Hudibras*, canto I, 147–8.

Frying-pan. Out of the frying-pan into the fire. In trying to extricate yourself from one evil you fall into a greater. The Greeks used to say, "Out of the smoke into the flame"; and the French say, "*Tomber de la poêle dans la braise*".

Fub. *See* FOB.

Fuchsia (fū' shà). A genus of highly ornamental flowering shrubs coming from Mexico and the Andes, though two species are found in New Zealand. They were so named in 1703 in honour of the German botanist Leonhard Fuchs (1501–1566).

Fuel. Adding fuel to the fire, or **flames.** Saying or doing something to increase the anger of a person already incensed.

Fugit irreparabile tempus (Lat.). Time, which cannot be retrieved, is flying. A classic reminder derived from VIRGIL's *Georgics* (III, 284).

Führer (fū' rėr) (Ger. leader). The title assumed by Adolf Hitler (1889–1945) when he acceded to supreme power in Germany on the death of Hindenburg in 1934.

Full. Full dress. Ceremonial dress; court dress, full uniform, academicals, evening dress, etc.

A full dress debate is one for which proper preparations and arrangements have been made, as opposed to one arising casually.

Full house. A term in the game of poker for a hand holding three of one kind and two of another, *e.g.* 3 tens and 2 sixes.

Full of beans. *See under* BEAN.

In full cry. Said of hounds that have caught the scent, and give tongue in chorus; hence hurrying in full pursuit.

In full fig. *See* FIG.

In full swing. *See under* SWING.

Fum, or **Fung-hwang.** The PHŒNIX of Chinese legend, one of the four symbolical creatures presiding over the destinies of China. It originated from fire, was born in the Hill of the Sun's HALO, and has its body inscribed with the five CARDINAL virtues. It is this curious creature that was embroidered on the dresses of certain MANDARINS.

Fum. *See* GEORGE IV.

Fun. To make fun of. To make a butt of; to ridicule.

A figure of fun. *See under* FIGURE.

Like fun. Thoroughly, energetically, with delight.

Fund. The Funds, or **The Public Funds.** Money lent at interest to Government or Government security.

The Sinking Fund. Money set aside by the Government for paying off the principal of the NATIONAL DEBT. According to Blackstone, it was intended "to sink and lower the National Debt". The first such fund was established at the end of the reign of Queen Anne.

To be out of funds. To be out of money.

Fundamentalism. The maintenance of traditional PROTESTANT Christian beliefs based upon a literal acceptance of the SCRIPTURES as fundamentals. Fundamentalism as a religious movement arose in the U.S.A. about 1919 among various denominations. What was new was not so much its ideas and attitudes, but its widespread extent and the zeal of its supporters. It opposed all theories of evolution and anthropology, holding that God transcends all laws of nature and that He manifests Himself by exceptional and extraordinary activities, belief in the literal meaning of the Scriptures being an essential tenet. In 1925, John T. Scopes, a science teacher of Rhea High School, Dayton, Tennessee, was convicted of violating the State laws by teaching evolution, an incident arousing interest and controversy far beyond the religious circles of the U.S.A. Their leader was William Jennings Bryan (1860–1925), the politician and orator. *Cp.* MODERNISM.

Funeral (Late Lat. *funeralis*, adj. from *funus*, a burial). *Funus* is connected with *fumus*, smoke, and the word seems to refer to the ancient practice of disposing of the dead by cremation. Roman funerals were conducted by torchlight at night, that magistrates and priests might not be made ceremonially unclean by seeing the corpse.

Most of our funeral customs derive from the Romans; as dressing in BLACK, walking in procession, carrying insignia on the bier, raising a mound on the grave (called *tumulus*, whence *tomb*), etc. The Greeks crowned the dead body with flowers, and also placed flowers on the tomb; the Romans had similar customs. In England the PASSING BELL or the *Soul Bell* used to be tolled from the church when a parishioner was dying and the funeral bell would be tolled as many times as the dead person's years of age.

Public games were held in Greece and Rome in honour of departed heroes; as the games instituted by HERCULES at the death of Pelops, those held by ACHILLES in honour of PATROCLUS (*Iliad*, Bk. xxiii), those held by ÆNEAS in honour of his father Anchises (Æneid, Bk. V), etc. The custom of giving a feast at funerals came to us from the Romans, who not only feasted the friends of the deceased, but also distributed meat to the persons employed. *See* ISTHMIAN GAMES; NEMEAN GAMES.

Funk. To be in a funk or **a blue funk,** may be the Walloon "*In de fonk zun*", literally to "be in the smoke". Colloquially, to be in a state of apprehensive fear or abject fear. The phrase first appears at Oxford in the first half of the 18th century.

Funny Bone. A pun on the word *humerus*, the Latin name for the arm bone. It is the inner condyle or knob at the end of the bone where the ulnar nerve is exposed at the elbow. A knock on this part is naturally painful and produces a tingling sensation.

Furcam et Flagellum (fĕr′kăm et flä jel′ ŭm) (Lat. gallows and whip). In the early MIDDLE AGES, the lowest form of tenure, that of the slave, whose life and limbs were at his lord's disposal. *Cp.* FORKS.

Furies, The. The Roman name (*Furiæ*) for the Greek ERINYES, said by Hesiod to have been the daughters of GÆA (the Earth) and to have sprung from the blood of URANUS, and by other accounts to be daughters of Night or of Earth and Darkness. They were three in number, Tisiphone (the Avenger of blood), ALECTO (the Implacable), and Megæra (the Jealous one).

They were merciless goddesses of vengeance and punished all transgressors, especially those who neglected filial duty or claims of kinship, etc. Their punishments continued after death. *See*

EUMENIDES.

Furphy. In World War I containers for sanitary purposes were supplied to Australian military camps by the firm of Furphy and Co., whose name appeared on all their products. Hence a "furphy" was a latrine rumour or a report of doubtful reliability. *Cp.* BARRACK-ROOM LAWYER.

Furry Dance. Part of the spring festival held at Helston, Cornwall, on 8 May (now the nearest Saturday). Furry Day, which is derived from the Lat. *Feriæ* (festivals, holidays), was incorrectly changed to *Flora* in the 18th century and in the 19th century the dance was called the *Floral Dance*, as in the well-known song. It is derived from a pre-Christian festivity and is copied in some other towns. In its present form prominent townsfolk dance through the town. There is a similar spring festival at Padstow beginning at midnight on 30 April. *See under* HOBBY.

Fustian. A coarse twilled cotton cloth with a velvety pile, probably so called from Fustat, a suburb of Cairo. It is chiefly used now in a figurative sense meaning inflated or pompous talk, CLAP-TRAP, BOMBAST, pretentious words. *Cp.* FLANNEL.

Futhorc (foo' thôrk). The ancient Runic alphabet of the Anglo-Saxons and other Teutons; so called (on the same principle as the A B C) from its first six letters, *viz., f, u, th, o, r, k.*

Futurism. An art movement which originated at Turin in 1909 under the influence of E.F.T. Marinetti. Its adherents sought to introduce into paintings a "poetry of motion" whereby, for example, the painted gesture should become actually "a dynamic condition". The Futurists tried to indicate not only the state of mind of the painter but also that of the figures in the picture. It was another movement to shake off the influence of the past. The original Futurists included Marinetti, Boccioni, Carra, Russolo, and Severini, and they first exhibited at Paris in 1912. *Cp.* CUBISM; DADAISM; FAUVISM; IMPRESSIONISM; ORPHISM; SURREALISM; SYNCHRONISM; VORTICISM.

Fylfot. A mystic sign or emblem known also as the SWASTIKA and GAMMADION, and in HERALDRY as the *cross cramponnée*, used (especially in Byzantine architecture and among the North American Indians) as an ornament of religious import. It has been found at Hissarlik, on ancient Etruscan tombs, CELTIC monuments, Buddhist inscriptions, Greek coins, etc. It has been thought to have represented the power of the SUN, of the four winds, of lightning, and so on. It is used nowadays in jewellery as an emblem of luck and was also adopted as the NAZI badge. (*See* diagram 21, p. 286.)

The name *fylfot* was adopted by antiquaries from a MS. of the 15th century, and is possibly *fill foot*, signifying a device to fill the foot of a stained-glass window.

G

G. This letter is a modification of the Latin C (which was a rounding of the Greek *gamma*, Γ); until the 3rd century B.C. the *g* and *k* sounds were both represented by the letter C. In the Hebrew and old Phœnician alphabets G is the outline of a camel's head and neck. Heb. *gimel*, a camel.

G.I. In World War II, American enlisted men called themselves G.I.s, from an abbreviation of Government Issue. After becoming accustomed to G.I. shirts, G.I. blankets, etc., the soldiers began to apply the term to themselves.

G-man, short for Government Man, an agent of the U.S. Federal Bureau of Investigation (F.B.I.)

G.O.M. The initial letters of "Grand Old Man", a nickname of honour given to W. E. Gladstone (1809–1898), in his later years. Lord Rosebery first used the expression in 1882.

Gab. The gift of the gab, or **gob.** Fluency of speech, also the gift of boasting. The word *gab* may be onomatopœic or derive from the identical Gaelic word for mouth.

Gabbara. The giant who, according to Rabelais, was "the first inventor of the drinking of HEALTHS".

Gabble Ratchet. *See* GABRIEL'S HOUNDS.

Gabelle (gȧ bel'). The French tax on salt, first levied in 1286 and abolished in 1790. The word was originally applied to any indirect tax. All the salt made in France had to be brought to the royal warehouses and was there sold at a price fixed by the government. The iniquity was that some provinces had to pay twice as much as others and everyone above the age of eight had to purchase a minimum quantity weekly.

Gaberlunzie. A Scottish term of uncertain origin for a mendicant; or one of the king's BEADSMEN. The name has also been given to the wallet carried by the gaberlunzie-man. *See* BLUE GOWN.

Gabriel (*i.e.* man of God). One of the ARCHANGELS, sometimes regarded as the ANGEL of death, the prince of fire and thunder, but more frequently as one of God's chief messengers, and traditionally said to be the only angel that can speak Syriac and Chaldee. The Mohammedans call him the chief of the four favoured angels and the spirit of truth. Milton makes him chief of the angelic guards placed over PARADISE (*Paradise Lost*, IV, 549).

In the TALMUD Gabriel appears as the destroyer of the hosts of Sennacherib, as the man who showed Joseph the way, and as one of the angels who buried MOSES.

According to the KORAN it was Gabriel who took MOHAMMED to heaven on Al BORAK and revealed to him his "prophetic love". In the OLD TESTAMENT Gabriel is said to have explained to DANIEL certain visions (*Dan*. viii. 16–26); in the NEW TESTAMENT he announced to Zacharias the future birth of JOHN THE BAPTIST (*Luke* i, 13, etc.) and appeared to Mary the mother of Jesus (*Luke* i, 26, etc.).

Gabriel Bell. In mediæval England, another name for the ANGELUS or AVE Bell, in remembrance of the archangel's salutation of the Virgin Mary.

Gabriel's horse. Haizum.

Gabriel's hounds, called also *Gabble Ratchet*. Wild geese. The noise of geese in flight is like that of a pack of hounds in full cry. The legend is that they are the souls of unbaptized children wandering through the air till the Day of JUDGMENT.

Gad. By Gad. A minced form of God, occurring also in *Gadzooks*, *Begad*, *Egad*.

Gæa (jē′ à) or **Ge.** The Greek goddess of the Earth who gave birth to sky, mountains, and sea. By URANUS she brought forth the TITANS, the CYCLOPS and other GIANTS and according to some legends she was the mother of the EUMENIDES.

Gaelic (gā′ lik). The language of the Gaelic branch of the CELTIC race. The name is now usually restricted to the Celtic language of the Scottish Highlands, but also includes that of Irish and Manx Celts. *See* ERSE.

Gaff. Slang for humbug; also for a cheap public entertainment or a low-class MUSIC HALL, often called *penny gaffs* from the price of admission. Such theatres were once common on the Surrey side of the Thames.

It is also the spar to which the upper edge of a fore-and-aft sail is bent such as the mainsail of a sloop.

Crooked as a gaff. Here a *gaff* is an iron hook at the end of a short pole, used for landing salmon, etc., or the metal spur of fighting-cocks (Span. and Port. *gafa*, a boat-hook).

To blow the gaff. *See under* BLOW.

To stand the gaff. To beat punishment or raillery with calmness.

Gaffer. An old country fellow; the boss, overseer, or foreman; a corruption of "grandfather". *Cp*. GAMMER.

Gag. In theatrical parlance, an interpolation. When SHAKESPEARE makes Hamlet direct the players to say no more "than is set down" (III, ii) he cautions them against gagging; also a joke.

To apply the gag. Said of applying the CLOSURE in the HOUSE OF COMMONS. Here *gag* is something forced into the mouth to prevent speech.

Gaiety. Gaiety Girl. One of the beauty chorus for which the Old Gaiety Theatre in the STRAND was famous in the '90s and Edwardian days. Several of them married into the peerage. *Cp*. GIBSON GIRL.

Gala Day. A festive day; a day when people put on their best attire (Ital. *gala*, festivity).

Galahad, Sir (găl′a hăd). In Arthurian legend the purest and noblest knight of the ROUND TABLE. He is a late addition and was invented by Walter Map in his *Quest of the San Graal*. He was the son of LANCELOT and ELAINE. At the institution of the Round Table one seat (the Siege Perilous) was left unoccupied for the knight who could succeed in the Quest. When Sir Galahad sat there it was discovered that it had been left for him. The story is found in Malory's *Morte d'Arthur*, Tennyson's *The Holy Grail*, etc.

Galatea (găl à tē′ a). A sea NYMPH, beloved by the monster POLYPHEMUS, but herself in love with the beautiful ACIS, who was killed by the jealous CYCLOPS. Galatea threw herself into the sea where she joined her sister nymphs. Handel has an opera entitled *Acis and Galatea* (1720). The Galatea beloved by PYGMALION was a different person.

Galaxy, The (Gr. *gala*, *galaktos*, milk). The "Milky Way". A long white luminous track of stars which seems to encompass the heavens like a girdle. It is composed of a vast collection of stars so distant that they are indistinguishable as separate stars, and they appear as a combined light. According to classic fable, it is the path to the palace of ZEUS.

Galen (gā′ len). A Greek physician and philosopher of the 2nd century A.D. For centuries he was the supreme authority in medicine. Hence *Galenist*, a follower of Galen's medical theories; *Galenical*, a simple, vegetable medicine.

Galen says "Nay" and Hippocrates "Yea". The doctors disagree, and who is to decide? HIPPOCRATES, born at Cos (460 B.C.), was the most celebrated physician of antiquity.

Galilee. A chapel or porch at the west end of some mediæval churches where penitents waited before admission to the body of the church and where clergy received women who had business with them. Examples remain at Durham, Ely and Lincoln cathedrals. The name derives from *Matt*. iv, 15.

Galilean. An inhabitant of Galilee, and specifically Jesus Christ, who was called "the Galilean". The term was also applied to Christians as his followers. The dying words attributed to the Roman Emperor Julian the Apostate were "*Vicisti, Galilæe*".

Galimatias (gắl i mā′ shiàs). Nonsense, unmeaning gibberish. The word first appeared in France in the 16th century, but its origin is unknown; perhaps it is connected with GALLIMAUFRY.

Gall (gawl). Bile; the very bitter fluid secreted by the liver; hence used figuratively as a symbol for anything of extreme bitterness.

Gall and wormwood. Extremely bitter and mortifying.

The gall of bitterness. The bitterest grief; extreme affliction. The ancients taught that grief and joy were subject to the gall as affection was to the heart, and knowledge to the kidneys. The "gall of bitterness" means the bitter centre of bitterness, as the "heart of hearts" means the innermost recesses of the heart or affections. In the *Acts* it is used to signify "the sinfulness of sin", which leads to the bitterest grief.

Gall of Pigeons. The story goes that pigeons have no gall, because the dove sent from the ark by Noah burst its gall out of grief, and none of the pigeon family has had a gall ever since.

Gallery. A gallery hit. In CRICKET is an exceptionally stylish stroke which arouses the crowd's enthusiasm.

To play to the gallery. An appeal to the lower elements of one's audience, to court popularity by such methods as an actor seeking popular applause from the patrons of the cheapest seats in the theatre, these being in the gallery.

Gallia. France, as in Thomson's

> Impending hangs o'er Gallia's humbled coast.
>
> *The Seasons: Summer.*

More properly the Latin name for Gaul, the much more extensive areas then populated by CELTIC peoples.

Gallicism. A phrase or sentence constructed after the French idiom; as, "When you shall have returned home you will find a letter on your table." *Cp. Mark* viii, 2. Also the use of a word in a sense peculiar to the French language, as "assist" in the sense of to "be present", using a word common to both languages in a French sense, etc.

Galligaskins. A loose wide kind of breeches worn by men in the 16th and 17th centuries.

The word is a corruption of Fr. *garguesque*, which is the Ital. *grechesca*, Greekish, referring to a Greek article of clothing.

Gallimaufry. A medley; any confused jumble of things; but strictly speaking, a HOTCH-POTCH made of all the scraps of the larder (Fr. *galimafrée*, the origin of which is unknown, though it is probably related to GALIMATIAS).

Gallio. A name applied to a person, particularly an official whose chief characteristic is one of indifference, especially to things outside his province.

Galloglass, or **Gallowglass.** An armed servitor or foot-soldier in ancient IRELAND (O.Ir. and Gael. *gall*, a stranger; *oglach*, a warrior). SHAKESPEARE speaks of *kerns and gallowglasses* as coming from the Western Isles of SCOTLAND. *See* KERN.

Gallup Poll. The best known of the public opinion surveys, instituted by Dr. George Gallup of the American Institute of Public Opinion in 1935. Trained interviewers interrogate a carefully selected but small cross-section of the population. For the British Parliamentary election of 1945, out of 25 million voters, 1,809 were interviewed, but the Gallup Poll forecast was within 1 per cent; but the forecast was wrong for the American Presidential Election of 1948. The LABOUR PARTY victory was forecast for the British Parliamentary Elections in 1964 and 1966. It is held that such polls in themselves influence the result. STRAW POLLS and market research surveys were the forerunners of the Gallup Poll. *Cp.* MASS OBSERVATION.

Galosh. The word comes from the Span. *galocha* (wooden shoes); Ger. *Galosche*; Fr. *galoche*, which is probably from Gr. *Kalopous*, a shoemaker's last.

It was originally applied to a kind of clog or patten worn as a protection against wet in the days when silk or cloth shoes were worn. It is used in this sense by Langland.

Galway Jury. An enlightened, independent jury. The expression has its origin when Thomas Wentworth, Lord Deputy of IRELAND, revived the king's claim to all the lands of Connaught. The juries of Mayo, Sligo, and Roscommon found verdicts in favour of the Crown, but that of Galway stood out against the plan; whereupon the SHERIFF was sentenced to a fine of £1,000 and each of the jurors £4,000.

Gambrel. Also known as cambrel, chambrel, chambren, gambril (O.Fr. *gambe*, the leg); the hock of a horse or other animal, also a crooked stick somewhat similarly shaped once used by butchers, from which they suspended carcases. *See* MANSARD ROOF.

Game. The game's afoot. The hare has started; the enterprise has begun.

> I see you stand like greyhounds in the slips,
> Straining upon the start. The game's afoot!
> Follow your spirit!
>
> SHAKESPEARE: *Henry V*, III, i.

The game is not worth the candle. *See under* CANDLE.

The game is up. The scheme, endeavour, plot, etc., has come to grief; all is at an end. In hunting it has the same significance as THE GAME'S AFOOT.

He's a game 'un. He's got some pluck, he's "a plucked 'un". Another allusion to gamecocks.

He's at his little games again, or **at the same old game.** He's at his old tricks; he's gone back to his old habits or practices.

To die game. To maintain a courageous attitude to the end. A phrase from COCK-FIGHTING.

To have the game in one's hands. To have such an advantage that success is assured; to hold the winning cards.

To play a waiting game. To bide one's time, knowing that that is the best way of winning; to adopt FABIAN TACTICS (*see under* FABIUS).

To play the game. To act in a straight-forward, honourable manner; to keep to the rules of fair play.

You are making game of me. You are bamboozling me, holding me up to ridicule. *Cp.* TO PULL SOMEONE'S LEG *under* PULL.

Game Laws. A series of enactments akin to the old FOREST LAW, designed to protect game for the landowner and to prevent poaching, and formerly noted for their harshness. In 1671 a Game Law was passed which prevented all freeholders killing game except those with lands worth £100 a year. *The Extraordinary Black Book* of 1831 pointed out that 50 times more property was required to kill a partridge than to vote for a KNIGHT OF THE SHIRE. In the reign of George III, 32 Game Laws were passed. The modern game licence for the killing of game stems from the Game Act of 1831, which also demarcated the seasons during which certain game might be taken. From 1671 to 1831 the sale of game was totally prohibited, thus providing a lucrative market for poachers.

Game leg. A lame leg. In this instance game is a dialect form of the CELTIC *cam*, meaning crooked. It is of comparatively modern usage. **Gammy** is also in this sense.

Gamesmanship. A term popularized by Stephen Potter, whose book *The Theory and Practice of Gamesmanship* (1947) defines the meaning in its sub-title. "The Art of Winning Games without actually Cheating".

Gamelyn, The Tale of (găm' lin). A Middle English metrical romance, found among the Chaucer MSS. and supposed to have been intended by him to form the basis of one of the unwritten *Canterbury Tales*, although the authorship is still in doubt. Gamelyn is a younger son to whom a large share of property has been bequeathed by his father. He is kept in servitude and tyrannically used by his elder brother until he is old enough to rebel. After many adventures during which he becomes a leader of outlaws in the woods, he comes to his own again with the help of the king, and justice is meted out to the elder brother. Thomas Lodge uses the story in his book, *Rosalynde, or Euphues' Golden Legacie* (1590), from which SHAKESPEARE drew a large part of *As You Like It*.

Gammadion (ga mā' di ón). The FYLFOT or SWASTIKA, so called because it resembles four Greek capital Gammas (Γ) set at right angles.

Gammer. A former rustic term for an old woman; a corruption of *grandmother*, with an intermediate form of *granmer*. *Cp.* GAFFER.

Gammer Gurton's Needle. The second earliest extant English comedy, which was probably written by William Stevenson of Christ's College, Cambridge, in the early 1550s but not published until 1575. The comedy is vigorous and it closes with the discovery of Gammer Gurton's missing needle in the seat of Hodge's breeches.

Gammon. This word derives from the same original as *game* and *gamble*, but in Victorian and later slang it means to impose upon, delude, cheat, or play a game upon. As an exclamation it means, "Nonsense, you're pulling my leg".

Gamp. Sarah Gamp is a disreputable monthly nurse in Dickens's *Martin Chuzzlewit*, famous for her bulky umbrella and perpetual reference to an imaginary Mrs. Harris, whose opinions always confirmed her own. Hence a *gamp* as a common term for an umbrella.

Gamut (găm' ŭt). Originally, the first or lowest note in Guido d'Arezzo's scale, corresponding to G on the lowest line of the modern bass stave; later the whole series of notes recognized by musicians; hence, the whole range or compass.

It is *gamma ut*; *gamma* (the third letter of the Greek alphabet) was used by Guido to mark the first or lowest note in the mediæval scale; and *ut* is the first word in the mnemonic stanza. *Ut queant laxis resonare fibris*, etc., containing the names of the hexachord. *See* ARETINIAN SYLLABLES.

Gandermonth. An old term for the month following a wife's confinement, when the husband was at a loose end, and sometimes went *gandermooning* or playing the GALLANT. The term possibly derives from the aimless meanderings of the gander when the goose is sitting.

Ganelon. A type of black-hearted treachery, figuring in Dante's *Inferno* and grouped by Chaucer (*Nun's Priest's Tale*, 407) with JUDAS Iscariot and—

> Greek Sinon,
> That broghtest Troye al outrely to sorwe.

He was Count of Mayence, and PALADIN of CHARLEMAGNE. Jealousy of ROLAND made him a traitor; and in order to destroy his rival, he planned with Marsil-lus, the Moorish king, the attack of RONCESVALLES.

Ganesha (găn' esh à). In Hindu mythology, the god of wisdom and good luck, lord of the Ganas, or lesser deities. He was the son of SIVA and is invoked at the beginning of a journey, or when commencing important work, and on the first pages of books, especially ledgers.

Gang. Gang of Four (1). Leaders of a Chinese radical group who unsuccessfully attempted to seize control after the death of Mao Tse-tung in 1976. The gang consisted of Jiang Qing (Mao's widow and third wife), Zang Chunjao, Wang Hungwen and Yao Wenyuan.

(2) In Great Britain the name was given to the four M.P.s who left the LABOUR PARTY in 1981 to form the Social Democratic Party (S.D.P.), namely Roy Jenkins (leader until 1983), David Owen, Shirley Williams and William Rodgers. Owen became leader in 1983 and was succeeded by Robert Maclennan in 1987. *See* LIBERAL.

Gang agley, To (Scot.). To go wrong. The verb *to glee*, or *gley*, means to look asquint, sideways.

> The best-laid schemes of mice and men
> Gang aft agley.
> BURNS: *To a Mouse*.

Gang-day. *See* ROGATION DAYS.

To gang up. To form a closely-knit group, usually in a spirit of antagonism.

Ganges, The (găn' jēz). So named from *ganga* or *gunga*, a river; as in *Kishen-ganga* (the black river), *Neelganga* (the blue river), *Naraingunga* (the river of Naranyana or VISHNU). The Ganges is the *Borra Ganga*, or great river. This sacred river of the Hindus is said to flow from the toe of Vishnu.

Gangway. Below the gangway. In the HOUSE OF COMMONS, on the farther side of the passageway between the seats which separate the Ministry from the rest of the Members. Thus "to sit below the gangway" is to sit among the members in general, and not among the Ministers or ex-Ministers and leaders of the OPPOSITION.

Gauntlet. *See* GAUNTLET.

Ganymede, or **Ganymedes.** In Greek mythology, the cup-bearer of ZEUS, successor to HEBE, and the type of youthful male beauty. This Trojan youth was taken up to OLYMPUS and made immortal. Hence a cup-bearer generally.

Gaora (gā ôr' a). According to Hakluyt this was a tract of land inhabited by people without heads, with eyes in their shoulders and their mouths in their breasts. *Cp.* BLEMMYES.

Gape. Looking for gape-seed. Gaping about and doing nothing. A corruption of "Looking agapesing"; *gapesing* (still used in Norfolk) is staring about with one's mouth open.

Garcia (gar' si à). **To take a message to Garcia** is to be resourceful and courageous, to be able to accept responsibility and carry one's task through to the end. The phrase originated in the exploit of Lieut. Andrew Rowan who, in the Spanish-American War of 1898, made his way through the Spanish blockade into Cuba, made contact with General Calixto Garcia, chief of the Cuban insurgent forces, and carried news from him back to Washington.

Garden, or **Garden Sect, The.** The disciples of EPICURUS, who taught them in his own garden.

The Garden of Eden. *See* EDEN. Traditionally supposed to be sited in Mesopotamia.

Garden of the Hesperides. *See* HESPERIDES.

Garden City. A name given to both Norwich and Chicago; also, as a general name, to model townships specially planned to provide attractive layouts for housing and industry with a surrounding rural belt and adequate open spaces. The term was first used by an American, A. T. Stewart, in 1869, and applied to an estate development on Long Island. The "garden city" movement in England was due to the social ideas of Sir Ebenezer Howard (1850–1928) set out in his book *To-morrow* (1898). His first garden city was founded at Letchworth, Hertfordshire, in 1903 and his second at Welwyn (1919–1920).

Garden Suburb. A name applied to certain models suburbs (*e.g.* Hampstead Garden Suburb) with certain characteristics of a GARDEN CITY.

The Garden Suburb. The nickname applied to Lloyd George's personal secretariat, of which he made increasing use after he became head of the War Cabinet (December 1916), to help him in effecting his policies. The name derives from the fact that they were accommodated in huts in St. James's Park. The "Garden Suburb" was dispersed when Bonar Law assumed the premiership in 1922.

Garden. A term commonly applied to the more fertile areas as:

Garden of England. Kent and Worcester are both so called.

To lead up the garden, or **garden path.** To deceive, to trick, to entice with false promises of fair prospects, etc.

Gardy loo. The cry of warning formerly given by Edinburgh housewives and servants when about to empty the contents of the slop-pail out of the window into the street below. It is a corruption of the Fr. *gare de l'eau*, beware of the water.

> At ten o'clock at night the whole cargo of the chamber utensils is flung out of a back window that looks into some street or lane, and the maid calls "Gardy loo" to the passengers.
> SMOLLETT: *Humphry Clinker.*

Gargantua. A giant of mediæval or possibly CELTIC legend famous for his enormous appetite (Sp. *garganta*, gullet), adopted by Rabelais in his great satire (1535), and made the father of PANTAGRUEL. One of his exploits was to swallow five pilgrims, complete with their staves, in a salad. He is the subject of a number of CHAP-BOOKS, and became proverbial as a voracious and insatiable guzzler.

Gargouille (gar goo ēl'). The great DRAGON that lived in the Seine, ravaged Rouen, and was slain by St. Romanus, Archbishop of Rouen, in the 7th century.

Garibaldi's red shirt. The famous red shirt worn by Garibaldi and his followers during the liberation of Italy was of accidental origin. When Garibaldi was raising an Italian legion at Montevideo in 1843 a number of red woollen shirts came on the market owing to the difficulties in trade due to the war with Argentina. The government of Uruguay bought them up cheaply and gave them to Garibaldi for his men. When the Italian Legion came over to Italy in 1848 they brought their red shirts with them.

The Garibaldi biscuit, in which currants are mixed in the pastry, was a form of food much favoured by the General on his farm in Caprera.

The name *Garibaldi* was also given to a loose-fitting blouse for women, fashionable in the late 19th century.

Garland. Primarily a wreath of flowers either worn or festooned around something. Its use has also been extended to apply to an anthology of prose or verse.

> What I now offer to your lordships is a collection of Poetry, a kind of Garland of Good Will.
>
> PRIOR'S dedication to his *Poems*.

Garlic. The old superstition that garlic can destroy the magnetic power of the LODE-STONE has the sanction of Pliny, Solinus, Ptolemy, Plutarch, Albertus, Mathiolus, Rueus, Rulandus, Renodæus, Langius, and others. Sir Thomas Browne places it among *Vulgar Errors* (Bk. II, ch. iii).

Garlic Wall. The satirical name applied by Gibraltarians to the Spanish barrier which closed the frontier to La Línea in 1969 as a consequence of Spain's claim to the Rock. GIBRALTAR was ceded to Great Britain by the Treaty of Utrecht, 1713. Spain reopened the frontier at La Linea in 1985. *See* ROCK SCORPION.

Garnish. In old prison slang, the entrance money, to be spent on drink, demanded by gaol-birds from new arrivals. *Garnish* means embellishment, extra decoration to dress, etc.; hence it was applied by prisoners to fetters, and the *garnish-money* was money given for the "honour" of wearing them; the bigger the "garnish", the lighter the fetters.

In its original meaning, to *garnish* was to warn (Fr. *garnir*), and it is in this sense still used in the legal term *garnishee*, one warned not to pay money he owes to another, because the latter is in debt to the *garnisher* who issues the warning.

Garter. The Most Noble Order of the Garter. The highest order of Knighthood in Great Britain, traditionally instituted by King Edward III about 1348, and reconstituted in 1805 and 1831. The popular legend is that the Countess of Salisbury accidentally slipped her garter at a court ball. It was picked up by the king who, noticing the significant looks of the spectators, rebuked them by binding the blue band round his own knee, saying as he did so, HONI SOIT QUI MAL Y PENSE. The lady has also been named as Joan the FAIR MAID OF KENT, her cousin, Alice Montague and Queen Philippa. The order is limited to the Sovereign, and other members of the Royal Family, with 25 knights, and such foreign royalties as may be admitted by statute. The only Ladies of the Garter are the Sovereign's Queen and his eldest daughter when she is heir presumptive to the throne. Until Viscount Grey (then Sir Edward Grey) was admitted to the order in 1912, no commoner for centuries had been able to put "K.G." after his name. Sir Winston Churchill received the Order of the Garter from Queen Elizabeth II in 1953.

St. GEORGE was from the outset the special patron of the Order; it is sometimes called the Order of St. George, and each Knight is allotted a stall in St. George's Chapel, Windsor. The habits and insignia are the garter, mantle, surcoat, hood, star, collar, and GEORGE.

Garters. Wearing the garters of a pretty girl either on the hat or knee was a common custom with our forefathers. Brides usually wore on their legs a host of gay ribbons, to be distributed after the marriage ceremony amongst the bridegroom's friends; and the piper at the wedding dance never failed to tie a piece of the bride's garter round his pipe.

Magic garters. In the old romances, etc., garters made of the strips of a young hare's skin saturated with motherwort. Those who wore them excelled in speed.

Flying-the-garter. Springing or jumping lightly over something. Flying-the-garter was a one-time children's game, in which the players jumped over the *garter* or line (usually of stones), and the back of another player. In circuses, the tapes held up for performers to jump over were called *garters*.

Garvies. Sprats; perhaps so called from Inch-garvie, the island in the Firth of Forth.

Gasconade. Absurd boasting, vainglorious BRAGGADOCIO. It is said that a Gascon, being asked what he thought of the Louvre in Paris, replied "Pretty well; it reminds me of the back part of my father's stables"; an especially boastful answer when the Gascons were proverbial for their poverty.

Gat. An American slang term for an automatic pistol. It is a contraction of *Gatling*, from the machine-gun invented (1861–1862) by Richard Jordan Gatling (1818–1903), of North Carolina.

Gat-tooth. Chaucer's "Wife of Bath" was *gat-toothed* (*see Prol.* to *Canterbury Tales*, 468, and *Wife of Bath's Prol.*, 603); this probably means that her teeth were set wide apart, with *gats*, *i.e.* openings or gaps between them. Some editors suggest it is *goat-toothed* (O.E. *gat*), *i.e.* lascivious, like a GOAT.

Gate. Gate of Tears. The passage into the Red Sea so called by the Arabs (*Bab-el-Mandeb*) from the number of shipwrecks that took place there.

Golden Gate. *See under* GOLD.

Traitors' Gate. *See* TRAITORS'.

Gate crasher. One who gains entrance to a social function without invitation or ticket of admission. The origin is obvious.

Gate money. Money paid at the door or gate for admission to an enclosure where some entertainment or contest, etc., is to take place.

Gate-post bargain. A "cash down" deal. An old country custom of placing the purchase money on the gate-post before the stock being sold left the field. *Cp.* LUCK MONEY; TO PAY ON THE NAIL *under* NAIL.

Between you and me and the gate-post. Strictly confidentially.

Gath. Tell it not in Gath. Don't let your enemies hear it. Gath was famed as the birthplace of the giant GOLIATH.

> Tell it not in Gath, publish it not in the streets of Askelon: lest the daughters of the Philistines rejoice, lest the daughters of the uncircumcised triumph.
> II *Sam*. i, 20.

Gatling Gun. *See* GAT.

Gaudeamus igitur (Lat). The opening words of the famous students' song of mediæval origin, the first line being —

Gaudeamus igitur juvenes dum sumus (Let us therefore rejoice while we are young). It has seven verses and was formerly often sung at student celebrations.

Gaudy, or **Gaudy-day** (gaw′ di) (Lat. *gaudium*, joy). A holiday, a feast-day; especially an annual celebration of some event, such as the foundation of a college.

Gaudy is also one of the beads in the ROSARY marking the five joys or JOYFUL MYSTERIES of the Virgin, and the name given to one of the tapers burnt at the commemoration of the same.

Gaul. The country inhabited by the Gauls. *See* GALLIA.

Gaunt. John of Gaunt (1340–1399), fourth son of Edward III; so called from his birthplace, Ghent in Flanders.

Gauntlet. To run the gauntlet. To be attacked on all sides, to be severely criticized. The word came into English at the time of the THIRTY YEARS WAR (1618–1648) as *gantlope*, meaning the passage between two files of soldiers. It is the Swedish *gata*, a way, passage (*cp.* GAT-TOOTH) and *lopp* (connected with our *leap*, a course). The reference is to the former punishment among soldiers and sailors; the company or crew, provided with rope ends, were drawn up in two rows facing each other, and the delinquent had to run between them, while every man dealt him as severe a punishment as he could. The spelling *gauntlet* (*gantlet*) here is a due to confused etymology with *gauntlet*, a glove (O.Fr. *gantelet*, a diminutive of *gant*, a glove).

To take up the gauntlet. To accept a challenge.

To throw down the gauntlet. To challenge. In mediæval times, when one KNIGHT challenged another, the custom was for the challenger to throw his gauntlet on the ground, and if the challenge was accepted the person to whom it was thrown picked it up. Such a challenge was used by the CHAMPION OF ENGLAND.

Gautama (gaw ta′ ma). The family name of BUDDHA. His personal name was

Siddhartha, his father's name Suddhodana, and his mother's name Maya. He assumed the title Buddha at about the age of 36, when, after seven years of seclusion and spiritual struggle, he believed himself to have attained to perfect truth.

Gauvaine. GAWAIN.

Gavelkind. A system of tenure, especially in Kent and Wales and also in other parts of England. It was based on the freemen who gave rent or *gafol* to their lord instead of services. Some of its principal features were that if a person died intestate his property was divided equally among his sons or his daughters in the absence of sons. The dower was half instead of a third of a husband's land; a widower's courtesy one half of the land while remaining unmarried. After the Norman conquest it was replaced in England by the custom of primogeniture, except in Kent. It was abolished in Wales during the reign of Henry VIII and completely by Acts of Parliament of 1922 and 1925.

Gawain (gà wān'). One of the most famous of the Arthurian knights, nephew of King ARTHUR and probably the original hero of the GRAIL quest. He appears in the Welsh Triads and in the MABINOGION as Gwalchmei, and in the Arthurian cycle is the centre of many episodes and poems. The Middle English poem *Sir Gawain and the Green Knight* (*c.* 1360) is a romance telling how Gawain beheads the Green Knight in single combat.

Gay (O.Fr. *gai*). Light-hearted, merry, in high good spirits; also bright looking, as "she wore a gay-coloured dress".

> Belinda smiled and all the world was gay.
> POPE: *The Rape of the Lock*, II, 52.

Gay also acquired the sense of "given to pleasure" and hence dissipated; thus we say "he's a bit of a gay dog" and a *gay house* was a once common term for a brothel. In common usage meaning homosexual, especially of men. The word has been adopted by homosexual men to convey a sense of shared identity, as in **Gay Pride** and **Gay Lib**.

A gay deceiver. A LOTHARIO, a LIBERTINE.

Gaze. To stand at gaze. To stand in doubt as to what to do. When a stag first hears the hounds it stands dazed, looking all round, and in doubt as to what to do. Heralds call a stag represented fullfaced, "a stag at gaze".

Gaze-hound. *See* LYME-HOUND.

Gazelle boy, The. In 1961, Jean-Claude Armen, travelling by camel through the Spanish Sahara in W. Africa, was told by nomad tribesmen of the whereabouts of a young boy living with a herd of gazelles. In due time he sighted the boy and eventually attracted him to close quarters by playing a Berber flute. The boy fed on the same plants as the animals, sometimes eating worms and lizards. On a subsequent expedition in 1963, this time in a jeep, the speed of the boy when galloping with the herd was established at over 30 m.p.h. *Cp.* PETER THE WILD BOY.

Gazette. A newspaper. A word of Italian origin derived from the government newspaper issued in Venice from about 1536. It may be a diminutive of *gazza*, a magpie, in the sense of gossip, tittle-tattle, chatter (*cp.* the English *Tatler*, *Chatterbox*, *Town Talk*), or from *gazetta*, a small coin charged as a fee for reading the Venetian newspaper.

The London Gazette, an official government organ, appeared first as the *Oxford Gazette* in 1665, when the Court was at Oxford. It was transferred to LONDON in 1666 and has appeared on Tuesdays and Fridays ever since. It contains announcements of pensions, promotions, bankruptcies, dissolutions of partnerships, etc. *Cp.* NEWS; YELLOW PRESS.

Similar journals are published at Edinburgh and Belfast, the latter being transferred from Dublin after the establishment of the Irish Free State.

Gazetted. Posted in the LONDON GAZETTE as having received some official appointment, service promotion, etc., or on being declared bankrupt, etc.

Gazetteer. A geographical and topographical index or dictionary; so called because the name of one of the earliest such works in English was Laurence Echard's *The Gazetteer's or Newsman's Interpreter* (1703), *i.e.* it was intended for the use of journalists, *gazetteer* being a word applied to writers of news.

Gazumping. A colloquial usage (derivation uncertain) from the early 1970s particularly with relation to the property market. It denotes the somewhat dubious practice of raising a selling price after agreement has been reached with an intending purchaser. After having fixed a price with the vendor the purchaser finds that he is *gazumped* by the vendor accepting an increased offer from another buyer before contracts have been signed and exchanged.

Ge. *See* GÆA.

Gear. In good gear. To be in good working order.

Out of gear. Not in working condition; out of health.

Gee-up! and **Gee-whoa!** Interjections addressed to horses meaning respectively "Go ahead!" and "Stop!" From them came the children's term "gee-gee", a horse, which was adopted by sporting men and others, as in "Backing the gee-gees".

Geese. *See* GOOSE.

Gehenna (ge hen' à) (Heb.). The place of eternal torment. Strictly speaking, it means the "Valley of Hinnom" (Ge-Hinnom), where sacrifices to BAAL and MOLOCH were offered (*Jer.* xix, 6, etc.). It came to be regarded as a place of unquenchable fire, possibly from the fires of Moloch.

> And made his grove
> The pleasant valley of Hinnom, Tophet thence
> And black Gehenna called, the type of hell.
>
> MILTON: *Paradise Lost*, I, 403.

Gelert (gel' ĕrt). Llewelyn's dog. *See* BEDD-GELERT.

Gemara (ge ma' rà) (Aramaic, completion). The second part of the TALMUD, consisting of annotations, discussions and amplifications of the MISHNA, which is the first part. The *Mishna* is the codification of the oral law, the *Gemara* is supplementary and commentary on the *Mishna*.

The Palestinian or Jerusalem *Gemara* was completed by the Palestinian academics in the 5th century A.D. and the much fuller Babylonian *Gemara* by the academics of Babylon during the 4th and 5th centuries A.D.

Gemini. Lat. the Twins, a constellation and one of the signs of the ZODIAC (21 May to 21 June); representing CASTOR AND POLLUX, the "great twin brethren" of classical mythology.

Gen (jen). **Give us the gen.** Tell us the news, give us the detailed information; hence **to gen up** means to inform oneself fully or to "swot up" a subject. A phrase from Service slang, especially in the R.A.F.; it comes from either "General information" or "Genuine".

Gendarmes (zhon' darm) (Fr. *gens d'armes*, men-at-arms), the armed police of France. The term was first applied to an armed KNIGHT or CAVALIER, then to the cavalry. In the time of Louis XIV it was applied to a body of horse charged with the preservation of order, and after the Revolution to a military police chosen from old soldiers of good character; and now to the ordinary police.

Gender Words. These are words which, prefixed to the noun, indicate an animal's sex, *e.g.*:

Bull, cow: elephant, rhinoceros, seal and whale.

Dog, bitch: ape, fox (the bitch is usually called a vixen), otter, wolf.

Buck, doe: hare, rabbit, deer.

He, she: general gender words for quadrupeds.

Cock, hen: gender words for most birds.

In many cases a different word is used for each of the sexes, *e.g.*: Boar, sow; cockerel, pullet; colt, filly; drake, duck; gander, goose; hart, roe; ram, ewe; stag, hind; stallion, mare; steer (in the U.S.A. used of beef cattle of any age), heifer.

General. General Issue. An old legal term for a plea of "not guilty"; the issue formed by a general denial of the plaintiff's charge.

General Warrants. Warrants issued for the arrest of unspecified persons, first by the Court of STAR CHAMBER and subsequently authorized by the Licensing Act of 1662, and continued after its lapse in 1695, when they were used against the authors and publishers of allegedly seditious or libellous writings.

They were declared illegal as a result of actions brought against the Crown (1763–1765) by John Wilkes, who was arrested with others after the publication of NUMBER 45 (*see under* FORTY) of the *North Briton*. The Incitement to Disaffection Act passed in 1934 to prevent Communist propaganda in the armed forces permitted the issue of a general warrant by a High Court Judge.

Generalissimo. The supreme commander, especially of a force drawn from two or more nations, or of a combined military and naval force; the equivalent of *Tagus* among the ancient Thessalians, *Brennus* among the ancient Gauls, and PENDRAGON among the ancient Welsh or Celts. The title is said to have been coined by Cardinal Richelieu on taking supreme command of the French armies in Italy, in 1629.

Generic Names. *See* BIDDY.

Generous. Generous as Hatim. An Arabian expression. Hatim was a Bedouin chief famous for his warlike deeds and boundless generosity. His son was a contemporary of MOHAMMED.

Geneva (je nē' và). *See* GIN.

Geneva Bible. *See* BIBLE, THE ENGLISH.

Geneva Convention. In 1862, Jean Henri Dunant, a Swiss, published an account of the sufferings of the wounded at the battle of Solferino in 1859. From this sprang the RED CROSS movement and an international conference at Geneva in 1864. The resulting Geneva Convention provided for the care of the wounded and the protection of the military medical services, under the international emblem of the RED CROSS (*see under* CROSS).

Geneva courage. The BRAGGADOCIO resulting from having drunk too much GIN or *geneva*. *Cp.* DUTCH COURAGE.

Geneva Cross. *See* THE RED CROSS *under* CROSS.

Geneva doctrines. CALVINISM.

Geneviève, St. (je nà věv) (422–512). Patroness of PARIS. Her day is 3 January, and she is represented in art with the keys of Paris at her girdle, a DEVIL blowing out her candle, and an ANGEL relighting it; or as restoring sight to her blind mother; or guarding her father's

sheep. She was born at Nanterre and was influential in saving Paris from the FRANKS and the threatened attack of ATTILA the Hun. Her church has since become the PANTHEON.

Genius (pl. *Genii*). In Roman mythology the tutelary spirit that attended a man from cradle to grave, governed his fortunes, determined his character. The *Genius* wished a man to enjoy pleasure in life, thus to *indulge one's Genius* was to enjoy pleasure. The *Genius* only existed for man, the woman had her JUNO. Another belief was that a man had two *genii*, one good and one evil, and bad luck was due to his *evil genius*. The Roman *genii* were somewhat similar to the guardian angels spoken of in *Matt*. xviii, 10. The word is from the Lat. *gignere*, to beget (Gr. *gignesthai*, to be born), from the notion that birth and life were due to these *dii genitales*. Thus it is used for birth-wit or innate talent; hence propensity, nature, inner man.

The Eastern *genii* (sing. *genie*) were JINNS, who were not attendant spirits but fallen angels under the dominion of EBLIS.

Genius loci. The tutelary deity of a place.

Genocide (jen' ō sīd). A word invented by Professor Raphael Lemkin, of Duke University, U.S.A., and used in the drafting of the official indictment of war criminals in 1945. It is a combination of Gr. *genos*, race; and Lat. *cædere*, to kill. It is defined as acts intended to destroy, in whole or in part, national, ethnical, racial, or religious groups, and in 1948 was declared by the United Nations General Assembly to be a crime in international law.

Genre Painter (zhon' rè) (Fr. mode, style). A term applied to those who paint scenes of everyday life in the home, the village, the countryside, etc. The Dutch artists of Rembrandt's time were particularly characteristic of this style. The term is sometimes used of drama in the same sense.

Gens (jenz) (Lat. pl. *gentes*). A CLAN or SEPT in ancient ROME; a number of families deriving from a common ancestor, having the same name, religion, etc.

Gens bracata, or **braccata** (Lat.).

Trousered people. Unlike the Gauls, Scythians, and Persians, the Romans wore no trousers or breeches.

Gens togata. *See* TOGA.

Gentle. Belonging to a family of position; well-born; having the manners of genteel persons. The word is from Lat. *gentilis*, of the same family or *gens*, through O.Fr. *gentil*, high-born.

> We must be gentle, now we are gentlemen.
> SHAKESPEARE: *The Winter's Tale*, V, ii.

The gentle craft. Shoe-making. CRISPIN and Crispianus, the patron saints of shoe-making, were said to be brothers of noble birth.

> As I am a true shoemaker, and a gentleman of the Gentle Craft, buy spurs yourselfes, and I'll find ye bootes these seven yeeres.
> DEKKER: *The Shoemaker's Holiday, or the Gentle Craft*, I, i (1599).

Angling is also known as "the gentle craft". It is a pun on *gentle*, the maggot of the flesh-fly or blue-bottle, used as a bait.

> Every little pitiful coarse fish in the Avon was on the alert for flies ... and every lover of the gentle craft was out to avenge the poor may-flies.
> T. HUGHES: *Tom Brown's Schooldays*, ch. ix.

The gentle sex. Women.

The Gentle Shepherd. A nickname given by the elder Pitt to George Grenville (1712–1770). In the course of a speech on the cider tax (1763) Grenville addressed the HOUSE somewhat plaintively: "Tell me where? Tell me where?" Pitt mimicked him with the words of the song "Gentle shepherd, tell me where?" The House burst into laughter and the name stuck to Grenville. The line is from a song by Samuel Howard (1710–1782).

Gentleman (from O.Fr. *gentilz hom*). Historically a man entitled to bear arms but not of the nobility; hence one of gentle birth, of some position in society, and with manners, bearing and behaviour appropriate to one in such a position.

In the *York Mysteries* (c. 1440) we read, "Ther schall a gentilman, Jesu, unjustely be judged."

A gentleman at large. A man of means, who does not have to earn a living, and is free to come and go as he pleases. Formerly the term denoted a gentleman attached to the court but having no special duties.

A gentleman of fortune. A pirate, an adventurer, etc.

A gentleman of the road. A highwayman.

A gentleman's agreement. An agreement or understanding as between gentlemen in which the one guarantee is the honour of the parties concerned.

A gentleman's gentleman. A manservant, especially a valet.

A nation of gentlemen. So George IV called the Scots when, in 1822, he visited their country and was received with great expressions of loyalty.

Gentleman Pensioner. *See* GENTLEMEN AT ARMS, *below*.

Gentleman-ranker. In the days of the small regular army before World War I, this term was applied to a well-born or educated man who enlisted as a private solider. It was considered as a last resort of one who had made a mess of things.

Gentlemen Ushers. Court attendants in the Royal Household. They comprise Gentlemen Ushers, Extra Gentlemen Ushers, the Gentleman Usher to the Sword of State, and the Gentleman Usher of the BLACK ROD.

Gentlemen at Arms, The Honourable Corps of. The Bodyguard of the sovereign (formerly called *Gentlemen Pensioners*), acting in conjunction with the *Yeomen of the Guard* (*see* BEEFEATERS). It has a Captain, Lieutenant, Standard Bearer, Clerk of the Cheque, Sub-officer, and 39 Gentlemen at Arms, chosen from retired officers of ranks from General to Major of the Regular Army and Royal Marines.

The gentleman in black velvet. It was in these words that the JACOBITES used to drink to the mole that made the molehill that caused William III's horse to stumble and so brought about his death.

The Old Gentleman. The DEVIL; Old Nick (*see under* NICK). Also a special card in a prepared pack, used for tricks or cheating.

To put a churl upon a gentleman. To drink beer just after drinking wine.

Geomancy (jē' ō măn si) (Gr. *ge*, the earth; *manteia*, prophecy). DIVINATION by means of the observation of points on the earth or by the patterns made by throwing some earth into the air and allowing it to fall on a flat surface.

Geopolitics. The name given to the German theories of applied political geography developed by Karl Haushofer in the 1920s and earlier by F. Ratzel, whose pupil Kjellen coined the term. Sir Halford Mackinder (1861–1947) and others formulated similar theories. These teachings were used by the NAZIS to support their demand for LEBENSRAUM.

George, St. George. The patron SAINT of ENGLAND since his "adoption" by Edward III (*see* GARTER). His day is 23 April. The popularity of St. George in England stems from the time of the early CRUSADES, for he was said to have come to the assistance of the Crusaders at Antioch in 1098. Many of the Normans under Robert CURTHOSE, son of WILLIAM THE CONQUEROR, took him as their patron.

Gibbon and others argued that George of Cappadocia, the Arian bishop of Alexandria, became the English patron saint but it is more generally accepted that he was a Roman officer martyred (*c.* 300) near Lydda during the Diocletian persecution. He is also the patron saint of Aragon and Portugal.

The legend of St. George and the DRAGON is simply an allegorical expression of the triumph of the Christian hero over evil, which St. JOHN THE DIVINE beheld under the image of a dragon. Similarly, St. MICHAEL, St. MARGARET, St. SYLVESTER, and St. MARTHA are all depicted as slaying dragons; the Saviour and the Virgin as treading them under their feet; St. John the Evangelist as charming a winged dragon from a poisoned chalice given him to drink; and Bunyan avails himself of the same figure when he makes CHRISTIAN prevail upon APOLLYON.

The legend forms the subject of the ballad *St. George for England* in PERCY'S RELIQUES.

St. George he was for England, St. Denis was for France. This refers to the battle-cries of the two nations—that of England was "St. George!" that of France, "MONTJOIE ST. DENIS!"

> St. George he was for England; St. Denis was for France;
> Sing, Honi soit qui mal y pense.
>
> PERCY: *Reliques: St. George for England*.

St. George's Cross. A red cross on a white background.

When St. George goes on horseback St. Yves goes on foot. In times of war it was supposed that lawyers have nothing to do. St. GEORGE is the patron of soldiers and St. YVES or Yvo patron of lawyers.

George. A jewelled pendant representing St. GEORGE and the DRAGON, part of the insignia of the GARTER.

George IV (1760, 1820–1830) was given many nicknames. As Prince Regent he was known as "Prinny", "Prince FLORIZEL" (the name under which he corresponded with Mrs. Robinson), "The First Gentleman of Europe", "The Adonis of Fifty". As King he was called, among less offensive titles, "Fum the Fourth", as by Byron in *Don Juan*, xi, 78.

George Eliot. The pseudonym of the author of *The Mill on the Floss*, *Silas Marner*, *Romola*, etc.—Mary Ann Evans (1819–1880). She lived with George Henry Lewes from 1854 until his death in 1878, and married her "second" husband John Walter Cross as Mary Ann Evans Lewes.

George Sand. The pen-name of the famous French novelist Amandine Lucile Aurore Dupin, baronne Dudevant (1804–1876). It was adopted during her liaison with Jules Sandeau.

George Cross and Medal. The George Cross is second only to the VICTORIA CROSS. It consists of a plain silver cross with a medallion showing St. GEORGE and the DRAGON in the centre. The words "For Gallantry" appear round the medallion, and in the angle of each limb of the cross is the royal cipher. It hangs from a dark blue ribbon. The George Cross was founded in 1940 for acts of conspicuous heroism, primarily by civilians. It is only awarded to service personnel for acts of heroism not covered by existing military honours.

The George Medal (red ribbon with five narrow blue stripes) is awarded for similar somewhat less outstanding acts of bravery.

George Cross Island. Malta is so called from the award of the George Cross to the island by King George VI in April 1942, in recognition of the steadfastness and fortitude of its people while under siege in World War II. It had suffered constant aerial attacks from Italian and German bombers.

As good as George-a-Green. Resolute-minded; one who will do his duty come what may. George-a-Green was the mythical *Pinder* (*Pinner* or *Pindar*) or pound-keeper of Wakefield, who resisted ROBIN HOOD, Will Scarlet, and LITTLE JOHN single-handed when they attempted to commit a trespass in Wakefield.

By George. An oath or exclamation. "St. George" was the battle-cry of English soldiers, and from this arose such expressions as "before George", "fore George". In American usage it is "George", which has additional meanings, one of which, applied to any person or thing, has the same significance as the CAT'S PYJAMAS (*see under* CAT).

Let George do it. Let someone else do it. Derived from Louis XII of France who, when an unpleasant task arose, was apt to say "Let Georges do it", referring to his minister, Cardinal Georges.

Geraint (ge rīnt'). In Arthurian legend, a tributory prince of Devon, and one of the Knights of the ROUND TABLE. In the MABINOGION, he is the son of Erbin, as he is in the French original *Erec et Enide*, from which Tennyson drew his *Geraint and Enid* in the *Idylls of the King*.

Geranium. The Turks say this was a common mallow changed by the touch of MOHAMMED's garment.

The word is Gr. *geranos*, a crane; and the wild plant is called "Crane's Bill", from the resemblance of the fruit to the bill of a crane.

Gerda, or **Gerdhr** (gĕr' dà). In Scandinavian mythology (the *Skirnismal*) daughter of the Frost-giant Gymir and wife of Frey. She was so beautiful that the

brightness of her naked arms illumined both air and sea.

Germain. St. Germain-en-Laye. The favourite summer residence of the Kings of France until Louis XIV moved the court to VERSAILLES. Situated some 13 miles S.W. of Paris, the chateau was the childhood home of Mary Queen of Scots and sheltered the exiled James II after the Revolution of 1688.

German, or **Germane.** Pertaining to, nearly related to, as *cousins-german* (first cousins), *germane to the subject* (bearing on or pertinent to the subject). The word is Lat. *germanus*, of the same germ or stock, and has no connection with the German nation.

> Those that are germane to him, though removed fifty times, shall all come under the hangman.
> SHAKESPEARE: *The Winter's Tale*, IV, iii.

Germany. The English name for *Deutschland* (Fr. *Allemagne*) is the Lat. *Germania*, the source of which is uncertain, but possibly a Roman form of a CELTIC or Gaulish name for the TEUTONS; in which case it may be connected with Celt. *gair*, neighbour, *gavin*, warcry, or with *ger*, spear.

Geoffrey of Monmouth says that Ebrancus, a mythological descendant of BRUTE, and founder of York (*Eboracum*), had twenty sons and thirty daughters by twenty wives. The twenty sons departed to Germany and obtained possession of it.

German comb. The four fingers and thumb. The Germans were late in adopting periwigs; and while the French were never seen without a comb in one hand, the Germans tidied their hair by running their fingers through it.

Gerrymander (jer i măn' dĕr). So to redraw the boundaries of electoral districts as to give one political party undue advantage over others. The word is derived from Elbridge Gerry (1744–1814), governor of Massachusetts, who did this in 1812 in order to preserve control for his party. Gilbert Stuart, the artist, looking at a map of the new distribution, with a little invention converted the outline of one district in Essex County to a salamander and showed it to Benjamin Russell, editor of the Boston *Sentinel*.

"Better say a gerrymander," said Russell, and the name caught on. The practice was not new.

Gertrude of Nivelles, St. The daughter of Pepin of Landen, aunt of Charles Martel's father, Pepin of Heristal. As abbess of Nivelles she was noted for her care of the poor and was reputed to have known most of the BIBLE by heart. In art she is usually represented as so rapt in contemplation that a mouse climbs her pastoral staff unnoticed. She died about 664 and her day is 17 March.

Geryon (gēr' i on). In Greek mythology, a monster with three bodies and three heads, whose oxen ate human flesh, and were guarded by Orthrus, a two-headed dog. HERCULES slew both Geryon and the dog.

Gessler, Hermann. The tyrannical Austrian governor of the three Forest Cantons of Switzerland who figures in the TELL legend.

Gesta Danorum or **Historica Danica.** *See* SAXO GRAMMATICUS.

Gesta Romanorum. A collection of popular tales in Latin, each with a moral attached, compiled at the end of the 13th century or beginning of the 14th. The name, meaning "Deeds of the Romans", is merely fanciful and some of the episodes are of Oriental origin. It was first printed at Utrecht and the earliest English edition is that of Wynkyn de Worde about 1510. It is the source of many stories used in later literature. Chaucer, Shakespeare, Rossetti, Longfellow and many others use tales and plots which are found in it. It seems to have been compiled for the use of preachers.

Gestapo (ge sta' pō). Shortened from the Ger. *Geheime Staatspolizei*, secret state police, which acquired such sinister fame in NAZI Germany after 1933. It was formed by Goering and later controlled by Himmler and was responsible for terrorizing both the Germans and the peoples of occupied territories. It was declared a criminal organization by the Nuremberg Tribunal in 1946.

Gestas (ges' tăs). The traditional name of the impenitent thief. *See* DYSMAS.

Get. How are you getting on? How do things fare with you? How are you prospering?

To get about. To travel about, to attend many social events. Also used to denote the spreading of news or rumour. **To get around,** an expression of American origin, has the same meanings.

To get at. To reach; to tamper with, bribe, influence to a wrong end; to attack, tease, to make a butt of, etc.

To get away with it. To do something dangerous, unlawful, wrong, etc., and escape the usual penalty.

To get by. To get along all right, to manage just satisfactorily, to pass MUSTER.

To get cracking. A popular expression with the same meaning as TO GET WEAVING.

To get down to it. To set about a task in downright earnest.

To get it in the neck. To receive a thorough dressing-down, beating, punishment, etc.

To get off. To escape, not to be punished; also (of a girl) to become engaged or to catch a man.

To get over it. To recover from illness, shock, or sorrow.

To get round someone. To persuade by coaxing or flattery.

To get there. To succeed, to "arrive", attain one's object.

To get up. To rise from one's bed. To learn, as, "I must get up my history". To organize and arrange, as "We will get up a bazaar".

To get weaving. To set about a task briskly. A colloquial Services expression in World War II. Weaving implies dexterous movement, as when aircraft make rapid directional changes to escape enemy fire.

To get well on, or **well oiled.** To become intoxicated.

Your get-up was excellent. Your style of dress was entirely suitable for the part you professed to enact. In the same way, "She was got up regardless". Her dress was splendid—regardless of expense.

For phrases such as **You got out of bed the wrong way, To get the mitten, To get the wind up,** etc., see the main word in the phrase.

Gethsemane (geth sem' à ni). The word

means "oil-press" and the traditional site of the Garden of Gethsemane, the scene of Our Lord's agony, is on the Mount of Olives, east of the ravine of the Kidron. There was presumably an oil-press on this plot of ground.

The *Orchis maculata* is called "geth-semane" from the legend that is was spotted by the blood of Christ.

Ghan, The. In Australia, a weekly train from Adelaide to Alice Springs. The construction of a railway line from Adelaide to the northern coast was begun in 1877 but got no further than Oodnadatta (472 km. from Alice Springs). For about 40 years camel trains conducted by Afghans carried goods and passengers from Oodnadatta to Alice. When the railway reached Alice in 1929 the train came to be known as "The Ghan".

Ghebers. *See* GUEBRES.

Ghibelline. *See* GUELPH.

Ghost. The Holy Ghost. *See under* HOLY.

The ghost of a chance. The least likelihood. "He has not the ghost of a chance of being elected", not the shadow of a probability.

The ghost walks. Theatrical slang for "salaries are about to be paid"; when there is no money available actors say "the ghost won't walk this time". The allusion is to SHAKESPEARE's *Hamlet*, I, i, where Horatio asks the ghost if it "walks" because—

Thou hast uphoarded in thy life
Extorted treasure in the womb of earth.

To give up the ghost. To die. The idea is that life is independent of the body, and is due to the habitation of the ghost or spirit in the material body.

To look like a ghost. To look deathly pale, pale as a ghost.

Ghost-word. A term invented by W. W. Skeat (*Philol. Soc. Transactions*, 1886) to denote words that had no real existence but are due to the errors of scribes, printers, or editors, etc. Like ghosts we may seem to see them, or may fancy that they exist; but they have no real being. ACRE-FIGHT (*see under* FIGHT) and SLUG-HORN are examples.

Intrusive letters that have no etymological right in a word but have been inserted through false analogy with words similarly pronounced (like the *gh* in *sprightly*, the *h* in *aghast* or the *h* in *ghost*) are sometimes called **ghost-letters**.

Ghost writer. The anonymous author who writes speeches, articles or books—especially autobiographies—for which another and better-known person gets the credit.

Giants, *i.e.* persons well above normal height and size, are found as "sports" or "freaks of nature"; but the widespread belief in pre-existing races of giants among primitive peoples is due partly to the ingrained idea that mankind has degenerated—"There were giants in the earth in those days" (*Gen*. vi, 4)—and partly to the existence from remote antiquity of cyclopæan buildings, gigantic SARCOPHAGI etc., and to the discovery from time to time in pre-scientific days of the bones of extinct monsters which were taken to be those of men. Among instances of the latter may be mentioned:

A 19 ft. skeleton was discovered at Lucerne in 1577. Dr. Plater is our authority for this measurement.

"Teutobochus", whose remains were discovered near the Rhône in 1613. They occupied a tomb 30 ft. long. The bones of another gigantic skeleton were exposed by the action of the Rhône in 1456. If this was a human skeleton, the height of living man must have been 30 ft.

Pliny records that an earthquake in Crete exposed the bones of a giant 46 cubits (*i.e.* roughly 75 ft.) in height; he called this the skeleton of ORION, others held it to be that of Otus.

Antæus is said by Plutarch to have been 60 cubits (about 90 ft.) in height. He furthermore adds that the grave of the giant was opened by Serbonius.

The "monster Polypheme". It is said that his skeleton was discovered at Trapani, in Sicily, in the 14th century. If this skeleton was that of a man, he must have been 300 ft. in height.

Giants of the Bible.

Anak. The eponymous progenitor of the Anakim (*see below*). The Hebrew spies said they were mere grasshoppers in comparison with these giants (*Josh*. xv, 14; *Judges* i, 20; and *Numb*, xiii, 33).

GOLIATH of Gath (I *Sam*. xvii, etc.). His height is given as 6 cubits and a span: the cubit varied and might be anything from about 18 in. to 22 in., and a span was about 9 in.; this would give Goliath a height of between 9 ft. 9 in. and 11 ft. 3 in.

OG, King of Bashan (*Josh*. xii, 4; *Deut*. iii, 10, iv, 47, etc.), was "of the remnant of the Rephaim". According to tradition, he lived 3,000 years and walked beside the Ark during the Flood. One of his bones formed a bridge over a river. His bed (*Deut*. iii, 11) was 9 cubits by 4 cubits.

The Anakim and Rephaim were tribes of reputed giants inhabiting the territory on both sides of the Jordan before the coming of the Israelites. The Nephilim, the offspring of the sons of God and the daughters of men (*Gen*. vi, 4), a mythological race of semi-divine heroes, were also giants.

Giants of Legend and Literature.

The giants of Greek mythology were, for the most part, sons of URANUS and GÆA. When they attempted to storm heaven, they were hurled to earth by the aid of HERCULES, and buried under Mount ETNA (*see* TITANS). Those of Scandinavian mythology dwelt in JOTUNHEIM and these "voracious ones" personified the unbridled forces of nature with superhuman powers against which man strove with the help of the gods. Giants feature prominently in nursery tales such as JACK THE GIANT-KILLER and Swift peopled BROBDING-NAG with giants.

Giants of Other Note.

Anak. *See* BRICE *below*.

Andronicus II, grandson of Alexius Comnenus, was 10 ft. in height. Nicetas asserts that he had seen him.

Bamford (Edward) was 7 ft. 4 in. He died in 1768 and was buried in St. Dunstan's churchyard, London.

Bates (Captain) was 7 ft. 11½ in. A native of Kentucky, he was exhibited in London in 1871. His wife, Anne Hannen Swan, a native of Nova Scotia, was the same height.

Blacker (Henry) was 7ft. 4 in. and most symmetrical. A native of Cuckfield, Sussex, he was called "the British Giant".

Bradley (William) was 7 ft. 9 in. Born in 1787 at Market Weight, Yorkshire, he died in 1820. His right hand is preserved in the museum of the Royal College of Surgeons.

Brice (M. J.), exhibited under the name of Anak, was 7 ft. 8 in. at the age of 26. He was born in 1840 at Ramonchamp in the Vosges and visited England 1862–1865. His arms had a stretch of 95½ in.

Brusted (Von) of Norway was 8 ft. He was exhibited at London in 1880.

Byrne. *See* O'BRIEN *below*.

Chang, the Chinese giant, was 8 ft. 2 in. He was exhibited in London in 1865–1866 and in 1880.

CHARLEMAGNE, according to tradition, was nearly 8 ft. and was so strong that he could squeeze together three horseshoes with his hands.

Cotter (Patrick), an Irish bricklayer, who exhibited as O'Brien, was 8 ft. 1 in. Born in 1761, he died at Clifton, Bristol, in 1806. A cast of his hand is preserved in the museum of the Royal College of Surgeons.

Daniel, the porter of Oliver Cromwell, was a man of gigantic stature.

Eleazer was 7 cubits (nearly 11 ft.). Vitellius sent this giant to Rome. He is mentioned by Josephus who also speaks of a Jew of 10 ft. 2 in.

Eleizegue (Joachim) was 7 ft. 10 in. A Spaniard, he was exhibited in the Cosmorama, Regent Street, London, in the mid-19th century.

Evans (William) was 8 ft. He was a porter of Charles I, and died in 1632.

Frank (Big) was 7 ft. 8 in. He was Francis Sheridan, an Irishman, and died in 1870.

Gabara, the Arabian giant, was 9 ft. 9 in. Pliny says he was the tallest man seen in the days of Claudius.

Gilly was 8 ft. This Swedish giant was exhibited at London in the early part of the 19th century.

Gordon (Alice) was 7 ft. She was a native of Essex, and died in 1737, at the age of 19.

Hale (Robert) was 7 ft. 6 in. and was born at Somerton, Norfolk in 1802. He died in 1862 and was called "the Norfolk Giant".

Hardrada (Harald) was nearly 7 ft. and was called "the Norway Giant". He was slain at Stamford Bridge in 1066.

Holmes (Benjamin) of Northumberland was 7 ft. 7 in. He became sword-bearer to the Corporation of Worcester and died in 1892.

McDonald (James) of Cork, Ireland, was 7 ft. 6 in. He died in 1760.

McDonald (Samuel) was 6 ft. 10 in. This Scot was usually called "Big Sam". He was the Prince of Wales's footman, and died in 1802.

Macgrath (Cornelius) was 7 ft. 10 in. at the age of 16. He was an orphan reared by Bishop Berkeley and died in 1760 at the age of 20.

Maximus I, Roman Emperor (235–238) was 8 ft. 6 in.

Middleton (John) was 9 ft. 3 in. He was born at Hale, Lancashire, in the reign of James I. "His hand was 17 in. long and 8½ in. broad" (Dr. Plot: *Natural History of Staffordshire*).

Miller (Maximilian Christopher) was 8 ft. His hand measured 12 in., and his forefinger 9 in. He died at London in 1734 at the age of 60.

Murphy, an Irish giant of the late 18th century, was 8 ft. 10 in. He died at Marseilles.

O'Brien, or Charles Byrne (1761–1783), was 8 ft. 4 in. He died in Cockspur Street, London and the skeleton of this Irish giant is preserved in the Royal College of Surgeons.

O'Brien (Patrick). *See* COTTER *above*.

Porus was 5 cubits in height (about 7½ ft.). He was an Indian king who fought against ALEXANDER the Great near the Hydaspes. (Quintus Curtius: *De rebus gestis Alexandri Magni*.)

Sam (Big). *See* MACDONALD *above*.

Sheridan. *See* FRANK *above*.

Swan (Anne Hannen). *See* BATES *above*.

Toller (James) was 8 ft. at the age of 24. He died in 1819.

Wadlow (Robert P.) of Illinois, U.S.A., was 8 ft. 11.1 in. (1918–1940), the tallest man of whose measurements there is complete certainty.

Winkelmaier (Josef), an Austrian, was 8 ft. 9 in. (1865–1887).

In addition to the above:

Del Rio tells us that he saw a Piedmontese in 1572 more than 9 ft. high.

M. Thevet published (1575) an account of a South American giant, the skeleton of which he measured. It was 11 ft. 5 in.

Gaspard Bauhin (1560–1624), the anatomist and botanist, speaks of a Swiss 8 ft. high.

A Mr. Warren (in *Notes and Queries*, 14 August 1875) said that his father knew a woman 9 ft. in height, and adds "her head touched the ceiling of a good-sized room".

There is a human skeleton 8 ft. 6 in. in height in the museum of Trinity College, Dublin.

There were over 100 applicants in response to an advertisement in *The Times* (25 July 1966) for "giants" of minimum height 6 ft. 7 in. for the premiere of *Cast a Giant Shadow* at the London Pavilion. The tallest was 7 ft. 3 in. *Cp.* DWARF; HEAVIEST MEN.

Giants' Cauldrons. *See* GIANTS' KETTLES.

Giant's Causeway. A formation of some 40,000 basaltic columns, projecting into the sea about 8 miles ENE of Portrush, Co. Antrim, on the north coast of IRELAND. It is fabled to be the beginning of a road to be constructed by the giants across the channel from Ireland to SCOTLAND. Here are to be found the *Giants' Loom*, the *Giants' Well* and the *Giants' Chair*. Other formations in the district are called the *Giants' Organ*, the *Giants' Peep-hole*, and the *Giants' Granny*, also reefs called the *Giants' Eye-glass*.

Giants' Dance, The. STONEHENGE, which Geoffrey of Monmouth says was removed from Killaurus, a mountain in IRELAND, by Uther PENDRAGON and his men under the direction of MERLIN.

Giants' Kettles, or **Giants' Cauldrons.** A name given to glacial pot-shaped cylindrical holes worn in rocks by the rotary currents of sub-glacial streams, often containing water-worn stones, boulders, etc. They are found in Norway, GERMANY, the U.S.A., etc.

Giants' Leap, The. A popular name in many mountainous districts given to two prominent rocks separated from each other by a wide chasm or stretch of open country across which some giant is fabled to have leapt and so baffled his pursuers.

Giants' Ring. A prehistoric circular mound near Milltown, Co. Down, IRELAND. It is 580 ft. in diameter and has a CROMLECH in the centre.

Giants' Staircase. The staircase which rises from the courtyard of the Doge's Palace, Venice. So named from the figures of two giants at its head.

Giants' War with Zeus. The War of the Giants and the War of the TITANS should be kept distinct. The latter was before ZEUS became god of HEAVEN and earth, the former was after that time. The Giants' War was a revolt by the giants against Zeus, which was readily put down by the help of the other gods and the aid of HERCULES.

Giaour (jour). A word used by the Turks for one who was not a Mohammedan, especially a CHRISTIAN. The word was popularized by Byron who wrote a poem called *The Giaour*.

Gib Cat (jib kăt). A tomcat. The male cat used to be called *Gilbert*. Tibert, or TYBALT, is the French form of Gilbert, and hence Chaucer, or whoever it was that translated that part of the *Romaunt of the Rose*, renders "Thibert le cas" by "Gibbe, our Cat" (line 6204). It is generally used of a castrated cat.

> I am as melancholy as a gib cat or a lugged bear.
> SHAKESPEARE: *Henry IV, Pt. I*, I, ii.

Gibeonite (gib' i on īt). A slave's slave, a workman's labourer, a farmer's understrapper, or Jack-of-all-work. The Gibeonites were made "hewers of wood and drawers of water" to the Israelites (*Josh*. ix, 27).

Gibraltar (jib rawl tàr). The "CALPE" of the ancients and one of the PILLARS OF HERCULES. The name is a corruption of *Gebel-al-Tarik*, the hill of Tarik, Tarik being the SARACEN leader, who utterly defeated RODERICK, the Gothic king of Spain in 711, and built a castle on the Rock. The Spaniards finally took it from the Moors in 1462. It was captured by a combined English and Dutch force under Sir George Rooke in 1704 and unsuccessfully besieged by the Spaniards and French in 1704, 1705 and subsequently, most memorably from 1779 to 1783, when it was heroically defended by General Eliott (later Lord Heathfield). *See also* GARLIC WALL; ROCK SCORPION.

Gibson Girl. A type of elegant female beauty characteristic of its period depicted by Charles Dana Gibson (1867–1944) in several series of black-and-white drawings dating from 1896. His delineations of the American girl enjoyed an enormous vogue and the series entitled *The Adventures of Mr. Pipp*, which appeared in *Collier's Weekly* (1899), formed the basis of a successful play. The Gibson Girl was portrayed in various poses and occupations, her individuality accentuated by the sweeping skirts and large hats of the period.

Her type was based on his wife Irene (neé Langhorne) and her sisters, among whom was the late Nancy, Viscountess Astor.

Gibus (jī'bùs). An opera-hat named after its inventor, a Parisian hat-maker of the early 19th century. It is a cloth top-hat with a collapsible crown that enables the wearer to fold it up when not in use.

Gideons. An international association of Christian business and professional men founded in 1899 and now functioning in over 65 countries. They seek to lead others to Christianity, particularly by the distribution of Bibles and New Testaments on a large scale. Bibles are provided in hotel bedrooms and hospitals and New Testaments are presented to pupils in schools. They are named after Gideon's men who overthrew the Midianites (*Judges* vii).

Giff Gaff. Give and take; good turn for good turn. A variant repetition from *give*.

Gift-Horse. Don't look a gift-horse in the mouth. When given a present do not inquire too minutely into its intrinsic value. The normal way of assessing the age of a horse is to inspect its front teeth. The proverb has its counterpart in many languages.

Gig-lamps. Once popular for spectacles, especially large round ones—an allusion to the lanterns attached to a gig. It is also a local nickname for a fire-fly.

Giglet, or **giglot.** A light, wanton woman.

Gigman. Used derisively or comtemptuously for a quite respectable person; hence *gigmanity*, smug respectability, a word invented by Carlyle.

Gilbertian. A term applied to anything humorously topsy-turvy, any situation such as those W. S. Gilbert (1836–1911) depicted in the Gilbert and Sullivan operas. Of these perhaps the *Mikado* furnishes the best examples.

Gilbertines. The only mediæval religious order of English origin, founded at Sempringham in Lincolnshire *c*. 1135 by Gilbert of Sempringham (*c*. 1083–1189). The monks observed the rule of the AUGUSTINIANS and the nuns that of the BENEDICTINES. There were some 25 houses at the Dissolution.

Gild. To gild the lily. To add superfluous ornament to that which is already beautiful.

To gild the pill. It was the custom of old-time doctors—QUACKS and genuine—to make their nauseous pills more attractive, at least to the sight, by gilding them with a thin coating of sugar. Hence to make an unattractive thing at least appear desirable.

Gilded Chamber, The. A familiar name for the HOUSE OF LORDS.

Gilded Youth. Wealthy and fashionable young men, principally engaged in the pursuit of pleasure. A parallel expression to the Fr. JEUNESSE DORÉE.

Gildas (*c*. 516–*c*. 570). The earliest British "historian", also called *Sapiens* and

Badonicus. Very little is known about him, but he was most probably an ecclesiastic and much of his writing consists of a tirade against his countrymen. His works contain much scriptural matter, and the history covers the period from the Roman invasion to his own times. Although vague and inaccurate, his sketch is important. Written *c*. 547, his treatise was first published in modified form by Polydore Virgil in 1525.

Gilderoy. A noted robber and cattle-stealer of Perthshire who was hanged with five of his gang in July 1638, at Gallowlee near Edinburgh. He was noted for his handsome person and his real name was said to be Patrick Macgregor. He is credited with having picked the pocket of Cardinal Richelieu, robbed Oliver Cromwell, and hanged a judge. There are ballads on him in PERCY'S RELIQUES, Ritson's *Collection*, etc., and a modern one by Campbell.

Giles. A mildly humorous generic name for a farmer; the subject of Bloomfield's poem *The Farmer's Boy* (1800) was so named.

Giles, St. Patron SAINT of cripples. The tradition is that Childeric, king of France, accidentally wounded the hermit in the knee when hunting; and he remained a cripple for life, refusing to be cured that he might the better mortify the flesh.

His symbol is a hind, in allusion to the "heaven-directed hind", which went daily to his cave near the mouth of the Rhône to give him milk. He is sometimes represented as an old man with an arrow in his hand and a hind by his side.

Churches dedicated to St. Giles were usually situated in the outskirts of a city, and originally outside the walls, cripples and beggars not being permitted to pass the gates. *Cp*. CRIPPLEGATE.

Gilgamesh Epic. A collection of ancient Babylonian stories and myths, older than HOMER, seemingly brought together around Gilgamesh, king of Erech, as the central hero. He was two-thirds a god, one-third a man. It appears to have covered 12 tablets (*c*. 3,000 lines), portions of which were found among the relics of the library of Assur-bani-pal, King of Assyria (668–626

B.C.). Some of the tablets date back to *c*. 2000 B.C. *See* DELUGE.

Gillie. A Gaelic word for a boy or lad, manservant or attendant, especially one who waits on a sportsman fishing or hunting.

Gillies' Hill. In the battle of Bannock-burn (1314), King Robert Bruce ordered all the gillies, drivers of carts, and camp followers to go behind a hill. Those, when the battle seemed to favour the Scots, desirous of sharing in the plunder, rushed from their concealment with such arms as they could lay hands on. The English, thinking them to be a new army, fled in panic. The height was ever after called the Gillies' Hill.

Gills. Humorous slang for the mouth.

Blue about the gills. Down in the mouth; depressed looking.

Pale about the gills. *See* WHITE *below*.

Rosy, or **red about the gills.** Flushed with liquor.

White about the gills. Showing unmistakable signs of fear or terror or sickness.

Gilpin, John, of Cowper's famous ballad (1782), is a caricature of a Mr. Beyer, a noted linendraper at the end of PATERNOSTER ROW, where it joins CHEAPSIDE. He died in 1791 at the age of 98. It was Lady Austin who told Cowper the story to divert him from his melancholy. The marriage adventure of Commodore Trunnion in Smollett's *Peregrine Pickle* is very similar to that of Gilpin's wedding anniversary.

Gilt. To take the gilt off the ginger-bread. *See under* GINGERBREAD.

Gilt-edged Investments. A phrase introduced in the last quarter of the 19th century to denote securities of the most reliable character, such as CONSOLS and other Government and Colonial Stock, first mortgages, debentures, and shares in first-rate companies, etc.

Gimlet-eyed. Keen-eyed, very sharp-sighted, given to watching or peering into things; eyes which bore through one. A squint is sometimes called a *gimlet-eye*.

Gimmick. The first use of this word in U.S.A. slang was to describe some device by which a conjurer or fairground

Gin

showman worked his trick. In later
usage it applied to some distinctive
quirk or trick associated with a film or
radio star, then to any such.

Gin. A contraction of *geneva*, the older
name of the spirit, from Fr. *genièvre*
(O.Fr. *genèvre*), juniper, the berries of
which are used to flavour the spirit. *See*
HOLLANDS.

Gin and It. A mixture of gin and Italian
vermouth.

Gin-palace. A garishly ornate gin-
shop, especially of Victorian and Edwardian times.

Gin-Sling. A long drink composed
mainly of gin and lemon. It has been attributed to JOHN COLLINS, famous bartender of Limmer's Hotel in London,
but it dates from before his time and was
found in the U.S.A. by 1800.

Ginger. A hot spicy root used in cooking
and in medicine, hence as a nickname
applied to someone with red hair.

Ginger group. A small group of people
whose object is to stir the more passive
majority into activity, especially in politics. The allusion to the spice is obvious.
The FOURTH PARTY is a notable example
of a political ginger group.

A stone ginger. A certainty, from the
New Zealand racehorse of this name
which (*c.* 1910) won every race for
which it entered.

Gingerbread. A cake mixed with treacle and flavoured with ginger made up
into toy shapes such as gingerbread
men, etc., and with gilded decorations
of DUTCH GOLD or gold leaf, it was commonly sold at FAIRS up to the middle of
the 19th century. Hence TAWDRY wares,
showy but worthless.

Gingerbread-work. A contemptuous
term for fanciful shapes, ornate carvings, etc., used to decorate furniture,
buildings, etc.

To take the gilt off the gingerbread.
To destroy the illusion; to appropriate
all the fun or profit and leave the dull
base behind; to rob something of its attraction.

Gingerly. Cautiously, with hesitating,
mincing, or faltering steps. The word is
over 400 years old in English and has
nothing to do with ginger. It is probably
from O.Fr. *gensour*, comparative of

gent, delicate, dainty.

Ginnunga gap. In Scandinavian mythology, the great abyss between NIFLHEIM,
the region of fogs and MUSPELHEIM, the
region of intense heat. It was without
beginning and without end, there was
neither day or night, and it existed before either land or sea, HEAVEN or earth.

Gioconda smile. An enigmatic smile, as
that of Mona Lisa. Leonardo da Vinci's
famous painting, also known as *La Gioconda* or *La Joconde*, is a portrait of the
wife of Francesco del Giocondo.

Giotto's O. The old story goes that the
POPE, wishing to employ artists from all
over Italy, sent a messenger to collect
specimens of their work. When the man
visited Giotto (*c.* 1267–1337) the artist
paused for a moment from the picture
he was working on and with his brush
drew a perfect circle on a piece of paper.
In some surprise the man returned to
the Pope, who, appreciating the perfection of Giotto's artistry and skill by his
unerring circle, employed Giotto forthwith.

Giovanni, Don. *See* DON JUAN.

Gipsy. *See* GYPSY.

Giralda (Sp. a weather-vane). The name
given to the great square tower of the
cathedral at Seville (formerly a Moorish
minaret) which is surmounted by a statue of Faith, so pivoted as to turn with
the wind.

Gird. To gird up the loins. To prepare
for hard work or for a journey. The Jews
wore a girdle only when at work or on a
journey.

To gird with a sword. To raise to a
peerage. It was the SAXON method of investiture to an earldom, continued after
the CONQUEST. Thus Richard I "girded
with the sword" Hugh de Pudsey, the
aged Bishop of Durham, making (as he
said) "a young earl of an old prelate".

**Girdle. A good name is better than a
good girdle.** A good reputation is better than money. It used to be customary
to carry money in the belt or in a purse
suspended from it, and a girdle of gold
meant a "purse of gold".

Children under the girdle. Not yet
born.

He has undone her girdle. Taken her
for his wife. The Roman bride wore a

436

chaplet of flowers on her head, and a girdle of sheep's wool about her waist. A part of the marriage ceremony was for the bridegroom to loose this.

If he be angry, he knows how to turn his girdle. A quotation from Shakespeare's *Much Ado About Nothing*, V, i. He knows how to prepare himself to fight. Before wrestlers engaged in combat, they turned the buckle of the girth behind them.

The Girdle of Venus. *See* CESTUS.

To put a girdle round the earth. To travel round it. PUCK says:

> I'll put a girdle round about the earth
> In forty minutes.
> SHAKESPEARE: *Midsummer Night's Dream*, II, i.

Girdle-cake. A cake cooked over the fire on a girdle or griddle, a circular iron plate, also called a bakestone.

Girl. The word first appears in Middle English and its etymology has given rise to many guesses. It was formerly applicable to a child of either sex (a boy was sometimes distinguished as a "knave-girl"), and is now applied particularly to a young female or young woman. It is probably a diminutive of some lost word cognate with Pomeranian *goer* and Old Low German *gor*, a child.

Girl Guides. The feminine counterpart to the BOY SCOUTS, organized in 1910 by General Baden-Powell, and his sister Miss Agnes Baden-Powell. Their training and organization is essentially the same as the Scouts and is based on similar promises and laws. The three sections of the movement were called Brownies, Guides, and Rangers, but the names and groupings have now been modified to Brownie Guides (7–11 years); Guides (10–16 years); Ranger Guides (14–19 years).

In the U.S.A., where they were formed in 1921, they are called Girl Scouts, with different age groupings and names, other than that of Brownie.

Girondists, or **The Gironde.** The moderate republicans in the French Revolution (1791–1793). So called from the department of the Gironde which elected for the Legislative Assembly men such as Vergniaud and Gensonné who championed its point of view. Condorcet,

Madame Roland, and Pétion were among them. Brissot became their chief spokesman, hence they were sometimes called *Brissotins*. They were the dominant party in 1792 but were overthrown in the Convention by the MOUNTAIN in 1793 and many of their leaders were guillotined.

Gis. A corruption of Jesus or J. H. S. Ophelia says "By Gis and by St. Charity" (*Hamlet*, IV, v).

Give. For such phrases as **Give the devil his due, Give a dog a bad name and hang him, I'll give him beans,** etc., see the principal noun.

A given name. A first or Christian name.

A give-away is a revealing or betraying circumstance.

To give and take. To be fair; to practise forbearance and consideration. In horse-racing *a give and take plate* is a prize for a race in which the runners which exceed a standard height carry more, and those who come short of it less, than the standard weight.

To give away. To hand the bride in marriage to the bridegroom, to act the part of the bride's father. Also, to let out a secret, inadvertently or on purpose; to betray an accomplice.

To give in. To confess oneself beaten, to yield.

To give it anyone, to give it him hot. To scold or thrash a person. As "I gave it him right and left", "I'll give it you when I catch you".

To give oneself away. To betray oneself by some thoughtless action or remark; to damage one's own cause by carelessly letting something out.

To give out. To make public. Also, to come to an end, to become exhausted; as, "My money has quite given out."

To give way. To break down; to yield.

To give what for. To administer a sound thrashing, to castigate thoroughly.

Gizzard. The strong, muscular second stomach of birds, where the food is ground, attributed humorously to man in some phrases.

That stuck in his gizzard. Annoyed him, was more than he could stomach, or digest.

Glad. To give the glad eye. *See* EYE.

Glad rags. A slang term for evening dress.

Gladiators (Lat. *gladius*, a sword). These combatants who fought to the death in Roman arenas were first drawn from condemned criminals and originally appeared at FUNERAL ceremonies in 164 B.C. Slaves and prisoners of war came to be employed as the taste for these revolting spectacles grew, and their employment as hired bodyguards by wealthy patrons became a threat to law and order. They were trained in special schools (*ludi*) and gladiatorial games spread throughout the provinces. Such combats were suppressed in the Eastern Empire by Constantine in A.D. 325 and in the West by Theodoric in A.D. 500. *See* THUMB.

Gladstone. A name given to cheap claret after W. E. Gladstone (1809–1898) when CHANCELLOR OF THE EXCHEQUER reduced the duty on French wines in his famous budget of 1860.

Gladstone bag. A kind of leather portmanteau made in various sizes and named after the great Victorian statesman, W. E. Gladstone.

Glamorgan. The southernmost county of Wales. Geoffrey of Monmouth says that Margan and Cunedagius, the sons of Gonorilla and Regan, divided the Kingdom of Britain between them after the death of their aunt Cordeilla. Margan, resolving to take the whole, attacked Cunedagius but was put to flight and killed "in a town of Kambria, which since his death has been by the country people called Margan to this day".

The name actually appears to be a corruption of *Gwlad Morgan*, the land or territory of Morgan, alternatively called *Morganwg* (or *Morgannwg*), the suffix *wg* after the name indicating the ruler's domain, Morgan probably being a native prince of the 10th century. Geoffrey of Monmouth wrote in the 12th century.

Glasgow, Arms of. *See* KENTIGERN, ST.

Glasgow magistrate. A salt herring. The phrase is said to have originated when some wag placed a salt herring on the iron guard of the carriage of a well-known magistrate who made up part of a deputation attending on King George IV.

Glasnost (Russ. openness). Mikhail Gorbachev became General Secretary of the Soviet Communist party in 1985 and in 1986 he introduced a policy of *glasnost* (in conjunction with PERESTROIKA) relaxing repression on human rights, but within the framework of socialism. The intention is to give more freedom in social and cultural affairs.

Glass. Glass breaker. A wine bibber. In the early part of the 19th century topers often threw the empty glass under the table or broke off the stand so that they might not be able to set it down and were compelled to drink it clean off, without HEEL-TAPS.

> We never were glass-breakers in this house, Mr. Lovel.
> SCOTT: *The Antiquary*, ch. ix.

Glass House. Army slang for a military prison. It was originally applied to the prison at North Camp, Aldershot, which had a glass roof.

To live in a glass house. To be in a vulnerable position morally, to be open to attack. An expression arising from the old proverb **those who live in glass houses should not throw stones.** It is found in varying forms from the time of Chaucer. *Cp. also Matt.* vii, 1–4.

Glass slipper (of Cinderella). *See* CINDERELLA.

Glasse, Mrs. Hannah. A name immortalized by the reputed saying in her cookery book, FIRST CATCH YOUR HARE (*see under* CATCH).

Glasites or **Glassites.** *See* SANDEMANIANS.

Glastonbury. An ancient town in Somerset, almost twelve miles from Cadbury Castle, "the many-towered CAMELOT". It is fabled to be the place where Joseph of Arimathea brought the Christian faith to Britain, and the Holy GRAIL in the year 63. It was here Joseph's staff took root and budded—the famous Glastonbury Thorn, which flowers every Christmas in honour of Christ's birth. The name is now given to a variety of *Cratægus* or hawthorn, which flowers about old Christmas Day. It is the isle of AVALON, the burial place of King ARTHUR.

Glauber Salts (glou' bèr). A strong purgative, so called from Johann Rudolph Glauber (1604–1668), a German chemist who discovered it in 1658 in his search for the PHILOSOPHER'S STONE. It is sodium sulphate, crystallized below 34°C.

Glaucus (glaw' kùs). The name of a number of heroes in classical legend, including:

(1) A fisherman of Bœotia, who became a sea-god endowed with the gift of prophecy by APOLLO. Milton alludes to him in *Comus* (1. 895), and Spenser mentions him in *The Faerie Queene* (IV, xi, 13):

> And Glaucus, that wise soothsayer understood,

and Keats gives his name to the old magician whom ENDYMION met in NEPTUNE'S hall beneath the sea (*Endymion*, Bk. III). *See also* SCYLLA.

(2) A son of SISYPHUS who would not allow his horses to breed; VENUS so infuriated them that they tore him to pieces. Hence the name is given to one who is so overfond of horses that he is ruined by them.

(3) A commander of the Lycians in the TROJAN WAR (*Iliad*, Bk. VI) who was connected by ties of ancient family friendship with his enemy, DIOMED. When they met in battle they not only refrained from fighting but exchanged arms in token of amity. As the armour of the Lycian was of GOLD, and that of the Greek of bronze, it was like bartering precious stones for FRENCH PASTE. Hence the phrase **A Glaucus swap**.

Gleek (Ger. *gleich*, like). An old card-game popular from the 16th to the 18th century, the object being to get three cards alike, as three aces, three kings, etc. Four cards all alike, as four aces, four kings, etc., is known as *mournival*.

Gleipnir (glīp' nèr) (Old Norse, the fetter). In Scandinavian legend the fetter by which the dwarfs bound the wolf FENRIR. It was extremely light and made of the miaul of a cat, the roots of a mountain, the sinews of a bear, the breath of a fish, the beard of a woman, and the spittle of a bird.

Gloria. Gloria in Excelsis (glôr i a in eksel' sis, ek shel' sis). The opening words of the ANGELIC HYMN, also called the Greater DOXOLOGY. The Latin *Gloria in Excelsis Deo*, etc., is part of the ORDINARY OF THE MASS and the English translation "Glory be to God on high" forms part of the CHURCH OF ENGLAND service for Holy Communion.

Gloria Patri. *See* DOXOLOGY.

Gloria Tibi (glôr i a ti bē). The brief DOXOLOGY, *Gloria tibi Domine*, Glory be to thee, O Lord. In the Roman Catholic Mass the Latin words are used after the announcement of the Gospel. In the CHURCH OF ENGLAND service for Holy Communion the English version is used similarly.

Gloria mundi, Sic transit (Lat.). So passes away the glory of the world. A quotation from *De Imitatione Christi* (Bk. I, ch. iii) by Thomas à Kempis (*c.* 1380–1471)—a classic statement on the transitory nature of human vanities. At the coronation ceremony of the POPE, a reed surmounted with flax is burnt, and as it flickers and dies the chaplain intones—*Pater sancte, sic transit gloria mundi*.

Gloriana. Spenser's name in *The Faerie Queene* for the typification of Queen Elizabeth I. Gloriana held an annual feast for twelve days, during which time adventurers appeared before her to undertake whatever task she chose to impose upon them. On one occasion twelve knights presented themselves before her, and their exploits form the scheme of Spenser's allegory of which only six and a half books remain.

Glory. Hand of Glory. In folk-lore, a dead man's hand, preferably one cut from the body of a man who has been hanged, soaked in oil, and used as a magic torch by thieves. Robert Graves points out that the *Hand of Glory* is a translation of the French *main de gloire*, a corruption of *mandragore*, the plant *mandragora* (mandrake), whose roots had a similar magic value to thieves. *Cp.* DEAD MAN'S HAND.

Glory-hole. A small room, cupboard, etc., where all sorts of odds and ends and junk are dumped.

Glorious. The Glorious First of June. 1 June 1794, when the Channel Fleet under Lord Howe gained a decisive victory over the French under Admiral Villaret Joyeuse. Off Ushant, six French ships were captured and one sunk but the convoy of corn ships, which they were escorting, got through to Brest.

Glorious Fourth, The. *See* INDEPENDENCE DAY.

Glorious Revolution, The. The revolution of 1688 which established parliamentary sovereignty, when James II, deserted by his followers, fled to France in December 1688 and William of Orange and his wife Mary (daughter of James II) were declared joint sovereigns.

Glorious Twelfth, The. 12 August, "St. Grouse's Day"; the day grouse-shooting begins, unless it be on a Sunday, when it is postponed until the Monday in accordance with the Game Act of 1831. Shooting ends on 10 December. *See* PARTRIDGE; SPORTING SEASONS.

Gloucestershire. As sure as God's in Gloucestershire. A strong asseveration. "As sure as God made little apples" is similarly used.

Glove. In the days of CHIVALRY it was customary for knights to wear a lady's glove in their helmets, and to defend it with their life.

On ceremonial occasions gloves are no worn in the presence of royalty, because one is to stand unarmed, with helmet and gauntlets off to show there is no hostile intention.

In mediæval times a folded glove was used as a gage or pledge to fulfil a judgment of a court of law. A glove was also thrown down as a challenge. (*See* HERE I THROW DOWN MY GLOVE *below*). VASSALS were often enfeoffed by investing them with a glove, and fiefs were held by presenting a glove to the sovereign. Gloves used to be worn by the clergy to indicate that their hands were clean and not open for bribes. BISHOPS were sometimes given gloves as a symbol of accession to their SEE. Anciently, judges were not allowed to wear gloves on the BENCH; so to give a judge a pair of gloves symbolized that he need not take his seat, and in a MAIDEN ASSIZE the SHERIFF presented the judge with a pair of white gloves.

The ancient Glovers Company of London was refounded in 1556.

Glove money. A bribe, a perquisite: so called from the ancient custom of a client presenting a pair of gloves to a counsel who undertook a cause.

A round with gloves. A friendly contest; a fight with gloves.

Hand in glove. Sworn friends; on most intimate terms, like glove and hand.

He bit his glove. He resolved on mortal revenge. On the BORDER, to bite the glove was considered a pledge of deadly vengeance.

Here I throw down my glove. I challenge you. *See* TO THROW DOWN THE GAUNTLET *under* GAUNTLET.

With the gloves off. Figuratively, to oppose without restraint. An allusion to the old pugilists who fought with bare fists.

Glubbdubdrib. The land of sorcerers and magicians visited by Gulliver in Swift's *Gulliver's Travels*.

Glumdalclitch. A girl, nine years old, and forty feet high, who, in Swift's *Gulliver's Travels*, had charge of Gulliver in BROBDINGNAG.

Glutton, The. Vitellius, the Roman Emperor, who reigned from 2 January to 22 December, A.D. 69. *Cp.* APICIUS.

Glyndebourne. The country estate, near Lewes in Sussex, where Mr. John Christie (1882–1962) opened the Glyndebourne Festival Theatre in 1934 for operatic and musical performancs which became an annual event.

Gnome (nōm). According to the ROSICRUCIAN system, a misshapen elemental spirit, dwelling in the bowels of the earth, and guarding the mines and quarries. Gnomes of various sorts appear in many FAIRY tales and legends. The word seems to have been first used (and perhaps invented) by PARACELSUS and is probably the Gr. *ge-nomos*, earth-dweller. *Cp.* SALAMANDER.

Gnomes of Zürich. An uncomplimentary name given to those financiers of Zürich controlling international monetary funds. The phrase became popular after its use in November 1964 by Mr. George Brown (then the Socialist Minister of Economic Affairs) at the time of a sterling crisis.

Gnomic Verse. Verse characterized by pithy expression of sententious or weighty maxims. The Gr. word *gnome*, (thought, judgment), acquired specialized meanings such as EPIGRAM, proverb, maxim; hence *gnomic verse*. A group of gnomic poets existed in Greece in the 6th century B.C. An English exemplar is Francis Quarles (1592–1644).

Gnostics (nos' tiks). Various sects, mainly of Christian inspiration, which arose and flourished in the 2nd century with offshoots which survived into the 5th century. The name derives from the Gr. word *gnosis*, knowledge, but it was usually used by the Gnostics in the sense of "revelation" which gave them certain mystic knowledge for salvation which others did not possess. It was essentially based on oriental DUALISM, the existence of two worlds, good and evil, the divine and the material. The body was regarded as the enemy of spiritual life. In most Gnostic systems there were seven world-creating powers, in a few their place was taken by one DEMIURGE. Christ was the final and perfect ÆON. The Gnostic movement caused the Christian Church to develop its organization and doctrinal discipline. In 1945 fifty-two Gnostic texts were found in Upper Egypt which underline its intellectual challenge to the early Church. *See also* MANICHÆANS; MARCIONITES.

Go (O.E. *gan*, start, depart, move, etc.). Both the verb and the noun are used in a wide range of expressions, some of which are recorded below. For others such as **to go by the board**, etc., *See under* the principal word.

A go. A fix, a scrape; as in **here's a go** or **here's a fine go**—here's a mess or awkward state of affairs. Also a share, a portion, or tot, as **a go of gin**; and an attempt, as **have a go at something.**

A go-between. One who acts as an intermediary; one who interposes between two parties.

A regular goer. One with plenty of dash, a man of mettle.

All the go. All the fashion, all the rage, quite in VOGUE.

Go along with you. A jocular expression of disbelief in what someone is saying, stop fooling, etc., used in the sense of "run off with you". Also, when someone agrees to participate in a course of action suggested by you, he is said to "go along with you".

Go as you please. Not bound by any rules; do as you like; unceremonious.

Go it! An exclamation of encouragement, sometimes ironical.

Go it alone. To play a lone hand; to carry on or do something without help; to assume sole responsibility.

Go to! An exclamation, often of impatience or reproof, or as an exhortation like "come".

I've been on the go all day. I have been very busy and active with no time to rest.

I've gone and done it! or **I've been and gone and done it!** There! I've done the very thing I ought not to have done! I've made a pretty mess of it.

I will go through fire and water to serve you. *See under* FIRE.

It is no go. It is not workable.

That goes for nothing. It doesn't count; it doesn't matter one way or the other.

That goes without saying. That is self-evident, that is well understood or indisputable. The French say *Cela va sans dire*.

To give one the go-by. To pass by and ignore someone, to disregard.

To go ahead. To make progress, to prosper, to start.

To give the go ahead. To give permission to proceed in an undertaking.

To go back on one's word. To fail to keep one's promise.

To go down. *See under* DOWN.

To go farther and fare worse. To take more pains and trouble and find oneself in a worse position.

To go for a man. To attack him, either physically or in an argument, etc.

To go hard with one. To prove a troublesome matter. "It will go hard with me before I give up the attempt", *i.e.* I won't give up until I have tried every means to success, however difficult, dangerous, or painful it may prove.

To go in for. To follow as a pursuit or occupation, as in "to go in for medicine".

To go into a matter. To explore or investigate it thoroughly.

To go it. To be fast, extravagant, head-strong in one's behaviour and habits.

To go off one's head, nut, onion, rocker, etc. Completely to lose control of oneself; to go mad, either temporarily or for good; to go out of one's mind.

To go off the rails. To behave abnormally, to go crazy.

To go on all fours. *See under* ALL FOURS.

To go round the bend. *See under* BEND.

To go the pace. *See* FAST.

To go through the motions. To make a pretence of doing something; to carry out an obligation or duty in a very half-hearted manner.

To go to Birmingham by way of Beachy Head. *See* BIRMINGHAM.

To go under. To become ruined; to fail utterly, to lose caste.

Also to pass as, to be known as; as, "She goes under the name of 'Mrs. Harlow', but we all know she is really 'Miss Smith'."

Godown (gō' down). In India, China, etc., a warehouse. It is a corruption of the Malay word *gadong* or *godong*. The English form of the name may have been influenced by the fact that these storehouses were often partly below ground level.

Go-getter. An enterprising, ambitious, person.

Go slow. The deliberate slowing down of work or production by employees engaged in an industrial dispute. In Canada and the U.S.A. the term is *Slow-down*.

Goat. From early times the goat has been associated with the idea of sin (*see* SCAPE- GOAT) and associated with devil-lore. The legend that the DEVIL created the goat may well be due to its destructiveness, and the Devil was frequently depicted as a goat. It is also a type of lust and lechery.

Don't play the giddy goat. Don't make a ridiculous fool of yourself; keep yourself within bounds. The derivation is obvious.

To get one's goat. An old Americanism for annoying one, making one wild.

To separate the sheep from the goats. To divide the worthy from the unworthy, the good from the evil, the favoured from the disfavoured. The allusion is to *Matt.* xxv, 32.

The Goat and Compasses. The origin of this PUBLIC-HOUSE SIGN is uncertain. A once popular suggestion was that it is a corruption of "God encompasseth us". Other suggestions are that it was derived from the arms of the Wine Cooper's Company of Cologne, or merely the addition of the masonic emblem of the compasses to an original sign of a goat.

Gobbledygook. A word invented by Henry Maverick of Texas to describe the convoluted, pretentious and often meaningless language of bureaucracy. It was an allusion to the gobble-gobble sound of a turkey.

Gobelin Tapestry (go' be lin). So called from a French family of dyers founded by Jehan Gobelin (d. 1476); their tapestry works in the Faubourg St. Marcel, Paris, were taken over by Colbert as a royal establishment in 1662.

Goblin. A familiar demon, dwelling, according to popular legend, in private houses, chinks of trees, etc. In many parts miners attributed to them the strange noises they heard in the mine. The word is Fr. *gobelin*, probably a diminutive of the surname *Gobel*, but perhaps connected with Gr. *kobalos*, an impudent rogue, a mischievous sprite, or with the Ger. *Kobold*. *Cp.* GNOME.

God. A word common, in slightly varying forms, to all Teutonic languages, probably from an Aryan root, *gheu*—to invoke; it is in no way connected with *good*.

It was VOLTAIRE who said, "*Si Dieu n'existait pas, il faudrait l'inventer*." For the various gods listed in this Dictionary see under their individual names.

Greek and Roman gods were divided into *Dii Majores* and *Dii Minores*, the greater and the lesser. The *Dii Majores* were twelve in number:

Greek	Latin
ZEUS	JUPITER (King)
APOLLON	APOLLO (the sun)
ARES	MARS (war)
HERMES	MERCURY (messenger)
POSEIDON	NEPTUNE (ocean)
HEPHAISTOS	VULCAN (smith)

HERA	JUNO (Queen)
DEMETER	CERES (tillage)
ARTEMIS	DIANA (moon, hunting)
ATHENE	MINERVA (wisdom)
APHRODITE	VENUS (love and beauty)
HESTIA	VESTA (home-life)

Their blood was ICHOR, their food was AMBROSIA, their drink NECTAR.

Four other deities are often referred to:

DIONYSOS	BACCHUS (wine)
EROS	CUPID (love)
PLUTON	PLUTO (the underworld)
KRONOS	SATURN (time).

Persephone (Greek) or PROSERPINE (Latin), was the wife of Pluto, CYBELE was the wife of Saturn, and RHEA of Kronos.

Hesiod says (i, 250):

Some thirty thousand gods on earth we find
Subjects of Zeus, and guardians of mankind.

The Greeks observed a *Feast of the Unknown Gods* that none might be neglected.

A god from the machine. *See* DEUS EX MACHINA.

Among the gods, or **up in the gods.** In the uppermost gallery of a theatre, just below the ceiling, which was frequently embellished with a representation of a mythological heaven. The French call this the *paradis*.

God helps those who help themselves. To this a wag has added "but God help those who are caught helping themselves". The French say AIDE-TOI, LE CIEL T'AIDERA.

God made the country and man made the town. So said Cowper in *The Task* (*The Sofa*, 749). *Cp.* Bacon's "God Almighty first planted a garden" (*Of Gardens*) and Cowley's "God the first garden made, and the first city Cain" (*On Gardens*). Varro says in *De Re Rustica*: "*Divina Natura dedit agros: ars humana aedificavit urbes.*" Marx and Engels say that the bourgeoisie "has created enormous cities ... and has thus rescued a considerable part of the population from the idiocy of rural life" (*Communist Manifesto*, I).

God save the King, or **Queen.** *See* NATIONAL ANTHEM.

God sides with the strongest. Fortune favours the strong. NAPOLEON said, "*Le bon Dieu est toujours du côté des gros bataillons*" (God is always on the side of the big battalions), but the phrase is of much earlier origin. Tacitus (*Hist.* IV, 17) has *Deos fortioribus adesse* (the gods are on the side of the strongest); the Comte de Bussy, writing to the Comte de Limoges, used it in 1677, as did VOLTAIRE in his *Epître à M. le Riche*, 6 February 1770.

God tempers the wind to the shorn lamb. The phrase comes from Sterne's *Sentimental Journey* (1768) but it was not original, for "*Dieu mesure le froid à la brebis tondue*" appears in Henri Estienne's *Les Prémices* (1594) and Herbert's *Jacula Prudentum* (1651) has "To a close-shorn sheep God gives wind by measure." Although Sterne's version is more poetical he did not improve the sense by substituting lamb for sheep—lambs are never shorn!

Man proposes, God disposes. An old proverb found in Hebrew, Greek, Latin, etc. In *Prov.* xvi, 9, it is rendered:

A man's heart deviseth his way; but the Lord directeth his steps;

and Publius Syrus (No. 216) has:

Homo semper aliud, Fortuna aliud cogitat.
(Man has one thing in view, Fate has another).

Whom God would destroy He first makes mad. A translation of the Latin version (*Quos Deus vult perdere, prius dementat*) of one of the *Fragments of Euripides. Cp.* also *Stultum facit fortuna quem vult perdere* (Publius Syrus, No 612), He whom Fortune would ruin she robs of his wits.

Whom the gods love die young. A translation of the Latin *Quem Di diligunt adolescens moritur* (Plautus, *Bacchides*, IV, vii, 18). For the popular saying "Only the good die young" *see under* GOOD.

God's Acre. *See under* ACRE.

Goddam, or **Godon** (gŏ dăm', gŏ-dǒn'). A name given by the French to the English at least as early as the 15th century, on account of the favourite oath of the English soldiers. JOAN OF ARC is reported to have used the word on a number of occasions in contemptuous reference to her enemies.

Godiva, Lady (gŏ dī' và). Patroness of

Coventry. In 1040 Leofric, Earl of Mercia and Lord of Coventry, imposed certain exactions on his tenants, which his lady besought him to remove. He said he would do so if she would ride naked through the town. Lady Godiva did so and the Earl faithfully kept his promise.

The legend is recorded by Roger of Wendover (d. 1236), in his *Flores Historiarum*, and this was adapted by Rapin in his *History of England* (1723–1727) into the story commonly known. An addition of the time of Charles II asserts that everyone kept indoors at the time, but a certain tailor peeped through his window to see the lady pass and was struck blind as a consequence. He has ever since been called "Peeping Tom of Coventry". Since 1768 the ride has been annually commemorated at Coventry by a procession in which "Lady Godiva" features centrally.

Goel (gō' el) (Heb. claimant). Among the ancient Hebrews the *goel* was the next of kin whose duty it was to redeem the property of a kinsman who had been forced to sell under stress of circumstances; he was also the AVENGER OF BLOOD.

Goemagot, or **Goemot** (gō em' à got or gō'mot). The names given in Geoffrey of Monmouth's *Historia Britonum* (I, xvi), and Spenser's *The Faerie Queene* (II, x, 10), etc. to the giant who dominated the western horn of England (CORNWALL or *Cornubia*). He was slain by CORINEUS. See GOG AND MAGOG.

Gog and Magog. In British legend, the sole survivors of a monstrous brood, the offspring of demons and the thirty-three infamous daughters of the Emperor Diocletian, who murdered their husbands. Gog and Magog were taken as prisoners to LONDON after their fellow giants had been killed by BRUTE and his companions, where they were made to do duty as porters at the royal palace, on the site of the Guildhall, where their effigies have stood at least from the reign of Henry V. The old giants were destroyed in the GREAT FIRE, and were replaced by figures 14 ft. high, carved in 1708 by Richard Saunders. These were subsequently demolished in an air raid in 1940 and new figures were set up in 1953. Formerly wickerwork models were carried in the LORD MAYOR'S SHOWS.

In the BIBLE Magog is spoken of as a son of Japhet (*Gen*. x, 2), in the *Revelation* Gog and Magog symbolize all future enemies of the Kingdom of God, and in *Ezekiel* Gog is prince of Magog, a ruler of hordes to the north of Israel.

Golconda (gol kon' dà). An ancient kingdom and city in India, west of Hyderabad, which was conquered by Aurangzeb in 1687. The name is emblematic of great wealth and proverbially famous for its DIAMONDS, but the gems were only cut and polished there.

Gold. According to the ancient alchemists, gold represented the SUN, and SILVER the MOON. In HERALDRY gold (called "or") is depicted by dots. The gold CARAT is the unit used by goldsmiths, assayers, etc., for expressing the proportion of gold in any article in gold. Gold coins were struck in England as regular currency from the reign of Edward III until 1917.

The gold of Nibelungen. *See* NIBELUNGENLIED.

Dutch gold. *See under* DUTCH.

Fool's Gold. A name given to iron pyrites or pyrite, which being of a brassy yellow colour was sometimes mistaken for gold. It is often found in coal-seams. Martin Frobisher returned with supposed "gold minerall" from his voyage of 1576 in search of the NORTH-WEST PASSAGE. Two further voyages were made in 1577 and 1578 for cargoes of the supposed ore which proved to be nothing but fool's gold.

Healing gold. Gold given to a monarch for "healing" the KING'S EVIL.

The Gold Standard. A currency system based upon keeping the monetary unit at the value of a fixed weight of gold.

Gold Stick. The gilt rod carried before the Sovereign on State occasions by the Colonel of the Life Guards or the Captain of the Gentlemen-at-arms; also the bearer of the Stick.

A gold brick. An American phrase descriptive of any form of swindling. It originated in the gold-rush days when a cheat would sell his dupe an alleged (or even a real) gold brick, in the latter case substituting a sham one before making his get-away.

All he touches turns to gold. All his ventures succeed; he is invariably lucky. The allusion is to MIDAS.

All that glistens is not gold. (Shakespeare: *Merchant of Venice*, II, vii.) Do not be deceived by appearances.

He has got gold of Tolosa. His ill-gotten gains will never prosper. Cæpio, the Roman consul, in his march, to *Gallia Narbonensis*, desecrated the temple of the Celtic APOLLO at Tolosa (Toulouse) and stole from it all the gold and silver vessels and treasure belonging to the Cimbrian DRUIDS. This, in turn, was stolen from him while it was being taken to Massilia (Marseilles). When he encountered the Cimbrians both he and his fellow-consul Maximus were defeated, and 112,000 of their men were left upon the field (106 B.C.).

To be worth its, or **his** (etc.), **weight in gold.** To be of great value or use. The phrase is applied both literally and metaphorically to persons and things.

Golden Age. An age in the history of peoples when life was idyllic, or when the nation was at its summit of power, glory, and reputation; the best age, as the *golden age of innocence*, the *golden age of literature*. *See* AGE.

Golden Apples. *See* APPLE OF DISCORD; ATALANTA'S RACE; HESPERIDES.

The Golden Ass, properly, *Metamorphoses*, a 2nd-century satirical romance by Apuleius, and seemingly called the *Golden Ass* because of its excellency. It tells the adventures of Lucian, a young man who, being accidentally metamorphosed into an ass while sojourning in Thessaly, fell into the hands of robbers, eunuchs, magistrates, and so on, by whom he was ill-treated; but ultimately he recovered his human form. It contains the story of CUPID AND PSYCHE.

The Golden Bull. In particular, an edict the Emperor Charles IV issued at the Diet of Nuremberg in 1356 for the purpose of regularizing the election to the throne of the Empire. It was sealed with a golden *bulla* or seal. *Cp.* PAPAL BULL *under* BULL.

Golden calf, To worship the. To bow down to money, to abandon one's principles for the sake of gain. The reference is to the golden calf made by AARON when Moses was absent on Mount Sinai. For their sin in worshipping the calf the Israelites paid dearly (*Exod.* xxxii).

The Golden Fleece. The old Greek story is that Ino persuaded her husband Athamus that his son Phryxus was the cause of a famine which desolated the land. Phryxus was thereupon ordered to be sacrificed but, being apprised of this, he made his escape over the sea on the winged ram, Chrysomallus, which had a golden fleece (*see* HELLESPONT). When he arrived at Colchis, he sacrificed the ram to ZEUS, and gave the fleece to king Æetes, who hung it on a sacred OAK. JASON subsequently set out to recover it.

Australia has been called "The Land of the Golden Fleece" from its abundant wool production.

Golden Fleece, The Order of the (Fr. *l'ordre de la toison d'or*). An historic order of knighthood once common to Spain and Austria, instituted in 1429, for the protection of the Church by Philip the Good, Duke of Burgundy, on his marriage with the Infanta Isabella of Portugal. It became two separate orders in 1713. Its badge is a golden sheepskin with head and feet attached, adopted in allusion to Greek legend. It has been suggested that it may also have been influenced by the fact that the manufacture of woollens had long been the staple industry of the Netherlands.

The Golden Gate. The strait forming the entrance to San Francisco Bay. San Francisco is hence called "The City of the Golden Gate". The name was given by John C. Frémont in 1846.

The state entrance to the city of Constantinople built of three arches to commemorate the victory of Theodosius I over Maximus (388), and incorporated in the walls built by Theodosius II, was called the Golden Gate. The 11th-century fortifications of Kiev also incorporated a Golden Gate.

Golden Handshake. A phrase applied to the often considerable terminal payments made to individuals, especially business executives, whose services are prematurely dispensed with. It has also been applied to the final grants made to colonial dependencies on attaining their independence. The phrase was coined by Frederick Ellis (d. 1979), City Editor of the *Daily Express*. *Cp.* TO BE BOWLER-HATTED *under* BOWLER HAT.

> This year promises to be an expensive one for the British taxpayer in "golden handshakes".
> *The Times*, 4 June 1964.

The Golden Hind. The famous ship in which Drake made his voyage of circumnavigation (1577–1580). Originally called the *Pelican*, it was renamed the *Golden Hind* at Port St. Julian, near the entrance to the Straits of Magellan, in 1578. Drake was knighted on board the *Golden Hind* in the presence of Queen Elizabeth I on 4 April 1581. *See* THE DRAKE BRASS PLATE *under* FORGERY.

Golden Horde. The Mongolian TARTARS who in the 13th century established an empire in S.E. Russia under Batu, grandson of Genghis Khan. They over-ran eastern Europe and parts of western Asia, being eventually defeated by TIMUR in 1395. The name golden derives from Batu's magnificent tent.

The Golden Horn. The inlet of the BOSPORUS around which Istanbul (formerly Constantinople) is situated. Some five miles long, it may have derived its name both from its shape and its abundance of fish which made it a real CORNUCOPIA.

The Golden Legend (*Aurea Legenda*). A collection of so-called lives of the SAINTS made by the Dominican, Jacobus de Voragine, in the 13th century; valuable for the picture it gives of mediæval manners, customs, and thought. It was translated from the Latin into most of the languages of western Europe and an English edition was published by CAXTON in 1483.

Longfellow's *The Golden Legend* is based on a story by Hartmann von Aue, a German MINNESINGER of the 12th century.

Golden Number. The number of the year in the METONIC CYCLE which may therefore consist of any number from 1 to 19. In the ancient Roman and Alexandrian CALENDARS this number was marked in gold, hence the name. The rule for finding the golden number is:

It is used in determining the EPACT and the date of EASTER.

Golden Rose. An ornament made of gold in imitation of a spray of roses, one rose containing a receptacle into which is poured balsam and musk. The rose is solemnly blessed by the POPE on LÆTARE SUNDAY, and is conferred from time to time on sovereigns and others, as well as churches and cities distinguished for their services to the ROMAN CATHOLIC CHURCH. The last to receive it was Princess Charlotte of Nassau, Grand Duchess of Luxembourg in 1956.

The Golden Rule. "Do as you would be done by."

> Whatsoever ye would that men should do to you, do ye even so to them: for this is the law and the prophets.
> *Matt.* vii, 12.

Golden Shower, or **Shower of Gold.** A bribe, money. The allusion is to the classical tale of ZEUS and DANAË.

The Golden State. California. So called from the gold discoveries of 1848. (*See* FORTY-NINERS *under* FORTY.)

The Golden Stream. St. JOHN DAMASCENE (d. *c.* 752), author of the first systematic treatise on dogmatic theology, was so called (*Chrysorrhoes*) for his flowing eloquence.

The Golden-tongued (Gr. *Chrysologos*). St. Peter, Archbishop of Ravenna (d. *c.* 450).

The Golden Town. Mainz or Mayence was so called in CARLOVINGIAN times.

Golden Vale or **Valley.** The rich plain of Munster in Ireland, of which Tipperary is the central town, is so called.

Golden Verses. Greek verses containing the moral rules of PYTHAGORAS, usually thought to have been composed by some of his scholars. He enjoins, among other things, obedience to God and one's rulers, deliberation before action, fortitude, and temperance in exercise and diet. He also suggests making a critical review each night of the actions of that day.

Golden Wedding. The fiftieth anniversary of marriage, husband and wife being both alive.

A good name is better than a golden

girdle. *See* GIRDLE.

The golden bowl is broken. Death. A Biblical allusion:

> Or ever the silver cord be loosed, or the golden bowl be broken, or the pitcher be broken at the fountain, or the wheel broken at the cistern; then shall the dust return to the earth as it was; and the spirit shall return unto God who gave it.
> *Eccles.* xii, 6, 7.

The golden section of a line. Its division into two such parts that the area of the rectangle contained by the smaller segment and the whole line equals that of the square on the larger segment (*Euclid*, ii, 11).

The Three Golden Balls. *See* BALLS.

To keep the golden mean. To practise moderation in all things. The wise saw of Cleobulus (*see* WISE MAN OF GREECE) and a virtue admired by the Romans, the *aurea mediocritas* of HORACE (*Odes* II, x, 5).

Golgotha (gol' goth à). The place outside Jerusalem where Christ was crucified. The word is Aramaic and means a "skull". It may have been a place of execution where bodies were picked clean by animals or named from the round and skull-like contour of the site. There is no Biblical evidence for supposing that it was a hillock. The traditional site is that recovered by Constantine. *Calvaria* is the Greek and Latin equivalent of Golgotha. *See* CALVARY.

Golgotha, at the University church, Cambridge, was the gallery in which the "heads of the houses" sat; so called because it was the place of skulls or heads. It has been more wittily than truly said that Golgotha was the place of empty skulls.

Goliards. Educated jesters and buffoons who wrote ribald Latin verse, and who were noted for riotous behaviour. They flourished mainly in the 12th and 13th centuries. The word comes from the Old Fr. *goliard* (glutton) which derived from the Lat. *gula* (gluttony).

Goliath (go lī' áth). The Philistine GIANT, slain by the stripling David with a small stone hurled from a sling (I *Sam.* xvii, 49–51). *See* GIANTS OF THE BIBLE.

Golosh. *See* GALOSH.

Gombeen Man. A village usurer, a money-lender. A word of Irish origin.

Gone. Gone with the Wind. Said of events or persons that have left no trace by which to be remembered. It is also the title of what probably remains America's most widely read novel, a story of the CIVIL WAR as seen through Southern eyes. It was written by Margaret Mitchell and published in 1936.

Goneril. One of LEAR's three daughters. Having received her moiety of Lear's Kingdom, the unnatural daughter first curtailed the old man's retinue, then gave him to understand that his company was troublesome. In Holinshed she appears as "Gonerilla". *Cp.* CORDELIA; REGAN.

Gong. A service nickname for a medal.

To be gonged. To be signalled to stop by motorized police for some breach of the traffic laws. A colloquial usage from the loud electric bell used to attract the offender's attention.

Gonnella's Horse. Gonnella, the domestic jester of the Duke of Ferrara, rode on a horse all skin and bone. The *Jests of Gonella* were printed in 1506. *See* COURT FOOLS *under* FOOL.

> His horse, whose bones stuck out like the corners of a Spanish real, being a worse jade than Gonela's *qui tantum pellis et ossa fuit*.
> CERVANTES: *Don Quixote*, ch. I.

Gonville and Caius. *See* CAIUS.

Good. Good Duke Humphrey. Humphrey, Duke of Gloucester (1391–1447), youngest son of Henry IV, said to have been murdered by Suffolk and Cardinal Beaufort (Shakespeare, *Henry VI*, *Pt. II*, III, ii); so called because of his devotion to the Church.

To Dine with Duke Humphrey. *See* HUMPHREY.

Good Friday. The Friday preceding EASTER Day, held as the anniversary of the Crucifixion. "Good" here means *holy*; CHRISTMAS, as well as SHROVE TUESDAY, used to be called "the Good Tide".

Born on Good Friday. According to old superstition, those born on CHRISTMAS Day or GOOD FRIDAY have the power of seeing and commanding spirits.

The Good Parliament. Edward III's

Parliament of 1376; so called because of the severity with which it pursued the unpopular party of the Duke of Lancaster.

Good Samaritan. *See* SAMARITAN.

For good and all. Permanently, finally, conclusively.

Never had it so good. *See under* NEVER.

Only the good die young. A popular saying derived ultimately from one of the Greek Gnomic poets (*see* GNOMIC VERSE), and echoed by several writers. Plautus says *Quem Di deligunt, adolescens moritur* (he whom the gods love dies young). Byron says "Heaven gives its favourites early death" (*Childe Harold*, iv, 102) and "Whom the gods love die young" (*Don Juan*, iv, 12), Defoe, in *Character of the late Dr. S. Annesley*, has "The good die early and the bad late", and Wordsworth "The good die first" (*The Excursion*, Bk. I).

There is a good time coming. A long established familiar saying in Scotland.

Good-bye. A contraction of *God be with you*. Similar to the French *adieu*.

Goodfellow. *See* ROBIN GOODFELLOW.

Goodman. A husband or master. In *Matt.* xxiv, 43, "If the goodman of the house had known in what watch the thief would come, he would have watched."

Goodman of Ballengeich. The assumed name of James V of Scotland when he made his disguised visits through the country districts around Edinburgh and Stirling, after the fashion of HAROUN-AL-RASCHID, Louis XI, etc.

Goodwife is the feminine counterpart of GOODMAN.

Goods. "He's got the goods on you!" He's got evidence against you.

That fellow's the goods. He's first class, just the man for the job.

To deliver the goods. To perform adequately; to carry out one's promise effectively; to deliver the "real thing".

Goodwin Sands. It is said that these dangerous sandbanks, stretching about 10 miles N.E. and S.W. some $5\frac{1}{2}$ miles off the East Kent coast, consisted at one time of about 4,000 acres of low land called Lomea (the *Infera Insula* of the Romans) fenced from the sea by a wall, and belonging to Earl Godwin. WILLIAM THE CONQUEROR gave them to the abbey of St. Augustine, Canterbury, but the abbot allowed the sea wall to decay and in 1099 the sea inundated the whole. *See* TENTERDEN.

Goodwood Races. So called from the park in which they are held in Sussex, the property of the Duke of Richmond. Racing at "Glorious Goodwood" dates from 1801 and the course was laid out under the direction of Lord George Bentinck.

Goody. A depreciative, meaning primly or sentimentally virtuous but with no strength of character or independence of spirit; NAMBY-PAMBY. It also denotes a sweet, jam tart, etc. The word is also a rustic variant of *goodwife* (*see* GOODMAN) and is sometimes used as a title, like GAMMER, as "Goody Blake", "Goody Dobson".

Goody-goody. A reduplication of GOODY, obtrusively virtuous.

Goody Two-shoes. This nursery tale first appeared in 1765. It was written for John Newbery (1713–1767), a notable publisher of children's books, probably by Oliver Goldsmith. She owned but one shoe and when given a pair she was so pleased that she showed them to everyone, saying "Two shoes!".

Googly. In CRICKET, a deceptive delivery depending on hand action by the bowler in which an off-break is bowled to a right-handed batsman with what appears to be a leg-break action. *Cp.* CHINAMAN.

It was invented and developed by B. J. T. Bosanquet from 1890 and he used it against the Australians in 1903. In Australia it is called a "BOSEY".

Goose. A foolish or ignorant person is called a goose beause of the alleged stupidity of this bird; a tailor's smoothing-iron is so called because its handle resembles the neck of a goose. The plural of the iron is *gooses* not geese. *Cp.* BOOBY.

Geese save the Capitol. When the Gauls attacked ROME in 390 B.C. it is said that a detachment advanced up the Capitoline Hill so silently that the foremost man reached the top unchallenged, but when climbing over the rampart disturbed some sacred geese whose cackle awoke the garrison. Marcus Manlius rushed to the wall and hurled the fellow over the precipice. To commemorate this event, the Romans carried a golden goose in procession to the Capitol every year. Manlius was given the name *Capitolinus*.

> Those consecrated geese in orders,
> That to the capitol were warders;
> And being then upon patrol,
> With noise alone beat off the Gaul.
> BUTLER: *Hudibras*, II, iii.

The Goose Bible. *See* BIBLE, SOME SPECIALLY NAMED EDITIONS.

Goose and Gridiron, The. A PUBLIC-HOUSE SIGN, probably in ridicule of the Swan and Harp, a popular sign for the early music-houses (*see* MUSIC HALL), but properly the coat-of-arms of the Company of Musicians—*viz*. azure, a *swan* with wings expanded argent, within *double tressure* [the gridiron] flory counterflory.

In the United States the name is humorously applied to the national coat-of-arms—the American EAGLE with a gridiron-like shield on its breast.

Goose-egg. *See* DUCK'S EGG under DUCK: in the U.S.A. a zero.

Goose Fair. A fair formerly held in many English towns about the time of MICHAELMAS, when geese were plentiful.

Goose flesh. A rough, pimply condition of the skin especially on the arms and legs like that of a plucked goose or fowl. It is usually occasioned by cold or shock.

Goose-month. The lying-in month for women. *Cp*. GANDERMONTH.

Goose-step. A military step in which the legs are moved from the hips, the knees being kept rigid, each leg being swung as high as possible. (It was introduced as a form of recruit drill in the British army but never became popular; it exists in a modified form in the slow march). The goose-step (*Stechschritt*) has been a full dress and processional march in the German army since the time of Frederick the Great. When the AXIS flourished it was adopted by the Italian army (*il passo romano*) but was

soon ridiculed into desuetude.

Michaelmas Goose. *See* MICHAELMAS DAY.

Mother Goose. Famous as giving the name to *Mother Goose's Nursery Rhymes*, which first seems to have been used in *Songs for the Nursery*: or, *Mother Goose's Melodies for Children*, published by T. Fleet in Boston, Mass., in 1719. The rhymes were free adaptations of Perrault's *Contes de ma mère l'oye* (Tales of My Mother Goose) which appeared in 1697.

Wayzgoose. *See* WAYZGOOSE.

All his geese are swans. He overestimates, he sees things in too rosy a light, he paints too rosy a picture.

He's cooked his goose. He's done for himself, he's made a fatal mistake, ruined his chances, "DISHED" himself. "To cook someone's goose" is to spoil his plans, to "fix" him, to "SETTLE HIS HASH" (*see* HASH). It is apparently of 19th-century origin.

At the time of the "Papal Aggression" when Cardinal Wiseman was designated Archbishop of Westminster and Administrator Apostolic of the Diocese of SOUTHWARK a street ballad of 1851 says:

> If they come here we'll cook their goose,
> The Pope and Cardinal Wiseman.

He can't say Bo! to a goose. *See* BO.

He killed the goose that laid the golden eggs. He grasped at what was more than his due and lost what was a regular source of supply; he has sacrificed future reward for present gain. The Greek fable says a countryman had a goose that laid golden eggs; thinking to make himself rich, he killed the goose to get the whole stock of eggs at once, thus ending the supply.

He steals a goose, and gives the giblets in alms. He amasses wealth by over-reaching, and salves his conscience by giving small sums for charity.

The old woman is plucking her goose. A children's way of saying "it is snowing".

To shoe the goose. To fritter away one's times on unnecessary work; to play about, to trifle.

What's sauce for the goose is sauce for the gander. What's good for one is good for the other; what the husband can do so can the wife.

Gooseberry. Gooseberry Fool. A dish essentially made of gooseberries, cream or custard, and sugar, the fruit being crushed through a sieve. Here the word *fool* comes from the Fr. *fouler*, to crush.

He played old gooseberry with me. He took great liberties with my property, and greatly abused it; in fact, he played the very deuce with me and my belongings.

To play, or **be gooseberry.** To act as chaperon; to be an unwanted third when lovers are together. The origin of the phrase is obscure but it may derive from the tact of the chaperon occupying the time in picking gooseberries while the others were more romantically engaged.

Goosebridge. Go to Goosebridge. "Rule a wife and have a wife." Boccaccio (ix, 9) tells us that a man who had married a shrew asked Solomon what he would do to make her more submissive; and the wise king answered, "Go to Goosebridge." Returning home, deeply perplexed, he came to a bridge which a muleteer was trying to induce a mule to cross. The beast resisted, but the stronger will of his master at length prevailed. The man asked the name of the bridge, and was told it was "Goosebridge".

Gopher wood. The wood of which Noah made his ark (*Gen.* vi, 14). It was probably some kind of cedar.

Gorboduc. *See* FERREX AND PORREX.

Gordian Knot. A great difficulty. Gordius, a peasant, being chosen king of Phrygia, dedicated his wagon to JUPITER, and fastened the yoke to a beam with a rope of bark so ingeniously that no one could untie it. ALEXANDER was told that "whoever undid the knot would reign over the whole East". "Well then," said the conqueror, "it is thus I perform the task," and, so saying, he cut the knot in twain with his sword; thus **To cut the Gordian Knot** is to get out of a difficult position by one decisive step; to resolve a situation by force or by evasive action.

Gorgon. Anything unusually hideous, especially such a woman. In classical mythology there were three Gorgons,

with serpents on their heads instead of hair. MEDUSA was their chief, the others, Stheno and Euryale, were immortal. They also had brazen claws and monstrous teeth. Their glance turned their victims to stone. *Cp.* PERSEUS.

Gospel. From O.E. *godspel* (good tidings), a translation of the Med. Lat. *bonus nuntius*. It is used to describe collectively the lives of Christ as told by the EVANGELISTS in the NEW TESTAMENT; it signifies the message of redemption set forth in those books; it is used to denote the entire Christian message; and it is also applied to any doctrine or teaching set forth for some specific purpose.

The first four books of the New Testament, known as **The Gospels,** are ascribed to MATTHEW, MARK, LUKE and JOHN, although their exact authorship is uncertain. The first three of these are called the **Synoptic Gospels** as they follow the same lines and may be readily brought under one general view or *synopsis*. The fourth Gospel stands apart as the work of one mind. There are many **Apocryphal Gospels,** examples of which are given below. *See* APOCRYPHA.

The Gospel of Nicodemus, or "The Acts of Pilate", is an apocryphal book of uncertain date between the 2nd and 5th centuries. It gives an elaborate and fanciful description of the trial, death, and resurrection of Our Lord; names the two thieves (DYSMAS and GESTAS); PILATE'S wife (Procla); the centurion (Longinus), etc., and ends with an account of the *descensus ad inferos* of Jesus, by Charinus and Leucius, two men risen from the dead. The title first appears in the 13th century and the Gospel was much used by the writers of Miracle and MYSTERY plays.

The Gospel of Peter is an apocryphal book in fragmentary form, first mentioned by Serapion, bishop of Antioch in the last decade of the 2nd century, and part of which was found in 1892.

The Gospel of Thomas is a GNOSTIC work, probably of the 2nd century, containing much that is fanciful.

The Gospel side of the altar is to the left of the celebrant facing the altar.

Gospeller. The priest who reads the

Gospel in the Communion Service; also a follower of Wyclif, called the "Gospel Doctor".

Hot Gospellers was an old nickname for PURITANS and is now frequently applied to the more energetic and colourful EVANGELISTS and revivalists.

Gossamer. According to legend, this delicate thread is the ravelling of the Virgin Mary's winding-sheet, which fell to earth on her ascension to HEAVEN. It is said to be *God's seam*, *i.e.* God's thread. Probably the name is from M.E. *gossomer*, goose-summer or ST. MARTIN'S SUMMER (early November), when geese are plentiful. Other suggestions are *God's summer* and *gaze à Marie* (gauze of Mary).

Gossip. A tattler; formerly a sponsor at baptism, a corruption of *God-sibb*, a kinsman in the Lord. (O.E. *sibb*, relationship, whence *sibman*, kinsman). *Cp.* ALL STUARTS ARE NOT SIB.

Also (archaic) a boon companion, a familiar friend.

Gotham. Wise men of Gotham—fools, wiseacres. The village of Gotham in Nottinghamshire was proverbial for the folly of its inhabitants and many tales have been fathered on them, one of which is their joining hands round a thorn-bush to shut in a cuckoo. *Cp.* COGGESHALL.

It is said that King John intended to make a progress through the town with the view of establishing a hunting lodge but the townsmen had no wish to be saddled with the cost of supporting the court. Wherever the royal messengers went they saw the people engaged in some idiotic pursuit and the king, when told, abandoned his intention and the "wise men" cunningly remarked, "We ween there are more fools pass through Gotham than remain in it." The nursery rhyme says:

Three wise men of Gotham
Went to sea in a bowl,
If the bowl had been stronger,
My story would have been longer.

Most nations have some locality renowned for fools; thus we have Phrygia as the fools' home of Asia Minor, ABDERA of the Thracians, BŒOTIA of the Greeks, Nazareth of the ancient Jews, Swabia of the Germans, etc.

Gothamites. Inhabitants of New York. The term was in use in 1800. The name of Gotham was given to New York by Washington Irving in his *Salmagundi*, 1807.

Goths. A Germanic barbarian tribe which invaded and devastated Europe in the 3rd to 5th centuries, establishing kingdoms in Italy, France, and Spain. Hence the use of the name to imply uncultured, uncivilized, destructive. *Cp.* VANDALS.

Gothic Architecture. The name for the style prevalent in Western Europe from the 12th to the 16th centuries. The name was given contemptuously to imply "barbaric" by the architects of the RENAISSANCE period who revived classical styles. A revival of Gothic architecture was started by wealthy dilettanti such as Horace Walpole in the 18th century and was further popularized by Sir Walter Scott and Ruskin. The works of A. W. Pugin (1812–1852) and Sir G. Gilbert Scott (1811–1878) are notable examples of 19th-century Gothic.

The last of the Goths. *See* RODERICK.

Gouk. *See* GOWK.

Gourmand. The gourmand's prayer. "O Philoxenos, philoxenos, why were you not Prometheus?" PROMETHEUS was the mythological creator of man, and Philoxenos was a great epicure, whose constant wish was to have the neck of a crane, that he might enjoy the taste of his food longer before it passed into his stomach (Aristotle, *Ethics*, III, x, 10).

Gout (Fr. *goutte*, Lat. *gutta*, a drop). This disease is so called from the belief that it was due to a "drop of acrid matter in the joints".

Goven. St. Goven's Bell. *See* INCHCAPE ROCK.

Government men. In Australia an early and customary name for convicts.

Government Stroke. A well-established Australian expression for taking a long time over very little work. It is probably derived from the way GOVERNMENT MEN worked.

Gowk. The cuckoo (from Icel. *gaukr*); hence a fool, a simpleton.

Hunting the gowk is making one an APRIL FOOL.

A gowk storm is one consisting of several days of tempestuous weather; believed by country-folk to take place periodically in early April, at the time that the gowk arrives in this country; it is also, curiously enough, a storm that is short and sharp, a "STORM IN A TEA-CUP".

Gown. Gown and town row. In university towns scrimmages between the students and citizens were once common.

Graal. *See* GRAIL.

Grace. A courtesy title used in addressing or speaking of dukes, duchesses, and archbishops. "His Grace the Duke of Devonshire", "My Lord Archbishop, may it please Your Grace", etc.

Act of Grace. A pardon; a general pardon granted by Act of Parliament, especially that of 1690, when William III pardoned political offenders; and that of 1784, when the estates forfeited for high treason in connexion with the FORTY-FIVE were restored.

Grace before, or **after meat.** A short prayer asking a blessing on, or giving thanks for, one's food; as the old college grace *Benedictus benedicat* before the meal followed by *Benedicto benedicatur* at the end. Here the word (which used to be plural) is a relic of the old phrase to *do graces* or to *give graces*, meaning to render thanks (Fr. *rendre grâces*; Lat. *gratias agere*), as in Chaucer's "yeldinge graces and thankinges to hir lord Melibee" (*Tale of Melibeus*, 71).

The Grace of God. The free and unmerited love and favour of God.

There but for the grace of God go I. A phrase used by the self-critical when others are faced with disaster, disgrace etc., through their actions or misdoings. It implies that most of us have committed the same follies, sins etc., or had similar temptations, but have been fortunate enough to escape the consequences.

Grace and Favour Residence. A residence belonging to the Crown bestowed upon a notable person as free accommodation.

Grace Cup, or **Loving Cup.** *See* LOVING CUP.

Grace Days, or **Days of Grace.** The three days over and above the time stated in a commercial bill. Thus, if a bill is drawn on 20 June, and is payable in one month, it is due on 20 July, but three "days of grace" are added, bringing the date to 23 July.

Grace Darling. *See* DARLING.

Grace Notes are musical embellishments not essential to the harmony or melody of a piece; more common in 16th-century music than in music of the present day.

Time of Grace. *See* SPORTING SEASONS.

To fall from grace. Apart from a theological implication, this means to relapse from a moral position attained or to fall from favour.

To get into ones' good graces. To insinuate oneself into the favour of.

With a good, or **bad grace.** Gracefully or ungracefully, willingly or unwillingly. *With a good grace* has an air of rather forced acquiescence.

Year of Grace. The year of Our Lord, *Anno Domini*. Also the favour of benefiting from a year's delay in resigning an appointment, etc. *Cp.* GRACE DAYS.

The Three Graces. In classical mythology, the goddesses who bestowed beauty and charm and were themselves the embodiment of both. They were the sisters AGLAIA, THALIA, and Euphrosyne. *Cp.* MUSES.

Grade. Grade crossing. The American equivalent of the British level crossing. From Lat. *gradus*, a step.

Grade separation. Where one road is an overpass or underpass.

To make the grade. To rise to the occasion, to reach the required standard or level, to overcome obstacles. From the analogy of climbing a hill or gradient.

Gradual. An antiphon sung between the Epistle and the GOSPEL as the deacon ascends the steps (Late Lat. *graduales*) of the altar or pulpit. Also the book containing the musical portions of the service at mass—the *graduals*, *introits*, *kyries*, GLORIA IN EXCELSIS, *credo*, etc.

The Gradual Psalms. Ps. cxx to cxxxiv inclusive; probably because they were sung when the priests made the ascent to the inner court of the temple at JERUSALEM. In the Authorized Version of the BIBLE they are called *Songs of Degrees*, and in the Revised Version *Songs of Ascents*. *Cp.* HALLEL.

Graffiti (grä fē' tē) (Ital. *graffito*, a scratching). A name applied originally to the "wall scribblings" found at Pompeii and other Italian cities, the work of schoolboys, idlers, etc., many of them obscene and accompanied by rough drawings. A collection of graffiti of Pompeii was published by Bishop Wordsworth in 1837 and it provides a useful insight into the life of the ancient Romans. Modern graffiti are found on walls, especially in lavatories, on posters, etc. They are usually crude and mostly erotic, but political graffiti are common.

Grahame's, Graham's, Grime's, or **Grim's Dyke.** A popular name for the remains of Antonine's wall between the Firth of Forth and Firth of Clyde. GRIM is an old name for the DEVIL. Scott in his *Tales of a Grandfather* (ch. i) says that when the Picts and Scots attacked, after the Romans left, Grahame was the first to climb over it.

Grail, The Holy. The cup or chalice traditionally used by Christ at the LAST SUPPER, the subject of a great amount of mediæval legend, romance, and allegory.

According to one account, JOSEPH OF ARIMATHÆA preserved the Grail and received into it some of the blood of the Saviour at the Crucifixion. He brought it to England, but it disappeared. According to others it was brought by angels from HEAVEN and entrusted to a body of knights who guarded it on top of a mountain. When approached by anyone not of perfect purity it vanished, and its quest became the source of most of the adventures of the knights of the ROUND TABLE. *See also* PERCEFOREST.

There is a great mass of literature concerning the Grail Cycle, and it appears to be a fusion of Christian legend and pre-Christian ritual origins. Part of the subject matter appears in the MABINOGION in the story of *Peredur son of Efrawg*. The first Christian Grail romance was that of the French TROUVÈRE Robert de Borron who wrote his *Joseph d'Arimathie* at the end of the 12th century, and it next became attached to the Arthurian legend. In Robert de Borron's work the Grail took the form of a dish on which the Last Supper was served.

Malory's *Le Morte d'Arthur* (printed by CAXTON in 1485) is an abridgement from French sources. The framework of Tennyson's *Holy Grail* (*Idylls of the King*) in which the poet expressed his "strong feeling as to the Reality of the Unseen" is based upon Malory.

Grain. To go against the grain. Against one's inclination. The allusion is to wood which cannot be properly planed the wrong way of the grain.

With a grain of salt. *See under* SALT.

Grand. Grand Alliance. The coalition against Louis XIV consisting of the Empire, Holland, Spain, Great Britain, etc., which fought the War of the Grand Alliance or War of the League of Augsburg (1689–1697) to check French aggression.

Grand Guignol. *See* GUIGNOL.

Grand Lama. *See* LAMA.

Grand National. The principal event in English steeplechasing, instituted at Liverpool in 1839, and now run at Aintree on a 4½-mile course of 30 jumps, including the famous Beecher's Brook. *See* RACES.

Grand Seignior. A term applied to the former Sultans of Turkey.

Grand Old Duke of York, The, of nursery rhyme fame was Frederick Augustus, Duke of York and Albany (1763–1827), second son of George III, who commanded the English Army in Flanders (1794–1795), co-operating with the Austrians against revolutionary France. His part in the campaign of 1794 was derisively summarized in the rhyme:

> The grand old Duke of York
> He had ten thousand men
> He marched 'em up to the top of the hill
> And he marched 'em down again.

In fact, there was no hill, he was young, and he commanded some 30,000 men. In variants of the rhyme he is the "brave" or "rare old Duke". He was made commander-in-chief in 1798.

Grandfather. Grandfather clock. The well-established name for the once commonly used weight and pendulum tall-case clock, or long-case clock. It derives from the popular song *My Grand-father's Clock* (1878) by Henry Clay Work (1832–1884) of Connecticut, author of the temperance song *Come Home Father* (1864) and *Marching through Georgia* (1865).

Grandison, Sir Charles, the hero of Samuel Richardson's *History of Sir Charles Grandison*, published in 1753. Sir Charles is the perfect hero and English Christian gentleman, aptly described by Sir Walter Scott as "a faultless monster that the world never saw". Richardson's model for Sir Charles may have been the worthy Robert Nelson (1656–1715), a religious writer and eminent non-juror, whose life was devoted to good works.

Grange. Properly the *granum* (granary) or farm of a monastery, where the corn was stored. Houses attached to monasteries where rent was paid in grain were also called granges, and in Lincolnshire and the northern counties the name is given to any lone farm.

Grangerize. To "extra-illustrate" a book; to supplement it by the addition of illustrations, portraits, autograph letters, caricatures, prints, broadsheets, biographical sketches, anecdotes, scandals, press notices, parallel passages, and any other matter directly or indirectly bearing on the subject. So called from James Granger (1723–1776), vicar of Shiplake, Oxon, who published his *Biographical History of England from Egbert the Great to the Revolution* ... "with a preface showing the utility of a collection of engraved portraits". The book went through several editions with added material and it was continued by Mark Noble in 1806. Collectors made this book a core around which to assemble great collections of portraits, etc., and in 1856 two copies were sold in London, one in 27 vols, with 1,300 portraits, the other in 19 vols. with 3,000 portraits. *Grangerizing* books became a fashion with the result that many excellent editions of biographies, etc., were ruined by having the plates removed for pasting in some dilettante's collection.

Granite. The Granite City. Aberdeen.

Granite Redoubt. The grenadiers of the Consular Guard were so called at the battle of Marengo in 1800, because when the French had given way they formed into a square, stood like a stone against the Austrians, and stopped all further advance.

The Granite State. New Hampshire, because the mountainous parts are chiefly granite.

Granny. Granny-knot. A knot that slips, a fumbled attempt at a reef-knot.

Granny Smith. A green-skinned, crisp-fleshed dessert apple, the best known Australian APPLE. Named after its first cultivator, Maria Ann Smith of Eastwood, New South Wales.

Grantchester. This village, of ancient origin, two miles south of Cambridge, has a fine old church with many interesting features but it owes its present celebrity to its associations with Rupert Brooke (1887–1915). He lived at the Old Vicarage, and saw active service in the Great War, his reputation being much enhanced by his last poems.

> But Grantchester! ah, Grantchester,
> There's peace and holy quiet there.
> RUPERT BROOKE: *The Old Vicarage, Grantchester.*

Grape. Sour grapes. Something disparaged because it is beyond one's reach. The allusion is to ÆSOP's well-known fable of the FOX who tried in vain to get at some grapes, but when he found they were beyond his reach went away saying, "I see they are sour."

Grapevine, or **Grapevine telegraph.** Somewhat the same as the BUSH TELEGRAPH, the mysterious means and covert whisperings by which information, rumours, etc., are spread around.

Grass. An old usage for spring or early summer, the time when the grass grows.

> ... she is five years old this grass ...
> MISS MITFORD: *Our Village, The Copse* 1819).

It is also the name given to the dried leaves and flowers of the cannabis plant or hemp (*cp.* HASH), also called marijuana and bhang. In criminal slang *to grass* is to inform, which may derive from rhyming slang "grasshopper" for COPPER. A *supergrass* is one who informs on a number of his associates. *See also*

GRASS HAND.

Not to let the grass grow under one's feet. To act with all dispatch, not to delay in taking steps to deal with a matter.

To go to grass, or to be put out to grass. Primarily to turn out an animal to pasture, especially an old horse too old to work. Hence, to be retired, to rusticate, to be sent on holiday, or even to go to the grave.

Grass roots. Used to denote that which is rooted in the earth, *i.e.* that which has its origins among the peasantry or common folk.

Grass widow. Formerly, an unmarried woman who has had a child. The origin of the term is uncertain but "grass" here may be the equivalent of "bed". It now implies a wife temporarily parted from her husband and in this sense it became current again in the days of British rule in India. By extension it also denotes a divorced woman or one deserted by her husband. Its counterpart is grass widower. *Cp.* TO GIVE A GIRL A GREEN GOWN *under* GREEN.

Grasshopper. The grasshoppers used on London signboards of goldsmiths, bankers, etc., commemorated the crest of Sir Thomas Gresham (1519–1579), founder of the ROYAL EXCHANGE, the original building being decorated with stone grasshoppers. The grasshopper still forms part of the crest of Martin's Bank.

Grattan's Parliament. The free Irish Parliament at Dublin between 1782 and 1800, so named after Henry Grattan (1746–1820), who obtained the repeal of Poynings' Law and the Declaratory Act of 1719, thereby theoretically abolishing English control. It came to an end with the Act of UNION (1800), which was a result of English bribery and influence.

Grave. Close as the grave. Very secret indeed.

It's enough to make him turn in his grave. Said when something happens to which the deceased person would have strongly objected.

Someone is walking over my grave. An exclamation when one is seized with an involuntary convulsive shuddering.

To carry away the meat from graves. *See under* MEAT.

With one foot in the grave. At the verge of death. The parallel Greek phrase is, "With one foot in the ferryboat", meaning that of Charon. *See* CHARON'S TOLL.

Graveyard Shift. In World War II the name given by shift workers in munitions factories, etc., to the shift covering the midnight hours.

Gravelled. I'm regularly gravelled. Nonplussed, like a ship run aground and unable to move.

> When you were gravelled for lack of matter.
> SHAKESPEARE: *As You Like It*, IV, i.

Gray. *See* GREY.

Gray-back. A Confederate soldier in the American CIVIL WAR. So called from the colour of the Confederate army uniform.

Gray's Inn. One of the four INNS OF COURT and formerly the residence of the de Greys, a family which, in the 13th century, had high-ranking legal associations. After the death of the first Lord Grey de Wilton (1308) the property was vacated and at some time in the 14th century it was occupied by the Society of Gray's Inn. In 1594 SHAKESPEARE'S *Comedy of Errors* was first acted in the hall of Gray's Inn and the walks and gardens were laid out by Sir Francis Bacon, Lord Verulam. The library containing some 30,000 vols, and MSS. and the original hall were destroyed in the air raids of 1940–1941.

Grease. Slang for money, especially that given as a bribe; "PALM-OIL".

Like greased lightning. Very quick indeed.

To grease one's palm, or **fist.** To give a bribe.

> Grease my fist with a tester or two, and ye shall find it in your pennyworth.
> QUARLES: *The Virgin Widow*, IV, i.

To grease the wheels. To make things run smoothly, usually by the application of a little money.

Great Bear, The. *See under* BEAR.

Great Bible, The. *See* BIBLE, THE ENGLISH.

Great Cham of Literature. So Smollett called Dr. Johnson (1709–1784).

Great Commoner. William Pitt, 1st Earl of Chatham (1708–1778).

Great Council. The *Magnum Concilium* of the Norman kings and their successors, the assembly of tenants-in-chief meeting at regular intervals with the king and his principal officers for consultation. It was the *curia regis* from which governmental, legal, and political institutions derived.

Great Dauphin. *See* DAUPHIN.

Great Divide. The Rocky Mountains. **To cross the Great Divide,** figuratively speaking, is to die.

Great Exhibition. The CRYSTAL PALACE exhibition of 1851.

Great Fire. *See under* FIRE.

Great Head. Malcolm III of Scotland (reigned 1057–1093); also called *Canmore* (Gael. *Ceann-mor*, Great Head).

Great Lakes. Lakes Erie, Huron, Michigan, Ontario, and Superior.

Great Mogul. The ruler of the former MOGUL Empire.

Great Plague (1665–1666). The last occurrence of the bubonic plague, which had frequently erupted in various localities since the Black Death but less disastrously. Outbreaks were particularly bad in London in 1603, 1625 and 1636, doubtless due to growing congestion. That of 1625 was known as the Great Plague until it was overshadowed by that of 1665. Deaths in London are estimated at *c*. 100,000, but the Lord Mayor remained at his post. *See* THE GREAT FIRE OF LONDON *under* FIRE.

Great Plains. The area east of the Rocky Mountains from the border of Canada to the mouth of the Arkansas river.

Great Rebellion. In English history the period of the CIVIL WARS, the time of the rebellion against Charles I; also called the PURITAN Revolution.

Great Schism. *See* SCHISM.

Great Scott, or **Scot!** An exclamation of surprise, wonder, admiration, indignation, etc. It seems to have originated in America in the late 1860s, perhaps evocative of General Winfield-Scott (1786–1866), a popular figure after his victorious Mexican campaign of 1847.

Great Seal. The chief seal of the Sovereign used to authenticate important state documents. It is always round in shape and one side shows the sovereign crowned and enthroned (*i.e.* in majesty) and the other the sovereign mounted. The seal is kept by the LORD CHANCELLOR (*see under* CHANCELLOR). *See also* E PLURIBUS UNUM.

Great Spirit. *See* MANITOU.

Great Trek. The exodus of some fifth part of the Dutch-speaking South Africans from Cape Colony from 1835 and into the 1840s, leading to the establishment of Boer Republics across the Orange and Vaal rivers and to British control of Natal.

The Great Unknown. Sir Walter Scott, who published *Waverley* (1814) and the subsequent novels as "by the author of Waverley". First so called by his publisher, James Ballantyne. It was not until 1827 that he admitted the authorship, though it was then well known.

The Great War. The war of 1914–18 was so called until that of 1939–1945, when the term World War I largely replaced it, the latter becoming World War II.

The Great White Way. A once popular name for Broadway, the theatrical district of New York City.

The Greatest Show on Earth. The name of the gigantic travelling combination of circus, menagerie and collection of human freaks in the U.S.A., displayed by the American showman Phineas T. Barnum (1810–1891) and his partners in 1871. In 1842 Barnum had exhibited General TOM THUMB and in 1850 had toured America with the SWEDISH NIGHTINGALE. He had a varied career of success and failure but the *Greatest Show* again made his fortune and that of his partner Bailey. In 1889 the show was presented at the LONDON OLYMPIA.

Grecian. Grecian bend. An affectation in walking with the body stooped slightly forward, assumed by English women in 1868. *Cp*. ALEXANDRA LIMP.

A Grecian nose, or **profile,** is one where the line of the nose continues that of the forehead without a dip.

Greco, El (grek' ō), or **The Greek.** Domenico Theotocopuli, a Cretan, who studied under Titian and MICHELANGE-

LO, and moved to Spain about 1570. He was the foremost 16th-century painter of the Castilian school.

Greegrees. The name given in Africa to AMULETS, CHARMS, FETISHES, etc.

A greegree man. One who sells these.

Greek. A merry Greek. In *Troilus and Cressida* (I, ii) SHAKESPEARE makes Pandarus, bantering Helen for her love to Troilus, say, "I think Helen loves him better than Paris", to which Cressida, whose wit is to parry and pervert, replies, "Then she's a merry Greek indeed", insinuating that she was a "woman of pleasure". *See* GRIG.

All Greek to me. Quite unintelligible; quite a foreign language. SHAKESPEARE'S Casca says, "For mine own part, it was Greek to me" (*Julius Cæsar*, I, ii).

Last of the Greeks. Philopœmen, of Megalopolis (252–182 B.C.), whose great object was to infuse into the Achæans a military spirit, and establish their independence.

To play the Greek. To indulge in one's cups. The Greeks have always been considered to have been addicted to CREATURE COMFORTS. The rule in Greek banquets was *E pithi e apithi* (Quaff, or be off!).

When Greek meets Greek, then is the tug of war. When two men or armies of undoubted courage fight, the contest will be very severe. The line is slightly altered from a 17th-century play, and the reference is to the obstinate resistance of the Greek cities to Philip and Alexander, the Macedonian kings.

> When Greeks joined Greeks, then was the tug of war.
> NATHANIEL LEE: *The Rival Queens*, IV, ii.

Greek Calends. Never. To defer anything to the Greek CALENDS is to defer it *sine die*. There were no Calends in the Greek months. *See* NEVER.

Greek Church. A name often given to the Eastern or ORTHODOX Church of which the Greek Church proper is an autocephalous unit, recognized as independent by the Patriarch of Constantinople in 1850.

Greek Cross. *See* CROSS.

Greek fire. A combination of nitre, sulphur, and naphtha used for setting fire to ships, fortifications, etc. Tow steeped in the mixture was hurled in a blazing state through tubes or tied to arrows. The invention is ascribed to Callinicus of Heliopolis, A.D. 668.

Greek gift. A treacherous gift. The reference is to the WOODEN HORSE OF TROY, or to VIRGIL's *Timeo Danaos et dona ferentes* (*Æneid* II, 49), "I fear the Greeks, even when they offer gifts".

Greek trust. No trust at all. *Græca fides* with the Romans was much the same as PUNIC FAITH.

Green. Young, fresh, as *green cheese*, cream cheese which is eaten fresh; *a green old age*, an old age in which the faculties are not impaired and the spirits are still youthful; *green goose*, a young or midsummer goose.

Hence, immature in age or judgment, inexperienced (*see* SALAD DAYS).

Simple, raw, easily imposed upon; the characteristic GREENHORN.

> "He is so jolly green," said Charley.
> DICKENS: *Oliver Twist*, ch, ix.

For its symbolism, etc., *see* COLOURS.

Do you see any green in my eye? *see under* EYE.

The green-eyed monster. So SHAKESPEARE called jealousy:

> *Iago:* O! beware my lord, of jealousy;
> It is the green-ey'd monster which doth mock
> The meat it feeds on.
> *Othello*, III, iii.

A greenish complexion was formerly held to be indicative of jealousy, and as all the green-eyed cat family "mock the meat they feed on", so jealousy mocks its victim by loving and loathing it at the same time.

Rub of the Green. An expression used in golf, and which has spread thence into ordinary life, meaning a piece of good or ill fortune which is outside the competence of the player (or individual). By way of example, *A* hits a shot to the green which glances off a stone into the woods; *B* hits the same stone at a different angle and his ball runs on to the green and into the hole. Since neither was aiming at, or aware of, the stone, the resulting disparity of fortune is "the rub of the green".

To be green with envy. To be extremely envious of someone's achievements, attainments, wealth, etc. Literally, to have one's face acquire a pale greenish hue as a result of envy.

To get the green light. To get permission to proceed with an undertaking, green being the "Go" sign on road and rail signals.

To give a girl a green gown. A 16th-century descriptive phrase for romping with a girl in the fields and rolling her on the grass so that her dress is stained green.

To look through green glasses. To feel jealous of one: to be envious of another's success. *Cp.* GREEN-EYED MONSTER.

You would have me believe that the moon is made of green cheese. *See under* MOON.

The wearing of the green. An Irish patriotic and revolutionary song dating from 1798. Green (*cp.* EMERALD ISLE) was the emblematic colour of Irish patriots.

> For they're hangin' men an' women there
> for wearin' o' the Green.

Green Belt. A stretch of country around a large urban area that has been scheduled for comparative preservation and where building development is restricted.

Green fingers. Said of a successful gardener.

Green hands. Inexperienced sailors. *Cp.* GREENHORN.

The Green Isle. Ireland. *Cp.* EMERALD ISLE.

Green Man. This common PUBLIC-HOUSE SIGN probably represents either a JACK-IN-THE-GREEN or a forester, who, like ROBIN HOOD, was once clad in green.

On a golf course the **green-man** is the club employee responsible for the putting greens.

Green Ribbon Day in IRELAND is 17 March, ST. PATRICK'S Day, when the SHAMROCK and green ribbon are worn as the national badge.

Green room. In a theatre the common waiting-room for the performers near the stage. Originally such rooms were painted green to relieve the eyes from the glare of the stage.

Green sickness. The old name for chlorosis, a form of anaemia once common in adolescent girls. It was characterized by a greenish pallor.

Greenbacks. Legal tender notes first issued in the United States in 1862, during the CIVIL WAR, as a war-revenue expedient. So called because the back is printed in green. The name is now applied to paper currency issued by any national American bank.

Greengage. A variety of plum introduced into England from France by Sir William Gage of Hengrave, Suffolk, about 1725, and named in his honour. Called by the French "reine-claude" out of compliment to the daughter of Anne of Brittany and Louis XII, first wife of Francis I.

Greenhorn. A novice at any trade, profession, sport, etc. In allusion to the "green horns" of a young horned animal. *Cp.* GREEN; GREEN HANDS.

Greenpeace. A movement originating in Canada in 1971, aiming to persuade governments to change industrial activities which threaten natural resources and the environment. It supports direct non-violent action and has gained wide attention by its efforts to protect whales and to prevent the killing of young seals. When acting against French nuclear tests in the South Pacific in 1985 their ship, *Rainbow Warrior* was sunk by a French saboteur. *Cp.* FRIENDS OF THE EARTH.

Greenshirt. A supporter of the Social Credit Movement established in England by Major Douglas in the 1920s, and so named from the green uniform shirt adopted.

Greensleeves. A very popular ballad in the time of Elizabeth I, published in 1581, given in Clement Robinson's *Handefull of Pleasant Delites* (1584) and mentioned by SHAKESPEARE (*Merry Wives*, II, i, and V, v). The air is of the same period and was used for many ballads. During the CIVIL WAR it was used by the CAVALIERS as a tune for political ballads, and Pepys (23 April 1660) mentions it under the title of *The Blacksmith*.

Greenlander. A native of Greenland, discovered by Eric the Red in 985 and called Grœnland "for he said it would make men's minds long to go there if it had a fine name". *Greenlander* is facetiously applied to a GREENHORN.

Greenwich. Greenwich barbers.

Greenwich Stars. The stars used by astronomers for the lunar computations in the nautical ephemeris.

Greenwich Time. Mean time for the meridian of Greenwich, *i.e.* the system of time in which noon occurs at the moment of passage of the mean sun over the meridian of Greenwich. It is the standard time adopted by astronomers and was used throughout the British Isles until 18 February, 1968, when clocks were advanced one hour and Summer Time became "permanent". The new system was designated British Standard Time (as from 27 October 1968), but the arguments against it duly prevailed and the country reverted to Greenwich Mean Time on 31 October 1971. *See* DAYLIGHT SAVING; STANDARD TIME.

Gregorian. Gregorian Calendar. A modification of the JULIAN CALENDAR, introduced in 1582 by Pope Gregory XIII. This is called "the New Style". *See* GREGORIAN YEAR.

Gregorian chant. Plainsong; the traditional ritual melody of the Christian Church of the West, so called because it was reformed and elaborated by GREGORY THE GREAT at the end of the 6th century.

Gregorian Epoch. The epoch or day on which the Gregorian CALENDAR commenced in October 1582. *See* GREGORIAN YEAR.

Gregorian telescope. The first form of the reflecting telescope, invented in 1663 by James Gregory (1638–1675), professor of mathematics at St. Andrews.

Gregorian tree. The gallows; so named from Gregory Brandon and his son Richard ("Young Gregory"), HANGMEN from the time of James I to 1649. Gregory was granted a coat of arms.

Gregorian Year. The civil year according to the correction introduced by Pope Gregory XIII in 1582. The equinox which occurred on 25 March in the time of Julius Cæsar fell on 11 March in the

year 1582. This was because the Julian calculation of 365¼ days to a year was 11 min. 14 sec. too long. Gregory suppressed 10 days by altering 5 October to 15 October, thus making the equinox fall on 21 March 1583. Further simple arrangements prevented the recurrence of a similar error in the future. The change was soon adopted by most CATHOLIC countries, but the PROTESTANT countries did not accept it until much later. The *New Style* was not adopted by ENGLAND and SCOTLAND until 1752. At the same time the beginning of the civil or legal year was altered from LADY DAY (25 March) to 1 January, a change adopted in Scotland in 1600. *See* ELEVEN DAYS.

Gregories. HANGMEN. *See* GREGORIAN TREE.

Gregory. A feast held on St. GREGORY's Day (12 March), especially in IRELAND.

Gregory the Great, or **St. Gregory** (540–604), the first Pope of this name, and DOCTOR OF THE CHURCH. The outstanding figure of his age, notable for church and monastic reform, for dealing with heresies, for wise administration, and kindness to the poor. He also refashioned the liturgy of the Church and made a lasting contribution to Church music (*see* GREGORIAN CHANT). He sent St. AUGUSTINE on his mission to the Anglo-Saxons, thus earning the title of *Apostle of England*.

Gremlin. One of a tribe of imaginary GNOMES or GOBLINS humorously blamed by the R.A.F. in World War II for everything that went wrong in an aircraft or an operation. The name was probably coined at the end of World War I or in the 1920s and was apparently in use on R.A.F. stations in India and the Middle East in the 1930s. The name is first traced in print in *The Aeroplane* (10 April 1929). A common explanation is that a gremlin was the goblin which came out of Fremlin's beer bottles (Fremlin being a brewer in Kent), although there are numerous other stories.

Grenadier. Originally a soldier, picked for his stature, whose duty in battle was to throw *grenades*. In time each regiment had a special company of them, and when in the 18th century the use of grenades was discontinued (not to be revived until World War I) the name was retained for the company composed of the tallest and finest men. In the British Army it now survives only in the Grenadier Guards, the First Regiment of Foot Guards, noted for their height, physique, traditions, and discipline.

Grendel. The mythical half-human monster killed by BEOWULF. Grendel nightly raided the king's hall and slew the sleepers.

Gresham. **Gresham's Law** can be briefly summarized as stating that bad money drives out good, and was promulgated by Sir Thomas Gresham to Elizabeth I in 1558, though the same law had been explained earlier by COPERNICUS.

Gretna Green Marriages. Runaway marriages. Elopers from England reaching Gretna, near Springfield, Dumfriesshire, 8 miles N.W. of Carlisle, could (up to 1856) get legally married without licence, banns, or priest. All that was required was a declaration before witnesses of the couple's willingness to marry. This declaration was generally made to a blacksmith, landlord, toll-keeper, etc. By an Act of 1856, the residence in Scotland for at least 21 days of one of the parties became essential before a marriage was possible. Gretna Green's prominence arose from the abolition of FLEET MARRIAGES. Although marriage by declaration ceased to be legal in July 1940, Gretna Green and other places in Scotland continue to attract young couples because minors may still marry there without parental consent. *Cp.* MAY-FAIR MARRIAGES.

Grève (Grev). **Place de Grève.** The TYBURN of old PARIS, where for centuries public executions took place, now called the *Place de l'Hôtel de Ville*. It is on the bank of the Seine, the word *grève* here meaning the strand of a river.

Grey. Grey as a badger. Said of one with dark hair thickly sprinkled with grey and white, from the resemblance to the grey brindled fur of the badger.

Grey Eminence. The name given to François Le Clerc du Tremblay (1577–1638), or Père Joseph, as he was

called, the CAPUCHIN agent and trusty counsellor of Cardinal Richelieu. It was inspired by his influence over Cardinal Richelieu's policies; he was, as it were, a shadowy CARDINAL in the background. Hence a close adviser who exercises power behind the scenes.

Grey Friars Grey. FRANCISCANS.

Grey Mare. *See under* MARE.

Grey Market. In World War II a transaction regarded as a lesser breach of the rationing regulations than the BLACK MARKET.

Grey matter. A pseudo-scientific name for the brain, for common sense. The active part of the brain is composed of a greyish tissue which contains the nerve-endings.

Grey Sisters. *See* FRANCISCANS.

Greybeard. An old man—generally a doddering old fellow; also an earthen pot for holding spirits; a large stone jar. *Cp.* BELLARMINE.

The Old Grey Whistle test. In TIN-PAN ALLEY song writers used to play their compositions to the "old greys", the elderly doorkeepers and suchlike workers in the offices of the music publishers. If the "old greys" were still whistling the tunes after a week or so, then they were likely to be worth publishing.

Gridiron. The emblem of St. LAWRENCE of ROME. One legend says that he was roasted on a gridiron; another that he was bound to an iron chair and thus roasted alive. He was martyred in 258, under Valerian. *See* ESCORIAL.

It is also the American term for a football playing field, from the fact that the field was marked with squares or grids. *See also* GOOSE AND GRIDIRON.

Griffin. A mythical monster; also called *Griffon*, *Gryphon*, etc., fabled to be the offspring of the LION and the EAGLE. Its legs and all from the shoulders to the head are like an eagle, the rest of the body is that of a lion. This creature was sacred to the sun and kept guard over hidden treasures. *See* ARIMASPIANS.

Among Anglo-Indians a newcomer, a GREENHORN, was called a *griffin*; and the residue of a contract feast, taken away by the contractor, half the buyer's and half the seller's, is known in the trade as *griffins*.

Grig. Merry as a grig. A grig is a small eel, a cricket or grasshopper; but grig here may be a corruption of Greek, "merry as a Greek". Both phrases were in use in the 16th century. *See* A MERRY GREEK *under* GREEK. Among the Romans *græcari* signified "to play the reveller".

Grim as an element in the naming of ancient earthworks and prehistoric sites derives from Old Norse *grimr*, a nickname of ODIN, supposedly from their size which made people attribute them to superhuman hands. From the 16th century they were often regarded as works of the DEVIL, with whom Grim was equated. *See* HAVELOCK THE DANE.

Grimaldi, Joseph (1779–1837). The most celebrated and irresistible clown of English PANTOMIME was born at LONDON, the son of an Italian actor. He appeared at Drury Lane theatre before he was two years old and at SADLER'S WELLS at the age of three. He was forced to retire in 1828, worn out by continuous overwork. He dressed in what became the traditional clown costume and the name "Joey the clown" attests his popularity and importance.

Grimalkin. An old she-cat, especially a wicked or eerie-looking one; from *grey* and MALKIN. In Shakespeare's *Macbeth* (I, i) a Witch says "I come, Graymalkin". The cat was supposed to be a witch.

Grimm's Law. The law of permutation of consonants in the Indo-Germanic, Low and High German languages. It was first comprehensively formulated by Jakob L. Grimm, the German philologist, in 1822. Thus what is *p* in Greek, Latin, or Sanskrit, becomes *f* in Gothic and *b* or *f* in the Old High German; what is *t* in Greek, Latin or Sanskrit, *th* in Gothic and *d* in Old High German, etc. Thus changing *p* into *f*, and *t* into *th*, "pater" becomes "father". Grimm's Law is of the greatest importance in philological studies.

Grin. To Grin like a Cheshire cat. *See under* CAT.

   You must grin and bear it. Resistance is hopeless; you may make a face if you like, but you must put up with things.

Grind. To work up for an examination.

He has an axe to grind. *See under* AXE.

To grind one down. To reduce the price asked; to oppress.

To grind to a halt. To gradually come to a standstill. From the clogging up of a piece of machinery until it can no longer function. In the days of the windmill, when the wind fell away, the grinding action of the millstones on the grain stopped the mill—it ground to a halt.

To take a grind. To walk for exercise.

Grindstone. To keep one's nose to the grindstone. *See* NOSE.

Griselda, or **Grisilda,** also called Patient Grisel, Grazel, etc. The model of enduring patience and wifely obedience. She was the heroine of the last tale in Boccaccio's *Decameron*. It was translated into Latin by Petrarch under the title *De Obidentia ac Fide uxoria Mythologia* and thence used by Chaucer for his *Clerkes Tale* and by Dekker, Chettle and Haughton for their *Patient Grissil* (1603). The story is of the Marquis of Saluzzo, who marries a poor girl of great beauty. He subjects her to almost unendurable trials, including the pretence that he has married another. At last convinced of her patience and devotion, Chaucer tells us:

> Ful many a yeer in heigh prosperitee
> Lyven thise two in concord and in reste.

Grist. All's grist that comes to my mill. All is appropriated that comes to me; I can make advantage out of anything or use all that comes my way. Grist is that quantity of corn which is to be ground at one time.

To bring grist to the mill. To bring profitable business or gain; to furnish supplies.

Groaning Chair. An old rustic name for a chair in which a woman sat after her confinement to receive congratulations.

Groat. The name given in mediæval times to all thick silver coins; derived from *denarii grossi*, large denarii. In ENGLAND the name was given specifically to the fourpenny piece first made in the reign of Edward I. Later it became a very small silver coin, the issue of which ceased in 1662 although they were still struck as MAUNDY MONEY. In 1836 the small fourpenny piece reappeared as the *Britannia Groat* (*see* JOEY).

Groats. Husked oat or wheat fragments rather larger than grits (O.E. *grut*, coarse meal).

Blood without groats is nothing. Family without fortune is worthless. The allusion is perhaps to black pudding which consists chiefly of blood and groats formed into a sausage.

Grog. Spirits. Properly rum diluted with water. In 1740 Admiral Vernon, when Commander-in-Chief West Indies, substituted watered-down rum for the neat spirit then issued to both officers and men. The Admiral was nicknamed *Old Grog* from his GROGRAM coat and the name was transferred to the new beverage.

> But Jack with smiles each danger meets,
> Casts anchor, heaves the log,
> Trims all the sails, belays the sheets,
> And drinks his can of grog.
> DIBDIN: *The Friendly Tars.*

Originally issued twice daily (a quarter of a pint of rum with a pint of water), the ration was cut to one issue in 1824 and reduced to a half-gill in 1850. The issue to officers was stopped in 1881 and to Warrant Officers in 1918. Grog ration to all ratings ended on 31 July 1970.

Grog-blossoms. Blotches or pimples on the face produced by heavy drinking.

Grogram. A coarse fabric made of silk and mohair or silk and wool, stiffened with gum. It is the Fr. *grosgrain*.

> Gossips in grief and grograms clad.
> PRAED: *The Troubadour*, c. i, st. v.

The Blood of the Grograms. *See under* BLOOD.

Groom of the Stole. *See* STOLE.

Groove. To get into a groove. To get into a rut, a narrow undeviating course of life or habit, to become restricted in outlook and ways.

To be in the groove or **groovy.** To be in the right mood, to be doing something successfully, to be up to the current style or "with it"; from the accurate reproduction of music by a needle set in the groove of a gramophone record or disc.

Gross. The French word *gros*, big, bulky, corpulent, coarse, in English has developed many additional meanings. Thus

a *gross* is twelve dozen; a *great gross*, twelve gross; *gross weight* is the entire weight without deductions; *gross average* is the general average. A VILLEIN *in gross* was the property of his master, and not part of the property of the manor; a *common in gross* is one which is entirely personal property. *Cp.* ADVOWSON IN GROSS.

Grotesque. Literally, in "Grotto style". The chambers of ancient buildings revealed in mediæval times in ROME were called *grottoes*, and as their walls were frequently decorated with fanciful ornaments and *outré* designs, the word grotesque (*grotesco*) came to be applied to similar ornamentations.

Grotto. Pray remember the grotto. This cry was raised in the streets (as late as the 1920s in the poorer parts of London) by small children, who collected old shells, bits of coloured stone or pottery, with leaves, flowers, etc., built a little "grotto" and knelt beside it with their caps ready for pennies. The custom should be restricted to 25 July (St. JAMES's Day), for it is a relic of the old shell grottoes which were erected with an image of the saint for the use of those who could not afford the pilgrimage necessary to pay a visit on that day to the shrine of St. James of COMPOSTELA. *See* COCKLE HAT.

Ground. Ground floor. The storey level with the ground, or, in a basement-house, the floor above the basement. In the U.S.A. known as the first floor.

To get in on the ground floor. To secure an advantageous position in an enterprise through participation at the outset, especially in securing investments before they are available to the general public.

Ground hog. The wood-chuck or North American marmot.

Ground-hog Day. CANDLEMAS (2 February), from the saying that the ground-hog first appears from hibernation on that day. If he sees his shadow, he goes back for another six weeks—indicating six more weeks of bad weather.

Ground swell. A long, deep rolling or swell of the sea, caused by a recent or distant storm, or by an earthquake.

That suits me down to the ground.
See under DOWN.

To break ground. To be the first to commence a project, etc.; to take the first step in an enterprise, as the first stage in siege operations was to break ground to dig trenches.

To gain ground. To make headway; to be improving one's position.

To have the ground cut from under one's feet. To see what one has relied on for support suddenly removed.

To hold one's ground. To maintain one's position, authority, etc. Not to budge or give way.

To lose ground. To become less successful or popular; to drift away from the object aimed at.

To shift one's ground. To try a different plan of attack; to change one's argument or the basis of one's reasoning.

To stand one's ground. Not to yield or give way; to stick to one's COLOURS; to have the courage of one's opinion.

Groundlings. Those who occupied the cheapest part of an Elizabethan theatre, *i.e.* the pit, which was the bare ground in front of the stage. The actor, who today "plays to the gallery", in Elizabethan times

> Split the ears of groundlings.
> SHAKESPEARE: *Hamlet*, III, ii.

Groundnut Scheme. Figuratively, an expensive failure or ill-considered enterprise; from a hastily organized and badly planned British government scheme (1947) to clear large areas of hitherto unprofitable land in Africa to grow groundnuts. The venture was abandoned three years later at considerable cost to the Taxpayer.

Growlers. The old four-wheeled horse-drawn cabs were called "growlers" from the surly attitude of their drivers, and "crawlers" from their slow pace.

Grub. To grub stake. A miner's term for equipping a gold prospector with his requirements in exchange for a share of his finds.

Grub Street. The former name of a London street in the ward of CRIPPLE-GATE Without, changed to Milton Street in 1830 after the carpenter and builder who was the ground landlord. It leads north out of Fore Street, Moorfields, to Chiswell Street.

The name is used allusively for needy authors, literary hacks, and their work. *Cp.* HACK.

Hermit of Grub Street. *See under* HERMIT.

Gruel. A gruelling time, gruelling heat, etc. Exhausting, overpowering.

He had a gruelling. He was given a pasting, he was punished severely (in boxing, etc.).

To take one's gruel. To accept one's punishment, to take what is coming to one.

Grundy. What will Mrs. Grundy say? What will our strait-laced neighbours say? The phrase is from Tom Morton's *Speed the Plough* (1798). In the first scene Mrs. Ashfield shows herself very jealous of neighbour Grundy, and farmer Ashfield says to her: "Be quiet, wool ye? Always ding dinging Dame Grundy into my ears—What will Mrs. Grundy zay? What will Mrs. Grundy think?"

Gryll. Let Gryll be Gryll and have his hoggish mind (Spenser: *The Faerie Queene*, II, xii, 87). Don't attempt to wash a blackamoor white; the leopard will never change his spots. Gryll is the Gr. *grullos*, a hog. When Sir Guyon disenchanted the forms in the BOWER OF BLISS some were exceedingly angry, and Gryll, who had been metamorphosed by ACRASIA into a hog, abused him most roundly.

Gryphon. *See* GRIFFIN.

Guardiana. According to the old legend the Spanish river was so called from Durandarte's Squire of this name. Mourning the fall of his master at RONCESVALLES, he was turned into a river (*see Don Quixote*, ii, 23). Actually, it is Arab. *wadi*, a river, and *Anas*, its classical name.

Guard. To be off one's guard. To be careless, to be caught unawares.

To be put on his guard. To "give him the tip", to show him where the danger lies.

Guards, The. *See* HOUSEHOLD TROOPS.

Guards of the Pole. *See* GREAT BEAR *under* BEAR.

Guarneri, or Guarnerius. The name of one of the famous violin-makers of CRE-

MONA of the 17th and 18th centuries. Andreas (*c.* 1626–1698) was a pupil of Nicolo AMATI. Giuseppe (1687–1745), known as Giuseppe del Gesù, from his habit of inscribing the sacred initials I.H.S. inside his violins, was held to be the greatest. *Cp.* STRAD.

Gubbins. The wild and savage inhabitants of the neighbourhood of Brentor, Devon, who according to Fuller in his *Worthies* (1661)—

> lived in cots (rather holes than houses) ..., having all in common, multiplying without marriage into many hundreds ... Their language is the dross of the dregs of the vulgar Devonian ... They held together like burrs.

As explanation of the name he says, "We call the shavings of fish (which are of little worth) *gubbins*".

Gudgeon. Gaping for gudgeons. Looking out for things extremely improbable. As a gudgeon is a small fish used as bait, it means here a snare, a lie, a deception.

To swallow a gudgeon. To be bamboozled with a most palpable lie, as silly fish are caught by gudgeons (Fr. *goujon*; whence the phrase *avaler le goujon*, to swallow the bait, to die).

Gudrun, or **Kudrun.** The heroine of the great 13th-century German epic poem of this name founded on a passage in the *Prose* EDDA. The third part describes how Gudrun, daughter of King Hettel, was carried off by Hochmut of Normandy and made to work like a menial in his mother's house, because she would not break her troth to Herwig, King of Zealand. She was eventually rescued by her brother. This poem is sometimes known as the German ODYSSEY.

Gudule, Gudula, or **Gudila, St.** Patron saint of Brussels, daughter of Count Witger, died 712. She is represented with a lantern, from a tradition that she was one day going to the church of St. Morzelle with a lantern which went out, but the Holy Virgin lighted it again with her prayers. Her feast day is 8 January.

Guebres, or **Ghebers** (gā' bĕrz). Followers of the ancient Persian religion, reformed by ZOROASTER; fire-worshippers, PARSEES. The name, which was given them by their Mohammedan conquerors, is now applied to fire-worshippers generally.

Guelphs and Ghibellines (gwelfs, gib' e lēnz). In mediæval Italy two rival factions whose quarrels occupy much of the political history of the period. The Guelphs were the papal and popular party, the Ghibellines, the imperial and aristocratic party. Both names are derived from two rival German factions of the 12th century. *Ghibelline* is an Italian form of *Waiblingen*, a small town in Württemberg and a possession of the Hohenstaufen Emperor Conrad III, the name of which is said to have been used as a war-cry by his followers at the battle of Weinsberg (1140). Their opponents similarly used the war-cry *Welf*, the personal name of their leader, Welf VI of Bavaria. *Guelph* is the Italian form of *Welf*.

The Guelph dynasty ruled in Hanover until 1866 and the reigning dynasty of Great Britain is descended from it. Guelphs ruled in Brunswick from its erection into a Duchy in 1235 until 1918.

Guenever. *See* GUINEVERE.

Guerinists (ger' i nists). An early 17th-century sect of French ILLUMINATI, founded by Peter Guérin.

Guernsey Lily. *See* MISNOMERS.

Guerrilla War (ge ril' à). Irregular warfare carried on by small groups acting independently; especially by patriots when their country is being invaded. From Span. *guerrilla*, diminutive of *guerra*, war. *See* F.F.I.

Gueux, Les (lā ger), or **The Beggars.** The name adopted by the confederates who rose against Spanish rule in the Netherlands in the 16th century. In 1556 Baron Berlaymont is said to have exclaimed to the Regent, Margaret of Parma: "Is it possible that your highness can entertain fear of these beggars?" (Motley, *Rise of the Dutch Republic*, II, vi). The name then became an honoured title.

Guides. *See* GIRL GUIDES.

Guignol (gē' nyol). The principal character in a popular 18th-century French puppet-show, similar to PUNCH. As the performance involved macabre and gruesome incidents the name came to be attached to short plays of this nature; hence **Grand Guignol,** a series of such plays, or the theatre in which they were performed.

Guilds, or **Gilds.** *See* LIVERY COMPANIES.

Guillotine (gil′ ō tēn). An instrument for inflicting capital punishment by decapitation, so named from Joseph Ignace Guillotin (1738–1814), a French physician, who proposed its adoption to prevent unnecessary pain. It was first used in the Place de GRÈVE, 25 April, 1792. For a time it was known as a *Louisette* after Antoine Louis (1723–1792), the French surgeon who devised it. Similar instruments had been used in some countries from the 13th century. *Cp.* MAIDEN.

It is also the name of a paper-cutting machine and a surgical instrument.

In British Parliamentary procedure, a development of the CLOSURE to arbitrarily cut delay by passing a *guillotine motion*, when, at the committee stage or report stage, a BILL is divided into compartments, each of which has to be dealt with in the specified time. It is also known as *closure by compartments*.

Guinea. A gold coin current in England from 1663 to 1817 (last struck 1813), originally made of gold from Guinea in West Africa. The early issues bore a small elephant below the head of the king. Its original LEGAL TENDER value was 20s. but from 1717 it was fixed at 21s. The actual value varied; in 1694 it was as high as 30s. Before the advent of DECIMAL CURRENCY, it was still customary for professional fees, subscriptions, the price of racehorses, pictures and other luxuries to be paid in guineas as money of account. *See also* SPADE GUINEA.

Guinea-dropper. A cheat. It alludes to an old cheating dodge of dropping counterfeit guineas which is of comparable significance to THIMBLE-RIGGING.

Guinea fowl. So called because it was introduced from Guinea, where it is common.

Guinea-hen. An Elizabethan synonym for a prostitute, who is won by gold.

> Ere ... I would drown myself for the love of a Guinea-hen, I would change my humanity with a baboon.
>
> SHAKESPEARE: *Othello*, I, iii.

Guinea-pig. Properly the cavy, a small South American rodent. A former Stock Exchange name for a person of standing who allowed his name to be put on a company director's list for a fee in guineas, but who was inactive. Guinea-pig is also an old name for a midshipman or a clergyman without a cure. The former because he was neither a fully-fledged officer nor a rating, as guinea-pigs are not pigs, nor do they come from Guinea; the latter because he did occasional duty for a guinea a sermon. Guinea-pigs are often used in scientific and medical experiments and the name is now applied to anyone used in this way or upon whom something is tried out.

Guinevere, Guinever, or **Guenever** (gwin′ e vēr). The wife of King ARTHUR. The name is a corruption of *Guanhumara* (from Welsh *Gwenhwyfar*) as she appears in Geoffrey of Monmouth's *Historia Britonum*, a principal source of ARTHURIAN ROMANCES.

Gule. The Gule of August. 1 August, LAMMAS DAY. The word is probably the Welsh *gwyl* (Lat. *vigilia*), a festival.

Gules. The heraldic term for red. In engraving it is shown by perpendicular parallel lines. From the plural of O.E. *gole, goule*, the mouth, the jaws; the reference is probably to the colour of the open jaws.

> With man's blood paint the ground, gules, gules.
>
> SHAKESPEARE: *Timon of Athens*, IV, iii.

Gulf. A great gulf fixed. An impassable separation. The allusion is to the parable of DIVES and LAZARUS (*Luke* xvi, 26).

Gulf Stream. The great warm ocean current which flows out of the Gulf of Mexico (whence its name) and, passing by the eastern coast of the United States, is, near the banks of Newfoundland, deflected across the Atlantic to modify the climate of Western Europe as far north as Spitzbergen and Novaya Zemlya. It washes the shores of the British Isles.

Gulistan (Pers. the garden of roses). The famous moral miscellany renowned for the quality of its prose and wit, written by Sadi (1194–1282 or 1292), the name adopted by Sheikh Muslih Uddin, the most celebrated Persian poet and writer

Gull

after OMAR KHAYYÁM. It contains sections on kings, dervishes, contentment, love, youth, old age, etc. with numerous stories and philosophical sayings.

Gull. An Elizabethan synonym for one who is easily duped, especially a high-born gentleman (*cp.* BEJAN).

Gum. To gum up the works. To clog up the proceedings, to throw an enterprise into confusion.

Up a gum tree. To be in real difficulty, unable to get any further with a project or task; to be virtually stuck. Possibly an allusion to the gum tree being a refuge for the opossum. (*See* POSSUM.)

Gun. This word was formerly used for a large stone-throwing military device of the catapult or mangonel type. In the *Legend of Good Women* (*Cleopatra*, 58) Chaucer seems to refer to the ballista:

> With grisley soun out goth the grete gonne,
> And hertely they hurtlen al at ones,
> And fro the top doun cometh the grete stones.

But in the *House of Fame* (iii, 553) he says:

> As swift as pelet out of gonne
> Whan fyr is in the poudre ronne.

The word is perhaps a shortened form of the old Scandinavian female name Gunnildr (*gunnr* is Icel. for war, and *hildr* for battle). The bestowing of female names on arms is not uncommon; there are the famous MONS MEG, Queen Elizabeth's pocket pistol (*see under* POCKET), as well as BIG BERTHA of World War I—the long-range gun that bombarded Paris, named after Bertha Krupp, wife of the head of the great armament factory at Essen.

Minute gun. The firing of a gun at minute intervals, generally as a salute at a royal or state funeral.

He's a great gun. A man of note or consequence.

Son of a gun. This familiar designation implying contempt but now used with jocular familiarity derives from the days when women were allowed to live in naval ships. The "son of a gun" was one born in the ship, often near the midship gun, behind a canvas screen. If paternity was uncertain the child was entered in the log as "Son of a gun".

To blow great guns. To be very boisterous, rough and windy, as the noise of great guns.

To jump the gun. To anticipate, to get started before the proper time, usually with a view to gaining an advantage; as when a competitor in a race starts just before the gun is fired.

To run away from one's own guns. To eat one's words; to desert what is laid down as a principle.

To stick to one's guns. To maintain one's position, argument, etc., in spite of opposition.

To gun for someone. To set out deliberately to get a person and do him a mischief or get even with him.

Gunboat. Gunboat Diplomacy. In the days of the Victorian colonial empire, gunboats and other naval vessels were often called upon to coerce local rulers in the interests of British traders, etc., usually in response to local clamour. Hence "gunboat diplomacy", to imply the settling of issues with weaker powers by the use or threat of force. *Cp.* PACIFICO.

Gun-cotton. A highly explosive compound, prepared by saturating cotton or other cellulose material with nitric and sulphuric acids. *Cp.* GREEK FIRE.

Gunman. An armed criminal prepared to use his gun recklessly. A term of American origin.

Gun money. Money issued in IRELAND by James II between 1689 and 1690 made from old brass cannon, bells, copper utensils, etc.

Gun room. In a large warship a room for the accommodation of junior officers, originally under the charge of the gunner. *Cp.* WARD ROOM.

Gun-runner. One who unlawfully smuggles guns into a country for belligerent purposes.

Gunnar. The Norse form of GUNTHER.

Gunner. Kissing the gunner's daughter. Being flogged on board ship. At one time sailors in the Royal Navy who were to be flogged were tied to the breech of a cannon.

Gunpowder Plot. A plan to destroy James I, with Lords and Commons at the opening of PARLIAMENT, 5 November 1605, as a prelude to a CATHOLIC rising. Barrels of powder were stored in a vault under the HOUSE OF LORDS and Guy Fawkes was to fire the train. Tresham, one of the plotters, warned his Catholic relative, Lord Monteagle, who revealed the plot to the authorities. The cellars were searched and Guy Fawkes was taken. The ceremony of searching the vaults of Parliament prior to the annual opening is a result of this plot. *See* GUY.

Gunter. According to Gunter. Carefully and correctly done; with no possibility of a mistake. It is the American counterpart of our "according to COCKER".

Gunter's Chain, for land surveying, is so named from Edward Gunter (1581–1626), the great mathematician and professor of astronomy at Gresham College. It is 66 ft. long, and divided into 100 links. As 10 square chains make an acre, it follows that an acre contains 100,000 square links.

Gunter's scale is a 2-ft. rule having scales of chords, tangents, logarithmic lines, etc., marked on it, used for the mechanical solving of problems in surveying, navigation, etc.

Gunther (gun' ter), or **Gunnar**. In the Nibelungen saga, a Burgundian king, brother of KRIEMHILD, the wife of SIEGFRIED. He resolved to wed the martial BRUNHILD (or Brynhild) who had made a vow to marry only the man who could ride through the flames that encircled her castle. Gunther failed, but Siegfried did so in the shape of Gunther, and remained with her three nights, his sword between them all the time. Gunther then married Brunhild, but later Kriemhild told Brunhild that it was Siegfried who had ridden through the fire, thus arousing her jealousy. Siegfried was slain at Brunhild's instigation, and she then killed herself, her dying wish being to be burnt at Siegfried's side. Gunther was slain by ATLI because he refused to reveal where he had hidden the hoard of the Nibelungs. Gundaharius, a Burgundian king, who, with his men, perished by the sword of the Huns in 436, is supposed to be the historical character around which these legends collected. *See also* NIBELUNGENLIED.

Gurney Light. *See* BUDE.

Guru (goo' roo). A Sanskrit word meaning venerable; it is now applied to a Hindu spiritual teacher and leader.

Guthlac, St., of Crowland, Lincolnshire, is represented in Christian art as a hermit punishing demons with a scourge, or consoled by ANGELS while demons torment him. He was a Mercian prince who died as a hermit in 714.

Gutter press. A term applied contemptuously to those widely circulating lowbrow newspapers, which indulge in sensationalism and scandal-mongering.

Guy. An effigy of a man stuffed with combustibles in mockery of Guy Fawkes, carried round and burnt on a BONFIRE on 5 November, in memory of the GUNPOWDER PLOT. Hence, any dowdy or fantastic figure. From American usage, the word as applied to a person is the equivalent of "CHAP".

Fall Guy. *See under* FALL.

To do a guy. To decamp.

To guy a person. To chaff him, to make fun of him.

Guy of Warwick. An English hero of legend and romance, whose exploits were first written down by an Anglo-Norman poet of the 12th century and were accepted as history by the 14th century.

To obtain the hand of the fair Félice or Phelis, daughter of the Earl of Warwick, he performed many doughty deeds abroad. Returning to England he married Phelis, but after forty days set off on pilgrimage to the HOLY LAND again performing deeds of prowess. Back in England he slew COLBRONDE, and then the DUN COW. After these achievements he became a hermit near Warwick and daily begged bread of his wife at his own castle gate. On his death-bed he sent her a ring, by which she recognized her lord, and she went to close his dying eyes. The story is told in the *Legend of Sir Guy* in PERCY'S RELIQUES.

Guy's Hospital. Founded in 1721 by Thomas Guy (*c*. 1645–1724), bookseller and philanthropist. He amassed an immense fortune in 1720 by speculations in South Sea Stock (*see* SOUTH SEA BUBBLE) and gave £238,295 to found and endow the hospital which is situated in SOUTHWARK.

Gwyn, Eleanor, or **Nell** (1651–1687). Popular actress and mistress of Charles II. She first became known when selling oranges at the Theatre Royal, DRURY LANE, and in 1665 appeared as Clydaria in Dryden's *Indian Emperor*. An illiterate child of the back streets, she was lively and infectious company. She had two sons by the king, the elder becoming Duke of St. Albans, and the younger James, Lord Beauclerk. She finally left the stage in 1682, and on his death-bed Charles said to his brother James, "Let not poor Nelly starve." James II fulfilled the request. She was buried in St. Martin-in-the-Fields and the funeral sermon was given by Thomas Tenison, later Archbishop of Canterbury.

Gyges (gī' jēz). A king of Lydia of the 7th century B.C., who founded a new dynasty, warred against Asurbanipal of Assyria, and is memorable in legend for his ring and for his prodigious wealth.

According to PLATO, Gyges went down into a chasm in the earth, where he found a brazen horse; opening the sides of the animal, he found the carcass of a man, from whose finger he drew a brazen ring which rendered him invisible.

It was by the aid of the ring that Gyges obtained possession of the wife of CANDAULES and through her, of his kingdom.

Gymnosophists (jim nos' o fists). A sect of ancient Hindu philosophers who went about with naked feet and almost without clothing. They lived in woods, subsisted on roots, and never married. They believed in the TRANSMIGRATION OF SOULS. (Gr. *gumnos*, naked; *sophistes*, sage.)

Gyp (jip). **To give a person gyp.** To give him a rough time, to make him suffer, as, "I'll give him gyp", "This tooth is giving me gyp", etc. An expression of unknown origin.

Gypsy, or **Gipsy.** A dark-skinned nomadic people which first appeared in England in the 16th century, called *Romanies* by George Borrow from their native name Rom (Fem. *Romni*). Their language is called *Romani*. Originally of low-caste Indian origin, they migrated to Persia and thence to Europe, reaching Germany and France in the 15th century. As they were first thought to have come from Egypt they were called *Egyptians*, which became corrupted to *Gyptians*, and so to the present form. The largest group of European Gypsies is *Atzigan*. In Turkey and Greece this became *Tshingian*, in the Balkans and Rumania *Tsigan*, in Hungary *Czigany*, in Germany *Zigeuner*, in Italy *Zingaro*, in Portugal *Cigano*, and in Spain *Zincalo*. The original name is said to mean "dark man". *See also* BOHEMIAN; ZINGARI.

Under the NAZIS they suffered the same fate as the Jews and large numbers were exterminated. Gypsies have an old reputation as smiths, tinkers, horse-dealers, fortune-tellers, and musicians. They practise a wide variety of crafts in many countries.

> That the Egyptians and Chaldean strangers,
> Known by the name of Gipsies, shall henceforth
> Be banished from the realm, as vagabonds.
> LONGFELLOW: *The Spanish Student*, III, ii.

Gyromancy. A kind of DIVINATION performed by walking round in a circle or ring until one fell from dizziness, the direction of the fall being of significance. (Gr. *guros*, ring; *manteia*, divination.)

Gytrash. A north of England spirit, which in the form of horse, mule, or large dog, haunts solitary ways, and sometimes comes upon belated travellers.

> I remember certain of Bessie's tales, wherein figured a ... spirit called a
>
> Gytrash.
> CHARLOTTE BRONTË: *Jane Eyre*, ch. xii.

H

H. The form of our capital **H** is through the Roman and Greek directly from the Phœnician (Semitic) letter *Heth* or *Cheth*, which, having two crossbars instead of one, represented a fence. The corresponding Egyptian HIEROGLYPH was a sieve, and the Anglo-Saxon RUNE is called hægl, hail.

Habeas Corpus (hā′ bē ås kôr′ pùs) (Lat. have the body). The name given to a prerogative writ (from the opening words) to one who detains a person in custody ordering him to produce or "have the body" of the accused before the Court. Various forms of this writ developed from the 13th century, and by Charles I's reign such writs were the established means of testing illegal imprisonment. The freedom of the subject from wrongful imprisonment was formally established by the *Habeas Corpus Act* of 1679 and the *Habeas Corpus Act* of 1816 provided for the issue of such writs in vacation as well as in term. By an Act of 1862 the writ of *Habeas Corpus* runs in all dominions of the Crown excepting such dominions where there is a court having authority to issue such a writ. An Irish *Habeas Corpus Act* was passed in 1782. In Scotland its place is taken by the *Wrongous Imprisonment Act* of 1701.

The *Habeas Corpus Act* has been suspended in times of political and social disturbance and its importance is that it prevents people being imprisoned on mere suspicion or left in prison an indefinite time without trial.

Habit is Second Nature. The wise saw of DIOGENES.

French: *L'habitude est une seconde nature.*

Latin: *Usus est optimus magister.*

SHAKESPEARE (*Hamlet*, III, iv) says: "Use almost can change the stamp of nature."

Habsburg, or **Hapsburg.** The name of the famous dynasty which ruled in Austria, Hungary, Bohemia, Spain, etc., is a contraction of *Habichts-burg* (Hawk's Castle). So called from the castle built in the 11th century near the junction of the Aar and the Rhine, in present-day Switzerland, by Werner, Bishop of Strassburg, whose nephew, Werner, was the first to assume the title of "Count of Hapsburg." *See* EMPEROR.

Habsburg Lip. *See* AUSTRIAN LIP.

Hack. Short for HACKNEY, a horse let out for hire; hence, one whose services are for hire, especially a literary drudge, compiler, furbisher-up of other men's work. *Cp.* GRUB STREET.

Hackney (O. Fr. *Haquenée*, ambling horse). Originally (14th century) the name given to a class of medium-sized horses, distinguishing them from warhorses. They were used for riding, and later the name was applied to a horse let out for hire, whence *hackney carriage*. *Cp.* HACK.

A hackneyed expression. One that is well-worn or over used.

Had it, To have. A colloquial expression widely popularized during World War II and possibly of Australian origin. It is applied to that which "finished with" or "done for". Thus a man seriously wounded was said to "have had it". At Roman gladiatorial combats the spectators cried *hoc habet* or *habet* (he has it, he is hit) when a gladiator was wounded or received his death-wound. It is also applied to one who has missed his chance or opportunity.

Never had it so good. *See under*

NEVER.

Haddock. Traditionally it was in a haddock's mouth that St. PETER found the piece of money, the *stater* or *shekel* (*Matt.* xvii, 27), and the two marks on the fish's neck are said to be impressions of the finger and thumb of the apostle. Haddocks, however, cannot live in the fresh water of the Lake of Gennesaret. *Cp.* JOHN DORY.

Hades (hā' dēz). In HOMER, the name of the god (PLUTO) who reigns over the dead; but in later classical mythology the abode of the departed spirits, a place of gloom but not necessarily a place of punishment and torture. As the state or abode of the dead it corresponds to the Heb. *Sheol*, a word which, in the Authorized Version of the BIBLE, has frequently been translated by the misleading HELL. Hence *Hades* is often used as a EUPHEMISM for Hell. *Cp.* INFERNO.

Hadith (hā'dith) (Arab., a saying or tradition). A 10th-century compilation by the Moslem jurists Moshin and Bokhari of the traditional sayings and doings of MOHAMMED. It forms a supplement to the KORAN, as the TALMUD does to the Jewish Scriptures. Originally the Hadith was not allowed to be committed to writing, but this became necessary later for its preservation.

Hadj (haj). The pilgrimage to the KAABA which every Mohammedan feels bound to make once at least before death. Those who neglect to do so "might as well die Jews or Christians". These pilgrimages take place in the twelfth month of each year, Dhu'l-Hijja, roughly corresponding to our AUGUST.

Until comparatively recent times none but a MOSLEM could make this pilgrimage except at risk of life, and the Hadj was only performed by Burckhardt, Burton, and a few other travellers in the guise of Moslems.

Hadji (ha' jē). A MOSLEM who has made the HADJ and who is therefore entitled to wear a green turban.

Hadrian's Wall. The Roman wall that runs for 73½ miles between Wallsend-on-Tyne and Bowness on the Solway Firth. It was built between A.D. 122 and 127, after the Emperor Hadrian had inspected the site, to keep back the PICTS. It was 16 ft. high with mile-castles and turrets between the castles. There were 17 forts on the south side and a parallel vallum or ditch (*c.* 10 ft. deep and 30 ft. wide) on the north. It was attacked and overrun in the 2nd and 3rd centuries and ceased to be an effective barrier by the latter part of the 4th century. *Cp.* ANTONINE'S WALL.

Hafiz. Shams-ud-din Mohammed, a 14th-century Persian poet, "the Persian ANACREON". His *ghazels* (*i.e.* songs, odes) tell of love and wine, nightingales, flowers, the instability of all things human, of ALLAH and the PROPHET, etc. He was a professed dervish and his tomb at Shiraz is still the resort of pilgrims. Hafiz is Arabic for one who knows the KORAN and HADITH by heart.

Hag. A witch or sorceress, an ugly old woman.

> How now, you secret, black, and midnight hags?
> SHAKESPEARE: *Macbeth*, IV, i.

Hag-knots. Tangles in the manes of horses and ponies, supposed to be used by witches for stirrups.

Hag's teeth. A seaman's term to express those parts of a matting, etc., which spoil its general uniformity.

Hagarenes (hăg a rēnz). An old name for the Saracens, Arabs, or Moors, who were supposed to be descendants of Hagar, ABRAHAM's bondswoman. *See* ISHMAEL.

Haganah. A clandestine Jewish militia organized in Palestine, when under British mandate, in preparation for the coming struggle for Zionist independence at the end of World War II. It formed the nucleus of the army of Israel which was established as an independent state in 1948.

Haggadah (Heb., narrative). The variety of MIDRASH which contains rabbinical interpretations of the historical and legendary, ethical, parabolic, and speculative parts of the Hebrew Scriptures. The variety devoted to law, practice, and doctrine is called *Halakhah* (rule by which to walk).

Haggis. A traditional Scottish dish (popular on BURNS' NIGHT) made from the heart, lungs, and liver of a sheep or calf chopped up with suet, oatmeal, onions and seasonings, and boiled like a big sausage in a sheep's stomach bag.

It was also an English dish until the 18th century.

Hail. An exclamation of welcome like the Lat. *salve*. It is from the Icel. *heill*, hale, healthy, and represents the O.E. greeting *wes hal* (may you) be in whole (or good) health. Hail (the frozen rain) is O.E. *hagol*. *Cp.* WASSAIL.

Hail fellow well met. One on easy, familiar terms; an intimate acquaintance.

Hail Mary. *See* AVE MARIA.

To hail a ship. To call to those on board.

To hail an omnibus, or **a cab,** etc. To attract the driver's attention in order to board or hire the vehicle.

To hail from. To come from or belong to a place by birth or residence. An expression of nautical origin from the custom of hailing passing ships to ascertain their port of departure.

Within hail. Within calling distance.

Hair. One single tuft is left on the shaven crown of a Moslem for MOHAMMED to grasp hold of when drawing the deceased to PARADISE.

The scalp-lock on the otherwise bald head of North American Indians is for a conquering enemy to seize when he tears off the scalp.

The ancients believed that till a lock of hair was devoted to PROSERPINE, she refused to release the SOUL from the dying body. When DIDO mounted the funeral pile, she lingered in suffering till JUNO sent IRIS to cut off a lock of her hair; THANATOS did the same for Alcestis when she gave her life for her husband; and in all sacrifices a forelock was first cut off from the head of the victim as an offering to the black queen.

It was an old idea that a person with red hair could not be trusted, from the tradition that JUDAS had red hair. Shakespeare says:

> *Rosalind:* His very hair is of the dissembling colour.
> *Celia:* Something browner than Judas's.
> *As You Like It*, III, iv.

See also RED-HAIRED PERSONS.

A man with black hair but a red beard was the worst of all. The old rhyme says:

> A red beard and a black head,
> Catch him with a good trick and take him dead.

BYRON says in *The Prisoner of Chillon:*

> My hair is grey, but not with years,
> Nor grew it white
> In a single night,
> As men's have grown from sudden fears.

It is a well-authenticated fact that this can happen, and has happened. It is said that Ludovico Sforza became grey in a single night; Charles I, also, while he was undergoing trial, and Marie Antoinette grew grey from grief during her imprisonment.

Hair-breadth escape. A very narrow escape from some danger or evil. In measurement, the forth-eighth part of an inch is called a "hair-breadth."

Hair by hair you will pull out the horse's tail. Slow and sure wins the race. Plutarch says that Sertorius, in order to teach his soldiers that "perseverance is irresistible", had two horses brought before them, one old and feeble, the other large and strong. Two men were set to pull at their tails. One of the men, robust and strong, pulled the tail of the weak HORSE with no effect; the other, a contemptible little fellow, plucked out the hairs from the great horse's tail one by one and soon stripped it bare.

The hair of the dog that bit you. The idea that the thing which causes the malady is the best cure or means of relief, as another drink in the morning is considered by some the best answer to a HANGOVER. The allusion is to the old notion that the burnt hair of a DOG is an antidote to its bite. *Simila similibus curantur.*

Keep your hair on! Don't lose your temper, don't get excited. *Keep your wool on* is an alternative form.

To a hair, or **To the turn of a hair.** To a nicety.

To let one's hair down. To behave in a free informal manner; to give free vent to private opinions, etc., among friends. The allusion is to the days when women wore long hair pinned up in various ways over their head for their public appearances, but occasionally "let it down" and let it flow freely in the privacy of their homes.

To make one's hair stand on end. To terrify. Dr. Andrews, once of Beresford Chapel, Walworth, who attended an execution said: "When the executioner put the cords on the criminal's wrists, his hair, though long and lanky, of a weak iron-grey, rose gradually and stood perfectly upright, and so remained for some time, and then fell gradually down again."

To split hairs. To argue over petty points, make fine, cavilling distinctions, quibble over trifles. The French equivalent is *couper les cheveux en quatre*.

To tear one's hair. To show signs of extreme vexation, anxiety, anguish, or grief. Tearing the hair was anciently a sign of mourning.

Without turning a hair. Without indicating any sign of distress or agitation, to be quite unruffled.

Hair-brained. *See* HARE-BRAINED.

Hair shirt. A garment of coarse haircloth (made from horsehair and wool or cotton) worn next to the skin by ascetics and penitents.

Hair-spring. The fine spiral spring in a clock or a watch for regulating the movement of the balance.

Hair Stane. *See* HOARSTONE.

Hair trigger. A trigger that allows the firing mechanism of a rifle or pistol to be operated by a very slight pressure. Invented in the 16th century.

Halakhah. *See* HAGGADAH.

Hal-an-tow. The song and procession at Helston which preceded the FURRY DANCE on Furry Day. Men and maids went into the country in early morning, returning with green boughs and flowers, with twigs in their hats and caps. Led by an elderly person riding a donkey they entered the decorated streets singing the *Morning Song,* the chorus being:

> Hal-an-Tow, jolly rumble -O
> And for to fetch the Summer home, the
>   Summer and the May-O,
> For Summer is acome-O and Winter is
>   agone-O.

Of considerable antiquity, the Hal-an-Tow eventually lapsed but was revived

in 1930. The name is possibly from Cornish *hayl* and *tyow*, which freely rendered would mean "in the moorland and in the town".

Halcyon Days (hăl′ si on). Times of happiness and prosperity. *Halcyon* is the Greek for a kingfisher, compounded of *hals* (the sea) and *kuo* (to brood on). The ancient Sicilians believed that the kingfisher laid its eggs, and incubated them for fourteen days on the surface of the sea, during which period, before the winter SOLSTICE, the waves were always unruffled.

> And wars have that respect for his repose
> As winds for halcyons when they breed
>   at sea.
>> DRYDEN: *Stanzas on Oliver Cromwell,*
>>   xxxvi.

Half. Half and half. A mixture of two liquors in equal quantities, such as PORTER and ALE, old and mild, mild and bitter, etc.

Half an eye. *See under* EYE.

Half a mind. To have half a mind. To be disposed to, to have an inclination towards doing something.

Half cock. To go off at half cock. To act or start unexpectedly, before one is ready; as a gun goes off when the hammer is set at half cock and supposedly secure.

Half is more than the whole. This is what Hesiod said to his brother Perseus, when he wished him to settle a dispute without going to law. He meant, "Half of the estate without the expense of law will be better than the whole estate after the lawyers have had their pickings." The remark, however, has a wide signification. Thus a large estate, to one who cannot keep it up, is impoverishing.

Half-seas over. Well on the way, pretty far gone. Usually applied to a person half drunk.

> Our Friend the Alderman was half Seas
>   over.
>> *Spectator,* No. 616 (5 Nov. 1714).

Half the Battle. *See under* BATTLE.

He is only half-baked. He is raw or soft, *i.e.* of weak mind, a noodle.

My better half. *See under* BETTER.

Not half. Very much; "Rather! I should think so." **Not half bad** means "not at all bad"; pretty good, in fact.

To do a thing by halves. To do it in a SLAPDASH manner, very imperfectly.

To go halves. To share something equally with another.

Half-life. As a scientific term, the time taken for half the atoms of a given amount of radioactive substance to decay. This time may vary from a fraction of a second to millions of years according to the given substance. A knowledge of this process has enabled archaeologists and geologists, etc., to date materials with considerable accuracy.

Half-timer. One engaged in some occupation for only half the usual time; the term formerly applied to a child attending school for half time and working the rest of the day. This practice was terminated by the Education Act passed in 1918.

Half-way House. A fairly common name for an inn situated midway between two towns or villages. It is figuratively used for a compromise or moderate policy.

Half-world. *See* DEMI-MONDE.

Go to Halifax. *See under* GO.

Hall Mark. The official mark stamped on gold and silver articles after they have been assayed, so called because the assaying or testing and stamping was done at the Goldsmiths' Hall. The hall mark includes (1) the standard mark, (2) the assay office, or "hall" mark, (3) the date letter, and sometimes (4) the duty mark. With it is found (5) the maker's mark.

(1) The standard mark. For GOLD, a *crown* in ENGLAND and a *thistle* in SCOTLAND; for 22 and 18 CARAT gold, followed by the number of carats in figures. In IRELAND a *crowned harp* for 22 carat, *three feathers* for 20 carat, and a *unicorn's head* for 18 carat. Lower standards of gold have the number of carats in figures, without the device.

For SILVER, a *lion passant* in England, a *thistle* in Edinburgh, a *thistle* and a *lion rampant* in Glasgow, and a *crowned harp* in Dublin. In 1697 Britannia Standard was introduced enforcing a higher proportion of silver to prevent the melting down of coins. *Britannia* and a *Lion's head erased* replaced the *lion passant* and *leopard*. Britannia Standard or New Sterling was abolished

in 1729 because the alloy was too soft.

(2) The Assay Office mark.

> London—a leopard's head (*see* LEOPARD).
> Sheffield—A York Rose for gold, a crown for silver.
> Edinburgh—a castle.
> Glasgow—the city arms: a tree, a bird, a bell, and a salmon with a ring in its mouth.
> Dublin—Hibernia.

Marks of Assay Offices now closed and dates of closing:

> Chester—three sheaves and sword (1962).
> Exeter—a castle (1883).
> Newcastle—castle over lion (1697).
> York—five lions on a cross (1856).

(3) The date letter. A letter of the alphabet indicates the date of an article. The London Assay Office used 20 letters of the alphabet, Glasgow 26 and most of the others 25. The letter is changed annually and a new type-face is adopted and the shape of the letter's frame is changed. Given the date letter and the Assay Office mark, the date of manufacture may be easily discovered on referring to a table.

(4) The duty mark was introduced in 1784 when a duty was imposed on silver plate. This was abolished in 1890. The mark was that of the head of the reigning sovereign (George III, George IV, William IV, Victoria).

(5) The maker's mark, originally a device, but since 1739 the maker's initials.

(6) Other marks.

> (a) A voluntary silver jubilee mark in 1935 consisting of the crowned heads of George V and Queen Mary.
> (b) A voluntary mark in 1952–1953 and 1953–1954 consisting of the crowned head of Queen Elizabeth II, to commemorate her coronation.

Hall Sunday. The Sunday before SHROVE TUESDAY; the next day is called *Hall Monday* or *Hall Night. Hall* is a contraction of *hallow* meaning holy. *Hall Monday* is also known as *Collop Monday* from the custom of celebrating with a dish of collops.

Hallel (hăl′ el). A Jewish hymn of praise recited at certain festivals, consisting of *Ps.* cxiii to cxviii inclusive, also called the *Egyptian* or *Common Hallel*. The name *Great Hallel* is given to *Ps.* cxxvi and sometimes to *Ps.* cxx-cxxxvi, thus including the GRADUAL PSALMS.

Hallelujah is the Heb. *halelu-Jah*, "Praise ye Jehovah". *Alleluia* is one of the several variant spellings.

Hallelujah Lass. In the early days of the SALVATION ARMY, a name given to female members.

Hallelujah Victory. A victory by the Britons in *c.* 429 over the combined Picts and Saxons probably somewhere in the North Midlands. The Britons, many newly baptized, were led by Germanus, Bishop of Auxerre, and when they raised the war-cry "Hallelujah", the Picts and Saxons, seeing themselves surrounded, fled without fighting.

Halloween (hăl ō ēn′). 31 October, which in the old CELTIC calendar was the last day of the year, its night being the time when all the witches and warlocks were abroad. On the introduction of Christianity it was taken over as the Eve of ALL HALLOWS or All Saints.

Hallstatt. The name given to a culture marking the transition between the Bronze and Iron Ages in central and western Europe and the Balkans. It takes its name from Hallstatt in Upper Austria, where between 1846 and 1899 over 2,000 graves were found, the earliest dating from *c.* 900 B.C.. They contained many objects typical of the earliest IRON AGE.

Halo. In Christian art, the same as a NIMBUS. The luminous circle round the SUN or MOON caused by the refraction of light through a mist is called a halo. Figuratively it implies the ideal or saintly glory surrounding a person and is often used derisively, as "you ought to be wearing a halo". It is the Gr. *halo*, originally a circular threshingfloor, then the sun or moon's disc. *Cp.* AUREOLE.

Ham Actor. A ranting, inferior actor. Among the suggested contributory origins of the terms are (1) that in the 19th century, theatrical make-up was removed with ham fat; (2) that one Hamish McCullough (1835–1885), who toured with his troupe in Illinois, was known as "Ham" and his company as "Ham's actors";(3) there was also a popular American minstrel song "The Hamfat Man", about an inept actor; (4) an allusion to the word "amateur"; (5) the tradition that down-at-heel actors had performed *Hamlet* in better days.

Shakespeare's *Hamlet* may well be the original source, since Hamlet in his speech to the players (III, ii) describes the essence of ham acting: to "saw the air too much with your hand", to "tear a passion to tatters" and to "strut and bellow".

Hamadryads. *See* DRYAD.

Haman. To hang as high as Haman. To be well and truly hanged, to be hoist with one's own PETARD. Haman, having gained favour with King Ahasuerus (XERXES) of Persia, was provoked by the Jew Mordecai's refusal to bow before him, and obtained permission to exterminate all Jews in the kingdom. He prepared a gallows fifty cubits high on which to hang Mordecai. Queen Esther, aware of the threat to her former guardian, secured the downfall of Haman, who was hanged on his own gallows. (*Esther*, vii, 9). *Cp.* HARM SET, HARM GET.

Hamet. *See* CID HAMET.

Hamlet. It's Hamlet without the Prince. Said when the person who was to have taken the principal place at some function is absent. SHAKESPEARE's *Hamlet* would lose all its meaning if the part of the Prince were omitted.

Hammer. The Hammer of the Scots. Edward I (1239–1307), nicknamed "Longshanks". The inscription on his tomb in Westminster Abbey reads "*Edwardus Primus Malleus Scotorum hic est*".

Hammer and Sickle. Since 1923, the emblem of the U.S.S.R., symbolic of productive work in the factory and on the land.

Knight of the Hammer. A blacksmith.

Throwing the hammer. An athletic contest involving the throwing of a 16 lb. hammer. The original hammer used was a blacksmith's sledge.

To come, or **sell under the hammer,** or **Gone to the hammer.** Said of goods and property sent for sale by auction; from the rap of the auctioneer's hammer to denote that a lot is sold.

To go at it hammer and tongs. To go at it with might and main, to fight or quarrel vigorously.

To hammer away at anything. To go at it doggedly; to persevere.

To hammer out. To arrive at the final form of a plan or scheme by effort, careful thought, and discussion. A META-PHOR from the blacksmith's shop.

Hampton Court Conference. Discussions held at Hampton Court in 1604 between James I, the BISHOPS, and four PURITAN clergy in the presence of the Council. The bishops would make no concessions of importance and their most valuable decision was to effect a new translation of the BIBLE, which became the Authorized Version of 1611.

Hanaper. *Hanap* was the mediæval name for a goblet or wine-cup, and the *hanaper* (connected with *hamper*) was the wicker-work case that surrounded it. Hence the name was given to any round wicker basket and especially to one kept in the Court of CHANCERY containing documents that had passed the GREAT SEAL. The office was under the charge of the Clerk of the Hanaper until its abolition in 1842.

Hancock. *See* JOHN HANCOCK.

Hand. A symbol of fortitude in Egypt, of fidelity in ROME. Two hands symbolize concord; by a closed hand ZENO represented dialectics and by an open hand eloquence.

In early art, the Deity was frequently represented by a hand extended from the clouds, with rays issuing from the fingers, but generally it was in the act of benediction, *i.e.* two fingers raised.

In card-games the word is used for the game itself, for an individual player (as "a good *hand* at WHIST") or the cards held.

> A saint in heaven would grieve to see such hand
> Cut up by one who will not understand.
> CRABBE: *The Borough.*

Also for style of workmanship, handwriting, etc. ("he is a good *hand* at carpentry", "he writes a good *hand*"). Workmen and sailors are also called

hands.

As a measure of length *a hand* equals 4 inches. Horses are measured up the foreleg to the withers, and their height is expressed in *hands*.

Dead Hand. *See under* DEAD.

Dead Man's hand. *See under* DEAD.

Hand of Glory. *See* GLORY.

The Red Hand, or **Bloody Hand,** in coat armour is the device of ULSTER and is carried as a charge on the coats of arms of English and Irish BARONETS (not on those of SCOTLAND or Nova Scotia). The "bloody hand" is also borne privately by a few families when its presence is generally connected with some traditional tale of blood. *Cp.* BLOODY HAND.

Hand gallop. A slow and easy gallop, in which the horse is kept well IN HAND.

Hand paper. A particular kind of paper well known in the Record Office, and so called from its watermark, which goes back to the early 16th century.

Also a hand-made paper.

A bird in the hand. *See under* BIRD.

A dab hand. One who is adept.

An empty hand is no lure for a hawk. You must not expect to receive anything without giving a return.

A note of hand. A promise to pay made in writing and duly signed.

An old hand at it. One who is experienced at it.

A poor hand. An unskilful one.

All hands. The nautical term for the whole crew.

It is believed on all hands. It is generally or universally believed.

At first, or **second, hand.** As the original (first) purchaser, owner, hearer, or (second) as one deriving, learning, etc., through another party.

At hand. Conveniently near. "Near *at hand*", quite close by.

By hand. Without the aid of machinery or an intermediate agent. A letter "sent by hand" is one delivered by a personal messenger, not sent through the post. But a child "brought up by hand" is one reared on the bottle instead of being breast-fed.

Cap in hand. *See under* CAP.

From hand to hand. From one person to another.

Hand and thigh. An ancient Irish form of inheritance of land by daughters in default of sons was known as *inheritance of hand and thigh*.

Hand in hand. In a friendly fashion; unitedly.

Hand-out. Primarily something handed out or given away, as oranges or buns at a children's party or gifts of food or clothing, etc., to tramps. It is now more commonly used to designate (1) free advertising material, brochures, etc., given to potential customers, (2) a press release by a news service, and (3) a prepared statement to the Press by a government, official body, publicity agent, etc.

Hand over hand. To put one hand above the other, as when climbing a rope or ladder; also to overtake or overhaul rapidly. Sailors when hauling a rope put one hand before the other alternately and rapidly. The French say *main sur main*.

Hands up! The order given by captors when taking prisoners, etc. The hands are to be held high above the head to preclude possibility of resistance, the use of firearms, etc.

He is my right hand. My principal assistant, my best and most trustworthy man.

In hand. Under control, in possession, in progress.

In one's own hands. In one's sole control, ownership, management, responsibility, etc.

Kings have long hands. *See under* KING.

Laying on of hands. In church usage, the imposition of hands is the laying on or touch of a BISHOP's hands in confirmation and ordination.

Among the Romans, a hand laid on the head of a person indicated the right of property, as when someone laid claim to a slave in the presence of the prætor. *Cp.* TO LAY HANDS ON, *below*.

Many hands make light work. An old proverb (given in Ray's *Collection*, 1670) enshrining the wisdom of the division of labour.

The Romans had a similar saying, *Multorum manibus magnum levatur onus*, by the hands of many a great load

is lightened.

My hands are full. I am fully occupied; I have as much work as I can manage.

My hands are tied. I am not free to act.

Offhand. In a casual, unceremonious fashiom, curt, rude; extempore, without premeditation.

Off one's hands. No longer one's responsibility. If something or somebody is **left on one's hands,** one has to take full responsibility.

On the one hand ... on the other hand. Expressions used to introduce contrasting viewpoints, etc., with the meaning of, "from this point of view ... from that point of view".

Out of hand. At once; done with, over.

Also meaning "beyond control", as in "These children are quite out of hand."

The hand that rocks the cradle rules the world. The line is from *The Hand that Rules the World* by the American poet, William Ross Wallace (1819–1881):

> They say that man is mighty,
> He governs land and sea,
> He wields a mighty sceptre
> O'er lesser powers that be;
> But a mightier power and stronger
> Man from his throne has hurled,
> And the hand that rocks the cradle
> Is the hand that rules the world.

To be hand in glove with. To be inseparable companions, of like tastes and affections; thick as thieves; to fit each other like hand and glove.

To ask, or **give the hand of so-and-so.** To ask or give her hand in marriage.

To bear a hand. To come and help.

To bite the hand that feeds you. To wound or upset one on whom you depend; to treat a benefactor cavalierly, as a surly dog snaps at the hand of a person offering food.

To change hands. To pass from one possessor to another.

To come to hand. To be received, to come within reach.

To come to one's hand. To do or perform with ease.

To force one's hand. To make a person reveal his intentions, plans, etc., earlier than intended, as in cardplaying.

To get one's hand in. To familiarize oneself with the task; to begin to take over a task or duty.

To get the upper hand. To obtain mastery.

To give one's hands upon something. To take one's oath on it; to pledge one's honour to keep the promise.

To hand down to posterity. To leave for future generations.

To hand in one's checks or **chips.** To die. A phrase of American origin derived from poker, etc. Checks (counters) were handed in when one had finished or was "cleaned out". Variants are, *to pass in* or *cash one's checks*.

To hand or **hand in** sail. To take in sail, to furl it.

To hand it to someone. To give well-merited credit to someone. A colloquial usage.

To hand round. To pass from one person to another, to distribute.

To have a free hand. To have freedom of action without the need of referring to others for agreement or approval.

To have a hand in the matter. To be associated with; to have a finger in the pie (*see under* FINGER).

To have clean hands. *See under* CLEAN.

To keep one's hand in. To maintain one's skill by practice.

To lay hands on. To apprehend; to lay hold of. *Cp.* LAYING ON OF HANDS, *above*.

To lend a hand. To help, to give assistance.

To live from hand to mouth. Improvidently, without thought for the morrow. The phrase implies the ready consumption of whatever one gets.

To play into someone's hands. To act unwittingly or carelessly, thus giving the advantage to the other party; to do just what will help him and not advance your own cause.

To play one's own hand. To look after NUMBER ONE; to act entirely for self-advantage.

To serve someone hand and foot. To be at someone's beck and call; to be someone's slave.

To shake hands. To greet by giving the hand clasped into your own a shake; to bid farewell.

> Fortune and Antony part here; even here
> Do we shake hands,
>   SHAKESPEARE: *Antony and Cleopatra*,
>   IV, xii.

It is customary to shake hands after settling a quarrel, also to confirm an agreement or a business deal, and before the commencement of a boxing context.

To show one's hand. To reveal one's intentions or resources, as when exposing a hand of cards to an opponent.

To strike hands. To make a contract, to become surety for another. *See Prov.* xvii, 18, and xxii, 26.

To take a hand. To play a part, especially in a game of cards.

To take in hand. To undertake to do something; to take charge of.

To take something off someone's hands. To relieve someone of something troublesome.

To wash one's hands of a thing. To have nothing to do with it after having been concerned in the matter; to abandon it entirely. The allusion is to PILATE's washing his hands at the trial of Jesus.

> When Pilate saw that he could prevail nothing, but that rather a tumult was made, he took water, and washed his hands before the multitude, saying, I am innocent of the blood of this just person: see ye to it.
>   *Matt.* xxvii, 24.

To win hands down. To win easily. A jockey rides with hands down when he is winning comfortably and easily.

With a heavy hand. Oppressively; without sparing.

With a high hand. Arrogantly.

Handfasting. A marriage "on approval", was formerly in vogue on the BORDER. A fair was at one time held in Dumfriesshire, at which a young man was allowed to pick a female companion to live with. If they both liked the arrangement after 12 months they became man and wife. This was called *handfasting* or *handfastening. Cp.* BUNDLING.

This sort of contract was common among the Romans and Jews.

Handiron. *See* ANDIRON.

Handkerchief. With handkerchief in

one hand and sword in the other.
Pretending to be sorry at a calamity, but
prepared to make capital out of it.

Handle. A handle to one's name. Some
title, as "lord", "sir", "doctor", etc.

To fly off the handle. *See under* FLY.

To give a handle to. To give grounds
for suspicion, as "He certainly gave a
handle to the rumour."

Dead Man's Handle. *See under* DEAD.

Handsel (O.E. *handselen*, delivery into
the hand). A gift for luck; earnest-
money; the first money received in a
day. Hence *Handsel Monday*, the first
MONDAY of the year, when small gifts
were given, before *Boxing Day* (*see*
CHRISTMAS BOX) took its place. To
"handsel a sword" is to use it for the first
time; to "handsel a coat", to wear it for
the first time, etc.

**Handsome. Handsome is as handsome
does.** It is one's actions that count, not
merely one's appearances or promises.
The proverb is in Ray's *Collection*, and
is also found in Goldsmith's *The Vicar of
Wakefield* (ch. i).

Handwriting on the wall. The sign of
impending calamity or disaster. The allusion is to the handwriting on Belshazzar's palace wall announcing the loss of
his kingdom (*Dan.* v).

Hang. Hang it all!, I'll be hanged! Exclamations of astonishment or annoyance; mild imprecations. A mincing
form of 'damned".

Hanged, drawn and quartered. *See
under* DRAW.

Hanging Day. *See* FRIDAY.

To get the hang of a thing. To understand the drift or connexion; to acquire
the knack.

**As well be hanged for a sheep as a
lamb.** *See under* SHEEP.

To hang a jury. To reduce them to disagreement so that they fail to bring in a
verdict.

To hang about, or **around.** To loiter,
loaf, wait about.

To hang back. To hesitate to proceed.

To hang by a thread. To be in a very
precarious situation. The allusion is to
the sword of DAMOCLES.

To hang fire. *See under* FIRE.

To hang in the balance. A state of
doubt or suspense with regard to the

outcome of a situation; not knowing on
which side the scales of fate may descend.

To hang on. To cling to; to persevere;
to be dependent on.

To hang on by the eyelids. To maintain one's position only with the greatest
difficulty or by the slightest holds.

To hang on like grim death. To cling
tenaciously, literally or metaphorically;
not to be shaken off, as death persists
having once marked down its victim.

Where do you hang out? Where are
you living or lodging? The phrase may
arise from the old custom of innkeepers,
shopkeepers, tradesmen, etc., hanging a
sign outside their premises.

> "I say old boy, where do you hang out?"
> Mr. Pickwick replied that he was at pre-
> sent suspended at the George and Vul-
> ture.
>
> DICKENS: *Pickwick Papers*, ch. xxx.

In the U.S.A. it implies, "Where do
you pass your spare time?"

Hangdog look. A guilty, shame-faced
look.

Hanging Gardens of Babylon. A
square garden (according to Diodorus
Siculus), 400 ft. each way, rising in a
series of terraces, and provided with
earth to a sufficient depth to accommodate trees of a great size. Water was
lifted from the Euphrates by a screw and
the gardens were irrigated from a reservoir at the top.

These famous gardens were one of the
SEVEN WONDERS OF THE WORLD (*see under* WONDERS) and were said to have
been built by Queen SEMIRAMIS and by
NEBUCHADNEZZAR, to gratify his wife
Amyitis, who felt weary of the flat plains
of Babylon, and longed for something to
remind her of her native Median Hills.
They may have been associated with the
great ziggurat of Babylon.

Hangmen and Executioners. Some
practitioners have achieved a particular
notice, *e.g.*:

BULL (*c.* 1593), the earliest hangman
whose name survives.

GREGORY BRANDON and his son
RICHARD (1640), who executed Charles
I, known as "the two Gregories". *See*
GREGORIAN TREE.

JACK KETCH (1663) executed Lord

Russell and the Duke of Monmouth. His name later became a generic word for a hangman.

EDWARD DENNIS (1780), introduced in Dicken's *Barnaby Rudge*.

WILLIAM MARWOOD (1820–1883), who invented the "long drop".

Hangover. Something remaining from a previous occasion; especially the headache and nausea experienced the "morning after the night before", *i.e.* the morning after an evening of alcoholic overindulgence.

Hanky-panky. Jugglery, underhand dealing. *Cp.* HOCUS POCUS.

Hannah. In World War II, a nickname given to a Wren serving with the Royal Marines, after Hannah Snell, the female MARINE.

Hansard. The printed official report of the proceeding and debates in the British Houses of PARLIAMENT and its standing committees and also those of some of the COMMONWEALTH parliaments.

The name is derived from T.C. Hansard (1776–1833), printer, then publisher, of the unofficial *Parliamentary Debates* begun by William Cobbett in 1803. After 1855 the firm was helped by government grants, until 1890, when the work was undertaken by several successive printers working at a loss. The name "Hansard" was omitted from the title page in 1891 and restored in 1943. Luke Hansard, the father of T.C. Hansard, was the printer of the HOUSE OF COMMONS Journals from 1774 until his death in 1828.

Hanse, or **Hanseatic League.** Originating in the 13th century as an organization of German merchants trading in northern Europe, it became a loose federation of nearly 100 towns by the mid-14th century, headed by Lübeck. It acquired a monopoly of the Baltic trade and dominated the North Sea routes until challenged by English, Dutch, and Scandinavian competitors in the 15th century. The last Diet of the Hanse met in 1669 and only Lübeck, Bremen and Hamburg remained in the League. Its London STEELYARD was sold in 1853 and its Antwerp premises in 1863.

Hanse Towns. Member towns of the HANSEATIC LEAGUE.

Hansel. *See* HANDSEL.

Hänsel and Gretel. The inseparables of the famous fairy story found among the tales of the brothers Grimm. Hänsel was a woodcutter's son and the little girl Gretel was found in the forest. When starvation threatened the household the woodcutter, at his wife's behest, abandoned the children in the forest. Hänsel laid a trail by which they found their way home, but they were subsequently again cast adrift. After several escapes from the machinations of a wicked fairy, Hänsel was at last transformed into a fawn and taken with Gretel to the king's castle, where Hänsel was restored to human form and enabled to marry Gretel. The story forms the basis of Humperdinck's opera (1893) of this name.

Hansom. A light two-wheeled cab, very popular in London before the introduction of taxicabs early in the 20th century. It was invented in 1834 by J. Aloysius Hansom (1803–1882), the architect of Birmingham Town Hall. The original vehicle had two very large wheels with sunk axle trees and a seat for the driver beside the passenger. The size of the wheels was subsequently reduced and the driver placed in a DICKEY at the rear.

Happy. Bomb Happy. A World War II expression to describe one in a state of near hysteria induced by bombing, which often took the form of wild elation of the spirits.

Call no man happy. Properly, "Call no man happy till he dies, he is at best fortunate". It implies that no man can be called happy until his life has ended happily. The saying is attributed by Herodotus (*Histories*, I, 32, to Solon) and is also used by Sophocles (*Œdipus Tyrannus*, 1195) and Aristotle.

Happy as a clam. *See* CLAM.

Happy as Larry. Very happy. An Australian expression. It is suggested that the original Larry may have been Larry Foley (1847–1917), the noted boxer.

Happy (jolly or **merry) as a sandboy.** Very happy or merry. An old-established expression from the days when sand-boys (or men) drove their donkeys through the streets hawking bags of sand, usually obtained from beaches. The sand was used by people for their gardens, by builders and by publicans for sanding their floors. The happiness of sand-boys was due to their habit of indulging in liquor with their takings.

Happy dispatch. See HARA-KIRI.

A happy expression. A well-turned phrase; one especially apt.

Happy Family. In travelling menageries, etc., the name given to an assortment of animals living together peaceably. The phrase is now more usually associated with the children's card game.

Happy-go-lucky. Thoughtless, indifferent, carefree.

Happy hunting ground. The North American Indians' HEAVEN. Figuratively, where one finds happy leisure occupation.

Happy is the country that has no history. The old proverb implies that such a nation avoids the wars, rebellions, etc., that forms so much of human history.

Hapsburg See HABSBURG.

Hara-Kiri (Jap. *Hara*, the belly; *kiri*, to cut). A method of suicide by disembowelling practised by Japanese military and governmental officials, daimios, etc., when in serious disgrace, or when their honour was positively impugned. *Hara-kiri* or *Happy dispatch* was practised from mediæval times but ceased to be obligatory in 1868. The act was performed with due ceremony. A law of 1870 granted the privilege of Hara-Kiri to the SAMURAI, in lieu of the death penalty. It was abolished as an official practice in 1873.

Hard. Hard and fast. Strict, unalterable, fixed. A "hard and fast rule" is one that must be rigidly kept. Originally a nautical phrase, used of a ship run aground.

Hard-bitten. Tough, doggedly stubborn, unyielding. Probably derived from *hard-bitten*, a term used of horses, hard-mouthed and difficult to control.

Hard-boiled. One who is toughened by experience, a person with no illusions or sentimentalities.

Hard by. In close proximity to. *Hard* here means close, pressed close together.

Hard cash. Money; especially actual currency as opposed to cheques or promises—"down on the nail" (*see* ON THE NAIL *under* NAIL); formerly coin as distinguished from banknotes.

Hard currency. Now usually refers to currency of a country which is hard to obtain by another country having an adverse balance of payments with it. The term has also been used to mean metallic money (*see* HARDS AND SOFTS) and to mean currency which is stable and unlikely to depreciate suddenly or change its value.

Hard-headed. Shrewd, intelligent, and businesslike. Not easily bamboozled.

Hard-hearted. Unfeeling, callous, pitiless.

Hard hit. Badly affected, especially by monetary losses.

Hard labour. A punishment of enforced labour additional to that of imprisonment, introduced by statute in 1706. For a long time it consisted of working the treadmill, stone-breaking, oakum picking, etc. Hard labour was abolished by the Criminal Justice Act of 1948.

Hard lines. A hard lot, hard luck. *Lines* here means one's lot or portion marked off as if by a line, "one's lot in life", as, "The lines are fallen unto me in pleasant places: yea, I have a goodly heritage." *Ps.* xvi, 6.

Hard of hearing. Somewhat deaf.

Hard tack. Ship's biscuit; coarse bread.

Hard up. Short of money. Originally a nautical phrase; when a vessel was forced by stress of weather to turn away from the wind the helm was put *hard up* to windward to alter course. So, when a man is "hard up" he has to weather the storm as best he may.

To go hard with. To fare ill with; to result in danger, hardship, etc.

Hardy. Kiss me, Hardy. These famous words, often used facetiously, if somewhat irreverently, were uttered by the dying Lord Nelson when taking leave of his Flag-Captain, Thomas Masterman Hardy, in the moment of victory. Hardy knelt down and kissed his cheek. They were preceded by the request, "Take care of poor Lady Hamilton."

Hare. See BURKE.

Hare. It is unlucky for a hare to cross your path, because witches were said to transform themselves into hares.

According to mediæval "science", the hare was a melancholy animal, and ate wild succory in the hope of curing itself; its flesh was supposed to generate melancholy in any who partook of it.

Another superstition was that hares are sexless, or that they change their sex annually.

Among the Hindus the hare is sacred to the MOON, because, as they affirm, the hare is distinctly visible in the full disc.

First catch your hare. *See under* CATCH.

Hare and Hounds. The name given to a form of cross-country running when one or two runners act as hares and set off in advance scattering a trail of paper; the remainder, the hounds, duly set off in pursuit. It is also a fairly common PUBLIC-HOUSE SIGN.

The Hare and the Tortoise. An allusion to the well-known fable of the race between them, which was won by the tortoise; the moral being, "Slow and steady wins the race."

Mad as a March Hare. Hares are unusually shy and wild in March, which is their rutting season.

> The March Hare will be much the more interesting, and perhaps, as this is May, it won't be raving mad—at least not so mad as it was in March.
> LEWIS CAROLL: *Alice in Wonderland*, ch. vi.

Erasmus in his *Aphorisms* says "Mad as a marsh hare", and adds, "Hares are wilder in marshes from the absence of hedges and cover."

To hold with the hare and run with the hounds, or **To run with the hare and hunt with the hounds.** To play a double game, to try to keep in with both sides.

To kiss the hare's foot. To be late for anything, to be a DAY AFTER THE FAIR. The hare has gone by and left its footprint for you to salute. A similar phrase is *to kiss the post*.

To start a hare. To introduce or raise an irrelevant issue in an argument or discussion. To start a hare in the literal sense is to rouse a hare from its form.

Hare-brained. Giddy, foolhardy, MAD AS A MARCH HARE (*see above*).

Hare-lip. A cleft lip; so called from its resemblance to the upper lip of a hare. It was fabled to be caused at birth by an ELF or malicious FAIRY.

Hare-stone. Another form of HOAR-STONE.

Harikiri. See HARA-KIRI.

Hark back, To. To return to the subject. A call to hounds in fox-hunting, when they have overrun the scent, "Hark, hounds, come back"; so "Hark forrard!", "Hark away!", etc.

Harlem. The main Negro district of New York City, so named by the original Dutch settlers after the town of Haarlem in the Netherlands.

Harlequin (har' le kwin). In British PANTOMIME, a mischievous fellow supposed to be invisible to all eyes but those of his faithful COLUMBINE. His function is to dance through the world and frustrate all the knavish tricks of the CLOWN, who is supposed to be in love with Columbine. He wears a tight-fitting spangled or parti-coloured dress and is usually masked. He derives from Arlecchino, a stock character of Italian comedy (like PANTALOON and SCARAMOUCH), whose name was in origin probably that of a sprite or HOBGOBLIN. One of the demons in Dante is named "Alichino", and another DEVIL of mediæval demonology was "Hennequin".

Harley Street. A street in Marylebone, London, which is generally regarded as the necessary address for leading and fashionable medical specialists.

Harm. Harm set, harm get. Those who lay traps for others get caught themselves.

Harmonia. Harmonia's Necklace. An unlucky possession, something that brings evil to all who possess it. Harmonia was the daughter of MARS and VENUS and she received such a necklace on her marriage to King CADMUS. VULCAN, to avenge the infidelity of her mother, also made the bride a present of a robe dyed in all sorts of crimes which infused wickedness and impiety into all her offspring. *Cp.* NESSUS. Both Harmonia and Cadmus, having suffered many misfortunes, were changed into serpents.

MEDEA, in a fit of jealousy, likewise sent Creusa a wedding robe, which burnt her to death. *Cp.* FATAL GIFTS.

Harmonists. A sect founded in Württemberg by George and Frederick Rapp. They emigrated to western Pennsylvania in 1803 and moved to Indiana, founding New Harmony in 1815. This was sold to Robert Owen in 1824 and they returned to Pennsylvania. They looked forward to the second ADVENT, practised strict economy and self-denial, amassed wealth, and favoured celibacy.

Harness. Out of harness. Not in practice, retired. A horse out of harness is one not at work.

To die in harness. To continue in one's work or occupation till death. The allusion is to a horse working and dying in harness, or to soldiers in armour or harness.

> At least we'll die with harness on our back.
> SHAKESPEARE: *Macbeth*, V, v.

Haro (hă' rō). **Clameur de haro.** To cry out haro to anyone (*haro* being in O.Fr. an exclamation or call for help). This cry is an ancient practice in the Channel Islands, usually as a form of protest against trespass, which must then cease until the matter is settled in court. It dates from the time of the first Duke of Normandy. The cry, *Haro, to my aid, my prince, wrong is being done to me*, was raised in the Guernsey PARLIAMENT in January 1966 by a government employee seeking redress.

Haroun al Raschid (hà roon' ăl răsh' id). CALIPH of Baghdad. *See* ABBASSIDES.

Harp. The cognizance of IRELAND. Traditionally, one of the early Irish kings was named David, and this king took the harp of the Psalmist as his badge. King John, to distinguish his Irish coins from the English, had them marked with a triangle, either in allusion to St. PATRICK'S explanation of the TRINITY, or to signify that he was king of England, Ireland, and France. The harp may have originated from this. Henry VIII was the first to adopt it as the Irish device, and James I placed it in the third quarter of the royal achievement of Great Britain.

To harp forever on the same string. To reiterate, to return continually to one point of argument.

Harpocrates (har pok' rà tēz). The Greek form of the Egyptian Harpa-Khruti (HORUS the child). Represented as a naked boy sucking his finger, the Greeks made him the god of silence and secrecy.

Harpy. In classical mythology, a winged monster with the head and breasts of a woman, very fierce, starved-looking and loathsome, living in an atmosphere of filth and stench and contaminating everything it came near. HOMER mentions but one harpy, Hesiod gives two, and later writers three. Their names, *Aello* (storm), *Celeno* (blackness), and *Ocypete* (rapid), indicate their early association with whirlwinds and storms.

Harry. Bell Harry. The splendid late-15th century central tower of Canterbury Cathedral is so called after the one bell "Harry" contained therein. It replaced the square Norman tower of Lanfranc's day known as the Angel Tower.

Old Harry. A familiar name for the DEVIL; probably from the personal name (*cp.* OLD NICK *under* NICK), but perhaps with some allusion to the word *harry*, meaning to plunder, harass, lay waste, from which comes the old *harrow*, as in the title of the 13th-century MIRACLE PLAY, *The Harrowing of Hell*.

Hart. In Christian art, the emblem of solitude and purity of life. It was the attribute of St. HUBERT, St. JULIAN, and St. Eustace. It was also the type of piety and religious aspiration (*Ps.* xlii, 1). *Cp.* HIND.

Hart Royal. A male red deer, when the crown of the antler has made its appearance, and the creature has been hunted by a king.

The White Hart, or **Hind,** with a golden chain in PUBLIC-HOUSE SIGNS, is the badge of Richard II, which was worn by his adherents. It was adopted by his mother, Joan of Kent, whose cognizance it was.

Harum Scarum. Giddy, HARE-BRAINED; or a person so constituted. From the old *hare*, to harass, and scare; perhaps with the additional allusion to the madness of a March hare (*see under* HARE).

Haruspex (pl. *haruspices*). A Roman official of Etruscan origins who interpreted the will of the gods by inspecting the entrails of animals offered in sacrifice (O. Lat. *haruga*, a victim; *specio*, I inspect). Cato said, "I wonder how one haruspex can keep from laughing when he sees another." *Cp.* AUSPICES. *See* DIVINATION.

Harvest Home. In former days the bringing in of the last load of the corn of the harvest with the harvesters singing the Harvest Home song; or the supper provided by the farmer followed by a general jollification. It is also a common PUBLIC-HOUSE SIGN.

Harvest Moon. The full moon nearest the autumnal equinox, which rises for several days at about the same time (nearly sunset) giving a longer proportion of moonlit evenings than usual.

Harvest Thanksgiving. On 1 October 1843, the Rev. R.S. Hawker, Vicar of Morwenstow in Cornwall, set aside that Sunday in order to thank God for the harvest. The popular CHURCH OF ENGLAND festival largely derives from this; the practice became widespread and nowadays churches are decorated with corn, fruit, vegetables and produce of all kinds, especially in country parishes. Hawker also reverted to the offering of the LAMMAS DAY bread at the EUCHARIST. *See* HARVEST HOME.

Hash. A mess, a muddle; as "a pretty hash he made of it". An allusion to the dish of re-cooked mixed-up meat and potatoes, etc. It is also the name given to the compacted resin of the cannabis plant, often mixed with molasses: an abbreviation of hashish. *Cp.* GRASS.

I'll soon settle his hash for him. I will soon deal with him; ruin his schemes; "cook his goose"; "put my finger in his pie" (*see* FINGER); "make mincemeat of him" (*see* MINCE). Our slang is full of such phrases. *See* COOKING.

> About earls as goes mad in their castles
> And females what settles their hash.
> G.R. SIMS: *The Dagonet Ballads.*

Hasideans (Heb. *Chasidim*, the pious). The forerunners of the PHARISEES. A religious party in Palestine, who, in the 2nd century B.C., sought to maintain strick adherence to the Hebrew law and Mosaism against Greek influences.

Hasmonæn. The family afterwards known as the MACCABEES.

Hassan-ben-Sabah, or **Hassan-ibn-Sabah.** The OLD MAN OF THE MOUNTAIN (*see under* MOUNTAIN), founder of the sect of the ASSASSINS.

Hat. A cockle hat. *See* COCKLE.

A white hat. A white hat used to be emblematical of RADICAL proclivities because the radical, Orator Hunt (1773–1835), wore one at the time of the Wellington administration.

Hats and Caps. In the 18th century two political factions in the Swedish Rikstag. The Hats (*Hattar*) favoured war with Russia to regain the provinces (Livonia, Esthonia, Ingria, and part of Karelia) surrendered by the Peace of Nystad (1721). The Caps (*Mussorna*) were the peace party, who were nicknamed the "Nightcaps" by their opponents because they were averse to action and war. The Hats were so named from their three-cornered officer's hats and controlled Sweden until the 1760s.

As black as your hat. Quite black, black being a common colour for hats.

At the drop of a hat. On a signal, immediately, without delay; from the American frontier practice of dropping a hat as a signal for a fight to begin, usually the only formality observed. Races are sometimes started by the downward sweep of a hat.

Hat in hand. *See* CAP IN HAND.

Knocked into a cocked hat. *See* COCKED.

Never wear a brown hat in Friesland. WHEN AT ROME DO AS ROME DOES (*see under* ROME). In Friesland the inhabitants used to cover the head with a knitted cap, a high silk skull-cap, then a metal turban, and over all a huge flaunting bonnet. A traveller once passed through the province with a common brown WIDE-AWAKE, and was hustled, jeered at, and pelted by the boys, because of his unusual attire.

Old hat. Outworn or obsolete. The expression probably arises from the fact that hats tend to date long before they are worn out.

To eat one's hat. Indicative of strong

emphasis. "I'd eat my hat first". "I'd be hanged first".

To hang up one's hat in a house. To make oneself at home; to become one of the family.

To keep something under one's hat. To keep something to oneself, not to divulge it; to keep it under cover.

To pass round the hat. To gather subscriptions into a hat.

To take off one's hat to someone. Figuratively, to express admiration for a person's achievements, etc. From the custom of removing the hat as a mark of deference.

To throw one's hat into the ring. To enter a contest or to become a candidate for office. From the custom of throwing one's hat into the ring as the sign of accepting a pugilist's challenge.

Where did you get that hat? A catchphrase of the early 1890s originating from J. Rolmaz's comic song of 1888, with the refrain:

> Where did you get that hat?
> Where did you get that tile?
> Isn't it a nobby one
> And just the proper style?

You are only fit to wear a steeple-crowned hat. To be burnt as a heretic. The victims of the INQUISITION were always decorated with such headgear.

You are talking through your hat. You are talking nonsense; what you say is rubbish; you don't know what you are talking about.

Hat-trick. In CRICKET, the taking of three wickets with three successive balls. A bowler who did this used to be entitled to a new hat at the expense of the club. The phrase is now also applied to a variety of thrice repeated successes or achievements.

Hatches. Batten down the hatches. Figuratively, to make oneself secure, to shut out the weather, etc., as the *hatches* of a ship are secured for sea by battens and wedges.

Hatches, Matches and Dispatches. A long established colloquialism for births, marriages and deaths.

Under hatches. Down in the world, depressed; under arrest; dead. The hatches of a ship are the coverings over the hatchways and to be *under hatches*

is to be below deck—with various implications.

These lines were inscribed on Dibdin's tombstone at St. Martin-in-the Fields.

Hatchet. To bury the hatchet. *See* BURY.

To throw the hatchet. To exaggerate heavily, to tell falsehoods. In allusion to an ancient game where hatchets were thrown at a mark. *Cp.* TO DRAW THE LONGBOW *under* BOW.

Hatter. In Australia, a lone dweller in the OUTBACK. Possibly from association with the phrase MAD AS A HATTER (*see under* MAD).

Hatto. A 10th-century archbishop of Mainz, a noted statesman and counsellor of Otto the Great, who, according to some, was noted for his oppression of the poor. In time of famine, that there might be more for the rich, he was supposed to have assembled the poor in a barn and burnt them to death, saying: "They are like mice, only good to devour the corn." Presently an army of mice came against the archbishop, who removed to a tower on the Rhine to escape the plague, but the mice followed in their thousands and devoured him. The tower is still called the MOUSE TOWER. Southey has a ballad on Bishop Hatto.

Many similar legends, or versions of the same legend, are told of the mediæval Rhineland:

Count Graaf raised a tower in the midst of the Rhine, and if any boat attempted to avoid payment of toll, the warders shot the crew with crossbows. In a famine year the count profiteered greatly by cornering wheat, but the tower was invaded by hungry rats who worried the old baron to death and then devoured him.

Widerolf, bishop of Strassburg (in 997), was devoured by mice because he suppressed the convent of Seltzen, on the Rhine.

Bishop Adolf of Cologne was devoured by mice or rats in 1112.

Freiherr von Güttingen collected the poor in a great barn and burnt them to death. He was pursued to his castle of Güttingen by rats and mice who ate him clean to the bones. His castle then sank to the bottom of the lake "where it may still be seen". *Cp.* PIED PIPER OF HAME-LIN.

Haussmannization. The demolition of buildings, whole districts, etc., and the construction on the site of new streets and cities; after Baron Haussman (1809–1891) who remodelled PARIS between 1835 and 1870. By 1868 he had saddled Paris with a debt of £34 million and was dismissed from his office of Prefect of the Seine in 1870.

Havelock (hăv' lok). A white cloth covering for a soldier's cap with a flap hanging down, worn in hot climates to protect the back of the neck from the sun. So called after General Sir Henry Havelock (1795–1857), who effected the first relief of Lucknow (1857) during the INDIAN MUTINY.

Havelock the Dane. A hero of mediæval romance, the orphan son of Birkabegn, King of Denmark. He was cast adrift on the sea through the treachery of his guardians and the raft bore him to the Lincolnshire coast. He was rescued by a fisherman called GRIM and brought up as his son. He eventually became King of Denmark and of part of England; Grim was suitably rewarded and with the money built Grim's town or Grimsby.

Haver-cakes. Oaten cakes (Icel. *hafr*; Ger. *hafer*, oat).

Haversack (Ger. *hafersack*, oat sack). Originally a bag to carry oats to feed a horse. Hence any small bag for rations, etc., slung over the shoulder.

Havock. An old military command to massacre without quarter. This cry was forbidden in the ninth year of Richard II's reign on pain of death. In a 14th-century tract entitled *The Office of the Constable and Mareschall in the Tyme of Werre* (contained in the *Black Book of the Admiralty*), one of the chapters is, "The peyne of hym that crieth havock, and of them that followeth him"—*Item si quis inventus fuerit qui clamorem inceperit qui vocatur havok.*

> Cry Havoc, and let slip the dogs of war.
> SHAKESPEARE: *Julius Cæsar*, III, i.

Hawcubites. Street bullies in the reign of Queen Anne who molested and ill-treated the old watermen, women, and children who chanced to be in the streets after sunset. The succession of these London pests after the RESTORATION was: The Muns, the TITYRE TUS, the Hectors, the SCOWERERS, the Nickers, then the Hawcubites (1711–1714), and worst of all the MOHOCKS. The name is probably a combination of Mohawk and JACOBITE. *Cp.* MODS AND ROCKERS.

Haw-haw, Lord. In World War II, the name given (originally by a FLEET STREET journalist, Jonah Barrington of the *Daily Express*, in allusion to his accent) to William Joyce, who broadcast anti-British propaganda in English from Germany. He was hanged for treason in 1946.

Hawk. Falconry, as a sport for kings and gentry, had a tremendous vogue and it retained its popularity until the advent of the shot-gun. The various hawks used in England mostly came from Norway and the chief market was the fair of St. Botolph, Boston, Lincs. Their maintenance was very expensive. In recent times there has been a serious revival of the sport.

The peregrine when full grown is called a *blue-hawk*.

Hawks and Doves. Politically, and generally, the Hawks are those who favour war and resolute military action, the Doves those who support peace or compromise and negotiation. In the U.S.A., the term *Warhawk* came into particular prominence for those agitating for war with Great Britain in 1811–1812.

I know a hawk from a handsaw (*Hamlet*, II, ii). Handsaw is probably a corruption of *hernshaw* (a young heron). I know a hawk from a heron, the bird of prey from the game flown at; I know one thing from another.

Neither hawk nor buzzard. Of doubtful social position—too good for the kitchen, and not good enough for the family; not hawks to be fondled and petted as the "tasselled gentlemen" of the days of falconry, nor yet buzzrds—a dull kind of falcon synonymous with dunce or plebeian. *Cp.* NEITHER FISH, FLESH, NOR GOOD RED HERRING *under*

HERRING.

Hawker's News. "PIPER'S NEWS", news known to all the world. *Un secret de polichinelle*.

Hawse-hole. He has a crept through the hawse-hole, or **hawse-pipe,** or **He has come in at the hawse-hole,** or **hawse-pipe.** A naval phrase meaning entered the service in the lowest grade; he has risen from the ranks. The hawse-hole of a ship is the hole in the bows through which the anchor cable runs.

Hawthorn. The symbol of "Good Hope" in the language of FLOWERS because it shows winter is over and spring is at hand. The Athenian girls used to crown themselves with hawthorn flowers at weddings, and the marriage-torch was made of hawthorn. The Romans considered it a charm against sorcery, and placed leaves of it on the cradles of new-born infants.

The hawthorn was chosen by Henry VII, as his device, because Richard III's crown was recovered from a hawthorn bush at Bosworth. *Haw* here is the O.E. *haga*, hedge. *Cp.* HAYWARD.

Hay. Antic Hay. The hay was an old English country dance (O.E. *haga*, hedge, bush), somewhat of the nature of a reel, with winding movements around other dancers or bushes, etc., when danced in the open.

Hay, Hagh, or **Haugh** (all pron. ha). An enclosed estate; rich pasture-land, especially a royal park; as Bilhagh (*Billahaugh*), Beskwood- or Bestwood-hay, Lindeby-hay, Welley-hay or Wel-hay.

Hay. In the following phrases hay (O.E. *hieg*) is the cut, dried grass used as fodder.

Between hay and grass. Too late for one and too soon for the other.

Neither hay nor grass. That awkward stage when a youth is neither boy nor man.

To look for a needle in a bottle of hay, or **in a haystack.** *See under* BOTTLE.

To make hay of something. To disorganize and throw things into confusion and disorder. Before the days of the hay-baler, hay was tossed around with a pitchfork before being gathered in.

To make hay while the sun shines. To strike while the iron is hot; to take advantage of the opportunity. *Cp.* TAKE TIME BY THE FORELOCK *under* TIME.

Haybote. The right of a tenant of an estate to take wood for repairing hedges and fences. Other estovers are HOUSE-BOTE and PLOUGHBOTE.

Hayseed. An American term for a rustic, a countryman.

Hayward (O.E. *haege, haga*, hedge; *weard*, keeper). A manorial and village officer whose duty it was to look after the hedges and boundaries and to impound straying livestock. He sometimes regulated the use of the common. *Cp.* HAWTHORN.

> Other haue an horne and be hawarde and liggen oute a nyghtes
> And kepe my corn in my croft fro pykers and theeves.
> *Piers Plowman (Text C),* vi, 16.

Haywire. To go haywire is to run riot, to behave in an uncontrolled manner. This American phrase probably arises from the difficulty of handling the coils of wire used for binding bundles of hay, which easily became entangled and unmanageable if handled unskilfully.

Hazazel. The scapegoat. *See* AZAZEL.

Haze. To bully, to punish by hard work. A nautical expression.

> Every shifting of the studding-sails was only to "haze" the crew.
> R.H. DANA: *Two Years Before the Mast* (1840), ch. viii.

In the U.S.A., to subject to horseplay or punishment in school or fraternity initiations.

He Bible. *See* BIBLE, SOME SPECIALLY NAMED EDITIONS.

Head. Cattle are counted by the *head*; labourers by *hands*, as "How many hands do you employ?"; soldiers once by their *arms*, as "so many rifles, bayonets, etc."; guests at dinner by the *cover*, "covers for ten", etc.

People are sometimes counted by *heads* as when a caterer undertakes to provide for a party at so much *a head*. *See also* SPEAKING HEADS *under* SPEAKING.

Better be the head of an ass than the tail of a horse. Better the foremost amongst commoners than the lowest of the aristocracy; "better to reign in hell than serve in Heav'n" (Milton: *Paradise Lost*, I, 263).

Get your head shaved. You are a dotard. Go and get your head shaved like other lunatics.

Head and shoulders. A phrase of sundry shades of meaning. Thus "head and shoulders taller" means considerably taller; "to turn one out head and shoulders" means to drive one out forcibly.

Heads I win, tails you lose. Descriptive of a one-sided arrangement. *See* HEADS OR TAILS *below*.

Heads or tails. Guess whether the coin spun will come down with head-side uppermost or not. The word *tail* includes all the various devices appearing on the reverse of a coin. The Romans said "Heads or ships".

He has a head on his shoulders. He is a clever fellow, he has got brains.

He has quite lost his head. He is so excited and confused that he does not know the right thing to do.

He has quite turned her head. She is so infatuated with him that she is unable to take a reasonable view of the situation.

I can make neither head nor tail or it. I cannot understand it at all. I can make nothing of it.

Off one's head. Deranged; delirious; extremely excited.

Over head and ears. *See under* EAR.

To bite a person's head off. A scathing or irritable answer to a mild remark or request.

To bury one's head in the sand. To shirk facing realities. Ostriches were popularly reputed to hide their head in the sand when pursued, and by thus not seeing their enemy believe that they themselves were not seen.

To come to a head. To reach a crisis. The allusion is to the ripening, or coming to a head, of a boil, ulcer, etc.

To eat its head off. *See under* EAT.

To give someone his head. To allow him complete freedom, let him go just as he pleases. A phrase from horse management.

To head off. To intercept; get ahead of and force to turn back.

To hit the nail on the head. To guess

aright; to arrive at the exact conclusion. The allusion is obvious. The French say, *Voux avez frappé au but* (You have hit the mark); the Italians, *Avete dato in brocca* (You have hit the pitcher), alluding to a game where a pitcher took the place of AUNT SALLY. The Lat. *rem acu tetigisti* (You have touched the thing with a needle), refers to the custom of probing sores.

To keep one's head. To remain calm in an emergency; to keep one's wits about one. *Not to lose one's head* is another way of saying the same thing.

To keep one's head above water. To avoid insolvency; to avoid being overwhelmed by one's tasks or commitments. The derivation is obvious.

To go to one's head. To be unduly influenced, to become conceited, etc., as a result of success, praise, etc. A figure based on the heady effect of intoxicating drinks.

To make head, or **headway.** To get on, to struggle effectually against something, as a ship makes headway against a tide or current.

To run one's head against a brick, or **stone wall.** To make fruitless attempts against insuperable difficulties.

To take it into one's head. To conceive a notion.

To talk a person's head off. To weary a person with so much talking that he is mentally benumbed; to talk incessantly.

Heal. To heal the breach. To effect a reconciliation.

Health. Drinking Healths. This custom, of immemorial antiquity, William of Malmesbury says, took its rise from the death of young Edward the Martyr (978), who was traitorously stabbed in the back while drinking a horn of wine presented by his mother Ælfthryth. (*See also* GABBARA.)

The Greeks handed the cup to the person toasted and said, "This to thee." Our holding out the wineglass is a relic of this Greek custom.

The Romans in drinking the health of a mistress used to drink a bumper to each letter of her name. Samuel Butler (*Hudibras*, II, i) satirizes this custom in the line, "And spell names over beerglasses." In Plautus (*Stich*. V, iv) we read of a man drinking to his mistress with these words: *Bene vos, bene nos, bene te, bene me, bene nostram etiam Stephanium* (Here's to you, here's to us all, here's to thee, here's to me, here's to our dear—) Martial, Ovid, HORACE, etc. refer to the same custom.

The Saxons were great health-drinkers, and Geoffrey of Monmouth (*Historia Britonum*, Bk. VI, xii) says that Hengist invited King Vortigern to a banquet to see his new levies. After the banquet, Rowena, Hengist's beautiful daughter, entered with a gold cup full of wine, and curtseying said to him "*Lauerd king wacht heil!*" (Lord King, your health). The king then drank and replied, "Drinc heil" (Here's to you). *See* WASSAIL.

Heap. Struck all of a heap. Struck with astonishment.

Hear, hear! An exclamation approving what a speaker says. Originally disapproval was marked by humming; those supporting the speaker protested by saying "Hear him", which eventually became "Hear, hear!"

Heart. In Christian art the heart is an attribute of St. TERESA of Avila.

The flaming heart is a symbol of charity, and an attribute of St. AUGUSTINE, denoting the fervency of his devotion. The heart of the Saviour is sometimes so represented.

Heart of Midlothian. The old TOL-BOOTH of Edinburgh. This old prison was demolished in 1817.

> "Then the tolbooth of Edinburgh is called the Heart of Midlothian?" said I. "So termed and reputed. I assure you." SCOTT: *Heart of Midlothian*, ch. i.

Heart of Oak. This famous sea song and naval march is from Garrick's pantomime, *Harlequin's Invasion*, with music by Dr. Boyce. It was written in 1759, "the year of victories" (Quiberon Bay, Quebec, Minden), hence the allusion to "this wonderful year" in the opening lines. "Heart of Oak" refers, of course, to the timber from which the ships were built.

> Come, cheer up my lads! 'tis to glory we steer,
> To add something more to this wonderful year.

The Immaculate Heart of Mary. In the ROMAN CATHOLIC CHURCH, devotion to the heart of Mary is a special form of devotion to Our Lady which developed from the 17th century. In 1947 Pius XII recognized 22 August as the Feast of the Immaculate Heart of Mary.

The Sacred Heart. In the ROMAN CATHOLIC CHURCH, devotion to the Sacred Heart of Jesus, essentially directed at the Saviour himself. It originated from a vision experienced by a French nun, Marguerite Marie Alacoque (1647–1690). This devotion in France was approved by Clement XIII in 1758 and extended to the whole church in 1856 by Pius IX. The festival is celebrated on the Friday after the Octave of CORPUS CHRISTI. There are various Congregations of the Sacred Heart. *Cp.* IMMACULATE HEART.

A heart to heart talk. A confidential talk in private; generally one in which good advice is offered, or a warning or reprimand given.

After my own heart. Just what I like; in accordance with my wish.

At heart. At bottom; substantially; in real character.

Be of good heart. Cheer up.

From the bottom of one's heart. Fervently; with absolute sincerity.

His heart is in the right place. He is kind and sympathetic, in spite, perhaps, of appearances.

His heart sank into his boots. In Latin, *Cor illi in genua decidet*. In French *Avoir la peur au ventre*. The last two phrases are very expressive: fear makes the knees shake, and it gives one a stomach-ache; but the English phrase suggests that his heart or spirits sank as low as possible short of absolutely deserting him.

His heart was in his mouth. That choky feeling in throat which arises from fear, conscious guilt, shyness, etc.

In one's heart of heart. In the innermost, most secure recesses of one's heart.

> Give me that man
> That is not passion's slave, and I will wear him
> In my heart's core, ay in my heart of heart.
> SHAKESPEARE: *Hamlet*, III, ii.

The phrase is often heard of as "heart of hearts", but this is incorrect, as will be seen from SHAKESPEARE's clear reference to the "heart's core". Cp. also:

> Even the very middle of my heart
> Is warmed.
>
> *Cymbeline*, I, vi.

Out of heart. Despondent; without sanguine hope.

Set your heart at rest. Be quite easy about the matter.

Take heart. Be of good courage. At one time moral courage was supposed to reside in the heart, physical courage in the stomach, wisdom in the head, affection in the REINS, melancholy in the BILE, spirit in the blood, etc.

To break one's heart. To waste away or die of disappointment. "Broken-hearted", hopelessly distressed. It is not impossible to die "of a broken heart".

To eat one's heart out. To brood over some trouble to such an extent that one wears oneself out with the worry of it; to suffer from hopeless disappointment in expectations.

To have at heart. To cherish as a great hope or desire; to be earnestly set on.

To learn by heart. By rote, to memorize.

To lose one's heart to. To fall in love with somebody.

To set one's heart upon something. To earnestly desire it.

To take heart of grace. To pluck up courage; not to be disheartened or downhearted when all seems to go against one. This expression may be based on the promise, "My grace is sufficient for thee" (II *Cor.* xii, 9); by this grace St. PAUL says, "When I am weak then am I strong." Take grace into your heart, rely on God's grace for strength.

To take to heart. To feel deeply pained at something which has occurred; to appreciate fully the implications of.

To warm the cockles of one's heart. *See under* COCKLE.

To wear one's heart upon one's sleeve. To expose one's secret thoughts or intentions to general notice.; to show plainly one's feelings. The reference is to the custom of tying one's lady's favour to one's sleeve, and thus exposing

the secret of the heart.

> For I come from Castlepatrick and me heart is on me sleeve,
> But a lady stole it from me on St. Gallowglass's Eve.
>
> G.K. CHESTERTON: *Me Heart*.

With all my heart, or **With my whole heart and soul.** With all the energy and enthusiasm of which I am capable.

With heart and hand. With enthusiastic energy.

Heart-breaker. A flirt. Also a particular kind of curl. A loose ringlet worn over the shoulders, or a curl over the temples.

Heartsease. The *Viola tricolor*. It has a host of fancy names; as the "Butterfly flower", "Kiss me quick", a "Kiss behind the garden gate", "LOVE-IN-IDLENESS", "Pansy", "Three faces under one hood", the "Variegated Violet", "Herba Trinitatis", etc.

Hearth money. *See* CHIMNEY MONEY.

Hearth-penny. An old name for PETER'S PENCE, a tax of one penny on every household.

Heat. One course of a race; that part of a race when the competitors are too numerous to run at the same time.

> Feign'd Zeal, you saw, set out the speedier pace,
> But, the last Heat, Plain Dealing won the Race.
>
> DRYDEN: *Albion and Albanius, Epilogue*.

A dead heat. When two or more competitors in a race cross the line together.

The heat of the day. The hottest part of the day; that part of the day when the heat is oppressive.

To turn the heat on. To subject to a severe cross-examination, to grill.

Heath Robinson, or **Heath Robinsonian,** is a phrase commonly applied to complicated, ingenious, and fantastic contraptions of machinery, etc., after W. Heath Robinson (1872–1944). His amusing drawings of such absurdities in *Punch* and elsewhere were distinctive of their kind.

Heaven (O.E. *heofon*). The word properly denotes the abode of the Deity and His ANGELS—"heaven is my throne" (*Is.* lxvi, 1, and *Matt.* v, 34)—but it is also used in the BIBLE and elsewhere for the air, the upper heights, as "the fowls of heaven", "the dew of heaven", "the clouds of heaven"; "the cities are walled up to heaven" (*Deut*. i, 28); and a tower whose top should "reach unto heaven" (*Gen*. xi, 4); the starry firmament, as "Let there be lights in the firmament of the heaven" (*Gen*. i, 14).

In the PTOLEMAIC SYSTEM, the heavens were the successive spheres surrounding the central earth. *See also* EMPYREAN; PARADISE.

The Seven Heavens (of the Mohammedans).

The first heaven is of pure SILVER, and here the stars, each with its ANGEL warder, are hung out like lamps on golden chains. It is the abode of ADAM and EVE.

The second heaven is of pure GOLD and is the domain of JOHN THE BAPTIST and Jesus.

The third heaven is of PEARL, and is allotted to JOSEPH. Here AZRAEL is stationed, and is forever writing in a large book (the names of the new-born) or blotting names out (those of the newly dead).

The fourth heaven is of white gold, and is Enoch's. Here dwells the angel of Tears, whose height is "500 days' journey", and who sheds ceaseless tears for the sins of man.

The fifth heaven is of silver and is AARON's. Here dwells the Avenging Angel, who presides over elemental fire.

The sixth heaven is composed of ruby and garnet, and is presided over by MOSES. Here dwells the Guardian Angel of heaven and earth, half-snow and half-fire.

The seventh heaven is formed of divine light beyond the power of tongue to describe, and is ruled by ABRAHAM. Each inhabitant is bigger than the whole earth, and has 70,000 heads, each head 70,000 faces and each face 70,000 mouths, each mouth 70,000 tongues and each tongue speaks 70,000 languages, all for ever employed in chanting the praises of the Most High.

To be in the seventh heaven. Supremely happy. The CABBALISTS maintained that there are seven heavens, each rising above the other, the seventh being the abode of God and the highest class of ANGELS.

Heavy. Heavy man. In theatrical parlance, an actor who plays foil to the hero, such as the King in SHAKESPEARE's *Hamlet*, or Iago to Othello.

Heaviest Men.

Robert Earl Hughes (1926–1958) of Illinois, U.S.A., was the heaviest recorded man. His greatest weight was 74 st. 5 lb.

William Campbell (1856–1878), born at Glasgow, was the heaviest man recorded in Great Britain. He attained 53 st. 8 lb.

Daniel Lambert (1770–1809) of Leicester was the previous record-holder at 52 st. 11 lb. He was a keeper at Leicester gaol.

There are others said to have been heavier, but their weights are not verified. *Cp.* DWARF; GIANTS.

Hebe (hē' bi). In Greek mythology, daughter of ZEUS and HERA, goddess of youth, and cup-bearer to the gods. She had the power of restoring youth and vigour to gods and men.

Hecate (hek' à ti). In Greek mythology, daughter of the TITAN Perses and of Asteria, and high in favour with ZEUS. Her powers extended over HEAVEN and HELL, the earth and the sea. She came to combine the attributes of SELENE, ARTEMIS, and PERSEPHONE and to be identified with them. She was represented as a triple goddess sometimes with three heads, one of a horse, one of a dog, and one of a boar; sometimes with three bodies standing back to back. As goddess of the lower world she became the goddess of magic, ghosts and WITCHCRAFT. Her offerings consisted of dogs, honey and black lambs, which were sacrificed to her at crossroads. SHAKESPEARE refers to the triple character of this goddess:

> And we fairies that do run
> By the triple Hecate's team.
> *Midsummer Night's Dream*, V, ii.

Hecatomb (hek' à tom, *or* toom). In ancient Greece, originally the sacrifice of a hundred head of oxen (Gr. *hekatombe*; *hekaton*, a hundred, *bous*, an ox); hence any large sacrifice or large number. Keats speaks of "hecatombs of vows", and Shelley of "hecatombs of broken hearts".

It is said that PYTHAGORAS, who, we know, would never take life, offered up 100 oxen when he discovered that the square of the hypotenuse of a right-angled triangle equals the sum of the squares of the other two sides. *See* DUL-CARNON.

Hector. Eldest son of PRIAM, the noblest and most magnanimous of all the Trojan chieftains in Homer's ILIAD. After holding out for ten years, he was slain by ACHILLES, who lashed him to his chariot, and dragged the dead body in triumph thrice round the walls of TROY.

Somewhat curiously his name has come to be applied to a swaggering bully, and "to hector" means to browbeat, bully, bluster.

You wear Hector's cloak. You are paid in your own coin for trying to deceive another. When Thomas Percy, Earl of Northumberland, was routed in 1569, he hid in the house of Hector Graham of Harlaw, who betrayed him for the reward offered. Fortune never favoured this traitor thereafter, and he eventually died a beggar on the roadside.

Hecuba (hek' ū bà). Second wife of PRIAM and mother of nineteen children, including HECTOR. When TROY was taken she fell to the lot of ULYSSES. She was afterwards metamorphosed into a bitch and finding she could only bark, threw herself into the sea. Her sorrows and misfortunes are featured in numerous Greek tragedies.

Hedge. To hedge, in betting, is to protect oneself against loss by cross bets. It is also to prevaricate.

The word is used attributively for persons of low origin, vagabonds who plied their trade in the open, under or between the hedges, etc.; hence *hedge-priest*, a poor or vagabond parson; *hedge-writer*, a GRUB-STREET author; *hedge-marriage*, a clandestine union, one performed by a hedge-priest; *hedge-born swain*, a person of mean or illegitimate birth (as in Shakespeare's *Henry VI, PT. I*, IV, i); *hedge-school*, a school conducted in the open air, as in IRELAND in former days.

To hedge-hop. An airman's term for flying so low as almost to skim the hedgetops.

Hedgers and Ditchers. In 1911, during the struggle against the PARLIAMENT Bill proposing to curtail the powers of the HOUSE OF LORDS, the Conservative majority in the Lords was split. The "Hedgers" under Lord Landsdowne were prepared to acquiesce rather than risk the creation of enough Liberal peers to ensure the bill's passage. The "Ditchers" led by Lord Halsbury were prepared to to die in the last ditch rather than yield. The Hedgers ("the JUDAS group") prevailed and the bill passed thus formally ending the power of the Lords over Money Bills and limiting that over other legislation to two years. *See* BALFOUR'S POODLE.

Hedonism. The doctrine of Aristippus, that pleasure or happiness is the chief good and end of man (Gr. *hedone*, pleasure). *Cp.* EPICURUS.

Heebie-jeebies. An American slang term descriptive of intense nervousness or JITTERS.

Heel. In American slang a *heel* is a CAD, a despicable fellow with no sense of decency or honour.

The heel of Achilles. *See under* ACHILLES.

Down, or **out at heels.** *See under* DOWN.

To cool, or **kick one's heels.** To be kept waiting a long time, especially after an appointment has been given one.

To lay by the heels. To render powerless. The allusion is to the stocks, in which vagrants and other petty offenders were confined by the ankles.

To show a clean, or **fair pair of heels.** To abscond, run away and get clear.

To take to one's heels. To run off.

Heeled in Western U.S.A. means supplied with all necessities, particularly money and firearms; hence well-heeled. It derives from metal spurs or "heels" fitted to the spurs of fighting cocks.

A heeler is the hanger-on of a political boss.

Heep, Uriah. An abject toady and a malignant hypocrite, making a great play of being "'umble", but in the end falling a victim of his own malice (Dickens: *David Copperfield*).

Hegira (hej' i ra, he jī' ra) (Arab. *hejira*, the departure). The flight of MO-HAMMED from MECCA to Yathrib, 16 July 622, which soon came to be called MEDINA, the City of the Prophet. The Islamic CALENDAR starts from this event.

Heidelberg Man. A type of Prehistoric man found near Heidelberg in 1907, possibly of the genus *Pithecanthropus*. A chinless jaw was found along with other extinct mammal fossils of the Pleistocene period.

Heimdall (hīm' dal). In Scandinavian mythology, a god of light who guards the rainbow bridge, BIFROST. He was the son of the nine daughters of ÆGIR, and in many attributes identical with TIW.

Heimskringla (hīm skring' là) (Orb of the world). An important collection of sixteen sagas on the lives of the early kings of Norway to 1184, the work of Snorri Sturluson (1179–1241). *See* EDDA.

Heir-apparent. The actual heir who will succeed if he outlives the present holder of the crown, title, etc., as distinguished from the *heir-presumptive*, whose succession may be broken by the birth of someone nearer akin, or of a son (who takes priority over daughters) to the holder. Thus the Princess Royal was heir-presumptive to Queen Victoria until the Prince of Wales (the future Edward VII), was born and became heir-apparent. At the death of his predecessor the heir-apparent becomes *heir-at-law*.

Hel. In early Scandinavian mythology the name of the abode of the dead and of its goddess; later, the home of those not slain in battle; slain warriors entered VALHALLA. Hel and her realm eventually acquired more sinister attributes after the advent of Christianity.

Heldenbuch (hel' den buk) (Ger., Book of Heroes). The name given to a collection of 13th-century German epic poetry. The stories are based upon national sagas, DIETRICH OF BERN being a central figure.

Helen. The type of female beauty. In Greek legend, she was the daughter of ZEUS and LEDA, and wife of MENELAUS,

King of Sparta. She eloped with PARIS and thus brought about the siege and destruction of TROY.

Helen's fire. *See* CORPOSANT.

St. Helena. Mother of Constantine the Great (*c.* 250–*c.* 330). She is represented in royal robes, wearing an imperial crown as an empress, sometimes carrying a model of the HOLY SEPULCHRE, sometimes carrying a large cross (*see* IN-VENTION OF THE CROSS *under* CROSS). Sometimes she also bears the three nails by which the Saviour was affixed to the cross. Her day is 18 August.

The island of St. Helena in the South Atlantic was discovered by the Portuguese on 21 May 1502 (St. Helena's Day as observed in the Eastern Church). It was the place of NAPOLEON's exile from 1815 until his death in 1821.

Helicon. The home of the MUSES, a part of PARNASSUS. It contained the fountains of AGANIPPE and HIPPOCRENE, connected by "Helicon's harmonious stream". The name is used allusively of poetic inspiration.

Heliopolis. The City of the Sun, a Greek form of (1) Baalbek, in Syria, and (2) On, in ancient Egypt (to the north-east of Cairo), where the sun was worshipped in the name of Re or RA or Aton.

Helios (Hē' li os). The Greek sun-god, who climbed the vault of HEAVEN in a chariot drawn by snow-white horses to give light, and in the evening descended into the Ocean. He is called HYPERION by HOMER, and in later times, APOLLO.

Heliotrope (Gr., "turn-to-sun"). for the story of the flower *see* CLYTIE.

The bloodstone, a greenish quartz with veins and spots of red, used to be called "heliotrope", the story being that if thrown into water it turned the rays of the sun to blood-colours. This stone also had the power of rendering its bearer invisible.

> Nor hope had they of crevice where to hide,
> Or heliotrope to charm them out of view.
>
> DANTE: *Vision, Hell*, xxiv (*Cary's Translation*).

Hell. The abode of the dead, then traditionally the place of torment or punishment after death (O.E. *hel*, hell, from root *hel-*, hide).

According to the KORAN, Hell has seven portals leading into seven divisions (*Surah* XV, 44).

True Buddhism admits of no Hell properly so called (*cp.* NIRVANA), but certain of the more superstitious Buddhists acknowledge as many as 136 places of punishment after death, where the dead are sent according to their deserts.

Classic authors tell us that the INFERNO is encompassed by five rivers: ACHERON, COCYTUS, STYX, PHLEGETHON, and LETHE. *See also* AVERNUS, GEHENNA, HADES, HEAVEN, PURGATORY, TARTARUS.

Hell and Chancery are always open. There's not much to choose between lawyers and the DEVIL. An old saying.

Hell is paved with good intentions. This occurs as a saying of Dr. Johnson (Boswell's *Life*, entry for 16 April 1775), but it is a good deal older. It is given by George Herbert (*Jacula Prudentum*, 1633) as "Hell is full of good meanings and wishings." The usual form today is, "The road to hell is paved with good intentions."

It was all hell broken loose. Said of a state of riot or disorder.

The road to hell is easy. *Facilis descensus Averno. See* AVERNUS.

The Vicar of Hell. *See* VICAR.

To give someone hell. To make things very unpleasant for someone.

To Hell or Connaught. This phrase arose after the Act for the Settlement of IRELAND, 1652, following the Cromwellian defeat of the Irish insurrection. After September 1653, every Irish CATHOLIC owning property over the annual value of £10, and not guiltless of involvement in the revolt, was to be dispossessed and transplanted to the poorer parts of Connaught. Those remaining had to speak English and rear their children as PROTESTANTS.

To lead apes in hell. *See under* APE.

To ride hell for leather. To ride with the utmost speed, "all out".

To work, play, etc., **like hell.** To do it with all the power at one's disposal, with the utmost vigour.

Hell broth. A magical mixture prepared for evil purposes (SHAKESPEARE:

Macbeth, IV, i).

Hell's Angels. Members of a group of unruly and trouble-making motorcyclists originating in California in the 1950s. Usually wearing leather jackets, their symbol is a winged DEATH'S HEAD.

In due course Hell's Angels appeared in Britain and Europe among devotees of the motor-cycle. Often tatooed and badge bestrewn, they still have a somewhat dubious image.

Hell's Corner. The triangle of Kent about Dover was so called in World War II from its being both under fire from German cross-channel gunnery and the scene of so much of the fiercest air combat during the BATTLE OF BRITAIN, 1940.

Hell Gate. A dangerous passage in the East River between Long Island and New York City. The Dutch settlers called it *Hoellgat* (whirling-gut), which was corrupted into Hell Gate. Flood Island, its most dangerous reef, was removed by mining and blasting in 1885.

Hellenes (hel' ēnz). "This word had in Palestine three different meanings: sometimes it designated the pagans; sometimes the Jews, speaking Greek and dwelling among the pagans; and sometimes proselytes of the gate, that is, men of pagan origin converted to Judaism, but not circumcised (*John* vii, 35, xii, 20; *Acts* xiv, 1, xvii, 4, xviii, 4, xxi, 28)" (Renan: *Life of Jesus*, xiv).

The Greeks were called *Hellenes*, from Hellen, son of DEUCALION AND PYRRHA, their legendary ancestors; the name has descended to the modern Greeks, and their sovereign was not "King of Greece", but "King of the Hellenes". After the abolition of the monarchy in 1973 a "Hellenic Republic" was instituted. The ancient Greeks called their country "Hellas"; it was the Romans who called it "Græcia", which, among the inhabitants themselves, referred only to Epirus.

Hellenic. The common dialect of the Greek writers after the age of ALEXANDER THE GREAT. It was based on the ATTIC.

Hellenistic. The dialect of the Greek language used by the Jews. It was full of Oriental idioms and METAPHORS. The term likewise particularly denotes Greek culture and art modified by foreign and oriental influences after the conquests of ALEXANDER THE GREAT.

Hellenists. Those Jews who used the Greek or Hellenic language; also a Greek scholar.

Hellespont (hel' es pont). The "sea of Helle"; so called because Helle, the sister of Phryxus, was drowned there. She was fleeing with her brother through the air to Colchis on the golden ram to escape from INO, her mother-in-law, who most cruelly oppressed her, but, turning giddy, she fell into the sea. It is the ancient name of the Dardanelles and is celebrated in the legend of HERO AND LEANDER. *See also* GOLDEN FLEECE.

Helmet. The helmet in Heraldry, resting on the chief of the shield, and bearing the crest, indicates rank.

The helmet of Mohammed. MOHAMMED wore a double helmet; the exterior one was called *al-mawashah* (the wreathed garland).

The helmet of Perseus rendered the wearer invisible. This was the "helmet of HADES", which, with winged sandals and magic wallet, he took from certain NYMPHS; but after he had slain MEDUSA he restored them again, and presented the GORGON's head to ATHENE, who placed it in the middle of her ÆGIS.

Heloïse. *See* ABELARD.

Helot. A drunken helot. The Spartans used to make a helot (slave) drunk as an object-lesson to the youths of the evils of intemperance.

Help-ale. *See* BID ALE.

Hemlock (*conium maculatum*). A poisonous biennial plant with umbels of small white flowers found in Britain, Europe and parts of Asia and W. Africa, also naturalized in North and South America. The roots and fruit are especially dangerous. Poisoning by hemlock was used in ancient Greece to kill condemned criminals and evil-doers. *See* SOCRATES.

Helve. To throw the helve after the hatchet. To be reckless, to throw away what remains because your losses have been so great. The allusions is to the fable of the wood-cutter who lost the head of his axe in a river and threw the handle in after it.

Hempe. When hempe is spun England is done. Bacon says he heard the prophecy when he was a child, and he interpreted it thus: Hempe is composed of the initial letters of Henry, Edward, Mary, Philip, and Elizabeth. At the close of the last reign "England was done", for the sovereign no longer styled himself "King of England", but, "King of Great Britain and Ireland". *See* NOTARIKON.

Hempen caudle, collar, etc. A hangman's rope.

Hempen fever. Death on the gallows, the rope being of hemp.

Hempen widow. The widow of a man that has been hanged.

Hen. A hen on a hot griddle. A Scottish phrase descriptive of a restless person.

A whistling maid and a crowing hen is fit for neither God nor men. A whistling maid is a WITCH, who whistles to call up the winds and was supposed to be in league with the DEVIL. The crowing of a hen was supposed to forbode a death. The usual interpretation is that masculine qualities in women are undesirable.

As fussy as a hen with one chick. Over-anxious about small matters; over-particular and fussy. A hen with one chick is for ever clucking it and never leaves it alone.

Hen and chickens. In Christian art this device is emblematical of God's providence. *See also* GREY HEN, *above*.

Hen-pecked. A man who submits to the lectures and nagging of his wife and is domineered by her. *See* CAUDLE LECTURE.

Tappit-hen. *See* TAPPIT.

Hengist and Horsa. The semi-legendary leaders who led the first Saxon war-band to settle in England. They are said to have arrived in KENT in 449 at the invitation of Vortigern, who offered them land on the understanding that they would help against the PICTS. Horsa is said to have been slain at the battle of Aylesford (*c.* 455), and Hengist to have ruled in Kent till his death in 488. The name Horsa is connected with our word *horse* and Hengist is the Ger. *hengst*, a stallion. The traditional badge of Kent is a white horse.

Henry the Navigator (1394–1460). The fourth son of King John I of Portugal. In 1415 he took part in the capture of Ceuta from the Moors and then settled at Sagres, Cape St. Vincent, where he built an observatory and training school for navigation. As a result the Madeiras were discovered in 1418 and systematic exploration of the Guinea coast began in 1430. Cape Verde was rounded in 1446 and the Azores reached in 1448, by which time Prince Henry had aroused a national interest in further exploration.

Hep, or **Hip**. Slang meaning "alive to, aware of, wise to". It is probably from the West African Wolof word *hipi*, meaning "to open one's eyes". *See* HIP-PIE.

Hep-cat. One who is fond of and moved by fast and noisy music. The use of *cat* here denotes "person". In Wolof, *hipi-kat* denotes "one who has opened his eyes".

Hepatoscopy. A very ancient form of DI-VINATION based upon inspection of the liver from the animal sacrificed (Gr. *he-par, hepatos*, liver). It rested on the belief that the liver was the seat of vitality and of the soul.

Hephæstus (hē fes' tus). The Greek VUL-CAN.

Heptameron, The. A collection of Italian and other mediæval stories written by, or ascribed to, Marguerite of Angoulême, Queen of Navarre (1492–1549), and published posthumously in 1558. They were supposed to have been related in seven days (Gr. *hepta*, seven; *hemera*, day). *Cp.* DECAMERON, HEXA-MERON.

Heptarchy (Gr., seven governments). The term is used of the seven English kingdoms of Kent, Sussex, Wessex, Essex, East Anglia, Mercia, and Northumbria during the period of their co-existence, *i.e.* from the 6th to the 8th centuries. This is the period when over-lordship was exercised by a BRETWALDA.

Heptateuch. (Gr. *hepta*, seven; *teuchos*, a tool, book). A name given to the first seven books of the BIBLE, the PENTA-TEUCH plus *Joshua* and *Judges*.

Hera (hē' rà) (Gr. *haireo*, chosen one). The Greek JUNO, the wife of ZEUS.

Herald (O.Fr. *heralt, heraut*). The herald was an officer whose duty it was to proclaim war or peace, carry challenges to battle, and messages between sovereigns, etc. Heralds had their attendants called PURSUIVANTS. Nowadays war or peace is still proclaimed by the heralds, but their chief duty as court functionaries is to superintend state ceremonies such as coronations, installations, etc., and also to grant arms, trace genealogies, attend to matters of precedence, honours, etc.

Edward III appointed two heraldic kings-at-arms for south and north—Surroy and Norroy. The English College of Heralds was incorporated by Richard II in 1483–1484. It consists of three Kings of Arms, six heralds and four Pursuivants, under the EARL MAR-SHAL, an hereditary office in the line of the Dukes of Norfolk.

Garter King of Arms is so called from his special duty to attend at the solemnities of election, investiture, and installation of Knights of the GARTER; he is Principal King of Arms for all England.

In Scotland heraldry is the function of the Lyon office and it consists of the *Lord Lyon King of Arms*, three Heralds (*Albany, Marchmont,* and *Rothesay*), three ordinary Pursuivants (*Unicorn, Carrick, Dingwell* or *Kintyre*) and two Pursuivants Extraordinary (*Linlithgow* and *Falkland*).

Heraldry. Originally a term applied to the science and functions of a HERALD but now more usually restricted to the knowledge or science of armorial bearings, formerly known as ARMORY.

A COAT OF ARMS consists of the *shield*, the HELMET, *crest, mantling* and *supporters*. The motto is not strictly part of the coat of arms or *armorial achievement*.

The *shield* is the main part of the *achievement* and the colours used upon it are *azure* (blue); *gules* (red); *purpure* (purple); *sable* (black); *vert* (green). *Argent* (silver) and *or* (gold) are known as *metals* and the other tinctures are called *furs* (*ermine, ermines, erminois, pean, potent*, and *vair*). The items put on the ground of the shield are called *charges* (*e.g. bends, chevrons, piles, fesses, bars, crosses*, animals, birds, reptiles, and inanimate objects, etc.).

Differencing is the alteration of a coat to distinguish between the various members and branches of a family.

Marshalling is the science of bringing together the arms of several families in one escutcheon.

In heraldry, punning on names and words is called *canting*.

The following are some of the principal terms used in heraldry:

Bars, horizontal bands (more than one) across the middle of the shield.

Bend, a diagonal stripe.

Bordure, an edge of a different colour round the whole shield.

Chevron, a bent stripe, as worn by non-commissioned officers in the army, but the point upwards.

Chief, the upper one-third of the shield divided horizontally.

Cinquefoil, a five-petalled formalized flower.

Couchant, lying down.

Counter-passant, moving in opposite directions.

Couped, cut straight at the stem or neck.

Coward, coué, with tail hanging between the legs.

Displayed (of birds), with wings and talons outspread.

Dormant, sleeping.

Endorse, a very narrow vertical stripe; *see* PALE.

Erased, with nothing below the stem or neck, which ends roughly as opposed to the sharp edge of *couped*.

Fesse, a broad horizontal stripe across the middle of the shield.

File, a horizontal bar from which normally depend one or more smaller bars called *labels*.

Gardant, full-faced.

Hauriant, standing on its tail (of fishes).

Issuant, rising from the stop or bottom of an *ordinary*.

Lodged, reposing (of stags, etc.).

Martlet, a swallow with no feet.

Mullet, a star of a stated number of points.

Naiant, swimming (of fishes).

Nascent, rising out of the middle of an ORDINARY.

Ordinary. A primary charge (*e.g.* bend, pale, fesse, chevron, pile, cross, lozenge, roundel*, etc.).

Pale, a wide vertical stripe down the centre of the shield.

Pallet, a narrow vertical stripe.

Passant, walking, the face in profile (emblematic of resolution).

Passant gardant, walking, with full face (emblematic of resolution and prudence).

Passant regardant, walking and looking behind.

Pile, a narrow triangle.

Rampant, rearing, with face in profile (emblematic of magnanimity).

Rampant gardant, erect on the hind legs, full face (emblematic of prudence).

Rampant regardant, erect on the hind legs, side face looking behind (emblematic of circumspection).

Regardant, looking back (emblematic of circumspection).

Salient, springing (emblematic of valour).

Sejant, seated (emblematic of counsel).

Statant, standing still.

Trippant, running (of stags, etc.).

Volant, flying.

Herb. Herb of Grace. Rue is so called probably because (owing to its extreme bitterness) it is the symbol of repentance.

Herba sacra. The "divine weed", vervain, said by the Romans to cure the bites of all rabid animals, to arrest the progress of venom, to cure the plague, to avert sorcery and WITCHCRAFT, to reconcile enemies, etc. So highly esteemed was it that feasts called *Verbenalia* were annually held in its honour. HERALDS wore a wreath of vervain when they declared war; and the DRUIDS are supposed to have held it in veneration.

Herb Trinity. A popular name for the pansy, *Viola tricolor. See* HEARTSEASE.

Hercules (hĕr' kū lēz). In Greek mythology, a hero of superhuman physical strength, son of ZEUS and ALCMENA. He is represented as brawny, muscular, short-necked, often holding a club and a lion's skin. In a fit of madness inflicted on him by JUNO, he slew his wife and children, and as penance was ordered by

APOLLO to serve for 12 years the Argive king, Eurystheus, who imposed upon him twelve tasks of great difficulty and danger:

(1) To slay the NEMEAN LION.

(2) To kill the Lernean HYDRA.

(3) To catch and retain the Arcadian stag.

(4) To destroy the Erymanthian boar.

(5) To cleanse the AUGEAN STABLES.

(6) To destroy the cannibal birds of the Lake Stymphalis.

(7) To take captive the Cretan bull.

(8) To catch the horses of the Thracian Diomedes.

(9) To get possession of the girdle of HIPPOLYTA, Queen of the Amazons.

(10) To capture the oxen of the monster GERYON.

(11) To obtain the apples of the HESPERIDES.

(12) To bring CERBERUS from the infernal regions.

After these labours and many other adventures he was rewarded with immortality.

Hercules' choice. Immortality, the reward of toil in preference to pleasure. Xenophon tells us that when Hercules was a youth he was accosted by Virtue and Pleasure, and asked to choose between them. Pleasure promised him all carnal delights, but Virtue promised immortality. Hercules gave his hand to the latter, and, after a life of toil, was received amongst the gods.

Hercules' horse. See FAMOUS HORSES under HORSE.

Hercules' Pillars. See under PILLAR.

Herculean knot (hĕr kū lē' ăn). A snaky complication on the rod or CADUCEUS of MERCURY, adopted by Grecian brides as the fastening of their woollen girdles, which only the bridegroom was allowed to untie. As he did so he invoked JUNO to render his marriage as those of Hercules, whose numerous wives all had families, among them being the 50 daughters of Thestius, all of whom conceived in one night. See TRUE LOVER'S KNOT under KNOT.

Heretic. From a Greek word meaning "one who chooses". A heretic is one who holds unorthodox opinions in matters of religion, *i.e.* he chooses his own creed.

Heriot. A feudal kind of death duty. The lord of the manor's right to the best beast or chattel of a deceased VILLEIN. Freemen also owed heriots to their overlords of horses and armour. The word is from the O.E. *here geatu*, military apparel, which was originally on loan to the tenant.

Hermæ. *See* HERMES.

Hermaphrodite (hĕr măf' rō dīt). A person or animal with indeterminate sexual organs, or those of both sexes; a flower containing both male and female reproductive organs. The word is derived from Hermaphroditus, son of HERMES and APHRODITE. The nymph Salmacis became enamoured of him, and prayed that she might be so closely united that "the twain might become one flesh". Her prayer being heard, the NYMPH and boy became one body (Ovid: *Metamorphoses*, IV, 347–88).

According to fable, all persons who bathed in the fountain Salmacis, in Caria, became hermaphrodites.

Hermas. One of the APOSTOLIC FATHERS (2nd century), author of *The Shepherd* which consists of Visions, Commandments, and Similitudes or Parables.

Hermes. The Greek MERCURY, whose busts, known as *Hermæ*, were affixed to pillars and set up as boundary marks at street corners, etc. The Romans also used them for garden ornaments.

Among alchemists, Hermes was the usual name for quicksilver or mercury (*see* Milton: *Paradise Lost*, III, 603).

Hermetic Art, or **Philosophy.** The art or science of ALCHEMY; so called from Hermes Trismegistus (the Thrice Greatest Hermes) the name given by the Neoplatonists to the Egyptian god THOTH, its hypothetical founder.

Hermetic books. Forty-two books fabled to have been written from the dictation of Hermes Trismegistus, dealing with the life and thought of ancient Egypt. They state that the world was made out of fluid; that the SOUL is the union of light and life; that nothing is destructible; that the soul transmigrates, and that suffering is the result of motion.

Hermetic powder. A sympathetic

powder, supposed to possess a healing influence from a distance; so called by mediæval philosophers out of compliment to Hermes Trismegistus (Sir Kenelm Digby: *Discourse Touching the Cure of Wounds by the Powder of Sympathy*, 1658).

Hermetically sealed. Closed securely; from sealing a vessel hermetically, *i.e.* as a chemist, a disciple of Hermes Trismegistus, would, by heating the neck of the vessel till it is soft, and then twisting it till the aperture is closed up.

Peter the Hermit. *See under* PETER.

Herne the Hunter. *See* WILD HUNTSMAN.

Hero. No man is a hero to his valet. An old saying. The idea is found in Plutarch and Montaigne (*Essays*, Bk. III, ii), but Bacon in his essay *Of Honour and Reputation* says, "Discreet followers and servants help much to reputation: '*Omnis fama a domesticis emanat*'." (All fame comes from one's own household.) *Cp. Matt.* xiii, 57, "A prophet is not without honour save in ... his own house."

Hero and Leander. The old Greek tale is that Hero, a priestess of VENUS, fell in love with Leander, who swam across the HELLESPONT every night to visit her. One night he was drowned, and heartbroken Hero drowned herself in the same sea. The story is told in one of the poems of Musæus, and in Marlowe and Chapman's *Hero and Leander*.

Lord Byron and Lieutenant Ekenhead repeated the experiment of Leander in 1810 and accomplished it in 1 hour 10 minutes. The distance, allowing for drifting, would be about four miles.

Heroic age. That age of a nation which comes between the purely mythical period and the historic. This is the age when the sons of the gods were said to take unto themselves the daughters of men, and the offspring partake of the twofold character.

Heroic size in sculpture denotes a stature superior to ordinary life, but not colossal.

Heroic verse. That verse in which epic poetry is generally written. In Greek and Latin it is HEXAMETER verse; in English it is ten-syllable IAMBIC verse, either in rhymes or not; in Italian it is

the ottava rima. So called because it is employed to celebrate heroic exploits.

Herod. To out-herod Herod. To outdo in wickedness, violence, or rant, the worst of tyrants. Herod, who destroyed the babes of Bethlehem (*Matt.* ii., 16), was made (in the old mediæval MYSTERIES) a ranting, roaring tyrant.

Herrenvolk. A German word meaning broadly "master race". In NAZI usage it implied the superiority of the German peoples.

Herring. A shotten herring. One that has shot off or ejected its spawn, and hence is worthless.

Drawing a red herring across the path. Trying to divert attention from the main question by some side issue. A red herring (*i.e.* one dried, smoked, and salted) drawn across a fox's path destroys the scent and sets the hounds at fault.

Neither barrel the better herring. Much of a muchness; not a pin to choose between them; SIX OF ONE AND HALF A DOZEN OF THE OTHER. The herrings of both barrels are so much alike that there is no choice whatever.

Neither fish, flesh, nor good red herring. *See under* FISH.

The Battle of the Herrings (12 February 1429). During the HUNDRED YEARS WAR Sir John Fastolf was conveying provisions to the English besiegers of Orleans and was unsuccessfully attacked by superior French forces seeking to intercept the supplies. The English used the barrels of herrings with which their wagons were loaded, as a defence; hence the name.

Herring-bone (in building). Courses of stone or brick laid angularly, thus: ◄ ◄ ◄ . Also applied to strutting placed between thin joists to increase their strength.

In needlework, an embroidery stitch, or alternatively a kind of cross-stitch used to fasten down heavy material.

The Herring-pond. The ocean or dividing seas, especially the Atlantic which separates America from the British Isles. Also called the "fishpond".

Hershey Bar. In the U.S.A. a Hershey Bar is a famous trade-marked chocolate bar which was only available to the troops in World War II. General L.B. Hershey was Director of the Selective Service System, 1941–1946. Hence in U.S. army slang the term was applied to the narrow gold bar worn by troops on the left sleeve to indicate that they had done six months' overseas service.

Hertha. *See* NERTHUS.

Hesperia (hes pēr' i à) (Gr. western). Italy was so called by the Greeks, because it was to them the "Western Land"; and afterwards the Romans, for a similar reason, transferred the name to Spain.

Hesperides (hes per' i dēz). Three sisters who guarded the golden apples which HERA received as a marriage gift. They were assisted by the dragon LADON. HERCULES, as the eleventh of his "twelve labours", slew the DRAGON and carried some of the apples to Eurystheus.

Many poets call the place where these golden apples grew the "Garden of the Hesperides". SHAKESPEARE (*Love's Labour's Lost*, IV, iii) speaks of "climbing trees in the Hesperides". (*Cp.* Milton's *Comus*, lines 393–7.)

Hesperus (hes' per us). The name given by the Greeks to the planet VENUS as an evening star. As a morning star it was called LUCIFER or *Phosphorus*. *See* HESPERIA.

The Wreck of the Hesperus. An episode made famous by Longfellow's ballad of 1840, formerly widely learnt by schoolchildren. The *Hesperus* was wrecked on Norman's Woe, near Gloucester, Massachusetts, in 1839.

Hesychasts. In the Eastern Church, supporters of the ascetic mysticism propagated by the monks of Mount Athos in the 14th century. Also called *Palamists* after Gregory Palamas (*c.* 1296–1350), who became the chief exponent of Hesychasm. The object of their exercises was to attain a vision of the "Divine Light" which they held to be God's "energy". Hesychasm lasted until the 17th century; the name is from the Gr. *hesychos*, quiet.

Hexameron (Gr). A period of six days, especially the six days of the Creation.

Hexameter. The metre in which Greek and Latin epics were written, and which has been imitated in English in such

poems as Longfellow's *Evangeline*, Clough's *Bothie*, Kingsley's *Andromeda* (probably the best), etc.

The line consists of six feet, dactyls or spondees for the first four, the fifth is almost always a dactyl (but sometimes a spondee), and the sixth a spondee or trochee.

Verse consisting of alternate hexameters and pentameters is known as ELEGIAC. Coleridge illustrates this in his:

> In the hexameter rises the fountain's silvery column;
> In the pentameter aye falling in melody back.
>
> *The Ovidian Elegiac Metre.*

Hexateuch. *See* ELOHISTIC; *cp.* HEPTATEUCH, PENTATEUCH.

Hiawatha. The Iroquois name of a hero of miraculous birth who came (under a variety of names) among the North American Indian tribes to bring peace and goodwill to man.

In Longfellow's poem (1855) he is an Ojibway, son of Mudjekeewis (the west wind) and Wenonah, and married Minnehaha, "Laughing Water". He represents the progress of civilization among his people. When the white man landed and taught the Indians the faith of Jesus, Hiawatha exhorted them to receive the words of wisdom, to reverence the missionaries who had come so far to see them.

Hibernia. The Latin name for IRELAND, a variant of the old CELTIC *Erin*, common in poetic usage.

Hic Jacets. Tombstones, so called from the first two words of the Latin inscription: *Hic Jacet* (Here lies ...)

> And by the cold Hic Jacets of the dead.
> TENNYSON: *Idylls of the King* (*Merlin and Vivien*).

Hickathrift, Tom. A hero of nursery rhyme and mythical strong man, fabled to have been a labourer at the time of the CONQUEST. Armed with an axle-tree and cartwheel he killed a GIANT who dwelt in a marsh at Tilney, Norfolk. He was knighted and made a governor of Thanet. *Cp.* JACK THE GIANT-KILLER.

Hickory. Hickory Mormons. MORMONS of half-hearted persuasions.

Old Hickory. General Andrew Jackson

(1767–1845), President of the United States (1829–1837). He was first called "Tough", from his great powers of endurance, then "Tough as hickory", and lastly, "Old Hickory". *Cp.* STONEWALL JACKSON.

Hicksites. QUAKERS in the U.S.A. who seceded from the main body in 1827 under the leadership of Elias Hicks.

Hide of land. In feudal England the term denoted the amount of land that was sufficient to support a family; usually varying between 60 and 120 acres according to the locality or quality of the land. A hide of good land was smaller than one of poorer quality. It was long used as the basis for assessing taxes. The name may derive from the possibility that the original tribute was payable in hides.

To hide one's light under a bushel. *See* BUSHEL.

Hieroglyphs (hī′ ėr ō glifs). The name applied to the picture characters of ancient Egyptian writing (Gr. *hieros*, sacred; *glyph*, what is carved). For many years these inscribed symbols of beasts and birds, men and women, etc. were indecipherable. Dr. Thomas Young (1773–1829) was the first to decipher part of the demotic text of the ROSETTA STONE in 1819, and prove the alphabetic nature of the signs. This provided a basis for the construction of a complete alphabet (1821–1822) by J.F. Champollion (1790–1832). Since then, our knowledge of ancient Egypt and its customs has been transformed.

High. An all-time high. A record achievement, an expression of American origin.

High and dry. Stranded, left out of the current of events. A nautical metaphor.

High and low. People of all estates and conditions.

High and mighty. Powerful, or more usually, arrogant and overbearing.

High days and holidays. Special occasions, a high day being a festival or great occasion. *See* HOLIDAY.

High falutin'. Oratorical bombast, affected pomposity.

To be on one's high horse. *See under* HORSE.

With a high hand. Arrogantly.

High Church. That section of the CHURCH OF ENGLAND distinguished by its "high" conception of Church authority, upholding sacerdotal claims and asserting the efficacy of the SACRAMENTS. It also stresses the historical links with CATHOLIC Christianity. It has its origins in the reign of Elizabeth I, although the name is of the late 17th century. Archbishop Laud was of this persuasion and High Church opinions were again strengthened and re-established by the OXFORD MOVEMENT. *Cp.* LOW CHURCH *under* LOW.

High German. Official and literary German, derived from the language of *High* or South Germany. Low German is the name applied to all other German dialects, or the language of *Low* or North Germany. *Cp.* LANGUE DO'OC; LANGUE D'OÏL.

High Heels and Low Heels. The names of two factions in Swift's tale of Lilliput (*Gulliver's Travels*), satirizing the HIGH and LOW CHURCH parties.

High places. In the Authorized Version of the BIBLE this is a literal translation of the Heb. *bamah* and applied to the local places of sacrifice where JEHOVAH was worshipped. Such sites were often on a hilltop or mound, which may account for the origin of the name. Because of their association with forms of idolatry, and sometimes immoral rites, they were denounced by Hosea. Hezekiah removed the high places. (II *Kings* xviii, 4), so did Asa (II *Chron.* xiv, 3) and others. *Cp.* HILLS.

High seas. As defined in international law, all the area of sea not under the sovereignty of any state. *Cp.* TERRITORIAL WATERS.

High table. In a college dining-hall, the table at which the dons sit.

High tea. A meal of a substantial character about the usual tea-time which can include fish, meats, pastry, etc. It is common in Scotland and the North of England and in agricultural areas.

High words. Angry words.

High-ball, the American term for whisky, diluted with water, soda-water or ginger ale and served in a tall glass with ice.

High-brow. A learned person, an intellectual. The term originated in the U.S.A. about 1911 and is also used to denote cultural, artistic, and intellectual matters above one's head. Derivatives are *low-brow* and *middle-brow*.

Highbinders. The name given to those rowdies, ruffians, and members of malevolent gangs who troubled New York and other American cities from the early 19th century.

Higher Criticism. Critical inquiry into the literary composition and sources, especially of the BIBLE, also called *historical criticism*. The term is used in contradistinction to textual or verbal criticism which is to establish the correctness of the text.

Highlands, The. That part of SCOTLAND lying north of the line approximately Dumbarton to Stonehaven. Stirling is known as the "gateway to the Highlands"; in the wars between ENGLAND and Scotland, possession of this strong point gave great advantage.

Highland bail. Fists and cuffs; to escape the constable by knocking him down with the aid of a companion.

Highland Mary. The most shadowy of Robert Burns's sweethearts, but the one to whom he addressed some of his finest poetry, including "The Highland Lassie, O", "Highland Mary", "'To Mary in Heaven", and perhaps "Will ye go to the Indies, my Mary?"

She is said to have been a daughter of Archibald Campbell, a Clyde sailor, and to have died young about 1784 or 1786.

Highness. Royal Highness. In Great Britain this title is now confined (since 1917) to the sovereign and his or her Consort, to the children of the sovereign, to grandchildren in the male line, and the eldest son of the eldest son of the PRINCE OF WALES. It was formerly granted to a somewhat wider group of relations.

Hijacker (hī' jāk ėr). A term of American origin denoting a bandit who preys on BOOTLEGGERS, and other criminals; now applied more generally to one who steals goods in transit, particularly lorries loaded with valuable merchandise. The name may derive from the gunman's command to his victom, "Stick 'em up high, Jack," meaning that the arms were to be raised well above the head. *Cp.* SKYJACKER.

Hilary Term. The former legal term, and the university term at Oxford and Trinity College Dublin corresponding to the LENT term elsewhere. It is named in honour of St. Hilary whose day is 13 January (14 January in the R.C. Church), near which day these terms begin.

The Hilary Law Sittings usually begin on 11 January, and end on the Wednesday before EASTER.

Hildebrand (hil' de brand). A celebrated character of German romance whose story is told in *Das Hildebrandslied*, an old German alliterative poem (written *c.* 800), and he also appears in the NIBELUNGENLIED, DIETRICH VON BERN, etc. He is an old man, who returns home after many years among the Huns through following his master Theodoric, only to be challenged to single combat by his own son Hadubrand.

The name is better known as that of the great reforming pope St. Gregory VII (*c.* 1020, 1073–1085) whose attempts to prohibit lay investiture brought Henry IV to CANOSSA and made him many enemies. He did much to remove abuses and to regenerate the Church.

Hildesheim (hil' des hīm). Legend relates that a monk of Hildesheim, an old city of Hanover, doubting how with God a thousand years could be as one day, listened to the singing of a bird in a wood, as he thought for three minutes, but found the time had been three hundred years. Longfellow makes use of the story in his *Golden Legend* (II), calling the monk Felix.

Hill. Hill-billy. An American rustic or countryman of the hilly regions; also applied to the characteristic traditional songs of the hill regions of the southeastern parts of the U.S.A.

Hill folk. So Scott calls the CAMERONIAN Scottish COVENANTERS, who met clandestinely among the hills. Sometimes the Covenanters generally are so called.

In Scandinavian tradition they are a type of being between elves and human beings. The "hill people" were supposed to dwell in caves and small hills.

Hills. Prayers were offered on the tops of high hills, and temples built on "HIGH PLACES", from the notion that the gods could better hear prayer on such places, as they were nearer HEAVEN. It will be remembered that Balak (*Num.* xxiii, xxiv) took BALAAM to the top of Peor and other high places when Balaam wished to consult God. We often read of "idols on every high hill' (*Ezek.* vi, 13).

Old as the hills. Very old indeed.

Hinc illæ lachrimæ (hink il ē lăk' ri mē) (Lat., "hence those tears", Terence: *Andria*, I, i, 99). This was the real offence; this was the true secret of the annoyance; the real source of the vexation.

Hind. Emblematic of St. Giles. *See under* GILES. *Cp.* HART.

The Hind of Sertorius. Sertorius (*c.* 122–72 B.C.), Marian governor of Hispania Citerior was proscribed by Sulla and forced to flee. Later he was invited to return by the Lusitani and held Spain against the Senatorial party until his death through treachery. He had a tame white hind, which he taught to follow him, and from which he pretended to receive the instructions of DIANA. By this artifice, says Plutarch, he imposed on the superstition of the people.

The milk-white hind, in Dryden's *Hind and the Panther,* means the RO-MAN CATHOLIC CHURCH, milk-white because "infallible". The panther, full of the spots of error, is the CHURCH OF ENGLAND.

Hinny. *See* MULE.

Hip. *See* HEP.

Hip. To have one on the hip. To have the mastery over him in a struggle, a term derived from a throw in wrestling.

> Now, infidel, I have thee on the hip.
> SHAKESPEARE: *Merchant of Venice*, IV, i.

To smite hip and thigh. To slay with great carnage. A Biblical phrase.

> An he smote them hip and thigh with a great slaughter.
> *Judges* xv, 8.

Hip! Hip! Hurrah! The old fanciful explanation of the origin of this cry is that hip is a NOTARIKON, composed of the initials *Hierosolyma est perdita*, and that when German knights headed a Jew-hunt in the MIDDLE AGES, they ran shouting "Hip! Hip!" as much as to say "Jerusalem is destroyed."

Hurrah was similarly derived from Slavonic *hu-raj* (to Paradise), so that Hip! Hip! Hurrah! would mean "Jerusalem is lost to the infidel, and we are on the road to Paradise."

Hipped. Melancholy, low-spirited, suffering from a "fit of the blues". *The hip* was formerly a common expression for morbid depression (now superseded by *the pip*); it is an abbreviation of *hypochondria.*

Hippie. A name derived from HEP. Hippies originated in San Francisco in the late 1960s among young people who sought personal freedom and self-expression but with regard for the environment. Their Bohemian lifestyle sometimes included the taking of drugs.

Hippocampus (hip' ō kăm' pús) (Gr. *hippos,* horse; *kampos,* sea monster). A sea-horse, having the head and forequarters resembling those of a horse, with the tail and hindquarters of a fish or dolphin. It was the steed of NEPTUNE.

Hippocras (hip' ō krăs). A cordial of the late MIDDLE AGES and down to Stuart times, made of Lisbon and Canary wines, bruised spices, and sugar; so called from being passed through HIPPO-CRATES' SLEEVE.

Hippocrates (hip ok' rà tēz). A Greek physician (*c.* 460–*c.* 375 B.C.), known as the FATHER of Medicine. He was a member of the famous family of priest-physicians, the Asclepidae, and was an acute and indefatigable observer, practising as both physician and surgeon. More than seventy treatises known as the *Hippocratic Collection* are extant, but their authorship is uncertain. In the MIDDLE AGES he was called "Ypocras" or "Hippocras".

Hippocratean School. The "Dogmatic" school of medicine, founded by HIP-POCRATES. *See* EMPIRICS.

Hippocrates' sleeve. A woollen bag of a square piece of flannel, having the opposite corners joined, so as to make it triangular. Used by apothecaries for straining syrups, decoctions, etc., and anciently by vintners, whence the name of HIPPOCRAS.

Hippocratic Oath. An outstanding

code of medical ethics contained in the *Hippocratic Collection* (*see* HIPPO-CRATES). The oath related particularly to the inviolability of secrecy concerning any communication made by a patient during consultation, and demanded absolute integrity concerning the patient's welfare. It also enjoined members of the profession not to aid a woman to procure an abortion.

Hippocrene (hip' ō krēn) (Gr. *hippos*, horse; *krene*, fountain). The fountain of the MUSES on Mount HELICON, produced by a stroke of the hoof of PEGA-SUS; hence, poetic inspiration.

> O for a beaker full of the warm South,
> Full of the true, the blushful Hippo-
> crene.
>> KEATS: *Ode to a Nightingale*.

Hippodamia. *See* BRISEIS.

Hippogriff (Gr. *hippos*, a horse; *gryphos*, a griffin). The winged horse, whose father was a GRIFFIN and mother a filly. A symbol of love (Ariosto: *Orlando Furioso*, iv, 18, 19).

Hippolyta (hip ol'i tà). Queen of the AMAZONS, and daughter of MARS. SHA-KESPEARE introduced the character in his *A Midsummer Night's Dream*, where he betroths her to THESEUS, Duke of Athens. In classic fable it is her sister Antiope who married Theseus, although some writers justify Shakespeare's account. Hippolyta was famous for a girdle given by her father, and it was one of the "twelve labours" of HER-CULES to possess himself of this prize.

Hippolytus (hip ol' it ùs). Son of THE-SEUS, King of Athens; when he repulsed his stepmother PILÆDRA's advances she accused him of attempting her seduction. In anger his father sought NEPTUNE's aid, who sent a sea monster which so terrified Hippolytus' horses that they dragged him to death. He was restored to life by ÆSCULAPIUS.

Hippomenes (hip om' en ēz). In Bœotian legend, the Greek prince who won the race with Atalanta. *See* ATALANTA'S RACE.

Hiram Abif (hī ràm a bif') is a central figure in the legend and ritual of FREE-MASONRY, the craftsman builder of King Solomon's TEMPLE who died rather than yield up the secrets of ma-

sonry. He appears as Huram, the alternative form of the name, in II *Chron*. ii and iv. He must not be confused with Hiram or Huram, King of Tyre, who supplied much of the material.

Hiroshima (hi rō shē' mà). A Japanese city and military base, the target of the first atomic bomb dropped in warfare (6 August 1945). Over 160,000 people were killed or injured and far more rendered homeless. The flash of the explosion was seen 170 miles away and a column of black smoke rose over the city to a height of 40,000 feet. Hiroshima remains a solemn portent of the fate overshadowing mankind in the event of major world conflict.

History. The Muse of History. CLIO.

To make history. To take part in events and actions that will shape the future, or which will be of such significance as to become part of the historical record.

Happy is the country that has no history. *See under* HAPPY.

Historical Materialism. *See under* MATERIALISM.

Hit. A capital, or **great hit.** A great success, a piece of good luck. From the game *hit and miss* or the game of backgammon, where "two *hits* equal a gammon".

Hit hard, or **hard hit.** Hurt or distressed by adversities of fortune.

Hitting on all six. Doing well, giving a fine performance. A motor-car engine when running well is described as having the pistons in all six cylinders *hitting* perfectly (*cp*. FIRING ON ALL FOUR).

Hit or miss. *See* HOB-NOB.

To hit below the belt. To hurt another unfairly, to ignore the rules of fair play; an allusion to the boxing ring.

To hit it off. To describe a thing tersely and epigrammatically; to make a sketch truthfully and quickly.

To hit it off together. To agree or get on well with each other.

To hit the high spots. To excel or to go to excesses in "gay living". In American parlance, to do something superficially.

To hit the nail on the head. *See under* HEAD.

To make a hit. To meet with great approval, to meet with unexpected success.

Hitch. Hitch your wagon to a star. Aim high; don't be content with low aspirations. The phrase is from Emerson's essay, *Civilization* (*Society and Solitude*). Young expressed much the same idea in his *Night Thoughts* (viii).

> Too low they build who build beneath the stars.

There is some hitch. Some impediment. A horse is said to have a hitch in his gait where he is lame.

To get hitched. To get married.

To go without a hitch. Entirely sucessfully or smoothly; without any obstruction or impediment.

To hitch. To get on smoothly; to fit in consistently; also on harness: as, "You and I hitch on well together"; "These two accounts do not hitch in with each other."

To hitch-hike. To travel from place to place by getting lifts from passing vehicles.

Hitched land. Part of the common field in which common rights were withdrawn or suspended to allow the cultivation of special crops such as turnips, clover, or potatoes. In Wiltshire, such land was said to be "hooked".

Hitlerism. A generic term for the whole doctrine and practice of Fascism as exemplified by the NAZI régime of Adolf Hitler (1889–1945), who became German Chancellor in 1933 and ruled until his death. His régime was marked by tyranny, aggression, and mass persecution of Communists and Jews.

Heil Hitler (Hail Hitler). The familiar salutation to the FÜHRER, often used derisively of one adopting dictatorial methods or attempting dictatorial policies.

Hoarstone. A stone marking out the boundary of an extate, properly an old, grey, lichen-covered stone. They are also called "Hour-stones", and in Scotland, "Harestanes". They have been wrongly taken for Druidical remains.

Hob. An abbreviated form of Robin.

Hobbism. The principles of Thomas Hobbes (1588–1679), author of *Leviathan* (1651). He was a sceptic noted for his MATERIALISM and ERASTIANISM. He emphasized the doctrine of state so-

vereignty based on the theory of a social contract which he used as a support for absolutism. Man, according to Hobbes, is motivated by self-interest and the urge for self-preservation. Many regarded *Hobbism* as subversive free-thinking.

Hobbit. A benevolent hospitable burrow people, two to four feet high, and fond of bright colours, the creation of Professor J.R.R. Tolkien. They are featured in his two works, *The Hobbit* (1937) and *The Lord of the Rings* (1954–1955).

Hobble Skirts. This women's fashion of skirts so tight around the ankles that the wearer was impeded in walking (much as a horse is hobbled) was at its height in 1912 and was gone by 1914.

Hobblers. A light-cavalry soldier, probably from his mount, a HOBBY or small horse. It was a feudal obligation for tenants of a certain class to provide hobblers for military service. They were often used to carry intelligence, to act as sentinels, and to reconnoitre.

Hobby. A favourite pursuit; a personal pastime that interests or amuses one. There are two words *hobby*. The earlier, meaning a smaller or medium-sized horse, is the M.E. *hoby* (*cp*. DOBBIN); the later, a small species of falcon, is the O.Fr. *hobé*, from Lat. *hobetus*, a falcon. It is from the first that our "hobby", a pursuit, comes. It is through *hobby-horse*, a light wickerwork frame, appropriately draped, in which someone gambolled in the old MORRIS DANCES. Padstow in Cornwall has its ancient Hobby Horse parade on May Day. The horse is preceded by men clad in white known as "teazers". The name is also applied to the child's plaything, consisting of a stick, across which he straddles, with a horse's head at one end.

To ride a hobby-horse was to play an infantile game of which one soon tired. It now implies to dwell to excess on a pet theory; the transition is shown in a sentence in one of John Wesley's sermons (No. lxxxiii):

> Every one has (to use the cant term of the day) his hobby-horse!

Hobgobiin. An impish, ugly, and mischievous sprite, particularly PUCK or RO-BIN GOODFELLOW. The word is a variant of Rob-goblin—*i.e.* the goblin Robin (*cp.* HODGE).

Hob-nob. A corruption of *Hab-nab*, meaning "have or not have". Hence, hit or miss, at random; and, give or take, whence also an open defiance.

To hobnob, or **hob and nob together.** To be on intimate terms of good fellowship, hold close and friendly conversation with, etc.; especially to drink together as cronies—probably with the meaning of "give and take".

Hobo. In American usage, a migratory worker who likes to travel, in contrast to a tramp, who travels without working, and a BUM, who neither travels nor works. It derives probably from *hoeboy*, which meant a migratory farm worker.

Hobson's Choice means no choice at all. The saying derives eponymously from Thomas Hobson (1544?–1631), a Cambridge carrier well known in his day (he is celebrated in Fuller's *Worthies* and in two epitaphs by Milton), who refused to let out any horse except in its proper turn.

Hobson-Jobson. An expression used by British soldiers in India in the 19th century for the Muharram festival. It was their corruption of the Shi'ites' cry *Ya Hasan! Ya Hosain!* Hasan and Hosain were the sons of Ali, the fourth Mohammedan CALIPH and his wife Fatima (MOHAMMED'S daughter).

Hock-day, or **Hock Tuesday.** The second Tuesday after EASTER Day, long held as a festival in England and observed until the 16th century. According to custom, on Hock Monday, the women of the village seized and bound men, demanding a small payment for their release. On the Tuesday of Hocktide the men similarly waylaid the women. The takings were paid to the churchwardens for parish work. This was later modified, as shown below:

> Hock Monday was for the men and Hock Tuesday for the women. On both days the men and women, alternately, with great merriment, intercepted the public roads with ropes, and pulled passengers to them, from whom they exacted money, to be laid out in pious uses.
>
> BRAND: *Antiquities*, vol. I.

Hock-shop. A pawnshop. In America *to hock* is to pawn. It derives from the earlier English Hocktide when small ransoms were demanded from those caught and bound.

Hockey, or **Horkey** is the old name in the eastern counties for the HARVEST-HOME feast.

Hocus Pocus (hō' kŭs pō' kŭs). Words formerly uttered by conjurers when performing a trick: hence the trick or deception itself, also the juggler himself.

The phrase dates from the early 17th century, and is the opening of a ridiculous string of mock Latin used by the performer (*Hocus pocus, toutous talontus, vade celerita jubes*), the first two words possibly being a parody of the words of consecration in the Mass (*Hoc est Corpus*), while the remainder was reeled off to occupy the attention of the audience.

Our word *hoax* is probably a contraction of hocus pocus, which also supplies the verb **to hocus,** to bamboozle, to cheat, etc.

Hodge. A familiar and condescending name for a farm labourer or peasant, a country clown or rustic; an abbreviated form of *Roger*. It was in use in the 16th century.

Hodge-podge. A medley, a mixed dish of "bits and pieces" all cooked together. The word is a corruption of HOTCH-POT.

Hodmandod. *See* DODMAN.

Hog. A swine, properly a male swine castrated, and, as it is raised solely for slaughter, killed young. The origin of the word is uncertain. The name is also applied to a gelded boar, a sheep in its first year unshorn, and yearling, colts and bullocks are also termed *hogs* or *hoggetts*. A *hog-steer* is a three-year-old boar.

In slang use, a *hog* is a gluttonous, greedy or unmannered person, thus a selfish, reckless, thrusting motorist is termed a *road-hog*.

Hog was also slang for a SHILLING or sixpence, or (in the U.S.A.) a ten-cent piece.

To drive one's hog to market. To snore very loudly.

To eat high off the hog. To be greedy, to have more than one's fair share.

To go the whole hog. To do the thing

completely and thoroughly; without compromise or reservation; to go the whole way. William Cowper says (*The Love of the World*; *or Hypocrisy Detected*, 1779) that the Moslem divines sought to ascertain which part of the hog was forbidden as food by the PROPHET.

> But for one piece they thought it hard
> From the whole hog to be debarred.

Unable to reach a decision, each thought to be excepted the portion of the meat he most preferred. As the tastes of the worthy IMAMS differed:

> Thus conscience freed from every clog,
> Mahometans eat up the hog.

A more probable origin of the phrase is that "to go the whole hog" was to spend the whole *hog* or SHILLING at one go.

To hog it, or **to pig it.** In colloquial usage means to live in a rough, uncouth fashion or to eat unceremoniously and greedily in a piggish fashion; also to act selfishly and greedily, to grasp everything for oneself.

You have brought your hogs to a fine market. You have made a pretty KETTLE OF FISH; said in derision when one's project turns out badly.

Hog and hominy (U.S.A.). Pork and maize, the latter being coarsely ground and boiled and considered poor food. In the Southern States it is often known as "Hog jowls and grits" or "Hog jowls and black-eyed peas". It is eaten on New Year's Day for good luck.

Hog-shearing. Much ado about nothing. "Great cry and little wool." (*See under* CRY.)

Hog wild. In American parlance to go berserk (*see* BERSERKER).

Hogen Mogen. Holland or the Netherlands; so called from *Hooge en Mogende* (high and mighty), the Dutch style of addressing the STATES-GENERAL. It has a secondary meaning, "Dutch".

Hogmanay. In SCOTLAND, the last day of the year, the day when children demanded gifts or *hogmanay* of oat-cake or oaten bread, etc.

> Hogmanay, Trollolay,
> Give us your white bread and none of your gray.

In olden times it was a kind of annual SATURNALIA. The word is of uncertain origin and of the numerous suggestions made, the most likely is that it is from the North French dialect word *hoginane*, O.Fr. *aguillaneuf* (to the mistletoe go this New Year).

Hoi Polloi (Gr., the many). The masses, usually used in a slighting sense.

Hoity-toity. A reduplicated word (like *harum-scarum, mingle-mangle, huggermugger*, etc.), probably formed from the obsolete verb *hoit*, to romp about noisily. It is used as an adjective, meaning "stuck up", haughty, or petulant; as a noun, meaning a good romp or frolic; and as an interjection expressing disapproval or contempt of someone's airs, assumptions, etc.

Hokey cokey. A light-hearted dance popular during the 1940s dependent on the song and tune of this name.

Hokey-pokey. An early form of cheap ice-cream sold by street-vendors until the 1920s with the cry "Hokey-pokey penny a lump". The name is derived from HOCUS POCUS although mistakenly said by some to be from the Ital. *Ecco un poco* (Here is a little). *Hokey-pokey* is also used to mean nonsense.

Hold. He is not fit to hold a candle to him. *See under* CANDLE.

Hold hard! Stop; go easy; keep a firm hold, seat, or footing, or else there is danger of being overthrown.

Hold off! Keep at a distance.

Hold the fort! Maintain your position at all costs. Immortalized as a phrase by General Sherman (During the American CIVIL WAR), who signalled it to General Corse from the top of Kennesaw in 1864.

To hold the fort. To be left to keep things running during the absence of others.

Hold your horses. *See under* HORSE.

To be left holding the baby, or **bag.** To be left in the LURCH, to carry the responsibility for faults committed by others, to carry the can (*see under* CARRY).

To cry hold. To give the order to stop; in the old TOURNAMENTS, when the umpires wished to stop the contest they cried out, "Hold!"

To hold the candle to someone, a candle to the devil. *See under* CAN-

DLE.

To hold forth. To speak in public, to harangue, to declaim. An author also *holds forth* certain opinions or ideas in his book, *i.e.* exhibits, or holds them out to view.

To hold good. To be valid, or applicable.

To hold in. To restrain. The allusion is to horses reined in tightly.

To hold in esteem. To regard with esteem.

To hold on one's way. To proceed steadily; to go on without heeding interruptions.

To hold someone guilty. To adjudge or regard as guilty.

To hold someone in hand, or **in play.** To keep control of; keep in expectation; to amuse in order to get some advantage.

To hold one's own. To maintain one's own position, opinion, advantage; to stand one's ground.

To hold one's tongue. To keep silence. In Coverdale's BIBLE, where the Authorized Version has, "But Jesus held his peace" (*Matt.* xxvi, 63), the reading is, "Jesus helde his tonge."

To hold out. To endure, persist, not to succumb.

To hold over. To keep back, retain in reserve, defer.

To hold the purse-strings. To be the one who controls the money and its expenditure. *See* CUTPURSE.

To hold up. To stop, as a highwayman did, with the intention of robbing. In this connexion the order "Hold 'em up!" or "Hold up your hands!" means that the victim must hold them above his head to ensure that he is not reaching for a weapon. *Cp.* HIJACKER. *A hold-up* is therefore an outdoor robbery where people or vehicles are held up. It also means a delay or obstacle.

To hold water. To bear close inspection; to be thoroughly sound and consistent, as a vessel that holds water is sound. In this sense it is usually used negatively, as "That statement will not hold water," *i.e.*, on examination it will be proved faulty. The expression also means to stay the progress of a boat by stemming the current with the oars.

Holdfast. That which is used to secure something in place, a cramp, a hook, etc.; a support.

Hole. A better 'ole. Any situation that is better than the present one. It originated in World War I from a drawing by Bruce Bairnsfather, depicting "Old Bill" taking cover in a wet and muddy shell-hole and rebutting the complaints of his companion with the remark, "If you know better 'ole, go to it."

A hold and corner business. Something clandestine and underhand.

In a hole. In an awkward predicament; in a mess.

To hole out. In golf, to drive the ball into the appropriate hole of the course.

To make a hole in something. To consume a considerable portion of it.

To pick holes in. To find fault with. The older phrase was to *pick a hole in one's coat*, thus a hole in one's coat is a blot on one's reputation.

Holger Danske. The national hero of Denmark. *See* OGIER THE DANE.

Holiday. Give the boys a holiday. A phrase attributed to Anaxagoras (*see* DYING SAYINGS). The old custom of so marking a noteworthy event has always been popular with pupils, but the unexpected holiday is less readily given now that most schools are subject to closer bureaucratic regulation.

Holidays, or **Holy days of Obligation.** Days on which Roman Catholics are bound to hear MASS and to abstain "from servile work". These *Feasts of Obligation* vary slightly in different countries. In ENGLAND and WALES they are: all SUNDAYS, CHRISTMAS DAY, the EPIPHANY (6 January), ASCENSION DAY (40th day after EASTER Sunday), CORPUS CHRISTI (Thursday after Trinity Sunday), SS. PETER and PAUL (29 June), the ASSUMPTION of B.V.M. (15 August), ALL SAINTS (1 November). St. JOSEPH (19 March) and St. PATRICK (17 March) are observed in IRELAND and SCOTLAND. The former and the feasts of the Octave Day of Christmas (1 January) and the IMMACULATE CONCEPTION (8 December) are not observed in England and Wales. Epiphany, Corpus Christi, SS. Peter and Paul, and St. Joseph are not kept in the U.S.A.

Holland, The cloth, so called because it was originally made in Holland; its full name was *holland cloth*.

Hollands, or properly Hollands gin, is the Dut. *Hollandsch genever*.

Hollow. I beat him hollow. Completely, thoroughly. *Hollow* here is perhaps a corruption of *Wholly*.

Holly. The custom of decorating churches and houses with holly at CHRISTMAS-time is of great antiquity and may derive from its earlier use by the Romans in the festival of the SATURNALIA, which occurred at the same season, or from the old Teutonic custom. It is held to be unlucky by some to bring it into the house before Christmas Eve. *See also* IVY; MISTLETOE.

Holmes. *See* SHERLOCK HOLMES.

Holy. Holy Alliance. A treaty signed originally by the rulers of Austria, Prussia, and Russia in 1815 (after the fall of NAPOLEON) and joined by all the kings of Europe, except Great Britain and the President of the Swiss Republic. Sponsored by the Tsar Alexander, the rulers undertook to base their relations "upon the sublime truths which the Holy religion of Our Saviours teaches". In effect it became a reactionary influence seeking to maintain autocratic rule.

Holy City. The city which the religious consider most expecially connected with their faith. Thus:

> *Benares* is the Holy City of the Hindus.
> *Cuzco* of the ancient Incas.
> *Fez* of the Western Arabs.
> *Jerusalem* of the Jews and Christians.
> *Mecca* and *Medina* as the places of the birth and burial of MOHAMMED.
>
> Figuratively, the Holy City is HEAVEN.

Holy Coat. Both the cathedral at Trèves (Trier) and the parish church of Argenteuil claim the ownership of Christ's seamless coat, which the soldiers would not rend and therefore cast lots for it (*John* xix, 23, 25). The traditions date from about the 12th century and the coat was supposed to have been found and preserved by the Empress HELENA in the 4th century. There are other places claiming this relic.

Holy Cross, or **Holy Rood Day.** 14 September, the day of the Feast of the EXALTATION OF THE CROSS, called by the Anglo-Saxons "Roodmass-day".

It was on this day that Jews in ROME used to be compelled to go to church and listen to a sermon—a custom abolished about 1840 by Pope Gregory XVI. It is the subject of Browning's *Holy-Cross Day* (1845).

Holy Door. The specially walled-up door of each of the four great basilicas at ROME (St. Peter's, St. John Lateran, St. Paul's-Outside-the-Walls, St. Mary's Major). That of St. Peter's is ceremoniously opened by the Pope on Christmas Eve, to inaugurate the Holy Year (*see* JUBILEE); the others are opened by Cardinals-Legate. They are similarly closed the following Christmas Eve. Many Pilgrims pass through these doors during the year to perform their devotions and receive INDULGENCES.

Holy Family. Properly, the infant Jesus, MARY, and JOSEPH; in art, the infant Saviour and His attendants, usually Joseph, Mary, Elisabeth, Anne the mother of Mary, and JOHN THE BAPTIST.

Holy Ghost. The third person of the TRINITY, the Divine Spirit, also called the Holy Spirit; represented in art as a dove.

The seven gifts of the Holy Ghost are: (1) Counsel, (2) the fear of the Lord, (3) fortitude, (4) piety, (5) understanding, (6) wisdom, and (7) knowledge.

The Procession of the Holy Ghost. *See* FILIOQUE CONTROVERSY.

The Sin against the Holy Ghost. Much has been written about this sin, the definition of which has been based upon several passages in the GOSPELS such as *Matt.* xii, 31, 32 and *Mark* iii, 29, and it has been interpreted as the wilful denouncing as evil that which is manifestly good, thus revealing a state of heart beyond the divine influence. Borrow in his *Lavengro* draws a graphic picture inspired by fear of this sin and its consequences, the danger of "eternal damnation".

Holy Grail. *See* GRAIL.

Holy Innocents, or **Childermas.** This Feast is celebrated on 28 December, to commemorate Herod's MASSACRE OF THE INNOCENTS. It used to be the custom on *Childermas* to whip the children (and even adults) "that the memory of Herod's murder of the Innocents might stick the closer". This practice forms the plot of several tales in the DECAMERON.

Holy Island, or Lindisfarne. In the North Sea, some 9 miles south-east from Berwick-on-Tweed, it became the SEE of St. Aidan in 635 and a missionary centre. St. CHAD, St. Oswy, St. Egbert, and St. WILFRID were among those educated there. It was the see of St. CUTH-BERT (685—687) and is now in the diocese of Newcastle. At low-water it can be reached across the sands by a causeway.

IRELAND was called the Holy Island on account of its numerous saints.

Guernsey was so called in the 10th century in consequence of the great number of monks residing there.

The Holy Land (1) Christians call Palestine the Holy Land, because it was the scene of Christ's birth, ministry, and death.

(2) Mohammedans call MECCA the Holy Land, because MOHAMMED was born there.

(3) The Chinese Buddhists call India the Holy Land, because it was the native land of Sakya-muni, the BUDDHA.

(4) The Greeks considered Elis as Holy Land, from the temple of Olympian ZEUS and the sacred festival held there. *See* OLYMPIC GAMES.

The Holy League. A combination formed by Pope Julius II in 1511 with Venice, Ferdinand of Aragon and the Emperor Maximilian of Germany to drive the French out of Italy. ENGLAND joined subsequently.

Among other leagues of the same name, that formed by Henry II of France in 1576, with the support of Henry of Guise and the JESUITS is noteworthy. It was formed to defend the Holy Catholic Church against the encoachments of the reformers, *i.e.* to destroy the HUGUENOTS.

The Holy Maid of Kent. Elizabeth Barton (*c.* 1506–1534) who incited the Roman Catholics to resist the REFORMATION, and imagined that she acted under inspiration. Having announced the doom and speedy death of Henry VIII

for his marriage with Anne Boleyn, she was hanged at TYBURN in 1534.

Holy of Holies. The innermost apartment of the Jewish temple, in which the Ark of the Covenant was kept, and into which only the High Priest was allowed to enter, and that but once a year on the Day of Atonement (*see* YOM KIPPUR). Hence, a private apartment, a *sanctum sanctorum*. *Cp.* ADYTUM.

The Holy Office. *See* INQUISITION.

Holy Orders. *See* ORDERS.

Holy Places. A name particularly applied to those places in Palestine and especially Jerusalem, associated with some of the chief events in the life of Christ, his death, and Resurrection. Jerusalem is also a HOLY CITY for Jews and MOSLEMS and in the course of history this has produced bitter quarrels. Christian pilgrimages to the Holy Places were a familiar feature of mediæval life and the CRUSADES began when Moslems interfered with pilgrims visiting the HOLY SEPULCHRE.

The Crimean War (1854–1856) had its origins in a dispute between orthodox and Roman Catholic rights over the Holy Places, which included the churches of the Holy Sepulchre and the Virgin in Jerusalem, GOLGOTHA, and the church of the Nativity at Bethlehem.

Holy Roman Empire. The mediæval Western Empire, said to be neither Holy, nor Roman, nor an Empire. *See* EMPEROR.

Holy Rood Day. *See* HOLY CROSS DAY.

Holy Saturday. *See* HOLY WEEK.

Holy See. The SEE of Rome. Often used to denote the Papacy and papal jurisdiction, authority, etc.

Holy Sepulchre. The cave in Jerusalem, where according to tradition Christ was entombed, said to have been found by St. HELENA. Successive churches have been built on the site which includes that of CALVARY.

The Holy Spirit. *See* HOLY GHOST.

Holy Thursday. In England an old name for ASCENSION DAY, the Thursday next but one before WHITSUN; by Roman Catholics and others MAUNDY THURSDAY, *i.e.* the Thursday before GOOD FRIDAY, is meant. *See also* IN CŒNA DOMINI.

Holy Trinity. *See* TRINITY.

Holy War. A war in which religious motivation plays, or is purported to play, a prominent part. The CRUSADES, the THIRTY YEARS WAR, the wars against the ALBIGENSES, etc., were so called.

The *Jehad*, or Holy War of the Moslems, is a call to the whole Islamic world to take arms against the Unbelievers.

John Bunyans's *Holy War*, published in 1682, tells of the capture of Mansoul by SATAN and its recapture by the forces of Shaddai (EMMANUEL).

Holy Water. Water blessed by a priest for religious purposes. It is particularly used in the ROMAN CATHOLIC CHURCH at the *Asperges*, the sprinkling of the altar and congregation before High MASS, and generally in the Church at blessings, dedications, etc., and kept in Holy Water stoups near church doors for the use of those entering.

Holy Week. The last week in LENT. It begins on PALM SUNDAY; the fourth day is called SPY WEDNESDAY; the fifth is MAUNDY THURSDAY; the sixth is GOOD FRIDAY; and the last "Holy Saturday", or the "Great Sabbath".

Holy Week has been called *Hebdomada Muta; Hebdomada Inofficiosa; Hebdomada Penitentialis; Hebdomada Indulgentiæ; Hebdomada Luctuosa; Hebdomada Nigra*; and *Hebdomada Ultima*.

Holy Writ. The BIBLE.

Holy Year. *See* JUBILEE.

Homburg. A soft felt hat popularized by Edward VII. It was originally made at Homburg in Prussia where the king "took the waters" (*see under* WATER).

Home. At home. At one's own home and prepared to receive visitors. An *at home* is a more or less informal reception for which arrangements have been made. *To be at home to somebody* is to be ready and willing to receive him; *to be at home with a subject* is to be quite conversant with it.

Not at home. A familiar locution for "not prepared to receive visitors", it does not necessarily mean "away from home". "Say I am not at home", is an instruction often given to the person sent to fob off a caller.

Home James, and don't spare the horses. An expression from the days when the well-to-do commanded their coachmen to drive them home as fast as possible. It is still used jocularly to imply "let us get home as fast as we can", or to tell the car-driver to proceed home without delay.

Home, sweet home. This popular English song first appeared in the opera *Clari, the Maid of Milan* (COVENT GARDEN, 1823). The words were by John Howard Payne (an American), and the music by Sir Henry Bishop, who professed to have founded it on a Sicilian air.

One's long home. The grave.

To come home to one. To reach one's heart; to become thoroughly understood or realized.

To come home to roost. Usually said of a lie, fault, misdeed, etc., which eventually rebounds or "catches up" on its perpetrator. "His chickens have come home to roost" is a common form of the expression, "his chickens" being his misdeeds, mistakes, etc.

To do one's homework. To make adequate preparation for the task facing one; especially to acquaint oneself thoroughly with the relevant material for a discussion, debate or speech, as a day-school pupil is expected to do preparation at home.

To make oneself at home. To dispense with ceremony in another person's house, to act as though one were at home.

Who goes home? When the HOUSE OF COMMONS adjourns at night the doorkeeper asks this question of the members. In bygone days, when danger lurked in the unlit streets from cutthroats and thieves, the cry was raised to enable them to depart in groups, and to escort the SPEAKER to his residence.

Home Counties. The counties nearest London; formerly Kent, Surrey, Essex, Middlesex; now Buckinghamshire, Berkshire, Hertfordshire and Sussex are usually included in the term, but Middlesex was swallowed up by the Greater London Council in 1965.

Home Guard. In Britain, the force of volunteers raised early in World War II and trained for defence against the threat of invasion. Originally known as the L.D.V. (Local Defence Volunteers), it was renamed the "Home Guard" at Winston Churchill's suggestion.

Home Rule. The name given by Isaac Butt, its first leader, to the movement for securing governmental independence for IRELAND under the British crown, after failures of earlier movements to secure the repeal of the Act of Union of 1800. *The Home Government Association* was founded in 1870 (renamed the *Home Rule Association* in 1873) and when C.S. Parnell became leader in 1879 its policy of obstruction in PARLIAMENT became a growing bugbear to English governments. A *Home Rule Bill* was eventually passed in 1914 but its implementation postponed by the advent of World War I. The Easter Rising in 1916, the activities of SINN FÉIN, and resistance in ULSTER led to the establishment of the Irish Free State in 1921, but Northern Ireland continues to be represented in the British Parliament.

Home truth. An unwelcome or uncomplimentary truth delivered by another person about oneself, which "goes home".

Homer. The traditional author of the ILIAD and the ODYSSEY. Estimates of his birth date vary between 685 B.C. and 1159 B.C.. In antiquity seven cities claimed the honour of being Homer's birthplace (Argos, ATHENS, Chios, COLPHON, Rhodes, Salamis in Cyprus, and Smyrna). *See also* MÆONIDES; SCIO'S BLIND OLD BARD.

PLATO has been called the Homer of philosophers, Milton the English Homer, and OSSIAN the Gaelic Homer. BYRON called Fielding the prose Homer of human nature, and Dryden said that "SHAKESPEARE was the Homer, or father, of our dramatic poets."

The Casket Homer. An edition corrected by ARISTOTLE, which ALEXANDER THE GREAT always carried about with him, and laid under his pillow at night with his sword. After the battle of Arbela, a golden casket richly studded with gems was found in the tent of DARIUS; and Alexander, being asked to what

purpose it should be assigned, replied, "There is but one thing in the world worthy of so costly a depository," saying which he placed therein his edition of Homer.

Homer, a cure for the ague. Among the old cures it was held that if the fourth book of the ILIAD was laid under the head of a patient, it would provide instant remedy. This book contains the cure of MENELAUS (when wounded by Pandarus) by Machaon, "a son of ÆSCULAPIUS".

Homer sometimes nods. Even the best of us is liable to make mistakes. The line is from HORACE'S *De Arte Poetica* (359):

> Indignor quandoque bonus dormitat Homerus,
> Verum operi longo fas est obrepere somnum.
> (I think it shame when the worthy Homer nods; but in so long a work it is allowable if drowsiness comes on.)

Honeysuckle. *See* MISNOMERS.

Hong Merchants. Those Chinese merchants who, under licence from the Imperial Government of China, held the monopoly of trade with Europeans, and under the Hong system, were restricted to Canton. The restriction was abolished in 1842 after the OPIUM WAR. *Hong* or *hang* means row, range; hence a warehouse, particularly one for foreign merchants.

Honi soit qui mal y pense (on' ē swa kēmăl ē pons). The motto of the Most Noble Order of the GARTER, usually rendered as "Evil be to him who evil thinks," although "shame to him" would be more accurate.

Honky-tonk. A disreputable night club or low roadhouse. A place of cheap entertainment. A *honky-tonk piano* is one from which the felts of the hammers have been removed, thus making the instrument more percussive and giving it a noticeably different tone quality. Such pianos are often used for playing ragtime and popular melodies in public houses.

Honor. A feudal term for a number of KNIGHT's fees administered as a unit, an aggregation of manors. It gave "honour" to its holder, hence the name.

Honorificabilitudinitatibus. A made-up

word on the Lat. *honorificabilitudo*, honourableness, found in SHAKESPEARE and elsewhere. *See* LONG WORDS.

> Thou are not so long by the head as honorificabilitudinitatibus.
> *Love's Labour's Lost*, V, i.

Honour. An affair of honour. A dispute to be settled by a duel.

Duels were generally provoked by offences against the arbitrary rules of courtesy and etiquette, not recognized at law and thus to be settled by private combat. *See* LAWS OF HONOUR, *below.*

Debts of honour. Debts contracted by betting or gambling, so called because these debts cannot be enforced as such by law.

Legion of Honour. *See under* LEGION.

Point of honour. An obligation which is binding because its violation would offend some scruple or notion of self-respect.

Word of honour. A pledge which cannot be broken without disgrace.

Honours. Titles, distinctions, civilities, etc.

Crushed by one's honours. The allusion is to the legend of the Roman damsel, Tarpeia, who agreed to open the gates of Rome to King Tatius, provided his soldiers would give her the ornaments which they wore on their arms (meaning their bracelets). As they entered, they threw their shields on her and crushed her, saying as they did so, "These are the ornaments worn by SABINES on their arms." *See also* TARPEIAN ROCK.

Draco, the Athenian legislator (*see* DRACONIAN CODE), was crushed to death in the theatre of Ægina, by the number of caps and cloaks showered on him by the audience, as a mark of their high appreciation of his merits. A similar story is told of the mad Emperor, ELAGABALUS, who smothered the leading citizens of Rome with roses.

Honours of war. The privilege, allowed to an enemy on capitulation, of being allowed to retain his weapons. This is the highest honour a victor can pay a vanquished foe. Sometimes the troops so treated are allowed to march with all their arms, drums beating, and colours flying.

Last honours. Funeral rites; last tributes of respect to the dead.

Military honours. Ceremonial marks of respect rendered by troops to royalty and high-ranking military and civil officials and also at military funerals.

To do the honours. To render necessary civilities, courtesies, hospitalities, etc., as at a reception or entertainment.

Honourable. As applied to the nobility, *see* COURTESY TITLES. This title of honour is also given to the children of life peers, to MAIDS OF HONOUR, and to Justices of the High Court, except Lord Justices and Justices of Appeal. In the HOUSE OF COMMONS one member speaks of another as "the honourable member for—". In the U.S.A. "honourable" is a courtesy title applied to persons of distinction in legal or civic life. The title was also borne by the East India Company (*see* JOHN COMPANY).

Most Honourable. The form of address for a MARQUESS.

Right Honourable. A prefix to the title of EARLS, VISCOUNTS, BARONS, and the younger sons of DUKES and MARQUESSES, Lord Justices and Justices of Appeal, all privy councillors, some lord mayors and lord provosts, and certain other civic dignitaries, and some COMMONWEALTH ministers.

Honourable Artillery Company. The oldest surviving unit in the British Army, having been founded by Henry VIII, in 1537, as the Guild of St. George.

Hooch. An American slang term for whisky or crude raw spirits, often made surreptitiously or obtained illegally. The word comes from the Alaskan Indian *hoochinoo*, a crude distilled liquor. *Cp.* MOONSHINE.

Hood. The hood, or cowl does not make the monk. It is a man's way of life, not what he professes to be, that really matters; from the Lat. *Cucullus non facit monachum*. The expression is probably derived from the lines in St. Anselm's *Carmen de Contemptu Mundi* (11th century):

> Non tonsura facit monachum, non horrida vestis; Sed virtus animi, perpetuusque rigor.

Hood, Robin. *See* ROBIN HOOD.

Hoodman Blind. A game now called BLINDMAN'S BUFF.

Hook. Above your hook. Beyond your comprehension; beyond your mark. Perhaps an allusion to hat-pegs fixed in rows, the higher ones being beyond the reach of small people.

By hook or by crook. Either rightfully or wrongfully; by some means or other; one way or another. It possibly derives from an old manorial custom which authorized tenants to take as much firewood as could be reached down by a shepherd's crook and cut down with a bill-hook.

He is off the hooks. Unhinged, out of spirits, put out, annoyed; also LAID ON THE SHELF, superseded, dead; the hooks being the pieces of iron on which gates hinges rest.

Hook it! Take your hook! Sling your hook! Be off! Buzz off! Go away! *Take your hook* refers to the practice in some Victorian MUSIC HALLS of the manager waiting in the wings with a long hooked pole ready to pull off a performer outrunning his time or welcome.

Hook, line and sinker. To swallow a tale *hook, line and sinker* is to be extremely gullible, like the hungry fish that swallows not only the baited hook, but the lead weight, and some of the line as well.

Let off the hook. To get out of a difficult situation. Also, of a married man, let out on his own, usually for a night with convivial male companions.

On one's own hook. On one's own responsibility or account. An angler's phrase.

To be hooked. To be caught, usually of a man "hooked" by a woman, *i.e.*, secured for marriage. More recently it also means to become addicted to the use of a drug.

With a hook at the end. Assent given with a mental reservation. It was a custom in some parts for a witness, when he swore the oath falsely, to crook his finger into a sort of hook with the idea of annulling the perjury. It is a crooked oath, an oath *with a hook at the end*.

A hook-up is a radio term for an arrangement of wiring for extended transmission or reception; it is applied to a network of radio stations connected for the transmission of the same programme.

Hookey, or **hooky. To play hookey.** To play truant, from the idea that "to hook" something is to make off with it.

Hooligan. A violent young rough; of late 19th-century origin from the name of a family of such people. Hence the word *hooliganism*.

Hooray. Normally used as an exclamation of joy, approbation, etc., but in Australia and New Zealand it is used as a farewell. Why this has come about is obscure, but it may have the implication of encouragement as a joyful send-off.

Hop Hop it. Be off with you, buzz off, go away.

To hop the twig. Usually to die; but sometimes to run away from one's creditors, as a bird eludes a fowler.

There are numerous phrases to express the cessation of life; for example, "to kick the bucket" (*see under* BUCKET); "to lay down one's knife and fork"; "to peg out" (from cribbage); "to snuff it" (*see under* SNUFF); "to fall asleep"; "to enter Charon's boat"; "to give up the ghost" (*see under* GHOST); etc.

Hopping mad. Very angry, jumping mad. So mad as to jump or hop about.

Hop-o'-my-thumb. A pygmy or dwarf. *Cp.* TOM THUMB.

Hope. *See* PANDORA'S BOX.

Band of Hope. *See* BAND OF HOPE *under* BAND.

Hope Diamond. A rare sapphire-blue Indian stone weighing 44¾ carats (now in America), which appeared on the market in 1830 and became the one-time property of Henry Thomas Hope. It is believed to be part of the large blue DIAMOND cut to 68 carats and sold to Louis XIV by Tavernier. Like the SANCY DIAMOND, it disappeared (1792) during the French Revolution.

Horace. Quintus Horatius Flaccus (65 B.C.– 8 B.C.), the Roman lyric poet.

Horae (hôr' ī) (Lat. hours, seasons). In classical mythology, the three sisters Eunomia (Good order), Dice (Justice), and Irene (Peace), who presided over spring, summer, and winter. According to Hesiod they were the daughters of JUPITER and THEMIS.

Horn. The horn was a symbol of power

and dominion and as such is found in classical writers and similarly in the OLD TESTAMENT. The original Hebrew SHO-FAR or trumpet was made of a ram's horn.

Astolpho's horn. Logistilla gave Astolpho at parting a horn that had the virtue of being able to appal and put to flight the boldest KNIGHT or most savage beast (ARIOSTO: *Orlando Furioso*, Bk. VIII).

The Horn Gate. *See* DREAMS, THE GATES OF.

Horn of Fidelity. MORGAN LE FAY sent a horn to King ARTHUR, which had the following "virtue": No lady could drink out of it who was not "to her husband true"; all others who attempted to drink were sure to spill what it contained. This horn was carried to King MARK, and "his queene with a hundred ladies more" tried the experiment, but only four managed to "drink cleane". ARISTO'S *enchanted cup* possessed a similar spell.

Horn of Plenty or **Cornucopia.** AMALTHEA'S horn, an emblem of plenty. CERES is drawn with a ram's horn in her left arm, filled with fruits and flowers; sometimes they are being poured on the earth, and sometimes they are piled high in the horn as in a basket.

The horns of a dilemma. *See* DILEMMA.

The horns of Moses' face. *See* MOSES.

My horn hath He exalted (I *Sam.* ii, 10; *Ps.* lxxxix, 24, etc). He has given me the victory, increased my sway. Thus, *Lift not up your horn on high* (*Ps.* lxxv, 5) means, do not behave scornfully, maliciously, or arrogantly. In these passages "horn" symbolizes power, and its exaltation signifies victory or deliverance. In DANIEL'S vision (*Dan.* vii, 7) the "fourth beast, dreadful and terrible, and strong exceedingly," had ten horns, symbolic of its great might.

To come, or **be squeezed out at the little end of the horn.** To come off badly in some affair; get the worst of it; fail conspicuously.

To draw in one's horns. To retrench, to curtail one's expenditure; to retract or mitigate an expressed opinion; to restrain pride. The allusion is to the snail.

To show one's horns. To let one's evil intentions appear. The allusion, like that in "to show the cloven hoof", is to the DEVIL—"Old Hornie" (*see under* AULD).

To take the bull by the horns. *See under* BULL.

To the horns of the altar. *Usque ad aras amicus*, Your friend even to the horns of the altar, *i.e.* through thick and thin. In swearing the ancient Romans held the horns of the altar, and one who did so in testimony of friendship could not break his oath without incurring the vengeance of the gods.

On heathen altars the horn was probably ornamental. In the TEMPLE OF SOLOMON the altar had a projection or horn at each of the four corners and they were regarded as especially sacred. Animals awaiting slaughter may have been bound to them and the horns were smeared with the blood of sacrifices (*Exod.* xxix, 12). Criminals were safe from vengeance if they grasped these horns.

To wear the horns. To be a CUCKOLD. This old term is connected with the chase. In the rutting season, one stag selects several females for his consorts. If challenged and beaten by another stag he is without associates unless he defeats another stag in turn. As stags are horned, and have their mates taken from them by their fellows, the application is palpable. *See also* ACTÆON.

Another explanation is that it is due to the former practice of engrafting the spurs of a castrated cock on the root of the excised comb, where they grew and became "horns." In support of this it is noteworthy that *Hahnrei*, the German equivalent for *cuckold*, originally signified a capon.

Auld Hornie. *See* AULD.

Cape Horn. So named by Schouten, a Dutch mariner, who first doubled it (1616). He was a native of Hoorn, in north Holland, and named the cape after his native town. To seamen it was simply known as "the Horn". *Cp.* CAPE.

Horn Childe. An early 14th-century metrical romance with a story closely related to that of KING HORN.

Horn Dance. *See* ABBOT'S BROMLEY.

Hornbook. A thin board about nine

inches long and five or six wide (with a handle) serving as backing to a leaf of vellum or sheet of paper on which was usually written (later printed) the alphabet, an exorcism, the Lord's Prayer, and the Roman numerals; the whole being covered by a thin piece of transparent horn. The handle had a hole in it so that it could be tied to a schoolchild's girdle. Hornbooks continued to be used in England until well into the 18th century. *See* CHRISS-CROSS.

Hornpipe. An obsolete wooden pipe with a reed mouthpiece at one end and horn at the other. The dance of this name, once particularly associated with mariners, was originally accompanied by this instrument.

Horner, Little Jack. *See under* JACK.

Horoscope (Gr. *horoskopos*, *hora*, an hour; *skopos*, observer). The observation of the heavens at the hour of a person's birth, used by astrologers for predicting the future events of his life. Also the figure or diagram of the twelve houses of HEAVEN, showing the positions of the planets at a given time as used by astrologers for calculating nativities and working out answers to horary questions. *See* HOUSES, ASTROLOGICAL.

Hors de combat (ô di kom' ba) (Fr. out of battle). Incapable of taking any further part in the fight; disabled.

Horsa. *See* HENGIST.

Horse. According to classical mythology, POSEIDON created the horse; and according to VIRGIL, the first person that drove a four-in-hand was ERICHTHONIUS. In Christian art, the horse is held to represent courage and generosity. It is an attribute of St. MARTIN, St. Maurice, St. GEORGE, and St. Victor, all of whom are represented on horseback.

It is a not uncommon emblem in the CATACOMBS and probably typifies the swiftness of life.

The use of *horse* attributively usually denotes something that is coarse, inferior, unrefined, as in *horse-parsley*, *horseradish*, *horse mushroom*. *See* COB; HAND.

The brazen horse. A magic horse given to Cambuscan by the king of Arabia and India. By giving it instructions and turning a pin in its ear it would carry its rider anywhere.

Flesh-eating horses. The horses of Diomedes, tyrant of Thrace, who fed his horses on the strangers who visited his kingdom. HERCULES vanquished the tyrant and gave the carcass to the horses to eat.

Hobby Horse. *See* HOBBY.

Iron horse. A steam locomotive.

The Pale Horse. Death. "I looked and behold a pale horse; and his name that sat on him was Death" (*Rev.* vi, 8). *See also* FOUR HORSEMEN OF THE APOCALYPSE *under* FOUR.

The White Horse. The standard of the ancient Saxons; hence the emblem of Kent.

The name is also given to the hillside figures formed by removing the turf, thus revealing the underlying chalk. The most famous of these is at Uffington, Berkshire, traditionally said to commemorate ALFRED THE GREAT's victory over the Danes in 871. It measures some 350 feet from nose to tail and gives its name to the *Vale of White Horse*, west of Abingdon. The scouring of the White Horse was once a local ceremony.

There are other white horses, that at Westbury, Wiltshire, being the best known.

A galloping white horse is the device of the House of Hanover and, during the reign of the first two Georges, the *White Horse* replaced the *Royal Oak* of Stuart fame on many PUBLIC-HOUSE SIGNS.

White horses. A poetic phrase for the white-capped breakers as they roll in from the sea.

O'Donohue's white horses. Waves which come on a windy day, crested with foam. The hero reappears every seventh year on MAY-DAY, and is seen gliding, to sweet but unearthly music, over the lakes of Killarney, on his favourite white horse. He is preceded by fairies who strew spring flowers in his path. Moore has a poem on the subject in his *Irish Melodies*.

Winged horse. *See* PEGASUS.

The Wooden Horse, called *Clavileno el Aligero*, in DON QUIXOTE, is governed by a peg in its forehead and has the same magical qualities as the BRAZEN HORSE given to Cambuscan. The similar *Magic Horse* in the ARABIAN NIGHTS was of ivory and ebony.

A former instrument of military punishment was called a *wooden horse*. The victim was seated on the horse's back, a beam of ridged oak, with a firelock tied to both feet to keep him in this painful position. This was known as **riding the wooden horse.**

Before the days of iron and steel construction, a ship was sometimes called a *wooden horse*.

The Wooden Horse of Troy. VIRGIL tells us that, after the death of HECTOR, ULYSSES had a monster wooden horse made by Epios and gave out that it was an offering to the gods to secure a prosperous voyage back to Greece. The Trojans dragged the horse within their city, but it was full of Grecian soldiers, including MENELAUS, who stole out at night, slew the guards, opened the city gates, and set fire to TROY.

Famous Horses of Myth and History.

In classical mythology the names give to the horses of HELIOS, the Sun, are:

> *Actæon* (effulgence); *Æthon* (fiery red); *Amethes* (no loiterer); *Bronte* (thunderer); *Erythreos* (red producer); *Lampos* (shining like a lamp); *Phlegon* (the burning one); and *Purocis* (fiery hot).

AURORA'S horses were:

> *Abraxa, Eoos* (dawn) and *Phæthon* (the shining one).

PLUTO'S horses were:

> *Abaster* (away from the stars); *Abatos* (inaccessible); *Æton* (swift as an eagle); and *Nonios*.

The ensuing list is arranged alphabetically:

> *Aarvak*, or *Arvak* ("early-waker"). In Norse mythology, the horse that draws the sun's chariot driven by the maiden Sol.
> *Alborak. See* BORAK.
> *Alfana* ("mare"). Gradasso's horse, in ORLANDO FURIOSO.
> *Alsvid*, or *Alswider* ("All-swift"). The horse that draws the chariot of the moon (Norse mythology).
> *Aquiline* ("like an eagle"). Raymond's steed, bred on the banks of the Tagus (Tasso: *Jerusalem Delivered*).
> *Arion* ("martial"). HERCULES' horse, given to ADRASTUS. Formerly the horse of NEPTUNE, brought out of the earth by striking it with his trident; its right

feet were those of a man, it spoke with a human voice and ran with incredible swiftness.
> *Arundel*. The horse of BEVIS OF HAMPTON. The word means "swift as a swallow" (Fr. *hirondelle*).
> *Balios* (Gr., "swift"). One of the horses given by NEPTUNE to Peleus. It afterwards belonged to ACHILLES. Like Xanthos (*see below*), its sire was the west wind, and its dam Swift-foot the HARPY.
> *Barbary. See* BARBARY ROAN.
> *Bavieca*. The CID's horse. He survived his master two years and a half, during which time no one was allowed to mount him; he was buried before the gates of the monastery at Valencia and two elms were planted to mark the grave.
> *Bayard. See* BAYARD.
> *Bayardo. See* BAYARDO.
> *Black Agnes*. A palfrey of Mary Queen of Scots given by her brother Moray, and named after Agnes of Dunbar.
> *Black Bess*. The mythical mare, created for Dick TURPIN by Harrison Ainsworth in his *Rookwood*, which carried Dick from London to York.
> *Black Saladin*. Warwick's famous coal-black horse. Its sire was Malech, and according to tradition, when the race of Malech failed, the race of Warwick would fail also. And thus it was.
> *Brigadore*, or *Brigliadore* ("Golden bridle"). Sir Guyon's horse in Spenser's *Faerie Queene* (V, iii, etc.). It had a distinguishing black spot on its mouth, like a horseshoe.
> ORLANDO's famous charger, second only to BAYARDO in swiftness and wonderful powers, was called *Brigiliadoro*.
> *Bucephalus* ("ox-head"). The famous charger of ALEXANDER THE GREAT, who was the only person who could mount him, and he always knelt down to take up his master. He was 30 years old at death and Alexander built the city of Bucephala for a mausoleum.
> *Carman*. The Chevalier BAYARD's horse, given to him by the Duke of Lorraine. It was a Persian horse from Kerman or Carmen (Laristan).
> *Celer* ("swift"). The horse of the Roman Emperor Lucius Versus. It was fed on almonds and raisins, covered with royal purple, and stalled in the imperial palace.
> *Cerus* ("fit"). The horse of ADRASTUS, swifter than the wind.
> *Clavileno. See* WOODEN HORSE *under* HORSE.
> *Copenhagen. See* COPENHAGEN.
> *Cyllaros*. Named from Cylla in Troas, a celebrated horse of CASTOR AND POLLUX.
> *Dapple. See* DAPPLE.
> *Dinos* ("the marvel"). DIOMEDES' horse.
> *Ethon* ("fiery"). One of the horses of HECTOR.

Fadda. MOHAMMED's white mule.

Ferrant d'Espagne ("The Spanish traveller"). The horse of OLIVER.

Galathe ("cream-coloured"). One of the horses of HECTOR.

Grani ("grey-coloured"). SIEGFRIED's horse, of marvellous swiftness.

Grizzle. All skin and bone, the horse of Dr. SYNTAX.

Haizum. The horse of the archangel GABRIEL (KORAN).

Harpagus ("one that carried off rapidly"). One of the horses of CASTOR AND POLLUX.

Hippocampus. One of NEPTUNE's horses. It had only two legs, the hind quarter being that of a dragon or fish.

Hrimfaxi ("frost-mane"). The horse of Night, from whose bit fall the "rimedrops" which nightly bedew the earth (Scandinavian legend).

Incitatus ("spurred-on"). The Roman Emperor CALIGULA's horse, made priest and consul. It had an ivory manger and drank wine from a golden pail.

Kantaka. The white horse of Prince GAUTAMA, the BUDDHA.

Lampon ("the bright one"). One of DIOMEDES' horses.

Lamri ("the curvetter"). King ARTHUR's mare.

Malech. See BLACK SALADIN, *above.*

Marengo. The white stallion which NAPOLEON rode at Waterloo. It is represented in Vernet's picture of *Napoleon Crossing the Alps.*

Marocco. See BANKS'S HORSE.

Pegasus. See PEGASUS.

Phallus ("stallion"). The horse of Heraclius.

Phrenicos ("intelligent"). The horse of Hiero of Syracuse, that won the prize for single horses in the 73rd OLYMPIAD.

Podarge ("swift-foot"). One of the horses of HECTOR.

Roan Barbary. See BARBARY ROAN.

Rosabelle. The favourite palfrey of Mary Queen of Scots.

Rosinante ("formerly a hack"). DON QUIXOTE's horse, all skin and bone. *Cp.* GRIZZLE, above.

Savoy. The favourite black horse of Charles VIII of France; so called from its donor, the Duke of Savoy. It had but one eye, and "was mean in stature".

Shibdiz. The Persian BUCEPHALUS, fleeter than the wind; charger of Chosroes II.

Skinfaxi ("shining-mane"). The horse of day (Norse legend). *Cp.* HRIMFAXI, *above.*

Sleipnir. ODIN's eight-footed grey horse which could traverse both land and sea. The horse typifies the wind which blows from the eight principal points.

Sorrel. The horse of William III was blind in one eye and "mean of stature" (*cp.* SAVOY, *above*). It stumbled over a mole-hill and the king's fall led to his death. *See* GENTLEMAN IN BLACK VELVET.

Strymon. The horse immolated by XERXES before he invaded Greece. It came from the vicinity of the river Strymon in Thrace.

Tachebrune. The horse of OGIER THE DANE.

Trebizond. The grey horse of Guarinos, one of the French Knights taken at RONCESVALLES.

Vegliantino ("the little vigilant one"). ORLANDO's famous steed, called in Fr. romance *Veillantif,* Orlando there appearing as ROLAND.

White Surrey. Richard III's favourite horse.

Saddle White Surrey for the field tomorrow.

SHAKESPEARE: *Richard III*, V, iii.

Xanthos. See XANTHUS.

A dark horse. One whose capabilities are not known to the general public; hence a person whose abilities are undisclosed or who conceals them till he can reveal them to the best advantage.

A horse of another colour. A different affair altogether.

A horse wins a kingdom. It is said that on the death of Smerdis (522 B.C.) the several competitors for the throne of Persia agreed that he should be king whose horse neighed first when they met on the following day. The groom of Darius showed his horse a mare on the place appointed, and as soon as it arrived at the spot the following day, the horse began to neigh and won the crown for DARIUS.

A nod is as good as a wink to a blind horse. However obvious a hint or suggestion may be, it is useless if the other person cannot see it or will not take the hint. Nowadays it is more generally used in the contrary sense and usually abbreviated to "a nod is as good as a wink",—the hint is sufficient, I understand, and MUM'S THE WORD. *Cp.* VERB SAP.

But you're a dutiful son, so I'll say no more about it—a nod's as good as a wink to a blind horse.

CAPTAIN MARRYAT: *Peter Simple*, ch. li.

As strong as a horse. Very strong. *Horse* is often used with intensive effect; as *to work,* or *to eat like a horse.*

A Trojan horse. A deception, a concealed danger. *See* WOODEN HORSE OF TROY, *above.*

Don't look a gift horse in the mouth. *See* GIFT-HORSE.

Flogging a dead horse. Trying to revive interest in a worn-out topic, matter, etc.

Hold your horses! Be patient, wait a moment; don't be too precipitate; hold up for a while on whatever you are doing.

Horse and foot. The cavalry and infantry; hence all one's forces; with all one's might.

I will win the horse or loose the saddle. NECK OR NOTHING; DOUBLE OR QUITS. The story is that a man made the bet of a horse that another could not say the Lord's Prayer without a wandering thought. The bet was accepted, but before being half-way through the reciter looked up and said, "By the by, do you mean the saddle also?"

One man may steal a horse, while another may not look over the hedge. Some people are specially privileged, and can take liberties, or commit offences, etc., with impunity, while others get punished for trivialities. An old proverb given by Heywood (1546).

Straight from the horse's mouth. Direct from the highest source, which cannot be questioned. The only certain way of discovering the age of a horse is by examining its front teeth, the incisors.

The grey mare is the better horse. *See under* MARE.

They cannot draw, or **set horses together.** They cannot agree together.

'Tis a good horse that never stumbles. Everyone makes mistakes sometimes; HOMER SOMETIMES NODS.

To back the wrong horse. To make an error in judgment. A phrase from THE TURF.

To be on one's high horse, to ride the high horse. To be overbearing and arrogant; to give oneself airs. Formerly people of rank rode on tall horses or chargers.

To lock the stable after the horse is stolen or **has bolted.** To take precautions after the mischief has happened.

To put the cart before the horse. *See* CART.

To ride on the horse with ten toes.

To walk; to ride on SHANKS'S MARE.

Working with a dead horse. Doing work which has already been paid for. Such work is a *dead horse*, because you can get no more out of it.

You can take a horse to the water but you cannot make him drink. There is always some point at which it is impossible to get an obstinate or determined man to proceed farther in the desired direction. The proverb is found in Heywood (1546).

Horse-chestnut. Gerard tells us in his *Herball* (1597) that the tree is so called —

> For that the people of the East countries do with the fruit thereof cure their horses of the cough ... and such like diseases.

Another explanation is that when a leaf-stalk is pulled off, it presents a miniature of a horse's hock and foot with shoe and nail marks.

Horse-laugh. A coarse, vulgar laugh.

Horse-leech. A type of insatiable voracity; founded on the blood-sucking habits of the worm and the passage in the BIBLE; "The horseleach hath two daughters, crying, Give, give" (*Prov.* xxx, 15).

Marbeck, commentating in 1581, explains the "two daughters"—

> That is, two forks in her tongue, which he heere calleth her two daughters, whereby she sucketh the bloud, and is never saciate

Horse Marines. Go and tell that to the horse marines! Said in derision to the teller of some "tall" yarn or unbelievable story, the horse marine being an apparent absurdity. The more common phrase is "tell that to the marines" (*see under* MARINES). To belong to the "Horse Marines" is the virtual equivalent of belonging to the "AWKWARD SQUAD". *Cp.* CREDAT JUDÆUS.

Horsemen. Four Horsemen of the Apocalypse. *See under* FOUR.

Horseshoes. The belief that it is lucky to pick up a horse shoe is from the idea that it was a protection against WITCHES and evil generally. According to Aubrey, the reason is "since MARS (iron) is the enemy of SATURN (God of the Witches)". Consequently they were nailed to the house door with two ends uppermost, so that the luck did not "run out". Nelson had one nailed to the mast of the *Victory*.

One legend is that the DEVIL one day asked St. DUNSTAN, who was noted for his skill as a farrier, to shoe his "single hoof". Dunstan, knowing who his customer was, tied him tightly to the wall, and proceeded with the job, but purposely put the devil to such pain that he roared for mercy. Dunstan at last agreed to release his captive on condition that he would never again enter a place where he saw a horseshoe displayed.

Horse-trading. Hard, shrewd, bargaining.

Hortus Siccus (Lat., a dry garden). A collection of plants dried and arranged in a book.

Horus. One of the major gods of the ancient Egyptians, originally a great sky-god and sun-god, who became merged with Horus the son of OSIRIS and ISIS, and Horus the Child (*see* HARPO-CRATES). He was also identified with the King himself and the Horus-name was the first of the five names of the Egyptian King. He was the most famous of the Falcon-gods and was represented in hieroglyphics by the winged sun-disc.

Hospital (Lat. *hospitale, hospitium*, from *hospes*, a guest). Originally a hospice or hostel for the reception of pilgrims; later applied to a charitable institution for the aged and infirm (as in Greenwich Hospital, Chelsea Hospital), to charitable institutions for the education of children (as in Christ's Hospital, Emmanuel Hospital, Greycoat Hospital), and finally to the present institutions for treatment of the sick and injured. *Hotel* and *spital* are related forms. *See also* LOCK HOSPITAL; MAGDALENE.

Hospital Sunday. The SUNDAY nearest St. LUKE's day (18th OCTOBER), when churches have special collections for hospitals. The practice began in London in 1873.

Hospitallers. First applied to those whose duty it was too provide *hospitium* (lodging and entertainment) for pilgrims. The most noted institution of the kind was founded at Jerusalem (*c.* 1048), which gave its name to an order

call the Knights Hospitallers or the Knights of St. John of Jerusalem; later they were styled the Knights of Rhodes; and then the Knights of MALTA; the islands of Rhodes (1310) and Malta (1529) being, in turn, their headquarters. The order became predominantly military in the 12th century but in late 18th century reverted to its earlier purposes of tending the sick and poor, moving to ROME in 1834.

The order came to an end in England after the REFORMATION but a branch was revived in 1831 which declared itself an independent order in 1858, now styled the Order of the Hospital of St. John of Jerusalem. It founded the St. John Ambulance Association in 1877.

Host (Lat. *hostia*, a sacrifice). The consecrated bread of the EUCHARIST regarded as the sacrifice of the Body of Christ.

The Elevation of the Host. At the EUCHARIST, the raising by the celebrant of the sacred elements immediately after consecration to symbolize the offering to God and to show them for adoration.

Host, as an army or multitude, is from the Lat. *hostis*, enemy. In Med. Lat. *hostem facere* came to mean "to perform military service". *Hostis* (military service) then came to mean the army that went against the foe, whence our word *host*.

The heavenly host. The ANGELS and ARCHANGELS.

The Lord God of Hosts, Lord of Hosts JEHOVAH, the hosts being the ANGELS and celestial spheres.

Host as one who entertains guests is from the Lat. *hospes*, a guest.

To reckon without your host. To reckon from your own standpoint only; not to allow for what the other man may do or think or decide.

Hostler, or **Ostler** (os′ lĕr). The name given to the man who looked after the horses of travellers at an inn was originally applied to the innkeeper (*hosteller*) himself. It has been jokingly said to be derived from *oat-stealer* for obvious reasons.

Hot. Hot air. Empty talk, boasting, threats, etc.; bombast. Hence *hot-air merchant*, one whose utterances are "full of sound and fury, signifying nothing"; a declamatory WINDBAG.

Hot cross buns. *See* BUN.

Hot-foot. With speed; rapidly.

Hot-pot. A dish of mutton or beef with sliced potatoes cooked in a tight-lidded pot in an oven. A popular dish in the North of England.

Hot rod. An old car stripped and tuned for speed, and, by transference, the owner of such a vehicle or other unruly youth.

Hot under the collar. Agitated, angry.

I'll give it him hot and strong. I'll rate him most soundly and severely. *To get it hot* is to get severe punishment.

I'll make this place too hot to hold him. I'll "show him up", or otherwise make things so unpleasant that he will not be able to endure it.

Like hot cakes. Very rapidly; as in "to sell like hot cakes".

Not so hot. Not so good, not very satisfactory.

Hotch-pot (Fr. *hochepot*; *hocher*, to shake, and *pot*). A thick broth containing meat and vegetables and other mixed ingredients; a confused mixture or jumble. *Hodge-podge* is another alternative form.

Hotspur. A fiery person of uncontrolled temper. Harry Percy (1364–1403), son of the first Earl of Nothumberland (*see* SHAKESPEARE's *Henry IV, Pt. I*), was so called. The 14th Earl of Derby, the CONSERVATIVE Prime Minister, was sometimes called the "Hotspur of Debate". *See also* RUPERT OF DEBATE.

Houdini, Harry. The stage name of Erik Weiz (1874–1926), the most celebrated illusionist and escapologist to date. Born at Budapest of Jewish parents, who emigrated to New York, he began his career as a magician in 1890 but world fame began with his appearance at London in 1900. No lock could hold him, even that of the condemned cell at Washington gaol. He escaped from handcuffs, ropes, safes, etc., etc., and was deservedly called "the Great Houdini". He died from a punch in the stomach, delivered before he had tensed his muscles. *Cp.* DAVENPORT-TRICK.

Hound. To hound a person is to harass and persecute him as hounds worry a fox or stag.

Hour. Book of Hours. A book of devotions for private use, especially during the CANONICAL HOURS (*see under* CANON). Such books in the later MIDDLE AGES were often beautifully and lavishly illuminated and have a particular importance in the history of the book arts.

Canonical Hours. *See under* CANON.

A bad quarter of an hour. A short disagreeable experience.

At the eleventh hour. Just in time; only just in time to obtain some benefit. The allusion is to the parable of the labourers hired for the vineyard (*Matt.* xx).

In an evil hour. Acting under an unfortunate impulse. In ASTROLOGY there are lucky and unlucky hours.

In the small hours (of the morning). One, two, and three, after midnight.

My hour is not yet come. The time for action has not yet arrived; properly, the hour of my death is not yet fully come; from the idea that the hour of one's death is pre-ordained.

Their finest hour. The famous phrase from Winston Churchill's speech (18 June 1940) given at the time when the collapse of France was imminent and the BATTLE OF BRITAIN about to begin.

> Let us therefore brace ourselves to our duties, and so bear ourselves that, if the British Empire and its Commonwealth last for a thousand years, men will say: "This was their finest hour."

Houri (hoo' ri). One of the black-eyed damsels of the Mohammedan PARADISE, possessed of perpetual youth and beauty, whose virginity is renewable at pleasure, and who are the reward of every believer; hence, in English use, any dark-eyed attractive beauty.

House. The House. A familiar name for the London Stock Exchange, the HOUSE OF LORD, HOUSE OF COMMONS, etc.

The House of ... denotes a royal or noble family with its ancestors and branches, as the *House of Windsor* (the British Royal Family), the *House of Hanover*, etc.; also a commercial establishment such as the *House of Rothschild*, the bankers, the *House of Cassell*, the publishers, etc.

House of Assembly. The lower legislative chamber in the Republic of South Africa.

House of Commons. The elected house of the British PARLIAMENT. It is also the lower house in the Canadian Parliament.

A house of correction. A jail. Originally a place where vagrants were made to work and offenders were kept in ward for the correction of small offences.

A or **The House of God.** A church or place of worship; also any place sanctified by God's presence. Thus JACOB in the wilderness, where he saw the ladder leading from earth to HEAVEN, said, "This is none other but the House of God, and this is the gate of heaven" (*Gen.* xxvii, 17).

House of ill fame, or **repute.** A brothel.

House of Keys. *See* TYNWALD.

House of Lords. The upper house of the British PARLIAMENT, consisting of the lords spiritual and temporal, namely: hereditary peers, life peers (Lords of Appeal and those created under the Life Peerages Act of 1958), Scottish Representative Peers, the archbishops and certain BISHOPS of the CHURCH OF ENGLAND.

House of Office. A 17th-century term for a privy.

House of Representatives. The lower legislative chamber in the U.S.A., Australia, and New Zealand.

The House that Jack built.

> This is the man, all tattered and torn,
> That kissed the maiden all forlorn,
> That milked the cow with the crumpled horn
> That tossed the dog
> That worried the cat ...
> That lay in the house that Jack built.

There are numerous similar constructions. For example the Hebrew parable of *The Two Zuzim*, the summation of which runs thus:

10. Then came the Most Holy, blessed be He, and slew
9. The angel of death who had slain
8. The slaughterer who had slaughtered
7. The ox which had drunk
6. The water which had extinguished
5. The fire which had burned
4. The staff which had smitten
3. The dog which had bitten
2. The cat which had devoured
1. The kid which my father had bought for two zuzim.

(Two zuzim was about a halfpenny.)

Cat house. American slang for a brothel.

Clearing House. *See* CLEARING HOUSE.

A disorderly house. A brothel.

The Lower House. The HOUSE OF COMMONS, a term in use in the 15th century; in the U.S.A., the HOUSE OF REPRESENTATIVES.

The Upper House. The HOUSE OF LORDS, in the 15th century termed the "higher house". It developed from the GREAT COUNCIL of magnates. The term is also used in the U.S.A. for the Senate.

House to house. Calling at every house, one after another; as a "house-to-house canvass".

Like a house on fire. Very rapidly. The old houses of timber and thatch burned very swiftly.

To bring down the house. *See under* BRING.

To cry, or **proclaim from the house-top.** To announce something in the most public manner possible. Jewish houses had flat roofs, where their owners often slept, held gatherings, and from which public announcements were made.

To eat one out of house and home. *See under* EAT.

To keep house. To maintain an establishment. "To go into housekeeping" is to start a private establishment.

To keep a good house. To supply a bountiful table.

To keep open house. To dispense hospitality freely and generously at all times.

House-bote. Under the manorial system, a form of estover, denoting the amount of wood that a tenant was allowed to take for fuel and for repairs to his dwelling. *Bote* is O.E. profit. *See* I WILL GIVE YOU THAT TO BOOT *under* BOOT.

House-leek. Grown formerly on house-roofs from the notion that it warded off lightning, fever, and evil spirits; also called *Jove's Beard.* An edict of CHARLEMAGNE ordered that every one of his subjects should have a house-leek on his roof (*Et habet quisque supra domum suum Jovis barbam*).

Houses, Astrological. In judicial ASTROLOGY, the whole HEAVEN is divided into twelve portions by means of great circles crossing the north and south points of the horizon, through which the heavenly bodies pass every twenty-four hours. Each of these divisions is called a *house*; and in casting a HOROSCOPE the whole is divided into two parts (beginning from the east), six above and six below the horizon. The eastern ones are called the *ascendant*, because they are about to rise; the other six are the *descendant*, because they have already passed the zenith. The twelve houses each have their special functions—(1) the house of life; (2) fortune and riches; (3) brethren; (4) parents and relatives; (5) children; (6) health; (7) marriage; (8) death; (9) religion; (10) dignities; (11) friends and benefactors; (12) mystery and uncertainty.

Three houses were assigned to each of the four ages of the person whose horoscope was to be cast, and his lot in life was governed by the ascendancy of these at the various periods, and by the stars which ruled in the particular "houses".

Houses of Life. In ancient Egypt, centres of priestly learning attached to the large temples where scribes copied religious texts, the art of medicine was furthered, etc.

Household gods. The LARNES AND PENATES who presided over the dwellings and domestic concerns of the ancient Romans; hence, in modern use, the valued possessions of home, all those things that go to endear it to one.

Household Troops. Those troops whose special duty it is to attend the sovereign.

Housel (hou' zel). To give the Sacrament (O.E. *husel*, sacrifice). *Cp.* UNANELED.

Unhouseled is without having had the EUCHARIST, especially at the hour of death.

Houssain, or **Housain,** etc. In the ARABIAN NIGHTS, brother of Prince AHMED and owner of the MAGIC CARPET (*see under* CARPET).

Houyhnhnms (whinims). In *Gulliver's Travels*, a race of horses endowed with reason and all the finer qualities of man.

Swift coined the word in imitation of "whinny".

Howleglass. An old form of *Owlglass*. *See* EULENSPIEGEL.

Hoyle. According to Hoyle. According to the best usage, on the biggest authority. Edmond Hoyle's *A Short Treatise on the Game of Whist* (1742) remained the standard authority on the game for many years. *Cp.* COCKER.

Hrimfaxi. *See* FAMOUS HORSES *under* HORSE.

Hub. The nave of a wheel; a boss; a centre of activity.

Up to the hub. Fully, entirely, as fas as possible. If a cart sinks in the mire up to the hub, it can sink no lower; if a quoit strikes the hub, it is not possible to do better.

Hubert, St. Patron saint of huntsmen (d. 727), reputedly son of Bertrand, Duke of Guienne. He so neglected his religious duties for the chase that one day a stag bearing a crucifix menaced him with eternal perdition unless he reformed. Upon this he entered the cloister and duly became Bishop of Liège, and the apostle of Ardennes and Brabant. Those who were descended of his race were supposed to possess the power of curing the bite of a mad dog.

In art he is represented as a BISHOP with a miniature stag resting on the book in his hand, or as a huntsman kneeling to the miraculous crucifix borne by the stag. His day is 3 November.

Hudson, Jeffrey (1619–1682). The famous DWARF served up in a pie at an entertainment given to Charles I by the Duke of Buckingham, who afterwards gave him to Queen Henrietta Maria for a page. He was 18 in. high until the age of thirty but afterwards reached 3 ft. 6 in. or so. He was a captain of horse in the CIVIL WAR, was captured by pirates, and imprisoned for supposed complicity in the POPISH PLOT. His portrait was painted by Van Dyck, and he is featured in Scott's *Peveril of the Peak*. His armour is on show in the TOWER.

Hue and Cry. An early system for apprehending suspected criminals. Neighbours were bound to join in a hue and cry and to pursue a suspect to the bounds of the manor. It became the old common law process of pursuing "with horn and with voice" (O.Fr. *huer*, to shout).

Huer (O.Fr. *hu*, a cry). In Cornwall, the man who directs fishermen to the pilchard shoals; a BALKER.

Hug. To hug the shore. To keep as close to the shore as is compatible with a ship's safety.

To hug the wind. To keep a ship close-hauled.

Hugh of Lincoln, St. There are two saints so designated.

(1) St. Hugh (*c*. 1140–1200), a Burgundian by birth, and founder of the first CARTHUSIAN house in England. He became bishop of Lincoln in 1186. He was noted for his charitable works and kindness to the Jews. His day is 17 November.

(2) St. Hugh (13th century), the boy of about ten years of age allegedly tortured and crucified in mockery of Christ. The story goes that the affair arose from his having driven a ball through a Jew's window while at play with his friends. The boy was finally thrown into a well from which he spoke miraculously. Eighteen Jews were purported to have been hanged. The story is paralleled at a number of other places in England and on the Continent (*cp*. WILLIAM OF NORWICH), and forms the subject of Chaucer's *The Prioress's Tale*. It is also found in Matthew Paris and elsewhere.

Huguenot. The French Calvinists (*see* CALVINISM) of the 16th and 17th centuries. The name is usually said to derive incorrectly from the Ger. *Eïdgenossen*, confederates, but according to Henri Estienne (*Apologie pour Hérodote*, 1566), it is from *Hugo*, from the fact that the PROTESTANTS of Tours used to meet at night near the gate of King Hugo. *See also* BARTHOLOMEW, MASSACRE OF ST.; CALAS.

Philippe de Mornay (1549–1623) called Duplessis-Mornay, their great supporter, was nicknamed "the Huguenot Pope".

Huitzilopochtli. *See* MEXITL.

Hulda. The old German goddess of marriage and fecundity. The name means "the Benignant".

Hulda is making her bed. It snows.

Hulks, The. Old dismasted men-of-war anchored in the Thames and off Portsmouth and used as prison ships, first established as a "temporary expedient" in 1778 and remaining until 1857. An impression of the Hulks is given by Dickens in the opening chapters of *Great Expectations*.

Hum, or **Hem and Haw, To.** To hesitate in giving a positive answer; to speak with frequent pauses and interjections of such sounds.

Huma (hū' má). A fabulous oriental bird which never alights, but is always on the wing. It is said that every head which it overshadows will wear a CROWN. The bird suspended over the throne of Tippoo Sahib at Seringapatam represented this poetical fancy.

Humanitarians. A name given to certain ARIANS who held that Christ was only man. The name was also used of the UNITARIANS and of the followers of Saint-Simon (1760–1825), an early exponent of socialism.

Nowadays the term is usually applied to philanthropists in general.

Humanities. Grammar, rhetoric, and poetry, with Greek and Latin (*literæ humaniores*); in contradistinction to divinity (*literæ divinæ*). Also of more general application to polite scholarship in general.

> The use of 'humanities' ... to designate those studies which are esteemed the fittest for training the true humanity in man.
> TRENCH: *Study of Words*, Lect. iii.

Humanity Martin. Richard Martin (1754–1834), one of the founders of the Royal Society for the Prevention of Cruelty to Animals. He secured the passage of several laws for the suppression of cruelty to animals.

Humber. The legendary king of the HUNS, fabled by Geoffrey of Monmouth to have invaded Britain about 1000 B.C. He was defeated in a great battle by LOCRIN near the river which bears his name. "Humber made towards the river in his flight, and was drowned in it, on account of which it has since borne his name."

Humble. A man of humble birth is one of low estate, born of the common people. Here "humble" is from the Lat. *humilis*, lowly.

A humble bee, a bumble bee, or dumbledor. Here "humble" is probably a derivative of *hum* in imitation of the droning noise of the bee. *Cp.* Ger. *Hummel*.

A humble cow is a polled cow, a cow without horns. Here "humble" is a variant of *hamble*, to mutilate.

To eat humble pie. *See under* EAT.

Humour, Good humour, ill, or **bad humour,** etc. According to the ancients there are four principal humours in the body: phlegm, blood, choler and black BILE. As any one of these predominates it determines the temper of the mind and body; hence the expressions sanguine, choleric, phlegmatic, melancholic humours. A just balance made a "good humour" and a preponderance of any one of the four an "ill" or "evil humour". See Ben Jonson's *Every Man Out of His Humour* (*Prologue*).

Humpback, The. Geronimo Amelunghi, *Il Gobbo di Pisa*, an Italian burlesque poet of the mid-16th century.

Cristoforo Solario (or Solari), Italian sculptor and architect, *Il gobbo* (1460–1527).

Humphrey. To dine with Duke Humphrey. To have no dinner to go to. The Good Duke Humphrey (*see under* GOOD) was renowned for his hospitality. At death it was reported that a monument would be erected to him in St. Paul's, but he was buried at St. Alban's. The tomb of Sir John Beauchamp (d. 1358), on the south side of the nave of old St. Paul's was popularly supposed to be that of the Duke, and when the promenaders left for dinner, the poor staybehinds who had no dinner to go to, or who feared arrest for debt if they left the precincts, used to say, when asked by the gay sparks if they were going, that they would "dine with Duke Humphrey" that day.

Humpty Dumpty. Short and broad, like the egg-shaped figure of the nursery rhyme; also a gypsy drink made of ale boiled with brandy.

Hun. An uncivilized brute; from the barbarian tribe of Huns who invaded the East Roman Empire in the 4th and 5th centuries. In World War I a slang name applied to the Germans.

Hundred. From pre-CONQUEST times, a division of the English shire, corresponding to the WAPENTAKE of Danish areas. Originally the Hundred probably consisted of 100 hides, hence the name (*see* HIDE). The Hundred Court or MOOT, which survived until late in the 19th century, met regularly in mediæval times to deal with private pleas, criminals, matters of taxation, etc.

The equivalent unit in Northumberland, Cumberland, Westmorland and Durham was called a WARD.

Yorkshire, Lincolnshire, Nottinghamshire, Derbyshire, Leicestershire and Rutland were divided into WAPENTAKES. Yorkshire had also three larger divisions called RIDINGS. Similarly Kent was divided into five LATHES and Sussex into six RAPES each with subordinate hundreds.

Chiltern Hundreds. *See* CHILTERN.

Great, or **Long hundreds.** Six score, a hundred and twenty.

The Hundred Days. The days between 20 March 1815, when NAPOLEON reached the TUILERIES (after his escape from Elba) and 28 June, the date of the second restoration of Louis XVIII. Napoleon left Elba, 26 February; landed near Cannes, 1 March; and finally abdicated 22 June.

The address of the prefect of PARIS to Louis XVIII on his second restoration begins: "A hundred days, sire, have elapsed since the fatal moment when your majesty was forced to quit your capital in the midst of tears." This is the origin of the phrase.

Hundred Years War. The long series of wars between England and France, beginning in the reign of Edward III, 1337, and ending in that of Henry VI, 1453.

The first battle was the naval victory of Sluys, 1340, and the last a defeat at Castillon, 1453. It originated in English claims to the French crown and results in the English losing all their possessions except Calais, which was held until 1558.

Old Hundred, or **Old Hundredth.** A famous and dignified Psalm tune that owes its name to its being so designated in the Tate and Brady *Psalter* of 1696 to indicate the retention of the setting of Kethe's version of the 100th Psalm in the *Psalter* of 1563 (by Sternhold and Hopkins). The tune is of older origin and is found as a setting to the 134th psalm in Marot and Beza's *Genevan Psalter* of 1551.

Hero of the hundred fights. Conn, a semi-legendary Irish king, of the 2nd century.

Hundred and thousands. A name given by confectioners to very tiny comfits.

It will all be the same a hundred years hence. An exclamation of resignation—it doesn't much matter what happens. It is an old saying and occurs in Ray's *Collection*.

Not a hundred miles off. An indirect way of saying "in this very neighbourhood" or "very spot". The phrase is used when it would be indiscreet or dangerous to refer more directly to the person or place hinted at.

The hundred-eyed. ARGUS in Greek and Latin fable. JUNO appointed him guardian of IO (the cow), but JUPITER caused him to be put to death; whereupon Juno transplanted his eyes into the tail of her peacock.

The Hundred-handed. Three of the sons of URANUS, namely, Ægæon or BRIAREUS, Cottys or COTTUS, and Gyges or Gyes. After the TITANS were overcome during the war with ZEUS and hurled into TARTARUS, the Hundred-handed ones were set to keep watch and ward over them.

CERBERUS is sometimes so called because from its three necks sprang writhing snakes instead of hair.

Hungary Water. Made of ROSEMARY flowers and spirit, said to be so called because a hermit gave the recipe to a Queen of Hungary.

Hunger. Hunger march. A march of the unemployed to call attention to their grievances, as that of 1932, the year in which Wal Hannington, the leader of the National Union of Unemployed Workers, led a march on London. The biggest of the marches organized by the N.U.W.M. was that against the MEANS TEST in 1936.

The march of the Blanketeers (*see under* BLANKET) was in effect the first such march.

Hunger Strike. The refusal of prisoners to take food in order to embarrass the authorities or to secure release; a notable SUFFRAGETTE tactic. *See* CAT AND MOUSE ACT.

Hungry. There are many common similes expressive of hunger, including— hungry as a hawk, a hunter, a church mouse, a dog. James Thomson (*The Seasons: Winter*) has "Hungry as the grave" and Oliver Wendell Holmes, "Hungry as the chap that said a turkey was too much for one, not enough for two."

The Hungry Forties. The 1840s in Great Britain, from the widespread distress among the poor, especially before 1843. Characterized by bad harvests, dear bread, and unemployment, it was the period of CHARTISM. 1847 and 1848 were also bad years; but the 1820s were probably worse than the 1840s. The situation was helped by the railway boom and Peel's financial measures.

Hunky. Hunky dory. An expression of approval, all's right or satisfactory. It is an elaborated form of 'hunky", derived from Dut. *honk*, goal, station, or "home" as in TAG and other games; hence, adjectivally, to be in a good or satisfactory position.

He who hunts two hares leaves one and loses the other. No one can do well or properly two things at once, he "falls between two stools". "No man can serve two masters."

To hunt with the hounds and run with the hare. *See under* HARE.

Hunters and Runners of classic renown:

ACASTUS who took part in the famous Calydonian hunt (*see under* BOAR).

ACTÆON, the famous huntsman who was transformed by DIANA into a stag, because he chanced to see her bathing.

ADONIS, beloved by VENUS, slain by a wild boar whil hunting.

ADRASTUS, who was saved at the siege of Thebes by the speed of his horse Arion, given him by HERCULES.

ATALANTA, who promised to marry the

man who could outstrip her in running.
CAMILLA, the swiftest-footed of all the
companions of DIANA.
LADAS, the swiftest-footed of all the
runners of ALEXANDER THE GREAT.
MELEAGER, who took part in the great
Calydonian boar-hunt (*see under*
BOAR).
ORION, the great and famous hunter,
changed into the constellation so con-
spicuous in November.
PHEIDIPPIDES, who ran 150 miles in
two days.

The mighty hunter. NIMROD was so
called (*Gen*. x, 9). The meaning seems
to be a conqueror. Jeremiah says, "I
[the Lord] will send for many hunters
[warriors], and they shall hunt [chase]
them [the Jews] from every mountain
... and out of the holes of the rocks."
(xvi, 16).

> Proud Nimrod first the bloody chase
> began—
> A mighty hunter, and his prey was man.
> POPE: *Windsor Forest.*

Hunting the gowk, snark, etc. *See*
these words.

Hurdy-gurdy. A stringed musical instrument, the music of which is produced
by the friction of a rosined wheel on the
strings, which are stopped by means of
keys. It had nothing to do with the
barrel-organ or piano-organ of the
streets which is sometimes so called,
probably from its being played by a
handle.

Hurlo-thrumbo. A ridiculous burlesque,
which in 1729–1730 had an extraordinary run at the Haymarket Theatre.

Husband. The word is from O.E. *hus*,
house, and Old Norse *bondi*, a free-
holder or yeoman, from *bua*, to dwell;
hence literally *husband* is a house-owner
in his capacity as head of the household,
and so it came to be applied to a married
man, who was the natural head of the
household. When Sir John Paston, writing to his mother in 1475, said:

> I purpose to leeffe alle heer, and come to
> you, and be your hosbonde and balyff,

he was proposing to come and manage
her household for her. We still use the
word in this sense in such phrases as **To
husband one's resources.**

Husbandry is merely the occupation of
the *husband* (in the original sense), the
management of the household; later re-

stricted to farm management, and the
husband became the *husbandman*.

Hush. Hush-hush. A term that came into
use in World War I to describe very secret operations, designs, or inventions;
from the exclamation "hush" enjoining
silence. *Cp.* TOP SECRET.

Hush-money. Money given as a bribe
for silence or "hushing" a matter up.

Hussites. Followers of John Hus, the Bohemian religious reformer (1369–1415),
sometimes called WYCLIFFITES from the
fact that many of the teachings of John
Hus were derived from those of Wyclif.

Hustings. A Norse word *hus-thing* (*Hus*,
house; *thing*, assembly); hence the assembly of a KING, EARL or chief. Hence
its application to open-air meetings connected with Parliamentary elections. In
many towns the *hustings court* transacted some legal business, particularly
that of the City of London, which still
exists and is presided over by the Lord
Mayor and sheriffs, although shorn of
most of its former powers. The use of
the word for the platform on which no-
minations, etc., of Parliamentary candidates were made (until the passing of
the Ballot Act of 1872) derives from its
first application to the platform in the
Guildhall on which the London court
was held. A realistic impression of the
old hustings at a Parliamentary election
is given by Dickens in *Pickwick Papers*
(ch. xiii).

To be beaten at the hustings. To
lose an election.

Hutber's Law. "Improvement means deterioration". A telling phrase coined by
Patrick Hutber (1928–1980), City Editor of the *Sunday Telegraph* from 1966
to 1979. It pin-pointed the growing tendency of officialdom to palm off reduced
services of poorer quality as "new and
improved". *Cp.* PARKINSON'S LAW.

Hyacinth (hī'ǎ sinth). According to
Greek fable, the son of Amyclas, a Spartan king. The lad was beloved by APOL-
LO and ZEPHYR and as he preferred the
sun-god, Zephyr drove Apollo's quoit at
his head, and killed him. The blood became a flower, and the petals are inscribed with the signature AI, meaning
woe (VIRGIL; *Eclogues*, iii, 106).

Hyades (hī'ǎ dēz) (Gr. *huein*, to rain).

Seven NYMPHS, daughters of ATLAS and Pleione, placed among the stars, in the constellation TAURUS, which threaten rain when they rise with the sun. The fable is that they wept at the death of their brother Hyas so bitterly that ZEUS out of compassion took them to HEAVEN. *Cp.* PLEIADES.

Hydra. A many-headed water-snake of the Lernaean marshes in Argolis. It was the offspring of TYPHON and ECHIDNA and was variously reputed to have one hundred heads, or fifty, or nine. It was one of the "twelve labours" of HERCULES to kill it, and, as soon as he struck off one of its heads, two shot up in its place. Hence **Hydra-headed** applied to a difficulty which goes on increasing as it is combated. The monster was eventually destroyed by Hercules with the assistance of his charioteer, who applied burning brands to its wounds as soon as each head was severed by his master.

Hyena (hī ē′ nà). Held in veneration by the ancient Egyptians, because it is fabled that a certain stone, called the "hyænia", is found in the eye of the creature, and Pliny asserts (*Nat. Hist.*, xxxvii, 60), that when placed under the tongue it imparts the gift of prophecy.

Hygeia (hī jē′ à). Goddess of health in Greek mythology, and the daughter of ÆSCULAPIUS. Her symbol was a serpent drinking from a cup in her hand.

Hyksos. The so-called "Shepherd Kings" who ruled Egypt from the end of the 18th century B.C. to the beginning of the 16th, the period between the Middle and New Kingdoms. They were Asiatic invaders, and the name derives from a mistranslation of the Egyptian word, which more correctly means "foreign princes".

Hylas (hī làs). A boy beloved by HERCULES, carried off by the NYMPHS while drawing water from a fountain in Mysia.

Hymen (hī′ men). Properly, a marriage song of the ancient Greeks; later personified as the god of marriage, represented as a youth carrying a torch and veil—a more mature EROS, or CUPID.

Hype. A slang abbreviation of *hypodermic* meaning a hypodermic needle or an injection from same. *Hyped up* is to be self-injected with a drug or to be artificially excited or stimulated. *Hype* used in the sense of a deception, racket or for misleading, inflated, or highly exaggerated advertising publicity, may be derived from the prefix *hyper*—meaning more than normal, excessive, or possibly from *hypodermic*.

Hyperboreans. In Greek legend, a happy people dwelling beyond the North Wind, BOREAS from which their name was supposedly derived. They were said to live for a thousand years under a cloudless sky, knowing no strife or violence. The word is applied in general to those living in the extreme north.

Hyperion. In Greek mythology, one of the TITANS, son of URANUS and GÆA, and father of HELIOS, SELENE, and Eos (the Sun, Moon, and Dawn). The name is sometimes given by poets to the sun itself, by not by Keats in his "Fragment" of this name.

Hypermnestra. Wife of LYNCEUS and the only one of the fifty daughters of Danaus who did not murder her husband on their bridal night. *See* DANAIDES.

Hypnotism. The art of producing trance-sleep, or the state of being hypnotized. Dr. James Braid of Manchester gave it this name (1843), after first calling it *neuro-hypnotism* (Gr., an inducing to sleep of the nerves).

Hypocrite. Prince of Hypocrites. Tiberius Cæsar (42 B.C., A.D. 14–37) was so called because he affected a great regard for decency, but indulged in the most detestable lust and cruelty.

Abdullah Ibn Obba and his partisans were called *The Hypocrites* by MOHAMMED, because they feigned to be friends, but were in reality foes.

Hypostatic Union. The union of three Persons in the TRINITY; also the union of the Divine and Human in Christ, in which the two elements, although inseparably united, each retain their distinctness. The *hypostasis* (Gr. *hypo*, under; *stasis*, standing; hence foundation, essence) is the personal existence as distinguished from both *nature* and *substance*.

Hyssop. David says (*Ps.* li, 7): "Purge me with hyssop, and I shall be clean." The reference is to the custom of ceremonially sprinkling the unclean with a bunch of hyssop (marjoram or the thorny caper) dipped in water in which had been mixed the ashes of a red heifer. This was done as they left the Court of the Gentiles to enter the Court of the Women (*Numb.* xix, 17, 18).

Hysteron proteron (his′ tĕr on prō′ tĕr on) from the Greek meaning "hinder foremost". A term used in rhetoric to describe a figure of speech in which the word that should come last is placed first or the second of two consecutive propositions is stated first, *e.g.* "*Moriamur, et in media arma ruamus*"—Let us die, and rush into the midst of the fray (VIRGIL, *Æneid*, ii, 353).

In logic, the offering of what is essentially an axiom as a proof of some theorem the proof of which depends upon the axiom. *Cp.* PETITIO PRINCIPII.

I

I. The ninth letter of the alphabet, also the FUTHORC, representing the Greek *iota* and Semitic *yod*. The written and printed *i* and *j* were for long interchangeable; it was only in the 19th century that in dictionaries, etc., they were treated as separate letters (in Johnson's Dictionary, *iambic* comes between *jamb* and *jangle*), and hence in many series—such as the signatures of sheets in a book, hallmarks on plate, etc.— either I or J is omitted. *Cp.* U. I is number one in Roman notation.

The dot on the small *i* was introduced about the 11th century as a diacritic in cases where two i's came together (e.g. *filii*), to distinguish between these and *u*.

I in logic denotes a particular affirmative.

To dot the i's and cross the t's. *See* DOT.

I.H.S. The Greek I H Σ, meaning IHΣους (Jesus), the long η (H) being mistaken for capital *H*, the abbreviation 'ihs' was often expanded as 'Ihsesus'. St. Bernadine of Siena in 1424 applied them to *Jesus Hominum Salvator* (Jesus, the Saviour of men). Other explanations were *In Hac Salus* (safety in this, *i.e.* the Cross) and *In Hoc Signo* [*vinces*] (in this sign [ye shall conquer]). *See* CONSTANTINE'S CROSS *under* CROSS.

I.N.R.I. The initial letters of the inscription affixed to the CROSS of Christ by order of Pontius Pilate—*Iesus Nazarenus, Rex Iudæorum*, Jesus of Nazareth, King of the Jews (*John* xix, 19). It was written in Greek, Latin, and Hebrew. (*Luke* xxiii, 38)

I.O.U., *i.e.* "I owe you". The acknowledgement of a debt given by the borrower to the lender. As such it requires no stamp. *See* HURRY.

I.R.A. The Irish Republican Army, a guerrilla force largely reorganized by Michael Collins from the former Irish Volunteers, which confronted the Royal Irish Constabulary and the BLACK AND TANS from 1919 to 1923. After the CIVIL WAR, extremists kept it in being as a secret organization and although proscribed in 1936, it continued to make occasional raids into ULSTER, its aim now being to establish a united Irish Republic. After a period of quiescence, violence steadily increased from the mid-1950s. Since 1969 its senseless acts of terrorism in Ulster, England and elsewhere have made a settlement of the Ulster problem increasingly difficult.

Iambic. An *iamb*, or *iambus*, is a metrical foot consisting of a short syllable followed by a long one, as *away*, *deduce*, or an unaccented followed by an accented, as *be gone!* Iambic verse is verse based on iambs, as for instance, the ALEXANDRINE measure, which consists of six iambuses:

> I think the thoughts you think; and if I
> have the knack
> Of fitting thoughts to words, you peradventure lack,
> Envy me not the chance, yourselves
> more fortunate!
> > BROWNING: *Fifine at the Fair*, lxxvi.

Ianthe. A Cretan girl who, as told in Ovid's METAMORPHOSES, ix, 714–797, married Iphis, who had been transformed for the purpose from a girl into a young man. The Ianthe to whom Lord BYRON dedicated his *Childe Harold* was Lady Charlotte Harley, born 1801, and only eleven years old at the time. Shelley gave the name to his eldest daughter.

Iapetus (ī ăp' ě tŭs). Son of URANUS and GÆA, father of ATLAS, PROMETHEUS,

Epimetheus, and Menœtius, and, for the Greeks, father of the human race, hence called *genus Iapeti*, the progeny of Iapetus.

Iberia (ī′ bēr′ i à). Spain, the country of the *Iberus*, the ancient name of the river Ebro.

Iberia's Pilot. Christopher Columbus (*c.* 1446–1506), a Genoese by birth but a servant of Spain from 1492.

Ibis (ī′ bis). A sacred bird of the ancient Egyptians, with white body and black head and tail. It was the incarnation of THOTH. It is still found in the Nile marshes of the upper Sudan. The sacred ibis was often mummified after death.

Iblis. *See* EBLIS.

Ibn Sina. *See* AVICENNA.

Ibraham. The ABRAHAM of the Koran.

Ibsenism. A concern in drama with social problems, realistically rather than romantically treated, as in the works of the Norwegian dramatist Henrik Ibsen (1828–1906), whose plays, translated by William Archer and championed by G. B. Shaw (1856–1950), infused new vigour into English drama.

Icarius. In Greek legend an Athenian who was taught the cultivation of the vine by DIONYSUS. He was slain by some peasants who had become intoxicated with wine he had given them, and who thought they had been poisoned. They buried him under a tree; his daughter Erigone, searching for her father, was directed to the spot by the howling of his dog Mœra, and when she discovered the body she hanged herself for grief. Icarius, according to this legend, became the constellation BOÖTES, Erigone the constellation VIRGO, and Mœra the star PROCYON, which rises in July, a little before the dog-star.

Icarus. Son of DÆDALUS. He flew with his father from Crete; but the sun melted the wax with which his wings were fastened on, and he fell into the sea. Those waters of the Ægean were thenceforward called the Icarian Sea.

Ice. Ice Age. This term is usually applied to the earlier part of the existing geological period, the Pleistocene, when a considerable portion of the northern hemisphere was overwhelmed by ice caps. PALÆOLITHIC man was contemporary with at least the latter periods of the Ice Age, his remains having been found, together with the mammoth and reindeer, in glacial deposits.

The Antarctic continent was also more completely ice-covered and glaciers existed on the heights of Hawaii, New Guinea, and Japan. The Ice Age is also called the *glacial epoch*.

Ice Saints, or Frost Saints. Those saints whose days fall in what is called "the blackthorn winter"—that is, the second week in May (between 11 and 14). Some give only three days, but whether 11, 12, 13, or 12, 13, 14, it is not agreed. 11 May is the day of St. Mamertus, 12 May of St. PANCRAS, 13 May of St. Servatius, and 14 May of St. BONIFACE.

Iceberg. The tip of an iceberg. That which is merely on the surface, a small or superficial manifestation of something with the implication that there is much more, or worse to follow of which the present is only a beginning.

The ice-blink. The mariner's name for a luminous appearance of the sky, caused by the reflection of light from ice. If the sky is dark or brown, the navigator may be sure there is water; if it is white, rosy, or orange-coloured he may be certain there is ice. The former is called a "water-sky", the latter an "ice-sky".

The Danish name for the great ice-cliffs of Greenland is "The Ice-blink".

To break the ice. *See under* BREAK.

To cut no ice. To make no impression on others or have no influence or effect.

To skate over thin ice. To take unnecessary risks, especially in conversation or argument; to touch on a dangerous subject very lightly.

Iceni. *See* BOADICEA.

Ich Dien (ish dēn) (Ger., I serve). The motto of the PRINCE OF WALES since the time of Edward, the BLACK PRINCE (1330–1376); said, without foundation, to have been adopted, together with the three white ostrich feathers, from John, King of Bohemia, who fell at the battle of Crécy in 1346.

According to Welsh tradition Edward I promised to provide WALES with a prince "who could speak no word of

English", and when his second son Edward (later Edward II) was born at Caernarvon he presented him to the assembly, saying in Welsh *Eich dyn* (Your Man).

Ichabod (ik′ ả bod). A son of Phinehas, born just after the death of his father and grandfather (I *Sam*. iv, 19). The name ("no glory") is translated "The glory has departed", hence the use of Ichabod as an exclamation.

Ichneumon. A species of mongoose venerated by the ancient Egyptians and called "Pharaoh's rat" because it fed on vermin, crocodiles' eggs, etc. The word is Gr. and means "the tracker".

Ichor (ī′ kôr). In classical mythology, the colourless blood of the gods (Gr. juice).

Ichthys (ik′ this) (Gr. *ichthus*, fish). From the 2nd century the fish was used as a symbol of Christ and the word is also an acronym formed from the initial letters of *Jesous CHristos, THeou Uios, Soter* (Jesus Christ, Son of God, Saviour). It is found on many seals, rings, urns and tombstones of the early Christian period and was believed to be a charm of mystical efficacy.

Icon, or **Ikon** (Gr. *eikon*, an image or likeness). A representation in the form of painting, low-relief sculpture or mosaic of Our Lord, The Blessed Virgin, or a SAINT, and held as objects of veneration in the EASTERN CHURCH. Excepting the face and hands, the whole is often covered with an embossed metal plaque representing the figure and drapery.

Icon Basilike. *See* EIKON BASILIKE.

Iconoclasts (Gr., image-breakers). In the 8th century reformers, essentially in the EASTERN CHURCH, opposed to the use of sacred pictures, statues, emblems, etc. The movement against the use of images was begun by the Emperor Leo III, the Isaurian, who was strongly opposed by the monks and also by Pope Gregory II and Pope Gregory III. The controversy continued under successive *Iconoclast Emperors*, notably Constantine V, called insultingly "Copronymus" by his opponents (he is said to have fouled the font at baptism). It was finally ended by the Empress Theodora in 843 in favour of the image-lovers, and Iconoclasm was proscribed.

Id, in Freudian psychology, is the whole reservoir of impulsive reactions that forms the mind, of which the EGO is a superficial layer. It is the totality of impulses or instincts comprising the true unconscious mind.

Id est. (Lat., that is). Normally abbreviated to *i.e.*

Ida. Mount Ida. A mountain or ridge of mountains in the vicinity of TROY; the scene of the Judgment of PARIS. *See* APPLE OF DISCORD.

Idæan Dactyls. *See* DACTYLS.

Ideal Commonwealths. *See* COMMONWEALTHS.

Idealism, as a philosophical theory, takes a variety of forms, all of which agree that the mind is more fundamental than matter and that mind does not originate in matter; also that the material world is less real than that of the mind or spirit. Modern idealism has its roots in the philosophy of Bishop Berkeley (1685–1753), sometimes called *theistic idealism*. The more important theories of idealism are:

Transcendental Idealism taught by I. Kant (1724–1804); *Subjective Idealism* taught by J. G. Fichte (1762–1814); *Absolute Idealism*, taught by G.ˉW. F. Hegel (1770–1831); and *Objective Idealism* taught by F. W. J. von Schelling (1775–1854).

Idealism in the general sense is applied to ethical and aesthetic concepts, etc., which adopt "ideal" or perfectionist standards. *Cp*. MATERIALISM.

Ides. In the ancient Roman CALENDAR the 15th of March, May, July, and October, and the 13th of all the other months; always eight days after the NONES.

Beware the Ides of March. Said as a warning of impending and certain danger. The allusion is to the warning received by Julius CÆSAR before his assassination:

> What is still more extraordinary, many report that a certain soothsayer forewarned him of a great danger which threatened him on the ides of March, and that when the day was come, as he was going to the senate-house, he called to the soothsayer, and said, laughing, "The ides of March are come"; to which he answered, softly, "Yes; but they are not gone."
>
> PLUTARCH: *Julius Cæsar (Langhorne trans.).*

Idiot. A mentally deficient or stupid person, originally (in Greece), a private person, one not engaged in any public office hence an uneducated, ignorant individual. The Greeks have the expressions, "a priest or an idiot" (layman), "a poet or an idiot" (prose-writer). In I *Cor.* xiv, 16, where the AUTHORIZED VERSION reads, "how shall he that occupieth the room of the unlearned say Amen...?" Wyclif's version reads, "who fillith the place of an idyot, how schal he seie amen...?"

Idle Bible, The. *See* BIBLE, SOME SPECIALLY NAMED EDITIONS.

Idomeneus. King of Crete and ally of the Greeks at TROY. After the city was burnt he made a vow to sacrifice whatever he first encountered if the gods granted him a safe return to his kingdom. He met his own son and duly sacrificed him, but a plague followed, and the king was banished from Crete as a murderer. *Cp.* IPHIGENIA.

Idris. Traditionally a Welsh giant, prince and astronomer. His rock hewn seat is on the summit of *Cader Idris* (the chair of Idris) in Gwynedd. According to legend, any person passing a night upon this will be either dead in the morning, in a state of frenzy, or endowed with the highest poetical inspiration.

Iduna. In Scandinavian mythology, daughter of the dwarf Svald and wife of BRAGI. She was guardian of the golden apples which the gods tasted whenever they wished to renew their youth. Iduna was lured away from ASGARD by LOKI, but eventually restored, and the gods were once more able to grow youthful again and Spring came back to the earth.

Ifreet. *See* AFREET.

If. If youth but knew and age could do. This probably derives from Louis VI of France (1081–1137), also called Louis the Fat. Abbot Suger, his friend and counsellor, said that it was the King's frequent regret never to be able to have knowledge and strength together: "In my youth had knowledge, and in my old age had strength been mine, I might have conquered many Kingdoms".

Ifs and Ans.

If ifs and ans
Were pots and pans
Where would be the tinker?

An old-fashioned jingle to describe wishful thinking; "if wishes were horses beggars could ride". The "ans", often erroneously written "ands", are merely the old use of "an" for "if".

Igerna. *See* IGRAINE.

Ignatius, St. According to tradition St. Ignatius was the little child whom our Saviour set in the midst of his disciples for their example. He was a convert of St. JOHN THE EVANGELIST, was consecrated Bishop of Antioch by St. PETER, and is said to have been thrown to the beasts in the amphitheatre by TRAJAN about 107. His day is 17 October and he is represented in art with lions, or chained and exposed to them.

Ignatius Loyola, St. *See* LOYOLA.

Ignis Fatuus. The "Will o' the wisp" or "Friar's lanthorn", a flame-like phosphorescence flitting over marshy ground (due to the spontaneous combustion of gases from decaying vegetable matter), and deluding people who attempt to follow it; hence any delusive aim or object, or some Utopian scheme that is utterly impracticable. The name means "a foolish fire" and is also called "Elf-fire", "Jack o'lantern", "Peg-a-lantern", "Kit o' the canstick", "Spunkie", "Walking Fire", "Fair Maid of Ireland", "John in the Wad".

According to Russian folklore, these wandering fires are the spirits of still-born children which flit between HEAVEN and the INFERNO.

Ignoramus (Lat., we take no notice of it. The grand jury used to write *ignoramus* on the back of indictments "not found" or not to be sent to court. This was often construed as an indication of the stupidity of the jury, hence its present meaning.

Ignorantines. A name given to the Brothers of the Christian Schools, A Roman Catholic religious fraternity founded at Reims by the Abbé de la Salle in 1680 for giving free education to the children of the poor. They now carry out teaching work in many countries. A clause in their constitution prohibited the admission of priests with theological training, hence the name, which was also given to a body of Augustinian mendicants, the Brothers of Charity, or Brethren of Saint Jean-de-Dieu, founded in Portugal in 1495.

Igraine, Igerna. In ARTHURIAN ROMANCE, the wife of Gerlois (Gorlois), Duke of Tintagel, in CORNWALL, and mother of King ARTHUR. His father, UTHER Pendragon, married Igraine the day after her husband was slain.

Ihram (i răm). The ceremonial garb of Mohammedan pilgrims to MECCA; also the ceremony of assuming it.

> We prepared to perform the ceremony of *Al-Ihram* (assuming the pilgrim garb) ... we donned the attire, which is nothing but two new cotton cloths, each six feet long by three and a half broad, white with narrow red stripes and fringes.... One of these sheets, technically termed the *Rida*, is thrown over the back, and, exposing the arm and shoulder, is knotted at the right side in the style *Wishah*. The *Izar* is wrapped round the loins from waist to knee, and knotted or tucked in at the middle, supports itself.
> BURTON: *Pilgrimage to Al-Madinah and Mecca*, xxvi.

Il Milione. *See* MILIONE.

Iliad (Gr. *Iliados*, of Ilium or Troy). The epic poem of twenty-four books attributed to HOMER, recounting the siege of TROY, PARIS, son of King PRIAM of Troy, when guest of MENELAUS, King of Sparta, ran away with his host's wife, HELEN. Menelaus induced the Greeks to lay siege to Troy to avenge the perfidy, and the siege lasted ten years. The poem begins in the tenth year with a quarrel between AGAMEMNON, King of Mycenae and commander-in-chief of the allied Greeks, and ACHILLES, the hero who had retired from the army in ill temper. The Trojans now prevail and Achilles sends his friend PATROCLUS to oppose them, but Patroclus is slain. Achilles in a desperate rage rushes into the battle and slays HECTOR, the commander of the Trojan army. The poem ends with the funeral rites of Hector.

Ilk, Of that (O.E. *ilca*, the same). This phrase is often misused to mean "of the same kind", but is only correctly used when the surname of the person spoken of is the same as the name of his estate; *Bethune of that ilk* means "Bethune of Bethune". Used adjectively it means

"every", "each"; as in "Ilka lassie has her laddie."

Ill-starred. Unlucky; fated to be unfortunate. In SHAKESPEARE's *Othello* (v, ii), Othello says of Desdemona, 'O ill-starr'd wench!" The allusion is to the astrological dogma that the stars influence the fortunes of mankind.

Illuminati. The baptized were at one time so called, because a lighted candle was given them to hold as a symbol that they were illuminated by the HOLY GHOST.

The name has been given to, or adopted by, several sects and secret societies professing to have superior enlightenment, especially to a republican society of deists founded by Adam Weishaupt (1748–1830), at Ingolstadt in Bavaria in 1776, to establish a religion consistent with "sound reasons". They were also called *Perfectibilists*.

Image-breakers, The. ICONOCLASTS.

Imagism. A school of poetry founded by Ezra Pound (1885–1972), derived from the ideas of the philosopher T. E. Hulme (1883–1917). The imagist poets were in revolt against excessive romanticism, and proclaimed that poetry should use the language of common speech, create new rhythms, be uninhibited in choice of subject, and present an image.

Imam. An Arabic word meaning "leader", *i.e.* one whose example is to be followed. The title is given to the head of the MOSLEM community but is more familiar through its application to those leading the prayers in the Mosques, the *lesser Imams*. The name is also given as an honorary title and to the ruler of the Yemen.

Hidden Imam. *See* MAHDI.

Imbroccata, or **imbrocata** (Ital.). An old fencing term for a thrust over the arm.

Immaculate Conception. This dogma, that the Blessed Virgin Mary was "preserved immaculate from all stain of original sin" from "the first moment of her conception" was not declared by the ROMAN CATHOLIC CHURCH to be an article of faith until 1854 when Pius IX issued the Bull *Ineffabilis Deus*. It has a long history as a belief and was debated by the SCHOOLMEN. It was denied by St. THOMAS AQUINAS (*see* THOMISTS), but upheld by Duns Scotus. (*See* DUNCE).

The Feast of the Immaculate Conception is on 8 December; it is a HOLIDAY OF OBLIGATION in some countries.

Immolate. To sacrifice (Lat. *immolare*, to sprinkle with meal). The reference is to the ancient Roman custom of sprinkling wine and fragments of the sacred cake (*mola salsa*) on the head of a victim to be offered in sacrifice.

Imp. Lincoln Imp. *See* LINCOLN.

Impanation. The dogma that the body and blood of Christ are locally present in the consecrated bread and wine of the EUCHARIST, just as God was present in the body and soul of Christ. The word means "putting into the bread" and is found as early as the 11th century. *Cp.* TRANSUBSTANTIATION.

Imperial Conference. The name given to the conferences held in London between the prime ministers of the various dominions of the British Empire between 1907 and 1946 inclusive. These conferences had their origin in the first Colonial Conference which met in 1887 on the occasion of Queen Victoria's JUBILEE. Since 1948 the COMMONWEALTH Prime Ministers' Conference has replaced the Imperial Conference.

Imposition. Imposition of hands. *See* LAYING ON OF HANDS *under* HAND.

Impositions, as duties levied on imports under royal prerogative, were a point of dispute between James I and the Commons. CHARLES I continued to levy them until the fall of Strafford in 1642, when he consented to an ACT OF PARLIAMENT rendering them illegal. Extra written work, lines, etc., given to schoolchildren as punishments are also called *impositions*.

Impossibilities. Examples of the many familiar expressions denoting the impossible are:

Gathering grapes from thistles.
Fetching water in a sieve.
Washing a blackamoor white.
Catching wind in cabbage nets.
Flaying eels by the tail.
Making cheese of chalk.
Squaring the circle.
Turning base metal into gold.
Making a silk purse of a sow's ear.

Impressionism. The first of the modern art movements, taking its name from a condemnatory criticism of Claude Monet's painting *Impression: Sunrise*, shown in 1874, Edouard Manet, Auguste Renoir, Camille Pissaro and Edgar Degas were the leading impressionist painters who upheld the new approach. As the name implies, they rejected the established conventions and sought to capture the impression of colour of transitory and volatile nature rather than its form. It broke down the distinction between a sketch and a finished painting. *See* SALON DES REFUSÉS.

Cp. CUBISM; DADAISM; FAUVISM; FUTURISM; ORPHISM; POINTILLISM; POST-IMPRESSIONISM; SURREALISM; SYNCHRONISM; VORTICISM.

Imprimatur (Lat., let it be printed). An official licence to print a book. Such a licence or *royal imprimatur* was required under the Licensing Act of 1662 to secure ecclesiastical conformity. The act was initially for two years, was not renewed after 1695, and was in abeyance from 1679 to 1685.

In the ROMAN CATHOLIC CHURCH, if a priest writes on theological and moral subjects the book has to receive an *imprimatur* and NIHIL OBSTAT. The former is granted by the BISHOP or his delegate. *Cp.* INDEX.

Impropriation (Lat. *impropriare*, to take as one's own). Profits of an ecclesiastical BENEFICE in the hands of a layman, who is called the *impropriator*. When the benefice is in the hands of a spiritual corporation it is called *appropriation*. At the REFORMATION, many appropriated monastic benefices passed into the hands of lay rectors, who usually paid only a small part of the TITHE to incumbents, hence the need for QUEEN ANNE'S BOUNTY.

In. Ins and outs. All the details of a subject, event, etc.

To be in for it. To be due for something unpleasant; to be due for a telling off; punishment is to be expected.

To have it in for a person is to be planning to work off a grudge against him; to be waiting the opportunity to get one's own back.

In Camera (Lat. vault or chamber). In judicial proceedings, the hearing of a case, either in the Judge's private room, or in Court, the public being excluded. Criminal cases may not be heard *in camera*.

In Cœna Domini (in chā' na dom' i ni) (Lat., on the Lord's Supper). A papal BULL issued from the 13th century until its suspension in 1773 owing to the opposition of the civil authorities. It contained excommunications and censures against heresies, schism, sacrilege, and the infringement of papal and ecclesiastical privileges by temporal powers, etc. Its publication came to be restricted to MAUNDY THURS- DAY and many of its ecclesiastical censures were incorporated in Pius IX's bull *Apostolicæ Sedis* (1869).

In commendam (in kom en' dâm) (Lat., in trust). The holding of church preferment for a time, during a vacancy; and later restricted to livings held by a BISHOP in conjunction with his SEE. There were many abuses, and the practice was ended in England in 1836.

In esse (in es' i) (Lat. *esse*, to be). In actual existence, as opposed to *in posse*, in potentiality. Thus a living child is "in esse", but before birth is only "in posse".

In extenso (Lat.). At full length, word for word, without abridgement.

In extremis (in eks trē' mis). At the very point of death; *in articulo mortis*.

In flagrante delicto (Lat., while the offence is flagrant). RED-HANDED; in the very act.

In gremio legis (in grē' mi ō lē' jis) (Lat., in the bosom of the law). Under the protection of the law.

In loco parentis (in lō' kŏ pa ren' tis) (Lat., in place of a parent). Usually applied to those having temporary charge of minors in some capacity and therefore taking over parental functions.

In medias res (in mē' di ās rāz) (Lat., in the middle of things). In novels and epic poetry, the author generally begins *in medias res*. *Cp.* AB OVO.

In memoriam (Lat.). In memory of.

In partibus (infidelium) (Lat., in the regions of the faithless.) A "bishop *in partibus*" was a Roman Catholic BISHOP in any country, Christian or otherwise and usually without a diocese, whose title was from some old SEE fallen away

from the Catholic faith. Pope Leo XIII abolished the designation in 1882 and substituted that of "titular bishop".

In pectore. *See* IN PETTO.

In petto (Ital.). Held in reserve, kept back, something done privately and not announced to the general public. (Lat. *in pectore*, in the breast.)

Cardinals in petto. CARDINALS chosen by the POPE, but not yet proclaimed publicly. Their names are in *pectore* [of the Pope].

In posse. *See* IN ESSE.

In propria persona (Lat.). Personally, and not by deputy or agents.

In re (in rē) (Lat.). In the matter of; on the subject of; as *In re* Jones *v.* Robinson.

In rem. against the property or thing referred to.

In situ (Lat.). In its original place.

> I at first mistook it for a rock *in situ*, and took my compass to observe the direction of its cleavage.
> CHARLES DARWIN: *The Voyage of the "Beagle"*, ch. ix.

In statu quo (in stăt' ū kwō) or, **In statu quo ante** (Lat.). In the state in which things were before the change took place.

To maintain the status quo is to keep things as they are.

In statu pupillari (L. Lat.). Under guardianship.

In toto (in tō' tō) (Lat.). Entirely, altogether.

In vacuo (in văk' ū ō) (Lat.). In a vacuum.

In vino veritas (Lat.). *See* VINO.

Inbread. *See* BAKER'S DOZEN.

Inca. A king or royal prince of the dynasty governing Peru before the Spanish conquest; a member of the tribe in Peru at that time. The capital of their extensive empire was at Cuzco, and the dynasty was mythologically descended from Manco Capac, who was high priest of the Sun. His brothers were Cachi (Salt), Uchu (Pepper), and Auca (Pleasure). It was prophesied that Manco's golden rod would sink into the ground on reaching their destined home. This happened at Cuzco—

> Here the children of the Sun ... soon entered upon their beneficent mission among the rude inhabitants of the coun-

try; Manco Capac teaching the men the art of agriculture and Mama Oello initiating her own sex in the mysteries of weaving and spinning.

H. M. PRESCOTT: *The Conquest of Peru*, I, i.

The last of the Inca dynasty Atahuallpa was murdered by the Spaniards in 1533.

Incarnation. The Christian doctrine that the Son of God took human flesh and that Jesus Christ is truly God and truly man (L.Lat. *incarnari*, to be made flesh).

Inchcape Rock. A dangerous rocky reef (also called the Bell Rock) about 12 miles from Arbroath in the North Sea (Inch or Innis means *island*). The abbot of Arbroath or "Aberbrothok" fixed a bell on a timber float as a warning to mariners. Southey's ballad of this name tells how the pirate Ralph the Rover cut the bell adrift and was himself wrecked on the very rock as a consequence.

A similar tale is told of St. Govan's bell in Pembrokeshire. In the chapel was a silver bell, which was stolen one summer evening by pirates, but no sooner had their boat put to sea than it was wrecked.

Incog.—*i.e.* **Incognito** (Ital. from Lat. *incognitus*, unknown). Under an assumed name or title. When a royal person, public figure, or a celebrity travels and does not wish to be treated ceremoniously or desires to avoid the public gaze he temporarily adopts another name and travels *incog*.

Incorruptible, The. Robespierre. *See* SEA-GREEN.

Incubus. A nightmare, anything that weighs heavily on the mind. In mediæval times it denoted an evil demon who was supposed to have sexual intercourse with women during their sleep (L.Lat. *incubus*, a nightmare). *Cp.* SUCCUBUS.

Incunabula (Lat., swaddling clothes; from *cunae*, a cradle). The cradle, birthplace, origins, or early stages of anything. The word is particularly and arbitrarily applied to early days of printing and book production up to 1500, although this date does not mark any significant change in these crafts. The middle of the 16th century is a much more satisfactory termination of the early period of printing and book production.

Independence Day. 4 July, which is kept as a national holiday in the United States of America, because the Declaration of Independence asserting the sovereign independence of the former British colonies was adopted on 4 July 1776.

Independents. A collective name for the various PROTESTANT separatist sects, especially prominent in 17th-century England, who rejected both Presbyterianism and EPISCOPACY, holding that each congregation should be autonomous or independent. The earliest were the BARROWISTS and BROWNISTS of Elizabeth I's reign, and the BAPTISTS and CONGREGATIONALISTS became the two main groups, but there were others more eccentric such as the FIFTH-MONARCHY MEN. They were notably strong in the Cromwellian army.

Index, The (Index Librorum Prohibitorum). The "List of Prohibited Books" of the ROMAN CATHOLIC CHURCH which members were forbidden to read except in special circumstances. The first Index was made by the INQUISITION in 1557, although Pope Gelasius issued a list of prohibited writings in 494 and there had been earlier condemnations and prohibitions. In 1571 Pius V set up a *Congregation of the Index* to supervise the list, and in 1917 its duties were transferred to the Holy Office. The Index was abolished 14 June 1966. In addition to the Index there was the *Codex Expurgatorius* of writings from which offensive doctrinal or moral passages were removed. Since 1897 diocesan bishops were given greater responsibility in the control of literature and the Index became less prominent.

All books likely to be contrary to faith and morals, including translations of the BIBLE not authorized by the Church, were formerly placed on the Index. Among authors wholly or partly prohibited were Chaucer, Bacon, Milton, Addison, Goldsmith, Locke, Gibbon; Montaigne, Descartes, VOLTAIRE, Hugo, Renan; Savonarola, Croce, D'Annunzio; and for a long time Galen, Copernicus, and Dante. *Cp.* IMPRIMATUR.

India. India paper. A creamy-coloured printing-paper originally made in China and Japan from vegetable fibre, and used for taking off the finest proofs of engraved plates; hence **India proof**, the proof of an engraving on India paper, before lettering.

The *India paper* (or *Oxford India paper*) used for printing Bibles and high- class "thin paper" and "pocket" editions is a very thin, tough, and opaque imitation. The name "India" given to these papers arises from their original importation through the "India trade" which brought in the products of the Far East.

Indian. American Indians. When Columbus left Spain in 1492 he set out to reach India and China, etc., by sailing west. When he reached the Bahamas the natives were called Indians in the belief that he had reached the fringes of the East. Hence the later name *West Indies*. *See* AMERINDIANS.

Indian file. Singly, one after another. From the American Indian practice of progressing in single file, each one of the column stepping in his predecessor's footprints, and the last man obliterating them. Thus neither the track nor the number of warriors could be traced.

Indian Mutiny. The name given to the revolt in parts of British India (1857–1859) which was primarily a mutiny of sepoys in the East India Company's Bengal army rather than a national revolt against British rule.

Indian ringworm. Dhobie itch.

Indian summer. A term of American origin now generally applied to a period of fine sunny weather in late autumn. In America it is applied to such a period of mild dry weather usually accompanied by a haze. The name arose from the fact that such weather was more pronounced in the lands formerly occupied by the Indians than in the eastern regions inhabited by the white population. *Cp.* St. MARTIN'S SUMMER.

Indo-European. A term invented by Thomas Young, the Egyptologist, in 1813, and later adopted by scientists, anthropologists, and philologists to describe the racial and linguistic origins of the main Indian and European peoples.

Philologists have classified the Indo-European languages in groups such as Indo-Iranian, Greek, Italic, CELTIC, Germanic, etc.

Indra. An ancient Hindu god of the sky, originally the greatest, who was the hurler of thunderbolts and giver of rain, a god of warriors and of nature. He is represented as four-armed and his steed is an elephant. He is the son of HEAVEN and Earth and lives on the fabulous Mount MERU, the centre of the earth, north of the Himalayas.

Induction (Lat., the act of leading in). When a clergyman is inducted to a living he is led to the church door, and his hand is laid on the key by the archdeacon. The new incumbent then tolls the bell.

Indulgence. In the ROMAN CATHOLIC CHURCH, the remission before God of the earthly punishment due for sins of which the guilt has been forgiven in the sacrament of Penance. Such indulgences are granted out of the TREASURY OF THE CHURCH; they are either plenary or partial. In the later MIDDLE AGES the sale of indulgences by PARDONERS became a grave abuse and it was the hawking of indulgences by Tetzel and the DOMINICANS in Germany that roused Luther and precipitated the REFORMATION.

Declarations of Indulgence. Declarations issued by Charles II (1662 and 1672) and James II (1687 and 1688) suspending the penal laws against DISSENTERS and Roman Catholics. Except for that of 1662, they were issued under royal prerogative; that of 1688 led to the trial of the SEVEN BISHOPS.

Industrial Revolution. A term popularized by Arnold Toynbee whose *Lectures on The Industrial Revolution of the 18th century in England* were published in 1884, although used half a century earlier by French observers. It generally denotes the whole range of technological and economic changes which transformed Great Britain from an essentially rural society into an urban industrialized state. The limiting dates usually assigned to this period of change vary somewhat, between 1750 to 1780 as the beginning and 1830 to 1850 as the end. The Industrial Revolution in this country occurred earlier than elsewhere.

Inexpressibles. A 19th-century EUPHEM-ISM for trousers, also called *unmentionables*. This absurdity is attributed to PETER PINDAR (*see* PINDAR) who used it in a biting LAMPOON on the DANDY Prince Regent.

Infallibility. In the ROMAN CATHOLIC CHURCH, the POPE, when speaking EX CATHEDRA on a question of faith and morals is held to be free from error. This dogma was adopted by the VATI-CAN COUNCIL of 1870 (many members dissenting or abstaining from voting) and was publicly announced by Pius IX at St. Peter's.

Infant (Lat. *infans*; ultimately from *in*, negative, and *fari*, to speak). Literally, one who is unable to speak; a child. It was used as a synonym of CHILDE, as "The Infant hearkened wisely to her tale" (Spenser, *The Faerie Queene*, VI, viii, 25). Hence **Infanta,** any princess of the royal blood in Spain and Portugal except an heiress of the crown; and **Infante,** any son of the sovereigns of Spain and Portugal except the crown prince who, in Spain, is called the Prince of the Asturias.

Infantry. Foot-soldiers. This is the same word as INFANT; it is the Ital. *infanteria*, from *infante*, a youth; hence one young and inexperienced who acted as a page to a KNIGHT, hence a foot-soldier.

Inferno. We have DANTE'S notion of the infernal regions in his *Inferno*: HOMER'S in the ODYSSEY, Bk. XI; VIRGIL'S in the ÆNEID, Bk. VI; Spenser's in THE FAERIE QUEENE, Bk. II, canto vii; Ariosto's in ORLANDO FURIOSO, Bk. XVII; Tasso's in JERUSALEM DELIVERED, Bk. IV; Milton's in PARADISE LOST; Fénelon's in *Télémaque*, Bk. XVIII; and Beckford's in his romance of VATHEK. *See* HELL; HADES.

Infra dig. Not befitting one's position and public character. Short for Lat. *infra dignitatem*, beneath (one's) dignity.

Infralapsarian. The same as SUBLAPSAR-IAN.

Ink. From Lat. *encaustus*, burnt in, encaustic.

Inkhorn terms. A common 16th-century term for pedantic expressions which smell of the lamp (*see under* LAMP). The inkhorn was the receptacle of horn, wood or metal which pedants and pedagogues carried with them.

Ink-slinger. A contemptuous term for a writer, especially a newspaper journalist.

Inn. The word is Old English and originally meant a private dwelling-house or lodging. Hence Clifford's Inn, once the mansion of De Clifford; Lincoln's Inn, the abode of the Earls of Lincoln; GRAY'S INN. The word then came to be applied to a public house giving lodging and entertainment, or a tavern.

Inns of Court. The four voluntary societies in London which have the exclusive right of calling to the English BAR. They are the Inner Temple, The Middle Temple, Lincoln's Inn and GRAY'S INN. Each is governed by a board of BENCHERS.

Innings. He has had a long, or **a good innings.** A good long run of luck, a long time in office, etc. An innings in cricket is the time that the eleven or an individual has in batting at the wicket.

Innocent, An. An idiot or born fool was formerly so called.

> Although he be in body deformed, in minde foolish, an innocent borne, a beggar by misfortune, yet doth he deserve a better then thy selfe.
>
> LYLY: *Euphues* (1579).

The Feast of the Holy Innocents. *See under* HOLY.

The massacre of the Innocents. *See* MASSACRE.

Ino. *See* LEUCOTHEA.

Inquisition, The (Lat. *inquisitio*, an enquiry). The name given to the ecclesiastical jurisdiction in the CATHOLIC Church dealing with the prosecution of heresy. In the earlier days of the Church excommunication was the normal punishment, but in the later 12th and early 13th centuries, disturbed by the growth of the Cathari (*see* ALBIGENSES), the Church began to favour seeking the aid of the State. The Inquisition as such was instituted by Pope Gregory IX in 1231, influenced by the activities of the Emperor Frederick II against HERETICS. Inquisitors were appointed, chiefly from the DOMINICAN and FRANCISCAN Orders to uphold the authority of the Church in these matters. They held court in the local monastery of their order. Proceedings were in secret, and torture, as a means of breaking the will of the accused, was authorized by Pope Innocent IV in 1252. Obstinate heretics were handed over to the secular authorities for punishment which usually meant death at the stake (*see* AUTO DA FÉ). In 1542 the *Congregation of the Inquisition* was set up as the final court of appeal in trials of heresy, and its title was changed to *The Congregation of the Holy Office* in 1908 and it was renamed *The Sacred Congregation for the Doctrine of the Faith* in 1965, concerned with the maintenance of ecclesiastical discipline.

The famous Spanish Inquisition was established in 1479, closely bound up with the State, and at first directed against "converts" from Judaism and IS-LAM. Its famous first Grand Inquisitor was Torquemada (1420–1498), and during his term of office some 2,000 heretics were burned. The Spanish Inquisition was abolished by Joseph Bonaparte in 1808, reintroduced in 1814 and finally terminated in 1834.

Inscription (on coins). *See* LEGEND.

Inspired Idiot, The. Oliver Goldsmith (1728–1774) was so called by Horace Walpole.

Installation. The correct term for the induction of a CANON or prebendary to his *stall* in a cathedral or collegiate church. Members of certain orders of CHIVALRY are also *installed*.

Institutes (Lat. *instituere*, to set up). A digest of the elements of a subject, especially law, as Coke's *Institutes of the Laws of England* and Erskine's *Institutes of the Laws of Scotland*.

Insult. Literally, to leap on (the prostrate body of a foe); hence, to treat with contumely (Lat. *insultare*, to leap upon). Terence says, *Insultare fores calcibus* (*Eunuchus*, II, ii, 54). The priests of BAAL, to show their indignation against their gods, "leaped upon the altar which they had made" (I *Kings* xviii, 26). *Cp.* DESULTORY.

Intelligence Quotient, or I.Q., is the ratio, expressed as a percentage, of a person's mental age to his actual age, the former being the level of test performance which is median for that age tested by the Binet type scale or some similar system. Thus if a 10-year-old has a mental age of 9, his I.Q. is 90. 100 indicates average intelligence. The term was introduced by William Stern and popularized by L. M. Terman.

Inter alia (Lat.) Among other things or matters.

Intercalary (Lat. *inter*, between; *calare*, to proclaim solemnly). An *intercalary day* is a day inserted between two others, as 29 February in a LEAP YEAR; so called because, among the Romans, this was a subject of solemn proclamation. *Cp.* CALENDS.

Interdict. In the ROMAN CATHOLIC CHURCH, an ecclesiastical punishment placed upon individuals, particular places, or a district, restrictions being placed upon participation in, or performance of, certain SACRAMENTS, solemn services and public worship. *Cp.* EXCOMMUNICATION.

Interest. In an interesting condition. Said of an expectant mother. The phrase came into use in the 18th century.

Interlingua. An international language consisting of the living Latin roots in all European languages. It dates from about 1908 and was the product of the former VOLAPÜK academy. *Cp.* ESPERANTO.

International, or **Internationale.** The recognized international socialist and communist anthem. The words were written in 1871 by Eugène Pottier, a woodworker of Lille, and set to music by P. Degeyter.

Internationals. The name usually applied to the international federations of Socialist and Communist parties (*see under* COMMUNISM), the first of which was set up under the auspices of Karl Marx in 1864 as the International Working Men's Association, lasting till 1872. The INTERNATIONALE was adopted as its anthem. The Second, or Social-Democratic International, was formed in 1889 and the Third or Communist International was set up by Lenin in 1919 and lasted until 1941. The abortive Trotskyite Fourth International dates from 1936.

Interregnum, The. In British history usually implies the period of the COMMONWEALTH and Protectorate from the execution of Charles I (30 Jan. 1649) until the RESTORATION (18 May 1660). The period between the flight of James II (22 Dec. 1688) and the accession of William and Mary (23 Feb. 1689; 20 April 1689 in Scotland) was also an Interregnum.

Intolerable Acts. The American name for a group of British measures directed against Massachusetts in 1774, after the BOSTON TEA PARTY. They consisted of the Boston Port Act, closing the port of Boston; the Massachusetts Government Act, increasing British control; the Transportation Act, permitting British officials accused of capital offences to be tried outside Massachusetts; and the Quartering Act, which stationed royal troops in the barracks of Boston.

Invalides (an' và lēd). *Hôtel des Invalides*. The great institution founded by Louis XIV at Paris in 1670 for infirm soldiers. It contains a museum of military objects and notably the parish church of Saint-Louis containing the tomb of NAPOLEON, whose body was brought thither from St. Helena in 1840. Close by are the tombs of his son, The Duc de Reichstadt (L'Aiglon), and Marshal Foch (1851–1929). Others buried there are Joseph Bonaparte (1768–1844), King of Naples and Spain; Jerome Bonaparte (1784–1860), King of Westphalia; Marshal Turenne (1611–1675); General Bertrand (1773–1844); Marshals Duroc (1772–1813) and Grouchy (1766–1847); General Kleber (1753–1800).

Invention of the Cross. *See under* CROSS.

Inventors. Among the inventors and innovators "hoist with their own petard" (*see* PETARD), the following examples are of interest, although some no doubt belong to the realm of fable.

Bastille. Hugues Aubriot, Provost of Paris, who built the BASTILLE (*c.* 1369), was the first person confined therein. The charge against him was heresy.

Brazen Bull. Perillus of Athens made a brazen bull for PHALARIS, Tyrant of Agrigentum, intended for the execution of criminals, who were shut up in the bull, fires being lighted under the belly. Phalaris admired the invention and tested it on Perillus, who was the first person baked to death in the horrible monster.

Eddystone Lighthouse. Henry Winstanley erected the first Eddystone lighthouse. It was a wooden polygon, 100 feet high, on a stone base. The architect perished in his own edifice when it was washed away by a storm in 1703.

Gallows and gibbet. We are told in the *Book of Esther* (vii, 9) that HAMAN devised a gallows 50 cubits high on which to hang Mordecai, by way of commencing the extirpation of the Jews; but the favourite of Ahasuerus was himself hanged thereon. Similarly Enguerrand de Marigny, Minister of Finance to Philip the Fair (1284–1314), was hanged on the gibbet which he had caused to be erected at Montfaucon for the execution of certain felons; four of his successors in office suffered the same fate.

Guillotine. Dr. J. B. V. Guillotin of Lyons was guillotined, but he was not the man after whom the GUILLOTINE was named.

Iron Cage. The Bishop of Verdun, who invented the Iron Cage, too small to allow the person confined in it to stand upright or lie at full length, was the first to be shut up in one. Cardinal La Balue, who recommended them to Louis XI, was himself confined in one for ten years.

Ostracism. Cleisthenes of Athens introduced the practice of OSTRACISM and was the first to be banished thereby.

Sanctuary. Eutropius induced the Emperor Arcadius to abolish the benefit of SANCTUARY; but a few days afterwards he committed some offence and fled for safety to the nearest church. St. Chrysostom told him that he had fallen into his own net, and he was put to death.

Turret-ship. Cowper Coles, inventor of the Turret-ship, perished in the *Captain* off Finisterre, 7 September 1870.

Witch-finding. Matthew Hopkins, the witch-finder, was himself tried by his own tests, and put to death as a WIZARD in 1647. *Cp.* DEATH FROM STRANGE CAUSES.

Investiture Controversy. The name given to disputes between the Church and the Emperor and other princes over the right to invest abbots and BISHOPS with the ring and staff and to receive homage.

Invincibles. An Irish secret society of FE-NIANS founded in Dublin in 1881 with the object of doing away with the English "tyranny" and killing the "tyrants". They were responsible for the PHŒNIX PARK MURDERS.

Invisibility, according to fable, was obtainable in many ways. For example:

Alberich's cap, "Tarnkappe", which SIEGFRIED obtained, rendered him invisible (NIBELUNGENLIED).

The helmet of PERSEUS, loaned by PLUTO and made by the CYCLOPS for the god of the underworld, rendered its wearer invisible.

JACK THE GIANT-KILLER had a cloak of invisibility as well as a cap of knowledge.

Otnit's ring. The ring of Otnit, King of Lombardy, according to the HELDEN-BUCH, rendered its wearer invisible.

Reynard's wonderful ring, according to REYNARD THE FOX, had three colours, one of which (green), made the wearer invisible.

Invulnerability. There are many fabulous instances of this having been acquired. According to Greek legend, a dip in the river STYX rendered ACHILLES invulnerable, and MEDEA rendered JASON, with whom she had fallen in love, proof against wounds and fire by anointing him with the PROMETHEAN UNGUENT.

SIEGFRIED was rendered invulnerable by anointing his body with dragon's blood.

Io. The priestess of JUNO of whom JUPITER became enamoured. When Juno discovered his liaison, Jupiter transformed Io into a heifer and she wandered over the earth, finally settling in Egypt, when she was restored to human form.

Ionic Order. One of the three Greek orders of architecture, so called from Ionia, where it took its rise. The capitals are decorated with volutes, which are

the characteristic feature of this order. *Cp.* CORINTHIAN ORDER; DORIC ORDER; TUSCAN ORDER.

Ionic School. A school of philosophy that arose in the 6th century B.C. in Ionia, notable as the nursery of Greek philosophy. It included Thales, Anaximander, Anaximenes, Heraclitus, Anaxagoras, and Archelaus. They sought a primal substance from which the infinite diversity of phenomena have evolved. Thales said it was water, Anaximenes thought it was air. Heraclitus maintained that it was fire. Anaxagoras developed a theory of fragments or particles from which all things emerged by process of aggregation and segregation.

Iota. *See* I; JOT.

Iphigenia. In classical legend, the daughter of AGAMEMNON and CLYTEMNESTRA. One account says that her father, having offended ARTEMIS by killing her favourite stag, vowed to sacrifice the most beautiful thing the year brought forth; this was his infant daughter. He deferred the sacrifice till the Greek fleet that was proceeding to TROY reached AULIS and Iphigenia had grown to womanhood. Then CALCHAS told him that the fleet would be wind-bound till he had fulfilled his vow; accordingly the king prepared to sacrifice his daughter, but Artemis at the last moment snatched her from the altar and carried her to HEAVEN, substituting a hind in her place. Euripides wrote a tragedy *Iphigenia in Tauris* and Gluck has an opera *Iphigénie en Tauride* (1779); the former's *Iphigenia in Aulis* was incomplete at his death. *Cp.* IDOMENEUS.

Ipse dixit (Lat., he himself said so). A mere assertion, wholly unsupported. "It is his *ipse dixit*" implies that there is no guarantee that what he says is so.

Ipso facto (Lat., by the very fact). Irrespective of all external circumstances of right or wrong; absolutely. It sometimes means the act itself carries the consequences. Thus by burning the PAPAL BULL (*see under* BULL), Luther *ipso facto* denied the POPE's supremacy.

Ireland. *Iar-en-land*, the land of the west. Called by the natives Erin, *i.e. Erinnis* or *Iar-innis*, west island; by the Welsh *Iwerddon*, west valley; by Apuleius Hibernia, which is *Iernia*, a corruption of *Iar-inni-a*; by Juvenal (ii, 160) Iuverna, the same as *Ierna* or *Iernia*; and by Claudian *Ouernia*.

The fair maid of Ireland. Another name for the IGNIS FATUUS.

The three great saints of Ireland. St. PATRICK, St. Columba, and St. Bridget.

Irene (I rē′ nē). The Greek goddess of peace and wealth (Gr. *Eïrene*). She is represented as a young woman carrying PLUTUS in her arms. Among her attributes are the OLIVE branch and CORNUCOPIA.

Iris. Goddess of the rainbow, or the rainbow itself. In classical mythology she was the messenger of the gods, and of JUNO in particular, and the RAINBOW is the bridge or road let down from heaven for her accommodation.

Besides being poetically applied to the rainbow, the name, in English, is given to the coloured membrane surrounding the pupil of the eye, and to a family of plants (Iridaceæ) having large, bright-coloured flowers and tuberous roots.

Iron. The Iron Age. An archæological term denoting the cultural phase conditioned by the introduction of the use of iron for edged-tools, implements, weapons, etc. In the Near East the preceding Bronze Age ended about 1200 B.C. and by 1000 B.C. the Iron Age was established. North of the Alps the first Iron Age, known as the HALLSTATT period, began about 750 B.C., in England about 500 B.C. and in Scotland the Bronze Age lasted till about 250 B.C. *See* LA TÈNE.

The era between the death of CHARLEMAGNE and the close of the Carlovingian dynasty (814–987) is sometimes so called from its ceaseless wars. It is sometimes called the *leaden age* for its worthlessness. *Cp.* DARK AGES. *See also* AGE.

Iron Chancellor. The name given to Prince Bismarck (1815–1898), the creator of the German Empire. *See* BLOOD AND IRON POLICY *under* BLOOD.

The Iron Cross. A Prussian military decoration (an iron Maltese CROSS, edged with silver), instituted by Frederick William III in 1813 during the struggle against NAPOLEON. Remodelled by William I in 1870 with three grades, in civil and military divisions, some 3,000,000 Iron Crosses were awarded in World War I.

Iron Curtain. The phrase denoting the barrier of secrecy created by the U.S.S.R. and her satellites along the Stettin-Trieste line, the Communist countries east of this line having cut themselves off from Western Europe after World War II. The phrase was popularized by Sir Winston Churchill in his Fulton Speech (5 March 1946) but it was used previously in Germany by Count Schwerin von Krosigk on 2 May 1945; and by Lord Conesford in February of that year. It has an earlier antecedent; Ethel Snowden used it in 1920 with reference to BOLSHEVIK Russia, Lord D'Abernon used it in 1925 with regard to the proposed Locarno Treaties, and the Queen of the Belgians, in 1914, spoke of a "bloody iron curtain", between her and the Germans. The phrase occurs in the Earl of Munster's journal as far back as 1817.

> From Stettin on the Baltic to Trieste on the Adriatic, an iron curtain has descended across Europe.
> SIR WINSTON CHURCHILL: *Fulton Speech*.

The Iron Duke. The Duke of Wellington (1769–1852) was so called from his iron will.

Iron Guard. The title adopted by the Rumanian FASCIST party of the 1930s.

The Iron Horse. The railway locomotive.

The Iron Lady. The name bestowed upon Mrs Margaret Thatcher, when leader of the Opposition in the HOUSE OF COMMONS, by the Soviet Defence Ministry newspaper *Red Star* (24 January 1976).

The Iron Maiden of Nuremberg. A mediæval instrument of torture used in Germany for traitors, heretics, parricides, etc. It was a box big enough to admit a man with folding doors, the whole studded with sharp iron spikes. When the doors were closed on him these spikes were forced into the body of the victim, and he was left to die.

Iron Mask, The Man in the. In the reign of Louis XIV, a mysterious state prisoner held for over forty years in various gaols until he finally died in the

BASTILLE on 19 November 1703. When travelling from prison to prison he always wore a mask of black velvet, not iron. His name was never revealed but he was buried under the name of "M. de Marchiel". Many conjectures have been made about his identity, one of them being that he was the Duc de Vermandois, an illegitimate son of Louis XIV. Dumas, in his romantic novel on the subject, adopted VOLTAIRE's suggestion that he was an illegitimate elder brother of Louis XIV with Cardinal Mazarin for his father. The most plausible suggestion is that of the historians Lord Acton and Funck-Brentano, who suggested a minister of the Duke of Mantua (Count Mattiolo, b. 1640), who, in his negotiations with Louis XIV, was found to be treacherous, and imprisoned at Pignerol.

Iron rations. Emergency rations, especially as provided in the army; usually tinned food, particularly BULLY BEEF and biscuit. Also, in World War I a popular name for hot shell-fire.

Ironside. Edmund II (c. 998–1016), King of England from April to November, 1016, was so called from his iron armour.

Ironsides. Cromwell's soldiers were so called after 1644. Their resolution at Marston Moor caused Prince Rupert to nickname Cromwell "Old Ironsides", and the name was thereafter applied to his men.

Shooting-iron. Slang for a small firearm, especially a pistol or revolver.

The iron entered his soul. This expression, used of one experiencing the pangs of anguish and embitterment, is found in the Prayer Book Version of *Ps.* cv (verse 18). It is a mistranslation of the Hebrew which appeared in the VULGATE. It was corrected in the Authorized Version of the BIBLE which says "whose feet they hurt with fetters: he was laid in iron", *i.e.* he was put in irons or fetters. Coverdale, following the Vulgate, says—"They hurte his feet in the stocks, the yron pearsed his herte."

The iron fist, or **hand in the velvet glove.** Ruthlessness, extreme severity, or tyranny covered by a polite and courteous manner.

In irons. In fetters. A sailing vessel is said to be *in irons* when head to wind without way and will not pay off on either tack. The vessel is temporarily unmanageable.

Strike while the iron is hot. Don't miss a good opportunity; take action while the situation lends chance of success. An allusion to the blacksmith's shop.

Too many irons in the fire. More affairs in hand than you can properly attend to. The allusion is to the smithy.

To rule with a rod of iron. To rule tyrannically.

Irony (ī' ron i) (Gr. *eironeia*, simulated ignorance). The use of expressions having a meaning different from the ostensible one; a subtle form of sarcasm understood correctly by the initiated.

Socratic irony. The assumption of ignorance as a means of leading on and eventually confuting an opponent.

The irony of fate. That which brings about quite the opposite of what might have been expected. Thus by an irony of fate Joseph became the saviour of his brethren who had cast him into the pit.

Iroquois (ir' ō kwa). The French form of the Indian name of the FIVE NATIONS.

Irredentism. The name given to national minority movements seeking to break away from alien rule and to join up with neighbours of their own nationality and language. It derives from *Italia Irredenta* (unredeemed Italy), the name given by the Italians, between 1861 and 1920, to those Italian-speaking areas still under foreign rule. When the kingdom of Italy was formed in 1861 Venetia, ROME, Trieste, the Trentino, Nice, etc., were not included.

Irresistible. ALEXANDER THE GREAT, before starting on his expedition against Persia, went to consult the Delphic ORACLE on a day when no responses were made. Nothing daunted he sought out PYTHIA and when she refused to attend took her to the temple by force. "Son," said the priestess, "thou art irresistible." "Enough,' cried Alexander, "I accept your words as an answer."

Irus. The gigantic beggar who carried out the commissions of the suitors of PENELOPE. When he sought to hinder the returning ULYSSES, he was felled to the ground by a single blow. "Poorer than Irus" was a classical proverb.

Isenbras, or **Isumbras, Sir**. A hero of mediæval romance who made visits to the HOLY LAND and slaughtered thousands of SARACENS. At first proud and presumptuous, when he was visited by all sorts of punishments; afterwards penitent and humble when his afflictions were turned into blessings. It was in this latter stage that he one day carried on his horse two children of a poor woodman across a ford.

Iseult. *See* YSOLDE.

Ishmael. An outcast. From the son of ABRAHAM and his concubine Hagar, handmaid of his wife Sarah. Hagar was driven into the wilderness by Sarah's harshness before her son was born. The Arabs regard Ishmael as their ancestor. *See* HAGARENES.

> And he will be a wild man; his hand will be against every man, and every man's hand against him.—
> *Genesis* xvi, 12.

Ishtar. The Babylonian goddess of love and war (Gr. *Astarte*), corresponding to the Phœnician ASHTORETH, except that, while the latter was identified with the moon, Ishtar was more frequently identified with the planet VENUS.

Isidorian Decretals. *See* DECRETALS.

Isis (ī' sis). The principal goddess of ancient Egypt, sister and wife of OSIRIS, and mother of HORUS, she typified the faithful wife and devoted mother. The cow was sacred to her, and she is represented as a queen, her head being surmounted by horns and the solar disc or by the double crown (*see* EGYPT). Her chief shrines were at Abydos and Busiris; later a splendid temple was built at Philæ. Proclus mentions a statue of her which bore the inscription "I am that which is, has been, and shall be. My veil no one has lifted. The fruit I bore was the Sun", hence **to lift the veil of Isis** is to pierce the heart of a great mystery.

She was worshipped as a nature goddess throughout the Roman world and was identified with JUNO, IO, APHRODITE, ASTARTE anda others, and in due course she became an embodiment of the universal goddess. Milton, in *Para-*

dise Lost (I, 478), places her among the fallen ANGELS.

Islam. The religion of Moslems, the whole body of the Moslems. The word means resignation or submission to the will of God.

Islam involves five duties:
(1) Recital of the creed (There is but one God and MOHAMMED is his Prophet).
(2) Reciting daily prayers.
(3) Fasting in the month of RAMADAN.
(4) Giving the appointed legal alms.
(5) Making a pilgrimage to MECCA at least once in a lifetime (*Hajj*).

Islands of the blest. *See* FORTUNATE ISLANDS.

Isle of Dogs. A peninsula on the left bank of the THAMES between LIMEHOUSE and Blackwall reaches, opposite Greenwich. Traditionally said to be named from the fact that Edward III kept hounds here for hunting in Waltham Forest. Another explanation is that it is a corruption of *Isle of Ducks*, from the number of wild fowl inhabiting the marshes. It has long been part of dockland.

Ismene. In Greek legend, daughter of ŒDIPUS and Jocasta. ANTIGONE was to be buried alive by order of King Creon for burying her brother Polynices (slain in combat with his brother Eteocles) against the tyrant's express command. Ismene declared that she had aided her sister and asked to share the same fate.

Isocrates (ī sok' rà tēz). One of the great orators of ATHENS, distinguished as a teacher of eloquence. He died 338 B.C.

Israfel. The angel of music for the Mohammedans. He possesses the most melodious voice of all God's creatures, and is to sound the Resurrection Trump which will ravish the ears of the saints in PARADISE. Israfel, GABRIEL, and MICHAEL were the three ANGELS that, according to legend, warned ABRAHAM of Sodom's destruction.

Issachar's ears. Ass's ears. The allusion is to *Gen*. xlix, 14: "Issachar is a strong ass couching down between two burdens."

> Is't possible that you, whose ears
> Are of the tribe of Issachar's ...
> Should be deaf against a noise

So roaring as the public voice?
SAMUEL BUTLER: *Hudibras to Sidrophel*.

Issue. At issue. Under dispute.
Side issues. Subsidiary issues; those of secondary importance to the main issue.
To join, or **take issue.** To dispute or take opposite views of a question, or opposite sides in a suit.
To join issues. In law is to leave a suit to the decision of the court because the parties interested cannot agree.
Istar. ISHTAR.
Isthmian Games. One of the four national festivals of the ancient Greeks, held every alternate spring, the second and fourth of each OLYMPIAD. They took place on the isthmus of Corinth, hence the name. According to one legend they were instituted as FUNERAL games in honour of MELICERTES. They included gymnastics, horse racing, and contests in music.
Isumbras. *See* ISENBRAS.
It. A humorous synonym for sex appeal, popularized by the novelist Elinor Glyn in *It* (1927), though Kipling had used the word earlier in the same sense in his story *Mrs. Bathurst* (*Traffics and Discoveries* 1904).
It. I'm it! I'm a person of some importance; also an expression used in children's games such as TAG by the one claiming the right to chase and touch the others, etc. It is also used as the name of the game.
In for it. About "to catch it" or be in trouble. In this phrase, and others, as to **come it strong, to rough it,** etc., *it* is the definite object of the verb.
To be with it. A much-used mid-20th century phrase meaning to be completely in with current trends, fashions, music etc., especially of the kind popular with certain sections of the young.
Its. One of the words by the use of which Chatterton betrayed his forgeries (*see* ROWLEY POEMS *under* FORGERY). In a poem, purporting to be the work of a 15th-century priest, he wrote, "Life and its goods I scorn," but the word was not in use till more than two centuries later, *it* (*hit*) and *his* being the possessive case.

For love and devocioun towards god also hath *it* infancie and it hath *it* comyng forewarde in groweth of age.

Udal's Erasmus: Luke, vii (1542).
Learning hath *his* infancy, when it is but beginning and almost childish; then *his* youth ... then *his* strength of years ... and, lastly, *his* old age.
BACON: *Essays; Of Vicissitudes of Things* (1625).

Its does not occur in any play of SHAKESPEARE published in his lifetime, but there is one instance in the First Folio of 1623 (*Measure for Measure*, I, ii), as well as nine instances of *it's*. Nor does it occur in the Authorized Version of the BIBLE (1611), the one instance of it in modern editions (*Lev*. xxv, 5) having been substituted for *it* in the Bible printed for Hills and Field in 1660.
Italia Irredenta. *See* IRREDENTISM.
Italian hand. I see his fine Italian hand in this may be said of a picture in which certain characteristics reveal the particular artist, or it may be remarked of an intriguer in which the characteristics of a particular plotter are apparent. The Italian hand was the *cancelleresca* type of handwriting used by the Apostolic Secretaries, and distinguishable by its grace and fineness from the Gothic styles of Northern Europe.
Italic. Pertaining to Italy, especially ancient Italy and the parts other than ROME.
Italic School of Philosophy. The Pythagorean, because PYTHAGORAS taught in Italy.
Italic type, or **italics.** The type in which the letters, instead of being erect, as in roman, slope from the left to right, *thus*. It was first used by Aldus Manutius in 1501, being the work of his type-designer, Francesco Griffo of Bologna, and based on the *cancelleresca corsiva* of the papal chancery. *Cp.* ITALIAN HAND.
Italic version. An old Latin version of the BIBLE, prepared from the SEPTUAGINT. It preceded the VULGATE.
The words italicized in the Bible have no corresponding words in the originals but were supplied by the translators to make the sense of the passage clearer.
Itch, To. Properly, to have an irritation of the skin which gives one a desire to scratch the part affected; hence, figuratively, to feel a constant teasing desire for

something. The figure of speech enters into many phrases; as, *to itch* or *to have an itch for gold*, to have a longing desire for money; *an itching palm* means the same thing.

> Let me tell you, Cassius, you yourself
> Are much condemned to have an itching palm.
>
> SHAKESPEARE: *Julius Cæsar*, IV, iii.

To have itching ears. To be very desirous for news or novelty.

My fingers itch to be at him. I am longing to give him a sound thrashing.

In popular belief, itching of various parts foretold certain occurrences; for instance, if your right palm itched you were going to receive money, the itching of the left eye betokened grief, and of the right pleasure. Itching of the lips foretold kissing; of the nose, that strangers were at hand, and the thumb, that evil approaches.

ITMA (initials of "It's That Man Again"). The famous and once most popular of British radio features, and one which did much to brighten up the dreariness of the BLACK-OUT years of World War II. It was devised and maintained by the comedian Tommy Handley (1896–1949), the script being written by Ted Kavanagh. It ran from 1939 until Handley's death in 1949. Mrs. Mopp and Funf were among the characters in this hilarious weekly skit on English life.

Ivan Ivanovitch. Used of a Russian, as Johnny CRAPAUD was of a Frenchman.

Ivan the Terrible. Ivan IV of Russia (1530, 1533–1584), infamous for his cruelties, but a man of great energy. He first adopted the title of Tsar (1547).

Ivory, Ivory Gate. *See* DREAMS, GATES OF.

Ivory shoulder. *See under* PELOPS.

Ivory tower (Fr. *tour d'ivoire*). To live in an ivory tower is to live in seclusion, divorced from everyday life, excluding the harsh realities of the outside world. Contemporaries of the French poet, Alfred de Vigny (1797–1863), often said that he shut himself up in an ivory tower (a common phrase in the literary circles of his time).

Ivories. Teeth; also dice, keys of the piano, billiard balls, dominoes, etc.

Ivy (O.E. *ifig*). Dedicated to BACCHUS from the notion that it is a preventive of drunkenness. In Christian symbolism ivy typifies the everlasting life, from its remaining continually green.

Like an owl in an ivy-bush. *See under* OWL.

Ixion. In Greek legend, a treacherous king of the LAPITHÆ who was bound to a revolving wheel of fire in the Infernal regions for boasting of having won the favours of HERA, ZEUS having sent a cloud to him in the form of Hera, and the cloud having become by him the mother of the CENTAURS.

J

J. The tenth letter of the alphabet, a modern introduction, only differentiated from I in the 17th century, and not completely separated till the 19th. It was a mediæval practice to lengthen the *I* when it was the initial letter, usually with the consonantal function now assumed by *J*. There is no roman *J* or *j* in the Authorized Version of the BIBLE. In the Roman system of numeration it was (and in medical prescriptions still is) used in place of *i* as the final figure in a series—iij, vij, etc., for iii, vii.

Jabberwocky. The eponymous central figure of a strange, almost gibberish poem in Lewis Carroll's *Through the Looking-glass*. It contains many significant PORTMANTEAU WORDS, as subsequently explained to Alice by HUMPTY DUMPTY.

Jachin and Boaz (jā'kin, bō'ăz). The two great bronze pillars set up at the entrance of the TEMPLE OF SOLOMON—*Jachin* being the right-hand (southern) pillar, the name probably expressing permanence, immovability, and *Boaz* being the left-hand (northern) pillar, typifying the Lord of all strength. *See* I *Kings* vii, 21; *Ezek.* xl, 49.

Jack. (1) A favourite name for JOHN, derived from *Jan* and *Jankin* which developed from *Johannes*; a generic name for a boy, man, husband, etc., and a familiar term of address among sailors, workmen and others.

Cheap Jack. *See* CHEAP.

Cousin Jack. *See under* COUSIN.

Finality Jack. *See* FINALITY.

Jack Adams. A fool.

Jack-a-Lent. A kind of AUNT SALLY which was thrown at in LENT; hence a puppet, a sheepish booby.

Jack and the Beanstalk. A nursery tale found among many peoples in varying forms. In the English version Jack exchanges his poor mother's cow for a handful of beans which miraculously produce stalks reaching the sky. Jack climbs up them and steals treasures from the ogre's castle—a bag of gold, a wonderful lamp, and the hen that lays the golden eggs, thus redeeming their poverty.

Jack and Jill. In the familiar nursery rhyme Jack and Jill who went up the hill "to fetch a pail of water" are probably generic names for lad and lass. Somewhat unconvincingly, attempts have been made to link them with Norse legend.

Jack-boot. A large boot extending over the knee, acting as protective armour for the leg, worn by troopers in the 17th and 18th centuries and later. It is still the type of boot worn by the Household Cavalry and was adopted by fishermen and others before the advent of gum boots. Figuratively, *to be under the jack-boot* is to be controlled by a brutal military regime. *Cp.* MAILED FIST; PRUSSIANISM.

Jack Frost. The personification of frost or frosty weather.

Jack the Giant-killer. The hero of the old nursery tale owed much of his success to his four marvellous possessions. When he put on his coat no eye could see him; when he had his shoes on no one could overtake him; when he put on his cap he knew everything he required to know and his sword cut through everything. The story is given by Walter Map (d. *c.* 1209), who obtained it from a French source.

Jack Horner. A very fanciful explanation of the old nursery rhyme "Little Jack Horner" is that Jack was steward to the Abbot of Glastonbury at the time of the Dissolution of the Monasteries, and that by a subterfuge he gained the deeds of the Manor of Mells. It is said that these deeds, with others, were sent to Henry VIII concealed, for safety, in a pasty; that "Jack Horner" was the bearer and that on the way, he lifted the crust and extracted this "plum".

Jack-in-the-box. A toy consisting of a box out of which "Jack" springs, when the lid is raised.

Jack in the cellar. Old slang for an unborn child: a translation of the Dutch expression for the same, *Hans in Kelder*.

Jack in office. A pompous overbearing official, usually with a RED-TAPE MIND, who uses his powers unimaginatively.

Jack Ketch. A notorious hangman and executioner, who was appointed about 1663 and died in 1686. He was the executioner of William, Lord Russell, for his share in the RYE HOUSE PLOT (1683), and of Monmouth (1685). In 1686 he was removed from office for insulting a SHERIFF and succeeded by a butcher named Rose, who was himself hanged within four months, when Ketch was reinstated. As early as 1678 his name had appeared in a ballad, and by 1702 was associated with the PUNCH AND JUDY puppet-play, which had recently been introduced from Italy.

Jack-knife. Phrases from the similitude of a jack-knife in which the big blade doubles up into the handle.
(1) In logging, where two logs join join to end and hold up the rest;
(2) In swimming, a form of fancy dive;
(3) In road transport, when the main chassis of an articulated lorry swings toards the cab;
a common cause of accidents.

Jack o' the bowl. The BROWNIE or house spirit of Switzerland; so called from the nightly custom of placing for him a bowl of fresh cream on the cowhouse roof. The contents are sure to disappear before morning.

Jack-o'-the clock, or **clock-house.** The figure which, in some old public clocks, comes out to strike the hours on the bell.

Must I strike like Jack o'th'clock-house, never but in season.
WM. STRODE: *Floating Island* I, ii (1655)

Jack-o'-lantern. The IGNIS FATUUS; in the U.S.A., the hollowed pumpkin of HALLOWEEN games.

Jack of cards. The knave or servant of the king and queen of the same suit.

Jack of Dover. Some unidentified eatable mentioned by Chaucer in the *Cook's Prologue*. "Our host," addressing the cook, says:

For many a pastee hastow laten blood,
And many a Jakke of Dover hastow sold
That hath been twyes hoot and twyes cold.

Skeat says that it is "probably a pie that has been cooked more than once", another suggestion is that is is some seafish (*cp.* JOHN DORY).

Jack out of Office. One no longer in office; one dismissed from his employment.

Jackpot. In poker, a pot which cannot be opened until a player has a pair of jacks, or better. Generally applied to the "pool" disgorged by ONE-ARMED BANDITS, etc.

Jack the Ripper. The name adopted by an unknown killer who murdered at least five prostitutes in Whitechapel in 1888 and mutilated their bodies.
Among suspects at the time were Michael Ostrog, a Russian doctor; Kosminski, a Polish Jew; and M.J. Druitt, unsuccessful son of a Dorsetshire surgeon. One recent fanciful theory was that the murders were planned by a group of high-ranking FREEMASONS, among them being Sir William Gull, the royal physician, their motive being to suppress scandals involving Prince Albert Victor, Duke of Clarence (1846–1892), elder son of the then Prince of Wales (later King Edward VII). Another theory was that it was the Duke of Clarence himself but a more likely candidate is J.K. Stephen, the Duke's lover.

Jack Russell. A white-coloured sporting terrier first bred by the Devonshire cleric John Russell (1759–1883). Much addicted to foxhunting and otter hunting, Jack Russell at one time kept his own pack of hounds and came to be known as "The Sporting Parson". *See* SQUARSON.

Jack Sprat. A DWARF; as if sprats were dwarf herrings. Children, by a similar METAPHOR, are called SMALL FRY.

Jack Sprat could eat no fat,
His wife could eat no lean,
And so, betwixt them both you see,
They licked the platter clean.
Nursery Rhyme.

Jack Straw. One of the leaders in the PEASANTS' REVOLT of 1381, mentioned in Chaucer's *Nonnes Preestes Tale* (line 628). The name came to signify a man of STRAW, a worthless sort of person.

Radical Jack. *See under* RADICAL.

A good Jack makes a good Jill. A good husband makes a good wife, a good master makes a good servant. Jill is a generic name for a woman. *See* JACK; *cp.* JACKEROO.

Before you can say Jack Robinson. Immediately, instantly. Grose says that the saying had its birth from a very volatile gentleman of that name who used to pay flying visits to his neighbours, and was no sooner announced than he was off again. Halliwell says (*Archaic Dictionary*, 1846):

> The following lines from "an old play" are elsewhere given as the original phrase—
>
> A warke it ys as easie to be done.
> As tys to saye Jacke! robys on.

But the "old play" has never been identified and both these accounts are palpably BEN TROVATO. The phrase was in use in the 18th century, and is to be found in Fanny Burney's *Evelina* (1778):

> "Done!" cried Lord Merton; "I take your odds!" "Will you?" returned he: "why then 'fore George, I'd do it as soon as say Jack Robinson".
> Letter Lxxxiii.

Sheridan, who became an M.P. in 1780, when attacking government bribery, retorted in response to shouts of "Name, Name", looking directly at John Robinson, Secretary of the Treasury; "Yes, I could name him as soon as I could say Jack Robinson".

Every Jack shall have his Jill. Every man shall have a wife of his own.

Jack shall have Jill
Nought shall go ill;

The man shall have his mare again, and all shall be well.
SHAKESPEARE: *Midsummer Night's Dream*, III, ii.

Every man Jack of them. All without exception.

I'm all right, Jack. *See* PULL UP THE LADDER, JACK, *below*.

Jack of all trades and master of none. One who turns his hand to everything is not usually expert in any one field. *Jack of all trades* is a contemptuous expression—more grandiloquently he is a *sciolist*.

Jack's as good as his master. An old proverb indicating the equality of man. *Cp.* WHEN ADAM DELVED *under* ADAM. It was the wise Agur (*see Proverbs*, xxx, 22) who placed "a servant when he reigneth" as the first of the four things that the earth cannot bear.

Jack system. An Australian phrase denoting the pursuit of one's own interests and welfare at the expense of others. *Cp.* PULL UP THE LADDER, JACK, *below*.

Pull up the ladder, Jack, I'm inboard. The nautical equivalent of *I'm all right, Jack* denoting the pursuit of self-interest and the complete disregard of the interest of others. The allusion is obvious. *Cp.* JACK SYSTEM.

To play the Jack. To play the rogue, the knave. To deceive or lead astray like Jack-o'-lantern, or IGNIS FATUUS.

Jack (2), applied to animals, usually denotes the male sex or smallness of size; hence, **Jackass; Jack-baker** (a kind of owl); **Jack**, or **dog fox; Jack hare; Jack rat; Jack shark; Jack snipe; Jack curlew**, the whimbrel, a small species of curlew. A young pike is called a *Jack*, so also were the male birds used in falconry.

Jack-rabbit. A large prairie-hare of North America; shortened from **Jackass-rabbit**, a name given to it on account of its very long ears and legs.

Jack (3) also forms part of the name of certain common wild plants, as in: **Jack-at-the-hedge** or cleavers; **Jack-by-the-hedge** or garlic mustard; **Jack-go-to-bed-at-noon** or goat's beard; etc. **Jack-in-the-pulpit** is a North American woodland plant, *Arisaema triphyllum*, so called from its upright spadix over-arched by the spathe.

Jack (4) when applied to certain articles usually implies smallness or inferiority of some kind. The *Jack* is the flag smaller than the ensign, worn on the jack-staff in the bows of a warship, although the Union flag is usually called the UNION JACK. The small waxed leather vessel for liquor was called a *jack* (*cp.* BLACK JACK). *Jack* was also the inferior kind of armour consisting of a leather surcoat worn by foot soldiers, formed by overlapping pieces of metal fastened between two layers of canvas, leather or quilted material. The *jack* at bowls is so called because it is small in comparison with the bowls themselves. A *jack* is an obsolete term for a FARTHING and a *jack* and *half-jack* were names given to counters, used in gambling, resembling a SOVEREIGN and half- sovereign.

To be upon their jacks. To have the advantage over one. The reference is to the *jack*, or jerkin worn by soldiers of olden times.

Jack rafter. A rafter in a hipped roof, shorter than a full-sized one.

Jack (5). Numerous appliances and contrivances which obviate the use of an assistant, etc., are called *Jacks*. A *jack* is used for lifting heavy weights and is also applied to the rough stool or horse used for sawing timber on; a **bottle-jack,** or **roasting-jack** was used for turning the meat when roasting before an open fire. Some others are:

Boot-jack. An appliance for pulling off boots by inserting the heel in a V-shaped opening.

Jack-roll. The cylinder round which the rope of a well coils; a windlass.

Jack-screw. A large screw rotating in a threaded socket, used for lifting heavy weights.

Smoke-jack. An apparatus in a chimney-flue for turning a spit, made to revolve by the upward drought.

Jackal. A toady. One who does the dirty work for another. It was once thought that the jackal hunted in troops to provide the lion with prey. *See* LION'S PROVIDER.

Jackanapes. A pert, vulgar, apish little fellow; a prig. It is uncertain whether the *-napes* is connected originally with the ape or with *Naples, Jackanapes* being a *Jack* (monkey) of (imported from) *Naples*, just as *fustian-a-napes* was fustian from Naples. By the 16th century *Jackanapes* was in use as a proper name for a tame ape. *See* JACK-A-NAPES *above*.

> I will teach a scurvy jackanape priest to meddle or make
> SHAKESPEARE: *Merry Wives of Windsor,*
> I, iv.

Jackass. An unmitigated fool

Jackdaw. A prating nuisance.

The Jackdaw of Rheims. One of the best known of the INGOLDSBY *Legends* in which the cardinal's ring mysteriously vanished and he solemnly cursed the thief by BELL, BOOK, AND CANDLE. The jackdaw's bedraggled appearance brought on by the curse revealed him as the culprit.

Jackeroo. A name used in Australia in the first half of the 19th century to describe a young Englishman newly arrived to learn farming, derived, according to some, from the Queensland *tchareroo,* the shrike, noted for its garrulity. Others derive it from *Jack Carew*; *Jack* and *Kangaroo*; etc. Later the name was applied simply to a station hand. **Jilleroo,** its feminine counterpart, was applied to the Australian land girls of World War II.

Jacket. Diminutive of *jack,* a surcoat. Potatoes when cooked unpeeled are said to be "cooked in their jackets".

To dust one's jacket, or **to give one a good jacketing.** *See* I'LL DUST YOUR JACKET FOR YOU *under* DUST.

Jackey. A monkey. *Cp.* JACKANAPES.

Jackstones. A children's game played with a set of small stones and a small ball or marble. They are thrown up and caught on the back of the hand in various ways, etc.

Jacob. Jacob's ladder. The ladder seen by Jacob leading up to HEAVEN (*Gen.* xxviii, 12); hence its application to steep ladders and steps, especially the rope ladder with wooden rungs slung from a ship's boom to the water. There is also a garden plant of this name so called from the ladder-like arrangement of its leaflets.

Jacob's staff. A pilgrim's staff; from

the Apostle JAMES (Lat. *Jacobus*), who is usually represented with a staff and SCALLOP SHELL.

Also a surveyor's rod, used instead of a tripod, and an obsolete instrument for taking heights and distances.

Jacob's stone. The Coronation stone of SCONE is sometimes called, from the legend that Jacob's head had rested on this stone when he had the vision of the ANGELS ascending and descending the ladder (*Gen*. xxviii, 11).

Jacobins. The DOMINICANS were so called in France from the "Rue St. Jacques", the location of their first house in PARIS. The famous French Revolutionary *Jacobin Club*, founded at Versailles in 1789 as the *Breton Club*, removed to Paris and met in a former Jacobin convent, hence the name. Among its famous members were Mirabeau, Robespierre, St. Just, Marat, and Couthon. It controlled the country at one stage through its hundreds of daughter societies in the provinces. The club was suppressed in November 1794, after the fall of Robespierre. Their badge was the Phrygian CAP OF LIBERTY.

Jacobites. A sect of Syrian MONOPHYSITES, so called from Jacobus Baradaeus, BISHOP of Edessa in the 6th century. The present head of their church is called the PATRIARCH of Antioch. The term is also applied to the Monophysite Christians in Egypt.

Jacobites. The name given to the supporters of James II (Lat. *Jacobus*) and of his descendants who claimed the throne of Great Britain and IRELAND. They came into existence after the flight of James II in 1688 and were strong in SCOTLAND and the north of ENGLAND. They were responsible for the risings of 1715 and 1745, the latter rising marking their virtual end as a political force. The last male representative of the Stuarts was Henry (IX), a cardinal and a pensioner of George III, who died in 1807.

Jacobus. The unofficial name of a hammered gold coin struck in the reign of James I, originally worth 20s. It was properly called a UNITE. (Lat. *Jacobus*, James.)

Jacquard Loom (jăk′ ard). So called from Joseph Marie Jacquard (1752–

1834), of Lyons, its inventor. Its particular importance was in facilitating the weaving of patterns, especially in silks.

Jacques (zhak) (Fr., James, Jim). A generic name for the French peasant, the equivalent of HODGE. *Jacques Bonhomme* is similarly used.

Jacquerie (zhăk′ e rē). An insurrection of the French peasantry in 1358, provoked by the hardships caused by the HUNDRED YEARS WAR, the oppressions of the privileged classes and Charles the BAD of Navarre. The Jacquerie committed many atrocities and savage reprisals followed. The name derives from JACQUES.

Jactitation of Marriage. A false assertion by a person of being married to another. This is actionable. *Jactitation* means literally "a throwing out", and here means "to utter", *i.e.* "to throw out publicly". The term comes from the old CANON LAW.

Jade. The fact that in mediaeval times this ornamental stone was supposed, if applied to the side, to act as a preservative against colic is enshrined in its name, for jade is from the Spanish *piedra de ijada*, stone of the side; and its other name, *nephrite*, is from Gr. *nephros*, kidney. Among the North American Indians it is still worn as an AMULET against the bite of venomous snakes, and to cure the gravel, epilepsy, etc.

Jade. A word of unknown etymology applied to a worthless horse, an old woman (contemptuously), and a young woman (often in the sense of "HUSSY" but not necessarily contemptuously).

Jagganath. *See* JUGGERNAUT.

Jahveh, or **Jahweh.** *See* JEHOVAH.

Jains. A sect of dissenters from Hinduism, of as early an origin as BUDDHISM. Jains, being largely traders, are usually wealthy, and therefore influential for their numbers.

Jakes. An old word for a privy.

Jam. Used colloquially for something really nice or which comes very easily, especially if unexpected.

Money for jam. Money (or money's worth) for nothing or very little; an unexpected bit of luck.

Jam session. A meeting of JAZZ musicians improvising spontaneously without rehearsal.

To be in a jam. To be in a predicament; from the verb *jam*, to compress, to squeeze or press down, to block, etc., akin to *champ*.

James. *See* JACOBUS.

St. James. The APOSTLE **St. James the Great** is the patron saint of Spain. One legend states that after his death in Palestine his body was placed in a boat with sails set, and that next day it reached the Spanish coast. At Padron, near COMPOSTELA, they used to show a huge stone as the veritable boat. Another legend says that it was the relics of St. James that were miraculously conveyed from Jerusalem, where he was BISHOP, to Spain, in a marble ship. A KNIGHT saw the ship entering port and his horse took fright and plunged into the sea but the knight saved himself by boarding the vessel and found his clothes entirely covered with SCALLOP SHELLS.

The saint's body was discovered in 840 by Bishop Theudemirus of Iria through divine revelation, and a church was built at Compostela for its shrine.

St. James is commemorated on 25 July and is represented in art sometimes with the sword by which he was beheaded, and sometimes attired as a pilgrim, with his cloak covered with shells. *Cp.* GROTTO.

St. James the Less, or **James the Little.** He has been identified both with the APOSTLE James, the son of Alphaeus, and with James the brother of the Lord. He is commemorated with St. PHILIP on 1 May. (3 May by Roman Catholics).

The Court of St. James. The British court to which foreign ambassadors are officially credited. St. James's Palace, PALL MALL, stands on the site of an ancient leper hospital dedicated to St. JAMES THE LESS. The palace was begun by Henry VIII in 1532 and was used as a residence by various monarchs and their children. After the burning of WHITEHALL in 1697, it came to be used for state ceremonies, hence the Court of St. James. It ceased to be a monarchical residence in 1837, but was used for LEVEES and other official functions. The office of the BOARD OF GREEN CLOTH was at St. James's.

Jesse James (1837–1882). A notorious American bandit. In 1867 he organized a band of bank and train robbers who perpetrated a number of infamous murders and daring crimes. A reward of $10,000 was put on his head. He retired to St. Joseph, Missouri, under the name of Howard and was shot by a reward-seeker while hanging a picture in his house. He undeservedly passed into legend as another ROBIN HOOD.

Jameson Raid. A foolhardy attempt by Dr. L. S. Jameson to overthrow the Transvaal government of Paul Kruger. On 29 December 1875, Jameson crossed the border with 470 men in the expectation of a simultaneous UITLANDER rising in the Transvaal. He was surrounded at Doornkop (2 January 1896) and subsequently handed over to the British authorities. Rhodes, the Cape Prime Minister, was involved and the Colonial Secretary, Joseph Chamberlain, almost certainly implicated.

Jamshid. In Persian legend, the fourth king of the Pishdadian, or earliest, dynasty who reigned for 700 years and had Devs or demons as his slaves. He was credited with 300 years of beneficent rule, but when he forgot God, was driven out and remained hidden for 100 years. He was eventually sawn apart. Among his magical possessions was a cup containing the ELIXIR OF LIFE which is mentioned in Fitzgerald's *Omar Khayyám* and Moore's *Lalla Rookh*.

Janissaries, or **Janizaries** (Turk, *yenitscheri*, new corps). Celebrated troops of the OTTOMAN EMPIRE, raised by Orchan in 1330; originally, and for some centuries, compulsorily recruited from Christian subjects of the Sultan. It was blessed by Hadji Becktash, a saint, who cut off the sleeve of his fur mantle and gave it to the captain, who put in on his head. Hence the fur cap worn by these footguards. In 1826 the Janissaries, long a tyrannical military caste, rebelled when their privileges were threatened, and they were abolished by total massacre.

Janissary music. Military music of the Turkish kind. Also called Turkish music.

Jannes, and **Jambres** (Jăn'ēz, jăm' brēz). The names under which St. PAUL (II *Tim*. iii, 8) referred to the two magicians of PHARAOH who imitated some of the miracles of MOSES (*Exod*. vii). The names are not mentioned in the OLD TESTAMENT, but they appear in the TARGUMS and other rabbinical writings, where tradition has it that they were sons of BALAAM, and that they perished either in the crossing of the Red Sea, or in the tumult after the worship of the GOLDEN CALF.

Jansenists. A sect of Christians, who held the doctrines of Cornelius Jansen (1585–1638), Bishop of Ypres. Jansen professed to have formulated the teaching of AUGUSTINE, which resembled CALVINISM in many respects. He taught the doctrines of "irresistible grace", "original sin" (*see under* SIN), and "the utter helplessness of the natural man to turn to God". Louis XIV took part against them and they were put down by Pope Clement XI, in 1713, in the famous Bull UNIGENITUS.

Januarius, St. The patron saint of Naples, a bishop of Benevento who was martyred during the Diocletian persecution, 304. He is commemorated on 19 September and his head and two vials of his blood are preserved in the cathedral at Naples. This congealed blood is said to liquefy several times a year.

January. The month dedicated by the Romans to JANUS, who presided over the entrance to the year and, having two faces, could look back to the year past and forward on the current year.

The Dutch used to call this month *Lauwmaand* (frosty-month); the Saxons *Wulf-monath*, because wolves were very troublesome then from the great scarcity of food. After the introduction of Christianity, the name was changed to *Se æfterageola* (the after-yule); it was also called *Forma monath* (first month). In the French Revoluntionary CALENDAR of the first French Republic it was called *Nivôse* (snow-month, 21, 22 or 23 December to 20, 21 or 22 January).

It's a case of January and May. Said when an old man marries a young girl. The allusion is to the *Merchant's Tale* in Chaucer's *Canterbury Tales*, in which May, a lovely girl, married January, a Lombard baron sixty years of age.

Janus (jā' nús). The ancient Roman deity who kept the gate of HEAVEN; hence the guardian of gates and doors. He was represented with two faces, one in front and one behind, and the doors of this temple in ROME were thrown open in times of war and closed in times of peace. The name is used allusively both with reference to the double-facedness and to war.

Japhetic. An adjective sometimes applied to the ARYANS, from their supposed descent from *Japheth*, one of the sons of Noah. *Cp.* JAVAN.

Jarkman. Sixteenth-century slang for an ABRAM-MAN, especially an educated beggar able to forge passes, licences, etc. *Jark* was rogues' CANT for a seal, whence also a licence of the Bethlehem Hospital to beg.

Jarnac. Coup de Jarnac. A treacherous and unexpected attack; so called from Guy Chabot, Sieur de Jarnac, who, in a duel with La Châteigneraie, on 1 July 1547, in the presence of Henry II, first "hamstrung" his opponent, and then, when he was helpless, slew him.

Jarndyce v. Jarndyce. An interminable CHANCERY suit in *Bleak House*. Dickens probably founded his story on the long-drawn-out Chancery suit of Jennens *v.* Jennens, which related to property in Nacton, Suffolk, belonging to an intestate miser who died in 1798. The case was only finally concluded more than eighty years after its start.

Jarvey. Old slang for a HACKNEY-coach driver; from the personal name *Jarvis*, with a possible allusion to St. Gervaise, whose symbol in art is a whip.

Jason. The hero of Greek legend who led the ARGONAUTS in the quest of the GOLDEN FLEECE, the son of Æson, King of Iolcus, brought up by the centaur CHIRON. When he demanded his kingdom from his uncle Pelias who had deprived him of it, and was told he could have it in return for the Golden Fleece, Jason gathered around him the chief heroes of Greece and set sail in the ARGO. After many tests and trials, including sowing the remaining dragon's teeth left unsown by CADMUS, he was successful through the help of MEDEA, whom he married. He later deserted her and subsequently killed himself through melancholy. Another account says he was crushed to death by the stern of his old ship Argo, while resting beneath it. *See* ÆSON'S BATH.

Jaundice. A jaundiced eye. A prejudiced eye which only sees faults. It was a popular belief that to the eye of a person who had jaundice (Fr. *jaune*, yellow), everything looked yellow.

Java man. *See* PITHECANTHROPUS.

Javan. In the BIBLE, the collective name of the Greeks (*Is*. lxvi, 19, and elsewhere), who were supposed to be descended from *Javan*, the son of Japheth (*Gen*. x, 2).

Jaw. To jaw, to annoy with words, to jabber, wrangle, cackle, etc.

Like a sheep's head, all jaw. Said of one who never stops talking but does little.

A break-jaw word; a jaw-breaker. A very long word, or one hard to pronounce.

Jaw-box, or **Jaw-hole** (Scots). A sewer or sink.

Pi jaw. A contemptuous term for pious talk, or for an ostentatious GOODY-GOODY.

Jay. Old slang for a frivolous person, a wanton.

Jaywalker. One who crosses a thoroughfare throughtlessly, regardless of passing traffic. A jay hops in an undulating fashion.

Jazey. A WIG; a corruption of *Jersey*, so called because wigs were once made of Jersey flax and fine wool.

Jazz. A type of dance music originating in the folk-music of the American Negro of the cotton fields. It first developed in New Orleans and reached Chicago by 1914 where it gained its name. It was slightly influenced by RAGTIME and is characterised by syncopation and the noisy use of percussion instruments, together with the trombone, trumpet and saxophone. Its impact grew steadily and it has had many notable exponents. The name has been somewhat loosely appropriated by popular dance orchestras playing their own conception of the jazz idiom. *Cp.* BLUES; BOOGIE-WOOGIE; SWING.

A load of jazz. A load of nonsense, a lot of CODSWALLOP.

Je ne sais quoi (zhe ne sā kwa) (Fr., I know not what). An indescribable something; as, "There was a *je ne sais quoi* about him which made us dislike him from the first."

Jeames. A flunkey. A former colloquial form of James. Thackeray's *Diary of C. Jeames de la Pluche, Esq.* first appeared in *Punch*).

Jean Crapaud. *See* CRAPAUD.

Jeddart, Jedburgh, or **Jedwood Justice.** Putting a person to death and trying him afterwards. From Jedburgh, the Scottish border town where MOSSTROOPERS were given this kind of treatment. The same as CUPAR JUSTICE and Abingdon law.

Jeep. A small all-purpose car first developed by the U.S.A. during World War II and known as G.P., *i.e.* General Purpose Vehicle, hence the name. Its four-wheel drive and high and low gearboxes gave it astonishing cross-country performance. The experimental models were also called Beeps, Peeps, and Blitz Buggies, but the name Jeep came to stay in 1941.

Jehad. *See* HOLY WAR.

Jehovah. The name *Jehovah* is an instance of the extreme sanctity with which the name of God was invested, for this is a disguised form of JHVH, the TETRAGRAMMATON which was too sacred to use, so the scribes added the vowels of ADONAI, thereby indicating that the reader was to say Adonai instead of JHVH. At the time of the RENAISSANCE these vowels and consonants were taken for the sacred name itself and hence *Jehovah* or *Yahweh*.

Jehovah's Witnesses. A religious movement founded in 1872 by Charles Taze Russel in Philadelphia, and known as International Bible Students until 1931. It does not ascribe divinity to Jesus Christ, regarding him as the perfect man and agent of God. Recognition of JEHOVAH as their sole authority involves the Witnesses in refusal to salute a national flag or to do military service. *The Watch Tower* is their official organ.

Jehovistic. *See* ELOHISTIC.

Jehu. A coachman, especially one who drives at a rattling pace.

Jekyll (jek' il). **Dr. Jekyll and Mr. Hyde.** Two aspects of one man. Jekyll is the "would do good," Hyde is "the evil that is present". The phrase comes from R. L. Stevenson's *The Strange Case of Dr. Jekyll and Mr. Hyde*, first published in 1886.

Jellyby, Mrs. The type of enthusiastic, unthinking philanthropist who forgets that charity should begin at home (Dickens: *Bleak House*).

Jemmy (a diminutive of *James*). Slang for a number of things, as a burglar's crowbar (*see* JIMMY); a sheep's head, boiled or baked, said to be so called from the tradition that James IV of Scotland breakfasted on one just before the battle of Flodden (1513); also, a greatcoat; and, as an adjective, spruce, dandified. *See* JEMMY JESSAMY.

Jenkins's Ear. The name given to an incident that largely helped to provoke war between England and Spain in 1739, which became merged into the War of the Austrian Succession (1740–1748) since Spain and Britain took opposite sides. Captain Robert Jenkins, of the brig *Rebecca*, claimed to have been attacked by a Spanish *guarda costa* off Havana in 1731, when homeward bound from the West Indies; and that his ship was plundered and his ear severed. He carried his complaint to the king on reaching London. The case was revived in 1738 and Walpole was forced to yield to the general clamour for war backed by the trading interests. The main incidents of this maritime war, basically caused by Spanish interference with British shipping, occasioned by large-scale illicit trading, were Vernon's capture of Portobello (1739) and Anson's voyage round the world (1740–1744).

Jeofail. An old legal term for an error, omission, or oversight in proceedings at law. The word is the Anglo-French, *jeo fail*, O.Fr. *je faille*, I am at fault. There were several statutes of Jeofail for the remedy of irregularities and mistakes.

Jeremiah. A doleful prophet; from allusion to the *Lamentations of Jeremiah*, the OLD TESTAMENT prophet.

Jeremiad. A pitiful tale, a tale of woe to produce compassion; so called from the *Lamentations of Jeremiah*.

Jerez. Jerez-de-la-Frontera, in southern Spain, once a frontier fortress between Moors and Christians, was the centre which produced the best SACK, which in the early 17th century came to be called "sherry", from *Scheris*, the Moorish rendering of Jerez. Drake brought home some 3,000 butts of Jerez wine when returning from the sack of Cadiz in 1587. *See* SINGEING THE KING OF SPAIN'S BEARD.

Jericho (Jer' i kō). Used in various phrases to give verbal location to some altogether indefinite place, possibly in allusion to II *Sam*. x, 5, and I *Chron*. xix, 5.

Go to Jericho. The equivalent of "GO TO HALIFAX," "Go and hang yourself," "Go to hell," etc.

Gone to Jericho. No one knows where.

Jerked Beef. "Jerked" is here a corruption of Chilian *charqui*, meat cut into strips and dried in the sun.

Jerkwater. An early American term for a small train on a branch railway; also a small township of little consequence, something of trifling importance. In such out of the way situations water was "jerked" by the bucketful into steam trains in need of replenishing their supply. *Cp*. ONE-HORSE TOWN.

Jeroboam. A very large wine bottle, flagon or goblet, so called in allusion to the "mighty man of valour" of this name who "made Israel to sin" (I *Kings* xi, 28, and xiv, 16). Its capacity is not very definite but it usually contains the equivalent of four bottles. An English wine bottle contains approximately one-sixth of a gallon or 26⅔ fluid ounces, also called a *reputed quart*. *Cp*. JORUM; MAGNUM; REHOBOAM; TAPPIT-HEN.

Jerome, St. A father of the Western Church, and compiler of the VULGATE (c. 340–420). He died at Bethlehem and is usually represented as an aged man in a cardinal's dress, writing or studying, with a lion seated beside him. His day is 30 September.

Jerrican. A 4½-gallon petrol or water container which would stand rough handling and stack easily, developed by the Germans for the Afrika Korps in World

War II. Borrowed by the British in Libya, it became the standard unit of fuel replenishment throughout the Allied armies. The name is an allusion to its origin. *See* JERRY.

Jerry. Since World War I a nickname for a German, or Germans collectively. Also an old colloquialism for a chamber-pot.

Jerry-built. Unsubstantial. A "jerry-builder" is a builder of cheap unsubstantial properties. Possibly the name may be connected with Jericho, the walls of which collapsed at the sound of a trumpet. The phrase, however, may have originated at Liverpool about 1830 and a possible suggestion is that it is a corruption of "jury" as used in "jury mast" and "jury rigging", the temporary or makeshift replacements in an emergency. This could be a natural usage in a major seaport such as Liverpool where the housing shortage was acute in the post-Waterloo years and much accentuated by the influx of Irish labourers. Rapid and cheap construction by small builders with inadequate resources was the inevitable consequence.

Jerrymander. *See* GERRYMANDER.

Jersey Lily, The. Emily Charlotte Langtry (1852–1929), or Lillie Langtry, was so called after her debut on the professional stage in 1881. A famous Edwardian beauty and one-time intimate of the Prince of Wales (later Edward VII), she was the wife of Edward Langtry and daughter of W. C. Le Breton, Dean of Jersey. After Langtry's death she married Sir Hugo Gerald de Bathe in 1899.

Jerusalem. JULIAN THE APOSTATE, the Roman Emperor (d.363), to please the Jews and humble the Christians, said that he would rebuild the temple and city, but was mortally wounded before the foundations were laid, and his work set at nought by "an earthquake, a whirlwind, and a fiery eruption" (*see* Gibbon's *Decline and Fall*, ch. dxiii).

Much has been made of this by early Christian writers, who dwell on the prohibition and curse pronounced against those who should attempt to rebuild the city. The fate of Julian is cited as an example of Divine wrath.

The New Jerusalem. The paradise of Christians, in allusion to *Rev.* xxi.

Jerusalem artichoke. Jerusalem is here a corruption of Ital. *girasole*. Girasole is the sunflower, which this vegetable resembles in leaf and stem. *Cp.* HELIOTROPE.

Jerusalem Cross. A CROSS potent.

Jerusalem Delivered. An Italian epic poem in twenty books by Torquato Tasso (1544–1595). Published in 1581, it was translated into English by Edward Fairfax in 1600. It tells the story of the First CRUSADE and the capture of Jerusalem by Godfrey of Bouillon in 1099.

Jess (through Fr. from Lat. *jactus*, a throw). A short strap of leather tied about the legs of a HAWK to hold it on the fist. Hence, metaphorically, a bond of affection, etc.

Jesse, or **Jesse Tree**. A genealogical tree, usually represented as a large vine or as a large brass candlestick with many branches, tracing the ancestry of Christ, called a "rod out of the stem of Jesse" (*Is.* xi, 1). Jesse is himself sometimes represented in a recumbent position with the vine rising out of his loins; hence a stained glass window representing him thus with a tree shooting from him containing the pedigree of Jesus is called a *Jesse window*.

Jesse James. *See under* JAMES.

Jesters. *See* COURT FOOLS *under* FOOLS.

Jesuit. The name given to members of the Society of Jesus, begun by Ignatius LOYOLA in 1534, and formally approved by Pope Paul III in 1540. It was founded to combat the REFORMATION and to propagate the faith among the heathen. Through its discipline, organization, and methods of secrecy it acquired such power that it came into conflict with both the civil and religious authorities. It was driven from France in 1594, from Portugal in 1759, and from Spain in 1767, was suppressed by Pope Clement XIV in 1773, but formally reconstituted by Pius VII in 1814.

Owing to the casuistical principles maintained by many of its leaders, the name Jesuit acquired an opprobrious signification and a *Jesuit* or *Jesuitical person* means (secondarily) a deceiver, a prevaricator, etc. Such associations have often obscured the extent of their achievements.

Jesuit's bark. *See* PERUVIAN BARK.

Jet. The Jet Set. A phrase applied to those affluent socialites who can afford to travel by jet aircraft to the various fashionable resorts around the world.

Jetsam, or **Jetson**. Goods cast into the sea to lighten a ship. *See* FLOTSAM.

Jettatura (Ital.). The evil eye, a superstition that certain persons have the power, by looking at one, of casting a malevolent spell.

Jeu d'esprit (zhĕr des prē) (Fr.) A witticism.

Jeu de mots (zhĕr dà mō) (Fr.). A pun; a play on some words or phrase.

Jeunesse Dorée (zhĕr nes′ dôr′ ā) (Fr.). The "gilded youth" of a nation; the rich, fashionable young bachelors.

Jew. A Hebrew. Used opprobriously to denote a mean or hard-fisted person.

Ebrew Jew. *See* EBREW.

Wandering Jew. *See* WANDERING.

Jew's ear. A fungus that grows on the JUDAS-TREE; its name is due to a mistranslation of its Latin name, *Auricula Judæ i.e.* Judas's ear.

Jew's harp. A simple musical instrument held between the teeth and twanged with the hand. The origin of the name is a matter of surmise, hence *Jaw's harp* as a popular supposition. It has also been called **Jew's trump**. Hakluyt uses the former term and the latter is used by Fletcher (*Humerous Lieutenant*, V, ii). It is also applied to a shackle from its similarity of shape.

Jew's myrtle. Butcher's Broom is so called, from the popular notion that it formed the crown of thorns placed by the Jews on the head of the Saviour.

Jezebel. The infamous wife of Ahab, King of Israel, who was denounced by Elijah for bringing in the worship of BAAL. Her name came to be used for an objectionable or abandoned woman, known to have used cosmetics. It is used for such a woman who paints her face, frequently referred to as a **painted Jezebel**.

> And when Jehu was come to Jezreel, Jezebel heard of it; and she painted her face, and tired her head, and looked out at a window.
>
> II *Kings*, ix, 30.

Jezreelites. A small sect founded in 1875

by James White (1849–1885), a one-time army private, who took the name James Jershom Jezreel. They were also called the "New and Latter House of Israel" and believed that Christ redeemed only souls, and that the body is saved by belief in the Law. Their object was to be numbered among the 144,000 (see *Rev*. vii, 4) who, at the Last JUDGEMENT, will be endowed with immortal bodies. Their headquarters were at Gillingham, Kent, where their Tower of Jezreel was formerly a familiar landmark.

Jib. The cut of his jib. The expression of a person's face. "Jib" here is the triangular foresail. Sailors used to recognize vessels at sea by the "cut of their jibs".

Jib is also applied to the lower lip. Thus **to hang the jib,** or **to make,** or **pull a jib** is to protrude the lower lip in an ill-tempered or discontented fashion.

To jib. To start aside, to back out; a "jibbing horse" is one that is easily startled. It is probably from the nautical *gybe*, which is with a fore-and-aft rig, is to bring a vessel so much by the lee (*i.e.* when the wind begins to blow on the same side as she is carrying her mainsail) that the mainsail swings to the other side. Accidental gybing can be dangerous.

Jiffy. In a jiffy. In a moment; in a brace of shakes; before you can say "Jack Robinson". (*See under* JACK). The origin of the word is unknown.

Jiggery-pokery. Fraud, "wangling", "fiddling", etc.

Jigot (jig′ ot). A Scots term for a leg of mutton or lamb. It is the Fr. *gigot*, and is one of the Scottish words arising from the close connection between the two countries in the 16th and 17th centuries.

Jill. A generic name for a lass, a sweetheart.

See JACK AND JILL *under* JACK.

Jilleroo. *See* JACKEROO.

Jingo. A word from the patter and jargon of 17th-century conjurers (*cp.* HOCUS-POCUS) probably substituted for *God*, in the same way as *Gosh*, *Golly*, etc. *See* JINGOISM, below.

Jingoism. Aggressive "patriotism", the equivalent of the Fr. *chauvinisme*. The term derives from the popular music-hall song by G. W. Hunt which appeared at the time of the Russo-Turkish War (1877–1878) when anti-Russian feeling ran high and Disraeli ordered the Mediterranean fleet to Constantinople.

> We don't want to fight, but by Jingo if we do,
> We've got the ships, we've got the men, and got the money too.
> We've fought the Bear before, and while we're Britons true,
> The Russians shall not have Constantinople.

The Russophobes became known as *Jingoes*, and a noisy war-mongering policy has been labelled jingoism ever since. *See* CHAUVINISM.

Jinks. High Jinks. Nowadays the phrase expresses the idea of pranks, fun, and jollity.

> The frolicsome company had begun to practise the ancient and now forgotten pastime of *high jinks*. This game was played in several different ways. Most frequently the dice were thrown by the company, and those upon whom the lot fell were obliged to assume and maintain for a time, a certain fictitious character, or to repeat a certain number of fescennine verses in a particular order. If they departed from the characters assigned...they incurred forfeits, which were...compounded for by swallowing an additional bumper...
> SCOTT: *Guy Mannering*, xxxvi.

Jinn. Demons of Arabian mythology fabled to dwell in the mountains of Kâf, which encompass the earth; they were created two thousand years before ADAM and assume the forms of serpents, dogs, cats, monsters and even human shape. The evil *jinn* are hideously ugly, but the good are singularly beautiful. The word is plural; its singular is *jinnee*; *genii* is a variant form.

Jitters. To have the jitters. A phrase of American origin meaning to be nervously apprehensive; in a state of nerves. *Jittery* is nervous or jumpy.

Jive. A canting name for the livelier and debased forms of JAZZ music, largely accomplished by the uninspired improvisations of short phrases. *Jive-talk* is the specialized vocabulary of its adepts. In Black American-English *jive* originally signified "misleading talk".

Joachim, St. (jō′ à kim). The father of the Virgin Mary. Generally represented as an old man carrying in a basket two turtledoves, an allusion to the offering made for the purification of his daughter. His wife was St. Anne.

Joan of Arc. St. (1412–1431), the Maid of Orleans (*La Pucelle d'Orléans*). Born at Domrémy in Lorraine, the daughter of a peasant, she was directed by heavenly voices to undertake her mission to deliver France, then undergoing the ravages of the HUNDRED YEARS WAR. She convinced the DAUPHIN of her sincerity, donned male dress, and inspired the French army in the relief of Orléans (1429) and then the advance to Rheims. She was captured by the Burgundians at Compiègne (May 1430) and sold to the English by the Count of Luxembourg for 10,000 livres. She was condemned to death by the Bishop of Beauvais for WITCHCRAFT and heresy and burned at the stake at Rouen (30 May 1431). Her last words were the name of Jesus repeated thrice. She was canonized in 1920 as the second patron of France but as such is not recognised by the State. There has been no official patron saint of France since the separation of Church and State in 1905. *See* TERESA, ST. (2).

Pope Joan. *See under* POPE.

Joanna Southcott. *See* SOUTHCOTTIANS.

Job (jōb). The personification of poverty and patience, in allusion to the PATRIARCH whose history is given in the BIBLE.

> I am as poor as Job, my lord, but not so patient.
> SHAKESPEARE: *Henry IV, Pt. II*, I, ii.

Job's comforter. One who means to sympathize with you in your grief, but says that you brought it on yourself, thus adding to your sorrow. An allusion to the rebukes Job received from his "comforters".

Job's post. A bringer of bad news.

Job's Pound. BRIDEWELL; prison.

Jobation. A scolding; so called from the patriarch JOB.

Job (job). Employment, work, something managed for undue private gain, etc.

A bad job. An unfortunate happening, a bad speculation.

A job lot. A collection of miscellaneous goods sold as one lot and usually bought as a speculation at a low price.

Jobs for the boys. A form of favouritism giving jobs and appointments to

John

friends and acquaintances or through the OLD BOY NETWORK—not by fair and open competition. *Cp.* NEPOTISM.

Just the job. Exactly what is needed or required.

To do a job. Colloquially, to commit a robbery.

Jocasta. *See* ŒDIPUS.

Jock. A popular nickname for a Scotsman.

Jockey. Properly "a little Jack". So the Scots say, "'Ilka Jeanie has her Jockie.'"

All fellows, Jockey and the laird. All fellows, man and master (Scots proverb).

To jockey for position. To manoeuvre for position, literally or figuratively, as in a horse race.

Jockey Club. The select body which controls the English TURF. Its headquarters are at Newmarket. It arose from a group of "noblemen and gentlemen" who first met in 1750 at the Star and Garter COFFEE-house in PALL MALL to remedy the abuses at Newmarket.

Jodhpurs. In the 1860s the Maharajah of the Rajputanian State of Jodhpur was an extreme devotee of polo which he played in breeches that were tight-fitting from near to the ankle and loose-fitting above. British army officers imported the game and the breeches.

Joe. American slang for the man in the street, and as a form of address for some-one whose name is unknown (*cp.* JACK). G.I. Joe was applied to an American soldier but G.I. is more general.

In Australian usage it was once an insult and a digger's name for a policeman, after Charles Joseph La Trobe, Lieutenant-Governor of Victoria in 1851, whose unpopularity was occasioned by setting the police to check up on every digger's licence.

Joe Soap. One who is imposed upon.

Joey. The small silver GROAT struck between 1836 and 1855 at the suggestion of Joseph Hume, M.P. (1777–1855), who advocated their usefulness for paying short cab fares, etc. The name was sometimes later colloquially applied to the silver threepenny piece.

In Australia a young kangaroo is called a *joey*.

Jog. Give his memory a jog. Remind him about it.

Jog-trot. A slow but regular pace.

Joggis, or **Jogges.** *See* JOUGS.

John. The English form of Lat. and Gr. *Johannes*, from Heb. *Jochanan*, meaning "God is gracious". The feminine form, *Johanna* or *Joanna*, is nearer the original. The French equivalent of "John" is *Jean* (formerly *Jehan*), the Italian *Giovanni*, Russian *Ivan*, Gaelic *Ian*, Irish *Sean* or *Shaun*, Welsh *Evan*, German *Johann* or *Johannes*, which is contracted to *Jan*, *Jahn*, and *Hans*. "John" is also American slang for water-closet.

For many centuries *John* has been one of the most popular of masculine names in England—probably because it is that of St. JOHN THE EVANGELIST, St. JOHN THE BAPTIST and many other saints.

The name *John* has been used by Popes more than any other, its last holder being John XXIII. The most famous "Johns" of history are probably King John of England (*c.* 1167, 1199–1216); John of Gaunt (1340–1399), the fourth son of Edward III; and Don John of Austria (1547–1478), illegitimate son of the Emperor Charles V, celebrated as a military leader, for his naval victory over the Turks at Lepanto (1571), and as Governor of the Netherlands.

Among the SAINTS of this name are:

St. John the Evangelist, or **the Divine.** The "beloved disciple". Tradition says that he took the Virgin Mary to Ephesus after the Crucifixion and that in the persecution of Domitian (A.D. 93–96) he was plunged into a cauldron of boiling oil but was delivered unharmed, and afterwards banished to the Isle of Patmos where he wrote the *Book of Revelation*. He died at Ephesus. His day is 27 December, and he is usually represented bearing a chalice from which a serpent issues, in allusion to his driving the poison from a cup presented to him to drink.

St. John the Baptist. The forerunner of Jesus, who was sent "to prepare the way of the Lord". His day is 24 June, and he is represented in a coat of sheepskin (in allusion to his life in the desert), either holding a rude wooden CROSS with a pennon bearing the words, *Ecce*

Agnus Dei; or with a book on which a lamb is seated; or holding in his right hand a lamb surrounded by a HALO, and bearing a cross on the right foot.

St. John of Beverley (*c.* 640–721). Bishop of Hexham and subsequently Archbishop of York. The Venerable BEDE was one of his pupils. His healing gifts are recorded by his biographers and his shrine at Beverley Minster (which he founded) became a favourite resort of pilgrims. His day is 7 May.

St. John Chrysostom (*c.* 347–407) (Golden tongued), Bishop of Constantinople and DOCTOR OF THE CHURCH, he did much to purify the life of his SEE. He was banished by his enemies in 403 and died in exile. He was noted for his holiness and liturgical reforms. His day is 13 September (formerly 27 January).

St. John of the Cross (1542–1591). Founder of the Discalced CARMELITES under the influence of St. TERESA. He is noted for his mystical writings, *The Ascent of Mount Carmel*, *The Dark Night*, *The Spiritual Canticle*, etc. He was canonized in 1726, his day being 14 December.

St. John Damascene (*c.* 675–*c.* 749). DOCTOR OF THE CHURCH and a defender of images during the Iconoclastic controversy. (*See* ICONOCLAST.) His day is 4 December (formerly 27 March).

St. John of God (1495–1550). Patron of hospitals, nurses and the sick, and a native of Portugal. In IRELAND he is also held popularly to be the patron of alcoholics, through association with the Dublin clinic devoted to their cure and bearing his name. He founded the Order of Charity for the Service of the Sick, or Brothers Hospitallers. His day is 8 March.

St. John of Nepomuk (*c.* 1340–1393). Patron saint of Bohemia, he was drowned by order of the dissolute King Wenceslaus IV, allegedly because he refused to reveal to the king the confessions of the queen. His day is 16 May.

John Barleycorn. *See under* BARLEY.

John Brown (1800–1859). An American abolitionist who led a body of men to free Negro slaves at Harper's Ferry, Virginia, 16 October 1859, and who was subsequently executed for treason. The famous Union song of the CIVIL WAR, *John Brown's Body*, made him a legend. It arose among the soldiers at Fort Warren, Boston, in 1861, around Sergeant John Brown of their regiment, who was jokingly connected with the "martyr" of Harper's Ferry.

John Bull. The nickname for an Englishman or Englishmen collectively. The name was used in Dr. John Arbuthnot's satire, *Law is a bottomless Pit* (1712), republished as *The History of John Bull*. Arbuthnot did not invent the name but established it.

John Chinaman. A Chinaman or the Chinese as a people.

John Collins. A long drink of gin, lemon or lime, and soda-water, sugar and a lump of ice. Curaçao is sometimes added. Possibly the name of the bartender who originally dispensed it. In the U.S.A. it is called a *Tom Collins*.

John Doe. *See* DOE.

John Hancock. American slang for one's own signature, derived from the fact that John Hancock (1737–1793), the first of the signatories to the Declaration of Independence (1776), had an especially large and clear signature.

John o' Groats. The site of a legendary house 1¾ miles west of Duncansby Head, Caithness, SCOTLAND. The story is that Malcolm, Gavin, and John o'Groat (or Jan de Groot), three Dutch brothers, came to this part of Scotland in the reign of James IV. There came to be eight families of the name and they met annually to celebrate. On one occasion a question of precedency arose, consequently John o'Groat built an eight-sided room with a door to each side and placed an octagonal table therein so that all were "head of the table". This building went ever after with the name of *John o'Groat's House*.

From Land's End to John o'Groats. From one end of Great Britain to the other; from DAN TO BEERSHEBA.

John-a-Dreams. A stupid, dreamy fellow, always in a BROWN STUDY and half asleep.

John-a-Nokes and John-a-Stiles. Names formerly given, instead of the very impersonal "A and B", to fictitious persons in an imaginary action at law;

hence either may stand for "just any-body". *Cp.* DOE.

> And doth the Lawyer lye then, when under the names of John a stile and John a noaks, hee puts his case?
> SIDNEY: *An Apologie for Poetrie* (1595).

John Company. The old Honourable East India Company. It is said that "John" is a pervision of "Hon"; but it is possible that "John Company" is allied to the familiar JOHN BULL. The Company was founded in 1600 and finally abolished in 1858.

John Dory. A golden yellow fish, the *Zeus faber*, common in the Mediterranean and round the south-western coasts of England. Its name was dory (Fr. *doré*, golden) long before the John was added.

There is a tradition that it was from this fish that ST. PETER took the stater or SHEKEL and it has an oval black spot on each side, said to be his finger-marks when he held the fish to extract the coin. It is called in France *le poisson de St. Pierre*, and in Gascon the *golden* or *sacred cock*, meaning St. Peter's cock. *Cp.* HADDOCK.

John in the Wad. The IGNIS FATUUS.

John Tamson's man. A henpecked husband; one ordered about here, there and everywhere. Tamson is a *Tame-son*, a spiritless character.

John Scotus. *See* ERIGENA.

Little John. *See* ROBIN HOOD.

Prester John. In mediaeval legend a fabulous Christian emperor of Asia who occurs in documents from the 12th century onwards. In Marco Polo's *Travels* he is lord of the TARTARS. From the 14th century he becomes the Emperor of Ethiopia or Abyssinia where he was apparently still reigning in the time of Vasco da Gama.

To wait for John Long, the carrier. To wait a long time.

Johnnie Cope, or **Hey, Johnnie Cope.** This famous Scottish song celebrates the Young PRETENDER'S victory at Prestonpans (20 September 1745). Sir John Cope, who led the Government troops, was surprised by the Highlanders at day-break and routed. He escaped and brought the news of his own defeat to Berwick.

> Hey, Johnnie Cope, are ye wauking yet?
> Or are ye sleeping, I would wit?
> Oh, haste ye, get up, for the drums do beat!
> O fye, Cope, rise in the morning.

The Scots attacked before the English were awake.

Johnny. A superfine, dandified youth was known as a *Johnny*, in the latter part of the 19th century.

Johnny Crapaud. A Frenchman. *See* FLEUR-DE-LIS.

Johnny Raw. A nervous novice, a raw recruit.

Johnny Reb. In the American CIVIL WAR a Federal name for a CONFEDERATE soldier, a *rebel* from the Northern standpoint.

Johnstone. St. Johnstone's Tippet. A halter; so called from Johnstone the HANGMAN.

Joint. In U.S.A. slang, originally a sordid place where illicit spirits were drunk, etc.; hence, disparagingly, any cheap restaurant, dive, etc.

To case a joint. *See under* CASE.

Out of joint. Figuratively, a disrupted or confused state of affairs, as a broken joint is out of order.

> The time is out of joint.
> SHAKESPEARE: *Hamlet*, I, v.

To put one's nose out of joint. *See under* NOSE.

Jolly. A sailor's nickname for a MARINE. A militiaman was called a *tame jolly*.

The noun is also slang for a man who bids at an auction with no intention of buying, but merely to force up the price.

To jolly is to chaff or banter and "to jolly someone along" is to wheedle him, to keep him in a good humour in order to coax something out of him.

The jolly god. BACCHUS. The BIBLE speaks of wine "that maketh glad the heart of man" (*Ps.* civ, 15).

A jolly good fellow. A very social, popular, or thoroughly commendable person. When toasts are drunk "with musical honours" the chorus usually is –

> For he's a jolly good fellow [thrice],
> And so say all of us [thrice],
> For he's a jolly good fellow [thrice],
> And so say all of us!

The Jolly Roger. *See under* ROGER.

Jolly-boat. A small clinker-built ship's boat. *Jolly* is probably the Dan. *jolle* or Dut. *jol*, our yawl.

Jonah. A person whose presence brings misfortune upon his companions as did Jonah to the mariners when he took ship to Tarshish to "flee from the presence of the Lord". (*Jon.*i.) *Jonas* is also similarly used, being an alternative name of the prophet Jonah.

Jonathan. *See* BROTHER JONATHAN.

Jonathan's arrows. They were shot to give warning, and not to hurt (I *Sam*. xx, 36).

Jones, Davy. *See* DAVY JONES.

Jones, Paul. *See* PAUL JONES.

Joneses, Keeping up with the. *See under* KEEP.

Jongleur (zhong' glĕr). A mediaeval minstrel who recited verses to his own musical accompaniment. They wandered from castle to castle performing the CHANSONS DE GESTE and are linked with the TROUBADOURS. The word is O. Fr. *jiglere*, Lat. *joculator*, our juggler.

Jophiel. *See* ARCHANGEL.

Jordan. A name anciently given to the pot used by alchemists and doctors, then tranferred to a chamber-pot. It was perhaps originally *Jordan-bottle*, *i.e.* a bottle in which pilgrims and crusaders brought back water from the River Jordan.

Jordan almond. Here Jordan has nothing to do with the river (*cp*. JERUSALEM ARTICHOKE), but is a corruption of Fr. *jardin*, garden. The Jordan almond is a fine variety which comes chiefly from Malaga.

Jordan passed. Death over. The Jordan separated the wilderness of the world from the PROMISED LAND, and thus came to be regarded as the Christian STYX.

Jorum. A large drinking-bowl, intended especially for PUNCH. The name is thought to be connected with King Joram (*cp*. JEROBOAM), who "brought with him vessels of silver, and vessels of gold, and vessels of brass" (II *Sam*. viii, 10).

Josaphat. *See* BARLAAM AND JOSAPHAT.

Joseph. One not to be seduced from his continency by the severest temptation is sometimes so called. The reference is to Joseph in Potiphar's house (*Gen*. xxxix). *Cp*. BELLEROPHON.

A form of great-coat used to be known by the same name, in allusion to Joseph's coat of many colours (*Gen*. xxxvii, 3).

Joseph, St. Husband of the Virgin Mary and the lawful father of Jesus. He is patron saint of carpenters, because he was of that craft.

In art Joseph is represented as an aged man with a budding staff in his hand. His day is 19 March, and in 1955 Pope Pius XII instituted the feast of St. Joseph the Workman on 1 May.

Joseph of Arimathea, St. The rich JEW, probably a member of the SANHEDRIN, who believed in Christ, but feared to confess it, and, after the Crucifixion, begged the body of the Saviour and deposited it in his own tomb (*see Matt*. xxvii, 57–60; *Mark* xv, 43–46). His day is 17 March.

Legend relates that he was imprisoned for 12 years and was kept alive miraculously by the holy GRAIL, and that on his release by Vespasian, about the year 63, he brought the Grail and the spear with which Longinus wounded the crucified Saviour to Britain, and founded the abbey of GLASTONBURY whence he commenced the conversion of Britain.

The origin of these legends is to be found in a group of APOCRYPHAL writings of which the *Evangelium Nicodemi* is the chief; these were worked upon at Glastonbury and further established by Robert de Borron in the 13th century, the latter version (by way of Walter Map) being woven by Malory into his *Morte d'Arthur*.

Josephus (*c*. A.D. 37–95). Flavius Josephus, the celebrated Jewish historian, and PHARISEE, took a prominent part in the last Jewish revolt against the Romans (A.D. 66–70) and later wrote his *History of the Jewish War*. According to his own account, his prophecy that Vespasian, the captor of Jerusalem, would become emperor of ROME, saved his life. The most important of his other writings was his *Jewish Antiquities*, dealing with the history of the Jews down to the end of Nero's reign.

Joss. A Chinese god or idol. The word is

probably a PIDGIN-ENGLISH corruption of Port. *deos*, Lat. *deus*, god. A temple is called a *joss-house*, and a *joss-stick* is a stick made from clay mixed with the powder of various scented woods burnt as incense.

Jot. A very little, the least possible. The iota ι (*see* **I**) is the smallest letter of the Greek alphabet, called the *Lacedaemonian letter*.

> This bond doth give thee here no jot of blood.
> SHAKESPEARE: *Merchant of Venice*, IV, i.

Jot or tittle. A tiny amount. The jot is ι or iota, and the tittle, from Lat. *titulus*, is the mark or dot over the *i*.

Jotunheim (jó' tŭn'hīm). The land of the Scandinavian *Jotuns* or GIANTS.

Jougs (joogz). The Scottish PILLORY, or more properly an iron ring or collar fastened to a wall by a short chain, and used as a pillory (O. Fr. *joug*, a yoke).

Journey-weight (Fr. *journée*, a day). Originally the quantity of coins that could be minted in a day. A *journey-weight* of gold is fifteen pounds troy, which was coined into 701 SOVEREIGNS or double that number of half-sovereigns. A *journey* of silver is sixty pounds troy, which, before the alteration in the silver coinage of 1920, was coined into 3,960 shillings. The trial of the Pyx (*see under* PYX) depends on these journey-weights.

Jove. Another name of JUPITER, being *Jovis pater*, father Jove. Milton, in *Paradise Lost*, makes Jove one of the fallen angels (I, 512).

Jovial. Merry and sociable, like those born under the planet JUPITER, which astrologers considered the happiest of the natal stars. *Cp.* SATURNINE.

> Our Jovial star reign'd at his birth.
> SHAKESPEARE: *Cymbeline*, V, iv.

Joy. To get no joy. Not to meet with any success.

The five Joyful Mysteries. The first chaplet of the ROSARY, made up of the ANNUNCIATION, the Visitation, the Nativity of Christ, the Presentation of Christ in the TEMPLE, and the finding of the Child Jesus in the Temple.

The seven joys of the Virgin. *See* MARY.

Joy-ride. A pleasure-ride or stolen ride in a motor-car or other vehicle, especi-

ally when driven fast.

Joy-stick. The control column of an aeroplane or glider, which is linked to the elevators and ailerons to control them.

Joyeuse (zhwa yĕrz). A name given to more than one famous sword in romance, especially to CHARLEMAGNE'S, which bore the inscription *Decem praeceptorum custos Carolus*, and was buried with him.

Joyeuse Garde, or **Garde-Joyeuse**. The estate given by King ARTHUR to Sir LANCELOT of the Lake for defending the Queen's honour against Sir Mador. It is supposed to have been at Berwick-on-Tweed.

Juan, Don. Don Juan Tenorio, the legendary hero of many plays, poems, stories and operas, was the son of a notable family in 14th-century Seville. The story is that he killed the commandant of Ulloa after seducing his daughter. He then invited the statue of the murdered man (erected in the FRANCISCAN convent) to a feast, at the end of which the sculptured figure delivered him over to HELL. He is presented as the complete profligate.

His name is synonymous with rake, roué and aristocratic libertine, and in Mozart's opera *Don Giovanni* (1787) the valet says that his master had "in Italy 700 mistresses, in Germany 800, in Turkey and France 91, in Spain 1,0003". Don Juan's dissolute life was dramatized by the monk Gabriel Tellez in the 17th century, followed by MOLIÈRE, Corneille, Shadwell and others. BYRON, the elder Dumas, Balzac, de Musset, and Shaw (*Man and Superman*) all utilized the story and helped to maintain its popularity.

Juan Fernandez. *See* ROBINSON CRUSOE.

Jubilate (joo bi la' ti) (Lat., Cry aloud) is the name given to two psalms which begin with this word in the VULGATE (lxv and xcix). In the English psalter they are *Psalms* lxvi and c.

Jubilate Sunday is the third Sunday after EASTER, when the introit at the MASS begins with two verses of the first of the Jubilate Psalms.

Jubilee. In Jewish history the year of *jubi-*

lee was every fiftieth year, which was held sacred in commemoration of the deliverance from Egypt. In this year the fields were allowed to lie fallow, land that had passed out of the possession of those to whom it originally belonged was restored to them, and all who had been obliged to let themselves out for hire were released from bondage. The jubilee was proclaimed with trumpets of ram's horn (*see Lev.* xxv, 11–34, 39–54, and xxvii 17–24).

Hence any fiftieth anniversary, especially one kept with great rejoicings, is called a *Jubilee*, and the name has been applied to other outbursts of joy or celebrations, such as the *Shakespeare Jubilee*, held at Stratford-upon-Avon in 1769, and the *Protestant Jubilee*, celebrated in Germany in 1617, the centenary of Luther's protest.

King George III's *Jubilee* was on 25 October 1809, the day before the commencement of the fiftieth year of his reign, Queen Victoria celebrated hers on 21 June 1887, and kept her *Diamond Jubilee* ten years later. George V celebrated the twenty-fifth year of his accession by a *Silver Jubilee* on 6 May 1935, and Queen Elizabeth II's Silver Jubilee was celebrated on 7 June 1977.

In the ROMAN CATHOLIC CHURCH Pope Boniface VIII instituted a *jubilee* in 1300 and INDULGENCES were granted to pilgrims visiting ROME. It was to be held at intervals of 100 years but in 1343 Clement VI altered it to 50 years and in 1389 Urban IV to 33. In 1470 Paul II reduced the interval to 25 years. The jubilee is the only occasion when the *Porta Santa* (HOLY DOOR) of St. Peter's Rome is opened. PILGRIMAGE to Rome ceased to be obligatory in 1500. A jubilee is also known as a *Holy Year*, and extends from Christmas to Christmas.

Judas. Judas Iscariot, who betrayed Christ, his Master; hence a traitor.

Judas Kiss. A deceitful act of courtesy or simulated affection. JUDAS betrayed his Master with a kiss (*Matt.* xxvi, 49).

Judas slits, or **holes.** The peep-holes in a prison door which the guard uncovers to check up on the prisoners.

Judas tree. A leguminous tree of southern Europe (*Cercis siliquastrum*) which flowers before the leaves appear, so called from a Greek tradition that Judas hanged himself on such a tree. *Cp.* ELDER-TREE, which is sometimes also so named. The American Judas tree is the *Cercis canadensis* or redbud.

Judas-coloured hair. Fiery red. In the MIDDLE AGES Judas Iscariot was represented with red hair and beard. *Cp.* CAIN-COLOURED BEARD

Jude, St. One of the twelve apostles, brother of James (*i.e.* the Lord's brother), also identified as brother of JAMES THE LESS. He is represented in art with a club or staff, and a carpenter's square in allusion to his trade. His day, 28 October, coincides with that of St. SIMON, with whom he suffered martyrdom in Persia. He is the author of the *Epistle of Jude* and nowadays is regarded as the patron of hopeless cases.

Judge. Judges' Rules. Rules concerning the questioning of suspects by the police, and the taking of statements. First formulated in 1912 and revised in 1918, they were re-formulated in 1964 by a committee of judges and approved by a meeting of all judges of the QUEEN'S BENCH.

Judgement, The Last, or **General Judgement,** is God's final sentence on mankind on the LAST DAY. The **Particular Judgement** is the judgement on each individual soul after death.

Judgement of Paris. *See* PARIS.

Judica Sunday (joo′ di kà). The fifth Sunday in LENT (formerly also known as Passion Sunday) is so called from the first word of the Introit at the MASS, *Judica me, Deus*, Give sentence with me, O God (*Ps.* xliii).

Judicial Astrology. *See* ASTROLOGY.

Judicium Crucis (jū dis′ i um kroo′ sis). Trial of the CROSS. A form of ORDEAL which consisted in stretching out the arms before a cross, till one party could hold out no longer, and lost his cause.

Judy. *See* PUNCH, MR.

Jug, or **Stone Jug.** A prison. *Cp.* JOUGS.

To be jugged, or **to be in the jug.** To be imprisoned.

Bottle and jug. A once common name for a public-house bar where beer was sold in bottles and draught beer could be collected in jugs for consumption off the premises.

Jugged hare. Hare stewed with wine and seasoning, properly in a jug or jar.

Juggernaut, or **Jagganath.** A Hindu god, "Lord of the World", having his temple at Puri in Orissa. It is a cult-title of VISHNU, and the pyramidal temple was erected in the 12th century and held the Golden Tooth of BUDDHA. The chief festival is the car festival when Jagganath is dragged in his car (35 feet square and 45 feet high) over the sand to another temple. The car has sixteen wheels, each seven feet in diameter. The belief that fanatical pilgrims cast themselves under the wheels of the car to be crushed to death on the last day of the festival is largely without foundation. However, it has led to the phrase the **car of the juggernaut,** used to denote customs institutions, etc., beneath which people are ruthlessly and unnecessarily crushed. The word *juggernaut* is also applied humorously to any wheeled "monster". More recently, juggernaut is the name given to the giant articulated lorries increasingly prevalent since Britain's entry into the Common Market, which pose another threat to the environment.

Juggler (Lat. *joculator,* a jester, joker). In the MIDDLE AGES, jugglers accompanied the MINSTRELS and TROUBADOURS and added to their musical talents sleight of hand, antics and feats of prowess to amuse their audience. In time the music was omitted and tricks became their staple. *Cp.* JONGLEUR.

Julian. Pertaining to Julius CAESAR (100–44 B.C.).

Julian the Apostate (332, 361–363). Flavius Claudius Julianus, Roman EMPEROR, and nephew of Constantine the GREAT. So called from his attempts to restore paganism, having abandoned Christianity at about the age of 20. He set an example by the austerity of his life and zeal for the public welfare and was notable for his literary and philosophical interests. Christians were not actively persecuted but there was discrimination against them. *See* GALILEAN.

Julian Calendar. The calendar instituted by Julius CAESAR in 46 B.C., which was in general use in Western Europe until the introduction of the GREGORIAN CALENDAR in 1582, and still used in England until 1752 and until 1918 in Russia. To allow for the odd quarter of a day, Cæsar ordained that every fourth year should contain 366 days, the additional day being introduced after the 6th before the CALENDS of March, *i.e.* 24 February. Cæsar also divided the months into the number of days they at present contain. It is now called "the Old Style". *See* JULY.

Julian Year. The average year of $365\frac{1}{4}$ days, according to the Julian Calendar.

Julian, St. A patron SAINT of travellers and of hospitality, looked upon in the MIDDLE AGES as the epicure of saints. Thus Chaucer says that the Franklin was "Epicurus owne sone", and:

> An house holdere, and that a greet was he;
> Seint Julian in his contree.
> *Canterbury Tales: Prologue*, 339.

He seems to be essentially a mythical saint. He is supposed to have unwittingly slain his parents and devoted his life to helping strangers by way of atonement.

Juliana (or **Mother Julian**) **of Norwich** (c. 1342–c. 1413). A religious recluse and mystic who recorded her visions in *XVI Revelations of Divine Love.*

Juliet. *See* ROMEO.

Julium Sidus. The comet which appeared at the death of Julius CAESAR, and which in court flattery was called the apotheosis of the murdered man.

July. The seventh month, named by Mark Anthony in honour of Julius CAESAR. It was formerly called *Quintilis,* as it was the fifth month of the Roman year. The old Dutch name for it was *Hooy-maand* (hay-month); the old Saxon, *Mædd-Monath* (because the cattle were turned into the meadows to feed) and *Lida æftevr* (the second mild or genial month). In the French Revolutionary CALENDAR it was called *Messidor* (harvest-month, 19 June to 18 July).

The July Monarchy. That of Louis Philippe, also called the Orleanist monarchy. *See* JULY REVOLUTION.

The July Revolution. The French revolution of 1830 (17–29 July) which overthrew Charles X and gave the throne to Louis Philippe, Duke of Orleans, the CITIZEN KING.

Jumbo. The name of an exceptionally large African elephant, which, after giving rides to thousands of children in the London Zoo, was sold to Barnum's "Greatest Show on Earth" in 1882. He weighed 6½ tons and was accidentally killed by a railway engine in 1885. His name is now synonymous with *elephant* in children's minds.

Jump. To jump at an offer. To accept eagerly.

To jump at, or **to conclusions.** To draw inferences too hastily from insufficient evidence.

To jump bail. To forfeit bail by absconding before trial.

To jump down a person's throat. See *under* THROAT.

To jump from the frying-pan into the fire. See FRYING-PAN.

To jump over the broomstick. To live together without the proper ceremony of marriage. To "jump the besom" is an alternative form. The derivation is uncertain.

To jump the gun. See *under* GUN.

To jump upon someone. To come down upon them heavily with a crushing remark, etc.

Jumping-off place. The edge of the earth, the end of civilization from which one leaped into nothingness. Thus used by settlers of any remote, desolate spot. Also a starting point from which to begin an enterprise, etc.

Jumpers. A nickname applied to the SHAKERS, and also to Welsh METHODISTS who were supposed to "jump for joy" during divine service.

June. The sixth month, named from the Roman *Junius*, a gens or clan name akin to *juvenis*, young. Ovid says *Junius a juvenum nomine dictus* (*Fasti*, v, 79). Alternatively, it may derive from JUNO.

The old Dutch name was *Zomermaand* (summer-month); the old Saxon, *Seremonath* (dry-month) and *Lida œrra* (joy time). In the French Revolutionary CALENDAR the month was called *Prairial* (meadow month, 20 May to 18 June).

June marriages lucky. "Good to the man and happy to the maid." This is an old Roman superstition. The festival of Juno Moneta was held on the CALENDS of JUNE, and JUNO was the great guardian of women from birth to death.

Junius. Junius Brutus. Son of M. Junius and Tarquinia and nephew of Tarquin. When his father and elder brother were murdered by Tarquin the Proud, he feigned insanity, thereby saving his life, and was called *Brutus* for his apparent stupidity. He later inspired the Romans to get rid of the Tarquins and became a consul. *Cp.* AMYRIS PLAYS THE FOOL.

The Letters of Junius. A series of anonymous letters, the authorship of which has never been finally settled, which appeared in the London *Public Advertiser* from 21 November 1768 to 21 January 1772. They were directed against Sir William Draper, the Duke of Grafton, and the Ministers generally. The author said in his Dedication, "I am the sole depository of my own secret, and it shall perish with me."

Junk. Nautically speaking is old, discarded or condemned cordage; **salt junk,** the salt meat supplied to ships for long voyages, from its toughness and likeness to old rope-ends. The term probably derives from Lat. *juncus*, a rush, once used in the making of cordage (*cp.* JUNKET). The word is now applied generally to a miscellany of cast-off or unwanted articles. It is now also the slang term for narcotic drugs such as heroin and cocaine and an addict of such is called a *junker* or *junkie*.

Junker (yung' ker). A German landowning aristocrat or squire, who formerly provided most of the officer class. Bismarck, the German chancellor, came frm the Prussian junker class. *See also* JUNK.

Juno. In Roman mythology "the venerable ox-eyed" wife and sister of JUPITER, and queen of HEAVEN. She is identified with the Greek HERA, was the special protectress of marriage and of women, and was represented as a war goddess. *Cp.* GENIUS.

Junonian Bird. The peacock, dedicated to the goddess-queen.

Junta (Sp. *juntar*, to join, congregate). In Spain a committee or council, especially a consultative or legislative assembly for the whole part of the country, the best known being the Junta of Regency set up under Murat's presidency after NAPOLEON had secured King Ferdinand's abdication, and the local Juntas, backed by a central Junta at Seville, formed to resist the French. A group of army officers who seize political power is called a "military junta".

The name was also applied by Sidney and Beatrice Webb to a group of TRADE UNION general secretaries in London who were influential in trade union affairs in the 1860s. Their contemporaries called them the "Clique".

Junto. A corruption of JUNTA, denoting a clique or faction. It is particularly used of the WHIG leaders of the reigns of William III and Anne. The lords of the Whig Junto were Wharton, Somers, Sunderland, Orford, and Halifax. *Cp.* CABAL.

Jupiter. Also called JOVE, the supreme god of Roman mythology, corresponding to the Greek ZEUS, son of SATURN or Kronos (whom he dethroned) and Ops or Rhea. He was the special protector of ROME, and as Jupiter Capitolinus (his temple being on the Capitoline Hill) presided over the Roman games. He determined the course of human affairs and made known the future through signs in the heavens, the flight of birds, etc. *See* AUGURY.

As Jupiter was lord of HEAVEN and bringer of light, white was the colour sacred to him; hence among the alchemists Jupiter designated tin. In HERALDRY Jupiter stands for AZURE, the blue of the heavens. *See* COLOURS.

His statue by Phidias at OLYMPIA was one of the Seven Wonders of the World (*see under* WONDER). It was removed to Constantinople by Theodosius I and destroyed by fire in 475. *See* THEMIS.

Jupiter is also the name of the largest of the planets.

Jupiter Ammon. A name under which JUPITER was worshipped in Libya where his temple was famous for its ORACLE which was consulted by HERCULES. *Cp.* AMMON.

Jupiter Scapin. A nickname of NAPOLEON, given him by the Abbé de Pradt. Scapin is a valet famous for his knavish tricks, in MOLIÈRE's comedy *Les Fourberies de Scapin*.

Jupiter tonans (the thundering Jupiter). A complimentary nickname given to *The Times* in the mid-19th century. *Cp.* PRINTING HOUSE SQUARE.

Jupiter's beard. HOUSE LEEK.

Jury mast. A temporary mast erected to replace one that has been carried away. Similarly *jury rudder*, *jury rig*, etc., and humorously *jury leg* for a wooden leg. The etymology of "jury" here is a matter of surmise.

Jus. Latin for law.

Jus civile (Lat.). Civil law; Roman law.

Jus divinum (Lat.). Divine law.

Jus gentium (Lat.). The law of nations or law common to all nations; used by moderns as an expression for international law for which the Roman term was *jus feciale*.

Jus mariti (Lat.). The right of the husband to the wife's property.

Jus naturae, or **naturale** (Lat.). Natural law, originally virtually the same as *Jus gentium*. The law of reason common to nature and man.

Jus primae noctis (Lat. right of the first night). The same as *droit du seigneur* (lord's right), the right of the lord to share the bed of the bride of any one of his vassals on the wedding night. The custom seems to have existed in early mediaeval Europe to a limited extent but was more often the excuse for levying dues in lieu.

Juste-milieu (zhoost mil yěr) (Fr.) The golden mean.

Le mot juste (lě mó zhoost) (Fr.). The word or phrase which exactly conveys the meaning desired.

Justice. *See* JEDDART.

Justices of the peace. Local lords and gentry were initially given judicial authority as Conservators of the Peace in 1361. As unpaid Justices of the Peace they acted firstly through the courts or QUARTER SESSIONS. Summary jurisdiction developed in the 16th century and they also carried out much administrative work until the Local Government Acts of 1888 and 1894. Today, as lay magistrates appointed by the Lord Chancellor, they largely deal summarily with the lesser offences, the licensing of premises, affiliation orders, etc.

Poetic justice. The ideal justice which poets exercise in making the good happy and the bad unsuccessful.

Juvenal (Lat. *juvenis*). A youth; common in SHAKESPEARE, as "The juvenal, the prince your master, whose chin is not yet fledged" (*Henry IV, Pt. II*, I, ii).

Juveniles. In theatrical parlance, actors playing young men's parts; in the journalistic and book-trade, periodicals or books intended for the young.

K

K. The eleventh letter of the alphabet, representing the Greek *kappa* and the Hebrew *kaph*. The Egyptian hieroglyphic for K was a bowl. The Romans, after the C was given the K sound, only used the latter for abbreviated forms of a few words from Greek; thus, false accusers were branded on the forehead with a K (*Kalumnia*), and the Carians, Cretans, and Cilicians were known as *the three bad K's*. K is the recognized abbreviation of *Knight* in British Orders but the abbreviation of KNIGHT *per se* is *Kt*.

K.B. or **Kt.Bach.** Knight Bachelor.

Ka me, ka thee. You scratch my back and I'll scratch yours; one good turn deserves another; do me a service, and I will give you a helping hand when you require one. It is an old proverb, and appears in Heywood's collection (1546).

Kaaba (ka' bả) (Arab. *kabah*, a cube). The ancient stone building said to have been first built by ISHMAEL and ABRAHAM and incorporated in the centre of the Great Mosque at MECCA. It forms a rough square and is about 40 feet high, containing the BLACK STONE in the east corner. The present Kaaba was built in 1626 and is covered with a cloth of black brocade that is replaced with annual ceremony.

Kabbalah. *See* CABBALA.

Kaf, Mount. *See* JINN.

Kaffir (kǎf' ûr) (Arab. *kafir*, an infidel). A name given to all Africans who were not MOSLEMS. The British and other Europeans restricted the term to the Bantu races.

Kailyard School. A school of writers flourishing in the 1890s, who took their subjects from Scottish humble life. It included Ian Maclaren, J. J. Bell, S. R. Crockett, and J. M. Barrie. The name is from the motto—"There grows a bonnie brier bush in our Kailyard"—used by Maclaren for his *Beside the Bonnie Brier Bush* (1894).

Kaiser (kī' zer). The German form of CÆSAR; the title formerly used by the head of the HOLY ROMAN EMPIRE, and by the Emperors of Austria and Germany. It was Diocletian (*c.* 284) who ordained that *Cæsar* should be the title of the EMPEROR of the West.

Kalevala. The national epic of the Finns, compiled from popular songs and oral tradition by the Finnish philologist, Elias Lönnroth (1802–1884), who published his first edition of 12,000 verses in 1835, and a second, of some 22,900 verses, in 1849. Its name is taken from the three sons of Kalewa (Finland), who are the heroes of the poem—Väinämöinen, Ilmarenin, and Lemminkäinen. Prominent in the action is the magical mill, the Sampo, an object that grants all one's wishes. The epic is influenced by Teutonic and Scandinavian mythology, and to a lesser extent by Christianity. It is written in unrhymed alliterative trochaic verse, and is the prototype both in form and content of Longfellow's *Hiawatha*.

Kali (ka' lē). The cult name of the Hindu goddess Durga, wife of SIVA goddess of death and destruction. Calcutta receives its name from her, Kali-ghat, the steps of Kali, by which her worshippers descended from the bank to the waters of the Ganges. It was to her that the THUGS sacrificed their victims. Her idol is black, besmeared with blood; she has red eyes, four arms, matted hair, huge fang-like teeth, and a protruding tongue that drips with blood. She wears a necklace of skulls, ear-rings of corpses, and is girdled with serpents.

Kalki. *See* AVATAR.

Kalyb (kă′ lib). The "Lady of the Woods", who stole St. GEORGE from his nurse, and endowed him with gifts. St. George enclosed her in a rock where she was torn to pieces by spirits. The story occurs in the *Famous History of the Seven Champions of Christendom*, Pt. I. *See* SEVEN CHAMPIONS.

Kami (ka′ mē). A god or divinity in SHINTOISM, the native religion of Japan; also the title given to daimios and governors, comparable to our "lord". Their respective ideographs are different.

Kamikaze (ka mi ka zi). A Japanese word meaning "divine wind", in reference to the providential typhoon which once balked a Mongol invasion. In World War II it was applied to the "suicide" aircraft attacks organized under Vice-Admiral Onishi in the Philippines between October 1944 and January 1945. Some 5,000 young pilots gave their lives when their bomb-loaded fighters crashed into their objectives.

Kamsa. *See* KRISHNA.

Kangaroo, or **Kangaroo Closure.** In British Parliamentary procedure, the process by which the SPEAKER (on the Report stage of a bill), or the Chairman of the Committee of the Whole House (or standing committee) selects the amendments to be debated. So named because the debate leaps from clause to clause.

Kangaroo Court. An irregular court or tribunal conducted in disregard of proper legal procedure, as a mock court held among prisoners in a gaol. "To kangaroo" means to convict a person on false evidence. The term, which probably arose from some likening of the "jumps" of the kangaroo to the progress of "justice" in such courts, was common in the U.S.A. during the 19th century. It obtained wide currency in England in 1966 when applied to the irregular punitive measures taken by certain TRADE UNIONS against their members.

Karaites. *See* SCRIPTURISTS.

Karma (Sans., action, fate). In Buddhist philosophy, the name given to the results of action, especially the cumulative results of a person's deeds in one stage of

his existence as controlling his destiny in the next.

Among Theosophists the word has a rather wider meaning, *viz*. the unbroken sequence of cause and effect; each effect being, in its turn, the cause of a subsequent effect.

Karmathians. A 9th-century Mohammedan sect in Iraq founded by Karmut, a labourer who professed to be a prophet. They were socialistic pantheists and rejected the forms and ceremonies of the KORAN, which they regarded as a purely allegorical work.

Karno. Fred Karno's army. A humorous nickname applied to the new British army raised during the war of 1914–1918 in allusion to the famous comedian and producer of stage burlesques, properly, Fred John Westcott (d. 1941). Fred Karno's company was a household name at the time from its merry and eccentric performances.

There are, of course, variants and in World War II "Old Hitler" was substituted for "The Kaiser". The name is also applied derisively to other nondescript bodies. *Cp*. HARRY TATE'S NAVY; MEREDITH.

Karttikeya. The Hindu god of war. He is shown riding on a peacock, with a bow in one hand and an arrow in the other, and is known also as *Skanda* and *Kumara*.

Kaswa, Al. MOHAMMED'S favourite camel, which fell on its knees when the prophet delivered the last clause of the KORAN to the assembled multitude at MECCA.

Katerfelto. A generic name for a QUACK or CHARLATAN. Gustavus Katerfelto was a celebrated quack who became famous during the influenza epidemic of 1782, when he exhibited his solar microscope at London and created immense excitement by showing the infusoria of muddy water.

Kathay. *See* CATHAY.

Kay, Sir. In ARTHURIAN ROMANCE, son of Sir Ector and foster-brother of King ARTHUR who made him his seneschal.

Keblah. *See* KIBLAH.

Kedar's Tents (kē dà). This world. Kedar was a son of ISHMAEL (*Gen*. xxv, 13), and was the ancestor of an important tribe of nomadic Arabs. The phrase means "houses in the wilderness of this world", and comes from *Ps.* cxx, 5: "Woe is me, that I sojourn in Mesech, that I dwell in the tents of Kedar!"

Keel. Keel-hauling. An old naval punishment consisting of dragging the offender under the keel of the ship from one side to the other by means of ropes and tackles attached to the yards. The result was often fatal. Figuratively it is "to haul over the coals" (*see under* COAL), to castigate harshly.

On an even keel. Figuratively, a state of stability or balance.

Keening. A weird lamentation for the dead, once common in Ireland, practised at funerals. It is from the Irish word *caoine*, pronounced *keen*, and was a similar musical dirge to the Scottish *coronach*.

Keep. One's *keep* is the amount that it takes to maintain one; heard in such phrases as **You're not worth your keep.** The *keep* of a mediæval castle was the main tower or stronghold of the donjon.

Keep, or **save your breath to cool your porridge.** Look after your own business, and do not put your SPOKE into another person's wheel.

Keep your hair on. *See under* HAIR.

Keep your powder dry. Keep prepared for action; keep your courage up. The phrase comes from a story told of Oliver Cromwell. During his campaign in IRELAND, he concluded an address to his troops, who were about to cross a river before attacking, with the words: "Put your trust in God; but be sure to keep your powder dry."

To keep, or **set a good table.** To provide a good and generous standard of fare at one's table.

To keep a stiff upper lip. To preserve a resolute appearance; not to give way to grief.

To keep at arm's length. To keep at a distance from one; to prevent another from being too familiar.

To keep at it. To continue hard at work; to persist.

To keep body and soul together. *See under* BODY.

To keep company with. A friendship preliminary to courtship.

To keep down. To prevent another from rising to an independent position; to keep in subjection; also to keep expenses low.

To keep good hours. *See under* HOUR.

To keep house, open house, etc. *See under* HOUSE.

To keep in. To repress, to restrain; also to confine pupils in the classroom as a punishment after school hours.

To keep in countenance, etc. *See under* COUNTENANCE.

To keep it dark, etc. *See under* DARK.

To keep oneself to oneself. To avoid the society of others; to keep aloof.

To keep one's hand in. *See under* HAND.

To keep one's terms. To reside in college, attend the INNS OF COURT, etc., during the recognized term times.

To keep tab, to keep tabs on. To keep a record; to keep a check on.

To keep the pot a-boiling. *See under* POT.

To keep up. To continue, as "to keep up a discussion"; to maintain, as, "to keep up one's courage", "to keep up appearances"; to continue PARI PASSU, as, "to keep up with the rest".

Keeper of the King's conscience. The LORD CHANCELLOR. (*See under* CHANCELLOR.)

Keeping up with the Joneses. Trying to keep up the social level or to keep up appearances with your neighbours. The phrase was invented by Arthur R. ("Pop") Momand, the comic-strip artist, for a series which began in the New York *Globe* in 1913, and ran in that and other papers for 28 years. It was originally based on the artist's own attempts to keep up with his neighbours.

Keeping-room. The common sitting-room of a family.

Kells, The Book of. Kells is an ancient Irish town in County Meath, and was the SEE of a BISHOP until the 13th century. Among its antiquities, but now preserved in Trinity College, Dublin, is the 8th-century *Book of Kells*, one of the finest extant illuminated manuscripts of the Gospels in Latin.

Kelly. As game as Ned Kelly. The phrase refers to the noted Australian desperado and BUSHRANGER, Ned Kelly

(1855–1880) who, after a legendary career of crime, was captured in a suit of armour of his own making, and hanged at Melbourne. He died bravely, his last words being, "Such is life."

Kelmscott Press. A private printing press founded in 1890 by William Morris (1834–1896) in a cottage adjoining his residence, Kelmscott House, Hammersmith. Assisted by Emery Walker, who initially gave Morris the inspiration, and Sidney Cockerell, the aim was to revive good printing as an art, and their publications made a serious impact on printing and book production.

Kelpie, or **kelpy.** A spirit of the waters in the form of a horse, in Scottish fairy-lore. It was supposed to delight in the drowning of travellers, but also occasionally helped millers by keeping the mill-wheel going at night.

Kelter or **Kilter.** Good condition, health, order or spirits. Of unknown origin, it occurs in various local dialects in such expressions as *out of kelter, in good kelter, to get into kelter.*

Kendal Green. Green cloth for foresters; so called from Kendal, Westmorland, formerly famous for its manufacture. LINCOLN was also famous for its green cloth.

Kenelm, St. An English SAINT, son of Kenwulf, King of Mercia in the early 9th century. He was only seven years old when, by his sister's order, he was murdered at Clent, Worcestershire. The murder, says Roger of Wendover, was miraculously notified at ROME by a white dove, which alighted on the altar at St. Peter's, bearing in its beak a scroll with

In Clent cow pasture, under a thorn,
Of head bereft, lies Kenelm, King-born.

His day is 17 July.

Kenne. A stone, fabled by mediæval naturalists to be formed in the eye of a stag. It was used as an antidote to poison. *Cp.* HYENA.

Kenno. A dialect name for a large rich cheese made by the women of the family for the refreshment of the GOSSIPS who were in the house at the birth of a child, any remnant being divided among them and taken home. Said to be derived from *ken*, to know, and so called because its making was kept secret. *Cp.*

GROANING CHAIR.

Kent. A man of Kent. One born east of the Medway. These men went out with green boughs to meet the CONQUEROR, and obtained in consequence a confirmation of their ancient privileges from the new King. *See* HENGIST AND HORSA.

A Kentish man. A native of West Kent.

The Fair Maid of Kent. *See under* FAIR.

The Holy Maid of Kent. *See under* HOLY.

Kentish Fire. Rapturous applause, or three times three and one more. The expression probably originated with the protracted cheers given in Kent to the No-Popery orators in 1828–1829. Lord Winchelsea, proposing the health of the Earl of Roden on 15 August 1834, said: "Let it be given with the Kentish Fire."

Kentigern, St. (kent' i jĕrn). The patron SAINT of Glasgow (*c.* 510–*c.* 600); apostle of north-west ENGLAND and southeast SCOTLAND, and traditional founder of Glasgow Cathedral. He is represented with his episcopal cross in one hand, and in the other a salmon and a ring in allusion to the popular legend:

> Queen Langoureth had been false to her husband, King Roderich, and had given her lover a ring. The king, aware of the fact, stole upon the knight in sleep, abstracted the ring, threw it into the Clyde, and then asked the queen for it. The queen, in alarm, applied to St. Kentigern, who after praying, went to the Clyde, caught a salmon with the ring in its mouth, handed it to the queen and was thus the means of restoring peace to the royal couple.

The Glasgow arms include the salmon with the ring in its mouth, an oak-tree with a bell hanging on one of the branches, and a bird at the top of the tree:

> The tree that never grew,
> The bird that never flew,
> The fish that never swam,
> The bell that never rang.

The oak and the bell are in allusion to the story that St. Kentigern hung a bell upon an oak to summon the wild natives to worship.

St. Kentigern is also known as "St. Mungo", for *Mungho* (dearest) was the name by which St. Servan, his first preceptor, called him.

His day is 13 January.

Kepler's Laws. Astronomical laws first enunciated by Johann Kepler (1571–1630). They formed the basis of Newton's work, and are the starting-point of modern astronomy.

Kermesse, Kermis, or **Kirmess.** Originally the *Kirkmass* or church mass held in most towns of the Low Countries on the anniversary of the dedication of the parish church. It was accompanied by processions, and by feasting, and sports and games often of a somewhat riotous nature. It still survives, essentially as a FAIR.

Kern (M.E. *kerne* from Ir. *ceithern*). In mediæval Ireland, a light-armed foot soldier, one of the lowest grade. *Cp.* GALLOGLASS.

Kern Baby. *See* CORN DOLLY.

Kernel. The kernel of the matter. Its gist, true import; the core or central part of it. The word is O.E. *cyrnel,* diminutive of *corn.*

Kersey. A coarse cloth, usually ribbed, and woven from long wool; said to be originally made at Kersey in Suffolk. Hence, figuratively, "homely", "homespun".

> Henceforth my wooing mind shall be expess'd
> In russet, yeas, and honest kersey noes.
> SHAKESPEARE: *Love's Labour's Lost,*
> V, ii.

Kestrel. A common European falcon, or small hawk, once regarded as of a mean or base variety; hence contemptuously, a worthless fellow.

> Ne thought of honour ever did assay
> His baser breast; but in his kestrell kynd
> A pleasing vaine of glory he did fynd.
> SPENSER: *The Faerie Queene,* II, iii, 4.

Ketch. *See* JACK KETCH *under* JACK.

Kettle. As well as meaning the vessel used for boiling water and cooking, it is old thieves' slang for a watch; a *tin kettle* is a silver watch and a *red kettle* a gold one.

A kettle of fish. An old Border name for a kind of *fête champêtre* or riverside picnic where a newly caught salmon is boiled and eaten. The discomfort of this sort of party may have led to the phrase, "A pretty kettle of fish", meaning an awkward state of affairs, a mess, a muddle.

> As the whole company go to the waterside today to eat a kettle of fish, there will be no risk of interruption.
> SCOTT: *St. Roman's Well,* ch. XII.

Kettledrum. A drum made of a thin hemispherical shell of brass or copper with a parchment top. Also an obsolete name for an afternoon tea party, on a somewhat smaller scale than the regular DRUM, and also in playful allusion to the presence of the tea kettle.

Kevin, St. An Irish saint of the 6th century, of whom legend relates that he retired to a cave on the steep shore of a lake where he vowed no woman should ever land. A girl named Kathleen followed him, but the saint flogged her with a bunch of nettles or, according to the more romantic story, hurled her from a rock and her ghost never left the place where he lived. A cave at Glendalough, Wicklow, is shown as the bed of St. Kevin. Moore has a poem on this tradition (*Irish Melodies,* IV).

Key. Metaphorically, that which explains or solves some difficulty, problem, etc., as *the key to a problem,* the means of solving it, *Keys to the Classics,* a well-known title for a series of CRIBS or literal translations. Also a place which commands a large area of land or sea, as Gibraltar is the **Key to the Mediterranean,** and, in the Peninsular War, Ciudad Rodrigo was known as the **Key to Spain.**

In music the lowest note of a scale is the **keynote,** and gives its name to the scale or key itself: hence the figurative phrases **in key, out of key,** in or out of harmony with.

St. Peter's Keys. The cross-keys, the insignia of the Papacy borne, saltirewise, one of gold and the other of silver, symbolizing the POWER OF THE KEYS.

The Cross Keys. The emblem of St. PETER.

The Ceremony of the Keys. When the gates of the TOWER OF LONDON are locked at 10 p.m. each night by the Chief Yeoman Warder and his escort the party is challenged on its return by the sentry with the words "Halt, who comes there?" The Chief Warder answers, "The Keys." The sentry asks, "Whose keys?" "Queen Elizabeth's keys", is the reply. The guard presents arms and the Chief Warder calls "God preserve Queen Elizabeth," to which the guard says "Amen," and the keys are deposited in the Queen's House. *See* BEEFEATERS.

The House of Keys. *See* TYNWALD.

The Power of the Keys. The supreme ecclesiastical authority claimed by the POPE as the successor of St. PETER. The phrase is derived from *Matt.* xvi, 19:

> And I will give unto thee the keys of the kingdom of heaven: and whatsoever thou shalt bind on earth shall be bound in heaven: and whatsoever thou shalt loose on earth shall be loosed in heaven.

To have the key of the door. A symbol of independence; much favoured on 21st and 18th birthday cards.

To have the key of the street. To be locked out of doors; to be turned out of one's home.

The key shall be on his shoulder. He shall have the dominion, shall be in authority, have the keeping of something. It is said of Eliakim that God would lay upon his shoulder the key of the house of David (*Is.* xxii, 22). The cumbersome wooden or iron keys of Bib- lical times were often carried across the shoulder.

Key-cold. Deadly cold, lifeless. A key, on account of its metallic coldness, is still sometimes used to stop bleeding at the nose.

> Poor key-cold figure of a holy king!
> Pale ashes of the house of Lancaster!
> Thou bloodless remnant of that royal blood!
> SHAKESPEARE: *Richard III*, I, ii.

Keystone Comedies. Mack Sennett's notable early film comedies made by the Keystone Comedy Company at Hollywood. The first of their slapstick burlesques appeared in 1913. Charlie Chaplin worked with this company between 1916 and 1918.

Keyne, St. A CELTIC saint of the 5th century, daughter of Brychan, King of Brecknock. St. Keyne's Well, near Liskeard, Cornwall, is reputed to give the upper hand to the first of the marriage partners to drink from it.

Khaki (ka' ki). A Hindu word, meaning dusty, or dust- coloured, from *khak*,

dust. Khaki uniform was first used by an irregular corps of Guides raised by the British at Meerut during the INDIAN MUTINY known as the *Khaki Risala* (khaki squadron), nicknamed "the Mudlarks". It was adopted as an active service uniform by several regiments and in the Omdurman campaign, etc., but was not generally introduced until the South African War of 1899–1902.

Khedive (ke dēv'). The title, meaning "prince" or "sovereign", by which the ruler of Egypt as viceroy of the Turkish Sultan was known from 1867 to 1914. In 1914, when Turkey joined the Central Powers, Khedive Abbas II was deposed by the British and Hussein Kamil set up as SULTAN. The title of King was adopted by Fuad in 1922 when the British terminated their Protectorate.

Kibbutz (Heb. a gathering). A Jewish communal settlement in Israel organised on socialist lines where land and property are shared. Work and meals are arranged collectively. Adults have private quarters but children are housed together. Originally agricultural only but later various factories and industries developed. The first Kibbutz was set up in the Jordan Valley in 1909 by Jewish immigrants from Europe. There are now c.280 *Kibbutzim* and they have played a considerable part in defending Jewish territory.

Kiblah. The point towards which Mohammedans turn when they worship, *i.e.* the KAABA at MECCA; also the niche or slab (called the *mihrab*) on the interior wall of a mosque indicating this direction.

Kibosh (kī' bosh). **To put the kibosh on.** To put an end to; to dispose of. It has been suggested that it is derived from the Irish *cie bais* (the last word being pronounced "bosh"), cap of death.

Kick. Former slang for a sixpence, but only in compounds, as, "Two-and-a-kick", two shillings and sixpence.

More kicks than ha'pence. More abuse than ha'pence. Called "monkey's allowance" in allusion to the monkeys once led about to collect ha'pence by performing tricks. The monkeys got kicks if they performed unsatisfactorily, but their owners collected the ha'pence.

To get a kick out of something. To derive pleasurable excitement from it. Young people today do things "for kicks".

To get the kick, or **kick out.** To be summarily dismissed; TO GET THE SACK (*see under* SACK) or the "order of the boot".

To kick against the pricks. To struggle against fate; to protest when the odds are against one. See *Acts* ix, 5, and xxvi, 14, where the reference is to an ox kicking when goaded, or a horse when pricked with the rowels of a spur. *Cp.* also I *Sam*. ii, 29—"Wherefore kick ye at my sacrifice and at mine offering?"

To kick one's heels. *See under* HEEL.

To kick over the traces. To break away from control; to throw off restraint; as a horse refusing to run in harness kicks over the traces.

To kick the bucket. *See* BUCKET.

To kick up a dust, row, etc. To create a disturbance.

Kick-off. In football, the start or resumption of a game by kicking the ball from the centre of the field.

Kickshaws. Made dishes, odds and ends, dainty trifles of small value. Formerly written "kickshose" (Fr. *quelque chose*).

Kicksy-wicksy. Full of whims and fancies, uncertain; hence, figuratively, a wife. Taylor, the WATER POET, calls it *kicksie-winsie*, but Shakespeare spells it *kicky-wicky*.

Kid. A faggot or bundle of firewood. **To kid** is to bind up faggots. In the parish register of Kneesal church there is the following item: "Leading kids to church, 2s. 6d.", that is, carting faggots to church.

Kid. A young child; in allusion to kid, the young of the goat, a very playful and frisky little animal.

The verb **to kid** means to make a fool of, to hoax, and to tease or banter.

Kidnapping. A slang word of 17th-century origin. "Nabbing" a "kid" or a child was the popular term for the stealing of young children and others who transported them to the colonial plantations. Usually, nowadays, people are kidnapped to be held to ransom, the kidnappers often being politically motivated. *Cp.* HIJACKER; SKYJACKER.

Kidd, Captain William Kidd (*c.* 1645–1701), famous privateer and pirate, about whom many stories and legends have arisen. Commissioned with LETTERS OF MARQUE in 1696 to attack the French and seize pirates, he turned the expedition into one of piracy. He was eventually arrested at Boston and subsequently hanged at Execution Dock, Wapping.

Kidney. Temperament, disposition, stamp, as **men of another kidney,** or **of the same kidney.** The REINS or kidneys were formerly supposed to be the seat of the affections.

Kildare's Holy Fane. Famous for the "Fire of St. Bridget" which the nuns never allowed to go out. Every twentieth night St. Bridget was fabled to return to tend the fire. St. Bridget founded a nunnery at Kildare in the 5th century. Part of the chapel still remains and is called "The Firehouse".

Kill. To kill by kindness. To overwhelm with benevolence, etc. It is said that Draco, the Athenian legislator, was killed by his popularity, being smothered in the theatre of Ægina by the number of caps and cloaks showered on him by the spectators (590 B.C.). Thomas Heywood wrote a play called *A Woman Killed by Kindness* (1607).

A killing pace. Too strong or hot to last; exhausting.

Killing no murder. A pamphlet published in Holland and sent over to England in 1657 advising the assassination of Oliver Cromwell. It purported to be by one William Allen, a JESUIT, and has frequently been attributed to Silas Titus (later made a colonel and Groom of the Bedchamber by Charles II), but it was actually by Col. Edward Sexby, a LEVELLER, who had gone over to the Royalists, and who, in 1657, narrowly failed in an attempt to murder Cromwell.

To kill time. To while away spare time with amusements or occupations of various kinds in order to avoid or relieve boredom.

Kilroy. During World War II, the phrase "Kilroy was here" was found written up wherever the Americans (particularly

Air Transport Command) had been. Its origin is a matter of conjecture. One suggestion is that a certain shipyard inspector at Quincy, Mass., chalked up the words on material he had inspected. *Cp.* CHAD; *see* GRAFFITI.

Kilter. *See* KELTER.

Kin. *See* KITH; FREMD.

Kindergarten, meaning in German "garden of children", is a name applied to schools for training young children where the child is led rather than taught through play materials, handwork, songs, etc. The system was initiated by Friedrich Froebel (1782–1852) when he opened his first kindergarten at Blankenburg in 1837.

Kindhart. A jocular name for a tooth-drawer in the time of Elizabeth I.

King. King Charles's head. A phrase applied to an obsession, a fixed fancy. It comes from Mr. Dick, the harmless half-wit in Dickens' *David Copperfield*, who, whatever he wrote or said, always got round to the subject of King Charles's head, about which he was composing a memorial—he could not keep it out of his thoughts.

King Charles's Spaniel. A small black and tan spaniel with a rounded head, short muzzle, and full eyes, silky coat and long, soft, drooping ears. The variety came into favour at the RESTORATION, but the colour of the dogs at that time was liver and white.

King Cole. *See* COLE.

King Cotton. Cotton, the staple of the American South, called at one time the Cotton Kingdom. The expression was first used by James H. Hammond in the United States Senate in 1858. *See* COTTON.

King Horn. The hero of a late 13th-century English metrical romance. His father, King of Sudenne, was killed by SARACEN pirates who set young Horn adrift in a boat with twelve other children. After many adventures he reconquers his father's kingdom and marries Rymenhild, daughter of King Aylmer of Westernesse. *Cp.* HORN CHILDE *under* HORN.

King James's Bible. *See* BIBLE, THE ENGLISH.

King Kong. A towering ape-like monster. From the gigantic character of this kind which played the title role in Cooper and Schoedsack's horror film of this name (1933).

King Log and King Stork. *See under* LOG.

King of Arms. *See* HERALD.

King of the Beasts. The lion.

King of the Beggars. *See under* BEGGARS.

The King of the Border. A nickname of Adam Scott of Tushielaw (executed 1529), a famous border outlaw and chief.

The King of the Dunces. In his first version of the *Dunciad* (1712), Pope gave this place of honour to Lewis Theobald (1688–1744); but in the edition of 1742 Colley Cibber (1671–1757) was put in his stead.

The King of the Forest. The OAK.

King of Kings. The Deity. The title has also been assumed by various Eastern rulers, especially the sovereigns of Ethiopia.

King of the King. Cardinal Richelieu (1585–1642) was so called, because of his influence over Louis XIII of France.

The King of Men. A title given to both ZEUS and AGAMEMNON.

The King of Metals. GOLD.

King of Misrule. In mediæval and Tudor times the director of the Christmas-time horseplay and festivities, called also the Abbot, or Lord, of Misrule, and in SCOTLAND the Abbot of Unreason. A King of Misrule was appointed at the royal court, and at Oxford and Cambridge one of the Masters of Arts superintended the revelries. Stow tells us that the Lord Mayor of London, the sheriffs, and the noblemen each had their Lord of Misrule. Philip Stubbs (*Anatomie of Abuses*, 1595) says that these mock dignitaries had from twenty to a hundred officers under them, furnished with HOBBY-HORSES, dragons, and musicians. They first paraded in church with such a babble of noise that no one could hear his own voice. Polydore Vergil says that the Feast of Misrule was derived from the Roman SATURNALIA. According to Stow, "this pageant potentate began his rule at ALL-HALLOWS' EVE, and continued the same till the morrow after the

Feast of the Purification."

The King of Painters. A title assumed by Parrhasius, the painter, a contemporary of Zeuxis (*c.* 400 B.C.). Plutarch says he wore a purple robe and a golden crown.

The King of Rome. A title conferred by NAPOLEON on his son Francis Charles Joseph Napoleon, Duke of Reichstadt (1811–1832), on the day of his birth. His mother was the Empress Marie Louise. He was called *L'Aiglon* (the young eagle) by Edmond Rostand in his play. His ashes were transferred to the INVALIDES in 1940.

The King of Spain's Trumpeter. A donkey. A pun on the word *don*, a Spanish magnate.

The King of Terrors. Death.

The King of Waters. The river Amazon, in South America. Although not as long as the Mississippi—Missouri (the longest river in the world), it discharges a greater volume of water.

The King of the World. The title (in Hindi *Shah Jehan*) assumed by Khorrum Shah, third son of Selim Jehangir, and fifth of the MOGUL Emperors of Delhi (reigned 1627–1658).

King of Yvetot. *See* YVETOT.

The King over the Water. The name given by JACOBITES to James II after his flight to France; to his son the Old PRETENDER (James III), and to his grandsons Charles Edward the Young Pretender (Charles III), and Henry, Cardinal of York (Henry IX).

The Three Kings of Cologne. THE MAGI.

King's, or **Queen's Bench.** *See under* QUEEN.

The King's Book. The usual name given to Henry VIII's *Necessary Doctrine and Evolution for any Christian Man* (1543) issued after presentation to Convocation. It was based on the *Bishops' Book* of 1537 and the royal supremacy was more strongly emphasized. Its doctrinal tone was more CATHOLIC than that of its predecessor. It was probably the work of Cranmer, although Henry VIII seems to have contributed the preface.

The King's Cave. On the west coast of the Isle of Arran; so called because it was here that King Robert Bruce and

his retinue are said to have lodged before they landed in Carrick (1307).

King's Champion. *See* CHAMPION OF ENGLAND.

King's, or **Queen's Colour.** *See under* QUEEN.

King's, or **Queen's Counsel.** *See under* QUEEN.

King's County in the province of Leinster in Eire was so called in 1556 when planted by English settlers, but is now called Offaly, its former name. Similarly *Queen's County* is once more called Leix.

King's Crag. Fife in SCOTLAND, so called because Alexander III of Scotland was killed there in 1286.

The King's or **Queen's English.** *See under* ENGLISH.

King's, or **Queen's Evidence.** *See* EVIDENCE.

King's Evil. Scrofula; supposedly cured by the royal touch, hence the name. The custom existed in France long before its introduction into England by Edward the Confessor. Ceremonial touching was introduced by Henry VII and the sufferers were presented with gold coins, although CHARLES I sometimes gave silver touch pieces instead of gold. The practice reached its height under Charles II, who, according to Macaulay (*History of England*, ch. xiv) touched nearly 100,000 people and in 1682 alone some 8,500. "In 1684, the throng was such that six or seven of the sick were trampled to death." William III called it "a silly superstition" and it was last practised by Queen Anne who touched Dr. Johnson without effecting a cure in 1712. Between the reign of Charles I and 1719 the *Book of Common Prayer* contained an office for the touching. The PRETENDERS also claimed this power.

King's Friends. In the early years of George III the name given to those politicians, mainly Tories, who for various reasons supported the crown and its ministries.

King's, or **Queen's Messenger.** *See under* QUEEN.

The King's Oak. The OAK under which Henry VIII sat in Epping Forest, while Queen Anne (Boleyn) was being executed.

The King's, or **Queen's picture.** Money; so called because it bears the portrait of the reigning sovereign.

King's or **Queen's Proctor.** A law official entitled to intervene in probate, divorce, or nullity cases where collusion or fraud is suspected.

King's, or **Queen's Regulations.** Regulations governing the organization and discipline of the Royal Navy, the Army and the Royal Air Force.

King's Scholar. One who holds a school or college scholarship in a royal foundation.

The King's, or **Queen's Shilling.** *See under* SHILLING.

The King's, or **Queen's Speech.** *See under* QUEEN.

The books of the four kings. A pack of cards.

A cat may look at a king. *See under* CAT.

A king of shreds and patches. In the old MYSTERIES, Vice used to be dressed in the motley of a clown or buffoon, as a mimic king in a parti-coloured suit.

The phrase has also been applied to HACKS who compile books for publishers but supply no originality of thought or matter. *Cp.* GRUB STREET.

A king should die standing. The reputed DYING SAYING of Louis XVIII.

A King's, or **Queen's bad,** or **hard bargain.** Said of a soldier who turns out to be a malingerer or to be of no use; in allusion to the SHILLING formerly given to the serviceman on enlistment.

The king's cheese goes half in paring. A king's income is half consumed by the numerous calls on his purse.

Kings have long hands. Do not quarrel with the king, as his power and authority reach to the end of his dominions. The Latin proverb is, *An nescis longas regibus esse manus* (Ovid, *Heroides*, XVII, 166).

Like a king. When Porus, the Indian prince, was taken prisoner, ALEXANDER THE GREAT asked him how he expected to be treated. "Like a king," he replied; and Alexander made him his friend, restoring Porus to his kingdom.

King-maker, The. Richard Neville, Earl of Warwick (1428–1471); so called

because when he supported Henry VI, Henry was King, but when he sided with Edward IV, Henry was deposed and Edward crowned. He was killed at the battle of Barnet after seeking to re-establish Henry VI. He was apparently first called "the king-maker" by John Major in his *History of Greater Britain, both England and Scotland*, 1521.

King-pin. In skittles, etc., the pin in the centre when all the pins are in place, or the pin at the front apex, because if struck successfully it knocks down the others. Figuratively the word is applied to the principal person in a company, enterprise, etc.

Kingdom come. The next world.

Kingsale. *See* HAT.

Kinless Loons. The judges whom Cromwell sent into SCOTLAND were so termed, because they had no relations in that country and so were free from temptations to nepotism.

Kismet. Fate, destiny; or the fulfilment of destiny; from Turk. *qismet*, portion, lot.

Kiss. Kiss it better, or **kiss the place and make it well.** Said to be a relic of the custom of sucking poison from wounds. St. MARTIN of Tours observed at the city gates of Paris a leper covered with sores; he went up to him and kissed the sores and the leper instantly became whole (Sulpicius Severus: *Dialogues*). There are many such stories.

Kiss of Life. The name applied to the mouth-to-mouth method of artificial respiration. SLEEPING-BEAUTY was awakened from her death-like sleep by the Prince's kiss.

Kissing the Pope's toe. Matthew of Westminster (15th century) says it was customary formerly to kiss the hand of his Holiness; but that a certain woman in the 8th century not only kissed the POPE'S hand but "squeezed it". Seeing the danger to which he was exposed, the Pope cut off his hand, and was compelled in future to offer his foot. In reality the Pope's foot (*i.e.* the cross embroidered on his right shoe) may be kissed by the visitor; BISHOPS kiss the knee as well. This is an old sign of respect and does not imply servility. It is customary to bend the knee and kiss the ring of a

CARDINAL, bishop, or abbot.

To kiss the book. To kiss the BIBLE, or the NEW TESTAMENT, after taking an oath; the kiss of confirmation or promise to act in accordance with the words of the oath and a public acknowledgment of its sanctity.

In the English courts, the Houses of PARLIAMENT, etc., non-Christians are permitted to affirm without kissing the book, as a result of the struggle waged by the atheist Charles Bradlaugh to take his seat in the HOUSE OF COMMONS. First elected in 1880 he was finally admitted to the House in 1886. Previously, in 1858, Baron Lionel de Rothschild, the first Jew to be admitted to Parliament, as a Jew, had been allowed to swear on the OLD TESTAMENT. He had been elected as WHIG M.P. for the City of London in 1847. The position was legalized by the Oaths Act of 1888.

In Roman Catholic churches it is customary for the priest to kiss the Bible after reading the Gospel.

To kiss, or **lick the dust.** To be completely overwhelmed and humiliated; to be slain.

His enemies shall lick the dust.
Ps. lxxii, 9.

To kiss the gunner's daughter. *See* GUNNER.

To kiss hands. To kiss the hand of the sovereign either on accepting or retiring from office.

Kissing the hand of, or one's own hand to, an idol, etc., was a usual form of adoration. God said he had in Israel seven thousand persons who had not bowed unto Baal, "every mouth which hath not kissed him" (I *Kings* xix, 18).

To kiss the hare's foot. *See under* HARE.

To kiss the rod. *See under* ROD.

Kist of Whistles. A church-organ (Scots). *Kist* is the same word as *cist* (a chest).

Kit and boodle. *See* CABOODLE.

Kit's Coty House. A great CROMLECH, 3½ m. north-west of Maidstone on the Rochester road, consisting of a 12-feet long block of sandstone resting on three standing blocks. The name may be British for "the tomb in the wood" (Wel. *coed*, a wood). It is near the ancient bat-tlefield where Vortigern is supposed to have fought HENGIST AND HORSA.

Kitchen. Kitchen cabinet. Originally an American term for an informal group of advisers used by a president and given more weight than the proper cabinet. The term was first used of such an unofficial group advising President Andrew Jackson (OLD HICKORY) in 1829.

Kitchen-middens. Prehistoric mounds (referred to the NEOLITHIC AGE) composed of sea-shells, bones, kitchen refuse, stone implements, and other relics of ancient man. They were first noticed on the coast of Denmark, but have since been found in the British Isles, North America, etc.

All but the kitchen sink. A comment on someone's excessive amount of luggage, particularly applicable to those travelling in motor cars crammed with bags, suitcases, etc.

Kite. Go fly a kite. The American equivalent to "buzz off".

To fly a kite. In commercial slang, to raise money by means of accommodation bills, etc. The phrase is more commonly used nowadays to denote an experiment to test public opinion.

Kith and Kin (O.E. *cyth*, relationship; *cynn*, kind, family). One's own people and kindred; friends and relations.

Kiwanis. An organization founded in the U.S.A. in 1915 aiming to improve business ethics and provide leadership for raising the level of business and professional ideals. There are many Kiwanis clubs in the U.S.A. and Canada.

Kiwi. A New Zealand bird incapable of flight. In flying circles the word is applied to a man of the ground staff of an aerodrome. It also denotes a New Zealander.

Klephts, or **Klepts** (Gr., robbers). The name given to those Greeks who maintained their independence in the mountains after the Turkish conquest in the 15th century. After the War of Independence (1821–1828) they relapsed into brigandage.

Klondike. A river and district of the Yukon, Canada. The rich gold-bearing gravel found at Bonanza Creek in 1896 resulted in a wild rush of prospectors. GOLD production reached its peak in 1900.

Knave (O.E. *cnafa*; Ger. *Knabe*). Originally a boy or male child, then a male servant, or one in low condition, and subsequently a dishonourable rascal.

In cards the *knave* (or *Jack*), the lowest court card of each suit, is the common soldier or servant of the royalties.

Knee. Knee tribute. Adoration or reverence by bending the knee; an act of homage. *Cp.* LIP-SERVICE.

> Coming to receive from us
> Knee-tribute yet unpaid, prostration
> vile.
>
> MILTON: *Paradise Lost*, V, 778-9.

Weak-kneed. Irresolute, infirm of purpose or conviction, as a *weak-kneed Christian*, a LAODICEAN, neither hot nor cold.

Knickerbockers, or **knickers.** Loose-fitting breeches, gathered in below the knees, once worn by boys, cyclists, sportsmen, etc., and by women as an undergarment. So named from George Cruickshank's illustrations of *Knickerbocker's History of New York* (1809) by Washington Irving, where the Dutch worthies wore such knee-breeches. The name probably signified a baker of *knickers*, *i.e.* clay marbles. *Cp.* BLOOMERS.

Knife. The emblem of St. AGATHA, St. Albert, and St. Christina.

The **flaying knife** is the emblem of St. BARTHOLOMEW, because he was flayed.

To live on a knife's edge. Metaphorically, to occupy such a precarious position that the slightest false move may result in disaster.

War to the knife. Deadly strife.

Knight (O.E. *cniht*). Originally a boy or servant, the word came to denote a man of gentle birth who, after serving at court or in the retinue of some lord as a page and ESQUIRE, was admitted with appropriate ceremonies at an honourable degree of military rank and given the right to bear arms. *See* BACHELOR; BANNERET; BARONET.

Since the disappearance of KNIGHT-SERVICE, knights, as men of standing in England, continued to give service as KNIGHTS OF THE SHIRE, SHERIFFS, etc. Titles have long been bestowed on administrative officials, professional men, politicians, scholars, artists, etc., as well as those serving in the armed forces, and trade union officials and professional sportsmen have joined the throng in the present century.

There are nine existing British *Orders of Knighthood*, the oldest being that of the GARTER, which takes precedence. The others are (in order of precedence): the THISTLE (1687); St. PATRICK (1788); the BATH (1399, but revived in 1715 and subsequently reorganized); the STAR OF INDIA (1861); St. MICHAEL AND St. GEORGE (1818); the Indian Empire (1877); the Royal Victorian Order (1896); the British Empire (1917-1918).

The modern *Knights Bachelor* do not constitute an order and rank lowest in precedence. The wife of a Knight is designated "Dame", or more usually "Lady".

Carpet-knight. *See under* CARPET.

Cross-legged Knights. *See* CROSS-LEGGED.

Knight Bachelor. *See* KNIGHT *above*; BACHELOR.

Knight Banneret. *See* BANNERET.

Knight Baronet. The original title of a BARONET.

Knight errant. A mediæval knight, especially a hero of those long romances satirized by Cervantes in *Don* QUIXOTE, who wandered about the world in quest of adventure and in search of opportunities of rescuing damsels in distress and performing other chivalrous deeds.

Knights Hospitallers. *See* HOSPITALLERS.

Knight Marshal. *See* MARSHALSEA.

Knight of Grace. A member of the lower order of the Knights of MALTA.

Knight of Industry. Slang for a sharper; one who lives on his wits.

Knights of Labor. An organization of working men (at first secret), founded at Philadelphia in 1869, which subsequently played an important part in the early development of the American TRADE UNION movement. It secured the recognition of LABOR DAY (*see under* LABOUR) and sought to organize all workers, but it was eclipsed by the American Federation of Labor (founded 1886) and rapidly declined.

Knights of the Round Table. *See* ROUND TABLE.

The Knight of the Rueful Countenance. Don QUIXOTE.

Knight of the Shire. The original name for the two men of the rank of knight who formerly represented a shire or county in PARLIAMENT. The boroughs were represented by burgesses.

Knight of the square flag. A knight BANNERET in allusion to cutting off the points of his pennon when he was raised to this rank on the battlefield.

The Knight of the Swan. LOHENGRIN.

Knights Templar. *See* TEMPLARS.

Knights of the White Camelia. *See* KU KLUX KLAN.

Knights of Windsor. Originally a small order of knights founded by Edward III in 1349 as the "Poor Knights of the Order of the Garter". It was formed of 26 veterans, but since the time of Charles I the numbers have been fixed at 13 for the Royal Foundation and 5 for the Lower (since abolished) with a Governor. The members are meritorious military officers who are granted apartments in Windsor Castle with small pensions. They have to be in residence for nine months of the year, attend St. George's Chapel on saints' days, and occasionally act as guards of honour. Every Knight of the GARTER on appointment has to give a sum of money for distribution among them. Their present uniform was designed by William IV, who made their title "Military Knights of Windsor". *See* POOR MAN.

Knight Service. The tenure of land in feudal times, on the condition of rendering military service to the Crown for 40 days, etc. By the reign of Edward III knights were paid for their military service.

Knight's fee (Lat. *feodum*). The amount of land for which, under the FEUDAL SYSTEM, the services of a knight were due to the Crown. It was probably determined by valuation rather than area, in any case the number of HIDES in a Knight's Fee varied.

Knightenguild. The guild of thirteen "cnihts" (probably youthful scions of noble houses attached to the court) to

which King Edgar, or, according to other accounts, Canute, gave that portion of the City of London now called PORTSOKEN WARD on the following conditions: (1) Each knight was to be victorious in three combats—one on the earth, and one under, and one in the water; and (2) each was, on a given day, to run with spears against all comers in East Smithfield. WILLIAM THE CONQUEROR, confirmed the same unto the heirs of these knights, whose descendants, in 1125, gave all the property and their rights to the newly founded Priory of the Holy Trinity.

Knipperdollings. ANABAPTIST followers of Bernard Knipperdolling (*c.* 1490 –1536), who was one of the leaders of the Munster theocracy (1532–1535). After the city was taken by the BISHOP and his supporters, Knipperdolling was tortured to death with red-hot pincers.

Knobstick. A knobstick wedding. The name given to an 18th-century practice whereby the churchwardens of a parish used their authority virtually to enforce the marriage of a pregnant woman, which they attended officially. The term "knobstick" was in allusion to the churchwarden's staff, his symbol of office. *Cp.* SHOTGUN WEDDING.

Knock, To. In slang of former days, to create a great impression, to be irresistible; as in Albert Chevalier's song "Knocked 'em in the Old Kent Road" (1892), *i.e.* astonished the inhabitants, filled them with admiration. *See* ALBERT THE GREAT.

In current colloquial usage it means to criticize adversely, to look for faults in someone or something, to disparage.

To be knocked into a cocked hat, or **into the middle of next week.** To be thoroughly beaten. *See under* COCK.

To get a knock, or **a nasty knock.** To receive a blow, literally or figuratively, that finishes one off.

To knock about, or **around.** To wander about the town "seeing life" and enjoying oneself; to be in the vicinity or in the neighbourhood.

To knock the bottom, or **the stuffing out of anything.** To confound, bring to naught; especially to show that some argument or theory is invalid and "won't hold water". (*See under* WATER.)

To knock down. To dispose of an article to the highest bidder at an auction when a sale is indicated by a knock of the auctioneer's gavel.

To knock for six. To completely demolish an argument or to completely defeat an opponent figuratively or literally. In CRICKET the ball is "knocked for six" when the batsman, by hitting it over the boundary of the cricket field, scores six runs, and shows, in that instance, an easy mastery of the bowling.

To knock off. To cease work; to purloin.

To knock out of the box. In baseball, to score so highly against a pitcher that he is replaced by another in the box. Figuratively, to achieve an easy and decisive victory over an opponent.

To knock out of time. To settle one's HASH, to double him up. A phrase from pugilism referring to disabling an opponent so that he is unable to resume when the referee calls, "Time".

To knock spots off someone, or **something.** To beat him soundly, to get the better of it. The allusion is probably to pistol-shooting at a playing-card, when a good shot will knock out the pips or spots.

To knock under. Virtually the same as to KNUCKLE UNDER.

You could have knocked me down with a feather. I was overcome with surprise.

A knock-about turn. A MUSIC HALL term for a noisy boisterous act usually involving horseplay and SLAPSTICK.

Knock-kneed. With the knees turned inwards so that they virtually knock or rub together in walking.

Knock-out. A disabling blow, especially in boxing, on the point of the chin, or under the ear, etc., which puts the receiver to sleep, thus finishing the fight. Hence a complete surprise is "a fair knock-out".

In the auction room a *knock-out* is a sale at which a ring of dealers combine to keep prices artificially low to obtain the goods for subsequent profit divided among themselves.

Knockers. GOBLINS or KOBOLDS who dwell in mines and indicate rich veins of ore by their presence. In Cardiganshire and elsewhere miners attributed the strange noises so frequently heard in mines to these spirits.

Knot. Gordian knot. *See* GORDIAN.

Knots of May. *See* HERE WE GO GATHERING NUTS IN MAY *under* NUT.

True lovers' knots. Sir Thomas Browne thinks the knot owes its origin to the *nodus Herculanus*, a snaky complication in the CADUCEUS or rod of MERCURY in which form the woollen girdle of the Greek brides was fastened (*Pseudodoxia Epidemica*, V, xxii). This interlacing knot is a symbol of interwoven affection.

Knotgrass. This plant, *Polygonum aviculare*, was formerly supposed, if taken in an infusion, to stop growth.

> Get you gone, you dwarf;
> You minimus of hindering knotgrass made.
> SHAKESPEARE: *Midsummer Night's Dream*, III, ii.

Know Thyself. The admonition of the oracle of APOLLO at DELPHI; also attributed (Diogenes Laertius, I, xl) to Thales; also to SOLON the Athenian lawgiver, SOCRATES, PYTHAGORAS, and others.

To know all the answers. To be well informed, resourceful, and intelligent. One who thinks he knows all the answers is one who conceitedly assumes a knowledge he does not really possess, a "CLEVER DICK".

To know the ropes. *See under* ROPE.

Knuckle. Near the knuckle. Said of a remark, story, joke, performance etc. that is bordering on the improper or indecent.

To knuckle down to. To submit to.

To knuckle down to it. To work away at it; to get on with it.

To knuckle under. To acknowledge defeat, to give in, to submit; in allusion to the old custom of striking the under side of a table with the knuckles when defeated in an argument. *Cp.* TO KNOCK UNDER.

Knuckle-duster. A loop of heavy, shaped brass, gripped in the hand and fitting over the knuckles, used as an offensive weapon. Its origin goes back to the days of Roman pugilism.

Knurr and Spell. An old English game

resembling trap ball and played with a *knurr* or wooden ball which is released from a little brass cup at the end of a tongue of steel called a *spell* or *spill*. After the player has touched the spring the ball flies into the air and is struck with the bat.

Knut. *See* NUT.

Kobold. A house-spirit in German folklore; similar to our ROBIN GOODFELLOW and the Scots BROWNIE. Also a GNOME who works in mines and forests. *Cp.* KNOCKERS.

Kochlani (kok la' ni). Arabian horses of royal stock, of which the genealogies have been preserved for more than 2,000 years. It is said that they are the offspring of SOLOMON's stud.

Koh-i-Noor (kó i nôr) (Pers., mountain of light). A famous DIAMOND, so called by Nadir Shah, and now kept in the TOWER OF LONDON. Its early history is uncertain, but when Aurangzeb (*d.* 1707), MOGUL Emperor of India, possessed the stone it was used for the eye of a peacock in his famous peacock throne at Delhi. In 1739 it was acquired by Nadir Shah of Persia and later passed to Afghanistan, but when Shah Shuja was deposed he gave it to Ranjit Singh of the Punjab for promised assistance towards his recovery of the Afghan throne. Ten years after Ranjit's death (1839) the Punjab was annexed to the British Crown and in 1849, by stipulation, it was presented to Queen Victoria. At this time it weighed 186$\frac{1}{16}$ carats, but was subsequently cut down to 106$\frac{1}{16}$ carats. There is a tradition that it always brings ill luck to its possessor.

Kon-Tiki Expedition. The unique voyage made by the Norwegian Thor Heyerdahl with five companions in 1947, who sailed a balsa raft from Callao in Peru to Tuamotu Island in the South Pacific. Their object was to support the theory that the Polynesian race reached the Pacific islands in this fashion and were descendants of the Incas of Peru. Their raft was called *Kon-Tiki* after the INCA sun-god.

Koppa. An ancient Greek letter, disused as a letter in classical Greek, but retained as the sign for the numeral 90.

Koran, or **Al Koran** (Arab. *qurān*, recitation). The sacred book of Islam, containing the religious teaching of the prophet with instructions on morality and Islamic institutions. The Koran, which contains 114 chapters or *Suras*, is said to have been communicated to the prophet at MECCA and MEDINA by an angel, to the sound of bells. It is written in Arabic and was compiled from MOHAMMED's own lips. The present text is of the 7th century, the chapters being arranged, except the first, in descending order of length.

Kosher (kō'sher). A Hebrew word denoting that which is "right", "fit" or "proper". It is applied usually to food—especially meat which has been slaughtered and prepared in the prescribed manner. Food must not be obtained from the animals, birds, and fish prohibited in *Lev.* xi and *Deut.* xiv and animals must be killed by cutting the windpipe.

Kowtow (Chin. knocking the head). A Chinese custom of kneeling down and knocking the head on the ground as a sign of reverence, homage, respect, etc. Hence in popular usage to behave obsequiously to someone, to fawn or grovel.

Kraken. A fabulous sea-monster supposed to have been seen off the coast of Norway and probably founded on an observation of a gigantic cuttle-fish. It was first described by Pontoppidan in his *History of Norway* (1752). It was supposed to be capable of dragging down the largest ships and when submerging could suck down a vessel by the whirlpool it created. *Cp.* LOCH NESS MONSTER.

Kralitz Bible. *See* BIBLE, SOME SPECIALLY NAMED EDITIONS.

Kratim. The dog of the SEVEN SLEEPERS, more correctly called Katmir or Ketmir, which according to MOHAMMED sleeps with them and is one of the ten animals to be admitted into his PARADISE.

Kremlin (Russ. *kreml*, a citadel). The Moscow Kremlin is on a scale of its own, comprising buildings of many architectural styles (Arabesque, Gothic, Greek, Italian, Chinese, etc.) enclosed by battlemented and many-towered walls 1$\frac{1}{2}$ miles in circuit. The Tsars and the PATRIARCH lived in the Kremlin until Peter the Great's reign when the court moved to St. Petersburg (Leningrad). Much of it was damaged in the revolution of 1917 but considerable repairs have been made. Its bells now ring out the INTERNATIONAL at 12 o'clock daily. The Imperial Palace was built in 1849.

As the seat of government of the U.S.S.R. the word is used symbolically of that government, just as the VATICAN is of the Papacy.

Kriegspiel. *See* WAR GAME.

Kriemhild (krēm' hild). The legendary heroine of the NIBELUNGENLIED, a woman of unrivalled beauty, daughter of King Dankrat, and sister of GUNTHER, Gernot, and Giselher. She first married SIEGFRIED and next Etzel (Attila), King of the Huns.

Krishna (the black one). A popular Hindu deity and an avatar of VISHNU. One myth says he was the son of Vasudeva and Devaki and was born at Mathura between Delhi and Agra. His uncle King Kamsa, who had been warned that one of his nephews would kill him, murdered Devaki's children on birth; accordingly Krishna was smuggled away and brought up among cow-herds and lived to kill his uncle. He was the APOLLO of India and the idol of women. He features in the MAHABHARATA, the BHAGAVAD-GITA and the *Bhagavata-Purana*. Another story is that Vishnu plucked out two of his own hairs, one white and one black, and the black one became Krishna.

Kronos, or **Cronos.** One of the TITANS of Greek mythology, son of URANUS and GE, father (by RHEA) of Hestia, DEMETER, HERA, HADES, POSEIDON, and ZEUS. He dethroned his father as ruler of the world, and was in turn dethroned by his son Zeus. By the Romans he was identified with SATURN.

Ku Klux Klan. An American secret society founded at Pulaski, Tennessee, in 1866 at the close of the CIVIL WAR as a social club with a fanciful ritual and hooded white robes. The name is a corruption of the Gr. *kuklos*, a circle. It soon developed into a society to overawe the newly emancipated Negroes, and similar societies such as the Knights of

the White Camelia, the White League, the Pale Faces and the Invisible Circle sprang up in 1867–1868. Its terroristic activities led to laws against it in 1870 and 1871. Although it had been disbanded by the Grand Wizard in 1869 local activities continued for some time.

In 1915 a new organization, The Invisible Empire, Knights of the Ku Klux Klan, was founded by the Rev. William Simmonds, preacher, near Atlanta, Georgia. He adopted much of the ritual of the original, adding further puerile ceremonies, titles, nomenclature, etc., of his own. *Klansmen* held *Klonvocations* and their local *Klaverns* were ruled by an *Exalted Cyclops*, a *Klaliff*, etc., etc. As well as anti-Negro it was anti-Catholic, anti-Jewish, and xenophobic. Advocating Protestant supremacy for the native-born whites, it grew rapidly from 1920 and gained considerable political control in the Southern States by unsavoury methods. By 1930 it had shrunk again to small proportions but a revival began before World War II and the Klan became noted for its FASCIST sympathies. In 1944 it was again disbanded but continued locally and in 1965 a Congressional Committee was set up to investigate Klan activities.

Kufic. Ancient Arabic letters, so called from Kufa, on the Hindiya branch of the Euphrates and capital of the CALIPHS before the building of Baghdad. It was noted for its skilled copyists. The KORAN was originally written in Kufic.

Kufic coins. Early Mohammedan coins inscribed in Kufic, which was superseded by Nashki characters in the 13th century A.D. Their inscriptions carry much useful information for the historian.

Kultur (Ger., civilization). When used in English it implies civilization as conceived by the Germans. The English word "culture" is translated by *Bildung*.

Kulturkampf (Ger. *Kampf*, struggle). The Kulturkampf, or so-called struggle for civilization, was the name used for Chancellor Bismarck's struggle with the Roman Catholic hierarchy in the 1870s to assert the supreme authority of the State over the individual and the Church, at a time when the latter, under

Pope Pius IX, was asserting CATHOLIC claims. The conflict began over the control of education and developed into a wider attack on the Church, but Bismarck eventually (1879) effected a reconciliation with the Catholic Centre Party in order to avoid control by the National Liberal Party.

Kuomintang, or **Guomindang** (kwō - min tăng). The National People's Party, a Chinese political party formed by Sun Yat-sen in 1905 which, after his death in 1925, passed under the control of General Chiang Kai-shek. From 1927 to 1949 the Kuomintang was the main government in China when it fled to Taiwan, driven out by the People's Liberation Army. It still governs Taiwan as the Republic of China.

Kurma. *See* AVATAR.

Kyrie Eleison (ki ri ā e lī' son) (Gr., "Lord have mercy"). The short petition used in the liturgies of the Eastern and Western Churches, as a response at the beginning of the MASS and in the Anglican Communion Service. Also, the musical setting for this..

Kyrle Society, The (kĕrl). Founded 1877 for decorating the walls of hospitals, schoolrooms, mission-rooms, cottages, etc.; for the cultivation of small open spaces, window gardening, the love of flowers, etc.; and improving the artistic taste of the poorer classes. *See* MAN OF ROSS *under* ROSS.

L

L. The twelfth letter of the alphabet. In Phœnician and Hebrew it represents an ox-goad, *lamedh*, and in the Egyptian hierogly̆hic a lioness.

L. For a pound sterling it is from the Lat. *libra*, a pound. In the Roman notation it stands for 50, and with a line drawn above the letter, for 50,000.

LL.D. Doctor of Laws—*i.e.* both civil and canon. The double L is the plural, as in MSS., the plural of MS., pp., pages, etc.

L.S. Lat. *locus sigilli*, that is, the place for the seal.

L.S.D. Lat. *libra*, a pound; *solidus*, a shilling; and *denarius*, a penny; introduced by the Lombard merchants, from whom we also have *Cr.*, creditor; *Dr.*, debtor, BANKRUPT, *do.* or DITTO, etc.

    L.S.D. also stands for Dextro-lysergic acid diethylamide 25, a powerful drug inducing hallucinations, used by certain drug addicts of today. Those who take this drug are said to "take a trip" and to have PSYCHEDELIC EXPERIENCES.

LXX. A common abbreviation for the SEPTUAGINT.

La Fontaine Jean de la Fontaine (1621–1695) essentially depends for his fame on his *Contes* (1664–1671) and his *Fables* (1668–1693), the first six books of the latter being dedicated to the DAUPHIN. The complete collection comprises twelve books.

La Mancha, The Knight of (la man' chà). Don QUIXOTE de la Mancha, the hero of Cervantes' romance *Don Quixote*. La Mancha was a province of Spain now the main part of Ciudad Real, an arid land with much heath and waste, and the most thinly populated part of Spain.

La Tène (la tän), or the Shallows. A site at the eastern end of the Lake of Neuchâtel, Switzerland, where extensive remains of the late IRON AGE have been found. The term covers a period of CELTIC culture from the 5th century B.C. to about the beginning of the Christian era.

La-di-da. A yea-nay sort of fellow, with no backbone; an affected fop with a drawl in his voice. Also used adjectively, as "in a la-di-da sort of way".

    The phrase was popularized by a song sung by the once famous Arthur Lloyd, the refrain of which was:

> La-di-da, la-di-do, I'm the pet of all the ladies,
> The darlings like to flirt with Captain La-di-da-di-do.

Labarum. The standard of the later Roman emperors. It consisted of a gilded spear with an eagle on the top, while from a cross-staff hung a splendid purple streamer, with a gold fringe, adorned with precious stones. *See also* CONSTANTINE'S CROSS *under* CROSS.

Labour. Independent Labour Party. A small socialist party formed by Keir Hardie in 1893 to establish independent labour candidates in PARLIAMENT. It played a prominent part in the early days of the LABOUR PARTY and continued to advocate more radical policies. In 1923 it had 46 members in the Commons. When James Maxton, then its Leader, died in 1946, it petered out as a parliamentary party. *See* CLYDESIDERS.

Labor Day. A legal holiday in the U.S.A. and some provinces of Canada, held on the first Monday in September (*see* KNIGHTS OF LABOR). Labour rallies in Great Britain and elsewhere are held on MAY DAY.

Labour Party. One of the major political parties of Great Britain and aiming to promote socialism; so called from 1906 but first formed as the Labour Representation Committee in 1900 from such elements as the INDEPENDENT LABOUR PARTY (*see above*), the TRADE UNIONS, and the FABIAN SOCIETY (*see under* FABIUS). The first Labour Government was that of Ramsay MacDonald in 1924, the second lasted from 1929 to 1931, when the party split over the cuts in unemployment benefit (*see* NATIONAL GOVERNMENT). It was not returned to power again until 1945 and was replaced by the CONSERVATIVES in October 1951. It was again in office from 1964 to 1970 and from 1974 to 1979.

A labour of love. *See under* LOVE.

The labourer is worthy of his hire (*Luke* x, 7). In Latin: *Digna canis pabulo.* "The dog must be bad indeed that is not worth a bone." Hence the Mosaic law, "Thou shalt not muzzle the ox that treadeth out the corn."

The Statute of Labourers. An attempt made in 1351 to fix the rates of wages consequent upon the demand for labour after the BLACK DEATH. It attempted to hold them at their pre-plague levels. The ensuing discontent helped to bring about the PEASANTS' REVOLT.

Labyrinth (lăb'i rinth). A Greek word of unknown (but probably Egyptian) origin, denoting a structure with complicated passages through which it is baffling to find one's way. The maze at Hampton Court, formed of high hedges, is a labyrinth on a small scale. The chief labyrinths of antiquity were:

(1) The Egyptian, by Petesuchis or Tithoes, near the Lake Mœris. It had 3,000 apartments, half of which were underground (1800 B.C.).—*Pliny*, xxxvi, 13; and *Pomponius Mela*, I, ix.

(2) The Cretan, by DÆDALUS, for imprisoning the MINOTAUR. The only means of finding a way out was by help of a skein of thread. (*see* Virgil: *Æneid*, V.)

(3) The Cretan conduit, which had 1,000 branches or turnings.

(4) The Lemnian, by the architects Smilis, Rholus, and Theodorus. It had 150 columns, so nicely adjusted that a child could turn them. Vestiges of this labyrinth were still in existence in the time of Pliny.

(5) The labyrinth of Clusium, made by Lars Porsena, King of Etruria, for his tomb.

(6) The Samian, by Theodorus (540 B.C.). Referred to by Pliny; by Herodotus, II, 145; by Strabo, X; and by Diodorus Siculus, I.

(7) The labyrinth at Woodstock, built by Henry II to protect Fair ROSAMOND.

Lacedæmonian Letter. The Greek ι (*iota*), the smallest of the letters. *See* JOT.

Laches (lăch' iz). A legal term for negligence and delay in enforcing a right, from the O.Fr. *laschesse*, negligence.

Lachesis (lăk' e sis). The Fate who spins life's thread and determines its length. *See* FATES.

Lack-learning, or **Unlearned Parliament.** The PARLIAMENT held at Coventry (October 1404) by Henry IV; so called because SHERIFFS were directed not to return any lawyers as members, in the hope that it would be more tractable.

Laconic. Pertaining to Laconia or Sparta; hence very concise and pithy, for the Spartans were noted for their brusque and aphoristic speech. When Philip of Macedon wrote to the SPARTAN magistrates, "If I enter Laconia, I will level Lacedæmon to the ground," the ephors sent back the single word, "If." CÆSAR's words "VENI, VIDI, VICI" and Sir Charles Napier's "PECCAVI" are well-known laconicisms.

Ladon. The name of the DRAGON which guarded the apples of the HESPERIDES, also one of the dogs of ACTÆON.

Ladrones (la' drōnz) (Thieves' Islands). The name given to the Marianas by Magellan's sailors in 1521, owing to the thievish habits of the natives.

Lady. Literally "the bread-maker", from O.E. *hlæfdige* (*hlaf*, loaf; and supposed root *dige*, to knead). The original meaning was simply the female head of the family, the mistress of the household. *Cp.* LORD. *See* COURTESY TITLES; COUSIN.

Dark Lady of the Sonnets. The woman about whom SHAKESPEARE wrote the sonnets numbered cxxvii-clii.

Among the candidates favoured by the critics for this claim to fame are Mary Fitton, Penelope Rich and Mrs. Davenant, wife of an Oxford innkeeper. Dr. Leslie Hotson arrives at Black Lucy or Luce, alias Lucy Negro, *née* Morgan, married to one Parker; she was a former gentlewoman to Queen Elizabeth I and had become a notorious bawd and brothel keeper at CLERKENWELL. More convincingly Dr. A.L. Rowse, with considerable supporting evidence, has identified her with Emilia Lanier (*née* Bassano), illegitimate daughter of a Venetian court musician. She was married to Alfonso Lanier, another court musician, in 1592, at the end of which year the affair with Shakespeare probably began. She had previously been a mistress of Lord Hunsdon, the Lord Chamberlain.

A lady of easy virtue. A "lady of the town", one who readily gives way to amorous advances, an unchaste woman.

Naked Lady. *See* NAKED BOY.

Lady Bountiful. The original character comes from Farquhar's *Beaux' Stratagem* (1706), and about a century later the term acquired the generic application of a village benefactress now in use.

Lady Chapel. *See under* CHAPEL.

Lady Day. 25 March, to commemorate the ANNUNCIATION of Our Lady, the Virgin Mary; formerly called "St. Mary's Day in Lent", to distinguish it from other festivals in honour of the Virgin which were also, properly speaking, "Lady Days". Until 1752, Lady Day was the legal beginning of the year and dates between 1 January and that day are shown with the two years, *e.g.* 29 January 1648/9, on present reckoning 29 January 1649. *See* GREGORIAN YEAR.

Our Lady of Mercy. A Spanish order of knighthood instituted in 1218 by James I of Aragon, for the deliverance of Christian captives among the Moors.

Our Lady of the Snows. A fanciful name given by Kipling in *The Five Nations* (1903) to Canada. Wordsworth has a poem *Our Lady of the Snow* (1820).

The Lady of England and Normandy. The Empress Maud, or Matilda (1102–1167), daughter of Henry I of England and wife of the Emperor Henry V of Germany, who died in 1125. She then married Geoffrey of Anjou and long contested Stephen's possession of the English crown on her father's death. She was acknowledged as "Lady of England and Normandy" by a council at Winchester in 1141, but finally withdrew to Normandy in 1145. Her son by Geoffrey of Anjou became king, as Henry II, in 1154. *See also* A.L.O.E.

The Lady of the Lake. In Arthurian legend, Vivien, the mistress of MERLIN. She lived in the midst of a lake surrounded by knights and damsels. *See* LANCELOT OF THE LAKE.

In Scott's poem of this name (1810), the lady is Ellen Douglas, who lived with her father near Loch Katrine.

The Lady of the Lamp. A name given to Florence Nightingale (1820–1910), from her nightly rounds of the hospital wards at Scutari during the Crimean War, carrying a lighted lamp.

The Lady of Shalott. *See* SHALOTT.

Lady's Man. One who is fond of the company of women and very attentive to them; usually without the more amorous implications of LADY-KILLER.

Lady's Mantle. *See* ALCHEMILLA.

Lady-Killer. A male flirt; a great favourite with the ladies, or one who devotes himself to their conquest.

Læstrygones. *See* LESTRIGONS.

Lætare Sunday (Lat., rejoice). The fourth Sunday in LENT, so called from the first word of the Introit, which is from *Is.* lxvi, 10: "Rejoice ye with Jerusalem, and be glad with her, all ye that love her."

It is also known as MOTHERING SUNDAY.

Lagado. In Swift's *Gulliver's Travels*, the capital of Balnibarbi, celebrated for its grand academy of projectors, where the scholars spend their time in such projects as making pincushions from softened rocks, extracting sunbeams from cucumbers, and converting ice into gunpowder.

Lagan, or **Ligan.** *See* FLOTSAM AND JETSAM.

Lais (lā' is). The name of three celebrated Greek courtesans. One flourished in Corinth in the 5th century B.C. and was visited by Aristippus the philosopher, but the best known was the daughter of Timandra, the mistress of Alcibiades. She was born *c.* 420 B.C. and came to Corinth as a child. She was patronized by princes, philosophers, and plebeians alike. Her charges were sufficiently exorbitant to deter Demosthenes. Her later success in Thessaly so enraged the women that they pricked her to death with their bodkins. There was a third Lais, contemporary with ALEXANDER THE GREAT, who sat for Apelles.

Laissez faire (lā sā fâr) (Fr., let alone). The principle of allowing things to look after themselves, especially the non-interference by government in economic affairs. The originator of the phrase may have been Legendre, a contemporary of Colbert, or possibly D'Argenson, a one-time minister of Louis XV. It became the accepted maxim of the French PHYSIOCRATS in the 18th century as a reaction against Colbertism and MERCANTILISM. Adam Smith was its advocate in Britain, as the prophet of FREE TRADE. The principle was extended to politics by Jeremy Bentham, the leader of the individualist school and philosopher of UTILITARIANISM. Since the 1870s the doctrine has steadily been eroded by collectivist policies which ever increasingly limit the freedoms and activities of the individual in the name of public good. *Laissez passer, laissez aller* are similar phrases.

Lake. Lake District. The picturesque and mountainous district of Cumbria and part of Lancashire (Furness) which contains the principal English lakes, including Windermere, Grasmere, Derwentwater and Ullswater. Noted as the home of the Lake Poets, Lowell called it Wordsworthshire, and it has many literary associations.

Lake Poets. *See* LAKE SCHOOL.

Lake School. The name applied derisively by the *Edinburgh Review* to Wordsworth, Coleridge, and Southey, who lived in the LAKE DISTRICT and sought inspiration in nature, and to the writers who followed them. Charles Lamb, Charles Lloyd and Christopher North (John Wilson) are sometimes placed among the "Lake Poets" or "Lakers".

Lady of the Lake. *See* LADY.

Lancelot of the Lake. *See* LANCELOT.

Laksmi, or **Lakshmi.** One of the consorts of VISHNU, and mother of Kama. She is the goddess of beauty, wealth and pleasure, and the RAMAYANA describes her as springing from the foam of the sea. *Cp.* APHRODITE.

Lamaism (Tibetan, *blama*, spiritual teacher, lord). A modified form of BUDDHISM, the religion of Tibet and Mongolia. The name is from the title given to monks in the higher ranks. The Grand Lama or Dalai Lama (the Sacred Lama) was the ruler of Tibet, although it came under Chinese control (1720) during the time of the 7th Dalai Lama. This control declined to nominal suzerainty, but the Chinese again invaded in 1950, and in 1959 the 14th Dalai Lama fled to India. There is another Grand Lama, the Tashi Lama or Panchen Lama, whose authority was confined to one province but who was supported by the Chinese as rival to the Dalai Lama. The priests are housed in *lamaseries*.

Lamb. In Christian art, the emblem of the Redeemer, in allusion to *John* i, 29, "Behold the Lamb of God, which taketh away the sins of the world."

It is also the attribute of St. AGNES, St. CATHERINE, St. GENEVIÈVE, and St. Regina. JOHN THE BAPTIST either carries a lamb or is accompanied by one.

Paschal Lamb. *See under* PASCH.

Lamb's wool. An old beverage consisting of the juice of apples roasted with ale, sugar, and nutmeg. Probably in allusion to its "softness".

The Vegetable, Tartarian, or **Scythian Lamb.** The woolly rootstalk of a fern (*Cibotium barometz*), found in Asia, and supposed in mediæval times to be a kind of hybrid animal and vegetable. The down is used in India for staunching wounds.

Lambert's Day, St. 17 September. St. Lambert, a native of Maestricht, lived in the 7th century. He supported the missionary work of St. Willibrord and was energetic in suppressing vice.

Lambeth. Lambeth Palace. The London residence of the archbishops of Canterbury since the 12th century.

Lambeth walk, a thoroughfare in

Lambeth leading from Black Prince Road to the Lambeth Road. It gave its name to an immensely popular "COCK-NEY" dance featured by Lupino Lane (from 1937) in the musical show *Me And My Gal* at the Victoria Palace.

Lamia. Among the Greeks and Romans a female demon who devoured children and whose name was used to frighten them. She was a Libyan queen beloved by JUPITER, but, robbed of her offspring by the jealous JUNO, she became insane and vowed vengeance on all children, whom she delighted to entice and devour. The race of *Lamiæ*, in Africa, were said to have the head and breasts of a woman and the body of a serpent and they enticed strangers into their embraces to devour them.

Witches in the MIDDLE AGES were called *Lamiæ*, and Keats' poem *Lamia* (1820) relates the story of how a bride, when recognized by APOLLONIUS as a serpent or lamia, vanished in an instant. Keats took the substance of his poem from Burton's *Anatomy of Melancholy* (Pt. III, sect. ii, memb. i, subsect. i) whose source was Philostratus (*De Vita Apollonii*, Bk. IV). *Cp.* LILITH.

Lammas Day. 1 August, one of the regular QUARTER-DAYS in SCOTLAND and a half-quarter or cross-quarter-day in ENGLAND, the day on which, in Anglo-Saxon times, the FIRST-FRUITS were offered. Formerly, bread for the Lammas Day EUCHARIST was made from the new corn of the harvest. So called from O.E. *hlaf-mæsse*, the loaf-mass. It is also the feast of St. PETER ad Vincula. *See* HAR-VEST THANKSGIVING.

At latter Lammas. Another way of saying "Never".

Lamourette's Kiss (la moo ret'). A French term (*baiser Lamourette*) to denote an insincere or ephemeral reconciliation. On 7 July 1792, the Abbé Lamourette induced the different factions of the Legislative Assembly to lay aside their differences and give the kiss of peace; but the reconciliation was unsound and very short-lived.

Lamp. The Lamp of Heaven. The MOON. MILTON calls the stars "lamps":

The Lady of the Lamp. *See under* LADY.

The Lamp of Phœbus. The sun. PHŒBUS is the mythological personification of the sun.

It smells of the lamp. Said of a literary composition that bears manifest signs of midnight study; one that is overlaboured. In Lat., *olet lucernam*.

Lampadion. The received name of a lively, petulant courtesan, in the later Greek comedy.

Lampoon. A sarcastic or scurrilous personal satire, so called from Fr. *lampons*, let us drink, which formed part of the refrain of a 17th-century French drinking song. According to Scott.

Lampos. One of the steeds of AURORA, also the name of one of the horses of DIOMEDES, and of HECTOR.

Lancastrian. An adherent of the Lancastrian line of kings, or one of those kings (*Henry IV, V, VI*), who were descendants of Edward III. *See* RED ROSE, WARS OF THE ROSES *under* ROSE; YORKIST.

Lance. A free lance. One who acts on his own judgment and is not bound to party; a journalist, musician, writer, etc., who is not definitely attached to, or on the salaried staff of, any one organization. The reference is to the FREE COMPANIES of the MIDDLE AGES which were free to sell themselves to any cause or master.

Lance-corporal. The lowest grade of N.C.O. in the army; a **lance-sergeant** is a corporal performing (on probation) the duties of a sergeant. Presumably formed on Ital. *lancia spezzata*, broken lance; *i.e.* an experienced soldier, one who has had his lance shivered in battle.

Lancers. The dance so called, an amplified kind of QUADRILLE, was introduced by Laborde in Paris in 1836 and brought over to England in 1850.

Lancelot du lac , or of the Lake. One of the Knights of the ROUND TABLE, son of King BAN of Brittany, and stolen in infancy by the LADY OF THE LAKE. She plunged with the baby into the lake (whence the cognomen *du Lac*), and when her protégé was grown to manhood, presented him to King ARTHUR. Sir Lancelot went in search of the GRAIL and twice caught sight of it. Though always represented in ARTHURIAN

ROMANCE as the model of CHIVALRY, bravery, and fidelity, Sir Lancelot was the adulterous lover of Queen GUINE-VERE, and it was through this liaison that war resulted which led to the disruption of the Round Table and the death of King Arthur.

Land. The Land of Beulah (*Is*. lxii, 4). In Bunyan's *Pilgrim's Progress* it is that land of heavenly joy where the pilgrims tarry till they are summoned to enter the CELESTIAL CITY.

The Land of Cakes. *See under* CAKE.

Land of Hope and Glory. Great Britain was so protrayed in the heyday of imperialism in Elgar's famous melody with words by A. C. Benson. Sung by Dame Clara Butt in 1902, and widely used at EMPIRE DAY celebrations and other occasions. The tune was taken from the first of the *Pomp and Circumstance* marches (1901). The words were originally used in Benson's *Coronation Ode* of 1902.

Land of My Fathers. In particular Wales, from the song *Hen Wlad fy Nhadau*, Land of My Fathers, which is the national anthem of Wales. The Welsh words are by Evan James and the tune by James James, first published in 1860.

Land of Nod. This was the land to which Cain was exiled after he had slain Abel (*Gen*. iv, 16). Swift, in *A Complete Collection of Genteel and Ingenious Conversation*, said that he was "going into the land of Nod", meaning that he was going to sleep, which meaning it has retained ever since.

The Land of Promise, or **the Promised Land.** Canaan, which God promised to give to Abraham for his obedience. *See Ex*. xii, 25, *Deut*. ix, 28, etc.

The Land o' the Leal. The land of the faithful or blessed; a Scotticism for a Happy Land or HEAVEN, as in Lady Nairn's song of this title:

I'm wearin' awa'
To the land o' the leal.

Land of the Midnight Sun. Norway. In the Arctic and Antarctic during summer the sun shines at midnight, a phenomenon observable from several lands within the high latitudes of the Arctic Circle. The name has been applied only to Norway where this phenomenon has been observed most by visitors.

Land of the Rising Sun. Japan.

Land of the White Eagle. Poland. The White Eagle, with a crown on its head, formed part of the Polish coat-of-arms. An old legend tells us that Prince Lech, when out hunting, came to a great oak-tree, where he saw a pair of huge white eagles over their nest. The prince regarded this as a prophetic sign and decided to establish his capital there. He called it *Gniezno* ("Nest-town"), saying, "Here shall be our nest."

Land League. An Irish association formed in 1879 under the leadership of Michael Davitt, with Parnell as president and two FENIANS as secretaries. It stimulated agrarian revolt and aimed to secure peasant proprietorship by forceful methods. It was declared illegal in 1881, but renewed as the National League in 1882.

See how the land lies. See whether things are propitious or otherwise; see in what state the land is that we have to travel over.

Land-girl. Girls or women recruited for farm-work during the two World Wars. In World War II they were organized as a "Women's Land Army".

Land-hunger. Desire to acquire land or to extend territory.

Land-loupers. Vagrants. *Louper* is from the Dut. *loopen*, to run. Persons who abscond for crime or debt and rove the country, vagabonds. Loafer, and luffer are variants of the Ger. *Läufer*, a vagrant, a runner.

Land-lubber. An awkward or inept sailor is so called, a mere landsman. A *lubber* is a heavy, clumsy fellow, a looby.

Land-slide. Used metaphorically of a crushing defeat at the polls, or a complete reversal of votes or support.

Landsturm (lant' shtoorm). German forces of the militia type not used as first-line troops but usually employed on garrison duties or as labour forces, etc. Usually formed from those unfit for full military service or from the older age-groups.

Landtag (lant' tak). The legislative assembly of a German state.

Lane. 'Tis a long lane that has no turn-

ing. Every calamity has an ending, things will eventually improve.

Lang syne (Scot., long since). In the olden time, in days gone by.

Auld Lang Syne. This song, commonly sung at the conclusion of dances and revelries and usually attributed to Robert Burns, is really a new version by him of a very much older song. In Watson's Collection (1711), it is attributed to Francis Sempill (d. 1682), but is probably older. Burns says in a letter to Thomson "It is the old song of the olden times, which has never been in print.... I took it down from an old man's singing."

Langtry, Lillie. *See* JERSEY LILY.

Language. Language was given to men to conceal their thoughts. *See* SPEECH.

The three primitive languages. The Persians say that Arabic, Persian, and Turkish are three primitive languages. Legend has it that the serpent that seduced EVE spoke Arabic, the most suasive language in the world; that ADAM and Eve spoke Persian, the most poetic of all languages; and that the angel GABRIEL spoke Turkish, the most menacing.

Langue d'oc; langue d'oïl (lang dok; lang doil) (Fr. *langue*, tongue). The former is the old Provençal language, spoken south of the River Loire; the latter, Northern French, spoken in the MIDDLE AGES to the north of that river, the original of modern French. So called because our "yes" was in Provençal *oc*, and in the northern speech *oil*, which later became *oui* (from Lat. *hoc illud*). *Cp.* HIGH GERMAN.

Lantern. In Christian art, the attribute of St. GUDULE and St. Hugh.

À la lanterne! (Fr., to the lamp-post). Hang him from the lamp-post! A cry and practice at Paris during the French Revolution. Many of the street lamp brackets were suitable for this purpose.

The Feast of Lanterns. A popular Chinese festival, celebrated annually at the first full moon. Tradition says that the daughter of a famous mandarin one evening fell into a lake. Her father and his neighbour took lanterns to look for her, and happily she was rescued. A fes-tival was ordained to commemorate the rescue, which in time developed into the "Feast of Lanterns".

Lantern jaws. Cheeks so thin and hollow that one may almost see daylight through them, as light shone through the horn of the lantern.

Lantern Land. The land of literary charlatans, pedantic graduates in arts, doctors, professors, prelates, etc., ridiculed as "Lanterns" by Rabelais (with a side alusion to the divines assembled in conference at the Council of Trent) in his *Pantagruel*, v, 33. *Cp.* CITY OF LANTERNS.

Laocoön. A son of PRIAM and priest of APOLLO, famous for the tragic fate of himself and his two sons, who were squeezed to death by serpents while he was sacrificing to POSEIDON. Their death was said to be in consequence of his having offended Apollo, or for having sought to prevent the entry of the WOODEN HORSE into TROY. The group representing these three in their death agony, now in the VATICAN, was discovered in 1506 at ROME. It is a single block of marble, and is attributed to Agesandrus, Athenodorus, and Polydorus of the School of Rhodes in the 2nd century B.C.

Laodamia. The wife of Protesilaus, who was slain before TROY by HECTOR. According to one account, she begged to be allowed to converse with her dead husband for only three hours, and her request was granted; she afterwards voluntarily accompanied the dead hero to the shades. Wordsworth had a poem on the subject (1814).

Laodicean. One indifferent to religion, caring little or nothing about the matter, like the Christians of that church mentioned in the *Book of Revelation* (iii, 14–18).

Lao-tse. *See* TAOISM.

Lap. In the lap of the gods. The unknown chances of the future, whatever may fall from the lap of the gods. **The lap of fortune** expresses the same idea.

To live in the lap of luxury is to have every material comfort and need supplied; "lap" here is a place for repose "in luxury".

Lapithæ. A people of Thessaly, noted in

Greek legend for their defeat of the CEN-TAURS at the marriage-feast of HIPPODA-MIA, when the latter were driven out of PELION. The contest was represented on the PARTHENON, the Theseum at ATHENS, the Temple of APOLLO at Bassæ, and on numberless vases.

Lapsus Linguæ (Lat.). A slip of the tongue, a mistake in uttering a word, an imprudent word inadvertently spoken. Similar adoptions from Latin are *lapsus calami*, a slip of the pen; and *lapsus memoriæ*, a slip of the memory.

Laputa. The flying island inhabited by scientific quacks, and visited by Gulliver on his "travels". These dreamy philosophers were so absorbed in their speculations that they employed attendants called "flappers", to flap them on the mouth and ears with a blown bladder when their attention was to be called off from "high things" to vulgar mundane matters.

Lapwing. SHAKESPEARE refers to two peculiarities of this bird; (1) to allure persons from its nest, it flies away and cries loudest when farthest from its nest; and (2) the young birds fly from their shells with part thereof still sticking to their heads.

The first peculiarity made the lapwing a symbol of insincerity, and the second that of a forward person, one who is scarcely hatched.

Lar. *See* LARES.

Larboard. *See* STARBOARD AND LARBOARD.

Larder. A place for keeping bacon (Lat. *laridum*), from O.Fr. *lardier* or *lardoir*, a storeroom for bacon. This shows that swine were the chief animals salted and preserved in olden times.

Robin Hood's Larder. *See* SOME FAMOUS OAKS *under* OAK.

Lares and Penates. Used as a collective expression for home, and for those personal belongings that make it homely and individual. In ancient ROME the *lares* (sing. *lar*) were the household gods, usually deified ancestors or heroes, and the *lar familiaris* was the spirit of the founder of the house which never left it. The *penates* were the gods of the storeroom and guardian deities of the household and the state, whose duty was

to protect and ward off dangers. Their images stood in a special shrine in each house and offerings were made to them of wine, incense, cakes and honey on special family occasions.

Large. By and large. *See under* BY.

Set at large. At liberty. It is a French phrase; *prendre le large* is to stand out to sea so as to free to move.

Lark. A spree or frolic. The word is a modern adaptation (*c*. 1800) of the dialectical *lake*, sport, from M.E. *laik*, play, and O.E. *lac*, contest. *Skylark*, as in *skylarking about*, etc., is a more recent extension.

If the sky falls we shall catch larks. *See under* SKY.

Larrikin. An Australian term dating from the 19th century denoting a young ruffian or rowdy given to acts of hooliganism. They flourished particularly in the 1880s and were known by their own style of dress, recognizable by its excessive neatness and severe colours. Possibly derived from the name *Larry* or from an Irishman's pronunciation of "larking".

Larvæ. Among the ancient Romans, a name for malignant spirits and ghosts. The larva or ghost of Caligula was often seen (according to Suetonius) in his palace.

Last. Last Day. The final day of the present dispensation when Christ is to return to earth for the last judgment; the day of judgment. *Cp.* BALANCE.

The Last Judgment. *See* JUDGMENT.

Last Light. *See* FIRST LIGHT.

The Last Man. CHARLES I was so called by the Parliamentarians, meaning that he would be the last king of Great Britain. His son, Charles II, was called *The Son of the Last Man*.

The Last Supper. The last meal Christ partook with his disciples on the night before the Crucifixion and the institution of the EUCHARIST.

Leonardo da Vinci's famous picture of this was painted on a wall of the refectory of the Convent of Santa Maria delle Grazie, Milan, in 1494–1497. Although the refectory was reduced to ruins by Allied bombs in August 1943, the wall on which the Last Supper is painted was practically undamaged and the picture left quite intact. It has worn badly with time and is now protected against further deterioration.

The Last Trump. *See* TRUMP.

The Last Word. That which is conclusive or definite; also, like the Fr. *le dernier cri* it has the meaning of the latest, most fashionable, and up-to-date style in anything.

To have the last word. To have the final say or decision; to make the last rejoinder in an argument.

Last Words. *See* DYING SAYINGS.

The Last of the English. Hereward the Wake (*fl.* 1070–1071) who led the rising of the English at Ely against William the Conqueror.

The Last of the Mohicans. The Indian chief Uncas is so called by Fenimore Cooper in his novel of this title (1826).

The Last of the Saxons. King Harold (1022–1066), who was defeated and slain at the Battle of Hastings. Lord Lytton has this as a sub-title for his novel *Harold* (1848).

Lateran. The ancient palace of the Laterani family which was appropriated by NERO (A.D. 66) and later given to Pope (St.) Sylvester by the Emperor Constantine. It remained the official residence of the Popes until the departure to AVIGNON in 1309. The present palace is now a museum. Fable derives the name from *lateo*, to hide, and *rana*, a frog, and accounts for it by saying that Nero once vomited a frog covered with blood, which he believed to be his own progeny, and had it hidden in a vault. The palace built on its site was called the "Lateran", or the palace of the hidden frog.

Lateran Council. The name given to each of five ŒCUMENICAL COUNCILS held in the Lateran church at ROME.

Lateran Treaty. A treaty concluded between the Holy SEE and the Kingdom of Italy in 1929, establishing the VATICAN CITY as a sovereign state, thus ending the "Roman Question" begun in 1870 when the temporal power of the papacy was finally abrogated and ROME became the capital of the Italian Kingdom. *See* PRISONER OF THE VATICAN *under* VATICAN.

St. John Lateran is called the *Mother and Head of all Churches* and is the cathedral church of ROME. It occupies part of the site of the old Lateran palace.

Lathe (O.E. *laeth*, estate, district). An ancient unit of local government in Kent, which was ultimately divided into five lathes. These still exist and the divisions for petty sessions are based on them. *Cp.* RAPE.

Spenser in his *View of the Present State of Ireland* (1596), uses *lathe* or *lath* for the division of a HUNDRED.

> If all that tything failed, then all that lath was charged for that tything; and if the lath failed, then all that hundred was demanded for them, and if the hundred, then the shire.

Latin. The language of the ancient inhabitants of Latium in Italy and spoken by the ancient Romans (Alba Longa was head of the Latin League and ROME was a colony of Alba Longa). According to one story Latium is from *lateo*, I lie hid, and was so called because SATURN lay hid there, when he was driven out of HEAVEN by the gods. According to Roman tradition the Latini were the aborigines. *See* LATINUS.

The earliest specimen of the Latin langauge is an inscription on the Præneste fibula (a gold brooch) found in 1886; it dates from the 6th century B.C.

Classical Latin. The Latin of the best authors centred around the Golden or AUGUSTAN AGE, as Livy, CICERO, etc. (prose); HORACE, VIRGIL, Ovid, etc. (poets).

Dog-Latin. *See under* DOG.

Late Latin. The period which followed the AUGUSTAN AGE to about A.D. 600; it includes the works of the Church FATHERS.

Law Latin. The debased Latin used in legal documents. *Cp.* DOG-LATIN.

Low Latin. MEDIÆVAL LATIN.

Mediæval, or **Middle Latin.** Latin from the 6th to the 16th century, both inclusive. In this Latin prepositions frequently supply the cases of nouns.

New Latin. Latin written since *c.* 1500, especially that used in scientific classifications, and in theological and philosophical works.

Thieves' Latin. Cant or jargon employed as a secret language by rogues and vagabonds.

The Latin Church. The Western Church, in contradistinction to the Greek or Eastern Church.

The Latin Cross. *See under* CROSS.

Latin Quarter. *See* QUARTERS.

The Latin Races. The peoples whose language is based on Latin; *i.e.* the Italians, Spanish, Portuguese, French, Rumanians, etc.

Latinus. Legendary king of the Latini, the ancient inhabitants of Latium (*see* LATIN). According to Virgil, he opposed ÆNEAS on his first landing, but later formed an alliance with him, and gave him his daughter, Lavinia, in marriage. Turnus, King of the Rutuli, declared that Lavinia had been betrothed to him and the issue was decided by single combat. Æneas, being the victor, became the husband of Lavinia and ancestor of ROMULUS and Remus (Virgil, *Æneid*, VII).

Latitudinarians. In the CHURCH OF ENGLAND a name applied, at first opprobriously, from the mid-17th century to those clergy attaching little importance to dogma and practice in religion, which in the 18th century encouraged laxity and indifference. The Cambridge Platonists were prominent among them. Latitudinarianism was checked by the advent of the EVANGELICALS and the OXFORD MOVEMENT. The term is widely applied to those attaching little importance to dogma and orthodoxy.

Latium. *See* LATIN.

Latona. The Roman name of the Gr. Leto, mother by JUPITER of APOLLO and DIANA. Milton (*Sonnet XII*) refers to the legend that when she knelt with her infants in arms by a fountain at Delos to quench her thirst, some Lycian clowns insulted her and were turned into frogs.

Latria and **Dulia.** Greek words adopted by the Roman Catholics; the former to express that supreme reverence and adoration which is offered to God alone; and the latter, that secondary reverence which is offered to saints. *Latria* is from the Greek suffix *-latreia*, worship, as in idol*atry*; *dulia* is the reverence of a *doulos* or slave. **Hyperdulia** is the special reverence paid to the Virgin Mary.

Latter-day Saints. *See* MORMONS.

Lauds. In the Western Church, the traditional morning prayer, so called from the repeated occurrence of the word *laudate* (praise ye) in *Pss.* cxlvii-cl which form part of the office. It is said in the early morning by religious orders who rise for the Night Office, otherwise it is nowadays coupled with MATINS and said overnight. It forms part of the BREVIARY of the ROMAN CATHOLIC CHURCH, and the service of Morning Prayer, in the BOOK OF COMMON PRAYER, is essentially composed of parts of Lauds and Matins.

Laugh. He laughs best that laughs last. Don't crow too soon, a game's not finished till it's won; to have the last laugh. In Ray's *Collection* (1742) is, "Better the last smile than the first laughter," and the French have the proverb *Rira bien qui rira le dernier*.

Laugh and grow fat. An old saw, expressive of the wisdom of keeping a cheerful mind.

To have the laugh on one. To be able to make merry at another's expense, generally to that other's surprise and confusion.

To laugh in one's sleeve. *See under* SLEEVE.

To laugh like a drain. To gurgle or laugh noisily, as water gurgles down a drain.

To laugh off. To dismiss a matter lightly; to shake off embarrassment with a jest.

To laugh on the wrong side, or **on the other side of one's face** or **mouth.** To be made to feel vexation and annoyance after mirth or satisfaction; to be bitterly disappointed; to cry.

To laugh out of court. To cover with ridicule, and so treat as not worth considering.

To laugh to scorn. To treat with the utmost contempt.

Laughing gas. Nitrous oxide (N_2O), discovered by Joseph Priestley in 1772 and suggested as an anaesthetic by Sir Humphry Davy in 1802. Formerly much used in dentistry and for minor operations. After inhalation it produces a feeling of exhilaration followed by unconsciousness, hence the name.

Laughing Murderer of Verdun. Friedrich Wilhelm, Crown Prince of Germany, who commanded the armies that tried to capture Verdun in World War I. He is said to have taken lightly the enormous casualties sustained on both sides, hence the nickname. British troops also called him "Little Willie".

Laughing Philosopher. Democrítus of ABDERA (5th century B.C.), who viewed with supreme contempt the feeble powers of man. *Cp.* WEEPING PHILOSOPHER.

Laughing stock. A butt for jokes.

No laughing matter. Something to be treated seriously. The expression is an example of LITOTES.

Launcelot. *See* LANCELOT.

Launfal, Sir. One of the Knights of the ROUND TABLE. His story is told in a metrical romance written by Thomas Chestre in the reign of Henry VI. James Russell Lowell has a poem entitled *The Vision of Sir Launfal* (1845).

Laura (la belle Laure). Laure de Noves (1308–1348) was immortalized by Petrarch (1304–1374) in his poems. He first saw her in the church of St. Clara, Avignon, on 6 April 1327, and it was this event which, he said, made him a poet.

Laureate. *See* POET LAUREATE.

Laurel. The Greeks gave a wreath of laurels to the victor in the PYTHIAN GAMES, but the victor in the OLYMPIC GAMES had a wreath of wild olives, in the NEMEAN GAMES, a wreath of green parsley, and in the ISTHMIAN GAMES, a wreath of dry parsley or green pine leaves.

The ancients held that laurel communicated the spirit of prophecy and poetry, hence the custom of crowning the Pytheness (the PYTHIA) and poets, and of putting laurel leaves under one's pillow to acquire inspiration. Another superstition was that the bay laurel (*see* DAPHNE) was antagonistic to the stroke of lightning; but Sir Thomas Browne, in his *Vulgar Errors*, tells us that Vicomereatus proves from personal knowledge that this is untrue.

The Laurel in modern times is a symbol of victory and peace, and of excellence in literature and the arts. St. GUDULE (patron saint of Brussels), in Christian art, carries a laurel crown. *See also* APOLLO.

To look to one's laurels. To have to try to maintain the lead in any field in which one has already excelled.

To rest on one's laurels. To be satisfied with the degree of success one has already achieved and to refrain from further effort.

Laurence, St. *See* LAWRENCE.

Laurin. The dwarf-king in the German folk-legend *Laurin*, or *Der Kleine Rosengarten*. He possesses a magic ring, girdle, and cap, and is attacked by DIETRICH OF BERN in his rose-garden, which no one may enter on pain of death. The poem belongs to the late 13th century and is attributed to Heinrich von Ofterdingen.

Lavender. Laid up in lavender. Taken great care of, laid away.

Lavinia. *See* LATINUS.

Lavolta (Ital., the turn). A lively dance, in which was a good deal of jumping or capering, whence its name.

Law. In-Laws. A way of referring to one's relations by marriage—mother-in-law, sisters-in-law, etc. *In-law* is short for in CANON LAW, the reference being to the degrees of a affinity within which marriage is allowed or prohibited.

Law Latin. *See under* LATIN.

Law Lords. The Lords of Appeal in Ordinary; also, additionally, those members of the HOUSE OF LORDS who are qualified to deal with the judicial business of the House, *i.e.* the Lord CHANCELLOR, the Lord Chief Justice, the Master of the ROLLS, and any peer who has held high judicial office. The Lords of Appeal in Ordinary were instituted in 1877 as life BARONS, being now seven to nine in number. Until 1873 the appellate jurisdiction of the Lords was open to the whole House.

The Law of Moses, or **Mosaic Law.** *See under* MOSES.

The law of the Medes and Persians. That which is unalterable.

> Now O King, establish the decree, and sign the writing, that it be not changed, according to the law of the Medes and Persians, which altereth not.
>
> *Dan.* vi, 8.

Possession is nine points of the law. *See under* NINE.

Quips of the law. *See* CEPOLA.

To give one law. A sporting term,

"law" meaning the chance of saving one-self. Thus a hare or a stag is allowed "law"—*i.e.* a certain start before any hound is permitted to attack it; and a tradesman allowed "law" is one to whom time is given to "find his legs".

To go to law, to have the law on someone. To take legal proceedings.

To take the law into one's own hands. To try to secure satisfaction by force or personal action; to punish, reward, etc., entirely on one's own resonsibility.

Lawless Parliament. *See* PARLIAMENT OF DUNCES *under* DUNCE.

Lawn. Fine, thin cambric, used for the rochets of Anglican BISHOPS, ladies' handkerchiefs, etc. So called from *Laon* (O.Fr. *Lan*), a town in the Aisne department of France, once noted for its linen manufacture.

Man of lawn. A BISHOP.

Lawn-market. The higher end of High Street, Edinburgh, once a place for executions; hence, **to go up the lawn-market** is to go to be hanged.

Lawrence, St. (of Rome). The patron saint of curriers, who was roasted on a GRID-IRON. He was archdecaon to Pope (St.) Sixtus II and was charged with the care of the poor, the orphans, and the widows. When summoned by the prætor to deliver up the treasures of the church, he produced the poor, etc., under his charge, and said, "These are the church's treasures." His day is 10 August. (*Cp* CORNELIA). Fragments of his relics were taken to the ESCORIAL.

The phrase **Lazy as Lawrence** is said to originate from the story that when being roasted over a slow fire he asked to be turned. "For", said he, "that side is quite done." This expression of Christian fortitude was interpreted by his torturers as evidence of the height of laziness, the martyr being too indolent to wriggle.

St. Laurence's tears or **The fiery tears of St. Laurence.** *See* SHOOTING STARS.

Lay. Pertaining to the people of laity (Lat. *laicus*) as distinguished from the clergy. Thus, a lay brother is one who, though not in HOLY ORDERS (*see under* ORDERS), is received into a monastery and is bound by its vows.

A layman is, properly speaking, anyone not in HOLY ORDERS; (*see under* ORDERS); it is also used by professional men, especially doctors and lawyers, to denote one not of their particular calling or specialized learning.

Lay Days. Days allowed under the terms of a charter party (the contract for hiring the whole or part if a ship for the delivery of cargo) for loading and unloading a ship; possibly from *delay* and *day*.

Lay figures. Wooden figures with free joints, used by artists chiefly for the study of how drapery falls. The word was earlier *layman* from Dut. *leeman*, a contraction of *ledenman* (*led*, a joint). Horace Walpole uses *layman* (1762), but *lay figure* had taken its place by the end of the 18th century. Hence, figuratively, a character who is a mere foil or puppet.

Lay investiture. *See* INVESTITURE CONTROVERSY.

Lay (the verb). **To lay about one.** To strike out lustily on all sides.

> He'll lay about him today.
> SHAKESPEARE: *Troilus and Cressida*,
> I, ii.

To lay into. To attack vigorously, either physically or verbally.

To lay it on thick. To flatter or over-praise.

To lay it on with a trowel. To flatter excessively.

> Well said; that was laid on with a trowel.
> SHAKESPEAR: *As You Like It*, I, ii.

To lay off. To dismiss workmen, usually temporarily; to cease to annoy, attack, tease, etc.

To lay on the table. *See under* TABLE.

To lay, or **put yourself out.** To go to a great deal of trouble; to go to especial pains.

To lay out. To disburse; to display goods, to arrange, etc.; to prepare a corpse for the coffin; to disable or render unconscious.

To lay to one's charge. To attribute an offence to a person; a Biblical phrase, see *Deut*. xxi, 8; *Rom*. viii, 33, etc.

> And he [Stephen] kneeled down, and cried with a loud voice, Lord, lay not this sin to their charge.

Acts vii, 60.

To lay up. The store away; to dismantle and berth a vessel for a period of disuse. A person temporarily incapacitated through injury or illness is said to be "laid up", especially if confined to bed.

Laylock. Ancient rustic name for lilac.

Lazar House, or **Lazaretto.** *See under* LAZARUS.

Lazarus. Any poor beggar; so called from the Lazarus of the parable, who was laid daily at the rich man's gate. *See* DIVES.

Lazar house, or **Lazaretto.** A house for lazars or poor persons affected with contagious diseases; so called from LAZARUS.

Lazy. Lazy man's load. One too heavy to be carried; so called because lazy people are apt to overload themselves to save a second journey.

L'état, c'est moi (lā ta sā mwa) (Fr., I am the State). The reply traditionally ascribed to Louis XIV when the President of the PARLEMENT of Paris objected "in the interests of the State" to the King's fiscal demands. This was in 1655, when Louis was only 17 years old. He acted on this principle with fair consistency throughout his long reign (1643–1715).

Le roy, or **La reyne le veult** (O.Fr., The King, or Queen, wills it). The form of royal assent to Parliamentary Bills. The dissent is expressed by *Le roy* (*La reyne*) *s'avisera*, the King (Queen) will give it consideration, but this has not been used since 1707.

Lead (led) was, by the ancient alchemists, called SATURN.

The *lead*, or *blacklead*, of a *lead* pencil contains no lead at all, but is composed of plumbago or graphite, an almost pure carbon with a touch of iron. It was so named in the 16th century when it was thought to be of or to contain the metal.

Swinging the lead. Malingering, usually by concocting some plausible yarn, or by feigning an indisposition. An allusion to the lazy leadsman idly swinging the line and protracting the job of taking soundings.

To strike lead. To make a good hit.

The Leads. The famous prison in Venice in which CASANOVA was incarcerated and from which he escaped.

Lead (lēd) (the verb) (O.E. *lædan*).

To lead apes in hell. *See under* APE.

To lead by the nose. *See* LED BY THE NOSE *under* NOSE.

To lead one a pretty dance. *See* DANCE.

Bear-leader. *See under* BEAR.

Leading article, or **Leader.** A newspaper article by the editor or a special writer. It takes the lead or chief place as commentary on current issues, and expresses the policy of the paper.

Leading case. A lawsuit that forms a precedent in deciding others of a similar kind.

Leading counsel in a case, the senior counsel on a circuit.

Leading Lady, or **man.** The actress or actor who takes the chief role in a play.

Leading note (music). The seventh note of the diatonic scale, which leads to the octave, only half a tone higher.

Leading question. A question so worded as to suggest an answer. "Was he not dressed in a black coat?" leads to the answer "Yes." In cross-examining a witness, leading questions are permitted, because the chief object of a cross-examination is to obtain contradictions.

To be in leading-strings is to be under the control of another. Infants just learning to walk are held up by "leading-strings".

Leaf. Before the invention of paper, leaves of certain plants were among the materials used for writing upon. The reverse and obverse pages are still called leaves; and the double page of a ledger is termed a "FOLIO", from Lat. *folium*, a leaf. *Cp.* the derivation of *paper* itself, from *papyrus*; and *book* from *boc*, a beech-tree.

To take a leaf out of my book. To imitate me; to do as I do. The allusion is to literary plagiarisms.

To turn over a new leaf. To amend one's ways, to start afresh.

League. The Holy League. Several leagues are so called. The best-known are: (1) 1511, between Pope Julius II, Ferdinand of Aragon, Henry VIII and Venice to drive the French out of Italy, and joined by the Emperor Maximilian and the Swiss; (2) 1526, the Holy League of Cognac between Clement VII and Francis I of France against the Emperor Charles V; (3) 1576, formed by Henry, Duke of Guise, and the JESUITS and joined by Henry III against the HUGUENOTS and for the defence of the CATHOLIC Church.

The League of Nations. A league, having at one time about 60 member nations with headquarters at Geneva, with the essential aim of preventing war as well as promoting other forms of international co-operation. It was formed on 10 January 1920, after the close of World War I, but was weakened from the outset by the refusal of the U.S.A. to participate (although President Woodrow Wilson had played a major part in its foundation), and the exclusion of Russia. Its achievements were considerable in many fields, but it failed in its primary purpose. It last met on 18 April 1946, being replaced by the UNITED NATIONS Organization which had been established on 24 October 1945.

Leak. To leak out. To come surreptitiously to public knowledge. As a liquid leaks out of an unsound vessel, so the secret filters through.

To spring a leak. Said of ships, etc., that open at the seams, etc., to admit water.

Leal. Anglo-French and O.Fr. *leel*, our *loyal*; trusty, law-abiding; now practically confined to SCOTLAND.

Land o' the leal. *See* LAND.

Leander. *See* HERO AND LEANDER.

Leaning Tower. While there are a number of leaning campanili, or bell-towers, in Italy, the most celebrated is that of the cathedral of Pisa which stands apart from the main building. It is 179 ft. high, $57\frac{1}{2}$ ft. in diameter at the base, and leans about 17 ft. from the perpendicular. It was begun in 1174 and the sinking commenced during construction, but it still stands because the centre of gravity is within its walls. Galileo availed himself of the overhanging tower to make his experiments in gravitation. Caerphilly Castle, Glamorganshire, has a tower which leans 10° from the perpendicular, due to attempts to dismantle the castle with gunpowder after the CIVIL

WARS. The church spires at Chesterfield, Derby, and Ermington, Devonshire, also lean.

Leap. The Leap in the Dark. The famous phrase used by Lord Derby, the Prime Minister, of his government's policy in promoting the Parliamentary Reform Act of 1867, He adopted the expression from Lord Cranborne who first "taunted the government with taking a leap in the dark" (Justin McCarthy, *Short History of Our Own Times*, ch. xxi). Thomas Hobbes is also supposed to have used it (*see* DYING SAYINGS).

Leap Year. A year of 366 days, a BISSEXTILE year: *i.e.*, in the Julian and Gregorian calendars (*see* CALENDAR), any year whose date is exactly divisible by 4 except those which are divisible by 100 but not by 400. Thus 1900 (though divisible by 4) was not a leap year, but 2000 will be.

In ordinary years, the day of the month which falls in Monday this year will fall on Tuesday next year, and Wednesday the year after; but the fourth year will *leap* over Thursday to Friday. This is because a day is added to February, the reason being that the astronomical year (*i.e.* the time that it takes the earth to go round the sun) is approximately $365\frac{1}{4}$ days (365·2422), the difference between ·25 and ·2422 being righted by the loss of the three days in 400 years.

It is an old saying that during leap year the ladies may propose, and, if not accepted, claim a silk gown. A Scottish law of 1288 says that "during the rein of hir maist blissit Megeste, for ilke yeare knowne as lepe yeare, ilk mayden ladye ... shal hae liberte, to bespeke ye man she like, albeit he refuses to taik hir to be his lawful wyfe, he shall be mulcted in ye sum of ane pundis...." There was a similar law passed in France and it became legal custom in Genoa and Florence in the 15th century.

Lear, King. A legendary king of Britain whose story is told by SHAKESPEARE. His immediate source was Holinshed, who in turn derived it from Geoffrey of Monmouth's *Historia Britonum*. It is also given in the GESTA ROMANORUM and in PERCE-FOREST. Spenser uses it in his *Faerie Queene* (ii, x) and Camden tells a similar story of Ina, King of the West Saxons. According to Shakespeare's version, King Lear in his old age divided his kingdom between his daughters GONERIL and REGAN, who professed great love for him but then harassed him into madness. CORDELIA, left portionless, succoured him and came with an army to dethrone her sisters, but was captured and slain. King Lear died over her body. See LIR.

Learn. To learn a person a thing, or to do something is now a provincialism or regarded as illiterate speech, but was formerly quite good English. In the Prayer Book version of the *Psalms* we have "Lead me forth in thy truth and learn me," and "such as are gentle, them shall he learn his way" (xxv, 4, 8). Other examples of this use of learn as an active verb will be found in *Ps*. cxic, 66, and cxxxii, 13.

> The new plague rid you
> For learning me your language.
> SHAKESPEARE: *Tempest*, I, ii.

"I'll learn you" or "I'll larn you" is still frequently used as a threat, especially by indignant housewives to troublesome children.

Leash. To strain at the leash. To be eager to be off; to be impatient of restraint or delay. From the lead used to restrain hounds in coursing.

Leather. Nothing like leather. The story is that a town in danger of a siege called together a council of the chief inhabitants to know what defence they recommended. A mason suggested a strong wall, a shipbuilder advised "WOODEN WALLS", and when others had spoken, a currier arose and said, "There's nothing like leather."

Another version is, "Nothing like leather to administer a thrashing."

It's all leather or prunella. Nothing of any moment, all rubbish; through a misunderstanding of the lines by Pope, who was drawing a distinction between the work of a cobbler and that of a parson.

> Worth makes the man, and want of it the fellow;
> The rest is all but leather or prunella.
> POPE: *Essay on Man*, iv, 203.

Prunella is a worsted stuff, formerly used for clergymen's gowns, etc., and for the uppers of ladies' boots, and is probably so called because it was the colour of a prune.

Leather medal. An American colloquial term for a BOOBY PRIZE.

To give one a leathering. To flog him with a leather strap; to give him a drubbing.

Leatherneck. A soldier or a MARINE.

Leatherstocking Novels. The novels by Fenimore Cooper (1789–1851) in which Natty Bumppo, nicknamed *Leatherstocking* and *Hawkeye*, is a leading character. They are *The Pioneers* (1823), THE LAST OF THE MOHICANS (1826), *The Prairie* (1827), *The Pathfinder* (1840), and *The Deerslayer* (1841). "Leatherstocking" was a hardy backwoodsman, a type of North American pioneer, ignorant of books but a philosopher of the woods.

Leave in the lurch. See LURCH.

Leave well alone. Do not try to alter a state of affairs which is reasonably satisfactory lest you make things worse. "Why not let it alone" was a maxim of Lord Melbourne, the WHIG Prime Minister (1835–1841); and the motto of his 18th-century predecessor, Sir Robert Walpole, was virtually the same— *Quieta non movere*, the equivalent of "let sleeping dogs lie".

To take French leave. See under FRENCH.

Lebensraum (lā bènz room'). A German phrase (room for living), somewhat akin to LAND HUNGER. It is applied especially to the territory required by a nation for overseas expansion, both for settlement and trade, to meet the population pressures in the mother country.

Leda. In Greek mythology, the wife of Tyndarus. JUPITER came to her in the guise of a swan when she was bathing, and in due time she brought forth two eggs, from one of which came CASTOR and CLYTEMNESTRA, and from the other POLLUX and HELEN. The two former are usually held to be the children of Tyndarus.

Leda Bible, The. See BIBLE, SOME SPECIALLY NAMED EDITIONS.

Lee (O.E. *helo, hleow*, a covering or shelter). Nautically, the side or quarter opposite to that against which the wind blows; the side away from the windward or weather side; the sheltered side.

Lee side. *See* LEEWARD.

Lee tide. A tide running in the same direction as the wind blows; if in the opposite direction is called a *tide under the lee*.

Under the lee of the land. Under the shelter of the land.

Under the lee of a ship. On the side away from the wind, so that the ship provides shelter and breaks the force of the wind.

Leeward (loo' àrd). Towards the LEE, or that part towards which the wind blows; *windward* is the opposite direction, the WEATHER side.

Leech. One skilled in medicine or "leech-craft", a doctor; the word, now obsolete, is the O.E. *læce*, one who relieves pain, from *lacnian*, to heal. The blood-sucking worm, the *leech*, gets its name, *the healer*, probably from the same word.

Leek. The national emblem of WALES. (*Cp*. DAFFODIL). The story is that St. DAVID, on one occasion, caused his countrymen under King Cadwaladr to distinguish themselves from their Saxon foes by wearing a leek in their caps.

SHAKESPEARE makes out that the Welsh wore leeks at the battle of Poitiers, for Fluellen says:

> If your majesties is remembered of it, the Welshmen did goot service in a garden where leeks did grow, wearing leeks in their Monmouth caps; which, your majesty knows, to this hour is an honourable padge of the service; and I do believe your majesty takes no scorn to wear the leek upon Saint Tavy's Day.
> *Henry V*, IV, vii.

To eat the leek. To be forced to eat your own words, or retract what you have said. Fluellen (in Shakespeare's *Henry V*, V, i) is taunted by Pistol for wearing a leek in his hat. "Hence," says Pistol, "I am qualmish at the smell of leek." Fluellen replies "I peseech you...at my desires...to eat...this leek." The ancient answers, "Not for Cadwallader and all his goats." Then the peppery Welshman beats him, nor desists till Pistol has swallowed the entire abhorrence.

Lees. There are lees to every wine. Everything has its dregs; the best things have some defect. A French proverb.

Settling on the lees. Making the best of a bad job; settling down on what is left, after having squandered the main part of one's fortune.

Leet. In East Anglia, a division of the HUNDRED formed of a group of vills for local government and taxation. The word occurs in DOMESDAY and is probably from the Dan. *lægd*, a division of the country for purposes of military service.

Court-leet. A court of record granted by the crown to a HUNDRED, lordship, MANOR, BOROUGH, etc. It took view of FRANKPLEDGE and dealt with minor criminal offences and a variety of administrative work. In its early days it was substantially the same as the COURT BARON.

Left. The *left* side of anything is frequently considered to be unlucky, of bad omen (*cp*. AUGURY; SINISTER), the *right* the reverse.

In politics the *left* denotes the more RADICAL political group, and today is usually applied to Socialists and Communists (*see* COMMUNISM). Within a particular party the *left wing* is made up of the "progressives" or "radicals". Communists are often known as the "extreme left". In many legislatures the radicals sit on the left-hand side (as seen from the chair) and in most of the British Commonwealth assemblies the opposition sits on the left.

In the French National Assembly of 1789, the reactionaries sat on the right, moderates in the centre, and democrats and extremists on the left, and this established the custom.

A left-handed compliment. A compliment which insinuates a reproach.

A left-handed marriage. A MORGANATIC MARRIAGE.

A left-handed oath. One not intended to be binding.

Over the left. In early Victorian days, a way of expressing disbelief, incredulity, or a negative.

Leg. In many phrases, *e.g.* "To find one's legs", "to put one's best leg foremost", leg is interchangeable with FOOT.

Leg and leg. Equal, or nearly so, in a race, game, etc. *Cp.* NECK AND NECK.

On its last legs. Moribund; obsolete; about to collapse or break up; practically worn out.

Shake a leg! Hurry up! Also, *to shake a leg* is to dance.

Show a leg. Jump out of bed and be sharp about it. A naval phrase, from the monologue used to call the hands from their hammocks, "Wakey Wakey, rise and shine, the morning's fine ... show a leg, show a leg, a show leg, etc." It comes from the days when women were allowed to sleep on board; they were allowed to "lie in" and had to "show a leg" to ensure that no rating was still turned in.

To give a leg up. To render timely assistance, "to help a lame dog over a stile". Originally from horsemanship—to help one into the saddle.

To have good sea-legs. To be a good sailor, to be able to stand up to the ship's motion without getting seasick.

To make a leg. To make a bow, especially an old-fashioned obeisance by advancing the right leg.

To set on his legs. To be independent, to be earning one's own living. The allusion is to being nursed, and standing "alone".

To stretch one's legs. To take a walk for exercise, particularly after long sitting.

Without a leg to stand on. Having no excuse; no hope of getting away with it.

Leg-bail. A runaway. **To give leg-bail,** to abscond, make a "get-away".

Leg-pulling means teasing, chaffing, or befooling.

Legal tender. Money which, by the law of a particular country, constitutes payment which a creditor is bound to accept; formerly in England the tender of gold, Bank of England notes, silver up to 40s., and bronze up to one shilling. Since decimalization amounts of legal tender are (1) all English banknotes in England and Wales, but only £1 notes in Scotland and Northern Ireland; (2) all gold coins; (3) "silver" or cupro-nickel of more than 10p face value up to £10; (4) "silver" up to 10p face value totalling £5; (5) bronze up to 10p.

Legem Pone (lē' jem pō ne). Old slang for money paid down on the NAIL, ready money; from the opening words of the first of the PSALMS appointed to be read on the twenty-fifth morning of the month—*Legem pone mihi, Domine, viam justificationum tuarum* (Teach me, O Lord, the way of thy statutes, *Ps.* cxix, 33). 25 March is the first QUARTER-DAY and Settlement Day of the year, and thus the phrase became associated with cash down.

Oremus (let us pray) occurs frequently in the Roman Catholic liturgy. Its application to a debtor who is suing for further time is obvious.

Legend (Lat. *legenda*; from *legere*, to read). Literally and originally "something to be read"; hence the narratives of saints and martyrs were so termed from their being read, especially at MA-TINS, and after dinner in monastic refectories. Exaggeration and a love for the wonderful so predominated in these readings, that the word came to signify a traditional story, a fable, a myth.

In numismatics the legend is the inscription impressed in letters on the edge or rim of a coin or medal and often used synonymously with *inscription*, which is strictly the words in the *field* of a coin. The *field* is the whole part of a coin not occupied by the device. Legend is also applied to the title on a map or under a picture.

Legenda Aurea. *See* GOLDEN LEGEND.

Leger. St. Leger Sweeptakes. One of the CLASSIC RACES, run at Doncaster early in September. It was instituted in 1776 by Colonel Anthony St. Leger, of Park Hill near Doncaster, and called the "St. Leger" two years later.

Legion. My name is Legion: for we are many (*Mark* v, 9). A proverbial expression somewhat similar to hydra-headed (*see* HYDRA). Thus we say of a plague of rats, "Their name is legion."

British Legion. An organisation for promoting the welfare of ex-service personnel, especially for the aged, sick and disabled. It was founded in 1921 largely through the exertions of Field Marshal Earl Haig (1861–1928) and it became the *Royal British Legion* in 1971. There are many local branches and much of the funds are raised by the sale of Flanders poppies. *See* ARMISTICE DAY; REMEMBRANCE DAY.

Foreign Legion. A body of volunteer sympathizers fighting to aid a foreign cause. The name is now particularly associated with the French Foreign Legion, a regular force composed of volunteers of many nationalities.

The Thundering Legion. *See* THUNDERING.

Legion of Honour. An order of distinction and reward instituted by NAPOLEON in 1802, for either military or civil merit.

The badge is a five-branched cross with a medallion bearing a symbolical figure of the republic and round it the legend, "République Française". This is crowned by a LAUREL wreath, and the ribbon is of red watered silk.

Leglen-girth. To cast a leglen-girth. To have made a *faux pas*, particularly by having an illegitimate child; to have one's reputation blown upon. *Leglen* is Scottish for a milk pail, and a *leglengirth* is the girth of a milk pail.

Leitmotiv (līt' mō tēf'). A German word meaning the "leading motive", and it is applied in music to a theme associated with a personality in an opera or similar work, repeatedly recurring to emphasize the dramatic situation. The term first came into use with Wagner. In general usage it describes any phrase or turn of thought that continually recurs with a certain association.

Lemnos. The island were VULCAN fell, when JUPITER flung him out of HEAVEN. Lemnos was mythically celebrated for two massacres. The men were said to have killed all the children of their abducted Athenian consorts, and the Lemnian women to have murdered their husbands; hence **Lemnian actions** signifies barbarous and inhuman actions. The ARGONAUTS were received with great favour by the women of Lemnos and as a result of their short stay the island was repopulated; the queen Hypsipyle became the mother of twins by JASON.

Lemnian earth. A kind of bole or clayey earth of reddish colour found in the island of Lemnos, said to cure festering wounds and snake bites. This medical earth was made into blocks and anciently stamped with the head of DIANA and hence called *terra sigillata* ("sealed earth"). It is still used locally, and a ceremonial digging of this earth took place on a particular day under the supervision of a priestess. The ceremony eventually became fixed on 6 August, the feast of Christ the Saviour in the GREEK CHURCH.

Lemon. Salts of Lemon. *See* MISNOMERS.

The answer's a lemon. Nothing doing; a suitable answer to an unreasonable or ridiculous request or question.

Lemures (lem' ū rēz). The name given by the Romans to evil spirits of the dead, especially spectres which wandered about at night-time to terrify the living. *Cp.* LARVÆ.

> The lars and lemures moan with midnight plaint.
> MILTON: *On the Morning of the Christ's Nativity* (*The Hymn* xxi).

Lemuria. The lost land that is supposed to have connected Madagascar with India and Sumatra in prehistoric times. The German biologist E. H. Haeckel (1834–1919) thought that it was the original habitat of the lemur. *See* W. Scott Elliott's *The Lost Lemuria* (1904). *Cp.* ATLANTIS; LYONESSE.

Lend-Lease. Reciprocal agreements made by the U.S.A. with Great Britain and the Allied Forces in World War II to foster the pooling of resources. The policy began with the destroyers (*see* RUM-RUNNERS) sent to Great Britain in return for naval and air bases in parts of the British Commonwealth, and was formalized by the Lend-Lease Act of March 1941. When Lend-Lease ended in 1945 the United States had received somewhat less than one-sixth, in monetary terms, of what she had expended in aid to her allies, over 60 per cent of which went to the British COMMONWEALTH.

Leningrad. The name given in 1924 to Petrograd which, until 1914, was known as St. Petersburg, the former capital of Tsarist Russia founded by Peter the Great in 1703.

Lent (O.E. *lencten*, the spring). The Saxons called MARCH *lencten monath* because in this month the days noticeably lengthen. As the chief part of the great fast, from ASH WEDNESDAY to EATER, falls in March, it received the name *Lencten-faesten* or Lent.

The fast of 36 days was introduced in the 4th century, but it did not become fixed at 40 days until the early 7th century, thus corresponding with Our Lord's fast in the wilderness.

Lent lily. The daffodil, which blooms in LENT.

Lenten. Frugal, stinted, as food in LENT. SHAKESPEARE has "lenten entertainment" (*Hamlet*, II, ii); "a lenten answer" (*Twelfth Night*, I, v); "a lenten pye" (*Romeo and Juliet*, II, iv).

Lenten curtain, or **Lenten veil.** In the mediæval Western Church, a white curtain hung down in parish churches between the altar and the nave, and parted on feast days kept during LENT. It was taken down in the last three days of HOLY WEEK and said to betoken "the prophecy of Christ's Passion, which was hidden and unknown till these days" (*Liber Festivalis*). Similarly, all crucifixes and images were covered, a practice still followed in some Anglican churches.

Leo. A constellation, and fifth sign of the ZODIAC.

Leonard, St. A Frank at the court of Clovis in the 6th century, founder of the monastery of Noblac and patron SAINT of prisoners, Clovis having given him permission to release all whom he visited. He is usually represented as a deacon holding chains or broken fetters in his hand. His day is 6 November.

Leonidas. King of Sparta, who defended the pass of THERMOPYLAE against the Persians in 480 B.C. Only one of the 300 SPARTANS survived.

Leonine (lē' ō nīn). Lion-like; also relating to one of the popes named Leo (especially Leo I); as **the Leonine City** the part of ROME surrounding the VATICAN, which was fortified by Leo IV in the 9th century.

Leonine contract. A one-sided agreement; so called in allusion to the fable of *The Lion and His Fellow Hunters. Cp.* GLAUCUS SWAP.

Leonine verses. Latin HEXAMETERS, or alternate hexameters and PENTAMETERS rhyming at the middle and end of each respective line. These fancies were common in the 12th century, and are said to have been popularized by and so called from Leoninus, a canon of the church of St. Victor, in Paris; but there are many such lines in the classic poets, particularly Ovid. In English verse, any metre which rhymes middle and end may be called Leonine verse.

Leopard. So called because it was thought in mediæval times to be a cross between the lion (*leo*) and the *pard*, which was the name given to a panther that had no white specks on it.

In Christian art, the leopard represents that beast spoken of in *Revelation* xiii, 1–8, with seven heads and ten horns; six of the heads bear a NIMBUS, but the seventh, being "wounded to death", lost its power, and consequently is bare.

> And the beast which I saw was like unto a leopard, and his feet were as the feet of a bear, and his mouth as the mouth of a lion.
>
> *Rev.* xiii, 2.

The leopard's head, or King's Mark, on silver is really a lion's head. It is called a leopard, because the O.Fr. heraldic term *leopard* means a lion passant gardant. *See also* THE LION IN HERALDRY *under* LION.

The leopard can never change its spots. A person's character never changes fundamentally; what's "bred in the BONE" remains. The allusion is to *Jeremiah* xiii, 23.

> *K. Richard:* Lions make leopards tame.
> *Norfolk:* Yea, but not change his spots.
> SHAKESPEARE: *Richard II*, I, i.

Leopolita Bible. *See* BIBLE, SOME SPECIALLY NAMED EDITIONS.

Leprechaun (lep' rà kawn). The fairy shoemaker of Ireland, so called because he is always seen working at a single shoe (*leith*, half; *brog*, a shoe or brogue). Another of his peculiarities is that he has a purse that never contains more than a single shilling.

He is also called lubrican, CLURICAUNE, etc.

Lernæan Hydra. *See* HYDRA.

Lesbian. Pertaining to Lesbos, one of the islands of the Greek Archipelago, or to SAPPHO, the famous poetess of Lesbos, and the homosexual practices attributed to her.

The Lesbian Poets. Terpander, Alcæus, Arion, and SAPPHO, all of whom came from Lesbos.

The Lesbian rule. A flexible rule used by ancient Greek masons for measuring curved mouldings, etc.; hence, figuratively, a pliant and accommodating principle or rule of conduct.

Lèse-majesté (lez mazh' estā) (Fr. from Lat. *læsa majestas*, injured or violated majesty). A phrase commonly applied to presumptuous conduct on the part of the inferiors who do not show sufficient respect for their "betters". The legal phrase **Lese-majesty** (lēz) denotes TREASON, a crime against the sovereign.

Lestrigons, or **Læstrygones.** A fabulous race of cannibal giants who lived in Sicily. ULYSSES (*Odyss.*, X) sent two sailors and a messenger to request that he might land, but the king of the place ate one for dinner and the other fled. The Lestrigons gathered on the coast and threw stones at Ulysses and his crew; they departed with all speed, but many men were lost. *Cp.* POLYPHEMUS.

Let. To let down. To disappoint; not to keep faith or trust; to fail in an obligation.

To let off steam. To give vent to pent up feelings in words, or to work off superabundant energy and high spirits in vigorous physical activity. From the noisy escape of steam from the safety valve of a steam locomotive.

To let up. To relax; to cease to act vigorously; to ease up.

Lethe (lē' thi). In Greek mythology, one of the rivers of HADES, which the souls of all the dead are obliged to taste, that they may forget everything said and done when alive. The word means "forgetfulness".

Letter. Letter of Bellerophon. *See* BELLEROPHON.

Letter of Credit. A letter written by a merchant or banker to another, requesting him to credit the bearer with certain sums of money. *Circular notes* are letters of credit carried by travellers.

Letter of the law. To keep to the letter of the law is to observe it strictly; to follow out the regulations thoroughly and to avoid breaking them.

Letter of Licence. An instrument in writing made by a creditor, allowing a debtor longer time for payment of his debt.

Letter of Marque. A commission from the crown making a merchantman a PRIVATEER or legalized ship of war able to take reprisals on a hostile nation. Without such authorization the vessel would be a pirate. Marque is from Provençal *marcar*, Med. Lat. *marcare*, to seize as a pledge.

Letter of safe conduct. A writ under the GREAT SEAL, guaranteeing safety to and from to the person named in the passport.

Letter of Slains. In old Scottish law, a petition to the crown from the relatives of a murdered person, declaring that they have received satisfaction (*assythment*), and asking pardon for the murderer.

Letter of Uriah. *See* URIAH.

Letter-lock. A lock that cannot be opened unless letters on exterior movable rings are arranged in a certain order.

> A strange lock that opens with A M E N.
> BEAUMONT and FLETCHER: *The Noble Gentleman*.

Letters Missive. An official letter from the Lord CHANCELLOR to a peer requesting him to put in an appearance to a bill filed in CHANCERY and sent in lieu of a summons; also a letter from the sovereign to a DEAN and CHAPTER nominating the person to be elected BISHOP.

Letters Patent, or **Overt.** *See* PATENT.

Letters of Administration. The legal instrument granted by the Probate Court to a person appointed administrator to one who has died intestate.

Letters of Credence, or **Letters Credential.** Formal documents with which a diplomatic agent is furnished accrediting him on his appointment to a post at the seat of a foreign government. They are signed by the sovereign or head of the state and he is not officially recognized until his letters have been presented.

Letters of Horning. In Scottish law, a process issued under the signet instructing a messenger to charge a debtor to pay under penalty of caption if he fails to do so. *Cp.* TO PUT TO THE HORN *under* HORN.

Letters of Junius. *See* JUNIUS.

Lettres de Cachet. *See* CACHET.

Leucothea (The White Goddess). So Ino, the mortal daughter of CADMUS and wife of Athamas, was called after she became a sea goddess. Athamas in a fit of madness slew one of her sons; she threw herself into the sea with the other, imploring assistance of the gods, who deified both of them. Her son, then renamed PALÆMON, was called by the Romans Portunus or Portumnus, and became the protecting genius of harbours.

Levant (le vănt'). **Levant and Couchant** (lev' ánt, kou' chánt) (Fr. rising up and lying down). In legal parlance, cattle which have strayed into another's field, and have been there long enough to lie down and sleep. The owner of the field can demand compensation for such intrusion.

Levant and Ponent Winds. The east wind is the Levant, and the west wind the Ponent. The former is from Lat. *levare*, to raise (sunrise), and the latter from *ponere*, to set (sunset).

> Forth rush the Levant and the Ponent winds.
>
> MILTON: *Paradise Lost*, X, 704.

Levant, the region, strictly applies to the eastern shore of the Mediterranean, but is often used to denote the lands from Greece to Egypt. In the 16th and 17th centuries the Far East was sometimes known as the High Levant.

Levee (le' vi) (Fr. *lever*, to rise). A morning assembly or reception. In Britain the word is particularly associated with the royal levees formerly held at St. James's Palace, official occasions when the sovereign received men only, most usually in the afternoon. Before the French Revolution, it was customary for the French monarch to receive visitors (court physicians, nobles, messengers, etc.) at the time of this *levée—i.e.* while making his morning toilet on rising from bed.

The word *levee* is also applied to an embankment.

Levée en masse (Fr.). A levy of all the able-bodied men of a country for its defence or other military service.

Level. On the level. Honest and sincere in whatever one is doing or saying. A term from FREEMASONRY.

To do one's level best. To do one's utmost. An expression originating in the Californian gold-diggings.

To find one's own level. To arrive at that position in society, or in an occupation, etc., best suited to one's gifts and attainments.

To level up, or **down.** To raise or lower to another level, status, or condition.

Level-headed. Shrewd, business-like, full of common sense; said of one who "has his head screwed on the right way".

Level pegging. To have even scores in a contest or an equality of achievements with another person. The expression is from those games (e.g. cribbage) in which a peg-board is used for scoring.

Levellers. In Cromwellian times, a group of RADICAL republicans who wanted the franchise for "freeborn Englishmen" (this did not necessarily include servants and labourers) and who were prominent at London and in the ranks of the Army until their power was broken by Cromwell, after the mutinies of 1647 and 1649. Their influence waned steadily, especially after the suppression (1652–1653) of their leader, John LILBURNE.

In Irish history, the WHITEBOYS were also called *Levellers*. *Cp.* ACEPHALITES.

Leviathan (le vī' á thàn). The Hebrew name for a monster of the waters. In *Job* xli, 1, and *Ps.* lxxiv, 14, it appears to refer to the crocodile; in *Ps.* civ, 26, it is probably the whale; and in *Is.* xxvii, 1, it is a sea-serpent.

Hence the name is applied to any huge sea-animal or ship of great size.

Hobbes took the name as the title for his famous treatise on "the Matter, Forme, and Power of a Commonwealth Ecclesiastical and Civil" (1651) from the Scriptures as he also did for his BEHEMOTH. His *Leviathan* is the absolute state.

Levitation is a term applied to the phenomenon of heavy bodies rising and floating in the air. It is frequently mentioned in Hindu and other writings, and is a not uncommon attribute of Roman Catholic saints. Joseph of Cupertino (1603–1663) was the subject of such frequent levitation that he was forbidden by his superiors to attend choir, and performed his devotions privately where he would not distract others.

Lex (Lat., law).

Lex non scripta (Lat., unwritten law). The COMMON LAW as distinct from STATUTE or written law. It does not derive its force from being recorded, such compilations being simply remembrancers.

Lex talionis (Lat.). The law of retaliation; TIT FOR TAT.

Lia-fail. The Irish name for the Coronation Stone, or Stone of Destiny, of the ancient Irish Kings. *See* SCONE; TANIST STONE.

Liars. Liars should have good memories. An old proverb in many languages, quoted by St. JEROME in the 4th century and traced to Quintilian's *Mendacem memorem esse oportet*, "It is fitting that a liar should be a man of good memory" (*Institutes*, IV, ii, 91).

Libel. Originally the word denoted a little book (Lat. *libellus*), as in *The Libel of English Policy* (*c.* 1436), the title of a poetical essay advocating a strong navy. Also a plaintiff's statement of his case, which often "defames" the defendant, was called a libel, for it made a "little book". Today it usually applies to a written defamation and is actionable.

Liber (Lat., a book).

Liber Albus (Lat., the white book). A compilation of the laws and customs of the City of LONDON, made in 1419 by John Carpenter, town clerk.

Liber Niger. *See* BLACK BOOK.

Liberal. as a political term, came to be applied to the more "advanced" Whigs in the early 19th century and acquired respectability after the Reform Act of 1832, when the name gradually supplanted that of WHIG. The first administration generally called Liberal was that of Gladstone (1868–1874), the last, that of Asquith (1908–1915). In March 1988 the Liberals merged with Social Democratic Party members to form the Social and Liberal Democrats. A minor-

ity of the S.D.P. continued under the leadership of David Owen.

Liberal Nationals, or **National Liberals**. Those Liberals who supported the NATIONAL GOVERNMENTS formed after the financial crisis of 1931 and who remained in close co-operation with the CONSERVATIVE party.

Liberal Unionists. Those Liberals who supported the maintenance of the parliamentary union with IRELAND and who opposed Gladstone's HOME RULE measures. From 1886, under Lord Hartington and Joseph Chamberlain, they supported the CONSERVATIVES.

Liberator, The. Simon Bolivar (1783–1830), who established the independence of Bolivia, Columbia, Ecuador, Panama, Peru and Venezuela from Spain in 1825.

Liberator of the World. A name given to Benjamin Franklin (1706–1790).

Libertine. A free-thinker in religion and morals, hence (more commonly) a debauchee, a profligate; one who puts no restraint on his personal indulgence. The application of the word to 16th-century ANABAPTIST sects in the Low Countries and certain of Calvin's opponents at Geneva had derogatory implications. In the NEW TESTAMENT (*Acts* vi, 9) it is probably used to mean a freedman (Lat. *libertinus*):

> Then there arose certain of the synagogue, which is called the synagogue of the Libertines, ... disputing with Stephen.

Liberty. Civil liberty. Freedom from arbitrary restraint in the citizen's conduct of his own affairs; limited only by the laws established on behalf of the community.

Press, Liberty of the. The right to publish without censorshop or restraint, subject to the laws of LIBEL and proper judicial processes.

Liberty Enlightening the World. The colossal statue standing on Bedloe's (or Liberty) Island at the entrance of New York Harbour, presented to the American people by the Republic of France in commemoration of the centenary of the American Declaration of INDEPENDENCE. It was unveiled in 1886 and is the work of the Alsatian sculptor Frédéric-Auguste Bartholdi (1834–

1904). The bronze, 151 ft. high (standing on a pedestal 154 ft. high) is of a woman, draped, and holding a lighted torch in her upraised hand.

The statue of Liberty, placed over the entrance of the Palais Royal, Paris, was modelled from Mme Tallien, "Notre-Dame-de-Thermidor".

The price of liberty is eternal vigilance. This oft-quoted maxim is found in a speech made in 1790 by the Irish judge John Philpot Curran (1750–1817), in which he said that "The condition upon which God hath given liberty to man is eternal vigilance." The phrase "eternal vigilance is the price of Liberty" was apparently first used by Wendell Phillips (1811–1884), the American reformer, in 1852.

Liberty boat. The boat taking seamen from a ship for shore leave, such passengers being designated **liberty men.**

Liberty Hall. The numerous applications of this descriptive phrase may be gathered from Goldsmith's definition—

This is Liberty-hall, gentlemen. You may do just as you please here.
She Stoops to Conquer, II, i

Liberty horses. Circus horses that perform evolutions without riders.

Liberty Ships. Standardized prefabricated cargo ships of about 10,000 tons much used by the U.S.A. during World War II.

Liberties. In mediæval England, areas of varying extent free from royal jurisdictions in whole or in part, such as the Marcher lordships (*see* MARCHES) and Palatine earldoms (*see* PALATINATE). The areas belonging to the City of London immediately without the City walls were called *liberties* and in course of time were attached to the nearest ward within the walls. *Cp.* TOWER LIBERTY.

The Liberties of the Fleet. *See under* FLEET.

To take liberties. To be unduly familiar, to over-presume; not to be over-scrupulous in handling facts or observing rules.

Libitina. In ancient Italy, the goddess who presided over funerals, her name often being a synonym for death itself. The Romans identified her with PROSERPINA.

Libra (Lat., the balance). The seventh sign of the ZODIAC and the name of one of the ancient constellations, which the SUN enters about 22 September and leaves about 22 October. At this time the day and night being "weighed" would be found equal.

Library. Before the invention of paper the thin inner bark of certain trees was used for writing on; this was in Lat. called *liber*, which came in time to signify also a "book". Hence our *library*, the place for books; and *librarian*, the keeper of books.

A circulating library. A library from which books may be borrowed and taken by members to their homes.

Famous libraries. Among the numerous great libraries of modern Europe, the VATICAN Library is especially notable for its antiquity and manuscript wealth. The present building was erected by Sixtus V in 1588 and it contains some 905,000 vols. and 60,000 MSS. The Biblioteca Mediceo-Laurenziana, Florence (opened to the public in 1571), has a particularly fine collection of precious classical MSS. Others are the great national libraries, such as the Biblioteca Nazionale Centrale at ROME, founded in 1875; the Biblioteca Nacional, Madrid (founded 1716, formerly the Royal Library); the Bibliothèque Nationale, PARIS (originating under Charles V and re-created under Louis XI); the Lenin State Library, Moscow (formerly the Rumyantzov Museum Collection), among the largest in the world with some 10,000,000 vols. The library of the Academy of Sciences in Leningrad is a noteworthy example of the specialized library.

The British Library, founded as the BRITISH MUSEUM library in 1753, is world-famous, with about 6,500,000 vols. and 75,000 MSS. The BODLEIAN LIBRARY, Oxford (1598), includes the original University Library based on the collection of Humphrey, Duke of Gloucester, and has *c.* 2,250,000 vols. and a large MSS. collection. Cambridge University Library (15th century) has 2,000,000 vols., 225,000 maps, and some 17,000 MSS. John Rylands Library, Manchester, founded 1888, has a notable collection of MSS. The oldest library in Scotland is that of St. Andrews University, founded in 1456. The National Library of Scotland was founded as the ADVOCATES LIBRARY. The National Library of Wales was founded at Aberystwyth in 1907. The Library of Trinity College, Dublin, possesses many valuable MSS. as well as the BOOK OF KELLS. All thse libraries (except John Rylands and St. Andrews) possess the copyright privilege.

The oldest library in the U.S.A. is that of Harvard University (1638) which has over 7,245,000 vols. The Library of Congress, founded in 1800, has some 14,000,000 books and pamphlets and over 18,000,000 MSS., plus maps (over 2,000,000) and music (over 3,000,000 volumes and pieces) and is probably the largest library in the world. New York Public Library has *c*. 7,000,000 vols. and 9,000,000 manuscript letters and documents. The Henry E. Huntington Library and Art Gallery, San Marino, California, is noted for rare books, and the Pierpont Morgan Library, New York, for INCUNABULA and MSS. Folger Shakespeare Library, Wahington, D.C., with 250,000 vols., has the largest collection of Shakespeareana in the world. It must, however, be stressed that figures for holdings of larger libraries can only be approximate and comparison is difficult due to different methods of computation.

Lich. A body (O.E. *lik*).

Lich fowls. Birds that feed on carrion, as night-ravens, etc.

Lich-gate. The covered entrance to churchyards intended to afford shelter to the coffin and mourners while awaiting the clergyman who is to conduct the cortège into church.

Lich-owl. The screech-owl, superstitiously supposed to foretell death.

Lich-wake, or **Lyke-wake.** The funeral feast or the *waking* of a corpse, *i.e.* watching it all night.

In a pastoral written by Ælfric in 998 for Wilfsige, Bishop of Sherborne, the attendance of the clergy at lyke-wakes is forbidden.

Lich-way. The path by which a funeral is conveyed to church, which not infrequently deviates from the ordinary road. It was long supposed that wherever a dead body passed became a public thoroughfare.

Lick. A lick and a promise. A superficial wash or clean up, as a cat might give a quick lick to its face.

I licked him. I flogged or beat him. A licking is a thrashing, or, in games, a defeat.

To go at a great lick, To run, ride, etc., at a great speed.

To lick a man's boots, shoes, etc. To CURRY FAVOUR, to be abjectly servile, to be a LICKSPITTLE or BOOTLICKER.

To lick into shape. To make presentable; to bring children up well, etc. Derived from the widespread mediæval belief that bear cubs are born shapeless and have to be licked into shape by their mothers. The story gained currency apparently from the Arab physician AVICENNA (979–1037) who tells it in his encyclopædia.

To lick one's lips. To give evident signs of the enjoyment of anticipation.

To lick the dust, or **the ground.** *See* TO KISS THE DUST *under* KISS.

Lickspittle. A toady; the meanest of sycophants.

Lictors. Binders (Lat. *ligo*, I bind or tie). These Roman officers were so called because they bound the hands and feet of criminals before they executed the sentence of the law.

Lie. The lie circumstantial, direct, etc. *See* COUNTERCHECK QUARRELSOME.

A lie hath no feet. Because it cannot stand alone. In fact, a lie wants twenty others to support it, and even then is in constant danger of tripping. *Cp.* LIARS SHOULD HAVE GOOD MEMORIES.

A white lie. A conventional lie, such as telling a caller that Mrs. X is not at home (*see under* HOME).

To give one the lie. To accuse him to his face of telling a falsehood.

To give the lie to. To show that such a statement is false; to belie.

The Father of Lies. SATAN (*John* viii, 44).

Lie (O.E. *licgan*, to bide or rest).

To lie at the catch. In Bunyan's *Pilgrim's Progress* (ch. xii), Talkative says

to Faithful, "You lie at the catch, I perceive." To which Faithful replies, "No,
not I; I am only for setting things
right." To lie at or on the catch is to lie
in wait or to lay a trap to catch one.

To lie in. To be confined in childbirth;
to stay in bed beyond one's usual time of
rising.

To lie in state. Said of a corpse of a
royal or distinguished person that is displayed to the general public.

To lie low. To conceal oneself or one's
intentions; to avoid notice.

To lie over. To be deferred; as, "This
question must lie over till next session."

To lie to. To stop the progress of a vessel at sea by reducing the sails and coun-
terbracing the yards (in a power-driven
vessel, to slow down the engines) and to
keep head to wind; hence to cease from
doing something.

To lie up. To refrain from work, especially through ill health; to rest.

To lie with one's fathers. To be buried in one's native place or with one's ancestors.

> I will lie with my fathers, and thou shalt
> carry me out of Egypt.
> *Gen.* xlvii, 30.

Life (O.E. *lif*). **Drawn from life.** Drawn
or described from some real person or
object.

For life. As long as life continues.

For the life of me. True as I am alive.
Even if my life depended on it.

High life. The life of high society.

Large as life. Of the same size as the
object represented, life size; in person,
in the flesh, "Here she is, large as life."

Low life. The life of the poor and lower
grades of society.

On my life. I will answer for it by my
life.

To bear a charmed life. To escape accidents or danger with amazing good
luck.

To see life. To "KNOCK ABOUT" town,
where life may be seen at its fullest; to
move in smart or fast society.

To the life. In exact imitation. "Done
to the life."

Life Guards. The senior cavalry regiment of the HOUSEHOLD TROOPS, the
members of which are not less than six
feet tall; hence a fine, tall, manly fellow

was called "a regular Life Guardsman".

Life preserver. A loaded short stick for
self-defence; also a buoyant jacket, belt,
etc., to support the human body in water.

Still life. In artistic representation, inanimate objects such as books, furniture, fruit, etc.

Lift. To have one at a lift is to have one
in one's power. When a wrestler has his
antagonist in his hands and lifts him
from the ground, he has him "at a lift",
or in his power.

> "Sirra," says he, "I have you at a lift.
> Now you are come unto your latest
> shift."
> PERCY: *Reliques* (*Guy and Amarant*).

Lifter. A thief, one who lifts to purloin.
We still speak of a "shop-lifter" and *lifter*
is a Scottish term for a cattle-stealer.

> Is he so young a man, and so old a lifter?
> SHAKESPEARE: *Troilus and Cressida*,
> I, ii.

In 18th-century English "a lifter" denoted a heavy drinker. *Cp.* ELBOW-
LIFTING.

Lifting the little finger. *See* FINGER.

Ligan, or **Lagan** *See* FLOTSAM AND JET-
SAM.

Light. Ancient lights. *See under* AN-
CIENT.

Inner Light. Inward or spiritual light;
knowledge divinely imparted; as used
by QUAKERS, the light of Christ in the
soul.

> Quakers (that, like to lanthorns, bear
> Their light within 'em) will not swear.
> BUTLER: *Hudibras*, II, ii.

The Light of Asia. Gautama BUDDHA.
*The Light of Asia, or the Great Renun-
ciation* was the name given by Sir Edwin Arnold to his famous narrative
poem dealing with the life and teachings
of Buddha (1879).

The Light of the World (Lat. *Lux
Mundi*). Jesus Christ; allegoricaly portrayed by Holman Hunt in his famous
picture (1854) showing Christ carrying
a lantern knocking at the door of the
soul.

The light of thy countenance. God's
smile of approbation and love.

> Lift thou up the light of thy countenance
> upon us.
> *Ps.* iv, 6.

According to his lights. According to

his information or knowledge of the matter; according to his way of looking at things.

Before the lights. In theatrical parlance, on the stage, *i.e.* before the footlights.

Light o' love. An inconstant capricious or loose woman; a harlot.

Light gains make a heavy purse. Small profits and a quick return is the best way of gaining wealth.

The light of one's eye. A much loved one.

To bring to light. To discover and expose; to reveal.

To light upon. To come across by chance; to discover by accident.

To make light of. To treat as of no importance; to take little notice of.

To put out one's light. To kill him, "send him into the outer darkness". SHA-KESPEARE's Othello says, "Put out the light and then put put out the light" (V, ii), meaning first the light in the room and then Desdemona's light (life).

To see the light. To be born; to be converted; to come to a full understanding or realization of something.

To stand in one's own light. To act in such a way as to hinder one's own advancement.

To throw, or **shed light upon.** To elucidate, to explain.

Light comedian. One who takes humorous, but not low parts.

Light-fingered. *See under* FINGER.

Light Infantry. In the British Army, infantry carrying less equipment than normal and trained to manœuvre at high speed. they were introduced into the British Army by Sir John Moore (1761–1809).

Light Year. A scientific unit for measuring stellar distances. Light travels at the rate of 186,000 miles per second; a light year, or the distance travelled by light in a year, is about 6 million million miles.

Lighthouse. *See* PHAROS.

Lightning. Chain lightning. Two or more flashes of lightning repeated without intermission.

Forked lightning. Zigzag lightning.

Globular lightning. A ball of fire which sometimes falls on the earth and

flies off with an explosion.

Sheet lightning. A diffuse discharge, caused by a flash of lightning in a cloud, or cloud to cloud discharge.

Lightning preservers. The EAGLE, the sea-calf, and the LAUREL were the most approved classical preservatives against lightning. JUPITER chose the first, Augustus CÆSAR the second, and Tiberius the third (Columella, x; Suetonius in *Vit. Aug.*, xc; ditto in *Vit. Tib.*, lxix). *Cp.* HOUSE-LEEK.

Liguria. The ancient name of a part of Cisalpine GAUL, and now a modern territorial division of Italy including the provinces of Genoa, Imperia, Savona, and Spezia. NAPOLEON founded a "Ligurian Republic" with Genoa as its capital, and embracing also Venetia and a part of Sardinia. It was annexed to France in 1805.

Like Billyo, or **Billio.** With great gusto or enthusiasm. Among the suggested origins of the slang term are (1) that Joseph Billio, rector of Wickham Bishops, ejected for nonconformity and first NON-CONFORMIST minister of Maldon (1696), was noted for his energy and enthusiasm; (2) one of Garibaldi's Lieutenants, a SWASHBUCKLER, Nino Biglio, used to dash enthusiastically into action shouting "I am Biglio! Follow me, you rascals, and fight like Biglio!" (3) that it has arisen from George Stephenson's locomotive "Puffing Billy" and "Puffing like Billy-o" and "running like Billy-o" were common phrases.

Lilith. A night monster and VAMPIRE, probably of Babylonian origin, supposed to haunt wildernesses in stormy weather, and to be especially dangerous to children. The name is from a Semitic root meaning "night" which was the special time of this demon's activities. In Rabbinical writings, she is supposed to have been the first wife of ADAM. *See* THE DEVIL AND HIS DAM *under* DEVIL. She is referred to in *Is.* xxxiv, 14, as the "screech-owl" in the Authorized Version; in the Revised Version as the "night-monster", and in the VULGATE as LAMIA. A superstitious cult of Lilith persisted among certain Jews until the 7th century. Goethe introduced her in his *Faust*, and Rossetti in his *Eden Bo-*

wer made the serpent the instrument of Lilith's vengeance—

> "Help, sweet snake, sweet lover of Lilith!
> (Alas the hour!)
> And let God learn how I loved and hated
> Men in the image of God created."

Lilliburlero (lil' i bĕr lēr' ō). The refrain of a piece of political doggerel written by Lord Thomas Wharton (1648–1716) which influenced popular sentiment at the time of the GLORIOUS REVOLUTION of 1688. Burnet says, "It made an impression on the [King's] army that cannot be imagined.... The whole army, and at last the people, both in city and country, were singing it perpetually ... never had so slight a thing so great an effect". The Orange Lily was the symbol of the Irish supporters of William of Orange and the words *Lilliburlero Bullenala* are apparently a corruption of the Erse *An lile ba léir é ba linn an lá* (the lily was triumphant and we won the day).

Lili Marlene. A German song of World War II (based on a poem written by a German soldier, Hans Leip, in 1917) composed by Norbert Schultze in 1938 and sung by the German singer Lale Andersen. It became increasingly popular during the 1940s, especially with the Afrika Korps, and the recorded version was played nightly by Radio Belgrade from the late summer of 1941 virtually until the end of hostilities. Other German stations plugged it and it was picked up and adopted by the British 8th Army, the English version of the lyric being by T. Connor. There were French, Italian and numerous other renderings of what became the classic song of the war.

> Underneath the lantern
> By the barrack gate,
> Darling I remember
> The way you used to wait
> ....
> My Lili of the lamplight,
> My own Lili Marlene.

Lilliput. The land of pigmies or Lilliputians (Swift: *Gulliver's Travels*).

Lily, The. There is a tradition that the lily sprang from the repentant tears of EVE as she went forth from PARADISE.

In Christian art the lily is an emblem of chastity, innocence, and purity, In pictures of the ANNUNCIATION, GABRIEL is sometimes represented as carrying a lily-branch, while a vase containing a lily stands before the Virgin who is kneeling in prayer. St. JOSEPH holds a lily-branch in his hand, indicating that his wife Mary was a virgin.

The lily in the field in *Matt.* vi, 29, "that even Solomon in all his glory was not arrayed like one of these", is the wild lily, probably a species of iris. Our "lily of the valley", with which this is sometimes confused, is a different plant, one of the genus *Convallaria*.

Lily of France. The device of Clovis was three black toads, but the story goes that an aged hermit of Joye-en-valle saw a miraculous light stream into his cell one night and an ANGEL appeared to him holding an azure shield of wonderful beauty, emblazoned with three gold lilies that shone like stars. This he was commanded to give to Queen Clothilde, who gave it to her husband, and his arms were everywhere victorious. The device thereupon became the emblem of France (*see Les Petits Bollandistes*, Vol. VI). *Cp.* FLEUR-DE-LIS.

Lily-livered. *See* LIVER.

To paint, or **gild the lily.** *See* PAINT.

Limbo (Lat. *limbus*, border, fringe, edge). The borders of HELL; that portion assigned by the SCHOOLMEN to those departed spirits to whom the benefits of redemption did not apply through no fault of their own.

Limbo of the Fathers (Lat. *limbus patrum*). The half-way house between earth and HEAVEN, where the PATRIARCHS and prophets who died before Christ's crucifixion await the last day, when they will be received into HEAVEN. Some hold that this is the "HELL" into which Christ descended after He gave up the ghost on the cross.

The Limbus of Fools, or **Limbus Fatuorum,** or **Paradise of Fools.** As fools or idiots are not responsible for their works, the SCHOOLMEN held that they were not punished in PURGATORY and could not be received into HEAVEN, so they were destined to go to a special "Paradise of Fools" (*cp.* FOOL'S PARADISE *under* FOOL).

Lime-light. A vivid light, giving off little heat, produced by the combustion of oxygen and hydrogen on a surface of lime. Also called *Drummond Light*, after Thomas Drummond (1797–1840) who invented it in 1826. It was tried at the South Foreland lighthouse in 1861, but its main use developed in the theatre, where it was used to throw a powerful beam upon one player on the stage to the exclusion of others. Hence the phrase **to be in the lime-light,** to be in the full glare of public attention.

Limerick. A nonsense verse in the metre popularized by Edward Lear in his *Book of Nonsense* (1846), of which the following is an example:

> There was a young lady of Wilts,
> Who walked up to Scotland on stilts;
> When they said it was shocking
> To show so much stocking,
> She answered, "Then what about kilts?"

The name has been said to come from the chorus "Will you come up to Limerick" which was supposed to follow each verse as it was improvised by a member of a convivial party, but there is no real evidence for this.

Limey. In American and Australian slang, a British sailor or ship, or just a Briton. It derives from the practice of issuing lime juice to a ship's crew to combat scurvy.

Limp. This word, formed from the initials Louis (XIV), James (II), his wife Mary (of Modena), and the Prince (of Wales) was used as a JACOBITE toast in the time of William III. *Cp.* NOTARIKON.

Lincoln. Lincoln Green. Lincoln was noted formerly for its light green, as was Coventry for its blue, and Yorkshire for its grey cloth. *Cp.* KENDAL GREEN.

Lincoln Imp. A grotesque carving having weird and prominent ears and nursing the right leg crossed over the left, in the ANGEL choir of Lincoln Cathedral. He is said to have been turned to stone by the angels for misbehaving in the Angel Choir. The Imp is now the county emblem.

Lincoln's Inn. One of the four INNS OF COURT in London. The inn takes its name from its landlord Thomas de Lincoln, king's serjeant, and is probably of late 14th-century origin. The Old Hall dates from the reign of Henry VII. The chapel was completed by Inigo Jones in 1643.

Lindor. One of the conventional names given by the classical poets to a rustic swain, a lover *en bergère*.

Line. The Line. The Equator; also in the British Army all regular infantry regiments except the Foot Guards, and the Rifle Brigade, are called line regiments. The term sometimes includes cavalry regiments.

All along the line. In every particular, as, "The accuracy of the statement is contested all along the line by persons on the spot."

Crossing the line. Sailing across the Equator; advantage is usually taken of this for ceremonial practical joking aboard ship. Those who have not previously crossed the line are summoned to the court of NEPTUNE for trial, and are usually ducked by "bears", sometimes lathered and roughtly shaved, given "soap pills" to swallow, etc. As at present practised the whole affair constitutes a good-humoured and amusing interlude, but in former days some of the buffoonery and horse-play was decidedly rough. Such performances have a long history and may have begun as propitiatory rites to the deities of the ocean. At one time similar ceremonies were performed when a ship crossed the thirty-ninth parallel (about the latitude of Lisbon) and also when passing through the Straits of GIBRALTAR and rounding the CAPE of Good Hope.

Hard lines. Hard luck, a hard lot. Here *lines* means an allotment measured out.

Line of battle. *See under* BATTLE.

Line of beauty. In art, a line of undulating curvature, usually in the form of a slender elongated letter S.

Line of country. One's business or occupation or specialization.

Line of life. In palmistry, the crease in the left hand beginning above the web of the thumb, and running towards or up to the wrist. The nearer it approaches the wrist, the longer will be the life, according to palmists. If long and deeply marked, it indicates long life with very little trouble; if crossed or cut with other marks, it indicates sickness.

The thin red line. British infantrymen in action. The old 93rd Highlanders were so described at the battle of Balaclava (1854) by W. H. Russell, because they did not take the trouble to form into a square. Their regimental magazine was later called *The Thin Red Line*.

To fall into line with. To agree with; to act in conformity with. Derived from the falling-in of soldiers into straight lines. *See also* TO FALL IN *under* FALL.

To lay it on the line. In American usage means "to give money"; "to give the information required", "to speak openly, or frankly about something".

To line one's pockets. *See under* POCKET.

To read between the lines. To discern the hidden meaning; to draw certain conclusions which are not apparent on the surface. One method of cryptography is to write so that the hidden message is revealed only when alternate lines are read.

To shoot a line. To exaggerate; to tell a tall story; to boast.

To toe the line. To obey orders; to conform with. Athletes awaiting the starting signal of a race line up with their toes just touching the starting line.

What line are you in? What is your trade or profession? Commercial travellers are said to be in the "grocery line", "the hardware line", etc. *Cp.* LINE OF COUNTRY *above*.

Line-up. A phrase with various meanings; a parade of persons, especially criminals, for inspection or recognition; an arrangment of players at the start of a game; the deploying of opposing forces before a battle.

Lingua Franca. A species of Italian mixed with French, Greek, Arabic, etc., spoken on the coasts of the Mediterranean; also any mixture of languages serving as a means of communication between different peoples. *Cp.* PIDGIN ENGLISH.

Lining. Lining of the Pocket. Money. When the court tailor wished to obtain the patronage of BEAU BRUMMEL, he made him a present of a dress-coat lined with bank-notes. Brummel wrote a letter of thanks stating that he quite approved of the coat, and especially admired the lining.

To be well-lined. Is to be rich, *i.e.* to have one's pockets well-lined with money.

Linnæan System. The system of classification adopted by the great Swedish botanist Linnæus (1707–1778), who arranged his three kingdoms of animals, vegetables, and minerals into classes, orders, genera, species, and varieties, according to certain characteristics.

Lion. An honourable nickname. Among its recipients are:

Ali, son of Abu Taleb, and son-in-law of MOHAMMED, called *The Lion of God* (*c*. 597–661). His mother called him at birth *Al Haidara*, "the Rugged Lion".

Richard I Cœur de Lion (*Lion's Heart*), so called for his bravery (1157, 1189–1199).

William of Scotland, *The Lion*, so called because he chose a *red lion rampant* for his cognizance (1143, 1165–1214).

A lion is the emblem of the tribe of Judah; Christ is called "the Lion of the tribe of Judah".

> Judah is a lion's whelp:...he couched as a lion, and as an old lion; who shall rouse him up?
>
> *Gen.* xlix, 9.

Among the titles of the Emperor of Ethiopia were *Conquering Lion of the tribe of Judah, Elect of God, King of Kings of Ethiopia*.

A lion is a symbol of Britain.

The Lion in Story and Legend.

CYBELE is represented as riding in a chariot drawn by two lions.

Hippomenes and ATALANTA (fond lovers) were metamorphosed into lions by Cybele.

HERCULES is sometimes represented clad in the skin of the NEMEAN LION.

The story of ANDROCLES and the lion has many parallels, the most famous of which are those related of St. JEROME and St. Gerasimus:

While St. Jerome was lecturing one day, a lion entered the schoolroom, and lifted up one of its paws. All his disciples fled; but Jerome, seeing that the paw was wounded, drew a thorn out if it and dressed the wound. The lion, out of gratitude, showed a wish to stay with its benefactor, hence the SAINT is represented as accompanied by a lion.

St. Gerasimus, says the story, saw on the banks of the Jordan a lion coming to him limping on three feet. When it reached the saint it held up to him the right paw, from which St. Gerasimus extracted a large thorn. The grateful beast attached itself to the saint, and followed him about as a dog.

Similar tales are told by the BOLLAND-ISTS in the *Acta Sanctorum*; and in more recent times a story was told of Sir George Davis, an English consul at Florence at the beginning of the 19th century, when he went to see the Duke of Tuscany's lions. There was one that the keepers could not tame; but no sooner did Sir George appear than it showed every symptom of joy. He entered its cage, and the lion licked his face and wagged his tail. Sir George told the duke that he had brought up the creature, but had sold it when it became older and more dangerous.

Sir Iwain de Galles, a hero of romance, was attended by a lion which he had delivered from the attacks of a serpent.

Sir Geoffrey de Latour was aided by a lion against the SARACENS, but it was drowned on attempting to board the vessel which was carrying Sir Geoffrey away from the HOLY LAND.

George Adamson, a game warden of Kenya, and his wife brought up the lion- ess Elsa. After returning to the jungle and rearing cubs she frequently visited the Adamsons. She died in 1961.

The Lion in Heraldry.

Ever since 1164, when it was adopted as a device by Philip I, Duke of Flanders, the lion has figured prominently as an emblem in HERALDRY and consequently in PUBLIC-HOUSE SIGNS. The earliest and most important attitude of the heraldic lion is *rampant* (the device of SCOTLAND), but it is also shown as *passant*, *passant gardant* (as in the shield of ENGLAND), *salient*, *sejant*, etc., and even *dormant*. A lion *statant gardant* is the device of the Duke of Norfolk; a lion *rampant*, with the tail between the legs and turned over its back, the badge of Edward IV as Earl of March; a sleeping lion, the device of Richard I; and a crowned lion the badge of Henry VIII.

The lions in the arms of England. Three lions *passant gardant*, *i.e.* walking and showing full face. The first was that of Rollo, Duke of Normandy, and the second that of Maine, which was added to Normandy. These were the two lions borne by WILLIAM THE CONQUEROR and his descendants. Henry II added a third to represent the Duchy of Aquitaine, which came to him through his wife Eleanor. Any lion not *rampant* is called a *lion leopardé*, and the French call the *lion passant* a *léopard; accordingly* NAPOLEON said to his soldiers "Let us drive these leopards (the English) into the sea."

Since 1603 the royal ARMS have been supported by (DEXTER) the English lion and (SINISTER) the Scottish UNICORN, but prior to the accession of James I the sinister supporter was a family badge. Edward III, with whom supporters began, had a lion and an EAGLE; Henry IV, an antelope and SWAN; Henry V, a lion and antelope; Edward IV, a lion and bull; Richard III, a lion and boar; Henry VII, a lion and DRAGON; Henry VIII, Mary I, and Elizabeth I, a lion and greyhound.

The lion in the arms of Scotland is derived from the earls of Northumberland and Huntingdon, from whom some of the Scottish monarchs were descended. *See* LYON KING OF ARMS.

The Lion as an emblem of the Resurrection. According to tradition, the lion's whelp is born dead, and remains so for three days, when the father breathes on it and it receives life.

A lion at the feet of crusaders, or **martyrs,** in effigy, signifies that they died for their cause.

The Lion of St. Mark, or of Venice. A winged lion *sejant*, holding an open book with the inscription *Pax tibi, Marce, Evangelista Meus*. A swordpoint rises above the book on the DEXTER side, and the whole is encircled by an AUREOLE.

Lions in Public-house Signs. *See* PUBLIC-HOUSE SIGNS.

The Lion will not touch the true prince (Shakespeare, *Henry IV, Pt. I*, II, iv). This is an old superstition, and has been given a Christian significance, the "true prince" being the MESSIAH. It is applied to any prince of blood royal, supposed at one time to be hedged around with a sort of divinity.

To lionize a person is either to show him the LIONS, or to make a lion of him by fêting him and treating him as a celebrity.

To meet a lion in one's path. To encounter a daunting obstacle.

To place oneself in the lion's mouth. To expose oneself to danger needlessly and recklessly.

To twist the Lion's tail. To insult or impose humiliating treatment on Great Britain when she is unable to retaliate; the lion being a British national emblem.

Lion-hunter. One who hunts up a celebrity, especially to adorn or give prestige to a party. Mrs. Leo Hunter in Dickens's *Pickwick Papers* is a good satire on the name and character of a lion-hunter.

Lion's Head. In fountains the water is often made to issue from the mouth of a lion, an ancient custom. The Egyptians thus symbolized the inundation of the Nile, which happens when the SUN is in LEO (23 July to 22 August), and the Greeks and Romans adopted the device for their fountains.

Lion's Provider. A JACKAL; a foil to another man's wit, a humble friend who plays into your hand to show you to the best advantage. The jackal feeds on the lion's leavings, and is said to yell to advise the lion that it has roused up his prey, serving the lion in much the same way as a dog serves a sportsman.

> ... the poor jackals are less foul,
> As being the brave lion's keen providers
> Than human insects catering for spiders.
>
> BYRON: *Don Juan*, ix, 27.

Lion's share. The larger part: all or nearly all. In *Æsop's Fables*, several beasts joined the lion in a hunt; but, when the spoil was divided, the lion claimed one quarter in right of his prerogative, one for his superior courage, one for his dam and cubs, "and as for the fourth, let who will dispute it with me". Awed by his frown, the other beasts silently withdrew.

Lions. The *lions* of a place are the sights worth seeing, or the celebrities; so called from the ancient custom of showing visitors the lions at the TOWER, as chief of LONDON sights. The Tower menagerie was abolished in 1834.

Lip. Lip homage, or **service.** Verbal devotion; insincere regard; honouring with the lips while the heart takes no part or lot in the matter. See *Matt.* xv, 8; *Is.* xxix, 13.

To bite one's lip. To express vexation and annoyance, or to suppress some emotion as anger or laughter.

To curl the lip. To express contempt or disgust with the mouth.

To keep a stiff upper lip. To be self-reliant; to bear difficulties and danger with fortitude.

To give someone lip. To be cheeky or abusive.

To hang the lip. To drop the under lip in sullenness or contempt.

To shoot out the lip. To show scorn.

Lir, King. The earliest known original of the king in SHAKESPEARE's *King Lear*, an ocean god of early Irish and British legend. He figures in the romance *The Fate of the Children of Lir* as the father of FIONNUALA. On the death of Fingula, the mother of his daughter, he married the wicked Aoife, who, through spite, transformed the children of Lir into swans.

Lir appears in the MABINOGION as *Llyr* and Geoffrey of Monmouth's *Historia Britonum* as *Leir*, the founder of Leicester, from which later source Shakespeare derived his plot. *See* LEAR, KING.

Lisbon. Camoëns, in the LUSIADS, derives the name from *Ulyssippo* (Ulysses' *polis*, or city), and says that it was founded by ULYSSES; it is in fact the Phœnician *Olisippo*, the walled town.

Lit de justice (lē dĕ zhus tēs) (Fr., bed of justice). Properly the bed on which the French king reclined when he attended the deliberations of a *parlement* (a judicial body, which also registered royal edicts, etc.); hence the session itself.

When the king was present he was the fount of authority. The first *lit de justice* is supposed to have been held by Louis XI and the last was that of Louis XVI in 1787.

Litotes (lī tō′ tēz). Understatement, especially emphasizing an affirmative by a negative of its contrary, as, "a citizen of no mean city", *i.e.* of a great or illustrious city.

Little. Little by little. Gradually; a little at a time.

Many a little makes a mickle. The real Scottish proverb is: "A wheen o'mickles mak's a muckle", where mickle means *little* and muckel *much*; but the O.E. *micel* or *mycel* means "much", so that if the Scots proverb is accepted we must give a forced meaning to the word "mickle".

Little Britain. The name given in the old romances to Armorica, now Brittany; also called Benwic.

Little Corporal. NAPOLEON Bonaparte. So called after the battle of Lodi in 1796, from his low stature, youthful age, and great courage. He was barely 5 ft. 2 in. in height.

Little-endians. *See* BIG-ENDIANS *under* BIG.

Little Englanders. An uncomplimentary term first applied in Victorian times to critics and opponents of imperialism and overseas expansion.

> That is why I distrust ... the late Government, because in their ranks were men who notoriously were "Little England" men, who took every opportunity of carping at and criticizing those brave Englishmen who have made for us homes across the sea, men who are opposed to any extension of the responsibilities and obligations of Empire, men who are unworthy sons of the ancestors who have made this country what it is.
>
> JOSEPH CHAMBERLAIN: *Speech at Walsall* (15 July 1895).

Little Entente. The name given to the political alliance formed between Czechoslovakia, Yugoslavia, and Rumania (1920–1922). Originally to prevent the restoration of HABSBURG power, it became broader in scope. It was brought to an end by the destruction of Czechoslovakia after the Munich Agreement (1938).

Little Gentleman in Velvet. A favour-ite JACOBITE toast in the reign of Queen Anne. The reference was to the mole that raised the molehill against which William III's horse Sorrel stumbled (21 February 1702). The king broke his collar-bone and died at Kensington (8 March).

Little Jack Horner. *See* JACK HORNER *under* JACK.

Little John. A character in the ROBIN HOOD cycle, a big stalwart man whose surname was also said to be Nailor. On his first encounter with Robin Hood he "tumbl'd him into the brook" and the outlaws changed the victor's name from John Little to "Little John".

Little Lord Fauntleroy. The title of an amazingly successful children's book by Frances E. Hodgson Burnett (1849–1924) which became a household name in late-Victorian and Edwardian days. First published in book form by Scribners in 1886, it was adapted as a play, *The Real Lord Fauntleroy*, in 1888. As a consequence many small boys, often to their embarrassment, were made to pattern themseles on the Fauntleroy image of polished manners, curly hair, and black velvet suits with lace collars. The garb was in vogue for at least a generation.

Little Master. A name applied to certain German designers who worked for engravers, etc., in the 16th century, because their designs were on a small scale, fit for copper or wood.

Little Parliament. BAREBONES PARLIAMENT.

Little People. Fairies (*see* FAIRY).

Little Red Ridinghood. This nursery story is also common to Sweden, Germany, and France. It comes from the French *Le Petit Chaperon Rouge*, in Charles Perrault's *Contes des Temps*, and was probably derived from Italy. The finale, which tells of the arrival of a huntsman who slits open the wolf and restores Little Red Ridinghood and her grandmother to life, is a German addition.

Liver. In the AUSPICES taken by the Greeks and Romans before battle, if the liver of the animals sacrificed was healthy and blood-red, the OMEN was favourable; but if pale it augured defeat.

The liver was anciently supposed to be the seat of love; hence in SHAKE-SPEARE'S *Love's Labour's Lost* (IV, iii), when Longaville reads the verses, Biron says in an aside. "This is the liver-vein, which makes flesh a deity." In the *Merry Wives of Windsor* (II, i) Pistol speaks of Falstaff as loving Ford's wife "with liver burning hot".

Another superstition was that the liver of a coward contained no blood; hence such expressions as **white-livered, lily-livered**, PIGEON-LIVERED, and Sir Toby's remark in Shakespeare's *Twelfth Night* (III, ii):

> For Andrew, if he were opened, and you find so much blood in his liver as will clog the foot of a flea, I'll eat the rest of the anatomy.

Liverpool. A native of Liverpool is called a *Liverpudlian*, a *Dicky Sam*, or SCOUSE.

Livery. What is delivered. The clothes of a manservant delivered to him by his master. The stables to which a horse is delivered for keep. Splendid uniforms were formerly given to members of royal households. BARONS and KNIGHTS gave them to their retainers, but in the reign of Edward IV a statute of 1468 forbade the latter practice and Henry VII prosecuted those giving or receiving liveries.

The colours of the livery of manservants were those of the field and principal charge of the armorial shield; hence the royal livery is scarlet trimmed with gold.

Livery Companies. The modern representatives of the City of LONDON of the old City Craft Gilds, which were originally associations for religious and social purposes and later trade organizations for fixing wages, standards of craftsmanship, etc. They also acted as Friendly Societies. Their members wore distinctive *livery* on special occasions, hence the name livery company.

The Weavers (1184) claim to be the oldest company. Many still have their halls in the City and contribute largely from their funds to charities, especially to almshouses and education. Merchant Taylors' School, the Haberdashers' schools, St. Paul's School, Goldsmith's College and numerous such institutions,

owe much to their benevolence. *See* AT SIXES AND SEVENS *under* SIX.

Liverymen. The freemen of the London LIVERY COMPANIES are so called because they were entitled to wear the livery of their respective companies.

Lizard. Supposed, at one time, to be venomous, hence a "lizard's leg" was an ingredient of the witches' cauldron in Shakespeare's *Macbeth*.

Lounge lizard. A popular phrase in the 1920s to describe a young man who spent his time, or often made his living, by dancing and waiting upon elderly women.

Lliannan-She. In the Isle of MAN, a spirit friend, a female FAIRY who waited to encounter men. If one spoke to her she followed him always, but remained invisible to everyone else.

Lloyd's. An international insurance market in the City of LONDON and the world centre of shipping intelligence that began in the 17th-century COFFEE house of Edward Lloyd in LOMBARD Street. Originally a market for marine insurance only, it now deals with nearly all forms of insurance. Lloyd's was incorporated by Act of PARLIAMENT in 1871. *Cp.* BALTIC.

Insurance is accepted at Lloyd's by individual underwriters, not by Lloyd's, which provides the premises, intelligence, and other facilities. Lloyd's Agents throughout the world send shipping information which is published in *Lloyd's List* and *Lloyd's Shipping Index*.

Load Line. Another name for the PLIMSOLL LINE.

Loaf. In sacred art, a loaf held in the hand is an attribute of St. PHILIP the Apostle, St. Osyth, St. Joanna, St. NICHOLAS, St. Godfrey, and other saints noted for their charity to the poor.

Half a loaf is better than no bread. If you can't get all you want, try to be content with what you do get; something is better than nothing.

Heywood (1546) says:

> Throw no gift at the giver's head;
> Better is half a loaf than no bread.

Never turn a loaf in the presence of a Menteith. An old Scottish saying. It was Sir John Menteith who betrayed WALLACE to the English. When he turned a loaf set on the table, his guests were to rush upon the patriot and secure him (Scott: *Tales of a Grandfather*, vii).

Use your loaf. A slang expression meaning "use your brains", use "your head". *loaf* (of bread) here means one's head.

With an eye to the loaves and fishes. With a view to the material benefits to be derived. The allusion is to the GOSPEL story of the crowd following Christ, not for His spiritual teachings but for the food He distributed among them.

Loamshire. An imaginary county of southern England used as a setting by writers of fiction to avoid identification with actual towns and villages. Hence the *Loamshires* as an equally fictitious regiment of the LINE.

Loathly Lady. A stock character of old romance who is so hideous that everyone is deterred from marrying her. When, however, she at last finds a husband her ugliness, the effect of enchantment, disappears, and she becomes a model of beauty. Her story is the feminine countepart of BEAUTY AND THE BEAST.

Lob. Old thieves' slang for a till. Hence *lobsneak*, one who robs the till; *lob-crawling*, on the prowl to rob tills.

Lobsters. Soldiers were popularly so called because they were "turned red" when they enlisted (*i.e.* they wore red coats). The name is also applied to Royal MARINES. The term was originally given to a troop of Parliamentary horse in the GREAT REBELLION.

Died for want of lobster sauce. Sometimes said of one who dies or suffers severely because of some trifling disappointment, pique, or wounded vanity. At a grand feast given by the great Condé to Louis XIV at Chantilly, Vatel, the chef, was told that the lobsters intended for sauce had not arrived, where upon he retired to his room and ran his sword through his body, unable to survive the disgrace thus brought upon him.

Local, The. In colloquial parlance, the local hostelry; also the local paper.

Local Defence Volunteers. *See* HOME GUARD.

Local option is the choice allowed to a local authority to decide what course it shall take on a given question, specifically the sale of liquor. In 1913 Scotland was given local option. Parishes, small towns, and wards of large towns were allowed to vote on liquor licensing—for no licence, reduction of licences, or no change. Very few places went "dry".

Loch Ness Monster. In April 1933, a motorist driving along the shore of Loch Ness, Scotland, saw a strange object at some distance out, subsequently described as being 30 ft. long with two humps, a snake-like head at the end of a long neck, and two flippers about the middle of the body. It was "seen" by others and much featured by the newspapers. Investigations showed no substantial evidence of the existence of the supposed prehistoric monster but more recent observations have increased the belief in its presence.

Lock hospital. A hospital for the treatment of venereal diseases. Such a hospital was established in the Harrow Road, London, in 1746, and that at Kingsland had a sundial which bore the inscription "*Post voluptatem misericordia*". The name was originally used in mediæval times for a leper hospital and probably comes from the word *lock* meaning to shut in or seclude, a necessary precaution with lepers.

Lock, Stock, and Barrel. The whole of anything; in entirety. The lock, stock, and barrel of a gun is the complete firearm.

Lockhart. Legend has it that the good Lord James, on his way to the HOLY LAND with the heart of the King Robert Bruce, was killed in Spain fighting against the MOORS. Sir Simon Locard of Lee was commissioned to carry the heart back to SCOTLAND and it was interred in Melrose Abbey. In consequence he changed his name to *Lockheart*, and adopted the device of *a heart within a fetterlock*, with the motto *Corda serrata pando* (Locked hearts I open).

Locksmith's Daughter. A key.

Locrin. Father of SABRINA, and eldest son of the mythical BRUTUS, King of

Britain. On the death of his father he became King of LOEGRIA (Geoffrey of Monmouth: *Historia Britonum*, ch. I-V).

Locum tenens, or **locum** (Med. Lat., one holding place). One acting temporarily for another, especially a doctor or a clergyman. *See* LIEUTENANT.

Locus Lat., a place).

Locus classicus (Lat.). The most cited or most authoritative passage on a subject.

Locus delicti. The place where a crime was committed (Lat. *delictum*, crime).

Locus in quo (Lat., the place in which). The place in question, the spot mentioned.

Locus pœnitentiæ (Lat., a place or opportunity of repentance). The interval when it is possible to withdraw from a bargain or course before being committed to it. In the interview between Esau and his father Isaac, St. PAUL says that the former "found no place of repentance, though he sought it carefully with tears" (*Heb*. xii, 17)—*i.e.* no means whereby Isaac could break his bargain with Jacob.

Locus sigilli (Lat., the place of the seal). The place where the seal is to be set; usually abbreviated in documents to "L.S.", or designated by a small circle.

Locus standi (Lat., a place of standing). Recognized position, acknowledged right or claim. In law, the right to be heard in court. We say of a person that he has no *locus standi* in society.

Locusta. A woman who murders those she professes to nurse, or those whom it is her duty to take care of. Locusta lived in the early days of the Roman Empire, poisoned Claudius and Britannicus, and attempted to destroy NERO. Being found out, she was put to death.

Lodestar. The North Star or Pole Star; the *leading-star* by which mariners are guided (*see* LODE). *Cp*. CYNOSURE.

> Your eyes are lodestars.
> SHAKESPEARE: *A Midsummer Night's Dream*, I, i.

Lodestone, Loadstone. The MAGNET or stone that guides, the magnetic oxide of iron. In the MIDDLE AGES pilots were called *lodesmen*.

Lodona. The Loddon, an affluent enter-

ing the Thames at Shiplake. Pope, in *Windsor Forest*, says it was a NYMPH, fond of the chase, like DIANA. It chanced one day that PAN saw her, and tried to catch her; but Lodona fled from him, imploring CYNTHIA to save her. No sooner had she spoken that she became "a silver stream" which "virgin coldness keeps".

Leogria, or **Logres** (lo eg'ri à, lō' gres). ENGLAND is so called by Geoffrey of Monmouth, from LOCRIN.

Log. An instrument for measuring the speed of a ship. In its simplest form it is a flat piece of wood, some 6 in. in radius, in the shape of a quadrant, and made so that it will float perpendicularly. To this is fastened the log-line, knotted at intervals. *See* KNOT.

A King Log. A king who rules in peace and quietness, but never makes his power felt. In allusion to the FABLE of *The Frogs desiring a King*: JUPITER first threw them down a log of wood, but they grumbled at so spiritless a King. He then sent them a stork, which devoured them eagerly. *See* KING STORK *under* STORK.

Log-book. In a ship, the journal in which the "logs" are entered (*see* LOG). It also contains the general record of proceedings on board, especially the navigational and meteorological records.

To be logged. To have one's name recorded in the ship's log for some misdemeanour or offence.

Log-rolling. Applied in politics to the "give and take" principle, by which one party will further certain interests of another in return for help given in passing its own measures.

In literary circles it means mutual admiration, the mutual admirers being called "log-rollers". The allusion, originally American, is to neighbours who assist a new settler to roll away the logs of his clearing.

Logan Stones. Rocking stones; large masses of stone so delicately poised by nature that they will rock to and fro at a touch. There are many such, especially in Cornwall, Derbyshire, Yorkshire and Wales; also in Scotland and Ireland.

Loggerheads. Fall to loggerheads, to squabbling and fisticuffs, perhaps with the idea of establishing which "block-head" was the harder. The word is used by SHAKESPEARE (*Taming of the Shrew*, IV, i.) *Logger* was the name given to the heavy wooden block fastened to the legs of grazing horses to prevent their straying, thus suggesting a block head, a thick head, a dolt.

To be at loggerheads with someone is to be in a state of disagreement or dispute.

Logres, Logria. *See* LOEGRIA.

Logris. Same as LOCRIN.

Lohengrin. A son of PERCIVAL in the German legend of the Knight of the Swan and attached to the GRAIL cycle. In France it was used to enhance the family of Godfrey of Bouillon. He appears at the close of Wolfram von Eschenbach's *Parzival* (*c.* 1210), and in other German romances, where he is the deliverer of Elsa, Princess of Brabant, who has been dispossessed by Tetramund and Ortrud. He arrives at Antwerp in a skiff drawn by a swan, champions Elsa, and becomes her husband on the sole condition that she shall not ask him his name or lineage. She is prevailed upon to do so on the marriage night, and he, by his vows to the Grail, is obliged to disclose his identity, but at the same time disappears. The swan returns for him, and he goes; but not before retransforming the swan into Elsa's brother Gottfried, who, by the wiles of the sorceress Ortrud, had been obliged to assume that form. Wagner's opera of this name was first produced in 1850.

Loins. Gird up our loins. Brace yourself for vigorous action, or energetic endurance. The Jews wore loose garments, which they girded about their loins when travelling or working.

> Gird up the loins of your mind.
>
> I *Pet.* i, 13.

My little finger shall be thicker than my father's loins (I *Kings* xii, 10). My lightest tax shall be heavier than the most oppressive tax of my predecessor. Rehoboam's arrogant answer to the deputation which waited on him to entreat an alleviation of "the yoke" laid on them by SOLOMON. The reply caused the revolt of all the tribes, except those of Judah and BENJAMIN.

Loki. The god of strife and spirit of evil in Norse mythology, son of the GIANT Farbauti and Laufey, and father of the MIDGARD snake, HEL, and FENRIR. It was he who artfully contrived the death of BALDER. He was finally chained to a rock and, according to one legend, there to remain until the Twilight of the Gods, when he will break his bonds; the heavens will disappear, the earth be swallowed up by the sea, fire shall consume the elements, and even ODIN, with all his kindred deities, shall perish. Another story has it that he was freed at RAGNAROK, and that he and HEIMDALL fought till both were slain.

Lollards. A name given to the followers of John Wyclif, and earlier to a sect in the Netherlands. It is probably from the Mid. Dut. *Lollaerd*, one who mumbles prayers or hymns. The word is recorded as having been used by William Courtenay, Archbishop of Canterbury, when he condemned their teachings in 1382.

The Lollards condemned TRANSUBSTANTIATION, INDULGENCES, clerical celibacy, the ecclesiastical hierarchy, and the temporal possessions of the church.

Lollipop man or lady. A schoolchildren's name for the traffic warden who conducts them across the road; from the striped pole, surmounted by a brightly coloured disc, which he or she carries.

Lombard. A banker or moneylender. In mediæval LONDON, Lombard Street became the home of Lombards and other Italian merchants who set up as goldsmiths, moneylenders, and bankers. From the 13th century they flourished as pawnbrokers and the three golden balls of the pawnshop are said to be taken from the armorial bearings of the MEDICI of Florence. *See* BALLS, THE THREE GOLDEN.

All Lombard Street to a China orange. An old saying, implying very long odds, Lombard Street being the great centre of banking and mercantile transactions. To stake the wealth of LONDON against an orange is to stake great wealth against a trifle.

> "It is Lombard Street to a China orange," quoth Uncle Jack.
>
> BULWER LYTTON: *The Caxtons*, IV, iii.

London. The first surviving reference to London is to be found in Tacitus (*Annals*, Lib. XIV, ch. xxxiii) written A.D. 115–117, and referring to events in A.D. 61. It is the Roman name *Londinium*, which is from a CELTIC name of uncertain derivation.

London Bridge was built upon woolpacks. An old saying commemorating the fact that in the reign of Henry II the construction of a new stone bridge over the THAMES was begun, to be paid for by a tax on wool.

London Gazette. The official organ of the British government and the appointed medium for all official announcements. It dates from 1665 when Henry Muddiman started it as a daily newsletter or newspaper. It is now published on Tuesdays and Fridays. The *Iris Oifigiuil* (Dublin) and the *Belfast Gazette* are similar official organs.

London Group. A society of artists founded in 1913 by some painters associated with Walter Sickert (1860–1942). Its aim was to break away from academic tradition and to draw inspiration from French Post-IMPRESSIONISM.

London Pride is the little red-and-white *Saxifraga umbrosa*, also called None-so-pretty and St. Patrick's Cabbage.

London Stone in Cannon Street is a most ancient relic of uncertain history. Camden thought it to be the point from which the Romans measured distances and another theory is that it is a Saxon ceremonial stone.

According to Holinshed, Jack CADE struck it with his sword when proclaiming himself master of the city and the incident is mentioned in Shakespeare's *Henry VI, Pt. II*, IV, vii. The stone was placed against the wall of St. SWITHIN's Church in 1798 as a safeguard against its destruction.

> Jack Straw at London-stone with all his rout
> Struck not the city with so loud a shout.
> DRYDEN: *The Cock and the Fox*, I, 742.

Londonderry. The Northern Ireland county and city of this name took their prefix "London" when in 1613 the confiscated lands of native chieftains were assigned to some of the London LIVERY COMPANIES and to the Corporation of LONDON.

Lone Star State. The State of Texas, U.S.A.

Long. Long chalk, dozen, odds, etc., *see these words.*

How long is a piece of string? *See under* STRING.

The long and the short of the matter. All that need be said; the essence or whole sum of the matter in brief.

So long. Good-bye, till we meet again.

To draw the longbow. *See under* BOW.

To make a long arm. To stretch for something, especially across the table.

Long Knives. *See under* NIGHT.

Long Meg of Westminster. A noted virago in the reign of Henry VIII, around whose exploits a comedy (since lost) was performed in LONDON in 1594.

Her name has been given to several articles of unusual size. Thus, the large blue-black marble in the south cloister of Westminster Abbey, over the grave of Gervasius de Blois, is called "Long Meg of Westminster". Fuller says the term is applied to things "of hop-pole height, wanting breadth proportionable thereunto", and refers to a great gun in the TOWER OF LONDON, so called, taken to Westminster in troublesome times; and in the *Edinburgh Antiquarian Magazine* (September 1769) we read of Peter Branan, aged 104, who was 6 ft. 6 in. high, and was commonly called *Long Meg of Westminster. See also* MAYPOLE; MEG.

Long Meg and her daughters. In the neighbourhood of Penrith, Cumbria is a prehistoric circle of 64 stones, some of them 10 ft. high. Some 17 paces off, on the south side, is a single stone, 15 ft. high, called *Long Meg*, the shorter ones being called *her daughters.*

Long Melford. A long stocking purse, such as was formerly carried by country folk. In boxing, according to Isopel Berners, it was a straight right-handed blow (Borrow: *Lavengro*, lxxxv). The village on Long Melford in Suffolk owes the epithet to the length of its main street.

Long Parliament. The most familiar of this name is the PARLIAMENT summoned by CHARLES I (3 November

1640), the remnant of which was not dissolved until 16 March 1660 (*see* RUMP). It was especially notable for its resistance to the king and its part in the GREAT REBELLION. The name is also applied to Henry IV's Parliament of 1406 (1 March–22 December), and to the CAVALIER PARLIAMENT (1661–1679) in Charles II's reign.

Long Range Desert Group. A British military force of volunteers in World War II who penetrated behind the enemy's lines in North Africa and carried out invaluable reconnaissance work through the uncharted desert. They helped to guide various forces to their objectives and facilitated the exploits of the *Special Air Service. Cp.* POPSKI'S PRIVATE ARMY.

Long stocking. To have a long stocking. To have a long purse; to have considerable monetary resources. *Cp.* LONG MELFORD.

Longchamps (long shong). The racecourse at the end of the Bois de Boulogne, Paris. An abbey formerly stood there, and it was long celebrated for the parade of smartly dressed Parisians which took place on the Wednesday, Thursday, and Friday of HOLY WEEK.

The custom dates from the time when all who could do so went to the abbey to hear the TENEBRÆ sung in HOLY WEEK; and it survives as an excellent opportunity to display the latest spring fashions.

Long-headed. Clever, sharp-witted. A long head was supposed to indicate shrewdness.

Longshanks. *See* HAMMER.

Longsword (*Longespée, Longepée, Longspée,* etc.). The surname of Wiliam, the first Duke of Normandy (d. 943). He was the great-great-grandfather of WILLIAM THE CONQUEROR. The name was also given to William, third Earl of Salisbury (d. 1226), a natural son of Henry II and (according to late tradition) Fair ROSAMOND.

Longtail, Cut and Longtail. One and another, all of every description. The phrase had its origin in the practice of cutting the tails of certain dogs and horses, and leaving others in their natural state, so that the cut and long-tail horses or dogs included all the species.

How about the long-tailed beggar? A reproof to one who is drawing the long-bow too freely (*see under* BOW). The tale is that a boy on returning from a short voyage pretended to have forgotten everything belonging to his home and asked his mother what she called that "long-tailed beggar", meaning the cat.

Long words. "Honorificabilitudinitatibus" has often been called the longest word in the English language; "quadra-dimensionality" is almost as long, and "antidisestablishmentarianism" beats it by one letter. While there is some limit to the coining of polysyllabic words by the conglomeration of prefixes, combining forms, and suffixes (*e.g.* deanthropomorphization, inanthropomorphizability), the chemists furnish us with such concatenations as "nitrophenylenediamine", and "tetramethyldiamidobenzhydrols". They are far surpassed, however, by the nonsense words found in Urquhart and Motteux's translation of Rabelais. The following comes from Ch. xv. of Bk. IV:

> He was grown quite esperruquanchure-lebublouzerireliced down to his very heel ... (J.M. Cohen in Penguin Classics ... bruisedblueandcontused ...)

The film *Mary Poppins* (1963) provides us with "supercalifragilisticexpialidocious".

The longest place-name in Britain is that of a village in Anglesey, Llanfairpwllgwyngyllgogerychwyrndrobwllllantysiliogogogoch (58 letters). It is usually shortened to Llanfair P.G. The meaning is, "The church of St. Mary in a hollow of white hazel, near to the rapid whirlpool and St. Tysilio church, near to a red cave".

The longest English surname is said to be Featherstonehaugh, often pronounced "Fanshaw".

The German language lends itself to extensive agglomerations and the following would be hard to beat—"Lebensmittelzuschusseinstellungskommissionsvorsitzenderstellvertreter", *i.e.* Deputy-President of the Food-Rationing-Winding-up-Commission.

Longevity (lon jev' i ti). Among the traditional stock cases of longevity are Harry Jenkins, who is reputed to have lived 169 years; Thomas PARR, who died at the age of 152; Catherine, Countess of Desmond, who died at the age of 140; and Thomas Carn of Shoreditch, listed by Dr. Brewer as living 207 years and in the reign of ten sovereigns. Carn's actual dates were 1471 to 1578 (107 years), a figure "2" having been superimposed over a "1" on his tombstone.

It must be noted that all these cases belong to the days before the Registration Act of 1836 ensured a really efficient system of recording births, marriages, and deaths.

The longest authenticated life in the United Kingdom is that of Ada Roe (née Giddings, 1858–1970), who lived 111 years 339 days. The French Canadian, Pierre Joubert (1701–1814), has been proved to have lived 113 years 124 days.

Longinus, or **Longius.** The traditional name of the Roman soldier who smote Our Lord with his spear at the Crucifixion. The only authority for this is the apocryphal *Acts of Pilate*, dating from the 6th century. According to Arthurian Legend, this spear was brought by JOSEPH OF ARIMATHEA to Listenise, when he visited King Pellam, "who was nigh of Joseph's kin". Sir Balim the Savage seized this spear, with which he wounded King Pellam and destroyed three whole countries with that one stroke. William of Malmesbury says the spear was used by CHARLEMAGNE against the SARACENS.

Longwood. The residence on the island of St. Helena where the Emperor NAPOLEON passed the last years of his life in exile, dying there 5 May 1821.

Look. Black looks, To look blue, daggers, a gift-horse, etc., *see these words.*

Look alive! Make haste; be on the alert.

Look before you leap. Consider well before you act.

> And look before you ere you leap.
> For as you sow, you're like to reap.
> BUTLER: *Hudibras*, Pt. II, canto ii, 502.

To look through blue glasses, or **coloured spectacles.** To regard actions in a wrong light; to view things distorted by prejudice.

To look through rose-coloured, or **rose-tinted spectacles.** To take an unduly favourable view of things which the circumstances do not warrant; to be over-optimistic.

To look up. To seek information in books; to visit an acquaintance; to pay a call. Things or persons are said to "look up" when they are improving.

It is unlucky to break a looking-glass. The nature of the ill-luck varies; thus, if a maiden, she will never marry; if a married woman, it betokens death, etc. This superstition arose from the use made of mirrors in former times by magicians, etc. If in their operations the mirror used was broken, the unlucky inquirer could receive no answer.

Looking-glass. As applied to words, a phrase implying that what is spoken or written is to be accepted in the reverse sense or turned upside down. Thus, as spoken by some, "We are prepared to negotiate" really means "We are willing to accept all our demands in full and concede nothing in return". Similarly "We believe in freedom of speech" really means "Only as long as you are on our side and say what we want to hear". The allusion is to Lewis Carroll's *Through the Looking-Glass. Cp.* MIRROR WRITING.

Loop. Looping the loop. The airman's term for the evolution which consists of describing a perpendicular circle in the air; at the top of the circle, or loop, the airman is upside down. The term is from a kind of switchback once popular at fairs in which a moving car or bicycle performed a similar evolution on a perpendicular circular track.

Loose. Figuratively, of lax morals; dissolute; dissipated.

A loose fish. *See under* FISH.

At a loose end. Without employment, or uncertain what to do next. **The loose ends** of any agreement or transaction are the final details requiring settlement, and **to tie up the loose ends** is to settle the outstanding points of detail.

Having a tile loose. *See under* TILE.

On the loose. Behaving in a dissolute fashion.

To cut loose. To break away from conventional restraints.

To play fast and loose. *See under* FAST.

Loose-strife. This name of several species of plants of the genera *Lysimachia* and *Lythrum* is due to mistranslation. The Greek name was *lusimachion*, from the personal name *Lusimachos,* and this was treated as though it were *lusi-*, from *luein*, to loose, and *mache*, strife. Pliny says that the plant has a soothing effect upon oxen that will not draw in the same yoke and that it keeps off flies and gnats, thus relieving horses and oxen from their irritation. Similarly in Fletcher's *Faithful Shepherdess* (II, ii) we read:

> Yellow Lysimachus, to give sweet rest
> To the faint shepherd, killing, where it comes,
> All busy gnats, and every fly that hums.

Lord. A nobleman, a peer of the realm; formerly (and in some connexions still), a ruler, a master, the holder of a manor. It is the O.E. *hlaford, hlaf,* loaf, and modern *ward, i.e.* the *bread-guardian* or *-keeper*, the head of the household (*cp.* LADY).

All members of the HOUSE OF LORDS are Lords; the archbishops and BISHOPS are Lords Spiritual, and the lay peers Lords Temporal. The word is used in COURTESY TITLES and as a title of honour to certain official personages, as the Lord Chief Justice and other Judges, the Lord Mayor, Lord Advocate, Lord Rector, etc. A BARON is called by his title of peerage (either a surname or territorial designation), prefixed by the title "Lord", as "Lord Dawson" or "Lord Islington". It may also be substituted in other than strictly ceremonial use for "MARQUESS", "EARL", or "VISCOUNT", the *of* being dropped, "Lord Salisbury" (for "The Marquess of Salisbury"), "Lord Derby" ("The Earl of Derby"), etc.; this cannot be done in the case of dukes.

Drunk as a lord. *See under* DRUNK.

In the year of our Lord. *See* ANNO DOMINI.

Lord Harry. *See* HARRY.

Lord Lieutenant. In the mid-16th century Lieutenants of the counties came into existence as Crown representatives for control of the military with the power of raising the MILITIA. Lords Lieutenant appointed by the Crown are now the chief executive authority in the counties with the right of recommending the appointment of magistrates. Their extensive control over the militia ended in 1871. Until 1922 the Viceroy was the Lord Lieutenant of Ireland.

Lord Look-on. A punning nickname given to Lord Lucan during the Crimean war for his cautiousness, particularly when he missed a splendid chance to charge a body of Russian cavalry on 5 October 1854.

Lord Lyon King of Arms. *See* HERALD.

Lord Mayor's Day. Originally the Lord Mayor of LONDON was elected on the Feast of St. SIMON and St. JUDE (28 October), and although the election day was altered, admittance to office continued to take place on that day until 1751. From 1752, owing to the adoption of the Gregorian CALENDAR, Lord Mayor's Day became 9 November. In recent years the Lord Mayor has been sworn in at Guildhall on the second Friday in November, being presented to the Lord Chief Justice on the following day (Saturday).

The Lord Mayor's Show. The annual procession which accompanies the Lord Mayor through the CITY to the Royal Courts of Justice on the second Saturday in November. It has developed in scale over the years, and from 1453 until 1856 a river pageant was part of the proceedings. A few days later the **Lord Mayor's Banquet** is held in the GUILDHALL where it is now customary for the Prime Minister to make a political speech. The bill for the Procession and Banquet is settled by the Lord Mayor and the Sheriffs.

Lord of the Ascendant. *See under* ASCENDANT.

Lord of Creation. Man.

> Replenish the earth, and subdue it: and have dominion over the fish of the sea, and over the fowl of the air, and over every living things that moveth upon the earth.... Behold, I have given you every herb bearing seed ... and every tree.
> *Gen.* i, 28, 29.

Lord of Hosts. In the Old Testament, a frequently used title for JEHOVAH, no doubt arising from the belief that He led their armies in battle.

Lord of the Isles. A title once borne by descendants of Somerled, Lord of Argyll, who ruled the Western Isles of Scotland as VASSALS of the King of Scotland in the 14th and 15th centuries.

The Lordship of the Isles was taken over by the Scottish crown in 1540 and it subsequently became one of the titles of the Prince of WALES. Scott has a poem called *The Lord of the Isles* (1814).

Lord of Misrule. *See* KING OF MISRULE.

The Lord of the Rings. Sauron the Great, the Dark Lord of Mordor in J.R.R. Tolkien's sequel (1954–55) the HOBBIT. Sauron's power depended on the possession of certain rings, especially the One Ring, the Ruling Ring, the Master Ring which he had lost many years ago and which he now sought to regain to give him strength to cover the land in a second darkness. This ring had eventually come into the hands of the Hobbit, Bilbo Baggins, who passed it on to Frodo Baggins, his adopted heir. If Sauron recovered it the Hobbits would be doomed and the only way to destroy the ring was to find the Cracks of Doom and cast it into the Fire-mountain. The saga essentially concerns Frodo's struggles, trials and adventures to achieve this.

The Lord's Day. SUNDAY.

The Lord's Prayer. The words in which Jesus taught his disciples to pray (*Matt.* vi, 9–13). *See* PATERNOSTER.

The Lord's Supper. A name given to the Holy Communion which commemorates the LAST SUPPER of Jesus with his disciples.

Lords and Ladies. The popular name of the wild arum. *Arum maculatum*. *See* CUCKOO FLOWERS *under* CUCKOO.

Lords Spiritual. The bishops who have seats in the HOUSE OF LORDS.

Lords Temporal. The lay members of the HOUSE OF LORDS.

My Lord. The correct form to use in addressing Judges of the Supreme Court (usually slurred to "M'Lud"), also the respectful form of address to BISHOPS, noblemen under the rank of DUKE, Lord Mayors, Lord Provosts, and the Lord Advocate.

The Lord knows who, what, where, etc. Flippant expressions used to denote one's own entire ignorance of the matter.

To live like a lord. To fare luxuriously; to live like a fighting-cock (*see under* COCK).

To lord it, or lord it over. To play the lord; to ruly tyrannically, to domineer.

When our Lord falls in our Lady's lap. When EASTER Sunday falls on the same date as LADY DAY (25 March). This is said to bode ill for England. In the 19th century this occured in 1883 and 1894; in the 20th, its sole occurrence has been in 1951.

Lord's. The Headquarters of the Marylebone Cricket Club (M.C.C.), and of CRICKET generally, is at St. John's Wood, London. The ground was opened by Thomas Lord (1757–1832) who was groundsman at the White Conduit Club, London, in 1780. In 1797 he started a cricket ground of his own on the site of what is now Dorset Square, moving the turf in 1811 to a new site near Regent's Canal, whence in 1814 he transferred to the present ground.

> I doubt if there be any scene in the world more animating or delightful than a cricket-match—I do not mean a set match at Lord's ground for money, hard money, between a certain number of gentlemen and players, as they are called.
>
> MISS MITFORD: *Our Village* (*A Country Cricket-Match*) (1832).

Lorel. Also *losel*, a worthless person; a rake or profligate. The word is from *loren*, also *losen*, from the old *lesen*, to lose. It is chiefly remembered through "Cock Lorell". *See* COCK LORELL'S BOTE.

Lorelie. The name of a steep rock, some 430 ft. high, on the right bank of the Rhine opposite St. Goar, noted for its remarkable echo. It is the traditional haunt of a SIREN who lures boatman to their death. Heine and others have poems on it, and Max Bruch made it the subject of an opera, *Die Lorelei*, produced in 1864. Mendelssohn has an incomplete opera of the same title.

Loreto. The house of Loreto. The Santa Casa or Holy House, the reputed house of the Virgin Mary at Nazareth. It was said to have been miraculously moved to Dalmatia in 1291, thence to Recanati in Italy in 1294, and finally to a site near Ancona in 1295. It was reputed to have been transported by ANGELS to prevent its destruction by the Turks. The name is from the Lat. *lauretum*, a grove of laurels, in which it stood in Recanati. The Holy House itself is a small stone building, now surrounded by a marble screen.

Losel. *See* LOREL.

Loss. To be at a loss. To be unable to decide. To be puzzled or embarrassed.

Lost causes, The Home of. Oxford. Referred to as such by the poet Matthew Arnold (1822–1888) in his *Essays in Criticism* (*Preface* to the 1st Series).

> Whispering from her towers the last enchantments of the Middle Ages.... Home of lost causes, and forsaken beliefs, and unpopular names, and impossible loyalties!

Lost Generation. A name sometimes applied to the young men, especially of the cultivated upper and middle classes, who lost their lives in World War I. Rupert Brooke became their symbol; he was 27 when he died (not in battle, but of blood-poisoning).

Lost Tribes. The term applied to the ten tribes of Israel who were carried away from North Palestine (721 B.C.) into Assyria, about 140 years before the BABYLONIAN CAPTIVITY (586 B.C.) exiled the tribes of Judah. Their disappearance has caused much speculation, especially among those who look forward to a restoration of the Hebrews as foretold in the OLD TESTAMENT. In 1649, John Sadler suggested that the English were of Israelitish origin. This theory was expanded by Richard Brothers, the half-crazy enthusiast who declared himself Prince of the Hebrews and Ruler of the World (1792), and has since been developed by others. The British Israelite theory is still held by some without any serious supporting evidence.

Lost Sunday. Another name for SEPTUAGESIMA SUNDAY, from its having no special name.

Lothario. A gay Lothario. A gay LIBERTINE, a seducer of women, a debauchee. The character is from Rowe's tragedy *The Fair Penitent* (1703). He probably got the name from Davenant's *Cruel Brother* (1630) in which there is a similar character with this name. *Cp.* LOVELACE.

> Is this that haughty, gallant, gay Lothario?
>
> *Fair Penitent*, V, i.

Lothian, in SCOTLAND, traditionally takes its name from King Lot, or Lothus Llew, the brother-in-law of ARTHUR, and father of MODRED.

Lots. Casting Lots. To obtain a decision by casting (or drawing from) a set of objects selected for the purpose was a very old form of DIVINATION and an established practice in WITCHCRAFT. Lots were used in ancient Israel in deciding the division of property, appointing to office, the discovering of culprits, etc. (*See Lev.* xvi, 7–10) with the presupposition of divine influence affecting the result.

> The lot is cast into the lap; but the whole disposing thereof is of the Lord.
>
> *Prov.* xvi, 33.

Lotus. A name given to many plants, *e.g.* by the Egyptians to various species of water-lily, by the Hindus and Chinese to the Nelumbo (a water-bean), their "sacred lotus", and by the Greeks to *Zizyphus lotus*, a North African shrub of the order *Rhamnaceæ*, the fruit of which was used for food.

According to MOHAMMED, a lotus-tree stands in the seventh HEAVEN, on the right hand of the throne of God, and the Egyptians pictured the creator springing from the heart of a lotus flower. Iamblichus says the leaves and fruit of the lotus-tree, being round, represent "the motion of intellect", its towering up through mud symbolizes the eminency of divine intellect over matter; and the Deity sitting on it implies His intellectual sovereignty (*On the Egyptian Mysteries*, sec. vii, cap. ii).

The classic myth is that *Lotis*, a daughter of NEPTUNE fleeing from PRIAPUS was changed into a tree, called *Lotus* after her. Another story is that Dryope of Œchalia and her infant son Amphisus were each changed into a lotus.

Lotus-eaters, or **Lotophagi,** in Homeric legend, are a people who ate of the lotus-tree, the effect of which was to make them forget their friends and homes, and to lose all desire of returning to their native country, their only wish being to live in idleness in Lotus-land (*Odyssey*, XI). Hence a *lotus-eater* is one living in ease and luxury. One of Tennyson's greatest poems is *The Lotos-Eaters*.

Louis, St. Louis IX of France (1214, 1226–1270) is usually represented as holding the Saviour's crown of thorns and the cross; sometimes he is pictured with a pilgrim's staff and sometimes with the standard of the cross, the allusion in all cases being to the CRUSADES. He was canonized in 1297, his feast day being 25 August. He is considered a saint offering special protection to France.

Louisette. *See* GUILLOTINE.

Louisiana in the U.S.A. was named in compliment to Louis XIV of France and was originally applied to the French possessions in the Mississippi valley.

Lounge Lizard. *See* LIZARD.

Lourdes (loord). A famous centre of pilgrimage situated in the south-west of France. In 1858 Bernadette Soubirous, a simple peasant girl, claimed that the Virgin Mary had appeared to her on eighteen occasions. Investigations failed to shake her narrative, and a spring with miraculous healing properties that appeared at the same time began to draw invalids from all over the world. The pilgrimage received ecclesiastical recognition in 1862 and Bernadette was canonized in 1933.

Louvre (loo' vrė). The former royal palace of the French kings in Paris. Dagobert is said to have built there a hunting seat, but the present buildings were begun by Francis I in 1541. Since the French Revolution, the greater part of the Louvre has been used for the national museum and art gallery.

Love. The Abode of Love. *See* AGAPEMONE.

Cupboard love. *See* CUPBOARD.

The God of Love. Generally implies either EROS or CUPID. Among the Scandinavians FREYJA was the goddess of sexual love, and among the Hindus Kama is the approximate equivalent of Eros.

Love's Girdle. The CESTUS.

A labour of love. Work undertaken for the love of the thing without regard to payment.

Love in a cottage. A marriage for love without sufficient means to maintain one's social status. "When povety comes in at the door, love flies out at the window."

Love is blind. Lovers cannot see each other's weaknesses and shortcomings. *See* CUPID.

Love me, love my dog. If you love anyone, you will like all that belongs to him. St. BERNARD quotes this proverb in Latin, *Qui me amat, amat et canem meam*.

Not for love or money. Unobtainable, either for payment or for entreaties; not under any circumstances.

There is no love lost between so and so. The persons referred to dislike each other. Formerly the phrase was used in exactly the opposite sense—it was all love between them, and none of it went amissing.

To play for love. To play without stakes.

Love-apple. The tomato. The name was given by the Spaniards who introduced it to Europe from South America. It was alleged to have aphrodisiac properties.

Love Feast. *See* AGAPE.

Love-in-a-mist. The fennel flower, *Nigella damascena*, also called devil-in-a-bush and love-in-a-puzzle.

Love-in-idleness. The HEARTSEASE, *Viola tricolor*. Fable has it that it was originally white, but was changed to purple by Cupid.

> Yet marked I where the bolt of Cupid fell.
> It fell upon a little western flower.
> Before, milk-white, now purple with love's wound;
> And maidens call it Love-in-idleness.
> SHAKESPEARE: *A Midsummer Night's Dream*, II, i.

Love-lies-bleeding. The red AMARANTHS from their hanging inflorescences of small crimson flowers.

Love-lock. A small curl worn by women, fastened to the temples, also called a BOW-CATCHER. At the end of the 16th century the love-lock was a long lock of hair hanging in front of the shoulders, curled and decorated with bows and ribbons.

Loving, or **Grace Cup.** A large cup, tankard or goblet passed round from guest to guest at formal banquets. Agnes Strickland (1786–1874) says that Margaret Atheling, wife of Malcolm Canmore, in order to induce the Scots to remain for grace, devised the grace cup, which was filled with the choicest wine, and of which each guest was allowed to drink *ad libitum*, after grace had been said.

The monks took over the WASSAIL bowl of their heathen predecessors and called it *poculum caritatis*, or the loving-cup. At the Lord Mayor's or City Companies' banquets the loving-cup is a silver bowl with two handles, a napkin being tied to one of them. Two persons stand up, one to drink and the other to defend the drinker. Having taken his draught, the first wipes the cup with the napkin and passes it to his "defender", when the next person rises up to defend the new drinker, and so on.

Lovel, the Dog. *See* RAT, CAT, AND DOG *under* RAT.

Low. To lay low is transitive, and means to overthrow or to kill; **to lie low** is intransitive, and means to be abased, or dead: and colloquially, to bide one's time, to do nothing for the moment.

In low water. Financially embarrassed; or in a bad state of health. The phrase comes from seafaring; *cp.* "stranded", "left HIGH AND DRY".

To give someone the lowdown. A colloquial expression meaning to impart inside information, to explain what the matter is really about. Possibly from the idea that it was mean, disreputable, or "low down" to give such information.

To lower your sail. To salute; to admit yourself submissive or conquered; to humble oneself. A nautical phrase which derives from the English sovereign's ancient claim to sovereignty of the British seas.

Low Church. The essentially PROTEST-ANT section of the CHURCH OF ENGLAND which gives a relatively low place to the claims of the priesthood, episcopate, etc., and has more in common with NONCONFORMIST than CATHOLIC teaching. It is used in contrast to HIGH CHURCH.

Low German. *See* HIGH GERMAN.

Low Latin. *See under* LATIN.

Low Mass. In the Western Church, MASS said by the celebrant without the assistance of other clergy. No part of the service is sung.

Low Sunday. The Sunday next after EASTER. So called probably because of the contrast to the "high" feast of EASTER Sunday. *Cp.* QUASIMODO SUNDAY.

Lower case. The printer's name for the small letters (minuscules) of a fount of type (*see* FONT), as opposed to the capitals; these were, in a type-setter's "case", on a *lower* level than the others.

Lower deck. In the Royal Navy, the rank and file of the ship's company as distinct from the officers. In the ships of former days the lower deck, above the orlop, was the lowest of the continuous gun decks where the crew had their messes and slung their hammocks.

Lower Empire. The later Roman, especially the Western Empire, from about the time of the foundation of the Eastern Empire in 330 to the fall of Constantinople in 1453.

The Lower House. The second of any two legislative chambers; in England, the HOUSE OF COMMONS.

Loyal. The Loyal Toast. This time-honoured toast to the King (or the Queen) is normally drunk while standing, but it is the Royal Navy's privilege to drink it sitting. The story is that this custom arose when George IV (or William IV), when acknowledging the toast in a ship, bumped his head on a beam as he stood up. However APOCRYPHAL such stories may be, it is probably due to the difficulty of standing upright between decks in the old wooden warships.

Loyola, St. Ignatius (1491–1556). Founder of the Society of Jesus, is depicted in art with the sacred monogram. I.H.S. on his breast, or as contemplating it, surrounded by glory in the skies, in allusion to his claim that he had a miraculous knowledge of the mystery of the TRINITY vouchsafed to him. He was the son of the Spanish ducal house of Loyola and, after being severely wounded at the siege of Pamplona (1521), left the army and dedicated himself to the service of the Virgin. *See* JESUIT.

Luce. Flower de Luce. A corruption of FLEUR-DE-LYS.

Lucian. The personification of the follies and vices of the age. Such was Lucian, the chief character in the GOLDEN ASS of Apuleius (2nd century A.D.).

Lucifer (Lat. lightbringer). VENUS, as the morning star. When she follows the SUN, and is an evening star, she is called HESPERUS.

Isaiah applied the epithet "Day-star" to the King of Babylon who proudly boasted he would ascend to the heavens and make himself equal to God, but who was fated to be cast down to the uttermost recesses of the pit. This epithet was translated into "Lucifer"—

> Take up this proverb against the king of Babylon and say, ... How art thou fallen from heaven, O Lucifer, son of the morning!
>
> *Is.* xiv, 4, 12.

By St. JEROME and other Fathers the name was applied to SATAN. Hence poets feign that Satan, before he was driven out of heaven for his pride, was called Lucifer. Milton, in *Paradise Lost* (X, 425), gives this name to the demon of "Sinful Pride", hence the phrase *Proud as Lucifer*.

Lucifer-match, or **Lucifer.** A match. The friction match was invented by John Walker in 1826 and first called a "friction light". The invention was copied by Samuel Jones of the STRAND and sold as the "Lucifer" (*c.* 1829). The term *match* was taken over from the name given to the spill used as secondary tinder in the days of the tinder-box. *Cp.* CONGREVES; LOCOFOCO; PROMETHEAN; SAFETY MATCHES.

Lucius. One of the mythical kings of Britain, the son of Coillus, and fabled as the first Christian British King according to Geoffrey of Monmouth.

Luck. He has the luck of the Devil, or **the Devil's own luck.** He is extraordinarily lucky; everything he attempts is successful.

Luck money, or **luck penny.** A trifle returned to a purchaser for good luck after a deal; also a penny with a hole in it, supposed to ensure good luck. Picking up a pin or a piece of coal is also supposed to be lucky.

Luckie, or **Lucky.** In Scotland a term of familiar but respectful endearment for any elderly woman; often used of the landlady of an ale-house; a *luckie dad* is a grandfather.

A Lucky dip, or **bag.** A tub or other container, in which are placed various articles covered with bran, etc., much in use at bazaars and children's parties. The visitors "dip" and take what they get.

A lucky stone. A stone with a natural hole through it. John Aubrey (1697) tells us that flints with holes in them were hung on a horse or in its stall as a preservative against its being hagridden. *Cp.* LUCKY PENNY.

The lucky bone. The small bone of a sheep's head; once prized by beggars and tramps as it was supposed to bring good luck for the day of its acquisition.

To strike lucky. *See* STRIKE.

Lucullus sups with Lucullus (lū-kŭl' ŭs). Said of a glutton who gourmandizes alone. Lucius Lucullus (*c.* 117–56 B.C.) was a successful Roman military leader and administrator whose latter years were given over to rich and elegant living. On one occasion a superb supper was prepared, and when asked who were to be his guests he replied, "Lucullus will sup tonight with Lucullus."

He was essentially a man of cultural tastes and more likely a *gourmet* than a GOURMAND.

Lucus a non lucendo (lū' kŭs ā non loosen' dō). An etymological contradiction; a phrase used by etymologists who accounted for words by deriving them from their opposites. It means literally "a grove (called *lucus*) from not being lucent" (*lux*, light; *luceo*, to shine). It was the Roman grammarian Honoratus Maurus (*fl.* end of 4th century A.D.) who provided this famous etymology. In the same way *ludus*, a school, may be said to come from *ludere*, to play, and our word *linen* from *lining*, because it is not used for linings.

Lucy, St. Patron SAINT for those afflicted in the eyes. She is supposed to have lived in Syracuse and to have suffered martyrdom there about 304. One legend relates that a nobleman wanted to marry her for the beauty of her eyes; so she tore them out and gave them to him, saying, "Now let me live to God." Hence she is represented in art carrying a palm branch and a platter with two eyes on it.

Lucy Stoner. An American colloquialism for a married woman who insists on using her maiden name; after Lucy Stone (1818–1893), a famous U.S. SUFFRAGETTE. Her married name was Blackwell.

Lud. A mythical king of Britain. According to Geoffrey of Monmouth, the beautifier of LONDON who was buried by the gate which bears his name. It is also suggested that the name is that of a CELTIC river god.

General Lud. *See* LUDDITES.

Lud's Town. LONDON; so called from King LUD.

> And on the gates of Lud's town set your heads.
> SHAKESPEARE: *Cymbeline*, IV, ii.

Luddites. The name given to the machine-breaking rioters in the manufacturing districts of Nottinghamshire, Lancashire, Cheshire, and Yorkshire, in the years 1811 to 1816. The textile workers blamed the new machinery for their unemployment and distress. They were called Luddites after their legendary leader, Ned Ludd, and the leadership of such rioters was often attributed to "General Ludd". *Cp.* CAPTAIN SWING *under* SWING.

Ludlam. *See* LAZY.

Luke, St. Patron SAINT of artists and physicians. Tradition says he painted a portrait of the Virgin Mary and *Col*. iv, 14, states that he was a physician. His day is 18 October. *See also* SYMBOLS OF SAINTS.

St. Luke's Summer. The latter end of autumn. *See* SUMMER.

As light as St. Luke's bird. Not light at all. In art St. LUKE is represented with an ox lying near him.

Luke's Iron Crown. A symbol of tyranny.

> The lifted axe, the agonising wheel,
> Luke's iron crown, and Damien's bed of steel,

> To men remote from power but rarely known,
> Leave reason, faith, and conscience all our own.
> GOLDSMITH: *The Traveller*, 435.

Lumber. Formerly a pawnbroker's shop (from LOMBARD). Thus Lady Murray (*Lives of the Baillies*, 1749) writes: "They put all the little plate they had in the lumber, which is pawning it, till the ships come home."

From its use as applied to old broken boards and bits of wood the word was extended to mean timber sawn and split, especially when the trees have been felled and sawn *in situ*.

Lump. If you don't like it, you may lump it. Whether you like to do it or not, no matter; you must take it as it is; you must put up with it, *i.e.* take it in a lump.

Lunar Month. From new moon to new moon, *i.e.* the time taken by the moon to revolve round the earth, about 29½ days. Popularly, the lunar month is 28 days. In the JEWISH and MOHAMMEDAN CALENDARS (*see under* CALENDAR), the lunar month commences at sunset of the day when the new moon is first seen after sunset, and varies in length, being sometimes 29 and sometimes 30 days.

Lunar Year. Twelve lunar months, *i.e.* about 354⅓ days.

Lunatics. Literally, moon-struck persons. The Romans believed that the mind was affected by the moon, and that lunatics grew more and more frenzied as the moon increased to its full (Lat. *luna*, moon).

Lupercal, The. (lū' pĕr kăl). In ancient ROME the spot where ROMULUS and Remus were suckled by the wolf (*lupus*).

An annual festival, the *Lupercalia* was held there on 15 February, in honour of Lupercus the Lycæan PAN (so called because he protected the flocks from wolves). The name *Lupercal* is sometimes, inaccurately, used for the Lupercalia. It was on one of these occasions that Antony thrice offered JULIUS CÆSAR the crown, but he refused, saying, "JUPITER alone is king of Rome."

> You all did see that on the Lupercal,
> I thrice presented him a kingly crown,
> Which he did thrice refuse.
> SHAKESPEARE: *Julius Cæsar*, III, ii

Lurch. To leave in the lurch. To desert a person in a difficulty. In cribbage, one is left in the position called the *lurch* when one's adversary has run out his score of fifty-one holes before one has oneself turned the corner (or pegged out one's thirty-first hole).

Lush. Beer and other intoxicating drinks. A word of uncertain origin, said by some to be derived from the name of a London brewer called Lushington. Up to about 1895, there was a convivial society of actors called "The City of Lushington," which met in the Harp Tavern, Russell Street, and claimed to be 150 years old. It may also be the O.Fr. *vin louche*, thick or unsettled wine. *Lush* is also slang for an alcoholic.

Lusiads, The. The Portuguese national epic, written by Camoëns, and published in 1572. It relates the stories of illustrious actions of the *Lusians* or Portuguese (*see* LUSUS), and primarily the exploits of Vasco da Gama and his comrades in their "discovery of India" (1497–1499). The intervention of VENUS and BACCHUS and other classical deities makes it far more than the narrative of a voyage. It has been said that Camoëns did for the Portuguese language what Dante did for Italian, and Chaucer for English. *See* LUSUS.

Lustral. Properly, pertaining to the LUSTRUM; hence purificatory, as *lustral water*, the water used in Christian as well as many pagan rites for aspersing worshippers. In ROME the priest used a small OLIVE or LAUREL branch for sprinkling infants and the people.

Lustrum. In ancient ROME the purificatory sacrifice made by the censors for the people once in five years, after the census had been taken (from *luere*, to wash, to purify); hence a period of five years.

Lusus. Pliny (III, i) tells us that Lusus was the companion of BACCHUS in his travels, and settled a colony in Portugal; whence the country was called *Lusitania*, and the inhabitants *Lusians*, or the sons of Lusus.

Lutetia (Lat. *lutum*, mud). The ancient name of PARIS, which, in Roman times, was a collection of mud hovels. CÆSAR called it *Lutetia Parisiorum* (the mud town of the Parisii), which gives the present name *Paris*.

Lutin. A GOBLIN in the folklore of Normandy; similar to the house-spirits of Germany. The name was formerly *netun*, and is said to be derived from NEPTUNE. When the *lutin* assumes the form of a horse ready equipped, it is called *Le Cheval Bayard. See* BAYARD.

To lutin. To twist hair into ELF-LOCKS. These mischievous urchins are said to tangle the mane of a horse or the locks of a child so that the hair must be cut off.

Lutine Bell. H.M.S. *Lutine*, a captured French warship, re-commissioned by the British, left Yarmouth for Holland on 9 October 1799 with bullion and specie to the value of some £500,000. The same night, she was wrecked on a sandbank off the Zuyder Zee with the loss of every soul on board save one, who died as soon as rescued. It was a black day for LLOYD'S underwriters. In 1858 some £50,000 was salvaged, as well as the *Lutine*'s bell and rudder, among other things. The latter was made into the official chair for Lloyd's chairman and a secretary's desk. The bell was hung at Lloyd's and is rung once whenever a total wreck is reported, and twice for an overdue ship.

It was rung in 1963 to signal the death of President Kennedy and in 1965 for that of Sir Winston Churchill, who was an honorary member of Lloyd's.

Luz (lŭz). The indestructible bone of the human body according to Rabbinical legend; the nucleus of the resurrection body. A bone in the spine and the sacrum (sacred bone) may have been so called in allusion to it.

Lycanthropy (lī kăn' thrō pi). The insanity afflicting one who imagines himself to be some kind of animal and exhibits the tastes, voices, etc., of that animal. Formerly, the name given by the ancients to those who imagined themselves to be wolves (Gr. *lukos*, wolf; *anthropos*, man). The WEREWOLF has sometimes been called a *lycanthrope*; and *lycanthropy* was sometimes applied to the form of witchcraft by which WITCHES transformed themselves into wolves.

Lycaon (lī kā' on). In classical mythology, a king of ARCADIA, who, desirous of testing the divine knowledge of JOVE, served up human flesh on his table; for which the god changed him into a wolf. His daughter, CALISTO, was changed into the constellation the Bear, which is sometimes called *Lycaonis Arctos*.

Lycopodium (lī kō pō′ di ùm). A genus of perennial plants comprising the club-mosses, so called from their fanciful resemblance to a wolf's foot (Gr. *lukos*, wolf; *pous, podos*, foot). The powder from the spore-cases of some of these is used in surgery as an absorbent and also (as it is highly inflammable) for stage-lighting. *Cp.* LIME-LIGHT.

Lyddite. A high explosive composed of picric acid and GUN-COTTON; so called from Lydd in Kent, where it was first tested on the artillery ranges in 1888.

Lydford Law. Punish first and try afterwards. Lydford was one of the four Saxon boroughs of Devon and its Norman castle became the prison of the STANNARIES. Offenders were confined in a dungeon so loathsome and dreary that they frequently died before they could be brought for trial. *Cp.* CUPAR JUSTICE; HULL; JEDDART; LYNCH LAW.

Lying for the whetstone. *See* WHETSTONE.

Lyke-wake. *See* LICH-WAKE.

Lyme-, or **Lyam-hound** (līm). The bloodhound, so called from *lyme*, or *lyam*, the leash (Lat. *ligare*, to tie). The *lymehound* was used by mediæval huntsmen for tracking down the wounded buck, and the *gaze-hound* for killing it.

Lynceus (lin′ sūs). One of the ARGONAUTS. He was so sharp-sighted that he could see through the earth, and distinguish objects that were miles off.

> Non possis oculo quantum contendere Lynceus.
> HORACE: I *Epistles*, i, 28.

Also the name of the husband of HYPERMNESTRA. *See* DANAIDES.

Lynch Law. Mob-law, law administered by private individuals, and followed by summary execution. The origin of the term is unknown; none of the suggested derivations from James Lynch, a 15th-century Mayor of Galway in Ireland, or Charles Lynch (1736–1796) of Virginia, has been substantiated. From the 18th century the practice was particularly associated with the more lawless districts of the U.S.A. *Cp.* CUPAR JUSTICE; JEDDART; LYDFORD LAW.

Lynx (lingks). The animal proverbial for its piercing eyesight is a fabulous beast, half dog and half panther, but not like either in character. The cat-like animal now called a lynx is not remarkable for keen-sightedness. The word is probably related to Gr. *lussein*, to see *Cp.* LYNCEUS.

Lyon King of Arms, Lord. The chief heraldic officer for SCOTLAND; so called from the *lion rampant* in the Scottish royal arms. *See* HERALDRY; THE LION IN HERALDRY *under* LION.

Lyonesse. A rich tract of land fabled to stretch between Land's End and the Scilly Isles on which stood the *City of Lions* and some 140 churches. King ARTHUR came from this mythical country. "That sweet land of Lyonesse" was, according to Spenser (*the Faerie Queene*), the birthplace of TRISTRAM, and, according to Tennyson, the scene of King Arthur's death.

> Of Faery damsels met in forest wide
> By knights of Logres, or of Lyones,
> Lancelot, or Pelleas, or Pellenore.
> MILTON: *Paradise Regained*, II, 359.

Lyre. The most ancient of all stringed instruments. That of Terpander and Olympus had only three strings; the Scythian lyre had five; that of Simonides had eight, and that of Timotheus had twelve. It was played either with the fingers or with a plectrum.

Hercules was taught music by Linus. One day, being reproved, the strong man broke the head of his master with his own lyre.

Orpheus charmed savage beasts, and even the infernal gods, with the music of his lyre. Mountains moved to hear his song and rivers ceased to flow.

Lysenkoism. *See* MICHURINISM.

M

M. The thirteenth letter of the English alphabet (the twelfth of the ancient Roman, and twentieth of the FUTHORC). M in the Phœnician character represented the wavy appearance of water, and is called in Hebrew *mem* (water). The Egyptian hieroglyphic represented the owl. In English M is always sounded, except in words from Greek in which it is followed by *n*, *as mnemonics*, *Mnason* (*Acts* xxi, 16).

In Roman numerals M stands for 1,000 (Lat. *mille*): MCMLXX = one thousand, nine hundred and seventy.

Persons convicted of manslaughter, and admitted to BENEFIT OF CLERGY, used to be branded with an M. It was burnt on the brawn of the left thumb.
What is your name? N or M. *See under* N.

M.C.C. The Marylebone Cricket Club, founded in 1787, which moved to LORD'S in 1814.

MS. (pl. **MSS**). Manuscript; applied to literary works, etc., in handwriting, but erroneously to typescript (Lat. *manuscriptum*, that which is written by hand).

Mab (perhaps the Welsh *maban*, a baby). The "fairies' midwife"—*i.e.* employed by the fairies as midwife to deliver man's brain of dreams. Thus whem ROMEO says, "I dreamed a dream tonight," Mercutio replies, "Oh, then, I see Queen Mab hath been with you." When Mab is called "queen" it does not mean sovereign, for TITANIA as wife of King OBERON was Queen of Faery, but simply "female" (O.E. *quén* or *cwén*, modern *quean*).

Mabinogion. A collection of eleven mediæval CELTIC stories of which the Four Branches of the Mabinogi are the most outstanding. Originally they were probably essentially concerned with the life and death of Pryderi, but a considerable amount of additional material has complicated the structure. The tales are basically Welsh mythology and folklore together with ARTHURIAN ROMANCE. The title "Mabinogion" was given by Lady Charlotte Guest to her translations of these stories (1838–1849); but this only properly applies to the Four Branches (*Pwyll*, *Branwen*, *Manawydan*, and *Math*) and not the remainder. The last three stories, *The Lady of the Fountain*, *Peredur*, and *Gereint son of Erbin*, show marked Norman-French influence, often attributed to Chrétien de Troyes, but it is now thought that his material may have derived from Welsh sources.

Mabinogi is derived from *mab* (youth) and was applied to a "tale of youth", then to any "tale". Lady Guest's translation long held the field, but the best and most complete English translation is now that of Gwyn Jones and Thomas Jones (1948).

Macaber, or **Macabre, The Danse**. *See* DANCE OF DEATH.

Macadamize. A method of road-making introduced after 1810 by John L. Macadam (1756–1836), consisting of layers of broken stones of nearly uniform size, each being separately crushed into position by traffic, or (later) by a heavy roller.

Macaire. A French CHANSON DE GESTE of the 12th century. Macaire was the name of the murderer of Aubry de Montdidier and he was brought to justice by the sagacity of AUBRY'S DOG (*see under* DOG). The story was transferred to the 14th century in another version and a 15th-century mural painting of the legend in the chateau of Montargis gave rise to Aubry's dog being called the "dog of Montargis".

Macaroni. A COXCOMB (Ital. *un maccherone, see* next entry). The word is derived from the Macaroni Club, instituted in London about 1760 by a set of flashy men who had travelled in Italy, and introduced at ALMACK's subscription table the newfangled Italian food, *macaroni*. The Macaronies were exquisite fops; vicious, insolent, fond of gambling, drinking and duelling, and were (*c.* 1773) the curse of VAUXHALL GARDENS. *Cp.* MOHOCKS.

Macaronic Latin. DOG-LATIN. From the Ital. *maccheroni* (macaroni), a mixture of coarse meal, eggs and cheese.

Macaroni verse. Verses in which foreign words are ludicrously distorted and jumbled together, as in Porson's lines on the threatened invasion of England by NAPOLEON or J. A. Morgan's "translation" of Canning's *The Elderly Gentleman*, the first two verses of which are—

> Prope ripan fluvii solus
> A senex silently sat
> Super capitum ecce his wig
> Et wig super, ecce his hat.
> Blew Zephyrus alte, acerbus,
> Dum elderly gentleman sat;
> Et a capite took up quite torve
> Et in rivum projecit his hat.

It seems to have been originated by Odaxius of Padua but was popularized by his pupil, Teofilo Folengo or Merlinus Coccaius (1491–1544), a Mantuan monk of noble family whose *Liber Macaronicorum* (1520), a poetical rhapsody, made up of words of different languages, treated of "pleasant matters" in a comical style.

Maccabæus. The surname given to Judas, the central figure in the Jewish struggle (*c.* 170–160 B.C.) against the SELEUCIDÆ, and hence to his family or clan. He was the third son of Mattathias the Hasmonæan. The most probable derivation of the name is from Heb. *makkabah*, hammer, just as Edward I was called '*Scotorum mallleus*'.

The Maccabees. The family of Jewish heroes descended from Mattathias the Hasmonæan and his five sons, John, Simon, Judas, Eleazar, and Jonathan, which delivered its race from the persecutions of the Syrian King, Antiochus Epiphanes (175–164 B.C.). It established a line of priest-kings which lasted till supplanted by Herod in 37 B.C. Their exploits are told in the four *Books of The Maccabees*, of which two are in the APOCRYPHA.

McCarthyism. Political WITCH-HUNTING; the hounding of Communist suspects to secure their removal from office and public affairs. So called after U.S. Senator Joseph McCarthy (1909–1957) who specialized in these activities somewhat unscrupulously.

McCoy, or **McKoy, The Real,** is used in the U.S.A., but formerly in Britain it was *the Real MacKay*. Various stories about an American boxer of the 1890s have been suggested as the origin of the phrase, but Eric Partridge in *From Sanskrit to Brazil* (1952), says with more probable truth that it dates from the 1880s and originated in SCOTLAND where it was applied to whisky, men, and things of the highest quality. The whisky was exported to both the U.S.A. and Canada where people of Scottish origin drank the whisky and kept the phrase alive. In the 1890s, however, there is no doubt that it was applied to an outstanding boxer whose name happened to be McCoy.

Mace. Originally a club armed with iron, and used in war; now a staff of office pertaining to certain dignitaries, as the SPEAKER of the HOUSE OF COMMONS, Lord Mayors, MAYORS, etc. Both sword and mace are symbols of dignity, suited to the times when men went about in armour, and sovereigns needed champions to vindicate their rights.

Macedonia's Madman. *See under* MAD.

Macedonians. A religious sect named after Macedonius (d. *c.* 362), Bishop of Constantinople, an upholder of semi-Arianism. He was deposed by the ARIAN Council of Constantinople in 360.

MacGregor (mà greg' òr). The MacGregors furnish the only instance of a clan being deprived of its family name. In 1603, as a result of their ruthless ferocity at the battle of Glenfruin against the Colquhouns of Luss, it was proscribed by James VI and the clan assumed the names of neighbouring families such as the Campbells, Buchanans, Grahams, Murrays, etc. The laws against them were annulled by Charles II in 1661 but in 1693, under William and Mary, similar measures were enacted against them. These penalties were finally abolished by the British PARLIAMENT and John Murray of Lanrick resumed the name MacGregor as chief of the clan in 1822. *See* ROB ROY.

Robert (Rob Roy) MacGregor. *See* ROB ROY.

Machiavelli, Niccolò (ma kyà vel' i) (1469–1527). The celebrated Florentine statesman and author of *Il Principe* (The Prince), a treatise on the art of government addressed to Lorenzo de' MEDICI, putting forward the view that only a strong and ruthless prince could free Italy from devastation by foreigners. In view of the distracted state of the country, he held that terrorism and deceit were justifiable means of achieving a peaceful and prosperous Italy. Hence the use of his name as an epithet or synonym for an unscrupulous politician; and *Machiavellianism* and *Machiavellism* to denote political deceit and intrigue and the use of unscrupulous methods generally.

> Am I politic? am I subtle? am I a Machiavel?
>
> SHAKESPEARE: *The Merry Wives of Windsor*, III, i.

Machismo (Sp. *Macho*, male). An American usage denoting assertive masculinity which emphasises such features as bravery, virility, and the domination of the opposite sex.

Mach Number. An expression of the ratio of flight speed to the speed of sound, devised by the Austrian physicist and psychologist, Ernst Mach (1838–1916). An aircraft flying at Mach 2 is travelling at twice the speed of sound.

Macintosh. Cloth waterproofed with rubber by a process patented in 1823 by Charles Macintosh (1766–1843); also a coat made of this or, loosely, any raincoat.

Mackerel. Mackerel Sky. A sky dappled with detached rounded masses of white cloud, something like the markings of a mackerel.

To throw a sprat to catch a mackerel. *See* SPRAT.

Mackworth's Inn. *See* BARNARD'S INN.

MacPherson (màc'fẽr' son). Fable has it that during the reign of David I of Scotland (1084, 1124–1153) a younger brother of the chief of the powerful clan Chattan became abbot of Kingussie. His elder brother died childless, and the chieftainship devolved on the abbot. He is supposed to have obtained a papal dispensation (a most improbable story) to marry the daughter of the thane of Calder. A swarm of little "Kingussies" was the result. The people of Invernessshire called them the Mac-phersons, *i.e.* the sons of the parson.

Macquarie Style. The late Georgian style of architecture favoured by General Lachlan Macquarie when Governor of New South Wales (1809–1821). His chief architect was Francis Howard Greenway, an ex-convict who designed St. James's Church, Sydney.

Macrocosm. (Gr., the great world). The ancients looked upon the universe as a living creature and the followers of PARACELSUS considered man a miniature representation of the universe. The one was termed the Macrocosm, the other the MICROCOSM.

Mad. Mad as a hatter. A phrase popularized by Lewis Carroll in *Alice in Wonderland* (1865). It is found in Thackeray's *Pendennis* (1850) and is recorded in America in 1836. Mercurous nitrate was used in the making of felt hats and its effects can produce St. VITUS'S DANCE or lesser tremulous manifestations, hence the likely origin of the phrase. It has also been suggested that the original "mad hatter" was Robert Crab, a 17th-century eccentric living at Chesham, who gave all his goods to the poor and lived on dock leaves and grass.

Mad as a March Hare. *See under* HARE.

The Mad Cavalier. Prince Rupert (1619–1682), noted for his impetuous courage and impatience of control as the Royalist cavalry leader during the English CIVIL WAR. He was the son of James I's daughter, Elizabeth, and Frederick, the Elector of the PALATINATE.

The Mad Parliament. The PARLIAMENT which met at Oxford in 1258 and which produced the Provisions of Oxford to limit the power of Henry III. The epithet "Mad" seems to have arisen through error, probably a substitution of *insance* for *insigne* (famous) in a contemporary description.

Madame. Madame Tussaud's. The widely known LONDON exhibition of wax models of prominent as well as notorious people established by Marie Tussaud (née Grosholtz) in 1802. She was born at Berne in 1760 and was taught the art of wax-modelling at Paris and in due course gave lessons to Louis XVI's sister, Elizabeth. After a short imprisonment during the French Revolution she came to London where she died in 1850. The famous Chamber of Horrors is filled with figures of notorious murderers and instruments of torture.

Mademoiselle from Armenteers (Armentières). In the GREAT WAR Armentières in northern France was held by the British until the great German offensive of 1918. The army song "Mademoiselle from Armenteers, Parlez-vous", which became so widely known, originated in 1916. It was a modification of the much earlier song and tune "Three Prussian Officers Crossed the Rhine". As before it readily lent itself to improvisation, especially of a scurrilous nature.

> 'O Madam, have you any good wine?
> Parlez-vous;
> O Madam, have you any good wine?
> Parlez-vous.
> O Madam, have you any good wine?
> Fit for a soldier of the line?
> Inky-pinky, parlez-vous.'

Madge. A MAGPIE; the abbreviated form of *Margaret. Cp.* MAG.

Madoc, or **Madog.** A Welsh prince, son of Owain Gwynedd, and legendary discoverer of America in 1170. He is supposed to have sailed from Aber-Cerrig-Gwynion near Rhos-on-Sea with two ships and reached Mobile Bay, Alabama. The Mandan Indians (extinct since the mid-19th century) have been held as the descendants of Madoc's voyagers, and there are fortifications north of Mobile Bay resembling Welsh pre-Norman castles. Madoc is also supposed to have made a second voyage to establish a col-

ony, supposedly setting out from Lundy.

Madonna (Ital., my lady). A title especially applied to the Virgin MARY.

Mæander. *See* MEANDER.

Mæcenas (mē sē' nàs). A patron of letters; so called from the Roman statesman G. Mæcenas (d. 8 B.C.), who kept an open house for men of letters in the reign of Augustus. He was the special friend and patron of HORACE and VIRGIL. Nicholas Rowe so dubbed the Earl of Halifax on his installation to the Order of the GARTER (1714). *See* AUGUSTAN AGE.

Maelduin, or **Maeldune, The Voyage of.** In early Irish romance, Maeldune was the son of Ailill, who had been killed by a robber from Leix. As a young man, he set sail to seek the murderer and voyaged for three years and seven months visiting many islands and seeing marvels hitherto unknown. He eventually found the culprit, but took no vengeance, out of gratitude to God for his deliverance from such a variety of great dangers. The story has much in common with the voyage of St. BRANDAN.

Mænads (frenzied women). The Bacchæ or Bacchantes, female attendants of BACHUS. The name arises from their extravagant gestures and frenzied rites.

Mæonides (mēon' i dēz), or **The Mæonian Poet.** HOMER either because he was the son of Mæon, or because he was born in Mæonia (Asia Minor).

Mæra, or **Mœra.** The dog of ICARIUS.

Maeve, or **Medb.** In Irish legend, a mythical queen of Connacht, wife of Ailill and mother of FINDABAIR who sought the downfall of CUCHULAIN and trained sorcerers to help bring this about. She instigated the Cattle Raid of Cuailnge, thus initiating the WAR OF THE BROWN BULL.

Mae West. The name given by aircraft personnel in World War II to the inflatable life-jacket or vest worn when there was danger of being forced into the sea. It was an allusion to the somewhat buxom charms of the famous film star of this name.

Mafficking. Extravagant and boisterous celebration of an event, especially on an occasion of national rejoicing. From the uproarious scenes and unrestrained exultation that took place in the centre of London on the night of 18 May 1900, when the news of the relief of Mafeking (besieged by the Boers for 217 days) became known. The "heroic" character of Baden-Powell's defence has been questioned, but the impact made at the time is not in dispute.

Mafia. A network of Sicilian criminal organizations which became increasingly powerful during the 19th century. "Protection" by blackmail, boycotting, terrorization and the vendetta are characteristic, and Sicilian politics came to be dominated by the *mafiosi*. Its power was largely broken under Mussolini in the 1920s but it has not been exterminated. Sicilian immigrants introduced it into the United States, where it became a growing nuisance from the 1890s, and Mussolini's firm measures caused a fresh influx to join the BOOTLEGGERS and gangsters of the AL CAPONE era. These groups eventually adopted the name Cosa Nostra (Ital. our thing, our affair) controlling much of the drug racket, gambling and prostitution in the big cities, although its use is mainly confined to the eastern seaboard.

Mafia is apparently an Arabic word denoting "a place of refuge", and is a result of the Arab conquest of Sicily in the 9th century, many Sicilian families found a *mafia* in the hills where they duly became peasant bandits, with patriotic and family loyalties. Their resistance continued after the Norman conquest of the 11th century and later control by Spain. After the liberation and unification of Italy the Mafia made crime a fulltime pursuit.

Nowadays *mafia* is frequently misused, becoming a vogue word loosely applied to any clique, exclusive circle, or influential group. *Cp.* CAMORRA.

Magazine. A place for stores (Arab., *makhzan*, a storehouse) and this meaning is still retained in military usage. The word now commonly denotes a periodical publication containing contributions by various authors. How this came about is seen from the *Introduction* to *The Gentleman's Magazine* (1731)—the first to use the word in this way:

This Consideration has induced several Gentlemen to promote a Monthly Collection to treasure up, as in a Magazine, the most remarkable Pieces on the Subjects above mention'd.

Magdalene (măg′ dà lēn). An asylum for reclaiming prostitutes; so called from Mary Magdalene, or Mary of Magdala, "out of whom He had cast seven devils" (*Mark* xvi, 9). It is probably a MISNOMER since the identification of Mary Magdalene with the sinner in *Luke* vii is very problematical. *See* MAUDLIN.

Magdalen College, Oxford (1458) and **Magdalene College, Cambridge** (1542), are pronounced mawd′ lin.

Magdalenian (măg dè lē′ nian). The name given to the late (upper) PALÆOLITHIC period from the district of La Madeleine, lower Vézère, France, where representative relics have been found. These people used wood and bone as well as flint, including bone needles and barbed harpoons. The cave paintings of Altamira in Spain belong to this period. In England, the Creswellian culture is akin to the Magdalenian.

Magdeburg Centuries. The first great PROTESTANT history of the Christian Church, compiled in Magdeburg under the direction of Matthias Flacius Illyricus (1520–1575). It was written in Latin and first published at Basle (1559–1574) as the *Historia Ecclesiæ Christi*, and takes the story to 1400.

Magenta (mà jen′tà). A brilliant red aniline dye derived from coal-tar, named in commemoration of the bloody battle of Magenta, when the Austrians were defeated by the French and Sardinians. This was just before the dye was discovered in 1859.

Maggot. There was an old idea that whimsical or crotchety persons had maggots in their brains:

Are you not mad, my friend? What time o' th' moon is't?
Have not you maggots in your brain?
JOHN FLETCHER: *Women Pleased*, III, iv (1620).

Hence *maggoty*, whimsical, full of fancies. Fanciful dance tunes used to be called *maggots*.

When the maggot bites. When the fancy takes us. Swift, making fun of the notion, says that if the bite is hexagonal it produces poetry; if circular, eloquence; if conical, politics.

Instead of maggots the Scots say, "His head is full of bees"; the French *Il a des rats dans la tête* (*cp*. our "rats in the garret" and "bats in the belfry"); and in Holland, "He has a mouse's nest in his head."

Magi (mā'jī) (Lat., pl. of *magus*). Literally "wise men"; specifically, the Three Wise Men of the East who brought gifts to the infant Saviour. Tradition calls them Melchior, Gaspar, and Balthazar, three kings of the East. The first offered GOLD, the emblem of royalty; the second, FRANKINCENSE in token of divinity; and the third, myrrh, in prophetic allusion to the persecution unto death which awaited the "Man of Sorrows".

> Melchior means "king of light"
> Gaspar or Caspar means "the white one".
> Balthazar means "the lord of treasures".

Mediæval legend calls them the *Three Kings of* COLOGNE, and the cathedral there claimed their relics. They are commemorated on 2, 3, and 4 January, and particularly at the Feast of the EPIPHANY.

Among the ancient Medes and Persians, the Magi were members of a priestly caste credited with great occult powers, and in Camoëns' LUSIAD (pub. 1572) the term denotes Indian BRAHMINS. Ammianus Marcellinus says the Persian magi derived their knowledge from the Brahmins of India (i, 23), and Arianus expressly calls the Brahmins "magi" (i, 7).

Maginot Line (ma' zhi no). A zone of fortifications built along the eastern frontier of France between 1929 and 1934 and named after André Maginot (1877–1932), Minister of War, who sponsored its construction. The line, essentially to cover the returned territories of Alsace-Lorraine, extended from the Swiss border to that of Belgium and lulled the French into a belief that they were secure from any German threat of invasion. In the event, Hitler's troops entered France through Belgium in 1940. *Cp*. SIEGFRIED LINE.

Magna Carta (Lat.). The Great Charter of liberties extorted from King John in 1215. Its main effect was to secure the liberties of the English Church, the rights of the baronial classes, and to restrict abuses of royal power. It gained a new, but historically inaccurate, importance in the constitutional quarrels of the 17th century as a charter of "English liberty".

Magnanimous, The. Alfonso V of Aragon (*c*. 1394, 1416–1458).

Magnet. The loadstone or LODESTONE; so called from Magnesia in Lydia, where the magnetic iron ore was said to abound.

Magnetic Island. An island in Halifax Bay, Queensland, Australia, so named by Captain Cook because he thought his compass was affected by metallic ore in the rocks, although later navigators found no confirmation of this.

Magnetic Mountain. A mountain of mediæval legend which drew out the nails of any ship that approached within its influence. It is referred to in MANDEVILLE's *Travels* and in other stories.

Magnificat. The hymn of the Virgin (*Luke i, 46–55*) beginning "My soul doth magnify the Lord" (*Magnificat anima mea Dominum*), used as part of the daily service of the Church since the beginning of the 6th century, and at Evening Prayer in England for over 800 years.

To correct Magnificat before one has learnt Te Deum. To try to do that for which one has no qualifications; to criticize presumptuously.

To sing the Magnificat at matins. To do things at the wrong time, or out of place. The Magnificat belongs to VESPERS, not to MATINS.

Magnificent, The. Lorenzo de' MEDICI (1449–1492), *Il Magnifico*, Duke of Florence.

C'est magnifique, mais ce n'est pas la guerre. A magnificent gesture, but not really warfare. Admirable, but not according to rule. The comment on the field made by the French General Bosquet to A. H. Layard on the charge of the Light Brigade at Balaclava. It has frequently been attributed to Marshal Canrobert.

Magnum. A wine bottle, twice the size of an ordinary bottle, or two "reputed quarts". A Double Magnum holds the contents of four ordinary bottles. *Cp*.

JEROBOAM.

Magnum opus (Lat. a great work). The chief or most important of one's learned or literary works.

Magog. *See* GOG.

Magpie. Formerly "maggot-pie", *maggot* representing *Margaret* (cp. *Robin* redbreast, *Tom*-tit, and the old *Phyllyp*-sparrow, and *pie* being *pied*, in allusion to its white and black plumage.

The magpie has generally been regarded as an uncanny bird; in Sweden it is connected with WITCHCRAFT; in Devonshire it was a custom to spit three times to avert ill luck when the bird was sighted; in SCOTLAND magpies flying near the windows of a house foretold death. The old rhyme about magpies seen in the course of a walk says:

One's sorrow, two's mirth,
Three's a wedding, four's a birth,
Five's a christening, six a dearth,
Seven's heaven, eight is hell,
And nine's the devil his ane sel'.

In target-shooting the score made by a shot striking the outermost division but one is called a *magpie* because it was customarily signalled by a black and white flag; and formerly BISHOPS were humorously or derisively called *magpies* because of their black and white vestments.

Magus. *See* SIMON MAGUS; MAGI.

Mahabharata (ma ha ba ra′ tà). One of the two great epic poems of ancient India, the other being the RAMAYANA. It is about eight times the combined length of the ILIAD and ODYSSEY. Its main story is the war between the Kauravas (descendants of Dhritarashtra) and the Pandavas (descendants of Pandu), but there are innumerable episodes. Dhritarashtra and Pandu were sons of Kuru, a descendant of Bharata from whom the poem gets its name. It contains the BHAGAVAD GITA.

Maha-pudma. *See* TORTOISE.

Mahâtma (mà hä t′ mà) (Sansk., "great soul").

Max Müller tells us that:

Mahâtma is a well-known Sanskrit word applied to men who have retired from the world, who, by means of a long ascetic discipline, have subdued the passions of the flesh, and gained a reputation for sanctity and knowledge. That these men are able to perform most startling feats, and to suffer the most terrible tortures, is perfectly true.
Nineteenth Century, May 1893.

By the Esoteric Buddhists the name is given to adepts of the highest order, a community of whom is supposed to exist in Tibet, and by Theosophists (*see* THEOSOPHY) to one who has reached perfection spiritually, intellectually, and physically. As his knowledge is perfect he can produce effects which, to the ordinary man, appear miraculous.

The title is particularly associated with Mohandas Karamchand Gandhi (1869–1948), the Hindu nationalist leader who identified himself with the poor, practised prayer and fasting, and sought to achieve his political ends by non-violence.

Mahayana ("Great Vehicle"). A development from the earlier form of BUDDHISM, which occurred about two thousand years ago. It enjoined, besides the pursuit of NIRVANA, that each individual should strive to become a Buddha, thereby becoming able to preach and serve the welfare of others.

Mahdi (Arab., "the divinely directed one"). The expected MESSIAH of the Mohammedans. There have been numerous bearers of this title since early on in the Mohammedan era and the Hidden IMAM (head of the true faith) of the Ismaelis was another such. The most popularly known to the British was Mohammed Ahmed, who led the revolt in the Sudan and who died in 1885. His tomb was destroyed after the battle of Omdurman in 1898. The most famous was Obaidallah al-Mahdi, first CALIPH of the Fatimite dynasty, who reigned from 909 to 933.

Mah-jongg. A Chinese game played with "tiles" like dominoes, made of ivory and bamboo, with usually four players. The tiles (136 or 144 in all) are made up of numbered *bamboos*, *circles*, and *characters*; *honours* (red, green and white dragons), *winds* (north, east, south and west), and additionally *flowers* and *seasons*.

It appears to be of 19th-century origin. The game was introduced to the U.S.A. by Joseph Babcock about 1919 under the trade name Mah-jongg, which he coined.

Mahomet. *See* MOHAMMED.

Maia. The eldest and most lovely of the PLEIADES and mother, by JUPITER, of MERCURY. *See* MAY.

Maid. Maid Marian. A female character in the old May games and MORRIS DANCES, usually as Queen of the May. In the later ROBIN HOOD ballads she became attached to the cycle as the outlaw's sweetheart, probably through the performance of Robin Hood plays at MAY-DAY festivities. The part of Maid Marian, both in the games and the dance, was frequently played by a man in female costume.

Maid of all work. A female servant doing work of all kinds.

Maid of Honour. An unmarried lady in attendance upon a queen or princess. Also the name of a small almond-flavoured cheesecake.

Maid of Norway. Margaret (*c.* 1283–1290), daughter of Eric II and Margaret of Norway, acknowledged Queen of Scotland on the death of her maternal grandfather, Alexander III of Scotland (1285). She was betrothed to Prince Edward, son of Edward I of England, but died on the voyage to Scotland (1290).

Maid of Orleans. JOAN OF ARC.

Old Maid. A spinster who remains unmarried, and also the name of a card game. The lapwing is so called, from the fancy that old maids are changed into lapwings after death.

Maiden. A form of GUILLOTINE used in SCOTLAND in the 16th and 17th centuries for beheading criminals; also called "the widow". It was introduced by Regent Morton for the purpose of beheading the laird of Pennycuik.

He who invented the maiden first hanselled it. Morton is erroneously said to have been the first to suffer by it; but Thomas Scott, one of Rizzio's murderers, was beheaded by it in 1566, and Morton not until 1581.

Maiden Assize. When there is nobody to be brought to trial. In a maiden assize, the sheriff of the county presented the judge with a pair of white gloves. We also have **maiden castle,** or **fortress,** one never taken; **maiden over,** an over

in CRICKET from which no runs are made; **maiden speech,** One's first public speech; **maiden tree,** one never lopped; **maiden voyage,** the initial voyage of a ship; etc. *Maiden* conveys the sense of unspotted, unpolluted, innocent; thus Hubert says to the king:

> This hand of mine
> Is yet a maiden and an innocent hand,
> Not painted with the crimson spots of blood.
>
> SHAKESPEARE: *King John,* IV, ii.

Maiden King, The. Malcolm IV of Scotland (1141, 1153–1165).

> Malcolm ... son of the brave and generous Prince Henry ... was so kind and generous in his disposition, that he was usually called Malcolm the Maiden.
>
> SCOTT: *Tales of a Grandfather,* iv.

Maiden, or **Virgin Queen.** Elizabeth I, Queen of England, who never married (1533, 1558–1603).

Maiden Town. A town never taken by the enemy, but specifically Edinburgh, from the tradition that the maiden daughters of a Pictish king were sent there for protection during an intestine war.

Mailed Fist, The. Aggressive military might; from a phrase (*gepanzerte Faust*) used by William II of Germany when bidding adieu to Prince Henry of Prussia as he was starting on his tour of the Far East (16 December 1897):

> Should anyone essay to detract from our just rights or to injure us, then up and at him with your mailed fist.

Cp. JACK-BOOT; PRUSSIANISM.

Maillotins (mī yō tan). Parisians who, in 1382, rose up against the taxes imposed by the regents early in the reign of Charles VI (1368–1422). They seized iron mallets (*maillets*) from the arsenal and killed the tax collectors but the insurrection was harshly suppressed.

Main. The main chance. Profit or money, probably from the game called hazard in which the first throw of the dice is called the *main,* which must be any number from 5 to 9 inclusive, the player then throwing his *chance,* which determines the main.

To have an eye to the main chance. *See under* EYE.

Main Plot. Lord Cobham's plot (1603)

to replace James I by his English-born cousin Arabella Stuart. Sir Walter Ralegh was one of the conspirators and there were contacts with Spanish agents. They were tried with the contrivers of Watson's plot (*see* BYE PLOT). The names *Main* Plot and *Bye* Plot arose from their supposed connection.

Mainbrace. To splice the mainbrace. A naval expression denoting an extra tot of GROG all round, a very rare occurrence. Probably from the issue of an extra rum ration to those who performed the hard and difficult task of splicing the mainbrace, the brace attached to the main yard. It is also used more generally for celebrating and indulging in strong drink.

Maize. American superstition had it that if a damsel found a blood-red ear of maize, she would have a suitor before the year was out.

> Even the blood-red ear to Evangeline brought not her lover.
> LONGFELLOW. *Evangeline*, II, iv.

Majesty. In mediæval England it was usual to refer to the king as "the Lord King". Henry VIII was the first English king styled "His Majesty", though it was not till the time of the Stuarts that this form of address became stereotyped, and in the Dedication to James I prefixed to the Authorized Version of the BIBLE (1611) the king is addressed also as "Your Highness".

> The Lord of Heaven and earth blesse your Majestie with many and happy dayes, that as his Heavenly hand has enriched your Highnesse, etc.

Henry IV was "His Grace"; Henry VI, "His Excellent Grace"; Edward IV, "High and Mighty Prince"; Henry VII, "His Grace" and "His Highness"; Henry VIII in the earlier years of his reign "His Highness". "His Sacred Majesty" was a title assumed by subsequent sovereigns, but was afterwards changed to "Most Excellent Majesty". The king of Spain was "His Catholic Majesty", and the king of France "His most Christian Majesty".

In HERALDRY, an eagle crowned and holding a sceptre is said to be "an eagle in his majesty".

Majority. He has joined the majority.

He is dead.

Make. Make or break. *This will either make or break you* means this will either bring you success or failure, ruin, etc.

On the make. Looking after one's own personal advantage or gain; intent on the MAIN CHANCE.

To make a book. To arrange or take bets on a particular event or occurrence.

To make a long arm. *See under* LONG.

To make away with. To take away, run off with; to squander; also, to murder; *to make away with oneself* is to commit suicide.

To make believe. To pretend; to play a game at. **Make-believe** is also a noun meaning "pretence".

To make bold. *See under* BOLD.

To make for. To conduce; as, "His actions make for peace"; also, to move towards; hence, in slang, to attack.

To make free with. To take liberties with, use as one's own.

To make good. To fulfil one's promises or to come up to expectations; to achieve success, often after an unpromising start.

Also to replace, repair, or compensate for; as, "My car was damaged through your carelessness and you will have to make it good".

To make heavy weather of. To make an undue labour of, from the labouring of a ship in rough seas.

To make it. To succeed in catching a train, keeping an appointment, etc., on time.

To make it up. To become reconciled.

To make off. To run away, to abscond.

To make out. To obtain an understanding of, as, "I can barely make out the meaning"; to assert, to establish by evidence or argument, as, "to make out one's case"; to draw up, prepare, as, "I am sick of making out income-tax returns." In the U.S.A., it is to achieve one's purposes, particularly amorous.

To make over. To transfer ownership; to refashion or renovate a garment.

To make tracks. To hurry away; to depart.

To make up to. To approach; to try to make friends with, usually for personal ends, to court.

Makeshift. A temporary improvisation

during an emergency.

Make-up. As a verb and a noun denoting face cosmetics and their application, the term is of theatrical origin; an actor is said to be *made-up* for the stage after the requisite applications of greasepaint, etc. Hence, colloquially, the sum of one's characteristics, idiosyncrasies, etc. In printing the *make-up* is the arrangement of the printed matter in columns, pages, etc.

Make-weight. A small addition is compensation or an "extra", as a piece of meat, cheese, etc., put into the scale to make the weight correct.

Malachi Malagrowther. The signature of Sir Walter Scott to a series of letters contributed to the *Edinburgh Weekly Journal* in 1826 upon the lowest limitation of paper money to £5. They caused a great sensation at the time. He had previously called a querulous old courtier in *The Fortunes of Nigel* (1822) Sir Mungo Malagrowther. *Cp.* DRAPIER'S LETTERS.

Malakoff. This fortification, which was captured by the French (8 September 1855) during the Crimean War, was named from a Russian, Alexander Ivanovitch Malakoff, who kept a liquorshop outside Sebastopol. Other houses sprang up round it and "Malakoff", as the settlement came to be called, was ultimately fortified.

Malaprop, Mrs. The famous character in Sheridan's *The Rivals*. Noted for her blunders in the use of words (Fr. *mal à propos*). "As headstrong as an *allegory* [alligator] on the banks of the Nile", (III, iii), is one of her grotesque misapplications. Hence the words *malaprop* and *malapropism* to denote such mistakes.

Malebolge (ma là bol' jä). The eighth circle of Dante's *Inferno* (Canto xviii), containing ten *bolge* or pits. The name is used figuratively of any cesspool of filth or iniquity.

Malice. In addition to its common meaning *malice* is a term in English law to designate a wrongful act carried out against another intentionally, without just cause or excuse—this is commonly known as *malice prepens* or *malice aforethought*. *Malicious damage* is a le-

gal term meaning damage done to property wilfully and purposely; *malicious prosecution* means the preferring a criminal prosecution or the presentation of a bankruptcy petition, maliciously and without reasonable cause.

Malignants. A term applied by the Parliamentarians to the Royalists who fought for CHARLES I and CHARLES II. They were also called DELINQUENTS.

Malkin. An old diminutive of Matilda; formerly used as a generic term for a kitchen-wench or untidy slut; also for a cat (*see* GRIMALKIN), and for a scarecrow or grotesque puppet, from which latter meaning derives the mop called a *malkin*, used especially for cleaning a baker's oven.

The name was also sometimes given to the Queen of the May (*see* MAID MARIAN).

Mall, The. A broad thoroughfare in St. James's Park, London, so called because the game of PALL-MALL used to be played there by Charles II and his courtiers. The *mall* was the mallet with which the ball was struck.

Malmsey (mam' zi or malm' zi). A strong, sweet wine from Greece, Spain, etc.; originally the wine of Malvasia (Gr. Monemvasia), in the Morea, which is the same name as *Malvoisie*.

George, Duke of Clarence, son of Richard, Duke of York, was, according to a London chronicle, put to death in the TOWER in 1478 by being drowned in a butt of malmsey by order of his brother, Edward IV. It is more likely that he was drowned in a bath.

Malta. *See* GEORGE CROSS ISLAND.

Knights of Malta, or **Hospitallers of St. John of Jerusalem.** *See* HOSPITALLERS.

Maltese Cross. Made thus: ✠. Originally the badge of the Knights of Malta, formed of four barbed arrow-heads with their points meeting in the centre. In various forms it is the badge of many well-known Orders, etc., as the British VICTORIA CROSS and Order of MERIT, and the German Iron Cross. *See* CROSS.

Malthusian Doctrine. The idea that population tends to outrun the means of subsistence put forward by the Rev. T.R. Malthus (1766–1834) in his *Essay* *on Population* (1798). It was not novel, but his systematic exposition drew attention to the population problem.

Malum. Malum in se (Lat.). What of itself is wrong, and would be even if no law existed against its commission, as lying, murder, theft.

Malum prohibitum (Lat.). What is wrong merely because it is forbidden, as eating a particular fruit was wrong in ADAM and EVE, because they were commanded not to do so.

Mambrino. A pagan king of old romance, introduced by Ariosto into ORLANDO FURIOSO. He had a helmet of pure gold which made the wearer invulnerable, and was taken possession of by RINALDO. This is frequently referred to in DON QUIXOTE, and we read that when the barber was caught in a shower, and clapped his brazen basin on his head, Don Quixote insisted that this was the enchanted helmet of the Moorish king.

Mamelukes (Arab. *mamluc*, a slave). The slaves brought from the Caucasus and Asia Minor to Egypt and formed into a bodyguard for the SULTAN, a descendant of SALADIN. In 1250 they set up one of their number as Sultan and the Mamelukes reigned until overthrown by the Turkish Sultan Selim I in 1517. The country was subsequently governed by twenty-four Mameluke beys under the PASHA but they retained virtual control. In 1811 they were exterminated by Mohammed Ali.

Mammet, or **Maumet.** An idol; hence a puppet, or doll (as in Shakespeare's *Romeo and Juliet*, III, v, and *Henry IV, Pt. I*, II, iii). The word is a corruption of *Mahomet*, hence to Christians it became a generic word to designate any false faith; even idolatry is called *mammetry*.

Mammon. The god of this world. The word in Syriac means riches, and it occurs in the BIBLE (*Matt.* vi, 24; *Luke* xvi, 13): "Ye cannot serve God and mammon." Spenser (*Faerie Queene*, II, vii), and Milton, who identifies him with VULCAN or MULCIBER (*Paradise Lost*, I, 738–51), both make Mammon the personification of the evils of wealth and miserliness.

Mammoth Cave. In Edmonson county,

Kentucky; the largest known in the world, reputedly discovered in 1809, but known earlier. It comprises many chambers with connecting passages said to total 150 miles, and covers an area of nearly 10 miles in diameter. Rivers, streams, and lakes, add to the majesty and scenic variety of this vast limestone cave.

Man. Man in the Moon, Man of Blood, Brass, December, Sin, Straw. etc. *See these words.*

Man about town. A fashionable idler.

Man Friday. *See under* FRIDAY.

The Man in the Street. The ordinary citizen, the man or woman who in the aggregate makes public opinion.

The Man of Destiny. NAPOLEON I (1769–1821). He regarded himself as an instrument in the hands of destiny.

Man of letters. An author, a literary scholar.

Man of Ross. *See* ROSS.

Man of Sorrows. Jesus Christ, from the prophecy in *Isaiah* liii, 3 that the MESSIAH would be "a man of sorrows, and acquainted with grief".

Man of the world. One versed in the ways of the world; no GREENHORN. Henry Mackenzie brought out a novel (1773) with this title and Charles Macklin a comedy (1871).

Man-of-war. A warship. Like other ships, a man-of-war is always referred to as "she". Formerly the term denoted a fighting man ("the Lord is a man of war", *Exod.* xv. 3).

The popular name of the marine hydrozoan, *Physalia pelagica*, is the *Portuguese man-of-war*, or simply, *man-of-war*.

The man on the Clapham omnibus. In legal parlance, "the reasonable man". Possibly the phrase was first used by Sir Charles Bowen, Q.C. (later Lord Bowen), who was junior council against the claimant in the TICHBORNE CASE (1871–4).

Man to man. Frankly, as one man to another; in a manly fashion, as when two individuals fight "man to man".

The man who broke the bank at Monte Carlo. Joseph Hobson Jagger, who, in 1886, won over 2,000,000 francs in 8 days. An expert on spindles, he suspected one of the roulette wheels of a faulty spindle and had it watched for a week. Thereafter he staked on the numbers which were turning up with much more than mathematical probability and won a fortune. He died in 1892, probably mainly from boredom. His exploit became the subject of the famous Victorian MUSIC HALL ballad in the repertoire of the inimitable Charles Coborn, written and composed by Fred Gilbert.

The New Man. The regenerated man. In scripture phrase the unregenerated state is called *the old man*.

The Threefold Man. According to Diogenes Laertius, the body was composed of (1) a mortal part; (2) a divine and ethereal part called the *phren*; (3) an ethereal and vaporous part, called the *thumos*.

According to the Romans, man has a threefold soul, which at the dissolution of the body resolves itself into (1) the MANES; (2) the *Anima* or *Spirit*; (3) the *Umbra*. The Manes went either to ELYSIUM or TARTARUS; the Anima returned to the gods; but the umbra hovered about the body as unwilling to quit it.

According to the Jews, man consists of body, SOUL and spirit.

To a man. Without exception, all together, everyone, unanimously, as, "The audience applauded to a man."

To be one's own man again. To fully recover good health after illness, shock, etc.

Man proposes but God disposes. So we read in the *Imitatio Christi* (*Homo proponit, sed Deus disponit*, I, xix, 2). Herbert (*Jacula Prudentum*) has nearly the same words; as also has Montluc: *L'homme propose et Dieu dispose* (*Comédie de Proverbes*, iii, 7); and there are others.

Man, Isle of. One explanation of the name is that given by Richard of Cirencester—"Midway between the two countries [Britain and Ireland] is the island called Monœda, but now Monavia", *i.e.* that it is from *menagh* or *meanagh* meaning *middle*. Another is that it is from *Mannanan*, a wizard who kept the Land of *Mann* under mists when marauders threatened it.

Mañana (măn ya′ na) (Span., tomorrow). A word frequently used to imply some vague unspecified future date.

Mancha, La. *See* LA MANCHA.

Manchester. The name is formed from the old British *Mamucion* and *ceaster*, O.E. form of Lat. *castra*, denoting that it was once a Roman walled town. A native of Manchester is a *Mancunian*, from *Mancunium*, the mediæval Latin name of the city. *See* COTTONOPOLIS.

Manchester Martyrs. The name given to the three Irishmen who were hanged for attempting to rescue two FENIAN prisoners in Manchester (November 1867). In the course of the struggle a policeman was killed.

The Manchester School. A term applied to a group of RADICALS and free traders originating from business men of the Manchester Chamber of Commerce and sponsors of the Anti-Corn Law League. They were supporters of LAISSEZ-FAIRE and against the growth of the colonial empire. Led by Cobden and Bright, they were derisively so called by Disraeli in 1848, and the name came to be applied to Victorian advocates of FREE TRADE and a pacific foreign policy generally.

Mancus. An Anglo-Saxon coin in both gold and silver. In the reign of Ethelbert of Kent, money accounts were kept in pounds, mancuses, shillings, and pence. Five pence = one shilling; 30 pence = one mancus.

Mandæans. A GNOSTIC sect, also called *Nasoreans* and *Christians of St. John* which arose in the 1st or 2nd century and still found near Baghdad. Their teachings were akin to those of the MANICHÆANS, and St. JOHN THE BAPTIST featured prominently in their writings. They favoured frequent baptism.

Mandamus (Lat., we command). A writ of QUEEN'S BENCH, commanding the person or corporation, etc., named to do what the writ directs. So called from the opening word.

Mandarin. A name given by the Portuguese to the official called by the Chinese *Kuan*. It is from the Malay and Hindu *mantri*, a counsellor, or minister of state. The word is sometimes used derisively for over-pompous officials, as,

"The mandarins of our Foreign Office."

The nine ranks of mandarins were distinguished by the button in the cap: (1) ruby, (2) coral, (3) sapphire, (4) an opaque blue stone, (5) crystal, (6) an opaque white shell, (7) wrought gold, (8) plain gold, (9) silver.

Mandeville, Sir John (or **Jehan De**). The name assumed by the compiler of a famous and influential 14th-century book of travels, originally written in French. The author claimed to have been born at St. Albans and from 1322 to have travelled through Turkey, Armenia, Tartary, Persia, Syria, Arabia, Egypt, Libya, Ethiopia, Amazonia, India, to have visited Prestor John and served under the Emperor of China. The work contains many stories of fabulous monsters and legends, but was essentially derived from the writings of others, especially such noted mediæval travellers as Friar Odoric and John de Plano Carpini. The book was probably the work of a Liège physician, Jean de Bourgogne or Jehan à la Barbe. An English version had appeared by the beginning of the 15th century. *Cp.* MÜNCHAUSEN.

Mandrake. The root of the mandrake, or mandragora, often divides in two, presenting a rough appearance of a man. In ancient times human figures were cut out of the root and wonderful virtues ascribed to them, such as the production of fecundity in women (*Gen.* xxx, 14–16). They could not be uprooted without supposedly producing fatal effects, so a cord used to be fixed to the root and round a dog's neck, and the dog when chased drew out the mandrake and died. A small dose was held to produce vanity in one's appearance, and a large dose, idiocy. The mandrake screamed when uprooted.

Of this latter property Thomas Newton, in his *Herball to the Bible*, says, "It is supposed to be a creature having life, engendered under the earth of the seed of some dead person put to death for murder."

> Shrieks like mandrakes, torn out of the earth.
> SHAKESPEARE: *Romeo and Juliet*, IV, iii.

He has eaten mandrake. Said of a very indolent and sleepy man, from the narcotic and stupefying properties of the plant, well-known to the ancients.

Mandrakes called love-apples. From the old notion that they were aphrodisiacs. Hence VENUS is called *Mandragoritis*, and the Emperor Julian, in his epistles, tells Calixenes that he drank its juice nightly as a love-potion.

Manes (mā' nēz). **To appease his Manes.** To do when a person is dead what would have pleased him or was due to him when alive. The spirit or ghost of the dead was called by the Romans his *Manes*, which never slept quietly in the grave while survivors left its wishes unfulfilled. 19 February was the day when all the living sacrificed to the shades of dead relations and friends—a kind of pagan ALL SOULS' DAY.

Mangi. The name used by Marco Polo for southern China. *Cp.* CATHAY.

Mani (ma' nē). The MOON. In Scandinavian mythology, the beautiful boy driver of the moon-car, the son of Mundilfœri. He is followed by a wolf, which, when time shall be no more, will devour both Mani and his sister SOL.

Mani, Manes, or **Manichæus.** The founder of MANICHÆISM, born in Persia (*c.* 215) and prominent in the reign of Shapur or Sapor I (*c.* 241–272). Mani began his teaching *c.* 240 and was put to death in 275.

Manichæans, or **Manichees.** Followers of Mani, who taught that the universe is controlled by two antagonistic powers, light or goodness (identified with God), and darkness, chaos, or evil. The system was based on the old Babylonian religion modified by Christian and Persian influences. St. AUGUSTINE was for nine years a Manichæan and Manichæism influenced many Christian heretical sects and was itself denounced as a heresy. One of Mani's claims was that, though Christ had been sent into the world to restore it to light and banish darkness, His APOSTLES had perverted his doctrine, and he, Mani, was sent as the PARACLETE to restore it. Manichæism survived in Turkestan until the 13th century.

Manitou (măn' i too). The Great Spirit of

certain American Indians, either the Great Good Spirit or the Great Evil Spirit. The word is Algonkian, meaning mystery, supernatural.

Manna. The miraculous food provided for the children of Israel on their journey from Egypt to the HOLY LAND.

> And when the children of Israel saw it, they said to one another, It is manna: for they wist not what it was. And Moses said unto them, This is the bread which the Lord hath given you to eat.
> *Exod.* xvi. 15.

The word is popularly said to be a corrupt form of *man-hu* (What is this?) but is probably Heb. *man*, a gift, and ultimately the Arab. *mann*, an exudation of the tamarisk.

> And the house of Israel called the name thereof Manna: and it was like coriander seed, white; and the taste of it was like wafers made with honey.
> *Exod.* xvi, 31.

Manoa. The fabulous capital of EL DORADO, the houses of which city were said to be roofed with gold. There was numerous attempts by Sir Thomas Roe, Ralegh and others to locate it during the reigns of Elizabeth I and James I.

Manor (O.Fr. *manoir*, from Lat. *manere*, to remain). A word introduced after the Norman Conquest and used of a dwelling of a man of substance, but not necessarily a large holding. It ultimately came to denote the self-contained estate in which the *demesne* (domain) land was worked for the lord's private benefit, the remainder being worked by free and unfree tenants (VILLEINS) who were subject to the COURT-BARON. *Cp.* MANSION; *See also* BOON WORK; COMMON; OPEN FIELD SYSTEM; WEEK-WORK.

Lord of the Manor. The person or corporation in whom the rights of a manor are vested.

Mansfield. The King and the Miller of Mansfield. This old ballad, given in PERCY'S RELIQUES, tells how Henry II, having lost his way, met a miller, who took him home to his cottage. Next morning the courtiers tracked the king, and the miller discovered the rank of his guest, who in merry mood knighted his host as "Sir John Cockle". On St. GEORGE's Day, Henry II invited the miller, his wife and son to a royal banquet, and after being amused with their rustic ways, made Sir John overseer of Sherwood Forest, with a salary of £300 a year.

Manticore (Pers. *mardkhora*, man-eater). A fabulous beast usually given as having the head of a man, the body of a lion, a porcupine's quills and the tail of a scorpion. It is mentioned by Ctesias, a Greek living in the late 5th and early 4th centuries B.C., who wrote a history of Persia. It features in mediæval BESTIARIES and also in HERALDRY where it generally has horns and the tail and feet of a DRAGON. Martinus SCRIBLERUS says that it was "the most noxious animal that ever infested the earth".

Mantle. The Mantle of Elijah. A symbol of authority or leadership; when someone succeeds to the established authority of a predecessor, he is said to assume "the mantle of Elijah". Elijah the prophet cast his mantle upon Elisha to show he was his chosen successor (I *Kings* xix, 19).

Mantle of Fidelity. The old ballad *The Boy and the Mantle* in PERCY'S RELIQUES tells how a little boy showed King ARTHUR a curious mantle which should become no wife "that hath once done amisse". Queen GUINEVERE tried it, but it changed from green to red, and red to black, and seemed rent into shreds. Sir KAY'S lady tried it, but fared no better; others followed, but only Sir Cradock's wife could wear it. The theme is a very common one in old story and was used by Spenser in the incident of Florimel's girdle. *Cp.* BRAWN.

Mantuan Swan, *or* **Bard.** VIRGIL.

Manu. In Hindu philosophy, one of a class of DEMIURGES of whom the first is identified with BRAHMA. Brahma divided himself into male and female, these produced *Viraj*, from whom sprang the first *Manu*, a kind of secondary creator. He gave rise to ten *Prajapatis* ("lords of all living"); from these came seven *Manus*, each of these presiding over a certain period, the seventh of these being *Manu Vaivasvata* ("the sun-born") who is now reigning and who is looked upon as the creator of the living races of beings. To him are ascribed the *Laws of Manu*, now called

Manavadharmashastra, a section of the VEDAS containing a code of civil and religious law compiled by the Manavans. *See* DELUGE.

Manual seal. A signet. *See* SIGN.

Manumit (măn′ ū mit). To set free; properly "to send from one's hand" (Lat. *e manu mittere*). One of the Roman ways of freeing a slave was to take him before the chief magistrate and say, "I wish this man to be free." The LICTOR or master then turned the slave round in a circle, struck him with a rod across the cheek and let him go. The ancient ceremony has a relic in the Roman Catholic rite of Confirmation when the BISHOP strikes the candidate lightly on the cheek, saying, "Peace be with you."

Manure (O.Fr. *manoverer*). Literally "handwork", hence tillage by manual labour, hence the dressing applied to land. Milton uses the word in its original sense in *Paradise Lost*, IV, 628:

> You flowery arbours...with branches overgrown
> That mock our scant manuring.

And in XI, 28, says that the repentant tears of ADAM brought forth better fruits than all the trees of PARADISE that his hands "manured" in the days of innocence.

Manx Cat. A tailless species of cat found in the Isle of MAN where it is popularly known as a *rumpee*. It was a practice to dock other cats in order to sell them to visitors as Manx cats. *See also* MODDEY DHOO.

Manxland (old Irish, *manu*). The Isle of Man.

Many a little makes a mickle. *See under* LITTLE.

Many men, many minds, *i.e.* there are as many opinions as there are men, as Terence says, *Quot homines tot sententiæ* (*Phormio*, II, iv, 14).

Too many for me, or **One too many for me.** More than a match. *Il est trop fort pour moi.*

Maquis (ma′ kē). The thick scrubland in Corsica and Mediterranean coastal lands to which bandits retreat to avoid capture.

In World War II French patriots, who formed guerilla groups in the countryside during the German occupation (1940– 1945), attacking their patrols, depots, etc., were known as *the Maquis*. *See* F.F.I.

Marabou. A large stork or heron of western Africa, from Arab. *murabit*, a hermit, because among the Arabs these birds were held sacred.

Marabouts. A priestly order of Morocco (Arab. *murabit*, a hermit) which in 1075 founded a dynasty and ruled over Morocco and part of Spain till it was put an end to by the Almohads in the 12th century.

Marais, Le. *See* PLAIN.

Maranatha (Syriac, the Lord will come—*i.e.* to execute judgement). A word which, with ANATHEMA, occurs in I *Cor.* xvi, 22, and has been erroneously taken as a form of anathematizing among the Jews; hence used for a terrible curse.

Marathon Race. A long-distance race, named after the battle of Marathon (490 B.C.), the result of which was announced at ATHENS by an unnamed courier who fell dead on his arrival, having run nearly 23 miles. This runner is sometimes cited as Pheidippides (or Philippides), who actually ran from ATHENS to Sparta to seek help against the Persians before the battle. In the modern OLYMPIC GAMES, the Marathon race was instituted in 1896, the distance being standardized at 26 miles 385 yards in 1924.

Maravedi (Span., ultimately from Arab. *Murabitin*, the name of a Moorish dynasty of Spain in the 11th and 12th centuries). Originally (11th century) a gold coin, later (16th–19th century) a very small Spanish copper coin worth less than a farthing.

Not worth a maravedi. Worthless.

Marbles. *See* ARUNDELIAN; ELGIN.

March[1]. The Month is so called from MARS.

The old Dutch name for it was *Lentmaand* (*see* LENT); the old Saxon name was *Hreth-monath* (rough-month, from its boisterous winds), subsequently changed to *Length-monath* (lengthening month); it was also called *Hlyd-monath* (boisterous month). In the French Republication CALENDAR it was called *Ventôse* (windy month, 20 February to 20 March).

A bushel of March dust is worth a king's ransom. Because we want plenty of dry windy weather in March for good tillage, it is worth much.

Mad as a March hare. *See under* HARE.

March borrowed three days from April. *See* BORROWED DAYS.

March comes in like a lion and goes out like a lamb. March begins with rough, boisterous weather and ends calmly.

March². **He may be a rogue, but he's no fool on the march.** Though his honesty may be in question he is a useful sort of person to have about.

To steal a march on one. *See* STEAL.

Marches. The O.E. *mearc*, a mark, border; O.Fr. *marche*, a frontier. The boundaries between ENGLAND and WALES, and England and SCOTLAND, were called *marches*. Hence *Marcher lords*, the powerful vassals with special rights who guarded the Welsh Marches at Hereford, Shrewsbury and Chester. The title *Earl of March* held by certain great feudal families is similarly derived. *Cp.* MARQUESS.

The word is still applied in the sense that a boundary is shared, *e.g.* Kent *marches* with Sussex, that is, the two counties are contiguous.

A territorial and historic division of Italy is called the *Marches*, which include Pesaro and Urbino, Ancona, Macerata, and Ascoli Piceno.

Riding the marches. In SCOTLAND, beating the BOUNDS of the parish.

Marchington (Staffordshire). Famous for a crumbling shortcake. Hence the saying that one of crusty temper is "as short as Marchington wake-cake".

Marchpane. The old name for the confection of almonds, sugar, etc., that we call *marzipan*, this being the German form of the original Ital. *marzapane*, which was adopted in the 19th century in preference to our well-established word because this confection was largely imported from Germany.

> *First Serv.* Away with the joint-stools, remove the court-cupboard, look to the plate. Good thou, save me a piece of marchpane.
> SHAKESPEARE: *Romeo and Juliet*, I, v.

Marcionites. An heretical sect founded by Marcion of Sinope in the 2nd century, and largely absorbed by the MANICHÆANS in the late 3rd century. They rejected the God of DEMI-URGE of the OLD TESTAMENT as a God of Law, and worshipped only Jesus Christ as the God of Love, whose mission was to overthrow the Demi-urge. Much of the NEW TESTAMENT was regarded by them as uncanonical and they had a certain kinship with Gnosticism (*see under* GNOSTICS).

Marcley Hill. Legend states that this hill in Herefordshire, at six o'clock in the evening on 7 February 1571, "roused itself with a roar, and by seven next morning had moved 40 paces". It kept on the move for three days, carrying all with it. It overthrew Kinnaston chapel and diverted two high roads at least 200 yards from their former route. Twenty-six acres of land are said to have been moved 400 yards (Speed: *Herefordshire*).

Mardi Gras (mar dē grái) (Fr., "fat Tuesday"). SHROVE TUESDAY, the last day of the LENT Carnival in France. At Paris, a fat ox, crowned with a fillet, used to be paraded through the streets. It was accompanied by mock priests and a band of tin instruments in imitation of a Roman sacrificial procession.

Marduk. The Babylonian god of HEAVEN and earth, light and life, and god of battle. He was identified with numerous other Babylonian dieties. *See* BEL.

Mare. Away with the mare. Off with the blue devils, goodbye to care. This mare is the INCUBUS, called the *nightmare*.

The grey mare is the better horse. The woman is paramount, "she wears the trousers"; said of a wife who "bosses" her husband.

Money will make the mare go. You can do anything if only you have the money.

Shanks's mare. One's legs or SHANKS.

The two-legged mare. The gallows.

To find a mare's nest is to make what you suppose to be a great discovery, but which proves to be no discovery or else all MOONSHINE. In some parts of SCOTLAND the expression is a *skate's nest*; in

CORNWALL, *you have found a wee's nest and are laughing over the eggs*; in Devon, nonsense is called *a blind mare's nest*.

To win the mare or lose the halter. To play DOUBLE OR QUITS; all or nothing.

Whose mare's dead? What's the matter?

Mare (mar' i). The Latin word for *sea*. *Mare Clausum* is a closed sea or one that is closed by a certain power or powers to the unrestricted passage of foreign shipping. *Mare liberum* is the free and open sea. In 1635 John Selden (1584–1654) published a treatise called *Mare Clausum*.

FASCIST Italy called the Mediterranean *Mare Nostrum*, "our sea", in their expansionist heyday.

Marforio. *See* PASQUINADE.

Margaret. St. Margaret. Virgin martyr of the 3rd century, known as St. Marina among the Greeks. It is said that Olybrius, governor of Antioch, captivated by her beauty, sought her in marriage but, being rejected, threw her into a dungeon, where the DEVIL came to her in the form of a DRAGON. She held up the cross and the dragon fled. Sometimes she is delineated as coming from the dragon's mouth, for one legend says that the monster swallowed her, but on her making the sign of the cross he suffered her to quit his maw.

She is the chosen type of female innocence and meekness, represented as a young woman of great beauty, bearing the martyr's palm and crown, or with the dragon as an attribute, sometimes standing upon it. She is the patron saint of the ancient borough of King's Lynn.

St. Margaret of Scotland (*c.* 1045–1093). The wife of Malcolm III of SCOTLAND and granddaughter of Edmund Ironside, King of England. She was noted for her services to the Church in Scotland and for her learning, piety and religious benefactions. She was canonized in 1250 and died on 16 November, which is her feast day.

Margin. In many old books a commentary was printed in the margin (as in the BIBLE); hence the word was often used for a commentary itself, as in

Shakespeare's—

His face's own margent did quote such amazes.

Love's Labour's Lost, II, i.

I knew you must be edified by the margent.

Hamlet, V, ii.

Mari Lwyd (ma ri loo ed). *Singing with Mari Lwyd* (Holy Mary) is an old Welsh Christmastide custom still surviving at Llangynwyd, Glamorganshire, and may have derived from the old miracle plays (*see* MYSTERIES). The chief character wears a white cowl and a horse's skull bedecked with ribbons and is accompanied by two or three fantastically dressed followers. They sing outside houses, demanding an entrance. This is, at first, refused until the callers give evidence of their worth in song and repartee. They are then made welcome and suitably refreshed or recompensed.

Maria Marten. *See* RED BARN.

Mariage de convenance (Fr., marriage of expediency). A marriage for money and position. *Cp.* KNOBSTICK; SHOTGUN WEDDING.

Marian Year. The method of reckoning 25 March, the Feast of the ANNUNCIATION, as the first day of the year. This was used until the reform of the CALENDAR in 1752. The beginning of the financial year follows this reckoning; the eleven days added in 1752 make it 5 April.

Marie Celeste. Properly MARY CELESTE.

Marigold. The plant *Calendula officinalis* with its bright yellow or orange flowers is so called in honour of the Virgin Mary.

In 17th-century slang a marigold (or "marygold") meant a SOVEREIGN.

Marine. A "Sea-soldier". In the Royal Navy.

Empty bottles were at one time called "marines" (because the seamen regarded them as useless) but now, more usually, *dead marines*, or, in the U.S.A., *dead soldiers*.

According to the story, the Duke of York, when dining in the mess, said to the servant, "Here, take away these marines." A marine officer present asked for an explanation, and the duke replied, "They have done their duty, and are prepared to do it again."

A GREENHORN or land-lubber afloat is sometimes contemptuously called "a marine" by seamen.

Tell that to the Marines. Said of a far-fetched yarn. The story is that Pepys, when re-telling stories gathered from the Navy to Charles II, mentioned flying fish. The courtiers were sceptical, but an officer of the Maritime Regiment of Foot said that he too had seen such. The king accepted this evidence and said, "From the very nature of their calling no class of our subjects can have so wide a knowledge of seas and lands as the officer and men of Our Loyal Maritime Regiment. Henceforward ere ever we cast doubts upon a table that lacks likelihood we will first 'Tell it to the Marines'." *Cp.* HORSE MARINES *under* HORSE.

Mariner's Compass. China traditionally claims the invention of the compass in 2634 B.C. but the earliest authentic reference to the LODESTONE is in A.D. 121, and not until the 12th century is there mention of a compass in a ship. Claims for its discovery have also been made for the Arabs, Greeks, Italians, etc., but it may have arrived independently in both Europe and China. The belief that Marco Polo introduced it from China in 1260 is unfounded, as it was in use in Europe a century before this. *See* FLEUR-DE-LIS.

Marinism. Excessive literary ornateness and affection. So named from Giambattista Marini (1569–1625), the Neapolitan poet, famous for his whimsical comparisons and pompous and overwrought descriptions.

Marjoram. As a pig loves marjoram. Not at all. "How did you like it?" "Well, as a pig loves marjoram." Lucretius tells us (VI, 974), *Amaricinum fugitat sus*, swine shun marjoram.

Mark. Government equipment of various kinds issued to the armed services in the original form is labelled Mark I. Subsequent modifications of the same are labelled Mark II, Mark III, etc.

A man of mark. A notable or famous man; one who has "made his mark" in some walk of life.

Beside the mark. Not to the point; a phrase from archery, in which the mark was the target.

God bless, or **save the mark!** A kind of apology for introducing a disagreeable subject. Hotspur, apologizing to the king for not sending the prisoners according to command (SHAKESPEARE: *Henry IV, Pt. I*, I, iii), says the messenger was a "popinjay", who made him mad with his unmanly ways, and who talked

> So like a waiting-gentlewoman
> Of guns and drums and wounds,—God save the mark!

Sometimes the phrase is used to avert ill fortune or an evil omen, as in *Merchant of Venice* (II, ii):

> To be ruled by my conscience, I should stay with the Jew my master, who God bless the mark! is a kind of devil.

It is suggested that the "mark" is possibly the sign of the cross and the phrase a kind of supplication.

The mark of the beast. To set the "mark of the beast" on an object of pursuit (such as dancing, gambling, drinking, etc.) is to denounce it as an EVIL. The allusion is to Rev. xvi, 2; xix, 20.

The coloured flashes worn on the lapels of a midshipman's jacket are jocularly known as "marks of the beast".

Mark time. Raising the feet alternately as in marching, but without advancing or retreating. Also, to keep things going whilst awaiting for something to happen or for an opportunity.

Near the mark. Nearly correct, fairly close to the truth; a phrase derived from archery.

To make one's mark. To distinguish oneself, to achieve note.

It is an ancient practice for persons who cannot write to "make their mark". In old documents, the mark was the sign of the CROSS, which was followed by the name of the person concerned.

To toe the mark. To line up abreast of the others; so, to "fall in" and do one's duty.

Up to the mark. Generally used in the negative as "Not quite up to the mark", not good enough, not quite well; not up to the standard fixed by the ASSAY office for gold and silver articles.

Marks of gold and silver. *See* HALL MARK.

Mark, *as a name.*

King Mark. In ARTHURIAN ROMANCE, a king of Cornwall, Sir TRISTRAM'S uncle. He lived at TINTAGEL, and is principally remembered for his treachery and cowardice, and as the husband of YSOLDE the Fair, who was passionately enamoured of Tristram.

Mark Twain. The pseudonym of the American novelist and humorist Samuel L. Clemens (1835–1910), who adopted it from the Mississippi river pilots' cry, "Mark twain!" when taking soundings.

St. Mark. The GOSPEL writer who died in prison *c.* 68 is represented in art as in the prime of life, sometimes habited as a BISHOP, and with a lion at his feet and scroll on which is written, "Peace be to thee, O Mark, My Evangelist." He is also represented with a pen in his right hand and in his left the Gospel. His day is 25 April.

St. Mark's Eve. An old custom in North-country villages was for people to sit in the church porch on this day (24 April) from 11 p.m. till 1 a.m. for three years running, in order to see on the third year the ghosts of those who were to die that year, pass into the church. In other parts this custom was observed on MIDSUMMER-eve.

Poor Robin's Almanack for 1770 refers to another superstition:

> On St. Mark's Eve, at twelve o'clock,
> The fair maid will watch her smock,
> To find her husband in the dark,
> By praying unto good St. Mark.

Market-penny. A toll surreptitiously exacted by servants sent out to buy goods for their master; secret commission on goods obtained for an employer.

Maro. VIRGIL.

Marocco, or **Morocco.** The name of BANKS'S HORSE.

Maronites. A UNIAT body, mainly in the Lebanon, in communion with ROME and having their own liturgy. Although probably of 7th century origin, according to tradition, they arose in the early 5th century as followers of Maro, an anchorite living near Antioch. They became MONOTHELITES, but recognized Rome's authority in the 12th century.

Marplot. An officious person who defeats some design by gratuitous meddling. The name is given to a silly, cowardly, inquisitive Paul PRY, in *The Busybody* (1709), by Mrs. Centlivre. Similarly we have SHAKESPEARE'S "Sir Oliver Martext", the clergyman in *As You Like It*, and "Sir Martin Mar-All", the hero of Dryden and the Duke of Newcastle's comedy of that name, which was based on MOLIÈRE'S *L'Etourdi*.

Marprelate Controversy. The name given to the vituperative pamphlet war between the PURITAN writer "Martin Marprelate" and the supporters of the established Church. The Marprelate Tracts (1587–1589) were scurrilous attacks on the BISHOPS, secretly printed and distributed. They threatened to establish a "young Martin" in every parish "to mar a prelate". The Church commissioned John Lyly, Thomas Nashe and Robert Greene to launch a counter-attack. The tracts led to a Conventicle Act and another against seditious writings and the presumed chief author, John Penry, was caught and hanged in 1593.

Marque. *See under* LETTER.

Marquess, or Marquis (O.Fr. *marchis*, warden of the marches). A title of nobility in England below that of DUKE. It was first conferred on Richard II's favourite, Robert de Vere, Earl of Oxford, who was created Marquess of Dublin in 1385. A marquess is addressed as "The Most Honourable the Marquess of—". *See* COURTESY TITLE; COUSIN; MARCH.

Marriage. The Marriage knot. The bond of marriage effected by the legal marriage ceremony. The Latin phrase is *nodus Herculeus*, and part of the marriage service was for the bridegroom to loosen (*solvere*) the bride's girdle, not to tie it. In the Hindu marriage ceremony the bridegroom knots a ribbon round the bride's neck. Before the knot is tied the bride's father may refuse consent, but immediately it is tied the marriage is indissoluble. The PARSEES bind the hands of the bridegroom with a sevenfold cord, seven being a sacred number. The ancient Carthaginians tied the thumbs of the betrothed with a leather lace. *See* RICE.

Close seasons for marriage. These were of old, from ADVENT to St. Hilary's Day (13 January); SEPTUAGESIMA to

LOW SUNDAY; ROGATION SUNDAY to TRINITY SUNDAY. They continued to be upheld in the English Church after the REFORMATION, but lapsed during the COMMONWEALTH.

The ROMAN CATHOLIC CHURCH does not allow nuptial MASS during what is left of the "close season", *i.e.* between the first Sunday of Advent and the Octave of the EPIPHANY, and from ASH WEDNESDAY to Low Sunday.

Marriages are made in Heaven. This implies that partners joined in marriage were foreordained to be so united. E. Hall (*c.* 1499–1547) says, "Consider the old proverbe to be true that saieth: Marriage is destinie." *Cp.* HANGING AND WIVING, etc. *under* HANG.

Down on your marrow-bones! Down on your knees! A good-humoured way of telling a person he had better beg pardon.

Marrow Controversy. A controversy in the CHURCH OF SCOTLAND arising from the General Assembly's condemnation in 1720 of *The Marrow of Modern Divinity*, a book by "E.F." which first appeared in 1645 and which was considered to uphold ANTINOMIAN doctrines and too free in its offer of salvation. Who "E.F." was is not known.

Marry! An oath, meaning by Mary, the Virgin.

Marry come up! An exclamation of surprise, disapproval or incredulity, etc. May Mary come up to my assistance, or to your discomfort!

Mars. The Roman god of war; identified in certain aspects with the Greek ARES. He was also the patron of husbandmen.

The PLANET of this name was early so called because of its reddish tinge, and under it, says the *Compost of Ptholomeus*, "is borne theves and robbers...nyght walkers and quarell pykers, bosters, mockers, and skoffers; and these men of Mars causeth warre, and murther, and batayle. They wyll be gladly smythes or workers of yron...lyers, gret swerers."

Among the alchemists *Mars* designated iron, and in Camoëns' LUSIADS typified divine fortitude. *See also* MARTIANS.

Marseillaise (Eng. mar se lāz'; Fr. mar sā yāz'). The hymn of the French Revolution and the national anthem of France. The words and music were written by Claude Rouget de Lisle (1760–1835), an artillery officer in the garrison at Strasbourg in 1792. It was first made known in Paris by troops from Marseilles, hence the name. *Cp.* CHANT DU DÉPART.

Marshall Plan. The popular name for the European Recovery Programme sponsored by U.S. Secretary of State G.C. Marshall, to bring economic aid to stricken Europe after World War II. It was inaugurated in June 1947. Most states other than Russia and her satellites participated. Britain ceased to receive Marshall Aid in 1950. *Cp.* LEND-LEASE.

Marshalsea Prison. An old prison in High Street, SOUTHWARK, the prison of the *Marshalsea Court*, which was originally a court of the HOUSEHOLD presided over by the *Earl Marshal*. The Court, with the *Knight-Marshal* for judge, existed until December 1849. From the 1430s, the prison also received admiralty prisoners and debtors. It moved to newer premises in 1799 and was closed in 1842. In 1381, its marshal was beheaded by the rebels under Wat Tyler; and Charles Dickens's father was imprisoned there in 1824.

> Necessarily, he was going out again directly, because the Marshalsea lock never turned upon a debtor who was not.
> DICKENS: *Little Dorrit*, ch. vi.

Marsyas (Mar' si ås). The Phrygian flute-player who challenged APOLLO to a contest of skill, and, being beaten by the god, was flayed alive for his presumption. From his blood arose the river so called. The flute on which Marsyas played had been discarded by MINERVA, and, being filled with the breath of the goddess, discoursed most beautiful music. The interpretation of this fable is as follows:

The DORIAN MODE, employed in the worship of Apollo, was performed on lutes; and the Phrygian mode, employed in the rites of CYBELE, was executed by flutes, the reeds of which grew on the river Marsyas. As the Dorian mode was preferred by the Greeks, they said that Apollo beat the flute-player.

Martel. The surname given to Charles (*c.* 688–741), son of Pippin II (MAYOR OF THE PALACE), probably because of his victory over the SARACENS, who had invaded France under Abd-el-Rahman in 732. It is said that Charles "knocked down the foe, and crushed them beneath his axe, as a martel or hammer crushes what it strikes."

Martello Towers. Round towers about 40 ft. high and of great strength. Many of them were built on the south-eastern coasts of England about 1803 against the threat of French invasion. They took their name from Mortella (Corsica), where a tower, from which these were designed, had proved extremely difficult to capture in 1794. *Cp.* PALMERSTON'S FOLLIES *under* FOLLY.

Mar-text. *See* MARPLOT.

Martha, St. Sister of St. LAZARUS and St. MARY MAGDALEN; patron saint of good housewives. She is represented in art in homely costume, bearing at her girdle a bunch of keys, and holding a ladle or pot of water in her hand. Like St. MARGARET she is accompanied by a DRAGON bound, for she is said to have destroyed one that ravaged the neighbourhood of Marseilles. She is commemorated on 29 July and is patron of Tarascon.

Martian Laws. Laws said to have been compiled by Martia, wife of King Guithelin of Brtain. According to Geoffrey of Monmouth (*Historia Britonum*) Martia was "a noble lady ... accomplished in all kinds of learning" and her work was translated into Saxon by King Alfred. *Cp.* MOLMUTINE LAWS.

Martians (mar′ shánz). The hypothetical inhabitants of the planet MARS, which has a much less dense atmosphere than the Earth. In 1898 H. G. Wells wrote *The War of the Worlds*, in which he recounted the adventures and horrors of a war between the men of Mars and the dwellers on Earth.

Martin. One of the swallow family; probably so called from the Christian name Martin (*see* St. MARTIN'S BIRD below), but possibly because it appears in ENGLAND about March (the *Martian* month) and disappears about MARTINMAS.

St. Martin (of Tours). The patron SAINT of innkeepers and reformed drunkards, usually shown in art as a young mounted soldier dividing his cloak with a beggar; in allusion to the legend that in midwinter, when a military tribune at Amiens, he divided his cloak with a naked beggar who sought alms and that at night Christ appeared to him arrayed in this very garment. This effected his conversion.

He was born of heathen parents in Pannonia but was converted at ROME and became Bishop of Tours in 371, dying at Candes *c.* 400. His day is 11 November, the day of the Feast of Bacchus; hence his purely accidental patronage and also the phrase MARTIN DRUNK.

St. Martin's goose. St. Martin's day (11 November) was at one time the great goose feast in France. The legend is that St. MARTIN was annoyed by a goose which he ordered to be killed and served up for dinner. Hence, the goose was "sacrificed" to him on each anniversary. *Cp.* GOOSE FAIR; MICHAELMAS DAY.

St. Martin of Bullions. The St. SWITHIN of SCOTLAND. His day is 4 July, and the saying is that if it rains then, rain may be expected for forty days.

St. Martin's summer. A late spell of fine weather. St. Martin's day is 11 November. *See* INDIAN SUMMER; SUMMER.

Martinmas. The feast of St. MARTIN, 11 November. **His Martinmas will come, as it does to every hog**—*i.e.* all must die. November was the great slaughtering time of the Anglo-Saxons when fodder was exhausted and oxen, sheep and hogs were killed and salted.

Martinet. A strict disciplinarian; so called from the Marquis de Martinet, colonel commanding Louis XIV's own regiment of infantry. The king required all young noblemen to command a platoon in this regiment before purchasing command of an infantry regiment. Martinet's system for training these wild young men in the principles of military discipline gained him lasting fame. He was slain at the siege of Duisburg in 1672.

Martyr (Gr.) simply means a witness, one who bears testimony; hence one who bears witness to his faith with his blood.

The Martyr King. CHARLES I of England, beheaded 30 January 1649.

Martyr to science. One who loses his health or life through his devotion to science.

Tolpuddle Martyrs. *See* TOLPUDDLE.

Marvedie. *See* MARAVEDI.

Marxism. The philosophical and political and economic theories or system propounded by Karl Marx (1818–1883) and Friedrich Engels (1820–1895) which form the basis of modern Communist dogma. It involves a materialist conception of history, a theory of class war, a belief in the ultimate destruction of capitalism and the formation of a classless society. *See* COMMUNISM; MATERIALISM.

Mary, the Mother of Christ, is represented in art as follows:

As *the Virgin*, with flowing hair, emblematical of her virginity.

As *Mater Dolorosa*. Somewhat elderly, clad in mourning, head draped, and weeping over the dead body of Christ.

As *Our Lady of Dolours*. Seated, her breast being pierced with seven swords, emblematic of her seven sorrows.

As *Our Lady of Mercy*. With arms extended, spreading out her mantle and gathering sinners beneath it.

As *The glorified Madonna*. Bearing a crown and sceptre, or an orb and CROSS, in rich robes and surrounded by angels.

Her seven joys. The ANNUNCIATION, VISITATION, NATIVITY, EPIPHANY, Finding in the Temple, Resurrection, Ascension.

Her seven sorrows. Simeon's Prophecy, the Flight into Egypt, the loss of the Holy Child, on meeting Our Lord on the way to CALVARY, the Crucifixion, the Taking Down from the CROSS, and the Entombment. Her festival is 8 September.

Bloody Mary. Queen Mary Tudor (1516, 1553–1558), for her persecution of PROTESTANTS. Some 300 suffered death, including Archbishop Cranmer. Also a COCKTAIL consisting of vodka and tomato juice.

Highland Mary. *See under* HIGHLANDS.

Little Mary. A euphemism for the stomach; from the play of that name by J. M. Barrie (1903).

The four Marys. The *Queen's Marys*, the companions of Mary Stewart, afterwards Queen of Scots. They were: Mary Beaton (or Bethune), Mary Livingstone (or Leuson), Mary Fleming (or Flemyng), and Mary Seaton (or Seyton). Mary Carmichael was not one of the four, although introduced in the well-known ballad.

> Yestre'en the queen had four Marys,
> This night she'll hae but three;
> There was Mary Beaton and Mary Seaton,
> Mary Carmichael, and me.

Mary Anne, or **Marianne**. A slang name for the guillotine, *see* MARY ANNE ASSOCIATIONS *below*.

Mary Anne Associations. Secret republican societies in France. The name was adopted by the Republican party because Ravaillac was moved to assassinate Henry IV in 1610 by his reading *De Rege et Regio Institutione* by *Mariana* (*see* LIVY OF SPAIN).

Mary of Arnhem. The name used by Helen Sensburg in her NAZI propaganda broadcasts to British troops in N.W. Europe, 1944–1945. Her melting voice made her programmes very popular with the British, but without the results for which she hoped.

Mary Celeste. A brigantine found abandoned, with sails set, between the Azores and Portugal on 5th December, 1872. The ship's one boat, sextant, chronometer, register and crew were missing and no trace of them was ever found. It remains one of the unsolved mysteries of the sea.

Mary Magdalene, St. Patron SAINT of penitents, being herself the model penitent of GOSPEL story. Her feast is 22 July. *See* MAGDALENE; MAUDLIN.

In art she is represented either as young and beautiful, with a profusion of hair, and holding a box of ointment, or as a penitent, in a sequestered place, reading before a CROSS or skull.

Marygold. *See* MARIGOLD.

Maryland (U.S.A.) was so named in compliment to Henrietta Maria, Queen of CHARLES I. In the Later charter it is called *Terra Mariæ*.

Masada. The great rock on the edge of the Judæan desert, the site of Herod the Great's palace, where the ZEALOTS made their last heroic stand against the Romans. When defeat was certain their leader Eleazar ben Ya'ir persuaded them to draw lots to select 10 men to kill the remaining 960 defenders. One of these finally slew his nine fellows and then pushed his sword through his own body. The story is told by JOSEPHUS. Among the relics revealed by Professor Yigael Yadin's excavation exhibited at London in 1966 were eleven small potsherds inscribed with names, on one of which was the name "ben Ya'ir". They are probably the lots in question. *See* LOT.

Masaniello (mäs ån yel'ō). A corruption of *Tommaso Aniello*, a fisherman's son who led the Neapolitan revolt of July 1647 and ruled Naples for nine days. He was finally betrayed and shot. His body was flung into a ditch but was reclaimed and interred with great pomp and ceremony. The discontent was caused by excessive taxation and Masaniello's immediate grievance was the seizure of his property because his wife had smuggled flour.

Auber's opera *La Muette de Portici* (1828) is based on these events.

Mascot. A person or thing that is supposed to bring good luck (*cp.* JETTATURA). The word is French slang (perhaps connected with Provençal *masco*, a sorcerer), and was popularized in England by Audran's opera, *La Mascotte* (1880).

> Ces envoyés du paradis
> Sont des Mascottes, mes amis,
> Heureux celui que le ciel dote d'une
>   Mascotte.

Masculine ending. The stress or accent falling on the final syllable of a line of verse. *Cp.* FEMININE ENDING.

> I must go down to the seas again, to the
>   lonely sea and the sky,
> And all I ask is a tall ship and a star to
>   steer her by.
>   MASEFIELD: *Sea Fever*, i.

Masochism. The name for the condition in which sexual gratification depends on the subject's self-humiliation and self-

inflicted pain; after Leopold von Sacher-Masoch (1836–1895), the Austrian novelist who described this aberration. *Cp.* SADISM.

Mason and Dixon Line. The southern boundary line which separated Pennsylvania from MARYLAND, fixed at 39° 43′ 26″ N., marked out (1763–1767) by two English surveyors, Charles Mason and Jeremiah Dixon. From about 1820 it was popularly used to signify the boundary between North and South, "free" and "slave" states.

Mass (Lat. *missa*, a dismissal). The EUCHARIST. In the early Church the unbaptized were dismissed before the Eucharist proper began and the remaining congregation were solemnly dismissed at the end. By the 8th century the name *missa* had become transferred to the service as a whole, and the original meaning of the word faded out. The name *Mass* is used by the ROMAN CATHOLIC CHURCH and by High Churchmen of the CHURCH OF ENGLAND.

High Mass, or *Missa solemnis*, in which the celebrant is assisted by a deacon and subdeacon, requires the presence of choir and acolytes. Sung Mass, or *Missa Cantata*, is a simplification in which the celebrant and congregation sing the musical parts of the service, but without the deacon and subdeacon. The plain form of Mass is called Low Mass. A Pontifical High Mass is one celebrated by a BISHOP or higher prelate with very full ritual. A Nuptial Mass follows the marriage service and Requiem Mass is one offered for the dead. There are also other special forms of Mass.

Massacre of the Innocents. The slaughter of the male children of Bethlehem "from two years old and under" when Jesus was born (*Matt*. ii, 16). This was done at the command of Herod the Great in order to destroy "the babe" who was destined to become "King of the Jews".

In parliamentary parlance, the phrase denotes the withdrawal at the close of the session of the bills which there has been no time to consider or pass.

Mast. To serve before the mast. To serve as a common sailor, whose quarters are in the forepart of the ship, the

FORECASTLE. An expression belonging to the days of sail.

Master (derived partly from O.E. *mæges-ter* and partly from O.Fr. *maistre*; from the Lat. *magister*).

Master of Arts, etc. One who holds a Master's degree of a university in arts. In the English universities it is the degree above that of Bachelor. At the modern universities it is awarded for further examination or research; at Oxford and Cambridge no further tests are required. In the Scottish universities it is a first degree. At most universities there are corresponding Master's degrees in other faculties.

Master of the Rolls. *See* ROLLS.

Master of the Sentences. *See* SENTENCES.

Master Mason. A FREEMASON who has been raised to the third degree.

Old Masters. The great painters (especially of Italy and the Low Countries) who worked from the 13th century to about the early 17th. Also their paintings.

Past Master. One who has held the office of dignity of *master*; hence an adept, one who is long-experienced in a craft, etc.

Matamore. A POLTROON, a swagger, a BOBADIL. It is composed of two Spanish words *matar-Moros* (a slayer of Moors). *See* MOOR-SLAYER.

Maté (măt'ā). Paraguay teá made from the leaves of Brazilian holly (*Ilex paraguay-enis*). Its full name is *Yerba de maté* (*yerba*, herb; *mate*, vessel) from the hollow gourd in which it was infused. It is also called *Brazil tea*, *Jesuit's tea* and *Yerba*.

The tea was drunk from the gourd through a *bombilla* or tube (S.Am. Span. *bomba*, a pump) and customarily the Paraguayan Indian host, after taking the first suck to signify that no treachery was possible, would pass the bombilla and gourd to his guests. *Cp.* CALUMET.

Mater Familias (mā' tĕr fă mi li ăs) (Lat.). The mother of a family.

Materia medica (mă tēr' i ă mĕd' i kà) (Med. Lat., medical material). That branch of medicine which deals with the remedial substances employed for the cure and alleviation of disease, including

their uses, properties and physiological effects. Dioscorides wrote his *Materia Medica* (1st century A.D.) giving the properties of some 600 medicinal plants and also animal products of medical and dietetic use which served to enlighten the herbalists of the 15th and 16th centuries.

Materialism. In philosophy, the doctrines of a *Materialist*, who maintains that there is nothing in the universe but matter, that mind is a phenomenon of matter, and that there is no ground for assuming a spiritual first cause. In general, Materialism is opposed to IDEALISM, free-will, and belief in God. In the ancient world, its chief exponents were EPICURUS and Lucretius, in modern times the 18th-century French philosophers La Mettrie and Holbach. In the 19th century Materialism was much influenced by the theory of evolution and became involved with problems of interpretation in science, while later Marx put forward DIALECTICAL MATERIALISM.

In everyday parlance "materialism" implies devotion to material things and interests.

Dialectical materialism. The Marxist adaptation of the Hegelian DIALECTIC to describe the way in which phenomena have, and therefore will, interact and develop; the general laws of motion which govern the evolution of nature and society. Every stage of history contains the germs of its own destruction, the thesis provokes its opposite or antithesis, and from the clash a new synthesis arises which preserves the best of both thesis and antithesis. The process then repeats itself. This conflict of opposites takes place gradually until a certain point, when quantitative change becomes qualitative change. By such processes is the classless society to be reached. It should be noted that ideas and institutions are the reflection of material conditions—the reverse of the Hegelian approach. *See* MARXISM.

Historical materialism. This is the application of DIALETICAL MATERIALISM to the evolution of society. Broadly it comes down to a materialist or economic interpretation of history in which all historical developments are basically due to economic phenomena and all social, political and intellectual life, as well as religion, are basically determined by the material conditions of life. Furthermore, historical development is part of the dialectical process.

Mathew, Father. Theobald Mathew (1796–1856), an Irish priest called *The Apostle of Temperance*. His work on behalf of total abstinence was truly remarkable. When the centenary of his death was celebrated in Cork (1956), 60,000 people gathered to honour his memory.

Matins. *See* MATTINS.

Matriculate (Lat. *matricula*, a roll or register). Students at universities matriculate when they enrol after fulfilling certain entrance requirements.

In common parlance, it used to mean to pass the entrance examination qualifying one to enter as a student at a university, although many sat for such examinations simply to obtain a qualification. This examination no longer exists.

In Scottish HERALDRY, when persons register their arms with the Lord LYON they are said *to matriculate*.

Matsya. *See* AVATAR.

Matter. A matter of course. Something one expects in the regular order of things; a natural consequence or accompaniment.

For that matter. As far as that is concerned.

No matter. It is of no consequence; regardless of, as in, "no matter what happens."

Matter-of-fact. Unvarnished truth; prosaic, unimaginative, as a "matter-of-fact swain".

Matterhorn. The German name of the mountain in the Pennine Alps known to the French as *Mont Cervin*, and to the Italians as *Monte Silvo*; so called from its peak (*Horn*) and the scanty patches of green meadow (*Matter*) which cluster round its base. Above a glacier-line, 11,000 ft. high, it rises in an almost inaccessible obelisk of rock to a total height of 14,703 ft. It was first scaled in 1865 by Edward Whymper (1840–1911), when four of his party lost their lives.

Figuratively used it applies to any danger, desperate situation threatening destruction, or LEAP IN THE DARK, as *the matrimonial Matterhorn*.

Matthew, St. Is represented in art as (1) an EVANGELIST, old and with a long beard, with an ANGEL generally standing near by dictating his GOSPEL; (2) an APOSTLE, bearing a purse in reference to his being a publican; sometimes carrying a spear, sometimes a carpenter's rule or square. His symbol is an angel or a man's face, and his day is 21 September.

One legend says that St. Matthew preached for 15 years in Judæa after the Ascension, and that he carried the Gospel to Ethiopia, where he was murdered.

Matthew Parker's Bible; Matthew's Bible. *See* BIBLE, THE ENGLISH.

Matthias, St. The APOSTLE chosen by lot to take the place left by the traitor Judas Iscariot (*Acts* i, 21–26). The name is a shortened form of *Mattathias*. His day is 14 May (formerly 24 February).

Mattins, or Matins. The BREVIARY office for the night called *Vigiliæ* until the 11th century, and originally held at midnight, but in the BENEDICTINE rule at 2 a.m. It is now anticipated and said the previous afternoon or evening. The name was retained in the BOOK OF COMMON PRAYER (1549) for the service of Morning Prayer which was derived from the ancient office. The name was discarded in the book of 1552.

Maudlin. Stupidly sentimental. *Maudlin drunk* is to be sentimentally drunk and inclined to tears. *Maudlin slip-slop* is sentimental chit-chat. The word is derived from the repentant tears of MARY MAGDALENE, who was often portrayed with eyes swollen after weeping. *Cp.* MAGDALENE.

Maul of Monks, The. Thomas Cromwell (1485–1540), VICAR-GENERAL (1535) who arranged for the visitation of the English monasteries and their subsequent dissolution.

Maumet, Maumetry. *See* MAMMET.

Maundy Thursday. The day before GOOD FRIDAY is so called from the first words of the antiphon for that day being *Mandatum novum do vobis*, a new commandment I give unto you (*St. John* xiii, 34), with which the ceremony of the washing of the feet begins. This is still carried out in Roman Catholic cathedrals and monasteries. It became the custom of popes, Catholic sovereigns, prelates, and priests to wash the feet of poor people. In England the sovereign did the same as late as the reign of James II. The word has been incorrectly derived from *maund* (a basket), because on the day before the great fast it was an ancient church custom to bring out food in maunds to distribute to the poor.

The Royal Maunds, or **Maundy Money.** Gifts in money given by the sovereign on MAUNDY THURSDAY to the number of aged poor men and women that corresponds with her (his) age. Broadcloth, fish, bread and wine were given in the reign of Elizabeth I, later clothing and provisions. The clothing was replaced by money in 1725 and the provisions in 1837. In due course the ceremony was transferred from the chapel at WHITEHALL to Westminster Abbey. Personal distribution of the doles ceased in 1688 until George V restarted it in 1932, as did Edward VIII in 1936. Queen Elizabeth II has made a personal distribution in most years since 1953 and the ceremony is no longer held at Westminster every year. Thus the 1979 service attended by the Queen and Prince Philip was held in Winchester Cathedral. The money is specially struck in silver pennies, twopennies, threepences, and fourpences and is unaffected by decimalization.

Mauretania, or **Mauritania.** Parts of Morocco and Algiers, the land of the *Mauri* or Moors. The kingdom of Mauritania was annexed to the Roman Empire in A.D. 42 and finally disintegrated when overrun by the VANDALS in 429.

The modern Islamic Republic of Mauritania is situated in the S.W. Sahara.

Mausoleum. Originally the name of the tomb of *Mausolus*, King of Caria, to whom his wife Artemisia erected a splendid monument at Halicarnassus (353 B.C.). Parts of the sepulchre, one of the SEVEN WONDERS OF THE WORLD (*see* WONDER), are now in the BRITISH MU-

SEUM. The name is now applied to any magnificent tomb, usually with a sepulchral chamber.

Mauthe Dog. *See* MODDEY DHOO.

Mauvais, mauvaise (mō va, mō vāz). Fr., bad.

Mauvais ton. Bad manners, illbreeding, vulgar ways.

Mauvaise honte (awnt). Bad or silly shame; false modesty, bashfulness, sheepishness.

Mauvaise plaisanterie. A rude or ill-mannered jest; a jest in bad taste.

Maverick. An unbranded animal, a stray, a masterless person or rover. Samuel A. Maverick, a Texan cattle-raiser, did not bother to brand his cattle, hence the practice arose of calling unbranded calves *mavericks*, and the usage extended to other animals. In the U.S.A. it acquired a political connotation from the 1880s, applying to politicians who did not acknowledge any party leadership. Kipling called an imaginary regiment "The Mavericks". **To maverick** is to seize or brand *mavericks*, hence to appropriate anything without legal claim.

Mavournin. Irish (*mo mhurnin*) for "My darling"; *Erin go bragh* is "Ireland for ever".

> Land of my forefathers, Erin go bragh!...
> Erin mavournin, Erin go bragh!
> THOMAS CAMPBELL: *Exile of Erin*, v.

Maxim's. The most famous and elegant French restaurant, a symbol of gastronomic perfection and gaiety. Situated in the rue Royale, Paris, it was opened by Maxime Gaillard in 1893. His rich and famous clientèle grew steadily, aided by the patronage of fashionable courtesans. Its characteristically opulent ART NOUVEAU décor is still maintained but it is now more noted for food than frolics.

May. The Anglo-Saxons called this month *thrimilce*, because then cows can be milked three times a day; the present name is the Lat. *Maius*, probably from *Maia*, the goddess of growth and increase, connected with *major*. It was the fifth month in the Julian and Gregorian CALENDAR. The old Dutch name was *Blou-maand* (blossoming month). In the French Republican Calendar it was called *Floréal* (the time of flowers, 20 April to 20 May).

Cast not a clout till May is out. An old warning not to shed winter clothing too early in the year. *Clout* here is a rag or patch, hence a piece of clothing. *May* is also another name for hawthorn, which blossoms in May. Thus some hold that the proverb means "do not discard clothing until the hawthorn blossoms" but more likely it means "wait until the end of May". F.K. Robinson's *Whitby Glossary* (1855) has:

> The wind at North and East
> was never good for man nor beast,
> so never think to cast a clout
> until the month of May be out.

Here we go gathering nuts in May. *See under* NUT.

It's a case of January and May. *See under* JANUARY.

May unlucky for weddings. This is a Roman superstition, and is referred to by Ovid. In this month were held the festivals of *Bona Dea* (the goddess of chastity), and the feasts of the dead called *Lemuralia*.

May-day. Polydore Virgil says that the Roman youths used to go into the fields and spend the CALENDS of May in dancing and singing in honour of FLORA, goddess of fruits and flowers. The English celebrated May-day with games and sports, particularly archery and MORRIS dancing and the setting up of the MAYPOLE. In due time ROBIN HOOD and MAID MARIAN came to preside as Lord and Lady of the May, and by the 16th century May-day was Robin Hood's day and Robin Hood plays became an integral part of the festivities.

May-day was also formerly the day of the London chimney-sweepers' festival. *See also* LABOR DAY.

Evil May Day. *See* DEVIL.

May-Fair Marriages. "The Rev. Alexander Keith's Chapel" in Curzon Street, Mayfair, was notorious for its traffic in weddings until the Act of 1753 stopped the trade. Here the younger of the two beautiful Miss Gunnings was married to the sixth Duke of Hamilton in 1752. The ring was from a bed-curtain and the ceremony took place half an hour after midnight. *Cp.* FLEET MARRIAGES; GRET-NA GREEN MARRIAGES.

Maypole, May Queen. etc. Dancing round the Maypole on MAY-DAY, "going-a-Maying", electing a May Queen, and lighting bonfires, are all ancient relics of nature-worship. In Cornhill, LONDON, before the Church of St. Andrew a great shaft or maypole was set up, round which the people danced, whence the church came to be called St. Andrew Undershaft. In the first May morning people went "a-maying" to fetch fresh flowers and branches of hawthorn (hence its name *may*) to decorate their houses, and the fairest maid of the locality was crowned "Queen of the May".

A very tall ungainly woman is sometimes called a "Maypole", a term which was bestowed as a nickname on the Duchess of Kendal, one of George I's German mistresses.

Maya. The mother of GAUTAMA who saw in a dream the future BUDDHA enter her womb in the shape of a little white elephant. Seven days after his birth she died from joy.

Mayflower. The 180-ton ship in which the PILGRIM FATHERS finally sailed from Plymouth, Devon, 6 September 1620. They arrived off Cape Cod, 11 November, and established their colony, although the original intention was to land on the shore of Delaware Bay. At Jordans, Buckinghamshire, the burial place of William Penn, there is a barn traditionally held to be built from the timber of this ship.

In 1957 a replica of the ship under the command of A. J. Villiers, and built of Devonshire oak and elm, sailed from Plymouth to Massachusetts following the route of its predecessor.

The Mayflower Compact. An agreement signed by 41 adults in the cabin of the *Mayflower* acknowledging their allegiance to the King of England and setting up a body politic "to frame just and equal laws" (21 November 1620).

Mayhem. An early form of *maim* and an archaic legal term for the crime of depriving a person of the use of an arm, leg, eye, etc. thus rendering him less able to defend himself in a violent struggle or to trouble his opponent. The word is now back in popular use for violent and injurious action.

Mayonnaise. A sauce made with pepper, salt, oil, vinegar, the yolk of egg, etc., beaten up together. When the Duc de Richelieu captured Port Mahon, Minorca, in 1756, he demanded food on landing; in the absence of a prepared meal, his chef took whatever he could find and beat it up together—hence the original form *mahonnaise*.

Mayor of the Bull-ring. In the Dublin of former times, this official and his sheriffs were elected on MAY-DAY and St. PETER Eve "to be captaine and guard- ian of the batchelers, and the unwedded youth of the civitie". For the year the "Mayor" had authority to punish those who frequented houses of ill-fame. He was termed "Mayor of the Bull-ring" because he conducted any bachelor who married during his term of office to an iron ring in the market place to which bulls were tied for baiting, and made him kiss it.

Mazarin, Cardinal Jules (1602–1661), Italian-born successor to Cardinal Richelieu and minister to the Queen-Regent during the minority of Louis XIV.

Mazarin Bible. See BIBLE, SOME SPECIALLY NAMED EDITIONS.

Mazarin Library. The first public LIBRARY (1642) at Paris. The great Cardinal Mazarin left his collection of 40,000 books to the city on his death in 1661, and himself composed the rules for its conduct.

Mazarinades. Pamphlets in prose or verse published against Cardinal Mazarin (1602– 1661) by supporters of the FRONDE.

Mazer. A large drinking vessel originally made of maple-wood, and so called from O.Fr. *masere*, O.H.Ger. *Masar*, a knot in wood, maple-wood.

Mazikeen, or **Shedeem.** A species of being in Jewish mythology resembling the Arabian JINN said to be agents of magic and enchantment. When ADAM fell, says the TALMUD, he was excommunicated for 130 years, during which time he begat demons and spectres.

Swells out like the Mazikeen ass. The allusion is to a Jewish tradition that

a servant, whose task it was to rouse the neighbourhood to midnight prayer, one night mounted a stray ASS and neglected his duty. As he rode along the ass grew bigger and bigger, till at last it towered as high as the tallest edifice, where it left the man, and there next morning he was found.

Meal. In meal or in malt. Directly or indirectly; in one way or another. If much money passes through the hand, some profit will be sure to accrue either "in meal or in malt", and a certain percentage of one or the other is the miller's perquisite.

Meal Tub Plot. In 1679 during the POPISH PLOT scare, Thomas Dangerfield pretended to have discovered a WHIG plot to prevent the Duke of York's succession to the throne. The evidence was claimed to be concealed under the meal tub of his associate Mrs. Cellier. The falsity of this was discovered and he next accused prominent Roman Catholics of promoting the conspiracy as cover for a popish plot. Dangerfield was convicted of perjury and Mrs. Cellier finally pilloried for libel in connection with her trial.

Mealy-mouthed is the Greek *melimuthos* (honey-speech), and means velvet-tongued, afraid of giving offence, hypocritical, "smarmy".

Meander. To wind, to saunter about at random; so called from the Mæander, a winding river of Phrygia. It is said to have given DÆDALUS his idea for a LABYRINTH. The term is also applied to an ornamental pattern of winding lines, used as a border on pottery, wall decorations, etc.

Measure (O.Fr. *mesure*; Lat. *mensura*).

Beyond measure, or **out of all measure.** Beyond all reasonable degree; exceedingly, excessively.

> Thus out of measure sad.
> SHAKESPEARE: *Much Ado about Nothing*,
> I, iii.

To measure one's length on the ground. To fall flat on the ground; to be knocked down.

To measure other people's corn by one's own bushel. *See under* BUSHEL.

To measure strength. To wrestle together; to fight, to contest.

To measure swords. To try whether

or not one is strong enough or sufficiently equally matched to contend against another. The phrase is from duelling, in which the seconds measure the swords to see that both are of the same length.

> So we measured swords and parted.
> SHAKESPEARE: *As You Like It*, V, iv.

To tread a measure. A poetic and archaic expression meaning "to dance", especially a slow stately dance.

Meat, Bread. Both words can connote food in general. For Italians and Asiatics *bread* stands for food, an indication of their lower consumption of animal food. The English being greater consumers of *meat*, which simply means food, use the word almost exclusively for animal food. In the banquet given to his brethren, Joseph commanded the servants "to set on bread" (*Gen.* xliii, 31). In *Ps.* civ, 27, it is said of fishes, creeping things, and crocodiles that God gives them *meat* in due season. In parts of Devonshire potatoes for the table are still called *meat* potatoes, as opposed to *seed* potatoes, and *feed* potatoes for livestock.

To carry off meat from the graves. To be as POOR as a church mouse; to be so poor as to descend to robbing the graves of offerings. The Greeks and Romans used to make feasts at certain seasons, when spirits were supposed to return to their graves, and the fragments were left on the tombs for them. Hence the Latin proverb *Eleemosynam sepulcri patris tui* (Alms on your father's grave).

Mebyon Kernow. (Sons of Cornwall). The society of Cornish nationalists, established in 1951. Their flag is the emblem of St. PIRAN—a white cross, which symbolises tin, on a black field which represents the ground rock from which it is extracted.

Mecca. The birthplace of MOHAMMED in Saudi Arabia. It is one of the two holy cities, the other being MEDINA and the most sacred pilgrimage for MOSLEMS. Hence, a place one ardently longs to visit, a place outstandingly frequented by the followers of a particular cult or pursuit. Thus Stratford-upon-Avon could be called a *Mecca* for the devotees of

Shakespeare as could Wimbledon for tennis players.

Mecklenburg Declaration. The first declaration of independence in the U.S.A. made at Mecklenburg, N. Carolina, on 20 May 1775.

Medal of Honor. In the U.S.A., a medal instituted in 1862 for conspicuous acts of gallantry in the CIVIL WAR. It is the premier decoration of the United States, the equivalent of the VICTORIA CROSS.

Médard, St. (mā' dar). The French St. SWITHIN; his day is 8 June.

> Quand il pleut à la Saint-Médard
> Il pleut quarante jours plus tard.

He was bishop of Noyon and Tournai in the 6th century and founded the Festival of the Rose at Salency, in which the most virtuous girl in the parish receives a crown of roses and a purse of money. Legend says that a sudden shower once fell which soaked everyone except St. Médard who remained dry as toast, for an EAGLE had spread its wings over him, and ever after he was termed *maître de la pluie*.

Medb. *See* MAEVE.

Medea (me dē' à). In Greek legend, a sorceress, daughter of Æetes, king of Colchis. She married JASON, the leader of the ARGONAUTS, whom she aided to obtain the GOLDEN FLEECE, and was the mother of Medus, regarded by the Greeks as the ancestor of the Medes.

Medea's kettle, or **cauldron.** A means of restoring lost youth. MEDEA cut an old ram into pieces, threw the bits into her cauldron, and a young lamb came forth. The daughters of Pelias accordingly killed and cut up their father thinking to restore him to youth in the same way, but Medea refused to save the situation.

> Get thee Medea's kettle and be boiled anew.
> CONGREVE: *Love for Love*, IV, vii.

Medes and Persians. *See under* LAW.

Mediæval times. *See* MIDDLE AGES.

Medici (med' i chi). A great and powerful family that ruled in Florence from the 15th to the 18th centuries, founded by Giovanni Medici, a banker, whose son Cosimo (1389–1464) was famous as a patron of art and learning. His grandson Lorenzo the Magnificent (1449–1492) was one of the outstanding figures of the

RENAISSANCE.

From Lorenzo, brother of Cosimo the Elder, came the line of Grand Dukes of Tuscany, the first being his great-grandson Cosimo (1519–1574), who was regarded by many as the original of MACHIAVELLI's *Prince*. The Medici family gave three Popes to the Church, Leo X (1475–1521; POPE 1513–1521), in whose pontificate the REFORMATION began; Clement VII (1478–1534; Pope 1523–1534), who refused Henry VIII's divorce from Katharine of Aragon; and Leo XI, who was Pope for only a few months in 1605.

Medicine. From Lat. *medicina*, which meant both the physician's art and his laboratory, and also a medicament. The alchemists applied the word to the PHILOSOPHER'S STONE and the ELIXIR OF LIFE; hence SHAKESPEARE'S.

> How much unlike art thou, Mark Antony!
> Yet, coming from him, the great medicine hath
> With his tinct gilded thee.
> *Antony and Cleopatra*, I, v.

The word was, and is, frequently used in a figurative sense, as

> The miserable have no other medicine
> But only hope.
> SHAKESPEARE: *Measure for Measure*,
> III, i.

Among the North American Indians *medicine* is a spell, charm, or FETISH, and sometimes even MANITOU himself, hence **Medicine-man,** a witch-doctor or magician.

The Father of Medicine. Aretæus of Cappadocia (2nd century A.D.) is sometimes so called, and especially HIPPOCRATES of Cos (*c.* 460–*c.* 377 B.C.).

Medicine Ball. A large, leather-covered, heavy ball tossed from one person to another as a form of exercise.

Medicine lodge. A tent or other form of structure used by North American Indians for ceremonial purposes.

Medicinal days. In ancient practice the 6th, 8th, 10th, 12th, 16th, 18th, etc., of a disease; so called because according to HIPPOCRATES no CRISIS occurs on these days and medicine may be safely administered.

Medicinal finger. Also the leech-finger or leechman. The finger next to the little

finger, the RING-finger; so called in mediæval times because of the notion that it contained a vein that led direct to the HEART.

Medina. The second holy city of Islam, called Yathrib before the Prophet fled thither from MECCA, but afterwards Medina-al-Nabi (the city of the prophet). *See* HEGIRA.

Mediterranean. The Key of the Mediterranean. The Rock of GIBRALTAR.

Medusa. In classical mythology, the chief of the GORGONS. Her face was so terrible that all who looked on it were turned to stone. Her head was struck off by PERSEUS. Medusa was the mother, by POSEIDON of Chrysaor and PEGASUS.

Meerschaum (mēr' shawm) (Ger., sea-froth). This mineral (used for making tobacco-pipes), from having been found on the seashore in rounded white lumps, was popularly supposed to be sea-froth petrified. It is a compound of silica, magnesia, lime, water and carbonic acid. When first dug it lathers like soap, and is used as soap by the Tartars.

Meg. Formerly slang for a GUINEA, and more recently for a halfpenny.

Mons Meg. A great 15th-century piece of ordnance in Edinburgh Castle, made at Mons in Flanders and much esteemed by the Scots. It was taken to London about 1757 and restored to Edinburgh in 1829. (Gr. *megas*, great.)

Roaring Meg. Formerly any large gun that made a great noise when fired was so called.

Megarians. The inhabitants of Megara and its territory, Megaris, Greece, were proverbial for their stupidity; hence the proverb "Wise as a Megarian", *i.e.* not wise at all; yet *see below*. *Cp.* ABDERA.

Megarian School. A philosophical school of the 4th-century B.C. founded by Euclid, a native of Megara, and disciple of SOCRATES. It combined the ethical doctrines of Socrates with the METAPHYSICS of the ELEATICS.

Meinie, or **Meiny** (mī' ni). A company of attendants; a household (from O.Fr. *meyné, mesnie,* from Lat. *mansio,* a house). Our word *menial* has much the same derivation and significance.

Mein Kampf (mīn kămf) Ger., My Struggle). The name adopted by Adolf

Hitler (1889–1945) for the book embodying his political and racial theories and misreadings of history, which in due course became the Nazi "Bible". The first part was written when he was in prison after the abortive "Beer Hall Putsch" of 1923. It was published in two parts (1925 and 1927). *Cp.* HITLERISM: MUNICH; NAZI.

Meiosis (mī ō sis). This word, coming from the Greek and meaning "lessening", denotes a figure of speech by which an impression is deliberately given that a thing is of less size or importance than it actually is. It is also used of LITOTES.

Meistersinger. (Mastersingers). Bürger poets of Germany, who, in the 14th to 16th centuries, attempted to revive the national minstrelsy of the MINNESINGER, which had fallen into decay. Hans Sachs, the cobbler (1494–1576), was the most celebrated. Wagner has an opera *Die Meistersinger von Nürnberg* (1868) in which he protested at his critics.

Melampode. Black Hellebore; so called from Melampus, a famous soothsayer and physician of Greek legend, who with it cured the daughters of Prœtus of their madness (VIRGIL: *Georgics*, iii, 550).

Melancholy (Gr. *melas chole*). Lowness of spirits, supposed at one time to arise from a superfluity of black BILE.

> Hence, loathed Melancholy,
> Of Cerberus and blackest midnight born.
>
> MILTON: *L'Allegro*.

Melba. Melba toast, narrow slices of thin toast.

Peach, or **Pêche Melba,** a confection of peach on vanilla ice-cream, covered with raspberry purée.

These take their name from Dame Nellie Melba (1861–1931), the colourful Australian operatic soprano.

Meleager (mel ē ā' ger). A hero of Greek legend, son of Œneus of Calydon and Althæa, distinguished for throwing the javelin, for slaying the Calydonian BOAR, and as one of the ARGONAUTS. *See* ALTHÆA'S BRAND.

Melibœan Dye. A rich purple. Melibœa, in Thessaly, was famous for the *ostrum*, a fish used in dyeing purple.

Melicertes (mel i sĕr' tēz). Son of Ino, a sea deity of Greek legend. Athamas imagined his wife Ino to be a lioness, and her two sons to be lion's cubs. In his frenzy he slew one of the boys and drove Melicertes and his mother into the sea. *See* LEUCOTHEA.

Mélisande. *See* MELUSINA.

Mell Supper. In the northern counties, Harvest supper; usually called Kern or Churn Supper in Scotland. *See also* CRYING THE NECK; CORN DOLLY; HARVEST HOME; HARVEST THANKSGIVING; HOCKEY.

> Mell is plainly derived from the French word *mesler*, to mingle together, the master and servant promiscuously at the same table. At the mell-supper, Bourne tells us, "the servant and his master are alike, and everything is done with equal freedom; they sit at the same table, converse freely together, and spend the remaining part of the night in dancing and singing, without any difference or distinction".
>
> STRUTT: *Sports and Pastimes*, Bk. IV, ch. iii, xxvii.

Melodrama (Gr. *melos*, a song). Properly (and in the early 19th century) a drama in which song and music were introduced, an OPERA. These pieces were usually of a sensational character and the musical parts were gradually dropped. The word now denotes a lurid, sensational and highly emotional play with a happy ending in which the villain gets all he richly deserves. *See* RED BARN.

Melon. The Mohammedans say that the eating of a melon produces a thousand good works. *See also* ELIJAH'S MELONS.

Melpomene (mel pom' e ni). The muse of TRAGEDY.

Melusina, or **Mélisande.** The most famous of all the fées of French romance, looked upon by the houses of Lusignan, Rohan, Luxembourg, and Sassenaye as their ancestor and founder. Having enclosed her father in a high mountain for offending her mother, she was condemned to become every Saturday a serpent from her waist downward. She married Raymond, count of Lusignan, and made her husband vow never to visit her on a Saturday; but the count hid himself on one of the forbidden days, and saw his wife's transformation. Melusina was now obliged to quit her husband, and was destined to wander about as a spectre till the day of doom, though some say that the count immured her in the dungeon of his castle.

A sudden scream is called *un cri de Mélusine*, in allusion to the scream of despair uttered by Melusina when she was discovered by her husband; and in Poitou certain gingerbread cakes bearing the impress of a beautiful woman *"bien coiffée"*, with a serpent's tail, made by confectioners for the MAY fair in the neighbourhood of Lusignan, are still called *Mélusines*.

Memento mori (Lat., remember you must die). An emblem of mortality, such as a skull; something to put us in mind of the shortness and uncertainty of life.

Memnon. The Oriental or Ethiopian prince who, in the TROJAN WAR, went to the assistance of his uncle PRIAM and was slain by ACHILLES. His mother Eos (the Dawn) was inconsolable for his death, and wept for him every morning. The Greeks called the statue of Amenophis III at Thebes that of Memmon. When first struck by the rays of the rising sun it is said to have produced a sound like the snapping asunder of a cord. Poetically, when Eos kissed her son at daybreak, the hero acknowledged the salutation with a musical murmur.

Memory. Memory Woodfall. William Woodfall (1746–1803), brother of the Woodfall who controlled the *Public Advertiser* in which the *Letters of* JUNIUS appeared. He established *The Diary* (1789), the first journal to report parliamentary proceedings the morning after the occurrence. He would attend a debate, and, without notes, report it accurately. *See also* HANSARD.

Memorial Day, 30 May, also known as Decoration Day, observed in most states of the U.S.A. as a holiday to honour those killed in war; originally to commemorate those who fell in the CIVIL WAR.

Menalcas. Any shepherd or rustic. The name figures in VIRGIL's *Eclogues* and the *Idylls* of Theocritus.

Mencius. *See* MENGZI.

Mendel's Law was promulgated in 1865 through experiments with peas. *Cp.* MICHURINISM.

Mendicant Orders, or **Begging Friars.** The orders of the FRANCISCANS (Grey Friars), DOMINICANS (Black Friars), AUGUSTINIANS (Austin Friars), CARMELITES (White Friars), Servites, and other lesser orders.

Menechmians. Persons exactly like each other; so called from the Menæchmi of Plautus, the basis of SHAKESPEARE's *Comedy of Errors*, in which not only the two Dromios are exactly alike but Antipholus of Ephesus is the facsimile of his brother, Antipholus of Syracuse.

Menelaus (men a lā' ŭs), son of Atreus, brother of AGEMEMNON, and husband of HELEN whose desertion of him brought about the TROJAN WAR. He was the king of Sparta or Lacadæmon.

Mengzi (d. 290 B.C.). The Chinese philosopher who ranks next to Confucius. After his death, his teachings were gathered by his disciples to form the *Mencius*, the fourth book of the corpus of Chinese Confucianism.

Mother of Meng. A Chinese expression, meaning, "an admirable teacher". Meng's father died soon after the birth of the sage and he was brought up by his mother—the pattern of all mothers to the Chinese.

Menippus, the CYNIC, was born at Gadara, Syria, in the 3rd century B.C. He was called by Lucian the greatest snarler and snapper of all the dogs (*cynics*).

Mennonites. Followers of Simon Menno (1492–1561), a parish priest of Friesland, who joined the ANABAPTISTS in 1536. They still exist in Holland, Germany, and America and some other places. They reject church organization, infant baptism, and usually military service and the holding of public office.

Mensheviks. A Russian word for a minority party. The name was applied to the moderate Russian social democrats who opposed the BOLSHEVIKS in the Russian Revolution of 1917.

Menthu. *See* BAKHA.

Mention in Dispatches. A reference by name to an officer in British naval, army and air force dispatches commending his conduct in action. An officer so mentioned is entitled to wear a small bronze oak leaf on the left breast or upon the medal ribbon for that particular campaign.

Mentor. A guide, a wise and faithful counsellor; so called from Mentor, a friend of ULYSSES, whose form MINERVA assumed when she accompanied TELMACHUS in his search for his father.

Menu. *See* MANU.

Meo periculo (Lat., at my peril). On my responsibility; at my own risk.

Mephistopheles. A manufactured name (possibly from three Greek words meaning "not loving the light") of a DEVIL or familiar spirit which first appeared in the late mediæval FAUST legend; he is well known as the sneering, jeering, leering tempter in Goethe's *Faust*.

Mercantilism. A term embracing a wide range of policies at different times in various countries and first popularized by Adam Smith's attack on Britain's "Mercantile System" in his *The Wealth of Nations* (1776). Mercantilism held sway in Britain between the mid-16th and the mid-18th centuries and was bound up with ideas of state power and security. National self-sufficiency, a favourable balance of trade which would bring an influx of the precious metals, and protection, were all basic to it, and colonial trade was primarily regulated in the interest of the mother country. Adam Smith taught that labour, not trade, was the real source of wealth and aimed to replace mercantilism by FREE TRADE and LAISSEZ-FAIRE.

Mercator's Projection is a Mercator's chart or map for nautical purposes. The meridian lines are at right angles to the parallels of latitude. It is so called after its inventor Gerhard Kremer (= merchant, pedlar) (1512–1594), whose surname is latinized is *Mercator*.

Merchant Adventurers. Local guilds of merchant adventurers were formed in the 14th century to develop English export of cloth to Europe and in 1407 a regulated company of Merchants Adventurers was formed at LONDON. It became a national organization with headquarters at Bruges, but political difficulties led to its removal at different times to other centres in the Low Countries and Germany. In the 16th century the company successfully rivalled the HANSE and it was not finally dissolved until 1808.

Mercia. One of the ancient Anglican Kingdoms of ENGLAND which first rose in importance under Penda in the first half of the 7th century; in the 8th century, under Ethelbald and Offa, it became the dominant kingdom of the HEPTARCHY, and Mercian kings were supreme south of the Humber; but in 829 it was temporarily incorporated with WESSEX under Egbert.

It was subjected to Danish attacks from 855. The Danes settled the eastern part and the remainder came under the control of Wessex by the early 10th century. The earldom of Wessex, created by Cnut (1016–1035), came to an end in 1070. The name is from O.E. *merce*, referring to the MARCH or frontier against the Britons (Welsh); Mercia occupied the land between the Humber and THAMES, WALES and East Anglia.

Mercury. The Roman counterpart of the Greek HERMES, son of MAIA and JUPITER, to whom he acted as messenger. He was the god of science and commerce, the patron of travellers and also of rogues, vagabonds and thieves. Hence, the name of the god is used to denote both a messenger and a thief.

> My father named me Autolycus; who being, as I am, littered under Mercury, was likewise a snapper-up of unconsidered trifles.
> SHAKESPEARE: *The Winter's Tale*, IV, iii.

Mercury is represented as a young man with winged hat and winged sandals (*talaria*), bearing the CADUCEUS, and sometimes a purse.

Posts with a marble head of Mercury used to be erected where two or more roads met, to point out the way (*Juvenal*, viii, 53).

In astrology, Mercury "signifieth subtill men, ingenious, inconstant: rymers, poets, advocates, orators, phylosophers, arithmeticians, and busie fellowes". The alchemists credited mercury (*cp.* QUICK-SILVER) with great powers and used it for many purposes, for which see Ben Jonson's masque, *Mercury Vindicated*.

Mercurial. Light-hearted, gay, volatile; such were supposed by the astrologers to be born under the planet Mercury.

Mercurial finger. The little finger, which, if pointed, denotes eloquence; if square, sound judgment.

Mercy. The seven corporal works of mercy are: (1) To tend the sick; (2) To feed the hungry; (3) To give drink to the thirsty; (4) To clothe the naked; (5) To harbour the stranger; (6) To minister to prisoners; (7) To bury the dead. *See Matt.* xxv, 35-45.

The seven spiritual works of mercy are: (1) To convert the sinner; (2) To instruct the ignorant; (3) To counsel those in doubt; (4) To comfort those in sorrow; (5) To bear wrongs patiently; (6) To forgive injuries; (7) To pray for the living and the dead.

The Merciless, or **Unmerciful Parliament** (3 Feburary to 3 June 1388). The PARLIAMENT in which the Lords Appellant secured the condemnation of Richard II's friends. Four knights of the King's chamber were executed and some of his supporters were exiled to Ireland.

Meredith. We're in, Meredith. A popular catch phrase derived from the very successful Fred KARNO sketch, *The Bailiff*, produced in 1907. It depicted the stratagems of a bailiff and his assistant Meredith attempting to enter a house for purposes of distraint. The phrase was used by the bailiff each time he thought he was on the verge of success.

Merit, Order of. A British order for distinguished achievement in all callings founded by Edward VII in 1902, with two classes, civil and military. The Order is limited to 24 men and women and confers no precedence; it is designated by the letters O.M., following the first class of the Order of the BATH and precedes all letters designating membership of other Orders. The badge is a red and blue CROSS patté, with a blue medallion in the centre surrounded by a LAUREL wreath, and bears the words "For Merit". The ribbon is blue and crimson. Crossed swords are added to the badge for military members.

Merlin. The historical Merlin was a Welsh or British BARD, born towards the close of the 5th century, to whom a number of poems have been very doubtfully attributed. He is said to have become a bard of king ARTHUR and to have perished after a terrible battle about 570 between the Britons and their Romanized compatriots.

His story has been mingled with that of the enchanter Merlin of the ARTHURIAN ROMANCE. This Prince of Enchanters was the son of a damsel seduced by a friend, but was baptized by Blaise, and so rescued from the power of SATAN. He became an adept in NECROMANCY, but was beguiled by the enchantress Nimue who shut him up in a rock; and later Vivien, the LADY OF THE LAKE, entangled him in a thornbush by means of spells, and there he still sleeps, though his voice may be sometimes heard.

He first appears in Nennius as the boy Ambrosius and in Geoffrey of Monmouth's *Historia Britonum* and the *Vita Merlini*.

Mermaid. The popular stories of this fabulous marine creature, half woman and half fish, allied to the SIREN of classical mythology, probably arose from sailors' accounts of the dugong, a cetacean whose head has a rude approach to the human outline. The mother while suckling her young holds it to her breast with one flipper, as a woman holds her infant in her arm. If disturbed, she suddenly dives under water, and tosses up her fish-like tail. *Cp.* MERROW.

In later 16th-century plays the term is often used for a courtesan. *See* Massinger's *Old Law*, IV, i, and SHAKESPEARE's *Comedy of Errors*, III, ii, etc.

The Mermaid Tavern. The famous meeting place (in Bread Street, Cheapside) of the wits, literary men, and men about town in the early 17th century. Among those who met there at a sort of early CLUB were Ben Jonson, Sir Walter Ralegh, Beaumont, Fletcher, John Selden, and in all probability SHAKESPEARE.

Mermaid's purses. The horny egg cases of the ray, skate, or shark, frequently cast up by the waves on the sea-beach.

Merope (mer' ō pi). One of the PLEIADES; dimmer than the rest, because, according to Greek legend, she married SISY-PHUS, a mortal. She was the mother of GLAUCUS.

Merops' Son. One who thinks he can set the world to rights, but can't. Agitators, demogogues, etc., are sons of Merops. The allusion is to PHÆTON, a reputed son of Merops (king of Ethiopia), who thought himself able to drive the car of PHŒBUS, but, in the attempt, nearly set the world on fire.

Merovingian Dynasty. The dynasty of Merovius, Merovech, or *Merwig* (great warrior), grandfather of Clovis, who ruled over the FRANKS in the 5th century. The dynasty rose to power under Clovis (d. 511) and gradually gave way before the MAYORS OF THE PALACE, until, in 751, the dynasty was brought to an end by Pippin the SHORT's usurpation.

Merrie England. *See* MERRY.

Merrow (Irish, *muirrúhgach*). A MER-MAID, believed by Irish fishermen to forebode a coming storm.

> It was rather annoying to Jack that, though living in a place where the merrows were as plenty as lobsters, he never could get a right view of one.
> W.B. YEATS: *Irish Folk Stories and Fairy Tales*.

Merry. The original meaning was pleasing, delightful; hence, giving pleasure; hence, mirthful, joyous.

The old phrase MERRIE ENGLAND (*Merry London*, etc.) merely signified it was pleasant and delightful, not necessarily full of merriment; and so with the *merry month* of MAY.

The phrase *merry men*, meaning the companions at arms of a KNIGHT, or outlaw (especially of ROBIN HOOD), is really for merry MEINIE.

Merry Andrew. A buffoon, jester, or attendant on a QUACK doctor at fairs. Said by Thomas Hearne (1678–1735)—with no evidence—to derive from Andrew Boorde (*c.* 1490–1549), physician to Henry VIII, who to his vast learning added great eccentricity. Prior has a poem on "Merry Andrew". *Cp.* ANDREW.

Merry as a cricket, grig. *See* GRIG.

Merry begot. An old name for a BAS-TARD.

Merry Dancers. The NORTHERN LIGHTS, so called from their undulatory motion. The French call them *chèvres dansantes* (dancing goats).

Merry Greek. *See* GRIG.

Merry Men. *See* MERRY.

Merry Monarch. Charles II. *Cp.* OLD ROWLEY *under* ROWLEY.

Merry Monday. An old name for the day before SHROVE TUESDAY.

Merrythought. The furcula or wishing-bone in the breast of a fowl; sometimes pulled asunder by two persons, the one holding the larger portion being supposed to have his wish.

To make merry. To be jovial, festive; to make merry over, to treat with amusement, to be joyful; to ridicule, to make fun of.

Meru. The "OLYMPUS" of the Hindus; a fabulous mountain in the centre of the world, 80,000 leagues high, the abode of VISHNU, and a perfect PARADISE.

Merveilleuse (mâr vä yĕrs) (Fr., marvellous). The sword of Doon of Mayence. It was so sharp that when placed edge downwards it would cut through a slab of wood without the use of force.

The term is also applied to the dress worn by the fops and ladies of the DI-RECTORY period in France, who were noted for their extravagance and aping of classical Greek modes.

Mesmerism. So called from Franz Anton Mesmer (1734–1815), an Austrian physician who introduced his theory of "animal magnetism" at PARIS in 1778. It was the forerunner of HYPNOTISM which is increasingly studied for therapeutic purposes by the medical and psychiatric professions. Mesmerism is commonly used as a synonym for *hypnotism*.

Mesolithic Age (Gr. *mesos*, middle; *lithos*, stone). The Middle Stone Age in Europe, between the PALÆOLITHIC and NEOLITHIC periods.

Mesopotamia (Gr., the land between the rivers, *i.e.* the Euphrates and the Tigris), one of the cradles of civilization. It is now called Iraq.

Mess. The usual meaning today is a dirty, untidy state of things, a muddle, a difficulty (*to get into a mess*); but the word originally signified a portion of food (Lat. *missum*, *mittere*, to send; *cp.* Fr. *mets*, viands, Ital. *messa*, a course of a meal); thence it came to mean mixed food, especially for an animal, and so a confusion, medley, jumble.

Another meaning was a small group of persons (usually four) who sat together at banquets and were served from the same dishes. This gave rise to army and navy *mess*, the place where meals are served and eaten, and to the Elizabethans using it in place of "four" or "a group of four".

Mess of pottage. For such Esau sold his birthright to JACOB (*Gen*. xxv, 29–34); hence, figuratively, to obtain some material comfort or advantage at the expense of something of much greater value or lasting worth.

Messalina. Wife of the Emperor Claudius of ROME, executed by order of her husband in A.D. 48. Her name has become a byword for lasciviousness and incontinency. Catherine II of Russia (1729–1796) has been called *The Modern Messalina*.

Messiah (Heb. *mashiach*, one anointed). It is the title of the expected leader of the Jews who shall deliver the nation from its enemies and reign in permanent triumph and peace. Equivalent to the Greek word Christ, it is applied by Christians to Jesus. *Messiah* (incorrectly *The Messiah*) is the title of an oratorio by Handel, first produced in Dublin in 1742.

Metals. Metals used to be divided into two classes, *Noble* and *Base*. The *Noble*, or *Perfect* metals were GOLD, SILVER and platinum, because they were not acted on by air (or oxygen) at any temperature. The *Base*, or *Imperfect* metals are subject to oxidation in air and change their character. The only metals used in HERALDRY are *or* (gold) and *argent* (silver).

The seven metals in alchemy:

Gold, APOLLO or the sun.
Silver, DIANA or the moon.
Quicksilver, MERCURY.
Copper, VENUS.
Iron, MARS.
Tin, JUPITER.
Lead, SATURN.

Metaphor (Gr., transference). A figure of speech in which a name or descriptive term is applied to an object, etc., to which it is not literally applicable as, "The ship spread its wings to the breeze."

A mixed metaphor is a figure of speech in which two or more inconsistent metaphors are combined, as "It is likely that the Government will bury its head in the sand and drive a bulldozer through the educational system."

Metaphysics (Gr., after-physics), so called because the name was posthumously given to ARISTOTLE'S "First Philosophy" which he wrote after his *Physics*. The science of metaphysics is that branch of speculation which deals with the first principles of existence, such as, being, substance, essence, the infinite, ultimate reality, etc.; the philosophy of being and knowing; the philosophy which establishes truth of existence by abstract reason. At various times the whole range of philosophical inquiry has been classed as metaphysics and the contrast between philosophy and science is comparatively modern.

Metaphysical Poets. A term used to describe certain poets of the 17th century, notably John Donne, George Herbert, Richard Crashaw, Henry Vaughan, and Andrew Marvell. They are characterized by subtlety of thought, expressed frequently in compressed though sometimes far-fetched images, and the use of complex versification. They mostly show strong religious feeling. The word *metaphysical* in relation to poetry was first used by William Drummond of Hawthornden about 1630, then applied to this particular group of poets by Dryden in 1693, and used derogatively of them by Dr. Johnson in 1781.

Metathesis (met à thē' sis). A Greek word meaning "transposition". A change in the relative order between sounds or letters in a word, as O.E. *bridd* becoming bird and *thrid* becoming third. *Cp*. SPOONERISM.

Methodists. A name given (1729) to the members of Charles Wesley's HOLY CLUB at Oxford, from the methodical way in which they observed their principles. They were originally members of the CHURCH OF ENGLAND and the separatist Methodist Church was not established until after John Wesley's death (1791). The movement was itself soon faced with secessions, the first being the Methodist New Connexion (1797), followed by the Independent Methodists (1805), Primitive Methodists (1810), the Bible Christians (1815), the Wesleyan Methodist Association (1835), and the Wesleyan Reformers (1849). Reunion began in 1857 with the formation of the United Methodist Free Church and was completed with the formation of the Methodist Church of Great Britain in 1932. Methodism was introduced into the U.S.A. in the 1760s and grew steadily in importance.

The name was at one time applied to the JESUITS, because they were the first to give systematic representations of the method of polemics.

Since 1965 the Church of England and the Methodist Church have been seeking reconciliation.

Methuselah (me′ thū zè lâ). **Old as Methuselah**. Very old indeed, almost incredibly old. He is the oldest man mentioned in the BIBLE, where we are told (*Gen.*, v, 27) that he died at the age of 969.

Metonic Cycle, The. A cycle of nineteen years at the end of which period the new moons fall on the same days of the year; so called because discovered by the Greek astronomer, Meton, 433 B.C. *See* CALLIPPIC PERIOD.

Metonymy (me ton′ i mi). The use of one thing for another related to it, as "the Bench" for the magistrates or judges sitting in court, "a silk" for a QUEEN'S COUNSEL, "the bottle" for alcoholic liquor. The word is Greek, meaning "a change of name".

Metropolitan. A BISHOP who controls a province and its SUFFRAGANS. The two metropolitans of England are the archbishops of Canterbury and York, and in Ireland the archbishops of Armagh and Dublin. The Archbishop of Canterbury is *metropolitanus et primus totius Angliæ*, and the Archbishop of York *primus et metropolitanus Angliæ*. In the early Church the bishop of the civil metropolis (mother city) was usually given rights over the other bishops (suffragans) of the province. In the GREEK CHURCH a metropolitan ranks next below a PATRIARCH and next above an archbishop.

Meum and tuum (mē′ ùm, tu′ ùm) (Lat.). Mine and thine: that which belongs to me and that which is another's. If a man is said not to know the difference between *meum* and *tuum*, it is another way of saying he is a thief.

Mews. Stables, but properly a cage for hawks when moulting (O.Fr. *mue*; Lat. *mutare*, to change). The word acquired its new meaning because the royal stables built in the 17th century occupied the site of the King's Mews where formerly the king's hawks were kept. It is now the site of the National Gallery in Trafalgar Square. With the development of fashionable LONDON in the 19th century, rows of stabling, with accommodation above for the coachman, were built and called Mews. Since the 1920s these have been steadily converted into garages with flats or maisonettes.

Mexitl, or Mextli. The principal god of the ancient Mexicans (hence the name of their country), to whom hundreds of human beings were offered annually as sacrifices. More usually called *Huitzilopochtli* (Humming-bird of the South, or He of the South), he was the god of war and storms and was born fully armed.

Micah Rood's Apples. Apples with a spot of red in the heart. The story is that Micah Rood was a prosperous farmer at Franklin, Pennsylvania. In 1693 a pedlar with jewellery called at his house, and next day was found murdered under an apple-tree in Rood's orchard. The crime was never brought home to the farmer, but next autumn all the apples of the fatal tree bore inside a red blood-spot, called "Micah Rood's Curse", and the farmer died soon afterwards.

Micawber. An incurable optimist; from Dickens's Mr. Wilkins Micawber (*David Copperfield*), a great speechifier and letter-writer and projector of BUBBLE SCHEMES sure to lead to fortune, but always ending in grief. Notwithstanding his ill success, he never despaired, but felt certain that something would "turn up" to make his fortune. Having failed in every adventure in the old country, he emigrated to Australia, where he became a magistrate.

Michael, St. The ARCHANGEL. The great prince of all the ANGELS and leader of the celestial armies.

> Go, Michael, of celestial armies prince,
> And thou, in military prowess next,
> Gabriel; lead forth to battle these my sons
> Invincible; lead forth my armed saints
> By thousands and by millions ranged for fight.
>
> MILTON: *Paradise Lost*, VI, 44.

His day (St. Michael and All Angels) is 29 September (*see* MICHAELMAS DAY). He appears in the BIBLE in *Dan*. x, 13, and xii, 1; *Jude*, verse 9; and *Rev*. xii, 7–9, where he and his angels fight the DRAGON. His cult was popular in the MIDDLE AGES and he was also looked on as the presiding spirit of the planet MERCURY, and bringer to man of the gift of prudence.

In art St. Michael is depicted as a beautiful young man with severe countenance, winged, and clad in either white or armour, bearing a lance and shield, with which he combats a dragon. In the final judgment he is represented with scales, in which he weighs the souls of the risen dead.

Michael Angelo or **Michelangelo.** The pre-eminent Italian sculptor, celebrated painter, also architect and poet (1475–1564). His full name was Michelangelo Buonarroti.

Michaelmas Day. 29 September, the Festival of St. MICHAEL and all Angels, one of the QUARTER DAYS when rents are due and the day when magistrates are chosen.

The custom of eating goose at Michaelmas (*see also* St. MARTIN'S GOOSE) is very old and is probably due to geese being plentiful and in good condition at this season. We are told that tenants formerly presented their landlords with one to keep in their good graces. The popular story is that Queen Elizabeth I, on her way to Tilbury Fort on 29 September 1588, dined with Sir Neville Umfreyville, and partook of geese, afterwards calling for a bumper of Burgundy, and giving as a toast "Death to the Spanish Armada!" Scarcely had she spoken when a messenger announced the destruction of the fleet by a storm. The Queen demanded a second bumper, and said, "Henceforth shall a goose commemorate this great victory." The tale is marred by the fact that the Armada was dispersed by winds in July and the thanksgiving sermon for victory was preached at St. Paul's on 20 August.

Michurinism. A genetic theory, named after the Soviet horticulturalist I. V. Michurin (1855–1935), repudiating the laws of Mendel and essentially claiming that acquired characteristics can be inherited. It is alternatively called *Lysenkoism*, after T.D. Lysenko, the Soviet agriculturalist, whose pamphlet *Heredity and its Variability* attempted to discredit orthodox genetics. Its revolutionary character was more due to Marxist wishful thinking than scientific proof, and the acceptability of such teaching to the Soviet Government. Lysenkoism replaced orthodox genetics in the U.S.S.R. in 1948 but after 1952 lost ground. Lysenko was dismissed from his key position in 1956. *Cp*. MENDELISM.

Mickey Finn. A draught or powder slipped into liquor to render the drinker unconscious. The term comes from a notorious figure in 19th-century Chicago.

To take the mickey out of someone is to tease, and humiliate him; to undermine his self-esteem.

Mickleton Jury. A corruption of *mickletourn* (*magnus turnus*), *i.e.* the jury of court LEETS which were visited at EASTER and CHRISTMAS by the county sheriffs in their *tourns*. In Anglo-Saxon times the Great Council of the kings was known as the *micklemote* (great assembly).

Microcosm (Gr., little world). So man is called by PARACELSUS. The ancients considered the world (*see* MACROCOSM) as a living being; the SUN and MOON being its *two eyes*, the earth its *body*, the ether its *intellect*, and the sky its *wings*. When man was looked on as the world in miniature, it was thought that the movements of the world and of man corresponded, and if one could be ascertained, the other could be easily inferred; hence arose the system of ASTRO-

Midas

LOGY, which professed to interpret the events of a man's life by the corresponding movements, etc., of the stars.

Midas (mī′ dăs). A legendary king of Phrygia who requested of the gods that everything that he touched might be turned to GOLD. His request was granted, but as his food became gold the moment he touched it, he prayed the gods to take their favour back. He was then ordered to bathe in the Pactolus, and the river ever after rolled over golden sands.

Another story told of him is, that when appointed to judge a musical contest between APOLLO and PAN, he gave judgment in favour of the SATYR; whereupon Apollo in contempt gave the king a pair of ass's ears. Midas hid them under his Phrygian cap; but his barber discovered them, and, not daring to mention the matter, dug a hole and relieved his mind by whispering in it "Midas has ass's ears", then covering it up again. Budæus gives a different version. He says that Midas kept spies to tell him everything that transpired throughout his kingdom, and the proverb "kings have long arms" was changed to "Midas has long ears".

A parallel of this tale is told of Portzmach, king of a part of Brittany. He had all the barbers of his kingdom put to death, lest they should announce to the public that he had the ears of a horse. An intimate friend was found willing to shave him, after swearing profound secrecy; but not able to contain himself he confided his secret to a river bank. The reeds of this river were used for panpipes and hautbois, which repeated the words, "Portzmach—King Portzmach has horse's ears".

Midden. A muck-heap, a kitchen refuse heap. See KITCHEN-MIDDENS.

Better marry over the midden than over the moor. Better seek a wife among your neighbours whom you know than among strangers of whom you know nothing.

Ilka cock craws loodest on its ain midden. The Scottish form of "Every COCK crows loudest on his own dunghill."

Middle. Middle Ages. A term used by historians to denote that period of European history between the downfall of the ancient classical civilization of Greece and Rome consequent upon the barbarian invasions and the Europe of the RENAISSANCE and REFORMATION, roughly a period of 1,000 years. It has no obvious beginning or end and is usually taken to begin about the 5th century and to extend to the late 15th. It is a term of convenience, but has resulted in popular misconceptions giving the mediæval period a spurious unity and distinctness which it did not really possess. Cp. DARK AGES.

Middle Kingdom. A term denoting that period of ancient Egyptian history covered by the XIIth-XIVth Dynasties from about 2130 to 1600 B.C. and essentially the period of the XIIIth Dynasty.

In the feudal period of Chinese history, the appellation *Chung Kwo*, "The Middle Kingdom", denoted the royal domain or the civilized states of China proper, and was not used in connexion with the idea that China was in the middle of the world.

Middle Temple. See TEMPLE.

Middle West. In the U.S.A., properly, the states of Ohio, Indiana, Illinois, Michigan, and Wisconsin. It is the industrial centre of the United States and in many ways the political pivot of the country.

Middlesex. The original territory of the Middle Saxons, which seems to have included the area of the later counties of Middlesex and Hertford, between Essex and WESSEX. It became a SHIRE in the 10th century, was much reduced in area by the Local Government Act of 1888, and was finally absorbed by the Greater London Council, Surrey, and Hertfordshire in 1965.

Midgard. In Scandinavian mythology, the abode of the first pair, from whom sprang the human race. It was midway between NIFLHEIM and MUSPELHEIM, formed from the flesh and blood of YMIR and joined to ASGARD by the rainbow bridge BIFROST. Cp. UTGARD.

Mid-Lent Sunday. The fourth Sunday in LENT. It is called *dominica refectionis* (Refreshment Sunday) because the first lesson is the banquet given by Joseph to

672

his brethren, and the GOSPEL of the day is the miraculous feeding of the five thousand. It is the day on which SIMNEL CAKES are eaten and it is also called MOTHERING SUNDAY.

Midnight Oil. Late hours.

Burning the midnight oil. Sitting up late, especially when engaged on literary work and study.

Smells of the midnight oil. *See* IT SMELLS OF THE LAMP *under* LAMP.

Midrash. Rabbinical commentary on, or exposition of, the OLD TESTAMENT writings, from the Heb. root meaning "to teach", "to investigate". *See* HAGGADAH. *Midrashim* of the 2nd century are the *Sifra* on *Leviticus*, the *Sifra* on *Numbers* and *Deuteronomy*, and the *Mekilta* on *Exodus*. *Cp.* MISHNAH.

Midsummer. The week or so round about the summer SOLSTICE (21 June). Midsummer Day is 24 June, St. JOHN THE BAPTIST'S DAY, and one of the QUARTERDAYS.

Midsummer madness. The height of madness. Olivia says to Malvolio in SHAKESPEARE's *Twelfth Night* (III,iv), "Why, this is very midsummer madness". The reference is to the heat of the sun or the wild celebrations on midsummer eve or possibly the midsummer moon when lunacy was held to be widespread. People who were inclined to be mad used to be said *to have but a mile to midsummer*.

Midsummer moon *"Tis midsummer moon with you"*; you are stark mad. Madness was supposed to be affected by the MOON, and to be aggravated by summer heat; so it naturally follows that the full moon at midsummer is the time when madness would be most pronounced.

Midwife (O.E. *mid*, with; *wif*, woman). The nurse who is with the mother in her labour.

Midwife of men's thoughts. So SOCRATES termed himself, and, as Grote observed, "No man ever struck out of others so many sparks to set light to original thought." Out of his intellectual school sprang PLATO and the DIALECTIC school; Euclid and the MEGARIAN; Aristippus and the Cyrenaic; Antisthenes and the CYNIC.

Mihrab. *See* KIBLAH.

Mikado (mik à' dō) (Jap. *mi*, exalted; *kado*, gate or door). The title used by foreigners for the Emperor of Japan. The Japanese title is *Tenno*. *Cp.* SHOGUN. One of Gilbert and Sullivan's most popular comic operas is *The Mikado* (1885).

Mike. To mike, or **to do a mike.** To idle away one's time, pretending to be waiting for a job or avoiding one. The word may be *miche*, to skulk. *See* MICHING.

Milan. The Edict of Milan. Proclaimed by Constantine after the conquest of Italy (313), to secure the Christians the restitution of their civil and religious rights.

Milanion. *See* ATALANTA'S RACE.

Mile. A measure of length; in the British Commonwealth and the United States, 1,760 yd.; so called from Lat. *mille*, a thousand, the Roman lineal measure being 1,000 paces, or about 1680 yd. The old Irish and Scottish miles were a good deal longer than the standard English, that in Ireland (still in use in country parts) being 2,240 yd., the Scottish 1,980 yd.

The Nautical, or **Geographical Mile** is supposed to be one minute of a great CIRCLE of the earth; but as the earth is not a true sphere the minute is variable, so a mean length of 6,080 ft. (2,026 yd. 2ft.) was adopted by the British Admiralty. The Geographical Mile varies slightly with different nations, so there is a further *International Nautical Mile* of 1,852 metres.

The Square Mile. The City of LONDON, so called from its area (677 acres). A square mile consists of 640 acres.

Milesians. Properly, the inhabitants of *Miletus*; but the name has been given to the ancient Irish because of the legend that two sons of Milesius, a fabulous king of Spain, conquered the country, and repeopled it after exterminating the Firbolgs (the aborigines).

Milesian Fables. A Greek collection of witty but obscene short stories by Antonius Diogenes, no longer extant, and compiled by Aristides of *Miletus* (2nd cent. B.C.), whence the name. They were translated into Latin by Sidenna about the time of the civil wars of Marius and Sulla, and were greedily read by luxurious SYBARITES. Similar stories are still sometimes called *Milesian Tales*.

Milione, Il (Ital., the million) or **Marco Milione**. The name given by the Venetians to Marco Polo and his writings. It may have been a reference to his stories of CATHAY and its wonders, millions, etc.

Military Knights of Windsor. *See under* KNIGHT.

Militia. A development of the fyrd in the form of a national levy for defence, organized by the Lords-Lieutenant on a county basis, and so called in the 17th century. The obligation to provide men and arms was placed on property owners and those called upon to serve were allowed to call upon substitutes. It was never properly trained and became essentially a volunteer force after 1852. It came to an end with the passing of the Territorial and Reserve Forces Act of 1907, but the name was applied to the Special Reserve in 1921 and revived by the Military Training Act of 1939.

Milk. To. Slang for to extract money out of somebody in an underhand way; also to plunder one's creditors, and (in mining) to exhaust the veins of ore after selling the mine.

A land of milk and honey. One abounding in all good things, or of extraordinary fertility. It is figuratively used to denote the blessings of HEAVEN.

> And I am come to deliver them out of the hand of the Egyptians, ... unto a land flowing with milk and honey.
>
> *Exod.* iii, 8.

Milk and water. Insipid, without energy or character, baby-pap, feeble stuff.

Milk teeth. The first, temporary teeth of a child.

The milk of human kindness. Sympathy, compassion.

> ... yet do I fear thy nature.
> It is too full o' th' milk of human kindness.
>
> SHAKESPEARE: *Macbeth*, I, v.

So that accounts for the milk in the coconut! Said when a sudden discovery of the reason for some action or state of things is made.

To cry over spilt milk. *See under* CRY.

Milk-run. An R.A.F. and R.A.A.F. expression of World War II for any sortie flown regularly day after day, or a sortie against an easy target on which inexperienced pilots could be used with impunity—as simple as delivering milk.

Milksop. An effeminate or babyish person; one without any backbone. The allusion is to young, helpless children, who are fed on pap.

Milky Way. *See* GALAXY.

To mill about is to move aimlessly in a circle, like a herd of cattle.

The mill cannot grind with water that is past. An old proverb, given in Herbert's *Collection* (1639). It implies that one must not miss one's opportunities and that it is no good *crying over spilt milk* (*see under* CRY).

The mills of God grind slowly. Retribution may be delayed, but it is sure to overtake the wicked. The *Adagia* of Erasmus puts it, *Sero molunt deorum molæ*, and the sentiment is to be found in many authors, ancient and modern.

To go through the mill. To undergo hardship; to have been through difficulties and hardships or subjected to a severe course of probationary training.

Millenary Petition. An appeal to James I in 1603 from some, 1000 PURITAN clergy asking for certain changes in liturgy and worship, and for the prevention of pluralities and non-residence of clergy, etc. Their requests included the discontinuance of the sign of the CROSS in baptism, of the RING in marriage, and of Confirmation; also optional use of the cap and surplice, more scope for preaching, simplification of music, etc. As a result James summoned the HAMPTON COURT CONFERENCE.

Millennium. A thousand years (Lat. *mille, annus*). In *Rev.* xx, 2, it is said that an angel bound SATAN a thousand years, and in verse 4 we are told of certain martyrs who will come to life again who "lived and reigned with Christ a thousand years". "This", says St. JOHN, "is the first resurrection"; and this is what is meant by the millennium—the period of a thousand years during which Christ will return to earth and live with His saints, and finally take them to heaven.

Millenarians, or **Chiliasts** (Lat. *mille*, Gr. *chilioi*, a thousand) is the name applied to early Christian sects who believed in a future MILLENNIUM. Such views were held by some post-REFORMATION sects and by some of the 17th-century Independents in England, and more recently by MORMONS, IRVINGITES, and ADVENTISTS.

Millennial Church. *See* SHAKERS.

Miller. A Joe Miller. A stale jest. A certain John Mottley compiled a book of facetiæ in 1739, which (without permission) he entitled *Joe Miller's Jest-Book*, from Joseph Miller (1684–1738), a popular comedian of the day who could neither read nor write. A "Joe Miller" is applied to a stale joke implying that it is stolen from Mottley's compilation. Byron, in *English Bards and Scotch Reviewers*, refers to critics who "take hackney'd jokes from Miller". *Cp.* CHESTNUT.

Every honest miller has a thumb of gold. *See under* THUMB.

More water glideth by the mill than wots the miller of (SHAKESPEARE: *Titus Andronicus*, II, i). Many things are done in a house which the master and mistress never dream of.

To drown the miller. To put too much water into spirits, or tea. The idea is that the supply of water is so great that even the miller, who uses a water wheel, is drowned with it.

Millerites. Followers of William Miller of Massachusetts (1782–1849). *See* SEVENTH-DAY ADVENTISTS.

Millstone. Hard as the nether millstone. Unfeeling, obdurate. The lower or "nether" of the two millstones is firmly fixed and very hard; the upper stone revolved round upon it on a shaft, and the corn, running down a tube inserted in the upper stone, was ground by the motion of the upper stone upon the lower one.

The millstones of Montisci. The stones produce flour of themselves, whence the proverb, "Grace comes from God, but millstones from Montisci" (Boccaccio: *Decameron*, day viii, novel iii).

To carry a millstone round one's neck. To be burdened with some heavy obligation, tie, etc.; to be handicapped by a dependant or companion who cannot be shaken off.

To look, or **see through a millstone.** To be wonderfully sharpsighted.

To weep millstones. Not weep at all.

Milo (mī'lō). A celebrated Greek athlete of Crotona in the late 6th century B.C. It is said that he carried through the stadium at OLYMPIA a heifer four years old, and ate the whole of it afterwards. When old, he attempted to tear in two an oak-tree, but the parts closed upon his hands, and while held fast he was devoured by wolves.

Mimosa (mi mō' zá). So called from the notion that it mimics the sensitivity of animals. The leaves fold upward at the slightest touch, hence the name *Sensitive Plant* for the most commonly cultivated variety, *M. pudica*.

Mince Pies at CHRISTMAS time are said to have been emblematical of the manger in which our Saviour was laid. The paste over the "offering" was made in the form of a cratch or hay-rack.

Mince pies is also RHYMING SLANG for "the eyes".

To mince matters. To avoid giving offence by speaking or censuring in mild terms. More commonly used in the negative to mean blunt speaking. From the mincing of meat to make it more digestible or pleasing.

A mincing manner. A prim manner, one of affected delicacy. Similarly we speak of *mincing ways*.

To make mincemeat of. Utterly to demolish; to completely defeat an opponent, literally or figuratively. Minced meat is meat cut up very fine.

Mind. In my mind's eye; Mind your eye. *See under* EYE.

Mind your own business; keep to your own affairs and don't intermeddle with those of other people; don't interfere or "POKE YOUR NOSE IN" (*see under* NOSE).

Mind your P's and Q's. *See under* P.

To be in two minds over a matter is to be in doubt.

To give a person a piece of one's mind. To express disapproval plainly and forcibly; to castigate.

To have a good mind to do some-

thing. To feel strongly inclined to do it.

To have a mind for it. To desire to possess it; to wish for it. *Mind* meaning desire, intention, is a common usage: "I mind to tell him what I think"; "I shortly mind to leave you", occur in SHAKESPEARE's *Henry VI, Pt. III.* IV, i.

To speak one's mind. To say clearly and emphatically what one thinks about the matter.

Minerva. The Roman goddess of wisdom and patroness of the arts and trades, fabled to have sprung, with a tremendous battle-cry, fully armed from the brain of JUPITER. She was subsequently identified by the Romans with the Greek ATHENE (Athena), the others being Jupiter and JUNO. She is represented as being grave and majestic, clad in a helmet and with drapery over a coat of mail, and bearing the ÆGIS on her breast. Phidias made a statue of her of ivory and gold 39 ft. high which was placed in the PARTHENON.

The Minerva Press. A printing establishment in Leadenhall Street, London, famous in the late 18th century for its trashy, ultra-sentimental novels, characterized by complicated plots, etc.

Miniature. Originally, a rubrication or a small painting in an illuminated MS., which was done with *minium* or red lead. Hence the word came to express any small portrait or picture on vellum or ivory. It is in no way connected with Lat. *minor* or *minimus*.

Minims (Lat. *Fratres Minimi*, least of the brethren). A term of self-abasement assumed by a mendicant order founded by St. Francis of Paula in 1453. They went barefooted, and wore a coarse black woollen stuff, which they never took off, day or night. The FRANCISCANS had already adopted the title of *Fratres Minores* (inferior brothers). The superior of the minims is called *corrector*.

Minister. Literally, an inferior person, in opposition to *magister*, a superior. One is connected with the Lat. *minus*, and the other with *magis*. Our Lord says, "Whosoever will be great among you, let him be your minister", where the antithesis is well preserved. Gibbon has:

> a multitude of cooks, and inferior ministers, employed in the service of the kitchen.
>
> *Decline and Fall*, ch. xxi.

The minister of a church is one who serves the parish or congregation; and a minister of the crown is the sovereign's or state's servant.

Minnesinger. The poet-musicians of 12th—14th century Germany were so called, because the subject of their lyrics was *Minne-sang* (love-ditty). The chief *Minnesinger* were Heinrich von Veldeke, Heinrich von Ofterdingen, Wolfram von Eshenbach, and Walter von der Vogelweide. All of them were men of noble birth and they were succeeded by the MEISTERSINGER.

Minoan. *See* MINOS.

Minoresses. *See* CLARE, ORDER OF ST.

Minorites, or **Minors.** *See* FRANCISCANS.

Minos (mī' nōs). A legendary king and lawgiver of Crete, made at death supreme judge of the lower world, before whom all the dead appeared to give an account of their stewardship, and to receive the reward of their deeds. He was the husband of PASIPHÆ and the owner of the LABYRINTH constructed by DÆDALUS. From his name we have the adjective *Minoan*, pertaining to Crete; the Minoan period is the Cretan bronze age, roughly about 2500–1200 B.C.

Minotaur (mīn' ō tôr). A mythical monster with the head of a bull and the body of a man, fabled to have been the offspring of PASIPHÆ and a bull that was sent to her by POSEIDON. MINOS kept it in his LABYRINTH and fed it on human flesh, seven youths and seven maidens being sent as tribute from Athens every year for the purpose. THESEUS slew this monster.

Minstrel. Originally, one who had some official duty to perform (Lat. *ministerialis*), but quite early in the MIDDLE AGES restricted to one whose duty it was to entertain his employer with music, storytelling, juggling, etc.; hence a travelling gleeman and entertainer.

Mint. The name of the herb is from Lat. *mentha* (Gr. *minthe*), so called from *Minthe*, a NYMPH of the COCYTUS, and beloved by PLUTO. This nymph was metamorphosed by PROSERPINE (Pluto's wife) out of jealousy, into the herb called after her.

The Mint, a place where money is coined, gets its name from O.E. *mynet*, representing Lat. *moneta*, money.

The chief seat of the Mint was at LONDON and was situated in the TOWER of London from its erection until 1810, when it moved to new premises upon Tower Hill and was one of the earliest public buildings lighted with gas. In Henry VIII's reign and in Saxon times, there was also a Mint at Southwark which later became a refuge or asylum for debtors and vagabonds, and a place for illicit marriages. (*Cp.* FLEET MARRIAGES; MAYFAIR MARRIAGES.) The Mint was removed to Llantrisant, west of Cardiff, in 1968. *See also* TRIAL OF THE PYX *under* PYX.

Minute. A Minute gun. A signal of distress at sea, or a gun fired at the death of some distinguished person; so called because a minute elapses between the discharges.

Minute-men. American militiamen who, at the onset of the War of Independence, promised to take arms at a *minute*'s notice. Hence one who is similarly vigilant and ready to take prompt action.

Miocene (mī′ō sēn). The geological period immediately preceding the Pliocene, when the mastodon, *Dinotherium*, *Protohippus* and other creatures flourished.

Miracle plays. *See* MYSTERIES.

Miramolin (Commander of the Faithful). The title in the MIDDLE AGES of the Emperor of Morocco.

Mirror. Cambuscan's mirror. Sent to CAMBUSCAN by the King of Araby and Ind; it warned of the approach of ill fortune, and told if love was returned (Chaucer: *Canterbury Tales*, "The Squires Tale").

Lao's mirror reflected the mind and its thoughts, as an ordinary mirror reflects the outward seeming (Goldsmith: *Citizen of the World*, xlv).

Merlin's magic mirror, given by MERLIN to King Ryence. It informed the king of treason, secret plots, and projected invasions (Spenser: *The Faerie Queene*, III, ii).

Reynard's wonderful mirror. This mirror existed only in the brain of Master Fox. He told the queen lion that whoever looked in it could see what was done a mile off. The wood of the frame was not subject to decay, being made of the same block as King Crampart's magic horse (REYNARD THE FOX, ch. xii).

Vulcan's mirror showed the past, the present, and the future. Sir John Davies tells us that CUPID gave it to ANTINOUS and Antinous gave it to PENELOPE, who saw therein "the court of Queen Elizabeth".

The Mirror for Magistrates. A large collection of poems (published 1555–1559) by William Baldwin, George Ferrers, and many others, with an "Induction" by Thomas Sackville. It contains in metrical form biographical accounts of British historical figures and the mirror reflects the falls of the great. It was much extended in four later editions up to 1587.

The Mirror of Diana. A lake in the Alban hills in the territory of ancient Aricia, in Italy, on the shores of which stood the earliest known temple of DIANA. The priest of this temple, called *Rex Nemorensis*, was either a gladiator or runaway slave who retained office until slain by a successor. The cult is described in the first chapter of Sir James Frazer's *Golden Bough*. The lake, *Nemorensis Lacus* (modern Nemi), is 110 ft. deep and some $3\frac{1}{2}$ miles in diameter.

The Mirror of Human Salvation. See SPECULUM HUMANÆ SALVATIONIS.

The Hall of Mirrors. The famous state apartments of the Palace of VERSAILLES. It was here that King William I of Prussia was acclaimed German Emperor (18 January 1871) after the defeat of France under NAPOLEON III.

Mirror writing. Writing which is reversed and which can only be read when held before a mirror. It sometimes occurs in left-handed people and those with certain derangements. The MSS. of Leonardo da Vinci were written from right to left. *Cp.* LOOKING-GLASS.

Mirza (Pers., royal prince). When prefixed to a surname it is a title of honour, but when annexed to the surname it means a prince of the blood royal.

Miscreant (Fr. *mécréant*). A false believer; a term first applied to the Mohammedans who, in return, call Christian infidels, and associate with this word all that we imply by "miscreants".

Mise (mēz) (O.Fr., expenses). A word used to denote a payment or disbursement, and in particular the payment made by the COUNTY PALATINE of Chester to a new EARL, or by the Welsh to a new lord of the MARCHES and subsequently to a new Prince of WALES, who is also Earl of Chester.

The word is also applied to the settlement of a dispute by agreement or arbitration, as in the *Mise of Amiens* (1264), when Louis IX of France arbitrated between Henry III and the Montfortians, and the subsequent *Mise of Lewes* "for re-establishment of peace in the realm of England and the reconciliation of the discords which have arisen...".

Mise en scène (Fr., setting on stage). The stage setting of a play, including the scenery, properties, etc., and the general arrangement of the piece. Also used metaphorically.

Miserere (miz e rē´ re). The fifty-first psalm is so called because its opening words are *Miserere mei*, Deus (Have mercy upon me, O God. *See* NECK-VERSE). One of the evening services of LENT is called *miserere*, because this penitential psalm is sung, after which a sermon is given. The under side of a folding seat in choirstalls is called a *mis-erere*, or more properly, a **misericord**; when turned up it forms a ledge-seat sufficient to rest the aged in a standing position. A shorter dagger used by knights to end the agony of a wounded man was also known as a *misericord* (Lat. *misereri*, to have pity; *cor*, *cordis*, heart).

Misers. Among the most renowned are:

Baron Aguilar, or Ephraim Lopes Pereira d'Aguilar (1740–1802), born at Vienna and died at Islington, worth £200,000.

Daniel Dancer (1716–1794). His sister lived with him, and was a similar character, but died before him, and he left his wealth to the widow of Sir Henry Tempest, who nursed him in his last illness.

Sir Hervey Elwes, who died in 1763 worth £250,000, but never spent more than £110 a year. His sister-in-law in-

herited £100,000, but actually starved herself to death, and her son John (1714–1789), M.P., an eminent brewer in SOUTHWARK, never bought any clothes, never suffered his shoes to be cleaned, and grudged every penny spent on food.

Thomas Guy (*c*. 1645–1724), founder of Guy's Hospital.

William Jennings (1701–1797), a neighbour and friend of Elwes, died worth £200,000.

Mishna, or **Mishnah** ((Heb., learning, instruction, from *shana*, to learn). The collection of moral precepts, traditions, etc., forming the basis of the TALMUD; the second or oral law (*see* GEMARA). It is divided into six parts: (1) agriculture; (2) Sabbaths, fasts, and festivals; (3) marriage and divorce; (4) civil and penal laws; (5) sacrifices; (6) holy persons and things.

Misnomers. There are many such in English which have arisen through ignorance, confusion of ideas, or from the changes that time brings about. *Catgut* for instance, was in all probability once made from the intestines of a *cat* but now never is, although the name remains.

Many misnomers are to be found in this book. *See* CLEOPATRA'S NEEDLE, FORLORN HOPE, GERMAN SILVER, GUINEA-PIG, HUMBLE PIE, INDIAN (American), JERUSALEM ARTICHOKE, MEERSCHAUM, MOTHER-OF-PEARL, POMPEY'S PILLAR, SAND-BLIND, SLUG-HORN, VENTRILOQUISM, and WORMWOOD.

Some others are:

Blacklead is plumbago or graphite, a form of carbon, and has no LEAD in its composition.

Blindworms are neither blind nor worms. They are legless lizards.

China, as a name for porcelain, gives rise to the contradictory expressions Chelsea china, Nantgarw china, Sèvres china, Dresden china, etc.; like wooden or iron mile*stones*; brass shoe-*horns*; sil-*ver* for our present cupro-nickel coins, etc.

Dutch clocks were of German (*Deutsch*), not Dutch, manufacture.

Elements. Fire, earth, air, and water, still often called "the four elements", are not elements at all.

Galvanized iron is not usually galvanized, but is simply iron dipped into molten zinc.

Guernsey lily (*Nerine sarniensis*) is not a native of Guernsey, but of South Africa. It is said that a ship bringing specimens to Europe was wrecked on the coast of Guernsey; some of the bulbs were washed ashore and took root, hence the misnomer.

Honeysuckle. So named from the old idea that bees extracted honey therefrom, but it is entirely useless to the bee.

India ink comes from China, not from India.

Isle of Portland, in Dorset, is a peninsula.

Japanese vellum is not vellum but a very costly handbeaten Japanese paper made from the inner bark of the mulberry tree.

Rice paper is not made from rice, but from the pith of a Formosan plant, *Fatsia papyrifera*.

Salts of lemon is in reality potassium acid oxalate, or potassium quadroxalate.

Slow-worm (or Blindworm). Is neither slow nor a worm.

Titmouse. Tit implies small and the second syllable represents O.E. *mase*, used of several small birds. It has no connexion with *mouse*.

Tonquin beans. A geographical blunder, for they are the seeds of *Dipteryx odorata*, from Tinka in Guyana, not Tonquin in Asia.

Turkeys do not come from Turkey, but from North America, and were brought to Spain from Mexico.

Turkish baths are not of Turkish origin though they were introduced from the Near East, which was associated with Turkish rule. The correct name of *Hammam* was commonly used in 17th-century England. HUMMUM's Hotel in COVENT GARDEN was on the site of a 17-century *Hammam*.

Whalebone is no bone at all but a horny substance (*baleen*) attached to the upper jaw of the whale which serves to strain the algæ, etc., which it consumes, from the water it takes into its mouth.

Misrule, Feast of. *See* KING OF MISRULE *under* KING.

Miss, Mistress, Mrs. (lady-master). Miss used to be written Mis, and is the first syllable of Mistress; Mrs. is the contraction of *mistress* and is called Mis'ess. As late as the reign of George II, unmarried women used to be styled Mrs., as, Mrs. Lepel, Mrs. Bellenden, Mrs. Blount, all unmarried women (*see* Pope's *Letters*).

Mistress was originally an honourable term for sweetheart or lover ("Mistress mine, where are you roaming"), and in the 17th century "Miss" was often used for a paramour, *e.g.* Charles II's "misses". Mistress has since come to mean a concubine.

The Mistress of the World. Ancient ROME was so called because it controlled all the known world.

To kiss the mistress. To make a good hit, to shoot right into the eye of the target; in bowls, to graze another bowl with your own; the JACK used to be called the "mistress", and when one ball just touches another it is said "to kiss it".

> Rub on, and kiss the mistress
> SHAKESPEARE: *Troilus and Cressida*,
> III, ii.

Miss. To fail to hit or—in such phrases as **I miss you now you are gone**—to lack, to feel the want of.

A miss is as good as a mile. A failure is a failure be it ever so little, and is no more be it ever so great; a narrow escape is an escape. An old form of the phrase was *An inch in a miss is as good as an ell*.

To miss the bus, or **boat.** To miss an opportunity; to be too late to participate in something.

The missing link. A popular term for that stage in the evolution of man when he was developing characteristics that differentiated him from the other primates with whom he shared a common ancestry; the link between man and the ape. The expression is sometimes applied disparagingly or jocularly.

Missal (Lat. *liber missalis*, book of the mass). The book containing the liturgy of the MASS with ceremonial instructions as used in the ROMAN CATHOLIC CHURCH. *See* BREVIARY.

Mississippi Bubble. The French counterpart of our SOUTH SEA BUBBLE and equally disastrous. In 1716, John Law (1671—1729), a Scottish financier, obtained permission to establish a *Banque générale* in France and in 1717 set up the *Compagnie de la Louisiane ou d'Occident* and was granted control of the mint and the farming of the revenue. For these concessions he undertook the payment of the NATIONAL DEBT and at one time shares were selling at nearly 40 times their nominal value. The crash came in 1720 and many people were ruined.

Mistletoe (mis' ĕl tō) (O.E. *mistiltan*; *mist* being both basil and mistletoe, and *tan*, a twig). The plant grows on various trees as a parasite, especially the apple-tree, and was held in great veneration by the DRUIDS when found on the OAK. Shakespeare calls it "the baleful mistletoe" (*Titus Andronicus*, II, iii), perhaps in allusion to the Scandinavian legend that it was with an arrow made of mistletoe that BALDUR was slain, or to the tradition that it was once a tree from which the wood of Christ's CROSS was formed; or possibly with reference to the popular belief that mistletoe berries are poisonous, or to the connexion of the plant with the human sacrifices of the Druids. It is probably for this latter reason it is excluded from church decorations. Culpeper says "some, for the virtues thereof, have called it *lignum sanctae crucis*, wood of the holy cross, as it cures falling sickness, apoplexy and palsy very speedily, not only to be inwardly taken, but to be hung at their neck". Mistletoe is said to have certain toxic qualities when taken in large doses.

Kissing under the mistletoe. An English CHRISTMAS-time custom, dating back at least to the early 17th century. The correct procedure, now seldom observed, is that a man should pluck a berry when he kisses a girl under the mistletoe, and when the last berry is gone there should be no more kissing.

Mistpoeffers. *See* BARISAL GUNS.

Mistress. *See* MISS.

Mithra, or **Mithras.** The god of light of the ancient Persians, one of their chief deities, and the ruler of the universe, sometimes used as a synonym for the SUN. The word means *friend*, and this deity is so called because he befriends man in this life, and protects him against evil spirits after death. He is represented as a young man with a Phrygian cap and plunging daggers into the neck of a bull that lies upon the ground.

Sir Thomas More called the Supreme Being of his *Utopia*, "Mithra" and the cult of Mithraism had certain affinities with Christianity.

Mithridate (mith' ri dāt). A concoction named from Mithridates VI, King of Pontus and Bithynia (d. *c.* 63 B.C.), who is said to have made himself immune from poisons by the constant use of antidotes. It was supposed to be an antidote against poisons and contained 46 or more ingredients.

Mitre (mī' ter) (Gr. and Lat. *mitra*, a headband, turban). The episcopal mitre is supposed to symbolize the cloven tongues of fire which descended on the apostles on the day of PENTECOST (*Acts* ii, 1—12).

Mitten. To give one the mitten. To reject a sweetheart, to jilt. Possibly with a punning allusion to Lat. *mittere*, to send (about your business), whence *dismissal*.

Mittimus (Lat., we send). A command in writing to a jailer, to keep the person named in safe custody. Also a writ for removing a record from one court to another. So called from the first word of the writ.

Mnemosyne (ne mos' i ni). Goddess of memory and mother by ZEUS of the nine MUSES of Greek Mythology. She was the daughter of heaven and earth. (URANUS and GÆA).

Moabite Stone, The. An ancient *stele*, bearing the oldest extant Semitic inscription, now in the LOUVRE, Paris. The inscription, of 34 lines in Hebrew-Phœnician characters, gives an account of the war of Mesha, King of Moab, who reigned about 850 B.C., against Omri, Ahab, and other kings of Israel (*see* II *Kings*, iii). Mesha sacrificed his eldest son on the city wall in view of the invading Israelites. The stone was found by F. Klein at Dibhan in 1868, and is 3 ft. 10 in. high, 2 ft. broad and 14½ in. thick. The Arabs resented its removal and splintered it into fragments, but it has been restored.

Moaning Minnie. A World War II term for a six-barrelled German mortar, from the rising shriek when it was fired. The name was also given to the air-raid warning siren from its repetitive wail and is colloquially applied to any constant moaner or habitual grumbler.

Mob-cap. A bag-shaped cap formerly worn indoors by women and useful for concealing hair that was not yet "done". It was originally called *mab-cap*, from the old verb *mab*, to dress untidily.

Mock. Mock-beggar Hall, or **Manor.** A grand, ostentatious house, where no hospitality is afforded, neither is any charity given.

Modality, in scholastic philosophy, means the *mode* in which anything exists. Kant divides our judgment into three modalities: (1) *Problematic*, touching possible events; (2) *Assertoric*, touching real events; (3) *Apodictic*, touching necessary events.

Moddey Dhoo (pronounced Mawther Doo; Manx, Black Dog). A ghostly black spaniel that for many years haunted Peel Castle in the Isle of MAN. It used to enter the guard room as soon as candles were lighted, and leave it at daybreak. While this spectre dog was present, the soldiers forebore all oaths and profane talk, but they always carried out their nightly duties of locking up and conveying the keys to the captain accompanied by one of their fellows. One night a drunken trooper, from bravado, performed the rounds alone but lost his speech and died in three days. The dog never appeared again.

During excavations in 1871 the bones of Simon, Bishop of Sodor and Man (died 1247) were uncovered, with the bones of a dog at his feet.

Model Parliament. Summoned by Edward I in 1295, it consisted of representatives of the clergy, nobility and commonalty. It included twenty bishops, sixty-seven abbots, seven earls and forty-one barons. In addition there were two knights from every SHIRE and two burgesses from each city or BOROUGH within a shire. It thus set the pattern for subsequent parliaments.

Modernism. A movement in the ROMAN CATHOLIC CHURCH which sought to interpret the ancient teachings of the Church with due regard to the current teachings of science, modern philosophy, and history. It arose in the late 19th century and was formally condemned by Pope Pius X in 1907 in the encyclical *Pascendi*, which stigmatized it as the "synthesis of all heresies".

The term **Modernist** is also applied to liberal and RADICAL critics of traditional theology in other churches. The Modern Churchmen's Union was founded in 1898 and was strongly critical of Anglo-Catholic and Roman Catholic ideals. Dean Inge (1860–1954) and Bishop Barnes (1874–1953) were prominent among its members.

Modred. In ARTHURIAN ROMANCE, one of the Knights of the ROUND TABLE, nephew and betrayer of King ARTHUR. He is represented as the treacherous knight. He revolted against the king, whose wife he seduced, was mortally wounded in the battle of CAMLAN and was buried in AVALON. The story is told, with a variation, in Tennyson's *Guinevere* (*Idylls of the King*).

Mods and Rockers. The *Mods* developed as a teenage cult in London in the early 1960s initially putting their emphasis on fastidiousness and extravagance in dress and fashion. The rise of CARNABY STREET as their dress centre was a consequence. Mainly devoid of social conscience, there was some association with homosexuality and PURPLE HEARTS and their mode of life reflected the less desirable results of the AFFLUENT SOCIETY. With the rise of the rival gangs of leather-jacketed *Rockers*, akin to the Teddy Boys (*see* EDWARDIAN) of the 1950s, trouble began. Bank holiday clashes between Mods and Rockers, who arrived in their hordes on scooters and motor-cycles, made certain seaside resorts hazardous places for the more responsible elements in society. Loutishness prevailed until the authorities took firm measures against them. They were temporarily outmoded by the more recent cult of the Flower-Children. *See* FLOWER POWER *under* POWER.

Modus operandi (Lat.). The mode of operation; the way in which a thing is done, or should be done.

Modus vivendi (Lat., way of living). A working arrangement whereby persons, not on friendly terms at the time, can be induced to live peacefully. The term may be applied to individuals, societies, and peoples.

Mogul (Mongol). **The Great Mogul.** The name given to the ruler of the Mohammedan-Tartar Empire in India which began in 1526 with Baber, great-grandson of Timur, or TAMERLANE. It disintegrated after the death of Aurang-zeb in 1707. Noteworthy among the Mogul emperors were Akbar, Jahangir and Shah Jahan. Wealthy business TY-COONS, etc., are sometimes called *moguls*.

Mohammed, Mahomet (Arab., "the praised one"). There are various spellings, the most correct being *Muhammad*. It is the titular name of the founder of ISLAM, adopted by him at the time of the HEGIRA; his original name is given both as Kotham and as Halabi. He was born at MECCA *c*. 570 and died at MEDINA in 632.

Angel of. When Mohammed was transported to HEAVEN, he said: "I saw there an angel, the most gigantic of all created beings. It had 70,000 heads, each head had 70,000 faces, each face had 70,000 mouths, each mouth had 70,000 tongues, and each tongue spoke 70,000 languages; all were employed in singing God's praises."

Banner of. Sanjaksherif, kept in the Eyab mosque at Istanbul.

Bible of. The KORAN.

Camel (swiftest). Adha.

Cave. The cave in which GABRIEL appeared to Mohammed (610) was in the mountain of Hira, near Mecca.

Coffin. Legend held that Mohammed's coffin was suspended in mid-air at Medina without any support.

> Sp'ritual men are too transcendent...
> To hang, like Mahomet, in the air,
> Or St. Ignatius at his prayer,
> By pure geometry.
> BUTLER: *Hudibras*, III, ii, 602.

Daughter (favourite). Fatima.

Dove. Mohammed had a dove which he fed with wheat out of his ear.

Father of. Abdullah of the tribe of

Koreish. He died just before or after the Prophet's birth.

Father-in-law of. Abu-Bekr (father of Ayesha) and the first CALIPH.

Flight from Mecca. The Hegira.

Horse of. Al Borak. *See* BORAK.

Miracles. Several are traditionally mentioned. The best known is that of the MOON. The story is that Habib the Wise asked Mohammed to prove his mission by cleaving the Moon in two. Mohammed raised his hands towards heaven and commanded the moon to do Habib's bidding. Accordingly it descended to the top of the KAABA, made seven circuits, and coming to the prophet, entered his right sleeve and came out of the left. It then entered the collar of his robe, descended to the skirt, and clove itself into two plaits, one of which appeared in the east of the skies and the other in the west. The two parts ultimately reunited.

Mother of. Amina, of the tribe of Koreish. She died when Mohammed was six years old.

Paradise of. The ten animals admitted to his paradise are:

(1) the dog Kratim, which accompanied the SEVEN SLEEPERS.

(2) BALAAM's ass, which spoke with the voice of a man to reprove the disobedient prophet.

(3) SOLOMON's ant, of which he said, "Go to the ant, thou sluggard ..."

(4) JONAH's whale.

(5) The ram caught in the thicket, and offered in sacrifice in lieu of Isaac.

(6) The calf of ABRAHAM.

(7) The camel of Saleb.

(8) The cuckoo of Bilkis.

(9) The ox of MOSES.

(10) Mohammed's steed, Al BORAK.

Stepping-stone. The stone upon which he placed his foot when he mounted Al Borak on his ascent to heaven. It rose as the beast rose, but Mohammed, putting his hand upon it, forbade it to follow him, whereupon it remained suspended in mid-air, where the True Believer, if he has faith enough, may still behold it.

Tribe. On both sides, the Koreish.

Uncle. Abu Tâlib, who took charge of Mohammed at the death of his grandfather.

Wives. Firstly, Kadija, a rich widow of the tribe of Koreish, who had been twice married already, and was forty years old. For twenty-five years she was his only wife, but he subsequently married a number of others, nine of whom survived him, the favourite being AYESHA. He also had concubines.

Year of Deputations. A.D. 630, the 8th of the Hegira.

If the mountain will not come to Mahomet, Mahomet must go to the mountain. When Mohammed was asked by the Arabs for miraculous proofs of his teaching he ordered Mount Safa to come to him, and as it did not move, he said, "God is merciful. Had it obeyed my words, it would have fallen on us to our destruction. I will therefore go to the mountain and thank God that He has had mercy on a stiffnecked generation." The phrase is often used of one who, unable to get his own way, bows before the inevitable.

Mohocks. A class of ruffians who in the 18th century infested the streets of London. So called from the Mohawk Indians. One of their "new inventions" was to roll people down Snow Hill in a tub; another was to overturn coaches on rubbish-heaps. (*See* Gay: *Trivia*, III.)

A vivid picture of the misdoings of these and other brawlers is given in the *Spectator*, No. 324. *Cp.* MODS AND ROCKERS; TITYRE TUS.

Moira. Fate or Necessity, supreme even over the gods of OLYMPUS.

Moke. A donkey. *See* DICKY.

Mole. A small animal which burrows underground throwing up small heaps of soil called *molehills*. The name is currently applied to spies and traitors obtaining positions of trust in organizations, especially government departments, intelligence and secret service. The most notorious of these moles was Kim Philby (1912–1988), who worked for the U.S.S.R. as did his fellow Cantabrigians Anthony Blunt, Guy Burgess and Donald Maclean.

To make mountains out of molehills. *See under* MOUNTAIN.

Molech. *See* MOLOCH.

Molinism. The system of grace and elec-

tion taught by the Spanish JESUIT, Louis Molina (1535–1600). His doctrine was that grace is a free gift to all, but consent of the will must be present before that grace can be effective. *Cp.* JANSENISTS.

Moll, Molly. Take away this bottle, it has Moll Thompson's mark on it. Moll Thompson is M.T. (*empty*).

Molly coddle. A pampered creature, a NAMBY PAMBY. To molly coddle is to fuss over or pamper.

Molly Maguires. An Irish secret society organized in 1843. Stout, active young Irishmen dressed up in women's clothes and otherwise disguised themselves to surprise rent-collectors. Their victims were ducked in bog-holes or more ruthlessly handled.

Molly Mog. This celebrated beauty was an innkeeper's daughter, at Oakingham, Berks. She was the toast of the gay sparks of the first half of the 18th century, and died unmarried in 1766, at the age of sixty-seven.

Molloch, May, or **The Maid of the Hairy Arms.** An ELF of folklore who mingles in ordinary sports, and will even direct the master of the house how to play dominoes or draughts. Like the WHITE LADY of Avenel, May Molloch is a sort of BANSHEE.

Molmutine Laws. According to Geoffrey of Monmouth, the laws of Dunwallo Molmutius, legendary king of Britain, son of Cloten, king of CORNWALL. *Cp.* MARTIAN LAWS.

Moloch (mō' lok), or **Molech** (Heb., king). Any influence which demands from us the sacrifice of what we hold most dear. Thus, *war* is a Moloch, the *guillotine* was the Moloch of the French Revolution, *king Mob* is a Moloch, etc. The allusion is to the god of the AMMONITES, to whom children were made "to pass through the fire" (II *Kings* xxiii, 10). Milton says he was worshipped in Rabba, in Argob, and Basan, to the stream of utmost Arnon (*Paradise Lost*, I, 392–8). His victims were slain and burnt.

Molotov. The alias of the Russian diplomat Vyacheslav Mikhailovich Skryabin was given in World War II to:

The **Molotov breadbasket.** A canister of incendiary bombs which, on being launched from a plane, opened and showered the bombs over a wide area. Also to the **Molotov cocktail**, a home-made anti-tank bomb, invented and first used by the Finns against the Russians in 1940 and developed in Britain as one of the weapons of the HOME GUARD. It consisted of a bottle filled with inflammable and glutinous liquid, with a slow match protruding from the top. When thrown at a tank the bottle burst, the liquid ignited and spread over the plating of the tank.

Moly. According to HOMER, the mythical herb given by HERMES to ULYSSES as an antidote against the sorceries of CIRCE.

> Black was the root, but milky white the flower,
> Moly the name, to mortals hard to find.
> POPE: *Odyssey*, X, 365.

Momus. (mō' mŭs). One who carps at everything. Momus was the god of ridicule and the son of Nox (Night), who was driven out of HEAVEN for his criticisms of the gods. VENUS herself was censured for the noise made by her feet, although he could find no fault with her naked body.

Monday. The second day of the week until 1971, called by the Anglo-Saxons *Monandæg*, i.e. the day of the Moon. It is now the first. *See* SUNDAY.

Monday's child. The traditional rhyme says:

> Monday's child is fair of face,
> Tuesday's child is full of grace,
> Wednesday's child is full of woe,
> Thursday's child has far to go;
> Friday's child is loving and giving,
> Saturday's child works hard for a living;
> But the child that is born on the Sabbath-day
> Is bonny and blithe and good and gay.

Another rhyme says:

> If you sneeze on Monday, you sneeze for danger;
> Sneeze on Tuesday, kiss a stranger;
> Sneeze on Wednesday, sneeze for a letter;
> Sneeze on Thursday, something better;
> Sneeze on Friday, sneeze for sorrow;
> Sneeze on Saturday, see your sweetheart tomorrow.

That Monday morning feeling. Disinclination to start work after the weekend break (often employed in more strenuous exertion in the garden, etc.).

The swing-it-till-Monday basket. A nickname for the desk tray or basket for non-urgent matter or that which can safely be put aside until after the weekend.

Money. Shortly after the Gallic invasion of ROME, in 344 B.C., Lucius Furius (or according to other accounts, Camillus) built a temple to JUNO Moneta (the *Monitress*) on the spot where the house of Manlius Capitolinus stood; and to this temple was attached the first Roman mint, as the public treasury (*ærarium*) was attached to the temple of SATURN. Hence the "ases" there coined were called *moneta*, and hence our word *money*.

Juno is represented on medals with instruments of coinage, as the hammer, anvil, pincers, and die. *See Livy*, VII, xxviii, and Cicero, *De Divinitate*, i, 15.

The oldest coin of Greece bore the impress of an ox. Hence a bribe for silence was said to be an "ox on the tongue". Subsequently each state had its own impress:

Athens, an owl (the bird of wisdom); *Bœotia*, BACCHUS (the vineyard of Greece); *Delphos*, a dolphin; *Macedonia*, a buckler (from its love of war); *Rhodes*, the disc of the sun (the COLOSSUS was an image to the sun).

Rome had a different impress for each coin:

For the *As*, the head of JANUS on one side, and the prow of a ship on the reverse; the *Semi-as*, the head JUPITER and the letter S; the *Sextans*, the head of MERCURY and two points to denote two ounces; the *Triens* the head of a woman (? Rome or MINERVA) and three points to denote three ounces; the *Quadrans*, the head of HERCULES and four points to denote four ounces.

In every country there are popular nicknames for common coins and sums of money. Thus a *bawbee* in SCOTLAND means a halfpenny and also is applied to money generally. In ENGLAND money is called *brass*, current colloquialisms being *bread* and *lolly*, and we had (before decimalization) a copper (1*d*.); a joey (4*d*. and 3*d*.); a tanner, a tizzy (6*d*.); a bob (1*s*.); half a dollar, two and a kick (2s. 6d.); a dollar, a cartwheel (5s.); a QUID (20s.); a jimmy o'goblin (a SOVEREIGN); a fiver (£5); a tenner (£10); a pony (£25); a monkey (£500).

In N. America: a penny, a Red Indian (1c.); a nickel (5c.); a dime (10c.); a quarter, two bits (25c.); four bits (50c.); a buck (in silver, a cartwheel, a smacker) ($1.00); a SAWBUCK ($10.00); a century ($100.00); a monkey ($500.00); a grand, a G ($1000.00).

Money for old rope, or **money for jam.** An easy job, yielding a profitable reward for little effort.

Money is the root of all evil. Many people will do anything, however unscrupulous it may be, if there is money to be gained.

Money of account is a monetary denomination used in reckoning and often not employed as actual coin. For example, a GUINEA as British money of account, when no coin of this value was in circulation. The U.S.A. *mill*, being one-thousandth of a dollar or one-tenth of a cent, is money of account.

Money talks. The moneyed have considerable influence in many ways.

Money will make the mare go. *See* MARE.

Pin Money. *See under* PIN.

Ready money. Cash down; money available for immediate payment.

Mongrel Parliament. The PARLIAMENT that Charles II summoned at Oxford in 1681 to deprive the WHIGS of the support of the City of LONDON in their struggle to alter the succession, *i.e.*, to exclude the Duke of York, a Roman Catholic.

Monism. (mo′ nizm). The doctrine of the oneness of mind and matter which explains everything in terms of a single reality, ignoring all that is supernatural; any one of the philosophical theories that denies the dualism of mind and matter and seeks to deduce all the varied spiritual and physical phenomena from a single principle.

Monitor (Lat. from *monere*, one who reminds or admonishes, a preceptor, a tutor, etc.). So the Romans called the nursery teacher. The *Military Monitor* was an officer to tell young soldiers of the faults committed against the service.

The *House Monitor* was a slave to rouse the family in the morning, etc. The term has long been applied to school pupils chosen to assist the staff in a variety of duties.

Monkey. Monkey jacket. A short jacket formerly worn by seamen. Possibly so called from its likeness to the jacket of the organ grinder's monkey of bygone days; or because it has no more tail than a monkey (or more strictly speaking, an ape).

Monkey puzzle. The Chilean pine, *Araucaria imbricata*, whose twisted and prickly branches puzzle even a monkey to climb.

Monkey spoons. Spoons having on the handle a heart surmounted by a monkey, at one time given in Holland at marriages to some immediate relative of the bride; at christenings and funerals to the officiating clergyman. *See* TO SUCK THE MONKEY, *below*.

Monkey suit. In the U.S.A. services, the term applied to full dress uniform, also to an aviator's overalls and sometimes to men's formal dress on important occasions.

Monkey tricks. Mischievous, ill-natured, or deceitful actions.

To get one's monkey up. To be riled or enraged; monkeys are often irritable and easily provoked. *Cp.* TO GET ONE'S GOAT *under* GOAT.

To monkey with, or **about.** To tamper with or play mischievous tricks. *To monkey with the cards* is to try to arrange them so that the deal will not be fair; *to monkey with the milk* is to add water to it and then sell it as pure and unadulterated.

To pay in monkey's money (Fr. *en monnaie de singe*). In goods, in personal work, in mumbling and grimace. In PARIS when a monkey passed the Petit Pont, if it was for sale four deniers' toll had to be paid; but if it belonged to a showman and was not for sale, it sufficed if the monkey went through his tricks.

To suck the monkey. Among the Dutch, drinking is called "sucking the monkey", because the early morning appetizer of rum and salt was taken in a MONKEY SPOON. In sailor's slang "to suck the monkey" is to suck liquor from a cask through a straw; and when milk has been taken from a coconut, and rum has been substituted, "sucking the monkey" is drinking this rum.

Monmouth's Rebellion. The disastrous last throw of the Duke of Monmouth, the son of Charles II's mistress Lucy Walter, to overthrow James II as champion of the Protestant religion. He landed at Lyme in 1685 and was hailed as King at Taunton and Bridgwater, but was routed by James II's army at Sedgemoor (6 July). Monmouth was executed and his rustic followers were dealt with at the BLOODY ASSIZES.

Monophysites (Gr. *monos*, one; *phusis*, nature). A religious sect in the Levant which maintained that Jesus Christ had only one nature, and that divine and human were combined in much the same way as body and soul were combined in man. It arose upon the condemnation of the EUTYCHIAN heresy at the Council of Chalcedon, 451, and is still represented by the Coptic (*see* COPTS), Armenian, Abyssinian, Syrian, and Malabar JACOBITE Churches.

Monothelites (Gr. *monos*, one; *thelein*, to will). A 7th-century heretical sect holding that Christ had only one will, the divine. Monothelitism was akin to the teaching of the MONOPHYSITES, and was an attempt to reconcile the latter to their fellow-Christians of the eastern Empire against Persian and Mohammedan invaders. It was condemned finally by the Council of Constantinople (680).

Monroe Doctrine (mùn rō'). The doctrine first promulgated in 1823 by James Monroe (President of the U.S.A., 1817–1825), to the effect that the American States would not entangle themselves in the broils of the Old World, nor suffer European powers to interfere in the affairs of the New. There was to be no future colonization by any European powers.

The Monroe Doctrine was invoked by the UNITED STATES during the Anglo-Venezuelan boundary dispute over the limits of British Guiana (1894–1896).

The capture of Manila and the cession of the Philippines to the United States in 1898, and still more the part the Americans took in the World Wars have abrogated a large part of this famous Doctrine.

Mons Meg. *See under* MEG.

Mons Star. The British war medal ("The 1914 Star") given for service in France or Belgium in 1914, is popularly so called. The battle of Mons was fought on 23 August 1914.

Monseigneur. The title given to the DAUPHIN from the time of Louis XIV.

Monsieur. The eldest brother of the King of France was so called from the time of Louis XIV (1643–1715).

Monsieur de Paris. The public executioner or JACK KETCH of France.

The Peace of Monsieur. The peace that the HUGUENOTS, the POLITIQUES, and the Duke d'Alençon ("Monsieur") obliged Henry III of France to sign in 1576. By it the Huguenots and the Duke gained great concessions.

Monsignor (mon sē' nyôr) (pl. *Monsignori*). A title pertaining to all prelates in the ROMAN CATHOLIC CHURCH, which includes all prelates of the Roman court, active or honorary. Used with the surname, as "Monsignor Newman", it does away with the solecism of speaking of Bishop so-and-so, which is like calling the Duke of Marlborough "Duke Churchill".

Mont. (Fr., hill). The technical term in PALMISTRY for the eminences at the roots of the fingers.

That at the root of the
thumb is the Mont de Mars.
index finger is the Mont de Jupiter.
long finger is the Mont de Saturne.
ring finger is the Mont du Soleil.
little finger is the Mont de Vénus.
The one between the thumb and the index finger is called the Mont de Mercure and the one opposite the Mont de la Lune.

Montagnards. *See* MOUNTAIN, THE.

Montanists. A short-lived 2nd-century heretical sect; so called from Montanus, a Phrygian, who asserted that he had received from the HOLY GHOST special knowledge that had not been vouchsafed to the APOSTLES. They were extreme ascetics and believed in the speedy coming of the Second ADVENT. *See* QUINTILIANS.

Monteer Cap. *See* MONTERO.

Montero, or **Monteer Cap.** So called

from the headgear worn by the *monteros de Espinosa* (mountaineers), who once formed the interior guard of the palace of the Spanish king. It had a spherical crown, and flaps that could be drawn over the ears, not unlike a Victorian shooting-cap.

Montessori Method. A system of training and educating young children evolved by the Italian educationist, Dr. Maria Montessori (1870–1952). Based on "free discipline", and the use of specially devised "educational apparatus" and "didactic material", it has exercised considerable influence on work with young children. *Cp.* FRŒBEL SYSTEM.

Month. One of the twelve divisions of a year. Anciently a new month started on the day of the new MOON, or the day after; hence the name (O.E. *monath*) which is connected with moon. For the individual months *see* their names; *see also* LUNAR MONTH.

The old mnemonic for remembering the number of days in each month runs:

Thirty days hath September,
April, June, and November,
February eight-and-twenty all alone
And all the rest have thirty-one,
Unless that Leap Year doth combine
And give to February twenty-nine.

This, with slight variations, is to be found in Grafton's *Chronicles* (1590), etc. In Harrison's *Description of England* (prefixed to Holinshed's *Chronicle*, 1577), is the Latin version:

Junius, Aprilis, Septemque, Novemque, tricenos,
Unum plus reliqui. Februus tenet octo vicenos,
At si bissextus fuerit superadditur unus.

A month of Sundays. An indefinite but long time; NEVER.

A month's mind. Properly the Requiem MASS said for the deceased on the 30th day after death or burial. The term often occurs in old wills in connection with charities to be disbursed on that day.

A *month's mind* was also used to denote an eager desire, as in:

I have a month's mind, instead of this damnable iteration of guesses and forebodings, to give thee the history of a little adventure which befell me yesterday.
SCOTT: *Redgauntlet, Letter* III.

Month in month out. Throughout all the months; constantly; all the time.

Montjoie St. Denis, or **Denys.** The war cry of mediæval France. *Montjoie* is a corruption of *Mons Jovis*, as the little mounds were called which served as direction-posts in ancient times; hence it was applied to whatever showed or indicated the way, as the banner of St. DENYS, called the ORIFLAMME. The Burgundians had for their war-cry, "Montjoie St. André"; the Dukes of Bourbon, "Montjoie Notre Dame"; and the Kings of England used to have "Montjoie St. George".

Montjoie was also the cry of the French heralds in the TOURNAMENTS, and the title of the French KING OF ARMS.

Where is Mountjoy the herald? speed him hence:
Let him greet England with our sharp defiance.
SHAKESPEARE: *Henry V*, III, v.

Montserrat (Lat. *mons serratus*, the mountain jagged like a saw). The Catalonians aver that this mountain was riven and shattered at the Crucifixion. Every rift is filled with evergreens. The monastery of Montserrat is famous for its printing-press and for its Black Virgin.

Monument. Monuments and effigies in churches. The following points usually apply:

Founders of chapels, etc., lie with their monument built into the wall.

Figures with their hands on their breasts, and chalices, represent *priests*.

Figures with armour represent *knights*.

Figures with legs crossed represent either *crusaders* or *married men*, but those with a SCALLOP SHELL are certainly *crusaders*.

Female figures with a mantle and large ring represent *nuns*.

In the age of CHIVALRY the woman was placed on the man's right hand; but when chivalry declined she was placed on his left hand.

It may usually be taken that ancient inscriptions in Latin, cut in capitals, are of the first twelve centuries; those in Lombardic capitals and French, of the 13th; those in Old English text, of the 14th; while those in the English language and roman characters are subsequent to the 14th century.

Tablets against the wall came in with the REFORMATION; and brasses are mostly post-13th century.

Moody and Sankey. Dwight Lyman Moody (1836–1899) was the son of a Massachusetts bricklayer who began his evangelical work in 1860. He was joined by Ira David Sankey (1840–1908) in 1870, who backed up Moody's preaching with singing and organ music. The famous "Sankey and Moody hymn book", first published in 1873, properly called *Sacred Songs and Solos*, was "compiled and sung" by Sankey. Their type of "Gospel Hymn" was partly popularized in Great Britain during their visits to this country and particularly by the SALVATION ARMY.

Moon. The word is probably connected with the Sanskrit root *me-*, to measure, because time was measured by it. It is common to all Teutonic languages (Goth. *mena*; O.Frisian *mona*; O.Norm. *mane*; O.E. *mona*, etc.) and is almost invariably masculine. In the EDDA the son of Mundilfœri is MANI (moon), and daughter SOL (sun); so it is still with the Lithuanians and Arabians, and so it was with the ancient Slavs, Mexicans, Hindus, etc., and the Germans still have *Frau Sonne* (Mrs. Sun) and *Herr Mond* (Mr. Moon).

The moon is represented in five different phases: (1) new; (2) full; (3) crescent or decrescent; (4) half; and (5) gibbous, or more than half. In pictures of the ASSUMPTION it is shown as a crescent under Our Lady's feet; in the Crucifixion it is eclipsed, and placed on one side of the CROSS, the SUN being on the other; in the Creation and Last JUDGMENT it is also depicted.

In classical mythology the moon was known as HECATE before she had risen and after she had set; as ASTARTE when crescent; as DIANA or CYNTHIA (she who "hunts the clouds") when in the open vault of heaven; as PHŒBE when looked upon as the sister of the sun (*i.e.* PHŒBUS); and was personified as SELENE or Luna, the lover of the sleeping ENDYMION, *i.e.* moonlight on the fields.

The moon is called *triform*, because it

presents itself to us either round, or waxing with horns towards the east, or waning with horns towards the west.

One legend connected with the moon was that there was treasured everything wasted on earth, such as misspent time and wealth, broken vows, unanswered prayers, fruitless tears, unfulfilled desires and intentions, etc. In ARIOSTO'S ORLANDO FURIOSO, Astolpho found on his visit to the moon (Bk. XXXIV, lxx) that bribes were hung on gold and silver hooks; princes' favours were kept in bellows; wasted talent was kept in vases, each marked with the proper name, etc.; and in *The Rape of the Lock* (canto V) Pope tells us that when the Lock disappeared—

> Some thought it mounted to the lunar sphere,
> Since all things lost on earth are treasured there,
> There heroes' wits are kept in pondr'ous vases,
> And beaux' in snuff-boxes and tweezer-cases.
> There broken vows and death-bed alms are found
> And lovers' hearts with ends of riband bound,
> The courtier's promises, and sick man's prayers,
> The smiles of harlots, and the tears of heirs,
> Cages for gnats, and chains to yoke a flea,
> Dried butterflies, and tomes of casuistry.

Hence the phrase, the **limbus of the moon.** *Cp.* LIMBO.

The cycle of the moon. *See under* CYCLE.

The island of the moon. Madagascar is so named by the natives.

Mahomet and the moon. *See* MOHAMMED.

The man in the moon. Some say it is a man leaning on a fork, on which he is carrying a bundle of sticks picked up on a Sunday. The origin of this fable is from *Numb.* xv, 32–36. Some add a dog also; thus SHAKESPEARE'S *Midsummer Night's Dream* (V, i) says:

> This man with lantern, dog, and bush of thorn,
> Presenteth moonshine.

Another tradition says that the man is Cain, with his dog and thorn bush; the thorn bush being emblematical of the thorns and briars of the fall, and the dog being the "foul fiend". Some poets make out the "man" to be ENDYMION, taken to the moon by DIANA.

Minions of the moon. Thieves who rob by night (*See* SHAKESPEARE: *Henry IV, Pt. I*, I, ii).

Moon's men. Thieves and highwaymen who ply their trade by night.

The Mountains of the Moon means simply White Mountains. The Arabs call a white horse "moon-coloured".

I know no more about it than the man in the moon. I know nothing at all about the matter.

Once in a blue moon. *See* BLUE MOON *under* BLUE.

To aim, or level at the moon. To be very ambitious, as to aim, in shooting, at the moon.

To be over the moon. To be highly excited, extremely delighted, in raptures over something.

To cast beyond the moon. *See* CAST.

To cry for the moon. To crave for what is wholly beyond one's reach. The allusion is to foolish children who "cry for the moon to play with". The French say *Il veut prendre la lune avec les dents* (He wants to take the moon between his teeth), alluding to the old proverb about the "moon" and a "green cheese".

You have found an elephant in the moon. You have found a MARE'S NEST. Sir Paul Neale, a conceited virtuoso of the 17th century, gave out that he had discovered "an elephant in the moon". It turned out that a mouse had crept into his telescope, and had been mistaken for an elephant in the moon. Samuel Butler has a satirical poem on the subject called *The Elephant in the Moon*.

You would have me believe that the moon is made of green cheese—*i.e.* the most absurd thing imaginable.

Moon-calf. An inanimate, shapeless abortion, formerly supposed to be produced prematurely owing to the malign influence of the moon; also a dolt or dunderhead.

Moon-drop. In Latin, *virus lunare*, a vaporous foam supposed anciently to be shed by the moon on certain herbs and objects, when influenced by incanta-

tions.

Moonies. A religious sect, properly called the *Unification Church*, founded by Sun Myung Moon in South Korea in 1954. It spread to the U.S.A. in the 1960s and subsequently to Great Britain, Australia, etc. Moon claims to be the Second MESSIAH and his devotees will save mankind from SATAN. Funds built up by his followers by selling artificial flowers and other items were used by Moon to create a large property and business organization in America where he has dwelt since 1972. Tax avoidance led to his prosecution and imprisonment (1984–1985).

Moonlight. A moonlight flit. A clandestine removal of one's furniture during the night, to avoid paying one's rent or having the furniture seized in payment thereof.

Moonlighting. In the Ireland of former days, the name given to acts of agrarian violence at night. In Australia, riding after cattle by night and, in the U.S.A., holding a night job in addition to one's regular employment. In Great Britain the term is now somewhat loosely applied to the additional employment outside regular working hours predominantly undertaken by building workers, craftsmen, electricians, etc.; also to undeclared employment by the registered unemployed. The employer usually pays in cash and tax evasion is thus possible.

Moonrakers. A nickname of Wiltshire folk; also of simpletons. From the story that Wiltshire yokels, with typical country guile, when raking a pond for kegs of smuggled brandy, feigned stupidity when surprised by the excise men, and said that they were trying to rake out the moon, which was reflected in the water.

Moonshine. In the U.S.A., especially Florida, a colloquial term for illicitly distilled liquor, the keeper of an illicit still being called a *moonshiner*. The liquor, called "corn", "shine", or "white lightning", is made from maize, sugar, and water. *See* BOOTLEGGER. In general colloquial usage the word means "nonsense", as in the phrase *It's all moonshine*; here the allusion is to the supposed effects of moonlight on mental stability. *Cp.* LUNATIC.

Moonstone. A variety of feldspar, so called on account of the play of light which it exhibits. It contains bluish-white spots, which, when held to the light, present a silvery play of colour not unlike that of the MOON.

Moor. The word is from Gr. and Lat. *Maurus*, an inhabitant of MAURITANIA. In the MIDDLE AGES, Europeans called all Mohammedans *Moors*, similarly the Eastern nations called all Europeans *Franks*. Camoëns, in the LUSIADS (Bk. VIII), gives the name to the Indians.

Moor-slayer, or **Mata-moros.** A name given to St. JAMES, the patron saint of Spain, because, as the legends say, in encounters with the Moors he came on his white horse to the aid of the Christians. *See also* MATAMORE.

Moot (O.E. *gemot*, a meeting). In Anglo-Saxon times, the assembly of freemen in a township, TITHING, etc. The main moots were those of the SHIRE and HUNDRED which served as units of local government. In a few towns, *e.g.* Aldeburgh, Suffolk, the town hall is still called the Moot Hall. *Cp.* WITENAGEMOT. In legal circles the name is given to the students' debates on supposed cases which formerly took place in the halls of the INNS OF COURT. The benchers and BARRISTERS took part, as well as the students.

Moot case, or **moot point.** A doubtful or unsettled question; one that is open to debate.

Mop, or **Mop Fair.** A statute or HIRING FAIR (*see under* FAIR). So called from the "mop" (a turf or tassel) worn as a badge by those seeking hire. Carters fastened a piece of whipcord to their hats; shepherds, a lock of wool; grooms, a piece of sponge, etc.

All mops and brooms. Intoxicated.

Mops and mows. Grimaces; here mop is connected with Dut. *moppen*, to pout.

Mopping-up operations. In military parlance means the final reduction of isolated pockets of enemy resistance.

Moral. Father of Moral Philosophy. St. THOMAS AQUINAS (*c.* 1225–1274).

Moral Re-armament (M.R.A.). A movement founded in 1938 by Frank Buchman, who had earlier founded the

OXFORD GROUP. Its purpose is to counter the MATERIALISM of present-day society by persuading people to live according to the highest standards of morality and love, to obey God, and to unite in a worldwide association according to these principles.

Morality Play. An allegorical dramatic form in vogue from the 15th to the 16th centuries in which the vices (*see* SEVEN DEADLY SINS) and VIRTUES were personified and the victory of the latter clearly established. It was a development from the earlier MYSTERY Plays. EVERYMAN, a 15th-century play translated from the Dutch *Elkerlijk*, is the best-known. *Cp.* PASSION PLAY.

Moran's Collar. In Irish folk-tale, the collar of Moran, the wise councillor of King Feredach the Just, which strangled the wearer if he deviated from the strict rules of equity.

Moravians. A PROTESTANT Church which is a direct continuation of the BOHEMIAN BRETHREN. Theirs is a simple and unworldly form of religion and John Wesley was influenced by them. They are now to be found in Denmark, Holland, Germany, Switzerland, Great Britain, and America.

More. More or less. Approximately; in round numbers, etc.; as, "It is ten miles, more or less, from here to there," *i.e.*, "it is about ten miles."

The more one has, the more one desires, or **wants.** In French, *Plus il en a, plus il en veut*. In Latin, *Quo plus habent, eo plus cupiunt*.

The more the merrier, the fewer the better cheer, or **fare.** The proverb is found in Heywood's *Collection* (1546) and Ray's (1670).

To be no more. To exist no longer; to be dead.

> Cassius is no more.
> SHAKESPEARE: *Julius Cæsar*, V, iii.

More of More Hall. *See* WANTLEY, DRAGON OF.

Morgan Le Fay. The fairy sister of King ARTHUR, a principal figure in CELTIC legend and ARTHURIAN ROMANCE, also known as *Morgane, Morganetta, Morgaine, Morgue la Faye* and (especially in ORLANDO FURIOSO) as *Morgana*. *See* FATA MORGANA.

It was Morgan le Fay who revealed to King Arthur the intrigues of LANCELOT and GUINEVERE. She gave him a cup containing a magic draught and he had no sooner drunk it than his eyes were opened to the perfidy of his wife and friend.

In *Orlando Furioso*, she is represented as living at the bottom of a lake, and dispensing her treasures to whom she liked. In ORLANDO INNAMORATO, she first appears as "Lady Fortune", but subsequently assumes her witch-like attributes. In TASSO, her three daughters, Morganetta, Nivetta, and Carvilia, are introduced.

In the romance of OGIER THE DANE she receives Ogier in the Isle of AVALON when he is over 100 years old, restores him to youth, and becomes his bride.

Morganatic Marriage. One between a man of high (usually royal) rank and a woman of lower station, as a result of which she does not acquire the husband's rank and neither she nor any children of the marriage are entitled to inherit the title or possessions; often called a "left-handed marriage" because the custom is for the man to pledge his troth with his left hand instead of his right. George William, Duke of Zell, married Eleanora d'Esmiers in this way, and she took the name and title of Lady Harburg; her daughter was Sophia Dorothea, the wife of George I. George, Duke of Cambridge (1819–1904), cousin of Queen Victoria, contracted a morganatic marriage in 1840. His children took the surname Fitz-George. The word comes from the Med. Lat. phrase *matrimonium ad morganaticam*, the last word representing O.H. Ger. *morgangeba*, the morning-gift, from husband to wife after the consummation of the marriage, and the wife's only claim to her husband's possessions.

Morgane, Morganetta. *See* MORGAN LE FAY.

Morgante Maggiore (môr gan' te mäjôr' ė). A serio-comic romance in verse by Pulci of Florence (1482). The characters had appeared previously in many old romances; Morgante is a ferocious giant, converted by ORLANDO (the real hero) to Christianity. After performing the most wonderful feats, he dies at last from the bite of a crab.

Pulci was practically the inventor of this burlesque form of poetry, called by the French BERNESQUE, from the Italian, Berni (1497–1535), who excelled in it.

Morgiana (môr ji ăn' à). In the ARABIAN NIGHTS (*Ali Baba and the Forty Thieves*), the clever, faithful slave of ALI BABA, who pries into the forty jars and discovers every jar but one contains a man. She takes the oil from the only jar containing it, and having made it boiling hot, pours enough into each jar to kill the thief therein. Finally she kills the captain of the gang and marries her master's son.

Morgue la Faye. The form of the name MORGAN LE FAY in OGIER THE DANE.

Morley, Mrs. The name under which Queen Anne corresponded with "Mrs. Freeman" (Sarah Churchill, Duchess of Marlborough).

Mormons. Properly the *Church of Jesus Christ of Latter-Day Saints* regarding itself as a restoration of the one and only Gospel of Christ.

Joseph Smith (1805–1844), a farmer's son of Western New York, claimed in 1820 that God the Father and his Son Jesus Christ had appeared to him and in 1823 that an account of the early inhabitants of America and of the everlasting Gospel inscribed on gold plates had been revealed to him and subsequently, in 1827, these plates were delivered to him. The result was the *Book of Mormon* produced at Palmyra, New York, in 1830, the book taking its name from the prophet Mormon, who had condensed earlier plates. In the same year Smith and his associates founded the Church. Smith was later murdered by a mob when imprisoned by his enemies in Carthage, Illinois, and his place was taken by Brigham Young (1801–1877), a carpenter. He led the persecuted "Saints" to the valley of the Salt Lake, 1,500 miles distant, generally called Utah, but by the Mormons, *Deseret* (Bee-country) the New Jerusalem where they have been settled since 1847, despite many disputes with the U.S. Government.

The Mormons accept the BIBLE as well as the *Book of Mormon* as authoritative, they hold doctrines of repentance and faith, that Zion will be built on the American continent, and believe in baptism, the EUCHARIST, the physical resurrection of the dead, and in the Second ADVENT when Christ will have the seat of His power in Utah. Marriage may be for "time and eternity". Popularly associated with polygamy the Mormons practised it until 1890 when the U.S. Supreme Court finally declared against it and this was accepted by the Church. Hence the expression **a regular Mormon** for a promiscuous or flighty person who cannot keep to one wife or sweetheart.

After Smith's death those who refused to recognize Brigham Young's presidency subsequently established the *Reorganized Church of Jesus Christ of Latter-Day Saints* at Wisconsin in 1852. Notably it rejected polygamy, claiming that it was introduced by Brigham Young, and also that it is the true successor of the original Church. Its headquarters are now at Independence, Missouri.

Mormon missionaries first arrived in Britain in 1837 and there are now some 350 congregations in the United Kingdom following a strict code of behaviour and self-sufficiency.

Moros. The name of the MOSLEM inhabitants of the island of Mindanao and the Sulu Archipelago in the Philippine Islands, and applied to them by the Spanish conquerors because of their supposed resemblance to MOORS.

Morpheus. Ovid's name for the son of Sleep, and god of dreams; so called from Gr. *morphe*, form, because he gives these airy nothings their form and fashion. Hence the name of the narcotic, *morphine*, or *morphia*.

Morrice, Gil, or **Childe.** The hero of an old Scottish ballad, a natural son of an earl and the wife of Lord Barnard, and brought up "in gude grene wode". Lord Barnard, thinking the Childe to be his wife's lover, slew him with a broadsword, and setting his head on a spear gave it to "the meanest man in a' his train" to carry to the lady. When she saw it she said to the baron, "Wi' that saim speir, O pierce my heart, and put me out o' pain"; but the baron replied, "Enouch of blood by me's bin spilt ... sair, sair I rew the deid," adding:

> I'll ay lament for Gill Morice,
> As gin he were mine ain;
> I'll neir forget the dreiry day
> On which the youth was slain.
> PERCY: *Reliques (Gil Morrice)*, xxvi.

Percy says this pathetic tale suggested to Home the plot of his tragedy, *Douglas*.

Morris Dance. A dance, popular in England in the 15th century and later, in which the dancers often represented characters from the ROBIN HOOD stories (*see* MAID MARIAN). Other stock characters were Bavian the fool, MALKIN the clown, the HOBBY-HORSE, or a DRAGON, and foreigners, probably MOORS or Moriscos. It was commonly part of the MAY-games and other pageants and festivals and the dancers were adorned with bells. It was brought from Spain in the reign of Edward III, and was originally a military dance of the Moors or Moriscos, hence its name.

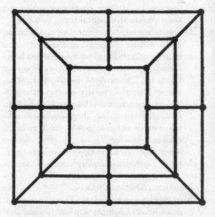

Nine Men's Morris. An ancient game (similar to draughts) once popular with shepherds, still found in East Anglia, and either played on a board or on flat greensward. Two persons have each nine pieces or "men" which they place down alternately on the spots (*see* diagram), and the aim of either player is to secure a row of three men on any line on the board, and to prevent his opponent achieving this by putting one of his own men on a line which looks like being completed, etc. Strutt says , "The rustics, when they have not materials at hand to make a table, cut the lines in the same form upon the ground, and make a small hole for every dot."

> The fold stands, empty in the drowned field,
> And crows are fatted with the murrain flock;
> The nine men's morris is fill'd up with mud.
>
> SHAKESPEARE: *A Midsummer Night's Dream*, II, ii.

It is also called *Merelles*.

Mortal. A mortal sin. A "deadly" sin, one which deserves everlasting punishment; opposed to VENIAL.

> Earth trembled from her entrails ... some sad drops
> Wept at completing of the mortal Sin
> Original; while Adam took no thought.
>
> MILTON: *Paradise Lost*, IX, 1003.

In slang and colloquial speech the word is used to express something very great or excessive, as, "He's in a mortal funk", "There was a mortal lot of people there", or as an emphatic expletive, "you can do any mortal thing you like."

Mortar-board. A college CAP surmounted by a square "board" usually covered with black cloth. The word is possibly connected with Fr. *mortier*, the cap worn by the ancient kings of France, and still used officially by the chief justice or president of the court of justice. It is perhaps more likely an allusion to the small square board or hawk on which a bricklayer or plasterer carries his mortar. *See* PHARISEES.

Morte d'Arthur, Le. *See* ARTHURIAN ROMANCES.

Morther. *See* MAUTHER.

Mortmain (O.Fr., Lat. *mortua manus*, dead hand). A term applied to land that was held inalienably by ecclesiastical or other corporations. In the 13th century, it was common for persons to make over their land to the Church and then receive it back as tenants, thus escaping their feudal obligations to the king or other lay lords. In 1279 the Statute of Mortmain was passed prohibiting the practice without the king's licence.

Morton's Fork. John Morton (*c.* 1420–1500), CARDINAL and Archbishop of Canterbury and minister of Henry VII, when levying forced loans or BENEVOLENCES from rich men so arranged that none should escape. Those who were ostentatiously rich were forced to contribute on the ground that they could well afford it, those who lived without display on the ground that their economies must mean they had savings. The argument was dubbed "Morton's fork", which was two-pronged.

Mortuary. Formerly a gift of the second best beast of the deceased to the incumbent of the parish church, later of the first or second best possession. In due course mortuaries became fees and in 1529 PARLIAMENT limited them to moderate amounts. The custom lingered on in some parishes into the 18th century.

Mosaic Law. The laws given in the PENTATEUCH including the Ten Commandments.

Moses. The horns of Moses' face. Moses is conventionally represented with horns, owing to a blunder in translation. In *Exod.* xxxiv, 29, 30, where we are told that when Moses came down from Mount Sinai "the skin of his face shone", the Hebrew for this *shining* may be translated either as "*sent forth beams*" or "sent forth *horns*"; and the VULGATE took the latter as correct, rendering the passage: *quod cornuta esset facies sua. Cp. Hab.* iii, 4, "His brightness was as the light; he had horns [rays of light] coming out of his hand."

MICHELANGELO followed the earlier painters in depicting Moses with horns.

Moses' rod. The DIVINING ROD is sometimes so called, after the rod with which Moses worked wonders before Pharaoh (*Exod.* vii, 9), or the rod with which he smote the rock to bring forth water (*Exod.* xvii, 6).

Moslem, or **Muslim** (moz' lem, mŭz' lim). A follower of ISLAM. The Arabic plural *Moslemin* is sometimes used, but *Moslems* is more common, and in English more correct.

Mosstrooper. A robber, a bandit; applied especially to the marauders who infested the borders of ENGLAND and SCOTLAND, who encamped on the *mosses* (O.E. *mos*, a bog).

Most. Most unkindest cut of all. Treachery from a friend; the proverbial "last straw". From SHAKESPEARE's *Julius Cæsar* (III, ii). When Mark Antony was showing the dagger cuts in Cæsar's mantle he thus referred to the thrust made by BRUTUS, whom he described as "Cæsar's angel".

> For when the noble Cæsar saw him stab,
> Ingratitude, more strong than traitor's arms,
> Quite vanquished him.

Mother. Mother Ann, Bunch, Goose, Shipton, etc. *See* these names.

Mother Carey's Chickens. Sailor's name for stormy petrels, probably derived from *mater cara* or *madre cara* ("mother dear", with reference to the Virgin Mary). Sailors also call falling snow *Mother Carey's Chickens*. See Marryat's *Poor Jack* for an account of sailors' superstitions on such matters.

Mother Carey's Goose. The great black petrel or fulmar of the Pacific.

Mother Carey is plucking her goose. It is snowing. *Cp.* HULDA.

Mother Church. The church considered as the central fact, the head, the last court of appeal in all matters pertaining to conscience or religion. St. John LATERAN, at ROME, is known as the *Mother and Head of all churches*. Also, the principal or oldest church in a country or district; the cathedral of a diocese.

Mother country. One's native country; or the country whence one's ancestors came to settle. England is the *Mother country* of Australia, New Zealand, Canada, etc. The German term is *Fatherland*.

Mother Earth. When Junius BRUTUS (after the death of Lucretia) formed one of the deputation to DELPHI to ask the ORACLE which of the three would succeed TARQUIN, the response was, "He who should first kiss his mother." Junius instantly threw himself on the ground, exclaiming, "Thus, then, I kiss thee, Mother Earth", and he was elected consul.

Mothering Sunday. MID-LENT SUNDAY, LÆTARE SUNDAY, when the POPE blesses the GOLDEN ROSE, children feast on mothering cakes and SIMNEL CAKES. A bunch of violets is emblematic of this day, and it is customary for children to give small presents to their mothers. It is said that it is derived from the pre-Reformation custom of visiting the MOTHER CHURCH on that day. Children away from home, especially daughters in service, normally returned to their family.

The Mother of Believers. Among Mohammedans, AYESHA, the second and favourite wife of MOHAMMED, who was called the "Father of Believers". Mohammed's widows are also sometimes called "mothers of believers".

Mother of Presidents. The state of Virginia. George Washington, first President of the U.S.A. (1789–1796), was a Virginian.

Mother's Day. In the U.S.A. the second Sunday in MAY is observed to remember one's mother by some act of grateful affection. In schools the preceding Friday is so observed. *Cp.* MOTHERING SUNDAY.

Mothers' meeting. A meeting of mothers held periodically in connection with some church or denomination, at which the women can get advice or religious instruction, drink tea, gossip, and sometimes do needlework. Hence, facetiously, a gossiping group of people—men as well as women.

Mother's ruin. A nickname for GIN.

Mother's Union. A CHURCH OF ENGLAND women's society to safeguard and strengthen Christian family life, to uphold the lifelong vows of marriage, and generally to play a proper part in the life of the Church. It was incorporated by Royal Charter in 1926 and generally operates as a parish institution.

Does your mother know you're out? A jeering remark addressed to a presumptuous youth or to a simpleton. It is the title of a comic poem published in the *Mirror*, 28 April 1838. It became a catch phrase both in England and America and occurs in Barham's *Ingoldsby Legends* (*Misadventures at Margate*).

Oh mother, look at Dick! Said in derision when someone is showing off, or doing something easy with the intent of being applauded for his skill.

Tied to one's mother's apron-strings. *See under* APRON.

Mother-of-pearl. The inner iridescent layers of the shells of many bivalve molluscs, especially that of the pearl oyster.

Mother-sick. Hysterical. Hysteria in women used to be known as "the mother". It also means "pining for one's mother".

Mother-wit. Native wit, a ready reply; the wit which "our mother gave us".

Motley. Men of Motley. Licensed fools; so called from their dress.

> Motley's the only wear.
> SHAKESPEARE: *As You Like It*, II, vii.

Motu proprio (Lat.). Of one's own motion; of one's own accord. Always applied to a rescript drawn up and issued by the POPE on his own initiative without the advice of others, and signed by him.

Mountain. The Mountain (Fr. *La Montagne*). The JACOBINS and extremists in the National Assembly at the time of the French Revolution, so called because they occupied the topmost benches on the left. Among its leaders were Robespierre, Danton, Marat, Collot-d'Herbois, Camille Desmoulins, Carnot, and St. Just. They gained ascendancy in the CONVENTION, supporting the execution of the king and the REIGN OF TERROR. The terms *Montagnard* and *Jacobin* were synonymous. Extreme RADICALS in France are still called *Montagnards Cp*. PLAIN.

> The Mountain, on the other hand, was resolved, less from ferocity than from calculation, that the king should die.
> LOUIS MADELIN: *The French Revolution*, ch. xxv.

Mountain Ash. *See* ROWAN.

Mountain dew. Scotch whisky; formerly that from illicit stills hidden away in the mountains. *Cp*. MOONSHINE.

The mountain in labour. A mighty effort made for a small effect. The allusion is to the celebrated line "*Parturient montes, nascetur ridiculus mus*" (Mountains will be in labour and the birth will be a funny little mouse) by HORACE (*Ars Poetica*, 139). A similar quotation occurs in ÆSOP. Creech translates Horace, "The travailing mountain yields a silly mouse"; and Boileau, "*La montagne en travail enfante une souris*".

There is a story that the Egyptian king, Tachos, sustained a long war against Artaxerxes Ochus, and sent to the Lace-dæmonians for aid. King Agesilaus went with a contingent, but when Tachos saw a little, ill-dressed, lame man, he said: "*Parturiebat mons; formidavat Jupiter; ille vero murem peperit.*" ("The Mountain laboured, JUPITER stood aghast, and a mouse ran out.") Agesilaus replied, "You call me a mouse, but I will soon show you I am a lion."

The Old Man of the Mountains (*Sheikh-al-Jebal*). Hasan ibn-al-Sabbah, or Hassan ben Sabbah, the founder of the ASSASSINS, who made his stronghold in the mountain fastnesses of Lebanon. He led an Ismaili revival against the SELJUKS and by the end of the 11th century his terrorists were well established throughout Persia and Iraq.

To make mountains out of mole-hills. To make a difficulty of trifles. Lat. *Arcem ex cloaca facere*. The corresponding French proverb is, *Faire d'une mouche un éléphant*.

Mountebank (Ital. *montambanco*). A vendor of quack medicines at FAIRS, etc., who attracts the crowd by his tricks and antics; hence any CHARLATAN or self-advertising pretender. The BANK, or bench, was the counter on which traders displayed their goods, and street-vendors used to *mount* on their *bank* to patter to the public.

Mourning. *Black*. To express the privation of light and joy, the midnight gloom of sorrow for the loss sustained. The colour of mourning in Europe; also in ancient Greece and the Roman Empire.

Black and white striped. To express sorrow and hope. The mourning of the South Sea Islanders.

Greyish-brown. The colour of the earth to which the dead return.

Pale brown. The colour of withered leaves. The mourning of Persia.

Sky blue. To express the assured hope that the deceased has gone to HEAVEN; used in Syria, Armenia, etc.

Deep blue. The colour of mourning in Bokhara, also that of the Romans of the Republic.

Purple and violet. To express royalty,

"kings and priests to God". The colour of mourning for CARDINALS and the kings of France; in Turkey the colour is violet.

White. Emblem of "white-handed hope". Used by the ladies of ancient ROME and Sparta, also in Spain till the end of the 15th century. Henry VIII wore white for Anne Boleyn.

Yellow. The sere and yellow leaf. The colour of mourning in Egypt and in Burma, where it is also the colour of the monastic order. In Brittany, widows' caps among the *paysannes* are yellow. Anne Boleyn wore yellow mourning for Katharine of Aragon. Some say yellow is in token of exaltation. *See also* BLACK CAP.

Mournival. *See* GLEEK.

Mouse. The soul was of often anciently supposed to pass at death through the mouth of man in some animal form, sometimes a mouse or rat. A red mouse indicated a pure soul; a black mouse, a polluted soul; a pigeon or dove, a saintly soul.

Mouse is also slang for a black eye, and was formerly a common term of endearment, like *bird, birdie; duckie* and *lamb*.

It's a bold mouse that nestles in the cat's ear. Said of one who is taking an unnecessary risk. The proverb appears in Herbert's *Collection* (1640).

Poor as a church mouse. *See* POOR.

The mouse that hath but one hole is quickly taken. Have two strings to your BOW. The proverb occurs in Herbert's *Collection* (1640) and in many European languages. In Latin *Mus non uni fidit antro*, the mouse does not trust to one hole.

When the cat's away the mice will play. *See under* CAT.

Mousterian. A name given to the epoch of NEANDERTHAL MAN, from the cave of Le Moustier near Les Eyzies, on the right bank of the Vézère in France, where PALÆOLITHIC remains were found.

Mouth, Down in the mouth. *See* DOWN.

His heart was in his mouth. *See under* HEART.

Hold your mouth! or **Stop your mouth!** A rougher equivalent of "hold

your tongue" be silent.

That makes my mouth water. The fragrance of appetizing food excites the salivary glands. The phrase means— that makes me long for it or desire it.

To be born with a silver spoon in one's mouth. *See under* BORN.

To laugh on the wrong side of one's face or **mouth.** *See under* LAUGH.

To live from hand to mouth. *See under* HAND.

To look a gift horse in the mouth. *See* GIFT-HORSE.

To make a mouth. To pull a wry face, to pout; to distort one's mouth in mockery.

To mouth one's words. To talk affectedly or pompously; to declaim.

> He mouths a sentence as curs mouth a bone.
> CHURCHILL: *The Rosciad*, 322.

To open one's mouth wide. To name too high a price; to strain after too big a prize.

To place oneself, or **one's head in the lion's mouth.** *See under* LION.

Moutons. Revenons à nos moutons (Fr., "Let us come back to our sheep"). A phrase used to express "Let us return to the subject". It is taken from the 14th century French comedy *La Farce de Maître Pathelin,* or *l'Avocat Pathelin* (line 1282), in which a woollen-draper charges a shepherd with ill-treating his sheep. In telling his story he continually ran away from the subject; and to throw discredit on the defendant's attorney (Pathelin), accused him of stealing a piece of cloth. The judge had to pull him up every moment, with *"Mais, mon ami, revenons à nos moutons"*. The phrase is frequently quoted by Rabelais. *See* ENFANTS SANS SOUCI *under* SANS SOUCI.

Movable. The first movable. *See* PRIMUM MOBILE.

Movable Feasts. Annual church feasts which do not fall on a fixed date but are determined by certain established rules. EASTER Day is a notable example.

Move. Give me where to stand, and I will move the world. So said ARCHIMEDES of Syracuse; and the instrument he would have used is the lever.

To move the adjournment of the

House (*i.e.* the HOUSE OF COMMONS). The House normally adjourns at the end of a day's sitting until the next day and motions of adjournment were formerly much used to hold up business. This form of obstruction is now prevented by STANDING ORDERS (*see under* STAND), etc. It is still open to a member "to move the adjournment on a definite matter of urgent public importance", although now a rare occurrence, and it can be disallowed by the SPEAKER. It is also customary to leave half an hour at the end of the day to allow M.P.s to raise matters "on the adjournment", thus giving scope for general debate and criticism. Occasionally the Government moves the adjournment after question-time as a concession to the Opposition and Private Members, thus leaving the day for discussion.

To move the previous question. *See under* QUESTION.

Much. The miller's son in the ROBIN HOOD stories. In the MORRIS-DANCE he played the part of the Fool, and his great feat was to bang the head of the gaping spectators with a bladder of peas.

Muckle. Many a mickle makes a muckle. *See under* LITTLE.

Muddied Oafs. Footballers. *See* FLANNELLED FOOLS.

Muff. One who is awkward at games and sports, or who is effeminate, dull or stupid; probably a sneering allusion to the use of muffs to keep one's hands warm. The term does not seem to be older than the early 19th century, but there is a Sir Harry Muff in Dudley's interlude, *The Rival Candidates* (1774), a stupid, blundering dolt.

Mufti. An Arabic word meaning an official, expounder of the KORAN and Mohammedan law: thus the Mufti of JERUSALEM is the chief religious official of the Moslems of Jerusalem; but used in English to denote civil, as distinct from military or official costume. Our meaning dates from the early 19th century, and probably arose from the resemblance that the flowered dressing-gown and tasselled smoking-cap, worn by off-duty officers in their quarters, bore to the stage get-up of an Eastern Mufti.

Mug. The word is used as slang for "face"

and also for one who is easily taken in, possibly coming from the GYPSY meaning, a simpleton or MUFF. **To mug up,** meaning to study hard for a specific purpose, *e.g.* to pass an examination, is an old university phrase. It has been suggested that it comes from the theatre where an actor, while making up his face or "mug", would hurriedly con over his lines.

Mugging. Now the common term for assault followed by robbery. From the old slang use of *mug* meaning to rob or swindle.

Mug-house. An ale-house was so called in the 18th century where many people gathered in the large tap-room to drink, sing and spout, one of their number being made chairman. Ale was served to the company in their own mugs, and the place where the mug was to stand was chalked on the table.

Muggins. Slang for a fool or simpleton—a juggins. Possibly an allusion to MUG.

Muggletonian. A follower of Lodovic Muggleton (1609–1698), a journeyman tailor, who, about 1651, set up for a prophet. He was sentenced for blasphemous writings to stand in the pillory, and was fined £500. The members of the sect, which maintained some existence until *c.* 1865, believed that their two founders, Muggleton and John Reeve, were the "two witnesses" spoken of in *Rev.* xi, 3.

Mugwump. An Algonkin word meaning a chief; in Eliot's Indian BIBLE the word "centurion" in the *Acts* is rendered *mugwump*. It is now applied in the U.S.A. to independent members of the Republican Party, those who refuse to follow the dictates of a CAUCUS, and all political PHARISEES whose party vote cannot be relied upon. It is also used in the sense of "big shot" or "BOSS".

Mulberry. Fable has it that the fruit was originally white and became blood-red from the blood of PYRAMUS and Thisbe. In the LANGUAGE OF FLOWERS, Black Mulberry (*Morus nigra*) means "I shall not survive you" and White Mulberry (*Morus alba*) signifies "widsom". Culpeper says that the tree is ruled by MERCURY and it is noted as a vermifuge. The old Gloucestershire proverb says, "After the mulberry-tree has shown green leaf, there will be no more frost". Silkworms are fed on the leaves of the mulberry, especially the white mulberry. The Paper Mulberry (*Broussonetia papyrifera*) is so called from its use in Japan and the Far East for making paper with the pulped shoots.

In the SEVEN CHAMPIONS (Pt. I, ch. iv), Eglantine, daughter of the King of Thessaly, was transformed into a mulberry-tree. *See* PYRAMUS.

Here we go round the mulberry bush. An old game in which children take hand and dance round in a ring, singing the song of which this is the refrain.

Mulciber. Among the Romans, a name of VULCAN; it means the softener, because he softened metals.

> And round about him [Mammon] lay on every side
> Great heaps of gold that never could be spent;
> Of which some were rude ore, not purified
> Of Mulciber's devouring element.
> SPENSER: *The Faerie Queene*, II, vii, 5.

Mule. Very stubborn or obstinate people are sometimes called *mules*, in allusion to the reputed characteristic of the beast.

Crompton's mule, or the **Spinning-mule,** was invented by Samuel Crompton (1753–1827) in 1779. His invention was pirated at the outset and he derived little financial benefit from his efforts. It was so called because it was.

To shoe one's mule. To appropriate moneys committed to one's trust.

> He had the keeping and disposall of the moneys, and yet shod not his own mule.
> *History of Francion*, III (1655).

Mull. To make a mull of a job is to fail to do it properly. It is either a contraction of *muddle*, or from the old verb *to mull*, to reduce to powder.

Anglo-Indians in the service of the Madras Presidency were known as *Mulls*. Here the word stands for *mulligatawny*.

Mulled ale. Ale spiced and warmed; similarly *mulled wine*, etc. Possibly from M.E. *mold-ale*, a funeral feast (*mold*, the earth, the grave), but the derivation is uncertain.

Mullah (Arab. *maula*). A title of respect given by Mohammedans to religious dignitaries versed in the sacred law.

The Mad Mullah. A nickname given to Mohammed bin Abdullah, a mullah who gave great trouble to the British in Somaliland at various times between 1899 and 1920. He claimed to be the MAHDI and made extensive raids on tribes friendly to the British. The DERVISH power was not finally broken until 1920 when the Mad Mullah escaped to Ethiopia, where he died in 1921.

Mulmutine Laws. *See* MOLMUTINE.

Mulready Envelope. An envelope resembling a half-sheet of letter-paper when folded, having on the front an ornamental design by William Mulready (1786–1863), the artist. These were the stamped penny postage envelopes introduced in 1840 but the Mulreadies remained in circulation for one year only owing to ridicule of their ludicrous design. They are prized by stamp-collectors.

Multipliers. So alchemists, who pretended to multiply GOLD and SILVER, were called. An act was passed (2 Henry IV, C. IV) making the "art of multiplication" a felony. In the *Canterbury Tales* (*Canon's Yeoman's Tale*), the Canon's YEOMAN says he was reduced to poverty by ALCHEMY, adding: "Lo, such advantage is't to multiply".

Multitude, Nouns of. Dame Juliana Berners, in her *Booke of St. Albans* (1486), says, in designating companies we must not use the names of multitudes promiscuously, and examples her remark thus:

> We say a congregacyon of people, a hoost of men, a felyshyppynge of yeomen, and a bevy of ladyes; we must speak of a herde of deer, swannys, cranys, or wrenys, a sege of herons or bytourys, a muster of pecockes, a watche of nyghtyngales, a flyghte of doves, a claterynge of choughes, a pryde of lyons, a slewthe of beeres, a gagle of geys, a skulke of foxes, a sculle of frerys, a pontificalitye of prestys, and a superfluyte of nonnes.

She adds that a strict regard to these niceties better distinguishes "gentylmen from ungentylmen", than regard to the rules of grammar, or even to the moral law. *See* ASSEMBLAGE, NOUNS OF.

Multum in parvo (Lat., much in little). Much "information" condensed into few words or into a small compass.

Mum. Mum's the word. Keep what is told you a profound secret. *See* MUMCHANCE.

To keep mum. To keep silent; not to speak or to tell anyone.

Mumbudget. An old exclamation meaning "Silence, please"; perhaps from a children's game in which silence was occasionally necessary. *Cp.* BUDGET; DRY; MUMCHANCE; NAY-WORD.

Mumchance. Silence. Mumchance was a game of chance with dice, in which silence was indispensable. *Mum* is connected with *mumble* (Ger. *mummeln*; Dan. *mumle*, to mumble). *Cp.* MUMBUDGET.

Also one who has nothing to say—

> Methinks you look like Mumchance,
>   that was hanged
> For saying nothing.
> > SWIFT: *Polite Conversation*, i.

Mumbo Jumbo. The name given by Europeans (possibly from some lost native word) to a BOGY or grotesque idol venerated by certain African tribes; hence any object of blind unreasoning worship.

Mungo Park, in his *Travels in the Interior of Africa* (1795–1797), says (ch. iii) that Mumbo Jumbo "is a strange bugbear, common to all Mandingo towns, and much employed by the Pagan natives in keeping their wives in subjection". When the ladies of the household become too quarrelsome, Mumbo Jumbo is called in. He may be the husband or his agent suitably disguised, who comes at nightfall making hideous noises. When the women have been assembled and songs and dances performed. "Mumbo fixes on the offender", she is "stripped naked, tied to a post, and severely scourged with Mumbo's rod, amidst the shouts and derision of the whole assembly."

Mummer. A contemptuous name for an actor; from the parties that formerly went from house to house at CHRISTMAS-time *mumming*, *i.e.* giving a performance of St. GEORGE and the DRAGON, and the like, in dumb-show.

Mummy is the Arabic *mum*, wax used for embalming; from the custom of anointing the body with wax and preparing it for burial.

Mummy wheat. Wheat (*Triticum compositum*) commonly grown on the southern shores of the Mediterranean, the seed of which is traditionally said to have been taken from ancient Egyptian tombs.

Mumpers. Beggars; from the old slang *to mump*, to cheat or to sponge on others; probably from Dut. *mompen*, to cheat. In Norwich, Christmas WAITS used to be called "Mumpers".

Mumping Day. St. THOMAS's Day, 21 December, is so called in some parts of the country, because on this day the poor used to go about begging, or, as it was called, "a-gooding", that is, getting gifts to procure good things for CHRISTMAS, or begging corn. In Lincolnshire the name used to be applied to BOXING DAY; in Warwickshire the term used was "going a-corning".

Mumpsimus. Robert Graves, in *Impenetrability*, gives this word as an example of the practice of making new words by declaration. With the meaning, "an erroneous doctrinal view obstinately adhered to", *mumpsimus* was put into currency by Henry VIII in a speech from the throne in 1545. He remarked, "Some be too stiff in their old mumpsimus, others be too busy and curious in their sumpsimus." He referred to a familiar story in the jest-books of a priest who always read in the MASS "*quod in ore mumpsimus*" instead of "*sumpsimus*", as his MISSAL was incorrectly copied. When his mistake was pointed out, he said that he had read it with an *m* for forty years, "and I will not change my old mumpsimus for your new sumpsimus." The word is now used to mean "an established manuscript-reading that, though obviously incorrect, is retained blindly by old-fashioned scholars".

Münchausen, Baron (min' chou zen). Karl Friedrich Hieronymus, Baron Münchausen (1720–1797) served in the Russian army against the Turks, and after his retirement told extraordinary stories of his war adventures. Rudolf Er-ich Raspe (1737–1794), a German scientist, antiquarian and writer, collected these tales, and when living in England as a mining engineer, published them in 1785 as *Baron Münchausen's Narrative of his Marvellous Travels and Campaigns in Russia*. The text of *Münchausen* as reprinted latterly contains *Sea Adventures*, an account of Baron de Tott (a character founded on a real French Hussar) partly written by Raspe, with much additional matter from various sources by other hands. *Cp.* MANDEVILLE.

Mungo, St. An alternative name for St. KENTIGERN.

A superior kind of shoddy, made from second-hand woollens, is known as *mungo*.

Muratorian Fragment. A fragment of a late 2nd-century document found embodied in an 8th-century codex. Written in Latin, it reveals the NEW TESTAMENT canon of the period as consisting of the four Gospels, thirteen Epistles of Paul, two Epistles of John, the Epistle of Jude, the Apocalypse of John, and the Apocalypse of Peter. It was discovered by L. A. Muratori, librarian of the Ambrosian Library at Milan.

Murderer's Bible, The. *See* BIBLE, SOME SPECIALLY NAMED EDITIONS.

Murphy. A POTATO, from its long established prominence as a staple crop in Ireland.

Murphy's Law. Of uncertain origin but with an Irish implication, Murphy's Law can be summed up by the saying "that anything that can go wrong, will go wrong". It has a good deal in common with CATCH-22.

Murrumbidgee Whaler. An Australian term for a tramp, the origin of which is obscure. Some derive the term from the fact that tramps camped for long periods by such rivers as the Murrumbidgee and then told lies about the fish or "whales" they had caught.

Muscadins. Parisian exquisites who aped those of London about the time of the French Revolution. They used musk as a perfume, wore top-boots with long tails, and a high stiff collar, and carried a thick cudgel called a "constitution".

Muses. In Greek mythology the nine daughters of ZEUS and MNEMOSYNE; originally goddesses of memory only, but later identified with individual arts and sciences. The paintings of Herculaneum show all nine in their respective attributes. Their names are: CALLIOPE, CLIO, EUTERPE, THALIA, MELPOMENE, TERPSICHORE, ERATO, POLYHYMNIA, URANIA. Three earlier Muses are sometimes given, *i.e.* Melete (Meditation), Mneme (Remembrance), and Aoide (Song).

Museum. Literally, a home or seat of the MUSES. The first building to have this name was the university erected at Alexandria by Ptolemy Soter about 300 B.C.

British Museum. *See under* BRITISH.

A museum piece. An object of historic or antiquarian interest and value, etc.; in a derogatory or facetious sense, any article which is antiquated or out of fashion, or an old-fashioned person.

Mushroom. Slang for an umbrella, on account of the similarity in shape; and as mushrooms are of very rapid growth, applied figuratively to anything that springs up "overnight", as a rapidly built housing estate, an upstart family, etc. In 1787, Bentham said, somewhat unjustly, "Sheffield is an oak, Birmingham is a mushroom."

To mushroom. To grow rapidly; to expand into a mushroom shape. Said especially of certain soft-nosed rifle bullets used in big-game shooting, or of a dense cloud of smoke that spreads out high in the sky, especially after an atomic explosion.

Music (Gr. *mousikē*, "art of the muses").

The music of the spheres. *See under* SPHERES.

To face the music. *See under* FACE.

Canned music. Recorded music on discs (records) or tapes for subsequent reproduction.

Live music. Music performed in one's presence, *i.e.* not reproduced.

Music Hall. This essentially popular form of variety entertainment had its origins in the "Free and Easy" of the public houses and in the song and supper rooms of early Victorian London. Food, drink, and the sing-song were its first ingredients and its patrons came from the working classes. The first music hall proper, the *Canterbury*, was opened in 1852 by Charles Morton (1819–1905), "the Father of the Halls", and a native of Hackney. It was specially built for the purpose, consequent upon the success of his musical evenings at the "Canterbury Arms", Lambeth, of which he became the landlord in 1849. Music Halls eventually became more numerous in London and the provinces than the regular theatres and such names as Palladium, Palace, Alhambra, Coliseum, Empire, Hippodrome, etc., proclaim their former glories. Their best days were before 1914, after which revue, the cinema, wireless and, later, television, helped to bring about their eclipse. They have left a legacy of popular ballad and song, and memories of a host of great entertainers whose fame depended upon the intrinsic qualities of their individual acts. *Cp.* EVANS'S SUPPER ROOMS.

Muslim. *See* MOSLEM.

Muspelheim. In Scandinavian mythology, the "Home of Brightness" to the south of NIFLHEIM, where Surt (black smoke) ruled with his flaming sword and where dwelt the sons of Muspel the fire giant.

Mussulman. A Mohammedan, a MOSLEM. The plural is Mussulmans.

Mustard. After meat, mustard. Expressive of the sentiment that something that would have been welcome a little earlier has arrived too late and is no longer wanted. *C'est de la moutarde après dîner.*

Muster. To pass muster. To pass inspection: to "get by", to be allowed to pass.

Mutantur. *See* TEMPORA MUTANTUR.

Mutatis mutandis (Lat. *mutare*, to change). After making the necessary changes; more literally, those things have been changed which were to be changed.

Mute, To stand. An old legal term for a prisoner who, when arraigned for treason or felony, refused to plead or gave irrelevant answers.

Mutton. Come and eat your mutton with me. Come and dine with me.

Dead as mutton. Absolutely dead.

Mutton Chops. Whiskers trimmed to the shape of mutton chops.

Mutton fist. A large, coarse red fist.

To return to our muttons. *See* MOUTONS.

Mutual Friends. Can people have mutual friends? Strictly speaking not; but since Dickens adopted the solecism in the title of his novel *Our Mutual Friend* (1864), many people have objected to the correct term *common friends*. *Mutual* implies reciprocity from one to another (Lat. *mutare*, to change); the friendship between two friends should be mutual, but this mutuality cannot be extended to a third party.

Myrmidons (lit. ant people, from Gk. *myrmix*) gained their name from the legend that when Ægina was depopulated by a plague, its king, Æacus, prayed to JUPITER that the ants running out of an OAK tree should be turned to men. According to one account they emigrated with Peleus to Thessaly, whence they followed ACHILLES to the siege of TROY. They were noted for their fierceness, diligence and devotion to their leader, hence their name is applied to a servant who carries out his orders remorselessly.

Myron. A famous Greek sculptor noted for his realistic statues of gods, heroes, athletes, and animals. It is said that he made a cow so lifelike that even bulls were deceived and made their approaches. He was an older contemporary of Phidias.

Myrrha. The mother of ADONIS, in Greek legend. She is fabled to have had an unnatural love for her own father, and to have been changed into a MYRTLE. The resinous juice called *myrrh* is obtained from the Arabian myrtle (*Balsamodendron myrrha*).

Myrrophores (Gr., myrrh-bearers). The Marys who went to see the sepulchre, bearing spices, are represented in Christian art as carrying vases of myrrh (*see Mark* xvi, i).

Myrtle. A leaf of myrtle, viewed in a strong light, is seen to be pierced with innumerable little punctures. According to fable, PHÆDRA, wife of THESEUS, fell in love with HIPPOLYTUS, her stepson. When Hippolytus went to the arena to exercise his horses, Phædra repaired to a myrtle-tree in Trœzen to await his return, and beguiled the time by piercing the leaves with a hairpin.

In ORLANDO FURIOSO Astolpho is changed into a myrtle-tree by Acrisia. *Cp.* MYRRHA.

The ancient Jews believed that the eating of myrtle leaves conferred the power of detecting witches; and it was a superstition that if the leaves crackled in the hands the person beloved would prove faithful.

The myrtle which dropped blood. ÆNEAS (Virgil's. *Eneid*, Bk. III) tells the story of how he tore up a myrtle to decorate a sacrificial altar, but was terrified to find it dripped blood, while a voice came from the ground saying, "Spare me, now that I am in my grave." It was that of Polydorus, the youngest son of PRIAM and HECUBA, who had been murdered with darts and arrows for the GOLD he possessed. The deed was perpetrated by Polymnestor, King of Thrace, to whose care Polydorus had been entrusted.

Mysteries of Udolpho. A romance by Mrs. Radcliffe (1764–1823), which was published in 1794 and founded the so-called "terror school" of English Romanticism, though Walpole's *Castle of Otranto* (1764) had broken the ground. *Cp.* FRANKENSTEIN.

Mysterium. The letters of this word, which, until the time of the REFORMATION, was engraved on the Pope's tiara, are said to make up the number 666. *See* NUMBER OF THE BEAST.

> And upon her forehead was a name written, MYSTERY, BABYLON THE GREAT, THE MOTHER OF HARLOTS AND ABOMINATIONS OF THE EARTH.
>
> *Rev.* xvii, 5.

Mystery. In English two distinct words are represented: *mystery*, the archaic term for a handicraft, as in *the art and mystery of printing*, is the same as the Fr. *métier* (trade, craft, profession), and is the M.E. *mistere*, from Med. Lat. *misterium*, *ministerium*, ministry. *Mystery*, meaning something hidden, inexplicable, or beyond human comprehension, is from Lat. *mysterium* (through French) and Gr. *mustēs*, from *muen*, to close the eyes or lips.

It is from this latter sense that the old miracle plays, mediæval dramas in which the characters and story were drawn from sacred history, came to be called **Mysteries,** though they were frequently presented by members of a guild or *mystery*. *Miracle plays* (as they were called at the time) developed from liturgical pageantry, especially in the CORPUS CHRISTI processions, and were taken over by the laity. They were performed in the streets on a wheeled stage or on stages erected along a processional route, and non-Biblical subjects were also introduced. They flourished in England from the 13th to the 15th century but MORALITY PLAYS continued into the 16th century. *Cp.* PASSION PLAY.

Mysteries of the Rosary. The fifteen subjects of meditation from the life of Christ and the Blessed Virgin Mary, connected with the decades of the ROSARY.

The three greater mysteries. The TRINITY, Original Sin, and the Incarnation.

N

N. The fourteenth letter of our alphabet; represented in Egyptian hieroglyphic by a water-line (∿). It was called *nun* (a fish) in Phœnician, whence the Greek *nu*.

N. A numeral; Gr. ν=50, but ‚ν=50,000. N (Med. Lat.)=90, or 900; but N̄=90,000, or 900,000.

n. The sign ~ (*tilde*) over an "n" indicates that the letter is to be pronounced as though followed by a "y", as *cañón=canyon*. It is used thus almost solely in words from Spanish. In Portuguese the accent (called *til*) is placed over vowels to indicate that they have a nasal value.

nth, or *nth* **plus one.** The expression is taken from the index of a mathematical formula, where *n* stands for any number, and $n+1$, one more than any number. Hence, *n-dimensional*, having an indefinite number of dimensions, *n-tuple* (on the analogy of *quadruple*, *quintuple* etc.), having an indefinite number of duplications.

n ephelkustic. The Greek *nu* (ν) added for euphony to the end of a word that terminates with a vowel when the next word in the sentence begins with a vowel.

N or M. The answer given to the first question in the CHURCH OF ENGLAND Catechism; and it means that here the person being catechized gives his or her *name* or *names*. Lat. *nomen vel nomina*. The abbreviation for the plural *nomina* was—as usual—the doubled initial (*cp.* "LL.D." for Doctor of Laws); and this when printed (as it was in old Prayer Books) in BLACK-LETTER and close together, N.N. came to be taken for M..

In the same way the M. and N. in the marriage-service ("I M. take thee N. to my wedded wife") merely indicate that the name is to be spoken in each case; but the M. and N. in the publication of banns ("I publish the BANNS OF MARRIAGE between M. of — and N. of —") stand for *maritus*, bridegroom, and *nupta*, bride.

N.B. (Lat. *nota bene*). Note well.

N.K.V.D. *See* OGPU.

Nabob (nā′ bob). Corruption of the Hind. *nawab*, deputy-governor; used of the governor or ruler of a province under the MOGUL Empire. Such men acquired great wealth and lived in splendour and eventually became independent princes. The name was sarcastically applied in the late 18th century to servants of the English East India Company who retired to England, having made their fortunes, bought estates and acquired seats in PARLIAMENT, etc.

Nabonassar, Era of. An era that was in use for centuries by the Chaldean astronomers, and was generally followed by Hipparchus and Ptolemy. It commenced at midday, Wednesday, 26 February, 747 B.C., the date of the accession of Nabonassar (d. 733 B.C.) as King of Babylonia. The year consisted of 12 months of 30 days each, with 5 complementary days added at the end. As no INTERCALARY day was allowed for, the first day of the year fell one day earlier every four years than the JULIAN year; consequently, to transpose a date from one era to another it is necessary to know the exact day and month of the Nabonassarian date, and to remember that 1,460 Julian years are equal to 1,461 Babylonian.

Naboth's Vineyard. The possession of another coveted by one who will use any means, however unscrupulous, to acquire it. (I *Kings* xxi.)

Nabu. *See* NEBO.

Nadir (nād´ ir). An Arabic word, signifying that point in the heavens which is directly opposite to the ZENITH, *i.e.* directly under our feet; hence, figuratively, the lowest point in one's fortunes, the lowest depths of degradation, etc.

Nævius. *See* ACCIUS NÆVIUS.

Naiad (nī´ ăd). In classical mythology, a NYMPH of lake, fountain, river, or stream.

Nail. In ancient ROME a nail was driven into the wall of the temple of JUPITER every 13 September. This was originally done to tally the year, but subsequently it became a religious ceremony for warding off calamities and plagues from the city. Originally the nail was driven by the *prætor maximus*, subsequently by one of the consuls, and lastly by the dictator (*see* LIVY, VII, iii).

In World War I patriotic Germans drove nails into a large wooden statue of Field-Marshal Hindenburg, buying each nail in support of a national fund.

The nails with which Our Lord was fastened to the Cross were, in the MIDDLE AGES, objects of great reverence. Sir John MANDEVILLE says, "He had two in his hondes, and two in his feet; and of on of theise the emperour of Constantynoble made a brydille to his hors, to bere him in bataylle; and throghe vertue thereof he overcam his enemyes" (*c.* viii). Fifteen are shown as relics. *See* IRON CROWN OF LOMBARDY *under* CROWN.

For want of a nail. "For want of a nail, the shoe is lost; for want of a shoe, the horse is lost; for want of a horse, the rider is lost." (Herbert: *Jacula Prudentum*).

Hard as nails. Stern, hard-hearted, unsympathetic; able to stand hard blows like nails. The phrase is used with both a physical and a figurative sense; a man in perfect training is "as hard as nails", and bigotry, straitlacedness, rigid puritanical pharisaism, make people "hard as nails".

Hung on the nail. Put in pawn. A reference to the old custom of hanging each pawn on a nail, with a number attached, and giving the customer a duplicate thereof.

I nailed him, or **it.** I pinned him, meaning I secured him, I fixed his attention or "got hold of him". *Is.* (xxii, 23) says, "I will fasten him as a nail in a sure place."

On the nail. Immediately, on the spot, as in, **to pay on the nail.** One meaning of nail (possibly from mediæval times) denoted a shallow vessel mounted on a stand and business was concluded by payment into the vessel. It may have been so named from the rough resemblance of the stand to a nail's shape.

Outside the Corn Exchange at Bristol such "nails" or pillars can still be seen and it is said that if a buyer was satisfied with the sample of grain shown on the nail he paid on the spot. (*Cp.* SUPERNACULUM.)

Nail drives out nail. A new interest or desire replaces what was previously felt for its predecessor; from the practice of using a new nail as a punch to drive out the old. An ancient proverb.

To drive a nail into one's coffin. *See under* COFFIN.

To hit the nail on the head. *See under* HEAD.

To nail to the counter. To convict and expose as false or spurious; as, "I nailed that lie to the counter at once." From the custom of shopkeepers nailing to the counter false money that was passed to them as a warning to others.

With colours nailed to the mast. *See under* COLOURS.

With tooth and nail. *See under* TOOTH.

Nail-paring. Superstitious people are particular as to the day on which they cut their nails. The old ryhme is:

> Cut them on Monday, you cut them for health;
> Cut them on Tuesday, you cut them for wealth;
> Cut them on Wednesday, you cut them for news;
> Cut them on Thursday, a new pair of shoes;
> Cut them on Friday, you cut them for sorrow;
> Cut them on Saturday, you see your true love tomorrow
> Cut them on Sunday, your safety seek,
> The devil will have you the rest of the week.

Another rhyme conveys an even stronger warning on the danger of nail-cutting on a Sunday:

> A man had better ne'er be born
> As have his nails on a Sunday shorn.

Naked. The Naked Boy Courts, and **Alleys,** of which there are more than one in the City of London, are named from the PUBLIC-HOUSE SIGN OF CUPID.

The naked truth. The plain, unvarnished truth; truth without trimmings. The fable says that Truth and Falsehood went bathing; Falsehood came first out of the water, and dressed herself in Truth's garments. Truth, unwilling to take those of Falsehood, went naked.

Namby-pamby. Wishy-washy; insipid, weakly sentimental; said especially of authors. It was the nickname of Ambrose Philips (1674–1749), bestowed on him by Henry Carey, the dramatist, for his verses addressed to Lord Carteret's children, and was adopted by Pope. It is also applied to a MOLLY CODDLE.

Name.

> What's in a name? That which we call a rose
> By any other name would smell as sweet.
> SHAKESPEARE: *Romeo and Juliet*, II, ii.

A name to conjure with. A very famous name, one of great influence. To conjure a name was to evoke a spirit. Thus Shakespeare says (*Julius Cæsar*, I, iii):

> Write them together, yours is as fair a name;
> Sound them, it doth become the mouth as well;
> Weigh them, it is as heavy; conjure with 'em,
> Brutus will start a spirit as soon as Cæsar.

Give a dog a bad name. *See under* DOG.

Give it a name. Tell me what it is you would like; said when offering a reward, a drink, etc.

In the name of. In reliance upon; or by the authority of.

Their name liveth for evermore. These consolatory words, frequently used on war memorials, are from the APOCRYPHA.

To call a person names. To blackguard him by derogatory nicknames, or hurling opprobrious epithets at him.

To lend one's name to. To authorize the use of one's name in support of a cause, venture, etc.

To name the day. To fix the day of the wedding—a privilege of the bride-to-be.

To take God's name in vain. To use it profanely, thoughtlessly, or irreverently.

Among primitive peoples, as well as the ancient Hebrews, the name of a deity is regarded as his manifestation, and is treated with the greatest respect and veneration. *See* ADONAI. Among savage tribes there is a reluctance in disclosing one's name because this might enable an enemy by magic to work one some deadly injury; the Greeks were particularly careful to disguise or reverse uncomplimentary names. *See* ERINYES; EUMENIDES; EUXINE.

Name-dropper. One who seeks to impress by casual reference to well-known or prominent people with the implication of friendly acquaintance.

Nana. In the story of PETER PAN, the gentle and faithful old dog who always looked after the children of the Darling family. When Mr. Darling played a trick on Nana by giving her unpleasant medicine, which he himself had promised to drink, the family did not appreciate his humour. This put him out of temper and Nana was chained up in the yard before he went out for the evening. As a consequence Peter Pan effected an entry into the children's bedroom. *See* IN THE DOGHOUSE *under* DOG.

Nantes Edict of Nantes. The decree of Henry IV of France, published from Nantes in 1598, giving guarantees to the HUGUENOTS and permitting them rights of worship in named towns, etc. The edict was revoked by Louis XIV in 1685. *See* CALAS; DRAGONNADES.

Nap. The doze or short sleep gets its name from O.E. *hnæppian*, to sleep lightly: the surface of cloth is so called from Mid. Dut. *noppe*; and *Nap*, the card game, is so called in honour of NAPOLEON III.

To be caught napping. *See under* CATCH.

To go nap. To set oneself to make five tricks (all one can) in the game of NAP;

hence, to risk all you have on some venture, to back it through thick and thin.

Naphtha (năf' thà). The Greek name for an inflammable, bituminous substance coming from the ground in certain districts; in the MEDEA legend it is the name of the drug used by the witch for anointing the wedding robe of Glauce, daughter of King Creon, whereby she was burnt to death on the morning of her marriage with JASON.

Napier's Bones. The calculating square rods of bone, ivory, or boxwood with numerical tables on each of their sides, invented by the Scottish mathematician John Napier (1550–1617), laird of Merchiston, in 1615. This ingenious arrangement was used for shortening the labour of multiplications and divisions. The previous year he had invented logarithms. *Cp.* ABACUS.

Naples. See Naples and (then) die. An old Italian saying, implying that nothing more beautiful remains to be seen on earth. There is also a pun involved since Naples was once a centre of typhoid and cholera. *See* PARTHENOPE.

Napoleon Bonaparte (1769–1821). Emperor of the French (1804–1815). His reign is known in French history as the *First Empire* and his name is sometimes used to denote supremacy in a particular sphere as in, *a Napoleon of finance*. *Cp.* BONEY.

Code Napoléon. The code of laws prepared (1800–1804) under his direction, based on work begun by a committee of the CONVENTION and so called in 1807. It forms the basis of modern French law and is only second in importance to the code of Justinian. Equality in the eyes of the law, justice, and common sense are its keynotes.

Napoleon II, King of Rome (1811–1832). Francis Joseph Charles, the son of Napoleon and Marie Louise of Austria, never reigned but was known to the Bonapartists as Napoleon II. He was given the compensatory title of Duke of Reichstadt in 1818.

Napoleon III (1808–1873). His reign (1852–1870) is called the *Second Empire*. He was the third son of Louis Bonaparte, King of Holland (brother of NAPOLEON BONAPARTE) and Napoleon

I's step-daughter Hortense de Beauharnais. Few men have had so many nicknames.

Napoo (na poo'). Soldier slang of World War I for something that is of no use or does not exist. It represents the French phrase *il n'y en a plus*, there is no more of it. It occurs in a popular song of 1917:

> Bonsoir old thing, cheerio, chin-chin,
> Nahpoo, toodle-oo, goodby-ee.
>
> WESTON and LEE: *Good-Bye-Ee.*

Nappy ale. Strong ale has been so called for many centuries, probably because it contains a *nap* or frothy head.

Naraka (nar' a kà). In Hindu mythology and BUDDHISM, the place of torture for departed evil-doers. It consists of many kinds of hells, hot and cold.

Narcissus (nar sis' us). In Greek mythology, the son of Cephisus; a beautiful youth who saw his reflection in a fountain, and thought it the presiding nymph of the place. He jumped in the fountain to reach it, where he died. The NYMPHS came to take up the body to pay it FUNERAL honours but found only flower, which they called by his name (Ovid: *Metamorphoses*, iii, 346, etc.).

Plutarch says the plant is called Narcissus from the Gr. *narkē*, numbness, and that it is properly *narcosis*, meaning the plant which produces numbness or palsy. ECHO fell in love with Narcissus.

> Sweet Echo, sweetest nymph that liv'st unseen...
> Canst thou not tell me of a gentle pair,
> That likest thy Narcissus are?
>
> MILTON: *Comus*, 230.

Narcissism is the psychoanalytical term for excessive love and admiration of oneself.

Nark, or **Copper's nark.** A police spy or informer; from a Romany word, *nak*, a nose, on the analogy of NOSEY Parker. The term is also applied to a policeman. In colloquial parlance, *to be narked* is to be angry or annoyed, and *nark it* means stop it, "give over".

Narrow. The Narrow Seas. The Irish Sea and the English Channel, especially the area around the Straits of Dover.

Narrowdale Noon. To do a thing *at Narrowdale noon* is to defer or delay it, to do it "late at noon". Narrowdale is in a deep limestone valley in Staffordshire near Dovedale, where for three months of the year there is virtually no sun at all and in the spring it does not appear until about one o'clock (2 p.m. B.S.T.). Hence *Narrowdale noon* as a proverbial expression when anything is delayed. *Cp.* GREEK CALENDS; NEVER.

Nasbys. A generic nickname in the U.S.A. for postal officials, particularly postmasters. The American humorist David Ross Locke (1833–1888) wrote a series of satirical articles in the form of letters which first appeared in 1861 in the *Jeffersonian*, published in Findlay, Ohio, and later in the *Blade*, published in Toledo, Ohio. These *Nasby Letters* purported to be those of a conservative, ignorant and whisky-drinking politician who hated Negroes and who was determined to be the postmaster of his little town. Comically spelled, and full of sly humour, the *Nasby Letters* were very popular, and soon gave rise to the generic title.

Naso (nā′ zō). Ovid (Publius Ovidius Naso, 43 B.C.–A.D. 18), the Roman poet, author of *Metamorphoses*. Naso means "nose", hence Holofernes' pun: "And why, indeed, Naso, but for smelling out the odoriferous flowers of fancy." (SHAKESPEARE: *Love's Labour's Lost*, IV, ii.)

Natheless, or **Nathless** (nāth′ les). An archaic form of nevertheless.

> Smote on him sore besides, vaulted with fire.
> Nathless he so endured.
> MILTON: *Paradise Lost*, I, 298.

National Anthem. The composition of "God Save the Queen", the British National Anthem, has been attributed to Dr. John Bull (d. 1628), organist at Antwerp Cathedral (1617–1628), and quite erroneously to Henry Carey, but the following, by Mme. de Brinon, was sung before Louis XIV in 1686:

> Grand Dieu sauvez le roi,
> Grand Dieu vengez le roi,
> Vive le roi!
> Qu'à jamais glorieux,
> Louis victorieux,
> Voie ses ennemis toujours soumis,
> Vive le roi!

The Authorized Version of the BIBLE has:

> And all the people shouted, and said,
> God save the king.
> I *Sam.* x, 24.

It became popular at the time of the FORTY-FIVE Rebellion as a demonstration of loyalty to George II and opposition to the JACOBITES, to whom the phrase "confound their politics" may well refer.

The following are examples of the National Anthems or principal patriotic songs of other nations:

Argentine: *Oíd, mortales, el grito sagrado Libertad.*

Australia: *God Save the Queen; Advance, Australia Fair.*

Austria: (After World War II) *Land der Berge, Land am Strome.*

Canada. *God Save the Queen; The Maple Leaf Forever; O Canada! terre de nos aïeux.*

Chile: *Dulce patria, recibe los votos.*

Denmark: *The Song of the Danebrog; Kong Christian stod ved højen Mast* (King Christian stood beside the lofty mast).

France: *The Marseillaise.*

Germany: (After World War I) *Deutschland über alles.*

German Democratic Republic: *Auferstanden aus Ruinen und der Zukunft zugewandt.*

German Federal Republic: *Einigkeit und Recht und Freiheit.*

Italy: *Inno di Mameli.*

Mexico: *Mexicanos, al grito de guerra.*

Netherlands: *Wilhelmus van Nassouwe.*

New Zealand: *God Defend New Zealand; God Save the Queen.*

Norway: *Ja, vi elsker dette Landet som det stiger frem* (Yes we love our country, just as it is).

Peru: *Somos libres, seámos lo siempre.*

Portugal: *Herois do mar.*

Russia (under the Tsars): *Bozhe Tsarya Khrani.*

Scotland: *Scots wha hae wi' Wallace bled.*

South Africa: *Die Stem van Suid-Afrika.*

Spain: *Marcha de Granaderos.*

Sweden: *Du gamla, du fria, du fjällhöga Nord, Du tysta, du glädjerika skōna Nord!* (Thou ancient, free, and mountainous North! Thou silent, joyous, and beautiful North!).

Switzerland: *Trittst im Morgenrot daher* (In the dawn you stride along).

U.S.A.: *The Star-spangled Banner.* See STARS AND STRIPES.

U.S.S.R.: *Soyuz nerushimy respublik svobodnykh.*

Wales: *Mae hen wlad fy nhadau* (Land of my Fathers); also *Men of Harlech.*

National Convention. For the French assembly of this name, *see* CONVENTION PARLIAMENTS.

In the U.S.A. the National Convention is the meeting of State delegates called by the national committees of the political parties which nominates candidates for President and Vice-President. The party platform is also drawn up.

National Debt. The public debt of the central government of a state and secured on the national revenue. The *Funded Debt* is the portion of the National Debt which is converted into bonds and annuities, etc. The remainder, essentially short-term debt, is called the *Floating Debt.*

The British National Debt assumed a permanent form in the reign of William III (1689–1702) and it has been managed by the Bank of England since 1750. The rapid increase of the National Debt has been mainly due to wars. *See* MISSISSIPPI BUBBLE; SINKING FUND; SOUTH SEA BUBBLE.

National Governments. As a result of the financial crises and the collapse of the labour Government in 1931, an all-party COALITION was formed under J. Ramsay MacDonald, the first of a series of governments called "National" which held office in succession until 1940, under MacDonald, then Baldwin, and lastly Chamberlain. Those LIBERAL and LABOUR M.P.s who supported these governments called themselves National Liberal candidates and National Labour candidates. The administrations became increasingly CONSERVATIVE in character.

National Guard. In France, the revolutionary leaders formed a National Guard at Paris in July 1789, and similar citizen armies were formed in the provinces. It supported Robespierre, but turned against the CONVENTION and was defeated by NAPOLEON with regular troops. Under Napoleon, a National Guard or militia was re-established which continued in existence until the Paris commune of 1871.

In the U.S.A., the National Guard is an organization of volunteer military units similar to the British Territorials. When called upon in a national emergency they become an integral part of the U.S. armed forces. The oldest unit is the 182nd infantry of Massachusetts which traces its origins back to 1636. *Cp.* MINUTE-MEN.

National Society. The shortened form of the name of the association formed in 1811 as the "National Society for the Education of the Poor in the Principles of the Established Church". It played a great part in the development of English education, especially before direct state participation and control. Principally known for the establishment of Church schools, or "National Schools", and teacher training colleges, it still continues its work. *See* MONITORIAL SYSTEM; VOLUNTARY SCHOOLS.

Nations, Battle of the. A name given to the battle of Leipzig (16–19 October 1813) which led to the first overthrow of NAPOLEON. Prussians, Russians, Austrians and Swedes took part against the French.

Native. To go native. To abandon civilized ways and to share the life and habits of a more primitive society.

Nativity, The. CHRISTMAS Day, the day set apart in honour of the Nativity or Birth of Christ.

The Cave of the Nativity. The "Cave of the Nativity" at Bethlehem, discovered, according to Eusebius, by the empress HELENA, is under the chancel of the BASILICA of the "Church of the Nativity". It is a hollow scraped out of rock, and there is a stone slab above the ground with a star cut in it to mark the supposed spot where Jesus was laid. There are no grounds for connecting the Nativity with a cave.

To cast a man's nativity. The astrologers' term for constructing a plan or map of the position of the twelve "houses" which belong to him and explaining its significance. *See* HOUSES, ASTROLOGICAL.

Nature. In a state of nature. Nude or naked.

A natural. A born idiot, *i.e.* someone who is born half-witted. The word is now commonly used to denote one who is naturally adept at some particular skill, especially at games.

A natural child. A BASTARD. The Romans called the children of concubines *naturales*, children according to nature and not according to law.

Natural increase. In population statistics, etc., the excess of births over deaths in a given period, usually a year. *Cp.* MALTHUSIAN DOCTRINE.

Natural Philosophy. *See* EXPERIMENTAL PHILOSOPHY.

Naught, Nought. These are merely variants of the same word, naught representing O.E. *na whil* and nought, *no whit*. In most senses they are interchangeable; but nowadays *naught* is the more common form, except for the name of the cipher, which is usually *nought*.

Naught was formerly applied to things that were bad or worthless, as in II *Kings* ii, 19, "The water is naught and the ground barren", and it is with this sense that Jeremiah (xxiv, 2) speaks of "naughty figs":

> One basket had very good figs, even like the figs that are first ripe...The other basket had very naughty figs, which could not be eaten.

The REVISED VERSION did away with the old "naughty" and substituted "bad"; and in the next verse, where the Authorized calls the figs "EVIL", the Douai Version has:

> The good figges, exceeding good and the naughtie figges, exceeding naught: which cannot be eaten because they are naught.

Naughty Nineties, The. The 1890s in England, when the puritanical Victorian code of behaviour and conduct gave way in certain wealthy and fashionable circles to growing laxity in sexual morals, a growing cult of hedonism, and a more light-hearted approach to life. MUSIC

HALLS were at the height of their popularity and the EMPIRE PROMENADE was in its heyday.

Nausicaa (naw sik ā' a). The Greek heroine whose story is told in the ODYSSEY. She was the daughter of Alcinous, king of the Phæacians, and the shipwrecked Odysseus found her playing ball with her maidens on the shore. Pitying his plight he conducted him to her father, by whom he was entertained.

Nautical mile. *See under* MILE.

Nay-word. A byword, a password.

Nazarene. A native of Nazareth; Our Lord is so called (*John* xviii, 5, 7). He was brought up in Nazareth, but was born in Bethlehem (*see Matt.* ii, 23). Hence the early Christians were called *Nazarenes* (*Acts* xxiv, 5); also an early sect of Jewish Christians, who believed Christ to be the MESSIAH, but who nevertheless conformed to much of the Jewish law.

Can any good thing come out of Nazareth? (*John* i, 46). A general insinuation against any family or place of ill repute. Can any great man come from such an insignificant village as Nazareth?

Nazarites (Heb. *'nazar*, to separate). A body of Israelites set apart to the Lord under vows. They refrained from strong drink, and allowed their hair to grow. (*See Numb.* vi, 1–21.)

Nazi (nat' zi, naz' i). The shortened form of *National-Sozialist*, the name given to Adolf Hitler's party. *See* FÜHRER; HITLERISM; MEIN KAMPF; NIGHT OF THE LONG KNIVES; SWASTIKA.

Ne plus ultra (nē plŭs ŭl' trà) (Lat., nothing further, *i.e.* perfection). The most perfect state to which a thing can be brought. *See* PLUS ULTRA.

Neæra (ne ē' rà). Any sweetheart or lady love. She is mentioned by HORACE, VIRGIL, and Tibullus.

Neanderthal Man (ni ăn' dĕr tal). A species of PALÆOLITHIC man inhabiting Europe during the MOUSTERIAN period. It was named from the bones discovered in a grotto of the Neanderthal ravine near Düsseldorf, in 1856. Similar remains have been found in many parts of Europe.

Near, meaning *mean*, is rather a curious

play on the word *close* (close-fisted). What is "close by" is near.

Near side, and **Off side.** In Britain, left side and right side when facing forward. "Near wheel" means that to the driver's left hand; and "near horse" (in a pair) means that to the left hand of the driver. In a four-in-hand the two horses on the left side of the coachman are the near wheeler and the near leader. Those on the right-hand side are "off" horses. This, which seems an anomaly, arose when the driver walked beside his team. The teamster always walks with his right arm nearest the horse, and therefore, in a pair of horses, the horse on the left side is nearer than the one on his right. *See* OFF.

Nebo (nē' bō). A god of the Babylonians (properly, *Nabu*) mentioned in *Is.* xlvi, 1. He was the patron of Borsippa, near Babylon, and was regarded as the inventor of writing, as well as the god of wisdom. The name occurs in many Babylonian royal names, as, Nebuchadrezzar, Nebushasban (*Jer.* xxxix, 13), Nebuzaradan (II *Kings* xxv, 8), etc.

Nebuchadnezzar (neb ū kăd nez' ăr). An incorrect form of *Nebuchadrezzar* (as it appears in *Jer.* xxi, 2, etc.). The name means NEBO *protects the crown*.

Nebuchadnezzar was the greatest king of Babylon and reigned from 604 to 561 B.C. He restored his country to its former prosperity and importance, practically rebuilt Babylon, restored the temple of BEL, erected a new palace, embanked the Euphrates, and probably built the HANGING GARDENS. His name became the centre of many legends.

Necessary. The 17th- and 18th-century term for a privy. In large houses the emptying and cleaning of this was carried out by a servant known as the *Necessary Woman*.

Necessitarians. Those who deny free will, holding that all action is determined by antecedent causes. Those who believe in free will are called *libertarians*.

Necessity. Necessity knows no law. These were the words used by the German Chancellor Bethmann-Hollweg in the Reichstag on 4 August 1914, as a justification for the infringement of Belgian neutrality.

Gentlemen, we are now in a state of necessity, and necessity knows no law. Our troops have occupied Luxembourg and perhaps have already entered Belgian territory.

The phrase is common to most languages. Publilius Syrus has *Necessitas dat legem, non ipsa accipit* (Necessity gives the law, but does not herself accept it), and the Latin proverb *Necessitas non habet legem* appears in Piers Plowman (14th century) as, "Neede hath no law."

To make a virtue of necessity. To grin and bear it; "what can't be cured must be endured".

Neck. Slang for cheek, impudence.

Neck and crop. Entirely. The crop is the gorge of a bird; a variant of the phrase is *neck and heels*, as, "I bundled him out neck and heels." There was once a punishment which consisted in bringing the chin and knees of the culprit forcibly together, and then thrusting him into a cage.

Neck and neck. Very close competitors, very near in merit. A phrase from the TURF, when two or more horses run each other very closely.

Neck of the woods. A settlement in the forest, or slang for any area.

Neck or nothing. Desperate. An all-out attempt; to win by a neck or to be nowhere; a racing phrase.

Oh that the Roman people had but one neck! The words of CALIGULA, the Roman Emperor. He wished that he could slay them all with one stroke.

Stiff-necked. Obstinate and self-willed. In the *Psalms* we read: "Speak not with a stiff neck" (lxxv, 5); and *Jer.* xvii, 23, "They obeyed not...but made their neck stiff'; and *Isaiah* xlviii, 4, says: "Thy neck is an iron sinew." The allusion is to a wilful horse, ox, or ass, which will not answer to the reins.

To get it in the neck. To be thoroughly castigated; to be severely reprimanded. The phrase is an Americanism—I got it where the chicken got the axe—"in the neck".

To stick one's neck out. To ask for trouble; to expose oneself to being hurt, as a chicken might stick out its neck for the axe.

To talk through the back of one's neck. To be utterly wrong or inaccurate, to talk rubbish, to be hopelessly wide of the mark.

Necking. A common expression for amorous "petting". In the Western States of the U.S.A., *necking* is to tie a restless animal by the neck to a tame one in order to render it more tractable. *Necking* is also part of a column between the shaft and capital, as the annulets of a DORIC capital.

Neck-tie party (U.S.A.). A hanging, particularly by LYNCH LAW.

Neck verse. The first verse of *Ps.* li. *See* MISERERE. "Have mercy upon me, O God, according to thy loving kindness: according unto the multitude of thy tender mercies blot out my transgressions."

> He [a treacherous Italian interpreter] by a fine cunny-catching corrupt translation, made us plainly to confesse, and cry *Miserere*, ere we had need of our necke-verse.
> NASH: *The Unfortunate Traveller* (1594).

This verse was so called because it was the trial-verse of those who claimed BENEFIT OF CLERGY, and if they could read it, the ORDINARY of the prison said, "*Legit ut clericus*" (he reads like a clerk) and the prisoner saved his neck, but by an Act of Henry VII convicted clerks were branded on the hand before release.

Necklace. Diamond Necklace. *See under* DIAMOND.

The Fatal Necklace. The necklace which CADMUS gave to HARMONIA; some say that VULCAN, and others that Europa, gave it to him. It possessed the property of stirring up strife and bloodshed. It is said to have eventually become the property of Phaÿllus, who gave it to his mistress. Her youngest son set fire to the house and mother, son, and the necklace were destroyed.

Necromancy (nek' rō man si) (Gr. *nekros*, the dead; *manteia*, prophecy). Prophesying by calling up the dead, as the WITCH OF ENDOR called up Samuel (I *Sam.* xxviii, 7 ff.). Also the art of magic generally, the BLACK ART. *See* DIVINATION.

Nectar. (Gr.). In classical mythology, the drink of the gods. Like their food AMBROSIA, it conferred immortality, hence the name of the *nectarine*, so called because it is as "sweet as nectar".

Need. Needfire. Fire obtained by friction; a beacon. It was formerly supposed to defeat sorcery, and cure diseases ascribed to WITCHCRAFT, especially cattle diseases. We are told in Henderson's *Agricultural Survey of Caithness* (1812), that as late as 1785 it was so used as a charm when stock were seized with the murrain.

Needs must. Necessity compels. A shortening of the old saying, "Needs must when the devil drives." *See under* DEVIL.

Needful, The. Ready money, cash.

Needham. You are on the high-road to Needham—to ruin or poverty. The pun is on *need* and there is no reference to Needham in Suffolk. *Cp.* LAND OF NOD.

Needle. Looking for a needle, etc. *See under* BOTTLE.

The eye of a needle. *See under* CAMEL.

To get the needle. To become thoroughly vexed, or even enraged, and to show it. A variant of the phrase is *to get the spike.*

To hit the needle. To hit the nail right on the head, to make a perfect hit. A term in archery, equivalent to hitting the bull's-eye.

To needle. To provoke, goad or tease.

Needle time. The time allocated to the broadcasting of recorded music and entertainment.

Negative. The answer is in the negative. The Parliamentary circumlocution for *No.*

Neiges d'Antan, Les (nāzh don tan) (Fr.). A thing of the past. Literally "last year's snows", from the refrain of François Villon's well-known *Ballade des Dames du Temps Jadis*:

> Prince, n'enquerez de sepmaine
> Ou elles sont, ne de cest an,
> Que ce reffrain ne vous remaine:
> Mais ou sont les neiges d'antan?
> (Where are the snows of yester-year?)

Neighbourhood Watch. *See under* WATCH.

Neither. Neither here nor there. Irrelevant to the subject under discussion; a matter of no moment.

Nelly. A popular name in Australia for MOTHER CAREY'S GOOSE.

Not on your Nellie or Nelly. Not likely, not on any account, not on your life or "puff". Probably from RHYMING SLANG, "Not on your Nellie Duff", Duff rhyming with "puff" which is old slang for "breath" and life itself.

Nelson's blood. *See under* BLOOD.

Nelson's Pillar. *See under* PILLAR.

Nemean (nem' ē àn). **Nemean Games.** One of the four great festivals of ancient Greece, held in the valley of Nemea in Argolis every alternate year, the first and third of each OLYMPIAD. Legend states that they were instituted in memory of Archemorus who died from the bite of a serpent as the expedition of the SEVEN AGAINST THEBES was passing through the valley. It was customary for the games to open with a funeral oration in his honour. After HERCULES had slain the NEMEAN LION the games were held in honour of ZEUS. Athletic contests were added after the model of the OLYMPIC GAMES. The victor's reward was at first a crown of OLIVES, later of green parsley. PINDAR has eleven odes in honour of victors.

The Nemean Lion. A terrible lion which kept the people of the valley of Nemea in constant alarm. The first of the Twelve Labours of HERCULES was to slay it; he could make no impression on the beast with his club, so he caught it in his arms and squeezed it to death. Hercules ever after wore the skin as a mantle.

My fate cries out,
And makes each petty artery in this body
As hardy as the Nemean lion's nerve.
SHAKESPEARE: *Hamlet*, I, iv.

Nemesis. The Greek goddess, daughter of Nox; a divinity of vengeance who rewarded virtue and punished the wicked and all kinds of impiety; the personification of divine retribution. Hence, retributive justice generally, as *the Nemesis of Nations*, the fate which, sooner or later, overtakes every great nation.

And though circuitous and obscure
The feet of Nemesis how sure!
SIR WILLIAM WATSON: *Europe at the Play*.

Nemine contradicente (usually contracted to **nem. con.**) (Lat.). No one opposing, unanimously.

Nemine dissentiente (**nem. diss.**) (Lat.). Without a dissentient voice.

Nemo me impune lacessit (Lat.). No one provokes me with impunity. The motto of the Order of the THISTLE and of the kings of SCOTLAND.

Neolithic Age (Gr. *neos*, new; *lithos*, stone). The later STONE AGE of Europe. Neolithic stone implements are polished, more highly finished and more various than those of the PALÆOLITHIC Age; man knew something of agriculture, kept domestic animals, used boats, slings, and bows and arrows. It was superseded by the Bronze Age.

Nepenthe, or **Nepenthes** (Gr. *ne*, not; *penthos*, grief). An Egyptian drug mentioned in the ODYSSEY (IV, 228) that was fabled to drive away care and make people forget their woes. Polydamna, wife of Thonis, King of Egypt, gave it to HELEN.

That nepenthes which the wife of Thone
In Egypt gave to Jove-born Helena.
MILTON: *Comus*, 675–6.

Nepomuk. *See* St. JOHN OF NEPOMUK *under* JOHN.

Nepotism (Ital. *nepote*, nephew). The practice of favouring relatives in matters of employment, promotion, etc. The usage derives from the days when Popes and high ecclesiastics gave preferment and advancement to their nephews as their illegitimate sons were euphemistically labelled.

Neptune. The Roman god of the sea corresponding to the Greek POSEIDON, hence, allusively, the sea itself. Neptune is represented as an elderly man of stately mien, bearded, carrying a trident, and sometimes astride a dolphin or horse. *See* HIPPOCAMPUS; PLANETS.

Nereus. "THE OLD MAN OF THE SEA", a sea-god of Greek mythology represented as a very old man. He was the father of the NEREIDS and his special dominion was the Ægean Sea.

Nereids. The sea-nymphs of Greek mythology, the fifty daughters of NEREUS and "grey-eyed" Doris. The best known are AMPHITRITE, THETIS, and

GALATEA. Milton refers to another, Panope, in his *Lycidas* (line 99):

The air was calm and on the level brine
Sleek Panope with all her sisters played.

And the names of all will be found in Spenser's *The Faerie Queene*, Bk. IV, c. xi, verses 48–51.

Neri. *See* BIANCHI.

Nero, A. Any bloody-minded man, relentless tyrant, or evil-doer of extraordinary cruelty; from the depraved and infamous Roman Emperor, C. Claudius Nero (A.D. 37, 54–68), whom contemporaries believed to be the instigator of the great fire that destroyed most of ROME in A.D. 64, and to have recited his own poetry and played his lyre while enjoying the spectacle. Nero blamed the Christians.

Nerthus, or **Hertha.** The name given by Tacitus to a German or Scandinavian goddess of fertility, or "Mother Earth", who was worshipped on the island of Rügen. She roughly corresponds with the classical CYBELE; and is probably confused with the Scandinavian god *Njorthr* or NIORDHR, the protector of sailors and fishermen. *Nerthus* and *Njorthr* alike mean "benefactor".

Nessus. Shirt of Nessus. A source of misfortune from which there is no escape. The shirt of Nessus killed HERCULES. *See* DEIANIRA; *cp.* HARMONIA.

Nest-egg. Money laid by. The allusion is to the custom of placing an egg in a hen's nest to induce her to lay her eggs there. If a person has saved a little money, it serves as an inducement to him to increase his store.

Nestor. King of Pylos, in Greece; the oldest and most experienced of the chieftains who went to the siege of TROY. Hence the name is frequently applied as an epithet to the oldest and wisest man of a class or company. Samuel Rogers, for instance, who lived to be 92, was called "the Nestor of English poets".

Nestorians. Followers of Nestorius, Patriarch of Constantinople, 428–431 (d. *c.* 451). He is traditionally supposed to have asserted that Christ had two distinct natures and that Mary was the mother of his human nature. His teaching was condemned by Pope Celestine I in 430. A separate Nestorian Church was established which spread to Asia where most of their churches were destroyed by Timur (TAMBURLAINE) about 1400. A small group called Assyrian Christians survived in parts of Asia Minor and Persia.

Nettle. To grasp the nettle. To face up firmly to a difficulty, to tackle a situation boldly. A nettle is less likely to sting when grasped firmly as the lines written by Aaron Hill (1685–1750) tell us:

Tender-handed stroke a nettle,
And it stings you for your pains;
Grasp it like a man of mettle,
And it soft as silk remains.

Never. There are numerous locutions to express this idea, as:

At the coming of the COCQCIGRUES.
At the Latter LAMMAS.
NARROWDALE NOON.
In the reign of QUEEN DICK.
On ST. TIB'S EVE.
In a MONTH OF SUNDAYS.
When two Fridays or three Sundays come together.
When Dover and Calais meet.
When pigs fly.
When the world grows honest.
When the Yellow river runs clear.

On the never never. To get or buy something on the never never is to obtain it on hire purchase, a system of deferred payment.

Never had it so good. Earlier current in the U.S.A., the phrase became popular in Britain after its use by Harold Macmillan, Conservative Prime Minister (1957–1964), in a speech at Bedford (20 July 1957). Referring to the overall prosperity and general improvement of living standards, he said, "Most of our people have never had it so good."

Never Never Land. The land where the Lost Boys and Red Indians lived, and where Pirates sailed up the lake in J. M. Barrie's PETER PAN (1904). The phrase was applied to the whole of the Australian outback, but since the publication of *We of the Never Never* (1908) by Mrs. Aeneas Gunn it was restricted to the Northern Territory.

New. New Atlantis. *See under* ATLANTIS.

New Deal. The name given to President Roosevelt's policy of economic reconstruction announced in his first presidential campaign (1932). "I pledge you, I pledge myself, to a new deal for the American people." A relief and recovery programme known as the "First New Deal" was inaugurated in March 1933, and a "Second New Deal" concerned with social reform in January 1935. The "Third New Deal" of 1938 sought to preserve such gains made by its predecessors.

New Jerusalem. The city of HEAVEN foretold in *Rev.* xxi, 2, "coming down from God out of heaven, prepared as a bride adorned for her husband". Hence, figuratively, the perfect society.

New Learning. The name given to the revival of Greek and Latin classical learning during the period of the 15th- and 16th-century RENAISSANCE.

New lease of life. Renewed health and vigour, especially applied to someone who appears to gain his "second wind" after a serious illness or change of circumstances.

New Look. The name given to the long-skirted women's dress of 1948. The style was reminiscent of Edwardian days and was short-lived.

New Model, The. In the CIVIL WAR, the Parliamentary army organized in 1645 under Sir Thomas Fairfax in place of a variety of local forces. Most of the officers were INDEPENDENTS and the troopers of the EASTERN ASSOCIATION became its backbone. Initially more than half of the infantry were pressed men. Regular pay (not available to the CAVALIERS) resulted in better discipline. Cromwell took command in 1650.

New Morality. A popular term of the 1960s implying that the hitherto publicly accepted canons of morality are no longer relevant to present-day society, owing to the rapid spread of social and technical change, the advent of the PILL, and more "enlightened" attitudes generally.

New Style. *See* GREGORIAN YEAR; STILO NOVO.

New Testament, The. The name given to the second group of sacred writings in the BIBLE comprising 27 books in all (the four Gospels, The Acts of the Apostles, 21 Epistles and the Revelation of St. John the Divine), but which more correctly could be called "The New Covenant" or "The New Dispensation".

The religion of Israel was regarded as a covenant between Jehovah and his chosen people and in due time a new covenant was promised by the prophets:

> Behold, the days come, saith the Lord, that I will make a new covenant with the house of Israel, and the house of Judah.—*Jeremiah* xxi, 31.

This new covenant, for the Christians, was established by the life and death of Christ, and towards the end of the 2nd century a generally accepted collection of new scriptures, worthy of complementing the OLD TESTAMENT, was evolving. The present canon is that established by the Council of Carthage in 397. The name *Testament* is from the Lat. *testamentum* which is an inaccurate rendering of the Gr. *diathēkē*, "disposition" or "covenant". Thus we have in the *Authorized Version* (*Luke* xxii, 20): "This cup is the new testament in my blood, which is shed for you." This in the *Revised Version* reads "This cup is the new covenant in my blood, even that which is poured out for you." *See* APOCRYPHA.

New Thought. A general term for a system of therapeutics based on the theory that the mental and physical problems of life should be met, regulated and controlled by the suggestion of right thoughts. This system has nothing in common with CHRISTIAN SCIENCE, auto-suggestion or psychotherapy.

New World. The Americas; the Eastern Hemisphere is called the Old World.

New Year's Day. 1 January. The Romans began their year in March; hence *September*, *October*, *November*, *December* for the 7th, 8th, 9th, 10th months. Since the introduction of the Christian era, CHRISTMAS Day, LADY DAY, EASTER Day, 1 March and 25 March have in turns been considered as New Year's Day. With the introduction of the GREGORIAN YEAR, 1 January was accepted as New Year's Day by most Christian countries, but not until 1600 in Scotland, and 1752 in England.

New Year's gifts. The giving of presents at this time was a custom among both the Greeks and the Romans, the latter calling them *strenæ*, whence the

French term *étrenne* (a New Year's gift). Nonius Marcellus says that Tatius, King of the SABINES, was presented with some branches of trees cut from the forest sacred to the goddess STRENIA (strength) on New Year's Day, and from this incident the custom arose.

Our forefathers used to bribe the magistrates with gifts on New Year's Day—a custom abolished by law in 1290, but even down to the reign of James II the monarchs received their "tokens".

Newcastle. To carry coals to Newcastle. *See under* COAL.

Newgate. Newgate Gaol. From its prominence, Newgate came to be applied as a general name for gaols, and Nash, in his *Pierce Pennilesse* (1592), says it is "a common name for all prisons, as *homo* is a common name for a man or woman".

News. The letters E $\frac{N}{S}$ W used to be prefixed to newspapers to show that they obtained information from the four quarters of the world, and the supposition that our word *news* is thence derived is an ingenious conceit but destroyed by the old spelling *newes*; it is from the Fr. *nouvelles*.

Newspeak. Language in which the words change their meaning to accord with the official party-political views of the state. Coined by George Orwell (1903–1950) in his *1984*. *Cp.* LOOKING-GLASS.

Newt. *See* NICKNAMES.

Newtonian Philosophy. The astronomical system that in the late 17th century displaced COPERNICANISM, and also the theory of universal gravitation. So called after Sir Isaac Newton (1642–1727), who established the former and discovered the latter.

Next of Kin. The legal term for a person's nearest relative, more especially where estate is left by an intestate. In English law the next of kin in priority is: Husband or wife; children; father or mother (equally if both alive); brothers and sisters; grandparents; uncles and aunts; half uncles and aunts; the Crown.

Next friend, in law, is an adult (usually a relation) who brings an action in a court of law on behalf of a minor or a person of unsound mind.

Nibelungenlied, The (nē be lung' en lēd). A great mediæval German epic poem founded on old Scandinavian legends contained in the *Volsunga Saga* and the EDDA.

Nibelung was a mythical king of a race of Scandinavian dwarfs dwelling in *Nibelheim* (*i.e.* "the home of darkness, or mist"). These *Nibelungs* or *Nibelungers* were the possessors of the wonderful "Hoard" of gold and precious stones guarded by the dwarf ALBERICH, and their name passed to later holders of the Hoard, SIEGFRIED's following and the Burgundians being in turn called "the Nibelungs".

Siegfried, the hero of the first part of the poem, became possessed of the Hoard and married KRIEMHILD, sister of GUNTHER, King of Worms, whom he helped to secure the hand of BRUNHILD of Iceland. After Siegfried's murder by Hagen at Brunhild's instigation, Kriemhild carried the treasure to Worms where it was seized by Gunther and his retainer Hagen. They buried it in the Rhine, intending later to enjoy it; but they were both slain for refusing to reveal its whereabouts, and the Hoard remains for ever in the keeping of the Rhine Maidens. The second part of the Nibelungenlied tells of the marriage of the widow Kriemhild with King Atli or ETZEL (Attila), her invitation of the Burgundians to the court of the Hunnish King, and the slaughter of all the principal characters, including Gunther, Hagen and Kriemhild.

Nic Frog. *See under* FROG.

Nicæa. The Council of Nicæa. The first ŒCUMENICAL COUNCIL of the Christian Church held under Constantine the Great in 325 at Nicæa in Bithynia, Asia Minor, primarily to deal with the ARIAN heresy, which it condemned. The second Council of Nicæa (787), the seventh General Council of the Church, was summoned by The Empress Irene to end the Iconoclastic Controversy (*see* ICONOCLASTS).

Nicene Creed. The creed properly so called was a comparatively short statement of beliefs issued in 325 by the COUNCIL OF NICÆA to combat the ARIAN heresy. The "Nicene Creed" commonly referred to is that properly called the *Niceno-Constantinopolitan Creed*, referred to in Article VIII of the THIRTY-NINE ARTICLES given in the BOOK OF COMMON PRAYER, which ultimately derives from the Baptismal Creed of JERUSALEM. It is used in the EUCHARIST of the ROMAN CATHOLIC CHURCH, the CHURCH OF ENGLAND, and the EASTERN CHURCH, where it still forms part of the service of Baptism. It was first used at Antioch in the late 5th century and gradually gained acceptance in both East and West. *See also* FILIOQUE CONTROVERSY. *Cp.* APOSTLES' CREED; ATHANASIAN CREED.

Nicholas, St. One of the most popular saints in Christendom, especially in the East. He is the patron SAINT of Russia, of Aberdeen, of parish clerks, of scholars (who used to be called clerks), of pawnbrokers (because of the three bags of gold—transformed to the three gold BALLS—that he gave to the daughters of a poor man to save them from earning their dowers in a disreputable way), of little boys (because he once restored to life three little boys who had been cut up and pickled in a salting-tub to serve for bacon), and is invoked by sailors (because he allayed a storm during a voyage to the HOLY LAND) and against fire. Finally he is the original of SANTA CLAUS.

Little is known of his life but he is said to have been Bishop of Myra (Lycia) in the early 4th century, and one story relates that he was present at the COUNCIL OF NICÆA (325) and buffeted Arius on the jaw. His day is 6 December, and he is represented in episcopal robes with either three purses of gold, three gold balls, or three small boys, in allusion to one or other of the above legends. *Cp.* LOMBARD.

St. Nicholas's Bishop. *See* BOY BISHOP.

Nick. Slang for to pilfer; in the 18th century those who delighted to break windows by throwing halfpence at them were called *nickers*.

Old Nick. The DEVIL. The term was in use in the 17th century, and is perhaps connected with the German *Nickel*, a GOBLIN, or in some forgotten way with St. NICHOLAS. Butler's derivation from

Niccolò Machiavelli is, of course, poetical licence:

> Nick Machiavel had ne'er a trick
> (Though he gave name to our old Nick).
> *Hudibras*, III, i.

In the nick. In prison, in custody.

In the nick of time. Just in time, at the right moment. The allusion is to tallies marked with nicks or notches. (*See* TALLY.)

Nickel. In the U.S.A. a *nickel* is a coin of 5 cents, so called from being made of an alloy of nickel and copper.

Nickelodeon. The first cinema theatre called a "Nickelodeon" (because the admission price was only five cents), was that opened by John P. Harris and Harry Davis at McKeesport, near Pittsburgh, Pennsylvania, in 1905. The picture shown was *The Great Train Robbery*. It was the first real motion-picture theatre and thousands more nickelodeons soon sprang up throughout the U.S.A. Hence, a cheap entertainment, and also its application to a juke-box.

Nicker, or **Nix.** In Scandinavian folklore, a water-wraith, or KELPIE, inhabiting sea, lake, river, and waterfall. They are sometimes represented as half-child, half-horse, the hoofs being reversed, and sometimes as old men sitting on rocks wringing the water from their hair. The female nicker is a *nixy*.

Nickname. Originally *an eke-name*, *eke* being an adverb meaning "also", O.E. *eac*, connected with *iecan*, to supply deficiencies in or to make up for. *A newt* was formed in the same way (*an ewt*). The "eke" of a beehive is a piece added to the bottom to enlarge the hive. *Cp.* APRON; NONCE. Surnames as such were not common in England before the 13th century; hence identification was helped by nicknames such as "Long", "Brown", "Bull", "Russell" (red-haired), "Sour milk", "Barefoot", etc.

National Nicknames. Among the best known are:

For an American of the U.S.A., "BROTHER JONATHAN", a "YANKEE"; for the U.S.A. personified, "UNCLE SAM" (*see under* SAM).

For an Australian, "AUSSIE", "DIGGER".

For a Dutchman, "NIC FROG" (*see un-*

Nightingale

der FROG) and "Mynheer Closh".

For an Englishman, "JOHN BULL", "LIMEY", "POMMIE".

For a Frenchman, "Crapaud" (*see* FLEUR-DE-LYS), "Froggie" or "FROG", "Johnny" or "Jean", "Robert MACAIRE", "Mossoo".

For a French Canadian, "Jean Baptiste", "CANUCK".

For French peasantry, "Jacques Bonhomme".

For French reformers, "BRISSOTINS".

For a German, "COUSIN MICHAEL" or "Michel", "Boche", "HUN", "Fritz", "Heinie", "Kraut", "JERRY."

For an Irishman, "PADDY".

For an Italian, "Antonio", or "Tony". *Cp.* WOP.

For a Scot, "Sandy", "Mac", or "Jock".

For a Spaniard or Portuguese, "Dago" (Diego).

For a Welshman, "TAFFY".

Traditional Nicknames of those with a particular surname are numerous. Among them are:

Dinger or Daisy Bell; Nobby Clark; Cocky Ducros (Austr.); Pincher Martin; Dusty Miller; Spud Murphy; Spud Thomson; Knocker White.

In Australia fair-headed people are called "Snowy" and red-headed "Blue".

Nickneven. A gigantic malignant hag of Scottish superstition. Dunbar has well described this spirit in his *Flyting of Dunbar and Kennedy*.

Nicodemus, Gospel of. *See under* GOSPEL.

Nicodemused into nothing. To have one's prospects in life ruined by a silly name; according to the proverb, "Give a DOG a bad name and hang him." It is from Sterne's *Tristram Shandy* (vol. I, 19):

> How many Cæsars and Pompeys...by mere inspiration of the names have been rendered worthy of them; and how many...might have done...well in the world...had they not been Nicodemused into nothing.

Niflheim (nif' ĕl hīm) (*i.e.* mist-home). In Scandinavian mythology, the region of endless cold and everlasting night, ruled over by the goddess HEL. It consisted of nine worlds, to which were consigned those who die of disease or old age; it existed in the north and out of its spring Hvergelmir flowed twelve ice-cold streams. *Cp.* MUSPELHEIM.

Nigger. A nigger in the woodpile. Originally a way of accounting for the disappearance of fuel; it now denotes something deceitful or underhanded; a concealed troublemaker or suspicious circumstance.

Night of the Long Knives, The. A descriptive phrase applied to the night of 30 June 1934 when Hitler, assisted by Göring and Himmler's GESTAPO, secured the murder of the leaders of the BROWNSHIRTS (S.A.) and some Catholic leaders. The shootings (mainly at Munich and Berlin) actually began on the Friday night of the 29th and continued through the Sunday. The estimates of those killed vary between 60 and 400 and Röhm and Schleicher were among them. Hitler had decided to rely on the *Reichswehr* rather than risk dependence on Röhm and the S.A. Himmler presented the assassins with "daggers of honour" inscribed with his name.

George Borrow, referring to a treacherous murder of South British chieftains by Hengist in 472, says:

> This infernal carnage the Welsh have appropriately denominated the treachery of the long knives. It will be as well to observe that the Saxons derived their name from the saxes, or long knives, which they wore at their sides, and at the use of which they were terribly proficient.
> *Wild Wales* (1862), ch. lii.

The phrase is now applied allusively to ruthless or relentless deeds and actions.

Nightingale. The Greek legend is that Tereus, King of Thrace, fetched Philomela to visit his wife, Procne, who was her sister; but when he reached the "solitudes of Heleas" he dishonoured her, and cut out her tongue that she might not reveal his conduct. Tereus told his wife that Philomela was dead, but Philomela made her story known by weaving it into a robe, which she sent to Procne. Procne, in revenge, cut up her own son and served him to Tereus, and as soon as the king discovered it he pursued his wife, who fled to Philomela; whereupon the gods changed all three into birds;

Tereus became the hawk, his wife the swallow, and Philomela, the nightingale, which is still called Philomel (lit., lover of song) by the poets.

> Youths and maidens most poetical...
> Full of meek sympathy must heave their sighs
> O'er Philomela's pity-pleading strains.
> COLERIDGE: *The Nightingale*.

The Swedish Nightingale. The operatic singer, Jenny Lind (1820–1887), afterwards Mme Goldschmidt. She was a native of Stockholm.

Nightmare. A sensation in sleep as if something heavy were sitting on one's breast, formerly supposed to be caused by a monster who actually did this. It was not infrequently called the *nighthag*, or the *riding of the witch*. The second syllable is the O.E. *mare* (old Norse *mara*), an INCUBUS, and it appears in the Fr. *cauchemar*, "the fiend that tramples". The word now usually denotes a frightening dream, a night terror.

The Nightmare of Europe. NAPOLEON BONAPARTE was so called.

Nihil. Nihil obstat. The words by which a Roman Catholic censor of books (*Censor Librorum*) declares that he has found nothing contrary to faith or good morals in the book in question. The full Latin phrase is *nihil obstat quominus imprimatur*, nothing hinders it from being printed.

The IMPRIMATUR is granted by the BISHOP or his delegate.

Nihilism (nī' hil izm) (Lat. *nihil*, nothing). The name given to an essentially philosophical and literary movement in Russia which questioned and protested against conventional and established values, etc. The term was popularized by Turgenev's novel *Fathers and Sons* (1862) and was subsequently confused with a kind of revolutionary anarchism. Although nihilism proper was basically non-political, it strengthened revolutionary trends. The term was not new having long been applied to negative systems of philosophy.

Nike (nī' kē). The Greek winged goddess of victory, according to Hesiod, the daughter of PALLAS and STYX. A U.S.A. army ground-to-air missile for use against high-flying attacking planes is so named from this goddess.

Nil admirari (Lat.). To be stolidly indifferent. Neither to wonder at anything, nor yet to admire anything. The tag is from HORACE (*Ep.* I, vi, 1):

> Nil admirari prope res est una, Numici,
> Solaque, quæ possit facere et servare beatum.

> (Not to admire, Numicius, is the best—
> The only way to make and keep men blest.)
> *Conington*.

Nil desperandum (Lat.). Never say die; never give up in despair; a tag from HORACE (*Carmen*, I, vii, 27):

> Nil desperandum Teucro duce et auspice Teucro.

> (There is naught to be despaired of when we are under Teucer's leadership and auspices.)

Nile. The Egyptians used to say that the rising of the Nile was caused by the tears of ISIS. The feast of Isis was celebrated at the anniversary of the death of OSIRIS, when Isis was supposed to mourn for her husband.

The Hero of the Nile. Horatio, Lord Nelson (1758–1805), from his great victory at Aboukir Bay (1798), for which he was made Baron Nelson of the Nile.

Nimbus (Lat., a cloud). In Christian art a HALO of light placed round the head of an eminent personage. There are three forms: (1) *Vesica piscis*, or fish form (*cp.* ICHTHYS), used in representations of Christ and occasionally of the Virgin Mary, extending round the whole figure; (2) a circular halo; (3) radiated like a star or sun. The enrichments are: (1) for our Lord, a CROSS; (2) for the Virgin, a circlet of stars; (3) for ANGELS, a circlet of small rays, and an outer circle of quatrefoils; (4) the same for SAINTS and martyrs, but with the name often inscribed round the circumference; (5) for the Deity the rays diverge in a triangular direction. Nimbi of a square form signify that the persons so represented were living when they were painted.

The nimbus was used by heathen nations long before painters introduced it into sacred pictures of saints, the TRINITY, and the Virgin Mary. PROSERPINE was represented with a nimbus; the Roman EMPERORS were also decorated in the same manner because they were *divi*. *Cp.* AUREOLE.

Nimini-pimini. Affected simplicity. Lady Emily, in General Burgoyne's *The Heiress*, III, ii (1786), tells Miss Alscrip to stand before a glass and keep pronouncing *nimini-pimini*—"The lips cannot fail to take the right plie."

A similar conceit is used by Dickens in *Little Dorrit* (Bk. II, ii), where Mrs. General tells Amy Dorrit:

> Papa gives a pretty form to the lips. Papa, *potatoes*, *poultry*, *prunes*, and *prism* are all very good words for the lips; especially *prunes* and *prism*.

W.S.Gilbert has the form (*Patience*, II):

> A miminy-piminy, *Je-ne-sais-quoi* young man.

Nimrod. Any daring or outstanding hunter; from the "mighty hunter before the Lord" (*Gen.* x, 9), which the TARGUM says means a "sinful hunting of the sons of men". Pope says of him, he was "a mighty hunter, and his prey was man" (*Windsor Forest*, 62); so also Milton interprets the phrase (*Paradise Lost*, XII, 24, etc.).

The legend is that the tomb of Nimrod still exists in Damascus, and that no dew ever falls upon it, even though all its surroundings are saturated.

Nimrod was the pseudonym of Major Charles Apperley (1779–1843), a devotee of hunting and contributor to the *Sporting Magazine*. His best-known works are *The Life of John Mytton Esq.*, *The Chase, the Turf, and the Road*, and the *Life of a Sportsman*.

Nine. Nine, FIVE, THREE are mystical numbers—the DIAPASON, *diapente*, and *diatrion* of the Greeks. Nine consists of a trinity of trinities. According to the Pythagoreans man is a full chord, or eight notes, and deity comes next. Three, being the TRINITY, represents a perfect *unity*; twice three is the perfect *dual*; and thrice three is the perfect *plural*. This explains why nine is a mystical number.

From ancient times the number nine has been held of particular significance. DEUCALION'S ark was tossed about for *nine* days when it stranded on the top of Mount PARNASSUS. There were *nine*

MUSES, *nine* Gallicenæ or virgin priestesses of the ancient Gallic ORACLE; and Lars Porsena swore by *nine* gods.

NIOBE'S children lay *nine* days in their blood before they were buried; the HYDRA had *nine* heads; at the *Lemuria*, held by the Romans on 9, 11, and 13 May, persons haunted threw black beans over their heads, pronouncing *nine* times the words: "Avaunt, ye spectres, from this house!" and the EXORCISM was complete (*see* Ovid's *Fasti*).

There were *nine* rivers of HELL, or, according to some accounts, the STYX encompassed the infernal regions in *nine* circles; and Milton makes the gates of HELL "thrice three-fold", "three folds were brass, three iron, three of adamantine rock". They had *nine* folds, *nine* plates, and *nine* linings (*Paradise Lost*, II, 645).

VULCAN, when kicked from OLYMPUS, was *nine* days falling to the island of LEMNOS; and when the fallen ANGELS were cast out of HEAVEN Milton says "*Nine* days they fell" (*Paradise Lost*, VI, 871).

In the early Ptolemaic system of astronomy, before the PRIMUM MOBILE was added, there were nine SPHERES; hence Milton, in his *Arcades*, speaks of

> The celestial siren's harmony,
> That sat upon the nine enfolded spheres.

In Scandinavian mythology there were *nine* earths, HEL being the goddess of the ninth; there were *nine* worlds in NIFLHEIM, and ODIN'S ring dropped eight other rings every *ninth* night.

In folk-lore *nine* appears frequently. The ABRACADABRA was worn *nine* days, and then flung into a river; in order to see the FAIRIES one is directed to put "*nine* grains of wheat on a four-leaved clover"; *nine* knots are made on black wool as a charm for a sprained ankle; if a servant finds *nine* green peas in a peascod, she lays it on the lintel of the kitchen door, and the first man that enters is to be her cavalier; to see *nine* magpies is most unlucky; a cat has *nine* lives (*see also* CAT-O'-NINE-TAILS); and the *nine* of Diamonds is known as the CURSE OF SCOTLAND.

The weird sisters in Shakespeare's *Macbeth* (I, iii) sang, as they danced round the cauldron, "Thrice to thine, and thrice to mine, and thrice again to make up nine"; and then declared "the charm wound up"; and we drink a *Three-times-three* to those most highly honoured.

Leases are sometimes granted for 999 years, that is *three* times *three-three-three*. Many run for 99 years, the dual of a trinity of trinities.

See also the NINE POINTS OF THE LAW *below*, and the NINE WORTHIES *under* WORTHIES. There are *nine* orders of angels; in HERALDRY there are *nine* marks of cadency and *nine* different crowns recognized.

Dressed up to the nines. *See* DRESSED.

Nine days' Queen. Lady Jane Grey. She was proclaimed queen in London on 10 July 1553; Queen Mary was proclaimed in London on 19 July.

Nine days' wonder. Something that causes a great sensation for a few days, and then passes into the LIMBO of things forgotten. An old proverb is: "A wonder lasts nine days, and then the puppy's eyes are open," alluding to dogs, which like cats, are born blind. As much as to say, the eyes of the public are blind in astonishment for nine days, but then their eyes are open, and they see too much to wonder any longer.

> *King:* You'd think it strange if I should marry her.
> *Gloster:* That would be ten days' wonder, at the least.
> *Clar.:* That's a day longer than a wonder lasts.
> SHAKESPEARE: *Henry VI, Pt. III*, III, ii.

The Nine First Fridays. In the ROMAN CATHOLIC CHURCH the special observance of the first FRIDAY in each of nine consecutive months, marked by receiving the EUCHARIST. The practice derives from St. Mary Alacoque (*see* SACRED HEART *under* HEART), who held that Christ told her that special grace would be granted to those fulfilling this observance.

Nine Men's Morris. *See under* MORRIS.

The Nine Worthies. *See* WORTHIES.

Nine times out of ten. Far more often than not.

Possession is nine points of the law. It is every advantage a person can have short of actual right. The "nine points of the law" have been given as: (1) a good deal of money; (2) a good deal of patience; (3) a good cause; (4) a good lawyer; (5) a good counsel; (6) good witnesses; (7) a good jury; (8) a good judge; and (9) good luck.

To look nine ways. To squint.

Ninepence. Commendation Ninepence. *See* COMMENDATION.

Nice as ninepence. A corruption of "Nice as nine-pins". In the game of nine-pins, the "men" are set in three rows with the utmost exactitude or nicety.

Nimble as ninepence. Silver ninepences were common till the year 1696, when all unmilled coin was called in. These ninepences were very *pliable* or "nimble", and, being bent, were given as love tokens, the usual formula of presentation being *To my love, from my love.* There is an old proverb, *A nimble ninepence is better than a slow shilling.*

Ninepence to a shilling. An old rustic phrase in the West of England meaning that the person referred to is deficient in common sense or intelligence.

Right as ninepence. Perfectly well; in perfect condition.

Ninus. Son of Belus, husband of SEMIRAMIS, and the reputed builder of Nineveh. It is at his tomb that the lovers meet in the PYRAMUS and Thisbe travesty:

> *Pyr.:* Wilt thou at Ninny's tomb meet me straightway?
> *This.:* 'Tide life, 'tide death, I come without delay.
> SHAKESPEARE: *Midsummer Night's Dream*, V, i.

Niobe (nī' o bē). The personification of maternal sorrow. According to Greek legend, Niobe, the daughter of TANTALUS and wife of AMPHION, King of THEBES, was the mother of fourteen children, and taunted LATONA because she had but two—APOLLO and DIANA. Latona commanded her children to avenge the insult and they consequently destroyed Niobe's sons and daughters. Niobe, inconsolable, wept herself to death, and was changed into a stone, from which ran water, "Like Niobe, all tears" (SHA-

KESPEARE: *Hamlet*, I, ii).

Niord, Niordhr, or **Njorthr.** A Scandinavian god, protector of wealth and ships, who dwelt at Noatun by the sea-shore. His wife Skadi lived in the mountains, for the gulls disturbed her sleep! *See* CUP OF VOWS; NERTHUS.

Nip. A nip of whisky, etc. Short for **Nipperkin.** A small wine and beer measure containing about half a pint, or a little under; now frequently called "a nip".

Nip and tuck. A NECK-AND-NECK race: a close fight.

To nip in the bud. To destroy before it has had time to develop; to stop something in its early stages, as a bud is nipped by frost or pests, etc., thus preventing further growth.

Nipper. Slang for a small boy.

Nippon. The Japanese name for Japan, "the great land of the rising sun".

Nirvana (Sansk., a blowing out, or extinction). In BUDDHISM, the cessation of individual existence; the attainment of a calm, sinless state of mind achieved by the extinction of passion, a state which can be attained during life.

Nisi (nī′ sī) (Lat., unless). In Law a "rule nisi" is a rule unless cause be shown to the contrary.

Decree nisi. A decree of divorce granted on the condition that it does not take effect until made *absolute*, which is done in due course, unless reasons why it should not have meantime come to light. Every decree of divorce is, in the first instance, a *decree nisi*.

Nisi prius (Lat., unless previously). Originally a writ commanding a SHERIFF to empanel a jury which should be at the Court of WESTMINSTER on a certain day unless the justices of assize have previously come to his county.

The second Statute of Westminster (1285) instituted Judges of *nisi prius*, who were appointed to travel through the shires three times a year to hear civil causes. A trial at *nisi prius* is now a trial by jury in a civil cause before a single judge.

Nisroch. The Assyrian god in whose temple Sennacherib was worshipping when he was slain (II *Kings* xix, 37). Nothing is known of this god but the name is probably a corruption of *Asur* or a by-form of *Asuraku. Cp.* ASSHER.

Nisus and Euryalus. An example of proverbial friendship comparable to that of PYLADES and Orestes. Nisus with a Trojan friend raided the camp of the Rutulians and slaughtered many of the enemy in their drunken sleep, but the youthful Euryalus was killed by Volscens. Nisus rushed to avenge his death and in slaying Volscens was himself killed (*Æneid*, IX).

Nitouch (ni toosh′). **Faire la Sainte Nitouche,** to pretend to great sanctity, to look as though BUTTER would not melt in one's mouth. Sainte Nitouche, a contraction of *n'y touche*, is a name given in France to a hypocrite.

Nivetta. *See* MORGAN LE FAY.

Nivôse (nē vōz) (Lat. *nivosus*, very snowy). The fourth month of the FRENCH REVOLUTIONARY CALENDAR (*see under* CALENDAR), lasting from 21 December to 19 January.

Nix. *See* NICKER. The word is also slang for "nothing" (Ger. *nichts*, nothing). "He won't work for nix" means he won't work without payment.

Nizam (ni zăm′). The title of sovereignty of the ruler of the former state of Hyderabad, India; contracted from *Nizam-ul-mulk* (regulator of the state), in 1713 the title of Asaf Jah, who later became independent of MOGUL control.

Njorthr. *See* NIORD.

No. No can do. I cannot do it.

No dice (U.S.A.). Nothing doing.

No Man's Land. The name given to the area between hostile lines of entrenchments or to any space contested by both sides and belonging to neither. In the OPEN FIELD system, odd scraps of land, also called "Jack's land" or "anyone's land".

Noah. Noah's Ark. A name given by sailors to a white band of cloud spanning the sky like a rainbow and in shape something like the hull of a ship. If east and west, expect dry weather, if north and south, expect wet. Noah's Ark is also used as a PUBLIC-HOUSE SIGN.

Noah's wife. According to legend she was unwilling to go into the ark, and the quarrel between the patriarch and his wife forms a prominent feature of

Noah's Flood, in the Chester and Townley MYSTERIES.

Noble. A former English gold coin, from the superior quality of its GOLD. First minted by Edward III (1344), possibly in commemoration of the Battle of Sluys (1340). It was originally valued at 6s. 8d. and replaced by the *royal* or *rose noble* in 1465.

The Noble Duke of York of nursery rhyme fame was George III's second son.

> The noble Duke of York,
> He had ten thousand men;
> He marched 'em up to the top of the hill,
> And he marched 'em down again.

The rhyme was a derisive commentary on his abortive operations in Flanders (1794) against the French. He was young at the time, although some versions refer to "the rare old Duke" or "the grand old Duke". The land was flat, otherwise the rhyme is fair comment. He was made Commander-in-Chief in 1798. *See* DUKE OF YORK'S COLUMN *under* COLUMN.

The Noble Science. The old epithet for fencing or boxing, sometimes called "The Noble Art of Self-Defence".

Noblesse oblige (nō bles' ō blēzh') (Fr.). Noble birth imposes the obligation of high-minded principles and noble actions.

Nod. A nod is as good as a wink to a blind horse. *See under* HORSE.

On the nod. On credit. To get a thing on the nod is to get it without paying for it at the time. The phrase is from the auction room where one signifies a bid by a mere nod of the head, the formalities of paying being attended to later. *Cp.* ON THE NEVER NEVER *under* NEVER.

The land of Nod. *See under* LAND.

A nodding acquaintance. A slight acquaintance, a person with whom one exchanges a nod for recognition when passing without seeking to become more closely acquainted. When used of one's acquaintance with literary works, etc., it means a superficial or slight knowledge.

Noel (nō' el). In English (also written *Nowell*), a Christmas CAROL, or the shout of joy in a carol; in French, Christmas Day. The word is Provençal *nadal*, from Lat. *natalem*, natal.

Nokes. *See* JOHN-A-NOKES.

Nolens volens (no' lenz vo' lenz). Whether willing or not. Two Latin participles meaning "being unwilling (or) willing". *Cp.* WILLY-NILLY.

Noli me tangere (nol' i mē tăn' jer i) (Lat., touch me not). The words Christ used to MARY MAGDALENE after his resurrection (*John* xx, 17) and given as a name to a plant of the genus *Impatiens*. The seed vessels consist of one cell in five divisions, and when the seed is ripe each of these, on being touched, suddenly folds itself into a spiral form, and leaps from the stalk. *See* Darwin's *Loves of the Plants*, II, iii.

Noll. Old Noll. Oliver Cromwell was so called, Noll being a familiar form of *Oliver*.

Nolle prosequi (nol' i prō sek' wi) (Lat., to be unwilling to prosecute). A petition from a plaintiff to stay a suit. *Cp.* NON PROS.

Nolo contendere (nō' lō kon ten' dè rē) (Lat., I am unwilling to contend). A plea in law by which the defendant, while not admitting guilt, declares he will not offer any defence. A plea tantamount to that of "guilty".

Nolo episcopari (nō' lō p isk ō pâ' ri) (Lat., I am unwilling to be made a BISHOP). The formal reply supposed to be returned to the royal offer of bishopric. Chamberlayne says (*Present State of England*, 1669) that in former times the person about to be elected modestly refused the office twice, and if he did so a third time his refusal was accepted.

Nom. Nom de guerre (Fr. "war name"). An assumed name. It was once customary for every entrant into the French army to assume a name, especially in the times of CHIVALRY, when knights were known by the device on their shields.

Nom de plume. English-French for "pen-name" or pseudonym, the name assumed by a writer, cartoonist, etc., who does not choose to use his own name; as Currer Bell (Charlotte Brontë); Stendhal (Marie Henri Beyle). *See* CARAN D'ACHE; GEORGE ELIOT; GEORGE SAND; PHIZ; VOLTAIRE.

Nominalism. The SCHOOLMEN'S name for the theory of knowledge which denies the objective existence of abstract ideas. A form of Nominalism was put forward by Roscelin in the 11th century, but in its more pronounced form by WILLIAM OF OCCAM in the 14th century. Those who held the opposite view were called Realists (*see* REALISM).

Non. The Latin negative, *not*; adopted in English and very widely employed as a prefix of negation, *e.g. non*-abstainer, *non*-conformist, *non*-existent, *non*-residence, *non*sense, etc.

Non amo te, Zabidi. *See* FELL.

Non Angli sed angeli. *See* ANGLES.

Non assumpsit (Lat., he has not undertaken). The legal term for a plea denying a promise or undertaking.

Non compos mentis (Lat., not of sound mind). Said of a lunatic, idiot, drunkard, or one who has lost memory and understanding by accident or disease.

Non est. A contraction of Lat. *non est inventus* (not to be found). They are the words which the sheriff writes on a writ when the defendant is not to be found in his bailiwick.

Non mi ricordo (I do not remember). A shuffling way of saying, "I don't choose to answer that question." It was the usual answer of the Italian witnesses when under examination at the trial of Queen Caroline, wife of George IV, in 1820.

Non placet (Lat., it is unpleasing). The formula used, especially by the governing body of a University, for expressing a negative vote.

Non pros. for Lat. *non prosequitur*, he does not follow up. Judgment *non pros.* for a defendant was pronounced in an action when the plaintiff failed to take the necessary steps in time.

Non sequitur (Lat., it does not follow). A conclusion which does not follow from the premises stated; an inconsequent statement, such as Artemus Ward's.

Nonce. M.E. for *than anes*, for the once. *Cp.* NICKNAME.

Nonce-word. A word coined for a particular occasion, such as BIRRELLISM, LIMEHOUSE, PUSEYITE.

Non-conformists. In England, members of PROTESTANT bodies who do not conform to the doctrines of the CHURCH OF ENGLAND. They had their origins in the BROWNISTS and BAPTISTS of Elizabeth I's reign and among the 17th-century PURITANS and sectaries. After the RESTORATION and the subsequent Act of Uniformity of 1662, which enforced strict observance of the BOOK OF COMMON PRAYER, some 2,000 clergy were ejected and a lasting division resulted. The DISSENTERS or Nonconformists were subjected to the CLARENDON CODE until relief came with the Toleration Act of 1689 and later measures. Nonconformity received further recruits particularly with the advent of the METHODISTS.

Nones (nōnz). In the ancient Roman CALENDAR, the *ninth* (Lat. *nonus*) day before IDES; in the ROMAN CATHOLIC CHURCH, the office for the *ninth* hour after sunrise, *i.e.* between noon and 3 p.m.

Non-jurors. Those HIGH CHURCH clergy who refused to take the oath of allegiance to William and Mary after the Revolution of 1688 and who were deprived of their livings in 1690. Their numbers included Archbishop Sancroft and five other bishops. They maintained their own episcopal succession until the death of their last bishop in 1805. *Cp.* SEVEN BISHOPS.

Non-resistance. In the CHURCH OF ENGLAND passive obedience to royal commands was a natural corollary of the DIVINE RIGHT OF KINGS but it acquired a particular importance after the RESTORATION, when TORY-minded clergy advocated non-resistance to combat NONCONFORMIST doctrines and WHIG policies. When James II tried to promote Roman Catholicism, many advocates of non-resistance abandoned their support of the monarchy and others became NON-JURORS after the accession of William of Orange.

Norman French. The old French dialect spoken in Normandy at the time of the CONQUEST and spoken by the dominant class in ENGLAND for some two centuries subsequently. Vestiges remain, particularly in legal terminology, and in other connections, such as "Fitz" (*fils*, son) that precedes certain family surnames. The royal assent to bills passed by PAR-

LIAMENT is still given in Norman French, *La Reine remercie ses bons sujets, accepte leur benevolence, et ainsi le veult*, etc.

Norns, The. The fates, dispensers of destiny in Norse mythology. They lived at the foot of the ash-tree YGGDRASIL which they watered daily from the fountain called Urd. These sisters eventually became three in number in imitation of the three FATES of classical legend.

Norroy (*i.e.* north *roy*, or king). The third King of Arms (*see* HERALD) is so called, because his jurisdiction is on the north side of the river Trent; that to the south is exercised by CLARENCEUX. In 1943, the office of ULSTER KING OF ARMS was united with that of Norroy.

North. There was an old belief that only evil-doers should be buried on the north side of a churchyard, which probably arose from the lack of sun on this side. The east was *God*'s side, where his throne is set; the west, *man*'s side, the GALILEE of the Gentiles; the south, the side of the "*spirits made just*", where the sun shines in his strength; and the north, the *devil*'s side. *Cp.* THE DEVIL'S DOOR *under* DEVIL.

North, Christopher. *See* AMBROSIAN NIGHTS.

North Briton. A periodical founded by John Wilkes in 1762 to air his animosity against Lord Bute and the Scottish nation. *See* NUMBER 45 *under* FORTY; GENERAL WARRANTS.

The North-East Passage. A hoped-for route to the East round the north extremity of Asia. It was first attempted by Willoughby and Chancellor (1553–1554) and its only practical result was the establishment of the Muscovy Company (1555). The passage was traversed by the Swedish ship *Vega* in 1897.

The North Pole was first reached on 6 April 1909, by the American explorer Robert Edwin Peary (1856–1920). In May 1933, the North Pole was claimed by the Russians and four years later they established a Polar station there under Prof. Otto Schmidt.

The North-West Frontier. Particularly, the north-west frontier of British India and the province of that name,

now part of PAKISTAN. Owing to the warlike nature of the local tribesmen and the Russian advance in central Asia, it gained an especial importance from the later 19th century, and was a constant drain in men and money.

The North-West Passage. The name given to the long-sought-for route to the East round the north of the American continent, the search for which began with Sebastian Cabot's voyage of 1509. Search continued through the centuries by men such as Frobisher, Davis, Hudson, Baffin and Bylot, Cook, and Vancouver. It was first traversed by the Norwegian Roald Amundsen (1903–1905).

The Northern Bear. Tsarist Russia was so called.

The Northern Gate of the Sun. The sign of CANCER, or summer SOLSTICE; so called because it marks the northern tropic.

The Northern Lights. The AURORA BOREALIS.

The Northern Wagoner. The genius presiding over the GREAT BEAR (*see under* BEAR) or CHARLES'S WAIN, which contains seven large stars.

Northamptonshire Poet. *See* PEASANT POET.

Northumbria. The Anglo-Saxon kingdom formed in the early 7th century, which included all ENGLAND north of the Humber, and S.W. and E. SCOTLAND to the Firth of Forth. For most of the 7th century it was the most powerful English kingdom and its kings Edwin, Oswald, and Oswy held the office of BRETWALDA. Its dominance was replaced by that of MERCIA. It was long noted as a centre of learning.

Norway, Maid of. *See* MAID.

Nose. As plain as the nose on your face. Extremely obvious, patent to all.

Bleeding of the nose. According to some, a sign that one is in love. Grose says if it bleeds one drop only it forebodes sickness, if three drops the omen is still worse; but Melton, in his *Astrologaster*, says, "If a man's nose bleeds one drop at the left nostril it is a sign of good luck, and vice versa."

Cleopatra's nose. *See under* CLEOPATRA.

Golden nose. Tycho Brahe (d. 1601), the Danish astronomer. He lost his nose in a duel, so adopted a golden one, which he attached to his face by a cement which he carried about with him.

The bloodthirsty Emperor Justinian II, nicknamed Rhinotmetus, had a golden nose in place of the nose that had been cut off by his general Leontius before he ascended the imperial throne. It used to be said that when Justinian cleansed this golden nose, those who were present knew that the death of someone had been decided upon.

Led by the nose. Said of one who has no will of his own but follows tamely the guidance of a stronger character, as horses, asses, etc., are led by the nose by bit and bridle. Hence SHAKESPEARE's Iago says of Othello, he was "led by the nose as asses are" (I, iii). Bulls, buffaloes, camels, and bears are led by a ring through their nostrils. *Isaiah* xxxvii, 29, says: "Because thy rage against me...is come up into mine ears, therefore will I put my hook in thy nose...and...I will turn thee back."

Nose tax. It is said that in the 9th century the Danes imposed a poll tax in IRELAND, and that this was called the "Nose Tax", because those who neglected to pay were punished by having their noses slit.

On the nose. An American expression meaning exactly on time. It originated in the broadcasting studio, where the producer, when signalling to the performers, puts his finger on his nose when the programme is running to schedule time.

The Pope's nose. The rump of a fowl, which is also called the *parson's nose*. The phrase is said to have originated during the years following James II's reign (1685–1688), when anti-Catholic feeling was high.

To bite, or **snap one's nose off.** To speak snappishly. To *pull* (or *wring*) *the nose* is to affront by an act of indignity; to *snap one's nose* is to affront by speech. Snarling dogs snap at each other's noses.

To count noses. A horse-dealer counts horses by the *nose*, as cattle are counted by the *head*; hence, the expression is sometimes ironically used of numbering votes, as in the Division lobbies.

To cut off your nose to spite your face, or **to be revenged on your face.** To act out of pique in such a way as to bring harm to yourself.

To follow one's nose. To go straight ahead; to proceed without deviating from the path.

To keep one's nose clean. To ensure that one does not get involved in dealings or practices of a dubious or shady character; to avoid any suspicion of malpractice.

To keep one's nose to the grindstone. To keep hard at work. Tools, such as scythes, chisels, etc., are constantly sharpened on a stone or with a grindstone.

To look down one's nose. To treat disdainfully, to regard with disapproval; from the customary attitude of disapproval of lowering one's eyelids and looking down one's nose.

To pay through the nose. To pay too much. Of many conjectured origins, the most likely is that this phrase derives from the NOSE TAX (*see above*).

To poke, or **thrust one's nose in.** Officiously to intermeddle with other people's affairs; to intrude where one is not wanted.

To put one's nose out of joint. To supplant a person in another's good grace; to upset one's plans; to humiliate or bring disgruntlement to someone.

To turn up one's nose. To express contempt. When a person sneers he turns up the nose by curling the upper lip.

To wipe one's nose. *See under* WIPE.

Unable to see beyond the end of one's nose. Totally lacking in foresight, perception and discernment; obtuse.

Under one's very nose. Right before one. In full view.

Nosey. Very inquisitive; overfond of poking one's nose into the business of others. One who does this is a **Nosey Parker,** possibly an allusion to Matthew Parker, Archbishop of Canterbury (1504, 1559–1575). He was noted for the detailed articles of inquiry concerning ecclesiastical affairs generally and the conduct of the clergy, which he issued for the Visitations of his province and diocese. The Duke of Wellington was called "Old Nosey" by his troops from his strongly accentuated aquiline nose. The nickname was also given to Oliver Cromwell. *See* COPPER NOSE.

Nostradamus. The name assumed by Michel de Nostradame, French physician and astrologer (1503–1566) who published an annual "Almanack" as well as the famous *Les Centuries* (1555) which suffered papal condemnation in 1781. His controversial prophecies were couched in very ambiguous language. Hence the saying *"as good a prophet as Nostradamus"*, *i.e.*, so obscure that your meaning cannot be understood.

Notarikon (Gr. *notarikon*; Lat. *notarius*, a shorthand writer). A cabalistic word denoting the old Jewish art of using each letter in a word to form another word, or using the initials of the words in a sentence to form another word, etc., as the word CABAL itself was fabled to have been from Clifford, Ashley, Buckingham, Arlington, and Lauderdale; and as the term ICHTHYS was applied to the Saviour. Other instances are: A.E.I.O.U.; CLIO; HEMPE; LIMP; SMECTYMNUUS. *Cp.* HIP! HIP! HURRAH!

Note. To compare notes. To exchange opinions, observations, etc., on a particular matter or subject, with someone else. Here the reference is to the written note.

To strike the right note. To say, write, or to do the particularly appropriate thing to suit the occasion; the allusion is to the note in music.

Notes of the Church. The four characteristic marks of the Church, *i.e.* one, *holy*, *catholic*, and *apostolic*, as set forth in the NICENE CREED. These "notes" were used by Roman Catholic theologians and others, and by the TRACTARIANS to demonstrate their claims.

Nothing. Mere nothings. Trifles; unimportant things or events.

Next to nothing. A very little, as, "It will cost next to nothing"; "He eats next to nothing."

Nothing doing! Used to imply that your request is refused; your wishes cannot be met, etc.

Nothing venture, nothing have, or

win. An old proverb, if you won't take a chance, you cannot expect to gain anything; if you daren't throw a SPRAT you mustn't expect to catch a mackerel.

Out of nothing one can get nothing; the Latin *Ex nihilo nihil fit*—*i.e.* every effect must have a cause. It was the dictum by which Xenophanes, founder of the ELEATIC School, postulated his theory of the eternity of matter. Persius (*Satires*, iii, 84) has *De nihilo nihilum, in nihilum nil posse reverti*, From nothing nothing, and into nothing can nothing return.

We now use the phrase as equivalent to "You cannot get blood from a stone", or expect good work from one who has no brains.

That's nothing to you, or **to do with you.** It's none of your business; it is not your concern.

There's nothing for it but to... There's no alternative, there is only one thing to do.

To come to nothing. To turn out a failure; to result in naught.

To make nothing of. To fail to understand; not to do anything with; not to make a fuss about.

To think nothing of. To regard as unimportant, or easy.

Nought. *See* NAUGHT.

Nous (nous) (Gr., mind, intellect). Adopted in English and used to denote "intelligence", "horse-sense", "understanding".

> Thine is the genuine head of many a house,
> And much divinity without a NOUS.
> POPE: *Dunciad*, IV, 244.

Nous was the Platonic term for mind, or the first cause, and the system of divinity referred to above is that which springs from blind nature.

Nous avons changé tout cela (noo ză-v on shon' zhā too sela) (Fr., We have changed all that). A facetious reproof to one who lays down the law upon everything, and talks contemptuously of old customs, old authors, old artists, etc. The phrase is taken from MOLIÈRE's *Médecin Malgré Lui*, II, vi.

Nouveaux riches (noo' vō rēsh') (Fr., the new rich). A phrase with derogatory implications applied to those who have newly acquired considerable affluence and who often seek to use their money for social climbing, etc.

Nova Scotia. *See* ACADIA.

Novel disseisin ("Seisin" is possession, hence "new dispossession"). A petty assize introduced by Henry II (*c.* 1166) to provide quick remedy for the man *disseised*, *i.e.* ejected from his FREEHOLD. If juries decided a man was wrongly disseised, he was restored to possession. It was particularly welcome after the anarchy of Stephen's reign and as time progressed the period covered by "novel" was increasingly extended until it lost meaning.

Novella. A diminutive from Lat. *novus*, new. A short story of the kind contained in Boccaccio's *Decameron*, and immensely popular in the 16th and 17th centuries. Such stories were the forerunners of the long novel and also of the short story of more recent times.

November (Lat. *novem*, nine). The ninth month in the ancient Roman CALENDAR, when the year began in MARCH; now the eleventh. The old Dutch name was *Slaghtmaand* (slaughter-month, the time when the beasts were slain and salted down for winter use); the old Saxon *Wind-monath* (wind-month, when the fishermen drew their boats ashore, and gave over fishing till the next spring); it was also called *Blot-monath*—the same as *Slaghtmaand*. In the French Republican Calendar it was called *Brumaire* (fog-month, 23 October to 21 November).

> No sun—no moon!
> No morn—no noon—
> No dawn—no dusk—no proper time of day.
> No warmth, no cheerfulness, no healthful ease,
> No comfortable feel in any member—
> No shade, no shine, no butterflies, no bees,
> No fruits, no flowers, no leaves, no birds!—November!
>
> T. HOOD: *No!* (1844).

Novena (nō vē′ nà) (Lat. *novenus*, nine each). In Roman Catholic devotions, a prayer for some special object or occasion extended over a period of nine days.

Nowell. *See* NOEL.

Noyades (nwa′ yad) (Fr., drownings).

During the REIGN OF TERROR in France (1793–1794), Carrier at Nantes drowned many of his victims in the Loire by stowing them in boats and removing the plugs. NERO, at the suggestion of Anicetus, attempted to drown his mother in the same manner.

Null and void. No longer of binding force; having no further validity.

Nulli secundus (Lat., second to none). The motto of the COLDSTREAM GUARDS, which regiment is hence sometimes spoken of as the *Nulli Secundus Club*.

Numbers, Numerals. PYTHAGORAS looked on numbers as influential principles; in his system:

1 was Unity, and represented Deity, which has no parts.
2 was Diversity, and therefore disorder; the principle of strife and all EVIL.
3 was Perfect Harmony; or the union of unity and diversity.
4 was Perfection; it is the first square (2 × 2 = 4).
5 was the prevailing number in Nature and Art.
6 was Justice.
7 was the CLIMACTERIC number in all diseases.

With the ancient Romans 2 was the most fatal of all the numbers; they dedicated the second month to PLUTO, and the second day of the month to the MANES.

In old ecclesiastical symbolism the numbers from 1 to 13 were held to denote the following:

1 The Unity of God.
2 The hypostatic union of Christ, both God and man.
3 The TRINITY.
4 The number of the EVANGELISTS.
5 The wounds of the Redeemer; two in the hands, two in the feet, one in the side.
6 The creative week.
7 The gifts of the HOLY GHOST and the seven times Christ spoke on the CROSS.
8 The number of BEATITUDES (*Matt.* v, 3–11).
9 The nine orders of ANGELS.
10 The number of the Commandments.
11 The number of the APOSTLES who remained faithful.
12 The original college.
13 The final number after the conversion of Paul.

All our numerals and ordinals up to a million (with one exception) are Anglo-Saxon. The one exception is *Second*, which is French. The Anglo-Saxon word was *other*, as First, Other, Third, etc., but as this was ambiguous, the Fr. *seconde* was early adopted. Million is from Lat. *mille*, a thousand.

The primitive method of counting was by the fingers (*cp.* DIGITS); thus, in the Roman system of numeration, the first four were simply i, ii, iii, iiii; five was the outline of the hand simplified into a v; the next four figures were the four combined, thus, vi, vii, viii, viiii; and ten was a double v, thus x. At a later period iiii and viiii were expressed by one less than five (i−v) and one less than ten (i−x); nineteen was ten-plus-nine (x+ix) etc. *See also* ARABIC FIGURES.

Apocalyptic number, 666. *See* NUMBER OF THE BEAST, *below*.

Back number. Any number of a paper or periodical previous to the current issue; hence an out-of-date or old-fashioned person or thing; one no longer IN THE SWIM (*see under* SWIM).

Book of Numbers. In the OLD TESTAMENT, the Fourth Book of Moses, from the "numbering" of the Israelites in chapters iii and xxvi.

Medical number. In the Pythagorean system (*see* NUMBER *above*), 7.

Number One. *See under* ONE.

The Number of the Beast. 666; a mystical number of unknown meaning but referring to some man mentioned by St. JOHN.

> Let him that hath understanding count the number of the beast: for it is the number of a man: and his number is Six hundred threescore and six.
> *Rev.* xiii, 18.

One of the most plausible suggestions is that it refers to Neron Cæsar, which in Hebrew characters with numerical value gives 666, whereas NERO, without the final "n", as in Latin, gives 616 (n=50), the number given in many early MSS., according to Irenæus.

Among the CABBALISTS, every letter represented a number, and one's number was the sum of these equivalents to the letters in one's name. If, as is probable, the *Revelation* was written in Hebrew, the number would suit either Nero, Hadrian, or Trajan—all persecu-

tors; if in Greek, it would fit Caligula or *Lateinos*, *i.e.* the Roman Empire; but almost any name in any language can be twisted into this number, and it has been applied to many persons assumed to have been ANTICHRIST or Apostates, Diocletian, Evanthas, JULIAN THE APOSTATE, Luther, Mohammed, Paul V, Silvester II, NAPOLEON Bonaparte, Charles Bradlaugh, William II of Germany, and several others; as well as to certain phrases supposed to be descriptive of "the Man of Sin", as Vicar-General of God, Kakos Odegos (bad guide), Abinu Kadescha Papa (our holy father the pope), *e.g.*—

M	a	o	m	e	t	i	s	
40	1	70	40	5	300	10	200	= 666

L	a	t	e	i	n	o	s	
30	1	300	5	10	50	70	200	= 666

One suggestion is that St. John chose the number 666 because it just fell short of the holy number 7 in every particular; it was straining at every point to get there, but never could. *See also* MYSTERIUM.

His days are numbered. They are drawing to a close; he is near death.

> God hath numbered thy kingdom, and finished it.
> *Dan.* v, 26.

Not to have one's number on it. An expression used by members of the armed forces when one has a narrow escape from a bullet or other missile, since it was not supposedly earmarked by fate for one's extinction. *Cp.* YOUR NUMBER'S UP.

There's luck in odd numbers. This is an ancient fancy. According to the Pythagorean system nine represents Deity. A major chord consists of a fundamental or tonic, its major third, and its just fifth. As the odd numbers are the fundamental notes of nature, the last being the Deity, it is understandable how they came to be considered the great or lucky numbers. *Cp.* DIAPASON; NUMBERS.

> Good luck lies in odd numbers...They say, there is divinity in odd numbers, either in nativity, chance or death.
> SHAKESPEARE: *The Merry Wives of Windsor*, V, i.

The odd numbers 1, 3, 5, 7, 9 (which

see), seem to play a far more important part than the even numbers. VIRGIL (*Eclogues*, viii, 75) says *Numero Deus impare gaudet* (the god delights in odd numbers). THREE indicates the "beginning, middle, and the end". The Godhead has three persons; so in classical mythology HECATE had threefold power; JOVE's symbol was a triple thunderbolt, NEPTUNE's a sea-trident, PLUTO's a three-headed dog; the Horæ three. There are SEVEN notes, NINE planets, nine orders of ANGELS, seven days a week, thirteen lunar months, or 365 days a year, etc.; FIVE senses, five fingers, five toes, five continents, etc.

To consult the Book of Numbers. A facetious way of saying "to put it to the vote".

Your number's up. You are caught, or about to die. A soldier's phrase; in the American army a soldier who has just been killed or has died is said to have "lost his mess number". An older phrase in the Royal Navy was "to lose the number of his mess". *Cp.* NOT TO HAVE ONE'S NUMBER ON IT, *above. See also* TO HAVE HAD IT *under* HAD.

Nunc dimittis. The Song of Simeon (*Luke* ii, 29), "Lord, now lettest thou thy servant depart in peace", so called from the opening words of the Latin version, *Nunc dimittis servum tuum, Domine*.

Hence, *to receive one's Nunc dimittis*, to be given permission to go; *to sing one's Nunc dimittis*, to show satisfaction at departing.

The Canticle is sung at Evening Prayer in the CHURCH OF ENGLAND, and has been anciently used at COMPLINE or VESPERS throughout the Church.

Nuremberg Laws. The infamous NAZI laws promulgated in September 1935. Jews, and all those of Jewish extraction, were deprived of all rights of German citizenship, and regulations were made against those of partial Jewish ancestry. Marriage between JEW and "German" was forbidden. Nuremberg was the centre of the annual Nazi Party convention.

Nuremberg Trials. The trial of 23 NAZI leaders conducted by an Inter-Allied tribunal at Nuremberg after World War II (September 1945—May 1946). Three were acquitted. Göring, Ribbentrop and nine others were condemned to death, and the remainder sentenced to various terms of imprisonment. Hitler, Himmler, and Goebbels avoided retribution by committing suicide, as did Göring.

Nurr and Spell. *See* KNURR.

Nursery. Nursery rhymes. The traditional metrical jingles learned by children "in the nursery" and frequently used in their games. They contain survivals of folklore, ancient superstitions, festival games, and local customs, history, etc. Most of them are very old, but some are more recent, such as OLD MOTHER HUBBARD and the NOBLE DUKE OF YORK.

Nursery slopes. Easy hillsides on which beginners learn to ski.

Nut. Slang for the head; perhaps from its shape. Also slang for a DUDE, a swell young man about town; in this sense it is sometimes spelled *Knut*, from an early 20th-century song featured by Basil Hallam, "I'm Gilbert the Filbert, the colonel of the K-nuts".

A hard nut to crack. A difficult question to answer; a hard problem to solve.

A nut case. Crazy, daft.

A tough nut. A difficult one to handle or convince.

He who would eat the nut must first crack the shell. The gods give nothing to man without great labour.

Here we go gathering nuts in May. This burden of the old children's game is a corruption of "Here we go gathering *knots* of may", referring to the old custom of gathering knots of flowers on MAY-DAY *i.e.* "to go a-maying". There are no nuts to be gathered in May.

It is time to lay our nuts aside (Lat. *relinquere nuces*). To leave off our follies, to relinquish boyish pursuits. The allusion is to an old Roman marriage ceremony, in which the bridegroom, as he led his bride home, scattered nuts to the crowd, as if to symbolize that he gave up boyish playthings.

That's nuts to him. A great pleasure, a fine treat, "meat and drink".

To edge his way along the crowded paths of life, warning all human sympathy to keep its distance, was what the

knowing ones call nuts to Scrooge.
DICKENS: *A Christmas Carol*, i.

To be dead nuts on, or **nuts on.** To be highly gratified with; to be very keen on.

My aunt is awful nuts on Marcus Aurelius; I beg your pardon, you don't know the phrase; my aunt makes Marcus Aurelius her Bible.
WILLIAM BLACK: *Princess of Thule*, xi.

To be off one's nut, to be nuts. Crazy, demented. Hence, **Nut house,** a lunatic asylum.

To use a sledgehammer to crack a nut. To take quite disproportionate steps to settle what is really a very small matter; virtually the same as "to break a butterfly on a wheel" (*see under* BREAK).

The "Iliad" in a nutshell. Pliny (vii, 21) tells us that the ILIAD was copied in so small a hand that the whole work could lie in a walnut shell; his authority is Cicero (*Apud Gellium*, ix, 421).

> Whilst they (as Homer's *Iliad* in a nut)
> A world of wonders in one closet shut.
> *On the Tradescant Monument,*
> *Lambeth Churchyard.*

To lie in a nutshell. To be explained in a few words; to be capable of easy solution.

Nymphs (nimfs) (Gr., young maidens). In classical mythology, minor female divinities of nature, of woods, groves, springs, streams, rivers, etc. They were young and beautiful maidens and well disposed towards mortals. They were not immortal, but their life span was several thousand years. Particular kinds of nymphs were associated with the various provinces of nature. *See* DRYADS; HAMADRYADS; NAIADS; NEREIDS; OCEANIDS; OREADS.

O

O. The fifteenth letter of our alphabet, the fourteenth of the ancient Roman, and the sixteenth of the Phœnician and Semitic (in which it was called "the eye"). Its name in O.E. was *oedel*, home. As a mediæval Latin numeral o represents 11.

The Seven O's, or **The Great O's of Advent.** The seven antiphons to the MAGNIFICAT sung during the week preceding CHRISTMAS. They commence respectively with *O Sapientia*, *O Adonai*, *O Radix Jesse*, *O Clavis David*, *O Oriens Splendor*, *O Rex gentium*, and *O Emmanuel*. They are sometimes called *The Christmas O's*.

O'. An Irish patronymic. (Gael. *ogha*; Ir. *oa*, a descendant.)

O' in *tam-o'-shanter*, *what's o'clock*? *cat-o'-nine-tails*, etc., stands for *of*; but in such phrases as *He comes home late o' night*, *I go to church o' Sundays*, it represents M.E. *on*.

O.K. All correct, all right; a reassuring affirmative that, coming from the U.S.A. to England, has spread colloquially throughout several European languages. Its first recorded use occurs in 1839. Commonly regarded as standing for "*Orl Korrect*" (all correct), it was said to derive from the political society called "Democratic O.K.", the "O.K." signifying "Old Kinderhook", a nickname of the Democratic leader, Martin Van Buren (1782–1862). Most probably it is from black American English *i.e.* of Afro-American origin. In Mandingo *O ke* signifies "all right", "that's it"; in Wolof *waw kay* means "yes indeed". Its use in New England in the late 1830s was probably due to the steady influx of refugees from the Southern slave states.

O tempora! O mores! (ō tem′ pôr à ó môr′ ēz) (Lat.). Alas! how the times have changed for the worse! Alas! how the morals of the people have degenerated! The tag is from Cicero's *In Catilinam*, i, 1.

O Yes! O Yes! O Yes! See OYEZ.

Oaf. A corruption of *ouph* (elf). A foolish lout or dolt is so called from the notion that idiots are CHANGELINGS, left by the FAIRIES in place of the stolen ones.

Oak. The oak was in ancient times sacred to the god of thunder because these trees are said to be more likely to be struck by lightning than any other. The DRUIDS held the oak in greatest veneration and the WOODEN WALLS of England depended upon it. About 3,500 full-grown oaks or 900 acres of oak forest were used in selecting the timber for a large three-decker line-of-battle ship. (*See* HEART OF OAK.) The strength, hardness, and durability of the timber, as well as the longevity of the tree, have given the oak a special significance to Englishmen, hence its name the *Monarch of the Forest*.

Heart of Oak. *See under* HEART.

Oak before the Ash. The old proverbial forecast, referring to whichever is in leaf first, says:

> If the oak's before the ash
> Then you'll only get a splash;
> If the ash precedes the oak,
> Then you may expect a soak.

i.e. a wet summer is to be expected.

To sport one's oak. An old university custom signifying that one is "not at home" to visitors by closing the *oak* or outer door of one's rooms.

Oak-apple Day (also called **Royal Oak Day**). 29 May, the birthday of Charles II and the day when he entered London at the RESTORATION; commanded by Act of PARLIAMENT in 1664 to be observed as a day of thanksgiving. A special service (expunged in 1859) was inserted in the BOOK OF COMMON PRAYER and people wore sprigs of oak with gilded oak-apples on that day.

It commemorates Charles II's concealment with Major Careless in the "Royal Oak" at Boscobel, near Shifnal, Salop, after his defeat at Worcester (3 September 1651).

Oak boys. Bands of PROTESTANT agrarian rioters in ULSTER in the 1760s, so called from the oak sprays worn in their hats. The main grievance was against the TITHE system. *Cp.* STEELBOYS.

Oakes's Oath (Austr.). Unreliable testimony delivered on oath. The phrase is said to derive from one, Oakes, who was asked in a Court of Law if he could identify a pair of horns as belonging to one of his own cattle. After hesitating a moment he is reported to have said, "I'll chance it; Yes!"

Oaks, The. The "Ladies' Race", one of the CLASSIC RACES of the turf; it is for three-year-old fillies, and is run at Epsom two days after the DERBY. It was instituted in 1779 and so called from an estate of the Earl of Derby near Epsom named "The Oaks".

Oannes (ō ăn′ ēz). A Babylonian god having a fish's body and a human head and feet. In the daytime he lived with men to instruct them in the arts and sciences, but at night returned to the depths of the Persian Gulf.

Oar. To put your oar into my boat. To interfere in my affairs.

To rest on one's oars. To take a rest or breathing space after hard work or strenuous effort. A boating phrase.

To toss the oars. To raise them vertically, resing on the handles. It is a form of salute.

Oaten pipe. A rustic musical pipe made of an oat straw so cut as to be stopped at one end with a knot, the other end being left open. A slit made in the straw near the knot was so cut as to form a reed.

Oatmeals. A 17th-century nickname given to profligate bands in the streets of London.

Oats. To sow one's wild oats. To indulge in youthful excesses and dissipa-

tions. The reference is to sowing bad grain (wild) instead of good (cultivated).

Obadiah. An old slang name for a QUAKER.

Obeah, Obi. The belief in and practice of *obeah*, *i.e.* a kind of sorcery or witchcraft prevalent in West Africa and formerly in the West Indies. *Obeah* is a native word and signifies something put into the ground, to bring about sickness, death, or other disaster. *Cp.* VOODOO.

Obelisk. A tapering pillar of stone, originally erected by the Egyptians, who placed them in pairs before temple portals. The base was usually one-tenth of the height and the apex was coppersheathed. Each of the four faces bore incised HIEROGLYPHS. The best known in England is CLEOPATRA'S NEEDLE.

The tallest obelisk (nearly 110 ft.) is at ROME, taken there from Heliopolis by the Emperor CALIGULA (37–41 A.D.) and later (1586) re-erected in the piazza of St. Peter's by order of Pope Sixtus V. Weighing some 320 tons, it was moved bodily on rollers. Spectators were forbidden to utter a sound on pain of death during the operation but when the ropes were straining to breaking point, one of the workmen, a sailor from San Remo, is said to have shouted *"Acqua alle funi"* (Water on the ropes), so saving the situation at risk of the death penalty.

The Obelisk of Luxor, in the Place de la Concorde, PARIS, came from Thebes, and was presented to Louis Philippe in 1831, by the then KHEDIVE of Egypt. Its hieroglyphs record the deeds of Rameses II (12th century B.C.). *Cp.* COLUMN.

Oberammergau. *See* PASSION PLAY.

Obermann. The impersonation of high moral worth without talent, and the tortures endured by the consciousness of this defect. From Senancour's psychological romance of this name (1804), in which Obermann, the hero, is a dreamer perpetually trying to escape the actual.

Oberon. King of the FAIRIES, husband of TITANIA. Shakespeare introduced them in his *Midsummer Night's Dream.* The name is probably connected with ALBERICH, the king of the elves.

He first appeared in the mediæval

French romance, *Huon de Bordeaux,* where he is the son of Julius CÆSAR and MORGAN LE FAY. He was only three feet high, but of angelic face, and was the lord and king of Mommur. At his birth, the fairies bestowed their gifts—one was insight into men's thoughts, and another was the power of transporting himself to any place instantaneously; and in the fullness of time legions of ANGELS conveyed his soul to PARADISE.

Obi. *See* OBEAH.

Obiter dictum (ob' i tèr dik' tùm) (Lat.). An incidental remark, something said in passing; a judge's expression of opinion backed by his knowledge and experience, but not forming part of a judgement and therefore not legally binding. *Obiter* means "in passing", the more common plural form of the phrase being *obiter dicta.*

Obolus. An ancient Greek bronze or silver coin of small value; also a mediæval silver coin of small value. *See* BELISARIUS.

Observantins. *See* FRANCISCANS.

Occam's Razor. *Entia non sunt multiplicanda praeter necessitatem* (entities ought not to be multiplied except from necessity), which means that all unnecessary facts or constituents in the subject being analysed are to be eliminated. These exact words do not appear in Occam's works but the principle expressed occurs in several other forms. Occam's razor cuts away superfluities.

William of Occam, the *Doctor Singularis et Invincibilis* (d. 1349), the great FRANCISCAN scholastic philosopher, was probably born at Ockham, Surrey, *Occam* being the latinized form of the name. *See also* SCHOLASTICISM.

Occasion. To improve the occasion. To draw a moral lesson from some event or occurrence.

To rise to the occasion. To show oneself equal to a demanding situation or task; to speak or act as the emergency requires.

Occult Sciences (Lat. *occultus*; related to *celare*, to hide). Magic, ALCHEMY, ASTROLOGY, palmistry, DIVINATION, etc.; so called because they were hidden mysteries.

Oceanids, or **Oceanides.** In Greek mythology, sea-NYMPHS, daughters of OCEANUS and Tethys, among whom were DORIS, Electra, and AMPHITRITE. Offerings were made to them by mariners.

Oceanus (ō sē' à nus). A Greek sea-god; also the river of the world which circles the earth and as such is represented as a snake with its tail in its mouth. As a sea-god, he is an old man with a long beard and with bull's horns on his head.

Ockham. *See* OCCAM.

October. The eighth month of the ancient Roman CALENDAR (Lat. *octo*, eight) when the year began in MARCH; the tenth of ours. The old Dutch name was *Wynmaand*; the O.E. *Winmonath* (Wine-month, or the time of vintage); also *Teomonath* (tenth month) and *Winter-fylleth* (winter full-moon). In the French Revolutionary Calendar it was *Vendémiaire* (time of vintage, 22 September to 21 October).

A tankard of October. A tankard of the best and strongest ale, brewed in October.

October Club. In the reign of Queen Anne, a group of High TORY M.P.s who met at a tavern near PARLIAMENT to drink October ALE and to abuse the WHIGS. It became politically prominent about 1710 although it had probably existed from the end of William III's reign.

Also a left-wing political club at Oxford in the 1930s of Communist sympathies, taking its name from the OCTOBER REVOLUTION.

Octobrists. A "constitutionalist" centre party in Russia supported by the landlords and wealthy mercantile interests, prominent in the dumas between 1907 and 1914, after the Tsar's famous liberal manifesto published in October 1905.

October Revolution. In Russian history, the BOLSHEVIK revolution of October 1917 (November in the western Calendar) which led to the overthrow of Kerensky and the MENSHEVIKS and the triumph of Lenin.

Od. *See* ODYLE.

Odal. *See* UDAL TENURE.

Odd. At odds. At variance.

By long odds. By a great difference; as, "He is the best man by long odds." In horse-racing, odds are the ratio by which the amount staked by one party to a bet exceeds that of the other; hence long odds indicates a big variance in this ratio.

Odd man out. The one of a group who fails to get selected or included when numbers are made up; one who does not fit into a group or gathering owing to difference of interests, temperament, position, etc.

Odds and ends. *see* END.

That makes no odds. No difference; never mind, that is no excuse. An application of the betting phrase.

To shout the odds. To make a noisy protest or fuss; as a bookmaker noisily proclaims the odds.

Odin (ō' din). The Scandinavian name of the GOD called by the Anglo-Saxons WO-DEN. He was god of wisdom, poetry, war, and agriculture. As god of the dead, he presided over banquets of those slain in battle. (*See* VALHALLA.) He became the All-wise by drinking of Mimir's fountain, but purchased the distinction at the pledge of one eye, and is often represented as a one-eyed man wearing a hat and carrying a staff. His remaining eye is the SUN, his horse Sleipnir. He was master of magic and discovered the RUNES.

The promise of Odin. The most binding of all oaths to a Norseman. In making it the hand was passed through a massive silver ring kept for the purpose; or through a sacrificial stone, like that called the "Circle of Stennis". *Cp.* THE STANDING STONES OF STENNESS *under* STONE.

The vow of Odin. A matrimonial or other vow made before the "Stone of Odin" in the Orkneys. This was an oval stone, with a hole in it large enough to admit a man's hand. Anyone who violated a vow made before this stone was held infamous.

Odium theologicum (ō' di ùm thē ō - loj' ikùm) (Lat.). The bitter hatred of rival theologians. No wars so sanguinary as holy wars; no persecutions so relentless as religious persecutions; no hatred so bitter as theological hatred.

Odor lucri (ō' dôr lū' krî) (Lat.). The sweets of gain; the delights of money-making.

Odour. In good odour; in bad odour. In favour, out of favour; in good repute, in bad repute.

The odour of sanctity. In the MIDDLE AGES it was held that a sweet and delightful odour was given off by the bodies of saintly persons at their death, and also when their bodies, if "translated", were distinterred. Hence the phrase, *he died in the odour of sanctity*, *i.e.* he died a saint. The SWEDENBOR-GIANS say that when the celestial AN-GELS are present at a deathbed, what is then cadaverous excites a sensation of what is aromatic.

Od's, used in oaths, as:

Od's bodikins! or *Odsbody!* means "God's body".

Od's pittikins! God's pity.

Od's plessed will! (*Merry Wives of Windsor*, I, i). God's blessed will.

Od rot'em! See DRAT.

Od-zounds! God's wounds.

Odyle (od' îl). The name formerly given to the hypothetical force which emanates from a medium to produce the phenomena connected with MESMERISM, spirit-rapping, table-turning, and so on. Baron von Reichenbach (1788–1869) called it *Od force*, and taught that it pervaded all nature, especially heat, light, crystals, magnets, etc., and was developed in chemical action; and also that it streamed from the fingers of specially sensitive persons.

> That od-force of German Reichenbach
> Which still from female finger-tips burns blue.
> MRS. BROWNING: *Aurora Leigh*, vii, 566.

Odyssey (od' i si). The epic poem of HOMER which records the adventures of Odysseus (ULYSSES) on his homeward voyage from TROY. The word implies the things or adventures of ULYSSES.

Œcumenical Councils (ē kū men' ik àl) (Gr. *oikoumenikos*, the whole inhabited world—*ge*, earth, being understood). Ecclesiastical councils whose findings are—or were—recognized as binding on all Christians.

Œcumenical Movement. The movement towards re-unity among the various Christian Churches, which has gathered strength in recent years, especially since the Second Vatican Council and the establishment of the World Council of Churches inaugurated at Amsterdam in 1948 which comprises most of the prominent Christian bodies.

Œdipus (ē di pủs) was the son of Laius, King of Thebes, and of Jocasta the Queen. To avert the fulfilment of the prophecy that he would murder his father and marry his mother, Œdipus was exposed on the mountains as an infant and taken in and reared by the shepherds. When grown to manhood he unwittingly slew his father; then, having solved the riddle of the SPHINX, he became King of THEBES, thereby gaining the hand in marriage of Jocasta, his mother, of whose relationship to himself they were both ignorant. When the facts came to light Jocasta hanged herself and Œdipus tore out his own eyes.

An **Œdipus complex** is the psychoanalytical term for the sexual desire (usually unrecognized by himself) of a son for his mother and conversely an equally unrecognized jealous hatred of his father.

Œil-de-Bœuf (ĕĕ de bĕrf) (Fr., "bull's-eye"). A large reception room (*salle*) in the Palace of VERSAILLES was so named from its round "bull's-eye" window. The ceiling, decorated by Van der Meulen, contains likenesses of Louis XIV's children. It was the ante-room where courtiers waited and gossiped, hence the name became associated with BACK-STAIRS intrigue.

Œnone (ēnō′ nē). A NYMPH of Mount IDA, the wife of PARIS before he abducted HELEN. She prophesied the disastrous consequences of his voyage to Greece and, on the death of Paris, killed herself.

Off. The off-side of a motor-car is that to the right hand of the driver (*cp.* NEAR); in Association Football the referee signals *Off-side* and awards a free kick when the ball is played and a player of the attacking side is nearer to his opponent's goal-line and there are not two of his opponents between himself and the goal.

Offa's Dyke. An earthwork running from the Wye, near Monmouth, to near Prestatyn (now in Clwyd), probably built by Offa of MERCIA (*c.* 784–796) as a boundary between him and the Welsh. *Cp.*

GRAHAME'S DYKE; GRIM'S DITCH; WANS-DYKE.

Office, The Divine. The obligatory prayers, etc., of the Church said by priests and the religious. The Divine Office (*horae canonicae*) of the ROMAN CATHOLIC CHURCH is contained in the BREVIARY.

Office, The Holy. *See* INQUISITION.

Offing. In the offing. Said of a ship visible at sea off the land. Such a ship is often approaching port, hence the phrase is used figuratively to mean "about to happen", "likely to occur" or "likely to take place", etc.

Og, King of Bashan, according to Rabbinical legend, was an antediluvian GIANT, saved from the Flood (*see* DELUGE) by climbing on the roof of the ark. After the passage of the Red Sea, MOSES first conquered Sihon, and then advanced against the giant Og whose bedstead, made of iron, was 9 cubits long and 4 cubits broad (*Deut*. iii, 11). The legend says that Og plucked up a mountain to hurl at the Israelites, but he got so entangled with his burden that Moses was able to kill him without much difficulty.

Ogam, or **Ogham.** The alphabet in use among the ancient Irish and British peoples. There were 20 characters, each of which was composed of a number (from one to five) of thin strokes arranged and grouped above, below, or across a horizontal line.

The word is connected with *Ogmius*, the name of a Gaulish god, likened to HERCULES by Lucian, who performed his feats through eloquence and the gift of languages. *Cp*. RUNE.

Ogier the Dane (ō′ ji ėr). One of the great heroes of mediaeval romance whose exploits are chronicled in the CHANSONS DE GESTE; son of Geoffrey, King of Denmark, of which country (as Holger Danske) he is still the national hero. In one account his son was slain by CHARLEMAGNE'S son Charlot and in revenge Ogier killed the king's nephew and was only prevented from slaying Charlemagne himself. He eventually returned from exile to defend France against the Saracen chief Brehus. In another romance, it is said, FAIRIES attended his birth, among them MORGAN

LE FAY, who eventually took him to AVA-LON where he dwelt for 200 years. She then sent him to defend France against invasion, after which she took him back to Avalon. William Morris gives a rendering of this romance in his *Earthly Paradise* (*August*).

Ogpu, or **G.P.U.** The secret political police of the U.S.S.R. which succeeded the Cheka in 1922. The initials stand for *Obedinennoe Gosudarstvennoe Politicheskoe Upravlenie* (United State Political Administration). It was renamed the N.K.V.D., *Narodnyi Komissariat Vnutrennykh Dyel* (People's Commissariat for Internal Affairs), in 1934. In 1944 it became the M.V.D., changing to the K.G.B. in 1954.

Ogres of nursery story are GIANTS of very malignant disposition, who live on human flesh. The word was first used (and probably invented) by Perrault in his *Histoires ou Contes du temps passé* (1697), and is thought to be made up from *Orcus*, a name of PLUTO.

Ogygia (ō jij′ i a). *See* CALYPSO.
  Ogygian Deluge. In Greek legend, a flood said to have occurred when Ogyges was King of Bœotia, some 200 years before DEUCALION'S flood. Varro says that the planet VENUS underwent a great change in the reign of Ogyges. It changed its diameter, its colour, its figure, and its course.

Oi Polloi, properly HOI POLLOI.

Oil. Oil of Angels. Money used as a bribe or douceur; in allusion to the old coin called an ANGEL.
  Burning the midnight oil. *See* MIDNIGHT OIL.
  To be well oiled. Pretty well drunk.
  To pour oil on troubled waters. To soothe by gentle words; to use tact and diplomacy to restore calm after excited anger and quarrelsome argument.
    The allusion is to the well-known fact that the violence of waves is much decreased when oil is poured upon them. In Bede's *Ecclesiastical History* (731) it is said that St. Aidan gave a young priest, who was to escort a maiden destined for the bride of King Oswy, a cruse of oil to pour on the sea if the waves became stormy. The priest did this when a storm arose and thereby calmed the waters.
  To strike oil. To make a lucky or valuable discovery; to come upon good fortune in some form or other. The phrase refers to the finding of mineral oil deposits, always a source of wealth.

Old. For names such as Old Grog, Harry, Noll, Nosey, Rowley, Scratch, Tom, etc., *see under these words*.

Old Bailey. The Central Criminal Court of the City of LONDON and of (approximately) the Greater London area, situated in the thoroughfare of this name. It is probably from Med. Lat. *ballium*, enclosure; the enclosure of the City wall between LUDGATE and NEWGATE. The area has historic associations with crime owing to the proximity of NEWGATE GAOL and its being the site of public executions, the last victim being a FENIAN executed by William Calcraft in 1868. It was also the site of a pillory.

Old Believers. Those members of the Russian ORTHODOX CHURCH who rejected the liturgical reforms of the patriarch Nikon and were excommunicated in 1667. They were subjected to violent persecution and eventually resolved into two groups, the *Popovtsy*, and the *Bespopovtsy*, the latter rejecting the priesthood altogether. The former attained state recognition in 1881.

Old Bill. *See* 'OLE, A BETTER.

Old Blood and guts. General G. S. Patton. *See* BLOOD AND GUTS.

Old Boots. *See under* BOOTS.

Old Boy. A friendly colloquial form of address between men of any age; the term also denotes a former pupil of a particular school, hence "old boys' clubs", "old boys' dinners", etc. *Old girl* is similarly used to denote old scholars, and by men as an affectionate term of address to members of the opposite sex. It is also applied to certain female animals, especially horses. Both terms are applied in the obvious sense to elderly men and women. *See* OLD SCHOOL TIE.

Old Boy net or **network.** To arrange something on the "Old Boy network" is to fix it through a social contact (properly someone from one's old school) instead of through the usual channels.

Old Bullion. Thomas Hart Benton (1782–1858), Jacksonian Democrat and statesman. He opposed the establishment of a national bank and was nicknamed "Old Bullion" for his championship of the virtues of "hard money" (*see* HARD CURRENCY).

Old Contemptibles. *See* CONTEMPTIBLES.

Old Country, The. In the days of the British Empire, Great Britain, the mother country.

Old Fox. A nickname of George Washington and Marshal Soult.

Old Glory. The United States Flag. *See* STARS AND STRIPES.

Old Guard. The veteran regiments of NAPOLEON's Imperial Guard, the flower of the French army. Devoted to their Emperor, the Old Guard could be relied upon in any desperate strait, and it was they who made the last charge of the French at Waterloo. Figuratively, the phrase *Old Guard* is used for the stalwarts of any party or movement.

Old hat. *See under* HAT.

Old Hickory. The nickname of General Andrew Jackson (1767–1845), 7th President of the U.S.A. (1828–1837); it arose from his staunchness and strength of character. *See* KITCHEN CABINET.

Old Hundredth. *See under* HUNDRED.

Old Ironsides. *See* IRONSIDES.

Old King Cole. *See* COLE.

Old Lady of the Bund. The nickname given by British residents in China to *The North China Daily News*, published at Shanghai (1855–1950).

Old Lady of Threadneedle Street. *See under* THREADNEEDLE STREET.

The name was also applied to John Quincy Adams (1767–1848), 6th President of the U.S.A. (1825–1829).

Old Man of the Mountain. *See under* MOUNTAIN.

Old Man of the Sea. In the story of *Sinbad the Sailor* (ARABIAN NIGHTS), the Old Man of the Sea hoisted himself on Sinbad's shoulders and clung there for many days and nights, much to the discomfort of Sinbad, who finally got rid of the Old Man by making him drunk. Hence, any burden, figurative or actual, of which it is impossible to free oneself without the greatest exertions is called an Old Man of the Sea. *Cp.* NEREUS.

Old Masters. *See under* MASTER.

Old Mother Hubbard. This lastingly popular NURSERY RHYME is one of definitely known origin and was first published in 1805. It was written by Sarah Catherine Martin (1768–1821) while staying with her brother-in-law, J. P. Bastard of Kitley, Yealmpton, South Devon. It is traditionally said that Mother Hubbard was the housekeeper at Kitley and there is a cottage at Yealmpton purporting to be her one-time residence.

> Old Mother Hubbard
> Went to the cupboard
> To fetch her poor dog a bone;
> But when she came there
> The cupboard was bare
> And so the poor dog had none.

Old Nick. *See under* NICK.

Old Pretender. *See* PRETENDER.

Old Reekie. *See* AULD REEKIE.

Old School Tie. Literally a distinguishing necktie worn by OLD BOYS of a particular school. Such ties being essentially associated with the public schools and the older grammar schools led to *old school tie* being given a pejorative use as a symbol of class distinction, *e.g.* "the old school tie brigade", meaning the members of a privileged class. *Cp.* OLD BOY NET.

Old stager. One of long experience, an old hand at the game; originally an experienced stage player.

The Galloping Major.

Old Style, New Style. Terms used in chronology. *Old Style* refers to dating by the JULIAN CALENDAR and *New Style* by the GREGORIAN CALENDAR. *See* STILO NOVO.

Old Testament, The. The collective name (*see* NEW TESTAMENT) of the first 39 books in the BIBLE inherited as sacred scripture from the Jewish church, and referred to by Christ and his disciples as "the Scriptures". *Matt*. xxi, 42 has:

> Jesus saith unto them, Did ye never read in the scriptures ...

The Hebrew canon, which is that of the Reformed churches and comprises the 39 books printed in most bibles, is substantially that adopted by a Jewish council at Jamnia (*c*. 90 A.D.). The Roman Catholic canon includes the APOCRYPHA.

Old wives' tales. Superstitious stories

and beliefs such as are kept alive and spread by credulous old women.

Old woman. Colloquially, a fusspot, an old ditherer, as, "he is a proper old woman."

Old World. So Europe, Asia, and Africa are called when contrasted with the NEW WORLD.

Oldenburg Horn. A horn long in the possession of the reigning princes of the House of Oldenburg, but now in the collection of the King of Denmark. According to tradition, Count Otto of Oldenburg, in 967, was offered drink in this silver-gilt horn by a "wild woman", at the Osenborg. As he did not like the look of the liquor, he threw it away, and rode off with the horn.

'Ole, A Better. Old Bill, a walrus-moustached, disillusioned old soldier in the 1914–1918 war, portrayed by Captain Bruce Bairnsfather (1887–1959), artist and journalist, in his publications *Old Bill* and *The Better 'Ole*. Cowering in a muddy shell-hole in the midst of a withering bombardment, he says to his grousing pal Bert, "If you know of a better 'ole, go to it." The joke and Old Bill struck the public fancy and Old Bill became the embodiment of a familiar type of simple, cynical, long-suffering, honest old grouser.

Olet lucernam (ō' let loo sĕr' năm). A Latin proverb, *see* IT SMELLS OF THE LAMP *under* LAMP.

Olive. In ancient Greece the olive was sacred to PALLAS, in allusion to the story that at the naming of ATHENS she presented it with an olive branch. It was the symbol of peace and fecundity, brides wearing or carrying an olive garland as ours do a wreath of ORANGE BLOSSOM. A crown of olive was the highest distinction of a citizen who deserved well of his country, and was the highest prize in the OLYMPIC GAMES.

In the OLD TESTAMENT, the subsiding of the FLOOD was demonstrated to Noah by the return of a DOVE bearing an olive leaf in her beak (*Gen*. viii, 11).

Olive branches. A facetious term for children in relation to their parents; the allusion is to "Thy wife shall be as a fruitful vine ... thy children like olive plants round about thy table" (*Ps*. cxxviii, 3).

To hold out the olive branch. To make overtures for peace; in allusion to the olive being an ancient symbol of peace. In some of Numa's medals the king is represented holding an olive twig, indicative of a peaceful reign.

Oliver. CHARLEMAGNE's favourite PALADIN, who, with ROLAND, rode by his side. He was the son of Regnier, Duke of Genoa (another of the paladins), and brother of the beautiful Aude. His sword was called *Hauteclaire*, and his horse *Ferrant d'Espagne*.

A Roland for an Oliver. *See under* ROLAND.

Olivet or **the Mount of Olives.** The range of hills to the east of Jerusalem, closely connected with ancient Jewish ceremonies and intimately associated with the events of the NEW TESTAMENT. Here Jesus retired for prayer and meditation and to talk to his disciples and here he came on the night of his betrayal.

> And in the daytime he was teaching in the temple, and at night he went out, and abode in the mount that is called the Mount of Olives.
> *Luke* xxi, 37.

Olympia. The ancient name of a valley in Elis, Peloponnesus, so called from the famous games held there in honour of the OLYMPIAN ZEUS. The ALTIS, an enclosure of about 500 ft. by 600 ft., was built in the valley, containing the temple of Zeus, the Herœum, the Metroum, etc., the STADIUM, with gymnasia, baths, etc. Hence the name is applied to large buildings for sporting events, exhibitions, etc., such as the Olympia at Kensington, London.

Olympiad. Among the ancient Greeks, a period of four years, being the interval between the celebrations of the OLYMPIC GAMES. The first Olympiad began in 776 B.C., and the last (the 293rd) in A.D. 392.

Olympian Zeus, or **Jove.** A statue by Phidias, one of the "Seven Wonders of the World" (*see under* WONDER). Pausanias (vii, 2) says when the sculptor placed it in the temple at OLYMPIA (433 B.C.), he prayed to the god to indicate whether he was satisfied with it, and immediately a thunderbolt fell on the floor of the temple without doing the slightest harm.

It was a chryselephantine statue, *i.e.* made of ivory and GOLD; and, though seated on a throne, was 60 ft. in height. The left hand rested on a sceptre, and the right palm held a statue of Victory in solid gold. The robes were of gold and so were the four lions which supported the footstool. The throne was of cedar, embellished with ebony, ivory, gold, and precious stones.

It was removed to Constantinople in the 5th century A.D., and perished in the great fire of 475.

Olympic Games. The greatest of the four sacred festivals of the ancient Greeks, held every fourth year at OLYMPIA in July. After suitable sacrifices, racing, wrestling, and other contests followed, ending on the fifth day with processions, sacrifices, and banquets and OLIVE garlands for the victors.

The games were revived in 1896 as international sporting contests, the first being held at Athens, and subsequently at Paris (1900), St. Louis (1904), London (1908), Stockholm (1912), Antwerp (1920), Paris (1924), Amsterdam (1928), Los Angeles (1932), Berlin (1936), London (1948), Helsinki (1952), Melbourne (1956), Rome (1960), Tokyo (1964), Mexico City (1968), Munich (1972), Montreal (1976), Moscow (1980), Los Angeles (1984), Seoul (1988).

Winter Olympic Games were inaugurated in 1924.

Olympus. The home of the gods of ancient Greece, where ZEUS held his court, a mountain about 9,800 ft. high on the confines of Macedonia and Thessaly. The name is used for any PANTHEON, as, "ODIN, HORT, BALDER, and the rest of the Northern Olympus."

Om. Among the BRAHMINS, the mystic equivalent for the name of the Deity; it has been adopted by modern occultists to denote absolute goodness and truth or the spiritual essence.

Om mani padme hum ("Omm, the jewel, is in the lotus: Amen"). The mystic formula of the Tibetans and northern Buddhists used as a charm and for many religious purposes. They are the first words taught to a child and the last uttered on the death-bed of the pious. The LOTUS symbolizes universal being, and the jewel the individuality of the utterer.

Omar Khayyam (ō' mar kī yăm'), Persian poet, astronomer, and mathematician, lived at Nishapur, where he died at about the age of 50 in A.D. 1123. He was known chiefly for his work on algebra until Edward Fitzgerald published a poetical translation of his poems in 1859. Little notice of this was taken, however, until the early '90s when the RUBAIYAT took Britain and America by storm. It is frankly hedonistic in tone, but touched with a melancholy that attunes with eastern and western pessimism alike. Fitzgerald never pretended that his work was other than a free version of the original; he made several revisions, but did not improve on his first text.

Ombre (om' bėr) (Span. *hombre*, man). A card-game, introduced into England from Spain in the 17th century, and very popular till it was supplanted by QUADRILLE, about 1730. It was usually played by three persons, and the eights, nines, and tens of each suit were left out. Prior has an epigram on the game; he was playing with two ladies, and Fortune gave him "success in every suit but hearts". Pope immortalized the game in his *Rape of the Lock*.

Ombudsman (om' boods man) (Swed. *ombudsman*, a commissioner). In Scandinavian countries, an official appointed by the legislature whose duty it is to protect the rights of the citizen against infringement by the government. Sweden has had once since 1809, Denmark since 1955, and Norway since 1962. New Zealand was the first COMMONWEALTH country to appoint such a commissioner (1962) and Great Britain appointed a Parliamentary Commissioner for Administration in 1967, commonly known as the "Ombudsman".

Omega (ō' meg à). *See* ALPHA.

Omelet (om'lėt). **You can't make omelets without breaking eggs.** Said by way of warning to one who is trying to "get something for nothing"—to accomplish some desired object without being willing to take the necessary trouble or make the necessary sacrifice. The phrase is a translation of the French *On ne saurait faire une omelette sans casser des œufs*.

Omens. Phenomena or unusual events taken as a prognostication of either good or EVIL; prophetic signs or auguries. *Omen* is a Latin word adopted in the 16th century. Some traditional examples of accepting what appeared to be evil omens, as of good AUGURY, are:

> Leotychides II, of Sparta, was told by his augurs that his projected expedition would fail because a viper had got entangled in the handle of the city key "Not so," he replied, "the key caught the viper."

> When Julius Cæsar landed at Adrumetum he tripped and fell on his face. This would have been considered a fatal omen by his army, but, with admirable presence of mind, he explained, "Thus I take possession of thee, O Africa!" A similar story is told of Scipio.

> When William the Conqueror leaped upon the English shore he fell on his face and a great cry went forth that it was an ill-omen; but the duke exclaimed, "I have taken seisin of this land with both my hands".

Omnibus (Lat., for all, dative pl. of *omnis*, all). The name was first applied to the public vehicle in France in 1828. In the following year it was adopted by Shillibeer for the vehicles which he started on the Paddington (now MARYLEBONE) Road, London. The plural is *omnibuses*, and the word is generally abbreviated to *bus*, without an initial apostrophe—just as *cabriolet* became *cab*, not *cab'*.

Omnibus Bill. The Parliamentary term for a BILL embracing clauses that deal with a number of different subjects, as a Revenue Bill dealing with Customs, Taxes, Stamps, Excise, etc.

Omnibus train. An old name for a train that stops at all stations—a train for all, as apart from the specials and the expresses that ran between only a few stations. *Cp.* JERKWATER.

Omnibus volume. A collection in one volume of an author's works, of short stories, essays, etc.

Omnium (Lat., of all). The particulars *of all* the items, or the assignment *of all* the securities, of a government loan.

Omnium gatherum. DOG-LATIN for a *gathering* or collection of *all* sorts of persons and things; a miscellaneous gathering together without regard to suitability or order.

Omphale (om' fả lē). In Greek legend, the Queen of Lydia of masculine inclinations to whom HERCULES was bound a slave for three years. He fell in love with her and led a submissive life spinning wool. Omphale wore the lion's skin while Hercules wore a female garment.

On. A little bit on. Slightly drunk.

It's not on. It cannot be done. A phrase from snooker, used when the object ball is obscured.

It's not on today. It's not on the menu, "it's off", *i.e.*, not available.

On the beach. Retired from naval service; in the Merchant Service it is to be without a ship, *i.e.* unemployed.

On the binge. ON THE SPREE.

On the loose. *See under* LOOSE.

On the shelf. *See* SHELF.

On the spree. Out for a frolic, *on the binge*, out carousing.

To have something on a person. To possess damaging evidence or information about him as, defiantly, "you've got nothing on me", meaning, "you know nothing that can incriminate me".

On dit (ong dē) (Fr., they say). A rumour, a report, a bit of gossip. "There is an *on dit* that the prince is to marry soon."

Once. Once and for all. Finally, emphatically, and decisively, as, "Let us settle this affair once and for all."

Once bitten twice shy. I am not to be caught again; I have learned by previous experience and am not going to be made a fool of twice.

Once in a while. Only occasionally.

Once upon a time. The traditional opening phrase in fairy stories, at some indefinite time long ago.

To give someone, or something the once-over. To make a quick examination or assessment of.

One. One is Deity. *The Evil One* is the DEVIL.

By one and one. Singly, one at a time; entirely by oneself.

He was one too many for me. He was a little too clever for me, he outwitted me.

Number one. Oneself; hence **to look after number one;** to be selfish; to seek one's own interest.

In the Royal Navy, the first lieutenant of a ship or establishment is colloquially known as "Number One" or "Jimmy the One".

One and all. Everybody, individually and jointly. The phrase is the motto of Cornishmen.

One for the road. *See under* ROAD.

One in the eye, on the nose, in the bread-basket, etc. A blow on the spot named—the last being slang for the stomach. *One in the eye* is also used figuratively, for a telling blow.

One of these days. Some day, at some unspecified time in the future.

There is One above. A reference to the Deity.

To go one better than he did. To improve upon another's lead, performance, action, story, etc. The phrase is from card-playing; at poker if one wishes to continue betting one has to "go" at least "one better", *i.e.* raise the stake.

One-armed bandit. A gambling or "fruit" machine operated by the insertion of coins and the pulling of an arm or lever. So called because it frequently "robs" one of loose change.

One-horse town. A very small town with few amenities. An expression of American origin when a small community might only boast of one horse. Now used figuratively of any small, amateurish affair as "a one-horse show", "a one-horse outfit". *Cp.* JERKWATER.

One-night stand. A single evening performance by a touring theatrical company, circus, etc., at a town only likely to provide an audience for one night.

One-track mind. A mind with one dominant preoccupation which constantly reverts to the one subject, as a single-track railway only allows traffic in one direction at a time.

Oneida Community, The. *See* PERFECTIONISTS.

Oneiromancy (Gr. *oneiros*, a dream; *manteia*, prophecy). DIVINATION from dreams.

Onomatopeia (on ō măt ōpē′ à) (Gr. *on-*

omatopoiia, word-making). The forming of a word by imitating the sound associated with the object designated, or a word that appears to suggest its nature or qualities. "Cuckoo", "murmur", "tingle" are examples.

Onus (ō′ nus) (Lat.). The burden, the responsibility; as, "The whole onus must rest on your shoulders."

Onus probandi (Lat., the burden of proving). The obligation of proving some proposition, accusation, etc.; as, "The *onus probandi* rests with the accuser."

Onyx (on′ iks) is Greek for a finger-nail; so called because the colour of the onyx resembles that of the finger-nail.

Oom Paul. "Uncle" Paul, the name familiarly applied to Paul Kruger (1825–1904), President of the Transvaal Republic and leader of Boer resistance to British rule in South Africa.

Op. cit. (Lat. *opere citato*). In the work quoted.

Opal (Gr. *opallios*; probably from Sansk. *upala*, a gem). This semi-PRECIOUS STONE, well known for its play of iridescent colours, a vitreous form of hydrous silica, has long been deemed to bring ill-luck. Alphonso XII of Spain (1857, 1874–1885) presented an opal ring to his wife on his wedding-day, and her death occurred soon afterwards. Before the funeral he gave the ring to his sister, who died few days later. The king then presented it to his sister-in-law, and she died within three months. Alphonso, astounded at these fatalities, resolved to wear the ring himself, and within a very short time he, too, was dead. The Queen Regent then suspended it from the neck of the Virgin of Almudena of Madrid.

Open. Open City. A city which is completely demilitarized and left open to occupation, either because of its historic treasures and importance or because it is a centre for hospitals and wounded.

Open diplomacy, as opposed to secret diplomacy, is defined in the first of Woodrow Wilson's FOURTEEN POINTS, "open covenants of peace openly arrived at, after which there shall be no private international understandings of any kind". It is perhaps significant that the

Treaty of VERSAILLES was an "open treaty" negotiated in secret, ultimately by President Wilson, Clemenceau and Lloyd George.

Open door. In political parlance, the principle of admitting all nations to a share in a country's trade, etc. Also any loophole left for the possibility of negotiation between contending parties, nations, etc.

Open field system. The old manorial common-field system of agriculture in which the villages cultivated their individual "strips" in the unfenced (open) arable fields. It was essentially a three-field system based on a triennial crop rotation. From the 15th century, and especially in the 18th and 19th centuries, the system gave way to enclosures. It still survives at Laxton in Nottinghamshire. *Cp.* COMMON; MANOR.

Open letter. A letter to a particular person but published in a newspaper or periodical so that its contents may be publicly known, usually of a critical nature or as a protest.

Open question. *See under* QUESTION.

Open secret. *See* SECRET.

Open Sesame. *See* SESAME.

Open shop. *See under* SHOP.

To keep open house. *See under* HOUSE.

Opera. Drama set to music, the latter being an integral part of the composition. Dialogue is mostly verse and sung to orchestral accompaniment; lyrics are an important element and in older operas a ballet was often included. The rise of opera dates from the end of the 16th century and it became popular after the first opera house was opened at Venice, in 1637. Alessandro Scarlatti (1659–1725) established the aria as a legitimate form of soliloquy, and introduced the recitativo. Henry Purcell (*c.* 1658–1695) was the father of English opera, writing some 42 musical works for the stage, including some semi-operas and one full opera, *Dido and Aeneas* (1689).

Grand opera. Opera in which the entire libretto is set to music.

Opéra bouffe (Fr. *bouffe*, buffoon) is a form of French comic opera or operetta light in construction and of slight musical value.

Opera buffa, a form of light Italian comedy with musical numbers and dialogue in recitative; comic opera.

Opéra comique is a French type of opera which contains spoken dialogue. It does not necessarily imply "comic opera".

Operetta. Short opera, light opera, usually with spoken dialogue. The works of Gilbert and Sullivan may be included in this category.

Ophir. An unidentified territory, famed in the OLD TESTAMENT for its fine GOLD, possibly in S.E. Arabia. (*See* I *Kings* ix, 26–28.)

Opinicus. A fabulous monster in HERALDRY, compounded from DRAGON, CAMEL and LION. It forms the crest of the Barber-Surgeons of London. The name seems to be corruption of *Ophinicus*, the classical name of the constellation, the serpent (Gr. *ophis*).

Opium-eater. Opium War. The name given to the war between Great Britain and China, the First Chinese War, 1839–1842. The British government did not contest the Chinese right to prohibit trade in opium, but the demand that foreign merchants should agree that if opium were found on a British ship the culprits would be handed over for execution and the ship or cargo confiscated. Hostilities began when the British refused to surrender an innocent British subject for execution after the death of a Chinaman in a brawl. *Cp.* HONG MERCHANTS.

The Opium of the People. A CATCHPHRASE applied to religion. It is derived from Karl Marx (*On Hegel's Philosophy of Law*).

> Religion is the sigh of the hard-pressed creature, the heart of a heartless world, as it is the soul of soulless circumstances. It is the opium of the people.

Oppidan (Lat. *oppidum*, town). At Eton College, all those who are not collegers (King's Scholars). Originally those not on the foundation boarded in the town.

Opposition. The constitutional term for whichever of the major political parties is out of power. The leader of the Opposition receives a salary as such. In the HOUSE OF COMMONS, the Opposition sits on the benches to the SPEAKER's left, its leader occupying the FRONT BENCH (*see under* BENCH).

Ops. The old SABINE fertility goddess and wife of SATURN. She was later identified with RHEA.

Optimism. The doctrine that "whatever is, is right", that everything which happens is for the best. It was originally set forth by Leibnitz (1646–1716) from the postulate of the omnipotence of God, and is cleverly travestied by VOLTAIRE in his CANDIDE. *See* PANGLOSS.

Opus (ō' pus) (Lat., a work). *See* MAGNUM OPUS.

Opus Anglicanum. Rich mediæval embroidery dominated by work in silver and gold thread; so called because the reputation of England was unrivalled in this art which revealed the skill of the English gold and silver wiresmiths. It was mostly employed on ecclesiastical vestments and frontals, but also on banners, palls, robes, and hangings.

Opus operantis, opus operatum; ex opere operato (Lat.). Theological terms long used in relation to the effectiveness of acts relating to the sacraments. *Opus operantis* means the "act of doer"; *opus operatum*, the "act done" irrespective of the qualities or disposition of the recipient. Thus baptism is held to convey regeneration to an infant. To hold that a SACRAMENT gives grace *ex opere operato* (from the act of being done) means that the sacrament, properly performed, itself conveys grace, irrespective of the merits of the performer or recipient.

Or. The heraldic term for the metal GOLD. *See* HERALDRY.

Oracle (Lat. *oraculum*; from *orare*, to speak, to pray). The answer of a god or inspired priest to an inquiry respecting the future; the deity giving responses; the place where the deity could be consulted, etc.; hence, a person whose utterances are regarded as profoundly wise and authoritative.

> I am Sir Oracle,
> And when I open my lips let no dog bark.
> SHAKESPEARE: *The Merchant of Venice*, I, i.

The most famous of the very numerous oracles of ancient Greece were those of:

APOLLO, at DELPHI, the priestess of which was called the Pythoness; at DELOS, and at Claros.
DIANA, at Colchis.
ÆSCULAPIUS, at Epidaurus, and at ROME.
HERCULES, at ATHENS and Gades.
JUPITER, at DODONA (the most noted), AMMON in Libya, and in CRETE.
MARS, in Thrace.
MINERVA, at Mycenæ.
PAN, in ARCADIA.
TROPHONIUS, in BŒOTIA, where only men made the responses.
VENUS, at Paphos, another at Aphæa, etc.

In most of the temples, women, sitting on a tripod, made the responses, many of which were ambiguous and so obscure as to be misleading; to this day, our word *oracular* is still used of obscure as well as of authoritative pronouncements. Examples are:

When CRŒSUS consulted the Delphic oracle respecting a projected war, he received for answer, *"Crœsus Halyn penetrans magnum pervertet opum vim"* (When Crœsus crosses over the river Halys, he will overthrow the strength of an empire). Crœsus supposed the oracle meant he would overthrow the enemy's empire, but it was his own that he destroyed when defeated by Cyrus.

Pyrrhus, being about to make war against Rome, was told by the oracle: *"Credo te, Æacide, Romanos vincere posse"* (I believe, Pyrrhus, that you the Romans can conquer), which may mean either "You, Pyrrhus, can overthrow the Romans", or "Pyrrhus, the Romans can overthrow you".

Another prince, consulting the oracle on a similar occasion, received for answer. *"Ibis redibis nunquam per bella peribis"* (You shall go you shall return never you shall perish by the war), the interpretation of which depends on the position of the comma; it may be "You shall return, you shall never perish in the war", or "You shall return never, you shall perish in the war", which latter was the fact.

Philip of Macedon sent to ask the oracle of Delphi if his Persian expedition would prove successful, and received for answer—

> The ready victim crowned for death

Before the altar stands

Philip took it for granted that the "ready victim" was the King of Persia, but it was Philip himself.

When the Greeks sent to Delphi to know if they would succeed against the Persians, they were told

> Seed-time and harvest, weeping sires shall tell
> How thousands fought at Salamis and fell.

But whether the Greeks or the Persians were to be the "weeping sires", no indication was given, nor whether the thousands "about to fall" were to be Greeks or Persians. *See also* WOODEN WALLS *under* WOOD.

When Maxentius was about to encounter Constantine, he consulted the guardians of the SIBYLLINE BOOKS as to the fate of the battle, and the prophetess told him, "*Illo die hostem Romanorum esse periturum*", but whether Maxentius or Constantine was the "enemy of the Roman people" the oracle left undecided.

In the BIBLE (I *Kings* xxii, 15, 35) we are told that when Ahab, King of Israel, was about to wage war on the King of Syria, and asked Micaiah if Ramoth-Gilead would fall into his hands, the prophet replied, "Go, for the Lord will deliver the city into the hand of the king." In the event, the city fell into the hands of the King of Syria.

The Oracle of the Church. St. BERNARD of Clairvaux (1091–1153). *Cp.* MELLIFLUOUS DOCTOR.

The oracle of the sieve and shears. *See* SIEVE.

To work the oracle. To succeed in persuading another to favour some plan or to join in a project, etc., when the chances seemed slender. Also, in slang, to raise money.

Orange. William III's territorial name originally came from Orange (anciently Arausio), a town on the Rhône north of Avignon; his ancestors acquired it through marriage. The House of Orange still reigns in the Netherlands.

Orange blossom. The conventional decoration for the bride at a wedding, introduced as a custom into ENGLAND from France about 1820. The *orange* is

said to indicate the hope of fruitfulness, few trees being more prolific; while the *white blossoms* are symbolic of innocence. Hence the phrase, **to go gathering orange blossoms,** to look for a wife.

Orange Lodges. *See* ORANGEMEN.

Orangemen, Orange Order. A society founded in 1795 in ULSTER to maintain "the PROTESTANT Constitution, and to defend the King and his heirs as long as they maintain the Protestant ascendancy". It was formed after an armed clash between Roman Catholics and Protestants in Armagh, known as the Battle of the Diamond. The name commemorated William of Orange (William III), who defeated James II and his Catholic supporters at the Battle of the Boyne in 1690. Orange Lodges or clubs of militant Protestants spread throughout the province, their members being known as *Orangemen*, an earlier association of this name having been formed in the reign of William III. Gladstone's championship of HOME RULE after 1886 led to a revival of the movement. The Orange Order still flourishes, imposing ethical obligations on its members.

Orange Peel. A nickname given to Sir Robert Peel when Chief Secretary for Ireland (1812–1818), on account of his PROTESTANT bias and opposition to Roman Catholic emancipation.

Orange-tawny. The ancient colour appropriated to clerks and persons of inferior condition, also the colour worn by Jews. Hence Bacon says: "Usurers should have orange-tawny bonnets, because they do judaise" (*Essay* xli).

Orator. Orator Hunt. Henry Hunt (1773–1835), RADICAL politician. He presided at the famous PETERLOO meeting, and as M.P. for Preston (1830–1833) presented the first petition to PARLIAMENT in favour of women's rights. *See* A WHITE HAT *under* HAT.

Oratorians. (Med. Lat. *oratorium*, a place of prayer). A congregation founded at ROME by St. Philip Neri (1515–1595), but with origins in the late 1550s. Now called the Institute of the Oratory of St. Philip Neri, membership consists of secular priests and lay brothers, who take no vows but live communally, and are free to leave if, and when, they wish. Each oratory is autonomous and its members work under the ORDINARY of their diocese. Dr. J. H. Newman was so impressed with the Oratory at Rome that he obtained papal permission to found the Birmingham Oratory in 1847 and in 1849 sent F. W. Faber to found the London Oratory, which moved to Brompton in 1854. *See* ORATORIO.

Oratorio is sacred story or drama set to music, in which solo voices, chorus, and instrumental music are employed. St. Philip Neri introduced the acting and singing of sacred dramas in his Oratory at ROME in the late 16th century, and it is from this that the term comes.

Orc. A sea-monster fabled by ARIOSTO, Drayton, Sylvester, etc., to devour men and women. The name was sometimes used for a whale.

Orcades. The Roman name for the Orkneys, probably connected with the old ORC, a whale.

Orcus. A Latin name for HADES. Spenser speaks of a DRAGON whose mouth was:

> All set with iron teeth in ranges twain,
> That terrified his foes, and armed him,
> Appearing like the mouth of Orcus grisely grim.
>
> *The Faerie Queene*, VI, xii, 26.

Ordeal (O.E. *ordel*, judgment). The ancient Anglo-Saxon and Teutonic practice of referring disputed questions of criminality to supernatural decision, by subjecting the accused to physical trials in the belief that God would defend the right, even by miracle if needful. Hence, figuratively, an experience testing endurance, patience, courage, etc. All ordeals, except that by battle and cold water for witches, were abolished in ENGLAND in the early 13th century when trial by jury took their place. Similar methods of trial are found among other races. *See* ACT OF TRUTH.

Ordeal, or **wager of battle.** The accused was obliged to fight his accuser. Lords often chose vassals to represent them and priests and women were allowed champions. It was legally abolished in 1818 when the right was claimed by a person charged with murder.

Ordeal of boiling water was usual for the common people and involved plunging the hand into hot water either up to the wrist or elbow and guilt was presumed if the skin was injured.

Ordeal by cold water. The accused was bound and tossed into water. If he floated he was guilty. If he sank he was hauled out. This became a common test for WITCHCRAFT.

Ordeal of fire was for persons of high rank. Carrying a red-hot iron or walking barefoot and blindfolded over red-hot plough-shares were the usual forms. If the accused showed no wound after three days he was adjudged innocent.

Ordeal of the bier. A suspected murderer was required to touch the corpse and was deemed guilty if blood flowed from the body.

Ordeal of the Corsned. *See* CORSNED.

Ordeal of the cross. The accuser and accused stood upright before a CROSS and he who moved first was adjudged guilty. *See also* JUDICIUM CRUCIS.

Ordeal of the Eucharist was for priests. It was believed that if the guilty partook of the SACRAMENT divine punishment would follow for the sacrilege commited.

Order! When members of the HOUSE OF COMMONS and other debators call out *Order!* they mean that the person speaking is in some way breaking the rule of *order* of the assembly, and has to be *called to order*.

The Order of the Day. The prevailing state of things.

The Orders of the Day. In the HOUSE OF COMMONS, the items of business set down for a particular day on the Order Papers, the main business of the day.

Architectural Orders. *See* ARCHITECTURE.

Holy Orders. A clergyman is said to be in *holy orders* because he belongs to one of the *orders* or ranks of the Church. In the CHURCH OF ENGLAND these are three, *viz.*, Deacon, Priest, and BISHOP; in the ROMAN CATHOLIC CHURCH there is a fourth, that of Sub-deacon.

In ecclesiastical use the term also denotes a fraternity of monks or friars (as the *Franciscan Order*), and also the Rule by which the fraternity is governed.

To take orders. To enter HOLY ORDERS by ordination.

Order of battle. See LINE OF BATTLE.

Orders in Council. Orders issued by the PRIVY COUNCIL with the sanction of the SOVEREIGN under the royal prerogative. In practice they are drawn up on the advice of Ministers who are answerable to PARLIAMENT, usually to deal with matters demanding immediate attention. Orders in Council are also issued on matters of administrative detail under certain Acts of Parliament.

Orders of Knighthood. See KNIGHT.

Ordinary. In the CHURCH OF ENGLAND, an ecclesiastic who has *ordinary* or regular jurisdiction in his own right and not by depute, usually the BISHOP of a diocese and the archbishops. The Chaplain of NEWGATE GAOL was called the Ordinary thereof. In the ROMAN CATHOLIC CHURCH, the POPE, diocesan bishops, abbots, apostolic vicars, etc., are classed as ordinaries. In SCOTLAND certain judges of the Court of Sessions are called *Lords Ordinary* and those legal experts appointed to aid the HOUSE OF LORDS in the determination of appeals are called *Lords of Appeal in Ordinary*.

A meal prepared at an eating-house at a fixed rate for all comers was called "an ordinary"; hence, the place providing such meals.

> 'Tis almost dinner; I know they stay for you at the ordinary.
> BEAUMONT and FLETCHER: *The Scornful Lady*, IV, i.

In HERALDRY the "ordinary" is a simple charge, such as the chief, pale, fesse, bend, bar, chevron, cross or saltire.

The Ordinary of the Mass. That part of the MASS which varies in accordance with the Church Calendar as opposed to the CANON OF THE MASS which does not change.

Oreads (ôr' ē adz) or **Oreades.** NYMPHS of the mountains (Gr. *oros*, mountain).

> The Ocean-nymphs and Hamadryades,
> Oreads and Naiads, with long weedy locks,
> Offered to do her bidding through the seas,
> Under the earth, and in the hollow rocks.
> SHELLEY: *Witch of Atlas*, xxii.

Orellana (or el ā' nà). A former name of the river Amazon, after Francisco do Orellana, lieutenant of Pizarro, who first explored it in 1541.

Oremus. See LEGEM PONE.

Orestes. See PYLADES.

Orgoglio (ôr gō' lyō) (Ital., Arrogant Pride, or Man of Sin). In Spenser's *Faerie Queene* (I, vii and viii), a hideous giant as tall as three men, son of Earth and Wind, who typifies the tyrannical power of the Church of ROME.

Oriana. The beloved of AMADIS OF GAUL, who called himself Beltenebros when he retired to the Poor Rock (*Amadis de Gaula*, ii, 6).

Queen Elizabeth I is sometimes called the "peerless Oriana", especially in the madrigals entitled the *Triumphs of Oriana* (1601).

Orientation (Lat. *oriens*, the east). The placing of the east window of a church due east so that the rising sun may shine on the altar. Anciently, churches were built with their axes pointing to the rising sun on the saint's day; so that a church dedicated to St. JOHN was not parallel to one dedicated to St. PETER, but in the building of modern churches the saint's day is not, as a rule, regarded.

Figuratively, *orientation* is the correct placing of one's ideas, mental processes, etc., in relation with each other and with current thought—the ascertainment of one's "bearings".

Oriflamme (Fr., "flame of gold"). The ancient banner of the Kings of France, first used in battle in 1124, which replaced the blue hood of St. MARTIN. It was the standard of the abbey of St. DENYS and was a crimson flag on a gilded staff, and said by some writers to have had three points or tongues with tassels of green silk. It was last used in the field at Agincourt (1415) and was replaced by a blue standard powdered with FLEUR-DE-LIS.

It is reputed that infidels were blinded by merely looking at it. In the *Roman de Garin* the Saracens cry, "If we only set eyes on it we are all dead men"; and Froissart records that it was no sooner unfurled at Rosbecq than the fog cleared away from the French, leaving their enemies in misty darkness.

Original Sin. *See under* SIN.

Orion (o rī' on). A giant hunter of Greek mythology, noted for his beauty. He was blinded by Œnopion, but VULCAN sent Cedalion to be his guide, and his sight was restored by exposing his eye-balls to the sun. Being slain by DIANA, he was made one of the constellations and is supposed to be attended with stormy weather. His wife was named Side and his dogs Arctophonus and Ptoophagus.

The constellation Orion is pictured as a giant hunter with belt and sword sur-rounded by his dogs and animals. Betel-geuse and Bellatrix are the "shoulder" stars and three bright stars in a line form the belt, below which is the sword-handle containing a remarkable nebula.

Orkneys. *See* ORCADES.

Orlando. The Italian form of ROLAND, one of the great heroes of mediaeval ro-mance, and the most celebrated of CHARLEMAGNE'S PALADINS.

Orlando Furioso (Orlando mad). An epic poem in 45 cantos, by ARIOSTO (published 1516–1533). Orlando's mad-ness is caused by the faithlessness of AN-GELICA, but the main subject of the work is the seige of PARIS by Agramant the MOOR, when the Saracens were over-thrown.

Ormulum. A long poem in Transition, or Early Middle, English, of which only a "fragment" of some 20,000 lines is ex-tant. It is so called from its author *Orm* or *Ormin*, an Austin canon who wrote about 1200. It consists of a simple narra-tive of the gospels appointed to be read in church each with a homily upon it and expositions out of Aelfric, BEDE, and St. AUGUSTINE. It is preserved in the BODLEIAN LIBRARY and its ortho-graphy makes it particularly valuable evidence of the vowel-length at the time.

This boc iss nemmed Ormulum
Forrthi that Orm itt wrohhte.

Ormuzd, or **Ahura Mazda.** In ZOROA-STRIANISM, the principle or ANGEL of light and good, and creator of all things and judge of the world. He is in perpet-ual conflict with AHRIMAN but in the end will triumph.

Orosius. An early 5th-century Spanish presbyter and historian whose *Historia*

Adversus Paganos, from the Creation to A.D. 417, was translated into Anglo-Saxon from the Latin by King ALFRED. It was a popular textbook of general his-tory in the MIDDLE AGES. He presented some of his works to St. AUGUSTINE when he visited him in 415.

Orpheus (ôr' fūs). In Greek legend, a Thracian poet, son of Œagrus and CALL-IOPE (held by some to be a son of APOL-LO), who could move even inanimate things by his music—a power that was also claimed for the Scandinavian ODIN. When his wife EURYDICE died he went into the infernal regions and so charmed PLUTO that she was released on the con-dition that he would not look back till they reached the earth. When about to place his foot on the earth he turned round and Eurydice vanished instantly.

The prolonged grief of Orpheus at his second loss so enraged the Thracian wo-men that in one of their Bacchanalian ORGIES they tore him to pieces. The fragments of his body were collected by the MUSES and buried at the foot of Mount OLYMPUS, but his head, thrown into the river Hebrus, was carried into the sea, and so to Lesbos, where it was buried.

The Orphic Egg. *See* MUNDANE EGG *under* EGG.

Orphism. A movement in painting started by Robert Delaunay (1885–1941), char-acterized by patches and swirls of in-tense and contrasting colours. *Cp.* CUB-ISM; DADAISM; FAUVISM; FUTURISM; IMPRESSIONISM; SURREALISM; SYN-CHRONISM; VORTICISM.

Orrery (or' ĕr i). A complicated piece of mechanism showing by means of clock-work the movements of the planets, etc., round the SUN. It was invented about 1700 by George Graham, who sent his model to Rowley, an instrument maker, to make one for Prince Eugene. Rowley made a copy of it for Charles Boyle (1676–1731), third Earl of Orr-ery, in whose honour it was named. One of the best is Fulton's, in Kelvin Grove Museum, Glasgow.

Orson (Fr. *ourson*, a little bear). Twin brother of Valentine in the old romance of VALENTINE AND ORSON.

Orthodox. The Orthodox Church. The

Eastern Church, properly, The Holy Orthodox Catholic Apostolic Eastern Church. Its separation from the Western Church was partly due to the historic division of the Empire by Constantine; but also to the differences arising between "Greek" and "Latin" Christianity which culminated in complete separation in 1054 over the FILIOQUE CONTROVERSY. The Eastern Church now consists of seven patriarchates and is oligarchical in structure. *See* CATHOLIC CHURCH; GREEK CHURCH.

Orthodox Sunday, or **Feast of Orthodoxy,** in the Eastern Church, is the First Sunday in LENT, to commemorate the restoration of the icons in 842. *See* ICONOCLASTS.

Orthos, or **Orthrus.** The dog of GERYON, destroyed by HERCULES. *See* ECHIDNA.

Orvietan, or **Venice Treacle,** once held to be a sovereign remedy against poison, an electuary of unknown composition. It took its name from a charlatan of Orvieto, Italy, who used to pretend to poison himself and effect a cure with his potion.

Orwell, George. The pseudonym adopted by Eric Arthur Blair (1903–1950), Old Etonian and socialist; author of *The Road to Wigan Pier*, ANIMAL FARM, *Nineteen Eighty-Four*, etc. *See* DOUBLE-THINK.

Os sacrum (Lat.). The sacred bone. A triangular bone at the lower part of the vertebral column. *See* LUZ.

Oscar. A gold-plated figurine awarded annually by the American Academy of Motion Picture Arts and Sciences for the best film-acting, writing, or production of the year. There are two claims for the origin of this name. One is that in 1931 the future executive secretary of the Academy, Mrs. Margaret Herrick, joined as librarian; on seeing the then nameless gold statue for the first time she exclaimed "it reminds me of my Uncle Oscar"—the name stuck.

The other claim is that it derives indirectly from Oscar Wilde. When on a lecture tour of the U.S.A. he was asked if he had won the Newdigate Prize for Poetry, and he replied, "Yes, but while many people have won the Newdigate, it is seldom that the Newdigate gets an Oscar." When Helen Hayes was presented with the award, her husband Charles MacArthur, a noted wit and playwright, said, "Ah, I see you've got an Oscar", and the name stuck.

Osiris (ō sī′ ris). One of the chief gods of ancient Egypt; son of Nut, brother of SET, his jealous and constant foe, and husband of ISIS. Set encompassed his death, but Osiris underwent resurrection with the aid of THOTH. His son HORUS became his avenger. He was the god of the dead and of the after-life and resurrection.

The name means *Many-eyed* and Osiris is usually depicted as a man wearing the White Crown and holding a sceptre and flail, as a mummy.

Osmand. A necromancer in *The Seven Champions of Christendom*, I, xix, who by enchantment raised an army to resist the Christians. Six of the Champions fell, whereupon St. GEORGE restored them; Osmand tore out his own hair, in which lay his magic power, bit his tongue in two, disembowelled himself, cut off his arms and then died. *See* SEVEN CHAMPIONS.

Ossa. *See* PELION.

Ossian, or **Oisin.** The legendary Gaelic bard and celebrated warrior hero of the 3rd century, the son of Fionn Mac Cumhail (FINGAL). He is best known from the publications (1760–1763) of James Macpherson born at Ruthven, Inverness (1736–1796), purporting to be translations of poems by Ossian, the son of Fingal, from original MSS. Macpherson became famous and his works were widely translated, but their authenticity was challenged by Dr. Johnson in his *Journey to the Western Islands of Scotland*, and others. They seem to have been essentially made up by Macpherson himself with some use of ancient sources.

> "I [Johnson] look upon M'Pherson's Fingal to be as gross an imposition as ever the world was troubled with."
> BOSWELL: *The Journal of a Tour to the Hebrides* (Wed., 22 Sept.).

Ostracism (Gr. *ostrakon*, a potsherd). Black-balling, boycotting; exclusion from society, etc. The word arose from the ancient Greek custom of banishing, by a popular vote, one whose power was a danger to the state, the citizens writing the name of one whose banishment was deemed desirable on a sherd. *Cp.* BLACK-BALLED; BOYCOTT.

Ostrich. At one time the ostrich was fabled, when hunted, to run a certain distance and then thrust his head into the sand, thinking because it cannot see that it cannot be seen (*cp.* CROCODILE); hence the application of *ostrich-like*, *ostrich-head*, *ostrich belief*, etc., to various forms of self-delusion.

The ostrich also has the habit of eating indigestible things such as stones and hard objects to assist the functions of its gizzard. This has given rise to such phrases as **to have a digestion like an ostrich** or **to have an ostrich-stomach**, *i.e.* to be able to digest anything.

Ostrich eggs are often suspended in Eastern churches as symbols of God's watchful care. It used to be thought that the ostrich hatches her eggs by gazing on them, and if she suspends her gaze even for a minute or so the eggs are addled. Furthermore, we are told that if an egg is bad the ostrich will break it; so will GOD deal with EVIL men.

Ostrog Bible, The. *See* BIBLE, SOME SPECIALLY NAMED EDITIONS.

Otium cum dignitate (ō′ ti ùm kūm dig ni tā′ ti) (Lat., leisure with dignity). Retirement after a person has worked and saved enough to live upon in comfort.

> *Otium cum dignitate* is to be had with £500 a year as well as with £5,000.
> BOLINGBROKE to Swift, 19 November 1729.

Ottava Rima (o ta′ và rē′ mà). A stanza of eight ten-syllable lines, rhyming *a b a b a b c c*, as used by Keats in his *Isabella*, BYRON in *Don Juan*, etc. It originated in Italy and was used by TASSO and ARIOSTO and many others, the lines being eleven-syllable.

Ottoman Empire. The Turkish empire founded by Othman or Osman I (1288–1320), which lasted until 1919.

Otus. *See* EPHIALTES.

Ouida (wē′ dà). The pseudonym of Maria Louise de la Ramée (1839–1908), originally Maria Louise Ramée, a prolific writer of romantic novels of high society, the best known being *Under Two Flags* (1867). She was an unconventional, and later eccentric character, herself unlucky in pursuit of romance. She was born at Bury St. Edmunds, the daughter of a French father and an English mother, the name *Ouida* being her early childhood attempt to produce "Louise".

Ouija (wē′ jà). A device employed by spiritualists for receiving spirit messages. It consists of a small piece of wood on wheels, placed on a board marked with the letters of the alphabet and certain commonly-used words. When the fingers of the communicators are placed on the Ouija board it moves from letter to letter and thus spells out sentences. The word is a combination of Fr. *oui* and Ger. *ja*, both meaning "yes". Ouija is a registered trade mark in the United States of America.

Out. Murder will out. The secret is bound to be revealed; "be sure your sins will find you out".

> O blisful god, that art so just and trewe!
> Lo, how that thou biwreyest mordre alway,
> Mordre wol out, that see we day by day.
> CHAUCER: *Nun's Priests's Tale*. 284.

Out and away. By far, incomparably, as, "He is out and away the best batsman."

Out and out. Thoroughly, absolutely, without qualification, thus an "out and out liar" is a complete and utter liar.

Out of it. Left on one side, not included.

Out on a limb. Isolated, stranded, cut off; as an animal on the end of a branch of a tree.

Outed. Expelled, ejected.

To be out for. To have one's mind set on achieving some particular end.

To go all out. To make every effort, to do one's utmost.

To have it out. To contest either physically or verbally with another to the utmost of one's ability; as, "I mean to have it out with him one of these days"; "I had it out with him"—*i.e.* "I spoke my mind freely and without reserve." The idea is that of letting loose pent-up disapprobation.

To out-Herod Herod. *See* HEROD.

Outback. The more remote and sparsely populated areas in the Australian interior, the bush.

Outsider, An. One who is not a member of a particular circle or group, one not considered a socially desirable companion; also a horse or person not thought to be in the running. The usage comes from coaching days when the humbler passengers travelled outside (other than on the box next to the coachman).

Ouzelum Bird. This fanciful bird is reputed to fly backwards and thus does not know where it is going but likes to know where it has been.

Oval, The. The famous cricket ground at Kennington, LONDON, the headquarters of the Surrey Cricket Club, a former market garden, was opened in 1846. It was after Australia's victory at the Oval in 1882 that the ASHES came into being.

Ovation. An enthusiastic display of popular favour, so called from the ancient Roman *ovatio*, a minor form of TRIUMPH in which the conqueror entered the city on horseback or on foot wearing a crown of MYRTLE instead of GOLD.

Over. Half seas over. *See under* HALF.

It's all over with him. He's finished, he can't go any farther, he's "shot his bolt". Said also of one who has been given up by the doctors.

Over and above. In addition to; besides.

Over and over again. Very frequently, repeatedly. In Lat., *Iterum iterumque*.

Over the left. *See under* LEFT.

Overlord. The famous code name given to the Allied operation for the invasion of N.W. Europe, which began on D-DAY 1944.

Overture (Fr. *ouvert*, O.F. *overt*, past part. of *ouvrir*, to open). An opening, a preliminary proposal; a piece of music for the opening of an OPERA. Independent pieces of instrumental music in overture style are called *concert overtures*.

To make overtures is to be the first to make an advance, as with a view to acquaintanceship, some business deal, or a reconciliation.

Overy, or Overie. The priory church of St. Mary Overy, renamed St. Saviour's in 1540, and which became SOUTHWARK Cathedral in 1905, was legendarily founded by a ferryman's daughter called Mary (or Mary Overs). Her miserly father Awdrey feigned death in the hope that sorrow would restrain his household's consumption of victuals. Instead they rejoiced and made merry, whereupon Awdrey rose up in anger, only to be slain as a ghost. Mary, now possessed of his fortune, sent for her lover, but he was thrown from his horse and was killed. In sorrow she founded the nunnery which she entered. *Overy* is probably a corruption of "over the river".

Owain. The hero of a 12th-century legend, *The Descent of Owain*, written by Henry of Saltrey, an English CISTERCIAN. Owain was an Irish KNIGHT of Stephen's court who, by way of penance for a wicked life, entered and passed through ST. PATRICK'S PURGATORY.

Owl. The emblem of ATHENS, where owls abounded. Hence MINERVA (ATHENE) was given the owl for her symbol. The Greeks had a proverb, **To send owls to Athens,** which meant the same as our *To carry coals to Newcastle* (*see under* COAL). *See also* MADGE.

I live too near a wood to be scared by an owl. I am too old to be frightened by a BOGY.

Like an owl in an ivy-bush. Having a sapient, vacant look, as some persons have when in their cups; having a stupid vacant stare. Owls are proverbial for their judge-like solemnity; IVY is the favourite plant of BACCHUS, and was supposed to be the favourite haunt of owls.

> Good ivy, say to us, what birds hast thou?
> None but the owlet that cries "How How!"
>
> *Carol* (15th century).

Gray, in his *Elegy*, and numerous other poets bracket the two:

> From yonder ivy-mantled tower
> The moping owl doth to the moon complain.

The owl was a baker's daughter. According to a Gloucestershire legend, our Saviour went into a baker's shop for something to eat. The mistress put a cake into the oven for Him, but her daughter said it was too large, and reduced it by half. The dough, however, swelled to an enormous size, and the daughter cried out, "Heugh! heugh! heugh!" and was transformed into an OWL. Ophelia alludes to the tradition:

> Well, God 'ield you! They say the owl
> was a baker's daughter.
>
> SHAKESPEARE: *Hamlet*, IV, v.

Owlglass. *See* EULENSPIEGEL.

Owl Jug. A large pot-bellied earthenware container with two ear-handles, once common in Dorset, used for carrying water, cider, etc.

Owl light. Dusk; the gloaming, "BLIND MAN'S HOLIDAY". Fr. *Entre chien et loup*.

Ox. One of the four figures which made up the cherubim in *Ezekiel* i, 10. It is the emblem of the priesthood, and was assigned to St. LUKE as his symbol because he begins his GOSPEL with the Jewish priest sacrificing in the TEMPLE.

It is also an emblem of St. Frideswide, St. LEONARD, St. Sylvester, St. MÉDARD, St. Julietta, and St. Blandina.

The dumb ox. *See under* DUMB.

Off-ox. A stupid or clumsy person. In an ox-team the off-ox is the one farthest away from the driver. *See* NEAR.

He has an ox on his tongue. *See* MONEY.

The black ox hath trod on your foot, or **hath trampled on you.** Misfortune has come to you or your house; sometimes, you are henpecked. A black ox was sacrificed to PLUTO, the infernal god, as a white one was to JUPITER.

Thou shalt not muzzle the ox when he treadeth out the corn (*Deut.* xxv, 4). In other words, do not grudge him the mouthful he may snatch when working for you; do not deprive a man of his little perquisites.

To play the giddy ox. To act the fool generally; to behave in an irresponsible or over-hilarious manner. There was an old phrase, *to make an ox of one*, meaning *to make a fool of one*; and in SHAKESPEARE's *Merry Wives of Windsor* (V, v) we have:

> *Fal.:* I do begin to perceive that I am
> made an ass.
> *Ford:* Ay, and an ox too; both the proofs
> are extant.

Ox-bow. A horseshoe bend in a river.

Ox-eye. A sailor's name for a cloudy speck which indicates the approach of a storm.

Oxgang. An Anglo-Saxon measure of no very definite quantity; as much as an ox could *gang* over or cultivate. Also called a *bovate*. Eight oxgangs made a *carucate*. An oxgang became a conventional unit varying from about 10 to 25 acres in different places. The Lat. *jugum* was a similar term, according to Varro, "Quod juncti boves uno die exarare possunt."

Oxbridge. A word widely used as an abbreviation for Oxford and Cambridge collectively, and for the type of historic English university. For some it is a convenient term, for others it has tendentious and snobbish implications. *Cp.* CAMFORD; REDBRICK.

Oxford. Oxford bags. Very widebottomed flannel trousers first fashionable among Oxford undergraduates in the 1920s.

Oxford frame. A picture frame the sides of which cross each other at the corners forming a cross-like projection; once much used for photographs of college groups, etc.

Oxford Group. The name first adopted in South Africa by the followers of Frank Buchman (1878–1961), also called *Buchmanism* which developed into the MORAL RE-ARMAMENT movement. He had a considerable following at Cambridge in the 1920s, but later wider support at Oxford. The movement was EVANGELICAL in character and also became concerned with social, industrial, and international questions.

Oxford Movement. A High Church revival movement in the CHURCH OF ENGLAND "started and guided" by Oxford clerics, especially John Keble, J. H. Newman, R. H. Froude, and E. B. Pusey (hence *Puseyism* as another name for the movement). They were dissatisfied with the decline of Church standards, and with the increase of liberal theology, and feared that the Catholic Emancipation Act of 1829 endangered the English Church. The movement began in 1833 with Keble's sermon against the suppression of ten Irish bishoprics.

It was published under the title of *National Apostasy*. Three tracts setting forth their views were published in 1833 and many *Tracts for the Times* followed, hence the name *Tractarianism*. They stressed the historical continuity of the Church of England and the importance of the priesthood and the sacraments. "PROTESTANT" and EVANGELICAL hostility was aroused, especially after Newman's reception into the ROMAN CATHOLIC CHURCH in 1845, but in spite of much official opposition the movement had a lasting influence on the standards and ceremonial of the Church.

Oxymoron. A rhetorical figure in which effect is produced by the juxtaposition of contradictory terms, such as "Make haste slowly", "Faith unfaithful kept him falsely true". The word is the Gr. for "pointedly foolish".

Oyez! Oyez! Oyez! (ō yes) (O. Fr., Hear ye!). The call made by the public crier, court officer, etc., to attract attention when a proclamation is about to be read out. Sometimes written *O yes!*

Oyster. And did you ever see an oyster walk upstairs? A satirical query sometimes addressed to one who has been telling unbelievable yarns about his own experiences.

Close as a Kentish oyster. Absolutely secret; hermetically sealed. Kentish oysters are proverbially good, and all good oysters are fast closed.

Never eat an oyster unless there's an R in the month. Good advice which limits the eating of native oysters to the months from September to April, the normal marketing time. The legal close time for oysters in ENGLAND and SCOTLAND, however, extends only from 15 June to 4 August. The advice does not necessarily apply to imported oysters.

> "I think oysters are more beautiful than any religion."
> SAKI: *The Chronicles of Clovis*.

The world's mine oyster. The world is the place from which to extract profit, etc., as a pearl can be extracted from an oyster. SHAKESPEARE uses the phrase (*The Merry Wives of Windsor*, II, ii).

Oz, Wizard of. *See under* WIZARD.

P

P. The sixteenth letter in the English alphabet called *pe*, "mouth", by the Phœnicians and ancient Hebrews, and represented in Egyptian hieroglyphs by a shutter.

In the 16th century, Placentius, a DOMINICAN friar, wrote a poem of 253 HEXAMETER verses, called *Pugna Porcorum*, every word of which begins with the letter *p*. It opens thus:

> Plaudite, Porcelli, porcorum pigra propago—

which may be translated:

> Piglets, praise pigs' prolonged progeny.

P as a mediæval numeral stands for 400, P̄ stands for 400,000. P is also the abbreviation for "new penny" in the British decimal currency.

p, pp, ppp (in music). *p=piano* (Ital., soft); *pp* and *ppp=pianissimo* (Ital., very soft).

P.C. The Roman *patres conscripti. See* CONSCRIPT FATHERS.

P.S. (Lat. *post-scriptum*). Written afterwards—*i.e.* after the letter or book was finished.

P's and Q's. Mind your P's and Q's. Be very circumspect in your behaviour. Most probably it derives from an admonition to children learning the alphabet to be careful to distinguish between the forms of *p* and *q* or to printers' apprentices in handling and sorting type. More fancifully it is suggested that in public houses accounts were scored up for beer "P" for pints and "Q" for quarts and a customer needed "to mind his P's and Q's" when the reckoning came. Another is that in the France of Louis XIV, when huge WIGS were fashionable, dancing masters would warn their pupils to "Mind your P's (*i.e. pieds*, feet) and Q's (*i.e. queues*, wigs)" lest the latter fall off

when bending low to make a formal bow.

Pace (pā′ si). From Lat. *pax*, meaning peace or pardon, is used in the sense of "with the permission of" when preceding the mention of some person who disagrees with what is being done.

Pace-eggs. *See under* PASCH.

Pace. To be put through one's paces. To test one's capabilities, as a horse might be tried out by an intending purchaser.

To set the pace. To set the standard of achievement for others to emulate or keep up with, as in a race.

Pacific Ocean. So named by MAGELLAN in 1520, because there he enjoyed calm weather, and a placid sea after the stormy and tempestuous passage of the Straits of Magellan. It was first sighted by Balboa in 1513.

Pack. Packing a jury. Selecting for a jury persons whose verdict is likely to be partial.

Pack up your troubles in your old kit-bag. The opening line of one of the most memorable choruses of World War I. It was written by George Asaf and composed by Felix Powell in 1915.

> Pack up your troubles in your old kitbag,
> And smile, smile, smile.
> While you've a lucifer to light your fag,
> Smile, boys, that's the style, etc.

To pack up. Slang for to take one's departure; to cease from a task; to have no more to do with the matter.

To send one packing. To dismiss summarily.

Packet. To stop a packet. Colloquially, to receive a severe injury, actually or figuratively; a packet of trouble.

Packstaff. *See* PIKESTAFF.

Pactolus. The golden sands of the Pac-

tolus. The Pactolus is a small river in Lydia, Asia Minor, once famous for the particles of GOLD in its sands, which legendarily was due to MIDAS having bathed there. Its gold was exhausted by the time of AUGUSTUS.

Paddington Fair. A public execution. TYBURN was in the parish of Paddington. Public executions were abolished in 1868.

Paddle your own canoe. *See under* CANOE.

Paddock. Cold as a paddock. A paddock is a toad or frog; and we have the corresponding phrases "cold as a toad" and "cold as a frog".

Paddy, Paddywhack. An Irishman; from PATRICK (Erse, *Padraig*). In slang both terms are used for a loss of temper, a childish temper; the latter also denotes the gristle in roast meat.

Padishah is the Turkish form of the Persian *Padshah*, a king or reigning sovereign. It was formerly applied exclusively to the SULTAN of Turkey.

Padre (pa' drā). A chaplain is so called by personnel of the armed forces. It is Spanish, Italian, and Portuguese for "father" and was adopted by the British Army in India, where it was introduced by the Portuguese.

Padua was long supposed in SCOTLAND to be the chief school of NECROMANCY, hence Scott says of the Earl of Gowrie:

He learned the art that none may name
In Padua, far beyond the sea.
Lay of the Last Minstrel, I, xi.

Pæan (pē' an). According to HOMER, the name of the physician to the gods. It was used in the phrase *Io Pæan* as the invocation in the hymn to APOLLO, and later in hymns of thanksgiving to other deities, hence *pæan* has come to mean any song of praise or thanksgiving, any shout of triumph or exultation.

Pagan (Lat. *paganus*, a rustic). Its present meaning of a heathen or non-Christian has usually been held to be derived from the fact that heathen practices lingered in the villages long after the Christian Church was established in the towns. The word was also a Roman contemptuous name for a civilian and it is likely that when the early Christians called themselves *milites Christi* (sold-

iers of Christ) they adopted the military usage, *paganus*, for those who were not "soldiers of Christ". (See the penultimate note to ch. xxi of Gibbon's *Decline and Fall of the Roman Empire*.)

Pagoda. A Buddhist temple or sacred tower in India, China, etc.; also the name of gold and silver coins formerly current in southern India, from the representation of a pagoda on the reverse. Hence the phrase **To shake the pagoda-tree**, to make money readily in the Far East.

The amusing pursuit of "shaking the pagoda-tree", once so popular in our Oriental possessions.
THEODORE HOOK: *Gilbert Gurney*, I.

Paid. *See* PAY.

Pain. Bill of Pains and Penalties. *See under* BILL.

For one's pains. In return for one's trouble or well-meant efforts.

On, or **under pain of.** Under the threat of punishment or penalty for non-compliance.

To be at pains. To take trouble, to make a positive effort.

Paint. To paint the lily. To indulge in hyperbolical praise, to exaggerate the beauties, good points, etc., of the subject.

To paint the lion. An old nautical term, meaning to strip a person naked and then smear his body all over with tar.

To paint the town red. To have a gay, noisy time; to cause some disturbance in town by having a noisy and disorderly spree. A phrase of American origin.

Painter. It is said that APELLES, being at a loss to delineate the foam of ALEXANDER's horse, dashed his brush at the picture in despair, and did by accident what he could not accomplish by art. Similar stories are told of many other artists and also of the living quality of their paintings. It is reputed that Apelles painted Alexander's horse so realistically that a living horse mistook it and began to neigh. Velasquez painted a Spanish ADMIRAL so true to life that Philip IV mistook the painting for the man and reproved the portrait for not being with the fleet. Birds flew at grapes painted by Zeuxis; and Mandyn tried to brush off a fly from a man's leg, both having been painted by Matsys. Parrhasios of Ephesus painted a curtain so well that Zeuxis told him to draw it aside to reveal the picture behind it; and Myron, the Greek sculptor, is said to have fashioned a cow so well that a bull mistook it for a living creature.

To cut the painter. To sever connection, as a boat is set adrift if the painter is cut which holds it fast to the mooring post, etc. The phrase was much used in the 19th century with reference to possible severance between Great Britain and her colonies.

Pair Off. When two members of PARLIAMENT of opposite parties agree to absent themselves, so that when a vote is taken the absence of one neutralizes the missing vote of the other, they are said to *pair off*. In the HOUSE OF COMMONS this is usually arranged by the WHIPS.

Pakeha. Any resident in New Zealand who is not a Maori. Thought by some to be a Maori word, but probably a native corruption of an abusive term used by early whaling crews.

Pakistan. The name of this state formed in 1947 was coined by Chaudrie Rahmat Ali in 1933 to represent the units which should be included when the time came: P—Punjab; A—Afghan border states; K—Kashmir; S—Sind; Tan for Baluchistan.

Pal. A gypsy word meaning brother or mate.

Palace originally meant a dwelling on the Palatine Hill (*see* PALATINATE) of ROME, where AUGUSTUS, and later Tiberius and NERO, built their mansions. The word was hence transferred to other royal and imperial residences; then to similar buildings, such as *Blenheim Palace*, *Dalkeith Palace*, and to the official residence of a BISHOP; and finally to a place of amusement as the CRYSTAL PALACE, the *People's Palace*, and—in irony—to a *gin palace* (*see under* GIN). *See also* ALLY PALLY.

In parts of Devonshire cellars for fish, storehouses cut in the rock, etc., are called *palaces* or *pallaces*; but this may be from the old word *palis*, a space enclosed by a palisade.

Paladin (păl' à din). Properly, an officer of, or one connected with, the PALACE, a

palatine; usually confined in romance to the Twelve Peers of CHARLEMAGNE'S court, and hence applied to any renowned hero or KNIGHT-ERRANT.

Palæmon (păl ē' mon). In Roman legend, a son of Ino (*see* LEUCOTHEA), and originally called MELICERTES. Palæmon is the name given to him after he was made a sea-god, and as Portumnus he was the protecting god of harbours. The story is given in Spenser's *Faerie Queene* (IX, xi); in the same poet's *Colin Clout* his name is used for Thomas Churchyard (*c.* 1520–1604), the poet.

Palæolithic Age (pā li ō lith' ik) (Gr. *palaios*, old; *lithos*, a stone). The first of the STONE AGES when man was essentially a hunter using somewhat primitive stone or flint implements and weapons. *Cp.* NEOLITHIC.

Palais Rose. The first of many international conferences after World War II was held in the rose-decorated chamber of a Parisian mansion. The monotonous reiteration by the Russian delegate of "No" to every suggestion put forward gave origin to the phrase "Another Palais Rose" to describe an abortive conference.

Palamedes (păl a mē' dēz). In Greek legend, one of the heroes who fought against TROY. He was the son of Nauplius and Clymene, and was the reputed inventor of lighthouses, scales and measures, the discus, dice, etc., and was said to have added four letters to the original alphabet of CADMUS. It was he who detected the assumed madness of ULYSSES, in revenge for which the latter encompassed his death. The phrase, *he is quite a Palamedes*, meaning "an ingenious person" is an allusion to this hero.

In ARTHURIAN ROMANCE, Sir Palamedes is a SARACEN knight who was overcome in single combat by TRISTRAM. Both loved YSOLDE, the wife of King Mark; and after the lady was given up by the Saracen, Tristram converted him to the Christian faith, and stood his godfather at the font.

Palamon and Arcite. *See* ARCITE.

Palatinate. The province of a *palatine*, who originally was an officer of the imperial palace at ROME. This was on the

Palatine Hill, which was so called from PALES.

In Germany *The Palatinate* was the name of a former state on the Rhine, and later that of a detached portion of Bavaria to the west of the Rhine which in 1946 became part of the newly formed *Land* Rhineland-Palatinate. *See also* COUNTY PALATINE.

Pale, The English. The name given in the 14th century to that part of IRELAND where English rule was effective resulting from the English settlement of Henry II's reign, *viz.* Louth, Meath, Trim, Dublin, Kilkenny, Wexford, Waterford and Tipperary. By the latter 15th century, it had shrunk to the four counties of Louth, Meath, Dublin, and Kildare, and this shrinking continued until the reconquest of Ireland was effected by the Tudors.

The word is from Lat. *palum*, a stake, hence a fence, a territory with defined limits. Hence the phrases **Within the pale** and **Beyond the pale**, *pale* here meaning "the bounds of civilization" or "civilized behaviour".

There was also an English pale around Calais (1347–1558), and in Imperial Russia, from 1792, a notorious Pale or Settlement for the Jews.

Paleface. A name for a white man, attributed to the North American Indians, as if a translation from an Indian expression, but largely owing its popularity to the novels of Fenimore Cooper.

Pales (pā' lēz). The Roman god (later a goddess) of shepherds and their flocks whose festivals, *Palilias*, were celebrated on 21 April, the "birthday of ROME", to commemorate the day when ROMULUS, the wolf-child, drew the first furrow at the foot of the hill, and thus laid the foundations of the "Rome Quadrata", the most ancient part of the city.

Palimpsest (Gr. *palin*, again; *psestos*, scraped). A parchment or other writing surface on which the original writing has been effaced and something else has been written, anciently common practice owing to the shortage of material. As the writing was not always entirely effaced, many works, otherwise lost, have been recovered. Thus Cicero's *De* *Republica* was restored, though partially erased to make way for a commentary of St. AUGUSTINE on the PSALMS.

Palindrome (Gr. *palin dromo*, to run back again). A word or line which reads backwards and forwards alike, as *Madam*, also *Roma tibi subito motibus ibit amor*. They have also been called *Sotadics*, from their reputed inventor, Sotades, a scurrilous Greek poet of the 3rd century B.C. Probably the longest palindrome in English is:

> Dog as a devil deified
> Deified lived as a god.

There is also NAPOLEON's reputed saying:

> Able was I ere I saw Elba.

Adam's reputed self-introduction to Eve:

> Madam, I'm Adam.

Also—Lewd did I live, evil I did dwel[l]; and there is the celebrated Greek palindrome:

> ΝΙΨΟΝΑΝΟΜΗΜΑΤΑΜΗΜΟΝΑΝΟΨΙΝ,

i.e. wash my transgressions, not only my face. 27.9.1972 is an example of palindromic date.

Palinode (Gr., singing again). A song or discourse recanting a previous one; such as that of Stesichorus to HELEN after he had been struck blind for singing EVIL of her, or HORACE's *Ode* (Bk. I, xvi), which ends:

> ...nunc ego mitibus
> Murare quæro tristia, dum mihi
> Fias recentatis amica
> Opprobrum animumque reddas.

It was a favourite form of versification among Jacobean poets, and the best known is that of Francis Quarles (1592–1644) in which man's life is likened to all the delights of nature, all of which fade, and man too dies.

Palinurus, or **Palinure**. Any pilot, especially a careless one; from the steersman in VIRGIL's ÆNEID who went to sleep at the helm, fell overboard and was swept ashore three days later, only to be murdered on landing.

Palissy Ware. Dishes and similar articles of pottery, covered with models of fish, reptiles, shells, flowers, leaves, etc., carefully coloured and enamelled in high relief; so called after Bernard Palissy (1510–1589), the French potter and enameller.

Pall (pawl). The small linen cloth stiffened by cardboard which covers the chalice at the EUCHARIST; also the covering thrown over a coffin. It is the Lat. *pallium*, a robe or mantle; also the long sweeping robe or pall worn by sovereigns at their coronation, by the POPE and archbishops. *See* PALLIUM.

> Sometimes let gorgeous Tragedy
> In sceptered pall come sweeping by.
> MILTON: *Il Penseroso*, line 97.

Pall Mall (păl măl). This dignified WEST-END thoroughfare, the centre of "clubland", takes its name from the old "alley" where Pall-mall was played long before Charles II introduced it in St. James's Park (*see* MALL). When the street was first built it was named Catherine Street, after Catherine of Braganza, Charles II's queen. "Pale-maille", says Cotgrave, "is a game wherein a round box ball is struck with a mallet through a high arch of iron, which he that can do at the fewest blows, or at the number agreed upon, wins" (Ital. *palla*, ball; *maglio*, mallet). *See* CROQUET.

Palladian. An architectural style based on the ancient classical, introduced by the Italian architect Andrea Palladio (1518–1580). It was first used in England by Inigo Jones, and the Banqueting Hall, WHITEHALL, and Lincoln's Inn Chapel built in 1622, are examples of his work.

Palladium. In classical legend, the colossal wooden statue of PALLAS in the citadel of TROY, which was said to have fallen from HEAVEN, and on the preservation of which the safety of the city was held to depend. It was said to have been taken by the Greeks and the city burned down; and later said to have been removed to ROME by ÆNEAS.

Hence the word is now figuratively applied to anything on which the safety of a people, etc., is supposed to depend.

> The liberty of the press is the palladium of all the civil, political, and religious rights of an English man.
> *Letters of Junius: Dedication.*

See also ANCILE.

Pallas, or **Pallas Athene.** A name of MINERVA, sometimes called *Pallas Minerva* daughter of JUPITER, perhaps so called from the spear which she brandished. Another suggestion is that she was named after Pallas, one of the TITANS, whom she flayed, using his skin as a covering.

Pallium. The Roman name for a square woollen cloak worn by men in ancient Greece, especially by philosophers and courtesans, corresponding to the Roman TOGA. Hence the Greeks called themselves *gens palliata*, and the Romans were *gens togata*. *Cp.* GALLIA BRACATA; GENS BRACATA; TOGA.

At the present time, the scarf-like vestment of white wool with red crosses, worn by the POPE and archbishops, is called the *pallium*. It is made from the wool of lambs blessed in the church of St. Agnese, ROME, and until he has received his pallium no Roman Catholic archbishop can exercise his functions. Its use in the Church of England (*see under* CHURCH) ended with the REFORMATION, although it is still displayed heraldically in the arms of the Archbishop of Canterbury in the shape of a letter Y. It is also called a PALL.

Palm. The well-known tropical and subtropical tree gets its name from the Lat. *palma*, the palm of the hand, from the spread-hand appearance of its fronds. The palm-tree is said to grow faster from its being washed down. Hence it is the symbol of resolution overcoming calamity. It is said by Orientals to have sprung from the residue of the clay of which ADAM was formed.

An itching palm. A hand ready to receive bribes. The old superstition is that if your palm itches you are going to receive money.

Palm-oil. Bribes, or rather money for bribes, fees, etc.

Palm Sunday. The Sunday next before EASTER. So called in memory of Christ's triumphant entry into JERUSALEM, when the multitude strewed the way (*John* xii., 12–19). In mediæval England "palms" were often made from willow, box, and yew.

Sad Palm Sunday. 29 March 1461, the day of the battle of Towton, the most fatal of all the battles of the WARS OF THE ROSES (*see under* ROSE) when well over 30,000 men were slain.

To bear the palm. To be the best. The allusion is to the Roman custom of giving the victorious GLADIATOR a branch of the palm-tree.

To palm off. To pass off fraudulently. The allusion is to jugglers, who conceal in the palm of their hand what they pretend to dispose of in some other way.

To yield the palm, *i.e.* to yield the palm of victory (*see* TO BEAR THE PALM, *above*). To admit another's superiority in a given field.

Palma Christi (Lat., Palm of Christ). The castor-oil plant (*Ricinus communis*).

Palmam qui meruit ferat (Lat., Let him bear the palm who has deserved it). Nelson's motto and that of the battleship H.M.S. *Nelson*. The line comes from Jortin's *Lusus Poetici* (1748), *Ad ventos*, stanza iv:

> Et nobis faciles parcite et hostibus,
> Concurrant pariter cum ratibus rates:
> Spectent numina ponti, et
> Palmam qui meruit ferat.

Palmer (Lat. *palmifer*, palm-bearer). A pilgrim to the HOLY LAND who was given a consecrated palm-branch to carry back which was usually laid on the altar of his parish church on his return.

> His sandals were with travel tore
> Staff, budget, bottle, scrip he wore;
> The faded palm-branch in his hand
> Showed pilgrim from the Holy Land.
> SCOTT: *Marmion*, i, 27.

Palmistry, or **Chiromancy** (Gr. *cheir*, the hand, *mantike*, DIVINATION). The art of reading the palm (of the hand) and deducing the character, temperament, fortune, etc., of the owner from the lines upon it. The art is ancient and was practised by the Greeks, Chaldean astrologers, GYPSIES, etc.

Palmy days. Prosperous or happy days, as those were to a victorious gladiator when he went to receive the palm-branch as the reward of his prowess.

Palmerin. The hero of a number of 16th-century Spanish romances of CHIVALRY, on the lines of AMADIS OF GAUL. The most famous are *Palmerin de Oliva*, and *Palmerin of England*. Southey published an abridged translation of the latter.

Palmerston's Follies. *See under* FOLLY.

Paludament. A distinctive mantle worn by a Roman general in the time of war. This was the "scarlet robe" in which Christ was invested (*Matt.* xxvii, 28).

Paly. In HERALDRY means divided perpendicularly into an even number of equal parts.

Pamphlet. A small written work of comparatively few sheets, often controversial and of only temporary interest. The word has been variously derived but is probably from *Pamphilet*, the French name of a 12th-century amatory Latin poem *Pamphilus seu de Amore*.

Pan (Gr. all, everything). In Greek mythology, the god of pastures, forests, flocks, and herds; also the universal deity. Another more probable etymology is that the name is derived from the same root as Lat. *pascere*, to graze. His parentage is variously given as born of JUPITER and CALISTO, HERMES and PENELOPE, etc., and he is represented with the upper part of a man and the body and legs of a goat. His lustful nature was a characteristic and he was the symbol of fecundity.

> Universal Pan,
> Knit with the Graces and the Hours in dance,
> Led on the eternal spring.
> MILTON: *Paradise Lost*, IV, 266.

Legend has it that at the time of the Crucifixion, just when the veil of the TEMPLE was rent in twain, a cry swept across the ocean in the hearing of a pilot, "Great Pan is Dead", and at the same time the responses of the ORACLES ceased for ever. (See E.B. Browning's poem of this name.) It has been suggested that what the mariner heard was a ritual lamentation in honour of ADONIS. *See also* PANIC.

Pan-pipes. A wind instrument of great antiquity, consisting of a series of pipes of graduated length, across the upper ends of which the player blows, obtaining a scale of thin, reedy notes. The story is that it was first formed by PAN from a reed into which the nymph SYRINX was transformed when fleeing from his amorous intentions.

Pan. To pan out. To turn out, to happen, as "it has panned out satisfactorily". From the pan used by a prospector to wash out GOLD from the gravel of streams and riverbeds.

Panacea (păn à sē' à) (Gr., all-healing). A universal remedy. Panacea was the daughter of ÆSCULAPIUS, and the medicine that cures is the daughter or child of the healing art.

In the MIDDLE AGES the search for the panacea was one of the self-imposed tasks of the alchemists. Fable tells of many panaceas, such as the PROMETHEAN UNGUENT which rendered the body invulnerable, ALADDIN'S ring, the balsam of FIERABRAS, and PRINCE AHMED'S APPLE (*see under* APPLE). *Cp.* ACHILLES'S SPEAR; MEDEA'S KETTLE, etc.

Panache (păn äsh'). The literal meaning of this French word is a plume of feathers flying in the wind as from the crest of a helmet. Figuratively, it is applied to one's courage or spirit, to keeping one's end up.

Pancake. A thin flat cake of batter fried in fat, traditionally cooked and eaten on **Pancake Day** (SHROVE TUESDAY). The ingredients are eggs, symbolic of creation, flour for the staff of life, salt for wholesomeness, and milk for purity. Shrove Tuesday became a day of revelry sounded off by the ringing of the **Pancake Bell**, which was the signal for the villagers to cease work and go home to make pancakes or join in the games and merry-making.

Panchæa (pan kē' à). A fabulous land, possibly belonging to ARABIA FELIX, renowned among the ancients for the quality of its perfumes, such as myrrh and incense.

Pancras, St. One of the patron saints of children (*cp.* NICHOLAS), martyred in the Diocletian persecution (304) at ROME at the age of 14. His day is 12 May, and he is usually represented as a boy with a sword in one hand and a palm-branch in the other.

The first church to be consecrated in England by St. AUGUSTINE, at Canterbury, was dedicated to St. Pancras.

Pandarus. In Greek legend, a Lycian leader and ally of the Trojans. Owing to his later connexion with the story of TROILUS and CRESSIDA, he was taken over by the romance-writers of the MIDDLE AGES

as a procurer. *See* PANDER.

Pandects of Justinian (Gr. *pandektes*, all-receiving, all-containing). The great compendium or DIGEST of Roman law made in the 6th century by order of Justinian, consisting of 50 books. These superseded all previous law books and decisions in his empire. *Cp.* CODE NAPOLÉON *under* NAPOLEON.

Pandemonium (Gr., all the demons). A wild, unrestrained uproar, a tumultuous assembly, the word was first used by MILTON as the name of the principal city in HELL. It was formed on the analogy of PANTHEON.

> The rest were all
> Far to the inland retired, about the walls
> Of Pandemonium city and proud seat
> Of Lucifer.
> *Paradise Lost*, X, 424 (*see also* I, 756).

Pander. To pander to one's vices is to act as an agent to them, and such an agent is termed a pander, from PANDARUS, who procures for TROILUS the love of CRESSIDA. In Shakespeare's *Much Ado About Nothing* it is said that Troilus was "the first employer of pandars" (V, ii).

Pandora's Box. A present which seems valuable, but which in reality is a curse; like that of MIDAS, who found his very food became GOLD, and so uneatable.

To punish PROMETHEUS, ZEUS ordered HEPHÆSTUS to fashion a beautiful woman who was named Pandora (*i.e.* the All-gifted), because each of the gods gave her some power which was to bring about the ruin of man. According to Hesiod, she was the first mortal female and was sent by Zeus as a gift to Epimetheus who married her, against the advice of his brother, Prometheus. She brought with her a large jar or vase (Pandora's box) which she opened and all the evils flew forth, and they have ever since continued to afflict the world. Hope alone remained in the box.

Pangloss, Dr. (Gr., all tongues). The pedantic old tutor to the hero in VOLTAIRE'S CANDIDE, *ou l'Optimisme* (1759). His great point was his incurable and misleading OPTIMISM; it did him no good and brought him all sorts of misfortune, but to the end he reiterated "all is for the best in this best of all possible worlds". This was an attack upon the current theories of Leibnitz.

Panhandle. In the U.S.A., a narrow strip of territory belonging to one State which runs between two others, such as the Texas Panhandle, the Panhandle of Idaho, etc.

A **panhandler**, however, is not an inhabitant of such territory, but American slang for a street-beggar, perhaps from carrying a pan or tin for the reception of any oddments he may be given.

Panic. The word comes from the god PAN because the sounds heard by night in the mountains and valleys, which give rise to sudden and unwarranted fear, were attributed to him. There are various legends accounting for the name; one is that BACCHUS, in his eastern expeditions, was opposed by an army far superior to his own, and Pan advised him to command all his men at dead of night to raise a simultaneous shout. The innumerable echoes made the enemy think they were surrounded on all sides, and they took to sudden flight. Another belief is that he could make men, cattle, etc., bolt in "Panic" terror. *Cp.* Judges vii, 18-21.

Panjandrum. A pretentious or pompous official, a local "potentate". The word occurs in Samuel Foote's farrago of nonsense which he composed to test old Macklin (*c.* 1697–1797), the actor, who said he had brought his memory to such perfection that he could remember anything by reading it over once. There is more than one version of the following test passage:

> So she went into the garden to cut a cabbage-leaf to make an apple-pie, and at the same time a great she-bear came running up the street and popped its head into the shop. "What! no soap?" So he died, and she—very imprudently— married the barber. And there were present the Picninnies, Jobillies, the Garyulies, and the Grand Panjandrum himself, with the little red button a-top, and they all fell to playing the game of catch-as-catch-can till the gunpowder ran out at the heels of their boots.

It is said that Macklin was so indignant at this nonsense that he refused to repeat a word of it.

Panope. *See* NEREIDS.

Panopticon (Gr. *pan*, all; *optikos*, of

sight). Jeremy Bentham's name for his proposed circular prison with a warder's well in the centre for the inspection of convicts. The Royal Panopticon of Science and Art, in Leicester Square, was opened in 1854 as a place of popular instruction and a home for the sciences and music. It was built in the Moorish style but failed in its original intention. It was renamed the ALHAMBRA in 1858 and became a theatre in 1871; it was burnt down in 1882 and finally demolished in 1936. *See* UTILITARIANISM.

Pantables. *See* PANTOFLES.

Pantagruel. The principal character in Rabelais' great satire *The History of Gargantua and Pantagruel* (the first part published in 1532, the last posthumously in 1564). He was King of Dipsodes and son of GARGANTUA and by some identified with Henri II of France. He was the last of the giants, and Rabelais says he got his name from the Gr. *panta*, all, and Arab. *gruel*, thirsty, because he was born during the drought which lasted thirty and six months, three weeks, four days, thirteen hours, and a little more, in that year of grace noted for having "three Thursdays in one week". Though he was chained in his cradle with four great iron chains, like those used in ships, he stamped out the bottom, which was made of weavers' beams. When he grew to manhood he knew all languages, all sciences, and all knowledge of every sort, out-Solomoning SOLOMON in wisdom. His immortal achievement was his voyage to UTOPIA in quest of the ORACLE OF THE HOLY BOTTLE. *See* PANURGE.

> Wouldst thou not issue forth ...
> To see the third part of this earthy cell
> Of the brave acts of good Pantagruel.
> RABELAIS: *To the Spirit of the Queen of Navarre.*

Pantagruelism. Coarse and boisterous buffoonery and humour, especially with a serious purpose—like that for which PANTAGRUEL was famous.

Pantaloon. Breeches, trousers, underdrawers or *pants*, get their name from *Pantaloon*, a lean and foolish old Venetian of 16th-century Italian comedy, who was dressed in loose trousers and slippers. His name is said to come from

San Pantaleone (a patron SAINT of physicians and very popular in Venice), and he was adopted in later harlequinades and PANTOMIMES as the butt of the clown's jokes.

Pantechnicon (păn tek' ni kòn) (Gr., belonging to all the arts). The name was originally coined for a bazaar for the sale of artistic work built about 1830 in Motcomb Street, Belgrave Square; as this was unsuccessful, the building was converted into a warehouse for storing furniture, and the name retained. It is now often used in place of *pantechnicon van*, a furniture-removing van.

Pantheism. The doctrine that God is everything and everything is God; a monistic theory elaborated by Spinoza, who by his doctrine of the Infinite Substance sought to overcome the opposition between mind and matter, body and soul. It also denotes PAGAN worship of all the gods. *Cp.* DUALISM.

Pantheon (Gr. *pan*, all; *theos*, god). A temple dedicated to all the gods; especially that at ROME built by Hadrian (*c.* 120 A.D.), its predecessor (begun by Agrippa in 27 B.C.) having been largely destroyed by fire. It is circular and over 140 ft. in diameter and of similar height. Since the early 7th century, as Santa Maria Rotunda, it has been used as a Christian Church. Among the national heroes buried there are Raphael, Victor Emmanuel II, and Humbert I. Hadrian also built the Pantheon at ATHENS. *See also* BARBARI.

The Panthéon at PARIS was originally the church of Ste. GENEVIÈVE, started by Louis XV in 1764 and completed in 1812. In 1791 the CONSTITUENT ASSEMBLY renamed it the Panthéon and decreed that men who had deserved well of their country should be buried there. Among them are Rousseau, VOLTAIRE, and Victor Hugo. Hence, a building to commemorate national heroes, or a MAUSOLEUM for such. Thus Westminster Abbey is sometimes called "The British Pantheon".

The Pantheon opened in Oxford Street in 1772 was built by Wyatt for musical promenades, and was much patronized by those of rank and fashion. It was converted into a theatre for Italian opera in 1791 and the orchestra included Cramer, La Motte, and Cervetto. It was burned down in 1792, rebuilt in 1795 as a theatre, etc., eventually becoming a bazaar in 1835 and subsequently being used for business premises. The original building was ornamented with Grecian reliefs, and statues of classical deities, Britannia, George III and Queen Charlotte.

Panther (earlier **Panthera**). In mediæval times this animal was supposed to be friendly to all beasts except the DRAGON, and to attract them by a peculiarly sweet odour it exhaled. Swinburne, in *Laus Veneris*, gives this characteristic a more sinister significance:

> As one who hidden in deep sedge and reeds
> Smells the rare scent made when the panther feeds,
> And tracking ever slotwise the warm smell
> Is snapped upon by the warm mouth and bleeds,
> His head far down the hot sweet throat of her—
> So one tracks love, whose breath is deadlier.

In the old *Physiologus*, the panther was the type of Christ, but later, when the savage nature of the beast became more widely known, it became symbolical of EVIL and hypocritical flattery; hence Lyly's comparison (in *Euphues, The Anatomy of Wit*) of the beauty of women to "a delicate bait with a deadly hook, a sweet panther with a devouring paunch, a sour poison in a silver pot".

The mediæval idea perhaps arose from the name which is taken from Gr. *panther*, all beasts. *See also* REYNARD'S WONDERFUL COMB *under* COMB.

Pantile. A roofing-tile curved transversely to an ogee shape. In the 18th century as DISSENTERS' chapels (and also cottages) were frequently roofed with these, such meeting-houses were sometimes called *pantile-shops*, and the word was used in the sense of dissenting. Mrs. Centlivre, in *A Gotham Election* (1715), contrasts the *pantile crew* with a good churchman.

Pantisocracy (Gr., all of equal power). The name given by Coleridge to the communistic, Utopian society that he, with Southey, George Burnett, and others intended (*c.* 1794) to form on the banks of the Susquehannah River. The scheme came to nothing owing chiefly to the absence of funds.

Pantomime. According to etymology this should be all dumb show, but the word was commonly applied to an adaptation of the old Commedia dell'Arte that lasted down to the 19th century. The principal characters are HARLEQUIN and COLUMBINE, who never speak, and Clown and PANTALOON, who keep up a constant fire of joke and repartee. The old Christmas pantomime or harlequinade as an essentially British entertainment was first introduced by John Weaver (1673–1760), a dancing-master of Shrewsbury, in 1702. It is now usually based on a nursery tale such as CINDERELLA, Mother Goose, JACK AND THE BEANSTALK, PUSS IN BOOTS, etc., enlivened by catchy songs, pretty chorus girls and considerable buffoonery.

Panurge (Gr. *pan*, all; *ergos*, worker); the "all-doer", *i.e.* the rogue, he who will "do anything or anyone". The roguish companion of PANTAGRUEL, and one of the principal characters in Rabelais's satire. A desperate rake, always in debt, he had a dodge for every scheme, knew everything and something more, and was a boon companion of the mirthfullest temper and most licentious bias; but was timid of danger and a desperate coward. He consulted LOTS, dreams, etc., and finally the ORACLE OF THE HOLY BOTTLE; and found insuperable objections to every one of its obscure answers.

Paper. Not worth the paper it is written on. Said of an utterly worthless statement, promise, etc.

On paper. In writing: as opposed to verbally.

Paper blockade. A blockade proclaimed but not backed up by suitable means of enforcement.

Paper credit. Credit allowed on the score of bills, promissory notes, etc., that show that money is due to the borrower.

Paper money, or **currency.** Bank notes as opposed to coin, or bills used as currency.

Paper profits. Hypothetical profits shown on a company's prospectus, etc.

Paper tiger. One who, or that which, seems strong, forceful or powerful, but is in fact feeble or ineffective—a balloon when pricked.

To paper a house. In theatrical phraseology, to fill the theatre with "deadheads", or non-paying spectators, admitted by paper orders.

To paper over the cracks. To prevent an open breach, by a temporary expedient or settlement unlikely to last, and to ignore the fundamental points at issue which require more radical treatment. So Bismarck alluded to the convention of Gastein of August 1865, after the defeat of Denmark, by which Austria was to administer Holstein, and Prussia, Denmark. "We have", he said, "papered over the cracks." The Austro-Prussian War broke out in June 1866. The allusion is to the decorator who papers over the cracks in a wall without bothering to repair them, thus only effecting a makeshift job.

To send in, to receive one's papers. To resign one's appointment, commission, etc., or to receive one's dismissal.

Paphian (pā' fi àn). Relating to VENUS, or rather to Paphos, a city of Cyprus, where Venus was worshipped; a Cyprian; a prostitute.

Paracelsus. The name coined for himself by Theophrastus Bombastus von Hohenheim (1490–1541) implying that he was superior to Celsus, the famous writer and physician of the 1st century. He studied chemistry and ALCHEMY and after experience of mining became a medical practitioner. He made many enemies owing to his disputatious temperament and flouting of academic traditions, and wrote numerous treatises propounding his theories which showed a keen concern for the development of medicine. He was essentially a Neoplatonist and held that, as man contained all elements, a knowledge of alchemy and the physical sciences was necessary for the treatment of disease. He did much to encourage innovation, but his work was marred by a certain element of charlatanism and superstition.

Paraclete. The advocate; one called to aid or support another; from Gr. *paraka-*

lein, to call to. The word is used as a title of the HOLY GHOST, the Comforter.

> O source of uncreated Light
> The Father's promised paraclete!
> DRYDEN: *Veni, Creator Spiritus.*

See also ABELARD AND HÉLOÏSE.

Paradise The Greeks borrowed this word from the Persians, among whom it denoted the enclosed and extensive parks and pleasure grounds of the Persian kings. The SEPTUAGINT translators adopted it for the garden of EDEN, and in the NEW TESTAMENT and by early Christian writers it was applied to HEAVEN, the abode of the blessed dead.

A fool's paradise. *See under* FOOL.

The Paradise of Fools. *See* LIMBUS OF FOOLS *under* LIMBO.

Paradise and the Peri. *See under* PERI.

Paradise Lost. MILTON's epic poem was first published in 1667. It tells the story:

> Of Man's first disobedience and the fruit
> Of that forbidden tree whose mortal taste
> Brought death into the World, and all our woe
> With loss of Eden.

Milton borrowed largely from the epic of Du Bartas (1544–1590), entitled *The First Week of Creation* which was translated into almost every European language; and he was indebted to St. Avitus (d. 523), who wrote in Latin hexameters *The Creation, The Fall*, and *The Expulsion from Paradise*, for his description of Paradise (Bk. I), of Satan (Bk. II), and other parts.

In 1671 *Paradise Regained* (in four books) was published. The subject is the Temptation. Eve, being tempted, fell, and lost Paradise; Jesus, being tempted, resisted, and regained Paradise.

Paradise shoots. The lign aloe; said to be the only plant descended to us from the Garden of EDEN. When ADAM left Paradise he took a shoot of this tree, and from it the lign aloes have been propagated.

The Earthly Paradise. It was a popular mediæval belief that paradise, a land or island where everything was beautiful and restful, and where death and decay were unknown, still existed somewhere on earth. It was usually located far away

to the east and in 9th-century maps it is shown in China, and the fictitious letter of PRESTER JOHN to the Emperor Emmanuel Comnenus states that it was within three days' journey of his own territory—a "fact" that is corroborated by MANDEVILLE. The Hereford map (13th century) shows it as a circular island near India. *Cp.* BRANDAN, ST.

Paraphernalia (păr á fĕr nā´ lyà) (Gr. *para*, beside; *pherne*, dowry). Literally, all that a married woman could legally claim as her own, *i.e.* personal articles, wearing apparel, jewellery, etc. Hence, personal attire, articles in general, anything for show or decoration.

Parcæ. *See* FATES.

Parchment. Made from the skins of animals and is so called from Pergamum, in Mysia, Asia Minor, where it was used for writing material when Ptolemy prohibited the exportation of PAPYRUS from Egypt.

Pardon Bell. The ANGELUS bell. So called because of the INDULGENCE once given for reciting certain prayers forming the Angelus.

Pardoner. A mediæval cleric licensed to preach and collect money for a definite object such as a CRUSADE or the building of a church, for contributing to which letters of INDULGENCE were exchanged. By many they were regarded as licences to sin and were denounced by Chaucer, Langland, and Wycliff.

The pardoner's mitten. Whoever put this mitten on would be sure to thrive in all things.

> He that his hondë put in this metayn,
> He shal have multiplying of his grayn,
> Whan he hath sowen, be it whete or otes,
> So that he offre pans [pence] or ellës grootes.
> CHAUCER: *Prologue to the Pardoner's Tale.*

Pari passu (Lat., at the same pace). At the same time; in equal degrees. Two or more schemes carried on at once and driven forward with equal energy are said to be carried on *pari passu*.

Pariah. A low-caste Hindu of southern India, from a native word meaning "a drummer", because such Hindus beat the drums at certain festivals. Europeans extended the term to those of no caste at all; hence its application to outcasts generally. *Cp.* UNTOUCHABLES.

Parian. Pertaining to the island of *Paros*, one of the Cyclades, renowned for its white marble; hence a fine white porcelain used for making statuettes, vases, etc.

Parian Chronicle. One of the ARUNDELIAN MARBLES, found on the island of *Paros*, and bearing an inscription which contains a chronological register of the chief events of the mythology and history of ancient Greece from the reign of Cecrops (*c.* 1580 B.C.) to the archonship of Diognetus (264 B.C.), of which approximately the last 100 years is missing.

Paris. In Greek legend, the son of PRIAM, King of TROY, and HECUBA; and through his abduction of HELEN the cause of the siege of Troy. Hecuba dreamed that she was to bring forth a firebrand, and as this was interpreted to mean that the unborn child would bring destruction to his house, the infant Paris was exposed on Mount IDA. He was, however, brought up by a shepherd and grew to perfection of beautiful manhood. At the judgment on the APPLE OF DISCORD, HERA, APHRODITE, and ATHENE had each offered him a bribe—the first power, the second the most beautiful of women, and the third martial glory. In return for her victory, Aphrodite assisted him in the abduction of Helen, for whom he deserted his wife ŒNONE, daughter of the river-god, Cebren. At Troy, Paris, having killed ACHILLES, was fatally wounded with a poisoned arrow by PHILOCTETES at the taking of the city.

Paris, the capital of France (*see* LUTETIA). Rabelais gives a whimsical derivation of the name. He tells (I, xvii) how GARGANTUA played a disgusting practical joke on the Parisians who came to stare at him, and the men said that it was a sport *"par ris"* (to be laughed at); wherefore the city was called Par'is.

The heraldic device of the city of Paris is a ship. As Sauval says, *"L'île de la cité est faite comme un grand navire enfoncé dans la vase, échoué au fil de l'eau vers le milieu de la Seine."* This form of a ship struck the authorities, who, in the later MIDDLE AGES, emblazoned it on the shield of the city.

The Parisian Wedding. The massacre of St. BARTHOLOMEW which took place (24 August 1572) during the festivities at the marriage of Henry of Navarre and Margaret of France.

Parkinson's Law. As satirically promulgated by C. Northcote Parkinson in his book with that title (1957), it states that the amount of work done is in inverse proportion to the number of people employed; in other words, something similar to the Law of Diminishing Returns takes effect. The "law" is directed mainly at public administration, but it is aimed also at inefficient business administration.

Parlement. Under the old régime in France, the sovereign court of justice at Paris, where councillors were allowed to plead, and where justice was administered in the king's name. It was a development of the *curia regis*.

Parliament (Fr. *parlement*, Med. Lat. *parliamentum*, a talk, meeting, discussion). Its application to assemblies of the king and his magnates, etc., becomes common in 13th-century England and a representative element was introduced at these meetings. It became an established institution during the 14th century.

A number of Parliaments have been given characteristic names for various reasons. *See under* ADDLED; BAREBONES; CAVALIER; CONVENTION; DEVIL'S; DRUNKEN; DUNCES; GOOD; GRATTAN'S; LONG; MAD; MERCILESS; MODEL; MONGREL; PENSIONARY; RUMP; SHORT; UNLEARNED; USELESS; WONDERMAKING, etc.

A hung Parliament. One in which no party has an overall majority and that which forms the government is dependent on the support of one or more of the smaller parties. Such a government is likely to prove unstable and is usually due to the existence of minority parties, especially where there is proportional representation.

Parliamentary language, *i.e.* restrained and seemly language, such as is properly required of any member speaking in Parliament.

Parlour. Originally the reception room in

a monastery, etc., where the inmates could see and speak (Fr. *parler*) to their friends.

Parlour tricks. Accomplishments that are useful in company, at parties, etc. "Don't try any of your parlour tricks here" is used in the sense of, "Don't try any of your games or nonsense with me".

Parnassus. A mountain near DELPHI, Greece, with two summits, one of which was consecrated to APOLLO and the MUSES, the other to BACCHUS. It is supposedly named from Parnassus, a son of NEPTUNE, and DEUCALION's ark came to rest there after the flood. Owing to its connexion with the Muses it came to be regarded as the seat of poetry and music, hence **To climb Parnassus** is "to write poetry".

Parnassian School. The name given to a group of French poets flourishing from about 1850 to 1890, from a collection of their poems entitled *Le Parnasse contemporain* (1866). They included Théophile Gautier, Leconte de Lisle, Baudelaire, François Coppée, Sully Prudhomme and Verlaine.

They were nicknamed *les impassibles* for their supposed devotion to "art for art's sake" and represented a reaction against the romanticism of Hugo and Lamartine.

In England, the group of poets following Rossetti and William Morris have sometimes been referred to as "the Parnassians". *Cp.* PRE-RAPHAELITE BROTHERHOOD.

Parolles (pà rol' ēz). **He was a mere Parolles.** A pretender, a man of words, and a pedant. The allusion is to the faithless, bragging, slandering villain who dubs himself "captain", pretends to knowledge which he has not, and to sentiments he never feels, in SHAKESPEARE's *All's Well That Ends Well*.

Parr. Thomas Parr, the "old, old, very old man", was said to have lived in the reigns of ten sovereigns, to have done penance for incontinence at the age of 105, to have married a second wife when he was 122 years old, and to have had a child by her. He was a husbandman, reputedly born at Alberbury, near Shrewsbury, in 1483, and died in 1635.

He was taken to the court of CHARLES I by the Earl of Arundel in 1635, and the change of his mode of life killed him. He was buried in the south transept of Westminster Abbey. There is no real evidence supporting his alleged age of 152, but he was doubtless a very old man. *See* LONGEVITY.

Parsees. GUEBRES or fire-worshippers; descendants of Persians who fled to India during the Mohammedan persecution of the 7th and 8th centuries, and still adherents of Zoroastrianism. The word means *People of Pars, i.e.* Persia. *See* TOWERS OF SILENCE *under* SILENCE.

Parsifal, Parsival. *See* PERCIVAL, SIR.

Parsley. He has need now of nothing but a little parsley, *i.e.* he is dead. A Greek saying; the Greeks decked tombs with parsley, because it keeps green a long time.

Parson's nose. The rump of a fowl. Also called the "POPE's nose".

Part. A portion, a piece, a fragment.

For my part. As far as concerns me.

For the most part. Generally, as a rule.

In good part. Favourably, graciously, not to be offended though one might well be. **To take in ill** or **bad part** has the opposite meaning.

Part and parcel. An essential part, portion, or element.

Parts of speech. A grammatical class of words of a particular character. The old rhyme by which children used to be taught the parts of speech is:

Three little words you often see
Are ARTICLES, *a, an*, and *the*.
A NOUN's the name of anything;
As *school* or *garden, hoop* or *swing*.
ADJECTIVES tell the kind of noun;
As *great, small, pretty, white*, or *brown*.
Instead of nouns the PRONOUNS stand;
Her head, *his* face, *our* arms, *your* hand.
VERBS tell of something being done;
To *read, count, sing, laugh, jump,* or *run*.
How things are done the ADVERBS tell;
As *slowly, quickly, ill,* or *well*.
CONJUNCTIONS join the words together;
As, men *and* women, wind *or* weather.
The PREPOSITION stands before
A noun, as *in* or *through* a door.
The INTERJECTION shows surprise;
As, *oh*! how pretty! *ah*! how wise!
The whole are called nine parts of speech,
Which reading, writing, speaking teach.

Lines 7 and 8 are now completely

misleading as the so-called "pronouns" here function as possessive adjectives; but it must be remembered that *her, his, our, your,* etc., were formerly regarded as personal pronouns of the possessive or genitive case.

Part up! Slang for "hand over", as in, "If you don't part up with the money, there will be trouble". An extension of the use is the old saying (George Buchanan, tutor to James VI), *A fool and his money are soon parted.*

Till death us do part. *See* DEPART.

To play a part. To perform some duty or pursue some course of action; also, to act deceitfully. The phrase is from the stage, where an actor's *part* is the words or the character assigned to him.

To take part. To assist; to participate.

To take the part of. To side with, to support the cause of.

A man of parts. An accomplished man; one who is clever, talented, or of high intellectual ability.

The parting of the ways. Said of a critical moment when one has to choose between two different courses of action. The allusion, of course, is to a place at which a road branches off in different directions.

Parthenon (par' the non) (Gr., "The maiden's chamber"). The great temple of ATHENE at ATHENS, many of the sculptured friezes and fragments of pediments of which are now in the BRITISH MUSEUM among the ELGIN MARBLES. The temple was begun by the architect Ictinus about 445 B.C. and was mainly embellished by Phidias, whose colossal chryselephantine statue of Athene was its chief treasure. The Parthenon was destroyed during the siege of Athens in 1687 by the Venetians, when the powder stored in it by the Turks exploded.

Parthenope (par then' ō pi). Naples; so called from Parthenope, the SIREN, who threw herself into the sea out of love for ULYSSES, and was cast up in the Bay of Naples. Parthenope was an early Greek settlement, later called *Palæopolis* (the old city), after subsequent settlers had established *Neapolis* (the new city), from which Naples derives its name.

Parthian shot, or **shaft.** A parting shot; a telling or wounding remark made on de-

parture, giving one's adversary no time to reply. An allusion to the ancient practice of Parthian horsemen turning in flight, to discharge arrows and missiles at their pursuers.

Parti pris (par' ti prē) (Fr., choice or side having been taken). A preconceived opinion, bias.

Particularists. Those who hold the doctrine of particular election and redemption, *i.e.* the election and redemption of some, not all, of the human race.

Partington. Dame Partington and her mop. A taunt against those who try to withstand progress or the inevitable. Sidney SMITH speaking at Taunton in October 1831, on the rejection of the Reform Bill by the Lords, compared them to Dame Partington, who, during a great storm at Sidmouth in 1824, tried to push back the Atlantic with her mop. "She was excellent at a slop, or a puddle," he said, "but she should not have meddled with a tempest. Gentlemen, be at your ease—be quiet and steady. You will beat Mrs. Partington."

Partlet (O.Fr. *Pertelote*, a feminine proper name). A neckerchief or ruff worn in the 16th century by women. Also used as the name of a hen with reference to the frill-like feathers round the neck of some hens. The hen in Chaucer's *Nun's Priest's Tale* is called Partlet.

Partridge, always partridge! *See* PERDRIX.

Parturient montes, etc. *See* THE MOUNTAIN IN LABOUR *under* MOUNTAIN.

Party. Party line. The official "line" or policy of a political party; also a telephone line shared by two or more subscribers. **To toe the party line** is to follow or be coerced into following party policy.

Parvenu (par' ve nū) (Fr., arrived). An upstart; one who has risen from the ranks. The word was made popular in France by Marivaux's *Paysan Parvenu* (1735).

Parvis (par' vis) (*Parvisus*, a Low Latin corruption of *paradisus*, a church close, especially the court in front of St. Peter's at ROME in the MIDDLE AGES). The "place" or court before the main entrance of a cathedral. In the parvis of St. Paul's lawyers used to meet for consultation as brokers do in exchange. The word is now applied to the room above the church porch.

> A sergeant of lawe, war and wys,
> That often hadde ben atte parvys.
> CHAUCER: *Canterbury Tales*, line 309.

Pasch. EASTER, from the Greek form of the Hebrew *Pesach*, PASSOVER.

Pasch eggs, or **Pace eggs.** EASTER eggs, given as an emblem of the Resurrection.

Paschal Lamb. The lamb sacrificed and eaten at the Jewish PASSOVER. For Christians, Jesus Christ is called the *Paschal Lamb* because He was called the "Lamb of God" by *John* (i, 29) and in allusion to I *Cor*. v, 7—"For even Christ our passover is sacrificed for us."

In HERALDRY, a white lamb *passant* carrying a banner of St. GEORGE.

Pasha (păsh′ a). A Turkish title borne by governors of provinces and certain military and civil officers of high rank. There were three grades of pashas, which were distinguished by the number of horsetails carried before them and planted in front of their tents. The highest rank were those of *three tails*; the grand VIZIER was always such a pasha, as also were commanding generals and admirals; generals of divisions, etc., were pashas of *two tails*; and generals of brigades, rear-admirals, and petty provincial governors were pashas of *one tail*. *Cp*. BASHAW.

Pasiphæ (păs′ i fē). In Greek legend, a daughter of the SUN and wife of MINOS, King of Crete. She was the mother of ARIADNE, and also through intercourse with a white bull (given by POSEIDON to Minos) of the MINOTAUR.

Pasque eggs. *See* PASCH EGGS.

Pasquinade (păs kwin ād′). A LAMPOON or political squib, having ridicule for its object; so called from Pasquino, an Italian tailor or barber of the 15th century, noted for his caustic wit. After his death, a mutilated statue was dug up and placed near the Piazza Navona. As it was not clear whom the statue represented, and as it stood opposite Pasquin's house, it came to be called "Pasquin". The people of ROME affixed their political, religious, and personal satires to it, hence the name. At the other end

of the city was an ancient statue of MARS, called *Marforio*, to which were affixed replies to the Pasquinades.

Pass. A pretty pass. A difficult or deplorable state of affairs.

To pass current. To be generally accepted as genuine or credible.

To pass the buck. To evade responsibility, to pass responsibility on to someone else. An American phrase, coming from the game of poker. The "buck", perhaps a piece of buckshot or a "bucktail", was passed from one player to another as a reminder that the recipient was to be the next dealer. The earliest recorded use of the phrase is by Mark Twain in 1872.

To pass the time of day. To exchange a greeting by some remark appropriate to the time of day or the weather, as "Good morning", "It's a lovely day", etc.

Passing Bell. *See under* BELL.

Passim (păs′ im) (Lat., here and there, in many places). A direction often found in annotated books which tells the reader that reference to the matter in hand will be found in many passages in the book mentioned.

Passion, The. The sufferings of Jesus Christ which had their culmination in His death on the CROSS.

Passion Flower. A plant of the genus *Passiflora*, whose flowers bear a fancied resemblance to the instruments of the PASSION. *Cp*. PIKE. It seems to have been given the name by 16th-century Spanish missionaries to South Africa.

> The *leaf* symbolizes the spear.
> The five *petals* and five *sepals*, the ten apostles
> (Peter who denied, and Judas who betrayed, being omitted).
> The five *anthers*, the five wounds.
> The *tendrils*, the scourges.
> The column of the *ovary*, the pillar of the cross.
> The *stamens*, the hammers.
> The three *stigmas*, the three nails.
> The *filaments* within the flower, the crown of thorns.
> The *calyx*, the glory or nimbus.
> The *white* tint, purity.
> The *blue* tint, HEAVEN.

It keeps open three days, symbolizing the three years' ministry.

Passion Play. A development of the mediæval MYSTERY play with especial reference to the story of our Lord's passion and death. The best-known survival of such plays, which were common in 14th-century France, is the Oberammergau Passion Play, which takes place every ten years. In 1633 the BLACK DEATH swept over the village of Oberammergau; when it abated the inhabitants vowed to enact the PASSION every ten years and this has been done with one or two exceptions. It is now a highly commercial undertaking although the cast is still taken from the villagers.

Passion Sunday. *See* JUDICA.

Passionists. Members of the Congregation of Discalced Clerks of the Most Holy Cross and Passion of Our Lord Jesus Christ, founded by St. Paul of the Cross in 1720. The first house, at Monte Argentario, an island off the coast of Tuscany, was opened in 1737. Their chief work is in the holding of retreats and missions. The fathers wear on the breast of their black habit a white heart with the inscription *Jesu Xpi Passio*, surmounted by a CROSS.

Passover. A Jewish festival to commemorate the deliverance of the Israelites, when the ANGEL of death (that slew the firstborn of the Egyptians) passed over their houses, and spared all who did as MOSES commanded them. The festival began on 14th of Nisan (*i.e.* about 12 April) when the PASCHAL LAMB was eaten, and the Festival of Unleavened Bread lasted seven days.

Patch. Cross-patch. An ill-tempered person.

Face patches. One of the more absurd fashions of the 17th and early 18th centuries was the wearing of face patches by women and sometimes by men. Round black patches were the most popular but diamond and other shapes were also used, sometimes to hide blemishes but usually intended as an adornment.

Not a patch upon. Not to be compared with; as, "His horse is not a patch upon mine."

To patch up a quarrel. To arrange the matter in a not very satisfactory way; a coat that has been torn and then "patched up" is pretty sure to break out again; so is a quarrel. *Cp.* PAPER OVER THE CRACKS.

Patent (through Fr. from Lat. *patentem*, lying open). Open to the perusal of anybody. A thing that is *patented* is protected by LETTERS PATENT.

Letters patent. Documents from the SOVEREIGN or a crown office conferring a title, right, privilege, etc., such as a title of nobility, or the exclusive right to make or sell for a given number of years some new invention. So called because they are written upon open sheets of parchment, with the seal of the sovereign or party by whom they were issued pendent at the bottom.

Patent Rolls. CHANCERY enrolment of LETTERS PATENT under the GREAT SEAL collected on parchment rolls and first dating from 1201. Each roll contains a year, though in some cases the roll is subdivided into two or more parts. Each sheet of parchment is numbered and called a membrane; for example the 8th sheet, say, of the 10th year of Henry III is cited thus: "Pat. 10 Hen. III, m.8". If the document is on the back of the roll it is called *dorso*, and "d" is added to the citation. Patents of invention were last enrolled in 1853 and they are now registered at the Patent Office. *Cp.* CLOSE ROLLS.

Paternoster (Lat., Our Father). The Lord's Prayer; from the first two words in the Latin version. Every eleventh bead of a ROSARY is so called, because at that bead the Lord's Prayer is repeated; the name is also given to a certain kind of fishing tackle, in which hooks and weights to suit them are fixed alternately on the line somewhat in rosary fashion.

Pathetic Fallacy. A term coined by John Ruskin (1819–1900) to describe the figure of speech that attributes human feelings to nature.

Patient Grisel. *See* GRISELDA.

Patmos. The island of the Sporades in the Ægean Sea (now called *Patmo* or *Patino*), to which St. JOHN retired—or was exiled (*Rev.* i, 9). Hence the name is used allusively for a place of banishment or solitude.

Patres Conscripti. *See* CONSCRIPT FATHERS.

Patriarch (Gr. *patria*, family; *archein*, to rule). The head of a tribe or family who rules by paternal right; applied specially

Patter

(after *Acts* vii, 8) to the twelve sons of
Jacob, and to ABRAHAM, Isaac, and Jacob and their forefathers. In one passage
(*Acts* ii, 29) David is spoken of as a patriarch.

In the early Church, "Patriarch", first
mentioned in the Council of Chalcedon,
but virtually existing from about the
time of the Council of Nicæa, was the
title of the highest Church officers. A
Patriarch ordained METROPOLITANS,
convened councils, received appeals,
and was the chief BISHOP over several
countries or provinces, as an archbishop
is over several dioceses. It was also the
title given by the POPES to the archbishops of Lisbon and Venice, in order
to make the patriarchal dignity appear
lower and distinct from the papal. It is
also the title of the chief bishop of various Eastern churches, as the JACOBITES,
Armenians and MARONITES.

In the ORTHODOX Eastern Church the
bishops of Constantinople, Alexandria,
Antioch, and JERUSALEM are patriarchs,
the Patriarch of Constantinople bearing
the style of Œcumenical Patriarch.
Within a religious order the title is given
to the founder, as St. Benedict, St.
FRANCIS, and St. DOMINIC.

Patrician. Properly, one of the *patres*
(fathers) or senators of ROME (*see* CON-
SCRIPT FATHERS), and their descendants. As for long they held all the honours of the state, the word came to signify the magnates or nobility of a nation,
the aristocrats or "patrician class". *Cp.*
PLEBEIAN; PROLETARIAT.

Patrick, St. The apostle and patron SAINT
of IRELAND (commemorated on 17
March) was not an Irishman but was
born at Bannavem (*c.* 389). Its location
is unknown but it may have been in Glamorgan and his father, Calpurnius, was
a Roman official and deacon. As a boy
he was captured in a Pictish raid and
sold as a slave in Ireland. He escaped to
GAUL where he probably studied in the
monastery of Lérins before returning to
Britain. After receiving a supernatural
call to preach to the heathen of Ireland,
he returned to Gaul and was ordained
deacon. He landed in Wicklow (432)
and going north converted the people of
ULSTER and later those of other parts of

Ireland. He established many communities and churches including the cathedral church of Armagh. He is said to
have died in 461 and to have been buried at Down in Ulster.

St. Patrick left his name to many
places and numerous legends are told of
his miraculous powers. Perhaps the best
known tradition is that he cleared Ireland of its vermin. The story goes that
one old SERPENT resisted him, so he
made a box and invited the serpent to
enter it. The serpent objected, saying it
was too small; but St. Patrick insisted it
was quite large enough to be comfortable. Eventually the serpent got in to
prove it was too small, whereupon St.
Patrick slammed down the lid and cast
the box into the sea.

In commemoration of this he is usually represented banishing the serpents,
and with a SHAMROCK leaf.

St. Patrick's Cross. The same shape as
St. Andrew's CROSS (X), only different
in colour, viz. red on a white ground.

St. Patrick's Purgatory. A cave on Station Island in Lough Derg, Co. Done-
gal, a resort of pilgrims from the 13th
century. The legend is that Christ revealed it to St. Patrick and told him that
all who visited it in penitence and faith
would gain a full INDULGENCE of their
sins and they would gain sight of the torments of HELL and the joys of HEAVEN.
Henry of Saltrey tells how Sir OWAIN visited it, and Fortunatus, of CHAP-BOOK
fame, was one of the adventurers. It
was blocked up by order of the POPE
on St. Patrick's Day, 1497. Calderón
(1600–1681) has a play on the subject,
El Purgatorio de San Patricio.

Patriots' Day. In the U.S.A. the anniversary of the battle of Lexington, 19 April
1775, the first battle in the War of Independence.

Patroclus. The gentle and amiable friend
of ACHILLES. When the latter refused to
fight in order to annoy AGAMEMNON, Patroclus appeared in the armour of
Achilles at the head of the MYRMIDONS
and was slain by HECTOR.

Patter. To chatter, to clack, also the running talk of CHEAP-JACKS, conjurers, entertainers and comedians, etc., is from
PATERNOSTER. When saying MASS the

769

priest often recited in a low rapid mechanical way until he came to the words "and lead us not into temptation", which he spoke clearly and deliberately.

The patter of feet, of rain, etc., is not connected with the above. It is a frequentative of *pat*, to strike gently.

Paul, St. Patron saint of preachers and tentmakers (see *Acts* xviii, 3). Originally called Saul, his name, according to tradition, was changed in honour of Sergius Paulus, whom he converted (*Acts* xiii, 6–12).

His symbols are a sword and open book, the former the instrument of his martyrdom and the latter indicative of the new law propagated by him as the apostle of the Gentiles. He is represented as of short stature, with bald head and grey, bushy beard; and legend relates that when he was beheaded at ROME (*c*. A.D. 66) after having converted one of NERO's favourite concubines, milk instead of blood flowed from his veins. He is commemorated on 25 January. *Cp.* WINIFRED.

St. Paul the Hermit. The first of the Egyptian hermits. When 113 years old, he was visited by St. ANTONY, himself over 90, and when he died in 341, St. Antony wrapped his body in the cloak given to him by St. Athanasius, and his grave was dug by two lions. He lived in a cave, and he is represented as an old man, clothed with palm-leaves, and seated under a palm-tree, near which are a river and loaf of bread.

A Paul's man. A braggart; a captain out of service, with a long rapier; so called because the Walk down the centre of Old St. Paul's LONDON, was at one time the haunt of stale knights and other characters. These loungers were also known as *Paul's Walkers*; Jonson called BOBADIL a Paul's man.

Paul's Cross. A pulpit in the open air situated on the north side of Old St. Paul's Cathedral, in which, from 1259 to 1643, eminent divines preached in the presence of the Lord Mayor and Aldermen every Sunday. The cross was demolished in 1643 by order of PARLIAMENT. A new pulpit and CROSS were erected on the site in 1910.

Paul Jones. A dance which became popular in Britain in the 1920s in which the ladies formed an outward facing circle moving in the opposite direction to the men, who faced inwards. The couples facing each other when the music stopped became partners for the next part of the dance, this pattern being repeated several times. It was earlier one of the "sets" in American barn-dancing, perhaps named after the naval adventurer John Paul Jones (1747–1792).

Paul Pry. *See* PRY.

To rob Peter to pay Paul. *See* ROB.

Pavan, or **Pavin** (pa' van). A stately Spanish dance of the 16th and 17th centuries, said to be so called because in it the dancers stalked like peacocks (Lat. *pavones*), the gentlemen with their long robes of office, and the ladies with trains like peacock's tails. The pavan, like the minuet, ended with a quick movement called the *galliard*, a sort of gavotte. The etymology is uncertain and it is also suggested that the name is from *Padova* (Padua).

Pawnbroker's Sign, The. *See* BALLS, THE THREE GOLDEN.

Pawnee (paw' nē). Anglo-Indian for water (Hind. *pani*, water). It is also the name of a North American Indian tribe.

Pax (păks) (Lat., peace). The "kiss of peace", which is given at MASS. It is omitted on MAUNDY THURSDAY.

Also a sacred utensil used when mass is celebrated by a high dignitary. It is sometimes a crucifix, sometimes a tablet, and sometimes a reliquary, and is handed round to be kissed as a symbolic substitute for the "kiss of peace".

The old custom of "kissing the bride", which took place immediately before the Communion of the newly married couple and still obtains in some churches, is derived from the Salisbury rubric concerning the Pax in the Missa Sponsalium:

> Tunc amoto pallio, surgant ambo sponsus et sponsa; et accipiat sponsus pacem a sacerdote, et ferat sponsæ osculans eam et neminem alium, nec ipse, nec ipsa; sed statim diaconus vel clericus a presbytero pacem accipiens, ferat aliis sicut solitum est.

Pax! The schoolboy's cry of truce.

Pax Britannica. The peace formerly imposed by British rule in her colonial empire. The phrase is modelled on the Latin **Pax Romana**, the peace existing between the different parts of the Roman empire.

> The *pax Britannica* was an umbrella that sheltered all colonists, one which they neither wished nor could afford to dispense with.
>
> A.P. THORNTON: *The Imperial Idea and Its Enemies*, iii.

Pax vobis(cum) (Peace be unto you). The formula used by a BISHOP instead of "The Lord be with you", wherever this versicle occurs in Divine service. They are the words used by Christ to His APOSTLES on the first EASTER morning.

Pay. He who pays the piper calls the tune. The one who foots the bill has the control. The allusion is obvious.

Here's the devil to pay, and no pitch hot. *See under* DEVIL.

I'll pay him out. I'll be a match for him, I'll punish him.

To pay in his own coin. To treat him as he has treated you; to settle with him by the methods he himself employs; a TIT FOR TAT.

To pay off old scores. *See under* SCORE.

To pay on the nail. *See under* NAIL.

To pay out a rope is to let it out gradually.

To pay with the roll of the drum. Not to pay at all. No soldier can be arrested for debt when on the march.

Who's to pay the piper? Who is to pay the score? When a piper amused guests at inns or on the green he expected payment for his efforts.

You can put paid to that. You can treat it as finished, it's all over and done with. A phrase from the counting-house; when "Paid" is put to an account it is settled. Similarly **that's put paid to him** means "that's settled him".

Pay dirt. A mining term for ground which pays for working.

Payload. The goods or passengers carried in a ship, aeroplane, etc., which pay for their carriage, as opposed to crew and equipment, etc.

Paynim (pā′ nim), from the O.Fr. *paienime*, Lat. *paganismus*, a heathen, was the recognized chivalric term for a MOSLEM.

Peace. A Bill of Peace. A bill intended to secure relief from perpetual litigation. It is brought by one who wishes to establish and perpetuate a right which he claims, but which, from its nature, is controversial.

Justices of the Peace. *See under* JUSTICE.

Peace at any price. Lord Palmerston sneered at the QUAKER statesman John Bright, as a "peace-at-any-price man". *Cp.* CONCHY.

> Though not a "peace-at-any-price" man, I am not ashamed to say I am a peace-at-almost-any-price man.
>
> LORD AVEBURY: *The Use of Life*, xi (1894).

Peace in our time. The unfortunate phrase used by Prime Minister Neville Chamberlain, on his return from MUNICH, 30 September 1938. It comes from the versicle in Morning Prayer, "Give peace in our time, O Lord."

Peace with honour. A phrase popularized by Lord Beaconsfield on his return from the Congress of Berlin (1878), when he said:

> Lord Salisbury and myself have brought you back peace—but a peace I hope with honour, which may satisfy our Sovereign and tend to the welfare of the country.

The Kiss of Peace. *See* PAX.

The Perpetual Peace. The peace concluded 24 June 1502 between ENGLAND and SCOTLAND, whereby Margaret, daughter of Henry VII, was betrothed to James IV of Scotland; but the Scots invaded England in 1513! The name has been given to other treaties, as that between Austria and Switzerland in 1474, and between France and Switzerland in 1516.

The Queen's, or **King's Peace.** The peace of law-abiding subjects; originally the protection secured by the king to those employed on his business.

If you want peace, prepare for war. A translation of the Latin proverb, *Si vis pacem, para bellum.* It goes a step further than the advice given by POLONIUS to his son (*Hamlet*, I, iii), for you are told, whether you are "in a quarrel" or not, always bear yourself so that all possible opposers "may beware of thee".

To hold one's peace. To keep silent, to refrain from speaking.

To keep the peace. To refrain from disturbing the public peace, to prevent strife or commotion. Wrongdoers are sometimes bound over to keep the peace for a certain time by a magistrate, subject to entering into a recognizance.

Peacock. A peacock in his pride. A peacock with his tail fully displayed.

By the peacock! An obsolete oath which at one time was thought to be blasphemous. The fabled incorruptibility of the peacock's flesh caused the bird to be adopted as a type of the resurrection.

There is a story that when George III had partly recovered from one of his bouts of "insanity" his Ministers got him to read the King's speech, and he ended every sentence with the word *peacock*. The Minister who drilled him said that *peacock* was an excellent word for ending a sentence, only kings should not let subjects hear it, but should whisper it softly. The resulting pause at the close of each sentence had an excellent effect.

The Peacock's feather. An emblem of vain-glory, and in some Eastern countries a mark of rank.

As a literary term the expression is used of a borrowed ornament of style spatchcocked into the composition; the allusion being to the fable of the jay who decked herself out in a peacock's feathers, making herself an object of ridicule.

The peacock's tail is an emblem of an EVIL EYE, or an ever-vigilant traitor; hence the feathers are considered unlucky. *Cp.* ARGUS-EYED.

Pearls. Dioscorides and Pliny mention the belief that pearls are formed by drops of rain falling into oyster-shells while open; the raindrops thus received being hardened into pearls by some secretions of the animal. They are actually a secretion forming a coating and repeated so often that they attain considerable thickness, caused by the attempts of marine and fresh-water molluscs to get rid of a foreign object (*e.g.* a grain of sand or tiny parasitic worm).

According to HORACE (II *Satires*, iii, 239), Clodius, son of Æsop the tragedian, drew a pearl of great value from his ear, melted it in vinegar, and drank to the health of Cecilia Metella. This story is referred to by Valerius Maximus, Macrobius, and Pliny. *Cp.* CLEOPATRA AND HER PEARL.

A pearl of great price. Something highly treasured or of especial value. One of the doctrinal works of the MORMONS is called *The Pearl of Great Price*.

To cast pearls before swine. To offer something of a quality which the uncultured PHILISTINE is unable to appreciate; to offer one's "pearls of wisdom" to an unappreciative audience.

> Give not that which is holy unto the dogs, neither cast ye your pearls before swine.
>
> *Matt.* vii, 6.

Pearl Mosque. At Agra, India; built of white marble at the orders of Shah Jehan, who also ordered the more famous Taj Mahal in the same city. There is another Pearl Mosque at Delhi, which was Aurangzeb's private place of prayer.

Pearlies. The coster "kings" and "queens", "princes" and "princesses" of the LONDON boroughs, so named from their glittering attire studded with innumerable pearl buttons. Since the Festival of Britain (1951), there has been a Pearly King of London. Originally elected by the street-traders of London to safeguard their rights from interlopers and bullies, they now devote their efforts to collecting and working for charities.

Their tradition is an old one and they are a reminder of the more colourful London when barrow-boys were more prevalent than supermarkets. *See* COSTERMONGER.

Peasant Poet. John Clare (1793–1864), the son of a labourer, who began work as a herd boy at the age of seven, was so called. His first publication, *Poems Descriptive of Rural Life and Scenery*, 1820, attracted attention and *The Village Minstrel* followed in 1821. His unsuccessful *Shepherd's Calendar* appeared in 1827 and *The Rural Muse* in 1835. He drifted through various occupations and was dogged by poverty. Mental disturbances began in 1836 and he eventually died in Northampton Asylum. He was born at Helpston, Huntingdonshire and was there buried. "Peasant Poet" is inscribed on his tombstone.

Peasants' Revolt. The name given to the English peasant risings of 1381 which were immediately occasioned by an unpopular poll-tax at a time when there was a growing spirit of social revolt. Its chief centre was south-eastern England, especially Kent and Essex. Wat Tyler's men beheaded the Archbishop of Canterbury (Sudbury) and temporarily held LONDON, and John Ball joined the Kentish rebels. King Richard II promised free pardon and redress of grievances (abolition of villeinage, etc.). Wat Tyler was slain by Walworth, the MAYOR of London, severe retribution followed, and the boy King's promises were not kept.

In Germany the *Peasants' Revolt* or *Peasant War* of 1524–1525 was caused by tyranny and oppression by the nobility and further stimulated by the seeming encouragement of religious reformers. Luther disowned the peasants and threw in his lot with the princes, and the risings were put down with great severity.

Peccavi. To cry peccavi. To acknowledge oneself in the wrong. Sir Charles Napier, in 1843, sent a preliminary despatch with the single word "Peccavi" (I have sinned, *i.e.* I have Sind) announcing his conquest by the victory of Miani.

Pecker. Keep your pecker up. As the mouth is in the head, *pecker* (the mouth) means the head; and to "keep your pecker up" means to keep your head up, or more familiarly, "keep your chin up", "never say die".

Going to Peckham. Going to dinner.

Pecksniff. A canting hypocrite, who speaks homilies of morality, does the most heartless things "as a duty to society", and forgives wrongdoing in nobody but himself (Dickens, *Martin Chuzzlewit*). *Cp.* PODSNAP.

Pecos Bill (pe′ kos). A cowboy of American legend who performed superhuman prodigies on the frontier in early days. One of his feats was to dig the Rio Grande river.

Pectoral Cross. *See* CRUX PECTORALIS.

Peculiar. A parish or group of parishes exempt from the jurisdiction of the OR-DINARY of the diocese. There were many such in mediæval England, e.g. monastic peculiars, royal peculiars, archiepiscopal, and diocesan, peculiars, peculiars belonging to Orders, and cathedral peculiars. In 1832 there were still over 300 peculiars which were abolished between 1838 and 1850, the exceptions being cathedral peculiars, Westminster Abbey and those of the royal residences including the Chapel Royal of the Savoy. *See also* DEAN OF THE ARCHES; DEANS OF PECULIARS.

Court of Peculiars. In particular, a branch of the Court of ARCHES which had jurisdiction over the PECULIARS of the Archbishop of Canterbury.

The Peculiar People. Properly, the Jews, the "Chosen people". The title was also assumed by a London sect, the "Plumstead Peculiars", founded in 1838. They refuse medical, but not surgical aid and rely on the efficacy of prayer and on anointing with oil by the elders. The name is based on *Titus* ii, 14—"Purify unto himself a peculiar people".

Pecuniary (Lat. *pecuniarius* from *pecunia*, money). The word is ultimately from Lat. *pecus*, cattle, sheep, etc. Varro says that sheep were the ancient medium of barter and standard of value. Ancient coin was commonly marked with the image of an ox or sheep.

Pedagogue (Gr. *pais*, boy; *agein*, to lead). A "boy-leader", hence a schoolmaster—now usually one who is pompous and pedantic. In ancient Greece the *pedagogos* was a slave whose duty it was to attend his master's son whenever he left home.

Pedestal. To set on a pedestal. To idolize or to idealize. From the custom of showing reverence to figures of SAINTS and others set on pedestals.

Pedlar. This word for an itinerant vendor of small wares is not from Lat. *pedes*, feet, but is probably from *ped*, basket, in which his goods were carried. In Norwich, Ped-market was where women used to display eggs, butter, cheese, etc., in open hampers.

Pedlars' French. The jargon or CANT of thieves, rogues, and vagabonds. "French" was formerly widely used to denote anything or anyone that was foreign.

Peel. A Peel Parish. In the CHURCH OF ENGLAND, a district taken out of an existing parish which may with due formalities be constituted a new parish. So called from the fact that Sir Robert Peel was Prime Minister when the ACT OF PARLIAMENT (1843) authorizing such changes was passed.

Peeler. Slang for a policeman; first applied to the Irish constabulary founded by Sir Robert Peel when Chief Secretary for IRELAND (1812–1818), and later to the Metropolitan Police which he established in 1829 when Home Secretary. *Cp.* BOBBY; *see* ORANGE PEEL.

In the 16th century the word was applied to robbers, from *peel* (later *pill*), to plunder, strip of possessions, rob. Holinshed, in his *Scottish Chronicle* (1570) refers to Patrick Dunbar, who "delivered the countrie of these peelers". *Cp. also* Milton's *Paradise Regained*, IV, 136:

Peelites. Those CONSERVATIVES who supported and remained loyal to Sir Robert Peel at the time of the Repeal of the Corn Laws. Among them were Aberdeen, Gladstone, Goulburn, Graham, and Sidney Herbert and they did not return to the Conservative party after the rift in 1846.

Peep-o'-Day Boys. The Irish PROTESTANT faction in ULSTER of the 1780s and 1790s; so called because they used to visit the houses of the DEFENDERS at "peep of day" searching for arms or plunder, etc. *Cp.* ORANGEMEN.

Peeping Tom of Coventry. *See* GODIVA, LADY.

Peers of the Realm. The five orders of DUKE, MARQUESS, EARL, VISCOUNT and BARON. The word peer is the Lat. *pares* (equals), and in feudal times all great vassals were held as equals.

Peewits' Pinch. The same as "BLACKTHORN WINTER", the short cold spell that usually occurs in MARCH, when peewits are about to begin nesting, and feel their "pinch" when frost and cold winds come upon them at this time. Peewits nest on the ground.

Peg. A square peg in a round hole. One who is doing (or trying to do) a job for which he is not suited; *e.g.* a BISHOP refereeing a prize-fight.

I am a peg too low. I am low-spirited, moody; I want another draught to cheer me up. Our Saxon ancestors used tankards with pegs inserted at equal intervals, so that when two or more drank from the same bowl no one might exceed his fair allowance (*cp.* IN MERRY PIN *under* PIN). We are told that St. DUNSTAN introduced the fashion to prevent brawling.

To peg a price. To fix or maintain a market price, as by buying, selling or subsidy.

To peg away at it. To stick at it persistently, often in spite of difficulties and discouragement. Probably derived from the use of the peg tankard.

To peg out. To die. From the game of cribbage where the game is ended by a player pegging out the last holes.

To take one down a peg. To take the conceit out of a braggart or pretentious person; to lower their self-esteem. The allusion is to a ship's colours, which used to be raised and lowered by pegs; the higher the colours are raised the greater the honour, and to take them down a peg would be to diminish the honour. An earlier explanation refers to the ancient practice of sharing drink from a pegged container down to one's allotted peg. *See above* I AM A PEG TOO LOW.

> Trepanned your party with intrigue,
> And took your grandees down a peg.
> BUTLER: *Hudibras*, II, ii.

Peg-leg. A wooden legged person; from the days when wooden legs were rods strapped at the knee.

Pegasus. The winged horse on which BELLEROPHON rode against the CHIMÆRA. When the MUSES contended with the daughters of Pieros, HELICON rose heavenward with delight; but Pegasus gave it a kick, stopped its ascent, and brought out of the mountain the soul-inspiring waters of HIPPOCRENE; hence, the name is used for the inspiration of poetry.

Peine forte et dure (pān fort ā dūr). A species of torture applied to contumacious felons who refused to plead; it usually took the form of pressing the accused between boards until he accepted a trial by jury or died. Juliana Quick (1442), Anthony Arrowsmith (1598), Walter Calverly (1605), and Major Strangeways (1657) suffered death in this way. Even in 1741 this torture was invoked at the Cambridge assizes. It was abolished in 1772. (Lat. *pœna*, punishment; *fortis et dura*, intense and severe.)

Peking Man (*Sinanthropus pekinensis*). The name given to remains of a skull found near Peking in 1929 which in many respects showed resemblances to that of PITHECANTHROPUS *erectus* and held as being intermediate between Java and NEANDERTHAL MAN.

Pelagians. Heretical followers of the British monk Pelagius (a Latinized form of his Welsh name *Morgan*, the sea). They denied the doctrine of ORIGINAL SIN (*see under* SIN) or the taint of ADAM, and maintained that we have power of ourselves to receive or reject the GOSPEL. They were opposed by St. AUGUSTINE and condemned by Pope Innocent I in 417 and again by Pope Zosimus in 418.

Pelf. Filthy Pelf. Money; usually with a contemptuous implication—as we speak of "filthy lucre", or "Who steals my purse steals trash".

The word is from O.Fr. *pelfre*, connected with our *pilfer*, and was originally used of stolen or pilfered goods, illgotten gains.

Pelican. In Christian art, a symbol of charity; also an emblem of Jesus Christ, by "whose blood we are healed". St. JEROME gives the story of the pelican restoring its young ones destroyed by serpents, and his own salvation by the blood of Christ. The popular fallacy that pelicans feed their young with their blood arose from the fact that the parent bird transfers macerated food from the large bag under its bill to its young. The correct term for the heraldic representation of the bird in this act is **a pelican in her piety,** *piety* having the classical meaning of filial devotion.

The mediæval BESTIARY tells us that the pelican is very fond of its brood, but, when they grow, they often rebel against the male bird and provoke his anger, so that he kills them; the mother

returns to the nest in three days, sits on the dead birds, pours her blood over them, revives them, and they feed on her blood.

Pelion (pē' li on). **Heaping Pelion upon Ossa.** Adding difficulty to difficulty, embarrassment to embarrassment, etc. When the giants tried to scale HEAVEN, they placed Mount Pelion upon Mount Ossa, two peaks in Thessaly, for a scaling ladder (*Odyssey*, XI, 315).

Pell-mell. Headlong; in reckless confusion. From the players of PALL-MALL, who rushed heedlessly to strike the ball.

Pelleas, Sir. One of the Knights of the ROUND TABLE, famed for his great strength. He is introduced in Spenser's *The Faerie Queene* (VI, xii) as going after the BLATANT BEAST. *See also* Tennyson's *Pelleas and Ettare*.

Pelmanism. A system of mind and memory training originated by W.J. Ennever in the closing years of the 19th century, and so called because it is an easy name to remember. Owing to its very extensive advertising, the verb *to pelmanize*, meaning to obtain good results by training the memory, was coined. It has also given its name to a card game, popular with children, which largely depends on mental concentration and memory.

Pelops. Son of TANTALUS, and father of Atreus and Thyestes. He was king of Pisa in Elis, and was cut to pieces and served as food to the gods. The Morea was called *Peloponnesus*, "the island of Pelops", from this mythical king.

The ivory shoulder of Pelops. The distinguishing or distinctive mark of anyone. The tale is that DEMETER ate the shoulder of Pelops when it was served by TANTALUS; when the gods put the body back into the cauldron to restore it to life, this portion was lacking, whereupon Demeter supplied one of ivory.

Penalty envelopes. In the U.S.A., envelopes franked for official use by government departments like those stamped O.H.M.S. (On Her Majesty's Service) in Britain. "Penalty" refers to the penalty for their misuse.

Penates. *See* DII PENATES; LARES AND PENATES.

Pendente lite (pen den' ti lī te) (Lat.). Pending the trial; while the suit is going on.

Pendragon. A title conferred on several British chiefs in times of great danger when they were invested with supreme power, especially (in ARTHURIAN ROMANCES) to UTHER Pendragon, father of King ARTHUR. The word is Welsh *pen*, head, and *dragon* (referring to the war-chief's dragon standard). It corresponded to the Roman *dux bellorum*.

Geoffrey of Monmouth relates that when Aurelius, the British king, was poisoned by Ambron, during the invasion of Pascentius, son of Vortigern, "there appeared a star of wonderful magnitude and brightness, darting forth a ray, at the end of which was a globe of fire in the form of a dragon, out of whose mouth issued forth two rays; one of which seemed to stretch itself beyond the extent of Gaul, the other towards the Irish Sea, and ended in seven lesser rays" (Bk. VIII, ch. xiv). Uther, brother of Aurelius and his predestined successor, ordered two golden dragons to be made, one of which he presented to Winchester Cathedral, and the other "to be carried along with him to his wars", whence he was called Uther Pendragon.

Penelope (pė nel' ō pi). The wife of ULYSSES and mother of TELEMACHUS in Homeric legend. She was a model of all the domestic virtues.

The Web of Penelope. A work "never ending, still beginning"; never done, but ever in hand. Penelope, according to HOMER, was pestered with suitors at Ithaca while ULYSSES was absent at the siege of TROY. To relieve herself of their importunities, she promised to make a choice of one as soon as she had finished a shroud for her father-in-law. Every night she unravelled what she had done in the day, and so deferred making any choice until Ulysses returned and slew the suitors.

Penetralia (pen e trā'li à) (Lat., the innermost parts). The private rooms of a house; the secrets of a family. Properly, the part of a Roman TEMPLE to which the priest alone had access, where the sacred images were housed, where the responses of the ORACLES made, and the sacred mysteries performed. The HOLY OF HOLIES was the *penetralia* of the Jewish Temple.

Penitential Psalms. The seven psalms expressive of contrition (vi, xxxii, xxxviii, li, cii, cxxx, cxliii). From TIME IMMEMORIAL they have all been used at the ASH WEDNESDAY services; the first three at MATINS, the 51st at the Commination, and the last three at Evensong.

Pennant, Pennon. *See* PENDANT.

Penny (O.E. *pening*). The English coin, before decimalization (*see* DECIMAL CURRENCY) worth one-twelfth of a SHILLING, was originally made of SILVER and was used by the Anglo-Saxons. A few silver pennies are still coined as MAUNDY MONEY, but they were last struck for general circulation in the reign of Charles II. A few GOLD pennies (worth 20 silver pennies) were struck in the reign of Henry III. The first English COPPER penny was made in 1797 by Boulton at the Soho Mint, Birmingham, hence *a copper* as a common synonym for a penny. In 1860 bronze coins were substituted for copper.

The plural *pennies* is used of the number of coins and *pence* of the value. A penny is sometimes used to denote low-value coins of other nations, such as in *Luke* xx, 24, where it stands for the Roman *denarius* from which the symbol *d* for a penny is derived. (*See also* P.)

A penny for your thoughts! Tell me what you are thinking about. Addressed humorously to one in a BROWN STUDY. The phrase occurs in Heywood's *Proverbs* (1546).

A penny saved is a penny gained, or **earned,** etc. An old adage intended to encourage thrift in the young.

A pretty penny. A considerable sum of money, an unpleasantly large sum.

He has got his pennyworth. He has got good value for his money; sometimes said of one who has received a good drubbing.

In for a penny, in for a pound. Once involved the matter must be carried through whatever obstacles or difficulties may arise—there can be no drawing back.

In penny numbers. In small amounts, or little by little. From the stories eked out in serial form in the penny periodicals of former days.

No penny, no paternoster. No pay, no work; you'll get nothing for nothing. The allusion is to pre-REFORMATION days, when priests would not perform services without payment.

Not a penny to bless himself with. *See* BLESS.

Penny plain, twopence coloured. A phrase originating in the shop of a maker of toy theatres in East London. The scenery and characters for the plays to be "acted" were printed on sheets of thick paper ready to be cut out, these being sold at 1*d*. if plain, 2*d*. if coloured.

Penny wise and pound foolish. Said of one who is in danger of "spoiling the ship for a ha'porth of tar". One who is thrifty in small matters and careless over large ones is said to be *penny wise*.

Take care of the pence and the pounds will take care of themselves. An excellent piece of advice, which Chesterfield records in his Letter to his son (5 February 1750) as having been given by "old Mr. Lowndes, the famous Secretary of the Treasury, in the reigns of King William, Queen Anne, and George I". Chesterfield adds:

> To this maxim, which he not only preached, but practised, his two grandsons, at this time, owe the very considerable fortunes that he left them.

The saying was parodied in the *Advice to a Poet*, which goes, "Take care of the *sense* and the *sounds* will take care of themselves".

To turn an honest penny. To earn an honest penny by working for it.

Penny-a-liner. The old name for a contributor to the newspapers who was not on the staff and was paid a penny a line. As it was in his interest to "pad" as much as possible, the word is still used in a contemptuous way for a second-rate writer or newspaper HACK.

Penny-dreadful, or **-horrible.** A cheap boy's paper full of crude situations and highly coloured excitement. Still used of such trashy periodicals although they are no longer available for a penny. A "shilling shocker" was a similar but more expensive publication.

Penny-father. A miser, a penurious person who "husbands" his pence.

Penny farthing. The nickname of what was also called the "ordinary" bicycle that came into vogue in 1872; the front wheel being sometimes as much as 5 ft. in diameter, while the rear was only 12 in., hence the name. The drive was on the front wheel, the seat being directly above it and slightly back from the perpendicular of the axle. The "Safety" bicycle, much on the lines of the usual cycle of today, was introduced in 1885.

Penny fish. A name given to the JOHN DORY because of the round spots on each side left by St. PETER'S FINGERS.

Penny gaff. A concert or crude music-hall entertainment for which the entrance charge was one penny.

Penny weddings. Weddings formerly in vogue among the poor in SCOTLAND and WALES at which each guest paid a small sum of money not exceeding a shilling. After defraying expenses, the residue went to the newly-weds to aid in furnishing their home.

Pension. Etymologically, that which is weighed out (Lat. *pensionem*, payment; from *pendere*, to weigh; also *to pay*, because payment was originally weighed out. *Cp.* our *pound*, both a weight and a piece of money).

Pensioner. Chelsea Pensioner. The popular name for the In-Pensioners of the Royal Hospital, Chelsea, founded by Charles II at the instigation of Sir Stephen Fox, the Paymaster General of the Forces. It is maintained for selected veterans of the regular army and was opened in 1692. The legend that Nell GWYN suggested the foundation is apparently imaginary.

The Pensioner, or **Pensionary Parliament.** The LONG PARLIAMENT or CAVALIER PARLIAMENT of Charles II (1661–1679), so called from the bribes or pensions accepted by many of its members and noted for the growth of party faction.

Pentacle. A five-pointed star, or five-sided figure, used in sorcery as a TALISMAN against WITCHES, etc., and sometimes worn as a folded headdress of fine linen, as a defence against demons in the act of conjuration. It is also called the *Wizard's Foot*, and is supposed to typify the five senses, though as it resolves itself into three triangles, its efficacy may spring from its being a triple symbol of the TRINITY.

It is also a candlestick with five branches. *Cp.* SOLOMON'S SEAL.

> And on her head, lest spirits should invade,
> A pentacle, for more assurance, laid.
> ROSE: *Orlando Furioso*, III, xxi.

The Holy Pentacles numbered forty-four, of which seven were consecrated to each of the planets SATURN, JUPITER, MARS, and the SUN; five to both VENUS and MERCURY; and six to the MOON. The divers figures were enclosed in a double circle, containing the name of God in Hebrew, and other mystical words.

Pentagon. A vast five-sided building erected in Washington, D.C., to house government officials. It now houses the U.S. Department of Defense, and the word Pentagon is a synonym for the official American attitude in military matters.

Pentameron. A collection of fifty folk tales modelled on the DECAMERON and written in the Neapolitan dialect by Giambattista Basile (*c.* 1575–1632) and first published at Naples in 1637. The stories were supposed to have been told by ten old women during five days, to a Moorish slave who had taken the place of the true princess.

The Pentameron (1837) of Walter Savage Landor (1775–1864) was a collection of five long imaginary conversations.

Pentameter (pen tăm′ i tẻr). In prosody, a line of five feet, DACTYLS or spondees divided by a cæsura into two parts of two-and-a-half feet each—the line used in alternation with the HEXAMETER in Latin elegiac verse. The name is sometimes wrongly applied to the English five-foot IAMBIC line.

> In the hexameter rises the fountain's silvery column,
> In the pentameter aye falling in melody back.
> COLERIDGE: *Example of Elegiac Metre*.

Pentateuch (pen′ ta tūk). The first five books of the OLD TESTAMENT, anciently attributed to MOSES (Gr. *penta*, five; *teuchos*, a tool, book).

The Samaritan Pentateuch. The He-

brew text of the Pentateuch as preserved by the Samaritans; said to date from the 4th century B.C.

Pentathlon. An athletic contest of five events, usually the jump, javelin throw, 200-metre race, discus throw, and 1,500-metre flat race. In the ancient OLYMPIC GAMES the contest consisted of running, jumping, throwing the discus and javelin, and wrestling.

Pentecost. (Gr. *pentecoste* fiftieth). The festival held by the Jews on the fiftieth day after the second day of the PASSOVER; our WHITSUNDAY.

Pentecostal Churches. PROTESTANT sects associated with manifestations of the gift of tongues such as had occurred at PENTECOST (*see Acts* ii, 1–4), and evangelical and healing campaigns.

Pentecostals. In mediæval England, offerings made to the parish priest at WHITSUNTIDE were called *Pentecostals*, or *Whitsun-farthings*. The term is also used of offerings paid by the parish church to the cathedral of the diocese. *Cp.* DOWELLING MONEY; PETER'S PENCE; SMOKE-FARTHINGS.

Penthesilea. Queen of the AMAZONS who, in the post-Homeric legends, fought for TROY; she was slain by ACHILLES. Hence any strong, commanding woman. Sir Toby Belch in SHAKESPEARE'S *Twelfth Night* (II, iii) calls Maria by this name.

Peony. According to fable, so called from Pæon, the physician who cured the wounds received by the gods in the Trojan war. The seeds were, at one time, worn round the neck as a charm against the powers of darkness.

> About an Infant's neck hang Peonie,
> It cures Alcydes cruell maladie.
> SYLVESTER: *Du Bartas*, I, iii, 712.

People. Chosen People. The Israelites, the Jews.

The good, or **little people.** FAIRIES, ELVES, etc.

People's Charter. *See* CHARTISM.

Pepper. To pepper one well. To give one a good basting or thrashing; also to sprinkle with pellets or shot.

To take pepper i' the nose. To take offence. The French say, *La moutarde lui monte au nez*.

When your daughter is stolen, close

Pepper Gate. The equivalent of "locking the stable door when the horse has bolted". Pepper Gate used to be on the east side of the city of Chester. It is said that the mayor's daughter eloped and the mayor ordered the gate to be shut.

Pepper-and-salt. A cloth mixture of light and dark wools making a pattern of light and dark dots.

Peppercorn rent. A nominal rent. A peppercorn is of very slight value and is a token rental; virtually free possession without the ownership of the freehold.

Cowper makes a figurative use of the custom.

> True. While they live, the courtly laureate pays
> His quit-rent ode, his pepper-corn of praise.
> *Table-talk*, 110.

Per contra (Lat.). A commercial term for "on the opposite side of the account". Used also of arguments, etc.

Per saltum (Lat., by a leap). A promotion or degree given without going through the usual stages; as the ordination of a man to the priesthood who is not yet a deacon. Such ordinations, now prohibited, were common in earlier times.

Perambulator. A wooden wheel which, when pushed along by a man on foot, records exactly the distance traversed. Such apparatuses were used by the employees of John Cary in the production of the first accurate *Itinerary of the Great Roads of England and Wales* (1798). The name, usually abbreviated "pram", has been attached to the vehicle in which babies are taken for walks.

Perceforest (pĕrs' for est). An early 14th-century French prose romance (said to be the longest in existence), belonging to the Arthurian cycle, but mingling with it the ALEXANDER romance. After Alexander's war in India, he comes to England, of which he makes Perceforest, one of his knights, king. The romance tells how Perceforest establishes the Knights of the Franc Palais, how his grandson brings the GRAIL to England, and includes many popular tales, such as that of the SLEEPING BEAUTY.

Percival, Sir. The Knight of the ROUND TABLE who, according to Malory's *Morte d'Arthur* (and Tennyson's *Idylls of the King*) finally won a sight of the Holy GRAIL. He was the son of Sir Pellinore and brother of Sir Lamerocke. In the earlier French romances (based probably on the MABINOGION and other CELTIC originals) he has no connexion with the Grail, but here (as in the English also) he sees the lance dripping with blood, and the severed head surrounded with blood in a dish. The French version of the romance is by Chrétien de Troyes (12th century), which formed the basis of Sebastian Evans's *The High History of the Holy Graal* (1893). The German version, *Parsifal* or *Parzival*, was written some 50 years later by Wolfram von Eschenbach and it is principally on this version that Wagner drew for his opera, *Parsifal* (1882).

Percy. When Malcolm III of SCOTLAND invaded ENGLAND and reduced the castle of Alnwick, Robert de Mowbray brought to him the keys of the castle suspended on his lance; and handing them from the wall, thrust his lance into the king's eye; from which circumstance, the tradition says, he received the name of "Pierce-eye", which has ever since been borne by the Dukes of Northumberland.

> This is all a fable. The Percies are descended from a great Norman baron, who came over with William, and who took his name from his castle and estate in Normandy.
> SCOTT: *Tales of a Grandfather*, iv.

Percy's Reliques. The famous collection of old ballads and poems published as *Reliques of Ancient English Poetry* by Thomas Percy in 1765. He became Bishop of Dromore in 1782 and died in 1811. He was encouraged in his project by Shenstone, Johnson, Garrick and others, and Scott acknowledged his debt to Percy's work: "To read and to remember was in this instance the same thing, and henceforth I overwhelmed my schoolfellows, and all who would hearken to me, with tragical recitations from the ballads of Percy."

Perdita. In SHAKESPEARE's *A Winter's Tale*, the daughter of Leontes and Hermione of Sicily. She was abandoned by order of her father, and put in a vessel which drifted to "the sea-coast of Bohemia" where the infant was discovered by a shepherd, who brought her up as his own daughter. In time, FLORIZEL, the son and heir of the Bohemian King Polixenes, fell in love with the supposed shepherdess. The match was forbidden by Polixenes and the young lovers fled to Sicily. Here the story is cleared up, and all ends happily in the restoration of Perdita to her parents, and her marriage with Florizel.

Mrs. Robinson, the actress and mistress of George IV when Prince of Wales, was specially successful in the part of Perdita, by which name she came to be known, the Prince being known as Florizel.

Perdrix, toujours perdrix (pâr′ drē, too zhoor pâr′ drē). Too much of the same thing. According to Horace Walpole, the confessor of one of the French kings reproved him for conjugal infidelity, and was asked by the king what he liked best. "Partridge", replied the priest, and the king ordered him to be served with partridge every day, till he quite loathed the sight of his favourite dish. When the king eventually visited him, and hoped he had been well served, the confessor replied, "*Mais oui, perdrix, toujours perdrix.*" "Ah! ah!", replied the amorous monarch, "and one mistress is all very well, but not '*perdrix, toujours perdrix*'."

> Soup for dinner, soup for supper, and soup for breakfast again.
> FARQUHAR: *The Inconstant*, V, ii.

Père Lachaise (pâr la shāz). This great Parisian cemetery is on the site of a religious settlement founded by the JESUITS in 1626, and later enlarged by Louis XIV's confessor, Père Lachaise. After the Revolution, the grounds were laid out as a cemetery and were first used in 1804. It was here that the Communards made their last stand in 1871.

Peregrine Falcon. A falcon of wide distribution, formerly held in great esteem for hawking, and so called (13th century) because taken when on passage or *peregrination*, from the breeding place, instead of straight off the nest, as was the case with most others (Lat. *peregrinus*, a foreigner, one coming from foreign parts). The hen is the *falcon* of fal-

coners; the cock the *tercel. See* HAWK.

The word *peregrine* was formerly used as synonymous with *pilgrim*, and (adjectivally) for one travelling about.

Perestroika (Russ. restructuring). A policy, linked with GLASNOST, much publicized since 1986 when it became Mikhail Gorbachev's intent to introduce economic and political reform and allow greater freedom of expression, which included the publication of formerly banned books. Gorbachev became President and Communist Party Leader in the autumn of 1988.

Perfect. Perfect rhyme is a rhyme of two words spelled or pronounced alike but with different meanings, as "rain" and "reign", "thyme" and "time".

Perfectibilist. *See* ILLUMINATI.

Perfectionists. Members of a communistic sect formed by J.H. Noyes (1811–1886) in Vermont about 1834, and removed by him and settled at Oneida, New York, 1847–1848. Its chief features were that the community was held to be one family, mutual criticism and public opinion took the place of government, and wives were— theoretically, at least—held in common, till 1879, when, owing to opposition, this was abandoned. In 1881 the sect, which had prospered exceedingly through its thrift and industry, voluntarily dissolved and was organized as a joint-stock company.

Perfide Albion. *See under* ALBION.

Peri (pē′ ri). Originally, a beautiful but malevolent sprite of Persian myth, one of a class which was responsible for comets, eclipses, failure of crops, etc.; in later times applied to delicate, gentle, fairy-like beings, begotten by fallen spirits who direct with a wand the pure in mind the way to HEAVEN. These lovely creatures, according to the KORAN, are under the sovereignty of EBLIS; and MOHAMMED was sent for their conversion, as well as for that of man.

The name used sometimes to be applied to any beautiful girl.

Paradise and the Peri. The second tale in Moore's *Lalla Rookh*. The Peri laments her expulsion from HEAVEN, and is told she will be readmitted if she will bring to the gate of heaven the "gift most dear to the Almighty". After a number of unavailing offerings she brought a guilty old man, who wept with repentance, and knelt to pray. The Peri offered the Repentant Tear, and the gates flew open.

Perillus and the Brazen Bull. *See under* INVENTORS.

Perilous Castle. The castle of "the good" Lord Douglas was so called in the reign of Edward I, because DOUGLAS destroyed several English garrisons stationed there, and vowed to be revenged on anyone who should dare to take possession of it. Scott calls it "Castle Dangerous" (*see* Introduction of *Castle Dangerous*).

Peripatetic School (per i på tet' ik). The school or system of philosophy founded by ARISTOTLE, who used to walk about (Gr. *peri*, about; *patein*, to walk) as he taught his disciples in the covered walk of the Lyceum. This colonnade was called the *peripatos*.

Periphrasis (pe rif' rà sis). A roundabout or long-winded form of expression (Gr. *peri*, around, about; *phrasis*, speech). A fair example is: "Persons prejudicial to the public peace may be assigned by administrative process to definite places of residence', *i.e.* breakers of the law may be sent to gaol.

Perish the thought! Do not entertain such an idea for a moment! A quotation from Colley Cibber's version of SHAKE-SPEARE'S *Richard III*, V, v.

Perk. To perk up. To get more lively, to feel better.

Permissive Society. A term widely used in Britain in the 1960s to denote the increasingly tolerant and liberal attitudes in society.

Perpetual Motion. The term applied to some theoretical force that will move a machine for ever of itself—a mirage which holds attractions for some minds much as did the search for the PHILOSO-PHER'S STONE, the ELIXIR OF LIFE, and the FOUNTAIN OF (perpetual) YOUTH. According to the laws of thermo-dynamics it is impossible.

Persecutions, The Ten Great. According to Orosius: (1) under Nero, A.D. 64; (2) Domitian, 95; (3) Trajan, 98–117; (4) Marcus Aurelius, 177; (5) Septimius

Severus, 193–211; (6) Maximinus Thrax, 235; (7) Decius, 250; (8) Valerian, 258; (9) Aurelian, 272; (10) Diocletian, 303–305. In fact neither Trajan nor Severus were active persecutors.

These were all persecutions of Christians, but Christians persecuted each other before they slowly learned toleration. *See* ALBIGENSES; BARTHOLOMEW, MASSACRE OF ST.; DRAGONNADES; HU-GUENOT; INQUISITION; WALDENSIANS; etc.

Jews, particularly, have suffered persecution for religious and other reasons, the worst of all being perpetrated by the NAZI régime, when possibly some 10 million were exterminated. Political persecutions have been common through the ages and in modern times totalitarian and Communist countries have relied on this weapon.

Persephone. *See* PROSERPINA.

Persepolis. The capital of the ancient Persian empire. It was situated some 35 miles N.E. of Shiraz. The palaces and other public buildings were some miles from the city and were approached by magnificent flights of steps.

Perseus. In Greek legend, the son of ZEUS and DANAE. He and his mother were set adrift in a chest but rescued by the intervention of Zeus. He was brought up by King Polydectes, who, wishing to secure DANAË, got rid of him by encouraging him in the almost hopeless task of obtaining the head of the MEDUSA. With the help of the gods, he was successful, and with the head (which turned all that looked on it into stone) he rescued AN-DROMEDA, and later metamorphosed Polydectes and his guests to stone.

Before his birth, an ORACLE had foretold that Acrisius, father of Danaë, would be slain by Danaë's son (hence Perseus being originally cast adrift to perish). This came to pass, for while taking part in the games at Larissa, Perseus accidentally slew his grandfather with a discus.

Person. From Lat. *persona*, which meant originally a mask worn by actors (perhaps from *per sonare*, to sound through), and later transferred to the character or personage represented by the actor (*cp.* our *dramatis personæ*), and so to any definite character, at which stage the word was adopted in English through O.Fr. *persone*.

Confounding the Persons. The heresy of Sabellius (*see* SABELLIANISM), who declared that Father, Son, and Holy Ghost were but three names, aspects, or manifestations of one God, the orthodox doctrine being that of the ATHANASIAN CREED.

Persona grata (Lat.). An acceptable person; one liked. When a diplomatic representative becomes no longer acceptable to the government to which he is accredited he is no longer *persona grata*, which virtually requests his recall. *Persona non grata* is the reverse of *persona grata*.

Perth. The Five Articles of Perth (1618) were imposed on the CHURCH OF SCOTLAND by James VI and I, enjoining kneeling at communion; the observance of CHRISTMAS, GOOD FRIDAY, EASTER, and PENTECOST; confirmation; communion for the dying; and early baptism of infants. They were ratified by the Scottish Parliament, 4 August 1621, called BLACK SATURDAY, and condemned by the General Assembly at Glasgow in 1638.

Peru. From China to Peru. From one end of the world to the other; worldwide. Equivalent to the biblical "from Dan to Beersheba". The phrase comes from the opening of Johnson's *Vanity of Human Wishes:*

Let observation with extensive view
Survey mankind from China to Peru.

Boileau (*Sat.* viii, 3) had previously written:

De Paris au Pérou, du Japon jusqu'à Rome.

Peruvian Bark, CHINCHONA bark, called also *Jesuit's Bark*, because it was introduced into Spain by the JESUITS. "Quinine", from the same tree, is called by the Indians *quinquina*.

Petard. Hoist with his own petard. Beaten with his own weapons, caught in his own trap; involved in the danger intended for others, as were some designers of instruments of torture. *See under* INVENTORS. The petard was a thick iron engine of war, filled with gunpowder, and fastened to gates, barricades, etc., to blow them up. The danger was lest the engineer who fired the petard should be blown up by the explosion.

Let it work;
For 'tis sport, to have the engineer
Hoist with his own petard; and it shall go hard
But I will delve one yard below their mines,
And blow them at the moon.
SHAKESPEARE: *Hamlet*, III, iv.

Peter. St. Peter. The patron saint of fishermen, being himself a fisherman; the "Prince of the APOSTLES". His feast is kept universally on 29 June, and he is usually represented as an old man, bald, but with a flowing beard, dressed in a white mantle and blue tunic, and holding in his hand a book or scroll. His peculiar symbols are the keys, and a sword (*Matt.* xvi, 19, and *John* xviii, 10).

Tradition tells that he confuted SIMON MAGUS, who was at NERO's court as a magician, and that in A.D. 65 he was crucified with his head downwards at his own request, as he said he was not worthy to suffer the same death as Our Lord. The location of his bones under the high altar of St. Peter's, ROME, was announced in 1950 and the POPE confirmed their authenticity in 1968.

St. Peter's Fingers. The fingers of a thief. The allusion is to the fish caught by St. Peter with a piece of money in its mouth. It is said that a thief has a fish-hook on every finger.

Peter's Pence. An annual tribute of one PENNY, paid at the feast of St. Peter to the see of ROME, collected at first from every family, but afterwards restricted to those "who had the value of thirty pence in quick or live-stock". This tax was collected in England from the late 8th century until its abolition by Henry VIII in 1534. It was also called *Rome-Scot, Rome fardynges*, or *Peter's farthings*. Much of it never got as far as Rome. *Cp.* PENTECOSTALS.

Peter's Pence now consists of voluntary offerings made to the HOLY SEE by Roman Catholics.

Great Peter. A bell in York Minster, weighing 10¾ tons, and hung in 1845.

Peter-boat; Peterman. A fishing boat made to go either way, with stem and stern alike. So called from *Peterman*, an old term for a fisherman.

Peter the Hermit (*c.* 1050–1115). Preacher of the first CRUSADE. He took part in the siege of Antioch (1098) and entered JERUSALEM with the victorious crusaders. He afterwards became Prior of Huy.

Peter Pan. The little boy who never grew up, the central character of Sir J.M. Barrie's famous play of this name (1904). One night Peter entered the nursery window of the house of the Darling family to recover his shadow. He flew back to NEVER NEVER LAND accompanied by the Darling children, to rejoin the Lost Boys. Eventually all were captured by the pirates, except Peter, who secured their release and the defeat of the pirates. The children, by now homesick, flew back to the nursery with their new friends but Peter refused to stay as he did not wish to grow up. In their absence Mr. Darling lived in the dog kennel as penance for having taken NANA away, thus making possible the children's disappearance in the first instance.

Peter the Wild Boy. In 1724 a boy was found walking on his hands and feet and climbing trees like a squirrel in a wood near Hameln, Hanover. He was taken to George I, who brought him to England and put him under the care of Dr. Arbuthnot, who had him christened "Peter". He never became articulate and eventually lived with a farmer who equipped him with a brass collar inscribed "Peter the Wild Boy, Broadway Farm, Berkhamsted". On the farmer's death (1785) Peter refused food and soon died. *Cp.* GAZELLE BOY.

To peter out. To come gradually to an end, to give out. A phrase from the American mining camps of the 1840s of unknown origin.

To rob Peter to pay Paul. *See* ROB.

Peterloo, or **the Manchester Massacre.** On 16 August 1819 a large crowd (about 50,000 to 60,000) gathered at St. Peter's Field, Manchester, to hear ORATOR HUNT address them on Parliamentary reform, and fearing a riot the magistrates ordered the YEOMANRY to disperse the assembly. Eleven people were killed including two women, and some

600 injured. Hunt was arrested and given three years' imprisonment. The "massacre" caused great indignation throughout England.

The name was founded on *Waterloo*, then fresh in the public mind.

Petitio principii (Lat.). A BEGGING OF THE QUESTION, or assuming in the premises the question you undertake to prove. In mediæval logic, a *principium* was an essential, self-evident principle from which particular truths were deducible; the assumption of this principle was the *petitio, i.e.* begging of it. It is the same as "arguing in a circle".

Petitioners and Abhorrers. Names given to political groupings in the reign of Charles II, eventually superseded by WHIGS and TORIES. When Charles II prorogued a newly elected Parliament in October 1679, Shaftesbury and the Country party *petitioned* the King to summon Parliament. The Court party *abhorred* this attempt to encroach on the royal prerogative. Hence the names as party labels.

Petrel. The stormy petrel. A small seabird. (*Procellaria pelagica*), traditionally so named from Ital. *Petrello*, little Peter, because during storms these birds seem to be able to fly patting the water with each foot alternately as though walking on it, reminiscent of St. PETER, who walked on the lake of Gennesareth. Sailors call them MOTHER CAREY'S CHICKENS. The term is used figuratively of one whose coming always portends trouble.

Petticoat Government is control by women, *i.e.* when women "wear the trousers".

Petto. In petto. In secrecy, in reserve (Ital., in the breast). The Pope creates cardinals *in petto, i.e.* in his own mind, and keeps the appointment to himself till he thinks proper to announce it. On the declaration of their names their seniority dates from their appointment *in petto*. It is claimed that the English historian Lingard was made cardinal *in petto* by Leo XII, who died before announcing the fact.

Peutingerian Table. A map on parchment of the military roads of the Western Roman Empire supposed to be a copy of one made in the 3rd century A.D. This copy was found by Konrad Celtes in 1494, who bequeathed it to his friend Konrad Peutinger (1465–1547) of Augsburg.

Phædra (fē' drà). Daughter of MINOS and PASIPILÆ, who became enamoured of her stepson HIPPOLYTUS. On her rejection by him she brought about his death by slandering him to her husband THESEUS. She subsequently killed herself in remorse. *See* MYRTLE.

Phædrus (fē' drùs). A freedman of AUGUSTUS, who, in the reign of Tiberius, translated ÆSOP'S FABLES into Latin verse, interspersing them with anecdotes of his own. A prose version of his work, written about the 10th century, served as a model for the mediæval fabulists.

Phaeton (fā' tòn). In classical myth, the son of PHŒBUS (the Sun); he undertook to drive his father's chariot, and was upset. He thereby caused Libya to be parched into barren sands, and all Africa to be more or less injured, the inhabitants blackened, and vegetation nearly destroyed; he would have set the world on fire had not ZEUS transfixed him with a thunderbolt.

The name was given to a light, four-wheeled open carriage usually drawn by two horses.

Phaeton's Bird. The swan. Cygnus, son of NEPTUNE, was the friend of PHAETON and lamented his fate so grievously that APOLLO changed him into a swan, and placed him among the constellations.

Phalanx (fǎl' ǎngks). The BATTLE order of the heavy infantry (hoplites) of ancient Greece, first used by the Spartans and made famous by Philip of Macedon and Alexander the Great. The hoplites with lances of 16 ft. length or longer and with shields joined, were drawn up in from 12 to 16 close parallel lines. Alexander used a 16-rank formation, the first five ranks carrying their spears horizontally and the remainder carrying theirs across the shoulder. Much resistant to hostile onset, the phalanx lacked mobility. Hence any number of people presenting an unyielding front or distinguished for firmness and solidity of union.

Phalaris (fǎl' a ris). **The brazen bull of Phalaris.** *See under* INVENTORS.

The Epistles of Phalaris. A series of 148 letters said to have been written by Phalaris, Tyrant of Agrigentum, Sicily, in the 6th century B.C. and edited by Charles Boyle in 1695. Boyle maintained them to be genuine, but Richard Bentley, applying methods of historical criticism, proved that they were forgeries, probably of the 2nd century A.D. *See* BOYLE CONTROVERSY; FORGERY.

Phantom. Phantom corn. The mere ghost of corn; corn that has as little body as a spectre.

Phantom fellow. One who is under the ban of some HOBGOBLIN; a half-witted person.

Phantom flesh. Flesh that hangs loose and flabby; formerly supposed to be bewitched.

Pharamond (fǎr' à mond). In the ARTHURIAN ROMANCES, a KNIGHT of the ROUND TABLE, said to have been the first king of France and to have reigned in the early 5th century. He was the son of Marcomir and father of Clodion.

Pharaoh (fâr' ō). An expression meaning the "great house", applied to the kings of ancient Egypt in much the same way as "the HOLY SEE" came to be used for the Pope, or "the Sublime PORTE" for the government of the Sultan of Turkey. Its popular use stems from the BIBLE but its use as a term for the King of Egypt begins during the 18th dynasty with Akhnaton. In hieroglyphics the old usage of four or five titles persisted.

The Pharaohs of the Bible are mostly not identifiable owing to vagueness of reference and absence of reliable chronological data, but the Pharaoh of the Oppression is usually taken to be Ramses II of the 19th dynasty, and his son Merenptah, the Pharaoh of the Exodus.

According to the TALMUD, the name of Pharaoh's daughter who brought up MOSES was Bathia.

In Dryden and Tate's *Absalom and Achitophel*, "Pharaoh" stands for Louis XIV of France.

Pharaoh's corn. The grains of wheat sometimes found in mummy cases. *Cp.*

MUMMY WHEAT.

Pharisees (făr′ i sēz) (Heb. *perusim*; from *perash*, to separate) means "those who have been set apart". The Jewish party of this name first appeared in Judea in the reign of John Hyrcanus I (135–104 B.C.) and strove to ensure that the state was governed in strict accordance with the TORAH. Their influence in the development of orthodox Judaism was profound. The condemnations of Jesus were essentially against the more extremist followers of the Pharisee Shammai, who were open to charges of narrow literalism and hypocrisy. The TALMUD mentions the following groups:

(1) The "Dashers" or "Bandy-legged" (*Nikfi*), who scarcely lifted their feet from the ground in walking, but "dashed them against the stones", that people might think them absorbed in holy thought (*Matt.* xxi, 44).

(2) The "Mortars", who wore a "mortier" or cap, which would not allow them to see the passers-by, that their meditations might not be disturbed. "Having eyes they saw not" (*Mark* viii, 18).

(3) The "Bleeders", who inserted thorns in the borders of their gaberdines to prick their legs in walking.

(4) The "Cryers", or "Inquirers", who went about crying out, "Let me know my duty, and I will do it" (*Matt.* xix, 16–22).

(5) The "Almsgivers", who had a trumpet sounded before them to summon the poor together (*Matt.* vi, 2).

(6) The "Stumblers", or "Bloody-browed" (*Kizai*), who shut their eyes when they went abroad that they might see no women, being "blind leaders of the blind" (*Matt.* xv, 14). Our Lord calls them "blind Pharisees", "fools and blind".

(7) The "Immovables", who stood like statues for hours together, "Praying in the market places" (*Matt.* vi, 5).

(8) The "Pestle Pharisees" (*Medinkia*), who kept themselves bent double like the handle of a pestle.

(9) The "Strong-shouldered" (*Shikmi*), who walked with their back bent as if carrying on their shoulders the whole burden of the law.

(10) The "Dyed Pharisees", called by Our Lord "Whited Sepulchres", whose externals of devotion cloaked hypocrisy and moral uncleanliness. (*Talmud of Jerusalem*, Berakoth, ix; *Sota*, v, 7; *Talmud of Babylon*, Sota, 22b.)

Pharos (făr′ os). A lighthouse; so called from the lighthouse (*see* SEVEN WONDERS OF THE WORLD *under* WONDER) built by Ptolemy Philadelphus on the island of Pharos, off Alexandria, Egypt. It was 450 ft. high, and according to JOSEPHUS could be seen at a distance of 42 miles. Part was blown down in 793 and it was totally destroyed by an earthquake in 1375.

Pharsalia (far sā′ lia). An epic in Latin hexameters by Lucan. It tells of the civil war between Pompey and CÆSAR, and of the battle of Pharsalus (48 B.C.) in which Pompey, with 45,000 legionaries, 7,000 cavalry, and a large number of auxiliaries, was decisively defeated by Cæsar, who had only 22,000 legionaries and 1,000 cavalry. Pompey's battle-cry was *Hercules invictus*: that of Cæsar, *Venus victrix*.

Pheidippides. See MARATHON.

Phigalian Marbles (fi gā′ li àn). A series of 23 sculptures in ALTO-RELIEVO, forming part of the ELGIN MARBLES. They were removed from the temple of APOLLO at Bassæ, near Phigalia, in 1812, and represent the combat of the CENTAURS and the LAPITHÆ, and that of the Greeks and AMAZONS.

Philadelphia lawyer. A lawyer of outstanding ability, with a keen scent for the weaknesses in an adversary's case, and a thorough knowledge of the intricacies of the law. "You will have to get a Philadelphia lawyer to solve that" is a familiar American phrase. It is said that in 1735, in a case of criminal libel, the only counsel who would undertake the defence was Andrew Hamilton, the famous Philadelphia barrister, who obtained his client's acquittal in face of apparently irrefutable evidence, and charged no fee. In NEW ENGLAND there was a saying that three Philadelphia lawyers were a match for the DEVIL.

Philandering (fi lăn′ dèr ing). Coquetting with a woman; paying court, and leading her to think you love her, but never declaring your preference. *Philander* literally means "a lover of men" (Gr. *philos*, loving; *andros*, man), but as the word was made into a proper noun and used for a lover by Ariosto in ORLANDO FURIOSO (followed by Beaumont and Fletcher in *The Laws of Candy*), it obtained its present significance.

Philemon and Baucis. Poor cottagers of

Phrygia (husband and wife), who, in Ovid's story (*Metamorphoses*, viii, 631), entertained JUPITER and MERCURY, in the guise of travellers, so hospitably that Jupiter transformed their cottage into a TEMPLE, making them its priest and priestess. They asked that they might die together, and it was so. Philemon became an OAK, Baucis a linden tree, and their branches intertwined at the top.

Philip, St., is usually represented bearing a large CROSS, or a basket containing loaves in allusion to *John* vi, 5–7. He is commemorated with ST. JAMES THE LESS on 1 May (since 1985, 11 May by Roman Catholics).

The name Philip is also applied to a sparrow.

Philip, remember thou art mortal. A sentence repeated to the Macedonian king every time he gave an audience.

Philippe Égalité. *See* ÉGALITÉ.

Philippic. A severe scolding; a speech full of acrimonious invective. So called from the orations of Demosthenes against Philip of Macedon, to rouse the Athenians to resist his encroachments. The orations of CICERO against Antony are called "Philippics".

Philistines. Properly, a warlike immigrant people of ancient Palestine or *Philistia* who contested its possession with the Israelites, hence a heathen foe. Its application to the ill-behaved and ignorant, those lacking culture and sensibility or of base and materialistic outlook stems from the term *Philister* as used by German university students to denote the townspeople, the "outsiders". This is said to have arisen at Jena, because of a TOWN AND GOWN row in 1693, which resulted in a number of deaths, when the university preacher took for his text, "The Philistines be upon thee" (*Judges* xvi, 12). Its use was much popularized in England by Matthew Arnold's frequent employment of the term in his *Culture and Anarchy* (1869).

Philoctetes. The most famous archer in the TROJAN WAR, to whom HERCULES, at death, gave his arrows. In the tenth year of the siege Odysseus (ULYSSES) commanded that he should be sent for, as an ORACLE had declared that TROY could

not be taken without the arrows of Hercules. Philoctetes accordingly went to Troy, slew PARIS and Troy fell.

The *Philoctetes* of Sophocles is one of the most famous Greek tragedies.

Philomel. *See* NIGHTINGALE.

Philopena. From the German *Viel-liebchen*, darling, sweetheart. A philopena is a double almond.

Philosopher. The sages of Greece used to be called *sophoi* (wise men), but PYTHAGORAS thought the word too arrogant, and adopted the compound *philosophos* (lover of wisdom), whence "philosopher", one who courts or loves wisdom.

The leading philosophers and Schools of Philosophy in Ancient Greece were:

Philosophers of the Academic sect. PLATO, Speusippos, Xenocrates (*see* XENOCRATIC), Polemo, Crates of Athens, Crantor, Arcesilaos, Carneades, Clitomachos, Philo, and Antiochos.

Philosophers of the Cynic sect. ANTISTHENES, DIOGENES of Sinope, Monimos, Onesicritos, Crates of Thebes, Metrocles, Hipparchia, MENIPPUS, and Menedemos of Lampsacos.

Philosophers of the Cyrenaic sect. Aristippos, Hegesias, Anniceris, Theodoros, and Bion.

Philosophers of the Eleac and Eretriac sects. Phædo, Plisthenes, and Menedemos of Eretria.

Philosophers of the Eleatic sect. Xenophanes, Parmenides, Melissos, ZENO of Tarsus, Leucippos, DEMOCRITUS, Protagoras, and Anaxarchos.

Philosophers of the Epicurean sect. EPICURUS, and a host of disciples.

Philosophers of the Heraclitan sect. Heraclitos; the names of his disciples are unknown.

Philosophers of the Ionic sect. Anaximander, Anaximenes, Anaxagoras, and Archelaos.

Philosophers of the Italic sect. PYTHAGORAS, EMPEDOCLES, Epicharmos, Archytas, Alcmæon, Hippasos, Philolaos, and Eudoxos.

Philosophers of the Megaric sect. Euclid, Eubulides, Alexinos, Euphantos, Apollonius Chronosis, Diodorus, Ichthyas, Clinomachos, and Stilpo.

Philosophers of the Peripatetic sect. ARISTOTLE, Theophrastos, Strato,

Lyco, Aristoxenus, Critolaos and Diodoros.

Philosophers of the Sceptic sect. Pyrrho (*see* PYRRHONISM) and Timon.

Philosophers of the Socratic sect. SOCRATES, Xenophon, Æschines, Crito, Simon, Glauco, Simmias, and Cebes.

Philosophers of the Stoic sect. ZENO, Cleanthes, CHRYSIPPUS, Zeno the Less, Diogenes of Babylon, Antipater, Panætios, Epictetus, Marcus Aurelius, Posidonios and Seneca.

Philosopher's Egg. A mediæval preservative against poison and a cure for the plague. The shell of a new egg was pricked, the white blown out, and the space filled with saffron or a yolk of an egg mixed with saffron.

Philosophers' Stone. The hypothetical substance which, according to the alchemists, would convert all baser metals into GOLD; by many it was thought to be compounded of the purest sulphur and mercury. Mediæval experimenters toiled endlessly in the search, thus laying the foundations of the science of chemistry, among other inventions. It was in this quest that Bötticher stumbled on the manufacture of DRESDEN porcelain, Roger Bacon on the composition of gunpowder, Geber on the properties of acids, Van Helmont on the nature of gas, and Dr. GLAUBER on the "salts" which bear his name.

In Ripley's treatise, *The Compound of Alchemie* (*c.* 1471), we are told the 12 stages or "gates" in the transmutation of metals are: (1) Calcination; (2) Dissolution; (3) Separation; (4) Conjunction; (5) Putrefaction; (6) Congelation; (7) Cibation; (8) Sublimation; (9) Fermentation; (10) Exaltation; (11) Multiplication; and (12) Projection. Of these the last two were much the most important; the former consisting of the ELIXIR, the latter in the penetration and transfiguration of metals in fusion by casting the powder of the philosophers' stone upon them, which is then called the "powder of projection". According to one legend, Noah was commanded to hang up the true philosophers' stone in the ark, to give light to every living creature therein; while another related that DEUCALION had it in a bag over his shoulder,

but threw it away and lost it. *Cp.* ALKAHEST: PARACELSUS.

Philter (Gr. *philtron*; from *philein*, to love). A draught or charm to incite in another the passion of love. The Thessalian philters were the most renowned, but both Greeks and Romans used these dangerous potions, which sometimes produced insanity. Lucretius is said to have been driven mad by one, and CALIGULA's death is attributed to some philters administered by his wife, Cæsonia. Brabantio says to Othello:

Phiz. The pseudonym assumed by the artist Hablot Knight Browne (1815–1882), who became well-known for his amusing and clever book illustrations. He adopted the name when he began illustrating the works of Charles Dickens (to match up with BOZ).

Phlegethon (Gr. *phlego*, to burn). A river of liquid fire in HADES, flowing into the ACHERON.

> Fierce Phlegethon,
> Whose waves of torrent fire inflame with Erage.
> MILTON: *Paradise Lost*, II, 580.

Phlogiston (flō jis' ton) (Gr., "combustible"). The inflammable substance that was supposed to be a constituent of all combustible material. A theory originated by German chemist J.J.Becher (1635–1682) and developed by G.E. Stahl in 1702. It held sway until overthrown in the 1770s by Lavoisier with the theory of oxygenation.

Phœbe (fē' bi). A female TITAN of classical myth, daughter of URANUS and GÆA; also a name of DIANA, as goddess of the MOON.

Phœbus (Gr., the Shining One). An epithet of APOLLO, god of the SUN. In poetry the name is sometimes used of the sun itself, sometimes of Apollo as leader of the MUSES.

Phœnix (fē' niks). A fabulous Egyptian (Arabian, or Indian, etc.) bird, the only one of its kind, according to Greek legend said to live a certain number of years, at the close of which it makes in Egypt (or ARABIA, etc.) a nest of spices, sings a melodious dirge, flaps its wings to set fire to the pile, burns itself to ashes, and comes forth with new life. It is to this bird that SHAKESPEARE refers in

Cymbeline (I, vi):

> If she be furnished with a mind so rare,
> She is alone the Arabian bird.

The Phœnix and Turtle (attributed to Shakespeare) is based on the legendary love and death of this bird and the turtledove.

The phœnix was adopted as a sign over chemists' shops through the association of this fabulous bird with ALCHEMY. PARACELSUS wrote about it, and several of the alchemists employed it to symbolize their vocation.

The phœnix is also a symbol of the Resurrection.

Phœnix, the son of Amyntor king of Argos, was tutor to ACHILLES.

Phœnix dactylifera. The date-palm; so called from the ancient idea that this tree, if burnt down or if it falls through old age, will rejuvenate itself and spring up fairer than ever.

Phœnix period, or **cycle,** generally supposed to be 500 years; Tacitus tells us it was 500 years; R. Stuart Poole that it was 1,460 Julian years, like the SOTHIC PERIOD; and Lipsius that it was 1,500 years. Opinions vary between 250 and 7,000 years. Tacitus (*Annales*, vi, 28) mentions four appearances of the bird in Egypt.

Phœnix Park. The Phœnix Park Murders. The assassination (6 May 1882) of Lord Frederick Cavendish, Chief Secretary for Ireland, and Mr. Burke, Under-Secretary, by Irish IN-VINCIBLES, when walking in Phœnix Park near the Vice-regal lodge. They were hacked to death by surgical knives on the day of Lord Spencer's arrival in Dublin as viceroy. James Carey, a Dublin councillor, one of the Invincibles, turned QUEEN'S EVIDENCE and five of the gang were hanged, others being given life sentences. Carey was shot later by an avenger. The affair aroused great horror and proved a great embarrassment to the Irish leader, Parnell.

Phoney, or **phony.** Fraudulent, bogus, insincere; an American colloquialism and slang term that became anglicized about 1920. It derives from *fawney*, an obsolete underworld CANT word meaning the imitation gold ring used by confidence tricksters. During World War

II, the period of comparative inactivity, from the outbreak to the invasion of Norway and Denmark, was characterized by American journalists as the "Phoney War".

Phrygians (frij' yànz). An early Christian sect of the late 2nd century, so called from Phrygia, where they abounded; also called MONTANISTS.

Phrygian mode. In music, the second of the "authentic" ecclesiastical modes. It had its "final" on E and its "dominant" on C, and was derived from the ancient Greek mode of this name, which was war-like.

Phryne (frī' nè). A famous Athenian courtesan of the 4th century B.C., who acquired so much wealth by her beauty that she offered to rebuild the walls of Thebes if she might put on them the inscription: "ALEXANDER destroyed them, but Phryne the hetæra rebuilt them." It is recorded of her that, when she was being tried on a capital charge, her defender, who failed to move the judges by his eloquence, asked her to uncover her bosom. She did so, and the judges, struck by her beauty, acquitted her on the spot.

Phylactery (Gr. *phylacterion*; from *phylasso*, I watch). A charm or amulet worn by conforming Jews on the forehead and arm during morning prayer. It consisted of four slips of parchment, each bearing a text of Scripture, enclosed in two black leather cases. One case contained *Exod.* xiii, 1–10, 11–16; and the other case *Deut.* vi, 4–9, xi, 13–21. The practice arose from the command of Moses, "Therefore shall ye lay up these my words in your heart ... and bind them for a sign upon your hand ... as frontlets between your eyes" (*Deut.* xi, 18).

Phynnodderee. A Manx HOBGOBLIN combining the properties of the Scandinavian TROLL, the Scottish BROWNIE and the Irish LEPRECHAUN. He drives home straying sheep and helps in the harvesting if a storm is brewing, and is possessed of great strength for his size.

Physiocrats. A school of French political economists in the second half of the 18th century founded by François Quesnay (1694–1774), a court physician. They attacked the economic regulations of

MERCANTILISM, and held that wealth consisted in the products of the soil, not in coin or bullion. They advocated a predominantly agricultural society, FREE TRADE, and LAISSEZ-FAIRE. All revenue was to be raised by a land tax. The word is from the Greek, meaning 'government according to nature".

Pica. *See* PIE.

Picards. An extremist early 15th-century sect prevalent in Bohemia and the VAUDOIS, said to be so called from Picard of Flanders, their founder, who called himself the New ADAM and tried to introduce the custom of living in the nude, like Adam in PARADISE. They were suppressed by Ziska in 1421. *Cp.* ADAMITES.

Picaresque (pik à resk'). The term applied to the class of literature that deals sympathetically with the adventures of clever and amusing rogues (Span. *picaresco*, roguish, knavish). The Spanish novel *Lazarillo de Tormes* (1553) is the earliest example of its kind and Le Sage's *Gil Blas* (1715) is perhaps the best known. Nash's *Jack Wilton* (1594) is the earliest English example, and others are Defoe's *Moll Flanders* and *Colonel Jack*.

Piccadilly. The famous London street takes its name after a *Piccadilly Hall* that existed in the vicinity in the early 17th century, the home of Robert Baker, a tailor. The name is derived from *pickadils* or *peccadilloes*, which, according to Blount's *Glossographia* (1656), were the round hems about the edge of a skirt or garment, also a kind of stiff collar or band for the neck and shoulders. The name may be in allusion to the tailor's source of wealth or that it was the "skirt house" or outermost house in the district.

Piccadilly Weepers. *See* WEEP.

Pickle. A rod in pickle. One ready to chastise with at any moment; one "preserved" for use.

I'm in a pretty pickle. In a sorry plight, or state of disorder.

> How cam'st thou in this pickle?
> SHAKESPEARE: *The Tempest*, V, i.

To be pickled. A colloquial term for being drunk.

Pickle-herring. The German term for

a CLOWN or buffoon, from a humorous character of that name in an early 17th-century play.

Pickwickian. In a Pickwickian sense. Said of words or epithets, usually of a derogatory or insulting kind, that, in the circumstances in which they are employed, are not to be taken as having quite the same force or implication as they naturally would have. The allusion is to the scene in ch. i. of *Pickwick Papers* when Mr. Pickwick accused Mr. Blotton of acting in "a vile and calumnious manner", whereupon Mr. Blotton retorted by calling Mr. Pickwick "a humbug". It finally was made to appear that both had used the offensive words only in a Pickwickian sense, and that each had, in fact, the highest regard and esteem for each other.

Picts. Ancient inhabitants of SCOTLAND before the coming of the Scots (Goidelic-speaking Celts) from Northern Ireland, in the 5th century. The Scots settled in Dalriada (Argyll) and the Pictish kingdom survived until the mid-9th century when it was conquered by Kenneth Mac Alpine, King of Dalriada. The name is the Lat. *picti*, painted, *i.e.* "tattooed men".

Picts' houses. Underground prehistoric dwellings found in the Orkneys and on the east coast of SCOTLAND, and attributed to the Picts.

Picture (Lat. *pictura*; from *pictus*, past participle of *pingere*, to paint). A model, or BEAU IDEAL, as, *He is the picture of health; The bride looked a picture*.

Picture Bible. A name given to the BIBLIA PAUPERUM.

To put someone in the picture. To inform someone of the proceedings or developments to date.

To see the picture whole. To be able to appreciate fully a situation, case, etc., in its entirety, based on a proper appreciation of its constituent elements.

Pidgin English. Originally a form of Anglo-Chinese jargon which developed on the China coast from the 17th century as a consequence of contact with English traders and businessmen. It is essentially a form of basic English with some Chinese, and additions from other tongues, but with certain Chinese constructions and a characteristic Chinese pronunciation, *i.e. ploper* for "proper", *solly* for "sorry", *makee* for "make", *tinkee* for "think", etc. Pidgin is a corruption of "business", hence, **this is not my pidgin,** this is not my business, not my responsibility, not my affair.

Similar forms, of largely independent growth, using the same basic words, have become widespread in the Pacific, Australia, Africa and elsewhere.

Pie or **Pi. Pie,** or **pi** is also an epithet applied to a smugly or irritatingly pious person.

Pie in the sky. The good time or good things promised which never come; that which will never be realized.

To eat humble pie. *See under* EAT.

Piece. Pièce de résistance (pi ās dè rā zēs tôns) (Fr., piece of resistance). The "substantial piece" *i.e.* the main dish of a meal; the joint or meat dish. Figuratively, the most important feature, the main event, the best part of the show, the outstanding item.

Pieces of Eight. The old Spanish silver *peso* (piastre) or DOLLAR of 8 reals of the 17th and 18th centuries. It was marked with an 8.

To give a person a piece of one's mind. *See under* MIND.

Piece work. A term used when an industrial worker is paid by the *piece* or job, instead of by the hour, etc.

Pied. Au pied de la lettre (Fr., to the foot of the letter). Quite literally, close to the letter.

Pied-à-terre (pē ā dà târ') (Fr. foot on the ground). A temporary lodging or a country residence, a footing.

Pied Piper of Hamelin. The legend is that the town of Hamelin (Westphalia) was infested with rats in 1284, that a mysterious piper in a parti-coloured suit appeared in the town and offered to rid it of vermin for a certain sum, which offer was accepted by the townspeople. The Pied Piper fulfilled his contract but payment was not forthcoming. On the following St. John's Day he reappeared, and again played his pipe. This time all the children followed him and he led them to a mountain cave where all disappeared save two—one blind, the other dumb, or lame. Another version is that

they were led to Transylvania where they formed a German colony. The story, familiar in ENGLAND from Robert Browning's poem, appeared earlier in James Howell's *Familiar Letters* (1645–1655). The legend has its roots in the story of the CHILDREN'S CRUSADE (*see under* CRUSADES).

Piepowder Court. A court of justice formerly held at FAIRS, which dealt with disputes between buyers and sellers. Literally a "wayfarer's court", piepowder being from F. *pied-poudreux*, dusty-footed (also a vagabond).

Pierrot (pē' rō) (*i.e.* "Little Peter"). A traditional character in French PANTO-MIME, a kind of idealized clown. He is generally tall and thin, has his face covered with white powder or flour, and wears a white costume with very long sleeves and a row of big buttons down the front. *Cp.* HARLEQUIN.

Piers Plowman. *See* VISION OF PIERS PLOWMAN.

Pietà (pē ā ta'). A representation of the Virgin embracing the dead body of her Son. Filial or parental love was called *pietas* by the Romans.

Pietists. A 17th-century Lutheran movement seeking to revive the life of the Lutheran Church in Germany. It was started by P.J. Spener (1635–1705) and the name was applied derisively by the orthodox in the same way as the term METHODIST was used in England.

Pig. The pig was held sacred by the ancient Cretans because JUPITER was suckled by a sow; it was immolated in the ELEUSINIAN MYSTERIES; was sacrificed to HERCULES, to VENUS, and to the LARES by all who sought relief from bodily ailments. The sow was sacrificed to CERES "because it taught men to turn up the earth". The pig is unclean to Jews and Moslems.

The five dark marks on the inner side of each of a pig's forelegs are supposed to be the marks of the DEVIL's claws when they entered the swine (*Mark* v, 11–15). *See also* HOG; SOW.

A pig in a poke. A blind bargain. The reference is to a common trick of yore of trying to palm off on a GREENHORN a cat for a sucking-pig. If he opened the poke or sack he "let the cat out of the bag", and the trick was disclosed. The use is referred to in Thomas Tusser's *Five Hundreth Good Pointes of Husbandrie* (1580). The French *chat en poche* refers to the fact, while our proverb refers to the trick. *Pocket* is a diminutive of *poke*.

A pig's whisper. A very short space of time; properly a grunt—which doesn't take long.

Bartholomew pig. *See under* BARTHO-LOMEW.

He has brought his pigs to a pretty market. He has made a very bad bargain; he has managed his affairs badly. Pigs were for long a principal article of sale among country folk.

Pig-a-back. *See* PICK-A-BACK.

Pig and Whistle. *See* PUBLIC-HOUSE SIGNS.

Pigs and whistles. Trifles. *To go to pigs and whistles* is to be ruined, to go to the DEUCE.

Pig's ear. IN RHYMING SLANG, beer.

Pig-headed. Obstinate, contrary.

Pig Iron. Iron cast in oblong ingots now called *pigs* but formerly *sows*. *Sow* is now applied to the main channel in which the molten liquid runs, the smaller branches which diverge from it being called *pigs*, and it is the iron from these which is called *pig iron*.

Pigs in clover. People who have money but don't know how to behave decently. Also, a game consisting of a box divided into recesses into which one has to roll marbles by tilting the box.

Please the pigs. If circumstances permit, *Deo volente*. An alliterative form which has been given several laboured explanations, such as "please the PYX", or "please the PIXIES".

St. Anthony's pig. *See under* AN-THONY.

The Pig and the Tinderbox. An old colloquial name for the ELEPHANT AND CASTLE public-house; in allusion to its sign of a pig-like elephant surmounted by the representation of a castle which might pass as a tinderbox.

To drive one's pigs to market. To snore very loudly.

To drive pigs. To snore.

To pig it. To eat in a greedy fashion, to bolt one's food; to live in a slovenly piggish fashion, in ill-kept and ill-provided circumstances.

To pig together. To huddle together like pigs in a sty. To share and share alike, especially in lodgings in a small way; formerly it meant to sleep two (or more) in the same bed.

To stare like a stuck pig. With open mouth and staring eyes, as a pig that is being killed; in the utmost astonishment, mingled sometimes with fear.

When pigs fly. NEVER.

Pigskin. A saddle, the best being made of pigskin. "To throw a leg across a pigskin" is to mount a horse.

Pigtail. In England the word first appeared (17th century) as the name of a tobacco that was twisted into a thin rope; and it was used of the plait of twisted hair worn by sailors till the early 19th century, as it is still used of that worn by schoolgirls (*see* FLAPPER).

When the Manchu invaded and conquered China in the 17th century the Chinese were required to wear queues or pigtails as a sign of servitude until the advent of the republic in 1912.

Pig-wife. A woman who sold crockery. A *piggin* was a small pail, especially a milkpail; and a *pig* a small bowl, cup or mug.

Piggy-bank. The traditional pig-shaped money-box, still manufactured, nowadays often in plastic but formerly of earthenware or glass. Such money-boxes, with a coin or coins inside, were given to apprentices in Tudor times as CHRISTMAS BOXES.

Pigeon. Slang for a dupe, an easily gullible person, a GULL. To *pigeon* is to cheat or gull one out of his money by fairly transparent hoaxes. Pigeons are very easily caught by snares, and in the sporting world rogues and their dupes are called "rooks and pigeons".

That's not my pigeon. That is not my responsibility; that's not my job; also used in the form, "That's someone else's pigeon". *Pigeon* here is an incorrect variant spelling of "pidgin". *See* PIDGIN ENGLISH.

To pluck a pigeon. To cheat a gullible person of his money; to fleece a GREEN-HORN.

To put the cat among the pigeons. *See under* CAT.

Pigeon, or **Pigeon's Blood.** Soy sauce; also the colour of a fine dark RUBY.

Pigeon English. An incorrect form of PIDGIN ENGLISH.

Pigeon Pair. Boy and girl twins. It was once supposed that pigeons always sit on two eggs which produce a male and a female, and these twin birds live together in love the rest of their lives.

Pigeon's milk. Partly digested food, regurgitated by pigeons for their young; also a non-existent liquid which gullible children and APRIL FOOLS are sometimes sent to fetch.

Pigeon-hole. A small compartment for filing papers; hence, a matter that has been put on one side is often said to have been *pigeon-holed*. In dovecots a small hole is left for the pigeons to walk in and out.

Pigeon-livered. Timid, easily frightened, like a pigeon. *See* LIVER.

Piggin. *See* PIG-WIFE.

Pigmies. *See* PYGMIES.

Pigott Forgeries. *See under* FORGERY.

Pigwidgin, or **Pigwiggen.** A FAIRY or DWARF; anything very small.

Pike. The Germans have a tradition that when Christ was crucified all fishes dived under the water in terror, except the pike, which, out of curiosity, lifted up its head and beheld the whole scene; hence the fancy that in a pike's head all the parts of the Crucifixion are represented, the CROSS, three nails, and a sword being clearly delineated. *Cp.* PASSION FLOWER.

Pikestaff. Plain as a Pikestaff. Quite clear, obvious, and unmistakable. The earlier form of the phrase (mid-16th century) was *plain as a packstaff, i.e.* the staff on which a pedlar carried his pack, which was worn plain and smooth.

> O Lord! what absurdities! as plain as any packstaff.
>
> DRYDEN: *Amphitryon*, III, i.

Pilate. One tradition has it that Pontius Pilate's later life was so full of misfortune that in CALIGULA'S time he committed suicide at ROME. His body was thrown into the Tiber, but evil spirits so disturbed the water that it was retrieved and taken to Vienne, where it was cast into the Rhône, eventually coming to rest in the recesses of a lake on Mount PILATUS. Another legend is that he committed suicide to avoid the sentence of death passed on him by Tiberius because of his having ordered the crucifixion of Christ. His wife is given as Claudia Procula, or Procla, and by some she has been identified with Claudia of II *Tim.* iv, 21: there is a story that they both became penitent and died peaceably in the faith.

In the Coptic Church he is regarded as a martyr, and his feast day is 25 June. Procla has been canonized in the GREEK CHURCH.

The Acts of Pilate. An apocryphal work, probably of the 4th century, recounting the trial, death, and resurrection of Christ. In combination with another treatise on the *Descent of Christ into Hades*, the two are known as the *Gospel of Nicodemus*.

Pilate voice. A loud ranting voice. In the old mysteries all TYRANTS were made to speak in a rough ranting manner. Similarly SHAKESPEARE has "outherods HEROD" (*Hamlet*, III, ii), and "This is Ercles' vein, a tyrant's vein" (*Midsummer Night's Dream*, I, ii).

Pilatus, Mount. In Switzerland, between the canton of Lucerne and Unterwalden. So called because during westerly winds it is covered with a white "cap" of cloud (Lat. *pileatus*, covered with the *pileus*, or felt cap). The similarity of the name gave rise to a fabled connection with PILATE. One tradition is that Pilate was banished to GAUL by Tiberius and threw himself into the lake near the summit of this mountain, where he appears annually. Whoever sees the ghost will die before the year is out. In the 16th century a law was passed forbidding anyone to throw stones into the lake for fear of bringing a tempest on the country.

Pilgarlic, or **Pill'd Garlic.** In the 16th and 17th centuries, a term for a bald-headed man, especially one who had lost his hair through disease, and left a head that was suggestive of peeled garlic. Stow says of one getting bald: "He will soon be peeled garlic like myself." The term was later used of any poor wretch forsaken by his fellows, and in a humorous and self-pitying way, of oneself.

Pilgrim Fathers. The term (first used in 1799) applied to the emigrants who founded the colony of Plymouth, NEW ENGLAND, in 1620. In 1608 a PURITAN congregation from Scrooby (Notts.) settled at Leiden and eventually decided to migrate to America. They finally left Plymouth in the MAYFLOWER. Of the 102 settlers, 24 were women, and only 35 of the party were Puritans. Their tradition is part of American folklore.

The Pilgrim's Progress. The allegorical masterpiece of John Bunyan, the first part of which appeared in 1678 and the second in 1684. It tells of Christian's pilgrimage, beset with trials and temptations, but with incidental encouragement, until he reached the Celestial City where he was later joined by his wife and children. The rustic simplicity and directness of its story gave it lasting appeal and many expressions have become part of the language. "The Slough of Despond", "Vanity Fair", "Mr. Worldly Wiseman" and "Mr. Facing-both-ways" are notable examples.

Pilgrimage. A journey to a sacred place undertaken as an act of religious devotion, either as an act of veneration or penance, or to ask for the fulfilment of some prayer. In the MIDDLE AGES the chief venues in the West were Walsingham and Canterbury (England), Fourvière, Le Puy, and St. Denis (France); ROME, Loreto, and Assisi (Italy); COMPOSTELA, Guadalupe, and Montserrat (Spain); Mariazell (Austria); Cologne, Trier (Germany); Einsiedeln (Switzerland). The pre-eminent pilgrimage was of course to the HOLY LAND. LOURDES became a noted place of pilgrimage for Roman Catholics after 1858.

Miraculous cures were sometimes effected upon those who worshipped at these shrines and spiritual and bodily welfare was the main concern of most pilgrims; for others a pilgrimage was an occasion for a holiday and an opportunity to visit distant parts or foreign lands. *Cp.* CANTERBURY TALES; COCKLE HAT; CRUSADES; PALMER.

> Whan that Aprille with his shoures soote
> The droghte of Marche hath perced to
> the roote...

Than longen folk to goon on pilgrimages,
(And palmers for to seken straunge strondes)...
CHAUCER: *Canterbury Tales (Prologue)*.

The Pilgrimage of Grace. A rising in Yorkshire (1536–1537) due to political unrest among the gentry occasioned by inclosures, etc., and the religious changes culminating in the dissolution of the monasteries. Under Robert Aske, the "pilgrims" took the five wounds of Christ as their banner and captured York and Hull. Among the insurgents were the Archbishop of York, Lords Darcy, Latimer, Lumley, Scrope, and Sir Thomas Percy. The Duke of Norfolk effected a truce based on promises of redress which were not kept. A full pardon was offered but further outbreaks in 1537 gave Henry VIII the excuse to execute some 220 rebels.

Pill, The. Since the introduction of the oral contraceptive in the early 1960s its impact has caused it to be known as *the pill*, to the exclusion of all others. In Victorian England pills were popular "universal remedies" for many maladies, but especially associated with liver complaints and constipation. Thomas Holloway and Thomas Beecham were the two richest pill magnates of the day, the former entering the market in 1837 and the latter in 1857. Aloes, ginger, and soap formed the basis of their products, and both became millionaires.

To gild the pill. To soften the blow; to make a disagreeable task less offensive, as pills used to be gilded (and are now sugar-coated) to make them more palatable.

Pillar. From pillar to post. Hither and thither; from one thing to another without definite purpose; harassed and badgered. The phrase was originally *from post to pillar*, and comes from the old tennis-courts in allusion to the banging about of the balls.

Nelson's Pillar. Formerly Dublin's most controversial monument, erected in honour of the great sailor by a committee of bankers and merchants in 1808–9, who raised the funds by public subscription. It was sited in Sackville Street (now O'Connell Street) and the statue of Nelson on the top was the work of Thomas Kirk. The column contained a spiral staircase leading to the top of the doric abacus and somewhat fresher air. The whole monument was 134 ft. high. It was blown up by young Republican extremists on 8 March 1966, and the 50 ft. of masonry left standing was demolished by army engineers. Nelson's head was removed to a Corporation depot whence it was taken by a group of art students and flown to London for subsequent sale to an antique dealer. *Cp.* NELSON'S COLUMN *under* COLUMN.

Pillar Saints. *See* STYLITES.

The Pillars of Hercules. The opposite rocks at the entrance to the Mediterranean, one in Spain and the other in Africa, anciently called Calpe and Abyla, now Gibraltar and Mount Hacho (on which stands the fortress of Ceuta). The tale is that they were bound together till HERCULES tore them asunder in order to get to Gades (Cadiz). Macrobius ascribes the feat of making the division to Sesostris (the Egyptian Hercules), Lucan follows the same tradition; and the Phœnicians are said to have set on the opposing rocks two large pyramidal columns to serve as seamarks, one dedicated to Hercules and the other to ASTARTE.

I will follow you even to the Pillars of Hercules. To the end of the world. The ancients supposed that these rocks marked the utmost limits of the habitable globe.

Pompey's Pillar. *See under* POMPEY.

Pillory. Punishment by the pillory was not finally abolished in England till 1837, but since 1815 it had been used only for cases of perjury.

Pilot. Pilot balloon. A small balloon sent up to find the direction of the wind; hence, figuratively, a feeler; a hint thrown out to ascertain public opinion on some point.

Pilot fish. The small sea-fish *Naucrates ductor*, so called because it is supposed to pilot the shark to its prey.

Pilot scheme, project. An experimental try-out.

The pilot that weathered the storm. William Pitt the younger, who as Prime Minister steered the country through much of the European storm stirred up by the French Revolution. It derives from Canning's *Song for the Inauguration of the Pitt Club.*

Pilpay, or **Bidpay.** The name given as that of the author of *Kalilah and Dimnah* (otherwise known as *The Fables of Pilpay*), which is the 8th-century Arabic version of the Sanskrit *Panchatantra.* The word is not a true name, but means "wise man" (Arab. *bidbah*), and was applied to the chief scholar at the court of an Indian prince.

Piltdown Man, or **Piltdown Skull.** *See under* FORGERY.

Pin. I don't care a pin, or **a pin's point.** I don't care in the least.

I do not pin my faith upon your sleeve. I am not going to take your IPSE DIXIT for gospel. In feudal times badges were worn on the sleeve by a leader's partisans and sometimes badges were changed for some reason, hence people were chary of judging by appearances and would say, "You wear the badge, but I do not intend to pin my faith on your sleeve."

Not worth a pin. Wholly worthless.

There's not a pin to choose between them. They're as like as two peas, practically no difference between them.

To pin a person down. To "nail him down", to compel him to reveal his intentions or to state clearly his views, etc.

To pin something on a person. To fasten the blame, guilt, or responsibility on him.

Weak on his pins. Weak in his legs, the legs being a man's "pins" or pegs.

You could have heard a pin drop. Said of a state—especially a sudden state in the midst of din—of complete silence.

Pin money. A woman's allowance of money for her own personal expenditure. Pins were once very expensive, and in 14th- and 15th-century wills there were often special bequests for the express purpose of buying pins; when they became cheap, women spent their allowances on other fancies but the term *pin money* remained in vogue.

Pins and needles. The tingling that comes over a limb when it has been numbed or is "asleep".

On pins and needles. On TENTER-

HOOKS; in a state of fearful expectation or great uneasiness.

Policy of pin pricks. A policy of petty annoyance to wear someone down. The term came into prominence during the period of strained relations between Britain and France in 1898 at the time of the Fashoda incident. It is an anglicization of a much older French phrase, *un coup d'épingle*.

Pin-up Girl. In World War II servicemen used to pin up in their quarters pictures of film stars and actresses (often scantily clad) or their own particular girl-friends. These were called "pin-up girls".

Pinch. At a pinch. In an urgent case; if hard pressed. There are things that one cannot do in the ordinary way, but that one may manage "at a pinch".

Peewits' pinch. *See* PEEWIT.

Pinch, punch, first of the month, and no returns. An old established children's trick, usually carried out fairly gently, on their fellows on the first of a month. The final phrase is a safeguard against retaliation. *Cp* APRIL FOOL.

To be pinched for money. To be in financial straits, hard up. Hence *to pinch and scrape* or *to pinch it*, to economize, to cheesepare.

To pinch. Slang for to steal.

Where the shoe pinches. *See under* SHOE.

Pinch-hitter. A person who substitutes for another in a crisis. The term is from baseball where the pinch-hitter—a man who always hits the ball hard—is put in to bat when the team is in desperate straits.

Pinchbeck. An alloy of copper (5 parts) and zinc (1 part), closely resembling GOLD, so called from Christopher Pinchbeck (1670–1732), a manufacturer of trinkets, watches, and jewellery in FLEET STREET, London. The term is used figuratively of anything spurious, of deceptive appearance, or low quality.

Pindar (*c.* 522–443 B.C.). A renowned lyric poet of THEBES who achieved great respect and public honour for his verse from his contemporaries.

Pindaric Verse (pin dar' ik). Irregular verse; a poem of various metres, and of lofty style; after the fashion started by Abraham Cowley in the mid-17th century, who inaccurately imitated in English the Greek versification of Pindar. He published fifteen *Pindarique Odes* in 1656 and the style was copied by many, including Dryden and Pope.

Pindar, Pinder, or **Pinner of Wakefield.** *See* AS GOOD AS GEORGE-A-GREEN *under* GEORGE.

Pine-tree shilling. A coin struck (1652–1684), contrary to English law, by the mint established by Massachusetts. Other shillings bore the devices of the oak-tree and willow. Charles II became aware of the practice, but as the royal OAK was used as a device took no action. The export of coins from Great Britain was forbidden and the early colonists relied on barter in wampum, beaver skins, corn, tobacco, etc., or on foreign coinage.

Pink. In pink. In the scarlet coat of a fox-hunter. The colour is not pink, but no hunting man would call it anything else. *Cp.* REDCOATS.

In the pink. In excellent health. An abbreviation of the modern phrase "in the pink of condition", deriving from SHAKESPEARE's "the very pink of courtesy" (*Romeo and Juliet*, II, iv), Steele's "the pink of courtesy" (*Tatler*, no. 204), Goldsmith's "the very pink of perfection" (*She Stoops to Conquer*, I), and Burns's "the pink o' womankind" (*The Posie*).

Pinkerton. Pinkerton's National Detective Agency was founded at Chicago (1852) by Allan Pinkerton (1819–1884), Glasgow-born deputy sheriff of Kane County, Illinois, who had proved himself a detective of some resource. It came to the forefront during the CIVIL WAR, when, in 1861, Pinkerton's men uncovered a plot to assassinate Lincoln, the President-elect. Pinkerton also found the means of obtaining military and political information from the Southern States during the war and eventually organized the Federal Secret Service. His most sensational coups were the discovery of the thieves of $700,000 stolen from the Adams Express in 1866, and the breaking-up of the MOLLY MAGUIRES (1877), an Irish-American secret society with many subversive and lawless deeds to their discredit.

Pinocchio (pē nō′ kiō). The mischievous hero of the famous puppet story *Le Avventure di Pinocchio* (1883) by G. Lorenzini, who wrote under the name of "Collodi", which was taken from his birthplace.

The story tells how a carpenter found a piece of wood that laughed and cried like a child and gave it to his friend Geppetto who fashioned from it the puppet Pinocchio. His creation proved unusually mischievous and had many bizarre adventures including having his feet burned off, his nose elongated, and being transformed into a donkey. Eventually he learned to show sympathy and goodness and "the fairy" changed him to a real boy back at home with Geppetto.

Pious. The Romans called a man who revered his father *pius*; hence Antoninus was called *pius*, because he requested that his adoptive father (Hadrian) might be ranked among the gods. ÆNEAS was called *Pius* because he rescued his father from the burning city of TROY. The Italian word PIETÁ has a similar meaning.

Pip. To be pipped is to be BLACKBALLED or defeated, the black ball being the pip. **To be pipped at the post** is to be defeated when victory seemed in sight.

Till the pips squeak. To put extreme pressure on someone, literally or metaphorically. An allusion to the squeezing of such fruits as oranges and lemons.

To have, or **to get the pip.** To be thoroughly "fed up", downhearted and miserable. Probably connected with *pip*, the poultry disease which causes fowls to pine away.

Pip emma. Military usage in World War I for P.M. Originally telephonese; "ten pip emma" avoids any possibility of misunderstanding. In the same way *ack emma* stands for A.M. *Cp.* TOC H.

Pipe. As you pipe, I must dance. I must accommodate myself to your wishes. "He who pays the piper calls the tune."

Pipe down! Stop being aggressive or noisy, stop talking. A naval colloquialism derived from the boatswain's call of this name meaning "hands turn in", *i.e.* "lights out".

Pipe dream. Originating with opium

smoking, an impossible, imaginary and fanciful hope or plan indulged in at one's ease when smoking a pipe.

Piping hot. Hot as water which pipes or sings; hence, new, only just out.

Piping times of peace (SHAKESPEARE, *Richard III*, I, i). Times when there was no thought of war, and the pastoral pipe instead of the martial trumpet was heard on the village greens.

Put that in your pipe and smoke it. Digest that if you can. "Swallow that one!" An expression used by one who has given an adversary a severe rebuke or given him "something to think about".

The pipe of peace. *See* CALUMET.

To pipe one's eye. To snivel, weep.

To put one's pipe out. To spoil his piping; to make him change his key or sing a different tune; "to take his shine out".

Pipe-laying (U.S.A.). Swaying the issue in an election by slipping in voters who are not on the electoral roll.

Pipeline. In the pipeline. Already under way; in process of manufacture or delivery, etc. From the transport of oil by pipeline.

Pipe Rolls, or **Great Rolls of the Pipe.** The name given to a class of EXCHEQUER records on account of their being kept in rolls in the form of a pipe. They begin in 1131 and continue till 1831, and contain the annual accounts of SHERIFFS with the Exchequer, county by county. They are now in the Public Record Office, Chancery Lane, London.

Piper. Piper's news. Stale news; FIDDLER'S NEWS.

The Pied Piper. *See* PIED.

Tom Piper. So the piper is called in the MORRIS DANCE.

Who's to pay the piper? *See under* PAY.

Pippin. *See* PIP.

Pippin the Short. *See under* SHORT.

Piran, St. (5th or 6th century). The patron saint of Cornish miners, said to have been sent to CORNWALL by St. PATRICK. According to another legend he was cast into the sea by his fellow Irishmen bound to a millstone and landed at Perranzabuloe (St.Piran in the

Sands) near Perranporth. He set up a hermitage and discovered tin when he saw it streaming from the stone of his fireplace. Two churches of St.Piran were buried in the sand dunes and the remains of one have been uncovered, hence legends of bells ringing in the sand. His day is 5th March. *See* MEBYON KERNOW.

Pis-aller (pēz ăl' ā) (Fr., worst course). A makeshift; something for want of a better; a last expedient.

Pisces (pis'kēz, pī'sēz) (Lat. the fishes). A constellation and the twelfth sign of the ZODIAC.

Piso's Justice (pī' zō). Verbally right, but morally wrong. Seneca says that Piso condemned a man on circumstantial evidence for murder; but when the execution was about to take place, the man supposed to have been murdered appeared. The centurion sent the prisoner to Piso, and explained the situation to him; whereupon Piso condemned all three to death, saying, *Fiat justitia* (Lat., let justice be done). The condemned man was executed because he had been sentenced, the centurion because he had disobeyed orders, and the man supposed to have been murdered because he had been the cause of death to two innocent men.

Pistol. To fire one's pistol in the air. Purposely to refrain from injuring an adversary. The phrase is often used of argument, and refers to the old practice of duellists doing this when they wished to discharge a "debt of honour" without incurring risks or wounding their opponent.

Pit-a-pat. My heart goes pit-a-pat. Throbs, palpitates. An echoic or a RI-COCHET word, as "fiddle-faddle", "harum-scarum", "ding-dong", etc.

Pitch. The devil to pay and no pitch hot. *See under* DEVIL.

He that touches pitch will be defiled. A rotten apple injures its companions. "Evil communications corrupt good manners." The saying occurs in *Ecclesiasticus* (xii, 1), "he that toucheth pitch shall be defiled therewith".

Pitch and pay. Pay up at once. There is a suppressed pun in the phrase: "to pay a ship" was to cover the oakum in the seams with pitch.

Pitch and toss. A game in which coins are pitched at a mark, the player getting nearest having the right to toss all the other's coins into the air and take those that come down with heads up. Hence, *to play pitch and toss* with one's money, prospects, etc., is to gamble recklessly, to play DUCKS AND DRAKES.

To pitch into one. To assail him vigorously; to give it him hot.

To queer one's pitch. *See under* QUEER.

A pitched battle. *See* BATTLE.

Pitcher. Little pitchers have long ears. Little folk or children hear what is said when you little think it. The *ear* of a pitcher is the handle, made somewhat in the shape of a man's ear.

The pitcher went once too often to the well. The dodge was tried once too often, and utterly failed. The sentiment is proverbial in most European languages.

Pithecanthropus (pith e kăn'throp ŭs) or **Java Man.** The name given by Haeckel in 1868 to the hypothetical MISSING LINK; from Gr. *pithekos*, ape, and *anthropos*, man. Later *pithecanthropus* was the generic name given to the remains of the extinct man-like ape discovered near Trinil, Java, in 1891. *Cp.* PEKING MAN.

Pitt Diamond. A DIAMOND of just under 137 CARATS found at the Parteal mines, India, and bought by Thomas Pitt (*see* DIAMOND PITT) in 1702 from a thief for a sum (said to have been £20,400) far below its real value. Hence Pope's reference:

> Asleep and naked as an Indian lay,
> An honest factor stole a gem away.
> *Moral Essays, Ep.* iii, 361.

Pitt sold the diamond in 1717 to the Regent Orleans (hence its alternative name the "Regent Diamond") for £135,000; it later adorned the sword-hilt of NAPOLEON, and is still in the possession of France. Its original weight before cutting was 410 carats.

Pitt's Pictures. "Blind" windows were so called because many window spaces were blocked up when Pitt the younger greatly increased the window tax in 1782 and 1797, although houses with fewer than seven windows were exempted in 1792.

Pixie, or **Pixy**. A sprite or FAIRY of folklore, especially in CORNWALL and Devon, where some held pixies to be the spirits of infants who died before baptism.

Place. Place-makers' Bible. *See* BIBLE, SOME SPECIALLY NAMED EDITIONS.

Placebo (plăs ē' bō) (Lat., I shall please, or be acceptable). VESPERS for the dead; because the first antiphon at Vespers of the office of the Dead began with the words *Placebo Domino in regione vivorum*, "I will walk before the Lord in the land of the living" (*Ps*. cxvi, 9).

As sycophants and those who hoped to get something out of the relatives of the departed used to make a point of attending this service and singing the *Placebo*, the phrase *to sing placebo* came to mean to play the flatterer or sycophant. Chaucer gives the name to such a parasite in the *Merchant's Tale* and in the *Parson's Tale* says, "Flattereres been the develes chapelleyns that singen evere *Placebo*" (§xl).

An innocuous medicine designed to humour a patient, and which may have a beneficial psychological and physical effect is called a *placebo*.

Placemen. A name given to those members of the HOUSE OF COMMONS who held "places" or offices of profit under the Crown. Their numbers grew steadily after the RESTORATION with the corrupt use of Crown patronage by the Treasury to gain support for the government of the day. (*See* WHIG BIBLE *under* BIBLE). Placemen included ministers, civil servants, court officials, contractors, army and navy officers, etc. Attempts to limit their influence by Place Bills excluding them from the Commons were frequent, particularly from the 1690s until the 1740s, but few were passed. The objective was mainly secured by administrative reforms (1782–1870) which abolished places. The problem of patronage, however, still exists.

Plaid Cymru (plīd kŭm rē) (W. Party of Wales). The Welsh nationalist party set up in 1925 with the object of achieving Welsh home rule. Support grew in the 1960s and the party gained three seats in the HOUSE OF COMMONS in 1974, but only two in 1979 and 1983 and three in 1987.

Plain, The. The GIRONDISTS were so called in the French Revolutionary National Convention, because they sat on the level floor or *plain* of the hall. After their overthrow this part of the House was called the *marais* or swamp, and included such members as were under the control of the MOUNTAIN.

The Cities of the Plain. *See under* CITY.

It's all plain sailing. It's perfectly straightforward; there need be no hesitation about the course of action. A nautical phrase which should be written *plane*, not *plain*. **Plane sailing** is the art of determining a ship's position on the assumption that the earth is flat and she is sailing, therefore, on a plane, instead of a spherical surface, which is a simple and easy method of determining the course and distance over short passages.

Plains Indians is the name given to the Indian tribes of the central prairie areas of North America from Alberta to Texas—once the land of the American bison or buffalo. They are the redskins of popular fame, with their feather head-dresses, teepees, and peace pipes. Among the numerous tribes are the Dakota, BLACKFEET, Cheyenne, Comanche, PAWNEE and APACHE.

Planets. The heavenly bodies that revolve round the SUN in approximately circular orbits; so called from Gr. *planes*, wanderer, because to the ancients, they appeared to wander about among the stars instead of having fixed places.

The *primary planets* are MERCURY, VENUS, the Earth, MARS, JUPITER, SATURN, URANUS, NEPTUNE and PLUTO (discovered in 1930); these are known as the *major planets*, the asteroids between the orbits of Mars and Jupiter being the *minor planets*.

The *secondary planets* are the satellites, or moons revolving round a primary.

Mercury and Venus are called *inferior planets* since their orbits are nearer to the sun than the Earth's; the remaining planets are *superior planets*. Only five of the planets were known to the ancients (the Earth not being reckoned), *viz.* Mercury, Venus, Mars, Jupiter, and Saturn; but to these were added the Sun and MOON, making seven in all.

For the relation of metals and precious stones to the planets *see* PRECIOUS STONES.

Planet-struck. A blighted tree is said to be planet-struck. Epilepsy, paralysis, lunacy, etc., are attributed to the malignant aspects of the planets. Horses are said to be *planet-struck* when they seem stupefied, whether from want of food, colic, or stoppage.

To be born under a lucky, or **unlucky planet.** According to ASTROLOGY, some planet, at the birth of every individual, presides over his destiny. Some of the planets, like JUPITER, are lucky; and others like SATURN, are unlucky. *See* HOUSES, ASTROLOGICAL.

Plank. Any one portion or principle of a political PLATFORM.

To walk the plank. To be put to the supreme test; also, to be about to die. Walking the plank was a mode of disposing of prisoners at sea, much in vogue among pirates in the 17th century.

Plantagenet (plăn tăj′ ė net). A name commonly given since the mid-17th century to the royal line now more properly called ANGEVIN and to the LANCASTRIAN and YORKIST kings from Henry IV to Richard III; the descendants of Geoffrey, Count of Anjou, and Matilda, daughter of Henry I. It may have arisen from Geoffrey of Anjou's habit of wearing a sprig of broom (*plante genêt*) in his cap, or that he planted BROOM to improve his hunting covers. Henry II was Geoffrey's son. The *House of Plantagenet* therefore includes the following kings: Henry II, Richard I, John, Henry III, Edward I, II, and III, Richard II, Henry IV, V, VI, Edward IV and V, and Richard III. It was historically only a nickname, first used as a surname by Richard Duke of York, father of Edward IV.

Plate. In horse-racing, the GOLD or SILVER cup forming the prize; hence the race for such a prize.

A lot on one's plate. Slang for having much to do or worry about.

Plates of meat. RHYMING SLANG for "feet"; often abbreviated to *plates*.

Selling plate. A race in which owners of starters have to agree beforehand that the winners shall be sold at a previously fixed price.

Platform. The policy or declaration of a political party, that on which the party stands (*cp.* PLANK). In this sense it is an Americanism dating from before the mid-19th century. It was, however, used in the late 16th century of a plan or scheme of church government, and Milton says, "some ... do not think it for the ease of their inconsequent opinions to grant that the Church-discipline is platformed in the Bible, but that it is left to the discretion of men" (*Church Government*).

Plato (*c.* 428–348 B.C.). The great Athenian philosopher, pupil of SOCRATES, and founder of the ACADEMY. Of his numerous writings the REPUBLIC has perhaps been the most influential. He was originally called Aristocles but the name Plato is said to have been bestowed by his gymnastic teacher, from his broad shoulders. Some say it arose from the breadth of his forehead.

Platonic bodies. An old name for the five regular geometric solids described by PLATO, *viz.* the tetrahedron, hexahedron, octahedron, dodecahedron, and icosahedron, all of which are bounded by like, equal, and regular planes.

Platonic love. Spiritual love between persons of opposite sexes; the friendship of man and woman, without any sexual implications. The phrase is founded on a passage towards the end of the *Symposium* in which PLATO was extolling not the non-sexual love of a man for a woman but the loving interest that SOCRATES took in young men—which was pure, and therefore noteworthy in the Greece of the period.

> I am convinced, and always was, that Platonic Love is Platonic nonsense.
>
> RICHARDSON: *Pamela*, III, lxxviii.

The Platonic Year. *See* PLATONIC CYCLE *under* CYCLE.

Platonism is characterized by the doctrine of pre-existing eternal ideas, and teaches the immortality and pre-existence of the soul, the dependence of virtue upon discipline, and the trustworthiness of cognition.

Plattdeutsch (plăt doich). Low German, which, until 1500, was the business language of northern Europe. *See* HIGH GERMAN.

Play. "This may be play to you, 'tis death to us." The allusion is to ÆSOP'S FABLE of the boys throwing stones at some frogs.

As good as a play. Intensely amusing. Said to have been the remark of Charles II at the HOUSE OF LORDS debate on Lord Ross's Divorce Bill (1670).

He played his cards well. *See under* CARD.

Played out. Exhausted; out of date; no longer in VOGUE.

Playing possum. *See* POSSUM.

To play for time. To prolong or delay negotiations, coming to a decision, in the hope of staving off defeat, failure, etc.; as in CRICKET, when victory for the batting team is no longer possible in the remaining time, but cautious play may lead to a drawn game instead of defeat.

To play into someone's hands. *See under* HAND.

To play someone up. To be a nuisance to them, to harass and annoy, to behave in a troublesome fashion, as schoolchildren are wont to "play up" certain of their teachers.

To play to the gallery, or **to the gods.** *See* GALLERY, *and* AMONG THE GODS *under* GOD.

To play up to someone. To seek to ingratiate oneself with a person by flattery, etc. Probably of theatrical origin.

Pleader, Pleading. *See* SPECIAL PLEADING.

Plebeian (ple bē' àn). One of, or appertaining to, the common people; properly a free citizen of ROME, neither PATRICIAN nor client. From Lat. *plebs*, the common people.

Plebiscite (pleb'i sit). In Roman history, a law enacted by the "comitia" or assembly of tribes; nowadays it means the direct vote of the whole body of citizens of a state on some definite question; thus Louis Napoleon's COUP D'ÉTAT (2 December 1851) was confirmed by a carefully "rigged" plebiscite and in No-

vember 1852 another plebiscite approved the re-establishment of the Empire.

Pledge. To sign, or **take the pledge.** To bind oneself by one's pledged word to abstain from intoxicating liquors. Such a pledge was taken by members of the BAND OF HOPE.

Pleiades (plī' a dēz). In classical myth, the seven daughters of ATLAS and Pleione, sisters of the HYADES. They were transformed into stars, one of which, MEROPE, is invisible, out of shame, because she married a mortal man; while others say it is ELECTRA who hides herself from grief for the destruction of TROY and its royal race. Electra is known as "the lost Pleiad".

The great cluster of stars in the constellation TAURUS, especially the seven larger ones, were called **the Pleiades** by the Greeks from the word *plein*, to sail, because they considered navigation safe at the rising of the constellation, and their setting marked the close of the sailing season.

The Pleiad. A name frequently given to groups of seven particularly illustrious persons.

The Pleiad of Alexandria. A group of seven contemporary poets in the 3rd century B.C., *viz*. Callimachus, Apollonius of Rhodes, Aratus, Philiscus (called HOMER the Younger), Lycophron, Nicander, and THEOCRITUS.

The French Pleiad of the 16th century, who wrote poetry in the metres, style, etc., of the ancient Greeks and Romans. Ronsard was their leader.

Plimsoll Line, or **Mark.** The mark fixing the maximum load line of a merchant vessel in salt water. It takes its name from Samuel Plimsoll (1824–1898), M.P. for Derby, who from 1870 led a campaign of protest against the overloading and over-insuring of unsafe shipping. His sensational outburst when Disraeli's government decided to drop the Shipping Bill in 1875 led to the Merchant Shipping (Plimsoll) Act of 1876.

Plonk. Also "RED BIDDY" or "Pinkie". An Australian term for cheap red wine fortified by methylated spirit. It is popularly applied to any cheap red wine.

Plough. Another name for the GREAT BEAR (*see under* BEAR).

Fond, Fool, or **White Plough.** The plough dragged about a village on PLOUGH MONDAY. Called *white*, because the MUMMERS were dressed in white, gaudily trimmed with flowers and ribbons. Called *fond*, or *fool*, because the procession is fond or foolish— *i.e.* not serious or of a business character.

Plough alms. In mediæval England, a payment of one penny for each plough team in the parish, paid to the priest a fortnight after EASTER.

Plough Monday. The first MONDAY after Twelfth Day is so called because it was the end of the CHRISTMAS holidays when men returned to their plough or daily work. It was customary for farm labourers to draw a plough (*see* FOND *above*) from door to door and solicit "plough-money" to spend in a frolic. The queen of the banquet was called Bessy. *Cp.* ST. DISTAFF'S DAY *under* DISTAFF.

Speed the plough, or **God speed the plough.** A wish for success and prosperity in some undertaking. It is a very old phrase, and occurs in the song sung by ploughmen on PLOUGH MONDAY.

To be ploughed. To fail to pass an examination (*see* PLUCK).

To plough the sands. To engage in some altogether fruitless labour.

To plough with another's heifer. To use information obtained by unfair means, *e.g.* through a treacherous friend. A Biblical phrase. When the men of Timnath gave Samson the answer to his riddle, he replied:

> If ye had not ploughed with my heifer, ye had not found out my riddle.
> *Judges* xiv, 18.

To put one's hand to the plough. To undertake a task; to commence operations in earnest. Only by keeping one's eyes on an object ahead is it possible to plough straight.

> And Jesus said unto him, No man, having put his hand to the plough, and looking back, is fit for the kingdom of God.
> *Luke* ix, 62.

To put the plough before the oxen. Another way of saying "to put the cart before the horse" (*see* CART).

Ploughbote. A bote or estover dating back to Saxon times, the tenant-right of taking wood from the estate for repairing the tools of husbandry; originally for the maintenance of the woodwork of the plough.

Plover. An old synonym for a dupe or GULL; also for a courtesan.

To live like a plover. To live on nothing, to live on air. Plovers, however, live on small insects and worms, which they hunt for in newly ploughed fields.

Plowden. "The case is altered," quoth Plowden. There is more than one story accounting for the origin of this old phrase—used by Jonson as the title of one of his comedies (1598). One is that Edmund Plowden (1518–1585), the great lawyer, was defending a gentleman who was accused of hearing MASS, and elicited the fact that the service was performed by a layman masquerading in priestly vestments for the purpose of informing against the worshippers. Thereupon the brilliant lawyer observed, "The case is altered, no priest, no mass", thus securing the acquittal of his client. Another version is that Plowden was asked what legal remedy there was against some hogs that trespassed on a complainant's ground. "There is a very good remedy," began the lawyer, but when informed that they were the complainant's own hogs, said, "Nay, then, the case is altered." *See* PUBLIC-HOUSE SIGNS.

Pluck, meaning courage, determination, was originally pugilistic slang of the late 18th century, and meant much the same as heart. A "pug" who was lacking in pluck was a coward; the *pluck* of an animal is the HEART, liver, and lungs, that can be removed by one pull or *pluck*. *Cp.* the expressions bold *heart*, lily-livered (*see* LIVER), a man of another KIDNEY, BOWELS OF MERCY, a *vein* of fun, it raised his BILE, etc.

A rejected candidate at an examination is said to be *plucked*, because formerly at the ancient universities, when degrees were conferred and the names were read out before presentation to the Vice-Chancellor, the PROCTOR walked once up and down the room, and anyone who objected might signify his dissent by plucking the proctor's gown. This was occasionally done by tradesmen to whom the candidate was in debt.

> "No, it isn't that, sir. I'm not afraid of being shot; I wish to God anybody would shoot me. I have not got my degree. I—I'm plucked, sir".
> THACKERAY: *Pendennis*, ch. xx.

A plucked pigeon. One fleeced out of his money; one plucked by a ROOK or sharper.

He's a plucked'un. He's a plucky chap; there's no frightening him.

I'll pluck his goose for him. I'll cut his crest, lower his pride, make him EAT HUMBLE PIE. Comparing the person to a GOOSE, the threat is to pluck off his feathers in which he prides himself.

Plug. Plug ugly. A rowdy, unpleasant character, a term said to have originated at Baltimore.

Plum. Old slang for a very large sum of money (properly £100,000), or for its possession. Nowadays the figurative use of the word means the very best part of anything, the prize, the "pick of the basket", a WINDFALL.

Plumes. In borrowed plumes. Assumed merit; airs and graces not merited. The allusion is to the fable of the jay who dressed up in peacock's feathers.

To plume oneself on something. To be proud of it, conceited about it; to boast of it. A plume is a feather, and *to plume oneself* is to feather one's own conceit.

Plus fours. Loose KNICKERBOCKERS overlapping the knee-band and thereby giving added freedom for active outdoor sports. They were particularly popular with golfers in the 1920s. The name derives from the four extra inches of cloth required below the knee in tailoring.

Plus ultra. The motto in the Spanish royal arms. It was once *Ne plus ultra* ("thus far and no farther") in allusion to the PILLARS OF HERCULES, the *ne plus ultra* of the world; but after the discovery of America, and when Charles V inherited the crown of Aragon and Castile, with all the vast American possessions, he struck out *ne*, and assumed the words *plus ultra* for the national motto, the suggestion being that Spain *could* go farther.

Pluto. In Roman mythology, the ruler of the infernal regions, son of SATURN, brother of JUPITER and NEPTUNE, and husband of PROSERPINE; hence, the grave, the place where the dead go before they are admitted into ELYSIUM or sent to TARTARUS.

In World War II, *Pluto* was the codename (from the initials of Pipe Line Under The Ocean) given to the pipelines to carry oil fuel laid across the bed of the English Channel—from Sandown to Cherbourg and from Dungeness to Boulogne.

Plutonian or **Plutonist.** *See* VULCANIST.

Plutonic Rocks. Granites, certain porphyries and other igneous unstratified crystalline rocks, supposed to have been formed at a great depth and pressure, as distinguished from the volcanic rocks which were formed near the surface. So called from PLUTO, as the lord of elemental fire. Richard Kirwan used the term in his *Elements of Mineralogy*, 1796.

Plutus. In Greek mythology, the god of riches. Hence, *rich as Plutus*, and *plutocrat*, one who exercises influence or possesses power through his wealth. The legend is that he was blinded by ZEUS so that his gifts should be equally distributed and not go only to those who merited them.

Plymouth Brethren. A sect of Evangelical Christians founded in IRELAND about 1828 by J.N. Darby, one-time Anglican priest (hence they are sometimes called Darbyites), and deriving their name from Plymouth, the first centre set up in England (1830). In 1849 they split up into "Open Brethren" and "Exclusive Brethren". They have no organized ministry and lay emphasis on the Breaking of Bread each SUNDAY.

Pocahontas (pok ả hon′ tăs). Daughter of Powhatan, an Indian chief of Virginia. She is said to have rescued Captain John Smith when her father was on the point of killing him. She subsequently married John Rolfe, the first Englishman to plant and cure tobacco. In 1616 she came to ENGLAND with her husband and infant son and was presented to James I and the Queen. She died off Gravesend

(21 March 1617) when about to return to Virginia, and was buried in St. George's Church. Curiously enough she passed her stay at the Bell-Savage (*see* LA BELLE SAUVAGE).

> The blessed
> Pocahontas, as the historian calls her,
> And great King's daughter of Virginia.
> BEN JONSON: *Staple of News*, II, v
> (1625).

Pocket. Pocket borough. Before the Reform Act of 1832, a borough where the electorate was so small that the local magnate had the borough "in his pocket", *i.e.* he was able to return his own nominee.

Pocket veto. When the President of the U.S.A. refuses to sign a Bill which has passed both Houses, he is said to *pocket* it.

Put your pride in your pocket. Lay it aside for the nonce.

To be in, or **out of pocket.** To be a gainer or loser by some transaction.

To have someone in one's pocket. To have complete influence over a person; to be sure of his ready complaisance in any matter.

To line one's pockets. To make a good deal of money, TO FEATHER ONE'S NEST (*see under* FEATHER); often with the implication of profiting at the expense of others. *See* LINING.

To pocket an insult. To submit to an insult without showing annoyance.

To put one's hand in one's pocket. To give money (often to a charity).

Pococurante (pō kō kū răn' ti). (Ital. *poco curante*, caring little). Insouciant, DEVIL-MAY-CARE (*see under* DEVIL PHRASES), easy-go-lucky. Hence, *pococurantism*, indifference to matters of importance but concern about trifles. Also used for one who in arguments leaves the main gist and rides off on some minor and indifferent point.

Podsnap. A pompous, self-satisfied man in Dickens's *Our Mutual Friend*, the type of one who is overburdened with stiff-starched etiquette and self-importance. Hence, *Podsnappery*. *Cp.* PECKSNIFF.

Podunk. A term for a little American ONE-HORSE TOWN; from the place near Hartford, Connecticut, of this name,

which is of American Indian origin.

Poet. Poet Laureate. A court official, now appointed by the PRIME MINISTER, who composes odes in celebration of royal birthdays and State occasions. The appointment essentially dates from the time of James I, but in earlier times there had been an occasional *Versificator Regis* and the universities gave the LAUREL wreath to graduates in rhetoric and Latin versification and to meritorious poets, among whom Skelton was styled *Laureatus*. The laurel crown was anciently a mark of distinction and honour. The following is the list of Poets Laureate:

> Ben Jonson, 1619–1637
> Sir William Davenant, 1638–1668
> John Dryden, 1670–1688
> Thomas Shadwell, 1688–1692
> Nahum Tate, 1692–1715
> Nicholas Rowe, 1715–1718
> Laurence Eusden, 1718–1730
> Colley Cibber, 1730–1757
> William Whitehead, 1757–1785
> Thomas Warton, 1785–1790
> Henry James Pye, 1790–1813
> Robert Southey, 1813–1843
> William Wordsworth, 1843–1850
> Alfred Tennyson, 1850–1892
> Alfred Austin, 1896–1913
> Robert Bridges, 1913–1930
> John Masefield, 1930–1967
> Cecil Day Lewis, 1968–1972
> John Betjeman, 1972–1984
> Ted Hughes, 1984–

Peasant Poet. *See* PEASANT.

Poeta nascitur, non fit. Poets are born, not made. *See under* BORN.

Poet's Corner. The southern end of the south transept of Westminster Abbey, first so called by Oliver Goldsmith because it contained the tomb of Chaucer. Addison had previously (*The Spectator*, No.26, 1711) alluded to it as the "poetical quarter", in which he says—

> I found there were Poets who had no Monuments, and Monuments which had no poets.

Among writers buried here are Spenser, Dryden, Dr. Johnson, Sheridan, Dickens, Browning, Tennyson, Macaulay, Hardy, and Kipling. There are many monuments to writers not buried here. Ben Jonson was buried in the north aisle of the Abbey, and Addison in Henry VII's Chapel.

Point. A point of honour. *See under* HONOUR.

A point of order. In a formal deliberative assembly, a question raised as to whether a particular proceeding is in accordance with the rules of the body itself.

A point-to-point race. A race, especially a STEEPLECHASE, direct from one point to another; a cross-country race.

Point of no return. The point in an aircraft's flight at which it has not enough fuel to return to its point of departure and must continue. Hence its figurative application, a point or situation from which there is no going back.

Armed at all points. Armed to the teeth; having no parts undefended.

In point of fact. A stronger way of saying "As a fact", or "As a matter of fact".

Not to put too fine a point upon it. Not to be over delicate in stating it; the prelude to a blunt though truthful remark. The allusion here is to the sharp end of a tool or weapon, etc.

To carry one's point. To attain the desired end; to get one's way.

To come to the point. To speak out plainly, to avoid circumlocution; to get to the gist of the matter; not TO BEAT ABOUT THE BUSH. (*See under* BEAT.)

To dine on potatoes and point. To have potatoes without any relish or extras, a very meagre dinner indeed. When viands were scarce parents used to tell their children to point their potato to the salt, cheese, bacon, etc. (as imaginary extras) and then eat the potato. *Bread and point* was a similar expression, akin to the more recent "bread and pull-it".

To give one points. To be able to accord him an advantage and yet beat him; to be considerably better than he.

To make a point of doing something. To treat it as a matter of duty, or to make it a special object. The phrase is a translation of the older French *faire un point de*.

To stand on points. On punctilios; delicacy of behaviour. SHAKESPEARE puns on the phrase in the following quotation, the side allusion being that Quince, in the delivery of his Prologue, had taken no notice of the stops, or *points*:

This fellow doth not stand upon points.

A Midsummer Night's Dream, V, i.

To stretch a point. To exceed what is strictly right or proper. It may allude to the tagged laces called *points*, formerly used in costume; to "truss a point" was to tie the laces that fastened the garment; to "stretch a point", to stretch these laces, so as to adjust for growth or the temporary fulness after good feeding.

Point-blank. Direct. A term from gunnery; when a cannon is so placed that the line of sight is parallel to the axis and horizontal, the discharge is point-blank, and was supposed to go direct, without curve, to an object within a certain distance. In French *point blanc* is the white mark or BULL'S-EYE of a target, to hit which the ball or arrow must not deviate in the least.

Point d'appui (pwăn dă pwē'). A standpoint, a fulcrum, a base for action; a pretext to conceal the real intention. Literally, the point of support.

Pointillism (pwăn' til izm) (Fr. *pointiller*, to dot, to stipple). A Neo-Impressionist technique of painting with dots of pure colour, popularized by the French painter Georges Seurat (1859–1891). It is also known as the Divisionist technique. *Cp.* IMPRESSIONISM.

Poison. *See* MITHRIDATE.

One man's meat is another man's poison. What is palatable or beneficial to one man is distasteful or harmful to another.

Poisson d'Avril (pwa' son dă vril) (Fr., April fish). The French equivalent of our APRIL FOOL.

Poke. A bag, pouch, or sack—from which comes our *pocket*, a little poke. The word is virtually obsolete except in the phrase *to buy* A PIG IN A POKE (*see under* PIG).

Poke bonnet. A long, straight, projecting bonnet, commonly worn by women in the early 19th century and later by SALVATION ARMY lassies and old-fashioned QUAKER women. Perhaps so called because it projects or pokes out in front.

To poke fun at one. To ridicule.

Poker face. An expressionless face characteristic of the good poker-player, who assumes it to conceal from his adversaries any idea of what cards he may be holding.

Polack (pō′ lăk). An inhabitant of Poland, a term now superseded by *Pole*, although derogatorily used in the U.S.A.

> So frowned he once, when, in an angry parle,
> He smote the sledded Polacks on the ice.
> SHAKESPEARE: *Hamlet*, I, i.

Poland. There are many legends of early Poland. One is that Prince Popiel invited all his family to a banquet and when they were drunk killed them off with poisoned wine. He was duly punished when millions of mice entered his castle and devoured him. The chiefs then elected one Piast, a wheelmaker, to be their ruler, it having been reported that when he had been sitting in the garden with his wife two young men with white wings on their shoulders were with them, and this was deemed a favourable omen. The two ANGELS were Cyril and Methodius, the APOSTLES of central Europe. The Piast dynasty ruled from 880 until 1370. *See also* LAND OF THE WHITE EAGLE.

The Polish Corridor. The territory given to Poland by the Treaty of VERSAILLES (1919) to give her access to the Baltic Sea west of Danzig. The Corridor cut off East Prussia from the rest of Germany and proved to be a bone of contention from the outset. It followed roughly the line of the Vistula.

Pole. Barber's pole. *See under* BARBER.

The Poles are the vintagers in Normandy. The Norman vintage consists of apples beaten down by poles. The French say *En Normandie l'on vendange avec la gaule*, a play on the words *Gaule* (Gaul) and *gaule*, meaning a pole. During the German occupation of Paris (1941–1944) students once marched through the streets carrying two posts (*deux gaules*) and it took the Germans some time to realise that this was a play on the name De Gaulle—then a symbol of French nationality and liberty.

Under bare poles. *See* BARE POLES.

Polichinelle, Un Secret de. *See under* SECRET.

Polish. Polish off. To finish out of hand.

In allusion to articles polished.

I'll polish him off in no time. I'll soon deal with him, give him a good drubbing.

To polish off a meal. To eat it quickly; to finish it off.

Spit and polish. *See* SPIT.

Politbureau, -buro. Formerly, the chief policy-making body of the Communist Party in the U.S.S.R., first formed in 1917. It examined matters before they were submitted to the government and consisted of five members. It was superseded by the PRESIDIUM of the Central Committee of the Communist Party in 1952.

Politeness of Kings. *See* PUNCTUAL.

Polka. A round dance said to have been invented about 1830 by a Bohemian servant girl, which soon took Europe by storm. It is danced by couples in 2/4 time, the characteristic feature being the rest on the second beat.

Poll (pōl) (of Teutonic origin) means the head; hence, the number of persons in a crowd ascertained by counting heads, hence the counting of voters at an election, and such phrases as **to go to the polls**, to stand for election, and POLL TAX, a tax levied on everybody.

Poll tax. A graduated tax levied per head in England in 1377 led to the PEASANTS' REVOLT in 1381. Another was imposed in 1513 and on subsequent occasions but it was abolished in 1689. In most of the Southern States of the U.S.A. it was used as a condition of suffrage from 1889 and was still imposed by a few well into the 20th century. A poll tax replaces domestic rates in Scotland in 1989 and in the remainder of Great Britain in 1990.

Clod poll. A blockhead, a stupid fellow.

> Therefore this letter, being so excellently ignorant, will breed no terror in this youth: he will find it comes from a clodpole.
> SHAKESPEARE: *Twelfth Night*, III, iv.

Pollux. In classical mythology the twin brother of CASTOR.

Polly, Mary. The change of M for P in pet names is by no means rare, *e.g.*—

> *Margaret.* Maggie or Meggy, becomes Peggie, and Pegg or Peg.

Martha. Matty becomes Patty.

In the case of *Mary—Polly* we see another change by no means unusual—that of *r* into *l* or *ll*. Similarly, *Sarah* becomes Sally; *Dorothea*, Dora, becomes Dolly; *Henry*, Hal.

Polonius. A garrulous old courtier in SHAKESPEARE'S HAMLET, typical of the pompous, sententious old man. He was the father of Ophelia and lord chamberlain to the king of Denmark.

Poltergeist (pol tĕr gīst). A household spirit well known to spiritualists, remarkable for throwing things about, plucking the bed-clothes, making noises, etc. It is a German term—*Polter*, noise; *Geist*, spirit. *See* SAMPFORD GHOST.

Polt-foot. A club-foot. Ben Jonson calls VULCAN, who was lame, the "polt-footed philosopher". Variant spellings are *poult* and *powlt*, and its literal meaning is chicken-foot.

> Venus was content to take the blake Smith [Vulcan] with his powlt foote.
> LYLY: *Euphues*.

Poltroon. A coward; from Ital. *poltro*, a bed, because cowards are sluggards and feign themselves sick a-bed in times of war.

In falconry the name was given to a bird of prey, with the talons of the hind toes cut off to prevent it flying at game, probably from the old idea that the word was the Lat. *pollice truncus*, maimed in the thumb.

Polycarp, St. One of the most noted martyrs of the 2nd century whose life was linked with the Apostolic age. Born *c.*69, he was probably converted to Christianity by ST. JOHN THE EVANGELIST and was Bishop of Smyrna for over 40 years where he became a staunch and vigorous leader. Persecution of Christians arose in Smyrna in 155 and the mob soon demanded Polycarp, "the father of the Christians" as their next victim. The proconsul, Statius Quadratus, had him arrested and he was burnt alive after refusing to deny his faith. His faithfulness to the Apostolic tradition is recorded by Irenæus, his disciple. Polycarp's only surviving writing is his *Epistle to the Philippians*. His day is 26 January.

Polycrates (pol i krā' tēz). *See* AMASIS.

Polyhymnia, or **Polymnia**. The Muse of lyric poetry and the inventor of the lyre. She invented harmony and presided over singing. *See* MUSES.

Polyphemus (pol i fē' mûs). One of the CYCLOPS, who ruled over Sicily. When ULYSSES landed on the island the monster made him and twelve of his crew captives; six of them he ate, and then Ulysses contrived to blind him and escape with the rest of the crew (*cp.* LESTRIGONS). *See also* ACIS; GALATEA.

Pommel. The pommel of a sword is the rounded knob terminating the hilt, so called from its apple-like shape (Fr. *pomme*, apple); and to *pommel* or *pummel* one, to pound him with your fists, was originally to beat him with the pommel of your sword.

Pommie, Pommy. An Australian and New Zealand term for an Englishman, used both affectionately and disparagingly. Of uncertain origin, it may derive ultimately from *pomme* (apple) or *pomegranate*, possibly in allusion to the pink and white complexions of the English in contrast to their own tanned countenances. Another possible suggestion is that it arose in the days when English convicts were transported to Australia and it was formed from the initials P.O.M.E. — Prisoner of Mother England.

Pomona (po mō' nà). The Roman goddess of fruits and fruit-trees (Lat. *pomum*), hence fruit generally.

Pompadour. The word is applied to a fashion of hairdressing in which the hair is raised (often on a pad) in a wave above the forehead.

Pompey (pom' pi). **Pompey's Pillar.** A Corinthian column of red granite, nearly 100 ft. high, erected at Alexandria by Publius, Prefect of Egypt, in honour of Diocletian and to record the conquest of Alexandria in 296. It was probably miscalled by travellers through ignorance. *Cp.* CLEOPATRA'S NEEDLE.

Pongo. In the old romance of THE SEVEN CHAMPIONS of Christendom he was an amphibious monster of Sicily who preyed on the inhabitants of the island for many years. He was slain by the three sons of St. GEORGE.

Pons Asinorum (ponz ăs i nôr' ùm).

(Lat., the asses' bridge). The fifth proposition, Bk. I, of EUCLID—the first difficult theorem, which dunces rarely got over for the first time without stumbling. It is anything but a "bridge"; it is really *pedica asinorum*, the "dolts' stumbling-block".

Pontiff. The term formerly applied to any BISHOP but now only to the POPE—the Supreme Pontiff. It means literally one who has charge of the bridges (Lat. *pons, pontis*, a bridge), and these were under the care of the principal college of priests in ancient Rome, the head of which was the *Pontifex Maximus*.

Pony. Pony Express. This was the U.S. government mail system across the continent just before the days of railways and telegraphs. It ran from St. Joseph, Missouri, to the Pacific Coast and was inaugurated in 1860; less than two years later it was superseded by the electric telegraph. The schedule time for the whole distance was ten days, but Lincoln's inaugural address was taken across the continent in 7 days 17 hours. Fleet horses were used, not ponies, ridden for stages of 10 to 15 miles, the rider doing three stages before handing over the wallet. The service was operated by the firm of Russell, Majors and Waddell.

Pooh Bah, A. One who holds numerous offices simultaneously, usually from motives of self-interest. Pooh Bah, The Lord High Everything Else, is a character in Gilbert and Sullivan's *Mikado*, who was First Lord of the Treasury, Lord Chief Justice, Commander-in-Chief, Lord High Admiral, Master of the Buckhounds, Groom of the Back Stairs, Archbishop of Titipu, and Lord Mayor.

Poor. Poor as a church mouse? In a church there is no cupboard or pantry where a mouse may take his pickings and he thus has a lean time.

Poor as Job. The allusion is to JOB being deprived by SATAN of everything he possessed.

Poor as Lazarus. This is the beggar LAZARUS, full of sores, who was laid at the rich man's gate and desired to be fed with crumbs that fell from DIVES' table. (*Luke* xvi, 19–31).

Poor Clares. *See* CLARE.

Poor Richard. The assumed name of Benjamin Franklin in a series of ALMANACS from 1732 to 1757. They contained maxims and precepts on temperance, economy, cleanliness, chastity, and other virtues; and several ended with the words "as poor Richard says".

Poor Robin's Almanack. A humorous ALMANAC, parodying those who seriously indulged in prophecy, published at intervals from 1662 to as late as 1828. The early issues were almost certainly the work of William Winstanley (*c.* 1628–1698). As a specimen of the "predictions", the following, for January 1664, may be cited:

> Strong Beer and good Fires are fit for this Season as a Halter for a Thiefe; and, when every Man is pleas'd, then 'twill be a Merry World indeed...This month we may expect to hear of the Death of some Man, Woman, or Child, either in Kent or Christendom.

There are none poor but those whom God hates. This does not mean that poverty is a punishment, but that those whom God loves are rich in his love. In this sense DIVES may be the poor man, and LAZARUS abounding in that "blessing of the Lord which maketh rich".

Pop goes the weasel. *See under* WEASEL.

Pope. The word represents the O.E. *papa*, from ecclesiastical Latin, and Gr. *pappas*, the infants' word for father.

In the early Church the title was given to many bishops; Leo I, the Great (440–461) was the first to use it officially, and in the time of Gregory VII (1073–1085) it was, by decree, specially reserved to the Bishop of Rome. *Cp.* PONTIFF.

According to Platina, Sergius II (844–847) was the first pope who changed his name on assuming office. Some accounts have it that his name was Hogsmouth, others that it was "Peter de Porca" and he changed it out of deference to St. PETER, thinking it arrogant to style himself Peter II. However, the first clear case of changed name was when Peter, Bishop of Pavia, on election (983) changed his name for that of John XIV.

Gregory the Great (590–604) was the first pope to adopt the title *Servus Ser-*

vorum Dei (the Servant of the Servants of God). It is founded on *Mark* x, 44.

The title *Vicar of Christ*, or *Vicar of God*, was adopted by Innocent III, 1198.

Including John Paul II, there are commonly 263 popes enumerated, and the nationality of two of them is unknown. Of the remainder, 209 were Italians, 15 Frenchmen, 12 Greeks, 6 Germans, 6 Syrians, 3 Africans, 3 Spaniards, 2 Dalmatians, and 1 each Dutch, English, Polish, Portuguese, and Jew (St. Peter).

The Black Pope. The General of the JESUITS.

The Pope of Geneva. A name given to Calvin (1509–1564).

The Pope's eye. The tender piece of meat (the lymphatic gland) surrounded by fat in the middle of a leg of an ox or a sheep. The French call it *Judas's eye*, and the Germans *the priest's tit-bit*.

The Pope's nose. Another name for the PARSON'S NOSE.

Pope Joan. A mythical female POPE first recorded in the 13th century by the Dominican Stephen de Bourbon (d. *c.* 1261) who is said to have derived the story from Jean de Mailly. It was widely and long accepted. She was said to have been born in Germany of English parents and eventually went to ROME after living with a monk at Athens. Passing under the name of Johannes Anglicus, her wide learning gained her election to the papacy in 855 as John VIII. She was supposed to have died in childbirth during a solemn procession. The Calvinist scholar David Blondel exploded the myth in 1647 and it was finally demolished by Döllinger in 1863. Emmanuel Royidis published his novel *Papissa Joanna* on the subject in 1886.

Popish Plot (1678). A fictitious JESUIT plot to murder Charles II and others, enthrone the Duke of York, fire the CITY of LONDON, after which, with the aid of French and Irish troops, a PROTESTANT massacre was to ensue. The plot was invented by the scoundrelly Titus Oates (1649–1705) and before the anti-Catholic panic abated in 1681 some 35 Catholics were judicially murdered, including the Roman Catholic Primate of

Ireland. Oates was eventually pilloried, whipped, and imprisoned when James II became king.

Popinjay. An old name for a parrot (ultimately of Arabic origin; Gr. *papagos*), hence, a conceited or empty-headed fop.

Poplar. The poplar was consecrated to HERCULES, because he destroyed Kakos in a cavern of Mount Aventine, which was covered with poplars. In the moment of triumph, the hero plucked a branch from one of the trees and bound it round his head. When he descended to the infernal regions, the heat caused a profuse perspiration which blanched the under surface of the leaves, while the smoke of the eternal flames blackened the upper surface. Hence the leaves of the poplar are dark on one side and white on the other.

The white poplar is fabled to have originally been the NYMPH Leuce, beloved by PLUTO. He changed her into this at death.

Poppy Day. *See* REMEMBRANCE DAY.

Popular Front. A political alliance of left-wing parties (communists, socialists, liberals, radicals, etc.) against reactionary government, especially dictatorship. The idea of an anti-FASCIST Popular Front was proposed by the Communist International in 1935. Such a government was set up in Spain in 1936, but CIVIL WAR soon followed. The French Popular Front government, set up by Blum in 1936, ended in 1938.

Populist. A term applied in the U.S.A. to a member of the People's Party, an agrarian protest movement formed at St. Louis in 1891. They demanded free and unlimited silver currency, the prohibition of alien land ownership, state control of transport, etc.

Porcelain. Ital. *porcellana*, from *porcella*, a little pig, the name given by the early Portuguese traders to cowrie-shells, the shape of which is not unlike a pig's back, and later to Chinese earthenware, which is white and glossy, like the inside of these shells.

Porch, The. A philosophic sect, generally called STOICS (Gr. *stoa*, a porch), because ZENO, the founder, gave his lectures in the public ambulatory, *Stoa poikile* (the painted colonnade), in the agora or market-place of ATHENS.

Pork, Pig. The former is Norman, the latter Saxon. As in the case of most edible domestic animals, the Norman word is used for the meat and the Saxon for the live animal. *See* PIG.

Pork Barrel. An American term applied to legislation, normally achieved by LOG-ROLLING which makes available Federal funds for local improvements or developments in the district of the congressman who promotes the measure to maintain popularity with the electorate. It is an allusion to old plantation days when slaves assembled at the pork barrel for the allowance of pork reserved for them and "pork barrel" for the congressman is a reward for party service.

Porphyrogenitus (pôr fi ro jen′ i tùs). A surname of the Byzantine Emperor, Constantine VII (905–959). It signifies "born in the purple" (Gr. *porphuros* purple; *genetos*, born), and a son born to a sovereign after his accession is so designated. It was specifically an epithet of the Byzantine emperors born while their father was reigning and the term refers to the purple room used by the empress for her accouchement.

Porridge. Everything tastes of porridge. However we may deceive ourselves, whatever CASTLES IN THE AIR we may construct, the facts of home life will always intrude.

He has supped all his porridge. Eaten his last meal; he is dead.

Keep, or **save your breath to cool your porridge.** A blunt remark to one who is giving unwanted or unsought advice.

Not to earn salt for one's porridge. To earn practically nothing; to be a "waster" or "layabout".

To do porridge. A slang expression for serving time in prison.

Port, meaning the left-hand side of a vessel when facing forward, is probably *port*, harbour, and it replaced the earlier *larboard* which was so easily confused with STARBOARD, so called from the days when the *steerboard* or rudder was carried over the right-hand side, and it was therefore necessary to come alongside on the larboard side. It is presumed the term *port* derives from the fact that the larboard was thus towards the side of the port.

Any port in a storm. Said when one is in a difficulty and has to take whatever refuge, literal or metaphorical, offers itself.

Port-Royal. A convent of CISTERCIAN nuns about 8 miles S.W. of VERSAILLES, which in the 17th century became a centre of the JANSENIST influence. In 1626 the community had moved to PARIS and Port-Royal des Champs was occupied mostly by laymen living a semi-monastic existence, among them many distinguished scholars. In 1648 some of the nuns returned and the hermits moved elsewhere in the neighbourhood.

From 1653 it came under papal condemnation for its adherence to Jansenism, and Louis XIV began active persecution from 1661. By 1669 the conformist nuns were all at the Paris house and the supporters of Jansen remained at Port-Royal des Champs until forcibly removed in 1709. The buildings were duly destroyed but Port-Royal-de-Paris remained in being till the French Revolution.

Porte, or **Sublime Porte.** Originally the official name of the OTTOMAN Court at Constantinople, and later used as a synonym for the Turkish government. The word is the French translation of an Arabic word for "gate", the gate in question being the Imperial Gate or "High" (sublime) gate of the SERAGLIO at Constantinople.

Porteous Riots. At Edinburgh, in September 1736, a smuggler awaiting death for robbing an excise-collector escaped with the aid of Andrew Wilson, a fellow culprit. At the latter's execution, Lieutenant Porteous ordered the town guard to fire on the mob, which had become tumultuous; about six people were killed and eleven injured. Porteous was condemned to death but temporarily reprieved; whereupon some citizens burst into the gaol and, dragging him to the Grassmarket, hanged him by torchlight on a barber's pole. The Lord Provost was dismissed as a consequence and the city fined £2,000. The episode is featured in Scott's *Heart of Midlothian*.

Portia (pôr′ shà). A rich heiress and "lady barrister" in Shakespeare's *Merchant of Venice*, in love with Bassanio. Her name is often used for a female advocate.

Portland Vase. A cinerary urn of transparent blue glass, coated with opaque white glass cut in cameo fashion, found in a tomb (supposed to be that of Alexander Severus) near ROME in the 17th century. In 1770 it was purchased from the Barberini Palace by Sir William Hamilton for 1,000 guineas, and came afterwards into the possession of the Duke of Portland, one of the trustees of the BRITISH MUSEUM, who placed it in that institution for exhibition. In 1845 a lunatic named Lloyd dashed it to pieces, but it was so skilfully repaired that the damage is barely visible. It is ten inches high, and six in diameter at the broadest part.

Portmanteau Word. An artificial word made up of parts of others, and expressive of a combination denoted by those parts—such as SQUARSON, a cross between a *squire* and *parson*. Lewis Carroll invented the term in *Through the Looking-glass*, ch. vi; *slithy*, he says means *lithe* and *slimy*, *mimsy* is *flimsy* and *miserable*, etc. So called because there are two meanings "packed up" in the one word.

Portreeve. In Saxon times and later, the chief magistrate of a town or BOROUGH, *port* here meaning town. *See also* REEVE.

Portsmouth. The Portsmouth Defence. This is a ploy whereby a man accused of assault pleads guilty but in defence says that he was outraged by a homosexual advance being made to him. It stems, of course, from Portsmouth being the chief port of the British Navy, where many men of all sorts and conditions are thrown together.

Portsoken Ward. The most easterly ward of the City of LONDON. (*Port*, town; *soke*, franchise.) It was the soke of the old KNIGHTENGUILD outside the wall in the parish of St. Botolph, Aldgate.

Portumnus. *See* PALÆMON.

Poseidon (pò sī′ don). In Greek mythology, the god of the sea, the counterpart of the Roman NEPTUNE. He was the son of CRONOS and RHEA, brother of ZEUS and HADES, and husband of AMPHI-

TRITE. It was he who, with APOLLO, built the walls of TROY, and as the Trojans refused to give him his reward he hated them and took part against them in the TROJAN WAR. Earthquakes were attributed to him, and he was said to have created the first HORSE.

Posh. This colloquialism for "grand", "SWELL", or "first rate" was supposed to have originated in the old days of constant steamship travel between England and India. Passengers travelling by the P. & O. (Peninsular and Oriental) would, at some cost, book their return passage with the arrangement "PORT Outward STARBOARD Homeward", thus ensuring cabins on the cooler side of the ship, as it was usually quite unbearably hot when crossing the Indian Ocean. Passages were booked "P.O.S.H." accordingly, and *Posh* soon came to be applied to a first-class passenger who could afford this luxury. This traditional explanation is apparently fictitious.

Positivism. A term originally applied to the system of Auguste Comte (1798–1857), which only recognized observable ("positive") facts scientifically established and disregarded metaphysical and theological considerations. Its chief English exponent was Frederic Harrison (1831–1923) who actively promoted it as a religious system centred on the worship of humanity.

In the wider sense, Positivism applies to any philosophical approach which rejects metaphysics and confines itself to the facts of experience.

Posse (pos′ i) (Lat., to be able). A body of men—especially CONSTABLES—who are armed with legal authority.

Posse Comitatus. The whole power of a county—that is, all male members of the county over 15 years of age with the exception of clergymen and peers, summoned by a SHERIFF to assist in preventing a riot, or enforcing process. In modern times assistance is provided by constables and special constables.

Possum. To play possum is to lie low, to feign quiescence, to dissemble. The phrase comes from the opossum's habitual attempt to avoid capture by feigning death. *See* GUM.

Post. Beaten on the post. Only just beaten: a racing term, the "post" being the winning-post.

By return of post. By the next mail in the opposite direction; originally the phrase referred to the messenger, or "post", who brought the dispatch and would return with the answer.

From pillar to post. *See* PILLAR.

Knight of the post. *See under* KNIGHT.

Post haste. With great speed or expedition. The allusion is to postal messengers galloping in to the inn yards with the cry "Post haste!", which gave them priority in the selection of horses available. The term was current by the early 16th century, signifying the quickest journey possible.

To be posted in a club is to have one's name put upon the notice board as no longer a member, for non-payment of dues or other irregularity. In the Army and R.A.F. it means to be assigned to a specific post or appointment; the naval term is to be *drafted*.

To be well posted. To be thoroughly acquainted with it, well informed. Originally an American colloquialism, probably from the counting-house, where ledgers are *posted*. In the U.S.A. it means that hunting and fishing are prohibited—*land posted with signs*.

To run your head against a post. To go ahead heedlessly and stupidly, or as if you had no eyes. *Cp.* TO RUN ONE'S HEAD AGAINST A BRICK WALL *under* HEAD.

Post (Lat., after). **Post factum** (Lat.). After the act has been committed.

Post hoc, ergo propter hoc (Lat.). After this, therefore because of this; expressive of the fallacy that because one thing follows another, the former is the cause of the latter. Because a man drinks a glass of beer and then falls over it does not follow that the beer was the cause of his fall. He *may* have actually slipped on a banana skin.

Post meridiem (Lat.). After noon; usually contracted to "P.M." *See* PIP EMMA.

Post mortem (Lat.). After death; as, a *post-mortem examination*, for the purpose of ascertaining the cause of death.

Post nati (Lat., those born after). Historically, a term referring to a judicial decision of 1607 which decided that all those born in SCOTLAND after James VI's accession as James I of ENGLAND (1603) were natural born subjects of the king of England. James unsuccessfully tried to bring about the union of England and Scotland and to get the English Parliament to agree to the naturalization of his Scottish subjects.

Post obit (Lat. *post obitus*, after decease, *i.e.* of the person named in the bond). An agreement to pay for a loan by a larger sum to be paid on the death of the person specified from whom the borrower has expectations.

Post-Impressionism. The name applied to the phase of painting that followed IMPRESSIONISM. The chief exponents were Cézanne, Gauguin, Van Gogh, and Seurat. It aimed at synthesis and the expression of the material and spiritual significance of the subject free from restraint. *Cp.* POINTILLISM.

Poste restante (pōst res tant′) (Fr., remaining post). A department at a post office to which letters may be addressed for callers, and where they will remain (within certain limits) until called for.

Posteriori. *See* A POSTERIORI.

Postman's knock. An old parlour kissing game. The girls are each given a number. The "postman" knocks on the door a certain number of times and the girl whose number corresponds with the number of knocks has to kiss the postman.

Posy properly means a verse or sentence inscribed on a ring or other object and is a contraction of *poesy*. The meaning of a bunch of flowers, a nosegay, probably comes from the custom of sending verses with gifts of flowers.

Pot. Apart from designating a variety of vessels and containers, the word *pot* is one of the many slang terms for the drug marijuana.

A big pot. An important person; also descriptive of a big belly.

A little pot is soon hot. A little person is quickly "riled". Grumio makes humorous use of the phrase in SHAKESPEARE's *The Taming of the Shrew* (IV. i).

A pot of money. A large amount of money; especially a large stake on a horse.

A watched pot never boils. Said as a mild reproof to one who is showing impatience; watching and anxiety won't hasten matters.

Gone to pot. Ruined, gone to the bad. The allusion is to the pot in which leftovers of cooked meat are put ready for their last appearance as a hash.

In the melting pot. Affairs are in a state of flux or transition; the outcome is still not apparent. The allusion is obvious.

The pot calling the kettle black. Said of one accusing another of faults similar to those committed by himself.

To keep the pot a-boiling. To keep things going briskly, to see that the interest does not flag; also to go on paying one's way and making enough to live on.

To take pot luck. To share a meal of whatever food is available, one that has not been specially prepared for visitors; to take a chance. It comes from the days when the family cooking pot, containing a variety of edibles, was kept boiling over the fire. When it was ladled out at meal-times what anyone received was "pot luck".

Pot-boiler. Anything done merely for the sake of the money it will bring in—because it will "keep the pot a-boiling", *i.e.* help to provide the means of livelihood; applied especially to work of small merit by artists and writers.

Pot-hook. The hook over an open fire on which hung the pot. The term was applied to a "hooked" stroke used in writing, especially to the stroke terminating in a curve formerly practised by children in learning to write, as in the second element of *n*.

Pot-hunter. One whose main aim is the collecting of prizes rather than enjoying a sport or activity for its own sake, the *pot* being the silver cup commonly awarded for sporting events, etc.

Pot-valour. Courage provided by liquor, DUTCH COURAGE; one so fortified is said to be *pot valiant*.

Pot-wallopers. Before the Reform Act of 1832, those who possessed a vote as householders because they had boiled their own *pot* at their own fireplace in the constituency for at least six months.

The earlier form was *pot-waller*, from O.E. *weallan*, to boil.

Potato. A set of circumstances or an issue which is difficult, risky, or disagreeable to handle is colloquially called a *hot potato*.

To think small potatoes of it. To think very little of it, to account it of very slight worth or importance.

Potato-bogle, tattie bogle. So the Scots call a scarecrow, the head of these bird-bogies being a big potato or turnip.

Poteen, Potheen (po tēn′) (Irish *poitín*, little pot). Illicitly distilled Irish whiskey, usually in small amounts. The practice arose in the late 18th century when the government refused to license small stills.

Potent. Cross potent. A heraldic CROSS each limb of which has an additional cross-piece like the head of an old-fashioned crutch; so called from Fr. *potence*, a crutch. It is also known as a *Jerusalem cross*.

Potichomania (po tēsh′ ō mā′ni à). The name is a combination of Fr. *potiche*, glass vase, and *manie*, craze or fad. It denotes the art of decorating plain glass vases, etc., on the inside with patterned paper designs to imitate decorated porcelain of various kinds. Glass panels, cheval-screens, chiffoniers, and other furniture was similarly dealt with. The art spread from France to ENGLAND in the early 19th century and is fully described in Cassell's *Household Guide* of 1875. A debased form of potichomania consisted in sticking figures on the outside of pottery jars and varnishing over the whole. Such jars were called "Dolly Varden" jars.

Potiphar's Wife (pot′ i fàr) is unnamed both in the BIBLE (*Gen.* xxxix, 7) and the KORAN. Some Arabian commentators have called her Rahil, others ZULEIKA, and it is this latter name that the 15th-century Persian poet gives her in his *Yusuf and Zulaikha*.

In C. J. Wells's poetic drama *Joseph and His Brethren* (1824), of which she is the heroine, she is named Phraxanor.

Potlatch. Among certain North American Indians of the north-west coast, a feast at which gifts are distributed lavishly to the guests while the hosts sometimes destroy some of their own valuable possessions. It is a social barbarity to refuse an invitation to a potlatch, or not to give one in return.

Potpourri (pō poo' rē) (Fr.). A mixture of dried sweet-smelling flower-petals and herbs preserved in a vase. *Pourri* means rotten and *potpourri* is literally the vase containing the "rotten" flowers. It is also a HOTCH-POTCH or OLLA PODRIDA; and in music, a medley of favourite tunes strung together.

Potter's Field. A name applied to a burial ground formerly reserved for strangers and the friendless poor. It is an allusion to the field bought by the chief priests with the thirty pieces of silver returned to them by the repentant JUDAS (*Matt.* xxvii, 7).

Poulaines (poo' lānz). The long pointed toes of the 14th century. They were put on the feet of suits of armour for purposes of defence. They appeared also on the fashionable *souliers à la poulaine*. The fashion is thought to have come from Poland—*poulaine* being O.Fr. for Polish.

Poulter's Measure. In prosody, a metre consisting of alternate ALEXANDRINES and fourteeners, *i.e.* twelve-syllable and fourteen-syllable lines. The name was given to it by Gascoigne (1576) because, it is said, poulterers—then called *poulters*—used sometimes to give twelve to the dozen and sometimes fourteen. The following specimen is from Surrey's *Complaint of the absence of her lover, being upon the sea:*

> Good ladies, ye that have your pleasure in exile.
> Step in your foot, come take a place, and mourn with me awhile,
> And such as by their lords do set but little price
> Let them sit still, it skills them not what chance come on the dice.

Pound. In for a penny, in for a pound. *See under* PENNY.

Pound of flesh. The whole of the bargain, to the last letter of the agreement, the bond *literatim et verbatim*. The allusion is to Shakespeare's *The Merchant of Venice* (IV, i), where Shylock bargained with Antonio for a "pound of flesh" but was foiled in his suit by PORTIA, who said the bond was expressly a pound of flesh, and therefore (1) the Jew must cut the exact quantity, neither more nor less than a just pound; and (2) in so doing he must not shed a drop of blood.

Pour. To pour down the drain. Figuratively, to waste one's resources, especially money, on useless, totally unproductive or unprofitable projects.

Poverty. When poverty comes in at the door, love flies out at the window. An old proverb, given in Ray's *Collection* (1742), and appearing in many languages. Keats says much the same in *Lamia* (Pt. II):

> Love in a hut, with water and a crust
> Is—Love forgive us—cinders, ashes, dust.

Powder. I'll powder your jacket for you. A corruption of Fr. *poudrer*, to dust. *Cp.* I'LL DUST YOUR JACKET FOR YOU *under* DUST.

Not worth powder and shot. Not worth the trouble; the thing aimed at is not worth the cost of the ammunition.

Power. Black Power. An emotive concept originating among certain sections of Negro opinion in the U.S.A. since 1966, whose advocates aim at redressing racial injustice by militant black nationalism that allows for violence and race war.

Flower Power. The power of the "Flower Children", based on the slogan "Make Love not War"; the Flower Children or Beautiful People being a new form of HIPPY movement whose adherents were characterized by the wearing of bells and flowers. The Flower Children appeared in Britain in 1967, taking their pattern from San Francisco.

The powers that be. A common expression applied to those in authority, especially those who exercise control of society as a whole. The phrase is taken from *Rom.* xiii, 1—"The powers that be are ordained of God."

Pow-wow. A consultation. Derived from the North American Indians.

Præmonstratensian. *See* PREMONSTRATENSIAN.

Præmunire (prē mū nī' rē). The title of numerous statutes passed from 1353, and especially that of 1393 designed to assert the rights of the Crown against encroachments from the Papacy, particularly rights of patronage, the removal of cases from the King's courts, and EX-COMMUNICATION. The name also denotes the offence, the writs, and the punishment under these statutes. The writ begins with the words *præmunire facias*, "that you cause to be forewarned". The most famous case of præmunire was when Henry VIII invoked the statute against Cardinal Wolsey in 1529 on account of his activities as Papal legate. A peer so charged cannot be tried by his peers, but must accept a jury. The last statute involving præmunire was the Royal Marriage Act of 1772.

Prætorian Guard, or **Prætorians.** Prætor was the title given to a provincial consul who had military powers and the general's bodyguard was the *cohors prætoria*. From the time of AUGUSTUS to that of Constantine, the Prætorians were the household guard of the Roman emperors. In due course they acquired a dangerous power of making and unmaking emperors in times of crisis and they were eventually (312) dispersed among the legions. *Cp.* JANISSARIES.

Pragmatic Sanction (Gr. *pragmatikos*, business-like, official). A term originating in the BYZANTINE EMPIRE to denote a public decree and later used by European sovereigns for important declarations defining their powers, settling the succession, etc. Prominent among such was the *Pragmatic Sanction* of St. Louis, 1269, and that of Charles VII in 1438, asserting the rights of the Gallican Church against the Papacy; that which settled the Empire of Germany in the House of Austria in 1439; the instrument by which Charles VI of Austria settled the succession of his daughter, Maria Theresa, in 1713; and that of Naples, 1759, whereby Charles III of Spain ceded the succession to the Kingdom of Naples to his third son and his heirs in perpetuity. The *Pragmatic Sanction* of 1713 is the most usually referred to unless some qualification is added.

Pragmatism (Gr. *pragma*, deed). The philosophical doctrine that the only test of the truth of human cognitions or phi-

losophical principles is their practical results, *i.e.* their workableness. It does not admit absolute truth, as all truths change their trueness as their practical utility increases or decreases. The word was introduced in this connection about 1875 by the American logician C.S. Peirce (1839–1914) and was popularized by William James, whose *Pragmatism* was published in 1907.

Praise the Lord and Pass the Ammunition. A World War II phrase said to have been used by an American Naval chaplain during the Japanese attack on Pearl Harbor, though the actual identity of the chaplain has since been in dispute. Made the subject of a popular song in 1942.

Prajapatis. *See* MANU.

Prayer wheel. A device used by the Tibetan Buddhists as an aid or substitute for prayer, supposedly founded on a misconception of the BUDDHA's instructions to his followers that they should "turn the wheel of the law"—*i.e.* preach BUDDHISM incessantly. It varies from a small pasteboard cylinder inscribed with prayers to a larger water-wheel. Among the many prayers is the mystic formula OM MANI PADME HUM, and each revolution represents one repetition of the prayers. *Cp.* ROSARY.

It is also another name for the mediæval WHEEL OF FORTUNE.

Pre-Adamites. The name given by Isaac de la Peyrère (1655) to a race of men whom he supposed to have existed before the days of ADAM. He held that only the Jews are descended from Adam, and that the Gentiles derive from these "Pre-Adamites".

Prebend (Late Lat. *præbenda*, a grant, pension). A cathedral BENEFICE, its holder being a *prebendary*. In the 19th century nearly all prebends became honorary offices only, and members of CHAPTERS came to be designated CANONS.

Precariæ. *See* BOON WORK.

Precarious (Lat. *precarius*, obtained by prayer) is applied to what depends on our prayers or requests. A *precarious tenure* is one that depends solely on the will of the owner to concede to our prayer; hence, uncertain, not to be depended on.

Preceptor. Among the Knights TEMPLAR a *preceptory* was a subordinate house or community (the larger being a *commandery*) under a *Preceptor* or *Knight Preceptor*. The *Grand Preceptor* was the head of all the preceptories in a province, those of Jerusalem, Tripolis, and Antioch being the highest ranking.

Précieuses, Les (prä sĕ ĕrz) (Fr.). The ladies of the intellectual circle that centred about the Hôtel de RAMBOUILLET in 17th-century Paris. It may be interpreted as "persons of distinguished merit". Their affected airs were the subject of MOLIÈRE'S comedy *Les Précieuses Ridicules* (1659), and they were further satirized in *Les Femmes Savantes* (1672).

Precious Stones. The ancients divided precious stones into male and female, the darker being the males and the light ones the females. Male sapphires approach indigo in colour, but the females are sky-blue. Theophrastus mentions the distinction.

> And the tent shook, for mighty Saul
> shuddered—and sparkles 'gan dart
> From the jewels that woke in his turban,
> at once with a start—
> All its lordly male-sapphires, and rubies
> courageous at heart.
>
> BROWNING: *Saul*, viii.

According to the Poles, each month is under the influence of a precious stone:

January	Garnet	*Constancy*
February	Amethyst	*Sincerity*
March	Bloodstone	*Courage*
April	DIAMOND	*Innocence*
May	Emerald	*Success in love*
June	Agate	*Health and long life*
July	Cornelian	*Content*
August	Sardonyx	*Conjugal felicity*
September	Chrysolite	*Antidote to madness*
October	Opal	*Hope*
November	Topaz	*Fidelity*
December	Turquoise	*Prosperity*

In relation to the signs of the ZODIAC:

Aries	Ruby	Libra	Jacinth
Taurus	Topaz	Scorpio	Agate
Gemini	Carbuncle	Sagittarius	Amethyst
Cancer	Emerald	Capricornus	Beryl
Leo	Sapphire	Aquarius	Onyx
Virgo	Diamond	Pisces	Jasper

In relation to the planets:

Saturn	Turquoise	*Lead*
Jupiter	Cornelian	*Tin*
Mars	Emerald	*Iron*
Sun	Diamond	GOLD
Venus	Amethyst	*Copper*
Moon	Crystal	SILVER
Mercury	Loadstone	*Quicksilver*

In HERALDRY:

> The topaz represents "or" (*gold*), or Sol, the Sun.
> The pearl or crystal represents "argent" (*silver*), or Luna, the Moon.
> The ruby represents "gules" (*red*), or the planet Mars.
> The sapphire represents "azure" (*blue*), or the planet Jupiter.
> The diamond represents "sable" (*black*), or the planet Saturn.
> The emerald represents "vert" (*green*), or the planet Venus.
> The amethyst represents "purpure" (*purple*), or the planet Mercury.

Many precious stones were held to have curative and magical properties, e.g. *loadstone* prevented quarrels between brothers; *jasper* worn by the ploughman ensured the fertility of a field; *turquoise* protected the wearer from injury if he fell; *jade* for the Chinese was the most pure and divine of natural materials and had many properties, including stimulating the flow of milk in nursing mothers when powdered and mixed with milk and honey.

Première (pre mi âr'). **Ce n'est que le premier pas qui coûte** (Fr.). It is only the first step that costs anything. An observation made by Mme. du Deffand (1697–1780) on hearing the Cardinal de Polignac's description of the miraculous walk of St. DENYS after decapitation. PYTHAGORAS used to say, The beginning is half the whole.

Premillenarians. *See* SECOND ADVENTISTS.

Premonstratensian (prē mon strà ten' sian) or *Norbertine Order*. An order founded by St. Norbert in 1120 in the diocese of Laon, France, which adopted the rule of St. AUGUSTINE. A spot was pointed out to him in a vision, hence the name *Pré montré* or *Pratum Monstratum* (the meadow pointed out). In England the order possessed 35 houses before the dissolution and its members were called "White Canons".

Prepense (prē pens'). **Malice prepense.** MALICE aforethought; malice designed or deliberate (Lat. *præ*, before; *pensare*, to think).

Pre-Raphaelite Brotherhood, The. A group of artists formed in London in 1848 consisting of Holman Hunt, Millais, D. G. Rossetti, and the sculptor Thomas Woolner. It was later joined by J. Collinson, W. H. Deverell, F. G. Stephen and W. M. Rossetti; Ford Madox Brown and Ruskin supported their movement, which espoused a closer study of nature than was practised by those tied to academical rules, and the study of the method and spirit of the artists before Raphael (1483–1520). Nevertheless, their works contained much artificiality of literary origins. The group was attacked by many artists and critics, especially by Charles Dickens in *Household Words* in 1850. From this date D. G. Rossetti ceased to exhibit publicly. Their works are characterized by exaggerated attention to detail and a high degree of finish, and their earlier lives, at least, by BOHEMIAN activities.

Presbyterians. Members of a church governed by elders or presbyters (Gr. *presbuteros*, elder), and ministers in a hierarchy of representative courts. Their doctrine is fundamentally Calvinistic. The CHURCH OF SCOTLAND (*see under* CHURCH) became presbyterian after the REFORMATION but the growth of Presbyterianism in 17th-century England was checked by the rise of the INDEPENDENTS and the Act of Uniformity of 1662. The Presbyterian Church of Wales is of 18th-century origin.

New Presbyter is but Old Priest writ large. There is no difference other than in the name; the name may be different but both things are essentially the same. The word *priest* actually derives from the same root as *presbyter*. The phrase is from Milton's *New Forcers of Conscience*.

Presence. *See* REAL PRESENCE.

Presidium. In the U.S.S.R. the Presidium of the Supreme Soviet, since 1936 a body elected by the Supreme Soviet which fulfils the role of constitutional head of the State. Its chairman is its representative in ceremonial affairs and it issues ordinances when the Supreme Soviet is not in session. *See* POLITBURO.

Press-gang. The name given particularly to those naval parties who carried out the task of *impressment*, an ancient and arbitrary method of obtaining men for military service dating back to the early

13th century. Individual captains of ships provided their own parties until the demands of the 18th-century Navy led to the establishment of an Impress Service with depots where seafarers abounded. Apart from seizing men from taverns, they seized merchant sailors from ships at sea, etc., and *Pressed men* formed about half of a ship's crew. The Royal Navy relied on this method until the 1830s, when improvements in pay and conditions encouraged adequate voluntary enlistment, although impressment has never been abolished. The word has nothing to do with "pressing" in the sense of "forcing" but derives from the *prest* or *imprest* money (Fr. *prêter*, to lend) advanced on enlistment, rather like the army's "KING'S SHILLING".

To be press-ganged into it. To be forced to do something or to take part against one's will or inclination.

Prester John. *See under* JOHN.

Prestige (pres tēzh). A word with a curiously metamorphosed meaning. The Lat. *præstigiæ*, from which it is derived, means juggling tricks, hence the extension to illusion, fascination, charm and so to the present meaning of standing, influence, reputation, based upon past achievements and associations, etc.

Presto. The name frequently applied to himself by Swift in his *Journal to Stella*. According to his own account (*Journal*, 1 August 1711) it was given him by the notorious Duchess of Shrewsbury, an Italian:

> The Duchess of Shrewsbury asked him, was not that Dr. —, Dr. —, and she could not say my name in English, but said Dr. Presto, which is Italian for Swift.

Pretender. The Old Pretender. James Francis Edward Stewart or Stuart (1688–1766), son of James II, the WARMING-PAN BABY, and known as the Old Chevalier. He was called James III by the JACOBITES on the death of his father in 1701. The word "Pretender" here denotes one who makes a claim or pretension to a title.

The Young Pretender. Charles Edward Stuart (1720–1788), son of the OLD PRETENDER, and popularly known as Bonnie Prince Charlie or the Young Chevalier. *See* THE FORTY-FIVE *under* FORTY.

Pretext. A pretence or excuse. From the Lat. *prætexta*, a dress embroidered in the front, worn by Roman magistrates, priests, and children of the aristocracy between the age of 13 and 17. The *prætextatæ* were dramas in which actors personated those who wore the *prætexta*; hence persons who pretended to be what they were not.

Prevarication. The Lat. word *varico* means I straddle, and *prævaricor*, I go zigzag or crooked. The verb, says Pliny, was first applied to men who ploughed crooked ridges, and afterwards to men who gave crooked answers in the law courts, or deviated from the straight line of truth. *Cp.* DELIRIUM.

Previous Question. *See under* QUESTION.

Priam (prī' ȧm). King of TROY when that city was sacked by the Greeks, husband of HECUBA, and father of 50 children, the eldest of whom was HECTOR. When the gates of Troy were thrown open by the Greeks who had been concealed in the wooden horse, Pyrrhus, the son of ACHILLES, slew the aged Priam.

Priapus (prī ā'pùs). In Greek mythology, the son of DIONYSUS and APHRODITE, the god of reproductive power and fertility (hence of gardens), the protector of shepherds, fishermen and farmers. He was later regarded as the chief deity of lasciviousness and obscenity and the phallus was his attribute.

Prick. The prick of conscience. Remorse; tormenting reflection on one's misdeeds. In the 14th century Richard of Hampole wrote a devotional treatise with this title.

To kick against the pricks. To strive against odds, especially against authority. *Prick* here is an ox-goad, and the allusion is to *Acts* ix, 5—"It is hard for thee to kick against the pricks."

To prick up one's ears. To pay particular attention; to do one's best to listen to what is going on. In allusion to the twitching of a horse's ears when its attention is suddenly attracted.

Pricking for sheriffs. The annual choosing of SHERIFFS used to be done by the king, who marked the names on a list by pricking them with a bodkin at random. Sheriffs are still "pricked" by the sovereign, but the names are chosen beforehand.

Prick-eared. Said of a dog with upstanding ears. The PURITANS or ROUNDHEADS were so called because they had their hair cut short and covered their heads with a black skull-cap drawn down tight, leaving the ears exposed.

Prick-song. Written music for singing as distinguished from music learnt by ear. So called because the notes were originally pricked in on parchment. The term has long been obsolete.

Pride. A pride of lions. A company or group of lions.

Fly pride, says the peacock (SHAKESPEARE, *Comedy of Errors*, IV, iii). A bird proverbial for pride, the POT CALLING THE KETTLE BLACK. *See under* POT.

The heraldic peacock is said to be *in his pride* when depicted with the tail displayed and the wings drooping.

Pride goes before a fall. An adaptation of *Proverbs* xvi, 18—"Pride goeth before destruction, and an haughty spirit before a fall."

The pride of the morning. The early mist or shower which promises a fine day. The morning is too proud to come out in her glory all at once—or the proud beauty being thwarted weeps and pouts awhile.

Pride's Purge (6 December 1648). When CHARLES I was a captive, after his defeat in the field, the LONG PARLIAMENT declared for a reconciliation (5 December), whereupon a body of soldiers under Colonel Pride arrested 45 M.P.s and debarred 78 others from entry. Another 20 refused to sit and the RUMP was prepared to serve the Army's purposes.

Prig. An old CANT word (probably a variant of PRICK) for to filch or steal, also for a thief. In SHAKESPEARE's *The Winter's Tale* (IV, ii) the clown calls AUTOLYCUS a "prig" who "haunts wakes, fairs, and bear-baitings".

Nowadays *prig* denotes a conceited, formal or didactic person—one who tries to teach others how to behave, etc., one of narrow-mindedly precise morals.

Prima Donna (prē' ma don' a) (Ital.,

first lady). The principal female singer in an opera.

Prima facie (Lat.). At first sight. A *prima facie* case is a case or statement which, without minute examination into its merits, seems plausible and correct.

Primate. The title of the BISHOP of the "first" or chief see of a state (Lat. *prima sedes*); originally the METROPOLITAN of a province. The Archbishop of York is called *Primate of England* and the Archbishop of Canterbury *Primate of All England*.

Prime (Lat. *primus*, first). In the Western Church, the office appointed for the first hour (6 a.m.), the first of the CANONICAL HOURS. Milton terms sunrise "that sweet hour of prime" (*Paradise Lost*, V, 170); and the word is used in a general way of the first beginnings of anything, especially of the world itself. *Cp.* Tennyson's "dragons of the prime" (*In Memoriam*, lvi).

In my prime. In my youth; at the best period of my life.

Prime Minister. The first minister of the Crown.

Primed. Fully prepared and ready to deliver a speech or to cope in an argument, etc. A man whose head is full of his subject is said to be "primed to the muzzle". The allusion is to firearms. Primed is also a euphemism for "drunk".

Primer. Originally the name of a book of devotions used by the laity in pre-REFORMATION England; this was used as a first reading book. The name was then applied to a small book by which children were taught to read and pray and hence to an elementary school book on any subject.

> This litel child his litel book lerninge
> As he sat in the scole at his prymer.
> CHAUCER: *Canterbury Tales*
> (*The Prioress's Tale*, I, 72).

Primrose. Primrose Day. 19 April, the anniversary of the death of Benjamin Disraeli, Earl of Beaconsfield, the season when primroses are at their best. *See* PRIMROSE LEAGUE.

The Primrose League. A Conservative party organization founded by members of the FOURTH PARTY in 1883, having as its objects "the maintenance of religion, of the estates of the realm, and of the imperial ascendancy". The name was taken in the mistaken belief that the primrose was Lord Beaconsfield's favourite flower, from the wreath of primroses sent to his funeral with the words, "His favourite flowers from Osborne, a tribute of affection from Queen Victoria". The league had its greatest influence and popularity in the days before World War I when imperial sentiment was at its height.

Primrose path. The easy way, the path of pleasure and self-indulgence. SHAKESPEARE refers to the "primrose path of dalliance" (*Hamlet*, I, iii), and to "the primrose way to the everlasting bonfire" (*Macbeth*, II, i).

Primum mobile (prī' mum mō' bile) (Lat., the first moving thing), in the PTOLEMAIC SYSTEM of astronomy, the ninth (later the tenth) sphere. It was supposed to revolve round the earth from east to west in 24 hours, carrying with it all the other spheres. Milton refers to it as "that first mov'd" (*Paradise Lost*, III, 483) and Sir Thomas Browne (*Religio Medici*) used the phrase, "Beyond the first movable", meaning outside the material creation. According to Ptolemy, the *primum mobile* was the boundary of creation, above which came the EMPYREAN, or seat of God.

The term is figuratively applied to any machine which communicates motion to others; and also to any great sources of motion or in the development of ideas, etc. Thus, SOCRATES may be called the *primum mobile* of the Dialectic, MEGARIAN, Cyrenaic, and CYNIC systems of philosophy.

Primus (prī' mus) (Lat., first). The presiding BISHOP of the Episcopal Church of Scotland. He is elected by the other six bishops, and presides in Convocation, and at meetings relative to Church matters.

Primus inter pares (Lat.). The first among equals.

Prince (Lat. *princeps*, chief, leader). A royal title which, in England, is now limited to the sons of the sovereign and their sons. *Princess* is limited to the sovereign's daughters and his sons' (but not daughters') daughters.

Black Prince. *See under* BLACK.

Crown Prince. The title of the heir-apparent to the throne in some countries, as Sweden, Denmark, and Japan (formerly also in Germany).

Prince Consort. A prince who is the husband of the reigning queen.

Prince Imperial. The title of the heir-apparent in the French Empire of NAPOLEON III (1852–1870).

Prince Regent. A prince ruling on behalf of the legal sovereign; in British history George, PRINCE OF WALES (*see under* WALES), who acted as regent for his father, George III. *See* REGENCY.

Prince of the Asturias. The traditional title of the heir-apparent to the Spanish throne.

Prince of the Church. A CARDINAL.

Prince of Darkness. The DEVIL; SATAN.

Prince of Peace. The MESSIAH; Jesus Christ.

> For unto us a child is born, unto us a son is given ... and his name shall be called Wonderful, Counsellor, The mighty God, The everlasting Father, The Prince of Peace.
>
> *Isaiah* ix, 6.

Prince of Wales. *See under* WALES.

Princess Royal. The title of an eldest daughter of a British sovereign. On the death of a Princess Royal the eldest daughter of the then reigning monarch customarily receives the title and retains it for life, no matter how many sovereigns with daughters may occupy the throne during her lifetime. George III's daughter Charlotte, Queen of Württemberg, was Princess Royal until her death in 1828; neither George IV nor William IV having daughters, the title was in abeyance until 1840 when Queen Victoria's daughter, Princess Victoria (later the Empress Frederick of Germany), succeeded to it. She remained Princess Royal until her death in 1901, when King Edward's daughter, Princess Louise, Duchess of Fife, succeeded. On her death in 1931 the title passed to Princess Mary, Countess of Harewood, daughter of George V. She died in 1965, and the title was given to Princess Anne on 13 June 1987.

Principalities. Members of one of the nine orders of angels in mediæval angelology. *See* ANGEL.

In the assembly next upstood
Nisroch, of Principalities the prime.
MILTON: *Paradise Lost*, VI, 447.

Printer. The Printer's Bible. *See* BIBLE, SOME SPECIALLY NAMED EDITIONS.

Printing House Square. Often used as synonymous with *The Times* newspaper, which was produced there from its inception until 1974. It began in 1785 as *The Daily Universal Register*, which became *The Times* in 1788. Printing House Square is at Blackfriars in the City of London and was earlier the site of the King's Printing House.

Priori. *See* A PRIORI.

Prisca, St. A Roman Christian maiden tortured and beheaded (*c.* 270) under the Emperor Claudius II. There is a church of St. Prisca at ROME. She is represented between two lions who, it is said, refused to attack her.

St. Priscilla, a Christian convert of the 1st century, and mentioned several times in the NEW TESTAMENT (*Acts* xviii, *Rom.* xvi, I *Cor.* xvi, 2 *Tim.* iv), is also known as St. Prisca.

Priscian's Head (prish' àn). **To break Priscian's head** (Lat. *diminuere Priscianis caput*). To violate the rules of grammar. Priscian was a great grammarian of the early 6th century, whose name is almost synonymous with grammar.

Privateer. A privately owned vessel commissioned under LETTERS OF MARQUE by a belligerent state to wage war on the enemy's commerce. The practice of issuing such commissions ceased as a result of the Declaration of Paris, 1856, but it did not finally become obsolete until the Hague Convention of 1907.

Privilege. In the Parliamentary sense applies to PARLIAMENT's right to regulate its own proceedings and in the case of the Commons the right to regulate membership; also the right to punish for *breach of privilege* or contempt, the right to freedom of speech, and freedom from civil arrest. In addition there is still the freedom of access as a body to the sovereign to present an address and the request for a favourable construction on its proceedings.

Privy Council. The council chosen by the SOVEREIGN originally to administer public affairs, but now never summoned to assemble as a whole except to proclaim the successor to the Crown on the death of the Sovereign, or to listen to the Sovereign's announcement of intention to marry. It usually includes Princes of the Blood, the two PRIMATES, the Bishop of London, the great officers of State and of the Royal Household, the Lord CHANCELLOR and Judges of the Courts of Equity, the Chief Justices of the Courts of COMMON LAW, the Judge Advocate, some of the PUISNE JUDGES, the SPEAKER of the HOUSE OF COMMONS, the Lord Mayor of London, Ambassadors, Governors of Colonies, and many politicians. The business of the Privy Council is nowadays to give formal effect to Proclamations and ORDERS-IN-COUNCIL; for this a quorum of three suffices. The CABINET and the Judicial Committee are, in theory, merely committees of the Privy Council. Privy Councillors are entitled to the prefix "the Right Honourable", and to the use of the initials "P.C." after their names; they rank next after Knights of the GARTER who may be commoners. The Lord President of the Council is the fourth great officer of State.

Privy Seal. The seal which the sovereign uses in proof of assent to a document, kept in the charge of a high officer of State known as the Lord Privy Seal. In matters of minor importance it is sufficient to pass the Privy Seal, but instruments of greater moment must have the GREAT SEAL also.

Prize Court. A court of law set up in time of war to examine the validity of capture of ships and goods made at sea by the navy.

Prize money. The name given to the net proceeds of the sale of enemy shipping and property captured at sea. Prior to 1914 the distribution was confined to the ships of the Royal Navy actually making the capture; since that date all prize money has been pooled and shared out among the navy as a whole. Prize money was paid at the end of World War II for the last time.

The prize ring is the boxing ring in which a *prize fight* takes place, a prize fight being a boxing match for a money prize or trophy.

Pro (Lat., for, on behalf of). *Pro* is also a common shortening of "professional" as, "He is a golf pro."

Pro and con (Lat.). For and against. "Con" is a contraction of *contra*. The *pros and cons* of a matter are all that can be said for or against it.

Pro bono publico (prō bō' nō pub' lik ō) (Lat.). For the public good or benefit.

Pro rata (prō rā' ta) (Lat.). Proportional or proportionally.

Pro tanto (Lat.). As an instalment, good enough as far as it goes, but not final; for what it is worth.

Pro tempore (Lat.). Temporarily; for the time being, till something is permanently settled. Contracted into *pro tem*.

Procne. *See* NIGHTINGALE.

Proconsul. A magistrate of ancient ROME who was invested with the power of a consul and charged with the command of an army or the administration of a province. The name has often been applied to some of the great colonial administrators of the former British Empire.

Procris (prok' ris). **Unerring as the dart of Procris.** When Procris fled from CEPHALUS out of shame, DIANA gave her a dog (Lælaps) that never failed to secure its prey, and a dart which not only never missed aim, but which always returned of its own accord to the shooter.

Procrustes' Bed (prō krus' tēz). Procrustes, in Greek legend, was a robber of Attica, who placed all who fell into his hands upon an iron bed. If they were longer than the bed he cut off the overhanging parts, if shorter he stretched them till they fitted it. He was slain by THESEUS. Hence, any attempt to reduce men to one standard, one way of thinking, or one way of acting, is called *placing them on Procrustes' bed.* Cp. DAMIENS' BED OF STEEL.

Procyon (prō' si on). The Lesser DOG-STAR (*see under* DOG(5)), *alpha* in *Canis Minor*, so called because it rises before the Dog-Star (Gr. *pro*, before; *kyon*, dog). It is the eighth brightest star in the heavens. *See* ICARIUS.

Prodigal. Festus the Latin lexicographer (2nd century A.D.) says the Romans called victims wholly consumed by fire *prodigæ hostiæ* (victims prodigalized), and adds that those who waste their substance are therefore called prodigals. This derivation is incorrect. Prodigal is Lat. *pro-ago* or *prod-igo*, I drive forth, and persons who had spent all their patrimony were "driven forth" to be sold as slaves to their creditors.

Profane means literally before or outside the temple (Lat. *pro fano*); hence *profanus* was applied to those persons who came to the temple and, remaining outside and unattached, were not initiated. Hence the idea of irreverence, disregard of sacred things, blasphemous, secular, etc.

Profile (prō' fīl) means shown by a thread (Ital. *profilo*; Lat. *filum*, a thread). A profile is an outline, but especially a view, or drawing or some other representation of the human face outlined by the median line. The term "profile", for an essay setting forth the outstanding characteristics of an individual—a verbal outline, so to speak—came into use in the 1940s.

Programme Music is instrumental music based on a literary, historical, or pictorial subject and intended to describe or illustrate this theme musically.

Projection. Powder of projection. A form of the PHILOSOPHERS' STONE, which was supposed to have the virtue of changing baser metals into GOLD. A little of this powder, being cast into the molten metal, was to *project* from it pure gold.

Proletariat (prō le târ' i ăt). The labouring classes; the unpropertied wage-earning classes. In ancient ROME the *proletarii* could hold no office, and were ineligible for the army and only served the State with their offspring (*proles*).

Prom, or **Promenade Concert.** A concert in which some of the audience stand in an open area of the concert-room floor. Promenade Concerts, familiarly called "Proms", date back to the days of the London pleasure gardens such as VAUXHALL and RANELAGH. Mansard had conducted similar concerts at Paris in the 1830s and from 1838 his example was followed at London. In 1895 Sir Henry Wood (1869–1944) began the concerts at the Queen's Hall which he conducted for over half a century and which became a regular feature of London life. In 1927 the B.B.C. took over their management from Chappell's. The destruction of the hall by enemy action in 1941 caused a break in the concerts but they were renewed at the Royal Albert Hall.

In the U.S.A. *going to a prom* means attending a dance given by members of a class at school or college.

Prometheus (prō mē' thūs) (Gr., Forethought). One of the TITANS of Greek myth, son of IAPETOS and the ocean-nymph Clymene, and famous as a benefactor to man. It is said that ZEUS, having been tricked by Prometheus over his share of a sacrificial ox, denied mankind the use of fire. Prometheus then stole fire from HEPHÆSTUS to save the human race. For this he was chained by Zeus to Mount Caucasus, where an EAGLE preyed on his liver all day, the liver being renewed at night. He was eventually released by HERCULES, who slew the eagle. It was to counterbalance the gift of fire to mankind that Zeus sent PANDORA to earth with her box of evils.

Promethean. Capable of producing fire; pertaining to PROMETHEUS.

Promethean fire. The vital principle; the fire with which PROMETHEUS quickened into life his clay images.

Promethean unguent. Made from a herb on which some of the blood of PROMETHEUS had fallen. MEDEA gave JASON some of it, and thus rendered his body proof against fire and warlike instruments.

Promised Land, or **Land of Promise.** Canaan; so called because God promised ABRAHAM, Isaac, and Jacob that their offspring should possess it. Figuratively, HEAVEN or any place of expected happiness or fulfilment.

Proof. The Proof Bible. *See* BIBLE, SOME SPECIALLY NAMED EDITIONS.

Proof spirit. A term applied to a standard mixture of alcohol and water used as a basis for customs and excise purposes. It is legally defined as having a specific gravity of $^{12}/_{13}$ at 51°F. When the mixture has more alcohol it is said to be *over proof*, and when less *under proof*.

In earlier days proof spirit was held to be that which if poured over gunpowder and ignited would eventually ignite the powder. If the spirit was under proof the water remaining would prevent the firing of the powder.

Prooshan Blue. A term of great endearment, when after the battle of Waterloo the Prussians were immensely popular in England. Sam Weller in *Pickwick Papers* (ch. xxxiii) addresses his father as "Vell, my Prooshan Blue." *See* PRUSSIAN BLUE.

Propaganda. The Congregation or College of the Propaganda (*Congregatio de propaganda fide*) is a committee of cardinals established at Rome by Gregory XV in 1622 for propagating the Faith throughout the world. Hence the term is applied to any scheme, association, publication, etc., for making PROSELYTES or influencing public opinion in political, social, and religious matters, etc.

Prophet, The. The special title of MOHAMMED. According to the KORAN there have been 200,000 prophets, but only six of them brought new laws or dispensations, *viz.* ADAM, Noah, ABRAHAM, MOSES, Jesus, and Mohammed.

The Great, or **Major Prophets.** Isaiah, JEREMIAH, Ezekiel, and DANIEL; so called because their writings are more extensive than the prophecies of the other twelve.

The Minor, or **Lesser Prophets.** Hosea, Joel, Amos, Obadiah, Micah, JONAH, Nahum, Habakkuk, Zephaniah, Haggai, Zechariah, and Malachi, whose writings are less extensive than those of the four GREAT PROPHETS.

Proscription. Outlawry, the denunciation of citizens as public enemies, etc.; so called from the Roman practice of writing the names of the *proscribed* on tablets which were posted up in the forum, sometimes with the offer of a reward for those who should aid in bringing them to court. If the proscribed did not answer the summons, their goods were confiscated and their persons outlawed. In this case the name was engraved on brass or marble, the offence stated, and the tablet placed conspicuously in the market-place.

Prose means straightforward speaking or

writing (Lat. *oratio prosa*), in opposition to foot-bound speaking or writing, *oratio vincta* (fettered speech, *i.e.* poetry).

It was Monsieur Jourdain, in MOLIÈRE'S comedy *Le Bourgeois Gentilhomme*, who suddenly discovered that he had been talking prose for forty years without knowing it.

Proselytes (pros' e līts). From Gr. *proselutos*, one who has come to a place; hence, a convert, especially (in its original application) to Judaism. Among the Jews proselytes were of two kinds—*viz.* "The proselyte of righteousness" and the "stranger that is within thy gates" (Hellenes). The former submitted to circumcision and conformed to the laws of MOSES; the latter went no farther than to refrain from offering sacrifice to heathen gods, and from working on the SABBATH.

Proserpina, or **Proserpine** (prosěr' pi nà, pros' er pīn). The Roman counterpart of the Greek goddess Persephone, queen of the infernal regions and wife of PLUTO (*see* DAFFODIL), and sometimes identified with HECATE.

Prosit (prō' sit) (Lat., "May it benefit you"). Good luck to you! A salutation used in drinking a person's health, and particularly associated with German university students.

Protean. *See* PROTEUS.

Protectionist. One who advocates the imposition of import duties, to "protect" home produce and manufactures. *Cp.* MERCANTILISM.

Protector, The. A title sometimes given in England to the regent during the sovereign's minority.

John of Lancaster, Duke of Bedford, was made Regent of France and Protector of England during the minority (1422–1442) of his nephew, Henry VI; and Humphrey, Duke of Gloucester, was Protector during Bedford's absence in France, which was, in fact, for most of the time.

Richard, Duke of Gloucester, was Protector from 1483 until his assumption of the crown as Richard III. He took Edward V into his custody on the death of Edward IV.

Edward Seymour, Duke of Somerset,

was Protector (1547–1550) and Lord Treasurer in the reign of his nephew, Edward VI.

The Lord Protector of the Common-wealth. Oliver Cromwell (1599–1658) was declared such in 1653. His son Richard succeeded to the title in 1658, but resigned in May 1659.

The Protectorate. *See* COMMON-WEALTH.

Protestant. A member of a Christian Church upholding the principles of the REFORMATION or (loosely) of any Church not in communion with ROME. In the time of Luther his followers called themselves "evangelicals". The name arose from the Lutheran *protest* against the recess of the Diet of Spires (1529) which declared that the religious STATUS QUO must be maintained.

The Protestant Pope. Clement XIV (1769–1775), who ordered the suppression of the JESUITS in 1773. He was a patron of art and a liberal-minded statesman but was under pressure from the BOURBON kings.

Proteus (prō' tūs). In Greek legend, NEP-TUNE'S herdsman, an old man and a prophet, famous for his power of assuming different shapes at will. Hence the phrase, *As many shapes as Proteus, i.e.* full of shifts, aliases, disguises, etc., and the adjective **protean**, readily taking on different aspects, ever-changing, versatile.

Proteus lived in a vast cave, and his custom was to tell over his herds of sea-calves at noon, and then to sleep. There was no way of catching him but by stealing upon him at this time and binding him; otherwise he would elude anyone by a rapid change of shape.

Protevangelium (prō te văn jē' li um). The first (Gr. *protos*) GOSPEL; a term applied to an apocryphal gospel which has been attributed to St. JAMES THE LESS. It was supposed by some critics that all the gospels were based upon this, but it appears to be the compilation of a Jewish Christian from a variety of sources and dates from the 2nd century. The name is also given to the curse upon the SERPENT in *Gen.* iii, 15, which has been regarded as the earliest utterance of the gospel.

See APOCRYPHA.

Prothalamion (prō thà lā' mi ùn). The term coined by Spenser (from Gr. *thalamos*, a bridal chamber) as a title for his "Spousall Verse" (1596) in honour of the double marriage of Lady Elizabeth and Lady Katharine Somerset, daughters of the Earl of Worcester, to Henry Gilford and William Peter, Esquires. Hence a song sung in honour of the bride and bridegroom before the wedding. *Cp.* EPITHALAMIUM.

Protocol (prō' tō kol). In diplomacy, the original draft of a diplomatic document such as a dispatch or treaty; from Gr. *protos*, first, *kolla*, glue, a sheet glued to the front of a manuscript, or the case containing it, giving certain descriptive particulars. The word also denotes the code of correct procedure, etiquette, and ceremonial to be observed in official international intercourse.

The Protocols of the Elders of Zion. Forged material published by Serge Nilus in Russia in 1905, based on an earlier FORGERY of 1903, purporting to outline secret Jewish plans for achieving world power by undermining Gentile morality, family life and health, and by securing a monopoly in international finance, etc. Their falsity was first exposed by Philip Graves, *The Times* correspondent in Constantinople, in 1921 and later judicially, at Berne (1934–1935). Their influence in inciting anti-semitism notably among the Russians, and later providing Hitler and his associates with an excuse they knew to be a myth, provide tragic evidence of the power of the "big lie".

Proto-martyr. The first martyr (Gr. *protos*, first). STEPHEN the deacon is so called (*Acts* vi, vii), and St. ALBAN is known as the proto-martyr of Britain.

Proud. To do someone proud. To treat them lavishly; to give them first-class hospitality, etc.

To stand proud. In engineering and the practical skills, said of something which sticks out further than it should or above a particular plane.

Proxime accessit (Lat. *proxime*, next; *accessit*, he approached). An expression used in prize lists, etc., for the runner-up, the one who came very near the winner.

Prud'homme (proo' dom) in O.Fr. meant a man endowed with all the knightly virtues (*preux homme*), but later implied a man of proven honesty, experience and knowledge in his craft or trade, whence its specialized meaning in Mod. Fr. for a member of an Industrial Arbitration Board.

Prunes and prisms. See NIMINI-PIMINI.

Prussian Blue. So called because it was discovered by a Prussian, Diesbach, a colourman of Berlin, in 1704. It was sometimes called *Berlin blue*. It is made by adding ferrous sulphate solution to one of potassium ferrocyanide to which ferric chloride is subsequently introduced. *Prussic acid* (hydrocyanic acid) can be made by distilling Prussian blue. *Cp.* PROOSHAN BLUE.

Prussianism. A term denoting the arrogance and overbearing methods associated with the Prussian military machine and governmental attitudes from the days of Frederick the Great (1712–1786) until World War I. Unfortunately there was a return to Prussianism in Germany under the NAZIS. *Cp.* JACK-BOOT; MAILED FIST.

Pry, Paul. An idle meddlesome fellow, who has no occupation of his own, and is always interfering with other folk's business. The term comes from the hero of John Poole's comedy, *Paul Pry* (1825).

Psalmanazar, George. A classical example of the impostor. A Frenchman whose real name is unknown to this day, he appeared in London in 1703 claiming to be a native of Formosa, at that time an almost unknown island. In 1704 he published an account of Formosa with a grammar of the language, which from beginning to end was a fabrication of his own. The literary and critical world of London was taken in, but his imposture was soon exposed by Roman Catholic missionaries who had laboured in Formosa, and after a time Psalmanazar publicly confessed his fraud. He turned over a new leaf and applied himself to the study of Hebrew and other genuine labours, ending his days in 1763 as a man of some repute and the friend of Dr. Johnson. *See* FORGERY; OSSIAN; PROTOCOLS OF THE ELDERS OF ZION.

Psalms. Of the 150 songs in the *Book of Psalms*, 73 are inscribed with David's name, 12 with that of Asaph the singer, 11 are attributed to the sons of Korah, a family of singers, and one (*Psalm* xc) to Moses. The whole compilation is divided into five books: Bk. 1, from i to xli; Bk. 2, from xlii to lxxii; Bk. 3, from lxxiii to lxxxix; Bk. 4, from xc to cvi; Bk. 5, from cvii to cl.

Much of the *Book of Psalms* was for centuries attributed to David (hence called the sweet psalmist of Israel) but it is doubtful whether he wrote any of them. The tradition comes from the author of *Chronicles*, and II *Sam.* xxii is a psalm attributed to David that is identical with *Ps.* xviii. Also, the last verse of *Ps.* lxxii ("The prayers of David the son of Jesse are ended") seems to suggest that he was the author up to that point.

In explanation of the confusion between the Roman Catholic and PROTESTANT psalters, it should be noted that *Psalms* ix and x in the BOOK OF COMMON PRAYER version (also in the BIBLE, AUTHORIZED VERSION and REVISED VERSION) are combined in the Roman Catholic Psalter to form *Psalm* ix, and *Psalms* cxiv and cxv in the *Book of Common Prayer* are combined in the Roman Catholic Psalter to form *Psalm* cxiii. Again, *Psalm* cxvi in the *Book of Common Prayer* is split to form *Psalms* cxiv and cxv in the Roman Catholic Psalter, and *Psalm* cxlvii in the *Book of Common Prayer* is split to form *Psalms* cxlvi and cxlvii in the Roman Catholic Psalter. Thus only the first eight and the last three *Psalms* coincide numerically in both psalters. *See also* GRADUAL PSALMS; PENITENTIAL PSALMS.

Pseudepigrapha (sū de pig' rả fả). (Gr., falsely inscribed or ascribed). In Bibl- ical scholarship, a term applied to certain pseudonymous Jewish writings such as the "Book of Enoch", the "Assumption of MOSES", the "Psalms of SOLOMON", the "Fourth Book of the MACCABEES" (*see under* MACCABÆUS), etc., which were excluded from the CANON of the OLD TESTAMENT and the APOCRYPHA.

Pseudonym. See NOM DE PLUME.

Psyche (sī' kē) (Gr., breath; hence, life,

or soul itself). In "the latest-born of the myths", *Cupid and Psyche*, an episode in the GOLDEN ASS, Psyche is a beautiful maiden beloved by CUPID, who visited her every night but departed at sunrise. Cupid bade her never seek to know who he was, but one night curiosity got the better of her; she lit the lamp to look at him, a drop of hot oil fell on his shoulder and he awoke and fled. The abandoned Psyche then wandered far and wide in search of her lover; she became the slave of VENUS, who imposed on her heartless tasks and treated her most cruelly. Ultimately she was united to Cupid and became immortal. The tale appears in Walter Pater's *Marius the Epicurean*.

Psychological Moment, The. The moment when the mind is readiest to receive suggestions from another. It is an inaccurate translation of the German *das Momentum*, which means *momentum*, not *moment*. It is incorrectly applied when the idea of mental receptivity is absent, but it is popularly used to mean "the opportune moment", "just at the right time", etc.

Ptolemaic System (to le mä' ik). The system to account for the apparent motion of the heavenly bodies expounded in the 2nd century by Ptolemy, the famous astronomer of Alexandria. He taught that the earth is fixed in the centre of the universe, and the heavens revolve round it from east to west, carrying with them the SUN, PLANETS, and fixed stars, in their respective spheres, which he imagined as solid coverings (like so many skins of an onion) each revolving at different velocities. The tenth or outer sphere was the PRIMUM MOBILE. This theory was an attempt to systematize theories long held by PLATO, ARISTOTLE, Hipparchus, and others, and it substantially held sway until replaced by the COPERNICAN SYSTEM.

Public. Public-house signs are in themselves a fascinating study and much of Britain's history may be gleaned from them, as well as folk-lore, HERALDRY, social customs, etc. Many are a compliment to the lord of the manor or a nobleman or his cognizance, as the *Warwick Arms*, the BEAR AND RAGGED STAFF.

Others pay tribute to distinguished warriors or their battles, as *The Marquis of Granby*, the *Duke of Wellington*, the *Waterloo*, the *Keppel's Head*, the *Trafalgar*. Royalty is conspicuously represented by the *Crown*, the *King's Arms*, the *Prince Regent*, the *Prince of Wales*, the *Victoria*, the *Albert*, the *George*, etc. Literary names are less conspicuous, but there is a *Shakespeare*, *Milton Arms*, *Macaulay Arms*, *Sir Richard Steele*, and *Sir Walter Scott*, as well as *The Miller of Mansfield, Pindar of Wakefield, Sir John Falstaff, Robinson Crusoe*, and *Valentine and Orson*. *Simon the Tanner*, *The Good Samaritan*, *Noah's Ark*, the *Gospel Oak*, the *Angel* have a Biblical flavour, and myth and legend are represented by *The Apollo, Hercules, Phœnix, King Lud, Merlin's Cave, The Man in the Moon, Punch, Robin Hood*, the *Moonrakers, Cat and the Fiddle*, etc.

Some signs indicate sporting associations, such as the *Cricketers*, the *Bat and Ball*, the *Bowling Green*, the *Angler's Rest*, the *Huntsman*; or trades associations as *Coopers', Bricklayers', Plumbers', Carpenters', Masons'* Arms, etc. Others show a whimsical turn as *The Who'd a Thought It, The Five Alls, The World Turned Upside Down, The Good Woman*.

The following list will serve to exemplify the subject:

The Bag o'Nails. From a tradesman's sign — that of an ironmonger. Said by some 19th-century writers to be a corruption of "Bacchanals".

The Bear. From the popular sport of bear-baiting.

The Bell. Mostly derived from the national addiction to bell-ringing.

The Bell Savage. See LA BELLE SAUVAGE.

The Blue Boar. See under BLUE.

The Blue Lion. Denmark (possibly a compliment to James I's queen, Anne of Denmark), also the badge of the Earl of Mortimer.

Bolt in Tun. The punning heraldic badge of Prior Bolton, last of the clerical rulers of St. Bartholomew's before the REFORMATION.

The Bull and Dog. From the sport of

bull-baiting.

The Bull and Gate. See under BULL.

The Case is Altered. Apart from the explanation that the circumstances of a particular inn have altered substantially, there are various supposed origins of the sign. One is (as at Ravensden, Bedfordshire) that it is from PLOWDEN's use of the expression. Another (as in Middlesex) is that it is a corruption of *Casa Alta* (Sp. High House), which was said to be used as a public house name when soldiers of the 57th Foot returned to Middlesex after the Peninsular War.

The Cat and Fiddle. See under CAT.

The Cat and Kittens. See under CAT.

The Cat and Wheel. A corruption of St. "CATHERINE'S Wheel".

The Chequers. See CHEQUERS.

The Coach and Horses. A favourite sign of a posting-house or stage-coach inn.

The Cock and Bottle. See under COCK.

The Cross Keys. See under KEY.

The Devil. See GO TO THE DEVIL *under* DEVIL.

Dirty Dick's. See under DIRT.

The Dog and Duck, or *The Duck in the Pond*, indicating that the sport so called could be seen there. A duck was put into the water, and a dog set to hunt it; the fun was to see the duck diving and the dog following it under water.

The Five Alls consists of a king (I rule all), a priest (I pray for all), a soldier (I fight for all), a JOHN BULL or a farmer (I pay for all), and a lawyer (I plead for all).

The Four Alls. The first four of the FIVE ALLS, above.

The Fox and Goose. Sometimes signifying that there were arrangements within for playing the game of Fox and Goose.

The Golden Fleece. An allusion to the fable of the GOLDEN FLEECE and to the woollen trade.

The Golden Lion. The badge of Henry I and the PERCYS of Northumberland.

The Goat and the Compass. See under GOAT.

The Golden Cross. A reference to the emblems carried by the crusaders.

The Goose and Gridiron. See under GOOSE.

The Green Man, The Green Man and Still. See under GREEN.

Hearts of Oak. A compliment to the British naval tradition. *See under* HEART.

The Hole in the Wall. Perhaps an allusion to the hole in the wall of a prison through which the inmates received donations, or a reference to the narrow alley or passage by which the tavern was approached.

The Horse and Jockey. An obvious allusion to the TURF.

The Man with a Load of Mischief. A sign in Oxford Street, London, nearly opposite Hanway Yard, said to have been painted by Hogarth, showing a man carrying a woman with a glass of gin in her hand, a magpie, and a monkey, etc.

The Marquis of Granby. In compliment to John Manners (*see* GRANBY), eldest son of John, third Duke of Rutland—a bluff, brave soldier, generous and greatly beloved by his men.

> What conquest now will Britain boast
> Or where display her banners?
> Alas! in Granby she has lost
> True courage and good Manners.

The Pig and Tinderbox. See under PIG.

The Pig and Whistle. Said by some to be a corruption of *pig and wassail, pig* being an abbreviation of *piggin*, an earthen vessel; or a facetious form of the BEAR AND RAGGED STAFF, etc.; but possibly a sign-painter's whimsy.

The Plum and Feathers. A corruption of *The Plume and Feathers*, the *Prince of Wales's Feathers* (*see under* WALES).

The Queen of Bohemia. In honour of James I's daughter Elizabeth who married Frederick, Elector of the Palatinate, who was chosen King of Bohemia in 1619.

The Red Cow. Possibly because at one time red cows were more esteemed in England than the more common "black".

The Red Lion. Rampant, Scotland; also the badge of John of Gaunt, Duke of Lancaster.

The Rising Sun. A badge of Edward III.

The Rose. A symbol of England.

The Rose and Crown. One of the "loyal" public-house signs.

The Running Footman. From the liveried servant who used to run before the nobleman's carriage.

St. George and the Dragon. In compliment to the patron saint of ENGLAND.

The Salutation. Refers to the angel saluting the Virgin MARY.

The Saracen's Head. Reminiscent of the CRUSADES.

The Seven Stars. An astrological sign.

The Ship and Shovel. Said to be a corruption of Sir Cloudesley Shovel, the admiral of Queen Anne's reign, but probably refers to the shovels used for unloading coal, etc.

The Star and Garter. The insignia of the Order of the Garter.

The Swan and Antelope. Supporters of the arms of Henry IV.

The Swan and Harp. *See* GOOSE AND GRIDIRON *under* GOOSE.

The Swan with Two Necks. *See under* SWAN.

The Tabard. A sleeveless coat, worn by noblemen and heralds, upon which a coat of arms was embroidered. The tavern with this sign at Southwark was where Chaucer's pilgrims "assembled".

The Talbot (a hound). The arms of the Talbot family.

The Three Kings. An allusion to the three kings of COLOGNE, the MAGI.

The Turk's Head. Like the Saracen's Head, an allusion to the CRUSADES.

The Two Chairmen. Found in the neighbourhood of fashionable quarters when sedan chairs were in vogue.

The Unicorn. The Scottish supporter in the royal arms of Great Britain.

The White Hart. The cognizance of Richard II.

The White Lion. The cognizance of Edward IV as Earl of March. Also the device of the Dukes of Norfolk, the Earls of Surrey, etc.

See also THE OLD CHAPEL *under* CHAPEL; A COCK AND BULL STORY *under* COCK; MERMAID TAVERN.

Publicans (Lat. *publicani*). In the Roman Empire, wealthy businessmen who contracted to manage State monopolies or to farm the taxes, which often led to abuses. Hence their unpopularity in the provinces and their being associated with sinners in the NEW TESTAMENT.

Pucelle, La (pū sel') (Fr., "The Maid"), *i.e.* of Orleans, JOAN OF ARC. Chapelain and VOLTAIRE wrote a poem with this title.

Puck. A mischievous sprite of popular folklore, also called ROBIN GOODFELLOW. In Spenser's *Epithalamion* he is an evil goblin:

> Ne let the Pouke, nor other evill sprights,

but SHAKESPEARE'S *Midsummer Night's Dream* (II,i) shows him as:

> that shrewd and knavish sprite
> Call'd Robin Goodfellow; are not you he
> That frights the maidens of the villagery;
> Skim milk, and sometimes labour in the quern
> And bootless make the breathless house-wife churn;
> And sometime make the drink to bear no barm;
> Mislead night wanderers, laughing at their harm?
> Those that Hobgoblin call you, and sweet Puck,
> You do their work, and they should have good luck.

Pudding. The proof of the pudding is in the eating. An old proverb meaning that performance is the true test, not appearances, promises, etc.; just as the best test of a pudding is to eat it, not just to look at it.

Puff. An onomatopœic word, suggestive of the sound made by puffing wind from the mouth; since at least the early 17th century, applied to extravagantly worded advertisements, reviews, etc., with the implication that they have as much lasting value as a "puff of wind".

Puffed up. Conceited; elated with conceit or praise; filled with wind. A *puff* is a tartlet with a very light or puffy crust.

Puisne Judges (pū' ni). Formerly justices and barons of the COMMON LAW courts at Westminster other than the Chief Justices; by the Judicature Act of 1877, Judges of the High Court other than the Lord CHANCELLOR, the Lord Chief Justice, the MASTER OF THE ROLLS, the Lord Chief Justice of the Common Pleas and the Lord Chief Baron (the last two offices becoming defunct). Since the Judicature Act of 1925 the term applies to Judges of the High Court other than the Lord Chancellor, the Lord Chief Justice, and the President of the Probate Division, but is not usually attached to the Master of the Rolls. *Puisne* is etymologically the same as *puny*; it is the O.Fr. *puisne*, subsequently born (Lat. *post natus*) and signifies "junior" or "inferior in rank".

Pulitzer Prizes, for literary work, journalism, drama, and music, are awarded annually from funds left for the purpose by Joseph Pulitzer (1847–1911), a prominent and wealthy American editor and newspaper proprietor.

Pull. Pull devil, pull baker. Said in encouragement of a contest, usually over the possession of something. *See under* DEVIL.

To have the pull of, or **over one.** To have the advantage over him; to be able to dictate terms or make him do what you wish.

To pull a fast one. To obtain an advantage by a trick or by somewhat questionable means.

To pull bacon. TO COCK A SNOOK (*see under* COCK).

To pull one's punches. Not to be as blunt as one could be; to soften the blow and to avoid offence by holding back a little. In boxing, blows delivered intentionally ineffectively are said to be "pulled".

To pull one's socks up. TO PULL ONESELF TOGETHER and endeavour to do better.

To pull one's weight. To do the very best one can, to play one's proper part. A phrase from rowing; an oarsman who does not put all his weight into the stroke is a drag on the rest of the crew and something of a passenger.

To pull oneself together. To rouse oneself to renewed activity; to shake off depression or inertia.

To pull out all the stops. To make a supreme effort to achieve one's objective. An expression derived from the organ player who has to be extremely dexterous to manipulate the many stops of his organ.

To pull someone's leg. To delude him in a humorous way, lead him astray by

chaff, exaggeration, etc.

To pull the chestnuts out of the fire. To retrieve a difficult situation for someone; to get someone out of an embarrassment. The allusion is to the fable of the monkey and the cat. *See* TO BE MADE A CATSPAW OF *under* CAT.

To pull the strings. To use private influence "behind the scenes". From the puppet-master who controls the movements of the puppets by the strings attached to them. *Cp.* TO PULL THE WIRES *under* WIRE.

To pull the wool over someone's eyes. To deceive or hoodwink; to blind him temporarily to what is going on.

To pull through. To get oneself well out of difficulty or serious illness.

To pull together. To co-operate harmoniously.

Pullman. Properly a well-fitted railway saloon or sleeping-car built at the Pullman Carriage Works, Illinois; so called from the designer, George M. Pullman (1831–1897) of Chicago. The word is now applied to other luxurious railway saloons and motor transport.

Pummel. *See* POMMEL.

Pump. To prime the pump. To give financial aid to an enterprise in the hope that it will become self-supporting. From starting a pump working by pouring in water to establish suction.

To pump someone is to extract information out of him by artful questions; to draw from him all he knows, as one draws water from a well by gradual pumping. Ben Jonson in *A Tale of a Tub* (IV, iii) has, "I'll stand aside whilst thou pump'st out of him his business."

Punch. The name of this beverage, which was introduced into England in the early 17th century, is usually held to derive from Hind. *panch*, five, because it has five principal ingredients (spirit, water, spice, sugar, and some acid fruit juice). It may equally derive from *puncheon*, the large wine cask.

Punch and Judy. The name of Mr. Punch, the hero of the puppet play, probably comes from Ital. *pulcinello*, a diminutive of *pulcino*, a young chicken. His identification with Pontius Pilate and of Judy with JUDAS is imaginary. The story roughly in its present form is attributed to an Italian comedian, Silvio Fiorillo (about 1600), and it appeared in ENGLAND about the time of the RESTORATION. Punch, in a fit of jealousy, strangles his infant child, whereupon his wife Judy belabours him with a bludgeon until he retaliates and beats her to death. He flings both bodies into the street, but is arrested and shut in prison whence he escapes by means of a golden key. The rest is an allegory showing how the light-hearted Punch triumphs over (1) Ennui, in the shape of a dog; (2) Disease, in the disguise of a doctor; (3) Death, who is beaten to death; and (4) the DEVIL himself, who is outwitted. In subsequent English versions JACK KETCH, instead of hanging Punch, gets hanged himself.

The satirical humorous weekly paper, *Punch*, or *The London Charivari*, is, of course, named after Mr. Punch, who naturally featured prominently on the cover design for very many issues. It first appeared in July 1841 under the editorship of Mark Lemon and Henry Mayhew.

Pleased as Punch. Greatly delighted. Punch is always singing with self-satisfaction at the success of his EVIL actions.

Punch line. A vivid, often startling climax to an anecdote, joke, story, etc., which gives point to the foregoing. The figurative "punch" suggests that the listener is struck by this line.

To be punch drunk. To experience a form of concussion to which boxers are liable, causing unsteadiness of gait resembling drunkenness, used figuratively of one "reeling from heavy punishment".

Punctual. No bigger than a point, exact to a point or moment (Lat. *ad punctum*). Hence the ANGEL, describing this earth to ADAM calls it, "This spacious earth, this punctual spot"—*i.e.* a spot not bigger than a point (Milton: *Paradise Lost*, VIII, 23).

Punctuality is the politeness of kings (Fr. *L'exactitude est la politesse des rois*). A favourite maxim of Louis XVIII, but erroneously attributed by Samuel Smiles to Louis XIV.

Pundit (Hind. *pandit*). In India, a

learned man, one versed in Sanskrit, law, religion, etc. We use the word for a learned man, an expert, an authority.

Punic Apple. A pomegranate or apple belonging to the genus *Punica*.

Punic Faith (Lat. *punica fides*). Treachery, violation of faith, the faith of the Carthaginians. The Phœnicians (Lat. *Punicus*, a Phœnician) founded Carthage and the long-drawn-out **Punic Wars** between Rome and Carthage ended in the latter's destruction. The Roman accusations of breach of faith were classic instances of the POT CALLING THE KETTLE BLACK. *Cp.* ATTIC FAITH.

> Our Punic Faith
> Is infamous, and branded to a proverb.
> ADDISON: *Cato*, II.

Punk. An old word for a harlot, a worthless person or thing. Currently applied to certain young people wearing bizarre clothes and hair style. *Cp.* HELL'S ANGELS; MODS AND ROCKERS; SKINHEADS.

Pup. To be sold a pup. To be swindled.

Pure, Simon. *See* SIMON PURE.

Purgatory. The doctrine of Purgatory, according to which the souls of the departed suffer for a time till they are purged of their sin, is of ancient standing, and in certain phases of Jewish belief GEHENNA seems to have been regarded partly as a place of purgatory.

The early Church Fathers developed the concept of purgatory and support for the doctrine was adduced from *2 Macc.* xii, 39–45; *Matt.* xii, 32; *1 Cor.* iii, 11–13; etc. The first decree on the subject was promulgated by the Council of Florence in 1439. It was rejected by the CHURCH OF ENGLAND in 1562 by the XXIInd of the *Articles of Religion*.

St. Patrick's Purgatory. *See under* PATRICK.

Purification, Feast of. *See* CANDLEMAS DAY.

Puritans. The more extreme PROTESTANTS inside and outside the CHURCH OF ENGLAND who found the Elizabethan religious settlement unacceptable and wished a further "purification" of religion. They looked more and more to the BIBLE as the sole authority, rejecting all tradition in matters of public worship, and were mainly Calvinist in outlook and theology. They feature in the 16th and 17th century as BROWNISTS, BARROWISTS, PRESBYTERIANS, BAPTISTS, SEPARATISTS, and Independents, and were sometimes called *Precisionists* from their punctiliousness over religious rules and observances. After the RESTORATION and the Act of Uniformity (1662), they became collectively known as DISSENTERS or NON-CONFORMISTS.

Purlieu (pĕr′ lū). The outlying parts of a place, the environs; originally the borders or outskirts of a forest, especially that which was formerly part of the forest. It is a corruption of the O.Fr. *pourallée*, a going through; the *lieu*, as though for *place*, being an erroneous addition due to English pronunciation and spelling of the French. Thus Henry III allowed certain portions around the forests, acquired by his predecessors by unlawful encroachment, to be freed from the forest-laws and restored to former owners. The boundaries were then settled by a perambulation or *pourallée*. *See* FOREST COURTS.

> In the purlieus of this forest stands
> A sheepcote fenced about with olive-trees.
> SHAKESPEARE: *As You Like It*, IV, iii.

Purple. A synonym for the rank of Roman emperor, derived from the colour of the emperor's dyed woollen robe, hence phrases such as "raised to the purple". Purple robes were a mark of dignity among the ancient Greeks and Romans and were worn by kings, magistrates, and military commanders, hence purple became a symbol of luxury and power. It was obtained from shellfish (*Buccinum, Murex*) and the deep colour was termed *purpura* (from the name of one of these molluscs). The famous *Tyrian purple* was made from a mixture of these shellfish and was very costly to produce. Differing shades were obtained by various combinations and methods. Since Roman times, purple was used in the insignia of emperors, kings and prelates, and a priest is said to be **raised to the purple** when he is created CARDINAL, though his insignia are actually red. *Purpure* is one of the tinctures used in HERALDRY, and in engravings it is shown by lines running diagonally from

sinister to dexter (*i.e.* from right to left as one looks at it). *See* COLOURS.

Born in, or **to the purple.** *See* PORPHYROGENITUS.

Purple Heart. A U.S. army medal awarded for wounds received by enemy action while on active service. It consists of a silver heart bearing the effigy of George Washington, suspended from a purple ribbon with white edges. The heartwood of *Copaifera pubiflora* and *C. bracteata* is called *Purple Heart* or *Purple Wood*. It is a native of Guyana and a rich plum colour, and was used in making ramrods for guns. *Purple Heart* is also the popular name of a stimulant pill (Drinamyl) favoured by youthful drugtakers, so called from its shape and colour.

Purple patches. Highly coloured or florid patches in a literary work which is generally undistinguished. The allusion is to Horace's *De Arte Poetica*, 14.

Pursuivant (pĕr′ swi vănt). The lowest grade of the officers of arms, comprising the Heralds' College, the others, under the EARL MARSHAL, being (1) the Kings of Arms, and (2) the HERALDS.

> ENGLAND has four Pursuivants, *viz. Rouge Croix, Bluemantle, Rouge Dragon,* and *Portcullis*; SCOTLAND has three, *viz. Carrick, Kintyre,* and *Unicorn*.

Puseyite (pū′zi īt). A HIGH CHURCH follower of E. B. Pusey (1800–1882), Professor of Hebrew at Oxford, one of the leaders of the OXFORD MOVEMENT, and a contributor to *Tracts for the Times*. Hence **Puseyism** as an unfriendly name for Tractarianism.

Push. To give one the push. To give him his CONGÉ, to give him the sack (*see under* SACK).

To push off. To depart, to commence the operations. A phrase from boating—one starts by pushing the boat off from the bank. Used imperatively, *Push off* means "Go away", "Get out of here".

To push the boat out. A popular expression meaning to celebrate by treating one's acquaintances to a drinking session. Of nautical origin, probably from the idea of a final celebration before sailing, to give impetus to one's departure.

Push-button, or **press-button war.** A war carried on with guided missiles controlled by pushing or pressing a button.

Puss. A conventional call-name for a cat, possibly imitative of a cat-like sound; also applied in the 17th century and since to hares. The derivation from Lat. *lepus*, a hare, Frenchified into *le pus*, is, of course, only humorous.

Puss in Boots. This nursery tale, *Le Chat Botté*, is from Straparola's *Nights* (1530), No. xi, where Constantine's cat procures his master a fine castle and the king's heiress. It was translated from the Italian into French, in 1585, and appeared in Perrault's *Les contes de ma Mère l'Oye* (1697), through which medium it reached England. In the story the clever cat secures a fortune and a royal partner for his master, who passes off as the Marquis of Carabas, but is in reality a young miller without a penny in the world.

Pussyfoot. A person with a soft, cat-like sneaking tread, and from PUSSY-FOOT JOHNSON (*below*), now applied as a noun to advocates of, and as an adjective to opinions, legislation, etc., promoting total abstinence.

Put. To put one's shoulder to the wheel. To make a determined effort; as a carter would put his shoulder to the wheel to assist his horses hauling his waggon out of a rut.

To put two and two together. To draw conclusions from facts, events, etc.; two and two make four, hence the suggestion of a simple and obvious deduction.

To stay put. To remain firmly in a position, literally or figuratively.

Putsch (pooch). A German word, the same as our *push*, applied to a COUP DE MAIN or political uprising.

Pygmalion (pig mā' li ŏn). In Greek legend, a sculptor and king of Cyprus. According to Ovid's *Metamorphoses*, he fell in love with his own ivory statue of his own ideal woman. At his earnest prayer the goddess APHRODITE gave life to the statue and he married it. The story is found in Marston's *Metamorphosis of Pygmalion's Image* (1598). Morris retold it in *The Earthly Paradise*

(*August*), and W. S. Gilbert adapted it in his comedy of *Pygmalion and Galatea* (1871), in which the sculptor is a married man. His wife, Cynisca, was jealous of the animated statue (Galatea), which, after considerable trouble, voluntarily returned to its original state. The name was used figuratively by G. B. Shaw for a play produced in 1912 from which the popular musical *My Fair Lady* was derived.

Pygmy (pig' mi). The name used by HOMER and other classical writers for a supposed race of DWARFS said to dwell in Ethiopia, Africa, or India; from Gr. *pugme*, the length of the arm from elbow to the knuckles. They cut down corn with hatchets and made war against cranes which came annually to plunder them. When HERCULES visited their country they climbed up his goblet by ladders to drink from it, and while he was asleep two whole armies of pygmies fell upon his right hand and two on his left and were rolled up by Hercules in the skin of the NEMEAN LION. Swift's debt to this legend is apparent in his *Gulliver's Travels*.

The term is now applied to certain dwarfish races of central Africa (whose existence was established late in the 19th century), Malaysia, etc.; also to small members of a species, as the *pygmy hippopotamus*.

Pylades and Orestes (pī' lă dēz, ō res' tēz). Two friends in Homeric legend, whose names have become proverbial for friendship, like those of DAMON AND PYTHIAS, DAVID AND JONATHAN. Orestes was the son, and Pylades the nephew, of AGAMEMNON, after whose murder Orestes was put in the care of Pylades' father (Strophius), and the two became fast friends. Pylades assisted Orestes in obtaining vengeance on Ægisthus and CLYTEMNESTRA, and afterwards married ELECTRA, his friend's sister.

Pyramid (pir' ă mid) (Gr. *pyramis*, a wheaten cake). The Greek name of these massive royal tombs of ancient Egypt was probably of humorous application. Zoser's step-pyramid at Saqqara (IIIrd Dynasty) was the forerunner of the true pyramid. The next stage was

Pyramus

when the step-pyramid at Meidum was covered with a uniform slope from base to top by filling in the steps (*c.* 2670 B.C.). The famous Great Pyramid at Giza, covering some 13 acres and originally rising to a height of 481 ft., was built by Cheops or Khufu (*c.* 2650 B.C.). That of Chephren or Khafra (*c.* 2620 B.C.), his son, is slightly smaller, and the third, the tomb of Mycerinius or Menkaura (*c.* 2600 B.C.), is 204 ft. high. Each contains entrances with passages leading to an antechamber and the burial chamber. Other pyramids are to be found at Abusir, Saqqara, Dahshur, Lisht, and in the Faiyum.

The kings of the XIth Dynasty built small brick pyramids at Thebes.

Pyramus (pir' à mùs). A Babylonian youth in classic story (*see* Ovid's *Metamorphoses*, iv), the lover of Thisbe. Thisbe was to meet him at the white MULBERRY-tree near the tomb of Ninus, but she, scared by a lion, fled and left her veil, which the lion besmeared with blood. Pyramus, thinking his lady-love had been devoured, slew himself, and Thisbe, coming up soon afterwards, stabbed herself also. The blood of the lovers stained the white fruit of the mulberry-tree into its present colour. The "tedious brief scene" and "very tragical mirth" presented by the rustics in SHAKESPEARE's *Midsummer Night's Dream* is a travesty of this legend.

Pyromancy (Gr. *pur*, fire; *manteia*, divination). DIVINATION by fire or the shapes observed in fire.

Pyrrha (pi' rà). The wife of DEUCALION.

Pyrrhic Dance (pi' rik). The famous wardance of the Greeks; so called from its inventor, Pyrrichos, a Dorian. It was a quick dance, performed in full armour to the flute, and its name is still used for a metrical foot of two short "dancing" syllables. The *Romaika*, still danced in Greece, is a relic of the ancient Pyrrhic dance.

Pyrrhic victory. A victory won at too heavy a price, like the costly victory won by Pyrrhus, King of Epirus, at Asculum in 279 B.C. ("One more such victory and we are lost."). Pyrrhus lost all his best officers and many men.

Pyrrhonism. Scepticism, or philosophic doubt; so named from Pyrrho (4th century B.C.), the founder of the first Greek school of sceptical philosophy. Pyrrho maintained that nothing was capable of proof and admitted the reality of nothing but sensations.

Pythagoras (pī thăg' or às). The Greek philosopher and mathematician of the 6th century B.C. (born at Samos), to whom was attributed the enunciation of the doctrines of the TRANSMIGRATION OF SOULS and of the harmony of the spheres, and also the proof of the 47th proposition in the 1st book of EUCLID, which is hence called the *Pythagorean proposition*. He taught that the SUN, MOON, and PLANETS have a motion independent of their daily rotation but seems to have held that the universe was earth-centred (*see* PYTHAGOREAN SYSTEM).

Pythagoras was noted for his manly beauty and long hair. Many stories are related of him, such as that he distinctly recollected previous existences of his own, having been (1) Æthelides, son of MERCURY; (2) Euphorbus the Phrygian, son of Panthous, in which form he ran PATROCLUS through with a lance, leaving HECTOR to kill him; (3) Hermotimus, the prophet of Clazomenæ; and (4) a fisherman. To prove his Phrygian existence he was taken to the temple of HERA, in Argos, and asked to point out the shield of the son of Panthous, which he did without hesitation. Rosalind alludes to this story in Shakespeare's *As You Like It* (III, ii) when she says:

I was never so be-rhymed since Pythagoras' time, that I was an Irish rat, which I can hardly remember.

It is also elaborated in *Twelfth Night* (IV, ii):

Clown: What is the opinion of Pythagoras concerning wild fowl?
Mal.: That the soul of our grandam might haply inhabit a bird.
Clown: What thinkest thou of his opinion?
Mal.: I think nobly of the soul, and no way approve his opinion.

Other legends assert that one of his thighs was of GOLD, and that he showed it to ABARIS, and exhibited it in the OLYMPIC GAMES.

It was also said that Pythagoras used

to write on a looking-glass in blood and place it opposite the MOON, when the inscription would appear reflected on the moon's disc; and that he tamed a savage Daunian bear by "stroking it gently with his hand", subdued an EAGLE by the same means, and held absolute dominion over beasts and birds by "the power of his voice" or "influence of his touch".

At Croton he became the centre of the *Pythagorean brotherhood* which sought the moral reformation of society, practising temperance and abstinence from fleshly food.

The letter of Pythagoras. The Greek letter upsilon, υ, so called because it was used by him as a symbol of the divergent paths of virtue and vice.

The Pythagorean System. The astronomical system so called which held the universe to be spherical in shape with fire at its centre, around which revolved the counter-earth, the earth, then the MOON, the SUN, the five PLANETS, and lastly the sphere of fixed stars. It is a forerunner of the COPERNICAN SYSTEM and seems to be a later hypothesis of the Pythagoreans and not to have been originated by Pythagoras himself.

The Pythagorean Tables. *See* TABLE OF PYTHAGORAS.

The Theorem of Pythagoras. That the square on the hypotenuse of a right-angled triangle is equal to the sum of the squares on the other two sides.

Pythia (pith′ i à). The priestess of APOLLO at DELPHI who delivered ORACLES. Inspiration was obtained by inhaling sulphureous vapours which issued from the ground from a hole over which she sat on a three-legged stool or tripod. Oracles were only available in the spring and were originally spoken in HEXAMETER verses.

Pythian Games. The Greek games held in honour of APOLLO at Pytho in Phocis, subsequently called DELPHI. They took place every fourth year, in the third year of each OLYMPIAD, and were next in importance to the OLYMPIC GAMES.

Pythias. *See* DAMON.

Python (pī′ thon). The monster serpent hatched from the mud of DEUCALION's deluge, and slain by APOLLO at DELPHI (Pytho).

Pyx (piks) (Gr. *pyxis*, a boxwood vessel). A small metal receptacle or box in which the reserved HOST is taken to sick people. It is also the vessel in which the Host is reserved in the Tabernacle in Roman Catholic (and some Anglican) churches.

Trial of the Pyx. In ENGLAND, out of every 15 lb. TROY WEIGHT of GOLD and every 60 lb. of "silver" minted a coin was put into the *pyx* or box for annual testing at Goldsmiths' Hall in the City of London. The *trial of the pyx* is conducted in the presence of the QUEEN's REMEMBRANCER and a jury of goldsmiths. Their verdict is delivered in the presence of the CHANCELLOR OF THE EXCHEQUER. The trial was initiated in the reign of Edward I and formerly took place in the Chapel of the Pyx in Westminster Abbey. Samples are now taken and coins are not assayed separately. Silver was replaced by cupronickel in 1947.

Q

Q. The seventeenth letter of the English alphabet, and nineteenth of the Phœnician and Hebrew. In English *q* is invariably followed by *u* except in transliteration of some Arabic words, as in *Qatar*. *Qu* in English normally represents the sound *kw* as in *quinquennial* but occasionally *k* as in *perique*, *grotesque*, and *quay* (pronounced kē). Without the *u* it is pronounced *k* as in *Iraq*. Formerly, in Scotland, *qu* replaced *hw* as in *quhat*, or *hwat* (what). Q as a mediæval Latin numeral represents 500.

"Q". In Biblical criticism, the symbol used for the theoretical document used by MATTHEW or LUKE or both. In the SYNOPTIC GOSPELS there is much material common to both Matthew and Luke, which is designated "Q" (usually held to be the German *Quelle*, source). These passages mainly consist of the sayings of Jesus.

Q. To mind one's P's and Q's. *See under* P.

Q.C. QUEEN'S COUNCIL.

Q.E.D. (Lat. *quod erat demonstrandum*, which was to be demonstrated). Appended to the theorems of EUCLID: Thus have we proved the proposition stated above, as we were required to do. In schoolboy parlance, "Quite easily done."

Q.E.F. (Lat. *quod erat faciendum*, which was to be done). Appended to the problems of EUCLID: Thus have we done the operation required.

Q.P. (Lat. *quantum placet*). Used in prescriptions to signify that the quantity may be as little or as much as you like. Thus, in a cup of tea we might say, "Milk and sugar *q.p.*"

Q ships. In World War I, the name given to war vessels camouflaged as tramps. These "mystery ships" were used to lure U-BOATS to their destruction.

Q.T. On the strict Q.T. With complete secrecy. "Q.T." stands for "quiet".

Q.V. (Lat. *quantum vis*). As much as you like, or *quantum valeat*, as much as is proper.

q.v. (Lat. *quod vide*). Which see.

Quack, or **Quack doctor;** once called *quacksalver*. A puffer of salves; an itinerant drug vendor at FAIRS who "quacked" forth the praises of his wares to the credulous rustics. Hence, a CHARLATAN.

Quad. The university contraction for quadrangle, the college ground; hence, *to be in quad* is to be confined to your college grounds. The word *quad* is also applied to one of a family of quadruplets. *Cp.* QUOD.

Quadragesima (kwod ra jes′ i mà). The forty days of LENT.

Quadragesima Sunday. The first Sunday in LENT; so called because it is, in round numbers, the fortieth day before EASTER.

Quadragesimals. The farthings or payments formerly made in commutation of a personal visit to the Mother-church on Mid-Lent Sunday. *Cp.* PENTECOSTALS.

Quadriga (kwod′ ri ga). A contraction of *quadrijugae* (Lat. *quattuor*, *quadri-*, four; *jugum*, yoke). In classical antiquity, a two-wheeled chariot drawn by four horses harnessed abreast. A spirited representation of Peace riding in a quadriga, executed in bronze by Adrian Jones in 1912, surmounts the arch at the west end of Constitution Hill, London.

Quadrilateral. The four fortresses of Peschiera and Mantua on the Mincio, with Verona and Legnago on the Adige.

Now demolished.

Quadrille (kwod ril'). An old card game played by four persons with an ordinary pack of cards from which the eights, nines, and tens have been withdrawn. It displaced OMBRE in popular favour about 1730, and was followed by WHIST.

The square dance of the same name was of French origin, and was introduced into England in 1813 by the Duke of Devonshire.

Quadrivium (kwod riv' i um). The collective name given by the SCHOOLMEN of the MIDDLE AGES to the four "liberal arts" (Lat. *quadri-*, four; *via*, way), viz., arithmetic, music, geometry, and astronomy. The quadrivium was the "fourfold way" to knowledge; the TRIVIUM, the "threefold way" to eloquence; both together comprehended the *Seven Liberal Arts* enumerated in the following hexameter:

Lingua, Tropus, Ratio, Numerus, Tonus, Angulus, Astra.

And in the two following:
Gram. loquitur, *Dia*. vera docet, *Rhet*. verba colorat;
Mus. cadit, *Ar*. numerat, *Geo*. ponderat, *Ast*. colit astra.

Quai d'Orsay (kā dôr sā). The quay in Paris running along the left bank of the Seine where are situated the departments of Foreign Affairs and other government offices. The name is applied to the French Foreign Office and sometimes to the French government as a whole.

Quail. This bird was formerly supposed to be of an inordinately amorous disposition, hence its name was given to a courtesan.

Here's Agamemnon, an honest fellow enough, and one that loves quails.
SHAKESPEARE: *Troilus and Cressida*, V, i.

Quaker. A familiar name for a member of the Society of Friends, a religious body having no definite creed and no regular ministry, founded by George Fox, who began his preaching in 1647. His followers created an organized society during the 1650s and 1660s. It appears from the founder's *Journal* that they first obtained the appellation (1650) from the following circumstances: "Justice Ben-

net, of Derby," says Fox, "was the first to call us Quakers, because I bid them Tremble at the Word of the Lord."

Quakers (that, like to lanterns, bear Their light within them) will not swear.
BUTLER: *Hudibras*, II, ii.

The name was previously applied to a sect whose adherents shook and trembled with religious emotion and was generally applied in the COMMONWEALTH period as an abusive term to religious and political radicals. *Cp*. SHAKERS.

Quaker guns. Dummy guns made of wood, for drill purposes or camouflage; an allusion to the Quaker reprobation of the use of force.

Quarantine (Ital. *quaranta*, forty). The period, originally forty days, that a ship suspected of being infected with some contagious disorder is obliged to lie off port. Now applied to any period of segregation to prevent infection.

In law, the term is applied to the forty days during which a widow who is entitled to a dower may remain in the chief mansion-house of her deceased husband. *See also* YELLOW ADMIRAL *under* ADMIRAL; YELLOW JACK.

Quare impedit (Lat., wherefore he hinders). A form of legal action by which the right of presentation to a Church of England BENEFICE is tried (from the opening words of the writ). When a BISHOP has failed to institute a clergyman presented by the patron of the benefice, the latter may apply for a writ of *Quare impedit* against the bishop. It is now only used where the bishop's objections relate to matters of doctrine and ritual.

Quarrel. To quarrel with your bread and butter. To act against your best nterest; to follow a course which may prejudice your livelihood.

Quarry. An object of chase, especially the bird flown at in hawking or the animal pursued by hounds or hunters. Originally the word (O.Fr. *cuirée*, skinned) denoted the entrails, etc., of the deer which were placed on the animal's skin after it had been flayed, and given to the hounds as a reward.

Quart d'heure (kar děr). **Un mauvais quart d'heure** (Fr., a bad quarter of an hour). Used of a short, disagreeable experience.

Quarter. The fourth part of anything, as of a year or an hour or any material thing. In weights a *quarter* is 28 lb., *i.e.* a fourth of a hundredweight; as a measure of capacity for grain it is 8 bushels, which used to be one-fourth, but is now one-fifth of a load. In the meat trade a *quarter* of a beast is a fourth part, which includes one of the legs. A *quarter* in the U.S. coinage is the fourth part of a DOLLAR; in a heraldic shield or on a flag the *quarters* are the divisions made by central lines drawn at right angles across them. When looking at a shield the 1st and 4th quarters are in the *dexter chief* and *sinister base* (left-hand top and right-hand bottom), and the 2nd and 3rd in the *sinister chief* and *dexter base*.

Quarter, as exemption from death upon surrender.

To cry quarter. To beg for mercy.

To grant quarter. To spare the life of an enemy in your power. The old suggestion that it derives from an agreement anciently made between the Dutch and Spaniards, that the ransom of a soldier should be the *quarter* of his pay, is not borne out. It is possibly due to the fact that the victor would have to provide his captive with temporary QUARTERS.

Quarter, Quarters. Residence or place of abode.

A district of a town or city is often known as a quarter, as the *poor quarter*, the *native quarter*. The **Quartier Latin** (Latin quarter) of Paris is the university area. Although popularly renowned as the cosmopolitan and BOHEMIAN quarter, it derives its name from its ancient fame as a centre of learning when Latin was the common language for the students, who came from all over Europe.

Winter quarters is the place where an army lodges during the winter months; *married quarters*, barrack accommodation, etc., for married service men and their families.

Quarter Days. (1) New Style LADY DAY (25 March), MIDSUMMER Day (24 June), MICHAELMAS DAY (29 Septem-

ber), and CHRISTMAS Day (25 December).

(2) Old Style—Lady Day (6 April), Old Midsummer Day (6 July), Old Michaelmas Day (11 October), and Old Christmas Day (6 January).

Quarter Days in Scotland. CANDLEMAS DAY (2 February), WHITSUNDAY (15 May), LAMMAS DAY (1 August), and MARTINMAS Day (11 November).

Quarter Sessions. From the mid-14th century JUSTICES OF THE PEACE sat four times a year in Quarter Sessions to deal with appeals from Petty Sessions, criminal charges, and some civil cases as well as administrative work. Generally trial was by jury before two or more justices, but in 1882 a qualified barrister known as a Recorder replaced them in the boroughs, and from 1962 the chairman in other courts of Quarter Sessions had to be a qualified lawyer. In 1842 the more serious criminal cases were transferred to the Assizes and most of their administrative work was lost to the County Councils by the Local Government Act of 1888. Quarter Sessions were abolished by the Courts Act of 1971.

Quartered. *See* DRAWN AND QUARTERED.

Quarterdeck. The upper deck of a ship from the mainmast to the stern. In the Royal Navy it is the promenade reserved for officers. Hence, *to behave as though he were on his own quarterdeck*, to behave as though he owned the place. The naval custom of saluting the quarterdeck is of uncertain origin, one suggestion being that anciently a shrine was kept in this part of the ship. *Cp.* FORECASTLE.

Quarterly, The. A common name for the *Quarterly Review*, a literary and political review first published by John Murray at Edinburgh in 1809. It was a TORY rival of the EDINBURGH REVIEW. Its first editor was William Gifford (1756—1826) and Scott and Southey were principal contributors. J. G. Lockhart took over the editorship from S. T. Coleridge in 1825 and continued in office until 1853. It ceased publication in 1967.

Quartermaster. In the army, the officer whose duty it is to attend to the QUARTERS of the soldiers. He superintends the issue of all stores and equipment.

In the navy, the rating or petty officer who supervises the steering of the ship at sea and in harbour keeps watch under the Officer of the WATCH.

Quarto. A size of paper made by folding the sheet twice, giving *four* leaves, or eight pages; hence, a book composed of sheets folded thus. *Cp.* FOLIO; OCTAVO. The word is often written "4to".

Quasi (kwā′ zī) (Lat., as if). Prefixed to indicate "seeming", "as it were", that what it qualifies is not the real thing but has some of its qualities. Thus a *quasi-historical account* is seemingly historical but not accurately so, or only partially so.

Quasimodo Sunday (kwā zī mō dō′). The first Sunday after EASTER or LOW SUNDAY; so called from the Introit at MASS on this day which begins *Quasi modo geniti infantes*, as newborn babes (I *Pet.* ii, 2). *Cp.* CANTATE SUNDAY.

Quasimodo was also the name of the hunchback in Victor Hugo's *Notre-Dame de Paris* (1831).

Quattrocento (Ital. from Lat. *quattuor*, four; *centum*, hundred). An abbreviation of *mille quattrocento*, 1400. The name given to the Fifteenth Century as a period of art and literature, especially with reference to Italy. *Cp.* CINQUEN-CENTO.

Que sçais-je? (kĕ sāzh) (Fr., What do I know?). The motto adopted by Michel-Eyquem de Montaigne (1533–1592), the great French essayist, as expressing the sceptical and inquiring nature of his writings.

Queen. Queen Anne. Daughter of James II and his first wife Anne Hyde. Her reign extended from 1702 to 1714 and her name is still used in certain phrases.

Queen Anne is dead. A slighting retort made to a teller of stale news.

Queen Anne style. The style in buildings, decoration, furniture, silverware, etc., characteristic of her period.

Queen Anne's Bounty. A fund established by Queen Anne in 1704 for the relief of the poorer clergy of the CHURCH OF ENGLAND.

Queen Consort. The wife of a reigning king.

Queen Dick. Richard Cromwell (1626–1712), son of Protector Oliver Cromwell, was sometimes so called; also known as "King Dick".

Queen Dowager. The widow of a deceased king.

Queen Mab. *See* MAB.

Queen Mother. The consort of a king is so called after her husband's death and when her son or daughter has succeeded to the throne.

Queen of the Blues. A nickname given by Dr. Johnson to Mrs. Elizabeth Montagu (1720–1800), a noted BLUE-STOCKING.

Queen of Glory. An epithet of the Virgin MARY.

Queen of Hearts. Elizabeth (1596–1662), daughter of James I, wife of the Elector of the PALATINATE, and ill-starred Queen of BOHEMIA; so called in the Low Countries from her amiable character and engaging manners, even in her misfortune.

Queen of Heaven. The Virgin MARY. In ancient times, among the Phœnicians, ASTARTE; Greeks, HERA; Romans, JUNO; HECATE; the Egyptian ISIS, etc., were also so called; but as a general title it applied to DIANA, or the MOON also called *Queen of the Night*, and *Queen of the Tides*. In *Jer.* vii, 18, we read: "The children gather wood...and the women knead dough, to make cakes to the queen of heaven", *i.e.* the Moon.

Queen of Love. APHRODITE or VENUS.

Queen of the May. *See under* MAY.

Queen Regnant. A queen who holds the crown in her own right, in contra-distinction to a QUEEN CONSORT.

Queen of Scots' Pillar. A column in the Peak Cavern, Derbyshire, as clear as alabaster. So called because on one occasion when going to throw herself on the mercy of Elizabeth I, the Queen of Scots proceeded thus far and then turned back.

Queen's or **King's Bench.** The Supreme Court of COMMON LAW; so called because at one time the SOVEREIGN presided in this court, and the court followed the sovereign when he moved from one place to another. Originally called the *Aulia Regia*, it is now a division of the High Court of Justice.

Queen's, or **King's Colour.** The UNION JACK, except in the case of foot guards, the first of the two colours borne by regiments. In the GUARDS it is a crimson flag bearing the royal cipher. The first colour was called "King's" in 1751, "Royal" in 1837, with the accession of Queen Victoria, and "Queen's" in 1892. *See also* REGIMENTAL COLOURS *under* COLOUR.

Queen's, or **King's Counsel.** In ENGLAND a member of the BAR appointed by the Crown or the nomination of the Lord CHANCELLOR; in SCOTLAND on the recommendation of the Lord Justice General. A Q.C. wears a silk gown and is thus often called a *silk*. He takes precedence over the junior Bar, and in a case must have a junior barrister with him.

Queen's Day. 17 November, the day of the accession of Queen Elizabeth I, first publicly celebrated in 1570, and for over three centuries kept as a holiday in Government offices and at Westminster School.

17 November at Merchant Taylors' School is a holiday also, now called Sir Thomas White's Founder's Day.

Queen's English. *See under* ENGLISH.

Queen's Evidence. *See* EVIDENCE.

Queen's, or **King's Messenger** is an official of the British Foreign Office whose duty it is to carry personally confidential messages from London to any embassy or legation abroad. He carries as his badge of office a silver greyhound, and though he receives courtesies and help in the countries across which he travels, he enjoys no diplomatic immunities or privileges except that of passing through the customs the "diplomatic bag" he is carrying.

Queen's or **King's Shilling.** *See under* SHILLING.

The Queen's or **King's Speech.** The speech from the throne in the HOUSE OF LORDS made at the opening of a parliamentary session outlining the government's programme for the session. It is always addressed to both Houses but the special clause relating to finance is addressed to the Commons alone.

Queen's ware. Glazed Wedgewood earthenware of a creamy colour.

Queen's weather. When a fête, etc., takes place on a fine day; so called because Queen Victoria was, for the most part, fortunate in having fine weather when she appeared in public.

The White Queen. Mary Queen of Scots; so called because she dressed in *white* mourning for her French husband, Francis II (1544–1560).

The Winter Queen. *See under* WINTER.

Queensberry Rules. The regulations governing boxing matches in which gloves were worn, formulated by John Sholto Douglas, eighth Marquess of Queensberry, and John G. Chambers (1843–1883) in 1867. They were first fully used at a London tournament in 1872. The present rules governing glove contests are those issued by the British Boxing Board of Control in 1929. *See* BELT.

Queer. Colloquial term for "out of sorts", "not up to the mark", also thieves' CANT for anything that is base and worthless, and a modern term for a homosexual.

A queer cove. An eccentric or strange person, a rum customer; the phrase *queer card* is also used.

In Queer Street. In financial difficulties. The punning suggestion has been made that the origin of the phrase is to be found in a query (?) with which a tradesman might mark the name of such a one on his ledger.

To come over all queer. To feel suddenly giddy, faint, etc.

To queer one's pitch. To forestall him; to render his efforts nugatory by underhand means; as a street or market vendor might find his trade spoilt by the interloper.

Querno (kwĕr′ nō). Camillo Querno, of Apulia, hearing that Pope Leo X (1475, 1513–1522) was a great patron of poets, went to ROME with a harp in his hand and sang a poem called *Alexias* containing 20,000 verses. He was introduced to the POPE as a buffoon, but was promoted to the LAUREL and became a constant frequenter of the Pope's table.

Querpo (kĕr′ pō). **In querpo.** In one's shirt-sleeves; in undress (Sp. *en cuerpo*, without a cloak).

> Boy, my cloak and rapier; it fits not a
> gentleman of my rank to walk the streets

in querpo.

BEAUMONT and FLETCHER: *Love's Cure*,
II, i.

Question. When members of the HOUSE OF COMMONS or other debaters call out *Question*, they mean that the speaker is wandering away from the subject under consideration.

A leading question. *See under* LEADER.

An open question. A statement, proposal, doctrine, or supposed fact where differences of opinion are permissible. In the HOUSE OF COMMONS every member may vote as he likes, regardless of party considerations, on an open question.

Out of the question. Not worth discussing, not to be thought of, or considered.

The previous question. The question whether the matter under debate shall be put to the vote or not. In the HOUSE OF COMMONS to "move the previous question" is to move "that the question be not now put". If the motion is carried the question that was previously before the house is abandoned, but if not carried the question concerned must be put forthwith. The motion is now rarely used. The previous question may not be moved on an amendment or business motion, nor in committee.

To beg the question. *See* BEG.

To pop the question. To propose or make an offer of marriage. As this request is supposedly unexpected, the question is said to be "popped".

Quetzalcoatl. An Aztec deity whose name means "feathered serpent", a god of the air or a sun-god and a benefactor of their race who instructed them in the use of agriculture, metals, etc. According to one account, he was driven from the country by a superior god and on reaching the shores of the Mexican Gulf promised his followers that he would return. He then embarked on his magic skiff for the land of Tlapallan. Prescott (*Conquest of Mexico*, ch. III) tells us that "He was said to have been tall in stature, with a white skin, long, dark hair, and a flowing beard. The Mexicans looked confidently to the return of the benevolent deity; and this remarkable

tradition, deeply cherished in their hearts, prepared...for the future success of the Spaniards."

Quey (kwā). A female calf, a young heifer (O.Scand. *kviga*).

Quey calves are dear veal. An old proverb, somewhat analogous to "killing the GOOSE which lays the golden eggs". Female calves should be kept and reared for milking.

Qui s'excuse, s'accuse (Fr.). He who excuses himself, accuses himself.

Qui vive (kē vēv) (Fr., who lives?). The French sentry's equivalent of Who goes there? which in French would be *Qui va là?*.

To be on the qui vive. On the alert; to be quick and sharp; to be expectantly on the lookout like a sentinel.

Quia Emptores (kwī′ à emp tôr ēz) (Lat., because purchasers). A statute passed in the reign of Edward I (1290), taking its name from its opening words, to insure the lord his feudal incidents when tenants sold lands held of them. It allowed free sale on condition that the purchaser should hold from the superior lord thus preventing subinfeudation. It resulted in a great increase of landowners holding direct from the Crown.

Quick. Living; hence, animated, lively; also, fast, active, brisk (O.E. *cwic*, living, alive). "Look alive" means "Be brisk."

Cut to the quick. Figuratively, deeply hurt. The reference here is to the sensitive flesh below the nails or skin, hence the seat of feeling.

The quick and the dead. The living and the dead.

Quicksand is sand which shifts its place as if it were alive. *See* QUICK.

Quickset is living hawthorn set in a hedge, instead of dead wood, hurdles, and palings. *See* QUICK.

Quicksilver is *argentum vivum* (living silver), silver that moves about like a living thing (O.E. *cwic seolfor*), i.e. mercury.

> That, swift as quicksilver, it courses through
> The natural gates and alleys of the body.
> SHAKESPEARE: *Hamlet*, I, v.

Quid. Slang for a SOVEREIGN (or a pound note). It occurs in Shadwell's *Squire of*

Alsatia (1688), but its origin is unknown.

In *a quid of tobacco*, meaning a piece for chewing, *quid* is another form of *cud*.

Quids. *See* QUIDDISTS.

Quids in. Extremely lucky, very profitable, to have everything turn out favourably.

Quidlibet. *See* QUODLIBET.

Quid pro quo (Lat., something for something). A return made for something, an equivalent, a TIT FOR TAT; in legal parlance, a consideration.

Quiddists, or **Quids.** In the U.S.A., sectionalists of the Democratic-Republican party under John Randolph who sought to maintain the ascendancy of Virginia and its planter aristocracy against the more democratic elements. Active between 1805 and 1811, they opposed Madison's succession to Jefferson as party leader. The name was from *tertium quid*, "a third something or other" opposed to the Federalists and administration Republicans.

Quiddity. The essence of a thing, or that which differentiates it from other things—"the Correggiosity of Correggio", "the Freeness of the Free". Hence used of subtle, trifling distinctions, quibbles, or captious argumentation. SCHOOLMEN say *Quid est?* (what is it?) and the reply is, the *Quid* is so and so, the *What* or the nature of the thing is as follows. The latter *quid* being formed into a barbarous Latin noun becomes *Quidditas*. Hence *Quid est?* (What is it?). Answer: *Talis est quidditas* (Its essence is as follows).

> He knew...
> Where entity and quiddity
> (The ghosts of defunct bodies) fly.
> BUTLER: *Hudibras*, I, i.

Quidnunc (Lat., What now?). One who is curious to know everything that's going on, or pretends to know it; a self-important newsmonger and gossip. It is the name of the leading character in Murphy's farce *The Upholsterer*, or *What News?*

Quién sabe? (kien sa' be) (Sp.). Who knows? Sometimes used as a response in the sense of "How should I know?"

Quieta non movere (Lat.). Literally, do not disturb the peace; *i.e.* let sleeping dogs lie (*see under* DOG). It was the favourite maxim of Sir Robert Walpole (1676–1745), traditionally regarded as the first prime minister (1721–1742). Lord Melbourne (1779–1848), the early Victorian prime minister, had a similar watchword, "Why not let it alone?".

Quietism. A form of religious mysticism based on the doctrine that the essence of religion consists in the withdrawal of the SOUL from external objects, and in fixing it upon the contemplation of God; especially that taught by Miguel Molinos (1640–1696), who taught the direct relationship between the soul and God. His followers were called Molinists or *Quietists*. Outward acts of mortification were held superfluous and when a person has attained the mystic state by mental prayer, even if he transgresses in the accepted sense, he does not sin, since his will has been extinguished. *See* MOLINISM.

Quietus (Late Lat. *quietus est*, he is quit). The writ of discharge formerly granted to those BARONS and KNIGHTS who personally attended the king on a foreign expedition, exempting them also from the claim of SCUTAGE or knight's fee. Subsequently the term was applied to the acquittance which a SHERIFF receives on settling his account at the EXCHEQUER; and, later still, to any discharge, as of an account, or even of life itself.

Quill-drivers. Writing clerks.

Quinapalus (kwin ăp' à lus). A high-sounding, pedantic name invented by Feste, the Clown in SHAKESPEARE'S *Twelfth Night*, when he wished to give some saying the weight of authority. Hence someone "dragged in" when one wishes to clench an argument by some supposed quotation.

> What says Quinapalus: "Better a witty fool, than a foolish wit."
> *Twelfth Night*, I, v.

Quinine. *See* CINCHONA.

Quinquagesima Sunday (kwin kwà jes' i mà) (Lat., fiftieth). Shrove Sunday, or the first day of the week which contains ASH WEDNESDAY. It is so called because in round numbers it is the fiftieth day before EASTER.

Quins, or **Quints** (U.S.A.), **The.** The popular name for the famous Dionne quintuplets, Marie, Emilie, Yvonne, Cécile, and Annette. Daughters born (1934) to a farmer's wife in Callander, Ontario, they became wards of King George VI, who, with his Queen, received them during his visit to Canada in 1939. There were seven other children in the family.

Quinsy. This is from the Med. Lat. *quinancia* derived from Gr. *kynagkhē*, dog-throttling, because those suffering from quinsy throw open the mouth like dogs, especially mad dogs. It appeared in English (14th century) as *qwinaci*, and later forms were *quynnancy* and *squinancy*. *Squinancy-wort* is still a name given to the small woodruff (*Asperula cynanchica*), which was used as a cure for quinsy by the herbalists.

Quintain (kwin' tin). **Tilting at the quintain.** An ancient military exercise and pastime, particularly practised by mediæval KNIGHTS. A dummy figure or just a head, often representing a Turk or SARACEN, was fastened to pivot or swing horizontally from an upright stake fixed in the ground. The knight tilted at the figure and if he did not strike it in the right place with his lance it moved round at speed and struck him in the back before he could pass on. There were various forms of quintain and in the 14th century Londoners used to tilt from boats, the quintain being fixed to a mast erected in the Thames. Tilting at the quintain remained a rustic sport, associated particularly with wedding festivities, until the outbreak of the English CIVIL WARS. The word is probably from Lat. *quintana*, fifth, a street in a Roman camp between the fifth and sixth maniples where the camp market was situated, supposedly a place for martial exercise.

Quintessence. The fifth essence. The ancient Greeks said that there are four elements or forms in which matter can exist—fire, air, water, and earth (*see* ELEMENTS); the Pythagoreans (*see* PYTHAGOREAN SYSTEM) added a fifth, the fifth essence—quintessence—ether, more subtle and pure than fire, and possessed of an orbicular motion, which flew upwards at creation and formed the basis of the stars. Hence the word stands for the essential principle or the most subtle extract of a body that can be procured. HORACE speaks of "kisses that Venus has imbued with the quintessence of her own nectar".

Quintilians (kwin'til'yàns). Members of a 2nd-century heretical sect of MONTANISTS, said to have been founded by one Quintilia, a prophetess. They made the EUCHARIST of bread and cheese, and allowed women to become priests and BISHOPS. *See* HERETIC.

Quipu (ke' poor or kwi' poo). An ancient Peruvian device used for keeping accounts, recording information, etc. The word means a knot, and the quipu was a length of cord, about two feet long, made of different coloured threads and tied with knots. The various threads and knots represented simple objects and numerical combinations.

Quirinal (kwi' ri nal). One of the seven hills of ancient ROME, named after Quirinus, the SABINE name of MARS, and given to ROMULUS after deification. It is now called Monte Cavallo. Also the name of the palace originally built on its slopes as a Papal summer residence and subsequently used by the Kings of Italy and now by the President. The term was applied emblematically to the Italian kingdom and government as opposed to the VATICAN, the seat of Papal authority and ecclesiastical government.

Quis (Lat). Who? Formerly commonly used, especially among schoolboys, when offering to give away something. When only one thing was being offered, the first to call *Ego*—I [do]—after the cry *Quis?*—Who [wants]—gained the reward.

Quis custodiet ipsos custodes? (Lat., Who will watch over the watchers themselves?) The shepherds keep watch over the sheep but who is there to keep watch over the shepherds? Said when one is uncertain of the person whom one has placed in a position of trust. The phrase is from Juvenal (*Satires*, VI, 347) and is used to question the wisdom of setting guards over wives to prevent infidelities.

Quis separabit? (Lat., Who shall separate us?) The motto adopted by the

Most Illustrious ORDER OF ST. PATRICK (*see under* PATRICK) when it was founded.

Quisling (kwiz' ling). A traitor or fifth columnist, from Vidkun Quisling, the Norwegian admirer of Mussolini and Hitler, who acted as advance agent for the German invasion of Norway in 1940. He duly became puppet Minister-President. He surrendered (9 May 1945) after the German defeat and was tried and shot (24 October).

Quit. Cry quits. When two boys quarrel, and one has had enough, he says, "Cry Quits", meaning "Let us leave off, and call it a drawn game". So in an unequal distribution, he who has the largest share restores a portion and "cries quits", meaning that he has made the distribution equal. Here *quit* means "acquittal" or discharge.

Double or quits. *See under* DOUBLE.

To be quit of. To be free from, to be rid of.

Quit rent. A rent formerly paid to the lord of a MANOR by freeholders and copy-holders which was an *acquittal* of all other services. Nowadays a token or nominal rent.

Quixote, Don (kwik' zot). The hero of the famous romance of this name by Miguel de Cervantes Saavedra (1547–1616). It was published at Madrid in 1605 with the continuation or second part in 1615. It ridicules the more tedious chivalric romances. Don Quixote is a gaunt country gentleman of La Mancha, gentle and dignified, affectionate and simple-minded, but so crazed by reading books of knight-errantry that he believes himself called upon to redress the wrong of the whole world. Hence a **quixotic** man is a romantic idealist, one with impractical ideas of honour or schemes for the general good. *See also* SANCHO PANZA.

Quiz. One who banters or chaffs another. The origin of the word, which appeared about 1780, is unknown; but fable accounts for it by saying that a Mr. Daly, manager of a Dublin theatre, laid a wager that he would introduce into the language within twenty-four hours a new word of no meaning. Accordingly on every wall, or all places accessible, were chalked up the four mystic letters, and all Dublin was inquiring what they meant. The wager was won and the word became part of the language. A monocular eyeglass with, or without, a handle was called a *quizzing-glass*, and any odd or ridiculous person or thing a *quiz*.

Quiz is also applied to a test, usually competitive, of knowledge, general or otherwise. Hence the American expression, **Quiz Kid**, from such children appearing on radio or television in *quiz programmes*.

Quo vadis? *See* DOMINE, QUO VADIS?

Quo warranto (kwō war ăn' tō) (Lat.). A writ against a defendant (whether an individual or a corporation) who lays claim to something he has no right to; so named because the offender is called upon to show *quo warranto* (*rem*) *usurpavit* (by what right or authority he lays claim to the matter of dispute).

Quoad hoc (kwō' ăd hok) (Lat.). To this extent, with respect to this.

Quod. Slang for prison. Probably the same word as QUAD, which is a contraction of *quadrangle*, the enclosure in which prisoners are allowed to walk, and where whippings used to be inflicted. The word was in use in the 17th century.

Quodlibet, or Quidlibet (Lat., what you please). Originally a philosophical or theological question proposed for purposes of scholastic debate; hence a nice and knotty point, a subtlety.

Quondam (Lat., former). We say, He is a quondam schoolfellow (a former schoolfellow); my quondam friend, the quondam chancellor, etc.

Quorum (kwôr' um) (Lat., of whom). The lowest number of members of a committee or board, etc., the presence of whom is necessary before business may be transacted; formerly, also certain JUSTICES OF THE PEACE (*See under* PEACE), hence known as Justices of the Quorum, chosen for their special ability, one or more of whom had to be on the Bench at trials before the others could act. SHAKESPEARE's Slender calls Justice Shallow "justice of the peace, and coram" (*Merry Wives of Windsor*, I, i).

I must not omit that Sir Roger is a justice of the quorum.

ADDISON: *Spectator*, No. 2.

Quos ego (kwōs eg' ō). A threat of punishment for disobedience. The words, from VIRGIL'S *Æneid* (I, 135), were uttered by NEPTUNE to the disobedient and rebellious winds, and are sometimes given as an example of aposiopesis, *i.e.* a stopping short for rhetorical effort. "Whom I—," said Neptune, the "will punish" being left to the imagination.

Quot. Quot homines, tot sententiæ (Lat.). As many minds as men; there are as many opinions as there are men to hold them. The phrase is from Terence's *Phormio* (II, iv, 14).

Quot linguas calles, tot homines vales (Lat.). As many languages as you know, so many separate individuals you are worth. Attributed to Charles V.

R

R. The eighteenth letter of the English alphabet (seventeenth of the Roman) representing the twentieth of the Phœnician and Hebrew. As a mediæval Roman numeral, R stood for 80 and Ṝ for 80,000. In England it was formerly used as a branding mark for rogues.

It has been called the "snarling letter" or "dog letter", because a dog in snarling utters a sound resembling *r-r-r-r*, etc., or *gr-r-r-r*.

> Irritata canis quod R R quam plurima dicat.
> LUCILIUS.

In his *English Grammar made for the benefit of all Strangers* Ben Jonson says:

> R is the dog's letter and hurreth in the sound; the tongue striking the inner palate, with a trembling about the teeth.

And see the Nurse's remark about R in SHAKESPEARE'S *Romeo and Juliet*, II, iv. Ṝ in prescriptions. The ornamental part of this letter is the symbol of JUPITER ( ), under whose special protection all medicines were placed. The letter itself (*Recipe*, take) and its flourish may thus be paraphrased: "Under the good auspices of JOVE, the patron of medicines, take the following drugs in the proportions set down."

The R months. *See under* OYSTER.

The three R's. Reading, writing, and arithmetic. The phrase is said to have been originated by Sir William Curtis (1752–1829), an illiterate alderman and Lord MAYOR of London, who gave this as a toast, *i.e.* "Riting, Reading and Rithmetic".

> Within the limits set by the code [The REVISED CODE, 1862], and by the ideal which most people then had of education for the poor, viz. an elementary knowledge of the three R's, Mr. Lowe had more than redeemed his promises.
> H. HOLMAN: *English National Education*, ch. viii (1898).

R.I.P. *Requiescat in pace.* Latin for "May he (or she) rest in peace"; a symbol used on mourning cards, tombstones, etc.

Ra, or Re. The sun-god of ancient Egypt, and from the time of Chephren (IVth Dynasty) the supposed ancestor of all the PHARAOHS. His chief centre was at HELIOPOLIS where he was also known as Atum. His great enemy was the serpent Apep with whom he fought continually, but always eventually defeated. According to one legend, Ra was born as a child every morning and died at night as an old man. His name and cult was assimilated with that of Amen (AMEN-RA) and many others and he was commonly represented with the head of a falcon surmounted by a solar disc surrounded with the Uræus, the sacred flame-spitting asp which destroyed his enemies.

Rabbit. To produce the rabbit out of the hat. To produce unexpectedly an answer or solution, etc., when success appears impossible or the situation seems hopeless. An allusion to the conjuror's art.

Rabelaisian. Coarsely and boisterously satirical; grotesque, extravagant and licentious in language; reminiscent in literary style of the great French satirist François Rabelais (1495–1553). When *Rabelaisian* is used it implies coarseness and complete frankness and ignores Rabelais's humanism. *See* PANTAGRUEL.

Raboin. *See* TAILED MEN.

Races. The principal horse-races in England are chiefly run at Newmarket, Doncaster, Epsom, Goodwood, and Ascot (*see* CLASSIC RACES). The GRAND NATIONAL is the greatest event in STEEPLE CHASING.

Rache (răch). In mediæval England, a hound that hunts by scent (O.E. *raecc*, a hound); they were later called "running hounds" (*canes currentes*). Cp. ALANS.

Rachmanism. RACK-RENTING, extortion, and general exploitation of tenants and purchasers of house-property. After Peter Rachman (1920–1962), a Polish immigrant whose undesirable activities of this kind in the Paddington area of London were brought to light in 1962–1963.

Rack. The instrument of torture so called (connected with Ger. *recken*, to strain) was a frame in which a man was fastened and his arms and legs stretched by windlass arrangements. Not infrequently the limbs were forced thereby out of their sockets. Its use in England was abolished in 1640. *See* THE DUKE OF EXETER'S DAUGHTER *under* DUKE.

Rack and ruin. Utter decay or destitution. Here "rack" is a variant of *wrack* and *wreck*.

Rack-rent. Legally regarded as the annual rent which can be reasonably charged for a property, being that which it can command in the open market; an excessive rent, one which is "racked" or stretched. *See* RACHMANISM.

To lie at rack and manger. To live without thought of the morrow, like cattle or horses whose food is placed before them without themselves taking thought; hence, to live at reckless expense.

To rack one's brains. To strain them to find out or recollect something; to puzzle about something.

Racketeer. From the practice (of American origin) of creating a noise, commotion or *racket* to enable a theft or crime to be carried out without attracting attention, the organizers of such came to be known as *racketeers*. The term was next applied to blackmailers and extortioners and their activities became *rackets*.

Radar. A name formed from Radio Detection and Ranging; a means of detecting the direction and range of aircraft, ships, etc., by the reflection of radio waves. It is particularly valuable at night or in fog when the eye is of no avail. It was first developed effectively for the purposes by Sir Robert Watson-Watt in 1934–1935 (and independently in the

U.S.A., France and Germany) and was of great importance during World War II, especially during the BATTLE OF BRITAIN.

Radegonde, or **Radegund, St.** (răd' e gond). Wife of Clotaire, King of the FRANKS (558–561). Disgusted with the crimes of the royal family, she founded the monastery of St. Croix at Poitiers. Her feast day is 13 August.

St. Radegonde's lifted stone. A stone 60 ft. in circumference, placed on five supporting stones, said by the historians of Poitou to have been so arranged in 1478, to commemorate a great FAIR held on the spot in October of that year. The country people insist that Queen Radegonde brought the impost stone on her head, and the five uprights in her apron, and arranged them all as they appear to this day.

Radevore (răd' e vôr). A kind of cloth, probably tapestry, known in the 14th century. It has been suggested (Skeat) that it was named from Vaur, in LANGUEDOC; *ras* (Eng. *rash*, a smooth—*rased*—textile fabric) *de Vor*.

Radical. A political label denoting an ultra-liberal which came into use about 1816 and is applicable to ORATOR HUNT, Major Cartwright, William Cobbett and many others of that period. The early radicals drew their inspiration mainly from the French Revolution but John Wilkes may be considered representative of a somewhat earlier tradition.

> If the Whigs most inclined to popular courses adhere steadily to their determination of having no communication with the Radicals of any description, I trust the session may pass over without any schism among Opposition ...
> *Letter from Mr. Allen to Mr. Creevey* (20 November 1816).

Radiocarbon dating. A scientific method of estimating the age of organic materials. Carbon dioxide from the atmosphere, which contains the radioactive isotope Carbon-14, is taken up by all living matter. After the organism has died the amount of Carbon-14 diminishes at a known rate, thus the age of the material can be approximately dated.

Rag. A tatter, hence a remnant (as "not a rag of decency", "not a rag of evidence"), hence a vagabond or RAGAMUF-

FIN.

> Lash hence these overweening rags of France.
>
> SHAKESPEARE: *Richard III*, V, iii.

The word was old CANT for a FARTH-ING, and was also used generally to express scarcity—or absence—of money:

> Money by me? Heart and goodwill you might,
> But surely, master, not a rag of money
>
> SHAKESPEARE: *Comedy of Errors*, IV, iv.

In university slang (now general) *a rag* is a boisterous escapade, jollification, etc., usually involving horseplay and practical jokes. **To rag** a person is to tease and torment him, TO BADGER him (*see under* BADGER).

The local rag. A colloquial term for the local newspaper.

The Rag Trade. The clothing and fashion industries.

Rag water. In thieves' jargon, whisky.

Glad rags. *See under* GLAD.

To chew the rag. A slang expression for "grousing", complaining, or talking at length on one particular subject. In the U.S.A., it means simply "to chat".

Rag-tag and bob-tail. The RIFF-RAFF, the rabble, "the great UNWASHED". The common expression in the 16th and 17th centuries was *the rag and tag*.

Ragtime. Medium tempo syncopated music of American Negro origin, properly solo piano music although also played by bands. Scott Joplin's *Maple Leaf Rag* (1899) was the first of its kind. *Cp.* BLUES; BOOGIE-WOOGIE; JAZZ; SWING.

Ragamuffin. A *muffin* is a poor thing of a creature, a "regular muff"; so that a *ragamuffin* is a sorry creature in rags.

> I have led my ragamuffins where they are peppered.
>
> SHAKESPEARE: *Henry IV, Pt. I*, V, iii.

Ragged Robin. A wild flower (*Lychnis floscuculi*), from the ragged appearance of its fringed petals. The word is used by Tennyson for a pretty damsel in ragged clothes.

> The prince
> Hath picked a ragged robin from the hedge.
>
> TENNYSON: *Idylls of the King* (*The Marriage of Geraint*).

Ragged schools. VOLUNTARY SCHOOLS for the education of destitute children, originated by John Pounds, a Portsmouth shoemaker, about 1818. Ragged Sunday Schools, Day Schools, and Evening Schools made an important contribution to the welfare of the STREET ARABS (*see under* ARABIA) of 19th-century LONDON and elsewhere. The seventh Earl of Shaftesbury was a notable benefactor.

Raglan. An overcoat which has no shoulder seams, the sleeves extending up to the neck. First worn by Lord Raglan, the British commander in the Crimean War.

Ragman Rolls. The returns of each HUNDRED to Edward I's inquest of 1274–1275, also called Hundred Rolls; their colloquial name is from the ragged appearance due to their numerous pendant seals. The roll of Homage and Fealty made by the Scottish clergy and barons to Edward I at Berwick in 1297 is likewise so called. *See* RIGMAROLE.

Ragnarok (răg′ na rok). The *Götterdämmerung* or Twilight of the Gods in Scandinavian mythology. The day of doom, when the old world and all its inhabitants were annihilated. Out of the destruction a new world was born, a world at peace. Of the old gods BALDER returned, and ODIN'S two sons VIDAR and Vail, Vili and Ve (Odin's brother's sons), Magni and Modi, sons of THOR, and Hœnir (Odin's companion).

Rahu (ra′ hū). The demon that, according to Hindu legend, causes eclipses. One day he quaffed some of the NECTAR of immortality, but was discovered by the SUN and MOON, who informed against him, and VISHNU cut off his head. As he had already taken some of the nectar into his mouth, the head was immortal, and he ever afterwards hunted the sun and moon, which he sometimes caught, thus causing eclipses.

Railroad. To railroad (U.S.A.). To hustle someone through (as of school) or out (as of an assembly) with unseemly haste and without reference to the proper formalities.

Underground Railroad. In the U.S.A. the name given (*c.* 1830) to the secret and changing system of hiding places and routes organized for helping runaway slaves to escape to the Northern States and Canada. An **Underground Road** was its forerunner.

What a way to run a railway! What an inefficient, chaotic or disorderly way of doing things.

Rain. It never rains but it pours. One occurrence is frequently the harbinger of many such; strokes of good or ill fortune are often accompanied by additional benefits or misfortunes. An 18th-century proverb.

To put something by for a rainy day. To save something against bad times.

To rain cats and dogs. In northern mythology the CAT is supposed to have great influence on the weather and "The cat has a gale of wind in her tail" is a seafarer's expression for when a cat is unusually frisky. Witches that rode on storms were said to assume the form of cats. The DOG is a signal of wind, like the WOLF, both of which were attendants of ODIN, the storm god.

Thus cat may be taken as a symbol of the down-pouring rain, and dog of the strong gusts of wind accompanying a rainstorm.

Rain Check (U.S.A.). A receipt or the counterfoil of a ticket entitling one to see another baseball game if the original match for which the ticket was purchased is rained off. The phrase is now in general use of a promise to accept an invitation at a later date, *e.g.* when invited and one cannot accept, one says, "I'll take a rain-check."

Raining-tree, or **Rain-tree.** Old travellers to the Canaries told of a linden tree from which sufficient water to supply all the men and beasts of the island of Hierro was said to fall. In certain weather conditions moisture condenses and collects on the broad leaves of many trees. The genisaro or guango, *Pithecolobium saman*, or ornamental tropical tree, one of the Leguminosæ, is known as the rain-tree. In this case ejections of juice by the cicadas are responsible for the "rain" under its branches. Another is the *Andira inermis*, found in tropical Africa and America.

Rainbow. The old legend is that if one reaches the spot where a rainbow touches the earth and digs there one will be sure to find a pot of GOLD. Hence visionaries, wool-gatherers, daydreamers, etc., are sometimes called *rainbow chasers*, because of their habit of hoping for impossible things.

Raison d'état (rä' zon dä' tǎ) (Fr., reason of state). The doctrine that the interests of the State take precedence even at the expense of moral considerations.

Raison d'être (rä' zon de tr) (Fr.). The reason for a thing's existence, its rational ground for being; as, "If crime were abolished there would be no *raison d'être* for the police."

Rajah (ra' ja). Sanskrit for king, cognate with Lat. *rex*. The title of an Indian king or prince, given later to tribal chiefs and comparatively minor rulers; also to Malayan and Javanese chiefs. *Maharajah* means the "great rajah".

Ralph Roister Doister. The name of the earliest English comedy on classical lines; so called from the chief character. It probably appeared in 1552 or 1553 and was written by Nicholas Udall, headmaster of Eton, 1534–1541, and headmaster of Westminster, 1555–1556.

Ram. Formerly, the usual prize at wrestling matches. Thus Chaucer says of his miller, "At wrastlynge he wolde bere awey the ram" (*Canterbury Tales: Prologue*, 548).

The Ram and Teazle. A PUBLIC-HOUSE SIGN, in compliment to the Clothworkers' Company. The *ram* is emblematical of wool and the *teazle* is used for raising the nap of woollen cloth.

The Ram of the Zodiac. This is the famous Chrysomallus, whose GOLDEN FLEECE was stolen by JASON. *See* ARIES.

Rama. The seventh incarnation of VISHNU (*see* AVATAR). His beautiful wife, Sita, was abducted by Ravana, the demon-king of Ceylon. With the aid of a nation of monkeys who collected trees and rocks, a bridge, Adam's bridge, was built across the straits. Rama and his invading army gradually overcame the enemy and Rama's arrow slew the demon-monster. The story is told in the RAMAYANA.

Ramachandra. *See* AVATAR.

Ramadan (rǎm á dǎn). The ninth month

of the Islamic year. It is the Holy Month in which the KORAN was revealed. The MOSLEM year being lunar sometimes means the Ramadan falls in midsummer when the fast causes much discomfort, since it involves abstinence from drinking.

Ramayana (ra' ma ya' na) (*i.e.* the deeds of Rama). The history of RAMA, the great epic poem of ancient India, ranking with the MAHABHARATA, and almost with the ILIAD. It is ascribed to the poet Valmiki and contains 24,000 verses in seven books.

Rambouillet, Hôtel de (răm bwē yā). The house in Paris where, about 1615, the Marquise de Rambouillet, disgusted with the immoral and puerile tone of the time, founded the salon out of which grew the Académie Française. Mme de Sévigné, Malherbe, Corneille, the Duchesse de Longueville, and La Rochefoucauld were among the members. They had a refinement of language of their own, but preciosity, pedantry, and affectation eventually led to disintegration of the coterie. The women were known as *Les* PRÉCIEUSES and the men as *Esprits doux*.

Ramilie, Ramillies (răm' i li). A name given to certain articles of dress in commemoration of the Duke of Marlborough's victory over the French at Ramillies in 1706. The *Ramillies hat* was the cocked hat worn between 1714 and 1740 with the brim turned up in three equal-sized cocks. The *Ramillies wig*, that lasted on until after 1760, had a long gradually diminishing plait, called the *Ramillies plait*, with a large bow at the top and a smaller one at the bottom.

Rampage. On the rampage. Acting in a violently excited or angry manner. The word was originally Scottish, and is probably connected with *ramp*, to storm and rage.

Rampallion (răm păl' yon). A term of contempt; probably a PORTMANTEAU WORD of *ramp* and *rapscallion*; in Davenport's *A New Trick to Cheat the Devil* (1639) we have: "and bold rampallion-like, swear and drink drunk."

Away, you scullion! you rampallion! you fustilarian! I'll tickle your catastrophe.

SHAKESPEARE: *Henry IV, Pt. II*, II, i.

Rampant. The heraldic term for an animal especially a LION, shown rearing up with the forepaws in the air; strictly, a LION RAMPANT should stand on the SINISTER hind-leg, with both forelegs elevated, and the head in profile.

Ran. *See* ÆGIR.

Ranch. A dude ranch. One run as a resort, where city-dwellers can spend their holidays playing at being COWBOYS.

Randan. On the randan or **ran-tan.** On the spree; having a high old time in town. *Randan* is a variant of *random*.

Formerly, at Cold Aston, Derbyshire, when a man was **ran-tanned**, a straw likeness was made and carried round the village on three successive nights, accompanied by people banging tin cans and making a general din. The image was burnt after the last parade. Matrimonial upsets usually provided the occasion for such performances. *Cp.* RIDING; SHALLAL; SKIMMINGTON; STANG.

Randem-tandem. Three horses driven TANDEM fashion.

Ranee, or **Rani.** A Hindu queen; the feminine of RAJAH.

Ranelagh (răn' ė lä). An old LONDON place of amusement on the site that now forms part of the grounds of Chelsea Hospital. It was named after Richard Jones, 1st Earl of Ranelagh, who built a house and laid out gardens there in 1690. From 1742 to 1803, Ranelagh rivalled VAUXHALL GARDENS for concerts, masquerades, etc. A notable feature was the Rotunda, built in 1742. It was not unlike the Albert Hall in design, and was 185 ft. across with numerous boxes in which refreshments were served, while the brightly lit floor formed a thronged promenade. There was also a Venetian pavilion in the centre of a lake.

Rank. A row, a line (especially of soldiers); also high station, dignity, eminence, as:

The rank is but the guinea's stamp,
The man's the gowd for a' that!
BURNS: *Is there for Honest Poverty?* 431.

Rank and fashion. People of high social standing; the "UPPER TEN" (*see under* TEN).

Rank and file. *See under* FILE.

Risen from the ranks. Said of a commissioned officer of the army who has worked his way up from a private soldier, often called a *ranker*. Hence applied to a SELF-MADE MAN in any walk of life.

Ransom. In origin the same word as *redemption*, from Lat. *redemptionem*, through O.Fr. *rançon*, earlier *redempçon*.

A king's ransom. A very large sum of money.

Ran-tan. *See* RANDAN.

Rantipole (răn' ti pōl). A HARUM-SCARUM fellow, a madcap. Probably from *ranty* or *randy*, riotous, disorderly, etc., and *poll*, a head or person. NAPOLEON III was called *Rantipole* for his escapades at Strasbourg and Boulogne.

Ranz des vaches (rans dā vash). Literally the air or tune for the cows. Simple melodies sung by the Swiss cowherds or played on the Alpenhorn when they drive their cows to pasture or bring them home.

Rap. Not worth a rap. Worth nothing at all. The rap was a base halfpenny, intrinsically worth about half a FARTHING circulated in Ireland in 1721, because small coin was so very scarce.

Why the coin was so called is not known.

To rap the knuckles. Figuratively, to administer a sharp rebuff. From the once common practice in schools, when children were punished for a misdemeanour in class by a sharp rap on the knuckles from the teacher's ruler.

Rape. One of the six divisions into which Sussex is divided, intermediate between HUNDRED and SHIRE; it is said that each had its own river, forest, and castle. *Herepp* is Norwegian for a parish district and *rape* in DOMESDAY BOOK is used for a district under military jurisdiction, but connexion between the two words is doubtful. *Cp*. LATHE.

Rape of the Lock. Lord Petre, in a thoughtless moment of frolic and gallantry, cut off a lock of Arabella Fermor's hair, and this liberty gave rise to the bitter feud between the two families which Alexander Pope worked up into the best heroic-comic poem of the language. The first sketch was published in 1712 in two cantos, and the complete work, including the most happily conceived machinery of SYLPHS and GNOMES, in five cantos in 1714. Pope, under the name of Esdras Barnevelt, apothecary, later pretended that the poem was a covert satire on QUEEN ANNE and the Barrier Treaty.

> Say what strange motive, goddess! could compel
> A well-bred lord t'assault a gentle belle?
> O say what stranger cause, yet unexplored,
> Could make a gentle belle reject a lord?
> *The Rape of the Lock*, Canto I, l.7.

Raphael (răf' ā el). One of the principal ANGELS of Jewish angelology. In the book of TOBIT we are told how he travelled with Tobias into Media and back again, instructing him on the way how to marry Sara and to drive away the wicked spirit. Milton calls him the "sociable spirit" and the "affable archangel" (*Paradise Lost*, VII, 40), and it was he who was sent by God to warn ADAM of his danger.

> Raphael, the sociable spirit that deigned
> To travel with Tobias, and secured
> His marriage with the seven-times-wedded maid.
> *Paradise Lost*, V, 221.

Raphael is usually distinguished in art by a pilgrim's staff or carrying a fish, in allusion to his aiding Tobias to capture the fish which performed the miraculous cure of his father's eyesight.

Raphaelesque. In the style of the great Italian painter Raphael (1483–1520), who was specially notable for his supreme excellence in the equable development of all the essential qualities of art—composition, expression, design, and colouring.

Rapparee (răp' á rē'). A wild Irish plunderer; so called from his being armed with a *rapaire*, or half-pike.

Rappee. A coarse kind of snuff manufactured from dried tobacco by an instrument called in French a *râpe*, or rasp; so called because it is *râpé*, rasped.

Rara avis (râr' à ā' vis) (Lat., a rare bird). A phenomenon; a prodigy; something quite out of the ordinary. First applied by Juvenal to the black swan, which until its discovery in Australia was unknown.

> Rara avis in terris nigroque simillima cygne (a bird rarely seen on the earth,

and very like a black swan).

JUVENAL, vi, 165.

Rare. Rare Ben. The inscription on the tomb of Ben Jonson (1573–1637), the dramatist, in the north nave aisle of Westminster Abbey. "O rare Ben Jonson", was, says Aubrey, "done at the charge of Jack Young (afterwards knighted), who, walking there when the grave was covering, gave the fellow eighteenpence to cut it." *Rare* here is Lat. *rarus*, uncommon, remarkable.

Raree Show. A peep-show; a show carried about in a box. In the 17th century, most of the travelling showmen were Savoyards, and perhaps this represents their attempt at pronunciation of *rare* or *rarity*.

Rascal. Originally a collective term for the rabble of an army, the commonalty, the mob, this word was early (14th century) adopted as a term of the chase, and for long almost exclusively denoted the lean, worthless deer of a herd. In the late 16th century it was retransferred to people, and so to its present meaning, a mean rogue, a scamp, a base fellow. SHAKESPEARE says, "Horns? the noblest deer has them as huge as the rascal" (*As You Like It*, III, iii); and "Come, you thin thing; come, you rascal" (*Henry IV, Pt. II*, V, iv).

Rascal counters. Pitiful £ s. d., "filthy lucre". Brutus calls money paltry compared with friendship, etc.

Raspberry, To give the. A 20th-century slang expression for showing contempt of someone. In action, *to give a raspberry* is to put one's tongue between the closed lips and expel air forcibly with a resulting rude noise. It is otherwise known as a BRONX CHEER. *Cp.* TO COCK A SNOOK *under* COCK; *see also* RHYMING SLANG.

Rasputin. Gregory Efimovitch (1871–1916), the Siberian monk notorious for his baneful influence over the Russian monarchy in its last years, was apparently so called by his fellow villagers. Rasputin means "the dissolute" and he lived up to his nickname until the end. His easy conquests over women were helped by his assertion that physical contact with him was itself a purification. His incredible indecencies and disgusting coarseness did not prevent his excessive familiarity with the Empress Alexandra and Tsar Nicholas II which arose from his undoubted success in healing and sustaining the Tsarevich Alexis, a tragic victim of hæmophilia. Rasputin was first called to the palace in 1905 and his power increased steadily until his murder by Prince Yusupov and associates in 1916—itself a story reminiscent of Hollywood rather than real life.

Rastafarians. Members of the *Ras Tafari*, a black political and religious group originating in the 1920s in Jamaica. They recognized Haile Selassie, Emperor of Ethiopia (1930–1974) as a god. They consider blacks are superior to whites, that Ethiopia is heaven, and that Haile Selassie will arrange that all of African origin will find a homeland in Ethiopia. *Ras* means duke and *Tafari* was a family name of Haile Selassie (Might of the Trinity). There are now Rastafarians in the West Indies, the U.S.A., Canada and Europe, conspicuous by their long matted curls (dreadlocks).

Rat. The Egyptians and Phrygians deified rats. In Egypt the rat symbolized utter destruction, and also wise judgement, the latter because rats always choose the best bread.

Pliny tells us (VIII, lvii) that the Romans drew presages from rats and to see a white rat foreboded good fortune. Clothing or equipment gnawed by rats presaged ill fortune.

It was an old superstition among sailors that rats deserted a ship before she set out on a voyage that was to end in her loss. Similarly rats were said to leave a falling house.

As wet as, or **like a drowned rat.** Soaking wet; looking exceedingly dejected.

I smell a rat. I perceive some underhand work or treachery afoot. The allusion is to a cat *smelling* a rat, while unable to *see* it.

Irish rats rhymed to death. It was once a common belief that rats in pasturages could be destroyed by anathematizing them in rhyming verse or by metrical charms. Thus Ben Jonson (*Poetaster, Apologetical Dialogue*) says: "Rhime them to death, as they do Irish rats." Sir Philip Sidney says (*Defence of Poesie*): "I will not wish unto you ... to be rimed to death, as is said to be done in Ireland"; and SHAKESPEARE makes Rosalind say (*As You Like It*, III, ii): "I was never so be-rhymed since Pythagoras' time, that I was an Irish rat."

Pharaoh's rat. *See* ICHNEUMON.

Rat, Cat, and Dog.

> The cat, the rat, and Lovel our dog,
> Rule all England under an hog.

The famous lines affixed to the door of St. Paul's and other places in the City of London in 1484 at the instigation of William Colyngburne, for which, according to the *Great Chronicle of London*, "he was drawn unto the Tower Hill and there full cruelly put to death, at first hanged and straight cut down and ripped, and his bowels cast into the fire". The rhyme implied that the kingdom was ruled by Francis, Viscount Lovel, the king's "spaniel" or dog; Sir Richard Ratcliffe, the Rat; and William Catesby, SPEAKER of the HOUSE OF COMMONS, the Cat. The Hog was the white boar or cognizance of Richard III. *See* BLUE BOAR.

Rats! Nonsense! etc.; or an exclamation of annoyance.

To rat. To forsake a losing side for the stronger party, as rats are said to forsake unseaworthy ships; to become a renegade; to "squeal" or to inform.

To take a rat by the tail (*prendre un rat par la queue*). An ancient French colloquialism for "to cut a purse". *See* CUT-PURSE.

Rat-killer. APOLLO received this derogatory title from the following incident: Apollo sent a swarm of rats against Crinis, one of his priests, for neglect of his office; but the priest seeing the invaders coming, repented and obtained pardon and the god annihilated the rats with his far-darting arrows.

Rat-race. The relentless struggle to get ahead of one's rivals, particularly in professional and commercial occupations. *Rat* is used generally as a derogatory epithet.

Rattening. Destroying or taking away another workman's tools, or otherwise incapacitating him from doing his work, with the object of forcing him to join a TRADE UNION or to obey its rules. The term was once common in Yorkshire and is of unknown origin.

Raven. A bird of ill omen; fabled to forbode death, and to bring infection and bad luck.

CICERO was forewarned of his death by the fluttering of ravens, and Macaulay relates the legend that a raven entered the chamber of the great orator the very day of his murder and pulled the clothes off his bed. Like many other birds, ravens indicate the approach of foul weather. When ravens forsake their normal abode we may look for famine and mortality, because ravens bear the characters of SATURN, the author of these calamities, and have a very early knowledge of the bad disposition of that planet.

According to Roman legend, ravens were once as white as swans and not inferior in size; but one day a raven told APOLLO that CORONIS, a Thessalian NYMPH whom he passionately loved, was faithless. The god shot the nymph with his dart; but hating the tell-tale bird:

> He blacked the raven o'er,
> And bid him prate in his white plumes no more.
> ADDISON: *Translation of Ovid*, Bk. II.

In Christian art, the raven is an emblem of God's Providence, in allusion to the ravens which fed ELIJAH. St. Oswald holds in his hand a raven with a ring in its mouth; St. Benedict has a raven at his feet; ST. PAUL THE HERMIT is drawn with a raven bringing him a loaf of bread.

The fatal raven, consecrated to ODIN, the Danish war-god, was the emblem of the Danish Standard, *Landeyda* (the desolation of the country), and was said to have been woven and embroidered in one noontide by the daughters of Ragnar Lodbrok, son of SIGURD. If the Danish arms were destined to defeat, the raven hung his wings; if victory was to attend them, he stood erect and soaring, as if inviting the warriors to follow.

> The Danish raven, lured by annual prey,
> Hung o'er the land incessant.

JAMES THOMSON: *Liberty*, Pt. IV.

The two ravens that sit on the shoulders of Odin are called Huginn and Muninn (Mind and Memory).

Raw. Johnny Raw. A raw recruit; a "new chum", a GREENHORN.

A raw deal. A transaction which is harsh or unfair to a person, perhaps from the idea that it leaves him feeling "raw" or hurt.

To touch one on the raw. To mention something that makes a person wince, like touching a horse on a raw place in currying him.

Rawhead and Bloody-bones. A BOGY at one time the terror of children.

Razor. On the razor's edge. To be in a hazardous position or a critical situation.

To cut blocks with a razor. *See under* CUT.

Razzia (ră' zi à). An incursion made by the military into enemy territory for the purpose of carrying off cattle or slaves, or for enforcing tribute. It is the French form of an Arabic word usually employed in connexion with Algerian and North African affairs.

Razzle-dazzle. On the razzle, or **razzle-dazzle.** On the spree, on a hilarious drunken frolic.

Read. To read between the lines. *See under* LINE.

To read oneself in. Said of an Anglican clergyman on entering upon a new incumbency, because one of his first duties is to give a public reading of the THIRTY-NINE ARTICLES in the church to which he has been appointed, and to make the Declaration of Assent.

Reader. Lay Reader. In the CHURCH OF ENGLAND, a layman licensed by the BISHOP to conduct church services; namely, Morning and Evening Prayer (except the absolution and the blessing) and the Litany. A Lay Reader may also publish BANNS OF MARRIAGE, preach, catechize children, etc. The modern office dates from 1866.

Ready. An elliptical expression for ready money.

> Lord Strutt was not flush in ready, either to go to law, or clear old debts.
> ARBUTHNOT: *History of John Bull.*

Real Presence. The doctrine that Christ Himself is present in the bread and wine of the EUCHARIST after consecration, as contrasted with doctrines that maintain the Body and Blood are only symbolically present.

Realism. In mediæval scholastic philosophy the opposite of NOMINALISM; the belief that abstract concepts or universals are real things existing independently of our conceptions and their expression. It was a development from PLATO'S metaphysic and was held in varying forms by ERIGENA, REMIGIUS, St. Anselm, ABELARD, Albertus Magnus, THOMAS AQUINAS, Duns Scotus, and others. *See* DUNCE; SCHOLASTICISM.

In literature and art it denotes the attempt to present life as it is, however unpleasant, ugly or distasteful. Zola and Maupassant were leaders of this school in France at the end of the 19th century. The brutality and outspokenness of their writings led to an outcry, thus Anatole France described Zola's novel *La Terre* as "a heap of ordure". Realism often tends to emphasize the crude, the perverted, and the immoral somewhat disproportionately, at the expense of the more balanced, admirable or beautiful.

Realpolitik (rē al po' li tēk') (Ger.). Practical politics, political realism; politics based on national "interests" or material considerations as distinct from moral objectives.

Reaper. The grim reaper. Death; often depicted, like Time, with a scythe.

Rearmouse, or **Reremouse.** The bat (O.E. *hreremus*, probably the fluttering-mouse; from *hrerean*, to move or flutter). The bat is not, of course, a flying mouse.

Reason. Age of Reason. *See under* AGE.

It stands to reason. It is logically manifest; this is the Lat. *constat* (*constare*, to stand together).

The Goddess of Reason. The central figure in an attempt to supersede Christianity during the French Revolution. The first Feast of Reason was held on 20th BRUMAIRE, 1793, when the "goddess" Mlle Candeille of the Opera was enthroned in the cathedral of Notre-Dame which became the Temple of Reason. She was dressed in white, with a red

Phrygian cap and the pike of Jupiter-Peuple in her hand. Mme Momoro, wife of a member of the CONVENTION, was later installed at St. Sulpice. Goddesses of Liberty and Reason were soon set up throughout France, one allegedly wearing a fillet bearing the words "Turn me not into Licence!" SATURNALIA of a disgusting kind accompanied these installations.

The woman's reason. I think so just because I *do* think so. (*See* SHAKESPEARE's *Two Gentlemen of Verona*, I, ii.)

> First then a woman will, or won't, depend on't;
> If she will do't, she will, and there's an end on't.
>
> AARON HILL: *Epilogue to "Zara".*

Rebeccaites (re bek' a īts). Bands of Welsh tenant-farmers dressed as women were responsible for the **Rebecca Riots** of 1839 and 1842–1843, which were suppressed with military aid. They demolished turnpike gates and were largely a reaction against tolls, rates, TITHES, rents and an unfair system of landholding. These riots occurred in Carmarthenshire, Pembroke, and Brecon, and the rioters took their name from *Gen.* xxiv, 60; when Rebecca left her father's house, Laban and his family "blessed her", and said, "Let thy seed possess the gate of those which hate them."

Rebellion, The Great. In English history, the period of the Civil Wars which ended in the execution of CHARLES I in 1649 (30 January). *See* RESTORATION; FIFTEEN; THE FORTY-FIVE *under* FORTY.

Rebus (rē' bŭs) (Lat., with things). A hieroglyphic riddle, *non verbis sed rebus*. The origin of the word has, somewhat doubtfully, been traced to the lawyers of Paris, who, during the carnival, used to satirize the follies of the day in SQUIBS called *De rebus quæ geruntur* (on the current events), and, to avoid libel actions, employed hieroglyphics either wholly or in part.

In HERALDRY the name is given to punning devices on a coat of arms suggesting the name of the family to whom it belongs; as the broken spear on the shield of Nicholas Breakspear (Pope Adrian IV).

Recessional. The music or words, or both, accompanying the procession of clergy and choir when they retire after a service.

Rechabites (rek' a bīts). Members of a teetotal benefit society (the Independent Order of Rechabites), founded in 1835, and so named from Rechab, who enjoined his family to abstain from wine and to dwell in tents (*Jer.* xxxv, 6, 7).

Reckon. Day of reckoning. Settlement day; when one has to pay up one's account or fulfil one's obligation; also used of the Day of JUDGMENT.

To reckon without your host. *See under* HOST.

Recollects. The name given (1) to a reformed branch of the FRANCISCAN Observants first formed in France; and (2) a reformed group of AUGUSTINIAN Hermits founded in Spain. Both orders were first formed in the late 16th century.

Record. That which is recorded, originally "got by heart" (Lat. *cor, cordis*, heart); hence the best performance or most striking event of its kind known, especially in such phrases as **to beat,** or **break the record, to do it in record time,** etc.

Court of Record. A court where proceedings are officially recorded and can be produced as evidence. The Supreme Court is a superior court of record.

For the record. To make a statement of one's views, etc., for public consumption or publication.

Off the record. Originally a legal term whereby a judge directs that improper or irrelevant evidence shall be struck off the record. This later became commonly synonymous with "in confidence", an unofficial expression of views.

Rector. *See* CLERICAL TITLES.

Recusants (rek' ū zănts). The name given from the reign of Elizabeth I to those who refused to attend the services of the CHURCH OF ENGLAND (Lat. *recusare*, to refuse). The term commonly denoted "popish recusants" although properly it included PROTESTANT dissenters. Fines were first exacted under statute in 1552 and 1559 at the rate of 1s. per Sunday but raised to the exorbitant sum of £20 per month in 1587. Fortunately they were intermittently imposed, and the last fines for recusancy were those in 1782 on two Yorkshire labourers and their wives.

Red. One of the primary colours; in HER-ALDRY said to signify magnanimity and fortitude; in liturgical use worn at certain seasons; and in popular folklore the colour of magic.

> Red is the colour of magic in every country, and has been so from the very earliest times. The caps of fairies and musicians are well-nigh always red.
>
> YEATS: *Fairy and Folk Tales of the Irish Peasantry (The Trooping Fairies—The Merrow)*.

Nowadays it is more often symbolical of anarchy and revolution—"Red ruin, and the breaking up of laws" (Tennyson: *Guinevere*, 421). In the French Revolution the *Red Republicans* were those extremists who never hesitated to dye their hands in blood. In Russia red is supposed to be the beautiful colour, but in general red is regarded as the colour of radicalism, socialism (*see* RED FLAG *under* FLAG), and revolution.

Red is the colour of the royal livery; and it is said that this colour was adopted by huntsmen because fox-hunting was declared a royal sport by Henry II. (*See* IN PINK *under* PINK.)

In the old ballads *red* was frequently applied to gold ("the gude red gowd"), and in thieves' CANT a gold watch is a *red kettle*, and the chain a *red tackle*. One of the names given by the alchemists to the PHILOSOPHER'S STONE was the *red tincture*, because with its help they hoped to transmute the base metals into gold.

In the red. Overdrawn at the bank; in debt; or said of a business running at a loss. From the banking practice of showing overdrawn accounts in red.

To paint the town red. *See under* PAINT.

To see red. To give way to excessive passion or anger; to be violently moved, TO RUN AMOK (*see under* RUN).

To see the red light. To be aware of approaching disaster; to realize it is time to desist; to take warning. From the railway signal, where the red light signifies danger.

Admiral of the Red. *See under* ADMIR-AL.

Red Barn, The murder in the. A sensational murder at Polstead, near Ipswich, that achieved lasting notoriety in melodrama and story. *The Red Barn* or *The Gypsy's Curse* was first performed at Weymouth in 1828 and gained immediate and widespread popularity. The theme, essentially that of the innocent village maiden, seduced, and later murdered, by a local man of property, next appeared in book form as *The Awful Adventure of Maria Monk*, and in other titles. They are all founded on the murder of Maria Marten, a mole-catcher's daughter of loose morals who first bore a child to Thomas Corder, the son of a prosperous farmer. Later William Corder, younger brother of Thomas, became enamoured of her with the inevitable consequences, but avoided marriage. In May 1827 it seems that arrangements were made for Maria to meet him at the Red Barn on his farm with the intention of going to Ipswich to be married. Maria was not seen alive again, but Corder decamped to London and married one Mary Moore, who kept a school. Eventually Maria's body was discovered in the Red Barn and William Corder was hanged for her murder at Bury St. Edmunds in August 1828.

Red Book. A directory relating to the court, the nobility, and the "UPPER TEN" (*see under* TEN) generally. *The Royal Kalendar*, published from 1767 to 1893, was known by this name, as also Webster's *Royal Red Book*, a similar work first issued in 1847.

The name is also given to certain special works covered in red, such as the official parliamentary records of the old Austro-Hungarian Empire, similar to our BLUE BOOKS, etc.

The Red Book of Hergest (*Llyfr Coch Hergest*). A Welsh manuscript of the late 14th or early 15th century containing the MABINOGION, poems by TALIE-SIN and Llywarch Hen, a history of the world from ADAM to 1318, etc. It is now in the library of Jesus College, Oxford.

Red Button. In the former Chinese Empire, a MANDARIN of the first class wore a button or knob of red coral or ruby as a badge of honour in his cap.

Cp. THE NINE RANKS OF MANDARIN *under* MANDARIN; PANJANDRUM.

Red cent. Not a red cent. No money at all; "stony broke". An Americanism; the cent used to be copper, but is now an alloy of copper, tin and zinc. Hence, *not worth a red cent*, worth nothing at all.

Red Comyn. Sir John Comyn the younger of Badenoch, nephew of John Balliol, king of SCOTLAND, so called from his ruddy complexion and red hair, and son of Black Comyn, John Comyn the elder, who was swarthy and black-haired. He was stabbed by Robert Bruce in 1306 in the church of the Minorites at Dumfries, and afterwards dispatched by Lindsay and Kirkpatrick.

The Red Crescent, Lion and Sun. The equivalent in non-Christian countries of the RED CROSS, *i.e.* the military hospital service.

Red Cross. *See under* CROSS.

The Red Cross Knight in Spenser's *Faerie Queene* (Bk. I) is a personification of St. GEORGE, the patron saint of ENGLAND. He typifies Christian holiness and his adventures are an allegory of the CHURCH OF ENGLAND. The knight is sent by the Queen to destroy a DRAGON which was ravaging the kingdom of Una's father. After many adventures and trials Una and the knight are united in marriage.

Red Dragon. Anciently the badge of the Parthians, it was introduced in Britain by the Romans. In the 7th century it became the standard of King Cadwaladr and later was one of the supporters of the Tudor arms. The present Welsh flag consists of a red dragon *passant* on a ground of two horizontal strips (white over green). *See* DRAGON.

Red Duster. The Red Ensign, the flag of British merchant ships since 1674, but also the senior ensign of the Royal Navy until 1864 where it was used as squadronal colour. Its use was solely reserved for the Merchant Navy in 1864. It is a red flag with a union device in the upper canton, but before 1707 it bore a St. GEORGE'S CROSS.

Red Eye (U.S.A.). Cheap whiskey.

Red Flag. *See under* FLAG.

Red Friday. Friday 31 July 1925, when a stoppage in the coal industry, planned to meet the threat of wage cuts, was averted by promise of government subsidies to support wages, etc. It was so called by the Labour press to distinguish it from BLACK FRIDAY of 15 April 1921, when union leaders called off an impending strike of railwaymen and transport workers designed to help the miners who were locked out.

Red Hand of Ulster. *See under* ULSTER.

The Red Hat. The flat broad-brimmed hat formerly bestowed upon cardinals, hence the office of CARDINAL.

Red Herring. *See* DRAWING A RED HERRING *under* HERRING.

Red Indians. The North American Indians; so called because of their copper-coloured skin; also called *Redskins* and *Red men*.

Red Lamp, or **Red Light district.** The brothel-quarter of a large town; from the red light frequently displayed outside a bawdy-house.

The Red Laws. The civil code of ancient ROME. Juvenal says, *Per lege rubras majoram leges* (*Satires*, xiv, 193). The civil laws, being written in vermilion, were called *rubrica*, and *rubrica vetavit* means: It is forbidden by the civil laws.

The prætor's laws were inscribed in white letters and imperial rescripts were written in purple.

The Red Letter. *See* THE ZINOVIEV LETTER *under* FORGERY.

Red-letter day. A lucky day; a day to be recalled with delight. In ALMANACS, and more commonly in ecclesiastical calendars, important FEAST days and saints' days were printed in red, other days in black.

Red Man. A term in ALCHEMY, used in conjunction with "white woman" to express the affinity and interaction of chemicals. In the long list of terms that Surly scoffingly gives (Ben Jonson's *The Alchemist*, II, iii) "your red man and your white woman" are mentioned.

The French say that a red man commands the elements, and wrecks off the coasts of Brittany those whom he dooms to death. The legend affirms that he appeared to NAPOLEON and foretold his downfall. *See also* RED INDIANS, *above*.

Red rag. Old slang for the tongue.

Also in the phrase **Like a red rag to a bull,** anything that is calculated to excite rage. Toreadors' capes are lined with red.

Red Sea. So called by the Romans (*Mare rubrum*) and by the Greeks, as a translation of the Semitic name, the reason for which is uncertain. One explanation is that it was the "sea of reeds", another that it is from the corals on its bed; or again, from the reflection of the eastern sky in its waters, etc.

Red Shirt. *See* GARIBALDI.

Red snow. Snow reddened by the presence of a minute alga, *Protococcus nivalis*, not uncommon in arctic and alpine regions where its sanguine colour formerly caused it to be regarded as a portent of evil.

Red tape. Official formality, or rigid adherence to rules and regulations, carried to excess; so called because lawyers and government officials tie their papers together with red tape. Charles Dickens is said to have introduced the expression; but the scorn poured on this EVIL of officialdom by Carlyle brought the term into popular use.

Redbrick. A term much favoured by journalists and often used in scholastic circles; it is loosely applied to all English universities other than those of Oxford and Cambridge. The name was introduced by Bruce Truscot (Professor E. Allison Peers: d. 1952) in his book *Redbrick University*, 1943). He was primarily dealing with the universities of Birmingham, Bristol, Leeds, Liverpool, Manchester, Reading, and Sheffield, and expressly excluded London. In his *Introduction* he says: "So unique has the University of London become and so essentially its own are the problems which it has to solve, that in this book very little specific mention will be made of it." Of the term itself: "Though red brick, rather than dingy stone, has been chosen as the symbol of the new foundations, it must be categorically stated that no one university alone has been in the author's mind." *Cp.* CAMFORD; OXBRIDGE.

Redcap. A colloquial term for British military police, who wear red covers to their caps; in the U.S.A., a porter at a railway- or bus-station.

Redcoats. British soldiers, from the colour of their uniforms in line regiments before the introduction of KHAKI. Cromwell's New Model Army was the first to wear red coats as a uniform. Regiments were distinguished by the colour of their facings—Blue, Green, Buff, etc. *See* REGIMENTAL AND DIVISIONAL NICKNAMES.

Red-haired persons. For centuries the red-haired have been popularly held to be unreliable, deceitful, and quick-tempered (*see* HAIR). The fat of a dead red-haired person used to be in demand as an ingredient for poisons (*see* Middleton's *The Witch*, V, ii) and Chapman says that flattery, like the plague—

> Strikes into the brain of man,
> And rageth in his entrails when he can,
> Worse than the poison of a red-hair'd man.
>
> *Bussy d'Ambois*, III, i.

Red-handed. To be caught red-handed is to be caught in the act, IN FLAGRANTE DELICTO, as if with blood on the hands.

Red-laced. A red-laced jacket. Old military slang for a flogging.

Redneck. In the U.S.A., a disparaging term for one of the "uneducated" masses. *Cp.* ROOINEK.

Redskins. *See* RED INDIANS.

Rede (O.E. *raed*). Archaic word meaning counsel, advice; also a verb.

To reck one's own rede. To be governed by one's own better judgment.

Ethelred II, King of England (968, 978–1016) was nicknamed the "Redeless" or "Unready", *i.e.* destitute of counsel.

Redemptioner. An immigrant who was obliged to pay back his passage money out of his earnings after landing in the new country, or who paid the master of the ship by his services.

Redemptionists. Members of a religious order whose object was to redeem Christian captives and slaves from the Mohammedans. They are also known as TRINITARIANS.

Redemptorists. Members of the Congregation of the Most Holy Redeemer, a religious order founded at Scala, Italy, in

1732 by St. Alphonsus Maria di Liguori. They are largely concerned with mission work among the poor and foreign missions.

Reductio ad absurdum (Lat.). Proof of the falsity of a principle by demonstrating that its logical consequence involves an absurdity. It is used loosely of taking an argument or principle to impractical lengths. "The more sleep one has the longer one lives. To sleep all the time ensures the longest possible life."

Reduplicated, or **Ricochet Words.** There are probably some hundreds of these words in English, which usually have an intensifying force, such as: chit-chat, click-clack, clitter-clatter, dilly-dally, ding-dong, drip-drop, fallal, fiddle-faddle, flim-flam, flip-flap, flip-flop, hanky-panky, harum-scarum, helter-skelter, higgledy-piggledy, hobnob, hodge-podge, hoity-toity, hubble-bubble, hugger-mugger, hurly-burly, mingle-mangle, mish-mash, namby-pamby, niminy-piminy, nosy-posy, pell-mell, ping-pong, pit-pat, pitter-patter, pribbles and prabbles, randem-tandem, randy-dandy, razzle-dazzle, riff-raff, roly-poly, shilly-shally, slip-slop, slish-slosh, tick-tack, tip-top, tittle-tattle, wibble-wobble, wig-wag, wiggle-waggle, wish-wash, wishy-washy.

Reed. A broken, or **bruised reed.** Something not to be trusted for support; a weak adherent. Egypt is called a broken reed, in which Hezekiah could not trust if the Assyrians made war on Jerusalem: "which broken reed if a man leans on, it will go into his hand and pierce it." *See* II *Kings* xviii, 21; *Is*. xxxvi, 6.

A reed shaken by the wind. A person blown about by every wind of doctrine. John the Baptist (said Christ) was not a "reed shaken by the wind", but from the very first had a firm belief in the Messiahship of the Son of MARY, and this conviction was not shaken by fear or favour. *See Matt*. xi, 7.

Reef. He must take in a reef or so. He must retrench; he must reduce his expenses. The reef of a sail is that part which is rolled and tied up by the reef points to reduce the area caught by the wind.

Reekie, Auld. *See* AULD REEKIE.

Reel. Right off the reel. Without intermission, continuously. From the use of a reel (O.E. *hreol*) for winding rope, etc.

The Scottish dance called a *reel* is from Gaelic *righil* or *ruidhil*, which may be from O.E. *hreol*.

Reeve (O.E. *gerefa*). The local officer and representative of his lord. The manorial reeve was generally a VILLEIN elected by his fellows. He was responsible for organizing the daily work of the MANOR and it was his duty to see that people were at their tasks. The *shire-reeve* or SHERIFF was an official of the SHIRE and the PORT-REEVE, of a town. There was a port-reeve in Tavistock as late as 1886.

Reformation, The. Specifically, the religious revolution of the 16th century which destroyed the religious unity of Western Europe and resulted in the establishment of "Reformed" or PROTESTANT churches. It aimed at reforming the abuses in the Roman Church and ended in schism, its chief leaders being Luther, Zwingli, and Calvin (*see* CALVINISM, ROMAN CATHOLIC CHURCH).

The Counter-Reformation. A name given by historians to the movement for reform within the Roman Church (much stimulated by the REFORMATION) and the measures taken to combat the spread of Protestantism and to regain lost ground. It is usually reckoned to extend from the mid16th century, when the Council of Trent (1545–1563) strengthened and reawakened the life and discipline of the Church, until the time of the THIRTY YEARS WAR (1618–48). The JESUITS played a major role, whilst the INQUISITION and the INDEX strengthened Papal influence.

Refresher. An extra fee paid to a BARRISTER during long cases in addition to his retaining fee, originally to remind him of the case entrusted to his charge.

Refreshment Sunday. *See* MID-LENT SUNDAY.

Regan. The second of King LEAR's unfilial daughters. In SHAKESPEARE's *King Lear* (IV, ii) called "most barbarous, most degenerate". She was married to the Duke of Cornwall, and in Geoffrey of Monmouth, from whose *Historia Britonum* the story originally comes, she is called *Regau*. See CORDELIA; GONERIL.

Regard, or **Reguard.** A forest visitation held triennially to review (regard) the forest boundaries, matters affecting the king's rights, and to inquire of dogs kept in the forest, which had to be lawed (*i.e.* to have the three talons cut from each front foot). Reguard was carried out by 12 selected KNIGHTS. See FOREST COURTS.

Regatta. A boat-race, or organized series of boat races; the name originally given to the races held between Venetian gondoliers, the Italian *regata* meaning "strife" or "contention".

Regency. In British history, architecture, and decoration the term is usually applied to the period 1811–1820 when George, PRINCE OF WALES (afterwards George IV), acted as regent during his father's (George III) illness. In French history it refers to the years from 1715 to 1723 when the Duke of Orleans was regent for the minor Louis XV.

Regicides. The name given to those 67 men who sat in judgment on CHARLES I in 1649 and especially the 58 who signed his death warrant. After the RESTORATION 10 were executed and 25 others imprisoned, the majority for life. The remainder escaped or were dead. The bodies of Cromwell, Ireton, and Bradshaw were disinterred, and after a solemn trial for treason were dismembered and exhibited at TYBURN and elsewhere.

Regimental and Divisional Nicknames. British Army

Black Watch. In 1725, six companies of clansmen loyal to the King were raised, and were stationed in small detachments to keep watch on the HIGHLANDS and the clans. Their tartan was dark, and their name was coined from a combination of this and their function, and was used to distinguish them from the English troops performing the same duty. These companies later became the 42nd Foot, now The Black Watch (Royal Highland Regiment). *Black Watch* has been a part of the official regimental title for over one hundred years.

Desert Rats. The name associated with the 7th Armoured Division, whose divisional sign was the desert rat (jerboa), which was adopted during its "scurrying

and biting" tactics in Libya. The final design of the badge was a red rat outlined on a black background. The division served throughout the North Africa campaign, and in North-West Europe from Normandy to Berlin.

Die-Hards. At the Battle of Albuera (1811), the 57th Foot, later 1st Battalion Middlesex Regiment, now 4th Battalion The Queen's Regiment, had three-quarters of the officers and men either killed or wounded. Colonel Inglis was badly wounded, but refused to be moved, instead he lay where he had fallen crying, "Die hard, my men, die hard."

Regium donum (Lat., royal gift). An annual grant paid by the Crown from 1670 until 1871 to help PRESBYTERIAN ministers in ULSTER. It was, however, withdrawn by James II and again in 1714. An English *regium donum* was introduced by Walpole in 1723 for the benefit of the widows of Dissenting ministers. NON-CONFORMIST unease led to its discontinuance in 1851.

Regius Professor (Lat. *regius*, royal). At Oxford and Cambridge, one who holds a professorship founded by Henry VIII and certain others of subsequent foundation. At the Scottish universities, any professorship instituted by the Crown.

Regnal Year. See under YEAR.

Regular (U.S.A.). In the early 19th century this meant thorough, well founded; in the 20th century, more often applied to people as, *a regular guy*, a straightforward, dependable person.

Regulars. All men of the British (and U.S.) armed forces who adopt their respective service as a career, as opposed to members of reserve forces, and conscripts.

Rehoboam (II *Chron*. xiii, 7). As a wine measure, the equivalent of six bottles. *See* BOTTLE; JEROBOAM; TAPPIT-HEN.

Charlotte Brontë—why is not known—applied the name to a clerical SHOVEL HAT.

> He [Mr. Helstone] was short of stature [and wore] a rehoboam, or shovel hat, which he did not ... remove.
> *Shirley*, ch. i.

Reign of Terror. The period in the French Revolution from April 1793 until July 1794, when supreme power was in the hands of the Committee of Public Safety, and the JACOBINS, dominated by Robespierre, St. Just, and Couthon. During this period, Taine estimated that 17,000 people were put to death, although this is perhaps an exaggeration, but some 2,600 were sentenced at Paris alone. The excuse was the external threat from the European coalition, "royalist plots", etc. Robespierre formulated the doctrine that "in times of peace the springs of popular government are in virtue, but in times of revolution, they are both in virtue and terror".

Reilly, To lead a life of. To live luxuriously. From a comic song, "Is That Mr. Reilly", by Pat Rooney, popular in the U.S.A. in the 1880s. The song described what the hero would do if he "struck it rich".

Rein. To draw rein. To tighten the reins; hence to slacken pace, to stop.

To give the reins, or **to give free rein to.** To let go unrestrained; to give licence.

To take the reins. To assume the guidance of direction; to assume control.

Reins (Lat. *renes*). The kidneys, supposed by the Hebrews and others to be the seat of knowledge, pleasure, and pain. The Psalmist says (xvi, 7), "My reins instruct me in the night seasons." SOLOMON (*Prov.* xxiii, 16), "My reins shall rejoice, when thy lips speak right things," and Jeremiah says (*Lam.* iii, 13), God "caused his arrows to enter into my reins," *i.e.* sent pain into my kidneys.

Relic, Christian. The corpse of a saint, or any part thereof; any part of his clothing; or anything ultimately connected with him. The veneration of Christian relics goes back to the 2nd century and led to many spurious relics being brought back from the HOLY LAND. Miracle-working relics brought wealth to many monasteries and churches and the remains of saints were often dismembered and trickery and violence were used to obtain them. Relics such as the tip of LUCIFER'S tail, the blood of Christ, the candle which the ANGEL of the Lord lit in Christ's tomb, were among the many accepted by the credulous.

Relief Church. A secession from the CHURCH OF SCOTLAND led in 1752 by Thomas Gillespie (1708–1774). He offered passive obedience respecting the settlement of ministers. The "Presbytery of Relief" was constituted in 1761; in 1847 the sect was embodied in the United Presbyterian Church of Scotland.

Religious. His Most Religious Majesty. The title by which the kings of England were formerly addressed by the POPE. It still survives in the BOOK OF COMMON PRAYER in the Prayer "for the High Court of Parliament under our most religious and gracious Queen at this time assembled" (which was written, probably by hand, in 1625), and in James I's *Act for Thanksgiving on the Fifth of November* occurs the expression "most great, learned, and religious King".

Similarly the Pope addressed the King of France as "Most Christian", the Emperor of Austria as "Most Apostolic", the king of Portugal as "Most Faithful", etc. *See* MAJESTY.

Reliquary. A receptacle of various kinds for RELICS. The smaller relics were preserved in monstrances, pyxes, pectoral reliquaries (usually in the form of a CROSS), shapes of arms and legs, etc. (*see* ARM-SHRINES). The entire remains of a saint were kept in shrines.

Reliques of Ancient English Poetry. *See* PERCY'S RELIQUES.

Remember! The mysterious injunction of CHARLES I, on the scaffold, to Bishop Juxon. Not his "last words". *See* DYING SAYINGS.

Remembrance Day, Remembrance Sunday. After World War I ARMISTICE DAY, or Remembrance Day, commemorating the fallen was observed on 11 November; also called "Poppy Day" from the artificial poppies (recalling the poppies of Flanders fields) sold by the British LEGION in aid of ex-servicemen. From 1945 to 1956 Remembrance Sunday was observed instead on the first or second Sunday of November, commemorating the fallen of World Wars I and II. In 1956 it was fixed on the second Sunday of November.

Remigius, or **Remy, St.** (re mij′ i ŭs,

re'mi) (438–533), BISHOP and confessor, and apostle of the FRANKS. He is represented as carrying a vessel of holy oil, or in the act of anointing therewith Clovis, who kneels before him. He is said to have given Clovis the power of touching for the KING'S EVIL. His day is 1 October.

Remittance men. In 19th-century Australia and other colonial territories, a name given to middle-class immigrants, well-connected Englishmen, and ne'er-do-wells who were often impractical, unsuccessful, and not at home in the BUSH; so called from their dependence on money sent from home. They were also called "colonial experiencers".

Remonstrants. Another name for the ARMINIANS. In Scottish history, the name is also given to those who presented a remonstrance to the Committee of Estates in 1650 refusing to acknowledge Charles II as king until he had established his good faith and devotion to the Covenant (see COVENANTERS).

Remus. See ROMULUS.

Renaissance, The (Fr., rebirth). The term applied to the intellectual movement characteristic of that period of European history marking the transition between the mediæval and modern. Chronologically it is usually taken to fall in the 15th and 16th centuries, occurring earliest in Italy and later in England. In a more limited sense it implies what was formerly called the REVIVAL OF LEARNING.

The period is particularly marked by a rediscovery of the classics, questioning of religious dogmas, the growth of a more scientific outlook, major developments in art and literature, new inventions and overseas discoveries, and a general assertion and emancipation of the human intellect.

The name is now also given to certain earlier periods, such as "the Twelfth-century Renaissance".

Renard (ren' ard). **Une queue de renard** (Fr., a fox's tail). A mockery. At one time it was a common practical joke to fasten a fox's tail behind a person against whom a laugh was designed. PANURGE never lost a chance of attaching a fox's tail, or the ears of a leveret, behind

a Master of Arts or Doctor of Divinity (*Gargantua*, II, xvi). *See also* REYNARD.

> C'est une petite vipère
> Qui n'épargneroit pas son père
> Et qui par nature ou par art
> Sçait couper la queue au renard.
> BEAUCAIRE: *L'Embarras de la Foire*.

Repenter Curls. The long ringlets of a lady's hair. *Repentir* is the French for penitence, and *les repenties* are the girls doing penance for their misdemeanours. MARY MAGDALENE had such long hair that she wiped off her tears from the feet of Jesus therewith. Hence the association of long curls and reformed (*repenties*) prostitutes.

Republic, The. The English name for PLATO'S best-known work, the *Politeia* (Commonwealth), written in the 4th century B.C. It is his ideal Commonwealth and *The Republic* is especially regarded for its philosophical and ethical teachings. It gave Sir Thomas More the inspiration for his UTOPIA. *See* IDEAL COMMONWEALTHS *under* COMMONWEALTH.

The Republic of Letters. The world of literature; authors generally and their influence. Goldsmith, in *The Citizen of the World*, No. 20 (1760), says "it is a very common expression among Europeans"; it is found in MOLIÈRE'S *Le Mariage Forcé*, Sc. vi (1664).

The Republican Queen. Sophia Charlotte (1668–1705), wife of Frederick I of Prussia, was so nicknamed on account of her advanced political views. She was the sister of George I of Britain, the friend of Leibniz, and a woman of remarkable culture. Charlottenburg was named after her.

Requests, Court of. A minor court of equity hearing poor men's causes, which fell into disuse at the time of the CIVIL WARS. Also certain local COURTS OF CONSCIENCE (*see under* CONSCIENCE).

Requiem (re' kwi em). The first word of the prayer *Requiem aeternam dona eis, domine, et lux perpetua luceat eis* (Eternal rest give them, O Lord, and let everlasting light shine upon them) used as the introit of a MASS for the Dead; hence a Requiem Mass.

Reremouse. See REARMOUSE.

Respects. To pay one's respects. To show polite regard for someone, usually by making a call.

To pay one's last respects. To show respect for one who is dead, particularly by being present at the funeral.

Rest. Laid to rest. Buried.

Restoration, The. In British history, the recall of the Stuarts to the throne in 1660 in the person of Charles II, thus bringing the Puritan COMMONWEALTH to an end. The Restoration period was marked by a relaxation in standards of conduct but scholarship, science, literature and the arts blossomed and flourished with the cessation of PURITAN restraints.

In France, the royal house of Bourbon was restored after the fall of NAPOLEON in 1815 in the person of Louis XVIII, brother of the late King Louis XVI, whose son, dynastically known as Louis XVII, did not survive to rule.

Resurrectionists, or **Resurrection Men.** Body-snatchers, those who broke open the coffins of the newly buried to supply the demands of the surgical and medical schools. The first recorded instance of the practice was in 1742 and it flourished particularly until the passing of the Anatomy Act of 1832. The Resurrectionist took the corpse naked, this being in law a misdemeanour, as opposed to a felony if garments were taken as well. Murders were sometimes committed for the same market. *See* BURKE.

Retiarius (rē ti ār' i us) (Lat.). A gladiator who made use of a net (*rete*), which he threw over his adversary. *See also* TRIDENT.

> As in the thronged amphitheatre of old
> The wary Retiarius trapped his foe.
> THOMSON: *Castle of Indolence*, canto ii.

Returned Letter Office. *See* BLIND DEPARTMENT.

Reuters. The premier international news agency, reputed for its integrity and impartiality, founded by Paul Julius Reuter (1816–1899), a native of Cassel, Germany. The agency was established at London in 1851, taking full advantage of the developing telegraph service, although links had to be completed by railway and pigeon-post. He developed a world-wide service in the ensuing

years and in 1871 was made Baron de Reuter by the Duke of Saxe-Coburg and Gotha. It became a private trust in 1916 and was later (1926–1941) taken over by the British Press Association, the Newspaper Publishers Association, the Australian Associated Press and the New Zealand Press Association, becoming a public company in 1984.

Reveille (re văl' i) (Fr. *réveiller*, to awaken). The bugle call used in the armed forces announcing that it is time to rise.

Revenant (rev' e non) (Fr., present participle of *revenir*, to come back). One who returns after long exile; an apparition, a ghost, one who returns from the dead.

Revenons à nos moutons. *See* MOUTONS.

Reverend. An archbishop is *the Most Reverend* (Father in God); a BISHOP, *the Right Reverend*; a DEAN, *the Very Reverend*; an archdeacon, *the Venerable*; all the other CLERGY, *the Reverend*. A person in orders should always be referred to as "the Reverend Mr. Jones", or "the Reverend John Jones"; never "Reverend", or "the Reverend Jones".

Revised code. The regulations governing English elementary education issued in 1862 when the many existing directives were gathered together and systematically arranged. It introduced the notorious system of "payment by results" whereby the grant to schools was dependent upon tests in THE THREE R'S (*see under* R) given to the pupils by H.M. Inspectors. Its effects on the teaching of grammar, geography, and history were disastrous as their teaching did not affect a school's revenues.

The Revised Version. *See* BIBLE, THE ENGLISH.

Revival of Learning, or **Letters.** A term applied to that aspect of the RENAISSANCE which involved the revival of classical learning, especially of Greek literature, freed from the cramping influences of mediæval SCHOLASTICISM and ecclesiastical restraint. Humanism, which demanded that human reason should be free to pursue its intellectual and æsthetic purposes, was its keynote. Marked by the enthusiastic pursuit of scholarship, the investigation of manuscript sources, and the establishment of libraries and museums, it received added impetus from the invention of printing (*c.* 1440). Italy was the centre of this European revival, where it was in evidence by the late 14th century, reaching its full development in the early 16th century.

Rexists. A Belgian political party formed by Léon Degrelle in 1936 advocating FASCIST methods. Markedly collaborationist during the German occupation of Belgium, it was accordingly suppressed when the Germans were expelled in 1944. The name is an adaptation of "Christus Rex", Christ the King, the watchword of a Catholic Young People's Action Society founded in 1925. *Cp.* QUISLING.

Reynard (rā' nard). A fox. Caxton's form of the name in his translation (from the Dutch) of the *Roman de Renart* (*see* REYNARD THE FOX, *below*). *Renart* was the Old French form, from Ger. *Reginhart*, a personal name; the M. Dutch was *Reynaerd* or *Reynaert*.

Reynard the Fox. A mediæval beast-epic satirizing contemporary life and events, found in French, Dutch, and German literature. Chaucer's *Nun's Priest's Tale* is part of the Reynard tradition. Most of the names in the Reynard cycle are German but it found its greatest vogue in France as the *Roman de Renart*. Caxton's *Hystorie of Reynart the Foxe* (1481) was based on a Dutch version published at Gouda in 1479. The oldest version (12th century) is in Latin.

Reynard's Globe of Glass. Reynard, in REYNARD THE FOX, said he had sent this invaluable treasure to her majesty the QUEEN as a present; but it never came to hand as it had no existence except in the imagination of the fox. It was supposed to reveal what was being done—no matter how far off—and also to afford information on any subject that the person consulting it wished to know. **Your gift was like the globe of glass of Master Reynard.** A great promise but no performance.

Reynard's Wonderful ring. *See* RINGS NOTED IN FABLE *under* RING.

Rhabdomancy. A form of DIVINATION by means of a rod or wand, dowsing (Gr. *rhabdomanteia*; *rhabdos*, rod; *manteia*, prophecy). *See* DOWSE.

Rhadamanthus. In Greek mythology, one of the three judges of HELL; MINOS and Æacus being the other two.

Rhapsody meant originally "songs strung together" (Gr. *rapto*, to sew or string together; *ode*, a song). The term was applied to portions of the ILIAD and ODYSSEY, which bards recited.

Rhea. In Greek mythology, Mother of the gods, daughter of URANUS and GÆA, and sister of KRONOS by whom she bore ZEUS, HADES, POSEIDON, HERA, Hestia, and DEMETER. She is identified with CYBELE and also known as AGDISTIS.

Rhea Sylvia. The mother of ROMULUS and Remus.

Rheims-Douai Version, The. *See* THE DOUAI BIBLE, *under* BIBLE, THE ENGLISH.

Rhetorical Question. A question asked for the sake of effect rather than demanding an answer as, "Who worries about that?" *i.e.* nobody worries.

Rhino (rī' nō). Slang for money; the term was in use in the 17th century. Its origin is uncertain but one plausible suggestion is that it derives from an Eastern belief that the powdered horn of the rhinoceros increased sexual potency and therefore commanded a high price.

> Some, as I know,
> Have parted with their ready rhino.
> *The Seaman's Adieu* (1670).

Rhodesia. Named after Cecil Rhodes (1853–1902), the former territories of Matabeleland and Mashonaland, which became part of the British Empire by 1894 through the enterprise of Rhodes and his British South Africa Company. In 1964 Northern Rhodesia was renamed Zambia and Southern Rhodesia became Zimbabwe in 1980. Both are independent republics within the COMMONWEALTH. *See* JAMESON RAID.

Rhodes Scholars. Students holding a scholarship at Oxford under the will of Cecil Rhodes, whose wealth largely accumulated from his mining activities in South Africa. These scholars are selected from candidates in the British COMMONWEALTH, the U.S.A. and Germany.

Rhodian Bully. The COLOSSUS of Rhodes.

> Yet fain wouldst thou the crouching world be stride,
> Just like the Rhodian bully o'er the tide.
> JOHN WOLCOT: *The Lousiad*, canto ii.

The Rhodian Law. The earliest system of maritime law known to history; compiled by the Rhodians about 900 B.C.

Rhopalic Verse (Gr. *rhopalon*, a club which is much thicker at one end than the other). Verse consisting of lines in which each successive word has more syllables than the one preceding it.

> Rem tibi confeci doctissime dulcisonorum
> Spes deus aeternæ stationis   conciliator
>   -est   AUSONIUS.
> Hope ever solaces miserable individuals.

Rhyme. Neither rhyme nor reason. Fit neither for amusement nor instruction. An author took his book to Sir Thomas More, CHANCELLOR of Henry VIII, and asked his opinion. Sir Thomas told the author to turn it into rhyme. He did so, and submitted it again to the Lord Chancellor. "Ay! ay!" said the witty satirist, "that will do, that will do. 'Tis rhyme now, but before it was neither rhyme nor reason."

See also WHAT! ALL THIS FOR A SONG? *under* SONG.

Rhyming slang. Slang, much used by the COCKNEY, in which the word intended is replaced by one that rhymes with it, as "plates of meat" for *feet*, "Rory O'More" for *door*, "dicky dirt" for *shirt*, "dicky-bird" for *word*. When the rhyme is a compound word the rhyming part is often dropped, leaving the uninitiated somewhat puzzled. Thus Chivy (Chevy) Chase rhymes with "face", by dropping "chase" *Chivy* remains. Similarly *daisies* are *boots*, from "daisy roots", the "roots" being dropped. Raspberry is *heart* (or vulgarly, *fart*), contracted from "raspberry tart". Numerous colloquial expressions derive from it, as "that's a fiddle", from "Yiddisher fiddle" (the musical instrument) which rhymed with *diddle*.

Rhyming to death. *See* IRISH RATS *under* RAT.

Thomas the Rhymer. Thomas Ercildoune, 13th-century border poet and seer, also called Thomas Learmont. He is the reputed author of a number of poems, including one on TRISTRAM (which Scott believed to be genuine), and is fabled to have predicted the death of Alexander III of SCOTLAND, the Battle of Bannockburn, the accession of James VI to the English throne, etc. He is not to be confused with Thomas Rymer (d. 1713), Historiographer Royal to William III.

Ribbon development. Single-depth building, chiefly houses, along main roads extending out of built-up areas. Such development was stopped by the Town and Country Planning Act of 1947.

Ribbonism. The activities, aims, etc., of the Ribbon or Riband societies, secret Irish CATHOLIC associations flourishing from *c.* 1820 to 1870, and at their peak *c.* 1835–1855. Ribbonism began in ULSTER to defend Catholics against ORANGEMEN, but spread south and by the 1830s was essentially agrarian; but its character and methods varied somewhat from district to district. It was basically a movement of the lower classes concerned with sporadic acts of outrage and took the place of the Whitefeet, MOLLY MAGUIRES, TERRY ALTS, etc. The name arose from the green ribbon worn as a badge.

Rice. The custom of throwing rice after a bride comes from India, rice being, with the Hindus, an emblem of fecundity. The bridegroom throws three handfuls over the bride, and the bride does the same over the bridegroom. *Cp.* MARRIAGE KNOT.

Rice Christians. Converts to Christianity for worldly benefits, such as a supply of rice to Indians. Profession of Christianity born of gain, not faith.

Rice-paper. *See* MISNOMERS.

Richard Roe. *See* DOE.

Richmond. Another Richmond in the field. Said when another unexpected adversary turns up. The reference is to SHAKESPEARE'S *Richard III*, V, iv, where the king, speaking of Henry of Richmond (afterwards Henry VII), says:

> I think there be six Richmonds in the field;
> Five have I slain to-day, instead of him.

Rick Mould. Fetching the rick mould.
An old catch played during the hay harvest. The GREENHORN was sent to borrow a rick-mould with strict injunctions not to drop it. Something very heavy was put in a sack and hoisted on to his back; when he had carried it carefully in the hot sun to the hayfield he was laughed at for his pains. *Cp.* ELBOW GREASE; PIGEON'S MILK.

Ricochet (rik′ ō shā). The bound of a bullet or other projectile after striking, the skipping of a flung stone over water ("DUCKS AND DRAKES"); hence applied to anything repeated again and again. Marshal Vauban introduced ricochet firing at Philipsburg in 1688.
Ricochet words. *See* REDUPLICATED.

Riddle. Josephus relates how Hiram, King of Tyre, and SOLOMON once had a contest in riddles, when Solomon won a large sum of money, but subsequently lost it to Abdemon, one of Hiram's subjects.

Plutarch says that HOMER died of chagrin because he could not solve a certain riddle. *See* SPHINX.
A riddle of claret. Thirteen bottles, a MAGNUM and twelve quarts; said to be so called because in certain old golf clubs, magistrates invited to the celebration dinner presented the club with this amount, sending it in a *riddle* or sieve.
Riddle me, riddle me ree. Expound my riddle rightly.

Ride. Riding. In Cornwall a "riding" was a practice similar to the SKIMMINGTON, designed to shame and publicize those guilty of marital infidelity. Two people, representing the offenders, were driven through the streets in a cart pulled by a donkey with a suitable accompanying din.

The three historic divisions of Yorkshire called **ridings**, because each formed a third part of the country, derive from the Danish occupation. Originally *thriding*; the initial *th-* of the word being lost through the amalgamation with *east*, *west*, or *north*. The divisions of Tipperary are (and those of Lincolnshire formerly were) also called ridings.
Riding the marches. *See* BOUNDS, BEATING THE.
To ride and tie. Said of a couple of tra-

vellers with only one horse between them. One rides on ahead and then ties the horse up and walks on, the other takes his turn on the horse when he has reached it.
To ride backwards up Holborn Hill. *See under* HOLBORN.
To ride for a fall. To proceed with one's business recklessly, usually regardless of the consequences; almost to invite trouble by thoughtless or reckless actions.
To ride roughshod. *See under* ROUGH.
To take for a ride. "To take for a trot", to pull someone's leg; to make the butt of a joke; but it has also become a gangster EUPHEMISM for murder. The victim is induced or forced into a vehicle and murdered in the course of the ride. Such methods were used by the NAZI régime in Germany.

Rider of the Shires, The. William Cobbett (1762–1835), the warm-hearted countryman and radical journalist, has been so designated. His journeys on horseback through many of the counties of England are described in his *Rural Rides*, which were written after days in the saddle.

Ridgeback. A native-born Rhodesian of white stock; probably from the native ridge-backed hunting dog, as a Britisher is sometimes similarly termed a "British BULLDOG". *See* RHODESIA.

Ridiculous. There is but one step from the sublime to the ridiculous. In his *Age of Reason* (1794), Pt. II, *note*, Tom Paine said, "The sublime and the ridiculous are often so nearly related that it is difficult to class them separately. One step above the sublime makes the ridiculous, and one step above the ridiculous makes the sublime again."

NAPOLEON, who was a great admirer of Tom Paine, used to say, "*Du sublime au ridicule il n'y a qu'un pas.*"

Ridotto (Ital.). A social assembly; a gathering for music and dancing (*cp.* Fr. *redoute*). In music, "reduced" from the full score, *i.e.* arranged for a smaller group of performers. It is ultimately from Lat. *reducere*, to bring back, reduce.

Riff-Raff. Sweepings, refuse; the offscourings of society, the rabble. The old

French term was *rif et raf*, whence the phrase *Il n'a laissé ni rif ni raf* (he has left nothing behind him). "Raff" may be Swed. *rafs*, sweepings, rubbish, etc.

Rift in the lute. A rift is a split or crack, hence a defect betokening the beginning of disharmony or incipient dissension.

Rig. A hoax or dodge; hence a swindle, and the phrase **to rig the market,** to arrange prices by underhand methods in order to make a profit.

To run the rig. To have a bit of fun, or indulge in practical jokes.

> He little thought when he set out
> Of running such a rig.
> COWPER: *John Gilpin*.

Rigadoon. A lively dance for two people, said to have been invented towards the close of the 17th century by a dancing-master of Marseilles called Rigaud.

Right. In politics the right is the CONSERVATIVE side. *See* LEFT.

Petition of Right (1628). A document presented by PARLIAMENT to CHARLES I which eventually gained his assent. It forbade the raising of gifts, loans, BENEVOLENCES and taxes without parliamentary consent and forbade arbitrary imprisonment, compulsory billeting of soldiers and sailors and the issue of commissions of martial law.

In one's right mind. Sane; in a normal state after mental excitement. The phrase comes from *Mark* v, 15:

> And they ... see him that was possessed with the devil, and had the legion, sitting and clothed, and in his right mind.

It'll all come right in the end. The cry of the optimist when things go wrong.

Miner's right. The Australian term for a licence to dig for GOLD.

Right as a trivet. Quite right; in an excellent state. The trivet was originally a three-legged stand—a tripod—and the allusion is to it standing firmly on its three legs.

Right foot foremost. It is considered unlucky to enter a house, or even a room, on the left foot, and in ancient ROME a boy was stationed at the door of a wealthy man's home to caution visitors not to cross the threshold with the left foot.

Right-hand man. An invaluable or chief assistant, as indispensable as one's right hand. A very old expression.

Right Honourable. *See under* HONOURABLE.

Right now. At this very moment. Immediately.

Righto! or Right ho! All right, a colloquial form of cheerful assent; *right you are* is a similar exclamation.

Right of way. The right of passing through the land of another. A highway is a public right. A private right is either customary or an easement (a legal right for the benefit of an adjoining owner). Rights of way may be for special purposes as an agricultural way, a way to church, a footway, a carriage way, etc.

To do one right. To be perfectly fair to him, to do him justice.

> King Charles, and who'll do him right now?
> BROWNING: *Cavalier Tunes*, II (*Give a Rouse*).

In Elizabethan literature the phrase is very common, and meant to answer when one's health had been drunk.

> *Falstaff* [To *Silence*, who drinks a bumper]: Why, now you have done me right.
> SHAKESPEARE: *Henry IV, Pt. II*, V, iii.

To send one to the right about. To clear him off, send him packing.

Rights. Declaration of Rights. An instrument submitted to William and Mary, after the GLORIOUS REVOLUTION, and accepted by them (13 February 1689). It sought to remove the specific grievances which arose from the arbitrary acts of James II such as the use of the dispensing and suspending power, the maintenance of a standing army in time of peace, taxation without parliamentary consent, freedom of elections, etc. The Declaration, together with a settlement of the succession, etc., was passed into law (October) as the **Bill of Rights.** It emphasized the importance of PARLIAMENT in the constitution which no king subsequently dared to question. *See also* RIGHTS OF MAN.

The Rights of Man. According to political philosophers of the 17th and 18th centuries, certain inalienable human rights—as stated by Locke—the right to life, liberty, and property. The social contract theorists also included the right to resistance from tyranny. Such rights were formally embodied in the French DECLARATION OF THE RIGHTS OF MAN and a *Declaration of Rights* was drawn up by the First American Continental Congress in 1774. The American Declaration of Independence, 1776, says:

> We hold these truths to be self-evident, that all men are created equal, that they are endowed by their Creator with certain inalienable Rights, that among these are Life, Liberty, and the pursuit of happiness.

Mazzini, the Italian republican idealist, preached a less popular doctrine:

> But I know, and you who are good and unspoiled by false doctrine and riches will understand before long, that every *right* you have can only spring from a *duty* fulfilled.
>
> *The Duties of Man (To the Italian Working Class).*

Declaration of the Rights of Man. A manifesto of the French National Assembly (August 1789) embodying the "principles" of the revolution. Thus, all citizens are born equal and are equal in the eyes of the law, with rights of liberty, property, and security, and the right to resist tyranny; the nation is sovereign and laws are the expression of the general will; every citizen has the right to freedom of opinion, speech, writing, etc. These rights were not, of course, honoured in practice, as the REIGN OF TERROR was to make manifest.

Universal Declaration of Human Rights. A document adopted by the General Assembly of the UNITED NATIONS in 1948 setting forth basic rights and fundamental freedoms to which all are entitled. They include the right to life, liberty, freedom from servitude, fair trial, marriage, ownership of property, freedom of thought and conscience, freedom of expression; the right to vote, work, education, etc.

To put things to rights. To tidy up, to put everything in its proper place.

Rigmarole (rig′ mȧ rōl). A rambling disconnected account, an unending yarn; said to be a popular corruption of RAGMAN ROLL. It is recorded from the early 18th century.

> You never heard such a rigmarole ... He said he thought he was certain he had seen somebody by the rick and it was

Tom Bakewell who was the only man he knew who had a grudge against Farmer Blaize and if the object had been a little bigger he would not mind swearing to Tom and would swear to him for he was dead certain it was Tom only what he saw looked smaller and it was pitch dark at the time ... etc.
> MEREDITH: *Richard Feverel*, ch. ix.

Rig-veda. *See* VEDAS.

Rile. A dialect word, common in Norfolk and other parts, for stirring up water to make it muddy; hence, to excite or disturb, and hence the colloquial meaning, to vex, annoy, make angry. It comes from O.Fr. *roillier*, to roll or flow (of a stream).

Rimmon. The Babylonian god who presided over storms. Milton identifies him with one of the fallen angels:

> Him followed Rimmon, whose delight-
> ful seat
> Was fair Damascus, on the fertile bank
> Of Abbana and Pharphar, lucid streams.
> *Paradise Lost*, Bk. I, 467.

To bow down in the house of Rimmon. To palter with one's conscience; to do that which one knows to be wrong so as to save one's face. The allusion is to Naaman obtaining Elisha's permission to worship the god when with his master (II *Kings* v, 18).

Rinaldo. One of the great heroes of mediæval romance (also called Renault of Montauban, Regnault, etc.), a PALADIN of CHARLEMAGNE, cousin of ORLANDO, and one of the four sons of AYMON. He was the owner of the famous horse BAYARDO, and is always painted with the characteristics of a borderer—valiant, ingenious, rapacious, and unscrupulous.

Tasso's romantic epic *Rinaldo* appeared in 1562 and his masterpiece JERUSALEM DELIVERED, in which Rinaldo was the ACHILLES of the Christian army, despising GOLD and power but craving renown, was published (without permission) in 1581.

In Ariosto's ORLANDO FURIOSO (1516), Rinaldo appears as the son of the fourth Marquis d'Este, Lord of Mount Auban or Albano, eldest son of Amon or Aymon, nephew of Charlemagne. He was the rival of his cousin Orlando.

Ring. A ring worn on the forefinger is supposed to indicate a haughty, bold, and overbearing spirit; on the long finger, prudence, dignity and discretion; on the marriage finger, love and affection; on the little finger, a masterful spirit. *Cp*. WEDDING FINGER.

The wearing of a wedding-ring by married women is now universal in Christian countries, but the custom varies greatly in detail. It appears to have originated in the betrothal rings given as secular pledges by the Romans. Until the end of the 16th century it was the custom in England to wear the wedding-ring on the third finger of the right hand.

As the forefinger was held to be symbolical of the HOLY GHOST, priests used to wear their ring on this in token of their spiritual office. Episcopal rings, worn by CARDINALS, BISHOPS and abbots, are of GOLD with a stone— cardinals a sapphire, bishops and abbots an AMETHYST— and are worn upon the third finger of the right hand. The POPE wears a similar ring, usually with a cameo, EMERALD, or RUBY. A plain gold ring is put upon the third finger of the right hand of a nun on her profession.

In ancient ROME, the free Roman had the right to wear an iron ring, only senators, chief magistrates and in later times KNIGHTS (*equites*), enjoyed the *jus annuli aurei*, the right to wear a ring of gold. The emperors conferred this upon whom they pleased and Justinian extended the privilege to all Roman citizens. *See also* CRAMP-RINGS.

Rings noted in Fable and Legend

Agramant's Ring. This enchanted ring was given by Agramant to the dwarf Brunello from whom it was stolen by BRADAMANT and given to Melissa. It passed successively into the hands of ROGERO and ANGELICA, who carried it in her mouth (ORLANDO FURIOSO).

The Ring of Amasis. See AMASIS.

Cambalo's Ring. See CAMBALO.

The Doge's Ring. See BRIDE OF THE SEA.

The Ring of Edward the Confessor. It is said that Edward the Confessor was once asked for alms by an old man, and gave him his ring. In time some English pilgrims went to the HOLY LAND and

happened to meet the same old man, who told them he was JOHN THE EVANGELIST, and gave them the identical ring to take to "Saint" Edward. It was preserved in Westminster Abbey.

The Ring of Gyges. See GYGES.

The Ring of Innocent. On 29 May 1205, Innocent III sent John, King of England, four gold rings set with precious stones, and explained that the *rotundity* signifies *eternity*—"remember we are passing through time into eternity"; the *number* signifies the *four* virtues which make up constancy of mind—*viz.* justice, fortitude, prudence, and temperance; the *material* signifies "the wisdom from on high", which is as gold purified in the fire; the *green* emerald is emblem of "faith", the *blue* sapphire of "hope", the *red* garnet of "charity", and the *bright* topaz of "good works" (Rymer: *Fœdera*, vol. I, 139).

Luned's Ring rendered the wearer invisible. Luned gave it to Owain, one of King ARTHUR'S knights.

> Take this ring and put it on thy finger, and put this stone in thy hand, and close thy fist over the stone; and so long as thou conceal it, it will conceal thee too.
> MABINOGION (*Lady of the Fountain*).

The Ring of Ogier was given him by MORGAN LE FAY. It removed all infirmities, and restored the aged to youth again.

Otnit's Ring of Invisibility belonged to Otnit, King of Lombardy, and was given to him by the queen-mother when he went to gain the soldan's daughter in marriage. The stone had the virtue of directing the wearer the right road to take in travelling (the HELDENBUCH).

Polycrates' Ring. See AMASIS.

Reynard's Wonderful Ring. This ring, which existed only in the brain of REYNARD, had a stone of three colours— red, white, and green. The red made the night as clear as day; the white cured all manner of diseases; and the green rendered the wearer invisible (*Reynard the Fox*, ch. xii).

Solomon's Ring enabled the monarch to overcome all opponents, to transport himself to the celestial spheres where he learned the secrets of the universe. It also sealed up the refractory JINN in jars and cast them into the Red Sea, and conferred upon the wearer the ability to understand and converse with the animal world.

The talking ring in Basque legend was given by Tartaro, the Basque CYCLOPS, to a girl whom he wished to marry. Immediately she put it on, it kept incessantly saying, "You there, and I here." In order to get rid of the nuisance, the girl cut off her finger and threw it and the ring into a pond. The story is given in Campbell's *Popular Tales of the West Highlands*, and in Grimm's *Tales* (*The Robber and His Sons*).

Ring a ring o'roses. *See* BLACK DEATH.

Ring of the Fisherman. *See* FISHERMAN'S RING *under* FISH.

Ring of the Nibelung, or **Ring Cycle.** The Festival cycle by Wagner first performed at Bayreuth in 1876. Its constituent parts are *Das Rheingold*, 1869; *Die Walküre*, 1870; *Siegfried*, 1876; *Götterdämmerung* (The Dusk of the Gods), 1876. *Cp.* NIBELUNGENLIED.

The Ring. Bookmakers or pugilists collectively, and the sports they represent, because the spectators at a prize-fight or race form a ring around the competitors. Specifically, *The Ring* was the hall for prize-fights in the Blackfriars Road.

In Australia in the early 19th century *The Ring* denoted a group of the most hard-bitten convicts at the Norfolk Island penitentiary, who exercised an EVIL influence over their fellows. This use antedates by some 30 years that of the U.S.A.

Also applied to unscrupulous dealers, as a group, who FORM, or MAKE A RING. Wagner's RING OF THE NIBELUNG is often called *The Ring*.

A ring of bells. A set of bells from 5 to 12 in number for CHANGE ringing.

It has the true ring. It has intrinsic merit; it bears the mark of real talent. A metaphor taken from the custom of judging genuine coin by its "ring" or sound.

Ring off. To end a telephone call.

Ring up. To make a telephone call.

To ring up the curtain. In the theatre, to order the curtain to be raised or opened; the signal originally being the ringing of a bell. Metaphorically, to initiate or inaugurate an enterprise, etc. Similarly **to ring down the curtain** is to terminate or bring to an end.

The Ringing island. Britain was once so called from the excellence of its church bellringers at CHANGE ringing.

Ringing the changes. *See* CHANGE.

Figuratively the phrase usually means to try many different ways of doing a thing for the sake of variety, but it also means to swindle someone over a transaction by confusing him in the changing of money. For example: a man bought a glass of beer for 1s. 4d. and gave the barmaid a ten-shilling note, receiving 8s. 8d. in change. "Oh!" said the man, "give me the note back, I have such a lot of change". He offered ten shillings in silver when handed the note, but before pocketing it put note and silver together and said: "There, let's have a QUID instead of the note and silver." If the barmaid was not quick enough to spot the trick she lost ten shillings by the deal.

That rings a bell. That recalls something to mind, that stirs a recollection.

To form, or **make a ring.** To act together in order to control the price of a given article, usually to enhance the price and ensure greater profit. Dealers at auctions sometimes form such a ring and do not outbid each other, thus ensuring articles being knocked down cheaply. After the auction, the dealers' ring then organizes a sale or distribution among its members.

To make rings, or **run rings round one.** To defeat him completely in some sport or competition, etc.; to outclass him easily. In Australia the fastest shearer in the shed is called a *ringer* as he is "the man who runs rings round the rest".

Ringer. The term *ringer* is applied on the racecourse, running-track, etc., to a runner who is entered for a race by means of a false return with regard to the detailed conditions of entry; to a person or thing which closely resembles another: hence, *dead ringer* (U.S.A.), for an exact resemblance.

Ringleader. The moving spirit, the chief in some enterprise, especially of a mutinous character; from the old phrase to *lead the ring*, the *ring* being a group of associated persons.

Riot. To read the Riot Act. Legally, when 12 or more persons are committing a riot it is the duty of the magistrates to command them to disperse in the Queen's name and anyone who obstructs or continues to riot for one hour afterwards is guilty of a felony. Such a proclamation is read in accordance with the Riot Act of 1715. Figuratively to *read the riot act* is to check noise, commotion and misbehaviour of children and others by vigorous and forceful protests, to threaten them with the consequences of disobedience, etc.

To run riot. To act without restraint or control; to act in a very disorderly way. The phrase was originally used of hounds which had lost the scent.

Rip. A regular rip. A thorough roisterer, rake, or debauchee; rip seems to be a perversion of *rep*, rep-robate. *Cp.* DEMI-REP.

> Some forlorn, worn-out old rips, broken-kneed and broken-winded.
> GEORGE DU MAURIER: *Peter Ibbetson*, Pt. VI.

Let her rip. Let it (an engine, etc.) go as fast as it can.

Rip Van Winkle. The famous character whose fabled adventures are recounted in Washington Irving's *Sketch Book* (1819). The tale is represented as being found among the papers of one Diedrich Knickerbocker, a Dutch antiquary of New York. Rip Van Winkle was a happy-go-lucky, hen-pecked husband of a "well-oiled" disposition. During a ramble on the Kaatskill Mountains he met some quaint personages dressed in the old Flemish style playing at ninepins. Unobserved he took a draught of their Hollands and soon fell asleep. He awoke to find himself alone, even his dog had disappeared and his firearm was heavy with rust. He made his way homewards in trepidation only to find his house deserted and none of his former companions about. He had apparently slept for 20 years and after establishing his identity became a village patriarch. He had set out as a subject of George III and returned as a free citizen of the United States!

Rise. On the rise. Going up in price; becoming more valuable, especially of stocks and shares.

To get a rise. To have an increase in salary or wages.

To take the rise out of one. To raise a laugh at his expense, to make him a butt. Hotten says this is a metaphor from fly-fishing; the fish *rise* to the fly, and are caught. In the U.S.A. a pay increase is called a *raise*, and to *get a raise* out of someone is to call forth the desired reaction or response.

Rising in the air. *See* LEVITATION.

Risorgimento (ri sôr ji men' tō) (Ital., resurrection). The name given to the 19th-century movement for Italian liberation. It can be said to have had its roots in the enlightened despotism of the 18th century and the influence of the French Revolution and French occupation. The CARBONARI in Naples and Sicily, the *Federati* in Sardinia, and Mazzini's YOUNG ITALY all played a part, and the *Risorgimento* was strengthened by the revolutionary events of 1848–1849. Its political aims were largely achieved by Cavour in the events of 1859–1860 and Garibaldi's radicalism made a further contribution, but the idealism of the *Risorgimento* was submerged by Cavour's realistic policies.

Ritzy. In colloquial usage, fashionable and luxurious. After the standards of the Ritz-Carlton Hotel, New York, the Ritz Hotel, Paris, and the Ritz Hotel, Piccadilly, London, which became identified with wealth. The latter hotel was established by the Swiss hotelier, César Ritz, in 1906. Hence "to dine at the Ritz" is the ultimate luxury in dining out.

Rivals. Originally "persons dwelling on opposite sides of a river" (Lat. *rivalis*, a river-man). Cælius says there was no more fruitful source of contention than river-right, both with beasts and men, not only for the benefit of its waters, but also because rivers are natural boundaries.

River. To be sent up the river. In American colloquial usage, to be sent to prison; from the fact that Sing Sing, one of the most widely known prisons, is up the Hudson River from New York.

To sell down the river. To let down,

to betray. From the days when American owners sold domestic slaves to plantation owners lower down the Mississippi, where harsh conditions often prevailed.

Road. All roads lead to Rome. All efforts of thought converge in a common centre. As from the centre of the Roman world roads radiated to every part of the Empire, so any road, if followed to its source, must lead to the great capital city, ROME.

Gentlemen of the road, or **knights of the road.** Highwaymen. In parts of North America a highwayman was called a *road agent* and the term is still sometimes applied to bandits who hold up trains, motorcars, etc.

One for the road. One last drink before departing, a popular call at the end of a night ON THE SPREE.

On the road. Progressing towards; as, "on the road to recovery"; said also of actors on tour and of commercial travellers.

Road hog. *See* HOG.

Roman roads. *See under* ROMAN.

The rule of the road.

> The rule of the road is a paradox quite,
> In riding or driving along;
> If you go to the left you are sure to go right,
> If you go to the right you go wrong.

This is still the rule in Great Britain, and IRELAND. In all other European countries and in the U.S.A. traffic keeps to the right.

To take to the road. To become a highwayman or a tramp.

Roadhouse. An inn, hotel, etc., by the roadside, usually at some distance outside a town, where parties can go out by car for meals, dancing, etc.

Roads or **Roadstead,** as "Yarmouth Roads", a place where ships can safely ride at anchor. *Road,* O.E. *rad*, comes from *ridan*, to ride.

Roan Barbary. *See* BARBARY ROAN.

Roar. Roarer. A broken-winded horse is so called from the noise it makes in breathing.

Bull-roarer. *See under* BULL.

He drives a roaring trade. He does a great business.

Roaring boys. The riotous blades of Ben Jonson's time, whose delight it was to annoy quiet folk. At one time their pranks in London were carried on to an alarming extent.

The Roaring Forties. *See under* FORTY.

The roaring game. Curling, so called because the Scots when playing or watching support their side with noisy cheering, and because the stones (made of granite or whinstone and shaped like a Dutch cheese) roar as they traverse the ice.

Roaring Meg. *See under* MEG.

Roast. To roast a person is to banter him unmercifully; also to give him a dressing-down.

To rule the roast. To have the chief direction, to be paramount. The phrase was common in the 16th century apparently deriving from the master of the household, as head of the table, carving the joint. It has been suggested that the expression is really *to rule the roost* (the common form nowadays) from the cock deciding which hen is to roost near him; but "roost" is more likely a corruption of "roast", the old spelling for which was "rost", or "roste". In Thomas Heywood's *History of Women* (*c.*1630) we read of "her that ruled the roast in the kitchen". *Cp.* TROUSERS.

Rob. To rob Peter to pay Paul. To take away from one person in order to give to another; or merely to shift a debt—to pay it off by incurring another one. Fable has it that the phrase alludes to the fact that on 17 December 1540 the abbey church of St. Peter, Westminster, was advanced to the dignity of a cathedral by LETTERS PATENT (*see under* PATENT); but ten years later was joined to the diocese of London, and many of its estates appropriated to the repairs of St. Paul's Cathedral. But it was a common saying long before and was used by Wyclif about 1380:

> How should God approve that you rob Peter, and give this robbery to Paul in the name of Christ.
>
> *Select Works*, III, 174.

Rob Roy (Robert the Red). Nickname of Robert M'Gregor (1671–1734), Scottish outlaw and FREEBOOTER, on account of his red hair. He assumed the name of Campbell about 1716, and was protected by the Duke of Argyll. He may be termed the ROBIN HOOD of Scotland.

> Rather beneath the middle size than above it, his limbs were formed upon the very strongest model that is consistent with agility ... Two points in his person interfered with the rules of symmetry:—his shoulders were so broad ... as ... gave him something the air of being too square in respect to his stature; and his arms, tough, round, sinewy, and strong, were so very long as to be rather a deformity.
>
> SCOTT: *Rob Roy*, ch. xxiii.

Robert. A name sometimes applied to a policeman, "the man in blue", in allusion to Sir Robert Peel. *Cp.* BOBBY; PEELER.

Highwaymen and bandits are called *Robert's men* from ROBIN HOOD.

King Robert of Sicily. A metrical romance taken from the *Story of the Emperor Jovinian* in the GESTA ROMANORUM, and borrowed from the TALMUD. It is also found in the ARABIAN NIGHTS, the Turkish *Tutinameh*, the Sanskrit *Panchatantra*, and was utilized by Longfellow in his *Tales of a Wayside Inn*.

Robert the Devil, or **Le Diable.** Robert, sixth Duke of Normandy (1028–1035), father of WILLIAM THE CONQUEROR. He supported the English athelings against Canute, and made the PILGRIMAGE to JERUSALEM. He got his name for his daring and cruelty. He is also called *Robert the Magnificent*. A Norman tradition is that his wandering ghost will not be allowed to rest till the Day of Judgment (*see* JUDGMENT, THE LAST) and he became a subject of legend and romance. Meyerbeer's opera *Roberto il Diavolo* (1831) portrays the struggle between the virtue inherited from his mother and the vice imparted by his father.

Robin. A diminutive of Robert.

Ragged Robin. *See under* RAG.

Robin Goodfellow. Another name for PUCK. His character and activities are given fully in the ballad of this name in PERCY'S RELIQUES, as exemplified in the following verse:

> When house or harth doth sluttish lye,
> I pinch the maidens black and blue;
> The bed-clothes from the bedd pull I,
> And lay them naked all to view.

> 'Twixt sleepe and wake,
> I do them take,
> And on the key-cold floor them throw.
> If out they cry
> Then forth I fly,
> And loudly laugh out, ho, ho, ho!

Robin Hood. This traditional outlaw and hero of English ballads is mentioned by Langland in the *Vision of Piers Plowman*, Bk. V, 402 (1377), and there are several mid-15th-century poems about him. The first published collection of ballads about him, *A Lytell Geste of Robyn Hode* was printed by Wynkyn de Worde (*c.* 1489). The earliest tales were set in Barnsdale, Yorkshire, or in Sherwood Forest, Nottinghamshire, and his adventures have been variously assigned from the reign of Richard I (1189–1199) to that of Edward II (1307–1327). One popular legend was that he was the outlawed Earl of Huntingdon, Robert Fitzooth, in disguise. The name may have been that of an actual outlaw around whose name the legends accumulated. He suffered no woman to be molested and he is credited with robbing the rich and helping the poor.

Robin's earlier companions included LITTLE JOHN, Will Scarlet, MUCH, the miller's son, Allen-a-dale, George-a-Green (*see* AS GOOD AS GEORGE-A-GREEN *under* GEORGE), and later FRIAR TUCK and MAID MARIAN.

The stories formed the basis of early dramatic representations and were later amalgamated with the MORRIS dancers' MAY-DAY revels. *Cp.* TWM SHON CATTI.

> Robyn was a proude outlawe,
> Whyles he walked on grounde,
> So curteyse an outlawe as he was one
> Was never none yfounde.
> *A Lytell Geste of Robyn Hode*, I.

Bow and arrow of Robin Hood. The traditional bow and arrow of Robin Hood are religiously preserved at Kirklees Hall, Yorkshire, the seat of the Armytage family; and the site of his grave is pointed out in the park.

Death of Robin Hood. He was reputedly bled to death treacherously by a nun, instigated to the foul deed by his kinswoman, the prioress of Kirklees, near Halifax (1247).

Many talk of Robin Hood who never shot with his bow. Many brag of deeds in which they took no part.

Robin Hood and Guy of Gisborne. A ballad given in PERCY'S RELIQUES. ROBIN HOOD and LITTLE JOHN, having had a tiff, part company, when Little John falls into the hands of the SHERIFF of Nottingham, who binds him to a tree. Meanwhile Robin Hood meets with Guy of Gisborne, sworn to slay the "bold forrester". The two bowmen struggle together, but Guy is slain and Robin Hood rides till he comes to the tree where Little John is bound. The sheriff mistakes him for Guy of Gisborne, and gives him charge of the prisoner. Robin cuts the cord, hands Guy's bow to Little John, and the two soon put to flight the sheriff and his men.

A Robin Hood wind. A thaw-wind which is particularly raw and piercing being saturated with moisture scarcely above freezing-point. Tradition runs that ROBIN HOOD used to say he could bear any cold except that which a thaw-wind brought with it.

Robin Hood's Bay, between Whitby and Scarborough, Yorkshire, is mentioned by Leland. Robin Hood is supposed to have kept fishing boats there to put to sea when pursued by the soldiery. He also went fishing in them in the summer.

Robin Hood's Larder. *See under* OAK.

To go round Robin Hood's barn. To arrive at the right conclusion by circuitous methods.

To sell Robin Hood's pennyworth is to sell things at half their value. As Robin Hood stole his wares he sold them under their intrinsic value, for what he could get.

Robin Redbreast. The tradition is that when Our Lord was on His way to CALVARY, a robin picked a thorn out of his crown, and the blood which issued from the wound falling on the bird dyed its breast red.

Another fable is that the robin covers the dead with leaves; this is referred to in Webster's *White Devil*, V, i (1612):

> Call for the robin-red-breast and the wren,
> Since o'er shady groves they hover,
> And with leaves and flowers do cover
> The friendless bodies of unburied men.

When so covering Christ's body, their white breasts touched his blood and they have ever since been red.

And in the ballad of the *Children in the Wood* (PERCY'S RELIQUES):

> No burial this pretty pair
> Of any man receives,
> Till Robin-red-breast piously
> Did cover them with leaves.

Robin and Makyne. An ancient Scottish pastoral given in PERCY'S RELIQUES. Robin is a shepherd for whom Makyne sighs. She goes to him and tells her love, but Robin turns a deaf ear, and the damsel goes home to weep. After a time the tables are turned, and Robin goes to Makyne to plead for her heart and hand; but the damsel replies:

> The man that will not when he may,
> Sall have nocht when he wald.

A round robin. *See under* ROUND.

Poor Robin's Almanack. *See under* POOR.

Robinson Crusoe. The ever-popular castaway of Defoe's novel of this name (1719) was suggested by the adventures of Alexander SELKIRK. Crusoe's Island was not Juan Fernandez in the South Pacific where Selkirk was put ashore, but an imaginary island near Trinidad; Defoe's description most nearly fits Tobago.

Robinson, Before you can say Jack. *See under* JACK.

Robot (rō′ bot) (Czech *robota*, forced labour). An automaton with semi-human powers and intelligence. From this the term is often extended to mean a person who works automatically without employing initiative. The name comes from the mechanical creatures in Karel Capek's play *R.U.R.* (Rossum's Universal Robots), which was successfully produced in London in 1923. The word was also applied to various forms of "flying bombs", "Buzz-bombs" or "Doodle-bugs" sent against England by the Germans in World War II.

Roc. In Arabian legend, a fabulous white bird of enormous size and such strength that it can "truss elephants in its talons", and carry them to its mountain nest, where it devours them. It is described in the ARABIAN NIGHTS (SINBAD THE SAILOR).

Roch, or **Roque, St.** (rōsh, rōk). Patron of those afflicted with the plague, because "he worked miracles on the plague-stricken, while he was himself smitten with the same judgment". He is depicted in a pilgrim's habit, lifting his dress, to display a plague-spot on his thigh, which an ANGEL is touching that he may cure it. Sometimes he is accompanied by a DOG bringing bread in his mouth, in allusion to the legend that a hound brought him bread daily while he was perishing of pestilence in a forest.

His feast day, 16 August, was formerly celebrated in England as a general HARVEST-HOME, and styled "the great August festival".

St. Roch et son chien (Fr., St. Roch and his dog). Inseparables; DARBY AND JOAN.

Rochdale Pioneers, The. The name given to the sponsors of the first financially successful co-operative store. In December 1844, a group of 28 weavers calling themselves the Equitable Pioneers opened their store in Toad Lane, Rochdale, Lancashire, with a capital of £28. They sold their wares at market prices and gave a dividend to purchasers in proportion to their expenditure. It was on this device that the co-operative movement grew.

Roche (rōsh). **Sir Boyle Roche's bird.** Sir Boyle Roche (1743–1807) was an Irish M.P., noted for his "BULLS". On one occasion in the House, quoting from Jevon's play, *The Devil of a Wife*, he said, "Mr. Speaker, it is impossible I could have been in two places at once, unless I were a bird." The phrase is probably of earlier origin.

Rock. A symbol of solidity and strength.

> Thou art Peter, and upon this rock I will build my church; and the gates of hell shall not prevail against it.
> *Matt.* xvi. 18.

It is the Lat. *petra*, rock, from which the name Peter is derived. *Cp.* ROCK OF AGES, below.

Gibraltar is commonly known as "The Rock" (*see* ROCK ENGLISH *below*).

Alcatraz Island in San Francisco Bay, the site of the former American prison for the most dangerous criminals, consists of 12 acres of solid rock and became known as "The Rock". It is now part of a recreation area.

In U.S.A. thieves' slang a *rock* is a diamond or other precious stone. *See also* ROCK DAY; ROCK 'N' ROLL.

A house builded upon rock. Typical of a person or a thing whose foundations are sure. The allusion is to *Matt.* vii, 24.

On the rocks. "Stony broke", having no money; a phrase from seafaring: a ship that is on the rocks will very quickly go to pieces unless she can be floated off.

People of the Rock. The inhabitants of Hejaz of ARABIA Petræa.

Rock Day. "St. Distaff's Day" (*see under* DISTAFF); *Cp.* PLOUGH MONDAY.

Rock Dove. The London Pigeon is a semi-domesticated Rock Dove. The wild *rock* is confined to cliffs, hence the name. It can be distinguished from the STOCK DOVE in that it has no black wing tips.

Rock English. The mixed patois of Spanish and English spoken by the native inhabitants of Gibraltar—colloquially referred to as *Rock Lizards* or ROCK SCORPIONS. Similarly, Malta or Mediterranean fever, which is common in Gibraltar, is also called *Rock fever*.

Rock of Ages. Christ, as the unshakeable and eternal foundation. In a marginal note to *Is.* xxvi, 4, the words "everlasting strength" are stated to be in Hebrew "rock of ages". In one of his hymns Wesley wrote (1788)—

> Hell in vain against us rages;
> Can it shock
> Christ the Rock
> Of eternal Ages?
> *Praise by all to Christ is given.*

Southey also has:

> These waters are the well of life and lo!
> The Rock of Ages, there, from whence they flow.
> *Pilgrimage to Waterloo*, Pt. II, iii.

The well-known hymn *Rock of ages, cleft for me*, was written by Augustus Montague TOPLADY (1740–1778) and first published in *The Gospel Magazine* (1775). One account says that he wrote it while seated by a great cleft of rock near Cheddar, Somerset; a more unlikely story is that the first verse was written on the ten of diamonds in the interval between two rubbers of WHIST at Bath.

It's like the Rock of Gibraltar. Said of something that is firmly fixed, solid and immovable; also sometimes applied to food that is hard and tough.

That is the rock you'll split on. That is the danger, or the more or less hidden or eventual difficulty. A phrase of nautical origin.

To rock the boat. To unsettle the stability of a situation; to create difficulties for one's associates, companions or partners.

Rock 'n' roll (Rock and Roll), or just *Rock*, was the "pop" music of the latter half of the 1950s, characterized by its swing or rhythm and the style of dancing that went with it. Its fans were called "rockers" and they belonged to the days of the *teddy boy* (*see* EDWARDIAN), before the advent of the Mods. *Cp*. MODS AND ROCKERS.

Rocking Stones. *See* LOGAN STONES.

Rocket. To give someone a rocket. To reprimand severely, "to blow him sky high".

Rococo (rō kō′ kō). A style in the fine and decorative arts, particularly characterized by motifs taken from shells, which developed in 18th-century France and spread to Germany, Austria and Spain. The name is from Fr. *rocaille*, rockwork, grotto work, as exemplified in the extravagances at VERSAILLES. At its best it was a lighter and more graceful development from Baroque as is seen in the furniture and architecture of France during the reign of Louis XV (1715–1774). At its worst, it was florid and ornate, hence the use of the word *rococo* to denote anything in art and literature that is pretentious and tasteless.

Rod. A rod in pickle. A scolding or punishment in store. Birch-rods used to be laid in brine to keep the twigs pliable.

> ... and therefore let everyone carry an even hand, and mind their hits, or else I would have them to know there are rods in pickle for them.
>
> CERVANTES: *Don Quixote*, ch. lxxi (Translation by Motteux).

Spare the rod and spoil the child. An old saying drawing attention to the folly of allowing childish faults to go unreproved; founded on *Prov*. xiii, 24, "He

that spareth his rod hateth his son; but he that loveth him chasteneth him betimes."

To kiss the rod. To submit to punishment or misfortune meekly and without murmuring.

To make a rod for one's own back. Doing something which will lead to trouble, difficulties or hardship for oneself in the future.

Rodeo (rō′ di ō, *or* rō dā′ ō) (Span. *rodear*, to go around). A contest or exhibition of skill among COWBOYS, a feature of the ROUND-UP. As a travelling show it was first introduced by BUFFALO BILL and depends for its popularity upon professional skill with the lasso, the riding of broncos and steers, etc.

Roderick, or **Rodrigo.** A Spanish hero round whom many legends have collected. He was the last of the Visigothic kings. He came to the throne in 710, and was routed, and probably slain, by the Moors under Tarik in 711. Southey took him as the hero of his *Roderick, the last of the Goths* (1814), where he appears as the son of Theodofred.

According to legend he violated Florinda, daughter of Count Julian of Ceuta, who called in the SARACENS by way of revenge. It is related that he survived to spend the rest of his life in penance and was eventually devoured by snakes until his sin was atoned for. It was also held that he would return in triumph to save his country.

Rodomontade. Bluster, brag, or a blustering and bragging speech; from Rodomont, the brave but braggart leader of the SARACENS in Boiardo's ORLANDO INNAMORATO and Ariosto's ORLANDO FURIOSO.

Roe, Richard. *See* DOE.

Rogation Days. Rogation Sunday is the SUNDAY before ASCENSION DAY, the Rogation days are the Monday, Tuesday, and Wednesday following Rogation Sunday. Rogation is the Latin equivalent of the Greek *litaneia*, supplication or litany (Lat. *rogatio*), and in the ROMAN CATHOLIC CHURCH on the three Rogation days "the Litany of the Saints" is appointed to be sung by the clergy and people in public procession.

The Rogation Days used to be called

Gang Days, from the custom of *ganging* round the country parishes to beat the BOUNDS at this time. Similarly the weed milkwort is called *Rogation* or *Gangflower* from the custom of decorating the pole carried on such occasions with these flowers.

Roger. The Jolly Roger. The black flag with skull and cross-bones, the pirate flag.

Sir Roger de Coverley. The simple, good, and lovable country squire created by Steele as the chief character in the club that was supposed to write for the *Spectator*, but essentially portrayed by Addison. Sir Roger de Coverley has left his name to a popular country dance which, he tells us, was invented by his great-grandfather. Coverley is intended for Cowley, near Oxford.

> As Sir Roger is landlord to the whole congregation, he keeps them in very good order, and will suffer no body to sleep in it besides himself.
> ADDISON: *A Sunday in the Country.*

Rogero, Ruggiero, or **Rizieri** (ro jâr' ō, rujâr' o, ritz i âr' i) of Risa (in Ariosto's ORLANDO FURIOSO), was brother of Marphisa, and son of Rogero and Galacella. His mother was slain by Agolant and his sons, and he was nursed by a lioness. He deserted from the Moorish army to CHARLEMAGNE, and was baptized. His marriage with BRADAMANTE, Charlemagne's niece, and election to the crown of Bulgaria conclude the poem.

Rogue. One of the "canting" words first used in the 16th century to describe sturdy beggars and vagrants (perhaps from some outstanding member of the class named Roger). There is a good description of them in Harman's *Caveat for Warening for Commen Corsetors, Vulgarely called Vagabones*, ch. iv. The expression *rogues and vagabonds* has since 1572 been applied in the Vagrancy Acts to all sorts of wandering, disorderly, or dissolute persons.

Rogue elephant. A vicious dangerous elephant that lives apart from the herd.

Rogue's badge. A race-horse or a hunter that becomes obstinate and refuses to do its work is known as a *rogue*, and the blinkers that it is made to wear are the *rogue's badge*.

Rogue's Latin. The same as thieves' Latin. *See under* LATIN.

Rogue's March. The tune played when an undesirable soldier was drummed out of his regiment; hence, an ignominious dismissal.

Roi Panade (Fr., King of Slops). Louis XVIII (1755, 1814–1824) was so nicknamed. Literally, panade is bread soup.

Roland, or (in Ital.) **Orlando.** The most famous of Charlemagne's PALADINS, called "the Christian THESEUS" and "the ACHILLES of the West". He was Count of Mans and knight of Blaives, and son of Duke Milo of Aiglant, his mother being Bertha, the sister of CHARLEMAGNE. Fable has it that he was eight feet high, and had an open countenance which invited confidence, but inspired respect. When Charlemagne was returning from his expedition against Pamplona and Saragossa the army fell into a natural trap at Roncesvalles, in the Pyrenees, and Roland, who commanded the rearguard, was slain with all the flower of the Frankish CHIVALRY (778).

His achievements are recorded in the Chronicle attributed to Turpin (d. 794), Archbishop of Rheims, which was not written till the 11th or 12th century. He is the hero of the SONG OF ROLAND (*see below*), Boiardo's ORLANDO INNAMORATO, and Ariosto's ORLANDO FURIOSO. He is also a principal character in Pulci's MORGANTE MAGGIORE and converts the giant Morgante to Christianity.

A Roland for an Oliver. A blow for a blow, TIT FOR TAT. The exploits of these two PALADINS are so similar that it is difficult to keep them distinct. What Roland did Oliver did, and what Oliver did Roland did. At length the two met in single combat, and fought for five consecutive days, but neither gained the least advantage. SHAKESPEARE alludes to the phrase: "England all Olivers and Rolands bred" (*Henry VI, Pt. I*, I, ii) and Edward Hall, the historian, almost a century before Shakespeare, writes:

> But to have a Roland to resist an Oliver, he sent solempne ambassadors to the King of Englande, offerying hym hys doughter in mariage.
> *Henry VI.*

Childe Roland. Youngest brother of

the "fair burd Helen" in the old Scottish ballad. Guided by MERLIN, he successfully undertook to bring his sister from Elfland, whither the fairies had carried her.

> Childe Roland to the dark tower came;
> His word was still "Fie, foh, fum,
> I smell the blood of a British man."
> SHAKESPEARE: *King Lear*, III, iv.

Browning's poem, *Child Roland to the Dark Tower Came*, is not connected, other than by the first line, with the old ballad.

Like the blast of Roland's horn. Roland had a wonderful ivory horn, named "Olivant", that he won from the giant Jutmundus. When he was attacked by the Saracens at Roncesvalles (Roncesvaux) he sounded it to give CHARLEMAGNE notice of his danger. At the third blast it cracked in two, but it was so loud that birds fell dead and the whole SARACEN army was panic-struck. Charlemagne heard the sound at St.-Jean-Pied-de-Port, and rushed to the rescue, but arrived too late.

Roland's sword. Duranda, Durindana or Durandal, etc., which was fabled to have once belonged to HECTOR, and which, like the horn, ROLAND won from the giant Jutmundus. It had in its hilt a thread from the Virgin Mary's cloak, a tooth of ST. PETER, one of ST. DENYS'S hairs, and a drop of St. Basil's blood. Legend relates that Roland, after he had received his death wound, strove to break Durandal on a rock to prevent it falling to the SARACENS; but it was unbreakable so he hurled it into a poisoned stream, where it remains for ever.

The Song (Chanson) of Roland. The 11th-century CHANSON DE GESTE ascribed to the Norman TROUVÈRE Théroulde or Turoldus, which tells the story of the death of ROLAND and all the PALADINS at Roncesvalles, and of CHARLEMAGNE's vengeance. When Charlemagne had been six years in Spain he sent GANELON on an embassy to Marsillus, the pagan king of Saragossa Ganelon, out of jealousy, betrayed to Marsillus the route which the Christian army designed to take on its way home, and the pagan king arrived at Roncesvalles just as Roland was conducting through the pass a rearguard of 20,000 men. He fought till 100,000 SARACENS lay slain, and only 50 of his own men survived, when another army of 50,000 men poured from the mountains. Roland now blew his enchanted horn. Charlemagne heard the blast but Ganelon persuaded him that Roland was but hunting deer. Thus Roland was left to his fate.

The *Chanson* runs to 4,000 lines, the oldest manuscript being preserved in the BODLEIAN LIBRARY, and Wace (*Roman de Rou*) tells us that the Norman minstrel sang parts of this to encourage William's soldiers at the Battle of Hastings.

> Taillefer, the minstrel-knight, bestrode
> A gallant steed, and swiftly rode
> Before the Duke, and sang the song
> Of Charlemagne, of Roland strong,
> Of Oliver, and those beside
> Brave knights at Roncesvaux that died.
> *A. S. Way's rendering.*

To die like Roland. To die of starvation or thirst. One legend has it that ROLAND escaped the general slaughter in the defile of Roncesvalles, and died of hunger and thirst in seeking to cross the Pyrenees. He was buried at Blayes, in the church of St. Raymond; but his body was removed afterwards to Roncesvalles.

Rolandseck Tower, opposite the Drachenfels on the Rhine, 22 miles above Cologne. The legend is that when ROLAND went to the wars, a false report of his death was brought to his betrothed, who retired to a convent in the isle of Nonnenwerth. When he returned flushed with glory and found she had taken the veil, he built the castle to overlook the nunnery, that he might gain a glimpse of his lost love.

Roll. The flying roll of Zechariah (v, 1-5). Predictions of evils to come on a nation are likened to the "flying roll of Zechariah" which was 20 cubits long and ten wide and full of maledictions, threats, and calamities about to befall the Jews. The parchment being unrolled fluttered in the air.

A rolling stone. *See under* STONE.

Rollright Stones. An ancient stone circle between the villages of Great and Little Rollright on the Oxfordshire-

Warwickshire border. The structure consists of the King Stone, a circle of about 70 stones called the King's Men, and a few others called the Whispering Knights. "The King" at this point could look over Oxfordshire and said:

> When Long Compton I shall see,
> King of England I shall be.

But he and his men were petrified by a witch.

Rolls. Chapel of the Rolls (Chancery Lane). Formerly the Chapel of the House of the Converts, founded by Henry III in 1232 for the reception of Jewish converts to Christianity. Edward I expelled the Jews and by 1377 the House of the Converts was allocated to the Keeper of the Rolls of CHANCERY, who was an ecclesiastic. The chapel remained a place of worship, but was also increasingly used for storing records. Most of the documents were transferred to the adjoining and newly-built Public Record Office in 1856 and it was replaced by the Museum of the Public Record Office. The name derives from the practice of keeping parchment documents in rolls for convenience of storing.

Master of the Rolls. A title of 15th-century origin for the keeper of CHANCERY records or rolls and legal assistant to the CHANCELLOR. In the 19th century he became the chief judge of the Chancery division and (since 1838) the custodian of all public records. In 1958 his jurisdiction again reverted to Chancery records only.

To be struck off the rolls. To be removed from the official list of qualified solicitors, and so prohibited from practising. This is done in cases of professional misconduct.

Roly-poly. A suet crust with jam rolled up into a pudding; a little fat child. *Roly* is a thing rolled with the diminutive added. In some parts of SCOTLAND the game of ninepins is called *rouly-pouly*.

Romaic. Modern or romanized Greek.

Roman. Pertaining to ROME, especially ancient Rome, or to the ROMAN CATHOLIC CHURCH.

Roman architecture. A style of architecture distinguished by its massive character and abundance of ornament, largely derived from the Greek and Etruscan. The Greek orders were adapted and the IONIC and CORINTHIAN were combined to form what came to be called the *Roman* or *Composite* order. Their greatest works were baths, amphitheatres, basilicas, aqueducts, bridges, triumphal arches and gateways.

Roman birds. Eagles; so called because the ensign of the Roman legion was an EAGLE.

Roman Catholic Church. A name introduced by "non-Catholics" for members of the CATHOLIC or western Church under the jurisdiction of the papacy. The term is a consequence of the REFORMATION and came into use at about the end of the 16th century. *See also* POPE.

Roman Empire. Properly, the Empire established by AUGUSTUS in 27 B.C., on the ruins of the Republic. It was finally divided into the Western or Latin Empire and the Eastern or Greek in A.D. 395. The Western Empire was eventually extinguished in 475, the last nominal emperor being Romulus Augustulus. The term "Roman empire" is also applied to the territories and dominions of the ROMAN REPUBLIC. *See* BYZANTINE EMPIRE.

Roman Empire, The Holy. *See under* HOLY.

Roman figures. *See* NUMBERS.

Roman holiday. An allusion to Byron's *Childe Harold's Pilgrimage*, IV, cxli, where he describes the death of a gladiator in the arena, "Butchered to make a Roman holiday".

The Roman Republic was established in 509 B.C. after the overthrow of the last of the seven kings, Tarquinius Superbus. It was superseded by the Empire (27 B.C.).

For a few months in 1849, after the flight of Pius IX, the people of Rome declared themselves a republic under the triumvirate of Mazzini, Saffi, and Armellini. *See also* YOUNG ITALY.

Roman roads. *See* ERMINE; FOSSE; WATLING.

Roman type. The first printing types were based upon the national or local handwriting. Roman type, the character in which this book is printed, developed from the *littera antiqua*, the conscious revival of the old Roman capital and the CAROLINGIAN minuscule which the Humanist scholars of the Italian RENAISSANCE considered more appropriate for the transcription of recently discovered Classical manuscripts than the everyday forms of Gothic handwriting. First used in print about 1465, Roman type had virtually superseded Gothic letter in less than 100 years in all parts of Europe except Germany, the British Isles, and Scandinavia. Roman type steadily took over in Britain from the late 16th century.

Romans. King of the Romans. The title usually assumed by the sovereign of the HOLY ROMAN EMPIRE previous to his actual coronation at ROME. NAPOLEON's son, afterwards the Duke of Reichstadt, was styled the *King of Rome* at his birth in 1811.

Last of the Romans. *See under* LAST.

Roman de la Rose. *See* ROSE, ROMANCE OF THE.

Romance. Applied in linguistics (*see* ROMANCE LANGUAGES, *below*) to the languages, especially Old French, sprung from the Latin spoken in the European provinces of the ROMAN EMPIRE; hence, as a noun, the word came to mean a mediæval tale in Old French or Provençal describing usually in mixed prose and verse the marvellous adventures of a hero of CHIVALRY. The modern application to a work of fiction containing incidents more or less removed from ordinary life, or to a love story or love affair, followed from this.

The mediæval romances fall into three main groups or cycles, *viz.* the Arthurian (*see under* ARTHUR), the CHARLEMAGNE cycle, and the cycle of ALEXANDER THE GREAT.

Romance languages. Those languages which are the immediate offspring of Latin, as Italian, Spanish, Portuguese, French, and Rumanian. Early French is emphatically so called; hence Bouillet says, "*Le roman était universellement parlé en Gaule au dixième siècle.*"

Romanesque Architecture (rō măn esk'). This term embraces the style of architecture in Western Europe from the virtual collapse of Roman rule in the 6th century until the emergence of the GOTHIC style in the late 12th century. A style with considerable regional variations, *e.g.* SAXON and Norman in England, CAROLINGIAN and Rhenish in Germany, it is characterized by the round arch, great thickness of walls, shallow (if any) buttressing, and in later phases by profuse decoration or arcades and other features.

Romantic Movement, The. The literary movement that began in Germany in the last quarter of the 18th century, having for its object a return from the AUGUSTAN or classical formalism of the time, to the freer fancies and methods of ROMANCE. It was led by Schiller, Goethe, Novalis, and Tieck, and spread to England where it influenced the work of Collins and Gray and received an impetus from the publication of PERCY'S RELIQUES and Macpherson's OSSIAN. It was immensely stimulated by the French Revolution and effected a transformation of English literature through the writings of Keats, Byron, Wordsworth, Shelley, Coleridge, Scott, etc. In France its chief exponents were Rousseau, Chateaubriand, Mme de Staël, Lamartine, Musset, Vigny, and Victor Hugo.

Romany. A GYPSY; or the gypsy language, the speech of the Roma or Zincali. The word is from Gypsy *rom*, a man, or husband.

> "Aukko to pios adrey Rommanis. Here is your health in Rommany, brother," said Mr. Petulengro; who having refilled the cup, now emptied it at a draught.
> BORROW: *Lavengro*, ch. liv.

Romany rye. One who enters into the GYPSY spirit, learns their language, lives with them as one of themselves, etc. *Rye* is gypsy for gentleman. George Borrow's book with this title (a sequel to *Lavengro*) was published in 1857.

Rome. The greatest city of the ancient world, according to legend founded in 753 B.C. by ROMULUS and named after him; but in all probability so called from Greek *rhoma* (strength), a suggestion supported by its other name Valentia (Lat. *valens*, strong). It acquired a new significance as the seat of the papacy.

All roads lead to Rome. *See under* ROAD.

Oh, that all Rome had but one head, that I might strike it off at a blow. Caligula, the Roman Emperor (A.D. 12, 37–41), is said to have uttered this sentiment.

Rome-Berlin Axis. *See* AXIS.

Rome penny, or **Rome scot.** The same as PETER'S PENCE.

Rome's best wealth is its patriotism. So said Mettius Curtius (*c.* 360 B.C.) who jumped into the wide gap which appeared in the Forum when the ORACLE gave out that it would never close till ROME threw therein its most precious possession.

Rome was not built in a day. Achievements of great moment, worthwhile tasks, etc., are not accomplished without patient perseverance and a considerable interval of time. It is an old saying, and occurs in Heywood's *Collection* (1562).

'Tis ill sitting at Rome and striving with the Pope. Don't TREAD ON SOMEONE'S CORNS when you are living with him or are in close touch with him—especially if he is powerful.

To fiddle while Rome burns. To trifle during an emergency or crisis. An allusion to NERO's reputed behaviour during the burning of ROME in A.D. 64 when he sang to his lyre and enjoyed the spectacle from the top of a high tower.

When at Rome, do as Rome does. Conform to the manners and customs of those amongst whom you live; "Don't wear a brown hat in Friesland." St. Monica and her son St. Augustine said to St. AMBROSE: "At Rome they fast on Saturday, but not at Milan; which practice ought to be observed?" To which St. Ambrose replied: "When I am at Milan, I do as they do at Milan; but when I go to Rome, I do as Rome does!" (*Epistle* xxxvi). *Cp.* II *Kings* v, 18.

The saying is to be found in that great storehouse of proverbs, Porter's *Two Angry Women of Abingdon* (1599).

Romeo and Juliet. A typification of romantic love as exemplified in SHAKESPEARE's famous play of this title. Romeo, of the house of Montague, falls in love with Juliet, one of the Capulet family, long-standing enemies of the Montagues. Romeo and Juliet are secretly married, but Romeo is banished from Verona before their wedding day is over as punishment for the unfortunate slaughter of a Capulet in an affray. Old Capulet now orders Juliet to prepare for marriage with Count Paris forthwith, and to avoid this, she drugs herself into a death-like trance. Romeo, hearing of her "death", returns, enters the tomb where Juliet lies, and kills himself. Juliet awakens, sees her lover dead, and dispatches herself with Romeo's dagger. Shakespeare closely based his play upon Arthur Brooke's long narrative poem, *The Tragicall History of Romeo and Juliet* (1562), which was derived ultimately from an earlier Italian story (1535) by Luigi da Porto, through a French version (1559) by Pierre Boisteau.

A regular Romeo. Said banteringly of one who fancies himself as a LADYKILLER.

Romulus (rom' ūlŭs). With his twin brother Remus, the legendary and eponymous founder of ROME. They were sons of MARS and Rhea Sylvia (Ilia), who, because she was a VESTAL virgin, was condemned to death, while the sons were exposed. They were, however, suckled by a she-wolf, and eventually set about founding a city, but quarrelled over the plans and Remus was slain by his brother in anger. Romulus was later taken to the heavens by his father, MARS, in a fiery chariot, and was worshipped by the Romans under the name of Quirinus.

The Second Romulus. Camillus was so called because he saved ROME from the Gauls, 365 B.C.

The Third Romulus. Caius Marius, who saved ROME from the Teutons and Cimbri in 101 B.C.

We need no Romulus to account for Rome. We require no hypothetical person to account for a plain fact.

Roncesvalles. *See* THE SONG OF ROLAND, *under* ROLAND.

Ronyon, or **Runnion** (ron' yŏn, rŭn' yŏn). A term of contempt for a woman. It is probably the Fr. *rogneux* (scabby, mangy). Shakespeare has:

> You hag, you baggage, you polecat, you ronyon! out, out!
> *The Merry Wives of Windsor*, IV, ii.

"Aroint thee, witch!" the rump-fed ronyon cries.

Macbeth, I, iii.

Rood (connected with *rod*). The Cross of the Crucifixion; or a crucifix, especially the large one that was formerly set on the stone or timber *rood-screen* that divides the nave from the choir in many churches. This is usually richly decorated with statues, and carvings of saints, emblems, etc., and frequently surmounted by a gallery called the *rood-loft*.

And then to see the rood-loft,
Zo bravely zet with saints.
PERCY: *Reliques* (*Plain Truth, and Blind Ignorance*).

By the rood: by the holy rood. Old expletives used by way of asseveration. In SHAKESPEARE's *Hamlet*, when the Queen asks Hamlet if he has forgotten her he answers "No, by the rood, not so" (III, iv).

Rood Day. HOLY ROOD DAY; 14 September, the EXALTATION OF THE CROSS; or 3 May, the INVENTION OF THE CROSS (*see under* CROSS).

Roof of the World. A name given to the Pamirs, the great region of mountains covering 30,000 square miles, devoid of trees and shrubs, and most of it in the Soviet Socialist Republic of Tadzhikistan. The name is a translation of *Bam-i-Dunya*, bestowed by the natives of this region. The name also applies to Tibet.

To raise the roof. To be very noisy; to make a real hullabaloo.

Rooinek (Afrikaans, "red-neck"). A name given by the Boers to the British in the South African War, and used later to mean any British or European immigrant to South Africa.

Rook, a cheat. "To rook", to cheat; "to rook a pigeon", to fleece a GREENHORN. Sometimes it simply means to win from another at a game of chance or skill.

Rook, the castle in CHESS, is through Fr. and Span., from Persian *rukh*, which is said to have meant a warrior.

Rookery. Any low, densely populated neighbourhood, especially one frequented by thieves and vagabonds. The allusion is to the way in which rooks build their nests closely together. Colonies of seals, and places where seals or seabirds collect in their breeding season are also known as *Rookeries*. *See* ALSATIA.

Rookie. In army slang, a recruit, a novice or GREENHORN. In the U.S.A., the name given to a raw beginner in professional sport. It is probably from *rook*, a rookie being a guileless greenhorn who is easily *rooked*, swindled, or "taken in".

Room. Your room is better than your company. Your absence is more to be wished than your presence. An old phrase; it occurs in Stanyhurst's *Description of Ireland* (1577), Greene's *Quip for an Upstart Courtier* (1592), etc.

Roost. To rule the roost. *See under* ROAST.

Root. Root and Branch. The whole of it without any exceptions or omissions; "LOCK, STOCK, AND BARREL". The Puritans who supported the Root and Branch Bill of 1641 to abolish EPISCOPACY were known as "Root-and-branch men", or "Rooters", and the term has since been applied to other political factions who are anxious TO GO THE WHOLE HOG (*see under* HOG).

The root of the matter. Its true inwardness, its actual base and foundation. The phrase comes from *Job* xix, 28:

But ye should say, Why persecute we him, seeing the root of the matter is found in me?

To root for. To support a sporting team. Also used of giving active support to a campaigning politician.

To take, or **strike root.** To become permanently or firmly established.

Rope. Fought back to the ropes. Fought to the bitter end. A phrase from the prize-ring, the "ropes" forming the boundary of the "ring". Hence the expression **on the ropes,** meaning on the verge of ruin or collapse.

It is a battle that must be fought game, and right back to the ropes.
BOLDREWOOD: *Robbery Under Arms*, ch. xxxiii.

Money for old rope. Easy money, money for nothing or very little; something which can be effected easily. The derivation is obvious.

Ropes of sand. *See* SAND.

She is on her high ropes. In a distant and haughty temper; "HIGH AND MIGHTY". The allusion is to a rope-dancer, who looks down on the spectators.

A taste of the rope's end. A flogging. A nautical expression, where it was formerly a routine punishment to administer a flogging with the end of a rope.

To come to the end of one's rope, or **tether.** *See* TETHER.

To fight with a rope round one's neck. To fight with a certainty of death if one loses.

> You must send in a large force; ... for, as he fights with a rope round his neck, he will struggle to the last.
> KINGSTON: *The Three Admirals*, ch. viii.

To give one rope enough. To allow a person to continue on a certain course of action (usually EVIL) till he reaps the consequences of his folly or wrongdoing. "Give him enough rope and he will hang himself" is the common saying.

To know the ropes. To be thoroughly familiar with what is to be done; to be up to all the tricks and dodges. It derives from the days of sail when a sailor or apprentice had to become thoroughly familiar with the details of the rigging and how to handle the ropes.

To rope one in. To get him to take part in some scheme, enterprise, etc. An expression from the cattle lands of America, where animals are roped in with a lasso.

The Rope-walk. Former barristers' slang for an OLD BAILEY practice. Thus "Gone into the Rope-walk" means, he has taken up practice in the OLD BAILEY. The allusion is to the murder trials there, and to the convicted murderer "getting the rope".

Ropeable. In Australia, a term now applied to one who is in a bad temper. Originally it meant cattle so wild that they could be controllable only by roping.

Ropey. A slang expression meaning inferior, worn-out, tatty, dubious, etc., as a "ropey outfit", a "ropey character".

Roque, St. *See* ROCH.

Roquelaure (rōk' lōr). A cloak for men, reaching to the knees. It was worn in the 18th century, and so named from Antoine-Gaston, Duc de Roquelaure (1656–1738), a Marshal of France.

Rory O'More. *See* RHYMING SLANG.

Rosabelle. The favourite palfrey of Mary Queen of Scots.

Rosalia, or **Rosalie, St.** (rō zā' li a, roz' a lē). The patron saint of Palermo, in art depicted in a cave with a CROSS and skull, or else in the act of receiving a ROSARY or chaplet of roses from the Virgin. She lived in the 13th century, and is said to have been carried by ANGELS to an inaccessible mountain, where she dwelt for many years in the cleft of a rock, a part of which she wore away with her knees in her devotions. A CHAPEL has been built there, with a marble statue, to commemorate the event.

Rosamond, The Fair (roz' amund). Higden, monk of Chester, writing about 1350, says: "she was the fayre daughter of Walter, Lord Clifford, concubine of Henry II, and poisoned by Queen Eleanor, A.D. 1177. Henry made for her a house of wonderful working, so that no man or woman might come to her. This house was named Labyrinthus, and was wrought like unto a knot in a garden called a maze. But the queen came to her by a clue of thredde, and so dealt with her that she lived not long after. She was buried at Godstow, in an house of nunnes, with these verses upon her tombe:

> Hic jacet in tumba Rosa mundi, non Rosa munda;
> Non redolet, sed olet, quæ redolere solet."
>
> Here Rose the graced, not Rose the chaste, reposes;
> The smell that rises is no smell of roses.
> E.C.B.

The legend of her murder by Queen Eleanor first appears in the 14th century and the story of the LABYRINTH even later. There is no evidence to support the stories that Fair Rosamond was the mother of William Longsword and Geoffrey, Archbishop of York. A subterranean labyrinth in Blenheim Park, near Woodstock, is still pointed out as "Rosamond's Bower".

> Jane Clifford was her name, as books aver:
> Fair Rosamond was but her *nom de guerre.*

DRYDEN: *Epilogue to Henry II*.

Rosary (rō' zår i) (Lat. *rosarium*, rose garden, garland). The bead-roll used by Roman Catholics for keeping count of the recitation of certain prayers; also the prayers themselves. The usual modern rosary consists of five decades of ten recitations, or one-third of the complete rosary known as a *corona* or *chaplet*. The full rosary comprises 15 decades of *Aves* (Hail Marys—small beads), each preceded by a *Pater* (Our Father—large bead), and followed by a *Gloria* (Glory be to the Father—large bead). While the first chaplet is being recited the five joyful MYSTERIES are contemplated; during the second chaplet, the five sorrowful mysteries; and during the third, the five glorious mysteries. Only one group of five mysteries is usually contemplated. Traditionally the devotion of the rosary is said to have begun with St. DOMINIC early in the 13th century but this is not established. Sometimes the Venerable BEDE is credited with its introduction but quite erroneously; the idea is based upon the fanciful derivation of bead from *Beda*. *Cp*. GAUDY; PATERNOSTER.

Roscius (ros' i us). A first-rate actor; after Quintus Roscius (d. *c*. 62 B.C.), the Roman actor unrivalled for his grace of action, melody of voice, conception of character, and delivery.

> What scene of death has Roscius now to act?
> SHAKESPEARE: *Henry VI, Pt. III*, V, vi.

Rose. Mediæval legend asserts that the first roses appeared miraculously at Bethlehem as the result of the prayers of a "fayre Mayden" who had been falsely accused and sentenced to death by burning. As Sir John MANDEVILLE tells the tale (*Travels*, ch. vi), after her prayer:

> sche entered into the Fuyer; and anon was the Fuyr quenched and oute; and the Brondes that weren brennynge, becomen red Roseres; and the Brondes that weren not kyndled, becomen white Roseres, fulle of Roses. And these weren the first Roseres and Roses, both white and rede, that evere any Man saughe. And was this Mayden saved be the Grace of God.

In Christian symbolism the *Rose*, as being emblematic of a paragon or one without peer, is peculiarly appropriated to the Virgin MARY, one of whose titles is "The Mystical Rose". It is also the attribute of St. DOROTHEA, who carries roses in a basket; of St. Casilda, St. Elizabeth of Portugal, and St. Rose of Viterbo, who carry roses in either their hands or caps; of St. Thérèse of Lisieux, who scatters red roses; and of ST. ROSALIE, St. Angelus, St. Rose of Lima, and St. Victoria, who wear crowns of roses.

The Rose is an emblem of ENGLAND and in HERALDRY is used as the mark of cadency for a seventh son. *See* RED ROSE; TUDOR ROSE; WHITE ROSE, *below*.

Golden Rose. *See under* GOLDEN.

The Red Rose was one of several badges of the House of Lancaster, but not especially the most prominent. It was used by Edmund, Earl of Lancaster (1245–1296), called Crouchback, second son of Henry III, and it was one of the badges of Henry IV and Henry V, but it does not appear to have been used by Henry VI. The rose-plucking scene in SHAKESPEARE's *Henry VI, Pt. I*, II, iv, is essentially a fiction.

The Tudor Rose. Henry of Richmond (1457–1509), son of Edmund Tudor, Earl of Richmond, and head of the House of Lancaster after the death of Henry VI, adopted the red rose to emphasize his LANCASTRIAN claims. After his victory at Bosworth (1485), he became king as Henry VII and in 1486 married Princess Elizabeth of York. The union of the two Houses gave rise to the Tudor Rose, a superimposition of the white rose on the red. *See* WARS OF THE ROSES, *below*.

The White Rose was used as a badge by Richard, Duke of York (1411–1460), and was derived from his Mortimer ancestors. It was one of the numerous badges used by his son Edward IV and was used by his descendants, but Richard III's badge was the white BOAR. It was also adopted by the JACOBITES as an emblem of the PRETENDER, because his adherents were obliged to abet him SUB ROSA (*see below*). Cecily Neville, wife of Richard, Duke of York, and grand-daughter of John of Gaunt, was known as *The White Rose of Raby*. *Cp*. RED ROSE, *above*; WARS OF THE ROSES, *below*.

The Rose Alley Ambuscade. The attack on Dryden by masked ruffians, probably in the employ of Rochester and the Duchess of Portsmouth, on 18 December 1679, in revenge for an anonymous *Essay on Satire* attacking King Charles II, Rochester, and the Duchesses of Cleveland and Portsmouth, which was erroneously attributed to Dryden but actually written by Lord Mulgrave.

Rose Noble. A gold coin, also called a *ryal*, or *royal*, so named because it bore a rose in a sun on the reverse. It was first minted in 1465 and was valued at 10s., but the issue ceased by 1470. It was revived by Henry VII and again by Mary and Elizabeth I. A *rose-ryal* was issued by James I.

The Rose of Jericho. The popular name of *Anastatica hierochuntina*, a small branching plant, native to the sandy deserts of ARABIA, Egypt, and Syria. When it is dry, if it is exposed to moisture, the branches uncurl. Also called the *rose of the Virgin,* or *Rosa Mariæ*.

Rose of Sharon. St. John's Wort, *Hypericum calycinum*, a small shrub-like plant with a yellow flower. The rose of Sharon in *The Song of Solomon* (II,i) was probably a bulbous plant.

Rose, The Romance of the. An early French poem of over 20,000 lines; an elaborate allegory on the Art of Love beneath which can be seen a faithful picture of contemporary life. It was begun by Guillaume de Lorris in the latter half of the 13th century, and continued by Jean de Meung in the early part of the 14th. The poet is accosted by Dame Idleness, who conducts him to the Palace of Pleasure, where he meets Love, accompanied by Sweet-looks, Riches, Jollity, Courtesy, Liberality, and Youth, who spend their time in dancing, singing and other amusements. By this retinue the poet is conducted to a bed of roses, where he singles out one and attempts to pluck it, when an arrow from CUPID'S bow stretches him fainting on the ground, and he is carried far from the flower of his choice. As soon as he recovers, he finds himself alone, and resolves to return to his rose. Welcome goes with him; but Danger, Shameface, Fear and Slander obstruct him at

every turn. Reason advises him to abandon the pursuit, but this he will not do; whereupon Pity and Liberality aid him in reaching the rose of his choice, and VENUS permits him to touch it with his lips. Meanwhile Slander rouses up Jealousy, who seizes Welcome, and casts him into a strong castle, giving the key of the castle door to an old hag. Here the poet is left to mourn over his fate, and the original poem ends.

In the second part—which is much the longer—the same characters appear, but the spirit of the poem is altogether different, the author being interested in life as a whole instead of solely love; and directing his satire especially against women.

An English version, *The Romaunt of the Rose*, was translated by Chaucer, but in the extant version (first printed in 1532) it is generally held that only the first 1,700 lines or so are his.

Rose Sunday. The fourth Sunday in LENT, when the POPE blesses the GOLDEN ROSE.

A rose by any other name would smell as sweet. The name is of little consequence, it does not affect the inherent qualities of the person or thing under consideration. Thus SHAKESPEARE's Juliet says:

> What's in a name? that which we call a rose,
> By any other name would smell as sweet;
> So Romeo would, were he not Romeo call'd.
>
> *Romeo and Juliet*, II, ii.

The expression is now commonly used sarcastically.

No rose without a thorn. There is always something to detract from pleasure—"every sweet has its sour", "there is a crook in every lot" (*see under* CROOK).

Sing Old Rose and burn the bellows. "Old Rose" was the title of a song now unknown; Isaak Walton refers to it:

> And now let's go to an honest alehouse, where we may have a cup of good barley wine, and sing "Old Rose", and all of us rejoice together.
>
> *The Compleat Angler*, Pt. I, ch. ii (1653).

Burn the bellows may be a schoolboys' perversion of *burn libellos*. At breaking-up time the boys might say,

"Let's sing *Old Rose* and burn our *libellos*" (school-books). This does not accord ill with the meaning of the well-known catch:

> Now we're met like jovial fellows,
> Let us do as wise men tell us,
> Sing *Old Rose* and burn the bellows.

Sub rosa (Lat.), or **Under the rose.** In strict confidence. The origin of the phrase is obscure but the story is that CUPID gave HARPOCRATES (the god of silence) a ROSE, to bribe him not to betray the amours of VENUS. Hence the flower became the emblem of silence and was sculptured on the ceilings of banquet-rooms, to remind the guests that what was spoken *sub vino* was not to be repeated SUB DIVO. In the 16th century it was placed over confessionals.

A bed of roses. *See under* BED.

The Wars of the Roses. The usual name given to the CIVIL WARS in England (1455–1485) between LANCASTRIANS and YORKISTS which ended in the triumph of Henry Tudor at Bosworth. The wars were partly dynastic and partly private wars of the nobility, occasioned by the weakness of government and the collapse of law and order. The name is not really historical and appears to derive from Scott.

> He now turned his eyes to the regaining of those rich and valuable foreign possessions which had been lost during the administration of the feeble Henry VI, and the civil discords so dreadfully prosecuted in the wars of the White and Red Roses.
>
> *Anne of Geierstein*, ch. vii.

There is no contemporary record of the use of the term for these struggles for political control. *See* THE RED ROSE; THE TUDOR ROSE; THE WHITE ROSE, *above*.

Rose-red City. Petra, ancient capital of the Nabatæan Kings from which Arabia Petræa took its name. It was occupied by the Romans in 105 A.D. and is noted for its ancient tomb and temple ruins as well as Roman remains. The epithet derives from the famous line of J. W. Burgon's Newdigate Prize poem of 1845:

> "A rose-red city half as old as time".

The local rocks are essentially red and much enhanced by red sunsets.

Rosemary (rōz' mà ri) (Lat. *Ros marinus*, sea-dew). The shrub (*Rosmarinus officinalis*) is said to be useful in love-making. As VENUS, the love goddess, was sprung from the foam of the sea, rosemary or sea-dew would have amatory qualities.

> The sea his mother Venus came on;
> And hence some rev'rend men approve
> Of rosemary in making love.
> BUTLER: *Hudibras*, Pt. II, Canto i, l. 843.

Rosemary, an emblem of remembrance. In SHAKESPEARE's *Hamlet* (IV, v) Ophelia says, "There's rosemary, that's for remembrance." According to Culpeper, "It quickens a weak memory, and the senses." As HUNGARY WATER, it was once extensively taken to quieten the nerves. It was much used in weddings, and to wear rosemary in ancient times was as significant of a wedding as to wear a white favour. When the Nurse in Shakespeare's *Romeo and Juliet* (II, iv) asks, "Doth not rosemary and Romeo begin both with a [*i.e.* the same] letter?" She refers to the emblematical characteristics of the herb. In the language of FLOWERS it means "Fidelity in love".

Rosetta Stone, The (rō zet' à). A stone found in 1799 by M. Boussard, à French officer of engineers, in an excavation made at Fort St. Julien, near Rosetta, in the Nile delta. It has an inscription in three different languages—the hieroglyphic, the demotic, and the Greek. It was erected (195 B.C.) in honour of Ptolemy Epiphanes, because he remitted the dues of the sacerdotal body. The great value of the stone is that it furnished the key whereby the Egyptian HIEROGLYPHS were deciphered.

Rosicrusians (roz i kroo' shánz). A secret society of CABBALISTS, occultists and alchemists that is first heard of in 1614 when the anonymous *Fama fraternitatis des löblichen Ordens des Rosenkreuzes* was published at Cassel, duly followed by the *Confessio* and *The Chemical Wedding of Christian Rosenkreutz*. The Rosicrucian Order was reputedly founded by the mythical Rosenkreutz (the cross of roses) in 1459. In FREEMASONRY there is still a degree known as the *Rose Croix*. Rosicrucian philosophy played a part in the early struggle for intellectual progress by clothing its progressive ideas in mystical guise. It seems to have influenced the Elizabethan, Dr. John Dee, and Sir Francis Bacon among others, and to have some links with the work of PARACELSUS.

Rosicrucian societies still exist.

Rosin Bible. *See* BIBLE, SOME SPECIALLY NAMED EDITIONS.

Rosinante. *See* ROZINANTE.

Ross, Betsy (1752–1836). She is said to have made the first STARS AND STRIPES in 1776. The story is that George Washington, with Robert Morris and General George Ross, visited Betsy's upholstery shop in Philadelphia and asked her to make a flag from their design. The stars had six points but Betsy said they would look better with five. This was agreed and in due course she produced the flag.

Ross. The Fair Maid of Ross. Amy, the daughter of Captain Browne, the warden of Ross Castle, Killarney, was known as "The Fair Maid of Ross" and attracted the attention of most of the young officers, especially Raymond Villiers whom her father wanted her to marry, but she was already in love with Donough McCarthy whose estates had been seized by the enemy. When the castle was beseiged by the Cromwellians in 1652, Villiers, having been refused by Amy, resolved to betray Ross Castle to Ludlow, Cromwell's general, but when engaged on this mission Amy followed him and learned of his treason. When Villiers finally left the castle Amy again followed him but was wounded by his pistol shot. In a subsequent skirmish McCarthy killed Villiers and Captain Browne surrendered the castle on honourable terms. In due course McCarthy recovered his land and married Amy.

The Man of Ross. John Kyrle (1637–1724) who spent most of his life at Ross, Herefordshire. He was famous for his benevolence and for supplying needy parishes with churches. The KYRLE SOCIETY was named in his honour.

Rosse. A famous sword which the dwarf ALBERICH gave to Otwit, King of Lombardy. It struck so fine a cut that it left

no "gap", shone like glass, and was adorned with gold.

Rostrum. A pulpit, or stand for public speakers. The Lat. *rostrum* is the bill or beak of a bird, also the beak or curved prow of a ship. In the Forum at ROME, the platform from which orators addressed the public was ornamented with *rostra*, or ship-prows taken from the Antiates in 338 B.C., hence this use of the word.

Rota. Rota Sacra Romana. A Roman Catholic ecclesiastical court of mediæval origin composed of auditors under the presidency of a DEAN. It was reconstituted by Pius X in 1908 and appears to take its name from the circular table originally used by the judges at Avignon. It tries cases and hears appeals from ecclesiastical tribunals.

Rotary Club. A movement among business men which takes for its motto "Service above Self". The idea originated with Paul Harris, a Chicago lawyer, in 1905. In 1911 it took root in Britain and there are now clubs in most towns, membership being limited to one member each of any trade, calling, or profession. Lectures are delivered at weekly meetings by guest speakers. The name derives from the early practice of holding meetings in rotation at the offices or business premises of its members. The Rotary Clubs are now members of one association called Rotary International.

Rote. To learn by rote is to learn by means of repetition, *i.e.* by going over the same beaten track or *route* again and again. *Rote* is really the same word as *route*.

Rothschild. I am not a Rothschild. I am not a millionaire. I am not "rolling in money". This and similar phrases are in allusion to the great wealth of the famous international banking family of Rothschild, whose name derives from the red shield by which their parent house at Frankfurt was known. The family banking business really stems from the activities of Meyer Amschel Rothschild (1743–1812) who made a fortune during the Napoleonic wars. His five sons separated, extending the business throughout Europe.

Rotten Row. The famous equestrian track

in Hyde Park, London, is said to be so called from O.Fr. *route le roi* or *route du roi*, because it formed part of the old royal route from the palace of the PLANTAGENET Kings at WESTMINSTER to the royal forests. Camden derives the word from *rotteran*, to muster, as the place where soldiers mustered. The reason for the name is obscure.

Roué (roo′ ā). The profligate Duke of Orleans, Regent of France, first used this word in its modern sense about 1720. It was his ambition to collect round him companions as worthless as himself, and he used facetiously to boast that there was not one of them who did not deserve to be broken on the *wheel*; hence these profligates went by the name of Orleans' *roués*. The most notorious *roués* were the Dukes of Richelieu, Broglie, Biron, and Brancas, together with Canillac and Nocé.

Rouen (roo′ on). **Aller à Rouen.** To go to ruin. A French pun comparable to our *You are on the road to* NEEDHAM (a market town in Suffolk), *i.e.* your courses will lead you to poverty.

The Bloody Feast of Rouen (1356). Charles the DAUPHIN (later Charles V) gave a banquet to his friends at Rouen, to which his brother-in-law Charles the BAD of Navarre was invited. While the guests were at table King John the Good entered the room with an escort, exclaiming, "Traitor, thou art not worthy to sit at table with my son!" Then, turning to his guards, he added, "Take him hence! By holy Paul, I will neither eat nor drink till his head be brought to me!" Then, seizing an iron mace from one of the men-at-arms, he struck another of the guests between the shoulders, saying, "Out, proud traitor! by the soul of my father, thou shalt not live!" Four of the guests were beheaded on the spot and Charles of Navarre was taken a prisoner to Paris.

Rouge (roozh) (Fr., red). **Rouge Croix.** One of the PURSUIVANTS of the Heralds' College. So called from the red cross of St. GEORGE, the patron saint of ENGLAND. Rouge Croix was instituted by Henry V.

Rouge Dragon. The PURSUIVANT established by Henry VII. The RED DRA-

GON was the ensign of the Welsh princes from whom Henry VII traced his ancestry.

Rouge et Noir (Fr., red and black). A game of chance; so called because of the red and black diamond-shaped compartments on the board. After the stakes have been placed on the table the cards are dealt in the prescribed manner and the player whose "pips" amount nearest to 31 is the winner. The game is also called *Trente-et-un* (31) or *Trente-et-Quarante* (30 and 40).

Rough. A rough diamond. *See under* DIAMOND.

A rough house. A disorderly scrimmage or brawl.

Rough music. A din or noisy uproar made by clanging together pots and pans and other noise-producing instruments usually as a protest outside the house of a person who has outraged propriety. In Somersetshire it was called skimmity-riding, by the Basques *toberac*, and in France CHARIVARI. *Cp.* SKIMMINGTON.

Rough and Ready. Rough in manner but prompt in action; not elaborate, roughly adequate. General Zachary Taylor (1784–1860), twelfth president of the United States, was called **Old Rough and Ready**, a name he won in the Seminole Wars.

To cut up rough. *See under* CUT.

To ride rough-shod over one. To treat one without the least consideration; to completely disregard another's interests or feelings, etc. The shoes of a horse that is *rough-shod* for slippery weather are equipped with points or calks.

Rough-hewn. Shaped in the rough, not finished, unpolished, ill-mannered, raw; as a "rough-hewn seaman".

> There's a divinity that shapes our ends,
> Rough-hew them how we will.
> SHAKESPEARE: *Hamlet*, V, ii.

Rouncival, or **Rounceval** (rown′ si val). Very large or strong; of gigantic size. Certain large bones said to have been dug up at Roncesvalles (*see* THE SONG OF ROLAND *under* ROLAND) were believed to have belonged to the heroes who fell with Roland, hence the usage. "Rouncival peas" are the large marrow-fat peas and a very big woman is called a *rouncival*.

Round. The Round Table. The Table fabled to have been made by MERLIN at Carduel for UTHER Pendragon. Uther gave it to King Leodegraunce of Cameliard, who gave it to King ARTHUR when the latter married GUINEVERE, his daughter. It was circular to prevent any jealousy on the score of precedency; it seated 150 knights, and a place was left in it for the SANGRAIL. The first reference to it is in Wace's *Roman de Brut* (1155); these legendary details are from Malory's *Morte d'Arthur*, III, i and ii.

The table shown at Winchester was recognized as ancient in the time of Henry III, but its anterior history is unknown. It is of wedge-shaped oak planks, and is 17 ft. in diameter and 2¾ in. thick. At the back are 12 mortice holes in which 12 legs probably used to fit. It was for the accommodation of 12 favourite knights. Henry VIII showed it to Francis I, telling him that it was the one used by the British king. The Round Table was not peculiar to the reign of Arthur. Thus the king of Ireland, father of the fair Cristabelle, says in the ballad given in PERCY'S RELIQUES:

Is there never a Knighte of my round table
This matter will undergo?
Sir Cauline (Part the Second).

In the eighth year of Edward I, Roger de Mortimer established a Round Table at Kenilworth for "the encouragement of military pastimes". At this foundation, 100 knights and as many ladies were entertained at the founder's expense. About 70 years later, Edward III erected a splendid table at Windsor. It was 200 ft. in diameter, and the expense of entertaining the knights thereof amounted to £100 a week. *Cp.* JOHN O'GROATS.

Knights of the Round Table. According to Malory (*Morte d'Arthur*, III, i and ii) there were 150 knights who had "sieges" at the table. King Leodegraunce brought 100 when he gave the table to King ARTHUR; MERLIN filled up 28 of the vacant seats, and the king elected GAWAIN and Tor; the remaining 20 were left for those who might prove worthy.

A list of the knights (151) and a description of their armour is given in the *Theatre of Honour* (1622) by Andrew Fairne. These knights went forth in quest of adventures, but their chief exploits were concerned with the quest of the Holy GRAIL.

SIR LANCELOT is meant for a model of fidelity, bravery, frailty in love, and repentance; Sir GALAHAD of chastity; Sir GAWAIN of courtesy; Sir KAY of a rude, boastful knight, and Sir MODRED of treachery.

There is still a "Knights of the Round Table" Club which claims to be the oldest social club in the world, having been founded in 1721. Garrick, Dickens, Toole, Sir Henry Irving, and Tenniel are among those who have been members.

A round table conference. A conference in which no participant has precedence and at which it is agreed that the question in dispute shall be settled amicably with the maximum amount of "give and take" on each side.

The expression came into prominence in connexion with a private conference in the house of Sir William Harcourt, 14 January 1887, with the view of trying to reunite the Liberal party after the split occasioned by Gladstone's advocacy of Irish Home Rule. Other politically notable Round Table Conferences were those on Indian government held in London (1931–1932).

A good round sum. A large sum of money.

Three thousand ducats; 'tis a good round sum.
SHAKESPEARE: *Merchant of Venice*, I, iii.

A round peg in a square hole. The same as a square peg in a round hole. *See* PEG.

A round robin. A petition or protest signed in a circular form, so that no name heads the list. The device is French, and the term seems to be a corruption of *rond* (round), *ruban* (a ribbon), and originally used by sailors.

At a round pace, or **rate.** Briskly, rapidly, smartly.

He cried again,
"To the wilds!" and Enid leading down

> the tracks...
> Round was their pace at first, but slack-
> en'd soon.
>
> TENNYSON: *Geraint and Enid.*

In round figures, or **numbers.** Disregarding fractions, units, etc., in tens, hundreds, etc., thus with the quantity ending in an o or round number. Thus we say, "His income in round figures was £5,000", although strictly accurately it may be £4,975, or, "The population of Haiti in 1962 was four millions in round numbers."

In the round. In the theatre, the production of plays on a central stage surrounded by the audience as in an arena, without proscenium arch or curtains.

Round dealing. Honest, straightforward dealing, without branching off into underhand tricks. The same as square dealing.

Round-up (Western U.S.A.). The gathering up of cattle by riding round them and driving them in. Hence, a gathering-in of scattered objects, or persons such as criminals. *See* RODEO.

To get round one. To take advantage of him by cajoling or flattery; to have one's own way through deception.

To round on one. To turn on him; to inform against him.

To walk the Round. Lawyers used frequently to give interviews to their clients in the Round Church in the TEMPLE; and "walking the Round" meant loitering about the church, in the hope of being hired for a witness.

Roundabout. A large revolving machine at FAIRS, circuses, etc., with wooden horses or the like which go round and round and are ridden by passengers to the strains of music, known in the U.S.A. as a *carousel.* From this arises the device at crossroads, whereby traffic circulates in one direction only.

What you lose on the swings you gain on the roundabouts. *See under* SWING.

Roundel, or **Roundle,** in HERALDRY, is a charge of a circular form. There are a number of varieties, distinguished by their colours or tinctures, as—a *Bezant,* tincture "or"; *Plate,* "argent"; *Torteau,* "gules"; *Hurt,* "azure"; *Ogress* or *Pellet,* "sable"; *Pomey* (because supposed to re-

semble an apple, Fr. *pomme*), "vert"; *Golpe,* "purpure"; *Guze,* "sanguine"; *Orange,* "tenney".

Roundheads. PURITANS of the time of the CIVIL WARS; especially Cromwell's soldiers. So called from their close-cropped hair as contrasted with the long hair fashionable among the Royalists or CAVALIERS. The name appears in 1641 in the affrays at WESTMINSTER when the mobs of apprentices were demonstrating against the EPISCOPACY.

Roundsmen. In the 18th century, the name given to those able-bodied paupers who were sent from house to house to find temporary employment. House occupiers and farmers paid the wages fixed by the parish but were reimbursed from the poor rate for all monies paid beyond a certain amount. Usually about half the wages came from the employer and half from the parish. The system was also known as the *billet* or *ticket* system from the chit for employment issued to the pauper by the parish overseer. This practice ended in 1834.

Roup, a name given to an auction in SCOTLAND. It is of Scandinavian origin and is connected with M. Swed. *ropa,* to shout.

Rout. A common term in the 18th century for a large evening party or fashionable assemblage. *Cp.* DRUM; HURRICANE, etc.

Routiers, or **Rutters** (roo' ti erz, rut' erz). Mediæval adventurers who made war a trade and let themselves out to anyone who would pay them. So called because they were always on the *route* or moving from place to place. (*Cp.* CONDOTTIERI.) Also the name given to early manuals of pilotage.

Rove. The original meaning was to shoot with arrows at marks that were selected at haphazard, the distance being unknown, with the object of practising judging distance.

Running at rovers. Running wild, at random, being without restraint.

To shoot at rovers. To shoot at random, without any distinct aim.

Rowan, or **Mountain Ash** (rou' an, rō' an). Called in Westmorland the "Wiggentree". It was greatly venerated by the DRUIDS and was formerly known as the "Witchen" because it was supposed to ward off WITCHES.

> Rowan-tree or reed
> Put the witches to speed.

Many mountain-ash berries are said to denote a deficient harvest. In Aberdeenshire it was customary to make crosses of rowan twigs on the eve of the INVENTION OF THE CROSS (*see under* CROSS) and to put them over doors and windows to ward off witches and evil spirits.

Rowley. Old Rowley. Charles II was so called after his favourite stallion. A portion of the Newmarket race-course is still called Rowley Mile and the Rowley Stakes are also held there.

> "Old Rowley himself, madam," said the King, entering the apartment with his usual air of easy composure.
> SCOTT: *Peveril of the Peak*, ch. xxxi.

The Rowley Poems. *See under* FORGERY.

Roxburghe Club, The (roks' brŏ). An association of bibliophiles founded in 1812 for the purpose of printing rare works or MSS. It was named after John, Duke of Roxburghe, a celebrated collector of ancient literature (1740–1804), and remains the most distinguished gathering of bibliophiles in the world.

Roy, Le, or **La Reine s'avisera** (The king (or queen) will consider it). This is the royal veto on a parliamentary bill, last put into force 11 March 1707, when Queen Anne refused her assent to a Scottish Militia Bill. *See* ROYAL ASSENT.

Royal. Royal Academy. Founded in 1768, with Sir Joshua Reynolds as the first president, "for the purpose of cultivating and improving the arts of painting, sculpture and architecture".

Royal and Ancient. The name by which the game of golf has been known since early days when the Scottish kings practised it. James IV of SCOTLAND is the first recorded royal patron and Mary, Queen of Scots, was playing golf when news was brought to her of Lord Darnley's death.

Royal Assent to parliamentary bills is still given in Norman French. The form of assent to public and private bills is *Le Roy*, or *La Reine le veult*; to personal bills *Soit fait comme il est désiré*; and to taxation and supply, *Le Roy* or *La Reine*

remercie ses bons sujets, accepte leur benevolence, et ainsi le veult. Cp. LE ROY S'AVISERA.

Royal Bounty. A part of the CIVIL LIST out of which the British sovereign makes gifts to charities and pays for official subscriptions.

Royal Exchange, Cornhill, London. The original exchange, founded by Sir Thomas Gresham, whose crest was a GRASSHOPPER, was opened by Queen Elizabeth I in 1568 and was modelled on the Bourse at Antwerp as a place for London Merchants to transact their business. It was burnt down during the GREAT FIRE and a new exchange was opened in 1670 but this was again destroyed by fire in 1838. It is said that before the bells fell they had chimed *There's nae luck aboot the hoose*. The third building was opened by Queen Victoria in 1844. In 1928 the building was taken over by the Royal Exchange Assurance Corporation which had occupied offices there since 1720.

Royal Flush. In poker, a hand consisting of the ace, king, queen, jack, and ten of one suit.

Royal Merchants. The wealthy, mediæval families such as the MEDICI of Florence and the Grimaldi of Genoa.

> Glancing an eye of pity on his losses,
> That have of late so huddled on his back,
> Enow to press a royal merchant down.
> SHAKESPEARE: *Merchant of Venice*, IV, i.

Sir Thomas Gresham, founder of the ROYAL EXCHANGE, was called a "royal merchant" from his wealth and influence.

Royal Oak. *See* OAK-APPLE DAY.

Royal road to learning, etc. A direct and easy way. Royal roads were generally straighter and better than most roads.

Royal Society. The premier scientific society in Great Britain. It was established in 1660 and incorporated as the Royal Society in 1662, but its origins can be traced to the meetings of philosophers and scientists held at Gresham College in 1645. It met at the college until 1710 and then moved to Crane Court, FLEET STREET. In 1780 it transferred to SOMERSET HOUSE and thence to Burlington House in 1857. Fellowship of the

Royal Society is the most coveted honour among scientists.

Royal Titles. *See* TITLES OF.

Royalists. *See* CAVALIERS.

Rozinante, Rocinante (roz i năn' ti). The wretched JADE of a riding-horse belonging to Don QUIXOTE. Although it was nothing but skin and bone—and worn out at that—he regarded it as a priceless charger surpassing "the BUCEPHALUS of ALEXANDER and the Babieca of the CID". The name, which is applied to similar hacks, is from Span. *rocin*, a jade, the *ante* (before) implying that once upon a time, perhaps, it had been a horse.

Rub. An impediment. The expression is taken from bowls where "rub" means that something hinders the free movement of your wood.

> We sometimes had those little rubs which Providence sends to enhance the value of its favours.
>
> GOLDSMITH: *The Vicar of Wakefield*, ch. i.

Don't rub it in! Yes, I know I've made a mistake, but you needn't go on emphasizing the fact.

Rub of the green. *See under* GREEN.

To rub shoulders with. To mix closely in company.

To rub up. To refresh the memory, to revive one's knowledge of a subject.

To rub up the wrong way. To annoy, to irritate by lack of tact, etc.; as a cat is irritated when its fur is rubbed the wrong way.

Rubaiyát (plural of *Ruba'i*), means quatrains, much used by Arabic poets, and familiar to English readers through Fitzgerald's *Rubaiyát* of OMAR KHAYYAM (1859).

Rubber. In WHIST, bridge, and some other games, a set of three games, the best two of three, or the third game of the set. The origin of the term is uncertain, but it may be a transference from bowls, in which the collision of two woods is a *rubber*, because they RUB against each other.

To rubber-stamp. To authorize as a matter of routine, to approve automatically, without any personal examination or check. From the use of rubber stamps on routine documents, etc., in place of a written authorization.

Rübezahl. A mountain spirit of German folk-lore, ruler of the weather, also called Herr Johannes, whose home is in the Riesengebirge (Giant Mountains), the mountain range which separates Prussian Silesia (now in Poland) and Bohemia (Czechodslovakia).

Rubicon. To cross the Rubicon. To take an irrevocable step; as when the Germans crossed the Belgian frontier in August 1914, which led to war with Great Britain. The Rubicon was a small river which separated ancient Italy from Cisalpine GAUL (the province allotted to Julius CÆSAR). When Cæsar crossed this stream in 49 B.C. he passed beyond the limits of his province and became an invader in Italy, thus precipitating war with Pompey and the Senate.

Rubric (roo'brik) (Lat. *rubrica*, red ochre or vermilion). The Romans called an ordinance or law a rubric, because it was written with vermilion.

The liturgical directions, titles, etc., in a Prayer Book are known as the *Rubrics* because these were (and sometimes still are) printed in red (*cp.* RED-LETTER DAY).

> No date prefix'd
> Directs me in the starry rubric set.
>
> MILTON: *Paradise Regained*, IV, 392.

The directions given on formal examination papers concerning the selection of questions to be answered, etc., are called the *rubrics*.

Ruby. The ancients considered the ruby to be an antidote to poison, to preserve persons from plague, to banish grief, to repress the ill effects of luxuries, and to divert the mind from EVIL thoughts.

It has always been a valuable stone, and even today a fine Burma ruby will cost more than a diamond of the same size.

> Who can find a virtuous woman? for her price is far above rubies.
>
> *Prov.* xxxi, 10; *cp.* also *Job* xxviii, 18, and *Prov.* viii, 11.

Marco Polo said that the king of Ceylon had the finest ruby he had ever seen. "It is a span long, as thick as a man's arm, and without a flaw." Kublai Khan offered the value of a city for it, but the king would not part with it, though all the treasures of the world were to be laid at his feet.

The perfect ruby. An alchemist's term for the ELIXIR, or PHILOSOPHER'S STONE.

Ruddock. The redbreast "sacred to the household gods": *see* ROBIN RED-BREAST. The word is ultimately from O.E. *rudu*, redness, whence *ruddy*. SHAKESPEARE makes Arviragus say over Imogen:

> Thou shalt not lack
> The flower that's like thy face, pale primrose; nor
> The azur'd hare-bell...the ruddock would,
> With charitable bill...bring thee all this.
> *Cymbeline*, IV, ii.

Rudolphine Tables, The (roo dol' fin). Astronomical calculations begun by Tycho Brahe, continued by Kepler, and published in 1627. They were named after Kepler's patron, Kaiser Rudolph II.

Rue (roo), called HERB OF GRACE, because it was employed for sprinkling holy water.

See also DIFFERENCE. Ophelia says:

> There's rue for you, and here's some for me! we may call it "herb of grace" o' Sundays.
> SHAKESPEARE: *Hamlet*, IV, v.

Ruff. An early forerunner of WHIST, very popular in the late 16th and early 17th centuries, later called *slamm*. The act of trumping at whist, etc., is still called "the ruff".

Rufus (The Red). William II of England (1056, 1087–1100).

Ruggiero. *See* ROGERO.

Rule, or **Regulus, St.** A priest of Patræ in Achaia, who is said to have come to SCOTLAND in the 4th century, bringing with him relics of ST. ANDREW, and to have founded the town and bishopric of St. Andrews. The name Killrule (*Cella Reguli*) perpetuates his memory.

Rule. Rule, Britannia. Words by James Thomson (1700–1748), author of *The Seasons*; music by Dr. Arne (1710–1778). It first appeared in a masque entitled *Alfred* produced in August 1740 at Maidenhead at Cliveden House. It was written at the command of the PRINCE OF WALES and performed before him. The original opening was:

> When Britain first, at Heaven's command,

> Arose from out the azure main,
> This was the charter of the land,
> And guardian angels sung this strain:
> "Rule, Britannia, rule the waves;
> Britons never will be slaves."

In the rising of 1745 "Rule, Britannia" was sung by the JACOBITES with modifications appropriate to their cause.

Rule nisi (nī' sī). A "rule" is an order from one of the superior courts, and a "rule nisi" (*cp.* NISI) is such an order "to show cause". That is, the rule is to be held absolute *unless* the party to whom it applies can "show cause" why it should not be so.

Rule of the Road. *See under* ROAD.

Rule of thumb. *See under* THUMB.

Rule the roost. *See under* ROAST.

Twelve Good Rules. (1) Urge no healths; (2) Profane no divine ordinances; (3) Touch no state matters; (4) Reveal no secrets; (5) Pick no quarrels; (6) Make no comparisons; (7) Maintain no ill opinions; (8) Keep no bad company; (9) Encourage no vice; (10) Make no long meals; (11) Repeat no grievances; (12) Lay no wagers.

The rules were framed and displayed in many taverns in the 18th century and derived from a broadside showing a rough-cut of the execution of CHARLES I and were said to have been "found in the study of King Charles the First, of Blessed Memory". Goldsmith refers to them in *The Deserted Village* (line 232).

Rulers, Titles of. The following titles are (1) designations that approximately correspond to our *King* or *Emperor* (*e.g. Bey, Mikado, Sultan*), and (2) appellatives that were originally the proper name of some individual ruler (*e.g. Cæsar*). Some are now, of course, obsolete.

Abgarus. A title of the kings of Edessa (99 B.C.-A.D. 217).

Abimelech (father of counsel). A title of the king of the ancient Philistines.

Akhoond. King and high priest of the Swat (N.W. provinces of India).

Ameer, Amir. Ruler of Afghanistan, Sind, and certain other Mohammedan princes.

Archon. Chief of the nine magistrates of ancient ATHENS. The next in rank was called *Basileus.*

Augustus. The title of the Roman Emperor when the heir-presumptive was styled *Cæsar*.

Beglerbeg. See BEY *below*.

Begum. A queen, princess, or lady of high rank in India.

Bey—of Tunis. In the Turkish Empire, a bey was usually a superior military officer, or the governor of a minor province or *sanjak*.

Brenn, or *Brenhin*. A war-chief of the ancient Gauls. A dictator appointed by the DRUIDS in times of danger.

Bretwalda. See BRETWALDA.

Cacique. See CAZIQUE, *below*.

Cæsar. Originally a surname of the Julian family, then assumed by successive Roman emperors and later by their heir-presumptive. *Cp.* AUGUSTUS, *above*.

Caliph, or *Calif* (successor). Successors of MOHAMMED in temporal and spiritual affairs. After the first four successors the caliphate passed to the Omayyad dynasty (660), thence to the ABBASSIDES (670–1538). The supposed transfer to the OTTOMANS is not authenticated and, in 1924, the caliphate was suppressed by the Turkish assembly.

Candace. A title of the queens of Meroe in Upper Nubia.

Caudillo. See CAUDILLO.

Cazique, or *Cacique*. A native prince of the ancient Peruvians, Cubans, Mexicans, etc., also applied to chiefs of Indian tribes in South America and the West Indies.

Chagan. The chief of the Avars.

Cham. See KHAN, *below*.

Czar. See TSAR, *below*.

Dey. Governor of Algiers before it was annexed to France in 1830; also the 16th-century rulers of Tunis and Tripoli.

Diwan. The native chief of Palanpur, India.

Doge (Duke). The ruler of the old Venetian Republic (*c.* 700–1797); also that of Genoa (1339–1797).

Duce. See DUCE.

Duke. The ruler of a duchy (Lat. *dux*, a leader); formerly in many European countries of sovereign rank.

Elector. A prince of the HOLY ROMAN EMPIRE of sovereign rank entitled to take part in the election of the Emperor.

Emir. The independent chieftain of certain Arabian provinces as Bokhara, Nejd, etc.; also given to Arab chiefs who claim descent from MOHAMMED.

Emperor. The ruler of an empire, especially of the HOLY ROMAN EMPIRE from Lat. *Imperator*, one who commands.

Exarch. The title of a viceroy of the BYZANTINE EMPIRE, especially the *Exarch* of Ravenna, who was *de facto* governor of Italy.

Führer. See FÜHRER.

Gaekwar. Formerly the title of the ruler of the Mahrattas; then that of the ruler of Baroda (his son being *Gaekwad*). The word is Marathi for a cowherd.

Gauleiter (Ger., "region leader"). The ruler of a province under the NAZI régime (1933–45).

Holkar. The title of the Maharajah of Indore.

Hospodar. The title borne by the princes of Moldavia and Wallachia before their union with Rumania (Slavic, "lord, master").

Imperator. See EMPEROR, *above*.

Inca. The title of the sovereigns of Peru up to the conquest by Pizarro (1532).

Kabaka. The native ruler in the Buganda province of Uganda.

Kaiser. The German form of CÆSAR (*see above*); the old title of the HOLY ROMAN EMPEROR and of the later Austrian and German Emperors.

Khan. The chief rulers of Tartar, Mongol, and Turkish tribes, as successors of Genghis Khan (d. 1227). The word means "lord" or "prince".

Khedive. The title meaning "prince" or "sovereign" conferred in 1867 by the SULTAN of Turkey on the viceroy or governor of Egypt. It was abandoned in favour of *Sultan* in 1914. *Cp.* VALI, *below*.

King. See KING.

Lama. See LAMA.

Maharajah (Hind., "the great king"). The title of many of the native rulers of Indian states.

Maharao. The title of the rulers of Cutch, Kotah, and Sirohi, India.

Maharao Rajah. The ruler of Bundi, India.

Maharawal. The rulers of Banswana, Dungarpur, Jaisalmer, and Partabgarh, India.

Mikado. See MIKADO. *Cp.* SHOGUN.

Mir. The ruler of Khairpur, India.

Mogul. See MOGUL.

Mpret. The old title of the Albanian rulers (from Lat. *imperator*), revived in 1913 in favour of Prince William of Wied, whose Mpretship lasted only a few months.

Nawab. The native rulers of Bhopal, Tonk, Jaora, etc.; and formerly of Bengal.

Negus (properly *Negus Negust*, "King of Kings"). The native name of the Emperor of Ethiopia.

Nizam. The title of the ruler of Hyderabad.

Padishah (Pers., "protecting lord"). A title of the former SULTAN of Turkey, the Shah of Persia, and of the former Great MOGULS.

Pendragon. See PENDRAGON.

Pharaoh. See PHARAOH.

Prince. Formerly in common use as the title of a reigning sovereign, and still used in a few cases, *e.g.* the Prince of Monaco, the Prince of Liechtenstein.

Rajah. Hindustani for "King" (*cp.* MAHARAJAH, *above*); the title of the rulers of Cochin, Ratlam, Tippera, Chamba, Faridkot, Mandi, Pudukota, Rajgarh, Rajpipla, Sailana, and Tehri (Garhwal). *Cp.* REX, *below*.

Rex. The Latin equivalent of "King", connected with *regere*, to rule, and with Sans. *rajan* (whence RAJAH), a king.

Sachem, Sagamore. Chieftains of certain tribes of Northern American Indians.

Satrap. The governor of a province in ancient Persia.

Shah (Pers., king). The supreme ruler of Persia and some other Eastern countries. *Cp.* PADISHAH, *above*.

Shaikh or *Sheikh*. An Arab chief, or head man of a tribe.

Shogun. See SHOGUN.

Sindhia. The special title of the Maharajah of Gwalior.

Sirdar. The commander-in-chief of the Egyptian army and military governor of Egypt (a British officer during the occupation, 1882–1922). Also applied to certain nobles in India (Pers. *sardar*, leader, officer).

Stadtholder. Originally a provincial viceroy in the Netherlands, later the chief executive officer of the United Provinces.

Sultan (also *Soldan*). The title of the rulers of certain Mohammedan states.

Tetrarch. The governor of the fourth part of a province in the ancient Roman Empire.

Thakur Sahib. The title of the native ruler of Gondal, India.

Tsar, or *Czar*. The common title of the former Emperors of Russia, first assumed by Ivan the Terrible in 1547 (Lat. *Cæsar*). His wife was the *Tsarina*, his son the *Tsarevitch*, and his daughter the *Tsarevna*. The latter titles were eventually reserved for the eldest son and his wife respectively.

Vali. The title of the governors of Egypt prior to their holding of the style KHEDIVE (*see above*).

Voivode, or *Vaivode* (Russ., "the leader of an army"). A title once used by the princes of Moldavia and Wallachia, later called HOSPODARS (*see above*).

Wali. A title of the ruler or Khan of Kalat, India.

It should be noted that many of these titles now refer to former rulers (*e.g.* those of Indian States and Persia).

Rum-Runners. During the prohibition era in the U.S.A., those engaged in smuggling illicit liquor by speedboats across the lakes from Canada or from ships outside the THREE-MILE LIMIT. The limit was subsequently increased to twelve miles by agreement with other powers and enforced by U.S.N. destroyers. These, when over-age, were passed to Great Britain in 1940 under the LEND-LEASE arrangements. *See* BOOTLEGGER; MOONSHINER.

Ruminate. To think, to meditate upon some subject; literally, "to chew the cud" (Lat. *rumino*; from *rumen*, the throat).

> He chew'd
> The thrice-turn'd cud of wrath, and cook'd his spleen.
> TENNYSON: *The Princess*, Pt. I, i.64.

Rump, The. The end of the backbone, with the buttocks. The term was applied contemptuously to the remnant of the LONG PARLIAMENT that was left after PRIDE'S PURGE. It first numbered less than 60 M.P.s and, when augmented, not more than 125. It abolished the HOUSE OF LORDS and the monarchy and declared England a COMMONWEALTH. It was dismissed by Cromwell in 1653, but resumed its sitting in 1659 and in 1660 Monck secured the recall of its purged members. It was finally dissolved in March 1660.

Rumpelstiltskin, or **Rumpelstilzchen** (rum pel stilts' kin). A passionate little deformed DWARF of German folk-tale. A miller's daughter was enjoined by a king to spin straw into GOLD, and the dwarf did it for her, on condition that she would give him her first child. The maiden married the king, and grieved so bitterly when the child was born that the dwarf promised to relent if within three days she could find out his name. Two days were spent in vain guesses, but the third day one of the queen's servants heard a strange voice singing:

> Little dreams my dainty dame
> Rumpelstilzchen is my name.

The child was saved, and the dwarf killed himself with rage.

Run. A long run, a short run. Said of a theatrical or film show. "It had a long run" means it was performed repeatedly over a long period, owing to its popularity. The allusion is to a long-distance run or race. A *short run* means that the show did not take on with the public and was soon withdrawn.

He that runs may read. The BIBLE quotation in *Hab.* ii, 2, is, "Write the vision, and make it plain upon tables, that he may run that readeth it."
Cowper says:

> But truths, on which depends our main concern ...
> Shine by the side of every path we tread
> With such a lustre, he that runs may read.
> *Tirocinium*, 1.77.

In the long run. Eventually, in the final result. The allusion is to the runner who may be outpaced at the start but who draws ahead before the finish. The hare got the start, but in the long run the patient perseverance of the tortoise won the race.

On the run. Moving from place to place and hiding from the authorities; said especially of criminals, etc.

Run of the mill. The expected or usual type, or sequence of events. Provided that a steady flow of water issued from the mill-pond, the mill would run smoothly and normally.

To be run in. To be arrested and taken to the lock-up.

To give someone a run for his money. To make him expend considerable effort, to lead him a pretty dance.

To go with a run. To go swimmingly; "without a HITCH". As a rope goes with a run when let go free, instead of being paid out gradually.

To have a run for one's money. To obtain satisfaction or pleasure from one's expenditure or efforts, even if the outcome is not entirely successful; as a bet on a horse may give the backer some excitement whether it wins or not.

To have the run of the house. To have free access and liberty to make full use of what it offers.

To run amok, or **amuck.** To indulge in physical violence while in a state of frenzy. *Amuck* or *amok* is the Malay *amog*, a state of frenzy.

To run down. To cease to go or act from lack of motive force, as a clock when the spring is fully unwound. *See also* TO RUN A MAN DOWN *under* DOWN.

To run into the ground. To pursue too far; to exhaust a topic.

To run rings round. To outclass completely. To be so much better than one's rival that one can run round him and still reach the winning post first.

To run riot. *See under* RIOT.

To run the show. To take charge of it, to make oneself responsible for its success.

To run through. "To run through one's inheritance" is to squander it at a rapid rate; "to run through one's part in a play" is to read or rehearse it; "to run through the accounts" is to make a quick general survey of them. "To run a person through" is to pass one's sword or rapier through his body.

To run to earth. To discover in a hiding-place; to get to the bottom of a matter. A METAPHOR from fox-hunting when the quarry is run to its "earth" or lair.

Runners. *See* REDBREASTS.

Runner-up. The competitor or team that finishes in second place; after the winner.

Runcible Hat, Spoon. In Edward Lear's *How Pleasant to know Mr. Lear* there is mention of a runcible hat and in the *Owl and the Pussycat* a runcible spoon. What *runcible* denotes is not apparent. Some who profess to know describe the spoon as a kind of fork having three broad prongs, one of which has a sharp cutting edge.

> They dined on mince and slices of quince
> Which they ate with a runcible spoon.
> *The Owl and the Pussycat.*

Rune (roon). A letter or character of the earliest alphabet in use among the Gothic tribes of northern Europe. Runic inscriptions most commonly occur in Scandinavia and parts of the British Isles. Runes were employed for purposes of secrecy, charms, or DIVINATION; and the word is also applied to ancient lore or poetry expressed in runes. *Rune* is related to O.E. *rūn*, secret. The deeds of warriors were recorded on runic staves and knowledge of rune writing was supposed to have been introduced by ODIN. *See* FUTHORC; OGAM.

Runic Staff, or **Wand.** *See* CLOG ALMANAC.

Running. Running footmen. Men servants in the early part of the 18th century whose duty was to run beside the slow-moving coach horses and advise the innkeeper of his approaching guests, bear torches, pay turnpikes, etc. The pole which they carried was to help the cumbrous coach out of the numerous sloughs. OLD Q (*see under* Q) was said to be the last to employ them. The "Running Footman" used as a PUBLIC-HOUSE SIGN derives from the old Tudor foot postmen.

Running the Hood, or **the Hood Game.** It is said that (in the 13th century) Lady Mowbray was passing over Haxey Hill (Lincolnshire) when the wind blew away her hood. It was recovered by 12 rustics who tossed it from one to the other. The event is celebrated annually on 6 January, when the participants called *boggans* play a curious kind of rugby with rolled canvas hoods.

Running Thursday. 13 December 1688, two days after the flight of James II. A rumour ran that the French and Irish papists had landed; panic ensued and many people ran for their lives into the country.

Running water. No enchantment can subsist in a living stream; if, therefore, a person can interpose a brook betwixt himself and the witches, sprites, or GOBLINS chasing him, he is in perfect safety. Burns's tale of *Tam o'Shanter* turns upon this superstition.

His shoes are made of running leather. *See under* SHOE.

Quite out of the running. Quite out of the competition; not worthy of consideration; like a horse that has been SCRATCHED for a race and is thus not "in the running".

To make the running. To set the pace or standard.

Rupert. Prince Rupert's drops. Bubbles made by dropping molten glass into water. Their form is that of a tadpole, and if the smallest portion of the "tail" is nipped off, the whole flies into fine dust with explosive violence. They were introduced into ENGLAND by Prince Rupert (1619–1682), grandson of James I and Royalist cavalry leader during the CIVIL WARS. *Prince's metal*, seemingly an alloy of brass or copper, was also his invention.

Ruritania (roo ri tā' nya). An imaginary kingdom in pre-World War I Europe where Anthony Hope placed the adventures of his hero in the novels *The Prisoner of Zenda* (1894) and *Rupert of Hentzau* (1898). The name is frequently applied to any small state where politics and intrigues of a melodramatic and romantic interest are the natural order of the day.

Rush. Friar Rush. *See under* FRIAR.

Not worth a rush. Worthless; not worth a STRAW. When floors used to be strewn with rushes, distinguished guests were given clean rushes, but those of inferior standing were left with used rushes or none at all, being considered "not worth a rush".

Keep your wisdom and your righteousness and piety for yourself. I do not value them a rush; but your love I will have.

S. BARING-GOULD: *In the Roar of the Sea*,
ch.xxxi.

Rush-bearing Sunday. A SUNDAY, generally near the festival of the SAINT to whom the church is dedicated, when anciently it was customary to renew the rushes with which the church floor was strewn. The custom is still observed at St. Mary Redcliffe, Bristol, on WHIT SUNDAY and at Ambleside, Grasmere, and elsewhere in Westmorland. At Ambleside, a rush-bearing procession is held on the Saturday nearest St. Anne's Day (26 July), the church being dedicated to St. Anne.

Russel. A common name given to a fox, from its russet colour.

And daun Russell the fox stirte up at ones
And by the gargat hente Chauntecleer,
And on his bak toward the wode hym beer.

CHAUCER: *The Nonnes Preestes Tale*,
l. 514.

Rustam, and **Rustem.** The Persian HERCULES, the son of Zal, prince of Sedjistan, famous for his victory over the white DRAGON Asdeev. His combat for two days with Prince Isfendiar is a favourite subject with the Persian poets. Matthew Arnold's poem *Sohrab and Rustam* gives an account of Rustam fighting with and killing his son Sohrab.

Let Zal and Rustrum bluster as they will,
Or Hatim call to Supper—heed not you.
FITZGERALD: *Omar Khayyám*, x.

Rusty. To turn rusty. Like a rusty bolt, which sticks and will not move; to become obstinate, or surly and ill-tempered. **To cut up rusty** is a similar expression.

Rye-house Plot. A conspiracy in 1683 to murder Charles II and his brother James on their return from Newmarket near the Rye House, Hoddesdon, Hertfordshire, the home of Rumbold, a Cromwellian, where the plot was hatched. It was the work of WHIG extremists and former Cromwellians but miscarried because the royal party left sooner than planned. Lord William Russell and Algernon Sidney, although not active participants, were executed for complicity.

Rymenhild. *See* KING HORN.

S

S. The nineteenth letter of the English alphabet (eighteenth of the ancient Roman), representing the Greek *sigma* from the Phoenician and Hebrew *shin*. As a mediæval Roman numeral S stood for 7, also 70; and S̄ for 70,000.

Collar of S.S., S's or **Esses.** *See under* COLLAR.

'S. A euphemistic abbreviation of *God's*, formerly common in oaths and expletives; as *'Sdeath* (God's death), *'Sblood* (God's blood), *'Sdeins* (God's *dignes*, *i.e.* dignity), *'Sfoot*, etc.

$ The typographical sign for the DOLLAR, is thought to be a variation of the 8 with which pieces of eight were stamped, and was in use in the United States before the adoption of the Federal currency in 1785. Another, perhaps fanciful, derivation is from the letters U.S.

S.A. *See* S.S.; NIGHT OF THE LONG KNIVES.

S.J. (*Societas Jesu*). The Society of Jesus; denoting that the priest after whose name those letters are placed is a JESUIT.

S O S. The Morse code signal (3 dots, 3 dashes, 3 dots, ...— — —...) used by shipping, etc., in distress to summon immediate aid; hence any urgent appeal for help.

The letters, in morse a convenient combination, have been popularly held to stand for *save our souls* or *save our ship*.

S.P.Q.R. S*enatus* P*opulusque* R*omanus* (The Roman Senate and People). Letters inscribed on the standards, etc., of ancient ROME. Facetiously, "small profits and quick returns".

S.S. (Ger.). *Schutz Staffeln*, an armed force that originated as part of Hitler's bodyguard in 1923 with the predominant S.A. (*Sturm Abteilung*). In 1929, Heinrich Himmler took on the S.S. and

defining its duties as "to find out, to fight and to destroy all open and secret enemies of the FÜHRER, the National Socialist Movement, and our racial resurrection", raised it to a position of dominating power and great numerical strength. During World War II, S.S. Divisions fought with fanatical zeal. *See also* NIGHT OF THE LONG KNIVES.

S.T.P. (*Sacræ Theologiæ Professor*). "Professor of Sacred Theology". "D.D."—*i.e.* Doctor of Divinity—is the English equivalent of "S.T.P."

Sabæans, Sabeans (sȧ bē' ȧnz). The ancient people of Yemen in south-western Arabia; from Arabic Saba', or SHEBA (*see Job* vi, 19).

Sabaism (sāb' ā izm). The worship of the stars, or the "host of heaven" (from Heb. *caba*, host). The term is also sometimes applied to the religion of the SABIANS.

Sabaoth (sȧ bā' oth). The Bible phrase *Lord God of Sabaoth* means *Lord God of Hosts* not *of the Sabbath*, *Sabaoth* being Hebrew for "armies" or "hosts". The epithet has been frequently misunderstood, as in the last stanza of Spenser's *Faerie Queene* (VII, viii, 21):

> All that moveth doth in change delight:
> But thenceforth all shall rest eternally
> With him that is God of Sabaoth hight:
> O! that great Sabaoth God, grant me
> that Sabbath's sight.

Sabbatæans. The disciples of Sabbatai Sebi (1626–1676) or Zebi of Smyrna who proclaimed himself MESSIAH in 1648. He was arrested at Constantinople in 1666 and accepted the MOSLEM faith. His learning and personal appeal were extraordinary and in his heyday he had thousands of followers. He was a Jew of Spanish descent.

Sabbath (săb′ăth) (Heb. *shabath*, to rest). Properly, the seventh day of the week, enjoined on the ancient Hebrews by the fourth Commandment (*Exod.* xx, 8–11) as a day of rest and worship; the Christian SUNDAY, "the Lord's Day", the first day of the week, is often inaccurately referred to as "the Sabbath". For Mohammedans, FRIDAY is the weekly day of rest.

A Sabbath Day's Journey (*Acts* i, 12) with the Jews was not to exceed the distance between the ark and the extreme end of the camp. This was 2,000 cubits, about 1,000 yards. It arose from the injunction (*Exod.* xvi, 29) against journeying on the Sabbath with that (*Jos.* iii, 4) providing for a distance of 2,000 cubits between the ark and the people when they travelled in the wilderness. As their tents were this distance from the ark, it was held that they might properly travel this distance, since the injunction could not have been intended to prevent their attendance at worship.

Sabbatarians. Those who observe the day of rest with excessive strictness, a peculiar feature of English and Scottish Puritanism enforced during the period of the COMMONWEALTH when sport and recreation was forbidden. Some relaxation occurred after the RESTORATION, but the Lord's Day Observance Act of 1782 closed all places of entertainment on a SUNDAY where an admission fee was charged. A Sunday Entertainments Act, 1932, empowered local authorities to license the Sunday opening of cinemas and musical entertainments; the opening of museums, etc., was permitted. The Bill was opposed by the Lord's Day Observance Society.

Sabbatians. Members of a 4th-century NOVATIAN sect, followers of Sabbatius. They followed the Quartodeciman rule.

Sabbatical Year (sà băt′ i kàl). One year in seven, when all the land, according to Mosaic law, was to lie fallow (*Exod.* xxiii, 10, etc.; *Lev.* xxv, 2–7; *Deut.* xv, 1–11). The term is used in universities, etc., for a specified period of freedom from academic duties, during which time a professor or lecturer is released to study or travel.

Sabean. *See* SABÆANS.

Sabians. A semi-Christian sect of Babylonia, akin to the MANDÆANS or Christians of St. John, a GNOSTIC sect which arose in the 2nd and 3rd centuries and still survives south of Baghdad.

Sabines, The (săb′ īnz). An ancient people of central Italy, living in the Apennines, N. and NE. of ROME, and subjugated by the Romans about 290 B.C.

The Rape of the Sabine Women. The legend, connected with the foundation of ROME, is that, as ROMULUS had difficulty in providing his followers with wives, he invited the men of the neighbouring tribes to a festival. In the absence of the menfolk, the Roman youths raided the Sabine territory and carried off all the women they could find. The incident has frequently been depicted in art; Rubens's canvas in the National Gallery, London, is one of the best known examples.

Sable. The heraldic term for *black*, shown in engraving by horizontal lines crossing perpendicular ones. The fur of the animal of this name is brown, but it is probable that in the 15th century, when the heraldic term was first used, the fur was dyed black, as seal fur is today. Sable fur was always much sought after, and very expensive.

Sabotage (săb′ ō tazh). Wilfull and malicious destruction of machinery, plant, disruption of plans and projects, etc., by strikers, rebels, fifth columnists, etc. The term came into use after the great French railway strike in 1912, when the strikers cut the shoes (*sabots*) holding the railway lines.

Sabres. *See* BAYONETS.

Sabrina (sa brī′ nà). The Roman name of the river Severn, but according to Geoffrey of Monmouth (*Historia Britonum*) it is from Sabre, daughter of Locrin and his concubine Estrildis, whom he married after divorcing Guendolœna. The ex-Queen gathered an army and Locrin was slain. Estrildis and Sabre were consigned to the waters of the Severn. NEREUS took pity on Sabre, or Sabrina, and made here the river goddess.

Sac and Soc. *Sac* is O.E. *sacu*, strife, contention, litigation; *soc* is O.E. *soc*, the inquiry or investigation, a jurisdiction. The expression was common both before and after the Norman CONQUEST and used in grants of land to denote the conveyance of rights in private jurisdiction to the grantee.

Sacco Benedetto, or **Saco Bendito** (săk′ ō ben ė det′ ō, ben dē′ tō) (Ital., Sp., blessed sack, or cloak). The yellow linen robe with two crosses on it, and painted over with flames and devils, worn by those going to the stake after condemnation by the Spanish INQUISITION. *See* AUTO DA FÉ. Penitents who had been taken before the Inquisition had to wear this habit for a stated period. Those worn by Jews, sorcerers, and renegades bore a St. Andrew's CROSS in red on back and front.

Sachem (sā′ chem). A chief among some of the North American Indian tribes. *Sagamore* is a similar title.

Sacheverell. The Sacheverell Affair. On 5 November 1709, the anniversary of William III's landing at Torbay, Dr. Henry Sacheverell (*c. 1674–1724*) preached a sermon in St. Paul's before the Lord Mayor of London reasserting the doctrine of non-resistance and by implication attacking the principles of the GLORIOUS REVOLUTION and the DISSENTERS. The sermon, *The Perils of False Brethren*, was subsequently printed and the WHIG ministry illadvisedly impeached him (1710). The affair aroused tremendous excitement; Queen Anne attended Westminster Hall daily, and the London mob burnt Dissenters' chapels. Sacheverell was declared guilty by 69 votes to 52 and sentenced to abstain from preaching for three years and to have his sermon burnt by the common hangman. It was substantially a moral victory for Sacheverell and his TORY adherents.

Sack (Lat. *saccus*). A bag. According to tradition, it was the last word uttered before the tongues were confounded at BABEL. Also applied to certain loose garments and ladies' gowns hanging from the shoulders.

Friars of the Sack (Lat. *fratres saccati*). Also known as *De Penitencia*, or friars of the Penance of Jesus Christ, and so called from their sackcloth garment. They were abolished in 1274 but some remained in England until 1317.

A sack race. A contest in which each runner is put up to the armpits in a sack to jump or run as well as the size of the sack permits.

To get the sack, or **To be sacked.** To be dismissed from employment. The phrase was current in 17th-century France (*On luy a donné son sac*); and the probable explanation of the term is that workmen carried their implements in a bag or sack, and when discharged took up their bag of tools and departed to seek a job elsewhere. The SULTAN used to put in a sack, and throw into the BOSPORUS any one of his harem he wished to be rid of; but this has no connexion with the phrase.

To wear sackcloth and ashes. Metaphorically, an expression of contrition and penitence. An allusion to the Hebrew custom of wearing sackcloth and ashes as suitably humble attire for religious ceremonies, mourning, penitence, etc. The sackcloth in question was a coarse dark haircloth from which sacks were made.

Sack. The old name for dry wines of the sherry type such as Madeira sack, Canary sack, Palm sack. It appears to be derived from span. *saca*, export, not from Fr. *sec*, dry.

Saco Bendito. *See* SACCO BENEDETTO.

Sacrament (Lat. *sacramentum*). Originally "a military oath" taken by the Roman soldiers not to desert their standard, turn their back on the enemy, or abandon their general. Traces of this meaning survive in early Christian usage but its present meaning comes from its employment in the Latin NEW TESTAMENT to mean "sacred mystery". Hence its application to baptism, confirmation, the EUCHARIST, etc.

The five sacraments are Confirmation, Penance, Orders, Matrimony, and EXTREME UNCTION. These are not counted "Sacraments of the GOSPEL". (*See Book of Common Prayer, Articles of Religion*, XXV.)

The seven sacraments are BAPTISM, Confirmation, the EUCHARIST, Penance, Orders, Matrimony, and EXTREME UNCTION.

The two sacraments of the PROTEST-

ANT Churches are BAPTISM and the Lord's Supper.

Sacramentarians. The name given by Luther to those who maintained that no change took place in the eucharistic elements after consecration but that the bread and wine are only the body and blood of Christ in a metaphorical sense. The name was thus applied in the 16th century to those who did not accept the REAL PRESENCE.

Sacred (Lat. *sacrare*, to consecrate). That which is consecrated or dedicated to religious use.

The Sacred Band. A body of 300 Theban "Ironsides" who fought against Sparta in the 4th century B.C. They specially distinguished themselves at Leuctra (371), and the Band was annihilated at Chæronea (338).

The Sacred City. *See* HOLY CITY.

The Sacred College. The College of Cardinals (*see under* CARDINAL).

A sacred cow. Any institution, long-cherished practice, custom, etc., treated as immune from criticism, modification, or abolition. An allusion to the fact that the cow is held sacred by the Hindus.

The Sacred Heart. *See under* HEART.

The Sacred Isle, or **Holy Island.** IRELAND was so called from its many SAINTS and Guernsey from its many monks. The island referred to by Moore in his *Irish Melodies* is Scattery, to which St. Senanus retired and vowed no woman should set foot thereon.

Enhallow (Norse *Eyinhalga*, holy isle) is a small island in the Orkney group where cells for the Irish anchorite fathers are still said to exist. *See also* HOLY ISLAND.

Sacred Majesty. *See* MAJESTY.

The Sacred War. In Greek history, one of the wars waged by the AMPHICTYONIC League in defence of the temple and ORACLE of DELPHI.

The Sacred Way. *See* SACRA VIA *under* VIA.

The Sacred Weed. VERVAIN (*see also* HERBA SACRA), or—humorously—tobacco, also called "divine."

Sacring Bell (săk' ring). From the obsolete verb to *sacre*, to consecrate, used especially of sovereigns and BISHOPS. The bell rung in churches to draw attention to the most solemn parts of the MASS. In mediæval times it served to announce to those outside that the Mass was in progress, and for this purpose often a handbell was rung out of a side window. It is more usually called the **Sanctus bell** because it was rung at the saying of the *Sanctus* at the beginning of the CANON OF THE MASS (*see under* CANON), and also at the Consecration and Elevation and other moments. It is still used in the ROMAN CATHOLIC CHURCH and certain other Churches.

Sacy's Bible. *See* BIBLE, SOME SPECIALLY NAMED EDITIONS.

Sad. Sad bread (Lat. *panis gravis*). Heavy bread, bread that has not risen properly. SHAKESPEARE calls it "distressful bread"—not the bread of distress, but the *panis gravis* or ill-made bread eaten by those who cannot get better. In America unleavened cakes are known as *sad cakes*.

Saddle. A saddle of mutton. The two loins with the connecting vertebræ.

Boot and saddle. *See under* BOOT.

I will lose the horse or win the saddle. *See under* HORSE.

Set the saddle on the right horse. Lay the blame on those who deserve it.

To be in the saddle. To be in office, to be in a position of authority; also to be ready for work and eager to get on with it.

To saddle with responsibility. To put the responsibility on, to make responsible for.

Sadducees (săd' ū sēz). A Jewish party opposed to the PHARISEES. They did not accept oral tradition, but only the written Law, denied the existence of ANGELS and spirits and rejected the idea of future punishments in an after-life, as well as the resurrection of the body. They were major opponents of Christ and His disciples and were involved in the events leading to His death. Substantially, they represented the interests and attitudes of the privileged and wealthy and nothing more is heard of them after the destruction of Jerusalem (A.D. 70).

The name is said to be from Zadok (*see* II *Sam*. viii, 17), who was high priest at the time of SOLOMON.

Sadism. The term for the obtaining of

sexual satisfaction through the infliction of pain or humiliation on another person, or even an animal; also the morbid pleasure those in certain psychological states experience in being cruel or in watching certain acts of cruelty. The name derives from the Marquis de Sade (1740–1814), a vicious pervert and writer of plays and obscene novels, notably *Justine* (1791), *Philosophie dans le boudoir* (1793), and *Les Crimes de l'amour* (1800). *Cp.* MASOCHISM.

Sadler's Wells. There was once a Holy Well at this place belonging to St. John's Priory, CLERKENWELL; it was blocked up at the REFORMATION but rediscovered by Mr. Sadler in 1683 when workmen were digging for gravel. The waters were pronounced to be chalybeate and the discovery was turned to immediate profit; when however attendance at the well declined, MUSIC HALL entertainment was provided, and from the 1690s this became the chief attraction under James Miles. In 1765, a builder named Rosoman erected a proper theatre which became famous for burlettas, musical interludes, and PANTOMIMES. Edmund Kean, Dibdin, and Grimaldi all appeared there. In 1844 Samual Phelps took over and produced SHAKESPEARE, but after his retirement the boom in WEST END theatres cast the Wells into the shade and it eventually became a cinema, which closed in 1916. A new theatre was built with the help of the Carnegie United Kingdom Trust which opened in 1931 under Lilian Baylis of the OLD VIC and it became one of the leading houses in London for the production of ballet and opera. In 1946 the ballet company transferred to the Royal Opera House, COVENT GARDEN, and in 1968 the opera company moved to the London Coliseum (*see* COLOSSEUM).

Sadler's Wells features in Smollett's *Humphry Clinker*.

Safari. On safari (Swahili from Arab. *safar*, journey). On a hunting expedition in Africa; often used in the sense of "on trek" in the wilds with a company of followers.

Safety. Safety bicycle. *See* PENNY FARTHING.

Safety Matches. Matches which only

light when struck on the specially prepared surface on the side of the box, *i.e.* the match head only contains part of the ingredients of combustion. They derive from the discovery of amorphous phosphorus by Anton von Schrotte in 1845. J.E. Lundstrom of Sweden is credited with their introduction. *Cp.* LUCIFER-MATCH; PROMETHEAN.

Saffron. He hath slept in a bed of saffron (Lat. *dormivit in sacco croci*). He has a very light heart, in reference to the exhilarating effects of saffron.

Saga (pl. *sagas*) (sa' gà). In Icelandic the word is applied to any kind of narrative, but in English it particularly denotes heroic biographies written in Iceland and Norway mainly during the 12th, 13th, and 14th centuries. From this comes its English application to a story of heroic adventure.

The sagas are a compound of history and myth in varying proportions, the *King's Sagas* being the oldest, the *First Saga of King Olaf* dating from 1180. Other notable examples are the *Saga of Hallfred*, the *Saga of Björn*, the *Grettis Saga*, the *Saga of Burnt Njáll*, the *Egils Saga* the *Islendinga Saga*, the *Ynglinga Saga*, the *Volsunga Saga*, *Tristram's Saga*, and the *Karlomagnus Saga*. Snorri Sturluson's *Heimskringla* (Orb of the World) is a collection of biographies of Norwegian kings from the 9th to the 12th century. *See* EDDA.

Sagamore. *See* SACHEM.

The Seven Sages. *See* WISE MEN OF GREECE.

Sagittarius (săj i târ' i ús) (Lat. the archer). One of the old constellations, the ninth sign of the ZODIAC, which the sun enters about 22 November. *See* CHIRON.

Sagittary (săj' i tà ri). The name given in mediæval romances to the CENTAUR, whose eyes sparkled like fire and struck dead like lightning, fabled to have been introduced into the TROJAN armies.

The "sagittary" referred to in *Othello* I, i:

> Lead to the Sagittary the raised search,
> and there will I be with him,

was probably an inn, but may have been the arsenal.

Sahib (sab, sa' ib) (Urdu, friend). A form of address used by Hindus to Europeans in India corresponding to our "Sir" in "Thank you, sir." Also an Englishman or European, a woman being *Memsahib*. The word is also used colloquially to describe a cultured, refined man. *Pukka sahib* denotes a gentleman.

Sail. Sailing under false colours. Pretending to be what you are not with the object of personal advantage. The allusion is to pirate vessels sailing under false colours to escape detection.

To sail against the wind. To swim against the tide, to oppose popular or current trends, opinions, etc.

To sail before the wind. To prosper, to go on swimmingly, to meet with great success, as a ship sails smoothly and rapidly with a following wind.

To sail close to the wind. To keep the vessel's head as near the quarter from which the wind is blowing as possible yet keeping the sails filled; figuratively to go to the verge of what decency or propriety allow; to act so as just to escape the letter or infringement of the law; to take a risk.

To sail into. "To sail into someone" is to attack or reprimand him forcefully, "to sail into a task", etc., is to set about it vigorously, as the attackers "sailing into" the enemy to commence a naval engagement.

To set sail. To start a voyage.

To trim one's sails. To modify or reshape one's policy or opinion to meet the circumstances, as the sails of a ship are "trimmed" or adjusted according to the wind.

You may hoist sail. Be off. Maria saucily says to Viola, dressed in man's apparel:

> Will you hoist sail, sir? Here lies your way.
>
> SHAKESPEARE: *Twelfth Night*, I, v.

Sailor King, The. William IV of England (1765, 1830–1837), also called *Silly Billy*, who entered the navy as a midshipman in 1779, and was made Lord High Admiral in 1827.

Saint. Individual saints are entered under their respective names.

The title of saint was from early Christian times applied to APOSTLES, EVANGELISTS, MARTYRS and Confessors of remarkable virtue, especially martyrs.

In due course the need arose for BISHOPS to intervene agains local recognition of the undeserving and eventually Pope Alexander III (1159–1181) asserted the exclusive right of the Papacy to add to the roll of saints. Nowadays canonization is dependent upon a lengthy legal process where the case for the canonization of a particular person is thoroughly explored and contested. JOAN OF ARC was canonized in 1920; Sir Thomas More (1478–1535) and John Fisher (1459–1535), Bishop of Rochester, in 1935.

In Christian art, saints are often depicted with a NIMBUS, AUREOLE, or glory and individual symbols by which they can be recognized. *See* SYMBOLS OF SAINTS, *below*.

Patron Saints. (1) a selected list of trades and professions with their patron saints:

Accountants, bankers, book-keepers	St. MATTHEW
Actors	St. Genesius
Advertising	St. Bernadine of Siena
Airmen	Our Lady of Loreto, SS. Thérèse of Liesiux, Joseph Cupertino
Architects	SS. THOMAS Ap., Barbara
Artists	St. LUKE
Athletes (and Archers)	St. SEBASTIAN
Authors and Journalists	St. Francis de Sales
Bakers	SS. ELIZABETH OF HUNGARY, NICHOLAS
Barbers	SS. Cosmas and, Damian Louis
Blacksmiths	St. DUNSTAN
Booksellers	St. JOHN OF GOD
Brewers	SS. AUGUSTINE of Hippo, Luke, NICHOLAS of Myra
Bricklayers	St. STEPHEN
Builders	St. Vincent Ferrer
Cab-drivers	St. Fiacre
Carpenters	St. JOSEPH
Children	St. Nicholas
Comedians	St. VITUS
Cooks	SS. LAWRENCE, Martha
Dentists	St. Apollonia
Dieticians (Medical)	St. MARTHA
Domestic Servants	St. Zita
Editors	St. John Bosco
Engineers	St. Ferdinand III
Farmers	SS. GEORGE, Isidore
Firemen	St. Florian
Florists	SS DOROTHEA, Thérèse
Funeral Directors	SS. JOSEPH OF

	ARIMATHEA, DYSMAS		Baptist de la Salle
Gardeners	SS. Dorothea, Adelard, Tryphon, Fiacre, Phocas	Television	St. CLARE
		Travellers	SS. ANTHONY OF PADUA, NICHOLAS, CHRISTOPHER, RAPHAEL
Goldsmiths and Metalworkers	SS. Dunstan, Anastasius		
Gravediggers	St. ANTHONY (Ab.)	Wine-growers	St. VINCENT
Grocers	St. MICHAEL	Workers	St. JOSEPH
Gunners	St. Barbara	Yachtsmen	St. Adjutor
Housewives	St. Anne		
Hunters	St. HUBERT		

Infantrymen St. Maurice

Innkeepers and St Amand
Wine merchants

Jewellers St. ELOI

Lawyers SS. Ivo, Genesius, Thomas More

Librarians St. JEROME

Lighthousekeepers St. Venerius

Miners St. Barbara

Motorcyclists Our Lady of Grace

Motorists SS. Frances of Rome, CHRISTOPHER

Musicians and SS. Gregory the Great, Singers CECILIA, Dunstan

Nurses SS. Camillus of Lellis, JOHN OF GOD, AGATHA, Alexius, RAPHAEL

Paratroopers St. Michael

Pawnbrokers St. Nicholas

Physicians SS. Pantaleon, Cosmas and Damian, LUKE, Raphael

Poets SS. DAVID, Cecilia

Policemen St. Michael

Postal, Radio, Tele- St. Gabriel
communications
and Telephone,
Telegraph and
Television Workers

Printers SS JOHN OF GOD, AUGUSTINE of Hippo

Sailors SS. CUTHBERT, Brendan, Eulalia, Christopher, Peter Gonzales, Erasmus

Scholars St. Bridget

Scientists St. Albert

Scouts St. GEORGE

Sculptors St. Claude

Secretaries SS. Genesius, Cassian

Shoemakers SS. CRISPIN and Crispinianus

Soldiers SS. Adrian, GEORGE, Ignatius, SEBASTIAN, MARTIN, JOAN OF ARC

Speleologists St. BENEDICT

Students SS. THOMAS AQUINAS, Catherine

Surgeons SS. Cosmas and Damian

Tailors St. Homobonus

Tax-collectors St. MATTHEW

Teachers SS. Gregory the Great, CATHERINE, John

(2) Some European and COMMON-WEALTH Countries with their patron saints:

Australia	Our Lady Help of Christians
Belgium	St. JOSEPH
Canada	SS. Joseph, Anne
Czechoslovakia	SS. Wenceslas, JOHN OF NEPOMUK, Procopius
Denmark	SS. Asgar, Canute
England	St. GEORGE
France	Our Lady of the ASSUMPTION, SS. JOAN OF ARC, DENYS, LOUIS, Thérèse (see TERESA). There is no official patron saint of France, those listed are recognised as patron saints by the Church.
Germany	SS. BONIFACE, Michael
Greece	SS. NICHOLAS, ANDREW
Holland	St. Willibrord.
Hungary	Our Lady, St. STEPHEN
India	Out Lady of the Assumption
Ireland	St. PATRICK
Italy	SS. FRANCIS of Assisi, Catherine of Siena
New Zealand	Out Lady Help of Christians
Norway	St. Olaf
Poland	Our Lady of Czestochowa, SS. Casimir, Stanislaus
Portugal	Immaculate Conception, SS. Francis Borgia, ANTHONY OF PADUA, George, VINCENT
Russia	SS. Andrew, NICHOLAS, Thérèse of Lisieux
Scotland	SS. Andrew, Columba
South Africa	Our Lady of the Assumption
Spain	SS. JAMES, Teresa
Sweden	SS. Bridget, Eric
Wales	St. DAVID
West Indies	St. Gertrude

Symbols of Saints. The symbol common to all saints is the NIMBUS which encircles the head. MARTYRS alone have the common symbols of the CROWN of eternal life won by their heroism and the PALM of triumph. With these is generally associated with some symbol peculiar to the individual saint, often the instrument of his martyrdom, such as the GRIDIRON of St. LAWRENCE or the windlass on which the bowels were drawn from St. Erasmus' body.

Saints not martyrs will be depicted with an object symbolizing their particular virtue (St. AMBROSE has the behive emblematic of eloquence) or relating to some incident in their lives (as St. DUNSTAN pinching the DEVIL's nose). All saints are depicted in their proper dress, as soldiers in armour, bishops or priests in appropriate vestments, kings robed and crowned, religious in the habits of their order.

The Battle of the Saints (12 April 1782). Rodney's victory over the French fleet during the American War of Independence which restored British supremacy in the West Indies. It was fought off Les Saintes near Gualdeloupe.

The City of Saints. See under CITY.

The Island of Saints. So IRELAND was called in the MIDDLE AGES.

The Latter-day Saints. See MORMONS.

Saint-Simonism. The social and political theories derived from the teachings of Claude Henri, Comte de Saint-Simon (1760–1825), the French utopian socialist. He advocated a social order based on large-scale industrial production controlled by benevolent industrial leaders. The aim of his society was to improve the lot of the poorest. His disciples advocated that the State should become the sole proprietor, and a form of socialism in which social groups were to manage the state properties. Each man was to be placed and rewarded in their social heirarchy according to his capacities.

Sake. A form of the obsolete word *sac*. See SAC AND SOC.

In the common phrases *For God's sake, for goodness' sake, for conscience's sake*, etc., it means "out of consideration for" God, goodness, etc.

For old sake's sake. For the sake of old acquaintance, past times.

For one's name's sake. Out of regard for one's reputation or good name.

Saki. The pseudonym of H. H. Munro (1870–1916), the author of *The Westminster Alice* (1902), *Reginald* (1904),

The Chronicles of Clovis (1911), *The Unbearable Bassington* (1912), etc., and numerous other short stories. His style was often bitingly satirical.

Sakuntala (så kun' ta la). The heroine of Kalidasa's great Sanskrit drama *Abhijnanasakuntala*. She was the daughter of a sage, Viswamita, and Menaka, a water-nymph, and was brought up by a hermit. One day King Dushyanta came to the hermitage during a hunt, and persuaded her to marry him; and later, giving her a ring, returned to his throne. A son was born and Sakuntala set out with him to find his father. On the way, while bathing, she lost the ring, and the king did not recognize her owing to enchantment. Subsequently it was found by a fisherman in a fish he had caught (*cp.* KENTIGERN), the king recognized his wife, she was publicly proclaimed his queen, and Bharata, his son and heir, became the founder of the glorious race of the Bharatus. Sir William Jones (1746–1794) translated it into English.

Sakya-Muni. One of the names of Gautama Siddartha, the BUDDAH.

Salad. Salad days. Days of inexperience, when persons are very immature or green.

> My salad days,
> When I was green in judgment.
> SHAKESPEARE: *Antony and Cleopatra*,
> I, v.

Saladin (Arab. *Salah ud-Din*, "Honour of the Faith") (1138–1193). SULTAN of Egypt and Syria and founder of the Ayubite dynasty, whose capture of JERUSALEM in 1187 led to the Third CRUSADE. He appears in Scott's *Talisman* as a chivalrous warrior.

Saladin tithe. The tax levied by Henry II in 1188 for the recovery of JERUSALEM after its capture by SALADIN.

Salamander (săl' å män der) (Gr. *salamandra*, a kind of lizard). The name is now given to a genus of amphibious Urodela (newts, etc.), but anciently to a mythical lizard-like monster that was supposed to be able to live in fire, which, however, it quenched by the chill of its body. Pliny refers to this belief (*Nat. Hist.* x, 86; xxix, 23). It was adopted by PARACELSUS as the name of the elemental being inhabiting fire

Salt

(GNOMES being those of the earth, SYLPHS of the air, and UNDINES of the water), and was hence taken over by the ROSICRUCIAN system, from which source Pope introduced salamanders into his *Rape of the Lock* (i, 60).

Francis I of France adopted as his badge a lizard in the midst of flames, with the legend *Nutrisco et extinguo* (I nourish and extinguish). The Italian motto from which it derived was *Nutrisco il buono e spengo il reo* (I nourish the good and extinguish the bad). Fire purifies good metal, but consumes rubbish.

Salary. Originally "salt rations" (Lat. *salarium* from *sal*, salt). The ancient Romans served out rations of salt and other necessaries to their soldiers and civil servants. These were collectively known as *salt*, and when money was substituted for the rations, the stipend went by the same name.

The salariat. Salaried employees collectively, such as civil servants, etc.

Salic (săl' ik). Pertaining to the Salian FRANKS, a tribe of Franks who in the 4th century established themselves on the banks of the Sala (now known as the Yssel), and from whom the MEROVINGIAN Kings of France descended.

> Which Salique, as I said, 'twixt Elbe and Sala,
> Is at this day in Germany called Meisen.
> SHAKESPEARE: *Henry V*, I, ii.

The Salic Law. The compilation of laws of the Salian Franks supposedly begun in the 5th century, with later additions. Several Latin texts of what was essentially a penal code still exist. *Lex Salica* LIX stated that a wife could not inherit the land of her husband. This proviso regarding Salic lands in no way applied to the succession to the French crown. The so-called "Salic Law" invoked in 1316 to exclude the daughters of Louis X and later Philip V from the throne of France never existed. Subsequent exclusions of females from European thrones rested on precedent rather than Salic Law. The so called "Spanish Salic Law", an Act of Philip V published in 1713 giving preference to male succession, was to satisfy European pressure and aimed at preventing the future union of the French and Spanish thrones. This law was abrogated by Charles IV in 1789, although the fact was not made public until 1830.

Salii, or **Saliens.** In ancient ROME, a college of twelve priests of MARS traditionally instituted as guardians of the ANCILE. Every year these young patricians paraded the city with song and dance, finishing the day with a banquet, insomuch that *saliares cœna* became proverbial for a sumptuous feast. The word *saliens* means dancing.

Sallee-man, or **Sallee rover.** A pirateship; so called from Sallee, a seaport near Rabat on the west coast of Morocco, formerly a notorious nest of pirates.

Sally Army. A nickname of the SALVATION ARMY. *See* POKE BONNET.

Sally Lunn. A tea cake; so called from a woman pastrycook of that name who used to cry them in the streets of Bath at the close of the 18th century. Dalmer, a baker and musician, bought her business and made a song about the buns. Sally Lunn's house still exists in Lilliput Alley.

Salmacis. *See* HERMAPHRODITE.

Salmagundi (săl' mă gŭn' di). A mixture of minced veal, chicken, or turkey, anchovies or pickled herrings, and onions, all chopped together and served with lemon-juice and oil. The word appeared in the 17th century; its origin is unknown, but fable has it that it was the name of one of the ladies attached to the suite of Marie de' MEDICI, wife of Henry IV of France, who either invented or popularized the dish.

Salon des Refusés. The exhibition of paintings opened at PARIS in 1863 at the instigation of NAPOLEON III, of works from artists (especially Claude Monet) rejected by the French Salon. Monet's picture *Impressions* gave rise to the term IMPRESSIONISM which was coined in derision by a journalist.

Salt. Flavour, smack. The "salt of youth" is that vigour and strong passion which then predominates.

> Though we are justices and doctors, and churchmen, Master Page, we have some salt of our youth in us.
> SHAKESPEARE:
> *The Merry Wives of Windsor, II, iii.*

Shakespeare uses the term on several

occasions for strong amorous passion. Thus Iago refers to it as "hot as monkeys, salt as wolves in pride" (*Othello*, III, iii). The Duke calls Angelo's base passion his "salt imagination", because he supposed his victim to be Isabella, and not his betrothed wife whom the Duke forced him to marry (*Measure for Measure*, V, i).

Salt lick. A place where salt is found naturally and in a position where animals which resort thither may lick it from the rocks. etc.

To salt away, or **down.** To store or preserve for future use, especially money.

A covenant of salt (*Numb.* xviii, 19). A covenant which could not be broken. As salt was a symbol of incorruption it symbolized perpetuity.

An old salt. A long-experienced sailor. One who has been well salted by the sea.

Attic salt. *See under* ATTIC.

The Pillar of Salt. Lot's wife, when escaping from Sodom with her husband and daughters, looked back on the cities of SODOM AND GOMORRAH against God's command and "She became a pillar of salt" (*Gen.* xix, 26). Our Lord, when teaching indifference to worldly affairs and material possessions, refers to the episode saying, "Remember Lot's wife" (*Luke* xvii, 32).

The salt of the earth. The perfeçt, the elect; the best of mankind. Our Lord told his disciples they were "the salt of the earth" (Matt. v, 13).

To eat a man's salt. To partake of his hospitality. Among the Arabs, to eat a man's salt created a sacred bond between host and guest. No one who has eaten of another's salt should speak ill of him or do him an ill turn.

If the salt have lost its savour, wherewith shall it be salted? (*Matt.* v, 13). If men fall from grace, how shall they be restored? The reference is to rock salt which loses its saltness if exposed to the hot sun.

Not worth your salt. Not worth your wages. The reference is to the SALARY issued to Roman soldiers, etc.

Put some salt on his tail. Catch or apprehend him. The phrase is from the advice given to young children to lay salt on a bird's tail if they want to catch it.

Spilling salt was held to be an unlucky omen by the Romans, and the superstition remains, but EVIL may be averted if he who spills the salt throws a pinch of it over the left shoulder with the right hand. In Leonardo da Vinci's picture of the LAST SUPPER, JUDAS Iscariot is known by the salt-cellar knocked over accidently by his arm. Salt was used in sacrifice by the Jews, as well as by the Greeks and Romans. It was an emblem of purity and the sanctifying influence of a holy life on others owing to its preservative quality; also a sign of incorruptibility. It is used for the preparation of HOLY WATER and it was not uncommon to put salt into a coffin; for it is said that SATAN hates salt. It was long customary to throw a handful of salt on the top of the mash when brewing to keep the witches from it.

To sit above the salt. To sit in a place of distinction. Formerly the family *saler* (salt cellar) was of massive silver, and placed in the middle of the table. Persons of distinction sat above the "saler"—*i.e.* between it and the head of the table; dependants and inferior guests sat below.

True to his salt. Faithful to his employers. Here *salt* means salary.

With a grain, or **pinch of salt.** (Lat. *cum grano salis*). With great reservations or limitation; allowing it a mere grain of truth. A pinch of salt with something may help one to swallow it.

Salutation, Salute (Lat. *salutare*, to keep safe, to greet). Military salutes take various forms according to the occasion, and include touching the CAP, presenting arms, the lowering of sword-points, lowering the FLAG, the firing of guns, etc. The number of guns fired for a Royal Salute in the Royal Navy is 21, in the Army 101. The lowering of swords indicates a willingness to put yourself in the power of the person saluted, as does the presenting of arms.

Other common forms of salutation are the kiss, rubbing noses, bowing, curtseying, shaking hands, the removal or touching of the hat, etc.

Salvation Army. A religious organization founded by William Booth (1829–1912), originally a METHODIST minister. Its origins are to be found in 1865 in his Christian Mission, WHITECHAPEL, and the movement took its present name in 1878. Booth himself became the "General" and the "Army" was planned on semi-military lines. The motto adopted was "Through Blood and Fire" and the activities were directed at the poor, outcast, and destitute. The movement became world-wide, and its brass bands and open-air meetings became a familiar feature of the street scene, as did the bonnets of the Salvation Army "lasses". Immense good has been done by the selfless devotion of its rank and file.

Salve. Latin, "hail", "welcome". The word is sometimes woven on door-mats.

Salve, Regina. An ancient antiphonal hymn recited at the end of some of the canonical hours and still widely used in Roman Catholic Churches. So called from the opening words, *Salve, regina mater misericordiæ* (Hail, O Queen, Mother of Mercy).

Sam. Uncle Sam. Nickname for the collective citizens of the U.S.A. It arose in the neighbourhood of Troy, N.Y., about 1812 partly from the frequent appearance of the initials U.S. on government supplies to the army, etc. The other contributory factor to the derivaton is puzzling, but some have maintained that there was someone in the district who had a connexion with army supplies and who was actually known as Uncle Sam.

Sam Browne belt. The leather belt with a strap over the shoulder and originally with a sword-frog, compulsory for officers and warrant officers in the British Army up to 1939, when it was declared optional. This belt was invented by General Sir Sam Browne, V.C. (1824–1901), a veteran of the INDIAN MUTINY. Its pattern has been adopted by almost every military power in the world.

Samanids. A Persian dynasty founded by Ismail at Samani. They ruled from 892 to 1005 and were notable patrons of Persian literature.

Samaritan. A good Samaritan. A philanthropist, one who helps the poor and needy (*see Luke* x, 30–7).

The Samaritans. An organization founded by the Rev. Chad Varah of St. Stephen, Walbrook, London, in 1953, to help the despairing and suicidal. It now has nearly 200 centres in the British Isles as well as some overseas. Trained volunteers give their help at any hour to those who make their needs known by telephone, letter, or by a personal visit.

Samian (sä'mi àn). **The Samian Letter.** The letter Y, the Letter of Pythagoras (*see under* PYTHAGORAS).

The Samian Poet. Simonides of Amorgos, Greek iambic poet and native of Samos, who flourished in the mid-7th century B.C.

The Samian Sage, or **The Samian.** PYTHAGORAS, who was born at Samos.

Samite (săm' ĭt). A rich silk fabric with a warp of six threads, generally interwoven with GOLD, held in high esteem in the MIDDLE AGES. So called after the Gr. *hexamiton*: *Hex*, six; *Mitos*, a thread. *Cp.* DIMITY.

Sampford Ghost. An uncommonly persistent POLTERGEIST which haunted a thatched house (destroyed by fire *c.* 1942) at Sampford Peverell, Devon, for about three years until 1810. Besides the usual knockings the inmates were beaten, curtains agitated and damaged, levitations occurred, and in one instance an "unattached arm" flung a folio Greek Testament from a bed into the middle of the room. The Rev. Charles Caleb Colton, rector of the Prior's Portion, Tiverton (credited as author of these freaks), offered £100 to anyone who could explain the matter except on supernatural grounds. No one claimed the reward.

Sampo. *See* KALEVALA.

Samson. Any man of unusual strength; so called from the ancient Hebrew hero (*Judges xiii—xvi*). The name has been specially applied to Thomas Topham, the "British Samson", son of a London carpenter. He lifted three hogsheads of water (1,836 lb.) in the presence of thousands of spectators at COLDBATH FIELDS, 28 May 1741. He stabbed his wife and committed suicide in 1749.

Samurai (săm' ū rī). The military class of old Japan. In early feudal times the term (which means "guard") was applied to all who bore arms, but eventually the

Samurai became warrior knights and administrators as retainers of the *daimyo* or nobles. From 1869 the rigid feudal stratification of society came to an end, and in 1876 they were forbidden to wear two swords, the symbol of a warrior. With the creation of a new nobility in 1884 they became *shizoku* ("gentry") and many took posts in administration and industry. The formal reorganization of society into *kazoku* (nobility), *shizoku* (gentry) and *heimin* (common people) set up in 1869, and subsequently modified, was abolished in 1947. *See also* HARA-KIRI.

San Benito. *See* SACCO BENEDETTO.

Sance Bell. The Sanctus bell. *See* SACRING BELL.

Sancho Panza (săn' chō păn' zà). The squire of Don QUIXOTE in Cervantes' romance. A short pot-bellied rustic, full of common sense, but without a grain of "spirituality", he became governor of BARATARIA. He rode upon an ass, DAPPLE, and was famous for his proverbs. *Panza*, in Spanish, means *paunch*. Hence a *Sancho Panza* as a rough-and-ready, sharp and humorous justice of the peace, an allusion to Sancho, as judge in the isle of Barataria.

Sanchoniathon (sang ko ni' à thon). The *Fragments of Sanchoniathon* are the literary remains of a supposed ancient Phœnician philosopher (alleged to have lived before the TROJAN WAR), which are incorporated in the *Phœnician History* by Philo of Byblos (1st and 2nd centuries A.D.), and which was drawn upon by Eusebius (*c*. 260–*c*. 340), the "Father of Church History". The name is Greek and may mean "the whole law of Chon" or alternatively may be a proper name. It is likely that the name was invented by Philo to give ancient authority to his writings.

Sanctuary, Right of. In Anglo-Saxon ENGLAND all churches and churchyards generally provided refuge for fugitives for 40 days; while permanent refuge was available at the great LIBERTIES of Beverley, Durham, and Ripon. Sanctuary for treason was disallowed in 1486 and most of the remaining rights were severely restricted by Henry VIII. Sanctuary for criminals was abolished in 1623

and for civil offenders by acts of 1697 and 1723.

Sanctum Sanctorum. Latin for HOLY OF HOLIES. *Cp*. ADYTUM.

Sanctus Bell. *See* SACRING BELL.

Sancy Diamond, The. A famous DIAMOND (55 carats), said to have once belonged to Charles the Bold of Burgundy, and named after the French ambassador in Constantinople, Nicholas de Harlay, Sieur de Sancy, who, about 1575, bought it for 70,000 francs. Later it was owned by Henri III and Henri IV of France, then by Queen Elizabeth I; James II took it with him in his flight to France in 1688 and sold it to Louis XIV for £25,000. Louis XV wore it at his coronation, but during the French Revolution it was stolen and, in 1828, sold to Prince Paul Demidoff for £80,000. In 1865, it was bought by Sir Jamsetjee Jeejeebhoy, but was on the market again in 1889 and rumoured to have been subsequently acquired by the Tsar of Russia. Its present fate is unknown.

Sand. A rope of sand. A proverbially weak link or tie, a union which is easily broken; that which is virtually worthless and untrustworthy.

Happy as a sand-boy. *See under* HAPPY.

The sands are running out. Time is getting short; there will be little opportunity for doing what you have to do unless you take the chance now. Often used in reference to one who has evidently not much longer to live. The allusion is to the hour-glass.

Sand-blind. Dim-sighted; not exactly blind, but with eyes of very little use. *Sand* here is a corruption of the obsolete prefix *sam-* meaning "half", as in the old *sam-dead*, *sam-ripe*, etc., and *sam-sodden*, which still survives in some dialects. In SHAKESPEARES *Merchant of Venice* (II, ii) Launcelot Gobbo connects it with *sand*, the gritty earth—

> This is my true-begotten father, who, being more than sand-blind, high gravel blind, knows me not.

The sand-man is about. A playful remark addressed to children who are tired and "sleepy-eyed". *Cp*. THE DUST-MAN HAS ARRIVED *under* DUST.

Sand, George Sand. *See under* GEORGE.

Sandabar, or **Sindibad.** Names given to a mediæval collection of tales much the same as those in the Greek *Syntipas the Philosopher* and the Arabic *Romance of the Seven Viziers* known in Western Europe as *The Seven Sages* (SEVEN WISE MASTERS), and derived from the *Fables of Bidpay.* These names probably result from Hebrew mistransliterations of the Arabic equivalent of Bidpay or PILPAY.

Sandal. A man without sandals. A prodigal; so called by the ancient Jews, because the seller gave his sandals to the buyer as a ratification of his bargain (*Ruth* iv, 7).

He wears the sandals of Theramenes. Said of a TRIMMER, an opportunist. Theramenes (put to death *c.* 404 B.C.) was one of the Athenian oligarchy, and was nicknamed *Cothurnus* (*i.e.* a sandal or boot which might be worn on either foot), because no dependence could be put on him. He "blew hot and cold with the same breath" (*see under* BLOW).

Sandemanians, or **Glasites** (sănd e' mān' i ănz). A religious party expelled from the CHURCH OF SCOTLAND under John Glas (1695–1773) for maintaining that national churches, being "kingdoms of this world" are unscriptural. He was suspended in 1728 and expelled in 1730. Eventually the leadership passed to his son-in-law Robert Sandeman, whence the more common name *Sandemanians.* They believe in salvation through grace and abstain from all animal food which has not been drained of blood. Love feasts (AGAPE) are held and the kiss of charity is enjoined.

Sandwich. Meat or other filling between two slices of bread, so called from the fourth Earl of Sandwich (1718–1792), the notorious "Jemmy TWITCHER". He passed whole days in gambling, bidding the waiter to bring him for refreshment a piece of ham between two slices of bread, which he ate without stopping play.

Sandwich man. A perambulating advertisement displayer, "sandwiched" between advertisement boards carried before and behind.

Sang-de-bœuf (săng de berf) (Fr., bullock's blood). The deep red with which ancient Chinese porcelain is often coloured.

Sang-froid (Fr., cold blood). Freedom from excitement or agitation. One does a thing "with perfect *sangfroid*" when one does it coolly and collectedly.

Sanger's Circus. One of the most spectacular entertainments of Victorian England. In 1845 the brothers John (1816–1889) and George (1827–1911) Sanger began a conjuring exhibition at Birmingham and from this they ventured into a travelling circus business.

Sangrail, or **Sangreal** (săn grāl). The Holy GRAIL. Popular etymology used to explain the word as meaning the real blood of Christ, *sang-real*, or the wine used in the LAST SUPPER; and a tradition arose that part of this wine-blood was preserved by JOSEPH OF ARIMATHÆA in the Saint, or Holy Grail.

Sanguine (săng' gwin) (Lat. *sanguis*, *sanguinis*, blood). The term used in HERALDRY for the deep red or purplish colour usually known as *murrey* (from the mulberry). In engravings it is indicated by lines of vert and purpure crossed, that is, diagonals from left to right. This is a word with a curious history. Its actual meaning is bloody, or of the colour of blood, hence it came to be applied to one who was ruddy, whose cheeks were red with good health and well-being. From this it was easy to extend the meaning to one who was full of vitality, vivacious, confident and hopeful. An artist's drawing in red chalk or crayon is called a *sanguine*, also the chalk itself.

Sanhedrin (săn i drin), or **Sanhedrim** (Gr. *syn*, together; *hedra*, a seat; *i.e.* a sitting together). The supreme council and highest court of justice of the ancient Jews held at JERUSALEM. It consisted of 70 priests and elders and a president, dealt with religious questions, and acted as a civil court for Jerusalem. It was the Sanhedrin that condemned Christ to death. The Sanhedrin proper came to an end with the fall of the Jewish state (A.D. 70). Some authorities, taking their evidence from the MISHNA, hold that there was a *Great Sanhedrin* of 71 members possessing civil authority and a little Sanhedrin of 23 with religious authority under the High priest.

In Dryden's *Absalom and Achitophel*, the *Sanhedrin* stands for the English PARLIAMENT.

Sans (Fr., without). SHAKESPEARE (*As You Like It*, II, vii) describes second childhood as "sans teeth, sans eyes, sans taste, sans everything".

Sans Culottes (Fr., without knee-breeches). A name given during the French Revolution to the extremists of the working classes. Hence *Sansculottism*, the principles, etc., of "red republicans".

Sans culottides. The five complementary days added to the 12 months of the Revolutionary Calendar (*see under* CALENDAR), each month being made to consist of 30 days. The days were named in honour of the *sans culottes*, and made idle days or holidays.

Sans-Gêne, Madame. The nickname of the wife of Lefebvre, Duke and Dantzic (1755–1820), one of NAPOLEON'S marshals. She was originally a washerwoman, and followed her husband—then in the ranks—as a VIVANDIÈRE. She was kind and pleasant, but her rough-and-ready ways and ignorance and etiquette soon made her the butt of the court, and earned her the nickname, which means "without constraint" or "free and easy".

Sans peur et sans reproche (Fr., without fear and without reproach). The Chevalier Bayard (*see under* BAYARD) was known as *Le chevalier sans peur et sans reproche*.

Sans Souci (Fr.). Free and easy, void of care. It is the name given by Frederick the Great to the palace he built near Potsdam (1747).

Sansei (săn' sā). An American citizen whose grandparents were immigrants to the U.S.A.; from a Japanese word meaning "third generation". *Cp.* NISEI.

Santa Casa. *See* LORETO.

Santa Claus. A contraction of Santa Nikolaus (St. NICHOLAS), the patron saint of German children. His feast-day is 6 December, and the vigil is still held in some places, but for the most part his name is now associated with Christmastide. The custom used to be for someone, on 5 December, to assume the costume of a BISHOP, and distribute small gifts to "good children". The present custom, introduced into England from Germany about 1840, is to put toys and other small presents into a stocking late on CHRISTMAS Eve, when the children are asleep, and when they wake on Christmas morn they find at the bedside the gifts brought by Santa Claus, who supposedly travels around in a sleigh pulled by reindeer.

Sapho (săf' ō). Mlle de Scudéry (1607–1701), the French novelist and poet, went by this name among her own circle.

Sappho (săf' ō). The Greek poetess of Lesbos, known as "the Tenth MUSE". She lived about 600 B.C., and is fabled to have thrown herself into the sea from the Leucadian promontory in consequence of her advances having been rejected by the beautiful youth Phaon.

Sapphics. A four-lined stanza-form of classical lyric poetry, named after SAPPHO of Lesbos, who employed it, the fourth line being an Adonic. There must be a cæsura after the fifth syllable of each of the first three lines which run thus:

—∪|——|—||∪∪|—∪|—∪

The Adonic is:

—∪∪|—∪ or ——

The first and third stanzas of the famous *Ode* of HORACE, *Integer vitæ* (i, 22), may be translated thus, preserving the metre:

> He of sound life, who ne'er with singers wendeth,
> Needs no Moorish bow, such as malice bendeth,
> Nor with poisoned darts life from harm defendeth. Fuscus, believe me.
> Once I, unarmed, was in a forest roaming,
> Singing love lays, when i' the secret gloaming
> Rushed a huge wolf, which though in fury foaming Did not aggrieve me.
>
> E.C.B.

Sapphism. Another name for Lesbianism. *See* LESBIAN.

Saracen (săr' à sen) (Late Gr. *Sarakenos*, possibly from Arab. *sharqi*, an "oriental"). Applied to Arabs generally by mediæval writers, especially those of Syria and Palestine; also applied to all

infidel nations who opposed the CRUSA-
DERS. The name was given by the
Greeks and Romans to the nomadic
tribes of the Syro-Arabian desert.

Saragossa, The Maid of. *See under*
MAID.

Sarah. The Divine Sarah. Sarah Bern-
hardt (1845–1923), French actress of international repute. Her original name
was Rosine Bernard.

Sarcenet. *See* SARSENET.

Sarcophagus (sar kof' á gus) (Gr. *sarx*,
flesh; *phagein*, to eat). A stone coffin; so
called because it was made of stone
which, according to Pliny, consumed
the flesh in a few weeks. The stone was
sometimes called *lapis Assius*, because it
was found at Assos in Lycia.

Sardanapalus. A name applied to any
luxurious, extravagant, self-willed tyrant. It is the Greek name of Asurbanipal
(mentioned in *Ezra* iv, 10, as *Asnap-
par*), king of Assyria in the 7th century
B.C.

Sardonic smile, or **laughter.** A smile of
contempt; bitter, mocking laughter; so
used by HOMER.

The *Herba Sardonia* (so called from
Sardis, in Asia Minor) is so acrid that it
produces a convulsive movement of the
nerves of the face, resembling a painful
grin; but the word is probably Gr. *sar-
danios*, a bitter laugh.

Sardonyx (sar' don iks). A precious stone
composed of white chalcedony alternating with layers of sard, which is an
orange-brown variety of cornelian. Pliny
says it is called *sard* from Sardis, in Asia
Minor, where it is found, and the *onyx*, the
nail, because its colour resembles that of
the skin under the nail (*Nat. Hist.
xxxvii*, 31).

Sarsen Stones (sar' sen). The sandstone
boulders of Wiltshire and Berkshire are
so called. The early Christian Saxons
used the word *Saresyn* (*i.e.* SARACEN) as
a synonym of pagan or heathen, and as
these stones were popularly associated
with DRUID worship, they were called
Saresyn (or heathen) stones.

Sarsenet (sar' sen et). A very fine, soft,
silk material, so called from its Saracenic
or Oriental origin. The word is sometimes used adjectivally of soft and gentle
speech.

Sassanides (săs ăn' i dēz). A powerful
Persian dynasty, ruling from about A.D.
225 to 641; so named because Ardeshir,
the founder, was son of Sassan, a lineal
descendant of XERXES.

Sassenach (săs' năk). The common form
of *Sassunnach*, Gaelic for "English" or
"an Englishman".

Satan (sā' tån), in Hebrew, means adversary or enemy, and is traditionally applied to the DEVIL, the personification of
EVIL.

> To whom the Arch-enemy
> (And thence in heaven called Satan).
> MILTON: *Paradise Lost*, Bk. I, 81. .

He appears as the SERPENT, tempter of
mankind in *Gen*. iii, 1, and the existence
of Satan as the centre of evil is part of
the teaching of bot the Old and NEW
TESTAMENT,

> But when they have heard, Satan co-
> meth immediately, and taketh away the
> word that was sown in their hearts.
> *Mark* iv, 15.

The name is often used of a tempter
or of a person of whom one is expressing
abhorrence. Thus the Clown says to
Malvolio:

> Fie, thou dishonest Satan! I call thee by
> the most modest terms; for I am one of
> those gentle ones that will use the devil
> himself with courtesy.
> SHAKESPEARE: *Twelfth Night*, IV, ii.

Satan rebuking sin. THE POT CALLING
THE KETTLE BLACK (*under* POT).

The Satanic School. So Southey called
BYRON, Shelley, and those of their followers who set at defiance the generally
received notions of religion. See the Preface to his *Vision of Judgment*.

Satire (săt' īr). Scaliger's derivation from
SATYR is quite untenable. It is Lat. *sa-
tura* (full of variety); originally *lanx sa-
tura*, a dish of varied fruits, a medley.
The term was applied to a medley or
hotchpotch in verse; later to compositions in verse or prose in which folly,
vice, or individuals are held up to ridicule. See Dryden's Dedication prefixed
to his *Satires*.

Father of Satire. Archilochus of Paros,
7th century B.C.

Father of Roman Satire. Lucilius
(*c.* 175–103 B.C.)

Saturday. The seventh day of the week
until 1971 when it became the sixth (see
Sunday); called by the Anglo-Saxons

Sœterdæg, after the Latin *Saturni dies*, the day of SATURN. *See* BLACK SATURDAY.

Saturn (săt' ŭrn). A Roman deity, identified with the Greek KRONOS (time). He devoured all his children except JUPITER (air), NEPTUNE (water), and PLUTO (the grave). These Time cannot consume. The reign of Saturn was celebrated by the poets as a "GOLDEN AGE". According to the old alchemists and astrologers Saturn typified LEAD, and was a very EVIL planet to be born under. He was the god of seedtime and harvest and his symbol was a scythe, and he was finally banished from his throne by his son Jupiter.

Saturn red. Red lead.

Saturn's tree. An alchemist's name for the Tree of DIANA, or PHILOSOPHER'S TREE.

Saturnalia. The ancient Roman festival of SATURN, celebrated on 19 December and eventually prolonged for seven days, was a time of freedom from restraint, merrymaking, and often riot and debauchery. During its continuance public business was suspended, the law courts and schools were closed and no criminals were punished.

Saturnian. Pertaining to Saturn; with reference to the "GOLDEN AGE", to the god's sluggishness, or to the baleful influence attributed to him by the astrologers.

Saturnian verses. A rude metre in use among the Romans before the introduction of Greek metres. Also a peculiar metre consisting of three iambics and a syllable over, joined to three trochees, as:

> The queen was in the par-lour...
> The maids were in the garden...

> The Fescennine and Saturnian were the same, for as they were called Saturnian from their ancientness, when Saturn reigned in Italy, they were called Fescennine, from Fescennia [*sic*] where they were first practised.
> DRYDEN: Essay on Satire.

Saturnine. Grave, phlegmatic, gloomy, dull and glowering. Astrologers affirm that such is the disposition of those who are born under the influence of the leaden planet SATURN.

Satyr (săt' ĭr). One of a body of forest gods or demons who, in classical mythology, were the attendants of BACCHUS. Like the FAUNS, they are represented as having the legs and hind-quarters of a GOAT, budding horns, and goat-like ears, and they were very lascivious.

Hence, the term is applied to a brutish or lustful man; and the psychological condition among males characterized by excessive venereal desire is known as *satyriasis*.

Sauce (Lat. *salsus*) means "salted food", for giving a relish to meat, as pickled roots, herbs, etc.

In familiar usage it means "cheek", impertinence, of the sort one expects from an impudent youngster or *sauce-box*.

The sauce was better than the fish. The accessories were better than the main part.

To serve the same sauce. To retaliate; to give as good as you get; to serve in the same manner.

What is sauce for the goose is sauce for the gander. The same principle applies in both cases; what is fitting for the husband, should be fitting for the wife.

Saucer. Originally a dish for holding sauce, the Roman *salsarium*.

Saucer eyes. Big, round, glaring eyes.

> Yet when a child (good Lord!) I thought
> That thou a pair of horns had'st got
> With eyes like saucers staring.
> PETER PINDAR: *Ode to the Devil*.

Saucer oath. When a Chinese is put in the witness-box, he says: "If I do not speak the truth may my soul be cracked and broken like this saucer." So saying, he dashes the saucer on the ground. The Jewish marriage custom of breaking a wineglass is of a similar character.

Flying saucers. Alleged mysterious objects resembling revolving, partially luminous discs that shoot across the sky at a high velocity and at a great height. "Flying saucers" have been reported on a number of occasions in recent years but their actuality remains as elusive as that of the LOCH NESS MONSTER. *Cp.* U.F.O.

Saul. Is Saul also among the prophets? (I *Sam*. x, 11). Said of one who unexpectedly bears tribute to a party or doctrine that he has hitherto vigorously assailed. At the conversion of Saul, afterwards called PAUL, the Jews said in substance, "Is it possible that Saul can be a convert?". (*Acts* ix, 21).

Sauve qui peut (sōv kē pėr) (Fr., save himself who can). One of the first uses of the phrase is by Boileau (1636–1711). The phrase thus came to mean a rout. Thackeray (*The Four Georges*, ch. 41) writes of "that general *sauve qui peut* among the Tory party".

Save. To save appearances. To do something to obviate or prevent embarrassment or exposure.

To save one's bacon, face, skin. *See under these words.*

Savoir-faire (săv' wa fâr) (Fr.). Readiness in doing the right thing; address, tact, skill.

Savoir-vivre (săv' wa vēvr). Good breeding; being at ease in society and knowing what to do.

Savonarola. *See* WEEPERS.

Savoy. Savoy Hill. The site of the first studios of the British Broadcasting Company (1922) and until 1932 the headquarters of the British Broadcasing Corporation, the original B.B.C. call-sign being 2LO.

Savoy Operas. The comic operas with words by W.S. Gilbert (1836–1911) and music by Arthur Sullivan (1842–1900), produced by R. D'Oyly Carte; most of them first appeared at the Savoy Theatre which D'Oyly Carte built specially for his productions. The players performing in these operas were known as the "Savoyards".

Saw. In Christian art an attribute of St. SIMON and St. JAMES THE LESS, in allusion to the tradition of their being sawn to death.

Saxifrage (săks' i frāj). A member of a genus of small plants (*Saxifraga*) probably so called because they grow in the clefts of rocks (Lat. *saxum*, a rock; *frangere*, to break). Pliny, and later writers following him, held that the name was due to the supposed fact that the plant had a medicinal value in the breaking up and dispersal of stone in the bladder.

Saxons. A Germanic people who invaded Britain in the late 5th and early 6th centuries; also the general name given by the Romans to the Teutonic raiders who from the 2nd century ravaged the coasts of Roman Britain. Essex, Sussex, Middlesex, and Wessex are names that commemorate their settlements.

Saxo Grammaticus (Saxo the Scholar or Grammarian). A famous Danish chronicler living in the latter part of the 12th century (died c. 1208). His *Gesta Danorum*, a chronicle of the early Danish kings to 1185 is a valuable source of the times nearer his own, the earlier parts, derived from old songs, traditions and Runic inscriptions (*see* RUNE), are less reliable.

Say. To take the say. To taste meat or wine before it is presented, in order to prove that it is not poisoned. *Say* is short for *assay*, a test; the phrase was common in the reign of Queen Elizabeth I.

Scævola (skē' vō là) (Lat., left-handed). So Gaius Mucius and his house were called because he had burnt off his right hand. Purposing to kill Lars Porsena, who was besieging ROME, he entered that king's camp but slew Porsena's secretary by mistake. He was captured and taken before the king and sentenced to the flames. He deliberately held his hand over the sacrificial fire till it was destroyed to show the Etruscan he would not shrink from torture. This fortitude was so remarkable that Porsena at once ordered his release and made peace with the Romans.

Scales. From time immemorial the scales have been one of the principal attributes of Justice, it being impossible to outweigh even a little Right with any quantity of Wrong.

> ...first the right he put into the scale,
> And then the Giant strove with puissance strong
> To fill the other scale with so much wrong
> But all the wrongs that he therein could lay,
> Might not it peise.
> SPENSER: *The Faerie Queene*, V, ii, 46.

According to the KORAN, at the Judgement Day everyone will be weighed in the scales of the archangel GABRIEL. The good deeds will be put in the scale called "Light", and the EVIL ones in the scale called "Darkness", after which they have to cross the bridge AL-SIRAT, not wider than the edge of a scimitar. The faithful will pass over in safety, but the rest will fall into the dreary realms of GEHENNA.

The scales fell from his eyes. The cause of his inability to recognise the truth having been removed, he now saw the facts clearly. *Scale* here is the shell or thin covering, a scab; it is cognate with the scale or dish of a balance.

After Ananias put his hands on Saul (St. PAUL) we are told:

> And immediately there fell from his eyes as it had been scales; and he received sight forthwith.
>
> *Acts* ix, 18.

To hold the scales even, or **true.** To judge impartially.

> King Providence attends with generous aid...
> And weighs the nations in an even scale.
>
> COWPER: *Table Talk*, 251.

To turn the scale. Just to outweigh the other side.

> Thy presence turns the scale of doubtful fight,
> Tremendous God of battles, Lord of Hosts!
>
> WORDSWORTH: *Ode* (1815), 112.

Scalp Lock. A long lock of hair allowed to grow on the scalp by men of certain North American Indian tribes as a challenge to their scalp-hunting enemies.

Scambling Days. *See* SKIMBLE-SKAMBLE.

Scammozzi's Rule (skȧ mot′ ziz). The jointed two-foot rule used by builders, and said to have been invented by Vincenzo Scammozzi (1552–1616), the famous Italian architect.

Scandal (Gr. *skandalon*) means properly a pitfall or snare laid out for an enemy; hence a stumbling-block, and morally an aspersion.

In *Matt*. xiii, 41–2, we are told that the angels "shall gather all things that offend...and shall cast them into a furnace"; here the Greek word is *skandalon*, and *scandals* is given as an alternative in the margin; the REVISED VERSION renders the word "all things that cause stumbling". Cp. also I *Cor*. i, 23.

The Hill of Scandal. So Milton (*Paradise Lost*, I, 415) calls the Mount of Olives, because King SOLOMON built

thereon "an high place for Chemosh, the abomination of the children of Ammon" (I *Kings* xi, 7).

Scandal broth. Tea. The reference is to the gossip held by some of the womenfolk over their tea. Also called "chatterbroth".

Scandalum Magnatum (skăn′ dȧ lum măg nā′ tùm) (Lat., scandal of magnates). Words in derogation of the Crown, PEERS, judges, and other great officers of the realm, made a legal offence in the time of Richard II. What St. PAUL calls "speaking evil of dignities"; popularly contracted to *scanmag*.

Scanderbeg. A name given by the Turks to George Castriota (1403–1468), the patriot chief of Epirus. The name is a corruption of *Iskander* (Alexander) *beg* or *bey*.

Scanderbeg's sword must have Scanderbeg's arm. None but ULYSSES can draw Ulysses' bow. MOHAMMED I wanted to see Scanderbeg's scimitar, but when presented no one could draw it; whereupon the Turkish emperor, deeming himself imposed upon, sent it back; Scanderbeg replied he had sent his majesty his sword, not the arm that drew it.

Scapegoat. Part of the ancient ritual among the Hebrews for the DAY OF ATONEMENT laid down by Mosaic Law (*see Lev*. xvi) was as follows: two goats were brought to the altar of the TABERNACLE and the high priest cast lots, one for the Lord, and the other for AZAZEL. The Lord's goat was sacrificed, the other was the scapegoat; and the high priest having, by confession, transferred his own sins and the sins of the people to it, it was taken to the wilderness and suffered to escape.

Scaphism (skă′ fizm) (Gr. *skaphe*, anything scooped out). A mode of torture formerly practised in Persia. The victim was enclosed in the hollow trunk of a tree, the head, hands, and legs projecting. These were anointed with honey to invite the wasps. In this situation the sufferer must linger in the burning sun for several days.

Scarab (skă′ rȧb). A trinket in the form of a dung-beetle, especially *Scarabæus sacer*. It originated in ancient Egypt as an

AMULET, being made of polished or glazed stone, metal, or glazed faience, and was perforated lengthwise for suspension. By the XIIIth Dynasty, scarabs became used as seals, worn as pendants, or mounted on signet rings. The insect was supposed to conceal in itself the secret of eternal life, since the scarab was believed to be only of the male sex, hence their use as amulets. They are still the most popular of Egyptian souvenirs.

Scaramouch (skăr' à mouch). The English form of Ital. *Scaramuccia* (through Fr. *Scaramouche*), a stock character in old Italian farce, introduced into England soon after 1670. He was a braggart and fool, very valiant in words, but a POLTROON, and was usually dressed in a black Spanish costume caricaturing the dons.

Scarborough Warning. No warning at all; blow first, warning after. In Scarborough robbers were said to be dealt with in a very summery manner by a sort of HALIFAX GIBBET-LAW, LYNCH LAW, or an *à la lanterne*. (*See under* LANTERN.)

Scarlet. The colour of certain official costumes as those of judges, CARDINALS, holders of certain academic qualifications, etc.; hence sometimes applied to these dignitaries. *Cp.* PINK; PURPLE.

Scarlet Hat. A CARDINAL; from his once traditional red hat.

Scarlet Letter. In the early days in Puritan New England a scarlet "A" for "adulteress" used to be branded or sewn on a guilty woman's dress.

Scarlet Pimpernel. A plant of the primrose family, *Anagallis arvensis*. The hero of Baroness Orczy's novel, *The Scarlet Pimpernel* (1905), and of several others in the series, took his nickname from the use of the pimpernel as his emblem.

The Scarlet Woman, or **Scarlet Whore.** The woman seen by St. JOHN in his vision "arrayed in purple and scarlet colour", sitting "upon a scarlet coloured beast, full of names of blasphemy, having seven heads and ten horns", "drunken with the blood of the saints, and with the blood of the martyrs", upon whose forehead was written "Mystery, Babylon the Great, The Mother of Harlots and Abominations of The Earth" (*Rev.* xvii, 1–6).

St. John was probably referring to ROME which, at the time he was writing, was "drunken with the blood of the saints; some controversial PROTESTANTS have applied the words to the Church of Rome, and some ROMAN CATHOLICS to the Protestant churches generally.

Will Scarlet. One of the companions of ROBIN HOOD.

Scat singing. In JAZZ a form of singing without words, using the voice as a musical instrument. Said to have been started by Louis Armstrong in the 1920s when he forgot the words or dropped the paper on which they were written while singing a number; Jelly Roll Morton, on the other hand, claimed to have sung scat as early as 1906.

Scavenger's Daughter. An instrument of torture invented by Sir Leonard Skevington, Lieutenant of the TOWER in the reign of Henry VIII. The machine compressed the body by bringing the head to the knees, and so forced blood out of the nose and ears.

Sceptic (skep' tik) literally means one who thinks for himself, and does not receive on another's testimony (from Gr. *skeptesthai*, to examine). Pyrrho founded the philosophic sect called "Sceptics", and Epictetus combated their dogmas. In theology we apply the word to those who do not accept revelation. *See* PYRRHONISM.

Sceptre (sep' ter) (Gr., a staff). The GOLD and jewelled wand carried by a SOVEREIGN as an emblem of royalty; hence, royal authority and dignity.

The sceptre of the kings and emperors of ROME was of ivory, bound with gold and surmounted by a golden EAGLE; the British sceptre is of richly jewelled gold, and bears immediately beneath the CROSS and ball the the great CULLINAN DIAMOND.

HOMER says that AGAMEMNON's sceptre was made by VULCAN, who gave it to the son of SATURN. It passed successively to JUPITER, MERCURY, PELOPS, Atreus and THYESTES till it came to Agamemnon. It was looked on with great reverence, and several miracles were attributed to it.

Schadenfreude (sha' den froi dĕ) (Ger.). A malicious delight in the bad luck of others (*Schaden*, damage; *Freude*, joy).

Scheherazade (she hēr' ȧ zad ȧ). The mouthpiece of the tales related in the ARABIAN NIGHTS, daughter of the grand VIZIER of the Indies. The SULTAN Schahriah, having discovered the infidelity of his sultana, resolved to have a fresh wife every night and have her strangled at daybreak. Scheherazade entreated to become his wife, and so amused him with tales for a thousand and one nights that he revoked his cruel decree, bestowed his affection on her, and called her "the liberator of the sex".

Schelhorn's Bible. *See* BIBLE, SOME SPECIALLY NAMED EDITIONS.

Schiedam (skĭ dăm'). Hollands gin, so called from Schiedam, a town where it is principally manufactured.

Schism, The Great. The split in the CATHOLIC CHURCH when there were rival popes at Avignon and ROME. It began in 1378 and ended in 1417. After the death of Gregory XI, the last of the AVIGNON POPES proper, Urban VI (1378–1389) alienated the French cardinals and their adherents, and they established an antipope, Clement VII, at Anagni. Clement soon retired to Avignon with his supporters, where the ANTI-POPE remained until the schism ended.

Schlemihl, Peter (shlem' il). The man who sold his shadow to the DEVIL, in Chamisso's tale so called (1814). The name is a synonym for any person who makes a desperate and silly bargain. *Schlemihl* is Yiddish for a clumsy person.

Scholasticism. The term usually denotes the philosophy and doctrines of the mediæval SCHOOLMEN from the 9th to the early 15th century. It was very much concerned with applying Aristotelian logic to Christian theology. On the whole, reason took second place to faith and the apparent reconciliation and harmony between the two established by St. THOMAS AQUINAS in his *Summa Theologica* was undermined by Duns Scotus and WILLIAM OF OCCAM. It taught men to discipline their thought and classify their knowledge. Scholasticism owed

much of its decline to its own internal quibblings, verbal subtleties, and intellectual exhaustion, but it never completely lost its vitality and still attracts theologians, especially in the ROMAN CATHOLIC CHURCH. *Cp.* NOMINALISM: REALISM; DIALECTIC.

Science. Literally "knowledge", it is Lat. *scientia* from *scire*, to know. SHAKESPEARE uses it in this old, wide meaning:

> Plutus himself,
> That knows the tinct and multiplying medicine,
> Hath not in nature's mystery more science
> Than I have on this ring.
> *All's Well That Ends Well*, V, iii.

The Science. Pugilism.

The Dismal Science. Economics, so named by Carlyle.

The Gay Science. *See under* GAY.

Hard and **Soft Science.** NATURAL SCIENCE, physics, etc. are sometimes called "hard science" as opposed to "soft science", a term applied to sociology, economics, psychology, political science and other social and behavioural sciences.

Natural Science. Empirical science as distinct from mathematics, logic, mental and moral science, etc. Its general principles are commonly called "the laws of nature".

The Noble Science. Boxing, or fencing; the "noble art of self-defence".

The Seven Sciences, or Seven Liberal Sciences. The same as the *Seven Liberal Arts. See* QUADRIVIUM.

Science persecuted. Anaxagoras of Clazomenæ (d. *c.* 430 B.C.) held opinions in NATURAL SCIENCE (*see above*) so far in advance of his age that he was accused of impiety and condemned to death. Pericles, with great difficulty, got his sentence commuted to fine and banishment.

Galileo (1564–1642) was imprisoned by the INQUISITION for maintaining that the earth moved, but recanted to gain his liberty. *See* EPPUR SI MUOVE.

Roger Bacon (*c.* 1214–1294) was excommunicated and imprisoned for diabolical knowledge, chiefly on account of his chemical researches. Dr. DEE was imprisoned under Queen Mary for using enchantments to compass the Queen's death. Averroes, the Arabian philosopher, who flourished in the 12th century, was denounced as a lunatic and degraded solely on account of his great eminence in natural philosophy and medicine.

Scire facias (sī' re fā' si as) (Lat., make [him] to know). A writ founded upon record (*i.e.* judgment, letters PATENT, etc.) directing the SHERIFF to make known (*scire facias*) to the person against whom it is brought to show why the person bringing the writ should not have the benefit of the record. It is now largely obsolete.

Sciron (sī' ron). A robber of Greek legend, slain by THESEUS. He infested the parts about Megara, and forced travellers over the rocks into the sea, where they were devoured by a sea monster.

Scissors. *See* KNIFE.

Scissors and paste. Compilation as distinct from original literary work. The allusion is obvious.

Scissors to grind. Work to do; purpose to serve. *I have my own scissors to grind* is a way of saying, "I've got my own work to do, or my own troubles, and can't be bothered with yours."

Scogan's Jests (skō' gan). A popular jest-book in the 16th century, said by Andrew Boorde (who published it) to be the work of one John Scogan, reputed to have been court fool to Edward IV. He is referred to (anachronously) by Justice Shallow in *Henry IV, Pt. II*, III, ii, and must not be confused with Henry Scogan (d. 1407), the poet-disciple of Chaucer to whom Ben Jonson alludes:

> Scogan? What was he?
> Oh, a fine gentleman, and a master of arts
> Of Henry the Fourth's times, that made disguises
> For the king's sons, and writ in ballad royal
> Daintily well.
>> *The Fortunate Isles* (1642).

Scold's bridle. *See under* BRIDLE.

Scone (skoon). **The Stone of Scone.** The great coronation stone, the Stone of Destiny, on which the Scottish kings were formerly crowned at Scone, near Perth. It was removed by Edward I in 1296 and brought to Westminster Ab-

bey, and has ever since been housed under the Chair of St. Edward. It was stolen on the night of 24–25 December 1950, but restored to its place in February 1952.

It is also, traditionally, called JACOB'S STONE. It is of reddish-grey sandstone and is fabled to have been once kept at Dunstaffnage in Argyll and removed to Scone by Kenneth MacAlpin in 843. *Cp.* TANIST STONE.

Scorched Earth Policy. A policy of burning and destroying crops and anything that may be of use to an invading force.

Score (O.E. *scoru*, a notch). Especially applied to a notch on a TALLY, hence a reckoning or account. As the number 20, probably from the special score or mark on a tally which indicated that figure. Drovers passing their animals through a toll-gate always based their counting on twenties or *scores*.

To pay off old scores. To settle accounts; used sometimes of money debts, but usually in the sense of revenging an injury, "getting even" with one.

Scorpio, Scorpion (skôr' pi ō). Scorpio is the eighth sign of the ZODIAC, which the sun enters about 24 October. ORION had boasted that he could kill any animal the earth produced. A scorpion was sent to punish his vanity and it stung Orion to death. JUPITER later raised the scorpion to HEAVEN.

Fable has it that scorpions carry with them an oil which is a remedy against their stings. *Cp.* THE TOAD, UGLY AND VENOMOUS *under* TOADS.

> 'Tis true, a scorpion's oil is said
> To cure the wounds the venom made,
> And weapons dress'd with salves restore
> And heal the hurts they gave before.
>> BUTLER: *Hudibras*, III, ii, 1029.

The oil was extracted from the flesh and given to the sufferer as a medicine; it was also supposed to be very useful to bring away the descending stone of the kidneys. Another belief was that if a scorpion was surrounded by a circle of fire it would sting itself to death with its own tail.

A lash, or **scourge of scorpions.** A specially severe punishment, in allusion to the Biblical passage:

> My father hath chastised you with

whips, but I will chastise you with scorpions.

I *Kings* xii, 11.

In the MIDDLE AGES a scourge of four or five thongs set with steel spikes and leaden weights was called a *scorpion*.

Scot. Payment, reckoning. The same word as SHOT; we still speak of *paying one's shot*.

Scot and lot. The rough equivalent of the modern rates, *i.e.* payments by householders for local and national purposes. They became in due course a qualification for the franchise. *Scot* is the tax and *lot* the allotment or portion alloted. Scot came from the Old Norse *skot*, a contribution, corresponding to O.E. *sceot. Cp.* CHURCH SCOT.

To go scot-free. To be let off payment; to escape payment or punishment, etc.

Scotch, Scots, Scottish. These three adjectives all mean belonging to, native of, or characteristic of SCOTLAND, but their application varies and the Scots usually prefer Scottish rather than Scotch, which is applied to whisky.

Broad Scotch (Braid Scots). The vernacular of the lowlands of SCOTLAND.

Scotch mist. Fine, misty, rain. The phrase *What do you think this is— Scotch mist?* is addressed sarcastically to one who cannot see or grasp what stares him in the face.

Scotch Plot. An alleged conspiracy, called the Queensberry Plot in SCOTLAND, for a JACOBITE rising and invasion of Scotland in 1703. Simon Fraser, Lord Lovat, after intriguing at St. GERMAIN and VERSAILLES, returned to Scotland with a letter from Mary of Modena (James II's widow) to be delivered to an unnamed nobleman. He addressed it to John Murray, Duke of Atholl, his pesonal enemy, and then took it to the Duke of Queensberry, Atholl's rival in the Scottish Ministry. This broke up the ministry and drove Atholl over to the Jacobites. It led to disputes between the English and Scottish parliaments but no punitive action was taken.

A pound Scots. English and Scottish coins were of equal value until 1355 after which the Scottish coinage steadily depreciated, and when James VI of SCOTLAND became James I of ENGLAND (1603) the pound Scots was worth 1s. 8d., one-twelfth the value of an English pound. A pound Scots was divided into 20 *Scots shillings* each worth an English penny. The Scottish Mint closed in 1709.

A Scots pint was about equivalent to three English imperial pints.

Scotch. To make a scotch is to cut with shallow incisions, to slash. SHAKESPEARE's *Macbeth* (III, ii) has, "We have scotch'd the snake, not killed it", but in the 1st Folio the word appears *scorch'd*. Isaac Walton's *Compleat Angler* tells us that to dress a chub, "Give him three or four scotches or cuts on the back with your knife, and broil him on charcoal." The derivation of the word is uncertain.

Out of all scotch and notch. Beyond all bounds; *scotch* was the line marked upon the ground in certain games, as **hopscotch.**

The word *scotch* is also applied to a wedge or block placed under a wheel, etc., to prevent it moving.

Scotists (skō' tists). followers of Duns Scotus (*see* DUNCE), who maintained the doctrine of the IMMACULATE CONCEPTION in opposition to THOMAS AQUINAS.

Scotland. St. ANDREW is the patron saint of Scotland and tradition says that his remains were brought by Regulus (St. RULE) to the coast of Fife in 368.

The old royal arms of Scotland were: Or, a lion rampant gules, armed and langued azure, within a double tressure flory counter-flory of fleur-de-lis of the second. *Crest.* An imperial crown proper, surmounted by a lion sejant affronté gules crowned or, holding in his dexter paw a naked sword and in the sinister a sceptre both proper. *Supporters.* Two UNICORNS argent, armed, crined, and unguled or, imperially crowned, gorged with open crowns with chains reflexed over the back of the last; the dexter supporting a banner charged with the arms of Scotland, the sinister supporting a similar banner azure, thereupon a saltire argent. *Mottoes.* NEMO ME IMPUNE LACESSIT and over the crest *In Defens.*

In Scotland now, the royal arms of

Great Britain are used with certain alterations; the collar of the THISTLE encircles that of the GARTER, the Scottish crest takes the place of the English, and the unicorn supporter crowned and gorged takes precedence of the lion (*see* HERALDRY).

The last Scottish coronation was that of Charles II at SCONE, 1 January 1651.

Scotland Yard. As commonly used it denotes the Criminal Investigation Department of the Metropolitan Police; from the fact that Great Scotland Yard, WHITEHALL, was the headquarters of the Metropolitan Police from *c.* 1842 to 1891 and thereafter New Scotland Yard, Parliament Street, until 1967 when "Scotland Yard" was transferred to Broadway, WESTMINSTER. The name of the original Scotland Yard comes from the fact that it was the residence of the kings of Scotland when they came to London.

Scotus, Duns. *See* DUNCE; SCOTISTS.

Scourge. A whip or lash; commonly applied to diseases that carry off great numbers, as "the scourge of influenza", etc., and to persons who seem to be the instruments of divine punishment, etc.

The Scourge of God (Lat. *flagellum Dei*). ATTILA (d. 453), king of the HUNS, so called by mediæval writers because of the widespread havoc and destruction caused by his armies.

Scouse (skous). A name applied to a native of the port of Liverpool; also to Liverpudlian speech and mannerisms. The word is the shortened form of *lobscouse*, a sailor's name for a stew, particularly of meat, vegetables, and ship's biscuit. Hence *lobscouser* as a name for a sailor.

Scout. This word comes from the old French *escoute*, a spy or eavesdropper, akin to the modern French *écouter*, to listen. It is applied to an individual, an aeroplane, warship, etc., sent to observe enemy movements or to obtain information. In the early days of CRICKET, the fielders were called scouts; college servants at Oxford are still called scouts; and it was also used for a member of the BOY SCOUTS whose association is now officially called the *Scout Association*.

Scowerers. A set of rakes (*c.* 1670–1720),

who with the Nickers (*see* NICK) and MOHOCKS, committed great annoyances in London and other large towns.

Scrap. The Scrap of Paper. The Treaty of 1839 maintaining the independence of Belgium; signed by Lord Palmerston for Great Britain; Count Sebastiani for France, Baron Bülow for Prussia; Count Pozzi di Borgo for Russia; Count Senfft for Austria; and M. Van de Weyer for Belgium. It was this treaty that the Germans violated when they invaded Belgium in August 1914. This brought Great Britain into the struggle and the German Chancellor Bethmann-Hollweg declared that Great Britain had entered the war "just for a scrap of paper".

Scrape. Bread and scrape. Bread and butter with the butter spread very thinly. *See* TO DINE ON POTATOES AND POINT *under* POINT.

I've got into a bad scrape. An awkward predicament, an embarrassing difficulty.

To scrape along. To get along in the world with difficulty, finding it hard to "make both ends meet".

To scrape an acquaintance with. To get on terms of familiarity with by currying favour and by methods of insinuation. The *Gentleman's Magazine* (N.S. xxxix, 230), says that Hadrian went one day to the public baths and saw an old soldier, well known to him, scraping himself with a potsherd for want of a flesh-brush. The emperor sent him a sum of money. Next day Hadrian found the bath crowded with soldiers scraping themselves with potsherds, and said, "Scrape on, gentlemen, but you'll not scrape acquaintance with me."

To scrape through. To pass an examination, etc., "by the skin of one's teeth" just to escape failure.

Scratch. Scratch cradle. Another form of CAT'S CRADLE. *See under* CAT.

A scratch crew, side, etc. One scraped together *ad hoc*; not a regular team.

Old Scratch. OLD NICK (*see under* NICK), the DEVIL. From *skratta*, an old Scandinavian word for a GOBLIN or monster (modern Icelandic *skratti*, a devil).

A scratch race. A race of horses, men,

boys, etc., without restrictions as to age, weight, previous winnings, etc., who all start from scratch.

To come up to (the) scratch. To be ready or good enough in any test; to make the grade. Under the London Prize Ring Rules, introduced in 1839, a round in a prize fight ended when one of the fighters was knocked down. After a 30-second interval this fighter was allowed eight seconds in which to make his way unaided to a mark scratched in the centre of the ring; if he failed to do so, he "had not come up to scratch" and was declared beaten.

Screw. Slang for wages, salary; possibly because in some employments it was handed out "screwed up in paper" or because it was "screwed out" of one's employer; it is also slang for a prison warder, from the days when the locks were operated with a screw-like movement.

An old screw. A skinflint; a miser who has amassed his wealth by "putting on the screw" (*see below*), and who keeps his money tight.

He has a screw loose. He is "not quite all there", he's "a little touched" or mad. His mind, like a piece of machinery, is in need of adjustment.

His head is screwed on the right way. He is clear-headed and right-thinking; he knows what he's about.

There's a screw loose somewhere. All is not quite right, there's something amiss. A figurative phrase from machinery, where one screw not tightened up may be the cause of a disaster.

To put on the screw. A phrase surviving from the days when the thumb-screw was used as a form of torture to extract confessions or money. To press for payment, as a screw presses by gradually increasing pressure. Hence *to apply the screw, to give the screw another turn*, to take steps (or additional steps) to enforce one's demands.

To screw oneself up to it. To force oneself to face it, etc.; to get oneself into the right frame of mind for doing some unpleasant or difficult job.

The Screw Plot. The story is that before Queen Anne went to St. Paul's in 1708 to offer thanksgiving for the victory of Oudenarde, conspirators re-

moved certain screw-bolts from the roof beams of the cathedral that the fabric might fall on the queen and her suite and kill them. In fact it appears that certain iron fastenings were omitted by one of the workmen as he thought the timbers were already sufficiently secured.

Screw-ball. A colloquial term for an erratic, eccentric, or unconventional person. It is also a baseball term for a ball pitched to break with a particular kind of slant away from the apparent curve of flight.

Screwed. Intoxicated. A playful synonym of *tight*.

Scribe. In the NEW TESTAMENT, it means a Jewish doctor of the law, and Scribes were generally coupled with the PHARISEES as upholders of the ancient ceremonial tradition. In *Matt.* xxii, 35, we read, "then one of them, which was a *lawyer*, asked Him...which is the great commandment in the law?" *Mark* (xii, 28) says, "And one of the *scribes* came, and...asked him, Which is the first commandment of all?"

In the OLD TESTAMENT the word has a wider application. In II *Sam.* viii, 17, it is used in the sense of "secretary", and again in *Jer.* xxxvi, 10, 12, 20, 21, etc. In II *Kings* xxv, 19, it applies to the military muster-master and *Is.* xxxiii, 18, a tax-official, etc. More commonly it denotes those occupied in literary study, copying and editing of the SCRIPTURES, and especially of the Law, this being akin to the New Testament usage.

Scriblerus, Martinus (mar ti nùs skrib lēr' ùs). A merciless satire on the false taste in literature current in the time of Pope, for the most part written by Arbuthnot, and published in 1741. Cornelius Scriblerus, the father of Martin, was a pedant, who entertained all sorts of absurdities about the education of his son. Martin grew up a man of capacity; but though he had read everything, his judgment was vile and taste atrocious. Pope, Swift, and Arbuthnot founded a *Scriblerus club* with the object of pillorying all literary incompetence.

Scriptores Decem (skrip tôr' ēz' dē - sem). A collection of ten ancient chronicles on English history edited by Sir Roger Twysden (1597–1672) and published in 1652 as *Historiæ Anglicanæ Scriptores Decem* with the "Glossary" of William Somner, the first Anglo-Saxon word-list. The chroniclers are Simeon of Durham, John of Hexham, Richard of Hexham, Ailred of Rieval, Ralph de Diceto (Archdeacon of London), John Brompton of Jorval, Gervase of Canterbury, Thomas Stubbs, William Thorn of Canterbury, and Henry Knighton of Leicester.

Thomas Gale (c. 1635–1702) published a similar collection of five chronicles, *Historiæ Anglicanæ Scriptores Quinque* in 1687, and in 1691 *Historiæ Britannicæ Saxonicæ Danicæ Scriptores Quindecim*.

Scriptorium (skrip tôr' i ŭm) (Lat. from *scriptus*, past part. of *scribere*, to write). A writing-room, especially the chamber set apart in the mediæval monasteries for the copying of MSS., etc. Sir James Murray (1837–1915) gave the name to the corrugated-iron outhouse in his garden at Mill Hill, in which he started the great *New English Dictionary*.

Scriptures, The, or **Holy Scripture** (Lat. *scriptura*, a writing). The BIBLE; hence appleid allusively to the sacred writings of other creeds, as the KORAN, *the Scripture of the Mohammedans*, the VEDAS and ZEND-AVESTA, of the Hindus and Persians, etc.

Scripturists. A name given to the Karaites ("Readers of the Scripture"), those Jewish literalists who kept Biblical injunctions, etc., to the letter. For them "an eye for an eye" meant just this, and "Ye shall kindle no fire throughout your habitations upon the sabbath day" (*Exod.* xxxv, 3) left them to shiver in the winter. The movement began in the 8th century under Anan ben David, and spread from Babylonia to Persia and Egypt. Its decline set in from the 10th century, although it has lingered on in isolated pockets.

Scrooge, A regular Scrooge. A miserable skinflint, a proper miser. The allusion is to Ebenezer Scrooge in Dickens's *Christmas Carol* (1843).

> Oh! But he was a tight-fisted hand at the grindstone, Scrooge! a squeezing, wrenching, grasping, scraping, clutching, covetous old sinner!

Christmas Carol, Stave One.

Scullabogue. The Barn of Scullabogue (skŭl á bōg'). In the Irish rebellion of 1798 which largely degenerated into a war between CATHOLICS and PROTESTANTS, revenge was taken after the repulse of the rebels at New Ross. The barn at Scullabogue, containing over 180 Protestant loyalists, was set on fire and all its inmates perished.

Scurry. Hurry-scurry. A confused bustle through lack of time; in a confused bustle. A RICOCHET word.

Scutage (skū' tij), or **Escuage.** In feudal times, a payment in commutation of KNIGHT-SERVICE (*i.e.* military service). It developed after the Norman CONQUEST but the term, from Lat. *scutum*, a shield, did not come into use until the beginning of the 12th century. The method of assessment was regularized in the reign of Henry II and TENANTS-IN-CHIEF passed on the levy to their tenants. Scutage came to an end in 1327.

Scuttle. To scuttle a ship in order to make it sink. This is from SCUTTLE in the sense of a hatch-opening or hole.

To scuttle off. To make off hurriedly. This was originally *to scuddle off*, scuddle being a frequentative of *scud*, to run or skim along.

Scylla. In Greek legend the name of a daughter of King Nisus of Megara; also a sea monster.

The daughter of Nisus promised to deliver Megara into the hands of her lover, MINOS, and, to effect this, cut off a golden hair on her father's head while he was asleep. Minos despised her for this treachery, and Scylla threw herself from a rock into the sea. Other accounts say she was changed into a lark by the gods and her father into a hawk.

Scylla, the sea monster, was a beautiful NYMPH beloved by GLAUCUS, who applied to CIRCE for a love-potion, but Circe became enamoured of him and metamorphosed her rival into a hideous creature with twelve feet and six heads, each with three rows of teeth. Below the waist her body was made up of hideous monsters, like dogs, which barked unceasingly. She dwelt on the rock of Scylla, opposite CHARYBDIS, on the Italian side of the Straits of Messina and was a terror to ships and sailors. Whenever a ship passed, each of her heads would seize one of the crew.

Avoiding Scylla, he fell into Charybdis. *See* CHARYBDIS.

Between Scylla and Charybdis. *See* CHARYBDIS.

To fall from Scylla into Charybdis—out of the FRYING-PAN into the fire. *See* CHARYBDIS.

Scythian (sith' i ăn). Pertaining to the peoples or region of Scythia, the ancient name of a great part of European and Asiatic Russia.

Scythian defiance. When DARIUS approached Scythia, an ambassador was sent to his tent with a bird, a frog, a mouse, and five arrows, then left without uttering a word. Darius, wondering what was meant, was told by Gobrias it meant this: Either fly away like a bird, hide your head in a hole like a mouse, or swim across the river like a frog, or in five days you will be laid prostrate by the Scythian arrows.

The Scythian or **Tartarian Lamb.** *See under* LAMB.

'Sdeath, 'Sdeins. *See* 's.

Sea. Any large expanse of water, more or less enclosed; hence the expression"molten sea" meaning the great brazen vessel which stood in SOLOMON'S TEMPLE (II *Chron*. iv, 2, and I *Kings*, vii, 23); even the NILE, the Euphrates, and the Tigris are sometimes called *sea* by the prophets. The world of water is the *Ocean*.

At sea, or **all at sea.** Wide of the mark, in a state of uncertainty or error; like one at sea who has lost his bearings.

The four seas. The seas surrounding Great Britain, on the north, south, east, and west.

Half-seas over. *See under* HALF.

The high seas. The open sea, the "main"; especially that part of the sea beyond "the THREE-MILE LIMIT, which forms a free highway to all nations.

The Old Man of the Sea. *See under* OLD.

The Seven Seas. *See under* SEVEN.

Sea Deities. In classical myth, besides the fifty NEREIDS, the OCEANIDS, the SIRENS, etc., there were numerous dei-

ties connected with the sea. Chief among them are: AMPHITRITE; GLAUCUS; Ino (*see* LEUCOTHEA); NEPTUNE; NEREUS and his wife TETHYS; Portumnus (*see* PALÆMON); POSEIDON (the Greek Neptune); PROTEUS; THETIS; TRITON.

Sea Lawyer. A seaman who is constantly arguing about his rights, a captious person, a troublemaker. It is also nautical slang for a shark.

Sea legs. To get one's sea legs. To acquire the ability to walk steadily in a ship at sea despite the rolling and pitching of the vessel.

Sea serpent. A serpentine monster supposed to inhabit the depths of the ocean. Many reports of such a creature have been made by mariners over the centuries but its existence has never been established; thus J. G. Lockhart (*Mysteries of the Sea: The Great Sea-Serpent*) writes: "We thus conclude with at least three sea-serpents, one in 1857, one in 1875, and one in 1905, for which we have reasonably satisfactory evidence ... Most of the witnesses agree on certain outstanding features; it is a long serpentine creature; it has a series of humps; its head is rather like a horse's; its colour is dark on the top and light below; it appears during the summer months; and unlike the sea monster it is harmless, for it never actually attacked anybody even under provocation". *Cp.* LOCH NESS MONSTER.

The Sea-born City. Venice.

The Sea-born goddess. APHRODITE.

The Sea-girt isle. ENGLAND. So called because, as SHAKESPEARE has it, it is "hedged in with the main, that water-walled bulwark" (*King John*, II, i).

> This precious stone set in the silver sea,
> Which serves it in the office of a wall,
> Or as a moat defensive to a house,
> Against the envy of less happier lands.
> *Richard II*, II, i.

Sea-green Incorruptible, The. So Carlyle called Robespierre in his *French Revolution*. He was of a sallow, unhealthy complexion.

Seal. The sire is called a *bull*, his females are *cows*, the offspring are called *pups*; the breeding-place is called a *rookery*, a group of young seals a *pod*, and a colony of seals a *herd*. The immature male is called a *bachelor*. A *sealer* is a seal-hunter, and seal-hunting is called *sealing*.

Seal (O.Fr. *seel* from Lat. *sigillum*). An impressed device, in wax, lead, etc.

Great Seal. *See under* GREAT.

Solomon's Seal. *See under* SOLOMON.

To set one's seal to. To give one's authority, to authenticate. From the affixing of seals to documents as an official sign of their authenticity.

Under my hand and seal. A legal phrase indicating that the document in question is both signed and sealed by the person on whose behalf it has been drawn up.

Sealed Orders. Orders delivered in a sealed package to naval and military commanders which they must not open before a certain time, or reaching a certain locality, etc.

Seamy side. The "wrong" or worst side; as the "seamy side of London", the "seamy side of life". In velvet, Brussels carpets, tapestry, etc., the "wrong" side shows the seams or threads of the pattern exhibited on the right side.

Seasons, The Four. Spring, Summer, Autumn, and Winter. *Spring* starts (officially) on 21 March, the Spring Equinox, when the sun enters ARIES; *Summer* on 22 June, the Summer SOLSTICE, when the sun enters CANCER; *Autumn* on 23 September, the Autumn Equinox, the sun entering LIBRA; the *Winter* on 22 December, when the sun enters CAPRICORN. *See* ZODIAC.

The ancient Greeks characterized Spring by MERCURY, Summer by APOLLO, Autumn by BACCHUS, and Winter by HERCULES.

James Thomson's poetic series *The Seasons* was not published as a collection until 1730. *Winter* first appeared in 1726 and fetched three guineas from the publisher, but gave Thomson a reputation. *Summer*, dedicated to Bob Dodington, was published in 1727, *Spring* in 1728, and *Autumn* in 1730.

In and out of season. Always or all the time, constantly.

The London Season. The part of the year when the Court and fashionable society generally is in town—May, June, July.

The silly season. *See under* SILLY.

Season-ticket. A ticket giving the holder certain specified rights (in connection with travelling, entrance to an exhibition, etc.) for a certain specified period.

Seat. To take a back seat. *See under* BACK.

Sebastian, St. Patron SAINT of archers, martyrd in 288. He was bound to a tree and shot at with arrows and finally beaten to death. As the arrows stuck in his body as pins in a pin-cushion, he was also made the patron saint of pinmakers. As he was a captain of the guard, he is the patron saint of soldiers. His feast, coupled with that of St. Fabian, is kept on 20 January.

Second. The next after the first (Lat. *secundus*).

In duelling the *second* is the representative of the principal; he carries the challenge, selects the ground, sees that the weapons are in order, and is responsible for all the arrangements.

A second of time is so called because the division of the minute into sixtieths is the second of the sexagesimal operations, the first being the division of the hour into minutes.

One's second self. One's ALTER EGO; one whose tastes, opinions, habits, etc., correspond so entirely with one's own that there is practically no distinction.

The Second Adam. Jesus Christ.

Second Adventists. Those who believe that the Second Coming of Christ (*cp.* 1 *Thess.* iv, 15) will precede the MILLENNIUM; hence sometimes also called Premillenarians.

Second Chamber. In a legislature of two houses the non-elected or indirectly elected house is so called. In Great Britain the HOUSE OF LORDS is the Second Chamber and in the U.S.A. it is the Senate.

Second Empire. *See* NAPOLEON III.

Second Floor. Two flights above the ground floor. In the U.S.A. the second floor is the English first floor.

Second-hand. Not new or original; what has been the property of another, as "second-hand" books, clothes, opinions, etc.

Second nature. Said of a habit, way of doing things, etc., that has become so ingrained that it is instinctive.

Second pair back. The back room on the floor two flights of stairs above the ground floor; similarly the front room is called the *second pair front*.

Second sight. The power of seeing things invisible to others; the power of foreseeing future events.

Second Wind. *See under* WIND.

To second an officer (accent on last syllable) is, in military parlance, to remove him temporarily from his present duties to take up another extra-regimental or staff appointment.

Secondary colours. *See under* COLOURS.

Secret. An open secret. A piece of information generally known, but not formally announced.

Un secret de polichinelle. No secret at all; an open secret. *Polichinelle* is the PUNCH of the old French puppet-shows, and his secrets are STAGE WHISPERS told to all the audience.

Secret Service. The popular name for governmental intelligence, espionage and counter-espionage organizations. The U.S. Secret Service, under the Treasury Department, is mainly concerned with Federal crime.

Secular. From Lat. *sæcularis*, pertaining to a *sæculum* or age, a generation; also a period of 100 years (the longest duration of man's life), any long period of indefinite length. This gives us our meanings of "occurring once in an age", "lasting indefinitely", "occurring once in a hundred years" and "lasting for a hundred years". The meaning "lay", "temporal", "of this world", is from Late Latin when *sæcularis* had acquired the meaning of "belonging to the world", "worldly".

Secular clergy. Clergy living "in the world" as opposed to the regular clergy of the cloister, who live under a rule. In the ROMAN CATHOLIC CHURCH secular clergy take precedence over the regular clergy.

Secular games (Lat. *Ludi sæculares*). In ancient ROME, the public games lasting three days and three nights, that took place once in an age (*sæculum*) or every 100 years (sometimes every 110 years).

They were instituted in obedience to the SIBYLLINE verses with the promise that "the empire should remain in safety so long as this admonition was observed". They derived from the Tarentine Games instituted in 249 B.C. to propitiate PLUTO and PROSERPINE.

> Date, quæ precamur
> Tempore sacro
> Quo Sibyllini monuere versus.
> HORACE: *Carmen Sæculare*, A.U.C. 737.

Secularism. The name given in 1846 by George Jacob Holyoake (1817–1906) to an ethical system founded on "natural morality" and opposed to the tenets of revealed religion and ecclesiasticism.

Sedan chair (se dăn'). The covered seat, so called, carried by two bearers back and front, originated in Italy in the late 16th century, and was introduced into England by Sir S. Duncombe in 1634.

The name is probably derived from Lat. *sedere*, to sit; but Johnson's suggestion that it is connected with the French town, *Sedan*, is a possibility.

Sedulous. To play the sedulous ape to. To study the style of another, and model one's own on his as faithfully and meticulously as possible; said, usually with more or less contempt, of literary men. The phrase is taken from R. L. Stevenson, who, in his essay, "A College Magazine" (*Memories and Portraits*), said that he had:

> Played the sedulous ape to Hazlitt, to Lamb, to Wordsworth, to sir Thomas Browne, to Defoe, to Hawthorne; to Montaigne, to Baudelaire, and to Obermann...That, like it or not, is the way to learn to write.

See[1] (Lat. *sedes*). The seat or throne of a BISHOP, hence the town or place where the bishop's cathedral is located and from which he takes his title; and so has to be distinguished from diocese, the territory over which he has jurisdiction.

The Holy See. *See under* HOLY.

See[2]. **To see a person through.** To help him through a difficulty.

To see into the matter. To investigate.

To see off. To accompany someone to the point of departure on a journey; also, colloquially, to outwit or get the better of someone by sharp practice,

Seljuks

etc.; or to get the better of someone physically, as a dog "sees off" unwanted prowlers.

To see through a person. To perceive his true character and motives, "not to be taken in".

To see to. To attend to.

Seeded players. Those players regarded by the organizers of a tournament (*e.g.* lawn tennis at the All England Club, Wimbledon) as likely to reach the final stages, and who are so placed in the order of play that they do not meet each other until the closing rounds. These players are numbered in the order of likelihood. Of course it sometimes happens that seeded players are defeated early in a tournament.

Seekers. A 17th-century PURITAN sect akin to the QUAKERS in their outlook who rejected the existing church and claimed to seek the true church which God would reveal in his own time. Roger Williams (*c.* 1603–1683) founded Providence, NEW ENGLAND, as a refuge for the sect.

Seel. To close the eyelids of a HAWK by running a thread through them; to hoodwink (Fr. *ciller*; *cil*, the eyelash).

> She that so young could give out such a seeming,
> To seel her fathers eyes up, close as oak.
> SHAKESPEARE: *Othello*, III, iii.

Seian Horse, The (sī an). A possession which invariably brought ill luck with it. Hence the Latin proverb *Ille homo habet equum Seianum*. Cneius Seius had an Argive horse, of the breed of Diomed, of a bay colour and surpassing beauty, but it was fatal to its possessor. Seius was put to death by Mark Antony. Its next owner, Cornelius Dolabella, who bought it for 100,000 sesterces, was killed in Syria during the civil wars. Caius Cassius, who next took possession of it, perished after the battle of Philippi by the very sword which stabbed CÆSAR. Antony had the horse next, and after the battle of Actium slew himself.

Likewise the gold of Tolosa (*see under* GOLD) *and* HARMONIA'S NECKLACE were fatal possessions. *Cp.* NESSUS; OPAL.

Selah (sē la). A Hebrew word occurring often in thd *Psalms* (and three times in *Habakkuk* iii), indicating some musical or liturgical direction, such as a pause, a repetition, or the end of a section.

Selene (se lē′ nē). The moon goddess of Greek mythology, daughter of HYPERION and Theia, corresponding approximately to the Roman DIANA. Selene had 50 daughters by ENDYMION and three by ZEUS, including Erse, the Jew. Selene is represented with a diadem and wings on her shoulders, driving in a chariot drawn by two white horses; Diana is represented with a bow and arrow running after a stag.

Seleucidæ (se lū′ si dē). The dynasty of Seleucus Nicator (*c.* 358–281 B.C.), one of ALEXANDER's generals who in 312 conquered Babylon and succeeded to part of Alexander's vast empire. The monarchy consisted of Syria, a large part of Asia Minor, and all the eastern provinces (Persia, Bacteria, etc.). The last of the line was dispossessed by the Romans in 64 B.C.

Self. The Self-denying Ordinance. The measure passed by the LONG PARLIAMENT (April 1645) providing that Members of either House should give up their military commands and civil offices within 40 days. Nothing was said to prevent their reappointment. The indecisive second battle of Newbury in 1644 led to this measure which was directed against incompetent commanders, particularly in the HOUSE OF LORDS.

Self-determination. In politics, the concept that every nation, no matter how small or weak, has the right to decide upon its own form of government and to manage its own affairs. The phrase acquired this significance during the attempts to resettle Europe after World War I.

A self-made man. One who has risen from poverty and obscurity to comparative opulence or a position of importance by his own efforts.

Seljuks (sel′ jūks). The name of several Turkish dynasties descended from Seljuk, a Ghuzz chieftain, and which ruled in Persia, Syria and Asia Minor between the 11th and 13th centuries. In 1055 Togrul Beg, grandson of Seljuk, was made "Commander of the Faithful" (*see* CALIPH) for coming to the assistance of

925

the ABBASSIDE Caliph of Baghdad. His successor Alp Arslan took Syria and Palestine, and a large part of Anatolia from the BYZANTINE Emperor. The territories were eventually partitioned among branches of the family, but were subject to Mongol onslaughts from 1243. Their power steadily declined and their place was eventually taken by the OTTOMANS.

Sell. Slang for a swindle, a hoax, a first-of-April trick; and the person hoaxed is said to be *sold*.

To sell down the river. *See* RIVER.

To sell a person up. To dispose of his goods by order of the court because he cannot pay his debts, the proceeds going to his creditors.

To sell short. *See under* SHORT.

A selling race. *See* SELLING PLATE *under* PLATE.

Selling the pass. Betraying one's own side. The phrase was originally Irish and applied to those who turned King's EVIDENCE, or who impeached their comrades for money. The tradition is that a regiment was sent by Crotha, "lord of Atha", to hold a pass against the invading army of Trathal, "King of Cael". The pass was betrayed for money; the Firbolgs (*see* MILESIANS) were subdued, and Trathal assumed the title of "King of Ireland".

Semele (sem' e lē). In Greek mythology, the daughter of CADMUS and HARMONIA. By ZEUS she was the mother of DIONYSUS and was slain by lightning when he granted her request to visit her in his majesty.

Semiramis (se mir' à mis). In ancient legend, daughter of the goddess Derceto and a young Assyrian. She married Menones, but he hanged himself when NINUS, king of Assyria and founder of Nineveh, demanded Semiramis from him. She forthwith married NINUS who was so enamoured that he resigned the CROWN to her. After this she put him to death, but was herself ultimately slain by her son Ninyas. She is sometimes identified with ISHTAR and her doves. These and other legends accumulated round an Assyrian princess of this name who lived *c*. 800 B.C.

Semitic (se mit' ic). Pertaining to the descendants of SHEM (*see Gen*. x), *viz*., the

Hebrews, Arabs, Assyrians, Aramæans, etc.; nowadays applied to the Jews.

The Semitic languages are the ancient Assyrian and Chaldee, Aramaic, Syriac, Arabic, Hebrew, Samaritan, Ethiopic, and old Phœnician. The great characteristic of this family of languages is that the roots of words consist of three consonants.

Senatus consultum (sen a' tus kon sŭl'tum). A decree of the Senate of Ancient ROME. The term was sometimes applied to a decree of any senate, especially that of the First Empire in France.

Send. That sends me. Amateurs of JAZZ use this phrase, meaning: The music sends me out of myself, or into ecstasies.

Se'nnight. A week; seven nights. *Fort'night*, fourteen nights. These words are relics of the ancient CELTIC custom of beginning the day at sunset, a custom observed by the ancient Greeks, Babylonians, Persians, Syrians, and Jews, and by the modern heirs of these peoples. In *Gen*. i, 5, we find the evening precedes the morning: as, "The evening and the morning were the first day", etc.

> He shall live a man forbid:
> Weary se'n-nights nine times nine
> Shall he dwindle, peak and pine.
> SHAKESPEARE: *Macbeth*, I, iii.

Sense. Common sense. *See under* COMMON.

Scared out of my seven senses. Utterly scared, scared out of my wits. *See* SEVEN SENSES.

Sensitive Plant. *See* MIMOSA.

Sentences, Master of the. The SCHOOLMAN, Peter Lombard (*c*. 1100–1160), and Italian theologian and BISHOP of Paris, author of *The Four Books of Sentences* (*Sententiarum libri IV*), a compilation from the Fathers of the leading arguments PRO AND CON, bearing on the hair-splitting theological questions of the MIDDLE AGES.

The mediæval graduates in theology, of the second order, whose duty it was to lecture on the *Sentences*, were called *Sententiatory Bachelors*.

Separatists. A name given to the BROWNISTS and Independents of the 17th century who separated from the Established

Church.

Sephardim. The Jews of Spain and Portugal, as distinct from those of Poland and Germany called *Ashkenazim* (from the location given in *Gen.* x, 3). The name is from *Sepharad* (*Obad.* 20) where Jews were in captivity. The TARGUM of Jonathan wrongly identified it with Spain, possibly from some similarity with Hesperis, hence the application of the name to Spanish Jews.

Sept, from O.Fr. *septe*, possibly a variant of *secte* or sect; a term especially applied to an Irish CLAN which was a division of the tribe. The freemen of the sept bore the clan name with the prefix "Ua", grandson, written in English as "O".

September. The seventh month from MARCH, where the year used to commence.

The old Dutch name was *Herstmaand* (autumn-month), the old Saxon, *Gerst-monath* (barley-month), or *Hæfest-monath*; and after the introduction of Christianity *Halig-monath* (holy-month, the nativity of the Virgin MARY being on the 8th, the EXALTATION OF THE CROSS or Holy Cross Day on the 14th and St. MICHAEL's Day on the 29th). In the French Republican CALENDER it was called *fructidor* (fruit-month, 18 August to 16 September).

September Bible. *See* BIBLE, SOME SPECIALLY NAMED EDITIONS.

September Massacres. An indiscriminate slaughter during the French Revolution, directed at the royalists confined in the Abbaye and other prisons, lasting from 2 to 7 September 1792. Over 1,500 were massacred with revolting brutalities. It was occasioned by the dismay at the fall of Verdun to the Prussians. Those taking part in the atrocities were called Septembrists.

Septentrional Signs (sep ten' tri ō nàl). The first six signs of the ZODIAC, because they belong to the *northern* celestial hemisphere. The north was called the *septentrion* from the seven stars of the Great Bear (Lat. *septem*, seven; *triones*, plough oxen). *Cp.* URSA MAJOR.

Septuagesima Sunday (sep tū à jes' i mà). The third Sunday before LENT; in round numbers, 70 (in fact 64) days (Lat. *septuagesima dies*) be-

fore EASTER.

Septuagint (sep' tū à jint) (Lat. *septuaginta*, seventy). The most important Greek version of the OLD TESTAMENT and APOCRYPHA, so called because it was traditionally said to have been translated from the Hebrew SCRIPTURES by 72 learned Jews in the 3rd century B.C., at the command of Ptolemy Philadelphus for the Alexandrian LIBRARY. They worked on the island of PHAROS and completed the task in 72 days.

The name Septuagint is commonly abbreviated as LXX. It is probably the work of Jewish scholars at Alexandria working over a long period of time.

Sepulchre, The Holy. The cave outside the walls of old JERUSALEM in which the body of Christ is believed to have lain between His burial and Resurrection. The tomb is said to have been discovered by St. HELENA and from at least the 4th century (*see* INVENTION OF THE CROSS *under* CROSS) the spot has been covered by a Christian Church, where today Greek, Catholic, Armenian, Syrian, and Coptic Christians have their rights of occupation.

Knights of the Holy Sepulchre. An order of military knights founded by Godfrey of Bouillon in 1099 to guard the Holy Sepulchre.

Seraglio (sè ra' lyō). The word is Italian and means "enclosure" and especially denotes the former palace of the SULTANS at Constantinople, situated on the GOLDEN HORN and enclosed by walls containing many buildings. The chief entrance was the Sublime Gate (*see* PORTE); and the chief edifice the Harem or "forbidden spot" which contained numerous dwellings, for the sultan's wives, and for his concubines. The Seraglio might be visited by strangers, not so the Harem.

Seraphic (se ráf' ik). **Seraphic Blessing.** The blessing written by St. FRANCIS OF ASSISI at the request of Brother Leo on Mt. Alverna in 1224. It is based on *Numbers* vi, 24: "May the Lord bless thee and keep thee. May he show His face to thee and have mercy on thee. May he turn his countanance on thee and give thee peace. May the Lord bless thee, Brother Leo."

Seraphim. The highest of the nine choirs of ANGELS, so named from the seraphim of *Is.* vi, 2. The word is probably the same as *saraph*, a serpent, from *saraph*, to burn (in allusion to its bite); and this connexion with burning suggested to early Christian interpreters that the seraphim were specially distinguished by the ardency of their zeal and love.

Seraphim is a plural form; the singular, *seraph*, was first used in English by Milton. ABDIEL was,

> The flaming Seraph, fearless, though alone,
> Encompassed round with foes.
> *Paradise Lost*, V, 875.

Serapis (se rā′ pis). The Ptolemaic form of APIS, an Egyptian deity who, when dead, was honoured under the attributes of OSIRIS and thus became "osirified Apis" or [O] Sorapis. He was lord of the underworld, and was identified by the Greeks with HADES.

Serat, Al. *See* AL-SIRAT.

Serbonian Bog, The (sĕr bō′ ni àn). A great morass, now covered with shifting sand, between the isthmus of Suez, the MEDITERRANEAN, and the delta of the Nile. In Strabo's time it was a lake stated by him to be 200 stadia long and 50 broad, and by Pliny to be 150 miles in length. TYPHON was said to dwell at the bottom of it, hence its other name, *Typhon's Breathing Hole*.

The term is used figuratively of a mess from which there is no way of extricating oneself.

Serendipity (se ren dip′ i ti). A happy coinage by Horace Walpole to denote the faculty of making lucky and unexpected "finds" by accident. In a letter to Mann (28 January 1754) he says that he formed it on the title of a fairy story, *The Three Princes of Serendip*, because the princes:

> were always making discoveries, by accidents and sagacity, of things they were not in quest of.

Serendip is an ancient name of Sri Lanka.

Sergeanty, or **Serjeanty.** Various forms of land tenure akin to KNIGHT service involving military service or some form of household service for the king or lord, sometimes nominal. *Serjeanty* comes from Norman French *serjantie* (Lat. *serviens*, a servant).

Serjeants-at-Arms. Officials of the Royal HOUSEHOLD with certain ceremonial functions, eight in number. In addition there is the SPEAKER's Serjeant-at-Arms in the HOUSE OF COMMONS, who carries the MACE and acts as the disciplinary officer, and another who carries the mace of the Lord CHANCELLOR in the HOUSE OF LORDS.

Serjeants-at-law. A superior order of barristers superseded by QUEEN'S COUNSEL in 1877. From the Low Latin *servientes ad legem*, one who serves the king in matters of law. They formed an Inn called Serjeants Inn which was in FLEET STREET and later Chancery Lane. *See* COIF.

Serpent. The serpent is symbolical of:

(1) Deity, because, says Plutarch, "it feeds upon its own body; even so all things spring from God, and will be resolved into deity again" (*De Iside et Osiride*, i, 2, p. 5; and *Philo Byblius*).

(2) Eternity, as a corollary of the former. It is represented as forming a circle, holding its tail in its mouth.

(3) Renovation and the healing art. It is said that when old it has the power of growing young again "like the eagle", by casting its slough, which is done by squeezing itself between two rocks. It was sacred to ÆSCULAPIUS, and was supposed to have the power of discovering healing herbs. *See* CADUCEUS.

(4) Guardian spirit. It was thus employed by the ancient Greeks and Romans, and not infrequently the figure of a serpent was depicted on their altars.

In the temple of Athena at ATHENS, a serpent, supposed to be animated by the soul of Erichthonius, was kept in a cage, and called "the Guardian Spirit of the Temple".

(5) Wisdom. "Be ye therefore wise as serpents, and harmless as doves" (*Matt.* x, 16).

(6) Subtlety. "Now the serpent was more subtil than any beast of the field" (*Gen.* iii, i).

(7) The DEVIL. As the Tempter (*Gen.* iii, 1–6). In early pictures the serpent is sometimes placed under the feet of the Virgin, in allusion to the promise made

to EVE after the fall (*Gen.* iii, 15).

In Christian art it is an attribute of St. CECILIA, St. Euphemia, St. PATRICK, and many other SAINTS, either because they trampled on SATAN, or because they miraculously cleared some country of snakes.

Fable has it that the cerastes (horned viper) hides in sand that it may bite the horse's foot and get the rider thrown. In allusion to this belief, Jacob says, "Dan shall be...an adder in the path, that biteth the horse heels, so that his rider shall fall backward" (*Gen.* xlix, 17). The Bible also tells us that the serpent stops up its ears that it may not be charmed by the charmers, "charming never so wisely" (*Ps.* lxiii, 4).

Another old idea about snakes was that when attacked they would swallow their young and not eject them until reaching a place of safety.

It was in the form of a serpent, says the legend, that Jupiter AMMON appeared to OLYMPIA and became by her the father of ALEXANDER THE GREAT. *See also* SNAKE.

The old Serpent. SATAN.

Pharaoh's serpent. *See under* PHARAOH.

Sea serpent. *See under* SEA.

The serpent of old Nile. CLEOPATRA, so called by Antony.

> He's speaking now,
> Or murmuring "Where's my serpent of
> old Nile?" for so he calls me.
> SHAKESPEARE: *Antony and Cleopatra*,
> I, v.

Their ears have been serpent-licked. They have the gift of foreseeing events, the power of seeing into futurity. This is a Greek superstition. It is said that CASSANDRA and Helenus were gifted with the power of prophecy, because serpents licked their ears while sleeping in the temple of APOLLO.

To cherish a serpent in your bosom. To show kindness to one who proves ungrateful. The Greeks say that a husbandman found a frozen serpent, which he put into his bosom. The snake was revived by the warmth, and stung its benefactor. SHAKESPEARE applies the tale to a serpent's egg:

Serpentine Verses. Such as end with the same word as they begin with. The following are examples:

> Crescit amor nummi, quantum ipsa pecunia crescit.
> (Greater grows the love of pelf, as pelf itself grows greater).
> Ambo florentes ætatibus, Arcades ambo.
> (Both in the spring of life, arcadians both).

The allusion is to the old representations of snakes with their tails in their mouths—no beginning and no end.

Serve. To serve a sentence. To undergo the punishment awarded.

To serve a writ on. To deliver into the hands of the person concerned a legal writ.

To serve its turn. Said of something which is used to satisfy a purpose or fulfil a need, and then discarded.

To serve one's time. To hold an office or appointment for the full period allowed; to go through one's apprenticeship; to go through one's length of service in the armed forces; to serve one's sentence in a prison.

Servus servorum (sĕr' vŭs sĕr vôr' ŭm) (Lat.). The slave of slaves, the drudge of a servant. *Servus servorum Dei* (the servant of the servants of God) is one of the honorific epithets of the POPE; it was first adopted by GREGORY THE GREAT (540, 590–604).

Sesame (ses' á mi). **Open, Sesame!** The password at which the door of the robbers' cave flew open in the tale of *The Forty Thieves* (ARABIAN NIGHTS); hence, a key to a mystery, or anything that acts like magic in obtaining favour, admission, recognition, etc.

Sesame is an East Indian annual herb, with an oily seed which is used as food, a laxative, etc. In Egypt they eat sesame cakes, and the Jews frequently add the seed to their bread.

Sesquipedalian (ses kwi pė dā' li ȧn) is sometimes applied in heavy irony to cumbersome and pedantic words. It comes from HORACE's *sesquipedalia verba*, words a foot and a half long.

Session, Court of. *See under* COURT.

Sestina (ses tē' nȧ). A set form of poem, usually rhymed, with six stanzas of six lines each and a final triplet. The terminal words of stanzas 2–6 are the same as those of stanza 1 but arranged differently. Sestinas were invented by the Provençal TROUBADOUR Arnaut Daniel (13th century); DANTE, Petrarch, and others employed them in Italy, Cervantes and Camoëns in the Peninsula, and an early use in English was by Drummond of Hawthornden. Swinburne's sestinas are probably the best in English.

Set, or Seth. The Egyptian original of the Greek TYPHON. He was the jealous brother of OSIRIS whom he murdered by tricking him into a coffer, nailing the lid, and having it sealed with molten lead. He was later castrated by HORUS and came to be regarded as the incarnation of evil. He is represented as having the body of a man with a thin curved snout and square shaped ears, and sometimes with a tail and the body of an animal which has not been identified with any certainty.

Set. All set. All ready to begin.

He'll never set the Thames on fire. *See under* THAMES.

A set scene. In theatrical parlance, a scene built up by the stage carpenters, or a furnished interior, as a drawing-room, as distinguished from an ordinary or shifting scene. **To set the scene** is to indicate to an audience where the action of the play is taking place, and what has prompted it.

A set to. A fight; a real tussle, literally or verbally. In pugilism the combatants were by their seconds "set to the scratch" or line marked on the ground (*see* TO COME UP TO (THE) SCRATCH *under* SCRATCH).

To set off to advantage. To display a thing in its best light.

To set one's face against something. *See under* FACE.

To set one's hand to. To sign; to begin a task.

To set one's heart upon. *See under* HEART.

Setting a hen. Giving her a certain number of eggs to hatch. The clutch of eggs is called a *sitting*.

Setting her cap at him. *See under* CAP.

The setting of a jewel. The frame or mount of GOLD or SILVER surrounding a jewel in a ring, brooch, etc.

The setting of the sun, moon, or **stars.** Their sinking below the horizon.

The Empire on which the sun never sets. This, and similar phrases applied to the British Empire in the imperialist heyday, was not original. Thus in the *Pastor Fido* (1590) Guarini speaks of Philip II of Spain as "that proud monarch to whom when it grows dark [elsewhere], the sun never sets."

Setebos (set' e bos). A god or DEVIL worshipped by the Patagonians, and introduced by SHAKESPEARE into his *Tempest* as the god of Sycorax, CALIBAN's mother.

The cult of Setebos was first known in Europe through MAGELLAN's voyage round the world, 1519–1521.

Seven. A mystic or sacred number; it is composed of four and three, which among the Pythagoreans were, and from time immemorial have been, accounted lucky numbers. Among the Babylonians, Egyptians, and other ancient peoples there were seven sacred planets; and the Hebrew verb to swear means literally "to come under the influence of seven things"; thus seven ewe lambs figure in the oath between Abraham and Abimelech at Beersheba (*Gen.* xxi, 28), and Herodotus (III, viii) describes an Arabian oath in which seven stones are smeared with blood.

There are seven days in creation, seven days in the week, seven VIRTUES, seven divisions in the Lord's Prayer, seven sages in the life of man, CLIMATERIC years are seven and nine with their multiples by odd numbers, and the seventh son of a seventh son was always held notable.

Among the Hebrews every seventh year was SABBATICAL, and seven times seven years was the JUBILEE. The three great Jewish feasts lasted seven days, and between the first and second were seven weeks. Levitical purifications lasted seven days. The number is associated with a variety of occurrences in the OLD TESTAMENT.

In the *Apocalypse* we have SEVEN CHURCHES OF ASIA, seven candlesticks, seven stars, seven trumpets, seven spirits before the throne of God, seven horns, seven vials, seven plagues, a seven-headed monster, and the Lamb with seven eyes.

The old astrologers and alchemists recognized seven PLANETS, each having its own "heaven":

The bodies seven, eek, lo hem heer anoon;
Sol gold is, and Luna silver we threpe,
Mars yren, Mercurie quyksilver we clepe;
Saturnus leed, and Jubitur is tyn;
And Venus coper, by my fader kyn.
            CHAUCER: *The Canon's Yeoman's Tale*, 472.

The Seven. Used of groups of seven people, especially (1) the "men of honest report" chosen by the APOSTLES to be the first Deacons (*Acts* vi, 5), *viz*. Stephen, Philip, Prochorus, Nicanor, Timon, Parmenas, and Nicholas; (2) the SEVEN BISHOPS (*see below*); or (3) the Seven Sages of Greece (*see* WISE MEN).

The original members of the European free Trade Association (EFTA) formed in 1959, namely, Denmark, Norway, Sweden, Austria, Portugal, Switzerland, and the UNITED KINGDOM, were known as "The Seven" as distinct from THE SIX.

The Seven against Thebes. The seven Argive heroes (ADRASTUS, Polynices, Tydeus, Amphiaraus, Capaneus, Hippomedon and Parthenopæus), who, according to Greek legend, made war on Thebes with the object of restoring Polynices (son of ŒDIPUS), who had been expelled by his brother Eteocles. All perished except Adrastus, and the brothers slew each other in single combat. The legend is the subject of one of the tragedies of ÆSCHYLUS. *See* NEMEAN GAMES.

The Seven Bishops. Archbishop Sancroft of Canterbury, and Bishops Lloyd of St. Asaph, Turner of Ely, Ken of Bath and Wells, White of Peterborough, Lake of Chichester, and Trelawney of Bristol, who petitioned James II against the order to have his second Declaration of Indulgence read in every church on two successive Sundays (May 1688). James foolishly sent them to the TOWER and had them duly tried on a charge of seditious libel; they were acquitted amidst universal rejoicing. Cf. NONJURORS.

The Seven Champions. The mediæval designation of the national patron SAINTS of ENGLAND, SCOTLAND, WALES, IRELAND, France, Spain, and Italy. In 1596 Richard Johnson published a chap-book *The Famous History of the Seven Champions of Christendom*. In this he relates that St. GEORGE of England was seven years imprisoned by the Almidor, the black king of Morocco; St. DENYS of France lived seven years in the form of a hart; St. JAMES of Spain was seven years dumb out of love for a fair Jewess; St. Anthony of Italy, with the other champions, was enchanted into a deep sleep in the Black Castle, and was released by St. George's three sons, who quenched the seven lamps by water from the enchanted fountain; St. ANDREW of Scotland delivered six ladies who had lived seven years under the form of white swans; St. PATRICK of Ireland was immured in a cell where he scratched his grave with his own nails; and St. DAVID of Wales slept seven years in the enchanted garden of Ormandine, and was redeemed by St. George.

The Seven Churches of Asia. Those mentioned in *Rev*. i, 11, viz.:

(1) Ephesus, founded by St. PAUL, 57, in a ruinous state in the time of Justinian.

(2) Smyrna. Polycarp was its first bishop.

(3) Pergamos, renowned for its library.

(4) Thyatira, now called Ak-hissar (the White Castle).

(5) Sardis, now Sart, a small village.

(6) Philadelphia, now called Allah Shehr (City of God).

(7) Laodicea, now a deserted place called Eski-hissar (the Old Castle).

Seven cities warred for Homer being dead. *See* HOMER.

The Island of the Seven Cities. A land of Spanish fable, where seven BISHOPS, who quitted Spain during the dominion of the MOORS, founded seven cities. The legend says that many have visited the island, but no one has ever quitted it.

The Seven Deacons. In *Acts* vi, 1–6, the "seven men of honest report, full of the Holy Ghost and wisdom" (*see* THE SEVEN). These are held to be the first deacons of the Church.

The Seven Deadly, or **Capital Sins.** Pride, Wrath, Envy, Lust, Gluttony, Avarice, Sloth.

The Seven Gifts of the Spirit, or **Holy Ghost.** Wisdom, Understanding, Counsel, Fortitude, Knowledge, Righteousness, Fear of the Lord.

The Seven Gods of Luck. In Japanese folklore, Benten, goddess of love; Bishamon, god of war; Daikoku, of wealth; Ebisu, of self-effacement; Fukurokuji and Jojorin, gods of longevity; and Hotei, of joviality.

The Seven Heavens. *See under* HEAVEN.

To be in the Seventh Heaven. *See under* HEAVEN.

The Seven Hills of Rome. The Palatine, Capitoline, Aventine, Cælian, Esquiline, Viminal, and QUIRINAL or Colline. The walls of ancient ROME were built about them.

The Seven Joys of Mary, or **the Virgin.** *See* MARY.

The Seven Liberal Arts. *See* QUADRIVIUM.

The Seven Planets. *See* PLANETS.

The Seven Sacraments. *See under* SACRAMENT.

The Seven Sages of Greece. *See* WISE MEN OF GREECE.

The Seven Sciences. The same as the *Seven Liberal Arts. See* QUADRIVIUM.

The Seven Seas. The Arctic and Antarctic, North and South PACIFIC, North and South ATLANTIC, and the Indian Oceans.

The Seven Senses. According to ancient teaching the SOUL of man, or his "inward holy body" is compounded of seven properties which are under the influence of the seven PLANETS. Fire animates, earth gives the sense of feeling, water gives speech, air gives taste, mist gives sight, flowers give hearing, and the south wind gives smelling. Hence the seven senses are animation, feeling, speech, taste, sight, hearing, and smelling (*see Ecclus.* xvii, 5).

The Seven Sisters. An old name of the PLEIADES; also given to a set of seven cannon, cast by one Robert Borthwick and used at Flodden (1513); and to the chalk cliffs between Cuckmere Haven and Beachy Head on the Sussex coast.

The Seven Sleepers. Seven Christian youths of Ephesus, according to the legend, who fled during the Diocletian persecution (250) to a cave in Mt. Celion. The cave was walled up by their pursuers and they fell asleep. In the reign of Theodosius II, some 200 years later, they awoke and one of them went into the city for provisions. They fell to sleep again, this time until the resurrection. Their names are given as Constantius, Dionysius, Joannes, Maximianus, Malchus, Martinianus, and Serapion. The legend was current in the 6th century and is referred to by Gregory of Tours.

The Seven Sorrows. *See* MARY.

The Seven Stars. Used formerly of the PLANETS; also of the PLEIADES and the GREAT BEAR (*see under* BEAR).

> *Fool:* The reason why the seven stars are no more than seven is a pretty reason.
> *Lear:* Because they are not eight?
> *Fool:* Yes, indeed; thou wouldst make a good fool
> SHAKESPEARE: *King Lear*, I, v.

The Seven Virtues. *See under* VIRTUE.

The Seven Wise Masters. A collection of oriental tales (*see* SANDABAR) supposed to be told to the king by his advisers. The king's son returned to court after being educated in the SEVEN LIBERAL ARTS by the Seven Wise Masters. By consulting the STARS, he learned that his life was in danger if he spoke before the elapse of seven days. One of the royal consorts then endeavoured to seduce him without success, whereupon she denounced him to the sovereign and the prince was condemned to death. The Wise Masters, by their tales against women, secured a suspension of the sentence for one day. The woman then told a contrary tale to secure the confirmation of Prince Lucien's punishment. The Wise Masters counteracted this with further tales and so on, until the seventh day, when the prince revealed the truth and his accuser was sentenced to death instead. There are numerous variant versions of these stories, which date from 10th century. *Cp.* SCHEHERAZADE.

The Seven Wonders of the World. *See under* WONDER.

The Seven Works of Mercy. *See* MERCY.

The Seven Years War (1756–1763). A war fought over European and colonial and commercial rivalries by France, Austria, the Empire, Russia, Poland and Sweden against Prussia, Great Britain, and Hanover. Spain joined in 1761 and attacked Portugal. It began with Frederick the Great's invasion of Saxony and was ended by the Treaty of Paris between Great Britain, France, Portugal, and Spain, which gave Canada and other colonial territories to Great Britain, New Orleans to Spain, etc. By the Peace of Hubertusburg between Austria and Prussia, the latter retained Silesia.

Seveners. The Isma'ilis, a SHI'ITE following of Isma'il, whom they hold to be the seventh IMAM; they include the ASSASSINS, Carmathians, DRUSES, and FATIMITES. *Cp.* TWELVERS.

Seventh-day Adventists. A sect of Adventists which grew out of a movement begun by William Miller in the United States in 1831. He preached that the present world would end about 1843. The Seventh-day Adventists adopted their name in 1860, and were formally organized from 1863. They observe Saturday as their SABBATH and insist on temperance and abstinence from alcohol, tobacco, etc., and a strict adherence to the SCRIPTURES.

Seventh-day Baptists. In the U.S.A., a group of German Baptist brethren who keep Saturday, the seventh day of the week, as their SABBATH.

Severn. *See* SABRINA.

Severus. The Wall of Severus. The Emperor Severus (146–211), who spent the last three years of his life in Britain, thoroughly strengthened the fortified line between the Tyne and Solway originally constructed by Hadrian. His work was so extensive that some ancient authorities speak of him as its original builder. *See* HADRIAN'S WALL.

Sexagesima Sunday (seks å jes' i må). The second Sunday before LENT so called because in round numbers it is 60 days (Lat. *sexagesima dies*) before EASTER.

Sextile (seks' tīl). The aspect of two PLANETS when distant from each other 60 degrees or two signs. This position is marked by astrologers thus ★.

> In sextile, square, and trine, and opposite
> Of noxious efficacy.
> MILTON: *Paradise Lost*, X, 659.

Shades. The abode of the departed or HADES; also the spirits or ghosts of the departed.

> Peter Bell excited his spleen to such a degree that he evoked the shades of Pope and Dryden.
> MACAULAY: *Moore's Life of Lord Byron*.

To put someone in the shade. To outdo him; eclipse him; to attract to yourself all the applause and encomiums he had been enjoying.

Shadow. A word with numerous figurative and applied meanings, such as, a ghost; Macbeth says to the ghost of Banquo:

> Hence, horrible shadow! unreal mockery, hence!
> SHAKESPEARE: *Macbeth*, III, iv.

An imperfect or faint representation, as, "I haven't the shadow of a doubt"; a constant attendant, as in Milton's "Sin and her shadow Death" (*Paradise Lost*, IX, 12); moral darkness or gloom, as, "He has outsoar'd the shadow of our night" (Shelley: *Adonais*, xl, 1); protecting influence:

> Hither, like yon ancient Tower,
> Watching o'er the River's bed,
> Fling the shadow of thy power,
> Else we sleep among the dead.
> WORDSWORTH: *Hymn (Jesu! bless)*.

May your shadow never grow less! May your prosperity always continue and increase. A phrase of Eastern origin. Fable has it that when those studying the black arts had made certain progress, they were chased through a subterranean hall by the DEVIL. If he caught only their shadow, or part of it, they lost all or part of it, but became first-rate magicians. This would make the expression mean, "May you escape wholly and entirely from the clutches of the devil", but a more simple explanation is, "May you never waste away, but always remain healthy and robust." *See* SCHLEMIHL.

To be reduced to a shadow. Of people, to become thoroughly emaciated; of things, to become an empty form from which the substance has departed.

To shadow. To follow about like a shadow, especially as a detective, with the object of spying out all one's doings.

Shady. A shady character. A person of very doubtful reputation; one whose character would scarcely bear investigation in the light of day.

Shaggy. A shaggy dog story. A would-be funny story told laboriously at great length with an unexpected twist at the end. So called from the shaggy dog featured in many stories of this genre popular in the 1940s.

Shagroon. In New Zealand, an original settler, other than those from England, who were called *Pilgrims*. The word is probably from the Irish *seachran*, wandering.

Shah. *See* RULERS, TITLES OF.

Shake. Give me a shake. Wake me up (at the requested time).

A good shake up. Something sudden that startles one out of one's lethargy and rouses one to action.

I'll do it in a brace of shakes. Instantly, as soon as you can shake the dice-box twice.

In two shakes of a lamb's tail. Instantly.

No great shakes. Nothing extraordinary or particularly clever; not very good. Commonly said to derive from gambling with dice; but Admiral Smyth's *Sailor's Word-Book* (1867) says it comes from "shaking a cask", which is to dismantle it and pick up the staves or shakes, a condition in which it has little value.

A shake of the head. An indication of refusal, disapproval, annoyance, etc.

To shake hands. A very old method of SALUTATION and farewell; when one was shaking hands one could not get at one's sword to strike a treacherous blow. When Jehu asked Jehonadab if his "heart was right" with him, he said, "If it be, give me thine hand", and Jehonadab gave him his hand (II *Kings* x, 15). NESTOR shook hands with ULYSSES on his return to the Grecian camp and the stolen horses of Rhesus; ÆNEAS, in the temple of DIDO, sees his lost companions

enter, who *avidi conjugere dextras ardebant* (*Æneid*, I, 514); and HORACE, strolling along the VIA SACRA, shook hands with an acquaintance: *Arreptaque manu, "Quid agis dulcissime rerum?"*

To shake in one's shoes. *See under* SHOE.

To shake one's sides. To be convulsed with laughter; *cp.* Milton's "Laughter holding both his sides" (*L'Allegro*).

To shake the dust from one's feet. *See under* DUST.

Shake-out. On the Stock Exchange, a crisis which drives the weaker speculators out of the market; also currently applied to the reduction of the labour force in an industry, trade, etc.

Shakers. A sect of Adventists started by James and Jane Wardley at Manchester in 1747 who seceded from the QUAKERS, and from their excited behaviour were derisively dubbed "Shakers". Ann Lee, known as Mother Ann, the "bride of the Lamb" and the "Female Christ", soon became their acknowledged leader and the sect left for America in 1774. They practised celibacy, temperance, communal living, etc., and a few small communities still survive.

Shakespeare, William (1564–1616). The greatest poetic dramatist. The Shakespearian canon comprises the 36 plays of the First Folio (1623), which include collaborative contributions that cannot be determined with certainty; the *Sonnets*, *The Rape of Lucrece*, *Venus and Adonis*, a few lyrics and the 16 lines contributed to the play of *Sir Thomas More*.

The theory that Shakespeare was not the writer of the works attributed to him, based on the assumption that he did not possess the knowledge and culture revealed in those works, was first put forward by Herbert Lawrence in 1769. In 1857 Willian Henry Smith suggested that the only writer of that age competent to produce such writings was Francis Bacon, thus the **Baconian theory** began its lengthy career. In 1887 Ignatius Donnelly published *The Great Cryptogram* which professed to show that cryptograms in the plays revealed Bacon as the undoubted author, and the cryptographic method was further advanced by Sir Edwin Durning-

Lawrence and others. The Baconians still persist and others have put forward many additional candidates, including a distributist school of thought which assigns Shakespear's work to a group of seven writers. *See also* DARK LADY OF THE SONNETS *under* LADY.

Shakuntala. *See* SAKUNTALA.

Shalott, The Lady of (shà lot'). A maiden in the ARTHURIAN ROMANCES (*see under* ARTHUR), who fell in love with Sir LANCELOT OF THE LAKE, and died because her love was not returned. Tennyson has a poem on the subject; and the story of ELAINE is substantially the same.

Shamanism (sha' mà nizm). A primitive form of religion, in which is is believed that the world is governed by good and EVIL spirits who can be propitiated through the intervention of a *Shaman*, a priest or sorcerer. The word is Slavonic, the cult being practised by the Samoyeds and other Siberian peoples.

Shamrock. The symbol of IRELAND, because it was selected by St. PATRICK to illustrate the Irish the doctrine of the TRINITY. According to the elder Pliny no serpent will touch this plant.

Shandean (shăn' dē ăn). Characteristic of Tristram Shandy or the Shandy family in Sterne's novel, *Tristram Shandy* (9 vols., 1759–1767). Tristram's father, Walter Shandy, is a metaphysical Don QUIXOTE in his way, full of superstitious and idle conceits. He believes in long noses and propitious names, but his son's nose is crushed, and his name becomes Tristram instead of Trismegistus. Tristram's Uncle Toby was wounded at the siege of Namur, and is benevolent and generous, simple as a child, brave as a lion, and gallant as a courtier. His modesty with Widow Wadman and his military tastes are admirable. He is said to be drawn from Sterne's father. The mother was the *beau idéal* of nonentity; and of Tristram himself we hear almost more before he was born than after he had burst upon an astonished world.

Shanghai, To (shang hī'). An old nautical phrase, meaning to make a man drunk or to drug him insensible and to get him on board an outward-bound vessel in need of crew. It originated on the west coast of the U.S.A. where Shanghai was a likely destination for a crimped sailor.

Shangri La (shăng gri la'). The hidden Buddhist lama PARADISE described in James Hilton's *Lost Horizon* (1933). The name was applied to F. D. Roosevelt's mountain refuge in Maryland, and to the secret "base" used for the great American air raid on Tokyo in 1942.

Shank's Mare. To ride Shank's mare or **pony** is to walk or go on foot, the shanks being the legs; the same as "Going by the MARROW-BONE STAGE" or by "Walker's bus".

Shannon. Dipped in the Shannon. One who has been dipped in the Shannon is said to lose all bashfulness. *Cp.* TO KISS THE BLARNEY STONE *under* BLARNEY.

Shanties, Chanties. Songs of the days of sail sung by a "shanty man" to help rhythmical action among sailors hauling on ropes, working the capstan, etc. The workers joined in the choruses. The word is probably from Fr. *chanter*, to sing. The chorus of one of the most popular runs thus:

> Then away, love, away,
> Away down Rio.
> O fare ye well my pretty young gel,
> For we're bound for the Rio Grande.

A *shanty* is also a small wooden house or hut, from Canadian-French *chantier*, log-hut, workshop (Fr., timber-yard).

Shark. A swindler, a pilferer, an extortionate dealer, landlord, etc.; one who snaps up things like a shark, which swallows its food alive or dead, regardlessly.

To shark up. To get a number of people, etc., together promiscuously, without consideration of their fitness.

> Now sir, young Fortinbras...
> Hath in the skirts of Norway here and there
> Shark'd up a list of lawless resolutes,
> For food and diet, to some enterprise
> That hath a stomach in't.
> SHAKESPEARE: *Hamlet*, I. i.

Sharp. Sharp practice. Over-smart, underhand or dishonourable dealing; low-down trickery intended to advantage oneself.

Sharp's the word! Look alive, there! No hanging about.

Sharp-set. Hungry; formerly used of

HAWKS when hungry for their food.

Shave. Just a grazing touch; *a near* or *close shave*, a narrow escape; *to shave through an examination*, only just to get through, narrowly to escape being *plucked* (*see* PLUCK).

A good lather is half the shave. Your work is half done if you've laid your plans and made your preparations properly.

To shave a customer. It was once a draper's expression for overcharging; it is said that when the manager saw a chance of doing this he stroked his chin as the sign to the assistant that he might fleece the customer.

To shave an egg. To attempt to extort the uttermost FARTHING; to "SKIN a flint".

Shaveling. Used in contempt of a young man and—especially after the REFORMATION—of a priest. At a time when the laity wore beards and moustaches the clergy were not only usually clean shaven but they also wore large shaven TONSURES.

Shavian (shā′vi ản). After the manner of George Bernard Shaw (1856–1950), or descriptive of his philosophy and style of humour.

She. The She Bible. *See* BIBLE, SOME SPECIALLY NAMED EDITIONS.

The She-Wolf of France. *See under* WOLF.

Shear. God tempers the wind to the shorn lamb. *See under* GOD.

Ordeal by sieve and shears. *See* SIEVE.

Sheathe. To sheathe the sword. To cease hostilities, make peace.

Sheba, The Queen of (shē′ bả). The queen who visited SOLOMON (I *Kings* x) is known to the Arabs as BALKIS, Queen of Sheba (KORAN, ch. xxvii). Sheba was thought by the Romans to have been the capital of what is now YEMEN; and the people over whom the queen reigned were the SABÆANS.

Shebang (she bảng′). **Fed up with the whole shebang.** Tired of the whole concern and everything connected with it. *Shebang* is American slang for a hut or one's quarters; also for a cart; and in a humorous depreciatory way, for almost anything.

Shebeen (she bēn′). A place (originally only in IRELAND) where liquor is sold without a licence; hence applied to any low-class public house. Possibly from Irish *sibin*, a little drinking mug.

Shedeem. *See* MAZIKEEN.

Sheep. The Black Sheep (*Kara-Koyunlu*) and the **White Sheep** (*Ak-Koyunlu*). Two rival confederacies among the Turkomans of Azerbaijan and Armenia in the late 14th and the 15th centuries. They were so called from the devices on their standards.

The black sheep of the family. The ne'er-do-well; the one who brings disgrace on the family.

There's a black sheep in every flock. In every group or community of people there is sure to be at least one shady character.

As well be hanged for a sheep as a lamb. Don't stop at half measures; in for a PENNY in for a POUND; if we are destined for trouble let's have our fling first.

Like a sheep's head, all jaw. Said of a tediously garrulous person.

Sheep dressed up as lamb. Said of a woman of some maturity who "dolls herself up" to give the appearance of being much younger.

To cast, or **make sheep's eyes.** To look askance, in a SHEEPISH way, at a person to whom you feel lovingly inclined.

Sheepish. Awkward and shy; bashful through not knowing how to deport oneself in the circumstances.

Sheep's head. A fool, a simpleton.

> What, no more compliment? Kiss her, you sheep's head!
> CHAPMAN: *All Fools,* II, i.

Sheer, or **Shere Thursday.** MAUNDY THURSDAY. It is generally supposed to be from M.E. *schere*, clean, *i.e.* free from guilt, from the custom of receiving absolution, or of cleansing the altars on this day. The *Liber Festivalis*, however, says:

> Hit is also in English tong "Schere Thursday", for in owr elde hardar days men wold on y^t day makon scheron hem honest, and dode here hedes ond clypon here berdes and poll here hedes, ond so makon hem honest agen Estur day.

Sheet. Three sheets in the wind. Very

drunk. The *sheet* is the rope attached to the clew of a sail used for trimming sail. If the sheet is quite free, leaving the sail free to flap without restraint, the sheet is said to be "in the wind", and "a sheet in the wind" is a colloquial nautical expression for being tipsy; thus to have "three sheets in the wind" is to be very drunk.

That was my sheet anchor. My best hope, chief stay, last refuge. The *sheet anchor*, once the heaviest anchor carried, but long since the same weight as the bower anchors, is a spare bower anchor available for use in emergency when the ship is moored. It is carried abaft the starboard bower anchor and in the days of sail abaft the fore rigging. Sheet is probably a corruption of *shoot* or *shot*, from the fact that it was shot, or let go, from the ship when needed.

Sheffield. A Sheffield whittle. So the general-purpose knife was often called in Chaucer's day.

Sheikh (shāk). A title of respect among the Arabs (Like the Ital. *signore*, Fr. *sieur*, Span. *señor*, etc.), but properly the head of a BEDOUIN clan, family, or tribe, or the headman of an Arab village.

Sheikh-ul-Islam. The Grand MUFTI, or supreme head of the Mohammedan hierarchy in Turkey.

Shekels (shek' ĕlz). Colloquial for money. It was anciently part of the Babylonian weight and monetary systems, and in general use among the peoples of Mesopotamia and Syria. The Hebrew heavy gold shekel weighed *c.* 252 grains TROY and the light gold shekel *c.* 126 grains; the heavy silver shekel weighed *c.* 224 grains troy and the light silver shekel *c.* 112 grains. The standard English gold SOVEREIGN was *c.* 123 grains troy. Phœnician shekels of *c.* 224 and *c.* 112 grains were also commonly found throughout the Near East.

Shekinah (she kī' nà) (Heb., that which dwells or resides). A word used frequently in the TARGUMS as an equivalent for the Divine Being or God. It does not occur in the BIBLE. The Shekinah is God's omnipresence and is everywhere. God is not identical with the world, He is of the world and yet afar off. Thus when Jacob says (*Gen.* xxviii, 16), "The Lord is in this place", the Targum says,

"The glory of the Shekinah of J is in this place."

Shelf. Laid, or **put on the shelf.** Put aside as of no further use; superannuated. Said of officials and others no longer actively employed; a project, etc., begun and set aside; also, a pawn at the brokers. A SPINSTER beyond the average age of marriage is said to be *on the shelf*.

Cockle shell. *See under* COCKLE.

Shell. Shellback. Nautical slang for a hardened and seasoned sailor, an "old salt'.

Shell jacket. A short tight-fitting undress military jacket reaching only to the waist at the back; also an officer's mess jacket.

Shell shock. An acute neurasthenic condition due to the explosion of a shell or bomb at close quarters. A term originating in World War I.

To lie in a nutshell. *See under* NUT.

To retire into one's shell. To become reticent and uncommunicative, to withdraw from the society of one's fellows. The allusion is to the tortoise, which, once it has "got into its shell", is quite unget-at-able. **To come out of one's shell** is the reverse process, *i.e.* to become friendly and communicative.

To shell out. To pay or "stump up", to "fork out"; as peas are shelled out of a pod.

Shem. The traditional ancestor of the Hebrews and other kindred peoples. *Semite* and SEMITIC derive from Shem, the eldest of the three sons of Noah (*Gen.* ix, 18).

Shemozzle (shi moz'l). **There was a bit of a shemozzle.** There was something of a fuss, a bit of a rumpus or a rough and tumble. *Shemozzle* (bad luck) is a YIDDISH term.

Sheol. *See* HADES.

Shepherd. The Good shepherd. Jesus Christ.

> I am the good shepherd: the good shepherd giveth his life for the sheep.
> *John* x, 11.

The Ettrick Shepherd. *See* ETTRICK.

The Shepherd Lord. Henry, fourteenth Baron Clifford (*c.* 1455–1523), sent by his mother to be brought up as a shepherd, in order to save him from the fury of the YORKISTS. At the accession of Henry VII he was restored to all his rights and seigniories. He is celebrated in Wordsworth's *The Song for the Feast of Brougham Castle*, and *The White Doe of Rylstone*.

The Shepherd of Banbury. The ostensible author of a Weather Guide (published 1744), written by John Claridge, which attained considerable popularity at the time.

The Shepherd of Hermas. An allegorical work of the mid-2nd century, essentially a collection of instructions and revelations from an angelic guide for the benefit of good Christians. It has been called "the Pilgrim's Progress of the Early Church". The identity of Hermas is largely a matter of conjecture.

The Shepherd of the Ocean. So Sir Walter Ralegh was called by Spencer.

The Shepherd's Sundial. The SCARLET PIMPERNEL, which opens at a little past seven in the morning and closes at a little past two. When rain is at hand, or the weather is unfavourable, it does not open at all. It is also called the Shepherd's Calendar, Clock, and Watch, and the Shepherd's Weatherglass.

The Shepherd's Warning.

> Red sky at night is the shepherd's delight,
> Red sky in the morning is the shepherd's warning.

The Italian saying is *Sera rossa e bianco mattino, allegro il pellegrino* (a red evening and a white morning rejoice the pilgrim).

Sheppard, Jack (1702–1724). A notorious thief, son of a carpenter in SMITHFIELD and brought up in Bishopsgate workhouse. He was famous for his prison escapes, especially when he broke out of "the Castle" of NEWGATE via the chimney. He was soon afterwards taken and hanged at TYBURN.

Shere Thursday. *See* SHEER.

Sherif (she rēf'). A descendant of the Prophet MOHAMMED through his daughter FATIMA, also formerly applied to the chief magistrate of MECCA. The title was also adopted by the rulers of Morocco, who claimed descent from the Prophet through his grandson Hasan.

Sheriff (sher' if) (O.E. *scirgerefa*). In mediæval and later times the sheriff (shire REEVE) was an official who looked after the royal demesne in the SHIRE and, by the 11th century, the chief official for local adminstration. After the 13th century, the sheriffs declined in importance with the rise of new courts and officials, and today they are largely of ceremonial and minor judicial importance. The sheriff is still the chief officer of the Crown in the County. The City of London has two sheriffs and certain ancient cities (Norwich, Bristol, York, Oxford, etc.) still have one. In the U.S.A. the sheriff, usually elected, has administrative and limited judicial functions. *See* PRICKING FOR SHERIFFS *under* PRICK.

Sheriffmuir. There was mair lost at the Shirramuir. Don't grieve for your losses, for worse have befallen others before now. The battle of Sheriffmuir, in 1715, between the JACOBITES and Hanoverians was very bloody; both sides sustained heavy losses, and both sides claimed the victory.

Sherlock Holmes. The most famous figure in detective fiction, the creation of Arthur Conan Doyle (1859–1930). His solutions of crime and mysteries were related in a series of 60 stories that appeared in the *Strand Magazine* between 1891 and 1927. The character was based on Dr. Joseph Bell of the Edinburgh Infirmary, whose methods of deduction suggested a system that Holmes developed into a science—the observation of the minutest details and apparently insignificant circumstances scientifically interpreted. Dr. Watson, Holmes's friend and assistant, was a skit on Doyle himself and Baker Street acquired lasting fame through his writings.

Sherrick. Yorkshire for something very small. Used in Australia for a small amount of anything, particularly money.

Sherry. *See* JEREZ; SACK.

Shewbread. The name adopted by Tyndale, modelled on Luther's *Schaubrot*; more correctly *presence-bread*. Tyndale explains it as "alway in the presence and sight of the Lorde". Shrewbread denotes the 12 loaves for the 12 tribes, arranged in two piles on the table of shittim wood set beside the altar each week and when they were removed only the priest was allowed to partake of them. This ancient oblation is referred to in *Exod*. xxv, 30; *Lev*. xxiv, 5–9, etc.

Shibboleth (shib′ ŏ leth). A test word; a catchword or principle to which members of a group adhere long after its original significance has ceased; hence a worn-out or discredited doctrine. *Shibboleth* (meaning "ear of wheat", "stream", or "flood") was the word the Ephraimites could not pronounce when they were challenged at the ford on the Jordan by their pursuers, Jephthah and the Gileadites. The Ephraimites could only say *Sibboleth*, thus revealing themselves to the enemy (*see Judges* xii, 1–6).

Shick-shack Day. Royal Oak Day, 29 May, also called *shig-shag*. The origin of the name is obscure. *See* OAK-APPLE DAY.

Shield. The clang of shields. When a CELTIC chief doomed a man to death, he struck his shield with the blunt end of his spear by way of notice to the royal BARD to begin his death-song.

> Cairbar rises in his arms,
> The clang of shields is heard.
> OSSIAN: *Temora*, I.

The Gold and Silver Shield. A mediæval allegory tells how two knights coming from opposite directions stopped in sight of a shield suspended from a tree branch, one side of which was GOLD and the other SILVER, and disputed about its metal, proceeding from words to blows. Luckily a third knight came up: the point was referred to him, and the disputants were informed that the shield was silver on one side and gold on the other. Hence the sayings, *The other side of the shield, It depends on which side of the shield you are looking at*, etc.

The Shield of David. *See* STAR OF DAVID.

The Shield of Expectation. The perfectly plain shield given to a young warrior on his maiden campaign. As he achieved glory, his deeds were recorded or symbolized on it.

Shi'ites (Arab. *shi'ah*, a sect). Those Mohammedans who regard ALI, MOHAMMED's son-in-law, as the first rightful

IMAM and CALIPH. They reject the first three Sunni caliphs and all SUNNITE tradition.

Shillelagh (shi lā′ la). The conventional cudgel of the Irishman made from OAK or blackthorn; so called from the village of this name in County Wicklow which is supposed to have supplied the roof timbers for WESTMINSTER Hall from its once extensive oak forest.

Shilling (O.E. *scilling*; which is connected with O.Teut *skel-*, to resound or ring, or *skil-*, to divide). The shilling, as such, dates from 1504, and was originally made with a deeply indented cross, and could be easily divided into halves and quarters.

Cut off with a shilling. *See under* CUT.

To take the Queen's or **King's shilling.** to enlist; in allusion to the former practice of giving each recruit a shilling when he was sworn in.

Shilling shocker. *See* PENNY-DREADFUL.

Shilly shally. To hesitate, act in an undecided, irresolute way; a corruption of "Will I, shall I," or "Shall I, shall I?"

Shindy. To kick up a shindy. To make a row or to create a disturbance. The word is probably connected with *shinty* or *shinny*, a primitive kind of hockey played in SCOTLAND and the north of ENGLAND.

Shine. To take the shine out of one. To humiliate him, "take him down a PEG or two"; to outshine him.

Shintoism ("The way of the Gods"). The ancient national religion of Japan, now partly supplanted by BUDDHISM. The chief of innumerable deities in Amaterasuōmikami, the sun goddess, from whom the imperial dynasty supposedly descended. In 1946 the Emperor divested himself of any divine attributes.

Ship. Ship of the line. A man-of-war with sufficient gun-power to take a place in "line of battle".

Losing, or **spoiling a ship for a ha'porth o' tar.** By saving a little to lose much. to mar a job, etc., in order to skimp. 'Ship' here is a dialect version of *sheep* and refers to the smearing of tar on sheep against various infections—a practice common in SHAKESPEARE's day, *e.g.*:

> And they [the hands] are often tarred
> over with the surgery of our sheep.
> *As You Like it*, III, ii.

Ships that pass in the night. Chance acquaintances only encountered once. The phrase is from Longfellow.

> Ships that pass in the night, and speak
> each other in passing,
> Only a signal shown and a distant voice
> in the darkness;
> So on the ocean of life we pass and speak
> one an other,
> Only a look and a voice; then darkness
> again and a silence.
> *Tales of a Wayside Inn*, III.
> *Theologian's Tale*.

When my ship comes home. When my fortune is made. The allusion is to the ARGOSY returning from foreign parts laden with rich freight, and so enriching the merchant who sent it forth.

Ship money. An old-established levy exacted from maritime towns and countries to strengthen the navy in time of need. CHARLES I extended the demand to inland areas in 1635, which resulted in John Hampden's famous refusal (1637) to pay his due of 20s. The judges decided against Hampden, contrary to the Petition of Right. Ship-money was made illegal by the LONG PARLIAMENT in 1641.

Shipshape. In proper order, as methodically as things in a ship. When a sailing vessel was properly rigged and equipped it was said to be "shipshape". *Cp.* ALL SHIPSHAPE AND BRISTOL FASHION *under* ALL.

Shipton, Mother. A prophetess and WITCH of legendary fame first recorded in a pamphlet of 1641, who is said to have foretold the death of Wolsey, Lord Percy, and others, and to have predicted the steam-engine and telegraph, etc. In 1677 Richard Head brought out a *Life and Death of Mother Shipton*. She was born in a cave at Knaresborough, Yorkshire, in 1488, baptized as Ursula Southiel and married Tony Shipton when she was 24. There is a fake "Mother Shipton's tomb" at Williton, Somerset.

Shire (O.E. *scir*). The main unit of local government in Anglo-Saxon England, presided over by an ealdorman but from the 10th century by a SHERIFF. Shires were divided into HUNDREDS or WAPENTAKES and after the Norman CONQUEST the name *county* was applied to shire.

The Shires. The English counties whose names terminate in *-shire*; but, in a narrower sense, the Midland counties noted for fox-hunting, especially Leicestershire, Northamptonshire, Rutland. The inhabitants of East Anglia, Kent, Sussex, Essex and Surrey apply this term to the rest of ENGLAND.

To come out of the shires. To come from a considerable distance; a phrase from Kent, which was surrounded by Surrey, Sussex, Middlesex, and Essex, none of which is suffixed with *shire*.

Knight of the Shire. *See under* KNIGHT.

The Rider of the Shires. *See* RIDER.

Shire horse. The old breed of large, heavily built cart-horse, originally bred in the Midlands.

Shire Moot. *See* MOOT.

Shirt. A boiled shirt. A white shirt, or more usually a dress shirt.

Hair shirt. A shirt made of haircloth worn by penitents. *See* TO WEAR SACKCLOTH AND ASHES *under* SACK.

The shirt of Nessus. *See* NESSUS.

A stuffed shirt. Said of a pompous nonentity; a bore.

Close sits my shirt, but closer my skin. An old proverb meaning that self-interest comes first.

Not a shirt to one's name. "Not a RAG to one's back." Penniless.

To give the shirt off one's back. All one has.

To keep one's shirt on. To keep one's temper.

To put one's shirt on a horse. To back it with all the money one possesses.

To take the shirt off someone's back. To strip him of all he has.

Shirts as party emblems. *See* BLACKSHIRTS; BLUE SHIRTS; BROWN SHIRTS; GARIBALDI'S RED SHIRT; GREENSHIRT.

Shirty. Bad-tempered; very cross and offended; in the state you are in when somebody has "got your shirt out".

Shiva. *See* SIVA.

Shivaree (shiv' ĕrē). the word is a corruption of CHARIVARI, and in the U.S.A. means the mocking serenade accorded to newly married people.

Shiver. Shiver my timbers. An imprecation used by "stage-sailors" and popular with children's story writers. Presumably of nautical origin, *shiver* here is used in the sense of "to shatter" or "splinter into pieces", the timbers being those of the ship.

Shoe. It was once thought unlucky to put on the left shoe before the right, or to put either shoe on the wrong foot.

It has long been a custom to throw an old shoe at the bride and bridegroom when the depart from the wedding breakfast or when they go to church to get married. Now it is more usual to tie an old shoe to their carriage or motorcar. To throw a shoe after someone is an ancient way of bringing good luck. The custom has been variously interpreted.

In Anglo-Saxon marriages, the father delivered the bride's shoe to the bridegroom who touched her on the head with it to show his authority.

Loosing the shoe (*cp. Josh*. v, 15) is a mark of respect in the East. The MOSLEM leaves his slippers outside the mosque. In *Deut*. xxv, 5–10, we read that the widow refused by her husband's surviving brother, asserted her independence by "loosing his shoe"; and in the story of *Ruth* (iv, 7) we are told that it was the custom in exchange to deliver a shoe in token of confirmation. "A man without sandals" was a proverbial expression among the Jews for a prodigal, from the custom of giving one's sandals in confirmation of a bargain.

Scot (*Discoverie of Witchcraft*, 1584) tells us that "many will go to bed again if they sneeze before their shoes be on their feet".

A shoe too large trips one up. A Latin proverb, *Calceus major subvertit*. An empire too large falls to pieces; a business too large comes to grief; an ambition too large fails altogether.

Another man's shoes. "To stand in another man's shoes" is to occupy the place of another. Among the ancient Northmen, when a man adopted a son, the person adopted put on the shoes of the adopter.

In REYNARD THE FOX, Reynard, having turned the tables on Sir Bruin the Bear, asked the queen to let him have the shoes of the disgraced minister; so Bruin's shoes were torn off and put upon the new favourite.

Another pair of shoes. A different thing altogether; quite another matter.

His shoes are made of running leather. He is given to roving.

Over Edom will I cast out my shoe (*Ps.* lx, 8; cviii, 9), *i.e.* will I march and triumph.

Over shoes, over boots. "In for a penny, in for a pound." *See under* PENNY.

> Where true courage roots
> The proverb says, "once over shoes, o'er boots."
> JOHN TAYLOR: *Workes*, ii, 145 (1630).

To die in one's shoes. To die a violent death, especially one on th escaffold. *Cp.* TO DIE IN HARNESS *under* HARNESS.

To shake in one's shoes. To be in a state of fear or nervous terror.

To shoe the anchor. To cover the flukes of an anchor with a broad triangular piece of a plank, in order that the anchor may have a stronger hold in soft ground.

To shoe the cobbler. To give a quick peculiar movement with the front foot in sliding.

To shoe a goose. To engage in a silly and fruitless task.

To shoe the wild colt. To exact a fine called "footing" from a newcomer, who is called the "colt". Colt is a common synonym for a GREENHORN, or a youth not broken in.

Waiting for dead men's shoes. Looking out for a legacy; waiting to take the place of another when he has passed on to retirement or death.

Where the shoe pinches. "No one knows where the shoe pinches like the wearer" is the reputed saying of a Roman sage who was blamed for divorcing his wife, with whom he seemed to live happily.

The cause of the trouble, or where the difficulty lies, is called "the place where the shoe pinches".

Whose shoes I am not worthy to bear (*Matt*. iii, 11). This means, "I am not worthy to be his humblest slave." It was the business of a slave recently purchased to loose and carry his master's sandals.

Shoestring. To live on a shoestring.
To manage on very little money.

Shofar (shō′ far). A Hebrew trumpet still
used in the modern SYNAGOGUE. It is
made of the horn of a ram or any ceremonially clean animal, and produces
only the natural series of harmonics
from its fundamental note.

Shogun (shō′ gŭn) ("Army leader"). The
Shoguns were hereditary commanders-
in-chief who seized political power in Japan at the end of the 12th century. The
MIKADO did not fully regain power until
1868. *Cp.* TYCOON.

Shoot (M.E. *shoten*, dart forth, rush). *See
also* SHOT.

Shoot! Go ahead; say what you have to
say. Let's have it! In film studios it is
the word used for the cameras to begin
turning.

To go the whole shoot. To do all there
is to do, go the whole HOG, run through
the gamut.

To shoot down in flames. To refute
the arguments of an opponent devastat-
ingly and completely. A METAPHOR from
aerial warfare.

To shoot a line. To boast extravagantly.

To shoot one's linen. To display an
unnecessary amount of shirt-cuff; to
show off.

To shoot the moon. To remove one's
household goods by night to avoid distraint; to "do a MOONLIGHT flit".

To shoot Niagara. To embark on a
desperate enterprise.

To shoot the sun. A nautical colloquialism meaning to take the sun's alti-
tude with a sextant.

Shooting-iron. Slang (originally American) for a firearm, especially a revolver.

Shooting stars. Incandescent meteors
shooting across the sky, formerly, like
comets, fabled to presage disaster:

> A little ere the mightiest Julius fell,
> The graves stood tenantless, and the
>   sheeted dead
> Did squeak and gibber in the Roman
>   streets;
> As stars with trains of fire and dews of
>   blood,
> Disasters with the sun.
>   SHAKESPEARE: *Hamlet*, I, i.

They were called in ancient legends

the "fiery tears of St. LAWRENCE", because one of the periodic swarms of
these meteors is between 9 and 14 AU-
GUST, about the time of St. Lawrence's
festival, which is on the 10th. Other periods are from 12 to 14 November, and
from 6 to 12 December.

Shooting stars are said by the Arabs
to be firebrands hurled by the ANGELS
against the inquisitive genii, who are
forever clambering up on the constellations to peep into HEAVEN.

Shooting war. A real war as distinct
from a COLD WAR.

Shop. All over the shop. Scattered in
every direction, all over the place; or
pursuing an erratic course.

Closed shop. A term, used to charac-
terize shops or factories from which
non-union labour is excluded.

On the shop floor. Among the industrial workers of a workshop, factory, etc.

Open shop. The reverse of a CLOSED
SHOP.

To shop a person. To put him in prison, or inform against him so that he is
arrested, similarly, a billiard player will
speak of "shopping the white", *i.e.* putting his opponent's ball down in the
pocket.

To shop around. To look for the "best
buy", to visit a variety of shops comparing prices and quality before making
one's choice.

To shut up shop. To retire or withdraw from participation in an undertaking.

To talk shop. To talk about one's
trade, occupation, business, etc.

You've come to the wrong shop. I
can't help you, I can't give you the information, and so on, you require.

Shop steward. The elected trade union
representative of a factory or workshop
who acts as the link with the local union
branch, keeps watch on union membership, etc., and has certain negotiating
functions with the management.

**Shopkeepers. A nation of shop-
keepers.** This phrase, applied to Englishmen by NAPOLEON in contempt,
comes from Adam Smith's *The Wealth
Nations* (iv, 7). This book, well known
to the Emperor, says:

> To found a great empire for the sole pur-

pose of raising up a people of customers, may at first sight appear a project fit only for a nation of shopkeepers.

Shorne, or **Schorne, John.** Rector of North Marston, Buckinghamshire (*c.* 1290–1314), in the church of which was once a shrine in his honour. He was renowned for his piety and miraculous powers. He blessed a local well giving it legendary healing properties and also "conjured the DEVIL into a boot". His shrine became so frequented by pilgrims that, in 1481, the DEAN and CHAPTER of Windsor, owners of the ADVOWSON, with papal permission, removed his shrine and relics to Windsor.

Short. Pepin, or **Pippin the Short.** Pippin III, MAYOR OF THE PALACE, father of CHARLEMAGNE and founder of the CAROLINGIAN dynasty of French kings. He deposed the last of the MEROVINGIANS, Childeric III, in 751 and reigned as King of the FRANKS until 768. He was the son of Charles Martel.

Short commons. *See* COMMONS.

Short Parliament (13 April–5 May 1640). The abortive PARLIAMENT summoned by CHARLES I after his ELEVEN YEARS TYRANNY to procure supplies to fight the Scots. The Commons insisted on redress of grievances and Charles dissolved Parliament.

A drop of something short. A tot of whisky, gin, etc., as opposed to a "long drink" such as a glass of beer.

Cut it short! Don't be so prolix, come to the point; "cut the cackle and come to the 'osses". Said to a speaker who goes round and round his subject.

My name is Short. I'm in a hurry and cannot wait.

The short cut is often the longest way round. It does not always pay to avoid taking a little trouble; short cuts don't always pay. Francis Bacon says:

> It is in life, as it is in ways, the shortest way is commonly the foulest, and surely the faire way is not much about.
> *Advancement of Learning.*

To break off short. Abruptly, without warning, but completely.

To make short work of it. To dispose of it quickly, to deal summarily with it.

To sell short. A STOCK EXCHANGE phrase meaning to sell stock that one does not at the moment possess, on the chance that it may be acquired at a lower rate before the date of delivery; the same as "selling for a fall", or "selling a BEAR".

To win by a short head. Only just to outdistance one's competitors, to win with practically nothing to spare. The phrase is from horse-racing.

To short-circuit. Metaphorically to take a short cut, especially when dealing with officialdom; a figure from electrics in which a short-circuit is a deviation of current along a path of lower resistance.

Shorter Catechism. One of the two Catechisms (the *Larger* and *Shorter*) drawn up by the WESTMINSTER ASSEMBLY in 1647 and adopted by the English PARLIAMENT and the Scottish General Assembly. The *Shorter Catechism* proved its instructional worth and came into regular use among PRESBYTERIANS, Baptists, and later, WESLEYANS.

Shot (O.E. *sceot*, arrow, dart, etc.). A missile weapon.

A big shot. An important person. A development of the 19th-century "great gun" or "big bug".

The fool's bolt is soon shot. *See under* BOLT.

He shot wide of the mark. He was altogether wrong. The allusion to target shooting is obvious.

I haven't a shot in the locker. My last resources are spent; I've run right out of food, drink, money, etc. The reference is to the ammunition locker of a warship.

Like a shot. With great rapidity; or, without hesitation; most willingly.

A long shot. A remote chance, such as hazarding a highly improbable guess.

Parthian shot. *See* PARTHIAN.

A shot in the arm. A drink of whisky, etc., something which puts new life into one; an allusion to hypodermic injections or morphine, cocaine, etc.

A shot in the dark. A wild guess, a random conjecture.

To have a shot at. To have a try, to make an attempt at something in which you make no particular claim to expertise.

To have shot one's bolt. *See under*

BOLT.

Shot. Akin to *Scot* (*see* SCOT AND LOT). A reckoning, share of an ale-house bill, etc.

Shotgun Wedding. One forced upon the couple, usually by the bride's parents, when the bride is pregnant.

Shotten Herring. A lean, spiritless creature, a JACK-O-LENT, like a herring that has *shot*, or ejected, its spawn. Herrings gutted and dried are likewise so called.

Shoulder. The government shall be upon his shoulder (*Is.* ix, 6). An allusion to the key slung on the shoulder of Jewish stewards on public occasions. *See* THE KEY SHALL BE UPON HIS SHOULDER *under* KEY.

Straight from the shoulder. With full force, physically, or verbally. A term from boxing.

To set, or put one's shoulder to the wheel. *See under* PUT.

Shout, To. To stand a round of drinks.

All over but the shouting. Success is so certain that only the applause is lacking. The phrase, perhaps, derives from elections.

Shovel Hat. A broad-brimmed black hat curved up at the sides producing a shovel-like projection at back and front; formerly favoured by CLERGY. Hence *shovel-hat* as a colloquialism for an ecclesiastic.

Show. To have a show-down. To reveal the strength of one's position; to have a final confrontation in a dispute to settle the matter or to clear the air. As in poker, cards are put face upwards on the table.

To show one's hand. To reveal one's motives or intentions, as in displaying one's hand at cards.

Shrew-mouse. This small insectivorous animal was fabled to have the power of harming cattle, etc., by running over their backs and to lame the foot over which it ran. Gilbert White tells of a shrew-ash, the twigs of which, if applied to the limbs of beasts harmed by the shrew-mouse, give relief. This tree was one in which a deep hole had been bored and a shrew-mouse thrust in alive; the hole was then plugged (*Natural History of Selbourne*, Letter xxviii). It was also ill luck to encounter a shrew-mouse when beginning a journey.

Shrift, Shrive. To shrive a person was to prescribe penance after confession and to absolve. *Cp.* SHROVETIDE.

To give short shrift to. To make short work of. *Short shrift* was the few minutes in which a criminal about to be executed was allowed to make his confession.

Shrovetide. The three days just before the opening of LENT, when people went to confession and afterwards indulged in all sorts of sports and merry-making.

Shrove Tuesday. The day before ASH WEDNESDAY; "PANCAKE DAY". It used to the great "DERBY DAY" of COCK-FIGHTING in England.

> Or martyr beat, like Shrovetide cocks, with bats.
> PETER PINDAR: *Subjects for Painters*: *Scene, The Royal Academy*, III.

Shut up. Slang for "HOLD your tongue"; shut up your mouth.

Shy. To have a shy at anything. To fling at it. To have a go, to take a chance and see how it turns out.

Shylock, A (shī' lok). A grasping, stony-hearted moneylender; in allusion to the Jew in SHAKESPEARE's *Merchant of Venice*.

Si (sē). *See* ARETINIAN SYLLABLES.

Si Quis (sī kwis) (Lat., if anyone). A notice to all whom it may concern, given in the parish church before ordination that a resident means to offer himself as a candidate for HOLY ORDERS (*see under* ORDERS); and if anyone knows any just cause or impediment thereto, he is to declare the same to the BISHOP.

Siamese twins. Identical twins physically joined together when born and often inseparable. The name originated with two children, Eng and Chang, born (1811) in Siam of Chinese parents. Joined in the area of the waist, they were duly sold by their mother and exhibited in America (where they eventually settled), England and Europe. They married two sisters and fathered offspring and died in 1874 within two and a half hours of each other.

Sibyl (sib'il). A prophetess of classical legend, who was supposed to prophesy under the inspiration of a deity; the name is now applied to any prophetess or woman fortune-teller. There were a number of sibyls, and they had their seats in widely separate parts of the world—Greece, Italy, Babylonia, Egypt, etc.

PLATO mentions only one, *viz.* the *Erythræan*—identified with AMALTHEA, the *Cumæan* sibyl, who was consulted by ÆNEAS and accompanied him into HADES and who sold the SIBYLLINE BOOKS to TARQUIN.

Sibylline Books, The. A collection of oracular utterances preserved in ancient ROME and consulted by the Senate in times of emergency or disaster. According to Livy, there were orginally NINE books offered to TARQUIN by the SIBYL of Cumæ but the offer was rejected, and she burnt three of them. She offered the remaining six at the same price. Again, being refused, she burnt three more. The remaining three were then bought by the King for the original sum.

The three books were preserved in a vault of the temple of JUPITER Capitolinus, and committed to the charge of custodians, ultimately 15 in number. These books were destroyed by fire in 83 B.C. A new collection of verses was made from those preserved in the cities of Greece, Italy, and Asia Minor, and deposited in the rebuilt temple. These were transferred to the temple of APOLLO by AUGUSTUS in 12 B.C. and were said to have been destroyed by Stilicho (*c.* 405).

Sibylline Oracles. A collection of 15 books, 12 of which are extant, of 2nd- and 3rd-century authorship, and written by Jews and Christians in imitation of the SIBYLLINE BOOKS. Their aim was to gain converts to their respective faiths.

Sic (sik) (Lat., thus, so). A word used by reviewers, quoters, etc., after a doubtful word or phrase, or a misspelling, to indicate that it is here printed exactly as in the original and to call attention to the fact that it is wrong in some way.

Sic transit gloria mundi. *See under* GLORIA.

Sicilies, The Two. The old name for the Spanish Bourbon Kingdom of Naples and Sicily formerly united under their Angevin rulers in the 13th century. The Two Sicilies were annexed to the Kingdom of Italy in 1860.

Sicilian Vespers. The massacre of the French in Sicily on EASTER Monday (30 March) 1282, which began on the stroke of the vesper-bell. It was occasioned by the brutality and tyranny of Charles of Anjou's rule.

Sick. Sick joke. A sadistic, gruesome joke — not really funny but the product of a warped sense of humour.

Sick Man, The. So Nicholas I of Russia (in 1844 and subsequently) called the Turkish Empire, which had long been in decline. His hints to Great Britain in 1853 of a partition were ignored.

Don John, Governor-General of the Netherlands, so spoke of his charge when writing to his master Philip II in 1579.

"Money is the gruel," said he, "with which we must cure this sick man."
MOTLEY: *Rise of the Dutch Republic,* Pt. V, ch. ii.

Side. On the side of the angels. The famous phrase with which Disraeli thought he had settled the problems raised by Darwin's theory of the origin of species. It occurred in his speech at the Oxford Diocesan Conference in 1864:

The quest is this: Is man an ape or an angel?
Now I am on the side of the angels.

It was the same statesman who said in the HOUSE OF COMMONS (14 May 1866), "Ignorance never settles a question."

Putting on side. Giving oneself airs; being bumptious. *To put on side* in billiards is to give your ball a twist or spin with the cue as you strike it.

To side-track. Originally an American RAIL-ROAD term; hence to divert, to put on one side, to shelve.

Sideburns. Short side-whiskers, originally called *burnsides* after the American Federal General Ambrose Everett Burnside (1824–1881) who wore side-whiskers.

Siege Perilous. In the cycle of ARTHURIAN ROMANCES a seat at the ROUND TABLE which was kept vacant for him who should accomplish the quest of the Holy GRAIL. For any less a person to sit in it was fatal. At the crown of his achievement Sir GALAHAD took his seat in the

Siege Perilous.

Siegfried (zēg′ frēd), or **Sigurd.** Hero of the first part of the NIBELUNGENLIED. He was the youngest son of Siegmund and Sieglind, King and Queen of the Netherlands.

Siegfried's cloak of invisibility, called "*Tarnkappe*" (*tarnen*, to conceal; *Kappe*, a cloak). It not only made the wearer invisible, but also gave him the strength of 12 men.

Siegfried Line. The defences built by the Germans on their western frontier before and after 1939 as a reply to France's MAGINOT LINE. The British song, popular in 1939, "We're gonna hang out the washing on the Siegfried Line" was somewhat premature. When Canadian troops penetrated the Line in 1945 they hung up a number of sheets with a large notice on which was written "The Washing".

Sieve and Shears. An ancient form of DIVINATION mentioned by THEOCRITUS. The points of the shears were stuck in the wooden rim of the sieve and two persons supported it upright with the tips of their two fingers. Then a verse of the BIBLE was read aloud, and St. PETER and St. PAUL were asked if the guilty person was A, B, or C (naming those suspected). When the guilty person was named the sieve would suddenly turn round. This method was also used to tell if a couple would marry, etc.

> Searching for things lost with a sieve and shears.
> BEN JONSON: *Alchemist*, I, i.

Sight. In archaic usage, it often denotes a "multitude" or large number of persons or objects.

Second sight. *See under* SECOND.

A sight for sore eyes. Something that it is very pleasurable to see or witness, especially something unexpected.

Though lost to sight, to memory dear. This occurs in a song by George Linley (*c.* 1835), but is found as an "axiom" in the *Monthly Magazine*, January 1827, and is probably earlier than this.

To do a thing on sight. At once, without any hesitation.

Sign. Royal Sign Manual. The signature of the monarch used on orders, commissions, and warrants. The earliest known royal signature is that of Edward III, prior to which marks or seals were used. Under certain restrictions a stamp is used for minor documents.

To sign off. In the 19th century this denoted finally leaving one religious organization for another. It is generally used to mean terminating attendances, registering when leaving work, finishing broadcasting, etc.

To sign on the dotted line. To fully accept the terms offered; from the space indicated by dots reserved for a person's signature on printed forms.

Sigurd. The SIEGFRIED of the Volsunga SAGA, the Scandinavian version of the NIBELUNGENLIED. He falls in love with BRUNHILD but under the influence of a love-potion marries GUDRUN, a union with fateful consequences.

Sikes, Bill. The type of a ruffianly housebreaker, from the character of that name in Dickens's *Oliver Twist*.

Silence. Amyclæan Silence. *See* AMYCLÆAN.

The Argument of Silence (Lat. *argumentum e silentio*). The conclusion that, if the works of an author omit all reference to a particular subject, the writer was unaware of it.

Silence gives consent. A saying, common to many languages, founded on the old Latin legal maxim—*Qui tacet consentire videtur* (who is silent is held to consent).

> But that you shall not say I yield, being silent,
> I would not speak.
> SHAKESPEARE: *Cymbeline*, II, iii.

Silence is golden. *See* SPEECH.

The rest is silence. The last words of the dying Hamlet (SHAKESPEARE: *Hamlet*, V, ii).

Towers of Silence. The small towers on which the PARSEES and ZOROASTRIANS place their dead to be consumed by birds of prey. The bones are picked clean in the course of a day, and are then thrown into a receptacle covered with charcoal.

Parsees do not burn or bury their dead, because they consider a corpse impure, and they will not defile any of the elements. They carry it on a bier to the tower. At the entrance they look their last on the body, and the corpse-bearers carry it within the precincts and lay it down to be devoured by vultures which are constantly on the watch.

Two-minute silence. The cessation of traffic and all other activities for two minutes at 11 a.m. on 11 November to commemorate those who died in World War I. First observed in 1919, it remained a central feature of REMEMBRANCE DAY.

William the Silent. Prince William of Orange (1533–1584), so called because when (1559) Henry II of France, thinking that he would be a ready accomplice, revealed to him the plans for a general massacre of PROTESTANTS:

> the Prince, although horror-struck and indignant at the Royal revelations, held his peace, and kept his countenance ... William of Orange earned the name of "the Silent", from the manner in which he received the communications of Henry without revealing to the monarch by word or look, the enormous blunder which he had committed.
> MOTLEY: *The Rise of the Dutch Republic*, Pt. II, i.

Silenus (sī lē′ nŭs). The drunken attendant and nurse of BACCHUS, represented as a fat, jovial old man, always full of liquor, riding an ass.

> Within his car, aloft, young Bacchus stood,
> Trifling his ivy-dart, in dancing mood,
> With sidelong laughing;...
> And near him rode Silenus on his ass,
> Pelted with flowers as he on did pass
> Tipsily quaffing.
> KEATS: *Endymion*, IV, 209.

Silhouette. A profile drawing of a person giving the outline only, and all within the outline in black; hence a shadow and, figuratively, a slight literary sketch of a person or other subject. Derived from the French minister of Finance, Etienne de Silhouette (1709–1767), noted for his parsimony in public expenditure. His name was applied to things made cheaply.

Silk. The Silk Road. The ancient caravan route along which silk was carried from China, through central Asia, thence to Antioch and the eastern Mediterranean and eventually to other parts of Europe It was in use for about 1500 years, particularly in the days of the Roman Empire. Parts of it were traversed by Marco Polo on his visits to China in the late 13th century.

To take silk. Said of a BARRISTER who has been appointed a QUEEN'S COUNSEL (Q.C.) because he then exchanges his stuff gown for a silk one.

You cannot make a silk purse out of a sow's ear. You cannot make something good of what is by nature bad or inferior in quality. "You cannot make a horn of a pig's tail."

Silly is the German *selig* (blessed) and used to mean in English "happy through being innocent"; whence the infant Jesus was termed "the harmless silly babe", and sheep were called "silly". As the innocent are easily taken in by worldly cunning, the word came to signify "gullible", "foolish".

Silly Billy. A nickname applied to William IV (1765, 1830–1837); also to William Frederick, Duke of Gloucester (1776–1834).

Silly-how. An old name—still used in SCOTLAND—for a child's caul. It is a rough translation of the German term *Glückshaube*, lucky cap. The caul has always been supposed to bring luck to its original possessor.

The silly season. An obsolescent journalistic expression for the part of the year when PARLIAMENT and the Law Courts are not sitting (about August and September), when, through lack of news, the papers had to fill their columns with trivial items—such as news of giant gooseberries and sea serpents—and long correspondence on subjects of evanescent (if any) interest.

Silurian. Of or pertaining to the ancient British tribe, the Silures, or the district they inhabited, *viz.* Monmouth, Glamorgan, Brecon, Radnor and Hereford. The "sparkling wines of the Silurian vats" are cider and perry.

Silurian rocks. A name given by Sir Roderick Murchison (1835) to what miners call *gray-wacke* and Werner termed *transition rocks*, because it was in the SILURIAN district (English-Welsh border) that he first investigated their structure.

Silver. Among the ancient alchemists silver represented the MOON or DIANA; in HERALDRY it is known by its French name ARGENT (which also gives its chemical symbol, Ag), and is indicated on engravings by the silver (argent) portion being left blank.

The Silver Age. According to Hesiod and the Greek and Roman poets, the second of the AGES of the World; fabled as a period that was voluptuous and godless, and much inferior in simplicity and true happinesss to the GOLDEN AGE.

The silver cooper. A kidnapper. "To play the silver cooper", to kidnap. A cooper is one who "coops up" another.

Silver of Guthrum. See GUTHRUM.

Silver Star. A United States military decoration for gallantry in action. It consists of a bronze star bearing a small silver star in its centre.

The Silver Streak. The English Channel.

Silver Wedding. The twenty-fifth anniversary, when presents of silver plate (in Germany a silver wreath) are given to the happy pair.

Thirty pieces of silver. The sum of money that JUDAS Iscariot received from the chief priests for the betrayal of his Master (*Matt.* xxvi, 5); hence used proverbially of a bribe or "BLOOD-MONEY" (*see under* BLOOD).

Born with a silver spoon in one's mouth. *See under* BORN.

A silver lining. The prospect of better things and happier times. The saying **Every cloud has a silver lining** is an old one; thus in Milton's *Comus* (I, 221–222) the lady lost in the wood resolves to hope on, and sees:

Was I deceiv'd, or did a sable cloud
Turn forth her silver lining on the night?

Speech is silver. *See under* SPEECH.

With silver weapons you may conquer the world. The Delphic ORACLE to Philip of Macedon, when he went to consult it. Philip, acting on this advice, sat down before a fortress which his staff pronounced to be impregnable. "You shall see," said the king, "how an ass laden with silver will find an entrance."

Simeon, St. (sim′ ē ŏn), the son of Cleophas, is usually depicted as bearing in his arms the infant Jesus or receiving Him in the TEMPLE. His feast day is 18 February.

St. Simeon Stylites. *See* STYLITES.

Similia similibus curantur (sim il′ ia simil′i bùs kū răn′ ter) (Lat.). Like cures like; or as we say. "Take a hair of the dog that bit you." (*See under* HAIR.)

Sim(p)kin. Anglo-Indian for champagne—of which word it is an Urdu mispronunciation.

Simnel Cakes. Rich cakes formerly eaten (especially in Lancashire) on MID-LENT SUNDAY (MOTHERING SUNDAY), EASTER, and CHRISTMAS DAY. They were ornamented with scallops, and were eaten at Mid-Lent in commemoration of the banquet given by Joseph to his brethren, which forms the first lesson of Mid-Lent Sunday, and the feeding of the five thousand, which forms the GOSPEL of the day.

The word *simnel* is through O.Fr. from Late Lat. *siminellus*, fine bread, Lat. *simila*, the finest wheat flour.

Simon, St. (Zelotes) is represented with a saw in his hand, in allusion to the instrument of his martyrdom. He sometimes bears fish in his other hand, in allusion to his occupation as a fisherman. His feast day is 28 October.

Simon Magus. Isidore tells us that Simon Magus died in the reign of NERO, and adds that he had proposed a dispute with PETER and PAUL, and had promised to fly up to HEAVEN. He succeeded in rising high into the air, but at the prayers of the two APOSTLES he was cast down to earth by the evil spirits who had enabled him to rise.

Milman, in his *History of Christianity* (ii) tells another story. He says that Simon offered to be buried alive, and declared that he would reappear on the third day. He was actually buried in a deep trench, "but to this day," says Hippolytus, "his disciples have failed to witness his resurrection".

His followers were known as *Simonians*, and the sin of which he was guilty, *viz.* the trafficking in sacred things, the buying and selling of ecclesiastical offices (*see Acts* viii, 18) is still called *simony*.

Simon Pure. The real man, the authentic article, etc. In Mrs. Centlivre's *Bold Stroke for a Wife*, a Colonel Feignwell passes himself off for Simon Pure, a QUAKER, and wins the heart of Miss

Lovely. No sooner does he get the assent of her guardian than the Quaker turns up, and proves beyond a doubt he is the "real Simon Pure". In modern usage, a hypocrite, making a great parade of virtue.

Simple Simon. A simpleton, a gullible booby; from the character in the well-known anonymous nursery tale, who "met a pie-man".

Simonism. *See* SAINT-SIMONISM.

Simple, The. Charles III of France (879, 893–929). He was dethroned in 923.

The simple life. A mode of living in which the object is to eliminate as far as possible all luxuries and extraneous aids to happiness, etc., returning to the simplicity of life as imagined by the pastoral poets.

Sin, according to Milton, is twin keeper with Death of the gates of HELL. She sprang full-grown from the head of SATAN.

Original Sin. That corruption which is born with us, and is the inheritance of all the offspring of ADAM. Theology teaches that as Adam was founder of his race, when Adam fell the taint and penalty of his disobedience passed to all posterity.

The Man of Sin (II *Thess.* ii, 3). Generally held to signify ANTICHRIST, and applied by the PURITANS to the POPE, by the FIFTH MONARCHY MEN to Cromwell, etc.

Mortal Sins. The same as deadly sins.

The seven deadly sins. *See under* SEVEN.

Sin-eaters. Poor persons hired at funerals in olden days, to eat beside the corpse and so take upon themselves the sins of the deceased, that the soul might be delivered from PURGATORY. In Carmarthenshire the sin-eater used to rest a plate of salt on the breast of the deceased and place a piece of bread on the salt. After saying an incantation over the bread the sin-eater consumed it and with it the sins of the dead.

"Sin on" Bible. *See* BIBLE, SOME SPECIALLY NAMED EDITIONS.

Sin rent. In mediæval England, a fine imposed upon the laity by the Church for living in sin, *i.e.*, for concubinage. *Cp.* CRADLE CROWN.

To earn the wages of sin. To be hanged or condemned to death.

The wages of sin is death.
Rom. vi, 23.

To sin one's mercies. To be ungrateful for the gifts of Providence.

Sinbad the Sailor. The hero of the story of this name in THE ARABIAN NIGHTS ENTERTAINMENTS. He was a wealthy citizen of Baghdad, called "The Sailor" because of his seven voyages in which, among many adventures, he discovered the ROC's egg and the Valley of Diamonds, and killed the OLD MAN OF THE SEA.

Sine (Lat.). Without.

Sine die (Lat.). No time being fixed; indefinitely in regard to time. When a proposal is deferred *sine die*, it is deferred without fixing a day for its reconsideration, which is virtually "for ever".

Sine qua non (Lat.). An indispensable condition. Lat. *Sine qua non potest esse* or *fieri* (that without which [the thing] cannot be, or be done).

Sinecure (Lat. *sine cura*, without cure, or care). An enjoyment of the emoluments attached to a benefice without having the trouble of the "cure"; applied to any office to which a salary is attached without any duties to perform. Government sinecures were a particular feature of 18th-century political life. *Cp.* PLACEMEN.

Sinews of War. Essential funds for the prosecution of a war. Troops have to be paid and fed and the materials of war are costly.

The English phrase comes from Cicero's *Nervos belli pecuniam* (*Phil.* V, ii, 5), money makes the sinews of war. Rabelais (I, xlvi) uses the same idiom—*les nerfs des batailles sont les pécunes*.

> Victuals and ammunition,
> And money too, the sinews of the war,
> Are stored up in the magazine.
> BEAUMONT and FLETCHER:
> *Fair Maid of the Inn*, I, i.

Sing. Singing bread (Fr. *pain à chanter*). An old term for the larger altar bread used in celebration of the MASS, because singing or chanting was in progress during its manufacture; also called *singing cake* and *singing loaf.*

Swans sing before they die. *See*

SWAN.

To make someone sing another tune. To make him change his behaviour altogether; to make him submit or humble himself.

To sing in agony, or **tribulation**. Old slang for to confess when put to the torture.

To sing out. To cry or squeal from chastisement; to shout or call out.

To sing small. To cease boasting and assume a quieter tone.

Singe. Singeing the King of Spain's beard. Sir Francis Drake's daring attack on the Spanish ships and stores at Cadiz (1587), which delayed the sailing of the Armada until 1588. He referred to it as his "singeing of the Spanish King's beard".

Sinis (sī' nis). A Corinthian robber of Greek legend, known as the *Pinebender*, because he used to fasten his victims to two pine-trees bent towards the earth, and then leave them to be rent asunder when the trees were released. He was captured by THESEUS and put to death in the same way.

Sinister (sin' is ter) (Lat., on the left hand). Foreboding of ill; ill-omened. According to AUGURY, birds, etc., appearing on the left-hand side forbode ill luck; but on the right-hand side, good luck. Plutarch, following PLATO and ARISTOTLE, gives as the reason that the west (or left side of the augur) was towards the setting or departing sun.

In HERALDRY it denotes the left side of the shield viewed from the position of its bearer, *i.e.* in illustrations it is the right-hand side.

Bar Sinister. *See under* BAR.

Cornix sinistra (Lat., a crow on the left hand) is a sign of ill luck which belongs to English superstitions as much as to the ancient Roman or Etruscan (VIRGIL, *Eclogues*, ix, 15).

> That raven on yon left-hand oak
> (Curse on his ill-betiding croak)
> Bodes me no good.
> GAY: *Fable* xxxvii, 27.

Sinking Fund. The name given to the government fund established in 1717, the interest from which was to "sink" or pay off the NATIONAL DEBT. The fund was re-established by Pitt the Younger in 1786, which, as a result of the French Revolutionary Wars, created a loss and was abandoned in 1828. A new fund was set up in 1875 which was remodelled in 1923 and 1928.

Sinn Fein (shin fān) (Irish, "Ourselves alone"). The Irish nationalist movement formed in 1905 which set up the Irish Republic (1919) under De Valera and carried on guerrilla warfare with the English until the treaty of 1922. Disagreements over this settlement disrupted the party, which still aims to bring ULSTER into the Republic.

Sinon (sī' non). The Greek who induced the Trojans to receive the WOODEN HORSE (VIRGIL, *Æneid*, II, 102, etc.). Anyone deceiving to betray is called "a Sinon".

Sir. Lat. *senex*; Span. *señor*; Ital. *signore*; Fr. *sieur*, sire.

As a title of honour prefixed to the Christian name of BARONETS and KNIGHTS, *Sir* is of great antiquity; and the CLERGY had at one time *Sir* prefixed to their name. This is merely a translation of the university word *dominus* given to graduates, as "Dominus Hugh Evans", etc. Spenser uses the title as a substantive, meaning a parson:

> But this good Sir did follow the plaine word.
> *Mother Hubberds Tale*, 390.

Sirat, Al. *See* AL-SIRAT.

Siren (sī' rèn). One of the mythical monsters, half woman and half bird, said by Greek poets (*see Odyssey*, XII) to entice seamen by the sweetness of their song to such a degree that the listeners forgot everything and died of hunger (Gr. *sirenes*, entanglers); hence applied to any dangerous, alluring woman.

In Homeric mythology there were but two sirens; later writers name three, viz. PARTHENOPE, Ligea, and Leucosia; and the number was still further augmented by others.

ULYSSES escaped their blandishments by filling his companions' ears with wax and lashing himself to the mast of his ship.

> What Song the Syrens sang, or what name Achilles assumed when he hid himself among women, though puzzling questions, are not beyond all conjecture.

SIR THOS. BROWNE: *Urn Burial*, v.

PLATO says there were three kinds of sirens—the *celestial*, the *generative*, and the *cathartic*. The first were under the government of JUPITER, the second under that of NEPTUNE, and the third of PLUTO. When the SOUL is in HEAVEN the sirens seek, by harmonic motion, to unite it to the divine life of the celestial host; and when in HADES, to conform it to the infernal regimen; but on earth they produce generation, of which the sea is emblematic (Proclus: *On the Theology of Plato*, Bk. VI).

In more recent times the word has been applied to the loud mechanical whistle sounded at a factory, etc., to indicate that work is to be started or finished for the day. Sirens with two or more recognizable notes were employed in World War II to give warning of the approach or departure of hostile aircraft.

Siren suit. A one-piece lined and warm garment on the lines of a boiler suit, sometimes worn in London during the air raids of World War II. It was much favoured by Sir Winston Churchill and so named from its being slipped on over night clothes at the first wail of the SIREN.

Sirius (sir' i ùs). The DOG-STAR; so called by the Greeks from the adjective *seirios*, hot and scorching. The Romans called it *canicula*, whence our CANICULAR DAYS, and the Egyptians *sept*, which gave the Greek alternative *sothis*. See SOTHIC YEAR.

Sirloin. Properly *surloin*, from Fr. *sur-longe*, above the loin. The mistaken spelling *sir-* has given rise to a number of stories of the joint having been 'knighted' because of its estimable qualities.

Sirocco. *See* AUSTER.

Sistine (sis' tin, sis' tĕn). **The Sistine Chapel.** The principal chapel in the VATICAN, reserved for ceremonies at which the POPE is present, so called because it was built by Pope Sixtus IV (1471–1484). It is decorated with frescoes by MICHELANGELO and others.

Sistine Madonna, The (*Madonna di San Sisto*). The Madonna painted by Raphael (*c*. 1518) for the church of St. Sixtus (San Sisto) at Piacenza; St. Sixtus is shown kneeling at the right of the Virgin. The picture is now in the Royal Gallery, Dresden.

Sisyphus (sis' i fùs) ("The Crafty"). In Greek legend, the son of ÆOLUS and husband of MEROPE; in post-Homeric legend, the father of Odysseus (ULYSSES). His punishment in the world of the SHADES was to roll a huge stone up a hill to the top. As it constantly rolled down again just as it reached the summit, his task was everlasting; hence "a labour of Sisyphus" or "Sisyphean toil" is an endless, heart-breaking job. The reasons given for this punishment vary. *See* AUTOLYCUS.

Sit. To make one sit up. To astonish or disconcert one considerably; to subject to punishment or hard work.

To sit down under. To submit tamely to; to put up with.

To sit like patience on a monument. To be exceptionally patient and long suffering. From the apparent patience of a statue.

> She sat like patience on a monument,
> Smiling at grief.
> SHAKESPEARE: *Twelfth Night*, II, iv.

To sit on, or **upon.** To snub, squash, smother, put in his place. *Sit on* has other meanings also; thus *to sit on a corpse* is to hold a coroner's inquest on it; *to sit on the bench* is to occupy a seat as a judge or magistrate.

To sit on the fence. *See under* FENCE.

To sit tight. Not to give up your seat; to keep your counsel; to remain in or as in hiding. The phrase is from poker, where, if a player does not want to continue betting and at the same time does not wish to throw in his cards, he "sits tight".

To sit under. To be one of the congregation of the clergyman named; to listen to.

Sit-down strike. A strike in which the workers remain at their factory, etc., but refuse to work themselves or allow others to do so. A tactic begun in the 1930s.

A Sit-in. Similar to a sit-down strike, currently applied to students occupying college premises, but boycotting lectures, etc., with the object of redressing

grievances or dictating policy. *See* BOY-
COTT.

Sitting Bull (*c.* 1834–1890). A famous
Sioux chief who resisted the governmental policy of reservations for his
tribe. He defeated Custer in 1876 (*See*
CUSTER'S LAST STAND) and later appeared in BUFFALO BILL's show. He was
killed while resisting arrest during the
Sioux rebellion of 1890.

Sitzkrieg (sits' krēg). The "sitting war",
the descriptive term applied (in contrast
to *Blitzkrieg*) to the period of comparative quiet and seeming military inactivity at the outset of World War II (September 1939–April 1940); the period of
the PHONEY war.

Siva, or **Shiva** (sē' va, shē' va). The third
member of the Hindu TRIMURTI, representing the destructive principle in life
and also the reproductive or renovating
power. He has other contrasting qualities, being a god of ascetics as well as of
music, dancing, and learning; in all a
god of many attributes and functions.
Siva, which means "The Benevolent", is
only one of his many names. He is generally represented with three eyes and
four arms and his symbol is the *lingam*.

Six. The Six. The six countries—
Belgium, France, Germany, Italy, the
Netherlands, and Luxemburg, who
were the original participants in three
economic communities. These are: the
European Coal and Steel Community,
1951 (ECSC); the European Economic
Community or Common Market
(EEC), set up by the Treaty of Rome,
1957; and the European Atomic Energy
Community or Euratom, 1957. *Cp.* THE
SEVEN.

Les Six. A group of French composers
formed at Paris in 1918 under the ÆGIS
of Jean Cocteau and Erik Satie, in order
to further their interests and those of
modern music generally. The group lost
its cohesion in the 1920s. Its members
were Honegger, Milhaud, Poulenc,
Durey, Auric, and Tailleferre.

The Six Articles. The so-called "Whip
with six strings", otherwise known as
the "Bloody Bill", the Statute of Six Articles passed in 1539 to secure uniformity in matters of religion. It was repealed
in 1547 under Edward VI. The articles

maintained (1) TRANSUBSTANTIATION;
(2) the sufficiency of Communion in one
kind; (3) clerical celibacy; (4) the obligation of monastic vows; (5) the propriety of private masses; (6) the necessity of auricular confession. Penalties
were imposed for non-observance including death at the stake for those who
spoke against transubstantiation.

Six Clerks Office. An old name for the
Court of CHANCERY, from the six clerks
who received and filed all Chancery proceedings, each of whom had ten subor-
dinates. The Six Clerks, who also had
charge of causes in court, were abolished in 1842.

The Six Counties. Another name for
ULSTER or Northern Ireland, *i.e.* Armagh, Antrim, Down, Derry, Fermanagh
and Tyrone.

The Six Nations. The FIVE NATIONS
together with the Tuscaroras.

The Six Points of Ritualism. Altar
lights, eucharistic vestments, the mixed
chalice, incense, unleavened bread, and
the eastward position. So called when
English Ritualists and upholders of the
OXFORD MOVEMENT sought to reintro-
duce them in the 1870s.

The six-foot way. The strip of ground
between two sets of railway lines.

A six-hooped pot. A two-quart pot.
Quart pots were bound with three
hoops, and when three men joined in
drinking, each man drank his hoop.

Six-Principle Baptists. A sect of Arm-
inian Baptists, founded about 1639, who
based their creed on the six principles
enunciated in *Heb.* vi, 1–2: repentance,
faith, BAPTISM, laying on of hands, the
resurrection of the dead, and eternal
judgment.

The Six-stringed Whip. The SIX ARTI-
CLES (*see above*).

At sixes and sevens. Higgledy-
piggledy, in a state of confusion; or of
persons, unable to come to an agreement, at LOGGERHEADS. The phrase
comes from dicing. Udall (*Erasmus'
Apothegmes,* 1542) says "There is a proverb *Omnem jacere aleam*, to cast all
dice by which is signified to set all on six
and seven ... assaying the wild chance of
fortune, be it good, be it bad".

It is also traditionally held that the expression arose out of a dispute between two of the great LIVERY COMPANIES, the Merchant Taylors and the Skinners as to which was sixth and which seventh in the order of the companies going in processions in THE CITY, both companies having been chartered in 1327 within a few days of each other. In 1484 they submitted the matter to the judgment of the Mayor, Sir Robert Billesden, and the Aldermen. The award was that the Master and Wardens of both companies were to dine each other annually and that the Skinners were to precede the Taylors in that year's procession. The next year the Taylors were to take the sixth place and this alternation was to continue "ever more".

Six of one and half a dozen of the other. There is nothing to choose between them, they are both in the wrong—ARCADES AMBO.

Six of the best. In the earlier decades of the present century, when corporal chastisement was still the normal way of punishing schoolboys for wrongdoing and bad behaviour, it meant six strokes of the cane across the delinquent's posterior given by the headmaster or one of his assistants.

Sixpence. *See* TANNER.

Sixty-four (or **Sixty-four thousand**) **dollar question** (U.S.A.). The last and most difficult question, the crux of the problem; from the stake money awarded in a QUIZ for answering the final question.

> Did that mean the whole area had extractable tin underneath it? "That's the 64,000 dollar question".
> *Sunday Telegraph* (5 August 1979).

Skanda. *See* KARTTIKEYA.

Skeleton. The family skeleton, or **the skeleton in the cupboard.** Some domestic source of worry or shame which the family conspires to keep to itself; every family is said to have at least one!

The story is that someone without a single care or trouble in the world had to be found. After long and unsuccessful search a lady was discovered who all thought would "fill the bill"; but to the great surprise of the inquirers, after she had satisfied them on all points and the quest seemed to be achieved, she took them upstairs and there opened a closet which contained a human skeleton. "I try", said she, "to keep my trouble to myself, but every night my husband compels me to kiss that skeleton." She then explained that the skeleton was once her husband's rival, killed in a duel. The expression was given literary use by Thackeray—

> And it is from these that we shall arrive at some particulars regarding the Newcome family, which will show us that they have a skeleton or two in their closets as well as their neighbours.
> *The Newcomes* (1855) ch. lv.

The skeleton at the feast. The thing or person that acts as a reminder that there are troubles as well as pleasures in life. Plutarch says in his *Moralia* that the Egyptians always had a skeleton placed in a prominent position at their banquets.

Skevington's daughter. *See* SCAVENGER'S.

Skid Row. An American expression applied to a district abounding in vicious characters and down-and-outs. In the lumber industry a *skid row* was a row of logs down which other felled timber was slid or skidded. Early on, Tacoma, near Seattle, flourished on its lumber production and in due course liquor and loose women became available for loggers descending the skid row. The usage may well derive from this situation.

Skidbladnir. In Scandinavian mythology, the magic ship made by the DWARFS for FREYR. It was big enough to take all the ÆSIR with their weapons and equipment, yet when not in use could be folded up and carried by Freyr in his pouch. It sailed through both air and water, and went straight to its destination as soon as the sails were hoisted. *Cp.* CARPET.

Skiffle. A name given to a style of JAZZ of the 1920s, and more recently to a type of jazz folk-music current in Britain in the late 1950s played by a skiffle group, consisting of guitar, drums, kazoo, washboard, and other improvised instruments.

Skimble-skamble. Rambling, worthless. "Skamble" is merely a variant of *scramble*, hence "scambling days", those days in LENT when no regular meals are provided, but each person "scrambles" or shifts for himself. "Skimble" is added to give force.

> And such a deal of skimble-skamble stuff
> As put me from my faith.
>
> SHAKESPEARE: *Henry IV*, *Pt*. I, III, i.

Skimmington. It was an old custom in rural ENGLAND and SCOTLAND to make an example of nagging wives by forming a ludicrous procession through the village accompanied by ROUGH MUSIC to ridicule the offender. A man, mounted on a horse with a distaff in his hand, rode behind the woman with his face to the horse's tail, while the woman beat him about the jowls with a ladle. As the procession passed a house where the woman was paramount the participants gave the threshold a sweep. The event was called *riding the Skimmington* (*cp*. To ride the STANG). The origin of the name is uncertain, but in an illustration of 1639 the woman is shown belabouring her husband with a skimming-ladle. Unfaithful husbands were similarly put to scorn. The procession is fully described in Butler's *Hudibras*, II, ii:

> Near whom the Amazon triumphant
> Bestrid her beast, and, on the rump on't,
> Sat face to tail and bum to bum,
> The warrior whilom overcome,
> Arm'd with a spindle and a distaff,
> Which, as he rode, she made him twist off:
> And when he loiter'd, o'er her shoulder
> Chastis'd the reformado soldier.

For another example see Hardy's *Mayor of Casterbridge*, ch. xxxix, where the *skimmity ride* causes the death of Lucetta Farfrae. *Cp*. RIDING; SHALLAL.

Skin. By the skin of one's teeth. Only just, by a mere hair's breadth. The phrase comes from the book of *Job* (xix, 20):

> My bone cleaveth to my skin, and to my flesh, and I am escaped with the skin of my teeth.

To get under one's skin. To irritate, to annoy. Probably an allusion to the activities of such larvæ as harvest-bugs, etc., which cause intense irritation "under the skin".

To have a thick skin. To be insensitive or indifferent to jibes, criticism or even insults; "to have a hide like a rhinoceros". Similarly **to have a thin skin** is

to be hypersensitive about such things.

To save one's skin. To get off with one's life.

To sell the skin before you have caught the bear. To count your chickens before they are hatched. SHAKESPEARE alludes to a similar practice:

> The man that once did sell the lion's skin
> While the beast lived, was killed with hunting him.
>
> *Henry V*, IV, iii.

To skin a flint. To be very exacting in making a bargain. The French say, *Tondre sur un œuf*. The Latin *lana caprina* (goat's wool) means something as worthless as the skin of a flint or fleece of an eggshell. Hence a **skinflint**, a pinchfarthing, a niggard.

Skin game. A swindling trick. Presumably from the sense of *skin* meaning to fleece or strip someone of their money by sharp practice or fraud. John Galsworthy has a play of this title (1920).

Skinhead. A young person, usually member of a gang, with hair very closely cropped or shaved off, making their appearance from the late 1960s. *Cp*. MODS AND ROCKERS; PUNK.

Skirt. A skirt, or **a piece of skirt** is English slang for a girl or young woman.

Skull. Skull and Crossbones. An emblem of mortality; specifically, the pirate's flag. The "crossbones" are two human thigh-bones laid across one another.

Sky. RHYMING SLANG for pocket, the missing word being *rocket*.

If tke sky falls we shall catch larks. A bantering reply to those who suggest some very improbable or wild scheme.

Lauded to the skies. Extravagantly praised; praised to the heights.

Out of a clear sky. Unexpectedly, without warning, "out of the blue".

Sky-pilot. A clergyman or padre. Originally a sailor's expression in use from late-Victorian days. The allusion is obvious.

Skyscraper. A very tall building, especially one in New York or some other American city. Some of them run to a hundred floors, and more. Also applied by sailors to a SKYSAIL.

To skylark about. To amuse oneself in a frolicsome way, jump around and be merry, indulge in mild horseplay. The phrase was originally nautical and referred to the sports of the boys among the rigging after work was done.

Slam. A term in card-playing denoting winning all the tricks in a deal. In bridge this is called *Grand slam*, and winning all but one, *Little or Small slam*. Cp. RUFF.

Slam. To slam the door (in someone's face). To refuse discussion; to dismiss abruptly; to put an end to the possibility of further negotiations.

Slang. As denoting language or jargon of a low or colloquial type the word first appeared in the 18th century; it is perhaps connected with *sling* (*cp. mud-slinging*, for hurling abuse). Slang is of various kinds, professional, sporting, schoolboy, nautical, thieves', etc., and usually has some element of humour about it. *See* BACK-SLANG; CANT; RHYMING SLANG.

A slanging match. A lengthy exchange of abuse and insulting language.

To slang a person. To abuse him, give him a piece of your mind.

Slap. Slap-bang. At once, without hesitation—done with a *slap* and a *bang*. The term was formerly applied to cheap eating-houses, where one *slapped* one's money down as the food was *banged* on the table.

> They lived in the same street, walked to town every morning at the same hour, dined at the same slap-bang every day.
> DICKENS: *Sketches by Boz*, iii, 36.

Slap-dash. In an off-hand manner, done hurriedly as with a *slap* and a *dash*. Rooms used to be decorated by *slapping* and *dashing* the walls so as to imitate paper, and at one time *slap-dash* walls were very common.

Slap-happy. Foolish and irresponsible, as one who is dazed, akin to PUNCH-DRUNK.

Slapstick. Literally the two or more laths bound together at one end with which HARLEQUINS, CLOWNS, etc., strike other performers with a resounding *slap* or *crack*; but more often applied to any broad comedy with knockabout action and horseplay.

Slap-up. First-rate, grand, stylish.

The more slap-up still have the two

shields painted on the panels with the coronet over.
THACKERAY: *The Newcomes*, xxxi.

Slate. On the slate. On the account, to be paid for later. From the custom of chalking up debts on a *slate* in shops and public houses.

To have a slate, or **tile loose.** *See under* TILE.

To slate one. To reprove, abuse, or criticize one savagely. It is not known how the term arose, but perhaps it is because at school the names of bad boys were chalked up on the *slate* as an exposure.

To start with a clean slate. To be given another chance, one's past misdeeds having been forgiven and expunged, as writing is sponged from a *slate*. **To wipe the slate clean** is a similar expression, meaning to cancel past debts or offences.

Slave. An example of the way words acquire changed meanings. The *Slavi* or *Slavs* were a tribe which once dwelt on the banks of the Dnieper; but as, in later days of the Roman Empire, many of them were spread over Europe as captives, the word acquired its present meaning.

The Slave Coast. The west coast of Africa around the Bight of Benin, between the River Volta and Mount Cameroon; for 350 years the chief source of African slaves.

The Slave States. A phrase current in the period before the American CIVIL WAR (1861–1865) and applied to the states where domestic slavery was practised, *i.e.* Delaware, Maryland, Virginia, North Carolina, South Carolina, Georgia, Florida, Alabama, Mississippi, Louisiana, Texas, Arkansas, Missouri, Kentucky, and Tennessee.

Chinese Slavery. *See* CHINESE.

Sledge-hammer. A sledge-hammer argument. A clincher; an argument which annihilates opposition at a blow. The sledge-hammer (O.E. *slecge*) is the largest hammer used by smiths, etc., and is wielded in both hands.

To use a sledge-hammer to crack a nut. *See under* NUT.

Sleep. To let sleeping dogs lie. *See under* DOG.

To put to sleep. Commonly used as a

EUPHEMISM for painlessly putting to death pet animals.

To sleep away. To pass away in sleep, to consume in sleeping; as "To sleep one's life away."

To sleep like a log, or **top.** To sleep very soundly, excellently, go the night through without waking or discomfort. When peg-tops are at the ACME of their gyration, they become so steady and quiet that they do not seem to move; in this state they are said to "sleep". Congreve plays on the two meanings:

> Hang him, no, he a dragon! If he be, 'tis a very peaceful one. I can ensure his anger dormant, or should he seem to rouse, 'tis but well lashing him and he will sleep like a top.
>
> *Old Bachelor*, I, v.

To sleep off. To get rid of by sleep, especially the after-effects of alcohol.

To sleep on a matter. To let a decision on it stand over until tomorrow.

The Sleeper. EPIMENIDES, the Greek poet, is said to have fallen asleep in a cave when a boy, and not to have waked for 57 years, when he found himself possessed of all wisdom.

In mediæval legend, stories of those who have gone to sleep and have been—or are to be—awakened after many years are very numerous. Such legends are associated with King ARTHUR, CHARLEMAGNE, and BARBAROSSA. *Cp.* also the stories of the SEVEN SLEEPERS of Ephesus, TANNHÄUSER, OGIER THE DANE, and RIP VAN WINKLE.

The Seven Sleepers. *See under* SEVEN.

The Sleeper Awakened. *See* SLY, CHRISTOPHER.

The Sleeping Beauty. This charming nursery tale comes from the French *La Belle au Bois Dormant*, by Charles Perrault (1628–1703) (*Contes de ma mère l'Oye*, 1697). The Princess is shut up by enchantment in a castle, where she sleeps a hundred years, during which time an impenetrable wood springs up around. Ultimately she is released by the kiss of a young prince, who marries her.

Sleeping partner. A partner in a business who takes no active share in running it beyond supplying capital; also called a *silent partner* in the U.S.A.

Sleeping sickness. A West African dis-

ease caused by a parasite, *Trypanosoma gambiense*, characterized by fever and great sleepiness, and often terminating fatally. The disease known in England, which shows similar symptoms, is usually called *Sleeping illness* or *Sleepy sickness* as a means of distinction; its scientific name is *Encephalitis lethargica*.

Sleepy. Said of pears and other fruits when they are beginning to rot.

Sleepy Hollow. Any village far removed from the active concerns of the outside world. From Washington Irving's story "The Legend of Sleepy Hollow" (*Sketch Book*), which deals with a quiet old-world village on the Hudson.

Sleepy sickness. *See* SLEEPING SICKNESS *above.*

Sleeve. To hang on one's sleeve. To listen devoutly to what one says; to surrender freedom of thought and action to the judgment of another.

To have up one's sleeve. To hold in reserve; to have ready to bring out in a case of emergency. The allusion is to conjurers, who frequently conceal in the sleeve the means by which they do the trick.

To laugh in, or **up one's sleeve.** To laugh inwardly; to hold in derision secretly. At one time it was quite possible to conceal amusement by hiding the face in the large loose sleeves then worn. The French say, *rire sous cape*.

To wear one's heart on one's sleeve. To expose all one's feelings to the eyes of the world; to be lacking in normal reserve.

> But I will wear my heart upon my sleeve
> For daws to peck at: I am not what I am.
> SHAKESPEARE: *Othello*, I, i.

Sleeveless. In the 16th and 17th centuries *sleeveless* was commonly used to signify fruitless, bootless, unprofitable, as *a sleeveless message, a sleeveless errand*, etc. The reason for this usage is uncertain.

Sleuth-hound. A blood-hound which follows the *sleuth* (Old Norse *sloth*, our more modern *slot*) or track of an animal. Hence used, especially in America, of a detective.

Slip. Many a slip 'twixt the cup and the lip. Everything is uncertain till you possess it. *Cp.* ANCÆUS.

To give one the slip. To steal off unperceived; to elude pursuit. Probably from the idea of a hound slipping its collar or from the slipping of an anchor when it is necessary to get away quickly from an uncomfortable berth. The normal practice in such circumstances is to buoy the cable before letting it slip through the hawse-pipe, so that anchor and cable are recoverable subsequently.

To let it slip through one's fingers. To fail to seize a chance at the favourable moment, as an unprepared fielder drops a catch in CRICKET.

To let slip. To tell unintentionally when off one's guard, as a hound might be let slip unintentionally in coursing.

To slip one over on. To deceive or hoodwink; to "put one over" on someone; to "pull a fast one" (*see under* FAST).

To slip the cable, To slip one's cable. *See under* CABLE.

To slip up. Metaphorically, to make a mistake, usually through an oversight.

Sloane Ranger. A young upper class person, living around Sloane Street, Holland Park and Kensington. The name was originated by Peter York, author of *Style Wear* (1982). *The Sloane Ranger Handbook* by Ann Barr and Peter York elaborated the theme.

Slogan (slō′gàn). The war-cry of the old Highland CLANS (Gael. *sluagh*, host; *ghairm*, outcry). Hence, any war-cry; and in later use, a political party cry, an advertising catchphrase, etc. *Cp.* SLUGHORN.

Slope. The slippery slope. The broad and easy way "that leadeth to destruction". *See* AVERNUS.

Slough of Despond. A period of, or fit of, great depression. In Bunyan's *Pilgrim's Progress*, Pt. I, it is a deep bog which Christian has to cross in order to get to the Wicket Gate. Help comes to his aid, but Neighbour Pliable turns back.

Slow. Slow-coach. A dawdler; also one who is mentally slow. A usage from the old coaching days.

Slow-worm. *See* MISNOMERS.

Slugabed. A late riser. To *slug* used to be quite good English for "to be thoroughly lazy".

Sly, Christopher. A keeper of bears and a tinker, son of a pedlar, and a sad drunken sot in the *Induction* of *The Taming of the Shrew.* SHAKESPEARE mentions him as a well-known character of Wincot, a hamlet near Stratford-on-Avon, and it is more than probable that in him we have an actual portrait of a contemporary.

Sly is found dead drunk by a lord, who commands his servants to put him to bed, and on his waking to attend upon him like a lord and bamboozle him into the belief that he is a great man; the play is performed for his delectation. The same trick was played by the Caliph HAROUN AL-RASCHID on ABOU HASSAN, the rich merchant, in *The Sleeper Awakened* (ARABIAN NIGHTS).

Sly. On the sly. In a sly, secretive manner.

You're a sly dog. You're a knowing one; you pretend to be discontented, but I can "read between the lines". (*See under* LINE).

Sly-boots. A cunning one, a WAG. A similar compound to *lazy-boots*, *clumsy-boots*, etc.

Smack. A slang term for heroin. *Cp.* GRASS.

Small. Small arms (Lat. *arma*, arms, fittings). Weapons fired from the hand or shoulder such as revolvers and rifles, also light portable machine-guns, etc.

Small-back. Death. So called because he is usually drawn as a skeleton.

Small beer. Properly, beer of only slight alcoholic strength; hence, trivialities, persons or things of small consequence.

Small clothes. Once a term for breeches, now for underclothes or "smalls".

Small coal. Coal in very small pieces, slack.

Small-endians. *See* BIG-ENDIANS.

Small fry. A humorous way of referring to a number of small children, from the numerous *fry* or young of fish and other creatures.

Small holding. A small plot of agricultural land bigger than an allotment, but not big enough to be called a farm.

The small hours. The hours from 1 a.m. to 4 or 5 a.m., when you are still in the *small*, or low numbers.

The small of the back. The slenderer, narrower part, just above the buttocks.

Small talk. Trifling conversation, social chit-chat.

To feel small. To feel humiliated, "taken down a PEG or two".

To sing small. To adopt a humble tone; to withdraw some sturdy assertion and apologize for having made it.

Smart Alec(k). An American term for a bumptious, conceited know-all. The name goes back to the 1860s, but no record now remains of Alec's identity.

Smart Money. Money paid by a person to obtain exemption from some disagreeable office or duty. It was applied to money paid by an army recruit to obtain release before being sworn in, and also to money paid to soldiers and sailors for wounds. In law it denotes heavy damages. It is something which makes the person "smart" (*i.e.* suffer), or which is received in payment for "smarting".

Smear. A smear campaign. A planned or organized attempt to tarnish someone's character or reputation.

Smectymnuus (smek tim' nū ús). The name under which was published (1641) an anti-episcopal tract in answer to Bishop Hall's *Humble Remonstrance*. The name was composed of the initials of its authors, *viz.* Stephen Marshall, Edward Calamy, Thomas Young, Matthew Newcomen, and William Spurstow.

Thomas Young was Milton's former tutor, and Milton seems to have had a part in it and wrote pamphlets in defence of the Smectymnuans.

> The handkerchief about the neck,
> Canonical cravat of Smec.
> BUTLER: *Hudibras*, I, iii, 1165.

Smell, To. Often used figuratively for to suspect, to discern intuitively, as in *I smell a rat, I smell treason*, etc.

SHAKESPEARE has, "Do you smell a fault?" (*King Lear*, I, i); and Iago says to Othello, "One may smell in such a will most rank" (III, iii). St. JEROME says that St. Hilarion had the gift of knowing what sins and vices anyone was inclined to by smelling either the person or his garments, and by the same faculty could discern good feelings and virtuous propensities.

It smells of the lamp. *See under* LAMP.

Smithfield. The smooth field (O.E. *smethe*, smooth), called in Latin *Campus Planus* and described by FitzStephen in the 12th century as a "plain field where every Friday there is a celebrated rendezvous of fine horses brought thither to be sold". It was originally outside the CITY wall and used for races, QUINTAIN-matches, TOURNAMENTS, etc., as well as a market. BARTHOLOMEW FAIR was held here until 1855, at which time the cattle market was transferred to the CALEDONIAN MARKET. Its less pleasant associations were the gibbet and the stake, and most of the Marian MARTYRS suffered death at Smithfield. It is now the central meat market of London.

The fires of Smithfield. An allusion to the burning of HERETICS at Smithfield during the Marian persecution of PROTESTANTS. Death at the stake was used at Smithfield as late as 1611.

Smoke, or **Big Smoke, The.** London. An old slang name of obvious origins. *Cp.* AULD REEKIE.

Smoke-farthings, smoke silver. An old church rate, the contribution of each house or hearth; also another name for PENTECOSTALS, the WHITSUNTIDE offering to the parish priest. Also called *smoke-money*, and *smoke-penny*, it appears in records as a contribution to the parochial purse as well as to the priest.

Much smoke, little fire. Said of one who makes a great fuss, commotion or protest but whose actions do not correspond.

No smoke without fire. Every slander or rumour has some foundation. The reverse proverb, **No fire without smoke,** means no good without some drawback.

Put that in your pipe and smoke it. *See under* PIPE.

To end in, or **up in smoke.** To come to no practical result; to come to nothing.

To smoke out. To drive someone out of hiding, literally or metaphorically.

To smoke the pipe of peace. *See* CALUMET.

To put up a smokescreen. To take steps to conceal one's basic motives from one's opponents or rivals, or from the public at large. The allusion is obvious.

Snag. To come against a snag. To encounter some obstacle in your progress.

Snake. RHYMING SLANG for a looking-glass, the missing portion being "in the grass".

It was an old idea that snakes in casting their sloughs annually gained new vigour and fresh strength; hence SHAKESPEARE's allusion:

> When the mind is quicken'd out of doubt,
> The organs, though defunct and dead before,
> Break up their drowsy grave, and newly move
> With casted slough and fresh legerity.
> *Henry V*, IV, i.

Another notion was that one could regain one's youth by feeding on snakes:

> You have eat a snake
> And are grown young, gamesome and rampant.
> BEAUMONT and FLETCHER:
> *Elder Brother*, IV, iv.

Snake stones. AMMONITES, from the old belief that these were coiled snakes petrified.

A snake in the grass. A hidden or hypocritical enemy, a disguised danger. The phrase is from VIRGIL (*Ecl.* iii, 93), *Latet anguis in herba*, a snake is lurking in the grass.

Great snakes! An exclamation of surprise.

To see snakes, to have snakes in one's boots, etc. To suffer from delirium tremens. This is one of the delusions common to those so afflicted.

Snake-eyes (U.S.A.). In throwing dice, a double one.

Snap. A snap vote. A vote taken unexpectedly, especially in PARLIAMENT. The result of a "snap vote" has, before now, been the overthrow of a ministry.

Not worth a snap of the fingers. Utterly worthless and negligible.

To snap a person's head off. Virtually the same as *To snap one's nose off. See* TO BITE ONE'S NOSE OFF *under* NOSE.

To snap one's fingers at. To brush aside contemptuously, to disregard authority.

To snap out of it. To shake off a fit of depression, to regain one's good humour, to pull oneself together, etc.

Snapdragon. The same as FLAPDRAGON; also a plant of the genus *Antirrhinum* with a flower opening like a dragon's mouth.

Snapshot. Formerly applied to a shot fired without taking aim, but now almost exclusively to an instantaneous photograph.

Snark. The imaginary animal invented by Lewis Carroll as the subject of his mock-heroic poem *The Hunting of the Snark* (1876). It was most elusive and gave endless trouble, and when eventually the hunters thought they had tracked it down, their quarry proved to be but a Boojum. The name (a "PORTMANTEAU WORD" of snake and shark) has sometimes been given to the quests of dreamers and visionaries.

It was one of Rossetti's delusions that in *The Hunting of the Snark* Lewis Carroll was caricaturing him.

Snarling Letter (Lat. *litera canina*). The letter *r, see* R.

Sneeze. St. GREGORY has been credited with originating the custom of saying "God bless you" after sneezing, the story being that he enjoined its use during a pestilence in which sneezing was a mortal symptom. ARISTOTLE, however, mentions a similar custom among the Greeks; and Thucydides tells us that sneezing was a crisis symptom of the great Athenian plague.

The Romans followed the same custom, their usual exclamation being *Absit omen!* The PARSEES hold that sneezing indicates that EVIL spirits are abroad, and we find similar beliefs in India, Africa, ancient and modern Persia, among the North American Indian tribes, etc.

We are told that when the Spaniards arrived in FLORIDA the Cacique sneezed, and all the court lifted up their hands and implored the sun to avert the evil omen. The nursery rhyme says:

> If you sneeze on Monday you sneeze for danger;
> Sneeze on Tuesday, kiss a stranger,

Sneeze on Wednesday, sneeze for a letter,
Sneeze on Thursday, something better,
Sneeze on Friday, sneeze for sorrow,
Sneeze on Saturday, see your sweetheart tomorrow.

It is not to be sneezed at. Not to be despised.

Snood. The lassie lost her silken snood. The snood was a ribbon with which a Scots lass braided her hair, and was the emblem of her maiden character. When she married, she changed the snood for the curch or coif; but if she lost the name of virgin before she obtained that of wife, she "lost her silken snood" and was not privileged to assume the curch.

In more recent times the word has been applied to the net in which women confine their hair.

Snooks. An exclamation of incredulity or derision.

To cock a snook. See under COCK.

Snottie. Naval slang for a midshipman; allegedly from their habit of wiping their noses on their sleeves; and it is said that the three buttons on the cuffs of their jackets were to prevent them doing this. New entries were called *warts* and the Lieutenant who overlooked the gunroom was known as the *snottie nurse*.

Snow. A slang term for cocaine, heroin or morphine.

Snow-line. The line above which a mountain is continually under snow.

Snuff. To be snuffed out. Put down, eclipsed, killed.

To snuff it is to die, the allusion being to the snuffing out of a candle.

'Tis strange the mind, that very fiery particle,
Should let itself be snuffed out by an article.
BYRON: *Don Juan*, xi, 60.

Up to snuff. Wide awake, knowing, sharp; not easily taken in or imposed upon. An allusion to the tobacco preparation.

So. So what? What of it? A colloquialism of American origin.

Soap, or **Soft soap.** Flattery, especially of an oily, unctuous kind.

How are you off for soap? A common street-saying of the mid-19th century, of indeterminate meaning. It may mean "What are you good for?" in the way of

cash, or anything else; and it was often just a general piece of cheek. *Cp.* "What! No soap?" in Foote's nonsense passage (*see* PANJANDRUM).

In soaped-pig fashion. Vague; a method of speaking or writing which always leaves a way of escape. The allusion is to the custom at FAIRS, etc., of soaping the tail of a pig before turning it out to be caught by the tail.

He is vague as may be; writing in what is called the "soaped-pig" fashion.
CARLYLE:
The Diamond Necklace, ch. iv (*Footnote*).

Soap-box oratory. Tub-thumping, demagogic utterance. From the use of a "soap-box" as a stand or platform. Soap was formerly packed in strong wooden boxes.

Soap-lock (U.S.A.). A lock of HAIR worn on the temple and kept in position with soap, a 19th-century fashion; any such lock of hair.

Soap opera. A somewhat disparaging term for a sentimental type of play, usually in episodic serial form, as used by commercial radio and television in advertising soap and other commodities.

Sob stuff. A phrase describing newspaper, film, or other stories of a highly sentimental kind; cheap or tear-jerking pathos.

Sob sister. A journalist who conducts an "answers to correspondents" column in a woman's magazine; one who writes tear-provoking sentimentalities.

Sobersides. A grave, steady-going, serious-minded person, called by some "a stick-in-the-mud"; usually **Old Sobersides.**

Socage (sok' aj). A free feudal non-military tenure, held in FEE SIMPLE (*see under* FEE), service being in the form of rent or some form of agricultural duty. It is from O.E. *soc*, jurisdiction, franchise.

Sociable. A horse-drawn carriage so named because its side seats faced each other; also a tricycle for two to ride side by side.

Social and Liberal Democrats. See GANG OF FOUR (2), LIBERAL.

Social Democratic Party. See GANG OF FOUR (2), LIBERAL.

Society. In the restricted sense, the world

of fashion, high society; the UPPER TEN (*see under* TEN).

Society of Friends. *See* QUAKERS.

Society verse. *See* VERS DE SOCIÉTÉ

Socinianism (so sin' yàn izm). A form of Unitarianism (*see* UNITARIANS) which, on the one hand, does not altogether deny the supernatural character of Christ, but, on the other, goes farther than Arianism (*see* ARIANS) which, while upholding His divinity denies that He is coequal with the Father. So called from the Italian theologians Laelius Socinus (1525–1562) and his nephew Faustus Socinus (1539–1604) who developed these tenets. Socinus is the latinized form of *Sozzini*.

Sock. The light shoe worn by the comic actors of Greece and ROME (Lat. *soccus*); hence applied to comedy itself.

> Then to the well-trod stage anon,
> If Jonson's learned sock be on.
>
> MILTON: *L'Allegro*.

The difference between the sock of comedy and the BUSKIN of tragedy was that the sock reached only to the ankle, but the buskin extended to the knee.

Put a sock in it. Be quiet, shut up, make less noise — a slang expression. In the late 19th century and earlier years of the 20th, when gramophones or phonographs amplified the sound through large horns, woollen socks were often stuffed in them to cut down the noise.

To pull one's socks up. *See under* PULL.

Socrates (sok' rà tēz). The great Greek philosopher of ATHENS (*c.* 470–399 B.C.). He used to call himself "the midwife of men's thoughts"; and out of his intellectual school sprang those of PLATO and the Dialectic system, Euclid and the MEGARIAN, Aristippus and the Cyrenaic, ANTISTHENES and the CYNIC, and the Elean and Eretrian schools. Phædo and Xenophon were also among his disciples. Cicero said of him, "he brought down philosophy from the heavens to earth"; and he was the first to teach that "the proper study of mankind is man". He was condemned to death for the corruption of youth by introducing new gods (thus being guilty of impiety) and drank hemlock in prison in the presence of his followers.

Socratic irony. Leading on your opponent in an argument by simulating ignorance, so that he "ties himself in knots" and eventually falls an easy prey—a form of procedure used with great effect by Socrates.

The Socratic method. The method of conducting an argument, imparting information, etc., by means of question and answer.

Sodom and Gomorrah. Figuratively, any town or towns regarded as exceptional centres of vice and immorality. An allusion to the cities which God destroyed (*see Gen.* xviii, xix).

Soft. A soft touch. One who is soft-hearted and easily imposed upon, especially one easy to "touch" for money.

Soft or **fair words butter no parsnips.** *See under* BUTTER.

Soho! An exclamation used by huntsmen, especially in hare-coursing when a hare has been started. It is a very old call dating from at least the 13th century, and corresponds to the "TALLY-HO!" of fox-hunters when the fox breaks cover. It was the pass-word used by Monmouth's forces in their ill-starred night attack at Sedgemoor in 1685. (*See* MONMOUTH'S REBELLION).

Soi-disant (swa dē' zon) (Fr.). Self-styled, would-be.

Soil. A son of the soil. One native to a district whose family has well-established local roots; one who works on the land.

To take soil. A hunting term, signifying that the quarry, usually a deer, has taken to the water. *Soil* here is Fr. *souille*, the mire in which a wild boar wallows.

Sol (Lat. *sol*, sun). The Roman SUN god; the sun itself. In Scandanivian mythology Sol was the maiden who drove the chariot of the sun.

The name was given by the alchemists to GOLD and in HERALDRY it represents *or* (gold). It is also the monetary unit of Peru. In music *sol* is the fifth note of the diatonic scale.

Sold down the river. *See* TO SELL DOWN THE RIVER *under* RIVER.

Soldier. An old soldier. An empty bottle.

Soldiers of fortune. Men who live by

their wits; *chevaliers d'industrie*. Referring to those men in mediæval times who let themselves for hire to any army.

To come the old(er) soldier over one. To dictate peremptorily and profess superiority of knowledge and experience; also to impose on one.

To soldier on. To keep going in spite of discouragements and difficulties; to plod on steadily like a good soldier.

Solecism (sō′ lĕ sizm). A deviation from correct idiom or grammar; from the Greek *soloikos*, speaking incorrectly, so named from Soloi, a town in Cilicia, the ATTIC colonists of which spoke a debased form of Greek.

The word is also applied to any impropriety or breach of good manners.

Solemn. The Solemn League and Covenant. An agreement between the English PARLIAMENT and the Scots in 1643 to strengthen their position in the struggle against CHARLES I. Presbyterianism was to be established in England and Ireland and the Scots undertook to provide an army in return for payment. Charles II swore to abide by the Covenant when he was crowned at SCONE in 1651, but after the RESTORATION it became a dead letter. *See* COVENANTERS.

Sol-fa. *See* TONIC SOL-FA.

Solicitor. *See* ATTORNEY.

Solicitor-General. The second law officer of the Crown and deputy of the ATTORNEY-GENERAL. He is a member of the HOUSE OF COMMONS and his period of office terminates with the fall of the ministry. It is customary to confer a knighthood on the holder of this office.

Solipsism (sō lip′ sizm) (Lat. *solus*, alone; *ipse*, self). Absolute egoism; the metaphysical theory that the only knowledge possible is that of oneself.

Solomon. King of Israel (d. *c*. 930 B.C.). He was specially noted for his wisdom, hence his name has been used for wise men generally.

The English Solomon. James I (1566, 1603–1625), who was a Scot, also called by Sully "the wisest fool in Christendom".

Solomon's Carpet. *See* CARPET.

Solomon's Ring. *See under* RING.

Solon. Athenian statesman and sage (*c*. 638–*c*. 558 B.C.), a great law giver and one of the Seven Sages of Greece (*see* WISE MEN).

Solstice (sol′ stis). The summer solstice is 21 JUNE; the winter solstice is 22 DECEMBER; so called because on or about these dates the sun reaches its extreme northern and southern points in the ECLIPTIC and appears to stand still (Lat. *sol*, sun; *sistit*, stands) before it turns back on its apparent course.

Soma (sō′ ma). An intoxicating drink anciently made, with mystic rites and incantations, from the juice of some Indian plant by the priests, and drunk by the BRAHMINS as well as offered as libations to their gods. It was fabled to have been brought from HEAVEN by a falcon, or by the daughters of the SUN; and it was itself personified as a god, and represented the MOON. The plant was probably a species of *Asclepias*.

To drink the Soma. To become immortal, or as a god.

Somerset House. The present building off the Strand, housing the Board of Inland Revenue, the Registrar-General (until 1974), and the Principal Probate Registry, was built (1776–1786) by Sir William Chambers. It occupies the site of the former princely mansion of Protector Somerset, brother of Jane Seymour and uncle of Edward VI.

Son. Son of God. Christ; one of the regenerate.

Son of a gun. *See under* GUN.

Sons of Liberty. American secret radical associations formed after the passing of the Stamp Act (1765) to resist British attempts at taxation. They had considerable influence in arousing revolutionary feeling.

Son of Man. In the GOSPELS, a title of Christ.

Every mother's son. All, without exception; every one of you.

Son et lumière (sô ā loo mē âr′) (Fr.). Sound and lights. Pageantry and dramatic spectacles presented after dark and, most advantageously, in an appropriate natural or historic setting. They are accompanied by, and dependent upon lighting effects, suitable music and narrative.

Song. A song or **an old song.** A mere trifle, something hardly worth reckoning, as "it went for a song", it was sold for practically nothing. It probably derives from the trifling cost of the old ballad sheets or the small change given to itinerant songsters outside inns and public houses.

The Songs of Degrees. Another name for the GRADUAL PSALMS.

The Song of Roland. *See under* ROLAND.

The Song of Songs. The *Song of Solomon* in the OLD TESTAMENT, also known as *Canticles*.

The Song of the Three Holy Children. An APOCRYPHAL book in the SEPTUAGINT and the VULGATE included as part of the *Book of Daniel*. It contains the prayer of Azarias and a narrative of the three Hebrews in the fiery furnace ending with the thanksgiving for their deliverance. The canticle known as the *Benedicite* is taken from this.

Don't make such a song about it! Be more reasonable in your complaints; don't make such a fuss about it.

What! all this for a song? The reputed comment of Lord Burghley, the Lord High Treasurer when he heard of Queen Elizabeth I's proposed bounty of £500 to Edmund Spenser, author of the *Faerie Queene*. The story is told by Edward Phillips in his *Theatrum Poetarum Anglicanorum* (1675), and he says that Burghley owed Spenser a grudge and had the grant cut to £100. An earlier account in Fuller's *Worthies of England* (1662) says that Elizabeth initially commanded the treasurer to give Spenser £100 but Burghley objected to the amount. So the Queen told him to give "what is reason". Payment was neglected so Spenser presented this petition to the Queen:

> I was promis'd on a time,
> To have reason for my rhyme;
> From that time unto this season,
> I receiv'd nor rhyme nor reason.

"Hereupon the queen gave strict order ... for the present payment of the hundred pounds the first intended unto him."

Sonnet. Dark Lady of the Sonnets. *See under* LADY.

Sooterkin. A kind of false birth fabled to be produced by Dutch women through sitting over their stoves; hence an abortive proposal or scheme, and, as applied to literature, an imperfect or a supplementary work.

Sop. A sop in the pan. A tit-bit, dainty morsel; a piece of bread soaked in the dripping of meat caught in the dripping pan; a bribe.

To give a sop to Cerberus. To give a bribe; to quiet a troublesome customer. CERBERUS is PLUTO's three-headed dog, stationed at the gates of the infernal regions. When persons died the Greeks and Romans used to put a cake in their hands as a sop to Cerberus to allow them to pass without molestation.

Soph. In American universities an abbreviation of *Sophomore*, a term applied to second-year students.

Sophia, Santa (sō fi' à). The great metropolitan cathedral of the ORTHODOX CHURCH at Istanbul. It was built by Justinian (532– 537), but since the capture of the city by the Turks (1453) has been used as a mosque and is now a museum. It was not dedicated to a saint named Sophia, but to the "Logos", or Second Person of the TRINITY, called *Hagia Sophia* (Sacred Wisdom).

Sophist, Sophistry, Sophism, Sophisticator, etc. These words have quite departed from their original meaning. The *seven sages* (*see* WISE MEN OF GREECE) were called *sophists* (wise men) and in the 5th and 4th centuries B.C. the term denoted those who made a profession of teaching the various branches of learning. PYTHAGORAS (*fl. c.* 540–*c.* 510 B.C.) out of modesty called himself a PHILOSOPHER (a wisdom-lover). A century later Protagoras of Abdera resumed the title and the sophists became hostile to the philosophers. Their hypercritical attitudes eventually led to sophistry falling into contempt, as the less able increasingly appeared as a set of quibblers. Hence *sophos* and its derivatives came to be applied to "wisdom falsely so called", and *philo-sophos* to the "modest search after truth". Current uses of *sophisticated* implying "worldly-wise", "disillusioned", "with the most technically up-to-date systems or devices", reveal a further drift in meaning of what is now a vogue word.

Sophy, The. An old title of the rulers of Persia, first given as an epithet to Sheik Junaid, whose grandson, Ismail I, founded the Safawid dynasty (1502–1736). It is derived from Arab. *Çafi-ud-din*, purity of religion. *See also* RULERS, TITLES OF.

Sorbonne. The usual name for the University of Paris, which derives from the ancient college of this name, the *Collegium Pauperum Magistrorum* founded by Robert de Sorbon *c.* 1257. He was confessor of St. LOUIS and the college was for the advanced study of theology. It was suppressed in 1792, but re-established by NAPOLEON in 1808 as a theological faculty which lasted until 1882.

Sorites (sò rī′ tēz). A "heaped-up" (Gr. *soros*, a heap) or cumulative SYLLOGISM, the predicate of one forming the subject of that which follows, the subject of the first being ultimately united with the predicate of the last. The following will serve as an example:

All men who believe shall be saved.

All who are saved must be free from sin.

All who are free from sin are innocent in the sight of God.

All who are innocent in the sight of God are meet for HEAVEN.

All who are meet for heaven will be admitted into heaven.

Therefore all who believe will be admitted into heaven.

The famous Sorites of Themistocles was:

That his infant son commanded the whole world, proved thus;

My infant son rules his mother.

His mother rules me.

I rule the Athenians.

The Athenians rule the Greeks.

The Greeks rule Europe.

And Europe rules the world.

Sorrow. The Seven Sorrows of the Virgin. *See* MARY.

Sort. Out of sorts. Not in good health and spirits. The French *être dérangé* explains the METAPHOR. If cards are out of sorts they are deranged, and if a person is out of sorts the health or spirits are out of order.

Sortes (sôr′ tēz) (Lat. *sors, sortis*, chance, lot). A species of DIVINATION performed by selecting passages from a book haphazard. VIRGIL's *Æneid* was anciently the favourite work for the purpose. (*Sortes Virgilianæ*), but the BIBLE (*Sortes Biblicæ*) has also been in common use.

The method is to open the book at random, and the passage you touch by chance with your finger is the oracular response. Severus consulted Virgil and read these words: "Forget not thou, O Roman, to rule the people with royal sway." Gordianus, who reigned only a few days, hit upon this verse: "Fate only showed him on this earth, and suffered him not to tarry"; and Dr. Wellwood gives an instance respecting CHARLES I and Lord Falkland. Falkland, to amuse the king, suggested this kind of AUGURY, and the king hit upon IV, 615–20, the gist of which is that "evil wars would break out, and the king lose his life". Falkland, to laugh the matter off, said he would show his Majesty how ridiculously the "lot" would foretell the next fate, and he lighted on XI, 152–81, the lament of Evander for the untimely death of his son Pallas. King Charles soon after mourned over his noble friend who was slain at Newbury (1643).

In Rabelais (III, x), PANURGE consults the *Sortes Virgilianæ et Homericæ* on the burning question, whether or not he should marry. In Cornelius Agrippa's *De Vanitate Scientiarum*, c. iv, there is a passage violently reprobating the *Sortes*.

Sothic Period, Year. The Sothic year was the fixed year of the ancient Egyptians, the CANICULAR year, determined from one heliacal rising of the DOG-STAR Sirius (*Sothis*) to the next. Since Sothis rose one day later every four years their CALENDAR did not accord with the solar year until after 1,460 (365 × 4) solar years when their first day of the year had worked through the seasons and come back into line. This was the Sothic or CANICULAR PERIOD.

Soul. The idea of the soul as the immaterial and immortal part of man surviving after death as a ghost or spirit was an ancient and widespread belief. The ancient

Egyptians represented it as a bird with a human head. With ARISTOTLE the soul is essentially the vital principle and the Neoplatonists held that it was located in the whole body and in every part. It has also been located in the blood, heart, brain, bowels, liver, kidneys, etc.

The MOSLEMS say that the souls of the faithful assume the forms of snow-white birds, and nestle under the throne of AL-LAH until the resurrection.

All Souls' Day. 2 November, the day following ALL SAINTS' Day, set apart by the ROMAN CATHOLIC CHURCH for a solemn service for the repose of the departed. In England it was formerly observed by ringing the soul bell (*see* PASSING-BELL *under* BELL), by making and distributing SOUL CAKES, blessing beans, etc.

Soul Cakes. Sweet cakes formerly distributed at the church door on ALL SOULS' DAY to the poor who went *a-souling, i.e.* begging for soul cakes. The words used were:

Soul, soul, for soul-cake,
Pray you, good mistress, a soul cake.

Soul-papers. Papers requesting prayers for the souls of the departed named thereon which were given away with SOUL CAKES.

Soup. In the soup. In a mess, in trouble.

Sour grapes. *See* GRAPES.

South Sea Bubble. The speculative mania associated with South Sea Company and other stock in 1720 which ended disastrously in the ruin of many. The South Sea Company, founded in 1711, was given the monopoly of trade with Spanish America in return for an undertaking to convert part of the NATIONAL DEBT to a lower rate of interest. In 1720 the company's monopoly was extended to the South Seas and at the same time it offered to take over the whole National Debt. This led to gross over-speculation and many other preposterous companies were floated. £100 shares of the company ran up to £890 and ultimately £1,000 with the inevitable consequences, and Ministers were involved. The South Sea Company continued its existence until 1856. *Cp.* MISSISSIPPI BUBBLE.

Southcottians. The followers of Joanna Southcott (1750–1814), one-time domestic servant at Exeter. Starting as a METHODIST, she became a prophetess and declared herself to be the "woman clothed with the sun, and the moon under her feet, and upon her head a crown of twelve stars" (*Rev*. xii, 1). At the age of 64 she announced that she was to be delivered of a son, the Shiloh of *Gen*. xlix, 10:

The sceptre shall not depart from Judah, nor a law-giver from between his feet, until Shiloh come; and unto him shall the gathering of the people be.

19 October 1814 was the date fixed for the birth, which did not take place, but the prophetess died in a trance soon afterwards and was buried in the churchyard of St. John's Wood Chapel. She left a locked wooden box usually known as **Joanna Southcott's Box** which was not to be opened until a time of national crisis, and then only in the presence of all the bishops in England. Attempts were made to persuade the episcopate to open it during the Crimean War and again in World War I. It was opened in 1927 in the presence of one reluctant prelate, and found to contain a few oddments and unimportant papers, and among them a lottery ticket. It is claimed by some that the box opened was not the authentic one. *Cp*. NUNAWADING MESSIAH.

Southpaw. In American usage, a left-handed baseball player, especially a pitcher; also meaning sometimes any left-handed person. In both American and British usage it describes a boxer who leads with his right hand.

Southwark. The ancient suburb on the south bank of the Thames annexed to the City of London in 1327 and once known as "The BOROUGH". It has a wealth of historical associations including the site of the TABARD INN of Chaucer's *Canterbury Tales*, the Globe Theatre on BANKSIDE, the CLINK, the MARSHALSEA, and PARIS GARDEN, as well as the church of St. Mary OVERIE, the George Inn, etc. Southwark possessed two MINTS and an annual fair (1550–1763), and it became an independent borough in 1899. As a DIOCESE, it was formed out of Rochester in 1905. The name means "Southern fort" and is of Saxon origin. *See* SOUTH BANK RELI-GION.

Sovereign. A strangely evolved word from Lat. *superanus*, supreme; the last syllable being assimilated to *reign*. The Fr. *souverain* is nearer the Latin; Ital. *sovrano*; Span. *soberano*.

The gold coin of this name valued at 20 shillings, first issued by Henry VII, was so called from its representation of the monarch enthroned and was replaced by the UNITE in the reign of James I. A smaller sovereign was issued from 1817 until 1917.

Sow (sou). **A pig of my own sow.** Said of that which is the result of one's own action.

A still sow. A cunning and selfish man; one wise in his own interest; one who avoids talking at meals that he may enjoy his food the better. So called from the old proverb, "The still sows eats the wash" or "draff".

To get the wrong sow by the ear. To capture the wrong individual, to take "the wrong end of the STICK", hit upon the wrong thing.

To send a sow to Minerva. To "teach your grandmother to suck eggs" (*see under* EGG), to instruct one more learned in the subject than oneself. From the old Latin proverb, *Sus Minervam docet* (a pig teaching MINERVA); Minerva being the goddess of wisdom.

You cannot make a silk purse out of a sow's ear. *See under* SILK.

Sow (sō). **Sow the wind and reap the whirlwind.** To provoke serious consequences through one's heedless actions.

Spade. The spade of playing-cards is so called from Span. *espada*, a sword, the suit in Spanish packs being marked with short swords; in French and British cards the mark—largely through similarity in name—has been altered to the shape of a pointed spade.

Spade guinea. An English gold coin, value 21s., minted 1787–1799, so called because it bears a shield shaped like the spade on playing-cards on the reverse. The legend is M.B.F. ET. H. REX. F.D. B. ET. L.D. S.R.I.A.T. ET. E.—Magnæ Britanniæ, Franciæ, et Hiberniæ Rex; Fidei Defensor; Brunsvicensis et Lunenburgensis Dux; Sacri Romani Imperii Archi Thesaurarius et Elector.

To call a spade a spade. To be outspoken, blunt, even to the point of rudeness; to call things by their proper names without any "beating about the bush" (*see under* BEAT).

Spagyric (spả jir' ik). Pertaining to ALCHEMY; the term seems to have been invented by PARACELSUS. Alchemy is "the spagyric art", and an alchemist a "spagyrist".

Spagyric food. CAGLIOSTRO's name for the ELIXIR of immortal youth.

Spain. Castles in Spain. *See* CASTLE.

Spanish fly. The cantharis, a coleopterous insect used in medicine. Cantharides are dried and used externally as a blister and internally as a stimulant to the genito-urinary organs; they were formerly considered to act as an aphrodisiac.

Spanish Inquisition. *See* INQUISITION.

The Spanish Main. Properly, the north-east coast of South America from the mouth of the Orinoco to the Isthmus of Panama; the mainland bordering the Caribbean Sea, called by the Spanish conquerors *Tierra Firme*. The term is often more loosely applied to the area of the Caribbean Sea and its islands.

To ride the Spanish mare. An old nautical punishment. The victim was put astride a boom with the stay slackened off when the ship was at sea. A hazardous position and of great discomfort.

To walk Spanish. To walk on tiptoe, being lifted and pushed by a more powerful person; to walk under compulsion; to walk GINGERLY. From the behaviour of pirates of the SPANISH MAIN towards captives. *Cp.* FROG MARCH.

Span New. *See* SPICK.

Spare the rod and spoil the child. *See under* ROD.

Sparker, or **Sparks.** A colloquial term for a ship's wireless operator; in the Royal Navy formerly called a Telegraphist, now called a Radio Operator. *Cp.* BUNTING-TOSSER.

Spartacists. An extreme Socialist group in Germany that flourished between 1916 and 1919. It was founded by Karl

Liebknecht who, with Rosa Luxemburg, led an attempted revolution in January of the latter year, in the suppression of which they were both killed. The movement was finally crushed by Ebert's government in the April. It took its name from the Thracian GLADIATOR, Spartacus, who in 73 B.C. led a slave rebellion against ROME, which was not suppressed until 71 B.C. During the uprising, he defeated five Roman armies and devastated whole tracts of Italy.

Spartan. The inhabitants of ancient Sparta, one of the leading city-states of Greece, were noted for their frugality, courage, and stern discipline; hence one who can bear pain unflinchingly is termed "a Spartan", a very frugal diet is "Spartan fare", etc. It was a Spartan mother, who, on handing her son the shield he was to carry into battle, said that he was to come back either with it or on it.

Spasmodic School, The. A name applied by W. E. Aytoun in 1854 to certain writers of the 19th century whose style was marked by sentimentality, forced conceits, and a certain lack of taste. Among them were P.J. Bailey, Sydney Dobell, Ernest Jones, Ebenezer Jones, and Alexander Smith.

Speak. It speaks for itself. There is no need for further explanation, evidence or discussion. It is sufficiently clear in itself.

Speak for yourself. Limit yourself to speaking about your own part in the matter or to expressing your own views. Don't involve or compromise other people.

To speak the same language. To understand each other perfectly, to hold the same views.

English as she is spoke. Used of ungrammatical or unidiomatic English. Andrew White Tuer (1838–1900) chose this as a title of a reprint of the English part of a book purporting to be a guide to conversation in English and Portuguese by Cavolino (first published at Paris, 1855). The gross distortions of English are said to have suggested the title.

Speak-easy. A place where alcoholic liquors are sold illegally. An American term widely current in the years of prohibition (1920–1934). *See* BOOTLEGGER; CAPONE.

Speaker. The title of the presiding officer and official spokesman of the British HOUSE OF COMMONS, the United States House of Representatives, and of some other legislative assemblies.

The Speaker of the House of Commons has autocratic power in the control of debates and internal arrangements of the House, etc.; he is elected by the members irrespective party, and ceases to be a "party man", having no vote—except in cases of a tie, when he can give a CASTING VOTE. He holds the office for the duration of that PARLIAMENT, but by custom (not law) is reappointed unless he wishes to resign (in which case he goes to the HOUSE OF LORDS).

The LORD CHANCELLOR (*see under* CHANCELLOR) is *ex officio* Speaker of the HOUSE OF LORDS.

To catch the Speaker's eye. The rule in the HOUSE OF COMMONS is that the member whose rising to address the House is first observed by the SPEAKER is allowed precedence.

Speaking. A speaking likeness. A very good and lifelike portrait; one that makes you imagine that the subject is just going to speak to you.

Properly speaking. Speaking in the strict and accurate meaning of the words: speaking without qualification.

Speaking Heads. Fables and romance tell of a variety of artificial heads that could speak: among the best known are:

The statue of MEMNON, in Egypt, which uttered musical sounds when the morning sun darted on it (*see* THEBES).

That of ORPHEUS, at Lesbos, which is said to have predicted the bloody death that terminated the expedition of Cyrus the Great into Scythia.

The head of MINOS, fabled to have been brought by ODIN to Scandinavia, and to have uttered responses.

The BRAZEN HEAD of Roger Bacon, and that of Gerbert, afterwards Pope Sylvester II (10th century).

An earthen head made by Albertus Magnus in the 13th century, which both spoke and moved. THOMAS AQUINAS broke it, whereupon the mechanist exclaimed: "There goes the labour of thirty years!"

Alexander's statue of ÆSCULAPIUS; it was supposed to speak, but Lucian says the sounds were uttered by a concealed man, and conveyed by tubes to the statue.

They are not on speaking terms. Said of those who have fallen out.

Spear. If a KNIGHT kept the point of a spear forward when he entered a strange land, it was a declaration of war; if he carried it on his shoulder with the point behind him, it was a token of friendship. In OSSIAN (*Temora*, I), Cairbar asks if FINGAL comes in peace, to which Morannal replies: "In peace he comes not, king of ERIN, I have seen his forward spear."

The spear of Achilles. *See* ACHILLES' SPEAR.

The spear side. The male line of descent, called by Anglo-Saxons *sperehealfe*. *Cp.* DISTAFF SIDE; SPINDLE SIDE.

To break a spear. To fight a TOURNAMENT.

To pass under the spear. To be sold by auction, sold "under the hammer". Writing to Pepys (12 August 1689), Evelyn speaks of "the noblest library that ever passed under the speare". The phrase is from the Lat. *sub hasta vendere*.

Special Pleading. Specious argument; making your own argument good by forcing certain words and phrases from their obvious and ordinary meaning. A pleading in law means a written statement of a cause PRO AND CON, and "special pleaders" are persons who have been called to the BAR, but do not speak as advocates. They advise on evidence, draw up affidavits, state the merits and demerits of a cause, and so on. After a time most special pleaders go to the bar and many get advanced to the BENCH.

Specie, Species, means literally "what is visible" (Lat. *species*, appearance). As things are distinguished by their visible forms, it has come to mean *kind* or *class*. As drugs and condiments at one time formed the most important articles of merchandise, they were called *species*—still retained in the French *épices*, and English *spices*. Again, as

banknotes represent money, money itself is called *specie*, the thing represented.

Spectre of the Brocken. An optical illusion, first observed on the Brocken (the highest peak of the Hartz range in Saxony), in which shadows of the spectators, greatly magnified, are projected on the mists about the summit of the mountain opposite. In one of De Quincey's opium-dreams, there is a powerful description of the Brocken spectre.

Speculum Humanæ Salvationis (The Mirror of Human Salvation). A similar book to the BIBLIA PAUPERUM on a somewhat more extensive scale, telling pictorially the BIBLE story from the fall of LUCIFER to the Redemption of Man, with explanations of each picture in Latin rhymes. Its illustrations were copied in church sculptures, wall paintings, altar-pieces and stained-glass windows. Copies of the 13th century and earlier are extant and it was one of the earliest of printed books (*c.* 1467). *See also* BLOCK BOOKS.

Speech. Speech Day. The annual prize-giving day at a school when it is customary to invite a guest to make a speech and to distribute the prizes. The Headmaster or Headmistress also makes a report on the school's record for the preceding year, and sundry other worthies manage to contribute (often lengthy) votes of thanks, etc.

The speech from the throne. *See* QUEEN'S OR KING'S SPEECH.

Speech is silver, or **silvern, silence is golden.** An old proverb, said to be of oriental origin, pointing to the advantage of keeping one's own counsel. The Hebrew equivalent is: "If a word be worth one shekel, silence is worth two."

Speech was given to man to disguise his thoughts. This epigram was attributed to Talleyrand by Barrère in his *Memoirs*; but though Talleyrand no doubt used it, he was not its originator. VOLTAIRE, in his XIVth Dialogue (*Le Chapon et la Poularde*), had said:

> Men use thought only as authority for their injustice, and employ speech only to conceal their thoughts.

and Goldsmith in *The Bee*, III (1759), has:

The true use of speech is not so much to express our wants as to conceal them.

Speenhamland System. The system of outdoor relief initiated by the magistrates of Speenhamland, Berkshire, in 1795 to counter distress among the agricultural labourers. Wages were to be supplemented by rate-aid according to a minimum-wage scale related to the price of bread and the size of the family. Outdoor relief was not new, but the Speenhamland System spread rapidly, particularly in the south. It tended to depress wages and demoralize its beneficiaries and sharply increased the poor rate. The Poor Law Amendment Act (1834) sought to terminate outdoor relief, but never wholly succeeded.

Speewah, The. A mythical cattle station somewhere in Australia where everything is bigger and better than anywhere else in the world. A series of legends comparable only with the adventures of Baron MÜNCHAUSEN are associated with it.

Spell. (O.E. *spel*, a saying, fable, etc.). Spells as charms and incantations are found the world over in folk-lore and superstition. They form part of the stock-in-trade of WITCHES, WIZARDS, magicians, sorcerers, GYPSY crones, etc., and many FAIRY stories revolve round their use.

The component words of the spells used by mediæval sorcerers were usually taken from Hebrew, Greek, and Latin, but mere gibberish was often employed. *Cp.* ABRACADABRA; ABRAXAS.

Spellbinders. Orators who hold their audience *spellbound*, that is fascinated, charmed. The word came into use in America in the presidential election of 1888.

Spencerian Handwriting is the name given to a style of calligraphy introduced by Platt Rogers Spencer (1800–1861), an American calligrapher. Written with a fine pen, with the down-strokes tapering from top to bottom and large loops, the writing has a forward slope and marked terminal flourishes. Spencer taught this style in many parts of U.S.A. and it is said to have had a marked influence on American calligraphy.

Spenserian Stanza. The stanza devised by Edmund Spenser for the *Faerie Queene* (1590). It may have been founded on the Italian *ottava rima*, or on Chaucer's stanza in the *Monk's Tale*. The Old French ballad has been suggested as another source. It is a stanza of nine IAMBIC lines, all of ten syllables except the last, which is an ALEXANDRINE. Only three different rhymes are admitted into a stanza and these are disposed: a b a b b c b c c.

Among those who used this stanza are Akenside (*Virtuoso*), Thomson (*Castle of Indolence*), Byron (*Childe Harold*), Shelley (*Adonais, The Revolt of Islam*), and Keats (*The Eve of St. Agnes*).

Spheres. In the PTOLEMAIC SYSTEM of astronomy the nine spheres were those carrying (1) DIANA or the MOON, (2) MERCURY, (3) VENUS, (4) APOLLO or the SUN, (5) MARS, (6) JUPITER, (7) SATURN, (8) the fixed stars—the Starry Sphere, and (9) the CRYSTALLINE SPHERE—introduced by Hipparchus, to account for the precession of the equinoxes. The PRIMUM MOBILE was added in the MIDDLE AGES.

The Music, or **Harmony of the Spheres.** PYTHAGORAS, having ascertained that the pitch of notes depends on the rapidity of vibrations, and also that the planets move at different rates of motion, concluded that the planets must make sounds in their motion according to their different rates; and that, as all things in nature are harmoniously made, the different sounds must harmonize; whence the old theory of the "harmony of the spheres". Kepler has a treatise on the subject.

> There's not the smallest orb which thou behold'st
> But in his motion like an angel sings,
> Still quiring to the young-eyed cherubims.
> SHAKESPEARE: *Merchant of Venice*, V, i.

Sphinx (sfingks). The sphinx of Greek mythology, quite distinct from the Egyptian sphinx, was a monster with the head and breasts of a woman, the body of a dog or LION, the wings of a bird, a SERPENT's tail, and lion's paws. It had a human voice and was said to be the daughter of Orthos and TYPHON (or the CHIMÆRA). She inhabited the vicinity of THEBES, setting the inhabitants riddles and devouring those unable to find solutions. The Thebans were told by the oracles that she would kill herself if the following riddle was solved:

> What goes on four feet, on two feet, and three,
> But the more feet it goes on the weaker it be?

It was at length solved by ŒDIPUS with the answer that it was a man, who as an infant crawls upon all fours, in manhood goes erect on two feet, and in old age supports his tottering legs with a staff. Thus were the Thebans delivered and this is the riddle of the sphinx.

The Egyptian sphinx was a lion, usually with a PHARAOH's head, symbolizing royal power and came to be associated with "HORUS in the Horizon" or Harmakhis. The famous Sphinx at Gizeh was hewn out of limestone rock by order of Khephren or Khafre (c. 2620 B.C.) and is some 60 ft. high and 180 ft. long.

Spice Islands. The Moluccas and most of the islands of the Malay Archipelago, whose chief products are spices of all kinds, much sought-after by 15th- and 16th-century navigators and traders when spices were highly prized commodities in Europe.

Spick and Span New. Quite and entirely new. A *spic* is a spike or nail, and a *span* is a chip. So that a spick and span new ship is one in which every nail and chip is new. The more common expression today is spick and span, meaning all neat, clean, bright, and tidy.

Spider. There are many old wives' tales about spiders, the most widespread being that they are venomous.

> Let thy spiders, that suck up thy venom,
> And heavy-gaited toads lie in their way.
> SHAKESPEARE: *Richard II*, III, ii.
> There may be in the cup
> A spider steep'd, and one may drink, depart,
> And yet partake no venom.
> SHAKESPEARE *The Winter's Tale*, II, i.

During the examination into the murder (1613) of Sir Thomas Overbury, one of the witnesses deposed "that the countess wished him to get the strongest poison that he could ...". Accordingly he brought seven great spiders. There

are few spiders poisonous to man, but the American Black Widow spider is a notable exception.

Other tales were that fever could be cured by wearing a spider in a nutshell round the neck, and a common cure for jaundice was to swallow a large live house-spider rolled up in butter. In IRELAND this was a remedy for ague. A spider on one's clothes was a sign of good luck or that money was coming and the very small spider is called a *money-spider*.

Yet another story was that spiders spin only on dark days.

> The subtle spider never spins,
> But on dark days, his slimy gins.
> S. BUTLER: *On a Nonconformist*, iv, 445.

Bruce and the spider. In 1306 Robert Bruce began a resistance to Edward I's domination of SCOTLAND and was crowned King at SCONE. The story is that, when in hiding in the island of Rathlin, he noticed a spider try six times to fix its web on a beam in the ceiling. "Now shall this spider (said Bruce) teach me what I am to do, for I also have failed six times." The spider made a seventh effort and succeeded. Bruce thereupon left the island (1307), with 300 followers, landed at Carrick, and at midnight surprised the English garrison in Turnberry Castle. His successes steadily grew until, in 1314, he routed the English at the great victory of Bannockburn.

Frederick the Great and the spider. While Frederick II was at SANS-SOUCI, he went into his ante-room to drink a cup of chocolate, but set his cup down to fetch a handkerchief. On his return he found a great spider had fallen from the ceiling into his cup. He called for fresh chocolate and the next moment heard the report of a pistol. The cook had been suborned to poison the chocolate and, supposing he had been found out, shot himself. On the ceiling of the room in Sans-Souci a spider has been painted (according to tradition) in remembrance of this event.

Mohammed and the spider. When MOHAMMED fled from MECCA he hid in a certain cave, with the Koreishites close upon him. Suddenly an acacia in full leaf sprang up at the mouth of the cave, a wood-pigeon had its nest in the branches, and a spider had WOVEN its net between the tree and the cave. When the Koreishites saw this, they felt persuaded that no one could have entered recently, and went on.

Spike. Slang for the workhouse; **to go on the spike,** to become a workhouse inmate. A *spike* is also a colloquialism for a high churchman, and the *Church Times* is colloquially known as *Spiky Bits.*

To spike a drink. To add strong spirits to increase the alcoholic content.

To spike one's guns for him. To render his plans abortive, frustrate the scheme he has been laying, "draw his teeth". The allusion is to the old way of making a gun useless by driving a spike into the touch-hole.

Spill. To spill the beans. To reveal a secret prematurely.

It's no good crying over spilt milk. *See under* CRY.

Spin a yarn, To. To tell a story. A nautical expression, from the days when sailors whiled away the time telling stories while sitting on the deck making spun yarn and other rope work.

Spindle side. The female line of descent. The spindle was the pin on which the thread was wound from the spinning-wheel. *Cp.* DISTAFF SIDE; SPEAR SIDE; SPINSTER.

Spinster. An unmarried woman. In Saxon times, spinning was a routine winter occupation of the female section of the household. ALFRED THE GREAT, in his will, calls the female part of his family the SPINDLE SIDE; and it was reckoned by our forefathers that no young woman was fit to be a wife till she had spun herself a set of body, table, and bed linen. Hence the maiden was termed a *spinner* or *spinster.*

It is said that the heraldic lozenge, in which the armorial bearings of a woman are depicted originally represented a spindle. Among the Romans the bride carried a DISTAFF, and HOMER tell us that Kryseis was to spin and share the king's bed.

Spirit. Properly, the breath of life, from

Lat. *spiritus* (*spirare*, to breathe, blow):

And the Lord God formed man of the dust of the ground, and breathed into his nostrils the breath of life; and man became a living soul.
Gen. ii, 7.

Hence, life or the life principle, the SOUL; a disembodied soul (a ghost or apparition), or an immaterial being that never was supposed to have had a body (sprite), as a GNOME, ELF, or FAIRY; also, the temper or disposition of mind as animated by the breath of life, as in *good spirits, high-spirited, a man of spirit.*

The mediæval physiological notion (adopted from Galen) was that spirit existed in the body in three kinds, *viz.* (1) the *Natural spirit,* the principle of the "natural functions"—growth, nutrition, and generation, said to be a vapour rising from the blood and having its seat in the liver; (2) the *Vital spirit,* which arose in the heart by a mixture of the air breathed in with the natural spirit and supplied the body with heat and life; and (3) the *Animal spirit,* which was responsible for the power of motion and sensation, and for the rational principle generally; this was a modification of the vital spirit, effected in the brain.

The **Elemental spirits** of PARACELSUS and the ROSICRUCIANS, *i.e.* those which presided over the four elements, were—the SALAMANDERS (or fire), GNOMES (earth), SYLPHS (air), and UNDINES (water).

Spirit also came to mean any volatile agent or essence; and hence, from the alchemists, is still used of solutions in alcohol and of any strong alcoholic liquor. The alchemists named four substances only as "spirits"—MERCURY, arsenic, sal ammoniac, and sulphur.

The first spirit quyksilver called is:
The second orpiment; the third y-wis
Sal armoniac; and the ferth bremstoon.
CHAUCER: *Canon's Yeoman's Tale,* 102.

Out of spirits. Depressed and despondent.

To spirit away. To kidnap, abduct; to make away with speedily and secretly. The phrase first came into use in the 17th century, in connexion with kidnapping youths and transporting them to the West Indian plantations.

Spiritualism. The belief that communication between the living and the spirits of the departed can and does take place, usually through the agency of a specially qualified person (a medium) and often by means of rapping, table-turning, or automatic writing; the system, doctrines, practice, etc., arising from this belief. *Cp.* OUIJA.

In philosophy, spiritualism—the antithesis of materialism—is the doctrine that the spirit exists as distinct from matter, or as the only reality.

Spit. The dead spit of his father, etc. The exact counterpart; the equivalent of SPIT AND IMAGE.

Spit and image, or **spitting image**. An exact likeness or resemblance—just as if one person were to spit out of another's mouth.

Spit and polish. To give something "a bit of spit and polish" is to clean it up, to make it shine, etc. To spit on leather, etc., and rub it to give it a shine was once common practice; an expression of army origin, the army being properly concerned with the maintenance of smartness of equipment. *See* BULL.

Spitting for luck. Spitting was a charm against enchantment among the ancient Greeks and Romans. Pliny says it averted WITCHCRAFT, and availed in giving an enemy a shrewder blow. People sometimes spit for luck on a piece of money given to them or found; boxers spit on their hands, and traders were wont to spit on the first money taken in the day. There are numerous other instances of spitting for luck and it was also common to spit for defiance or as a challenge, etc.

Spitting image. *See* SPIT AND IMAGE.

Spiv. A shady character who lives by his wits without working. A word used by race-course gangs since the 1890s. Probably an abbreviation of *spiffing*, an old slang word meaning "fine", "excellent"; an allusion to the flash, dandified appearance of the characteristic spiv.

Spleen. The soft vascular organ placed to the left of the stomach and acting on the blood, once believed to be the seat of melancholy and ill humour. The fern *spleenwort* was supposed to remove splenic disorders.

Splice. To marry, to join together. A phrase of nautical origin. *Splice* is probably derived from Ger. *spleissen*, to split, as ropes are split or unlayed prior to their being united or interwoven or "spliced".

To splice the main brace. *See* MAINBRACE.

Split. Colloquially, to give away one's accomplices, to betray secrets, to tell tales, to PEACH.

To split hairs. *See under* HAIR.

To split the infinitive. To interpose words between *to* and the verb, as, "to thoroughly understand the subject". This construction is branded as a SOLECISM by pedants and purists, but it is long established and has been used by many accomplished writers.

To split with laughter. To laugh uproariously or unrestrainedly; to "split one's sides".

Spoil. To spoil the Egyptians. To plunder one's enemies by force or trickery, as the Jewish women were instructed to do (*Exod.* iii, 22) before their departure from Egypt.

To spoil the ship for a ha'porth o' tar. *See under* SHIP.

Spoke. To put a spoke in one's wheel. To interfere with one's projects and frustrate them; to thwart one. When solid wheels were used, the driver was provided with a pin or spoke, which was thrust into one of the three holes made to receive it, to skid the cart when it went down-hill. "To put a sprag in one's wheel" is the same thing and has the same meaning.

Sponge. To sponge on someone. To live on someone like a parasite, sucking up all he has as a dry sponge will suck up water.

To throw up the sponge. Give up; confess oneself beaten. The METAPHOR is from boxing matches, for when a second tossed a sponge (used to refresh a contestant) into the air it was a sign that his man was beaten.

A sponger is a mean parasite who is always accepting the hospitality of those who will give it and never makes any adequate return.

A Sponging House. A house where persons arrested for debt were kept for 24 hours, before being sent to prison.

They were generally kept by a bailiff, and the person lodged was "sponged" of all his money before leaving.

Spoon. Love spoons. The giving of elaborately carved love spoons by a lover to his lady as a token during courtship was common in 18th-century Wales and later.

Born with a silver spoon in his mouth. *See under* BORN.

The Wooden Spoon. *See under* WOOD.

He needs a long spoon who sups with the Devil. You will want all your wits about you if you ally or associate yourself with EVIL. SHAKESPEARE alludes to this proverb in the *Comedy of Errors*, IV, iii, and again in *The Tempest*, II, ii, where Stephano says: "Mercy! mercy! this is a devil … I will leave him, I have no long spoon."

Spoonerism. A form of METATHESIS that consists of transposing the initial sounds of words so as to form some ludicrous combination, often the accidental result of mental tiredness or absent-mindedness; so called from the Rev. W. A. Spooner (1844–1930), Warden of New College, Oxford. Some of the best attributed to him are: "We all know what it is to have a half-warmed fish within us" (for "half-formed wish"); "Yes, indeed; the Lord is a shoving leopard"; and "Kinkering Kongs their titles take." Sometimes the term is applied to the accidental transposition of whole words, as when the tea-shop waitress was asked for "a glass bun and a bath of milk". *Cp.* MALAPROP.

Sport. To sport one's oak. *See under* OAK.

Sporting Seasons in England. The lawful season for venery, which began at Midsummer and lasted till HOLY ROOD DAY, used to be called the *Time of Grace*. The fox and wolf might be hunted from the NATIVITY to the ANNUNCIATION; the roebuck from EASTER to MICHAELMAS; the roe from Michaelmas to CANDLEMAS; the hare from Michaelmas to Midsummer; and the boar from the Nativity to the PURIFICATION.

The times for hunting and shooting are now fixed as follows: those marked thus (*) are fixed by Act of Parliament.

BLACK GAME*, from 20 August to 10 December; but in Somerset, Devon, and the New Forest, from 1 September to 10 December.

Deer, about 12 August to 12 October for stags and from 10 November to 31 March for hinds.

Fox-hunting, early November until April.

Grouse shooting*, 12 August to 10 December.

Otter hunting, mid-April to mid-September.

Partridge shooting*, 1 September to 1 February.

Pheasant shooting*, 1 October to 1 February.

There is no close season for the shooting of rabbits, hares, woodcock, snipe, quail, etc., but it is illegal for shops to sell hares between 1 March and 31 July.

There are special game laws for IRELAND and SCOTLAND and permitted seasons for the taking of trout, salmon, oysters, chub, carp, etc.

Spot. In a spot. In a jam or difficulty, up against it.

On the spot. Immediately, then and there, ready and alert; without having time to move away or do anything else. "He answered on the spot", immediately, without hesitation. **To put on the spot** (U.S.A.), to mark down for assassination; to give one a grilling; to put one in a very difficult position, or virtually inextricable situation.

To knock spots off someone. To excel someone completely in something; originally an Americanism.

Spot cash. Ready money, money down.

Spot check. A surprise check on the spot without notice being given; a random check to serve as a basis for conclusions on a wider basis.

Spot on. Exactly right, right on the mark.

Spouse, one who has promised (Lat. *sponsus*, past part. of *spondere*, to promise). In ancient ROME, the friends of the parties about to be married met at the house of the woman's father to settle the marriage contract. This contract was called *sponsalia* (espousal); the man, *sponsus*, and the woman, *sponsa*.

The spouse of Jesus. St. TERESA of Avila (1515–1582) was given this title by some of her contemporaries.

> All thy good works ... shall
> Weave a constellation
> Of Crowns with which the King thy
>   spouse
> Shall build up thy triumphant brows.
> CRASHAW: *Hymn to St. Theresa*
(1652).

Spout. To spout. To utter in a bombastic, declamatory manner; to declaim.

Up the spout. At the pawnbroker's or more usually nowadays "down the drain", gone, lost, ruined, etc. An allusion to the "spout" up which brokers sent the articles ticketed. When redeemed they returned down the spout—*i.e.* from the storeroom to the shop. It is also a vulgarism meaning "pregnant".

Sprag. To put a sprag in one's wheel. *See* SPOKE.

Sprat. To throw a sprat to catch a mackerel. To give a trifle, to make a concession, etc., in the hope of a bigger return.

Spread-eagle,   spread-eaglism, spread-eagled. *See under* EAGLE.

Spring. The season of young growth between WINTER and SUMMER. In the Northern hemisphere, March, April and May; astronomically from 21/22 March to 21/22 June.

> Sweet spring, full of sweet days and
>   roses,
> A box where sweets compacted lie.
> GEORGE HERBERT: *Virtue*.

Spring Tides. The tides that *spring* or rise up higher than other tides. They occur just after new and full MOON, when the gravitational attraction of both SUN and moon acts in a direct line. *Cp.* NEAP TIDES.

Sprite. *See* SPIRIT.

Spunging House. *See* SPONGING HOUSE.

Spur. On the spur of the moment. Instantly; without stopping to take thought.

Spur money. A small fine formerly imposed on those who entered a church wearing spurs, because of the interruption caused to divine service by their ringing. It was collected by the choir-boys or the BEADLES.

To dish up the spurs. In SCOTLAND, during the times of the BORDER feuds, when any of the great families had come to the end of their provisions, the lady of the house sent up a pair of spurs for the last course, to intimate that it was time to put spurs to the horses and make a raid upon ENGLAND for more cattle.

To ride whip, or **switch and spur.** To ride with all possible speed; to trample down obstacles ruthlessly.

To win his spurs. To gain the rank of knighthood; hence to win entitlement to recognition by one's efforts. When a man was knighted, the person who dubbed him presented him with a pair of gilt spurs.

Sputnik (Russ. travelling-companion). A Russian man-made earth satellite. Sputnik 1, launched 4 October 1957, was the first satellite to be projected successfully into orbit round the earth.

Spy Wednesday. A name given in IRELAND to the Wednesday before GOOD FRIDAY, when JUDAS bargained to become the spy of the Jewish SANHEDRIN (*Matt*. xxvi, 3–5, 14–16).

Squalls. Look out for squalls. Expect to meet with difficulties. A nautical term, a squall being a succession of sudden violent gusts of wind (Icel. *skvata*).

Square, A. In modern slang, one who likes orthodox music and not JAZZ and its derivatives; one of "bourgeois" tastes; one who is not in with current trends, fashions, and hence old-fashioned. There are several suggestions for the origin of these usages none of which is particularly convincing, the most likely being associated with the patrons of the traditional square dance as opposed to the devotees of rocking and rolling, jiving and twisting, etc.

A square deal. A fair deal, one that is straight and above board. Similarly **a square meal** is one that is adequate and satisfying. In both these expressions "square" conveys the idea of "straight", "right", and hence "satisfying".

To square an account. To settle it; to pay the amount owing.

To square accounts with a person. To get even with; to be revenged upon.

To square the circle. To attempt an impossibility. The allusion is to the impossibility of exactly determining the precise ratio (π) between the diameter and the circumference of a circle, and thus constructing a circle of the same area as a given square. Approximately π

is 3·14159, but the next decimals would be 26537, and the numbers would go on *ad infinitum*.

To square a person. To bribe him, or to pay him for some extra trouble he has taken.

To square up to a person. To put oneself in a fighting attitude.

Square-bashing. A slang expression used by the armed services for parade-ground drill.

Square rig. *See* FORE AND AFT.

Squarson. A 19th-century usage for a clergyman who was both squire and parson of the parish. The Revd. Sabine Baring-Gould (1834–1924), Vicar of Lew Trenchard, Devon, was a classic example of this combination. He was also a novelist, investigator of prehistoric sites, collector of West-country songs and author of the hymn *Onward Christian Soldiers*. *Cp.* JACK RUSSELL.

Squib. A damp squib. Said of an enterprise or joke, etc., that fails to come off or satisfy the expectations aroused, just as a damp squib disappointingly fails to explode.

Squinancy. *See* QUINSY.

Squire. In mediæval times a youth of gentle birth attendant on a KNIGHT (*see* ESQUIRE). From the later 16th century the term is applied to country landowners who exercised sway, mostly paternal, over a district. The squirearchy as such has largely been extinguished by the rise of a more democratic urbanized society on the one hand and rapacious taxation on the other. Addison's benevolent Sir ROGER DE COVERLEY, Fielding's Squire Western in *Tom Jones* and Squire Jawleyford, the creation of Surtees, himself a Northumbrian squire, provide lively portraits of varying traditions.

Stabat Mater (sta′ băt ma′ ter) (Lat., The Mother was standing). The Latin hymn reciting the SEVEN SORROWS of the Virgin at the CROSS, so called from its opening words, forming part of the service during Passion week in the ROMAN CATHOLIC CHURCH. It is of unknown authorship and in addition to its traditional plainsong there are settings by Palestrina, Pergolesi, Haydn, Rossini, and others.

Stable. To lock the stable door, etc. *See* *under* HORSE.

Stadium. This word is from Gr. *stadion*, a length of 600 Greek feet (about 606 English feet), which was the length of the foot-race course at OLYMPIA; hence applied to the race, then the place where it was run. The Olympic stadium had terraced seats along its length and the length of the course was traditionally said to have been fixed by HERCULES.

Staff. I keep the staff in my own hand. I keep possession; I retain the right. The staff was the ancient SCEPTRE, and therefore, figuratively, it means power, authority, dignity, etc.

> Give up your staff, sir, and the king his realm.
> SHAKESPEARE: *Henry VI, Pt. II*, ii, iii.

The staff of life. Bread, which is the support of life.

> "Bread," says he, "dear brothers, is the staff of life."
> SWIFT: *Tale of a Tub*, iv.

To put down one's staff in a place. To abide for a while, to set down one's staff, as a traveller at an inn. The phrase introduced by Thomas Adams (*fl.* 1612–1653), a divine, called by Southey "the prose SHAKESPEARE of PURITAN theologians".

To strike staff. To lodge for the time being.

Stag. A male deer or hart.

The Stag in Christian art. The attribute of St. JULIAN Hospitaller, St. Felix of Valois, and St. Aidan. When it has a crucifix between its horns it alludes to the legend of St. HUBERT. When luminous it belongs to St. Eustachius.

Stag party. A gathering of men only—usually out on the spree, and especially on the eve of a wedding.

Stags, in Stock Exchange phraseology, are persons who apply for an allotment of new shares, not because they wish to hold the shares, but because they hope to sell the allotment at a premium.

Stage whispers. A "whisper" intended to be heard by other than those to whom it is addressed, as one on the stage is heard by the audience.

Stagirite, or **Stagyrite, The** (stăj′ i rīt). ARISTOTLE, who was born at Stagira, in Macedon (4th century B.C.).

> And rules as strict his laboured work

975

confine
As if the Stagirite o'erlooked each line.
POPE: *Essay on Criticism*, I. 137.

Stairs. Below stairs. In the basement among the servants. In most of the town houses built from the end of the 18th century for the well-to-do, the kitchens and servants' day-time quarters were in the basement, hence the phrase. **Above stairs** has the opposite implications and associations. *Cp.* UPSTAIRS.

Stakhanovism (stăk ăn' ō vizm). In the U.S.S.R., a movement for specially raising the output of labour on a basis of specialized efficiency, after Alexei Stakhanov, a Donetz coal-miner who substantially increased his daily output by rationalization. In 1935 Stalin held a conference of Stakhanovites in which he extolled the working-man.

Stalemate. To stalemate a person. To bring him to a standstill, render his projects worthless or abortive. The phrase is from CHESS, *stalemate* being the position in which the king is the only moveable piece and he, though not in CHECK, cannot move without becoming so. *Stale* in this word is probably from O.Fr. *estal* (our *stall*), a fixed position.

Stalingrad. Formerly Tsaritsyn, on the Volga, renamed to commemorate its defence by Stalin, in 1917, against the WHITE RUSSIANS. Stalin died in 1953 and in 1962 the name was changed to Volgograd. In 1943 it was the scene of the decisive defeat of the German VI Army.

Stalking-horse. A mask to conceal some design; a person put forward to mislead; a sham. Sportsmen often used to conceal themselves behind horses, and go on stalking step by step till they got within shot of the game.

> He uses his folly like a stalking-horse, and under the presentation of that he shoots his wit.
> SHAKESPEARE: *As You Like It*, V, iv.

Stand. To let a thing stand over. To defer consideration of it to a more favourable opportunity.

To stand by. To be ready to give assistance in case of need. A *stand-by* is a person or thing on which one can confidently rely.

To stand for a child. To be sponsor

for it; to stand in its place and answer for it.

To stand it out. Persist in what one says. A translation of "persist" (Lat. *per-sisto* or *per-sto*).

To stand Sam, stand to reason, stand treat, etc. *See these words*.

To stand to one's guns. To persist in a statement; not to give way. A military phrase.

To stand up for. To support, to uphold.

To stand up for one's privilege, or on **punctilios.** Quietly to insist on one's position, etc., being recognized; this is the Latin *insisto*.

A stand-in. A substitute.

Stand-offish. Unsociable, rather snobbishly reserved.

Standing orders. Rules or instructions constantly in force, as those of a commanding officer or those rules of the Houses of PARLIAMENT for the conduct of proceedings which stand in force till they are rescinded or superseded. The suspension of the latter is generally caused by a desire to hurry through a BILL with unusual expedition.

The Standing Fishes Bible. *See* BIBLE, SOME SPECIALLY NAMED EDITIONS.

Standard. Properly a large flag tapering towards the fly, slit at the end and flown by personages of rank. It bore the owner's badges and its length depended upon the owner's rank.

The personal *Royal Standard* of the British Sovereign is a banner in shape and quarterings. The word is from Lat. *extendere*, to stretch out, through O.Fr. *estandard*. *See* THE BATTLE OF THE STANDARD, *below*.

The Battle of the Standard. Between the English and Scots at Cowton Moor, near Northallerton (22 August 1138). Here David I, fighting on behalf of Matilda, was defeated by King Stephen's army under Thurstan, Archbishop of York, and Raoul, Bishop of Durham. It received its name from the mast (erected on a wagon) carrying the banners of St. PETER of York, St. JOHN OF BEVERLEY, and St. WILFRED of Ripon, surmounted by a PYX containing the HOST. It was this occasion which introduced the word *standard* into the English language.

Gold Standard. *See under* GOLD.

The standard of living. A conventional term to express the supposed degree of comfort or luxury usually enjoyed by a man, a family, or a nation: this may be high or low according to circumstances.

Standard Time, or **Zone Time.** A system of time-keeping in most parts of the world based on 24 meridians, each 15° apart, starting from Greenwich, thus giving an exact difference of an hour between any two adjacent zones (certain countries have adopted zones involving half-hour differences). Such a system was first adopted by the chief railway companies of Canada and the U.S.A. in 1883 to overcome the obvious inconveniences causd by the differing local times on their routes. *Cp.* DAYLIGHT SAVING; GREENWICH TIME.

Stang. To ride the stang. At one time in SCOTLAND and the north of ENGLAND a man who ill-treated his wife (or sometimes a HEN-PECKED husband) was made to sit on a *stang* (O.E. *staeng*, a pole) hoisted on men's shoulders. On this uneasy conveyance the "stanger" was carried in procession amidst the hootings and jeerings of his neighbours. *Cp.* RANDAN; RIDING; ROUGH MUSIC; SHALLAL; SKIMMINGTON.

Stannaries, The. The tin-mining areas of Devon and Cornwall (Lat. *stannum*, tin), an appanage of the Crown, and after 1337 of the Duchy of Cornwall. There were four in Cornwall and four in Devon (covering Dartmoor and surrounding areas). A warden was appointed in 1198 and in 1201 King John issued their first charter confirming the tinners' privileges and making the Warden the only magistrate to have jurisdiction over them. The tinners had their own representative meetings or "parliaments" as late as 1752 and were subject to special *Stannary Courts* which were not finally abolished until 1897. The courts, under the Lord Warden, vice-warden, and stewards were also concerned with regulation of the trade. The miners were anciently called *stannators*; their privileges arose from the king's aim to increase tin production.

Star. In ecclesiastical art a number of SAINTS are depicted with a star; thus, St. Bruno bears one on his breast, St. DOMINIC, St. Humbert, St. Peter of Alcantara, one over the head, or on the forehead, etc. *See also* BLAZE.

A star of some form constitutes part of the insignia of every order of Knighthood; the *Star and Garter*, a common PUBLIC-HOUSE SIGN, being in reference to the Most Noble Order of the GARTER.

Star is also figuratively applied to a noted performer, especially a film actor; hence the **star part,** the part taken by the leading actor; who is the **star turn.**

The stars were said by the old astrologers to have almost omnipotent influence on the lives and destinies of man (*cp. Judges* v, 20: "The stars in their courses fought against Sisera"), and to this belief is due a number of phrases as: **Bless my stars! You may thank your lucky stars; star-crossed** (not favoured by the stars, unfortunate); **to be born under an unlucky star,** etc.

Star Chamber. A court of mediæval origin, composed of the King's Council, reinforced by judges, which developed criminal jurisdiction. So named from its meeting place, the Star Chamber in the Palace of WESTMINSTER, the ceiling or roof of which was decorated with stars. The reputation it acquired for harshness was largely unjustified and it was frequently attacked by the Common Lawyers who resented its jurisdiction. It was abolished by the LONG PARLIAMENT in 1641.

Star of David, or **Shield of David.** A symbol of obscure origin (also called SOLOMON'S SEAL) made up of two superimposed equilateral triangles thus: ✡. It was adopted by the first Zionist Conference in 1897 and is the symbol on the flag of Israel. It is found as early as the 3rd century but is not mentioned in the BIBLE or the TALMUD. Jews were made to wear such a cloth star under the NAZI régime and, to show his disapproval of this racial indignity, King Christian X of Denmark wore a Star of David during the German occupation of his country.

Star of India. A British order of knighthood, The Most Exalted Order of the Star of India, instituted by Queen

Victoria in 1861. Its motto is "Heaven's Light our Guide" and it was a means of recognizing services to India and the loyalty of its princely rulers. No appointments have been made since 1947 and it is now obsolescent.

Star of South Africa. A pear-shaped DIAMOND discovered near the Orange River in 1869, also called the *Dudley diamond* after the Earl of Dudley, its first purchaser. It weighs 47.7 carats but was 85.75 carats when uncut.

Stars and Bars. The flag of the 11 CONFEDERATE STATES of America which broke away from the UNION in 1861. It consisted of two horizontal red bars with a narrow white bar between them; in the top left corner a blue union bearing eleven white stars arranged in a circle.

Stars and Stripes, or **the Star-spangled Banner.** The flag of the United States of America. The *stripes* are emblematic of the original 13 states, and the *stars*—of which there are 50—of the States that now constitute the UNION. It is also popularly called *Old Glory*, a name said to have been given by William Driver, a Salem skipper, in 1831.

At the outset of the American Revolution each state adopted its own flag, that of Massachusetts bearing a pine tree and that of South Carolina a rattlesnake with the words "Don't tread on me". In 1776 a national flag of 13 red and white stripes with crosses of St. GEORGE and St. ANDREW in a canton was adopted.

By act of Congress, 14 June 1777, a flag of 13 alternate red and white stripes, with a union of 13 white stars on a blue field was adopted, the stars arranged in a circle representing "a new constellation". It was apparently designed by Francis Hopkinson and the story that it was first embroidered by Betsy Ross is now discredited.

In 1794 (after the admission of Vermont and Kentucky), the stripes and stars were increased to 15, but in 1818 it was decided that the original 13 stripes should be restored, and stars added to signify the number of States in the Union. The stars were also squared up for the first time.

The *Stars and Stripes forever* is the name of Sousa's most popular military band tune, and the *Star-Spangled Banner* was adopted as the official anthem of the United States in 1931. The words were written by Francis Scott Key in 1814, the tune being that of 'ANACREON in Heaven", a popular drinking song composed by J. S. Smith for the Anacreontic Society of London.

His star is in the ascendant. He is in luck's way; said of a person to whom some good fortune has fallen and who is very prosperous. According to ASTROLOGY, those leading stars which are above the horizon at a person's birth influence his life and fortune; when those stars are in the ASCENDANT, he is strong, healthy, and lucky; but when they are in the descendant below the horizon, his stars do not shine on him, he is in the shade and subject to ill fortune. *Cp.* HOUSES, ASTROLOGICAL.

I'll make you see stars! "I'll put you through it"; literally, will give you such a blow in the eye with my fist that, when you are struck, you'll experience the optical illusion of seeing brilliant streaks, radiating and darting in all directions.

Star-gazy, of **Starry-gazy pie.** An old Cornish dish of pilchards baked in a pie with their heads poking through the crust.

Starboard and Larboard. *Star-* is the O.E. *steor*, paddle, rudder, and *bord*, side. Larboard is perhaps from *lade-bord*, the lading side. *See* PORT.

Stare. To stare like a stuck pig. *See under* PIG.

States. States General. In France, the national consultative assembly (*États Généraux*), of 14th-century origin, but not summoned between 1614 and 1789. It consisted of three estates, Clergy, Nobility and Third Estate (*le tiers état*) or commoners (the vast majority of deputies being from the bourgeoisie when the Revolution began in 1789).

The name is still applied to the PARLIAMENT of the Netherlands consisting of two chambers, the upper elected by members of the Provincial States and the second chamber elected by the people.

Station. The Stations of the Cross; known as the *via Calvaria* or *via Cru-*

cis. Each station represents, by fresco, picture, or otherwise, some incident in the passage of Christ from the judgment hall to CALVARY, and at each one prayers are offered up in memory of the event represented. They are as follows:

(1) The condemnation to death.
(2) Christ is made to bear His CROSS.
(3) His first fall under the cross.
(4) The meeting with the Virgin.
(5) Simon the Cyrenean helps to carry the cross.
(6) Veronica wipes the sacred face.
(7) The second fall.
(8) Christ speaks to the daughters of Jerusalem.
(9) The third fall.
(10) Christ is stripped of His garments.
(11) The nailing to the cross.
(12) The giving up of the Spirit.
(13) Christ is taken down from the cross.
(14) The deposition in the sepulchre.

Stator (stā′ tôr) (Lat., the stopper or arrester). When the Romans fled from the SABINES, they stopped at a certain place and made terms with the victors. On this spot they afterwards built a temple to JUPITER, and called it the temple of Jupiter Stator, or Jupiter who caused them to stop in their flight.

Status quo (stā′ tŭs kwō) (Lat.). The state in which, the existing state or condition.

Status quo ante (Lat.). The previous position.

In statu quo (Lat.). In the same state (as before).

Status symbol. A possession, privilege, etc., which is a mark of one's social standing; generally used caustically of a fashionable, expensive, material object, the possession of which is designed to impress others and to flatter one's own self-esteem. *Cp.* KEEPING UP WITH THE JONESES *under* KEEP.

Statute. On the statute book. Included among the laws of the nation; the *statute book* is the whole body of the laws.

Steal. To steal a march on one. To obtain an advantage by stealth, as when an army appears unexpectedly before an enemy.

To steal the show. To win the greatest applause or acclamation; to surpass or outshine all other performers or players. An expression at first limited to performers in stage shows.

Stolen sweets are always sweeter. Things procured by stealth, and game illicitly taken, have the charm of illegality to make them the more palatable. SOLOMON says, "Stolen waters are sweet, and bread eaten in secret is pleasant" (*Prov.* ix, 17).

Steam. To let off steam. To give vent to anger; to work off one's feelings; to work off energy; as steam pressure is released from an engine or boiler.

Steelboys. Bands of ULSTER insurgents who committed agrarian outrages in protest against the TITHE system in the early 1770s. Probably named from their "hearts of steel". *Cp.* OAK BOYS; WHITEBOYS.

Steenie. A nickname given by James I to his handsome favourite, George Villiers, Duke of Buckingham, with whom he was infatuated. "Steenie" is a Scotticism for STEPHEN, the allusion being to *Acts* vi, 15, where those who looked on Stephen the martyr "saw his face as it had been the face of an angel".

Steeplechase. Originally a horse race across fields, hedges, ditches and other obstacles, now run over a prepared course. The term is said to have originated from the frolic of a party of fox-hunters in IRELAND (1803) who decided to race in a straight line to a distant steeple. The term is also applied to a cross-country race of this kind on foot. *See* RACES.

Steeple house. An old PURITAN epithet for a church.

Steering committee. A committee which decides the programme and order of business. A term of American origin.

Stentor (sten′ tôr). **The Voice of a Stentor.** A very loud voice. Stentor was a Greek herald in the Trojan war. According to HOMER (*Iliad*, V, 783), his voice was as loud as that of 50 men combined; hence *stentorian*, loud-voiced.

Stephen, St. (d. *c*. 35). The first Christian martyr—the "protomartyr". He was accused of blasphemy and stoned to death (*see Acts* vi–viii). He is commemorated on 26 December; the name means "wreath" or "crown" (Gr. *stephanos*).

The Crown of St. Stephen. The crown of Hungary, this St. Stephen being the first King of Hungary (975, 998–1038). He became a Christian in 985 and set out to convert his country. He was canonized in 1083 and his day is 16 August. The existing crown is probably of 13th-century origin. It was removed to the U.S.A. in 1944.

St. Stephen's. PARLIAMENT is still sometimes so called, because for nearly 300 years prior to its destruction by fire in 1834, the Commons used to sit in the Chapel of St. Stephen in the Palace of WESTMINSTER. *See* BIG BEN.

St. Stephen's loaves. Stones.

Fed with St. Stephen's bread. Stoned.

Sterling. A term applied to British money and also to GOLD and SILVER plate denoting that they are of standard value or purity; hence applied figuratively to anything of sound intrinsic worth, as *A man of sterling qualities*. The word, first met with in the 12th century, has been held to be a corruption of *Easterling*, a name given to the HANSE merchants trading with England; but it is probably from O.E. *steorling*, a coin with a star, from the fact that some of the early Norman pennies had a small star on them.

Sternold and Hopkins. The old metrical version of the Psalms that used to be bound up with the BOOK OF COMMON PRAYER and sung in churches. They were mainly the work of Thomas Sternhold (d. 1549) and John Hopkins (d. 1570). The completed version appeared in 1562.

> Mistaken choirs refuse the solemn strain
> Of ancient Sternhold.
> CRABBE: *The Borough*, III, 1. 130.

Stetson. A large-brimmed hat habitually worn by cattle-men in the U.S.A., so called from the best-known manufacturer, John B. Stetson.

Stevenographs. Coloured silk pictures woven on a special Jacquard loom, first made in 1879 by Thomas Stevens, a Coventry silk weaver. Some 180 designs were produced on popular subjects including Dick TURPIN on Black Bess, and the London-York stagecoach. The factory was destroyed by bombing in 1940.

Stew. In a stew. In a fix, a flurry; in a state of mental agitation.

Irish stew. A stew of mutton, onions, and potatoes; called "Irish" from the predominance of potatoes, regarded as the Irishman's staple diet.

To stew in one's own juice. To suffer the natural consequences of one's own actions; to reap as one has sown. Chaucer has:

> In his own gress I mad him frie
> For anger and for very jalousie.
> *Wife of Bath's Tale (Prologue)*, 1. 487.

Stick. An old stick-in-the-mud. A dull, unprogressive person, sometimes but not always "old". *Cp.* SQUARE.

It sticks out a mile! It is absolutely obvious, one cannot miss it, there is no mistake about it, as, "Anyone can see he's a rogue—it sticks out a mile!"

It sticks out like a sore thumb. It hits you in the eye, it looks very much out of place.

Over the sticks. Over the hurdles; hence a hurdle-race or a STEEPLECHASE.

The policy of the big stick. One backed by threat of force. *See* BIG STICK DIPLOMACY *under* BIG.

The wrong end of the stick. Not the true facts; a distorted version. To *have got hold of the wrong end of the stick* is to have misunderstood the story.

To have, or **get the dirty end of the stick.** To come off badly; to be left to bear the brunt of things; not to be treated fairly.

To stick at it. To persevere.

To stick at nothing. To be heedless of all obstacles in accomplishing one's desire; to be utterly unscrupulous.

To stick in one's gullet. Something difficult to swallow or digest, literally or metaphorically; something repugnant or unacceptable. **To stick in one's gizzard** and **to stick in one's craw** (a bird's crop) are similar expressions.

To stick to, or **in his fingers.** To appropriate improperly or unlawfully (usually money); to embezzle.

To stick up. To waylay and rob a coach, etc.; originally Australian BUSHRANGER'S slang; in common use nowadays for armed robbery when the victims are covered with revolvers and told to "stick 'em up", *i.e.* to hold their hands above their heads.

The sticking-place. The point at which a screw becomes tight; hence, the point aimed at. SHAKESPEARE's use of the word is probably an allusion to the peg of a musical instrument, which is not much use unless it is actually in the "sticking-place".

> We fail!
> But screw your courage to the sticking-place,
> And we'll not fail.
>
> *Macbeth*, I, vii.

The sticks. An American colloquialism meaning "countryside"; "rural area"; "wilds", etc. *Cp.* OUTBACK.

Stuck up. Said of pretentious people who give themselves airs, nobodies who assume to be somebodies. The allusion is to the peacock, which sticks up its train allegedly to add to its "importance" and overawe antagonists.

Stickit. A Scotticism for "stuck (*stick-ed*) half-way", as a *stickit job*, one that is unfinished or unsatisfactory; hence, applied to persons who have given up their work through lack of means or capacity or some other reason, as a *stickit minister*, one who has failed to get a pastoral charge, or to obtain preferment. S. R. Crockett wrote a novel called *The Stickit Minister* (1893).

Stickler. A stickler over trifles. One particular about things of no moment. *Sticklers* were the umpires in tournaments, or seconds in single combats, very punctilious about the minutest points of etiquette. The word is connected with O.E. *stihtan*, to arrange, regulate.

Stiff. Slang for a corpse; also for a horse that is sure to lose in a race; also (with reference to the stiff interest exacted by moneylenders) an I O U, a bill of acceptance.

> His "stiff" was floating about in too many directions, at too many high figures.
>
> OUIDA: *Under Two Flags*, ch. vii.

Stigmata (stig´ mà tà). Marks developed on the body of certain persons, which correspond to some or all of the wounds received by our Saviour in His trial and crucifixion. It is a well-known psychological phenomenon and has been demonstrated in many modern instances. From Gr. *stigma*, the brand with which slaves and criminals in ancient Greece and ROME were marked; hence our verb

stigmatize, to mark as with a brand of disgrace.

Among those who are said to have been marked with the stigmata are: (1) *Men.* St. PAUL, who said "I bear in my body the marks of the Lord Jesus" (*Gal.* vi, 17); Angelo del Paz (all the marks); Benedict of Reggio (the CROWN OF THORNS), 1602; Carlo di Saeta (the lance-wound); FRANCIS of Assisi (all the marks), 15 September 1224; and Nicholas of Ravenna. Francesco Forgione (1887– 1968), who became a Capuchin friar in 1902 taking the name of brother Pio, is said to have received stigmata on his hands in 1902. (2) *Women.* Bianca de Gazeran; Catherine of Siena; Catharine di Raconisco (the CROWN OF THORNS), 1538; Cecilia di Nobili of Nocera, 1655; Clara di Pugny (mark of the spear), 1514; "Estatica" of Caldaro (all the marks), 1842; Gabriella da Piezolo of Aquila (the spear-mark), 1472; Hieronyma Carvaglio (the spear-mark, which bled every Friday); Joanna Maria of the Cross; Maria Razzi of Chio (marks of the thorny crown); Maria Villani (ditto); Mary Magdalen di Pazzi; Mechtildis von Stanz; Ursula of Valencia; Veronica Giuliani (all the marks), 1694; Vincenza Ferreri of Valencia; Anna Emmerich of Dülmen, West phalia (d. 1824); Maria von Mörl (in 1839); Louise Lateau (1868), and Anne Girling, the foundress of the English SHAKERS. Theresa Neumann, of Kounersreuth, Germany (1898–1962), received her first stigmata on the tops of her hands and feet, on GOOD FRIDAY, 1926. In subsequent years more marks appeared, on her side, shoulders, and brow. Stigmata as studied in her case, never heal and never suppurate.

Stilo Novo (stī´ lō nō´ vō) (Lat., in the new style). Newfangled notions. When the CALENDAR was reformed by Gregory XIII (1582), letters used to be dated *stilo novo*, which grew in time to be a CANT phrase for any innovation. *See* OLD STYLE.

> And so I leave you to your *stilo novo*.
>
> BEAUMONT and FLETCHER: *Woman's Prize*, IV, iv.

Stir Up Sunday. The last SUNDAY after TRINITY. So called from the first two words of the collect: "Stir up, we beseech thee, O Lord, the wills of thy faithful people ...".

Stirrup cup. A "parting cup" given to guests on leaving, when their feet were in the stirrups. *Cp.* DOCH-AN-DORIS.

Among the ancient Romans a "parting cup" was drunk to ensure sound sleep (*see* Ovid, *Fasti*, ii, 35).

Stiver (stī' vẻr). **Not a stiver.** Not a penny, not a cent. The stiver (*stuiver*) was a Dutch coin, equal to about a penny.

Stock. Originally a tree-trunk, or stem (connected with *stick*); hence, in figurative use, something fixed, also regarded as the origin of families, groups, etc.; as **He comes of a good stock,** from a good stock, of good line of descent, **Languages of Indo-Germanic stock,** etc. **To worship stocks and stones** is to worship idols, *stock* here being taken as a type of a motionless fixed thing like a tree-stump. The village **stocks,** in which petty offenders were confined by the wrists and ankles, are so called from the stakes or posts at the side. *Stock* in the sense of a fund or capital derives from that part of the old wooden TALLY which the creditor took with him as evidence of the king's debt, the other portion, known as the *counterstock*, remaining in the EXCHEQUER. The word was then applied to the money which this tally represented, *i.e.* money lent to the government.

His stocks are good. His reputation is sound, he is held in good estimation. An allusion to stocks as investments.

It is on the stocks. It is in hand, but not yet finished. The stocks is the frame in which a ship is placed during building and so long as it is in hand it is said to be, or to lie, *on the stocks*.

Live stock. In colloquial usage, lice or other parasitic vermin.

Lock, stock, and barrel. *See* LOCK.

Stock in trade. The goods kept for sale by a shopkeeper; the equipment, tools, etc., for a trade or profession.

To take stock. To ascertain how one's business stands by taking an inventory of all goods and so on on hand, balancing one's books, etc.; hence, to survey one's position and prospects.

Stock-broker, Stock-jobber. The *bro-ker* was engaged in the purchase of stocks and shares for clients on commission; the *jobber* speculated in stocks and shares so as to profit by market fluctuations, acting as an intermediary between buying and selling brokers. The jobber had to be a member of the Stock Exchange but a broker not necessarily; if the latter was not, he was known as an "outside broker" or "kerbstone operator". These differentiations were markedly changed by the BIG BANG. *See also* BUCKET-SHOP.

Stock Dove. Also called a blue rock, very similar to a ROCK DOVE; so called from its nesting in old tree stumps or from the erroneous idea that it was the ancestor of varieties of the domestic pigeon.

Stock Exchange. A market in which stocks and shares are bought and sold.

Stockfish. Dried cod, cured without salt, supposed to derive the name from its being beaten with a stock or club to make it more tender. Till beaten it was very tough and was called *buckhorn*. Hence the expression **I will beat thee like a stockfish.**

> Peace, thou'lt be beaten like a stockfish else.
>
> JONSON: *Every Man in His Humour*, III, i.

Stock-rider. The Australian term for one in charge of cattle, *i.e.* stock. He uses a *stock-whip*, and herds his beasts in a *stockyard*.

Stockwell Ghost. A supposed ghost that created a great sensation in Stockwell (London) in 1772, then a village. The author of the strange noises was Anne Robinson, a servant. *Cp.* COCK LANE GHOST; SAMPFORD GHOST.

Stoic. (stō' ik). A school of Greek philosophers founded by ZENO (*c.* 308 B.C.) who held that virtue was the highest good, and that the passions and appetites should be rigidly subdued. *See* PORCH. The later Stoic school of the Romans is represented by Seneca, Epictetus, and Marcus Aurelius.

Stole (Lat. *stola*). An ecclesiastical vestment, also called the Orarium. Deacons wear the stole over the left shoulder like a sash. Priests normally wear it round the neck, both ends hanging loose in front. With Eucharistic vestments the ends are crossed over the chest.

Stole, Groom of the. Formerly, the first lord of the bedchamber, a high officer of the Royal HOUSEHOLD ranking next after the vice-chamberlain. In the reign of Queen Anne it was held by a woman, and on the accession of Queen Victoria the office was replaced by that of the *Mistress of the Robes*.

Stole here is not connected with Lat. *stola*, a robe, but refers to the King's *stool* or privy. As late as the 16th century, when the king made a royal progress his close-stool formed part of the baggage and was in charge of a special officer or groom.

Stolen sweets. *See under* STEAL.

Stomach. An army marches on its stomach. The troops need to be well provisioned if they are to be fighting fit.

To stomach an insult. To swallow or put up with an insult.

Stone. Used figuratively when some characteristic of a stone is implied as, *stone blind*, *stone cold*, *stone dead*, *stone deaf*, *stone still*, etc., as blind, cold, dead, deaf, or still as a stone.

> I will not struggle; I will stand stone still.
> SHAKESPEARE: *King John*, IV, i.

In all parts of the world primitive peoples have set up stones, especially those of meteoric origin (fabled to have fallen from HEAVEN), in connexion with religious rites. Anaxagoras mentions a stone that fell from JUPITER in Thrace, a description of which is given by Pliny. The Ephesians asserted that their image of DIANA came from Jupiter. The stone at Emessa, in Syria, worshipped as a symbol of the SUN, was a similar meteorite, and there were similar stones at Abydos and Potidæa. At Corinth one was venerated as ZEUS, and Tacitus describes one in Cyprus dedicated to VENUS. The famous BLACK STONE set in the KAABA is also a meteorite.

The great stone circles of Avebury, STONEHENGE, and the STANDING STONES OF STENNESS, are particularly noteworthy examples of the industry and ingenuity of early man, each having their mythological and religious associations. *See also* ÆTITES; PHILOSOPHER'S STONE; PRECIOUS STONES; TOUCHSTONE; etc.

Hag-stones. Flints naturally perforated used in country places as charms against witches, the EVIL EYE, etc. They are hung on the key of an outer door, round the neck for luck, on the bed-post to prevent nightmare, on a horse's collar to ward off disease, etc.

The Standing Stones of Stenness, in Orkney, some 4 miles from Stromness, comprise a NEOLITHIC stone-circle 340 ft. in diameter of which only 13 stones of a probable 60 are still standing, the tallest being 14 ft. high. Scott in a note (*The Pirate*, ch. xxxviii) says "One of the pillars ... is perforated with a circular hole, through which loving couples are wont to join hands when they take the *Promise of* ODIN." The *Eyrbiggia Saga* gives an account of the setting apart of the Helga Fels, or Holy Rock, by the pontiff Thorolf for solemn meetings.

The Stone Age. The period when stone implements were used by primitive man, before the discovery of metals. Its dating varies considerably over the continents, the use of bows and arrows, stone axes, bone tools, etc., persisting in Papua, New Guinea, etc., in the present century. *See* PALÆOLITHIC; NEOLITHIC.

The Stone of Destiny. *See* SCONE.

Stone lilies. *See* St. CUTHBERT'S BEADS.

Stone soup, or **St. Bernard's soup.** The story goes that a beggar asked alms at a lordly mansion, but was told by the servants that they had nothing to give him. "Sorry for it," said the man, "but will you let me boil a little water to make some soup of this stone?" This was so novel a proceeding, that the curiosity of the servants was aroused, and the man was readily furnished with a saucepan, water, and a spoon. In he popped the stone, and begged for a little salt and pepper for flavouring. Stirring the water and tasting it, he said it would be the better for any fragments of meat and vegetables they might happen to have. These were supplied, and ultimately he asked for a little ketchup or other sauce. When ready the servants tasted it, and declared that "stone soup" was excellent.

This story, which was a great favourite in the 16th and 17th centuries, was told with many variations, horseshoes, nails, ram's-horns, etc., taking the place of the stone as narrated above.

A rolling stone gathers no moss. One who is always on the move and does not settle down will never become prosperous or wealthy. A common proverb. Tusser in his *Five Hundred Points of Good Husbandrie* (1573) has:

> The stone that is rolling can gather no moss.
> For master and servant oft changing is loss.

To cast the first stone. To take the lead in criticizing, fault-finding, quarrelling, etc. The phrase is from *John* viii, 7:

> He that is without sin among you, let him first cast a stone at her.

To kill two birds with one stone. *See under* BIRD.

To leave no stone unturned. To spare no trouble, time, expense, etc., in endeavouring to accomplish your aim. After the defeat of Mardonius at Platæa (477 B.C.), a report was current that the Persian general had left great treasures in his tent. Polycrates the Theban sought long, but found them not. The ORACLE of Delphi, being consulted, told him "to leave no stone unturned", and the treasures were discovered.

You have stones in your mouth. Applied to one who stutters or speaks very indistinctly. Demosthenes cured himself of stuttering by putting pebbles in his mouth and declaiming on the seashore.

Stony Arabia. A mistranslation of *Arabia Petræa*, where Petræa is supposed to be an adjective formed from Gr. *petros*, a stone. The name really derives from the city of Petra, the capital of the Nabathæans. *Cp.* YEMEN.

Stonehenge. The most famous prehistoric monument in Britain, although covering a smaller area than Avebury. It is situated on Salisbury Plain, 2 miles west of Amesbury. The name is from O.E. *hengen*, in reference to something hung up, in this case the horizontal lintel stones. At various times regarded as having been built by the DRUIDS, the Romans and the Danes, it is originally of late NEOLITHIC construction and was later reconstructed by the Beaker folk and subsequently. It seems to have last been used *c.* 1400 B.C. It finally consisted of an outer circle of local SARSEN STONES and two inner circles of Blue Stones, apparently from the Prescelly Mountains in Pembrokeshire. The first and third circles are capped with stone lintels. The whole is surrounded by a ditch, inside the bank of which are 56 pits known as *Aubrey holes*. The Hele Stone, over which the sun rises on MIDSUMMER Day, stands in isolation outside the circles. It is certain that Stonehenge was a centre of worship, probably connected with the sun, and it has recently been suggested that it was a massive kind of astronomical clock. Scientific examination of the site did not begin until 1901.

Stonewall, To. A cricketer's term for adopting purely defensive measures when at the wicket, blocking every ball and not attempting to score. It was originally Australian political slang and was used of obstructing business. In general usage, *stonewalling* is to employ obstructive or delaying tactics.

Stonewall Jackson. Thomas J. Jackson (1824–1863), one of the Confederate generals in the American CIVIL WAR; so called from his firmness at the Battle of Bull Run (1861), when a fellow officer observed him with his brigade standing "like a stone wall".

Stool. Stool Pigeon. A police spy or informer; a decoy.

Stool of Repentance. The cutty stool, a low stool placed in front of the pulpit in Scottish churches, on which persons who had incurred ecclesiastical censure were placed during divine service. When the service was over the penitent had to stand on the stool and receive the minister's rebuke.

Store. Store is no sore. Things stored up for future use are no EVIL. *Sore* means grief as well as wound, our *Sorrow*.

To set store by. To value highly.

Stork. According to Swedish legend, the stork received its name from flying round the cross of the crucified Redeemer, crying *Styrka! styrka!* (Strengthen, strengthen!).

Lyly in his *Euphues* (1580) says of this bird:

> Ladies use their lovers as the stork doth her young ones who pecketh them till they bleed with her bill, and then healeth them with her tongue.

Also:

> Constancy is like unto the stork, who wheresoever she fly cometh into no nest but her own.

And:

> It fareth with me ... as with the stork, who, when she is least able, carrieth the greatest burden.

It is an old tale to children that babies are brought by storks and they still feature prominently on cards of congratulation to a baby's parents. It was also a belief that a stork will kill a snake "on sight".

King Stork. A tyrant that devours his subjects, and makes them submissive with fear and trembling. The allusion is to the fable of *The Frogs desiring a King*. *See* A KING LOG *under* LOG.

Storm. A Brain-storm. A sudden and violent upheaval in the brain, causing temporary loss of control, or even madness. *Nervestorm* is used in much the same way of the nerves.

The Cape of Storms. So Bartholomew Diaz named the south cape of Africa in 1486, but John II of Portugal (d. 1495) changed it to the *Cape of Good Hope*.

Storm and Stress. *See* STURM UND DRANG.

A storm in a teacup. A mighty to-do about a trifle; making a great fuss about nothing.

To take by storm. To seize by a sudden and irresistible attack; a military term used figuratively, as of one who becomes suddenly famous or popular; an actor, suddenly springing to fame, "takes the town by storm".

Stormy Petrel. *See* PETREL.

Storting or **Stirthing**, (stôr' ting). The Norwegian PARLIAMENT, elected every fourth year (*stor*, great; *thing*, assembly).

Stovepipe Hat. An old-fashioned tall silk hat, a chimney-pot hat. A name of American origin.

Strad. A colloquial name for a violin made by Antonio Stradivarius (1644–1737) of CREMONA, now much prized. His best violins were made between 1700 and 1723. *Cp.* AMATI.

Strafe (straf) (Ger. *strafen*, to punish). A word borrowed in good-humoured contempt from the Germans during World War I. One of their favourite slogans was *Gott strafe England!* The word was applied to any sharp and sudden bombardment, and also used by Americans in World War II for the machine-gunning of troops or civilians by low-flying aircraft.

Strain. The quality of mercy is not strained (SHAKESPEARE: *Merchant of Venice*, IV, i)—not constrained or forced, but comes down freely as the rain, which is God's gift.

To strain a point. To go beyond one's usual, or the proper limits; to give way a bit more than one ought.

To strain at a gnat and swallow a camel. To make much fuss about little peccadilloes, but commit offences of real magnitude. The proverb comes from *Matt.* xxiii, 24, which in Tyndale's, Coverdale's, and other early versions of the BIBLE reads *strain out, i.e.* to filter out a gnat before drinking the wine. The REVISED VERSION also adopts this form but the AUTHORIZED VERSION's rendering is *which strain at a gnat*, which was not a mistake but established usage at the time. Greene in his *Mamillia* (1583) speaks of "straining at a gnat and letting pass an elephant".

Stranger. Originally, a foreigner; from O.Fr. *estrangier* (Mod. Fr. *étranger*), which is the Lat. *extraneus*, one without.

It is said that BUSIRIS, King of Egypt sacrificed to his gods all strangers who set foot on his territories. DIOMEDES gave strangers to his horses for food.

Floating tea-leaves in one's cup, charred pieces of wick that make the candle gutter, little bits of soot hanging from the grate, etc., are called "strangers", because they are supposed to foretell the coming of visitors.

I spy strangers! The recognized form of words by which a Member of PARLIAMENT conveys to the SPEAKER the information that there is an unauthorized person in the House.

The little stranger. A new-born infant.

The stranger that is within thy gates. *See* PROSELYTES.

Strap. A taste of the strap. A strapping or flogging, properly with a leather strap.

A strapping young fellow. A big sturdy chap; just as we speak of a "thumping" or "whacking great chap"; a vigorous young woman is similarly called a *strapper*.

Straphanger. One who stands in a bus, train, etc., when the seats are fully occupied, holding on to the strap hanging from the roof.

Strappado (strå på′ dō) (Ital. *strappare*, to pull). A mode of torture formerly practised for extracting confessions, retractions, etc. The hands were tied behind the back, and the victim was pulled up to a beam by a rope tied to them and then let down suddenly; by this means a limb was not infrequently dislocated.

> An I were at the strappado, or all the racks in the world, I would not tell you on compulsion.
> SHAKESPEARE: *Henry IV, Pt. I,* II, iv.

Strasbourg Goose. A goose fattened, crammed, and confined in order to enlarge its liver, from which is made true pâté de foie gras.

Straw. Straw was proverbially regarded as worthless, something blown about by the wind; hence used in phrases as, **Not worth a straw,** quite valueless, not worth a RAP, a FIG, etc.; **to care not a straw,** not to care at all.

Straw Polls. An early form of public opinion poll sponsored by the American press as early as 1824 when reporters of the *Harrisburg Pennsylvanian* were sent to inquire from the townsfolk of Wilmington which candidate they favoured for the presidency. Such polls were subsequently used on a much larger scale and postal voting came to be employed. The name derives from the idea of a straw "showing which way the wind blows". *Cp.* GALLUP POLL.

Straw vote. A vote of no official value taken casually at a meeting, etc., as an indication of opinion.

I have a straw to break with you. I have something to quarrel with you about; I am displeased with you; I have a reproof to give you. An obsolete expression.

In the straw. Applied to women in childbirth. The allusion is to the straw with which beds were once stuffed before the introduction of feather beds.

The last straw. "This is the last straw that breaks the camel's back." There is an ultimate point of endurance beyond which calamity breaks a man down.

A man of straw. A man without means, with no more substance than a straw doll; also, an imaginary or fictitious person put forward for some reason.

A straw shows which way the wind blows. Mere trifles often indicate the coming of momentous events. They are shadows cast before coming events.

To catch at a straw. A FORLORN HOPE. A drowning man will catch at a straw.

To make bricks without straw. To attempt to do something without the proper or necessary materials. The allusion is to the exaction of the Egyptian taskmasters mentioned in *Exod.* v, 6–14.

To pick straws. To show fatigue or weariness, as birds pick up straws to make their nests (or bed).

To stumble at a straw. To be pulled up short by a trifle.

To throw straws against the wind. To contend uselessly and feebly against what is irresistible; to "sweep back the Atlantic with a besom". *Cp.* PARTINGTON.

Strawberry. The strawberry leaves. A dukedom; the honour, rank, etc., of a DUKE. The ducal CORONET is ornamented with eight strawberry leaves.

Strawberry mark. A birthmark something like a strawberry. In J. M. Morton's BOX AND COX the two heroes eventually recognize each other as long-lost brothers through one of them having a strawberry mark on his left arm.

Strawberry preachers. So Latimer called the non-resident country clergy, because they "come but once a year and tarie not long" (*Sermon on the Plough*, 1549).

Stream of Consciousness. A technique

of novel writing, first deliberately employed by Dorothy Richardson in *Pointed Roofs* (1915) and developed by James Joyce and Virginia Woolf. By this technique the writer presents life as seen through impressions on the mind of one person.

To swim with the stream. *See under* SWIM.

Street. Right up my street. "Just my handwriting", in my particular province or field; "just my line of country". As familiar to a person as his own street.

Streets ahead. Well ahead; much in advance. The phrase conveys the idea of long distance.

Street Arab. *See under* ARABIA. *Cp.* BEDOUINS.

To be in easy street. In a very comfortable situation and of considerable affluence.

Strenia (strē′ ni à). A SABINE goddess identified with the Roman Salus, to whom gifts (*strenæ*) were taken at the New Year, consisting of figs, dates, and honey. The custom is said to have been instituted by the Sabine King Tatius, who entered ROME on NEW YEAR'S DAY and received from some augurs palms cut from the sacred grove dedicated to her. The French *étrenne*, a New Year's gift, is from this goddess.

Strephon (stref′ òn). A stock name for a rustic lover; from the languishing lover of that name in Sidney's *Arcadia*.

Strike. It strikes me that ... It occurs to me that ..., it comes into my mind that ...

Strike-a-light. The flint formerly used with tinder-boxes for striking fire; also, the shaped piece of metal used to strike the flint. The latter's similarity with the links of the collar of the Order of the GOLDEN FLEECE gave rise to the nickname "the collar of strike-a-lights". *Strike a light* is also commonly used as an exclamation.

Strike, but hear me! (Lat. *verbera, sed audi*). Carry out your threats—if you must—but at least hear what I have to say. The phrase comes from Plutarch's life of Themistocles. He strongly opposed the proposal of Eurybiades to quit the Bay of Salamis. The hot-headed SPARTAN insultingly remarked that

"those who in the public games rise up before the proper signal are scourged". "True," said Themistocles, "but those who lag behind win no laurels." On this, Eurybiades lifted up his staff to strike him, when Themistocles earnestly exclaimed, "Strike, but hear me!"

Bacon (*Advancement of Learning*, ii) calls this "that ancient and patient request".

Strike me dead! blind! etc. Vulgar expletives, or exclamations of surprise, dismay, wonder, and so on. *Strike me dead* is also sailor's slang for thin, wishy-washy beer.

Strike while the iron is hot. Act while the time or the opportunity presents; a METAPHOR from the blacksmith's shop. Similar proverbs are: "Make hay while the sun shines", "Take time by the forelock".

To be struck all of a heap. *See* HEAP.

To be struck on a person. To like or be much interested in, or inclined to be enamoured of a person.

To strike an attitude. To pose, to assume an exaggerated or theatrical attitude.

To strike a balance. *See under* BALANCE.

To strike a bargain (*Cp.* Lat. *fœdus ferire*). To make or conclude a transaction; "I have just struck a bargain" is also used in the sense, "I have just come across an advantageous purchase".

To strike at the foundations. To attempt to undermine the whole thing, to overthrow it utterly.

To strike camp. To take down the tents and move off.

To strike the flag. *See under* FLAG.

To strike hands upon a bargain is to confirm it by shaking or "striking hands".

To strike lucky. To have unexpected good fortune; a phrase from the miners' camps. *Cp.* TO STRIKE OIL *under* OIL.

To strike out in another direction. To open up a new way for oneself, to start a new approach, to open out into a new line of business.

To strike sail. *See under* SAIL.

To strike up. To begin, start operations; as to *strike up an acquaintance*, to set acquaintanceship going. Originally of an orchestra or company of singers, who "struck up" the music.

Willing to wound, and yet afraid to strike. Said of one who dare not do the injury or take the revenge that he wishes. The "tag" is from Pope's *Epistle to Dr. Arbuthnot*, 1.204 (1735).

Strike-breaker. A "BLACKLEG", a "scab"; a worker induced by the employer to carry on working when the other employees are on strike.

String. Always harping on one string. Always talking on the same subject; always repeating or referring to the same thing. The allusion is obvious.

He has two strings to his bow. *See under* BOW.

How long is a piece of string? Who knows? How can one tell? Said to someone who asks a question to which there is no accurate or worthwhile answer.

To pull the strings. *See under* PULL.

To string along with. To accompany; to join up with, *i.e.* to join the line or "string".

Stringy-bark. *See* SETTLER'S MATCHES.

Strip. To tear someone off a strip. To give one a severe castigation; to reprimand angrily.

Strip-tease. A theatrical or cabaret performance in which an actress slowly and provocatively undresses herself. One who does this is called a *stripper*.

Strong. Going strong. Prospering, getting on famously; in an excellent state of health.

To come it strong. *See under* COME.

Struldbrugs (strŭld' brŭgz). Wretched inhabitants of Luggnagg (in Swift's *Gulliver's Travels*), who had the privilege of immortality without having eternal vigour, strength, and intellect.

Stuck up. *See under* STICK.

Stuff. Stuff Gown. A BARRISTER who has not yet taken SILK.

Stuffed shirt. *See under* SHIRT.

Stumer (stū' mer). A swindle, or a swindler, a forged banknote or "dud" cheque; a fictitious bet recorded by the bookmakers, and published in the papers, to deceive the public by running up the odds on a horse which is not expected to win. From 1914, in military parlance, a dud shell was called a *stumer*. The word

is of unknown origin.

Stump. The Black Stump. *This side of the Black Stump* or *The other side of the Black Stump* are Australian expressions implying "a long way off", "a considerable, but unspecified distance". The *Black Stump* refers to the undefined stump left after a bush fire. There is an actual place bearing the name, south of Hillston in New South Wales.

A stump speaker, or **orator.** A speaker who harangues all who will listen to him from some improvised vantage point; often with the implications of rant and bombast of the tub-thumping variety. The phrase is of American origin, where it has not necessarily derogatory implications. It originates from the days when a tree stump was often the most readily available platform for political speeches. Hence such phrases as *to stump the country*, *to take to the stump*, to go from place to place making inflammatory or provocative speeches, etc. So-called **stump speeches** were once favoured by entertainers, minstrel shows, etc., and usually somewhat laboured in their humour.

To be stumped. Outwitted; at a loss, defeated. A term borrowed from CRICKET.

To stir one's stumps. To get on faster; to set about something expeditiously. *Stumps* here are one's legs; also the wooden stump or peg-leg once fastened to mutilated limbs, or the mutilated limbs themselves.

To stump up. To pay one's reckoning, to pay what is due. Ready money is called *stumpy* or *stumps*. An Americanism, meaning money paid down on the spot—*i.e.* on the stump of a tree. *Cp. On the* NAIL.

Stupor Mundi (Lat., "The amazement of the world"). So the Emperor Frederick II (1194, 1215–1250) was called as being the greatest sovereign, soldier, and patron of artists and scholars in the 13th century.

Sturm und Drang (shtoorm unt drŭng) (Ger., storm and stress). The name given to the German literary movement of the late 18th century with which Goethe, Schiller, and Herder were closely associated, from a tragedy of this title (1776) by Frederick Maximilian von Klinger (1752–1831). The dramas of the period are typified by the extravagant passion of the characters, and the movement had considerable effect upon the subsequent ROMANTIC MOVEMENT.

Stygian (sti′ ji àn). Infernal, gloomy; pertaining to the river STYX.

> At that so sudden blaze the Stygian throng
> Bent their aspect.
>
> MILTON: *Paradise Lost*, X, 453.

Style. New Style, Old Style. *See* OLD STYLE *under* OLD; STILO NOVO.

The style is the man. A mistranslation of "Le style est l'homme même" from the discourse of Buffon (1707–1788) on his reception into the French Academy.

To do a thing in style. To do it splendidly, regardless of expense.

Styles. Tom Styles, or **John a Styles,** connected with JOHN-A-NOKES, an imaginary plaintiff or defendant in a lawsuit in the same way as John DOE and Richard Roe.

Stylites, or **Pillar Saints** (stī lī′ tēz). A class of ascetics found especially in Syria, Mesopotamia, Egypt and Greece between the 5th and 10th centuries. They took up their abode on the tops of pillars, which were sometimes equipped with a small hut, from which they never descended. They take their name from St. Simeon Stylites of Syria (390–459) who spent some 30 years on a pillar which was gradually increased to the height of 40 cubits. St. Daniel, his most famous disciple, spent 33 years on a pillar near Constantinople. Tennyson wrote a poem on St. Simeon Stylites.

Stymie. A golfing term, obsolete since 1952. A player was *laid a stymie* if, on the putting-green, the opponent's ball fell in the line of his path to the hole (providing the balls were not within 6 in. of each other). To hole out could only be achieved by a very difficult lofting stroke. Hence several still current expressions. **A stymie** is a frustrating situation, a discouragingly difficult position and **to be stymied** is to be in such a position; and **to stymie** is to hinder or thwart; also to put one in the position of having to negotiate.

Styx (stiks). The river of Hate (Gr. *stu-*

gein, to hate)—called by Milton "abhorred Styx, the flood of deadly hate" (*Paradise Lost*, II, 577)—that, according to classical mythology, flowed nine times round the infernal regions. Some say it was a river in ARCADIA whose waters were poisonous and dissolved any vessel put upon them. When a god swore falsely by the Styx, he was made to drink a draught of its water which made him lie speechless for a year. The river was said to take its name from Styx, the eldest daughter of OCEANUS and TETHYS, and wife of Pallas, by whome she had three daughters. Victory, Strength, and Valour. *See* ACHERON; CHARON.

> By the black infernal Styx I swear
> (That dreadful oath which binds the Thunderer)
> 'Tis fixed!
>
> POPE: *Thebais of Statius*, I, 411.

Suaviter (swā vi ter) **in modo, fortiter in re** (Lat.). Gentle in manner, resolute in action. Said of one who does what is to be done with unflinching firmness, but in the most inoffensive manner possible.

Sub divo (Lat. *divum*, sky). Under the open sky; in the open air.

Sub hasta (sŭb hăs tà) (Lat.). By auction. When an auction took place among the Romans, it was customary to stick a spear in the ground to give notice of it to the public; literally, under the spear. *See* SPEAR.

Sub Jove (Lat.). Under Jove; in the open air. JUPITER is the god of the upper regions of the air, as JUNO is of the lower regions, NEPTUNE of the waters of the sea, VESTA of the earth, CERES of the surface soil, and HADES of the invisible or underworld.

Sub judice (sŭb joo′ di sē) (Lat.). Under consideration; not yet decided in a court of law.

Sub rosa. *See under* ROSE.

Subject and Object. In METAPHYSICS the *Subject* is the ego, the mind, the conscious self, the substance or substratum to which attributes must be referred; the *Object* is an external as distinct from the ego, a thing or idea brought before the consciousness. Hence **subjective criticism, art,** etc., is that which proceeds from the individual mind and is consequently individualistic, fanciful, imaginative; while **objective criticism** is that which is based on knowledge of the externals.

Subject-object. The immediate object of thought, the thought itself as distinct from the *object-object*, the real object as it is in fact.

Sublapsarian, or **Infralapsarian** (sŭb lăp sâr′ i ăn). A Calvinist who maintains that God devised His scheme of redemption after he had permitted the "lapse" or fall of ADAM, when He elected some to salvation and left others to run their course. The *supra*lapsarian maintains that all this was ordained by God from the foundation of the world, and therefore before the "lapse" or fall of Adam.

Sublime. There is but one step from the sublime to the ridiculous. *See under* RIDICULOUS.

Submerged. The Submerged Tenth. The very poor; sunk or submerged in poverty.

Subpœna (sŭb pē′ nà) (Lat., under penalty) is a writ commanding a man to appear in court, usually unwillingly, to bear witness or give evidence on a certain trial named. It is so called because the party summoned is bound to appear *sub pœna centum librorum* (under a penalty of £100). We have also the verb *to subpœna*.

Subtopia. A word coined (from *suburb* and *Utopia*) by Ian Nairn in 1954 to denote the sprawling suburban housing estates built to satisfy the town workers' yearning for country surroundings while clinging to the amenities of the town. The term includes all the paraphernalia of concrete posts, lamp standards, chain link fencing, and other uglinesses associated with a disfigured landscape.

Succoth, or **Sukkoth** (Heb. *sukkoth*, booths). The Jewish name for the feast of the Tabernacles (*see under* TABERNACLE).

Succubus (suk′ ū bus) (Med. Lat. masculine form of Late Lat. *succuba*, from *succumbere*, to lie under). A female demon fabled to have sexual relations with sleeping men. *Cp.* INCUBUS.

Suck, or **Suck-in.** A swindle, hoax, deception, fiasco. **To be sucked in** is to be taken in, deceived, tricked, and one who is thus gulled is said to be a *sucker*. A **suck-up** or **sucker-up** is a TOADY or creep.

Teach your grandmother to suck eggs. *See under* EGG.

Suffering. The Meeting for Sufferings. The standing representative committee of the Yearly Meeting of the Society of Friends, so called because originally its chief function was to relieve the sufferings imposed upon QUAKERS by distraint of TITHES and other petty persecutions.

Suffragan (sŭf′ rà gàn). An auxiliary BISHOP; one who has not a see of his own but is appointed to assist a bishop in a portion of his SEE. In relation to a METROPOLITAN or archbishop all bishops are suffragans; and they were so called because they could be summoned to a synod to give their SUFFRAGE.

Suffrage. One's vote, approval, consent; or one's right to vote, especially at parliamentary and municipal elections. The word is from Lat. *suffragium*, voting tablet, probably from *suffrago*, the hock or ankle-bone of a horse, which may have been used by the Romans for balloting.

Hence **Suffragettes** as the name for the militant women who agitated for the parliamentary vote, in the period 1906–1914. *See* CAT AND MOUSE ACT.

Sugar. Sugar Daddy. An elderly, wealthy man who lavishes expensive gifts on a much younger woman. From U.S. slang.

Sui generis (sū′ i jen′ er is) (Lat., of its own kind). Having a distinct character of its own; unlike aything else.

Sui juris (Lat.). Of one's own right; the state of being able to exercise one's legal rights—*i.e.* freedom from legal disability.

Suicide (Lat. *sui*, of oneself; *-cidium*, from *cædere*, to kill). Until 1823, a suicide was buried at the CROSS-ROADS with a stake thrust through the body.

Suit. To follow suit. To follow the leader; to do as those do who are taken as your exemplars. The term is from games of cards.

Sukkoth. *See* SUCCOTH.

Sultan (Arab., King). Until 1923 the title of the ruler of the former Turkish Empire and, until 1957, of the King of Morocco. It is still in use in certain lesser Mohammedan states, as Muscat and Oman, Kishen and Socotra, etc. In mediæval writings *sultan* is often corrupted to **Soldan** or **Sowdan**. The wife (also mother, sister or concubine) of the sultan is called **Sultana**, a name which is also sometimes applied to a mistress.

Summer. The warmest season of the year. In Britain, June, July, and August; astronomically, from the summer SOLSTICE to the autumn equinox (*c.* 22 September).

St. LUKE's little summer is a period of mild weather around mid-October, St. Luke's Day being 18 October. *See also* ALL-HALLOWS SUMMER; INDIAN SUMMER; St. MARTIN'S SUMMER.

Summer Time. *See* DAYLIGHT SAVING.

Summit. A summit conference. One between the chief representatives of the participating powers.

Summum bonum (sŭm′ ŭm bō′ nŭm). (Lat., the highest good). The chief excellence; the highest attainable good. The STOIC School held that virtue and its attainment was the highest end.

SOCRATES said knowledge is virtue, and ignorance is vice.

ARISTOTLE said that happiness is the greatest good.

Bernard de Mandeville and *Helvetius* contended that self-interest is the perfection of the ethical end.

Bentham and *Mill* were for the greatest happiness of the greatest number.

Herbert Spencer placed it in those actions which best tend to the survival of the individual and the race; and

Robert Browning (see his poem of this name) "in the kiss of one girl".

Sumptuary Laws. Laws to limit the expenses of food and dress, or any luxury.

Sun. The source of light and heat, and consequently of life to the whole world; hence regarded as a deity and worshipped as such by all primitive peoples and having a leading place in their mythologies. *Shamash* was the principal sun-god of the Assyrians and Babylonians, MITHRAS of the Persians, RA of the Egyptians, *Tezcatlipoca* (Smoking Mirror) of the Aztecs, HELIOS of the Greeks, known to the Romans as SOL and usually identified with PHŒBUS and APOLLO.

The Southern Gate of the Sun. The sign Capricornus or winter SOLSTICE. So called because it is the most southern limit of the sun's course in the ECLIPTIC.

The Sun of Righteousness. Jesus Christ (*Mal.* iv. 2).

The empire on which the sun never sets. *See under* SET.

Heaven cannot support two suns, nor earth two masters. So said ALEXANDER the Great when DARIUS (before the battle of Arbela) sent to offer terms of peace.

More worship the rising than the setting sun. More persons pay honour to ascendant than to fallen greatness. The saying is attributed to Pompey.

A place in the sun. A favourable position that allows for development; a share in what one has a natural right to. The phrase achieved a particular significance when William II of Germany spoke of his nation taking steps to ensure that "no one can dispute with us the place in the sun that is our due."

Out of God's blessing into the warm sun. One of Ray's proverbs, meaning from good to less good. In Shakespeare's *Hamlet* (I, ii), when the king says to Hamlet, "How is it that the clouds still hang on you?" the prince answers, "Not so, my lord; I am too much i' the sun", meaning, "I have lost God's blessing, for too much of the sun"—*i.e.* this far inferior state.

The sun is over the foreyard or **yardarm.** An expression among naval officers indicating that the time has come to have a drink. In home waters and northern latitudes the sun would be over the yardarm towards noon.

To make hay while the sun shines. *See under* HAY.

Sundowner. In Australia, a tramp. In the early days one who went from one settlement to another arriving at *sundown*, so it is said, to be too late for work, but in time for food. In Africa and India, a *sundowner* denotes a drink of spirits, etc., taken just after sundown; in the

U.S.A., an official who works late at the office.

Sunday (O.E. *sunnen dæg*). For centuries the first day of the week, anciently dedicated to the sun. In 1971 it became the seventh when Britain adopted the decision of the International Standardisation Organisation to call MONDAY the first day. *See* WEEK, DAYS OF THE; SABBATH.

Sunday Letters. *See* DOMINICAL LETTERS.

Sunday School. Nowadays, classes for children organized by church and chapel for a fairly short time on Sundays for religious instruction. They were first established in the 18th century to teach working class children their letters in order that they might learn to read the BIBLE, to improve their behaviour through moral instruction and to keep them off the streets all day. The movement gained considerable impetus when Robert Raikes founded his school in Gloucester in 1780 and William Fox set up the Sunday School Society in 1785. Sunday Schools became particularly strong in Wales.

Not in a month of Sundays. Not in a very long time.

One's Sunday best, Sunday suit, Sunday-go-to-meeting togs. One's best clothes, as worn on Sundays.

Sunday saint. One who observes the ordinances of religion, and goes to church on a Sunday, but is worldly, grasping, "indifferent honest", the following six days.

When three Sundays come together. NEVER.

Sunflower State. Kansas.

Sunna (Arab., custom, divine law). The traditional sayings and example of MOHAMMED and his immediate followers as set forth in the HADITH.

Sunnis, Sunnites. Orthodox MOSLEMS who consider the SUNNA as authentic as the KORAN itself and acknowledge the first four CALIPHS to be the rightful successors of MOHAMMED. They form by far the largest section of Mohammedans. *Cp.* SHI'ITES.

Supererogation, Works of. A theological expression for good works which are not enjoined or of obligation and therefore "better" (Lat. *super*, over, above; *erogare*, to pay out). The phrase is commonly applied to acts performed beyond the bounds of duty.

Superman. A hypothetical superior human being of high intellectual and moral attainment, fancied as evolved from the normally existing type. The term (*Übermensch*) was invented by the German philosopher Nietzsche (d. 1900), and was popularized in England by George Bernard Shaw's play, *Man and Superman* (1903).

The wide popularity of the term gave rise to many compounds, such as *superwoman*, *super-critic*, *super-tramp*, *super-Dreadnought*, and *super-tax*.

Supply. The law of supply and demand. The economic statement that the competition of buyers and sellers tends to make such changes in price that the demand for any article in a given market will become equal to the supply. In other words, if the demand exceeds the supply the price rises, operating so as to reduce the demand and so enable the supply to meet it, and VICE VERSA.

Supralapsarian. *See* SUBLAPSARIAN.

Surloin. *See* SIRLOIN.

Surname. The name added to, or given over and above, the Christian name (O. Fr. *sur-*; from Lat. *super-*, over, above). Surnames, as names passed from father to son, were not widespread until the 13th century, and grew from the custom of adding the place of domicile or provenance, trade or some descriptive characteristic, to the Christian name to assist identification, *e.g.* York, Butcher, Large, Russell (red-haired), etc. Yet another category derives from family relationship, *e.g.* Williamson, Macgregor, O'Brien.

Surplice. Over the *pelisse* or fur robe (Lat. *superpellicium*, from *pellis*, skin). The white linen vestment worn by CLERGY, acolytes, choristers, etc., so fashioned for its ease of wearing over fur dress worn in northern Europe in mediæval times. The shorter *cotta* is a development from this.

Surplice fees. The fees for marriage and burials which are the right of the incumbent of a BENEFICE.

Surrealism. A movement in art and the

literary world which began in 1924 and flourished between the two World Wars under the leadership of the poet André Breton. In painting it falls into two groups: hand-painted dream scenes as exemplified by Chirico, Dali, and Magritte: and the creation of abstract forms by the practice of complete spontaniety of technique as well as subject-matter by the use of contrast as with Arp, Roy, Mirò and Dali. They sought to express thought uncontrolled by reason and aesthetic and moral concepts. *Cp.* CUBISM; DADAISM; FAUVISM; FUTURISM; IMPRESSIONISM; ORPHISM; SYNCHRONISM; VORTICISM.

Susanna and the Elders. *See* DANIEL.

Sutras (sū' tràz) (Sansk, *sutra*, a thread). In Sanskrit literature, certain aphoristic writings giving the rules of systems of philosophy, grammar, etc.; and in Brahmanic use, directions concerning religious ritual and ceremonial customs which are part of the VEDA.

Suttee (Sansk. *sati*, a virtuous wife). The Hindu custom of burning the widow on the funeral pyre of her deceased husband; also, the widow so put to death. Women with child and mothers of children not yet of age could not perform suttee. This ancient practice was prohibited in British India by Lord William Bentinck in 1829, but was practised as late as 1877 in Nepal.

Sutton Hoo Treasure. An Anglo-Saxon ship-burial of the early 7th century, discovered at Sutton Hoo near Woodbridge, Suffolk, in 1939. It is one of the richest ever found and the treasure, consisting of a sword and sheath, helmet, bowls and other objects in precious metals, is now in the BRITISH MUSEUM. The find is of considerable archæological and historical importance.

Swaddlers. An early nickname for Wesleyans, and applied later by Roman Catholics to DISSENTERS and PROTESTANTS generally. Southey (*Life of Wesley*, ii) explains its origin as follows:

> It happened that Cennick, preaching on Christmas Day, took for his text these words from St. Luke's Gospel: "And this shall be a sign unto you; ye shall find the babe wrapped in swaddling clothes lying in a manger." A Catholic who was present, and to whom the language of

scripture was a novelty, thought this so ridiculous that he called the preacher a swaddler in derision, and this unmeaning word became a nickname for "Protestant", and had all the effect of the most opprobrious appellation.

Swag (connected with Norwegian *svagga*, to sway from side to side). One's goods carried in a pack or bundle; hence the booty obtained from a burglary, often carried away in a sack. **To get away with the swag** is used figuratively to imply profiting by one's cleverness or sharp practice.

Swagman. The Australian term for the numerous itinerant labourers who tramped from sheep station to sheep station in former times carrying their "swag" (*i.e.* bundle of clothes, blankets, etc.), seeking employment from the squatters. *Cp.* SUNDOWNER.

Swag-shop. A place kept by a "FENCE"; where thieves can dispose of their "SWAG"; also, a low-class shop where cheap and trashy articles are sold.

Swagger-stick. The small cane a soldier was formerly obliged to carry when walking out.

Swallow. According to Scandinavian tradition, this bird hovered over the cross of our Lord, crying "*Svala! svala!*" (Console! console!), whence it was called *svalow* (the bird of consolation).

Ælian says that the swallow was sacred to the PENATES or household gods, and therefore to injure one would be to bring wrath upon your own house. It is still considered a sign of good luck if a swallow or martin builds under the eaves of one's house.

> Perhaps you failed in your foreseeing skill,
> For swallows are unlucky birds to kill.
> DRYDEN: *Hind and Panther*, Pt. III.

Longfellow refers to another old fable regarding this bird:

> Seeking with eager eyes that wondrous stone which the swallow
> Brings from the shore of the sea to restore the sight of its fledglings.
> *Evangeline*, Pt. I, 119.

One swallow does not make a summer. You are not to suppose summer has come to stay just because you have seen a swallow; nor that the troubles of life are over because you have sur-

Swan

mounted one difficulty. The Greek proverb, "One swallow does not make a spring", is to be found in ARISTOTLE's *Nicomachœan Ethics* (I, vii, 16).

Swan. The fable that the swan sings beautifully just before it dies is very ancient, but baseless. The only one for which a song of any kind can be claimed is the Whistling Swan (Cygnus musicus). The superstition was credited by PLATO, ARISTOTLE, Euripides, Cicero, Seneca, Martial, etc., and doubted by Pliny and Ælian. SHAKESPEARE refers to it more than once; Emilia, just before she dies, says:

> I will play the swan,
> And die in music.
> *Othello*, V, ii.

Spenser speaks of the swan as a bird that sings:

> He, were he not with love so ill bedight,
> Woulde mount as high, and sing as soote
> [sweetly] as Swanne.
> *Shephearde's Calendar* (*October*, 89).

Coleridge (*On a Volunteer Singer*), referring to poetasters of the time, gives the old superstition an epigrammatic turn:

> Swans sing before they die; 'twere no bad thing
> Did certain persons die before they sing.

One Greek legend has it that the soul of APOLLO, the god of music, passed into a swan, hence the Pythagorean fable that the souls of all good poets passed into swans (*See* SWAN OF AVON, MANTUA etc., *below*).

The male swan is called a *cob*, the female, a *pen*; a young swan, a *cygnet. See also* FIONNUALA; LEDA; LOHENGRIN.

The Knight of the Swan. LOHENGRIN.

The Order of the Swan. An order of knighthood founded by Frederick II of Brandenburg in 1440 (and shortly after in Cleves) in honour of the LOHENGRIN legend.

The Swan of Avon. SHAKESPEARE; so called (Ben Jonson) in allusion to his birthplace at Stratford-upon-Avon and the legend that APOLLO was changed into a swan.

The Swan of Lichfield. The name given to Anna Seward (1747–1809) the poetess.

The Swan of Mantua. VIRGIL, who

was born at Mantua.

The Swan of Meander. HOMER, who is supposed to have lived on the banks of the MEANDER.

The Swan with Two Necks. An old tavern sign, said to be a corruption of "two nicks" with which the Vintners' Company mark the beaks of their swans.

All your swans are geese. All your fine promises or expectations have proved fallacious. "Hope told a flattering tale." The converse, **All your geese are swans,** means all your children are paragons, and whatever you do is in your own eyes superlative work.

To swan about, or **around.** To move around aimlessly.

Swan-maidens. Fairies of northern folklore, who can become maidens or swans at will by means of the *swan shift*, a magic garment of swan's feathers. Many stories are told of how the swan shift was stolen, and the FAIRY was obliged to remain thrall to the thief until rescued by a KNIGHT.

Swan song. The song fabled to be sung by a dying swan; hence, the last work or appearance of a poet, composer, actor, etc.

Swan-upping. A taking up of swans and placing the marks of ownership on their beaks. The term is specially applied to annual expeditions for this purpose up the THAMES, when the marks of the owners (*viz.* the Crown and the Dyers' and Vintners' Companies) are made. The royal swans are marked with five nicks—two lengthwise, and three across the bill—and the Companies' swans with two nicks. Also called *swan-hopping*.

Swap. To swap, or **change horses in midstream.** To change leaders at the height of a crisis. Abraham Lincoln, in an address, 9 June 1864, referring to the fact that his fellow Republicans, though many were dissatisfied with his conduct of the CIVIL WAR, had renominated him for President, said that the Convention had concluded "that it is best not to swap horses while crossing the river".

Swashbuckler. A ruffian; a swaggerer. "From swashing," says Fuller (*Worthies*, III, 1662), "and making a noise on the buckler." The sword-players used to "swash" or tap their shield as fencers tap their foot upon the ground when they attack. *Cp.* SWINGE-BUCKLER.

Swastika. The GAMMADION or FYLFOT, an elaborate cross-shaped design (*see* CROSSES) used as a charm to ward off evil and bring good luck. It was adopted by Hitler as the NAZI emblem about 1920, probably from the German Baltic Corps, who wore it on their helmets after service in Finland, where it was used as a distinguishing mark on Finnish aeroplanes. It is from Sanskrit *svasti*, good fortune.

Swear to. Originally used only for solemn affirmations by the invocation of God or some sacred personage, etc.; hence to take an oath. Later extended to profanities and bad language by the use of sacred expressions as intensives and expletives.

To swear black and blue. To assert vigorously and emphatically.

To swear black is white. To swear to any falsehood.

To swear like a trooper. To indulge in very strong blasphemy or profanity, as a soldier sometimes does.

Sweat. An old sweat. An experienced soldier of long service, an old soldier.

To sweat a coin was to shake up GOLD or SILVER coins to remove particles of metal from them without the diminution of weight being noticeable.

To sweat a person is to exact the maximum amount of labour out of a person for a minimum wage. Also to bleed or fleece a person. Hence **sweating system** to denote the overworking of operatives in the clothing trades, etc., of earlier days. In the U.S. **to sweat it out of a person** is to extort a confession by threats and violence.

Sweating sickness, or **English sweat.** A fatal disease characterized by its symptoms—the onset of shivers followed by intense sweating, etc., which brought death in a few hours. It first appeared in England in 1485, and the last outbreak was in 1551. Although infrequent in its occurrence (five visitations in all), the mortality was considerable. It first reached the Continent in 1528. *Cp.* BLACK DEATH.

Swedenborgians. Followers of Emanuel Swedenborg (1688–1772), distinguished Swedish scientist and mystic, who in middle life came to hold himself appointed to reveal the Lord's teachings to mankind. He taught that Christ is the one God and that the Divine Trinity was present in him. The New Jerusalem Church or New Church was set up in ENGLAND in 1787 to propagate his teachings, which differ considerably from those of accepted Christianity.

Sweep. To sweep the board. In gaming, to win everything, to pocket all the stakes. Hence applied to one who carries all before him, wins all the prizes, etc.

To sweep the threshold. To announce to the world that the woman of the house is paramount. *See* SKIMMINGTON.

To sweep under the carpet. *See under* CARPET.

Sweepstakes. A race in which stakes are made by the owners of horses engaged, to be awarded to the winner or other horse in the race. Entrance money has to be paid to the race fund. If the horse runs, the full stake must be paid; but if it is withdrawn, a forfeit only is imposed.

Also a gambling arrangement in which a number of persons stake money on some event (usually a horse-race), each of whom draws a lot for every share bought, the total sum deposited being divided among the drawers of winners (or sometimes of starters).

Sweet. The sweet singer of Israel. King David, traditional author of the PSALMS.

To be sweet on. To be enamoured of, in love with.

To have a sweet tooth. To be very fond of dainties and sweet things generally.

Sweetness and light. A phrase much favoured by Matthew Arnold, particularly in his *Culture and Anarchy*:

> What we want is a fuller harmonious development of our humanity, a free play of thought upon our routine notions, spontaneity of consciousness, sweetness and light, and these are just what culture generates (ch. V).

The phrase was used by Swift (BATTLE OF THE BOOKS, 1697) in an imaginary fable by ÆSOP as to the merits of the bee (the ancients) and the spider (the moderns). It concludes:

> The difference is that instead of dirt and poison, we have rather chosen to fill our hives with honey and wax, thus furnishing mankind with the two noblest of things, which are sweetness and light (*Preface*).

Swell. A person showily dressed; one who puffs himself out beyond his proper dimensions, like the frog in the fable; hence, a fashionable person, one of high standing or importance. In American usage as an adjective, fine, stylish, first rate, just right.

Swelled head. An exaggerated sense of one's own dignity, usefulness, importance, etc.

Swim. In the swim. In a favourable position in SOCIETY of any kind; in with those who matter or from whom advantages may be gained; a phrase from angling. A lot of fish gathered together is called a *swim*, and when an angler can pitch his hook in such a place he is said to be "in a good swim".

Sink or swim. No matter what happens; convicted WITCHES were thrown into the water to "sink or swim"; if they sank they were drowned; if they swam it was clear proof they were in league with the Evil One; so it did not much matter, one way or the other.

To swim with the stream. To allow one's actions and principles to be guided solely by the force of prevailing public opinion.

Swing, with reference to JAZZ music is to play, either solo or ensemble, in such a manner over a regular pulse beat as to give the impression of a forward-moving rhythmic momentum. *To swing* is to play jazz music in this particular way and the term swing, although not new, gained a wide currency in the early 1930s from a popular number beginning "It don't mean a thing if it ain't got that swing". *Cp.* BOOGIE-WOOGIE; RAGTIME.

I don't care if I swing for him! A bitterly vengeful remark implying that the speaker will go to any length to get even—even if hanging be the consequence!

In full swing. Going splendidly; everything prosperous and in perfect order.

It went with a swing. Said of a ceremony, function, entertainment, etc., that passed off without a hitch and was a great success.

The swing-it-till-Monday basket. *See under* MONDAY.

What you lose on the swings you gain on the roundabouts. What you lose on one venture you recoup on another. A way of stating the law of averages.

Swiss. Swiss Guard. The Bourbon kings of France maintained a Guard of Swiss mercenaries until the Revolution. Pope Julius II (1503–13) instituted a Swiss Guard supplied by the cantons of Lucerne and Zürich. Some 100 men are still maintained as a papal escort drawn from the various Swiss cantons. Their formal uniform is still of MICHELANGELO's design.

No money—no Swiss—*i.e.* no assistance. The Swiss were for centuries the mercenaries of Europe—willing to serve anyone for pay—and were usually called in England *Switzers*, as in SHAKESPEARE's "Where are my Switzers? Let them guard the door" (*Hamlet*, IV, v).

Switched on. AU FAIT with contemporary fashionable and popular cults, thoroughly up to date and responsive to current trends and tendencies. The expression is also applied to someone under the influence of drugs.

Swithin, St. If it rains on St. Swithin's Day (15 July), **there will be rain for forty days.**

> St. Swithin's day, gif ye do rain, for forty days it will remain;
> St. Swithin's day an ye be fair, for forty days 'twill rain nae mair.

The legend is that St. Swithin (or Swithun), Bishop of Winchester and adviser of Egbert of Wessex, who died in 862, desired to be buried in the churchyard of the minster, that the "sweet rain of heaven might fall upon his grave". At CANONIZATION, the monks thought to honour the SAINT by removing his body into the cathedral choir and fixed 15 July 971 for the ceremony, but it rained day after day for 40 days, thereby, according to some, delaying the proceedings. His shrine was destroyed during the REFORMATION and a new one was dedicated in 1962. Those who hold to this superstition ignore the fact that it is based upon the dating of the JULIAN Calendar and therefore could not hold for 40 days from the current 15 July which is based on the GREGORIAN YEAR.

Switzers. *See* SWISS.

Sword. In the days of CHIVALRY and romance a KNIGHT's horse and sword were his two most carefully prized possessions and it was customary to give each a name.

Sword dance. A Scottish dance performed over two swords laid crosswise on the floor, or sometimes danced among swords placed point downwards in the ground; also a dance in which the men brandish swords and clash them together, the women passing under them when crossed.

The Sword of Damocles. *See* DAMOCLES.

The Sword of God. Khaled-ibn-al-Walid (d. 642), Mohammedan leader, was so called for his prowess at the battle of Muta (629), when he defeated the Emperor Heraclius, after a fierce two days' engagement.

The Sword of Rome. Marcellus, who opposed Hannibal (216–214 B.C.).

The Sword of the Spirit. The Word of God (*Eph.* vi, 17). Also the name of a Roman Catholic social movement founded in 1940.

At sword's point. In deadly hostility, ready to fight each other with swords.

Fire and sword. Rapine and destruction perpetrated by an invading army.

Flaming swords. *See* FLAMING.

Poke not fire with a sword. This was a precept of PYTHAGORAS, meaning add not fuel to fire, or do not irritate an angry man by sharp words which will only increase his rage. (*See* Iamblichus: *Protrepticus*, symbol ix.).

Sword and buckler. An old epithet for brag and bluster; as *a sword and buckler voice, sword and buckler men*, etc. Hotspur says of the future Henry V:

> And that same sword and buckler Prince of Wales,
> . . . .
> I'd have him poisoned with a pot of ale.
>
> SHAKESPEARE: *Henry IV, Pt. I*, I, iii.

To put to the sword. To slay.

To sheathe the sword. Figuratively, to put aside enmity, to make peace.

Your tongue is a double-edged sword. Whatever you say wounds; your argument cuts both ways. The allusion is to the double-edged sword out of the mouth of the Son of Man—one edge to condemn, and the other to save (*Rev.* i, 16).

Yours is a Delphic sword—it cuts both ways. Erasmus says a Delphic sword is that which accommodates itself to the PRO OR CON of a subject. The reference is to the double meanings of the Delphic ORACLES.

Sybarite (sĭ' bår ĭt). A self-indulgent person; a sensualist. The inhabitants of Sybaris, in south Italy, were proverbial for their luxurious living and self-indulgence. A tale is told by Seneca, of a Sybarite who complained that he could not rest comfortably at night, and being asked why, replied that, "He found a rose-leaf doubled under him, and it hurt him."

Sybil. A perverted spelling of SIBYL, in classical mythology a prophetess, especially the prophetesses of APOLLO (*see* SIBYLLINE BOOKS). GEORGE ELIOT was known to her friends as *The Sybil*.

Sycophant (sik' ō fănt). A SPONGER, parasite or servile flatterer; the Greek *sukophantes* (*sukon*, fig; *phainein*, to show), which is said to have meant one who informed against those who exported figs contrary to law or robbed the sacred fig-trees. Hence, by extension, a tale-bearer, flatterer, etc. This explanation is difficult to substantiate.

At ATHENS, *sycophantes* were a class of professional prosecutors who often blackmailed the wealthy with threats of prosecution or litigation and thus their name may include the added allusion of "shaking a fig-tree" to expose the fruit, as a blackmailer might shake his wealthy victim to produce the cash. This has no direct connexion with our use of the word.

Sydney or the Bush. An Australian expression meaning you either go for the very best or its the worst, there is no half-way house.

Syllogism (sil' ō jizm). A form of argument consisting of three propositions, a *major premise* or general statement, a *minor premise* or instance, and the *con-*

clusion, which is deducted from these.

Sylph (silf). An elemental spirit of air; so named in the MIDDLE AGES by the ROSICRUCIANS and CABBALISTS, from the Greek *silphe*, beetle or larva. *Cp.* SALAMANDER.

Any mortal who has preserved inviolate chastity might enjoy intimate familiarity with these gentle spirits, and deceased coquettes were said to become sylphs, "and sport and flutter in the fields of air".

> Whoever, fair and chaste,
> Rejects mankind, is by some sylph embraced.
> POPE: *The Rape of the Lock*, i, 67.

Symbolists. A group of French writers who, towards the end of the 19th century, revolted against Naturalism and Parnassianism (*see* PARNASSIAN SCHOOL *under* PARNASSUS). Their aim was to suggest rather than to depict or transcribe, and their watchword was Verlaine's, "Pas de couleur, rien que la nuance." Their precursors were Baudelaire, Banville, G. de Nerval and Villiers de l'Isle-Adam. Chief Symbolists: in verse, Verlaine, Rimbaud, Mallarmé; in prose, Huysmans.

Symbols of Saints. *See under* SAINTS.

Symplegades. Another name for the CYANEAN ROCKS.

Symposium. The Symposium is the title given to a dialogue by PLATO, and another by Xenophon, in which the conversation of SOCRATES and others is recorded.

Synagogue (Gr. *synagoge*, assembly or place of assembly). In Jewish communities, the institution for worship, the study of Judaism, and social life and service which had its origins at the time of the BABYLONIAN CAPTIVITY. The most notable of its special symbols are the Ark, in which scrolls of the Law are kept, the ever-burning lamp, and the Reading Desk, usually in the middle of the building. It is managed by a board of elders. *See* TABERNACLE; TEMPLE.

The Great Synagogue. According to Jewish tradition a body of 120 men in the time of Ezra and Nehemiah (5th century B.C.) who were engaged in remodelling the religious life of the Jews after the return from exile and in establishing the text and canon of the Hebrew SCRIPTURES.

Synchronism. A form of abstract art resembling ORPHISM begun by two Americans, Morgan Russell and S. MacDonald Wright, in 1913, characterized by movements of pure colour moving by gradations or rhythms from the primaries to the intermediary colours. Their painting depended on colour and its immediate effects. *Cp.* CUBISM; DADAISM; FAUVISM; FUTURISM; IMPRESSIONISM; SURREALISM; VORTICISM.

Syndicalism (Fr. *syndicalisme*, trade unionism). A trade-union movement originating in France about 1890 where it was known as *Syndicalisme révolutionnaire*. It was opposed to State socialism, the means of production being taken over by the TRADE UNIONS and not by the State, and government was to be by a federation of trade-union bodies.

Synecdoche (si nek' dō ki). The figure of speech which consists of putting a part for the whole, the whole for the part, a more comprehensive for a less comprehensive term, or *vice versa*. Thus, *a hundred bayonets* (for *a hundred soldiers*), *the town was starving* (for *the people in the town*).

Synoptic Gospels. Those of MATTHEW, MARK, and LUKE; so called because, taken together and apart from that of JOHN, they form a *synopsis* (Gr., a seeing together), *i.e.* a general and harmonized account of the life of Christ.

The Synoptic Problem. The problems of the origin and relationship of the three SYNOPTIC GOSPELS arising from large sections of material, and often phrasing, being common to them. There is general agreement that MARK is the earliest of the GOSPELS, and that it provides much of the material for MATTHEW and LUKE. The latter two contain material not found in Mark (*see* "Q"). There are varying theories among Biblical scholars to account for this parallelism, etc.

Syntax, Dr. (sin' tăks). The pious, henpecked clergyman, very simple-minded, but of excellent taste and scholarship, created by William Combe (1741–1823) to accompany a series of coloured comic illustrations by Rowlandson. His adventures are told in eight-syllabled verse in the *Three Tours of Dr. Syntax* (1812, 1820, and 1821).

Syrinx (sī' ringks). An Arcadian NYMPH of Greek legend. On being pursued by PAN she took refuge in the river Ladon, and prayed to be changed into a reed; the prayer was granted, and of the reed Pan made his pipes. Hence the name is given to the PAN-PIPE, or reed mouth-organ, and also to the vocal organ of birds.

T

T. The twentieth letter of the alphabet, representing Semitic and Greek *tau*, which meant "a sign or a mark". Our T is a modification of the earlier form, X. *See also* TAU.

As a mediæval numeral T represents 160, and T̄ 160,000.

It fits to a T. Exactly. The allusion is to the use of a *T-square* for the accurate drawing of right-angles, parallel lines, etc.

Marked with a T. Notified as a felon. Persons convicted of felony, and admitted to the BENEFIT OF CLERGY, were branded on the thumb with the letter T (thief). The law authorizing this was abolished in 1827.

Tab. To keep tabs on someone is to keep check on him.

Tabard. An outer coat of rough, heavy material once worn by poor people; also a loose outer garment, with or without short sleeves, worn like a cloak by KNIGHTS over their armour—what Chaucer called *cote-armour* often emblazoned with heraldic devices. It survives in the tabard worn by Heralds and PURSUIVANTS.

The Tabard Inn. The inn where pilgrims from LONDON used to set out on their journey to Canterbury; it was on the London estate of the abbots of Hyde (near Winchester), and lay in the SOUTHWARK (now BOROUGH) High Street, a little to the south of LONDON BRIDGE. The site is marked by a commemorative plaque. The inn and its host Harry Baily are immortalized in Chaucer's *Canterbury Tales*.

Tabby. Originally the name (from Arabic) of a silk material with a "watered" surface, giving an effect of wavy lines; applied to the brownish cat with dark stripes, because its markings resemble this material.

Tabernacle. (Lat. *tabernaculum*, a tent). The portable shrine instituted by MOSES during the wanderings of the Jews in the wilderness. It was divided by a veil or hanging, behind which, in the "HOLY OF HOLIES", was the Ark. The outer division was called the Holy Place. When set up in camp the whole was surrounded by an enclosure. *See Exod.* xxv–xxxi; xxxiii, 7–10; xxxv–xl.

In Roman Catholic churches, the tabernacle is the ornamental receptacle on the High Altar, in which the vessels containing the Blessed Sacrament are reserved. The name derives from the application of the word *tabernaculum* in church ornamentation to a variety of canopied forms.

The Feast of the Tabernacles. One of the three main feasts of the Jewish year lasting seven days followed by an eighth day of "holy convocation" (see *Lev.* xxiii. 34–43; *Numb.* xxix, 12–34). It commemorates the way the Jews dwelt in booths or tents in the wilderness and also celebrates the final in-gathering of the harvest and the vintage. It begins on the 15th Tishri (September—October).

Tin Tabernacles. The name given to the corrugated iron Nonconformist chapels and other churches which were erected in the 19th and early 20th centuries to meet the needs of developing or scattered Christian communities.

Table. Archbishop Parker's Table. The table of prohibited degrees within which marriage was forbidden, published in 1563, and to be found as the *Table of Kindred and Affinity* in the BOOK OF COMMON PRAYER. Matthew Parker was Archbishop of Canterbury from 1559 to 1575 (*See* NAG'S HEAD CONSECRATION; VESTIARIAN CONTROVERSY.)

The Lord's Table. The communion table or ALTAR.

The Round Table, or **Table Round.** *See under* ROUND.

Table d'hôte (Fr., the host's table). The "ORDINARY" at an hotel or restaurant; the meal for which one pays a fixed price whether one partakes of all the courses or not. In the MIDDLE AGES, and even down to the reign of Louis XIV, the landlord's or host's table was the only public dining place known in Germany and France.

Table of Pythagoras. The common multiplication table, carried up to ten. The table is divided into a hundred little squares. The name is taken from a corrupt text of Boethius, who was really referring to the ABACUS.

Table of Cebes. Cebes was a Theban philosopher and disciple of SOCRATES. His *Tabula* presents a picture of human life depicted with great accuracy of judgment and splendour of sentiment.

The Twelve Tables. The tables of the Roman laws engraved on brass, brought from ATHENS to ROME by the decemvirs.

Table Mountain. A flat topped mountain, especially that overlooking Cape Town.

Table-rapping. The occurrence of knocking sounds on a table without apparent source but coming from the departed, according to spiritualists, who use them as a supposed means of contacting the dead.

Table-talk. Small talk, chit-chat, familiar conversation.

Table-turning. The turning of tables without the application of mechanical force, which in the early days of SPIRITUALISM was commonly practised at seances, and sank to the level of a parlour trick. It was said by some to be the work of departed spirits, and by others to be due to a force akin to MESMERISM.

To fence the tables. In Scottish usage, to debar those unworthy from communion.

To lay on the table. The parliamentary phrase for postponing consideration of a motion, proposal, BILL, etc., indefinitely. Hence *to table a matter* is to defer it *sine die*. It is also used to mean submitting something for discussion.

To turn the tables. To reverse the conditions or relations; as, for instance, to rebut a charge by bringing forth a counter-charge. The phrase comes from the old custom of reversing the *table* or board, in games such as CHESS and draughts, so that the opponent's relative position is altogether changed.

Tableaux vivants (Fr., living pictures). Representations of statuary groups by living persons; said to have been invented by Madame de Genlis (1746–1830) while she had charge of the children of the Duc d'Orléans.

Taboo, tabu. A Polynesian word signifying that which is banned; the prohibition of the use of certain persons, animals, things, etc., or the utterance of certain names and words. Thus a temple is *taboo*, and so is he who violates a temple and everyone and everything connected with what is taboo becomes taboo also. Captain Cook was made *taboo* when he tried to set up an observatory in the Sandwich Islands. The idea of taboo is not, of course, peculiar to the Polynesians and is found among the ancient Egyptians, Jews, etc. Hence a person who is ostracized or an action, custom, etc., that is altogether forbidden by society, is said to be *taboo* or *tabooed*.

Tabula rasa (tăb′ ū là rā′ zà) (Lat., a scraped tablet). A clean slate—literally and figuratively—on which anything can be written. Thus, we say that the mind of a person who has been badly taught must become a *tabula rasa* before he can learn anything properly.

Tace is Latin for candle. Silence is most discreet. "MUM'S THE WORD". *Tace* is Latin for "be silent", and *candle* is symbolical of light. The phrase means "keep it dark", do not throw light upon it. Fielding, in *Amelia* (ch. x), has—"*Tace*, madam," answered Murphy, "is Latin for a candle".

It was customary at one time to express disapprobation of a play or an actor by throwing a candle on to the stage thus sometimes causing the curtain to be drawn.

Tack. On the right tack, or **on the**

Taffeta

wrong tack. Taking the right (or wrong) line or course of action. A nautical phrase, *tack* here being the course of a ship when "tacking", *i.e.* steering a zigzag course when sailing to windward.

Taffeta, or **taffety. Taffeta phrases.** Smooth, sleek phrases, EUPHEMISMS. We also use the words FUSTIAN, *stuff, silken, shoddy,* BUCKRAM, *velvet,* etc., to qualify phrases and literary compositions spoken or written.

> Taffeta phrases, silken terms precise,
> Three-piled hyperboles.
>> SHAKESPEARE: *Love's Labour's Lost,*
>> V, ii.

Taffy. A Welshman, from *Davy (Dafydd,* David), a common name in Wales; perhaps it is best known among the English from the old rhyme in allusion to the days of border cattle raids.

> Taffy was a Welshman,
> Taffy was a thief,
> Taffy came to my house
> And stole a leg of beef.

Tag. A children's game of catch in which from the outset each person touched or "caught" joins the line to catch those remaining.

Tag Days. The American equivalent of British FLAG DAYS.

Tag, rag and bobtail. *See* RAG-TAG AND BOBTAIL.

Tages (tā´ jēz). In Etruscan mythology, a mysterious boy with the wisdom of an old man who was ploughed up, or who sprang from the ground, at Tarquinii. He is said to have been the grandson of JUPITER and to have instructed the Etruscans in the art of AUGURY. The latter wrote down his teaching in 12 books, which were known as "the books of Tages", or "the Acherontian books".

Tail. According to an old fable lions wipe out their footsteps with their tail, that they may not be tracked.

Out of the tail of one's eye. With a side-long glance; just to see a thing "out of the corner of your eye."

Tail male, tail female. *See* ENTAIL.

To put salt on the tail. *see* PUT SOME SALT ON HIS TAIL *under* SALT.

To tail a person is to follow someone and not to lose sight of them.

To turn tail. To turn one's back and make off.

To twist the lion's tail. *See under* LION.

With his tail between his legs. Very dejected, quite downcast. The allusion is to dogs.

With a sting in its tail. In speech or writing, that which contains a sting or rebuke at the end: an unexpected catch, snag or hurt at the end of the matter. The bee has a sting in its tail, so have the sting-ray and the scorpion. *See* TELEGONUS.

Tailed men. It was an old belief in mediæval times that such creatures existed and among continentals Englishmen were once reputed to have tails. It was long a saying that the men of Kent were born with tails, as a punishment for the murder of Thomas á Becket.

Jews and Cornishmen were also held to have tails, the appendage also being borne by the DEVIL. In the former case from a confusion of *rabbi* with *raboin* or *rabuino,* the devil, from Span. *rabo,* a tail.

Tail-end Charlie. An R.A.F. phrase in World War II for the rear-gunner in the tail of an aircraft; also for the aircraft at the rear of a group, or the last ship in a flotilla.

Taillefer (tī a fâr). The Norman TROUVÈRE who accompanied William of Normandy's army to England in 1066. He begged leave to strike the first blow and rode far ahead of the other horsemen singing of CHARLEMAGNE and ROLAND and playing like a juggler with his sword. After overcoming his first two opponents he charged into the Saxon host and was cut to pieces.

Tailor. The Three Tailors of Tooley Street. Canning says that three tailors of Tooley Street, SOUTHWARK, addressed a petition of grievances to the HOUSE OF COMMONS, beginning: "We, the people of England". Hence the phrase is used of any pettifogging côterie that fancies it represents the nation.

Tai-ping. The word means "Great peace", and the Tai-pings were the Chinese followers of Hung Hsiu-ch'uan (Heavenly Prince) in the rebellion of 1851–1864 against the Manchu dynasty. Hung, a Christian of a kind, who claimed to be the Younger Brother of

Christ, set out to establish the "Great Peace" and captured Nanking in 1853. The rebellion was finally crushed, after millions had been killed by the Emperor's forces aided by CHINESE GORDON and his EVER-VICTORIOUS ARMY.

Take. To be taken aback. *See* ABACK.

To have taking ways. To be of an ingratiating disposition; readily able to make oneself liked. *Fetching ways, winning ways* amount to the same thing.

To take after. To have a strong resemblance to, physically, mentally, etc. "Doesn't little Johnny take after his father?" "Most of Lawrence's paintings seem to take after Romney."

To take back one's words. To withdraw them; to recant.

To take in. To deceive, gull. Hence, *a regular take-in*, a hoax, swindle.

To take in one's stride. Effortlessly or unflurriedly, without disrupting one's normal activities or routine.

To take it. To withstand suffering, hardship, punishment, insult, etc. "Britain can take it" was a popular slogan during the air attacks of World War II.

To take it lying down. To submit to insult or oppression without protest or resistance, like a dog when it is cowed.

To take it out of someone. To exact the utmost from, to give someone a real drubbing; to exact satisfaction from, to get one's own back. Also to become thoroughly exhausted, as, "Working after midnight does take it out of me."

To take it out on someone. Colloquially, to work off one's irritation, frustration, etc., by being unpleasant to someone else.

To take it upon oneself. To make oneself responsible (perhaps unwarrantably), to assume control.

To take off. To mimic or ridicule; also to start, especially of an aeroplane or of one in an athletic contest, as jumping or racing.

To take on. To undertake to perform, to assume, or, colloquially, to be upset or considerably affected as in, "Don't take on so" (*i.e.* don't distress yourself so); to make a fuss.

To take one down a peg. *See under* PEG.

To take over. To assume the management, control, or ownership.

To take someone at his word. To regard what he has said as trustworthy.

To take to. To develop an immediate liking for someone; to begin to develop a habit, as, "He has taken to drink since his wife absconded."

To take to task. To blame or censure, to call to account.

To take up. To pick up, to raise; to arrest; to begin to cultivate a hobby, study, etc.; also used of beginning to patronize or "adopt" people, usually for their advancement in society or business, etc.

To take up with. To commence to associate with.

You can't take it with you, *i.e.* to the grave; in other words make use of your resources, material and financial, while you have the chance.

You must take us as you find us. Said to an unexpected visitor before whose arrival there has been no time to make special preparations.

Take-home pay. That which is left to the wage earner after the depredations of the CHANCELLOR OF THE EXCHEQUER and the exaction of the various levies for social insurance.

A take-over bid. A favourable offer to the shareholders of a company by another company which wishes to secure control of it.

Tale. An old wives' tale. Legendary lore, or a story usually involving the marvellous, and only accepted by the credulous. George Peele has a play *The Old Wives' Tale* (1595) and Arnold Bennett a novel (1908) of the same title.

A tale of a tub. *See under* TUB.

To tell tales out of school. To utter abroad affairs not meant for the public ear; to reveal confidential matters.

Talent. Ability, aptitude, a "gift" for something or other. The word is borrowed from the parable in *Matt.* xxv, 14–30, and was originally the name of a weight and piece of money in Assyria, Greece, ROME, etc. (Gr. *talanton*, a balance). The value varied, the later Attic talent weighing about 57 lb. troy, and being worth about £250.

The Ministry of all the Talents. *See* ALL THE TALENTS.

Tales (tā' lēz). Persons in the court from whom selection is made to supply the place of jurors who have been empanelled, but are not in attendance. It is the first word of the Latin sentence providing for this contingency—*Tales de circumstantibus, i.e.* "from such (persons) as are standing about". Those who supplement the jury are called *talesmen* and their names are set down in the *talesbook*.

> To serve for jurymen or tales.
> BUTLER: *Hudibras*, III, viii.

Taliesin (tăl i ēs' in). A Welsh BARD of the late 16th century about whom very little is known. The so-called *Book of Taliesin* is of the 13th century and its contents are the work of various authors. The village of Taliesin in Cardiganshire is named after him. The story is that Prince Elphin, son of the King of Gwynedd, was given the right to net a certain weir near the mouth of the Dovey once a year, and on this occasion his net was brought ashore without a single salmon in it. While bewailing his constant misfortune, he noticed a leather wallet suspended from the timber of the weir and upon opening it found therein a youth of such lustrous brow that Elphin named him Taliesin (radiant brow). Taliesin brought wonderful prosperity to Elphin and became the greatest of the British bards at the court of King ARTHUR at CAERLEON.

Talisman. A charm or magical figure or word, such as the ABRAXAS which is cut on metal or stone under the influence of certain planets; it is supposed to be sympathetic and to communicate to the wearer influence from the planets.

In order to free a place of vermin, a talisman consisting of the obnoxious creature was made in wax or consecrated metal, in a planetary hour.

The word is the Arabic *tilsam* from late Greek *telesma*, mystery.

Tall. A tall story. An incredible tale.

To walk tall. *See under* WALK.

Tally, To. To correspond. In England the tally, a notched piece of wood (Fr. *taille* a notch or incision) used for reckoning, had a particular importance as an EXCHEQUER record and receipt down to 1826 (usually of money loaned to the Government). The notch on one side was an acknowledgement of the sum paid, two other sides were marked with the date, the name of the payer, etc., and the whole was cleft longitudinally so that each half contained one written side and the half of every notch. One part was retained at the Exchequer (the *counterstock*) and the other (the *stock*) was issued. When payment was required the two parts were compared if they "tallied" all was in order.

In 1834, the mass of these valuable records were burnt in the stoves which heated the HOUSE OF LORDS; an unintelligent action causing the disastrous fire which destroyed the old PARLIAMENT buildings.

Tallyman. A travelling hawker who calls at private houses to sell wares on the *tally system*—that is, part payment on account, and other parts when the man calls again, so called because he keeps a *tally* or SCORE of his transactions.

To live tally, or **make a tally bargain.** Said of a couple who live together as man and wife without being married—presumably because they do so as their tastes *tally*, and not from any reason of compulsion. *Cp.* COMMON LAW WIFE.

Tally-ho! The cry of fox-hunters on catching sight of the fox. It is an English form of Fr. *taiaut*, which was similarly used in deer-hunting.

Talmud, The (tăl' mŭd) (Heb., instruction). The collection of Jewish civil and religious law, religious and moral doctrine, and ritual founded on SCRIPTURE. It consists of the MISHNAH and the GEMARA and there are two recensions, the Babylonian and the Palestinian, or Jerusalem. The Babylonian Talmud, about three times the volume of the Palestinian, is held to be the more important and it was completed towards the end of the 5th century A.D.. The Palestine Talmud was produced in the mid-4th century A.D. After the BIBLE, the Talmud is the most important influence in Jewish life.

Talus (tā' lùs). *See* MAN OF BRASS *under* BRASS.

Tamberlane, Tamerlane. Names under

which the renowned Tartar conqueror Timur, or Timur i Leng, *i.e.* Timur the Lame (1336–1405), is commonly known. He had his capital at Samarkand, and conquered most of Persia and India, Georgia and other Caucasian lands, and was preparing to conquer China when he died. The story of his confinement of the Sultan Bayezid, or Bajazet, in an iron cage is probably legendary. He is the hero of Marlowe's blank verse tragedy *Tamburlaine the Great* (acted 1587). In Rowe's play *Tamerlane* (1702), the warrior appears as a calm philosophic prince—out of compliment to William III.

Tammany Hall. The headquarters (in 14th Street, New York) of the Democratic Party organization in New York City and State. In the 19th century, it became a powerful influence in the party as a whole and in the 1870s, under W.M. Tweed, was associated with widespread corruption, and this and other incidents led to *Tammany Hall* being used figuratively for wholesale and widespread political or municipal malpractice.

Tammuz. *See* THAMMUZ.

Tam-o'-Shanter. The hero of Burns's poem of that name; the soft cloth headdress is so called from him.

Tancred (d. 1112). One of the chief heroes of the First CRUSADE, and a leading character in TASSO'S JERUSALEM DELIVERED. He was the son of Otho the Good and Emma (sister of Robert Guiscard). In the epic he was the greatest of all Christian warriors except RINALDO.

Disraeli's strange romance, *Tancred* (1847), tells of an early-19th-century heir to a dukedom who went on a "New Crusade" to the HOLY LAND.

Tangie. A water-spirit of the Orkneys appearing as a man covered with seaweed (Dan. *tang*, seaweed) or as a little seahorse.

Tanist (Ir. and Gael., *tanaiste*). The lord or chief of a territory, or his elected heir. It was an ancient custom in IRELAND and among CELTIC peoples for the family or CLAN to elect a successor to the lands from among their number, usually the nearest male relative of the existing chieftain unless he were a minor or

otherwise unsuitable. This mode of tenure is called **tanistry**.

Tanist Stone. The monolith erected by the ancient GAELIC kings at their coronation, especially that called LIA-FAIL, which, according to tradition, is identical with the famous Stone of SCONE. It is said to have been set up at Icolmkil for the coronation of Fergus I of SCOTLAND, a contemporary of ALEXANDER THE GREAT and son of Ferchard, King of Ireland.

Tank. The heavily armoured motorized combat vehicle running on caterpillar tracks was first introduced on the battlefield by the British in the Battle of the Somme (1916). It owes its name to *tank* being used as a code word for these vehicles in order not to arouse enemy suspicions and to achieve a complete surprise.

Tanner. Slang for a sixpenny piece. Originally a silver coin, first minted in 1551. It survived after the introduction of DECIMAL CURRENCY with a value of 2½p. until its withdrawal in 1980. It was so called after John Sigismund Tanner (d. 1775), an engraver at the MINT. *Cp.* TESTER.

Tannhäuser (tăn' hoi zer). A lyrical poet, or MINNESINGER of Germany, who flourished in the second half of the 13th century. He led a wandering life, and is said even to have visited the Far East; this fact, together with his *Busslied* (song of repentance), and the general character of his poems, probably gave rise to the legend about him—which first appeared in a 16th-century German ballad. This related how he spends a voluptuous year with VENUS, in the VENUSBERG, a magic land reached through a subterranean cave; at last he obtains leave to visit the upper world, and goes to POPE Urban IV for absolution. "No", says His Holiness, "you can no more hope for mercy than this dry staff can be expected to bud again." Tannhäuser departs in despair; but on the third day the papal staff bursts into blossom; the Pope sends in every direction for Tannhäuser, but the KNIGHT is nowhere to be found, for, mercy having been refused, he has returned to end his days in the arms of Venus. *See* ECKHARDT THE

FAITHFUL.

Wagner's opera of this name was first produced in 1845.

Tantalus (tăn' tà lus). In Greek mythology, the son of ZEUS and a NYMPH. He was a Lydian king, highly honoured and prosperous; but, because he divulged to mortals the secrets of the gods, he was plunged up to the chin in a river of HADES, a tree hung with clusters of fruit being just above his head. As every time he tried to drink the waters receded from him, and as the fruit was just out of reach, he suffered agony from thirst, hunger, and unfulfilled anticipation.

Hence, our verb, *to tantalize*, to excite a hope and disappoint it; and hence the name *tantalus* applied to a lock-up spirit chest in which the bottles are visible but un-get-at-able without the key.

Tantivy, or **Tantivy Man** (tăn tiv' i). A name given TORY High churchmen in the time of James II. They were caricatured as being mounted on the CHURCH OF ENGLAND riding "tantivy" to ROME. *To ride tantivy* is a hunting term meaning to ride at full gallop.

Tantony pig. The smallest pig of a litter, which, according to the old proverb, will follow its owner anywhere. So called in honour of St. ANTHONY, who was the patron SAINT of swineherds, and is frequently represented with a little pig at his side.

Tantony is also applied to a small church bell—or to any hand bell—for there is usually a bell round the neck of St. Anthony's pig or attached to the TAU CROSS he carries.

Tantras, The. Sanskrit religious books (6th and 7th century A.D.) of the Shaktas, a Hindu cult whose adherents worship the female principle, usually centring round Siva's wife, Parvati. They are mostly in the form of a dialogue between SIVA and his wife.

Tantra is Sanskrit for thread, or warp, and hence is used of groundwork, order or doctrine of religion.

Taoism (tā' ō izm) (*tao*, the way). One of the three religious systems of China along with Confucianism and BUDDHISM. It derives from the philosophical system of Lao-tsze (6th century B.C.).

Tap. On tap. Available, ready for use; as

liquor is from a cask when it has been tapped.

Taped. To have a person taped. Fully appraised or summed up, completely "weighed up" or assessed; as if measured with a tape. When one has a situation "taped" it also implies having things under control.

Tapley, Mark. Martin's servant and companion in Dickens's *Martin Chuzzlewit,* sometimes taken to typify anyone cheerful under all circumstances.

Tappit-hen. A Scots term, properly for a hen with a crest or tuft on its head, but generally used for a large beer or wine measure. *Cp.* JEROBOAM.

Tar. All tarred with the same brush. All alike to blame, all having the same faults; all sheep of the same flock. The allusion is to the former treatment of sores, etc., on sheep, with a brush dipped in tar.

Losing or **spoiling a ship for a ha'porth o' tar.** *See under* SHIP.

Tarred and feathered. Stripped to the skin, daubed with tar, and then rolled in feathers so that the feathers adhere; a common popular punishment in primitive communities, and still occasionally resorted to.

The first record of this punishment is in 1189 (1 Rich. I). A statute was made that any robber voyaging with the crusaders "shall be first shaved, then boiling pitch shall be poured on his head, and a cushion of feathers shook over it". The wretch was then to be put on shore at the very first place the ship came to (Rymer: *Fœdera*, I, 65).

Tara. The Hill of Tara, County Meath, some 20 miles north of Dublin, was the ancient seat of the High Kings of IRELAND until the 6th century A.D. Only a series of earthworks now remain to mark the site of "Tara's halls". Here were held a national assembly, the Feis of Tara, and gatherings for music, games and literary contests. Here too was the LIA-FAIL which is supposed to have been Jacob's pillow taken from Tara to SCOTLAND. *See* TANIST STONE.

Tarantella (tăr ėn tel' à). A very quick Neapolitan dance (or its music) for one couple, said to have been based on the gyrations practised by those whom the

TARANTULA had poisoned.

Tarantula (tà răn′ tū là). A large and hairy venomous spider (so called from *Taranto*, Lat. *Tarentum*, a town in Apulia, Italy, where they abound), whose bite was formerly supposed to be the cause of the dancing mania hence known as *tarantism*. This was an hysterical disease, common, epidemically, in Southern Europe from the 15th to the 17th centuries.

Targums (Aramaic, interpretations). The name given to the various Aramaic (Chaldean) interpretations and translations of the OLD TESTAMENT, made in Babylon and Palestine when Hebrew was ceasing to be the everyday speech of the Jews. They were transmitted orally and the oldest, that of Oneklos on the PENTATEUCH, is probably of the 2nd century A.D.

Tarot, or **Tarok Cards.** Italian playing cards, first used in the 14th century and still occasionally employed in fortune-telling. The pack originally contained 78 cards: four suits of numeral cards with four COAT CARDS, *i.e.* king, queen, chevalier, and valet, and in addition to the four suits 22 *atutti* cards, or trumps, known as *tarots*.

The modern pack contains 54 cards: 32 suit cards, 21 tarots, and 1 joker.

Tarpeian Rock (tar pē′ àn). An ancient rock or peak (no longer in existence) of the Capitoline Hill, ROME; so called from Tarpeia, the faithless daughter of the governor of the citadel (*see* CRUSHED BY HIS HONOURS *under* HONOUR), who was flung from this rock by the SABINES. It became the traditional place from which traitors were hurled.

Tarquin (tar′ kwin). The family name of a legendary line of early Roman kings. Tarquinius Priscus, the fifth king of ROME is dated 617–578 B.C. His son, Tarquinius Superbus, was the seventh (and last) king of Rome, and it was his son, Tarquinius Sextus, who committed the rape on Lucretia, in revenge for which the Tarquins were expelled from Rome and a Republic established.

Tarquin is also the name of a "recreant knight" figuring in the ARTHURIAN ROMANCES.

Tarroo-Ushtey. In MANXLAND, an amphibious bull which frequented the curraghs (fens) and sometimes mingled with the cattle in the fields to lure the finest heifer to death.

Tartar, or **Tatar.** The Asiatic tribes of this name are properly called *Tatars*, the form *Tartar* probably deriving from association with TARTARUS, HELL, the Tatars being part of the Asiatic host under Jenghiz Khan which threatened 13th-century Europe. Hence a savage, irritable or excessively severe person is called a *tartar*; when applied to a woman it denotes a VIXEN or shrew.

To catch a tartar. *See under* CATCH.

Tartarian Lamb. *See under* LAMB.

Tartarus. The infernal regions of classical mythology; used as equivalent to HADES by later writers, but by HOMER placed as far beneath Hades as Hades is beneath the earth. It was here that ZEUS confined the TITANS. *Cp.* HELL.

Tassies. Tasmanians. *See* APPLE-ISLANDERS.

Tasso, Torquato (1544–1595). The celebrated Italian poet, author of *Rinaldo* (1562) and JERUSALEM DELIVERED (1575). He became the idol of the brilliant court of Ferrara but his exhausting literary labours and the excitement and stresses of court life caused mental breakdown, and he spent most of the rest of his life in confinement, exile, and poverty. His *Jerusalem Delivered* was pirated in 1580 and he received no payment for his masterpiece. He died as a pensioner of Pope Clement VIII.

Tattoo. The beat of the drum at night to recall soldiers to barracks is from Dutch *taptoe*, and "to beat the taptoe" was the signal to put the tap to, *i.e.* shut, public houses. When the word came into use in the mid-17th century it was written *taptoo, tapp-too*, etc.

Tattoo, as the indelible marking of the skin, is one of our few words from Polynesian. It is the Tahitian *tatau*, mark, and was introduced by Captain Cook in 1769.

Beating the devil's tattoo. *See under* DEVIL (phrases).

Torchlight tattoo. A military entertainment, carried out at night in the open air with illuminations, evolutions, and martial music.

Tau. The letter T in Greek and the SEMI-
TIC languages. Anciently it was the last
letter of the Greek alphabet (as it still is
of the Hebrew); and in Middle English
literature the phrase *Alpha to Omega*
was not infrequently rendered *Alpha to
Tau*.

Tau cross. A T-shaped CROSS, especially St. ANTHONY's cross.

Taurus (taw' rŭs) (Lat., the bull). The
second zodiacal constellation, and the
second sign of the ZODIAC, which the
sun enters about 21 April.

Taverner's Bible. *See* BIBLE, THE ENG-
LISH.

Tawdry. A corruption of St. Audrey (*Audrey* itself being a corruption of *Ethel-
drida*). At the annual fair of St. Audrey,
in the Isle of Ely, cheap jewellery and
showy lace called *St. Audrey's lace* were
sold; hence *tawdry*, which is applied to
anything gaudy, in bad taste, and of little value. *Cp.* TANTONY.

Taxi, Short for *taximeter*, is the accepted
term for a motor-cab, which takes its
name from the meter which was installed on French horse-drawn cabs or
fiacres long before motor-cabs appeared
on the road. In Britain it only became
common with the introduction of
motor-cabs and was thus associated with
them.

Te Deum, The (tē dē' ŭm). So called
from the opening words *Te Deum lau-
damus* (Thee, God, we praise). This
Latin hymn was traditionally assigned
to SS. AMBROSE and AUGUSTINE, and
was supposed to have been improvised
by St. Ambrose while baptizing St. Augustine (386). Hence it is sometimes
called "the Ambrosian Hymn" and in
some early psalters it is entitled "*Canti-
cum Ambrosii et Augustini*". It is now
generally thought to have been written
by Niceta, Bishop of Remesiana (d. *c.*
414). It is used in various offices and at
MATTINS.

Te Igitur (Lat.) "Thee therefore". In
the ROMAN CATHOLIC CHURCH, the first
words of the old form of the CANON OF
THE MASS, and consequently the name
for the first section of the canon.

Oaths upon the Te Igitur. Oaths
sworn on this part of the MISSAL, which
were regarded as especially sacred.

Tea. Not for all the tea in China. Under
no circumstances, not for any consideration.

Not my cup of tea. Not at all in my
line, not what I want or am suited for.

A storm in a teacup. *See under*
STORM.

That's another cup of tea. That is a
very different matter.

Teapoy (tē' poi). A small, three- or
four-legged occasional table. Though
largely used for standing a tea-tray
upon, the teapoy has really nothing to
do with tea, the name coming from Hindustani *teen*, three, and the Persian *pae*,
a foot.

Teague. A contemptuous name for an Irishman (from the Irish personal name),
rarely used nowadays but common in
the 17th and 18th centuries.

Tear (târ). **To tear Christ's body.** To
use imprecations. The common oaths of
mediæval times were by different parts
of the Lord's body; hence the preachers
used to talk of "tearing God's body by
imprecations".

To tear someone off a strip. *See under* STRIP.

Tear (tēr). St. LAWRENCE's tears. *See*
SHOOTING STARS.

Tears of Eos. The dewdrops of the
morning were so called by the Greeks.
Eos was the mother of MEMNON, and
wept for him every morning.

The Vale of Tears. This world. *Cp.*
BACA.

Tear-jerker. A novel, play, or film
with a very sad or sentimental theme.

Ted, or Teddy. A pet-form of Edward.

A ted, teddy boy, teddy girl. *See* ED-
WARDIAN.

Teddy-bear. A child's toy bear, said to
have been named after Theodore (Teddy) Roosevelt, who was fond of bear-
hunting.

Teeth. *See* TOOTH.

Teetotal. A word expressive of total abstinence from alcoholic liquors. The origin
of the word has two explanations. Dick
Turner, a Lancashire artisan of Preston,
coined it about 1833 (some accounts say
that he stuttered!) and his tombstone
bears the inscription:

> Beneath this stone are deposited the re-
> mains of Richard Turner, author of the

word *Teetotal* as applied to abstinence from all intoxicating liquors, who departed this life on the 27th day of October, 1846, aged 56 years.

The word also seems to have arisen independently in America, perhaps a little earlier, from the practice introduced by a New York Temperance Society of getting members to sign the pledge. "O.P." against a name stood for "Old Pledge" (abstinence from distilled spirits only) and "T" for total abstinence. Frequent reference to "T-total" gave rise to the word.

Teian Muse, The (tī' an). ANACREON, who was born at Teos, Asia Minor.

Telamones (tel a mō' nēz). Large, sculptured male figures (*cp.* ATLANTES; CARYATIDES) serving as architectural columns or pilasters. So called from the Greek legendary hero Telamon (father of AJAX) who took part in the Calydonian hunt (*see* CALYDONIAN BOAR *under* BOAR), and the expedition of the ARGONAUTS.

Telegonus (tē leg' on us). The son of ULYSSES and CIRCE, who was sent to find his father. On coming to Ithaca, he began to plunder the fields when Ulysses and TELEMACHUS appeared in arms to prevent him. Telegonus killed his father, who was unknown to him, with a lance pointed with the spine of a trygon, or sting-ray which Circe had given him. He subsequently married PENELOPE.

Tel el Amarna Tablets. Cuneiform tablets found in 1887 at Tel el Armarna, the modern name for the abandoned site of Akhetaton, the short-lived capital built (*c.* 1360 B.C.) by Ikhnaton (Amenophis IV) in place of THEBES. These important sources of historical evidence concern a period before the exodus of the Israelities from Egypt and consist of letters from Egyptian governors in Syria and Palestine, from the kings of Assyria and Babylon, and others. About two-thirds of the 230 or so tablets went to the Berlin Museum, the remainder to the BRITISH MUSEUM.

Telemachus (tel lem'akus). The only son of ULYSSES and PENELOPE. After the fall of TROY he went, attended by ATHENE in the guise of MENTOR, in quest of his father. He ultimately found him, and the two returned to Ithaca and slew Penelope's suitors.

Telepathy (tē lep' a thi). The word invented in 1882 by F.W.H. Myers to describe "the communication of impressions of any kind from one mind to another independently of the recognized channels of sense". The term "thought-transference" is often used for this phenomenon and more nearly expresses its implications, for it indicates the communication of thought from one person to another without the medium of speech.

Telephus. *See* ACHILLEA.

Tell, William. The legendary national hero of Switzerland whose deeds appear to be an invention of the 15th century and are paralleled in numerous European myths and legends.

The story is that Tell was the champion of the Swiss in the struggle against Albert I (slain 1308), Duke of Austria. Tell refused to salute the cap of Gessler, Albert's tyrannical steward, and for this act of independence was sentenced to shoot with his bow and arrow an apple from the head of his own son. He achieved this feat and Gessler demanded what his second arrow was for, whereupon Tell boldly replied, "To shoot you with, had I killed my son." Gessler had him conveyed to Küssnacht castle, but he escaped on the way and later killed Gessler in ambush. A rising followed which established the independence of Switzerland.

The story has been systematically exposed as having no foundation in fact, and similar feats are recorded in the Norse legend of Toki. The popularity of tales of the "master shot" is evidence by the stories of Adam Bell, CLYM OF THE CLOUGH, WILLIAM CLOUDESLEY and EGIL.

Telstar. The name given to the satellite launched in 1962 for relaying transatlantic telephone messages and television pictures.

Temperance, The Apostle of. *See* MATHEW.

Templars, or **Knights Templar.** In 1119, nine French KNIGHTS bound themselves to protect pilgrims on their way to the HOLY PLACES and took monastic vows. They received the name

TEMPLARS because they had their headquarters in a building on the site of the old TEMPLE OF SOLOMON at JERUSALEM.

Their habit was a long white mantle ornamented with a red cross on the left shoulder. Their seal showed two knights riding on one horse, the story being that the first Master was so poor that he had to share a horse with one of his followers. Their banner, called *Le Beauseant* or *Bauceant* (an old French name for a piebald horse), was half black, half white, and charged with a red CROSS.

Their bravery in the field was unquestionable, as was in due course the wealth and power of the Order which had houses throughout Europe, but the fall of Acre (1291) marked the ultimate failure of their efforts. Jealousy of their power and wealth rather than the internal corruption of their Order resulted in their suppression and extinction in 1312, in France accompanied by particular cruelties.

Temple. This is the Lat. *templum*, from Gr. *temenos*, a sacred enclosure, *i.e.* a space cut off from its surroundings (Gr. *temnein*, to cut). The Lat. *templum* originally denoted the space marked out by the augurs within which the sign was to occur.

Temple, The. The site between FLEET STREET and the THAMES formerly occupied by the building of the TEMPLARS (*c.* 1160–1312) of which the Temple Church, one of the four circular churches built in England by them, is the only portion remaining. On the suppression of the Order, the site was granted to the Knights HOSPITALLERS and, from 1346, it has been occupied by practitioners and students of law who, since 1609, have formed two separate INNS OF COURT known as the Inner and Middle Temples. The badge of the former is the Winged Horse (*Pegasus*), that of the latter the Lamb (*Agnus Dei*).

Anacreon of the Temple. *See under* ANACREON.

The Temple of Reason During the REIGN OF TERROR (1793–1794) the Paris Commune enthroned a dancer on the high altar of Notre Dame Cathedral as the Goddess of Reason. She was draped in a tricolour flag and the cathedral became the *Temple of Reason*. There was much desecration and plundering of Notre Dame by the Paris mob.

The Temple of Solomon. The national shrine of the Jews at JERUSALEM, erected by SOLOMON and his Tyrian workmen on Mount Moriah in the 10th century B.C.. It was destroyed in the siege of Jerusalem by NEBUCHADNEZZAR (558 B.C.), and some 70 years later the new **Temple of Zerubbabel** was completed on its site. The third building, the **Temple of Herod** begun in 20 B.C., was the grandest and was that of NEW TESTAMENT times. It is said to have covered 19 acres. In the holy place were kept the golden candlestick, the altar of incense, and the table of the SHEWBREAD; within the HOLY OF HOLIES, the ark of the covenant and the mercy-seat. It was destroyed by fire by the Romans under Titus, A.D. 70. The site has long been covered by a MOSLEM shrine. *See* JACHIN AND BOAZ.

Tempora mutantur (Lat., the times are changed). The tag is founded on *Omnia mutantur, nos et mutamur in illis* (all things are changed, and we with them), a saying of Nicholas Borbonius, a Latin poet of the 16th century. Lothair, EMPEROR of the HOLY ROMAN EMPIRE, had, it is stated, already said, *Tempora mutantur, nos et mutamur in illis.*

Tempus fugit (tem' pus fū' jit) (Lat.). Time flies.

Ten. The Ten Commandments. *See* COMMANDMENT; DECALOGUE.

Ten to one. The chances are very much in favour of; there is a very strong probability that, as, "It's ten to one that it will rain tonight," *i.e.* there is a ten to one chance of rain.

The Upper Ten. The aristocracy, the cream of society. Short for *the upper ten thousand*. The term was first used by N.P. Willis (1806–1867), a spirited American journalist, in speaking of the fashionables of New York.

Ten-cent Jimmy. James Buchanan (1791–1868), fifteenth President of the U.S.A. (1857–1861), was so nicknamed on account of his advocacy of low tariffs and low wages.

Ten-gallon hat. The original tall-crowned, wide-brimmed hat worn by cowboys. Doubtless a jocular allusion to its capacity.

Tenant. Tenant at will. One who at any moment can be dispossessed of his tenancy at the will of the landlord or lessor.

Tenant in chief. One who held land direct from the king.

Tenant-right. The right of an outgoing tenant to claim compensation from an incoming tenant for improvements, manuring, crops left in the ground, etc. In earlier times, the term denoted the right of passing on a tenancy, at decease, to the eldest surviving issue. It is also applied to the right of a well-behaved tenant to compensation if deprived of his tenancy.

Tender. *See* LEGAL TENDER.

Tendon of Achilles. *See* ACHILLES TENDON.

Tenebrae (ten' ē brē) (Lat., darkness, gloom). In the Western Church the MATTINS and LAUDS of the following day sung on the Wednesday, Thursday, and Friday of HOLY WEEK. The lights of 15 candles are extinguished one by one at the end of each psalm, the last after the *Benedictus*. The MISERERE is then sung in darkness. This ritual goes back to the 8th century and symbolizes dramatically Christ's PASSION and Death.

Tennis-Court Oath, The (20 June 1789). The famous oath taken by the Third ESTATE in the Tennis Court at VERSAILLES—never to separate, and to meet wherever circumstances might make it necessary for it to meet, until the Constitution had been established and set on a firm foundation. The occasion was when Louis XVI excluded the deputies from their assembly hall and they met in the neighbouring building, the royal tennis court. It was another step towards revolution.

Tenson. A contention in verse between rival TROUBADOURS before a court of love; a metrical dialogue consisting of smart repartees, usually on women and love; also a subdivision of the troubadours' love lyrics (Lat. *tensio*, a struggle).

Tenterden. Tenterden steeple was the cause of Goodwin Sands. A satirical remark when some ridiculous reason is

given for a thing. The story, according to one of Latimer's sermons, is that Sir Thomas More, being sent into Kent to ascertain the cause of the GOODWIN SANDS, called together the oldest inhabitants to ask their opinion. A very old man said, "I believe Tenterden steeple is the cause," and went on to explain that in his early days there was no Tenterden steeple, and there were no complaints about the sands. This reason seems ridiculous enough, but the fact seems to be that the Bishops of Rochester applied to the building of Tenterden steeple moneys raised in the county for the purpose of keeping Sandwich haven clear, so that when they found the harbour was getting blocked up there was no money for taking the necessary counter-measures.

Tenterhooks. To be on tenterhooks. In suspense, most curious or anxious to hear the outcome. An allusion to newly-woven cloth being stretched or "tentered" on hooks passed through the selvedges (Lat. *tentus*, stretched, hence "tent", canvas stretched).

Tenth. The Submerged, or **Tenth legion.** *See* SUBMERGED.

The Tenth Muse. A name given originally to SAPPHO, there being *nine* true MUSES and afterwards applied to older literary women.

The tenth wave. *See* WAVE.

Tenths. In English ecclesiastical usage, the tenth part of the annual profit of every living originally paid to the POPE and transferred to the Crown after the breach with ROME, later to QUEEN ANNE'S BOUNTY. *Cp.* ANNATES. Also, in former days, a tax levied by the Crown of one-tenth of every man's personal property.

Teocalli (Mexican, house of a god). A temple of earth and stone or brick used by the aborigines of Mexico, built like a four-sided truncated pyramid on a platform at the top of terraces. The best known is the pyramid of Cholula which is 177ft. high.

Teraphim (ter' á fim). The idols or images of the ancient Hebrews and other Semitic peoples, worshipped by them as household gods or individual protecting deities (*see Judges* xviii, 5;

Hosea iii, 4). It was her father Laban's teraphim that Rachel stole and hid in the camel's saddle in *Gen.* xxxi, 17–35. *Cp.* LARES AND PENATES. That they were also used for DIVINATION and soothsaying seems apparent. *See Ezek.* xxi, 21; *Zec.* x.2.

Teresa, St. The name of two Carmelite nuns of remarkable qualities: (1) St. Teresa of Avila (1515–1582) or St. Teresa of Jesus, whose life combined great practical achievement with continual prayer and religious sanctity in which she reached a state of "spiritual marriage". She was responsible for the reform of the Carmelite Order and founded 32 convents as well as writing outstanding works on prayer and meditation. She was canonized in 1622 and in 1970 the first woman to be made a DOCTOR OF THE CHURCH. Her day is 15 October. (*See* ST. JOHN OF THE CROSS *under* JOHN.) (2) St. Teresa of Lisieux (1873–1897), a Carmelite nun, professed in 1890, who died of tuberculosis, and who is associated with miracles of healing and prophecy. Her autobiography, *L'Histoire d'une âme*, made her famous and she was canonized in 1925. She was associated with JOAN OF ARC as patroness of France in 1947 and in England she is known as "The Little Flower".

Term. To be on good (or **bad**) **terms** with a person is to be on a good (or bad) footing with them.

To come to terms. To make an agreement with; decide the terms of a bargain.

Termagant. The name given by the Crusaders, and in mediæval romances, to an idol or deity that the SARACENS were popularly supposed to worship. He was introduced into the MORALITY PLAYS as a most violent and turbulent person in long, flowing Eastern robes, a dress that led to his acceptance as a woman, whence the name came to be applied to a shrewish, violently abusive VIRAGO. The origin of the word is uncertain.

> 'Twas time to counterfeit, or that hot termagant Scot [Douglas] had paid me scot and lot too.
> SHAKESPEARE: *Henry IV, Pt. I*, V, iv.

O'erdoing Termagant (*Hamlet*, III,

ii). In old drama, the degree of rant was the measure of villainy. TERMAGANT and HEROD, being considered the BEAU IDEAL of all that is bad, were represented as settling everything by CLUB-LAW, and bawling so as to split the ears of the groundlings.

That beats Termagant. Your ranting, raging pomposity, or exaggeration, surpasses that of TERMAGANT of the old MORALITY PLAYS.

Terpsichore (tĕrp sik' ôr i). One of the nine MUSES of ancient Greece, the Muse of dancing and the dramatic chorus, and later of lyric poetry. Hence *Terpsichorean*, pertaining to dancing. She is usually represented seated, and holding a lyre.

Terra firma (Lat.). Dry land—in opposition to water; the continents as distinguished from islands. The Venetians so called the mainland of Italy under their sway, and the continental parts of America belonging to Spain were called by the same term.

Terror, The, or **The Reign of Terror.** *See* REIGN.

Terry Alts. One of the numerous secret societies of Irish insurrectionists similar to the Blackfeet, Lady Clares, and MOLLY MAGUIRES, etc. It was active in County Clare in the early 19th century. *See* WHITEBOYS.

Ter-Sanctus. *See* TRISAGION.

Tertiaries. Members of "a third order", an institution which began with the FRANCISCANS in the 13th century for lay folk who wished to strive for Christian perfection in their day-to-day life in accordance with the spirit and teaching of St. FRANCIS. The name *Third Order* arises from the Friars and Nuns being classed as the First and Second Orders.

Tertium quid. A third party which shall be nameless; a third thing resulting from the combination of two things, but different from both. Fable has it that the expression originated with PYTHAGORAS, who, defining bipeds, said:

> Sunt bipes homo, et avis, et tertium quid.
> A man is a biped, so is a bird, and a third thing (which shall be nameless).

Iamblichus said this third thing was Pythagoras himself.

In chemistry, when two substances chemically unite, the new substance is called a *tertium quid*, as a neutral salt produced by the mixture of an acid and an alkali.

Terza Rima. An Italian verse-form in triplets, the second line rhyming with the first and third of the succeeding triplet. In the first triplet lines 1 and 3 rhyme, and in the last there is an extra line, rhyming with its second.

Dante's *Divine Comedy* is in this metre: it was introduced into ENGLAND by Sir Thomas Wyatt in the 16th century, and was largely employed by Shelley, as also by Byron in *The Prophecy of Dante*.

Test Acts. A name given to the various Acts of PARLIAMENT designed to exclude Roman Catholics, Protestant NONCONFORMISTS, and "disaffected persons" from public offices, etc. They include Acts of Abjuration, Allegiance, and Supremacy, the Corporation Act, 1661, the Act of Uniformity, 1662, as well as those specifically named *Test Acts*. Those named "Test Acts" were: (1) that of 1673 which insisted that all holders of civil and military office must be communicants of the CHURCH OF ENGLAND as well as taking the oaths of Allegiance and Supremacy; (2) that of 1678 which excluded all Roman Catholics, other than the Duke of York, from Parliament; (3) that for Scotland (1681) which made all state and municipal officials affirm their belief in the PROTESTANT faith. These Acts were repealed in 1828. *See also* UNIVERSITY TESTS ACT.

Test Match. In CRICKET one of the matches between selected national teams arranged by the International Conference, which replaced the Imperial Cricket Conference (1909–1965) after South Africa left the COMMONWEALTH (1961). *See* THE ASHES *under* ASHES.

Testudo. *See* TORTOISE.

Tête-à-tête (Fr., head to head). A confidential conversation, a heart-to-heart talk.

Tête-de-mouton (Fr., sheep's head). A 17th-century head-dress, the hair being arranged in short, thick curls.

Tête du pont. The barbican or watchtower placed on the head of a drawbridge.

Tether He has come to the end of his tether. He has come to the end of his resources; he has exhausted his fortune etc. The reference is to a tethered animal which can only graze as far as the rope allows.

HORACE calls the end of life *ultima linea rerum*, the final goal, referring to the white chalk mark at the end of a racecourse. *Cp.* BITTER END.

Tethys. A sea goddess, wife of OCEANUS hence, the sea itself. She was the daughter of URANUS and GÆA, and mother of the OCEANIDES.

Tetragrammaton. A word of four letters, especially the Jewish name of the Deity JHVH, which the Jews never pronounced but substituted the word ADONAI instead (usually rendered in the BIBLE as *Lord*). Its probable pronunciation was *Yahweh* and from the 16th century was corrupted into JEHOVAH by combining the vowels of Adonai with JHVH.

PYTHAGORAS called Deity a Tetrad or Tetracys, meaning the "four sacred letters". The Greek *Zeus* and θεος, in Latin *Jove* and *Deus*; Fr. *Dieu*, Ger. *Gott*, Sansk. *Deva*, Span. *Dios*, Scand. *Odin*, and our *Lord* are tetragrams.

> Such was the sacred Tetragrammaton.
> Things worthy silence must not be revealed.
> DRYDEN: *Britannia Rediviva*, 197.

Tetrarch (tet' rark). Originally meaning the rule of one of four parts of a region (Gr. *tettares*, four; *archein*, to rule), under the Roman Empire the term came to be applied to minor rulers, especially to the princes of Syria subject to the Roman Emperor.

Teucer. In the ILIAD, the son of Telamon, and stepbrother of AJAX; he went with the allied Greeks to the siege of TROY, and on his return was banished by his father for not avenging on Odysseus (ULYSSES) the death of his brother.

Teutons. The name of an ancient tribe of northern Europe called by the Romans *Teutones* or *Teutoni*. The adjective *Teutonic* is also applied to the Germanic peoples generaly and in the widest sense includes both Scandinavians and Anglo-Saxons.

Teutonic Cross. A CROSS potent, the badge of the order of TEUTONIC KNIGHTS. *See* POTENT.

Teutonic Knights. The third great military crusading Order which has its origin in the time of the Third CRUSADE. It developed from the provision of a hospital service by Germans at the siege of Acre (1190) which became the German Hospital of St. Mary at JERUSALEM. It was made a Knightly Order in 1198, thenceforward confined to those of noble birth. In 1229 they began the conquest of heathen Prussia and after 1291 their contact with the East ceased. They survived as a powerful and wealthy body until their disastrous defeat by the Poles and Lithuanians at Tannenberg in 1410. The Order lingered on until its suppression in 1809, but was revived in Austria in 1840 but with HABSBURG associations.

Texas Rangers. A constabulary force first organized in Texas in 1835 and much developed by General Sam Houston a few years later. They wore no uniform and especially proved their worth in 1870 against rustlers and raiders. Their resourcefulness in the saddle, their toughness, and colourful exploits have given them legendary fame.

Th (θ, *theta*). The sign given in the verdict of the AREOPAGUS of condemnation to death (THANATOS).

Thais (thā' is). The Athenian courtesan who, it is said, induced ALEXANDER THE GREAT when excited with wine, to set fire to the palace of the Persian kings at Persepolis. After Alexander's death, she married Ptolemy Lagus, king of Egypt, by whom she had seven children.

Thales. *See* WISE MEN OF GREECE.

Thalestris (thà les' tris). A queen of the AMAZONS who went with 300 women to meet ALEXANDER THE GREAT, in the hope of raising a race of Alexanders.

Thalia (thà lī' à). One of the MUSES who presided over comedy and pastoral poetry. She also favoured rural pursuits and is represented holding a comic mask and a shepherd's crook. Thalia is also the name of one of THE THREE GRACES (*see under* GRACE) or *Charites*.

Thames. He'll never set the Thames on fire. He'll never make any figure in the world; never do anything wonderful and print his footsteps on the sands of time. The popular explanation is that the word Thames is a pun on the word *temse*, a corn-sieve; and that the parallel French locution *He will never set the Seine on fire* is a pun on *seine*, a dragnet; but these solutions are not tenable. There is a Latin saw, *Tiberum accendere nequaquam potest*, which is probably the *fons et origo* of other parallel sayings; and the Germans had *Den Rhein anzünden* (to set the Rhine on fire) as early as 1630.

Thammuz (thăm' ŭz). A Sumerian, Babylonian and Assyrian god who died every year and rose again in the spring. He is identified with the Babylonian MARDUK and the Greek ADONIS. In *Ezek.* viii, 14, reference is made to the heathen "women weeping for Tammuz".

Thamyris (thăm' i ris). A Thracian bard mentioned by HOMER (*Iliad*, II, 595). He challenged the MUSES to a trial of skill, and, being overcome in the contest, was deprived by them of his sight and powers of song. He is represented with a broken lyre in his hand.

Thanatos. The Greek personification of death, twin brother of Sleep (*Hypnos*). Hesiod says he was born of Night with no father.

Thane. The name given in Anglo-Saxon England to a class of soldiers and landholders ranking between the earl and the churl. The rank of thane could be obtained by a man of lower degree. After the Norman Conquest the word disappeared in ENGLAND, giving place to KNIGHT. In SCOTLAND, a thane ranked with an earl's son, holding his land direct from the king; the title was given also to the chief of a CLAN who became one of the king's barons.

Thanksgiving Day. An annual holiday in the U.S.A. usually held on the last Thursday in NOVEMBER and observed as an acknowledgement of the divine favours received during the year. It was first celebrated by the Plymouth Colony in 1621. After the Revolution, its observance became general and from 1863 it was annually recommended by the President. In 1941 it was fixed as a public holiday for the fourth Thursday in November. Pumpkin pies and turkey are part of the traditional fare.

That And that's that! A colloquial way of emphatically and triumphantly making one's point, closing the argument, etc.

Thaumaturgus (thaw ma tĕr' gus) (Gr., a wonder-worker). A miracle-worker; applied to SAINTS and others who are reputed to have performed miracles, and especially Gregory, Bishop of Neo-Cæsarea, called Thaumaturgus (*c.* 213–*c.* 270) whose miracles included the moving of a mountain. St BERNARD of Clairvaux (1090–1153) was called "The Thaumaturgus of the West".

Thé dansant. An afternoon tea party with dancing.

Thebes, called *The Hundred-Gated*, was not Thebes of Bœotia, but the chief town of the Thebaid, on the Nile in Upper Egypt, said to have extended over 23 miles of land. HOMER says out of each gate the Thebans could send forth 200 war-chariots.

It is here that the vocal statue of MEM-NON stood. The sound was caused by internal vibrations resulting from a split in the statue after an earthquake. Here too is the VALLEY OF THE KINGS, including the tomb of TUTANKHAMUN, the Temple of Luxor and those of Karnak. It is now a favourite tourist centre.

The Seven Against Thebes. An expedition in Greek legend fabled to have taken place against Thebes of Bœotia before the TROJAN WAR. The Seven were the Argive chiefs ADRASTUS, Polynices, Tydeus, Amphiaraus, Hippomedon, Capaneus and Parthenopæus.

When ŒDIPUS abdicated, his two sons agreed to reign alternate years; but at the expiration of the first year, the elder, Eteocles, refused to give up the throne, whereupon Polynices, the younger brother, induced the six chiefs to espouse his cause. The allied army laid siege to Thebes, but without success, and all the heroes perished except Adrastus. Subsequently, seven sons of the chiefs, resolved to avenge their fathers' deaths, marched against the city, took it, and placed Terpander, one of their number on the throne. These are known as the *Epigoni* (Gr., descen-

dants). The Greek tragic poets ÆSCHY-LUS and Euripides dramatized the legend.

Theban Bard, or **Eagle, The.** PINDAR, born at Thebes (*c.* 522–443 B.C.).

Theban Sphinx, *See* SPHINX.

Thecla, St. (thek' là). One of the most famous saints of the 1st century, the first woman martyr. All that is known of her is from the *Acts of Paul and Thecla*, pronounced APOCRYPHAL by Pope Gelasius. According to the legend, she was born of a noble family at Iconium and was converted by St. PAUL.

Theist, Deist, Atheist, Agnostic. A *theist* believes there is a God who made and governs all creation; Christians, Jews, and Mohammedans are included among *theists*.

A *deist* believes there is a God who created all things, but does not believe in His superintendence and government. He thinks the Creator implanted in all things certain immutable laws, called the *Laws of Nature*, which act *per se*, as a watch acts without the supervision of its maker. He does not believe in the doctrine of the TRINITY, nor in a divine revelation.

The *atheist* disbelieves even the existence of a God. He thinks matter is eternal, and what we call "creation" is the result of natural laws.

The *agnostic* believes only what is knowable. He rejects revelation and the doctrine of the Trinity as "past human understanding". He is neither theist, deist, nor atheist, as all these subscribe to doctrines that are incapable of scientific proof.

Theme song. A song which recurs during the course of a musical play or film which generally reflects the mood or *theme* of the production.

Themis. A daughter of URANUS and GÆA and a wife of JUPITER, mother of the HORÆ and PARCÆ. With Jupiter she presides over law and order. She also is protector of hospitality and the oppressed and has oracular powers.

Theocritus. A Greek poet of Syracuse (3rd century B.C.), the creator of pastoral poetry, whose verse was imitated by VIRGIL.

Theodoric (thē od' ō rik). King of the

Ostrogoths (*c*. 454–526), who became celebrated in German legend as DIE-TRICH OF BERN, and also has a place in the Norse romances and the *Nibelungen Saga*. He invaded Italy, slew Odoacer (493), and became sole ruler.

Theon (thē' on). A satirical poet of ancient ROME, noted for his mordant writings. Hence **Theon's tooth**, the bite of an ill-natured or carping critic. Thus:

> *Dente Theonino circumroditur* (HOR-ACE: I *Epist*. xviii, 82), meaning "is slandered, calumniated".

Theosophy (Gr., the wisdom of God). The name adopted by the Theosophical Society (founded in 1875 by Mme Blavatsky, Col. H.S. Olcott, William Q. Judge, and others) to define their religious or philosophical system, which aims at the knowledge of God by means of intuition and contemplative illumination, or by direct communion. *Esoteric Buddhism* is another name for it; and its adherents claim that the doctrines of the great world religions are merely the *exoteric* expressions of their own *esoteric* traditions.

The name was formerly applied to the philosphical system of Jakob Boehme (1575–1624).

Théot, Catherine. *See under* CATHER-INE.

Theramenes. *See* HE WEARS THE SANDALS OF THERAMENES *under* SANDAL.

Therapeutæ (thēr a pū' tē) (Gr., servants, ministers). A sect of Jewish ascetics in Egypt described in Philo's *De Vita Contemplativa*. They lived in a community near Alexandria run on monastic lines which was developed long before the rise of Christianity. *Cp.* ESSENES.

Thermidor (thĕr' mi dôr). The eleventh month of the French Republican CA-LENDAR 20 July—18 August. So named from Gr. *therme*, heat; *doron*, a gift.

Thermidorians. The French Revolutionaries who took part in the COUP D'ETAT which effected the fall of Robespierre, on 9th Thermidor of the second Republican year (27 July 1794), thus ending the REIGN OF TERROR.

Thermopylæ (thĕr mop' i li). The famous pass from Thessaly to Locris, only 25 ft. wide at its narrowest part, cele-

brated for its heroic defence (480 B.C.) by LEONIDAS, with some 300 Spartans and 700 Thespians against XERXES and the Persian Host. Eventually, treachery allowed the Persians to get to the rear of the Greeks and the Spartan king and his band were all slain. The pass took its name from the hot baths nearby.

Thersites (thĕ sī' tēz). A deformed, scurrilous officer in the Greek army at the siege of TROY. He was always railing at the chiefs; hence the name is applied to any dastardly, malevolent, impudent railer against the powers that be. ACHILLES felled him to the earth with his fist and killed him.

In SHAKESPEARE's *Troilus and Cressida* (I, iii) he is "A slave whose gall coins slanders like a mint."

Theseus (thē' sūs). The chief hero of Attica in ancient Greek legend; son of ÆGEUS, and the centre of countless exploits. Among them are the capture of the Marathonian bull, the slaying of the MINOTAUR, his war against the AMA-ZONS, and the hunting of the CALYDO-NIAN BOAR (*see under* BOAR). He was eventually murdered by Lycomedes in Scyros. *See* SINIS.

Theseus is also the name of the Duke of Athens in Chaucer's *Knight's Tale*. He married Hippolita, and as he returned home with his bride, and Emily her sister, was accosted by a crowd of female suppliants who complained of Creon, King of Thebes. The Duke forthwith set out for Thebes, slew Creon, and took the city by assault. Many captives fell into his hands, amongst whom were the two knights, Palamon and ARCITE.

SHAKESPEARE gives the same name to the Duke of Athens in *A Midsummer Night's Dream*.

Thespians (thes' pi ánz). Actors; so called from Thespis, an Attic poet of the 6th century B.C., reputed to be the father of Greek TRAGEDY.

Thestylis (thes' ti lis). A stock poetic name for a rustic maiden; from a young female slave of that name in the *Idylls* of THEOCRITUS.

Thetis (thē' tis). The chief of the NEREIDS of Greek legend. By Peleus she was the mother of ACHILLES.

Thick. As thick as a doorpost. Dull-witted, unintelligent.

As thick as two short planks. Very obtuse.

It's a bit thick. More than one can be expected to tolerate.

Those two are very thick. They are very good friends, on excellent terms with one another. **As thick as thieves** is a similar saying.

Through thick and thin. Despite all difficulties; under any conditions; unwaveringly.

To be thick. Not to be very bright or intelligent; to be slow on the uptake.

To lay it on thick. To flatter extravagantly; also to blame or punish excessively.

Thick-skinned. Not sensitive; not irritated by rebukes or slanders. *Thin-skinned*, on the contrary means impatient of reproof or censure, having skin so thin that it is an anoyance to be touched.

Thief, The Penitent. *See* DYSMAS.

Thieves' Latin. Slang; gibberish.

Thimble. Just a thimble or **thimbleful.** A very little drop, just a taste—usually with reference to spirits.

Thimble-rigging. A form of cheating, carried on with three thimbles and a pea, formerly mainly practised on or about race-courses. A pea is put on a table, and the manipulator places three thimbles over it in succession, and then, setting them on the table, asks you to say under which thimble the pea is. You are sure to guess wrong.

The term *thimble-rigging* is used allusively of any kind of mean cheating or JIGGERY-POKERY.

Thin. It's a lot too thin! Said of an excuse, explanation, story, etc., that sounds plausible but is quite unacceptable. The idea is that it is so thin as to be transparent—it is easily seen through.

The thin end of the wedge. An action, innovation, etc., of apparently small consequence which may lead to major undesirable developments. The reference is to wedges used for splitting blocks of stone or wood.

The thin red line. *See under* LINE.

Thin-skinned. *See* THICK-SKINNED.

Thing. The Old Norse word for the assembly of the people, PARLIAMENT, etc. It is etymologically the same word as our *thing* (an object), the original meaning of which was a discussion (from *thingian*, to discuss), hence a cause, an object.

The Parliament of Norway is still called the *Storting* which divides itself into the *Lagting* and the *Odelsting*.

Just the thing, or **the very thing.** Just what I was wanting; exactly what will meet the case.

Old thing. A dated mode of address between friends.

One's things. One's minor belongings, especially clothes, or personal luggage.

A poor thing. A person (or sometimes an inanimate object) that is regarded with pity or disparagement. Touchstone's remark about Audrey—"An ill-favoured thing, sir, but mine own" (SHAKESPEARE: *As You Like It*, V, iv)—is frequently misquoted, "A poor thing, but mine own", when employed in half-ironical disparagement of one's own work.

The thing. The proper thing to do; as, "it's not the thing to play leapfrog down Bond Street in a top-hat and spats."

To do the handsome thing. To treat generously.

To know a thing or two. To be sharp, shrewd, not easily taken in; knowing, experienced.

To make a good thing of. To make a success of; to develop into something worthwhile; to make a profit out of.

You can have too much of a good thing. "Enough is as good as a feast."

Think-tank. A popular term for a group of people with specialized knowledge and ability, set up to carry out research into particular problems (usually social, political and technological) and to provide ideas and possible solutions.

Third. *See also* THREE.

Third Degree. In the U.S.A. the term is applied to the use of exhaustive questioning and cross-questioning by the police in an endeavour to extort a confession of compromising information from a criminal, accomplice, or witness.

Third Estate. *See under* ESTATE.

Third Order. *See* TERTIARIES.

Third Republic. The French Republic

established in 1870 after the capitulation of NAPOLEON III at Sedan (4 September). It came to an end with another French capitulation to Germany in 1940, when a collaborationist government was set up under Marshal Pétain at VICHY.

Third World. *See under* WORLD.

Thirteeen. It is said that the origin of sitting down 13 at a table being deemed unlucky is because, at a banquet in VALHALLA, LOKI once intruded, making 13 guests, and BALDER was slain.

In Christian countries, the superstition was confirmed by the LAST SUPPER of Christ and His twelve APOSTLES.

Addison, *On Popular Superstitions* (*Spectator*), says:

> I remember I was once in a mixed assembly that was full of noise and mirth, when on a sudden an old woman unluckily observed there were thirteen of us in company. This remark struck a panic terror into several who were present, insomuch that one or two of the ladies were going to leave the room; but a friend of mine, taking notice that one of our female companions was big with child, affirmed there were fourteen in the room, and that, instead of portending one of the company should die, it plainly forebode one of them should be born. Had not my friend found this expedient to break the omen, I question not but half the women in the company would have fallen sick that night.

It is traditionally regarded as unlucky for a ship to begin a voyage on the 13th, especially if it happens to be FRIDAY.

Thirteenpence-halfpenny. A hangan. So called because thirteenpence-halfpenny was at one time his wages for hanging a man.

Thirty. The Thirty Tyrants. *See under* TYRANT.

The Thirty Years War. The wars in Germany which began in Bohemia in 1618 and were terminated by the peace of Westphalia in 1648. Traditionally regarded as a struggle initially between German PROTESTANTS and Catholics, which was exploited by foreign powers, it was more essentially part of a contest between BOURBON and HABSBURG dynastic interests combined with constitutional struggles inside the Habsburg Empire waged under the cloak of religion. The idea that "Germany" was uni-

versally devastated is largely a myth.

The Thirty-nine Articles. The *Articles* of Religion in the BOOK OF COMMON PRAYER largely defining the CHURCH OF ENGLAND's position in certain matters of dogma which were in dispute at the time. They were first issued in 1563, based on the Forty-two Articles of 1553, and revised in 1571. Clergy had to subscribe to them, but since 1865 a more general affirmation has been substituted.

Thirty-six-Line Bible. *See* BIBLE, SOME SPECIALLY NAMED EDITIONS.

A man at thirty must be either a fool or a physician. A saying attributed by Tacitus (*Annals*, VI, xlvi) to the Emperor Tiberius, who died at the age of 78 in A.D. 37 (Plutarch gives the story, but changes the age to 60). The idea seems to be that if a man has not learned to look after his health by the time he is 30 he must be a fool.

Thisbe. *See* PYRAMUS.

Thistle. The heraldic emblem of SCOTLAND which seems to have been adopted by James III (1451, 1460–1488), possibly as a symbol of defence. The motto *Nemo me impune lacessit*, "Nobody touches (or provokes) me with impunity", first appeared on the coinage of James VI (1566, 1567–1603).

Thistles, especially "Our Lady's Thistle", are said to be a cure for stitch in the side. According to the doctrine of signatures, Nature has labelled every plant, and the prickles of the thistle tell us that the plant is efficacious for *prickles* or the stitch. The species called *Silybum marianum*, we are told, owes the white markings on its leaves to milk from Our Lady's breast, some of which fell thereon and left a white mark behind.

The "Most Ancient" Order of the Thistle. This Scottish Order of knighthood (ranking second to the Order of the GARTER) is not very ancient, being instituted by James VII and II in 1687. It is inaccurately said to have been "refounded" then; legend has it that it was founded by Achaius, King of the Scots in 787. It fell into abeyance after 1688 but was revived by QUEEN ANNE in 1703.

It is sometimes called the Order of St.

Andrew.

Thomas. St. Thomas. The Apostle who doubted (*John* xx, 25); hence the phrase, **a doubting Thomas,** applied to a sceptic. The story told of him in the APOCRYPHAL *Acts of St. Thomas* is that he was deputed to go as a missionary to India, and, on refusing, Christ appeared and sold him as a slave to an Indian prince who was visiting JERUSALEM. He was taken to India, where he baptized the prince and many others, and was finally martyred at Mylapore.

Another legend has it that Gundaphorus, an Indian king, gave him a large sum of money to build a palace. St. Thomas spent it on the poor, "thus creating a superb palace in heaven". On account of this he is the patron SAINT of masons and architects, and his symbol is a builder's square.

Another story is that he once saw a huge beam of timber floating on the sea near the coast, and the king unsuccessfully endeavouring, with men and elephants, to haul it ashore. St. Thomas desired leave to use it in building a church, and, his request being granted, he dragged it easily ashore with a piece of packthread.

His feast day is 3 July (formerly 21 December). His relics are now said to be at Ortona in the Abruzzi.

Christians of St. Thomas. According to tradition, St. THOMAS founded the Christian churches of Malabar and then moved on to Mylapore (Madras), thus Christian communities were there to welcome the Portuguese when Vasco da Gama arrived in 1498. They called themselves "Christians of St. Thomas" and may be descendants of Christians converted by NESTORIAN missions, although the claim that they were evangelized by St. Thomas is not entirely improbable.

Thomasing. Collecting small sums of money or obtaining drink from employers on St. Thomas's Day.

Thomas Aquinas, St. (*c.* 1225–1274). DOMINICAN scholastic philosopher and theologian, of outstanding authority and intellectual distinction among his contemporaries, and whose teachings have been a major influence on the doctrines

of the ROMAN CATHOLIC CHURCH. He was the youngest son of Count Landulf of Aquino (midway between ROME and Naples) and became a Dominican in the face of strong family opposition. He was a pupil of Albertus Magnus and subsequently taught at PARIS, ROME, Bologna and Pisa. First nicknamed the DUMB OX he became *Doctor Angelicus* and "the Fifth Doctor of the Church". Among his many writings his *Summa Theologica* is his classic work. He drew a clear distinction between Faith and Reason and was considerably influenced by the philosophy of ARISTOTLE. He was canonized in 1323 and his feast day is 28 January.

Thomists. Followers of St. THOMAS AQUINAS (*c.* 1225–1274). They were opponents of the SCOTISTS, or followers of Duns Scotus (*see* DUNCE).

> Scotists and Thomists now in peace remain.
> POPE: *Essay on Criticism*, 444.

Thomas the Rhymer. *See under* RHYME.

Thone, or **Thonis.** In Greek mythology, the governor of a province of Egypt to which, it is said by post-Homeric poets, PARIS took HELEN, who was given by Polydamnia, wife to Thone, the drug NEPENTHES, to make her forget her sorrows.

Thopas, Rime of Sir (thō′ păs). A burlesque on contemporary metrical romances, told as Chaucer's own tale in the *Canterbury Tales*.

Thor (thôr). Son of WODEN, god of war, and the second god in the PANTHEON of the ancient Scandinavians—their VULCAN, and god of thunder. He had three principal possessions, a Hammer (*Mjolnir*), typifying thunder and lightning, and having the virtue of returning to him after it was thrown; a Belt (*Meginjardir*) which doubled his strength; and Iron Gloves to aid him in throwing his hammer.

He was a god of the household, and of peasants, and was married to Sif, a typical peasant woman. His name is still perpetuated in our THURSDAY, and in a number of place-names such as *Thorsby* (Cumberland), *Torthorwald* (Dumfries), and *Thurso* (Caithness).

Thorn. The Crown of Thorns. That with which Our Saviour was crowned in mockery (*Matt.* xxvii, 29); hence sometimes used of a very special affliction with which one is unjustly burdened.

Calvin (*Admonitio de Reliquiis*) gives a long list of places claiming to possess one or more of the thorns which composed the Saviour's crown. *See* GLASTONBURY.

Glastonbury Thorn. *See* GLASTONBURY.

A thorn in the flesh. A source of constant irritation, annoyance, or affliction; said of objectionable and parasitical acquaintances, obnoxious conditions, etc. There was a sect of the PHARISEES which used to insert thorns in the borders of their gaberdines to prick their legs in walking and make them bleed. The phrase is taken from St. PAUL'S reference to some physical complaint or misfortune (II *Cor.* xii, 7).

Thorough. The name given to the methods of government associated with Strafford and Laud, especially the former's policy in IRELAND (1632–1639). It was characterized by firm, efficient and orderly government, but was also associated with corruption and tyrannical methods. *Through* and *thorough* were then interchangeable terms.

Thoth. The Egyptian lunar god, usually with the head of an IBIS but sometimes that of a baboon. His chief centre was Hermapolis (modern Ashmunein) and he was identified with HERMES by the Greeks. He was the master over writing, languages, laws, annals, calculations, etc., and patron of scribes and magicians. He made the CALENDAR and his control over HIEROGLYPHS and divine words enhanced his magical powers. He acted as secretary of the gods. At the judgement after death he weighed the heart.

Thousand. Thousand and One Nights. *See* ARABIAN NIGHTS.

He's one in a thousand. Said of a man who is specially distinguished by his excellent qualities; similarly, *a wife in a thousand*, a perfect wife, or one that exactly suits the speaker's ideas of what a wife should be.

Thrash. To thrash out. To decide and settle by discussion and argument the points at issue. A METAPHOR from the threshing of corn to separate the grain from the chaff.

Thread. The thread of destiny. That on which destiny depends; the imaginary thread or span of life provided by the FATES.

The Triple Thread. Brahminism. The ancient Brahmins wore a symbol of three threads, reaching from the right shoulder to the left. João de Faria says that their religion sprang from fishermen, who left the charge of the temples to their successors on the condition of their wearing some threads of their nets in remembrance of their vocation.

To lose the thread. To lose the train of thought or issue of argument, etc., owing to a digression, interruption, mental aberration, etc.

To pick up the threads. To resume one's line of argument, etc., also to get back into the way of things after absence, illness, etc.

The Old Lady of Threadneedle Street. A synonym for the BANK of England, which stands in this street.

Three. PYTHAGORAS calls three the perfect number, expressive of "beginning, middle, and end", wherefore he makes it a symbol of Deity.

A TRINITY is by no means confined to the CHRISTIAN creed. The BRAHMINS represent their god with three heads; the world was supposed by the ancients to be under the rule of three gods, *viz.* JUPITER (HEAVEN), NEPTUNE (sea), and PLUTO (HADES). Jove is represented with three-forked lightning, Neptune with a trident, and Pluto with a three-headed dog. The FATES are three, the FURIES three, the Graces three (*see under* GRACE), the Harpies three (*see* HARPY), the SIBYLLINE BOOKS three times three (of which only three survived); the fountain from which HYLAS drew water was presided over by three NYMPHS; the MUSES were three times three; in Scandinavian mythology we hear of "the Mysterious Three", *viz* "Har" (High), "Jafenhar" (Equally High), and "Thridi" (the third), who sat on three thrones in ASGARD.

Man is threefold (body, mind, and

spirit); the world is threefold (earth, sea, and air); the enemies of man are threefold (the world, the flesh, and the DEVIL); the Christian graces are threefold (Faith, Hope, and Charity); the Kingdoms of Nature are threefold (animal, vegetable and mineral).

Rule of Three. The method of finding the fourth term of a proportion where three are given, the numbers being such that the first is to the second as the third is to the fourth. By multiplying the second and third terms together and dividing the result by the first, the fourth term is arrived at.

Three Emperors. The Battle of the Three Emperors. The Battle of Austerlitz (2 December 1805), when the French Emperor NAPOLEON routed the Emperors of Austria and Russia, all three being personally present on the field.

The Three Estates of the Realm. *See* ESTATES OF THE REALM.

The Three F's. Fair rent, free sale, and fixity of tenure, which were demanded by the Irish LAND LEAGUE and conceded by Gladstone's Land Act of 1881.

Three Kings' Day. EPIPHANY or Twelfth Day, designed to commemorate the visit of the "three kings" or Wise Men of the East to the infant Jesus. *See* MAGI.

Three-Mile Limit. The usual limit of territorial waters around their coasts claimed by maritime states including Great Britain and the U.S.A. Some states claim much wider jurisdiction and disputes over territorial waters are not infrequent.

The Three Musketeers. Athos, Porthos, and Aramis, the three heroes of Dumas's novels *The Three Musketeers*, 1844; *Twenty Years After*, 1845; and *Vicomte de Bragelonne*, 1848–1850. The Musketeers were a mounted guard of gentlemen in the service of the kings of France from 1661 until the Revolution caused their abolition in 1791. They formed two companies, called the Grey and the Black from the colour of their horses. The uniform was scarlet, hence their quarters were known as *La Maison Rouge*. In peacetime the Musketeers formed the king's bodyguard, but in war they fought on foot or on horseback with the army. Their ranks included many Scots, either JACOBITE exiles or mere soldiers of fortune.

The Three R's. *See under* R.

The Three Tailors of Tooley Street. *See under* TAILOR.

The Three Tongues. Those in which the inscription on the CROSS was written, *viz.* Hebrew, Greek, and Latin. In the MIDDLE AGES it was considered that a thorough knowledge of these was necessary before one could begin to understand theology.

A three-cornered fight. A parliamentary (or other) contest in which there are three participants.

A three-decker. Properly, in the days of sail, a warship having three gun decks. Also applied to other triplicates arranged in tiers; and to the three-volume novel—the usual way of publishing the 19th-century novel.

The name is also given to a sandwich with three slices of bread.

Three-field system. The system of crop rotation under the old OPEN-FIELD SYSTEM of agriculture which persisted from manorial times until well into the reign of George III. The three open arable fields were successively used for wheat or rye, then peas, beans, barley, oats, etc., and left fallow for the third season.

The three-legged mare. In obsolete slang, the gallows, which at TYBURN was a triple erection in triangular plan.

Three score years and ten. A ripe old age—not necessarily (in allusive use) exactly 70 years. The reference is to *Ps.* xc, 10:

> The days of our years are three score years and ten; and if by reason of strength they be fourscore years, yet is their strength labour and sorrow; for it is soon cut off, and we fly away.

Three sheets in the wind. *See* SHEET.

To give one three times three. To give him a rousing ovation, cheer after cheer.

We three. "Did you never see the picture of We Three?" asks Sir Andrew Aguecheek (SHAKESPEARE: *Twelfth Night*, II, iii)—not meaning himself, Sir Toby Belch, and the clown, but referring to a PUBLIC-HOUSE SIGN of *Two LOGGERHEADS* with the inscription, "We three loggerheads be," the third being the spectator.

Throat. To cut one's own throat. Figuratively, to adopt a policy, or take action that ruins one's own chances, plans, etc. Similarly, **to cut one another's throat** is to ruin one another by excessive competition.

To have a bone in one's throat. A pretended excuse for being unwilling to talk.

To jump down a person's throat. To interrupt and affront him, suddenly, sharply, and decisively.

To lie in one's throat. To lie most outrageously, well knowing that you are lying, and meaning to do so.

To ram, or **thrust down a person's throat.** To force an opinion or point of view upon another which he may be reluctant to accept or "swallow"; to assert insistently without allowing an opportunity for reply or being prepared to listen.

The words stuck in his throat. *See under* WORD.

Throgmorton Street. The financial world at large, or the STOCK EXCHANGE, which is situated in this narrow LONDON street. So named from Sir Nicholas Throckmorton (1515–1571), head of the ancient Warwickshire family, and ambassador to France in the reign of Elizabeth I.

Throne, The. The Speech from the Throne. *See* QUEEN'S SPEECH.

Thrones, Principalities, and Powers. According to Dionysius the Areopagite, three of the nine orders of ANGELS. These names or their liguistic counterparts occur frequently in Jewish-Christian writings around NEW TESTAMENT times.

Through. *See* THOROUGH.

Throw. To throw a spanner in the works. To deliberately sabotage a plan or enterprise or spoil a scheme by creating difficulties, obstructions, etc., designed to promote failure, as some machinery can be wrecked by literally throwing a spanner or a piece of metal into moving parts.

To throw away one's money. to spend it carelessly, recklessly, extravagantly.

To throw back. To revert to ancestral traits; *a throw-back* is one who does this. "To throw back at someone" is to retort.

To throw good money after bad. Having already lost money on a scheme, investment or project, to continue to spend more on what is bound to result in loss.

To throw in one's hand. To abandon a project; to give up. A METAPHOR from card-playing.

To throw oneself on someone. to commit oneself to his protection, favour, mercy, etc.

To throw the helve after the hatchet. *See* HELVE.

To throw to the wolves. *See under* WOLF.

To throw up the sponge. *See* SPONGE.

Thug. A worshipper of KALI, who practised *thuggee*, the strangling of human victims in the name of religion. Robbery of the victim provided the means of livelihood. They were also called *Phansigars* (Noose operators) from the method employed. Vigorous suppression was begun by Lord William Bentinck in 1828, but the fraternity did not become completely extinct for another 50 years or so.

In common parlance the word is used for any violent "tough".

Thule. The name given by the ancients to an island, or point of land, six days' sail north of Britain, and considered by them to be the extreme northern limit of the world. The name is first found in the account by Polybius (*c.* 150 B.C.) of the voyage made by Pytheas in the late 4th century B.C. Pliny says, "It is an island in the Northern Ocean discovered by Pytheas, after sailing six days from the Orcades." Others, like Camden, consider it to be Shetland, in which opinion they agree with Marinus, and the descriptions of Ptolemy and Tacitus; and still others that it was some part of the coast of Norway. The etymology of the word is unknown.

Ultima Thule. The end of the world; the last extremity.

Tibi serviat Ultima Thule.

Thumb. In the ancient Roman combats, when a GLADIATOR was vanquished it rested with the spectators to decide whether he should be slain or not. If they wished him to live, they shut up their thumbs in their fists (*pollice compresso favor judicabatur*); if to be slain they turned out their thumbs. *See* Juvenal, iii, 36; Horace, I *Epist*, xviii, 66.

Our popular saying **Thumbs up!** expressive of pleasure or approval is probably a development from this custom.

Rule of thumb. A rough, guesswork measure; practice or experience, as distinguished from theory; in allusion to the use of the thumb for rough measurements.

Thumb index. Grooves cut in the pages of a book showing initial letters or other particulars to enable the reader to find a reference easily.

Thumb-nail. Used attributively of various things, especially sketches, portraits, and so on, that are on a very small scale.

Tom Thumb. *see under* TOM.

Every honest miller has a thumb of gold. Even an honest miller grows rich with what he filches; for he simply cannot help some of the flour that ought to go into the loaf sticking to his thumb! Chaucer says of his miller:

> Wel koude he stelen corn and tollen thries,
> And yet he hadde a thombe of gold pardee.
>
> *Canterbury Tales: Prologue*, 562.

The pricking of one's thumb. In popular superstition, a portent of evil. The Second Witch in SHAKESPEARE's *Macbeth* (IV, i) says:

> By the pricking of my thumbs
> Something wicked this way comes.

And Macbeth enters.

Another proverb says, **My little finger told me that.** When your *ears tingle* it is to indicate that someone is speaking about you; when a sudden fit of *shivering* occurs, it is because someone is treading over the place which is to form your grave; when the *eye twitches*, it indicates the visit of a friend; when the *palm itches* it shows that a present will shortly be received; and when the *bones ache* a storm is prognosticated.

Sudden pains and prickings are the warnings of evil on the road; sudden glows and pleasurable sensations are the couriers to tell us of joy close at hand.

In ancient ROME, the augurs (*see* AUGURY) took special notice of the palpitation of the heart, the flickering of the eye, and the pricking of the thumb. In regard to the last, if the pricking was on the left hand it was considered a very bad sign, indicating mischief at hand.

To bite one's thumb at one. To insult him. Formerly a way of expressing defiance and contempt by snapping the finger or putting the thumb in the mouth. Both these acts are terms a FICO. *Cp.* HE BIT HIS GLOVE *under* GLOVE.

To thumb a lift. to ask for or to "scrounge" a ride from a passing vehicle by holding out the hand with the thumb pointing upwards and moving in the direction of intended travel.

To thumb the nose. To COCK A SNOOK.

To twiddle one's thumbs. To sit in a state of bored inactivity, often against one's inclination; to be wasting time or to have to waste one's time. An allusion to the habit at such times, of sitting with the hands interlaced in one's lap idly rotating the thumbs round each other.

Under one's thumb. Under the influence or power of the person named.

Thumbikins, Thumbscrew. An instrument of torture used largely by the INQUISITION, whereby the thumbs are compressed between two bars of iron, by means of a screw. William Carstares (1649–1715) was the last person put to the torture in Britain; as the Law of ENGLAND would not permit torture, he was sent by the PRIVY COUNCIL for examination in Edinburgh, to elicit the names of the accomplices in the RYE HOUSE PLOT.

Thunder. Used figuratively of any loud noise, also of vehement denunciations or threats, as, "the thunders of the VATICAN", meaning the anathemas and denunciations of the POPE.

THOR was the Scandinavian god of thunder, and JUPITER in Roman mythology; hence Dryden's allusion to the inactivity of Louis XIV:

> And threatening France, placed like a

painted Jove,
Kept idle thunder in his lifted hand.
Annus Mirabilis, XXXIX.

Sons of Thunder. *See* BOANERGES.

To steal one's thunder. To forestall him; or to adopt his own special methods as one's own. The phrase comes from the anecdote of John Dennis (1657–1734), the critic and playwright who invented an effective device for producing stage thunder for his play *Appius and Virginia*. The play was a failure and was withdrawn, but shortly afterwards Dennis heard his thunder used in a performance of *Macbeth*. "My God," he exclaimed, "The villains will play my thunder but not my plays!"

Thunderbolt. A missile or mass of heated matter that was formerly supposed to be discharged from thunder-clouds during a storm; used figuratively of an irresistible blow, a sudden and overwhelming shock. *cp.* A BOLT FROM THE BLUE *under* BOLT.

JUPITER was depicted by the ancients as a man seated on a throne, holding a sceptre in his left hand and thunderbolts in his right.

Be ready, gods, with all your thunder-
bolts;
Dash him to pieces!
SHAKESPEARE: *Julius Cæsar*, IV, iii.

Thunderday. *See* THURSDAY.

Thunderer, The. A name facetiously applied to *The Times* newspaper in the mid-19th century, in allusion to an article by the assistant editor, Edward Sterling (1773–1847), which began, "We thundered forth the other day an article on the subject of social and political reform." *See* PRINTING HOUSE SQUARE.

Thundering Legion, The. The XIIth Legion of the Roman army; probably so called because its ensign was a representation of JUPITER TONANS.

The name *Fulminata* dates from the time of Augustus (31 B.C.—A.D. 14) but fable relates it to the time of Marcus Aurelius. The story is that in this emperor's expedition against the Marco-manni, Quadi, etc. (172), the XIIth Legion, consisting of Christians, saved the whole army from a disastrous drought by praying for rain. A terrible thunder-storm burst and not only provided abundance of water but dispersed the enemy with lightning and THUNDER-BOLTS. Hence the legion's name.

Thursday. The fifth day of the weeek until 1971, now the fourth (*see* SUNDAY). The day of the god THOR, called by the French *jeudi*, that is, Jove's day. Both JOVE and THOR were gods of thunder, and formerly Thursday was sometimes called *Thunderday*. *See also* BLACK, HOLY, MAUNDY THURSDAY.

When three Thursdays come together. One of the many circumlocutions for NEVER.

Thyestes (thī′ es tēz). Brother of Atreus, and son of PELOPS and HIPPODAMIA. He seduced his brother's wife and also contrived a situation which led to Atreus slaying his own son. By way of revenge, Atreus invited Thyestes to a banquet in which the limbs of two of his sons, slain by Atreus, were served as a dish. Hence a *Thyestean feast*: one at which human flesh is served.

Thyrsus (ther′ sus). The staff carried by DIONYSUS and his attendants, topped with a pine cone and decorated with vine and ivy leaves. *See* TORSO.

Ti. *See* ARETINIAN SYLLABLES.

Tiara (tē ar′ à). Anciently the turban-like head-dress worn erect by the Persian kings and turned down by lords and priests; now applied to a coronet-like head ornament, especially to the triple CROWN of the POPE. The latter resembles the old-style beehive in shape and is worn on other than liturgical occasions. It typifies the temporal or sovereign power of the Papacy and is composed of GOLD cloth encircled by three crowns and surmounted by a golden globe and CROSS. It is first mentioned in the early 8th century and was a kind of cap called *camelaucum*. By the 11th century, a coronet had been added to the rim with two pendants or lappets hanging down at the back. The second circlet was added by Boniface VIII (1294–1303), perhaps to symbolize both temporal and spiritual powers, and the third coronet seems to have been added either by Benedict XI (1303–1304) or Clement V (1305–1314).

Tib. St. Tib's Eve. NEVER. There is no such SAINT in the CALENDAR, her eve is nonexistent like the GREEK CALENDS.

Tich. A diminutive person; from celebrated dwarfish music-hall comedian Harry Ralph (1868–1928), known as Little Tich. As a podgy infant at the time of the TICHBORNE CASE, he was nicknamed "Tichborne" or "Tich" in allusion to the Tichborne claimant, who was very corpulent. As he remained a "TOM THUMB" he came to be called "Little Tich", a name he used professionally.

Tichborne Case. The most celebrated impersonation case in English law. In March 1853, Roger Charles Tichborne, heir to an ancient Hampshire baronetcy, sailed for Valparaiso, and after travelling a while in S. America embarked on 20 April 1854 in a sailing ship named the *Bella*, bound for Jamaica. The ship went down and nothing more was heard or seen of Roger Tichborne. In October 1865, "R.C. Richborne" turned up at Wagga Wagga, in Australia, in the person of a man locally known as Tom Castro. On Christmas Day 1866, he landed in England as a claimant to the Tichborne baronetcy, asserting that he was the lost Roger. Lady Tichborne, the real Roger's mother, professed to recognize him, but the family could not be deceived. The case came into the courts where the fellow's claims were proved to be false and he himself identified as Arthur Orton, the son of a Wapping butcher. A further trial for perjury, lasting 188 days, ended in his being sentenced to 14 years' penal servitude. *See* B. OF B.K..

Tichborne Dole. An ancient charity maintained by the Tichborne family said to have been instituted by Lady Mabel Tichborne in 1150. The legend is that, when dying, she begged her husband to provide for the poor from the produce of the estate and he promised to give the value of the land she could encircle while holding a burning torch. She rose from her deathbed and encompassed 23 acres and prophesied that if the charity were allowed to lapse, seven sons would be born to the family followed by seven daughters and the title would lapse. The dole was stopped after 644 years and the then baronet had seven sons and his heir seven daughters. The third son changed his name to Doughty and revived the dole and escaped the full consequences of the curse. The title became extinct in 1968 with the death of Sir Anthony Doughty-Tichborne, the fourteenth baronet.

Tick. To get, or **go on tick.** To get on credit, to owe for what one buys. In the 17th century *ticket* was the ordinary term for the written acknowledgment of a debt, and one living on credit was said to be living *on ticket* or *tick*.

To tick someone off. To rebuke or "tell off" sharply; both "tick off" and "tell off" involve the idea of enumerating or checking off a list of complaints or offences.

What makes it tick? The child's question, asked about a watch or clock, has given rise to a figurative use: "What makes him (her or it) tick?" meaning, "What keeps him on the go?" Sometimes the question is asked with wider implications, such as, what are a person's beliefs and interests?

Ticket (U.S.A.). The party list of candidates in an election. "I intend to vote for the straight Republican ticket."

Ticket of leave. A warrant given to convicts to have their liberty on condition of good behaviour; hence, *Ticket-of-leave man*, a convict freed from prison but obliged to report himself to the police from to time until his sentence was completed. The system is now discontinued.

That's the ticket, or **that's the ticket for soup.** That's the right thing, that's just what is wanted, from the custom among 19th-century charities of issuing to the needy tickets exchangeable for soup, clothing, coal, etc.

To get one's ticket. In the Merchant Service the expression denotes becoming a qualified mate or master, etc., of a ship, *i.e.* to get one's certificate as such. Thus **to lose one's ticket** is to have one's certificate withdrawn as a result of incompetence causing the hazarding of a ship etc.

To work one's ticket. An army expression meaning to secure one's discharge before the contract of service has expired.

All tickety-boo. Everything is in order, everything is fine and as it should be. An expression of uncertain origin, possibly from *ticket* as in THAT'S THE TICKET (*above*).

Tide (O.E. *tid*, time, season, tide of the sea). The word is cognate with TIME. *See also* TIDY. It is used figuratively of a tendency, a current or flow of events, etc., as in a tide of feeling, and in SHAKESPEARE'S:

> There is a tide in the affairs of men,
> Which, taken at the flood, leads on to fortune.
>
> *Julius Cæsar*, IV, iii.

Time and tide wait for no man. *See under* TIME.

To tide over a difficulty, hard times, etc. To surmount the difficulty, to get by.

Tidy. The word is used in the sense of a thing being worth consideration: **a tidy penny,** quite a good sum; **a tidy fortune,** an inheritance worth having.

Tied House. A retail business, especially a public house *tied* by agreement to obtain its supplies from a particular firm.

Tiffin. An old north of ENGLAND provincialism for a small draught of liquor; also a lunch or slight repast between breakfast and dinner. In Anglo-Indian usage it denotes a light meal or lunch, especially of curried dishes, chutney and fruit.

Tiger. A liveried servant who rides out with his master used to be called a *tiger*, also a boy in buttons, a page. In America it is applied to a final yell in a round of cheering.

In poker, *tiger* is the lowest hand that can be drawn—six high, ace low, without pair, straight or flush. Great nerve is required to hold and bluff on such a hand, and the expression is responsible for the title of the famous JAZZ classic *Tiger Rag*. *Cf.* YARBOROUGH.

Paper Tiger. *See under* PAPER.

Tike, or **Tyke.** A provincial word (from Old Norse) for a dog or cur; hence used of a low or rough-mannered fellow, as in the contemptuous insults, "you dirty tike", "you measly tyke".

A Yorkshire tike. An established name for a Yorkshireman, nowadays without any derogatory implications; it formerly specially denoted a clownish rustic of that county.

Tilbury. A once fashionable well-sprung, two-wheeled horse carriage or gig, without top or cover. Designed by John Tilbury of London in the early 19th century. He was a horse-dealer and later a job-master and both NIMROD and John Mytton used his mounts.

Tile. Old slang for a hat, this being to the head what tiles are to a house.

Out on the tiles. On a late night spree, on the loose, on a nocturnal drinking bout.

To have a tile loose. To be not quite *compos mentis*, not "all there".

Tilt. At full tilt. At full speed. From the encounter at full gallop of KNIGHTS in a tilt. *See* QUINTAIN.

To tilt at windmills. *See under* WINDMILL.

Tim Bobbin. A native of Lancashire.

Timbuctoo, or **Timbuktu.** An ancient African city on the southern edge of the Sahara, "the part of the Sudan in the Sahara", which first began as a settlement in the 11th century and subsequently developed as a mart for GOLD, etc., and achieved legendary repute. It was the last great goal of 19th century European travellers searching for fabulous wealth and splendour. Major Gordon Laing having reached it from Tripoli in 1826 was put to death, but René Caillé of Bordeaux, to whom its then ruinous condition became apparent, made a safe return in 1828. It was occupied by the French in 1894 and is now in the Republic of Mali.

Time. Greenwich Time. *See under* GREENWICH. **Summer Time.** *See* DAYLIGHT SAVING.

Time lag. The term given to the pause that elapses between a cause and its effect.

Time of Grace. *See* SPORTING SEASONS.

Time of Troubles. In Russian history, the years 1584–1613, a period of monarchical instability, foreign intervention, social disorder and economic crises. It began with the accession of Ivan IV's son Feodor, who was incapable of exercising his office, with resultant intrigues among the boyars, and did not end until the accession of Michael Romanov in 1613. Boris Godunov was proclaimed Tsar in 1598 and ruled until his death in 1605, but from 1604 various Pretenders intrigued for the throne. In 1609 King Sigismund of Poland intervened until Patriarch Hermogen stimulated national resistance, which led to the election of Michael by the Zemsky Sobor, and the expulsion of the Poles.

Time zone. *See* STANDARD TIME.

Take time by the forelock. Seize the present moment; CARPE DIEM. Time, called by SHAKESPEARE "that bald sexton" (*King John*, *III*, i), is represented with a lock of hair on his forehead but none on the rest of his head, to signify that time past cannot be used, but time present may be seized by the forelock. The saying is attributed to Pittacus of Mitylene, one of the SEVEN SAGES OF GREECE. It is also suggested that the statue of Opportunity by Lysippus inspired the phrase.

Time and tide wait for no man. One of many sayings pointing the folly of procrastination. It appears in Ray's *Scottish Proverbs* as, "Time bides na man."

Time, gentlemen, please! The traditional announcement for closing time in bars and public houses.

Time Immemorial. Since ancient times, beyond memory. In English law, beyond "legal memory", *i.e.* before the reign of Richard I (1189–1199), because the Statute of Westminister of 1275 fixed this reign as the time limit for bringing certain types of action.

Time is, Time was, Time's past. *See* BRAZEN HEAD.

Time out of mind. TIME IMMEMORIAL; time longer than anyone can remember.

To have had one's time. In World War II, a British soldier's expression for being ripe for death, to expect imminent disaster. In the Royal Navy, part of the traditional "Wakey, Wakey" chant when calling the hands is, "You've had your time", *i.e.* your allotted period of rest.

To know the time o'day. to be smart, wide awake.

Time-expired. Applied to soldiers whose term of service is completed. Also

used of convicts who have served their sentences.

Timeo Danaos. *See* GREEK GIFT.

Timoleon (tī mō' lē ŏn). The Greek general and statesman (d. *c.* 336 B.C.) who so hated tyranny that he voted for the death of his own brother Timophanes when he attempted to make himself absolute in Corinth.

Timon of Athens (tī' mon). An Athenian misanthrope of the late 5th century B.C., and the principal figure in SHAKE-SPEARE's play so called.

Tin. Money. A depreciating synonym for SILVER, called by alchemists "JUPITER".

Tin fish. Naval slang for a torpedo.

Tin hat. A soldier's name for his protective metal helmet. **To put the tin hat on it,** to bring something to an abrupt and conclusive end.

Tin-pan Alley. The district of New York City, originally in the area of 14th Street, where popular music is published. In England, Denmark Street, off CHARING CROSS Road, was so called as the centre of the popular music industry. The name has been said to derive from the rattling of tins by rivals when a performance was too loud and too protracted. The "Alley" is now largely deserted by song writers and music publishers who have moved to bigger premises. *See* OLD GREY WHISTLE TEST under GREY.

Tin Tabernacle. *See under* TABERNA-CLE.

Tintype. A positive photograph taken on a sensitized sheet of enamelled tin. Tintypes were cheap and very popular at FAIRS, amusement parks, etc.

Tincture. In HERALDRY, the hues or colours of the shield and its charges. It include metals, colours, and furs.

Tinker. Not worth a tinker's damn, or **curse.** Absolutely worthless. It has been suggested that the term derives from the old-time tinker's custom of blocking up the hole in the article he was mending with a pellet of bread, thus making a dam which would prevent the solder from escaping. This pellet was discarded as useless when the job was finished.

Tintagel (tin tăj' ĕl). The castle on the north coast of Cornwall fabled as King

ARTHUR's Castle and according to Geoffrey of Monmouth (*Historia Britonum*, XIX) the birthplace of King Arthur. The present ruin upon the cliff is of mid-12th century origin.

Tip. A small present of money, such as that given to a waiter, porter, or schoolboy; from the CANT verb (common in the 16th and 17th centuries) *to tip*, meaning to hand over, which also gives rise to the other signification of the verb, *viz*. private warning, such secret information as may guide the person *tipped* to make successful bets or gain some other advantage. *A straight tip* comes straight or direct from the owner or trainer of a horse, or from one in a position to know.

Tip and Run raid. A phrase used in World War II to denote a hurried and often indiscriminate air raid when the enemy sped homeward after jettisoning their bombs. So called from the light-hearted form of CRICKET in which the batsman is forced to run every time he hits the ball.

Tip-off. To warn or give a hint, especially timely warning of a police raid.

To have a thing on the tip of one's tongue. *See under* TONGUE.

To tip one the wink. To give a signal to another by a wink; to tip one off, *i.e.* to give him a hint or warning.

Tip-top. First rate, capital, splendid.

Tiphany. The name given in the old romances to the mother of the MAGI. It is a corruption of EPIPHANY.

Tiphys. The pilot of the ARGONAUTS, hence a generic name for pilots.

"Tipperary". This song, inseparably associated with World War I, was composed by Jack Judge (d. 1938), of Oldbury, Birmingham. The words were by Harry J. Williams of Temple Balsall, Warwickshire, and the first line of the refrain was engraved on his tombstone. It was composed in 1912 and was already popular in the MUSIC HALL by 1914; it was sung by troops embarking for France and on the front.

> It's a long way to Tipperary,
> It's a long way to go,
> It's a long way to Tipperary,
> To the sweetest girl I know;
> Goodbye, Piccadilly; farewell, Leicester Square;

> It's a long, long way to Tipperary,
> But my heart's right there.

Tipperary Rifle. A SHILLELAGH or stick made of blackthorn.

Tippling House. A contemptuous name for a tavern or public house. A *tippler* was formerly a tavern-keeper or tapster, and the tavern was called a *tippling house*.

Tipstaff. A constable, BAILIFF, or SHERIFF'S officer; so called because he carried a staff tipped with a bull's horn or with metal. In the documents of Edward III allusion is often made to his staff.

Tirant lo Blanch. A romance of CHIVALRY by Johannot Martorell and Johan de Galba, written in Catalan and produced at Valencia in 1490. A favourite book of Cervantes, and one which figures in Don QUIXOTE'S library.

Tiresias (tī rē' si ás). A Theban of Greek legend, who by accident saw ATHENE bathing, and was therefore struck with blindness by her splashing water in his face. She afterwards repented, and, as she could not restore his sight, conferred on him the power of soothsaying and of understanding the language of birds, giving him a staff with which he could walk as safely as if he had his sight. He found death at last by drinking from the well of Tilphosa.

Another story is that he had been temporarily changed into a woman (for seven years) and was therefore called upon by JUPITER and JUNO to settle an argument as to which of the sexes derived the greatest pleasure from the married state. Tiresias, speaking from experience, declared in favour of the female, whereupon Juno struck him blind.

Tirl. A Scottish variant of *twirl*.

To tirl at the pin. To twiddle or rattle the latch before opening the door. The pin was part of the door-latch and it was a signal that one wished to enter.

Tironian (ti rō' ni án). Pertaining to a system of shorthand said to have been invented by Tiro, the freedman and amanuensis of CICERO. Our "&" (*see* AMPERSAND) is still sometimes called the *Tironian sign*, for it represents the contraction of Latin *et* introduced by Tiro.

Tisiphone. *See* FURIES.

Tit for Tat. Retaliation; probably representing *tip for tap, i.e.* blow for blow. J. Bellenden Ker says this is the Dutch *dit vor dat* (this for that), Lat. QUID PRO QUO. Heywood uses the phrase *tit for tat*, perhaps the French *tant pour tant*.

Titania (tĭ tan′ yà). Wife of OBERON, and Queen of the Fairies. SHAKESPEARE uses the name in his *A Midsummer Night's Dream*.

Titans (tĭ′tànz). In Greek mythology, children of URANUS and GÆA, of enormous size and strength, and typical of lawlessness and the power of force. There were 12, six male (OCEANUS, Cœus, Crius, CRONUS, HYPERION, and Japetus or IAPETOS) and six female (Theia, RHEA, THEMIS, MNEMOSYNE, PHŒBE, and TETHYS). This is according to Hesiod, but the number is variously given by other writers.

Incited by their mother, they overthrew Uranus and emasculated him, and set up Cronus as king. Cronus was in turn overthrown by his son ZEUS. After the long struggle which some of the Titans carried on against Zeus, they were finally hurled down into TARTARUS. *See* GIANTS' WAR WITH ZEUS.

By VIRGIL and Ovid the SUN was sometimes surnamed *Titan*; hence SHAKESPEARE'S:

> And flecked Darkness like a drunkard reels
> From forth Day's path and Titan's fiery wheels.
>
> *Romeo and Juliet*, II, iii.

Tithes. One-tenth of the produce of the land given to the Church, at first voluntarily but made compulsory by the end of the 8th century. The *great* tithes were those of the major crops, the *small* consisting of lesser produce. With the growth of the parochial system, they became an important item in the income of the parson and source of friction between clergy and their parishioners. With the rise of the PURITANS and later Nonconformity a new grievance arose. Commutation of tithes began before 1600, and an attempt to commute tithes to a single rent charge was begun by an Act of 1836. Acts of 1937 and 1951 commuted them to a lump sum redeemable by instalments up to A.D. 2000. *Cp.* TENTHS; *see* VICAR.

Tithing. King Cnut (1017–1035) provided that all free men over the age of 12 should be put in a tithing, a group of ten upon which rested the responsibility of securing the good behaviour of the group, etc.

Tithonus (tĭ thō′ nŭs). A beautiful Trojan of Greek legend, brother to Laomedon, and beloved by Eos (AURORA). At his prayer, the goddess granted him immortality, but as he had forgotten to ask for youth and vigour he grew old, and life became insupportable. He now prayed Eos to remove him from the world; this, however, she could not do, but she changed him into a GRASSHOPPER.

Titles of Kings. *See* RULERS; RELIGIOUS.

Title-Role, in a play, opera or film, is the part or role from which the title is taken, *e.g.* HAMLET, *Carmen,* KING KONG.

Titmouse. *See* MISNOMERS.

Titular Bishops. The Roman Catholic dignitaries formerly known as bishops IN PARTIBUS.

Titus (tĭ′ tŭs). An alternative name for DYSMAS. Also the name of one of St. PAUL'S disciples to whom he wrote one of his *Epistles*. The latter is traditionally regarded as the first bishop of Crete, where he died. His head was eventually carried off by the Venetians and the skull was returned to the ORTHODOX CHURCH in Crete in 1964.

The Arch of Titus. The arch built in ROME in commemoration of the capture of JERUSALEM (A.D. 70) by Titus and his father Vespasian. Titus became Emperor in A.D. 79. The arch is richly sculptured, and the trophies taken at the destruction of the TEMPLE are shown in relief.

Tityre Tus (tit′ i rē tūz). Dissolute young scapegraces of the late 17th century (*cp.* MOHOCKS) whose delight was to annoy the watchmen, upset SEDANS, wrench knockers off doors, and insult pretty women. The name comes from the first line of VIRGIL'S first *Eclogue*, *Tityre, tu patulæ recubans sub tegmine fagi,* because the Tityre Tus loved to lurk in the dark night looking for mischief.

Tityrus (tit′ i rus). A poetical surname for a shepherd; from its use in Greek idylls and VIRGIL'S first *Eclogue*.

Tityus (tit′ i ůs). In Greek mythology, a gigantic son of ZEUS and GÆA whose body covered nine acres of land. He tried to defile LATONA, but APOLLO cast him into TARTARUS, where a vulture fed on his liver which grew as fast as it was devoured (*cp*. PROMETHEUS).

Tiu, Tiw, or **Tyr.** In Scandinavian mythology, son of ODIN and a younger brother of THOR. He had his hand bitten off when chaining up the wolf FENRIR. He was identified with MARS, the Roman god of war, and his name is found in our *Tuesday* (Fr. *mardi*). Philologists have generallly equated the name with Gr. ZEUS, Lat. *Deus*, Sansk. *devas*.

Tmesis (tmē′ sis). The grammatical term for the separation of the parts of a compound word by inserting between them other words, or the rearrangement in this manner of the words of a phrase; *e.g. A large meal and rich*, instead of, "A large, rich meal"; *The greatness of his power to us-ward* (*Eph*. i, 19), instead of, "The greatness of his power toward us".

Toads. The device of Clovis was three toads (or *botes*, as they were called in O. Fr.); legend relates that after his conversion and BAPTISM the ARIANS assembled a large army under King Candat against him. While on his way to meet the heretics, Clovis saw in the heavens his device miraculously changed into three lilies *or* on a banner *azure*. He instantly had such a banner made, and called it his ORIFLAMME, and even before his army came in sight of King Candat, the host of the HERETIC lay dead, slain, like the army of Sennacherib, by a blast from the God of Battles (Raoul de Presles, *Grans Croniques de France*).

The toad, ugly and venomous, wears yet a precious jewel in its head. Nashe (*Anatomie of Absurditie*, 1589) says, "It fareth with finer wits as it doth with the pearl, which is affirmed to be in the head of the toad", and SHAKESPEARE says:

> Sweet are the uses of adversity,
> Which, like the toad, ugly and venomous,
> Wears yet a precious jewel in its head.

As You Like It, II, i.

Thomas Lupton, in his *One Thousand Notable Things* (1579), speaks of the virtues of the *toadstone* which the toad carried inside its head. "A toad-stone (*crapaudina*) touching any part envenomed, hurt, or stung with rat, spider, wasp, or any other venomous beast, ceaseth the pain or swelling thereof." Such stones, toad-like in shape or colour, believed to have come from the toad, were used as amulets and set in rings.

Toads were also generally held to be poisonous.

Toads unknown in Ireland. It is said that St. PATRICK cleared the island of all vermin by his malediction.

Toad-eater or **Toady.** A cringing parasite, an obsequious lickspittle. The old MOUNTEBANKS used to take around with them a boy who ate—or pretended to eat—toads, then believed to be poisonous. This gave the master the chance to exhibit his skill in expelling poison.

> Be the most scorn'd Jack-Pudding of the pack,
> And turn toad-eater to some foreign quack.
>
> TOM BROWN: *Satire on an Ignorant Quack* (*Works* I, 71).

Toad-in-the-hole. A piece of beef, sausage, chop, etc., baked in batter.

Toast. The person, cause, object, etc., to which guests are invited to drink in compliment, as well as the drink itself. The word is taken from the piece of toast which used at one time to be put into the tankard, and which still floats in the LOVING-CUPS at the ancient universities.

The story goes that, in the reign of Charles II, a certain beau pledged a noted beauty in a glass of water taken from her bath; whereupon another roysterer cried out he would have nothing to do with the liquor, but would have the toast—*i.e.* the lady herself (*Tatler*, No. 24).

Toast-master. The official who announces the after-dinner speakers at a formal banquet.

Tobit. The central character of the popular story in the *Book of Tobit*, in the Old Testament APOCRYPHA. Tobit is a scrupulous and pious Jew who practised good works, but, while sleeping in his courtyard, being unclean from burying a Jew found strangled in the street, was blinded by sparrows which "muted warm dung in his eyes". His son Tobias was attacked on the Tigris by a fish, which leapt out of the water and which he caught at the bidding of the angel RAPHAEL, his mentor. Tobit's blindness was cured by applying to his eyes the gall of the fish. Father and son prepared to reward Azarias (Raphael), whereupon the ANGEL revealed his identity and returned to HEAVEN.

Tobit's dog. *See* CAMEL.

Toby. The dog in the puppet-show of PUNCH AND JUDY. He wears a frill garnished with bells to frighten away the DEVIL from his master.

The high toby, the high road; **the low toby,** the by-road. A highwayman is a "high tobyman"; a mere footpad is a "low tobyman". This is probably from the Shelta (*i.e.* tinkers' jargon) word for road, *tobar*.

Toby jug. A small jug in the form of a squat old man in 18th-century dress, wearing a three-cornered hat, one corner of which forms the lip. The name comes from a poem (1761) about one "Toby Philpot", adapted from the Latin by Francis Fawkes; and the design of the jug from a print sold by Carrington Bowles, a London print-seller, to Ralph Wood, the potter, who turned out a great number of Toby Jugs.

Toc H. The morse pronunciation of the letters T.H., the initials of Talbot House. The term was used in World War I, when the first Talbot House was founded, in December 1915, at Poperinghe, in memory of Gilbert Talbot, son of the Bishop of Winchester, who had been killed at Hooge in the preceding July. The Rev. P.B. Clayton, M.C., made it a famous rest and recreation centre. In 1920, he founded a similar centre in London, also known as Toc H, which developed into an interdenominational association for Christian social service. *See* PIP EMMA.

Tod. To be on one's tod. To be alone; a contraction of Tod Sloan in cockney rhyming slang. (Tod Sloan was a famous jockey).

Toddy. Properly the juice obtained by tapping certain palms, fermented so as to become intoxicating (Hindu *tadi*; from *tar*, a palm). It is also applied to a beverage compounded of spirits, hot water, and sugar, a kind of PUNCH.

Toe. From top to toe. From head to foot.

To toe the line. To submit to discipline or regulations, to come into line with the rest. In foot races the runners are made to assemble with toes up to the start line.

To tread on someone'e toes. To upset, to offend; to vex or annoy.

To turn up one's toes. To die.

Tofana. *See* AQUA TOFANA.

Toga. The distinctive public garb of the Roman citizen consisting of a single semicircular piece of white woollen cloth worn in a flowing fashion round the shoulders and body. The Romans were hence the *Gens togata*, the "togaed people". It was also worn by freedwomen and prostitutes. Respectable women wore the *stola*. *Cp.* GALLIA BRACATA; GENS BRACATA; PALLIUM.

Toga candida. A new toga whitened with chalk, worn by candidates for public office when they appeared before the people.

Toga picta. The toga embroidered with golden stars that was worn by the emperor on special occasions, by a victorious general at his "TRIUMPH", etc.

Toga prætexta. The toga bordered (*prætexta*) with purple that was worn by children, by those engaged in sacred rites, magistrates on duty, etc.

Toga virilis. The toga worn by men (*virilis*, manly), assumed at the age of 15.

Togs. Slang for clothes; hence *togged out in his best*, dressed in his best clothes; *toggery*, finery. The word may be connected with TOGA.

Token payment. A small payment made as a formal and binding acknowledgment of indebtedness. The word "token" is often used to describe some action or phrase used in lieu of—but acknowledging—a greater obligation.

Tolbooth, or **Tollbooth** (tōl' boo*th*). Originally a booth or stall where taxes were collected.

In SCOTLAND, the term was applied

to the town gaol, from the custom of confining offenders against the laws of a fair or market in the booth where market dues were collected.

Tolpuddle Martyrs. Six agricultural labourers of Tolpuddle, Dorset, who formed a TRADE UNION to resist wage cuts. They were sentenced to seven years' transportation to Australia in 1834 on a concocted charge of administering illegal oaths. After continuous protests they were pardoned in 1836.

Tom. Tommy. Short for *Thomas*; used for the male of certain animals (especially the cat), and generically, like JACK, for a man. It sometimes has a somewhat contemptuous implication, as in TOM O'BEDLAM, TOM-FOOL.

Great Tom of Lincoln. A bell at Lincoln Cathedral weighing 5 tons 12 cwt.

Great Tom of Oxford. A bell in TOM GATE Tower, Oxford, tolled every night. It weighs 7 tons 12 cwt.

Tom Collins. *See* JOHN COLLINS.

Tom, Dick and Harry. A Victorian term for the "MAN IN THE STREET", more particularly persons of no note; persons unworthy of notice. BROWN, JONES AND ROBINSON are for other men; they are the vulgar rich, who give themselves airs, especially abroad, and look with scorn on all foreign manners and customs which differ from their own.

Tom Fool. A clumsy, witless fool, fond of stupid practical jokes; hence *tom-foolery*.

Tom Long. Any lazy, dilatory man.

Tom Noddy. A puffing, fuming, stupid creature.

Tom o'Bedlam. A mendicant who levies charity on the plea of insanity. In the 16th and 17th centuries many harmless inmates of BEDLAM were let out to beg and such a beggar was called an ABRAM-MAN.

Tom Thumb. Any dwarfish or insignificant person is so called from the tiny hero of the old nursery tale, popular in the 16th century. *The History of Tom Thumb* was published by Richard Johnson in 1621, and there was a similar tale by Perrault, *Le Petit Poucet*, 1697.

Tom Tiddler's Ground. A place where it is easy to pick up a fortune or make a place in the world for oneself; from the old children's game in which a base-keeper, who is called *Tom Tiddler*, tries to keep the other children who sing:

> Here we are on Tom Tiddler's ground
> Picking up gold and silver,

from crossing the boundary into his base.

Tom Tiler, or **Tyler.** A hen-pecked husband.

Uncle Tom. *See* UNCLE TOM'S CABIN under UNCLE.

Tomboy. A romping girl. The word was also used of a loose or immodest woman, whence the slang, *Tom*, applied to a prostitute.

Tommy, or **Tommy Atkins.** A British army private soldier as a JACK TAR is a British sailor. From 1815 and throughout the 19th century *Thomas Atkins* was the name used in the specimen form, accompanying the official manual issued to all army recruits, supplied to show them how their own form requiring details of name, age, date of enlistment, etc., should be filled in.

Tommy Dodd. The "odd" man who, in tossing up, either wins or loses according to agreement with this confederate.

Tommy gun. A Thompson short-barrelled sub-machine-gun.

Tommy rot. Utter nonsense, rubbish; a COCK AND BULL STORY.

Tommy shop. A shop where vouchers, given by an employer in lieu of money, can be exchanged for goods; commonly run by large employers of labour before the TRUCK SYSTEM was made illegal. *Tommy* here is a slang term for bread, provisions, etc.

Tomahawk (tom' à hawk). The war axe of the North American Indians, pre-historically made of stone or deer-horn, but after the coming of the white man, of iron or steel with a wooden handle. Sometimes the blunt end of the head was hollowed into a pipe-bowl, the handle being bored to form a stem. *See* BURY THE HATCHET.

Tongue. Confusion of tongues. According to the BIBLE (*Gen*. xi, 1–9), the people of the earth originally spoke one language and lived together. They built a city and a tower as a rallying point, but

God, seeing this as the beginning of ambition, "did confound the language of all the earth" and scattered them abroad and hence the town was called BABEL. This was taken as an explanation of the diversity of languages and the dispersal of mankind and the origin of the name BABYLON.

The gift of tongues. Command of foreign languages; also the power claimed by the early church and by some later mystics (as the IRVINGITES) of conversing in and understanding unknown tongues (from the miracle at PENTECOST—*Acts* ii, 4, the implications of which are obscure).

One's mother tongue. One's native language.

The tongue of the trump. The spokesman or leader of a party. The trump here is the Jew's HARP and the tongue is its most important part.

A lick with the rough side of the tongue. A severe reprimand, a good slating.

To bite one's tongue. To repress one's speech, to remain silent under provocation.

To find one's tongue. To speak after recovery from initial shyness.

To give someone the length of one's tongue. To tell him in unmeasured language what you really think of him.

To give tongue. Properly used of a dog barking when on the scent; hence sometimes applied to people. Thus POLONIUS says to his son:

To have a long tongue. To be talkative or indiscreet in one's utterance.

To have something on the tip of one's tongue. To be just about to utter it or to have it on the verge of one's memory but escaping utterance.

To hold one's tongue. To keep silent when one might speak; to keep a secret.

To lose one's tongue. To become tongue-tied or speechless through shyness, fear, etc.

To speak with one's tongue in one's cheek. Insincerely; saying one thing and meaning another.

To wag one's tongue. To talk continuously or indiscreetly.

You've got a tongue in your head (or **mouth**). Why did you not speak or say something at the time and miss the opportunity? It is no good complaining now.

Tonic Sol-fa. A system of musical notation and sight singing in which diatonic scales are written always in one way (the keynote being indicated), the tones being represented by syllables or initials, and time and accents by dashes and colons. *Tonic* is a musical term denoting pertaining to or founded on the keynote; *sol* and *fa* are two of the ARETINIAN SYLLABLES. *See also* DOH; GAMUT.

The system was developed about 1850 by the Rev. John Curwen (1816–1860), a CONGREGATIONALIST minister who made use of the earlier work of Miss Sarah Ann Glover (1785–1867).

Tonnage or **Tunnage.** From the 12th century English imports of Bordeaux wine increased steadily and the ships carried it in huge casks or *tuns* containing 252 gallons, occupying some 60 cubic feet in the holds. In due course this became the unit of measurement of the stowage or tonnage of a ship.

Tonnage and Poundage. Customs duties levied from the early years of the 14th century and granted to the sovereign by PARLIAMENT from 1373 until their abolition in 1787 (except during the reign of Charles I when they were levied without Parliamentary consent).

Tonquin Bean. *See* MISNOMERS.

Tonsure (Lat. *tonsura*, a shearing). The shaving of part of the head among CATHOLIC clergy became customary in the 6th and 7th centuries as a mark of the clerical state. It is not retained in such countries as Britain and the U.S.A. where it is not in accordance with custom. The western form of tonsure leaving a circle of hair around the head is supposed to symbolize the CROWN OF THORNS. The CELTIC tonsure consisted of shaving off all the hair in front of a line extending over the head from ear to ear. In the East the whole head was shorn. The modern Roman Catholic tonsure varies among the different Orders and that of the secular clergy is a small circle on the crown of the head.

Tontine (ton' tēn). A form of annuity shared by several subscribers, in which the shares of those who die are added to the holdings of the survivors till the last survivor inherits all. So named from Lorenzo Tonti, a Neopolitan banker who introduced the system into France in 1653.

Toom Tabard. (Scot. empty jacket). A NICKNAME given to John Baliol (1249—1315), because of his poor spirit, and sleeveless appointment to the throne of Scotland. The honour was an "empty jacket", which he enjoyed only from 1292 to 1296. He died in Normandy.

Tooth, Teeth. Milk teeth. A child's first set of teeth.

By the skin of one's teeth. *See* SKIN.

From the teeth outwards. Merely talk; insincerity, not from the heart. An archaic expression.

He has cut his eye-teeth. He is "wide awake"; he has acquired wordly wisdom, is quite sophisticated. The eye-teeth are cut late, the first set about 16 months, the second set at 12 years. *Cp.* WISDOM TEETH under WISDOM.

His teeth are drawn. His power of doing mischief is taken from him. The phrase comes from the fable of the LION in love, who consented to have his teeth drawn and his claws cut, in order that a fair damsel might marry him. When this was done the girl's father fell on the lion and slew him.

In spite of his teeth. In opposition to his settled purpose or resolution; even though he snarl and show his teeth like an angry dog.

In the teeth of the wind. With the wind dead against one, blowing in or against one's teeth.

> To strive with all the tempest in my teeth.
>
> POPE: *Epistles of Horace*, II, ii.

To cast into one's teeth. To utter reproaches; to throw it back at him.

To draw one's eye-teeth. To take the conceit out of a person; to fleece without mercy.

To get one's teeth into something. To get to grips with it, to set to work with energy and determination.

To have a sweet tooth. To be addicted to sweet things.

To lie in one's teeth. To lie flagrantly.

To put teeth into. Said of a law regulation, etc., when steps are taken to make it effective.

To set one's teeth on edge. *See under* EDGE.

To show one's teeth. To adopt a menacing tone or attitude; as a dog shows its teeth when it snarls.

To take the bit between one's teeth. *See* BIT.

With tooth and nail. In right good earnest, with one's utmost power; as though biting and scratching.

Tooth and egg. An obsolete corruption of *tutenag* (from Arab. *tutiya*), an alloy rich in zinc, coming from the East Indies, much used for the lining of tea chests.

Top. *See also* MIZZENTOP.

The Big Top. The great circus tent in which the main performance takes place.

Can you top that? (U.S.A.) Can you beat or surpass that, especially in the telling of outlandish stories.

Out of the top drawer. *See under* DRAWER.

The top o'the morning to ye! A cheery greeting on a fine day, especially in IRELAND. It is about the same as, "The best of everything to you!"

To be on top of the world. Said of the feeling of elation experienced when one is in the best of care-free good health and when all one's affairs are flourishing.

To blow one's top. To lose one's temper excessively; to lose all self-control.

To go over the top. To take the final plunge. A phrase from the trench warfare of World War I, when, at ZERO HOUR, troops climbed over the parapet of the front-line trenches to advance across NO-MAN'S LAND to attack the enemy front line.

To sleep like a top. *See under* SLEEP.

Top dog. The one who by skill, personality or violence obtains the mastery, as the dog who is on top of his adversary in a fight.

Top-heavy. Liable to tip over because the centre of gravity is too high; intoxicated.

Top secret. Service or governmental information about which the greatest secrecy is to be observed. *Cp.* HUSH-HUSH.

Topping out. Traditional drinking ceremony when the framework of a building is completed.

Tophet (tō' fet). The valley of the children of Hinnom through which children were made "to pass through the fire of MOLECH" (II *Kings* xxiii, 10). Isaiah (xxx, 31), in prophesying the destruction of the Assyrians, foretold that their king would be destroyed by fire in Tophet. It is a loathsome place associated with horror and defilement, a place of human sacrifice, but its location is a matter of surmise. The name is taken as symbolical of HELL and it may mean "a place to be spat upon" or "the place of burning".

> The pleasant valley of Hinnom, Tophet thence
> And black Gehenna call'd the Type of Hell.
> MILTON: *Paradise Lost*, I, 404.

Topsy. The little slave girl in Harriet Beecher Stowe's UNCLE TOM'S CABIN (1852); chiefly remembered because when asked by "Aunt Ophelia" about her parents she maintained that she had neither father nor mother, her solution of her existence being, "I 'spect I grow'd."

Topsy-turvy. Upside down; probably *top*, with *so* and obsolete *terve*, connected with O.E. *tearflian*, to turn or roll over. SHAKESPEARE says (*Henry IV*, *Pt. I*, iv, i), "Turn it topsy-turvy down."

Torah (tôr' à) (Heb., the law). The Jewish term for the PENTATEUCH which contains the Mosaic Law; the revealed will of God as contained in the Jewish SCRIPTURES.

Torch. The code-name for the Allied plan for the North African landings which began on 8 November 1942.

To carry the torch (U.S.A.). To suffer unrequited love, the torch being the torch of love. *A torch singer* is a female who sings sentimental ditties of such love.

To hand on the torch. To maintain and transmit knowledge, learning, etc., to the succeeding generation. The allusion is to the runners at ancient Greek festivals passing on the torch in relays.

Torso. The Torso Belvedere, the fa-

mous torso of HERCULES in the VATICAN, was discovered in the 15th century. It is said that MICHAELANGELO greatly admired it.

Tortoise. This animal is frequently taken as the type of plodding persistence—"slow but sure".

In Hindu myth, the tortoise Chukwa supports the ELEPHANT Maha-pudma, which in its turn supports the world.

The name *tortoise* (Lat. *testudo*) is also given to the ancient Roman protective shelter formed by soldiers with shields overlapping above their heads when attacking a fort.

Achilles and the tortoise. *See under* ACHILLES.

The hare and the tortoise. *See under* HARE.

Tory (tôr'i) (Irish *toiridhe*, *toruidhe*, a pursuer, plunderer). The name applied in the 17th century to Irish ROMAN CATHOLIC outlaws and bandits who harassed the English in IRELAND. In the reign of Charles II, the name came to be applied as an abusive term to the supporters of the Crown and its prerogatives at the time of the struggle over the Exclusion Bills. As supporters of the CHURCH OF ENGLAND they opposed NONCONFORMIST and Roman Catholic alike, but most of them acquiesced in the Revolution of 1688. Tory extremists remained JACOBITES at the time of the Hanoverian succession which led to a WHIG monopoly of political power during the reign of George I and George II, after which they regained office under Pitt the Younger and remained dominant throughout the period of the French Revolutionary and Napoleonic Wars. From about 1830, the Tory party under the leadership of Peel came to be called CONSERVATIVE, the older name being associated with reaction. Nowadays *Tory* and *Conservative* are essentially interchangeable terms. *Cp.* DIEHARD; LIBERAL; UNIONIST.

Toss. A toss-up. An even chance; a matter of heads or tails as in the spinning of a coin.

Totem (tō' tem). A North American Indian (Algonkian) word for some natural object, usually an animal, taken as the EMBLEM of a person or CLAN on account of a supposed relationship. Persons bearing the same totem were not allowed to marry, thus totemism prevented intermarriage between near relations. The animal borne as one's totem must neither be killed nor eaten. Totemism is common among primitive peoples.

Totem pole. The post standing before a dwelling on which grotesque and frequently brilliantly coloured representations of the TOTEM were carved or hung. It is often of great size, and sometimes so broad at the base that an archway is cut through it.

Touch. A soft touch. *See under* SOFT.

Not to touch it with a barge pole. Not to have anything to do with it under any circumstances, to avoid it at all costs, the pole used for propelling a barge being a very lengthy one.

To be in, or **keep in touch.** To maintain contact with someone either in person, or by correspondence, etc.

To touch wood. *See under* WOOD.

Touch and go. A very narrow escape; a METAPHOR derived, perhaps, from driving when the wheel of one vehicle touches that of another passing vehicle without doing mischief. It was a touch, but neither vehicle was stopped, each could go on.

Touch down. In Rugby and American football, to score by touching the ball on the ground within a certain defined area behind the opponent's goal posts.

When an aircraft lands it is said to *touch down*.

Touch pieces. *See* KING'S EVIL.

Touché (too′ shā) (Fr., touched). An acknowledgment of a telling remark or rejoinder by one's opponent in an argument. It is the fencing term denoting a hit or touch.

Touchstone. A dark, flinty schist, jasper, or basanite (the *Lapis Lydius* of the ancients); so called because GOLD was assayed by comparing the streak made on it by the sample of gold with those made by *touch-needles* of known gold content, after all the streaks had been treated with nitric acid. The needles were made of varying proportions of gold and SILVER, gold and copper, or of all three metals. Hence the use of *touchstone* as any

criterion or standard.

Ovid (*Metamorphoses*, Bk. II, xi) tells us that Battus saw MERCURY steal APOLLO'S oxen, and Mercury gave him a cow to secure his silence, but, being distrustful of the man, changed himself into a peasant, and offered him a cow and an ox if he would tell him where he got the cow. Battus, caught in the trap, told the secret, and Mercury changed him into a touchstone.

Touchstone is the name given to the clown in SHAKESPEARE'S *As You Like It*.

Tour. The Grand Tour. In the 17th, 18th, and early 19th centuries it was the custom of families of rank and substance to finish their sons' education by sending them under the guardianship of a tutor or BEAR-LEADER on a tour through France, Switzerland, Italy, and home through western Germany. This was known as the Grand Tour and sometimes a couple of years or more were devoted to it. The young men were supposed to study the history, language, etc., of each country they visited and such travel was a distinguishing mark between the great landowners and the ordinary squire.

Tour de force (Fr.). A feat of strength or skill.

Tournament (O.Fr. *torneiement*; from Lat. *tornare*, to turn). In the days of CHIVALRY, a martial sport or contest among knights of jousting or tilting; the chief art being to manœuvre or turn your horse away to avoid the adversary's blow. Usually blunted weapons were used and the contests came to be associated with elaborate pageantry. *See* QUINTAIN.

Tours (toor). Geoffrey of Monmouth (*Historia Britonum*, xvi) says that BRUTUS had a nephew called Turonus who slew 600 men before being overwhelmed by the Gauls. "From him the city of Tours derived its name, because he was buried there." The name, in fact, derives from the Turones, a people of Gallia Lugdunensis.

Tower, The. Specifically, the Tower of LONDON, the oldest part of which is the great keep known as the WHITE TOWER (*see below*) built by WILLIAM THE CONQUEROR, traditionally on the site of a fort erected by Julius CÆSAR.

> Ye Towers of Julius, London's lasting shame,
> With many a foul and midnight murther fed.
>
> GRAY: *The Bard*.

As well as a fortress, it has a special place in English history, both as a royal residence down to the reign of James I, and as a state prison. It has also housed the Royal MINT (until 1810), a menagerie and the Public Records, and is still the home of the Crown Jewels. Among those buried in its chapel are Protector Somerset, the Duke of Northumberland, Anne Boleyn, Katharine Howard, Lord Guildford Dudley, Lady Jane Grey, the Duke of Monmouth, and Lords Kilmarnock, Balmerino, and Lovat (supporters of the FORTY-FIVE REBELLION). State prisoners confined there range from Ralf Flambard to Sir Walter Ralegh, Sir Roger Casement, and Rudolf Hess. W. Harrison Ainsworth's novel *The Tower of London* was first published in 1840. *See also* BEEF-EATERS; CEREMONY OF THE KEYS *under* KEY; TRAITORS' GATE.

The Bloody Tower. Built as the *Garden Tower*, this addition to the TOWER of London dates from the reign of Richard II (1377–1399). It had won its present name by 1597 from the supposition that it witnessed the murder of the PRINCES IN THE TOWER. It subsequently housed such famous prisoners as Sir Walter Ralegh, Archbishop Laud and Judge Jeffreys.

Leaning Tower. *See under* LEANING.

The Princes in the Tower. The boy King Edward V and his younger brother Richard, Duke of York, who were lodged in the TOWER (May—June 1483), after which their uncle Richard, Duke of Gloucester, assumed the CROWN as Richard III. The princes disappeared at this time and are generally presumed to have been murdered by their uncle, but there is no conclusive evidence. Bones found during excavations near the WHITE TOWER in 1674 were transferred to Westminster Abbey. In 1933, experts proclaimed them to be bones of children of ages corresponding to those of the princes.

Tower of Babel. *See* BABEL; CONFUSION OF TONGUES *under* TONGUE.

Towers of Silence. *See under* SILENCE.

Tower pound. The legal pound of 5,400 grains (11¼ oz. TROY WEIGHT), used in England until the adoption of the Troy pound in 1526. So called from the standard pound kept in the TOWER of London. *See* PENNYWEIGHT.

Town. Town and Gown. The two sections of a university town, composed of those not connected with the university and those who are members of it; hence *a town and gown row*, a collision or brawl between the students and non-gownsmen. *See* PHILISTINES.

Town crier, also called a bellman, a town official, usually in a robe, ringing a bell and crying OYEZ! OYEZ! to attract attention to his public announcements and proclamations. The earlier bellman was a night watchman whose duty was to parade the streets at night and call out the hours, etc.

Going to town. Letting oneself go in a lighthearted fashion. To go to town on something is to GO THE WHOLE HOG (*see under* HOG), to exploit the situation to the full. The expression is of American origin, probably originating among those in the backwoods who went to town for a spree.

A man about town. *See under* MAN.

A woman of the town. A prostitute.

Trachtenberg System. A system of speedy mathematical calculations based upon simple counting according to prescribed keys or formulæ which need to be memorized. There is no division or multiplication as such, and complicated calculations can be more easily and rapidly handled than by normal processes. The system was devised by Jakow Trachtenberg (b. 1888) during his seven long years in a NAZI concentration camp. He was born at Odessa and trained as an engineer and became a refugee in German after the Russian Revolution. *See* CALCULATOR.

Tractarians. *See* OXFORD MOVEMENT.

Tracy. All the Tracys have the wind in their faces. Those who do wrong will always meet with punishment. William de Tracy was the most active of the four

KNIGHTS who slew Thomas à Becket, and for this misdeed all who bore the name were saddled by the Church with this ban:

> Wherever by the sea or land they go
> For ever the wind in their face shall blow.

Trade. The Trade. Usually the liquor trade, especially those engaged in brewing and distilling; also applied to those engaged in the particular trade under consideration.

The Balance of Trade. *See under* BALANCE.

Board of Trade. A government department concerned with the various aspects of trade, first set up in 1786. It developed from the various PRIVY COUNCIL Committees of Trade appointed from 1622 onwards which were then much concerned with colonial matters. In 1974 most of its functions were absorbed by the Department of Trade and Industry.

Free Trade. *See under* FREE.

Trade board. A committee representing workers and management set up under Act of PARLIAMENT to regulate conditions of labour in a particular industry.

Trade mark. The name or distinctive device for an article made for sale indicating that it was made by the holder of that device. Trade marks are usually registered and protected by law.

Trade Union. An association of employees formed for the promotion and protection of their working conditions, wages, etc., by collective bargaining, and sometimes also acting as Friendly Societies to their members. Nowadays they constitute powerful pressure groups. They are essentially a by-product of the INDUSTRIAL REVOLUTION. *Cp.* TOLPUDDLE MARTYRS.

Trade winds. Winds that *blow trade*, *i.e.* regularly in one track or direction (Low Ger. *Trade*, track). In the Northern Hemisphere they blow from the *northeast*, and in the Southern Hemisphere from the *south-east*, about 30 degrees each side of the Equator. In some places they blow six months in one direction, and six months in the opposite.

To blow trade. *See* TRADE WINDS *above*.

To trade something in. To hand over a part-worn article (*e.g.* a cooking stove or motor-car) in part payment for a new one.

To trade something off. To barter or exchange it; to sell it as a "JOB LOT".

To trade upon. To make use of so as to gain some advantage, as in making unscrupulous use of private knowledge, or using a personal affliction to arouse sympathy, other people's kindness and generosity, etc.

Trade follows the flag. Wherever the flag flies trade with the mother country develops and prospers; where the flag is established trade will grow up.

Tragedy. Literally, a goat-song (Gr. *tragos*, goat; *ode*, song), though why so called is not clear. HORACE (*Ars Poetica*, 220) says, because the winner at choral competitions received a goat as a prize, but the explanation has no authority. *Cp.* COMEDY.

It was ARISTOTLE (in his *Poetics*) who said that tragedy should move one "by pity and terror":

> The plot ought to be so constructed that, even without the aid of the eye, he who hears the tale told will thrill with horror and melt to pity at what takes place.
> ARISTOTLE: *Poetics*, xix (*Butcher*).

The Father of Tragedy. A title given to ÆSCHYLUS (d. 456 B.C.), author of the Orestean trilogy and many other tragedies, and to Thespis. *See* THESPIANS.

Trahison des clercs (tra ēz ôn dā klär) (Fr. the treason or treachery of the intellectuals). The incursion of the intelligentsia, who should be concerned with the pursuit of truth and guided by abstract principle, into the field of partisan politics and propaganda.

Trail. To trail one's coat. *See under* COAT.

Train-bands. Locally-raised bodies of citizen soldiers or MILITIA of little military value, with the exception of those of London. They derived from an order of Elizabeth I (1573) that a "convenient number" in every county were to be organized in bands and trained. They were not willing to leave their districts and were seldom suitably trained.

Traitors' Gate. The old water gate under St. Thomas's Tower to the THAMES under which many state prisoners were brought to imprisonment or death in the TOWER of London. An old proverb says:

> A loyal heart may be landed at the Traitors' Gate.

Trajan (trā' jàn). Marcus Ulpius Trajanus, Roman Emperor (*c.* 53, 88–117), notable for his campaigns against the Dacians and Parthians, and for his buildings and public works.

Trajan's Arch. There are two arches known by this name, commemorating the triumphs of Trajan. One, the finest ancient arch in existence, was erected in A.D. 114 over the APPIAN WAY at Benevento, and the other in 112 at Ancona. Both are of white marble.

Trajan's Column. *See under* COLUMN.

Trajan's Wall. A line of fortifications stretching across the Dobrudja from Czernavoda to the BLACK SEA.

Tram. The old "popular" derivation of this word from the name of Benjamin Outram, who ran vehicles on stone rails at Little Eaton, Derbyshire, in 1800, is discredited. The word is connected with Low Ger. *Traam*, a baulk or beam, and was applied as early as the 16th century to trucks used in coal mines, and run on long wooden beams as rails.

Tramontana (tra mon ta' na). The north wind; so called by the Italians, because to them it comes from over the mountains (Lat. *trans*, across; *montem*, mountain).

Tramontane (tra mon' tān). Beyond the mountain, *i.e.* on the other side of the Alps from ROME; hence, barbarous, foreign; as a noun, a barbarian or foreigner. *See* ULTRAMONTANE.

Transept. An architectural term (from the Lat. *trans*, across; *septum*, enclosure) for the transverse portion of any building lying across the main body of that building. The transept became common in ecclesiastical architecture in the MIDDLE AGES and almost universal in the GOTHIC period. The CROSS is often surmounted by a tower, spire, or dome. In a BASILICA church the transept is the transverse portion in front of the choir.

Transfiguration. The word applied to the miraculous transformation of Christ's appearance which occurred on a

mountain where He was praying. It was witnessed by PETER, JAMES and JOHN and is celebrated on the 6th of August.

Transmigration of Souls. An ancient belief concerning the transition of the soul after death to another body or substance, usually human or animal; also known as metempsychosis. BRAHMINS and Buddhists accept human descent into plants as well as animals, and the BUDDHA underwent 550 births in different forms. The ancient Egyptians held to a form of transmigration in which the soul could inhabit another form to allow temporary revisiting the earth. *See* PYTHAGORAS.

Transubstantiation (trăn sub stan-shi ā'shon). A change from one substance into another. Theologically, the change of the whole substance of the bread and wine in the EUCHARIST to the body and blood of Christ, only their outward form or ACCIDENTS remaining.

Trap. Slang for the mouth; also old slang for a policeman; **shut your trap,** be quiet.

Trappists. Properly, the CISTERCIANS of the French abbey at Soligny La Trappe (founded 1140) after their reform and reorganization in 1664. They were absorbed by the CISTERCIANS of the Strict Observance in 1892, to whom the name is now applied. They are noted for extreme austerity, their rule including absolute silence, a common dormitory, and no recreation.

Traskites. A sect of Puritan SABBATARIANS founded by John Trask, a Somerset man, about 1620. They believed that the law as laid down for the ancient Hebrews was to be taken literally and applied to themselves and all men. Trask was brought before the STAR CHAMBER and pilloried. He is said to have recanted later and to have become an ANTINOMIAN, and his followers became absorbed by the SEVENTH-DAY BAPTISTS.

Tre, Pol, Pen. *See* CORNISH NAMES.

Treacle properly means an antidote against the bite of wild beasts (Gr. *theriake*; from *ther*, a wild beast). The ancients gave the name to several sorts of antidotes, but ultimately it was applied chiefly to Venice treacle (*theriaca an-*

drochi), a compound of some 64 drugs in honey.

Sir Thomas More speaks of "a most strong treacle [*i.e.* antidote] against these venomous heresies". *See also* TREACLE BIBLE, *under* BIBLE, SOME SPECIALLY NAMED EDITIONS.

Tread. To tread on someone's corns. *See under* CORN.

To tread on someone's neck. To oppress or tyrannise over a person.

To tread the boards. To perform on the stage; to be an actor; the *boards* being the planks of the stage.

To tread the light fantastic. To dance.

> Come and trip it as ye go
> On the light fantastic toe.
> MILTON: *L'Allegro*.

Treason. Betrayal of a trust or of a person.

High treason is an act of treachery against the SOVEREIGN of the State, a violation of one's allegiance. **Petty treason** is the same against a subject, as the murder of a master by his servant. *See also* MISPRISION OF TREASON.

Treasure. These are my treasures; meaning the sick and the poor. So said St. LAWRENCE when the Roman prætor commanded him to deliver up his treasures. *See also* CORNELIA.

Treasure trove (O. Fr. *trove*, found). The term applied to coins and other valuables of GOLD or SILVER found in the ground or other place of concealment. Gold ornaments, etc., found in tombs where there is no purpose of concealment are not treasure trove. Treasure trove belongs to the Crown, but in practice the finder is usually given the market value of his find.

Treasury, Treasury Bills are a form of British government security issued in multiples of £1,000 and repayable in 3, 6, 9, or 12 months.

Treasury Bonds are for money borrowed for a number of years.

Treasury Notes were issued by the Treasury from 1924 to 1928 for £1 and 10s. Their place was taken by notes issued by the Bank of England. *See* BRADBURY.

Treasury of the Church, Treasury of Merits, or **Satisfactions.** The theological term for the superabundant store of merits and satisfactions of Christ which were beyond the needs of the salvation of the human race. To these are added the excess of merits and satisfactions of the B.V.M. and the SAINTS. It is by drawing on this treasury that the Church grants INDULGENCES.

Treat. To stand treat. To pay the expenses of some entertainment; especially to pay for drinks consumed by others.

Tree. For particulars of some famous and patriarchal trees *see under* OAK *and* YEW.

In the Natural History Museum, South Kensington, is the section of a *Sequoia gigantea* with 1,335 rings, representing that number of years, and the Jardin des Plantes at Paris has a similar section. There are yet older trees still in full life in the forests of America.

The CROSS on which Our Lord was crucified is frequently spoken of in hymns and poetry as *the tree*. *See Acts* v, 30, "... Jesus, whom ye slew and hanged on a tree'; and I *Pet*. ii, 24, "Who his own self bare our sins in his own body on the tree".

The gallows is also called *the tree*, or *the fatal tree*. *See* TYBURN TREE.

One proverb says, "If on the trees the leaves still hold, the coming winter will be cold," and another, "When caught by the tempest, wherever it be, if it lightens and thunders beware of a tree." *See also under* WOOD.

The Tree of Buddha, or **of Wisdom.** The BO-TREE.

The Tree of Diana. *See* PHILOSOPHER'S TREE.

The Tree of Knowledge. The tree which God planted, together with the *Tree of Life*, in the Garden of EDEN.

"But of the tree of the knowledge of good and evil, thou shalt not eat of it; for in the day that thou eatest thereof thou shalt surely die" (*Gen*. ii, 17). EVE partook of the forbidden fruit and gave some to ADAM; "And the Lord God said, Behold, the man is become as one of us, to know good and evil: and now, lest he put forth his hand, and take also of the tree of life, and eat, and live for ever" (*Gen*. iii, 22); and so the first man and the first woman were driven from the garden and the woes of mankind began.

The Tree of Liberty. A post or tree set up by the people, hung with flags and devices and crowned with a CAP OF LIBERTY. In the United States, poplars and other trees were planted during the War of Independence "as growing symbols of growing freedom". The JACOBINS in Paris planted their first trees of liberty in 1790, and used to decorate them with tri-coloured ribbons, circles to indicate unity, triangles to signify equality, and Caps of Liberty. Trees of liberty were also planted by the Italians in the revolution of 1848.

The Tree of Life. *See* TREE OF KNOWLEDGE.

The Tree of the Universe. YGGDRASIL.

At the top of the tree. At the highest position attainable in one's profession, calling, etc.

The tree is known by its fruit. One is judged by what one does, not by what one says. The saying is from *Matt.* xii, 33.

A tree must be bent while it is young. "You can't teach an old dog new tricks." (*See under* DOG). The Scots say, "Thraw the wand while it is green."

The treeness of the tree. The essential qualities that compose a tree; in the absence of which the tree would cease to be a tree. Hence, the absolute essentials of anything. The phrase is evidently modelled on Sterne's "Correggiosity of Correggio" (*Tristram Shandy*, III, xii).

Up a tree. In a difficulty, in a mess, nonplussed. An American phrase, from 'coon hunting. As soon as the 'coon is driven up a tree he is helpless.

You cannot judge of a tree by its bark. Don't go by appearances; an old proverb.

Tregeagle (Trĕ gā' gul). A kind of Cornish BLUEBEARD who sold his soul to the DEVIL and married and murdered numerous rich heiresses, and whose ghost haunts various parts of Cornwall.

Trench fever. A remittent or relapsing fever affecting men living in trenches, dug-outs, etc., and transmitted by the excrement of lice. It first appeared in World War I, in the static warfare on the Western Front.

Trencher. Trencher cap. The MORTARBOARD worn at college; so called from the trenchered or split boards which form the top.

Trencher friends. Persons who cultivate the friendship of others for the sake of sitting at their board, and the good things they can get.

Trencher knight. A table KNIGHT, a suitor from CUPBOARD LOVE.

A good trencher-man. Usually said of a good eater, his opposite being a *poor trencher-man*. The trencher was the platter on which food was cut (Fr. *trancher*, to cut) or served, and the term *trencher-man* is sometimes applied to a cook or table companion.

He that waits for another's trencher eats many a late dinner. He who is dependent on others must wait, and wait, and wait, happy if after waiting he gets anything at all.

Trenchmore. A popular dance in the 16th and 17th centuries.

Trente et quarante. *See* ROUGE ET NOIR.

Tressure. A border within an heraldic shield and surrounding the bearings. The origin of the "double-tressure flory-counterflory gules" in the royal arms of SCOTLAND is traced by old heralds to the 9th century. They assert that CHARLEMAGNE granted it to King Achaius of Scotland in token of alliance, and as an assurance that "the lilies of France should be a defence to the lion of Scotland".

Trèves. The Holy Coat of Trèves. *See under* HOLY.

Tria Juncta in Uno (Lat., three combined in one). The motto of the Order of the BATH. It refers to the three classes of which the order consists, *viz.* Knights Grand Cross, Knights Commander, and Companions.

Triads. Three subjects more or less connected, treated as a group; as the Creation, Redemption, and Resurrection; BRAHMA, VISHNU, and SIVA; ALEXANDER THE GREAT, JULIUS CÆSAR, and NAPOLEON; Law, Physic, and Divinity.

The Welsh *Triads* are collections of historic facts, mythological traditions, moral maxims, or rules of poetry disposed in groups of three for mnemonic purposes.

The anciently established Chinese secret society known as "The Hung" or "The Society of Heaven and Earth", is also called "The Triad" from the trinity of HEAVEN, earth and man, and the use of the triangle in its ritual.

Trial at Bar. *See under* BAR.

Trial of the Pyx. *See under* PYX.

Tribune (trib′ ūn). A chief magistrate and very powerful official among the ancient Romans. During the revolt of the plebs in 494 B.C. they appointed two tribunes as protectors against the PATRICIANS' oppression; later the number was increased to ten and their office put on a proper footing. They were personally inviolable, and could separately VETO measures and proceedings.

As a military title *tribune* denoted the commander of a cohort.

A tribune of the people. A democratic leader.

Trice. In a trice. In an instant; in a twinkling.

It is probably *trice*, to haul, to tie up; the idea being "at a single tug". The older expression was *at a trice*.

> The howndis...pluckid downe deere all
> at a tryse.
> *Ipomydon*, 392 (*c.* 1440).

Tricolour. A FLAG of three broad stripes of different COLOURS, especially the national standard of France, blue, white, and red. The first flag of the Republicans was *green*. The tricolour was adopted 11 July 1789, when the people were disgusted with the king for dismissing Necker; the popular tale is that the insurgents had adopted for their flag the two colours, *red* and *blue* (the colour of the city of Paris), but that Lafayette persuaded them to add the BOURBON *white*, to show that they bore no hostility to the king.

Tricoteuses (trē kot ĕrz′). Parisian women who, during the French Revolution, used to attend the meetings of the CONVENTION and, while they went on with their *tricotage* (knitting), encouraged the leaders in their bloodthirsty excesses. They gained for themselves the additional title, *Furies of the Guillotine*.

Trident. In Greek mythology, the three-pronged spear which POSEIDON (Roman NEPTUNE), god of the sea, bore as the symbol of his sovereignty. It has come to be regarded as the emblem of sea power and as such is borne by BRITANNIA. In gladiatorial combats in ROME, the trident was used by the RETIARIUS, whose skill lay in entangling his opponent in a net, and then despatching him with his trident.

Trigon (trī′ gon). In ASTROLOGY, the junction of three signs. The ZODIAC is partitioned into four trigons, named respectively after the four elements: the *watery* trigon includes CANCER, SCORPIO, and Pisces; the *fiery*, ARIES, Leo, and SAGITTARIUS; the *earthly*, TAURUS, Virgo (*see* VIRGIN), and CAPRICORN; and the *airy*, GEMINI, LIBRA, and AQUARIUS.

Trilogy (tril′ ō ji). A group of three tragedies. Everyone in Greece who took part in the poetic contest had to produce a trilogy and a satiric drama. The only complete specimen extant contains the *Agamemnon*, the *Choephorœ*, and the *Eumenides*, by ÆSCHYLUS.

Hence, any literary, dramatic, or operatic work consisting of three self-contained parts but related to a central theme, such as SHAKESPEARE's *Henry VI* or Schiller's *Wallenstein*.

Trimurti (Sansk. *tri*, three; *mirti*, form). The Hindu TRIAD of BRAHMA, VISHNU, and SIVA as a unity, represented as one body with three heads. It bears only a forced resemblance to the idea of a TRINITY.

Trine (Lat. *trinus*, threefold). In ASTROLOGY, a PLANET distant from another one-third of the circle is said to be in trine; one-fourth, it is in square; one-sixth or two signs, it is in sextile; but when one-half distant, it is said to be "opposite".

Planets distant from each other six signs or half a circle have opposite influences, and are therefore opposed to each other.

Trinitarians. Believers in the doctrine of the Holy TRINITY as distinct from UNITARIANS. Also, members of the Order of the Most Holy Trinity, or Mathurins, founded by St. John of Matha and St. Felix of Valois in 1198, concerned with the ransoming of captives and slaves and sometimes known as REDEMPTIONISTS. Their rule is an austere form of the AUGUSTINIAN.

Trinity, The. The three Persons in one God—God the Father, God the Son, and God the HOLY GHOST. *See also* CONFOUNDING THE PERSONS *under* PERSON; THREE.

> And in this Trinity none is afore, or after other; none is greater, or less than another; but the whole three Persons are co-eternal together: and co-equal.
> *The Athanasian Creed.*

The term TRIAD was first used by Theophilus of Antioch (*c.* 180) for this concept; the term *Trinity* was introduced by Tertullian about 217 in his treatise *Adversus Praxean.*

Trinity, or **Trinity Sunday.** The SUNDAY next after WHIT SUNDAY; widely observed as a feast in honour of the Trinity since the MIDDLE AGES, its general observance was enjoined by Pope John XXII in 1334. The EPISTLE and GOSPEL used in the CHURCH OF ENGLAND on this day are the same as those in the Lectionary of St. JEROME, and the Collect comes from the Sacramentary of St. GREGORY. The Church of England followed the Sarum Use in reckoning Sundays after Trinity, the ROMAN CATHOLIC CHURCH reckons them after PENTECOST (now adopted in the ALTERNATIVE SERVICES BOOK).

Trinobantes (trin ō băn' tēz). A tribe, referred to in Cæsar's Gallic Wars, inhabiting the area of Essex and the southern part of Suffolk. The name was corrupted into *Trinovantes. See* TROYNOVANT.

Tripitaka (trip it' a ka) (Pali, "the threefold basket"). The three classes into which the sacred writings of the Buddhists are divided—viz. the *Vinayapitaka* (Basket of Disciplinary Directions for the monks), the *Sutrapitaka* (Basket of Aphorisms or Discourses), and the *Abhidhammapitaka* (Basket of Metaphysics).

Tripos (trī' pos) (Lat. *tripus,* a three-footed stool). A Cambridge term, meaning the three honour classes in which candidates are grouped at the final examination, whether of Mathematics, Law, Theology, or Natural Science, etc.

So called because the B.A. who disputed with the "Father" in the Philosophy School on ASH WEDNESDAY sat on a three-legged stool and was called "Mr. Tripos".

Triptolemus (trip tol' ē mùs). A Greek hero and demi-god who was born at Eleusis and was taught the arts of agriculture by CERES. He established the ELEUSINIAN MYSTERIES and festivals.

Trisagion (tris ăg' i on) (Gr., thrice holy). A hymn in the liturgies of the Greek and Eastern Churches in which (after *Is.* v, 3) a threefold invocation to the Deity is the burden—"Holy God, Holy and Mighty, Holy and Immortal, have mercy on us."

The name is sometimes applied to Bishop Heber's hymn for Trinity Sunday—

> Holy, Holy, Holy! Lord God Almighty,
> Early in the morning our song shall rise to Thee;

which is more properly called the *Ter-Sanctus.*

Triskelion (tri skel' i on) (Gr., three-legged). The emblem of the Isle of MAN, and of Sicily; three human legs, bent at the knee, and joined at the thigh.

Trismegistus. *See* HERMETIC ART.

Tristram, Sir (Tristam, Tristan, or **Tristem).** A hero of mediæval romance whose exploits, though originally unconnected with it, became attached to the ARTHURIAN cycle, he himself being named as one of the KNIGHTS of the ROUND TABLE. There are many versions of his story, which is, roughly, that he was cured of a wound by Iseult, or YSOLDE, daughter of the king of IRELAND, and on his return to CORNWALL told his uncle, King MARK, of the beautiful princess. Mark sent him to solicit her hand in marriage, and was accepted. Tristram escorted her to ENGLAND, but on the way they both unknowingly partook of a magic potion and became irretrievably enamoured of each other. Iseult married the king, and on Mark's discovering their liaison Tristram fled to Brittany and married Iseult, daughter of the Duke of Brittany. Wounded by a poisoned weapon, he sent for Iseult of Ireland to come and heal him. The vessel in which she was to come had orders to hoist a white sail if she was on board, otherwise a black sail. Tristram's wife, seeing the vessel approach, told her husband, from jealousy, that it bore a black sail. In despair Tristram died; Iseult of Ireland, arriving too late, killed herself.

The name was originally *Drystan*, from the Pictish name *Drostan*, and the initial was changed to *T* apparently to connect it with Lat. *tristis*, sad. Wagner's opera *Tristan and Isolde* was first produced in 1865.

Triton. Son of POSEIDON and AMPHITRITE, represented as a fish with a human head. It is this sea-god that makes the roaring of the ocean by blowing through his shell.

A Triton among the minnows. A great man among a host of inferiors.

Triumph. A word formed from Gr. *thriambos*, the Dionysiac hymn, *Triumphe* being an exclamation used in the solemn processions of the ARVAL BROTHERS.

> Some...have assigned the origin of...triumphal processions to the mythic pomps of Dionysus, after his conquests in the East, the very word triumph being...the Dionysiac hymn.
> PATER: *Marius the Epicurean*, ch. xii.

The old Roman *triumphus* was the solemn and magnificent entrance of a general into ROME after having obtained a great or decisive victory. *Cp.* OVATION.

Triumvir (trī'ŭm'vėr). In ancient ROME, one of a group of three men (Lat. *trium*, gen. of *tres*, three; *vir*, man) acting as joint magistrates for some special purpose or function. In Roman history the most famous triumvirate was that of Octavian, Antony, and Lepidus (43 B.C.), which was known as the *Second Triumvirate* to distinguish it from the combination of CÆSAR, Pompey and Crassus in 60 B.C., which is known as the *First Triumvirate*.

Trivet. Right as a trivet. *See under* RIGHT.

Trivia. Gay's name for his invented goddess of streets and ways (Lat. *trivius*, of three roads). His burlesque in three books so entitled (1716) is a mine of information on the outdoor life of QUEEN ANNE's time.

Trivium (Lat. *tres*, three; *via*, a road). In the MIDDLE AGES, the three roads to

learning, *i.e.* Grammar, Rhetoric, and Logic; forming the lower division of the seven liberal arts. *See* QUADRIVIUM.

Trochilus. A small Egyptian bird said by the ancients to enter with impunity the mouth of the CROCODILE and to pick its teeth, especially of a leech which greatly tormented the creature.

It is now known as the Crocodile-bird, *Pluvianus ægyptus*, a species of plover which not only picks the crocodile's teeth but by its cry gives warning of an approaching foe.

Troglodytes (Gr. *trogle*, cave; *duein*, to go into). A name given by the ancient Greeks to races of uncivilized men who dwelt in caves or holes in the ground. Strabo mentions troglodytes in Syria and Arabia, and Pliny (v, 8) asserts that they fed on serpents. The best-known were those of southern Egypt and Ethiopia. The term is applied to other cave-dwellers, and, figuratively, to those who dwell in seclusion.

In ornithology, wrens, which mostly build their nests in holes, are named *troglodytes*.

Troilus. The prince of CHIVALRY, one of the sons of PRIAM, killed by ACHILLES in the TROJAN WAR.

The loves of Troilus and CRESSIDA, celebrated by Chaucer and SHAKESPEARE, form no part of the old classic tale. This story appears for the first time in the *Roman de Troie* by the 12th century TROUVÈRE Benoit de Ste. More. Guido delle Colonne included it in his *Historia Trojana* (1287), it thence passed to Boccaccio, whose *Il Filostrato* (1338)—where Pandarus first appears—was the basis of Chaucer's *Troilus and Criseyde*.

As true as Troilus. Troilus is meant by SHAKESPEARE to be the type of constancy, and Cressida the type of female inconstancy.

Trojan. Trojan Horse. *See* WOODEN HORSE OF TROY.

Trojan War. The legendary war sung by HOMER in the ILIAD as having been waged for ten years by the confederated Greeks against the men of TROY and their allies, in consequence of PARIS, son of PRIAM, the Trojan king, having carried off HELEN, wife of MENELAUS. The last year of the siege is the subject of the *Iliad*; the burning of Troy and the flight of ÆNEAS is told by VIRGIL in his ÆNEID.

There is no doubt that the story of the siege of Troy, much doubted in the 19th century, has an historical basis and probably took place during the 13th and 12th centuries B.C.

He is a regular Trojan. A fine fellow, with courage and spirit, who works very hard, usually at some uncongenial task, indeed, doing more than could be expected of him. The Trojans in Homer's ILIAD and Virgil's ÆNEID are described as truthful, brave, patriotic, and confiding.

Troll-madam, or **Troll-my-dames.** A popular indoor game in the 16th and 17th centuries (also known as *trunks*, *pigeon-holes*, or *nine-holes*), borrowed from the French and called by them *trou* (hole) *madame*. It resembled bagatelle, and was played on a board having at one end a number of arches, like pigeon-holes, into which the balls were rolled. SHAKESPEARE has a reference to it in *The Winter's Tale* (IV, ii).

Trolls. In Icelandic myth, malignant one-eyed giants; in Scandinavian folklore, mischievous DWARFS, some cunning and treacherous, some fair and good to men, akin to the Scottish BROWNIE. They were wonderfully skilled in working metals and lived in the hills, and had a propensity for stealing, even carrying off women and children. They were especially averse to noise, from a recollection of the time when THOR used to be forever flinging his hammer after them.

Trompe l'oeil (trômp lēē') (Fr.). A trick of the eye, a visual deception. It is applied to art which gives a distinct impression of reality, as, for example, perspective art which can give a sense of distance, solidity and space. The apparent dimensions of an interior can be imagnified by such decorative effects.

Trooping. Trooping the Colour. The annual ceremony on Horse Guards Parade, WHITE-HALL, in which the colour or regimental FLAG is carried between files of troops and received by the sovereign. It takes place on the sovereign's official birthday.

The ceremony dates from the 18th century (probably from Marlborough's time), and was originally a guard-mounting ceremony, the battalion providing the guards for the day "trooping" the colour to be carried on King's guard.

Trophonius (trō fō' ni us). An architect, celebrated in Greek legend as the builder of the TEMPLE of APOLLO at DELPHI. After his death he was deified, and had an ORACLE in a cave near Lebadeia, Bœotia, which was so awe-inspiring that those who entered and consulted the oracle never smiled again. Hence a melancholy or habitually terrified man was said to have visited the cave of *Trophonius*.

Trophy. Originally the arms of a vanquished foe, collected and set up by the victors on the field of battle. The captured standards were hung from the branches of an OAK-tree, a portion of the booty being laid at the foot of the tree and dedicated to the tutelary deity. The Romans frequently bore their trophies to ROME; under the Empire the triumphs of the victorious generals were also celebrated with arches and columns.

Troubadours. Poets of the south of France in the 11th to 14th centuries whose works were often performed and sung by wandering minstrels or JONGLEURS; so called from the Provencal verb *trobar*, to find or invent (*cp.* "poet", which means "a maker"). They wrote in the LANGUE D'OC or Provencal, principally on love and CHIVALRY. *Cp.* TROUVÈRES.

Trouble-shooter. An American coinage for one expert in locating and mending "trouble", mechanical or otherwise; hence its application to those brought into industry to mend relations between employer and employee.

Trousers. She's the one who wears the trousers. Said of a married woman who lords it over her husband, from the days when only men normally wore trousers and were more usually the dominant partners.

Trouvères (troo' vâr). Court poets in central and northern France in the 12th to 14th centuries, writing chiefly of love.

So called from F. *trouver*, to find or invent (*cp.* TROUBADOURS). They wrote in the LANGUE D'OÏL or *langue d'oui*.

Trows, or **Drows.** DWARFS of Orkney and Shetland mythology, similar to the Scandinavian TROLLS. There are land-trows and sea-trows.

Troy. The fortress city of Homer's ILIAD in the extreme north-west corner of Asia Minor overlooking the strait of the Dardanelles; also the land of Troy or the *Troad*, with Ilium as its chief city.

The siege of Troy. *See* ACHILLES; ILIAD; HELEN; TROJAN WAR; ULYSSES; WOODEN HORSE OF TROY (*under* HORSE), etc.

Troy weight. The system of weights used in weighing precious metals and gems, the pound of 12 ounces weighing 5,760 grains as compared with the pound *avoirdupois* which weighs 7,000 grains and is divided into 16 ounces. Why it is so called is not certainly known, but probably it was the system used at the great FAIRS at Troyes, in France. 1 lb. troy = 0·822861 lb.av., rather over four-fifths. *See* TOWER POUND.

Troynovant. The name given by the early chroniclers to LONDON, anciently the city of the TRINOBANTES; a corruption of *Trinovant*, *Troynovant* was assumed to mean *The New Troy*, which Geoffrey of Monmouth (*Historia Britonum*, Bk. I, ch. xvii) tells us was built by BRUTUS, a Trojan refugee (from whom is derived the name *Britain*). Afterwards LUD surrounded it with walls and called it *Caer-Lud*, or the City of Lud (London).

> For noble Britons sprong from Trojans bold,
> And Troynovant was built of old Troyes ashes cold.
>
> SPENSER: *The Fairie Queene*, III, ix, 38.

Truce of God. In the MIDDLE AGES, a suspension of private warfare decreed by the CHURCH on certain days or for certain seasons such as ADVENT and LENT. In 1027 hostilities between Saturday night and Monday morning were forbidden and the *Truce of God* was reaffirmed and extended by various Councils including the LATERAN COUNCIL of 1179. It was only partly effective and was eventually superseded by the King's peace.

Truck System, The. The system of paying employees wholly or in part in goods and tokens valid only at a TOMMY SHOP connected with their employers. The system was controlled and essentially abolished by insisting on payment in coin by Acts of 1831, 1881, and 1896. An Act of 1960 authorized payment other than in current coin, *i.e.*, by cheque, or bank transfer.

True. A true bill. *see under* BILL.

True blue, *i.e.* lasting blue; hence a type of constancy. A true blue is one who is constant, steadfast, loyal, faithful, etc.

True-lovers' knot. A complicated double KNOT with two interlacing bows on each side and two ends, used as a symbol of love.

> Three times a true-love's knot I tie secure;
> Firm be the knot, firm may his love endure.
>
> GAY: *Pastorals, The Spell*, 506.

True Thomas. THOMAS THE RHYMER (*see under* RHYME).

Trump. This word in such phrases as *a trumped-up affair* (falsely concocted, etc.), *trumpery* (showy finery, worthless stuff), etc., is the same word as *trumpet*; from Fr. *trompe*, a trumpet, whence *tromper*, which, originally meaning "to play on a trumpet", came to mean to beguile, deceive, impose upon.

Trump in cards, is from Fr. *triomphe* (triumph), the name of an old variant of écarté.

Jew's trump. A JEW'S HARP.

The last trump. The final end of all things earthly; the Day of JUDGMENT.

> We shall not all sleep, but we shall all be changed, in a moment, in the twinkling of an eye, at the last trump.
>
> *I Cor.* xv, 51, 52.

To play one's last trump. To be reduced to one's last expedient; a phrase from card-playing.

To turn up trumps. Unexpectedly to prove very friendly and helpful; to be much better than anticipated. An allusion to card-playing.

Trumpet. *See* TRUMP.

The Feast of Trumpets. A Jewish festival held on the first two days of Tishri (about mid-SEPTEMBER to mid-OCTOBER), the beginning of the Jewish ecclesiastical year, at which the blowing of trumpets formed a prominent part of the ritual. *See Num.* xxix, 1.

A flourish of trumpets. An ostentatious introduction, preliminary, or arrival. From the fanfare announcing the arrival of one of high rank or distinction.

To blow one's own trumpet. To indulge in self-advertisement, to publish one's own praises, etc. The allusion is to HERALDS, who used to announce with a flourish of trumpets the KNIGHTS who entered a list. Similarly, **Your trumpeter is dead** means that you are obliged to sound your own praises because no one will do it for you.

Trunk road is a main highway between two principal towns.

Trust. A combination of a number of companies or businesses doing similar trade, for the purpose of defeating competition or creating a monopoly, under one general control. So called because each member is *on trust* not to undersell the others, but to remain faithful to the terms agreed on.

Truth. PILATE said, "What is truth?" (*John* xviii, 38). This was the great question of the Platonists. PLATO said we could know truth if we could sublimate our minds to their original purity. Arcesilaus said that man's understanding is not capable of knowing what truth is. Carneades maintained that not only our understanding could not comprehend it, but even our senses are wholly inadequate to help us in the investigation. Gorgias the SOPHIST said "What is right but what we prove to be right? and what is truth but what we believe to be truth?"

> "What is truth?" said jesting Pilate, and would not stay for an answer.
> BACON: *Essays, Of Truth.*

Act of Truth. *See under* ACT.

Truth drug. Alkaloid scopolamine. An American doctor, R. E. House (1875–1930), used this drug to induce a state of lethargic intoxication in which the patient lost many of his defences and spoke the truth concerning matters about which he would normally have lied or prevaricated. The value of this and other truth drugs in penology has by no means been established.

Truth lies at the bottom of the well. This expression has been attributed to Heraclitus, Cleanthes, DEMOCRITUS the Derider, and others.

Trygon. *See* TELEGONUS.

Tu autem (tū aw' tem) (Lat., But thou). A hint to leave off; "hurry up and come to the last clause". In the long Latin grace at St. John's College, Cambridge, the last clause used to be *Tu autem miserere mei, Domine, Amen*, and it was not unusual, when a scholar read slowly, for the senior Fellow to whisper *Tu autem, i.e.* Skip all the rest and give us only the last sentence.

Tu quoque (tū kwo' kwē) (Lat., You too). A retort implying that the one addressed is in the same case as the speaker—no better and no worse.

The tu quoque style of argument. Personal invective; the argument of personal application; *argumentum ad hominem.*

Tuatha De Danann (twa' thà de dăn' àn). A legendary race of superhuman heroes which invaded IRELAND, overthrew the Firbolgs and Fomors, and were themselves overthrown by the MILESIANS, who later worshipped them as gods.

Tub. A tale of a tub. A COCK-AND-BULL STORY, a RIGMAROLE; a nonsensical romance.

There is a comedy of this name by Ben Jonson (produced 1633), and a prose satire by Swift (1704) which portrays allegorically the failings of the English, Roman, and PRESBYTERIAN Churches.

To throw a tub to the whale. To create a diversion in order to avoid a real danger; to bamboozle or mislead an enemy. In whaling, according to Swift, when a ship was threatened by a school of whales, it was usual to throw a tub into the sea to divert their attention.

A tub of naked children. Emblematical in religious paintings of St. NICHOLAS.

Tub-thumper. A ranter, a SOAP-BOX ORATOR or STUMP ORATOR; in allusion to the upturned tub once used as a platform at open-air meetings.

Tuck. In the sense of eatables *tuck* is a mid-18th-century slang word, especially used by boys in boarding schools whose *tuck-box*, supplied from home, supplemented the school fare. **To tuck in** is to eat heartily and with relish. In Australia the word became **tucker** for any kind of food, especially that carried on journeys in one's *tucker bag*.

To tuck one up. To finish him, do for him. Possibly from the duellist's rapier formerly called a *tuck* (O. Fr. *estoc*, stock), or from *tuck up* in the sense of to draw up, this being old slang meaning to hang a person.

Tuck, Friar. See FRIAR TUCK.

Tucker. The ornamental frill of lace or muslin worn by women in the 17th and 18th centuries round the top of their dresses to cover the neck and shoulders. Hence, **with clean,** or **best bib and tucker,** dressed in one's best, looking fresh and spruce. *See also* TUCK.

Tuesday. The third day of the week until 1971 when it became the second. *See* SUNDAY; TIU.

Tuffet. A small grassy mound or hillock.

> Little Miss Muffet
> Sat on a tuffet
> Eating her curds and whey.
> *Nursery Rhyme.*

Tug. Tug of war. A sporting activity in which a number of men, divided into two teams, lay hold of a strong rope and pull against each other till one side has tugged the other over the dividing line.

When Greek meets Greek then is the tug of war. *See under* GREEK.

Tuileries (twē' lė rē). A former palace in Paris, so named from the tile-yards (*tuileries*) once on the site. It stood between the LOUVRE and the Place de la Concorde. The palace was designed by Philibert de l'Orme for Catherine de' MEDICI, 1564, and long served as a residence for the sovereigns of France. In 1871 it was burned down by the Communards, but the gardens remain as a pleasant public open space.

Tulchan Bishops. Certain titular Scottish BISHOPS introduced by the PRESBYTERIANS in 1572 and whose office had ceased by 1580. A *tulchan* is a stuffed calf-skin placed under a cow that holds her milk to deceive her into yielding into the pail. The bishops were contemptuously so called because their title was but an empty one, their revenues being mainly absorbed by nobles as lay patrons.

Tulip Mania. A reckless mania for the purchase of tulip-bulbs that arose in Holland in the 17th century and was at its greatest height about 1633–1637. A bulb of the species called *Viceroy* sold for £250; *Semper Augustus* more than double that sum. The mania spread all over Europe, and became a mere stock-jobbing speculation. *La Tulipe Noire* (1850) by Alexandre Dumas the elder, centres around the black tulip and a tulip-fancier, Cornelius van Baerle, of the period of the "tulipo-mania". He succeeded in growing a black tulip thereby winning a prize of one hundred thousand florins.

To number the streaks of the tulip. To devote too much attention to minute details—characteristic, in the view of 18th-century critics, of a bad poet. The phrase comes from Imlac's dissertation on poetry in Johnson's *Rasselas* (ch. x) where the principle is laid down that a poet must examine not the individual but the species, and concern himself with the general rather than the particular.

Tumbledown Dick. *See under* DICK.

Tumbler. The flat-bottomed stemless glass derives its name from the fact that it was originally made with a rounded bottom which made it tumble over if set down on a table; hence requiring that it should be held till emptied.

Tune. The man who pays the piper calls the tune. He who foots the bill decides what is to be done. An old proverb.

To change one's tune, or **to make one sing another tune.** *See under* SING.

The tune the old cow died of. Advice instead of relief; remonstrance instead of help.

To the tune of. To the amount of; as, "I had to pay up to the tune of £500."

Tuneful Nine, The. The nine MUSES.

Tunkers, Dunkers, or **Dunkards** (Ger., dippers). A religious sect also known as the German Baptists, founded in Germany in 1708 by Alexander Mack. In 1719 they emigrated to Pennsylvania and spread westwards and into Canada. They reject infant baptism, the taking of oaths or bearing of ARMS, and practise triple immersion, the AGAPE, etc. They are now called the Church of the Brethren. The SEVENTH-DAY BAPTISTS (1728) are an offshoot.

Tunnage. *See* TONNAGE.

Turf, The. The race-course, horse-racing; the horse-racing world; in allusion to the *turf* or grass of the course.

Turk. Formerly applied to the barbarous, savage, and cruel, from the European association of the Old Ottoman Empire with barbaric practices, from mediæval times until the early years of the 20th century; now usually applied to mischievous and unruly children; as, *You little Turk!* or, *You young Turk!*

The Young Turks. A Turkish reforming party seeking to transform the decadent Turkish Empire into a modern European state and to give it a parliamentary constitution. It had its origins in a committee formed at Geneva in 1891 and the party, considerably supported by students, raised the standard of revolt at Salonika in 1908, deposed Sultan Abdul Hamid, and replaced him by his brother as Mohammed V (1909). Their "liberalism" was not dominant but they remained the major force in Turkish politics until the end of World War I, when the party was dissolved. Turkey was proclaimed a republic in 1923.

Turk Gregory. Falstaff's *ne plus ultra* of military valour—a humorous combination of the SULTAN with Gregory VII (HILDEBRAND), probably the strongest of all the POPES.

> Turk Gregory never did such deeds in arms as I have done this day.
> SHAKESPEARE: *Henry IV, Pt. I*, V, iii.

Turkey. *See* MISNOMERS.

To talk turkey (U.S.A.). To talk plainly or seriously. Also, **that's cold turkey,** the frank details, the straight truth.

Turn. Done to a turn. Cooked exactly right; another turn on the spit would be too much.

He felt that the hour for the upturn-

ing of his glass was at hand. He knew that the sand of life was nearly run out, and that death was about to turn his hourglass upside down.

One good turn deserves another. A benefit received ought to be repaid.

To serve its turn. To answer the purpose; to be sufficient for the occasion; sometimes with the implication of being a makeshift or barely meeting requirements.

To turn down. To reject, as, "She turned down his marriage proposal", or, "His application for the post was turned down."

In Eastern countries a glass is turned down at convivial gatherings as a memento of a recently departed companion.

To turn in. Colloquially, to go to bed.

To turn the tables. *See under* TABLE.

To turn to. To carry on with one's work; to get to work.

To turn turtle. To turn completely over, upside down, TOPSY-TURVY. Usually said of boats, from the fact that a turtle, when turned on its back, is quite helpless.

To turn up. To arrive, often unexpectedly; to appear.

A turn-up for the book. A bit of good luck, unexpected good fortune.

Waiting for something to turn up. Expectant that luck will change, that good fortune will arrive without much effort on one's own part. Mr. MICAWBER's philosophy of life:

> "And then", said Mr. Micawber, who was present, "I have no doubt I shall, please Heaven, begin to be beforehand with the world, and to live in a perfectly new manner, if—in short, if anything turns up."
> DICKENS: *David Copperfield*, ch. xi.

Turncoat. A renegade; one who deserts his principles or party.

Fable has it that a certain Duke of Saxony, whose dominions were bounded in part by France, hit upon the device of a coat *blue* one side, and *white* the other. When he wished to be thought in the French interest he wore the white outside; otherwise the blue. Hence a SAXON was nicknamed *Emmanuel Turncoat*.

Turnspit. One who has all the work but none of the profit; he *turns* the *spit* but eats not of the roast. The allusion is to the turnspit, a small dog which was used to turn the roasting-spit by means of a kind of tread-wheel.

Turnip. Common slang for a large, old-fashioned silver watch.

Turpin. Archbishop of Rheims, who appears in several CHANSONS DE GESTE as a friend and companion of CHARLEMAGNE. He was formerly supposed to be the writer of the *Historia de vita Caroli et Rolandi*. In the *Chanson de Roland* Turpin dies with the hero and is buried with him. He is most likely the same as Tilpin, archbishop of Rheims in the 8th century (*c*. 753–*c*. 800).

Dick Turpin (1705–1739). The "King of the Road" was born at the Bell Inn, Hempstead, Essex, and apprenticed to a butcher at WHITECHAPEL at the age of 16. He soon became a footpad to supplement his earnings and, after his marriage in 1728, set up as a butcher in Essex. He took to stocking his shop with stolen cattle and sheep and, on discovery, joined a gang of smugglers near Canvey Island and there turned to housebreaking with Gregory's Gang in Epping Forest. In 1735 he became a highwayman working around the south of LONDON, and in 1736 began his partnership with Tom King; his effrontery became a public legend as did his activities in Epping Forest and Hounslow Heath. After the death of King in 1737, he shifted to Lincolnshire and thence to Yorkshire where he was finally apprehended and hanged at the Mount, outside the walls of York. The legend of Black BESS and the ride to York derives from Harrison Ainsworth's *Rookwood* (1834) although that of the ride has historical precedents.

> And the fame of Dick Turpin had been something less
> If he'd ne'er rode to York on his bonnie Black Bess.
> ELIZA COOK: *Black Bess*.

Tuscan Order. In architecture, essentially a simplified form of Roman DORIC, plain and lacking in ornament. The columns are never fluted. *See* CORINTHIAN; IONIC.

Tusitala. Teller of tales; the name given by the Samoans to R. L. Stevenson.

Tutankhamun. *See* VALLEY OF THE KINGS.

Tutankhamun's Curse. *See under* CURSE.

Tutivillus, or **Titivil** (tū ti vil' ŭs). The demon of mediæval legend who collects all the words skipped over or mutilated by priests in the celebration of the MASS. These scraps or shreds he deposits in that pit which is said to be paved with "good intentions" never brought to effect.

Twain, Mark. The pen-name of Samuel Langhorne Clemens (1835–1910), the famous humorist, creator of Tom Sawyer and Huckleberry Finn. The name "Mark Twain" is from the calls used by Mississippi pilots when taking soundings—in this case the two-fathom mark on the lead-line.

Tweed. The origin of this name of a woollen cloth used for garments is to be found in a blunder. It should have been *tweel*, the Scots form of *twill*; but when the Scottish manufacturer sent a consignment to James Locke of London, in 1826, the name was badly written and misread; and as the cloth was made on the banks of the Tweed, *tweed* was accordingly adopted. *Twill* like DIMITY, means "two-threaded".

Tweedledum and Tweedledee. Names invented by John Byrom (1692–1763) to satirize two quarrelling schools of musicians between whom the real difference was negligible. Hence used of people whose persons or opinions are "as like as two peas".

> Some say compared to Bononcini
> That mynheer Handel's but a ninny;
> Others aver that he to Handel
> Is scarcely fit to hold a candle.
> Strange all this difference should be
> 'Twixt Tweedledum and Tweedledee.
> J. BYROM: *Feud between Handel and Bononcini*.

The Duke of Marlborough and most of the nobility took the side of G. B. Bononcini (d. *c*. 1752), but the Prince of Wales, with Pope and Arbuthnot, was for Handel. *Cp.* GLUCKISTS.

Lewis Carroll uses the names for two fat little men in his *Through the Looking-Glass*.

Twelve, Twelfth. The Glorious Twelfth. *See* GLORIOUS.

Two

Twelfth man. The reserve chosen for a team of 11, especially in CRICKET, hence, anyone who just misses distinction.

Twelfth Night. 5 January, the eve of the Twelfth Day after CHRISTMAS or Feast of the EPIPHANY. Formerly this was a time of great merrymaking when the BEAN-KING was appointed, and the celebrations and festivities seemingly derive from the SATURNALIA of old Roman times which were held at the same season. By the JULIAN CALENDAR Twelfth Day is Old CHRISTMAS Day.

SHAKESPEARE's play of this name (produced 1600–1601) was so called because it was written for acting at the Twelfth Night revels.

The Twelve Tables. The earliest code of Roman law, compiled by the Decemviri (451–450 B.C.), and engraved on 12 tablets. Originally ten, to which two were added, they were supposed to comprise the basis of all Roman law. In CICERO's boyhood it was still customary for them to be learnt by heart (Livy: III, lvii; Diodorus, xii, 56).

Each English archer carries twelve Scotsmen under his girdle. This was a common saying at one time, because the English were unerring archers, and each carried 12 arrows in his belt.

The Twelvers. A sect of SHI'ITES who accept *twelve* of the descendants of ALI as Imams. The 12th IMAM, MOHAMMED, it is held, disappeared (*c.* 874) but is still alive and will return at the end to set up the Shi'ite faith through the world.

Twickenham. The Bard of Twickenham. Alexander Pope (1688–1744), who lived there for 25 years. Contemporaries sometimes called him the *Wasp of Twickenham* because of his acerbity.

Twig. I twig you. I catch your meaning; I understand (Irish *tuigim*, I understand). The Irish word is pronounced *tigim*.

Twilight Twilight of the Gods. *See* RAGNAROK.

Twilight Sleep. A state of semiconsciousness produced by injection of scopolamine and morphia in which a woman can undergo childbirth with comparatively little pain. *See also* TRUTH DRUG.

Twins, The. *See* GEMINI.

Twirl. In prison parlance, the same as a SCREW, and for a similar reason.

Twist. The twist. A dance popular about 1962, so called from the contortions performed.

Like Oliver Twist, asking for more. Oliver Twist, the workhouse-boy hero of Dickens's famous novel of that name (1838), astonished the workhouse-master and caused general consternation by once actually asking for more gruel (*see* chap. ii).

To twist a person. Slang for to swindle him or to bamboozle him to one's own advantage. Also (with allusion to giving the screw another twist), to extract from a person all one can and a bit over.

To twist a person's arm. To coerce or persuade a person to do something against their inclination.

To twist a person round one's (little) finger. To be able to influence him at will; to have him in complete subjection.

To twist the lion's tail. *See under* LION.

Twm Shon Catti (tum shŏn kati). A kind of Welsh ROBIN HOOD who was born about 1530. He is mentioned in George Borrow's *Wild Wales*. There are many tales of his exploits and he is said to have eventually married an heiress and ended up as a squire and magistrate.

Two. The evil principle of PYTHAGORAS. Accordingly the second day of the second month of the year was sacred to PLUTO, and was esteemed unlucky.

Two bits. American term for 25 cents, otherwise known as a *quarter*. The origin of the term is in British slang "bit" (*e.g.* threepenny bit), which was adopted in the south and west of the U.S.A. for the old Mexican *real* worth 12½ cents.

The Two cultures. *See* CULTURES.

The two eyes of Greece. ATHENS and Sparta.

He has two strings to his bow. *See under* BOW.

To put two and two together. To come to an inference or conclusion (usually fairly obvious) from the facts of the matter.

Two heads are better than one. Another's advice is often very useful. To the saying is sometimes added—*or why do folks marry?*

Two is company, three is none. An old saying, much used by lovers; it is given in Heywood's collection of proverbs (1546).

Two may keep counsel–if one of them's dead. A caustic saying expressive of the great difficulty of being certain that the secret is not told once it is imparted to someone else.

When two Fridays come together. One of a number of circumlocutions for NEVER!

Twopenny. Often used slightingly of things of very little value.

Twopenny Damn. *See* DAMN.

The Twopenny Tube. The Central London Railway was so called, because for some years after its opening (1900) the fare between any two stations was 2*d*.

Tybalt (tib' ålt). An old name given to a cat (*see* GIB CAT). Hence the allusions to cats in connexion with Tybalt, one of the CAPULET family in SHAKESPEARE'S *Romeo and Juliet* (III, i). Mercutio says, "Tybalt, you rat-catcher, will you walk?"; and again, when Tybalt asks, "What wouldst thou have with me?" Mercutio answers, "Good King of Cats! nothing but one of your nine lives."

Tyburn (tī' běrn). A famous tributary of the THAMES rising at Hampstead, which gave its name to the village that was later called MARYLEBONE and to a place of execution. Hence **Tyburn tree,** the gallows (at Tyburn); **to take a ride to Tyburn,** to go to one's hanging; **Lord of the Manor of Tyburn,** the common hangman, etc.

The site of the gallows is marked by three brass triangles let into the pavement at the corner of Edgware Road and Bayswater Road. The last criminal to be hanged there was John Austin in 1783; after that executions were carried out at NEWGATE until its demolition.

Tyburn ticket. A certificate which, under a statute of William III (10 W. III, c.12), 1698, was granted to prosecutors who had secured a capital conviction against a criminal, exempting them from all parish and ward offices within the parish in which the felony had been committed. This, with the privilege it conferred, might be sold once, and once only, and the *Stamford Mercury* for 27 March 1818 announced the sale of one for £280. The Act was repealed in 1818, but as late as 1856 Mr Pratt of Bond Street claimed exemption from serving on an OLD BAILEY jury on the strength of the possession of a Tyburn Ticket and was successful.

Tyke. *See* TIKE.

Tyler's Insurrection. The main rebellion of the English PEASANTS' REVOLT.

Tylwyth Teg (tŭl with tăg) (Welsh *tylwyth*, family; *teg*, fair). The fairies of Welsh folklore, friendly but mischievous, who live in caves and on the mountains, who communicate by signs and never speak. They are versed in country lore, but if they touch iron, vanish away.

Tyndale's Bible. *See* BIBLE, THE ENGLISH.

Tynwald. The Court of Tynwald constitutes the governing body of the Isle of MAN. It consists of the Lieutenant-Governor, a Crown appointment; the Legislative Council, consisting of the Bishop of Sodor and Man, two DEEMSTERS, the Attorney-General, two of the Governor's nominees, and five members of the House of Keys; and the House of Keys, which is composed of 24 members elected by adult suffrage. No British Act of PARLIAMENT applies to the island unless specifically stated. The House of Keys was self-elected until 1866. *Tyn* is from THING and *Wald*, the *wold* or down on which it assembled. The origin of *Keys* is a matter of conjecture; in the 15th century the 24 keys are referred to as *Keys of Man and Keys of the Law*.

Typhœus (tī fē' us), or **Typhon** (tī' fon). A monster of Greek mythology, son of GÆA and TARTARUS, with a hundred heads, each with a terrible voice. He made war on ZEUS, who killed him with a THUNDERBOLT. According to one legend, he lies buried under Mount ETNA. By ECHIDNA he fathered ORTHOS, CERBERUS, the Lernæan HYDRA, the CHIMÆRA, the Theban SPHINX, and the NEMEAN LION. *See* SET.

Tyr. *See* TIU.

Tyrant. In ancient Greece the *tyrant* was merely the absolute ruler, the *despot*, of a state, and at first the word had no implication of cruelty or what we call tyranny. Many of the Greek tyrants were pattern rulers, as Pisistratus and Pericles of ATHENS. The word (*turannos*) soon, however, obtained much the same meaning as it has with us.

The Thirty Tyrants. The 30 magistrates appointed by Sparta over ATHENS, at the termination of the Peloponnesian War. This "reign of terror", after one year's continuance, was overthrown by Thasybulus (403 B.C.).

In Roman history, those military leaders who endeavoured in the reigns of Valerian and Gallienus (A.D. 253–268) to make themselves independent princes are also known as *the Thirty Tyrants*, although the number is loosely applied.

Tyrian Purple. *See* PURPLE.

Tyrtæus (tĕr tē ŭs). A lame schoolmaster and elegiac poet of ATHENS who is said to have so inspired the Spartans by his songs that they defeated the Messenians (7th century B.C.). The name has hence been given to many martial poets who have urged on their countrymen to deeds of ARMS and victory.

U

U. The twenty-first letter of the English alphabet; in form a modification of V with which for many centuries it was interchangeable. Words beginning with U and V were (like those in I and J) not separated in English dictionaries till about 1800 and later. *A Dictionary of the English Language* published by Henry Washbourne, London, 1847, still adhered to the old practice. In 16th- and early 17th-century books spellings such as *vpon* and *haue* are the rule rather than the exception.

U.F.O. Unidentified flying object; the name given to objects claimed to have been sighted in the sky such as FLYING SAUCERS (*see under* SAUCER) etc., or picked up on radar screens, the exact nature of which is uncertain. Study and observation of U.F.O.s is termed *ufology* by enthusiasts.

U and Non-U. A semi-humorous mark of distinction between social classes in England based on the usage of certain words. "U" is Upper Class, "Non-U" being non-Upper Class. It is "U" to say "luncheon" for what "Non-U" folk call "lunch"; "napkin" and "serviette", "cycle" and "bike" are samples of this snobbism. The terms owe their popularity to Nancy Mitford, who quoted them in an article in the magazine *Encounter* in September 1955; but they were invented by Professor A.S.C. Ross in 1954 and appear in his article "Linguistic class indicators in present-day English".

U-boat. A German submarine; the term is adapted from the German *Unterseeboot* (under-water vessel). *Cp.* E-BOAT.

Uberrimæ fidei (Lat., of the fullest confidence, complete faith). A legal expression used of contracts in which the fullest and frankest information must be disclosed by the applicant or promisee. All insurance contracts are governed by this principle in order that the insurers may judge whether or not to accept the proposal.

Udal Tenure (Icel. *othal*). More correctly *odal* tenure, the same as "allodial tenure", a sort of FREEHOLD tenure depending on attested long-term undisturbed possession, as in the ORKNEYS and Shetlands. It was quite distinct from feudal forms of tenure. A *Udaller* is one holding such a tenure.

Ugly Duckling. An unpromising child who develops into a beautiful or handsome adult; also anything of an unprepossessing character that may change with time into something attractive. The expression is taken from Hans Andersen's story of the *Ugly Duckling* that endured many embarrassments but grew into a beautiful swan.

Uisnech. *See* USNECH.

Uitlander (oit lan' dĕr). The Boer term for a foreigner (Outlander), and especially those Europeans resident in the Transvaal and Orange Free State (mostly British subjects) after the discoveries of GOLD, who were not given political rights.

Ulema (ū lē' mà). The learned classes in Mohammedan countries, interpreters of the KORAN and the law, from whose numbers came the MULLAHS, MUFTIS, IMAMS, cadis, etc. (teachers of religion, of law, and administrators of justice). *Ulema* is the plural of Arab. *alim*, a wise man.

Ullage (ŭl' àj). The difference between the amount of liquid a vessel can contain and what it actually does contain (O.Fr. *œiller*, to fill up). The term is applied to a bottle of wine of which part of the contents have evaporated. Colloquially it is applied to *dregs*, or *rubbish* generally.

Ulster. The northernmost province of IRELAND which was forfeited to the Crown in James I's reign in consequence of the rebellions of Tyrconnell and Tyrone and planted by English and Scottish settlers (1609– 1612). Under Acts of 1920 and 1922, as Northern Ireland, it was made a separate political division of the United Kingdom while still sending 12 M.P.s to WESTMINSTER.

The Red, or **Bloody Hand of Ulster.** The badge of ULSTER, a sinister hand, erect, open, and couped at the wrist, gules; the Red Hand of the O'Neills. *See* BARONET.

Ultima Thule. *See under* THULE.

Ultimus Romanorum (ŭl′ ti mùs rō mà nôr′ ùm) (Lat.). The LAST OF THE ROMANS.

Ultor (ŭl′ tôr) (Lat., the Avenger). A title given to MARS when, after defeating the murderers of Julius CÆSAR at Philippi, Augustus built a temple to him in the Forum at ROME.

Ultra vires (ŭl′ tra vī′ rēz) (Lat. *ultra*, beyond; *vires*, the powers). In excess of the authority given by law, hence invalid in the legal sense. Thus if the BANK of England were to set up a MINT on its premises it would be acting *ultra vires*.

Ultramontane Party. The extreme party in the Church of ROME. *Ultramontane* opinions or tendencies are those which favour the high "Catholic" party. *Ultramontane* (beyond the mountains, *i.e.* the Alps) means Italy or the old Papal States. The term was first used by the French, to distinguish those who look upon the POPE as the fountain of all power in the Church, in contradistinction to the Gallican school, which maintained the right of self-government by national churches. *Cp.* TRAMONTANE.

Ulysses, or **Odysseus** (ū′ lis ēz, o dis′ūs) ("the hater"). A mythical king of Ithaca, a small rocky island of Greece, one of the leading chieftains of the Greeks in HOMER'S ILIAD, and the hero of his ODYSSEY, represented by Homer as wise, eloquent, and full of artifices.

According to VIRGIL, it was he who suggested the device of the WOODEN HORSE (*see under* HORSE) through which TROY was ultimately taken. *See* TELEGONUS.

Ulysses' Bow. Only ULYSSES could draw his own bow, and he could shoot an arrow through 12 rings. By this sign PENELOPE recognized her husband after an absence of 20 years. He was also recognized by his dog, Argus.

The bow was prophetic. It belonged at one time to Eurytus of Œchalia.

Umble pie. *See* TO EAT HUMBLE PIE *under* EAT.

Umbrage. To take umbrage (Lat. *umbra*, shade). Originally to feel overshadowed, slighted, and hence to take offence.

Umbrella. Under the umbrella of So-and-so. Under his dominion, regimen, influence, protection. The allusion is to the umbrella carried over certain African potentates as an EMBLEM of sovereignty. In 1876, the sacred umbrella of King Koffee of the Ashantis was captured and placed in the South Kensington Museum.

Unam sanctam (Lat., One holy). The opening words of Boniface VIII's BULL of 1302 declaring that there was "One holy Catholic and Apostolic Church", membership of which was necessary for salvation.

Unaneled. Unanointed; without having had extreme unction (O.E. *ele*, oil; from Lat. *oleum*). *See* HOUSEL.

Unhouseled, disappointed, unaneled.
SHAKESPEARE: *Hamlet*, I, v.

Uncials (ŭn′ si àlz). A form of majuscule (large) script used in MSS. dating from about the 4th century A.D. to the 8th century; so called from Lat. *uncia*, twelfth part, inch, because the letters were about an inch high. There were also half-uncials.

Uncle. Slang for a pawnbroker, in use as early as 1756. Its origin is unknown. An article that has *gone to uncle's* is in pawn.

Old Uncle Tom Cobleigh. The last named of the seven village worthies who borrowed Tom Pearce's grey mare on which to ride to WIDECOMBE FAIR and whose names form the refrain of the famous ballad of that name which has become as much the county song of Devon as "D'ye ken John Peel" is of Cumberland.

> When the wind whistles cold on the moor of a night,
> All along, down along, out along lee,
> Tom Pearce's old mare doth appear gashly white,
> Wi' Bill Brewer, Jan Stewer, Peter Gurney,
> Peter Davy, Dan'l Whidden, Harry Hawk,
> Old Uncle Tom Cobleigh and all,
> Old Uncle Tom Cobleigh and all.

Uncle Joe. A British (World War II) nickname for Joseph Stalin, head of the Government of the U.S.S.R. (1941–1953).

Uncle Remus (rē′ mŭs). The old plantation negro whose quaint and proverbial wisdom, and stories of Br'er Rabbit and BR'ER FOX, were related by Joel Chandler Harris (1848–1908) in *Uncle Remus, his Songs and Sayings* (1880), and *Nights with Uncle Remus* (1883).

Uncle Sam. *See under* SAM.

Uncle Tom's Cabin. A story by Mrs. Harriet Beecher Stowe (1811–1896) that appeared in 1852. It tells of the sale of a pious and faithful old Negro slave to a bad owner. By its emphasis on the worst sides of Negro slavery, the book helped in no small degree to arouse the American nation to an understanding of the iniquities of the system. The original of Uncle Tom was a slave subsequently ordained as the Rev. J. Henson. He came to London in 1876 and was presented to Queen Victoria. **Uncle Tom** is now used by Black Nationalists to denote Negroes who are over-subservient to the white ESTABLISHMENT.

Welsh uncle. The husband of a parent's cousin; sometimes a parent's first cousin.

Don't come the uncle over me. In Latin, *Ne sis patruus mihi* (HORACE, II *Sat.*, iii, 88), *i.e.* do not overdo your privilege of reproving or castigating me. The Roman notion of a *patruus* or uncle acting as guardian was that of a severe castigator.

To talk like a Dutch uncle. *See under* DUTCH.

Unconscious, The. In psychology, the mental processes which the individual cannot bring into consciousness—they are, indeed, often unknown to him.

Undecimilla *See* URSULA, St.

Under. Under the counter. Said of actions that are surreptitious and savouring of dishonest practice; in World War II, rationing led to considerable "under the counter" transactions by some shopkeepers who kept back goods for privileged customers or BLACK MARKET transactions "under the counter".

Under cover. Working out of sight, in secret. An under-cover agent is one who pursues his inquiries or work unknown to any but his employer.

Underground. A political or military movement carried on in secret against an oppressor government of an occupying enemy administration, especially in World War II.

Undertaker. Originally any contractor. The application of this word to one who carries out funerals—in the U.S.A. termed a mortician—dates from the 17th century.

Undine (ŭn′ dēn). One of the elemental spirits of PARACELSUS, the spirit of the waters. She was created without a soul; but had this privilege, that by marrying a mortal and bearing him a child she obtained a soul, and with it all the pains and penalties of the human race. She is the subject of a tale (*Undine*, 1811) by Friedrich de la Motte Fouqué (1777–1843). *Cp.* SYLPH.

Unfinished Symphony. Schubert's Symphony No. 8 in B Minor (1822), of which only two movements were completed. The phrase is applied figuratively and humorously to various unfinished compositions.

Unguem (ŭn′ gwem). **Ad unguem.** To a nicety, exactly. To finish a statue *ad unguem* is to finish it so smoothly and perfectly that when the nail is run over the surface it can detect no imperfection. *See* TO HAVE IT AT ONE'S FINGERS' ENDS *under* FINGER.

Unhinged. To be quite unhinged. To have one's nerves badly shaken, one's balance of mind disturbed; like a door which has lost one of its hinges.

Unhouseled. *See under* HOUSEL.

Uniat, or **Uniate Churches** (Lat. *unus*, one). Churches of Eastern Christendom which are in communion with ROME but retain their own rights, languages, and canon law.

Unicorn (ū' ni kôrn) (Lat. *unum cornu*, one horn). A mythical and heraldic animal, represented by mediæval writers as having the legs of a buck, the tail of a LION, the head and body of a HORSE, and a single horn, white at the base, black in the middle, and red at the tip, in the middle of its forehead. The body is white, the head red, and eyes blue. The earliest author that describes it is Ctesias (400 B.C.).

Another popular belief was that the unicorn by dipping its horn into a liquid could detect whether or not it contained poison. In the designs for GOLD and SILVER plate made for the Emperor Rudolph II by Ottavio Strada is a cup on which a unicorn stands as if to assay the liquid.

The supporters of the old royal ARMS of SCOTLAND are two Unicorns; when James VI of Scotland came to reign over ENGLAND (1603) he brought one of the Unicorns with him, and with it supplanted the RED DRAGON which, as representing WALES, was one of the supporters of the English shield, the other being the Lion.

The animosity which existed between the lion and the unicorn referred to by Spenser in his *Faerie Queene* (II, v, 10):

> Like as a lyon, whose imperiall powre
> A prowd rebellious unicorn defyes—

is allegorical of that which once existed between England and Scotland.

Unigenitus (ū ni jen' i tus) (Lat., the Only-Begotten). A Papal BULL, so called from its opening sentence *Unigenitus, Dei Filius*, issued in 1713 by Clement XI in condemnation of Quesnel's *Réflexions Morales*, which favoured Jansenism. It was a *damnatio in globo*—*i.e.* a condemnation of the whole book without exception. It was confirmed in 1725, but in 1730 the bull was condemned by the civil authorities of PARIS and this clerical controversy died out.

Union, The. A short term for the United States of America; in ENGLAND, a once familiar colloquialism for the workhouse, from its being maintained by a group of parishes formed into a *Union* in accordance with the Poor Law Amendment Act of 1834.

The Act of Union. Specifically the Act of Union of 1707 declaring that on and after 1 May 1707 ENGLAND and SCOTLAND "for ever after be united into One Kingdom by the Name of Great Britain". It provided for one PARLIAMENT for both countries. There had been a common sovereign since 1603.

The term also applies to the Act of 1536, incorporating WALES with England, and the Act of 1800, which united the Kingdoms of Great Britain and IRELAND on and after 1 January 1801, a union which came to an end in 1922.

Union Jack. The national banner of the UNITED KINGDOM. It consists of three united crosses—that of St. GEORGE for ENGLAND, the saltire of St. ANDREW for Scotland (added by James I), and the CROSS of St. PATRICK for Ireland (added at the Union in 1801).

The white edging of St. George's cross shows the white field. In the saltire the cross is reversed on each side, showing that the other half of the cross is covered over. The broad white band is the St. Andrew's cross and should be uppermost at the top left-hand corner of the flag (*i.e.* the hoist). The narrow white edge is the white field of St. Patrick's cross.

Union of South Africa. The union of the former self-governing colonies of the Cape of Good Hope, Natal, the Transvaal, and the Orange River Colony, with its PARLIAMENT at Cape Town. The title was changed to the Republic of South Africa on 31 May 1961, when South Africa left the British COMMONWEALTH.

The Union Rose. The Tudor Rose. *See under* ROSE.

Union is strength (Lat. *unitate fortior*). The wise saw of Periander, tyrant of Corinth between *c.* 627 and 586 B.C.

Unionists. In 1886, when Gladstone introduced his first Home Rule Bill for Ireland, 78 LIBERALS under Joseph Chamberlain and Lord Hartington allied with the CONSERVATIVES as Liberal Unionists to uphold the union with IRELAND (*see* ACT OF UNION, *above*). From 1886, the Conservative Party was also called the Unionist Party; it adopted the official name of *Conservative and Un-*

ionist Party in 1909.

Unitarians. Originally Christians who denied the existence of the TRINITY, maintaining that God existed in one person only. Many of the early heretical sects were unitarian in belief if not in name, and at the time of the REFORMATION unitarianism had numerous exponents who may be regarded as the founders of the modern movement.

In ENGLAND, John Biddle (1615–1662) is generally regarded as the founding father and among the famous men who have been Unitarians are Dr. Samuel Clarke, Joseph Priestley, Dr. Lardner, James Martineau, Sir Edgar Bowring, and Joseph Chamberlain. Modern Unitarianism is not based on Scriptural authority, but on reason and conscience and includes AGNOSTICS and humanists among its members. There is no formal dogma or creed.

United. United Empire Loyalists. Many of those American colonists who remained loyal to the mother country during the American War of Independence subsequently migrated to Ontario and the Maritime Provinces. They formed the nucleus of British Canada and were given the honourable title of *United Empire Loyalists*.

United Irishmen. A society formed by Theobald Wolfe Tone in 1791 with its first headquarters at Belfast and with the objects of securing a representative national PARLIAMENT, to unite all Irishmen against British influence, etc. Membership included both PROTESTANTS and Roman Catholics, but it soon became revolutionary and was largely responsible for the rebellion of 1798.

United Kingdom. The name adopted on 1 January 1801, when Great Britain and IRELAND were united. *See* ACT OF UNION *under* UNION.

United Nations. The successor to the LEAGUE OF NATIONS as a world organization primarily concerned with the maintenance of peace but with numerous other functions and agencies. It sprang from the Dumbarton Oaks conversations (1944) between the UNITED STATES, Great Britain, and Soviet Russia, and was formally inaugurated in 1945. Its headquarters is in New York City.

United Provinces. Guelderland, Utrecht, Friesland, Overyssel, Groningen, Zeeland, and Holland; the seven provinces whose independence was recognized by Spain in 1648 and who first came together in the *Union of Utrecht* (1579), thus laying the foundation of the United Kingdom of the Netherlands. They became the Batavian Republic in 1795 and the Kingdom of Holland under Louis Bonaparte in 1806. At the end of the Napoleonic Wars (1814), the Kingdom of the Netherlands was reconstituted with the addition of the Southern Netherlands. Belgium secured its independence after the revolt in 1830 and was formally recognized in 1839.

The United Provinces of Agra and Oudh (1902) were entitled the United Provinces in 1935, changed to Uttar Pradesh in 1950.

United Reformed Church. The church formed in 1972 from the union of the Congregational Church of England and Wales (*see* CONGREGATIONALISTS) with the English PRESBYTERIAN Church.

United States of America. The Federal republic of 50 States and one Federal District which has developed from the original 13 States (marked with an asterisk in the list below) which secured their independence from Great Britain in 1783. Its government is based upon the Constitution of 1787. *See also* UNCLE SAM *under* SAM; YANK.

All States except three have official abbreviations and NICKNAMES which are shown below, together with the dates of admission to the UNION.

Alabama (Ala.), Cotton. (1819).
Alaska. (1959).
Arizona (Ariz.), Apache. (1912).
Arkansas (Ark.), Wonder. (1836).
California (Calif.), Golden. (1850).
Colorado (Colo.), Centennial. (1876).
*Connecticut (Conn.), Nutmeg. (1788).
*Delaware (Del.), Diamond. (1787).
Florida (Fla.), Peninsula. (1845).
*Georgia (Ga.), Empire State of the South. (1788).
Hawaii. (1959).

Idaho (Id., Ida.), Gem. (1890).

Illinois (Ill.), Prairie. (1818).

Indiana (Ind.), Hoosier. (1816).

Iowa (Ia., Io.), Hawkeye. (1846).

Kansas (Kans.), Sunflower. (1861).

Kentucky (Ky.), Blue Grass. (1792).

Louisiana (La.), Pelican. (1812).

Maine (Me.), Pine Tree. (1820).

*Maryland (Md.), Old Line. (1788).

*Massachusetts (Mass.), Bay. (1788).

Michigan (Mich.), Wolverine. (1837).

Minnesota (Minn.), Gopher. (1858).

Mississippi (Miss.), Magnolia (1817).

Missouri (Mo.), Show-me. (1821).

Montana (Mont.), Treasure. (1889).

Nebraska (Nebr.), Cornhusker. (1867).

Nevada (Nev.), Sagebrush. (1864).

*New Hampshire (N.H.), Granite. (1788).

*New Jersey (N.J.), Garden. (1787).

New Mexico (N. Mex.), Sunshine. (1912).

*New York (N.Y.), Empire. (1788).

*North Carolina (N.C.), Tar Heel. (1789).

North Dakota (N.D.), Flickertail. (1889).

Ohio (O.), Buckeye. (1803).

Oklahoma (Okla.), Sooner. (1907).

Oregon (Ore., Oreg.), Beaver. (1859).

*Pennsylvania (Pa.), Keystone. (1787).

*Rhode Island (R.I.), Little Rhody. (1790).

*South Carolina (S.C.), Palmetto. (1788).

South Dakota (S.D.), Coyote. (1889).

Tennessee (Tenn.), Volunteer. (1796).

Texas (Tex.), Lone Star. (1845).

Utah, Mormon. (1896).

Vermont (Vt.), Green Mountain. (1791).

*Virginia (Va.), Old Dominion.

Washington (Wash.), Evergreen. (1889).

West Virginia (W. Va.,), Panhandle. (1863).

Wisconsin (Wis.), Badger. (1848).

Wyoming (Wyo.), Equality. (1890).

District of Columbia (D.C.). (1791).

There are other outlying territories and other nicknames.

Unities, The Dramatic. *See under* DRA-MA.

Unknown. The Great Unknown. *See under* GREAT.

The Unknown Prime Minister. A name given to A. Bonar Law (1858–1923), who held office as CONSER-VATIVE leader in 1922–1923.

The Unknown Warrior. The body of an unknown British soldier of World War I brought home from one of the battlefields of the Western Front and "buried among the kings" in Westminster Abbey (11 November 1920). Part of the inscription on the gravestone reads: "Thus are commemorated the many multitudes who during the Great War of 1914–1918 gave the most that man can give, Life itself...."

Unlearned Parliament, The. Henry IV's second PARLIAMENT of 1404, also called the *Lawless Parliament*, and *Parliament of Dunces*, because the king hoped for a more tractable assembly by directing the sheriffs not to return any lawyers.

Unmentionables. One of the 19th-century humorous colloquialisms for trousers, pantaloons, breeches; also known as *inexpressibles*. *See* GENS BRA-CATA.

Unmerciful Parliament, The. The MER-CILESS PARLIAMENT (*see under* MERCY); also called the WONDERFUL PARLIA-MENT.

Unready, The. Ethelred II, King of England (978–1016), called the *redeless*, or deficient in counsel. *Unready* is a modern corruption. Ethelred means "noble-counsel". His nickname is first found in the 13th century.

Unrighteous Bible, The. *See* BIBLE, SOME SPECIALLY NAMED EDITIONS.

Untouchables. The lowest CASTE in India, excluded from social and religious contact with Hinduism and subjected to many indignities. Their touch was supposed to sully the higher castes. Largely through the teaching of Mahatma Gandhi, untouchability was legally ended in 1949. *Cp.* PARIAH.

Unwashed, The Great. Usually a derogatory reference to the lower classes of former days or to the less hygienic habits of our ancestors.

Unwritten Law. Uncodified custom which rests for its authority on the supposed right of the individual to take into his hands the avenging of personal wrongs; also applied to understood and long-standing custom or convention. COMMON LAW is sometimes so called, which rests upon judicial decision as opposed to written statute.

Up. It is up to him. It is for him to take the initiative or decide what is to be done.

Up country. In the interior, away from the coast, inland. The term is sometimes used in America and Australia with slighting implications, meaning unsophisticated, rustic.

"Up, Guards, and at them!" The somewhat APOCRYPHAL order attributed to Wellington as his order to the Guards at the battle of Waterloo (18 June 1815). Creasy gives this rendering in his *Fifteen Decisive Battles*.

Up stage. As a technical theatrical direction this means at the back of the stage which in many theatres slopes down slightly to the footlights. Colloquially the phrase *up-stage* means aloof, putting on airs of consequence or superiority; an actor up stage of another has the advantage, the latter having to act with his back to the audience.

Up State. In the U.S.A., the part of a State farthest north or distant from the coast; the term is used more particularly of the northern parts of New York State.

Upper storey or **story. Not quite right in his upper storey.** Somewhat mentally unsound, not quite *all there*; something wrong *up top*, *i.e.* in the head or brain.

The Upper House. *See under* HOUSE.

The Upper Ten. *See under* TEN.

Down on or **on one's uppers.** Impoverished; as typified by the worn-out condition of one's footwear. *Cp.* DOWN AT HEEL.

Upanishads (ū păn' i shădz). Part of the oldest speculative literature of the Hindus, a collection of treatises on the nature of the universe, the deity, and man. They form the VEDANTA, or last part of

the VEDA, and date from about 500 B.C. The name is Sanskrit, and means "a sitting down" (at another's feet), hence "a confidential talk", "esoteric doctrine".

Upas Tree (ū' păs). The Javanese tree, *Antiaris toxicaria*, the milky juice of which contains a virulent poison and is used for tipping arrows.

Fable has it that a putrid steam rises from it, and that whatever the vapour touches dies. Foersch, a Dutch physician, wrote in 1783, "Not a tree, nor blade of grass is to be found in the valley or surrounding mountains. Not a beast or bird, reptile or living thing, lives in the vicinity." He adds that on "one occasion 1,600 refugees encamped within 14 miles of it, and all but 300 died within two months". This "traveller's tale" has given rise to the figurative use of *upas* for a corrupting or pernicious influence.

Upstairs. To kick upstairs. To get rid of an embarrassing colleague in the CABINET or HOUSE OF COMMONS by giving him a peerage, thereby removing him to the HOUSE OF LORDS. Thus any promotion given to get rid of someone.

Urania (ū rā' ni à). One of the MUSES in Greek mythology who presides over ASTROLOGY; usually represented pointing at a celestial globe with a staff. Also an epithet of APHRODITE or VENUS. The name means "heavenly" or "celestial". Milton (*Paradise Lost*, VII, 1–39) makes her the spirit of the loftiest poetry, and calls her "heavenly born" and the sister of Wisdom.

Uranus (ū' rà nus). In Greek mythology, the personification of HEAVEN, son and husband of GÆA (Earth), and father of the TITANS, the CYCLOPS, etc. He hated his children and confined them in the body of Earth who begged them to avenge her, and his son KRONOS unmanned him with a sickle and dethroned him.

The planet Uranus was discovered in 1781 by Herschel, and named by him *Georgium Sidus* in honour of George III. Its five satellites are named *Ariel*, *Umbriel*, *Titania*, *Oberon*, and *Miranda*.

Urbanists. *See* FRANCISCANS.

Urbi et Orbi (ĕr' bī et ôr' bī). (Lat., to the city [Rome] and the world). A phrase applied to the solemn blessing publicly given by the POPE from the balcony of St. Peter's on special occasions, such as his election. The custom fell into abeyance after 1870 but was revived by Pope Pius XI after his election in 1922.

Urdu. The form of Hindustani spoken by Mohammedans and Hindus in contact with them; from *urdu zaban*, "the language of the camp", which grew up as the means of communication between the MOSLEM conquerors and their subject population.

Uriah (ū rī´ à). **Letter of Uriah.** A treacherous letter, importing friendship but in reality a death warrant. (*See* II *Sam*. xi, 15.)

Uriel (ū´ ri ĕl). One of the seven ARCHANGELS of rabbinical angelology, sent by God to answer the questions of Esdras (II *Esdras* iv). In Milton's *Paradise Lost* (III, 690) he is the "Regent of the Sun", and "sharpest-sighted spirit of all in HEAVEN".

Urim and Thummim (ū´ rim, thŭm´ im). Sacred LOTS of unknown nature used for DIVINATION by the ancient Hebrews as a means of ascertaining the will of God. They are mentioned in *Exod*. xxviii, 30; *Deut*. xxxiii, 8; I *Sam*. xxviii, 6; *Ezra* ii, 63, etc., but fell out of use as more spiritual conceptions of the Deity developed and there is no mention of them after the time of David.

Ursa Major. The GREAT BEAR (*see under* BEAR), or CHARLES'S WAIN, the most conspicuous of the northern constellations.

Ursa Minor. The Little Bear; the northern constellation known also as Cynosura or Dog's tail, from its circular sweep. The Pole star is α in the tail. *See* CYNOSURE; GREAT BEAR *under* BEAR.

Ursula, St. A 5th-century British princess, according to legend, who went with 11,000 virgins on a pilgrimage to ROME and was massacred with all her companions by the Huns at Cologne. One explanation of the story is that *Undecimilla* (mistaken for *undecim millia*, 11,000) was one of Ursula's companions.

Ursulines. An order of nuns founded by St. Angela Merici of Brescia in 1535, from their patron SAINT, St. URSULA. They were primarily concerned with the education of girls.

Use. To have no use for a person. Used idiomatically, implies active dislike mingled with contempt—one is not prepared to make use of him for any purpose. "To have no time for a person" is a similar expression.

Useless Parliament, The. The PARLIAMENT convened by CHARLES I, on 8 June 1625; adjourned to Oxford, 1 August; and dissolved 12 August; having done nothing but quarrel with the KING.

Usher. From Fr. *huissier*, a door-keeper.
Gentleman Usher of the Black Rod. *See* BLACK ROD.
Usher of the Green Rod. An officer in attendance on the Knights of the Thistle at their chapters.

Usnech, or **Uisnech, The Sons of.** Naoise (or Noisi), Ainle, and Ardan. DEIRDRE was told by her foster-father that she would fall in love with a man who had hair as black as a raven, cheeks as red as blood, and a body white as snow. Naoise was such a man and Deirdre eloped with him.

Usquebaugh (us´ kwē baw). Whisky (Ir. *uisgebeatha*, water of life). Similar to the Lat. *aqua vitæ* and Fr. *eau de vie*.

Utgard. In Scandinavian mythology, the abode of the giants, where Utgard-LOKI had his castle.

Uther. According to Geoffrey of Monmouth (*Historia Britonum*), King of Britain and father of King ARTHUR by an adulterous amour with Igerna, wife of Gorlois, Duke of Cornwall, at TINTAGEL. *See* PENDRAGON.

Uti possidetis (ū´ tī pos i dē´ tis) (Lat., as you possess). The principle that the property remains with its present possessor; in international law that the belligerents retain possession of their acquisitions in war.

Uticensis (ū ti sen´ sis). Cato the Younger (95–46 B.C.) was so called from Utica, the place of his death.

Utilitarianism. The ethical doctrine that actions are right in proportion to their usefulness or as they tend to promote happiness; the doctrine that the end and criterion of public action is "the greatest happiness of the greatest number".

The term originated with Jeremy Bentham (1748–1832), whose ideas were expounded by his disciple James Mill (1773–1836) and by the latter's son John Stuart Mill (1806–1873), in his *Utilitarianism* (1869), who also introduced quantitative and qualitative distinctions in pleasures. *See* PANOPTICON.

Utnapishtim. The Babylonian counterpart of Noah, whose story is told in the GILGAMESH EPIC, and which has many notable resemblances to the BIBLE story. The Hebrews almost certainly derived their account from Babylonia.

Utopia. Nowhere (Gr. *ou*, not; *topos*, a place). The name given by Sir Thomas More to the imaginary island in his political romance of the same name (1516), where everything is perfect—the laws, the morals, the politics, etc., and in which the evils of existing laws, etc., are shown by contrast. *See* IDEAL COMMONWEALTHS *under* COMMONWEALTH.

Hence *Utopian*, applied to any idealistic but impractical scheme.

Utraquists (Lat. *utraque specie*, in both kinds). HUSSITES or CALIXTENES, so called because they insisted that both elements should be administered to communicants in the EUCHARIST.

Uzziel. One of the principal ANGELS of rabbinical angelology, the name meaning "Strength of God". He was next in command to GABRIEL, and in Milton's *Paradise Lost* (IV, 782) is commanded by Gabriel to "coast the south with strictest watch".

V

V. The twenty-second letter of the alphabet formerly sharing its form with U.

In the Roman notation it stands for 5 and represents ideographically the four fingers and thumb with the latter extended. V̄ represents 5,000.

V for Victory. On 14 January 1941, M. Victor de Lavaleye, a member of the exiled Belgian government in London, proposed in a broadcast to Belgium that the letter V, standing for Victory in all European languages, be substituted for the letters R.A.F. which were being chalked up on walls, etc., in Belgium. The plan was immediately adopted and the Morse Code V (···—) was featured in every B.B.C. broadcast to Europe followed by the opening bar of Beethoven's 5th Symphony which has the same rhythm. "Colonel Britton" (D. E. Ritchie), director of the B.B.C. European news service, was responsible for the diffusion of the V-sign propaganda which gave hope to those under the NAZI yoke. Sir Winston Churchill greatly popularized the sign of two upraised fingers in the form of a V.

V.C. *See* VICTORIA CROSS.

V.E. Day. The end of hostilities in Europe after World War II, 8 May 1945.

V.I.P. Very Important Person. This well-established usage was coined by a Station Commander of Transport Command in 1944 who was responsible for the movement of a plane-load of important individuals, including Lord Mountbatten, to the Middle East and so described them in his movement orders to avoid disclosing their identity.

VXL. A punning monogram on lockets, etc., standing for UXL (you excel). U and V were formerly interchangeable.

Vacuum. Nature abhors a vacuum.

This maxim is used by Spinoza in his *Ethics* (1677) and by Rabelais in its Latin form, *natura abhorret vacuum*, in his GARGANTUA (ch. V). *See* TORRICELLI.

Vade mecum (vā′ dē mē′ kŭm) (Lat., go-with-me). A pocket-book, memorandum-book, pocket cyclopædia, lady's pocket companion, or anything else which contains many things of daily use in a small compass.

Væ Victis! (vē vik′ tis) (Lat.). Woe to the vanquished! So much the worse for the conquered! This was the exclamation of Brennus, the Gaulish chief, on throwing his sword into the balance as a makeweight, when determining the price of peace with ROME (390 B.C.).

Vagitanus. *See* BABES, PROTECTING DEITIES OF.

Vails, or **Vales,** an obsolete term for a tip given to servants, from Fr. *valoir*, Lat. *valere*, to be worth. The older form was *avails*.

Vale! Farewell! 2nd pers, sing. imp. of Lat. *valere*, to be worth, or to fare well.

Ave atque vale! Hail and farewell! The words of Catullus at his brother's tomb.

Vale of the White Horse. *See under* HORSE.

Valentine, St. A priest of ROME who was imprisoned for succouring persecuted Christians. He became a convert and, although he is supposed to have restored the sight of the gaoler's blind daughter, he was clubbed to death (*c.* 270). His day is 14 February, as is that of St. Valentine, bishop of Terni, who was martyred a few years later. There are several other saints of this name.

The ancient custom of choosing *Valentines* has only accidental relation to either SAINT, being essentially a relic of the old Roman *Lupercalia* (*see* LUPER-CAL), or from association with the mating season of birds. It was marked by the giving of presents and nowadays by the sending of a card on which CUPIDS, transfixed hearts, etc., are depicted.

Chaucer refers to this in his *Assembly of Fowls* (310):

> For this was on Saint Valentine's Day,
> When ev'ry fowl cometh to choose her make.

Valentine and Orson. An old French ROMANCE connected with the Carolingian cycle.

The heroes, from whom it is named, were the twin sons of Bellisant, sister of King Pepin, and Alexander, and were born in a forest near Orléans. Orson (Fr. *ourson*, a little bear) was carried off by a bear and became a wild man and the terror of France. While the mother was searching for him, Valentine was carried off by his uncle, the KING. The brothers had many adventures and Orson was reclaimed by Valentine. Orson married Fezon, daughter of Duke Savary of Aquitaine, and Valentine, Clerimond, sister of the Green Knight.

Valhalla. In Scandinavian mythology, the hall in the celestial regions whither the souls of heroes slain in battle were borne by the VALKYRIES, to spend eternity in joy and feasting (*valr*, the slain, and *hall*).

Valkyries (Old Norse, the choosers of the slain). The nine (or seven, or twelve) handmaidens of ODIN, who, mounted on swift horses and holding drawn swords, rushed into the *mêlée* of battle and selected those destined to death. These heroes they conducted to VALHALLA, where they waited upon them and served them with mead and ALE in the skulls of the vanquished.

Vallary Crown (Lat. *vallum*, a mound, rampart). The same as a *mural* CROWN.

The Valley of the Kings. A site in the Theban Hills, north-west of THEBES, Egypt, containing the tombs of PHARAOHS of the New Kingdom. Thutmosis I (1530–1520 B.C.) was the first to build his tomb there. The wadi was guarded by small forts and the tombs were walled up with rubble, but pillaging began as the New Kingdom declined. The many tombs uncovered include that of Tutankhamun, revealed with its remarkable treasures in 1922–3 by Howard Carter who, with Lord Carnarvon, had been engaged in excavations there since 1906. *See* CURSE OF TUTANKHAMUN.

The Valley of the Queens. The less spectacular cemetery of the wives and daughters of Pharaohs of the XXth Dynasty. It lies to the south of the VALLEY OF THE KINGS.

Valois (văl' wa). The reigning dynasty in France from 1328 to 1589, taking its name from Philip, Duke of Valois, the first of the line. They were a branch of the CAPET family and were succeeded by the BOURBON line when Henry of Navarre, husband of Marguerite of Valois, became King as Henry IV in 1589.

Vamana. *See* AVATAR.

Vampire. A fabulous being, supposed to be the ghost of a heretic, criminal, etc., who returned from the grave in the guise of a monstrous bat to suck the blood of sleeping persons who usually became vampires themselves. The only way to destroy them was to drive a stake through their body. The superstition is essentially Slavonic.

The word is applied to one who preys upon his fellows—a "blood-sucker".

One of the classic horror stories, Bram Stoker's *Dracula* (1897), centres on vampirism. The Dracula of Transylvanian legend appears to originate from Vlad V of Wallachia (1456–1476), known as Vlad the Impaler, although he was not a vampire. It is suggested that Stoker's Count Dracula was a composite figure derived from Vlad the Impaler and the Countess Báthori, who was arrested in 1610 for murdering girls. It was her habit to wash in the blood of her several hundred girl victims in order to maintain her skin in a youthful condition. The name comes from Vlad's membership of the Order of the Dragon, although *dracul* in Rumanian also means *devil*.

Van Diemen's Land. The former name for Tasmania, given by its Dutch discoverer Abel Jans Tasman in 1642 in honour of his patron, the Dutch Governor-General of Batavia. It became a British settlement in 1803, and its name was changed to Tasmania in 1853, to obliterate memories of its associations with BUSHRANGERS and convicts, transportation having ceased at that time.

Vandals. A Teutonic race first recorded in north-east Germany which in the 5th century ravaged GAUL, Spain, and North Africa, and in 455 ROME itself, when they despoiled it of its treasures of art and literature.

The name is hence applied to those who wilfully or ignorantly indulge in destruction of works of art, etc. *Vandalism* is now applied to most forms of wanton damage.

Vandyke. Vandyke beard. A pointed beard such as those frequently shown in Van Dyck's portraits, especially of CHARLES I.

Vanessa (và nes' à). Dean Swift's name for his friend and correspondent, Esther Vanhomrigh, made by compounding Van, the first syllable of her surname, with Essa, the pet form of Esther. Swift called himself Cadenus, an anagram on Decanus (Lat. for DEAN).

Vanguard. *See* AVANT-GARDE.

Vanir. A Scandinavian race of gods of peaceful and benevolent functions in contrast to the ÆSIR, who were essentially warriors. Among them were NJÖRD, FREYR, and FREYJA.

Vanity Fair. In Bunyan's *Pilgrim's Progress*, a fair established by BEELZEBUB, Apollyon, and Legion, in the town of Vanity, and lasting all the year round. Here were sold houses, lands, trades, places, honours, preferments, titles, countries, kingdoms, lusts, pleasures, and delights of all sorts.

Thackeray adopted the name for the title of his novel (1847) satirizing the weaknesses and follies of human nature.

Vantage loaf. The thirteenth loaf of a baker's dozen.

Varaha. *See* AVATAR.

Variety is the spice of life. It is variety in all its aspects that makes life interesting.

Variorum Edition (Lat. *variorum*, of various persons). An edition of a literary text giving the variant readings, notes, and comments of different scholars.

Varuna. In Hindu mythology, the brother of Mitra, one of the ADITYAS. Varuna shines at night and is linked with the MOON. He is represented as a white man riding on a sea monster, is the witness of everything, orders the seasons and controls the rains. Mitra is linked with the sun and shines or sees by day.

Vassal. A feudal TENANT with military obligations to his superior; hence, a dependant, retainer, servant, etc.

Vatican (văt' i kàn). The palace of the POPE; so called because it stands on the *Vaticanus Mons* (Vatican Hill) of ancient ROME, which got its name through being the headquarters of the *vaticinatores*, or soothsayers.

The Vatican City State. The area of ROME occupied by the city of the VATICAN, recognized by the LATERAN TREATY (1929) as constituting the territorial extent of the temporal power of the HOLY SEE. It consists of the Papal palace, the LIBRARY, archives, and museums, the Piazza of St. PETER, and contiguous buildings including a railway station, in all an area of just under a square mile. It has about 900 inhabitants and its own coinage. Certain other buildings outside the Vatican enjoy extraterritorial rights.

The Vatican Council. The twentieth ŒCUMENICAL COUNCIL of the ROMAN CATHOLIC CHURCH (1869–1870), summoned by Pius IX and suspended when the Italians occupied ROME after the withdrawal of the French garrison. It was notable for its definition of Papal INFALLIBILITY which was limited to when the Pope speaks *ex cathedra* regarding faith or morals.

A second Vatican Council was opened by Pope John XXIII in October 1962 and concluded by Paul VI in December 1965. Among numerous controversial proposals for change, it was notably concerned with the need for Christian unity, liturgical reforms, and matters of church government. One special feature was the presence of observers from non-Roman Catholic Churches. *See* ŒCUMENICAL COUNCILS.

The Prisoner of the Vatican. The POPE was so called after 1870, when Pius

IX retired into the VATICAN after the occupation of ROME. He proclaimed himself a prisoner for conscience' sake and his successors remained in the precincts of the Vatican until the LATERAN TREATY of 1929.

Vaudeville (vō' divil). A corruption of *Val de vire* or in O.Fr. *Vau de vire*, valley of the Vire, the native valley of Olivier Basselin, a Norman poet (d. 1418) and author of convivial songs which were so named from the place where he composed them. It is now applied to variety entertainment made of songs, dances, sketches, etc.

Vaudois. *See* WALDENSIANS. *Cp.* VOODOO.

Vauxhall. Vauxhall Gardens. A very popular pleasure resort for Londoners, first laid out in 1661 as Spring Gardens and finally closed in 1859. Pepys refers to it as Fox Hall. It finds mention in the *Spectator*, Dickens's *Sketches by Boz*, Thackeray's *Vanity Fair*, etc. It provided ample refreshment, musical entertainment, fireworks, displays of pictures and statuary, etc., and at night was lit by over 1,000 lamps. *Cp.* CREMORNE GARDENS; ROSHERVILLE GARDENS.

Vedanta (Sansk., "The end of the Veda"). The UPANISHADS, the philosophy of the Upanishads; the system of Hindu philosophy based on the VEDAS.

Vedas. The four sacred books of the BRAHMINS, comprising (1) the *Rigveda*; (2) the *Samaveda*; (3) the *Yajurveda*; and (4) the *Atharvaveda*. The first consists of hymns, the second of chants, the third mainly of sacrificial prayers in prose and verse, and the fourth largely of hymns and spells concerned with superstitious practices.

The word *Veda* means knowledge.

Vehmgerichte (fām' gė rich tė). Also *Fehmgerichte*. Courts or tribunals conducted by groups of free men under the presidency of a *Freigraf* (free count) which flourished in Germany (especially in Westphalia) between the 12th and 16th centuries. They were restricted to Westphalia in the 16th century and their last vestiges abolished in 1811. They dealt with serious crimes (punishable by death), heresy and witchcraft. Generally portrayed as sinister institutions, for the most part they did not abuse their power. In secret session the only punishment awarded was the death sentence which was carried out on the guilty forthwith.

Veil. Beyond the veil. The unknown state of those who have departed this life.

To take the veil. To become a nun; from the traditional head-dress of women in religious orders.

Velvet. The iron hand in the velvet glove. Absolute firmness concealed by mildness of approach.

The little gentleman in velvet. The MOLE. *See under* LITTLE.

Vendémiaire (von dā mē âr). The first month in the FRENCH REVOLUTIONARY CALENDAR (*see under* CALENDAR); from 22 SEPTEMBER to 21 OCTOBER. The word means "Vintage month".

Venerable (Lat. *venerabilis*, worthy of honour). The title applied to archdeacons in formally addressing them ("The Venerable the Archdeacon of Barset", or "The Venerable E. L. Brown"); and in the ROMAN CATHOLIC CHURCH, the title of one who has attained the first of the three degrees of CANONIZATION.

It belongs especially to BEDE, the monk of Jarrow, an English ecclesiastical historian (d. 735), and to William of Champeaux (d. 1121), the French scholastic philosopher and opponent of ABELARD.

Veni, Creator Spiritus (vā nē' krā a'tôr spē' ri tůs). A hymn to the HOLY GHOST in the Roman BREVIARY, probably of the 9th century and often attributed to Rabanus Maurus (d. 856), Archbishop of Mainz. It is sung at VESPERS and Terce during PENTECOST and on other occasions such as the consecration of a church or of a BISHOP. The popular English version beginning "Come, Holy Ghost, our souls inspire" is by John Cosin (1594–1672), Bishop of Durham.

Veni, Sancte Spiritus (Lat., Come, Holy Spirit). A mediæval Latin hymn, used as a sequence at PENTECOST in the ROMAN CATHOLIC CHURCH.

Veni, vidi, vici (Lat., I came, I saw, I conquered). According to Plutarch, it was thus that Julius CÆSAR announced to his friend Amintius his victory at Zela

(47 B.C.), in Asia Minor, over Pharnaces, son of Mithridates, who had rendered aid to Pompey.

Venial Sin. One that does not forfeit grace. In the ROMAN CATHOLIC CHURCH sins are of two sorts, MORTAL and venial (Lat. *venia*, grace, pardon). *See Matt.* xii, 31.

Venice Glass. The drinking-glasses of the MIDDLE AGES, made at Venice, were said to break into shivers if poison were put into them.

Venire facias (Lat., cause to come). An ancient writ directing a SHERIFF to assemble a jury.

Venite (vē nī' tē). Psalm 95, from its opening words *Venite, exultemus Domino*, "O come, let us sing unto the Lord". It is said or sung at MATTINS.

Venner's Rising. The last futile attempt of some 80 men under Thomas Venner to set up the FIFTH MONARCHY in January 1661. They fought desperately and Venner and 16 of his accomplices were executed.

Venom. The Venom is in the tail. The real difficulty is the conclusion; *with a sting in its tail* is a similar expression. (*See* TAIL).

Ventôse (von' tōz) (Fr., windy). The sixth month of the FRENCH REVOLUTIONARY CALENDAR (*see under* CALENDAR).

Ventre-saint-Gris (vontr săng grē). The usual oath of Henri IV of France, *Gris* being a euphemism for Christ, and *ventre*, stomach. Oaths not infrequently took this form of blasphemy—*God's nails*, *God's teeth*, etc., were common in England.

Ventriloquism. The trick of producing vocal sounds so that they appear to come, not from the person producing them, but from some other quarter. So called from Lat. *venter*, belly, *loqui*, to speak (speaking from the belly), with the erroneous notion that the voice of the ventriloquist proceeded from his stomach.

Venus. The Roman goddess of beauty and sensual love, identified with APHRODITE, in some accounts said to have sprung from the foam of the sea, in others to have been the daughter of JUPITER and DIONE, a NYMPH. VULCAN was her husband, but she had amours with MARS and many other gods and demigods. By MERCURY she was the mother of CUPID, and by the hero Anchises, the mother of ÆNEAS, through whom she was regarded by the Romans as the foundress of their race. Her chief festival is 1 April. *See* VENUS VERTICORDIA, *below*.

Her name is given to the second planet from the SUN (*see* HESPERUS), and in ASTROLOGY "signifiethe white men or browne ... joyfull, laughter, liberall, pleasers, dauncers, entertayners of women, players, perfumers, musitions, messengers of love".

Venus loveth ryot and dispence.
CHAUCER: *Wife of Bath's Prol.*, 700.

By the alchemists *copper* was designated *Venus*, probably because mirrors were anciently made of copper. A mirror is still the astronomical symbol of the planet Venus.

Venus Anadyomene. VENUS rising from the sea, accompanied by dolphins. The name is given to the famous lost painting by APELLES, and to that by Botticelli in the Accademia delle Belle Arti at Florence.

Venus Callipyge (Gr., with the beautiful buttocks). The name given to a late Greek statue in the Museo Nazionale at Naples. There is no real ground for connecting the statue with VENUS.

Venus de' Medici. A famous statue, since 1860 in the Uffizi Gallery, Florence, ranking as a canon of female beauty. It is supposed to date from the time of AUGUSTUS, and was dug up in the 17th century in the villa of Hadrian, near Tivoli, in 11 pieces. It was kept in the MEDICI Palace at ROME till its removal to Florence by Cosimo III.

Venus Genetrix (Lat., she that has borne). VENUS worshipped as a symbol of marriage and motherhood. CÆSAR erected a temple to Venus Genetrix in the Forum at ROME and there are several statues of this name. She is represented as raising her light drapery and holding an apple, the emblem of fecundity.

Venus of Cnidus. The nude statue of Praxiteles, purchased by the ancient Cnidians, who refused to part with it, although Nicomedes, king of Bithynia, offered to pay off their national debt as its price. It was subsequently removed to Constantinople, and perished in the great fire during the reign of Justinian (A.D. 532); but an ancient reproduction is in the VATICAN.

Venus of Milo, or **Melos.** This statue, with three of HERMES, was discovered by the French admiral Dumond d'Urville in Milo or Melos, one of the Greek islands. It dates from the 2nd century B.C. and is probably the finest single work of ancient art extant. It is now in the LOUVRE.

Venus Verticordia. One of the surnames of VENUS because she was invoked to "turn the hearts" of women to virtue and chastity (Lat. *vertere*, to turn; *cor, cordis*, heart).

Venus Victrix. VENUS, as goddess of victory, represented on numerous Roman coins.

Venus's Fly-trap. A plant (*Dionæa muscipula*) which feeds on insects, and is found in Carolina.

Venus's girdle. The CESTUS.

Venusberg. The Hörselberg, or mountain of delight and love, situated between Eisenach and Gotha, in the caverns of which, according to mediæval German legend, the Lady Venus held her court. Human visitors were sometimes allowed in, such as Thomas of Ercildoune and TANNHÄUSER, but they ran the risk of eternal perdition. ECKHARDT the Faithful sat outside to warn them against entering.

Vera causa (vē' rà kaw' zà) (Lat., a true cause). A cause in harmony with other causes already known. A fairy godmother may be assigned in story as the cause of certain marvellous effects, but is not a *vera causa*. The revolution of the earth round the sun may be assigned as the cause of the four seasons, and is a *vera causa*.

Verb. sap., or **Verb. sat.** The abbreviations of the Lat. *verbum sapienti sat est*, a word to the wise is enough. A hint is sufficient to any intelligent person.

Verbatim et litteratim (Lat.). "Word for word and letter for letter." Accurately rendered.

Verderer. In English forest law (*see under* FOREST COURTS), an official having jurisdiction in the royal forests with especial charge of trees and undergrowth.

Vere adeptus (Lat., one who has truly attained). A title assumed by one admitted to the fraternity of the ROSICRUCIANS.

Verger. The BEADLE in a church who carries the rod or staff, which was formerly called the *verge* (Lat. *virga*, a rod).

Vergil. *See* VIRGIL.

Vermeer Forgery. *See under* FORGERY.

Veronica, St. According to late mediæval legend, a woman of JERUSALEM who handed her head-cloth to Our Lord on His way to CALVARY. He wiped His brow and returned it to the giver when it was found to bear a perfect likeness of the Saviour impressed upon it and was called *Vera-Icon* (true likeness); the woman became St. *Veronica*. It is one of the relics at St. Peter's, ROME. In Spanish bull-fighting the most classic movement with the cape is called the *Veronica*, the cape being swung so slowly before the face of the charging bull that it resembles St. Veronica's wiping of the Holy Face.

Vers de société (Fr., Society verse). Light poetry of a witty or fanciful kind, generally with a slight vein of social satire running through it.

Vers libre. *See* FREE VERSE.

Versailles (vâr sī'). The great palace built by Louis XIV, in the town of that name to the S.W. of Paris. It was begun by Louis XIII, but in 1661 the great enlargement was started that made it the greatest palace in Europe. The gardens were planned by Le Nôtre and the original park contained the Grand Trianon and the Petit Trianon. Its fountains, water-courses, statuary, and shrubberies were all on a grand scale.

It was the scene of many historic occasions including the signing of the armistice between Great Britain and the United States with their French allies in 1783, and the taking of the TENNIS COURT OATH by the States General in 1789. Here, too, in the famous Galerie des Glaces, William I of Prussia was crowned first German Emperor, and the Treaty of Versailles between the Allied Powers and Germany was signed after World War I. *See also* ŒIL-DE-BŒUF.

Versi Berneschi. *See* BERNESQUE.

Vert (vĕrt). The heraldic term (from French) for *green*, said to signify love, joy, and abundance; in engravings it is indicated by lines running diagonally across the shield from right to left.

Vertumnus (vĕr tŭm' nus). The ancient Roman god of the seasons, and the deity presiding over gardens and orchards. He was the husband of POMONA. 12 August was his festival.

Vesica Piscis (ves' i ka pis'is). (Lat., fish-bladder). The ovoidal frame or glory which, in the 12th century, was much used, especially in painted windows, to surround pictures of the Virgin Mary and of Our Lord. It is meant to represent a fish, from the acronym ICHTHUS. *See* ICHTHYS.

Vespers. The sixth of the canonical hours in the Greek and Roman Churches; sometimes also used of the Evening Service in the English Church. From Lat. *vesperus*, the evening, cognate with HE-SPERUS, Gr. *Hesperos*, the evening star.

The Sicilian Vespers. *See* SICILIAN.

Vesta. The virgin goddess of the hearth in Roman mythology, corresponding to the Greek Hestia, one of the 12 great Olympians. She was custodian of the sacred fire brought by ÆNEAS from TROY, which was never permitted to go out lest a national calamity should follow.

Wax matches are named from her.

Vestals. The six spotless virgins who tended the sacred fire brought by ÆNEAS from TROY, and preserved by the state in a sanctuary in the Forum at ROME. They were chosen by lot from maidens between the ages of six and ten and served under strict discipline for 30 years, after which they were free to marry, although few took this step. In the event of their losing their virginity they were buried alive.

The word *vestal* has been figuratively applied by poets to any woman of spotless chastity. SHAKESPEARE bestowed the epithet on Elizabeth I.

A fair vestal enthroned by the west.
A Midsummer Night's Dream, II, i.

Vestiarian Controversy. The name given to the dispute about the wearing of clerical vestments raised by puritan-minded clergy in the reign of Edward VI and again in the reign of Elizabeth I. The simplest vestments such as the surplice and gown were described as the livery of ANTICHRIST. Archbishop Parker sought to enforce conformity by his *Advertisements* of 1566 ordering the wearing of the four-cornered cap, scholar's gown, and surplice, but many refused and deprivations followed. Diversity of practice remained and the controversy became merged with the puritan agitation against EPISCOPACY.

Vestry (Lat. *vestiarium*, robing-room). A room in a church in which the vestments, registers, altar vessels, etc., are kept and used as a robing-room by the clergy. Some larger churches contain a priests' vestry, wardens' vestry, and choir vestry. From the habit of parishioners meeting to conduct parish business in the vestry, both the body of parishioners and the meeting were called the *Vestry*.

Up to 1894 the Vestry was the final authority in all parish matters, civil and ecclesiastical. The parish priest presided over the meeting which elected churchwardens and other parish officers and the property of the parish was usually vested in the churchwardens. The *Common Vestry* consisted of the general assembly of ratepayers and the *Select Vestry* of a body of *vestrymen* elected to represent the parish, the usual procedure in many of the larger parishes. With the passing of the Local Government Act of 1894, secular Parish Councils were elected to take over the civil administrative functions of the rural parishes and in the towns such work was subsequently transferred to Urban Councils. In 1921 ecclesiastical administration passed to the newly created Parochial Church Councils, although the meeting which elects the churchwardens is still called a *Vestry Meeting*.

Veteran. In Britain this word is applied only to soldiers with long experience under arms, but in the U.S.A. it is bestowed upon one who has had any service, however brief, in some field of warfare.

Veto (vē' tō) (Lat., I forbid). Louis XVI and Marie Antoinette were called *Mon-*

sieur and *Madame Veto* by the Republicans, because the CONSTITUENT ASSEMBLY (1791) allowed the king to have the power, which he abused, of putting his veto upon any decree submitted to him.

Vexillum (veks il' ŭm) (Lat., a standard). The standard borne by troops of the Roman army. In particular it was the red flag flown on the general's tent as a signal for marching or for battle.

Via (Lat., a way). Our use of the word, in *I'll go via Chester*, *i.e.* "by way of Chester", is the ablative of *via*.

Sacra Via (Lat., The Holy Street). The street in ancient ROME where ROMULUS and Tatius (the SABINE) swore mutual alliance.

Via Appia. The APPIAN WAY.

Via Dolorosa (Lat., Dolorous way). The route Our Lord went from the place of judgment to CALVARY, now marked by the fourteen STATIONS OF THE CROSS.

Via Flaminia. The FLAMINIAN WAY.

Via Lactea (Lat.). The Milky Way. *See* GALAXY.

Via Media (Lat., The Middle Way). The mean between two extremes. The Elizabethan Church Settlement of the 16th century is often so called, the CHURCH OF ENGLAND being regarded as the mean between extreme Protestantism and Roman Catholicism.

Vial. Vials of wrath. Vengeance, the execution of wrath on the wicked. The allusion is to the seven ANGELS who pour out upon the earth their vials full of wrath (*Rev.* xvi).

Viaticum (Lat.). The EUCHARIST administered to the dying. The word means "provision for a journey", and its application is obvious.

Vicar (Lat. *vicarius*, a substitute). The priest of a parish where the TITHES were appropriated in pre-REFORMATION times, usually to monasteries. The monastery retained the *Rectorial* or great tithes and reserved the small tithes (*Vicarial* tithes) for the incumbent. After the Dissolution such Rectorial tithes were granted to CHAPTERS, COLLEGES, laymen, etc., known as impropriators (*see* IMPROPRIATION), who were under obligation to appoint vicars to carry out the ecclesiastical duties. The title is also given to Perpetual Curates. *Cp.* CLERICAL TITLES.

In the U.S. Episcopal Church a vicar is head of a chapel dependent on a parish church. In the ROMAN CATHOLIC CHURCH he is an ecclesiastic representing a BISHOP.

Lay Vicar. A cathedral officer who sings those portions of the liturgy not reserved for the clergy. Formerly called a *clerk vicar*.

Vicar Apostolic. In the ROMAN CATHOLIC CHURCH, a titular BISHOP appointed to a place where no episcopate has been established, or where the succession has been interrupted. In 1585 the English hierarchy came to an end and until 1594 Catholics came under the jurisdiction of Cardinal Allen, then that of archpriests from 1599 until 1621; but from 1623 until 1850 the Roman Catholic Church in ENGLAND was governed by vicars apostolic. The term formerly denoted a bishop to whom the POPE delegated some part of his jurisdiction.

Vicar Choral. One of the minor clergy, or a layman, attached to a cathedral for singing certain portions of the service.

Vicar Forane. A priest appointed by a Roman Catholic BISHOP to exercise limited (usually disciplinary) jurisdiction in a particular part of his diocese. The office is similar to that of RURAL DEAN (*see under* DEAN). *Forane* is a form of "foreign", hence outlying, rural.

Vicar-General. An ecclesiastical functionary assisting a BISHOP or archbishop in the exercise of his jurisdiction. In 1535 Thomas Cromwell was appointed Vicar-General to carry out Henry VIII's ecclesiastical policies.

The Vicar of Bray. This popular (probably early 18th-century) song depicting a time-serving VICAR of the 17th–18th century is based upon a 16th-century Vicar of Bray, Berkshire, who managed to retain his living during the religious changes of the reigns of Henry VIII, Edward VI, Mary, and Elizabeth.

> And this is the law I will maintain,
> Until my dying day, Sir,
> That whatsoever king shall reign,
> I'll still be the Vicar of Bray, Sir.

The Vicar of Christ. A title given to the POPE, an allusion to his claim to be the representative of Christ on earth.

The Vicar of Hell. A name playfully given by Henry VIII to John Skelton, his "poet laureate", perhaps because Skelton was rector of Diss, in Norfolk, the pun being on *Dis* (PLUTO). Milton refers to the story in his *Areopagitica*:

> I name not him for posterity's sake, whom Henry the Eighth named in merriment his vicar of hell.

Vice. The buffoon in the old English MORALITY PLAYS. He wore a cap with ass's ears, and was generally named after some particular vice, Gluttony, Pride, etc.

Vice versa (vī′ si vĕr′ sà) (Lat. *vicis*, change; *versa*, turned). The reverse; the terms of the case being reversed.

Vichy (vē shē). A town in the Department of Allier, in central France, formerly fashionable on account of its thermal and medicinal springs, *Vichy water* being a considerable export and taken for various forms of indigestion, catarrh, etc.

Vichy acquired a new significance during World War II as the seat of Marshal Pétain's collaborationist government (1940–1944), after the German occupation.

Vicious circle. A chain of circumstances, in which the solving of a problem creates a new problem, which makes the original problem more difficult of solution.

In logic, the fallacy of proving one statement by another which itself rests on the first for proof.

Vicisti, Galilæe. *See* GALILEAN.

Victoria Cross. The premier British award for conspicous bravery in the presence of the enemy, instituted by Queen Victoria in 1856. The ribbon is now claret coloured, but was formerly blue for the Royal Navy and red for the Army. It is a bronze Maltese CROSS with the royal crown surmounted by a LION in its centre under which is a scroll bearing the words "For Valour". It is worn on the left breast and takes precedence over all other decorations. The crosses were made from the metal of guns captured in the Crimean War at Sebastopol

(1855).

Victory Medal (World War I). A bronze medal with a winged figure of Victory on the obverse; awarded in 1919 to all allied service personnel who had served in a theatre of war, also to certain women's formations.

Vidar. In Scandinavian mythology, a son of ODIN, noted for his taciturnity and fearless destruction of FENRIR.

Videlicet (vi del′ i set) (Lat. *videre licet*, it is permitted to see). To wit, that is to say, namely. Abbreviated to VIZ.

Vigilance Committee. A privately formed citizen group taking upon themselves to assist in the maintenance of law and order, etc.; sometimes found in the Southern States of the U.S.A. as a body intimidating Negroes. During the CIVIL WAR (1861–1865) they also strove to suppress the activities of loyalists to the Northern cause. Members of such committees are called *Vigilantes*.

Vigiliæ. *See* MATTINS.

Villain, or **Villein** (Late Lat. *villanus*, a farm-servant, from *villa*, a farm). Originally the unfree peasant of feudal times was called a *villein*. He was bound to the MANOR and owed service to its lord. As the latter's personal chattel, he could be sold or transferred, but he had shares in the village fields. From the time of the BLACK DEATH shortage of labour led to the villein improving his status into that of a copyholder. *Cp.* BORDAR; COTTAR. *See* BOON WORK; WEEK-WORK.

The notion of rascality, wickedness, and worthlessness now associated with *villain* is a result of aristocratic condescension and sense of superiority.

Vim. Slang for energy, force, "go"; usually in the phrase *vim and vigour*. It is the accusative of Lat. *vis*, strength.

Vinalia. Roman wine festivals in honour of JUPITER and also associated with VENUS as a goddess of vineyards. The first such festival was held on 23 APRIL when the wine of the previous season was broached and the second on 19 AUGUST when the VINTAGE began (Lat. *vinalis*, pertaining to wine).

Vinayapitaka. *See* TRIPITAKA.

Vincent, St. A deacon of Saragossa, martyred in *c.* 304 during the persecution under Diocletian. His day is 22 January. He is a patron SAINT of drunkards for no apparent reason; an old rhyme says:

> If on St. Vincent's Day the sky is clear
> More wine than water will crown the year.

Vincentian. A Lazarist or Lazarite, a member of the Congregation of Priests of the Mission founded (1625) by St. Vincent de Paul (c. 1580–1660).

Vine. The Rabbis say that the fiend buried a LION, a LAMB, and a hog at the foot of the first vine planted by NOAH; and that hence men receive from wine ferocity, mildness, or wallowing in the mire.

Vinegar. Livy tells us that when Hannibal led his army over the Alps from Spain into Italy in 218 B.C. he splintered the rocks with fire and vinegar to create a zigzag road for the descent. The vinegar or sour wine may have been used for lack of water.

The Vinegar Bible. See BIBLE, SOME SPECIALLY NAMED EDITIONS.

Vingt-et-un (vant′ ā ŭn′) (Fr., twenty-one). A card game in which the object is to get as near as possible to 21 without exceeding it. The court cards count as ten and the ace as one or 11.

Vinland. The name (Wineland) given to that portion of North America known to the Norsemen and first discovered by Leif Ericsson about A.D. 1000. Its location is uncertain and is generally held to have been in the region of Newfoundland, but its estimated position ranges between Labrador and VIRGINIA. Some account for much of the discrepancy in Scandinavian writings by positing a Vinland I and Vinland II. *Vinland* may well refer to pasture-land, thus obviating the difficulties presented by the association of the name with the vine.

Vinland Map. See under FORGERY.

Vino. In vino veritas (Lat.). In wine is truth, meaning when persons are intoxicated they utter many things they would at other times seek to conceal or disguise.

Violet. A flower usually taken as the type of modesty, but fabled by the ancients to have sprung from the blood of the boaster AJAX.

The colour indicates the love of truth and the truth of love. For ecclesiastical

and symbolical uses, *see* COLOURS.

In the language of FLOWERS the white violet is emblematical of innocence, and the blue violet of faithful love.

The City of the Violet Crown. *See under* CITY.

Corporal Violet. NAPOLEON Bonaparte; because when banished to Elba he told his friends he would return with the violets. "Corporal Violet" became a favourite toast of his partisans, and when he reached Fréjus a gang of women assembled with violets, which were freely sold. The SHIBBOLETH was, "Do you like violets?" If the answer given was "*Oui*," the person was known not to be a confederate; but if the answer was "*Eh bien*", the respondent was recognized as an adherent.

Violin. See AMATI; CREMONA; STRAD; FIDDLE.

Viper. Viper and File. The biter bit. ÆSOP says a viper found a file, and tried to bite it, under the supposition that it was good food; but the file said that its province was to bite others, and not to be bitten.

Virago (vi ra′ gō). Literally, a man-like woman, but a term usually employed to designate a turbulent or scolding shrew.

Viraj. See MANU.

Virgil (vĕr′ jil). The greatest poet of ancient ROME, Publius Virgilius Maro (70–19 B.C.), born near Mantua (hence called *The Mantuan Swan*), a master of epic, didactic, and idyllic poetry. His chief works are the ÆNEID, the *Eclogues* or *Bucolics*, and the *Georgics*. From the *Æneid*, grammarians illustrated their rules and rhetoricians selected the subjects of their declamations; and even Christians looked on the poet as half inspired; hence the use of his poems in DIVINATION. *See* SORTES.

In the MIDDLE AGES Virgil came to be represented as a magician and enchanter, hence Dante's conception in his *Divina Commedia* of making Virgil, as the personification of human wisdom, his guide through the infernal regions.

Virgil was wise, and as craft was considered a part of wisdom, especially over-reaching the spirit of EVIL, so he is represented by mediæval writers as outwitting the demon. Much of this legend grew out of Neapolitan folklore and one story says that he beguiled the DEVIL into a glass bottle and kept him there until he had learned the devil's magic arts. The tale has much in common with that of the *Fisherman and the Genie* in the ARABIAN NIGHTS. Virgil's magical exploits are recounted in numerous mediæval romances and poems and there is an account of Virgil's NECRO-MANCY in the *Gesta Romanorum*.

Virgin. The Virgin Birth. The belief that Christ had no human father and that His miraculous birth did not impair the virginity of his mother, the Blessed Virgin Mary (*see Matt.* i, 18; *Luke* i, 27–35).

The Virgin Queen. Elizabeth I (1558–1603); also called by SHAKESPEARE "the fair Vestal" (*see* VESTALS).

Virginal. A quilled keyboard instrument of the harpsichord family in use in the 16th and early 17th century; often referred to as *a pair of virginals*. It has been suggested that it was so called because it was used in convents to lead the *virginals* or hymns to the Virgin, but its name probably arises from the fact that it was mostly played by girls.

Virginia. The first securely established English colony in North America, founded at Jamestown in 1607. It took its name from the earlier attempt (1584–1587) of Sir Walter Ralegh to found a colony on Roanoke Island (now in North Carolina) which was named after the VIRGIN QUEEN. In the early days of settlement, the name *Virginia* was applied to the whole coast between FLORIDA and NOVA SCOTIA.

Virgo (Lat., Virgin). One of the ancient constellations and the sixth sign of the ZODIAC (23 August–22 September). The constellation is the metamorphosis of ASTRÆA. *See also* ICARIUS.

Virtue. Moral virtue. An ethical virtue as opposed to the *theological* virtues. *See below.*

The Seven Virtues. Faith, Hope, Charity, Justice, Fortitude, Prudence, and Temperance. The first three are called the *supernatural*, *theological* or *Christian* virtues; the remaining four are PLATO's *cardinal* or *natural* virtues. *Cp.* SEVEN DEADLY SINS.

Virtuoso (vĕr tū ō′ zō). An Italian word meaning one who excels; it is applied to those with expert knowledge or appreciation for works of art or *virtu*. It is especially applied to instrumental performers of the highest ability; hence *virtuoso music*, that which demands exceptional skill from the performer.

Vis à vis (vēz′ a vē′) (Fr., face to face). Properly applied to persons facing one another, as in a railway carriage; also an old name for a carriage or coach which enables the occupants to face one another. The phrase is now often used in the sense of "in relation to", "as regards".

Vis inertiæ (vis in ĕr′ shē) (Lat., the power of inactivity). It is a common mistake to imagine that *inertia* means absence of motion; *inertia* is that property of matter which makes it resist any change. Thus it is hard to set in motion what is still, or to stop what is in motion. Figuratively, it applies to that unwillingness to change which makes men rather bear those ills they have than fly to others that they know not of.

Viscount (vī′ kount) (O. Fr. *viconte* from Lat. *vice*, *comes*, the deputy of a count). In Britain, a peer ranking next below an EARL and above a BARON. The title was first granted to John Lord Beaumont in 1440. The CORONET of a Viscount bears 16 pearls set around the rim. He is styled "Right Honourable" and addressed by the Sovereign as "Our right trusty and well-beloved Cousin". *See also* COURTESY TITLES.

Vishnu. The Preserver; the second in the Hindu TRIMURTI, though worshipped by many Hindus as the supreme deity. He originally appears as sun-god. He is beneficent to man and has made numerous incarnations or "descents", ten being the number most generally reckoned. (*See* AVATAR). He is usually represented as four-armed and carrying a mace, a conch-shell, a disc, and a LOTUS, and often riding the EAGLE Garuda. His wife is LAKSHMI, born from the sea.

Vision of Piers Plowman, The. A long allegorical poem in Middle English alliterative verse, written by William Langland (*c.* 1332–*c.* 1400), who was born probably in the West Midlands. The poet's dream or vision gives a vivid insight into 14th-century conditions and the current social and religious evils. Properly, *The Vision of William concerning Piers the Plowman*; in the earlier part Piers typifies the simple, pious English labourer, and in the latter, Christ Himself. Piers is the subject, not the author of the poem. There are several texts.

Visitation, The, or **The Visitation of Our Lady.** The Blessed Virgin's visit to her cousin St. Elisabeth before the birth of St. JOHN THE BAPTIST (*Luke* I, 39–56). It is celebrated on 2 July.

The Order of the Visitation, or **Visitandines.** A contemplative Order for women founded by St. Francis de Sales and St. Jane Frances de Chantal in 1610. They adopted a modification of the AUGUSTINIAN Rule and their chief work is now concerned with education.

Vital Statistics. Properly, population statistics concerned with births, marriages, deaths, divorces, etc. (Lat. *vita*, life). It is now applied humorously to a woman's bust, waist, and hip measurements.

Vitus, St. (vī′ tús). A Sicilian youth who was martyred with Modestus, his tutor, and Crescentia, his nurse, during the Diocletian persecution, *c*. 303.

St. Vitus's Dance. In Germany in the 17th century it was believed that good health for the year could be secured by anyone who danced before a statue of St. VITUS on his feast-day; such dancing to excess is said to have come to be confused with chorea, hence its name, *St. Vitus's Dance*, the SAINT being invoked against it.

Viva! (vī′ và, vē′ và). An exclamation of applause or joy; Italian, meaning (long) live. A VIVA VOCE examination is usually called a "*viva*".

Viva voce (Lat., with the living voice). Orally; by word of mouth. A *viva voce* examination is one in which the respondent gives spoken answers.

Vivat regina, or **rex!** (Lat.). Long live the Queen, or King! At the coronation of British sovereigns the boys of Westminster School have the privilege of acclaiming the King or Queen with shouts of "*Vivat Rex*, or *Regina!*".

Vivien. An enchantress of ARTHURIAN ROMANCE, the LADY OF THE LAKE.

Vixen (O.E. *fyxen*). A female fox. Metaphorically, a shrewish woman, one of villainous and ungovernable temper.

Vixere fortes ante Agamemnona. *See under* AGAMEMNON.

Viz. A contraction of VIDELICET. The *z* represents 3, a common mark of contraction in writing in the MIDDLE AGES; as oṁib 3—*omnibus*.

Vizier (vi zēr′, viz′ i ĕr) (Arab. *wazir*, bearer of the burden). A name given to the chief minister of the ABBASSIDE caliphs and to officials serving other MOSLEM rulers. The title was also formerly given to Turkish ministers and governors; the chief minister (until 1878) was called the *Grand Vizier*.

Vogue. Vogue la galère (Fr., lit., row the galley). Let the world go how it will; let us keep on, whatever happens; *advienne que pourra*.

Volapük (vol′ à pūk). An artificial language invented in 1879 by a German pastor, J. M. Schleyer. It was based on European languages, about one-third from English, and the remainder from Latin, German, and the ROMANCE LANGUAGES. The words were cut down so that no original is recognizable: *Volapük* is supposed to be *Vol*, from "English" *world*; *pük*, from "English" *speech*. After about ten years its place was taken by ESPERANTO. *See also* INTERLINGUA.

Voltaire. The assumed name of François Marie Arouet (1694–1778), the great French philosopher, poet, dramatist, and author. He began to use the name on his release from imprisonment in the Bastille in 1718. It is probably an anagram of Arouet l(e) j(eune). *See* CANDIDE.

Volte-face (volt′ fas) (Fr., a turning of the head, a turn-about). Used of a complete about-face or change of front in argument, opinions, views, etc.

Volund. *See* WAYLAND.

Voluntary Schools. The name for schools established by the Voluntary Societies such as the NATIONAL SOCIETY and the British and Foreign Schools Society, religious bodies, etc., as opposed to those established by local public authorities which were formerly called *council schools*, and until 1902, BOARD SCHOOLS. All primary and secondary schools maintained by a local education authority are still classified as county or voluntary schools according to their origins, although the voluntary principle in education has largely been submerged.

Voodoo, or **Voodooism.** A mixture of superstition, magic, WITCHCRAFT, serpent-worship, etc., derived from African rites and some Christian beliefs. It still survives among some Negro groups in Haiti, and other parts of the West Indies and the Americas.

The name is said to have been first given to it by missionaries, from Fr. *Vaudois*, a WALDENSIAN, as these were accused of sorcery; but Sir Richard Burton derived it from *vodun*, a dialect form of Ashanti *obosum*, a fetish or tutelary spirit. *Cp.* OBEAH.

Vorticism. An artistic movement which began in England in 1914, somewhat akin to CUBISM and FUTURISM and embracing art and literature. It was iconoclastic and regarded the question of representation as irrelevant; its designs are in straight lines and angular patterns. Concern with machinery was also a feature. Among its representatives, P. Wyndham Lewis and Edward Wadsworth were the most notable. The name was bestowed by Ezra Pound. *Cp.* DADAISM; FAUVISM; IMPRESSIONISM; ORPHISM; SURREALISM; SYNCHRONISM.

Votive offerings. *See* ANATHEMA.

Vox. Vox et præterea nihil (Lat., a voice, and nothing more). Empty words—"full of sound and fury, signifying nothing"; a threat not followed out. When the Lacedæmonian plucked the nightingale, on seeing so little substance he exclaimed, *Vox tu es, et nihil præterea* (Plutarch, *Apophthegmata Laconica*).

Vox populi vox Dei (Lat., the voice of the people is the voice of God). This does not mean that the voice of the

many is wise and good, but only that it is irresistible. After Edward II had been dethroned by the people in favour of his son (Edward III), Walter Reynolds (d. 1327), Archbishop of Canterbury, preached at the coronation of Edward III with these words as his text.

Vulcan. A son of JUPITER and JUNO, and GOD of fire, and the working of METALS, and patron of handicraftsmen in metals, identified with the Gr. Hephæstus, and called also MULCIBER, *i.e.* the softener.

His workshops were under Mount ETNA and other volcanoes where the CYCLOPS assisted him in forging thunderbolts for JOVE. It is said that he took the part of Juno against Jupiter who hurled him out of HEAVEN. He was nine days in falling and was saved by the people of Lemnos from crashing to earth, but one leg was broken, hence his lameness. VENUS was his wife and, in consequence of her amour with MARS, he came to be regarded as the special patron of CUCKOLDS. He was the father of CUPID and the Cecrops, and created PANDORA from clay.

Vulcanist. One who supports the Vulcanian or Plutonian theory, which ascribes the changes on the Earth's surface to the agency of fire. These theorists say the earth was once in a state of igneous fusion, and that the crust has gradually cooled down to its present temperature.

Vulgate, The. The Latin translation of the Bible, made about 384–404 by St. JEROME, originally to establish a standard text. The first printed edition was the MAZARIN BIBLE (1456) (*see* BIBLE, SOME SPECIALLY NAMED EDITIONS). A revised edition was issued by Clement VIII in 1592 and a new edition was commissioned by Pius X in 1908. *Genesis* was published in 1926 and the work is still in progress. The name is the Lat. *editio vulgata*, the common edition sanctioned by the ROMAN CATHOLIC CHURCH.

W

W. The twenty-third letter of the English alphabet. The form is simply a ligature of two Vs (VV); hence the name; for V was formerly the symbol of U (*q.v.*) as well as of V.

Waac (wăk). The familiar name of a member of the Women's Army Auxiliary Corps, a body of women raised for non-combatant army service in World War I. In World War II they were termed A.T.S., Auxiliary Territorial Service. This became the W.R.A.C. (Women's Royal Army Corps) in 1949.

Waaf (wăf). The familiar name of a member of the Women's Auxiliary Air Force, or the force itself, which was established in 1939. It became the W.R.A.F. (Women's Royal Air Force) in 1949. There was an earlier W.R.A.F. in World War I.

W.A.C. (U.S.A.). In World War II the Women's Army Corps, equivalent to the British A.T.S. *Cp.* WAVES.

W.V.S. The Women's Voluntary Service set up in 1938, primarily to help with air raid precautions. It became the W.R.V.S. (Women's Royal Voluntary Service) in 1949. It continues to do valuable social and welfare work with the aged and infirm and gives help in emergencies. It is particularly noted for its "Meals on Wheels" service.

Wad. A roll of paper money, and hence the money itself.

Wade. General Wade. The old rhyme:

> Had you seen but these roads before they were made,
> You would hold up your hands and bless General Wade,

refers to Field-Marshal George Wade (1673–1748), famous for his construction of military roads in the HIGHLANDS (c. 1724–1730) as a precaution against JACOBITE insurrection.

Wafer. Ecclesiastically a thin disc of unleavened bread used in the EUCHARIST.

Before the device of gummed envelope flaps was introduced, thin round discs of dried paste or gelatine were inserted between the flap and the envelope—or earlier still, between the outer sides of the folded letter—and having been moistened and pressed with a seal served the same purpose of keeping the paper closed.

Wag. Meaning a humorous person, one given to jest, is the O.E. *wagge*, probably from the facetious use of *waghalter*, a droll, a rascal—one who wags or shakes a halter.

To hop, or **play the wag.** To play truant—probably some allusion to *waghalter* (*see* WAG *above*).

Wager (wā′ jĕr). Anything staked or hazarded on the event of a contest, etc. Connected with *gage* and *wage* (Low Lat. *wadiare*, to pledge).

Wager of battle. *see* ORDEAL OF BATTLE.

Wagoner. *See* BOÖTES.

Wahabis, or **Wahabites.** Adherents of a MOSLEM movement seeking to purify ISLAM and restore it to its primitive simplicity; so called from the founder Ibn-abd-ul-Wahab who began his activities about 1760. The sect centres upon Saudi Arabia.

Wailing Wall. The length of high stone wall at Jerusalem, said to be a relic of the TEMPLE OF HEROD which was destroyed in A.D. 70. After the Jews returned, it eventually became a tradition to gather there every FRIDAY for prayer and lamentations for the Dispersion and lost glories of Israel.

Wait. Wait and See. A phrase often humorously used with reference to H. H. Asquith (Earl of Oxford and Asquith), thus "What did Asquith say?" is another way of saying "Wait and see." Asquith used the phrase in answer to a question in the HOUSE OF COMMONS, 4 April 1910, and took to repeating it—subsequently when faced with an awkward question.

Lords in Waiting, Gentlemen in Waiting, Grooms in Waiting, etc., are functionaries in the Royal HOUSEHOLD for personal attendance upon the sovereign.

Ladies in Waiting (in the Queen's Household) are officially styled *Ladies of the Bedchamber, Bedchamber Women*, and MAIDS OF HONOUR.

Waits. A name now given to parties of singers and musicians who perform outside people's houses at CHRISTMAS-time. They derive their name from those watchmen of former times called *waits* who sounded a horn or played a tune to mark the passing hours. Waits were employed at the royal court "to pipe the watch" and also by town corporations.

Waits duly came to provide a uniformed band for their town for civic occasions, and played to the public at Christmas-time, hence the current usage. The hautboy was also called a *wayte* or *wait*, from its being their chief instrument.

Waitangi Day. 6th February; since 1960 celebrated as NEW ZEALAND's national day. It is a public holiday and commemorates the day on which the Treaty of Waitangi was made in 1840 by the British governor, William Hobson, with the Maori chiefs. They recognised British sovereignty in return for the tribes being guaranteed possession of their lands.

Wake. A watch or vigil. The name was early applied to the all-night watch kept in church before certain holy days and to the festival kept at the annual commemoration of the dedication of a church. In due course the festive element predominated and the name came to be associated with annual FAIRS and revelries held at such times. Some towns in the North country still observe local holidays called *wakes*.

In IRELAND, the term denotes the

watching of the body of the deceased before the funeral, and the feasting which follows, a custom formerly also common in WALES and SCOTLAND.

Waking a witch. If a witch were obdurate, the most effectual way of obtaining a confession was by what was termed *waking* her. An iron bridle or hoop was bound across her face with prongs thrust into her mouth; this was fastened to the wall by a chain in such a manner that the victim was unable to lie down; and men were constantly by to keep her awake, sometimes for several days. *See* WITCHCRAFT.

Waldensians, or **Waldenses** (wol-den'siȧnz, wol den' sēz). Also known by their French name as the *Vaudois*. Followers of Peter Waldo of Lyons who sought to govern their life by the teaching of the GOSPELS and who came to be known as the "Poor Men of Lyons". The movement began about 1170 and papal prohibition of their preaching culminated in Waldo's EXCOMMUNICATION. Various heretical teachings followed and papal authority was completely rejected. Active persecution scattered them to other parts of France, Italy, and Spain, etc., and it continued till the late 17th century.

Their doctrinal descendants still exist, principally in the Alpine Valleys of Piedmont.

Wales. From O.E. *Wealas*, plural of *wealh*, foreigner, applied to the Britons by the Anglo-Saxons. The WELSH name for their own land is CYMRU (kŭm' rē).

The Prince of Wales. When Edward I extinguished WELSH independence (1282– 1283) he is popularly said to have presented WALES with a new prince in the form of his son Edward who was born at Caernarvon (1284). In fact Edward was created Prince of Wales in 1301. The last native prince, Llywelyn ap Gruffydd, was killed at Builth in 1282.

Since 1337 the king's or queen's eldest son has been born Duke of Cornwall and the title Prince of Wales has been conferred upon him subsequently.

The Prince of Wales's feathers. *See* ICH DIEN.

Walhalla. *See* VALHALLA.

Walk

Walk. Cock of the Walk. *See under* COCK.

To make a man walk Spanish. *See under* SPANISH.

To walk into. To attack vigorously, to thrash; also to eat heartily of, as, "He walked into the apple tart." *To wade into* has similar meanings. *To walk into a trap*, either verbal or physical, is to be caught unsuspectingly.

To walk off with. To filch and decamp with.

To walk out with. To court, as a preliminary to marriage.

To walk tall. To hold one's head high, to maintain one's proper sense of pride and self-respect.

To walk the chalk. An old-established method of testing sobriety by making the suspected inebriate walk between two parallel lines chalked on the floor without stepping on either line. Hence, figuratively, to keep on the straight and narrow path of rectitude.

To walk the hospitals. To attend the hospitals as a medical student; from the practice of accompanying the hospital doctors when visiting patients in the wards.

To walk the plank. *See under* PLANK.

To walk through one's part. To repeat one's part at rehearsal verbally, but without dressing for it or acting it; to do anything appointed you in a listless, indifferent manner.

Walk not in the public ways. The fifth symbol of the *Protreptics* of Iamblichus, meaning, follow not the multitude in their EVIL ways; or, wide is the path of sin and narrow the path of virtue, few being those who find it.

> Broad is the way that leadeth to destruction.
>
> *Matt.* vii, 13.

A walk-out. To down tools and go on strike.

A walk-over. Properly, an uncontested race, won by the only competitor perambulating the course; hence applied to a very easy victory with little serious competition.

To go by Walker's bus. To walk. Similar expressions are, "To go by the MARROWBONE stage", "To ride SHANKS'S MARE or pony".

Walkie-Talkie. A small portable short-range wireless containing receiver and transmitter as used by the fighting services, the police, etc.

A walking-on part. A part in a play in which the actor has only to walk about on the stage, sometimes with a word or two to say.

Wall. The Roman Wall. *See* ANTONINE'S WALL; GRAHAME'S DYKE; HADRIAN'S WALL; SEVERUS.

Wall Street. The street in New York City which contains the STOCK EXCHANGE and offices of major banking and insurance concerns etc. It is the financial centre of the U.S.A., hence the name is a synonym for the American Stock market and "big business" generally. The street is on the site of a *wall* or palisade built in 1652 by the Dutch against a possible English attack.

To drive someone up the wall. *See under* DRIVE.

To drive to the wall. *See under* DRIVE.

To give the wall. To allow another, as a matter of courtesy, to pass by on the pavement at the side furthest from the gutter; hence, to be courteous. At one time pedestrians *gave the wall* to persons of a higher rank than themselves. Nathaniel Bailey says (1721) it is:

> a compliment paid to the female sex, or those to whom one would show respect, by letting them go nearest the wall or houses, upon a supposition of its being the cleanest. This custom is chiefly peculiar to England, for in most parts abroad they will give them the right hand, though at the same time they thrust them into the kennel.

Cp. TO TAKE THE WALL, *below*.

To go to the wall. To be put on one side; to be shelved. This is in allusion to another phrase, **laid by the wall**, *i.e.* dead but not buried; put out of the way.

To hang by the wall. To hang up neglected; not to be made use of.

To run one's head against a brick or stone wall. *See under* HEAD.

To take the wall. To take the place of honour.

> I will take the wall of any man or maid of Montague's
>
> . SHAKESPEARE: *Romeo and Juliet*, I, i.

Cp. TO GIVE THE WALL, *above*.

The weakest go to the wall. The saying is explained by Halliwell as deriving from the placing of beds along the side of the room and putting the youngest or feeblest in the safest place—*i.e.* against the wall. Another explanation is that, in the days when few churches had pews, except maybe for the gentry, there were benches along the walls for the aged. Pews were not installed generally until the late 17th century and subsequently.

The Writing on the wall. *See under* WRITE.

Walls have ears. Things uttered in secret get rumoured abroad; there are listeners everywhere, and you'd better be careful. Certain rooms in the LOUVRE were said to be so constructed in the time of Catherine de' MEDICI, that what was said in one room could be heard distinctly in another. It was by this contrivance that the suspicious queen became acquainted with state secrets and plots. The tubes of communication were called the *auriculaires*. *Cp.* DIONYSIUS'S EAR *under* EAR.

Wall-eyed. The M.E. *wald-eyed*, a corruption of Icel. *vald eygthr*, having a beam in the eye (*vagl*, beam). Persons are wall-eyed when the white is unusually large, and the sight defective, due to opacity of the cornea, or when they have a divergent squint.

Wallflower. So called because it grows on old walls, etc. Similarly *wall-cress*, *wall creeper*, etc., are plants which grow on dry, stony places, or on walls. *Wall fruit* is fruit trained against a wall. *Cp.* WALNUT.

Girls who sit along the wall without partners during a dance are called wallflowers.

Wallace, Sir William (*c.* 1274–1305). The Scottish hero who won a great victory over the English at Stirling Bridge in 1297 but was eventually hanged, disembowelled, beheaded and quartered at West SMITHFIELD.

Wallace's Larder. *See under* LARDER.

Wallah (wol' à). Anglo-Indian for a man of specified attributes or duties, as *dhobi-wallah*, the Indian washerman; *bathroom-wallah*, the man who looks after the bathrooms in an hotel; *punka-wallah*, the man who waves a fan, etc. A *Competition wallah* was the old nick-

name for a successful competitor in the Indian Civil Service examinations introduced in 1856, in contrast to those who obtained their appointments under the old system of influence. *Wallah* is a Hindu suffix denoting an agent, as *-er* in English.

Walnut. The foreign nut; called in M.E. *walnote*, from O.E. *wealh*, foreign, since it came from Persia.

> Some difficulty there is in cracking the name thereof. Why walnuts, having no affinity to a wall, should be so called. The truth is, *gual* or *wall*, in the old Dutch signifieth "strange" or "exotic" (whence *Welsh* foreigners); these nuts being no natives of England or Europe.
> FULLER: *Worthies of England*.

It is said that the walnut tree thrives best if the nuts are beaten off with sticks, and not picked. There is an old saying that:

> A woman, a dog, and a walnut tree,
> The more you beat them the better they be.

Walpurgis Night (wol pēr' gis). The eve of MAY DAY, when the witch-world was supposed to hold high revelry under its chief, the DEVIL, on certain high places, particularly the Brocken, the highest point of the Harz Mountains. Walpurgis was an English nun who went as a missionary to Germany and became abbess of Heidenheim (d. *c.* 788). Her day is 1 May, hence her coincidental association with the rites of an earlier pagan festival.

Walpurgis oil. A bituminous kind of oil exuding from the rock at Eichstatt in which the relics of St. Walpurgis were deposited. It was supposed to have miraculous healing and curative properties.

Walstan, St. In ENGLAND, the patron SAINT of husbandmen. He worked as a farm labourer in Norfolk and was noted for the austerity and piety of his life and for his charity. He died in 1016 and is usually depicted with a scythe in his hand and cattle in the background.

Waltham Blacks. *See* BLACK ACT.

Waltzing Matilda. An Australian phrase made famous by the Australian poet A. B. (Banjo) Paterson (1864–1941). It means carrying or humping one's bag or pack as a tramp does. Henry Lawson (*The Romance of Song*) says, "Travelling with SWAG in Australia is variously and picturesquely described as 'humping bluey', 'walking Matilda', 'humping Matilda', 'humping your drum', 'being on the wallaby' ..."

The reason for the tramp's roll being called a "Matilda" is obscure; to *waltz* conveys the impression of tramping along with one's pack jogging up and down with one's steps. *See* BILLABONG.

> Once a jolly swagman camped by a bill-
> abong
> Under the shade of a coolibah tree,
> And he sang as he watched and waited
> till his billy boiled,
> "You'll come a-waltzing Matilda with
> me."

Wampum (wom' pům). Shell beads made and strung for ornament, currency, ceremonial gift belts, etc., by North American Indian tribes. They were used as money as late as the 19th century, but machine-made mass-produced "wampum" with resultant inflation first caused its obsolescence in the eastern states. The name comes from the Algonkian *wompi*, white.

> When he came in triumph homeward
> With the sacred Belt of Wampum.
> LONGFELLOW: *The Song of Hiawatha*,
> II.

Wandering Jew, The. The central figure of the widespread later-mediæval legend which tells of a JEW who insulted or spurned Christ when He was bearing the cross to CALVARY, and was condemned to wander over the face of the earth till JUDGMENT Day.

The usual form of the legend says that he was AHASUERUS, a cobbler, who refused to allow Christ to rest at his door, saying, "Get off! Away with you, away!" Our Lord replied, "Truly I go away, and that quickly, but tarry thou till I come."

An earlier tradition has it that the Wandering Jew was Cartaphilus, the doorkeeper of the judgment hall in the service of Pontius Pilate. He struck our Lord as he led Him forth, saying, "Go on faster, Jesus"; whereupon the MAN OF SORROWS replied, "I am going, but thou shalt tarry till I come again." (*Chronicle of St. Alban's Abbey*, 1228). The same Chronicle, continued by Matthew Paris, tells us that Cartaphilus was baptized by Ananias, and received the name of Joseph. At the end of every hundred years he falls into a trance, and wakes up a young man about 30.

In German legend he is associated with John Buttadæus, seen at Antwerp in the 13th century, again in the 15th, and the third time in the 16th. His last appearance was in 1774 at Brussels. In the French version he is named Isaac Laquedom or Lakedion; another story has it that he was Salathiel ben-Sadi, who appeared and disappeared towards the close of the 16th century at Venice, in so sudden a manner as to attract the notice of all Europe; and another connects him with the WILD HUNTSMAN.

Wansdyke. Woden's dyke. A system of dykes, perhaps built by the Romano-Britons, stretching some 60 miles from Inkpen in Berkshire to Maesbury in Somerset. It was probably a defence against the English invaders. *See* GRAHAME'S DYKE; GRIM'S DITCH; OFFA'S DYKE.

Wantley, The Dragon of. An old story, preserved in PERCY'S RELIQUES, tells of this monster who was slain by More of More Hall. He procured a suit of armour studded with spikes, and kicked the DRAGON in the backside, where alone it was vulnerable. Percy says the Dragon stands for a greedy renter of the TITHES of the Wortley family who attempted to take the tithes in kind from the parishioners and More was the man who conducted the suit against him. There are other theories. Wantley is Wharncliffe in Yorkshire.

Wapenshaw, Wappenshaw, or **Wapinshaw,** etc. A weapon show, the early spelling being *Wappinschaw*. Formerly the Scottish term for the review of men under ARMS to check that they were properly equipped according to rank. It is now used of a rifle-shooting competition.

Wapentake (wop' en tāk). A subdivision of a county similar to a HUNDRED, found in Yorkshire and other areas of once strong Danish influence—Derbyshire, Leicestershire, Lincolnshire, Nottinghamshire and the former county of Rutland. The word is of Scandinavian origin meaning "a taking" or "grasping of weapons" signifying the clash of ARMS made by an assembly to signify assent.

War. Civil War. *See under* CIVIL.

Cold War. *See under* COLD.

A Holy war. Properly a war undertaken from religious motives, such as the CRUSADES. As such wars were fiercely and often bitterly contested the expression is often colloquially applied to relentless crusades of various kinds.

Hundred Years War. *See* HUNDRED.

Thirty Years War. *See under* THIRTY.

The War of the Brown Bull. Also known as the "Cattle raid of Cooley" or "Cuailnge". In Irish legend, the struggle provoked by Queen MAEVE (Medb) of Connaught who led the forces of four provinces to capture the great bull, the Brown One of Cuailnge belonging to an ULSTER chief. Her husband Ailill had a great white bull called Finnbennach and she wished to equal his possessions. The Brown Bull was taken by strategem but Maeve's forces were driven into retreat by CUCHULAIN and the men of Ulster. The Brown One fought the White Bull all over IRELAND until the latter was slain, and the Brown Bull then rushed northwards until its heart burst.

The Wars of the Roses. *See under* ROSE.

War baby. A baby born in wartime; especially the illegitimate offspring of a serviceman.

War game. Originally known by its German name *Kriegsspiel*, it was introduced by a Prussian officer, Lieutenant von Reiswitz, in 1824, who completed and improved upon his father's design. It depends upon the use of maps as battlefields in miniature and blocks or counters representing troops, etc., for the purpose of instructing officers in military tactics. In modern times the computer is used to this end.

War-hawk (U.S.A.). One who is eager for war. *See* HAWKS AND DOVES.

War-head. The explosive head of a torpedo or bomb.

War-horse. A veteran or old warrier; a "FIRE-EATER". An allusion to the charger formerly used in battle.

War-paint. The paint applied to their faces by RED INDIANS and other peoples to make their appearance terrifying before going out ON THE WARPATH. Putting on one's war paint is a phrase applied figuratively to getting ready to enter energetically into a dispute or, of a woman, to putting on lipstick, powder, etc., in order to overcome her rivals.

On the warpath. Thoroughly roused and incensed; looking for one's adversary or victim with every intention of exacting retribution.

War of nerves. Planned measures to undermine morale by threats, rumours, SABOTAGE, etc.

Ward (O.E. *weard*, keeping watch, guard, etc.). A district under the charge of a warden. The word is applied to subdivisions of Cumberland, Westmorland, and Durham, also in some counties of SCOTLAND. In mediæval times, the Wardens were appointed by the English and Scottish governments to watch over the border districts.

The word is also applied to administrative divisions of a town or city, a large room or division of a hospital; a part of a lock or of a key which prevents the door being opened by the wrong key; a minor placed under the care of a guardian, etc. *See* WATCH AND WARD.

Wardour Street English. The affected use of archaic words and phrases. A term first applied by William Morris in 1888 to a translation of the ODYSSEY, couched in language which reminded him of the pseudo-antique furniture that in those days was sold in Wardour Street, LONDON.

Warlock. An evil spirit; a WIZARD. O.E. *wærloga*, a traitor, one who breaks his word.

Warm. A house-warming. An entertainment given by new occupiers of a house; a first welcoming of friends to a fresh residence.

Warming the bell. *See under* BELL.

Warming-pan. One who holds a place temporarily for another; sometimes applied to a clergyman who officiates while the actual holder of the living is qualifying. In public schools it used to be the custom to make a FAG warm his "superior's" bed by lying in it till the proper occupant was ready to turn him out.

The Warming-pan baby. The Old PRETENDER, because of the widely circulated story that he was introduced into the lying-in chamber of Mary of Modena, queen of James II, in a warming-pan, and that her own child was still-born. Hence **warming-pans** as a nick-name for JACOBITES.

Warrior Queen, The. BOADICEA.

Wart. Warts and all. Said of a description, biography, etc., which seeks to give the rounded portrait, including the blemishes and defects. Oliver Cromwell, whose face was not without blemishes, when having his portrait painted by Lely, apparently told him to "Remark all these roughnesses, pimples, warts, and everything as you see me".

Warwick the King-maker. *See* KING-MAKER *under* KING.

Wash. It will all come out in the wash. Everything will turn out all right in the end, as dirt and stains, etc., are removed by washing.

It's got lost in the wash. It has just disappeared in the welter of things, in the proceedings, etc., as items get lost in the laundry. The expression is also sometimes punningly used with reference to King John's loss of royal treasure and baggage when his convoy of horses and waggons was caught and swallowed up by the incoming tide on the sands of the Wash in 1216.

That (story) won't wash. That story or excuse won't do at all; you'll have to think of a better tale than that! Said of an explanation or excuse that is palpably false, far-fetched, or exaggerated.

To take in one another's washing. To do each other reciprocal favours; to help each other out.

To wash one's dirty linen in public. To expose the family SKELETON to the public gaze; openly to discuss private affairs that are more or less discreditable.

To wash one's hands of a thing. *See under* HAND.

Washed out. Exhausted, done up, with no strength or spirit left. **Washed up** has similar implications.

Head-washing. An old provincialism for drinking a new infant's health. *To wet the baby's head* is a colloquialism for the same thing.

A wash-out. A fiasco, a failure. As an imperative verb, it means cancel, disregard, from the times when naval signal messages were taken down on a slate which was washed clean when the message had been transmitted to the proper quarters.

Wassail (O.E. *wæs hael*, be whole, be well). A salutation, especially over the spiced ale cup at the New Year, hence called the "wassail bowl". *See also* HEALTH.

Strutt (*Sports and Pastimes of the People of England*, III, iv) says: "Wassail, or rather the wassail bowl, which was a bowl of spiced ale, formerly carried about by young women on New-year's eve, who went from door to door in their several parishes singing a few couplets of homely verses composed for the purpose, and presented the liquor to the inhabitants of the house where they called, expecting a small gratuity in return ..."

> The King doth wake tonight and takes his rouse, keeps wassail.
> SHAKESPEARE: *Hamlet*, I, iv.

Hence *Wassailers*, those who join a wassail; revellers, drunkards.

Wat. An old name for a hare, short for *Walter*.

Watch. In nautical usage, the time during which part of a ship's complement is on duty; usually four hours except during the DOG WATCHES of two hours each, by which the variation in the watches kept by any individual is effected. Ship's companies are arranged in two watches, port and starboard, each of which is usually subdivided thus providing four groups for normal watch-keeping duties.

Historically, *the Watch* refers to the body of men in towns who patrolled the streets at night before the introduction of police forces, which, in the boroughs, were under the control of the Watch Committee until their amalgamation with the County Police in 1967. *See also* COCK-CROW; WAKE; WATCH AND WARD.

The Black Watch. *See under* BLACK.

Neighbourhood Watch. As a result of increasing crime, especially burglary, residents in particular areas began organising *Neighbourhood Watch* groups from the early 1980s with police co-operation. Suspicious activities and circumstances are reported to the police and some worthwhile impact on burglary has resulted. The idea was copied from similar schemes in the U.S.A.

Watch Night. 31 December, to see the Old Year out and the New Year in by a religious service. John Wesley introduced it among the METHODISTS and it has been adopted by other Christian denominations.

The Watch on the Rhine (*Die Wacht am Rhein*). A German national song which achieved a place of honour with *Deutschland über Alles* (Germany over all) in the former German Empire. It was written by Max Schneckenburger in 1840 at a time when French policies were suspect.

Watch and Ward. Continuous vigilance; *watch* and *ward* being the terms formerly used to denote guard by *night* and by *day* respectively. Townships were made responsible for appointing watchmen in the 13th century. *See* WATCH.

Watchword. A word given to sentries as a signal that one has the right of admission, a password; hence, a motto, word, or phrase symbolizing or epitomizing the principles of a party, etc. *Cp.* SHIBBOLETH.

Water. The Water of Jealousy. If a woman was known to have committed adultery she was to be put to death, according to the Mosaic law (*Deut.* xxii, 22). If, however, the husband had no proof, but only suspected his wife of infidelity, he might take her before the SANHEDRIN to be examined, and "bitter water" was prepared from holy water and the dust of the floor of the tabernacle. The priest then said to the woman, "If thou hast not gone aside to uncleanness with another instead of thy husband, be thou free from this bitter water that causeth the curse." If she had "gone aside" the priest wrote the curses on a roll, sprinkled it with water, and gave the woman the "water of jealousy" to drink (*Numb.* v, 11–29).

The Father of the Waters. The Mississippi, the chief river of North America. The Missouri is its child. The Irrawaddy (in Burma) is also thus named.

Territorial Waters. *See* THREE-MILE LIMIT.

Blood is thicker than water. *See under* BLOOD.

I am for all waters (SHAKESPEARE, *Twelfth Night*, IV, ii). I am a JACK OF ALL TRADES, can turn my hand to anything. Like a fish which can live in salt or fresh water.

In deep water. In difficulties; in great perplexity; similarly, *in smooth water* means all is PLAIN SAILING, one's troubles and anxieties are things of the past.

In low water. *See under* LOW.

It makes my mouth water. It is very alluring; it makes me long for it. Saliva is excited in the mouth by appetizing food.

More water glideth by the mill than wots the miller. The Scots say, "Mickle water goes by the miller when he sleeps". *See under* MILLER.

Of the first water. Of the highest type, superlative. *See* DIAMOND OF THE FIRST WATER *under* DIAMOND.

Smooth, or still waters run deep. Deep thinkers are persons of few words; he (or she) thinks a good deal more than is suspected; silent conspirators are the most dangerous; BARKING DOGS SELDOM BITE. A calm exterior is far more to be feared than a tongue-doughty BOBADIL.

That won't hold water. That is not correct; it is not tenable. It is a vessel which leaks. *Cp.* THAT WON'T WASH *under* WASH.

To back water. To row backwards in order to reverse or stay a boat's motion; hence, to go easy, to retrace one's steps, to retreat.

To carry water to the river. To carry coals to Newcastle. *See under* COAL.

To fish in troubled waters. *See under* FISH.

To get into hot water. *See under* HOT.

To keep one's head above water. *See under* HEAD.

To pour oil on troubled waters. *See under* OIL.

To take the waters. To visit a spa for health reasons, a common routine among fashionable folk in the 18th and 19th centuries.

To throw cold water on a scheme. To discourage the proposal; to dwell upon its weaknesses and disadvantages;

to speak slightingly of it.

To tread water. In swimming, to keep the body erect moving the hands and feet up and down, thus keeping one's head above water.

To turn on the waterworks. To cry, to blubber.

Water-gall. The dark rim round the eyes after much weeping; a peculiar appearance in a rainbow which indicates more rain at hand.

Watergate. In the U.S.A. an area of flats and offices, etc. beside the river Potomac, Washington, which gave its name to a major political scandal. An illegal bugging attempt was made by Republicans at the Watergate headquarters of the Democratic Party during the 1972 elections followed by attempts to cover-up the affair. The subsequent resignation and prosecution of senior WHITE HOUSE officials and further evidence of corruption eventually led to the resignation of the Republican President Richard Nixon when threatened with impeachment.

Water-sky. The term used by Arctic navigators to denote a dark or brown sky, indicating an open sea. An ice-sky is a white one, or a sky tinted with orange or rose-colour, indicative of a frozen sea (*cp*. ICE-BLINK).

Water-witch. Another name for a dowser (*see* DOWSE).

Waterman. A boatman, especially one who rows a boat for hire. The Thames watermen were a feature of old LONDON. *See* DOGGET.

Hackney-coach stands and cab ranks were each supplied with a licensed waterman whose duty it was to water the cab-horses, etc.

Watermark. A design impressed into paper by fine wire during manufacture and while the paper is still wet. Watermarks were used as early as 1282 and served to identify the products of each paper mill.

Waterloo. He met his Waterloo. He came up against it; he suffered a crushing defeat; an allusion to the final defeat of NAPOLEON by WELLINGTON and Blücher (*see* FORWARDS, MARSHAL) at Waterloo (1815).

Watling Street. The great Roman road

beginning at Dover and running through Canterbury to LONDON, thence through St.Albans and Dunstable, along the boundary of Leicester and Warwick to Wroxeter on the Severn. In the late 9th century it became the boundary between English and Danish territory. There are several other sections of road so called.

The name is from O.E. *Wæclingastraet*, the road leading to *Wæclingaceaster* (now St. Albans).

Watson, Dr. *See* SHERLOCK HOLMES.

Watson's Plot. *See* BYE PLOT.

Wattle. Australian settlers built wattle-and-daub huts after the English manner from twigs of the abundant acacia trees which hence became known as *wattles*. *Wattle Day* is a national festival in Australia, held on 1 August or 1 September, according to the peak of the flowering of the wattle in each State.

Wave. The tenth wave. A notion prevails that the waves keep increasing in regular series till the maximum arrives, and then the series begins again. No doubt when two waves coalesce they form a large one, but this does not occur at fixed intervals.

Wavy Navy. The popular name for the former Royal Naval Volunteer Reserve (R.N.V.R.), whose officers wore gold distinction lace made in wavy lines instead of straight, as worn on the sleeves of regular officers belonging to the "Straight Navy". The R.N.V.R. lost its separate existence, after a brilliant wartime record, in December 1957, when it was combined with the Royal Naval Reserve (R.N.R.). *Cp*. WRENS; WAVES.

Waverley Novels. The novels of Sir Walter Scott (1771–1832), which took their name from the first of the series, the title of which was derived from the ruined Waverley Abbey, near Farnham, Surrey. *See* GREAT UNKNOWN.

Wax. Slang for temper, anger; *he's in an awful wax*, he's in a regular rage. Hence **waxy**, irritated, vexed, angry.

A man of wax. A model man; like one fashioned in wax. HORACE speaks of the "waxen arms of Telephus", meaning model arms, or of perfect shape and colour; and in SHAKESPEARE'S *Romeo and Juliet* (I, iii), the nurse says of

Paris, "Why, he's a man of wax," which she explains by saying, "Nay, he's a flower, i' faith a very flower."

A nose of wax. Of a pliable and yielding character; mutable and accommodating. A waxen nose may be twisted in any way.

Way. In the family way. With child, pregnant.

The way of all flesh. To die, Samuel Butler (1835–1902) has a novel of this title published posthumously in 1903.

The Way of the Cross. See STATIONS OF THE CROSS.

To mend one's ways. To improve one's hitherto unsatisfactory habits and behaviour; TO TURN OVER A NEW LEAF (see under LEAF).

Under way. Said of a ship in motion, one which is making headway. *To lose way* is to lose speed when sailing and *to gather way* is to pick up speed.

Ways and means. Methods and means of accomplishing one's purposes; resources; facilities.

The Committee of Ways and Means. The name given in the HOUSE OF COMMONS to a Committee of the whole House which authorizes the Government to raise money for the upkeep of public services and approves new, altered, or revised forms of taxation. It also authorizes payments from the CONSOLIDATED FUND for these purposes. The uses to which the money is put are controlled by the *Committee of Supply*.

Wayland Smith. The English form of the Scandinavian Volund (Ger. *Wieland*), a wonderful and supernatural smith and lord of the elves (see ELF), a kind of VULCAN. The legend is found in the EDDA and is alluded to in BEOWULF. He was bound apprentice to Mimir, the smith. King Nidung cut the sinews in his feet in order to retain his services but he eventually flew away in a feather robe which had been first tested out by his brother EGIL. The legend has much in common with that of DÆDALUS.

Tradition has placed his forge in a megalithic monument known as *Wayland Smith's Cave* near the WHITE HORSE in Berkshire, where it was said that if a traveller tied up his horse there, left sixpence for fee, and retired from

sight, he would find the horse shod on his return.

Wayzgoose. An annual dinner, picnic, or BEANFEAST especially one given to, or held by, those employed in a printing-house. *Wayz* (*wase*) is an obsolete word for a bundle of hay, straw, stubble; hence a "STUBBLE GOOSE", a harvest goose or fat goose, which is the crowning dish of the entertainment.

We. Used of himself by a Sovereign, the "royal we", said to have been used first by Richard I. His Charter to Winchester (1190) reads, "Sciatis *nos* concessisse civibus *nostris* Wintoniæ..." while an earlier charter of his father, Henry II, reads "Sciatis *me* concessisse civibus *meis* Wyntoniæ...".

We is also used by the editor of a newspaper or the writer of unsigned articles, as representing the journal for which he is writing and to avoid the appearance of egotism.

"We are not amused!" A reproof attributed to Queen Victoria and frequently used as an ironical rebuke. There appears to be no evidence that Queen Victoria ever used the expression.

Weapon Salve. A salve said to cure wounds by sympathy; applied not to the wound, but to the instrument which gave the wound. The direction "Bind the wound and grease the nail" is still common. Sir Kenelm Digby says the salve is sympathetic, and quotes several instances to prove that "as the sword is treated the wound inflicted by it feels. Thus, if the instrument is kept wet, the wound will feel cool; if held to the fire, it will feel hot", etc.

Weapon-schaw. See WAPENSHAW.

Wearing of the Green, The. See under GREEN.

Pop goes the Weasel. Now regarded as a children's song, was obviously originally intended for their parents:

Up and down the City Road,
In and out the Eagle.
That's the way the money goes,
Pop goes the weasel.

The Eagle was a tavern and old-time MUSIC HALL in the City Road, LONDON, and a popular rendezvous for singing and Saturday night drinking, which explains the need to "pop" or pawn the "weasel". Whatever the "weasel" was is not clear, but it may have been slang for a tailor's iron.

To catch a weasel asleep. To deceive a very vigilant person or to catch him off his guard.

Weasel words. Words of convenient ambiguity, or a statement from which the original meaning has been sucked or retracted. Theodore Roosevelt popularized the term by using it in a speech in 1916 when criticizing President Wilson. A quotation from the speech provides a good example: "You can have universal training, or you can have voluntary training, but when you use the word *voluntary* to qualify the word *universal*, you are using a weasel word; it has sucked all the meaning out of *universal*. The two words flatly contradict one another."

Roosevelt was indebted to a story by Stewart Chaplin, "Stained-Glass political Platform", which appeared in the *Century Magazine* in June 1900, and in which occurs the sentence: "Why, weasel words are words that suck the life out of the words next to them, just as a weasel sucks the egg and leaves the shell." In the U.S.A. a politician who sits on the fence is sometimes called a *weasler*.

Weather. A-weather. To windward.

Clerk of the Weather. *See under* CLERK.

Fair weather friends. Those that stick to you when you are flourishing but desert as soon as your fortunes change.

I have my weather-eye open. I have my wits about me, I am keeping a good look out, I am on my guard. The weather-eye is towards the wind, supposedly to observe the weather and to be on the look out for squalls.

The peasant's, or **shepherd's weatherglass.** Another name for the SHEPHERD'S SUNDIAL.

Queen's weather. *See under* QUEEN.

To make fair weather. To flatter, conciliate; to make the best of things.

To make heavy weather of something. To find it a trial, to make a burden of it; to make heavy going of it.

Under the weather. To feel unwell or out of sorts; a condition affected by the weather. Also a colloquialism for being tipsy.

A weather breeder. A day of unusual fineness coming suddenly after a series of damp, dull days, especially at the time of year when such a genial day is not looked for. Such a day is generally followed by foul weather.

Weathercock. By a Papal enactment made in the middle of the 9th century, the figure of a cock was set up on every church steeple as the EMBLEM of St. PETER. The emblem is in allusion to his denial of our Lord thrice before the cock crew twice. On the second crowing of the cock the warning of his Master flashed across his memory, and the repentant apostle "went out and wept bitterly".

A person who is always changing his mind is, figuratively, a *weathercock*.

Web. The Web of Life. The destiny of an individual from the cradle to the grave. An allusion to the three FATES who, according to Roman mythology, spin the thread of life, the pattern being the events which are to occur.

Wed, Wedding. *Wed* is Old English, and means a pledge. The ring is the pledge given by the man to avouch that he will perform his part of the contract. *See* MARRIAGE.

The Blood-red wedding. The marriage of Henry of Navarre and Margaret of Valois (18 August 1572), which was followed a week later by the Massacre of St. BARTHOLOMEW.

Penny Weddings. *See under* PENNY.

Wedding anniversaries. Fanciful names have been given to many wedding anniversaries, the popular idea being that they designate the nature of the gifts suitable for the occasion. The following is not without variants for the lesser anniversaries. Most of them are observed by few other than the twenty-fifth and fiftieth.

First	...	Cotton Wedding.
Second	...	Paper Wedding.
Third	...	Leather Wedding.
Fourth	...	Flower or Fruit Wedding.
Fifth	...	Wooden Wedding.
Sixth	...	Iron or Sugar-candy Wedding.
Seventh	...	Woollen Wedding.

Weep

Eighth	...	Bronze or Electrical Appliances Wedding.
Ninth	...	Copper or Pottery Wedding.
Tenth	...	Tin Wedding.
Eleventh	...	Steel Wedding.
Twelfth	...	Silk and Fine Linen Wedding.
Thirteenth	...	Lace Wedding.
Fourteenth	...	Ivory Wedding.
Fifteenth	...	Crystal Wedding.
Twentieth	...	China Wedding.
Twenty-fifth	...	Silver Wedding.
Thirtieth	...	Pearl Wedding.
Thirty-fifth	...	Coral Wedding.
Fortieth	...	Ruby Wedding.
Forty-fifth	...	Sapphire Wedding.
Fiftieth	...	Golden Wedding.
Fifty-fifth	...	Emerald Wedding.
Sixtieth	...	Diamond Wedding.
Seventy-fifth	...	Diamond Wedding.

The sixtieth anniversary is often reckoned the "Diamond Wedding" in place of the seventy-fifth, as the sixtieth anniversary of Queen Victoria's accession was her "Diamond Jubilee".

Wedding Finger. The fourth finger of the left hand. Macrobius says the thumb is too busy to be set apart, the forefinger and little finger are only half protected, the middle finger is called *medicus*, and is too opprobrious for the purpose of honour, so the only finger left is the *pronubus*.

Aulus Gellius tells us that Appianus asserts in his Egyptian books that a very delicate nerve runs from the fourth finger on the left hand to the heart, on which account this finger is used for the marriage ring.

In the ROMAN CATHOLIC CHURCH, the thumb and next two fingers represent the TRINITY; thus the bridegroom says, "In the name of the Father," and touches the thumb; "in the name of the Son," and touches the index finger; and "in the name of the Holy Ghost," and he touches the long or third finger; with the word "Amen" he then puts it on the fourth finger and leaves it there. In some countries the wedding ring is worn on the right hand; this was the custom generally in ENGLAND until the end of the 16th century, and among Roman Catholics until much later.

No herring, no wedding. A bad fishing season discourages marriage among fisherfolk.

Wedge, The Wooden. *See under* WOOD. *Cp.* WOODEN SPOON.

The thin end of the wedge. *See under* THIN.

Wedlock. This word comes from O.E. *wed*, a pledge, and *lac*, action, the whole meaning the marriage vow and hence the married state. It does not imply the unopenable lock of marriage, as has sometimes been supposed.

Wednesday. The fourth day of the week until 1971 when it became the third (*see* SUNDAY); Woden's Day or ODIN's Day, called by the French *mercredi*, Mercury's Day. The Persians regard it as a "RED-LETTER DAY" because the MOON was created on the fourth day (*Gen.* i, 14–19).

Wee Frees. *See under* FREE.

Weeds. Widow's weeds. The mourning worn by a widow; from O.E. *wæde*, a garment. Spenser (*Fairie Queene*, II, iii, 21) speaks of "A goodly lady clad in hunter's weed".

SHAKESPEARE (*Midsummer Night's Dream*, II, i) has:

> And there the snake throws her enamell'd skin,
> Weed wide enough to wrap a fairy in.

And in *Titus Andronicus* (I, i) we get the modern meaning:

> Hail, Rome, victorious in thy mourning weeds!

Week, Days of the. The names of these days are of Anglo-Saxon origin while those of the months are derived from the Romans. See the individual entries SUNDAY, MONDAY, etc., also JANUARY, FEBRUARY, etc.

A week of Sundays. A long time, an indefinite period. *See* SUNDAY.

Week-work. Under FEUDALISM, compulsory work by the unfree TENANT on his lord's land for so many days a week, usually three days. It was the chief mark of serfdom or villeinage. *Cp.* BOON WORK. *See* VILLEIN.

Weep. Weeper. In the more elaborate and formal funeral ceremonial of the 19th century, undertakers attending (called *mutes*) and the principal male mourners wore long black streamers hanging from the hatband; these were commonly known as weepers, as was also the widow's long black veil. In humorous allusion to the former, the long side whiskers in fashion in the 1860s were called *Piccadilly weepers*.

Weeping. A notion long prevailed in this country that it augured ill for future married happiness if the bride did not weep profusely at the wedding.

As no WITCH could shed more than three tears, and those from her left eye only, a copious flow of tears gave assurance to the husband that the lady had not "plighted her troth" to SATAN, and was no witch.

Weeping Cross. A cross set up by the roadside for penitential devotions.

To come home, or **to return by Weeping Cross.** To suffer grievous disappointment, defeat, or failure; hence, to repent of one's actions.

The Weeping Philosopher. Heraclitus (d. *c.* 475 B.C.), so called because he grieved at the folly of man.

The Weeping Saint. St. SWITHIN, because of the tradition of forty days' rain if it rains on his day (15 July).

Weigh (O.E. *wegan*, to carry). **To weigh anchor.** To haul up the anchor preparatory to sailing.

Weighed in the balance and found wanting. Tested and proved to be at fault, or a failure. The phrase is from Daniel's interpretation of the vision of Belshazzar (*Dan.* v, 27).

Dead weight. *See under* DEAD.

Weimar Republic, The. The German federal republic established under the Constitution of 1919, which lasted until it was overthrown by Hitler in 1933. So called from the Thuringian town, particularly associated with Goethe, where the constitution was adopted by the National Assembly.

Welcome Nugget. One of the largest nuggets of GOLD ever discovered. It was found at Baker's Hill, Ballarat, 11 June 1858, and weighed 2,217 oz.

Welcome Stranger. The largest gold nugget found to date. It weighed 2,520 oz. and was found in Victoria, Australia, in 1869.

To wear out one's welcome. To visit too frequently or to stay too long so that one's presence is no longer appreciated or desired.

Welfare State, The. A term applied to

Britain after the implementation of the *Beveridge Report* (1942) providing for nation-wide social security services for sickness, unemployment, retirement, want, etc., and essentially based upon the National Insurance Act of 1946. The system depends upon compulsory contributions and taxation and was built up on the less sweeping Liberal legislation of 1908–14.

Well. Well heeled. Materially prosperous as indicated by one's being well shod; the reverse of DOWN-AT-HEEL.

Wellington. The Duke of Wellington (1769–1852) is commemorated in the name of types of riding-boots and top-boots, a tree of the sequóia family (the *Wellingtonia*), and as a term in cards. Thus in "Nap" a call of *Wellington* doubles *Napoleon—i.e.* the caller has to take all five tricks and wins (or loses) double stakes. Wellington College (opened 1853, as a public school for the sons of officers) was also named after him, as were also many thoroughfares, public-houses, etc.

Wells-Fargo. The famous American company founded by William George Fargo (1818–1881) and Henry Wells (1805–1878) in 1852. It carried on the stage express business between New York and San Francisco via the isthmus of Panama. It absorbed the PONY EXPRESS and took over the Overland Mail Company in 1866, and was also an agency for the transport of bullion. It amalgamated with the Adams Express in 1918 as the American Railway Express Company. *Cp.* COBB AND CO.

Welsh. *See* WALES; TAFFY.

Welsh, welsher. *To welsh* is to decamp from a racecourse without settling one's debts; to avoid settling a debt. A *welsher* is one who does this. The origin of the term is uncertain.

Welsh cake. A small, flat cake or GIRDLE CAKE cooked on a bakestone, or an iron pan. It is made from flour, fat, currants, egg, milk, salt, and sugar.

Welsh harp. The musical instrument of the ancient Welsh bards; a large harp with three rows of strings, two tuned diatonically in unison, the third supplying the chromatic sharps and flats.

Also applied loosely to the Brent Reservoir, in Middlesex, from the public-house of that name in the vicinity.

Welsh mortgage. A pledge of land in which no day is fixed for redemption.

Welsh rabbit. Cheese melted with butter, milk, Worcester sauce, etc., spread on buttered toast. *Rabbit* is not a corruption of *rare-bit*; the term is on a par with "mock-turtle", "BOMBAY DUCK", etc.

Welter-weight. A boxer between light and middle weight, about 147 lb. In racing the term is applied to any extra heavy weight.

Weltpolitik (velt′ pol i tēk). The German phrase (world politics) for the policy a nation pursues in its relations with the world at large.

Wen, The, or **The Great Wen.** London. A name used by William Cobbett (1762–1835) in his *Rural Rides*, meaning that it was an abnormal growth or blotch on the land. To him the sprawl and growth of any town was "a wen".

Wenceslas, St. (*c.* 907–929). The Bohemian martyr-prince made famous in ENGLAND by the 19th-century carol *Good King Wenceslas*. He was noted for his piety and was murdered by Boleslav, his brother. He became recognized as the patron of Bohemia and his day is 28 September.

Werewolf. *See* WERWOLF.

Wergild. The BLOOD-MONEY (*wer*, man; *gild*, payment) paid in Anglo-Saxon times by the kindred of the slayer to the kindred of the slain to avoid a blood-feud in cases of murder or manslaughter. There was a fixed scale, as 1,200 shillings for a thegn, 200 shillings for a ceorl, etc.

Werwolf. A "man-wolf" (O.E. *wer*, man), *i.e.* a man who, according to ancient superstition, was turned—or could at will turn himself—into a WOLF (the *loupgarou* of France). It had the appetite of a wolf, and roamed about at night devouring infants and sometimes exhuming corpses. Its skin was proof against shot or steel, unless the weapon had been blessed in a chapel dedicated to St. HUBERT.

Ovid tells the story of LYCAON, King of ARCADIA, turned into a wolf because he tested the divinity of JUPITER by serving up to him a "hash of human flesh"; Herodotus describes the Neuri as having the power of assuming once a year the shape of wolves; Pliny relates that one of the family of ANTÆUS was chosen annually, by lot, to be transformed into a wolf, in which shape he continued for nine years; and St. PATRICK, we are told, converted Vereticus, King of WALES, into a wolf.

Hence the term *lycanthropy* (Gr. *lukos*, wolf; *anthropos*, man) for this supposed transformation and for the form of insanity in which the subject exhibits depraved animal traits.

Tigers, hyenas, and leopards had the same associations in other parts of the world, and after the disappearance of the wolf in England WITCHES were commonly "transformed" into cats.

Wesleyan. A member of the NONCONFORMIST church which grew out of the evangelical movement started by John Wesley (1703–1791) and his associates, although there was no real break with the CHURCH OF ENGLAND until 1795. *See* METHODISTS.

Wessex. The ancient kingdom of the West Saxons, founded by Cerdic in the 6th century. Its nucleus was the modern Berkshire and Hampshire, and it later spread to CORNWALL in the west and to Kent and Essex in the east. The Danish invasions of the 9th century destroyed the other English kingdoms and ALFRED THE GREAT came to be recognized as King of all the English outside the Danish areas. The subsequent reconquest of the DANELAW resulted in the king of Wessex becoming king of ENGLAND.

West. To go west. Of persons, to die; of things, to be lost, rendered useless or unattainable, as, "My chance of promotion has gone west." The reference is to the setting sun, which "goes west", and then sinks and expires, or possibly TYBURN.

The Western Church. The CATHOLIC CHURCH.

The Western Empire. The western division of the ROMAN EMPIRE with ROME as its capital, after the division into the Eastern and Western Empire by Theodosius in 395.

Westerns. *See* WILD WEST.

Westminster. The seat of government in ENGLAND since the time of Canute (1016–35). From the time of WILLIAM THE CONQUEROR the sovereign has been crowned in Westminster Abbey and it later became the home of the Mother of Parliaments. Hence, like WHITEHALL and DOWNING STREET, it is sometimes used as a synonym for government or PARLIAMENT.

The Palace of Westminster. Until 1512, a royal residence and the place to which PARLIAMENT was summoned; now the seat of Parliament. In 1547 St. Stephen's Chapel within the Palace became the home of the HOUSE OF COMMONS until the fire of 1834, when new buildings were erected. The House of Commons Chamber was again destroyed by enemy bombing in 1940. The LORDS occupied other parts of the Palace which ceased to be a royal residence after a serious fire in 1512. STAR CHAMBER stood in these precincts, but the only ancient building now remaining is Westminster Hall, parts of which date from 1097.

The Westminster Assembly. The assembly appointed by the LONG PARLIAMENT to reform the English Church. It consisted of 30 laymen and 120 clergy and met in Westminster Abbey precincts (1643–53). Its most important achievement was the WESTMINSTER CONFESSION. *See also* ERASTIANISM.

The Westminster Confession. The PRESBYTERIAN Confession of faith adopted by the WESTMINSTER ASSEMBLY in 1646 and approved by PARLIAMENT in 1648. It became a standard definition of Presbyterian doctrine.

Wet. Slang for a drink; hence **to have a wet** is to have a drink, and **to wet one's whistle** means the same thing; Chaucer has, "So was her joly whistle wel y-wet" (*Reeve's Tale*, 235).

In the U.S.A. *wet* States were those which did not support the prohibition of the sale of alcoholic drinks.

In colloquial speech *wet* also denotes stupidity, foolishness, thus **he is pretty wet** means he is fairly stupid and **don't talk wet** means don't talk such nonsense, don't be silly. The more liberal element in the TORY party, which does not favour all the IRON LADY's policies, are called "wets".

A wet blanket. *See under* BLANKET.

Wetback. An illegal immigrant to the U.S.A. from Mexico. The term originates in the fact that such interlopers usually had to swim the Rio Grande.

Wet nurse. A woman employed to suckle children not her own.

To wet the baby's head. To celebrate a baptism with a social gathering to drink to the health of the newly born baby.

W. H., Mr. When SHAKESPEARE's *Sonnets* appeared in 1609 they were dedicated to a Mr. W. H., called their "onlie begetter". The identity of Shakespeare's friend is uncertain. Various names have been put forward and for long the most favoured were William Herbert, third Earl of Pembroke, to whom (with his brother) the First Folio Shakespeare was dedicated, and Henry Wriothesley, third Earl of Southampton, to whom *Venus and Adonis* and *Lucrece* were dedicated. In 1964 Dr. Leslie Hotson put forward a case for William Hatcliffe of Lincolnshire, "Prince of Purpoole" in the GRAY'S INN revels of 1588. According to Dr. A. L. Rowse, Master W. H. is Sir William Harvey, the Earl of Southampton's stepfather.

Very like a whale. Very much like a COCK-AND-BULL STORY. In SHAKESPEARE's *Hamlet* (III, ii), the Prince chaffs POLONIUS by comparing a cloud to a camel, and then to a weasel, and when the courtier assents Hamlet adds, "Or like a whale"; to which Polonius answers, "Very like a whale."

A whale of a lot. A great amount. Colloquially *whale* is used of something very fine or big as *we had a whale of a time*, a fine time, or *a whale of a job*, a very considerable task.

Whalebone. *See* MISNOMERS.

What. He knows what's what. He is a shrewd fellow, not to be imposed upon. One of the senseless questions of logic was *Quid est quid*?

What makes it tick. *See under* TICK.

What-not. A small stand with shelves for photographs, knick-knacks, china ornaments, and "what-not" (*i.e.* etc.), popular in Victorian and Edwardian times.

Wheel. Emblematical of St. CATHERINE, who was broken on a spiked wheel.

Broken on the wheel. *See under* BREAK.

To break a butterfly on a wheel. *See under* BREAK.

To put a spoke in one's wheel. *See* SPOKE.

To put one's shoulder to the wheel. *See under* PUT.

The wheel is come full circle. Just retribution has followed. The line is from SHAKESPEARE's *King Lear*, V, iii.

The wheel of Fortune. Fortuna, the goddess, is represented on ancient monuments with a wheel in her hand, emblematical of her inconstancy.

Wheels within wheels. A complex of motives and influences and circumstances at work which are not always apparent. The allusion is to *Ezekiel* i, 16.

Praying-wheel. A revolving wheel or cylinder, used for purposes of prayer among Buddhists, upon which written prayers are set, each turn of the wheel being reckoned as a prayer. In Europe, a wheel with bells (sometimes called a WHEEL OF FORTUNE), used as a means of DIVINATION, a favourable or unfavourable response being indicated by the position at which it came to rest.

Wheel-horse, or **Wheeler.** Figuratively, one who does the hard work or bears the brunt. The wheel-horse is the one nearest the front wheels of a vehicle and is harnessed to the pole or shafts, as distinct from the leader who is the front horse.

Wheeler-dealer. One who "wheels and deals". Wheel in American slang signifies a leader, one who takes charge, a "big shot". Hence one of great influence in a particular field (usually business or politics); a shrewd and influential operator and manipulator.

Wherewithal. In older writings this is a form of *wherewith* as in:

Wherewithal shall a young man cleanse his way?

Ps. cxix, 9.

It is now used as a noun in the sense of *means, money.*

Whetstone. *See* ACCIUS NAEVIUS.

Lying for the whetstone. Said of a person who is grossly exaggerating or falsifying a statement. One of the WHITSUN amusements of our forefathers was the lie-wage or lie-match; he who could tell the greatest lie was rewarded with a whetstone to sharpen his wit. The nature of these contests may be illustrated by the following: one of the combatants declared he could see a fly on the top of a church steeple; the other replied, "Oh, yes, I saw him wink his eye."

Whig. A name applied to Scottish cattle rustlers and horse thieves, then to the Presbyterian COVENANTERS and later, in the reign of Charles II (1660–1685), to those seeking to exclude the Duke of York from succession to the throne. The name was used abusively by their TORY opponents. From the time of the GLORIOUS REVOLUTION the Whigs were upholders of parliamentary supremacy and toleration for NONCONFORMISTS. They supported the Hanoverian succession and enjoyed a monopoly of political power until the reign of George III, when they were superseded by the Tories after 1783 and did not recover the ascendancy until 1830, the time of the Reform Bill. By 1868 the name LIBERAL had largely replaced that of Whig.

The origin of the word is obscure but it is probably a shortened form of *whiggamore*, a horse drover.

In American usage, *Whig* denotes a supporter of the American Revolution; also a member of the American Whig party formed in 1834 from the old National Republican Party against President Andrew Jackson and "executive tyranny". The part disintegrated by 1854 over the question of "free soil" and slavery.

The Whig Bible. *See* BIBLE, SOME SPECIALLY NAMED EDITIONS.

Whip. In British parliamentary usage, M.P.s appointed by a party, whose duty it is to see that the members of their party vote at important divisions and to discipline them if they do not attend, or vote against the party.

Whip also denotes the notice sent by party whips to members requesting their attendance in the HOUSE, and the degree of urgency is indicated by one, two, or three lines shown under the summons. The name derives from the *whipper-in* at a fox-hunt.

A whip-round. An impromptu collection for some benevolent object.

To whip-saw. To have or take the advantage over an opponent; especially in faro, to win two different bets at one turn.

Whip-sawing is also an American term for accepting bribes from two opposing interests at the same time. The whip-saw is a long narrow frame-saw with a handle at either end so that it cuts both ways.

Whipper-snapper. An inexperienced, insignificant and often intrusive young person. The word probably derives from *whip snapper*, one who has nothing to do but crack a whip.

Whipping Boy. A boy kept to be whipped when a prince deserved chastisement. Fuller (*Church History*, II) says Barnaby Fitzpatrick so stood for Edward VI, and Mungo Murray for CHARLES I. When Henry IV of France abjured Protestantism and was received into the ROMAN CATHOLIC CHURCH in 1593, Bishop Duperron and Cardinal d'Ossat were sent to ROME to obtain the King's absolution. They knelt in the portico of St. Peter's singing the MISERERE. At each verse a blow with a switch was given on their shoulders.

Whisky. SCOTCH. In Ireland and the U.S.A. spelt *whiskey*. See USQUEBAUGH. The light one-horse gig called a whisky is from *whisk*, to move briskly.

Whisper. Pig's whisper. *See under* PIG.

To give the whisper. To give the tip, the warning; to pass some bit of secret information.

Whist. The card game originated in England (16th century) and was first called *Triumph* (whence *trump*), then *Ruff* or *Honours*, and then, early in the 17th century, *Whisk*, in allusion to the sweeping up of the cards. Whist, the later name, appears in Butler's *Hudibras* (1663), and was adopted through confusion with *Whist!* meaning Hush! Silence!

Whistle. To wet one's whistle. *See* WET.

To whistle down the wind. To abandon; to talk or argue purposelessly. From the releasing of a HAWK down wind.

To whistle for it. It was an old superstition among sailors that when a ship was becalmed a wind could be raised by whistling, but to many seamen whistling was "the Devil's music" which could raise a gale. It was, therefore, not tolerated. More rationally the phrase "you can whistle for it" now means "You won't get it".

Worth the whistle. Worth calling; worth inviting; worth notice. The dog is worth the pains of whistling for. Thus Heywood, in one of his dialogues consisting entirely of proverbs, says, "It is a poor dog that is not worth the whistling." Goneril says to Albany:

I have been worth the whistle.
SHAKESPEARE: *King Lear*, IV, ii.

You paid too dearly for your whistle. You paid dearly for something you fancied, but found that it did not answer your expectation. The allusion is to a story told by Benjamin Franklin of his nephew, who set his mind on a common whistle, which he bought of a boy for four times its value.

Whistle-stop tour. In the U.S.A., to conduct a brief campaign, usually political, by travelling the country visiting the smaller communities, often talking from the rear platform of a train. A *whistle-stop* being a small town on a rail-road where the train only stopped on a given signal. *Cp.* JERKWATER.

Whitsunday. *White* Sunday. The seventh SUNDAY after EASTER, to commemorate the descent of the HOLY GHOST on the day of PENTECOST. It was one of the great seasons for baptism and the candidates wore white garments, hence the name.

Whitsuntide. The whole week following WHIT SUNDAY.

Whitsun farthings. *See* PENTECOSTALS.

Whitsun-ale. The most important CHURCH-ALE, celebrated with much revelry.

White denotes purity, simplicity, and candour; innocence, truth, and hope. For its ecclesiastical use, symbolism, etc., *see* COLOURS.

Generally, the priests of antiquity wore white vestments, and Bardic costume, supposedly derived from the DRUIDS, is always white. OSIRIS, the ancient Egyptian god, wore a white crown; the priests of JUPITER were clad in white, and at the death of a CÆSAR the national mourning was white. The Persians affirm that the divinities are clothed in white.

The white bird. Conscience, or the SOUL of man. The Mohammedans have preserved the old idea that the souls of the just lie under the throne of GOD, like white birds, till the resurrection morn. *Cp.* DOVE.

White Canons. *See* PREMONSTRATENSIAN.

The White Cockade. The badge worn by the followers of Charles Edward, the Young PRETENDER.

The White Company. In 13th-century France, a band of cut-throats organized by Folquet, bishop of Toulouse, to extirpate heretics in his diocese. The name is better known for its association with the FREE COMPANIES of the late 14th century: that which Bertrand du Guesclin led against Pedro the Cruel of Castile in 1367, whose members wore a white CROSS on the shoulder; and that under Sir John Hawkwood in Italy. Sir Arthur Conan Doyle's notable story, *The White Company*, was first published in 1891. *See also* CONDOTTIERI.

White elephant. *See under* ELEPHANT.

White Ensign. A St. George's CROSS on a white ground with the UNION JACK in a canton, since 1864 the ensign of the Royal Navy but also used by members of the Royal Yacht Squadron who have the requisite warrant.

White Fathers. Members of the French Society of Missionaries of Africa established at Algiers in 1868. So called from their white tunic.

White flag. An all-white flag is universally used as the signal of surrender or desiring to parley and its bearer is by international custom immune from harm.

White Friars. The CARMELITES, so called from their white mantle worn over a brown habit. One of their houses founded in LONDON on the south side of FLEET STREET in 1241 gave its name to the district called *Whitefriars* or ALSATIA which was long a SANCTUARY.

White harvest. A late harvest, when the ground is white of a morning with hoar frost.

The White Horse. *See under* HORSE.

White horses. *See under* HORSE.

The White House. The Presidential mansion at Washington, D.C. It is a building of freestone, painted white. The cornerstone was laid by George Washington. Figuratively it means the Presidency of the U.S.A.

White Lady. A kind of spectre, the appearance of which generally forebodes death in the house. It is a relic of Teutonic mythology, representing HULDA or BERCHTA, the goddess who received the SOULS of maidens and young children. She is dressed in white and carries a bunch of keys at her side.

The first recorded instance of this apparition was in the 15th century, and the name given to the lady is Bertha von Rosenberg. She last appeared, it is said, in 1879. German legend says that when the castle of Neuhaus, Bohemia, was being built a white lady appeared and promised the workmen a sweep soup and a carp on the completion of the castle. In remembrance thereof, these dainties were for long given to the poor on MAUNDY THURSDAY.

White Ladies. A popular name for the CISTERCIAN nuns in mediæval ENGLAND, from the colour of their habit, and for the Magdalenes. Also applied to the French Order of the Sisters of the Presentation of Mary (1796).

White League. A name for the KU KLUX KLAN.

A white lie. *See under* LIE.

White magic. Sorcery in which the DEVIL is not invoked and plays no part, as distinct from *black* magic.

A white man. A thoroughly straightforward and honourable man.

The White Man's Burden. In the days of imperialism, the duty supposed to be imposed upon the white races, especially the British, to govern and to educate the less-civilized or backward coloured peoples.

> Take up the White Man's Burden—
> Send forth the best you breed,
> Go bind your sons to exile
> To serve the captives' need.

KIPLING: *The White Man's Burden*.

The White Man's Grave. The unhealthy areas of equatorial West Africa, especially Sierra Leone.

White Monks. The CISTERCIAN monks, whose habit was made from white wool.

A white night. A sleepless night; the French have the phrase *Passer une nuit blanche*.

White Paper. A government publication printed for the information of PARLIAMENT. Such a report, statement of policy, etc., is not bulky enough to warrant the protective covers of a BLUE BOOK. White Papers are available to the public through H.M. Stationery Office.

The White Rose. *See under* ROSE.

White Russian. An inhabitant of White Russia or Byelorussia (Russ. *byely*, white), one of the republics of the U.S.S.R. A *"White"* Russian also denotes a counter-revolutionary or *émigré* at the time of the BOLSHEVIK revolution, and their army was known as the **White Army.**

White sheep. *See* BLACK SHEEP *under* SHEEP.

The White Ship. The ship carrying Henry I's son William from Normandy to ENGLAND, which struck a rock off Barfleur (25 November 1120) and sank. William was drowned with the resultant conflict for the crown between Stephen and Matilda. The disaster was due to the drunken laxity of the crew.

White Sisters. The Congregation of the Daughters of the HOLY GHOST, founded in Brittany in 1706, so called from the colour of their habit. Also the Congregation of the Missionary Sisters of Our Lady of Africa (1869), the counterpart of the WHITE FATHERS.

White Slave. A woman who is sold or forced into prostitution, especially when taken abroad.

White tincture. The alchemist's name for a preparation that should convert any base metal into SILVER. It is also called the Stone of the Second Order, the Little Elixir, and the Little Magisterium. *See* RED.

White wedding. A wedding in which the bride wears the traditional white wedding dress and veil, white symbolizing purity and virginity. For the same reason, grey horses were formerly used for the wedding carriage and the postboys wore white hats. Wedding cake is coated with white icing and invitations, etc., are usually printed in silver. It is also said to be unlucky to be married in anything but white.

White witch. One who practises WHITE MAGIC only.

Days marked with a white stone. Days to be remembered with gratification. The Romans used a white stone or piece of chalk to mark their lucky days on the calendar. Unlucky days were marked with charcoal. *Cp.* RED-LETTER DAY.

To hit the white. To be quite right, make a good shot. The phrase is from the old days of archery, the white being the inner circle of the target—the BULL'S EYE.

To show the white feather. To show cowardice; a phrase from COCKFIGHTING, a white feather in a gamecock's tail being taken as a sign of degenerate stock, not a true game-bird.

To stand in a white sheet. Part of the ancient penance for incontinence was to stand before the congregation at MASS robed in a white sheet. The term now designates the utmost penitence.

White-collar worker. The professional or clerical worker, whose calling demands a certain nicety of attire typified by the wearing of a white shirt and collar. *Cp* BLACK-COATED WORKER.

A white tie affair. A social function at which the men wear formal evening dress with a white bow-tie and swallow-tailed coat.

A whited sepulchre. A hypocrite, especially one who conceals wickedness under a cloak of virtue.

In Biblical times, Jewish sepulchres were whitened to make them conspicuous so that passers-by might avoid ritual defilement by near approach. Thus Jesus (*Matt.* xxiii, 27) says: "Ye are like unto whited sepulchres, which indeed appear beautiful outward, but are within full of dead men's bones, and of all uncleanness."

White-livered. Cowardly, from the old notion that the livers of cowards were bloodless.

Whiteboys. Irish Catholic peasant organizations first appearing in Munster in the 1760s, whose outrages were a protest against RACK-RENTING, TITHES, enclosures, etc. They again terrorized southern IRELAND from the late 1780s until the end of the century. So called because they wore white frocks over their clothing. In the Isle of MAN, Christmas mummers were known as *White Boys*.

Whitechapel. A district of Stepney in the East END of London, east of Aldgate, and a noted Jewish quarter. It contains part of PETTICOAT LANE and was the scene of the notorious **Whitechapel Murders** by JACK THE RIPPER. It is also notable for its bell-foundry. It takes its name from the colour of the original chapel-of-ease to Stepney built there.

Whitechapel cart. A light, two-wheeled spring cart, once used by tradesmen for delivering goods.

Whitehall. This famous thoroughfare takes its name from the royal palace sited there, which was in use from the time of Henry VIII to William III. It was mostly destroyed by fire in 1698 and only the banqueting hall, built by Inigo Jones, still stands. The palace was formerly Wolsey's mansion called York Place, but was named *White Hall* after its confiscation by Henry VIII.

> You must no more call it York Place,
>   that's past:
> For, since the cardinal fell, that title's
>   lost;
> 'Tis now the King's, and call'd White-
>   hall.
>
>   SHAKESPEARE: *King Henry VIII*, IV, i.

From its being the site of the major Government offices the name is often used as a synonym for the British government.

Whitewash. Figuratively, excuses made in palliation of bad conduct; a false colouring given to a person's character or memory, a stained reputation, etc.

The term is also applied to the clearance by a bankrupt of his debts, not by paying them but by judicial process.

Whitsun. *See under* WHIT.

Whittington, Dick. According to the popular legend and PANTOMIME story, a poor boy who made his way to LONDON when he heard that the streets were paved with GOLD and SILVER. He found shelter as a scullion in the house of a rich merchant who permitted each of his servants to partake in sending a cargo of merchandise to Barbary. Dick sent his CAT, but subsequently ran away owing to ill-treatment below STAIRS. He was recalled by BOW BELLS seeming to say:

> Turn again Whittington
> Thrice Lord Mayor of London.

He returned to find his cat had been purchased for a vast sum by the King of Barbary, who was much plagued by rats and mice. He married his master's daughter Alice, prospered exceedingly, and became thrice Lord Mayor.

In fact, he was the youngest son of Sir William Whittington of Pauntley in Gloucestershire and duly became a mercer of London, having married Alice, the daughter of Sir Ivo Fitzwaryn. He became very wealthy, the richest merchant of his day, and was made Lord MAYOR of London in 1397–1398, 1406–1407, and 1419–1420. He died in 1423 leaving his vast wealth for charitable and public purposes.

The part of the cat in the story has been carefully explained: that he traded in coals brought to London in *cats* (a type of sailing-vessel), and that it is a confusion with Fr. *achat*, "purchase" (a term then used for trading at a profit). Whatever be the truth, Dick Whittington and his cat are now inseparables.

Whizz or **Whiz Kid.** A highly intelligent young person, one who achieves rapid success, the onomatopoeic word *whizz* being the sound of something moving through the air with great rapidity.

Who dun it. A colloquialism originating in the U.S.A. for a detective story (in American usage, a mystery).

Whoopee (woo pē'). **To make whoopee.** To enjoy oneself uproariously, to go on the RAZZLE or spree.

Wicked. Probably connected with O.E. *wicca*, a WIZARD.

The Wicked Bible. *See* BIBLE, SOME SPECIALLY NAMED EDITIONS.

The Wicked Prayer Book. Printed 1686, octavo. In the Epistle for the Fourteenth Sunday after TRINITY the following passage occurs:

Now the works of the flesh are manifest, which are these, adultery, fornication, uncleanness, idolatry...they who do such things shall inherit the kingdom of God.

("shall inherit" should be "shall not inherit".)

Wicket. To bat on a sticky wicket. To be confronted with a difficult situation which demands coolness and judgment. An allusion to the game of CRICKET when a soft pitch causes greater difficulties for the batsman when the ball is delivered.

Widdershins. *See* WITHERSHINS.

Wide. Slang for cunning, artful, or for one who is very wide-awake. Hence **wide boy,** a plebeian type of SMART-ALEC who needs watching, one who tries "to see you off." *Cp.* SPIV.

Wideawake. Types of felt hat, with a low crown and wide brim, common in Victorian times. Punningly so called because they never had a *nap*.

Widecombe Fair. The famous fair held annually on the second Tuesday of September at Widecombe-in-the-Moor. The long established sheep and pony fair in this DARTMOOR parish became widely known from the old folk song telling the story of UNCLE TOM COBLEIGH. He still appears in the modern carnival dressed in an old linen smock astride the old grey mare giving rides to young children.

Widow, The. Old slang for the gallows.

The Widow at Windsor. A name applied to Queen Victoria whose husband Albert, the PRINCE CONSORT, died at the end of 1861. Her remaining 39 years were largely spent in seclusion and she never ceased to mourn her loss. The name *The Widow at Windsor* was applied by Rudyard Kipling in his *Barrack-Room Ballad* of that name (1892).

The widow's cruse. A small supply of anything which, by good management, is made to go a long way and to be apparently inexhaustible. In allusion to the miracle of the cruse of oil in II *Kings* iv.

Widow's mite. An offering, small in itself but representing self-sacrifice on the part of the giver; a small contribution

from one who is unable to give much. An allusion to *Mark* xii, 42. Lord John Russell, 1st Earl Russell (1792–1878), of Reform Bill fame was nicknamed the *Widow's mite* from his small stature and his marriage in 1835 to the widow of the 2nd Lord Ribblesdale.

Widow's peak. A V-shaped point of hair over the forehead reminiscent of the front cusp of the cap formerly worn by widows.

Widow's weeds. *See* WEEDS.

Wieland *See* WAYLAND SMITH.

Wife. O.E. *wif*, a woman. The ultimate root of the word is obscure; but it is "certainly not allied to *weave* (O.E. *weafn*), as the fable runs" (Skeat).

The old meaning, a *woman*, still appears in such combinations as *fish-wife*, *house-wife*, etc., and **old-wives' tales** for unconvincing stories or proverbial legend.

> But refuse profane and old wives' fables, and exercise thyself rather unto godliness.
>
> I *Tim.* iv, 7.

The Wife-hater Bible. *See* BIBLE, SOME SPECIALLY NAMED EDITIONS.

Wig. A shortened form of *periwig* (earlier, *perwig*), from Fr. *perrugue*. The long flowing wig of Louis XIV's time was called the *allonge* (lengthening) and in the 18th century there were thirty or forty different styles and names: as the artichoke, bag, barrister's, bishop's, Blenheim, brush, buckle, busby, bush (buzz), campaigning, cauliflower, chain, chancellor's corded, Count Saxe's mode, crutch, cut bob, Dalmahoy (a bob wig worn by tradesmen), detached buckle, drop, Dutch, full, half natural, Jansenist bob, judge's, ladder, long bob, Louis, pigeon's wing, rhinoceros, rose, she-dragon, small back, spinach seed, staircase, wild boar's back, wolf's paw.

A bigwig. A magnate, someone of importance; in allusion to the large wigs that in the 17th and 18th centuries encumbered the head and shoulders of the aristocracy of England and France, etc. They are still worn by the Lord CHANCELLOR, judges, and the SPEAKER of the HOUSE OF COMMONS; BISHOPS continued to wear them in the HOUSE OF LORDS until 1880.

Scratch wig. A small one just large enough to cover the bald patch, as opposed to the full-bottomed wig.

Tie-wig. The small wig as worn by barristers.

Welsh wig. A worsted cap.

Wigging. A scolding, a reprimand. Possibly from the idea of dislodging or ruffling someone's wig, or from a reproof by a BIGWIG or a *wigged* superior.

Wild. Wild Bill. James Butler Hickok (1837–1876) American soldier and scout was so called. A renowned pistol shot in his early days he served as a stage driver and later in the Union army during the Civil War as a scout and sharpshooter. He became a deputy marshal in 1866 and served as a scout for General CUSTER and others. From 1869–1871 he was marshal in Kansas. Of great strength and courage he shot many thieves and outlaws and in 1872–1873 toured in the east with BUFFALO BILL. He was killed from behind, at Deadwood, Dakota in 1876.

Wild Boy. *See* GAZELLE BOY; PETER THE WILD BOY.

Wildcat. A female of fierce and uncontrolled temper is often called a wildcat for obvious reasons and the expression is variously applied to reckless, uncontrolled, and unsound activities, ventures, etc. Thus, *wildcat strike*, an impromptu or unofficial strike; *wildcat scheme*, a rash and hazardous scheme, especially financial; *wildcat banking*, financially unsound; etc. The usage is of colloquial American origin and in the U.S.A. a prospect well for oil or natural gas is also called a *wildcat*.

The Wild Huntsman. A spectral hunter of mediæval legend, who with a pack of spectral dogs frequents certain forests and occasionally appears to mortals. It takes numerous forms in Germany, France, and England, and the wild huntsman is often identified with various heroes of national legend.

A wild-goose chase. An impracticable or useless pursuit of something; an absurd enterprise. A wild-goose is very difficult to catch. *Cp.* WILDCAT.

To sow one's wild oats. *See* OATS.

Wildfire. A very old English description of a composition of inflammable materials that catch fire quickly. It is now used figuratively in the phrase **To catch like wildfire,** to take on with the public instantaneously.

Wild men. A term often applied in politics to party intransigents or extremists. Women who took part in the campaign for women's rights, especially the militant SUFFRAGETTES, were sometimes called **wild women.**

Wild West. In 19th-century America, the moving western frontier, before orderly settlement was established under governmental control. It was an area of action and adventure, of desperadoes and cattle rustlers, noted for hard drinking, gambling, and violence and crime generally. Since romanticized in stories and films (called *Westerns*), it has its own folk heroes varying from the Lone Ranger to Deadwood Dick.

Wilderness. To go into the Wilderness. A figurative description of being deprived of political office through a change of government.

Wilfrid, St. (*c.* 634–709). A Northumbrian, educated at Lindisfarne, he subsequently visited Canterbury and ROME, learning the Roman liturgy. He became Abbot of Ripon and was largely responsible for the adoption of Roman usages in preference to CELTIC at the Synod of Whitby, 664. Soon afterwards he became BISHOP of York and finally of Hexham. His day is 12 October.

St. Wilfrid's Needle. A narrow passage in the crypt of Ripon cathedral, built by Odo, Archbishop of Canterbury, and said to have been used to test a woman's chastity, as none but a virgin was able to squeeze through.

Wilgefortis. *See* UNCUMBER.

Will-o'-the-wisp. *See* IGNIS FATUUS.

William. St. William of Norwich (1132–1144). A tanner's apprentice of Norwich, alleged to have been crucified and murdered by Jews during the PASSOVER. It was said at the time that it was part of Jewish ritual to sacrifice a Christian every year. (*See* Drayton's *Polyolbion*, song xxiv.)

St. William of York (d. 1154). William Fitzherbert, chaplain to King Stephen and Archbishop of York (1142). He was canonized by Honorius III in

1227, largely on account of the miracles reported to have been performed at his tomb.

William of Malmesbury (c. 1080–1143). A monk and librarian of Malmesbury Abbey and noted chronicler and historian. Among his numerous works his two most important are his *De Gestis Regum Anglorum* (Chronicle of the Kings of England, to 1125) and *De Gestis Pontificum Anglorum* (The History of the Prelates of England, to 1122).

William of Occam (c. 1300–c. 1349). The famous NOMINALIST philosopher, a native of Ockham, Surrey; also called *Doctor Invincibilis*. *See* OCCAM'S RAZOR

William of Wykeham. *See* WYKEHAMIST.

William Rufus (the Red). King William II of England (c. 1056, 1087–1100); so called from his ruddy complexion.

William the Conqueror. King William I of England (c. 1027, 1066–1087), who as Duke of Normandy invaded and conquered the English in 1066. Also called William the Bastard, from his parentage.

William the Lyon. King of SCOTLAND (1143, 1165–1214). The reason for this appellation is not known, but it is popularly supposed that he was the first Scottish king to adopt the LION as his achievement.

William the Silent. *See under* SILENCE.

William Tell. *See* TELL.

Willow. Willow Pattern. This celebrated design for porcelain in blue and white was introduced by Thomas Turner of Caughley in 1780. It imitated the Chinese style of decoration but was not an exact copy of any Chinese original. It takes its name from the willow tree being a main feature of the design.

To handle, or **wield the willow.** To play CRICKET, cricket-bats being made of willow; hence the game is sometimes called *King Willow* (*see* the Harrow School song of that name).

To wear the willow. To go into mourning, especially for a sweetheart or bride, to bewail a lost lover.

The willow, especially the weeping willow, has anciently been associated with sorrow and ever since the BABYLONIAN CAPTIVITY the latter is said to have drooped its branches. *Psalm* cxxxvii says:

> By the rivers of Babylon, there we sat down, yea, we wept, when we remembered Zion.
> We hanged our harps upon the willows in the midst thereof.

Willy-nilly. *Nolens volens*; willing or not. Will-he, nill-he, *nill* being *n'* (negative) *will*, just as Lat. *nolens* is *n'-volens*.

Wimbledon. A name synonymous with lawn tennis and tennis championships; a London suburb, and home of the All England Croquet Club. In the middle of the 1870s the Club, being in low water, added "Lawn Tennis" to its title, this being then a new game increasing in popularity. On the Club's courts, the first lawn tennis Championship in the world was held in 1877. The annual tournament run by the All England Club at Wimbledon ranks as the premier championship.

Win, To. Colloquially, to acquire, often by dubious means, to filch surreptitiously; a somewhat more questionable form of "scrounging", which does not always bear inspection.

Winchester. Identified by Malory and other old writers with the CAMELOT of ARTHURIAN ROMANCE. It was King Alfred's capital. *See also* SWITHIN; WYKEHAMIST.

Wind. According to classical mythology, the north, south, east, and west winds (BOREAS, *Notus*, EURUS, and ZEPHYRUS) were under the rule of ÆOLUS, who kept them confined in a cave on Mount Hæmus, Thrace. Other strong winds of a more destructive nature were the brood of TYPHŒUS.

The story says that Æolus gave ULYSSES a bag tied with a silver string, in which were all the hurtful and unfavourable winds, so that he might arrive home without being delayed by tempests. His crew, however, opened the bag in the belief that it contained treasure, the winds escaped, and a terrible storm at once arose, driving the vessel out of its course and back to the island of Æolus.

Aquilo is another Latin name for the north wind, as AUSTER is of the south and FAVONIUS of the west. *Thrascias* is a north-north-west wind and *Libs* a west-south-west wind, CAURUS or *Corus* a north-west wind (also personified as *Argestes*), *Volturnus* a south-east wind and *Africus* and *Afer ventus* a south-west wind. *See also* ETESIAN WIND; SOLANO; TRADE WINDS; WILLY-WILLY.

A rasher of wind. A phrase widely current in late-Victorian times and subsequently, used to describe a very slight or thin person or something of very little account.

A wind egg. An egg without a shell, or with a soft shell, or an unfertilized one; from the old superstition that the hen that lays it was impregnated, like the "Thracian mares", by the wind.

Wind of change. A new current of opinion, a markedly reformist or novel trend, etc. A phrase popularized by Harold Macmillan in his speech to the South African Parliament (3 February 1960), with reference to the social and political ferment in the African continent.

> The wind of change is blowing through this continent, and, whether we like it or not, this growth of national consciousness is a political fact.

In the wind's eye. *See under* EYE.

There's something in the wind. There are signs that something is about to happen; something is being prepared or concocted without one's knowledge.

Three sheets in the wind. *See* SHEET.

'Tis an ill wind that blows nobody any good. Someone profits by every loss; someone usually benefits by every misfortune.

To get one's second wind. To recover and go about one's pursuits with renewed vigour; as a runner, after initial breathlessness, warms up and regains more regular respiration known as his second wind.

To get the wind up. To become thoroughly alarmed, nervous, over-anxious, and frightened.

To get wind of something. To get advance knowledge of something which has not yet happened. From an animal's ability to detect the approach of others by their scent on the wind.

To have the wind. *See* TO TAKE, etc., *below.*

To know which way the wind blows. To be aware of the true state of affairs.

To raise the wind. To obtain necessary money or funds.

To sail against, or **before the wind, To sail close to the wind,** etc. *See under* SAIL.

To take, or **have the wind.** To get or keep the upper hand. *To have the wind* also means to have flatulence.

To take the wind out of one's sails. To forestall him, "to steal his thunder" (*see under* THUNDER), frustrate him by utilizing his own material or methods. Literally, it is to sail to windward of a ship and so rob its sails of the wind.

To temper the wind to the shorn lamb. To exercise forbearance and moderation towards someone who is vulnerable and likely to be hurt. Shorn lambs are obviously more susceptible to rough weather than well-coated sheep. It is ultimately from the French proverb "*A brebis tondue Dieu mesure le vent.*"

To whistle down the wind. *See under* WHISTLE.

Windbag. A long-winded, bombastic speaker, who uses inflated phrases and promises far more than he can perform.

Windfall. An unexpected piece of good luck, especially an unexpected legacy; something worth having that comes to one without any personal exertion—like fruit which has fallen from the tree and so does not have to be picked.

Windjammer. A sailing ship, or one of its crew. The term is a modern one, born since steam superseded sail.

Windy City. Chicago.

Windmill. To have windmills in your head. To be full of fancies; TO HAVE A BEE IN YOUR BONNET (*see under* BEE). SANCHO PANZA says:

> Did I not tell you they were windmills, and that nobody could think otherwise, unless he had also windmills in his head? CERVANTES: *Don Quixote*, Pt. I, ch. viii.

To tilt at windmills. To face imaginary adversaries, combat CHIMÆRAS. The allusion is to *Don* QUIXOTE (Pt. I, ch. viii) when the crazy knight imagines them to be GIANTS and gives battle.

Window. Window Dressing. Properly

the display of goods in a shop window for the purpose of attracting customers. Figuratively, a specious display to present oneself or one's case, etc., in a favourable light.

Window Tax. A tax first imposed in 1691 and abolished in 1851, which accounts for the blocked-up window spaces in many old houses. It took the place of the Hearth Tax and was greatly increased in 1782 and 1797, and reduced in 1823. Houses with less than seven windows were exempt in 1782 and with less than eight in 1825.

All his goods in the window is much the same as WINDOW DRESSING, implying that a man is displaying all his superficial merits, etc., to view with nothing substantial to back them up.

Windsor. The House of Windsor. The style of the British Royal House adopted in 1917 in deference to anti-German sentiment to replace the then existing style of Saxe-Coburg-Gotha derived from Albert the PRINCE CONSORT. It was changed in 1960 to Mountbatten-Windsor for the descendants of Queen Elizabeth II, other than those entitled to the style of Royal Highness or of Prince and Princess.

After his abdication, 11 December 1936, King Edward VIII was created Duke of Windsor.

The Knights of Windsor. *See under* KNIGHT.

Windsor Herald. One of six heralds of the College of Arms, and others being Chester, Lancaster, Richmond, Somerset and York. *See* HERALDRY.

The Widow at Windsor. *See under* WIDOW.

Wine. Wine of Ape. In Chaucer's Prologue to the *Manciple's Tale*, the Manciple says, "I trow that ye have drunken wine of ape"—*i.e.* wine to make you foolishly drunk; in French *vin de singe*. According to Rabbinical tradition SATAN came to Noah when he was planting vines, and slew a *lamb*, a *lion*, a *pig*, and an *ape*, to teach Noah that man, in turn, reveals the characteristics of all four according to the amount of liquor consumed.

To put new wine in old bottles. To impose new practices, principles, etc.,

on people or things too old or unfit to stand the strain. A reference to the unwisdom of putting new fermentations in old wine-skins which are bound to crack under the pressure.

Wing. Don't try to fly without wings. Attempt nothing you are not fit for or until you are properly equipped to do so. A Latin saying; Plautus has (*Pœnulus*, IV, ii, 47): *Sine pennis volare haud facile est*, It is by no means easy to fly without wings.

On the wing. Flying, in motion, or about to depart or take flight.

To clip one's wings. To take down one's conceit; to hamper one's freedom of action.

To lend wings. To spur one's speed.

To take one under your wing. To assume patronage of, to protect. The allusion is to a hen gathering her chicks under her wing.

To take wing. To fly away; to depart without warning.

Winifred, or **Winefride, St.** Patron SAINT of North Wales and virgin martyr. According to the story she was the daughter of a Welsh chieftain and was instructed by St. Beuno. Prince Caradoc made violent advances to her and she fled to the church for safety. Caradoc pursued her and struck off her head, but it was replaced on her body by St. Beuno who breathed life into her again. She died a second time about 660. The miraculous healing spring of Holywell (Flintshire) gushed forth where her head had come to rest, and it became a regular resort of pilgrims. *Cp.* PAUL, St.

Wink. Forty winks. A short nap, a doze.

Like winking. Very quickly, in a flash.

A nod is as good as a wink to a blind horse. *See* NOD.

To tip one the wink. To give him a hint privately; to give a signal or secret hint.

To wink at. To connive at, or to affect not to notice.

> He knows not how to wink at human frailty
> Or pardon weakness that he never felt.
> ADDISON: *Cato*, 102.

Winkle, Rip Van. *See* RIP VAN WINKLE.

Winkle-pickers. Shoes with very elongated and pointed toes, affected by some in the early 1960s. The allusion is to the use of a pin for picking winkles out of their shells.

Winter. The coldest part of the year. In the Northern Hemisphere DECEMBER, JANUARY, FEBRUARY; astronomically from 21/22 December to 21/22 March.

> From winter, plague and pestilence, good lord, deliver us!
>
> THOMAS NASHE: *Summer's Last Will and Testament.*

Winter's King and Queen. Frederick V, Elector Palatine, and his wife Elizabeth, who reigned in Bohemia from November 1619 to November 1620. Elizabeth was the daughter of James I of England and her beauty inspired Sir Henry Wotton's lyric, *Elizabeth of Bohemia.*

Wipe. Old slang for a pocket-handkerchief.

To wipe one's nose. To affront him; to give him a blow on the nose. Similarly, **to wipe a person's eye,** to steal a march on him; **to fetch one a wipe over the knuckles,** to give him a good rap.

To wipe the floor with someone. To defeat him completely and ignominiously, literally or figuratively; to demolish utterly all his arguments, to floor him absolutely.

Wiped out. Destroyed, annihilated; quite obliterated.

Wire. A live wire. A wire charged with electricity; hence, a very lively person abounding with energy.

To pull the wires, wire-pulling. The same as TO PULL THE STRINGS (*see under* PULL).

Wisdom. The Wisdom of Solomon. A book of the Old Testament APOCRYPHA, probably written by an Alexandrian Jew between 100 B.C. and A.D. 50. It seems to be a reply to the Stoicism and Epicureanism reflected in the Book of *Ecclesiastes*, and is designed to reawaken loyalty and zeal for the old Jewish faith among apostates and waverers.

The wisdom of many and the wit of one. Lord John Russell (1792–1878) thus defined a proverb.

Wisdom tooth. The popular name for the third molar in each jaw. Wisdom teeth usually appear between the ages of 17 and 25, hence the name from association with years of discretion.

To cut your wisdom teeth. To reach the years of discretion.

Wise, The. The following have been thus surnamed:

Wise Men of the East. *See* MAGI.

Wise Men of Gotham. *See* GOTHAM.

The Wise Men of Greece. Also known as *The Seven Sages*, all of whom flourished in the 6th century B.C..

Bias of Priene, one of whose sayings was: "Most men are bad."

Chilo of Sparta. "Consider the end." *See* DE MORTUIS.

Cleobulus of Lindos. "The golden mean" or "Avoid extremes."

Periander of Corinth. "Nothing is impossible to industry."

Pittacus of Mitylene. "Seize time by the forelock."

Solon of Athens (*c.* 640–*c.* 558 B.C.). "Know thyself."

Thales of Miletus. "Who hateth suretyship is sure."

The Wisest Man of Greece. So the Delphic ORACLE pronounced SOCRATES to be, and Socrates modestly made answer: "'Tis because I alone of all the Greeks know that I know nothing."

The Wisest fool in Christendom. James I of ENGLAND (1566, 1603–1625); so called by Henry IV of France.

Wiseacre (Ger. *Weissager*, a soothsayer or prophet). This word, like SOPHIST, has quite lost its original meaning and is applied to dunces, wise only in their own conceit.

There is a story told that Ben Jonson, at the *Devil*, in FLEET STREET, said to a country gentleman who boasted of his estates, "What care we for your dirt and clods? Where you have an acre of land, I have ten acres of wit." The landed gentleman retorted by calling Ben "Good Mr. Wiseacre." The story may pass for what it is worth.

Wisecrack. A colloquialism for a facetious or witty remark.

Wish. Wish Hounds, or **Yell Hounds.** Spectral hounds that hunt the wildest parts of Dartmoor on moonless nights, urged on by the "Midnight Hunter of the Moor" on his huge horse which breathes fire and flame. The baying of these hounds, held by some to be headless, if heard, spells death to the hearer within the year. The Abbot's Way, an ancient track across the southern part of the moor, is said to be their favourite path. *See* WILD HUNTSMAN.

The wish is father to the thought. We are always ready to believe what we most want to believe. When the Prince says to his dying father, "I never thought to hear you speak again," Henry IV replies:

> Thy wish was father, Harry, to that thought.
> I stay too long for thee, I weary thee.
> SHAKESPEARE: *Henry IV, Pt. II*, IV, iv.

To wish one farther. To prefer his room to his company; to wish him gone.
Wishful thinking. A popular psychoanalytical term describing the unconscious expression of one's desire in accordance with one's wishes; the thinking of a thing to be true because one wants it to be so.
Wishing bone. *See* MERRYTHOUGHT.
Wishing Cap. *See* FORTUNATUS.
Wit. Understanding, from O.E. *witan*, to know.
The five wits. *See under* FIVE.
At one's wits' end. Quite at a loss as to what to say or what to do next; "flummoxed".
To live on one's wits. To live by temporary shifts and expedients rather than by honest work.
To have one's wits about one. To be wide awake; observant of all that is going on and prepared to take advantage of any opportunity that offers.
To wit. Namely; that is to say.
Witch. Waking a witch. *See* WAKING.
Witchcraft. (O.E. *wiccian*, to practise sorcery). Belief in witchcraft, prevalent into the 18th century and later, was a legacy from pagan times and is found in the BIBLE (*see* WITCH OF ENDOR). DIVINATION of all kinds was a fundamental aspect of witchcraft. Even St. AUGUSTINE believed in it; in 1258, Pope Alexander IV instructed the INQUISITION to deal with witchcraft when allied to heresy and Innocent VIII's celebrated bull (*Summis Desiderantes*, 1484) encouraged the Inquisition to severe measures against witches. Countless people suf-

fered death from this superstition, especially old women. Witchcraft was made a felony in ENGLAND in 1542, causing death by witchcraft became a capital offence in 1563, and in the same year witchcraft became subject to the death penalty in SCOTLAND.

Witch-hunting was a particular pastime of 17th-century PRESBYTERIANS until after the RESTORATION. The notorious "witch-finder" Matthew Hopkins travelled through the eastern counties in the 1640s to hunt out witches and is said to have hanged 60 in one year in Essex alone. In 1647 he was tested by his own methods; when cast into the river, he floated, and so was hanged as a WIZARD. *Cp.* MCCARTHYISM.

The last trial for witchcraft in ENGLAND occurred in 1712, and in SCOTLAND in 1722. English and Scottish laws against witchcraft were repealed in 1736.
Witch balls. The popular name for the lustred glass globes in use since the 16th century as domestic ornaments. They mirror in miniature the contents of a room, and the name is probably a fanciful corruption of *watch* ball. The inside of the ball was usually coated with a preparation largely made up of mercury.
The Witch of Endor. The woman who had "a familiar spirit" through whom Saul sought communication with the dead Samuel. She brought Samuel up "out of the earth" (a classic case of NECROMANCY) having first secured a promise from Saul that he would take no action against her as a witch (*see* I *Sam*. xxviii).
The Witch of Wookey. *See* WOOKEY HOLE.
Witches' Sabbath. A midnight meeting of witches, demons, etc., supposed to have been held annually. Mediæval devotees of the witchcraft cult held sabbaths at CANDLEMAS, Roodmas, LAMMAS, and ALL HALLOWS' EVE, and their celebrations lasted until dawn. The rites were lead by the "Coven", a group of 12 members and one DEVIL.
Witch-hunting. In political usage it denotes the searching out and exposure of opponents alleged to be disloyal to the State, often amounting to persecution.

See MCCARTHYISM.

Witchen. *See* ROWAN.

Witenagemot (wit′ ė na gė mōt). The Anglo-Saxon national assembly of higher clerics and laymen (ealdormen, thegns, etc.) which gave advice and consent on legislation, taxation, important judicial matters, etc., and which formally elected a new king. *Witan* is O.E. for *wise men* (connected with *wit*, knowledge); *gemote* is *ge-*, together; *moot*, meet hence "an assembly of wise men".

Withershins or **Widdershins** (O.E. *wither*, against; *sith*, journey). An old English word, still in use in SCOTLAND and in north-country dialects, denoting a movement in a contrary direction to that of the SUN—as of a clock whose hands are going backwards. Witches and warlocks were supposed to approach the DEVIL *withershins*.

The opposite of withershins is *deasil* meaning righthandwise or sunwise (Gael. *deiseil*).

Wivern (wī′ vern). A fabulous creature of HERALDRY consisting of a winged DRAGON ending in a barbed, serpent's tail.

Wizard. A magician, one adept in the black arts; the male counterpart of a WITCH. It is derived from *wise*.

Wizard is popularly used to express admiration, etc., as, *a wizard performance*, a wonderful performance; *absolutely wizard*, absolutely splendid.

The Wizard of the North. A nickname given to Sir Walter Scott.

The Wizard of Oz. The central figure in the very popular children's book, *The Wonderful Wizard of Oz* (1900), by Lyman Frank Baum (1856–1919), a well-known American journalist. The musical comedy of the same name (1901) was a great success, which was carried on to the film of some years later.

Woden. *See* ODIN; WEDNESDAY.

Woden's dyke. *See* WANSDYKE.

Woebegone. Overwhelmed by woe, especially applied to the appearance—*a woebegone countenance*. It does not mean "woe, go away, be gone"; *begone* here is from the O.E. verb *began*, to beset, surround. It thus means "beset with woe."

Wolf. WILLIAM OF MALMESBURY (*Chroni-*

cles of the Kings of England, Bk. ii, ch. viii) says that the tribute of 300 wolves payable yearly by the king of WALES to Edgar the Peaceful (959—975) ceased after the third year because "he could find no more"; but they are recorded in ENGLAND as late as the 15th century and in IRELAND and SCOTLAND they seem to have lingered on until the 18th century.

The She-wolf of France. Isabella of France (1292–1358), daughter of Philip the Fair and adulterous wife of Edward II. She executed the Despensers and procured her husband's death (1327) at Berkeley Castle. His murderers are said to have thrust a hot iron into his bowels.

> She-wolf of France, with unrelenting fangs
> That tear'st the bowels of thy mangled Mate.
>
> GRAY: *The Bard*, II, i.

Wolf Cub. The long-established and original name for a member of the Junior branch of the SCOUT Movement, now called Cub Scouts (age range 8–11 years). The conception owes much to Kipling's *Jungle Books*.

Wolf month, or **Wolf-monath.** *See* JANUARY.

A wolf pack. A term applied in World War II to German submarines in a group.

Wolf whistle. An oafish call made by a male at the sight of a female. It implies admiration.

Between dog and wolf. Neither daylight nor dark, the BLIND MAN'S HOLIDAY. Generally applied to the evening dusk. In Latin, *Inter canem et lupum*; in French, *Entre chien et loup*.

Dark as a wolf's mouth. Pitch dark.

He has seen a wolf. Something or other has frightened him, formerly said of a person who had lost his voice. Our forefathers believed that if a man saw a wolf before the wolf saw him, he became dumb, at least for a time.

To see a wolf was also a good sign, inasmuch as the wolf was dedicated to ODIN, the giver of victory. *Cp.* FENRIR.

He put his head into the wolf's mouth. He exposed himself to needless danger. The allusion is to ÆSOP's fable of the crane that put its head into a wolf's (or fox's) mouth in order to extract a bone.

Holding a wolf by the ears. An old Greek saying; AUGUSTUS used it of his situation at ROME, meaning it was equally dangerous to keep hold or to let go.

To cry "Wolf!" To give a false alarm. The allusion is to the fable of the shepherd lad who so often called "Wolf!" merely to make fun of the neighbours, that when at last the wolf came no one would believe him. This fable appears in almost every nation the world over.

To keep the wolf from the door. To ward off starvation. We say of a ravenous person, "He has a wolf in his stomach", and one who eats voraciously is said *to wolf* his food. French *manger comme un loup* is to eat voraciously.

To throw to the wolves. To sacrifice someone (a companion, colleague, subordinate), usually to divert criticism or opposition from the "thrower"; to make someone the SCAPEGOAT. As a traveller in a sleigh, pursued by a pack of wolves, might throw food or other objects in the hope of gaining his escape.

Wake not a sleeping wolf! (SHAKESPEARE: *Henry IV, Pt. II*, I, ii). A variant of "Let sleeping dogs lie!"—Let well alone.

A wolf in sheep's clothing. An enemy posing a a friend. The phrase is taken from the well-known fable of ÆSOP.

Women. Hell hath no fury like a woman scorned. A popular saving derived from Congreve's *The Mourning Bride* (1697), III, viii.

> Heav'n has no rage, like love to hatred turn'd,
> Nor Hell a fury, like a woman scorn'd.

Wonder. The Seven Wonders of the World. In the ancient world:

The PYRAMIDS of Egypt.
The HANGING GARDENS OF BABYLON.
The Tomb of Mausolus (MAUSOLEUM).
The Temple of DIANA at Ephesus.
The COLOSSUS of Rhodes.
The Statue of JUPITER by Phidias.
The PHAROS of Alexandria.

A later list gives:

The Coliseum of Rome (*see* COLOSSEUM).
The Catacombs of Alexandria.
The Great Wall of China.
STONEHENGE.

The LEANING TOWER of Pisa.
The Porcelain Tower of Nanking.
The Mosque of San Sophia at Constantinople (Istanbul).

The Wonder of the World. The title given to Otto III, Holy Roman EMPEROR (980, 983–1002), on account of his brilliant intellectual endowment. The title was also applied to Frederick II (*see* STUPOR MUNDI).

The Wonderful Doctor. Roger Bacon, also called the ADMIRABLE DOCTOR.

The Wonderful, or Wondermaking Parliament. Also called the MERCILESS PARLIAMENT (1388), when Richard II's favourites were condemned for treason.

Wonder-worker. *See* THAUMATURGUS.

Wood. Don't cry, or halloo till you are out of the wood. Do not rejoice for having escaped danger till the danger has passed away. "Don't count your CHICKENS before they are hatched"; "there's many a slip 'twixt the CUP and the lip."

Drawn from the wood. Said of beer and wines served directly from the cask. Beer barrels have now largely been supplanted by metal containers and their contents dispensed through pressurized beer-engines, a matter of regret to connoiseurs of good ALE.

One can't see the wood for the trees. It is difficult to pick out the essentials from the surrounding mass of detail; the main issues are not readily apparent.

To touch wood. An old superstition to avert bad luck or misfortune or to make sure of something good; also when feeling pleased with one's achievement or when bragging. Traditionally, certain trees such as the OAK, ash, hazel, HAWTHORN and willow had a sacred significance, and thus protective powers. Properly these should be the ones touched but this detail has largely passed into oblivion and any wood is put to use. Often, jocularly, the forehead is touched.

Wooden. Used of one who is awkward or ungainly; or of a spiritless, emotionless person.

The Wooden Horse. *See under* HORSE.

The Wooden Horse of Troy. *See under* HORSE.

The Wooden Mare. An instrument

used for military punishments, also called the WOODEN HORSE (*see under* HORSE).

The wooden spoon. A booby prize.

Wooden Walls. When the Greeks consulted the Delphic ORACLE to ask how they were to defend themselves against XERXES, who had invaded their country, the evasive answer was to this effect:

> Pallas hath urged, and Zeus, the sire of all,
> Hath safety promised in a wooden wall;
> Seed-time and harvest, weeping sires shall tell
> How thousands fought at Salamis and fell.

Themistocles interpreted "wooden wall" to mean the Greek ships in the Bay of Salamis and so won a decisive victory over the Persians.

Woodcock. Old slang for a simpleton; from the ease with which he is ensnared. POLONIUS tells his daughter that protestations of love are "springes to catch woodcocks" (SHAKESPEARE: *Hamlet*, I, iii).

Wood's Halfpence. The copper coinage which William Wood began to introduce into IRELAND (1723) under a patent purchased from the Duchess of Kendal, George I's mistress, to whom it had been granted. The outcry against Wood's Halfpence, supported by Swift in his DRAPIER'S LETTERS, led to the withdrawal of the patent in 1725. The Irish PARLIAMENT and government were not informed of the scheme in advance and it was feared that the flood of COPPER coins would drive out the existing small stocks of GOLD and SILVER.

Wookey Hole. A famous cavern near Wells in Somerset, which has given rise to numerous legends. *Wicked as the Witch of Wookey* is an old local simile. Her repulsiveness led to her directing her spells against "the youth of either sex" as well as blasting every plant and blistering every flock. She was turned into a stone by a "lerned wight" from "Glaston" but left her curse behind, since the girls of Wookey found "that men are wondrous scant".

Wool. All wool and a yard wide. Genuine, of real quality; no sham or substitute.

Dyed in the wool. Cloth which is wool-dyed, not piece-dyed, and true throughout. Hence the phrase is used to mean through and through, genuine, out and out, as "dyed-in-the-wool teetotaller", a completely convinced and genuine teetotaller. *Cp.* A KNAVE IN THE GRAIN *under* GRAIN.

Great cry and little wool. *See under* CRY.

No wool is so white that a dyer cannot blacken it. No one is so free from faults that slander can find nothing to say against him; no book is so perfect as to be free from adverse criticism.

To be wool-gathering. To let one's mind wander from the matter in hand; to be absent-minded. As children sent to gather wool from hedges wander hither and thither, apparently aimlessly.

To go for wool and come home shorn. To have the tables turned on one.

To pull the wool over one's eyes. To delude or deceive; from the idea of obscuring one's vision.

Burial in Woollen. Under Acts of 1666 and 1678 corpses were not to be buried "in any shirt, shift, sheet, or shroud" other than of wool nor was the coffin to be lined with any other material. It was intended for the encouragement of English woollen manufacturers and was eventually repealed in 1814, after it had largely fallen into abeyance; it had long been ignored by those able and willing to pay the fines for its non-observance:

The Woolsack. The official seat of the Lord CHANCELLOR as SPEAKER of the HOUSE OF LORDS. It is a large red square bag of wool, rather like an enlarged hassock. There were originally four, probably introduced in the reign of Edward III as symbols of England's staple trade, on which sat the Judges, the Barons of the EXCHEQUER, the SERJEANTS-AT-LAW, and the Masters in CHANCERY. The woolsacks were technically outside the precincts of the House, as these officials had no voice in the proceedings; thus when the Lord Chancellor wishes to speak as a peer he goes to his place in the House.

The term *woolsack* is often applied to the office of Lord Chancellor.

Woomera. The name of the rocket testing

range in South Australia, appropriately an aborigine word for a spear-throwing stick.

Word. The Word. The SCRIPTURES; Christ as the Logos.

> In the beginning was the Word, and the Word was with God, and the Word was God.
>
> _John_ i, 1.

By word of mouth. Orally. As, "the message was passed by word of mouth", _i.e._ spoken, not written.

I take you at your word. I accept what you say and rely on what you tell me.

A man of his word. One whose word may be depended on; trustworthy; "he is as good as his word" and "his word is as good as his bond".

Many words will not fill a bushel. Mere promises will not help the needy. If we say to a beggar, "Be thou filled," is he filled?

The object of words is to conceal thoughts. _See_ SPEECH WAS GIVEN TO MAN TO DISGUISE HIS THOUGHTS.

Put in a good word for me, please! Do your best to get me some privilege or favour; put my claims, my deeds, etc., in the best light possible.

Soft words butter no parsnips. _See_ BUTTER.

To eat one's words. _See under_ EAT.

To give, or **pass one's word.** To give a definite undertaking, make a binding promise.

To have words with one. To quarrel; to have an angry discussion. **To have a word with one** is to have a brief conversation with him.

To take the words out of one's mouth. When someone else says what one is about to say oneself.

Upon my word. Assuredly; by my troth. As an exclamation it implies outraged surprise or irritation.

Upon my word and, or **of honour.** A strong affirmation of the speaker as to the truth of what he asserts.

Weasel words. _See under_ WEASEL.

A word to the wise! Said when giving advice as a hint that it would be well for the recipient to follow it. _See_ VERB. SAP.

The words stuck in his throat. He was unable to utter them owing to nervousness or great reluctance.

Work. Seven Works of Mercy. _See_ MERCY.

To give someone the works. To subject a person to rigorous or extreme treatment, either verbally or physically, even to the point of murder. A slang phrase of American origin.

To have one's work cut out. To have difficulty in completing or carrying out a task owing to circumstances.

To shoot the works. To stake one's all in a game of chance; to make an all-out effort. A slang phrase from the U.S.A.

Working to rule. In trade-union parlance, to fulfil all the regulations relating to one's work literally and pedantically, in order to bring about delays in working, and frustration generally; another form of GO-SLOW tactics.

World. All the world and his wife. Everyone without exception.

A man, or **woman of the world.** One who is acquainted with the "ways of the world", a socially experienced, practical person. **A worldly man,** or **woman,** denotes one who only cares for the material things of this world.

In SHAKESPEARE's time _a woman of the world_ signified a married woman.

Out of this world. Something quite exceptional, quite out of the ordinary, indescribably luxurious, beautiful, etc. A 20th-century vogue phrase.

To be on top of the world. _See under_ TOP.

To go to the world. To be married.

The world, the flesh, and the devil. "The world" is the material things of this world as opposed to the things of the spirit; "the flesh", sensual pleasures; the DEVIL", EVIL of every kind.

The Third World. An expression coined in France (_le Tiers-Monde_) and applied to those less developed countries of Africa, Asia and Latin America which are not substantially aligned with the capitalist or communist "worlds" or political groupings.

The Workshop of the World. England in its 19th century heyday as the leading industrial nation. In the days of CHARTISM F.D.Maurice and Charles Kingsley produced a poster in 1848 addressing the workers "...Englishmen! Saxons! Workers of the great cool-headed, strongheaded nation of England, the workshop of the world..."

The World Turned Upside Down.
An inn sign illustrating an unnatural state of affairs, and also an allusion to the antipodes. It often took the form of a man walking at the South Pole.

World Wars. The name given to the wars of 1914–1918 (The Great War or World War I) and of 1939–1945 (World War II) in which participation was world-wide.

Worm. The word was formerly used of DRAGONS and great SERPENTS especially those of Teutonic and old Norse legend; it is now figuratively applied to miserable, grovelling creatures; also to the ligament under a dog's tongue.

Even a worm will turn. The most abject of creatures will turn upon its tormentors if driven to extremity.

Idle worms. It was once supposed that little worms were bred in the fingers of idle servants. To this SHAKESPEARE alludes:

> A round little worm
> Pricked from the lazy finger of a maid.
> *Romeo and Juliet*, I, iv.

To be food for worms. To be dead.

> Your worm is your only emperor for diet: we fat all creatures else, to fat us; and we fat ourselves for maggots.
> SHAKESPEARE: *Hamlet*, IV, iii.

To have a worm in one's tongue. To be cantankerous; to snarl and bite like a mad dog.

To satisfy the worm. To appease one's hunger.

To worm oneself into another's favour. To insinuate oneself into the good graces of another.

To worm out information. To extract it piecemeal or indirectly.

Wormwood. The common name for the aromatic herbs of the genus *Artemisia*, especially *A. absinthium*, from which absinthe and vermouth are concocted. Culpeper recommends it as a specific against worms. It is said to have been so called because this plant, according to legend, sprang up in the track of the SERPENT as it writhed along the ground when driven out of PARADISE. The word is also used figuratively to denote bitterness or its cause.

Worship. Literally "worth-ship", honour, dignity, reverence; in its highest and now usual sense, the respect and reverence man pays to God.

At one time the word carried a sense of personal respect, as in, "Thou shalt have worship in the presence of them that sit at meat with thee" (*Luke* xiv, 10), and in the marriage service (*Book of Common Prayer*), the man says to the woman: "With my body I thee worship, and with all my worldly goods I thee endow."

Magistrates and MAYORS are addressed as *Your Worship* and referred to as *the Worshipful Mayor of*...

Worst. If the worst comes to the worst. Even if the very worst occurs.

To get the worst of it. To be beaten, defeated; to come off second best.

Worsted (wus' ted). This varity of woollen thread formed of regular parallel strands takes its name from Worsted (now Worstead) near Norwich, once an important woollen centre. The name occurs as early as the 13th century.

Worthies, The Nine. Nine heroes—three from the BIBLE, three from the classics, and three from romance; or three pagans, three Jews, and three Christians, who were bracketed together by writers like the SEVEN WONDERS OF THE WORLD (*see under* WORLD). They are usually given as HECTOR, ALEXANDER, and Julius CAESAR; Joshua, DAVID, and Judas MACCABÆUS; ARTHUR, CHARLEMAGNE, and Godfrey of Bouillon. SHAKESPEARE's Pageant of the Nine Worthies in *Love's Labour's Lost* (V, ii) has an incomplete list of five which includes Pompey and Hercules, who are not on the traditional list.

> Nine worthies were they called, of different rites,
> Three Jews, three pagans, and three Christian Knights.
> DRYDEN: *The Flower and the Leaf*, 535.

The Nine Worthies of London. A kind of chronicle-history in mixed verse and prose of nine prominent citizens of LONDON, published in 1592 by Richard Johnson, author of *The* SEVEN CHAMPIONS *of Christendom*. His worthies are:

Sir William Walworth, who stabbed Wat Tyler the rebel, and was twice Lord

Mayor of London (1374, 1381).

Sir Henry Pritchard, who (in 1357) feasted Edward III (with 5,000 followers), Edward the BLACK PRINCE, John, King of France, the King of Cyprus, and David, King of SCOTLAND.

Sir William Sevenoke, who fought with the DAUPHIN of France and was Lord Mayor in 1418 and who endowed a grammar school.

Sir Thomas White, a merchant tailor, who was Lord Mayor in 1553 and founder of St. John's College, Oxford; also a founder of Merchant Taylors' School.

Sir John Bonham, entrusted with a valuable cargo for the Danish market, and made commander of an army raised to stop the progress of the great Solyman.

Christopher Croker, famous at the siege of Bordeaux, and companion of the Black Prince when he helped Don Pedro to the throne of Castile.

Sir John Hawkwood, famous soldier and commander of the WHITE COMPANY in Italy. He died in 1394 and is known in Italian history as *Giovanni Acuto Cavaliero*.

Sir Hugh Calveley (d. 1393), soldier and commander of FREE COMPANIES. He fought under the Black Prince against the French and became governor of the Channel Islands and famous for ridding Poland of a monstrous bear.

Sir Henry Maleverer, generally called Henry of Cornhill, who lived in the reign of Henry IV. He was a crusader, and became the guardian of "Jacob's well".

The above are essentially noted for military rather than civic achievement.

Wound. Bind the wound, and grease the weapon. A Rosicrucian maxim. *See* WEAPON SALVE.

Wraith (rāth). The phantom or spectral appearance of one still living, usually taken as a warning that this person's death is imminent. It appears to persons at a distance and forewarns them of the event. In general, a spectre, a ghost.

Wrath money. *See* WROTH.

Wren. A member of the Women's Royal Naval Service.

Write. To write down, to commit to writing, also to criticize unfavourably, to depreciate. Contrariwise **to write up** is to puff, to bring into public notice or estimation by favourable criticism or accounts.

To write off a debt. To cancel it.

Writer to the Signet. A member of an anciently-established society of solicitors in SCOTLAND who still have the sole right of preparing crown writs.

The writing on the wall. Said of something foreshadowing trouble or disaster. The reference is to *Dan.* v, 5–31, when a mysterious hand appeared writing on the wall while Belshazzar was feasting. Daniel interpreted the words to him as portending his downfall and that of his kingdom. Belshazzar was slain that night.

Wrong. The king can do no wrong. The legal and constitutional principle that the Crown acts on the advice and consent of ministers and therefore the Sovereign cannot be held responsible. It is another way of expressing the principle of ministerial responsibiity. Nor, according to Dicey (*Law of the Constitution*), "can the king be made personally responsible at law for any act done by him."

Wrong'un. A swindler, a cheat, a palpably dishonest person; also applied to false coin and other fakes.

Wroth Money, or **Wroth Silver.** Money paid to the lord in lieu of castleward, *i.e.* a feudal obligation in return for protection, *castle ward* or *guard* being KNIGHT SERVICE for defending the lord's castle. It was a local name for what is also called *warth money* or *ward silver.* Such a feudal rent was collected by the Duke of Buccleuch as lord of the HUNDRED of Knightlow in Warwickshire.

Wulfstan, or **Wulstan.** There are two English saints of this name. (1) Wulfstan, Archbishop of York (d. 1023), and formerly Bishop of Worcester, best known for his homily in Old English prose *Lupi Sermo ad Anglos*, etc., portraying the miseries of the year 1014 during the Danish onslaught. (2) Wulfstan, Bishop of Worcester (d. 1095), noted, in association with Lanfranc, for suppression of the slave trade between ENGLAND and IRELAND.

Wuyck's Bible. *See* BIBLE, SOME SPECI-
ALLY NAMED EDITIONS.

Wycliffite (wik′ lif īt). A LOLLARD, a follower of Wyclif (*c.* 1320–1384), who was
called "The Morning Star of the REFOR-
MATION". He condemned TRANSUB-
STANTIATION, and monasticism, and
held that only the righteous have the
right to dominion and property. He at-

tacked the Papacy and the BISHOPS, and
advocated the use of the BIBLE in English.

Wysiwyg. Computer slang for "What you
see is what you get" *i.e.* what you see on
the screen is exactly what will appear in
computer-printed form.

Wyvern. *See* WIVERN.

X

X. The twenty-fourth letter of the alphabet, representing the twenty-second letter of the Greek alphabet (*chi*), and denoting in Roman numeration 10, or, on its side ( ) 1,000 and with a dash over it (X̄) 10,000.

In algebra and mathematics generally *x* denotes an unknown quantity. The reason for this is that algebra came into use in Europe from Arabia and that the Arab. *shei*, a thing, a something, used to designate the mathematically "unknown" was transcribed as *xei*. (*Cp.* COSS)

X as an abbreviation stands for Christ as in Xmas.

Xanthian Marbles, The (zăn' thi ån). A collection of ancient sculptures and friezes discovered by Sir Charles Fellows in 1838 at Xanthus, a Greek city of Lycia, Asia Minor, and now in the BRITISH MUSEUM.

Xanthippe, or **Xantippe** (zăn tip' i). Wife of the philosoper SOCRATES. Her bad temper shown towards her husband has rendered her name proverbial for a conjugal scold.

Xanthus, or **Xanthos** (zăn' thŭs) (Gr., reddish-yellow). ACHILLES' wonderful HORSE brother of Balios, Achilles' other horse, and offspring of ZEPHYRUS and the harpy, Podarge. Being chid by his master for leaving PATROCLUS on the field of battle, Xanthus turned his head reproachfully, and told Achilles that he also would soon be numbered with the dead, not from any fault of his horse, but by the decree of inexorable destiny (ILIAD, XIX).

Xanthus is also the ancient name of the Scamander, and of a city on its banks. Ælian and Pliny say that HOMER called the Scamander "Xanthos", or the

"Gold-red river", because it coloured with such a tinge the fleeces of sheep washed in its waters. Others maintain that it was so called because a Greek hero of this name defeated a body of TROJANS on its banks, and pushed half of them into the stream.

Xaverian Brothers, The (zăv ēr' i ån). A Roman Catholic congregation founded at Bruges in 1839, concerned chiefly with the education of youth. It was founded by Theodore James Ryken who took the name Brother Francis Xavier after St. Francis Xavier (1506–1552), one of the earliest of the JESUITS, celebrated as the "Apostle of the Indies" and "the Apostle of Japan".

Xenocratic (zen ō krăt' ik). Pertaining to the doctrine of Xenocrates (396–314 B.C.), a disciple of PLATO, noted for his continence and contempt of wealth. He combined Pythagoreanism with Platonism. Even the courtesan LAIS failed to tempt him from the path of virtue.

Xerxes (zĕrks' ēz). A Greek way of writing the Persian *Ksathra* or *Kshatra*. Xerxes I, the great Xerxes, King of Persia (485–465 B.C.), is identical with the Ahasuerus of the BIBLE.

When Xerxes invaded Greece he constructed a pontoon bridge across the Dardanelles, which was swept away by the force of the waves; this so enraged the Persian despot that he "inflicted 300 lashes on the rebellious sea, and cast chains of iron across it". This story is a Greek myth, founded on the peculiar construction of Xerxes' second bridge, which consisted of 300 boats, lashed by iron chains to two ships serving as supporters.

Another story tells us that when he reviewed his enormous army before starting for Greece, he wept at the thought of the slaughter about to take place. "Of all this multitude, who shall say how many will return?"

Ximena (zim ē′ nȧ). The CID's bride.

Xiphias (zif′ i ȧs) (Gr. *xiphos*, a sword). The name used in mediæval times for a sword-shaped comet; also for the southern constellation now called Dorado; and a poetical name given to the swordfish (genus *Xiphias*).

Xylomancy (zī′ lō măn si). A form of DIVINATION using twigs, rods, etc. (Gr. *xylon*, wood; *manteia*, prophecy).

Y

Y. The twenty-fifth letter of the alphabet, derived from the Greek Y (*upsilon*), added by the Greeks to the Phœnician alphabet. *See* SAMIAN LETTER. It is used to represent both consonantal and vowel sounds.

As a mediæval numeral Y represents 150 and $\overline{Y}$, 150,000.

In algebra it denotes the second unknown quantity (*cp.* X). *See also* YE.

Yachtsman, The Noble. *See under* NOBLE.

Yahoo (ya hoo'). Swift's name, in *Gulliver's Travels*, for brutes with human forms and vicious propensities. They are subject to the HOUYHNHNMS, the horses with human reason. Hence applied to coarse, brutish or degraded persons.

Yahweh. *See* JEHOVAH.

Yama. In Hindu mythology, the first of the dead, born from the SUN, judge of men and king of the dead. His kingdom is the PARADISE for the worthy where friends and relations are reunited. His twin sister is called Yami and he is usually represented as four-armed and riding a buffalo.

Yank, Yankee (yăng' ki). A citizen of the U.S.A., properly a New Englander. The derivation is uncertain but probably from Dut. *Janke*, a diminutive of John, perhaps used originally of the Dutch of New Amsterdam. The word was popularized by the song YANKEE DOODLE. America is often referred to as *Yankee-land*.

Yankee Doodle. A popular mid-18th-century song perhaps first introduced by British troops during the Anglo-French war (1755–63). It is now a quasi-national air of the United States.

There are several suggested origins of the tune which was first printed in England in 1778 and in America in 1794, but none is conclusive.

Yclept (i klept'). An old English word meaning called, named, styled. It is now only used in a sort of arch facetiousness that Fowler calls "Worn-out Humour".

Ye. An archaic way of writing *the*, the *y* representing O.E.3. Early printers used *y* as a substitute for the letter Þ, the character representing our *th*, hence the use of *ye* for *the* and *yt* as an abbreviation for *that*. It was always pronounced *the*.

Ye is also, of course, the archaic nominative plural of the second person.

Year (connected with Gr. *horos*, a season, and Lat. *hora*, an hour). The period of time occupied by the revolution of the Earth round the SUN.

The Astronomical, Equinoctial, Natural, Solar, or Tropical year is the time taken by the Sun in returning to the same equinox, in mean length, 365 days 5 hours 48 min. and 46 sec.

The Astral or Sidereal year is the time in which the Sun returns from a given star to the same star again: 365 days 6 hours 9 min. and 9·6 sec.

The Platonic, Great, or Perfect year (*Annus magnus*), a great cycle of years (estimated by early Greek astronomers at about 26,000 years) at the end of which all the heavenly bodies were imagined to return to the same places as they occupied at the Creation. *See also* CALENDAR; CANICULAR PERIOD; EMBOLISMIC; LEAP YEAR; SOTHIC PERIOD; SABBATICAL YEAR.

Academic Year. The university year, usually beginning in October.

Financial Year. In the United Kingdom, the year ending 31 March. The taxation year, however, ends on 5 April as a consequence of the transition to the Gregorian CALENDAR. Until 1752, the year began on 25 March and the transition from the JULIAN Calendar was effected by omitting Eleven Days from the September of that year. Taxpayers objected to paying on a year thus shortened and so the taxation was correspondingly adjusted to end on 5 April.

Gregorian Year. *See* GREGORIAN.

Julian Year. *See* JULIAN.

Regnal Year. The year beginning with a monarch's accession. In Great Britain Acts of PARLIAMENT are still referred to by the regnal year in which they were passed; thus the Local Government Act 1929, is also dated 19 Geo. 5, the 19th year of the reign of George V.

Year Book. Historically, the term denotes the unique series of reports of cases decided in the courts of COMMON LAW, written in Norman French, and covering the period 1292–1534.

Year of Confusion. A.D. 46, when the JULIAN CALENDAR was introduced, a year of 445 days.

Year of Grace. *See under* GRACE.

Year of Our Lord. A year of the Christian era.

For a year and a day. In law the period of time which in certain matters determines a right or liability. Thus the Crown formerly had the right to hold the land of felons for a year and a day, and if a person wounded does not die within a year and a day, the assailant is not guilty of murder.

Year in year out. Continuously, all the time.

Yell Hounds. *See* WISH HOUNDS.

Yellow (O.E. *geolo*, connected with Gr. *chloros*, green, and with *gall*, the yellowish fluid secreted by the liver). In symbolism it indicates jealousy, inconstancy, adultery, perfidy, and cowardice. In France, the doors of traitors used to be daubed with yellow and in some countries the laws ordained that Jews must be clothed in yellow, because they betrayed Jesus, and in mediæval pictures JUDAS is arrayed in yellow. In Spain at an AUTO DA FE, the victims wore yellow, to denote heresy and treason. *See* COLOURS.

In HERALDRY and ecclesiastical symbolism yellow is frequently used in place of GOLD.

Yellow Books. Official documents, Government reports, etc., in France, corresponding to British BLUE BOOKS; so called from the colour of their covers.

Yellow dog contracts. An American name for agreements made by the employers with employees to prevent the latter from joining labour unions. Such contracts became invalid under an Act of 1932.

Yellow fever. A tropical fever accompanied by jaundice and black vomit; also called YELLOW JACK. In Australia the name was given to the gold-prospecting mania of colonial days.

Yellow Jack. The YELLOW FEVER; also the yellow flag displayed from lazarettos and commonly, but somewhat inaccurately, called the QUARANTINE flag, probably because it was the flag usually flown by vessels liable to the performance of quarantine. By an act of 1825, the yellow flag was adopted as one of three quarantine flags and when flown signified a clean bill of health. A yellow flag with a black ball in the centre signified the converse, and the yellow and black quartered flat meant dangerous plague or disease on board. In the current International Code of Signals (1931), the yellow (Q) flag, when flown by a ship entering territorial waters from abroad, still has the same meaning—"My ship is healthy and I request free PRATIQUE". Flag Q flown over the first substitute (QQ) means, in short, "My ship is suspect", and Flag Q flown over L (QL) means "My ship is infected".

The Yellow Peril. A scare, originally raised in Germany in the late 1890s, that the yellow races of China and Japan would rapidly increase in population and overrun the territories occupied by the white races with fearful consequences.

The Yellow Press. The sensationalist newspapers. The name arose in the United States when W. R. Hearst's *Journal*, during the circulation battle with Pulitzer's *World*, introduced a comic picture feature called "The Yellow Kid". This rivalry was dubbed "yellow journalism" and came to be characterized by scare headlines, sensational articles, lavish illustrations, comic features, Sunday supplements, etc.

The Yellow River. The Hwang-Ho in China, so called from the yellow earth or loess that it carries in suspension. It is also an epithet of the Tiber.

Yellow-back. A cheap novel, especially of the sensational kind. So called from the yellow board binding familiar on the railway bookstalls of Victorian days.

Yellow-hammer. A bunting with yellowish head, neck, and breast (O.E. *amore*; Ger. *Ammer*, a bunting). The tradition is that the bird fluttered about the CROSS, and got its plumage stained with the Blood; by way of punishment its eggs were doomed ever after to bear marks of blood. Because the bird was "cursed", boys were taught that it was right and proper to destroy its eggs.

Yen. To have a yen for. An expression of American origin, to have an intense desire or longing for. From the Chinese *yen*, opium smoke.

Yeoman. Historically, a middle class of small freeholders, variously defined at different periods and later applied to the class of "forty-shilling freeholders".

Yeoman service. Effectual service, characterized by hard and steady work. The reference is to the service of yeomen in the English armies of former days.

Yeoman of the Guard. *See* BEEFEATERS.

Yeomanry. British volunteer cavalry units were so called from 1761, although not effectively formed until 1794. In the 19th century they were largely used for suppressing riots and were essentially maintained by private benevolence and voluntary efforts. Most of them were former members of the regular cavalry. The Yeomanry were absorbed in the Territorial Army in 1907. *See* TERRIER.

Yes-man. An expressive colloquialism for one who always expresses agreement with his superior, irrespective of his private opinions.

Yeti. Tibetan name for the ABOMINABLE SNOWMAN.

Yew. The yew is a native British tree (*Taxus baccata*), and is commonly planted in churchyards because, as an evergreen, it is a symbol of immortality. The practice was also encouraged to provide a supply of bow-staves from the hard, elastic wood resulting from the slow growth of this tree, which lives to a great age. To decorate the house with yew was held to lead to a death in the family. Yew leaves and berries are poisonous.

Yggdrasil (ig drá sil). The world tree of Scandinavian mythology that, with its roots and branches, binds together HEAVEN, earth, and HELL. It is an ash, and is evergreen, and at the root is a fountain of wonderful virtues. In the tree, which drops honey, sit an EAGLE, a squirrel, and four stags. It is the tree of life and knowledge, and of time and space.

Yiddish (Ger. *jüdisch*, Jewish). A Middle German dialect developed in Poland under Hebrew and Slavonic influence, written in Hebrew characters, and used as a language by Eastern European Jews. As a result of the latter's widespread dispersal Yiddish became the *lingua franca* of world Jewry. Hence *Yid* as a term for a JEW.

Ymir (im ir). The primæval being of Scandinavian mythology, father of all the GIANTS. He was nourished by the four milky streams which flowed from the cow Audhumla. From his body the world was created and his skull became the vault of the heavens.

Yob. *See* BACK-SLANG.

Yodel (yō' dèl). To sing with frequent alternations between the ordinary voice and falsetto. It is properly peculiar to Switzerland and is a development of Switzerland and the Tyrolese.

Yoga (yō' gà). A practice of Hindu philosophy, the withdrawal of the physical senses from external objects. Adepts in yoga are able to hold their breath for protracted periods and do other things in apparent contravention of natural requirements. Hypnotism and self-mortification are part of the cult. Union with the Deity became its object (Sans. *yoga*, union, devotion). A *yogi* is one who practises yoga.

Yoke. To pass under the yoke. To make a humiliating submission; to suffer the disgrace of a vanquished army. The Romans made a yoke of three spears—two upright and one resting on them. When an army was vanquished, the soldiers had to lay down their arms and pass under this archway of spears.

Yom Kippur (yom ki pĕr'). *See* DAY OF ATONEMENT *under* ATONEMENT.

Yorkist. A partisan of the House of York in the WARS OF THE ROSES (*see under* ROSE).

Young. Young England. A group of young TORY politicians of the early 1840s who sought to revive a somewhat romantic concept of paternal feudalism and to idealize the functions of the territorial aristocracy. They saw their movement as a safeguard against revolution and the triumph of the LAISSEZ FAIRE doctrines of the MANCHESTER SCHOOL. Their leaders were Lord John Manners and George Smythe; Disraeli also joined their ranks.

Young Germany. A German school of the 1830s whose aim was to liberate politics, religion and manners from the old conventional trammels. Heinrich Heine was its most prominent representative.

Young Ireland. An Irish nationalist movement of the 1840s taking its name in imitation of Mazzini's YOUNG ITALY. There aims included the revival of Irish language and literature and national independence. Including both Protestants and Catholics, they were responsible for the futile rising of 1848. Their leaders included Smith O'Brien, Gavan Duffy, John Mitchel, Thomas Francis Meagher, and Fintan Lalor.

Young Italy. (*Giovine Italia*). A republican nationalist movement inspired by the exiled Mazzini and seeking to promote an Italian revolution. Founded in 1831 and imbued by its leader with fervent idealism, it never gained the support of the masses, but it

did much to develop the spirit of nationalism in the 1830s and 1840s. *See* CARBONARI.

Young Pretender. *See under* PRETENDER.

The Young Turks. *See under* TURK.

Ysolde (Yseult, Isolde, etc.**).** The name of two heroines of ARTHURIAN ROMANCE, *Ysolde the Fair*, daughter of the king of IRELAND, wife of King MARK and lover of TRISTRAM, the other *Ysolde of the White Hands* or *Ysolde of Brittany*.

Yuga. One of the four ages of the world into which, according to Hindu cosmogony, mundane time is divided.

Yule, Yuletide. CHRISTMAS-TIME. O.E. *gēol*, from Icel. *jōl*, the name of a heathen festival at the winter SOLSTICE.

Yule log, or **Yule clog.** A great log of wood formerly laid across the hearth with great ceremony on Christmas Eve and lit with a brand from the previous year's log. There followed drinking and merriment.

Yuppie. A young urban (or upwardly mobile) professional person. A popular acronym from the 1980s. *Cp.* CLIMBING THE LADDER.

Yves, or **Yvo, St.** (ēv, ē' vō) (1253–1303). Patron SAINT of lawyers, being himself a lawyer. He became an ecclesiastical judge at Rennes and in 1285 entered the priesthood. His work for orphans and widows earned him the title of "Advocate of the Poor". He was canonized in 1347 and his day is 19 May.

Yvetot (ēv' tō). **The King of Yvetot.** A man of mighty pretensions but little merit. Yvetot is a town in Normandy; the "King" was the lord of the town, and the title was in use from the 14th to the 16th century. The ballad of this title by Béranger, with satirical allusions to NAPOLEON, appeared in 1813 and became a type of the "*roi bon enfant*".

Z

Z. The last letter of the alphabet, called *zed* in England, but in America *zee*. Its older English name was *izzard*. It was the seventh letter of the Greek alphabet, *zeta*.

> Thou whoreson zed! thou unnecessary letter!
>
> SHAKESPEARE: *King Lear*, II, ii.

In mathematics it denotes the third unknown quantity; and as a mediæval numeral it represents 2,000. It is also used as a contraction mark as in *viz.*, *oz*.

Zadkiel (zăd' ki el). In Rabbinical angelology, the ANGEL of the planet JUPITER.

Zany (zā' ni). The buffoon who mimicked the clown in the Commedia dell'Arte; hence, a simpleton, one who "acts the goat". The name is the Ital. *zanni*, a buffoon, a familiar form of *Giovanni* (*i.e.* John).

Zarathustra. *See* ZORASTRIANS.

Zealots, or **Cananæans.** A Jewish sect founded by Judas of Gamala in the early years of the 1st century A.D., who fiercely opposed Roman domination. They fought fanatically during the great rebellion which ended in the destruction of Jerusalem in A.D. 70. *See* MASADA.

Zebi. *See* SABBATÆANS.

Zeitgeist (zīt' gīst) (Ger. *Zeit*, time; *Geist* spirit). The spirit of the time.

Zem Zem. The sacred well near the KAABA at MECCA. According to Arab tradition, this is the very well that was shown to Hagar when ISHMAEL was perishing of thirst.

Zemindar. Under the MOGUL emperors of India, one of a class of tax farmers, responsible for the revenues of land held in common. They were treated as landlords by the British and made proprietors paying a fixed annual tax. This change, introduced by Lord Cornwallis in Bengal in 1793, did not prevent RACK-RENTING of the peasantry by the zemindars.

Zemstvo (Russ. *zemlya*, land). The name given to the elected District Assemblies and provincial councils (elected by the District Assemblies) in Russia, introduced by Alexander II in 1864.

Zen. A Japanese Buddhist sect which believes that the ultimate truth is greater than words and is therefore not to be wholly found in the sacred writings, but must be sought through the "inner light" and self-mastery. It originated in the 6th century in China.

Zend-Avesta. The sacred writings of Zoroaster that formed the basis of the religion that prevailed in Persia from the 6th century B.C. to the 7th century A.D. *Avesta* means the lore, or sacred writings, and *Zend*, the commentary. Hence the application of *Zend* to the ancient Iranian language in which the *Zend-Avesta* is written. *See* ZOROASTRIANS.

Zenith, Nadir (Arab.). *Zenith* is the point of the heavens immediately over the head of the spectator. NADIR is the opposite point immediately beneath the spectator's feet. Hence, *to go from the zenith of one's fortunes to the nadir* is to fall from the height of fortune to the depth of poverty.

Zeno. The name of several PHILOSOPHERS. Zeno of Elia, who flourished about 500 B.C., was a disciple of Parmenides and one of the ELEATIC school. He is said to have been the inventor of DIALECTIC. When tortured for conspiring against the tyrant Nearchus he bit off his tongue and spat it in the tyrant's face.

Zeno of Citium (342–270 B.C.) was founder of the STOIC school at ATHENS.

One of his maxims was that we are given two ears, and only one mouth, to tell us that we should listen more than we should speak.

Zephyr (zef' ir). **Zephyrus**. In classical mythology, the west wind, son of Astræus and AURORA, and lover of Flora, identified with the Roman FAVONIUS; hence, any soft, gentle wind.

Zero (zē' rō) (Arabic, a cipher). The figure o; nothing; especially the point on a scale (such as that of a thermometer) from which positive and negative quantites are measured; on the Centigrade and Réaumur thermometers fixed at the freezing-point of water; on the Fahrenheit 32° below freezing-point.

Absolute zero is the point at which it would be impossible to get any colder; *i.e.* that at which it is totally devoid of heat (estimated at about —273° C).

Zero hour. A military term (first used in World War I) for the exact time at which an attack, etc., is to be begun.

Zeugma (zūg' mà) (Gr. *zeugnumi*, yoke). In grammar and logic, a term for a phrase in which one word modifies or governs two or more not connected in meaning. A well-known example is, "Miss Bolo went straight home in a flood of tears and a sedan chair." (Dickens, *Pickwick Papers*, xxxv.)

Zeus (zūs). The Greek equivalent of JUPITER. The root meaning of the word is "bright".

Zingari. Gypsies; so called in Italy. The name is thought to derive from *Sinte* or *sind* (India) and *calo* (black).

Zinoviev Letter. *See under* FORGERY.

Zion (Heb. *Tsiyon*, a hill). Figuratively, the chosen people, the Israelites; the church of God, the kingdom of HEAVEN. The city of David stood on Mount Zion.

In *Pilgrim's Progress* Bunyan calls the Celestial City (*i.e.* heaven) *Mount Zion*.

Daughter of Zion. JERUSALEM or its people.

Zionism. The Jewish movement for the establishment of the "national home" in Palestine. The Zionist movement was founded by Dr. Theodore Herzl of Vienna in 1895 and the Balfour Declaration of 1917 recognized Zionist aspirations. From 1920 to 1948 Palestine was a British mandate, administered under great difficulties arising from the friction between Jews and Arabs. The independent state of Israel was established in 1948.

Zip code. In the U.S.A., the system used to differentiate the mail delivery zones based on five-digit numbers. The name 'Zip' is derived from the initial letters of the name of the system, Zone Improvement Plan. The British Post Code composed of letters and numbers is a similar system.

Zodiac (Gr. *zodiakos*, pertaining to animals; from *zoon*, an animal). The imaginary belt or zone of the heavens, extending about eight degrees each side of the ECLIPTIC, which the SUN traverses annually.

Signs of the Zodiac. The zodiac was divided by the ancients into 12 equal parts, proceeding from west to east, each part of 30 degrees, and distinguished by a sign; these originally corresponded to the zodiacal constellations bearing the same names, but now, through the precession of the equinoxes, they coincide with the constellations bearing the names next in order.

Beginning with ARIES, we have first six on the north side and six on the south side of the Equator; beginning with CAPRICORNUS, we have six ascending and then six descending signs—*i.e.* six which ascend higher and higher towards the north, and six which descend lower and lower towards the south. The six northern signs are: *Aries* (the ram), TAURUS (the bull), GEMINI (the twins), spring signs; CANCER (the crab), *Leo* (the lion), VIRGO (the virgin), summer signs. The six southern are: LIBRA (the balance), SCORPIO (the scorpion), SAGGITARIUS (the archer), autumn signs; *Capricornus* (the goat), AQUARIUS (the water-bearer), and *Pisces* (the fishes), winter signs.

Zoilus. A Greek rhetorician of the 4th century B.C., a literary THERSITES, shrewd, witty, and spiteful, nicknamed *Homeromastix* (Homer's scourge), because he mercilessly assailed the epics of HOMER, and called the companions of ULYSSES in the island of CIRCE "weeping porkers". He also attacked PLATO and ISOCRATES. His name is applied to a spiteful and carping critic. *See* THRACIAN DOG *under* DOG.

Zombie. The python god of certain West African tribes. Its worship was carried to the West Indies with the slave trade, and still somewhat covertly survives in VOODOO ceremonies in Haiti and some of the Southern States of the U.S.A.

The word *zombie* is also applied to an alleged dead body brought to life in a more or less cataleptic or automaton state by Voodoo magic; also, colloquially, to a half-wit or thick-head.

Zone time. *See* STANDARD TIME.

Zoroastrians. Followers of Zoroaster or Zarathustra, founder of the ancient Persian religion called Zoroastrianism. Zoroaster's teachings are contained in the AVESTA and he taught that ORMUZD, the creator and ANGEL of GOOD, will triumph over AHRIMAN, the spirit of EVIL. Man's state after death will depend on the good and evil in his life. Sacred fire-altars were used in their ritual, hence their inaccurate appellation of "fire-worshippers". *See* GUEBRES; PARSEES.

Zounds! A minced oath, euphemistic for *God's wounds*.

Zucchetto (zu ket' ō). The small skullcap worn by Roman Catholic clergy; white for the POPE, red for a CARDINAL, purple for a BISHOP, and black for others.

Zuleika. The name traditionally ascribed to POTIPHAR'S WIFE, and a very common name in Persian poetry.

Zürich. The Zürich Bible. *See* BIBLE, SOME SPECIALLY NAMED EDITIONS.

Gnomes of Zurich. *See under* GNOME.

Zwickau Prophets, The. An early sect of ANABAPTISTS at Zwickau in Saxony, who sought to establish a Christian commonwealth. *See also* ABECEDARIAN.

Zwinglian. Pertaining to the teachings of Ulrich (Huldreich) Zwingli (1484–1531), the Swiss religious reformer and minister at Zurich. The term **Zwinglianism** refers especially to his teachings on the EUCHARIST. He maintained a completely symbolic interpretation and rejected all forms of local or corporeal presence, including Luther's doctrine of Consubstantiation. *see* IMPANATION; TRANSUBSTANTIATION.

A.M.D.G.

THE USBORNE LITTLE
SCHOOL
ATLAS

Stephanie Turnbull

Designers: Stephen Moncrieff and Helen Wood
Consultant cartographic editor: Craig Asquith

Cartography by European Map Graphics Ltd
Map design by Laura Fearn and Keith Newell

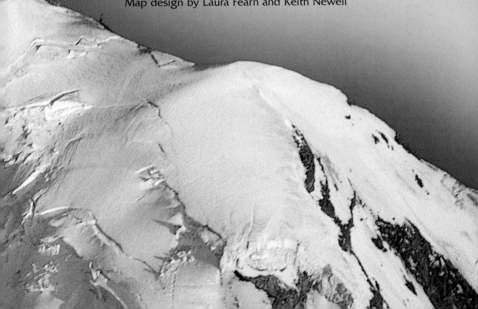

CONTENTS

This page: African elephants graze on plains south of the Sahara Desert.

Title page: Evening sunlight shines on Mount Rainier, in Washington, northwestern U.S.A.

Endpapers: This picture of the world at night has been made by combining many satellite images.

INTERNET LINKS

This book contains descriptions of many interesting websites where you can find out more about maps and places around the world. For links to these sites, go to the Usborne Quicklinks Website at **www.usborne-quicklinks.com** and enter the keywords "essential atlas". There you will find links to take you to all the sites.

Site availability

The links on the Usborne Quicklinks Website will be reviewed and updated regularly. If any sites become unavailable, we will, if possible, replace them with suitable alternatives.

Occasionally, you may get a message saying that a website is unavailable. This may be temporary, so try again a few hours later, or even the next day.

Internet links

For links to all the websites described in this book, go to **www.usborne-quicklinks.com** and enter the keywords "essential atlas".

Help

For general help and advice on using the Internet, go to the Usborne Quicklinks Website and click on "Net Help".

To find out more about using your web browser, click on your browser's Help menu and choose "Contents and Index". You'll find a searchable dictionary containing tips on how to find your way around the Internet easily.

What you need

The websites described in this book can be accessed using a standard home computer and a web browser (the software that enables you to display information from the Internet). Here's a list of the basic requirements:

- A PC with Microsoft® Windows® 98 or a later version, or a Macintosh computer with System 9.0 or later

- 64Mb RAM

- A web browser such as Microsoft® Internet Explorer 5, or Netscape® 6, or later versions

- Connection to the Internet via a modem (preferably 56kbps) or a faster digital or cable line

- An account with an Internet Service Provider (ISP)

- A sound card to hear sound files

Computer not essential

If you don't have use of the Internet, don't worry. This atlas is a complete, self-contained reference book on its own.

4

Extras

Some websites need additional free programs, called plug-ins, to play sounds, or to show videos, animations or 3-D images. If you go to a site and you do not have the necessary plug-in, a message should come up on the screen.

There is usually a button on the site that you can click on to download the plug-in. Alternatively, go to Usborne Quicklinks and click on "Net Help". There you can find links to download plug-ins. Here is a list of plug-ins that you might need:

- **QuickTime** – lets you play video clips.

- **RealOne**™ **Player** – lets you play video clips and sound files.

- **Flash**™ – lets you play animations.

- **Shockwave**® – lets you play animations and enjoy interactive sites.

Computer viruses

A computer virus is a program that can damage your computer. A virus can get into your computer when you download programs from the Internet, or in an attachment (an extra file) that arrives with an email. We strongly recommend that you buy anti-virus software to protect your computer and that you update the software regularly. You can buy anti-virus software at computer stores or download it from the Internet. To find out more about viruses, go to Usborne Quicklinks and click on "Net Help".

Macintosh and QuickTime are trademarks of Apple computer, Inc., registered in the U.S.A. and other countries.

RealOne Player is a trademark of RealNetworks, Inc., registered in the U.S.A. and other countries.

Flash and Shockwave are trademarks of Macromedia, Inc., registered in the U.S.A. and other countries.

Internet safety

When using the Internet, make sure you follow these simple safety rules.

- Ask your parent's or guardian's permission before you connect to the Internet. They can then stay nearby if they think they should do so.

- If you write a message in a website guest book or on a website message board, do not include your email address, real name, address or telephone number.

- If a website asks you to log in or register by typing your name or email address, ask the permission of an adult first.

- If you receive email from someone you don't know, tell an adult and do not reply to the email.

- Never arrange to meet anyone you have talked to on the Internet.

Note for parents

The websites described in this book are regularly checked and reviewed by Usborne editors and the links in Usborne Quicklinks are updated. However, the content of a website may change at any time and Usborne Publishing is not responsible for the content of any website other than its own.

We recommend that children are supervised while on the Internet, that they do not use Internet chat rooms and that you use Internet filtering software to block unsuitable material. Please ensure that your children follow the safety guidelines above. For more information, go to the Net Help area on the Usborne Quicklinks Website at **www.usborne-quicklinks.com**

MAPS AND ATLASES

An atlas is a collection of maps, along with useful information about the areas shown. The maps in this atlas cover the whole world and are grouped by continent.

What maps show

A map is an image that represents an area of the Earth's surface, usually from above. Unlike a photograph, which shows exactly what an area looks like, a map can show features of the area in a clear, simplified way. It can also give different information, such as place names. Symbols are often used to mark features such as volcanoes and waterfalls.

Wolf volcano

Darwin volcano

Fernandina

Alcedo volcano

La Cumbre volcano

San Salvador

Isabela

Santa Cruz

Sierra Negra volcano

Cerro Azul volcano

This simple map of the central Galapagos Islands names the main islands and their volcanoes.

Floreana

This is a satellite image of part of the Galapagos Islands. Using the map on this page, can you identify the islands shown in the satellite photo?

Which way is up?

Although the Earth doesn't have a top and a bottom, north is usually at the top of maps. But it is sometimes more convenient to reposition a map, so north might not necessarily be at the top. Some maps have a compass symbol that indicates where north lies.

Physical and political

Physical maps indicate natural features such as mountains, deserts, rivers and lakes. Political maps focus on the division of the Earth's surface into different countries. Look on pages 16–17 for a political map of the world, and on pages 18–19 for a physical map. Most of the maps in this atlas show physical features as well as country borders, cities and towns.

Using satellites

Today, scientists can make more accurate maps of the world than ever before, using information from artificial satellites in space. These devices travel around, or orbit, the Earth, and send back pictures of its surface. Satellite images provide detailed views of the Earth, and are often artificially shaded to highlight certain features, for example forests or deserts, so they are easier to see. They are used for a variety of purposes, such as monitoring weather conditions and natural hazards.

Map scales

The size of a map in relation to the area it shows is called its scale. Some maps have a scale bar, which is a rule with measurements. It tells you how many miles or km are represented by a certain distance on the map. Other maps show these relative distances just as numbers. For example, the figure 1:100 means that 1cm on the map represents 100cm on the Earth's surface.

The scale of a map depends on its purpose. A map showing the whole world is on a very small scale, but a town plan is on a much larger scale so that features such as roads can be shown clearly.

Internet links

For links to the following websites, go to **www.usborne-quicklinks.com**

Website 1 Find physical and political maps of different countries.

Website 2 Look at detailed satellite pictures of any part of the world.

This illustration shows a satellite that monitors weather conditions on Earth. It collects data using powerful radar.

1:110,700,000

| 0 | 1,000 | 2,000 | 3,000km |

| 0 | 1,000 | 2,000 miles |

This map of Europe is on a small scale so that it all fits onto one small map.

1:9,700,000

| 0 | 100 | 200 | 300km |

| 0 | 100 | 200 miles |

This map of Denmark is on a larger scale to show more detail.

DIVIDING LINES

The Earth is divided up with imaginary lines that help us measure distances and find where places are. There are two sets of lines, called latitude and longitude.

This arctic fox lives in northern Canada, very near the Arctic Circle line of latitude.

Latitude lines

Lines of latitude run around the globe. They are parallel to each other and get shorter the closer they are to the two poles. The latitude line that runs around the middle of the Earth is called the Equator. It is the most important line of latitude as all other lines are measured north or south of it.

Longitude lines

Lines of longitude run from the North Pole to the South Pole. All the lines are the same length, and they all meet at the North and South Poles.

The most important line of longitude is the Prime Meridian Line, which runs through Greenwich, in England. All other lines of longitude are measured east or west of this line.

Other lines

The Equator is not the only named line of latitude. The Tropic of Cancer is a line north of the Equator. The Tropic of Capricorn is at the same distance south of the Equator. Between these lines are the hottest, wettest parts of the world. This region is called the tropics.

The Arctic Circle is a latitude line far north of the Equator. The area north of this includes the North Pole and is called the Arctic. On the other side of the globe is the Antarctic Circle. The area south of this includes the South Pole and is known as the Antarctic.

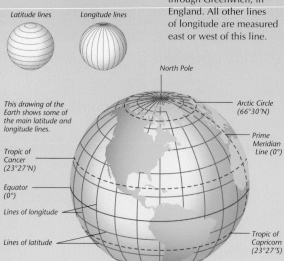

Latitude lines   Longitude lines

This drawing of the Earth shows some of the main latitude and longitude lines.

Tropic of Cancer (23°27'N)

Equator (0°)

Lines of longitude

Lines of latitude

North Pole

Arctic Circle (66°30'N)

Prime Meridian Line (0°)

Tropic of Capricorn (23°27'S)

Internet link

For a link to a website where you can find out more about the Earth's lines of latitude and longitude, and test your knowledge with a great latitude and longitude quiz, go to **www.usborne-quicklinks.com**

Using the lines

Lines of latitude and longitude are measured in degrees (°). The positions of places are described according to which lines of latitude and longitude are nearest to them. For example, a place with a location of 50°S and 100°E has a latitude 50 degrees south of the Equator, and a longitude 100 degrees east of the Prime Meridian Line.

Exact locations

The distance between degrees is divided up to give even more precise measurements. Each degree is divided into 60 minutes ('), and each minute is divided into 60 seconds ("). The subdivisions allow us to locate any place on Earth. For example, the city of New York, U.S.A., is at 40°42'51"N and 74°00'23"W.

The steamy rainforests of Malaysia lie near the Equator. Many apes, like the one shown here, live in these rainforests.

Using a grid

Lines of latitude and longitude form grids on maps. The maps in this book look similar to the one on the left. The columns that run from top to bottom are formed by lines of longitude and marked with letters. The rows running across the page are formed by lines of latitude and are numbered.

All the places listed in the map index on page 98 have a letter and a number reference that tell you where to find them on a particular page. For example, on the map on the left, the city of Christchurch would have a grid reference of C3.

This is a map of New Zealand, with a grid formed by lines of latitude and longitude.

HOW MAPS ARE MADE

The process of making maps is called cartography. Map-makers, or cartographers, compile each map by gathering information about the area and representing it as an image as accurately as possible.

Internet link

For links to websites with lots more about map projections and an interactive guide to how maps are made, go to **www.usborne-quicklinks.com**

Creating maps

Many sources are used to create maps. These include satellite images and aerial photographs. Cartographers often visit the area to be mapped, where they take many extra measurements.

In addition, cartographers use statistics, such as population figures, from censuses and other documents. As the maps are being made, many people check them to make sure they are accurate and up to date.

Map projections

Cartographers can't draw maps that show the world exactly as it is, because it is impossible to show a curved surface on a flat map without distorting (stretching or squashing) some areas. A representation of the Earth on a map is called a projection. Projections are worked out using complex mathematics.

There are three basic types of projections – cylindrical, conical and azimuthal, but there are also variations on these. They all distort the Earth's surface in some way, either by altering the shapes or sizes of areas of land or the distance between places.

A cartographer uses an electronic distance measurer to check the measurements of an area of land.

Cylindrical projections

A cylindrical projection is similar to the image created by wrapping a piece of paper around a globe to form a cylinder and then shining a light inside the globe. The shapes of countries would be projected onto the paper. Near the middle they would be accurate, but farther away they would be distorted.

Cartographers often alter the basic cylindrical projection to make the distortion less obvious in certain areas, but they can never make a map that is completely accurate.

This picture of a piece of paper wrapped around a globe illustrates how a cylindrical projection is made.

Below is a type of cylindrical projection called the Mercator projection, which was invented in 1596 by a cartographer named Gerardus Mercator. It makes countries the right shape, but makes those near the poles too big.

This cylindrical projection makes countries the right size in relation to each other, but some parts are too long. The projection was created in 1973 by Arno Peters. It is called the Peters Projection.

Conical projections

A conical projection is similar to the image you would get if you wrapped a cone of paper around part of a globe, then shone a light inside the globe. Where the cone touches the globe, the projection will be most accurate.

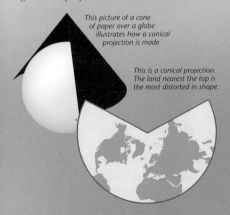

This picture of a cone of paper over a globe illustrates how a conical projection is made.

This is a conical projection. The land nearest the top is the most distorted in shape.

Azimuthal projections

An azimuthal projection is like an image made by holding paper in front of a globe, and shining a light through it. Land projected onto the middle of the paper would be accurate, but areas farther away would be distorted.

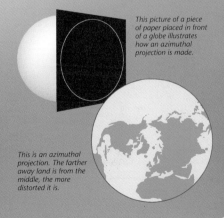

This picture of a piece of paper placed in front of a globe illustrates how an azimuthal projection is made.

This is an azimuthal projection. The farther away land is from the middle, the more distorted it is.

THEMATIC MAPS

Maps that represent information on particular themes, like the ones on these pages, are known as thematic maps. They help you to identify patterns and make comparisons between the features of different areas.

Earth's resources

The Earth contains all kinds of useful resources. Rocks and minerals can be used as building materials, and fuels such as coal, oil and gas contain energy that can be turned into heat and electricity.

Countries with large amounts of natural resources can become very rich. For example, Saudi Arabia, in western Asia, has large oil and gas reserves, which it exports all over the world.

This is an oil field, where oil is extracted from the ground using pumps. It is then piped to refineries and turned into products such as motor fuel.

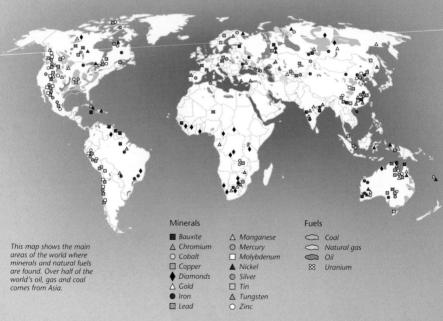

This map shows the main areas of the world where minerals and natural fuels are found. Over half of the world's oil, gas and coal comes from Asia.

Minerals

- ■ Bauxite
- △ Chromium
- ○ Cobalt
- □ Copper
- ◆ Diamonds
- △ Gold
- ● Iron
- □ Lead
- △ Manganese
- ○ Mercury
- □ Molybdenum
- ▲ Nickel
- ◉ Silver
- □ Tin
- △ Tungsten
- ○ Zinc

Fuels

- ⬭ Coal
- ⬭ Natural gas
- ⬭ Oil
- ⊠ Uranium

Different climates

The long-term or typical pattern of weather in a particular area is known as its climate. Climates vary across the world and depend largely on each area's latitude. The hottest parts of the world are those closest to the Equator.

Climate is also affected by other factors, such as wind and the height of the land. Oceans influence climate too – places near the sea normally have a milder, wetter climate than areas farther inland.

On this map, land is divided into five climate types. Dry areas are generally hot, but temperatures there can fall very low too. Some dry places, such as the Gobi Desert in eastern Asia, are extremely cold in winter.

- ☐ Polar
- ☐ Cold
- ☐ Temperate
- ☐ Dry
- ■ Tropical

World population

There are more than six billion people in the world, and the population is still growing. Experts think it may reach more than nine billion by 2050. The number of people living in a given area is known as its population density. Europe and Asia are the most densely populated continents in the world. About a third of the world's population lives in China and India alone.

Internet link

For a link to a website where you can discover how many people there were on Earth when you were born, and find out about the effects of population growth, go to **www.usborne-quicklinks.com**

This map shows the average population density by country. The shading indicates the number of people per sq km (0.386 sq miles).

- ■ Over 500 people
- ■ 200–500 people
- ☐ 100–200 people
- ☐ 50–100 people
- ☐ 10–50 people
- ☐ Fewer than 10 people

HOW TO USE THE MAPS

E ach continent section in this atlas begins
with a political map showing the whole
continent. The rest of the maps are larger
scale maps showing the various parts of the
continent in more detail.

Political maps

The shading on the political
maps in this atlas is there to
help you see clearly the
different countries that make
up each continent. The main
purpose of these maps is to
show country borders and
capital cities. Alongside
them there are facts and
figures about the continents
and their features.

*This is a section of the political map of
South America. You can see the whole
map on pages 28–29.*

Environmental maps

The majority of the maps in
this atlas are environmental
maps, like the one on the right.
The shading on these maps
shows different types of land,
or environments, such as
desert, mountain or wetland.

The main key on the opposite
page shows what the different
shading means. It also shows
the symbols used to represent
towns, cities and other
features. There is a smaller key
on each environmental map
repeating the most important
information from this key.

Finding places

To find a particular place or
feature on the environmental
maps, look up its name in
the index on pages 98–111.
Its page number and grid
reference is given next to the
name. You can find out how
to use the grid on page 9.

*The map on the right is part of the
environmental map of the U.S.A. The
numbered labels at the top explain some
important features of these maps.*

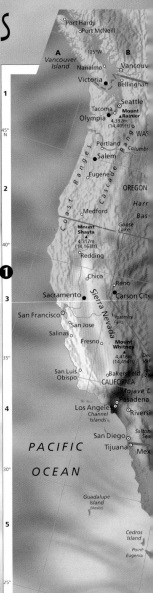

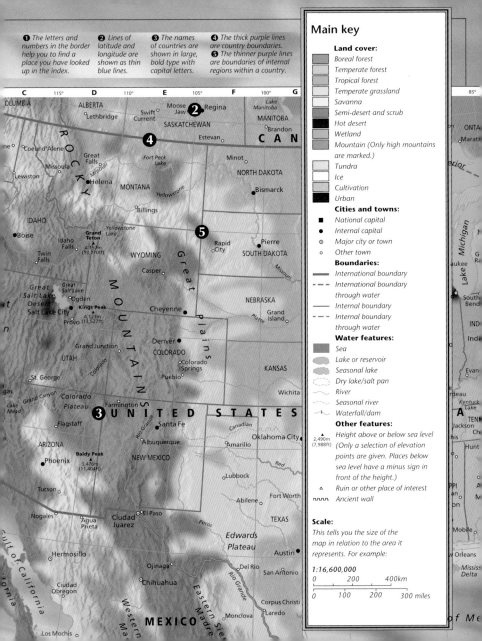

Main key

Land cover:
- Boreal forest
- Temperate forest
- Tropical forest
- Temperate grassland
- Savanna
- Semi-desert and scrub
- Hot desert
- Wetland
- Mountain (Only high mountains are marked.)
- Tundra
- Ice
- Cultivation
- Urban

Cities and towns:
- ■ National capital
- ● Internal capital
- ⊙ Major city or town
- ○ Other town

Boundaries:
- ——— International boundary
- – – – International boundary through water
- ——— Internal boundary
- – – – Internal boundary through water

Water features:
- Sea
- Lake or reservoir
- Seasonal lake
- Dry lake/salt pan
- River
- Seasonal river
- Waterfall/dam

Other features:
- ▲ 2,490m (7,988ft) Height above or below sea level (Only a selection of elevation points are given. Places below sea level have a minus sign in front of the height.)
- ∴ Ruin or other place of interest
- ⌐⌐⌐ Ancient wall

Scale:
This tells you the size of the map in relation to the area it represents. For example:

1:16,600,000

| 0 | 200 | 400km |
| 0 | 100 | 200 | 300 miles |

❶ The letters and numbers in the border help you to find a place you have looked up in the index.

❷ Lines of latitude and longitude are shown as thin blue lines.

❸ The names of countries are shown in large, bold type with capital letters.

❹ The thick purple lines are country boundaries.

❺ The thinner purple lines are boundaries of internal regions within a country.

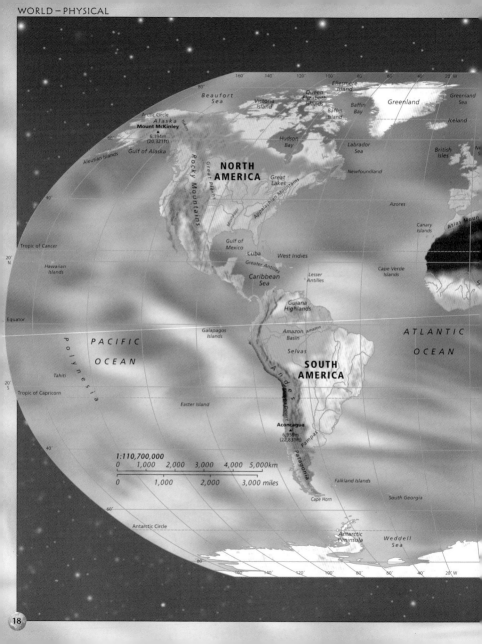

North America

Beaufort Sea
Victoria Island
Queen Elizabeth Islands
Ellesmere Island
Greenland
Greenland Sea
Iceland
Arctic Circle
Alaska
Mount McKinley
▲ 6,194m (20,321ft)
Baffin Island
Baffin Bay
British Isles
Gulf of Alaska
Aleutian Islands
Rocky Mountains
Great plains
Hudson Bay
Labrador Sea
Newfoundland
NORTH AMERICA
Great Lakes
Appalachian Mountains
Mississippi
Azores
Canary Islands
Atlas Mountains
Tropic of Cancer
20° N
Hawaiian Islands
Gulf of Mexico
Cuba
Greater Antilles
West Indies
Caribbean Sea
Lesser Antilles
Cape Verde Islands
Equator
Polynesia
PACIFIC OCEAN
Galapagos Islands
Guiana Highlands
Amazon Basin
Amazon
ATLANTIC OCEAN
Selvas
SOUTH AMERICA
Andes
Tahiti
20° S
Tropic of Capricorn
Easter Island
Aconcagua
▲ 6,959m (22,831ft)
Pampas
40°
1:110,700,000
0   1,000   2,000   3,000   4,000   5,000km
0   1,000   2,000   3,000 miles
Patagonia
Falkland Islands
South Georgia
Cape Horn
60°
Antarctic Circle
Antarctic Peninsula
Weddell Sea
80°

18

ARCTIC OCEAN

North Cape
Svalbard
Novaya Zemlya
Kara Sea
Severnaya Zemlya
Laptev Sea
New Siberia Islands
East Siberian Sea
Barents Sea

Arctic Circle

Scandinavia
Ural Mountains
Ob
Siberia
Verkhoyansk Range

EUROPE
Volga
ASIA
Lake Baikal
Sea of Okhotsk
Kamchatka Peninsula

Danube
Black Sea
Mount Elbrus
5,642m
(18,510ft)
Aral Sea
Caspian Sea
Altai Mountains
Gobi Desert
Huang He (Yellow)
Yellow Sea
Sea of Japan
Hokkaido

Mediterranean Sea
Zagros Mountains
Himalayas
Chang Jiang (Yangtze)
Honshu

Red Sea
Arabian Peninsula
Ganges
▲ Mount Everest
8,850m
(29,035ft)
East China Sea
Tropic of Cancer
20° N

AFRICA
Arabian Sea
Deccan Plateau
Bay of Bengal
Mekong
South China Sea
Philippine Islands
Micronesia
PACIFIC
OCEAN

Ethiopian Highlands
Sri Lanka
Taiwan

Lake Victoria
Seychelles
Sumatra
Celebes Sea
Equator

Congo Basin
▲ Kilimanjaro
5,895m
(19,340ft)
INDIAN
Borneo
Greater Sunda Islands
New Guinea
▲ Mount Wilhelm
4,509m
(14,793ft)
Melanesia
Solomon Islands

Rift Valley
Comoro Islands
OCEAN
Java
Arafura Sea

Madagascar
Mauritius
Reunion
Lesser Sunda Islands
Coral Sea
New Caledonia
Fiji Islands
20°

Kalahari Desert
Great Sandy Desert
AUSTRALASIA AND OCEANIA
Great Victoria Desert
Great Dividing Range
Great Barrier Reef
Tropic of Capricorn

Drakensberg
Cape of Good Hope
Tasman Sea
North Island
40°

Kerguelen Islands
Tasmania
South Island

SOUTHERN OCEAN
Antarctic Circle
60°

ANTARCTICA
See page 15 for key.
80°

40 60 80 100 120 140 160 180

NORTH AMERICA

The name "North America" can be used to mean several different things. In this atlas, North America includes Greenland, Canada, the U.S.A., the Caribbean, and the countries of Central America, which run along the narrow strip of land between the U.S.A. and South America. The continent has over 20 countries, including Canada, the second-largest country in the world.

ARCTIC OCEAN

Arctic Circle

Beaufort Sea

Bering Sea

Yukon

ALASKA (U.S.A.)

Anchorage

Victoria Island

CANADA

Vancouver

Columbia

These are columns of rock called hoodoos in Bryce Canyon National Park, U.S.A.

PACIFIC

OCEAN

Hawaiian Islands (U.S.A.)

UNITED STATES

Colorado

Los Angeles

Rio Grande

Tropic of Cancer

MEXICO

Mexico Ci

The shading on this map is there to help you see clearly the different countries that make up the continent.

GREENLAND
(Denmark)

Internet link

For links to websites with interactive maps of U.S. states and Canada's landscape, go to **www.usborne-quicklinks.com**

smere
nd
on
sbeth
ds

Baffin
Island

Godthab ■

Hudson
Bay

Newfoundland

St. Lawrence

Montreal
Ottawa ■ ○

Great
Lakes

New York

Chicago ○

Washington D.C. ■

AMERICA

Mississippi

Houston

Gulf of
Mexico

Havana ■
CUBA

THE
BAHAMAS

Puerto Rico
(U.S.A.)

Guadeloupe
(France)

DOMINICA
Martinique (France)

BARBADOS

HAITI
DOMINICAN
REPUBLIC

JAMAICA

BELIZE
GUATEMALA
HONDURAS
EL SALVADOR
NICARAGUA
COSTA RICA
PANAMA

Caribbean Sea

TRINIDAD
AND TOBAGO

ATLANTIC
OCEAN

Arctic Circle

Tropic of Cancer

Facts

Total land area 22,656,190 sq km (8,745,289 sq miles)
Total population 487 million
Biggest city Mexico City, Mexico
Biggest country Canada 9,970,610 sq km (3,849,653 sq miles)
Smallest country Saint Kitts and Nevis 269 sq km (104 sq miles)

Highest mountain Mount McKinley, Alaska, U.S.A. 6,194m (20,321ft)
Longest river Mississippi/Missouri, U.S.A. 6,019km (3,741 miles)
Biggest lake Lake Superior, between the U.S.A. and Canada 82,414 sq km (31,820 sq miles)
Highest waterfall Yosemite Falls, on the Yosemite Creek, California, U.S.A. 739m (2,425ft)
Biggest desert Great Basin Desert, U.S.A. 492,000 sq km (190,000 sq miles)
Biggest island Greenland 2,175,600 sq km (840,000 sq miles)

Main mineral deposits Silver, gold, copper, lead, zinc, graphite, molybdenum, nickel
Main fuel deposits Oil, coal, natural gas, uranium

The bald eagle is the national bird of the U.S.A. It is not really bald, but has white feathers on its head.

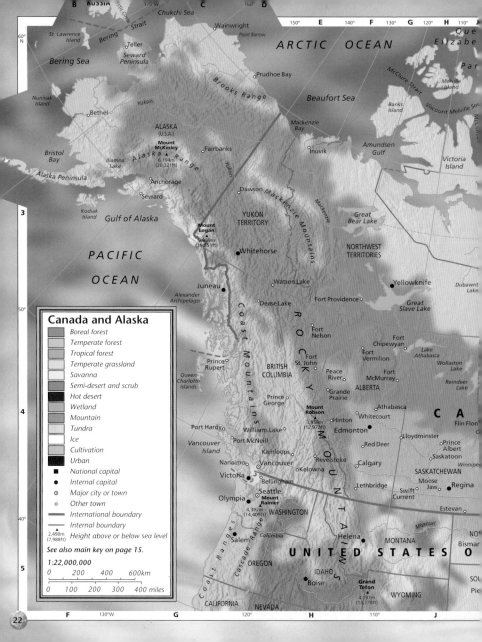

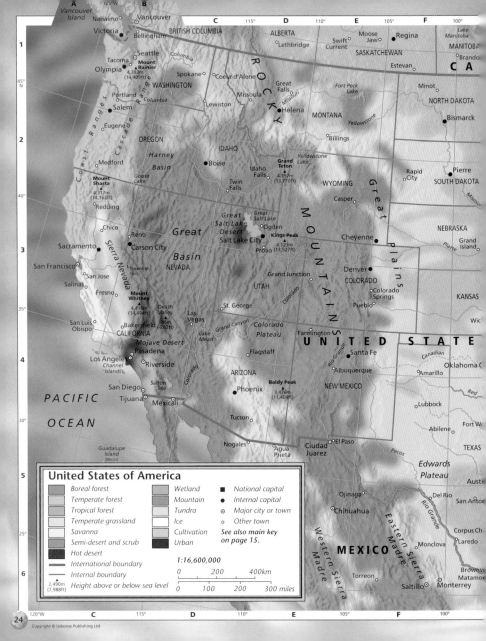

120°W A 115° B 110° C 105° D 100° E 95° F 90°

San Diego
Tijuana
Mexicali
CALIFORNIA
Phoenix
ARIZONA
Tucson
Nogales
Agua Prieta
Ciudad Juarez
El Paso
NEW MEXICO
Lubbock
OKLAHOMA
Little Rock
ARKANSAS
Tupelo
MISSISSIPPI
Texarkana
Shreveport
Jackson
Hattiesburg
LOUISIANA
Baton Rouge
New Orleans

UNITED STATES OF AMERICA

Fort Worth
Dallas
Abilene
Waco
Austin
Houston
San Antonio
Galveston
TEXAS
Edwards Plateau

Guadalupe Island (Mexico)

Cedros Island
Point Eugenia

Gulf of California

Lower California

Hermosillo

Ciudad Obregon

Western Sierra Madre

Los Mochis
Culiacan

La Paz

Cape San Lucas

Mazatlan

Chihuahua
Ojinaga
Rio Grande
Pecos

Plateau
of
Mexico

Durango

MEXICO

Aguascalientes
Puerto Vallarta
Guadalajara
Colima
Colima
Morelia
Uruapan

Torreon
Saltillo
4,054m (13,300ft)
Matehuala
San Luis Potosi
Leon
Celaya
Teotihuacan
Mexico City
Puebla
Orizaba 5,610m (18,405ft)

Monclova
Monterrey
Laredo
Nuevo
Ciudad Victoria

Tampico

Matamoros
Brownsville
Corpus Christi

Eastern Sierra Madre

Gulf of Mexico

Bay of Campeche

Merida
Yucata Peninsu
Campeche

Tropic of Cancer

Tehuacan
Veracruz
Coatzacoalcos
Ciudad del Carmen
Villahermosa
Oaxaca
Acapulco
Southern Sierra Madre
Isthmus of Tehuantepec
Gulf of Tehuantepec
Juchitan
Tuxtla Gutierrez
Tajumulco 4,220m (13,845ft)
Belmopan
Tikal
BELI
GUATEMALA
Quezaltenang
Tapachula
Guatemala City
San Salvador
EL SALVAD

PACIFIC OCEAN

L 65°W M 60° N

Virgin Islands (U.K.)
ATLANTIC OCEAN

San Juan
Puerto Rico (U.S.A.)
Anguilla (U.K.)
Virgin Islands (France and Netherlands)
St. Martin (France/Netherlands)

Basseterre
ST. KITTS AND NEVIS
Montserrat (U.K.)

ANTIGUA AND BARBUDA
St. John's

Leeward Islands

Guadeloupe (France)
Basse-Terre

DOMINICA
Roseau

Martinique (France)
Fort-de-France

Windward Islands

1:11,000,000

0   100   200km
0   50   100 miles

Caribbean Sea

Lesser Antilles

Castries
ST. LUCIA

Kingstown
ST. VINCENT AND THE GRENADINES

BARBADOS
Bridgetown

St. George's
GRENADA

Margarita Island
Porlamar
Cumana
VENEZUELA

Tobago

Port-of-Spain
TRINIDAD AND TOBAGO
Trinidad

Equator

Galapagos Islands (Ecuador)

Puerto Ayora

115°W B 110° C 105° D 100° E 95°

26

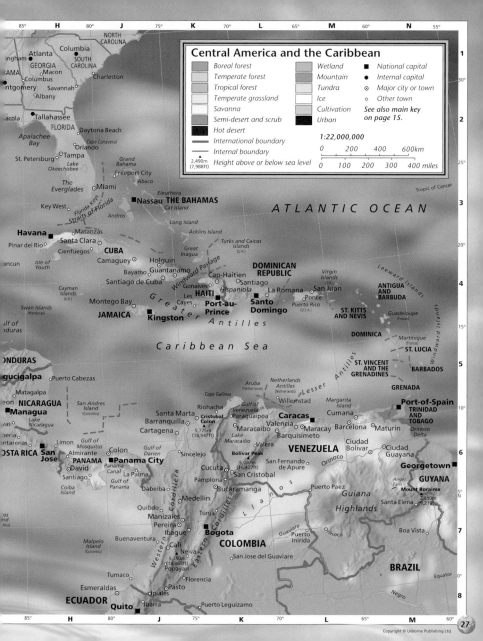

Central America and the Caribbean

Key:
- Boreal forest
- Temperate forest
- Tropical forest
- Temperate grassland
- Savanna
- Semi-desert and scrub
- Hot desert
- Wetland
- Mountain
- Tundra
- Ice
- Cultivation
- Urban
- International boundary
- Internal boundary
- 2,490m (7,988ft) Height above or below sea level
- ■ National capital
- ● Internal capital
- ⊙ Major city or town
- ○ Other town

See also main key on page 15.

1:22,000,000

0   200   400   600km
0   100   200   300   400 miles

NORTH CAROLINA
SOUTH CAROLINA
GEORGIA
Columbia
Atlanta
Macon
Columbus
Charleston
Savannah
Albany
Montgomery
Tallahassee
FLORIDA
Daytona Beach
Cape Canaveral
Orlando
Apalachee Bay
Tampa
St. Petersburg
Lake Okeechobee
The Everglades
Miami
Key West
Straits of Florida
Florida Keys

ATLANTIC OCEAN
Tropic of Cancer

THE BAHAMAS
■Nassau
Eleuthera
Cat Island
Grand Bahama
Freeport City
Abaco
Andros
Long Island
Acklins Island
Great Inagua
Turks and Caicos Islands (U.K.)

CUBA
■Havana
Pinar del Rio
Matanzas
Santa Clara
Cienfuegos
Camaguey
Holguin
Bayamo
Guantanamo
Santiago de Cuba
Isle of Youth
Cayman Islands (U.K.)

Cap-Haitien
Gonaives
HAITI
Les Cayes
■Port-au-Prince
DOMINICAN REPUBLIC
Santiago
Hispaniola
La Romana
■Santo Domingo
Virgin Islands (U.K.)
San Juan
Ponce
Puerto Rico (U.S.A.)

JAMAICA
Montego Bay
■Kingston

Greater Antilles

ATLANTIGUA AND BARBUDA
Guadeloupe (France)
ST. KITTS AND NEVIS
DOMINICA
Martinique (France)
ST. LUCIA
ST. VINCENT AND THE GRENADINES
BARBADOS
GRENADA

Leeward Islands
Windward Islands
Lesser Antilles

Caribbean Sea

Port-of-Spain
TRINIDAD AND TOBAGO

HONDURAS
■gucigalpa
Puerto Cabezas
Matagalpa
NICARAGUA
■Managua
Lake Nicaragua
San Andres Island (Colombia)

Gulf of Honduras
Swan Islands (Honduras)

COSTA RICA
■San Jose
Limon
Gulf of Mosquitos
Almirante
PANAMA
Colon
■Panama City
David
Panama Canal
La Palma
Santiago
Coiba Island
Gulf of Panama
Malpelo Island (Colombia)

Cape Gallinas
Riohacha
Gulf of Venezuela
Paraguaipoa
Santa Marta
Barranquilla
Cristobal Colon 5,775m (18,947ft)
Cartagena
Maracaibo
Lake Maracaibo
Valera
Sincelejo
Dabeiba
Quibdo
Medellin
Manizales
Pereira
Ibague
Buenaventura
Cali
Neiva 5,750m (18,865ft)
Popayan
Tumaco
Esmeraldas
Ipiales
ECUADOR
Quito
Ibarra
Pasto
Florencia
Puerto Leguizamo

COLOMBIA
■Bogota
Tunja
Bucaramanga
Pamplona
San Cristobal
Cucuta
Bolivar Peak 5,007m (16,427ft)
San Fernando de Apure
Valencia
Maracay
Caracas
Barquisimeto
Maturin
Barcelona
Cumana
Margarita Island
Netherlands Antilles (Netherlands)
Aruba (Netherlands)
Willemstad

VENEZUELA
Ciudad Bolivar
Ciudad Guayana
Orinoco
Puerto Paez
Llanos
San Jose del Guaviare
Guaviare
Puerto Inirida

Georgetown■
GUYANA
Angel Falls
Mount Roraima 2,810m (9,219ft)
Santa Elena
Guiana Highlands
Boa Vista

BRAZIL
Negro
Equator

Western Cordillera
Central Cordillera
Eastern Cordillera

SOUTH AMERICA

South America is made up of 12 independent countries, along with French Guiana, which belongs to France. The continent's biggest and most industrialized country is Brazil, which covers about half of the total land. Brazil is also home to half of South America's population.

This is a guanaco. Guanacos are members of the camel family that live in South America. Guanaco hair is used to make textiles.

Caribbean Sea

Caracas

VENEZUELA

Medellín ○ ● Bogota

COLOMBIA

Orinoco

Quito ○

Equator

ECUADOR

Galapagos Islands (Ecuador)

Guayaquil ○

Mar

PERU

Lima ■

BOLIVIA

■ La Paz

● Sucr

Tropic of Capricorn

CHILE

PACIFIC

OCEAN

Santiago ● ○ Mendoza

ARGENT

Cape Horn

Drake Passe

The shading on this map is there to help you see clearly the different countries that make up the continent.

Georgetown
Paramaribo
ANA   Cayenne
URINAM FRENCH
        GUIANA
         (France)

Equator

Amazon

B R A Z I L

°Recife

■ Brasilia

Belo Horizonte

Parana

°Rio de Janeiro

RAGUAY   Sao Paulo

°Asunción

Tropic of Capricorn

°Porto Alegre

ATLANTIC

RUGUAY
■ Montevideo
enos Aires

OCEAN

alkland Islands
(U.K.)

This is a red-eyed tree frog. These frogs live in rainforests in South and Central America.

Facts

Total land area 17,866,130 sq km (6,898,113 sq miles)
Total population 346 million
Biggest city Sao Paulo, Brazil
Biggest country Brazil 8,547,400 sq km (3,300,151 sq miles)
Smallest country Surinam 163,270 sq km (63,039 sq miles)

Highest mountain Aconcagua, Argentina 6,959m (22,831ft)
Longest river Amazon, mainly in Brazil 6,440km (4,000 miles)
Biggest lake Lake Maracaibo, Venezuela 13,312 sq km (5,140 sq miles)
Highest waterfall Angel Falls, on the Churun River, Venezuela 979m (3,212ft)
Biggest desert Patagonian Desert, Argentina 673,000 sq km (260,000 sq miles)
Biggest island Tierra del Fuego 46,360 sq km (17,900 sq miles)

Main mineral deposits Copper, tin, molybdenum, bauxite, emeralds
Main fuel deposits Oil, coal

Internet link
For links to websites with a clickable map of South America and sounds of the Amazon, go to www.usborne-quicklinks.com

GRENADA

TRINIDAD AND TOBAGO

Port-Spain

Riohacha
Cape Gallinas
Santa Marta
Cristobal
Colon
5,775m
(18,947ft)

Netherlands Antilles (Netherlands)

Paraguaipoa
Coro
Willemstad
Lesser Antilles

Tortuga
Island

Margarita
Island

Barranquilla
Cartagena
Maracaibo
Maracay

Caracas
Cumana
Guiria
Maturin

Sincelejo
Magangue
Barquisimeto
Valencia
Barcelona

Liberia
Limon
Turbo
Caceres
Lagunillas
Lake
Maracaibo
Valera

Araure
Zaraza
Tucupita

Orin

Gulf of
Mosquitos
Colon
Gulf of
Darien

Panama City
La Palma

Bolivar Peak
5,007m
(16,427ft)

Barinas

Ciudad
Bolivar
Ciudad
Guayana

San Jose

COSTA RICA

Puerto
Armuelles
David
Santiago
Penonome

Dabeiba
Pamplona
San Cristobal

San Fernando
de Apure

VENEZUELA

Angel
Falls

Almirante
PANAMA
Panama
Canal
Gulf of
Panama

Medellin
Duitama

Cravo
Norte

Caicara

Coiba
Island

Nuqui
Quibdo
Manizales
Tunja

Puerto
Paez

Mount Roraima
2,810m
(9,219ft)

Malpelo Island
(Colombia)

Pereira

Bogota

Buga
Ibague

Santa Elena

Buenaventura
Cali
Neiva
5,750m
(18,865ft)

COLOMBIA

Guaviare

Puerto
Inirida

Boa Vist

Tumaco
Popayan

Florencia
San Jose del Guaviare

Guiana Highlands

Esmeraldas
Cape
San Francisco
Ipiales
Pasto

Orinoco

Ibarra
Nueva Loja
Puerto Leguizamo

Equator

Quito
Santo Domingo de los Colorados

La Chorrera

Negro

Manta
Quevedo

Japura

ECUADOR
Ambato
6,310m
(20,702ft)
Montalvo

Amazon

Babahoyo

Guayaquil

La Libertad
Cuenca

Iquitos
Leticia

Gulf of
Guayaquil
Machala

Atalaia do Norte

Tumbes
Loja

Amazon

Talara
Zumba
Maranon

Sullana
Chulucanas

S e l v a s

Cape Negro
Piura

Yurimaguas
Ucayali

Jurua
Purus
Madeira

Chiclayo
Moyobamba

Cruzeiro do Sul

Porto Velho

Pacasmayo
Cajamarca

PERU
Pucallpa

Trujillo
Huacrachuco

Rio Branco

Chimbote
Mount Huascaran
6,746m
(22,132ft)
Huanuco

Cerro de Pasco

Riberalta

PACIFIC OCEAN

A N D E S

La Oroya
Cobija

Lima
Huancayo

Puerto
Maldonado

Mala
Quillabamba

Machu Picchu

Magdalena

Chincha Alta
Ayacucho

Cusco

Rurrenabaque
Trinidad

Ica
Sicuani

Mount Coropuna
6,425m
(21,079ft)
Juliaca

Lake
Titicaca

Chala
Puno
La Paz
Concepcion

BOLIVIA

Mollendo
Arequipa
Mount Illimani
6,402m
(21,004ft)
Cochabamba
Santa
Cruz
San Jose
Chiqui

Oruro

Arica
Lake
Poopo
Challapata
Camiri

CHILE
Gulf of
Arica
Sucre

Potosi
Charagua

Same scale as main map

N
90°W
P

Galapagos Islands
(Ecuador)

Fernandina
San Salvador
Santa Cruz
San Cristobal

Isabela
Equator

Puerto
Ayora

PACIFIC OCEAN

N
90°W
P

9

9

10

10

Western Cordillera
Central Cordillera
Eastern Cordillera

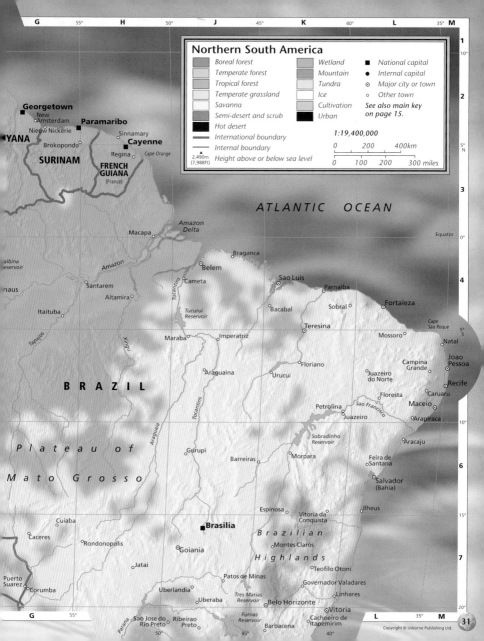

Northern South America

■	Boreal forest		Wetland	■ National capital
	Temperate forest		Mountain	● Internal capital
	Tropical forest		Tundra	⊙ Major city or town
	Temperate grassland		Ice	○ Other town
	Savanna		Cultivation	*See also main key*
	Semi-desert and scrub	■	Urban	*on page 15.*
	Hot desert			

International boundary
Internal boundary

▲ 2,490m (7,988ft) *Height above or below sea level*

1:19,400,000

0   200   400km

0   100   200   300 miles

ATLANTIC   OCEAN

Georgetown
New
Amsterdam
Nieuw Nickerie
Brokopondo
Sinnamary
Paramaribo
Cayenne
YANA
SURINAM
Regina
Cape Orange
FRENCH
GUIANA
(France)

albina
reservoir

naus

Macapa
Amazon
Delta
Braganca
Belem
Sao Luis
Parnaiba
Fortaleza
Cape
Sao Roque

Santarem
Amazon
Cameta
Altamira
Tocantins
Bacabal
Sobral
Teresina
Mossoro
Natal

Itaituba
Tucurui
Reservoir
Maraba
Imperatriz
Joao
Pessoa

Tapajos
Xingu
Floriano
Urucui
Juazeiro
do Norte
Campina
Grande
Recife

BRAZIL
Araguaina
Tocantins
Petrolina
Sao Francisco
Floresta
Caruaru
Maceio

Araguaia
Juazeiro
Arapiraca

Plateau   of
Gurupi
Sobradinho
Reservoir
Aracaju

Mato   Grosso
Barreiras
Morpara
Feira de
Santana

Cuiaba
Espinosa
Vitoria da
Conquista
Salvador
(Bahia)
Ilheus

Caceres
Brasilia
Brazilian

Rondonopolis
Goiania
Montes Claros
Highlands

Jatai
Teofilo Otoni

Puerto
Suarez
Corumba
Patos de Minas
Governador Valadares
Linhares

Uberlandia
Tres Marias
Reservoir
Belo Horizonte
Vitoria

Uberaba
Furnas
Reservoir
Teofilo Otoni

Parana
Sao Jose do
Rio Preto
Ribeirao
Preto
Barbacena
Cachoeiro de
Itapemirim

Equator

10°
5°N
0°
5°S
10°
15°
20°

1
2
3
4
5
6
7

BRAZIL

Brasilia

Brazilian Highlands

Plateau of Mato Grosso

PERU

BOLIVIA

La Paz
Mount Illimani 6,462m (21,004ft)

Sucre

Lake Titicaca
Lake Poopó

Mount Ojos del Salado 6,908m (22,664ft)

Aconcagua 6,959m (22,831ft)

A N D E S

Gran Chaco

PARAGUAY

Asuncion

URUGUAY

CHILE

Santiago

Valparaiso

Tropic of Capricorn

Rio Branco
Cobija
Riberalta
Puerto Maldonado
Juliaca
Puno
Rurrenabaque
Trinidad
Magdalena
Cochabamma
Oruro
Challapata
Potosi
Uyuni
Tupiza
Olloque
Ollague
Lake Poopó
San Pedro de Atacama
Calama
Antofagasta
Taltal
Chañaral
Copiapo
Vallenar
Coquimbo
Ovalle
Illapel
San Felipe
Rancagua

Arica
Iquique

Santa Cruz
San Josede Chiquitos
Puerto Suarez
Corumba
Concepcion
Caceres
Cuiaba
Rondonopolis
Jatai
Goiania
Gurupi
Barreiras

Tocantins
Araguaia

Sobradinho Reservoir
Feira de Santana
Morpará
Espinosa
Montes Claros
Barbacena
Belo Horizonte
Patos de Minas
Uberaba
Uberlandia
Campo Grande
Sao Jose do Rio Preto
Dourados
Ponta Porã
Pedro Juan Caballero
Concepcion
Paraguay
Vilharrica
Formosa
Reconquista
Corrientes
Santiago del Estero
San Miguel de Tucuman
Salta
San Salvador de Jujuy
Tartagal
Camiri
Charagua
Tarija
Catamarca
La Rioja
San Juan
Mendoza
San Luis
Villa Mercedes
Merlo
San Francisco
Rio Cuarto
Villa Maria
Cordoba
Rosario
Venado Tuerto
San Nicolas
delos Arroyos
Gualeguaychu
San Fe
Santa Fe
Concordia
Salto
Paysandu
Tacuarembo
Durazno
Rivera
Melo
Bage
Pelotas
Rio Grande
Caxias do Sul
Porto Alegre
Santa Maria
Passo Fundo
Uruguaiana
Criciuma
Florianopolis
Itajai
Joinville
Curitiba
Paranagua
Guarapuava
Londrina
Marilia
Presidente Prudente
Itapetininga
Campinas
Sao Paulo
Poços de Caldas
Ribeirao Preto
Araraquara
Furnas Reservoir
Tres Marias Reservoir
Juiz de Fora
Campos
Macae
Nova Iguacu
Rio de Janeiro
Mount Aguihas Negras 2,787m (9,144ft)
Vitoria
Cachoeiro de Itapemirim
Governador Valadares
Teofilo Otoni
Vitoria da Conquista
Ilheus
Linhares
Cascavel
Foz do Iguacu
Ciudad del Este
Eldorado
Posadas
Encarnacion
Pilcomayo
Parana
Paraná
Salado

Mirim Lake
Patos Lagoon

Tropic of Capricorn

D 70°W

32

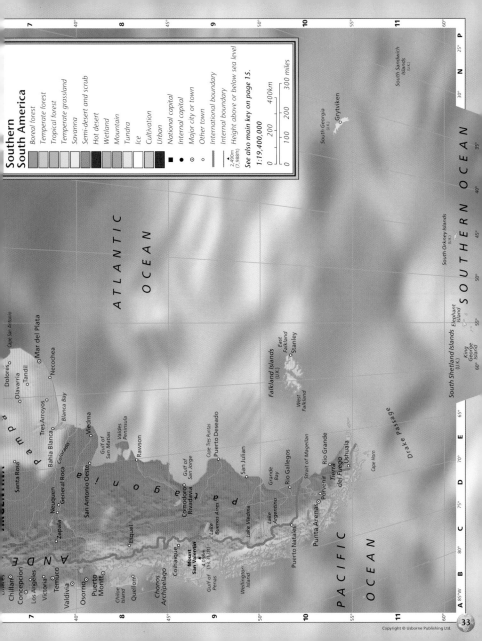

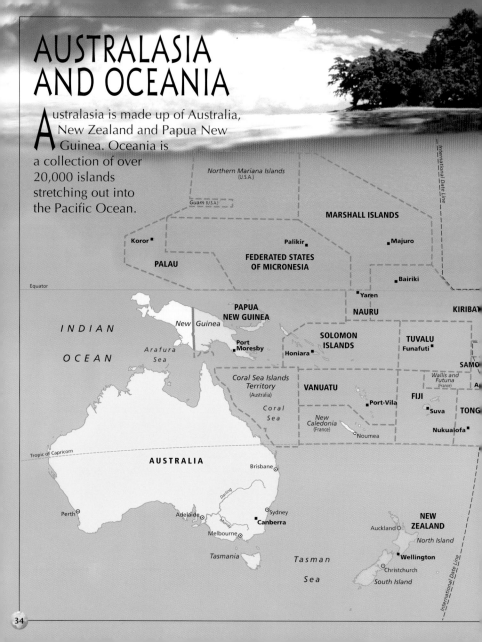

AUSTRALASIA AND OCEANIA

Australasia is made up of Australia, New Zealand and Papua New Guinea. Oceania is a collection of over 20,000 islands stretching out into the Pacific Ocean.

International Date Line

Northern Mariana Islands
(U.S.A.)

Guam (U.S.A.)

MARSHALL ISLANDS

Koror ■

Palikir ■

■ Majuro

PALAU

FEDERATED STATES OF MICRONESIA

■ Bairiki

Equator

■ Yaren

NAURU

KIRIBA

INDIAN

New Guinea

PAPUA NEW GUINEA

OCEAN

Arafura Sea

Port Moresby ■

SOLOMON ISLANDS

Honiara ■

TUVALU

Funafuti ■

SAMO

Coral Sea Islands Territory
(Australia)

VANUATU

Wallis and Futuna
(France)

A

Coral Sea

New Caledonia
(France)

Port-Vila ■

FIJI

■ Suva

TONG

Noumea ○

Nukualofa ■

Tropic of Capricorn

AUSTRALIA

Brisbane ○

Darling

Perth ○

Adelaide ○

Murray

■ Sydney
Canberra

Auckland ○

NEW ZEALAND

North Island

Melbourne ○

Tasmania

Tasman

■ Wellington

Sea

○ Christchurch

South Island

International Date Line

This small island belongs to Papua New Guinea.

PACIFIC OCEAN

The shading on this map is there to help you see clearly the different countries that make up the continent.

Line Islands

Equator

kelau
(Zealand)
erican
noa
(S.A.)
Niue
(New Zealand)
Cook Islands
(New Zealand)

Marquesas Islands

Society Islands

French Polynesia (France)

Pitcairn Islands (U.K.)

Tropic of Capricorn

Internet link

For a link to a website where you can take a virtual tour of New Zealand and find out all about its sights, cities and landscape, go to
www.usborne-quicklinks.com

Facts

Total land area 8,564,400 sq km (3,306,715 sq miles)
Total population 31 million
Biggest city Sydney, Australia
Biggest country Australia 7,686,850 sq km (2,967,124 sq miles)
Smallest country Nauru 21 sq km (8 sq miles)

Highest mountain Mount Wilhelm, Papua New Guinea 4,509m (14,793ft)
Longest river Murray/Darling River, Australia 3,718km (2,310 miles)
Biggest lake Lake Eyre, Australia 9,000 sq km (3,470 sq miles)
Highest waterfall Sutherland Falls, on the Arthur River, New Zealand 580m (1,904ft)
Biggest desert Great Victoria Desert, Australia 388,500 sq km (150,000 sq miles)
Biggest island New Guinea 800,000 sq km (309,000 sq miles) (Australia is counted as a continental land mass and not as an island.)

Main mineral deposits Iron, nickel, precious stones, lead, bauxite
Main fuel deposits Oil, coal, uranium

The Moorish idol fish is found in shallow waters throughout the Pacific. It has very bold stripes and a long, distinctive snout.

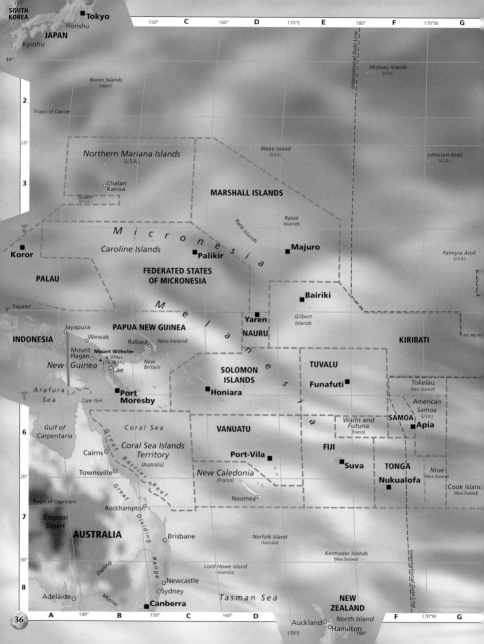

SOUTH
KOREA
Tokyo
Honshu
JAPAN
Kyushu

150° C 160° D 170°E E 180° F 170°W G

30°

2 Tropic of Cancer

Bonin Islands (Japan)

Midway Islands (U.S.A.)

20°

Northern Mariana Islands (U.S.A.)

Wake Island (U.S.A.)

Johnston Atoll (U.S.A.)

3 Chalan Kanoa
Guam (U.S.A.)

MARSHALL ISLANDS

10° N

M i c r o n e s i a

Ratak Islands

Raluk Islands

Palmyra Atoll (U.S.A.)

Koror *Caroline Islands* **Palikir**

Majuro

PALAU

FEDERATED STATES OF MICRONESIA

Bairiki

0° Equator

M e l a n e s i a

Jayapura
INDONESIA Wewak
Mount Hagen **Mount Wilhelm** ▲ 4,509m (14,793ft)
New Guinea Lae
Rabaul *New Ireland*

PAPUA NEW GUINEA

Yaren

NAURU

Gilbert Islands

KIRIBATI

TUVALU

SOLOMON ISLANDS

Funafuti

10° S

Arafura Sea Cape York
Port Moresby

Honiara

Tokelau (New Zealand)

American Samoa (U.S.A.)

SAMOA **Apia**

6 Gulf of Carpentaria
Coral Sea
Coral Sea Islands Territory (Australia)
Cairns

VANUATU

Wallis and Futuna (France)

FIJI

Port-Vila

Suva

TONGA

20° Townsville

New Caledonia (France)

Nukualofa

Niue (New Zealand)

Cook Islands (New Zealand)

Noumea

7 Tropic of Capricorn Rockhampton

Simpson Desert

Brisbane

Norfolk Island (Australia)

Kermadec Islands (New Zealand)

AUSTRALIA

30°

Lord Howe Island (Australia)

Darling
Newcastle
Sydney
Adelaide
Murray
Canberra

Tasman Sea

NEW ZEALAND

8

Auckland
North Island
Hamilton

36 A 140° B 150° C 160° D 170°E E F 170°W G

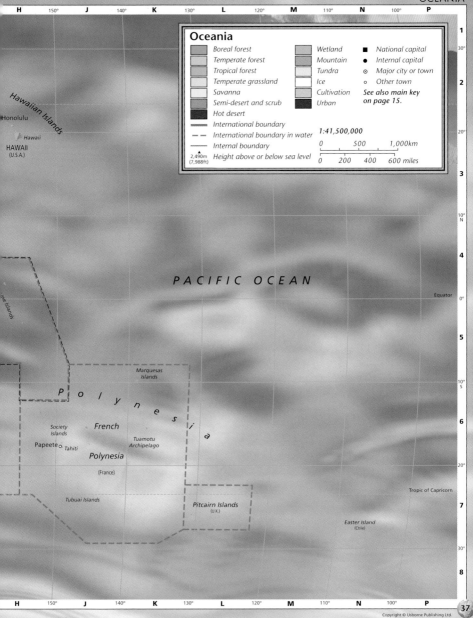

Oceania

- Boreal forest
- Temperate forest
- Tropical forest
- Temperate grassland
- Savanna
- Semi-desert and scrub
- Hot desert
- Wetland
- Mountain
- Tundra
- Ice
- Cultivation
- Urban

- ■ National capital
- ● Internal capital
- ⊙ Major city or town
- ○ Other town

See also main key on page 15.

International boundary
International boundary in water
Internal boundary
▲ 2,490m (7,988ft) Height above or below sea level

1:41,500,000

0   500   1,000km

0   200   400   600 miles

Hawaiian Islands

Honolulu

Hawaii

HAWAII
(U.S.A.)

PACIFIC OCEAN

Equator

ine Islands

Marquesas
Islands

Polynesia

Society
Islands

French

Papeete   Tahiti

Tuamotu
Archipelago

Polynesia

(France)

Tubuai Islands

Pitcairn Islands
(U.K.)

Tropic of Capricorn

Easter Island
(Chile)

30°
20°
10° N
0°
10° S
20°
30°

37

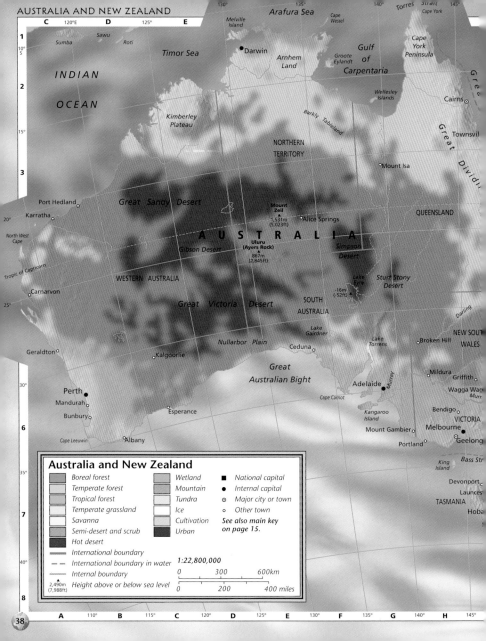

Arafura Sea

Torres Strait

Cape Wessel

Cape York

Timor Sea

INDIAN

OCEAN

Sumba

Sawu

Roti

Melville Island

Darwin

Arnhem Land

Groote Eylandt

Gulf of Carpentaria

Cape York Peninsula

Kimberley Plateau

NORTHERN TERRITORY

Wellesley Islands

Cairns

Barkly Tableland

Great

Townsvil

Port Hedland

Great Sandy Desert

Mount Isa

QUEENSLAND

Great Dividi

Karratha

North West Cape

Mount Zeil 1,531m (5,023ft)

Alice Springs

Gibson Desert

Uluru (Ayers Rock) 867m (2,845ft)

Simpson Desert

Tropic of Capricorn

Carnarvon

WESTERN AUSTRALIA

Lake Eyre -16m (-52ft)

Sturt Stony Desert

SOUTH AUSTRALIA

Darling

Great Victoria Desert

Lake Gairdner

Lake Torrens

NEW SOUT WALES

Broken Hill

Geraldton

Kalgoorlie

Nullarbor Plain

Ceduna

Mildura

Griffith

Wagga Wag

Murr

Great Australian Bight

Adelaide

Murray

Bendigo

Perth

Mandurah

Bunbury

Esperance

Cape Carnot

Kangaroo Island

Mount Gambier

VICTORIA

Melbourne

Cape Leeuwin

Albany

Portland

Geelong

King Island

Bass Str

Devonport

Launces

TASMANIA

Hoba

Australia and New Zealand

- Boreal forest
- Temperate forest
- Tropical forest
- Temperate grassland
- Savanna
- Semi-desert and scrub
- Hot desert
- Wetland
- Mountain
- Tundra
- Ice
- Cultivation
- Urban

- ■ National capital
- ● Internal capital
- ⊙ Major city or town
- ○ Other town

See also main key on page 15.

International boundary

International boundary in water

Internal boundary

▲ 2,490m (7,988ft) Height above or below sea level

1:22,800,000

0   300   600km

0   200   400 miles

SOLOMON ISLANDS

Rennell Island

Santa Cruz Islands

TUVALU

Coral Sea

Coral Sea Islands Territory (Australia)

VANUATU

Banks Islands

Espiritu Santo

○ Luganville

Malakula

FIJI

Vanua Levu

Efate ■ **Port-Vila**

Lautoka ○

Viti Levu ■ **Suva**

Chesterfield Islands

New Caledonia (France)

Noumea ○ *Loyalty Islands*

arrier Reef

○ Mackay

khampton ○

Gladstone ○

Bundaberg ○

Gympie ○

Toowoomba ○

Fraser Island

○ Brisbane
○ Gold Coast

Moree ○

Dubbo ○

PACIFIC OCEAN

Tropic of Capricorn

○ Grafton

○ Armidale

○ Port Macquarie

Norfolk Island (Australia)

Lord Howe Island (Australia)

○ Newcastle

○ Sydney
○ Wollongong

■ **Canberra**
AUSTRALIAN CAPITAL TERRITORY

Mount sciuszko

29m 13ft)

Kermadec Islands (New Zealand)

Tasman Sea

North Cape

linders land

○ Whangarei

○ Auckland

North Island

Hamilton ○

East Cape

New Plymouth ○

○ Rotorua

Lake Taupo

Cape Farewell

○ Napier

Nelson ○

South Island

Wellington

Aoraki
(Mount Cook)
▲
3,754m
(12,316ft)

○ Christchurch

NEW ZEALAND

Sutherland Falls

Cape Providence

○ Dunedin

Invercargill ○

Stewart Island

South West Cape

Chatham Islands (New Zealand)

Copyright © Usborne Publishing Ltd.

39

ASIA

A sia is the largest continent and has over 40 countries, including Russia, the biggest country in the world. As well as large land masses, it has thousands of islands and inlets, giving it over 160,000km (100,000 miles) of coastline. Turkey and Russia are partly in Europe and partly in Asia, but both are shown in full on the map on the right.

The shading on this map is there to help you see clearly the different countries that make up the continent.

Internet link

For a link to a website where you can take a tour of the Great Wall of China and see a photo of it taken from space, go to www.usborne-quicklinks.com

This is a type of Chinese boat called a junk, sailing in the sea off Singapore.

ARCTIC OCEAN

Franz Josef Land

Novaya Zemlya

Barents Sea

Kara Sea

Moscow

R U S

Ob

Yenisey

Volga

Black Sea

Ankara

TURKEY

GEORGIA

Astana

KAZAKHSTAN

CYPRUS

ARMENIA

Caspian Sea

Aral Sea

LEBANON   SYRIA

AZERBAIJAN

UZBEKISTAN

Beirut Damascus

TURKMENISTAN

Tashkent

Bishkek

Jerusalem   Amman

Ashgabat

KYRGYZSTAN

ISRAEL   JORDAN

Baghdad

Tehran

Dushanbe

TAJIKISTAN

IRAQ

IRAN

KUWAIT

Kabul

Islamabad

SAUDI ARABIA

AFGHANISTAN

Tropic of Cancer

BAHRAIN

PAKISTAN

Riyadh   QATAR

Indus

New Delhi

NEPAL

Doha   Abu Dhabi

Kathmandu

UNITED ARAB EMIRATES

Muscat

Ganges

Thimp

Sana

OMAN

BANGLADES

YEMEN

Arabian Sea

INDIA

Socotra (Yemen)

Bay of Bengal

INDIAN OCEAN

Equator

SRI LANKA

Sri Jayewardenepura Kotte   Colombo

MALDIVES

Male

A

Wrangel Island

New Siberian Islands

East Siberian Sea

Bering Sea

Severnaya Zemlya

Laptev Sea

Lena

Sea of Okhotsk

Lake Baikal

Hokkaido

Ulan Bator ■

MONGOLIA

Sea of Japan

NORTH KOREA

JAPAN

Pyongyang ■

■Tokyo

Beijing ■

Seoul

Honshu

SOUTH KOREA

Huang He (Yellow)

East China Sea

C H I N A

Tropic of Cancer

Chang Jiang (Yangtze)

■Taipei

TAIWAN

PACIFIC

OCEAN

TAN

Irrawaddy

aka

BURMA (MYANMAR)

LAOS

■Hanoi

PHILIPPINES

ngoon

Vientiane ■

South China Sea

Mekong

■Manila

THAILAND

VIETNAM

Philippine Sea

Bangkok ■

CAMBODIA

Andaman Islands (India)

Phnom Penh ■

Nicobar Islands (India)

BRUNEI

Equator

MALAYSIA

New Guinea

■Kuala Lumpur

SINGAPORE

Borneo

Celebes

Sumatra

INDONESIA

Dili

Arafura Sea

■Jakarta

■ EAST TIMOR

Java

Facts

Total land area 44,537,920 sq km (17,196,090 sq miles)
Total population 3.8 billion (including all of Russia)
Biggest city Tokyo, Japan
Biggest country Russia *Total area: 17,075,200 sq km (6,592,735 sq miles) Area of Asiatic Russia: 12,780,800 sq km (4,934,667 sq miles)*
Smallest country Maldives 300 sq km *(116 sq miles)*

Highest mountain Mount Everest, Nepal/China border 8,850m (29,035ft)
Longest river Chang Jiang (Yangtze), China 6,380km (3,964 miles)
Biggest lake Caspian Sea, western Asia 370,999 sq km (143,243 sq miles)
Highest waterfall Jog Falls, on the Sharavati River, India 253m (830ft)
Biggest desert Arabian Desert, in and around Saudi Arabia 2,230,000 sq km (900,000 sq miles)
Biggest island Borneo 751,100 sq km (290,000 sq miles)

Main mineral deposits Zinc, mica, tin, chromium, iron, nickel
Main fuel deposits Oil, coal, uranium, natural gas

These are lotus flowers, a type of water lily. In China they are associated with purity and for Buddhists they are sacred.

41

A 100°E B 105° C 110° D 115°

Southern Southeast Asia

Boreal forest
Temperate forest
Tropical forest
Temperate grassland
Savanna
Semi-desert and scrub
Hot desert
International boundary
Internal boundary
2,490m (7,988ft) Height above or below sea level

Wetland
Mountain
Tundra
Ice
Cultivation
Urban

■ National capital
● Internal capital
⊙ Major city or town
○ Other town

See also main key on page 15.

1:16,600,000

0 200 400km
0 100 200 300 miles

Qui Nhon
VIETNAM
Nha Trang

South China Sea

Spratly Islands

THAILAND Hat Yai
Yala
Kota Bharu
Alor Setar
George Town (Penang)
Taiping
Gunung Tahan 2,187m (7,175ft)
Ipoh
Kuantan

MALAYSIA

Kota Kinabalu
Bandar Seri Begawan
BRUNEI
Miri
Tarak

Banda Aceh
Lhokseumawe
Langsa
Medan
Pematangsiantar
Lake Toba
Sibolga
Simeulue

Kuala Terengganu
Seremban
Kuala Lumpur
Melaka
Johor Bahru
Singapore
SINGAPORE
Pekanbaru

Natuna Islands
Anambas Islands

Bintulu
Sibu
Kuching

2,968m (9,803ft)
Tanjungrede

Nias

Equator 0°

Padang
Gunung Kerinci 3,805m (12,483ft)
Jambi

Riau Islands
Bangka
Pangkalpinang

Karimata Strait
Pontianak

Borneo
Samarinda
Balikpapan

Mentawai Islands

Palembang
Belitung
Palangkaraya

Banjarmasin

Bengkulu
Lahat
Baturaja

Martapura

Greater Sunda Islands

5° S

Tanjungkarang-Telukbetung
Krakatoa 813m (2,667ft)
Serang
Bogor
Bandung

INDONESIA
Jakarta
Java Sea

Tegal
Semarang
Surakarta
Surabaya

Lesse

INDIAN OCEAN

Cilacap
Yogyakarta
Malang
Denpasar

Jember
Bali
Lombok
Matara
Sumba

Christmas Island (Australia)

Simeulue
Sumatra
Strait of Malacca
Java

Andaman Sea

A 100°E B 105° C 110° D 115°

PHILIPPINES

120° *Luzon* Cabanatuan
Olongapo○ ○Quezon City
Manila ■
○Lucena
Calapan○ ○Naga Legaspi
Mindoro ○Lucena Naga Legaspi
Masbate○
Masbate
○Calbayog
Calamian Masbate○ Samar
Group Panay ○Roxas ○Tacloban
○Taytay Iloilo○ ○Bacolod
○Puerto Princesa *Negros* ○Cebu *Bohol* ○Surigao
lawan Dumaguete○ ○Butuan
○Cagayan de Oro
○Pagadian ○Iligan
Mindanao
Sulu Sea ○Zamboanga ○Davao
○Jolo
Sulu
Archipelago
○General Santos

Philippine Sea

PACIFIC OCEAN

PALAU

Celebes Sea
Talaud Islands
Sangihe Islands
○Manado *Morotai*
○Gorontalo *Ternate*○ *Halmahera*
Molucca Sea
○Palu
Celebes *Sula Islands* *Ceram Sea* *Misool*
○Palopo *Buru* *Ceram* ○Fakfak
arepare○ ○Kendari ○Ambon
○Watampone *Buton*
○Ujung Pandang *Banda Sea*
Flores Sea *Aru Islands*
unda Islands *Wetar*
Flores ○Ende ■**Dili**
○Kupang **EAST TIMOR**
Sumba *Sawu Sea* *Timor*
○Sawu *Roti*
Timor Sea

○Sorong
Biak
Yapen
Jayapura○
Maoke Range
New Guinea
Puncak Jaya ▲
5,030m
(16,502ft)

Tanimbar islands
Dolak

Arafura Sea

Torres Strait

AUSTRALIA
NORTHERN TERRITORY
●Darwin

Inset map

J 140°E K 145° L 150° M Equator N 155°E N

Jayapura○
Admiralty Islands
PACIFIC OCEAN
Wewak○ *Bismarck Sea* *New Ireland*
Mount Wilhelm ○Rabaul
4,509m
New Guinea Mount Hagen○ ▲ Madang○ *New Britain*
Lae○
PAPUA NEW GUINEA
○Kerema *Solomon Sea*
Gulf of Papua
D'Entrecasteaux Islands
■**Port Moresby**
Torres Strait 1:24,900,000
Cape York 0 400km
6 *Cape York Peninsula* 0 200 miles
AUSTRALIA

43
Copyright © Usborne Publishing Ltd.

A 90°E B 95° C 100° D 105° E

Himalayas

Brahmaputra
Lhasa

Chengdu
Wanxian
Ensh

Gongga Shan
7,556m
(24,790ft)
Leshan

Neijiang
Chongqing

Mount Everest
8,850m
(29,035ft)
NEPAL
Darjeeling
Biratnagar
Thimphu
BHUTAN

INDIA

Xichang
Luzhou
Yibin
Zunyi
Huai

Darbhanga
Rangpur
Bhagalpur
Ganges
Guwahati
Shillong
Dibrugarh
Jorhat
Brahmaputra

Zhaotong
Panzhihua

CH

Rajshahi
Asansol
Sylhet
Dali
Baoshan
Kunming
Anshun
Guiyang

BANGLADESH
Dhaka
Khulna
Imphal
Myitkyina
Liuzhou

Jamshedpur
Kolkata
(Calcutta)
Chittagong
Aizawl
Lashio
Kaiyuan
Gejiu
Simao
Ha Giang
Nann

Mouths of the Ganges
Monywa
Mandalay
Mount Victoria
3,053m
(10,016ft)
BURMA
(MYANMAR)
Meiktila
Taunggyi
Phongsali
Lao Cai
Son La
Thai Nguyen
Hanoi
Hai Phong
Qinzhou

Sittwe
Pyinmana
Pye
Salween
Irrawaddy
Mekong
Louangphrabang
Thanh Hoa
Gulf of Tonkin
Sany

Bay of Bengal
Sandoway
Henzada
Pathein
Rangoon
Thaton
Pegu
Moulmein
Chiang Mai
LAOS
Vientiane
Vinh
Da Nar

Mouths of the Irrawaddy

INDIAN OCEAN

Udon Thani
Savannakhet
Hue

Phitsanulok
Khon Kaen
Ubon Ratchathani
Pakxe
Attapu
VIETNA

Nakhon Sawan
THAILAND
Nakhon Ratchasima

Tavoy
Bangkok
Pattaya
Angkor
Tonle Sap
Stoeng Treng
Qui Nhon
Buon Me Thuot

Andaman Islands
(India)
Andaman Sea
Mergui
Batdambang
CAMBODIA
Da Lat

Port Blair
Little Andaman
Prachuap Khiri Khan
Kampong Chhnang
Kampong Cham
Bien Hoa

Mergui Archipelago
Krong Kaoh Kong
Phnom Penh
Mekong
Ho Chi Minh City
(Saigon)

Ten Degree Channel
Chumphon
Kampong Saom
Long Xuyen
Can Tho

Gulf of Thailand
Bac Lieu
Con Son

Nicobar Islands
(India)
Nakhon Si Thammarat

Hat Yai
Yala
Banda Aceh
Alor Setar
Kota Bharu
Kuala Terengganu

Lhokseumawe
Langsa
George Town
(Penang)
Taiping
Ipoh
Gunung Tahan
2,187m
(7,175ft)
Kuala Terengganu
Natuna Islands
(Indonesia)

Sumatra
INDONESIA
MALAYSIA

44

A 90°E B 95° C 100° D 105° E

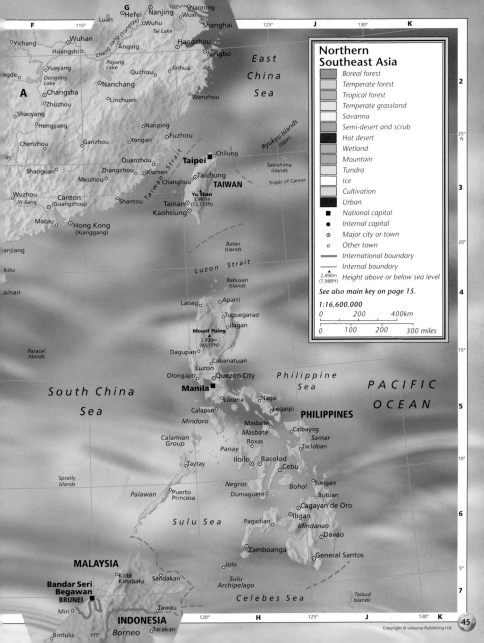

F **G** Nantong
Luan oHefei Nanjing oWuxi
Yichang oWuhu Tai Lake Shanghai
Wuhan Anqing Hangzhou
Huangshi Chang Jiang (Yangtze)
gde o Yueyang Poyang oNingbo
Dongting Lake East
Lake Quzhou oJinhua China
A Changsha Nanchang Sea
Zhuzhou Linchuan
Shaoyang oHengyang oWenzhou
Chenzhou oNanping
in Ganzhou oYongan oFuzhou Ryukyu Islands (Japan)
Shaoguan Quanzhou Chilung 25°
Zhangzhou Xiamen Taipei N
Wuzhou Meizhou Changhua Taichung Sakishima
Canton Shantou Islands
Xi Jiang (Guangzhou) Tainan TAIWAN Tropic of Cancer 3
Macau Kaohsiung Yu Shan
anjiang Hong Kong 3,997m
(Xianggang) (13,113ft)
kou Batan 20°
Islands
ainan Luzon Strait
Babuyan
Islands 4

Northern
Southeast Asia
Boreal forest
Temperate forest
Tropical forest
Temperate grassland
Savanna
Semi-desert and scrub
Hot desert
Wetland
Mountain
Tundra
Ice
Cultivation
Urban
■ National capital
● Internal capital
⊙ Major city or town
○ Other town
— International boundary
— Internal boundary
▲ 2,490m Height above or below sea level
(7,988ft)
See also main key on page 15.

1:16,600,000
0   200   400km
0   100   200   300 miles

Paracel Laoag Aparri 15°
Islands Tuguegarao
Mount Pulog Ilagan
2,930m
(9,613ft)
Dagupan Cabanatuan
Luzon
Olongapo Quezon City Philippine
South China Manila ■ Sea PACIFIC
Sea Lucena OCEAN
Calapan Naga
Mindoro Legaspi 5
Masbate PHILIPPINES
Calamian Masbate Calbayog
Group Roxas Samar
Panay Tacloban
Taytay Iloilo Bacolod
Negros Cebu 10°
Sulu Bohol Surigao
Spratly Palawan Dumaguete Butuan
Islands Puerto Cagayan de Oro
Princesa Iligan 6
Sulu Sea Pagadian Mindanao
Davao
Zamboanga
MALAYSIA General Santos
Jolo
Kota Sulu
Bandar Seri Kinabalu Sandakan Archipelago Talaud 7
Begawan Islands
BRUNEI Celebes Sea
Miri Tawau
INDONESIA 120° **H** 125° **J** 130° **K**
Bintulu Tarakan Borneo
115°

A   80°E   B   85°   C   90°   D   95°   E   100°   F   105°   G   110°

KAZAKHSTAN

Bulgan

■ Ulan Bator

2   Almaty   Karamay   Dzungarian Basin

Yining   Kuytun   Shihezi   Altay

Lake Issyk   KYRGYZSTAN   Urumqi   Altai Mountains

Pik Pobedy   7,439m   (24,406ft)   Tien   Shan   MONGOLIA

Aksu   Korla   Turpan   Bosten -154m   Lake (-505ft)   Turpan Depression   Hami

40° N

Erer

3   Hotan   Tarim Basin   Lop Lake   Gobi   Desert   Baotou   Hohh

Taklimakan Desert   Altun Mountains   Mogao Caves   Yumen   The Great Wall of China   Wuhai

35°   Kunlun   Mountains   5,547m   (18,199ft)   Yinchuan   Tai

Qaidam Basin   Qinghai Lake   Xining   Lanzhou

Plateau of Tibet   Golmud   CHINA   Huang He (Yellow)

30°   Siling Lake   Yushu   Baoji   Mount Li Terracotta   Xian

TIBET   Nam Lake   Chang Jiang (Yangtze)   Shiyan

Himalayas   Brahmaputra   Xiang

5   NEPAL   Lhasa   Salween   Mekong   Gongga Shan   7,556m   (24,790ft)   Chengdu   Yichang

Kathmandu   Mount Everest   8,850m   (29,035ft)   Darjeeling   Thimphu   Leshan   Chongqing   Changde

Darbhanga   Biratnagar   BHUTAN   Luzhou

Patna   Rangpur   Brahmaputra   Dibrugarh   Xichang   Chang Jiang (Yangtze)   Huaihua

Ganges   Bhagalpur   Guwahati   Zunyi   Heng

INDIA   Shillong   Panzhihua   Guiyang

Ranchi   Asansol   Rajshahi   Sylhet   Guilin

6   Tropic of Cancer   BANGLADESH   Imphal   Myitkyina   Dali   Kunming   Liuzhou

Kolkata (Calcutta)   Dhaka   Aizawl   Irrawaddy   Red   Wuzhou

Khulna   Chittagong   Lashio   Gejiu   Nanning   Yulin

20°   Cuttack   Mouths of the Ganges   Monywa   Mandalay   Simao   Lao Cai   Zhanjia

Bay of Bengal   Mount Victoria   3,053m   (10,016ft)   BURMA (MYANMAR)   Taunggyi   Phongsali   Son La   Thai Nguyen   Hanoi   Hai Phong   Haikou

Sittwe   Pyinmana   Mekong   Louangphrabang   Thanh Hoa   Gulf of Tonkin   Haina

7   INDIAN   OCEAN   Sandoway   Pye   Irrawaddy   Chiang Mai   Salween   LAOS   VIETNAM

Henzada   THAILAND   Vientiane   Vinh   Sanya

15°   Pathein   Pegu   Rangoon   Udon Thani

C   90°E   D   Mouths of the Irrawaddy   95°   Moulmein   100°   F   105°   G   110°

46

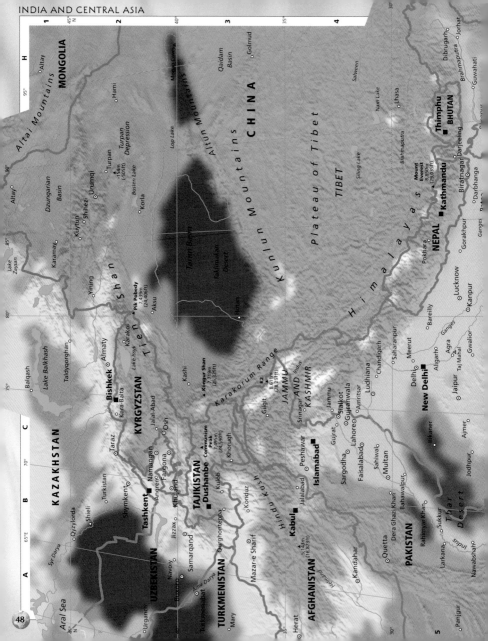

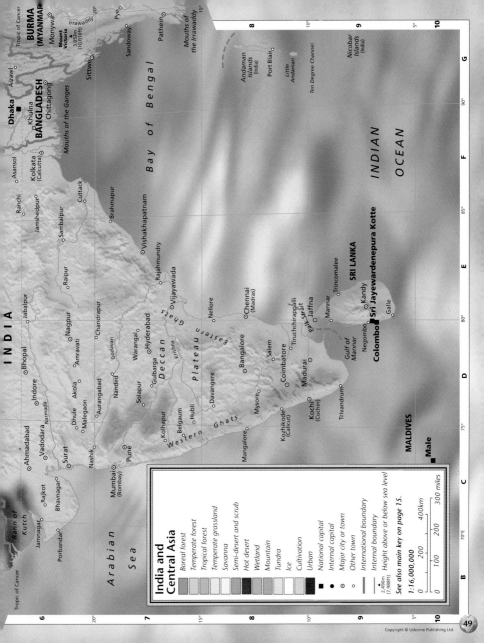

India and Central Asia

Boreal forest
Temperate forest
Tropical forest
Temperate grassland
Savanna
Semi-desert and scrub
Hot desert
Wetland
Mountain
Tundra
Ice
Cultivation
Urban

■ National capital
● Internal capital
⊙ Major city or town
○ Other town

International boundary
Internal boundary
▲ 2,490m (7,988ft) Height above or below sea level

See also main key on page 15.

1:16,000,000

0   100   200   300   400km
0   100   200   300 miles

Copyright © Usborne Publishing Ltd.

49

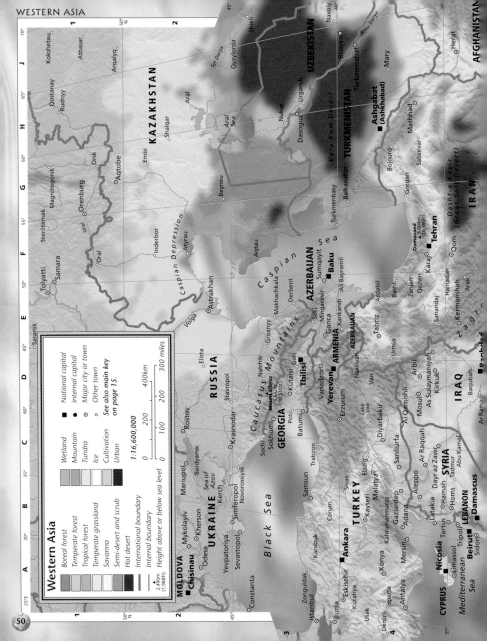

Western Asia

Boreal forest	
Temperate forest	
Tropical forest	
Temperate grassland	
Savanna	
Semi-desert and scrub	
Hot desert	

■ National capital
● Internal capital
○ Major city or town
○ Other town

See also main key on page 15.

1:16,600,000

0	100	200	400km
0	100	200	300 miles

International boundary
Internal boundary

Height above or below sea level

2,490m
(7,988ft)

KAZAKHSTAN

UZBEKISTAN

TURKMENISTAN

AFGHANISTAN

RUSSIA

GEORGIA

AZERBAIJAN

ARMENIA

UKRAINE

MOLDOVA

TURKEY

SYRIA

LEBANON

CYPRUS

IRAQ

IRAN

Kokshetau
Atbasar
Qostanay
Rudnyy
Arqalyq
Shieli
Navoiy
Amu Darya
Herat
Bukoro
Syr Darya
Qyzylorda
Urganch
Mary
Ashgabat
(Ashkhabad)
Mashhad
Aral
Aral Sea
Nukus
Dasoguz
Kara Kum Desert
Turkmenabat
Shalqar
Embi
Sazevar
Bojnurd
Orsk
Aqtobe
Beyneu
Balkanabat
Turkmenbasy
Gorgan
Dasht-e Kavir
(Great Salt Desert)
Magnitogorsk
Orenburg
Sterlitamak
Inderbor
Caspian Depression
Atyrau
Aqtau
Damavand
5,604m
(18,386ft)
Tehran
Tolyatti
Samara
Oral
Astrakhan
Volga
Caspian Sea
Baku
Sumqayit
Qom
Karaj
Saransk
Elista
Stavropol
Naltik
Kutaisi
Tbilisi
Makhachkala
Derbent
'Ali Bayramli
Ardabil
Zanjan
Qazvin
Hamadan
Arak
Sandandaj
Kermanshah
Zagros
Rostov
Krasnodar
Sochi
Sokhumi
Batumi
Poti
Gori
Vanadzor
Yerevan
Grozny
Saki
Ganca
Mingacevir
Xankandi
Naxcivan
Urmia
Tabriz
Mariupol
Berdyansk
Kerch
Sea of Azov
Novorossiysk
Trabzon
Erzurum
Van
Lake Van
Arbil
Mosul
As Sulaymaniyah
Kirkuk
Mykolayiv
Kherson
Simferopol
Sevastopol
Samsun
Sivas
Diyarbakir
Al Qamishli
Baqubah
Chisinau
Odesa
Yevpatoriya
Corum
Ankara
Kayseri
Kahramanmaras
Gaziantep
Sanliurfa
Ar Raqqah
Aleppo
Dayr az Zawr
Tadmur
Abu Kamal
Ar Ramadi
Karabuk
Eskisehir
Kutahya
Konya
Adana
Mersin
Hamah
Homs
Latakia
Tartus
Tripoli
Beirut
Sidon
Damascus
Zonguldak
Istanbul
Bursa
Usak
Denizli
Isparta
Antalya
Nicosia
Limassol
Mediterranean Sea
Constanta
Black Sea

Caucasus Mountains
Mount Elbrus
5,642m
(18,510ft)

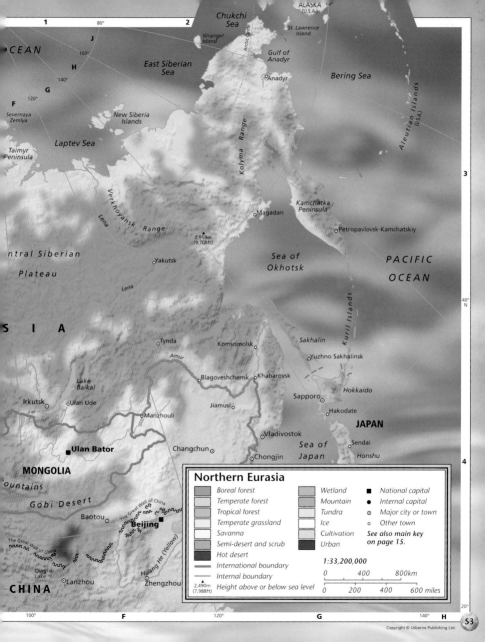

Northern Eurasia

Legend		
Boreal forest	Wetland	■ National capital
Temperate forest	Mountain	● Internal capital
Tropical forest	Tundra	⊙ Major city or town
Temperate grassland	Ice	○ Other town
Savanna	Cultivation	*See also main key*
Semi-desert and scrub	Urban	*on page 15.*
Hot desert		

International boundary
Internal boundary
2,490m (7,988ft) Height above or below sea level

1:33,200,000

0   400   800km
0   200   400   600 miles

EUROPE

Europe is a small continent, packed with over 40 countries and more than 700 million people. Russia is an enormous country, spanning two continents. Its western part is in Europe, while its eastern part is in Asia. The European part of Russia is larger than any other country in Europe.

The shading on this map is there to help you see clearly the different countries that make up the continent.

Internet link

For links to websites where you can find out about the European Union and try online games to test your knowledge about Europe, go to **www.usborne-quicklinks.com**

Arctic Circle

ARCTIC OCEAN

Reykjavik
ICELAND

Faroe Islands
(Denmark)

Norwegian
Sea

Shetland
Islands

Orkney
Islands

North
Sea

SWEDEN

NORWAY
Oslo

Stockholm

DENMARK
Copenhagen

Bal...
Sea

IRELAND
Dublin

**UNITED
KINGDOM**
The
Hague
London

Amsterdam
NETHERLANDS
Brussels
BELGIUM
Paris

Berlin

GERMANY

POLAN...

LUXEMBOURG
Luxembourg

Prague
**CZECH
REPUBLIC**

Vienna
Bratislava
AUSTRIA Budapes...

LIECHTENSTEIN
Bern Vaduz

Bay
of
Biscay

FRANCE **SWITZERLAND**

SLOVENIA
Ljubljana

HUNGA...

Zagreb
CROATI...

ATLANTIC

OCEAN

MONACO

ANDORRA
Andorra
la Vella

SAN MARINO

**BOSNIA AND
HERZEGOVIN...**
Sarajevo

PORTUGAL
Lisbon

Madrid

SPAIN

Corsica

ITALY

Rome

VATICAN CITY

ALBAN...
Tira...

Balearic
Islands

Sardinia

Mediterranean Sea

Sicily

MALTA
Valletta

Rhine

Barents Sea

Murmansk

Arctic Circle

Arkhangelsk

FINLAND

isinki

Tallinn
ESTONIA

St. Petersburg

R U S S I A

Riga LATVIA

Nizhniy Novgorod

Kazan

LITHUANIA
Vilnius

Moscow

SIA

Minsk

BELARUS

Volga

Warsaw

Kiev

Volgograd

Dnieper

UKRAINE

VAKIA

MOLDOVA

Chisinau

ROMANIA

grade

Bucharest

Danube

RBIA AND
NTENEGRO

Black Sea

Sofia

BULGARIA

Skopje
ACEDONIA

TURKEY

REECE

Athens

Crete

Facts

Total land area 10,205,720 sq km (3,940,428 sq miles) (including European Russia)

Total population 727 million (including all of Russia)

Biggest city Moscow, Russia

Biggest country Russia *Total area: 17,075,200 sq km (6,592,735 sq miles) Area of European Russia: 4,294,400 sq km (1,658,068 sq miles)*

Smallest country Vatican City *0.44 sq km (0.17 sq miles)*

Highest mountain Elbrus, Russia *5,642m (18,510ft)*

Longest river Volga *3,700km (2,298 miles)*

Biggest lake Lake Ladoga, Russia *17,700 sq km (6,834 sq miles)*

Highest waterfall Utigard, on the Jostedal Glacier, Norway *800m (2,625ft)*

Biggest desert No deserts in Europe

Biggest island Great Britain *234,410 sq km (90,506 sq miles)*

Main mineral deposits Bauxite, zinc, iron, potash, ìluorspar

Main fuel deposits Oil, coal, natural gas, peat, uranium

A cow in Devon, in the south of England

F 50° G 55° H 60° J 65° K 70° L

West Siberian Plain

Kotlas
Syktyvkar
Ivdel
Uray

Serov
Tobolsk

Solikamsk
Berezniki

Kama Reservoir

Nizhniy Tagil
Tyumen

Kirov
Glazov
Perm
Yekaterinburg

R U S S I A

Izhevsk
Votkinsk

Yoshkar-Ola
Sarapul
Kurgan

Cheboksary
Kazan
Naberezhnyye Chelny
Zlatoust
Chelyabinsk

Belaya

Buinsk
Kuybyshev Reservoir
Almetyevsk
Ufa
Ershovka

Yamantau
1,640m
(5,381ft)

Ulyanovsk
Oktyabrskiy
Beloretsk
Komsomolets

Qostanay
Rudnyy
Semiozernoe

Sterlitamak
Magnitogorsk
Tobyl

Volga
Tolyatti

Belaya

Syzran
Samara
Buzuluk

Saratov Reservoir

Zhetiqara
Zhayylma

Balakovo

Orenburg
Ural
Orsk

aratov
Engels

Oral
Aqsay
Tolybay

olgograd servoir
Aqtobe
Torghay

KAZAKHSTAN

Kaztalovka
Chapaev

Zhanibek
Ural

Inderbor

Topoli

Balkuduk

Caspian Depression

Atyrau

Volga

Astrakhan
Caspian Sea

55° H 60° J 45°N

Ural Mountains

Irtysh

Tobol

Uy

55°N

50°

Eastern Europe

- Boreal forest
- Temperate forest
- Tropical forest
- Temperate grassland
- Savanna
- Semi-desert and scrub
- Hot desert
- International boundary
- Internal boundary

2,490m
(7,988ft) Height above or below sea level

- Wetland
- Mountain
- Tundra
- Ice
- Cultivation
- Urban

■ National capital
● Internal capital
⊚ Major city or town
○ Other town

See also main key on page 15.

1:9,700,000

0   100   200   300km
0   100   200 miles

Copyright © Usborne Publishing Ltd.

57

Barents Sea
Kola Peninsula
White Sea
Arctic Circle
North Cape
Soroya
Vadso
Kirkenes
Murmansk
Severomorsk
Monchegorsk
Apatity
1,191m (3,907ft)
Kandalaksha
Belomorsk
Lake Vyg
Lake Onega
Lake Seg
Medvezhyegorsk
Petrozavodsk
Lake Pya
Lake Top
Lake Kuyto
Kostomuksha
Lieksa
R U S S I A
Lake Ladoga
Vyborg
Zelenogorsk
St. Petersburg
Pushkin
Gatchina
Volkhov
Tikhvin
Kirishi
Borovichi
Lake Ilmen
Novgorod
Kingisepp
Narva
Lake Peipus
Kohtla-Jarve
Tallinn
ESTONIA
Haapsalu
Hiiumaa
Gulf of Finland
Helsinki
Espoo
Kotka
Kouvola
Lahti
Lappeenranta
Saimaa Lake
Pihlaja Lake
Hauki Lake
Puula Lake
Mikkeli
Paijanne Lake
Jyvaskyla
Varkaus
Kuopio
Pielis Lake
Kuhmo
Kajaani
Oulu Lake
Kiuruvesi
FINLAND
Oulu
Raahe
Kokkola
Saarijarvi
Alavus
Tampere
Nasi Lake
Hameenlinna
Turku
Pori
Rauma
Kurikka
Vaasa
Lokan Reservoir
Kuusamo
Sodankyla
Rovaniemi
Tornio
L a p l a n d
Lake Inari
Utsjoki
Sevettijarvi
Kaamanen
Hammerfest
Alta
Tromso
Narvik
Kebnekaise
2,114m (6,935ft)
Kiruna
Stora Lule Lake
Boden
Horn Lake
Storavan Lake
Ume
Skelleftea
Umea
Gulf of Bothnia
Sundsvall
Hudiksvall
Aland Islands
Stockholm
Sodertalje
Gavle
Uppsala
Eskilstuna
Lake Malar
Dal
Borlange
Orebro
Karlstad
Lake Vaner
Klar
SWEDEN
Ostersund
Indals
Stor Lake
Vesteralen
Lofoten
Svolvaer
Vestfjorden
Bodo
Mo i Rana
Namsos
Steinkjer
Trondheim
Vikna
Norwegian Sea
Froya
Hitra
Smola
Kristiansund
Oppdal
NORWAY
Galdhopiggen
2,469m (8,100ft)
Lillehammer
Glama
Oslo
Honefoss
Drammen
Fredrikstad
Larvik
Arendal
Alesund
Bergen
Odda
Stavanger
Sula
Sotra
Karmoy
Varhaug
ICELAND
Isafjordhur
Siglufjordhur
Seydhisfjordhur
Langanes
Vatnajokull
Hvannadalshnukur
2,119m (6,952ft)
Reykjavik
Keflavik
Faxafloi
ATLANTIC OCEAN
Same scale as main map

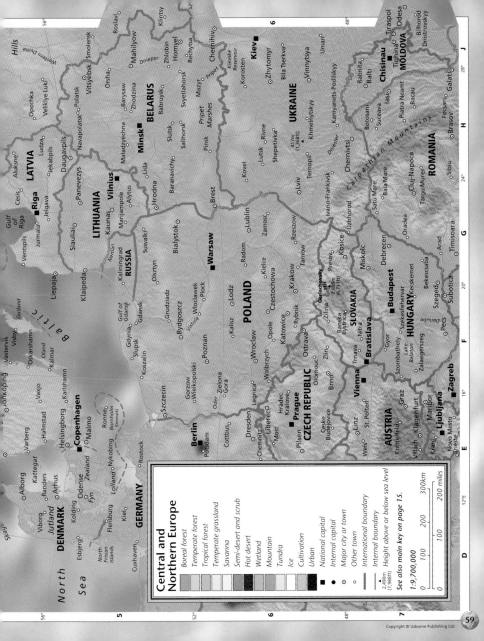

Central and Northern Europe

Boreal forest
Temperate forest
Tropical forest
Temperate grassland
Savanna
Semi-desert and scrub
Hot desert
Wetland
Mountain
Tundra
Ice
Cultivation
Urban

■ National capital
● Internal capital
◉ Major city or town
○ Other town

International boundary
Internal boundary

2490m (7,988ft) Height above or below sea level

See also main key on page 15.

1:9,700,000

0   100   200   300km
0   100   200 miles

Copyright © Usborne Publishing Ltd.

59

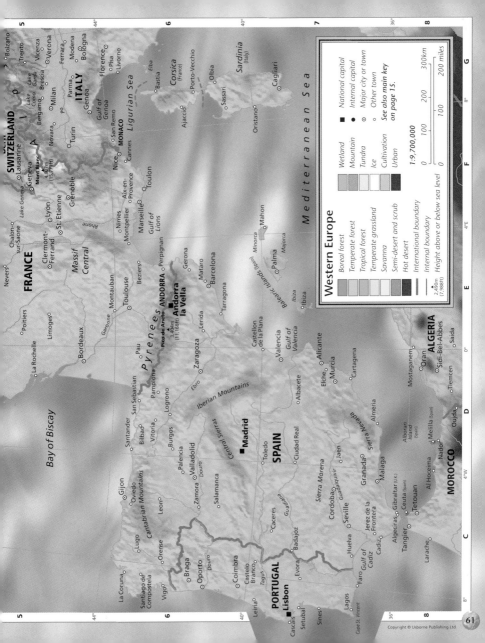

Western Europe

Legend:
- Boreal forest
- Temperate forest
- Tropical forest
- Temperate grassland
- Savanna
- Semi-desert and scrub
- Hot desert

- Wetland
- Mountain
- Tundra
- Ice
- Cultivation
- Urban

■ National capital
● Internal capital
● Major city or town
○ Other town

See also main key on page 15.

International boundary
Internal boundary

▲ 2,490m (7,988ft) Height above or below sea level

1:9,700,000

0   100   200   300km
0   100   200 miles

Bozano, Trento, Vicenza, Verona, Modena, Ferrara, Bologna, Parma, Florence, Pisa, Livorno, **ITALY**, Milan, Bergamo, Brescia, Lake Como, Lake Garda, Genoa, Gulf of Genoa, Elba, Corsica (France), Bastia, Sardinia (Italy), Olbia, Sassari, Oristano, Cagliari, Porto-Vecchio, Ajaccio, Ligurian Sea, San Remo, MONACO, Cannes, Nice, Turin, Novara

Mediterranean Sea

SWITZERLAND, Lausanne, Lake Geneva, Geneva, Mont Blanc 4,807m (15,771ft), Grenoble, Lyon, St. Etienne, Chalon-sur-Saone, Nevers, Aix-en-Provence, Toulon, Marseille, Montpellier, Nîmes, Gulf of Lions

FRANCE, Clermont-Ferrand, Massif Central, Poitiers, Limoges, Montauban, Toulouse, Béziers, Perpignan, Gerona, Mataro, Barcelona, Tarragona, ANDORRA, Andorra la Vella, Pico de Aneto 3,404m (11,168ft), Pyrenees, Pau, Pamplona, Lerida, Zaragoza, Gironde, Bordeaux, La Rochelle

Balearic Islands (Spain), Minorca, Mahon, Majorca, Palma, Ibiza, Gulf of Valencia, Valencia, Castellón de la Plana, Alicante, Elche, Murcia, Cartagena, Albacete

Bay of Biscay, La Coruña, Santiago de Compostela, Lugo, Orense, Vigo, Braga, Oporto, Gijón, Oviedo, Cantabrian Mountains, Santander, Bilbao, San Sebastian, Vitoria, Logroño, Iberian Mountains, Ebro, Palencia, Burgos, Leon, Zamora, Valladolid, Douro, Salamanca, **SPAIN**, Madrid, Central Sierras, Toledo, Ciudad Real, Sierra Morena, Jaén, Córdoba, Sierra Nevada, Granada, Almería, Málaga, Guadalquivir

PORTUGAL, Lisbon, Braga, Oporto, Coimbra, Castelo Branco, Cáceres, Badajoz, Evora, Setúbal, Cascais, Leiria, Lagos, Sines, Faro, Cape St. Vincent, Gulf of Cadiz, Cádiz, Jerez de la Frontera, Seville, Huelva, Algeciras, Gibraltar (U.K.), Ceuta (Spain), Tangier, Tarifa, Larache, Tetouan, Al Hoceima, Nador, Melilla (Spain), Alboran Island (Spain)

MOROCCO, ALGERIA, Oran, Mostaganem, Sidi-Bel-Abbes, Tlemcen, Oujda, Saida

Copyright © Usborne Publishing Ltd.

61

A 0° B 4°E C 8°E D 12°E E 16°E

Cherbourg Le Havre Charleroi Namur BELGIUM Koblenz Erfurt Gera Dresden Liberec Wroclaw Walbrzych
Caen Rouen Amiens LUXEMBOURG Frankfurt Chemnitz Most Hradec Kralove Prague
Le Mans Seine Paris Reims Luxembourg Mannheim Wurzburg GERMANY Karlovy Vary Pilsen CZECH REPUBLIC
48°N Evry Metz Saarbrucken Nuremberg Olomouc Brno Zlir
Angers Tours Orleans Troyes Nancy Karlsruhe Regensburg Ingolstadt Linz Vienna Trna
Poitiers Dijon Strasbourg Rhine Stuttgart Danube Ulm Augsburg Wels St. Polten Bratisla
Nevers Freiburg Munich Salzburg AUSTRIA Knittelfeld Gyor
FRANCE Besancon Basel Winterthur Kempten Innsbruck Grossglockner Graz Szombathely
Limoges Chalon-sur-Saone Bern Zurich Lucerne Vaduz 3,798m Villach Klagenfurt Zalaegersz
Clermont-Ferrand Geneva SWITZERLAND LIECHTENSTEIN (12,461ft) Kranj Maribor
St. Etienne Lausanne Lake Geneva Bolzano Trento SLOVENIA Ljubljana Novo Mesto Zagreb
Massif Lyon Mont Blanc Lake Como Bergamo Lake Garda Vicenza Trieste Karlovac CROATIA
Central 4,807m Novara Brescia Verona Rijeka Slavon Br
Montauban Grenoble (15,771ft) Milan Po Venice Pula Banja Luka
Toulouse Turin Parma Ferrara Zadar BOSNIA
Montpellier Nimes Genoa Modena Bologna Pula AND Zen
Beziers Aix-en-Provence MONACO Gulf of Ravenna HERZEGOVIN
Andorra la Vella Gulf of Marseille Nice Genoa San Remo ITALY Rimini Split Most
Lions Toulon Cannes Pisa Livorno Florence SAN MARINO Ancona
Ligurian Sea Bastia Elba Perugia Pescara
Corsica Terni Foggia
(France) Bari
Ajaccio VATICAN CITY Rome Naples Pompeii Salerno Taranto
Porto-Vecchio Olbia Sardinia Tyrrhenian Cosenza
Oristano (Italy) Sea Catanzar
Sassari Lipari Islands
Mediterranean Sea Palermo Messina
Cagliari Trapani Mount Etna Catania
Annaba Menzel Bizerte Sicily 3,323m Syracuse
Guelma Bourguiba Carthage (10,902ft) Agrigento Ragusa
Souk Ahras Tunis Pantelleria MALTA Valletta
TUNISIA Nabeul (Italy)
Tebessa Kairouan Sousse Monastir Pelagian Islands
Kasserine El Jem (Italy)

Southern Europe

- Boreal forest
- Temperate forest
- Tropical forest
- Temperate grassland
- Savanna
- Semi-desert and scrub
- Hot desert
- Wetland
- Mountain
- Tundra
- Ice
- Cultivation
- Urban
- ■ National capital
- ● Internal capital
- ◉ Major city or town
- ○ Other town
- International boundary
- Internal boundary
- 2,490m (7,988ft) Height above or below sea level

See also main key on page 15.

1:9,700,000

0 100 200 300km
0 100 200 miles

B 4°E C 8°E D 12°E E 16°E

POLAND
Czestochowa
Kielce
Zamosc
Lutsk
Rivne
Zhytomyr
Kiev
Lubny
Poltava
Slovyansk
towice
Rybnik
Krakow
Tarnow
Rzeszow
Lviv
Shepetivka
Bila Tserkva
Cherkasy
Kremenchukske Reservoir
Kremenchuk
Kramatorsk
strava
Zilina
Ternopil
Khmelnytskyy
UKRAINE
Dniprodzerzhynsk
Dnipropetrovsk
417m (1,368ft)
Gerlachovsky stit 2,655m (8,711ft)
Banska Bystrica
Presov
Ivano-Frankivsk
Dniester
Vinnytsya
Uman
Oleksandriya
Kirovohrad
Zaporizhzhya
48° N
LOVAKIA
Kosice
Uzhhorod
Chernivtsi
Kamyanets-Podilskyy
Kryvyy Rih
Nikopol
Kakhovske Reservoir
a
Miskolc
Satu Mare
Botosani
Balti
Rabnita
Yuzhnoukrayinsk
Berdyansk
Budapest
Debrecen
Baia Mare
Suceava
MOLDOVA
Mykolayiv
Melitopol
2
ekesfehervar
Bala Mare
Iasi
Chisinau
Kherson
Sea of Azov
HUNGARY
Oradea
Cluj-Napoca
Piatra Neamt
Tighina
Tiraspol
Odesa
Dzhankoy
Kerch
cskemet
Targu Mures
Bacau
Bilhorod-Dnistrovskyy
Crimea
Feodosiya
Bekescsaba
Szeged
Arad
ROMANIA
Focsani
Yevpatoriya
Simferopol
cs
Subotica
Timisoara
Mount Moldoveanu 2,544m (8,346ft)
Sibiu
Brasov
Galati
Sevastopol
44°
Osijek
Novi Sad
Transylvanian Alps
Ramnicu Valcea
Braila
Buzau
Tulcea
Mouths of the Danube
Tuzla
Belgrade
Pitesti
Ploiesti
Black Sea
SERBIA AND MONTENEGRO
Drobeta-Turnu Severin
Bucharest
Constanta
Sarajevo
Craiova
Danube
Kragujevac
Ruse
Dobrich
Kraljevo
Vratsa
Pleven
Shumen
Varna
Niksic
Leskovac
Nis
Balkan Mountains
BULGARIA
Sliven
rovnik
Pristina
Vranje
Sofia
Stara Zagora
Burgas
Bosporus
Zonguldak
Karabuk
igorica
Tetovo
Kumanovo
Plovdiv
Corum
Shkoder
Skopje
Blagoevgrad
Edirne
Istanbul
Adapazari
MACEDONIA
Prilep
Serres
Tekirdag
Sea of Marmara
Ankara
Kirikkale
40°
Durres
Tirana
Bitola
Kavala
Thasos
Bursa
Eskisehir
ALBANIA
Korce
Thessaloniki
Canakkale
Kutahya
Lake Tuz
TURKEY
Aksaray
ce
Vlore
Pindus Mountains
Mount Olympus 2,917m (9,570ft)
Larisa
Limnos
Balikesir
Akhisar
Usak
Corfu
Corfu
Ioannina
Volos
Aegean Sea
Lesvos
Manisa
Izmir
Odemis
Konya
Karaman
4
GREECE
Lamia
Euboea
Skyros
Chios
Ephesus
Aydin
Denizli
Isparta
Beysehir Lake
Preveza
Kefallonia
Patra
Chalkida
Peiraias
Athens
Cyclades
Antalya
Taurus Mountains
nian Sea
Pyrgos
Kalamata
Kythira
Dodecanese
Rhodes
Rhodes
Alanya
Gulf of Antalya
Chania
Crete
Irakleio
Karpathos
Nicosia
Kyrenia
CYPRUS
Larnaca
Paphos
Limassol
Ierapetra

AFRICA

Africa is the second-biggest continent in the world, and has 53 countries. These range from the vast, dry Sudan, to small, tropical islands such as the Seychelles. More than a quarter of Africa's countries are landlocked, with no access to the sea except through other countries.

Here is a group of Masai people from East Africa, silhouetted against a sunset over the flat grasslands of Africa.

Madeira (Portugal)

Canary Islands (Spain)

Tropic of Cancer

Rabat
MOROCCO

Algiers Tunis
TUNISIA Tripoli

ALGERIA

LIBYA

Laayoune
WESTERN SAHARA (Morocco)

MAURITANIA
Nouakchott

MALI

Niger

NIGER

CHAD

Ndjamena

CAPE VERDE
Praia

Dakar
SENEGAL
THE GAMBIA Banjul
Bissau
GUINEA-BISSAU GUINEA
Conakry
Freetown
SIERRA LEONE
Monrovia
LIBERIA Yamoussoukro
IVORY COAST
Bamako
BURKINA FASO
Ouagadougou
Niamey

BENIN
TOGO
GHANA Porto-Novo
Accra Lome

NIGERIA
Abuja

CENTRAL AFRICAN REPUBLIC
Bangui

CAMEROON
Malabo
EQUATORIAL GUINEA
SAO TOME AND PRINCIPE

Yaounde

Equator

Libreville
GABON CONGO

Brazzaville Kinshasa

ATLANTIC

OCEAN

Luanda

ANGOLA

NAMIBIA

Tropic of Capricorn

Windhoek

Orange

Cape Town

Facts

Total land area 30,311,690 sq km (11,703,343 sq miles)
Total population 794 million
Biggest city Lagos, Nigeria
Biggest country Sudan *2,505,810 sq km (967,493 sq miles)*
Smallest country Seychelles *455 sq km (176 sq miles)*

Highest mountain Kilimanjaro, Tanzania *5,895m (19,340ft)*
Longest river Nile, running from to Burundi to Egypt *6,671km (4,145 miles)*
Biggest lake Lake Victoria, between Tanzania, Kenya and Uganda *69,215 sq km (26,724 sq miles)*
Highest waterfall Tugela Falls, on the Tugela River, South Africa *610m (2,000ft)*
Biggest desert Sahara, North Africa *9,100,000 sq km (3,500,000 sq miles)*
Biggest island Madagascar *587,040 sq km (226,656 sq miles)*

Main mineral deposits Gold, copper, diamonds, iron ore, manganese, bauxite
Main fuel deposits Coal, uranium, natural gas

The shading on this map is there to help you see clearly the different countries that make up the continent.

INDIAN

OCEAN

Internet link

For links to websites where you can take a tour of African states, and find out about the wildlife of Madagascar, go to **www.usborne-quicklinks.com**

This greater flamingo is from the Transvaal National Park, South Africa.

GREECE   Ath

Sicily (Italy)   Catania   Syracuse

Annaba   Menzel   Bizerte   Carthage
Bourguiba   ■Tunis   Pantelleria (Italy)

Saida   Djelfa   Batna   Tebessa   Kairouan   Sousse
Monastir   El Jem   MALTA   ■Valletta

Atlas Mountains   Biskra   Gafsa   Tozeur   Sfax   Kerkenah Islands
Pelagian Islands (Italy)

El Oued   Touggourt   Chott el Jerid   Gulf of Gabes   Jerba
Ghardaia   Ouargla   Tataouine   TUNISIA   Tripoli■   Al Khums   Misratah
Leptis Magna   Gharyan   Surt   Benghazi   Cyrene   Al Bayda   Darnah

M e d i t e r r a n e a

30°N   Tademait Plateau   Ghadamis   Gulf of Sidra   Ajdabiya   Tubruq   Libya

Great Eastern Erg

ALGERIA   Illizi   Sabha   LIBYA   25°

Ahaggar Mountains   Ghat   Murzuq   Libya

Mount Tahat   2918m   (9,573ft)   20°

Tamanrasset   Al Jar

Djado Plateau   Tibesti Mountains

Emi Koussal   3,415m   (11,204ft)

MALI   S   A   H   A   R   A

Agadez   NIGER   Faya-Largeau   Ennedi Plateau

15°   Bodele Depression

Tahoua

CHAD   Mount M   3,08   (10,1

Dosso   Maradi   Zinder   Mao   Abeche
Sokoto   S   A   H   E   L   Nya
Birnin-Kebbi   Katsina   Lake Chad   Mongo
Kandi   Gusau   Kano   Maiduguri   ■Ndjamena   Am Timan
Zaria   Potiskum   Kumo   Mongo
10°   Kainji Reservoir   Kaduna   NIGERIA   Maroua   Bongor   Birao
Saki   Bida   Minna   Jos   CAMEROON
Niger   Abuja■

B   5°E   C   10°   D   15°   E   20°   F

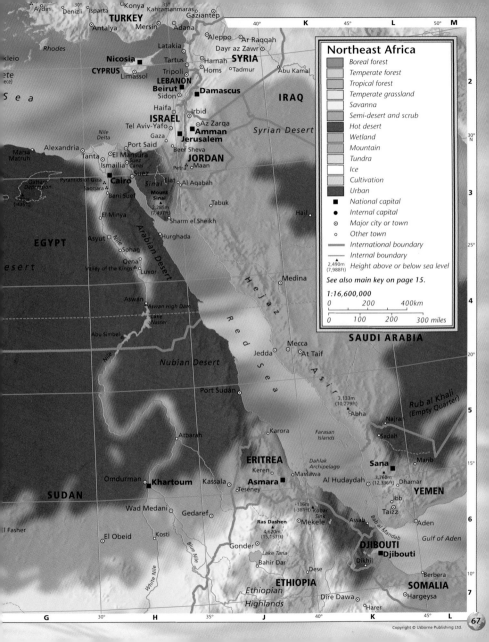

Northwest Africa

Boreal forest
Temperate forest
Tropical forest
Temperate grassland
Savanna
Semi-desert and scrub
Hot desert

Wetland
Mountain
Tundra
Ice
Cultivation
Urban

■ National capital
● Internal capital
◉ Major city or town
○ Other town

See also main key on page 15.

International boundary
Internal boundary

▲2,490m (7,988ft)
Height above or below sea level

1:16,600,000

| 0 | 100 | 200 | 300 miles |
| 0 | 200 | 400km | |

NIGER
Maradi
Tahoua
Katsina
Gusau
Zaria
Kaduna
Sokoto
Minna
Birnin-Kebbi
Bida
Abuja
Dosso
Niamey
Tillaberi
Kainji Reservoir
Ilorin
Enugu
Niger
NIGERIA
Ogbomoso
Owo
Onitsha
Ibadan
Abeokuta
Benin City
Saki
Lagos
Warri
Porto-Novo
Port Harcourt
BENIN
Kandi
Natitingou
Cotonou
Lome
Bight of Benin
Niger Delta
Gao
Djougou
Parakou
Abomey
Sokode
Accra
Gulf of Guinea
Tombouctou (Timbuktu)
Dori
Ouahigouya
BURKINA FASO
Fada-Ngourma
Tenkodogo
Bawku
White Volta
TOGO
GHANA
Cape Coast
Gourma-Rharous
Mopti
Ouagadougou
Koudougou
Wa
Tamale
Wenchi
Koforidua
Sekondi-Takoradi
Cape Three Points
SAO TOME AND PRINCIPE
Principe
Sao Tome ■ Equator
Goundam
San
Tougan
Bobo Dioulasso
Black Volta
Bouna
Tamale
Damongo
Lake Volta
Kumasi
Tarkwa
Niono
Segou
Sikasso
Bondoukou
Koutiala
Bougouni
Bouake
Adzope
Divo
Nioro du Sahel
Bamako
Bafoula
Banfora
Korhogo
Katiola
Odienne
IVORY COAST
Yamoussoukro
Gagnoa
Abidjan
San Pedro
Ayoun el Atrous
Kita
Kayes
Siguiri
Man
1750m (5,748ft)
Daloa
Harper
Cape Palmas
Selibabi
Kedougou
Labe
Nzerekore
Tubmanburg
Kolda
Tambacounda
GUINEA
Kankan
Gueckedou
Zorzor
LIBERIA
Bignona
Kindia
Boke
SENEGAL
St. Louis
Louga
Thies
Dakar
Kaolack
Dara
Bissau
GUINEA-BISSAU
Bissagos Archipelago
Conakry
Makeni
Bo
Sefadu
Kenema
SIERRA LEONE
Monrovia
Freetown
Ziguinchor
Banjul
THE GAMBIA

ATLANTIC OCEAN

CAPE VERDE
ATLANTIC OCEAN
Santo Antao
Sao Nicolau
Mindelo
Sal
Boa Vista
Sao Tiago
Maio
Praia
Fogo

Same scale as main map

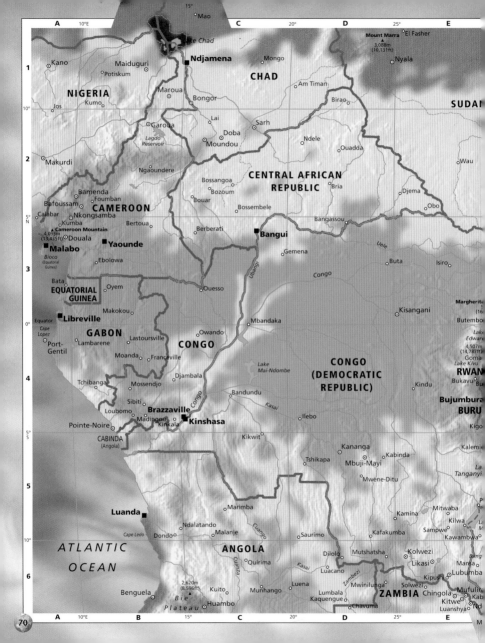

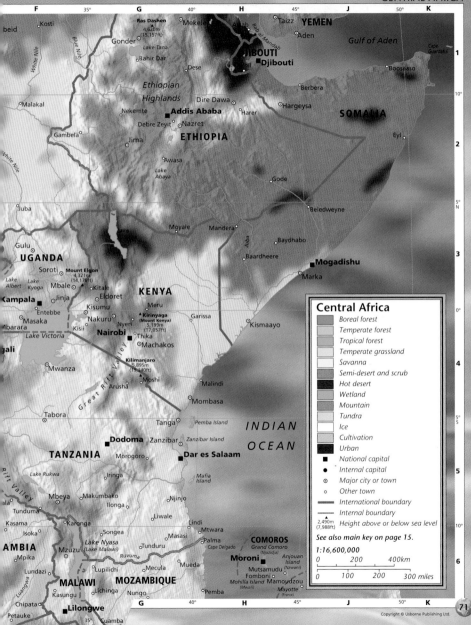

beid
Kosti °

Ras Dashen
4,620m
(15,157ft) ▲
Mekele °

Alaba °
Bab al Mandab

Taizz °   YEMEN

Gonder °

Lake Tana
Bahir Dar °

Aden °

Gulf of Aden

Cape
Guardafui

1

White Nile

Blue Nile

Dese °

DJIBOUTI

■ Djibouti

Boosaaso °

Ethiopian
Highlands

Dire Dawa °

Berbera °

10°

Malakal °

Nekemte °

Addis Ababa ●

Harer °

Hargeysa °

SOMALIA

Gambela °

Debre Zeyit °   ● Nazret

ETHIOPIA

Jima °

Eyl °

2

Juba °

Awasa °

Lake
Abaya

Gode °

5°
N

White Nile

Gulu °

Moyale °

Mandera °

Beledweyne °

UGANDA

Soroti °

Mount Elgon
4,321m
(14,176ft) ▲

Mbale °

Kitale °
Eldoret °

KENYA

Meru °

Juba

Baydhabo °

Baardheere °

Auba

3

Lake
Albert

Lake
Kyoga

Kampala ■

Jinja °

Kisumu °

Nakuru °

Kirinyaga
(Mount Kenya)
5,199m ▲
(17,057ft)

Garissa °

Marka °

Mogadishu ■

Entebbe °

Masaka °

Mbarara °

Kisii °

Nyeri °
Nairobi ●

Thika °
Machakos °

Kismaayo °

0°

gali

Lake Victoria

Mwanza °

Kilimanjaro
5,895m ▲
(19,340ft)

Moshi °

Arusha °

Malindi °

4

Tabora °

Tanga °

Pemba Island

Mombasa °

INDIAN

Dodoma ■

Zanzibar °

Zanzibar Island

OCEAN

5°
S

TANZANIA

Morogoro °

Dar es Salaam ■

Great Rift Valley

Lake Rukwa

Iringa °

Mafia
Island

Mbeya °

Makumbako °

Ilonga °

Njinjo °

5

Tunduma °

Liwale °

Rift Valley

Kasama °

Songea °

Lindi °
Mtwara °

Isoka °

Karonga °

Masasi °

COMOROS
Grand Comoro
(Njazidja)

Luangwa

AMBIA

Mzuzu °

Lake Nyasa
(Lake Malawi)

Tunduru °

Ruvuma

Palma °

Cape Delgado

Anjouan
Island
(Nzwani)

10°

Mpika °

Lupilichi °

Mecula °

Mueda °

Moroni ■

Mayotte
(France)

6

Lundazi °

Lichinga °

Nungo °

MALAWI

MOZAMBIQUE

Mutsamudu
Fomboni °
Mohilla Island
(Mwali)   Mamoudzou
(Meali)

Chipata °

Kasungu °

Lilongwe ■

Quamba °

Pemba °

Petauke °

Central Africa

- Boreal forest
- Temperate forest
- Tropical forest
- Temperate grassland
- Savanna
- Semi-desert and scrub
- Hot desert
- Wetland
- Mountain
- Tundra
- Ice
- Cultivation
- Urban
- ■ National capital
- ● Internal capital
- ⊙ Major city or town
- ○ Other town
- ━━━ International boundary
- ━ ━ Internal boundary
- ▲ 2,490m (7,988ft) Height above or below sea level

See also main key on page 15.

1:16,600,000

0   200   400km

0   100   200   300 miles

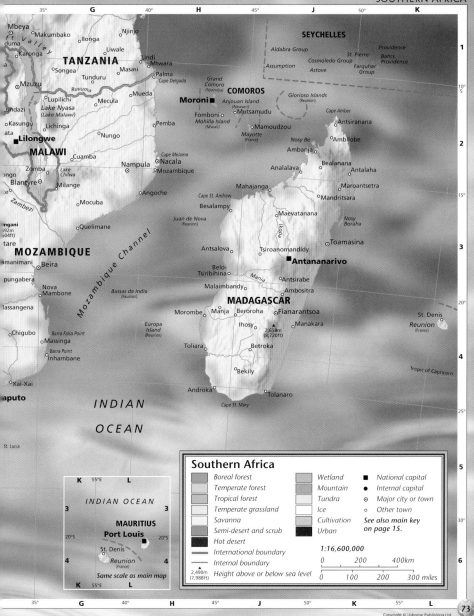

Southern Africa

Boreal forest	Wetland
Temperate forest	Mountain
Tropical forest	Tundra
Temperate grassland	Ice
Savanna	Cultivation
Semi-desert and scrub	Urban
Hot desert	

- National capital
- Internal capital
⊙ Major city or town
○ Other town

See also main key on page 15.

International boundary
Internal boundary
Height above or below sea level

1:16,600,000

0   200   400km
0   100   200   300 miles

Mauritius inset:

INDIAN OCEAN

MAURITIUS
Port Louis
St. Denis
Reunion (France)

Same scale as main map

2,490m (7,988ft)

Map labels:

Mbeya, Makumbako, Ilonga, Njinjo, duma, Karonga, Liwale, Lindi, TANZANIA, Mtwara, Songea, Tunduru, Masasi, Palma, Cape Delgado, Mzuzu, Ruvuma, Mueda, Grand Comoro (Njazidja), COMOROS, Lupilichi, Mecula, Moroni, Anjouan Island (Nzwani), Mutsamudu, Lake Nyasa (Lake Malawi), Lichinga, Nungo, Pemba, Fomboni, Mohilla Island (Mwali), Glorioso Islands (Reunion), Cape Amber, Lilongwe, MALAWI, Cuamba, Mamoudzou, Antsiranana, Zomba, Lake Chilwa, Nacala, Nampula, Mayotte (France), Nosy Be, Ambilobe, Blantyre, Milange, Mozambique, Ambanja, Analalava, Bealanana, Antalaha, Zambezi, Mocuba, Angoche, Cape St. Andrew, Mahajanga, Maroantsetra, ngani, 92m (04ft), tare, Quelimane, Besalampy, Juan de Nova (Reunion), Maevatanana, Nosy Boraha, MOZAMBIQUE, Mozambique Channel, Antsalova, Tsiroanomandidy, Toamasina, manimani, Beira, Antananarivo, Belo-Tsiribihina, Mania, Antsirabe, pungabera, Nova Mambone, Bassas da India (Reunion), Malaimbandy, Ambositra, lassangena, Europa Island (Reunion), MADAGASCAR, Morombe, Manja, Beroroha, Fianarantsoa, Chigubo, Barra Falsa Point, Ihosy, Manakara, St. Denis, Reunion (France), Massinga, 2,658m (8,720ft), Barra Point, Inhambane, Toliara, Betroka, Tropic of Capricorn, Xai-Xai, Bekily, aputo, Androka, Tolanaro, Cape St. Mary, INDIAN OCEAN, St. Lucia

SEYCHELLES, Aldabra Group, St. Pierre, Providence, Cosmoledo Group, Bancs, Providence, Assumption, Astove, Farquhar Group

THE ARCTIC

The Arctic is not a continent. It is a region north of the Arctic Circle line of latitude, around the North Pole. The Arctic consists of the Arctic Ocean, islands such as Greenland and the most northerly parts of mainland Europe, North America and Asia. The Arctic region is covered in ice and snow almost all year round.

The large white area in this satellite image is ice covering the Arctic Ocean and Greenland. At the top left of the image is the edge of Russia and at the top right is part of Europe.

These Inuit people are wearing thick, animal-skin coats, boots and gloves to keep warm.

Internet link

For a link to a website where you can discover more about the Arctic, including its wildlife, climate and native peoples, go to **www.usborne-quicklinks.com**

Facts

Size of Arctic Ocean
14,056,000 sq km (5,426,000 sq miles)

Highest point Gunnbjorns Mountain, Greenland *3,700m (12,139ft)*

Lowest point Fram Basin, Arctic Ocean *-4,665m (-15,305ft)*

Lowest recorded temperature -67.8°C (-90°F)

Main mineral deposits Diamonds, gold

Main fuel deposits Oil, natural gas

Seals living in Arctic regions have a thick layer of fat under their skin to keep them warm in the freezing weather.

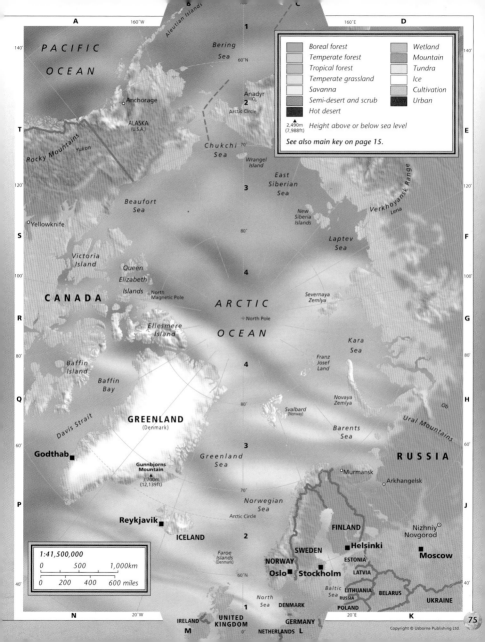

A | 160°W | B | C | 160°E | D

140°

PACIFIC
OCEAN

1

Bering
Sea

60°N

Aleutian Islands

Anadyr

Arctic Circle

2

Anchorage

ALASKA
(U.S.A.)

T

E

Rocky Mountains

Yukon

Chukchi
Sea

70°

Wrangel
Island

East
Siberian
Sea

Verkhoyansk Range

Lena

140°

120°

S

Beaufort
Sea

Yellowknife

80°

New
Siberia
Islands

3

Laptev
Sea

120°

F

100°

Victoria
Island

Queen
Elizabeth
Islands

North
Magnetic Pole

ARCTIC

4

Severnaya
Zemlya

100°

CANADA

North Pole

Kara
Sea

R

OCEAN

Ellesmere
Island

G

80°

Baffin
Island

Baffin
Bay

4

80°

Franz
Josef
Land

Ob

Q

Davis Strait

GREENLAND
(Denmark)

80°

Novaya
Zemlya

Svalbard
(Norway)

Ural Mountains

H

60°

Godthab

3

Greenland
Sea

Barents
Sea

RUSSIA

60°

P

Gunnbjorns
Mountain
3,700m
(12,139ft)

70°

Murmansk

Arkhangelsk

J

Reykjavik

Norwegian
Sea

Arctic Circle

Nizhniy
Novgorod

ICELAND

2

FINLAND

Moscow

SWEDEN

Helsinki

Faroe
Islands
(Denmark)

NORWAY

ESTONIA

40°

North
Sea

DENMARK

1

Oslo Stockholm

Baltic
Sea

LATVIA

LITHUANIA

RUSSIA

BELARUS

40°

POLAND

UKRAINE

N | 20°W | GERMANY | 20°E | K

IRELAND
M

UNITED
KINGDOM

0°

NETHERLANDS
L

Key (legend box):

- Boreal forest
- Temperate forest
- Tropical forest
- Temperate grassland
- Savanna
- Semi-desert and scrub
- Hot desert
- Wetland
- Mountain
- Tundra
- Ice
- Cultivation
- Urban

2,490m
(7,988ft) Height above or below sea level

See also main key on page 15.

1:41,500,000

0   500   1,000km

0   200   400   600 miles

75

Copyright © Usborne Publishing Ltd.

ANTARCTICA

Antarctica is a huge, frozen continent within the Antarctic Circle. It is almost completely covered by an enormous ice sheet, which is more than 3km (2 miles) deep in some places. Nobody lives permanently in Antarctica, though many scientists visit to study the area. No plants grow in the ice, and the only land animals are tiny mites. But many animals, including penguins, seals, whales and fish, live in the seas around Antarctica.

This ship takes tourists on Antarctic expeditions. Visitors can see animals such as these gentoo penguins, which come onto land to breed.

Internet link

For a link to a website where you can find out more about Antarctica and the creatures that live in the seas around it, go to **www.usborne-quicklinks.com**

Facts

Total land area 14,000,000 sq km (5,405,442 sq miles), of which 13,720,000 sq km (5,297,333 sq miles) are covered in ice
Highest point Vinson Massif *5,140m (16,863ft)*
Lowest point Bentley Subglacial Trench *-2,555m (-8,382ft)*
Lowest recorded temperature -89.2°C (-128.6°F)

Main mineral deposits Iron ore, chromium, copper, gold, nickel, platinum

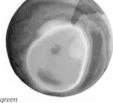

The green area in this satellite photograph is a hole in the ozone layer over Antarctica. The hole is caused by atmospheric pollution.

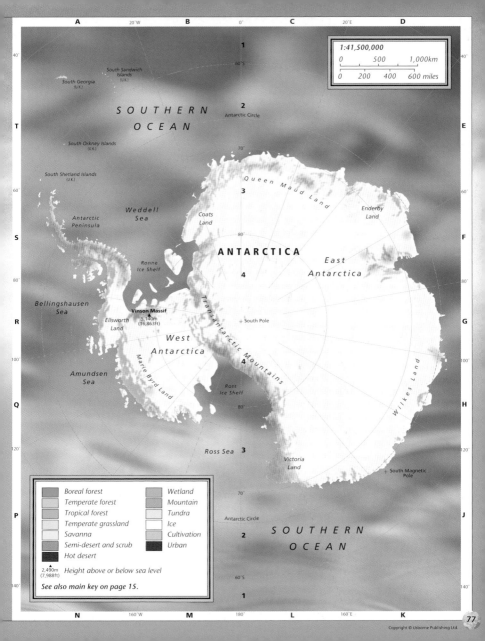

A | B | C | D

20°W | 0° | 20°E

1
60°S

1:41,500,000

| 0 | 500 | 1,000km |
| 0 | 200 | 400 | 600 miles |

South Sandwich
Islands
(U.K.)

South Georgia
(U.K.)

2
Antarctic Circle

S O U T H E R N
O C E A N

T · E

South Orkney Islands
(U.K.)

70°S

South Shetland Islands
(U.K.)

Queen Maud Land

3

Weddell
Sea

Coats
Land

Enderby
Land

60°

Antarctic
Peninsula

S · F

ANTARCTICA

80°S

Ronne
Ice Shelf

East
Antarctica

80°

4

Bellingshausen
Sea

Vinson Massif
5,140m
(16,863ft)

Transantarctic Mountains

R · G

Ellsworth
Land

+ South Pole

100°

West
Antarctica

4

Amundsen
Sea

Marie Byrd Land

Wilkes Land

100°

Ross
Ice Shelf

Q · H

80°S

Ross Sea **3**

120°

Victoria
Land

+ South Magnetic
Pole

120°

	Boreal forest		Wetland
	Temperate forest		Mountain
	Tropical forest		Tundra
	Temperate grassland		Ice
	Savanna		Cultivation
	Semi-desert and scrub		Urban
	Hot desert		

70°S

Antarctic Circle

2

S O U T H E R N
O C E A N

P · J

▲ 2,490m
(7,988ft) *Height above or below sea level*

60°S

See also main key on page 15.

1

N | M | L | K

160°W | 180° | 160°E

140° · 140°

WORLD RECORDS

Here are some of the Earth's longest rivers, highest mountains and other amazing world records. But the world is always changing; mountains wear down, rivers change shape, and new buildings are constructed. Ways of measuring things can also change. That's why you may find slightly different figures in different books.

Highest mountains	
Everest, Nepal/China	8,850m (29,035ft)
K2, Pakistan/China	8,611m (28,251ft)
Kanchenjunga, India/Nepal	8,597m (28,208ft)
Lhotse I, Nepal/China	8,511m (27,923ft)
Makalu I, Nepal/China	8,481m (27,824ft)
Lhotse II, Nepal/China	8,400m (27,560ft)
Dhaulagiri, Nepal	8,172m (26,810ft)
Manaslu I, Nepal	8,156m (26,760ft)
Cho Oyu, Nepal/China	8,153m (26,750ft)
Nanga Parbat, Pakistan	8,126m (26,660ft)

Longest rivers	
Nile, Africa	6,671km (4,145 miles)
Amazon, South America	6,440km (4,000 miles)
Chang Jiang (Yangtze), China	6,380km (3,964 miles)
Mississippi/Missouri, U.S.A.	6,019km (3,741 miles)
Yenisey/Angara, Russia	5,540km (3,442 miles)
Huang He (Yellow), China	5,464km (3,395 miles)
Ob/Irtysh/Black Irtysh, Asia	5,411km (3,362 miles)
Amur/Shilka/Onon, Asia	4,416km (2,744 miles)
Lena, Russia	4,400km (2,734 miles)
Congo, Africa	4,374km (2,718 miles)

Biggest natural lakes	
Caspian Sea	370,999 sq km (143,243 sq miles)
Lake Superior	82,414 sq km (31,820 sq miles)
Lake Victoria	69,215 sq km (26,724 sq miles)
Lake Huron	59,596 sq km (23,010 sq miles)
Lake Michigan	58,016 sq km (22,400 sq miles)
Lake Tanganyika	32,764 sq km (12,650 sq miles)
Lake Baikal	31,500 sq km (12,162 sq miles)
Great Bear Lake	31,328 sq km (12,096 sq miles)
Lake Nyasa	29,928 sq km (11,555 sq miles)
Aral Sea	28,600 sq km (11,042 sq miles)

Deepest ocean
The Mariana Trench, part of the Pacific Ocean, is the deepest part of the sea at 10,911m (35,797ft) deep.

Deepest lake
Lake Baikal in Russia is the deepest lake in the world. At its deepest point it is 1,637m (5,370ft) deep.

Biggest islands	
Greenland	2,175,600 sq km (840,000 sq miles)
New Guinea	800,000 sq km (309,000 sq miles)
Borneo	751,100 sq km (290,000 sq miles)
Madagascar	587,040 sq km (226,656 sq miles)
Baffin Island	507,451 sq km (195,928 sq miles)
Sumatra	437,607 sq km (184,706 sq miles)
Great Britain	234,410 sq km (90,506 sq miles)
Honshu	227,920 sq km (88,000 sq miles)
Victoria Island	217,290 sq km (83,896 sq miles)
Ellesmere Island	196,236 sq km (75,767 sq miles)

Tallest inhabited buildings	
Petronas Towers, Malaysia	452m (1,483ft)
Sears Tower, U.S.A.	443m (1,454ft)
Jin Mao Building, China	420m (1,378ft)
CITIC Plaza, China	391m (1,283ft)
Shun Hing Square, China	384m (1,260ft)
Plaza Rakyat, Malaysia	382m (1,254ft)
Empire State Building, U.S.A.	381m (1,250ft)
Central Plaza, China	373m (1,227ft)
Bank of China, China	368m (1,209ft)
Emirates Tower, U.A.E.	350m (1,148ft)

Biggest cities/urban areas	
Tokyo, Japan	26.4 million
Mexico City, Mexico	18.1 million
Bombay, India	18.1 million
Sao Paulo, Brazil	17.8 million
New York, U.S.A.	16.6 million
Lagos, Nigeria	13.4 million
Los Angeles, U.S.A.	13.1 million
Calcutta, India	12.9 million
Shanghai, China	12.9 million
Buenos Aires, Argentina	12.6 million

Famous waterfalls	Height
Angel Falls, Venezuela	979m (3,212ft)
Sutherland Falls, New Zealand	580m (1,904ft)
Mardalfossen, Norway	517m (1,696ft)
Jog Falls, India	253m (830ft)
Victoria Falls, Zimbabwe/Zambia	108m (355ft)
Iguacu Falls, Brazil/Argentina	82m (269ft)
Niagara Falls, Canada/U.S.A.	57m (187ft)

Natural disasters

Natural disasters can be measured in different ways. For example, some earthquakes score highly on the Richter scale, while others cause more destruction. The earthquakes, volcanic eruptions, floods, hurricanes and tornadoes listed here are among the most famous and destructive disasters in history.

Earthquakes	Richter scale	Disastrous effects
San Francisco, U.S.A., 1906	7.9	3,000 died in resulting fire
Messina, Italy, 1908	7.5	More than 70,000 people died
Tokyo-Kanto, Japan, 1923	8.3	Great Tokyo Fire; 142,807 died
Quetta, Pakistan, 1935	7.5	30–60,000 died; city destroyed
Concepcion, Chile, 1960	8.7	2,000 died; strongest quake ever
Alaska, U.S.A., 1964	8.6	125 died; strongest U.S. quake ever
Tangshan, China, 1976	7.9	More than 655,000 people died
Manjil-Rudbar, Iran, 1990	7.7	50,000 died; cities destroyed
Kobe, Japan, 1995	6.8	6,400 died; over $147bn damage
Gujarat, India, 2001	8.0	20,085 died; 2nd strongest Indian quake

Volcanic eruptions	Disastrous effects
Mount Vesuvius, Italy, AD79	Pompeii flattened; up to 20,000 died
Tambora, Indonesia, 1815	92,000 people starved to death
Krakatau, Indonesia, 1883	36,500 drowned in resulting tsunami
Mount Pelee, Martinique, 1902	Nearly 30,000 people buried in ash flows
Kelut, Indonesia, 1919	Over 5,000 people drowned in mud
Agung, Indonesia, 1963	1,200 people suffocated in hot ash
Mount St. Helens, U.S.A., 1980	Only 61 died but a large area was destroyed
Ruiz, Colombia, 1985	25,000 people died in giant mud flows
Mt. Pinatubo, Philippines, 1991	800 killed by collapsing roofs and disease
Island of Montserrat, 1995	Volcano left most of the island uninhabitable

Floods	Disastrous effects
Holland, 1228	100,000 drowned by a sea flood
Kaifeng, China, 1642	300,000 died after rebels destroyed a dyke
Johnstown, U.S.A., 1889	2,200 killed in a flood caused by rain
Italy, 1963	Vaiont Dam overflowed; 2–3,000 killed
East Pakistan, 1970	Giant wave caused by cyclone killed 250,000
Bangladesh, 1988	1,300 died, 30m homeless in monsoon flood
Southern U.S.A., 1993	$12bn of damage after Mississippi flooded
China, 1998	Chang Jiang overflow left 14m homeless
Papua New Guinea, 1998	Tsunamis killed 2,000 people
Venezuela, 1999	Floods and mudslides killed 5,000–20,000

Storms	Disastrous effects
Caribbean "Great Hurricane", 1780	Biggest ever hurricane killed over 20,000
Hong Kong typhoon, China, 1906	10,000 people died in this giant hurricane
Killer tornado, U.S.A., 1925	Up to 700 people died in Ellington, Missouri
Tropical Storm Agnes, U.S.A., 1972	$3.5bn damage, 129 dead
Hurricane Fifi, Honduras, 1974	8,000 people died and 100,000 left homeless
Hurricane Georges, U.S.A., 1998	Caribbean and U.S.A. hit; $5bn of damage
Hurricane Mitch, C. America, 1998	Over 9,000 killed across Central America

Amazing Earth facts

The Earth is 12,103km (7,520 miles) across. Its circumference (the distance around the Equator) is 38,022km (23,627 miles) and it is 149,503,000 km (92,897,000 miles) away from the Sun.

To make one complete orbit around the Sun, the Earth has to travel 938,900,000km (583,400,000 miles). To do this in just a year, it has to travel very fast. Because of the atmosphere surrounding the Earth, you can't feel it moving. But in fact you are zooming through space faster than any rocket.

• **Orbit speed** The Earth travels around the Sun at a speed of about 106,000kph (65,868mph).

• **Spinning speed** The Earth also spins around an axis, but the speed you are spinning at depends on where you live. Places on the Equator move at 1,600kph (995mph). New York moves at around 1,100kph (684mph). Near the poles, the spinning is not very fast at all. (You can see how this works by looking at a spinning globe.)

• **Solar System speed** The whole Solar System, including the Sun, the Earth and its moon, and the other planets and their moons, is moving at 72,400kph (45,000 mph) through the galaxy.

• **Galaxy speed** Our galaxy, the Milky Way, whizzes through the universe at a speed of 2,172,150kph (1,350,000mph).

TIME ZONES

The Earth is divided into different time zones.
Within each zone, people usually set their clocks
to the same time. If you fly between two zones,
you change your watch to the time in the new zone.

Dividing up time

There are 25 time zones. They
are separated by one-hour
intervals and there is a time
zone every 15 degrees of
longitude. There are 12
one-hour zones both ahead
of and behind Greenwich
Mean Time (GMT), the time
at the Prime Meridian Line.

For convenience, whole
countries usually keep the
same local time instead of
sticking to the zones exactly.
For example, China could
be divided into several
time zones, but instead the
whole country has the same
time. A few places, such
as India, use non-standard
half hour deviations.

Summer time

Some places adjust their clocks
in summer. For example,
in the U.K. all clocks go forward
one hour. It is a way of getting
more out of the days by
having an extra hour of light.

Changing dates

The International Date Line
runs mostly through the
Pacific Ocean and bends
to avoid the land. Places to
the west of it are 24 hours
ahead of places to the east.
This means that if you travel
east across it you lose a
day and if you travel west
across it you gain a day.

*This map shows the time zones. The times at the top of the map tell you the time in the different zones when it is
noon at the Prime Meridian Line. There are two midnight zones, one for each day on either side of the International
Date Line. The numbers in circles tell you how many hours ahead of or behind Greenwich Mean Time an area is.*

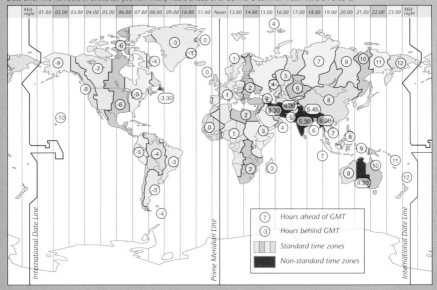

TYPES OF GOVERNMENTS

Most states have one main leader along with a parliament or assembly of politicians. The main types of governments are listed and explained below. A state can have a combination of more than one of these types of governments. For example, the United States of America is a federal republic.

Anarchy
Anarchy means a situation where there is no government. This can happen after a civil war, when a government has been destroyed and rival groups are battling to take its place.

Capitalist state
In a Capitalist or free-market state, people can own their own businesses and property, and buy services such as healthcare privately. However, most Capitalist governments also provide national health, education and welfare services.

Commonwealth
This word is sometimes used to mean a democratic republic, in which all the state's citizens are seen as having an equal interest in the functioning of the state.

Communist state
Under Communism, the state owns things like factories, farms and businesses, and provides healthcare, welfare and education for its people.

Democracy
In a democracy, the government is elected by the people, using a voting system.

Dictatorship
This is a state run by a single, unelected leader, who may use force to keep control. In a military dictatorship, the army is in power.

Federal government
In a federal system, such as that of the U.S.A., a central government shares power with a number of smaller regional governments.

Monarchy
A monarchy is a state with a king or queen. In some traditional monarchies, the monarch has complete power. A constitutional monarchy, however, also has a separate, usually democratic, government and the monarch's powers are limited.

Regional or local government
A government that controls a smaller area within a state. Some regional governments have very limited powers, and are largely directed by the central government. Others, such as the regional governments in the U.S.A., have much more power and can make their own laws.

Republic
A republic is a state with no monarch. The head of state is usually an elected president.

Revolutionary government
After a revolution, when a government is overthrown by force, the new regime is sometimes called a revolutionary government.

Totalitarian state
This is a state with only one political party, in which individuals are forced to obey the government and may also be prevented from leaving the country.

Transitional government
A government that is changing from one system to another is known as a transitional government. For example, a dictatorship may become a democracy after the dictator dies, but the transition between the systems can take several years.

GAZETTEER OF STATES

Afghanistan

Algeria

This gazetteer lists the world's 193 independent states, along with key facts about each one. In the lists of languages, the language that is most widely spoken is given first, even if it is not the official language. In the lists of religions, the one followed by the most people is also placed first. Every state has a national flag, which is usually used to represent the country abroad. A few states also have a state flag which they prefer to use instead. The state flags appear here with a dot • beside them.

Armenia

Australia

Austria

Azerbaijan

Bahamas, The

Bahrain

Andorra

Angola

Antigua and Barbuda

• Argentina

AFGHANISTAN (Asia)
Area: 647,500 sq km (249,935 sq miles)
Population: 27,755,775
Capital city: Kabul
Main languages: Dari, Pashto
Main religion: Muslim
Government: transitional
Currency: 1 afghani = 100 puls

ALBANIA (Europe)
Area: 28,750 sq km (11,100 sq miles)
Population: 3,544,841
Capital city: Tirana
Main language: Albanian
Main religions: Muslim, Albanian Orthodox
Government: emerging democracy
Currency: 1 lek = 100 qintars

ALGERIA (Africa)
Area: 2,381,740 sq km (919,589 sq miles)
Population: 32,277,942
Capital city: Algiers
Main languages: Arabic, French, Berber dialects
Main religion: Sunni Muslim
Government: republic
Currency: 1 Algerian dinar = 100 centimes

ANDORRA (Europe)
Area: 468 sq km (181 sq miles)
Population: 68,403
Capital city: Andorra la Vella
Main languages: Catalan, Spanish
Main religion: Roman Catholic
Government: parliamentary democracy
Currency: 1 euro = 100 cents

ANGOLA (Africa)
Area: 1,246,700 sq km (481,351 sq miles)
Population: 10,593,171
Capital city: Luanda
Main languages: Kilongo, Kimbundu, other Bantu languages, Portuguese
Main religions: indigenous, Roman Catholic, Protestant
Government: transitional
Currency: 1 kwanza = 100 lwei

ANTIGUA AND BARBUDA (North America)
Area: 442 sq km (171 sq miles)
Population: 67,448
Capital city: Saint John's
Main languages: Caribbean Creole, English
Main religion: Protestant
Government: constitutional monarchy
Currency: 1 East Caribbean dollar = 100 cents

ARGENTINA (South America)
Area: 2,766,890 sq km (1,068,305 sq miles)
Population: 37,812,817
Capital city: Buenos Aires
Main language: Spanish
Main religion: Roman Catholic
Government: republic
Currency: 1 peso = 100 centavos

ARMENIA (Asia)
Area: 29,800 sq km (11,506 sq miles)
Population: 3,336,100
Capital city: Yerevan
Main language: Armenian
Main religion: Armenian Orthodox
Government: republic
Currency: 1 dram = 100 luma

AUSTRALIA (Australasia/Oceania)
Area: 7,686,850 sq km (2,967,124 sq miles)
Population: 19,546,792
Capital city: Canberra
Main language: English
Main religion: Christian
Government: federal democratic monarchy
Currency: 1 Australian dollar = 100 cents

AUSTRIA (Europe)
Area: 83,858 sq km (32,378 sq miles)
Population: 8,169,929
Capital city: Vienna
Main language: German
Main religion: Roman Catholic
Government: federal republic
Currency: 1 euro = 100 cents

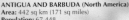

Bangladesh

Barbados

Belarus

Belgium

Belize

Benin

Bhutan

• **Bolivia**

AZERBAIJAN (Asia)
Area: 86,600 sq km (33,436 sq miles)
Population: 7,798,497
Capital city: Baku
Main language: Azeri
Main religion: Muslim
Government: republic
Currency: 1 manat = 100 gopiks

BAHAMAS, THE (North America)
Area: 13,940 sq km (5,382 sq miles)
Population: 300,529
Capital city: Nassau
Main languages: Bahamian Creole, English
Main religion: Christian
Government: parliamentary democracy
Currency: 1 Bahamian dollar = 100 cents

BAHRAIN (Asia)
Area: 665 sq km (257 sq miles)
Population: 656,397
Capital city: Manama
Main languages: Arabic, English
Main religion: Muslim
Government: traditional monarchy
Currency: 1 Bahraini dinar = 1,000 fils

BANGLADESH (Asia)
Area: 144,000 sq km (55,598 sq miles)
Population: 133,376,684
Capital city: Dhaka
Main languages: Bengali, English
Main religions: Muslim, Hindu
Government: republic
Currency: 1 taka = 100 poisha

BARBADOS (North America)
Area: 430 sq km (166 sq miles)
Population: 276,607
Capital city: Bridgetown
Main languages: Bajan, English
Main religion: Christian
Government: parliamentary democracy
Currency: 1 Barbadian dollar = 100 cents

BELARUS (Europe)
Area: 207,600 sq km (80,154 sq miles)
Population: 10,335,382
Capital city: Minsk
Main language: Belarusian
Main religion: Eastern Orthodox
Government: republic
Currency: 1 Belarusian ruble = 100 kopecks

BELGIUM (Europe)
Area: 30,510 sq km (11,780 sq miles)
Population: 10,274,595
Capital city: Brussels
Main languages: Dutch, French
Main religions: Roman Catholic, Protestant
Government: constitutional monarchy
Currency: 1 euro = 100 cents

BELIZE (North America)
Area: 22,960 sq km (8,865 sq miles)
Population: 262,999
Capital city: Belmopan
Main languages: Spanish, Belize Creole, English, Garifuna, Maya

Main religions: Roman Catholic, Protestant
Government: parliamentary democracy
Currency: 1 Belizean dollar = 100 cents

BENIN (Africa)
Area: 112,620 sq km (43,483 sq miles)
Population: 6,787,625
Capital city: Porto-Novo
Main languages: Fon, French, Yoruba
Main religions: indigenous, Christian, Muslim
Government: republic
Currency: 1 CFA* franc = 100 centimes

BHUTAN (Asia)
Area: 47,000 sq km (18,146 sq miles)
Population: 2,094,176
Capital city: Thimphu
Main languages: Dzongkha, Nepali
Main religions: Buddhist, Hindu
Government: monarchy
Currency: 1 ngultrum = 100 chetrum

BOLIVIA (South America)
Area: 1,098,580 sq km (424,162 sq miles)
Population: 8,445,134
Capital cities: La Paz, Sucre
Main languages: Spanish, Quechua, Aymara
Main religion: Roman Catholic
Government: republic
Currency: 1 boliviano = 100 centavos

BOSNIA AND HERZEGOVINA (Europe)
Area: 51,129 sq km (19,741 sq miles)
Population: 3,964,388
Capital city: Sarajevo
Main languages: Bosnian, Serbian, Croatian
Main religions: Muslim, Orthodox, Roman Catholic
Government: emerging federal democracy
Currency: 1 marka = 100 pfenninga

BOTSWANA (Africa)
Area: 600,372 sq km (231,743 sq miles)
Population: 1,591,232
Capital city: Gaborone
Main languages: Setswana, Kalanga, English
Main religions: indigenous, Christian
Government: parliamentary republic
Currency: 1 pula = 100 thebe

BRAZIL (South America)
Area: 8,547,400 sq km (3,300,151 sq miles)
Population: 176,029,560
Capital city: Brasilia
Main language: Portuguese
Main religion: Roman Catholic
Government: federal republic
Currency: 1 real = 100 centavos

BRUNEI (Asia)
Area: 5,770 sq km (2,228 sq miles)
Population: 350,898
Capital city: Bandar Seri Begawan
Main languages: Malay, English, Chinese
Main religions: Muslim, Buddhist
Government: constitutional sultanate (a type of monarchy)
Currency: 1 Bruneian dollar = 100 cents

Bosnia and Herzegovina

Botswana

Brazil

Brunei

Bulgaria

Burkina Faso

Burma (Myanmar)

*CFA = Communaute Financiere Africaine

Burundi

Cambodia

Cameroon

Canada

Cape Verde

Central African Republic

Chad

BULGARIA (Europe)
Area: 110,910 sq km (42,822 sq miles)
Population: 7,621,337
Capital city: Sofia
Main language: Bulgarian
Main religions: Bulgarian Orthodox, Muslim
Government: parliamentary democracy
Currency: 1 lev = 100 stotinki

BURKINA FASO (Africa)
Area: 274,200 sq km (105,869 sq miles)
Population: 12,603,185
Capital city: Ouagadougou
Main languages: Moore, Jula, French
Main religions: Muslim, indigenous
Government: republic
Currency: 1 CFA* franc = 100 centimes

BURMA (MYANMAR) (Asia)
Area: 678,500 sq km (261,969 sq miles)
Population: 42,238,224
Capital city: Rangoon
Main language: Burmese
Main religion: Buddhist
Government: military dictatorship
Currency: 1 kyat = 100 pyas

BURUNDI (Africa)
Area: 27,830 sq km (10,745 sq miles)
Population: 6,373,002
Capital city: Bujumbura
Main languages: Kirundi, French, Swahili
Main religions: Christian, indigenous
Government: republic
Currency: 1 Burundi franc = 100 centimes

CAMBODIA (Asia)
Area: 181,040 sq km (69,900 sq miles)
Population: 12,775,324
Capital city: Phnom Penh
Main language: Khmer
Main religion: Buddhist
Government: constitutional monarchy
Currency: 1 new riel = 100 sen

CAMEROON (Africa)
Area: 475,440 sq km (183,567 sq miles)
Population: 16,184,748
Capital city: Yaounde
Main languages: Cameroon Pidgin English,
Ewondo, Fula, French, English
Main religions: indigenous, Christian, Muslim
Government: republic
Currency: 1 CFA* franc = 100 centimes

CANADA (North America)
Area: 9,970,610 sq km (3,849,653 sq miles)
Population: 31,902,268
Capital city: Ottawa
Main languages: English, French
Main religions: Roman Catholic, Protestant
Government: federal democracy
Currency: 1 Canadian dollar = 100 cents

CAPE VERDE (Africa)
Area: 4,033 sq km (1,557 sq miles)
Population: 408,760
Capital city: Praia
Main languages: Crioulo*, Portuguese

Main religions: Roman Catholic, Protestant
Government: republic
Currency: 1 Cape Verdean escudo = 100
centavos

CENTRAL AFRICAN REPUBLIC (Africa)
Area: 622,984 sq km (240,536 sq miles)
Population: 3,642,739
Capital city: Bangui
Main languages: Sangho, French
Main religions: indigenous, Christian, Muslim
Government: republic
Currency: 1 CFA* franc = 100 centimes

CHAD (Africa)
Area: 1,284,000 sq km (495,752 sq miles)
Population: 8,997,237
Capital city: Ndjamena
Main languages: Arabic, Sara, French
Main religions: Muslim, Christian,
indigenous
Government: republic
Currency: 1 CFA* franc = 100 centimes

CHILE (South America)
Area: 756,626 sq km (292,133 sq miles)
Population: 15,498,930
Capital city: Santiago
Main language: Spanish
Main religions: Roman Catholic, Protestant
Government: republic
Currency: 1 Chilean peso = 100 centavos

CHINA (Asia)
Area: 9,596,960 sq km (3,705,386 sq miles)
Population: 1,284,303,705
Capital city: Beijing
Main languages: Mandarin Chinese, Yue, Wu
Main religions: Taoist, Buddhist
Government: Communist state
Currency: 1 yuan = 10 jiao

COLOMBIA (South America)
Area: 1,138,910 sq km (439,733 sq miles)
Population: 41,008,227
Capital city: Bogota
Main language: Spanish
Main religion: Roman Catholic
Government: republic
Currency: 1 Colombian peso = 100 centavos

COMOROS (Africa)
Area: 2,170 sq km (838 sq miles)
Population: 614,382
Capital city: Moroni
Main languages: Comorian*, French, Arabic
Main religion: Sunni Muslim
Government: republic
Currency: 1 Comoran franc = 100 centimes

CONGO (Africa)
Area: 342,000 sq km (132,046 sq miles)
Population: 2,958,448
Capital city: Brazzaville
Main languages: Munukutuba, Lingala,
French
Main religions: Christian, animist
Government: republic
Currency: 1 CFA* franc = 100 centimes

Chile

China

Colombia

Comoros

Congo

Congo (Democratic Republic)

Costa Rica

*CFA = Communaute Financiere Africaine; Comorian = a blend of Swahili
and Arabic; Crioulo = a blend of Portuguese and West African

Croatia

CONGO (DEMOCRATIC REPUBLIC) (Africa)
Area: 2,345,410 sq km (905,563 sq miles)
Population: 55,225,478
Capital city: Kinshasa
Main languages: Lingala, Swahili, Kikongo, Tshiluba, French
Main religions: Roman Catholic, Protestant, Kimbanguist, Muslim
Government: transitional
Currency: 1 Congolese franc = 100 centimes

COSTA RICA (North America)
Area: 51,100 sq km (19,730 sq miles)
Population: 3,834,934
Capital city: San Jose
Main language: Spanish
Main religions: Roman Catholic, Evangelical
Government: democratic republic
Currency: 1 Costa Rican colon = 100 centimos

Cuba

CROATIA (Europe)
Area: 56,538 sq km (21,829 sq miles)
Population: 4,390,751
Capital city: Zagreb
Main language: Croatian
Main religions: Roman Catholic, Orthodox
Government: parliamentary democracy
Currency: 1 kuna = 100 lipas

Cyprus

CUBA (North America)
Area: 110,860 sq km (42,803 sq miles)
Population: 11,224,321
Capital city: Havana
Main language: Spanish
Main religion: Roman Catholic
Government: Communist state
Currency: 1 Cuban peso = 100 centavos

Czech Republic

CYPRUS (Europe)
Area: 9,250 sq km (3,571 sq miles)
Population: 767,314
Capital city: Nicosia
Main languages: Greek, Turkish
Main religions: Greek Orthodox, Muslim
Government: republic with a self-proclaimed independent Turkish area
Currency: Greek Cypriot area: 1 Cypriot pound = 100 cents; Turkish Cypriot area: 1 Turkish lira = 100 kurus

CZECH REPUBLIC (Europe)
Area: 78,866 sq km (30,450 sq miles)
Population: 10,256,760
Capital city: Prague
Main language: Czech
Main religion: Roman Catholic
Government: parliamentary democracy
Currency: 1 koruna = 100 haleru

Denmark

DENMARK (Europe)
Area: 43,094 sq km (16,639 sq miles)
Population: 5,368,854
Capital city: Copenhagen
Main language: Danish
Main religion: Evangelical Lutheran
Government: constitutional monarchy
Currency: 1 Danish krone = 100 oere

Djibouti

Dominica

DJIBOUTI (Africa)
Area: 23,200 sq km (8,957 sq miles)
Population: 472,810
Capital city: Djibouti
Main languages: Afar, Somali, Arabic, French
Main religion: Muslim
Government: republic
Currency: 1 Djiboutian franc = 100 centimes

DOMINICA (North America)
Area: 751 sq km (290 sq miles)
Population: 70,158
Capital city: Roseau
Main languages: English, French patois
Main religions: Roman Catholic, Protestant
Government: democratic republic
Currency: 1 East Caribbean dollar = 100 cents

DOMINICAN REPUBLIC (North America)
Area: 48,730 sq km (18,815 sq miles)
Population: 8,721,594
Capital city: Santo Domingo
Main language: Spanish
Main religion: Roman Catholic
Government: democratic republic
Currency: 1 Dominican peso = 100 centavos

EAST TIMOR (Asia)
Area: 15,007 sq km (5,794 sq miles)
Population: 952,618
Capital city: Dili
Main languages: Tetum, Portuguese, Indonesian
Main religions: Roman Catholic, animist
Government: republic
Currency: 1 U.S. dollar = 100 cents

ECUADOR (South America)
Area: 283,560 sq km (109,483 sq miles)
Population: 13,447,494
Capital city: Quito
Main languages: Spanish, Quechua
Main religion: Roman Catholic
Government: republic
Currency: 1 sucre = 100 centavos

EGYPT (Africa)
Area: 1,001,450 sq km (386,660 sq miles)
Population: 70,712,345
Capital city: Cairo
Main language: Arabic
Main religion: Sunni Muslim
Government: republic
Currency: 1 Egyptian pound = 100 piasters

EL SALVADOR (North America)
Area: 21,040 sq km (8,124 sq miles)
Population: 6,353,681
Capital city: San Salvador
Main language: Spanish
Main religion: Roman Catholic
Government: republic
Currency: 1 Salvadoran colon = 100 centavos

EQUATORIAL GUINEA (Africa)
Area: 28,050 sq km (10,830 sq miles)
Population: 498,144
Capital city: Malabo

• **Dominican Republic**

East Timor

• **Ecuador**

Egypt

• **El Salvador**

Equatorial Guinea

Eritrea

85

Estonia

Main languages: Fang, Bubi, other Bantu
languages, Spanish, French, Pidgin English
Main religion: Christian
Government: republic
Currency: 1 CFA* franc = 100 centimes

ERITREA (Africa)
Area: 121,320 sq km (46,842 sq miles)
Population: 4,465,651
Capital city: Asmara
Main languages: Tigrinya, Afar, Arabic
Main religions: Muslim, Coptic Christian,
Roman Catholic, Protestant
Government: transitional
Currency: 1 nafka = 100 cents

Ethiopia

ESTONIA (Europe)
Area: 45,226 sq km (17,462 sq miles)
Population: 1,415,681
Capital city: Tallinn
Main languages: Estonian, Russian
Main religions: Evangelical Lutheran, Russian
and Estonian Orthodox, other Christian
Government: parliamentary democracy
Currency: 1 Estonian kroon = 100 senti

**Federated States
of Micronesia**

ETHIOPIA (Africa)
Area: 1,127,127 sq km (435,184 sq miles)
Population: 67,673,031
Capital city: Addis Ababa
Main languages: Amharic, Tigrinya, Arabic
Main religions: Muslim, Ethiopian
Orthodox, animist
Government: federal republic
Currency: 1 birr = 100 cents

Gambia, The

Main religion: Roman Catholic
Government: republic
Currency: 1 euro = 100 cents

GABON (Africa)
Area: 267,670 sq km (103,347 sq miles)
Population: 1,233,353
Capital city: Libreville
Main languages: Fang, Myene, French
Main religions: Christian, animist
Government: republic
Currency: 1 CFA* franc = 100 centimes

GAMBIA, THE (Africa)
Area: 11,300 sq km (4,363 sq miles)
Population: 1,455,842
Capital city: Banjul
Main languages: Mandinka, Fula, Wolof,
English
Main religion: Muslim
Government: democratic republic
Currency: 1 dalasi = 100 butut

Georgia

GEORGIA (Asia)
Area: 69,700 sq km (26,911 sq miles)
Population: 4,960,951
Capital city: Tbilisi
Main languages: Georgian, Russian
Main religions: Georgian Orthodox, Muslim,
Russian Orthodox
Government: republic
Currency: 1 lari = 100 tetri

Germany

Fiji

**FEDERATED STATES OF MICRONESIA
(Australasia/Oceania)**
Area: 702 sq km (271 sq miles)
Population: 135,869
Capital city: Palikir
Main languages: Chuuk, Ponapean, English
Main religions: Roman Catholic, Protestant
Government: democracy
Currency: 1 U.S. dollar = 100 cents

GERMANY (Europe)
Area: 357,021 sq km (137,846 sq miles)
Population: 83,251,851
Capital city: Berlin
Main language: German
Main religions: Protestant, Roman Catholic
Government: federal republic
Currency: 1 euro = 100 cents

Ghana

Finland

FIJI (Australasia/Oceania)
Area: 18,270 sq km (7,054 sq miles)
Population: 856,346
Capital city: Suva
Main languages: Fijian, Hindustani, English
Main religions: Christian, Hindu
Government: republic
Currency: 1 Fijian dollar = 100 cents

GHANA (Africa)
Area: 239,460 sq km (92,456 sq miles)
Population: 20,244,154
Capital city: Accra
Main languages: Twi, Fante, Ga, Hausa,
Dagbani, Ewe, Nzemi, English
Main religions: indigenous, Muslim, Christian
Government: democratic republic
Currency: 1 new cedi = 100 pesewas

Greece

France

FINLAND (Europe)
Area: 337,030 sq km (130,127 sq miles)
Population: 5,183,545
Capital city: Helsinki
Main language: Finnish
Main religion: Evangelical Lutheran
Government: republic
Currency: 1 euro = 100 cents

GREECE (Europe)
Area: 131,940 sq km (50,942 sq miles)
Population: 10,645,343
Capital city: Athens
Main language: Greek
Main religion: Greek Orthodox
Government: parliamentary republic
Currency: 1 euro = 100 cents

Grenada

FRANCE (Europe)
Area: 547,030 sq km (211,208 sq miles)
Population: 59,765,983
Capital city: Paris
Main language: French

Gabon

GRENADA (North America)
Area: 340 sq km (131 sq miles)
Population: 89,211
Capital city: Saint George's
Main languages: English, French patois
Main religions: Roman Catholic, Protestant
Government: constitutional monarchy
Currency: 1 East Caribbean dollar = 100 cents

Guatemala

*CFA = Communaute Financiere Africaine

Guinea

Guinea-Bissau

Guyana

• Haiti

Honduras

Hungary

Iceland

GUATEMALA (North America)
Area: 108,890 sq km (42,042 sq miles)
Population: 13,314,079
Capital city: Guatemala City
Main languages: Spanish, Amerindian languages including Quiche, Kekchi, Cakchiquel, Mam
Main religions: Roman Catholic, Protestant, indigenous Mayan beliefs
Government: democratic republic
Currency: 1 quetzal = 100 centavos

GUINEA (Africa)
Area: 245,860 sq km (94,927 sq miles)
Population: 7,775,065
Capital city: Conakry
Main languages: Fuuta Jalon, Mallinke, Susu, French
Main religion: Muslim
Government: republic
Currency: 1 Guinean franc = 100 centimes

GUINEA-BISSAU (Africa)
Area: 36,120 sq km (13,946 sq miles)
Population: 1,345,479
Capital city: Bissau
Main languages: Crioulo*, Balante, Pulaar, Mandjak, Mandinka, Portuguese
Main religions: indigenous, Muslim
Government: republic
Currency: 1 CFA* franc = 100 centimes

GUYANA (South America)
Area: 214,970 sq km (83,000 sq miles)
Population: 698,209
Capital city: Georgetown
Main languages: Guyanese Creole, English, Amerindian languages, Caribbean Hindi
Main religions: Christian, Hindu
Government: republic
Currency: 1 Guyanese dollar = 100 cents

HAITI (North America)
Area: 27,750 sq km (10,714 sq miles)
Population: 7,063,722
Capital city: Port-au-Prince
Main languages: Haitian Creole, French
Main religions: Roman Catholic, Protestant, Voodoo
Government: republic
Currency: 1 gourde = 100 centimes

HONDURAS (North America)
Area: 112,090 sq km (43,278 sq miles)
Population: 6,560,608
Capital city: Tegucigalpa
Main language: Spanish
Main religion: Roman Catholic
Government: republic
Currency: 1 lempira = 100 centavos

HUNGARY (Europe)
Area: 93,030 sq km (35,919 sq miles)
Population: 10,075,034
Capital city: Budapest
Main language: Hungarian
Main religions: Roman Catholic, Calvinist
Government: parliamentary democracy
Currency: 1 forint = 100 filler

ICELAND (Europe)
Area: 103,000 sq km (39,768 sq miles)
Population: 279,384
Capital city: Reykjavik
Main language: Icelandic
Main religion: Evangelical Lutheran
Government: republic
Currency: 1 Icelandic krona = 100 aurar

INDIA (Asia)
Area: 3,287,590 sq km (1,269,339 sq miles)
Population: 1,045,845,226
Capital city: New Delhi
Main languages: Hindi, English, Bengali, Urdu, over 1,600 other languages and dialects
Main religions: Hindu, Muslim
Government: federal republic
Currency: 1 Indian rupee = 100 paise

INDONESIA (Asia)
Area: 1,919,440 sq km (741,096 sq miles)
Population: 231,328,092
Capital city: Jakarta
Main languages: Bahasa Indonesia, English, Dutch, Javanese
Main religion: Muslim
Government: republic
Currency: 1 Indonesian rupiah = 100 sen

IRAN (Asia)
Area: 1,648,000 sq km (636,293 sq miles)
Population: 66,622,704
Capital city: Tehran
Main languages: Farsi and other Persian dialects, Azeri
Main religions: Shi'a Muslim, Sunni Muslim
Government: Islamic republic
Currency: 10 Iranian rials = 1 toman

IRAQ (Asia)
Area: 437,072 sq km (168,754 sq miles)
Population: 24,001,816
Capital city: Baghdad
Main languages: Arabic, Kurdish
Main religion: Muslim
Government: republic under a military regime
Currency: 1 Iraqi dinar = 1,000 fils

IRELAND (Europe)
Area: 70,280 sq km (27,135 sq miles)
Population: 3,883,159
Capital city: Dublin
Main languages: English, Irish (Gaelic)
Main religion: Roman Catholic
Government: republic
Currency: 1 euro = 100 cents

ISRAEL (Asia)
Area: 20,770 sq km (8,019 sq miles)
Population: 6,029,529
Capital city: Jerusalem
Main languages: Hebrew, Arabic
Main religions: Jewish, Muslim
Government: parliamentary democracy
Currency: 1 Israeli shekel = 100 agorot

India

Indonesia

Iran

Iraq

Ireland

Israel

Italy

*CFA = Communaute Financiere Africaine;
Crioulo = a blend of Portuguese and West African

GAZETTEER OF STATES

Ivory Coast

ITALY (Europe)
Area: 301,230 sq km (116,305 sq miles)
Population: 57,715,625
Capital city: Rome
Main language: Italian
Main religion: Roman Catholic
Government: republic
Currency: 1 euro = 100 cents

IVORY COAST (Africa)
Area: 322,460 sq km (124,502 sq miles)
Population: 16,804,784
Capital city: Yamoussoukro
Main languages: Baoule, Dioula, French
Main religions: Christian, Muslim, animist
Government: republic
Currency: 1 CFA* = 100 centimes

Jamaica

JAMAICA (North America)
Area: 10,990 sq km (4,243 sq miles)
Population: 2,680,029
Capital city: Kingston
Main languages: Southwestern Caribbean Creole, English
Main religion: Protestant
Government: parliamentary democracy
Currency: 1 Jamaican dollar = 100 cents

Japan

JAPAN (Asia)
Area: 377,835 sq km (145,882 sq miles)
Population: 126,974,628
Capital city: Tokyo
Main language: Japanese
Main religions: Shinto, Buddhist
Government: constitutional monarchy
Currency: 1 yen = 100 sen

Jordan

JORDAN (Asia)
Area: 92,300 sq km (35,637 sq miles)
Population: 5,307,470
Capital city: Amman
Main languages: Arabic, English
Main religion: Sunni Muslim
Government: constitutional monarchy
Currency: 1 Jordanian dinar = 1,000 fils

Kazakhstan

KAZAKHSTAN (Asia)
Area: 2,717,300 sq km (1,049,150 sq miles)
Population: 16,741,519
Capital city: Astana
Main languages: Kazakh, Russian
Main religions: Muslim, Russian Orthodox
Government: republic
Currency: 1 Kazakhstani tenge = 100 tiyn

Kenya

KENYA (Africa)
Area: 582,650 sq km (224,961 sq miles)
Population: 31,138,735
Capital city: Nairobi
Main languages: Swahili, English, Bantu languages
Main religions: Christian, indigenous
Government: republic
Currency: 1 Kenyan shilling = 100 cents

Kiribati

KIRIBATI (Australasia/Oceania)
Area: 811 sq km (313 sq miles)
Population: 96,335
Capital city: Bairiki (on Tarawa island)

Main languages: Gilbertese, English
Main religions: Roman Catholic, Protestant
Government: republic
Currency: 1 Australian dollar = 100 cents

Kuwait

KUWAIT (Asia)
Area: 17,820 sq km (6,880 sq miles)
Population: 2,111,561
Capital city: Kuwait City
Main languages: Arabic, English
Main religion: Muslim
Government: monarchy
Currency: 1 Kuwaiti dinar = 1,000 fils

Kyrgyzstan

KYRGYZSTAN (Asia)
Area: 198,500 sq km (76,641 sq miles)
Population: 4,822,166
Capital city: Bishkek
Main languages: Kyrgyz, Russian
Main religions: Muslim, Russian Orthodox
Government: republic
Currency: 1 Kyrgyzstani som = 100 tiyin

Laos

LAOS (Asia)
Area: 236,800 sq km (91,428 sq miles)
Population: 5,777,180
Capital city: Vientiane
Main languages: Lao, French, English
Main religions: Buddhist, animist
Government: Communist state
Currency: 1 new kip = 100 at

Latvia

LATVIA (Europe)
Area: 64,589 sq km (24,938 sq miles)
Population: 2,366,515
Capital city: Riga
Main languages: Latvian, Russian
Main religions: Lutheran, Roman Catholic, Russian Orthodox
Government: parliamentary democracy
Currency: 1 Latvian lat = 100 santims

Lebanon

LEBANON (Asia)
Area: 10,400 sq km (4,015 miles)
Population: 3,677,780
Capital city: Beirut
Main languages: Arabic, French, English
Main religions: Muslim, Christian
Government: republic
Currency: 1 Lebanese pound = 100 piasters

LESOTHO (Africa)
Area: 30,350 sq km (11,718 sq miles)
Population: 2,207,954
Capital cities: Maseru, Lobamba
Main languages: Sesotho, English, Zulu, Xhosa
Main religions: Christian, indigenous
Government: constitutional monarchy
Currency: 1 loti = 100 lisente

Lesotho

LIBERIA (Africa)
Area: 111,370 sq km (43,000 sq miles)
Population: 3,288,198
Capital city: Monrovia
Main languages: Kpelle, English, Bassa
Main religions: indigenous, Christian, Muslim
Government: republic
Currency: 1 Liberian dollar = 100 cents

Liberia

*CFA = Communaute Financiere Africaine

Libya

LIBYA (Africa)
Area: 1,759,540 sq km (679,358 sq miles)
Population: 5,368,585
Capital city: Tripoli
Main languages: Arabic, Italian, English
Main religion: Sunni Muslim
Government: military rule
Currency: 1 Libyan dinar = 1,000 dirhams

Liechtenstein

LIECHTENSTEIN (Europe)
Area: 160 sq km (62 sq miles)
Population: 32,842
Capital city: Vaduz
Main languages: German, Alemannic
Main religion: Roman Catholic
Government: constitutional monarchy
Currency: 1 Swiss franc = 100 centimes

Lithuania

LITHUANIA (Europe)
Area: 65,200 sq km (25,174 sq miles)
Population: 3,601,138
Capital city: Vilnius
Main languages: Lithuanian, Polish, Russian
Main religions: Roman Catholic, Lutheran, Russian Orthodox
Government: democracy
Currency: 1 Lithuanian litas = 100 centas

Luxembourg

LUXEMBOURG (Europe)
Area: 2,586 sq km (998 sq miles)
Population: 448,569
Capital city: Luxembourg
Main languages: Luxemburgish, German, French
Main religion: Roman Catholic
Government: constitutional monarchy
Currency: 1 euro = 100 cents

Macedonia

MACEDONIA (Europe)
Area: 25,333 sq km (9,781 sq miles)
Population: 2,054,800
Capital city: Skopje
Main languages: Macedonian, Albanian
Main religions: Macedonian Orthodox, Muslim
Government: emerging democracy
Currency: 1 Macedonian denar = 100 deni

Madagascar

MADAGASCAR (Africa)
Area: 587,040 sq km (226,656 sq miles)
Population: 16,473,477
Capital city: Antananarivo
Main languages: Malagasy, French
Main religions: indigenous beliefs, Christian
Government: republic
Currency: 1 Malagasy franc = 100 centimes

Malawi

MALAWI (Africa)
Area: 118,480 sq km (45,745 sq miles)
Population: 10,701,824
Capital city: Lilongwe
Main languages: Chichewa, English
Main religions: Protestant, Roman Catholic, Muslim
Government: parliamentary democracy
Currency: 1 Malawian kwacha = 100 tambala

MALAYSIA (Asia)
Area: 329,750 sq km (127,316 sq miles)
Population: 22,662,365
Capital city: Kuala Lumpur
Main languages: Bahasa Melayu, English, Chinese dialects, Tamil
Main religions: Muslim, Buddhist, Daoist
Government: constitutional monarchy
Currency: 1 ringgit = 100 sen

MALDIVES (Asia)
Area: 300 sq km (116 sq miles)
Population: 320,165
Capital city: Male
Main languages: Maldivian, English
Main religion: Sunni Muslim
Government: republic
Currency: 1 rufiyaa = 100 laari

MALI (Africa)
Area: 1,240,000 sq km (478,764 sq miles)
Population: 11,340,480
Capital city: Bamako
Main languages: Bambara, Fulani, Songhai, French
Main religion: Muslim
Government: republic
Currency: 1 CFA* franc = 100 centimes

MALTA (Europe)
Area: 316 sq km (122 sq miles)
Population: 397,499
Capital city: Valletta
Main languages: Maltese, English
Main religion: Roman Catholic
Government: republic
Currency: 1 Maltese lira = 100 cents

MARSHALL ISLANDS (Australasia/Oceania)
Area: 181 sq km (70 sq miles)
Population: 73,630
Capital city: Majuro
Main languages: Marshallese, English
Main religion: Protestant
Government:
Currency: 1 U.S. dollar = 100 cents

MAURITANIA (Africa)
Area: 1,030,700 sq km (397,953 sq miles)
Population: 2,828,858
Capital city: Nouakchott
Main languages: Arabic, Wolof, French
Main religion: Muslim
Government: republic
Currency: 1 ouguiya = 5 khoums

MAURITIUS (Africa)
Area: 2,040 sq km (788 sq miles)
Population: 1,200,206
Capital city: Port Louis
Main languages: Mauritius Creole French, French, Hindi, Bhojpuri, Urdu, Tamil, English
Main religions: Hindu, Christian, Muslim
Government: parliamentary democracy
Currency: 1 Mauritian rupee = 100 cents

MEXICO (North America)
Area: 1,972,550 sq km (761,602 sq miles)
Population: 103,400,165
Capital city: Mexico City
Main languages: Spanish, Mayan, Nahuatl

Malaysia

Maldives

Mali

Malta

Marshall Islands

Mauritania

Mauritius

*CFA = Communaute Financiere Africaine

Mexico

Main religion: Roman Catholic
Government: federal republic
Currency: 1 Mexican peso = 100 centavos

MOLDOVA (Europe)
Area: 33,843 sq km (13,067 sq miles)
Population: 4,434,547
Capital city: Chisinau
Main languages: Moldovan, Russian, Gagauz
Main religion: Eastern Orthodox
Government: republic
Currency: 1 Moldovan leu = 100 bani

Moldova

MONACO (Europe)
Area: 1.95 sq km (0.75 sq miles)
Population: 31,987
Capital city: Monaco
Main languages: French, Monegasque, Italian
Main religion: Roman Catholic
Government: constitutional monarchy
Currency: 1 euro = 100 cents

MONGOLIA (Asia)
Area: 1,565,000 sq km (604,247 sq miles)
Population: 2,694,432
Capital city: Ulan Bator
Main language: Khalkha Mongol
Main religion: Tibetan Buddist Lamaist
Government: republic
Currency: 1 tugrik = 100 mongos

Monaco

Mongolia

MOROCCO (Africa)
Area: 446,550 sq km (172,413 sq miles)
Population: 31,167,783
Capital city: Rabat
Main languages: Arabic, Berber, French
Main religion: Muslim
Government: constitutional monarchy
Currency: 1 Moroccan dirham = 100 centimes

Morocco

MOZAMBIQUE (Africa)
Area: 801,590 sq km (309,494 sq miles)
Population: 19,607,519
Capital city: Maputo
Main languages: Makua, Tsonga, Portuguese
Main religions: indigenous, Christian, Muslim
Government: republic
Currency: 1 metical = 100 centavos

Mozambique

NAMIBIA (Africa)
Area: 825,418 sq km (318,694 sq miles)
Population: 1,820,916
Capital city: Windhoek
Main languages: Afrikaans, German, English
Main religions: Christian, indigenous
Government: republic
Currency: 1 Namibian dollar = 100 cents

Namibia

NAURU (Australasia/Oceania)
Area: 21 sq km (8 sq miles)
Population: 12,329
Capital city: Yaren
Main languages: Nauruan, English
Main religion: Christian
Government: republic
Currency: 1 Australian dollar = 100 cents

NEPAL (Asia)
Area: 140,800 sq km (54,363 sq miles)
Population: 25,873,917
Capital city: Kathmandu
Main languages: Nepali, Maithili
Main religions: Hindu, Buddhist
Government: constitutional monarchy
Currency: 1 Nepalese rupee = 100 paisa

Nauru

NETHERLANDS (Europe)
Area: 41,532 sq km (16,036 sq miles)
Population: 16,067,754
Capital cities: Amsterdam, The Hague
Main language: Dutch
Main religion: Christian
Government: constitutional monarchy
Currency: 1 euro = 100 cents

Nepal

NEW ZEALAND (Australasia/Oceania)
Area: 268,680 sq km (103,737 sq miles)
Population: 3,908,037
Capital city: Wellington
Main languages: English, Maori
Main religion: Christian
Government: parliamentary democracy
Currency: 1 New Zealand dollar = 100 cents

Netherlands

NICARAGUA (North America)
Area: 129,494 sq km (49,998 sq miles)
Population: 5,023,818
Capital city: Managua
Main language: Spanish
Main religion: Roman Catholic
Government:
Currency: 1 gold cordoba = 100 centavos

New Zealand

NIGER (Africa)
Area: 1,267,000 sq km (489,189 sq miles)
Population: 10,639,744
Capital city: Niamey
Main languages: Hausa, Djerma, French
Main religion: Muslim
Government: republic
Currency: 1 CFA* franc = 100 centimes

Nicaragua

NIGERIA (Africa)
Area: 923,768 sq km (356,667 sq miles)
Population: 129,934,911
Capital city: Abuja
Main languages: Hausa, Yoruba, Igbo, English
Main religions: Muslim, Christian, indigenous
Government: republic
Currency: 1 naira = 100 kobo

Niger

NORTH KOREA (Asia)
Area: 120,540 sq km (46,540 sq miles)
Population: 22,224,195
Capital city: Pyongyang
Main language: Korean
Main religions: Buddhist, Confucianist
Government: authoritarian socialist
Currency: 1 North Korean won = 100 chon

Nigeria

NORWAY (Europe)
Area: 324,220 sq km (125,181 sq miles)
Population: 4,525,116
Capital city: Oslo
Main language: Norwegian

North Korea

Main religion: Evangelical Lutheran
Government: constitutional monarchy
Currency: 1 Norwegian krone = 100 oere

OMAN (Asia)
Area: 212,460 sq km (82,031 sq miles)
Population: 2,713,462
Capital city: Muscat
Main languages: Arabic, English, Baluchi
Main religion: Muslim
Government: monarchy
Currency: 1 Omani rial = 1,000 baiza

Norway

PAKISTAN (Asia)
Area: 803,940 sq km (310,401 sq miles)
Population: 147,663,429
Capital city: Islamabad
Main languages: Punjabi, Sindhi, Urdu, English
Main religion: Muslim
Government: federal republic
Currency: 1 Pakistani rupee = 100 paisa

Oman

PALAU (Australasia/Oceania)
Area: 459 sq km (177 sq miles)
Population: 19,409
Capital city: Koror
Main languages: Palauan, English
Main religions: Christian', Modekngei
Government: democratic republic
Currency: 1 U.S. dollar = 100 cents

Pakistan

PANAMA (North America)
Area: 78,200 sq km (30,193 sq miles)
Population: 2,882,329
Capital city: Panama City
Main languages: Spanish, English
Main religions: Roman Catholic, Protestant
Government: democracy
Currency: 1 balboa = 100 centesimos

PAPUA NEW GUINEA
(Australasia/Oceania)
Area: 462,840 sq km (178,703 sq miles)
Population: 5,172,033
Capital city: Port Moresby
Main languages: Tok Pisin, Hiri Motu, English
Main religions: Christian, indigenous
Government: parliamentary democracy
Currency: 1 kina = 100 toea

Palau

PARAGUAY (South America)
Area: 406,750 sq km (157,046 sq miles)
Population: 5,884,491
Capital city: Asuncion
Main languages: Guarani, Spanish
Main religion: Roman Catholic
Government: republic
Currency: 1 guarani = 100 centimos

Panama

PERU (South America)
Area: 1,285,220 sq km (496,223 sq miles)
Population: 27,949,639
Capital city: Lima
Main languages: Spanish, Quechua, Aymara
Main religion: Roman Catholic
Government: republic
Currency: 1 nuevo sol = 100 centimos

Papua New Guinea

PHILIPPINES (Asia)
Area: 300,000 sq km (115,830 sq miles)
Population: 84,525,639
Capital city: Manila
Main languages: Tagalog, English, Ilocano
Main religion: Roman Catholic
Government: republic
Currency: 1 Philippine peso = 100 centavos

POLAND (Europe)
Area: 312,685 sq km (120,727 sq miles)
Population: 38,625,478
Capital city: Warsaw
Main language: Polish
Main religion: Roman Catholic
Government: democratic republic
Currency: 1 zloty = 100 groszy

PORTUGAL (Europe)
Area: 92,391 sq km (35,672 sq miles)
Population: 10,084,245
Capital city: Lisbon
Main language: Portuguese
Main religion: Roman Catholic
Government: parliamentary democracy
Currency: 1 euro = 100 cents

QATAR (Asia)
Area: 11,437 sq km (4,416 sq miles)
Population: 793,341
Capital city: Doha
Main languages: Arabic, English
Main religion: Muslim
Government: monarchy
Currency: 1 Qatari riyal = 100 dirhams

ROMANIA (Europe)
Area: 237,500 sq km (91,699 sq miles)
Population: 22,317,730
Capital city: Bucharest
Main languages: Romanian, Hungarian, German
Main religion: Romanian Orthodox
Government: republic
Currency: 1 leu = 100 bani

RUSSIA (Europe and Asia)
Area: 17,075,200 sq km (6,592,735 sq miles)
Population: 144,978,573
Capital city: Moscow
Main language: Russian
Main religions: Russian Orthodox, Muslim
Government: federal government
Currency: 1 ruble = 100 kopeks

RWANDA (Africa)
Area: 26,338 sq km (10,169 sq miles)
Population: 7,398,074
Capital city: Kigali
Main languages: Kinyarwanda, French, English, Swahili
Main religions: Roman Catholic, Protestant, Adventist
Government: republic
Currency: 1 Rwandan franc = 100 centimes

SAINT KITTS AND NEVIS
(North America)
Area: 261 sq km (101 sq miles)
Population: 38,736

Paraguay

• **Peru**

Philippines

Poland

Portugal

Qatar

Romania

91

Russia

Capital city: Basseterre
Main language: English
Main religions: Protestant, Roman Catholic
Government: constitutional monarchy
Currency: 1 East Caribbean dollar = 100 cents

SAINT LUCIA (North America)
Area: 620 sq km (239 sq miles)
Population: 160,145
Capital city: Castries
Main languages: French patois, English
Main religion: Roman Catholic
Government: parliamentary democracy
Currency: 1 East Caribbean dollar = 100 cents

Rwanda

SAINT VINCENT AND THE GRENADINES (North America)
Area: 389 sq km (150 sq miles)
Population: 116,394
Capital city: Kingstown
Main languages: English, French patois
Main religions: Protestant, Roman Catholic
Government: parliamentary democracy
Currency: 1 East Caribbean dollar = 100 cents

Saint Kitts and Nevis

SAMOA (Australasia/Oceania)
Area: 2,860 sq km (1,104 sq miles)
Population: 178,631
Capital city: Apia
Main languages: Samoan, English
Main religion: Christian
Government: constitutional monarchy
Currency: 1 tala = 100 sene

Saint Lucia

SAN MARINO (Europe)
Area: 61 sq km (24 sq miles)
Population: 27,730
Capital city: San Marino
Main language: Italian
Main religion: Roman Catholic
Government: republic
Currency: 1 euro = 100 cents

Saint Vincent and the Grenadines

SAO TOME AND PRINCIPE (Africa)
Area: 1,001 sq km (386 sq miles)
Population: 170,372
Capital city: Sao Tome
Main languages: Crioulo* dialects, Portuguese
Main religion: Christian
Government: republic
Currency: 1 dobra = 100 centimos

Samoa

SAUDI ARABIA (Asia)
Area: 1,960,582 sq km (756,987 sq miles)
Population: 23,513,330
Capital city: Riyadh
Main language: Arabic
Main religion: Muslim
Government: monarchy
Currency: 1 Saudi riyal = 100 halalah

SENEGAL (Africa)
Area: 196,190 sq km (75,749 sq miles)
Population: 10,589,571
Capital city: Dakar
Main languages: Wolof, French, Pulaar
Main religion: Muslim
Government: democratic republic
Currency: 1 CFA* franc = 100 centimes

• San Marino

SERBIA AND MONTENEGRO (Europe)
Area: 102,350 sq km (39,517 sq miles)
Population: 10,656,929
Capital city: Belgrade
Main language: Serbian
Main religions: Orthodox, Muslim
Government: republic
Currency: 1 Yugoslavian new dinar = 100 paras

SEYCHELLES (Africa)
Area: 455 sq km (176 sq miles)
Population: 80,098
Capital city: Victoria
Main languages: Seselwa, English, French
Main religion: Roman Catholic
Government: republic
Currency: 1 Seychelles rupee = 100 cents

SIERRA LEONE (Africa)
Area: 71,740 sq km (27,699 sq miles)
Population: 5,614,743
Capital city: Freetown
Main languages: Mende, Temne, Krio, English
Main religions: Muslim, indigenous, Christian
Government: constitutional democracy
Currency: 1 leone = 100 cents

SINGAPORE (Asia)
Area: 692 sq km (267 sq miles)
Population: 4,452,732
Capital city: Singapore
Main languages: Chinese, Malay, English, Tamil
Main religions: Buddhist, Muslim
Government: parliamentary republic
Currency: 1 Singapore dollar = 100 cents

SLOVAKIA (Europe)
Area: 48,845 sq km (18,859 sq miles)
Population: 5,422,366
Capital city: Bratislava
Main languages: Slovak, Hungarian
Main religion: Roman Catholic
Government: parliamentary democracy
Currency: 1 koruna = 100 halierov

SLOVENIA (Europe)
Area: 20,273 sq km (7,827 sq miles)
Population: 1,932,917
Capital city: Ljubljana
Main language: Slovenian
Main religion: Roman Catholic
Government: democratic republic
Currency: 1 tolar = 100 stotins

SOLOMON ISLANDS (Australasia/Oceania)
Area: 28,450 sq km (10,985 sq miles)
Population: 494,786
Capital city: Honiara
Main languages: Solomon pidgin, Kwara'ae, To'abaita, English
Main religion: Christian
Government: parliamentary democracy
Currency: 1 Solomon Islands dollar = 100 cents

SOMALIA (Africa)
Area: 637,657 sq km (246,199 sq miles)
Population: 7,753,310
Capital city: Mogadishu
Main languages: Somali, Arabic, Oromo

Sao Tome and Principe

Saudi Arabia

Senegal

Serbia and Montenegro

Seychelles

Sierra Leone

Singapore

Slovakia

Main religion: Sunni Muslim
Government: currently has no government
Currency: 1 Somali shilling = 100 cents

SOUTH AFRICA (Africa)
Area: 1,219,912 sq km (471,008 sq miles)
Population: 43,647,658
Capital cities: Pretoria, Cape Town, Bloemfontein
Main languages: Zulu, Xhosa, Afrikaans, Pedi, English, Tswana, Sotho, Tsonga, Swati, Venda, Ndebele
Main religions: Christian, indigenous
Government: republic
Currency: 1 rand = 100 cents

SOUTH KOREA (Asia)
Area: 98,480 sq km (38,023 sq miles)
Population: 48,324,000
Capital city: Seoul
Main language: Korean
Main religions: Christian, Buddhist
Government: republic
Currency: 1 South Korean won = 100 chun

SPAIN (Europe)
Area: 504,782 sq km (194,898 sq miles)
Population: 40,077,100
Capital city: Madrid
Main languages: Castilian Spanish, Catalan
Main religion: Roman Catholic
Government: constitutional monarchy
Currency: 1 euro = 100 cents

SRI LANKA (Asia)
Area: 65,610 sq km (25,332 sq miles)
Population: 19,576,783
Capital cities: Colombo, Sri Jayewardenepura Kotte
Main languages: Sinhala, Tamil, English
Main religions: Buddhist, Hindu
Government: republic
Currency: 1 Sri Lankan rupee = 100 cents

SUDAN (Africa)
Area: 2,505,810 sq km (967,493 sq miles)
Population: 37,090,298
Capital city: Khartoum
Main languages: Arabic, English
Main religions: Sunni Muslim, indigenous
Government: Islamic republic
Currency: 1 Sudanese dinar = 100 piastres

SURINAM (South America)
Area: 163,270 sq km (63,039 sq miles)
Population: 436,494
Capital city: Paramaribo
Main languages: Sranang Tongo, Dutch, English
Main religions: Christian, Hindu, Muslim
Government: constitutional democracy
Currency: 1 Surinamese guilder = 100 cents

SWAZILAND (Africa)
Area: 17,363 sq km (6,704 sq miles)
Population: 1,123,605
Capital cities: Mbabane, Lobamba

Main languages: Swati, English
Main religions: Christian, indigenous, Muslim
Government: monarchy
Currency: 1 lilangeni = 100 cents

SWEDEN (Europe)
Area: 449,964 sq km (173,731 sq miles)
Population: 8,876,744
Capital city: Stockholm
Main language: Swedish
Main religion: Lutheran
Government: constitutional monarchy
Currency: 1 Swedish krona = 100 oere

SWITZERLAND (Europe)
Area: 41,290 sq km (15,942 sq miles)
Population: 7,301,994
Capital city: Bern
Main languages: German, French, Italian
Main religions: Roman Catholic, Protestant
Government: federal republic
Currency: 1 Swiss franc = 100 centimes

SYRIA (Asia)
Area: 185,180 sq km (71,498 sq miles)
Population: 17,155,814
Capital city: Damascus
Main languages: Arabic, Kurdish
Main religions: Muslim, Christian
Government: republic under military regime
Currency: 1 Syrian pound = 100 piastres

TAIWAN (Asia)
Area: 35,980 sq km (13,892 sq miles)
Population: 22,548,009
Capital city: Taipei
Main languages: Taiwanese, Mandarin Chinese, Hakka Chinese
Main religions: Buddhist, Confucian, Daoist
Government: democracy
Currency: 1 New Taiwan dollar = 100 cents

TAJIKISTAN (Asia)
Area: 143,100 sq km (55,251 sq miles)
Population: 6,719,567
Capital city: Dushanbe
Main languages: Tajik, Russian
Main religion: Sunni Muslim
Government: republic
Currency: 1 somoni = 100 dirams

TANZANIA (Africa)
Area: 945,087 sq km (364,898 sq miles)
Population: 37,187,939
Capital cities: Dar es Salaam, Dodoma
Main languages: Swahili, English, Sukuma
Main religions: Christian, Muslim, indigenous
Government: republic
Currency: 1 Tanzanian shilling = 100 cents

THAILAND (Asia)
Area: 514,000 sq km (198,455 sq miles)
Population: 62,354,402
Capital city: Bangkok
Main languages: Thai, English, Chaochow
Main religion: Buddhist
Government: constitutional monarchy
Currency: 1 baht = 100 satang

Sri Lanka

Sudan

Surinam

Swaziland

Sweden

Switzerland

Syria

• Slovenia

Solomon Islands

Somalia

South Africa

South Korea

• Spain

GAZETTEER OF STATES

Taiwan

Tajikistan

Tanzania

Thailand

Turkmenistan

Togo

Tonga

TOGO (Africa)
Area: 56,785 sq km (21,925 sq miles)
Population: 5,285,501
Capital city: Lome
Main languages: Mina, Ewe, Kabye, French
Main religions: indigenous, Christian, Muslim
Government: republic
Currency: 1 CFA* franc = 100 centimes

TONGA (Australasia/Oceania)
Area: 748 sq km (289 sq miles)
Population: 106,137
Capital city: Nukualofa
Main languages: Tongan, English
Main religion: Christian
Government: constitutional monarchy
Currency: 1 pa'anga = 100 seniti

TRINIDAD AND TOBAGO (North America)
Area: 5,128 sq km (1,980 sq miles)
Population: 1,163,724
Capital city: Port-of-Spain
Main languages: English, French, Spanish, Hindi
Main religions: Christian, Hindu
Government: parliamentary democracy
Currency: 1 Trinidad and Tobago dollar = 100 cents

TUNISIA (Africa)
Area: 163,610 sq km (63,170 sq miles)
Population: 9,815,644
Capital city: Tunis
Main languages: Arabic, French
Main religion: Muslim
Government: republic
Currency: 1 Tunisian dinar = 1,000 millimes

TURKEY (Europe and Asia)
Area: 780,580 sq km (301,382 sq miles)
Population: 67,308,928
Capital city: Ankara
Main language: Turkish
Main religion: Muslim
Government: democratic republic
Currency: 1 Turkish lira = 100 kurus

TURKMENISTAN (Asia)
Area: 488,100 sq km (188,455 sq miles)
Population: 4,688,963
Capital city: Ashgabat (Ashkhabad)
Main languages: Turkmen, Russian
Main religion: Muslim
Government: republic
Currency: 1 Turkmen manat = 100 tenesi

TUVALU (Australasia/Oceania)
Area: 26 sq km (10 sq miles)
Population: 11,146
Capital city: Funafuti
Main languages: Tuvaluan, English
Main religion: Congregationalist
Government: constitutional monarchy
Currency: 1 Tuvaluan dollar or 1 Australian dollar = 100 cents

UGANDA (Africa)
Area: 236,040 sq km (91,135 sq miles)
Population: 24,699,073

Capital city: Kampala
Main languages: Luganda, English, Swahili
Main religion: Christian, Muslim, indigenous
Government: republic
Currency: 1 Ugandan shilling = 100 cents

UKRAINE (Europe)
Area: 603,700 sq km (233,089 sq miles)
Population: 48,396,470
Capital city: Kiev
Main languages: Ukrainian, Russian
Main religion: Ukrainian Orthodox
Government: republic
Currency: 1 hryvnia = 100 kopiykas

UNITED ARAB EMIRATES (Asia)
Area: 82,880 sq km (32,000 sq miles)
Population: 2,445,989
Capital city: Abu Dhabi
Main languages: Arabic, English
Main religion: Muslim
Government: federation
Currency: 1 Emirati dirham = 100 fils

UNITED KINGDOM (Europe)
Area: 244,820 sq km (94,525 sq miles)
Population: 59,778,002
Capital city: London
Main language: English
Main religions: Anglican, Roman Catholic
Government: constitutional monarchy
Currency: 1 British pound = 100 pence

UNITED STATES OF AMERICA (North America)
Area: 9,629,091 sq km (3,717,792 sq miles)
Population: 280,562,489
Capital city: Washington D.C.
Main language: English
Main religions: Protestant, Roman Catholic
Government: federal republic
Currency: 1 U.S. dollar = 100 cents

URUGUAY (South America)
Area: 176,220 sq km (68,039 sq miles)
Population: 3,386,575
Capital city: Montevideo
Main language: Spanish
Main religion: Roman Catholic
Government: republic
Currency: 1 Uruguayan peso = 100 centesimos

UZBEKISTAN (Asia)
Area: 447,400 sq km (172,741 sq miles)
Population: 25,563,441
Capital city: Tashkent
Main languages: Uzbek, Russian
Main religions: Muslim, Eastern Orthodox
Government: republic
Currency: 1 Uzbekistani sum = 100 tyyn

VANUATU (Australasia/Oceania)
Area: 12,189 sq km (4,706 sq miles)
Population: 196,178
Capital city: Port-Vila
Main languages: Bislama, French, English
Main religion: Christian
Government: republic
Currency: 1 vatu = 100 centimes

Trinidad and Tobago

Tunisia

Turkey

Turkmenistan

Tuvalu

Uganda

Ukraine

VATICAN CITY (Europe)
Area: 0.44 sq km (0.17 sq miles)
Population: 900
Capital city: Vatican City
Main languages: Italian, Latin
Main religion: Roman Catholic
Government: led by the Pope
Currency: 1 euro = 100 cents

VENEZUELA (South America)
Area: 912,050 sq km (352,143 sq miles)
Population: 24,287,670
Capital city: Caracas
Main language: Spanish
Main religion: Roman Catholic
Government: federal republic
Currency: 1 bolivar = 100 centimos

VIETNAM (Asia)
Area: 329,560 sq km (127,243 sq miles)
Population: 81,098,416
Capital city: Hanoi
Main languages: Vietnamese, French,
English, Khmer, Chinese
Main religion: Buddhist
Government: Communist state
Currency: 1 new dong = 100 xu

YEMEN (Asia)
Area: 527,970 sq km (203,849 sq miles)
Population: 18,701,257
Capital city: Sana
Main language: Arabic
Main religion: Muslim
Government: republic
Currency: 1 Yemeni rial = 100 fils

ZAMBIA (Africa)
Area: 752,614 sq km (290,584 sq miles)
Population: 9,959,037
Capital city: Lusaka
Main languages: Bemba, Tonga, Nyanja,
English
Main religions: Christian, Muslim, Hindu
Government: republic
Currency: 1 Zambian kwacha = 100 ngwee

ZIMBABWE (Africa)
Area: 390,580 sq km (150,803 sq miles)
Population: 11,376,676
Capital city: Harare
Main languages: Shona, Ndebele, English
Main religions: Christian, indigenous
Government: republic
Currency: 1 Zimbabwean dollar = 100 cents

**United
Arab Emirates**

United Kingdom

**United States
of America**

Uruguay

Vanuatu

Vatican City

Venezuela

Vietnam

Yemen

Zambia

Zimbabwe

The United Nations

The United Nations (U.N.) is
an organization which aims
to bring countries together
to work for peace and
development. Of the world's
193 states, 191 belong to the
U.N. Those that
don't belong
are Taiwan
and the
Vatican City.

Internet link
For a link to a website where you
can match countries and their flags
in a great game, go to
www.usborne-quicklinks.com

*Kofi Annan,
the Secretary-
General of the
U.N., with U.N.
ambassador
Pele*

Uzbekistan

USEFUL WEBSITES

On these pages, there are descriptions of websites that have information, photographs and games on the theme of maps and geography. For links to these sites, go to the Usborne Quicklinks website at **www.usborne-quicklinks.com** and enter the keywords "essential atlas". There you will find links to take you to all the sites.

Map resources

Website 1
Find street maps of any town or city in the world.

Website 2
See maps of the Earth in daylight or darkness at this very moment, plus the latest weather conditions around the world.

Website 3
Download clip art of world's countries, maps, flags, globes and more.

Website 4
Find maps of any country in the world, with informative country profiles.

Website 5
Follow an interactive guide about maps and mapmakers, past and present.

This is part of Kluane National Park, in Yukon Territory, Canada. A huge mass of ice known as a glacier flows slowly downhill, cutting valleys through the mountains.

World wildlife

Website 1
Discover some of the weird and wonderful creatures that live in the world's oceans and seas.

Website 2
Learn about the world's endangered animals and find out what can be done to stop them from becoming extinct.

Website 3
Find out about amazing animals and watch videos of them in the wild.

Website 4
Learn about the unusual animals that live in the Galapagos Islands, including iguanas and giant tortoises.

Website 5
Read about animals that live in the Arctic, such as walruses, snowy owls, polar bears and arctic foxes.

Amazing Earth

Website 1
Read fascinating facts about some of the world's most interesting locations, including the Amazon Rainforest, Greenland and Madagascar. This site also has short films to watch and quiz questions to answer.

Website 2
Find out about earthquakes, hurricanes, tornadoes, and volcanoes and see what happens when the forces of nature take over.

Website 3
Take an interactive tour of Everest, the highest mountain in the world.

Website 4
Read up-to-date information about all the current volcanic eruptions around the world.

Website 5
Explore the vast Sahara Desert and learn about its landscape and peoples.

Website 6
Discover all kinds of underground caves and find out how they were formed.

A birdwing butterfly feeds from a tropical flower. Birdwings are the world's largest butterflies and live in the rainforests of Asia and Australasia.

Quizzes and games

Website 1
See if you can identify and name countries and capital cities.

Website 2
Try all kinds of geography quizzes and have a go at some online crosswords.

Website 3
Find lots of online games about maps and see if you can solve a jigsaw of the world.

Website 4
Online quizzes of places around the world.

MAP INDEX

This is an index of the places and features named on the maps. Each entry consists of the following parts: the name (given in bold type), the country or region within which it is located (given in italics), the page on which the name can be found (given in bold type), and the grid reference (also given in bold type). For some names, there is also a description explaining what kind of place it is – for example a country, internal administrative area (state or province), national capital or internal capital. To find a place on a map, first find the map indicated by the page reference. Then use the grid reference to find the square containing the name or town symbol. See page 9 for help with using the grid.

Atalaia do Norte, *Brazil,* 30 D4
Atar, *Mauritania,* 68 C4
Atbarah, *Sudan,* 67 H5
Atbasar, *Kazakhstan,* 50 J1
Athabasca, *Canada,* 22 H3
Athabasca, Lake, *Canada,* 22 J3
Athens, *Greece, national capital,* 63 G4
Atka Island, *U.S.A.,* 23 B3
Atlanta, *U.S.A., internal capital,* 25 K4
Atlantic City, *U.S.A.,* 25 M3
Atlantic Ocean, 18
Atlas Mountains, *Africa,* 68 D2
At Taïf, *Saudi Arabia,* 51 D7
Attapu, *Laos,* 44 E5
Attu Island, *U.S.A.,* 23 A3
Atyrau, *Kazakhstan,* 57 G4
Auckland, *New Zealand,* 39 P7
Augsburg, *Germany,* 60 G4
Augusta, *U.S.A., internal capital,* 25 N2
Aurangabad, *India,* 49 D7
Austin, *U.S.A., internal capital,* 24 G4
Australasia and Oceania, 19
Australia, *Australasia, country,* 38 E4
Australian Capital Territory, *Australia, internal admin. area,* 39 J6
Austria, *Europe, country,* 62 E2
Awasa, *Ethiopia,* 71 G2
Ayacucho, *Peru,* 30 D6
Aydin, *Turkey,* 63 H4
Ayers Rock, *Australia,* 38 F5
Ayoun el Atrous, *Mauritania,* 69 D5
Azerbaijan, *Asia, country,* 50 E3
Azores, *Atlantic Ocean,* 68 K10
Azov, Sea of, *Europe,* 63 K2
Az Zarqa, *Jordan,* 51 C5

b

Baardheere, *Somalia,* 71 H3
Babahoyo, *Ecuador,* 30 C4
Bab al Mandab, *Africa/Asia,* 67 K6
Babruysk, *Belarus,* 59 J5
Babuyan Islands, *Philippines,* 45 H4
Babylon, *Iraq,* 50 C4
Bacabal, *Brazil,* 31 K4
Bacau, *Romania,* 63 H2
Bac Lieu, *Vietnam,* 44 E6
Bacolod, *Philippines,* 45 H5
Badajoz, *Spain,* 61 C7
Baffin Bay, *Canada,* 23 N1
Baffin Island, *Canada,* 23 M2
Bafoussam, *Cameroon,* 70 B2
Bage, *Brazil,* 32 H6
Baghdad, *Iraq, national capital,* 50 D5
Bahamas, The, *North America, country,* 25 L5
Bahawalpur, *Pakistan,* 48 C5
Bahia, *Brazil,* 31 H6
Bahia Blanca, *Argentina,* 33 F7
Bahir Dar, *Ethiopia,* 71 G1
Bahrain, *Asia, country,* 51 F6
Baia Mare, *Romania,* 63 G2
Baie-Comeau, *Canada,* 23 N4
Baikal, Lake, *Russia,* 53 F3
Bairiki, *Kiribati, national capital,* 36 H4
Bakersfield, *U.S.A.,* 24 C3
Baku, *Azerbaijan, national capital,* 50 E3
Balakovo, *Russia,* 57 F3
Balaton, Lake, *Hungary,* 59 F7
Balbina Reservoir, *Brazil,* 31 G4
Baldy Peak, *U.S.A.,* 24 E4
Balearic Islands, *Spain,* 61 E7
Bali, *Indonesia,* 42 E5
Balikesir, *Turkey,* 63 H4
Balikpapan, *Indonesia,* 42 E4
Balkanabat, *Turkmenistan,* 50 F4
Balkan Mountains, *Europe,* 63 G3
Balkhash, Lake, *Kazakhstan,* 48 D1
Balkuduk, *Kazakhstan,* 57 F4
Balqash, *Kazakhstan,* 48 D1
Balti, *Moldova,* 63 H2
Baltic Sea, *Europe,* 59 F4
Baltimore, *U.S.A.,* 25 L3
Bamako, *Mali, national capital,* 69 D6
Bamenda, *Cameroon,* 70 B2
Bancs Providence, *Seychelles,* 73 K1
Banda Aceh, *Indonesia,* 42 A2

Bandar-e Abbas, *Iran,* 51 G6
Bandar Seri Begawan, *Brunei, national capital,* 42 D2
Banda Sea, *Indonesia,* 43 G5
Bandundu, *Democratic Republic of Congo,* 70 C4
Bandung, *Indonesia,* 42 C5
Banfora, *Burkina Faso,* 69 E6
Bangalore, *India,* 49 D8
Bangassou, *Central African Republic,* 70 D3
Bangka, *Indonesia,* 42 C4
Bangkok, *Thailand, national capital,* 44 D5
Bangladesh, *Asia, country,* 49 F6
Bangor, *U.S.A.,* 25 N2
Bangui, *Central African Republic, national capital,* 70 C3
Bangweulu, Lake, *Zambia,* 72 E2
Banja Luka, *Bosnia and Herzegovina,* 62 F2
Banjarmasin, *Indonesia,* 42 D4
Banjul, *The Gambia, national capital,* 69 B6
Banks Island, *Canada,* 22 G1
Banks Islands, *Vanuatu,* 39 N2
Banska Bystrica, *Slovakia,* 59 F6
Baoding, *China,* 47 J3
Baoji, *China,* 46 G4
Baotou, *China,* 46 G2
Baqubah, *Iraq,* 50 D5
Baranavichy, *Belarus,* 59 H5
Barbacena, *Brazil,* 32 K4
Barbados, *North America, country,* 26 N5
Barcelona, *Spain,* 61 G6
Barcelona, *Venezuela,* 30 F1
Bareilly, *India,* 48 D5
Barents Sea, *Europe,* 52 B2
Bari, *Italy,* 62 F3
Barinas, *Venezuela,* 30 D2
Barkly Tableland, *Australia,* 38 G3
Barnaul, *Russia,* 52 E3
Barquisimeto, *Venezuela,* 30 E1
Barra Falsa Point, *Mozambique,* 73 G4
Barranquilla, *Colombia,* 30 D1
Barra Point, *Mozambique,* 73 G4
Barreiras, *Brazil,* 32 J2
Barrow, Point, *U.S.A.,* 22 D1
Barysaw, *Belarus,* 59 J5
Basel, *Switzerland,* 62 C2
Basra, *Iraq,* 51 E5
Bassas da India, *Africa,* 73 G4
Basse-Terre, *Guadeloupe,* 26 M4
Basseterre, *St. Kitts and Nevis, national capital,* 26 M4
Bass Strait, *Australia,* 38 J7
Bastia, *France,* 61 G6
Bata, *Equatorial Guinea,* 70 A3
Batan Islands, *Philippines,* 45 H3
Batdambang, *Cambodia,* 44 D5
Bathurst, *Canada,* 23 N4
Bathurst, *U.S.A.,* 25 N1
Bathurst Island, *Canada,* 23 K1
Batna, *Algeria,* 68 G1
Baton Rouge, *U.S.A., internal capital,* 25 H4
Batumi, *Georgia,* 50 D3
Baturaja, *Indonesia,* 42 C4
Bawku, *Ghana,* 69 E6
Bayamo, *Cuba,* 27 J3
Baydhabo, *Somalia,* 71 H3
Bealanana, *Madagascar,* 73 J2
Beaufort Sea, *North America,* 22 F1
Beaufort West, *South Africa,* 72 D6
Beaumont, *U.S.A.,* 25 H4
Bechar, *Algeria,* 68 E2
Beer Sheva, *Israel,* 51 B5
Beijing, *China, national capital,* 47 J3
Beira, *Mozambique,* 73 G3
Beirut, *Lebanon, national capital,* 50 C5
Bejaia, *Algeria,* 68 F1
Bekescsaba, *Hungary,* 59 G7
Bekily, *Madagascar,* 73 J4
Belarus, *Europe, country,* 59 J5
Belaya, *Russia,* 57 G2
Belcher Islands, *Canada,* 23 L3
Beledweyne, *Somalia,* 71 J3

Belem, *Brazil,* 31 J4
Belfast, *United Kingdom, internal capital,* 60 C3
Belgaum, *India,* 49 C7
Belgium, *Europe, country,* 60 E4
Belgrade, *Serbia and Montenegro, national capital,* 63 G2
Belitung, *Indonesia,* 42 C4
Belize, *North America, country,* 26 G4
Bellingham, *U.S.A.,* 24 B1
Bellingshausen Sea, *Antarctica,* 77 R2
Belmopan, *Belize, national capital,* 26 G4
Belo Horizonte, *Brazil,* 32 K3
Belomorsk, *Russia,* 58 K2
Beloretsk, *Russia,* 57 H3
Belo-Tsiribihina, *Madagascar,* 73 H3
Bendigo, *Australia,* 38 H7
Bengal, Bay of, *Asia,* 49 F7
Benghazi, *Libya,* 66 F2
Bengkulu, *Indonesia,* 42 B4
Benguela, *Angola,* 72 B2
Beni Mellal, *Morocco,* 68 D2
Benin, *Africa, country,* 69 F6
Benin, Bight of, *Africa,* 69 F7
Benin City, *Nigeria,* 69 G7
Beni Suef, *Egypt,* 67 H3
Ben Nevis, *United Kingdom,* 60 C2
Benoni, *South Africa,* 72 E5
Berbera, *Somalia,* 71 J1
Berberati, *Central African Republic,* 70 C3
Berdyansk, *Ukraine,* 56 D4
Berezniki, *Russia,* 57 H2
Bergamo, *Italy,* 62 D2
Bergen, *Norway,* 58 C3
Bering Sea, *North America,* 22 C2
Bering Strait, *U.S.A.,* 22 B2
Berlin, *Germany, national capital,* 60 H3
Bern, *Switzerland, national capital,* 62 C2
Beroroha, *Madagascar,* 73 J4
Bertoua, *Cameroon,* 70 B3
Besalampy, *Madagascar,* 73 H3
Besancon, *France,* 61 F5
Bethel, *U.S.A.,* 22 C2
Bethlehem, *South Africa,* 72 E5
Betroka, *Madagascar,* 73 J4
Beyneu, *Kazakhstan,* 50 G2
Beysehir Lake, *Turkey,* 63 J4
Beziers, *France,* 61 E6
Bhagalpur, *India,* 48 F5
Bhavnagar *India,* 49 C6
Bhopal, *India,* 49 D6
Bhutan, *Asia, country,* 48 G5
Biak, *Indonesia,* 43 K4
Bialystok, *Poland,* 59 G5
Bida, *Nigeria,* 69 G7
Biel, *Switzerland,* 62 C2
Bielefeld, *Germany,* 60 G3
Bien Hoa, *Vietnam,* 44 E5
Bie Plateau, *Angola,* 72 B2
Bignona, *Senegal,* 69 B6
Bikaner, *India,* 48 C5
Bila Tserkva, *Ukraine,* 59 J6
Bilbao, *Spain,* 61 D6
Bilhorod Dnistrovskyy, *Ukraine,* 56 C4
Billings, *U.S.A.,* 24 E1
Bindura, *Zimbabwe,* 73 F3
Binga, *Zimbabwe,* 72 E3
Bintulu, *Malaysia,* 42 D3
Bioco, *Equatorial Guinea,* 70 A3
Birao, *Central African Republic,* 70 D1
Biratnagar, *Nepal,* 48 F5
Birjand, *Iran,* 50 G5
Birmingham, *United Kingdom,* 60 D3
Birmingham, *U.S.A.,* 25 J4
Birnin-Kebbi, *Nigeria,* 69 F6
Biscay, Bay of, *Europe,* 61 C5
Bishkek, *Kyrgyzstan, national capital,* 48 C2
Bisho, *South Africa,* 72 E6
Biskra, *Algeria,* 68 G2
Bismarck, *U.S.A., internal capital,* 24 F1
Bismarck Sea, *Papua New Guinea,* 43 L4
Bissagos Archipelago, *Guinea-Bissau,* 69 B6
Bissau, *Guinea-Bissau, national capital,* 69 B6

Bitola, *Macedonia,* 63 G3
Bitterfontein, *South Africa,* 72 C6
Bizerte, *Tunisia,* 66 C1
Blackpool, *United Kingdom,* 60 D3
Black Sea, *Asia/Europe,* 52 B3
Black Volta, *Africa,* 69 E6
Blagoevgrad, *Bulgaria,* 63 G3
Blagoveshchensk, *Russia,* 53 G3
Blanca Bay, *Argentina,* 33 F7
Blanc, Cape, *Africa,* 68 B4
Blanc, Mont, *Europe,* 61 F5
Blantyre, *Malawi,* 73 F3
Blida, *Algeria,* 68 F1
Bloemfontein, *South Africa, national capital,* 72 E5
Blue Nile, *Africa,* 67 H6
Bo, *Sierra Leone,* 69 C7
Boa Vista, *Brazil,* 30 F3
Boa Vista, *Cape Verde,* 69 M11
Bobo Dioulasso, *Burkina Faso,* 69 E6
Bodele Depression, *Africa,* 66 E5
Boden, *Sweden,* 58 G2
Bodo, *Norway,* 58 E2
Bogor, *Indonesia,* 42 C5
Bogota, *Colombia, national capital,* 30 D3
Bohol, *Philippines,* 45 H6
Boise, *U.S.A., internal capital,* 24 C2
Bojnurd, *Iran,* 50 F4
Boke, *Guinea,* 69 C6
Bolivar Peak, *Venezuela,* 30 D2
Bolivia, *South America, country,* 32 E3
Bologna, *Italy,* 62 D2
Bolzano, *Italy,* 62 D1
Bombay, *India,* 49 C7
Bondoukou, *Ivory Coast,* 69 E7
Bongor, *Chad,* 70 C1
Bonin Islands, *Japan,* 36 B2
Bonn, *Germany,* 60 F4
Boosaaso, *Somalia,* 71 J1
Boothia, Gulf of, *Canada,* 23 K1
Boothia Peninsula, *Canada,* 23 K1
Bordeaux, *France,* 61 D5
Bordj Bou Arreridj, *Algeria,* 68 F1
Borlange, *Sweden,* 58 E3
Borneo, *Asia,* 42 D4
Bornholm, *Denmark,* 59 E5
Borovichi, *Russia,* 58 K4
Bosnia and Herzegovina, *Europe, country,* 62 F2
Bosporus, *Turkey,* 63 J3
Bossangoa, *Central African Republic,* 70 C2
Bossembele, *Central African Republic,* 70 C2
Bosten Lake, *China,* 48 F2
Boston, *U.S.A., internal capital,* 25 M2
Bothnia, Gulf of, *Europe,* 58 F3
Botosani, *Romania,* 63 H2
Botswana, *Africa, country,* 72 D4
Bouake, *Ivory Coast,* 69 E7
Bouar, *Central African Republic,* 70 C2
Bougouni, *Mali,* 69 D6
Boujdour, *Western Sahara,* 68 C3
Bouna, *Ivory Coast,* 69 E7
Bozoum, *Central African Republic,* 70 C2
Braga, *Portugal,* 61 B6
Braganca, *Brazil,* 31 J4
Brahmapur, *India,* 49 E7
Brahmaputra, *Asia,* 48 G5
Braila, *Romania,* 63 H2
Brandon, *Canada,* 23 K4
Brandon, *U.S.A.,* 24 G1
Brasilia, *Brazil, national capital,* 32 J3
Brasov, *Romania,* 63 H2
Bratislava, *Slovakia, national capital,* 59 F6
Brazil, *South America, country,* 31 H5
Brazilian Highlands, *Brazil,* 32 K2
Brazzaville, *Congo, national capital,* 70 C4
Bremen, *Germany,* 60 G3
Bremerhaven, *Germany,* 60 G3
Brescia, *Italy,* 62 D2
Brest, *Belarus,* 59 G5
Brest, *France,* 60 C4
Bria, *Central African Republic,* 70 D2
Bridgetown, *Barbados, national capital,* 26 N5

Florencia, *Colombia*, 30 C3
Flores, *Azores*, 68 J10
Flores, *Indonesia*, 43 F5
Flores Sea, *Indonesia*, 43 F5
Floresta, *Brazil*, 31 K5
Floriano, *Brazil*, 31 K5
Florianopolis, *Brazil*, 32 J5
Florida, *U.S.A., internal admin. area*, 25 K5
Florida Keys, *U.S.A.*, 25 K6
Florida, Straits of, *North America*, 25 K6
Focsani, *Romania*, 63 H2
Foggia, *Italy*, 62 E3
Fogo, *Cape Verde*, 69 M12
Fomboni, *Comoros*, 73 H2
Formosa, *Argentina*, 32 G5
Fort Albany, *Canada*, 23 J3
Fortaleza, *Brazil*, 31 L4
Fort Chipewyan, *Canada*, 22 H3
Fort-de-France, *Martinique*, 26 M5
Fort Lauderdale, *U.S.A.*, 25 K5
Fort McMurray, *Canada*, 22 H3
Fort Nelson, *Canada*, 22 G3
Fort Peck Lake, *U.S.A.*, 24 E1
Fort Providence, *Canada*, 22 H2
Fort St. John, *Canada*, 22 G3
Fort Severn, *Canada*, 23 L3
Fort Vermilion, *Canada*, 22 H3
Fort Wayne, *U.S.A.*, 25 J2
Fort Worth, *U.S.A.*, 24 G4
Foumban, *Cameroon*, 70 B2
Foxe Basin, *Canada*, 23 M2
Fox Peninsula, *Canada*, 23 M2
Fox Islands, *U.S.A.*, 23 C3
Foz do Cunene, *Angola*, 72 B3
Foz do Iguacu, *Brazil*, 32 H5
France, *Europe, country*, 61 E5
Franceville, *Gabon*, 70 B4
Francistown, *Botswana*, 72 E4
Frankfort, *U.S.A., internal capital*, 25 K3
Frankfurt, *Germany*, 60 G4
Franz Josef Land, *Russia*, 52 C1
Fraser Island, *Australia*, 39 K5
Fredericton, *Canada, internal capital*, 23 N4
Fredrikstad, *Norway*, 58 D4
Freeport City, *The Bahamas*, 25 L5
Freetown, *Sierra Leone, national capital*, 69 C7
Freiburg, *Germany*, 60 F4
French Guiana, *South America, dependency*, 31 H3
French Polynesia, *Oceania, dependency*, 37 J6
Fresno, *U.S.A.*, 24 C3
Frisian Islands, *Europe*, 60 F3
Froya, *Norway*, 58 D3
Fuerteventura, *Canary Islands*, 68 B3
Fuji, Mount, *Japan*, 47 N3
Fukui, *Japan*, 47 N3
Fukuoka, *Japan*, 47 M4
Fukushima, *Japan*, 47 P3
Funafuti, *Tuvalu, national capital*, 36 E5
Funchal, *Madeira*, 68 B2
Furnas Reservoir, *Brazil*, 32 J4
Fushun, *China*, 47 K2
Fuxin, *China*, 47 K2
Fyn, *Denmark*, 59 D5

g

Gabes, *Tunisia*, 66 D2
Gabes, Gulf of, *Africa*, 66 D2
Gabon, *Africa, country*, 70 B4
Gaborone, *Botswana, national capital*, 72 E4
Gafsa, *Tunisia*, 66 C2
Gagnoa, *Ivory Coast*, 69 D7
Gairdner, Lake, *Australia*, 38 F6
Galapagos Islands, *Ecuador*, 30 N9
Galati, *Romania*, 63 J2
Galdhopigen, *Norway*, 58 D3
Galle, *Sri Lanka*, 49 E9
Gallinas, Cape, *Colombia*, 30 D1
Galveston, *U.S.A.*, 25 H5
Galway, *Ireland*, 60 B3
Gambela, *Ethiopia*, 71 F2

Gambia, The, *Africa, country*, 69 B6
Ganca, *Azerbaijan*, 50 E3
Gander, *Canada*, 23 P4
Ganges, *Asia*, 48 E5
Ganges, Mouths of the, *Asia*, 49 F6
Ganzhou, *China*, 47 H5
Gao, *Mali*, 69 F5
Garda, Lake, *Italy*, 62 D2
Garissa, *Kenya*, 71 G4
Garonne, *France*, 61 E5
Garoua, *Cameroon*, 70 B2
Gaspe, *Canada*, 23 N4
Gatchina, *Russia*, 58 J4
Gavle, *Sweden*, 58 F3
Gaza, *Israel*, 51 B5
Gaziantep, *Turkey*, 50 C4
Gdansk, *Poland*, 59 F5
Gdansk, Gulf of, *Poland*, 59 F5
Gdynia, *Poland*, 59 F5
Gedaref, *Sudan*, 67 J6
Geelong, *Australia*, 38 H7
Gejiu, *China*, 46 F6
Gemena, *Democratic Republic of Congo*, 70 C3
General Roca, *Argentina*, 33 E7
General Santos, *Philippines*, 45 J6
General Villegas, *Argentina*, 32 F7
Geneva, *Switzerland*, 62 C2
Geneva, Lake, *Europe*, 62 C2
Genoa, *Italy*, 62 D2
Genoa, Gulf of, *Italy*, 62 D2
Gent, *Belgium*, 60 F3
Georgetown, *Guyana, national capital*, 31 G2
George Town, *Malaysia*, 42 B2
Georgia, *Asia, country*, 50 D3
Georgia, *U.S.A., internal admin. area*, 25 K4
Gera, *Germany*, 60 H4
Geraldton, *Australia*, 38 B5
Gerlachovsky stit, *Slovakia*, 59 G6
Germany, *Europe, country*, 60 G4
Gerona, *Spain*, 61 E6
Ghadamis, *Libya*, 66 C2
Ghana, *Africa, country*, 69 E7
Ghardaia, *Algeria*, 68 F2
Gharyan, *Libya*, 66 D2
Ghat, *Libya*, 66 D3
Gibraltar, *Europe*, 61 C7
Gibson Desert, *Australia*, 38 E4
Gijon, *Spain*, 61 C6
Gilbert Islands, *Kiribati*, 36 E5
Gilgit, *Pakistan*, 48 D2
Girardeau, Cape, *U.S.A.*, 25 J3
Giza, Pyramids of, *Egypt*, 67 H3
Gladstone, *Australia*, 39 K4
Glama, *Norway*, 58 D3
Glasgow, *United Kingdom*, 60 C3
Glazov, *Russia*, 57 G2
Glorioso Islands, *Africa*, 73 J2
Gloucester, *United Kingdom*, 60 D4
Gobabis, *Namibia*, 72 C4
Gobi Desert, *Asia*, 46 F2
Gochas, *Namibia*, 72 C4
Godavari, *India*, 49 D7
Gode, *Ethiopia*, 71 H2
Goiania, *Brazil*, 32 J3
Gojra, *Pakistan*, 48 C3
Gold Coast, *Australia*, 39 K5
Golmud, *China*, 48 G3
Goma, *Democratic Republic of Congo*, 70 E4
Gonaives, *Haiti*, 27 K4
Gonder, *Ethiopia*, 71 G1
Gongga Shan, *China*, 46 F5
Good Hope, Cape of, *South Africa*, 72 C6
Goose Lake, *U.S.A.*, 24 B2
Gorakhpur, *India*, 49 E5
Gorgan, *Iran*, 50 F4
Gori, *Georgia*, 50 D3
Gorki Reservoir, *Russia*, 56 E2
Gorontalo, *Indonesia*, 43 F3
Gorzow Wielkopolski, *Poland*, 59 E5
Gothenburg, *Sweden*, 59 F4
Gotland, *Sweden*, 59 F4
Gottingen, *Germany*, 60 G4

Gouin Reservoir, *Canada*, 25 L1
Goundam, *Mali*, 69 E5
Governador Valadares, *Brazil*, 32 K3
Graaff-Reinet, *South Africa*, 72 D6
Grafton, *Australia*, 39 K5
Grahamstown, *South Africa*, 72 E6
Granada, *Spain*, 61 D7
Gran Canaria, *Canary Islands*, 68 B3
Gran Chaco, *South America*, 32 F4
Grand Bahama, *The Bahamas*, 25 L5
Grand Canal, *China*, 47 J6
Grand Canyon, *U.S.A.*, 24 D3
Grand Comoro, *Comoros*, 73 H2
Grande, *Argentina*, 33 E10
Grande Prairie, *Canada*, 22 H3
Grand Forks, *U.S.A.*, 25 G1
Grand Island, *U.S.A.*, 24 G2
Grand Junction, *U.S.A.*, 24 E3
Grand Rapids, *Canada*, 23 K3
Grand Rapids, *U.S.A.*, 25 J2
Grand Teton, *U.S.A.*, 24 D2
Graskop, *South Africa*, 72 F5
Graz, *Austria*, 62 E2
Great Australian Bight, *Australia*, 38 F6
Great Barrier Reef, *Australia*, 38 J3
Great Basin, *U.S.A.*, 24 C2
Great Bear Lake, *Canada*, 22 G2
Great Dividing Range, *Australia*, 39 J6
Great Eastern Erg, *Algeria*, 68 G2
Greater Antilles, *North America*, 27 J4
Greater Khingan Range, *China*, 47 J1
Greater Sunda Islands, *Asia*, 42 C4
Great Falls, *U.S.A.*, 24 D1
Great Inagua, *The Bahamas*, 27 K3
Great Karoo, *South Africa*, 72 D6
Great Plains, *U.S.A.*, 24 F2
Great Rift Valley, *Africa*, 71 F5
Great Salt Desert, *Iran*, 50 F5
Great Salt Lake, *U.S.A.*, 24 D2
Great Salt Lake Desert, *U.S.A.*, 24 D2
Great Sandy Desert, *Australia*, 38 D4
Great Slave Lake, *Canada*, 22 H2
Great Victoria Desert, *Australia*, 38 D5
Great Wall of China, *China*, 46 F3
Great Western Erg, *Algeria*, 68 E2
Greece, *Europe, country*, 63 G4
Green Bay, *U.S.A.*, 25 J2
Greenland, *North America, dependency*, 75 P3
Greenland Sea, *Atlantic Ocean*, 75 M3
Greensboro, *U.S.A.*, 25 L3
Greenville, *U.S.A.*, 25 K4
Grenada, *North America, country*, 26 M5
Grenoble, *France*, 61 F5
Griffith, *Australia*, 38 J6
Groningen, *Netherlands*, 60 F3
Groot, *South Africa*, 72 D6
Groote Eylandt, *Australia*, 38 G2
Grossglockner, *Austria*, 62 D2
Groznyy, *Russia*, 50 E3
Grudziadz, *Poland*, 59 F5
Grunau, *Namibia*, 72 C5
Grytviken, *South Georgia*, 33 L10
Guadalajara, *Mexico*, 26 D3
Guadalquivir, *Spain*, 61 C7
Guadalupe Island, *Mexico*, 26 A2
Guadeloupe, *North America*, 26 M4
Guadiana, *Europe*, 61 C7
Gualeguaychu, *Argentina*, 32 G6
Guam, *Oceania*, 36 B3
Guangzhou, *China*, 47 H6
Guantanamo, *Cuba*, 27 J3
Guarapuava, *Brazil*, 32 H5
Guardafui, Cape, *Somalia*, 71 K1
Guatemala, *North America, country*, 26 F4
Guatemala City, *Guatemala, national capital*, 26 F5
Guaviare, *Colombia*, 30 E3
Guayaquil, *Ecuador*, 30 C4
Guayaquil, Gulf of, *Ecuador*, 30 B4
Gueckedou, *Guinea*, 69 C7
Guelma, *Algeria*, 62 E4
Guiana Highlands, *Venezuela*, 30 E2
Guilin, *China*, 46 H5
Guinea, *Africa, country*, 69 C6

Guinea-Bissau, *Africa, country*, 69 B6
Guinea, Gulf of, *Africa*, 69 F8
Guiria, *Venezuela*, 30 F1
Guiyang, *China*, 46 G5
Gujranwala, *Pakistan*, 48 C4
Gujrat, *Pakistan*, 48 C4
Gulbarga, *India*, 49 D7
Gulf, The, *Asia*, 51 F6
Gulu, *Uganda*, 71 F3
Gunnbjorns Mountain, *Greenland*, 75 N2
Gunung Kerinci, *Indonesia*, 42 B4
Gunung Tahan, *Malaysia*, 42 B3
Gurupi, *Brazil*, 32 J2
Gusau, *Nigeria*, 69 G6
Guwahati, *India*, 48 G5
Guyana, *South America, country*, 31 G2
Gwalior, *India*, 48 D5
Gweru, *Zimbabwe*, 72 E3
Gympie, *Australia*, 39 K5
Gyor, *Hungary*, 59 F7

h

Haapsalu, *Estonia*, 58 G4
Haarlem, *Netherlands*, 60 F3
Hadhramaut, *Yemen*, 51 E9
Ha Giang, *Vietnam*, 44 E3
Hague, The, *Netherlands, national capital*, 60 F3
Haifa, *Israel*, 50 B5
Haikou, *China*, 46 H6
Hail, *Saudi Arabia*, 51 D6
Hailar, *China*, 47 J1
Hainan, *China*, 46 H7
Hai Phong, *Vietnam*, 44 E3
Haiti, *North America, country*, 27 K4
Hakodate, *Japan*, 47 P2
Halifax, *Canada, internal capital*, 23 N4
Halmahera, *Indonesia*, 43 G3
Halmstad, *Sweden*, 59 E4
Hamadan, *Iran*, 50 E5
Hamah, *Syria*, 50 C4
Hamamatsu, *Japan*, 47 N4
Hamburg, *Germany*, 60 G3
Hameenlinna, *Finland*, 58 H3
Hamhung, *North Korea*, 47 L3
Hami, *China*, 48 G2
Hamilton, *Canada*, 23 M4
Hamilton, *New Zealand*, 39 Q7
Hammerfest, *Norway*, 58 G1
Handan, *China*, 47 H3
Hangzhou, *China*, 47 K4
Hannover, *Germany*, 60 G3
Hanoi, *Vietnam, national capital*, 44 E3
Happy Valley-Goose Bay, *Canada*, 23 N3
Haradh, *Saudi Arabia*, 51 E7
Harare, *Zimbabwe, national capital*, 72 F3
Harbin, *China*, 47 L1
Harer, *Ethiopia*, 71 H2
Hargeysa, *Somalia*, 71 H2
Harney Basin, *U.S.A.*, 24 C2
Harper, *Liberia*, 69 D8
Harrisburg, *U.S.A., internal capital*, 25 L2
Harrismith, *South Africa*, 72 E5
Hartford, *U.S.A., internal capital*, 25 M2
Hatteras, Cape, *U.S.A.*, 25 L3
Hattiesburg, *U.S.A.*, 25 J4
Hat Yai, *Thailand*, 44 D6
Hauki Lake, *Canada*, 27 H3
Havana, *Cuba, national capital*, 27 H3
Hawaii, *Pacific Ocean, internal admin. area*, 25 P7
Hawaiian Islands, *Pacific Ocean*, 25 P7
Hebrides, *United Kingdom*, 60 C3
Hefei, *China*, 47 J4
Hegang, *China*, 47 M1
Hejaz, *Saudi Arabia*, 51 C6
Helena, *U.S.A., internal capital*, 24 D1
Helmand, *Asia*, 48 B4
Helsingborg, *Sweden*, 59 E4
Helsinki, *Finland, national capital*, 58 H3
Hengyang, *China*, 46 H5
Henzada, *Burma*, 44 C4
Herat, *Afghanistan*, 48 A4
Hermosillo, *Mexico*, 26 B2
Hiiumaa, *Estonia*, 58 G4
Hilo, *U.S.A.*, 25 P8

102

Himalayas, *Asia,* **48 E4**
Hindu Kush, *Asia,* **48 B3**
Hinton, *Canada,* **22 H3**
Hiroshima, *Japan,* **47 M4**
Hispaniola, *North America,* **27 K4**
Hitra, *Norway,* **58 D3**
Hobart, *Australia, internal capital,* **38 J8**
Ho Chi Minh City, *Vietnam,* **44 E5**
Hohhot, *China,* **46 H2**
Hokkaido, *Japan,* **47 P2**
Holguin, *Cuba,* **27 J3**
Homs, *Syria,* **50 C5**
Homyel, *Belarus,* **59 J5**
Honduras, *North America, country,* **27 G4**
Honduras, Gulf of, *North America,* **27 G4**
Honefoss, *Norway,* **58 D3**
Hong Kong, *China,* **47 H6**
Honiara, *Solomon Islands, national capital,* **36 D5**
Honolulu, *U.S.A., internal capital,* **25 P7**
Honshu, *Japan,* **47 N3**
Horlivka, *Ukraine,* **56 D4**
Hormuz, Strait of, *Asia,* **51 G6**
Horn, Cape, *Chile,* **33 D11**
Horn Lake, *Sweden,* **58 F2**
Hotan, *China,* **48 D3**
Hotazel, *South Africa,* **72 D5**
Houston, *U.S.A.,* **25 G5**
Hradec Kralove, *Czech Republic,* **62 E1**
Hrodna, *Belarus,* **59 G5**
Huacrachuco, *Peru,* **30 C5**
Huaihua, *China,* **46 H5**
Huambo, *Angola,* **72 C2**
Huancayo, *Peru,* **30 C6**
Huang He, *China,* **47 H3**
Huanuco, *Peru,* **30 C5**
Huascaran, Mount, *Peru,* **30 C5**
Hubli, *India,* **49 D7**
Hudiksvall, *Sweden,* **58 F3**
Hudson Bay, *Canada,* **23 L3**
Hudson Strait, *Canada,* **23 M2**
Hue, *Vietnam,* **44 E4**
Huelva, *Spain,* **61 C7**
Hull, *United Kingdom,* **60 D3**
Hulun Lake, *China,* **47 J1**
Hungary, *Europe, country,* **59 F7**
Huntsville, *Canada,* **23 M4**
Huntsville, *U.S.A.,* **25 J4**
Hurghada, *Egypt,* **67 H3**
Huron, Lake, *U.S.A.,* **25 K2**
Hvannadalshnukur, *Iceland,* **58 P2**
Hwange, *Zimbabwe,* **72 E3**
Hyderabad, *India,* **49 D7**
Hyderabad, *Pakistan,* **48 B5**
Hyesan, *North Korea,* **47 L2**

i
Iasi, *Romania,* **63 H2**
Ibadan, *Nigeria,* **69 F7**
Ibague, *Colombia,* **30 C3**
Ibarra, *Ecuador,* **30 C3**
Ibb, *Yemen,* **51 D9**
Iberian Mountains, *Spain,* **61 D6**
Ibiza, *Spain,* **61 E7**
Ica, *Peru,* **30 C6**
Iceland, *Europe, country,* **58 P2**
Idaho, *U.S.A., internal admin. area,* **24 C2**
Idaho Falls, *U.S.A.,* **24 D2**
Ierapetra, *Greece,* **63 H5**
Iguacu Falls, *South America,* **32 H5**
Ihosy, *Madagascar,* **73 J4**
Ikopa, *Madagascar,* **73 J3**
Ilagan, *Philippines,* **45 H4**
Ilebo, *Democratic Republic of Congo,* **70 D4**
Ilheus, *Brazil,* **32 L2**
Iliamna Lake, *U.S.A.,* **22 D2**
Iligan, *Philippines,* **45 H6**
Illapel, *Chile,* **32 D6**
Illimani, Mount, *Bolivia,* **32 E3**
Illinois, *U.S.A., internal admin. area,* **25 J2**
Illizi, *Algeria,* **68 G3**
Ilmen, Lake, *Russia,* **58 J4**
Iloilo, *Philippines,* **45 H5**
Ilonga, *Tanzania,* **71 G5**
Ilorin, *Nigeria,* **69 F7**

Imperatriz, *Brazil,* **31 J5**
Imphal, *India,* **49 G6**
Inari, Lake, *Finland,* **58 H1**
Inchon, *South Korea,* **47 L3**
Indals, *Sweden,* **58 E3**
Inderbor, *Kazakhstan,* **57 G4**
India, *Asia, country,* **49 D6**
Indiana, *U.S.A., internal admin. area,* **25 J2**
Indianapolis, *U.S.A., internal capital,* **25 J3**
Indian Ocean, **19**
Indonesia, *Asia, country,* **42 C5**
Indore, *India,* **49 D6**
Indus, *Asia,* **48 B5**
Ingolstadt, *Germany,* **60 G4**
Inhambane, *Mozambique,* **73 G4**
Inner Mongolia, *China,* **47 H2**
Innsbruck, *Austria,* **62 D2**
Inukjuak, *Canada,* **23 M3**
Inuvik, *Canada,* **22 F2**
Invercargill, *New Zealand,* **39 N9**
Inyangani, *Zimbabwe,* **73 F3**
Ioannina, *Greece,* **63 G4**
Ionian Sea, *Europe,* **63 F4**
Iowa, *U.S.A., internal admin. area,* **25 H2**
Ipiales, *Colombia,* **30 C3**
Ipoh, *Malaysia,* **42 B3**
Ipswich, *United Kingdom,* **60 E3**
Iqaluit, *Canada, internal capital,* **23 N2**
Iquique, *Chile,* **32 D4**
Iquitos, *Peru,* **30 D4**
Irakleio, *Greece,* **63 H5**
Iran, *Asia, country,* **50 F5**
Iranshahr, *Iran,* **51 H6**
Iraq, *Asia, country,* **50 D5**
Irbid, *Jordan,* **50 C5**
Ireland, *Europe, country,* **60 B3**
Iringa, *Tanzania,* **71 G5**
Irish Sea, *Europe,* **60 C3**
Irkutsk, *Russia,* **53 F3**
Irrawaddy, *Burma,* **44 C4**
Irrawaddy, Mouths of the, *Burma,* **44 B4**
Irtysh, *Asia,* **52 D3**
Isabela, *Ecuador,* **30 N10**
Isafjordhur, *Iceland,* **58 N2**
Isiro, *Democratic Republic of Congo,* **70 E3**
Islamabad, *Pakistan, national capital,* **48 C4**
Isle of Man, *Europe,* **60 C3**
Isle of Wight, *United Kingdom,* **60 D4**
Ismailia, *Egypt,* **67 H3**
Isoka, *Zambia,* **73 F2**
Isparta, *Turkey,* **63 J4**
Israel, *Asia, country,* **51 B5**
Issyk, Lake, *Kyrgyzstan,* **48 D2**
Istanbul, *Turkey,* **63 J3**
Itaituba, *Brazil,* **31 H4**
Itajai, *Brazil,* **32 J5**
Italy, *Europe, country,* **62 D2**
Itapetininga, *Brazil,* **32 J4**
Ivano-Frankivsk, *Ukraine,* **59 H6**
Ivanovo, *Russia,* **56 E2**
Ivdel, *Russia,* **57 J1**
Ivory Coast, *Africa, country,* **69 D7**
Ivujivik, *Canada,* **23 M2**
Izhevsk, *Russia,* **57 G2**
Izmir, *Turkey,* **63 H4**

j
Jabalpur, *India,* **49 D6**
Jackson, *Mississippi, U.S.A., internal capital,* **25 H4**
Jackson, *Tennessee, U.S.A.,* **25 J3**
Jacksonville, *U.S.A.,* **25 K4**
Jaen, *Spain,* **61 D7**
Jaffna, *Sri Lanka,* **49 E9**
Jaipur, *India,* **48 D5**
Jakarta, *Indonesia, national capital,* **42 C5**
Jalalabad, *Afghanistan,* **48 C4**
Jalal-Abad, *Kyrgyzstan,* **48 C2**
Jamaica, *North America, country,* **27 J4**
Jambi, *Indonesia,* **42 B4**
James Bay, *Canada,* **23 L3**
Jamestown, *U.S.A.,* **25 L2**

Jammu, *India,* **48 C4**
Jammu and Kashmir, *Asia,* **48 D4**
Jamnagar, *India,* **49 C6**
Jamshedpur, *India,* **49 F6**
Japan, *Asia, country,* **47 N3**
Japan, Sea of, *Asia,* **47 M2**
Japura, *Brazil,* **30 E4**
Jatai, *Brazil,* **32 H3**
Java, *Indonesia,* **42 C5**
Java Sea, *Indonesia,* **42 C5**
Javapura, *Indonesia,* **43 K4**
Jedda, *Saudi Arabia,* **51 C7**
Jefferson City, *U.S.A., internal capital,* **25 H3**
Jekabpils, *Latvia,* **59 H4**
Jelgava, *Latvia,* **59 G4**
Jember, *Indonesia,* **42 D5**
Jerba, *Tunisia,* **66 D2**
Jerez de la Frontera, *Spain,* **61 C7**
Jerusalem, *Israel, national capital,* **51 C5**
Jhansi, *India,* **48 D5**
Jiamusi, *China,* **47 M1**
Jilin, *China,* **47 L2**
Jima, *Ethiopia,* **71 G2**
Jinhua, *China,* **47 J5**
Jining, *China,* **47 J3**
Jinja, *Uganda,* **71 F3**
Jinzhou, *China,* **47 K2**
Jixi, *China,* **47 M1**
Jizzax, *Uzbekistan,* **48 B2**
Joao Pessoa, *Brazil,* **31 M5**
Jodhpur, *India,* **48 C5**
Johannesburg, *South Africa,* **72 E5**
Johnston Atoll, *Oceania,* **36 A3**
Johor Bahru, *Malaysia,* **42 B3**
Jolo, *Philippines,* **45 H6**
Jonesboro, *U.S.A.,* **25 H3**
Jonkoping, *Sweden,* **59 E4**
Jordan, *Asia, country,* **51 C5**
Jorhat, *India,* **48 G5**
Jos, *Nigeria,* **70 A2**
Juan de Nova, *Africa,* **73 H3**
Juazeiro, *Brazil,* **31 K5**
Juazeiro do Norte, *Brazil,* **31 L5**
Juba, *Africa,* **71 F3**
Juba, *Sudan,* **71 F3**
Juchitan, *Mexico,* **26 E4**
Juiz de Fora, *Brazil,* **32 K4**
Juliaca, *Peru,* **30 D7**
Juneau, *U.S.A., internal capital,* **22 F3**
Jurmala, *Latvia,* **59 G4**
Jurua, *Brazil,* **30 E5**
Jutland, *Europe,* **59 D4**
Jyvaskyla, *Finland,* **58 H3**

k
K2, *Asia,* **48 D3**
Kaamanen, *Finland,* **58 H1**
Kabinda, *Democratic Republic of Congo,* **70 D5**
Kabul, *Afghanistan, national capital,* **48 B4**
Kabunda, *Democratic Republic of Congo,* **70 E6**
Kabwe, *Zambia,* **72 E2**
Kadoma, *Zimbabwe,* **72 E3**
Kaduna, *Nigeria,* **69 G6**
Kaedi, *Mauritania,* **69 C5**
Kafakumba, *Democratic Republic of Congo,* **70 D5**
Kafue, *Zambia,* **72 E3**
Kagoshima, *Japan,* **47 M4**
Kahramanmaras, *Turkey,* **50 C4**
Kahului, *U.S.A.,* **25 P7**
Kainji Reservoir, *Nigeria,* **69 F6**
Kairouan, *Tunisia,* **66 D1**
Kajaani, *Finland,* **58 H2**
Kakhovske Reservoir, *Ukraine,* **56 C4**
Kalahari Desert, *Africa,* **72 D4**
Kalamata, *Greece,* **63 G4**
Kalemie, *Democratic Republic of Congo,* **70 E5**
Kalgoorlie, *Australia,* **38 D6**
Kaliningrad, *Russia,* **59 F6**
Kalisz, *Poland,* **59 F6**
Kalkrand, *Namibia,* **72 C5**

Kalmar, *Sweden,* **59 F4**
Kaluga, *Russia,* **56 D3**
Kamanjab, *Namibia,* **72 B3**
Kama Reservoir, *Russia,* **57 H2**
Kamativi, *Zimbabwe,* **72 E3**
Kamchatka Peninsula, *Russia,* **53 H3**
Kamenka, *Russia,* **56 E3**
Kamina, *Democratic Republic of Congo,* **70 E5**
Kamloops, *Canada,* **22 G3**
Kampala, *Uganda, national capital,* **71 F3**
Kampong Cham, *Cambodia,* **44 E5**
Kampong Chhnang, *Cambodia,* **44 D5**
Kampong Saom, *Cambodia,* **44 D5**
Kamyanets-Podilskyy, *Ukraine,* **59 H6**
Kamyshin, *Russia,* **56 F3**
Kananga, *Democratic Republic of Congo,* **70 D5**
Kanazawa, *Japan,* **47 N3**
Kandahar, *Afghanistan,* **48 B4**
Kandalaksha, *Russia,* **58 K2**
Kandi, *Benin,* **69 F6**
Kandy, *Sri Lanka,* **49 E9**
Kang, *Botswana,* **72 D4**
Kangaroo Island, *Australia,* **38 G7**
Kanggye, *North Korea,* **47 L2**
Kankan, *Guinea,* **69 D6**
Kano, *Nigeria,* **69 G6**
Kanpur, *India,* **48 E5**
Kansas, *U.S.A., internal admin. area,* **24 G3**
Kansas City, *U.S.A.,* **25 H3**
Kanye, *Botswana,* **72 E4**
Kaohsiung, *Taiwan,* **47 K6**
Kaolack, *Senegal,* **69 B6**
Kara-Balta, *Kyrgyzstan,* **48 C2**
Karabuk, *Turkey,* **63 K3**
Karachi, *Pakistan,* **49 B6**
Karaj, *Iran,* **50 F4**
Karakol, *Kyrgyzstan,* **48 D2**
Karakorum Range, *Asia,* **48 D3**
Kara Kum Desert, *Turkmenistan,* **50 G3**
Karaman, *Turkey,* **63 K4**
Karamay, *China,* **48 E1**
Kara Sea, *Russia,* **52 D2**
Kariba, *Zimbabwe,* **72 E3**
Kariba, Lake, *Africa,* **72 E3**
Karibib, *Namibia,* **72 C4**
Karimata Strait, *Indonesia,* **42 C4**
Karlovac, *Croatia,* **62 E2**
Karlovy Vary, *Czech Republic,* **62 E1**
Karlshamn, *Sweden,* **59 E4**
Karlsruhe, *Germany,* **60 G4**
Karlstad, *Sweden,* **58 E4**
Karmoy, *Norway,* **58 C4**
Karonga, *Malawi,* **73 F1**
Karora, *Eritrea,* **67 J5**
Karpathos, *Greece,* **63 H5**
Karratha, *Australia,* **38 C4**
Kasai, *Africa,* **70 C4**
Kasama, *Zambia,* **73 F2**
Kashi, *China,* **48 D3**
Kassala, *Sudan,* **67 J5**
Kassel, *Germany,* **60 G4**
Kasungu, *Malawi,* **73 F2**
Kataba, *Zambia,* **72 E3**
Kathmandu, *Nepal, national capital,* **48 F5**
Katiola, *Ivory Coast,* **69 D7**
Katowice, *Poland,* **59 F6**
Katsina, *Nigeria,* **69 G6**
Kattegat, *Europe,* **59 D4**
Kauai, *U.S.A.,* **25 P7**
Kaukau Veld, *Africa,* **72 C4**
Kaunas, *Lithuania,* **59 G5**
Kavala, *Greece,* **63 H3**
Kawambwa, *Zambia,* **72 E1**
Kayes, *Mali,* **69 C6**
Kayseri, *Turkey,* **50 C4**
Kazakhstan, *Asia, country,* **52 C3**
Kazan, *Russia,* **57 F2**
Kaztalovka, *Kazakhstan,* **57 F4**
Kebnekaise, *Sweden,* **58 F2**
Kecskemet, *Hungary,* **59 F7**
Kedougou, *Senegal,* **69 C6**
Keetmanshoop, *Namibia,* **72 C5**

Minneapolis, U.S.A., **25 H2**
Minnesota, U.S.A., internal admin. area,
    25 G1
Minorca, Spain, **61 E6**
Minot, U.S.A., **24 F1**
Minsk, Belarus, national capital, **59 H5**
Miri, Malaysia, **42 D3**
Mirim Lake, Brazil, **32 H6**
Miskolc, Hungary, **59 G6**
Misool, Indonesia, **43 H4**
Misratah, Libya, **66 E2**
Mississippi, U.S.A., **25 H4**
Mississippi, U.S.A., internal admin. area,
    25 H4
Mississippi Delta, U.S.A., **25 J5**
Missoula, U.S.A., **24 D1**
Missouri, U.S.A., **24 G2**
Missouri, U.S.A., internal admin. area,
    25 H3
Mistassini, Lake, Canada, **23 M3**
Mitwaba, Democratic Republic of Congo,
    70 E5
Mkushi, Zambia, **72 E2**
Mmabatho, South Africa, **72 E5**
Moanda, Gabon, **70 B4**
Mobile, U.S.A., **25 J4**
Mochudi, Botswana, **72 E4**
Mocuba, Mozambique, **73 G3**
Modena, Italy, **62 D2**
Mogadishu, Somalia, national capital,
    71 J3
Mogao Caves, China, **46 E2**
Mohilla Island, Comoros, **73 H2**
Mo i Rana, Norway, **58 E2**
Mojave Desert, U.S.A., **24 C4**
Moldova, Europe, country, **63 J2**
Moldoveanu, Mount, Romania, **56 C4**
Molepolole, Botswana, **72 E4**
Mollendo, Peru, **30 D7**
Molokai, U.S.A., **25 P7**
Molopo, Africa, **72 D5**
Molucca Sea, Indonesia, **43 F4**
Mombasa, Kenya, **71 G4**
Monaco, Europe, country, **61 F6**
Monastir, Tunisia, **66 D1**
Monchegorsk, Russia, **58 K2**
Monclova, Mexico, **26 D2**
Moncton, Canada, **23 N4**
Mongo, Chad, **66 F6**
Mongolia, Asia, country, **46 F1**
Mongu, Zambia, **72 D3**
Monrovia, Liberia, national capital, **69 C7**
Montalvo, Ecuador, **30 C4**
Montana, U.S.A., internal admin. area,
    24 E1
Montauban, France, **61 E5**
Montego Bay, Jamaica, **27 J4**
Monterrey, Mexico, **26 D2**
Montes Claros, Brazil, **32 K3**
Montevideo, Uruguay, national capital,
    32 G6
Montgomery, U.S.A., internal capital,
    25 J4
Montpelier, U.S.A., internal capital,
    25 M2
Montpellier, France, **61 E6**
Montreal, Canada, **23 M4**
Montserrat, North America, **26 M4**
Monywa, Burma, **44 C3**
Moose Jaw, Canada, **22 J3**
Mopti, Mali, **69 E6**
Moree, Australia, **39 J5**
Morelia, Mexico, **26 D4**
Morocco, Africa, country, **68 D2**
Morogoro, Tanzania, **71 G5**
Morombe, Madagascar, **73 H4**
Moroni, Comoros, national capital,
    73 H2
Morotai, Indonesia, **43 G3**
Morpara, Brazil, **32 K2**
Moscow, Russia, national capital, **56 D2**
Moshi, Tanzania, **71 G4**
Mosquitos, Gulf of, North America, **27 H5**
Mossendjo, Congo, **70 B4**
Mossoro, Brazil, **31 L5**
Most, Czech Republic, **62 E1**

Mostaganem, Algeria, **68 F1**
Mostar, Bosnia and Herzegovina, **62 F3**
Mosul, Iraq, **50 D4**
Moulmein, Burma, **44 C4**
Moundou, Chad, **70 C2**
Mount Gambier, Australia, **38 H7**
Mount Hagen, Papua New Guinea,
    43 K5
Mount Isa, Australia, **38 G4**
Mount Li, China, **46 G4**
Moyale, Ethiopia, **71 G3**
Moyobamba, Peru, **30 C5**
Mozambique, Africa, country, **73 F3**
Mozambique, Mozambique, **73 H3**
Mozambique Channel, Africa, **73 G4**
Mpika, Zambia, **72 F2**
Mtwara, Tanzania, **71 H6**
Mudanjiang, China, **47 L2**
Mueda, Mozambique, **73 G2**
Mufulira, Zambia, **72 E2**
Multan, Pakistan, **48 C4**
Mumbai, India, **49 C7**
Mumbue, Angola, **72 C2**
Munhango, Angola, **72 C2**
Munich, Germany, **60 G4**
Munster, Germany, **60 F4**
Murcia, Spain, **61 D7**
Murmansk, Russia, **58 K1**
Murom, Russia, **56 E2**
Murray, Australia, **38 G6**
Murzuq, Libya, **66 D3**
Muscat, Oman, national capital, **51 G7**
Mutare, Zimbabwe, **73 F3**
Mutoko, Zimbabwe, **72 F3**
Mutsamudu, Comoros, **73 H2**
Mutshatsha, Democratic Republic of
    Congo, **70 D6**
Mwali, Comoros, **73 H2**
Mwanza, Tanzania, **71 F4**
Mwene-Ditu, Democratic Republic of
    Congo, **70 D5**
Mweru, Lake, Africa, **72 E1**
Mwinilunga, Zambia, **72 D2**
Myanmar, Asia, country, **44 C3**
Myitkyina, Burma, **44 C2**
Mykolayiv, Ukraine, **56 C4**
Mysore, India, **49 D8**
Mzuzu, Malawi, **73 F2**

n

Naberezhnye Chelny, Russia, **57 G2**
Nabeul, Tunisia, **62 D4**
Nacala, Mozambique, **73 H2**
Nador, Morocco, **61 D8**
Naga, Philippines, **45 H5**
Nagasaki, Japan, **47 L4**
Nagoya, Japan, **47 N3**
Nagpur, India, **49 D6**
Naha, Japan, **23 N3**
Nairobi, Kenya, national capital, **71 G4**
Najran, Saudi Arabia, **51 D8**
Nakhodka, Russia, **47 M2**
Nakhon Ratchasima, Thailand, **44 D5**
Nakhon Sawan, Thailand, **44 D4**
Nakhon Si Thammarat, Thailand, **44 D6**
Nakuru, Kenya, **71 G4**
Nalchik, Russia, **50 D3**
Namangan, Uzbekistan, **48 C2**
Namib Desert, Africa, **72 B3**
Namibe, Angola, **72 B3**
Namibia, Africa, country, **72 C4**
Nam Lake, China, **48 G4**
Nampo, North Korea, **47 L3**
Nampula, Mozambique, **73 G3**
Namsos, Norway, **58 D2**
Namur, Belgium, **60 F4**
Nanaimo, Canada, **22 G4**
Nanchang, China, **47 J5**
Nancy, France, **60 F4**
Nanded, India, **49 D7**
Nanjing, China, **47 J4**
Nanning, China, **46 G6**
Nanping, China, **47 J5**
Nantes, France, **61 D5**
Napier, New Zealand, **39 Q7**
Naples, Italy, **62 E3**

Narmada, India, **49 C6**
Narva, Estonia, **58 J4**
Narvik, Norway, **58 F1**
Nashik, India, **49 C6**
Nashville, U.S.A., internal capital, **25 J3**
Nasi Lake, Finland, **58 G3**
Nassau, The Bahamas, national capital,
    25 L5
Nasser, Lake, Egypt, **67 H4**
Natal, Brazil, **31 L5**
Natitingou, Benin, **69 F6**
Natuna Islands, Indonesia, **42 C3**
Nauru, Oceania, country, **36 D5**
Navapolatsk, Belarus, **59 J5**
Navoiy, Uzbekistan, **48 B2**
Nawabshah, Pakistan, **48 B5**
Naxcivan, Azerbaijan, **50 E4**
Nazca, Peru, **30 D6**
Nazret, Ethiopia, **71 G2**
Ndalatando, Angola, **72 B1**
Ndele, Central African Republic, **70 D2**
Ndjamena, Chad, national capital, **66 E6**
Ndola, Zambia, **72 E2**
Near Islands, U.S.A., **23 A3**
Nebraska, U.S.A., internal admin. area,
    24 F2
Necochea, Argentina, **33 G7**
Negombo, Sri Lanka, **49 D9**
Negro, Brazil, **30 F4**
Negro, Cape, Peru, **30 B5**
Negros, Philippines, **45 H6**
Neiva, Colombia, **30 C3**
Nekemte, Ethiopia, **71 G2**
Nellore, India, **49 E8**
Nelson, New Zealand, **39 P8**
Nelspruit, South Africa, **72 F4**
Nema, Mauritania, **69 D5**
Neman, Europe, **59 G5**
Nepal, Asia, country, **48 E5**
Netherlands, Europe, country, **60 F3**
Netherlands Antilles, North America,
    dependency, **27 L5**
Nettilling Lake, Canada, **23 M2**
Neuquen, Argentina, **33 E7**
Nevada, U.S.A., internal admin. area,
    24 C3
Nevers, France, **61 E5**
New Amsterdam, Guyana, **31 G2**
Newark, U.S.A., **25 M2**
New Britain, Papua New Guinea, **43 M5**
New Brunswick, Canada,
    internal admin. area, **23 N4**
New Caledonia, Oceania, **39 N4**
Newcastle, Australia, **39 K6**
Newcastle upon Tyne, United Kingdom,
    60 D3
New Delhi, India, national capital, **48 D5**
Newfoundland, Canada, **23 P4**
Newfoundland, Canada,
    internal admin. area, **23 N3**
New Hampshire, U.S.A.,
    internal admin. area, **25 M2**
New Ireland, Papua New Guinea, **43 M4**
New Jersey, U.S.A., internal admin. area,
    25 M3
New Mexico, U.S.A., internal admin. area,
    24 E4
New Orleans, U.S.A., **25 J5**
New Plymouth, New Zealand, **39 P7**
Newport, United Kingdom, **60 D4**
New Siberia Islands, Russia, **53 H2**
New South Wales, Australia, internal
    admin. area, **38 H6**
New York, U.S.A., **25 M2**
New York, U.S.A., internal admin. area,
    25 M2
New Zealand, Australasia, country, **39 Q8**
Ngami, Lake, Botswana, **72 D4**
Ngaoundere, Cameroon, **70 B2**
Ngoma, Zambia, **72 E3**
Nha Trang, Vietnam, **44 E5**
Niagara Falls, North America, **23 M4**
Niamey, Niger, national capital, **69 F6**
Nias, Indonesia, **42 A3**
Nicaragua, North America, country, **27 G5**

Nicaragua, Lake, Nicaragua, **27 H5**
Nice, France, **61 F6**
Nicobar Islands, India, **49 G9**
Nicosia, Cyprus, national capital, **63 K5**
Nieuw Nickerie, Surinam, **31 G2**
Niger, Africa, **69 G7**
Niger, Africa, country, **66 D5**
Niger Delta, Nigeria, **69 G8**
Nigeria, Africa, country, **69 F7**
Niigata, Japan, **47 N3**
Nikopol, Ukraine, **56 C4**
Niksic, Serbia and Montenegro, **63 F3**
Nile, Africa, **67 H3**
Nile Delta, Egypt, **67 H2**
Nimes, France, **61 E6**
Ningbo, China, **47 K5**
Niono, Mali, **69 D6**
Nioro du Sahel, Mali, **69 D5**
Nipigon, Lake, Canada, **23 L4**
Nis, Serbia and Montenegro, **63 G3**
Nitra, Slovakia, **59 F6**
Niue, Oceania, **36 G6**
Nizhniy Novgorod, Russia, **56 E2**
Nizhniy Tagil, Russia, **57 H2**
Njazidja, Comoros, **73 H2**
Njinjo, Tanzania, **71 G5**
Nkongsamba, Cameroon, **70 A3**
Nogales, Mexico, **26 B1**
Nokaneng, Botswana, **72 D3**
Norfolk Island, Australia, **39 N5**
Norilsk, Russia, **52 E2**
Norrkoping, Sweden, **58 F4**
North America, **2**
North Bay, Canada, **23 M4**
North Cape, New Zealand, **39 P6**
North Cape, Norway, **58 J1**
North Carolina, U.S.A.,
    internal admin. area, **25 K3**
North Dakota, U.S.A., internal admin.
    area, **24 F1**
Northern Ireland, United Kingdom,
    internal admin. area, **60 C3**
Northern Mariana Islands, Oceania, **36 B3**
Northern Territory, Australia,
    internal admin. area, **38 F3**
North European Plain, Russia, **56 C2**
North Frisian Islands, Europe, **60 F3**
North Island, New Zealand, **39 Q7**
North Korea, Asia, country, **47 L2**
North Sea, Europe, **60 E2**
North West Cape, Australia, **38 B4**
Northwest Territories, Canada,
    internal admin. area, **22 G2**
Norway, Europe, country, **58 D3**
Norwegian Sea, Europe, **58 D2**
Norwich, United Kingdom, **60 E3**
Nosy Be, Madagascar, **73 J2**
Nosy Boraha, Madagascar, **73 J3**
Nottingham, United Kingdom, **60 D3**
Nouadhibou, Mauritania, **68 B4**
Nouakchott, Mauritania, national capital,
    68 B5
Noumea, New Caledonia, **39 N4**
Nova Iguacu, Brazil, **32 K4**
Nova Mambone, Mozambique, **73 G4**
Novara, Italy, **62 D2**
Nova Scotia, Canada, internal admin. area,
    23 N4
Novaya Zemlya, Russia, **52 C2**
Novgorod, Russia, **58 J4**
Novi Sad, Serbia and Montenegro, **63 F2**
Novocherkassk, Russia, **56 E4**
Novo Mesto, Slovenia, **62 E2**
Novorossiysk, Russia, **50 C3**
Novosibirsk, Russia, **52 E3**
Novyy Urengoy, Russia, **52 D2**
Nubian Desert, Africa, **67 H4**
Nuevo Laredo, U.S.A., **26 D2**
Nukualofa, Tonga, national capital, **36 F7**
Nukus, Uzbekistan, **50 G3**
Nullarbor Plain, Australia, **38 E6**
Nunavut, Canada, internal admin. area,
    23 K2
Nungo, Mozambique, **73 G2**
Nunivak Island, U.S.A., **22 C3**
Nuqui, Colombia, **30 C2**

Nuremberg, *Germany*, 60 G4
Nyala, *Sudan*, 66 F6
Nyasa, Lake, *Africa*, 71 F6
Nyeri, *Kenya*, 71 G4
Nykobing, *Denmark*, 59 D5
Nzerekore, *Guinea*, 69 D7
Nzwani, *Comoros*, 73 H2

O
Oahu, *U.S.A.*, 25 P7
Oaxaca, *Mexico*, 26 E4
Ob, *Russia*, 52 D2
Obi, *Indonesia*, 43 G4
Obninsk, *Russia*, 56 D2
Obo, *Central African Republic*, 70 E2
Odda, *Norway*, 58 C3
Odemis, *Turkey*, 63 J4
Odense, *Denmark*, 59 D5
Oder, *Europe*, 59 E5
Odesa, *Ukraine*, 56 C4
Odienne, *Ivory Coast*, 69 D7
Ogbomoso, *Nigeria*, 69 F7
Ogden, *U.S.A.*, 24 D2
Ohio, *U.S.A.*, 25 J3
Ohio, *U.S.A.*, internal admin. area,
    25 K2
Ojinaga, *Mexico*, 26 D2
Ojos del Salado, Mount, *South America*,
    32 E5
Oka, *Russia*, 56 E2
Okahandja, *Namibia*, 72 C4
Okahandja, *Namibia*, 72 C3
Okavango, *Africa*, 72 D3
Okavango Swamp, *Botswana*, 72 D3
Okayama, *Japan*, 47 M4
Okeechobee, Lake, *U.S.A.*, 25 K5
Okhotsk, Sea of, *Asia*, 53 H3
Okinawa, *Japan*, 47 L5
Oklahoma, *U.S.A.*, internal admin. area,
    24 G4
Oklahoma City, *U.S.A.*, internal capital,
    24 G3
Oktyabrskiy, *Russia*, 57 G3
Oland, *Sweden*, 59 F4
Olavarria, *Argentina*, 33 F7
Olbia, *Italy*, 62 D3
Oleksandriya, *Ukraine*, 56 C4
Ollague, *Chile*, 32 E4
Olomouc, *Czech Republic*, 62 F1
Olongapo, *Philippines*, 45 H5
Olsztyn, *Poland*, 59 G5
Olympia, *U.S.A.*, internal capital, 24 B1
Olympus, Mount, *Greece*, 63 G4
Omaha, *U.S.A.*, 25 G2
Oman, *Asia*, country, 51 G7
Oman, Gulf of, *Asia*, 51 G7
Omdurman, *Sudan*, 67 H5
Omsk, *Russia*, 52 D3
Ondangwa, *Namibia*, 72 C3
Onega, Lake, *Russia*, 58 K3
Onitsha, *Nigeria*, 69 G7
Ontario, *Canada*, internal admin. area,
    23 L3
Ontario, Lake, *U.S.A.*, 25 L2
Opochka, *Russia*, 59 J4
Opole, *Poland*, 59 F6
Oporto, *Portugal*, 61 B6
Oppdal, *Norway*, 58 D3
Opuwo, *Namibia*, 72 B3
Oradea, *Romania*, 63 G2
Oral, *Kazakhstan*, 57 G3
Oran, *Algeria*, 68 E1
Orange, *Africa*, 72 C5
Orange, Cape, *Brazil*, 31 H3
Orapa, *Botswana*, 72 E4
Orebro, *Sweden*, 58 F4
Oregon, *U.S.A.*, internal admin. area,
    24 B2
Orel, *Russia*, 56 D3
Orenburg, *Russia*, 57 H3
Orense, *Spain*, 61 C6
Orinoco, *Venezuela*, 30 F2
Orinoco Delta, *Venezuela*, 30 F2
Oristano, *Italy*, 62 D4
Orizaba, *Mexico*, 26 E4
Orkney, *South Africa*, 72 E5

Orkney Islands, *United Kingdom*, 60 D2
Orlando, *U.S.A.*, 25 K5
Orleans, *France*, 60 E5
Orsha, *Belarus*, 59 J5
Orsk, *Russia*, 57 H3
Oruro, *Bolivia*, 32 E3
Osaka, *Japan*, 47 N4
Osh, *Kyrgyzstan*, 48 C2
Osijek, *Croatia*, 63 F2
Oskarshamn, *Sweden*, 59 F4
Oslo, *Norway*, national capital, 58 D4
Osnabruck, *Germany*, 60 G3
Osorno, *Chile*, 33 D8
Ostersund, *Sweden*, 58 E3
Ostrava, *Czech Republic*, 63 F1
Otavi, *Namibia*, 72 C3
Otjiwarongo, *Namibia*, 72 C4
Ottawa, *Canada*, national capital, 23 M4
Ouadda, *Central African Republic*, 70 D2
Ouagadougou, *Burkina Faso*,
    national capital, 69 E6
Ouahigouya, *Burkina Faso*, 69 E6
Ouargla, *Algeria*, 68 G2
Ouarzazate, *Morocco*, 68 D2
Oudtshoorn, *South Africa*, 72 D6
Ouesso, *Congo*, 70 C3
Oujda, *Morocco*, 68 E2
Oulu, *Finland*, 58 H2
Oulu Lake, *Finland*, 58 H2
Ovalle, *Chile*, 32 D6
Oviedo, *Spain*, 61 C6
Owando, *Congo*, 70 C4
Owen Sound, *Canada*, 23 L4
Owo, *Nigeria*, 69 G7
Oxford, *United Kingdom*, 60 D4
Oyem, *Gabon*, 70 B3
Ozark Plateau, *U.S.A.*, 25 H3

P
Paarl, *South Africa*, 72 C6
Pacasmayo, *Peru*, 30 C5
Pacific Ocean, 18
Padang, *Indonesia*, 42 B4
Pafuri, *Mozambique*, 72 F4
Pagadian, *Philippines*, 45 H6
Paijanne Lake, *Finland*, 58 H3
Pakistan, *Asia*, country, 48 B5
Pakxe, *Laos*, 44 E4
Palangkaraya, *Indonesia*, 42 D4
Palau, *Oceania*, country, 36 A4
Palawan, *Philippines*, 45 G6
Palembang, *Indonesia*, 42 B4
Palencia, *Spain*, 61 C6
Palermo, *Italy*, 62 E4
Palikir, *Federated States of Micronesia*,
    national capital, 36 C4
Palk Strait, *Asia*, 49 D9
Palma, *Mozambique*, 73 H1
Palma, *Spain*, 61 E7
Palmas, Cape, *Africa*, 69 D8
Palmyra Atoll, *Oceania*, 36 G4
Palopo, *Indonesia*, 43 F4
Palu, *Indonesia*, 43 E4
Pampas, *Argentina*, 33 F7
Pamplona, *Colombia*, 30 D2
Pamplona, *Spain*, 61 D6
Panama, *North America*, country, 27 H6
Panama Canal, *Panama*, 27 J6
Panama City, *Panama*, national capital,
    27 J6
Panama, Gulf of, *North America*, 27 J6
Panay, *Philippines*, 45 H5
Panevezys, *Lithuania*, 59 H5
Pangkalpinang, *Indonesia*, 42 C4
Panjgur, *Pakistan*, 48 A5
Pantelleria, *Italy*, 62 E4
Panzhihua, *China*, 46 F5
Papeete, *French Polynesia*, 37 J6
Paphos, *Cyprus*, 63 K5
Papua, Gulf of, *Papua New Guinea*,
    43 K5
Papua New Guinea, *Oceania*, country,
    43 L5
Paraguaipoa, *Venezuela*, 30 D1
Paraguay, *South America*, 32 G4

Paraguay, *South America*, country, 32 F4
Parakou, *Benin*, 69 F7
Paramaribo, *Surinam*, national capital,
    31 G2
Parana, *South America*, 32 G6
Paranagua, *Brazil*, 32 J5
Parepare, *Indonesia*, 43 E4
Paris, *France*, national capital, 60 E4
Parma, *Italy*, 62 D2
Parnaiba, *Brazil*, 31 K4
Parnu, *Estonia*, 58 H4
Parry Islands, *Canada*, 22 J1
Pasadena, *U.S.A.*, 24 C4
Passo Fundo, *Brazil*, 32 H5
Pasto, *Colombia*, 30 C3
Patagonia, *Argentina*, 33 E9
Pathein, *Burma*, 44 B4
Patna, *India*, 48 F5
Patos de Minas, *Brazil*, 32 J3
Patos Lagoon, *Brazil*, 32 H6
Patra, *Greece*, 63 G4
Pattaya, *Thailand*, 44 D5
Pau, *France*, 61 D6
Pavlodar, *Kazakhstan*, 52 D3
Paysandu, *Uruguay*, 32 G6
Peace River, *Canada*, 22 H3
Pecos, *U.S.A.*, 24 F4
Pecs, *Hungary*, 59 F7
Pedro Juan Caballero, *Paraguay*, 32 G4
Pegu, *Burma*, 44 C4
Peipus, Lake, *Europe*, 58 H4
Peiraias, *Greece*, 63 G4
Pekanbaru, *Indonesia*, 42 B3
Pelagian Islands, *Italy*, 62 E5
Peleng, *Indonesia*, 43 F4
Pelotas, *Brazil*, 32 H6
Pematangsiantar, *Indonesia*, 42 A3
Pemba, *Mozambique*, 73 H2
Pemba Island, *Tanzania*, 71 G5
Penang, *Malaysia*, 42 B2
Penas, Gulf of, *Chile*, 33 C9
Pennsylvania, *U.S.A.*, internal admin. area,
    25 L2
Pensacola, *U.S.A.*, 25 J4
Penza, *Russia*, 56 F3
Penzance, *United Kingdom*, 60 C4
Peoria, *U.S.A.*, 25 J2
Pereira, *Colombia*, 30 C3
Perm, *Russia*, 57 H2
Perpignan, *France*, 61 E6
Persepolis, *Iran*, 51 F6
Persian Gulf, *Asia*, 51 F6
Perth, *Australia*, internal capital, 38 C6
Peru, *South America*, country, 30 C5
Perugia, *Italy*, 62 E3
Pescara, *Italy*, 62 E3
Peshawar, *Pakistan*, 48 C4
Petauke, *Zambia*, 72 F2
Petra, *Jordan*, 51 C5
Petrolina, *Brazil*, 31 K5
Petropavlovsk-Kamchatskiy, *Russia*, 53 H3
Petrozavodsk, *Russia*, 58 K3
Philadelphia, *U.S.A.*, 25 L3
Philippines, *Asia*, country, 45 J5
Philippine Sea, *Asia*, 45 H5
Phitsanulok, *Thailand*, 44 D4
Phnom Penh, *Cambodia*, national capital,
    44 D5
Phoenix, *U.S.A.*, internal capital, 24 D4
Phongsali, *Laos*, 44 D3
Piatra Neamt, *Romania*, 63 H2
Pica, *Chile*, 32 E4
Pico, *Azores*, 68 K10
Pielis Lake, *Finland*, 58 J3
Pierre, *U.S.A.*, internal capital, 24 F2
Pietermaritzburg, *South Africa*, 72 F5
Pietersburg, *South Africa*, 72 E4
Pihlaja Lake, *Finland*, 58 J3
Pik Pobedy, *Asia*, 48 E2
Pilcomayo, *South America*, 32 F4
Pilsen, *Czech Republic*, 62 E1
Pinar del Rio, *Cuba*, 27 H3
Pindus Mountains, *Greece*, 63 G4
Pingdingshan, *China*, 47 H4
Pisa, *Italy*, 62 D3

Pitcairn Islands, *Oceania*, 37 L7
Pitesti, *Romania*, 63 H2
Pittsburgh, *U.S.A.*, 25 L2
Piura, *Peru*, 30 B5
Platte, *U.S.A.*, 24 F2
Pleven, *Bulgaria*, 63 H3
Plock, *Poland*, 59 F5
Ploiesti, *Romania*, 63 H2
Plovdiv, *Bulgaria*, 63 H3
Plumtree, *Zimbabwe*, 72 E4
Plymouth, *United Kingdom*, 60 C4
Po, *Italy*, 62 D2
Pocos de Caldas, *Brazil*, 32 J4
Podgorica, *Serbia and Montenegro*, 56 C4
Podolsk, *Russia*, 56 D2
Pointe-Noire, *Congo*, 70 B4
Poitiers, *France*, 61 E5
Pokhara, *Nepal*, 48 E5
Poland, *Europe*, country, 59 F6
Polatsk, *Belarus*, 59 J5
Poltava, *Ukraine*, 56 C4
Polynesia, *Oceania*, 36 G5
Pompeii, *Italy*, 62 E3
Ponta Delgada, *Azores*, 68 K10
Ponta Pora, *Brazil*, 32 G4
Pontianak, *Indonesia*, 42 C3
Poole, *United Kingdom*, 60 D4
Poopo, Lake, *Bolivia*, 32 E3
Popayan, *Colombia*, 30 C3
Porbandar, *India*, 49 B6
Pori, *Finland*, 58 G3
Porlamar, *Venezuela*, 26 M5
Port-au-Prince, *Haiti*, national capital,
    27 K4
Port Blair, *India*, 49 G8
Port Elizabeth, *South Africa*, 72 E6
Port-Gentil, *Gabon*, 70 A4
Port Harcourt, *Nigeria*, 69 G8
Port Hardy, *Canada*, 22 G3
Port Hedland, *Australia*, 38 C4
Portland, *Australia*, 38 H7
Portland, *Maine*, *U.S.A.*, 25 M2
Portland, *Oregon*, *U.S.A.*, 24 B1
Port Louis, *Mauritius*, national capital,
    73 L4
Port Macquarie, *Australia*, 39 K6
Port McNeill, *Canada*, 22 G3
Port Moresby, *Papua New Guinea*,
    national capital, 43 L5
Porto Alegre, *Brazil*, 32 H5
Port-of-Spain, *Trinidad and Tobago*,
    national capital, 26 M5
Porto-Novo, *Benin*, national capital,
    69 F7
Porto-Vecchio, *France*, 61 G6
Porto Velho, *Brazil*, 30 F5
Port Said, *Egypt*, 67 H2
Portsmouth, *United Kingdom*, 60 D4
Port Sudan, *Sudan*, 67 J5
Portugal, *Europe*, country, 61 B7
Port-Vila, *Vanuatu*, national capital,
    39 N3
Porvenir, *Chile*, 33 D10
Posadas, *Argentina*, 32 G5
Poti, *Georgia*, 50 D3
Potiskum, *Nigeria*, 66 D6
Potosi, *Bolivia*, 32 E3
Potsdam, *Germany*, 60 H3
Poyang Lake, *China*, 47 J5
Poznan, *Poland*, 59 F5
Prachuap Khiri Khan, *Thailand*, 44 C5
Prague, *Czech Republic*, national capital,
    62 E1
Praia, *Cape Verde*, national capital,
    69 M12
Presidente Prudente, *Brazil*, 32 H4
Presov, *Slovakia*, 59 G6
Pretoria, *South Africa*, national capital,
    72 E5
Preveza, *Greece*, 63 G4
Prieska, *South Africa*, 72 D5
Prilep, *Macedonia*, 63 G3
Prince Albert, *Canada*, 22 J3
Prince Edward Island, *Canada*,
    internal admin. area, 23 N4
Prince George, *Canada*, 22 G3

109

t

Tabora, *Tanzania*, 71 F5
Tabriz, *Iran*, 50 E4
Tabuk, *Saudi Arabia*, 51 C6
Tacloban, *Philippines*, 45 J5
Tacna, *Peru*, 30 D7
Tacoma, *U.S.A.*, 24 B1
Tacuarembo, *Uruguay*, 32 G6
Tademait Plateau, *Algeria*, 68 F3
Tadmur, *Syria*, 50 C5
Taegu, *South Korea*, 47 L3
Taejon, *South Korea*, 47 L3
Tagus, *Europe*, 61 B7
Tahat, Mount, *Algeria*, 68 G4
Tahiti, *French Polynesia*, 37 J6
Tahoua, *Niger*, 66 C6
Taian, *China*, 47 J3
Taichung, *Taiwan*, 47 K6
Tai Lake, *China*, 47 J4
Taimyr Peninsula, *Russia*, 53 F2
Tainan, *Taiwan*, 47 K6
Taipei, *Taiwan, national capital*, 47 K5
Taiping, *Malaysia*, 42 B3
Taiwan, *Asia, country*, 47 K6
Taiwan Strait, *Asia*, 47 J6
Taiyuan, *China*, 46 H3
Taizz, *Yemen*, 51 D9
Tajikistan, *Asia, country*, 48 B3
Taj Mahal, *India*, 48 D5
Tajumulco, *Guatemala*, 26 F4
Taklimakan Desert, *China*, 48 E3
Talara, *Peru*, 30 B4
Talaud Islands, *Indonesia*, 43 G3
Talca, *Chile*, 33 D7
Taldyqorghan, *Kazakhstan*, 48 D1
Tallahassee, *U.S.A., internal capital*, 25 K4
Tallinn, *Estonia, national capital*, 58 H4
Taltal, *Chile*, 32 D5
Tamale, *Ghana*, 69 E7
Tamanrasset, *Algeria*, 68 G4
Tambacounda, *Senegal*, 69 C6
Tambov, *Russia*, 56 E3
Tampa, *U.S.A.*, 25 K5
Tampere, *Finland*, 58 G3
Tampico, *Mexico*, 26 E3
Tana, Lake, *Ethiopia*, 71 G1
Tandil, *Argentina*, 33 G7
Tanga, *Tanzania*, 71 G5
Tanganyika, Lake, *Africa*, 70 E5
Tangier, *Morocco*, 68 D1
Tangshan, *China*, 47 J3
Tanimbar Islands, *Indonesia*, 43 H5
Tanjungkarang-Telukbetung, *Indonesia*, 42 C5
Tanjungredeb, *Indonesia*, 42 E3
Tanta, *Egypt*, 67 H2
Tan-Tan, *Morocco*, 68 C3
Tanzania, *Africa, country*, 71 F5
Tapachula, *Mexico*, 26 F5
Tapajos, *Brazil*, 31 G5
Tarakan, *Indonesia*, 42 E3
Taranto, *Italy*, 62 F3
Taraz, *Kazakhstan*, 48 C2
Targu Mures, *Romania*, 63 H2
Tarija, *Bolivia*, 32 F4
Tarim Basin, *China*, 48 E3
Tarkwa, *Ghana*, 69 E7
Tarnow, *Poland*, 59 G6
Tarragona, *Spain*, 61 E6
Tartagal, *Argentina*, 32 F4
Tartu, *Estonia*, 58 H4
Tartus, *Syria*, 50 C5
Tashkent, *Uzbekistan, national capital*, 48 B2
Tasmania, *Australia, internal admin. area*, 39 J8
Tasman Sea, *Australasia*, 39 L7
Tataouine, *Tunisia*, 66 D2
Taunggyi, *Burma*, 44 C3
Taupo, Lake, *New Zealand*, 39 Q7
Taurus Mountains, *Turkey*, 63 J4
Tavoy, *Burma*, 44 C5
Tawau, *Malaysia*, 43 E3
Taytay, *Philippines*, 45 G5
Taza, *Morocco*, 68 E2
Tbilisi, *Georgia, national capital*, 50 D3

Tchibanga, *Gabon*, 70 B4
Tebessa, *Algeria*, 68 G1
Tegal, *Indonesia*, 42 C5
Tegucigalpa, *Honduras, national capital*, 27 G5
Tehran, *Iran, national capital*, 50 F4
Tehuacan, *Mexico*, 26 E4
Tehuantepec, Gulf of, *Mexico*, 26 E4
Tehuantepec, Isthmus of, *Mexico*, 26 E4
Tekirdag, *Turkey*, 63 H3
Tel Aviv-Yafo, *Israel*, 51 B5
Teller, *U.S.A.*, 22 C2
Temuco, *Chile*, 33 D7
Ten Degree Channel, *India*, 49 G9
Tenerife, *Canary Islands*, 68 B3
Tenkodogo, *Burkina Faso*, 69 E6
Tennessee, *U.S.A.*, 25 J3
Tennessee, *U.S.A., internal admin. area*, 25 J3
Teofilo Otoni, *Brazil*, 32 K3
Teotihuacan, *Mexico*, 26 E4
Terceira, *Azores*, 68 K10
Teresina, *Brazil*, 31 K4
Ternate, *Indonesia*, 43 G3
Terni, *Italy*, 62 E3
Ternopil, *Ukraine*, 59 H6
Terracotta Army, *China*, 46 G4
Terra Firma, *South Africa*, 72 D5
Teseney, *Eritrea*, 67 J5
Tete, *Mozambique*, 73 F3
Tetouan, *Morocco*, 68 D1
Tetovo, *Macedonia*, 63 G3
Texarkana, *U.S.A.*, 25 H4
Texas, *U.S.A., internal admin. area*, 24 G4
Thailand, *Asia, country*, 44 D4
Thailand, Gulf of, *Asia*, 44 D6
Thai Nguyen, *Vietnam*, 44 E3
Thames, *United Kingdom*, 60 D4
Thanh Hoa, *Vietnam*, 44 E4
Thar Desert, *Asia*, 48 B5
Thasos, *Greece*, 63 H3
Thaton, *Burma*, 44 C4
Thessaloniki, *Greece*, 63 G3
Thies, *Senegal*, 69 B6
Thika, *Kenya*, 71 G4
Thimphu, *Bhutan, national capital*, 48 F5
Thompson, *Canada*, 23 K3
Three Points, Cape, *Africa*, 69 E8
Thunder Bay, *Canada*, 23 L4
Tianjin, *China*, 47 J3
Tibesti Mountains, *Africa*, 66 E4
Tibet, *China*, 48 F4
Tibet, Plateau of, *China*, 48 F4
Tidjikja, *Mauritania*, 68 C5
Tien Shan, *Asia*, 48 D2
Tierra del Fuego, *South America*, 33 E10
Tighina, *Moldova*, 63 J2
Tigris, *Asia*, 51 E5
Tijuana, *Mexico*, 26 A1
Tikal, *Guatemala*, 26 G4
Tikhvin, *Russia*, 56 D3
Tillaberi, *Niger*, 69 F6
Timbuktu, *Mali*, 69 E5
Timisoara, *Romania*, 63 G2
Timor, *Asia*, 43 F5
Timor Sea, *Asia/Australasia*, 43 G6
Tindouf, *Algeria*, 68 D3
Tirana, *Albania, national capital*, 63 F3
Tiraspol, *Moldova*, 63 J2
Tiruchchirappalli, *India*, 49 D8
Titicaca, Lake, *South America*, 30 E7
Tlemcen, *Algeria*, 68 E1
Toamasina, *Madagascar*, 73 J3
Tobago, *Trinidad and Tobago*, 26 M5
Toba, Lake, *Indonesia*, 42 A3
Tobol, *Asia*, 57 K2
Tobolsk, *Russia*, 57 K3
Tobyl, *Kazakhstan*, 57 J3
Tocantins, *Brazil*, 31 J4
Togo, *Africa, country*, 69 F7
Tokelau, *Oceania*, 36 F5
Tokyo, *Japan, national capital*, 47 N3
Tolanaro, *Madagascar*, 73 J5
Toledo, *Spain*, 61 D7

Toledo, *U.S.A.*, 25 K2
Toledo Bend Reservoir, *U.S.A.*, 25 H4
Toliara, *Madagascar*, 73 H4
Tolyatti, *Russia*, 57 F3
Tolybay, *Kazakhstan*, 57 J3
Tomakomai, *Japan*, 47 P2
Tombouctou, *Mali*, 69 E5
Tomsk, *Russia*, 52 E3
Tonga, *Oceania, country*, 36 F6
Tongliao, *China*, 47 K2
Tonkin, Gulf of, *Asia*, 44 E4
Tonle Sap, *Cambodia*, 44 D5
Toowoomba, *Australia*, 39 K5
Topeka, *U.S.A., internal capital*, 25 G3
Top, Lake, *Russia*, 58 K2
Topoli, *Kazakhstan*, 57 G4
Torghay, *Kazakhstan*, 57 J3
Tornio, *Finland*, 58 H2
Toronto, *Canada, internal capital*, 23 M4
Torrens, Lake, *Australia*, 38 G6
Torreon, *Mexico*, 26 D2
Torres Strait, *Australasia*, 38 H2
Tortuga Island, *Venezuela*, 30 H1
Toubkal, *Morocco*, 68 D2
Tougan, *Burkina Faso*, 69 E6
Touggourt, *Algeria*, 68 G2
Toulon, *France*, 61 F6
Toulouse, *France*, 61 E6
Tours, *France*, 60 E5
Townsville, *Australia*, 38 J3
Toyama, *Japan*, 47 N3
Tozeur, *Tunisia*, 66 C2
Trabzon, *Turkey*, 50 C3
Tralee, *Ireland*, 60 B3
Transantarctic Mountains, *Antarctica*, 77 S4
Transylvanian Alps, *Romania*, 63 G2
Trapani, *Italy*, 62 E4
Trento, *Italy*, 62 D2
Trenton, *U.S.A., internal capital*, 25 M2
Tres Arroyos, *Argentina*, 33 F7
Tres Marias Reservoir, *Brazil*, 32 J3
Tres Puntas, Cape, *Argentina*, 33 E9
Trieste, *Italy*, 62 E2
Trincomalee, *Sri Lanka*, 49 E9
Trinidad, *Bolivia*, 32 F2
Trinidad, *Trinidad and Tobago*, 26 M5
Trinidad and Tobago, *North America, country*, 26 M5
Tripoli, *Lebanon*, 50 C5
Tripoli, *Libya, national capital*, 66 D2
Trivandrum, *India*, 49 D9
Trnava, *Slovakia*, 59 F6
Trois-Rivieres, *Canada*, 23 M4
Tromso, *Norway*, 58 F1
Trondheim, *Norway*, 58 D3
Troyes, *France*, 60 F4
Trujillo, *Peru*, 30 C5
Tsau, *Botswana*, 72 D4
Tses, *Namibia*, 72 C5
Tshabong, *Botswana*, 72 D5
Tshane, *Botswana*, 72 D4
Tshikapa, *Democratic Republic of Congo*, 70 D5
Tshwane, *Botswana*, 72 D5
Tsimlyansk Reservoir, *Russia*, 56 F4
Tsiroanomandidy, *Madagascar*, 73 J3
Tsumeb, *Namibia*, 72 C3
Tuamotu Archipelago, *French Polynesia*, 37 K6
Tubmanburg, *Liberia*, 69 C7
Tubruq, *Libya*, 66 F2
Tubuai Islands, *French Polynesia*, 37 J7
Tucson, *U.S.A.*, 24 D4
Tucupita, *Venezuela*, 30 J2
Tucurui Reservoir, *Brazil*, 31 J4
Tugela Falls, *South Africa*, 72 E5
Tuguegarao, *Philippines*, 45 H4
Tula, *Russia*, 56 D3
Tulcea, *Romania*, 63 J2
Tulsa, *U.S.A.*, 25 G3
Tumaco, *Colombia*, 30 C3
Tumbes, *Peru*, 30 B4
Tunduma, *Tanzania*, 71 F5
Tunduru, *Tanzania*, 71 G6
Tunis, *Tunisia, national capital*, 66 D1

Tunisia, *Africa, country*, 66 C2
Tunja, *Colombia*, 30 D2
Tupelo, *U.S.A.*, 25 J4
Tupiza, *Bolivia*, 32 F4
Turbat, *Pakistan*, 51 H6
Turbo, *Colombia*, 30 C2
Turin, *Italy*, 62 C2
Turkana, Lake, *Africa*, 71 G3
Turkey, *Asia, country*, 50 C4
Turkistan, *Kazakhstan*, 48 B2
Turkmenabat, *Turkmenistan*, 50 H4
Turkmenbasy, *Turkmenistan*, 50 F3
Turkmenistan, *Asia, country*, 50 G4
Turks and Caicos Islands, *North America*, 27 K3
Turku, *Finland*, 58 G3
Turpan, *China*, 48 F2
Turpan Depression, *China*, 48 G2
Tuscaloosa, *U.S.A.*, 25 J4
Tuvalu, *Oceania, country*, 36 E5
Tuxtla Gutierrez, *Mexico*, 26 F4
Tuzla, *Bosnia and Herzegovina*, 63 F2
Tuz, lake, *Turkey*, 63 K4
Tver, *Russia*, 56 D2
Twin Falls, *U.S.A.*, 24 D2
Tynda, *Russia*, 53 G3
Tyrrhenian Sea, *Europe*, 62 D3
Tyumen, *Russia*, 57 K2

u

Ubangi, *Africa*, 70 C3
Uberaba, *Brazil*, 32 J3
Uberlandia, *Brazil*, 32 J3
Ubon Ratchathani, *Thailand*, 44 D4
Ucayali, *Peru*, 30 D5
Udaipur, *India*, 49 C6
Uddevalla, *Sweden*, 58 D4
Udon Thani, *Thailand*, 44 D4
Uele, *Democratic Republic of Congo*, 70 D3
Ufa, *Russia*, 57 H3
Uganda, *Africa, country*, 71 F3
Uitenhage, *South Africa*, 72 E6
Ujung Pandang, *Indonesia*, 43 E5
Ukhta, *Russia*, 52 C2
Ukraine, *Europe, country*, 56 C4
Ulan Bator, *Mongolia, national capital*, 46 G1
Ulanhot, *China*, 47 K1
Ulan Ude, *Russia*, 53 F3
Ulm, *Germany*, 62 D5
Uluru, *Australia*, 38 F5
Ulyanovsk, *Russia*, 57 F3
Uman, *Ukraine*, 59 J6
Ume, *Sweden*, 58 F2
Umea, *Sweden*, 58 G3
Umnak Island, *U.S.A.*, 23 C3
Umtata, *South Africa*, 72 E6
Unalaska Island, *U.S.A.*, 23 C3
Ungava Bay, *Canada*, 23 N3
Ungava Peninsula, *Canada*, 23 M2
Unimak Island, *U.S.A.*, 23 C3
United Arab Emirates, *Asia, country*, 51 F7
United Kingdom, *Europe, country*, 60 D3
United States of America, *North America, country*, 24 F3
Upington, *South Africa*, 72 D5
Uppsala, *Sweden*, 58 F4
Ural, *Asia*, 57 G4
Ural Mountains, *Russia*, 57 H2
Uray, *Russia*, 57 J1
Urganch, *Uzbekistan*, 48 A2
Urmia, *Iran*, 50 E4
Uruapan, *Mexico*, 26 D4
Urucui, *Brazil*, 31 K5
Uruguaiana, *Brazil*, 32 G6
Uruguay, *South America, country*, 32 G6
Urumqi, *China*, 48 F2
Usak, *Turkey*, 63 J4
Ushuaia, *Argentina*, 33 E10
Uskemen, *Kazakhstan*, 48 E2
Utah, *U.S.A., internal admin. area*, 24 D3
Utsjoki, *Finland*, 58 H1
Utsunomiya, *Japan*, 47 N3
Uy, *Asia*, 57 J3

Uyuni, *Bolivia*, 32 E4
Uzbekistan, *Asia, country*, 52 D3
Uzhhorod, *Ukraine*, 59 G6

V
Vaasa, *Finland*, 58 G3
Vadodara, *India*, 49 C6
Vadso, *Norway*, 58 J1
Vaduz, *Liechtenstein, national capital*, 62 D2
Valdai Hills, *Russia*, 59 K4
Valdes Peninsula, *Argentina*, 33 F8
Valdivia, *Chile*, 33 D7
Val-d'Or, *Canada*, 23 M4
Valdosta, *U.S.A.*, 25 K4
Valencia, *Spain*, 61 D7
Valencia, *Venezuela*, 30 E1
Valencia, Gulf of, *Spain*, 61 D7
Valera, *Venezuela*, 30 D2
Valladolid, *Spain*, 61 C6
Vallenar, *Chile*, 32 D5
Valletta, *Malta, national capital*, 62 E5
Valley of the Kings, *Egypt*, 67 H3
Valparaiso, *Chile*, 32 D6
Van, *Turkey*, 50 D4
Vanadzor, *Armenia*, 50 D3
Vancouver, *Canada*, 22 G4
Vancouver Island, *Canada*, 22 G4
Vaner, Lake, *Sweden*, 58 E4
Van, Lake, *Turkey*, 50 D4
Vannes, *France*, 60 D5
Vanua Levu, *Fiji*, 39 Q3
Vanuatu, *Oceania, country*, 39 M3
Varanasi, *India*, 48 E5
Varberg, *Sweden*, 59 E4
Varhaug, *Norway*, 58 C4
Varkaus, *Finland*, 58 H3
Varna, *Bulgaria*, 63 H3
Vastervik, *Sweden*, 59 F4
Vatican City, *Europe, country*, 62 E3
Vatnajokull, *Iceland*, 58 P2
Vatter, Lake, *Sweden*, 59 E4
Vaxjo, *Sweden*, 59 E4
Velikiye Luki, *Russia*, 59 J4
Venado Tuerto, *Argentina*, 32 F6
Venezuela, *South America, country*, 30 E2
Venezuela, Gulf of, *Venezuela*, 30 D1
Venice, *Italy*, 62 E2
Ventspils, *Latvia*, 59 G4
Veracruz, *Mexico*, 26 E4
Verkhoyansk Range, *Russia*, 53 G2
Vermont, *U.S.A., internal admin. area*, 25 M2
Verona, *Italy*, 62 D2
Vesteralen, *Norway*, 58 E1
Vestfjorden, *Norway*, 58 E2
Viborg, *Denmark*, 59 D4
Vicenza, *Italy*, 62 D2
Vicksburg, *U.S.A.*, 25 H4
Victoria, *Australia, internal admin. area*, 38 H7
Victoria, *British Columbia, Canada, internal capital*, 22 G4
Victoria, *Chile*, 33 D7
Victoria Falls, *Africa*, 72 E3
Victoria Island, *Canada*, 22 J1
Victoria, Lake, *Africa*, 71 F4
Victoria Land, *Antarctica*, 77 L3
Victoria, Mount, *Burma*, 44 B3
Viedma, *Argentina*, 33 F8
Viedma, Lake, *Argentina*, 33 D9
Vienna, *Austria, national capital*, 62 F1
Vientiane, *Laos, national capital*, 44 D4
Vietnam, *Asia, country*, 44 E5
Vigo, *Spain*, 61 B6
Vijayawada, *India*, 49 E7
Vikna, *Norway*, 58 D2
Villach, *Austria*, 62 E2
Villahermosa, *Mexico*, 26 F4
Villa Maria, *Argentina*, 32 F6
Villa Mercedes, *Argentina*, 32 E6
Villarrica, *Paraguay*, 32 G5
Vilnius, *Lithuania, national capital*, 59 H5
Vinh, *Vietnam*, 44 E4
Vinnytsya, *Ukraine*, 59 J6
Vinson Massif, *Antarctica*, 77 R3

Virginia, *U.S.A., internal admin. area*, 25 L3
Virginia Beach, *U.S.A.*, 25 L3
Virgin Islands (U.K.), *North America*, 26 M4
Virgin Islands (U.S.A.), *North America*, 26 M4
Visby, *Sweden*, 59 F4
Viscount Melville Sound, *Canada*, 22 H1
Vishakhapatnam, *India*, 49 E7
Vistula, *Poland*, 59 F5
Viti Levu, *Fiji*, 39 Q3
Vitoria, *Brazil*, 32 K4
Vitoria, *Spain*, 61 D6
Vitoria da Conquista, *Brazil*, 32 K2
Vitsyebsk, *Belarus*, 59 J5
Vladimir, *Russia*, 56 E2
Vladivostok, *Russia*, 47 M2
Vlore, *Albania*, 63 F3
Volga, *Russia*, 57 F4
Volga Uplands, *Russia*, 57 F3
Volgodonsk, *Russia*, 56 E4
Volgograd, *Russia*, 56 E4
Volgograd Reservoir, *Russia*, 57 F3
Volkhov, *Russia*, 58 K4
Vologda, *Russia*, 56 D2
Volos, *Greece*, 63 G4
Volta, Lake, *Ghana*, 69 E7
Vorkuta, *Russia*, 52 D2
Voronezh, *Russia*, 56 D3
Voru, *Estonia*, 59 H4
Votkinsk, *Russia*, 57 G2
Vranje, *Serbia and Montenegro*, 63 G3
Vratsa, *Bulgaria*, 63 G3
Vyborg, *Russia*, 58 J3
Vyg, Lake, *Russia*, 58 K3

W
Wa, *Ghana*, 69 E6
Waco, *U.S.A.*, 25 G4
Wad Medani, *Sudan*, 67 H6
Wagga Wagga, *Australia*, 38 J7
Wainwright, *U.S.A.*, 22 C1
Wakayama, *Japan*, 47 N4
Wake Island, *Oceania*, 36 D3
Walbrzych, *Poland*, 59 F6
Wales, *United Kingdom, internal admin. area*, 60 C3
Wallis and Futuna, *Oceania, dependency*, 36 E6
Walvis Bay, *Namibia*, 72 B4
Warangal, *India*, 49 D7
Warmbad, *South Africa*, 72 E5
Warri, *Nigeria*, 69 G7
Warsaw, *Poland, national capital*, 59 G5
Washington, *U.S.A., internal admin. area*, 24 B1
Washington D.C., *U.S.A., national capital*, 25 L3
Waskaganish, *Canada*, 23 M3
Watampone, *Indonesia*, 43 F4
Waterford, *Ireland*, 60 C3
Watson Lake, *Canada*, 22 G2
Wau, *Sudan*, 70 F2
Weddell Sea, *Antarctica*, 77 T3
Weifang, *China*, 47 K3
Welkom, *South Africa*, 72 E5
Wellesley Islands, *Australia*, 38 G3
Wellington, *New Zealand, national capital*, 39 Q8
Wellington Island, *Chile*, 33 C9
Wels, *Austria*, 62 E1
Wenchi, *Ghana*, 69 E7
Wenzhou, *China*, 47 K5
Werda, *Botswana*, 72 D5
Wessel, Cape, *Australia*, 38 G2
West Antarctica, *Antarctica*, 77 Q4
Western Australia, *Australia, internal admin. area*, 38 D5
Western Cordillera, *Colombia*, 30 C3
Western Cordillera, *Peru*, 30 C6
Western Dvina, *Europe*, 59 J4
Western Ghats, *India*, 49 C7
Western Isles, *United Kingdom*, 60 E2
Western Sahara, *Africa, dependency*, 68 C3

Western Sierra Madre, *Mexico*, 26 C2
West Falkland, *Falkland Islands*, 33 F10
West Siberian Plain, *Russia*, 52 D2
West Virginia, *U.S.A., internal admin. area*, 25 K3
Wetar, *Indonesia*, 43 G5
Wewak, *Papua New Guinea*, 43 K4
Whangarei, *New Zealand*, 39 P7
Whitecourt, *Canada*, 22 H3
Whitehorse, *Yukon, Canada, internal capital*, 22 F2
White Lake, *Russia*, 56 D1
White Nile, *Africa*, 67 H6
White Sea, *Russia*, 58 K2
White Volta, *Africa*, 69 E6
Whitney, Mount, *U.S.A.*, 24 C3
Wichita, *U.S.A.*, 24 G3
Wick, *United Kingdom*, 60 D2
Wight, Isle of, *United Kingdom*, 60 D4
Wilhelm, Mount, *Papua New Guinea*, 43 L5
Wilkes Land, *Antarctica*, 77 H2
Willemstad, *Netherlands Antilles*, 27 L5
Williams Lake, *Canada*, 22 G3
Windhoek, *Namibia, national capital*, 72 C4
Windsor, *Canada*, 23 L4
Windward Islands, *North America*, 27 N5
Windward Passage, *North America*, 27 K3
Winnipeg, *Canada, internal capital*, 23 K3
Winnipeg, Lake, *Canada*, 22 K3
Winnipegosis, Lake, *Canada*, 22 J3
Winterthur, *Switzerland*, 62 D2
Wisconsin, *U.S.A., internal admin. area*, 25 H2
Wloclawek, *Poland*, 59 F5
Wollaston Lake, *Canada*, 22 J3
Wollongong, *Australia*, 39 K6
Wonsan, *North Korea*, 47 L3
Woods, Lake of the, *Canada*, 23 K4
Worcester, *South Africa*, 72 C6
Wrangel Island, *Russia*, 53 K2
Wroclaw, *Poland*, 59 F6
Wuhai, *China*, 46 G3
Wuhan, *China*, 47 H4
Wurzburg, *Germany*, 60 G4
Wuxi, *China*, 47 K4
Wuzhou, *China*, 46 H6
Wyoming, *U.S.A., internal admin. area*, 24 E2

X
Xai-Xai, *Mozambique*, 73 F5
Xangongo, *Angola*, 72 B3
Xankandi, *Azerbaijan*, 50 E4
Xiamen, *China*, 47 J6
Xian, *China*, 46 G4
Xiangfan, *China*, 46 H4
Xianggang, *China*, 47 H6
Xichang, *China*, 46 F5
Xi Jiang, *China*, 46 H6
Xilinhot, *China*, 47 J2
Xingu, *Brazil*, 31 H5
Xining, *China*, 46 F4
Xuzhou, *China*, 47 J4

Y
Yakutsk, *Russia*, 53 G2
Yala, *Thailand*, 44 D6
Yamantau, *Russia*, 57 H3
Yamoussoukro, *Ivory Coast, national capital*, 69 D7
Yancheng, *China*, 47 K4
Yangtze, *China*, 47 J4
Yanji, *China*, 47 L2
Yantai, *China*, 47 K3
Yaounde, *Cameroon, national capital*, 70 B3
Yapen, *Indonesia*, 43 J4
Yaren, *Nauru, national capital*, 36 D5
Yarmouth, *Canada*, 23 N4
Yaroslavl, *Russia*, 56 D2
Yazd, *Iran*, 51 F5
Yekaterinburg, *Russia*, 57 J2
Yelets, *Russia*, 56 D3

Yellow, *China*, 47 J3
Yellowknife, *Canada, internal capital*, 22 H2
Yellow Sea, *Asia*, 47 K3
Yellowstone, *U.S.A.*, 24 E1
Yellowstone Lake, *U.S.A.*, 24 D2
Yemen, *Asia, country*, 51 E8
Yenisey, *Russia*, 52 E2
Yerevan, *Armenia, national capital*, 50 D3
Yevpatoriya, *Ukraine*, 63 K2
Yichang, *China*, 46 H4
Yichun, *China*, 47 L1
Yinchuan, *China*, 46 G3
Yining, *China*, 48 E2
Yogyakarta, *Indonesia*, 42 D5
Yongan, *China*, 47 J5
York, Cape, *Australia*, 38 H2
Yosemite Falls, *U.S.A.*, 24 C3
Yoshkar-Ola, *Russia*, 57 F2
Youth, Isle of, *Cuba*, 27 H3
Yucatan Peninsula, *Mexico*, 26 G3
Yukon, *North America*, 22 D2
Yukon Territory, *Canada, internal admin. area*, 22 F2
Yulin, *China*, 46 H6
Yumen, *China*, 46 E3
Yurimaguas, *Peru*, 30 C5
Yu Shan, *Taiwan*, 47 K6
Yushu, *China*, 46 E4
Yuzhno Sakhalinsk, *Russia*, 53 H3
Yuzhnoukrayinsk, *Ukraine*, 56 C2

Z
Zabol, *Iran*, 51 H5
Zadar, *Croatia*, 62 F2
Zagreb, *Croatia, national capital*, 62 F2
Zagros Mountains, *Iran*, 50 E5
Zahedan, *Iran*, 51 H6
Zalaegerszeg, *Hungary*, 59 F7
Zambezi, *Africa*, 73 F3
Zambia, *Africa, country*, 72 E2
Zamboanga, *Philippines*, 45 H6
Zamora, *Spain*, 61 C6
Zamosc, *Poland*, 59 G6
Zanjan, *Iran*, 50 E4
Zanzibar, *Tanzania*, 71 G5
Zanzibar Island, *Tanzania*, 71 G5
Zapala, *Argentina*, 33 E7
Zaporizhzhya, *Ukraine*, 56 D5
Zaragoza, *Spain*, 61 D6
Zaraza, *Venezuela*, 30 E2
Zaria, *Nigeria*, 69 G6
Zaysan, Lake, *Kazakhstan*, 48 E1
Zealand, *Denmark*, 59 D5
Zeil, Mount, *Australia*, 38 F4
Zelenogorsk, *Russia*, 58 J3
Zelenograd, *Russia*, 56 D2
Zenica, *Bosnia and Herzegovina*, 62 F2
Zhangjiakou, *China*, 47 H2
Zhanibek, *Kazakhstan*, 57 F4
Zhanjiang, *China*, 46 H6
Zhavylma, *Kazakhstan*, 57 J3
Zhengzhou, *China*, 47 H4
Zhetiqara, *Kazakhstan*, 57 J3
Zhlobin, *Belarus*, 59 J5
Zhodzina, *Belarus*, 59 J5
Zhuzhou, *China*, 47 H5
Zhytomyr, *Ukraine*, 59 J6
Zibo, *China*, 47 J3
Zielona Gora, *Poland*, 59 E6
Ziguinchor, *Senegal*, 69 B6
Zilina, *Slovakia*, 59 F6
Zimba, *Zambia*, 72 E3
Zimbabwe, *Africa, country*, 72 E3
Zinder, *Niger*, 66 C6
Zlatoust, *Russia*, 57 H2
Zlin, *Czech Republic*, 62 F1
Zomba, *Malawi*, 73 G3
Zongdaak, *Turkey*, 63 J3
Zorzor, *Liberia*, 69 D7
Zouerat, *Mauritania*, 66 C4
Zumba, *Ecuador*, 30 C4
Zumbo, *Mozambique*, 72 F3
Zunyi, *China*, 46 G5
Zurich, *Switzerland*, 62 D2
Zvishavane, *Zimbabwe*, 72 F4

GENERAL INDEX

Acknowledgements

Every effort has been made to trace the copyright holders of the material in this book. If any rights have been omitted, the publishers offer to rectify this in any subsequent edition, following notification. The publishers are grateful to the following organizations and individuals for their contributions and permission to reproduce material (t=top, m=middle, b=bottom, l=left, r=right):

© **AFP Photos** 95bm (Henry Ray Abrams). © **Agripicture** 55br (Peter Dean). © **Craig Asquith** 11 projections, 12b, 13, 80. © **Corbis** 8tr (Dan Guravich), 9tr (W. Perry Conway), 10 (Christopher Cormack), 12tr (Bill Ross), 20bl (Richard Cummins), 21br (W. Perry Conway), 28b (Galen Rowell), 29tr (Eye Ubiquitous), 35br (Bates Littlehales), 40–41b (Michael S. Yamashita), 41br (Keren Su), 64–65b (Tom Brakefield), 65br (Gallo Images), 74bl (Galen Rowell), 76b (Wolfgang Kaehler). © **Digital Vision** cover globe, 1, 2–3, 4–5 background, 7tr Earth, 14 background, 54–55 background, 74br, 82–95 background, 96–97b, 97tr. © **European Map Graphics Ltd** 7bm & br, 9bl, 14–19, 20–21 map, 22–27, 28–29 map, 30–33, 34–35 map, 36–39, 40–41 map, 42–53, 54–55 map, 56–63, 64–65 map, 66–73, 75, 77. © **Flag Enterprises Ltd** 82–95 all flags except Afghanistan, Bahrain, Comoros, East Timor, Rwanda, Turkmenistan. © **Stephen Moncrieff** 6mr, 8bl globes, 11 globes. © **NASA** cover background, endpapers (data by Marc Imhoff, NASA GSFC, & Christopher Elvidge, NOAA NGDC; image by Craig Mayhew & Robert Simmon, NASA GSFC), 7tr satellite (JPL). © **Science Photo Library** 4tr (Geospace), 6bl (CNES, 1988 Distribution SPOT image), 74tr (Worldsat International), 76mr (NASA). © **Shipmate Flags, Vlaardingen, The Netherlands** 82 Afghanistan & Bahrain flags, 84 Comoros flag, 85 East Timor flag, 92 Rwanda flag, 94 Turkmenistan flag. © **Still Pictures** 34–35t (Pascal Kobeh).

Managing editor: Gillian Doherty   Managing designer: Mary Cartwright   Cover design by Zöe Wray